Pocket Oxford
Polish Dictionary

OXFORD
UNIVERSITY PRESS

OXFORD
UNIVERSITY PRESS

Great Clarendon Street, Oxford OX2 6DP

Oxford University Press is a department of the University of Oxford.
It furthers the University's objective of excellence in research, scholarship,
and education by publishing worldwide in

Oxford New York

Auckland Cape Town Dar es Salaam Hong Kong Karachi
Kuala Lumpur Madrid Melbourne Mexico City Nairobi
New Delhi Shanghai Taipei Toronto

with offices in

Argentina Austria Brazil Chile Czech Republic France Greece
Guatemala Hungary Italy Japan Poland Portugal Singapore
South Korea Switzerland Thailand Turkey Ukraine Vietnam

Oxford is a registered trade mark of Oxford University Press
in the UK and in certain other countries

Published in the United States
by Oxford University Press Inc., New York

First published in Poland by Wydawnictwo Naukowe PWN SA as
Nowy słownik angielsko-polski polsko-angielski, 2005

Wydawnictwo Naukowe PWN SA
00-251 Warszawa, ul. Miodowa 10, Poland

www.pwn.pl
http://en.pwn.pl/rights

British Library Cataloguing in Publication Data
Data available

Library of Congress Cataloging in Publication Data
Data available

Printed in Great Britain by Clays Ltd, Bungay, Suffolk

ISBN 978-0-19-921491-4

Contents

Editors and contributors

**Redaktorzy Naukowi/
Chief Editors**
Jadwiga Linde-Usiekniewicz
Phillip G. Smith

**Autorzy haseł/
Entry Compilers**
Agnieszka Andrzejewska
Paweł Beręsewicz
Danuta Hołata-Lötz
Zuzanna Łubkowska
Regina Mościcka
Jerzy Pilawski
Agnieszka Płudowska
Sherill Howard Pociecha
Bogna Piotrowska
Krystyna Rabińska
Katarzyna Zawadzka

**Współpraca ze strony OUP/
OUP Contributors**

**Redaktor prowadzący/
Managing Editor**
Della Thompson

Proprietary names

This dictionary includes some words which have, or are asserted to have, proprietary status as trademarks or otherwise. Their inclusion does not imply that they have acquired for legal purposes a non-proprietary or general significance, nor is any other judgment implied concerning their legal status. In cases where the editorial staff have some evidence that a word has proprietary status, this is indicated in the entry for that word by the symbol ®, but no judgment concerning the legal status of such words is made or implied thereby.

Nazwy zastrzeżone

Słownik zawiera słowa posiadające status nazw zastrzeżonych (lub uznawane za nazwy zastrzeżone), na przykład znaki firmowe. Ich włączenie do słownika nie sugeruje zmiany tego statusu. W przypadkach, gdy redaktorzy mieli do dyspozycji materiał wskazujący na to, że dany wyraz jest nazwą zastrzeżoną, zostało to zaznaczone w haśle symbolem ®, nie jest to jednak sugestia dotycząca statusu prawnego takiej nazwy.

Preface

The *Pocket Oxford-PWN Polish Dictionary* combines the authority of the *Oxford-PWN Polish-English English-Polish Dictionary* with the convenience of a smaller format and quick-access layout. It is an easy-to-use pocket dictionary and is the ideal reference tool for all those requiring quick and reliable answers to their translation questions. It provides guidance on selecting the most appropriate translation and numerous examples to help with problems of usage and construction.

Geared to the needs of a wide range of users, from the student at intermediate level and above to the enthusiastic traveller and business professional, the *Pocket Oxford-PWN Polish Dictionary* is an invaluable practical resource for learners of modern, idiomatic Polish at the start of the twenty-first century.

The whole of the dictionary has been checked throughout by Polish and English native speakers, to ensure that the information given is more accurate and up to date than in any comparable dictionary. The *Pocket Oxford-PWN Polish Dictionary* has been awarded the European Medal – a prestigious award of the Business Centre Club for the best products in their respective categories.

Wstęp

Pocket Oxford-PWN Polish Dictionary łączy wiarygodność i niezawodność *Wielkiego słownika polsko-angielskiego i angielsko-polskiego PWN-Oxford* z poręcznością mniejszego formatu i przystępnego opracowania graficznego. Prosty w użyciu, jest idealnym źródłem informacji dla użytkowników poszukujących szybkich i jednoznacznych odpowiedzi na pytania dotyczące polskich lub angielskich tłumaczeń. Słownik pomaga w wyborze najbardziej trafnych odpowiedników i, wraz z informacją na temat składni, podaje liczne przykłady typowych użyć i konstrukcji gramatycznych.

Przeznaczony dla szerokiej grupy użytkowników, od średnio zaawansowanych uczących się danego języka po osoby podróżujące w celach turystycznych lub służbowych, *Pocket Oxford-PWN Polish Dictionary* jest niezbędny w nauce współczesnego języka angielskiego.

Całość materiału włączonego do słownika została sprawdzona przez rodzimych użytkowników języka polskiego i angielskiego, gwarantując jego dokładność i aktualność.

Pocket Oxford-PWN Polish Dictionary otrzymał Medal Europejski – prestiżową nagrodę dla najlepszych produktów w swojej kategorii przyznawaną przez Business Centre Club.

Abbreviations used in the Dictionary

Subject

English		Polish
accountancy	Accts	księgowość
administration	Admin	administracja
advertising	Advertg	reklama
aerospace	Aerosp	kosmonautyka
agriculture	Agric	rolnictwo
anatomy	Anat	anatomia
anthropology	Anthrop	antropologia
antiquity	Antiq	starożytność
archaeology	Archeol	archeologia
architecture	Archit	architektura
	Art	sztuka
	Audio	audiotechnika
astrology	Astrol	astrologia
astronomy	Astron	astronomia
automobile	Aut	motoryzacja
aviation	Aviat	lotnictwo
	Bible	Biblia
biology	Biol	biologia
botany	Bot	botanika
chemistry	Chem	chemia
cinema	Cin	kino
civil engineering	Civ Eng	inżynieria lądowa
commerce	Comm	handel
computing	Comput	informatyka
construction	Constr	budownictwo
cosmetics	Cosmet	kosmetyka
culinary	Culin	kulinaria
	Dance	taniec
dentistry	Dent	stomatologia
ecology	Ecol	ekologia
economics	Econ	ekonomia
electricity	Elec	elektryka
electronics	Electron	elektronika
equestrianism	Equest	jeździectwo
fashion	Fashn	moda
finance	Fin	finanse
fishing	Fishg	rybołówstwo
	Games	gry
geography	Geog	geografia
geology	Geol	geologia
heraldry	Herald	heraldyka
history	Hist	historia
horticulture	Hort	ogrodnictwo
hunting	Hunt	myślistwo

Abbreviations used in the Dictionary

English		Polish
industry	Ind	przemysł
insurance	Insur	ubezpieczenia
journalism	Journ	dziennikarstwo
law	Jur	prawo
linguistics	Ling	językoznawstwo
literature	Literat	literatura
mathematics	Math	matematyka
measure, units etc.	Meas	jednostki miary
mechanics	Mech	mechanika
medicine	Med	medycyna
meteorology	Meteorol	meteorologia
management	Mgmt	zarządzanie
military	Mil	wojskowość
Navy	Mil Naut	marynarka wojenna
mineralogy	Miner	mineralogia
music	Mus	muzyka
mythology	Mythol	mitologia
nautical	Naut	nautyka
nuclear physics	Nucl	fizyka jądrowa
pharmacology	Pharm	farmakologia
philosophy	Philos	filozofia
photography	Phot	fotografia
physics	Phys	fizyka
physiology	Physiol	fizjologia
politics	Pol	polityka
postal services	Post	poczta
printing	Print	drukarstwo
psychology	Psych	psychologia
publishing	Publg	edytorstwo
	Radio	radio
railway	Rail	kolejnictwo
	Sport	sport
	Sewing	krawiectwo
religion	Relig	religia
school	Sch	szkolnictwo
sciences	Sci	nauki ścisłe
sociology	Sociol	socjologia
statistics	Stat	statystyka
technology	Tech	technika
telecommunications	Telecom	telekomunikacja
textiles	Tex	włókiennictwo
theatre	Theat	teatr
transport	Transp	transport
	Turf	wyścigi konne
television	TV	telewizja
university	Univ	szkolnictwo wyższe
veterinary medicine	Vet	weterynaria
winemaking	Wine	winiarstwo
zoology	Zool	zoologia

Abbreviations used in the Dictionary

Style

English		Polish
archaic	arch	archaiczne
Australian	Austral	australijskie
	baby talk	mowa dzieci
Canadian	Can	kanadyjskie
controversial	controv	kontrowersyjne
dated	dat	przestarzałe
dialect	dial	dialektalne
euphemistic	euph	eufemizm
figurative	fig	przenośne
formal	fml	książkowe, oficjalne
British English	GB	angielszczyzna brytyjska
humorous	hum	żartobliwe
informal	infml	potoczne, nieoficjalne
Irish	Ir	irlandzkie
ironic	iron	ironiczne
journalese	journ	dziennikarskie
literary	liter	literackie
	offensive	obraźliwe
pejorative	pej	pejoratywne
proverb	Prov	przysłowie
rare	ra	rzadkie
Scottish	Scot	szkockie
slang	sl	slangowe
specialist	spec	specjalistyczne
American English	US	angielszczyzna amerykańska
very informal	vinfml	pospolite
vulgar or taboo	vulg	wulgarne

English Grammar

English		Polish
adjective	adj	przymiotnik
adjectival phrase	adj phr	fraza przymiotnikowa
adverb	adv	przysłówek
adverbial phrase	adv phr	fraza okolicznikowa
auxiliary	aux	posiłkowy
comparative	comp	stopień wyższy
conjunction	conj	spójnik
conjunction phrase	conj phr	spójnik złożony
determiner	det	określnik
definite article	def art	przedimek określony
exclamation	excl	wykrzyknik
indefinite article	indef art	przedimek nieokreślony
	linking verb	spójka

Abbreviations used in the Dictionary

English		Polish
modal auxiliary verb	modal aux	czasownik posiłkowomodalny
modifier	modif	przydawka rzeczowna
noun	n	rzeczownik
noun plural	npl	rzeczownik w liczbie mnogiej
onomatopoeia	onomat	onomatopeja
person	pers.	osoba
past participle	pp	imiesłów przeszły
past participle adjective	pp adj	imiesłów przymiotnikowy bierny
preposition	prep	przyimek
prepositional phrase	prep phr	przyimek złożony
present tense	pres	czas teraźniejszy
proper noun	prn	nazwa własna
pronoun	pron	zaimek
present participle	prp	imiesłów czasu teraźniejszego
present participle adjective	prp adj	imiesłów przymiotnikowy czynny
past tense	pt	czas przeszły
quantifier	quantif	kwantyfikator
singular	sg	liczba pojedyncza
superlative	superl	stopień najwyższy
verb	v	czasownik
auxiliary verb	v aux	czasownik posiłkowy
impersonal verb	v impers	czasownik nieosobowy
intransitive verb	vi	czasownik nieprzechodni
reflexive verb	vr	czasownik zwrotny
transitive verb	vt	czasownik przechodni

Polish Grammar

English		Polish
feminine	f	żeński
masculine	m	męski
neuter	n	nijaki
plural	pl	liczba mnoga
	plt	plurale tantum

Other Symbols

English		Polish
trade mark	®	znak handlowy
European Community	EC	Wspólnota Europejska
somebody	sb	ktoś
something	sth	coś
	also	także
	or	lub

Jak korzystać ze słownika

Alfabetyczna kolejność haseł.	**gaf|a** *f* blunder, gaffe **gag** *m* gag
Homonimy traktowane są jako oddzielne hasła opatrzone cyfrą arabską podniesioną o pół wiersza.	**gro|t**[1] *m* (strzały) (arrow)head; (włóczni) tip **gro|t**[2] *m* Żegl. mainsail
W niektórych przypadkach we wspólne hasła połączono: • **męskie i żeńskie formy** rzeczowników osobowych • **wymiennie** stosowane warianty wyrazów.	**geode|ta** *m*, **~tka** *f* geodesist, (geodetic) surveyor **peł|zać, peł|znąć** *impf vi* [1] *[gad, owad, osoba]* to crawl [...] **perli|czka, ~ca** *f* guineafowl
Wspólne hasło **dla dokonanej i niedokonanej** postaci czasownika, jeżeli różnią się od siebie przyrostkiem.	**dobud|ować** *pf* — **dobud|owywać** *impf vt* to build on, to add *[piętro, garaż]*
Jeżeli w jakimś znaczeniu dany czasownik **nie ma pary aspektowej**, to jest traktowany jako homonim.	**dochodzić**[1] *impf→* **dojść** **dochodz|ić**[2] *pf vi* [1] (prowadzić) *[droga, ulica]* to lead (**do czegoś** to sth) [...]
Pionowa kreska oddzielająca część wyrazu niezmienną w czasie odmiany, wewnątrz hasła zastępowaną tyldą.	**gotów|ka** *f* cash; zastrzyk **~ki** a cash injection; **w ~ce** in cash [...]
Wymowę zapisano międzynarodowym alfabetem fonetycznym (**IPA**) w przypadkach odstępstw od ogólnych reguł.	**dancing** /ˈdansiŋ/ *m* dance, dancing [...]
Numerowane cyframi rzymskimi **podhasła** o różnych cechach **gramatycznych**.	**gdzieś I** *pron.* (nieokreślone miejsce) somewhere [...] **II** *part.* pot. (w przybliżeniu) somewhere
Symbole gramatyczne opisujące wyraz hasłowy (patrz lista skrótów na str. vi-ix).	**gener|ować** *impf vt* to generate także przen. **genety|ka** *f* genetics
Forma podstawowa dla podhasła.	**gniewa|ć** *impf* **I** *vt* to anger **II gniewać się** [1] (złościć się) to be angry (**na kogoś** with a. at sb) [...]
Cyframi arabskimi wyróżniamy **znaczenia** danego wyrazu.	**gam|a** *f* [1] Muz. scale [2] przen. range
Kwalifikatory wskazują na ograniczenia w użyciu danego wyrazu, a także na dziedzinę życia, której on dotyczy (patrz lista skrótów na str. vi-ix). Kwalifikator może dotyczyć: hasła, podhasła, znaczenia, odpowiednika, zwrotu lub przykładowego zdania polskiego lub angielskiego.	**goryl** *m* [1] Zool. gorilla [2] pot. (o osobie) bodyguard; minder GB pot. **heroin|a**[2] *f* książk. [1] Teatr leading lady przest. [2] (powieści, filmu) heroine, main character
Minidefinicje pokazują różnice pomiędzy poszczególnymi znaczeniami lub odpowiednikami znaczenia.	**grusz|ka** *f* [1] (owoc) pear; (drzewo) pear tree [2] (kształt) bulb; **w kształcie ~ki** pear-shaped [3] Sport (worek treningowy) punchbag GB, punching bag US
Słowa, z którymi wyraz hasłowy typowo się łączy: • **podmioty** lub **dopełnienia** czasowników • **wyrazy określane** przez przymiotniki i przysłówki.	**gaworz|yć** *impf vi* *[niemowlę]* to babble **gło|sić** *impf vt* to promote *[pogląd, zasadę]*; to deliver *[kazanie]* [...] **gotowan|y** *adi.* *[warzywa, mięso]* cooked; *[mleko]* boiled

● ●

● ●

Angielski odpowiednik wyrazu hasłowego.	**grzał⏐ka** *f* immersion heater
Przybliżony odpowiednik wyrazu hasłowego.	**garmażeri⏐a** *f* ≈ delicatessen
Wyjaśnienie zastępujące odpowiednik.	**dyngus** *m Easter Monday custom of throwing water over people*
Wyjaśnienie precyzujące znaczenie odpowiednika.	**andrzej⏐ki** *plt* St Andrew's Eve party *(traditionally involving fortune telling)*
Przecinkami rozdzielono odpowiedniki w pełni **wymienne** lub należące do jednej z geograficznych odmian języka angielskiego. Informacje towarzyszące takiej parze dotyczą obu elementów. **Średnikami** rozdzielono odpowiedniki **różniące** się odcieniem znaczeniowym, łączliwością lub stylem.	**ginekolo⏐g** *m.* Med. gynaecologist GB, gynecologist US **aproba⏐ta** *f* książk. approval; approbation książk. **bezmyśln⏐y** *adi. [osoba, postępowanie]* mindless; *[naśladownictwo]* slavish
Schemat składniowy pokazuje przyimki, z jakimi wyraz hasłowy i jego odpowiednik najczęściej występują.	**gap⏐ić się** *impf v refl.* pot. to gawk pot. (**na coś** at sth)
Typowe **zwroty i przykładowe zdania** polskie.	**garaż⏐ować** *impf vt* to garage; ~**owany samochód** a car housed in a garage
Wymiennie używane części wyrażeń i odpowiedników.	**ależ** *part.* [1] (wyraz zdziwienia) but; ~ **tak!** but of course; ~ **nie** a. **skąd** a. **gdzie tam!** of course not!, why, no! [...] **golf¹** *m* [1] (sweter) polo neck a. roll-neck (sweater) GB [...]
Zwroty o różnym znaczeniu łączące się z wyrazem hasłowym oddzielono **ukośnikami**.	**artyleri⏐a** *f* (the) artillery; **ciężka/lekka** ~**a** heavy/light artillery
Elementy, które **można pominąć**.	**garbnik** *m* tanning agent; (roślinny) (vegetable) tannin
Wyodrębniona część hasła zawierająca **zestawienia** (terminy wielowyrazowe).	**gał⏐ka** *f* [1] (uchwyt, pokrętło) knob [2] (porcja) ~**ka lodów** a scoop of ice cream ❑ ~**ka oczna** Anat. eyeball
Wyodrębniona część hasła zawierająca **związki frazeologiczne** (idiomy).	**gap⏐a** *m, f* pot. butterfingers pot. ■ **jeździć na** ~**ę** pot. to dodge fares
Odsyłacz do innego hasła.	**gorzej** *adv. comp.* → **źle**
Oznaczenie **pozycji dopełnienia** wewnątrz grupy czasownikowej.	**gips⏐ować** *impf vt* [1] (tynkować) to plaster *[ścianę]*; to patch [sth] with plaster, to spackle US *[dziurę, pęknięcie]* [2] Med. to put [sth] in a (plaster) cast *[nogę, rękę]*

Jak korzystać ze słownika

Alfabetyczny układ haseł. Złożenia są oddzielnymi hasłami włączonymi w porządek alfabetyczny słownika.

oddity /'ɒdɪtɪ/ *n* osobliwość *f*
odd job *n* praca *f* dorywcza [...]

Homonimy traktowane są jako oddzielne hasła opatrzone cyfrą arabską podniesioną o pół wiersza.

foil[1] /fɔɪl/ *n* folia *f* aluminiowa; **silver ~** (wrapping) sreberko
foil[2] /fɔɪl/ *n* Sport floret *m*

Warianty pisowni brytyjskiej (GB) i amerykańskiej (US).

odour GB, **odor** US /'əʊdə(r)/ *n* woń *f*

Wymowa brytyjska i amerykańska w międzynarodowym alfabecie fonetycznym.

frizzy /'frɪzɪ/ *adj [hair]* mocno kręcony
frog /frɒg, US frɔːg/ *n* żaba *f*

Numerowane cyframi rzymskimi podhasła należące do różnych części mowy.

oblong /'ɒblɒŋ, US -lɔːŋ/ **I.** *n* wydłużony prostokąt *m*
II *adj* podłużny

Symbole części mowy (patrz lista skrótów na str. vi-ix).

orchestra /'ɔːkɪstrə/ *n* orkiestra *f*

Różnice w wymowie wyrazu hasłowego w zależności od części mowy.

overnight **I** /'əʊvənaɪt/ *adj* [1] *[journey, train]* nocny [...]
II /ˌəʊvə'naɪt/ *adv* [1] **to stay ~** zostać na noc [...]

Forma podstawowa, w której wyraz hasłowy występuje w danej kategorii gramatycznej.

fry /fraɪ/ **I** *vt* u|smażyć
II *vi* smażyć się
III **fried** *pp adj [fish, potatoes]* smażony

Warianty, w których wyraz hasłowy może występować.

obituary /ə'bɪtʃʊərɪ, US -tʃʊerɪ/ *n* (also **~ notice**) nekrolog *m*

Numery znaczeń – w obrębie podhasła cyframi arabskimi wyróżniamy różne znaczenia danego wyrazu.

outer /'aʊtə(r)/ *adj* [1] *[limit]* najdalszy [2] (outside) zewnętrzny

Kwalifikatory – wskazują na ograniczenia w użyciu danego wyrazu, a także na dziedzinę życia, której on dotyczy (patrz lista skrótów na str. vi-ix). Kwalifikator może dotyczyć: całego hasła, podhasła, znaczenia, odpowiednika, zwrotu lub przykładowego zdania.

gobbledygook /'gɒbldɪguːk/ *n* infml bełkot *m* infml
grate /greɪt/ **I** *n* ruszt *m*
II *vt* Culin ze|trzeć, u|trzeć, -cierać *[cheese, carrot]* [...]

Minidefinicje pokazujące różnice pomiędzy poszczególnymi znaczeniami lub różnice między odpowiednikami w obrębie jednego znaczenia.

oaf /əʊf/ *n* (clumsy) niezdara *m/f*, (loutish) prosta|k *m*, -czka *f*

Słowa, z którymi wyraz hasłowy typowo się łączy:
• podmioty lub dopełnienia czasowników lub zwrotów czasownikowych
• wyrazy określane przez przymiotniki i przysłówki oraz wyrażenia o funkcji przydawki lub okolicznika.

obsess /əb'ses/ *vt [fears]* prześladować; **to be ~ed by** or **with sb** mieć obsesję na punkcie kogoś
organize /'ɔːgənaɪz/ *vt* z|organizować *[event, meeting]*; u|porządkować *[books, papers]*; załatwi|ć -ać *[babysitter]*
organic /ɔː'gænɪk/ *adj* organiczny; *[produce, farming]* naturalny

Polski odpowiednik wyrazu hasłowego.

obedient /ə'biːdɪənt/ *adj* posłuszny

Przybliżony odpowiednik wyrazu hasłowego.

BA *n* = **Bachelor of Arts** ≈ licencjat *m* w dziedzinie nauk humanistycznych

Jak korzystać ze słownika

• •

Dodatkowe wyjaśnienie precyzujące znaczenie odpowiednika.

sitcom /'sɪtkɒm/ *n* infml sitcom *m* *(serial komediowy nagrywany z udziałem publiczności)*

Rodzaj gramatyczny polskich rzeczowników.

octave /'ɒktɪv/ *n* oktawa *f*

Męskie i żeńskie rzeczowniki osobowe.

teacher /'tiːtʃə(r)/ *n* nauczyciel *m*, -ka *f*

Postać dokonana i niedokonana polskich odpowiedników czasownikowych.

invest /ɪn'vest/ ▯ *vt* za|inwestować *[money]*; w|łożyć, -kładać *[effort]* (**in sth** w coś) [...]

Przecinkami rozdzielono **odpowiedniki w pełni wymienne. Średnikami** rozdzielono **odpowiedniki różniące się** odcieniem znaczeniowym, łączliwością lub stylem.

offer /'ɒfə(r), US 'ɔːf-/ *n* ▯ oferta *f*, propozycja *f* (**to do sth** zrobienia czegoś) [...]
sick note *n* infml (for school) usprawiedliwienie *n*; (for work) zwolnienie *n* lckarskic

Schemat składniowy – pokazuje przyimki, z jakimi wyraz hasłowy najczęściej występuje.

opportunity /ˌɒpə'tjuːnəti, US -'tuːn-/ *n* okazja *f*, sposobność *f* (**for sth** do czegoś) [...]

Typowe **zwroty i przykładowe zdania** angielskie. **Tylda** zastępuje w nich wyraz hasłowy.

jellied /'dʒelɪd/ *adj* ~ **eels** węgorz w galarecie

Tłumaczenia zwrotów i przykładowych zdań angielskich.

kite /kaɪt/ *n* latawiec *m*; **to fly a** ~ puszczać latawca

Wymiennie używane części wyrażeń.

jet-black /ˌdʒet'blæk/ *adj* *[hair]* kruczoczarny; *[eyes]* czarny jak węgiel or jak smoła

Zwroty o różnym znaczeniu łączące się z wyrazem hasłowym, a także ich tłumaczenia, oddzielono **ukośnikami.**

bearing /'beərɪŋ/ ▯ *n* ① (posture) postawa *f*; (behaviour) zachowanie *n* ② (relevance) **to have no/little** ~ **on sth** nie mieć związku/mieć niewielki związek z czymś [...]

Elementy, które **można pominąć** (w nawiasach okrągłych).

paintbox /'peɪntbɒks/ *n* pudło *n* farb (wodnych)

Oznaczenie **czasownika złożonego** (frazowego).

■ **opt out**: *[person, country]* wycof|ać, -ywać się

Wyodrębnienie różnych **kategorii czasownika złożonego**: nieprzechodniego, przechodniego rozłącznego, przechodniego nierozłącznego.

■ **open up**: ¶ ~ **up** ① *[gap]* powsta|ć, -wać ② *[person]* otw|orzyć, -ierać się ③ *[shop, branch]* rozpocz|ąć, -ynać działalność ¶ ~ **[sth] up** otw|orzyć -ierać

Pozycję **dopełnienia** w czasownikach frazowych przechodnich zaznaczono **zaimkiem w nawiasach kwadratowych.**

■ **search out**: ~ **[sb/sth] out**, ~ **out [sb/sth]** odszuk|ać, -iwać

Wyodrębniona część hasła zawierająca **związki frazeologiczne** (idiomy).

dagger /'dægə(r)/ *n* sztylet *m*
IDIOMS **to look** ~**s at sb** rzucać komuś mordercze spojrzenie

Odsyłacz **do innego hasła.**

CAD *n* → **computer-aided design**

Guide to the use of the Dictionary

Entries are listed in alphabetical order.

gaf|a *f* blunder, gaffe
gag *m* gag

Homographs are treated as separate entries differentiated by raised numbers.

gro|t[1] *m* (strzały) (arrow)head; (włóczni) tip
gro|t[2] *m* Żegl. mainsail

Feminine and masculine forms of nouns, as well as interchangeable variant forms are in some cases listed under the same entry.

geode|ta *m*, **~tka** *f* geodesist, (geodetic) surveyor
peł|zać, peł|znąć *impf vi* [1] *[gad, owad, osoba]* to crawl [...]
perli|czka, ~ca *f* guineafowl

One entry for both perfective and continuous aspects of a verb.

dobud|ować *pf* — **dobud|owywać** *impf vt* to build on, to add *[piętro, garaż]*

Verb senses with no aspectual pair are treated as homographs.

dochodzić[1] *impf→* **dojść**
dochodz|ić[2] *pf vi* [1] (prowadzić) *[droga, ulica]* to lead (**do czegoś** to sth) [...]

Vertical bar separates out the stem of a headword that is replaced with a swung dash within entry.

gotów|ka *f* cash; **zastrzyk ~ki** a cash injection; **w ~ce** in cash [...]

Pronunciation, where it does not follow general rules, is given in the International Phonetic Alphabet (IPA).

dancing /ˈdansiŋg/ *m* dance, dancing [...]

Roman numerals mark grammatical categories.

gdzieś I *pron.* (nieokreślone miejsce) somewhere [...]
II *part.* pot. (w przybliżeniu) somewhere

Abbreviated grammatical labels (see Abbreviations list on pages vi–ix).

gener|ować *impf vt* to generate także przen.
genety|ka *f* genetics

Base form of a sub-entry.

gniewa|ć *impf* [I] *vt* to anger
II gniewać się [1] (złościć się) to be angry (**na kogoś** with a, at sb) [...]

Arabic numbers indicate different senses within entry.

gam|a *f* [1] Muz. scale [2] przen. range

Register symbols and field labels indicate specialist or restricted use of a word (see Abbreviations list on pages vi–ix). Such symbols and labels may refer to an entire entry, sub-entry, sense, translation, or Polish or English examples.

goryl *m* [1] Zool. gorilla [2] pot. (o osobie) bodyguard; minder GB pot.
heroin|a[2] *f* książk. [1] Teatr leading lady przest. [2] (powieści, filmu) heroine, main character

Sense indicators illustrate differences between senses, or indicate alternative translations within a single sense.

grusz|ka *f* [1] (owoc) pear; (drzewo) pear tree [2] (kształt) bulb; **w kształcie ~ki** pear-shaped [3] Sport (worek treningowy) punchbag GB, punching bag US

Words typically used with a headword:
• object or subject collocates
• words modified by adjectives or adverbs.

gaworz|yć *impf vi [niemowlę]* to babble
gło|sić *impf vt* to promote *[pogląd, zasadę]*; to deliver *[kazanie]* [...]
gotowan|y *adi. [warzywa, mięso]* cooked; *[mleko]* boiled

English translation.

grzał|ka *f* immersion heater

≈ indicates approximate equivalence.

garmażeri|a *f* ≈ delicatessen

Explanatory gloss where there is no direct equivalent translation.

dyngus *m* *Easter Monday custom of throwing water over people*

Explanatory gloss for English speaker.

andrzej|ki *plt* St Andrew's Eve party *(traditionally involving fortune telling)*

Commas separate equivalent (fully interchangeable) translations or regional variations. Any syntax or collocation information given refers to all variants or translations.
Semicolons separate alternative translations (of different meaning, collocation pattern or register).

ginekolo|g *m* Med. gynaecologist GB, gynecologist US
aproba|ta *f* książk. approval; approbation książk.
bezmyśln|y *adi.* *[osoba, postępowanie]* mindless; *[naśladownictwo]* slavish

Syntactical pattern showing typical prepositions used with headword.

gap|ić się *impf v refl.* pot. to gawk pot. **(na coś** at sth)

Example of a Polish collocate.
Swung dash substitutes headword in examples.

garaż|ować *impf vt* to garage; **~owany samochód** a car housed in a garage

Interchangeable forms of translation.

ależ *part.* 1 (wyraz zdziwienia) but; **~ tak!** but of course; **~ nie** a. **skąd** a. **gdzie tam!** of course not!, why, no! [...]
golf¹ *m* 1 (sweter) polo neck a. roll-neck (sweater) GB [...]

Phrases syntactically interchangeable, but with different meanings, are separated with slashes.

artyleri|a *f* (the) artillery; **ciężka/lekka ~a** heavy/light artillery

Translation elements that can be omitted.

garbnik *m* tanning agent; (roślinny) (vegetable) tannin

Separate compound block within entry.

gał|ka *f* 1 (uchwyt, pokrętło) knob 2 (porcja) **~ka lodów** a scoop of ice cream
❏ **~ka oczna** Anat. eyeball

Separate idiom block within entry.

gap|a *m, f* pot. butterfingers pot.
■ **jeździć na ~ę** pot. to dodge fares

Cross-reference to another headword.

gorzej *adv. comp.* → **źle**

Object position indicator within English verb group.

gips|ować *impf vt* 1 (tynkować) to plaster *[ścianę]*; to patch [sth] with plaster, to spackle US *[dziurę, pęknięcie]* 2 Med. to put [sth] in a (plaster) cast *[nogę, rękę]*

Entries are listed in alphabetical order.
Compounds are treated as separate entries,
and appear in alphabetical order.

oddity /'ɒdɪtɪ/ *n* osobliwość *f*
odd job *n* praca *f* dorywcza [...]

Homographs are treated as separate entries
differentiated by raised numbers.

foil[1] /fɔɪl/ *n* folia *f* aluminiowa; **silver ~** (wrapping) sreberko
foil[2] /fɔɪl/ *n* Sport floret *m*

British (GB) and North American (US) variant spellings.

odour GB, **odor** US /'əʊdə(r)/ *n* woń *f*

British and North American pronunciation given in the International Phonetic Alphabet (IPA).

frizzy /'frɪzɪ/ *adj [hair]* mocno kręcony
frog /frɒg, US frɔːg/ *n* żaba *f*

Roman numerals are used as part of speech indicators.

oblong /'ɒblɒŋ, US -lɔːŋ/ **I** *n* wydłużony prostokąt *m*
II *adj* podłużny

Abbreviated part of speech
(see Abbreviations list on pages vi–ix).

orchestra /'ɔːkɪstrə/ *n* orkiestra *f*

Variant pronunciations for different parts of speech.

overnight **I** /'əʊvənaɪt/ *adj* [1] *[journey, train]* nocny [...]
II /əʊvə'naɪt/ *adv* [1] **to stay ~** zostać na noc [...]

Base form is given for each grammatical category of headword.

fry /fraɪ/ **I** *vt* u|smażyć
II *vi* smażyć się
III **fried** *pp adj [fish, potatoes]* smażony

Variant use of headword.

obituary /ə'bɪtʃʊərɪ, US -tʃʊerɪ/ *n* (also **~ notice**) nekrolog *m*

Arabic numbers indicate different senses within entry.

outer /'aʊtə(r)/ *adj* [1] *[limit]* najdalszy [2] (outside) zewnętrzny

Register symbols and field labels indicate specialist or restricted use of word (see Abbreviations list on pages vi–ix). Such symbols and labels may refer to entire entry, sub-entry, sense, translation, or Polish or English examples.

gobbledygook /'gɒbldɪguːk/ *n* infml bełkot *m* infml
grate /greɪt/ **I** *n* ruszt *m*
II *vt* Culin ze|trzeć, u|trzeć, -cierać *[cheese, carrot]* [...]

Sense indicators illustrate differences between senses, or indicate alternative translations within one sense.

oaf /əʊf/ *n* (clumsy) niezdara *m/f*; (loutish) prosta|k *m*, -czka *f*

Words typically used with a headword:
• object or subject collocates
• words modified by adjectives or adverbs.

obsess /əb'ses/ *vt [fears]* prześladować; **to be ~ed by** or **with sb** mieć obsesję na punkcie kogoś
organize /'ɔːgənaɪz/ *vt* z|organizować *[event, meeting]*; u|porządkować *[books, papers]*; załatwi|ć -ać *[babysitter]*
organic /ɔː'gænɪk/ *adj* organiczny; *[produce, farming]* naturalny

Polish translation of headword.

obedient /ə'biːdɪənt/ *adj* posłuszny

≈ indicates approximate equivalence.

BA *n* = **Bachelor of Arts** ≈ licencjat *m* w dziedzinie nauk humanistycznych

Explanatory gloss where there is no direct translation equivalent.	**sitcom** /ˈsɪtkɒm/ *n* infml sitcom *m* *(serial komediowy nagrywany z udziałem publiczności)*
Gender of translation.	**octave** /ˈɒktɪv/ *n* oktawa *f*
Masculine and feminine form of translation.	**teacher** /ˈtiːtʃə(r)/ *n* nauczyciel *m*, -ka *f*
Perfective and imperfective aspects of Polish verbs.	**invest** /ɪnˈvest/ **[]** *vt* zainwestować *[money]*; włożyć, -kładać *[effort]* (**in sth** w coś) [...]
Commas separate equivalent (fully interchangeable) translations.	**offer** /ˈɒfə(r), US ˈɔːf-/ *n* **[]** oferta *f*, propozycja *f* (**to do sth** zrobienia czegoś) [...]
Semicolons separate alternative translations (of different meaning, collocation pattern or register).	**sick note** *n* infml (for school) usprawiedliwienie *n*; (for work) zwolnienie *n* lekarskie
Syntactical pattern showing typical prepositions used with headword.	**opportunity** /ˌɒpəˈtjuːnətɪ, US -ˈtuːn-/ *n* okazja *f*, sposobność *f* (**for sth** do czegoś) [...]
Example of English collocate. Swung dash substitutes headword in examples.	**jellied** /ˈdʒelɪd/ *adj* ~ **eels** węgorz w galarecie
Translations of English examples.	**kite** /kaɪt/ *n* latawiec *m*; **to fly a** ~ puszczać latawca
Interchangeable forms of translation.	**jet-black** /ˌdʒetˈblæk/ *adj* *[hair]* kruczoczarny; *[eyes]* czarny jak węgiel or jak smoła
Phrases and their translations, syntactically interchangeable but of different meanings, are separated with slashes.	**bearing** /ˈbeərɪŋ/ **[]** *n* [1] (posture) postawa *f*; (behaviour) zachowanie *n* [2] (relevance) **to have no/little** ~ **on sth** nie mieć związku/mieć niewielki związek z czymś [...]
Translation elements that can be omitted.	**paintbox** /ˈpeɪntbɒks/ *n* pudło *n* farb (wodnych)
Symbol used to denote phrasal verbs.	■ **opt out**: *[person, country]* wycof|ać, -ywać się
Transitive and intransitive forms of phrasal verbs.	■ **open up**: ¶ ~ **up** [1] *[gap]* powsta|ć, -wać [2] *[person]* otw|orzyć, -ierać się [3] *[shop, branch]* rozpocz|ąć, -ynać działalność ¶ ~ **[sth] up** otw|orzyć -ierać
Pronouns in square brackets denote transitive phrasal verb objects.	■ **search out**: ~ **[sb/sth] out**, ~ **out [sb/sth]** odszuk|ać, -iwać
Idioms section.	**dagger** /ˈdægə(r)/ *n* sztylet *m* IDIOMS **to look** ~**s at sb** rzucać komuś mordercze spojrzenie
Cross-reference to another headword.	**CAD** *n* → **computer-aided design**

Numbers

Cardinal numbers	Liczebniki główne	Ordinal numbers	Liczebniki porządkowe
1 one	1 jeden	1st first	1. pierwszy
2 two	2 dwa	2nd second	2. drugi
3 three	3 trzy	3rd third	3. trzeci
4 four	4 cztery	4th fourth	4. czwarty
5 five	5 pięć	5th fifth	5. piąty
6 six	6 sześć	6th sixth	6. szósty
7 seven	7 siedem	7th seventh	7. siódmy
8 eight	8 osiem	8th eighth	8. ósmy
9 nine	9 dziewięć	9th ninth	9. dziewiąty
10 ten	10 dziesięć	10th tenth	10. dziesiąty
11 eleven	11 jedenaście	11th eleventh	11. jedenasty
12 twelve	12 dwanaście	12th twelfth	12. dwunasty
13 thirteen	13 trzynaście	13th thirteenth	13. trzynasty
14 fourteen	14 czternaście	14th fourteenth	14. czternasty
15 fifteen	15 piętnaście	15th fifteenth	15. piętnasty
16 sixteen	16 szesnaście	16th sixteenth	16. szesnasty
17 seventeen	17 siedemnaście	17th seventeenth	17. siedemnasty
18 eighteen	18 osiemnaście	18th eighteenth	18. osiemnasty
19 nineteen	19 dziewiętnaście	19th nineteenth	19. dziewiętnasty
20 twenty	20 dwadzieścia	20th twentieth	20. dwudziesty
21 twenty-one	21 dwadzieścia jeden	21st twenty-first	21. dwudziesty pierwszy
30 thirty	30 trzydzieści	30th thirtieth	30. trzydziesty
40 forty	40 czterdzieści	40th fortieth	40. czterdziesty
50 fifty	50 pięćdziesiąt	50th fiftieth	50. pięćdziesiąty
60 sixty	60 sześćdziesiąt	60th sixtieth	60. sześćdziesiąty
70 seventy	70 siedemdziesiąt	70th seventieth	70. siedemdziesiąty
80 eighty	80 osiemdziesiąt	80th eightieth	80. osiemdziesiąty
90 ninety	90 dziewięćdziesiąt	90th ninetieth	90. dziewięćdziesiąty
100 one hundred	100 sto	100th [one] hundredth	100. setny
101 one hundred and one	101 sto jeden	101st [one] hundred and first	101. sto pierwszy
1,000 one thousand	1 000 tysiąc	1,000th [one] thousandth	1 000. tysięczny
1,001 one thousand and one	1 001 tysiąc jeden	1,001st one thousand and first	1 001. tysiąc pierwszy
10,000 ten thousand	10 000 dziesięć tysięcy	10,000th ten thousandth	10 000. dziesięciotysięczny
13,438 thirteen thousand, four hundred and thirty-eight	13 438 trzynaście tysięcy czterysta trzydzieści osiem	13,438th thirteen thousand, four hundred and thirty-eighth	13 438. trzynaście tysięcy czterysta trzydziesty ósmy
100,000 one hundred thousand	100 000 sto tysięcy	100,000th [one] hundred thousandth	100 000. stutysięczny
1,000,000 one million	1 000 000 milion	1,000,000th [one] millionth	1 000 000. milionowy
2,000,000 two million	2 000 000 dwa miliony	2,000,000th two millionth	2 000 000. dwumilionowy
1,000,000,000 one thousand million (Brit.); one billion (Amer.)	1 000 000 000 miliard	1,000,000,000th [one] thousand millionth (Brit.); one billionth (Amer.)	1 000 000 000. miliardowy

A

A, a *n inv.* ① (litera) A, a ② Muz. A
- **od a do zet** from A to Z; **znać coś od a do z** to know something inside out a. from beginning to end

a [] *conj.* ① (przyłączające) and; **między Warszawą a Krakowem** between Warsaw and Cracow; **dziś, a nie jutro** today, (and) not tomorrow; **ja idę, a ty?** I'm going, what about you? ② (przeciwstawne) while, whereas; **masz osiemnaście lat, a on dopiero pięć** you're eighteen, whereas a. while he's only five ③ (w powtórzeniach) **nic a nic z tego nie rozumiem** I don't understand a bit of it; **w takim a takim dniu, o tej a o tej godzinie** on such-and-such a day, at such-and-such a time
[] *part.* ① (wprowadzające) and; **a jak tam twoje egzaminy?** and how are your exams going?; **a widzisz!** (you) see?; **a niech sobie idzie** oh, let him/her go ② (emfatyczne) **a to łajdak!** what a swine! pot.; **a nie mówiłem?** didn't I say so?, I told you (so)!

abażu|r *m* (lamp)shade

abdykacj|a *f* abdication

abdyk|ować *pf, impf vi* to abdicate

abecad|ło *n* ① (the) alphabet ② przen. the ABC

abiturien|t *m*, **~tka** *f* a secondary-school pupil *about to take his/her school-leaving exams*

abonamen|t *m* (telefoniczny) rental (charge), standing charge; (telewizyjny) licence fee GB, license fee US; (na koncerty, mecze) season ticket; **~t na coś** subscription to sth

abonen|t *m*, **~tka** *f* subscriber

abon|ować *impf vt* to subscribe (**coś** to sth)

aborcj|a *f* abortion

absencj|a *f* książk. absence; **~a w szkole** absence from school; **wysoka ~a uczniów** a high rate of non-attendance among pupils; **~a nieusprawied-liwiona** absenteeism

absolutnie *adv., part., inter.* absolutely

absolutn|y *adi.* ① *[cisza, zaufanie]* absolute; **masz ~ą rację** you are absolutely right ② Polit. *[monarchia, władca]* absolute

absolwen|t *m* (szkoły średniej) former pupil GB, alumnus US; (uczelni) graduate; **~ci kursu komputerowego** those who have completed a computer course

absolwent|ka *f* (szkoły średniej) former pupil GB, alumna US; (uczelni) graduate

absorb|ować *impf vt* to absorb *[osobę]*; **~ować kogoś swoimi sprawami** to occupy sb with one's problems; **~ować czyjeś myśli** to occupy sb's mind a. thoughts; **~ująca rozmowa** an absorbing conversation

abstrah|ować *impf vi* to disregard, to leave aside (**od czegoś** sth); **~ując od...** leaving aside..., quite apart from...

abstrakcj|a *f* abstraction

abstrakcyjn|y *adi.* abstract

abstynencj|a *f* abstinence; (od alkoholu) abstinence from alcohol, teetotalism

abstynen|t *m*, **~tka** *f* teetotaller, teetotaler US

absur|d [] *m* absurdity; **doprowadzić coś do ~du** to take sth to absurd levels
[] *inter.* that's absurd!

absurdaln|y *adi.* absurd

aby [] *conj.* książk. → **żeby**
[] *part.* (wyrażająca wątpliwość) **czy te informacje są ~ pewne?** is this information really reliable?; **czy on ~ się nie przeziębił?** are you sure he hasn't caught a cold?
- **aby-aby** pot. (byle jak) any old how pot.; **na nasze pytania odpowiadał ~ zbyć** pot. he answered our questions offhandedly

aczkolwiek *conj.* książk. although, though; albeit książk.

adaptacj|a *f* ① (utworu) adaptation; (budynku) conversion (**na coś** into sth) ② (przystosowanie) adaptation (**do czegoś** to sth)

adapte|r *m* record player

adapt|ować *pf, impf* [] *vt* to adapt *[utwór]*; to convert *[budynek]* (**na coś** into sth); **~ować powieść na scenę** to adapt a novel for the stage
[] **adaptować się** to adapt (oneself), to adjust (**do czegoś** to sth)

adekwatn|y *adi.* książk. appropriate (**do czegoś** to sth); (o ilości) commensurate, proportional (**do czegoś** to sth)

adidas *m* trainer GB, sneaker US

administracj|a *f* ① (zarządzanie) (the) management, (the) administration ② (zespół) (the) management, (the) administration; **~a państwowa** the civil service ③ Polit. (w USA) administration, government; **~a Reagana** the Reagan administration

administracyjn|y *adi.* administrative

administrato|r *m*, **~rka** *f* administrator, manager

administr|ować *impf vt* to administer, to manage (**czymś** sth)

admira|ł *m* ① Wojsk. admiral ② Zool. red admiral

adnotacj|a *f* książk. annotation książk.; **robić ~e do tekstu** to annotate a text

adopcj|a *f* adoption

adopt|ować *pf, impf vt* to adopt *[dziecko]*

adorato|r *m*, **~rka** *f* książk. admirer

adrenalin|a *f* Med. adrenalin(e)

adres *m* address; **~ domowy** home address; **~ e--mailowy** Komput. e-mail address; **~ zwrotny** return address; **zmieniać ~** to move (house) ∎ **robić aluzje pod czyimś ~em** to make insinuations about sb; **z tymi pretensjami trafiłeś pod niewłaściwy ~** pot. you've come to the wrong place a. you're knocking at the wrong door with those complaints

adresa|t *m*, **~tka** *f* addressee

adres|ować *impf vt* to address *[list, paczkę, uwagę]* (**do kogoś** to sb)

adresow|y *adi. [dane, książka]* address; **kod ~y** postcode GB, zip code US

adwen|t *m* Advent

adwokac|ki *adi. [praktyka, zawód]* legal; **kancelaria ~ka** law firm

adwoka|t *m* (w sądzie) barrister GB, (trial) lawyer US; (doradca) lawyer, solicitor GB, attorney (at law) US; **~t z urzędu** court-appointed lawyer GB, public defender US ∎ **~t diabła** devil's advocate

aerobik *m* aerobics

aerozol *m* ① (substancja) aerosol ② pot. (pojemnik) spray, aerosol; **dezodorant w ~u** spray deodorant

afek|t *m* **w ~cie** in a fit of passion, in the heat of the moment; **zabójstwo w ~cie** crime of passion, crime passionnel

afe|ra *f* scandal; (gospodarcza) swindle, fraud; **ale ~ra!** pot. what a busines! pot.

aferzy|sta *m*, **~stka** *f* swindler

afisz *m* poster; **nie schodzić z ~a** to be running; **wejść na ~** *[sztuka]* to open, to be staged; *[film]* to be out, to be on release; **zdjąć coś z ~a** to take sth off *[sztukę]*; to withdraw sth (from general release) *[film]*

aga|t *m* agate

agencj|a *f* agency; (przedstawicielstwo) office, agent(s); **~a prasowa** news a. press agency

agen|da *f* branch (office)

agen|t *m*, **~tka** *f* ① (reklamowy) agent; (handlowy) representative; rep pot. ② (szpieg) secret agent

agitacj|a *f* (prasowa) campaigning, publicity; (wyborcza) canvassing; **prowadzić ~ę na rzecz czegoś/ przeciwko czemuś** to campaign a. agitate for/ against sth

agitato|r *m*, **~rka** *f* Polit. campaigner, agitator

agit|ować *impf* ⓘ *vt* to canvass *[wyborców]*; **~ować ludzi do głosowania** to urge people to vote ⓘ *vi* to campaign, to agitate (**za czymś/przeciwko czemuś** for/against sth)

aglomeracj|a *f* książk. ① (miasto) urban(ized) area, conurbation ② (skupisko) agglomeration

agoni|a *f* Med. death throes także przen.

agraf|ka *f* safety pin; **zapięty na ~kę** fastened with a safety pin

agrega|t *m* Techn. unit; **~t chłodniczy** refrigeration unit

agresj|a *f* ① aggression; **wyładować ~ę na kimś** to take out one's anger on sb ② Polit. invasion, aggression

agre|st *m* gooseberry

agresywn|y *adi. grad. [postawa, ton, polityka]* aggressive

AIDS */ejts/ m inv., n inv.* Med. AIDS; **chorzy na ~** AIDS victims

ajencj|a *f* ① (placówki handlowej, usługowej) concession; **wziąć sklep w ~ę** to obtain a concession to run a shop ② (agencja) branch (office), agent(s)

ajen|t *m*, **~tka** *f* ① (placówki handlowej, usługowej) concessionaire, concession holder ② (ubezpieczeniowy, handlowy) agent

akacj|a *f* acacia

akademi|a *f* ① (instytucja) academy; **Polska Akademia Nauk** the Polish Academy of Science(s) ② Uniw. college, academy; **~a medyczna/wojskowa** medical/military college; **Akademia Sztuk Pięknych** Academy of Fine Arts ③ (uroczystość) celebration(s)

akademic|ki *adi. [środowisko]* academic; *[nauczyciel, zajęcia]* university; *[klub]* students'; *[rozważania, spory]* academic; **młodzież ~ka** (university) students

akademi|k *m* pot. hall (of residence) GB, student hostel GB, dorm US pot.

akapi|t *m* paragraph; **zacząć od nowego ~tu** to start a new paragraph

akcen|t *m* ① Jęz. (przycisk) stress, accent; (znak graficzny) accent; **~t pada na przedostatnią sylabę** the stress falls on the penultimate syllable ② (wymowa) accent; **mówić z obcym ~tem** to speak with a foreign accent ③ (nacisk) emphasis, stress; **kłaść na coś ~t** to emphasize sth, to lay stress on sth ④ (element) note, tone; **główny ~t obchodów** the main focus of the celebrations ⑤ Muz. accent, stress

akcent|ować *impf vt* ① Jęz., Muz. to stress, to accent; **sylaba ~owana/nieakcentowana** a stressed/an unstressed syllable ② przen. to emphasize, to accentuate

akcept|ować *impf vt* książk. (zatwierdzić) to accept, to approve *[dokument, kandydaturę]*; (zgadzać się) to accept, to agree to *[plan, warunki]*

akcesori|a *plt* accessories

akcj|a *f* ⊡ (działanie) campaign (**na rzecz czegoś/ przeciwko czemuś** for/against sth); ~**a charytatywna** charity drive; ~**a protestacyjna** protest campaign; ~**a ratunkowa** rescue operation a. mission; ~**a strajkowa** industrial action GB ② Wojsk. operation, action; ~**a bojowa** combat mission ③ Sport attack; ~**a na bramkę przeciwnika** an attack on the opponents' goal ④ (w filmie, książce) action, plot; ~**a powieści rozgrywa się w Paryżu** the novel is set in Paris ⑤ Ekon. share; **jego** ~**e idą w górę/spadają** przen. he's on the way up/down

akcjonariusz *m*, ~**ka** *f* shareholder

akcyjn|y *adi.* Ekon. *[spółka]* joint-stock; *[fundusz]* share

akcyz|a *f* Ekon. excise (duty) (**na coś** on sth)

aklimatyzacj|a *f* acclimatization, acclimation US

aklimatyz|ować się *impf v refl.* to acclimatize, to acclimate US

akompaniamen|t *m* Muz. accompaniment także przen.; **przy** ~**cie gitary** to the accompaniment of a guitar

akompaniato|r *m*, ~**rka** *f* Muz. accompanist

akompani|ować *impf vi* Muz. to accompany (**komuś** sb)

akor|d *m* ⊡ Muz. chord ② Ekon. piecework; **pracować na** ~**d** to do piecework, to be on piecework

akordeon *m* accordion

akredytacj|a *f* accreditation

akredyt|ować *pf, impf vt* to accredit; ~**owany przy ONZ** accredited to the UN

akrobacj|a *f* acrobatic feat, acrobatic manoeuvre GB a. maneuver US; ~**e lotnicze** aerial acrobatics

akroba|ta *m*, ~**tka** *f* acrobat

aksami|t *m* velvet

aksamitn|y *adi.* *[sukienka, wstążka]* velvet; *[skóra, głos]* velvet(y)

ak|t ⫿ *m* ⊡ (czyn) act; **akt agresji** an act of aggression ② (dokument) certificate, deed; **akt ślubu/urodzenia/zgonu** marriage/birth/death certificate; **akt darowizny/własności** deed of gift/ ownership; **akt oskarżenia** bill of indictment ③ (in theatre) act; **komedia w pięciu aktach** a comedy in five acts ④ Szt. nude

⫿⫿ **akta** *plt* records, files; (dotyczące osoby, sprawy) dossier

akto|r *m* actor

aktor|ka *f* actress

aktors|ki *adi.* *[kariera, warsztat, zdolności]* acting; **szkoła** ~**ka** drama school, school of acting

aktorstw|o *n* acting, the acting profession

aktów|ka *f* document case

aktualnoś|ć ⫿ *f* topicality, relevance; **stracić** ~**ć** a. **na** ~**ci** to go out of date

⫿⫿ **aktualności** *plt* (polityczne, prasowe) current events, news

aktualn|y ⫿ *adi. grad.* (na czasie) topical; **wciąż** ~**y film** a film that is still relevant (today)

⫿⫿ *adi.* ⊡ (ważny) *[umowa]* valid; **czy oferta jest** ~**a?** is the offer still standing? ② (teraźniejszy) *[cena, moda, potrzeby]* current, present; ~**y mistrz świata** current a. reigning world champion

aktyw|a *plt* Ekon. assets

aktywacj|a *f* activation

aktywnoś|ć *f* activity, activeness

aktywn|y *adi.* active

akumulacj|a *f* accumulation

akumulato|r *m* Elektr. storage battery, accumulator GB; Aut. battery

akurat ⫿ *adv.* just; ~ **wróciliśmy** we've just come back

⫿⫿ *part.* exactly, just; **czemu** ~ **my?** pot. why us exactly?; **w tym** ~ **przypadku** in this particular case

⫿⫿⫿ *inter.* (yeah,) sure!, yeah, right! pot., iron.

akustyczn|y *adi.* ⊡ *[właściwości, instrument, płytka]* acoustic; *[izolacja]* sound ② pot. *[ściany]* paperthin

akusty|ka *f* acoustics

akusze|rka *f* przest. midwife

akwarel|a *f* watercolour GB, watercolor US

akwari|um *n* aquarium

akwen *m* body of water

akwizycj|a *f* canvassing (for business), soliciting custom

akwizyto|r *m*, ~**rka** *f* salesperson, sales representative

alarm *m* ⊡ (sygnał) alarm; **fałszywy** ~ false alarm także przen.; ~ **lotniczy** air-raid warning ② (urządzenie) alarm; ~ **przeciwwłamaniowy/samochodowy** burglar/car alarm ③ (stan gotowości) alert; ~ **powodziowy** flood alert; ~ **bojowy** battle a. combat alert; ~ **bombowy** bomb scare; ~ **próbny** emergency drill; **bić** a. **uderzać na** ~ to sound the alarm także przen.; **podnieść** ~ przen. to raise a. give the alarm

alarm|ować *impf vt* ⊡ (wzywać) to call *[policję, straż pożarną]*; to place a. put *[sb]* on alert *[wojsko]* ② (ostrzegać) to alarm *[opinię publiczną]*

alarmow|y *adi. [sygnał, system]* alarm; **telefony** ~**e** emergency telephone numbers

albinos *m*, ~**ka** *f* albino

albo ⫿ *coni.* or; **dziś** ~ **jutro** today or tomorrow; ~**... ~** either... or; ~ **on, ~ ja** it's either him or me; **tysiąc złotych** ~ **więcej** a thousand zlotys or more; ~ **i lepiej** pot. or (even) more; ~ **i nie** or not; ~ **co** or something; ~ **co?** pot. or what? pot.; ~ **też** or else; **zabieraj się do pracy** ~ **pożałujesz** get to work, or (else) you'll be sorry

⫿⫿ *part.* pot. (czyż) ~ **on cokolwiek z tego rozumie?** can he really understand any of this?; ~ **ja wiem?** I don't really know; „**tylko tyle?**" – „~ **to mało?**" 'only so much?' – 'why, isn't that enough?'

III albo, albo *inter.* (either) one thing or the other!, it's either-or!

albowiem *coni.* książk. because, since; for książk.

album *m* album

ale I *coni.* but; **powiem ci,** ~ **nie teraz** I'll tell you, but not now; **nie tylko...,** ~ **i...** not only..., but also...; **niewiarygodne,** ~ **prawdziwe** it's incredible, but a. yet true; **nikt,** ~ **to nikt** nobody, but nobody; **wcale,** ~ **to wcale mi się to nie podoba** I don't like it in the least little bit **II** *part.* ① (wyraz zdziwienia) but; ~ **dlaczego?** but why?; ~ **skąd** a. **gdzie tam!** of course not!, why, no! ② (emfatyczne) ~ **samochód!** what a car!, that's some car! pot.; ~ **głupiec ze mnie!** what a fool I am!; ~ **mnie urządziłeś!** you've really landed me in it! pot. **III** *n inv.* (zastrzeżenie) but; **tylko bez żadnych** ~ no buts, now!; **mam wobec niej jedno** ~ I have one reservation about her ■ ~, ~! hold a. hang on! pot.; ~ **heca** a. **numer!** pot. what a gas! a. scream! pot.; ~ **już!** pot. right now!, pronto! pot.

ale|ja *f* (w parku) alley; (w mieście) avenue, boulevard

alej|ka *f* path

alergi|a *f* allergy także przen. (**na coś** to sth)

alergiczn|y *adi.* allergic

alergi|k *m,* ~**czka** *f* allergy sufferer

ależ *part.* ① (wyraz zdziwienia) but; ~ **tak!** but of course; ~ **nie** a. **skąd** a. **gdzie tam!** of course not!, why, no!; ~ **to absurd!** but that's absurd!; why, that's absurd! ② (emfatyczne) ~ **ona piękna!** she's so beautiful!; ~ **się umorusał!** (but) he's absolutely filthy!

alfabe|t *m* alphabet; ~**t Braille'a** the Braille alphabet; ~**t głuchoniemych** sign language; ~**t Morse'a** the Morse code; **według** ~**tu** in alphabetical order, alphabetically

alfabetyczn|y *adi.* alphabetical

algebra *f* algebra

alibi *n inv.* alibi

aligato|r *m* Zool. alligator

aliment|y *plt* (separate) maintenance GB, alimony US; **zasądzić** ~**y na rzecz kogoś** to award sb alimony

alkohol *m* alcohol, alcoholic drink a. beverage; **być pod wpływem** ~**u** to be under the influence of alcohol

alkoholi|k *m,* ~**czka** *f* alcoholic

alkoholizm *m* alcoholism

alkoholow|y *adi.* alcoholic

alkoma|t *m* breathalyser GB, Breathalyzer® US

aloes *m* Bot. aloe

alpejs|ki *adi.* ① [kraj] Alpine; [krajobraz] alpine ② Sport [narciarstwo, konkurencje] alpine, downhill

alpini|sta *m,* ~**stka** *f* (mountain) climber, mountaineer

alpinizm *m* mountaineering, mountain-climbing

al|t *m* Muz. alto

altan|a *f* (domek) garden house; (ażurowa) arbour GB, arbor US

alternatyw|a *f* alternative (**dla czegoś** to sth)

alternatywn|y *adi.* [medycyna, teatr] alternative

altów|ka *f* Muz. viola

altrui|sta *m,* ~**stka** *f* książk. altruist

altruistyczn|y *adi.* książk. altruistic

altruizm *m* książk. altruism

aluminium *n inv.* aluminium GB, aluminum US

aluzj|a *f* allusion, hint; **robić** ~**ę do czegoś** to allude to sth, to hint at sth

aman|t *m,* ~**tka** *f* Kino, Teatr romantic lead

amato|r *m,* ~**rka** *f* ① (miłośnik) lover, enthusiast ② (nieprofesjonalista) amateur; **fotograf** ~**r** an amateur photographer ③ Sport amateur, non-professional ④ (chętny) customer; **znalazłem** ~**ra na nasz samochód** I've found a buyer for the car

amators|ki *adi.* ① (niezawodowy) [sport, teatr] amateur ② (niefachowy) amateur, amateurish; **po** ~**ku** amateurishly

amatorstw|o *n* amateurism

ambasa|da *f* embassy

ambasado|r *m* ambassador także przen.; ~**r Francji w Polsce** the French ambassador to Poland

ambicj|a *f* ① (duma) pride, self-respect; **zranić** a. **urazić czyjąś** ~**ę** to hurt sb's pride ② (aspiracje) ambition; **mieć** ~**ę dokonania czegoś** a. **żeby czegoś dokonać** to have an ambition to do sth

ambitn|y *adi. grad.* [osoba, plan, repertuar] ambitious

ambon|a *f* pulpit

ambulans *m* Med. ambulance

ambulatori|um *n* outpatient a. outpatients' clinic

ameb|a *f* Zool. amoeba, ameba US

amen *inter.* amen ■ **jak** ~ **w pacierzu** pot. as sure as anything; **na** ~ pot. absolutely, completely

amety|st *m* amethyst

amfetamin|a *f* amphetamine

amnesti|a *f* amnesty

amnezj|a *f* amnesia

amok *m* **dostać** ~**u** a. **wpaść w** ~ to run amok; **w** ~**u** in a frenzy

amortyzacj|a *f* ① Ekon. depreciation, amortization ② Techn. (shock) absorption

amortyz|ować *impf* **I** *vt* ① Ekon. to amortize, to write off [koszty] ② Techn. to cushion [uderzenie, wstrząs]; to break [upadek] **II amortyzować się** Ekon. [maszyna, urządzenie] to pay for itself

amor|y *plt* pot., żart. flirtation

amplitu|da *f* ① amplitude; ~**da dobowa** Meteo. diurnal range ② przen. fluctuation (**czegoś** of a. in sth)

ampuł|ka *f* ampoule

amputacj|a *f* amputation

amput|ować *pf, impf vt* to amputate *[rękę, nogę]*; to remove *[pierś]*

amunicj|a *f* ammunition; **ostra** ~a live ammunition; **ślepa** ~a blank cartridges

anachroniczn|y *adi.* anachronistic

anachronizm *m* anachronism

anakon|da *f* Zool. anaconda

analfabe|ta *m*, ~**tka** *f* ① illiterate; ~**ci** the illiterate; **wtórny** ~**ta** adult a. functional illiterate ② przen. ignoramus

analfabetyzm *m* ① illiteracy ② przen. ignorance

analityczn|y *adi. [metoda, podejście, umysł]* analytical; *[język]* analytic(al)

anality|k *m*, ~**czka** *f* analyst

analiz|a *f* analysis

analiz|ować *impf vt* to analyse GB, to analyze US

analogi|a *f* analogy; **przez** ~**ę** by (way of) analogy

analogiczn|y *adi.* analogous (**do czegoś** to a. with sth)

ananas *m* ① Bot. pineapple ② pot. (osoba) scamp pot.

anarchi|a *f* anarchy

anarchiczn|y *adi.* anarchic

anarchi|sta *m*, ~**stka** *f* anarchist

anatomi|a *f* anatomy

anatomiczn|y *adi.* anatomical

andru|t *m* wafer

andrzej|ki *plt* St Andrew's Eve party *(traditionally involving fortune telling)*

anegdo|ta *f* anecdote

aneks *m* ① (w książce) appendix; (do dokumentu) annexe GB, annex US ② (budynek) annexe GB, annex US; ~ **jadalny/kuchenny** dinette/kitchenette, dining/kitchen annexe

anemi|a *f* anaemia, anemia US

anemiczn|y *adi.* anaemic GB, anemic US także przen.

anestezjolo|g *m* anaesthetist GB, anesthetist US

anestezjologi|a *f* anaesthesiology GB, anesthesiology US

angaż|ować *impf* **Ⅰ** *vt* ① (zatrudnić) to employ, to engage *[pracownika]* ② (zajmować) to engage, to absorb *[osobę, uwagę]* ③ (włączać) to involve *[instytucję, osobę]* (**w coś** in sth)
Ⅱ angażować się ① (zatrudnić się) to take up a job ② (włączać się) to become involved (**w coś** in sth); to commit oneself (**w coś** to sth); ~**ować się uczuciowo** to become a. get emotionally involved

angiels|ki **Ⅰ** *adi.* English
Ⅱ *m* (język) English
■ **wyjść po** ~**ku** to take French leave

angielszczy|zna *f* English; **łamana/płynna** ~**zna** broken/fluent English

angin|a *f* tonsillitis, quinsy

anglisty|ka *f* English studies

anglojęzyczn|y *adi. [ludność]* English-speaking; *[prasa]* in English; *[pisarz]* English-language

ango|ra *f* angora (wool)

ani **Ⅰ** *coni.* nie mówię ani po hiszpańsku, ani po włosku I can speak neither Spanish nor Italian; klucza nie było ~ w jednej, ~ w drugiej szufladzie the key wasn't in either of the drawers; nie zadzwonił ~ nie napisał he didn't call, and he didn't write (either); ~ **to ładne**, ~ **potrzebne** it's neither pretty nor useful; ~ **nie potwierdził**, ~ **nie zdementował tej informacji** he neither confirmed, nor denied this information; „**nie idę z nimi**" – „~ **ja**" 'I'm not going with them' – 'neither am I'; **nie mam czasu** ~ **pieniędzy** I don't have the time or the money
Ⅱ *part.* ① (przed rzeczownikiem) not a (single); ~ **śladu** not a trace; ~ **żywego ducha** not a (living) soul; ~ **trochę** not (even) a bit; ~ **razu** not (even) once; ~ **przez chwilę się nie zawahał** he didn't hesitate for a moment; **nie uwierzył w** ~ **jedno jej słowo** he didn't believe a single word she said ② (przed czasownikiem) not even, not as much as; **śruba** ~ **drgnęła** the screw didn't even budge; ~ **pisnął** there wasn't so much as a squeak out of him; ~ **się spostrzeżesz** a. **obejrzysz** in no time at all; ~ **myślę** a. ~ **mi się śni!** like hell I will! pot.; ~ **myślę ustąpić** I haven't the slightest intention of giving way; ~ **mi się waż!** don't you dare!; don't even think about it! pot.

aniels|ki *adi.* angelic także przen.

animacj|a *f* Kino, Komput. animation

anim|ować *impf vt* ① Kino, Komput. to animate *[film, postacie]* ② Teatr to manipulate, to work *[lalki]*

animowan|y *adi. [film]* animated

animusz *m* zest, spirit

ani|oł *m* Relig. angel także przen.; **Anioł Pański** angelus; **Anioł stróż** guardian angel

anioł|ek *m* cherub

aniżeli *coni.* książk. than; **bogatszy**, ~ **przypuszczano** wealthier than was thought; (**on**) **raczej zginie**, ~ **się podda** he'd rather die than surrender

ankie|ta *f* ① (kwestionariusz) questionnaire (form), survey form ② (sondaż) (public opinion) survey a. poll

ankiete|r *m*, ~**rka** *f* pollster

ankiet|ować *impf vt* to poll

annał|y *plt* annals

anomali|a *f* anomaly

anonim *m* (osoba) unknown person; (autor) anonymous author; (dzieło) anonymous work; (list) anonymous letter

anonimow|y *adi. [autor, dzieło, list]* anonymous

anons *m* książk. (w prasie) advertisement, (newspaper) announcement

anons|ować *impf vt* książk. to announce *[gości, wydarzenie]*

anoreksj|a *f* Med. anorexia

antagoni|sta *m*, **~stka** *f* książk. adversary, antagonist

anten|a *f* aerial, antenna US; **~a nadawcza/odbiorcza** transmitter/receiver; **~a satelitarna** satellite aerial a. dish
■ **być na ~ie** Radio, TV to be on the air; **wejść na ~ę** Radio, TV to go on the air

antidot|um *n* antidote także przen. (**na coś** to sth)

antologi|a *f* anthology

antonim *m* Jęz. antonym

antrak|t *m* interval GB, intermission

antropologi|a *f* anthropology

anty [] *adi. inv.* pot. anti pot.; **zawsze i wszędzie był ~** he's always been anti everything
[II] **anty-** *w wyrazach złożonych* anti-; **antybodziec** anti-stimulant; **antygen** antigen

antybiotyk *m* antibiotic

antyczn|y *adi.* [] (starożytny) [*epoka, świat*] ancient; [*tradycja*] classical [2] (zabytkowy) [*mebel, zegar*] antique

antyk *m* [] (starożytność) antiquity [2] (zabytek) antique [3] przen. piece of junk pot.

antykoncepcj|a *f* contraception

antykwaria|t *m* (z używanymi książkami) second-hand bookshop GB a. bookstore US; (z cennymi książkami) antiquarian bookshop GB a. bookstore US

antylop|a *f* Zool. antelope

antypati|a *f* antipathy (**do kogoś** to a. towards sb)

antypatyczn|y *adi.* [*wygląd, zachowanie*] awful, repulsive

antyseptyczn|y *adi.* antiseptic

antyterrory|sta *m* counter-terrorist

antyterrorystyczn|y *adi.* [*akcja, brygada*] anti-terrorist, counter-terrorist

antywłamaniow|y *adi.* [*alarm, blokada*] anti-burglar

anul|ować *pf, impf vt* [] to annul [*głosowanie, małżeństwo, umowę*]; to revoke, to rescind [*przepis*]; to cancel [*dług, zamówienie*] [2] Komput. to cancel

anyż *m* Bot. anise; Kulin. aniseed

apara|t *m* [] (urządzenie) apparatus, device; **~t fotograficzny** camera; **~t ortodontyczny** brace GB, braces US; **~t słuchowy** hearing a. deaf aid GB; **~t telefoniczny** telephone [2] (instytucje) apparatus, machine

aparatu|ra *f* (laboratoryjna, diagnostyczna) apparatus; (oświetleniowa, nagłaśniająca, pomiarowa) equipment

apartamen|t *m* [] (mieszkanie) luxury apartment [2] (hotelowy) suite, apartment

apasz|ka *f* (damska) scarf, neckerchief; (męska) cravat

apati|a *f* apathy

apatyczn|y *adi.* apathetic; **~y wyraz twarzy** a dull expression (on sb's face)

apel *m* [] (odezwa) appeal (**o coś** for sth); **zwrócić się z ~em do kogoś** to make an appeal to sb [2] (uczniów) assembly; (żołnierzy) parade, muster

apelacj|a *f* Prawo appeal (**od czegoś** against sth); **złożyć ~ę** to lodge an appeal

apel|ować *impf vi* to appeal (**do kogoś/o coś** to sb/for sth); to call (**do kogoś/o coś** on sb/for sth); **~ować do czyichś uczuć** to appeal to sb's feelings

apetyczn|y *adi. grad.* [] [*potrawa*] appetizing [2] przen. [*kobieta*] attractive, appealing

apety|t *m* appetite także przen.; **mieć ~t na coś** to fancy sth; **odebrać komuś ~t** to spoil sb's appetite; **stracić ~t** to lose one's appetite; **mieć dobry ~t** to have a good appetite; **z ~tem** with relish
■ **~t rośnie w miarę jedzenia** przysł. appetite comes with eating przysł.

aplauz *m* książk. applause

aplikacj|a *f* [] (wzór) appliqué design [2] Prawo legal training a. apprenticeship, pupilage GB [3] Komput. application (program)

aplik|ować *impf vt* książk. to administer [*kurację, lekarstwo*] (**komuś** to sb)

apodyktyczn|y *adi.* [*osoba, charakter*] overbearing, domineering; [*głos, ton*] peremptory

aport *inter.* fetch!

aport|ować *impf vt* to retrieve [*zwierzynę*]; to fetch [*patyk*]

apostols|ki *adi.* apostolic

aposto|ł *m* apostle także przen.

apostrof *m* apostrophe

aproba|ta *f* książk. approval; approbation książk.

aprob|ować *impf vt* książk. to approve, to (give) consent to [*projekt, wydatki*]; to approve of [*działalność, pomysł*]

aprowizacj|a *f* książk. [] (zaopatrywanie) supply(ing); (w żywność) provision(ing) [2] (żywność) provisions, (food) supplies

aptecz|ka *f* (domowa) medicine cabinet a. chest; (podręczna, samochodowa) first-aid kit

apte|ka *f* chemist GB, chemist's GB, drugstore US, pharmacy

apteka|rz *m*, **~rka** *f* (dispensing) chemist GB, druggist US, pharmacist

arab *m* Zool. Arab

aranżacj|a *f* [] Muz. arrangement; **melodie ludowe w ~i na orkiestrę** folk melodies arranged for orchestra [2] (układ) arrangement; (mieszkania) decor; (obrazu) composition; **~a wnętrz** interior decoration a. design; **~a wystaw sklepowych** window dressing

aranż|ować *impf vt* [] książk. (organizować) to arrange [*spotkanie*] [2] książk. (urządzać) to design [*wnętrze*]; to arrange [*wystawę*] [3] Muz. to arrange [*piosenkę*]; **~ować utwór na orkiestrę** to arrange a piece for orchestra

arbit|er *m* [] książk. (autorytet) arbiter; **~er mody** an arbiter of fashion [2] książk. (rozjemca) mediator, arbiter [3] Sport referee

arbitraln|y *adi.* książk. *[decyzja, ocena, postępowanie]* arbitrary; *[osoba]* despotic, dictatorial; *[ton]* peremptory, imperious

arbuz *m* Bot. watermelon

archaiczn|y *adi.* *[język, kultura]* ancient, archaic; *[metody, przepisy]* archaic; *[sprzęt, urządzenie]* antiquated

archani|oł *m* archangel

archeolo|g *m* archaeologist GB, archeologist US

archeologi|a *f* archaeology GB, archeology US

archeologiczn|y *adi.* archaeologic(al) GB, archeologic(al) US

archidiecezj|a *f* archdiocese

architek|t *m* architect; **~t wnętrz** interior designer a. decorator

architektu|ra *f* architecture; **~ra wnętrz** interior design a. decoration

archiwaln|y *adi.* *[materiały, źródła]* archival; *[film, zdjęcia]* archive

archiwiz|ować *impf vt* to archive *[akta, dokumenty]*

archiw|um *n* archive(s); **~um policyjne** police files a. records

arcy- *w wyrazach złożonych* [1] książk. (wzmocnienie) extremely; **arcyciekawy** extremely interesting [2] (w tytułach i funkcjach) arch-, archi-; **arcyksiążę** archduke; **arcyłotr** arch-villain

arcybiskup *m* archbishop

arcybiskupstw|o *n* archbishopric, archdiocese

arcydzie|ło *n* masterpiece, masterwork

arcykapłan *m* archpriest; (w judaizmie) high priest

arcymistrz *m*, **~yni** *f* grand master

aren|a *f* arena także przen.; **na ~ie międzynarodowej** in the international arena

aresz|t *m* [1] (zatrzymanie) arrest, custody; **~t domowy** house arrest [2] (pomieszczenie) jail, prison

aresztan|t *m* prisoner

areszt|ować *pf, impf vt* to arrest; **być ~owanym** to be under arrest

argumen|t *m* argument (**za czymś/przeciwko czemuś** for/against sth); **~t nie do odparcia** an irrefutable argument; **poprzeć coś ~tami** to support a. back up sth with arguments

argumentacj|a *f* argumentation

argument|ować *impf* **[]** *vt* to justify, to defend; **~ować coś czymś** to plead sth as a/the reason for sth; **jak ~ował swoją odmowę?** how did he justify his refusal?

[] *vi* to argue (**za czymś/przeciwko czemuś** for/against sth)

ari|a *f* aria

arktyczn|y *adi.* *[ekspedycja, klimat]* Arctic

arkusz *m* [1] (papieru, blachy) sheet [2] (zestawienie) report; **~ kalkulacyjny** spreadsheet; **~ ocen** Szkol. mark GB a. grade US sheet

arlekin *m* [1] Teatr Harlequin [2] Zool. harlequin Great Dane

arma|ta *f* cannon, (heavy) gun

armat|ka *f* cannon, gun; **~ka śnieżna** a. **śniegowa** snow cannon; **~ka wodna** water cannon

armato|r *m* shipowner

armatu|ra *f* [1] Techn. fittings; **~ra łazienkowa** bathroom fittings [2] Budow. reinforcement

armi|a *f* (wojsko) the armed forces; (lądowa) the army; **~a bezrobotnych** przen. an unemployed army

arogancj|a *f* arrogance

aroganc|ki *adi.* arrogant

aroma|t *m* [1] (zapach) aroma, fragrance [2] (substancja) essence; **~ty spożywcze** cooking essences; **~t identyczny z naturalnym** nature identical flavour

aromatyczn|y *adi.* aromatic

arsena|ł *m* arsenal także przen.

arszenik *m* arsenic (trioxide)

arteri|a *f* artery

artretyzm *m* Med. arthritis

artyku|ł *m* [1] (tekst) article (**o czymś** on a. about sth); **~ł wstępny** editorial [2] (rzecz) article; **~ły gospodarstwa domowego** household articles a. goods; **~ły pierwszej potrzeby** basic necessities; **~ły spożywcze** groceries

artykuł|ować *impf vt* to articulate *[dźwięki, głoski, poglądy]*

artyleri|a *f* (the) artillery; **ciężka/lekka ~a** heavy/light artillery

arty|sta *m*, **~stka** *f* [1] (twórca) artist [2] (aktor) artist; (cyrkowy) artiste; **~sta estradowy** entertainer [3] przen. (mistrz) artist, master

artystyczn|y *adi.* *[talent, twórczość, prądy]* artistic; *[forma]* art; **rzemiosło ~e** handicraft, craftwork

arystokracj|a *f* aristocracy

arystokra|ta *m*, **~tka** *f* aristocrat

arystokratyczn|y *adi.* aristocratic

arytmety|ka *f* arithmetic

arytmi|a *f* Med. arrhythmia

as *m* ace także przen.; **as atutowy** the ace of trumps; **as lotnictwa** a flying ace

■ **mieć asa w rękawie** to have an ace up one's sleeve; **wyciągnąć asa z rękawa** to play one's trump card

asce|ta *m*, **~tka** *f* ascetic

ascetyczn|y *adi.* ascetic

ascez|a *f* asceticism

asekuracj|a *f* [1] (zabezpieczenie) safeguard, precautionary measure (**przed czymś** against sth) [2] Sport (urządzenia) safety gear, safety device(s); (osoba, grupa osób) back-up (team) [3] (ubezpieczenie) insurance (**od czegoś** against sth)

asekuracyjn|y *adi.* [1] *[środki, urządzenia]* safety [2] *[polisa, towarzystwo]* insurance, assurance

asekuranc|ki *adi.* *[postawa, zachowanie]* overcautious; play-safe pot.

asekuranctw|o *n* overcautiousness

asekuran|t *m* hedger

asekur|ować *impf* **[]** *vt* to protect; (podczas wspinaczki) to belay

[] **asekurować się** **[1]** to protect oneself (**przed czymś** against sth); to play safe pot. **[2]** Sport (jeden drugiego) to back one another up; (podczas wspinaczki) to belay

aseptyczn|y *adi.* aseptic, sterile

asertywn|y *adi.* assertive

asfal|t *m* asphalt, tarmac

asfalt|ować *impf* *vt* to asphalt, to tarmac, to blacktop US *[drogę, ulicę]*

asfaltow|y *adi. [nawierzchnia, szosa]* asphalt, tarmac

asortymen|t *m* range (of products)

aspek|t *m* aspect, facet

aspiracj|e *plt* aspirations; **mieć ~e artystyczne** to have artistic aspirations

aspiran|t *m* **[1]** książk. (kandydat) aspirant, candidate (**do czegoś** for sth) **[2]** (w policji) ≈ inspector; (w straży pożarnej) ≈ fire officer

aspir|ować *impf* *vi* to aspire (**do czegoś** to sth)

aspiryn|a *f* aspirin

aspołeczn|y *adi.* asocial

ast|er *m* Bot. aster

astm|a *f* Med. asthma

astmaty|k *m*, **~czka** *f* asthmatic (sufferer)

astrolo|g *m* astrologer, astrologist

astrologi|a *f* astrology

astronau|ta *m*, **~tka** *f* astronaut

astronauty|ka *f* astronautics

astronom *m* astronomer

astronomi|a *f* astronomy

astronomiczn|y *adi.* **[1]** astronomical *przen.* *[koszty, suma]* astronomic(al) pot.

asymetri|a *f* asymmetry

asymilacj|a *f* assimilation

asymil|ować *impf* **[]** *vt* to assimilate

[] **asymilować się** to become assimilated, to assimilate

asy|sta *f* książk. entourage; **w ~ście kogoś** accompanied by sb, in the company of sb; **król w ~ście dworzan** a king attended by his courtiers

asysten|t *m*, **~tka** *f* **[1]** Uniw. junior a. assistant lecturer **[2]** (pomocnik) assistant; **~t reżysera** assistant director; **~tka stomatologa** dental assistant

asyst|ować *impf* *vi* **[1]** (towarzyszyć) to accompany (**komuś** sb) **[2]** (pomagać) to assist (**komuś** sb)

atak *m* **[1]** (napaść) attack, assault (**na coś** on a. against sth); **~ bombowy** bomb raid; **do ~u!** attack! **[2]** (choroby) attack, seizure; (kaszlu, śmiechu) fit; **dostać ~u szału** to get in a rage **[3]** Sport attack; **grać w ~u** to play in attack

atak|ować *impf* *vt* to attack *także przen.*

atawizm *m* atavism

atei|sta *m*, **~stka** *f* atheist

ateizm *m* atheism

atelier /ˌateˈlje/ *n inv.* studio, atelier

ate|st *m* seal of approval, certificate; **produkt z ~stem/bez ~stu** a product with/without a seal of approval

atlas *m* **[1]** atlas; **~ świata** a world atlas, an atlas of the world **[2]** Sport multigym

atle|ta *m* **[1]** (siłacz) strongman **[2]** Sport heavyweight athlete

atlety|ka *f* athletics; **lekka ~ka** athletics GB, track and field US

atłas *m* (jedwabny) satin; (bawełniany) sateen

■ **szkoda czasu i ~u** przysł. it's a waste of time and effort

atłasow|y *adi. [obrus, suknia]* (z jedwabiu) satin; (z bawełny) sateen; przen. *[skóra]* satiny

atmosfe|ra *f* **[1]** atmosphere; **~ra ziemska** the (earth's) atmosphere **[2]** przen. atmosphere; **oczyścić ~rę** to clear the air; **rozładować ~rę** to ease the tension

atmosferyczn|y *adi.* atmospheric

atom *m* Chem., Fiz. atom

atomow|y *adi.* atomic

atrakcj|a *f* attraction; **główna ~a programu** the highlight of the programme

atrakcyjn|y *adi. grad. [osoba, cena, nagroda, towar]* attractive

atramen|t *m* ink; **~t sympatyczny** invisible ink

atramentow|y *adi. [plama]* ink; przen. *[chmury, noc]* inky

atrap|a *f* (bomby, towaru) dummy

atropin|a *f* atropine

atrybu|t *m* attribute

atu|t *m* **[1]** Gry (kolor) trumps; (karta) trump (card) **[2]** przen. chief asset, trump card

■ **mieć wszystkie ~ty w ręku** to hold all the aces

audiencj|a *f* audience (**u kogoś** with sb)

audio *adi. inv.* audio

audiowizualn|y *adi.* audio-visual

audycj|a *f* programme GB, program US, broadcast; **~a na żywo** a live programme a. broadcast

audytori|um *n* książk. **[1]** (słuchacze) audience **[2]** (sala) lecture theatre, auditorium US

aukcj|a *f* auction

aul|a *f* lecture hall

au|ra *f* książk. **[1]** (pogoda) weather **[2]** (nastrój) aura, air

aureol|a *f* halo, aureole

austriac|ki *adi.* Austrian

■ **~kie gadanie** pot. (a lot of) nonsense, fiddle-faddle

au|t /awt/ *m* Sport **posłać piłkę na aut** to send the ball out of play; **stać na aucie** to stand on the sidelines; **rzut z autu** (w piłce nożnej) a throw-in

■ **znaleźć się na aucie** pot. to be left on the sidelines

autentyczn|y *adi.* **[1]** (prawdziwy) *[fakt, relacja]* authentic; **film oparty na ~ych wydarzeniach**

a film based on true events [2] (oryginalny) *[dokument, obraz, podpis]* authentic, genuine [3] (szczery) *[radość, zainteresowanie]* genuine
autentyk *m* original
au|to [] *n* car
[] **auto-** *w wyrazach złożonych* [1] (samo-) self-; **autocenzura** self-censorship [2] (samochodowy) car; **autoalarm** car alarm
autobiografi|a *f* autobiography
autobus *m* bus; ~ **dalekobieżny** coach GB, long-distance bus US; ~ **piętrowy/przegubowy** double-decker/articulated bus; ~ **pośpieszny** express bus
autocasco /ˌawto'kasko/ *n inv.* ≈ comprehensive motor insurance
autograf *m* autograph
autoka|r *m* coach GB, bus US
automa|t *m* [1] (urządzenie) (automatic) machine; (z biletami, napojami) slot a. vending machine; ~**t telefoniczny** public telephone, payphone; ~**t do gry** gaming machine [2] pot. (pralka) automatic (washing machine) [3] pot. (pistolet) sub-machine gun [4] (robot) robot, automaton *także przen.*
automatyczn|y *adi. [broń, urządzenie]* automatic *także przen.*
autonomi|a *f* autonomy
autoportre|t *m* self-portrait
autopsj|a *f* Med. post-mortem, autopsy; **znać coś z ~i** przen. to know sth from experience
auto|r *m*, ~**rka** *f* [1] (dzieła) author [2] (planu, pomysłu) author, initiator
autorstw|o *n* authorship
autorytatywn|y *adi.* książk. [1] (wiarygodny) *[decyzja, opinia, źródła]* authoritative [2] (nieznoszący sprzeciwu) *[rządy, ton]* authoritarian
autoryte|t *m* [1] (prestiż) authority, standing; **cieszyć się ~tem** to have considerable standing; **zdobyć ~t** to gain authority a. respect; **powoływać się na czyjś ~t** to cite a. quote sb as an authority [2] (osoba, instytucja) authority; **być ~tem w czymś** to be an authority on sth
autoryzacj|a *f* authorization
autoryz|ować *pf, impf vt* to authorize *[przekład, wywiad]*; ~**owany** *[dealer, serwis]* authorized
autoserwis *m* (obsługa techniczna) garage services, car servicing; (punkt) garage, service station
autostop *m* hitch-hiking; **podróżować ~em** to hitch-hike; to hitch pot.
autostopowicz *m*, ~**ka** *f* hitch-hiker
autostra|da *f* motorway GB, expressway US, freeway US
autow|y *adi.* Sport **linia ~a** (w tenisie) (boczna) the sideline; (na końcu kortu) the baseline; (w piłce nożnej) the touchline; **piłka ~a** a ball that has gone out of play; **sędzia ~y** (w tenisie) line judge; (w piłce nożnej) linesman; **kopnął piłkę poza linię ~ą** he kicked the ball into touch a. out of play

autyzm *m* autism
awangar|da *f* avant-garde, vanguard; **w ~dzie** at the forefront, in the vanguard
awangardow|y *adi.* avant-garde
awans *m* (na wyższe stanowisko) promotion; (społeczny) advance(ment); **dostać ~ na dyrektora** to be promoted to director; **wywalczyć ~ do finału** Sport to fight one's way through to the final
■ ~**em** *[otrzymać, zapłacić]* in advance
awans|ować *pf, impf* [] *vt* to promote; ~**ować kogoś na kapitana** to promote sb to captain
[] *vi* [1] to be promoted, to advance; ~**ować na stanowisko dyrektora** to advance a. rise to the position of director [2] Sport to advance, to go through; ~**ować do finału** to go through a. advance to the final
awantu|ra *f* [1] (kłótnia) row [2] (bójka) brawl, fight
awanturni|k *m* [1] pejor. (wszczynający awantury) troublemaker [2] książk. (lubiący przygody) adventurer [3] (w polityce) adventurist
awantur|ować się *impf v refl.* (kłócić się) to (kick up a) row; (bić się) to fight, to brawl (**o coś** about sth)
awari|a *f* failure, breakdown; ~**a sieci elektrycznej** failure in the power supply, power failure; ~**a elektrowni atomowej** nuclear accident
awaryjn|y *adi. [lądowanie, wyjście]* emergency; **światła ~e** Aut. hazard (warning) lights
awers *m* obverse
awersj|a *f* książk. aversion, dislike (**do czegoś** to sth)
awionet|ka *f* light aircraft
awiz|o *n* advice (note)
awokado *n inv.* avocado (pear)
azo|t *m* nitrogen
azyl *m* (political) asylum; przen. refuge
azymu|t *m* azimuth *także przen.*
aż [] *coni.* [1] (dopóki nie) until, till; **poczekaj, aż wrócę** wait until a. till I get back; **aż tu (nagle)** (when) all of a sudden, (when) suddenly [2] (tak bardzo, że) **pioruny waliły, aż cały dom trząsł się** the thunder was so loud that the whole house shook; **wrzeszczał, aż uszy puchły** he was screaming his head off pot.
[] *part.* [1] (z policzalnymi) as many as, no fewer than; (z niepoliczalnymi) as much as, no less than; (z określeniem odległości) as far as; **aż dziewięciu uczniów** as many as a. no fewer than nine pupils; **aż 70%** as much as a. no less than 70 per cent; **aż tak wielu/dużo?** as many/much as that?; **aż za dużo** more than enough; **aż do/z Berlina** all the way to/from Berlin; **aż po szyję** right up to the neck; **aż do XVI wieku** (right) up until the sixteenth century; **nie powinieneś aż tyle pracować** you shouldn't work as hard as that [2] (określające stopień nasilenia)

ostrożny aż do przesady cautious to a fault; **zimno aż nie do wytrzymania** unbearably cold; **aż do skutku** for as long as it takes, to the bitter end; **zajadał, że aż miło** the way he was eating it was a pleasure to watch; **ciemno/zimno (że) aż strach** terribly a. awfully dark/cold; **aż strach pomyśleć** it doesn't bear thinking about, one shudders to think; **aż nadto** more than enough; **znała go aż nadto dobrze** she knew him only a. all too well; **wcale nie jest aż tak zimno** it's not that cold

ażeby *coni., part.* książk. → **żeby**

ażu|r *m* openwork pattern a. design

ażurow|y *adi.* openwork

B

B, b *n inv.* [1] (litera) B, b [2] Muz. B

bab|a *f* pot. [1] (kobieta) woman; (żona) old lady pot. [2] mężczyzna) sissy pot.

■ **~a z wozu, koniom lżej** przysł. that solves that (problem), that's that problem out of the way

bab|cia *f* (babka) grandmother; grandma pot.; (stara kobieta) old lady

bab|ka *f* [1] (babcia) grandmother [2] pot. (kobieta) chick pot. [3] (ciasto) cake [4] (z piasku) sandcastle

■ **na dwoje ~ka wróżyła** przysł. your guess is as good as mine

bab|rać *impf* **I** *vt* (brudzić) to get [sth] messy **II** *vi* (grzebać) to mess about a. around (**w czymś** with sth) **III** **babrać się** [1] (brudzić się) to get oneself messy [2] (grzebać się) to mess about

bacho|r *m* pot. brat

bacznie *adv. grad.* [słuchać, obserwować] closely

baczno|ść *f* stać na **~ć** to stand at a. to attention

■ **mieć się na ~ci** to be on one's guard (**przed kimś/czymś** against sb/sth)

baczn|y *adi. grad.* [widz, obserwator] attentive

b|ać się *impf v refl.* [1] (czuć strach) to be afraid (**kogoś/czegoś** of sb/sth); **bać się coś zrobić** to be afraid to do sth; **bać się czegoś jak ognia** a. **diabeł święconej wody** to be scared stiff of sth; **nie pójdę, boję się** I'm not going, I'm scared [2] (niepokoić się) to worry (**o kogoś/coś** about sb/sth)

badacz *m*, **~ka** *f* (prowadzący badania) researcher; (naukowiec) scholar

bada|ć *impf* **I** *vt* [1] Med. to examine [pacjenta]; **~ć komuś puls** to take a. feel sb's pulse; **~ć sobie krew/wzrok** to have a blood/an eye test [2] (sprawdzać) to examine [problem, zjawisko]; to test [teorię]; to explore [teren]; **~ć coś na zwierzętach** to test sth on animals [3] (zadawać pytania) to question [świadka] **II** **badać się** Med. (być badanym) to have a check-up

bada|nie *n* (rentgenowskie, mikroskopowe) examination; (antydopingowe, krwi, moczu) test; **~nia naukowe** research; **prowadzić ~nia** to carry out a. conduct research

badawcz|y *adi.* [zespół, ośrodek, praca] research; [wzrok] searching

bagateliz|ować *impf vt* (nie doceniać) to underestimate [niebezpieczeństwo]; (lekceważyć) to ignore [opinie]; to make light of [chorobę]

bagaż *m* luggage GB, baggage US; **~ ręczny** hand luggage; **nadać ~** (na lotnisku) to check in one's luggage

bagażnik *m* boot GB, trunk US

bagażow|y I *adi.* [wagon, wózek] luggage, baggage **II** *m* [1] (na kolei) porter [2] (w przechowalni) left luggage attendant GB, baggage clerk US

bagienn|y *adi.* [roślinność] marsh; [teren] marshy

bagiet|ka *f* baguette, French loaf a. stick

bagne|t *m* bayonet

bag|no *n* [1] (teren) bog; **ugrzęznąć w ~nie** to get bogged down [2] przen. (dirty) business pot.

baje|r *m* pot. tall story

bajeranc|ki *adi.* pot. snazzy pot.

bajer|ować *impf vt* pot. to have GB a. put US [sb] on pot.; **nie ~uj!** you're making it up!

baj|ka *f* [1] (baśń) fairy tale; **~ka na dobranoc** a bed-time story [2] Literat. fable; **~ki Ezopa** Aesop's Fables [3] (plotka) story; (kłamstwo) fib

bajkopisarz *m* writer of fables

bajo|ro *n* (overgrown) pond

baj|t *m* Komput. byte

bajz|el *m* posp. tip pot.

bak *m* (petrol) tank

bakali|e *plt* Kulin. nuts and dried fruit

bakcyl *m* bacillus

■ **połknąć ~a teatru/żeglarstwa** to catch the theatre/sailing bug pot.

bakłażan *m* aubergine GB, eggplant US

bakteri|a *f* Biol. bacterium; **~e chorobotwórcze** pathogenic bacteria

bakteriobójcz|y *adi.* antibacterial

bakteryjn|y *adi.* bacterial; **zakażenie ~e** bacterial infection

bal *m* (zabawa taneczna) ball; **~ kostiumowy** a fancy dress ball, a costume ball US; **~ maturalny** ≈ an end of school ball; ≈ a prom US pot.; **wydać ~** to organize a ball

■ **i po ~u!** pot. and that's it!

balan|ga *f* pot. bash pot.; **wyprawić ~gę** to put on a bash

balans|ować *impf vi* [1] (utrzymywać równowagę) to balance (**na czymś** on sth); **~ować ciałem** to keep one's balance [2] przen. **~ować na granicy prawa** to operate on the edge of the law

bala|st *m* ballast; przen. burden

baldachim *m* baldachin; **łoże z** ~**em** a four-poster bed

baleron *m* ≈ cured pork shoulder

bale|t *m* ballet; (zespół) ballet (company); **wystawić** ~**t** to put on a ballet

balet|ka *f* ballet shoe

baletni|ca *f* ballet dancer

baletow|y *adi. [zespół, szkoła]* ballet

bali|a *f* washtub; ~**a wody** a tub(ful) of water

balistyczn|y *adi.* ballistic

balisty|ka *f* ballistics

balkon *m* [1] balcony; **wyjść na** ~ to go (out) on to the balcony [2] (w teatrze) (pierwszy) dress circle, mezzanine US; (drugi) upper circle, balcony US; (trzeci) gallery; (w kinie) balcony, circle

balla|da *f* ballad

balon *m* [1] Lotn. (hot-air) balloon; ~**-sonda** Meteo. a sounding balloon [2] (do zabawy, dekoracji) balloon; **nadmuchać** ~ to blow up a balloon [3] (szklane naczynie) balloon (flask)
■ **robić z kogoś** ~**a** a. **kogoś w** ~**a** pot. (nabierać) to make a fool (out) of sb; (oszukiwać) to put one over on sb pot.

balonik *m* pot. (alkomat) breathalyser GB, Breathalyzer® US; drunkometer US pot.

bal|ować *impf vi* pot., żart. [1] (tańczyć) ~**ować do białego rana** to dance the night away [2] (bawić się) to go partying pot. (**z kimś** with sb)

balow|y *adi.* ball; **sala** ~**a** a ballroom; **suknia** ~**a** a ballgown

balsam *m* [1] Farm. balsam [2] Kosmet. lotion; ~ **do ciała** body lotion

balsam|ować *impf vt* to embalm *[zwłoki]*

balustra|da *f* balustrade; (na schodach) banister(s)

bałagan *m* mess; **narobić** ~**u** to make a mess

bałagania|rz *m*, ~**ra** *f* pot. (niedbający o porządek) slob pot.; (roztrzepany) scatterbrain pot.

bałaga|nić *impf vi* pot. to make a mess

bałwan *m* [1] (śniegowy) snowman [2] (figura bożka) pagan idol [3] (fala) breaker [4] pot. (o osobie) blockhead pot.

bambus *m* bamboo; **stolik/laska z** ~**a** a bamboo table/cane

banaln|y *adi. grad.* [1] (nieoryginalny) *[frazes, rozmowa]* trite [2] (nieistotny) *[szczegół]* trivial; *[sprawa]* banal [3] (łatwy) *[zadanie]* straightforward

bana|ł *m* banality

banan *m* banana; **skórka (od)** ~**a** a banana skin

bananow|iec *m* Bot. banana tree a. palm

ban|da *f* [1] (złodziei, włamywaczy) gang [2] pot. (chuliganów, kibiców) bunch pot. [3] Sport (lodowiska) board; (toru wyścigowego) rail; (stołu bilardowego) cushion

bandaż *m* bandage; **obwiązać** a. **owinąć komuś rękę** ~**em** to bandage sb's hand

bandaż|ować *impf vt* to bandage *[ranę, nogę]*

bande|ra *f* ensign; **pod polską/angielską** ~**rą** under the Polish/British flag

banderol|a *f* band; (na alkoholu, papierosach) excise band

bandy|ta *m*, ~**tka** *f* thug; **jednoręki** ~**ta** pot. one-armed bandit pot.

banicj|a *f* książk. banishment; **skazać kogoś na** ~**ę** to banish a. exile sb

bani|ta *m* książk. exile

bank *m* [1] Fin. bank; **napad na** ~ a bank raid; **podjąć pieniądze z** ~**u** to withdraw money from the bank [2] (zbiór, zapas) bank; ~ **krwi/spermy/szpiku kostnego** a blood/sperm/bone marrow bank [3] Gry bank; **rozbić** ~ to break the bank
■ **oddam ci jutro, na** ~ pot. I'll give it back tomorrow, honest pot.

bankie|r *m* banker

bankie|t *m* banquet

bankno|t *m* (bank)note GB, bill US; ~**t dwudziestozłotowy** a twenty-zloty banknote

bankoma|t *m* cash machine a. dispenser GB

bankowoś|ć *f* banking

bankow|y *adi. [pożyczka]* bank; *[usługi]* banking

bankructw|o *n* bankruptcy; **ogłosić** ~**o firmy** to declare a company bankrupt

bankru|t *m* bankrupt także przen.; **życiowy** ~**t** a failure (in life)

bankrut|ować *impf vi [osoba, firma]* to go a. become bankrupt

ba|ńka *f* [1] (pojemnik) can [2] Med. cupping-glass przest. [3] (pęcherzyk) bubble
■ **na bańce** pot. tanked up pot.

ba|r *m* bar; **bar kawowy** a coffee bar a. shop; **bar szybkiej obsługi** a fast-food bar; **usiąść przy barze** to sit at the bar a. counter

barak *m* hut

Baran *m* Astrol., Astron. Aries, the Ram

baran *m* [1] Zool. ram; **leźć za kimś jak stado** ~**ów** to follow sb like (a flock of) sheep; **liczyć** ~**y** (żeby zasnąć) to count sheep [2] pot. (o osobie) idiot pot.; **ty** ~**ie jeden!** you (damn) fool!
■ **wziąć/nieść kogoś na** ~**a** to give sb a piggyback/to carry sb piggyback

baran|ek *m* [1] (jagnię) lamb; **Baranek Boży** Relig. the Lamb (of God); **łagodny jak** ~**ek** as meek a. mild as a lamb [2] Meteo. cirrus cloud [3] pot. (fryzura) frizz

barani *adi.* [1] *[runo]* sheep's; *[rogi]* ram's; **trząść się jak** ~ **ogon** to shake like a jelly a. leaf [2] *[czapka, kołnierz]* sheepskin; *[kotlety]* mutton; **udziec** ~ leg of lamb
■ ~**a głowa** a. ~ **łeb** pot. muttonhead pot.; **patrzeć na kogoś/coś** ~**m wzrokiem** pot. to gawp at sb/sth pot.

baranin|a *f* Kulin. mutton

barbarzyńc|a *m* [1] (nieokrzesany) barbarian [2] (okrutny) savage

barbarzyńs|ki *adi.* [1] (nieokrzesany) barbarous [2] (okrutny) barbaric

barbarzyństw|o n [1] (postępowanie) barbarity [2] (brak kultury) barbarism

Barbór|ka f ≈ Miner's Day *(in Poland St Barbara's Day, 4 December)*

barczy|sty *adi. [mężczyzna]* broad-shouldered

bardz|o [] *adv. grad. [wysoki, uprzejmie]* very; *[lubić, cieszyć się]* very much; **w ~o podobny sposób** in a very similar way; **~o coś zachwalać** to praise sth (very) highly; **~o starać się** to try very hard; **~o potrzebować czegoś** to be badly in need of sth; **~o płakał** he cried a lot pot.; **~o boli?** does it hurt much?; **~o proszę o spokój** could everyone please be quiet?; **~o dziękuję** thank you very much; **przepraszam ~o,** excuse me, what time is it?; **tak ~o** so much; **za ~o** too much; **za ~o zmęczony/śpiący, żeby...** too tired/sleepy to...; **nie (za) ~o** not really; **nie ~o rozumiem** I don't quite understand; **najbardziej lubię banany/matematykę** I like bananas/maths most of all; **najbardziej interesujący/kontrowersyjny** the most interesting/controversial; **jak najbardziej!** pot. of course!

[] **bardziej** *adv. comp.* more; **~iej interesujący niż...** more interesting than...; **dużo ~iej interesujący** much more interesting; **coraz ~iej** more and more; **tym ~iej, że...** (all) the more so (in) that a. because...; **nigdy go nie widziałem, a tym ~iej nie rozmawiałem z nim** I've never even seen him, let alone spoken to him; **im ~iej nalegali, tym ~iej...** the more they insisted, the more...

bar|ek m (stolik na kółkach) trolley; (szafka) drinks cabinet a. cupboard

barie|ra f (przegroda) barrier; (wzdłuż drogi) crash barrier GB, guard rail US; **~ra naturalna** a natural barrier; **~ra językowa** a language barrier; **~ry architektoniczne** architectural barriers; **przełamać ~ry psychiczne** to overcome a psychological barrier; **~ra dźwięku** the sound barrier

bark m Anat. shoulder; **spoczywać na czyichś ~ach** przen. to rest on sb's shoulders; **złożyć coś na czyjeś ~i** przen. to burden sb with sth

bar|ka f barge; **~ka desantowa** a landing craft

barman m barman GB, bartender US

barok m (the) baroque; **muzyka ~u** baroque music

baromet|r m barometer; **~r idzie do góry** a. **na pogodę** the barometer is rising; **~r spada** a. **idzie na niepogodę** the barometer is falling

barometryczn|y *adi.* barometric; **ciśnienie ~e** atmospheric a. barometric pressure

baron m baron; **~ narkotykowy** przen. a drug baron

barszcz m Kulin. borsch(t)

■ **tani jak ~** dirt cheap pot.

barw|a f [] f [1] (kolor) colour GB, color US; hue książk.; **~a ochronna** Zool. protective coloration; Wojsk.

camouflage; **natężenie/intensywność ~y** colour intensity [2] Muz. tone (colour); **~a głosu** timbre

[] **barwy** *plt* (państwa, stowarzyszenia) colours GB, colors US; **~y narodowe** national colours; **grać w ~ach Anglii** to play in England's colours

■ **widzieć coś w różowych** a. **jasnych ~ach** to see sth through rose-coloured spectacles; **przedstawiać coś w ciemnych** a. **czarnych ~ach** to paint a gloomy picture of sth

barw|ić *impf* [] *vt* to colour GB, to color US *[szkło, policzki]*; to dye *[tkaninę]*; **~ić coś na zielono** to dye sth green

[] **barwić się** to take on a colour GB a. color US; **~ić się na czerwono** to turn red

barwnik m dye; **~ spożywczy** a food colouring

barwn|y *adi. grad.* [1] (kolorowy) colourful GB, colorful US; *[zdjęcia, odbitka]* colour GB, color US [2] (o określonej barwie) coloured GB, colored US; *[filtr]* colour GB, color US [3] przen. (interesujący) colourful GB, colorful US; *[opis, język]* vivid

bar|y *plt* (broad) shoulders; **szeroki w ~ach** broad-shouldered

baryka|da f barricade; **postawić ~dę** to set up a. erect a barricade; **stanąć po drugiej** a. **przeciwnej stronie ~dy** przen. to go over to the other camp

barykad|ować *impf vt* to barricade (**coś czymś** sth with sth)

barył|ka f [1] (beczka) keg [2] (ropy) barrel

baryton m baritone

bas m bass

basen m [1] (pływalnia) (swimming) pool; **~ kryty/odkryty** an indoor/outdoor swimming pool; **iść na ~** to go to the pool [2] Sport (długość basenu) length [3] (dmuchany) paddling pool a. wading US pool [4] (zbiornik) basin [5] Med. bedpan [6] Geog., Geol. basin

basse|t /'baset/ m basset (hound)

bastion m bastion; **ostatni ~ cywilizacji** przen. the last bastion of civilization

basz|ta f tower

baśniow|y *adi. [rycerze, świat]* fairy-tale

baś|ń f fairy tale

ba|t [] m whip; **zdzielić kogoś batem** to lash sb

[] **baty** *plt* [1] (uderzenie batem) whipping [2] pot. (klęska) hiding

batali|a f (bitwa) battle; (ciąg bitew) campaign; **rozpocząć ~ę przeciwko czemuś** przen. to launch a campaign against sth

batalion m battalion

bateri|a f [] f [1] Elektr. battery; **~a słoneczna** a solar battery; **~a się wyczerpała** the battery has run down [2] (wodociągowa) mixer tap GB, (mixing) faucet US [3] Wojsk. battery

baton m (chocolate) bar

batu|t m trampoline

batu|ta f baton; **pod ~tą Lutosławskiego** *[grać]* under the baton of Lutosławski; *[orkiestra]* conducted by Lutosławski

bawełn|a *f* cotton; (krzew) cotton plant
■ **bez owijania w ~ę** without beating about the bush; **nie owijać w ~ę** to not mince one's words
baw|ić *impf* **[]** *vt* [1] (uprzyjemniać czas) to entertain *[gości, dzieci]* [2] (interesować, zajmować) *[czynność, przedmiot]* to amuse; **~i mnie chodzenie po sklepach** I enjoy shopping; **to mnie nie ~i** it's not (really) my idea of fun
[] *vi* książk. (przebywać) to stay
[] **bawić się** [1] (uprzyjemniać sobie czas) to play (**czymś** with sth); **~ić się w chowanego** to play (at) hide-and-seek; **~ić się w kucharza/ogrodnika** przen. to try one's hand at cooking/gardening; **~ się dobrze!** have fun! a. a good time! [2] (mieć uciechę) to enjoy oneself; **~ić się kimś** to toy with sb [3] (poruszać bez celu) to play (around); **~ić się ołówkiem** to play around a. fiddle with a pencil
baw|ół *m* Zool. buffalo
baz|a *f* [1] (podstawa) base; **~a danych** Komput. a database; **na ~ie czegoś** on the basis of sth [2] (lotnicza, zaopatrzeniowa) base; (alpinistów) base (camp); **~a wojskowa** a military base
bazal|t *m* basalt
baza|r *m* (targowisko) market (place); (ze starociami) bazaar
bazg|rać *impf vt* pot. to scrawl; **ale ~rzesz!** your handwriting is terrible!
bazgroł|y *plt* pot. scribble
bazi|a *f* catkin; pussy-willow pot.
baz|ować *impf vi* **~ować na czymś** *[osoba]* to rely on sth; *[metoda, polityka]* to be based on sth
bazyli|a *f* Bot., Kulin. (sweet) basil
bazyli|ka *f* Archit. basilica
bażan|t *m* Zool. pheasant
bąb|el *m* [1] (na ciele) blister; **pokryty ~lami** *[skóra, ręce]* blistered [2] (w cieczy) bubble
bądź **[]** → **być**
[] *coni.* or; **chodził na wycieczki ~ (to) samemu, ~ (to** a. **też) z kolegami** he used to go hiking – either by himself or with his friends
[] *part.* any; **co ~** anything (at all); **kto ~** anybody a. anyone at all; **gdzie ~** anywhere at all; **kiedy ~** any time; **jak ~** anyhow; **jaki ~** any; **~ co** after all
bąk *m* [1] (giez) horsefly [2] (trzmiel) bumblebee [3] (ptak) (European) bittern [4] (zabawka) (spinning) top
■ **opić się jak ~** to drink one's fill; **puścić ~a** pot. to break wind euf.; **zbijać ~i** pot. to fool around
bąk|nąć *pf* — **bąk|ać** *impf* **[]** *vt* to mumble *[słowo, powitanie]*; **~nąć coś pod nosem** to mumble a. mutter sth under one's breath
[] *vi* (napomknąć) **~nąć o czymś** to mention sth casually
beczeć¹ *impf* → **beknąć¹**
becz|eć² *impf vi* pot. [1] (płakać) to blubber pot. [2] (brzydko śpiewać) to sing out of tune a. off-key

becz|ka *f* [1] (naczynie) barrel [2] Lotn. (figura) barrel-roll
■ **~ka śmiechu** a barrel of laughs pot.; **a tak z innej ~ki...** oh, by the way...
beczkow|óz *m* water cart
befsztyk *m* Kulin. (kotlet) (beef) steak; (z mielonego mięsa) rissole
bejc|a *f* (do drewna) wood stain
bejc|ować *impf vt* to stain *[drewno]*
bek *m* [1] (głos kozy, barana) bleat [2] pot. (głośny płacz) blubbering pot.
be|knąć¹ *pf* — **be|czeć¹** *impf vi [owca, koza]* to bleat
bek|nąć² *pf* — **bek|ać** *impf vi* pot. to burp pot.
bekn|ąć³ *pf vi* pot. (ponieść karę) to pay (the price); **on grubo ~ie za to** he'll pay dearly for that
bekon *m* Kulin. bacon
beks|a *m, f* pot. cry-baby pot.
bel|a *f* [1] (zwój) roll; **~a tkaniny** a roll of fabric [2] (sprasowany materiał) bale; **wełna w ~ach** bales of wool
■ **pijany jak ~a** pot. (as) drunk as a lord
beletrysty|ka *f* fiction
belf|er *m* pot. teacher
bel|ka *f* [1] (drewniana, metalowa) beam; (w konstrukcjach, maszynach) girder [2] Wojsk. stripe
bełko|t *m* [1] (niewyraźna mowa) mumbling [2] przen. (niezrozumiała wypowiedź) gibberish
bełko|tać *impf vi* [1] (mówić niewyraźnie) to mumble [2] pot. (mówić nielogicznie) to gabble (on)
benefis *m* (koncert) benefit concert; (przedstawienie) benefit performance
benzyn|a *f* petrol GB, gas(oline) US; **~a bezołowiowa** unleaded petrol
ber|ek *m* (zabawa) tag
bere|t *m* beret; **czerwone ~ty** pot. ≈ paratroopers; paras pot.
ber|ło *n* [1] (królewskie) sceptre GB, scepter US; (rektorskie) staff (of office) [2] przen. (władza) reins of power a. government
bernardyn *m* (pies) St Bernard (dog)
bess|a *f* fall a. decline in the market, slump
besti|a *f* [1] (zwierzę) (wild) beast [2] (okrutnik) animal [3] pot., żart. beast pot., żart.
bestials|ki *adi.* *[napad, czyn]* savage; *[zbrodniarz]* brutal; **po ~ku** brutally
bestialstw|o *n* [1] (okrucieństwo) bestiality [2] (brutalny czyn) bestial act
bestselle|r *m* best-seller
beszta|ć *impf vt* pot. to tell [sb] off pot.
beton *m* [1] Budow. concrete; **nawierzchnia z ~u** a concrete surface [2] pot. (o osobie) hardliner; **partyjny ~** the party hardliners a. diehards
betoniar|ka *f* (urządzenie) concrete a. cement mixer; (samochód) cement mixer
beton|ować *impf vt* to concrete
b|ez¹ *m* common lilac; **krzak bzu** a lilac bush

bez² [] *praep.* [1] (wyrażające brak) without; ~ **wysiłku** without (any) effort; ~ **żadnej pomocy** without any help; ~**e mnie** without me; ~ **końca** endlessly; ~ **przerwy** non-stop; ~ **smaku** tasteless; **sukienka** ~ **rękawów** a sleeveless dress; **mięso** ~ **kości** boned meat; **sok** ~ **cukru** sugar-free juice; **dzień** ~ **samochodu** a car-free day; ~ **środków do życia** with no means of subsistence; **ujść** ~ **kary** to go unpunished; **obchodzić** a. **obywać się** ~ **kogoś/czegoś** to make do a. manage without sb/sth; ~ **atu** Gry no trumps [2] (wyrażające zaniechanie) without; **odejść** ~ **pożegnania** to leave without saying goodbye; **wziąć coś** ~ **pytania** to take something without asking [3] (wyrażające pomniejszenie, pozbawienie) minus; **trzy miesiące** ~ **dwóch dni** three months less a. minus two days [4] (w wyrażeniach wykrzyknikowych) ~ **paniki!** don't panic!; **tylko** ~ **wygłupów!** pot. no messing (around) though! pot.; ~ **dyskusji!** no arguing!; ~ **obaw!** no problem a. sweat pot.; ~ **przesady!** don't exaggerate!
[II] **nie bez** not without; **nie** ~ **znaczenia jest fakt, że...** it is not without significance that...

bez|a *f* meringue

bezalkoholow|y *adi.* [*piwo, dzień*] alcohol-free; **napoje** ~**e** soft drinks, non-alcoholic beverages

bezapelacyjn|y *adi.* [*przewaga*] decided; **odnieść** ~**e zwycięstwo** to score a decisive a. an unqualified victory; ~**y wyrok** a sentence without right of appeal

bezbarwn|y *adi.* [1] (przezroczysty) [*gaz, ciecz*] colourless GB, colorless US; [*pasta do butów*] neutral [2] przen. [*tłum*] faceless; [*postać*] bland; [*budynek*] grey; [*styl, proza*] dull

bezbłędn|y *adi.* [1] (niezawierający błędów) [*odpowiedź, rozwiązanie*] correct [2] pot. (świetny) great pot.

bezbole|sny *adi.* [*poród*] pain-free; [*wspomnienia, przemiany*] painless

bezbronn|y *adi.* [*osoba, pisklę*] defenceless GB, defenseless US; [*spojrzenie*] helpless

bezbrzeżn|y *adi.* [*morze, przestrzeń*] boundless

bezcelow|y *adi.* [1] (daremny) [*wysiłki, starania*] pointless [2] (bez określonego celu) [*błądzenie*] aimless

bezcen *m* pot. **za** ~ for next to nothing

bezchmurn|y *adi.* [*niebo, dzień*] cloudless

bezczelnoś|ć *f* insolence

bezczeln|y *adi.* grad. [*osoba, list, śmiech*] insolent; ~**e kłamstwo** a blatant lie

bezcze|ścić *impf vt* książk. to desecrate

bezczynnoś|ć *f* inactivity

bezczynn|y *adi.* inactive; ~**e siedzenie w domu** sitting at home doing nothing

bezdomn|y [] *adi.* [1] [*osoba*] homeless [2] [*zwierzę*] stray
[II] **bezdomn|y** *m*, ~**a** *f* homeless person; ~**i** the homeless

bezdroż|e *n* roadless tract

bezduszn|y *adi.* [*biurokrata*] heartless; [*twarz, przepisy*] impersonal

bezdzietn|y *adi.* [*małżeństwo*] childless

bezdźwięczn|y *adi.* [1] [*głos, szept*] muffled; ~**y śmiech** a silent laugh [2] [*głoski, spółgłoski*] voiceless

bezgotówkow|y *adi.* [*transakcja, kredyt*] cashless

bezgraniczn|y *adi.* [1] (rozległy) [*pustynia, ocean*] boundless [2] (całkowity) [*zaufanie*] utter; ~**a cześć** unbounded respect; **ich głupota jest** ~**a** their stupidity knows no limits

bezimienn|y /beziˈmjennɨ/ *adi.* [*żołnierz, bohater*] unknown; [*datek, broszura*] anonymous; ~**a mogiła** a nameless a. an unknown grave

bezinteresown|y /bezinteˈresɔvnɨ/ *adi.* [*osoba*] unselfish; [*uczucie, parada*] disinterested; [*pomoc, przyjaźń*] selfless

bezkarn|y *adi.* **być** ~**ym** [*występek, chuligan*] to go unpunished

bezkompromisow|y *adi.* [*osoba, krytyka*] uncompromising

bezkonfliktow|y *adi.* [*stosunki, osoba*] peaceful

bezkonkurencyjn|y *adi.* [*zawodnik, produkt*] unrivalled

bezkresn|y *adi.* [*ocean, puszcza*] boundless

bezkręgow|iec *m* Zool. invertebrate

bezkrwaw|y *adi.* [*rewolucja, walka*] bloodless

bezkrytyczn|y *adi.* [*czytelnik, widz*] uncritical; [*miłość, uwielbienie*] blind

bezkształtn|y *adi.* [*postać, nos*] shapeless

bez liku countless

bezlito|sny *adi.* [*sędzia, los*] merciless

bezludn|y *adi.* [*ulica, teren*] deserted; ~**a wyspa** a desert island

bezładn|y *adi.* chaotic; ~**e krzyki** confused shouts

bezmię|sny *adi.* [*dieta, dzień*] meat-free

bezmyśln|y *adi.* [*osoba, postępowanie*] mindless; [*naśladownictwo*] slavish

beznadziejn|y *adi.* hopeless; ~**a pogoda** awful weather

beznamiętn|y *adi.* [*gracz*] unemotional; ~ **wyraz twarzy** an impassive a. a detached expression

bezobjawow|y *adi.* Med. asymptomatic

bezokolicznik *m* infinitive; **czasownik w** ~**u** a verb in the infinitive

bezowocn|y *adi.* fruitless

bezpań|ski *adi.* ownerless; ~**ki pies** a stray dog

bezpartyjn|y [] *adi.* (nienależący do żadnej partii) politically non-aligned; (nienależący do partii komunistycznej) non-Party
[II] **bezpartyjn|y** *m*, ~**a** *f* (nienależący do żadnej partii) independent; (nienależący do partii komunistycznej) non-Party member

bezpieczeństw|o *n* [1] (brak zagrożenia) safety; ~**o i higiena pracy** work safety and hygiene; ~**o publiczne** public safety; ~**o narodowe** national security [2] Polit. **aparat** a. **służba** ~**a** the security services; **siły** ~**a** security forces

bezpiecznik *m* [1] Elektr. fuse; ~ **automatyczny** an automatic cut-out; **przepalił się** ~ a fuse has blown [2] Wojsk. safety catch [3] Techn. safety valve

bezpieczn|y *adi. grad.* safe; **czuć się przy kimś** ~**ym** to feel safe with sb; ~**a ulica/odległość** a safe street/distance; ~**y dla środowiska** environment-friendly

bezpłatn|y *adi.* free (of charge); **urlop** ~**y** unpaid leave

bezpłodn|y *adi.* [1] Med., Wet. infertile, sterile [2] *[krzew, roślina]* fruitless; *[ziemia]* barren [3] *[spory, dyskusja]* fruitless

bezpodstawn|y *adi. [pretensje, zarzuty]* groundless; *[przesłanka, twierdzenie]* unsubstantiated; *[działanie, pytanie]* unreasonable

bezpośredni *adi.* [1] (wprost) direct; **mieć** ~ **związek z czymś** to be directly linked to sth; **brać w czymś** ~ **udział** to be directly a. actively involved in sth [2] (najbliższy) *[otoczenie, sąsiedztwo]* immediate [3] (szczery) *[osoba]* direct

bezpośrednio *adv.* [1] (wprost, osobiście) *[stykać się]* directly [2] (tuż) directly; ~ **za mną** directly a. immediately behind me; ~ **po wojnie** directly after the war

bezprawi|e *n* [1] (anarchia) anarchy [2] (czyn sprzeczny z prawem) unlawful act

bezprawn|y *adi.* unlawful

bezradn|y *adi. [gest, uśmiech]* helpless; **być** ~**ym wobec przemocy** to be helpless in the face of violence

bezrękawnik *m* [1] (sukienka) sleeveless dress; (zakładana na inne ubranie) pinafore (dress) [2] (kamizelka) sleeveless cardigan; (ocieplana) body warmer

bezroboci|e *n* unemployment; **strukturalne/ ukryte** ~**e** structural/hidden unemployment; **wzrost/spadek** ~**a** a rise/fall in unemployment

bezrobotn|y [] *adi. [robotnik, kobieta]* unemployed [] **bezrobotn|y** *m*, ~**a** *f* unemployed person; ~**i** the unemployed; **zasiłek dla** ~**ych** unemployment benefit

bezsenno|ść *f* sleeplessness; (chroniczna) insomnia

bezsenn|y *adi. [noc, podróż]* sleepless

bezsens *m* absurdity; ~ **życia** the pointlessness a. meaninglessness of life

bezsensown|y *adi. grad. [pomysł]* absurd; ~**e pytania** nonsensical a. pointless questions

bezsiln|y *adi.* helpless; *[władza]* powerless

bezskuteczn|y *adi. [poszukiwania, usiłowania]* fruitless

bezsoln|y *adi. [dieta]* salt-free

bezsporn|y *adi. [dowód, fakt]* indisputable, incontrovertible

bezstronn|y *adi. [ocena, opinia, obserwator]* impartial

beztalenci|e *n pot.* (osoba) nonentity

beztros|ka *f* [1] (pogoda ducha) serenity [2] (niefrasobliwość) carefree manner a. attitude

beztros|ki *adi.* [1] (pogodny) *[zabawa]* light-hearted; *[życie]* serene; *[dziecko, młodzież]* carefree [2] (niefrasobliwy) casual

bez ustanku incessantly

bezustann|y *adi. [deszcz, kłótnia, praca]* continuous

bezużyteczn|y *adi. [ubranie, rupieć, książka]* useless; **czuć się** ~**ym** to feel worthless a. useless

bezwartościow|y *adi. [dokument, dzieło]* worthless

bezwarunkow|y *adi. [kapitulacja]* unconditional; *[posłuszeństwo]* absolute

bezwła|d *m* [1] (osoby, instytucji) inertia [2] Med. paralysis

bezwładnoś|ć *f* [1] Med. numbness, paralysis; ~**ć nóg/rąk** paralysis of the legs/hands [2] Fiz. inertia także przen.

bezwładn|y *adi. [kończyna]* paralysed GB, paralyzed US; *[osoba, ciało]* limp

bezwoln|y *adi. [osoba]* submissive

bezwstydn|y *adi. [osoba, zachowanie]* shameless; *[kłamstwo]* barefaced

bezwzględn|y [] *adi. grad.* (okrutny) *[osoba, zachowanie]* ruthless [] *adi. [zakaz, posłuszeństwo]* absolute; ~**e prawdy/ wartości** absolute truths/values; ~**a większość w parlamencie** Polit. an absolute majority in parliament

bezzasadn|y *adi. [twierdzenie, żądanie]* groundless; *[niepokój]* unjustified

bezzwłoczn|y *adi. [działanie, decyzja]* immediate

bezzwrotn|y *adi. [zaliczka]* non-returnable; *[zapomoga]* non-repayable

beż *m, adi. inv.* beige

beżow|y *adi.* beige

bęb|en *m* [1] Muz. drum; ~**en wielki** a bass drum; ~**en mały** a side a. snare drum [2] pot. (duży brzuch) pot-belly [3] (część maszyny) (betoniarki, pralki) drum; (drukarskiej) cylinder; ~**en hamulcowy** a brake drum [4] Techn. (do nawijania) drum; ~**en wyciągarki** a winding drum

bęben|ek *m* [1] (zabawka) (toy) drum [2] pot. (błona bębenkowa) eardrum; **hałas, że** ~**ki pękają** an earsplitting noise [3] Techn. (w rewolwerze) cylinder; (w maszynie do szycia) bobbin case; (w kołowrotku) spool

bębni|ć *impf vi* [1] (uderzać) to drum; (walić, łomotać) to pound; ~**ć palcami po stole** to drum one's fingers on the table [2] (grać na bębnie) to drum [3] pot. (rozgłaszać) ~**ć o czymś** to broadcast sth żart.

bęcwa|ł *m pot.* lummox pot.

bękar|t *m* [1] (nieślubne dziecko) bastard [2] Druk. widow

biadol|ić *impf vi pot.* to bellyache pot.; ~**ić nad czymś** a. **na coś** to moan about sth

białacz|ka *f* Med. leuk(a)emia

biał|ko *n* [1] (część jaja) (egg) white, albumen [2] Anat. white of the eye [3] Biol., Chem. protein

bi|ało *adv. grad.* **ubrana na biało** dressed in white

biało-czerwon|y [I] *adi.* white and red; **flaga biało-czerwona** a red-and-white flag

[II] **biało-czerwoni** *plt* pot. (o sportowcach) the Poles

bi|ały [I] *adi. grad.* [1] (kolor) white; **biały jak śnieg** (as) white as snow; **bielszy od śniegu** whiter than snow [2] (blady) *[osoba]* pale; **biały jak ściana** a. **płótno** (as) white as a sheet

[II] *m* (osoba) white (man)

■ **białe plamy** (na mapie) uncharted territory; (w dziejach) blank pages (of history); **białe szaleństwo** skiing

bibelo|t *m* knick-knack; ~**ty** bric-a-brac

Bibli|a *f* (Pismo Święte) the (Holy) Bible; (egzemplarz) bible

biblijn|y *adi.* biblical

bibliografi|a *f* bibliography

bibliotecz|ka *f* (mebel) bookcase; **przeszklona** ~**ka** a glass bookcase

bibliote|ka *f* [1] (instytucja, pokój, księgozbiór) library; ~**ka szkolna/publiczna** a school/public library; **Biblioteka Narodowa** the National Library; **mieć coś w swojej** ~**ce** to have sth in one's book collection [2] (mebel) bookcase

biblioteka|rz *m*, ~**rka** *f* librarian

bibu|ła *f* [1] (do atramentu) blotting paper; (do filtrowania) filter paper; (do odsączania) absorbent paper [2] pot. (druki, ulotki) underground pamphlets a. publications [3] (krepina) crêpe paper

biceps *m* biceps; **prężyć** ~**y** to flex one's biceps

bicz *m* horsewhip; **strzelić z** ~**a** to crack a whip

■ **jak z** ~**a trzasnął** a. **trzasł** pot. in (less than) no time; **ukręcić** ~ **na siebie** to make a rod for one's own back

bicz|ować *impf* [I] *vt* to scourge; Relig. to flagellate

[II] **biczować się** to flagellate oneself

bi|ć *impf* [I] *vt* [1] (zadawać ciosy) (ręką, kijem) to hit; (pięścią) to punch; (batem) to whip; (pasem) to beat [2] (zabijać) to slaughter *[bydło, świnie]*; to kill *[muchy]* [3] (wyciskać w metalu) to mint *[monety]*; to strike *[medal]* [4] Kulin. to whip *[krem, jajka]*; **bić białko a. pianę** to whisk a. beat egg whites [5] (zwyciężać) *[wojsko, kraj]* [6] (przewyższać) to beat; **bić na głowę kogoś/coś** to beat sb/sth hands down pot. [7] (w kartach) to beat; (w szachach, warcabach) to take

[II] *vi* [1] (uderzać) to strike (**czymś w coś** sth with sth); **bić kilofem w skałę** to strike (at) rock with a pickaxe; **bić pięścią w stół** to bang one's fist on the table [2] (wydawać dźwięk) *[dzwon]* to ring; *[zegar]* to strike [3] pot. *[licznik]* to run [4] (tętnić) *[puls]* to beat [5] (wydobywać się gwałtownie) *[woda, źródło]* to spurt; *[ogień]* to spout; *[zapach, blask]* to be given off [6] Wojsk. to fire; **bić z dział do czegoś** to shell sth

[III] **bić się** to fight (**z kimś o coś/kogoś** with sb

over sth/sb); **bić się za ojczyznę** to fight for one's country; **bić się na szable** to duel with swords

■ **bić się z myślami** to be in two minds, to not be able to make up one's mind

bide|t *m* bidet

bie|c, ~gnąć *impf vi* [1] (poruszać się) to run; ~**c komuś na pomoc** a. **z pomocą** to run a. rush to sb's aid [2] (rozciągać się) *[ścieżka, linia]* to run [3] (trwać) *[czas, życie]* to pass [4] książk. (kierować się) to turn

bie|da *f* [1] (ubóstwo) poverty; **żyć w** ~**dzie** to live in poverty [2] (kłopot) trouble; **(cała)** ~**da w tym, że...** the problem a. trouble is that...; **napytać sobie** ~**dy** to make trouble for oneself; **napytać komuś** ~**dy** to cause sb trouble

■ **od** ~**dy** (w braku czegoś lepszego) for want of anything better; **to jeszcze pół** ~**dy** that's the least of our worries; **prawdziwych przyjaciół poznaje się w** ~**dzie** przysł. a friend in need is a friend indeed przysł.

biedactw|o *n* pot. poor thing

bieda|k *m* [1] (cierpiący biedę) poor man [2] (nieszczęśliwy) poor man a. devil

biedni|eć *impf vi* to become poor a. impoverished

biedn|y *adi. grad.* [1] (ubogi) poor; ~**y jak mysz kościelna** (as) poor as a church mouse [2] (skromny, lichy) *[mieszkanie]* modest, humble; *[ubranie]* shabby [3] (nieszczęśliwy) poor; **o ja** ~**a!** poor me!

biedron|ka *f* ladybird, ladybug US

bie|dzić się *impf v refl.* ~**dzić się nad czymś** to toil over sth *[pracą, książką]*; ~**dzili się nad tym, skąd wziąć pieniądze** they racked their brains trying to work out where to get the money from

bieg [I] *m* [1] (osoby, zwierzęcia) run; **poranny** ~ a morning run; **puścić się** ~**iem** to set off a. run; **poruszać się szybkim** ~**iem** to run fast; **zwolnić/przyspieszyć** ~ a. ~**u** to slow down/ speed up; **w pełnym** ~**u** in full flight [2] (pojazdu) **wyskoczyć w** ~**u (z autobusu/pociągu)** to jump off a moving bus/train [3] Sport race; ~ **sztafetowy** a relay race; ~ **przez płotki** the hurdles; ~ **zjazdowy** a downhill race; ~ **na 100 metrów** the 100 meters sprint a. 100-meter dash US [4] Techn. gear; ~ **wsteczny** reverse gear; **jechać na drugim/trzecim** ~**u** to drive in second/third gear; **wrzucić drugi/trzeci** ~ pot. to get a. shift into second/third gear; **dźwignia zmiany** ~**ów** a gear lever GB, a gear shift US [5] (nurt) course; **w górnym/ dolnym** ~**u rzeki** in the upper/lower reaches of the river [6] (ciąg wydarzeń) course; **naturalny** ~ **rzeczy** the natural course of events; **z** ~**iem lat** a. **czasu** over the course of the years, in a. over the course of time

[II] **biegiem** *adv.* pot. in a hurry; at a. on the double pot.

[III] **w biegu** *adv.* pot. on the run pot.

■ **nadać** ~ **sprawie** (w sądzie, urzędzie) to set the

wheels in motion; **zostawić sprawy własnemu** ∼**owi** to let matters take their own course

biegacz *m* Sport runner

biega|ć *impf vi* to run; ∼**ć na krótkie dystanse** to do sprinting

biegle *adv. grad. [czytać]* fluently; *[grać]* skilfully GB, skillfully US; *[pisać na maszynie]* proficiently; **mówić** ∼ **po angielsku** to speak English fluently

biegłoś|ć *f* proficiency (**w czymś** at a. in sth); expertise (**w czymś** in sth); (w obcym języku) fluency (**w czymś** in sth)

bieg|ły [I] *adi. grad.* proficient (**w czymś** at a. in sth); (w obcym języku) fluent (**w czymś** in sth)

[II] *m* (specjalista) ∼**ły sądowy** expert witness

biegnąć → **biec**

biegun *m* [1] (płoza) rocker; **fotel/koń na** ∼**ach** a rocking chair/horse [2] Elektr., Fiz., Geog. pole; ∼ **północny/południowy** the North/South Pole; ∼ **dodatni/ujemny** the positive/negative (pole)

■ **dwa** ∼**y** polar opposites

biegun|ka *f* Med. diarrhoea GB, diarrhea US

biegunow|y *adi.* Elektr., Fiz., Geog. polar

biel *f* white; ∼ **śniegu/alabastru** the white(ness) of snow/alabaster; **w** ∼**i** *[osoba]* (dressed) in white

biel|eć *impf vi* [1] (stawać się białym) *[lis, sierść]* to turn white; *[włosy]* to turn grey GB a. gray US [2] (wyróżniać się bielą) *[śnieg, budynek]* to show white

biel|ić *impf* [I] *vt* [1] (malować) to whitewash *[ściany, budynek]*; to treat *[sth]* with limewash *[drzewa]* [2] Chem., Techn. to bleach *[papier, materiał]*; to refine *[cukier]* [3] Techn. (cynować) to blanch

[II] **bielić się** *[żagle, pola]* to show white

bieli|zna *f* [1] (ubranie) underwear; (damska) lingerie; ∼**zna osobista** underwear; ∼**zna nocna** nightclothes [2] (domowa) linen; ∼**zna pościelowa/stołowa** bedlinen/table linen

bier|ki *plt* Gry spillikins, jackstraws GB

biern|y *adi.* [1] (pasywny) *[osoba]* passive; ∼**a znajomość języka** a reading knowledge of a language [2] Jęz. passive; **strona** ∼**a** the passive (voice)

bierzmowa|nie *n* Relig. confirmation

bieżąc|y *adi.* [1] (obecny) *[rok, stulecie]* current; **list z 3** ∼**ego miesiąca** a letter dated the 3rd of this month a. the 3rd instant przest. [2] (aktualny, teraźniejszy) *[sprawy]* current; ∼**e prace/negocjacje** work/negotiations currently in progress; ∼**e naprawy** running repairs; **rachunek** ∼**y** a current account GB, a checking account US [3] (płynący) ∼**a woda** running water

bieżni|a *f* [1] (na stadionie) (running) track [2] (przyrząd do ćwiczeń) treadmill

bieżnik *m* [1] (serweta) (table) runner [2] Techn. (warstwa opony) tread

bigos *m* [1] Kulin. stewed dish made of sauerkraut and/or fresh cabbage, meat and mushrooms [2] przen. mess; **narobić** ∼**u** to make a mess of things

bijaty|ka *f* pot. brawl; punch-up pot.; **wszcząć** ∼**kę** to start a fight

bikini *n inv.* bikini

bil|a *f* ball

bilans *m* [1] (zestawienie) balance; (dokument) balance sheet; ∼ **otwarcia/zamknięcia** an opening/a closing balance; **sporządzić** ∼ to draw up a balance sheet [2] (podsumowanie) assessment; (efekt) outcome

bilar|d *m* billiards; ∼**d elektryczny** pinball

bile|t *m* ticket; ∼**t do teatru** a theatre ticket; ∼**t na pociąg** a train ticket; ∼**t miesięczny** a monthly season ticket; ∼**t ulgowy** a reduced-fare ticket; ∼**t powrotny** a return ticket, a round trip ticket US; ∼**t wizytowy** a visiting card GB, a calling card US

bilete|r *m* usher

bilion *m* [1] (milion milionów) trillion; billion GB przest. [2] (tysiąc milionów) billion, thousand million

billboar|d /'bilbord/ *m* billboard

billing *m* Telekom. (rejestracja połączeń) telephone billing; (wydruk) itemized (tele)phone bill

bilon *m* coin; **100 złotych w** ∼**ie** 100 zlotys in coin(s)

bimba|ć *impf vi* pot. to not give a hoot pot.; ∼**ć (sobie) z czegoś** to make light of sth; ∼**ć sobie z kogoś** to snub sb

biochemi|a *f* biochemistry

biod|ro *n* hip; **sukienka za ciasna w** ∼**rach** a dress too tight at the hips

biografi|a *f* biography

biolo|g *m* biologist

biologi|a *f* biology

biologiczn|y *adi.* biological

biopsj|a *f* Med. biopsy

biorc|a *m* Med. recipient; ∼**a krwi/narządu** a blood/an organ recipient

bis *m* encore; **wykonać coś na** ∼ to perform sth as an encore; **brawo,** ∼**!** bravo, encore!

biskup *m* bishop

bis|ować *impf* [I] *vt* to give an encore of *[utwór, piosenkę]*

[II] *vi* to give a. perform an encore

biszkop|t *m* [1] (ciasto) sponge (cake) [2] (ciastko) sponge finger

bi|t *m* Komput. bit

bit|wa *f* battle; **wydać/stoczyć** ∼**wę** to give/do battle; ∼**wa pod Grunwaldem** the Battle of Grunwald; ∼**wa na śnieżki** a snowball fight; ∼**wa o klientów/głosy wyborców** przen. the battle for customers/votes

bit|y *adi.* [1] (ubity) *[śmietana]* whipped [2] pot. (cały) whole; **czekać** ∼**y kwadrans** to wait a whole fifteen minutes

biur|ko *n* desk; **siedzieć za** ∼**kiem** a. **przy** ∼**ku** to sit at a. behind a desk

biu|ro *n* (instytucja) office; (dział) bureau; ∼**ro matrymonialne** a marriage agency a. bureau; ∼**ro podróży** a travel agency a. bureau; ∼**ro prasowe** a press office; ∼**ro rzeczy znalezionych** a lost property office; **pracować w** ∼**rze** to work in an office

biurokracj|a *f* bureaucracy, red tape

biurow|iec *m* pot. office block

biurow|y *adi. [praca, meble]* office

biu|st *m* ① (piersi) bust; **obfity** ∼**st** an ample a. a full bust ② (rzeźba) bust

biustonosz *m* bra; **rozpiąć/zapiąć** ∼ to unfasten/to fasten one's bra

biwak *m* camp; **rozłożyć się** ∼**iem** to set up camp

biwak|ować *impf vi* (pod gołym niebem) to bivouac; (w namiotach) to camp

biznes *m* ① (działalność gospodarcza) business; **ludzie** ∼**u** business people ② pot. (firma) business; **prowadzić mały** ∼ to run a small business ③ pot. (korzyść) profit ④ pot. (sprawa) business; **to nie twój** ∼! that's none of your business!; **mam do ciebie** ∼ there's something I want to ask you

biznesmen *m* businessman

biznesplan *m* business plan

biżuteri|a *f* jewellery GB, jewelry US; **sztuczna** ∼**a** costume jewellery

bla|cha *f* ① (wyrób metalowy) metal sheet; (cynowa) tin; **okuć coś** ∼**chą** to plate sth (with metal) ② (wierzch pieca) hob; **postawić coś na** ∼**sze** to put sth on the stove ③ Kulin. (do ciasta) baking tin; (do ciasteczek) baking tray; (do mięsa) roasting tin ④ pot. (karoseria samochodowa) (car) shell
■ **wykuć coś na** ∼**chę** pot. to learn sth inside out a. by heart

blacharz *m* ① (samochodowy) panel beater GB, autobody mechanic US ② (wyrabiający przedmioty) metalsmith; (specjalizujący się w cynie) tinsmith; (kryjący dachy) roofer

bla|do *adv. grad. [uśmiechnąć się]* weakly; **wyglądać** ∼ **do** *[osoba]* to look pale; **wypaść** ∼**do** to give a weak a. lame performance

bl|ady *adi. grad.* ① *[twarz, policzki, cera]* pale, pallid; **blady jak ściana** (as) white as a sheet; **padł na nich blady strach** they were scared out of their wits, they were quaking in their boots ② (słaby) *[uśmiech]* pale, wan; **wyruszyć bladym świtem** to set off at the crack of dawn; **nie mieć bladego pojęcia o czymś** to not have the slightest a. foggiest pot. idea about sth
■ **blada twarz** paleface

blak|nąć *impf vi [kolory, wspomnienia]* to fade

blankie|t *m* (do wypełnienia) form; (z nadrukiem firmy) headed writing paper a. notepaper

blask *m* ① (jasność) (bright) light; **w** ∼**u słońca** in bright sunlight; **w** ∼**u dnia** in the full light of day ② przen. (splendor) splendour GB, splendor US; **dodawać czemuś** ∼**u** to add lustre a. a bit of glamour to sth; **w** ∼**u chwały** in a blaze of glory
■ ∼**i i cienie czegoś** the good side and the bad side of sth

bla|t *m* (stołu, biurka) top; (w kuchni, w warsztacie) work surface; **stolik ze szklanym** ∼**tem** a glass-topped coffee table

bl|ednąć *impf vi* ① *[twarz]* to go a. turn pale ② (tracić intensywność) *[kolor, wspomnienie]* to fade

blef *m* bluff

blef|ować *impf vi* to bluff

bleze|r *m* cardigan

blich|r *m* książk. show; ∼**r wielkiego miasta** the glitter a. lights of the big city

bli|ski *adi. grad.* ① (sąsiedni) close; ∼**scy sąsiedzi** close neighbours; **najbliższe okolice miasta** the city's immediate environs; **w** ∼**skim sąsiedztwie** in the (immediate) vicinity ② (niedaleki w czasie) **w** ∼**skich odstępach** at short intervals; **najbliższa przyszłość** the near(est) a. immediate future; **najbliższe lata/godziny** the next few years/hours ③ *[przyjaźń, rodzina]* close; **być** ∼**skim czyjemuś sercu** to be close to sb's heart; **być** ∼**skim płaczu/zwycięstwa** to be close to a. on the verge of tears/winning; **przy** ∼**ższym poznaniu** on closer acquaintance

bli|sko ① *adv. grad.* ① (w przestrzeni) (w pobliżu) close; ∼**sko (od) parku/stadionu** close to a. near a park/stadium; **nie podchodź za** ∼**sko** don't come too close a. near; **stąd masz a. jest już** ∼**sko** it's not far from here ② (w czasie) not far off; **jesień już** ∼**sko** autumn's not far off; ∼**sko północy** close on a. just before midnight ③ (o związkach) *[związany, spokrewniony]* closely; **wpółpracować z kimś** ∼**sko** to work closely a. in close cooperation with sb; **być z kimś** ∼**sko** to be (very) close to sb; **ludzie, którzy są** ∼**sko prezydenta** people close to the president ④ przen. close; **być** ∼**sko prawdy** to be close to a. not far from the truth
② *part.* (prawie) close on; ∼**sko godzinę/tydzień/rok** close on a. nearly an hour/a week/a year; ∼**sko pięć milionów** close on a. nearly five million; **mieć** ∼**sko 50 lat** to be almost a. approaching fifty
③ **bliżej** *adv. comp.* (lepiej) better; **zapoznać się** ∼**żej ze sprawą** to take a closer look at a problem; ∼**żej nieznany** unidentified; **sprawy** ∼**żej mi nieznane** things I know very little about
④ **z bliska** *adv.* (z małej odległości) *[patrzeć, widzieć]* from close up; **przyjrzeć się z** ∼**ska czemuś** to take a good a. close look at sth

bliskoznaczn|y *adi.* close in meaning; **wyrazy** ∼**e** synonyms

bli|zna *f* scar

Bliźnia|k *m* pot. Gemini

bliźnia|k *m* [1] (osoba) twin; **brat** ~**k** a twin brother [2] (dom) semi-detached (house) GB

bliźnię *n* twin; ~**ęta jednojajowe/dwujajowe** identical/fraternal twins

blocz|ek *m* [1] (zeszyt) (note)pad, block GB [2] Techn. block

blok *m* [1] (budynek) block (of flats) GB, (apartment) block US [2] (bryła) block; ~ **granitu** a. **granitowy** a block of granite, a granite block [3] (wydzielone miejsce) block; (w obozie) barracks (block); ~ **operacyjny** an operating block a. wing [4] (seria, całość) block [5] (zeszyt) pad, block GB; ~ **rysunkowy** a drawing a. sketch pad [6] Polit. bloc [7] Techn. block; ~ **napędowy samochodu** a car's cylinder a. engine block [8] Sport (w siatkówce) block; (na bieżni) (starting) block

bloka|da *f* [1] (izolacja) blockade; ~**da ekonomiczna** an economic embargo a. blockade; ~**da drogi** a roadblock [2] Med. nerve block; ~**da chemiczna** (a) chemical blockade [3] Techn. (urządzenie) block; ~**da zapłonu** Aut. an immobilizer; ~**da kierownicy** Aut. a steering lock

blok|ować *impf* **I** *vt* [1] (utrudniać) to block *[przejście, dojazd]* [2] Sport to block *[podanie, strzał]*; to stop *[piłkę, krążek]* [3] (utrudniać) to block *[ustawę, projekt, decyzję]* [4] (unieruchamiać) to stop *[licznik, urządzenie]*; to jam *[mechanizm, drzwi]* [5] (izolować) to blockade *[państwo, terytorium]* [6] (w bankowości) to block, to freeze *[konto]*
II *vi* Sport (w siatkówce) to block

blond *adi. inv. [włosy]* blond(e); *[osoba]* blond(e); **zrobić się na** ~ to dye one's hair blonde

blondyn *m* blonde (man)

blondyn|ka *f* blonde

bluszcz *m* Bot. ivy

bluz|a *f* [1] (sportowa) sweatshirt; (dresowa) tracksuit top [2] (robocza) top; ~**a harcerska** a scout shirt

bluz|ka *f* (jedwabna, bawełniana) blouse; (sportowa) top; ~**ka koszulowa** a shirt-blouse

bluźni|ć *impf vi* [1] (uwłaczać) to blaspheme (**przeciwko komuś/czemuś** against sb/sth) [2] (przeklinać) to swear

bluźnierc|a *m* blasphemer

bluźnierstw|o *n* blasphemy

błaga|ć *impf vt* to beg, to implore ~**ć kogoś o przebaczenie** to beg sb for forgiveness; ~**ć pomocy** to beg for help

błagaln|y *adi.* beseeching

błahost|ka *f* trifle

błah|y *adi. grad. [przyczyna, sprawa]* trivial

błazen *m* [1] (w cyrku) clown [2] (zachowujący się niepoważnie) clown; **wyjść na** ~**zna** to make a fool of oneself [3] (trefniś) fool; **nadworny** ~**zen** a court jester

błazn|ować *impf vi* to clown about a. around

bł|ąd *m* [1] (pomyłka) mistake, error; **błąd ortograficzny** a spelling mistake; **błąd rachunkowy** a. **w obliczeniach** a miscalculation; **błąd zecerski**

a typo pot.; **zrobić** a. **popełnić błąd** to make a mistake a. an error; **roić się od błędów** to be full of mistakes [2] (złe postępowanie) mistake; **błędy młodości** the sins of youth; **przyznać się do błędu** to admit to a mistake; **uczyć się na błędach** to learn by a. from one's (own) mistakes; **przyczyną wypadku był błąd człowieka** the accident was caused by human error [3] (fałszywe przekonanie) misconception, misapprehension; **być w błędzie** to be under a misapprehension; **wprowadzić kogoś w błąd** to mislead sb; **wyprowadzić kogoś z błędu** to put sb right [4] (zły wynik) error; **błąd statystyczny** a statistical error; **błąd odczytu** a misreading; **margines błędu** a margin of error

błą|dzić *impf vi* [1] (szukając drogi) to wander about a. around; ~**dzić po lesie** to wander around in the forest [2] (chodzić bez celu) to roam; ~**dzić gdzieś myślami** przen. to let one's thoughts wander a. roam [3] (mylić się) to be mistaken; ~**dzić jest rzeczą ludzką** to err is human

błąka|ć się *impf v refl.* to roam; ~**ć się od wsi do wsi** to roam from village to village

błędnik *m* Anat. labyrinth

błędn|y *adi.* [1] (niepoprawny) *[odpowiedź]* incorrect; *[założenie, hipoteza]* false, erroneous; *[rozumowanie]* unsound, fallacious; ~**e mniemanie** a misguided opinion; ~**e obliczenie** a. ~**y wynik** a miscalculation, a faulty calculation [2] (nieprzytomny) *[spojrzenie]* vacant; **chodzić jak** ~**y** to walk around in a daze

błęki|t *m* blue; ~**t morza/jej oczu** the blue of the sea/her eyes

błękitn|y *adi.* sky a. light blue

bło|gi *adi. [nastrój, sen]* blissful

błogosław|ić *impf* **I** *vt* [1] (czynić znak krzyża) to bless [2] (być wdzięcznym) to be grateful (**kogoś za coś** to sb for sth)
II *vi* (życzyć szczęścia) to give one's blessing (**komuś** to sb)

błogosławieństw|o *n* [1] (obrzęd, życzenie) blessing, benediction; **udzielić komuś** ~**a** to bless sb; **prosić kogoś o** ~**o** to ask for sb's blessing; **osiem** ~ the Beatitudes [2] (dobrodziejstwo) blessing [3] pot. (zgoda) blessing; okay pot.; **mieć czyjeś** ~**o na zrobienie czegoś** to have sb's blessing to do sth

błogosławi|ony **I** *adi.* [1] (pomyślny) *[czas, chwila]* blessed; (zbawienny) beneficial [2] Relig. blessed; ~**eni ubodzy duchem** Bibl. blessed are the poor in spirit; ~**onej pamięci** of blessed memory książk.; **w** ~**onym stanie** książk. pregnant
II **błogosławi|ony** *m*, ~**ona** *f* Relig. a blessed person; ~**eni** the Blessed

błon|a *f* [1] Anat., Biol. membrane; ~**a dziewicza** the hymen; ~**a komórkowa** cell membrane; ~**a śluzowa** mucous membrane [2] Fot. film

błonnik *m* Biol. fibre GB, fiber US, cellulose; **dieta bogata w ~** a high-fibre diet

błotnik *m* (w rowerze, motocyklu) mudguard; (w samochodzie) wing GB, fender US

błotni|sty *adi.* [*droga, łąka, kolor*] muddy

bło|to 🔲 *n* mud; **ugrzęznąć w ~cie** to get bogged down a. stuck in the mud

🔳 **błota** *plt* marsh(land)

■ **obrzucić kogoś ~tem** to throw a. sling mud at sb; **wyrzucać pieniądze w ~to** to throw money down the drain; **zmieszać kogoś z ~tem** (naubliżać) to hurl abuse a. insults at sb; (oczernić) to drag sb through the mud

błysk *m* 🔲 (odblask światła) flash; **~ pioruna** a lightning flash; **~ wrogości/radości w czyichś oczach** przen. a flash a. glint of hostility/joy in sb's eyes 🔢 pot. (szybkość) **~iem sprzątnąć mieszkanie** to clean the flat in a flash 🔢 (połysk) shine; **wypolerować coś na ~** to polish sth to a shine 🔢 Ryboł. spinner

błyskać *impf* → **błysnąć**

błyskawic|a *f* (flash of) lightning; **szybki jak ~a** as quick as lightning; **ale z niego ~a!** przen. he's like greased lightning!

błyskawiczn|y *adi.* [*refleks, reakcja*] lightning; **z ~ą szybkością** with lightning speed

błyskotliw|y *adi. grad.* [*osoba, kariera*] brilliant; [*rozmowa*] sparkling

błys|nąć *pf* — **błys|kać** *impf* 🔲 *vi* 🔲 (zaświecić) to flash; [*oczy*] to sparkle; **na niebie ~nął piorun** lightning flashed in the sky 🔢 (wyróżnić się) to shine; **~nąć w matematyce** to shine at maths 🔢 (wyrażać uczucie) **~kać czymś** [*oczy*] to shine with sth [*podnieceniem*]; to burn with sth [*gniewem*]

🔳 **błysnąć się — błyskać się** *v imp.* **~nęło się** there was a flash of lightning

błyszcz|eć *impf vi* to shine

błyszczyk *m* 🔲 Kosmet. lipgloss 🔢 Ryboł. spinner

bo 🔲 *coni.* 🔲 (ponieważ) because; for książk.; **niepraktyczna, bo jasna, suknia** an impractical dress, because it's a light colour 🔢 (w przeciwnym razie) or (else); **uważaj, bo zrobisz sobie krzywdę** be careful or you'll hurt yourself

🔳 *part.* pot. 🔲 (przeczące) **bo ja wiem?** I don't really know; **a bo to źle być dzieckiem?** is it that bad (then), being a child? 🔢 (wyrażające bezcelowość) **nie odpowiedziałem mu, bo i po co?** I didn't answer him – what's the point?

🔳 (a) **bo co?** *inter.* pot. why; „**mówił coś o mnie?**" – „**a bo co?**" 'did he say something about me?' – 'why, what if he did?'; „**nie stój tutaj**" – „**a bo co?**" 'don't stand there' – 'why's that?'

boa 🔲 *m inv.* Zool. (wąż) boa

🔳 *n inv.* (szal) boa

❑ **~ dusiciel** Zool. boa constrictor

boazeri|a *f* wood(en) panelling; **ściana wyłożona ~ą** a panelled wall

bochen|ek *m* loaf (of bread)

bocian *m* Zool. stork

■ **wierzyć w ~y** to believe that storks bring babies

bocz|ek *m* bacon

boczn|y *adi.* [*ulica, wejście, kieszeń*] side; **~y wiatr** a crosswind; **lusterko ~e** a wing mirror; **~a linia boiska** a sideline; **nawa ~a** an aisle

bocz|yć się *impf v refl.* pot. to be cross (**na kogoś o/ za coś** with sb about/for sth)

bodaj 🔲 *part.* 🔲 (chyba) perhaps; **był wtedy ~(że) nauczycielem** I think he was a teacher at the time 🔢 (przynajmniej) at least 🔢 pot. (żeby) **~by wszyscy byli tacy** if only we were all like that

🔳 *coni.* (chociażby) say; **masz coś do czytania, ~ gazetę?** have you got anything to read, like a newspaper?

bo|dziec *m* 🔲 (czynnik) stimulus; **reagować na bodźce** to respond to stimuli 🔢 (zachęta) incentive (**do czegoś** to sth)

bogactw|o *n* 🔲 (zamożność) wealth; **żyć w ~ie** to live in affluence a. opulence 🔢 przen. (skarb) asset; **~a naturalne** natural resources a. wealth 🔢 (myśli) wealth; (towarów, barw) (rich) variety; (form, kształtów) multiplicity; (języka, dźwięków) richness; (przyrody) lushness

bogacz *m* rich a. wealthy man

bogat|ka *f* Zool. great tit

boga|ty 🔲 *adi. grad.* 🔲 (majętny) wealthy 🔢 (kosztowny) [*strój, wystrój*] rich 🔢 (obfity, różnorodny) rich (**w coś** in sth); abounding (**w coś** in a. with sth); **~te słownictwo** a rich a. extensive vocabulary; **potrawy ~te w wapń** calcium-rich meals

🔳 *m* rich man; **~ci** the rich

bogi|ni *f* goddess także przen.; **~ni miłości/wojny** the goddess of love/war

bohate|r *m* 🔲 (narodowy, wojenny) hero 🔢 (powieści, filmu) main character; **~r negatywny** a villain 🔢 (zdarzenia) central figure; **~r dnia/wieczoru** the hero of the day/evening

bohaters|ki *adi.* [*czyn, postawa*] heroic

bohaterstw|o *n* heroism

boisk|o *n* (piłkarskie, hokejowe) pitch; (siatkarskie) court; (szkolne) (sports) field

bo|ja *f* Żegl. buoy

bojaźliw|y *adi. grad.* (lękliwy) [*dziecko*] timid, timorous; [*spojrzenie*] apprehensive; (tchórzliwy) faint-hearted

bojaź|ń *f* książk. fear; **~ń Boża** the fear of God

bojko|t *m* boycott; **~t wyborów** a boycott of an election; **~t towarzyski** social ostracism

bojle|r *m* boiler

bojow|y *adi.* 🔲 (związany z walką) battle; **okrzyk ~y** a war a. battle cry 🔢 [*postawa, nastrój*] militant

bok 🔲 *m* 🔲 (osoby, zwierzęcia) side; **przewrócić się na prawy/lewy ~** to turn over onto one's right/left side; **robić ~ami** [*koń*] to pant; przen. to cope with difficulty [2] (strona) side; **porozmawiać z kimś na ~u** to have a quiet word with sb; **zjechać na ~** to pull over to the side; **na ~!** step aside! [3] (szafy, stołu, kwadratu) side

[II] boki *plt* pot. money earned on the side pot.

[III] bokiem *adv.* sideways; **ominąć coś ~iem** to bypass sth; **patrzeć na kogoś/coś ~iem** to look askance at sb/sth

■ **zrywać ~i (ze śmiechu)** pot. to split one's sides (laughing); **mieć coś pod ~iem** pot. to have sth close at hand a. close by; **mieć kogoś na ~u** pot. to have sb on the side pot.; **stać z ~u** to stand on the sidelines

boks[1] *m* Sport boxing

boks[2] *m* (pomieszczenie) box; (stajenny) (loose) box, stall; (w szatni) cubicle; (w pracy) section, partition

bokse|r *m* [1] Sport boxer [2] (pies) boxer

boksers|ki *adi.* Sport boxing

boks|ować *impf* **[I]** *vt* (okładać pięściami) to pummel

[II] *vi* (uprawiać boks, walczyć) to box

[III] boksować się to box (**z kimś** with sb)

bol|ec *m* Techn. pin

bol|eć *impf vi* to hurt także przen.; **~i mnie noga** my leg hurts a. is aching; **~i mnie głowa/brzuch/ząb** I have a headache/stomach ache/toothache; **~i mnie gardło** I have a sore throat

■ **oczy ~ą patrzeć** it's a real eyesore; **uszy ~ą słuchać** it's enough to give you a headache; **~eć nad czymś losem/nieszczęściem** to bemoan someone's fate/bad luck

bole|sny *adi. grad.* [1] [kuracja] painful; [rana] painful, sore [2] [temat, wspomnienie] painful; [słowa] hurtful

boleści *plt* (stomach) pains

■ **przywódca/lekarz od siedmiu ~ci** żart. a poor leader/doctor

bomb|a [I] *f* [1] (pocisk, materiał wybuchowy) bomb; **~a atomowa** an atom bomb; **~a głębinowa** a depth charge a. bomb; **~a wodorowa** a hydrogen bomb, H-bomb; **~a zegarowa** a time bomb także przen.; **podłożyć ~ę** to plant a bomb; **zrzucać ~y** to drop bombs; **wpaść/wypaść jak ~a** to storm in/out [2] pot., przen. (sensacyjna wiadomość) bombshell

[II] *inter.* pot. (that's) fantastic! pot.

■ **~a (poszła) w górę** they're off!

bombard|ować *impf vt* [1] (zrzucać bomby) to bomb [2] (pociskami artyleryjskimi) to bombard; **~ować kogoś pytaniami/skargami** przen. to bombard sb with questions/complaints

bombastyczn|y *adi. grad.* książk. [metaforyka, styl] bombastic, pompous

bomb|ka *f* (gaudy) bauble

bombonier|ka *f* box of chocolates

bombow|iec *m* Lotn. bomber

bombow|y *adi.* [1] [zamach] bomb [2] [dywizjon] bomber [3] pot. [fryzura, książka, wiadomość] fantastic pot.

bon *m* [1] (talon) voucher; **~ książkowy** a book token [2] (papier wartościowy) bond, debenture US

bonifika|ta *f* (price) reduction; **udzielać ~ty na coś** to give a discount on sth; **sprzedawać coś z ~tą** to sell sth at a discount a. reduced price

bordo *n inv.* Wina Bordeaux (wine)

bor|ować *impf vt* to drill [ząb]

borsuk *m* Zool. badger

bos|ki *adi.* [1] (dotyczący Boga) [opieka, wszechmoc] divine; **na litość a. miłość ~ką!** for God's a. heaven's sake!; **niech cię ręka ~ka broni!** God a. heaven forbid! [2] (dotyczący bóstwa lub boga) [pochodzenie, moc] divine [3] przen. (wspaniały, cudowny) super pot.; divine przest., pot.

bosko *adv.* pot. fabulously pot.; divinely przest., pot.

boso *adv.* [chodzić, biegać] barefoot(ed)

bos|y *adi.* [osoba] barefoot(ed); **~e nogi** bare feet

botani|ka *f* botany

bot|ek *m* (lined) boot

bowiem *coni.* książk. because; for książk.

b|ób *m* broad bean

■ **zadać komuś bobu** pot. to give sb what for pot.

b|óbr *m* Zool. beaver; **płakać jak bóbr** to cry one's eyes out

b|óg *m* [1] Relig. **Bóg** God; **Bóg Ojciec** God the Father; **Bóg Zastępów** Lord (God) of hosts; **Bóg zapłać** (podziękowanie) God bless you; **bój a. bójcie się Boga!** for the love of God!; **broń (Panie) Boże** a. **niech Bóg broni!** God a. heaven forbid!; **chwała Bogu!** praise the Lord!, praise be to God!; **dzięki Bogu!** thank God!; **jak Boga kocham!** honest to God! pot.; I swear to God!; **tak mi dopomóż Bóg** so help me God!; **niech cię Bóg ma w swojej opiece** God be with you; **(wielki) Boże!** good God a. Lord! [2] Relig. (istota) god także przen.; (wizerunek) idol także przen.

■ **człowiek strzela, Pan Bóg kule nosi** przysł. man proposes, God disposes przysł.; **kto rano wstaje temu Pan Bóg daje** przysł. the early bird catches the worm przysł.

bój|ka *f* scuffle; scrap pot.; **wdać się w ~kę** to get into a fight a. scuffle

ból *m* [1] pain; (lekki) discomfort; **~ w klatce piersiowej** (a) chest pain; **~ głowy** a headache; **~ zęba/ucha/żołądka** (a) toothache/(an) earache/(a) stomach ache; **~ gardła** a sore throat [2] (cierpienie) pain; **sprawiać komuś ~** to hurt sb

b|óść *impf* **[I]** *vt* [1] [krowa, byk] to gore; [baran, koza] to butt [2] (kłuć) to poke; **bóść konia ostrogą** to dig in one's spurs

[II] bóść się to butt each other

bractw|o *n* [1] (znajomi) company [2] Relig. brotherhood

brać *impf* → **wziąć**

brak [I] *m* [1] (pieniędzy, żywności) shortage; (doświadczenia, dowodów, snu) lack; (witamin) deficiency; **odczuwać ~ czegoś** to lack sth; **odczuwać ~**

kogoś to miss sb; **cierpieć na** ~ **pieniędzy/czasu** to be pressed for money/time; **z** ~**u czegoś** for want of sth [2] (produkt wybrakowany) reject

[II] *praed.* ~ **mi słów** I'm at a loss for words; **ludzi tu nie** ~ there are plenty of people here; **nie** ~ **mu niczego** he has everything; **nie** ~ **jej pomysłów** she's full of ideas

[III] **braki** *plt* (w wykształceniu) gaps; (jakościowe) defects; **mieć poważne** ~**i w matematyce** to be way behind in maths

brak|nąć *pf, impf v imp.* ~**ło mu sił** he was exhausted; ~**ło nam pieniędzy** we were short of money; ~**ło mi jednego punktu na egzaminie** I needed (just) one more point in the exam

brak|ować *impf v imp.* ~**uje mi czasu** I don't have enough time; ~**uje mu dobrego wychowania** he lacks (good) manners; **w tym tekście** ~**uje przecinków** there are no commas in the text; **stołowi** ~**uje jednej nogi** the table is missing a leg; ~**uje mi pięciu lat do emerytury** I have five years left a. to go before I retire; ~**uje tu tylko...** pot. all that's missing is... ; **nic mu nie** ~**uje** there's nothing wrong with him; **niewiele** ~**owało** it was a close shave a. thing pot.; **tylko tego** ~**owało!** that's all we need a. needed!

bram|a *f* [1] (drzwi) gate; (wjazd, wejście) gate(way) (**do czegoś** to sth) [2] przen. gateway; ~**a do sławy/sukcesu** a gateway to fame/success

bram|ka *f* [1] gate; (przy stadionie sportowym) turnstile [2] Sport (w grach zespołowych) goal; **stać na** ~**ce** to be in a. to keep goal; **strzelić** ~**kę** to score a goal [3] Sport (w kajakarstwie, narciarstwie) gate [4] pot. (wejście) entrance; **stać na** ~**ce** to stand on the door post.

bramkarz *m* [1] (gracz) goalkeeper [2] pot. (ochroniarz) bouncer pot.

bransole|ta *f* bracelet

branż|a *f* business; **człowiek z** ~**y** pot. a person in the same line of business a. trade

bra|t *m* [1] (krewny) brother; ~**t cioteczny** a cousin; **przyrodni** ~**t** a half-brother [2] pot. (sposób zwracania się) mate GB pot., buddy US pot. [3] przen. (bliźni) brother [4] (zakonnik) brother

■ **on dla mnie ani** ~**t, ani swat** he's nothing to do with me

bratan|ek *m* nephew

bratanic|a *f* niece

brat|ek *m* Bot. pansy

braters|ki *adi.* brotherly

braterstw|o *n* brotherhood, camaraderie

■ ~**o broni** brotherhood in arms; ~**o krwi** blood brotherhood

bratow|a *f* sister-in-law (*brother's wife*)

braw|o [I] *n* applause; **bić** ~**o** to applaud; „**a teraz duże** ~**a dla...**" 'and now let's have a big hand for a. give a big hand to...'

[II] *inter.* bravo!

brawu|ra *f* bravado

brąz *m* [1] (stop) bronze; **epoka** ~**u** the Bronze Age [2] (kolor) brown, bronze

brązowo *adv.* **na** ~ *[farbować]* brown; *[ubierać się]* in brown

brązow|y *adi.* [1] (zrobiony z brązu) bronze [2] (kolor) brown

bredni|a *f* pot. rubbish pot.; **opowiadać** ~**e** to talk rubbish

bre|dzić *impf vi* [1] (w gorączce) to rave; ~**dzić przez sen** to ramble a. rave in one's sleep [2] pejor. (mówić rzeczy głupie) to blather GB pot.; to babble

brelo|k *m* (do zegarka) pendant

br|ew *f* (eye)brow; **zmarszczyć brwi** to knit one's brows, to frown; **ołówek do brwi** an eyebrow pencil

brezen|t *m* tarpaulin

brn|ąć *impf vi* [1] (iść z trudem) to wade [2] przen. ~**ąć w długi/kłamstwa** to get bogged down in debt/lies

br|oda *f* [1] (część twarzy) chin [2] (zarost na twarzy) beard; **nosić brodę** to wear a beard; **zapuścić brodę** to grow a beard

■ **kawał z brodą** an old chestnut pot.

broda|ty *adi. [mężczyzna, zwierzę]* bearded

bro|dzić *impf vi* to paddle; (głęboko) to wade

brodzik *m* [1] (płytki basen) paddling pool GB, wading pool US [2] (płytka wanna) footbath; (z prysznicem) shower base, shower-tray US

bro|ić *impf vi [dzieci]* to misbehave

broku|ł *m* Bot., Kulin. (sprouting) broccoli

bro|nić *impf* [I] *vt* [1] (walcząc) to defend (**coś przed kimś/czymś** sth from sb/sth) [2] Prawo (przed sądem) to defend; ~**nić w procesie** to act as defence counsel [3] (zakazywać) to forbid (**czegoś** sth) [4] Sport (w piłce nożnej, hokeju) to defend; (stać na bramce) to keep goal

[II] **bronić się** [1] (w walce, w sądzie) to defend oneself [2] Uniw. to defend a thesis/dissertation

bro|ń *f* [1] (do walki) weapon; (zbiorowo) arms; ~**ń masowego rażenia** weapons of mass destruction; **chwycić za** ~**ń** to take up arms; **składać** ~**ń** to lay down one's arms; **zawieszenie** ~**ni** a ceasefire, a truce; **rzuć** ~**ń!** throw down your weapon!; **napad z** ~**nią w ręku** (an) armed robbery [2] (formacja) arm [3] przen. weapon przen.; **kłamstwo to niebezpieczna** ~**ń** lies are a dangerous weapon; **wytrącić komuś** ~**ń z ręki** to leave sb without a leg to stand on

■ **to nie moja** ~**ka** pot. it's nothing to do with me, it's none of my business

brosz|ka *f* brooch; ~**ka z brylantem** a diamond brooch

broszu|ra *f* (książeczka) booklet; (z ilustracjami) brochure; (propagandowa) pamphlet

browa|r *m* [1] (przedsiębiorstwo) brewery; **właściciel** ~**ru** a brewer [2] pot. (piwo) beer; brew pot.

bru|d *m* [1] (zanieczyszczenie) dirt; (intensywny, trwały) filth; **żyć w** ~**dzie** to live in filth; **zarastać** ~**dem** to

get filthy; ~**d moralny** przen. moral depravity
2 **brudy** *plt* 1 (brudna bielizna) (dirty) laundry
2 (śmieci, odpadki) rubbish 3 (zło, złe uczynki) dirty
dealings; **wyciągać** a. **wywlekać** ~**dy o kimś** to
dig up some dirt on sb pot.; **prać swoje** ~**dy**
publicznie to wash one's dirty linen in public

brudas *m* pot. slob pot.

brudn|o 2 *adv. grad.* **w pokoju było** ~**o** the room
was dirty
2 na brudno *adv.* **pisać na** ~**o** to do a (first) draft

brudnopis *m* (rough) draft

brudn|y *adi. grad.* 1 (zabrudzony) dirty; **buty** ~**e od**
błota muddy shoes; ~**a robota** dirty work także
przen.; ~**y interes** przen. a dirty business; **mieć** ~**e**
myśli przen. to have a dirty mind; **prać** ~**e**
pieniądze przen. to launder dirty money 2 [kolor]
muddy

bru|dzić *impf* **1** *vt* to get [sth] dirty [ubranie]; to soil
[książki]
2 brudzić się to get dirty

bruk *m* (nawierzchnia) (z kamienia) cobbled (road)
surface; (z kostki) stone sett surface a. paving;
układać ~ to pave a road with cobbles/setts
■ **szlifować** ~**i** (próżnować) to roam the streets; (być
bezrobotnym) to walk the streets looking for work;
wyrzucić kogoś na ~ (z mieszkania, domu) to throw
sb out onto the street; (z pracy) to throw sb out of
work

brukowan|y *adi.* paved; (kamieniem naturalnym) cob-
bled

brukow|iec *m* 1 (kamień) cobble(stone) 2 (czaso-
pismo) tabloid; rag pot.

bruksel|ka *f* Bot., Kulin. (Brussels) sprout

brulion *m* 1 (zeszyt) exercise book GB, notebook
2 (pierwsza wersja) (rough) draft

brunatn|y *adi.* (dark) brown

brune|t *m* black-haired man

brunet|ka *f* black-haired woman

brutal *m* brute

brutaln|y *adi. grad.* [osoba, napad, słowa] brutal

brutto 1 *adi. inv.* gross; **cena** ~ gross price
2 *adv.* [zarabiać] gross

bru|zda *f* 1 (w ziemi) furrow 2 (na twarzy) furrow
3 (wyżłobienie) groove

bru|ździć *impf* **1** *vt* to furrow [ziemię]; to wrinkle
[twarz]
2 *vi* pot. (przeszkadzać) ~**ździć komuś** to thwart sb

brydż *m* Gry bridge

bryga|da *f* 1 Wojsk. brigade 2 (robotników) gang;
(remontowa, monterów) team; (transportowa) crew

bryk *m* (ze streszczeniami) abstract; (z rozwiązaniami zadań)
maths aid pot.

bryk|a *f* pot. (samochód) motor GB pot.

brylan|t *m* 1 (kamień) diamond; **pierścionek**
z ~**tem** a diamond ring 2 przen. (osoba) gem;
diamond pot.

bry|ła *f* 1 (kawałek) lump; ~**ła lodu** an ice block
2 Mat., Fiz. solid 3 (kształt) shape; **ciężka** ~**ła zamku**
the bulky mass of the castle

bry|znąć *pf* — **bry|zgać** *impf* *vi* [woda, błoto] to
splash

brzask *m* daybreak; **o** ~**u** at the break of day

brzdąc *m* pot. kiddie pot.; toddler

brzdąk|nąć *pf* — **brzdąk|ać** *impf* *vi* 1 pot. (na
gitarze) to strum (away); (na fortepianie) to plonk (away)
2 (wydać dźwięk) [monety, klucze] to jingle; [garnki,
pokrywki] to clang

brzeg *m* 1 (rzeki) bank; (jeziora, morza) shore; **nad**
~**iem rzeki/jeziora** on the river bank/lake shore;
spacerować ~**iem morza** to walk along the
shore; **wystąpić z** ~**ów** to overflow 2 (stołu, pola,
monety, książki) edge; (szklanki, filiżanki, krateru) rim;
napełnić coś po ~**i** to fill sth to the brim; **spał**
z ~**u** he slept on the outside (of the bed)

brzęcz|eć *impf* *vi* 1 [mucha, pszczoła] to buzz;
[dzwonek] to ring; [szyby] to rattle 2 pot. [osoba] to
drone (on)

brzęczyk *m* Techn. buzzer

brzęk *m* 1 (metalu) clank; (szkła) clink; (monet) jingle
2 (owada) buzz(ing), drone

brzęk|nąć *pf* — **brzęk|ać** *impf* *vi* 1 ~**ać czymś**
[osoba] to rattle sth [talerzami, łyżkami]; to jingle sth
[kluczami] 2 [talerze, łyżki] to rattle; [klucze] to
jingle; [metal] to clang; [szklanki, kieliszki] to clink
3 pot. (na gitarze) to strum (away); (na fortepianie) to
plonk (away)

brzmi|eć *impf* *vi* 1 (być słyszanym) [głos, muzyka,
instrument] to sound; [dzwon] to ring; [kroki, echo] to
resound 2 (wyrażać treść) [zdanie, tekst] to read;
zdanie powinno ~**eć następująco...** the sentence should read as follows...; **odpowiedź** ~ **nie!**
the answer is no!

brzoskwi|nia *f* peach

brz|oza *f* (drzewo) birch (tree); (drewno) birch

brzuch *m* Anat. abdomen, stomach; belly pot.; **ból**
~**a** a stomach ache; **ćwiczyć z pełnym** ~**em** to
exercise on a full stomach; **leżeć na** ~**u** to lie on
one's stomach; **wciągnąć** ~ to hold in one's
stomach

brzyd|ki *adi. grad.* 1 (nieładny) ugly; ~**ka pogoda**
nasty a. foul weather; ~**ki dzień** a miserable day;
~**ki jak noc** as ugly as sin a. night 2 (zły, niemoralny)
[czyn] mean (nieprzyzwoity) [słowa, wyrazy] foul
■ **płeć** ~**ka** the sterner a. rougher sex

brzyd|nąć *impf* *vi* 1 (stawać się brzydkim) [budynek,
miejsce] to become ugly; [osoba] to lose one's looks
2 (budzić niechęć) **już mi to** ~**nie** I'm getting tired
of it

brzydo|ta *f* ugliness

brzydul|a *f* pot. plain Jane pot.

brzy|dzić się *impf* *v refl.* ~**dzić się czymś** to find
sth repulsive

brzyt|wa f cut-throat razor GB, straight razor US; **ostry jak** ∼**wa** razor-sharp

■ **tonący** ∼**wy się chwyta** przysł. a drowning man clutches at straws przysł.

bub|el m pot. (piece of) trash pot.

buch|nąć pf — **buch|ać** impf vi to burst; ∼**nąć ogniem** to burst into flames

bucz|eć impf vi ① [syrena] to wail; [owad] to buzz ② (z dezaprobatą) to boo ③ pot. (głośno płakać) to blubber pot.

bu|da f ① (na narzędzia, sprzęt) shed; (zaniedbany dom) ramshackle house; (jarmarczna) stall ② (psia) kennel GB, doghouse US ③ pot., Szkol. school ④ (nakrycie pojazdu) (folding) hood GB, (folding) top US ⑤ pot. (samochód policyjny) Black Maria GB pot., paddy wagon US pot.

buddyzm m Buddhism

bud|ka f ① (małe pomieszczenie) box; ∼**ka telefoniczna** a phone booth GB, a phone box ② (kiosk) kiosk ③ (dla ptaków) nesting box

bud|owa f ① Budow. (działalność) building; (być) **w** ∼**owie** (to be) under construction ② Budow. (obiekt z terenem) building site ③ (komórki, wyrazu) structure; (urządzenia) design; **mieć atletyczną** ∼**owę** to have an athletic build

bud|ować impf Ⅰ vt ① to build [drogę, most]; to construct [silnik, urządzenie, trójkąt] ② to build (up) [ustrój, zaufanie, atmosferę] ③ przen. to inspire, to edify; ∼**ować kogoś swoim przykładem** to inspire sb with one's example; ∼**ujące słowa** inspiring a. uplifting words; ∼**ujące jest, że...** it's (very) heartening a. reassuring that...

Ⅱ **budować się** ① (stawiać sobie dom) to build a house ② (być budowanym) [dom, most, droga] to be built

budowl|a f (budynek, fabryka) building; (most, tunel, wieża) structure

budowlan|y adi. [materiały, działka] building

budownictw|o m ① (budowanie) building; ∼**o mieszkaniowe** housing construction; ∼**o okrętowe** shipbuilding ② Archit. architecture; **nowoczesne** ∼**o** modern architecture

budownicz|y m ① Budow. builder; ∼**y skrzypiec** a violin-maker ② przen. (twórca, organizator) architect

budul|ec m ① Budow. building material(s) ② przen. (składnik) ingredient

budyn|ek m building

budy|ń m Kulin. ≈ blancmange

budzeni|e n wake-up call; **zamówić** ∼**e na siódmą** to book a wake-up call for seven

bu|dzić impf Ⅰ vt ① (przerywać sen) to wake (up); **budzić kogoś ze snu** to wake sb from their sleep ② (stymulować) to rouse; **budzić kogoś z zadumy** to rouse sb from their meditations ③ (wywoływać) to arouse [litość, podejrzenia]; to raise [wątpliwości, nadzieję]; to inspire [zaufanie, zapał]

Ⅱ **budzić się** ① (przestawać spać) to wake (up) ② przen. [tęsknota, marzenia] to awake

budzik m alarm clock; **nastawić** ∼ **(na szóstą)** to set the alarm (clock) (for six)

budże|t m budget; ∼**t domowy** the household budget; **przekroczyć** ∼**t** to go over budget

buf|a f puff(ed) sleeve

bufe|t m ① (pracowniczy) canteen; (dworcowy) snack bar; (teatralny) buffet ② (lada w sklepie, restauracji) counter; **przy** ∼**cie** at the counter ③ (posiłek na przyjęciu) buffet; (zastawiony stół) buffet table; ∼**t z sałatkami** (w restauracji) a salad bar

bufo|r Ⅰ m ① Kolej. buffer także przen. ② Komput. buffer (memory)

Ⅱ **bufory** plt pot. (piersi) knockers pot.

bujać[1] impf → **bujnąć**

buja|ć[2] impf Ⅰ vi (w powietrzu) to soar; **ptaki** ∼**jące w przestworzach** birds soaring in the air

Ⅱ **bujać się** pot. (kochać się) to have a crush pot. (**w kimś** on sb)

buj|da f pot. fib pot.; ∼**da na resorach** a whopping (great) lie pot.

buj|nąć pf — **buj|ać**[1] impf Ⅰ vt pot. ① (w kołysce) to rock; (na huśtawce) to swing; ∼**ać nogami** to swing one's legs ② (kłamać) to kid pot.; ∼**asz!** you're making it up a. kidding! pot.

Ⅱ **bujnąć się** — **bujać się** (kołysać się) to rock

buk m ① (drzewo) beech (tree) ② (drewno) beech(wood)

bukie|t m ① (pęk kwiatów) bunch; (starannie ułożony) bouquet; ∼**t róż** a bouquet of roses ② (zapach wina) bouquet

buldog m (English) bulldog

buldoże|r m bulldozer

bulgo|tać impf vi ① [płyn] to gurgle ② [indyk] to gobble

bulion m Kulin. bouillon; (wywar, koncentrat) stock; (zupa) broth; ∼ **z mięsa** meat consommé; **kostka** ∼**u** a stock cube

bulw|a f ① (podziemna łodyga) bulb ② (roślina) Jerusalem artichoke ③ pot. (zgrubienie) lump

buł|ka f (bread) roll; (okrągła, słodka) bun; ∼**ka paryska** a French loaf a. stick; ∼**ka tarta** breadcrumbs

■ ∼**ka z masłem** pot. a piece of cake pot.

bunk|ier m ① (schron) bunker ② (zbiornik) (na węgiel) bunker; (na ziarno) silo

bun|t m ① (wewnętrzny sprzeciw) rebellion (**przeciwko czemuś** against sth) ② (akcja) revolt; (na statku, w armii) mutiny; ∼**t więźniów** a prison riot; **podnieść** ∼**t przeciwko komuś** to rise in revolt against sb; **podburzać do** ∼**tu** to stir up a revolt

bunt|ować impf Ⅰ vt to incite [sb] to revolt [chłopów, robotników]; to incite [sb] to mutiny [marynarzy, żołnierzy]

Ⅱ **buntować się** [uczniowie, syn] to rebel; [żołnierze, marynarze] to mutiny

buntownicz|y adi. [gest, odpowiedź] defiant; [idee, zachowanie] rebellious

buntowni|k *m* rebel; (na statku, w armii) mutineer

burak *m* (roślina) beet; (jadalny korzeń) beetroot; ~ **cukrowy** sugar beet; ~ **pastewny** mangold; **czerwony jak** ~ as red as a beetroot

burcz|eć[1] *impf* → **burknąć**

burcz|eć[2] *impf vi* [1] (wydawać dźwięk) *[żołądek]* to rumble; *[rury, silnik]* to rattle [2] pot. (narzekać) to grumble (**na kogoś** at sb)

bur|da *f* (bójka) brawl; (kłótnia) row; **urządzać uliczne** ~**dy** to brawl in the streets

bur|knąć *pf* — **bur|czeć**[1] *impf vi* (powiedzieć) (niewyraźnie) to mumble; (opryskliwie) to growl

burmistrz *m* mayor

bursztyn *m* amber

bur|ta *f* [1] Żegl. (ship's) side; **lewa/prawa** ~**ta** port/starboard (side); **ląd z prawej** ~**ty** land to starboard; **ster prawo na** ~**tę!** helm to starboard!; **człowiek za** ~**tą!** man overboard! [2] Lotn. (prawa) starboard; (lewa) port [3] (w samochodzie ciężarowym) (tył) back; (bok) sideboard

bur|y *adi. [zwierzę]* brownish grey; *[niebo]* dark grey

burz|a *f* [1] Meteo. storm; tempest książk.; ~**a gradowa** a hailstorm; **śnieżna** ~**a** a snowstorm; ~**a z piorunami** a thunderstorm; ~**a piaskowa** a sandstorm; **zanosiło się na** ~**ę** a storm was gathering; **zerwała się** ~**a** a storm broke; ~**a przeszła bokiem** the storm passed over; **wpadł do domu jak** ~**a** przen. he stormed into the house [2] przen. (wstrząsy dziejowe) turmoil; **wojenna** ~**a** the turmoils of war [3] przen. (gwałtowna reakcja) storm; ~**a oklasków/protestów** a storm of applause/protest ■ ~**a mózgów** (metoda) brainstorming; (sesja) brainstorming session; (burzliwa dyskusja) stormy discussion; ~**a w szklance wody** a storm in a teacup GB, a tempest in a teapot US

burzliw|y *adi. [pogoda, debata]* stormy; *[życie, romans]* tempestuous; *[czasy, okres]* turbulent

burz|yć *impf* **[]** *vt* [1] to demolish *[budynek]* [2] przen. to shatter *[szczęście, spokój]* [3] (poruszać) to agitate *[wodę]*; to ruffle *[włosy]*
[] **burzyć się** [1] (gwałtownie się poruszać) *[woda]* to be churned up; *[włosy]* to be ruffled [2] (buntować się) to rebel

burżuazj|a *f* bourgeoisie

busol|a *f* [1] (przyrząd) compass [2] przen. lodestar; (czyjaś) **życiowa** ~**a** the lodestar of sb's life

busz *m* the bush

busz|ować *impf vi* to rummage about a. around; ~**ować po szufladach** to rummage a. root through some drawers

bu|t *m* shoe; (z cholewą) boot; **siedmiomilowe buty** seven-league boots
■ **głupi jak but (z lewej nogi)** (as) thick as a brick a. as two (short) planks GB pot.; **to takie buty!** pot. so that's it! pot.; **wchodzić komuś z butami w życie** pot. to wade into sb's private life

bu|ta *f* arrogance

butel|ka *f* bottle; ~**ka na mleko/na wodę** a milk/water bottle; **karmić kogoś** ~**ką** to bottle-feed sb
■ **nabić kogoś w** ~**kę** pot. to take sb in

butelk|ować *impf vt* to bottle *[piwo, sok]*

butl|a *f* [1] (duża butelka) demijohn [2] (z gazem) cylinder

by **[]** *coni.* [1] (dla wyrażenia celu, skutku) (przed bezokolicznikiem) (in order) to, so as to; (przed zdaniem) so (that); **biegł przez całą drogę, by zdążyć na pociąg** he ran all the way so as to catch the train; **załóż czapkę, byś się nie zaziębił** put your hat on so (that) you don't catch cold; ~ **nie** in case; lest książk. [2] (dla wyrażenia woli, sądu) **chcą, byś przyszedł na zebranie** they want you to come to the meeting [3] książk. (wyrażające następstwo) only to; **wrócił z wyprawy, by wkrótce...** he returned from the expedition, only to... [4] (dla wyrażenia intensywności) to; **była zbyt zmęczona, by...** she was too tired to... [5] (z wtrąceniem) to; **... by użyć dzisiejszego pojęcia** ... to use today's terminology
[] *part.* (w formach trybu warunkowego) would; **bez parasola by zmokła** she would get/would have got wet without an umbrella; **kurs ukończono by we wrześniu** the course would have ended in September; **trzeba by już wracać** we should go back now; **cokolwiek by o nim powiedzieć...** whatever you might a. may say about him...; **jak by nie liczyć ...** however you add it up ...; **jak by nie było** after all, when all's said and done

być *impf* **[]** *vi* [1] (istnieć, żyć) to be; **być albo nie być** to be or not to be; **myślę, więc jestem** I think, therefore I am; **są sprawy, które...** there are (certain) things that...; **był sobie król** there was once a. there once lived a king; **nie ma nikogo** there's no one there/here; **nie ma obaw** a. **strachu** pot.! no problem! pot., not to worry! pot.; **nie ma co płakać/gadać** it's no use crying/talking; **nie ma co** a. **czego żałować** it's no great loss; **nie ma o co się kłócić** there's nothing to quarrel about; **nie ma się czemu dziwić, że...** it's not surprising a. no wonder that...; **nie ma za co** (po podziękowaniu) you're welcome; (po przeprosinach) that's all right [2] (przebywać, znajdować się) to be; **być w pracy/szkole** to be at work/at school; **będę w domu o piątej** I'll be home at five; **w pokoju nikogo nie było** there was no one in the room; „**czy jest Robert?**" – „**nie, nie ma go**" 'is Robert in?' – 'no, he's not'; „**są jeszcze bilety?**" – „**niestety, już nie ma**" 'are there any tickets left?' – 'no, I'm afraid not'; **nigdy nie byłem w Rosji** I've never been to Russia; „**skąd jesteś?**" – „**(jestem) z Krakowa/Polski**" 'where are you from?' – '(I'm) from Cracow/Poland'; „**jestem!**" (przy odczytywaniu listy) 'here!', 'present'; **biblioteka jest w budynku głównym** the library is in the main building; **wczoraj na kolację był dorsz** we had cod for dinner yesterday [3] (trwać, stawać się) to be; **jest godzina druga po południu** it's two in the afternoon a. two p.m.; **był maj** it was (in) May; **jest piękny ranek** it's a beautiful morning; **wczoraj był deszcz** it was raining yesterday; **będzie z niego dobry pracownik** he'll make a good worker; **nic z tego nie będzie** it's hopeless 4 (odbywać się, zdarzać się) to be; **egzamin jest jutro** the exam is tomorrow; **czy były do mnie jakieś telefony?** did anyone call (me)?; **co będzie, jeśli...** what happens if...; **co będzie, jeśli ktoś nas zobaczy?** supposing a. what if someone sees us?; **opowiedziałem jej wszystko, tak jak było** I told her everything just as it happened; **co ci jest?** what's the matter with you?; **nic mu nie będzie** he'll be fine 5 (uczestniczyć, uczęszczać) to be; **być na weselu/zebraniu** to be at a. attend a wedding/meeting; **być w liceum/na uniwersytecie** to be at secondary school/at university; **być na prawie** to be studying law; **był na trzecim roku** he was in his third year 6 (przybyć) to come; **być pierwszym/drugim** to be the first/second to arrive; **był na mecie trzeci** he finished a. came third; **czy był już listonosz?** has the postman been a. come yet? 7 (znajdować się w jakimś stanie) to be; **być pod wrażeniem kogoś/czegoś** to be impressed by sb/sth; **bądźmy dobrej myśli** let's hope for the best; **jestem przed obiadem** I haven't had lunch yet; **wody było do kostek** the water was ankle-deep; **jeszcze chwila i byłoby po mnie** another second and I'd have had it pot.

II *v aux.* 1 (łącznik w orzeczeniu złożonym) to be; **być nauczycielem** to be a teacher; **być Polakiem** to be Polish; **pojemnik był z plastiku** the container was made of plastic; **czyj jest ten samochód?** whose car is this?; **bądź sobą** be yourself; **są małżeństwem od dziesięciu lat** they've been married for ten years; **bądź tak miły i otwórz okno** would you mind opening the window?; **nie bądź głupi!** don't be stupid!; **cicho bądź!** be quiet!; **być w kapeluszu/spodniach** to be wearing a hat/trousers; **być za kimś/czymś** (opowiadać się) to be for sb/sth 2 (w stronie biernej) to be; **artykuł jest dobrze napisany** the article is well written; **to musi być zrobione do czwartku** it must be done by Thursday 3 (w czasie przyszłym złożonym) shall, will; **będziemy długo go wspominali** a. **wspominać** we shall a. will long remember him 4 (w trybie warunkowym) **byłbym napisał** a. **napisałbym do ciebie, gdybym znał twój adres** I would have written to you, if I had known your address; **byłaby spadła ze schodów** (omal nie) she almost fell down the stairs; **byłbym zapomniał!** I almost a. nearly forgot! 5 (w zwrotach nieosobowych) **było już późno** it was (already) late; **nie było co jeść** there was nothing to eat; **trzeba było coś z tym zrobić** something had to be done about it; **trzeba było od razu tak mówić** why didn't you say so in the first

place?; **za ciepło ci będzie w tym swetrze** you'll be too hot in that jumper; **byłoby przyjemnie zjeść razem obiad** it would be nice to have lunch together; **żeby nie było na mnie** as long as you/ they don't blame me; **nie ma z kim się bawić** there's no one to play with

■ **co będzie, to będzie** what will be, will be; **co było, to było** let bygones be bygones; **co jest?** pot. what's up? pot.; **było siedzieć w domu** pot. you should have stayed at home; **nie ma co!** well, well!; **nie ma (to) jak kuchnia domowa** there's nothing like a. you can't beat home cooking; **nie może być!** (niedowierzanie) I don't believe it!; **tak jest!** (owszem) (that's) right!; Wojsk. yes, sir!

byd|ło *n* 1 (zwierzęta) cattle 2 pot. (ludzie) animals pot.

Byk *m* Astrol., Astron. Taurus, the Bull

byk *m* 1 (buhaj, łoś) bull; (jeleń) stag; **walki ~ów** bullfights; **silny jak ~** (as) strong as a horse; **uderzyć kogoś ~iem** pot. to butt sb in the stomach 2 pot. (błąd) slip-up pot., boob GB pot.; (w maszynopisie, druku) typo pot.; **zrobić ~a** to slip up; (w druku) to make a typo; **palnąć** a. **strzelić ~a** pot. to put one's foot in it pot.

■ **chwycić ~a za rogi** to take the bull by the horns; **tu jest jak ~ napisane, że...** it says here in black and white that...; **działać na kogoś jak (czerwona) płachta na ~a** to be like a red rag to a bull to sb; **z ~a spadłeś?** pot. are you off your head a. rocker? pot.

byle 1 *coni.* 1 (wyrażające warunek) providing a. provided (that), (just) as long as; **wyjdzie za każdego, ~ miał pieniądze** she'll marry anyone, providing a. as long as he's got money; **każdy, ~ nie on** anybody but him 2 (wyrażające cel) (przed bezokolicznikiem) (in order) to; (przed zdaniem) so that; **gadać, ~ gadać** to talk for the sake of talking; **on zrobi wszystko, ~ osiągnąć swój cel** he'll do anything to achieve his goal

II *part.* 1 (wyrażające życzenie) **~ dojechać do skrzyżowania!** if we could just get to the crossroads; **~śmy się nie spóźnili!** I just hope we won't be late; **zrób to, ~ szybko!** do it, (and) just be quick about it! 2 (dowolny) any; (kiepski) any old pot.; **~ dziecko/głupiec to potrafi** even a child/ any old fool can do that; **z ~ powodu** for the slightest reason; **pod ~ pretekstem** at the slightest excuse; **przy ~ sposobności** whenever an opportunity presents itself 3 (z zaimkami) **~ co** (cokolwiek) (just) anything; any old thing pot.; **mówić ~ co** to say any old thing; **śmiać się z ~ czego** to laugh at anything a. for the slightest reason; **~ nie ~ co** it's no small thing a. no joke pot.; **~ kto** anyone, anybody; **to nie ~ kto** he's not just anybody; **~ gdzie** anywhere; any old where a. place pot.; **~ kiedy** any time; any old time pot.; **~ jaki** (pierwszy z brzegu) any; (kiepski) rotten pot.; **to nie**

~ **jaki wyczyn** that's no mean feat; ~ **jak** anyhow; any old how pot.

by|ły **[I]** *adi. [prezydent, wojskowy, współmałżonek]* former, ex-; **kraje byłego ZSRR** the countries of the former USSR

[II] by|ły *m*, była *f* pot. ex pot.

bystroś|ć *f* (mental) acuity

byst|ry *adi. grad.* **[1]** *[rozum, umysł]* quick; *[osoba]* bright; *[odpowiedź]* clever **[2]** *[wzrok, ucho, obserwator]* keen **[3]** ~**ry nurt/strumień** a swift a. rapid current/stream

by|t *m* **[1]** (warunki materialne) standard of living **[2]** (istnienie) existence; **walka o byt** the struggle for survival a. to survive; **stracić rację bytu** to lose one's raison d'être

bytow|y *adi.* **warunki** ~**e** living standards

bywa|ć *impf* **[I]** *vi* **[1]** (w jakimś miejscu) to be; ~**ć na koncertach/zebraniach** to go to concerts/meetings; **puby, w których** ~**ją żołnierze** pubs frequented a. patronized by soldiers; **on rzadko tu** ~ he doesn't come here often **[2]** (w jakimś stanie, położeniu) to be; **rzadko** ~**li tego samego zdania** they were rarely of the same opinion **[3]** (utrzymywać kontakty towarzyskie) to go out; ~**ć u kogoś** to visit sb;

ona często u nas ~ she often comes to see us; ~**ć w świecie** a. **między ludźmi** to lead an active social life **[4]** (zdarzać się) to be; **ranki** ~**ją chłodne** the mornings are sometimes cold; ~**, że...** it sometimes happens that...; ~**ło, że całą noc nie spałem** sometimes a. there were times when I didn't sleep the whole night

[II] *v aux.* to be; ~**ło gorzej!** we've seen worse

[III] bywaj!, bywajcie! *inter.* **[1]** (pożegnanie) goodbye!; farewell! książk.; ~**j zdrów!** take care! **[2]** (powitanie) welcome!

bywal|ec *m* **[1]** (stały gość) regular, habitué; **stały** ~**ec** a regular (customer); ~**ec wyścigów** a regular racegoer **[2]** (światowiec) well-travelled person GB, well-traveled person US

bzdu|ra *f* pot. **[1]** (brednia) rubbish GB pot.; **opowiadać** a. **pleść** ~**ry** to talk rubbish a. rot **[2]** (błahostka) rubbish pot.; trifle

bzik *m* pot. **[1]** (mania) **mieć** ~**a na punkcie czegoś** to have a thing about sth pot. **[2]** (niezrównoważenie psychiczne) **ona ma** ~**a** she's nuts a. crazy pot.

bzy|knąć *pf* — **bzy|czeć, bzyk|ać**[1] *impf vi [owad, mechanizm]* to buzz; *[pocisk]* to whiz(z)

C

C, c *n inv.* ① (litera) C, c ② Muz. C
cacka|ć się *impf v refl.* pot. ~ć się z kimś/czymś to make a fuss of sb/sth
cac|ko *n* ornament; **elektroniczne** ~**ko** an electronic gadget
cal *m* inch
■ **gentleman w każdym** ~**u** every inch a gentleman
cał|ka *f* Mat. integral
całkiem *adv. [zapomnieć]* completely; *[przystojny]* quite; ~ **możliwe** (it's) quite possible
całkowicie *adv.* ① (do końca) completely ② (w pełni) entirely
całkowi|ty *adi. [cisza, kwota]* total; *[dyskrecja]* absolute; *[zakaz, brak]* complete
cało *adv.* in one piece; **wyjść** ~ **z katastrofy** to walk away from an accident in one piece
całodobow|y *adi. [dyżur, praca]* round-the-clock, 24-hour; *[sklep]* ~**y** an all-night shop
cało|dzienny, ~**dniowy** *adi. [kurs, wycieczka]* all-day, day-long; *[utrzymanie, zarobek]* daily; ~**dzienne wyżywienie** full board
całokształ|t *m* (problemów, sytuacji) entirety; ~**t twórczości** lifetime a. career achievement
całonocn|y *adi. [podróż, dyżur, czuwanie]* all-night; *[dyskusje]* night-long
całoroczn|y *adi. [pobyt, choroba]* year-long; *[dochód, opad]* annual; ~**a odzież** clothes for all seasons
całościow|y *adi. [ujęcie]* comprehensive, exhaustive; ~**y obraz czegoś** an overall a. global picture of sth
cało|ść *f* ① (całokształt) whole, entirety; **tworzyć zamkniętą** ~**ć** to form a self-contained whole ② (nienaruszalność) integrity
cał|ować *impf* **Ⅰ** *vt* to kiss; ~**ować kogoś na pożegnanie** to kiss sb goodbye; ~**ować kogoś w policzek/rękę** to kiss sb on the cheek/hand
Ⅱ całować się to kiss (z kimś sb)
całun *m* shroud
całus *m* pot. kiss; **dać komuś** ~**a** to give sb a kiss
cał|y **Ⅰ** *pron.* ① (wszystek) *[dzień, świat, prawda]* all, whole; **cały czas** all the time, the whole time; **całymi godzinami/dniami** for hours/days on end; **jesteś cały mokry** you're all wet; **iść na całego** pot. to go the whole way a. whole hog pot.; **na całe gardło** a. **cały głos** at the top of one's voice

② (pełny) whole; **całe wiadro wody** a whole bucket(ful) of water ③ (kompletny) *[zbiór, zestaw]* entire, complete ④ (jedyny) all, only; **to moja cała pociecha** it's all the comfort I have
Ⅱ *adi.* ① (nieuszkodzony) (o osobie, ubraniu) in one piece; **wazon spadł, ale jest cały** the vase fell, but it's intact; **wrócił cały i zdrów** he returned safe and sound ② (całkowity) complete; **z całą pewnością** with complete certainty; **z całą szczerością** in all sincerity ③ pot. (przejawiający typowe cechy) all over pot.; **to cały Marek** that's Marek all over
■ **całe szczęście, że...** luckily, I...
capn|ąć *pf vt* pot. to grab, to snatch; ~**ąć kogoś za kołnierz** to collar sb pot.
ca|r *m* Hist. tsar, czar
cars|ki *adi. [urzędnik, policja]* tsarist, czarist; *[pałac, dwór]* tsar's, czar's
caryc|a *f* Hist. tsarina, czarina, tsaritsa
cąż|ki *plt* nail clippers
cebul|a *f* ① (warzywo) onion ② (bulwa) bulb ③ pot. (zegarek) pocket watch; (kopuła) onion dome
■ **ubierać się na** ~**ę** to wear several layers of clothing
cebul|ka *f* (włosa) root
cech *m* guild
ce|cha *f* ① (właściwość) feature, quality; (osoby) characteristic, trait ② (znak) (urzędu) (official) stamp; (fabryki) trademark; **cecha probiercza** a hallmark
cech|ować *impf* **Ⅰ** *vt* to characterize; ~**ują ją spokój i opanowanie** her chief qualities are calmness and level-headedness
Ⅱ cechować się to be marked a. characterized (czymś by sth)
cedzak *m* pot. strainer; (z dwoma uchwytami) colander
ce|dzić *impf vt* ① (odsączać) to strain *[mleko, ziemniaki, makaron]*; **cedzić coś przez sito** to strain sth through a sieve ② (mówić wolno) to drawl; **cedzić słowa** to drawl (out) one's words
cegielni|a *f* brickyard
cegieł|ka *f* (datek) donation (**na coś** for a. to sth); (dowód wpłaty) donation certificate; **dołożyć** ~**kę do czegoś** to make one's contribution to sth
ceglan|y *adi. [mur, dom]* brick
cegla|sty *adi.* (kolor) brick-red, brick
ceg|ła *f* brick
cekin *m* sequin, spangle

cel **[]** *m* [1] Sport, Wojsk. target; **mierzyć do** ~**u** to aim at a target; **trafić w** ~ a. **do** ~**u** to hit the target; **brać kogoś/coś na** ~ to aim at sb/sth [2] (przedmiot działań) aim, goal; **jaki jest** ~ **twojej wizyty?** what's the purpose of your visit?; **w tym** ~**u musisz...** in order to do that, you need to...; **postawić sobie jakiś** ~ to set oneself a target, to set one's sights on sth [3] (miejsce) destination; **dotrzeć/dojść do** ~**u** to reach one's destination; **bez** ~**u** *[chodzić, włóczyć się]* aimlessly [4] (obiekt działań) target; **wziąć** a. **obrać sobie kogoś za** ~ **kpin** to make sb the butt a. target of one's jokes **[]** *inter.* Wojsk. ~**! pal!** aim! fire!

■ **mijać się z** ~**em** to be pointless, to defeat the purpose; ~ **uświęca środki** przysł. the end justifies the means

cel|a *f* cell

celebr|ować *impf vt* to celebrate także przen. *[mszę, święto]*; ~**ować posiłek** to make a ritual of a meal

celiba|t *m* celibacy; **żyć w** ~**cie** to be celibate

cellulitis /ˌtselu'litis/ *m, m inv.* cellulite

celni|k *m*, ~**czka** *f* customs officer

celn|y[1] *adi. grad.* [1] *[strzał, strzelec]* accurate; ~**y rzut!** good shot!; ~**e oko** a good eye [2] *[uwaga, przykład]* apt; **mieć** ~**y dowcip** to have a sharp wit

celn|y[2] *adi. [urząd, przepisy]* customs

celofan *m* cellophane®

cel|ować *impf vi* [1] (mierzyć) to aim (**do kogoś/czegoś** at sb/sth) [2] (być skierowanym) *[palec]* to point (**w kogoś/coś** at sb/sth) [3] (przodować) to excel (**w czymś** at a. in sth)

celownik *m* [1] Techn., Wojsk. sight(s) [2] Fot. (view)finder [3] Jęz. the dative (case)

celowo *adv. [zrobić]* intentionally, on purpose

celow|y *adi. [postępowanie]* (zamierzony) intentional, deliberate; (stosowny) appropriate

Celsjusz *m* skala ~**a** Celsius, the Celsius scale; **39 stopni** ~ **a** 39° Celsius a. centigrade

celująco *adv.* **zdać egzamin** ~ to pass an exam with flying colours

celując|y[] *adi. [odpowiedź]* excellent; ~**y uczeń** a model a. first-class student

[] *m* Szkol. ≈ starred A (grade)

celuloi|d *m* celluloid

celuloz|a *f* Chem. cellulose

cembrowin|a *f* (studni) (well) casing; (rzeki) embankment, reinforced bank; (kanału, basenu) lining

cemen|t *m* cement

cement|ować *impf vt* to cement także przen.

cementowni|a *f* cement plant a. works

cen|a *f* price także przen.

■ **za każdą** a. **wszelką** ~**ę** at all costs, at any cost; **za żadną** ~**ę** not at any price

ce|nić *impf* **[]** *vt* [1] (szanować) to value; **wysoko kogoś/coś cenić** to think highly of sb/sth; **cenić kogoś za coś** to value sb for sth [2] (szacować) to price *[towar, usługę]*

[] **cenić się** [1] (znać swoją wartość) to know one's own worth; **cenić się wysoko/nisko** to have a high/low opinion of oneself [2] pot. (wyznaczać cenę za swoją pracę) to charge

ceni|ony *adi. [towary]* (highly) valued, sought-after; *[artysta, fachowiec]* highly-regarded

cennik *m* price list

cenn|y *adi. grad. [biżuteria, obraz, czas]* valuable, precious; *[rada, uwaga, współpracownik]* valuable; *[pamiątka]* treasured, precious

cen|t *m* cent

central|a *f* (instytucja) head a. central office; headquarters; (magazyn) main depot a. warehouse; ~**a telefoniczna** (budynek) telephone exchange; (urządzenie) (telephone) switchboard

centralizacj|a *f* (władzy, gospodarki) centralization

centraliz|ować *impf vt* to centralize *[państwo, produkcję]*

centraln|y **[]** *adi. [miejsce, baza danych, urząd, ogrzewanie]* central; *[zarządzanie, gospodarka]* centralized

[] **centralne** *n* pot. central heating

centr|um *n* centre GB, center US; ~**um (miasta)** the city centre GB, downtown US; **znajdować się w** ~**um uwagi** to be the centre of attention; ~**um handlowe** a shopping centre

centymet|r *m* [1] Miary centimetre GB, centimeter US; ~**r kwadratowy/sześcienny** a square/cubic centimetre [2] (taśma) tape measure, measuring tape

cenzu|ra *f* [1] censorship [2] Szkol. school report

cenzur|ować *impf vt* [1] to censor *[filmy, gazety, książki]* [2] przen. to criticize; to censure książk. *[osobę, postępek, zachowanie]*; **być na** ~**owanym** książk. ≈ to be in the spotlight a. public eye; **czuć się jak na** ~**owanym** to be in the hot seat pot.

ce|ra *f* complexion, skin

cerami|ka *f* ceramics, pottery

cera|ta *f* oilcloth, plastic cloth

ceregiel|e *plt* pot. fuss; performance pot.; **robić** ~**e** to make a fuss; **robić z kimś/czymś** ~**e** to make a fuss over a. of sb/sth; **bez (żadnych/zbędnych)** ~**i** (bezceremonialnie) without ceremony a. further ado; (bez skrupułów) without thinking twice, without any qualms

ceremoni|a **[]** *f* ceremony; ~**a chrztu/koronacji** a christening/coronation ceremony

[] **ceremonie** *plt* ceremony; **robić z kimś/czymś** ~**e** pot. to make a fuss over a. of sb/sth

cerk|iew *f* Relig. (prawosławna) the (Eastern) Orthodox Church; (greckokatolicka) the Uniat(e) Church

cer|ować *impf vt* to darn *[skarpetki, dziurę]*

certyfika|t *m* (zaświadczenie pisemne) certificate, written certification; Ekon. (obligacja państwowa) government bond

cesarstw|o *n* (państwo) empire; (system) imperial rule

cesarz *m* emperor

cesarzow|a *f* empress

cesj|a *f* (majątku, nieruchomości) transfer, conveyance; (terytorium, miasta) cession

cew|ka *f* 1 Anat. tubule; (łzowa, wydalnicza) duct; ~**ka moczowa** the urinary tract 2 Elektr. coil

cewnik *m* Med. catheter

cęg|i *plt* Techn. pincers

cęt|ka *f* spot; **w** ~**ki** spotted

cętkowan|y *adi.* (o zwierzęciu) spotted

cha|ła *f* 1 (bułka) plait GB, challah US 2 pot. trash, rubbish pot.

chał|ka *f* plait GB, challah US

chałtu|ra *f* pot. 1 (praca) work on the side pot.; sideline 2 (efekt) potboiler pot.; (piece of) hackwork

chałup|a *f* 1 (wiejska chata) peasant cottage 2 pot. (zniszczony dom) ramshackle dwelling 3 pot., żart. (dom) home

chałupnictw|o *n* outwork

chałw|a *f* halva

cham *m* pot., obraźl. lout, boor

■ **robić coś na** ~**a** pot. to do sth without any regard for anyone else

chams|ki *adi.* pot. (grubiański) loutish, boorish; **po** ~**ku** like a lout

chamstw|o *n* loutishness, boorishness

chand|ra *f* pot. the blues, the hump GB pot.; **mieć** ~**rę** to feel down, to have the blues pot.

chaos *m* chaos, turmoil

chaotyczn|y *adi. grad.* (bezładny) *[działanie, wypowiedź]* chaotic, disjointed; (niezorganizowany) *[osoba]* disorganized, chaotic

charakte|r *m* 1 (usposobienie) character, nature; ~**r pisma** handwriting 2 (funkcja) capacity; **pracować w** ~**rze doradcy** to work as an aide

charakterystyczn|y *adi.* 1 (typowy) characteristic, typical (**dla kogoś/czegoś** of sb/sth) 2 (szczególny) distinctive, distinguishing; **cecha** ~**a** a distinguishing a. distinctive feature

charakterysty|ka *f* 1 (opis) characterization, description 2 (wypracowanie szkolne) character study, character description

charakteryzacj|a *f* make-up

charakteryz|ować *impf* **I** *vt* 1 (opisywać) to describe, to characterize 2 (cechować) to mark; to be characteristic (**coś** of sth); ~**owała go odwaga** courage was one of his chief qualities 3 (zmieniać wygląd) to make [sb] up

II charakteryzować się 1 (cechować się) to be characterized a. distinguished (**czymś** by sth) 2 (zmieniać wygląd) *[aktor]* to make (oneself) up

charcz|eć *impf vi [osoba, zwierzę, urządzenie]* to wheeze

char|t *m* greyhound; ~**t afgański** an Afghan hound

charytatywn|y *adi. [działalność, organizacja]* charity, charitable; *[przedstawienie]* charity, benefit

charyzm|a *f* charisma

charyzmatyczn|y *adi.* charismatic

chaszcz|e *plt* (krzaki) thick bushes, thicket; (zarośla) scrub, undergrowth

cha|ta *f* 1 (chłopska) (peasant) cottage, cabin 2 pot. (mieszkanie) place pot.

chcąc|y *m* anyone wishing a. inclined; **dla** ~**ych studiować oferujemy stypendia** we offer grants for those wishing to study a. those who want to study

■ **dla** ~**ego nie ma nic trudnego** przysł. where there's a will there's a way przysł.

chc|ieć *impf vt* to want; ~**ę iść do kina** I want to go to the cinema; ~**ecie może herbaty?** maybe you'd like some tea?; ~**ę/**~**iałam/**~**iałabym cię o coś prosić** I want/I wanted/I'd like to ask you a favour; ~**iał, żebym mu towarzyszył** he wanted me to accompany him; **rana nie** ~**e się goić** the wound doesn't want to heal up a. won't heal up; **nie** ~**e mu się uczyć** he's not interested in school; ~**ieć dobrze** to mean well; ~**ieć jak najlepiej** to want what's best (**dla kogoś** for sb)

■ ~**ąc nie** ~**ąc** willy-nilly

chciwoś|ć *f* greed

chciw|y *adi. grad.* greedy (**na coś** for sth); ~**y na pieniądze** money-grubbing pot.

chełp|ić się *impf vi* to boast; to brag pot.; ~**ić się czymś** to boast of a. about sth

chemi|a *f* 1 Nauk. chemistry 2 pejor. chemicals; **niektóre produkty spożywcze to sama** ~**a** some foodstuffs are nothing but chemicals 3 pot. (chemioterapia) chemo pot.

chemiczn|y *adi. [analiza, reakcja]* chemical; **czyszczenie** ~**e** dry-cleaning

chemi|k *m* chemist

chemikali|a *plt* chemicals

chemioterapi|a *f* Med. chemotherapy

cherla|k *m* pot. weakling; weed pot.

cherlaw|y *adi.* (słaby) *[osoba]* sickly, frail; *[zdrowie]* poor; *[drzewka, rośliny]* sickly, puny; ~**a gospodarka** przen. an ailing economy

chę|ć *f* 1 (ochota) willingness (**do czegoś** to do sth); **mieć** ~**ć na lody** to feel like some ice cream; **mieć** ~**ć zrobić coś** to feel like doing sth 2 (zamiar) intention; **mieć dobre** ~**ci** to have good intentions

chęt|ka *f* pot. itch pot.; **mieć** ~**kę coś zrobić** to be itching to do sth; **naszła mnie** ~**ka na lody** I suddenly fancied some ice cream

chętnie I *adv. grad.* willingly, readily; ~ **się uczyć** to like a. enjoy studying

II *inter.* with pleasure; „**może wpadniesz jutro?**" – „**bardzo** ~" 'perhaps you could drop in tomorrow?' – 'yes, I'd be glad to'; „**kawy?**" – „~" 'coffee?' – 'I'd love some'

chętn|y *adi. grad.* willing, eager (**do czegoś** to do sth); ~**y uczeń** a keen pupil; ~**y do pomocy** willing to help

chicho|t *m* (wesoły) giggle, titter; (do siebie) chuckle; (nieprzyjemny) snigger, snicker

chicho|tać *impf* **[]** *vi* (nerwowo) to giggle, to titter; (kpiąco, szyderczo) to snigger, to snicker; (do siebie) to chuckle (**z czegoś** at a. over sth); ~**tać z byle czego** to giggle at anything
[] **chichotać się** pot. (nerwowo) to giggle, to titter; (kpiąco, szyderczo) to snigger, to snicker; (do siebie) to chuckle (**z czegoś** over sth)

chimeryczn|y *adi. grad. [natura, usposobienie]* capricious, whimsical; *[plany, marzenia]* chimeric(al); *[idee, nadzieje]* fanciful

chinin|a *f* Chem., Farm. quinine

chińczyk *m* (gra) ludo; **rozłożyć** ~**a** to set up a ludo board

chips /tʃips/ *m* Kulin. (potato) crisp GB, (potato) chip US

chirur|g *m* surgeon

chirurgi|a *f* **[]** (dział medycyny) surgery **[]** pot. (oddział) surgical ward

chirurgiczn|y *adi. [gabinet]* surgeon's; *[narzędzia]* surgical

chlap|nąć *pf* — **chlap|ać** *impf* **[]** *vt* pot. (powiedzieć niepotrzebnie) to blab (out) pot., to babble (out) pot.; ~**ać językiem** a. **ozorem** to wag one's tongue
[] *vi* (rozpryskać) to splash (**czymś na coś** sth on sth); **woda** ~**nęła mi na rękaw** the water splashed (onto) my sleeve

chleb *m* **[]** bread; **bochenek** ~**a** a loaf (of bread); **kup dwa** ~**y** buy two loaves; ~ **powszedni** (jedzenie) one's daily bread; (codzienna rzecz) quite a normal thing, nothing unusual **[]** przen. (utrzymanie) bread and butter, livelihood; **zarabiać na** ~ to work for one's living, to earn one's daily bread

chlebak *m* knapsack, haversack

chlew *m* pigsty, pigpen US

chlip|nąć *pf* — **chlip|ać** *impf* **[]** *vt* (głośno pić) *[osoba]* to slurp pot. *[zupę, herbatę]*; *[zwierzę]* to lap (up) *[wodę, mleko]*
[] *vi* (popłakiwać) to snivel

chlo|r *m* chlorine

chlorofil *m* Biol. chlorophyll

chlub|a *f* **[]** (duma) pride, boast; ~**a polskiego sportu** the pride of Polish sport **[]** (zaszczyt) credit, honour; **przynosić** ~**ę rodzinie** to bring credit a. honour to one's family

chlub|ić się *impf v refl.* to pride oneself (**czymś** on sth); to take pride (**czymś** in sth)

chlubn|y *adi. grad. [tradycje, zwycięstwo]* glorious; *[czyn, postawa]* commendable książk.; praiseworthy; ~**y wyjątek** a notable a. commendable exception

chlup|nąć *pf* — **chlup|ać** *impf* *vi [woda]* to splash; *[błoto]* to squelch; ~**ie mi w butach** my shoes are squelching; **kamień** ~**nął w wodę** the stone plopped into the water

chlupo|t *m* (wody) splash(ing); (mleka w bańkach) slosh(ing); splosh(ing) GB pot.; (błota) squelch(ing), slurp; (fal) wash, lap(ping)

chlupo|tać *impf vi [ciecz]* to lap, to splash (**o coś** against sth)

chlu|snąć *pf* — **chlu|stać** *impf* **[]** *vt* to fling, to throw (**czymś na coś** sth on sth); ~**snąć wodą na podłogę** to fling a. slosh water over the floor
[] *vi [woda, krew]* to gush, to spout (**z czegoś** from sth)

chłodni|a *f* cold store; **samochód** ~**a** a refrigerator truck

chłodnic|a *f* radiator

chłodn|y *adi. grad.* cool, chilly; ~**e powitanie** a cool a. cold a. chilly welcome

chłodziar|ka *f* refrigerator, cooler US

chł|odzić *impf vt* to cool (down) *[zupę]*; to chill *[wino]*

chło|nąć *impf vt* to absorb

chłonn|y *adi. grad. [gąbka, pieluchy]* absorbent; *[umysł]* receptive; *[rynek]* ready

chłop *m* **[]** (rolnik) peasant; ~ **pańszczyźniany** serf **[]** pot. (mężczyzna) bloke GB, guy pot.; man; **równy** a. **swój** a ~ a nice bloke a. guy

chłopa|k *m* pot. **[]** (dziecko) boy **[]** (młodzieniec) youngster, boy; lad pot. **[]** (sympatia) boyfriend

chłop|iec *m* **[]** (dziecko) boy **[]** pot. (młodzieniec) boy; lad pot. **[]** pot. (sympatia) boyfriend

chłopięc|y *adi. [wdzięk, figura]* boyish, boylike; *[lata]* boyhood; *[obuwie, ubranie]* boys'

chłop|ka *f* peasant (woman)

chłops|ki *adi. [pochodzenie, gwara, partia]* peasant

chłopstw|o *n* peasantry

chło|sta *f* **[]** (bicie) flogging; (batem) whipping, lashing **[]** przen. (verbal) lashing, pasting

chło|stać *impf vt* **[]** (bić) to flog, to lash *[skazańca, konia]* (**za coś** for sth); to cane, to whip *[ucznia]* (**za coś** for sth) **[]** przen. to lambast(e), to castigate książk. *[wady, głupotę]*

chł|ód *m* **[]** (niska temperatura) coolness, chill **[]** przen. (obojętność) coldness (of manner), coolness

chma|ra *f* (owadów) swarm, cloud; (ludzi) crowd, horde(s); (dzieciaków) swarm(s); (ptactwa) swarm, flock; (psów) pack

chmiel *m* (roślina) hop; (szyszki) hops

chmu|ra *f* cloud

chmurn|y *adi.* książk. **[]** *[dzień, niebo]* cloudy, overcast **[]** *[mina, twarz, wzrok]* sulky, surly

chmurz|yć się *impf v refl.* **[]** *[niebo]* to cloud over, to become overcast **[]** przen. *[osoba]* to sulk, to scowl

choch|la *f* ladle

chochlik *m* goblin, imp; ~ **drukarski** printing gremlin

chociaż **[]** *coni.* although, (even) though
[] *part.* at least; ~ **tyle mogłem dla niej zrobić** it was the least I could do for her

choćby **I** *coni.* [1] (nawet gdyby) even if; **skończę książkę, ~m miał czytać całą noc** I'll finish the book, even if I have to read all night [2] (na przykład) say; **sprawdź to gdzieś, ~ w encyklopedii** check it somewhere, in an encyclopaedia, say; **połóż to byle gdzie, ~ na stole** just put it anywhere, like on the table

II *part.* [1] (przynajmniej) if only, even; **~ miesiąc/dwa dni** if only (for) a. even (for) a month/two days; **wstąp do nas ~ na chwilę** drop in on us, even if it's just a. only for a moment; **~ nie wiem gdzie/jak/co** no matter where/how/what [2] (na przykład) for instance, say; **porozmawiajmy ~ o polityce** let's talk about politics, say a. for instance

chodliw|y *adi.* pot. [towar, książki] fast-selling; **kawalerki są bardziej ~e niż duże mieszkania** one-room flats sell faster a. are in greater demand than large apartments

chodnik *m* [1] (część ulicy) pavement GB, sidewalk US; **ruchomy ~** travelator [2] (dywanik) runner [3] Górn. drift, gallery

chodzia|rz *m*, **~rka** *f* Sport race walker

cho|dzić *impf* **I** *vi* [1] (osoba, zwierzę) to walk, to go; **zaczął ~dzić, gdy miał rok** he started walking when he was a year old; **~dzić piechotą** a. **na piechotę** to go on foot; **~dzić po lesie/górach** walk in the forest/mountains; **~dzić po drzewach** to climb trees; **~dzić na czworakach** to crawl on all fours; **~dzić o lasce** to use a walking stick; **~dzić o kulach** to walk on a. go about on crutches; **~dzić z kimś** to go out with sb; **ta piosenka ~dzi za mną cały dzień** pot. that song's been going around in my head all day; **od rana ~dzi za mną coś słodkiego** pot. I've been dying for something sweet to eat since this morning pot.; **~dzić za czymś** pot. to be looking for sth; **~dziłem za butami** I've been looking for some shoes [2] (uczęszczać, bywać) to go; **~dzić do pracy/szkoły/biura** to go to work/school/the office; **~dzić na wykłady** to go to a. attend lectures; **~dzić na basen** to go swimming; **~dzić na wagary** to play truant; **~dzić po kawiarniach/dyskotekach** to go round coffee bars/discos; **~dzić po znajomych** to go round visiting friends; **~dzić na jagody/grzyby** to go berry-picking/mushroom-picking; **~dzić na ryby** to go fishing; **on często do nich ~dzi** he often visits them [3] (kursować) [autobus, pociąg] to go, to run; [statek] to sail; **metro ~dzi do północy** the metro runs until midnight [4] (funkcjonować) to work; **zegar źle ~dzi** the clock doesn't keep good time [5] (krążyć) [plotki, wieści] to go around; **~dzą słuchy, że...** everyone's saying that... [6] (nosić) to wear; **~dzić w płaszczu** to wear a coat; **~dzić w żałobie** to be in a. to be wearing mourning [7] (dbać, zabiegać) pot. **~dzić koło kogoś** to look after sb; **ona umie ~dzić koło dzieci** she's (very) good with children

II *v imp.* **~dzi o to, że(by)...** the point is that...; **nie ~dzi o to, żeby...** it's not that...; **o co ~dzi?** what's up? pot.; what's the problem a. matter?; **nie rozumiem, o co ~dzi w tym filmie** I don't get a. understand that film at all; **o co ci ~dzi?** what do you mean?; **~dzi o nasze zarobki...** it's about our earnings...; **jeśli o mnie ~dzi...** as far as I'm concerned...

III **chodź/chodźcie** *inter.* come on, let's go; **~dź, pokażę ci całe mieszkanie** come on, I'll show you the whole flat; **~dźcie jeść!** let's (go and) get something to eat; **~dź no tutaj!** come here, will you!

■ **~dzić po świecie** (wędrować) to roam the world; przen. (istnieć) to walk the earth; **~dzić własnymi drogami** przen. to do things a. go one's own way; **po ile ~dzą teraz dolary?** what's the going rate for the dollar? pot.

choin|a *f* [1] (sosna) pine (tree) [2] (las) pine wood [3] (ścięta gałąź) pine branch

choin|ka *f* Christmas tree; **co dostałeś pod ~kę?** what did you get for Christmas?

chole|ra **I** *f* [1] Med. cholera [2] posp. (o osobie) jerk pot., obraźl.; (o rzeczach) damn(ed) thing pot.; bloody thing posp.

II *inter.* posp. (przekleństwo) damn (it)! pot., oh, hell! pot.; **~ra jasna!** a. **jasna ~ra!** bloody hell! GB posp.; goddammit! US pot.; **do (jasnej) ~ry!** for Christ's sake! pot.

■ **zły jak ~ra** posp. angry as hell; **idź do ~ry!** posp. go to hell! pot.

cholern|y *adi.* pot. damn(ed) pot.; bloody posp.; **~y świat!** damn (it)!; **miałeś ~e szczęście** you were incredibly a. damn lucky; **miał ~ego pecha** he was terribly a. damn unlucky

cholery|k *m*, **~czka** *f* hothead, spitfire

cholesterol *m* cholesterol

cholew|ka *f* upper

chomą|to *n* (horse) collar

chomik *m* Zool. hamster

chomik|ować *impf vt* żart. to hoard, to squirrel away

chorąg|iew *f* (flaga) flag, ensign; (sztandar) standard; (proporzec) banner, streamer; **biała ~iew** a white flag, a flag of truce

chorągiew|ka *f* (flaga) flag, ensign; **~ka sygnalizacyjna** a signal(ling) flag; **~ka na wietrze** weathercock; pejor. trimmer

chorąż|y *m* [1] Wojsk. (osoba, stopień, tytuł) warrant officer, ensign [2] (w procesji) standard-bearer

choreograf *m*, **~ka** *f* choreographer

choreografi|a *f* choreography

chor|oba **I** *f* [1] (zły stan zdrowia) illness, sickness; (schorzenie) illness, disease; (dolegliwość) complaint; (zaburzenie) disorder; **~oba gardła** a throat condition; **~oba nowotworowa** cancer; **~oba serca** a heart disease a. condition; **~oba wątroby** a liver disease a. complaint; **nawrót** ∼**oby** a relapse; **historia** ∼**y** Med. sb's medical record, sb's case history; **być na** ∼**obie** pot. to be off sick ② przen. (negatywne zjawisko) disease, malady

II *inter.* pot., euf. (przekleństwo) heck pot., euf.; sugar euf.; ∼**oba, gdzie ja to położyłem?** where the heck did I put it?

chorobliwie *adv. [ciekawy]* morbidly; *[ambitny]* pathologically, unhealthily; *[zazdrosny]* insanely

chorobliw|y *adi. [apetyt]* abnormal; *[lęk, wstręt]* morbid, pathological; ∼**a zazdrość** insane jealousy

chorobow|y *adi. [zmiany]* pathological, morbid; *[ubezpieczenie]* sickness, health; **karta** ∼**a** a patient's chart; **torebka** ∼**a** a sick bag; **zwolnienie** ∼**e** sick leave

chor|ować *impf vi* ① (być chorym) to be ill GB, to be sick US; ∼**ować na grypę** to have (the) flu; ∼**ować na nerki/wątrobę** to have a kidney/liver complaint a. condition; ∼**ować obłożnie** to be bedridden ② pot., przen. (bardzo chcieć) to be dying pot. **(na coś** for sth a. to do sth)

chorowi|ty *adi. [osoba]* sickly, frail; *[wygląd, cera]* sickly, unhealthy

cho|ry **I** *adi.* ① *[osoba, zwierzę]* ill, sick; *[noga, oczy]* bad; *[nerka]* diseased; *[gardło]* sore; ∼**ry umysłowo** psychiatric patient; **być** ∼**rym na gruźlicę/raka** to have TB/cancer; **być** ∼**rym na serce** to have a. to suffer from a heart condition; **być** ∼**rym na żołądek** to have a stomach complaint; **być** ∼**rym z zazdrości** to be sick with jealousy; **być psychicznie/śmiertelnie** ∼**rym** to be mentally/terminally ill; **obłożnie** ∼**ry** bedridden; ∼**ry z miłości/tęsknoty** przen. lovesick/homesick ② pot., przen. (zdenerwowany) sick; **być** ∼**rym na myśl o czymś** to be sick at the very thought of (doing) sth ③ przen. (źle funkcjonujący) *[wyobraźnia]* sick; **żyjemy w** ∼**rej rzeczywistości** we live in a sick world

II cho|ry *m,* ∼**ra** *f* (osoba) sick person; (pacjent) patient; ∼**rzy** the sick, patients

chowa|ć *impf* **I** *vt* ① (kłaść) to put (away); (głęboko) to stow (away); ∼**ć coś na miejsce** to put sth back a. away; ∼**ć coś do kieszeni/szafy** to put sth in one's pocket/in the cupboard ② (przechowywać) to keep, to put; ∼**ć coś w szafie/pod łóżkiem** to keep sth in the cupboard/under the bed ③ (ukrywać) to hide *[biżuterię, pieniądze]*; to harbour, to hide *[zbiega, przestępcę]* ④ (nie ujawniać) to keep, to hide *[tajemnicę]*; ∼**ć coś w tajemnicy** to keep sth (a) secret ⑤ (zasłaniać) to bury *[twarz]* ⑥ pot. (wychowywać) to bring up, to raise US; ∼**ć kogoś surowo** to bring sb up strictly ⑦ (trzymać, hodować) to rear, to raise *[świnie, drób]*; to keep *[psa]* ⑧ (składać do grobu) to bury ⑨ książk. (żywić uczucia) to harbour *[gniew, żal]* **(do kogoś** towards sb)

II chować się ① (znikać z pola widzenia) to disappear, to go; (chronić się) to (take) shelter; **słońce** ∼ **się za**

lasem the sun is going down behind the forest; ∼**ć się do cienia** to try and find some shade ② (ukrywać się) to hide ③ pot. (wychowywać się) to be brought up, to be raised US; ∼**ć się u ciotki** to be brought up by an aunt ④ (rozwijać się) *[dziecko, zwierzę]* to thrive

ch|ód **I** *m* ① (sposób chodzenia) walk; gait książk.; **poznałam go po chodzie** I recognized him by his walk ② Sport race walking; **chód na 20 kilometrów** a 20-kilometre walking race ③ Gry move ④ (zegarka) movement; **(być) na chodzie** pot. *[urządzenie]* (to be) in working a. running order; *[osoba]* to be in good form; **trzymać motor na chodzie** to keep the engine running

II chody *plt* pot. connections; **mieć chody w ministerstwie** to have connections at the ministry

III chodu *inter.* pot. run for it!; **złapał czapkę i chodu za drzwi** he grabbed his hat and ran out pot.

ch|ór *m* ① (zespół) choir; ∼**r męski/chłopięcy** a male/boys' choir; ∼**r szkolny/kościelny** a school/church choir ② (śpiew) choral singing; (utwór) choral piece a. work, chorus ③ przen. (dźwięków, głosów) chorus; ∼**r ptaków/syren fabrycznych** a chorus of birds/factory sirens; **mówić/odpowiadać** ∼**rem** to speak/answer in chorus, to chorus

chóraln|y *adi. [pieśń, zespół]* choral; *[śmiech, wrzask]* general

chórzy|sta *m,* ∼**stka** *f* choir a. chorus singer, chorister

ch|ów *m* (bydła, drobiu) breeding; (ptaków) aviculture

chrabąszcz *m* Zool. cockchafer, May bug

chrapać *impf* → **chrapnąć**

chrapliw|y *adi.* grad. *[głos]* hoarse, husky; *[oddech]* wheezy

chrap|nąć *pf* — **chrap|ać** *impf vi* to snore

chrom *m* Chem. chromium, chrome

chromosom *m* Biol. chromosome

chromowan|y *adi. [zderzak]* chrome, chromium-plated

chroniczn|y *adi. [katar, ból głowy]* chronic

chro|nić *impf* **I** *vt* (strzec) to protect; ∼**nić kogoś przed czymś/od czegoś** to protect sb against/from sth; ∼**nić oczy przed słońcem** to shield one's eyes from the sun

II chronić się ① (strzec się) to protect oneself; ∼**nić się przed czymś** a. **od czegoś** to protect oneself against a. from sth; ∼**nić się przed grypą** to guard against flu ② (chować się) to shelter, to take shelter a. cover **(przed czymś** from sth)

chroni|ony *adi. [gatunki, rośliny, zwierzęta]* protected

chronologi|a *f* sequence, chronology

chronologiczn|y *adi. [porządek, opis]* chronological

chropowa|ty *adi.* ① (grudkowaty) lumpy, nodular; (nierówny, szorstki) coarse, rough ② (matowy, niemelodyjny) harsh, hoarse ③ (niedoskonały) coarse, crude; **~ty styl powieści** the novel's uneven style

chrupać¹ *impf* → **chrupnąć**

chrup|ać² *impf vt* to crunch, to munch *[jabłko, grzankę]*

chrup|ki *adi. [pieczywo]* crisp(y); *[sałata, wafle]* crisp; *[śnieg, marchewki]* crisp, crunchy; *[lód]* crunchy

chrup|nąć *pf* — **chrup|ać**¹ *impf vi* (zatrzeszczeć) to crunch, to crack; **w stawach mu ~nęło** his joints cracked a. made a cracking noise; **~iące bułeczki** crispy a. crusty bread rolls; **~iąca marchewka** a crunchy carrot

chryp|a *f* hoarseness; **mieć ~ę** to be hoarse, to have a sore throat; to have a frog in one's throat pot.

chryp|ieć *impf vi [osoba]* to speak in a hoarse voice, to croak; *[głośnik, megafon]* to crackle, to rasp

chrystianizm *m* Christianity

Chryst|us *m* Christ; **(Jezu) ~e!** Christ Almighty!, (Jesus) Christ!

chryzantem|a *f* Bot. chrysanthemum

chrzan *m* Bot., Kulin. horseradish

■ **zły jak ~** pot. (absolutely) livid, foaming at the mouth pot.; **być do ~u** pot. to be hopeless a. lousy pot.; **życie jest do ~u** life is shitty wulg.

chrza|nić *impf posp.* [I *vt* ① (pleść bzdury) to bullshit GB posp.; **nie ~ń!** don't give me that crap! posp. ② (partaczyć) to cock up GB pot., to screw up pot. *[robotę]* ③ (lekceważyć) to not give a monkey's posp.; **~nię to, znajdę inną robotę!** sod this, I'll find another job! posp.

[II **chrzanić się** ① (cackać się) to mess about a. around (**z czymś** with sth); to bugger about a. around posp. (**z czymś** with sth) ② (plątać się) **~nią mi się daty powstań** I get the dates of the uprisings mixed up ③ (psuć się) to turn crappy posp.

chrząk|nąć *pf* — **chrząk|ać** *impf vi* ① *[osoba]* (charkać) to hawk, to clear one's throat; (dla przyciągnięcia uwagi) to (give a slight) cough; to hem przest.; (z zakłopotania, niezdecydowania) to hum and haw ② *[świnia]* to grunt, to oink

chrząknięci|e *n* ① (charknięcie) hawk; (dla przyciągnięcia uwagi) slight cough, hem; (z zakłopotania, niezdecydowania) slight cough ② (świni) grunt, oink

chrząst|ka *f* ① Anat. cartilage ② (w mięsie) gristle

chrząszcz *m* Zool. beetle, cockchafer

chrz|cić *impf* [I *vt* ① Relig. to baptize, to christen *[dziecko]* ② przen. (nadawać nazwę) to christen, to name *[statek]* ③ pot., żart. (rozcieńczać wodą) to water down *[wino]*

[II **chrzcić się** Relig. to be baptized

chrzcielnic|a *f* Relig. (baptismal) font

chrzcin|y *plt* christening party

chrz|est *m* baptism, christening

chrzestn|y [I *adi. [imię]* Christian, baptismal; *[obrzęd]* baptismal; **córka ~a** a goddaughter; **matka ~a** a godmother a. sponsor; **ojciec ~y** a

godfather a. sponsor; **rodzice ~i** godparents; **syn ~y** a godson

[II *m* pot. godfather

[III **chrzestna** *f* pot. godmother

[IV **chrzestni** *plt* pot. godparents

chrześcijan|in *m*, **~ka** *f* Christian

chrześcijańs|ki *adi. [wartości, filozofia, teolog]* Christian

chrześcijaństw|o *n* Christianity

chrzę|st *m* (żwiru, piasku) crunch(ing); (kluczy uderzających o siebie) jangle, jangling; (klucza w zamku) grating, grinding

chrzę|stnąć, **chrzę|snąć** *pf* — **chrzę|ścić** *impf vi [żwir, szkło, śnieg]* to crunch; *[mechanizm]* to grind; *[kości]* to grate, to crunch

chuchać¹ *impf* → **chuchnąć**

chuch|ać² *impf vi* pot., przen. (troszczyć się) to lavish care (and attention) (**na kogoś/coś** on sb/sth); **~ała na swojego jedynaka** she pampered a. mollycoddled her only son; **~ają na swój nowy samochód** they're extremely fussy about their new car

chuch|nąć *pf* — **chuch|ać**¹ *impf vi* to breathe; **~nęła w zgrabiałe dłonie** she blew a. breathed on her numb hands

chuch|ro *n* pot. weakling, frail individual

chud|nąć *impf vi* to grow thin

chudoś|ć *f* thinness

chu|dy [I *adi. grad. [osoba, ręka]* thin; *[książka]* slim; *[mięso]* lean; *[ser]* low-fat; **~de mleko** skimmed a. low-fat milk

[II *m* thin person

chuligan *m*, **~ka** *f* hooligan, hoodlum

chuligańs|ki *adi.* loutish; **~kie wybryki** acts of hooliganism

chuligaństw|o *n* hooliganism

chu|sta *f* scarf

chustecz|ka *f* ① (do użytku osobistego) **~ka (do nosa)** (z tkaniny) handkerchief; (jednorazowa) tissue ② (na głowę) headscarf

chwal|ić *impf* [I *vt* ① (oceniać dodatnio) to praise *[dziecko, książkę]* ② książk. (wielbić) to praise *[Pana, Stwórcę]*; to sing the praises of książk.

[II **chwalić się** (chełpić się) to boast (**czymś** about sth); **nie ma się czym ~ić** it's nothing to be proud of a. to boast about

■ **~ić Boga** książk. thank heavens; praise be (to God) przest.; **~ić sobie życie na wsi** to be happy living in the country; **to jej się ~i** książk. she deserves credit for it, it's to her credit

chwalipię|ta *m*, *f* pot. show-off pot.; braggart

chwa|ła *f* (cześć) glory; (chluba) pride (**kogoś/ czegoś** of sb/sth); **przynosić komuś ~łę** to do sb credit, to do credit to sb

chwa|st *m* weed

chwi|ać się *impf v refl.* ① *[stół, szafka]* to wobble; *[konstrukcja, rusztowanie]* to be rickety; *[łódź]* to rock; *[ząb]* to be loose; *[płomień]* to flicker, to waver; ~**ać się na wietrze** to sway in the wind; ~**ać się na nogach** to be unsteady on one's legs, to be shaky on one's feet ② przen. (wahać się) to waver; to vacillate książk.

chwiejn|y *adi.* ① *[drabina]* unstable, wobbly; *[chód]* unsteady; *[konstrukcja, kładka]* rickety, shaky; *[pismo]* shaky; **iść** ~**ym krokiem** to totter ② przen. *[osoba]* (niestabilny) fragile; (niezdecydowany) wavering, irresolute; ~**a równowaga polityczna** the fragile political balance

chwil|a ① *f* ① (moment) moment, instant; **co** ~**a** every now and then a. again; **przed** ~**ą** just now, a minute ago; **za** ~**ę** in a minute a. moment; **pod wpływem** ~**i** on the spur of the moment ② (okres, pora) time; **dobre/szczęśliwe** ~**e** good/happy times; **ciężkie** a. **trudne** ~**e** difficult times a. moments

② **chwilami** *adv.* at times, now and then

chwilecz|ka ① *f* second; **to potrwa tylko** ~**kę** it'll only take a second

② **chwileczkę** *inter.* just a minute!; ~**kę! jeszcze nie skończyłem** just a minute, I haven't finished yet!; ~**kę! nie odpowiedział pan na pytanie** hold on (a minute), you haven't answered the question!; ~**kę, już idę** one second, I'm just coming; **zaraz,** ~**kę** okay, just (give me) a minute

chwil|ka *f* moment, second; **wrócę za** ~**kę** I'll only be a second

chwilowo *adv.* ① (tymczasowo) temporarily ② (przez chwilę, na chwilę) *[wypogodzić się, zapomnieć]* for a moment ③ (w tej chwili) *[zajęty]* at a. for the moment

chwilowoś|ć *f* temporary nature, temporariness

chwilow|y *adi.* ① (trwający chwilę) *[wahanie, uczucie]* momentary; ~**y nastrój** a passing mood; ~**e wrażenie** a fleeting impression; ~**a przerwa** a short break ② (tymczasowy) *[ulga, poprawa]* temporary

chwy|cić *pf* — **chwy|tać** *impf* ① *vt* ① (złapać) to get a. take hold of *[torbę, dziecko]*; to catch *[piłkę, jabłko]*; to seize, to grasp *[nóż, szablę]*; ~**tać (za) czapkę** to grab one's cap; ~**cić kogoś za włosy/kark** to grab sb by the hair/(the scruff of) the neck; ~**cić kogoś za rękę** to grip sb's hand, to grasp sb by the hand; ~**cić kogoś w objęcia** to grasp a. clasp sb in an embrace; ~**tać konia na lasso** to lasso a. rope a horse ② przen. (postrzegać) to catch *[dźwięki, spojrzenia]* ③ przen. (pojmować) to grasp; to get pot.; ~**tać coś w lot** to grasp sth immediately; to catch on (to sth) at once a. immediately pot. ④ przen. (ogarnąć) ~**tały go bóle/konwulsje** he was gripped by pain/seized by convulsions; ~**cił go kaszel** he had a coughing fit; ~**ciły ją dreszcze** she started shivering

② *vi* ① przen. (przywrzeć) *[farba, emulsja]* to take; *[klej]* to set, to stick; *[cement]* to set ② pot., przen. (zyskać uznanie) *[pomysł, reklama]* to catch on pot.; *[towar, film]* to take off pot.; *[propozycja]* to be accepted

③ **chwycić się** — **chwytać się** ① (siebie samego) to clutch, to grasp ② (jeden drugiego) to grasp a. hold one another ③ (dla utrzymania równowagi) to hold on to, to cling to *[poręczy, płotu]* ④ (dać się złapać) *[ryba, zwierzę]* to be caught ⑤ przen. (robić wszystko) to try (out), to resort to; ~**tać się różnych pomysłów** to try (out) different ideas; ~**tać się różnych sposobów** to resort to various methods a. means; ~**tać się różnych zajęć** to take on a. up various activities ⑥ pot. (spostrzegać w sobie) to catch oneself (**na czymś** doing sth)

■ ~**cić wiatr** *[pies]* to catch a. get the scent; ~**tać coś na gorąco** pot. (w mediach) to be where the action is pot.; ~**cić za broń/pióro/pędzel** to take up arms/writing/painting

chwy|t *m* ① (chwycenie, złapanie) grip(ping), grasp-(ing); (piłki) catch ② Sport (w zapasach, judo) hold; (we wspinaczce) handhold ③ (manewr) trick, dodge; (środek) device; **tani** ~**t** a cheap a. dirty trick; ~**t reklamowy** a sales gimmick; ~**t literacki/stylistyczny** a literary/stylistic device; **wszystkie** ~**ty (są) dozwolone** no holds barred ④ (na instrumencie) fingering

chyba ① *part.* ① (przypuszczenie) ~ **wreszcie doszliśmy do porozumienia** it seems we've finally reached an agreement; **miał** ~ **ze sto lat** he must have been a hundred; ~ **tutaj zostawiłem klucze** I think I left my keys here; ~ **tak/nie** I think so/I don't think so ② (emfatyczne) surely; ~ **w to nie wierzysz!** surely you don't believe that!; ~ **żartujesz!** you must be joking!, you're joking, of course!

② **chyba że/żeby** *coni.* unless; **wieczorami nie wychodzę z domu,** ~ **że muszę** I don't go out at night, unless I have to

chybi|ć *pf* — **chybi|ać** *impf vi* to miss; ~**ć celu** (**o włos**) to miss the target (by a hair's breadth); ~**ać celu** przen. to miss a. fall wide of the mark, to be off target

■ **ani** ~ książk. for certain; **awans go za to czeka ani** ~ he's bound a. sure to be promoted for that; **na** ~**ł trafił** at random

chybi|ony *adi.* *[wysiłek]* fruitless; vain książk.; *[uwaga, porównanie]* inept, inappropriate; *[plan, pomysł]* abortive; *[decyzja]* unwise, poor; ~**ony strzał** a. **rzut** a miss; **ten film jest całkowicie** ~**ony** the film's a complete disaster

chybo|tać *impf v refl.* *[żyrandol]* to swing; *[mostek]* to sway; *[konstrukcja, drzewo]* to shake, to sway; *[łódź]* to rock; *[płomień]* to flicker, to waver

chyl|ić *impf* ① *vt* to bow *[głowę]*; to bend (down) *[gałęzie]*; **wiatr** ~**ił łódź na bok** the wind pushed the boat to one side

② **chylić się** ① (zginać się) *[drzewa]* to bend (down); *[chata]* to lean over; ~**ić się w ukłonie** to bow ② przen. (kończyć się) to decline; ~**ić się ku upadkowi** to be on the decline ③ przen. (skłaniać się) to tip; **szala zwycięstwa ∼i się na ich stronę** the scales of victory are tipping a. are tipped in their favour

chyłkiem *adv.* [1] (ukradkiem) stealthily; **wymknąć się ∼ z przyjęcia** to sneak away from a party; **zakraść się ∼ do budynku** to sneak into a building [2] (potajemnie) quietly; on the quiet pot.; **∼ wycofać się ze sprawy** to withdraw quietly from an affair

chytrus *m*, **∼ka** *f* pot., pejor. [1] (sprytny) sly one; cunning so-and-so pot.; **a to ∼!** that sly old devil! [2] (chciwiec) greedy so-and-so pot.; (skąpiec) stinge pot.; miser

chyt|ry *adi. grad.* [1] (przebiegły) *[osoba]* wily, sly; *[spojrzenie, uśmiech]* sly; *[wybieg, sztuczka]* cunning [2] pot., żart. (pomysłowy) crafty, artful; **∼re urządzenie** an ingenious device [3] pot. (chciwy) stingy pot.; mean; **∼ry na pieniądze** mean with money

cia|ło *n* Biol. body; **∼ka tłuszczowe** fatty bodies; **białe/czerwone ∼ka krwi** white/red blood cells

ci|ało *n* [1] (organizm) body; **części ciała** body parts [2] książk. (grupa osób) body; **ciało ustawodawcze** a legislative body [3] (zwłoki) (dead) body, corpse; **złożyć ciało do grobu** to lower a coffin into a grave [4] Chem., Fiz. body

❏ **Boże Ciało** Relig. Corpus Christi; **ciało niebieskie** celestial a. heavenly body, celestial object

ciamka|ć *impf vi* pot. to smack one's lips

ciar|ki *plt* shivers

ciasno|ta *f* [1] (ograniczona przestrzeń) cramped conditions; **mieszkać/podróżować w ∼cie** to live/travel in cramped conditions [2] przen. parochialism, insularity; **∼ta umysłowa** narrow-mindedness

cia|sny *adi. grad.* *[ubranie, buty]* tight(-fitting); *[pomieszczenie]* cramped; *[krąg, szeregi]* tight; *[ścieg, szyk]* close; *[definicja, program]* narrow, restricted; *[poglądy, pojęcia]* narrow(-minded), parochial

ciastkar|nia *f* cake shop

ciast|ko *n* [1] (nieduży słodki wypiek) cake [2] (wypiek z kruchego ciasta) (miękkie) (small) pastry; (twarde) biscuit GB, cookie US

ci|asto *n* [1] (gęsta masa) dough; (na wypieki słodkie) pastry, paste; (na placki) batter [2] (wypiek) cake; **ciasto biszkoptowe** sponge (cake); **ciasto drożdżowe** a raised cake

ciastowa|ty *adi.* doughy, pasty

ci|ąć¹ *impf* **[]** *vt* [1] (krajać) to cut *[materiał, szkło]* (**czymś** with sth); **ciąć coś na kawałki** to cut sth up a. into pieces; **ciąć coś na plasterki** to slice sth (up); **ciąć drzewo piłą** to saw wood [2] (kąsać, kłuć) *[komar]* to bite; *[pszczoła]* to sting

[] *vi* przen. *[wiatr]* to lash, to sting (**w coś** sth); *[mróz, śnieg]* to sting (**w coś** sth); **deszcz ciął ostro** the rain was pelting a. driving down (hard)

ci|ąć² *pf, impf vt* (uderzyć) *[nożem, szablą]* to slash, to cut; (batem) to lash, to slash

ciąg *m* [1] (w przestrzeni) row, stretch; **∼ handlowy** a shopping precinct; **∼ pieszy** a pedestrian way a. precinct; **∼ sklepów** a row a. stretch of shops [2] (w czasie) (wydarzeń) chain, sequence; (nieszczęść, wypadków) series, string; (scen, zdjęć) sequence; **w ∼u rozmowy** during the course of conversation; **odpowiedzieć w ∼u czterech dni** to answer within four days; **∼ przyczynowo-skutkowy** cause and effect; **∼ dalszy** (przedłużenie) continuation; (następny film, książka) sequel; **∼ dalszy nastąpi** to be continued; **jednym ∼iem** pot. *[oglądać, czytać]* in one go; *[wypić]* in one gulp; **w dalszym ∼u** still [3] Techn. (powietrza) current of air; (w kominie) draught GB, draft US; (wody, gazu) flow [4] pot. (okres pijaństwa, brania narkotyków) bender pot.

ciąga|ć *impf vt* pot. [1] (włóczyć) to drag, to pull; **∼ć coś po podłodze** to drag a. pull sth along the floor [2] (zabierać ze sobą) to drag [sb] around a. along *[dzieci, męża]* [3] (szarpać) to pull; **∼ć kogoś za włosy/ brodę** to pull sb's hair/beard; **∼ć kogoś za uszy** to pull sb by the ears

■ **∼ć kogoś po sądach** to drag sb through the courts

ciągle *adv.* [1] (bez przerwy) *[zmieniać się, pracować]* continuously [2] (bardzo często) *[kłócić się, chorować]* constantly, continually [3] (wciąż) still; **∼ to samo** the same old story, it's always the same

ciągłoś|ć *f* continuity; **∼ć pracy** continuous employment

ciąg|ły *adi.* *[hałas, ruch]* continuous; *[strach, za-grożenie]* continual, constant; *[przerwy, podróże]* constant; *[linia]* unbroken, continuous; **∼ła za-budowa** ribbon development

ciągn|ąć *impf* **[]** *vt* [1] (przesuwać, wlec) to drag, to pull *[osobę, zwierzę]*; to draw, to pull *[wóz, wagon]*; to tow *[przyczepę]* [2] (zabierać ze sobą) to drag [sb] along [3] (prowadzić, wieść) to carry out *[prace]*; to carry on *[naukę]*; to run, to carry on *[gospodarstwo]*; **on ledwo ∼ie** pot. he just gets by [4] (wydobywać) to draw; **∼ąć wodę ze studni** to draw water from a well [5] (wchłaniać) to consume *[elektryczność]*; **∼ąć lemoniadę przez słomkę** to drink a. suck lemonade through a straw; **∼ąć wódkę** pot. to knock back vodka pot.; **∼ąć dym z fajki** to draw on a pipe [6] (przyciągać) to draw; **wir rzeki ∼ął go na dno** the river eddy was sucking him under [7] (pociągać, wabić) *[lektura, sport]* to draw [8] (szarpać, targać) to pull, to tug; **∼ąć kogoś za rękaw/włosy** to pull sb's sleeve/hair [9] (rozciągać) to draw out, to stretch (out) *[sznur, gumę]* [10] (przedłużać) to carry on, to continue *[roboty, poszukiwanie]* [11] (uzyskiwać) to derive *[zyski, korzyści]* (**z czegoś** from sth) [12] (zakładać) to run, to lay *[kabel, linię kolejową]*; (budować) to build, to run (up) *[mur, ścianę]*

[] *vi* [1] (wiać, dmuchać) **chłód ∼ął od rzeki** there was a cool breeze off the river; **piec dobrze ∼ie** the chimney draws well; **ależ tu ∼ie** it's so draughty in here ② (przemieszczać się) to head ③ (nad-chodzić) *[burza, chmury]* to draw near, to near ④ (być amatorem) ~**ąć do czegoś** to be drawn to *[sportu, lekkiego życia]* ⑤ (mówić dalej) to continue, to go on ⑥ pot. (jechać) *[samochód]* to do pot.; ~**ąć setką** to be doing a hundred

III ciągnąć się ① (zajmować obszar) *[las, pustynia]* to stretch (out) ② (wlec się) to trail; ~**ąć się z tyłu** to trail behind ③ (szarpać jeden drugiego) to pull one another; ~**ąć się za włosy** to pull each other's hair ④ (trwać długo) *[spotkanie, film]* to drag on; *[dzień, wieczór]* to wear on; ~**ąć się bez końca** to go on forever ⑤ (unosić się) *[zapach]* to waft ⑥ *[pasek, sznurowadła]* to trail ⑦ (być ciągliwym) *[substancja]* to be stringy; *[cukierek]* to be chewy

ciągnie|nie n ① (w loterii) draw; ~**nie losów** the drawing of lots, a ballot ② Techn. (rur, prętów) drawing ③ (w górnictwie) haulage

ciągnik m tractor

ciąż|a f pregnancy

ciążeni|e n ~**e powszechne** (universal) gravita-tion; **siła** ~**a** the force of gravity

ciąż|yć *impf vi* ① (przytłaczać ciężarem) ~**yć komuś** to press heavily on sb, to weigh sb down ② przen. (skłaniać się) to lean (**ku czemuś** towards sth) ③ (dawać się we znaki) *[obowiązki, odpowiedzialność]* to be a burden, to get [sb] down ④ (moralnie) *[obowiązek, odpowiedzialność]* to rest (**na kimś** with sb); ~**y na nim zarzut morderstwa** he stands accused of murder ⑤ (zagrażać) *[niebezpieczeństwo, groźba]* to hang (**nad kimś/czymś** over sb/sth)

cich|aczem, ~**cem** adv. *[wymknąć się, zakraść się]* quietly, silently; *[wyjechać, działać]* secretly, clan-destinely

cich|nąć *impf vi* (milknąć) *[dźwięki, kroki]* to die away; *[osoba]* to fall silent, to quieten down; *[miejsce]* to become quiet; **ujadanie psów powoli** ~**ło** the barking of the dogs slowly ceased

ci|cho I adv. grad. (mówić, poruszać się) quietly; *[odbywać się]* quietly, with little fanfare; **tu jest tak cicho** it's so quiet here

II adv. przen. (dyskretnie) *[popierać]* quietly, tacitly

III inter. quiet!; **cicho, sza** hush!

IV z cicha *[uśmiechać się, szumieć]* quietly

■ **być cicho** to keep a. stay quiet; **siedzieć cicho** pot. to keep quiet; **z cicha pęk** a dark horse; **żartowniś z cicha pęk** a bit of a joker on the quiet

ci|chy I adi. grad. *[głosy, muzyka]* quiet, soft; *[urzą-dzenie]* noiseless; *[pukanie]* gentle; *[dom, dzielnica]* quiet; *[morze]* calm; *[osoba]* quiet, gentle; *[uroczy-stość, ślub]* quiet, low-key; **po cichu** quietly; **czytać po cichu** to read quietly a. to oneself

II adi. przen. (niejawny) *[zmowa, układ]* tacit, un-spoken; *[poplecznik]* tacit; *[transakcje, interesy]* se-cret, under-the-counter; *[adorator, wielbiciel]* secret; *[rozpacz]* quiet; **cichy wspólnik** a sleeping partner GB, a silent partner US; **ciche współzawodnictwo**

hidden rivalry; **mam cichą nadzieję, że...** I'm secretly hoping that...; **po cichu** on the quiet

■ **cicha woda** a deep one; **cicha woda brzegi rwie** przysł. still waters run deep przysł.

cie|c, cie|knąć *impf vi* ① (spływać) *[woda, płyn]* to run; (kroplami) to drip; ~**c po czymś** to run a. roll down sth; **krew mu** ~**knie z nosa** his nose is bleeding; **cały czas** ~**knie mi z nosa** my nose keeps running ② (przeciekać) *[rynna, zbiornik]* to leak; ~**knący kran** a dripping a. leaking tap

ciecz f liquid, fluid; **krew jest** ~**ą** blood is a fluid

ciecz|ka f Zool. heat, oestrus

ciekaw|ić *impf* **I** vi to interest; **bardzo/mało kogoś** ~**ić** to be of great/little interest to sb; ~**i mnie, dlaczego/jak...** I'm curious to know why/how...; ~**i mnie, co będzie dalej** I wonder what will happen next

II ciekawić się to take an interest, to be interested (**czymś** in sth)

ciekawost|ka f (przedmiot) curiosity; (informacja) titbit GB, tidbit US

ciekawoś|ć f curiosity; ~**ć czegoś** curiosity about sth, interest in sth; **z** ~**ci** a. **przez** ~**ć** out of curiosity; **z (czystej)** ~**ci spytam** I'm just curious (that's all)

■ ~**ć pierwszy stopień do piekła** przysł. curiosity killed the cat przysł.

ciekaws|ki pot. **I** adi. *[reporter, pytania]* nosy pot.; prying; ~**ki wzrok** prying eyes

II ciekaws|ki m, ~**ka** f rubberneck pot.; inquisi-tive onlooker

ciekaw|y I adi. grad. *[osoba]* curious; *[umysł, spojrzenie]* inquisitive, inquiring; *[książka, przedsta-wienie]* interesting, engaging; *[postać, pomysł]* inter-esting; ~**a rzecz, jak/że...** it's interesting a. curious how/that...

II ciekaw adi. praed. curious (**czegoś** about sth); ~**a jestem, jak on wygląda** I wonder what he looks like; **wcale nie jesteśmy tego** ~**i** we're not the slightest bit interested

III ciekawe adi. praed. interesting; **a to** ~**e** now that's (very) interesting; ~**e, czy zdam** I wonder if I'll pass; **i co najciekawsze, okazał się moim dalekim krewnym** and the oddest thing of all is that he turned out to be a distant relative of mine

IV ciekaw|y m, ~**a** f onlooker; **ślub zgromadził mnóstwo** ~**ych** the wedding attracted a crowd of onlookers

ciek|ły adi. *[substancja]* liquid, fluid; *[paliwo]* liquid; *[gaz]* liquefied, liquid; *[metal]* molten

cieknąć → **ciec**

ciela|k m (krowa, byk) calf; (sarna, łoś, łania) fawn

cielesn|y adi. książk. *[potrzeby, cierpienia]* bodily; *[kara]* corporal; *[miłość, przyjemności]* carnal książk.; **pociąg** ~**y** physical a. sexual attraction; **tortury** ~**e** physical torture

ciel|ę *n* [1] (krowa, byk) calf; (sarna, łoś, łania) fawn [2] pot. (osoba) ninny pot.; **głupie ~ę z ciebie** you silly billy pot.

cielęcin|a *f* Kulin. veal

cielęc|y *adi.* [1] (z cielaka) veal; **nóżki ~e w galarecie** calf's-foot jelly; **skóra ~a** calf(skin) [2] przen. childish; **~e spojrzenie** a. **~y wzrok** goo-goo eyes pot.

■ **~y wiek** a. **~e lata** książk. salad days; **~y zachwyt** a. **~e uwielbienie** blind admiration

ciel|ić się *impf v refl.* [krowa] to calve; [sarna, łania, łosza] to fawn

cieli|sty *adi.* [rajstopy, pończochy] flesh-coloured; **kolor ~sty** flesh colour

ciemi|ę *n* crown, top of the head

■ **być nie w ~ę bitym** pot. to be no(body's) fool; **potrzebny nam ktoś nie w ~ę bity** we need someone with their wits about them

ciemię|zca, **~życiel** *m* książk. oppressor, tyrant

ciemni|a *f* darkroom

ciemnia|k *m* pot. ignoramus

ciemni|eć *impf* **[I]** *vi* [1] (tracić jasność) [niebo] to darken, to grow dark; [kolor, włosy] to grow darker [2] (odcinać się ciemnym kolorem) to stand out dark(ly), to show dark; **las ~ał na horyzoncie** a forest showed dark on a. against the horizon [3] (o wzroku, oczach) to cloud over

[II] *v imp.* **na dworze ~eje** it's getting a. growing dark outside

ciemn|o *adv. grad.* [1] (bez światła) dark; **robi się ~o** it's getting dark; **zrobiło mu się ~o przed oczami** he felt dizzy; **~o widzę przyszłość** przen. the future looks bleak to me [2] (w ciemnym kolorze) dark, darkly; **~o zabarwiony** dark-coloured

■ **~o, choć oko wykol** (as) dark as pitch, pitch-dark; **randka w ~o** a blind date pot.; **kupować coś w ~o** to buy sth on spec pot.; **jechałem tam zupełnie w ~o** I went there without any idea of what to expect; **można w ~o założyć, że...** you can bet your life that...

ciemnoskó|ry *adi.* [rasa, ludy] dark-skinned, black; **~ra miss Ameryki** a black Miss America

ciemnoś|ć *f* darkness, (the) dark; **~ć zapadła** darkness fell; **bać się ~ci** to be afraid of the dark; **poruszać się** a. **błądzić w ~ciach** to grope in the dark także przen.; **siły ~ci** the forces of darkness

ciemno|ta *f* [1] (brak oświaty) ignorance; **tam panuje zabobon i ~ta** the place is rife with superstition and ignorance [2] (środowisko) ignoramuses [3] pot. (niedorzeczność) drivel, hogwash pot.; **przestań wciskać mi ~tę!** don't give me that drivel a. hogwash!

ciemnowłos|y *adi.* dark-haired

ciemn|y **[I]** *adi. grad.* [noc, pokój, oczy] dark; [oświetlenie, światło] dim; [interes, sprawa] shady pot.; [karnacja, cera] dark, brown; [myśli] dark, gloomy; **~y chleb** brown bread; **~e okulary** dark glasses, sunglasses; **~e piwo** brown ale; **~y**

typ a shady customer; **~y rumieniec** a deep flush; **~a opalenizna** a deep tan; **o ~ej cerze** dark-complexioned

[II] *adi. pot.* (ograniczony) [osoba, lud] illiterate, ignorant

[III] **ciemn|y** *m*, **~a** *f* pot. dimwit pot.

[IV] **ciemne** *n* pot. (piwo) brown (ale)

■ **~a masa** pot. thickhead pot.; **~y jak tabaka w rogu** pot. (as) thick as a brick a. two short planks pot.

cieni|ować *impf vt* [1] to shade (in) [rysunek, detale] [2] przen. (modulować) to modulate [ton, nastrój] [3] (strzyc) to layer [włosy]

cieni|sty *adi. grad.* [1] (zacieniony) [aleja, weranda] shaded, shady [2] (rzucający cień) [lipa] shady, shade-giving

cie|nki *adi. grad.* [1] (niegruby) [drut, warstwa] thin; [nić, linia] fine [2] (lekki) [sweter, rajstopy] thin [3] (chudy) [nogi, ręce] thin [4] (wysoki) [głos, ton] high and thin, reedy [5] (mało pożywny) [kawa, zupa] thin, watery; [posiłek, obiad] meagre [6] pot. (marny) [film, impreza] poor; rop(e)y GB pot.; [dowcip, fabuła] weak, thin

cien|ko *adv. grad.* [1] (niegrubo) [kroić, smarować] thinly; [ubierać się] lightly [2] pot. (niepomyślnie) tight; **u mnie ~ko z forsą** things are a bit tight money-wise; **~ko z nim było** he was in a tight spot

■ **~ko prząść** pot. (biedować) to live from hand to mouth; (chorować) to be on one's last legs; **~ko śpiewać** pot. (biedować) to have a hard a. thin time of it; (pokornieć) to sing small

cienkopis *m* (flamaster) fine felt-tip pen; (długopis) fine ballpoint pen

cie|ń *m* [1] (ciemne odbicie) shadow [2] (zacienione miejsce) shade; **30 stopni w ~niu** 30 degrees in the shade [3] przen. (odrobina) trace, shadow; **~ń szansy** the slightest chance; **~ń uśmiechu** a flicker of a smile; **bez ~nia uśmiechu** without the ghost a. a trace of a smile; **bez ~nia wątpliwości** without a. beyond a shadow of (a) doubt; **nie ma w tym ~nia prawdy** there isn't a grain of truth in it [4] (ciemność) darkness, shadows; **gra świateł i ~ni** the play of light and shade a. shadow [5] (niewyraźny zarys) (dark) shape, shadow [6] książk. (zjawa, duch) ghost; shade książk. [7] (do powiek) eyeshadow

■ **blaski i ~nie** the pros and cons; **być** a. **pozostawać** a. **trzymać się w ~niu** to be a. stay in the background; **~ń ~nia** the slightest trace; **kłaść się ~niem na czymś** książk. to cast a shadow over sth; **rzucać ~ń na kogoś** książk. to cast suspicion on sb, to put sb under a cloud

cieplar|nia *f* (heated) greenhouse; (większa) hot-house, (heated) glasshouse

cieplarnian|y *adi.* [1] [rośliny, kwiaty] greenhouse, hothouse [2] przen. over-protective; **~a atmosfera w rodzinnym domu** an over-protective atmosphere at home

ciepł|o[1] *n* [1] (temperatura dodatnia) warmth; (pogoda) warm weather; **miłe** ~**ło** a pleasant warmth; **trzymać coś w** ~**le** to keep sth warm; **na zewnątrz jest 20 stopni** ~**ła** it's 20 degrees outside [2] przen. (serdeczność) warmth (of feeling); ~**ło domowego ogniska** hearth and home [3] (ogrzewanie) central heating [4] Fiz. heat

ciepł|o[2] *adv. grad.* [1] (o temperaturze) warm; **dzisiaj jest** ~**ło** warm today; **czy jest ci** ~**ło?** are you warm (enough)?; **„podawać na** ~**ło"** Kulin. 'serve hot' [2] przen. (serdecznie) *[odezwać się, uśmiechnąć się]* warmly [3] (zabezpieczając przed zimnem) warmly; **ubrać się** ~**ło** to dress warmly

■ ~**ło,** ~**ło...** you're getting warmer; **trzymaj się** ~**ło** pot., żart. take it easy! pot.; ~**ło jak w uchu** (as) warm as toast

ciepło|ta *f* Med. ~**ta ciała** body temperature

ciepłowni|a *f* thermal power station

ciepłownictw|o *n* Techn. heat engineering

ciepł|y *adi. grad.* [1] *[dzień, wiatr, klimat]* warm; **mieć** ~**ły stosunek do ludzi** to be very warmhearted [2] pot. (przynoszący zyski) ~**ła posada** a cushy job pot. [3] pot. (dopiero wydany) *[gazeta, książka]* hot off the press

cierni|k *m* Zool. three-spined stickleback

cierni|sty *adi. [krzew, gałąź]* thorny; *[kaktus, płetwa]* spiny; ~**sta droga do sławy** the thorny road to success

cier|ń *m* [1] (kolec) thorn, prickle [2] książk., przen. (zadra) thorn; **nosić** ~**ń w sercu** to have a thorn in one's side a. flesh

cierpiąc|y [] *adi.* książk. *[osoba]* ill, suffering; ~**a mina** an expression of pain

[] **cierpiąc|y** *m,* ~**a** *f* sufferer; **nieść ulgę** ~**ym** to bring relief to the suffering

cierp|ieć *impf* [] *vt* książk. to endure, to suffer *[głód, nędzę]*; to put up with, to suffer *[niewygody]*; **nie** ~**ieć kogoś/czegoś** to detest a. not be able to stand sb/sth

[] *vi* [1] (doznawać bólu) to suffer, to be in pain; ~**ieć z powodu rany w nodze** to be suffering with a leg wound; ~**ieć za popełnione winy** to suffer for one's sins; **on bardzo** ~**i** he's in great pain [2] (chorować) to suffer (**na coś** from sth) [3] (odczuwać brak) to suffer; ~**ieć na chroniczny brak pieniędzy** to suffer from an acute shortage of money [4] (smucić się) to be mortified (**nad czymś** by sth) [5] (ponosić stratę) to suffer (**na czymś** from sth); **na tej zmianie** ~**iały jego interesy** his business interests suffered as a result of the change

[] **cierpieć się** (znosić) **nie** ~**ieć się** not to be able to stand one another

cierpie|nie *n* [1] (nieszczęście) suffering, anguish; **przysporzyć komuś** ~**ń** to cause suffering to sb [2] (ból) suffering, pain; **ulżyć komuś w** ~**niach** to ease sb's suffering; **umierać w** ~**niach** to die in great pain

cierp|ki *adi. [owoc, smak]* tart; *[zapach]* pungent, acrid; *[uwaga, ton]* acrid, tart; *[mina]* sour; *[uśmiech, humor]* sardonic; *[doświadczenie, prawda]* bitter

cierpliwie *adv. grad. [tłumaczyć, czekać]* patiently

cierpliwoś|ć [] *f* patience

[] **cierpliwości** *inter.* patience; ~**ci, przyjdzie na nas kolej** just be patient, our turn will come

cierpliw|y *adi. grad.* patient

cierp|nąć *impf vi* to go numb

■ **skóra mi** ~**nie na jego widok** he makes my flesh creep

ciesz|yć *impf* [] *vi* to please; ~**y mnie, że wróciłeś** I'm pleased a. glad that you're back; ~**yć oko** a. **oczy** a. **wzrok** to delight a. gladden the eye; ~**yć oko krajobrazem** to feast one's eyes on the landscape

[] **cieszyć się** [1] (odczuwać radość) to be pleased, to be glad; ~**ę się, że cię widzę** I'm glad to see you; ~**ę się tym, co mam** I'm happy with what I've got; ~**yć się na coś** to look forward to sth [2] (mieć) to enjoy (**czymś** sth); ~**yć się dobrym zdrowiem** to enjoy good health; ~**yć się popularnością wśród młodzieży** to be popular with young people; ~**yć się złą sławą** to have a bad reputation

cieśl|a *m* carpenter

cieśnin|a *f* strait

cietrzew *m* black grouse; (samiec) blackcock; (samica) greyhen

cię|cie *n* [1] (noża, szabli) slash, cut; (szpady, miecza) stroke; (batem) lash, slash [2] Med. incision, cut [3] (rana) cut; (długa) slash; (głęboka) gash, deep cut [4] (budżetowe) cut(back); ~**cia inwestycyjne** cuts in investment, investment cuts; ~**cia kadrowe** staff cuts

❑ **cesarskie** ~**cie** Med. Caesarean (section)

cięciw|a *f* [1] (łuku, kuszy) (bow)string [2] (w geometrii) chord

cięg|i *plt* książk. [1] (bicie) tanning, belting pot.; **dać** a. **sprawić komuś** ~**i** to give sb a belting a. tanning, to tan sb's hide (**za coś** for sth) [2] przen. knocks, blows; **dostałem niezłe** ~**i od życia** I've taken some hard knocks in (my) life

ciętoś|ć *f* (języka) sharpness; (stylu) pungency

cię|ty *adi.* [1] (ostry) *[satyryk, publicysta]* biting; *[pisarz]* caustic; *[uwaga, riposta]* cutting, caustic; *[odpowiedź, dowcip]* scathing, caustic; *[język]* sharp [2] pot. (rozgniewany) snappish; **shirty** GB pot.; **szef coś dzisiaj na mnie** ~**ty** the boss seems to have it in for me today pot.

cięża|r [] *m* [1] (waga) weight [2] (ciężki przedmiot) weight, heavy object [3] przen. burden; **być/stać się dla kogoś** ~**rem** to be/become a burden to sb

[] **ciężary** *plt* pot. weights; **trenować** ~**ry** to lift weights

ciężar|ek [] *m* (do obciążania) weight

[] **ciężarki** *plt* (gimnastyczne) dumb-bells

ciężarn|a *f* pregnant woman
ciężarow|iec *m* Sport weightlifter
ciężarów|ka *f* pot. lorry GB, truck
cięż|ki *adi. grad.* *[worek, bagaż, chmury]* heavy; *[ubrania, zasłony]* heavy, thick; *[czasy, obowiązki, praca]* hard, difficult; *[styl, książka]* heavy(-going); *[cios, strata]* heavy, serious; *[choroba, zarzut]* serious; *[atmosfera, milczenie]* heavy, oppressive; *[potrawa, kolacja]* heavy, stodgy; *[powietrze]* heavy, stuffy
■ **zarabiać** ~**kie pieniądze** pot. to earn oodles of money pot.
cięż|ko *adv. grad.* heavily; *[pracować]* hard; *[oddychać]* with difficulty; *[obrazić, zawinić]* seriously, gravely; ~**ko chory/ranny** seriously a. gravely ill/injured; **zamek w drzwiach** ~**ko chodzi** the door lock's rather stiff
ciężkoś|ć *f* heaviness, weight; **siła** ~**ci** the force of gravity, gravitation; **środek** ~**ci** the centre of gravity
cio|cia *f* pot. auntie, aunty pot.
cios *m* (uderzenie) blow; (pięścią) punch; (siekierą) blow, stroke; (nożem) thrust, stab; **zadać** ~ to deal a. strike a blow; **zasłonić się przed** ~**em** to shield oneself from a blow także przen.
■ ~ **poniżej pasa** (w boksie) blow a. punch below the belt, low blow; **iść za** ~**em** pot., przen. to keep going, to follow sth up
ciosa|ć *impf vt* to hew *[drewno, kamień]*
■ ~**ć komuś kołki na głowie** to browbeat a. bully sb
cioteczn|y *adi.* **jej** ~**y brat** her first cousin; **jego** ~**a siostra** his first cousin; **moja** ~**a babka** my great-aunt; **twój** ~**y dziadek** your great-uncle
ciot|ka *f* ① aunt ② wulg. (miesiączka) the curse pot.; **mieć** ~**ę** to have got the curse
cis *m* Bot. yew (tree)
ci|snąć¹ *pf* — **ci|skać** *impf* **I** *vt* (rzucać) to hurl, to fling; **ciskać w kogoś kamienie** a. **kamieniami** to fling a. hurl stones at sb
II ciskać się ① pot. (złościć się) to rant and rave (o coś about a. over sth); to fume ② (poruszać się gwałtownie) to thrash around
ci|snąć² *impf* **I** *vt* ① (dławić) to press; **coś mnie ciśnie za gardło** I have a lump in my throat ② pot. (zmuszać) to force, to press; **cisną mnie, żebym się wreszcie oświadczył** they're trying to press me into proposing; **cisnąć kogoś o oddanie długu** to press sb to pay back their debt ③ (gnębić) to oppress, to grind down; **cisnąć kogoś podatkami** to overburden sb with taxes
II *vi* (o obuwiu, ubraniu) to pinch
III cisnąć się ① (tłoczyć się) to swarm, to throng ② przen. to fill; **łzy cisnęły się mu do oczu** his eyes filled with tears
cisz|a *f* **I** ① (brak dźwięków) silence; **martwa/grobowa** ~**a** a deathly hush a. silence; **prosić o** ~**ę** to ask for quiet a. silence; **co taka** ~**a?** why is everyone so

quiet? ② przen. (spokój) (peace and) quiet; ~**a domowego ogniska** the tranquillity of domestic life ③ (brak wiatru) calm; ~**a morska** a. **na morzu** a calm at sea
II *inter.* silence!, quiet!
ciśnie|nie *n* pressure
ciśnieniomierz *m* manometer
ciuch pot. **I** *m* piece of clothing; **modne** ~**y** fashionable clothes
II ciuchy *plt* pot. (bazar) second-hand clothes market
ciuchci|a *f* pot. narrow-gauge (steam) train
ciuciubab|ka *f* ① (zabawa) blind man's buff GB, blind man's bluff US; **bawić się w** ~**kę** to play blind man's buff ② (gracz) it
■ **bawić się** a. **grać z kimś w** ~**kę** to lead sb up the garden path pot.
ciułacz *m*, ~**ka** *f* hoarder; **drobni** ~**e** small-(time) savers
ciuła|ć *impf vt* to scrimp (and save)
ciurka|ć *impf vi* to trickle
ciurkiem *adv.* ① (gęstymi kroplami) in a stream ② pot., przen. (bez przerwy) non-stop
ciut *adv.* pot. a bit; ~ **więcej** a bit more
ckliw|y *adi. grad.* mawkish
cl|ić *impf vt* to impose a customs duty on *[towary]*
c|ło *n* customs (duty), tariff; **towary zwolnione od cła** duty-free goods
cmentarz *m* cemetery; (przykościelny) graveyard, churchyard
cmok|nąć *pf* — **cmok|ać** *impf* pot. **I** *vt* ① (pocałować) to kiss; ~**nąć kogoś w rękę** to kiss sb's hand; ~**nąć kogoś w policzek** to give sb a peck on the cheek ② (ssać) ~**ać fajkę** to suck at a. on a pipe
II *vi* (mlasnąć) to smack one's lips
III cmoknąć się — **cmokać się** to kiss
cn|ota *f* książk. ① (prawość) virtue ② (dziewictwo) chastity
cnotliw|y *adi. grad.* książk. *[życie, osoba]* virtuous, righteous książk.; *[kobieta]* innocent, virtuous
co **I** *pron.* ① (w pytaniach) what; **co to (jest)?** what's this/that?; **co robisz?** what are you doing?; **co się dzieje?** what's going on a. happening?; **o co chodzi?** what's the problem a. matter?, what's going on?; **w co się ubierzesz?** what are you going to wear?; **czego szukasz?** what are you looking for?; **czego on chciał?** what did he want?; **do czego służy ten guzik?** what is this button for?; **z czego jest ta koszula?** what is this shirt made of?; **czemu się tak przyglądasz?** what are you looking at?; **czym mam otworzyć tę puszkę?** what should I open this tin with?; **czym to się skończy?** how will it (all) end?; **o czym oni mówią?** what are they talking about?; **co ty na to?** what do you say a. think?; **co u ciebie?** what's new?, how's life (treating you)?, don't you feel well?; **co z tego?** a.

no to co? what about it?, what of it? pot.; **co ty mi tu przyniosłeś?** what on earth have you brought me?; **czemu płaczesz?** what are you crying for?; **„idziesz z nami?" – „czemu nie"** 'are you coming with us?' – 'why not?' [2] (w mowie zależnej) what; **powiedz, co chcesz na śniadanie** tell me what you want for breakfast; **nie wiem, co to była za ryba** I don't know what kind of fish it was; **powiem mu jutro, co i jak** I'll tell him tomorrow what's what; **wiesz co?...** (do) you know what?..., (I'll) tell you what... pot. [3] (w zdaniu podrzędnym zawężającym) that; **mam coś, co cię zainteresuje** I've got something that'll interest you; **rób, co chcesz** do what you want [4] (w zdaniu podrzędnym rozwijającym) which; **powiedział, że pożyczył mi pieniądze, co nie było prawdą** he said he had lent me some money, which wasn't true; **zdał egzamin, czym bardzo ucieszył rodziców** he passed the exam, which made his parents delighted [5] (ile, jak, jaki) as; **mam dwa razy tyle pracy, co ty** I have twice as much work as you (have) [6] pot. (kto, który) who; **znam kogoś, co to chętnie zrobi** I know someone who'll be glad to do it [7] pot. (dlaczego) why; **co się tak kręcisz?** why can't you sit still?; **coś taki wesoły?** what are you so happy about? [8] (emfatycznie) what (a); **co za niespodzianka!** what a surprise!

II praep. every; **co dziesięć minut/dwa tygodnie** every ten minutes/two weeks; **przystawał co krok** he stopped with each step; **co jakiś czas** every now and then; **opuszczał co drugą stronę** he skipped every other page

III adv. (bardziej) **co ciekawsze książki** some of the more interesting books; **co wytrwalsi zostali do końca sztuki** only the most persevering stayed till the end of the play

IV coni. (jak) as; **(ona) pracuje w tej samej firmie co ja** she works for the same company as me; **ten sam/to samo co zawsze** the same as always; **to już nie ten człowiek, co dawniej** he's not the man he used to be; **co ciekawe/dziwne...** what's interesting/strange...; **co gorsza...** what's worse...; **co więcej...** what's more...

V part. pot. (jako równoważnik zdania) **ale ona urosła, co?** she's really grown, hasn't she?; **będziemy w kontakcie, co?** we'll be in touch, right? pot.; **miłe dzieciaki, co nie?** nice kids, eh? pot.; **wszyscy gdzieś jadą na wakacje, a my co?** everyone's going on holiday somewhere, and what about us?

VI **co do** praep. [1] (jeśli chodzi o) as for, as far as [sb/sth] is concerned; **co do mnie...** as for me...; **co do pańskiego artykułu...** as for your article..., as far as your article is concerned... [2] (w sprawie) regarding, concerning; **jego uwagi co do nowelizacji ustawy** his remarks regarding a. concerning amendment of the law [3] (pod względem) regarding,

concerning; **ustalenia co do zakresu prac** details regarding a. concerning the scope of the work; **druga co do wielkości partia polityczna** the second largest political party [4] (dokładnie) **co do godziny/dnia** to the hour/day; **o siódmej co do minuty** at seven o'clock sharp pot.; **oddał mi wszystko co do grosza** he gave me back every (single) penny; **zginęli wszyscy co do jednego** not one of them survived

VII **co..., (to)...** coni. [1] (ile razy) each time; **co strzelił, to chybił** every time he fired, he missed; **co premiera, to sukces** each new production is/was a success [2] (dla podkreślenia) **co praca, to praca** work is work (after all); **co chłop, to chłop** you can't beat a man (about the place); **co głowa, to głowa** you can't beat brains

VIII **czym..., tym...** coni. **czym starszy, tym głupszy** the older he gets, the more foolish he becomes

■ **a co tam** what do I care?, what does it matter?; **chciała pokazać, co to nie ona** she wanted to show what she was made of; **co jak co, ale ciasto robisz pyszne** say what you like, but you make delicious cake; **czego jak czego, ale pieniędzy im nie brakuje** whatever they're short of, it's not money; **co najmniej** at least; **co najwyżej** at most; **co to, to nie!** pot. that's out of the question!; no way! pot.; **co (takiego)?** (wyrażające zdziwienie) what?, really?; **dopiero a. tylko a. ledwo co** only just

codziennie adv. every day, daily

codzienność f daily life, everyday life; **szara ~ć** the everyday humdrum

codzienn|y adi. [praca, gazeta] daily; [zajęcia, obowiązki, życie] everyday; **artykuły ~ego użytku** everyday items

cof|nąć pf — **cof|ać** impf **[]** vt to reverse a. back up [samochód]; to rewind [taśmę]; to reverse [decyzję]; to take back [obietnicę]; to cancel [rozkaz]; to lift [zakaz]; to withdraw [oskarżenie, zgodę, koncesję]; to withdraw, to cut off [stypendium, zasiłek, kredyt]; **~nąć zegarek** to put one's watch back; **~nąć zegarki** to put back the clocks

[] **cofnąć się** — **cofać się** [1] to move back; [wojska] to fall back, to retreat; [choroba] to recede; [kryzys] to ease; **~nąć się o krok** to take a step backwards; **~nijcie się!** stand a. get back!; **samochód ~nął się** the car reversed a. backed up [2] (osłabnąć) [choroba] to recede; [kryzys] to ease [3] (powracać) to go back (**do czegoś** to sth); **~nąć się myślą a. pamięcią do czegoś** to think back to sth; **~ać się w rozwoju** to regress [4] (powstrzymać się) to shrink; to refrain książk. (**przed czymś** from sth); **nie ~ać się przed niczym** to stop at nothing

cokolwiek **[]** pron. [1] (obojętnie co) anything; **nie macie czegokolwiek do picia?** have you got anything to drink? [2] (byle co) anything, whatever;

any old thing pot.; **~ powiesz/zrobisz** whatever you say/do

II *adv.* (trochę) somewhat, slightly

cok|ół *m* base, pedestal

comb|er *m* Kulin. saddle; **~er z sarny** a saddle of venison

comiesięczn|y *adi.* monthly

co niemiara no end; plenty, lots pot.; **kłopotów mieli ~** they had no end of problems

coraz *adv.* more and more; **~ ładniejszy** prettier and prettier, ever prettier; **~ lepiej** better and better, ever better

coroczn|y *adi.* annual

c|oś **I** *pron.* (rzecz nieokreślona) something; (w pytaniach) anything; **mieć coś do zrobienia/czytania** to have something to do/read; **czy w tym pudełku coś jest?** is there anything inside this book?; **czegoś tu nie rozumiem** there's something I don't understand here; **coś innego** something else; **coś innego niż...** something other than...; **coś w rodzaju kanapy/rewolucji** something like a sofa/revolution, a kind of sofa/revolution; **(lub) coś w tym rodzaju** a. **coś podobnego** (or) something of the kind, (or) something like that; **coś jak** a. **jakby** a. **jak gdyby** something like; **ona ma w sobie coś** she's got a certain something; **to było coś!** that was (really) something!; **dojść do czegoś w życiu** to achieve something in life; **coś około 100 kilogramów** somewhere around a hundred kilos; **coś ponad 200 złotych** something over 200 zlotys; **dwadzieścia kilometrów z czymś** twenty something kilometres; **1000 złotych lub coś koło tego** a thousand zlotys or thereabouts GB a. thereabout US

II *part.* pot. **coś małe to mieszkanie** it's a bit on the small side, this flat; **coś mi dzisiaj praca nie idzie** I can't get down to work today somehow; **coś mi się widzi, że...** something tells me that...

III **czegoś** *part.* pot. (bez powodu) for some reason, somehow

IV **czemuś** *part.* pot. (z nieznanych powodów) for some reason

■ **coś niecoś** a little, a bit; **coś niecoś wiem na ten temat** I know a thing or two about that; **coś takiego** a. **podobnego!** that's amazing a. incredible! pot.; **coś ty!** pot. (zaskoczenie) you're kidding! pot; (oburzenie) don't be ridiculous!

cór|ka *f* daughter

c|óż **I** *pron.* pot. (dlaczego) why; **czemuż mnie nie zapytałeś?** why didn't you ask me?

II *inter.* (oh) well; **cóż, to się zdarza** oh well, it happens

cuchn|ąć *impf vi* to stink, to reek (**czymś** of sth); **to mięso ~ie** that meat smells bad; **~ący oddech** foul a. bad breath

cu|cić *impf* **I** *vt* to revive, to bring [sb] round GB, to bring [sb] around US

II **cucić się** książk. to come to, to revive

cu|d **I** *m* miracle; **nie wierzę w cuda** I don't believe in miracles; **liczyć na cud** to hope for a miracle; **cuda przyrody/techniki** the wonders a. marvels of nature/modern technology

II **cuda** *plt* pot. amazing things pot.; **dokonywać cudów męstwa** to perform amazing deeds of valour; **nie ma cudów** pot. there's no getting away from it pot.; **cuda niewidy** pot. (all sorts of) weird and wonderful things pot.

III **cudem** *adv.* miraculously, by a miracle; **jakim cudem** how come?, how can that be?; **nie wiem, jakim cudem, ale się udało** I don't know how, but we did it

cudaczn|y *adi. grad.* [wygląd, ubiór] bizarre, weird

cuda|k *m* pot. freak pot.

cudn|y *adi. grad.* [kobieta, kwiat] gorgeous, beautiful; [książka, krajobraz, zapach] marvellous GB, marvelous US, wonderful

cu|do *n* pot., żart. knockout, stunner pot.; **jego nowy samochód to prawdziwe cudo** his new car's a real beauty; **jak to cudo działa?** how does this box of tricks work? pot.

cudotwór|ca *m*, **~czyni** *f* miracle-worker, wonder-worker także przen.

cudown|y *adi. grad.* [kobieta, krajobraz] beautiful; [pomysł, artysta] wonderful, marvellous GB, marvelous US; [wydarzenie, ocalenie] miraculous; **~y lek** a miracle a. wonder drug

cudzoł|ożyć *pf, impf vi* książk. to commit adultery

cudzołóstw|o *n* książk. adultery

cudzoziem|iec *m*, **~ka** *f* foreigner, alien

cudzoziems|ki *adi.* foreign

cudz|y **I** *adi.* other people's, someone else's; **żyć z ~ej pracy** to live on a. off other people

II **cudze** *n* other people's property; **nie sięgaj po ~e** do not touch what doesn't belong to you

■ **~e chwalicie, swego nie znacie** przysł. the grass is always greener on the other side of the fence przysł.

cudzysł|ów *m* quotation marks, inverted commas GB; **ująć coś w ~ów** to put sth in quotation marks; **w ~owie** in quotes, in inverted commas także przen., iron.; **to dzieło, oczywiście w ~owie, sztuki** this work of art, quote unquote

cugl|e *plt* rein(s); **ściągnąć ~e** to draw the reins; **popuścić koniowi ~e** a. **~i** to give a horse its head

■ **popuścić komuś ~i** to give (a) free rein to sb; **popuścić ~i fantazji** to give free rein to one's imagination; **wziąć kogoś w ~e** a. **trzymać kogoś w ~ach** to keep a tight rein on sb, to keep sb on a tight rein

cuk|ier *m* sugar; **migdały w** ~**rze** sugared a. candied almonds; **owoce w** ~**rze** candied a. crystallized fruit

cukier|ek *m* sweet GB, (sugar) candy US

cukier|nia *f* cake shop, patisserie

cukiernicz|ka *f* sugar bowl

cukierni|k *m* confectioner

cukini|a *f* courgette GB, zucchini US

cukrowni|a *f* sugar factory

cukrzyc|a *f* Med. diabetes

cukrzy|k *m* pot. diabetic

cum|a *f* Żegl. hawser; (do mocowania do nabrzeża) mooring line; (do holowania) towing line

cum|ować *impf* **I** *vt* to moor *[łódź]* (**do czegoś** to sth); to berth, to moor *[statek]*; to dock *[statek kosmiczny]*
II *vi [łódź]* to be moored; *[statek]* to be at berth, to be moored; *[statek kosmiczny]* to dock

cwa|ł *m* gallop; **puścić się** ~**łem** a. **w** ~**ł** to break into a gallop

cwał|ować *impf vi* to gallop

cwania|k *m* pot. con man, sharp operator pot.

cwa|ny *adi. grad.* pot. sharp, wily

cybernety|ka *f* cybernetics

cyferbla|t *m* clock face, dial

cyf|ra *f* digit, figure; ~**ry arabskie/rzymskie** Arabic/Roman numerals

cyfrow|y *adi. [kod, szyfr]* numerical, number; *[zegar, technika]* digital

Cygan *m* gypsy; **czarny jak** ~ (as) dark as a gypsy

cygan *m* pot. [1] (o śniadej cerze) dark(-looking) man, swarthy man [2] (włóczęga) vagabond, tramp; **żyć jak** ~ to live like a gypsy [3] pejor. (krętacz) (lying) cheat pejor.; twister GB pot.

cyganeri|a *f* Bohemia

Cygan|ka *f* gypsy (woman)

cygan|ka *f* pot. [1] (o śniadej cerze) dark(-looking) woman, dark-complexioned woman [2] (włóczęga) vagabond, tramp [3] pejor. (krętaczka) (lying) cheat

cygańs|ki *adi.* [1] (dotyczący Cyganów) *[pieśń, kapela]* gypsy; *[uroda]* gypsy, gypsyish; *[życie]* vagabond; **mówić po** ~**ku** to speak Romany [2] (dotyczący cyganerii) bohemian

cygarnicz|ka *f* cigarette-holder

cyga|ro *n* cigar

cyjan|ek *m* cyanide

cyka|da *f* Zool. cicada

cykl *m* [1] (powtarzający się) cycle; ~ **produkcyjny** production cycle [2] (jednorazowy) series; ~ **koncertów/wykładów** a concert/lecture series, a series of concerts/lectures

cykliczn|y *adi. [proces, praca]* cyclic(al); *[program, audycja]* weekly/monthly

cyklin|ować *impf vt* to sand *[podłogę]*

cyklon *m* [1] Meteo. cyclone, hurricane [2] Chem. Zyklon B

cyk|nąć *pf* — **cyk|ać** *impf* **I** *vt* pot. [1] (dać) ~**ać komuś po kilka złotych** to let sb have a few zlotys at a time; ~**ać po jednym słowie** to hardly utter a. say a word [2] (sfotografować) ~**nąć kogoś/coś** to take a snap of sb/sth, to snap sb/sth
II *vi* [1] *[zegar, licznik]* to tick [2] *[świerszcz, cykada]* to chirp

cykori|a *f* [1] Bot. chicory, succory; ~**a sałatowa** witloof [2] (ekstrakt) chicory

cyku|ta *f* [1] Bot. cowbane, water hemlock [2] (trucizna) hemlock

cylind|er *m* [1] (kapelusz) top hat [2] Techn. cylinder

cylindryczn|y *adi.* cylindrical

cymba|ł *m* pot. dope pot.; oaf

cymbałk|i *plt* Muz. chimes

cymbał|y *plt* Muz. dulcimer

cyn|a *f* (metal) tin

cynad|ry, ~**erki** *plt* Kulin. kidneys

cynamon *m* Kulin. cinnamon

cynfoli|a *f* tinfoil

cyng|iel *m* trigger; **pociągnąć za** ~**iel** to pull the trigger

cyni|a *f* Bot. zinnia

cyniczn|y *adi.* [1] *[osoba, metody, uwaga]* cynical [2] Filoz. Cynic

cyni|k *m* [1] cynic [2] Filoz. Cynic

cynizm *m* [1] cynicism [2] Filoz. Cynicism

cynk[1] *m* Chem. zinc

cynk[2] *m* pot. (wiadomość) tip-off pot.; **dać komuś** ~ to tip sb off

cynk|ować *impf vt* to galvanize

cynow|y *adi. [związki, kwas]* tin; *[rura]* tinplated, tinned; *[łyżka]* tin

cyp|el *m* Geog. headland, promontory

cyprys *m* Bot. cypress (tree)

cyranecz|ka *f* Zool. (green-winged) teal

cyran|ka *f* Zool. garganey

cyrk *m* [1] (instytucja, widowisko) circus [2] pot. (heca) lark pot.; (zamieszanie) scene; **ale** ~! what a lark/farce!; **nie rób** ~**u** don't make a scene
❏ ~ **lodowcowy** Geol. cirque, corrie

cyrk|iel *m* compass(es)

cyrk|owiec *m*, ~**ówka** *f* circus performer

cyrkulacj|a *f* circulation

cyrograf *m* bond; **podpisać** ~ **własną krwią** to sign a pact in one's own blood

cyrylic|a *f* Cyrillic (alphabet)

cy|sta *f* Med. cyst

cystern|a *f* [1] (zbiornik) tank [2] (samochód) tanker (lorry) GB, tank truck US

cytadel|a *f* Wojsk. citadel

cyta|t *m* quotation; quote pot.; **koniec** ~**tu** end of quote

cytologi|a *f* [1] (nauka) cytology [2] pot. (badanie) (cervical) smear GB, Pap smear US

cyt|ować *impf vt* [1] (przytaczać) to quote *[przysłowie, aforyzmy]*; to cite *[książk.]*; **premier powiedział,**

~**uję**... the Prime Minister said, quote... 2 (wymieniać) to quote *[tytuły, nazwiska]*; to cite książk.; **wykaz** ~**owanych prac** a list of references a. works cited

cytrus *m* citrus (fruit)

cytryn|a *f* lemon

cytryn|ek *m* Zool. brimstone (butterfly)

cywil *m* civilian; civvy pot.; **wracać do** ~**a** pot. to return to civilian life; to return to Civvy Street pot., przest.; **w** ~**u był nauczycielem** he was a teacher in civilian life

cywilizacj|a *f* civilization

cywilizacyjn|y *adi. [postęp, zdobycze]* of civilization

cywiliz|ować *impf* **I** *vt* to civilize *[dzikie plemiona]* **II cywilizować się** to become civilized

cywilizowan|y *adi. [kraj, społeczeństwo]* civilized

cywiln|y *adi.* 1 (niewojskowy) civilian; **obrona** ~**a** civil defence; **(ubrany) po** ~**emu** *[żołnierz]* (dressed) in civilian clothes; *[policjant]* (dressed) in plain clothes 2 *[kodeks, odpowiedzialność, powództwo, sprawa]* civil; **stan** ~**y** marital status; **urząd stanu** ~**ego** register office GB, office of vital statistics US; registry office GB pot.; **odwaga** ~**a** moral courage

cyzel|ować *impf vt* 1 Techn. to polish 2 przen. to polish (up), to put the finishing touches to *[wiersz, utwór]*

cza|d *m* 1 (gaz) carbon monoxide 2 pot. (zapach) smell of burning 3 pot. (o muzyce rockowej) **więcej** ~**du!** pot. rock it!, let it rock! pot.; **dać** ~**du** to rock out pot.

cza|ić się *impf v refl.* 1 (czekać w ukryciu) *[osoba, zwierzę]* to lurk; to lie in wait (**na kogoś/coś** for sb/ sth); ~**ić się do skoku** to be poised for the leap 2 (zbliżać się) **w jej oczach** ~**ił się śmiech** there was a hint of laughter in her eyes

czaj|ka *f* Zool. (northern) lapwing, peewit GB, green plover GB

czajnicz|ek *m* teapot

czajnik *m* kettle

czap|ka *f* hat; (z daszkiem) cap; ~**ka z papieru** a paper hat; ~**ka z pomponem** a bobble hat

czap|la *f* Zool. heron; ~**la siwa** grey heron

cza|r *m* 1 (magia) sorcery, magic; (zaklęcie) spell, charm; **rzucić** ~**r** to cast a. put a spell (**na kogoś** on sb) 2 (wdzięk) charm; ~**r prysł** the spell broke a. was broken

czarn|o *adv. grad.* 1 (najciemniej) ~**o nakrapiana sierść** a black spotted coat; **na** ~**o** *[farbować]* black; *[ubierać się]* in black; **w kuchni było** ~**o od sadzy** the kitchen was black with soot 2 (pesymistycznie) darkly; ~**o widzieć swoją przyszłość** to see a black future before one

■ ~**o na białym** *[napisane]* in black and white; **widział** ~**o na białym, że...** he could see plainly that...

czarnoksiężni|k *m* wizard, sorcerer

czarnorynkow|y *adi.* black-market

czarnoskó|ry **I** *adi.* black

II czarnoskó|ry *m,* ~**ra** *f* black

czarnowidz *m* prophet of doom

czarnowidztw|o *n* doom and gloom

czarnoziem *m* black earth, chernozem

czarn|y **I** *adi. grad.* 1 (kolor) *[farba, kot]* black; *[oczy]* dark, black 2 (ciemny) *[chmury, drzewa]* dark, black 3 (nieoświetlony) *[noc, ulica, wnętrze]* black, dark 4 (ubrudzony) black, filthy; ~**y od sadzy** black with soot 5 (niegodziwy) *[niewdzięczność]* foul, black 6 (złowieszczy) *[myśli, rozpacz]* black, dark; *[wizja]* dark, bleak; (smutny) *[wieści, rok]* bad, sad

II czarn|y *m,* ~**a** *f* pot. black (person)

❏ **mała** ~**a** a. **pół** ~**ej** (kawa) small black coffee; **mała** ~**a** (sukienka) little black dress

czarodzie|j *m* wizard, magician

czarodziej|ka *f* enchantress, sorceress

czar|ować *impf* **I** *vt* 1 (wzbudzać zachwyt) to charm, to enchant 2 pot., iron. (zwodzić) to sweet-talk pot.; to beguile książk.

II *vi* (czynić czary) to cast spells, to work magic

III czarować się pot. (łudzić się) to fool oneself; to kid oneself pot.; **nie ma się co** ~**ować...** let's not kid ourselves...

czarownic|a *f* witch

czarowni|k *m* 1 (w bajkach) sorcerer 2 (szaman) witch doctor, medicine man

czarown|y *adi. [widok, uśmiech]* charming, enchanting; *[moc, chwila]* magic(al), enchanted

czarte|r *m* charter; **lecieć** ~**rem** to take a charter flight

czarterow|y *adi. [lot, umowa]* charter; *[samolot]* charter(ed)

czarując|y *adi.* charming

czar|y-mar|y **I** *plt* pot., iron. hocus-pocus; mumbo-jumbo pot.

II *inter.* (formułka) abracadabra!, hey presto!

czas **I** *m* 1 (trwanie) time; ~ **płynie** time passes a. goes by; ~ **mijał im na rozmowach o życiu** they whiled away the time talking about life; **z** ~**em** a. **z biegiem** a. **upływem** ~**u** with (the passing of) time 2 (moment, pora) the time; ~ **żniw** harvest time; ~ **odjazdu/przyjazdu** arrival/departure time; **co jakiś** ~ once in a while; **od** ~**u do** ~**u** from time to time, every now and then; **od tego** ~**u** since then a. that time; **do** ~**u naszego wyjazdu** (w przyszłości) before we leave; (w przeszłości) before we left; **o** ~**ie** on time a. schedule; **przyszliśmy po** ~**ie/przed** ~**em** we arrived late/ahead of time; **póki** ~ while there's still time 3 (odcinek czasu) time, duration; **po jakimś** ~**ie** after some time; **w tym** ~**ie** at that time; **od dłuższego** ~**u** for a long time; **przez cały** ~ all the time; **w** ~**ie** during; **w** ~**ie wakacji/podróży** during the holiday/journey; **na** ~ **leczenia** for the duration of the treatment [4] (ilość czasu) time; **mieć mało** ~**u** to be pressed for time; **mieć dużo** ~**u** to have lots of time; **zabrakło nam** ~**u** we ran out of time [5] Sport (wynik) time; **jaki masz** ~ **na 100 metrów?** what's your time for the 100 metres? [6] Sport (przerwa) timeout; **trener poprosił o** ~ the coach asked for a timeout [7] Astrol., Geog. time; ~ **letni** summer time GB, daylight-saving time US; ~ **zimowy** standard time; ~ **miejscowy** local time [8] Jęz. tense; **w** ~**ie przeszłym/przyszłym/teraźniejszym** in the past/future/present (tense)

[II] *praed.* (pora) **nie** ~ **na żarty** this is no time for jokes; ~ **spać** it's bedtime, it's time to go to bed; ~ **na mnie** it's time I went a. was off; **najwyższy** a. **wielki** ~ iron. (it's) about time (too) iron.

[III] czasy *plt* (okres) times, days; **ciężkie** ~**y** hard times; **to były** ~**y!** those were the days!; **od niepamiętnych** ~**ów** since time immemorial książk.; since time out of mind; **po wieczne** a. **wsze** a. **wszystkie** ~**y** książk. for ever (and a day); **w** ~**ach minionych** in days gone by; **w dzisiejszych** ~**ach** nowadays, in this day and age; **w ostatnich** ~**ach** a. **ostatnimi** ~**y** przest. lately; **z** ~**ów** czegoś dating back to sth; **za czyichś** ~**ów** in sb's time a. day; **za dawnych** ~**ów** in days of old; **pamiętać lepsze** ~**y** przen. to have seen better days

[IV] czasami *adv.* (niekiedy) sometimes

[V] czasem *adv.* [1] (niekiedy) sometimes [2] (przypadkiem) by any chance; **nie masz** ~**em zapalniczki?** do you have a lighter by any chance?, do you happen to have a lighter?

■ **grać na** ~ to play for time; **w swoim** ~**ie** (niegdyś) once, in one's time a. day; (w odpowiednim momencie) in due time a. course; **aktor/serial wszech** ~**ów** an all-time favourite actor/series; **na** ~**ie** (modny) fashionable; (aktualny) topical; ~ **leczy** a. **goi rany** przysł. time is a great healer przysł.; ~ **to pieniądz** przysł. time is money przysł.

czasochłonn|y *adi.* time-consuming

czasopi|smo *n* magazine, periodical; ~**smo fachowe** a professional journal

czasownik *m* verb

czasow|y *adi.* [granice] temporal [pobyt, zatrudnienie] temporary

czasz|ka *f* Anat. cranium, skull

czat|ować[1] *impf vi* [1] (czaić się) to lie in wait a. ambush (**na kogoś/coś** for sb/sth) [2] (wyczekiwać) to wait (**na coś** for sth)

czat|ować[2] *impf vi* pot., Komput. to talk a. chat on the Web

cząb|er *m* Bot., Kulin. savory

cząstecz|ka *f* [1] Chem. molecule [2] Fiz. particle [3] (mała cząsteczka) fraction, small part

cząst|ka *f* [1] (część) particle; (pomarańczy) segment; **dzielić coś na** ~**ki** to divide sth into pieces;

człowiek jest ~**ką przyrody** man is a part of nature [2] Fiz., Jęz. particle

cząstkow|y *adi.* partial

czciciel *m*, ~**ka** *f* worshipper

cz|cić *impf vt* [1] (oddawać cześć) to worship, to adore; (otaczać szacunkiem) to revere, to venerate [2] (świętować) to celebrate [rocznicę]

czcigodn|y *adi.* książk. [gość] honoured książk., esteemed książk.; [starzec] venerable książk.

czcion|ka *f* Druk. [1] (materiał zecerski) type, character [2] (krój pisma) type(face), font

czczo *adv.* **na** ~ on an empty stomach

czcz|y *adi.* [1] [żołądek] empty [2] [słowa] empty

czeczot|ka *f* Zool. redpoll

czek *m* cheque GB, check US; **wystawić** ~ to make out a. write a cheque; **płacić** ~**iem** to pay by cheque; **zrealizować** ~ to cash a cheque; ~ **bez pokrycia** bounced cheque GB, rubber check US pot.; ~ **in blanco** blank cheque

czeka|ć *impf* **[I]** *vi* [1] (być w stanie gotowości) to wait (**na kogoś/coś** for sb/sth); **jak długo pani** ~? how long have you been waiting?; **on tylko na to** ~ that's just what he's waiting for; ~**ć, aż ktoś coś powie** to wait for sb to say sth; **nie każ na siebie** ~**ć** don't keep me/us waiting; ~**ać na kogoś do późna** to wait for sb [2] (mieć w perspektywie) [przykrości, obowiązki] to wait (**kogoś** a. **na kogoś** for sb); ~ **go więzienie** he's facing a prison sentence; ~ **ją przykra niespodzianka** she's in for an unpleasant surprise pot. [3] (zwlekać) to wait (**z czymś** with sth); ~**ć na kogoś z kolacją** to wait with dinner until sb arrives

[II] czekaj, czekajcie *inter.* pot. hold on!, wait!; ~**j no, łobuzie!** pot. just you wait, you bum! pot.

■ ~**j tatka latka** iron. that'll be the day iron.

czekola|da *f* chocolate

czekolad|ka *f* chocolate; **pudełko** ~**ek** a box of chocolates

czekoladow|y *adi.* [lody, cukierki] chocolate; [kolor, sukienka] chocolate(-brown); [opalenizna] dark-brown; **o smaku** ~**ym** chocolate-flavoured

czelnoś|ć *f* książk. audacity; **mieć** ~**ć coś zrobić** to have the audacity to do sth

czep|ek *m* [1] (pielęgniarski, kąpielowy) cap [2] Hist. mob cap, bonnet; **nocny** ~**ek** a nightcap [3] (dziecięcy) bonnet [4] Med. caul

■ **w** ~**ku urodzony** born with a silver spoon in one's mouth

czep|ić się *pf* — **czep|iać się** *impf v refl.* [1] (chwycić się) to cling (**kogoś** (on) to sb); ~**iać się nadziei** to cling to hope [2] pot. (krytykować) ~**iać się kogoś** to get at sb pot.; ~**iać się każdego słowa** to pick at every word

czerem|cha *f* Bot. bird cherry

czereśni|a *f* (owoc) cherry; (drzewo) cherry (tree)

czerniak *m* Med. melanoma

czer|nić *impf* **[]** *vt* to darken, to blacken *[brwi, rzęsy, wąsy]*

[] **czernić się** to show black

czerni|eć *impf vi* [] (ciemnieć) to turn black, to blacken [] (wyróżniać się) to show black

czer|ń *f* [] (kolor) black; sable książk.; **kobieta w ~ni** a woman in black [] książk. (ciemność) pitch-blackness, pitch-darkness

czerp|ać *impf vt* [] (nabierać) to draw *[wodę]*; to ladle *[zupę]*; to scoop *[mąkę]* [] (pobierać) to draw *[prąd, wodę]*; to obtain *[gaz, energię]* [] przen. to obtain, to get *[wiadomości]*; to draw *[wiedzę]*; to derive *[korzyści]*

czerstw|y *adi.* [] (suchy) *[chleb, bułka]* stale [] (zdrowy) hale and hearty; *[starzec]* robust; *[twarz, policzki]* ruddy

czerw|iec *m* June

czerwie|nić się *impf v refl.* [] (pąsowieć) to turn a. go red; **~nić się ze wstydu** to go red with embarrassment [] (wyróżniać się) to show red

czerwieni|eć *impf vi* [] (stawać się czerwonym) to turn a. go red, to redden [] (mieć czerwony kolor) to show red

czerwie|ń *f* red; **kobieta w ~ni** a woman in red

czerwon|ka *f* Med. dysentery

czerw|ono *adv. grad.* **na ~ono** *[malować, farbować]* red; *[ubrać się]* in red

czerwonoskó|ry *m*, **~ra** *f* redskin przest., pejor.

czerw|ony **[]** *adi. grad.* red; **~ony na twarzy** red-faced; **~ony ze złości** red with anger

[] *adi.* pot., pejor. red, commie pot., pejor.

cze|sać *impf* **[]** *vt* [] (grzebieniem) to comb; (szczotką) to brush; **~sać włosy** to comb/brush one's hair [] (robić fryzurę) to do a. style [sb's] hair; **~sała córkę w koński ogon** she did her daughter's hair in a ponytail

[] **czesać się** [] (grzebieniem) to comb one's hair; (szczotką) to brush one's hair; **~sać się w warkocz** to wear one's hair in a plait; **~sać się z grzywką** to wear a bang [] (u fryzjera) to have one's hair done

czesn|e *n* tuition fee(s)

cz|eść **[]** *f* [] (szacunek) reverence, veneration książk.; (uwielbienie) adoration, worship; **z czcią** with reverence; **otaczać kogoś czcią** to venerate sb książk.; **cześć bohaterom!** may the names of these heroes live on!; **cześć ich pamięci!** may they rest in peace!; **na cześć** a. **ku czci kogoś** in honour of sb, in sb's honour; **pomnik ku czci powstańców** a monument in honour of the insurgents [] książk. (godność) honour GB, honor US; (cnota) virtue książk.

[] *inter.* (na powitanie) hello!; hi! pot.; (na pożegnanie) bye!, cheers! GB pot.

■ **i cześć** pot. and that's that

czę|sto *adv. grad.* often, frequently, oftentimes US; **~sto powtarzający się motyw** a (frequently) recurring motif

częstotliwoś|ć *f* frequency

częst|ować *impf* **[]** *vt* (proponować) **~ować kogoś kawą** to give a. offer sb some coffee

[] **częstować się** [] (przyjmować poczęstunek) to help oneself (**czymś** to sth); **~uj się ciastem** have some cake [] (jeden drugiego) **~owali się wzajemnie kanapkami** they offered one another their sandwiches; **~owali się wyzwiskami** przen. they exchanged a. traded insults with each other

czę|sty *adi. grad. [błąd, objaw]* frequent, common; *[klient, gość]* frequent, regular

częściowo *adv.* partly, partially; **~ odpowiedzialny** partly responsible; **~ sparaliżowany** partially paralyzed

częściow|y *adi.* partial; **to tylko ~a prawda** that's only (a) part of the truth

częś|ć *f* [] (wycinek całości) part, portion; (książki, sztuki) part; Muz. movement [] (element) part, piece; **~ci zamienne** spare parts; **~ć garderoby** a piece a. item of clothing; **~ć składowa** a constituent (part), a component; **rozłożyć rower na ~ci** to take a bike apart, to strip down a bike; **w przeważającej ~ci** for the most part; **sprostał wymaganiom tylko w znikomej ~ci** he only carried out a fraction of what was required of him; **po** a. **w ~ci** in part, partly; **po ~ci tego się spodziewał** he half-expected it

❏ **intymne ~ci ciała** private parts; **~ć mowy** Jęz. part of speech; **~ć zdania** Jęz. part of a sentence

■ **pewna ~ć ciała** euf. sit-upon pot., żart.; behind pot.

czkać *impf* → **czknąć**

czkaw|ka *f* hiccup

■ **odbijać się (komuś) ~ką** to leave its mark (on sb)

czk|nąć *pf* — **czk|ać** *impf vi* to hiccup

człap|ać *impf vi* pot. to trudge, to plod

człekokształtn|y *adi.* anthropoid

człon *m* element, segment; Zool. segment; (rakiety) module

człon|ek **[]** *m* [] (osoba) member [] (penis) member, penis

[] **członki** *plt* limbs

członkostw|o *n* membership

człowieczeństw|o *n* książk. humanity

człowiek **[]** *m* [] (istota ludzka) person, human (being); **dwoje ludzi** two people; **prawa człowieka** human rights; **w końcu jesteśmy tylko ludźmi** after all we're only human [] (mężczyzna) man; **starszy człowiek** an elderly man; **dwóch ludzi** two men; **człowieku, patrz, gdzie idziesz** pot. look where you're going, man! pot. [] (wartościowa jednostka) man, decent person; **wyjść na ludzi** to turn out all right (in the end) [] pot. (osoba zaufana) man; **ludzie prezydenta** the president's people a. men; **zostaw ją, to nasz człowiek** leave her alone, she's one of us [] pot. (pracownik) man, worker; **wziąć paru ludzi do naprawy dachu** to hire some men to repair the roof 6 pot. (jako zaimek osobowy) you; one książk.; **człowiek całe życie się uczy** one lives and learns

II ludzie *plt* people; **ludzie mówią, że...** they a. people say (that)...; **co ludzie powiedzą?** what will people say?; **przy ludziach** in public, in front of other people

■ **być podobnym do ludzi** pot. to look halfway human pot.; **zachowuj się jak człowiek** pot. behave yourself (properly)

czmych|nąć *pf* — **czmych|ać** *impf vi* to dart, to make off

czołg *m* tank

czołga|ć się *impf v refl.* 1 to crawl; ~ć się **po podłodze** to crawl along the floor 2 przen. to grovel pejor.; to crawl pot. (**przed kimś** to sb); ~ć się **u czyichś stóp** to grovel at sb's feet

cz|oło II *n* 1 (część twarzy) forehead, brow; **kapelusz zsunięty na czoło** a hat pulled down over one's eyes; **czesać się z czoła** to wear one's hair swept back 2 (przód) head; **czoło pochodu/lodowca** the head of a parade/glacier; **stać na czele czegoś** przen. to head a. lead sth, to come to the fore

II **czołem** *inter.* (na powitanie) hello; (na pożegnanie) see you pot.

■ **chylić czoło** a. **czoła przed kimś** to take one's hat off to sb; **stawić czoła** a. **czoło komuś/czemuś** to face (up to) sb/sth; **puknij** a. **stuknij się w czoło** pot. you must be off your rocker a. out of your mind! pot.

czołow|y *adi.* 1 (główny) *[przedstawiciel, ośrodek]* foremost, leading; *[miejsce, pozycja]* leading; ~y **zawodnik drużyny** the top player in the team 2 (przedni) *[elewacja]* front; **zderzenie** ~**e** a head-on collision 3 Anat. *[kość, płaty, zatoki]* frontal

czołów|ka *f* 1 (grupa wiodąca) ~**ka francuskich aktorów** leading a. the top French actors; **należeć do światowej** ~**ki w dziedzinie...** to be among the world leaders in the field of ... 2 Kino opening credits, title sequence 3 (w gazecie) lead story; **trafić na** ~**ki gazet** to hit the headlines 4 Sport lead; **nasi zawodnicy biegną w** ~**ce** our runners are in the lead

czop|ek *m* Farm. suppository

czor|t *m* pot. 1 (zły duch) (the) devil, evil spirit; **idź do** ~**ta!** go to the devil! a. to blazes! pot.; ~**t wie gdzie/dlaczego** the devil knows where/why; **ki** a. **jaki** ~**t!?** what the devil!? pot.; ~**t z nim!** to hell with him!; **jeden** ~**t!** it's all the same a. przen. (young) devil pot.; (dziecko) (little) devil pot.

czosn|ek *m* garlic

czółen|ko *n* 1 (small) canoe 2 (pantofel) court shoe GB, pump US 3 Włók. shuttle

czół|no *n* dugout (canoe)

czterdziest|ka *f* forty

czterdzie|sty *num. ord.* fortieth

czterdzie|ści *num.* forty

czterechsetn|y *num. ord.* four-hundredth

czternast|ka *f* fourteen

czternast|y *num. ord.* fourteenth

czterna|ście *num.* fourteen

czterokrotnie *adv.* *[wzrosnąć, zmaleć]* fourfold; *[powtórzyć]* four times

czterokrotn|y *adi.* *[wzrost, spadek]* fourfold, quadruple; *[zwycięzca]* four-times GB, four-time US

czterowiersz *m* quatrain

czter|y II *num.* four

II *n* (ocena) ≈ B

■ ~**y litery** pot., euf. (pośladki) bum GB, behind pot.; (osoba) wimp pot., pejor.; prat GB posp., pejor.

czteryst|a *num.* four hundred

czub *m* 1 (o włosach) topknot; (o piórach) crest 2 (o osobie) nutter, nutcase pot.

■ **mieć w** ~**ie** pot. to be well oiled pot.

czuba|ty *adi.* *[ptak]* crested, tufted; *[łyżka]* heaped; *[talerz]* heaped-up

czub|ek *m* 1 (wierzchołek) tip, top; ~**ek nosa** the tip of one's nose; ~**ek głowy** the top of one's head; ~**ek buta** the tip a. toe of a shoe; ~**ek drzewa** the top of a tree; ~**ek noża** the point of a knife; **chodzić na** ~**kach palców** to walk on tiptoe 2 pot. (o osobie) nutcase, head case pot.

■ **po** ~**ek głowy** from head to toe, from top to toe

czuci|e *n* (the sense of) feeling, sensation

czu|ć *impf* II *vt* 1 (doznawać wrażeń zmysłowych) to feel; (węchem) to smell; ~**ć głód/pragnienie** to feel hungry/thirsty; ~**ć zapach czegoś** to smell sth; ~**jesz, jak pachnie jaśmin?** can you smell jasmine?; ~**ła od niego alkohol** she could smell alcohol on his breath; **nie** ~**ć rąk/nóg** przen. to be dead tired 2 (doznawać uczuć) to feel; ~**ć miłość/nienawiść do kogoś** to feel love/hatred towards a. for sb; ~**ć do kogoś żal** to bear a grudge against sb; ~**ł, że się czerwieni** he felt himself blushing 3 (uświadamiać sobie) to feel; ~**łem, że coś jest nie tak** I had a feeling that something was wrong 4 (przeczuwać) to feel, to sense; ~**łem tylko jego obecność** I just sensed his presence 5 pot. (rozumieć) to have a feel(ing) (**coś** for sth); **ten reżyser** ~**je aktorów** this director has a feel for actors

II *praed.* 1 (śmierdzieć) to smell (**czymś** of sth); ~**ć go było czosnkiem** he smelt of garlic 2 przen. (przejawiać cechy) to smell (**czymś** of sth); ~**ć od niego szpiclem na kilometr** you can tell he's a spy

III **czuć się** 1 (być w jakimś stanie) to feel; **jak się pan** ~**je?** how are you feeling?; ~**ję się dobrze** I'm (feeling) fine; ~**ł się nieswojo** he felt ill at ease 2 (mieć świadomość) to feel, to consider oneself; ~**ła się Polką** she considered herself (to be) a Pole

czujnik *m* sensor, detector

czujnoś|ć *f* vigilance książk.; **obudzić czyjąś ~ć** to put sb on their guard; **uśpić czyjąś ~ć** to lull sb into a false sense of security

czujn|y *adi. grad.* [1] (uważny) vigilant książk.; alert; **pod czyimś ~ym okiem** under sb's vigilant a. watchful eye [2] (wrażliwy) sensitive; **~e ucho** a sharp ear; **mieć ~y sen** to be a light sleeper

czule *adv. grad.* [uśmiechać się, żegnać się] affectionately, tenderly; **~ kogoś wspominać** to remember sb with affection

czul|ić się *impf v refl.* to cuddle, to caress; **~ić się do kogoś** to cuddle up to sb

czułostkowoś|ć *f* mawkishness, sentimentality

czułoś|ć [] *f* [1] (uczuciowość) tenderness, affection; **z ~cią** with affection, affectionately [2] (precyzyjność) (termometru) sensitivity [3] Fot. (film) speed **[] czułości** *plt* (pieszczoty) caresses; (słowa) endearments

czu|ły *adi. grad.* [1] (serdeczny) [gest, spojrzenie] tender, affectionate; **~ła opieka** tender loving care; **~łe słówka** endearments, sweet nothings; **~ły mąż** a loving husband [2] (wrażliwy) sensitive (**na coś** to sth); **~łe miejsce** a. **~ły punkt** przen. a weak point, a weakness [3] (precyzyjny) [termometr, waga] sensitive; **~ły film** a high-speed film

czupryn|a *f* mop (of hair), shock of hair

czupurn|y *adi. grad.* [osoba, mina] truculent, pugnacious książk.

czusz|ka *f* [1] Bot. hot red pepper [2] Kulin. ≈ cayenne (pepper)

czuwa|ć *impf vi* [1] (być czujnym) to be on the alert a. lookout [2] (pilnować) to watch; [wartownik] to stand guard, to keep watch; **~ć nad kimś/czymś** to watch (over) sb/sth [3] (nie spać) to stay awake a. up

czuwa|nie *n* [1] (całonocne) (all-night) vigil [2] (stan urządzenia) stand-by (mode); **przechodzić w stan ~nia** to go into stand-by mode

czwart|ek *m* Thursday; **Wielki Czwartek** Maundy a. Holy Thursday; **tłusty ~ek** the last Thursday of carnival

czwar|ty *num. ord.* fourth

czworaczk|i *plt* quadruplets

czwor|o *num. mult.* four

czworobok *m* quadrilateral

czworoką|t *m* quadrangle

czworon|óg *m* quadruped

czwórb|ój *m* Sport four-event competition

czwór|ka *f* [1] (liczba) four [2] (grupa) four; **~ka koni** a four-horse team; **maszerować ~kami** to march in fours [3] pot., Aut. fourth; **wrzuć ~kę** change into fourth [4] Sport (łódka, załoga) four [5] (ocena) ≈ B; **dostał ~kę z matematyki** he got a B for maths [6] Druk. quarto

czy [] *part.* [1] (w pytaniu) **~ pada deszcz?** is it raining?; **~ możesz wyłączyć radio?** can a. could you turn the radio off?; **~ście** a. **~ wyście**

powariowali? pot. are you all out of your minds? pot. [2] (w zdaniu złożonym) if, whether; **ciekawe, ~ przyjdą** I wonder if they'll come; **nie wiem, ~ pisać do niego, ~ nie** I don't know if a. whether I should write to him or not

[] coni. or; **tak ~ nie** yes or no; **prędzej ~ później** sooner or later; **~..., ~...** (zarówno) whether... or...; **~ to autobusem, ~ to pociągiem** whether (it's) by bus or by train; **w taki ~ inny sposób** one way or the other a. another; **z tego ~ innego powodu** for one reason or another; **~ co a. jak** pot. or what?, or something?; **zgłupiałeś ~ co** a. **jak?** are you stupid or what? a. something?; **~ co tam jeszcze** pot. or whatever pot.; **~ coś takiego** pot. or something (like that) pot.; **... ~ jak mu/jej tam** pot. ...or whatever his/her name is pot.; **tak ~ inaczej** a. **tak ~ owak** a. **tak ~ tak** a. **tak ~ siak** one way or the other a. another

czyha|ć *impf vi* [1] (czaić się) to lurk; to lie in wait (**na kogoś** for sb); **~ć na czyjeś życie** to be out to kill sb pot. [2] książk. (zagrażać) to await książk. (**na kogoś** sb); **śmierć ~ła na nich na każdym kroku** death lay in wait for them at every turn

czy|j *pron.* whose; **~ja to książka?** whose book is this?

czy|jkolwiek *pron.* anyone's, (just) anybody's

czy|jś *pron.* (osoby nieznanej) somebody's, someone's; (cudzy) somebody else's, someone else's

czyli *coni.* [1] or, that is [2] (wprowadzające wniosek) which means (that), in other words; **nie poszedł do dentysty, ~ stchórzył** he didn't go to the dentist, in other words a. which means he chickened out pot.

czyn *m* książk. [1] (uczynek) act, deed; **~y bohaterskie** heroic deeds a. exploits; **słowem i ~em** in word and deed; **przejść od słów do ~ów** to put a. translate words into action(s); **wprowadzać** a. **wcielać coś w ~** to put sth into action a. practice; **~ zbrojny** armed action; **~ społeczny** community action [2] (występek) act, offence GB, offense US; **~ karalny** a punishable offence

czy|nić *impf* książk. **[] *vt*** (robić) to make; **~nić postępy** to make progress; **~nić przygotowania do czegoś** to make a. carry out preparations for sth; **~nić honory domu** to do the honours; **~nić cuda** [osoba] to work a. perform miracles także przen.; [lek, kuracja, osoba] to do a. work wonders; **wiara ~ni cuda** faith works miracles

[] *vi* (postępować) to do, to act; **~nił tak zawsze** he always did that

■ mieć z kimś/czymś do ~nienia to deal with sb/sth; **nigdy nie miał do ~nienia z bronią** he'd never handled a gun before; **nie ~ń drugiemu, co tobie niemiło** przysł. do as you would be done by przysł.

czynnie *adv.* [uczestniczyć, przeciwstawiać się] actively; **opanować język ~** to learn to speak a language; **znać język** ~ to be able to speak a language

czynnik *m* ☐ (element) factor; **rozłożyć coś na ~i pierwsze** (przeanalizować) to break sth down into its constituent parts; pot., żart. (rozebrać) to strip sth down (to its component parts) ☐ książk. (instytucja) authority; **~i państwowe** the state authorities; **~i rządowe** governmental bodies ☐ Mat. factor; **~i pierwsze** prime numbers; **rozłożyć liczbę na ~i pierwsze** to factorize a number

czynność *f* ☐ / ☐ (działanie, praca) activity, action; **jest to ~ć pracochłonna** it's painstaking work ☐ (obowiązek) duty; **zawiesić kogoś w ~ciach** to suspend sb from their duties **☐ czynności** *plt* (oficjalne działania) action, measures

czynny ☐ *adi.* grad. (aktywny) [osoba, postawa, pierwiastek] active

☐ *adi.* ☐ (funkcjonujący) [sklep] open; [urządzenie] working; [wulkan] active; [lekarz, prawnik] practising GB, practicing US ☐ Jęz. [imiesłów] active; **strona ~a** the active (voice)

czynsz *m* rent; **płacić 400 zł ~u** to pay 400 zlotys (in) rent

czyrak *m* Med. boil

czysto ☐ *adv.* grad. ☐ (starannie) neatly; **~sto utrzymany ogród** a neatly a. nicely kept garden; **przepisać coś na ~sto** to make a clean a. fair copy of sth ☐ (bez zniekształceń) [brzmieć, dźwięczeć] pure; **śpiewać ~sto** to sing in tune ☐ (bez domieszek) purely; **niebo ~sto niebieskie** a clear blue sky; **to ~sto osobista sprawa** it's a purely personal matter ☐ (uczciwie) [grać] fair; [postępować, rywalizować] fairly

☐ **do czysta** pot. **pokój wymieciony do ~sta** a room swept clean

■ **wyjść na ~sto** to break even; **zarabiać na ~sto 2000 dolarów** pot. to earn $2,000 clear a. a clear $2,000

czystopis *m* fair copy

czystość *f* ☐ (brak brudu) cleanness, cleanliness; **środki ~ci** household detergents a. cleansing agents; **koszula nie pierwszej ~ci** a none too clean shirt; **nauczyć kota ~ci** to house-train a cat ☐ (brak zniekształceń) purity, pureness; **~ć stylu/głosu** purity of style/voice ☐ (brak domieszek) purity; **~ć języka** purity of language ☐ (uczciwość) fairness, integrity; **~ć czyichś intencji** the purity of sb's intentions

czysty ☐ *adi.* grad. [paznokcie, woda] clean; [głos, dźwięk] pure, clear; [niebo, kolor] clear; [zamiary, myśli] pure; [walka] fair, clean; [gra] fair; **przez ~sty przypadek** by pure chance a. sheer accident; **z ~stej ciekawości** out of sheer curiosity; **koń ~stej krwi arabskiej** a pure-bred Arab horse

☐ *adi.* [wełna, jedwab] pure; [dyskietka, formularz] blank; **~sta forma** Szt. pure form; **~sty dochód/zysk** net income/profit; **mieć ~stą hipotekę** [nieruchomość] to be unencumbered; przen., pot. [osoba] to have a clean record; **mieć ~ste konto** przen., pot. to have a clean sheet

☐ **czysta** *f* pot. (wódka) (pure) vodka

■ **~stej wody** [idealizm, idealista] of the first order; **brylant ~stej wody** a diamond of the first water

czyścić *impf* ☐ *vt* ☐ (usuwać brud) to clean; **~ścić buty** to polish one's shoes; **~ścić coś chemicznie** a. **na sucho** to dry-clean sth ☐ Kulin. to dress [kurczaka, rybę]

☐ *v imp.* Med. **~ści go** he's got diarrhoea; **leki ~szczące** laxatives, purgative medicines

☐ **czyścić się** to clean (oneself) up; **~ścić się z błota** to clean the mud off oneself

czyściec *m* purgatory

czyścioch *m* pot. stickler for cleanliness

czytać *impf* ☐ *vt* ☐ to read; **~ć coś po angielsku/w oryginale** to read sth in English/in the original; **to się ~ jak dobrą powieść** it reads like a good novel; **to nie daje się ~ć** it's unreadable; **to słowo inaczej się ~ po angielsku** you pronounce a. say this word differently in English ☐ (interpretować symbole) to read [schemat, ślady]; **~ć nuty** to read music; **~ć przyszłość** to read the future ☐ Komput. to read [dyskietkę, program]

☐ *vi* to (be able to) read; **on już ~** he can already read

czytadło *n* pejor. easy read pot.; trashy novel pejor.

czytanie *n* reading; **pierwsze/drugie ~nie ustawy** Polit. the first/second reading of a bill

czytelnia *f* reading room

czytelnik *m*, **~czka** *f* reader; **biblioteka ma wielu ~ków** the library has a large membership

czytelny *adi.* grad. [pismo, napis] legible, readable; [aluzja, reguły] clear, distinct

czytnik *f* Techn. reader; **~ kodu paskowego** a light pen

czytywać *impf vt* to read; **nie ~uję gazet** I don't read newspapers

czyż[1] *part.* książk. **~ to nie piękny widok?** isn't this a magnificent view?; **~ można było przyglądać się temu obojętnie?** how could one possibly look on with indifference?; **~byście już o tym zapomnieli?** (surely) you can't have forgotten about it?!

czyż[2], **~yk** *m* Zool. siskin

czyżby książk. ☐ *part.* **~ się myliła?** can she have made a mistake?

☐ *inter.* iron. oh, really?, is that so? iron.

Ć

ćma *f* Zool. moth

ćmi|ć *impf* **I** *vt* (palić) to smoke *[papierosa, fajkę]*
II *vi* 1 (tlić się) *[papieros, ognisko]* to glow; *[lampa, gwiazdy]* to glimmer 2 (boleć) *[ząb]* to nag; ~ **mnie w głowie** I've got this dull headache
III **ćmić się** (żarzyć się) *[papieros, ognisko]* to smoulder GB, to smolder US, to glow; *[lampa]* to glimmer
■ ~ **mi się w oczach** a. **głowie** I feel a. I'm feeling dizzy

ćpa|ć *impf* pot. **I** *vt* (jeść) to wolf (down), to gobble (up)
II *vi* (używać narkotyków) to do drugs pot.; to be on drugs

ćpun *m* pot. junkie, druggy pot.

ćwiart|ka *f* 1 (czwarta część) quarter 2 pot. (wódki) quarter-litre bottle of vodka 3 Muz. crotchet GB, quarter note US 4 Druk. quarto

ćwiart|ować *impf vt* to cut up (into quarters) *[mięso]*

ćwicze|nie **I** *n* 1 (gimnastyczne) exercise 2 Szkol., Uniw. (zadanie) exercise; ~**nie z angielskiego** an English exercise
II **ćwiczenia** *plt* 1 Uniw. (rodzaj zajęć) classes; (godzina zajęć) class; **mam teraz** ~**nia z logiki** I have a logic class now 2 Wojsk. exercises, manoeuvres GB, maneuvers US

ćwicz|yć *impf* **I** *vt* 1 (kształcić) to train *[dzieci]*; to train, to drill *[żołnierzy]*; to train, to exercise *[umysł]* 2 (trenować) to practise GB, to practice US; ~**yć gamy** to practise one's scales
II *vi* (gimnastykować się) to (take) exercise, to work out
III **ćwiczyć się** to practise GB, to practice US (**w czymś** sth); ~**yć się we francuskim** to practise one's French

ćwier|ć *f* quarter

ćwierćfina|ł *m* (the) quarter-final(s)

ćwierka|ć *impf vi [dzieci, młode kobiety]* to twitter (away), to chirp

ćwierk|nąć *pf* — **ćwierk|ać** *impf vi [ptaki]* to chirrup, to chirp; *[świerszcze]* to chirp

ćwik|ła *f* Kulin. cold beetroot and horseradish relish

D

D, d *n inv.* [1] (litera) D, d [2] Muz. D

dach *m* roof; **mieć ∼ nad głową** to have a roof over one's head; **pod jednym ∼em** under one roof **dachów|ka** *f* (pojedyncza) roof tile; (pokrycie) roof tiling

da|ć *pf* — **da|wać** *impf* **I** *vt* [1] (ofiarować) to give; **dać komuś coś** to give sth to sb, to give sb sth; **dać komuś jeść/pić** to give sb something to eat/drink; **dać z siebie wszystko** to give one's all; **dane mi było współpracować z...** książk. I had the opportunity of working with... [2] (podać) to give, to pass; **daj mi rękę** give me your hand; **daj mi sól** pass (me) the salt; **dajcie mi tu Malinowskiego** pot. get Malinowski in here pot.; **daj mi ojca do telefonu** pot. put your father on pot. [3] (udzielić) to give [odpowiedź, rozwód, korepetycje]; to give, to grant [kredyt, zezwolenie] [4] (oddać) **dać buty do naprawy** to take one's shoes in to be mended; **dać ogłoszenie do gazety** to put an advert in the paper [5] (przynieść) to give, to bring [rezultat, wynik]; to yield [dochód, zysk]; (wytworzyć) to produce [effect, mleko]; **dwa plus dwa daje cztery** two plus two makes a. equals four; **to nic nie da** that's no use a. good [6] (wystąpić) to give [koncert, wykład, przedstawienie] [7] pot. (zapłacić) to give; **ile dałaś za ten płaszcz?** how much did you give for that coat?; **kto da więcej?** any advance on that?

II *vi* [1] (pozwolić) **dać komuś coś zrobić** to let sb do sth, to allow sb to do sth [2] (uderzyć) **dać komuś w twarz** to give sb one in the face pot.; **dać komuś po łapach** to rap sb's knuckles

III dać się — **dawać się** pot. (być możliwym) to be possible; **ile się da** as much/many as possible; **robić co się da** to do what one can; **tego nie da się przewidzieć** that's impossible to predict; **tego nie da się wyjaśnić** it can't be explained; **drzwi nie dają się otworzyć** the door won't open

IV daj *inter.* daj, pomogę ci here, let me help you **■ dałbym jej 40 lat** I'd say she was 40; **dać nogę** a. drapaka a. dyla pot. to do a runner pot.; **dajmy na to** (na przykład) (let's) say; (przypuśćmy) suppose, supposing; **ja ci dam!** pot. I'll teach a. show you!; **nie dajcie się** don't give in a. up

daktyl *m* Bot. date

dal *f* distance; **w ∼i** [znajdować się] in the distance; [zniknąć] in(to) the distance; **z ∼a** from afar; **z ∼a** od czegoś far away from sth; **trzymać się z ∼a od czegoś** przen. to keep well away from sth

dal|eki I *adi. grad.* [kraje, strony] distant, faraway; [odgłos, krewny, przeszłość] distant; [podróż] long **II** *adi.* (niepodobny) far (**od czegoś** from sth); **∼eki od doskonałości** far from perfect

III dalszy *adi. comp.* (następny) [badania, rozmowy] further; **w ∼szych rozdziałach** in subsequent chapters; **∼szy ciąg nastąpi** to be continued

dale|ko I *adv. grad.* [1] (w przestrzeni) far, a long way; **∼ko od centrum** a long way from the town centre; **mieć ∼ko do szkoły** to have a long way to go to school; **jak ∼ko jest (stąd) do dworca?** how far is it (from here) to the railway station? [2] przen. far; **∼ko zajść** to go far; **∼ko mu do ciebie/do doskonałości** he's nowhere near you/perfect; **∼ko idące skutki** far-reaching results [3] (w czasie) far; **do świąt jeszcze ∼ko** Christmas is still a long way off

II *adv.* (znacznie) far; **∼ko lepiej** far better

III dalej *adv. comp.* [1] (nadal) **mów ∼j** go on; **brawo, oby tak ∼j** well done, keep it up [2] (potem) then, afterwards [3] (poza tym) further, furthermore

IV najdalej *adv. sup.* (najpóźniej) at the (very) latest

V z daleka *adv.* from afar, from a distance; **z ∼ka od czegoś** far away from sth; **trzymać się z ∼ka od czegoś** przen. to keep well away from sth

■ i tak ∼j and so on a. so forth, and so on and so forth; **nie ∼j niż wczoraj** only yesterday

dalekobieżn|y *adi.* [pociąg, autobus] long-distance **dalekomors|ki** *adi.* [rybołówstwo, połowy] deep-sea; [statek] ocean-going

dalekowidz *m* long-sighted GB a. far-sighted US person

dalekowroczn|y *adi.* [osoba] long-sighted GB, far-sighted US; przen. [polityk, plan] far-sighted

dali|a *f* dahlia

dalmatyńczy|k *m* Dalmatian

daltoni|sta *m,* **∼stka** *f* colour-blind GB a. color-blind US person

daltonizm *m* colour GB a. color US blindness

dam|a *f* [1] (kobieta) lady; **∼a dworu** lady-in-waiting [2] (w kartach, szachach) queen; (w warcabach) king

dam|ka *f* [1] (w warcabach) king [2] pot. (rower) lady's a. woman's bike pot.

dams|ki *adi.* [fryzjer, garderoba, obuwie] women's, lady's; **krawiec ∼ki** dressmaker; **∼kie towarzy-**

stwo female company; ~**ka toaleta** the Ladies GB, the ladies' room US

dancing /'dansiŋ/ m dance, dancing; **pójść na** ~ to go to a dance, to go dancing

dan|e plt data; **baza** ~**ych** database; **przetwarzanie** ~**ych** data processing; ~**e personalne** personal details; **mieć wszelkie** ~**e ku temu, żeby wygrać** to have every reason to believe that one will win

da|nie n (potrawa) dish; (część obiadu) course; **obiad z trzech dań** a three-course dinner; **drugie danie** the main course GB, entrée US; **na pierwsze danie** for the first course

daniel m fallow deer

dan|y adi. given; **w** ~**ej chwili** at a given moment; **w** ~**ym wypadku** in the case in question

da|r m [1] (prezent) gift; **w darze** as a gift [2] (talent) gift (**do czegoś** for sth); **dar słowa** a silver tongue

daremnie adv. in vain

daremn|y adi. vain, futile

darmo adv. [1] (bezpłatnie) **za** ~ for free; **bilety są za** ~ the tickets are free; **kupić coś (za) pół** ~ to buy sth for a song [2] (daremnie) in vain; **(na)** ~ **tracicie czas** you're just wasting your time; ~ **o tym mówić** there's no point (in) talking about it; **nie (na)** ~ not for nothing

darmow|y adi. [posiłek] free

darmozja|d m pot. scrounger pot.

dar|owywać pf — **dar|owywać** impf vt [1] (dać) to give (**komuś coś** sth to sb, sb sth); ~**owywać komuś wolność** przen. to set sb free [2] (nie egzekwować) to waive, to remit; ~**owywać komuś karę** to let sb off; ~**owywać komuś życie** to spare sb (their life) [3] (przebaczyć) to forgive (**komuś coś** sb for sth); **nigdy bym sobie nie** ~**owywał, gdybym...** I'd never forgive myself if I...; ~**uj, ale...** forgive me but...

darowi|zna f donation (**na rzecz kogoś** to sb)

darz|yć impf vt ~**yć kogoś sympatią** to like sb; ~**yć kogoś szacunkiem** to hold sb in high esteem; ~**yć kogoś uczuciem** to feel affection for sb

dasz|ek m [1] roof; **ganek z** ~**kiem** a covered porch [2] (czapki) peak GB, visor US; **czapka z** ~**kiem** peaked cap

da|ta f date; **data urodzenia** date of birth; **data ważności** expiry date; **być człowiekiem starej daty** to be old-fashioned

■ **być pod dobrą datą** pot. to be well oiled pot.

dat|ek m donation (**na coś** to a. for sth)

dat|owywać pf, impf [] vt to date [dokument, pismo]
[] **datować się** to date back; ~**owywać się od od XIX w.** to date back to the 19th century

datownik m date stamp

dawać impf → **dać**

daw|ca m, ~**czyni** f donor; ~**ca krwi/serca** blood/heart donor

daw|ka f dose także przen.; **śmiertelna** ~**ka** lethal dose; ~**ka uderzeniowa** megadose; **w małych** ~**kach** in small doses

dawk|ować impf vt to administer [lekarstwo]

dawn|o [] adv. grad. a long time ago, long ago; ~**o,** ~**o temu** once upon a time
[] adv. (długo) for a long time; **jak** ~**o tu mieszkasz?** how long have you been living here?
[] **dawniej** adv. comp. (kiedyś) before, formerly; **wszystko jest jak** ~**iej** everything's like it used to be
[] **od dawna** adv. for a long time; **od** a. **z dawien** ~**a** from time immemorial

dawn|y [] adi. grad. [1] (stary) [zabytki] ancient; [przyjaciel] old; ~**e, dobre czasy** the good old days; **od najdawniejszych czasów** since a. from time immemorial [2] (poprzedni) [nazwa, adres] former, previous
[] adi. (były) former

d|ąb m [1] (drzewo) oak (tree) [2] (drewno) oak

■ **stawać dęba** [koń] to rear up; [osoba] to bristle; **włosy stanęły mu dęba** his hair stood on end

d|ąć impf vi [wiatr] to blow; **dąć w trąbkę** to blow a trumpet

dąsa|ć się impf v refl. to sulk (**o** a. **za coś** over a. about sth); ~**ć się na kogoś** to be cross with sb

dąs|y plt the sulks pot.

dąże|nie n aspiration, aim

dąż|yć impf vi to aspire (**do czegoś** to sth); to strive (**do czegoś** after a. for sth); ~**yć do celu** to pursue one's goal

dba|ć impf vi [1] (troszczyć się) ~**ć o kogoś/coś** to look after sb/sth, to take care of sb/sth; ~**ć o porządek** to keep things in order; ~**ć o siebie** to take good care of oneself, to look after oneself [2] (przywiązywać wagę) to care (**o coś** about sth); **nie** ~**m, co ludzie powiedzą** I don't care what people will say

deale|r /'diler/ m [1] Handl. dealer [2] pot. (narkotyków) pusher pot.

deba|ta f debate (**nad czymś** on a. about sth)

debat|ować impf vi to debate (**nad czymś** (about) sth)

deb|el m Sport doubles

debe|t m [1] (dług) overdraft; **być na** ~**cie** to be overdrawn [2] Ekon. debit; **zapisać coś na** ~**t** a. ~**cie** to debit sth

debil m, ~**ka** f pot., obraźl. moron pot., obraźl.

debiu|t m debut

debiutan|t m novice, debutant

debiutant|ka f novice, debutante

debiut|ować pf, impf vi to make one's debut, to debut

dech m breath; **nie móc złapać tchu** to be short of breath; **zapierający dech widok** a breathtaking view; **bez tchu** (tracąc oddech) out of breath, breathless; (bez przerwy) without stopping; **co** a. **ile tchu** as quickly as one can; **jednym tchem** *[przeczytać]* at one sitting; *[wypić]* in one gulp; **z zapartym tchem** with bated breath

de|cha *f* plank

■ **w dechę** pot. awesome pot.; **wcisnąć gaz do dechy** pot. to step on it pot.

decybel *m* decibel

decyd|ować *impf* **[]** *vi* [] (postanawiać) to decide (**o czymś** about sth); ~**ować za kogoś** to decide for sb; ~**ować o sobie** to make one's own decisions [] (przesądzać) to decide, to determine (**o czymś** sth) **[]] decydować się** [] (dokonywać wyboru) to decide, to make up one's mind; ~**ować się na coś** to opt for sth [] (rozstrzygać się) to be decided a. determined

decydując|y *adi. [atak, krok]* decisive; ~**y głos** the final word; ~**y punkt** a decider; ~**y mecz** a decider, a deciding match; **w** ~**ym momencie** at a crucial moment

decyzj|a *f* decision (**o czymś** on a. about sth); **podjąć a. powziąć** ~**ę** to make a. take a decision; ~**a należy do ciebie** the decision rests with you; **czyjąś** ~**ą** by (the) decision of sb

dedukcj|a *f* deduction; **drogą** a. **metodą** ~**i** by a process of deduction

deduk|ować *impf vt, vi* to deduce

dedykacj|a *f* dedication (**dla kogoś** to sb)

dedyk|ować *pf, impf vt* to dedicate *[utwór, kompozycję]* (**komuś** to sb); **tę książkę** ~**uję mojej matce** this book is dedicated to my mother

defek|t *f* defect; **towary z** ~**tami** defective goods

defensyw|a *f* defence GB, defense US; **być w** ~**ie** to be on the defensive; **przejść do** ~**y** to go on the defensive

defensywn|y *adi. [akcja, broń, gra, postawa]* defensive; *[linia]* defence GB, defense US

deficy|t *m* [] Ekon. deficit; ~**t budżetowy** budget deficit [] (niedobór) shortage; ~**t siły roboczej** manpower shortage

deficytow|y *adi. [gospodarka, przedsiębiorstwo]* loss-making; *[towar]* scarce

defila|da *f* parade; (lotnicza) fly-past GB, fly-by US; (piechoty) march past; **przyjmować** ~**dę** to take the salute

defil|ować *impf vi* to parade także przen.

definicj|a *f* definition; **z** ~**i** by definition

defini|ować *impf vt* to define

deformacj|a *f* deformation; ~**a rzeczywistości** distortion of reality; **ulec** ~**i** to become misshapen

deform|ować *impf* **[]** *vt* to deform *[kształt]*; to distort *[znaczenie, odbicie]* **[]] deformować się** *[część ciała]* to become deformed; *[przedmiot]* to lose one's shape

defraudacj|a /ˌdefrawˈdatsja/ *f* książk. embezzlement

defraud|ować /ˌdefrawˈdovatɕ/ *impf vt* książk. to embezzle

degeneracj|a *f* książk. degeneration

degener|ować się *impf v refl.* to degenerate

degradacj|a *f* [] (w hierarchii) demotion [] (upadek) decline [] (zniszczenie) degradation

degrad|ować *impf vt* [] to demote *[żołnierza]*; to downgrade *[pracownika]* [] to degrade *[środowisko]*

degustacj|a *f* książk. tasting, savouring

degust|ować *impf vt* książk. to taste, to sample *[wino, potrawy]*

deka|da *f* książk. (dziesięć dni) ten days; (dziesięć lat) decade; **w drugiej** ~**dzie kwietnia** in mid April

dekadenc|ki *adi.* decadent

dekadentyzm *m* the Decadent movement

dekagram *m* ten grams, ten grammes GB; decagram

Dekalog *m* the Decalogue

dekarz *m* roofer

dek|iel *m* [] Aut. hubcap [] (pokrywka) lid, cover

deklamacj|a *f* declamation, recitation

deklam|ować *impf vt* to recite, to declaim

deklaracj|a *f* [] (oświadczenie) declaration [] (dokument) declaration; ~**a akcesyjna** Polit. declaration of accession; ~**a celna** customs declaration; ~**a podatkowa** tax return; (formularz) tax return form

deklar|ować *impf* **[]** *vt* [] (ogłaszać) to declare [] (obiecywać) to pledge; ~**ować poparcie dla kogoś** to pledge one's support for sb; ~**ować pomoc** to offer assistance **[]] deklarować się** to declare oneself (**za czymś/przeciwko czemuś** for/against sth)

deklinacj|a *f* Jęz. declension

dekode|r *m* decoder

dekol|t *m* (wycięcie) neckline; **głęboki** ~**t z przodu** a low a. plunging neckline; **bluzka z** ~**tem** a low-cut blouse; **sweter z** ~**tem w szpic** a V-necked jumper, a V-neck

dekoncentracj|a *f* [] (uwagi) lack of concentration [] Ekon. decentralization [] Wojsk. scattering, dispersal

dekoncentr|ować *impf* **[]** *vt* to distract *[osobę]*; to decentralize *[produkcję]* **[]] dekoncentrować się** to become distracted

dekoracj|a *f* [] (ozdoby) decoration [] (teatralna, filmowa) set; **zmiana** ~**i** a change of scenery [] (odznaczanie) decorating; **dokonać** ~**i żołnierzy Krzyżem Walecznych** to decorate soldiers with the Cross of Valour

dekoracyjn|y *adi. [motywy, sztuka]* decorative; *[rośliny]* ornamental

dekorato|r *m*, ~**rka** *f* decorator; ~**r teatralny** stage a. scene designer; ~**r wnętrz** interior decorator a. designer; ~**r wystaw sklepowych** window dresser

dekor|ować *impf vt* to decorate

dekre|t *m* decree (**o czymś** on a. sth); ~**tem królewskim** by royal decree

delegacj|a *f* [] (grupa) delegation [] (wyjazd) business trip; **pojechać w** a. **na** ~**ę** to go on a business trip; **być w** ∼**i** to be away on business ③ pot. (wydatki) expenses

delegalizacj|a f ban (**czegoś** on sth), banning (**czegoś** of sth)

delegaliz|ować impf vt to ban, to make [sth] illegal

delega|t m, ∼**tka** f delegate; ∼**ci na zjazd** delegates to the convention

deleg|ować pf, impf vt to delegate

delekt|ować się impf v refl. to savour GB, to savor US (**czymś** sth)

delfin¹ m ① Zool. dolphin ② Sport butterfly (stroke)

delfin² m Hist. dauphin

delfinari|um n dolphinarium

delikates|y plt ① (sklep) delicatessen ② (przysmaki) delicacies

delikatn|y adi. grad. ① (taktowny) considerate ② (mało odporny) [zdrowie, budowa ciała] delicate; [porcelana] delicate, fragile; [tkanina] fine ③ (lekki) [dotyk, podmuch, światło] delicate, soft; [odcień, smak] delicate ④ (drażliwy) [sprawa, misja] delicate, sensitive

delirium n inv. delirium; **być w** ∼ to be delirious

del|ta f delta

demago|g m demagogue GB, demagog US

demagogi|a f demagoguery, demagogy

demakijaż m make-up removal; **preparat do** ∼**u** a make-up remover

demaskato|r m, ∼**rka** f exposer, unmasker

demaskators|ki adi. [publikacja] investigative; ∼**ki artykuł w prasie** an exposé

demask|ować impf **Ⅰ** vt to expose

Ⅱ demaskować się to drop one's disguise

dement|ować impf vt książk. to deny

demilitaryzacj|a f demilitarization

demobilizacj|a f ① Wojsk. demobilization ② przen. lethargy, lassitude

demografi|a f demography

demograficzn|y adi. demographic(al)

demokracj|a f democracy

demokra|ta m, ∼**tka** f democrat

demokratyczn|y adi. democratic

demol|ować impf vt to wreck, to vandalize

demon m demon

demoniczn|y adi. demoni(a)c

demonstracj|a f ① (manifestacja) demonstration ② (prezentacja) demonstration, display; ∼**a siły a** show a. display of strength

demonstracyjn|y adi. [zachowanie, gest] ostentatious

demonstran|t m, ∼**tka** f demonstrator

demonstr|ować impf **Ⅰ** vt ① to present, to show [kolekcję, ubiory, umiejętności] ② to show, to display [uczucia, niezadowolenie]

Ⅱ vi (manifestować) to demonstrate (**przeciw czemuś/na rzecz czegoś** against sth/in favour of sth)

demontaż m disassembly; dismantling także przen.

demont|ować impf vt to dismantle; to disassemble także przen.

demoralizacj|a f (moral) corruption, moral decay

demoraliz|ować impf **Ⅰ** vt to corrupt, to deprave

Ⅱ demoralizować się to become corrupt a. depraved

dena|t m, ∼**tka** f ① Prawo the deceased; (ofiara zabójstwa, wypadku) victim ② pot., żart. wreck pot.

denatura|t m methylated spirit(s)

denerw|ować impf **Ⅰ** vt to irritate, to annoy; **hałas mnie** ∼**uje** noise gets on my nerves

Ⅱ denerwować się ① (martwić się) to be anxious a. worried (**czymś** about sth) ② (złościć się) to be irritated a. annoyed (**czymś** by sth)

denerwując|y adi. irritating, annoying

den|ko n (spód) bottom; (góra) top; (kapelusza) crown

denn|y adi. ① [ryby, erozja] bottom ② pot. [film, książka] crummy pot.

denty|sta m, ∼**stka** f dentist

dentystyczn|y adi. [fotel] dentist's; [zabieg, nici] dental; **gabinet** ∼**y** dental surgery GB, dentist's office US

denucj|ować impf vt książk. to denounce; to inform on

departamen|t m department

depesz|a f ① (telegram) telegram, cable; wire pot. ② (prasowa) dispatch

depesz|ować impf vi to send a telegram; ∼**ować do kogoś** to cable a. wire US pot. sb

depilato|r m (kosmetyk) depilatory; (urządzenie) depilator

deport|ować impf vt to deport

depozy|t m deposit; **oddać coś do** ∼**tu** to put sth in safe deposit

depresj|a f ① Astron., Ekon., Geog. depression ② Med. depression; ∼**a poporodowa** post-natal depression; ∼**a sezonowa** seasonal affective disorder; **mieć** ∼**ę** to suffer from depression ③ Meteo. depression, low-pressure area

dep|tać impf vt ① (następować) to tread (**coś** a. **po czymś** on sth); to trample (**coś** a. **po czymś** on sth); „**nie** ∼**tać trawników!**" 'keep off the grass!' ② przen. to trample on [prawa]

deptak m pot. promenade

deputowan|y m, ∼**a** f deputy; ∼**y do Parlamentu Europejskiego** a Member of the European Parliament

derkacz m corncrake

dermatolo|g m dermatologist

dermatologi|a f dermatology

desan|t m ① (operacja) landing operation ② (oddziały) landing force

dese|ń m pattern, design; **kwiatowy** ∼**ń** a floral pattern

■ **w ten** ∼**ń** pot. like that

dese|r n dessert, pudding GB

deserow|y *adj.* dessert
des|ka *f* ⟨1⟩ (kawałek drewna) plank, board; ~**ka podłogowa** floorboard ⟨2⟩ (do krojenia) (chopping) board; ~**ka do chleba/serów** breadboard/cheese-board ⟨3⟩ pot. (narta) ski; (deskorolka) skateboard; (snowbordowa) snowboard; (surfingowa) surfboard; (wind-surfingowa) sailboard, windsurfer® US
❑ ~**ka do prasowania** ironing board; ~**ka kreślarska** drawing board; ~**ka rozdzielcza** control panel; ~**ka sedesowa** toilet seat
■ **dziura zabita** ~**kami** the back of beyond pot.; ~**ki sceniczne** a. **teatralne** the stage; **do grobowej** ~**ki** pot. till death, to the end of one's days; **ostatnia** ~**ka ratunku** the last resort; **od** ~**ki do** ~**ki** from cover to cover
deskorol|ka *f* skateboard
desperacj|a *f* desperation, despair
desperac|ki *adj.* desperate
despo|ta *m*, ~**tka** *f* despot
despotyczn|y *adj.* despotic
despotyzm *m* despotism
destrukcj|a *f* destruction
destrukcyjn|y *adj.* destructive
destylacj|a *f* distillation
destyl|ować *impf vt* distil GB, distill US
deszcz *m* rain; ~ **ze śniegiem** sleet; **przelotne** ~**e** showers; **ulewny** ~ heavy rain; **kwaśne** ~**e** acid rain; **pada** ~ it's raining; ~ **obelg/pochwał** przen. a shower of abuse/praise
■ **trafić z** ~**u pod rynnę** pot. to fall out of the frying pan into the fire pot.
deszczow|y *adj.* [dzień, pora] rainy; [chmura] rain; **woda** ~**a** rainwater
deszczów|ka *f* rainwater
detal *m* ⟨1⟩ (szczegół) detail; **wdawać się w** ~**e** to go into details; **z** ~**ami** in detail ⟨2⟩ Handl. retail; **cena w** ~**u** retail price
detaliczn|y *adj.* retail; **punkt sprzedaży** ~**ej** retail outlet; **cena** ~**a** retail price
detektyw *m* detective; **prywatny** ~ private detective a. investigator US; private eye pot.
detektywistyczn|y *adj.* [agencja, film, powieść] detective
detergen|t *m* detergent
determinacj|a *f* determination; **z** ~**ą** doggedly
determin|ować *impf vt* książk. to determine
detonacj|a *f* explosion, detonation
dewaluacj|a *f* ⟨1⟩ Ekon., Fin. devaluation ⟨2⟩ przen. debasement
dewalu|ować *impf* **[]** *vt* to devalue także przen.
[][] **dewaluować się** to become devalued
dewastacj|a *f* devastation
dewast|ować *impf vt* to vandalize [wagony, ławki]; to devastate [lasy]
dewiacj|a *f* deviation; ~**e psychiczne** deviant behaviour

dewiz|a **[]** *f* motto
[] **dewizy** *plt* foreign currency
dewo|t *m*, ~**tka** *f* bigot
dezaktualizacj|a *f* książk. **ulec** ~**i** to become outdated a. outmoded
dezaktualiz|ować *impf* książk. **[]** *vt* to cancel out [plany, projekty]
[] **dezaktualizować się** [sprawa] to become irrelevant
dezaproba|ta *f* książk. disapprobation, disapproval (**dla czegoś/wobec kogoś** of sb/sth); **z** ~**tą** disapprovingly, reprovingly
dezercj|a *f* desertion
dezerte|r *m* deserter
dezerter|ować *impf vi* to desert; ~**ować z wojska/z pola bitwy** to desert (from) the army/from the battlefield
dezodoran|t *m* Kosmet. deodorant; (odświeżacz powietrza) air-freshener
dezorganizacj|a *f* disorganization
dezorganiz|ować *impf vt* to disrupt, to disorganize
dezynfekcj|a *f* disinfection
dezynfek|ować *impf vt* to disinfect
dezynsekcj|a *f* pest control, extermination of insects
dębow|y *adj.* [las, aleja] oak; [stół, klepka] oak, oaken
dęt|ka *f* (rowerowa, samochodowa) (inner) tube; (w piłce) bladder
dę|ty *adj.* [instrument] wind; **orkiestra dęta** brass band
diabels|ki *adj.* ⟨1⟩ [moc, sztuczka] devil's, devilish ⟨2⟩ pot. [hałas] infernal pot.
■ ~**ki młyn** big wheel, Ferris wheel
diab|eł *m* devil; ~**eł wcielony** the devil incarnate
■ **do** ~**ła z nim/tym!** pot. to hell with him/it! pot.; **idź do** ~**ła** a. **w** ~**ły** pot. go to hell! pot.; **po** ~**ła?** pot. why the devil a. hell? pot.; ~**li (go) wiedzą** pot. who the hell knows pot.; **jak** ~**li** pot. like hell pot.; **jeden** ~**eł** pot. makes no difference! pot.; **tam, gdzie** ~**eł mówi dobranoc** in the middle of nowhere; ~**eł tkwi w szczegółach** the devil's in the detail; **co nagle, to po** ~**le** przysł. more haste, less speed; **gdzie** ~**eł nie może, tam babę pośle** przysł. ≈ where the Devil can't go himself, he'll send a woman; **nie taki** ~**eł straszny (jak go malują)** przysł. the devil's not so black as he's painted
diagnoz|a *f* diagnosis; **postawić** ~**ę** to make a diagnosis
diagram *m* ⟨1⟩ (wykres) diagram, graph ⟨2⟩ (krzyżówka) grid
dialek|t *m* dialect
dializ|a *f* dialysis
dialog *m* dialogue GB, dialog US
diamen|t *m* diamond; **pierścionek z** ~**tem** a diamond ring

didaskali|a *plt* Teatr stage directions

didżej /ˈdidʒej/ *m*, **~ka** *f* deejay pot.; DJ

diecezj|a *f* diocese

dies|el /ˈdizel/ *m* (silnik) diesel (engine); (samochód) diesel (car)

die|ta¹ *f* (odżywianie się) diet; **~ta odchudzająca/ niskotłuszczowa** a slimming/low-fat diet; **~ta bezmięsna** a meat-free diet; **być na ~cie** to be on a diet; **przestrzegać ~ty** to stick to a diet

die|ta² *f* (zwrot kosztów) daily allowance a. expenses

dietetyczn|y *adi.* ① *[potrzeby, wymagania]* dietary ② (zdrowy) healthy; (nietuczący) low-fat, diet

dinozau|r *m* dinosaur także przen.

disco /ˈdisko/ *n inv., adi. inv.* disco

dla *praep.* (przeznaczony) for; (wobec) for, to; **film ~ dorosłych** a film for adults, an adult film; **„~ panów/pań"** (na drzwiach toalety) 'ladies/gentlemen'; **~ kogo są te kwiaty?** who are these flowers for?; **~ własnego dobra** for one's own good; **podziw/szacunek ~ kogoś** admiration/ respect for sb; **miły/uprzejmy ~ kogoś** nice/ kind to sb; **to był ~ niej szok** it was a shock to a. for her; **(jak) ~ mnie** as far as I'm concerned; **porzuciła go ~ jakiegoś cudzoziemca** she dropped him for some foreigner

dlaczego *pron.* why; **~ jesteś smutny?** why are you sad?; **~ jej nie lubisz?** why don't you like her?; **nie wiem, ~ wyjechała** I don't know why she went away; **nie pytaj mnie ~** don't ask me why; **~ (by) nie?** why not?

dlatego ① *pron.* that is why, therefore; **~ przyszedłem** that's why I came; **czy to ~ dzwoniła?** is that why she phoned?; **właśnie ~!** that's just why!

② **dlatego że** *coni.* because; **„dlaczego?" – „~ że ja tak mówię"** 'why?' – 'because I say so'

dław|ić *impf* ① *vt* ① (tamować oddech) to choke; **~i go w gardle** he's choking ② (powstrzymywać) to stifle *[krzyk, płacz]* ③ przen. to suppress *[powstanie, opozycję]*; **~ić protesty** to stifle protests

② **dławić się** ① (jedzeniem) to choke; **~ić się ością** to choke on a fish bone ② przen. **~ić się ze śmiechu** to choke with laughter

dło|ń *f* (wewnętrzna strona ręki) palm; (ręka) hand; **wierzch ~ni** the back of the hand; **trzymać coś w ~ni** to hold sth in one's hand; **uścisnąć komuś ~ń** to shake hands with sb

■ **(jasne) jak na ~ni** as plain as a pikestaff; **podać komuś pomocną** a. **przyjazną ~ń** to lend a. give sb a helping hand; **mieć serce na ~ni** to be open-hearted; **prędzej włosy mi na ~ni wyrosną, niż wygracie** all the hell will freeze over before you win

dłub|ać *impf vi* ① (drążyć) to pick, to poke; **~ać w nosie** to pick one's nose ② pot. (majstrować) to tinker (**przy czymś** with sth)

dług *m* debt; **mieć ~i** to be in debt; **mieć ~ wobec kogoś** przen. to be in sb's debt

dłu|gi *adi. grad.* long; **~gie buty** high a. long boots; **~gi na 5 metrów** 5 metres long; **przez ~gie miesiące** for months and months; **jak dzień ~gi** all day long

■ **upadł jak ~gi** he fell flat on his face

dłu|go *adv. grad.* long; **jak ~go?** how long?; **~żej tego nie wytrzymam!** I can't stand it any longer!; **tak ~go jak...** (for) as long as...

długodystansow|iec *m* long-distance runner

długodystansow|y *adi. [bieg]* long-distance; *[odrzutowiec]* long-range, long-distance

długofalow|y *adi. [program, planowanie]* longterm; *[promieniowanie]* long-wave

długoletni *adi. [przyjaźń]* long(-standing); *[pracownik]* long serving; **~e doświadczenie** many years of experience

długopis *m* ballpoint (pen)

długoś|ć *f* length; **most (o) ~ci 800 m** a bridge 800 metres long a. in length; **mieć 5 metrów ~ci** to be 5 metres long; **średnia ~ć życia człowieka** the average human life-span; **wygrać o dwie ~ci** to win by two lengths

❑ **~ć fali** wavelength; **~ć geograficzna** longitude

długotrwa|ły *adi.* long-lasting; *[przyjaźń]* lasting; *[rywalizacja, konflikt]* long-standing

dłu|to *n* chisel

dłużni|k *m*, **~czka** *f* debtor; **być czyimś ~kiem** przen. to be indebted to sb

dłuży|ć się *impf v refl.* to drag (on)

dmuchać *impf → dmuchnąć¹*

dmuchaw|iec *m* pot. dandelion; (przekwitły) clock GB, blow-ball pot.

dmuch|nąć¹ *pf – dmuch|ać* *impf vi* to blow (**na coś** on sth)

dmuchn|ąć² *pf vt* pot. (ukraść) to pinch GB pot.

dni|eć *impf v imp.* to dawn; **na dworze ~ało** it was getting light (outside)

dniów|ka *f* (dzień pracy) working day; (wynagrodzenie) daily rate; **na ~kę** on a daily basis

d|no *n* ① (morza, jeziora, rzeki) bottom, bed; (doliny) floor; (zbiornika, łodzi) bottom; **iść na dno** to go down a. under; **do dna!** bottoms up! pot. ② przen. **na dnie duszy** in one's heart of hearts; **dno nędzy** extreme a. abject poverty; **spaść** a. **stoczyć się na dno** to end up in the gutter a. on skid row US pot.; **zupełne dno!** pot. it's the pits! pot.

■ **beczka** a. **studnia** a. **worek bez dna** a bottomless pit

do *praep.* ① (w kierunku) to; **pojechać do Warszawy** to go to Warsaw; **pójść do kina** to go to the cinema; **chodzić do szkoły** to go to school; **podejść do kogoś** to come up to sb; **pójść do lekarza** to go to the doctor's ② (do środka) in, into; **włożyć coś do kieszeni** to put sth in(to) one's pocket ③ (z określeniami czasu) till, until; **zostanę tutaj do soboty** I'll be here till a. until Saturday; **skończę tłumaczenie do środy** I'll finish the translation by Wednesday; **do śmierci** to the end of one's life; **do jutra!** see you a. till tomorrow!; **do widzenia** a. **zobaczenia!** goodbye!; **wpół do drugiej/szóstej** half past one/five ④ (do określonej granicy) up to; (o wysokości) down/up to; **do dwudziestu pacjentów** up to twenty patients; **do tamtego drzewa** up to a. as far as that tree ⑤ (przeznaczenie) for; **telefon do ciebie** a phone call for you; **piłka do metalu** a saw for (cutting) metal; **pasta do butów** shoe polish; **do czego to jest?** what is it for?; **coś do jedzenia/picia** something to eat/drink ⑥ (z wyrażeniami uczucia) for, to; **miłość/ szacunek do kogoś** love/respect for sb; **niena- wiść do kogoś** hatred for a. of sb; **być wzru- szonym do łez** to be moved to tears

■ **co ci do tego?** what business is it of yours?; **jemu nic do naszych spraw** he has no business interfering in our affairs; **był przystojny, do tego jeszcze nie stary** he was good looking, and not so old either; **do tego wszystkiego** (na domiar złego) on top of all that

d|oba f twenty-four hours, day (and night); **24 godziny na dobę** twenty-four hours a day, round the clock; **czynne całą dobę** open 24 hours; **doba romantyzmu** przen. the age a. era of romanticism

doberman m Dobermann (pinscher)

dobi|ć pf — **dobi|jać** impf [] vt (zabić) to finish off pot.; (skrócić cierpienia) to put [sth] out of its misery; **ta wiadomość go ~je** przen. he'll be devastated by the news

[] vi [statek, łódź] to pull in; **~ć do brzegu/celu** to reach the shore/one's destination

[] **dobijać się** (uderzać) **~jać się do drzwi** to hammer a. bang on the door

dobie|c, dobie|gnąć pf — **dobie|gać** impf vi ① (dotrzeć) [osoba] to run (up) (**do czegoś** to sth); [dźwięk, zapach] to come; **~c do mety** to reach the finish(ing) line; **~gł go płacz dziecka** he could hear a child crying ② (nadejść) **~ga czwarta** it's close on a. it's almost four (o'clock) ③ (osiągać) **~c końca** to come to an end; **~gać końca** to be drawing a. coming to an end; **~gać sześćdzie- siątki** to be getting on for sixty

dobierać impf → **dobrać**

dobijać impf → **dobić**

dobit|ka f Sport rebound shot

■ **na ~kę** a. **na ~ek** to make matters a. things worse

dobitnie adv. grad. [powiedzieć] explicitly; [świad- czyć, wykazać] clearly

dobitn|y adi. grad. [głos] forceful; [przykład] blatant; [dowód] clear

dob|ór m selection; **~ór słów** choice of words; **~ór naturalny** natural selection

dob|rać pf — **dob|ierać** impf [] vt to choose, to select [dodatki, słowa]; **~rać coś do czegoś** to match sth with sth

[] **dobrać się** — **dobierać się** ① (dopasować się) to make a perfect match; **~rać się w pary** to pair up (**z kimś** with sb) ② (znaleźć dostęp) **~rać się do czegoś** to get at sth [skarbca, spiżarni]; **~rać się do kogoś** to get a. lay one's hands on sb ③ pot. (napastować) **~ierać się do kogoś** to make a pass at sb

dobranoc inter. goodnight!; **pocałować kogoś na ~** to kiss sb goodnight; **bajka na ~** a bedtime story

dobran|y adi. [para] well-matched, well-suited

dobrn|ąć pf vi to get (**do czegoś** to sth)

d|obro [] n ① (wartość) good; **dobro i zło** good and evil ② (cecha) goodness, kindness; **czynić dobro** to do good; **wyświadczyć komuś wiele dobra** to show sb a good deal of kindness ③ (pomyślność) good; **dla jej (własnego) dobra** for her (own) good; **dla dobra sprawy** for the sake a. good of the cause

[] **dobra** plt ① (towary) goods; (majątek) possessions ② książk. (posiadłości) estate; **dobra królewskie** Crown lands, royal demesnes

dobroby|t m prosperity, well-being

dobroczynnoś|ć f charity

dobroczynn|y adi. ① [bal, koncert] charity; [orga- nizacja, praca] charitable; **na cele ~e** for charity ② [wpływ, klimat] beneficial

dobro|ć f [] ① goodness, kindness; **okazywać komuś ~ć** to be kind to sb; **z ~ci (serca)** out of the goodness a. kindness of one's heart

[] **po dobroci** pot. (dobrowolnie) voluntarily, peace- fully; **radzę ci po ~ci: nie ruszaj tego** I'm telling you for your own good – leave it alone

dobroduszn|y adi. good-natured, kind-hearted

dobrowoln|y adi. voluntary

dobry [] adi. grad. ① (spełniający oczekiwania) good; **dobry/najlepszy gatunek** good/best quality; **zmienić się na lepsze** to change for the better; **wyjść komuś na dobre** to do sb good; **nic dobrego z tego nie będzie** no good will come of it; **nie wróżyć nic dobrego** to not augur well książk.; **w najlepszym razie** a. **wypadku** at best; **każdy pretekst jest dobry** any excuse will do; **może to będzie dobre zamiast młotka?** maybe this will do instead of a hammer?; **wszystkiego dobrego/ najlepszego** all the best; **wszystkiego dobrego w dniu urodzin** Happy Birthday! [osoba, uczynki] good, kind; **dobre zamiary** good intentions; **mimo najlepszych chęci** despite my best intentions; **mieć dobre serce** to be kind- hearted; **być dobrym dla zwierząt** to be good to animals; **zasługiwać na lepsze traktowanie** to deserve better treatment; **bądź tak dobry i podaj mi książkę** would you be so kind as to pass me that book, please? książk. ③ (kompetentny) [lekarz, *nauczyciel]* good; **być dobrym z matematyki/w tenisie** to be good at maths/tennis; **być dobrym w swoim fachu** to be good at one's job a. trade ④ (bliski) *[przyjaciel, kolega]* good ⑤ (pozytywny) *[opinia, wrażenie]* good; **dobrej oceny** good marks; **dać się poznać od dobrej/najlepszej strony** to reveal a. show one's good side/one's finest qualities ⑥ (smaczny) good, tasty ⑦ Szkol. good; **ocena dobra/bardzo dobra** ≈ a B/an A

II *adi.* pot. (znaczny) good; **dobre pięć kilogramów** a good five kilos; **dobrą godzinę** for a good hour

III *m* Szkol., Uniw. ≈ grade B; **bardzo dobry** ≈ grade A

IV **lepszy** *adi.* comp. pot. iron. **obraca się teraz w lepszym towarzystwie** he keeps better company nowadays iron.; **lepszy z niego cwaniak** he's a sly one

V **na dobre** *adv.* *[osiąść, wyprowadzić się]* for good; *[zakochać się, rozpadać się]* really

VI **w najlepsze** *adv.* *[bawić się]* oblivious to everything; **kłamać w najlepsze** to lie through one's teeth

VII **dobra** *inter.* pot. okay pot.; **dobra, dobra!** yeah, yeah! pot.

■ **być z kimś na dobre i na złe** to stick with sb through thick and thin; **dobre** a. **dobry sobie!** iron. that's a good one pot., iron.; **dość tego dobrego!** pot. that's enough!; **coś ty zrobił najlepszego!** why did you have to do it?; **nic dobrego** (osoba) good-for-nothing; **być już dobrym** a. **być pod dobrą datą** pot. to be well oiled a. far gone pot.; **tłumaczyć coś komuś jak komu dobremu** pot. to explain sth to sb as best one can; **wszystko dobre, co się dobrze kończy** przysł. all's well that ends well przysł.

dobrze **I** *adv.* grad. ① (właściwie, umiejętnie) *[zachowywać się, ubierać, gotować]* well; **jeśli wszystko dobrze pójdzie** if all goes well; **chciał dobrze** he meant well; **dobrze zrobiłeś** you did the right thing; **lepiej być nie może** things couldn't be better; **szło mu całkiem dobrze** he was doing really well; **dobrze ci w tej sukience** you look good in that dress; **równie dobrze mógłby studiować w Paryżu** he could just as easily study in Paris; **najlepiej będzie, jeśli...** it'll be best if...; **dobrze mówię?** pot. am I right?; **mieć dobrze w głowie** to have one's head screwed on the right way pot. **nie mieć dobrze w głowie** to be not right in the head pot. ② (dokładnie) *[pamiętać]* well; *[przeczytać]* right; **dobrze się znamy** we know each other well; **dobrze wiesz, o co mi chodzi!** you know very well what I mean!; **trzeba by dobrze się zastanowić** we/you need to think about it carefully ③ (zdrowo) *[czuć się, wyglądać]* well; **już jest z nim lepiej** he's feeling better now; **było z nią nie najlepiej** she wasn't feeling too good; **poranna gimnastyka dobrze mi robi** morning exercise does me good ④ (przyjemnie) **dobrze się**

bawić to have a good time; **dobrze mi tutaj** I'm fine right here; **z nikim mi nie było tak dobrze, jak z tobą** nobody ever made me feel as good as you did; **tobie to dobrze, nie musisz chodzić do pracy** you're lucky, you don't have to go to work; **gdzie ci będzie lepiej niż tu?** where else would you be this well off? ⑤ (pozytywnie) *[skończyć się, układać się]* well; **dobrze komuś życzyć** to wish sb well; **mówić dobrze o kimś** to speak well of sb; **dobrze jest mieć sąsiadów** it's good to have neighbours; **dobrze, że...** it's a good thing that...; **byłoby dobrze, gdyby...** it would be good if...; **uda im się wygrać, to dobrze, nie uda się, to drugie dobrze** if they win, all well and good, and if they don't, that's okay too; **to nie jest dobrze widziane** it's not the done thing; **nie będzie dobrze widziane, jeśli...** it won't go down too well if...

II *adv.* pot. (sporo) well pot.; **dobrze po pierwszej** well past one

III *inter.* ① (zgoda) okay pot.; all right; **dobrze, dobrze!** all right, all right! ② (aprobata) good, right

IV **lepiej** *adv.* comp. ① (raczej) better; **lepiej się zastanów** you'd better think about it ② pot. (więcej) more; **dziesięć lat albo i lepiej** a. **jak nie lepiej** ten years or more a. if not more

■ **wyjść na czymś dobrze/lepiej/najlepiej** pot. to come off well/better/best out of sth; **mieć się dobrze** (być bogatym) to be well-off; (być zdrowym) to be a. feel well; **mieć dobrze w głowie** a. **czubie** to be well away a. far gone pot.; **dobrze ci tak** pot. serves you right; **dobrze ci tak mówić** that's easy for you to say; **nie ma tak dobrze** pot. it's not as simple a. easy as that; **lepiej nie mówić** pot. it doesn't bear talking about; **lepiej późno niż wcale** a. **nigdy** przysł. better late than never przysł.

dobud|ować *pf* — **dobud|owywać** *impf vt* to build on, to add *[piętro, garaż]*

dobudów|ka *f* extension

dobyt|ek *m* belongings, possessions

docelow|y *adi.* *[rynek, port]* destination; *[program, wydajność]* target

doce|nić *pf* — **doce|niać** *impf vt* to appreciate; **nie ~niać czegoś** to underestimate sth

docen|t *m* ≈ Reader GB, ≈ associate professor US

dochodow|y *adi.* *[interes, przedsiębiorstwo]* profitable; **podatek ~y** income tax

dochodze|nie *n* inquiry, investigation; **wszcząć ~nie** to launch an inquiry a. investigation

dochodzić¹ *impf* → **dojść**

dochodz|ić² *pf vi* ① (prowadzić) *[droga, ulica]* to lead (**do czegoś** to sth) ② (kursować) *[pociąg, autobus, winda]* to go (**do czegoś** as far as sth) ③ (zbliżać się) **~i północ** it's getting on for midnight; **~i piąta** it's almost five (o'clock)

dochow|ać *pf* — **dochow|ywać** *impf vt* to keep *[tajemnicy, przyrzeczenia]*; **~ać wierności żonie** to remain faithful to one's wife

doch|ód *m* (zarobki) income; (zysk) profit; **miesięcz-
ne ∼ody** monthly earnings; **∼ód narodowy**
national income

do|ciąć *pf* — **do|cinać** *impf vi* to make a cutting
remark (**komuś** about sb)

docie|c *pf* — **docie|kać** *impf vi* książk. ∼**c** czegoś
to find out sth; ∼**kać czegoś** to inquire into sth

dociekliw|y *adi.* [czytelnik, badacz] inquisitive;
[pytania] probing; [umysł] inquiring

docierać *impf* → **dotrzeć**

docinać *impf* → **dociąć**

docin|ek *m* cutting remark

doczek|ać *pf* — **doczek|iwać** *impf* **[]** *vi*
[1] (dotrwać) to wait; ∼**ać, aż...** to wait until a. till...;
nie ∼ała do końca filmu she left before the film
was over [2] (dożyć) to live (**czegoś** to see sth); ∼**ać**
późnej starości to live to a ripe old age
[] **doczekać się** to wait; **nie mogę się ∼ać**
powrotu brata I can't wait for my brother to come
back; ∼**ać się czternastu wydań** to run to
fourteen editions

docze|sny *adi.* książk. [życie, szczątki] mortal;
[sprawy] worldly

doda|ć *pf* — **doda|wać** *impf* **[]** *vt* [1] (dołożyć,
dopowiedzieć) to add; **pragnę ∼ć, że...** I'd like to add
that...; **nie mam nic do ∼nia** I've nothing more to
add; ∼**wać sobie lat** to pretend that one is older;
∼**ć komuś pewności siebie/odwagi** to bolster
sb's confidence/courage [2] (zsumować) to add up, to
sum up [kolumnę cyfr]; ∼**ć trzy do siedmiu** to add
three and seven
[] **dodać** *coni.* plus; **dwa ∼ć dwa** two plus two

dodat|ek **[]** *m* [1] (uzupełnienie) addition (**do czegoś**
to sth); (do gazety, czasopisma) supplement; ∼**ek**
nadzwyczajny special supplement; **z ∼kiem**
witamin with added vitamins; **na ∼ek** a.
w ∼ku in addition [2] (do wynagrodzenia) bonus;
∼**ek rodzinny** family allowance [3] (do potraw)
additive
[] **dodatki** *plt* (do ubrania) accessories

dodatkow|y *adi.* additional; [opłata, wydatki,
wyposażenie] extra

dodatni *adi.* positive; ∼**a temperatura** temperature above zero; **wynik badania był ∼** the test was
positive

dodawać *impf* → **dodać**

dodawani|e *n* addition, sum

dodzw|onić się *pf* — **dodzw|aniać się** *impf*
v refl. to get through (**do kogoś** to sb)

dog *m* Great Dane

dogad|ać *pf* — **dogad|ywać** *impf* **[]** *vt* (ustalić) to
agree on [szczegóły]; **wszystko jest już ∼ane**
everything's been agreed
[] *vi* (zrobić uwagę) to make a gibe (**komuś** at sb)
[] **dogadać się** — **dogadywać się** [1] (dojść do
porozumienia) to come to an agreement (**z kimś** with

sb) [2] (w obcym języku) to make oneself understood (**z
kimś** to sb)

dogadzać¹ *impf* → **dogodzić**

dogadza|ć² *impf vi* książk. (odpowiadać) to be conveni-
ent (**komuś** for sb); to suit (**komuś** sb)

doganiać *impf* → **dogonić**

doga|snąć *pf* — **doga|sać** *impf vi* [ognisko, pożar]
to burn out, to die down

dogodn|y *adi.* grad. [1] [położenie, termin] conveni-
ent [2] [oferta, propozycja, cena] attractive; [warunki]
favourable GB, favorable US

dog|odzić *pf* — **dog|adzać¹** *impf vi* ∼**adzać**
komuś to indulge sb; ∼**adzać sobie** to overindulge (oneself); ∼**odzić czyimś zachciankom**
to indulge sb's whims; **niczym mu nie można**
było ∼odzić he was impossible to please

dog|onić *pf* — **dog|aniać** *impf vt* to catch [sb]
up, to catch up with

dogryw|ka *f* (część meczu) extra time GB, overtime
US; (mecz) play-off

dogry|źć *pf* — **dogry|zać** *impf vi* pot. to taunt
(**komuś** sb)

d|oić *impf vt* [1] to milk [krowę, kozę] [2] pot. to guzzle
pot. [piwo, wino]
■ **doić kogoś** a. **doić od kogoś pieniądze** pot. to
milk sb

doj|azd *m* [1] (podróż) journey; ∼**azd do pracy**
zajmuje mi godzinę it takes me an hour to get to
work; **tracić czas na ∼azdy do pracy** to waste
time travelling to (and from) work; **mieć dobry**
∼**azd** to have good transport connections [2] (droga)
road; (do domu, garażu) drive(way)

dojazdow|y *adi.* [droga, trasa] approach, access

doj|echać *pf* — **doj|eżdżać** *impf vi* to arrive, to
get; ∼**echać gdzieś na czas** to arrive a. get
somewhere on time; ∼**eżdżać codziennie do**
pracy to commute to work; **osoby ∼eżdżające do**
pracy commuters; **już ∼eżdżamy** we're almost
there

dojrzałoś|ć *f* (człowieka, zwierzęcia) maturity; (owocu)
ripeness

dojrza|ły **[]** *adi.* grad. [1] [owoce, zboże] ripe
[2] [osobnik, postępowanie] mature
[] *adi.* [ser, wino] mature, ripe

dojrz|eć¹ *pf* — **dojrz|ewać** *impf vi* [1] [owoce,
zboża] to ripen [2] [osoba] to mature; **nie ∼ał do**
tego, aby być ojcem he's not mature enough to be
a father [3] [ser, wino] to mature, to ripen

dojrz|eć² *pf vt* (zauważyć) to spot; (odczytać) to make
out; ∼**eć w kimś ukryty talent** to see hidden
talent in sb

dojś|cie *n* access (**do czegoś** to sth); **mieć ∼cia**
w ministerstwie pot. to have connections in the
ministry

do|jść *pf* — **do|chodzić¹** *impf* **[]** *vi* [1] (dotrzeć)
[osoba] to reach (**do czegoś** sth); to arrive (**do**
czegoś at a. in sth); [dźwięk, zapach] to come; [list,

przesyłka] to arrive; **dojść do domu** to arrive a. get home; **jak mogę dojść do dworca?** how can I get to the railway station?; **uliczny hałas tu nie dochodzi** you can't hear the traffic here; **doszło do moich uszu, że...** I heard a. hear that...; **doszły mnie słuchy, że wyszłaś za mąż** I hear you got married; **wreszcie doszło do niego, że...** it finally got through to him that... 2 *(dołączyć)* to join (**do czegoś** sth); **do pensji dochodzi premia** on top of the salary there's a bonus; **dojdą nam nowe obowiązki** we'll have additional responsibilities 3 *[liczba, temperatura, cena]* to amount, to come (**do czegoś** to sth); **kurs dolara doszedł do 4 zł** the exchange rate for the dollar went up to 4 zlotys; **upał dochodził do 40°C** the temperature was approaching 40°C 4 *(osiągnąć)* **dojść do czegoś** to achieve something; **dojść do perfekcji w czymś** to achieve a. attain perfection in sth; **dojść do bogactwa/sławy** to become rich/famous; **dojść do pieniędzy** to come into money; **dojść do władzy** to come a. rise to power; **dojść z kimś do porozumienia** to reach a. come to an agreement with sb 5 *(domagać się)* to demand; **dochodzić swoich praw na drodze sądowej** to pursue one's rights in a court of law; **dochodzić sprawiedliwości** to seek a. demand justice 6 *(ustalić)* to find out; **dojść prawdy** to find out the truth; **trudno dojść, kto** it's hard to find out who; **dojść do wniosku** a. **przekonania** to come to a. reach a conclusion 7 *(ugotować się)* **ziemniaki zaraz dojdą** the potatoes will be ready in a minute

II *v imp.* *(zdarzyć się)* to happen, to come about; **często dochodzi tu do wypadków** accidents often occur here; **doszło do tego, że...** it came to the point where...; **do czego to doszło!** what are things coming to!

■ **dojść do siebie** *(po chorobie)* to recover; *(po zemdleniu)* to come round a. to

dokańczać *impf* → **dokończyć**

dokarm|ić *pf* — **dokarm|iać** *impf vt* to feed *[zwierzęta, ptaki]*

doka|zać *pf* — **doka|zywać**[1] *impf vi* *(osiągnąć)* to achieve, to accomplish; **~zać cudu** a. **cudów** to work a. perform miracles a. marvels

dokaz|ywać[2] *impf vi* *(psocić)* to romp, to frolic

dokąd *pron.* *(cel)* where (to); *(odległość)* how far; **idź, ~ chcesz** go wherever you want; **nie miała ~ pójść** she had nowhere to go

dokądkolwiek *pron.* wherever

dokądś *pron.* somewhere

dokładać *impf* → **dołożyć**

dokład|ka *f* second helping; seconds *pot.*

■ **na ~kę** *pot.* *(dodatkowo)* for good measure; *(na domiar)* on top of that

dokładnie **I** *adv. grad. [opisać, pamiętać]* precisely, accurately; *[obejrzeć, umyć]* carefully; *[omówić, zbadać]* thoroughly

II *part.* precisely, exactly; **~ dwadzieścia minut** precisely twenty minutes; **rok temu, ~ 21 lipca** a year ago, on 21 July to be precise a. exact

dokładnoś|ć *f* 1 *(precyzja)* accuracy, precision 2 *(skrupulatność)* meticulousness

dokładn|y *adi. grad.* 1 *[opis, pomiary]* accurate, precise; *[wymiary, adres, czas]* exact; *[mapa, informacja]* accurate; **~a kopia** an exact copy 2 *(skrupulatny)* *[osoba]* thorough, meticulous

dokoła *adv., praep.* → **dookoła**

dokon|ać *pf* — **dokon|ywać** *impf* **I** *vt* książk. to make *[odkrycia, wyboru, rezerwacji]*; to commit *[zbrodni, morderstwa]*; to carry out *[napadu, zamachu]*; **~ywać cudów** to work a. perform miracles

II **dokonać się** — **dokonywać się** *[rewolucja, przemiany, reformy]* to take place, to occur; *[zbrodnia]* to be committed a. perpetrated

dokona|nie *n* achievement, accomplishment

dokonan|y *adi.* Jęz. perfective

dokonywać *impf* → **dokonać**

dokończe|nie *n* conclusion, ending

dok|ończyć *pf* — **dok|ańczać** *impf vt* to finish (off), to complete

dokrę|cić *pf* — **dokrę|cać** *impf vt* to tighten (up) *[śrubę]*; to turn off (properly) *[kran]*

dokształ|cić się *pf* — **dokształ|cać się** *impf v refl.* to train, to improve one's skills

dokto|r *m* 1 Uniw. Doctor; **~r filozofii** Doctor of Philosophy; **~r prawa** Doctor of Law 2 *pot.* *(lekarz)* doctor; **pójść do ~ra** to go and see a doctor

doktora|t *m* Uniw. 1 *(stopień)* doctorate 2 *(praca)* doctoral thesis

dokuczać *impf* → **dokuczyć**

dokuczliw|y *adi. grad. [mróz]* biting; *[ból]* nagging; *[osoba]* exasperating, annoying

dokucz|yć *pf* — **dokucz|ać** *impf vi* 1 *(sprawić przykrość)* to tease, to annoy (**komuś** sb) 2 *(doskwierać)* *[głód, pragnienie]* to nag (**komuś** at sb); *[serce, reumatyzm]* to bother, to trouble (**komuś** sb)

dokumen|t *m* 1 *(akt)* document 2 *(dowód tożsamości)* document, paper 3 *pot.* *(film)* documentary 4 Komput. document

dokumentacj|a *f* documentation; **~a techniczna** specification sheet

dokumentaln|y *adi.* documentary

dokument|ować *impf vt* *(być świadectwem)* to testify (**coś** to sth); *(dowodzić)* to prove; *(potwierdzać)* to substantiate

dokup|ić *pf* — **dokup|ywać, dokup|ować** *impf vt* to buy (some) more *[farby, krzeseł, ziemi]*

dol|a *f* 1 *(los)* lot; **~a i niedola** a. **~e i niedole** life's ups and downs 2 *pot.* *(łup)* whack GB *pot.*

dol|ać[1] *pf* — **dol|ewać** *impf vt* to pour (some) more; **~ać komuś wina** to top sb up with wine *pot.*

dol|ać[2] *pf vi pot.* to bash *pot.* (**komuś** sb)

dola|r *m* dollar

dol|ecieć pf — **dol|atywać** impf vi 1 [ptak, samolot, osoba] to reach; **kula ~eciała do celu** the bullet hit the target 2 [dźwięk, zapach] to reach 3 pot. (dobiec) to run up (**do kogoś** to sb)

dolega|ć impf vi [ręka, żołądek] to bother (**komuś** sb); **co ci ~?** what seems to be the trouble?; **nic mi nie ~** I'm all right

dolegliwoś|ć f 1 (ból) complaint 2 przen. inconvenience

dolewać impf → **dolać**¹

dolew|ka f (zupy) second helping; seconds pot.; (herbaty) refill

dolicz|yć pf — **dolicz|ać** impf 1 vt (dodać) to add (**coś do czegoś** sth to sth); **do ceny ~ono podatek VAT** the price includes VAT

II vi (skończyć liczenie) **~yć do dziesięciu** to count (up) to ten

III doliczyć się (ustalić) to count up; **nie mogę się ~yć trzech książek** I'm three books short

dolin|a f valley; **w ~ie** in a valley

doln|y adi. 1 (znajdujący się u dołu) [szuflada, półka] bottom; [pokład, warga, powieka] lower; **~a Wisła** the Lower Vistula; **~y Śląsk** Lower Silesia 2 (minimalny) [próg, granica wieku] lower, minimum

dołącz|yć impf — **dołącz|ać** impf 1 vt (dodać) to attach (**do czegoś** to sth); **do wniosku należy ~yć życiorys** please enclose your CV with the application

II vi (przyłączyć się) to join (**do kogoś** sb)

III dołączyć się — **dołączać się** to join (**do kogoś** sb)

doł|ek m 1 (zagłębienie) hole 2 (na policzku, w brodzie) dimple 3 pot. (brzuch) **boli go w ~ku** he's got a tummy ache; **ze wzruszenia ściska mnie w ~ku** I have a knot in the pit of my stomach; **ze strachu ściskało ją w ~ku** she had butterflies in her stomach pot. 4 pot. (zła sytuacja) bad patch GB pot.; **być w (psychicznym) ~ku** to be feeling low pot.; **być w ~ku finansowym** to be in financial doldrums ❑ **~ek startowy** Sport ≈ starting mark

■ **kopać pod kimś ~ki** pot. to plot behind sb's back; **kto pod kim ~ki kopie, sam w nie wpada** przysł. ≈ (it is a case of) the biter bit

do|łożyć pf — **do|kładać** impf 1 vt (dodać) to add; **dołożył drew do ogniska** he put some more wood on the fire; **dołożyć starań** a. **wysiłków, żeby coś zrobić** przen. to make an effort to do sth

II vi 1 (dopłacić) to contribute (**do czegoś** to sth); **dokładać do interesu** to run a business at a loss 2 pot. (zbić) to wallop pot. (**komuś** sb); **nasi piłkarze dołożyli im 5:0** our team thrashed them 5-0 pot.

III dołożyć się — **dokładać się** (dopłacić) to contribute (**do czegoś** to sth)

dom m 1 (budynek) building; (mieszkalny) house; **~ jednorodzinny** detached house 2 (mieszkanie) home; **w ~u** at home; **pójść do ~u** to go home;

przebywać poza ~em to be away from home 3 (rodzina) home, family; **z dobrego ~u** from a good home a. family; **być bogatym z ~u** to come from a rich family; **z ~u Kowalska** née Kowalska; **z ~u nazywała się...** her maiden name was... 4 (instytucja) house; **~ mody** fashion house 5 (ród) house; **~ Habsburgów** the house of Habsburg ❑ **Biały Dom** the White House **~ akademicki** hall of residence GB, dormitory US **~ dziecka** children's home; **~ gry** gaming house; **~ kultury** ≈ community centre; **~ maklerski** brokerage (firm); **~ poprawczy** young offenders' institution; **~ publiczny** brothel; **~ starców** old people's home

■ **~ wariatów** pot. madhouse pot.; **czuj się jak u siebie w ~u** make yourself at home; **gość w ~,** **Bóg w ~** przysł. you're very welcome; **wszędzie dobrze, ale w ~u najlepiej** przysł. there's no place like home przysł.

domaga|ć się impf v refl. to demand (**czegoś** sth); **~ł się, żeby winni zostali ukarani** he demanded that the culprits be punished

domato|r m, **~rka** f stay-at-home, home bird GB, homebody US pot.

domia|r m **na ~r złego** to make matters worse

domiesz|ka f admixture; **z ~ką ironii** przen. with a touch of irony

domieśniow|y adi. intramuscular

dominacj|a f dominance, predominance (**nad czymś** over sth)

domin|o n dominoes; **grać w ~o** to play dominoes

domin|ować impf vi to dominate (**nad kimś** over sb)

dom|knąć pf — **dom|ykać** impf 1 vt to close (to), to shut; **nie ~knęła drzwi** she left the door ajar

II domykać się to close properly

domnieman|y adi. książk. alleged

domofon m entryphone® GB, intercom

domokrążc|a m pot. hawker, pedlar GB, peddler US

domoro|sły adi. self-taught, home-grown

domostw|o n książk. homestead

domowni|k m household member; **traktować kogoś jak ~ka** to treat sb like family

domow|y adi. 1 [adres, telefon] home; [budżet, obowiązki] household; [ciasto, dżem] home-made 2 [tradycje, atmosfera] family 3 [zwierzęta, ptactwo] domestic; **rośliny ~e** house plants

domykać impf → **domknąć**

domy|sł m guess; **snuć ~sły** to speculate (**na temat czegoś** on sth); **wszystko to opiera się na ~słach** all this is pure guesswork

domyśl|ić się pf — **domyśl|ać się** impf v refl. to guess (**czegoś** (at) sth); **~ić się prawdy** to work out the truth; **czegoś się ~ają** they suspect something; „**to był koszmar**" – „**~am się**" 'it was a nightmare' – 'I can imagine'

domyśln|y [I] *adi. grad. [osoba]* quick-witted

[II] *adi.* [1] *[uśmiech, mrugnięcie]* knowing [2] *[wartość, ustawienie]* default

doni|czka *f* flowerpot, plant pot

doniczkow|y *adi. [kwiaty, rośliny]* pot GB, potted

doniesie|nie *n* [1] *(powiadomienie)* notification (**o czymś** of a. about sth); **złożyć ~nie na kogoś** to inform on sb [2] *(wiadomość)* (news) report

don|ieść *pf* — **don|osić** *impf* **[I]** *vt (dostarczyć)* (to manage) to carry

[II] *vi* [1] *(przekazać wiadomość)* to inform; *[reporter, prasa]* to report (**o czymś** on sth); **jak ~osi agencja Reutera...** according to a Reuter's report... [2] *(złożyć donos)* to report (**na kogoś** sb); to inform (**na kogoś** on a. against sb)

[III] donieść się — donosić się *[dźwięki]* to be heard

donikąd *pron.* nowhere; **prowadzić ~** to lead nowhere *także przen.*; **droga ~** a road leading nowhere *także przen.*

doniosłoś|ć *f* importance, significance

donio|sły *adi. grad.* significant, important; **~słe wydarzenie** a momentous occasion

donos *m* denunciation (**na kogoś** of sb); **złożyć na kogoś ~** to inform on sb

donosiciel *m*, **~ka** *f* informer

donosić *impf* → **donieść**

donośn|y *adi. grad.* resonant

dookoła [I] *adv.* around, round GB; **rozglądać się ~** to look (all) around; **obejść coś ~** to go around sth

[II] *praep.* around, round GB; **~ stołu** around a. round a table; **rejs ~ świata** a round-the-world cruise

■ **~ Wojtek** over and over (again), all over again

dopadać *impf* → **dopaść**

dopas|ować *pf* — **dopas|owywać** *impf* **[I]** *vt (kształtem)* to adjust (**coś do czegoś** sth to sth); *(kolorem, stylem)* to match (up) (**coś do czegoś** sth to sth)

[II] dopasować się — dopasowywać się to adapt (**do czegoś** to sth)

dopasowan|y *adi. [suknia, ubranie]* fitted

dopasowywać *impf* → **dopasować**

dopa|ść *pf* — **dopa|dać** *impf* **[I]** *vt* [1] *(schwytać)* to catch *[zbiega, ofiarę]*; **jeszcze cię ~dnę!** *pot.* I'll get you one day! *pot.* [2] *(dogonić)* to catch up (**kogoś** with sth)

[II] *vi (dobiec)* **~ść do kogoś** to run up to sb

dopat|rzyć, dopat|rzeć *pf* — **dopat|rywać** *impf* **[I]** *vi (dopilnować)* **~rzyć czegoś** to see to sth

[II] dopatrzyć się — dopatrywać się *(znaleźć)* **~rzyć się czegoś (w czymś)** to find sth (in sth); **~rywać się czegoś (w czymś)** to look for sth (in sth)

dopełniacz *m* Jęz. genitive (case); **rzeczownik w ~u** a noun in the genitive (case)

dopeł|nić *pf* — **dopeł|niać** *impf* **[I]** *vt* to complete, to go through *[formalności]*; to discharge *[obowiązku, zobowiązania]*

[II] dopełnić się — dopełniać się *(dobiec końca) [uroczystość]* to come to an end

dopełnie|nie *n* Jęz. object; **~nie bliższe/dalsze** direct/indirect object

dopędz|ić *pf* — **dopędz|ać** *impf* *vt (złapać)* to catch; *(dogonić)* to catch up (**kogoś** with sb)

dopi|ąć *pf* — **dopi|nać** *impf* **[I]** *vt (dołączyć)* to attach (**coś do czegoś** sth to sth)

[II] dopiąć się — dopinać się *(zapiąć się) [osoba]* to button (up) one's clothes; **marynarka się na nim nie ~ina** the jacket's too tight for him

■ **~iąć celu** to achieve one's objective; **~iąć swego** to get one's own way

dopi|ć *pf* — **dopi|jać** *impf vt* to drink up

dopieprz|yć *pf* — **dopieprz|ać** *impf vi posp.* **~yć komuś** to lay into sb *pot.*

dopiero *part.* [1] *(nie wcześniej)* only; **~ wczoraj** only yesterday; **~ wtedy, gdy** only when; **~ co** only just; **wyjeżdżam ~ jutro** I'm not leaving till tomorrow; **wróci ~ za dwa tygodnie** he won't be back for another two weeks [2] *(zaledwie)* only; **ona ma ~ dwa lata** she's only two

■ **a to ~!** well, I never!; **a co** a. **cóż ~...** to say nothing of...

dopiln|ować *pf* — **dopiln|owywać** *impf vt* **~ować czegoś** to see to sth; **~ować, żeby...** to see to it that...

dopinać *impf* → **dopiąć**

doping *m* [1] *(zachęta)* encouragement (**do czegoś** to sth); *(publiczności)* cheering, cheers [2] Med., Sport doping; **stosować ~** to take drugs

doping|ować *impf vt* to encourage (**kogoś do czegoś** sb to do sth); *[kibice]* to cheer on *[zawodnika, drużynę]*

dopingow|y *adi. [afera]* doping; **kontrola ~a** dope test

dopingując|y *adi. [czynnik]* motivating; **środki ~e** Med., Sport performance enhancing drugs

dopi|sać *pf* — **dopi|sywać** *impf vt* [1] *(dodać)* to add *[zdanie, uwagę]*

[II] *vi* **apetyt mu ~suje** he has a good appetite; **zdrowie mu ~suje** he is in good health; **szczęście nam ~sało** we were lucky

[III] dopisać się — dopisywać się to add a note (**do czegoś** to sth)

dopis|ek *m (uwaga)* note; *(w liście)* postscript

dopisywać *impf* → **dopisać**

dopła|cić *pf* — **dopła|cać** *impf vt* [1] *(zapłacić dodatkowo)* to pay extra (**do czegoś** for sth) [2] *(dotować)* **~cać do czegoś** to subsidize sth

dopła|ta *f* [1] *(dodatkowy koszt)* extra charge (**do czegoś** for a. on sth); **~ta do biletu/przesyłki**

excess fare/postage; **za** ~**tą** for an extra charge
[2] (dodatek); ~**ta do wczasów** holiday bonus; ~**ty
dla rolników** subsidies for farmers

dopły|nąć *pf* — **dopły|wać** *impf vi* [1] (przypłynąć)
[osoba, ryba] to swim (**do czegoś** (up) to sth); *[łódź,
statek]* to sail (**do czegoś** (up) to sth); ~**nąć do
brzegu** to reach the shore [2] *[gaz, prąd]* to run (**do
czegoś** to sth)

dopływ *m* [1] (cieczy, prądu, gazu) inflow; **odciąć** ~
wody do budynku to cut off the water supply to a
building [2] przen. inflow, influx; ~ **taniej siły
roboczej** an influx of cheap labour [3] (rzeki) tributary

dopływać *impf* → **dopłynąć**

dopóki *coni.* książk. as long as, while; ~ **nie** until,
till; **zaczekaj,** ~ **nie wrócę** wait till I come back

dopóty *coni.* książk. ~, **dopóki** (for) as long as,
while; ~, **dopóki nie** until

doprac|ować *pf* — **doprac|owywać** *impf vt*
to polish up *[artykuł]*; to refine *[szczegóły]*; **niedo-
pracowane projekty** rough designs; **wymagać**
~**owania** to require (some) more work

doprawdy *part.* książk. really, truly; ~**?** really?

dopraw|ić *pf* — **dopraw|iać** *impf* [] *vt* to season
[potrawę] (**czymś** with sth); ~ **do smaku** season to
taste

[] **doprawić się** — **doprawiać się** pot., żart. to get
plastered a. sloshed pot.

doprowa|dzić *pf* — **doprowa|dzać** *impf* [] *vt*
[1] (przyprowadzić) to lead, to take (**kogoś do czegoś**
sb to sth) [2] (dostarczyć) to supply *[krew, prąd, wodę]*
(**do czegoś** to sth) [3] (spowodować) to bring; ~**dzić
coś do skutku** to bring sth to a successful
conclusion; ~**dzić kogoś do rozpaczy/łez** to
reduce sb to despair/tears; ~**dzić coś do porządku** to tidy sth up; ~**dzić się do porządku** to
tidy oneself up; ~**dzać kogoś do szału** to drive sb
mad pot.; **nie** ~**dzaj mnie do ostateczności!**
don't drive a. push me too far! pot.

[] *vi* ~**dzić do czegoś** to lead to sth, to bring
about sth; **to do niczego dobrego nie** ~**dzi** no
good will come of it

dopuszczać *impf* → **dopuścić**

dopuszczaln|y *adi.* (akceptowalny) acceptable; (moż-
liwy) permissible

dopu|ścić *pf* — **dopu|szczać** *impf* [] *vt*
[1] (pozwolić się zbliżyć) ~**ścić kogoś do kogoś** to
let sb see sb; ~**ść mnie do zlewu** let me get to the
sink [2] (zezwolić) ~**ścić kogoś do egzaminu** to
allow sb to sit an exam; ~**ścić kogoś do głosu** to
allow sb to speak; ~**ścić kogoś do tajemnicy** to
let sb in on a secret; **nie** ~**szczę do tego** I won't let
it happen; ~**ścić coś do eksploatacji** to pass sth
as being fit for use; ~**ścić coś do obrotu** to allow
sth onto the market [3] (uznać za możliwe) to allow (for)
[wyjątki, możliwość] [4] (przyjąć do wiadomości) **nie**
~**szczać do siebie przykrych myśli** to reject
unpleasant thoughts

[] **dopuścić się** — **dopuszczać się** (popełnić) to
commit, to perpetrate *[zbrodni, zdrady]*

dorabiać *impf* → **dorobić**

doradc|a *m* adviser; ~**y prezydenta do spraw
bezpieczeństwa narodowego** national security
advisers to the President; **gniew jest złym** ~**ą**
przen. anger is poor counsel

doradcz|y *adi. [organ, zespół]* advisory; **z głosem**
~**ym** in an advisory capacity

dora|dzić *pf* — **dora|dzać** *impf vt* to advise
(**komuś coś** sb sth); ~**dzić komuś zrobienie
czegoś** to advise sb to do sth

dorasta|ć *impf vi* to grow up

■ **nie** ~**ć komuś do pięt** pot. to be no match for sb

dorastając|y *adi. [syn, córka]* adolescent, teenage;
~**a młodzież** teenagers, adolescents

doraźn|y *adi.* [1] *[rozwiązanie, środek]* temporary;
[cel, korzyść] short-term; *[potrzeby, sprawy]* immediate; ~**a pomoc** relief; (pierwsza pomoc) first aid
[2] *[postępowanie, sąd]* summary; **rozpatrywać
sprawę w trybie** ~**ym** to try a case summarily

doręczać *impf* → **doręczyć**

doręczyciel *m* postman GB, mailman US, letter-
carrier US

doręczyciel|ka *f* postwoman GB, letter-carrier US

doręcz|yć *pf* — **doręcz|ać** *impf vt* to deliver
[przesyłkę] (**komuś** to sb); ~**yć komuś wezwanie
do sądu** to serve sb with a summons

dorob|ek *m* [1] (mienie) possessions; ~**ek (całego)
życia** all (of) one's possessions; **ten samochód to
cały mój** ~**ek** this car is all I have [2] (twórczość)
work, output, oeuvre; (w nauce) achievements,
accomplishments

■ **być na** ~**ku** pot. to be working one's way up pot.

dor|obić *pf* — **dor|abiać** *impf* [] *vt* (wykonać) to
make; ~**obić klucz** to have another key cut

[] *vi* pot. (zarobić) to earn some extra cash pot.;
~**abiać tłumaczeniami** to earn extra money by
doing translations

[] **dorobić się** — **dorabiać się** pot. [1] (wzbogacić
się) to make a pile pot.; ~**obić się majątku** to
make a fortune [2] (osiągnąć) to acquire *[przewiska]*;
~**obić się autorytetu** to gain authority [3] (nabawić
się) to give oneself *[kataru, grypy]*

dorodn|y *adi. [osoba, zwierzę]* fine-looking, healthy-
looking; *[owoc]* ripe

doro|sły [] *adi. [osoba]* adult, grown-up; *[zwierzę]*
adult, full-grown; *[zachowanie]* mature

[] **doro|sły** *m*, ~**sła** *f* adult, grown-up; **tylko dla**
~**słych** adults only

dorówn|ać *pf* — **dorówn|ywać** *impf vi* ~**ać
komuś** to equal a. rival sb (**w czymś** in sth); **nie**
~**ywać czemuś** to not compare with sth

dorsz *m* cod(fish)

dor|wać *pf* — **dor|ywać** *impf* pot. [] *vt* to get a. lay
one's hands on pot.

[] **dorwać się** — **dorywać się** (dobrać się) ~**wać**

się do władzy to seize power; **~wać się do cukierków** to have a go at the sweets pot.

dorywcz|y *adi. [działanie, pomoc]* occasional; *[praca]* casual

dorzecz|e *n* catchment area, river basin

dorzu|cić *pf* — **dorzu|cać** *impf* **[I]** *vt* [1] (dołożyć) to throw in, to add; **~cić polan do ogniska** to throw more logs onto the fire [2] (do celu) to throw (**coś do czegoś** sth as far as sth) [3] (dopowiedzieć) to throw in, to add

[II] dorzucić się — **dorzucać się** pot. (dołożyć się) to chip in (**do czegoś** towards sth)

dosadn|y *adi.* (wymowny) *[zdanie, sformułowanie]* blunt; (wulgarny) *[język, słowo]* crude

dosi|ąść *pf* — **dosi|adać** *impf* **[I]** *vi* to mount *[konia]*; to get on *[motocykla, roweru]*

[II] dosiąść się — **dosiadać się** to sit (down) (**do kogoś** next to sb); **~adł się do naszego stolika** he joined us at the table; **czy mogę się ~ąść?** may I join you?

dosięg|nąć *pf* — **dosięg|ać** *impf vt* [1] (dotknąć) to reach ((**do) czegoś** sth); to get at ((**do) czegoś** sth) [2] przen. (doświadczyć) to affect; **~nie cię kara** you won't escape punishment

doskonale [I] *adv.* znać się **~ na czymś** to be an expert on sth; **mówić ~ po polsku** to speak excellent Polish; **czuć się ~** to feel great pot.; **~ o tym wiesz** you know that perfectly well; **znam go ~** I know him very well; **~, że...** it's great that...

[II] *inter.* excellent!, fine!

doskonal|ić *impf* **[I]** *vt* to perfect *[umiejętność, grę]*

[II] doskonalić się *[technika, umiejętności]* to develop; *[osoba]* to improve

doskona|ły *adi. grad. [metoda, wino, zawodnik]* excellent; *[wynik]* outstanding; *[słuch, wzrok]* perfect; **zbrodnia ~ła** the perfect crime

dosłownie *adv.* literally; *[tłumaczyć]* word for word

dosłown|y *adi.* literal; *[przekład]* word for word

dosłysz|eć *pf vt* to hear, to catch; **nie ~ałem, co mówił** I didn't catch what he was saying

dosta|ć *pf* — **dosta|wać** *impf* **[I]** *vt* [1] (otrzymać) to get *[prezent]*; to get, to receive *[list, odpowiedź]*; **~ć jeść/pić** to get a. be given something to eat/drink; **na chrzcie ~ł imię Stefan** he was christened Stefan; **~ł dwa lata za włamanie** he got two years for breaking and entering; **nie mógł ~ć pracy** he couldn't get a job; **~liśmy trzy dni na przeprowadzkę** we've been given three days to move house [2] (kupić) to get; **nie mogę ~ć ich pierwszej płyty** I can't find their first record [3] (złapać) to get, to catch; **~ć kogoś w swoje ręce** to get a. lay one's hands on sb pot.; **żywego mnie nie ~ną** they won't take me alive

[II] *vi* [1] pot. (odebrać cios) to get one pot.; **~ć w twarz** to get one a. it in the face pot.; **~ć po głowie** to get hit on the head; **~ć za swoje** to get what one

deserves [2] (nabawić się) **~ć grypy/gorączki** to come down with the flu/a fever; **~ć zawału** to have a heart attack; **cholery można ~ć!** przen., posp. it's enough to drive you up the wall! pot. [3] (sięgać) to reach (**do czegoś** sth); **głową prawie ~wał sufitu** his head almost touched the ceiling

[III] dostać się — **dostawać się** to get (**do czegoś** (in)to sth); **ledwo ~łam się do autobusu** I barely managed to get on (the bus); **jak ~ć się stąd na dworzec** how do I get to the station from here?; **~ć się do niewoli** to be taken captive a. prisoner; **~ć się na studia** to be admitted to university

dostarcz|yć *pf* — **dostarcz|ać** *impf vt* [1] (przywieźć) to deliver (**coś komuś** sth to sb); to supply (**komuś czegoś** sb with sth) [2] (być źródłem) to provide (**komuś czegoś** sb with sth)

dostatecznie *adv.* sufficiently, adequately; **jesteś ~ dorosły** you're old enough

dostateczn|y [I] *adi.* [1] *[ilość, powód]* sufficient, adequate [2] Szkol. **ocena ~a** ≈ pass mark, ≈ C

[II] *m* Szkol. ≈ pass mark, ≈ C

dostat|ek *m* [1] (dobrobyt) affluence; **żyć w ~ku** to be wealthy; **opływać w ~ki** to live in the lap of luxury [2] przest. (obfitość) abundance (**czegoś** of sth); **pod ~kiem** in abundance

dostatni *adi. grad.* affluent

dostaw|a *f* [1] (zaopatrzenie) delivery; (gazu, prądu, wody) supply [2] (dostarczane produkty) supplies

dostawać *impf* → **dostać**

dostaw|ca *m*, **~czyni** *f* supplier; **~ca Internetu** Internet provider

dost|ąpić *pf* — **dost|ępować** *impf vi* książk. to gain, to attain *[łaski, zbawienia]*

dostęp *m* access (**do czegoś** to sth); **kraj bez ~u do morza** a landlocked country

dostępn|y *adi. grad.* [1] *[towar, informacje]* accessible; **lek ~y bez recepty** a drug available over the counter [2] *[miejsce]* accessible, easy to reach

dostępować *impf* → **dostąpić**

dostojni|k *m* dignitary; **wysoki ~k kościelny** a high-ranking church official

dostojn|y *adi. grad. [osoba, ruchy]* dignified, stately; *[gość]* honourable GB, honorable US

dostos|ować *pf* — **dostos|owywać** *impf* **[I]** *vt* to adapt (**coś do czegoś** sth for a. to sth); to adjust (**coś do czegoś** sth to sth)

[II] dostosować się — **dostosowywać się** to adapt (oneself) (**do czegoś** to sth); to adjust (**do czegoś** to sth)

dostrze|c *pf* — **dostrze|gać** *impf vt* [1] (dojrzeć) to spot [2] przen. (uświadomić sobie) to discern, to perceive

dostrzegaln|y *adi.* discernible, perceptible

dosu|nąć¹ *pf* — **dosu|wać** *impf vt* (przysunąć) **~nąć coś do czegoś** to push sth up to sth; **akapit ~nięty do lewego marginesu** a paragraph aligned with a. to the left margin

dosu|nąć² *pf vi* (uderzyć) pot. **~nąć komuś** to work sb over pot.

dosyć → **dość**

doszczętnie *adv.* completely

doszuk|ać się *pf* — **doszuk|iwać się** *impf v refl.* **~ać się czegoś** to discern sth *[podobieństw, prawdy]*; to detect sth *[błędów]*; **~iwać się czegoś** to suspect sth

dościg|nąć *pf* — **dościg|ać** *impf vt* [1] (dogonić) to catch up (**kogoś** with sb) [2] przen. (dorównać) to equal (**kogoś w czymś** sb in sth)

dość [1] *adv.* [1] (w pewnym stopniu) quite, rather; **~ dawno temu** quite a long time ago; **~ łatwo można udowodnić, że...** it's fairly easy to prove that...; **ona ~ dobrze zna niemiecki** she knows German quite well [2] (wystarczająco) enough; **~ długi** long enough; **nie ~ wysoko** not high enough [2] *pron.* enough; **mam ~ zmartwień bez tego** I've got enough worries as it is [3] *praed.* **~ powiedzieć, że...** suffice it to say (that)... [4] *inter.* (that's) enough!; **~ tego dobrego!** enough's enough! [5] **~ że** *coni.* **nie ~, że..., to jeszcze...** not only..., but also... ■ **mieć kogoś ~** to be fed up with sb, to have had enough of sb

dośrodkowa|nie *n* Sport centre GB, center US, cross

doświadczaln|y *adi.* experimental

doświadcze|nie *n* [1] (praktyka) experience; **mieć ~nie w czymś** to be experienced in sth; **pracownik z piętnastoletnim ~niem** an employee with fifteen years' experience; **wiedział z ~nia, że...** he knew from experience that... [2] (przeżycie) experience; **nauczona smutnym ~niem...** taught by bitter experience... [3] (eksperyment) experiment; **przeprowadzić ~nie** to carry out an experiment; **~nia na zwierzętach** animal experiments

doświadcz|ony *adi.* *[lekarz, kierowca]* experienced; *[oko, ręka, ucho]* practised GB, practiced US

doświadcz|yć *pf* — **doświadcz|ać** *impf vt* to experience *[bólu, głodu]*; **los go ciężko ~ył** książk. life has tried him sorely książk.

dotacj|a *f* subsidy (**na coś** to a. for sth), grant (**na coś** for a. towards sth)

dotąd *pron.* [1] (do tego momentu) (up) until a. till now, up to now; (do tamtego momentu) (up) until a. till then, up to then; **jak ~** so far; (w przeszłości) until a. till then; **~ prosił, aż się zgodziła** he kept on asking her until she agreed [2] (wciąż jeszcze) still; **~ jest za granicą** he is still abroad [3] (do tego miejsca) this far; (do tamtego miejsca) that far; **przeczytaj ~** read up to here; **odległość stąd ~** the distance from there to here

dotkliw|y *adv. grad.* *[ból, brak, strata]* acute; *[zimno, wiatr]* biting

dot|knąć *pf* — **dot|ykać** *impf vt* [1] (ręką, palcem) to touch (**czegoś** sth) [2] (poruszyć w rozmowie) to touch (up)on *[problemu, sprawy]* [3] (urazić) to hurt, to wound; **~knąć kogoś do żywego** to cut sb to the quick [4] (doświadczyć) *[choroba, klęska]* to afflict

dotle|nić *pf* — **dotle|niać** *impf* [1] *vt* to oxygenate *[wodę, krew]*; to ventilate *[pacjenta]* [2] **dotlenić się** — **dotleniać się** pot. *[osoba]* to get some fresh air

dot|ować *pf, impf vt* to subsidize

dotrwa|ć *pf vi* to survive; **~ć do naszych czasów** to survive to this day

do|trzeć *pf* — **do|cierać** *impf* [1] *vt* to run in *[silnik, samochód]* [2] *vi* to reach (**do czegoś** sth); to get (**do czegoś** to sth); **dotrzeć do finału** to get through to the finals; **dotrzeć do źródła informacji** to get to the source of the information; **dotarła do nas pogłoska, że...** we heard a rumour that...; **dotarło do niego, że...** he realized that... [3] **dotrzeć się** — **docierać się** *[silnik, samochód]* to be run in

dotrzym|ać *pf* — **dotrzym|ywać** *impf vt* to fulfil GB, to fulfill US *[umowy]*; to meet *[warunków]*; **~ać słowa/obietnicy** to keep one's word/promise; **~ać terminu** to meet the deadline

dotychczas *adv.* up to now, so far; **jak ~** so far, to date; **więcej niż ~** more than before

dotychczasow|y *adi.* (ten, co dotąd) current; (poprzedni) former, previous; **jego ~e osiągnięcia** his achievements to date a. up to now; **na ~ych zasadach** on the same basis as before

dotycz|yć *pf vi [dyskusja, wykład]* to relate (**kogoś/czegoś** to sb/sth); to concern (**kogoś/czegoś** sb/sth); *[przepis, prawo]* to apply (**kogoś/czegoś** to sb/sth)

dotyk *m* [1] (dotknięcie) touch; **miękki w ~u** soft to the touch [2] (zmysł) (the sense of) touch

dotykać *impf* → **dotknąć**

doustn|y *adi. [lekarstwo, szczepionka]* oral

dowartości|ować *pf* — **dowartości|o-wywać** *impf* [1] *vt* **~ować kogoś** to boost a. bolster sb's confidence [2] **dowartościować się** — **dowartościowywać się** to feel (more) appreciated

dowcip *m* [1] (żart) joke; **~ rysunkowy** a cartoon; **opowiedzieć ~** to tell a joke; **zrobić komuś ~** to play a joke a. trick on sb; **sypać ~ami** to crack jokes pot. [2] (poczucie humoru) wit; **mieć cięty ~** to have a sharp wit ■ **~ (cały) polega na tym, że...** the snag a. hitch is that... pot.

dowcipk|ować *impf vi* to joke, to crack jokes

dowcipni|ś *m* joker

dowcipn|y *adi. grad.* witty

dowi|edzieć się *pf* — **dowi|adywać się** *impf*
v refl. to learn, to find out (**o czymś** about sth);
~**edzieć się czegoś** to learn a. find out sth;
jak się o tym ~**edziałeś?** how did you find that
out?; ~**edziałem się, że wyjeżdżasz** I hear you're
leaving; ~**adywać się o kogoś** to ask about sb

dow|ieść *pf* — **dow|odzić**[1] *impf* **[]** *vt* to prove
[teorii, zarzutów]; to prove, to establish *[winy,
niewinności, słuszności]*; ~**ieść, że ktoś ma rację/
myli się** to prove sb right/wrong; **autor** ~**odzi,
że...** the author argues that...

[] *vi* (świadczyć) to prove, to show; **badania** ~**odzą,
że...** research shows that...; **ich zachowanie**
~**odzi braku wyobraźni** their behaviour demon-
strates a lack imagination

dow|ieźć *pf* — **dow|ozić** *impf vt* to bring

dowodzić[1] *impf* → **dowieść**

dow|odzić[2] *impf vt* to command, to be in
command of *[oddziałem, armią]*; to lead *[powsta-
niem]*

dowoln|y *adi.* [1] (swobodny) *[temat, przekład]* free
[2] (jakikolwiek) *[liczba, miejsce]* any

dow|ód *m* [1] (potwierdzenie) proof, evidence; ~**ody
poszlakowe** circumstantial evidence; ~**ód rzeczowy** material evidence; **dać** ~**ód odwagi** to
prove one's courage; **na** ~**ód przytoczył kilka
przykładów** as evidence he cited several examples;
w a. **na** ~**ód uznania** as a token a. in token of one's
appreciation [2] (dokument) certificate; (dostawy, zakupu)
receipt; ~**ód tożsamości** identification; ~**ód
osobisty** identity card; ~**ód rejestracyjny** (vehicle) registration document, logbook GB

dowódc|a *m* (wódz) commander; (oficer dowodzący)
commanding officer; **naczelny** ~**a** commander-
in-chief

dowództw|o *n* [1] (władza) command; **objąć** ~**o
czegoś** to take command of sth; **sprawować** ~**o
czegoś** to be in command of sth; **pod** ~**em kogoś**
under sb's command [2] (zespół dowódców) command
[3] (siedziba) headquarters

doz|a *f* dose; **pewna** ~**a nieufności** a certain
amount of mistrust; **z dużą** ~**ą prawdopodobieństwa** in all likelihood

dozna|ć *pf* — **dozna|wać** *impf vt* [1] to experi-
ence *[bólu, radości]*; ~**ć olśnienia** to have a flash of
insight [2] to suffer *[porażki, kontuzji, obrażeń]*

dozna|nie *n* experience

doznawać *impf* → **doznać**

dozorc|a *m* [1] (gospodarz domu) caretaker, janitor US
[2] (na parkingu) attendant; (na budowie) watchman; (w
więzieniu) warder GB, guard US; (w parku, zoo) keeper

dozorczy|ni *f* caretaker, janitor US

doz|ować *impf vt [automat]* to dispense; *[lekarz]* to
dose

doz|ór *m* [1] książk. (nadzór) supervision (**nad kimś/
czymś** over sb/sth); **sprawować** ~**ór nad czymś**
to supervise a. oversee sth; **pozostawić kogoś bez**

~**oru** to leave sb unattended [2] (instytucja) supervis-
ory staff; **pracownik** ~**oru technicznego** a
technical supervisor

doży|ć *pf* — **doży|wać** *impf vi* to live to see
[spełnienia, sukcesu]; to reach *[starości, późnego wieku]*;
on nie ~**je jutra** he won't last a. live through the
night; ~**ć osiemdziesiątki** to live to be eighty;
~**wać swoich lat na wsi** to live out one's days in
the country; **jeśli** ~**ję** if I live that long

dożyln|y *adi.* intravenous

dożyn|ki *plt* harvest festival a. home

dożywać *impf* → **dożyć**

dożywoci|e *n* pot. (kara) life pot.; **dostać** ~**e** to get
life

dożywotni *adi. [więzienie, renta]* life; *[stanowisko,
dyskwalifikacja]* lifetime

d|ół **[]** *m* [1] (w ziemi) hole; (głębszy) pit [2] (dolna część)
(schodów, szafy) bottom; (budynku) downstairs, ground
floor; (twarzy, pleców, ściany) lower part; **na dole** a. **u
dołu strony** at the bottom of the page; **zejść na
dół** (po schodach) to go downstairs; (zboczem) to go
downhill; **schodzić/zjeżdżać w dół** to go down, to
descend; **mieszkać na dole** (niżej) to live downstairs; (na parterze) to live on the ground floor;
zadzwonić z dołu to phone from downstairs; **ból
w dole pleców** a pain in the lower back; **dół
spódnicy** the hem of a skirt; **leżeć w dole rzeki** to
lie downstream; **z góry do dołu** *[przeczytać]* all the
way through; *[sprawdzić]* from top to bottom;
zmierzyć kogoś wzrokiem od góry do dołu to
look sb up and down; **ceny idą** a. **lecą w dół** prices
are going down; **wynagrodzenie płatne z dołu**
salary paid in arrears

[] **doły** *plt* pot. (społeczne) hoi polloi; riffraff pot.;
(partyjne, związkowe) grass roots

drabin|a *f* (ze szczeblami) ladder także przen.; (składana,
ze stopniami) stepladder; **wchodzić po** ~**ie** to climb
a. go up a ladder; **schodzić po** ~**ie** to go down a
ladder; ~**a społeczna** the social ladder

drabin|ka *f* (gimnastyczna) wall bars

dra|ka *f* pot. rumpus pot.; **zrobić coś dla** ~**ki** to do
sth for laughs pot.

drama|t *m* [1] drama [2] przen. tragedy; **robić** ~**t
z czegoś** to make a big thing out of sth

dramatur|g *m* dramatist, playwright

dramatyczn|y *adi. grad.* dramatic

dra|ń *m* bastard posp.

drapacz *m* ~ **chmur** skyscraper

drap|ać *impf* **[]** *vt* [1] (skrobać) to scratch [2] (drażnić)
dym ~**ie mnie w oczy** smoke makes my eyes itch;
~**ie mnie w gardle** I have a tickle in my throat

[] **drapać się** [1] (skrobać się) to scratch oneself; ~**ać
się w głowę** to scratch one's head [2] (wspinać się)
~**ać się na coś** to scramble up sth

drapak *m* pot. [1] (choinka) thin, shabby Christmas
tree [2] (szczotka) worn-out brush

■ dać ~**a** to skedaddle pot.

drapieżni|k *m* (zwierzę) predator, beast of prey; (ptak) bird of prey

drapieżn|y *adi. grad.* predatory; **ptaki/zwierzęta** ~**e** birds/beasts of pray

dra|snąć *pf* **[I]** *vt* [pocisk, strzała] to graze; [osoba] to nick
[II] drasnąć się to nick oneself; ~**snąć się w palec** to cut one's finger

drastyczn|y *adi. grad.* [1] [opis, scena] graphic [2] [środki, redukcja] drastic

draśnię|cie *n* graze

drażet|ka *f* [1] (cukierek) drop [2] (tabletka) (coated) tablet; (do ssania) lozenge

drażliw|y *adi. grad.* [kwestia, sytuacja] touchy; [misja] sensitive; [osoba, charakter] (over)sensitive, touchy

drażni|ć *impf* **[I]** *vt* [1] (irytować) to annoy, to irritate [2] (dokuczać) to tease [osobę, zwierzę] [3] (szkodzić) to irritate [oczy, skórę]
[II] drażnić się to tease (**z kimś** sb)

drąg *m* pole, bar

drąż|ek *m* [1] (pręt) rod [2] Sport, Taniec bar
❏ ~**ek sterowy** Lotn. control column; joystick pot.

drąż|yć *impf vt* [1] to sink [szyb, studnię]; to bore [tunel] [2] to core [jabłko, gruszkę]; to pit [oliwki, wiśnie]; to hollow (out) [drewno] [3] to go a. delve (deeper) into [temat, kwestię]
■ **kropla** ~**y skałę** przysł. ≈ little by little does the trick

drelich *m* [1] (tkanina) drill [2] (ubranie robocze) work clothes; (strój więzienny) prison garb a. clothes

dren *m* drain

dren|ować *impf vt* to drain [grunt, ranę]; ~**ować rynek** przen. to drain the market

drep|tać *impf vi* [dziecko] to toddle around; [dorosły] to take short steps; (nienaturalnie) to mince (about a. around)

dres *m* tracksuit, sweatsuit; (ortalionowy) shell suit

dreszcz *m* shiver; **mieć** ~**e** to be shivering; **przyprawiać kogoś o** ~**e** to send shivers up a. down sb's spine; ~ **mnie przechodzi na samą myśl, że...** I shiver at the thought that...

dreszczow|iec *m* thriller

drewniak *m* clog

drewnian|y *adi.* [1] [beczka, dom, mebel] wooden; [belka, konstrukcja] timber [2] [dźwięk] wooden; [głos, śmiech] hollow [3] przen. [nogi, palce, ruchy] stiff

drew|no *n* [1] wood; (budowlane) timber; ~**no na opał** firewood; **szafa z dębowego** ~**na** an oak wardrobe [2] (tkanka) xylem

dręcz|yć *impf* **[I]** *vt* to torment; ~**yć kogoś pytaniami** to pester a. plague sb with questions; ~**y go poczucie winy** he's (w)racked with guilt; ~**ące pytanie** a persistent question; ~**ący strach** gnawing fear
[II] dręczyć się [1] (siebie samego) to agonize (**czymś**

over sth); to torment oneself (**czymś** with sth) [2] (jeden drugiego) to torment each other

drętwi|eć *impf vi* [kończyna] to become numb; [kark] to stiffen (up)

drętw|y *adi.* [1] [kończyna] numb [2] pot. [osoba, przemówienie, przyjęcie] dull, boring; [zachowanie] stiff, formal

drgać¹ *impf* → **drgnąć¹**

drga|ć² *impf vi* [1] [światło, blask] to shimmer; [głos, dźwięk] to tremble [2] Fiz. [fala, wahadło] to oscillate

drgaw|ki *plt* convulsions; **dostać** ~**ek** to go into convulsions

drg|nąć¹ *pf* — **drg|ać¹** *impf vi* [powieka, mięsień] to twitch; [budynek, grunt] to shudder

drg|nąć² *pf vi* to twitch; **ani** ~**nąć** to not (even) budge

drink *m* (alcoholic) drink

drobiazg *m* [1] (przedmiot) knick-knack, nick-nack [2] (błahostka) trifle; „**dziękuję ci bardzo**" –„~" 'thanks a lot' – 'don't mention it'

drobiazgow|y *adi.* [1] [badania, przygotowania] meticulous, painstaking; [opis, analiza] detailed [2] [osoba] pedantic

drobiow|y *adi.* [filety, farma] poultry; **podroby** ~**e** giblets

drobn|o *adv. grad.* [kroić, siekać] fine(ly); [zmielony, pocięty] finely; ~**o zadrukowany** in fine a. small print

drobnomieszczańs|ki *adi.* petit a. petty bourgeois pejor.

drobnomieszczaństw|o *n* the petite a. petty bourgeoisie, the lower middle class

drobnost|ka *f* mere trifle

drobnoustr|ój *m* micro-organism

drobn|y **[I]** *adi. grad.* [1] [przedmiot, suma, ilość] small; [deszcz, pył, siatka] fine; [piasek, sól] fine-grained; **pieniądze na** ~**e wydatki** pocket money [2] [osoba, budowa] slight; [kobieta] petite; [figura] diminutive [3] [inwestor, przedsiębiorca] small; [oszust] petty, small-time [4] [szansa] slight; [błąd, zmiana] minor
[II] drobne *plt* small change; **rozmienić banknot na** ~**e** to change a banknote

dr|oga **[I]** *f* [1] road; (wąska, wiejska) lane; (leśna) track; **droga szybkiego ruchu** a. **ekspresowa** through route GB, clearway GB, throughway US, expressway [2] (szlak komunikacyjny) **droga wodna** waterway; **drogą morską/lotniczą/kolejową** by sea/air/rail; **drogą lądową** overland [3] (kierunek) way; (trasa) route; **po drodze** on the a. one's way, along the way; **po** a. **w drodze do Dublina** on the way a. en route to Dublin; **to mi nie po drodze** it's out of my way; **pytać kogoś o drogę** to ask sb the way; **wskazać komuś drogę** to show sb the way; **pomylić drogę** to go the wrong way; **planować drogę ucieczki** to plan an escape route; **droga do sławy/sukcesu** przen. the road to fame/success; **ich drogi się rozeszły** przen. they've drifted apart [4] (podróż) way;

dzień drogi od miasta (piechotą) a day's march from town; (samochodem) a day's drive from town; **być w drodze** to be on one's a. the way; **jedzenie na drogę** food for the journey; **ruszać w drogę** to set off a. out (on a journey); **być gotowym do drogi** to be ready to set off a. out; **w drodze powrotnej** on the way back; **w drogę!** time to go!; **szerokiej drogi!** have a safe journey a. trip! ⑤ (możność poruszania się) **ustąpić komuś drogi** to give way to sb; **odciąć komuś drogę** to cut sb off; **z drogi!** get out of the way!; **droga wolna!** przen. (rób jak chcesz) suit yourself! ⑥ (sposób) way; (tryb) channel; **najlepsza droga do zrobienia czegoś** the best way to do sth; **drogą dyplomatyczną/służbową** through diplomatic/official channels; **wstąpić na drogę prawną** to take legal action; **w drodze wyjątku** by way of exception, as an exception; **drogą radiową** over the radio; **choroby przenoszone drogą płciową** sexually transmitted diseases

Ⅱ drogi plt Med. (moczowe, łzowe, żółciowe) ducts; **drogi oddechowe** airway

❑ **Droga Krzyżowa** Relig. the Way of the Cross; **Droga Mleczna** Astron. the Milky Way

■ **swoją drogą...** (and) anyway... pot.; **być na dobrej/złej drodze** to be on the right/wrong track; **chadzać własnymi drogami** to go one's own way; **sprowadzić kogoś na złą drogę** to lead sb astray; **zejść na złą drogę** to stray from the straight and narrow; **komu w drogę, temu czas** time to hit the road a. trail US pot.; **wstąpił do piekieł, po drodze mu było** przysł. ≈ he couldn't have gone a longer way round; **wszystkie drogi prowadzą do Rzymu** przysł. all roads lead to Rome przysł.

drogeri|a f ≈ chemist GB, ≈ drugstore US

dro|gi adi. grad. ① (kosztowny) [towar, usługa, hotel] expensive; **~gie kamienie** precious stones; **każda chwila jest ~ga** every moment is precious ② (bliski) dear; **ludzie, którzy są nam ~dzy** those dear to us, **rzeczy, które są mu ~gie** things he holds dear ③ (w zwrotach grzecznościowych) dear; **~dzy przyjaciele** (my) dear friends; **Drogi Adamie!** (w liście) Dear Adam; **~dzy państwo!** ladies and gentlemen!; **moja ~ga** my dear; **mój najdroższy** my darling

dro|go adv. grad. [kupić, sprzedać] at a high price; [kosztować, zapłacić] a lot; **~go za coś zapłacić** przen. to pay dearly for sth; **~go kogoś kosztować** przen. to cost sb dear a. dearly

drogocenn|y adi. grad. valuable, precious

drogowskaz m signpost

drogow|y adi. [mapa, transport, wypadek] road; [policja, zator] traffic; **roboty ~e** roadworks; **światła ~e** full beam headlights GB, high beams US; **wykroczenie ~e** a driving a. traffic offence; **znaki ~e** traffic a. road signs

drogów|ka f pot. traffic police

dromade|r m dromedary

drops m (owocowy) fruit drop; (miętowy) mint

dro|zd m thrush; **~zd śpiewak** song thrush

drożdż|e plt yeast

■ **rosnąć jak na ~ach** to shoot up

drożdżow|y adi. Kulin. [ekstrakt] yeast; [zapach, smak] yeasty; **babka ~a** a leavened pound cake

drożdżów|ka f ≈ teacake, ≈ bun

droż|eć impf vi [towar, usługi] to become dearer, to go up (in price); [koszty] to rise, to go up

droży|zna f pot. high prices

dr|ób m poultry

dróż|ka f track, path

dróżni|k m, **~czka** f level GB a. grade US crossing attendant

drucian|y adi. [szczotka, siatka] wire

dru|gi Ⅰ num. ord. second; **co ~gi dzień** every other a. second day; **na ~gi dzień/tydzień** the following a. next day/week; **a na ~gi raz...** pot. next time...; **po ~gie...** secondly...

Ⅱ adi. ① (jeden z dwóch) [brzeg, strona, koniec] (the) other; (wspomniany później) the latter ② (mniej ważny) second; **obywatel ~giej kategorii** a second-class citizen

Ⅲ pron. (inny) the other; **bronić ~gich** to defend the others

Ⅳ **drugie** n (danie) main course GB, entrée US; **na ~gie było** risotto the main course was risotto

■ **moja ~ga ojczyzna** my adopted country; **moje ~gie ja** my alter ego; **~gie tyle** (o ludziach, przedmiotach) the same number (again); (o substancjach, zjawiskach) the same amount (again)

drugoplanow|y adi. [szczegół] background; [rola, aktor] supporting

drugorzędn|y adi. ① (mniej ważny) secondary, minor ② (gorszy) second-class, second-rate

druh m ① (harcerz) ≈ scout; **~ zastępowy/drużynowy** ≈ a patrol/troop leader ② książk. (przyjaciel) familiar

druh|na f ① (na weselu) bridesmaid ② (harcerka) ≈ girl guide GB, ≈ girl scout US

druk m ① (proces) press, printing; **tekst jest gotowy do ~u** the text is ready to go to press; **ukazać się ~iem** to appear in print; **wydać a. ogłosić coś ~iem** to print a. publish sth ② (czcionka) print, type ③ (technika) printing; **~ wielobarwny** colour a. process printing ④ (powielony materiał) printed matter; (formularz) form; (odbitka) print; **stare ~i** old prints; **~i reklamowe** handbills, flyers; **„~"** (na kopercie) 'Printed matter'

drukar|ka f printer; **~ka atramentowa/igłowa/laserowa** ink-jet/dot matrix/laser printer

drukar|nia f printing house; (mniejsza) print shop

drukars|ki adi. [maszyna, przemysł] printing; **błąd ~ki** misprint

drukarz m printer

druk|ować *impf vt* [1] *(osoba, drukarka)* to print [2] *[gazeta, wydawca, autor]* to publish; **powieść** ~**owana w odcinkach** a serialized novel, a novel in instalments

drukowan|y *adi. [książka, tekst, wzór]* printed; **pisać** ~**ymi literami** to write in block capitals

dru|t *m* [1] (metalowy) wire; ~**t kolczasty** barbed wire; ~**ty wysokiego napięcia** high tension a. voltage wire [2] (do robienia swetrów) knitting needle; **robić szalik na** ~**tach** to knit a scarf; **sweter zrobiony na** ~**tach** a hand-knitted sweater

■ **pogoda jak** ~**t** pot. fantastic a. brilliant weather pot.; **prosty jak** ~**t** pot. (as) easy a. simple as ABC

drużb|a *m* best man

druż|ka *f* bridesmaid

drużyn|a *f* [1] (sportowa) team; (ratownicza) party, team; (harcerska) ≈ troop; ~**a gospodarzy/gości** the home/visiting team [2] Wojsk. squad

drwal *m* woodcutter, lumberjack US

drwiąc|y *adi.* sneering, derisive

drwi|ć *impf vi* to mock (**z czegoś** sth); to sneer (**z czegoś** at sth); ~**ć (sobie) z niebezpieczeństwa** to laugh in the face of danger

drwin|a *f* mockery, derision; **być przedmiotem** ~ to be a laughing stock

drybl|ować *impf* Sport **I** *vt* to dribble past, to outdribble *[obrońców]*
II *vi* to dribble

dryf|ować *impf vi* to drift

dryl *m* (w wojsku) drill; (w domu, szkole) strict discipline

dryl|ować *impf vt* to stone GB, to pit US

drzaz|ga *f* splinter; (do rozpalania) splint

■ **strzaskać** a. **rozbić coś na** a. **w** ~**gi** to reduce sth to matchwood

d|rzeć *impf* **I** *vt* [1] (niszczyć) to tear *[papier, materiał]* [2] (zużywać) to wear out *[ubrania, buty]* [3] pot., przen. **drzeć z kogoś skórę** a. **pieniądze** to rip sb off pot. [4] pot. (boleć) *[staw]* to throb with pain
II **drzeć się** [1] (niszczyć się) *[materiał, papier]* to tear [2] (zużywać się) *[ubrania, buty]* to wear out [3] pot. (krzyczeć) to bawl; (ze złością) to bellow (**na kogoś** at sb); **drzeć gębę** a. **mordę** to bowl a. head one's head off pot.

drzem|ać *impf vi* [1] to doze; to snooze pot. [2] przen. *[siły, talent]* to lie dormant (**w kimś** in sb); ~**iące w nim możliwości** his latent talents

drzem|ka *f* (cat)nap; snooze pot.; **uciąć sobie** ~**kę** to take a little nap; **zapaść w** ~**kę** to doze off

drzewn|y *adi. [przemysł]* timber; *[wióry]* wood

drzew|o *n* [1] Bot. tree; ~**a iglaste/liściaste** coniferous/deciduous trees [2] (materiał) wood; ~**o bukowe/dębowe** beech/oak; ~**o na opał** firewood

❑ ~**o genealogiczne** family a. genealogical tree

■ ~**o wiadomości dobrego i złego** Bibl. the tree of knowledge (of good and evil); **na pochyłe** ~**o**

wszystkie kozy skaczą przysł. ≈ it's easy to kick someone when they're down

drzewory|t *m* woodcut, wood engraving

drzwi *plt* [1] (zamknięcie) door; ~ **do kuchni** kitchen/stable door; **dwoje/troje** ~ two/three doors; **otworzyć komuś** ~ to open the door for sb; **mieszkać z kimś** ~ **w** ~ to live across from a. opposite sb; **zamknąć/zatrzasnąć komuś** ~ **przed nosem** to shut/slam the door in sb's face; **zamknąć przed kimś** ~ to shut the door on sb także przen.; **wyrzucić kogoś za** ~ to throw a. turn sb out; „**nie trzaskać** ~**ami**" 'don't slam the door'; **przy** ~**ach otwartych** *[rozprawa]* in open court; **przy** ~**ach zamkniętych** a. **za zamkniętymi** ~**ami** behind closed doors, in camera [2] (otwór) doorway; **stanąć w** ~**ach** to stand in the doorway

■ **cisnąć się** ~**ami i oknami** pot. to flock; **dostać się tylnymi** ~**ami** to sneak in by a. through the back door; **pokazać komuś** ~ to show sb the door; **nie kładź palca między** ~ don't stick your neck out

drż|eć *impf vi [osoba]* to tremble, to shiver; *[dom, samolot]* to shudder; *[głos]* to quaver, to quiver; *[światło, płomień]* to waver, to flicker; ~**ącym głosem** in a trembling a. shiver with cold; ~**ącym głosem** in a tremulous a. tremulous voice; ~**eć o kogoś** to fear for sb; ~**eć przed kimś** to be terrified of sb

dubbing /'dabiŋ/ *m* dubbing; **filmy z** ~**iem** dubbed films

dubbing|ować /dabiŋ'govatɕ/ *impf vt* to dub

duble|r *m*, ~**rka** *f* Kino double, stand-in; Teatr understudy

dubl|ować *impf vt* [1] Teatr to understudy; Kino to stand in for [2] Sport to lap [3] (podwajać) to double *[stawkę, liczbę]*

duch *m* [1] (zjawa) ghost, spirit; **w** ~**y wierzysz!** iron. you'll believe anything! [2] Relig. spirit; ~**y przodków** ancestral spirits; **on jest twoim złym** ~**em** he's a bad influence on you; **wyzionąć** ~**a** pot. to give up the ghost [3] (usposobienie) spirit, mind; (nastrój) spirits; **śmiać się w** ~**u** to laugh up one's sleeve; **młody** ~**em** young at heart; **podnieść kogoś na** ~**u** to raise sb's spirits [4] (nastawienie) spirit; ~ **współpracy/wspólnoty** team/community spirit; **w** ~**u** *[wierzyć, sądzić]* in one's heart of hearts; **człowiek wielkiego/małego** ~**a** a courageous/faint-hearted person a. individual; **okazać hart** ~**a** to show spirit; **tracić** ~**a** to lose spirit a. heart; **upadać na** ~**u** to become dispirited; ~ **czasu** the spirit of the times a. age; **iść z** ~**em czasu** to move with the times

❑ **Duch Święty** Relig. the Holy Spirit a. Ghost

■ **ani żywego** ~ not a soul

ducho|ta *f* (w pomieszczeniu) stuffiness; (na dworze) sultry weather

duchowieństw|o *n* clergy

duchown|y [I] *adi. [stan, szaty]* clerical; *[funkcje, obowiązki]* priestly; **seminarium** ~**e** a seminary [II] *m* (ksiądz) clergyman; (zakonnik) monk

duchow|y *adi.* spiritual; **czyjś stan** ~**y** sb's frame of mind

dud|ek *m* hoopoe
■ **wystrychnąć kogoś na** ~**ka** to make a fool of sb

dudni|ć *impf vi [pociąg, koła, grzmot]* to rumble; *[deszcz, grad]* to beat; *[głos, krzyki]* to boom; *[głośnik, muzyka]* to blare

due|t *m* [1] Muz. duet, duo [2] (para) pair

duka|ć *impf vt, vi* (mówić) to stammer (out); (czytać) to falter, to stumble

dum|a *f* pride (**z czegoś** in sth); **być** ~**ą miasta** to be the pride of the town; **rozpierała ją** ~**a** she was bursting with pride; ~**a nie pozwala jej prosić o pomoc** she's too proud to ask for help

duma|ć *impf vi* książk. to ponder (**nad czymś** over sth); to muse (**nad czymś** on sth)

dumn|y *adi.* proud (**z czegoś** of sth)

dup|a *f* wulg. [1] (pośladki) arse GB, ass US posp.; **dać komuś w** ~**ę** to kick sb's arse; **nogi mu z** ~**y powyrywam!** I'll kick the shit out of him! wulg.; **mam to w** ~**ie** I don't give a shit about it posp.; **wsadź to sobie w** ~**ę!** stick a. shove it up your arse! wulg.; **do** ~**y z tym!** screw it! posp.; **to jest do** ~**y** this is just hopeless [2] obraźl. (kobieta) nice bit (of stuff) GB pot., obraźl.; piece of ass US posp., obraźl. [3] pejor. (oferma) arsehole GB, asshole US posp.

duplika|t *m* duplicate; ~**t prawa jazdy** a duplicate driving license

du|r *m* **dur plamisty** typhus, spotted fever; **dur brzuszny** typhoid (fever)

dur|eń *m* pot. fool; **robić z kogoś** ~**nia** to make a fool of sb

durn|y *adi. grad.* pot. dumb pot.

durszlak *m* colander

dusiciel *m* [1] (osoba) strangler [2] Zool. **boa** ~ boa constrictor

du|sić *impf* [I] *vt* [1] (ściskać szyję) to strangle; (zatykać usta i nos) to smother [2] (utrudniać oddychanie) *[dym, zapach]* to stifle, to choke [3] Kulin. to stew *[mięso, warzywa, grzyby]*
[II] **dusić się** [1] to suffocate także przen. [2] Kulin. *[wołowina, jarzyny]* to stew

dusigrosz *m* pot. skinflint, cheapskate pot.

dusz|a *f* soul; **ile** ~**a zapragnie** to one's heart's content; **z całej** ~**y** a. **całą** ~**ą** with all one's heart; **w głębi** ~**y czuł, że...** in his heart of hearts he felt that...; **oddać się czemuś** ~**ą i ciałem** to throw oneself into sth heart and soul; **widzieć coś oczyma** ~**y** to see sth in one's mind's eye; **miałem** ~**ę na ramieniu** my heart was in my mouth; **bratnia** ~**a** a soulmate; ~**a towarzystwa** the life and soul of the party

duszkiem *adv.* **wypić coś** ~ to down sth in one draught GB a. gulp

duszności *plt* breathlessness; **mieć** ~ to be short of breath

duszn|y *adi. [pomieszczenie]* stifling, stuffy; *[dzień]* muggy; przen. *[atmosfera]* stifling, oppressive

dusz|ony *adi.* stewed

duszpasterz *m* priest; ~ **akademicki** university chaplain

dużo [I] *adv. grad. [pić, mówić]* a lot; **za dużo jeść/ mówić** to eat/talk too much; **powinieneś więcej pracować** you should work harder
[II] *adv.* far; **dużo więcej osób** far a. many more people; **dużo więcej miejsca** far a. much more space; **dużo mniej samochodów** far fewer cars; **dużo mniej czasu** far a. much less time; **dużo lepszy/gorszy** far a. much better/worse; **dużo wiesz!** pot., iron. a fat lot you know!
[III] *pron.* (z policzalnymi) many, a lot; (z niepoliczalnymi) much, a lot; **coraz więcej** more and more; **trochę a bit** more; **nie więcej niż sto złotych** 100 zlotys at the most; **więcej niż ładna** more than pretty
[IV] **więcej** *adv. comp.* **więcej tam nie pójdę** I won't a. shan't go there any more; **lubię ją i nic więcej** I like her and that's all
[V] **więcej** *part.* **co więcej...** what's more...
■ **co za dużo, to niezdrowo** przysł. ≈ all things in moderation przysł.

du|ży [I] *adi. grad.* [1] (rozmiarem) *[miasto, przedmiot, posiłek, osoba]* big, large; **kiedy będę duży...** when I grow up... [2] (poważny) *[błąd]* serious; *[skandal]* major; *[zainteresowanie]* great
[II] *adi. [litera]* capital; **duże A/B** a capital A/B

dw|a [I] *num.* two; **zrobić coś dwa razy** to do sth twice; **dwa razy większy/szybszy** twice as big/fast
[II] *n inv.* Szkol. (ocena niedostateczna) ≈ F; (ocena mierna) ≈ E
■ **jeść za dwóch** to eat enough for two; **pracować za dwóch** to do the work of two; **wytłumaczyć coś w dwóch słowach** to explain sth in a couple of words; **bez dwóch zdań** without a doubt; **to dwa kroki stąd** it's just a stone's throw from here; **to proste jak dwa razy dwa cztery** it's as simple as two plus two

dw|adzieścia *num.* twenty

dw|anaście *num.* twelve

dwanaścior|o *num. mult.* twelve

dw|ieście *num.* two hundred

dw|oić się *impf v refl.* **dwoi mi się w oczach** I'm seeing double; **dwoić się i troić, żeby coś zrobić** to go to no end of trouble to do sth

dwojaczk|i *plt* twins

dwoja|ki *adi.* **w** ~**ki sposób** in two ways; **produkty** ~**kiego rodzaju** two kinds of products

dwojako *adv.* in two ways

dwoj|e *num. mult.* two; **wakacje dla** ~**ga** a holiday for two; **robić coś we** ~**e** to do sth together; **złożyć coś na** ~**e** to fold sth in half; **przełamać coś na** ~**e** to break sth in two a. in half; **zgiąć się we** ~**e** to bend double; **jedno z** ~**ga!** one or the other

■ **na** ~**e babka wróżyła** it's anybody's guess

dwo|rzec m station; ~**rzec kolejowy** railway station; ~**rzec autobusowy** bus station a. terminal; ~**rzec lotniczy** airport; **na** ~**rcu** at the station; **wyjść po kogoś na** ~**rzec** to meet sb at the station

dwój|a f pot., Szkol. (niedostateczn) ≈ F; (mierny) ≈ E

dwój|ka f [1] (cyfra) two [2] (niedostateczny) ≈ F; (mierny) ≈ E [3] pot., Aut. second (gear); **jechać** ~**ką** to be in second [4] Sport ~**ka podwójna** a double scull

dwójkow|y adi. [1] Komput., Mat. binary [2] Szkol. ~**y uczeń** a very poor student

dw|ór m [1] (dom) manor house; (majątek) (landed) estate [2] (królewski) court; **na dworze cesarskim** at the imperial court [3] (świeże powietrze) **na dworze** outside, outdoors; **wyjść na dwór** to go outside; **wrócić z dworu** to come (back) in

dwub|ój m combined event; ~**ój klasyczny** the Nordic combined; ~**ój zimowy** the biathlon

dwuczęściow|y adi. [kostium] two-piece; [książka, film] two-part

dwudziest|ka f twenty

dwudziestoleci|e n ~**e (międzywojenne)** the interwar period (1919-1939)

dwudzie|sty num. ord. twentieth

dwuizbow|y adi. [mieszkanie] two-room; [parlament] two-chamber, bicameral

dwujajow|y adi. **bliźnięta** ~**e** fraternal twins

dwujęzyczn|y adi. bilingual

dwukolorow|y adi. two-coloured GB, two-colored US

dwukołow|y adi. two-wheeled

dwukrop|ek m colon

dwulicow|y adi. two-faced, double-faced

dwunast|ka f twelve

dwunastnic|a f duodenum

dwuna|sty num. ord. twelfth

■ **robić coś za pięć** ~**sta** to do sth at the last minute

dwuosobow|y adi. [pokój] double; [kajak, załoga] two-man; ~**a wycieczka** a trip for two

dwupasmow|y adi. ~**a droga** dual carriageway GB, divided highway US

dwurzędow|y adi. [kurtka, marynarka] double-breasted

dwusetn|y num. ord. two hundredth

dwustronn|y adi. [1] [taśma klejąca, dyskietka] double-sided; [tkanina] reversible, double-faced [2] [umowa, stosunki] bilateral

dwuszereg m two lines (one behind the other)

dwutlen|ek m dioxide; ~**ek węgla/siarki** carbon/sulphur dioxide

dwutygodnik m fortnightly, biweekly

dwuwiersz m couplet

dwuwymiarow|y adi. two-dimensional

dwuznaczn|y adi. [1] (niejasny) ambiguous [2] (nieprzyzwoity) suggestive

dydaktyczn|y adi. [1] [praca, teorie] teaching; **talent** ~**y** a gift for teaching; **zajęcia** ~**e** (teaching) classes [2] (pouczający) didactic

dydakty|ka f theory of teaching

dyftery|t m diphtheria

dygnitarz m dignitary

dygo|tać impf vi to tremble, to shiver; ~**tać z zimna/ze strachu** to tremble a. shiver from the cold/with fear

dygresj|a f digression

dykcj|a f diction, enunciation

dyk|ta f plywood

dyktafon m Dictaphone®

dyktan|do n (ćwiczenie) dictation (exercise); (sprawdzian) spelling test

■ **robić coś pod czyjeś** ~**do** to do sth at sb's bidding

dyktato|r m dictator; ~**r mody** fashion dictator

dyktatu|ra f dictatorship

dykt|ować impf vt to dictate [list, ceny, warunki]; ~**ować tempo** to set the pace

dylema|t m dilemma; **stanąć przed** ~**tem** to face a dilemma

dyletan|t m, ~**tka** f książk. dilettante

dym m smoke; (drażniący, szkodliwy) fume; **pójść z** ~**em** [budynek, praca, marzenia] to go up in smoke; **puścić coś z** ~**em** to send sth up in smoke

■ **iść** a. **walić do kogoś jak w** ~ pot. to go straight to sb; **nie ma** ~**u bez ognia** przysł. there's no smoke without fire przysł.

dym|ek m (w komiksie) balloon

dym|ić impf **[]** vi [1] [piec, komin] to smoke [2] (parować) [potrawa, garnek] to steam

[II] dymić się [1] [drewno] to smoke [2] (parować) [zupa, obiad] to steam

dymisj|a f (zwolnienie) dismissal; (ustąpienie) resignation; **podać się do** ~**i** a. **złożyć** ~**ę** to hand in one's resignation

dymisjon|ować pf, impf vt to dismiss

dym|ka f spring onion

dynamiczn|y adi. grad. dynamic

dynami|ka f [1] (tempo) dynamics; (żywiołowość) dynamism [2] Fiz. dynamics; **zasady** ~**ki Newtona** Newton's laws of motion

dynami|t m dynamite także przen.

dynasti|a f dynasty

dyngus m Easter Monday custom of throwing water over people

dy|nia f pumpkin

dyplom m [1] (dokument) diploma, certificate [2] Uniw. (stopień) degree (**z czegoś** in sth); (egzamin) final a. graduation exam; (projekt) diploma/degree project [3] (wyróżnienie) diploma of merit

dyplomacj|a f diplomacy także przen.

dyploma|ta m diplomat także przen.

dyplomatyczn|y adi. diplomatic

dyplomowan|y adi. [pielęgniarka] registered GB, qualified; ~**y księgowy** chartered accountant

dyplomow|y adi. [egzamin, koncert, praca] graduation

dyrekcj|a f [1] (kierownictwo) management; **za jego** ~**i** under his management [2] Muz. **orkiestra pod czyjąś** ~**ą** an orchestra conducted by sb

dyrekto|r m director, manager; ~**r szkoły** headmaster GB, principal US; ~**r naczelny** managing director; ~**r departamentu** head of a department; ~**r do spraw sprzedaży** sales manager

dyrektor|ka f ~**ka szkoły** headmistress GB, principal US; ~**ka przedszkola** head of a nursery school

dyrygen|t m, ~**tka** f conductor

dyryg|ować impf vt to conduct [orkiestrą, chórem]; ~**ować kimś** pot. to boss sb about a. around pot.

dyscyplin|a f [1] (rygor) discipline; ~**a wewnętrzna** self-discipline [2] (dziedzina) discipline, branch [3] Sport sport

dyscyplinarn|y adi. [kara, postępowanie] disciplinary; **zwolnienie** ~**e** dismissal on disciplinary grounds

dysharmoni|a /dɪsxarˈmɔnja/ f disharmony

dysk m [1] Sport discus; **rzut** ~**iem** discus throwing [2] (kształt) disc, disk US [3] Komput. (hard) disk [4] Anat. intervertebral disc a. disk US

dyskiet|ka f floppy (disk), diskette

dyskobol m, ~**ka** f discus thrower

dyskomfor|t m książk. discomfort; **odczuwać** ~**t psychiczny** to feel uneasy

dyskopati|a f slipped disk

dyskote|ka f disco(theque); **pójść na** ~**kę** to go to a disco

dyskrecj|a f discretion

dyskretnie adv. grad. discreetly

dyskretn|y adi. [1] [osoba, pytanie] discreet [2] [makijaż] discreet; [muzyka, światło] soft

dyskryminacj|a f discrimination; ~**a kobiet** discrimination against women; ~**a etniczna** discrimination on ethnic grounds

dyskrymin|ować impf vt to discriminate (**kogoś** against sb)

dyskusj|a f (debata) discussion, debate (**o** a. **nad czymś** about a. on sth); (spór) argument, dispute (**o** a. **nad czymś** about a. over sth); **prowadzić** a. **toczyć z kimś** ~**ę** to have a. hold a discussion with sb; **sprawa do** ~**i** a matter open to discussion; **być przedmiotem** ~**i** to be under discussion a. debate; **nie podlegać** ~**i** to be indisputable; **bez** ~**i!** that's final!

dyskusyjn|y adi. [1] [kółko, klub] discussion, debating [2] [zagadnienie] disputable, arguable; **kwestia** ~**a** a moot point

dyskut|ować impf [] vt to discuss, to debate [kwestię]

[] vi to discuss (**o** a. **nad czymś** sth); to debate (**o** a. **nad czymś** (about) sth); ~**ować z kimś na temat czegoś** to have a discussion with sb about sth; **z tym można** ~**ować** that's debatable; **nie** ~**uj!** don't argue!

dyskwalifikacj|a f disqualification

dyskwalifik|ować impf vt to disqualify

dysleksj|a f dyslexia

dysonans n książk. dissonance, discord

dyspon|ować impf vt książk. (mieć) to possess, to have (at one's disposal) (**czymś** sth)

dyspozycj|a f order, instruction; **szczegółowe** ~**e co do czegoś** exact instructions regarding sth ■ **mieć coś do** ~**i** książk. to have sth at one's disposal; **pozostawać w** a. **do czyjejś** ~**i** książk. to be at sb's disposal

dyspozycyjn|y adi. [osoba] flexible; **ośrodek** ~**y** headquarters

dysproporcj|a f disproportion

dystans m distance; **pokonać** ~ **100 km** to cover a distance of 100 km ; **długie/krótkie** ~**e** long/ short distances; **bieg na** ~**ie 3000 m** a 3,000 metre run; **trzymać kogoś na** ~ to keep sb at a distance; **zachowywać** ~ **wobec kogoś** to keep one's distance from sb

dystans|ować się impf v refl. książk. to distance oneself (**od czegoś** from sth)

dystrybucj|a f distribution

dystrybuto|r m [1] (osoba) distributor [2] (benzyny) petrol GB a. gas US pump [3] (automat) dispenser; ~**r soków** juice dispenser

dysyden|t m (polityczny) dissident; (religijny) dissenter

dysz|a f nozzle

dysz|eć impf vi to pant; ~**eć nienawiścią** to be fuming with hatred ■ **ledwo** a. **ledwie** ~**eć** to be on one's last legs

dysz|el m (wozu, bryczki, sań) shaft, pole; (przyczepy) tow bar

dywan m carpet; (mniejszy) rug; ~ **mchów** a carpet of moss; **latający** ~ magic a. flying carpet

dywanik m rug, mat ■ **wziąć** a. **wezwać kogoś na** ~ pot. to carpet sb GB pot.

dywersan|t m, ~**tka** f saboteur

dywersj|a f sabotage

dywiden|da f dividend

dywiz m hyphen

dywizj|a f division; ~**a piechoty** infantry division

dywizjon m (w wojskach lądowych) battalion; (w lotnictwie) squadron; (w marynarce) division

dyzenteri|a f dysentery

dyżu|r *m* duty; **nocny** ∼**r** night duty; **mieć** ∼**r** to be on duty; **zawieźć kogoś na ostry** ∼**r** to take sb to the casualty department

dyżur|ka *f* (w szpitalu) staffroom; (strażnika) guardroom

dyżurn|y [] *adi.* **lekarz** ∼**y** the doctor on call a. on duty; ∼**a pielęgniarka** duty nurse; **oficer** ∼**y** duty officer; ∼**y temat** iron. a standby topic iron. [] dyżurny *m*, ∼**a** *f* (w szkole) monitor

❏ ∼**y ruchu** train dispatcher

dyżur|ować *impf vi* to be on duty a. call; ∼**ujący szpital** a hospital on standby (duty)

dzban|ek *m* (naczynie) jug GB, pitcher US; (zawartość) jug(ful) GB, pitcher US; ∼**ek do kawy** coffee pot; ∼**ek do herbaty** teapot

dziab|nąć *pf* — **dziab|ać** *impf vt* pot. [] (ugryźć) to bite; (użądlić) to sting [] (zadać cios) to stab; ∼**nąć kogoś nożem** to stab sb (with a knife)

dzi|ać się *impf* [] *vi* to happen; **akcja powieści** ∼**eje się w...** the novel is set in...; **co się tu** ∼**eje?** what's going on here?; **nie wiem, co się z nim teraz** ∼**eje** I don't know what he's up to these days; **co się z tobą** ∼**eje?** pot. what's the matter with you? [] *v imp.* ∼**ało się coraz gorzej** the situation was getting worse and worse; ∼**eje się tak dlatego, że...** it's because (of the fact that)...; **niech się** ∼**eje, co chce** come what may

dzia|d *m* [] książk. (dziadek) grandfather; (przodek) forefather; **Polak z** ∼**da pradziada** a Pole born and bred [] (biedak) pauper; (żebrak) beggar ■ ∼**da z babą** a. ∼**da i baby tylko tu brakuje** pot. all that's missing is the kitchen sink; **mówił** ∼**d do obrazu** pot. it's like talking to a brick wall; **zejść na** ∼**dy** pot. to go to the dogs pot.

dziad|ek *m* grandfather; grand(d)ad, grandpa pot.; ∼**kowie** (babcia i dziadek) grandparents

❏ ∼**ek do orzechów** nutcracker

dziadostw|o *n* pot. (tandeta) rubbish pot.

dziadows|ki *adi.* pot. (tandetny) shoddy

dzia|ł *m* [] (nauki, sztuki) branch [] (w czasopiśmie, książce) section [] (instytucji, sklepu) department; ∼**ł personalny/meblowy** the personnel/furniture department

❏ ∼**ł wodny** a. **wód** watershed, divide US

działacz *m*, ∼**ka** *f* activist; ∼ **związkowy** trade union activist

działa|ć *impf vi* [] (wykonywać czynności) to act; ∼**ć na własną rękę** to act on one's own; ∼**ć w konspiracji** to be active in the underground; ∼**ć na czyjąś korzyść/niekorzyść** to work to sb's advantage/disadvantage; **czas** ∼ **na naszą korzyść** time is on our side [] (funkcjonować) *[urządzenie, maszyna]* to work; ∼**ć na baterie** to run on batteries; **nie** ∼**ć** to be out of order [] (wywierać wpływ) to have an effect (**na coś** on sth); ∼**ć moczopędnie** to have a diuretic effect; ∼**ć na**

wyobraźnię to stimulate the imagination; **proszki nasenne zaczęły** ∼**ć** the sleeping pills began to take effect; **zastrzyk przeciwbólowy przestał** ∼**ć** the analgesic has stopped working; ∼**ć czymś na coś** to treat sth with sth

działalnoś|ć *f* activity; **rozpocząć** ∼**ć** to start one's activities

działa|nie [] *n* [] Mat. calculation, (mathematical) operation [] Farm., Med. effect; **lek o** ∼**niu przeciwzapalnym** anti-inflammatory medication; ∼**nia uboczne** side effects [] **działania** *plt* action, activities; **podjąć** ∼**nia** to take action

dział|ka *f* [] (parcela) plot GB, lot US; ∼**ka budowlana/rekreacyjna** a building/garden plot [] (ogródek) allotment GB [] pot. (zadanie) **gotowanie to twoja** ∼**ka** cooking is your department pot. [] pot. (część) cut pot. [] pot. (kokainy) line pot.; (heroiny, amfetaminy) fix pot.

dział|ko *n* small cannon; ∼**ko wodne** water cannon

dzia|ło *n* gun, cannon; **bić z** ∼**ł** to fire one's guns

działow|y *adi. [ścianka, linia]* partition

dzianin|a *f* knitwear; **suknia z** ∼**y** a knitted dress

dzią|sło *n* gum

dziczy|zna *f* game

dzi|da *f* spear

dzidziu|ś *m* pieszcz. baby

dziecięc|y *adi. [głos, uśmiech]* child's; *[książki, odzież, szpital]* children's; *[lata, przyjaźń, zażyłość]* childhood; *[ufność, zachowanie]* childlike

dziecinni|eć *impf vi* to become childish

dziecinn|y *adi.* [] (dotyczący dziecka) child's; ∼**y pokój** nursery [] (niedojrzały) *[osoba, pomysł]* childish; **nie bądź** ∼**a!** don't be so childish!

dzieciństw|o *n* childhood; **przyjaciel z** ∼**a** a childhood friend; **w** ∼**ie wiele chorował** he was a sickly child

dzie|cko *n* [] child; **dorosłe** ∼**ci** grown-up children; **od** ∼**cka** since childhood; **płakać jak** ∼**cko** to cry like a baby; **spodziewać się** ∼**cka** to be expecting (a baby); ∼**cko z probówki** a test-tube baby pot.; ∼**cko natury/epoki** przen. a child of nature/the times; ∼**cko szczęścia** a lucky person; ∼**ci-kwiaty** flower children [] przen. brainchild ■ **wylać** ∼**cko z kąpielą** to throw the baby out with the bathwater; ∼**ci i ryby głosu nie mają** przysł. children should be seen and not heard przysł.

dziedzictw|o *n* [] książk. (spadek) inheritance, legacy [] (dorobek) legacy, heritage; ∼**o kulturowe** cultural heritage; ∼**o po okresie kolonializmu** a legacy from the colonial period

dziedziczn|y *adi.* hereditary

dziedzicz|yć *impf vt* to inherit; ∼**yć coś po kimś** to inherit sth from sb; ∼**yć tron po ojcu** to succeed one's father to the throne

dziedzin|a *f* field, sphere; **w** ~**ie medycyny** in the field of medicine; **jaką** ~**ę sportu uprawiasz?** what sport do you practise?; **książka z** ~**y chemii** a book on chemistry

dziedzi|niec *m* court(yard); **na** ~**ńcu** in the courtyard

dziej|e *plt* książk. history; ~**e narodu** the history of a nation; **od zarania** ~**ów** from the dawn of history; **na przestrzeni** ~**ów** through the ages; **stare** ~**e!** that's ancient history!

dziejow|y *adi.* książk. historic

dziekan *m* Uniw. dean

dziekana|t *m* Uniw. dean's a. faculty office

dziele|nie *n* Mat. division

dziel|ić *impf* **[]** *vt* **1** (wyodrębniać części) to divide; ~**ić coś na części** to divide sth into parts; ~**enie wyrazów** word division **2** (rozdawać) to divide, to share out; ~**ić coś pomiędzy kilka osób** to divide a. share out sth among several people; ~**ić czas pomiędzy pracę a obowiązki domowe** to divide one's time between work and running the household **3** (rozgraniczać) to divide, to separate (**od czegoś** from sth); ~**iło ich 30 metrów** they were 30 metres apart; ~**ą nas poglądy na tę sprawę** our views differ on this matter **4** (korzystać, przeżywać wspólnie) to share *[obowiązki, przeżycia]*; ~**ić z kimś pokój** to share a room with sb **5** Mat. to divide; ~**ić 20 przez 5** to divide 20 by 5

[]] dzielić się 1 (na części) to divide, to split **2** (składać się) to be divided (**na coś** into sth); to be composed (**na coś** of sth) **3** (oddawać część) ~**ić się czymś z kimś** to share sth with sb; ~**ić się z kimś wrażeniami** przen. to share one's impressions with sb **4** Mat. *[liczba]* to be divisible; **8** ~**i się przez 2 i przez 4** 8 is divisible by 2 and 4

dzieln|a *f* Mat. dividend

dzielnic|a *f* district, quarter; (kraju) province, region

dzielnicow|y [] *adi.* **1** Admin. *[rada]* district **2** Hist. **książęta** ~**i** local princes; **rozbicie** ~**e** feudal disintegration

**[]] ** *m* pot. neighbourhood a. community policeman

dzielnie *adv. grad.* bravely

dzielnik *m* Mat. divisor

dzieln|y *adi.* brave

dzie|ło *n* **1** (utwór) work; ~**ło sztuki** a work of art; ~**ła zebrane Dickensa** the collected works of Dickens; **obraz jest** ~**łem nieznanego artysty** the painting is the work of an unknown artist **2** książk. (praca) work; **wziąć się** a. **zabrać się do** ~**ła** to get down to work; **do** ~**ła!** let's get (down) to work!; ~**ło zniszczenia/zbawienia** an act of destruction/redemption

dzienniczęk *m* Szkol. ≈ pupil's record book, ≈ grade book US

dziennie *adv.* a day, daily; **50 euro** ~ 50 euros a day; **dwa razy** ~ twice a day

dziennik *m* **1** (gazeta) daily (paper) **2** Radio, TV the news; **słyszałem o tym w** ~**u** I heard it on the news **3** (pamiętnik) diary, journal; **prowadzić** ~ to keep a diary a. journal **4** (księga urzędowa) register; ~ **lekcyjny** a. **klasowy** Szkol. (class) register

❑ ~ **okrętowy** log(book); ~ **ustaw** law gazette

dziennikars|ki *adi. [praca]* journalist's; *[gatunek, styl, studia]* journalistic; **żargon** ~**ki** journalese pot.

dziennikarstw|o *n* journalism

dziennika|rz *m,* ~**rka** *f* journalist; ~ **„Gazety Wyborczej"** a journalist from a. for 'Gazeta Wyborcza'

dzienn|y *adi.* **1** (całodobowy) daily; ~**y utarg** daily takings **2** (w ciągu dnia) *[połączenie, patrol]* daytime; **przy świetle** ~**ym** in daylight; ~**a zmiana** a day a. daytime shift; **studia** ~**e** full-time courses *(in higher education)*

dzień *m* **1** (doba) day; **pewnego dnia** one day; **co dzień** every day; **co drugi dzień** every other day; **co cztery dni** every four days; **lada dzień** any day now; **w tych dniach** one of these days; **dzień w dzień** day in day out; **do dnia dzisiejszego** a. **do dziś dnia** until now a. today; **z dnia na dzień** (nagle) overnight; (stopniowo) day by day, by the day; **jak co dzień** as usual; **dzień jak co dzień** a day like any other; **na co dzień** (zwykle) usually; **ubranie na co dzień** everyday clothes; **temat dnia** the topic of the day **2** (od wschodu do zachodu) day; **słoneczny/deszczowy dzień** a sunny/rainy day; **dzień powszedni/świąteczny** a weekday/ holiday; **dzień pracy** a. **roboczy** a working day, a workday; **dzień i noc** a. **dniami i nocami** day and night; **(przez) cały dzień** the whole day, all day long; **całymi dniami** a. **po całych dniach** all day long; **dzień dobry** good day książk.; (rano) good morning; (po południu) good afternoon **3** (światło dzienne) daylight; **za dnia** by day, in a. during the daytime; **wrócimy za dnia** we'll be back before nightfall; **w biały** a. **jasny dzień** in broad daylight; **dzień wstaje** a. **budzi się** dawn is breaking **4** (data, termin) day; **dzień wczorajszy/dzisiejszy/jutrzejszy** yesterday/today/tomorrow; **czyjś dzień urodzin/imienin** sb's birthday/name day; **jaki dziś dzień?** what day is it today?; **w dniu ślubu** on the day of the wedding; **umowa z dnia 31 marca 1994** a contract dated 31 March 1994 **5** (odległość) day; **(o) dwa dni drogi stąd** two days' journey from here ❑ **dzień polarny** Astron. polar day; **dzień rektorski** Uniw. *a day free of classes*; **Dzień Dziecka** Children's Day; **Dzień Matki** Mother's Day; **Dzień Kobiet** Women's Day

■ **żyć z dnia na dzień** to live from hand to mouth, to live a hand-to-mouth existence; **twoje dni są policzone** your days are numbered; **podobni jak dzień do nocy** as different as chalk and cheese

dzierżaw|a *f* **1** (użytkowanie) lease, tenancy; **mieć coś w** ~**ie** to have sth on lease; **oddać coś w** ~**ę**

to lease sth out; **wziąć coś w** ~**ę** to take out a lease on sth ② (opłata) rent

dzierżaw|ca *m*, ~**czyni** *f* (użytkownik) leaseholder, lessee

dzierżawcz|y *adi.* Jęz. possessive; **zaimek** ~**y** (rzeczowny) possessive pronoun; (przymiotny) possessive adjective

dzierżaw|ić *impf vt* to lease *[ziemię, budynek, las]* (**komuś** to sb); ~**ić coś od kogoś** to lease sth from sb

dzierż|yć *impf vt* książk. ① to hold *[łyżkę, miecz]* ② przen. to wield *[władzę, rządy]*; ~**yć ster** to be at the helm

dziesiąt|ka ① *f* ten

② **dziesiątki** *plt* (duża ilość) tens, dozens; ~**ki tysięcy ludzi** tens of thousands of people

■ **trafić** a. **strzelić w** ~**kę** to score a bullseye

dziesiątk|ować *impf vt* książk. to decimate

dziesią|ty *num. ord.* tenth

■ **za** ~**tą górą, za** ~**tą rzeką** far, far away

dziesięciob|ój *m* decathlon

dziesięcioleci|e *n* ① (rocznica) tenth anniversary ② (okres) decade, ten years; **w drugim** ~**u XIX wieku** in the 1820s

dziesięcioletni *adi. [dziecko, zwierzę]* ten-year-old; *[okres, plan]* ten-year

dziesięcior|o *num. mult.* ten

dziesię|ć *num.* ten

dziesiętn|y *adi.* decimal; **ułamek** ~**y** decimal (fraction)

dziewann|a *f* mullein

dziewczęc|y *adi.* girlish

dziewczyn|a *f* ① (młoda kobieta) girl ② (sympatia) girl(friend)

dziewczyn|ka *f* girl

dziewiąt|ka *f* nine

dziewią|ty *num. ord.* ninth

dziewic|a *f* virgin

dziewicz|y *adi. [las, krajobraz]* virgin; ~**y rejs** maiden voyage

dziewięcior|o *num. mult.* nine

dziewię|ć *num.* nine

dziewięćdziesią|t *num.* ninety

dziewięćdziesią|ty *num. ord.* ninetieth

dziewię|ćset *num.* nine hundred

dziewięćsetn|y *num. ord.* nine hundredth

dziewiętna|sty *num. ord.* nineteenth

dziewiętna|ście *num.* nineteen

dziewiętnaścior|o *num. mult.* nineteen

dzięcio|ł *m* woodpecker

dziękczynn|y *adi.* książk. *[modlitwa, hymn]* thanksgiving; **list** ~**y** a letter of thanks

dzięki ① *plt* książk. thanks; **składać komuś** ~ (**za coś**) to thank sb (for sth); ~ **Bogu!** thank God! a. heaven!

② *inter.* pot. thanks!; cheers! GB pot.; **serdeczne/ stokrotne** ~! thanks a lot!/million!

③ *praep.* thanks (**komuś/czemuś** to sb/sth); ~ **temu, że...** thanks a. owing to the fact that...

dzięk|ować *impf vi* to thank (**komuś za coś** sb for sth); ~**uję bardzo** thank you very much; „**zjesz coś?**" – „~**uję, chętnie/nie,** ~**uję**" 'would you like something to eat?' – 'yes, please/ no, thank you'; **nie wiem, jak ci (mam)** ~**ować** I don't know how to thank you

dzik *m* (wild) boar

dzi|ki *adi. grad.* ① *[zwierzę, roślina, okolica]* wild; ~**ka plaża** an unguarded beach ② *[lud]* primitive; savage daw. ③ *[osoba]* unsociable ④ *[namiętność, radość]* wild; *[wrzask]* terrible

dziko *adv. [śmiać się, krzyczeć]* wildly

dziobać[1] *impf → dziobnąć*

dziob|ać[2] *impf* ① *vt* ① *[ptak]* to peck (at) ② pot., przen. (jeść) to pick a. peck at pot.

② **dziobać się** *[ptaki]* to peck one another

dziobak *m* (duck-billed) platypus

dzioba|ty *adi.* pockmarked, pocked

dzi|obek *m* ① (ptasi) bill, beak ② (dzbanka, czajnika) lip, spout

dzi|obnąć *pf* — **dzi|obać**[1] *impf vt [ptak]* to peck (at)

dziobow|y *adi. [ster, fala]* bow

dzi|ób ① *m* ① (ptasi) beak, bill ② pot. (usta) gob GB, trap pot.; **zamknij** ~**ób** shut your trap ③ (statku, łodzi) bow, prow

② **dzioby** *plt* pot. pockmarks, pocks; **twarz miał całą w** ~**obach** his face was all pockmarked

dzi|siaj, ~ś ① *adv.* ① (danego dnia) today; ~**siaj wieczorem** tonight, this evening ② (teraz) today, nowadays; **po** ~**ś dzień** to this day

② *n inv.* ① (dzień dzisiejszy) today; **od** ~**siaj** starting (from) today; **dość na** ~**ś** enough for today ② (teraźniejszość) today, the present

dzisiej|szy *adi.* ① (bieżący) *[gazeta, mecz]* today's; **dzień** ~**szy** today; ~**szy ranek** this morning ② (współczesny) *[obyczaje]* present-day; *[młodzież, pokolenie]* today's; **w** ~**szych czasach** today, nowadays

dziś → **dzisiaj**

dziupl|a *f* ① (w pniu) hole, hollow ② pot. (kryjówka) hid(e)y-hole pot.

dziu|ra *f* ① (otwór) hole (**w czymś** in sth); (w nawierzchni) pothole; (w zębie) cavity; ~**ra na kolanie** a hole in the knee of sb's trousers ② przen. (brak) gap; ~**ra budżetowa** a budget gap; **mieć** ~**ry w pamięci** to have memory gaps ③ pot. (miejscowość) hole pot.; **w jakiejś zapadłej** ~**rze** in some godforsaken hole

■ ~**ry w niebie nie będzie** the sky won't fall in; **potrzebny nam jak** ~**ra w moście** we need it like a hole in the head pot.; **szukać** ~**ry w całym** to nit-pick pot.

dziuraw|ić *impf vt* to make holes (**coś** in sth)

dziuraw|iec *m* St John's wort

dziuraw|y *adi. [sweter, chodnik]* full of holes; *[dach, garnek, wiadro]* leaky; ~**a droga** a road full of (pot)holes; **polskie prawo jest** ~**e** przen. Polish law is full of loopholes
■ **mieć** ~**ą kieszeń** pot. to spend money like water; **mieć** ~**e ręce** pot., pejor. to be a butterfingers pot.

dziur|ka *f* small hole; ~**ki w nosie** nostrils; ~**ka od klucza** keyhole
■ **mieć czegoś po** ~**ki w nosie** pot. to be fed up (to the back teeth) with sth pot.

dziurkacz *m* punch

dziurk|ować *impf vt* to perforate, to punch

dziw *m* wonder, marvel; *(aż)* ~ **(bierze), że...** it's a wonder (that)...; **nie** ~, **że...** it's a small wonder (that)...

dziwactw|o *n* ① (zachowanie) eccentricity, peculiarity ② (rzecz) oddity

dziwaczn|y *adi. grad.* bizarre

dziwa|k *m*, ~**czka** *f* freak, oddball pot.; **stary** ~**k** an old crank

dziw|ić *impf* ① *vt* to surprise; **nic mnie już nie** ~**i** nothing surprises me any more
■ ① **dziwić się** to be surprised; ~**ię ci się, że...** I'm surprised (that)...; ~**ić się czemuś** to wonder a. be surprised at sth

dziwn|y *adi. grad.* strange, odd; ~**y zbieg okoliczności** a strange coincidence; **to** ~**e, że...** (it's) strange a. odd that...; ~**ym trafem** just a. purely by chance; **nic** ~**ego** no wonder, small wonder

dziwoląg *m* (osoba) weirdo, freak pot.; (rzecz) oddity

dzwon ① *m* bell; ~**y pogrzebowe** a. **żałobne** (death) knell; **bić** a. **uderzać w** ~**y** to ring the bells
② **dzwony** *plt* pot. (spodnie) flares pot.; bell-bottoms
■ **od wielkiego** ~**u** pot. once in a blue moon pot.; **serce jak** ~ pot. a heart as sound as a bell

dzwon|ek ① *m* ① (urządzenie) bell; ~**ek do drzwi** a doorbell ② (dźwięk) ring, ringing; **trzy krótkie** ~**ki** three short rings; **nie słyszał** ~**ka do drzwi** he didn't hear the doorbell (ring) ③ Bot. campanula, bellflower
② **dzwonki** *plt* Muz. glockenspiel
■ ~**ek alarmowy** an alarm bell, a warning signal; **ostatni** ~**ek** the last chance

dzwo|nić *impf vi* ① (dzwonkiem) to ring; ~**nić do drzwi** to ring the (door)bell; ~**nić na alarm** to sound the alarm ② (metalowym przedmiotem) to jingle *[kluczami, monetami]* ③ (telefonować) to ring (up) GB, to phone, to call (up) **(do kogoś** sb) ④ (dźwięczeć) *[telefon, alarm]* to ring; *[dzwon]* to ring, to peal;

[klucze] to jingle
■ ~**ni mi w uszach** my ears are ringing

dzwonnic|a *f* belfry, bell tower

dzwonni|k *m* bell-ringer

dźg|nąć *pf* — **dźg|ać** *impf* ① *vt* ① (zranić) to stab **(kogoś czymś** sb with sth) ② (ukłuć) to jab **(kogoś czymś** sb with sth); ~**nął konia ostrogą** he spurred his horse; ~**nąć kogoś w żebro** to poke a. prod sb in the ribs
② **dźgnąć się** — **dźgać się** (samego siebie) to stab a. jab oneself **(czymś** with sth)

dźwięcz|eć *impf vi* *[alarm, dzwonek, sygnał]* to sound; *[dzwon, dzwonek]* to ring; *[klucze, monety]* to jingle; **jego słowa** ~**ą mi w uszach** his words ring in my ears

dźwięczn|y *adi. grad.* ① *[okrzyk]* resounding; *[głos, instrument]* resonant; *[śmiech]* ringing ② *[spółgłoska]* voiced

dźwięk *m* ① sound ② Muz. tone

dźwiękonaśladowcz|y *adi.* onomatopoeic

dźwiękoszczeln|y *adi.* soundproof

dźwiękow|y *adi. [efekty, fale, film]* sound; **ścieżka** ~**a filmu** soundtrack

dźwig *m* ① (na budowie, portowy) crane ② (winda) lift GB, elevator US

dźwiga|ć¹ *impf vt* to carry, to lug *[walizki, ciężary]*

dźwig|nąć *pf* — **dźwig|ać²** *impf* ① *vt* (podnieść) to lift; ~**ać ciężar czegoś** przen. to bear the burden of sth; ~**nąć gospodarkę z kryzysu** to lift the economy out of crisis; ~**nąć miasto z gruzów** a. **ruin** to raise a city from (the) rubble
② **dźwignąć się** — **dźwigać się** (powstać) to rise; ~**nąć się z nędzy** przen. to struggle out of poverty

dźwigni|a *f* lever także przen.; ~**a zmiany biegów** gear lever GB, gear shift US

dźwigow|y *m* crane operator

dżdżownic|a *f* earthworm

dżdży|sty *adi.* drizzly, rainy

dżem *m* jam; ~ **truskawkowy** a. **z truskawek** strawberry jam

dżentelmen *m* gentleman

dżentelmeńs|ki *adi.* gentlemanly; ~**ka umowa** a gentleman's a. gentlemen's agreement

dżins ① *m* denim, jean
② **dżinsy** *plt* jeans

dżokej *m* jockey

dżoke|r *m* joker

dżum|a *f* the plague

dżungl|a *f* jungle; ~**a przepisów** przen. the jungle of red tape

E

E, e *n inv.* ① (litera) E, e ② Muz. E

ech|o ⫶ *n* ① (dźwięk) echo ② (rozgłos) news; **odbić się szrokim ~em** to attract a lot of publicity; **minąć bez ~a** to go unnoticed

edukacj|a *f* education; **uzupełnić luki w ~i** to fill in the gaps in one's education; **~a permanentna** continuing a. ongoing education; **~a seksualna** sex education

edukacyjn|y *adi. [broszura, program, telewizja]* educational

edycj|a *f* ① (wydanie) edition; **~a kieszonkowa/dwutomowa** a pocket/two-volume edition; **książka w luksusowej ~i** a de luxe edition ② (konkursu, festiwalu) edition

edyto|r *m* editor; **~r tekstów** Komput. word processor

edytors|ki *adi. [plany, zamierzenia]* editorial

efek|t *m* ① (wrażenie) effect; **~t cieplarniany** the greenhouse effect; **~ty dźwiękowe** sound effects; **niezamierzony ~t komiczny** an unintentionally comic effect; **wywołać ~t** to produce an effect ② (wynik) result; **w ~cie** in the end; **w ~cie czegoś** as a result of sth; **bez ~tu** to no avail

efektown|y *adi. grad. [strój, występ, dziewczyna]* striking

efektywn|y *adi.* ① (skuteczny) effective; (wydajny) efficient ② (rzeczywisty) effective; **~y czas pracy** effective work time

egi|da *f* książk. aegis; **pod czyjąś ~dą** under the aegis of sb

ego *n inv.* ① (jaźń) ego ② (godność) ego; **zranić czyjeś ~** to hurt sb's pride

egocentryczn|y *adi.* książk. *[osoba, zachowanie]* egocentric

egoi|sta *m*, **~stka** *f* egoist

egoistyczn|y *adi. [zachowanie, osoba]* egoistic

egoizm *m* egoism

egzaltacj|a *f* exaltation; **popadać w ~ę** to go into raptures a. ecstasies (**z powodu czegoś** about a. over sth)

egzaltowan|y *adi.* książk. *[usposobienie, zachowanie]* effusive; *[okrzyk]* rapturous

egzamin *m* ① (sprawdzenie wiedzy). exam(ination), exam; **~ końcowy** a final exam(ination); **~ ustny/pisemny** an oral/a written exam(ination); **~ poprawkowy** a resit; **~y (wstępne) na studia** university entrance exams; **~ z fizyki** a physics exam; **~ dojrzałości** a. **maturalny** Szkol. *Polish school-leaving examination*; **~ na prawo jazdy/kartę pływacką** a driving/swimming test; **zdawać ~** to take an exam; **zdać** a. **zaliczyć ~** to pass an exam; **nie zdać ~u** to fail an exam ② pot. (praca egzaminacyjna) exam(ination) paper ③ przen. (sprawdzian) test; **poddać kogoś/coś ~owi** to put sb/sth to the test; **zdać ~** pot. *[urządzenie, procedura]* to work (well); to do the job pot.

egzaminacyjn|y *adi.* exam(ination); **komisja ~a** an examination board; **praca ~a** an exam(ination) paper

egzaminato|r *m*, **~rka** *f* examiner; **~r zewnętrzny** Szkol., Uniw. an external examiner

egzamin|ować *impf vi* ① to examine *[uczniów, studentów]*; **~ujący i ~owani** examiners and examinees ② przen. to cross-examine przen.

egzekucj|a *f* ① (wykonanie wyroku) execution; **publiczna ~a** a public execution ② Prawo execution; **~a prawa** law enforcement; **~a długów** debt collecting a. recovery

egzekucyjn|y *adi.* ① (wykonujący wyrok śmierci) **pluton ~y** a firing squad ② Prawo enforcement; **nakaz ~y** a warrant of execution

egzekw|ować *impf vt* (wymagać) to enforce *[decyzję, prawo, przepisy]*; to exact *[należność, obietnicę]*; **~ować swoje polecenia** to make sure that one's instructions are carried out; **~ować swoje prawa** to exercise one's rights

egzem|a *f* eczema

egzemplarz *m* ① (książka, czasopismo) copy; **umowa sporządzona w dwóch/trzech ~ach** an agreement drawn up in duplicate/triplicate ② (okaz) specimen

egzorcy|sta *m* exorcist

egzorcyzm *m* exorcism; **odprawiać ~y** to perform an exorcism

egzotyczn|y *adi. [strój, roślina, zwierzę]* exotic

egzoty|ka *f* exoticism

egzystencj|a *f* książk. ① (istnienie) existence ② (życie ludzkie) life; **zmagać się z codzienną ~ą** to struggle through life ③ (byt) standard of living

egzystencjalizm *m* Filoz. existentialism

egzyst|ować *impf vi* książk. to exist; **~ować na granicy nędzy** to live on the brink of poverty

ekier|ka *f* set square GB, (drafting) triangle US

ekip|a *f* 1 (zespół) team; ∼**a sportowa** a sports team; ∼**a ratunkowa** a rescue team a. party; ∼**a robotników/monterów** a crew of workers/fitters; ∼**a telewizyjna** a TV a. camera crew 2 pot. (rząd) government; ∼**a rządząca** the present government

ekle|r *m* 1 (suwak) zip (fastener) GB, zipper US; **zapiąć kurtkę na** ∼**r** to zip up a jacket; **kurtka zapinana na** ∼**r** a zip jacket GB, a zip-up jacket US 2 Kulin. eclair

ekolo|g *m* 1 (specjalista) ecologist 2 (działacz) environmentalist

ekologi|a *f* ecology

ekologiczn|y *adi.* 1 (dotyczący ekologii) *[równowaga, warunki, badania]* ecological; **katastrofa** ∼**a** an ecological catastrophe 2 (związany z ochroną środowiska) *[problemy, edukacja]* environmental; **ruch** ∼**y** the ecology a. green movement 3 (przyjazny dla środowiska) *[produkty, paliwo, opakowanie]* eco-friendly; *[żywność]* organic; **warzywa z upraw** ∼**ych** organically grown vegetables

ekonomi|a *f* 1 (nauka) economics; ∼**a polityczna** political economy 2 (oszczędność) economy; ∼**a gestu/słowa** economy of gesture/words

ekonomi|sta *m*, ∼**stka** *f* economist

ekran *m* 1 (kinowy, telewizyjny, komputerowy) screen; **telewizor z 24-calowym** ∼**em** a 24-inch TV set 2 przen. (kino) the screen; **gwiazdy** ∼**u** film a. screen stars; **przenieść powieść na** ∼ to adapt a novel for the screen 3 Techn. screen; ∼**y dźwiękochłonne** acoustic screens; ∼ **ochronny** a protective screen

ekranizacj|a *f* 1 (opracowanie) adaptation 2 (film) adaptation, version

ekraniz|ować *impf vt* to adapt [sth] for the screen *[opowiadanie, sztukę]*

ekscelencj|a *f* excellency; **Jego Ekscelencja ambasador Francji** His Excellency the Ambassador of France

ekscentryczn|y *adi. grad. [osoba, wygląd, zachowanie]* eccentric

ekscentry|k *m* eccentric

ekscyt|ować *impf* książk. **I** *vi* to excite **II ekscytować się** to be excited (**czymś** about a. over sth); **nie ma się czym** ∼**ować** there's nothing to get excited about

ekshibicjonizm *m* exhibitionism także przen.

ekshumacj|a *f* exhumation

ekshum|ować *pf, impf vt* to exhume *[zwłoki]*

ekskluzywn|y *adi. grad. [szkoła, sklep, dzielnica, klub]* exclusive

eksmisj|a *f* eviction; **nakaz** ∼**i** an eviction order

eksmit|ować *impf vt* to evict *[mieszkańców]*

ekspansj|a *f* expansion; ∼**a terytorialna/gospodarcza** territorial/economic expansion

ekspedien|t *m*, ∼**tka** *f* shop assistant GB, (sales) clerk US

ekspedycj|a *f* 1 (wyprawa) expedition; ∼**a naukowa/wojskowa** a scientific/military expedition; ∼**a karna** 2 (dział) shipping department; ∼**a kolejowa** railway dispatch 3 (wysyłanie) shipping

eksper|t *m* expert (**w dziedzinie czegoś** in a. on sth); **komisja** ∼**tów** a panel of experts

ekspertyz|a *f* książk. (expert) opinion; ∼**a lekarska** a medical opinion; **grafologiczna** ∼**a pisma** a graphological analysis

eksperymen|t *m* 1 (doświadczenie) experiment; **przeprowadzać** ∼**t** to carry out a. perform an experiment 2 (próba) experiment; ∼**t literacki** a literary experiment; **tytułem** ∼**tu** on a trial basis

eksperymentaln|y *adi. [teatr, dowód, dane]* experimental

eksperyment|ować *impf vi* 1 (robić doświadczenia) to experiment (**na kimś/czymś** on sb/sth) 2 (podejmować próby) to experiment (**z czymś** with sth)

eksploatacj|a *f* książk. 1 (wydobywanie) extraction 2 (urządzeń, sprzętu) use; **oddać coś do** ∼**i** to put sth into service; **wycofać coś z** ∼**i** to withdraw sth from use 3 (wyzysk) exploitation

eksploat|ować *impf* książk. **I** *vt* 1 (wydobywać) to mine *[złoże]* 2 (użytkować) to utilize *[budynki, sprzęt]*; to operate *[maszyny, urządzenia]* 3 (wyzyskiwać) to exploit *[pracownika, niewolników]* 4 (nadużywać) to overuse *[pomysły, sprzęt]* **II eksploatować się** to slave (away)

eksplod|ować *pf, impf* **I** *vt* to detonate *[pocisk, ładunek]* **II** *vi* to explode także przen.

eksplozj|a *f* explosion także przen.; ∼**a atomowa** a nuclear a. an atomic explosion; ∼**a demograficzna** a population explosion; ∼**a uczuć** an outburst of feeling

ekspona|t *m* exhibit

ekspon|ować *impf vt* 1 (prezentować) to exhibit *[obraz, rzeźbę]* 2 (podkreślać) to emphasize 3 Fot. to expose *[błonę fotograficzną]*

eksponowan|y *adi.* 1 (nieosłonięty) *[posterunek, placówka, odcinek frontu]* exposed; *[plakat, położenie]* prominent; **wyraźnie** ∼**y napis** a prominently-displayed sign 2 (ważny) *[stanowisko, pozycja społeczna]* prominent

ekspor|t *m* export(ation); ∼**t węgla/żywności** the export of coal/food; **produkować coś na** ∼**t** to produce sth for export; **dochody z** ∼**tu** export revenue(s)

eksporte|r *m* exporter; **ważny** ∼**r kawy** a major exporter of coffee

eksport|ować *impf vt* to export *[odzież, węgiel, zboże]*

eksportow|y *adi. [produkty, handel, agent]* export

ekspozycj|a *f* 1 (wystawa) exhibition, exhibit US; ∼**a prac polskich plastyków** an exhibition of Polish art 2 książk. (budynku, stoku) exposure;

południowa ~a a southern exposure ③ Fot. exposure

ekspres m ① pot. (usługa) express (service) ② (przesyłka) express delivery (letter/parcel) ③ (pociąg) express (train) ④ (do parzenia kawy) espresso (machine a. coffee maker); **kawa z** ~u espresso (coffee)

ekspresj|a f książk. ① (wyrażenie) expression; **środki** ~**i artystycznej** modes of artistic expression; ~**a słowna** verbal expression ② (ekspresyjność) expressiveness; **z** ~**ą** with expression; **siła** ~**i** power of expression

ekspresjonizm m expressionism

ekspresow|y adi. [usługa, pociąg, przesyłka] express; ~**e czyszczenie odzieży** express dry-cleaning; **nowe połączenie** ~**e** a new express service; **herbata** ~**a** tea bags

ekspresy|jny, ~**wny** adi. [barwa, głos, aktorstwo] expressive

ekstaz|a f ① (uniesienie) ecstasy; **być w stanie** ~**y** to be in (a state of) ecstasy; **wpaść w** ~**ę** to go into ecstasies ② (narkotyk) Ecstasy; E pot.

eksterminacj|a f extermination

ekstra adi., adv. pot. ① (dodatkowy) [fundusze, wydatki] extra ② (świetny) great pot.; **zapłacić/zarobić** ~ to pay/earn extra; ~**!** great!

ekstradycj|a f extradition

ekstrakcj|a f extraction

ekstraklas|a f Sport top a. first league GB, major league US; ~**a piłkarska** ≈ the premier league GB; **koszykarze** ~**y** major-league basketball players US

ekstrak|t m ① (substancja) extract (**z czegoś** of sth); ~**t bulionu** beef extract ② książk., przen. essence

ekstrawagancj|a f extravagance; **ubierać się bez** ~**i** to dress unpretentiously

ekstrawaganc|ki adi. [wygląd, strój, zachowanie] extravagant

ekstremaln|y adi. książk. [poglądy, warunki, polityka, ugrupowanie] extreme; **sporty** ~**e** extreme sports

ekstremistyczn|y adi. extremist

ekumeniczn|y adi. Relig. [ruch, nabożeństwo] ecumenical

ekwipun|ek m equipment; ~**ek turystyczny** camping a. hiking equipment

ekwiwalen|t m książk. ① (równowartość) equivalent; ~**t w naturze/gotówce** the equivalent in kind/in cash ② (odpowiednik) equivalent (**czegoś** of sth)

elastyczn|y adi. [kostium, tkanina] stretchy GB, stretch US; [krok, chód, ruchy] springy; przen. [polityka, poglądy, plan] flexible; ~**y system cen** flexible pricing

elegancj|a f elegance; **ubierać się z** ~**ą** to dress elegantly

eleganc|ki adi. ① [kobieta, strój, ukłon] elegant; ~**ki wobec kobiet** gallant towards women ② [bal,

sklep, mieszkanie] elegant; posh pot. ③ (sprytny) [plan, rozwiązanie] elegant

elegan|t m, ~**tka** f fashionable dresser także iron.

elek|t m the elect; **prezydent** ~**t** the president-elect

elektora|t m electorate; **niezdecydowany** ~**t** floating voters GB, swing voters US; ~**t socjalistów** the socialist vote

elektrociepłowni|a f (combined) heat and power station a. plant

elektro|da f electrode; ~**da dodatnia/ujemna** a positive/negative electrode

elektron m electron

elektroni|ka f ① (nauka) electronics ② pot. (sprzęt) (home/office) electronics; (w samochodzie) high-tech gadgetry

elektrowni|a f power station a. plant; ~**a atomowa** a. **jądrowa** an atomic a. a nuclear power station; ~**a cieplna** a thermal power station; ~**a wodna** a hydroelectric power station

elektrowstrząs m Med. electric shock; **leczenie** ~**ami** electroshock therapy

elektryczność f electricity

elektryczn|y adi. [prąd, obwód, czajnik] electric; [energia, urządzenie] electric(al); **gniazdko** ~**e** an electricity a. power socket; **ogrzewanie** ~**e** electric heating; **sklep** ~**y** an electrical shop; **zegar** ~**y** an electric(al) clock

elektryfikacj|a f electrification

elektryfik|ować impf vt to electrify [linię kolejową]

elektry|k m ① (technik) electrician, wireman US ② (inżynier) electrical engineer

elektryz|ować impf **Ⅰ** vt ① to charge (up) [bursztyn] ② przen. to electrify [widzów, słuchaczy] **Ⅱ** **elektryzować się** [materiał, włosy] to pick up static

elemen|t m ① (składnik) element; **obce** ~**ty w języku** foreign elements in a language; ~**t składowy** a component part; **istnieje tu także** ~**t ryzyka** there's also an element of risk involved ② książk., pejor. (grupa ludzi) element; ~**t przestępczy/ wywrotowy** criminal/subversive elements

elementarn|y adi. [potrzeby, oczekiwania] basic; [wiedza, pojęcia, cząstki] elementary; **brak mu** ~**ej kultury** he has no manners at all

elementarz m ① Szkol. primer ② przen. ABC

elewacj|a f elevation; ~**a frontowa/tylna/boczna** the front/back/side elevation

elewato|r m silo, grain elevator US

eliksi|r m elixir; ~**r młodości/życia** the elixir of youth/life

eliminacj|a f ① (usuwanie) elimination ② (wstępny etap konkursu) preliminary; (w sporcie) qualifier; ~**e do biegu na 100 m** the 100 m qualifiers; ~**e do mistrzostw świata w piłce nożnej** the World Cup qualifiers

elimin|ować *impf vt* ① (usuwać) to eliminate ② (wykluczać) *[kara, kontuzja]* to disqualify *[zawodnika]* ③ (wygrywać) *[drużyna, zawodnik]* to eliminate *[rywala]*

elips|a *f* ① Mat. ellipse ② Jęz., Literat. ellipsis

eli|ta *f* elite; ~**ty władzy** the ruling elite

elitarn|y *adi. [sztuka, literatura]* elitist; *[dzielnica, klub]* exclusive

elokwencj|a *f* ① (krasomówstwo) eloquence ② iron. verbosity

elokwentn|y *adi.* książk. ① (wymowny) eloquent ② iron. verbose

emali|a *f* ① (szkliwo) enamel ② (farba) gloss paint; ~**a do paznokci** nail polish a. varnish GB

emaliowan|y *adi. [czajnik, broszka]* enamel; **naczynia** ~**e** enamelware

emancypacj|a *f* emancipation; ~**a kobiet** women's liberation a. emancipation

emancypant|ka *f* women's rights advocate; Hist. suffragette

emancyp|ować się *impf v refl.* ① *[kobieta]* to become emancipated a. liberated ② książk. (usamodzielniać się) to emancipate oneself; ~**ujące się narody** emerging nations

eman|ować *impf* ① *vt* książk. (emitować) to radiate *[ciepło, światło]* ② *vi* przen. to emanate

embarg|o *n* Handl. embargo (**na coś** on sth); **nałożyć** ~**o** to impose an embargo; **znieść** ~**o** to lift a. end an embargo

emblema|t *m* emblem

embrion *m* embryo

emery|t *m*, ~**tka** *f* senior citizen, (old age) pensioner GB

emerytaln|y *adi. [fundusz, system, świadczenia]* pension; **wiek** ~**y** retirement age

emerytu|ra *f* ① (świadczenie) (retirement) pension; **otrzymywać** a. **pobierać** ~**rę** to receive a. draw a pension ② (okres) retirement; **pójść na** ~**rę** to retire; **przejść na wcześniejszą** ~**rę** to take early retirement; **być na** ~**rze** to be retired

emigracj|a *f* ① (opuszczenie ojczyzny) emigration; (niedobrowolna) exile; ~**a zarobkowa** emigration for economic reasons; ~**a sezonowa** seasonal migration; **przebywać na** ~**i** to be an expatriate a. émigré; (niedobrowolnie) to be in exile ② (ludzie) expatriate a. émigré community

emigran|t *m*, ~**tka** *f* emigrant; (polityczny) émigré

emigr|ować *pf, impf vi* to emigrate

emisj|a *f* ① Ekon. issue; ~**a akcji/papierów wartościowych** an issue of shares/securities; ~**a nowej serii znaczków** an issue of a new series of stamps ② Radio, TV broadcast(ing); TV transmission; **przerwa w** ~**i** a break in transmission ③ Fiz. emission; ~**a cząstek/elektronowa** particle/electron emission ④ Ekol. emission; ~**a dwutlenku węgla do atmosfery** carbon dioxide emission a. discharge (into the atmosphere) ⑤ Muz. emission

emit|ować *impf vt* ① Ekon. to issue *[akcje, pieniądze, znaczki]* ② Radio, TV to broadcast *[program]* ③ Fiz. to emit *[ciepło, energię, promienie]* ④ Ekol. to discharge *[gaz, pyły, zanieczyszczenia]*

emocj|a *f* emotion; **dreszczyk** ~**i** a thrill of emotion; **bez** ~**i** unemotionally; **opanować** ~**e** to control a. contain one's emotions; **dać się ponieść** ~**om** to be a. get carried away by one's emotions

emocjonaln|y *adi. [reakcja, stan, zaburzenia]* emotional

emocjon|ować *impf* ① *vt* to excite ② **emocjonować się** to be excited (**czymś** about sth)

emulsj|a *f* emulsion; (farba) emulsion (paint); ~**a do opalania** a suntan lotion; ~**a światłoczuła** a light-sensitive emulsion

encyklopedi|a *f* encyclop(a)edia; ~**a podręczna/powszechna** a concise/popular encyclopedia; ~**a wojskowa** a military encyclopedia

encyklopedyczn|y *adi. [hasło, publikacja, wydawnictwo]* encyclop(a)edic; **słownik** ~**y** a lexicon; ~**a pamięć** przen. an encyclopedic memory

endokrynolo|g *m* Med. endocrinologist

endokrynologi|a *f* Med. endocrinology

energetyczn|y *adi.* energy; **zasoby** ~**e** energy resources; **światowy kryzys** ~**y** a world energy crisis; **przemysł** ~**y** the power industry; **zakład** ~**y** a power plant

energi|a *f* ① (żywotność) energy; **przypływ** ~**i** a burst a. surge of energy; **być pełnym** ~**i** to be full of energy a. vitality ② Fiz. energy; ~**a chemiczna/cieplna** chemical/thermal energy; ~**a atomowa/jądrowa** atomic/nuclear energy; ~**a słoneczna** solar power a. energy; ~**a wiatrowa/wodna** wind/water power; **przerwa w dostawie** ~**i elektrycznej** a power cut a. failure

energiczn|y *adi. grad. [osoba, działanie]* energetic; ~**y chód/ruch** a brisk gait/movement

energooszczędn|y *adi. [oświetlenie, technologia]* energy-efficient; *[żarówka]* energy-saving

enigmatycznie *adv. [powiedzieć, uśmiechać się]* enigmatically

enigmatyczn|y *adi. [mina, odpowiedź, uśmiech]* enigmatic

entuzja|sta *m*, ~**stka** *f* enthusiast

entuzjastyczn|y *adi. grad. [powitanie, recenzja, tłum]* enthusiastic; **zbyt** ~**y** overenthusiastic

entuzjazm *m* enthusiasm; **z** ~**em** enthusiastically; **bez** ~**u** without enthusiasm

entuzjazm|ować się *impf v refl.* to be enthusiastic (**czymś** about sth); „**to wspaniały pomysł!**" – ~**ował się** 'that's great idea!' – he enthused

enzym *m* enzyme; ~**y trawienne** digestive enzymes

epicentr|um *n* epicentre GB, epicenter US

epidemi|a *f* epidemic także przen.; ~**a grypy/cholery** a flu/cholera epidemic; **osiągnąć rozmiary** ~**i** to reach epidemic proportions

epi|ka *f* epic

epilepsj|a *f* Med. epilepsy; **atak** a. **napad** ~**i** an epileptic fit

epilepty|k *m*, ~**czka** *f* Med. epileptic

epilog *m* Literat., Teatr epilogue; Muz. coda; **jaki był** ~ **tej awantury?** przen. what was the outcome of the row?

episkopa|t *m* [1] Relig. (biskupi) episcopate; **polski** ~**t** the Polish Episcopate [2] (godność) episcopate; **sprawować** ~**t** to hold a bishopric a. an episcopate

epite|t *m* [1] Literat. epithet [2] pot. (wyzwisko) name; **obrzucać kogoś** ~**tami** to hurl abuse a. insults at sb

epizo|d *m* [1] (zdarzenie) episode; **godny ubolewania** ~**d** a lamentable episode a. incident [2] Kino, Literat., Teatr (fragment) episode; **film złożony z** ~**dów** an episodic film [3] Kino, Teatr (rola) bit part

epo|ka *f* [1] (okres) era; **miniona** ~**ka** a bygone era a. age; ~**ka Napoleona** the Napoleonic era a. period; ~**ka lotów kosmicznych** the space age; **umeblowanie z** ~**ki** authentic period furniture; **wyprzedzać** ~**kę** to be ahead of one's time [2] Archeol. age [3] Geol. epoch
■ **być nie z tej** ~**ki** żart. to be a relic (of a bygone age)

epokow|y *adi.* [odkrycie, wydarzenie] epoch-making

e|ra *f* [1] (okres) age, era; **era telewizji** the age a. era of television; **nasza era** the modern age [2] Geol. era; **era paleozoiczna/mezozoiczna/kenozoiczna** the Paleozoic/Mesozoic/Cenozoic (era)

erekcj|a *f* erection

er|ka *f* pot. [1] (karetka) ambulance *(equipped for cardiopulmonary resuscitation)* [2] (oddział szpitalny) intensive-care unit, ICU [3] (rządowa linia telefoniczna) hotline

erotoman *m* erotomaniac; pot. sex maniac pot.

erotyczn|y *adi.* [1] (zmysłowy) [doświadczenie, perwersja] sexual; [film, sen] erotic; **scena** ~**a** an erotic a. a sex scene; **życie** ~**e** sex life [2] (miłosny) [utwór, wiersz] erotic

erotyzm *m* erot(ic)ism

erozj|a *f* [1] Geol. erosion [2] Techn. abrasion

erudycj|a *f* erudition książk.

erudy|ta *m*, ~**tka** *f* erudite person książk.

erupcj|a *f* Geol. eruption także przen.; ~**a uczuć** an eruption a. outburst of feeling; ~**a talentu** an explosion of talent

esej *m* essay; ~ **historyczny/filozoficzny** a historical/philosophical essay

esencj|a *f* [1] (roztwór, wywar) essence; ~**a rumiankowa** camomile essence a. extract [2] (napar) infusion

[3] książk. (istota) essence; ~**a bytu** the essence of existence

eskad|ra *f* Wojsk. (w lotnictwie) flight; (w marynarce) squadron; ~**ra bombowców/myśliwców** a bomber/fighter flight; ~**ra krążowników** a cruiser squadron

eskapa|da *f* (przygoda) escapade; (wycieczka) jaunt; **wybrać się na kilkudniową** ~**dę w góry** to take off for the mountains for a few days pot.

eskor|ta *f* [1] (konwój) (armed) escort; ~**ta policyjna** a police escort; **pod** ~**tą** under escort a. guard; **bez** ~**ty** unescorted [2] (asysta) entourage; ~**ta prezydencka** the president's entourage [3] Wojsk. (zespół okrętów) escort

eskort|ować *impf vt* [1] (pilnować) to escort [konwój, więźnia]; ~**ować pieniądze** to transport money under escort [2] (towarzyszyć) to escort [głowę państwa]

esperan|to *n, n inv.* Esperanto

estaka|da *f* (wiadukt) flyover GB, overpass; (pomost) gantry

este|ta *m*, ~**tka** *f* aesthete, esthete US

estetyczn|y [I] *adi.* [dociekania, poglądy, postawa] aesthetic, esthetic US; **medycyna** ~**a** a cosmetic surgery

[II] *adi. grad.* (ładny) [ubiór, wygląd] aesthetic(ally pleasing), esthetic(ally pleasing) US

estra|da *f* [1] (podium) stage; **wejść na** ~**dę** to come on (to the) stage [2] (przemysł rozrywkowy) show business; **gwiazda** ~**dy** a show-business star

etap *m* [1] (część drogi) stage; **ostatni** ~ **podróży** the last stage a. leg of the journey [2] (stadium) stage; **wczesny** ~ **rozwoju** an early stage of development; ~**ami** in a. by stages; **zacząć nowy** ~ **w życiu** to begin a new phase a. stage in one's life; **wprowadzić/wycofywać coś** ~**ami** to phase sth in/out; **na tym** ~**ie** at this stage

eta|t *m* (stałe zatrudnienie) (permanent) job; **pełny** ~**t** a full-time job; **wolny** ~**t** a (job) vacancy; **redukcja** ~**tów** job cuts; **pracować na całym** ~**cie/na części** ~**tu** to work full-time/part-time

etatow|y *adi.* ~**y pracownik** (na stałe) a permanent a. regular employee; (na pełnym etacie) a full-time employee

ete|r *m* [1] Chem. ether [2] Radio the ether; **cisza w** ~**rze** radio silence

etol|a *f* stole; ~**a z norek** a mink stole

etui /ˌetu'i/ *n inv.* (na okulary, pierścionki) case; (na klucze, płyty CD) holder

etyczn|y *adi.* [zagadnienie, norma] ethical; **kodeks** ~**y naukowca** a scientist's code of ethics

ety|ka *f* ethic(s); ~**ka lekarska/zawodowa** medical/professional ethics; **naruszenie zasad** ~**ki** a breach of ethics

etykie|ta *f* [1] (na produkcie) label [2] Komput. label [3] (normy zachowania) etiquette; **zasady** ~**ty** the rules of etiquette

■ **przypięto** a. **przyczepiono mu** ~**tę buntownika** he was labelled a rebel

etymologi|a f etymology

eucharysti|a /ˌewxaˈrɪstja/ f Relig. the Eucharist; **sprawować/przyjmować** ~**ę** to celebrate/receive the Eucharist

eufemistyczn|y /ˌewfemisˈtɪtʃnɪ/ adi. [wyrażenie] euphemistic

eufemizm /ewˈfemizm/ m euphemism

eufori|a /ewˈforja/ f euphoria; **ogarnęła go** ~**a** he became euphoric

eukaliptus /ˌewkaˈliptus/ m Bot. eucalyptus, gum tree

euro /ˈewro/ n inv. euro

europejs|ki /ewroˈpejski/ adi. [język, cywilizacja, kultura] European

eutanazj|a /ˌewtaˈnazja/ f euthanasia

ewakuacj|a f evacuation

ewakuacyjn|y adi. [droga, plan] evacuation

ewaku|ować pf, imp [I] vt to evacuate [ludzi]
[II] **ewakuować się** [1] (z zagrożonych terenów) to be evacuated [2] pot., żart. to take off pot.; to bail out US pot., żart.

Ewangeli|a f Gospel; ~**a według św. Jana** the Gospel according to St John

ewangelic|ki adi. evangelical

ewangeli|k m, ~**czka** f evangelical

ewentualnie [I] adv. if need be; **czy i** ~ **jakie działania przedsięwziąć** what action, if any, should be taken; **Anglia, Francja i** ~ **Niemcy** England, France, and possibly Germany
[II] coni. or

ewentualn|y adi. [zmiany, szkody] possible

ewidencj|a f record(s); ~**a wydatków** a record a. account of expenses; ~**a ludności** population records; ~**a gruntów** land records; ~**a pacjentów** patients' records

ewidentn|y adi. książk. [błąd, nonsens, dowód] evident; [przykład, znak] clear

ewolucj|a f [1] (przemiana) evolution [2] Biol. evolution; ~**a człowieka** human evolution; **teoria** ~**i** the theory of evolution [3] (trudna figura) acrobatic manoeuvre GB, acrobatic maneuver US; (łyżwiarza, tancerza) evolution; ~**e lotnicze** a. **powietrzne** aerial acrobatics

ewolu|ować impf vi książk. to evolve

F

F, f *n inv.* ① (litera) F, f ② Muz. F

fabry|ka *f* (zakład) factory; **~ka samochodów** a car factory a. plant; **~ka papieru** a paper mill; **~ka absolwentów** przen., pejor. (o uczelni) a degree factory przen., pejor.

fabryk|ować *impf vt* (podrabiać) to fabricate *[dowody]*; to forge *[dokumenty, zaświadczenia, dzieła sztuki]*

fabularn|y *adi.* fictional; **proza ~a** fiction; **film ~y** a feature film

fabu|ła *f* story(line)

face|t *m* pot. bloke GB, guy pot.; **porządny z niego ~t** he's a decent bloke GB a. regular guy US

fach *m* trade; **kolega po ~u** a colleague in the same line of work; **nauczyć się (jakiegoś) ~u** to learn a trade; **znać swój ~** to know one's job

fachow|iec *m* ① (specjalista) expert ② pot. (rzemieślnik) repairman

fachow|y *adi.* ① (specjalistyczny) *[terminologia, wykształcenie]* specialist ② (kompetentny) *[firma, usługa]* professional

fago|t *m* Muz. bassoon

fajans *m* (ceramika) earthenware; faience spec.

fajerwerk *m* ① (sztuczny ogień) firework; **puszczać ~i** to let off GB a. set off US fireworks ② przen. (błyskotliwa uwaga) flash of wit; wisecrack pot.

faj|ka *f* ① pipe; **palić ~kę** to smoke a pipe ② pot. (papieros) fag GB pot. ③ (do oddychania) snorkel ④ pot. (znak) tick GB, check (mark) US

■ **~ka pokoju** a peace pipe także przen.

fajn|ie, ~o *adv. grad.* pot. *[śpiewać, pisać]* great pot.; **~ie wyglądać** to look great a. cool pot.; **~ie, że jesteś** it's great that you're here

fajn|y *adi. grad.* pot. *[osoba, książka, samochód]* great pot.

faks *m* (urządzenie) fax (machine); (wiadomość) fax (message); **przesłać coś ~em** to send sth by fax

faks|ować *impf vt* to fax

fak|t *m* fact; **suche ~ty** dry facts; **~t dokonany** a fait accompli; **po ~cie** after the fact; **oparty na ~tach** based on fact a. the facts; **literatura ~tu** non-fiction; **~t ~tem**... a. **(to) ~t, że...** it's true a. it's a fact that...; **liczyć się z ~tami** to face the facts

faktu|ra *f* ① (rachunek) invoice; **wystawić ~rę na zakupiony towar** to make out an invoice for goods purchased ② (powierzchnia, budowa) texture także przen.

faktyczn|y *adi.* actual

fakultatywn|y *adi.* książk. optional

fakulte|t *m* ① (wydział) faculty GB, department a. school US; **robić drugi ~t** (kolejne studia) to do a second degree; (studia równoczesne) to be on a joint-degree programme GB a. in a dual-degree program US ② pot., Szkol., Uniw. option GB, elective US

fal|a *f* ① (na wodzie) wave; **~a powodziowa** a flood wave; **~a przypływu** high tide; **płynąć z ~ą/przeciw ~i** to swim with/against the current; **kołysać się na ~ach** to be rocked by the waves ② przen. (zjawisko) wave; **~a mrozów/upałów** a cold wave/heatwave; **~a imigrantów** a wave of immigrants; **~a meksykańska** Sport a Mexican wave ③ przen. (przypływ uczuć) wave; (złości) surge ④ Fiz. wave; **długość ~i** a wavelength; **nadawać na tych samych ~ach** to transmit on the same wavelength; przen. to be on the same wavelength ⑤ (w wojsku) bullying , ≈ hazing US

■ **być na ~i** (odnosić sukcesy) to be riding high pot.; (być modnym) to be in vogue; **na ~ach eteru** Radio on the air

fali|sty *adi.* ① (w kształcie fal) *[włosy, linia]* wavy; **blacha ~sta** corrugated iron ② (pagórkowaty) *[krajobraz]* rolling

falochron *m* ① (na brzegu) breakwater ② (na statku) bulwark

fal|ować *impf* **Ⅰ** *vt* ① (poruszać) *[wiatr]* to ripple *[powierzchnię wody]* ② (nadawać kształt fali) to corrugate *[blachę]*

Ⅱ *vi* ① (poruszać się) *[zboże]* to wave; *[woda]* to ripple *[drzewa, tłum]* to sway ② (tworzyć fale) *[włosy]* to wave; *[teren, droga]* to undulate ③ przen. (zmieniać się) *[nastroje, sympatie]* to fluctuate

falow|y *adi.* ① (rytmiczny) regular ② Fiz., Radio *[ruch]* wave

falsyfika|t *m* (dzieło sztuki) forgery; (banknot) counterfeit; **~t paszportu/podpisu** a forged passport/signature

fał|da *f* ① (zakładka) pleat; **spódnica (układana) w ~dy** a pleated skirt ② (nierówność) fold; **~da skóry/tłuszczu** a fold of skin/fat

fałsz *m* ① (kłamstwo) lie ② (obłuda) falseness; **wyczuć ~ w czyichś słowach** to sense a false note in sb's words [3] Muz. false note; **wpadać w** ~ to slip out of tune a. off key [4] Filoz. falsity

fałszerstw|o *n* (podrabianie) falsification; (oszustwo) fraud; ~**o wyborcze** electoral fraud

fałszerz *m* forger; ~ **obrazów** an art forger; ~ **pieniędzy** a counterfeiter

fałsz|ować *impf* **[]** *vt* [1] (podrabiać) to forge *[dokument, podpis, obraz]* [2] (przeinaczać) to falsify *[dane, wyniki]*; to distort *[historię, prawdę]*

[] *vi* Muz. (w śpiewie) to sing out of tune a. off-key; (na instrumencie) to play out of tune a. off-key

fałszyw|y *adi.* [1] (podrobiony) fake; ~**y paszport** a fake a. false passport; ~**e pieniądze** counterfeit money [2] (nieprawdziwy, niewłaściwy) false; ~**y alarm** a false alarm [3] (obłudny) *[osoba]* insincere; *[uśmiech]* false; ~**a skromność** false modesty [4] Muz. *[nuta]* false; ~**e brzmienie** discordance

fanatyczn|y *adi.* *[zwolennik, nienawiść]* fanatic(al)

fanaty|k *m*, ~**czka** *f* [1] (ślepo oddany idei) fanatic; ~**k polityczny/religijny** a political/religious fanatic [2] (wielbiciel) fanatic pot.; ~**k komputerów/ żeglowania** a computer/sailing fanatic a. freak pot.

fan|t *m* [1] (na loterii) prize [2] (w grach towarzyskich) forfeit; **dać/wykupić** ~**t(a)** to give/buy back a forfeit

■ **co z tym** ~**tem zrobić?** what can I do about it?

fantastycznonaukow|y *adi.* *[literatura, opowiadanie]* science fiction

fantastyczn|y *adi.* [1] (dziwaczny, nierealny) *[wizje, kształty]* fantastic(al) [2] pot. (wyjątkowy) fantastic pot. [3] Kino, Literat. fantasy

fantasty|ka *f* Literat., Szt. fantasy; ~**ka naukowa** science fiction

fantazj|a *f* [1] (zmyślenie) fantasy; **świat** ~**i** a world of fantasy [2] (wyobraźnia) imagination; **puścić wodze** ~**i** to indulge in fantasizing [3] (zuchwałość) daring; **ułańska** ~**a** a swashbuckling a. daredevil streak; **robić coś z** ~**ą** to do sth with panache a. dash [4] (kaprys) caprice; **miewać swoje** ~**e** to have one's whims a. caprices [5] Muz. fantasy

fantazj|ować *impf* *vi* to fantasize; **dość tego** ~**owania** stop fantasizing

faraon *m* pharaoh

farb|a *f* [1] (do malowania) paint; (do barwienia) dye; ~**a drukarska** printing ink; ~**a do drewna** wood stain; ~**a olejna** oil paint; ~**y plakatowe** poster paints a. colours; ~**y wodne** watercolours; ~**a do włosów** hair dye [2] pot. blood; **puścić komuś** ~**ę z nosa** pot. to give sb a bloody nose

■ **puścić** ~**ę** pot. to spill the beans pot.

farb|ować *impf* **[]** *vt* [1] (zabarwiać) to dye *[tkaninę]*; ~**ować włosy na czarno/rudo** to dye one's hair black/red [2] (plamić) to stain

[] *vi* (puszczać kolor) to run; **sukienka** ~**owała w praniu** the (colours of the) dress ran in the wash

[] **farbować się** [1] (zabarwiać się) *[materiał, włókno]* to dye [2] (farbować włosy) to dye one's hair

farm|a *f* farm

farmaceu|ta /ˌfarmaˈtsewta/ *m*, ~**tka** *f* pharmacist

farmaceutyczn|y /ˌfarmatsewˈtɪtʃnɪ/ *adi.* *[przemysł, rynek]* pharmaceutical

farmacj|a *f* pharmacy, pharmaceutics

fars|a *f* farce także przen.

farsz *m* Kulin. stuffing; ~ **mięsny** forcemeat (stuffing), meat stuffing

fartuch *m* [1] (chroniący przód ubrania) apron; (z karczkiem) pinafore [2] (ubranie ochronne) gown; ~ **lekarski** a (doctor's) white a. lab coat [3] (osłona) apron; ~**y przeciwbłotne** mudflaps

■ **trzymać się czyjegoś** ~**a** to be tied to sb's apron strings

fasa|da *f* facade także przen.; **jego grzeczność to tylko** ~**da** his politeness is just a facade

fascynacj|a *f* fascination; ~**a sztuką/muzyką** fascination with art/music

fascyn|ować *impf* **[]** *vi* to be fascinated; **to mnie** ~**uje** it fascinates me

[] **fascynować się** to be fascinated (**czymś** by sth)

fascynując|y *adi.* *[przygoda, zjawisko, osoba]* fascinating

fasol|a *f* (roślina) bean; (nasiona, strąki) beans

fasolów|ka *f* pot. bean soup

fason *m* [1] (krój) cut; ~ **płaszcza/kołnierzyka** the cut of a coat/collar; **stracić** ~ to lose shape [2] (animusz) dash; **mieć** ~ to have style; **z** ~**em** with great panache; **trzymać** ~ to keep one's chin up, to keep a stiff upper lip

fastry|ga *f* [1] (ścieg) tack(ing) [2] (nić) tacking thread a. cotton GB, basting thread

fastryg|ować *impf* *vt* to tack; ~**ować mankiety do rękawów** to tack a. baste the cuffs to the sleeves

faszer|ować *impf* **[]** *vt* [1] Kulin. to stuff *[kaczkę, paprykę]* (**czymś** with sth) [2] pot., przen. to stuff pot.; ~**ować dziecko słodyczami** to stuff a child with sweets

[] **faszerować się** pot. (jeść zbyt dużo) to stuff oneself pot. (**czymś** with sth)

faszerowan|y *adi.* *[kaczka, papryka]* stuffed

fatalnie *adv. grad.* [1] (źle) *[grać]* terribly; *[czuć się, wyglądać]* awful; ~ **mówi po francusku** his French is terrible; **koncert wypadł** ~ the concert was a dismal failure [2] (tragicznie w skutkach) *[potłuc się]* badly; *[skończyć się]* disastrously; ~ **skończyć** to come to a bad end

fataln|y *adi.* [1] (nieodpowiedni) *[warunki, organizacja]* awful, dreadful; **co za** ~**a pogoda** what awful a. dreadful weather; **zrobić** ~**e wrażenie** to make a terrible impression [2] (zły, niekorzystny) *[błąd, krok]* fatal; **mieć** ~**e skutki** to have disastrous results

fatamorgan|a *f* [1] (obraz, zjawisko) mirage [2] przen. (wytwór wyobraźni) illusion

fatum *n inv.* ① (zły los) fate; **ciążyło na niej jakieś ~** she was doomed ② Mitol. Fate

faty|ga *f* trouble; **zadali sobie wiele ~gi, żeby...** they went to a lot of trouble (in order) to...; **to dla pana, za ~gę** this is for you, for your trouble; **szkoda ~gi** it's not worth the bother

fatyg|ować *impf* **[]** *vt* to bother; **nie chciała go tym ~ować** she didn't want to bother him with it **[]** **fatygować się** to bother; **proszę się nie ~ować** don't bother about a. with that; **niepotrzebnie pan się ~ował** you needn't have bothered

faul /fawl/ *m* Sport foul; **~ na kimś** a foul against a. on sb

faul|ować /faw'lovatɕ/ *impf vt* Sport to foul

faun|a /ˈfawna/ *f* fauna

fawory|t *m*, **~tka** *f* ① (prawdopodobny zwycięzca) favourite GB, favorite US; **~t do złotego medalu** the favourite to win the gold medal ② książk. (ulubieniec) favourite GB, favorite US, darling

faworyz|ować *impf vt* to favour GB, to favor US; **~ować kogoś kosztem kogoś** to favour sb over sb

faz|a *f* ① (etap) phase; **początkowa ~a projektu** the initial phase of a project; **wejść w ostateczną ~ę** to reach the final phase a. stage ② Astron. phase; **Księżyc w pierwszej ~ie** the Moon in its a. the first quarter ③ Elektr. phase

feb|ra *f* pot. ① (gorączka) fever; (dreszcze) shivers ② (malaria) malaria

federacj|a *f* federation

fele|r *m* pot. defect; (w sprzęcie) bug pot.

felern|y *adi.* pot. *[buty, urządzenie]* duff GB pot.; *[towar]* tenth-rate pot.

felieton *m* (newspaper/magazine) column; **~y polityczne** political commentaries

femini|stka *f* feminist

feminizm *m* feminism

fenomen *m* ① (osobliwość) phenomenon ② książk. (zjawisko) phenomenon; **~ aktorski** a phenomenal actor

fenomenaln|y *adi.* *[wynik, głos, sukces]* phenomenal

feraln|y *adv.* *[liczba, rok]* unlucky; **tego ~ego dnia** on that fateful day

feri|e *plt* (szkolne) holiday(s) GB, vacation US; (uniwersyteckie) vacation; **wyjechać na ~e** to go away for the holidays

ferm|a *f* farm; **~a drobiu** a. **drobiowa** a poultry farm

fermen|t *m* ① (niepokój) unrest ② Biol., Chem. enzyme

fermentacj|a *f* fermentation

ferment|ować *impf vi* (wino, sok) to ferment

ferwo|r *m* fervour GB, fervor US; **gestykulować w ~rze** to gesture fervently

festiwal *m* festival; **~ filmowy/muzyczny** a film/music festival; **na ~u w Cannes** at the Cannes Film Festival

festyn *m* fête GB, fair

fe|ta *f* gala

feto|r *m* stench

fet|ować *impf vt* to fête *[zwycięzców, bohatera]*; to celebrate *[zwycięstwo, jubileusz]*

fetysz *m* ① Antrop. fetish ② przen. (obiekt kultu) totem, icon ③ pot. (talizman) talisman; (maskotka) mascot ④ Med., Psych. fetish

fiask|o *n* fiasco

fi|ga **[]** *f* ① (owoc) fig ② (drzewo) fig (tree) ③ pot. (nic) zilch pot.; **figa z makiem** sweet Fanny Adams a. FA GB pot.; **figę mnie to obchodzi** I don't care a. give a fig; **figa! no way! **[]** **figi** *plt* panties

fig|iel *m* trick; **życie często płata ~le** przen. life often plays tricks on us; **o mały ~iel** within an inch a. inches

figlarn|y *adi.* *[zachowanie, uśmiech]* playful

figla|rz *m*, **~rka** *f* prankster

figl|ować *impf vi* to frolic

figu|ra *f* ① (rzeźba) statue ② (kształt ciała) figure; **kostium dopasowany do ~ry** a close-fitting suit ③ (osobistość) figure; **~ra urzędowa** a public figure ④ (osoba) character pot.; **podejrzana/malownicza ~ra** a shady/colourful character ⑤ Gry (w kartach) court card GB, face card US; (w szachach) (chess) piece ⑥ Sport figure ⑦ Mat. figure ⑧ Literat. **~ra retoryczna** a. **stylistyczna** rhetorical figure

figur|ować *impf vi* to appear

fikcj|a *f* ① (nierzeczywistość) fiction; (złudzenie, mrzonka) illusion; **~a literacka** literary fiction; **bezpłatne studia to ~a** free education is a myth a. pure fiction ② (pozór) pretence GB, pretense US; **cała ta reforma to czysta ~a** the entire reform is mere window-dressing

fikcyjn|y *adi.* *[postać, bohater]* fictional; *[nazwisko, adres]* fictitious

fiks|ować *impf vi* pot. ① (wariować) to be going mad a. crazy pot.; **~ować z radości/ze szczęścia** to be deliriously happy ② (szwankować) to act up pot.; **od czasu tej stłuczki samochód ~uje** the car has been acting up since that crash we had

fikuśn|y *adi.* grad. pot. fancy

filantropi|a *f* książk. philanthropy

filantropijn|y *adi.* *[działalność, organizacja]* philanthropic

fila|r *m* ① (słup) pillar; **~ry mostu** the piers of a bridge ② przen. (podpora) pillar; **jest ~rem naszej rodziny** he's the pillar of our family

filateli|sta *m* stamp collector

filatelistyczn|y *adi.* *[sklep, wystawa]* philatelic

filatelisty|ka *f* stamp collecting

filc *m* felt; **kapelusz z ~u** a felt hat

file|t *m* fillet; ~**t z łososia** (a) salmon fillet; ~**ty cielęce** veal fillets
filharmoni|a /ˌfilxar'monja/ *f* 1 (instytucja) Philharmonic (Society) 2 (budynek) (Philharmonic) concert hall
fili|a *f* branch
filiżan|ka *f* cup; ~**ka herbaty** a cup of tea
film *m* 1 (w kinie) film, movie US; ~ **długometrażowy** a. **pełnometrażowy** a full-length feature (film); ~ **dokumentalny** a documentary film; ~ **fabularny** a feature film; ~ **tylko dla dorosłych** an adult a. adults-only film 2 (kinematografia) the cinema, the movies US; **interesować się** ~**em** to be interested in film a. (the) cinema 3 (klisza) film; **włożyć nowy** ~ **do aparatu** to put a new (roll of film) in one's camera 4 (taśma filmowa) film 5 (warstwa ochrona) film
■ ~ **mu/mi się urwał** pot. he/I got completely blotto pot.
film|ować *impf vt* 1 (utrwalać na taśmie) to film 2 (ekranizować) to make [sth] into a film; ~**ować powieść** to make a film version of a novel
filmow|iec *m* film-maker
filmow|y *adi.* 1 [aktor, reżyser] film, movie US 2 [książka, proza] cinematic 3 pot. (jak z filmu) **to była** ~**a scena** it was like a scene from some film pot.
filologi|a *f* 1 (dyscyplina uniwersytecka) language and literature studies; (badania naukowe) philology; ~**a angielska/klasyczna** English/Classical studies 2 (wydział) school of (foreign) languages
filozof *m* philosopher
filozofi|a *f* philosophy
filozof|ować *impf vi* to philosophize (**nad czymś** on a. about sth)
filt|r *m* 1 (urządzenie) filter; **stacja** ~**rów** a filtration plant 2 (papierosa) filter (tip) 3 Kosmet. filter
filtr|ować *impf vt* to filter [wodę, powietrze]
finali|sta *m,* ~**stka** *f* finalist
finaliz|ować *impf vt* książk. to finalize [umowę, transakcję, rozmowy]
fina|ł *m* 1 (koniec) end; **mieć tragiczny** ~**ł** to end in tragedy; **sprawa znalazła swój** ~**ł w sądzie** the dispute ended up in court 2 (konkursu, zawodów) final; **wejść do** ~**łu** to reach the final 3 (filmu, książki) ending; (koncertu, opery) finale
finałow|y *adi.* Sport final; [monolog, scena] concluding
finans|e *plt* 1 (środki pieniężne) funds; (zarządzanie) finances; ~**e publiczne** public finance; **Ministerstwo Finansów** the Ministry of Finance 2 pot. (pieniądze) funds; ~**e rodziny** the household budget
finansi|sta *m,* ~**stka** *f* 1 (bogacz) tycoon 2 (ekspert) financier
finans|ować *impf vt* to finance; **szpital** ~**owany przez państwo** a state-funded hospital; ~**ować kluby piłkarskie** to sponsor football clubs

finansow|y *adi.* [polityka, plan, doradca] financial
finezj|a *f* książk. finesse
finisz *m* 1 Sport (wyścigu, biegu) home straight GB, home stretch US 2 pot. (zakończenie) the home straight GB., the home stretch US przen.
finisz|ować *impf vi* Sport [zawodnik] to finish 2 pot. (kończyć) to complete (**z czymś** sth)
fiole|t *m* (kolor) purple
fioletow|y *adi.* purple
fiol|ka *f* phial
fioł|ek *m* Bot. violet
fior|d *m* fjord
firan|ka *f* net curtain
firm|a *f* 1 (przedsiębiorstwo) company; **renomowana/ solidna** ~**a** a reputable/reliable company; **firma- krzak** przen. a fly-by-night company a. business pejor.; **wizerunek** ~**y** the corporate image 2 (nazwa przesiębiorstwa) company name 3 pot., przen. (o osobie) **solidna** ~**a** a reliable person
firm|ować *impf vt* 1 (użyczać nazwiska, nazwy) ~**ować program własnym nazwiskiem** to lend one's name to a programme; **koncert** ~**owała znana agencja** the concert was organized under the auspices of a well-known agency 2 (wspierać autorytetem) to endorse [transakcje, reformy] 3 (podpisywać) to sign; ~**ować przelew** to sign a transfer
firmow|y *adi.* 1 (dotyczący danej firmy) company; **nazwa** ~**a** a proprietary a. brand name; **papier** ~**y** letterhead(ed) paper; **znak** ~**y** a trademark 2 (dobrej firmy) [komputer, sprzęt] name-brand
fiskaln|y *adi.* fiscal; **polityka** ~**a** fiscal policy; **przepisy** ~**e** tax regulations; **kasa** ~**a** a cash register
fiskus *m* 1 (skarb państwa) ≈ the Exchequer GB, ≈ the Treasury (Department) US 2 pot. (urząd podatkowy) tax office
fistasz|ek *m* peanut
fisz|ka *f* 1 (katalogowa) (index) card 2 Gry chip; **płacić** ~**kami** to pay with chips
fizjologi|a *f* Biol., Med. physiology
fizjologiczn|y *adi.* Med. [procesy, zmiany, potrzeby] physiological; **sól** ~**a** saline solution
fizyczn|y *adi.* 1 (dotyczący fizyki) physics; **prawa** ~**e** the laws of physics; **wzory** ~**e** physics a. physical formulae 2 (materiały) physical 3 (dotyczący ciała ludzkiego) physical; **siła** ~**a** physical strength; **pociąg** ~**y** physical attraction; **wychowanie** ~**e** physical education 4 [mapa, geografia] physical
fizy|k *m* physicist
fizy|ka *f* physics
fla|ga *f* flag; ~**ga amerykańska** the American flag, the Stars and Stripes; ~**ga brytyjska** the British flag, the Union Jack
flak [**I**] *m* pot. 1 (jelito) gut(s) 2 (na kiełbasie) (sausage) skin a. casing 3 (opona) flat (tyre) GB, flat (tire) US
[**II**] **flaki** *plt* Kulin. (wołowe) tripe; (wieprzowe) chitterlings

■ **nudny jak** ∼**i z olejem** pot. (as) dull as dishwater a. ditchwater; ∼**i się we mnie/w nim przewracają na ten widok** pot. the sight makes my/his gorge rise a. turns my/his stomach; **wypruwać komuś** ∼**i** pot. to nag sb to death pot.; ∼**i ci/mu wypruję!** pot. I'll have your/his guts for garters! GB pot.; **wypruwać z siebie** a. **sobie** ∼**i** pot. to work one's guts out pot.

flakon m ① (na perfumy) flacon ② (wazon) vase

flamast|er m felt-tip (pen)

flanel|a f flannel

flasz|ka f pot. bottle; (smukła) flask; **płaska** ∼**ka** a hip flask; **puste** ∼**ki** empties pot.; **kupić dwie** ∼**ki** to buy two bottles of alcohol

fląd|ra f ① Zool. flounder ② pot., obraźl. (o kobiecie) slut obraźl.; slag GB pot., obraźl.

flegm|a f ① Med. (wydzielina) phlegm ② pot., przen. (zimna krew) cool-headedness; **angielska** ∼**a** British phlegm ③ pot., pejor. (osoba powolna) sluggard pejor.

flegmatyczn|y adi. ∼**y temperament** a phlegmatic temperament

flegmaty|k m, ∼**czka** f ① Psych. phlegmatic type ② (osoba powolna) sluggard

flejtuch m pot. scruff GB pot.

flek m heel tip

■ **być na** ∼**u** pot. to be well-oiled pot.

flesz m Fot. flash; **błyski** ∼**y** camera flashes

fle|t m Muz. flute; (prosty) recorder

flircia|ra, ∼**rka** f pot. flirt

flirciarz m pot. ladykiller pot.

flir|t m flirtation także przen.; **krótki** ∼**t z polityką** a brief flirtation with politics

flirt|ować impf vi ① (zalecać się) to flirt (**z kimś** with sb) ② przen. to have a flirtation (**z czymś** with sth)

flo|ra f Bot. flora

flore|t m Sport ① (broń) foil ② (dyscyplina) foil (fencing)

flo|ta f ① (statki, okręty) fleet; ∼**ta rybacka/ pasażerska** a fishing/passenger fleet ② pot. (pieniądze) cash pot.

flui|d m ① (energia) vibrations; (atmosfera) aura; **wydzielać dobroczynne** ∼**dy** to give off good vibrations ② Kosmet. liquid make-up a. foundation

fluo|r m Chem. fluorine; **pasta do zębów z** ∼**rem** a fluoride toothpaste

fluor|ować impf vt ① Chem. to fluorinate [metal, substancję] ② (dodawać związki fluoru) to fluoridate [wodę, sól] ③ Stomat. to fluoridate [zęby]

fluoryzacj|a f fluoridation

fobi|a f phobia

foch|y plt the sulks pot.; **stroić** ∼**y** to have the sulks

fo|ka f Zool. seal

foksterie|r m fox terrier

folde|r m brochure, folder US; ∼**r reklamowy/ turystyczny** an advertising/a travel brochure

foli|a f ① (metalowa) foil; (plastikowa) (plastic) wrap; ∼**a aluminiowa** aluminium foil; ∼**a do żywności** food wrap; ∼**a samoprzylegająca** shrinkwrap, cling film GB ② (tunel ogrodniczy) plastic tunnel

foli|ować impf vt to laminate [dokument, papier, trening]

folklo|r m (legendy i mity) folklore; (zwyczaje) folk customs; (rękodzieło) folk handicraft

fonety|ka f ① (nauka) phonetics ② (system dźwięków) sound system ③ (wymowa) pronunciation

foni|a /ˈfɔnja/ f Radio, TV sound

fontann|a f fountain także przen.

forem|ka f ① Kulin. (do pieczenia) mould GB, mold US; (do wycinania) pastry cutter, cookie cutter US ② (zabawka) (sandcastle) mould

foremn|y I adi. grad. [nos, ciało] shapely; [budynek] well-proportioned

II adi. [wielokąt, wielościan] regular

form|a f ① (postać, sposób) form; (kształt) shape; ∼**a i treść** form and content; **różne** ∼**y współpracy** different forms of cooperation; **wydać coś w** ∼**ie książkowej** to publish sth in book form; **przybierać różne** ∼**y** to take (on) various forms ② (utwór, dzieło sztuki) form; ∼**y przestrzenne** spatial forms ③ Jęz. form; ∼**y czasu przeszłego** past tense forms; ∼**a dopełniacza** the genitive form ④ Kulin. tin; ∼**a do ciasta** a cake tin; ∼**a chlebowa** a bread pan ⑤ Techn. mould GB, mold US ⑥ (wykrój) pattern ⑦ (sprawność) form; **być w dobrej/złej** ∼**ie** to be in good/poor form a. shape; **nie być w** ∼**ie** to be off form ⑧ (konwenanse) form; ∼**y towarzyskie** social conventions; **robić coś wyłącznie dla** ∼**y** to do sth purely as a matter of form

formacj|a f ① książk. (środowisko) background ② Polit. (ugrupowanie) group; ∼**a prawicowa/lewicowa** the right/left wing ③ Wojsk. (rodzaj broni) arm; (jednostka) unit; (szyk) formation

formali|sta m, ∼**stka** f stickler for rules; (urzędnik) jobsworth GB pot.

formaliz|ować impf vt książk. to formalize [kryteria, opis, umowę]

formalnoś|ć f formality; ∼**ci prawne/celne** legal/customs formalities; **ten egzamin to czysta** ∼**ć** the exam is a mere formality

formaln|y adi. formal

forma|t m ① format; **książka dużego** ∼**tu** a large format book ② przen. (klasa) stature; **pisarz wielkiego** ∼**tu** a writer of the first order

form|ować impf **I** vt ① (nadawać kształt) to shape; ∼**ować kulki z gliny** to shape clay into balls ② (kształtować) to form [osobę, charakter, upodobania] ③ (tworzyć) to form [rząd, armię, system] ④ (ustawiać się) to form [szereg, kolumnę]

II formować się ① (powstawać) [chmury, stalaktyty] to form ② (kształtować się) [osobowość] to be formed ③ (tworzyć się) [rząd, organizacja] to be formed

⁴ (ustawiać się) to form up; **~ować się w szereg/ krąg** to form into a row/circle

formularz *m* form; **~ zamówienia** an order-form; **wypełnić ~** to fill in GB a. out US a form

formu|ła *f* ① (sformułowanie, zasada) formula; **magiczne ~ły** magic formula ② Chem., Fiz., Mat. (wzór) formula; **~ła chemiczna/matematyczna** a chemical/mathematical formula ③ (charakter) format; **~ła programu/czasopisma** the format of a programme/magazine ④ Sport Formula; **kierowca ~ły pierwszej** a Formula One driver

formuł|ować *impf vt* to formulate *[myśli, przepisy]*

fors|a *f pot.* dosh pot.; **być bez ~y** to be out of cash; **być przy ~ie** to be in the money pot.; **leżeć** a. **siedzieć** a. **spać na ~ie** to be rolling in it pot.

fors|ować *impf* **❶** *vt* ① Wojsk. to cross *[rzekę, kanał]* ② (wyważać) to force *[drzwi, bramę]* ③ (popierać) to push a. force through *[kandydata, rozwiązanie]* ④ (męczyć) to strain *[struny głosowe, mięśnie]*; **~ować drużynę nadmiernym treningiem** to push a team too hard through too much training ⑤ Sport (narzucać) **~ować tempo** to force the pace **❷** **forsować się** to strain oneself

forsown|y *adi. grad. [marsz, wysiłek]* strenuous

fortec|a *f* Wojsk. fortress także przen.; **~a nie do zdobycia** an impregnable fortress; **latająca ~a** Wojsk. a flying fortress

fortel *m* książk. stratagem, ruse

fortepian *m* Muz. (grand) piano

fortun|a *f* ① (majątek) fortune; **dorobić się ~y** a. **zbić ~ę** to make a fortune; **rodzinna ~a** the family fortune ② (los) fortune; **~a się do nas uśmiechnęła** fortune smiled upon us ■ **~a kołem się toczy** fortune is fickle

fortyfikacj|a Wojsk. **❶** *f* (umacnianie) fortification **❷** **fortyfikacje** *plt* fortifications; **otoczyć miasto ~ami** to fortify a town

fortyfik|ować *impf vt* Wojsk. to fortify *[miasto, teren, obóz]*

for|um *n* forum także przen.; **postawić sprawę na ~um międzynarodowym** to raise an issue in the international arena; **wystąpić na ~um zjazdu** to speak at a convention

fos|a *f* moat; **~a orkiestrowa** Muz. the orchestra pit

fosfo|r *m* Chem. phosphorus

fotel *m* ① (mebel) armchair; **~ z wikliny** a wicker chair; **~ bujany** a. **na biegunach** a rocking chair; **~ obrotowy** a swivel chair; **siedzieć w ~u** to sit in an armchair ② (w samochodzie, samolocie, teatrze) seat; **~ kierowcy/pasażera** the driver's/passenger's seat ③ (do zabiegów) chair; **~ dentystyczny** a dentist's chair ④ (stanowisko) post; **~ dyrektorski/ministerialny** a managerial/ministerial post; **ubiegać się o ~ prezydencki** to run for President a. the presidency

fotogeniczn|y *adi. [osoba, twarz]* photogenic

fotograf *m* (osoba) photographer; (zakład fotograficzny) photographer's (shop)

fotografi|a *f* ① (zdjęcie) photograph; **czyjaś ~a** a photograph of sb ② (technika) photography; **~a barwna/czarno-biała** colour/black-and-white photography; **~a artystyczna/reklamowa** art/commercial photography

fotograficzn|y *adi.* ① *[papier, wystawa, agencja]* photographic; **błona ~a** a (photographic) film; **aparat ~y** a camera; **album ~y** a photo(graph) album ② przen. *[pamięć, wierność]* photographic; **z ~ą dokładnością** with photographic accuracy

fotograf|ować *impf* **❶** *vt* to photograph; „**zakaz ~owania**" 'no photography' **❷** **fotografować się** (robić sobie zdjęcia) to take a photo of oneself ② (być fotografowanym) to have one's photo a. picture taken

fotokomór|ka *f* photocell

fotokopi|a *f* photocopy; **zrobić ~ę czegoś** to photocopy sth

fotomontaż *m* photomontage

fotoreportaż *m* picture story

fotoreporte|r *m*, **~rka** *f* photojournalist

fotos *m* (sceny z filmu) still; (gwiazdy) publicity photograph

fragmen|t *m* passage; (wiersza, piosenki) excerpt

fragmentaryczn|y *adi. [notatki, wiedza]* fragmentary

fraj|da *f pot.* fun; **sprawić komuś wielką ~dę** to please sb no end

frak *m* tailcoat; tails pot.

frakcj|a *f* ① Polit. faction; **~a lewicowa/prawicowa** a left-/right-wing faction ② Chem., Geol. fraction

framu|ga *f* ① (rama) casing; **~ga drzwi** a doorcase; **~ga okienna** a window casing ② (otwór) doorway; (okna) window recess

frasz|ka *f* ① Literat. epigram ② (błahostka) trifle; (łatwa praca) cinch pot.

frazes *m* platitude; **wyświechtane ~y** hackneyed a. well-worn platitudes; **mieć usta pełne ~ów na temat czegoś** to mouth platitudes about sth

frekwencj|a *f* ① Szkol. attendance; **mieć słabą ~ę** *[klasa, uczeń]* to have a poor attendance record ② (udział) attendance; (w wyborach) turnout; **niska/ wysoka ~a wyborcza** a low/high voter turnout; **film bije rekordy ~i** the film is breaking box-office records

fresk *m* fresco

frędz|el *m*, **~la** *f* (pojedynczy) tassel; (obszycie) fringe; **zasłony z ~lami** tasselled curtains

fron|t *m* ① (przód) front; **~t budynku/pochodu** the front of a building/procession; **mieszkanie od ~tu** a flat at the front; **wejście od ~tu** a front entrance; **stać ~tem do kogoś/czegoś** książk. to stand facing sb/sth ② Meteo. front; **ciepły/zimny ~t** a warm/cold front ③ Wojsk. (rejon walk) front także przen.; **~t wschodni/zachodni** the eastern/western front; **linia** ~**tu** the front line; **wysłać kogoś na** ~**t** to send sb to the front; **na** ~**cie gospodarczym/reform** on the economic/reform front; **na wszystkich** ~**tach** on all fronts także przen.; **działać na dwa** ~**ty** to be playing a double game [4] (organizacja) front; ~**t narodowy** a national front

■ **zmienić** ~**t** to make an about-turn pot.

frontaln|y adi. [szturm, ostrzał, natarcie] frontal; **przypuścić** ~**y atak na kogoś** przen. to launch a head-on attack on sb

froter|ować impf vt to polish [podłogę, parkiet]

frotté /'frote/ adi. inv. [ręcznik, skarpetki, szlafrok] terry

fru|nąć [] pf vi [ptak, owad] (unieść się) to fly up; (polecieć) to fly (off); [pierze, piłka] to fly (up)

[] impf vi [ptak, owad] to be flying

frustracj|a f frustration

frustr|ować impf [] vt to frustrate

[] **frustrować się** to be frustrated (**czymś** over a. about sth)

fryt|ka f Kulin. chip GB; ~**ki** chips, (French) fries US

fryzje|r m [1] (osoba) hairdresser; (męski) barber [2] (zakład) hairdressing salon

fryzjer|ka f hairstylist

fryzu|ra f hairstyle; (damska) hairdo pot.; **krótka** ~**ra** short hair; **zmienić** ~**rę** to change one's hairstyle

fu|ga f [1] Muz. fugue [2] Budow. (szczelina) joint; (zaprawa) (między cegłami) mortar; (między kafelkami) grout

fundacj|a f [1] (instytucja) foundation; ~**a badań nad rakiem** a cancer research foundation [2] (ufundowanie) foundation; **biblioteka** ~**i naszej rodziny** a library founded by our family [3] (darowizna) donation

fundamen|t m foundation także przen.; **położyć** ~**t pod coś** to lay the foundations for sth

fundato|r m, ~**rka** f [1] (założyciel) founder; (darczyńca) donor; (sponsor) sponsor [2] żart. (w restauracji, kinie) **być czyimś** ~**rem** to treat sb; **być** ~**rem czegoś** to pay for sth

fund|ować impf vt [1] (budować, zakładać) to found [kościół, szpital]; to endow [nagrodę, stypendium] [2] pot. (płacić) ~**ować sobie/komuś coś** to treat oneself/sb to sth; **ja** ~**uję** this is on me pot.; **nie chcą** ~**ować sobie nowej wojny** przen. they don't want to risk getting into a new war

fundusz [] m fund; ~ **emerytalny** a pension fund; ~ **pomocy ofiarom katastrof** a disaster fund; **Międzynarodowy Fundusz Walutowy** the International Monetary Fund

[] **fundusze** plt funds; ~**e prywatne/publiczne** private/public funds; ~**e na badania naukowe** funds for scientific research; **gromadzić** ~**e** to raise funds

funkcj|a f [1] (zastosowanie) function; **pełnić** ~**ę czegoś** to function as sth [2] (stanowisko) post; **sprawować** ~**ę dyrektora** to hold the post of director; **pełnić** ~**ę przewodnika** to act as an interpreter [3] (działanie) function; ~**a nagrywania/ suszenia** a recording/drying function; ~**e życiowe** bodily functions [4] Log., Mat. function

funkcjonariusz m [1] (urzędnik) functionary [2] (policjant) (police) officer

funkcjon|ować impf vi [1] (pracować) to function; (być sprawnym) to be functional [2] pot. (być rozpowszechnionym) [mit, pogląd] to function, to prevail

funkcyjn|y adi. [1] (spełniający funkcję) **klawisz** ~**y** Komput. a function key; **wyraz** ~**y** a function word [2] (związany ze stanowiskiem) **dodatek** ~**y** a managerial a. an executive bonus [3] Mat. [zależność] functional

fun|t m [1] Fin. pound [2] Miary pound

furgonet|ka f van; ~**ka pocztowa** a mail van

furi|a f [1] fury; **w** ~**i** in a fury; **z** ~**ą** furiously; **dostać** ~**i** to fly into a rage [2] Mitol. Fury; ~**e** the Furies

furt|ka f [1] (w ogrodzeniu) gate; (w bramie) wicket [2] przen. loophole; **znaleźć** ~**kę** to find a loophole; **zostawić sobie** ~**kę** to leave one's options open

fus|y plt (po herbacie) dregs; (po kawie) (coffee) grounds; (na dnie butelki) sediment

futbol m (association) football GB, soccer; ~ **amerykański** American football GB, football US

futera|ł m case; ~**ł na aparat fotograficzny** a camera case

fut|ro n [1] (sierść) fur [2] (wyprawiona skóra) pelt; **płaszcz podbity** ~**rem** a fur-lined coat [3] (ubranie) fur (coat); **sztuczne** ~**ro** an artificial a. fake fur coat

futryn|a f (drzwiowa) doorcase; (okienna) window casing

futrzan|y adi. [dywan, czapka, kołnierz] fur

fuzj|a f Ekon. merger

G

G, g /gje/ n inv. ① (litera) G, g ② Muz. G
gabary|t m Techn. dimension
gabine|t m ① (w domu) study; (w pracy) office ② (dentystyczny, lekarski) surgery GB, office US; ~t kosmetyczny a beauty parlour ③ (z eksponatami) room; ~t osobliwości a cabinet of curiosities ④ Polit. cabinet
gabinetow|y adi. [kryzys] cabinet
gablo|ta f ① (szafka) display case; ~ta informacyjna a noticeboard GB, a bulletin board US ② pot. (samochód) motor GB pot.
ga|d m reptile także przen.
gada|ć impf vi pot. ① (mówić) to jabber pot.; ~ć głupstwa to talk rubbish; ~ć na kogoś to run sb down; ludzie ~ją, że... the word on the street is (that)...; nie mieć nic do ~nia to have no say ② (rozmawiać) to chat; ~ć z kimś o czymś to chat to a. with sb about sth
gadanin|a f pot. idle chatter
gadatliwoś|ć f talkativeness
gadatliw|y adi. talkative
gad|ka f pot. (rozmowa) chinwag GB, rap US pot.; ~ka szmatka twaddle pot.
gadulstw|o n garrulousness książk.
gadu|ła m, f pot. chatterbox pot.
gadże|t m gadget
gaf|a f blunder, gaffe
gag m gag
gagat|ek m pot. scamp pot.
gaj m grove
gal|a f ① (uroczystość) gala ② (uroczysty strój) formal dress; (oficjalny strój) full dress ③ Żegl. full ceremonial colours GB a. colors US
galakty|ka f galaxy
galanteri|a f ① książk. (kurtuazja) chivalry ② (dodatki) (krawieckie) haberdashery GB, notions US; (do ubioru) accessories
galare|ta f Kulin. aspic, jelly; karp w ~cie carp in aspic; trząść się jak ~ta to shake like a (bowl of) jelly
galeri|a f ① (sztuki) (art) gallery; ~a postaci przen. a collection of characters przen. ② (część budynku) gallery; (pasaż handlowy) shopping arcade
galon m (gold/silver) braid, galloon
galop m gallop także przen.; jechać ~em to gallop; zrobić coś ~em przen. to do sth in a rush; wziąć kogoś do ~u przen. to ride sb hard pot.
galop|ować impf vi [osoba, zwierzę] to gallop także przen.; ~ować z robotą pot. to rush through one's work (at a gallop)
galow|y adi. [koncert] gala; [strój] formal
gał|ąź f ① Bot., Med. branch; podcinać ~ąź, na której się siedzi przen. to saw off the branch one's sitting on ② (nauki, rodu) branch
gałgan m pot. ① (szmata) rag ② (o osobie) scamp pot.
gał|ka f ① (uchwyt, pokrętło) knob ② (porcja) ~ka lodów a scoop of ice cream
□ ~ka oczna Anat. eyeball
gam|a f ① Muz. scale ② przen. (kolorów, zachowań) range
gamo|ń m pot. clod pot.
gan|ek m porch
gang m gang
gangren|a f Med. gangrene
gangste|r m gangster
gania|ć impf Ⅰ vt (ścigać) to chase; ~ć za kimś to chase after sb; ~ć za dziewczynami pot., przen. to run after girls
Ⅱ vi pot. (biegać) (dla zabawy) to romp; (bez celu) to run about a. around
ga|nić impf vt to criticize [osobę, postępowanie]; to reprove książk. [osobę] (za coś for sth)
gap m gawker pot.
gap|a m, f pot. butterfingers pot.
■ jeździć na ~ę pot. to dodge fares
gap|ić się impf v refl. pot. to gawk pot. (na coś at sth)
gapowicz m, ~ka f pot. fare dodger
ga|r m pot. (large) pot; (objętość) pot(ful); myć gary to do the dishes; stać przy garach to slave over a hot stove
garaż m garage
garaż|ować impf vt to garage; ~owany samochód a car housed in a garage
garb m ① Anat. hump ② (w terenie) hump; (na drodze) bump
garba|ty adi. [osoba] hunchbacked; [zwierzę] humpbacked; [nos] humped; [powierzchnia] bumpy; [teren] undulating
garb|ić się impf v refl. to stoop; nie ~ się! sit up/ stand up straight!
garbnik m tanning agent; (roślinny) (vegetable) tannin
garb|ować impf vt to tan [skóry]

garbus *m* pot. [1] obraźl. (o osobie) hunchback obraźl. [2] (samochód) beetle pot.

garder|oba *f* [1] (ubiory) wardrobe [2] (w domu, teatrze) dressing room

gard|ło *m* throat także przen.; **boli mnie ~ło** I have a sore throat; **wąskie ~ło** przen. bottleneck; **stanąć komuś kością w ~le** przen. to stick in sb's throat; **śmiać się na całe ~ło** to laugh one's head off

gar|dzić *impf vi* to despise (**czymś** sth); **~dzić niebezpieczeństwem** to be scornful of danger; **nie ~dzić czymś** iron. to not be averse to sth

gardziel *f* [1] Anat. throat [2] przen. narrow passage

garmażeri|a *f* ≈ delicatessen

garn|ąć się *impf v refl.* [1] (przytulać się) to cling (**do kogoś** to sb) [2] (lgnąć) to feel attracted (**do kogoś** to sb); **~ąć się do nauki** to be eager to study

garncarstw|o *n* pottery

garn|ek *m* (do gotowania) pot; (płytki) pan; (z rączką) saucepan; (zawartość) pot(ful)

garnitu|r *m* [1] (ubranie) suit [2] (zestaw) set; **drugi ~r polityków** second-rate politicians

garnizon *m* garrison

garsonie|ra *f* przest. studio flat GB, studio apartment US

garson|ka *f* woman's suit

garś|ć *f* cupped hand; (ilość) handful; **ściskać coś w ~ci** to clutch sth; **mieć kogoś w ~ci** przen. to have sb in one's grasp; **wziąć się w ~ć** przen. to pull oneself together

ga|sić *impf vt* [1] (przerywać palenie się) to put out *[ogień, pożar]*; (zdmuchnąć) to blow out *[świecę, zapałkę]*; to switch off *[lampę]*; to turn off *[gaz, światło, silnik]* [2] przen. (tłumić) to extinguish *[entuzjazm, nadzieję]* [3] pot., przen. (onieśmielać) to overawe [4] przen. (przyćmiewać) to outshine [5] Techn. to slake *[wapno]*

ga|snąć *impf vi* [1] *[ognisko, płomień]* to be dying (down); *[lampa, światło]* to be going out; *[gwiazda]* to fade (away); *[samochód, silnik]* to be stalling [2] książk. *[osoba]* to fade away; *[oczy]* to glaze (over) [3] przen. *[entuzjazm, nadzieja]* to fade; *[uczucie, zapał]* to drain away; *[dźwięk, kolor]* to fade (away)

gastronomi|a *f* [1] (sztuka kulinarna) gastronomy książk. [2] (działalność usługowa) catering

gaśnic|a *f* fire extinguisher

gatun|ek *m* [1] (rzeczy, ludzi, zjawisk) kind [2] (towarów) quality [3] Biol. species

gatunkow|y *adi.* [1] Biol. species [2] (dobrej jakości) *[artykuły spożywcze]* choice; *[tytoń]* fine; *[piwo]* quality

gawę|da *f* tale

gawędzia|rz *m*, **~rka** *f* (opowiadający) raconteur; (autor) storyteller

gawę|dzić *impf vi* to chat

gaworz|yć *impf vi [niemowlę]* to babble

gawron *m* Zool. rook

gaz [] *m* [1] (substancja) gas; **~ ziemny** natural gas; **gotować na ~ie** to cook with gas; **postawić coś na ~ie** to put sth on the stove [2] pot. accelerator; gas (pedal) US pot.; **(do)dać ~u** to put one's foot down GB, to step on the gas US pot. [] **gazy** *plt* (w jelitach) wind, gas US ■ **~u!** pot. get a move on! pot.

gaz|a *f* gauze

gazel|a *f* gazelle

gaze|ta *f* (news)paper; **trafić na pierwsze strony ~t** to make the front pages

gazet|ka *f* news-sheet; **~ka ścienna** ≈ a newsletter

gazik[1] *m* ≈ jeep®

gazik[2] *m* Med. gauze pad

gazociąg *m* (gas) pipeline

gazomierz *m* gas meter

gazowni|a *f* gasworks

gąb|ka *f* [1] (do mycia) sponge [2] (do izolacji) foam rubber, sponge rubber GB [3] Zool. sponge

gąsienic|a *f* [1] Zool. caterpillar [2] Techn. caterpillar (track); track; **pojazd na ~ach** a tracked vehicle

gbu|r *m* pot. boor

gda|kać *impf vi [kura]* to cluck

gdera|ć *impf vi* pot. to gripe pot. (**na coś** about sth)

gdy *coni.* [1] (o jednoczesnym zdarzeniu) when; **podczas ~** while; (w przeciwstawieniu) whereas [2] (o wcześniejszym wydarzeniu) when, after; **~ tylko** as soon as [3] (rozwijające) when; **z chwilą ~ – wylądowali w Rzymie** the moment they touched down in Rome; **teraz, ~ jesteś już żonaty...** now that you are a married man... [4] (określające warunek) when; **otrzymam dyplom, ~ zdam ostatni egzamin** I'll receive my diploma when I pass my last exam

gdyby [] *coni.* (w trybie warunkowym) if; **~ nadarzyła się sposobność** should the opportunity arise; **~ nie to, że...** if it weren't for the fact that...; **~ nawet** a. **nawet ~** even if [] *part.* [1] (wyrażające możliwość) what if; **a ~ posadzić go koło Adama?** and what if we seat him next to Adam? [2] (wyrażające pragnienie) if only; **~m to ja wiedział!** if only I knew/had known! [3] (wyrażające prośbę) if; **~ pan był taki uprzejmy i zamknął okno** if you would be kind enough to close the window

gdzie [] *pron.* [1] (pytajny) where; **~ są klucze?** where are the keys?; **~ on nie był! w Indiach, Australii...** he's been everywhere – India, Australia... [2] (względny) where; **kryli się, ~ kto mógł** they hid wherever they could; **~ tylko człowiek pójdzie, wszędzie tłumy** wherever one goes, there are always crowds of people; **~ spojrzeć...** wherever you look... [3] (nieokreślony) somewhere; someplace US pot.; (w pytaniu) anywhere; (w przeczeniu) nowhere; **masz ~ spać?** do you have anywhere a. somewhere to sleep?; **mało ~** hardly anywhere

II *part.* ~ **mi staremu do żeniaczki?** (będzie trudno) where's an old man like me going to get married? pot.; (nie chcę) what would an old man like me want with marriage?; ~ **mi do niego?** I'm not a patch on him pot.

gdziekolwiek *pron.* ① (gdzie bądź) anywhere (at all) ② (wszędzie) wherever; ~ **poszedł** wherever he went

gdzieniegdzie *adv.* here and there

gdzieś **I** *pron.* (nieokreślone miejsce) somewhere; someplace US pot.; (w pytaniu) anywhere; ~**, gdzie...** somewhere where...; **mieć kogoś/coś (głęboko)** ~ posp. to not give a monkey's about sb/sth GB posp. **II** *part.* pot. (w przybliżeniu) somewhere; ~ **około godziny dziesiątej** somewhere around ten o'clock

gej *m* pot. gay

gejze|r *m* geyser także przen.

gekon *m* Zool. gecko

gen *m* gene

gencjan|a *f* Bot. gentian; (płyn) gentian violet

genealogi|a *f* książk. ① (rodu) genealogy ② (miasta, utworu) origin(s)

generacj|a *f* książk. generation

generaliz|ować *impf* książk. **I** *vt* to extrapolate *[doświadczenia, zjawiska]* **II** *vi* to generalize

generaln|y *adi.* ① (ogólny) *[przegląd, strajk]* general ② (naczelny) *[dyrektor, sekretarz]* general

genera|ł *m* general

generato|r *m* generator

gener|ować *impf vt* to generate także przen.

genety|ka *f* genetics

genez|a *f* książk. genesis książk.

genialn|y *adi. grad.* ① (wybitny) *[artysta, wynalazek]* brilliant; ~**e dzieło** a work of genius ② pot. (świetny) fantastic pot.

genitali|a *plt* genitals

geniusz *m* genius

geode|ta *m*, ~**tka** *f* geodesist

geodezj|a *f* geodesy

geografi|a *f* geography

geograficzn|y *adi.* geographic(al)

geologi|a *f* geology

geometri|a *f* ① Mat. geometry ② (kształt) geometry; ~**a kół** wheel alignment

geometryczn|y *adi.* geometric(al)

geriat|ra *m* geriatrician

geriatri|a *f* geriatrics

germanisty|ka *f* Germanic studies

germanizacj|a *f* Germanization

ge|st *m* ① (ruch) gesture ② (czyn) gesture; **mieć (szeroki) gest** to be open-handed

gestapo *n inv.* the Gestapo

gestapow|iec *m* Gestapo officer

gesti|a *f* authority; **w czyjejś** ~**i** under sb's authority; **decyzja leży w** ~**i prezydenta** the decision rests with the President

gestykulacj|a *f* gesticulation

gestykul|ować *impf vi* to gesticulate, to gesture

getr|y *plt* leggings

g|ęba *f* ① posp. (twarz) mug pot.; **zamknij gębę!** shut your face! pot.; **aktor całą** a. **pełną gębą** an actor through and through; **trzymać gębę na kłódkę** to keep one's trap shut pot.; **wyskoczyć na kogoś z gębą** pot. to bawl sb out ② (pysk zwierzęcia) mouth

gęga|ć *impf vi* ① *[gęś]* to gaggle ② pot. *[osoba]* (przez nos) to talk through one's nose; (nudno) to rattle on a. away

gęstni|eć *impf vi [dym, mgła, sos]* to thicken; *[tłum]* to grow thicker

gę|sto *adv. grad. [zaludniony]* densely; **w pokoju zrobiło się gęsto** the room got crowded; **na ścianach jest gęsto od obrazów** the walls are thick with paintings; **gęsto się tłumaczyć** pot. to explain oneself in great detail

gęstwin|a *f* thicket

gę|sty *adi. grad. [ciecz, las, włosy, sieć]* thick; *[tłum, mgła]* dense; *[cień]* deep; *[woń]* heavy

gę|ś *f* ① Zool., Kulin. goose; **niech cię/to gęś kopnie** pot. damn you/it! pot. ② pot., obraźl. (kobieta) goose pot.

g|iąć *impf* **I** *vt* to bend *[drut, gałąź]* **II** **giąć się** *[blacha, drut, gałąź]* to bend; **giąć się w ukłonach** *[osoba]* to bow

gieł|da *f* ① Ekon. stock exchange a. market; **na** ~**dzie** on the stock exchange ② (targi) fair; (bazar) market; ~**a komputerowa** a second-hand computer sale; ~**da pracy** a job fair

giełdow|y *adi. [obroty, spekulacje]* stock exchange a. market

gię|tki *adi. grad. [gałąź, łodyga]* pliant; *[pręt]* flexible; *[osoba, ruchy]* supple; przen. *[charakter, osoba]* pliable

gigan|t *m* ① giant także przen.; **pomidory** ~**ty** giant(-sized) tomatoes ② Sport the giant slalom

gigantyczn|y *adi. grad.* gigantic

gil *m* ① Zool. bullfinch ② pot. (w nosie) snot pot.

gilotyn|a *f* guillotine

gimnastyczn|y *adi. [ćwiczenia, sprzęt]* gymnastic; (w szkole) *[zajęcia]* gym; **sala** ~**a** the gym(nasium); **strój** ~**y** a gym kit

gimnasty|ka *f* ① (dyscyplina) gymnastics ② (ćwiczenia) (physical) exercises ③ Szkol. gym

gimnastyk|ować *impf* **I** *vt* to exercise *[mięśnie, umysł]* **II** **gimnastykować się** to exercise

gimnazjali|sta *m*, ~**stka** *f* ≈ secondary school pupil

gimnazj|um *n* (trzyletnia szkoła średnia) ≈ middle school

gi|nąć *impf vi* ① (tracić życie) to die; **ginąć w walce** to be killed in action ② (gubić się) to be lost ③ (zamierać) *[przyjaźń, lojalność]* to die out a. away; **ginąca tradycja** a vanishing tradition ④ (zostać ukradzionym) to be stolen ⑤ (znikać) to disappear; (stawać się niesłyszalnym) *[dźwięk]* to die away; **ginąć w hałasie** *[głos]* to be lost in the noise; **powoli ginąć z oczu** to fade out of sight

ginekolo|g *m* gynaecologist GB, gynecologist US

ginekologi|a *f* gynaecology GB, gynecology US

gips *m* ① (minerał) gypsum ② (materiał) plaster ③ (opatrunek) (plaster) cast; **włożyć komuś rękę w** ~ to put sb's arm in a cast

gips|ować *impf vt* ① (tynkować) to plaster *[ścianę]*; to patch [sth] with plaster, to spackle US *[dziurę, pęknięcie]* ② Med. to put [sth] in a (plaster) cast *[nogę, rękę]*

gita|ra *f* guitar

gitarzy|sta *m*, ~**stka** *f* guitarist, guitar player

glazu|ra *f* ① (polewa) glaze ② (kafelki) tiles, tiling

gleb|a *f* soil także przen.

glę|dzić *impf vi* pot. to ramble (**o czymś** about sth)

gliceryn|a *f* glycerine, glycerin US

glin *m* aluminium GB, aluminum US

glin|a¹ *f* clay; **być ulepionym z tej samej** ~**y** przen. to be cut from the same cloth

glin|a² *m* pot. cop pot.

gli|sta *f* ① Med., Wet. roundworm ② pot. (dżdżownica) caterpillar

gliwie|ć *impf vt [ser]* to go bad

glizda → **glista**

glob *m* globe

globaln|y *adi.* książk. ① (światowy) global ② (całkowity) total

globus *m* globe

glon|y *plt* algae

glori|a *f* ① (aureola) halo ② książk. (sława) glory; **chodzić w** ~**i** to be famous ③ książk. (zwycięstwo) victory

gloryfikacj|a *f* książk. (słuszna) extolling książk. (**czegoś** of sth); (niesłuszna) glorification

gloryfik|ować *impf vt* książk. (słusznie) to extol książk.; (niesłusznie) to glorify

gład|ki ① *adi. grad.* ① (bez nierówności) *[skóra]* smooth; *[droga, powierzchnia]* smooth, level; **psy o** ~**kiej sierści** short-haired dogs ② (łatwy) *[sukces]* easy; *[życie]* simple ③ przen. *[przemówienie]* elegant; *[maniery, osoba]* suave; ~**kie pochlebstwa** smooth flattery

Ⅱ *adi.* (bez wzorów) *[materiał]* (in a) plain colour GB, (in a) plain color US; *[papier]* unruled; (bez ozdób) *[papier, ubranie]* plain

gła|dzić *impf vt* ① (usuwać nierówności) to smooth *[powierzchnię]* ② (głaskać) to stroke

gła|skać *impf vt* ① (gładzić) to stroke *[dziecko, zwierzę]* ② przen. (chwalić) to flatter *[osobę, dumę]*

głaz *m* boulder; **zimny jak** ~ (as) cold as stone; **milczeć jak** ~ to be as quiet as the grave

głąb¹ *m* ① Bot. stalk ② pot., obraźl. (o osobie) dimwit pot., obraźl.

głąb² ① *f* książk. depths książk.

Ⅱ w głąb *adv.* deep into; **na sześć metrów w głąb** to a depth of six metres

głębi|a ① *f* książk. ① (oceanu, morza) depths książk. ② (filmu, wypowiedzi) depth ③ (procesu, zjawiska) extent

Ⅱ w głębi *adv.* (w samym środku) deep in(side); (w tylnej części) in a. at the back; **w** ~ **lądu** inland; **w** ~ **sceny** upstage; **w** ~ **ducha** deep down (inside); **w** ~ **serca** in one's heart (of hearts)

Ⅲ z głębi *adv.* (z wnętrza) from (deep) inside

głęb|oki ① *adi. grad.* ① (niepłytki) *[rzeka, studnia, wdech]* deep; ~**oki dekolt** a low a. plunging neckline; ~**oki na dwa metry** two metres deep ② przen. (zamierzchły) *[średniowiecze]* early; *[przeszłość]* distant ③ przen. (niepowierzchowny) *[przeświadczenie, myśl, uczucie, wiara]* deep; *[wiedza]* profound ④ przen. (poważny) *[konflikt, kryzys]* deep(-seated) ⑤ przen. (intensywny) *[cień, kolor]* deep ⑥ przen. (niski) *[dźwięk]* deep ⑦ przen. (całkowity) *[ciemność, cisza]* deep; **w** ~**okiej tajemnicy** in complete secrecy

Ⅱ głębszy *m* pot. shot (of vodka) pot.

głębokoś|ć *f* ① (rozmiar) depth; **mieć 28 metrów** ~**ci** to be 28 metres deep a. in depth ② (uczucia, zjawiska) depth

głodn|y ① *adi. grad.* (odczuwający głód) *[osoba, zwierzę, spojrzenie]* hungry

Ⅱ *adi.* książk. (pragnący) hungry (**czegoś** for sth); starved (**czegoś** of sth)

głodom|ór *m* pot. glutton

głod|ować *impf vi [osoba, zwierzę]* (cierpieć głód) to starve; (jadać niedostatecznie) to go hungry

głodów|ka *f* ① (protest głodowy) hunger strike ② (brak żywności) hunger ③ (lecznicza) hunger cure

gł|odzić *impf* ① *vt* to starve *[osobę, zwierzę]*

Ⅱ głodzić się to starve oneself

głos *m* ① (osoby) voice; **nie móc (wy)dobyć z siebie** ~**u** to be unable to get a word out; ~ **uwiązł mu w krtani** he couldn't get the words out; **zawiesić** ~ to pause (for effect); **na** ~ *[czytać, liczyć]* aloud; **na cały** ~ *[wrzeszczeć]* at the top of one's voice; **iść za** ~**em serca** przen. to follow one's heart ② (zwierząt) cry; ~**y ptaków** bird calls ③ książk. (zdanie) opinion ④ (wypowiedź w dyskusji) comment; **zabrać** ~ to speak; **dojść do** ~**u** to take the floor; **dopuścić kogoś do** ~**u** to let sb say something; **udzielić komuś** ~**u** to give sb the floor ⑤ (udział w głosowaniu) vote; **oddać** ~ **na kogoś** to vote for sb; **wstrzymać się od** ~**u** to abstain (from voting) ⑥ Muz. (linia melodyczna) voice; **utwór na dwa** ~**y** a piece for two voices

gło|sić *impf vt* to promote *[pogląd, zasadę]*; to deliver *[kazanie]*; ~**sić słowo Boże** to preach the word of God; **fama** ~**si, że...** rumour has it that...

głos|ka *f* sound

głos|ować *impf* ① *vt* to vote on *[projekt, ustawę]*

Ⅱ *vi* to vote; ~**ować na kogoś** to vote for sb; ~**ować za czymś** to vote for a. in favour of sth;

~**ować przeciwko czemuś** to vote against sth; ~**ować nogami** przen. to vote with one's feet przen.

głośnik *m* (loud)speaker

głośn|y [I] *adi. grad.* ① (słyszalny) *[rozmowa, śmiech]* loud ② (hałaśliwy) *[osoba, zachowanie, ulica]* noisy ③ przen. (sławny) *[osoba, dzieło]* well-known **[II]** *adi.* (wypowiadany na głos) ~**e czytanie** reading aloud

gł|owa *f* ① (część ciała) head; **ból głowy** a headache; **głową naprzód** *[upaść, skoczyć]* head first; **przerastać kogoś o głowę** (być wyższym) to be a head taller than sb; przen. to be head and shoulders above sb; **chodzić z gołą głową** to not wear a hat; **kręciło się jej w głowie** she felt dizzy; **mieć mocną/słabą głowę** to have/to not have a strong head (for alcohol); **uderzać komuś do głowy** *[alkohol]* to go to sb's head ② (umysł) head, mind; **z głowy** (bez sprawdzania) off the top of one's head; **nie mieścić się komuś w głowie** to be unbelievable; **nie wchodzić komuś do głowy** *[wiedza]* to not come easily to sb; **wylecieć komuś z głowy** to slip sb's mind; **wbijać coś komuś do głowy** to hammer sth into sb's head; **mącić komuś w głowie** to mix sb up; **moja w tym głowa, żeby...** it's up to me to...; **mieć coś z głową** pot. to have a screw loose pot., **mieć dobrze w głowie** pot. to have one's head screwed on pot.; **mieć głowę na karku** to have one's head screwed on right ; **mieć głowę do czegoś** to have a (good) head for sth *[interesów, matematyki]*; **nabić sobie głowę czymś** to stuff one's head with sth; **zaświtać komuś w głowie** *[myśl, pomysł]* to dawn on sb; **tracić głowę** pot. to lose one's head; **wyjazd na wycieczkę zaplanowany z głową** a well-planned trip; **nic mi nie przychodzi do głowy** I can't think of anything; **nie przyszło jej do głowy, żeby...** it didn't occur to her to...; **nie mam teraz głowy do tego** I've got too many other things on my mind to think about that right now ③ (człowiek inteligentny) **mądra głowa** a brain pot. ④ (w wyliczeniach) **na głowę** a. **od głowy** each; **dochód na głowę mieszkańca** per capita income ⑤ (przywódca) head

■ **zawracać komuś głowę** to bother a. pester sb; **suszyć komuś głowę** to nag sb; **przewracać komuś w głowie** *[pochlebstwa, sukcesy, zaszczyty]* to go to sb's head; **mieć kogoś z głowy** pot. to get rid of sb; **mieć coś z głowy** to get sth over (and done) with pot.; **wybić coś sobie z głowy** to get sth out of one's head pot.; **zwalić się komuś na głowę** pot. to descend on sb; **chować głowę w piasek** to bury one's head in the sand; **stawać na głowie** (żeby coś zrobić) pot. to bend over backwards (to do sth); **zmyć komuś głowę** pot. to give sb what for pot.; **spokojna głowa** pot. not to worry pot.; don't worry; **co dwie głowy to nie jedna** przysł. two heads are better than one przysł.

głowic|a *f* ① Techn. head ② Wojsk. (war)head ③ (rękojeść broni siecznej) hilt ④ Archit. capital, head

gł|owić się *impf v refl.* to (w)rack one's brain(s) (**nad czymś** over sth)

gł|ód *m* ① (łaknienie) hunger; **klęska głodu** famine ② przen. (pragnienie) craving (**czegoś** for sth); **być na głodzie** pot. to be going through withdrawal

gł|óg *m* ① Bot. hawthorn ② (owoce) haws, hawthorn berries

głów|ka *f* ① (część ciała) (little) head; **skoczyć na** ~**kę** to dive (head first) ② (część rośliny) head; ~**ka czosnku** a garlic bulb; ~**ka kapusty/sałaty** a (head of) cabbage/lettuce ③ (część kapelusza) crown ④ (górna część) head; ~**ka szpilki** a pinhead ⑤ Sport header

główk|ować *impf vi* pot. ① (zastanawiać się) to (w)rack one's brain(s) (**nad czymś** over sth) ② Sport to head

głównie *adv.* mainly, chiefly

główn|y *adi.* *[posiłek, problem, wyjście]* main; *[cel, powód, księgowy]* chief; *[miasto, rzeka]* principal

głuch|nąć *impf vi* ① (tracić słuch) *[osoba, zwierzę]* to be going deaf ② (cichnąć) *[odgłos]* to fade away

głucho *adv.* ① (w sposób przytłumiony) dully ② przen. (cicho) ~ **o...** there's been no mention of...

głuchoniem|y *adi.* (profoundly) deaf

głucho|ta *f* deafness także przen.

głu|chy *adi.* ① (niesłyszący) deaf; hearing-impaired euf.; ~**che telefony** pot. dead calls ② (obojętny) deaf (**na coś** to sth) ③ (przytłumiony) *[odgłos]* dull ④ przen. (cichy, milczący) silent

głup|i *adi. grad.* (nieinteligentny) stupid; (niepoważny) silly; daft GB pot.; ~**i błąd** a silly a. stupid mistake; ~**i jak but (z lewej nogi)** (as) daft as a brush GB pot.; ~**iego robota!** soul-destroying work; **jak** ~**i** (nieinteligentnie) like an idiot; (jak obłąkany) like a lunatic; **pracować jak** ~**i** to work like mad pot.; **udawać** ~**iego** to act dumb pot.; **nie ma** ~**ich!** who do you think you're fooling?!; ~**i ma zawsze szczęście** fortune favours fools

głup|iec *m* fool, idiot

głupi|eć *impf vi* pot. to turn stupid

głupi|o *adv. grad.* *[odpowiadać, uśmiechać się]* foolishly, stupidly; *[brzmieć, wyglądać]* stupid, foolish; **zrobiło mu się** ~**o** he felt stupid

głupo|ta *f* ① (tępota) stupidity ② pot. (bzdura, głupstwo) nonsense

głupstw|o *n* ① (bzdura) nonsense; **gadać** ~**a** to talk rubbish ② (nierozważny czyn) stupid thing (to do); (gafa) boob GB, goof(-up) US pot. ③ (drobnostka) trifle

głuptas *m* pot. dummy pot.

gmach *m* building; edifice książk.; ~ **sądu** a courthouse

gmatwa|ć *impf* **[I]** *vt* to complicate *[sprawy, wywód]*; to muddle (up) *[myśli]*

[II] gmatwać się ① *[sprawa]* to get complicated

2 (popadać w sprzeczność) *[świadek, oskarżony]* to trip oneself up

gmin|a *f* 1 (obszar) (administrative) district 2 (wspólnota) community

gna|ć *impf* **I** *vt* 1 (zmuszać do pośpiechu) to drive *[bydło]* 2 (zmuszać do działania) to make (**kogoś do czegoś** sb do sth); ~**ny ambicją** driven by ambition
II *vi* (pędzić) to race, to rush

gna|t *m* pot. 1 (kość) bone 2 (pistolet) pistol; piece US pot.

gnęb|ić *impf vt* 1 (prześladować) *[osoba, reżim]* to oppress 2 (martwić) *[problem]* to depress, to trouble; **co cię ~i?** what's troubling you?

gniazd|ko *n* 1 (mieszkanie) nest; **uwić własne ~ko** to set up home 2 Techn. socket, (power) point GB

gni|azdo *n* 1 (schronienie zwierząt) nest; **bocianie ~azdo** a stork's nest; Żegl. a crow's nest; **uwić ~azdo** to build a nest; **wyfrunąć z ~azda** to fly the nest także przen. 2 książk., przen. (dom rodzinny) hearth książk., przen. 3 (siedlisko) ~**azdo buntu** a hotbed of revolt 4 Techn. socket

gni|ć *impf vi* to decay; *[żywność, zwłoki]* to rot

gni|eść *impf* **I** *vt* 1 (miażdżyć) to crush; (rozgniatać) to mash *[owoce, warzywa]* 2 (miąć) to crumple *[papier, tkaninę]*; (marszczyć) to crease, to wrinkle *[tkaninę]* 3 (wyrabiać) to knead *[ciasto, glinę]* 4 (ściskać) to press, to squeeze 5 (uwierać) **te buty mnie ~otą** these shoes are too tight; **kołnierzyk ~ół go w szyję** the collar was chafing his neck
II **gnieść się** 1 (tłoczyć się) to be squeezed a. crushed 2 (miąć się) *[ubranie, materiał]* to wrinkle, to crease

gniew *m* anger, rage; **wpaść w ~** to get angry, to fly into a rage

gniewa|ć *impf* **I** *vt* to anger
II **gniewać się** 1 (złościć się) to be angry (**na kogoś** with a. at sb) 2 (być w złych stosunkach) ~**ć się z kimś** to be on bad terms with sb

gniewn|y *adi. grad. [osoba, gest]* angry

gnie|ździć się *impf v refl.* 1 *[zwierzę]* to nest 2 przen. *[osoby, rodzina]* to be crowded together

gn|ój *m* pot. 1 (odchody) dung; (jako nawóz) manure 2 obraźl. (o osobie) shit posp., obraźl.

god|ło *n* emblem; (handlowe) logo, trademark

godnie *adv. grad.* 1 (stosownie) duly 2 (z dumą) proudly

godnoś|ć *f* 1 (duma) dignity; **pełen ~ci** dignified; **uwłaczający ~ci** demeaning 2 książk. (nazwisko) (sur)name 3 książk. (urząd) office; (tytuł) rank

godn|y **I** *adi. grad.* (szlachetny) ~**a kobieta** a woman of dignity; ~**a sprawa** a worthy cause
II *adi. praed.* (zasługujący) worth (**czegoś** sth); worthy (**czegoś** of sth); ~**y pochwały** commendable; ~**y podziwu** admirable; ~**y pogardy** contemptible; ~**y polecenia** recommendable; ~**y potępienia** reprehensible; ~**y pożałowania** regrettable; ~**y**

szacunku estimable; ~**y uwagi** noteworthy; ~**y zaufania** trustworthy

g|odzić¹ *impf* **I** *vt* 1 (jednać) to reconcile (**kogoś z kimś** sb with sb) 2 (łączyć) to combine (**coś z czymś** sth with sth)
II **godzić się** 1 (jednać się) to be reconciled (**z kimś** with sb) 2 (łączyć się) to be combined (**z czymś** with sth) 3 (przyzwalać) to agree (**na coś** to sth) 4 (akceptować) to reconcile oneself (**z czymś** to sth)
III **godzi się** *v imp.* książk. to befit książk.; **nie godzi się tak traktować ludzi** it ill befits you to treat people this way

g|odzić² *impf vi* książk. 1 (uderzać) to smite książk. 2 przen. (szkodzić) to harm (**w coś** sth)

godzin|a **I** *f* 1 Miary hour; **pół ~y** half an hour; **półtorej ~y** an hour and a half; **za ~ę/dwie ~y** in an hour/two hours; ~**ę/dwie ~y temu** an hour/two hours ago; **w ~ę** a. **w ciągu ~y** within an hour; **co ~ę/pół ~y** every hour/half hour; **jechać 100 kilometrów na ~ę** to drive at 100 kilometres an hour; **20 dolarów za ~ę** 20 dollars an hour 2 (moment dnia) **która (jest) ~a?** what time is it?, what's the time?; **o której ~ie wróciłeś?** at what time did you come back? 3 (pora) hour; **w ~ach porannych/wieczornych** in the morning/ evening; **do późnych ~ nocnych** until all hours; **wybiła ~a próby/zemsty** książk. the hour of trial/ vengeance has come 4 (odległość) hour; **to dwie ~y marszu stąd** it's two hours' walk from here 5 Szkol. (lekcja) hour; ~**a lekcyjna** forty-five minutes
II **godziny** *plt* hours; ~**y urzędowania** opening a. business hours; ~**y przyjęć** (lekarza) surgery hours; **w ~ach pracy** during working hours; **pracować po ~ach** to work after hours a. overtime
❑ ~**a policyjna** curfew; ~**a wychowawcza** Szkol. form period GB; ~**a zegarowa** sixty minutes; ~**y nadliczbowe** overtime; ~**a** a. ~**y szczytu** rush hour

godzinn|y *adi.* hour-long

godziw|y *adi. grad.* książk. *[cena, proces]* fair; *[rozrywka]* wholesome; *[praca]* (uczciwa) honest; (odpowiednia) decent

gof|r *m* waffle

gogl|e *plt* goggles

g|oić *impf* **I** *vt* to heal *[ranę]*
II **goić się** to heal

goj *m*, ~**ka** *f* Gentile; goy pot., obraźl.

gol *m* Sport goal; **strzelić ~a** to score a goal; **puścić ~a** to let in a goal

golas *m* pot. naked person; **chodzić na ~a** to walk around naked

gole|ń *f* shin

golf¹ *m* 1 (sweter) polo neck a. roll-neck (sweater) GB, turtleneck US 2 (kołnierz) (obcisły) polo neck GB, roll-neck GB, turtleneck US; (luźny) cowl neck a. collar

golf² *m* Sport golf

g|olić[1] *impf* **[]** *vt* to shave (off) *[włosy, zarost]*; to shave *[osobę, twarz, głowę]*; **krem/pędzel do golenia** shaving cream/a shaving brush; **płyn po goleniu** aftershave (lotion)

[] **golić się** to shave

g|olnąć *pf* — **g|olić**[2] *impf vt* pot. to down, to swig pot.; **golnąć sobie kielicha** to knock back a glass a. shot

goli|zna *f* pot. nudity

golon|ka *f* pork hock a. knuckle

goł|ąb *m* pigeon, dove; **~ąb pocztowy** a racing pigeon; (przenoszący wiadomości) a carrier pigeon

gołąb|ek *m* **[1]** Kulin. stuffed cabbage **[2]** Bot. russula mushroom

gołole|dź *f* black ice

go|ły *adi.* **[1]** (bez ubrania) *[ramiona, plecy, skóra]* bare; *[osoba, ciało]* naked; **z gołą głową** bareheaded **[2]** (niezakryty) *[głowa]* bald; *[pisklę, młode]* naked; *[pień, pole, ściana, żarówka]* bare; **goła prawda** the naked truth; **gołe fakty** the bare facts **[3]** pot. (biedny) broke pot.

■ **gołym okiem** with the naked eye; **pod gołym niebem** outdoors

gondol|a *f* gondola

gong *m* gong; (przy drzwiach) doorbell

go|nić *impf* **[]** *vt* **[1]** (ścigać) to chase *[złodzieja, zwierzynę]* **[2]** (starać się dorównać) to try to catch up (**kogoś/coś** with sb/sth) **[3]** pot. (ponaglać) to pressure, to prod; **goni nas czas** we're running out of time **[]** *vi* **[1]** przen. to chase (**za czymś** after sth) **[2]** pot. (biec) to rush, to race

■ **gonić w piętkę** to be at sixes and sevens pot.

go|niec *m* **[1]** (osoba) (w biurze) messenger; (w wojsku) orderly, runner **[2]** (w szachach) bishop

gonitw|a *f* **[1]** (bieganie) chase **[2]** Sport race

gończ|y *adi.* **pies ~y** a tracking dog; **list ~y** an arrest warrant

gorąc *m* pot. heat, heatwave

gorąc|o **[]** *n* heat

[] *adv.* **[1]** (ciepło) hot; **~o mi** I'm hot; **podawać coś na ~o** to serve sth hot **[2]** (serdecznie) *[witać, pozdrawiać]* warmly; *[polecać, gratulować, dziękować]* heartily; *[przyjmować, oklaskiwać]* enthusiastically

■ **na ~o** *[nadawać, transmitować]* live

gor|ący *adi. grad.* *[powietrze, żelazko]* hot; *[powitanie, pozdrowienia, życzenia]* warm; *[podziękowania]* heartfelt, sincere; *[gratulacje]* hearty; *[miłość, pragnienie]* burning; *[debata, spór]* heated; *[patriotyzm, pragnienia]* fervent; *[poparcie, zwolennik]* ardent; *[wiadomość]* breaking, latest; *[temat]* hot

■ **być w ~ącej wodzie kąpanym** to be hot-headed; **złapać kogoś na ~ącym uczynku** to catch sb in the act; **kuć żelazo, póki ~ące** to strike while the iron is hot

gorącz|ka *f* **[1]** Med. temperature, fever; **dostać ~ki** to come down with a fever; **zmierzyć komuś ~kę** to take sb's temperature **[2]** przen. fever; **pracować w ~ce** to be working at fever pitch

gorączk|ować *impf* **[]** *vi* to have a. run a fever **[]** **gorączkować się** to be (all) keyed a. wound up (**czymś** about sth)

gorliwoś|ć *f* (polityczna, religijna) zeal; (nadmierna) zealotry; (do pracy, pomocy) eagerness

gorliw|y *adi. grad.* **[1]** (sumienny) *[student, pracownik]* eager **[2]** (żarliwy) *[zwolennik, modlitwa]* ardent

gorse|t *m* **[1]** (przedłużony stanik) corselette GB, long line bra **[2]** (opinający talię i biodra) (elastyczny) corset **[3]** (w stroju ludowym) bodice **[4]** (pas ortopedyczny) (elastyczny) corset; (sztywny) brace

gorszy *adi. comp.* → **zły**

gorsz|yć *impf* **[]** *vt* **[1]** (oburzać) to shock; (zawstydzać) to scandalize **[2]** (demoralizować) to deprave *[nieletnich, młodzież]*

[] **gorszyć się** to be scandalized (**czymś** by sth)

gorycz *f* bitterness także przen.

goryl *m* **[1]** Zool. gorilla **[2]** pot. (o osobie) bodyguard; minder GB pot.

gorza|łka *f* pot. booze pot.

gorzej *adv. comp.* → **źle**

gorz|ki *adi.* bitter także przen.; *[czekolada]* plain GB, bitter US; *[herbata, kawa]* unsweetened

[] **gorzka** *f* (wódka) bitters

gorzkn|ieć *impf vi* **[1]** *[herbata, mleko]* to turn bitter **[2]** przen. *[osoba]* to become bitter a. embittered

gosp|oda *f* inn

gospodarcz|y *adi.* **[1]** Ekon. economic **[2]** Roln. *[zabudowania, prace]* farm **[3]** (porządkowy) *[sprawy]* administrative; **pomieszczenie ~e** a utility room

gospodar|ka *f* **[1]** Ekon. economy **[2]** (zarządzanie) management **[3]** pot. (gospodarstwo) farm

gospodarn|y *adi. grad.* thrifty, economical

gospodar|ować *impf vi* **[1]** (na wsi) to run a farm; **~ować na 200 hektarach** to farm 200 hectares of land **[2]** (używać) to manage *[pieniędzmi, zasobami]*

gospodarstw|o *n* **[1]** (rolne) farm **[2]** (dom) **~o domowe** a household

gospodarz *m* **[1]** (rolnik) farmer **[2]** (pan domu) host **[3]** (właściciel) homeowner; (wynajmujący innym) landlord **[4]** (programu, audycji) presenter, frontman GB; (imprezy) host; **~e miasta** local dignitaries; **drużyna ~y** Sport the home team

gospody|ni *f* **[1]** (własnego domu) housewife; (przyjęcia, imprezy) hostess; (własnej kamienicy, mieszkania) homeowner; (wynajmująca innym) landlady **[2]** (programu, audycji) presenter

❏ **~ni domowa** housewife

gospo|sia *f* housekeeper

go|ścić *impf* **[]** *vt* **[1]** (udzielać gościny) **gościć kogoś** to have sb staying **[2]** (częstować) to treat (**kogoś czymś** sb to sth)

[] *vi* (być gościem) to stay; **gościć u kogoś** to stay with sb

gościn|a *f* shelter; **udzielić komuś** ~**y** to give shelter to sb; **dziękujemy za** ~**ę** thank you for having us

gościnn|y **I** *adi. grad. [osoba, okolica]* hospitable **II** *adi.* ① *[wykład]* guest ② *[pokój]* guest

goś|ć **I** *m* ① (osoba zaproszona) guest; **być u kogoś częstym** ~**ciem** to visit sb often; **pójść do kogoś w** ~**ci** to visit sb ② (w restauracji) customer; ~**ć hotelowy** a hotel guest ③ pot. guy pot., bloke GB pot.; **równy** ~**ć** a great bloke a. regular guy US **II** **goście** *plt* Sport visitors

■ ~**ć w dom, Bóg w dom** przysł. ≈ our house is your house

got|ować *impf* **I** *vt* ① (przyrządzać posiłek) to cook ② (podgrzewać) to boil *[jajko, ziemniaki, bieliznę]*; ~**ować coś na parze** to steam sth ③ (szykować) to prepare *[wojnę, zagładę]*

II **gotować się** ① *[makaron, obiad]* to be cooking; *[jajko, ziemniaki, woda]* to be boiling; ~**owało się w całym kraju** przen. the entire country was seething ② pot. (pocić się) to swelter pot.

gotowan|y *adi. [warzywa, mięso]* cooked; *[mleko]* boiled

gotowoś|ć *f* ① (stan pogotowia) readiness; **być w** ~**ci** to be ready a. on standby ② (chęć) willingness, readiness

got|owy **I** *adi.* ① (zakończony, wykonczony) *[projekt, budynek, osoba]* ready; **być** ~**owym do czegoś** to be ready to do sth; **jestem** ~**ów przyznać, że...** I'm ready a. willing to admit that...; ~**ów pomyśleć, że...** he's liable to think that...; **...i nieszczęście** ~**owe** ...and you've got an accident waiting to happen ② (nie na zamówienie) *[żakiet, sukienka]* ready-to-wear; **dania** ~**owe do spożycia** ready-made meals

II **gotowe** *inter.* pot. ready!

gotów|ka *f* cash; **zastrzyk** ~**ki** a cash injection; **w** ~**ce** in cash; **płacić** ~**ką** to pay (in) cash

gotówkow|y *adi.* cash

gotyk *m* ① (styl) Gothic (style) ② (pismo) Gothic lettering a. type, Gothic script

goździk *m* ① Bot. (kwiat) carnation, (garden) pink ② Kulin. clove

gó|ra **I** *f* ① (wzniesienie) (wysokie) mountain; (niskie) hill; **wspiąć się na górę** to climb a mountain; **schodzić z góry** to be going downhill; **nieść coś pod górę** to carry sth uphill ② (sterta) pile, mountain ③ (górna część) top; **od góry do dołu** from top to bottom; **na górze** at the top ④ (w budynku) upstairs; **iść na górę** to go upstairs; **zejść z góry** to come downstairs ⑤ (miejsce, położenie) **tam, na górze** up there; **poruszać się w górę** a. **do góry** a. **ku górze** to move up a. upwards; **do samej góry** to the very top; **twarzą do góry** face up; **w górze** (w powietrzu) up in the air; **w górze rzeki** upriver; **wejść do czegoś od góry** to enter sth from above;

patrzeć na coś z góry to watch sth from above ⑥ pot. (zwierzchnicy) the authorities; **rozkaz z góry** an order from above

II *adv.* pot. (co najwyżej) at (the) most; max pot.

III **górą** *adv.* (powyżej) overhead, up above

IV **z górą** *adv.* (ponad, przeszło) over

V **z góry** *adv.* (zawczasu) *[wiedzieć]* in advance, beforehand

❏ **góra lodowa** iceberg

■ **do góry nogami** upside down, wrong side up; **głowa do góry!** chin up! pot.; **brać górę nad kimś** to get the upper hand over sb; **być górą** to have the upper hand; **patrzeć na kogoś z góry** to look down on sb

góral *m* highlander

górals|ki *adi. [styl, taniec]* highland

gór|ka *f* ① (wzniesienie) hill; **zbiegać z** ~**ki** to run downhill; **iść pod** ~**kę** to walk uphill ② pot. (mięso) loin

górnicz|y *adi. [sprzęt, region]* mining; *[strój, lampka]* miner's; *[święto]* miners'

górni|k *m* miner

górnolotn|y *adi.* high-flown; grandiloquent książk.

górn|y *adi.* ① (na górze) upper; ~**e światło** overhead light ② (maksymalny) *[pułap, granica]* upper ③ Muz. high; ~**e C** a top C

gór|ować *impf vi* ① (być wyższym) ~**ować nad kimś/czymś** to tower over sb/sth ② (dominować) to predominate (**nad kimś** over sb)

górs|ki *adi.* mountain

górzy|sty *adi.* mountainous

gów|no *n* wulg. shit wulg., także przen.; **awanturować się o byle** ~**no** to kick up a row over bugger-all posp.; ~**no mnie to obchodzi!** I don't give a shit about that!; **a** ~**no prawda!** bullshit!

g|ra *f* ① (rozrywka) game; **gry komputerowe/planszowe** computer/board games ② (granie) play; **wykluczyć kogoś z gry** to send sb off ③ (partia) game ④ (na instrumencie) playing ⑤ (aktorska) acting; **jego zdumienie było tylko grą** his surprise was just put on ⑥ (rozgrywka) game; **gra idzie o nasze zdrowie** our health is at stake

❏ **gra słów** play on words, pun; **gra wstępna** foreplay

■ **to nie wchodzi w grę** that's out of the question; **w grę wchodzą trzej kandydaci** there are three candidates worth considering

grab *m* hornbeam

graba|rz *m* gravedigger

grab|ić *impf vt* ① (zgarniać) to rake (up) *[liście]*; to rake *[ścieżki]* ② (okradać) to plunder *[mienie]*; to rob *[ludzi]*

grabi|e *plt* rake

grabi|eć *impf vi [ręce, palce]* to go a. grow numb

grabież *f* książk. plunder

gracj|a *f* ① **Gracja** (w mitologii) Grace ② przen., żart. (kobieta) graceful woman ③ (wdzięk) grace; **z** ~**ą** gracefully

gracz *m* ① (uczestnik gry) player; (hazardzista) gambler ② (strateg) strategist ③ (przebiegła osoba) schemer

gra|ć *impf* **Ⅰ** *vt* ① (rozgrywać) to play *[partię, mecz]*; ~**ć w piłkę nożną/karty** to play football/cards; ~**ć na wyścigach** to bet at the races; ~**ć w Bayernie/ reprezentacji** to play for Bayern/one's country ② Muz. to play *[utwór, Mozarta]*; ~**ć na skrzypcach/gitarze** to play the violin/guitar; ~**ć na czyichś emocjach** przen. to play on sb's emotions ③ *[aktor]* to play *[rolę, Hamleta]*; **aktorzy** ~**li fatalnie** the acting was terrible; ~**ć przed kimś komedię** przen. to put on an act for sb; ~**ć rolę czegoś** przen. (spełniać funkcję) to serve as sth; **pieniądze nie** ~**ją roli** money is no object ④ (mieć w repertuarze) **co** ~**ją w kinie?** what's on at the cinema?

Ⅱ *vi* ① (dźwięczeć) *[muzyka, instrument, radio]* to play ② pot. (być włączonym, działać) *[telewizor, radio]* to be on; **magnetofon nie chce** ~**ć** the tape recorder isn't working ③ pot. (współgrać) to match (**z czymś** sth)

gra|d *m* hail także przen.; (kulki) hailstones; **pada** ~**d** it's hailing; **zasypać kogoś** ~**dem pytań** to shower sb with questions

graf *m* (diagram) graph

graficzn|y *adi.* ① (w postaci rysunku) graphic(al) ② *[dzieło, interfejs, dane]* graphic ③ (ilustratorski) **szata** ~**a książki** the design of a book; **układ** ~**y strony** the layout of a page

grafi|k *m* ① (osoba) graphic designer; (artysta) graphic artist ② (plan) schedule; (podział obowiązków) rota, roster

grafi|ka *f* ① (dział sztuki) ~**ka (artystyczna)** graphic arts; ~**ka komputerowa** computer graphics ② (odbitka) engraving, print ③ (rysunek) drawing ④ (układ) design; Komput. graphics

grafi|t *m* ① (minerał) graphite ② (w ołówku) lead; (wymienny) refill

grafomani|a /ˌgrafoˈmanja/ *f* pejor. worthless writing; **ten wiersz to czysta** ~**a** the poem's just a piece of drivel

grafomańs|ki *adi.* pejor. *[książka, powieść]* worthless

graham *m* graham bread

gram *m* gram, gramme GB

gramatyczn|y *adi.* grammatical

gramaty|ka *f* (nauka) grammar; (podręcznik) grammar textbook

gramol|ić się *impf v refl.* pot. to clamber

grana|t *m* ① (owoc) pomegranate; (roślina) pomegranate (tree) ② (kolor) dark a. deep blue; **jasny** ~**t** ≈ royal blue; **ciemny** ~**t** ≈ navy blue ③ (kamień szlachetny) garnet ④ (pocisk) grenade

granatow|y *adi.* (ciemnoniebieski) navy (blue), deep a. dark blue

graniastosłup *m* prism

granic|a *f* ① (państwowa) border; (obszaru) boundary; ~**a polsko-niemiecka** the Polish-German border; ~**a z Czechami** the Czech border; **poza** ~**ami miasta** outside (the) city limits; **przekroczyć** ~**ę** to cross the border; **być za** ~**ą** to be abroad; **wyjechać za** ~**ę** to go abroad ② przen. (linia podziału) borderline, boundary ③ (zasięg, zakres) limit; **dolna/górna** ~**a wieku** the lower/upper age limit; **być na** ~**y wytrzymałości nerwowej** to be on the brink of a nervous breakdown; **temperatury w** ~**ach 10-15 stopni** temperatures in the 10-15 degree range; **koszt w** ~**ach 1000 złotych** a cost of around 1,000 zlotys; **w** ~**ach rozsądku** within reason

graniczn|y *adi.* ① *[słup, kontrola, przejście]* border ② książk. (ostateczny) *[termin, data]* final

granicz|yć *impf vi* ① (przylegać) *[kraj, obszar, ogród]* to border (**z czymś** on sth); *[pokój, pomieszczenie]* to adjoin (**z czymś** sth) ② przen. (przypominać) to verge a. border (**z czymś** on sth)

grani|t *m* granite

granul|ka *f* granule

gra|ń *f* ridge

gra|t *m* pot. (mebel, urządzenie) piece of junk pot.; (pojazd) (rust)heap pot.

gratulacj|e *plt* congratulations (**z okazji czegoś** on sth); **składać komuś** ~**e** to congratulate sb

gratul|ować *impf vi* to congratulate (**komuś czegoś** sb on sth)

grawe|r *m* engraver

grawitacj|a *f* gravity

grejpfru|t *m* (owoc) grapefruit; (drzewo) grapefruit (tree)

gre|ka *f* (ancient a. classical) Greek

grekokatoli|k *m*, ~**czka** *f* Greek Catholic

gremi|um *n* książk. (kierownictwo) executive committee; ~**um doradcze** the advisory committee

grobow|iec *m* tomb

grobow|y *adi.* *[krypta, kaplica]* sepulchral książk.; tomb; przen. *[nastrój, mina, głos]* sepulchral książk.; *[milczenie]* dead, deathly

groch **Ⅰ** *m* pea; **dwa ziarnka** ~**u** two peas **Ⅱ** **grochy** *plt* (wzór) polka dot; **sukienka w żółte** ~**y** a yellow polka dot dress

grochów|ka *f* pot. pea soup

gr|odzić *impf vt* to fence (off) *[ogród, plac]*

grom *m* thunderbolt; **ciskać** ~**y na kogoś** przen. to lambast(e) sb; **jak** ~ **z jasnego nieba** like a bolt out of a. from the blue

■ mieć czegoś od ~**a** pot. to have loads a. tons of sth pot.

groma|da *f* ① (ludzi) bunch; (ptaków, owiec) flock; (psów, wilków) pack ② (gwiazd) cluster ③ Zool. class

groma|dzić *impf* **Ⅰ** *vt* ① (zbierać) to stock up on *[zapasy]*; to collect *[książki, dzieła sztuki]*; to amass *[pieniądze]*; to gather *[dane]* ② (skupiać) to concen-

trate *[wojsko]*; *[serial, koncert]* to attract *[widzów]*
II gromadzić się to gather
grom|ki *adi.* książk. *[śmiech, oklaski]* thunderous
gromnic|a *f* blessed candle
gronkow|iec *m* staphylococcus
gron|o *n* ① (grupa osób) circle; **w ~ie rodzinnym** in the family circle ② (kiść) bunch ③ Bot. cluster
grosz *m* ① (moneta polska) grosz ② pot. (pieniądze) money; **co do ~a** down to the last penny; **za ~e** for next to nothing; **liczyć się z każdym ~em** to count a. watch one's pennies; **nie mieć ~a przy duszy** to not have a penny to one's name; **nie mieć wstydu/rozumu za ~** to have no shame/sense whatsover
grosz|ek II *m* ① (ziarna grochu) peas ② (kwiat) sweet pea
II groszki *plt* (deseń) (polka) dots, spots; **sukienka w ~ki** a polka-dot(ted) dress
gro|t¹ *m* (strzały) (arrow)head; (włóczni) tip
gro|t² *m* Żegl. mainsail
gro|ta *f* cave
grotes|ka *f* grotesque piece
groteskow|y *adi.* grotesque także przen.
grotołaz *m* (sportowiec) caver; (badacz) speleologist
groz|a *f* terror; **budzić ~ę** to be terrifying
gro|zić *impf vi* ① (straszyć) to threaten ② książk. (stwarzać niebezpieczeństwo) **budynek ~zi zawaleniem** the building is in danger of collapsing; **~zi mu więzienie** he faces a prison sentence
gr|oźba *f* threat; **pod groźbą utraty stanowiska** under threat of losing one's job
groźn|y *adi.* grad. ① (niebezpieczny) *[przeciwnik, działalność]* dangerous; *[choroba, rana]* serious ② (niepokojący) *[spojrzenie]* menacing; *[wieści]* ominous
gr|ób *m* grave; **po grób** for the day one dies; **przewracać się w grobie** pot. to turn in one's grave
grubas *m*, **~ka** *f* pot. fat person; fatso pot., obraźl.
grubiańs|ki *adi.* przest. (niemiły) churlish książk.; (ordynarny) boorish pejor.
grubi|eć *impf vi* *[przedmiot, warstwa]* to thicken; *[osoba]* to get fatter; *[skóra, rysy]* to coarsen; *[głos]* to get deeper
grub|o II *adv.* grad. ① *[smarować]* thickly; *[trzeć, szatkować]* coarsely; *[ubrać]* warmly ② *[wyglądać]* fat
II *adv.* pot. (znacznie) **~o się mylić** to be way off the mark pot.; **~o przed czasem** way too early pot.
gruboskórn|y *adi.* thick-skinned; *[zachowanie, postępek]* callous
grub|y II *adi.* grad. *[nogi, palce, osoba]* fat; *[krata, warkocz, deska]* thick; *[głos]* deep; *[cukier, kasza]* coarse; *[ciepły]* *[sweter, kurtka]* thick, heavy
II *adi.* pot. ① (prostacki) *[żart]* coarse ② (duży) *[przesada, błąd]* gross
III grub|y *m*, **~a** *f* pot., obraźl. fatso pot., obraźl.
IV z grubsza *adv.* pot. (w przybliżeniu) roughly

grucha|ć *impf vi [gołąb]* to coo; żart. *[osoby]* to bill and coo przen.
grucho|t *m* ① (łoskot) clatter ② pot. (pojazd) banger GB, crate US pot.
gruczo|ł *m* gland
gru|da *f* lump
■ **iść jak po ~dzie** *[nauka]* to be hard work a. hard going
grud|ka *f* (small) lump; **~ka ziemi** a clod of earth
gru|dzień *m* December
grun|t II *m* ① (gleba) soil ② (teren) land; **przygotować ~t pod coś** przen. to lay the ground for sth; **spotkać się na neutralnym ~cie** to meet on neutral ground; **trafić na podatny ~t** przen. to be well received ③ (dno) bottom; **masz ~t?** can you touch (the) bottom? ④ (podkład) primer ⑤ (podstawa, zasada) basis ⑥ pot. (najważniejsze) the main thing
II do gruntu *adv.* (zasadniczo) through and through
III z gruntu *adv.* (zupełnie) completely; (zasadniczo) thoroughly
■ **w ~cie rzeczy** in (actual) fact
gruntown|y *adi.* *[zmiana, reforma]* thorough
grup|a *f* group; **~a operacyjna** an operational group; **~a przestępcza** a gang of criminals
□ **~a krwi** blood group
grup|ować *impf* **II** *vt* ① (łączyć w grupy) to group *[ludzi]*; to sort, to classify *[fakty, dane, dokumenty]*; **~ować coś według czegoś** to sort sth according to sth ② (skupiać wokół siebie) to gather *[zwolenników, członków]*
II grupować się to gather
grupow|y *adi.* group
grusz|a *f* pear (tree)
grusz|ka *f* ① (owoc) pear; (drzewo) pear tree ② (kształt) bulb; **w kształcie ~ki** pear-shaped ③ Sport (worek treningowy) punchbag GB, punching bag US
■ **obiecywać komuś ~ki na wierzbie** pot. to promise sb the earth; **ni z ~ki, ni z pietruszki** pot. out of the blue
gruz *m* rubble, debris; **~y** ruins także przen.; **lec w ~ach** przen. *[plany, nadzieje]* to come to nothing
gruźlic|a *f* tuberculosis
grymas II *m* grimace
II grymasy *plt* (narzekanie) moans
gryma|sić *impf vi* ① (narzekać) to sulk ② (kaprysić) to be fussy
gryp|a *f* flu
grysik *m* grits
gryząc|y *adi.* ① *[dym, smak]* acrid ② książk. *[wstyd, żal]* bitter
gryzmol|ić *impf vt* to scribble *[litery, rysunek]*; **strasznie ~isz!** you have terrible handwriting!
gryzmo|ły *plt* scribbles
gryzo|ń *m* rodent
gry|źć *impf* **II** *vt* ① (chwytać zębami) to bite (into); (żuć) to chew *[chleb, mięso]*; *[pies]* to gnaw (on) *[kość]* ② (zadawać rany) *[pies, komar]* to bite ③ (podrażniać)

[dym] to sting; *[materiał, sweter]* to itch 4 (niepokoić) *[tęsknota]* to nag (at); **co cię ~zie?** what's eating you?

II gryźć się 1 (walczyć) *[psy]* to bite each other 2 (kłócić się) to bicker 3 (nie pasować) *[elementy, kolory]* to clash 4 (martwić się) to fret (**czymś** over sth)

grz|ać *impf* **I** *vt* 1 (podgrzewać) to heat up *[zupę, wodę]*; to warm (up) *[ręce, nogi]*; to mull *[wino, piwo]* 2 *[ubranie, kołdra]* to keep [sb] warm 3 (przygotowywać do działania) to warm up *[silnik]*

II *vi* 1 (dostarczać ciepło) to heat; **~ać w samochodzie** to have the heating on in the car 2 pot. (pędzić) *[osoba, pojazd]* to tear (along) pot.

III grzać się 1 (ogrzewać się) to warm oneself; **~ać się piecykiem elektrycznym** to have an electric stove on 2 *[zupa, obiad]* to heat up

grzał|ka *f* immersion heater

grzan|ka *f* 1 (tost) piece a. slice of toast; **~ka z serem** cheese on toast 2 (dodatek do zupy) crouton

grząd|ka *f* bed; **~ka kwiatowa** a flower bed

grzbie|t *m* 1 (u ludzi, zwierząt) back 2 (dłoni, piły) back; (nasypu) ridge; (książki) spine; (fali) crest; **~t górski** a mountain ridge 3 pot. (styl pływacki) the backstroke

grzeb|ać *impf* **I** *vt* *[osoba, lawina]* to bury; **~ać czyjeś szanse** przen. to ruin sb's chances

II *vi* (w ziemi) to dig (around) (**w czymś** in sth); (w śmieciach, kieszeni, szufladzie) to rummage (around a. about) (**w czymś** in sth);

III grzebać się pot. (nie śpieszyć się) to dawdle

grzebie|ń *m* 1 (do włosów) comb 2 (zakończenie, wyrostek) crest; (u koguta) comb

grzech *m* sin także przen.; **~ ciężki** a cardinal sin; **~ pierworodny** original sin; **popełnić ~** to commit a sin; **odpuścić komuś ~y** to absolve sb's sins; **za jakie ~y...?** przen. what have I done to deserve...?

grzechot|ka *f* rattle

grzechotnik *m* rattlesnake

grzeczność|ć I *f* 1 (uprzejmość) politeness (**wobec kogoś** to sb); **przez ~ć** out of politeness 2 (przysługa) favour

II grzeczności *plt* polite words

grzeczn|y *adi. grad.* 1 (uprzejmy) *[osoba, uśmiech]* polite 2 (posłuszny) *[dziecko]* well-behaved; **bądź ~y!** be a good boy! 3 (konwencjonalny) *[film, płyta]* run-of-the-mill

grzejnik *m* heater

grzeszni|k *m*, **~ca** *f* sinner

grzesz|yć *impf vi* to sin także przen. (**przeciw czemuś** against sth); **nie ~ą inteligencją** iron. they're not exactly blessed with intelligence

grzę|da *f* roost, perch

grzmi|eć *impf vi [armata, oklaski]* to thunder; **~eć na kogoś** *[osoba]* to thunder at sb; **~ało** it was thundering

grzmocić *impf →* **grzmotnąć¹**

grzmo|t *m* 1 (huk) thunderclap 2 pot. (duży przedmiot) hulk pot.; **baba-grzmot** a hulk of a woman

grzmo|tnąć¹ *pf —* **grzmo|cić** *impf* pot. **I** *vt* 1 (uderzyć) to whack pot. 2 (rzucić) to hurl

II grzmotnąć się — grzmocić się (uderzyć się) **~tnąć się w głowę o coś** to bang one's head against sth

grzmotn|ąć² *pf vi* pot. (upaść) to thump pot.

grzyb *m* 1 Biol. fungus; (z kapeluszem i nóżką) mushroom; **zbierać ~y** to pick mushrooms; **~ na ścianach** mould on the walls; **wyrastać jak ~y po deszczu** to spring up like mushrooms 2 (o osobie) old fogey pot.

grzybic|a *f* mycosis; **~a skóry** dermatomycosis

grzybobra|nie *n* mushroom picking

grzyw|a *f* 1 (włosy) mane 2 (na falach) crest

grzyw|ka *f* (damska) fringe GB, bangs US

grzyw|na *f* fine; **wymierzyć komuś ~nę** to fine sb

gubernato|r *m* governor

gub|ić *impf* **I** *vt* 1 (tracić) to lose *[pieniądze, rękawiczki, pogoń]*; **~ić pióra/sierść** *[ptaki, zwierzęta]* to shed one's feathers/hair, to moult 2 (o ludzi) **~i nadmierna pewność siebie** excessive self-confidence leads to disaster

II gubić się 1 (tracić rozeznanie) to get lost 2 (tracić się z oczu) to lose sight of each other 3 (zapodziewać się) to be lost

gulasz *m* goulash, stew

gulgo|tać *impf vi [lejący się płyn]* to gurgle; *[wrzątek]* to bubble; *[indyk, osoba]* to gobble

gum|a *f* 1 (tworzywo) rubber; **~a do żucia** chewing gum 2 (do wycierania) rubber GB, eraser US 3 (taśma) elastic 4 pot. (opona) tyre GB, tire US; **złapać ~ę** to get a flat (tyre) pot. 5 pot. (prezerwatywa) johnny GB, rubber US pot.

gumiak *m* pot. welly GB pot.; rubber boot US

gum|ka *f* 1 (do wycierania) rubber GB, eraser US 2 (taśma) elastic; **~ka recepturka** a rubber band

gumow|y *adi.* rubber

gu|st *m* taste; **być w dobrym/złym guście** to be tasteful/in bad taste; **jak na mój gust...** to my mind a. taste...; **być w czymś guście** *[piosenka, sukienka]* to be sb's kind of thing; *[osoba]* to be sb's type

gust|ować *impf vi* książk. to have a liking (**w czymś** for sth)

gustown|y *adi. grad.* tasteful

guz *m* 1 Anat. protuberance 2 Med. tumour GB, tumor US 3 (obrzmienie) bump, lump; **nabić sobie ~a na głowie** to give oneself a bump on the head; **szukać ~a** przen. to be looking for trouble

guzd|rać się *impf v refl.* pot. to dawdle

guzik *m* 1 (zapięcie) button; **zapiąć ~i koszuli** to button up one's shirt; **rozpiąć ~i** to undo the buttons; **zapiąć coś na ostatni ~** przen. to button sth up przen. 2 (przycisk) (push-)button; **nacisnąć ~** to press a button 3 pot., euf. (nic) **a ~ (z pętelką)!**

(odmowa) forget it!, nothing doing! pot.; (przeczenie) like hell! pot.

gwał|cić *impf vt* ⒈ to rape *[kobietę]* ⒉ przen. to violate *[prawo]*

gwał|t *m* ⒈ (zmuszanie do stosunku) rape; **~t zbiorowy** a gang rape; **usiłowanie ~tu** (an) attempted rape ⒉ (przemoc) violence ⒊ pot. (pośpiech) rush; **~tem** a. **na ~t** at once

gwałtown|y *adi. grad.* ⒈ (porywczy) violent ⒉ (nagły) *[zmiana, wzrost]* sudden

gwa|r *m* hubbub

gwa|ra *f* (dialekt) (local) dialect; (żargon) jargon, slang

gwarancj|a *f* guarantee; **posiadać ~ę banku** to be underwritten by a bank; **na ~i** under guarantee a. warranty; **mieć trzyletnią ~ę** to come with a three-year warranty a. guarantee

gwarancyjn|y *adi.* guarantee; **karta ~a** a warranty a. guarantee card

gwarant|ować *impf vt* to assure, to guarantee

gwardi|a *f* (wojsko) guard; (oddziały ochotnicze) militia; **~a narodowa** the national guard

gwi|azda *f* ⒈ (ciało niebieskie, kształt) star; **w kształcie ~azdy** star-shaped; **urodzić się pod szczęśliwą ~azdą** to be born under a lucky star ⒉ przen. (osoba popularna) star ⒊ Sport cartwheel

❑ **Gwiazda Betlejemska** Bibl. the Star of Bethlehem; Bot. poinsettia; **Gwiazda Dawida** the Star of David; **Gwiazda Polarna** the North a. Pole Star

gwiazd|ka *f* ⒈ (small) star; **~ki śniegowe** snowflakes; **hotel z trzema ~kami** a three-star hotel ⒉ (znak drukarski) asterisk ⒊ pot. (Boże Narodzenie) Christmas; **dostać coś na ~kę** to get sth for Christmas ⒋ pot. (młoda aktorka) starlet

gwiazdkow|y *adi. [prezent, zakupy]* Christmas

gwiazdo|r *m* (artysta) star

gwiazdozbi|ór *m* constellation

gwiaździ|sty *adi.* ⒈ *[niebo]* starry; *[tkanina]* starred; **~ste oczy** starry eyes ⒉ (w kształcie gwiazdy) star-shaped; (promienisty) radial

gwiezdn|y *adi.* stellar; **pył ~y** stardust; **wojny ~e** star wars

gwin|t *m* (screw) thread; **przekręcić ~t** to strip the thread; **pić z ~ta** pot. to drink straight from the bottle

gwi|zd *m* whistle; **~zd pocisku** the whiz(z) of a bullet; **na widowni rozległy się ~zdy** the audience started hissing and booing

gwizd|ek *m* whistle; **czajnik z ~kiem** a whistling kettle

■ **cała para poszła w ~ek** it was all just a lot of hot air; **pracować na pół ~ka** pot. *[zakład, załoga]* (nie na pełnych obrotach) to work at half capacity; (miernie) to work below par pot.

gwi|zdnąć[1] *pf* — **gwi|zdać** *impf vt, vi [osoba, czajnik, wiatr, ptak]* to whistle; (gwizdkiem) to (blow a) whistle; *[pocisk]* to whiz(z), to whistle; **~zdać na psa** to whistle for one's dog; **~zdać na coś** to not care a. give a hoot about sth pot.

gwizdn|ąć[2] *pf vt* pot. ⒈ (ukraść) to lift pot. ⒉ (uderzyć) to bash pot.

gw|óźdź *m* nail; **wbić gwóźdź w deskę** to drive a nail into a plank; **zabić drzwi gwoździami** to nail up a door; **(ostatni) gwóźdź do trumny** przen. (the final) nail in the coffin

■ **gwóźdź programu** the main attraction

gzyms *m* ⒈ (występ) cornice; **~ nad kominkiem** a mantelpiece ⒉ (skała) ledge

H

H, h *n inv.* ① (litera) H, h ② Muz. B

habilitacj|a *f* Uniw. ① (proces) habilitation *(qualification as a university professor)* ② (rozprawa) postdoctoral thesis

habilitacyjn|y *adi.* Uniw. postdoctoral

habilit|ować *impf* Uniw. **[]** *vt* ~**ować kogoś** to confer on sb their qualification as a university professor

[] **habilitować się** to qualify as a university professor

habi|t *m* habit, frock

haczyk *m* ① (do zawieszania) hook ② (do zamykania) catch, latch ③ (na ryby) (fish-)hook; **łowić na** ~ to fish with a rod and line, to angle; **połknąć** ~ przen. to swallow a. rise to the bait ④ pot. (kruczek) catch ⑤ (część haftki) hook

hafciar|ka *f* embroiderer

hafciarstw|o *n* embroidery

haf|t *m* embroidery; ~**t angielski** broderie anglaise; ~**t ażurowy** open-work embroidery

haft|ka *f* hook and eye

haft|ować *impf* **[]** *vt* to embroider *[serwetę, wzór]*

[] *vi* pot. (wymiotować) to puke, to throw up pot.

hak *m* ① (zgięty pręt) hook ② (do wspinaczki) piton ③ (cios) uppercut

■ **tydzień z** ~**iem** pot. a week and a bit pot.; **mieć na kogoś** ~**a** pot. to have something on sb; **znaleźć na kogoś** ~**a** pot. to dig up some a. the dirt on sb pot.

hake|r *m* hacker

hal|a¹ *f* (budynek, pomieszczenie) hall; ~**a sportowa** a sports hall; ~**a dworcowa** a (railway) station concourse; ~**a fabryczna** a shop floor; ~**a montażowa** an assembly room; ~**a targowa** a (covered) market

hal|a² *f* (pastwisko) mountain pasture

hal|ka *f* slip, petticoat

haln|y *m* foehn, föhn (wind) *(in the Carpathians)*

halo¹ *inter.* ① (dla zwrócenia uwagi) excuse me! ② (przez telefon) hello, hallo GB, hullo GB; ~, **kto mówi?** hello, who's speaking?

■ **wielkie mi** ~! pot. big deal! pot.; **zrobić wokół czegoś wielkie** ~ pot. to make a big fuss over a. about sth

halo² *m inv.* Fot., Meteo. halo

halow|y *adi.* Sport *[zawody, mistrzostwa]* indoor

halucynacj|a *f* hallucination

hałas *m* noise także przen.; **wejść z** ~**em** to enter noisily; **wiadomość narobiła** ~**u w prasie** there was a lot of noise about it in the press; **wiele** ~**u o nic** much ado about nothing

hałas|ować *impf vi* to make a noise, to be noisy

hałaśliw|y *adi. grad.* *[osoba, muzyka]* noisy; *[kampania, reklama]* aggressive, noisy

hał|da *f* slag heap

hamak *m* hammock

ham|ować *impf* **[]** *vt* ① (zatrzymywać) to rein in *[konia]* ② (powstrzymywać) to hold back, to suppress *[łzy, płacz]*; to curb *[inflację, proces]* ③ (utrudniać) to hinder, to hamper *[wzrost, rozwój]*

[] *vi* (zmniejszać prędkość) *[osoba, pojazd]* to brake

[] **hamować się** *[osoba]* to restrain oneself

hamul|ec **[]** *m* brake także przen.; ~**ec nożny/ręczny** a footbrake/handbrake; **być** ~**cem postępu** to act as a brake on progress

[] **hamulce** *plt* restraints; ~**ce moralne/wewnętrzne** moral/inner restraints

hand|el *m* (wymiana) trade (**czymś** in sth); (dział gospodarki) commerce; (nielegalny) trafficking; ~**el uliczny** street trading; ~**el obnośny** peddling, itinerant trading; ~**el wymienny** barter

handlar|ka *f* trader; (na bazarze) stallholder; ~**ka zieleniną** a vegetable seller

handlarz *m* (kupiec) tradesman, dealer; (na bazarze) stallholder; ~ **bydłem/drewnem** a cattle/timber dealer a. merchant; ~ **narkotyków** a drug dealer a. pedlar; ~ **niewolników** a slave trader; ~ **żywym towarem** a white slave trader

handl|ować *impf vi* to trade, to deal (**czymś** in sth); ~**ować na bazarze** to be a market trader

handlow|iec *m* (pracownik) salesman; (specjalista) sales specialist

handlow|y *adi.* *[stosunki, transakcje]* commercial, trade; **attaché** ~**y** a commercial attaché; **centrum** ~**e** a shopping centre a. mall; **dział/przedstawiciel** ~**y** a sales department/representative; **kursy** ~**e** business courses; **statek** ~**y** a merchant ship

hanga|r *m* (dla samolotów) hangar; (portowy) cargo shed

haniebn|y *adi. grad.* książk. *[czyn, myśl, zbrodnia]* disgraceful

hantl|e *plt* dumb-bells

hańb|a **[]** *f* książk. dishonour GB, dishonor US, disgrace; **to** ~**a, że...** it's a disgrace that...

II *inter.* ∼**a zdrajcom!** shame on the traitors!; **wstyd i** ∼**a!** shame!, shame!

hańb|ić *impf* książk. **II** *vt* to dishonour GB, to dishonor US, to disgrace *[nazwisko, dobre imię, rodzinę]*

II hańbić się to disgrace oneself

haracz *m* ① Hist. tribute ② (gangsterski) protection money; (okup) ransom; **ściągać** ∼ to extort protection money ③ (wygórowana opłata) exorbitant charge

harcer|ka *f* (Girl) Guide, Girl Scout *(in Poland)*

harcerstw|o *n* scouting/guiding *(in Poland)*; **należeć do** ∼**a** to be in the scouts/guides

harcerz *m* (Boy) Scout *(in Poland)*

har|dy *adi.* ① (dumny) proud, haughty ② (zuchwały) impertinent

harf|a *f* harp

harmid|er *m* racket

harmoni|a *f* ① (ład, zgoda) harmony ② Muz. (instrument) concertina; (współbrzmienie) harmony; (nauka) harmonics

harmonij|ka *f* Muz. ∼**ka (ustna)** harmonica, mouth organ; **złożony/zwinięty w** ∼**kę** concertinaed

harmoniz|ować *impf* książk. **II** *vt* to harmonize *[kolory, melodię]*

II *vi* to harmonize (**z czymś** with sth)

harmonogram *m* schedule

har|ować *impf vi* pot. to slog away pot.

harów|ka *f* pot. slog pot.

harpun *m* harpoon

har|t *m* książk. fortitude

hart|ować *impf* **II** *vt* ① Techn. to temper, to harden *[żelazo, stal, szkło]* ② (uodparniać) to toughen up *[dziecko, organizm]*; to harden off *[rośliny]* ③ przen. (psychicznie) to strengthen *[wolę, charakter]*

II hartować się ① Techn. *[stal, szkło]* to harden ② *[osoba]* to build up one's resistance; *[organizm]* to toughen up

hasa|ć *impf vi* ① (bawić się) *[dziecko]* to cavort (around), to romp (around) ② (tańczyć) to dance wildly pot.

ha|sło *n* ① (patriotyczne) watchword, motto; (chwytliwe) catchword; (reklamowe, wyborcze) catchphrase, slogan ② (wezwanie do działania) battle cry przen.; rallying cry a. call ③ Komput., Wojsk. password; **wpisać hasło** to enter one's password ④ (w słowniku) (tekst) entry; (tytuł) headword

hau|st *m* gulp, swig; **jednym** ∼**stem** in one gulp, at a gulp

hazar|d *m* ① Gry gambling; **uprawiać** ∼**d** to gamble ② (ryzyko) risk, gamble

hazardzi|sta *m*, ∼**stka** *f* gambler

hebl|ować *impf vt* to plane *[deski]*

hec|a *f* pot. lark GB pot.; **dla** ∼**y** for a lark, for laughs

hejna|ł *m* bugle call; **odegrać** ∼**ł** to sound a bugle call

hekta|r *m* Miary hectare; ∼**ry** pot. acreage

helikopte|r *m* helicopter

hełm *m* ① (nakrycie głowy) helmet ② Archit. cupola, dome

hełmofon *m* headset

hemoglobin|a *f* Biol. haemoglobin GB, hemoglobin US

hemoroid|y *plt* Med. haemorrhoids GB, hemorrhoids US, piles

henn|a *f* (do włosów) henna; (do brwi i rzęs) eyebrow and eyelash dye

herb *m* ① (państwa, miasta) coat of arms, emblem ② (rodu) coat of arms, family crest

herbaciar|nia *f* tea room a. shop

herba|ta *f* ① Bot., Kulin. tea; ∼**ta z rumem** tea laced with rum; ∼**ta ekspresowa** (tea in) teabags ② (wizyta) tea; **proszona** ∼**ta** a tea party

■ **po** ∼**cie** pot. it's too late

herbatni|k *m* Kulin. biscuit GB, cookie US

herety|k *m*, ∼**czka** *f* heretic także przen.

herezj|a *f* heresy także przen.

hermetyczn|y *adi.* *[zamknięcie, naczynie]* hermetic; *[pomieszczenie, pojemnik]* hermetically sealed; *[grupa]* hermetic, insular; *[utwór, język]* hermetic, esoteric

heroiczn|y *adi.* książk. *[czyn, wysiłek]* heroic

heroin|a[1] *f* Chem. heroin

heroin|a[2] *f* książk. ① Teatr leading lady przest. ② (powieści, filmu) heroine, main character

heroizm *m* książk. heroism

hersz|t *m* (ring)leader

heteroseksuali|sta *m* heterosexual

hetman *m* ① Hist., Wojsk. hetman ② (w szachach) queen

hiacyn|t *m* ① Bot. hyacinth ② Miner. jacinth, hyacinth

hien|a *f* ① Zool. hy(a)ena ② przen. vulture przen.; ∼**a cmentarna** ghoul, grave robber

hierarchi|a *f* hierarchy

hieroglif *m* Antrop., Archeol., Jęz. (egipski) hieroglyph; (Majów, Azteków) ideogram, (hiero)glyph; (chiński) character, ideogram; ∼**y** żart. (nieczytelne pismo) hieroglyphics żart.

higien|a *f* hygiene

higieniczn|y *adi.* hygienic, sanitary; **warunki** ∼**e** sanitation

hipnotyze|r *m*, ∼**rka** *f* hypnotist

hipnotyz|ować *impf vt* to hypnotize; przen. to hypnotize, to mesmerize

hipnoz|a *f* hypnosis; **wprowadzić kogoś w stan** ∼**y** to put sb into a hypnotic trance

hipochondry|k *m*, ∼**czka** *f* hypochondriac

hipokry|ta *m*, ∼**tka** *f* hypocrite

hipokryzj|a *f* hypocrisy, insincerity

hipopotam *m* hippopotamus

hipote|ka *f* ① (zabezpieczenie) mortgage; **wziąć pożyczkę pod** ∼**kę czegoś** to mortgage sth, to take out a mortgage on sth; **mieć czystą** ~**kę** *[nieruchomość]* to be unencumbered; przen., pot. to have a good (track) record, to have a clean copybook ② (księga) mortgage register; (wpis) mortgage register entry ③ (biuro) mortgage a. land registry

hipoterapi|a *f* hippotherapy

hipotez|a *f* hypothesis; **postawić** ~**ę** to construct a. formulate a hypothesis

hippiczny *adi.* horse-riding, equestrian

histeri|a *f* ① Med. hysteria ② przen. hysterics; **dostać** ~**i** to have hysterics

histeryczn|y *adi.* hysterical

histery|k *m*, ~**czka** *f* hysteric

histeryz|ować *impf vi [osoba]* to be hysterical

histori|a *f* ① (dzieje) history; ~**a Polski** the history of Poland; ~**a powszechna** world history; ~**a choroby** Med. a case history; ~**a jej życia** the story of her life; **przejść** a. **wejść do** ~**i** to go down in history; **to już należy do** ~**i** that's ancient a. past history ② Szkol. (lekcja) history (class) ③ pot. (opowiadanie) story; ~**e o duchach** ghost stories; ~**a wyssana z palca** pot. a cock-and-bull story pot. ④ (zdarzenie) (**ciągle**) **ta sama** ~**a** the same old story; **ładna** ~**a!** pot. a fine old mess pot.

historyczn|y *adi.* ① (odnoszący się do przeszłości) *[badania, powieść]* historical ② (z przeszłości) *[wydarzenie, epoka]* historical, historic; **meble** ~**e** period furniture ③ (odnoszący się do historii) history, historical; **olimpiada** ~**a** a (school) history competition ④ (ważny) *[wydarzenie]* historic, history-making; **w tym** ~**ym momencie** at this historic moment

historyj|ka *f* ① (opowiadanie) story, tale; ~**ka obrazkowa** a picture story, a story in pictures ② (plotka) gossip, story

history|k *m* historian; pot. (nauczyciel) history teacher

hobbi|sta *m*, ~**stka** *f* hobbyist

hochsztaple|r *m*, ~**rka** *f* pejor. swindler, impostor pejor.

hochsztaplers|ki *adi.* pejor. *[metody, sposoby]* fraudulent pejor.

hod|ować *impf* Ⅰ *vt* ① to breed, to raise *[zwierzęta]*; to grow, to cultivate *[rośliny]*; to culture *[bakterie, tkankę]*; (jako hobby) to keep *[kota, papugi]* ② przen. to harbour GB, to harbor US, to nurture *[zazdrość, złość]*

Ⅱ **hodować się** *[zwierzęta]* to breed, to reproduce

hodowc|a *m* (zwierząt) breeder; (roślin) grower

hodowl|a *f* ① (zajęcie) (zwierząt) breeding; (roślin) growing, cultivation; (tkanek, bakterii) culture; ~**psów** dog breeding; ~**a ryb** fish farming ② (gospodarstwo, ferma) (zwierząt) (breeding) farm; (roślin) farm, plantation; ~**a psów** kennels; ~**sadzonek** a nursery ③ Nauk. breeding, husbandry

hodowlan|y *adi. [zwierzęta, rasa]* farm; **odmiana** ~**a** a breed; **stawy** ~**e** fish ponds

hojn|y *adi. grad. [osoba, dar]* generous; **mieć** ~**ą rękę** to be open-handed a. free-handed

hokej *m* Sport ~ **na lodzie** ice hockey GB, (ice) hockey US; ~ **na trawie** (field) hockey GB, field hockey US

hol[1] *m* (przedpokój) hall; (poczekalnia) lounge (area); (w hotelu, w teatrze) foyer, lobby

hol[2] *m* ① Aut., Żegl. tow(ing) rope, towline; **wziąć samochód na** ~ to take a car in tow; **dotrzeć na** ~**u do portu** to be towed into port ② Ryboł. haul

hol|ować *impf vt* to tow *[pojazd, statek, szybowiec]*

holownik *m* tug(boat)

hoł|d *m* homage, tribute; **oddawać komuś** ~**d** to pay tribute a. homage to sb

hołd|ować *impf vi* książk. ~**ować czemuś** to uphold sth, to adhere to sth *[ideałom, tradycjom]*; to follow sth *[modzie, zwyczajom]*

hoło|ta *f* obraźl. rabble, riff-raff pejor.

homa|r *m* lobster

homeopa|ta *m* hom(o)eopath

homeopati|a *f* hom(o)eopathy

homeopatyczn|y *adi.* hom(o)eopathic

homili|a *f* homily

homogeniczn|y *adi.* książk. homogeneous

homogenizowan|y *adi. [mleko]* homogenized; **serek** ~**y** ≈ cream cheese

homologacj|a *f* ① (test) official prototype test ② (atest) certification of approval

homonim *m* homonym

homoseksuali|sta *m* homosexual

homoseksualizm *m* homosexuality

hono|r Ⅰ *m* honour GB, honor US; **ująć się** ~**rem** to do the honourable thing; **unieść się** ~**rem** to take offence; **wyjść z** ~**rem** to emerge with one's honour intact, to save face

Ⅱ **honory** *plt* ceremony, honour GB, honor US; **z należnymi** ~**rami** with all due ceremony; **pochowany z** ~**rami wojskowymi** buried with full military honours; **oddawać** ~**ry wojskowe** to salute (**komuś** sb)

■ **na słowo** ~**ru** pot. just barely; by the skin of one's teeth pot.; **pełnić** ~**ry domu** książk. to do the honours

honorari|um *n* fee, remuneration; ~**um autorskie** author's fee

honor|ować *impf vt* ① (uznawać) to honour GB, to honor US, to recognize *[dokumenty, zaświadczenie]*; to accept, to honour GB, to honor US *[kartę płatniczą]* ② książk. (czcić) to honour GB, to honor US *[bohaterów]*

honorow|y *adi.* ① (zgodny z honorem) *[osoba, postępowanie]* honourable GB, honorable US ② (zaszczytny) **nagroda** ~**a** a merit award; ~**y gość** a guest of honour ③ (tytularny) *[członek, obywatelstwo]* honorary [4] (bez zapłaty) *[zajęcie]* volunteer, voluntary; *[konsultant]* honorary, volunteer

hormon *m* hormone

hormonaln|y *adi. [zaburzenia, leki]* hormone, hormonal; *[zmiany, substancje]* hormonal

horoskop *m* horoscope

horro|r *m* [1] (koszmar) horror, nightmare [2] Kino horror film a. movie US

hortensj|a *f* hydrangea

horyzon|t [I] *m* [1] (widnokrąg) horizon; **linia** ~**tu** the skyline; **na** ~**cie** on the horizon [2] (zakres zainteresowań) horizon; **mieć ciasne** a. **wąskie** ~**ty** to have narrow horizons, to be narrow-minded

[II] **horyzonty** *plt* (perspektywy) horizons, vistas

hospicj|um *n* hospice

hospitalizacj|a *f* hospitalization

hospitaliz|ować *pf, impf vt* to hospitalize *[pacjenta]*

hoss|a *f* run (**na coś** on sth); ~**a na giełdzie** a bull market

hosti|a *f* the Host

hotel *m* hotel; ~ **robotniczy/pracowniczy** a workers' hostel

hotelarstw|o *n* the hotel trade a. industry

hotelarz *m* hotelier; (prowadzący) hotel manager; (właściciel) hotel owner

hoż|y *adi.* książk. *[chłopak, dziewczyna]* robust; *[cera]* ruddy, sanguine

hrabi|a *m* count, earl GB; **jak** ~**a** like a lord a. king

hrabian|ka *f* count's daughter, earl's daughter GB

hrabin|a *f* countess

hub|a *f* bracket fungus

hub|ka *f* touchwood

huczeć[1] *impf →* **huknąć**[3]

hucz|eć[2] *impf* [I] *vi [działa, wystrzały]* to boom (out); *[morze, wiatr]* to roar; **sala** ~**ała od oklasków** the hall resounded with applause; ~**y mi w głowie** a. **uszach** my head is thumping

[II] *v imp.* **w mieście aż** ~**y od plotek** the town is buzzing a. abuzz with rumours

huczn|y *adi. grad.* [1] (okazały) *[wesele, bankiet]* grand [2] (głośny) *[oklaski]* thunderous; *[śmiechy]* raucous

huf|iec *m* [1] (harcerski) (scout) troop [2] Wojsk. regiment

huk *m* [1] (łoskot) thud; (dział, pioruna) rumble; (fal, maszyn) roar, roaring; **z** ~**iem** *[upaść]* with a thud; *[eksplodować]* with a bang [2] pot. (zamieszanie) stir, commotion; **narobić wiele** ~**u** to cause a great stir; **z wielkim** ~**iem** (uroczyście) in grand style [3] pot. (dużo) load(s) pot.; **mam** ~ **roboty** I've got loads of work to do

hukać[1] *impf →* **huknąć**[1]

huka|ć[2] *impf vi* (nawoływać) to shout, to yell

huk|nąć[1] *pf —* **huk|ać**[1] *impf vi [sowa]* to hoot

huk|nąć[2] *pf* [I] *vt* pot. (uderzyć) to bash, to whack pot.; ~**ąć kogoś w głowę** to bash sb on the head; ~**ąć pięścią w stół** to thump the table with one's fist

[II] *vi [strzały, działo]* to boom; *[piorun]* to strike; ~**ął drzwiami** he slammed the door

[III] **huknąć się** pot. ~**ąć się w głowę** to bump a. bang one's head

hu|knąć[3] *pf —* **hu|czeć**[1] *impf vi* (krzyknąć) to yell (**na kogoś** at sb)

hula|ć *impf vi* [1] *[wiatr]* to rage [2] przest. (bawić się) to have a good time; to revel książk.

hulajno|ga *f* scooter

hulta|j *m* przest. ne'er-do-well przest.

humani|sta *m* [1] (naukowiec) scholar [2] Hist. humanist

humanist|ka *f* scholar

humanistyczn|y *adi. [ideały, postawa]* humanistic, humane; *[poeta, ruch]* humanist; *[nauki, studia]* liberal; humane książk.; **przedmioty** ~**e i przedmioty ścisłe** the (liberal) arts and the sciences

humanitarn|y *adi. [organizacja]* humanitarian; *[osoba, postępek]* humane; **pomoc** ~**a** humanitarian a. relief aid

humo|r [I] *m* [1] (usposobienie) humour GB, humor US [2] (komizm) humour GB, humor US; ~**r sytuacyjny/ słowny** situational/verbal humour [3] (dobry nastrój) good humour GB, good humor US, good mood; **tryskać** ~**rem** to be in a brilliant mood [4] (nastrój) mood; **być w dobrym/złym** ~**rze** to be in a good/ bad mood; **poprawić komuś** ~**r** to cheer sb up

[II] **humory** *plt* (dąsy) moodiness, moods

humorystyczn|y *adi. [sytuacja, historia]* humorous, comical

humorza|sty *adi.* pot. moody

huragan *m* [1] (wiatr) gale, windstorm US; **wpadł do domu jak** ~ he stormed into the house [2] przen. (wybuch) storm, outburst; ~ **braw/śmiechu** a storm of applause/laughter

hur|t [I] *m* wholesale

[II] **hurtem** *adv.* pot. [1] *[kupić, sprzedać]* wholesale, in bulk [2] (za jednym razem) at a. in one go

hurtowni|a *f* (przedsiębiorstwo) wholesale company; (magazyn) warehouse; (sklep) wholesale outlet

hurtowni|k *m* wholesaler

hurtow|y *adi. [handel, kupiec]* wholesale

huśta|ć *impf* [I] *vt* to rock; (na wiszącej huśtawce) to swing

[II] **huśtać się** to rock; (na wiszącej huśtawce) to swing; (na podpartej desce) to play on a see-saw

huśtaw|ka *f* [1] (wisząca) swing; (podparta deska) see-saw, teeter-totter US [2] przen. see-saw przen.; ~**ka nastrojów** an emotional see-saw, mood swings

hu|ta *f* steelworks; **huta miedzi** a copper smelter a. smelting plant; **huta szkła** a glassworks

hutnictw|o *n* metallurgy; ~**o żelaza** the iron and steel industry; ~**o metali kolorowych** nonferrous metallurgy; ~**o szkła** glass-making

hutnicz|y *adi. [kombinat, przemysł]* smelting; **odpady** ~**e** smelter waste

hutni|k *m* mill a. foundry worker; ~k żelaza
a steelworker
hydran|t *m* ⒈ (zawór) hydrant; ~t przeciw-
pożarowy a fire hydrant, a fireplug US ⒉ pot. (wąż)
hose
hydrauli|k *m* plumber
hydroelektrowni|a *f* hydroelectric power plant

hydrofo|r *m* water pump
hydroplan *m* seaplane, hydroplane US
hymn ⒈ *m* ⒈ (kraju, grupy) anthem; ~ **państwowy**
the national anthem ⒉ (pochwalny) hymn
⒒ **hymny** *plt* przen. paeans książk. (**na cześć kogoś**
in praise of sb)
hyś *m* **mieć hysia** pot. to be nuts a. bonkers pot.

I

I, i *n inv.* I, i

i [] *coni.* and; **filiżanki i spodki** cups and saucers; **i w lecie, i w zimie** both in summer and in winter; **myślał i myślał o tym** he thought and thought about it; **to i to** this and that; **tego i tego dnia, o tej i o tej godzinie** on such and such a date, at such and such an hour; **trzydzieści osiem i pięć (stopni)** thirty eight point five (degrees); **mieć dwa i pół roku** to be two and a half; **on tylko śpi i śpi** all he does is sleep

[] *part.* [1] (także) too, also; **i ciebie może to spotkać** it could happen to you, too; **intratna, ale i niebezpieczna praca** a lucrative, but also dangerous job [2] (z wyrażeniem wtrąconym) and; **zastanawiał się, i nie bez powodu, czy...** he was wondering, and not without reason, whether... [3] (w nawiązaniach) and; **i co?** and what?; **i jeszcze jedna sprawa** (and) one more thing [4] (nawet) even; **i ty możesz się pomylić** even you can make a mistake

[] **i tak** [1] (mimo to) still, anyway [2] (na przykład) and thus książk.; and so

ich *pron.* [1] (osobowy) → **oni** [2] (dzierżawczy) (przed rzeczownikiem) their; (bez rzeczownika) theirs; **~ pokój/samochód** their room/car; **jestem ~ krewnym** I'm a relative of theirs

ide|a *f* idea; **robić coś dla ~i** to do sth for idealistic reasons

ideali|sta *m*, **~stka** *f* idealist

idealiz|ować *impf vt* to idealize *[osobę, rzeczywistość]*

idealn|y *adi. [warunki, nauczyciel, świat]* ideal

ideal|ł *m* [1] (wzór) ideal, model; **~ł wszelkich cnót** a paragon of virtue; **być bliskim ~łu** to be close to perfection, to be nearly perfect [2] (cel dążeń) ideal; **~ły społeczne** social ideals

identyczn|y *adi. [tekst, głos]* identical

identyfikacj|a *f* [1] (rozpoznanie) identification; **dokonać ~i ofiary** to establish the victim's identity [2] (utożsamianie się) identification (**z kimś/czymś** with sb/sth)

identyfikacyjn|y *adi. [karta]* identity, identification, ID; *[kod, numer]* identification; *[znak, cecha]* identifying, distinguishing

identyfikato|r *m* [1] (plakietka) ID badge [2] Komput., Techn. identifier

identyfik|ować *impf* [] *vt* [1] (stwierdzać tożsamość) to identify *[sprawcę, przedmiot]* [2] (utożsamiać) to identify (**z kimś/czymś** with sb/sth)

[] **identyfikować się** to identify (**z kimś/czymś** with sb/sth)

ideologi|a *f* ideology

ideologiczn|y *adi. [walka, różnice]* ideological

idiom *m* idiom

idio|ta *m* pot., obraźl. idiot pot., obraźl.

idiotyczn|y *adi. grad.* pot. *[śmiech, dowcip, uwaga]* idiotic pot.

idol *m* idol

igla|sty *adi. [drzewo, las]* coniferous

igliwi|e *n* conifer needles

ig|ła *f* needle; **wyglądać jak spod igły** to be dressed (up) to the nines pot.; **robić z igły widły** pot. to make a mountain out of a molehill; **szukać igły w stogu siana** to look for a needle in a haystack

ignor|ować *impf* [] *vt* to ignore *[osobę]*; to ignore, to disregard *[fakty, rady]*

[] **ignorować się** (nawzajem) to ignore each other

igra|ć *impf vi* [1] **~ć ze śmiercią** to dice with death przen.; **~ć z ogniem** to play with fire przen. [2] książk. *[uśmiech, promień]* to play książk.; **na jego ustach ~ł ironiczny uśmiech** an ironic smile played on his lips

Igrek *m* (osoba) Y *(as opposed to X)*

igrzysk|a *plt* games; **~a olimpijskie** the Olympic Games, the Olympics

ikon|a *f* [1] Relig., Szt. icon, ikon [2] Komput. icon

ik|ra *f* [1] Zool. spawn, eggs; Kulin. roe [2] pot. gumption, spunk pot.; **mieć ikrę** to be full of spunk pot.; **robić coś z ikrą** to do sth with gusto

Iks *m* (osoba) X, so-and-so

Iksińs|ki *m*, **~ka** *f* pot. X, so-and-so, (Mr/Ms) X

il|e [] *pron.* [1] (pytajny) (z policzalnymi) how many; (z niepoliczalnymi) how much; **ile razy?** how many times?; **ile to kosztuje?** how much is this/it?; **po ile są pomidory?** how much are the tomatoes?; how much for the tomatoes? pot.; **ile jestem ci winien?** how much do I owe you?; **ile czasu wam to zajmie?** how long will it take you?; **ile jest siedem razy sześć?** what's seven times six?; **ile masz lat?** how old are you?; **ile tu ludzi!** what a crowd!; **ile jest stąd do Krakowa?** how far is it from here to Cracow?; **ile jeszcze mam czekać?**

how much longer do I have to wait? pot. [2] (względny) (przed policzalnymi) as many; (przed niepoliczalnymi) as much; **weź, ile chcesz** take as many/much as you like

[II] **ile razy** (zawsze kiedy) each a. every time, whenever; **ile razy prosił ją o pomoc, zawsze odmawiała** every time he asked her for help, she refused

[III] **na ile** how far, to what extent a. degree; **na ile sprawa jest poważna?** how serious a matter is it?

[IV] **o tyle, o ile** a. **na tyle, na ile** pot. to the extent that, in so far as; (only) inasmuch as książk.

[V] **o ile** (jeśli) as long as, provided, providing; (z przeczeniem) unless; **o ile firma nie zbankrutuje** as long as a. provided the firm doesn't go bankrupt, unless the firm goes bankrupt; **o ile to będzie możliwe** if possible; (z powątpiewaniem) if it's a. that's (at all) possible; **o ile wiem** a. **o ile mi wiadomo...** as far as I know...; **o ile dobrze pamiętam...** as far as I remember..., if I remember correctly...; **o ile się nie mylę...** if I'm not mistaken...; **tysiące, o ile nie miliony** thousands, if not millions

[VI] **o ile..., o tyle...** a. **o ile..., to...** while...; **o ile on lubi westerny, o tyle ona woli melodramaty** he likes westerns, whereas a. while she prefers melodramas

■ **o tyle o ile** pot. *[interesować się, znać]* to a degree, up to a point

il|eś *pron.* (z policzalnymi) a (certain) number of; (z niepoliczalnymi) a certain amount of; **ileś lat temu** a. **przed iluś laty** some years ago; **(ona) ma siedemdziesiąt ileś lat** she's seventy-something

iloczyn *m* Mat. product

iloraz *m* Mat. quotient; **~ inteligencji** Psych. intelligence quotient, IQ

ilościow|y *adi.* quantitative; **stosunek ~y soli do wody** the ratio of salt to water

iloś|ć *f* amount, quantity; **~ć wody/cukru** the amount of water/sugar

iluminacj|a *f* książk. [1] (oświetlenie) illumination, lighting [2] przen. (oświecenie) enlightenment, illumination

ilustracj|a *f* [1] (rysunek) illustration [2] (przykład) illustration, example

ilustrato|r *m*, **~rka** *f* illustrator

ilustr|ować *impf vt* to illustrate

iluzj|a *f* [1] (złudzenie) illusion [2] (błędne przekonanie) delusion, illusion; **nie mieć ~i co do czegoś** to have no illusions about sth

iluzjoni|sta *m* conjuror; illusionist książk.

im¹ *conj.* im..., tym... the... the...; **im więcej/ szybciej, tym lepiej** the more/the sooner the better

im² *pron.* → **oni**

imad|ło *n* Techn. vice, vise US

imbi|r *m* ginger

imbrycz|ek *m* teapot

imbryk *m* kettle

imienin|y *plt* [1] (święto) name day; **wszystkiego najlepszego z okazji ~** all the best on your name day [2] (przyjęcie) name day party

imienni|k *m*, **~czka** *f* namesake

imienn|y *adi.* **lista ~a** a list of names; **głosowanie ~e** a vote by roll-call, a roll-call vote; **akcje ~e** registered shares; **zaproszenie ~e** a personal invitation

imiesł|ów *m* participle; **~ów czynny/bierny** the active/passive participle; **~ów przeszły** the past participle; **~ów przysłówkowy uprzedni/współczesny** the perfect(ive)/present participle

imi|ę *n* [1] (osoby) (first a. given) name; **drugie ~ę** middle name; **dać komuś na ~ę Jan** to name sb Jan; **nosić ~ę po dziadku** to be named after one's grandfather; **jak ci na ~ę?** what's your name?; **mam na ~ę Maria** my name is Maria; **być z kimś po ~eniu** to be on first-name terms with sb; **zwracać się do kogoś po ~eniu** to call sb by their first name; **człowiek ~eniem Robert** a man by the name of Robert; **nazwać szkołę ~eniem kogoś** to name a school after sb; **fundacja ~enia Fryderyka Chopina** the Frederic Chopin Foundation [2] przen. (opinia) name; **(czyjeś) dobre ~ę** sb's good name; **szargać dobre ~ę rodziny** to besmirch the family's good name

■ **w ~ę Ojca i Syna** in the name of the Father and of the Son; **w czyimś ~niu** on sb's behalf GB, in sb's behalf US; **nazywać rzeczy po ~eniu** to call a spade a spade

imigracj|a *f* [1] (proces) immigration [2] (imigranci) immigrants, immigration

imigran|t *m*, **~tka** *f* immigrant

imigr|ować *pf, impf vi* to immigrate

imitacj|a *f* [1] (naśladowanie) imitation, imitating [2] (kopia) imitation; **~a skóry** imitation leather

imitato|r *m*, **~rka** *f* imitator, mimic

imit|ować *impf vt* to imitate, to mimic

immunite|t *m* immunity

immunologi|a *f* immunology

impas *m* impasse, deadlock

imperi|um *n* empire także przen.

impertynencj|a *f* książk. impertinence, impudence; **~e** impertinent a. impudent remarks

impertynenc|ki *adi.* książk. impertinent, impudent

impertynen|t *m*, **~tka** *f* książk. impertinent person

impon|ować *impf vi* [1] (budzić podziw) to impress (komuś sb) [2] pot. (pysznić się) to flaunt, to show off *[bogactwem]*

imponując|y *adi.* *[wygląd, zwycięstwo]* impressive; *[budowla, wielkość]* imposing; *[przyjęcie, uroczystość]* grand

impor|t *m* import, importation; **towary z ~tu** imported goods, imports

importe|r *m* importer
import|ować *impf vt* to import
impoten|t *m* impotent man
impregn|ować *impf vt* to impregnate; (przeciw wilgoci) to (water)proof; (przeciw czynnikom atmosferycznym) to weatherproof
impresjoni|sta *m*, **~stka** *f* Impressionist
impresjonizm *m* Impressionism
imprez|a *f* [1] (sportowa, rozrywkowa, kulturalna) event [2] pot. (towarzyska) party; do GB pot. [3] pot. (przedsięwzięcie) game pot., business pot.
imprez|ować *impf vi* pot. to party pot.
improwizacj|a *f* [1] Muz. improvisation [2] przen. slapdash a. slipshod affair
improwiz|ować *impf vt, vi* to improvise; *[jazzman]* to jam pot.
impuls *m* [1] (bodziec) impulse; **pod wpływem ~u** on (an) impulse [2] (zewnętrzny czynnik) impetus; **dać komuś ~ do czegoś/do zrobienia czegoś** to spur sb to sth/into doing sth [3] Fiz. impulse, pulse [4] Med. impulse [5] Telekom. call unit
impulsywn|y *adi. grad. [charakter, odpowiedź]* impulsive
inaczej **[1]** *pron.* (w inny sposób) differently, another way; **~ niż ktoś** in a different way to sb, unlike sb; **zrób to ~** do it another way; **los chciał ~** fate decreed otherwise książk.; **nie ~** (na pewno) that's it a. right; **tak czy ~** (w każdym razie) anyway, in any event; **tak czy ~ trzeba coś postanowić** one way or another we need to decide something; **~ mówiąc...** in other words...; **(to) może ~...** (well,) let me put it another way...
[II] *coni.* [1] (w przeciwnym razie) otherwise, or (else); **pośpiesz się, (bo) ~ się spóźnimy** hurry up, or (else) we'll be late [2] (innymi słowy) or, also known as
inauguracj|a *f* książk. inauguration
inauguracyjn|y *adi.* książk. *[przemówienie, koncert]* inaugural
inaugur|ować *pf, impf vt* książk. to inaugurate, to open *[sesję, sezon]*
incyden|t *m* książk. incident
indeks *m* [1] (spis) index; **~y rzeczowe/nazwisk** subject/name indexes a. indices [2] Uniw. ≈ student record book, ≈ (grade) transcript US; **dostać ~** to be admitted to a university [3] Druk. **~ górny/dolny** superscript/subscript [4] Ekon., Fin. index; **~ giełdowy** a share index, a stock exchange index
industrializacj|a *f* książk. industrialization
industrializ|ować *impf* książk. **[1]** *vt* to industrialize *[kraj, region]*
[II] industrializować się to undergo industrialization
indycz|ka *f* turkey hen
indyk *m* turkey
indywiduali|sta *m*, **~stka** *f* individualist
indywidualizm *m* individualism

indywidualnoś|ć *f* [1] (wyjątkowość) individuality [2] (osoba) personality; **wybitna ~ć** an outstanding personality a. individual
indywidualn|y *adi.* [1] (wyjątkowy) *[styl]* individual; *[odczucie, wrażenie]* personal [2] (pojedynczy) *[turysta, terapia]* individual
indywidu|um *n* [1] książk. (jednostka) individual [2] pejor. (podejrzany) character pot.
indziej *adv.* **gdzie(ś) ~** somewhere else; **gdzie ~ (mogą być)?** where else (can a. could they be)?; **gdziekolwiek ~** anywhere else; **nigdzie ~** nowhere else; **codziennie gdzie ~** every day in a different place; **spotkajmy się kiedy ~** let's meet some other time; **dziś jest to ważniejsze niż kiedykolwiek ~** today it's more important than ever
infantyln|y *adi.* infantile
infekcj|a *f* infection
infek|ować *impf vt* książk. to infect *[osobę, bydło]*
inflacj|a *f* inflation
informacyjn|y *adi. [agencja, biuletyn]* information
informato|r *m* [1] (o osobie) (źródło informacji) source; (policyjny) informer, informant; (w sondażu) informant [2] (publikacja) guide; (uniwersytecki) prospectus; **~r o Warszawie** a guide to Warsaw
informator|ka *f* (źródło informacji) source; (policyjna) informer, informant; (w sondażu) informant
informaty|k *m*, **~czka** *f* computer specialist
informaty|ka *f* computer a. information science
inform|ować *impf* **[1]** *vt [osoba, znak]* to inform; **~ować kogoś na bieżąco** to keep sb informed
[II] informować się (zasięgać informacji) to inquire, to enquire
ingerencj|a *f* interference; (wojskowa, policyjna) intervention
inger|ować *impf vi* to interfere
inhalacj|a *f* inhalation
inhalato|r *m* inhaler, inhalator
inicjacj|a *f* książk. initiation
inicja|ł *m* initial
inicjatyw|a *f* initiative; **człowiek z ~ą** a man of initiative
inicj|ować *impf vt* to initiate *[badania, budowę]*
inkasen|t *m* meter reader
inkas|ować *impf vt* to collect *[pieniądze, należność]*; **~ować czeki** to cash cheques
inkubato|r *m* incubator
innowacj|a *f* książk. innovation
inn|y *pron.* [1] (odmienny) other, different; **nie mamy ~ego wyboru** we have no other choice; **lekarze, pielęgniarki i ~i** doctors, nurses, and others; **ceny są takie, a nie ~e** prices are as they are; **spojrzeć na coś ~ymi oczami** to see sth in a different light [2] (nie ten) (the) other; **koleżanka z ~ej szkoły** a friend from another school; **może ~ym razem** maybe some other time; **kto/nikt ~y** somebody/nobody else; **co/nic ~ego** something/

nothing else; **co ~ego, gdyby...** it would/might have been different if...; **wszystko ~e** everything else; **wszystko ~e się nie liczy** nothing else counts; **w ten czy ~y sposób** one way or another, somehow or other; **z tego czy ~ego powodu** for one reason or another ③ (o ludziach) somebody a. someone else; (w pytaniu, przeczeniu) anybody else; **on kocha ~ą** he loves somebody else; **~i** other people, others; **robić coś dla ~ych** to do something for others ■ **~ymi słowy** in other words; **między ~ymi** (z żywotnymi) among others; (z nieżywotnymi) among other things; inter alia książk.

inscenizacj|a f Teatr ① (wystawienie) staging, (stage) adaptation ② (spektakl) stage production

inscenizato|r m, **~rka** f Teatr producer

insceniz|ować impf vt ① Teatr to stage [operę, sztukę] ② (aranżować) to arrange [spotkanie]; (pozorować) to fake [porwanie]

inspekcj|a f ① (kontrola) inspection ② (urząd) inspectorate

inspek|t m frame, hotbed US

inspekto|r m ① (urzędnik) inspector ② (w policji) ≈ superintendent

inspicjen|t m, **~tka** f stage manager

inspiracj|a f inspiration

inspirato|r m, **~rka** f initiator, guiding spirit; **~r spisku** the instigator of a plot

inspir|ować ▮ vt to inspire ▮▮ **inspirować się** to be inspired

instalacj|a f installation; **~a gazowa** gas fittings

instal|ować impf ▮ vt ① (montować) to instal(l) [aparaturę, licznik] ② pot. (lokować) to instal(l) ▮▮ **instalować się** to instal(l) oneself, to settle in

instancj|a f ① Prawo **sąd pierwszej ~i** a court of first instance, a trial court US; **sąd niższej/wyższej ~i** a lower/higher court ② (organizacja) authority, body; **odwołać się do wyższych ~i** to appeal to a higher authority ■ **być ostatnią ~ą** to have the last a. final word

instrukcj|a f instruction; **postępować według ~i** to follow the instructions; **~a obsługi telewizora** a TV-set operating manual; **~a przeciwpożarowa** fire regulations

instruktaż m ① (szkolenie) briefing, training ② (instrukcje) instructions; **~ obsługi sprzętu** instructions on how to operate the equipment

instrukto|r m, **~rka** f instructor

instrumen|t m instrument także przen. **~t władzy** an instrument a. a tool of the authorities

instru|ować impf vt to instruct, to brief

instynk|t m instinct; **~t macierzyński** maternal instinct(s); **~t (samo)zachowawczy** the survival instinct, the instinct for self-preservation

instynktown|y adi. [zachowanie, reakcja] instinctive

instytucj|a f institution

instytu|t m institute

insulin|a f insulin

insynu|ować impf vt książk. to insinuate; to impute (coś komuś sth to sb)

integracj|a f książk. integration

integralnoś|ć f książk. integrity

integraln|y adi. książk. [składnik, część] integral

integr|ować impf książk. ▮ vt to integrate, to bring together [rodzinę, środowisko] ▮▮ **integrować się** to integrate

intelek|t m intellect, mental powers

intelektuali|sta m, **~stka** f intellectual

intelektualn|y adi. [elita, rozwój] intellectual

inteligencj|a f ① (intelekt) intelligence, cleverness; **test na ~ę** an intelligence test ② (grupa) the intelligentsia

inteligen|t m, **~tka** f educated person

inteligentn|y adi. [osoba, odpowiedź] intelligent

intencj|a f ① (zamiar) intention; **mieć dobre ~e** to have good intentions, to mean well ② Relig. **modlić się w czyjejś ~i** to pray for sb

intenden|t m ① (w firmie, biurze) ≈ purchasing manager; (zakupujący żywność) steward ② Wojsk. ≈ quartermaster

intensyfik|ować impf książk. ▮ vt to intensify [procesy, działania] ▮▮ **intensyfikować się** [działanie, ból] to intensify, to become more intense

intensywnoś|ć f intensity, intensiveness

intensywn|y adi. grad. [zapach, światło] intense, strong; [kurs, trening] intensive; **~e opady śniegu** a heavy snowfall

interes m ① (sprawa) business; **załatwiać ~** a. **~y** to see to some business; **to nie twój ~!** pot. it's none of your business; **mam do ciebie ~** I've got something I'd like to talk to you about ② (korzyść) interest ③ (przedsięwzięcie) business, dealing; **mieć głowę do ~ów** to have a good head for business; **podróżować w ~ach** to travel on business; **zrobić na czymś (dobry) ~** to make a profit on sth; **ubić ~** to make a deal ④ pot. (firma) business; **założyć własny ~** to start up a. establish one's own business

interesan|t m, **~tka** f (w urzędzie) enquirer, inquirer; (w biurze) client; (składający podanie) applicant; „**przyjmowanie ~tów w godzinach 10.00 – 13.00**" 'office a. business hours: 10 am to 1 pm'

interes|ować impf ▮ vt to interest; **sława jej nie ~uje** she's not interested in fame; **w ~ującym nas okresie** in the period in question ▮▮ **interesować się** to be interested (**kimś/czymś** in sb/sth), to take an interest (**kimś/czymś** in sb/sth)

interesown|y adi. [osoba, czyn] self-interested, self-seeking; [przyjaźń, grzeczność] self-interested

interesując|y adi. [osoba, książka] interesting

intern|a f [1] (dział medycyny) internal medicine [2] pot. (oddział) internal medicine ward

interna|t m boarding house, (boarding school) dormitory; **szkoła z ~tem** a boarding a. residential school

Interne|t m the Internet

internetow|y adi. [łącze] Internet; [bank, zakupy] online

interni|sta m, **~stka** f specialist in internal medicine, internist

internistyczn|y adi. **badania ~e** internal (medical) examination

intern|ować pf, impf vt to detain, to intern

internowan|y m, **~a** f internee; **obóz dla ~ych** an internment camp

interpelacj|a f Admin., Polit. (parliamentary) question

interpretacj|a f [1] (wytłumaczenie) interpretation [2] Muz., Teatr interpretation, rendition

interpret|ować impf vt to interpret; **błędnie coś ~ować** to misinterpret sth

interpunkcj|a f punctuation

interwa|ł m interval

interwencj|a f książk. intervention; **prosić kogoś o ~ę (w swojej sprawie)** to ask sb to intervene on one's behalf

interweni|ować pf, impf vi książk. to intervene; **~ować w czyjeś sprawie** to intervene on sb's behalf

intonacj|a f intonation

inton|ować impf vt to intone [pieśń, modlitwę]

intratn|y adi. grad. książk. [posada] well paid; [handel, inwestycja] lucrative, profitable

introligato|r m bookbinder

introwerty|k m, **~czka** f introvert

intruz m intruder, interloper; **czuć się ~em** to feel like an outsider a. intruder

intry|ga f [1] (knowanie) intrigue, scheme; **dworskie ~gi** courtly intrigue(s) [2] Literat. (sub)plot

intrygan|t m, **~tka** f intriguer, schemer

intryg|ować impf vi [1] (spiskować) to intrigue, to scheme (**przeciw komuś** against sb) [2] (zaciekawiać) to intrigue

intrygując|y adi. [osoba, zagadka] intriguing

intuicj|a f intuition

intuicyjn|y adi. [podejście, zdolności] intuitive

intymnoś|ć f intimacy

intymn|y [] adi. grad. [zwierzenia, myśli] intimate

inwali|da m, **~dka** f invalid, disabled person; **~da wojenny** a war-disabled person

inwalidz|ki adi. **wózek ~ki** a wheelchair, an invalid chair; **renta ~ka** an invalidity pension

inwalidztw|o n disablement, invalidity GB

inwazj|a f książk. [1] (agresja) invasion [2] (plaga) invasion; **~a szczurów** an invasion of rats

inwektyw|a f książk. insult; **~y** invective

inwencj|a f książk. invention, ingenuity; **~a twórcza** creative imagination

inwentaryzacj|a f (towarów) stocktaking; (majątku) inventorying

inwentaryz|ować impf vt to inventory [majątek, zabytki]; to catalogue GB, to catalog US [książki, pisma]

inwentarz m [1] (zwierzęta) (live)stock [2] (mienie) stock [3] książk. (rejestr) inventory; **~ zabytków** an inventory of historic monuments

inwesto|r m investor

inwest|ować impf vt to invest (**w coś** in sth)

inwestycj|a f investment

inwigil|ować impf vt książk. to keep [sb] under surveillance

inżynie|r m engineer; **skończyć studia z tytułem magistra ~ra** to have an engineering degree

inżyniers|ki adi. [dyplom, tytuł] engineering; [pensja] engineer's; **wyższa szkoła ~ka** ≈ a college of advanced technology

inżynieryjn|y adi. [prace, wydział] engineering

ir|cha f chamois (leather)

ironi|a f irony; **z ~ą** with irony; **jak na ~ę** ironically (enough); **czy to nie ~a, że...?** isn't it ironic that...?

ironiczn|y adi. [uwaga, uśmiech] ironic

ironiz|ować impf vi to be ironic

irracjonaln|y adi. książk. irrational

irygato|r m Med. douche

irys m [1] Bot. iris, flag [2] (cukierek) ≈ toffee

irytacj|a f irritation, annoyance

iryt|ować impf [] vt to irritate, to annoy; **to mnie ~uje** I find it irritating
[] **irytować się** to be irritated

isk|ra f spark; **żywy jak ~ra** as lively as a cricket
■ **mieć ~rę bożą** to have a talent a. gift; **robić coś z ~rą w oku** to do sth with one's whole heart

iskrz|yć impf [] vi [przewód, maszyna] to spark
[] v imp. przen. **~y między nimi** there's a lot of friction between them
[][] **iskrzyć się** [brylant, śnieg] to sparkle

islam m Islam

istni|eć impf vi to exist

istnie|nie n being; **katastrofa pochłonęła sto ~ń ludzkich** the crash caused the death(s) of a hundred people

isto|ta [] f [1] (stworzenie) being, creature; **~ta ludzka** a human being; **~ty pozaziemskie** extraterrestrial beings; **~ty żywe** living beings a. creatures [2] (najważniejszy element) essence; **~ta rzeczy** the heart of the matter
[] **w istocie** [1] (w gruncie rzeczy) in (actual) fact [2] (naprawdę) really

istotnie książk. [] part. (rzeczywiście) indeed, sure enough
[] adv. (bardzo) [wzrosnąć, zmienić się] significantly, substantially

istotn|y *adi. grad. [szczegół, element]* essential, vital; *[różnica, wzrost]* substantial, significant

i|ść *impf vi* [1] (przemieszczać się) *[osoba]* to go, to walk; **iść ulicą** to go along a. down/up the street; **idziemy?** shall we go?; **statek szedł na dno** the ship was going under [2] (udawać się) to go; **iść do domu** to go home; **iść do pracy/szkoły** to go to work/school; **iść na koncert** to go to a concert; **iść na film** to go to see a film; **iść na spacer** to go for a walk; **iść na zakupy** to go shopping; **iść popływać** to go swimming; **iść na grzyby** to go mushroom picking; **iść do lekarza** to go to a doctor, to go and see a doctor; **iść do szpitala/więzienia** to go into hospital/to prison; **iść do ataku** to go on the attack [3] (rozpocząć nowy okres) to go; **iść na studia** pot. to go to university; **iść na emeryturę** to retire; **iść na urlop** to go on leave; **iść na zwolnienie** to take sick leave [4] (być pokazywanym) *[film, sztuka]* to be on; **program idzie na żywo** pot. the programme is going out live [5] (odbywać się) to go; **wszystko szło sprawnie** everything went smoothly; **interes idzie dobrze** pot. business is going well; **w szkole nauka szła mu kiepsko** pot. he didn't do well at school; **jak ci idzie?** pot. how's it going? pot., how are you doing? pot. [6] (zbliżać się) to approach, to come; **idzie burza** there's a storm coming, a storm is approaching; **chyba idzie na deszcz** it looks like rain [7] przen. (dochodzić) *[zapach, dźwięk]* to come; **jak długo idzie list do Berlina?** how long does it take for a letter to get to a. reach Berlin? [8] (pracować) *[fabryka, maszyna]* to run, to work; **iść pełną parą** to run a. work at full speed [9] (być przeznaczonym) *[pieniądze]* to go (**na coś** on sth) [10] *[droga, szlak]* (ciągnąć się) to run; (prowadzić) to go, to lead [11] (podążać) to follow; **iść za kimś** to follow sb;

iść z duchem czasu to move with the times [12] (mijać) to go by; **czas idzie nieubłaganie naprzód** time goes marching on ■ **a co za tym idzie...** and consequently a. in consequence...; **idzie o to, że...** the point is that...; **idzie mi o to, że...** what I mean is that...; **iść jak po maśle** a. **jak z płatka** to go swimmingly a. like clockwork; **iść na coś** to agree to sth; **iść na kompromis** to reach a compromise; **iść sobie** to go away; **iść w górę/dół** to go up/down; **szybko szedł w górę** (awansował) he advanced rapidly; **idź precz** a. **do diabła** pot. go to hell! pot.

izb|a *f* [1] (pokój) room [2] (stowarzyszenie) association, society; **~a handlowa** a chamber of commerce [3] (urząd) chamber, office; **~a skarbowa** a treasury office [4] (w parlamencie) house, chamber; **~a niższa/wyższa** the lower/upper house a. chamber; **Izba Gmin/Lordów** the House of Commons/Lords ❏ **~a porodowa** Med. ≈ delivery room; **~a przyjęć** Med. ≈ admissions; **~a wytrzeźwień** detoxification detention centre; drunk tank US pot.

izolacj|a *f* [1] (odosobnienie) isolation, seclusion [2] (zabezpiecznie) insulation [3] (materiał izolacyjny) insulation, insulating material

izolacyjn|y *adi. [taśma, warstwa]* insulating, insulation

izolat|ka *f* (w szpitalu) isolation ward; (w więzieniu) isolation a. seclusion cell

izol|ować *pf, impf* **[]** *vt* [1] (oddzielać) to isolate, to separate [2] (pokrywać izolacją) to insulate *[ściany, przewód]* **[]** *vi* (nie przepuszczać) to insulate; **warstwa ~ująca** an insulating layer **[]]** **izolować się** to seclude oneself

izotop *m* isotope

J

J, j *n inv.* J, j

ja **[I]** *pron.* (jako podmiot) I; (w pozostałych przypadkach) me; „wyjdź z pokoju!" – „ja?" 'leave the room!' – '(who,) me?'; „kto to?" – „to ja" 'who is it?' – 'it's me'; **ona jest starsza ode mnie** she's older than I am a. than me
[II] *n inv.* (one's) self, the I; **świadomość własnego ja** a person's sense of self; **jego drugie ja** his alter ego
[III] *mi part.* **idźże mi stąd!** (just) go away! iron.; **ładny mi (z niego) przyjaciel!** iron. some friend a. a fine friend he is! iron.

jabłecznik *m* pot. [1] (wino) apple wine [2] (ciasto) ≈ apple pie

jabł|ko *n* [1] (owoc) apple [2] (królewskie) orb [3] pot. (w kolanie) kneecap

jabło|ń *f* apple tree

jach|t *m* yacht

ja|d *m* venom także przen.

jada|ć *impf vt* to eat

jadalni|a *f* (pokój) dining room

jadaln|y **[I]** *adi. [grzyb, olej]* edible
[II] *m* (pokój) dining room

jadłodajni|a *f* eating place

jadłospis *m* menu

jadowi|ty *adi. [wąż, pająk]* venomous; *[owoc, roślina]* poisonous; *[spojrzenie, uwaga]* venomous przen.; *[czerwień, żółć]* garish

jagni|ę *n* (owcy) lamb; (kozy) kid

jag|oda *f* (czarna jagoda) bilberry GB, blueberry US; (owoc) berry; **~ody jarzębiny** rowan berries

jagodzian|ka *f* bilberry GB a. blueberry US bun

jagua|r *m* Zool. jaguar

jajeczkowani|e *n* ovulation

jajecznic|a *f* scrambled eggs

jaj|ko *n* egg; **~ko na miękko/na twardo** a soft-boiled/hard-boiled egg; **~ko sadzone** a fried egg; **~ka w koszulkach** poached eggs
■ **obchodzić się z kimś jak z ~kiem** to handle a. treat sb with kid gloves

jajnik *m* ovary

jaj|o *n* [1] Kulin., Zool. egg [2] Biol. (komórka) ovum, egg [3] wulg. (jądro) ball, bollock GB posp.
■ **dla ~** posp. (just) for the hell of it pot.

jajow|ód *m* Fallopian tube, oviduct

jak¹ **[I]** *pron.* how; **~ to zrobiłeś?** how did you do it a. that?; **~ było w Londynie?** how was (it in) London?, what was it like in London?; **~ ona wygląda?** what does she look like?; **~ mu tam** pot. what d'you call him, what's his name pot.; **~ tu gorąco!** it's so hot (in) here!; **~ ty wyglądasz!** (just) look at you!
[II] *praep.* as, like; **czarny ~ węgiel** as black as coal; **oczy ~ gwiazdy** eyes like stars; **b ~ Barbara** 'B' as in 'Barbara'; **płakała ~ dziecko** she cried like a baby; **taki (sam) ~...** the same as...
[III] *coni.* [1] (porównanie) like, as; **ciepło ~ w lecie** as warm as (in) summer; **(tak) ~ co roku, pojechał do Londynu** he went to London, as he did every year, just as; **~ gdyby** as if, as though; **nie dalej ~ dwa dni temu** only two days ago [2] pot. (kiedy) when, as; **porozmawiamy o tym, ~ wrócę** we'll talk about it when I get back [3] pot. (odkąd) since; **już dwa miesiące, ~ wyjechał** it's (been) two months since he left [4] pot. (jeżeli) if; **~ nie dziś, to jutro** either today or tomorrow; if not today, then tomorrow [5] pot. (skoro) as, since; **zrób to sam, ~ jesteś taki mądry** do it yourself if a. as you're so clever [6] (w dopowiedzeniach) as; **~ się okazało** as it turned out; as it transpired książk.; **~ się zdaje** as it seems; **~ również** as well as; **zarówno w sobotę, ~ i w niedzielę** on Saturday as well as on Sunday [7] (w powtórzeniach) **na wojnie ~ na wojnie** war's war pot.; **komu ~ komu, ale jemu możesz zaufać** you can trust him more than anyone pot.
[IV] *part.* pot. (emfaza) **~ to!?** what do you mean?!, how come?; **~ to, już czwarta?** what, is it four (o'clock) already?
[V] *adv.* **~ najkrótszy/najdłuższy** the shortest/longest possible; **~ najtaniej/najbliżej** as cheap/close as possible; **miał o niej ~ najlepszą opinię** he had a very high a. the highest opinion of her

jak² *m* Zool. yak

jakby **[I]** *coni.* [1] (jak gdyby) as if, as though [2] (warunek) if; **~m miał psa...** if I had a dog...
[II] *part.* kind of pot., sort of pot.; **~ mimochodem** sort of casually; **praca jest tak ~ skończona** the job is more or less finished
[III] *pron.* how; **~m mógł!** how could I?!

ja|ki **[I]** *pron.* [1] (w pytaniach) what; **jakiego koloru są ściany?** what colour are the walls?; **jaka jest pogoda?** what's the weather like?; **jaki to samochód?** what kind of car is that?; **jaka ona jest?**

what is she like?; **w jaki sposób?** in what way?, how?; **po jakiemu oni mówią?** what language are they speaking? ② (w zdaniach względnych) which, that; **powieści, jakie pisał pod koniec życia** the novels (which a. that) he wrote towards the end of his life ③ (emfatyczne) (przed przymiotnikiem) how; (przed rzeczownikiem) what; **jakie to ładne!** how pretty (this is)!; **jakiś ty miły!** you're so nice!; **"podobno masz psa?" – "jakiego psa? kota!"** 'I hear you have a dog?' – 'what dog? cat, you mean' pot. ④ pot. (nieokreślony) some; **weź się do jakiej pracy** why don't you get down to some work!

ja|kikolwiek pron. any; **jakikolwiek inny** any other; **w jakikolwiek sposób** in any way (whatsoever); **jeśli, z jakiegokolwiek powodu, zrezygnujesz...** if you should resign for any reason at all a. whatsoever...; **jakąkolwiek cenę przyjdzie nam zapłacić** whatever (the) price we have to pay

ja|kiś pron. ① (nieokreślony) some; (w pytaniu, przeczeniu) any; **jakaś dziewczyna/jacyś chłopcy** some girl/boys; **przez jakiś czas** for some time; **czy masz jakieś pytania?** do you have any questions?; **jakiś pan Kwiatkowski/jakiś Adam** a Mr Kwiatkowski/someone called Adam ② (około) some; **jakieś dziesięć tygodni** some ten weeks; **w jakiś tydzień potem** a week or so later ③ (trochę) kind of, sort of pot.; **on jest dzisiaj jakiś markotny** he's out of sorts

jakkolwiek ① pron. ① (obojętnie jak) no matter how, however; ~ **sprawa się zakończy** no matter how it all ends; ~ **potoczą się rozmowy** how ever the talks a. negotiations go; ~ **postąpisz** whatever you do ② (byle jak) anyhow

② coni. książk. (chociaż) although, though; ~ **bardzo się starał** (al)though he tried extremely hard

jako ① praep. ① (w okresie życia) as; ~ **młody człowiek** as a young man; **nauczył się francuskiego** ~ **dziecko** he learnt French when he was a child ② (w charakterze) as książk.; ~ **gospodarz/nauczyciel** as host/teacher; ~ **lekarz uważam, że...** in my capacity as (a) doctor, I believe that...

② coni. as; **stany określane** ~ **depresyjne** conditions described as depressive; **przyszła** ~ **pierwsza** she was the first to arrive; **urodził się** ~ **ostatni z siedmiorga rodzeństwa** he was born the youngest of seven children; ~ **taki** as such

③ **jako że** a. **iż** książk. as, since

④ **jako tako** pot. [czuć się] so-so pot.; [zachowywać się] tolerably; [inteligentny] fairly

jakoś ① pron. somehow; ~ **sobie poradzę** I'll manage somehow; **czuł się** ~ **niewyraźnie** he felt out of sorts; ~ **to będzie** things will work out; it'll be all right

② part. ~ **na początku przyszłego tygodnia** somewhere around the beginning of next week

jakoś|ć f quality

jakże ① pron. książk. how; ~ **mógłbym zapomnieć?** how could I possibly forget?; ~ **się cieszę!** I'm so happy!; ~ **go nie lubić?!** you can't but like him!

② inter. **a** ~**!** yes, indeed!; ~ **to?** how's that?

jałmużn|a f alms przest.; **prosić o** ~**ę** to beg for alms

jałowców|ka f juniper vodka

jałow|iec m juniper

jałowi|eć impf vi [gleba, ziemia] to turn barren

jałowoś|ć f (gleby) barrenness; (bezskuteczność) futility; (sterylność) sterility

jałow|y adi. [ziemia, step] barren, infertile; [rozmowa, dyskusja] futile; [gaza, igła] sterile; [kuchnia, potrawa] bland; [koło, przebieg] idle; **bieg** ~**y** neutral (gear)

jałów|ka f heifer

jam|a f ① (zagłębienie) hollow; (nora) burrow; **smocza** ~**a** a dragon's lair ② Anat. cavity

jamnik m dachshund

jamochłon m coelenterate

ja|r m ravine

jarmark m (targ) (farmer's) market; (kiermasz) fair; **na** ~**u** at the market/fair

jarosz m vegetarian

jars|ki adi. [danie, dieta] vegetarian

jarzą|b m Bot. mountain ash

jarząb|ek m Zool. hazel grouse a. hen

jarzeniow|y adi. [światło, lampa] fluorescent

jarzeniów|ka f pot. glow tube pot.

jarzębiak m rowan-berry vodka

jarzębin|a f ① (drzewo) rowan (tree) ② (owoc) rowanberry

jarz|yć się impf v refl. ① (tlić się) [papieros, węgle] to glow ② (lśnić) to gleam ③ przen. [oczy] to glow, to glimmer

jarzyn|a f vegetable

jarzynow|y ① adi. [sałatka, zupa] vegetable

② **jarzynowa** f pot. (zupa) vegetable soup

jaseł|ka plt ① (widowisko) nativity play ② (szopka) crib

ja|siek m ① (poduszka) (small) pillow ② (fasola) butter beans

jask|ier m Bot. buttercup

jaski|nia f cave; ~**nia lwa** a lion's den

jaskiniow|iec m caveman także przen.

jaskół|ka f ① Zool. swallow; ~**ka brzegówka** sand martin, bank swallow; ~**ka dymówka** common swallow; ~**ka oknówka** house martin ② Sport (w łyżwiarstwie) arabesque

■ **pierwsza** ~**ka czegoś** the harbinger of sth; **jedna** ~**ka nie czyni wiosny** przysł. one swallow doesn't make a summer przysł.

jask|ra f glaucoma

jaskraw|y adi. [kolor, strój] bright; lurid, garish pejor.; [światło] glaring, garish pejor.; [przykład, różnica] glaring

ja|sno *adv. grad.* ① *[palić się, świecić]* brightly; **w pokoju było jasno** it was (very) bright in the room; **ufarbować włosy na jasno** to dye one's hair a light colour; **ubierać się jasno** a. **na jasno** to wear light-coloured clothes ② *przen. [mówić, pisać]* clearly, plainly; **wyrażać się jasno** to express oneself clearly, to make oneself clear ③ *przen.* (radośnie) brightly, cheerfully

jasnoś|ć *f* ① (światło) brightness; ~**ć dnia** the brightness of the day ② *przen.* (zrozumiałość) clarity, lucidity; ~**ć umysłu** clarity of mind; **mieć** ~**ć w czymś** a. **co do czegoś** to be (absolutely) clear about a. on sth

jasnowidz *m* clairvoyant

ja|sny ① *adi. grad.* ① *[lampa, słońce, dzień]* bright; *[pomieszczenie]* bright, light ② (o odcieniu) *[kolor]* light; *[włosy]* fair, blond(e); *[skóra, cera]* pale, light ③ *przen. [styl]* clear, lucid; *[umysł, uśmiech, twarz]* bright; **jasne strony czegoś** the bright(er) side of sth

③ najjaśniejszy *adi. sup.* (w tytułach) **najjaśniejszy pan/najjaśniejsza pani** His/Her Majesty; **najjaśniejszy panie/najjaśniejsza pani** Your Majesty

④ jasne *n* (piwo) lager

⑤ jasne *inter.* pot. of course; sure pot.; **jasne, że wiem** of course I know

■ **jasna sprawa** a. **rzecz** of course; **rzecz jasna, że...** of course...; **cholera jasna!** posp. damn it!, bloody hell! GB pot.

jaspis *m* Miner. jasper

jastrz|ąb *m* Zool. hawk także przen.

jaszczur|ka *f* lizard

ja|ś *m* (fasola) butter beans

jaśmin *m* Bot. jasmine

jaśni|eć *impf* ① *vi* ① (świecić) *[słońce, gwiazdy]* to shine ② (odcinać się od tła) to stand out; ~**eć w mroku** to stand out in the darkness ③ (blednąć) *[kolor, włosy]* to fade

② *v imp.* (świtać) to grow light

■ ~**eć czystością** książk. to be sparkling clean; ~**eć urodą** to glow a. sparkle with beauty

jat|ka *f* ① *przen.* bloodbath ② *przest.* (rzeźnia) butchery GB

jaw *m inv.* **wyjść na** ~ *[tajemnica, kłamstwo]* to come to light

jaw|a *f* real world a. life, wakefulness; **na** ~**ie** in reality; **sen na** ~**ie** a daydream; **śnić na** ~**ie** to daydream

jawnie *adv. grad.* ① (otwarcie) openly, overtly ② (ewidentnie) blatantly, openly

jawnoś|ć *f* openness, overtness

jawn|y *adi. grad.* ① (otwarty) open, overt; **głosowanie** ~**e** (an) open ballot ② (oczywisty) blatant; ~**e pogwałcenie prawa** a flagrant a. patent violation of the law

jawo|r *m* sycamore

j|azda ① *f* ① (samochodem, autobusem, pociągiem) (jako kierowca) drive; (jako pasażer) ride; **jazda konna** horse riding GB, horseback riding US; **jazda na łyżwach/ wrotkach** ice/roller skating; **jazda na nartach** skiing; **jazda na rowerze/motorze** cycling/ motorcycling; **egzamin z jazdy** a driving test ② Hist., Wojsk. cavalry

② *inter.* pot. clear off a. out! pot.; jazda stąd! get away from a. out of here! pot.; no to jazda, ruszamy! come on, let's go!

jazgo|t *m* (głosów) yapping pot.; (dźwięków) racket pot.; din; (karabinu) rattle

jazgo|tać *impf vi* pot. *[osoba]* to yammer pot.; *[pies]* to yap; *[karabin]* to clatter

jaź|ń *f* Psych. ego, self

jąd|ro *n* ① Anat. testicle ② Bot. kernel ③ przen. crux, heart; ~**ro sprawy** the crux a. heart of the matter ④ Astron., Biol., Chem., Fiz. nucleus ⑤ Komput. kernel

jądrow|y *adi. [broń, energia]* nuclear

jąka|ć się *impf v refl.* ① (zacinać się) to stutter ② (mówić niewyraźnie) to stammer

jąka|ła *f, m* pot. stutterer

jątrz|yć *impf* ① *vt* ① Med. to inflame *[ranę]* ② książk. (drażnić) to incense

② jątrzyć się ① Med. *[rana]* to fester ② książk. (wzmagać się) to fester; ~**ące się spory** festering disputes

j|echać *impf* ① *vi* ① *[osoba]* to go, to travel; **jechać autobusem/pociągiem** to go a. travel by bus/ train, to ride on a bus/on a train; **jechać samochodem** *[kierowca]* to drive, to go by car; *[pasażer]* to go a. travel by car, to ride in a car; **jechać rowerem** a. **na rowerze** to go by bike, to cycle; **jechać konno** a. **na koniu** to ride, to go on horseback; **jechać windą** to go by lift, to take the lift; **jechać na wycieczkę/na urlop** to go on a trip/on holiday; **jechać nad morze/w góry** to go to the seaside/to the mountains; **jechać czterdziestką** to be doing forty pot. ② *[autobus, pociąg, samochód]* to go, to travel; **winda już jedzie** the lift is just coming ③ pot. (korzystać) to use; **jechać na opinii dobrego ucznia** to use one's reputation as a good pupil pot.

② *v imp.* pot. (brzydko pachnieć) to stink, to reek; jedzie od niego czosnkiem he reeks of garlic

■ **jechać na kogoś** pot. to have a go at sb, to tear sb off a strip GB pot.; **jedziemy jeszcze raz!** pot. let's do it again

jed|en ① *num.* one; ~**en z nas** one of us; **po** ~**nym** one each; **wszyscy co do** ~**ego** each and every one of them

② *adi.* ① (pierwszy z wielu) one; **przyjechał ~**en autobus, potem drugi** one bus came, then another ② (taki sam) same; ~**en i ten sam** one and the same; **byliśmy w** ~**nej klasie** we were in the same class ③ (emfatyczne) one pot.; ~**en wielki bałagan** one great mess; **sam** ~**en** all alone ④ pot. (w wyzwiskach)

leniu ~**en!** you lazy so-and-so! pot.

III _pron._ ~**na pani** a certain a. some lady; **przeczytałem to w** ~**nej książce** I read it in some a. a book; ~**ni klaskali, drudzy gwizdali** some (people) clapped, others booed; ~**en drugiemu pomagał** one helped the other/another; ~**en po a. za drugim** one after another a. the other; ~**en na drugim** one on top of another a. the other; **wynoście się,** ~**en z drugim!** pot. off you go, both/all of you! pot.; **był tu taki** ~**en** pot. some guy was here pot.; **co to za** ~**na?** pot. who's that?; who's she?

IV _m_ pot. (kieliszek wódki) quick one, snifter pot.; ~**en głębszy** a drop of the hard stuff pot.; **wpaść (gdzieś) na** ~**nego** to drop in (somewhere) for a quick one

■ **jak** ~**en mąż** as one man, to a man; **numer** ~**en** number one

jedenast|ka _f_ ① eleven ② Sport (drużyna) (football) team; (rzut karny) penalty

jedenastolat|ek _m_, ~**ka** _f_ eleven-year-old

jedenastoletni _adi._ _[dziecko]_ eleven-year-old; _[okres]_ eleven-year

jedena|sty _num. ord._ eleventh

jedena|ście _num._ eleven

jedenaścior|o _num. mult._ eleven

jedna|ć _impf_ **I** _vt_ książk. ① (zdobywać) ~**ć sobie kogoś** to win sb over; ~**ć sobie ludzką przychylność** to win people's favour ② (godzić) to reconcile _[ludzi]_

II jednać się to make peace (**z kimś** with sb)

jednak I _coni._ but, yet; **niewiarygodne,** ~ **prawdziwe** incredible but a. yet true

II _part._ however; **gdybyś** ~ **wolał przyjechać w sobotę...** if, however, you'd prefer to come on Saturday...; **a** ~ **ona mówi po francusku** she can speak French, after all

jednakowo _adi._ _[ubrany, umeblowany]_ identically; _[cenić, traktować]_ equally; _[szybko, mało]_ equally; **wyglądają** ~ they look the same

jednakow|y _adi._ _[przedmioty, powody]_ identical; _[traktowanie, kryteria]_ equal

jednoaktów|ka _f_ Teatr one-act play

jednobarwn|y _adi._ _[fotografia, rysunek]_ monochromatic; _[krawat, sukienka]_ plain

jednobrzmiąc|y _adi._ _[wyroki, zeznania]_ identical; _[wyrazy]_ homophonous

jednocze|sny _adi._ _[działanie, wymarsz]_ simultaneous

jednocześnie _adv._ _[występować, odbywać się]_ at the same time, simultaneously; **robić kilka rzeczy** ~ to do several things at the same time a. at once; **odbywać się** ~ **z czymś** to take place at the same time as sth

jednoczęściow|y _adi._ _[kostium, kombinezon]_ one-piece

jednocz|yć _impf_ **I** _vt_ to unite, to unify _[kraj, naród]_; ~**yć wysiłki** to combine efforts; ~**yć w sobie coś** to unite a. combine sth _[cechy, elementy]_

II jednoczyć się to unite (**z kimś/czymś** with sb/sth)

jednogłośnie _adv._ _[uznać, wybrać]_ unanimously

jednogłośn|y _adi._ _[wybór, potępienie]_ unanimous

jednokierunkow|y _adi._ _[ruch, ulica]_ one-way; _[proces]_ unidirectional; _[wykształcenie]_ one-sided; _[zainteresowania]_ narrow; _[myślenie, polityka]_ single-track, one-track

jednokrotn|y _adi._ _[pukanie, występ]_ single; _[zwycięzca]_ one-time

jednoli|ty _adi._ _[system, standardy]_ uniform; _[społeczeństwo]_ homogeneous

jednomyślnoś|ć _f_ unanimity

jednomyśln|y _adi._ _[werdykt, wybór]_ unanimous

jednoosobow|y _adi._ _[firma, patrol]_ one-man; _[łóżko, pokój]_ single

jednopartyjn|y _adi._ _[system, rząd]_ one-party

jednorazowo _adv._ (za jednym razem) at a time; (raz) once, on a one-off basis pot.

jednorazow|y _adi._ _[premia, wysiłek]_ one-time; _[przejazd]_ single; _[pieluszka, strzykawka]_ disposable; **do** ~**ego użytku** for use once only

jednorazów|ka _f_ pot. (igła) disposable needle; (strzykawka) disposable syringe

jednoroczn|y _adi._ _[dziecko, psiak]_ one-year-old; _[kredyt, przerwa]_ one-year; **roślina** ~**a** Bot. an annual (plant)

jednorodn|y _adi._ _[masa, skała]_ homogeneous

jednorodzinn|y _adi._ _[dom, budownictwo]_ (single-)-family

jednoroż|ec _m_ Mitol. unicorn

jednorzędow|y _adi._ _[marynarka, płaszcz]_ single-breasted

jednostajn|y _adi._ _grad._ _[hałas, cykanie]_ monotonous; _[ciemność, zieleń]_ uniform

jednost|ka _f_ ① (osoba) individual; **wybitne** ~**ki** outstanding individuals ② Miary, Wojsk. unit ③ Żegl. ~**ka (pływająca)** a vessel

jednostkow|y _adi._ ① (indywidualny) individual ② (na jednostkę) _[ciężar, koszt]_ unit ③ (sporadyczny) _[przypadek, zdarzenie]_ isolated

jednostronn|y _adi._ _[ruch]_ one-way; _[moneta, druk]_ one-sided; _[opinia, podejście]_ one-sided; _[decyzja, zobowiązanie]_ unilateral

jednoś|ć I _f_ ① (spójność) unity ② (jednomyślność) unanimity

II jedności _plt_ Mat. (single) digits

jednośla|d _m_ pot. two-wheel(ed) vehicle

jednoznaczn|y _adi._ ① (niebudzący wątpliwości) _[polecenie]_ explicit, unambiguous; _[sytuacja]_ clear(-cut) ② (synonimiczny) _[określenie, zwrot]_ synonymous ③ (równoznaczny) tantamount (**z czymś** to sth)

jedwab _m_ silk

jedwabi|sty *adi.* silky; silken książk.
jedwabnik *m* Zool. silkworm
jedwabn|y *adi. [bielizna, przędza]* silk
jedyna|k *m*, **~czka** *f* only child
jedynie książk. **[]** *adv.* only; **~ słuszny pogląd** the only correct view
[] *part.* [1] (tylko) only; **~ w piątki** only on Fridays; **wiemy ~, że wyjechał** all we know is that he left [2] (zaledwie) just, merely; **to ~ hipoteza** it's just a. merely a hypothesis
jedyn|ka *f* [1] (cyfra) one [2] Szkol. (ocena) ≈ E [3] (pokój) single room pot. [4] pot., Aut. first (gear) [5] Sport single; **wyścig ~ek** a singles race
jedyn|y [] *adi.* [1] (tylko jeden) *[przyjaciel, egzemplarz]* only; **~y w swoim rodzaju** the only one of its kind; **to był człowiek ~y w swoim rodzaju** he was one in a thousand [2] (optymalny) *[sposób, metoda]* best, only [3] (ukochany) *[córka, syn]* dearest przest.; darling pot.
[] **jedyne** *n* pot. the only thing; **~e, co możesz zrobić** the only thing you can do
jedzeni|e *n* food
jego *pron.* (o osobie) his; (o zwierzęciu) its, his; (o rzeczy) its; **~ garnitur** his suit; **ta książka jest ~** this book is his; **Kraków i ~ okolice** Cracow and its environs; **Jego Wysokość** His Royal Highness
jej *pron.* (dzierżawczy) (o osobie) (przed rzeczownikiem) her; (bez rzeczownika) hers; (o zwierzęciu) its, her; (o rzeczy) its; **~ sukienka** her dress; **ten komputer jest ~** this computer is hers; **Warszawa i ~ mieszkańcy** Warsaw and its inhabitants; **Jej Królewska Mość Elżbieta II** Her Majesty Queen Elizabeth II
jele|ń *m* Zool. (red) deer; (samiec) stag
■ **~ń na rykowisku** a kitschy painting
jeli|to *n* Anat. intestine, bowel
jelon|ek *m* Zool. [1] (jeleń) fawn [2] (owad) stag beetle
jełcz|eć *impf vi [masło, tłuszcz]* to go rancid
jemio|ła *f* mistletoe
jemiołusz|ka *f* waxwing
je|niec *m* prisoner of war, POW
jeno|t *m* raccoon dog
jerzyk *m* swift
jesienn|y *adi. [krajobraz, pogoda]* autumn GB, fall US; autumnal książk.
jesie|ń *f* autumn GB, fall US; **~nią** a. **na ~ni** in autumn
jesion *m* [1] (drzewo) ash (tree) [2] (drewno) ash
jesion|ka *f* spring coat
jesiot|r *m* sturgeon
jest → **być**
jeszcze [] *adv.* (wciąż) still; (z przeczeniem) yet; **zostańcie ~** stay a bit longer; **~ nie** not yet; **to ~ nie koniec** (o wydarzeniu) it's not over yet; (o opowieści) that's not all
[] *part.* [1] (nie dalej jak) still, only; **~ wczoraj padał śnieg** it was still snowing yesterday; **~ dwa lata temu** only two years ago [2] (już) still; (tak dawno jak) as

early as, as far back as; **poznali się ~ jako dzieci** they met when they were still children [3] (dodatkowo, ponadto) more, still; **~ jeden** one more; **~ raz** one more time, once more a. again; **daj mi ~ trochę czasu** give me a little a. a bit more time; **czy są ~ jakieś pytania?** are there any more questions?; **kto/co ~?** who/what else? [4] (nawet) even, still; **~ większy** even a. still bigger; **~ gorzej** even a. still worse [5] (zapowiedź) **~ pożałujesz!** one day a. one of these days you'll be sorry!
■ **~ czego!** forget it! pot.; some a. fat chance! pot., iron.; **~ jak!** and how! pot.; **„czy on jest przystojny?" – „~ jak!"** 'is he good looking?' – 'he sure is!' pot.
j|eść *impf* **[]** *vt* to eat *[bułkę, obiad]*; **chce mu się jeść** he's hungry
[] *n inv* pot. **dać komuś jeść** to give sb something to eat; **daj psu jeść** could you feed the dog?
jeśli *coni.* [1] (określające warunki) if; **pomogę ci, ~ ładnie poprosisz** I'll help you, if you ask nicely; **w środę, ~ nie wcześniej** on Wednesday, if not sooner; **a ~...?** what if...?, supposing...?; **~ to możliwe** if it's possible; **~ się nie mylę** if I'm not mistaken, unless I'm mistaken; **pan Kowalski, ~ się nie mylę** Mr Kowalski, I believe?; **~ o mnie chodzi** as far as I'm concerned [2] (skoro) if, since
jezdni|a *f* roadway GB, pavement US; **po drugiej stronie ~** on the other side of the road a. street
jezio|ro *n* lake
je|ździć *impf vi* [1] (środkiem lokomocji) to go, to travel; **jeździć samochodem** *[kierowca]* to go by car, to drive; *[pasażer]* to go a. travel by car, to ride in a car; **jeździć autobusem/pociągiem** to go a. travel by bus/train; **jeździć rowerem** to go by bike, to cycle; **jeździć taksówką** to go by taxi, to take a taxi; **jeździć windą** to go by lift GB, to take the lift GB; **jeździć na wózku inwalidzkim** to use a wheelchair; **jeździć za granicę** to go a. travel abroad; **jeździć nad morze/w góry** to go to the seaside/to the mountains [2] (kursować) *[autobus, pociąg]* to run, to go; **tramwaje jeżdżą co pięć minut** the trams run every five minutes [3] (prowadzić pojazd) to drive; **jeździć dobrze/słabo** to drive well/to not drive very well [4] Sport to ride; **jeździć konno** a. **na koniu** to ride a horse; **jeździć na rowerze** to ride a bike; **jeździć na nartach/łyżwach** to ski/skate [5] pot., przen. (przesuwać) to run; **jeździć palcem po mapie** to run one's finger over a map [6] pot., przen. (ślizgać się) *[dywanik]* to slide, to slip
■ **jeździć komuś po głowie** pot. to walk all over sb pot.
jeź|dziec *m* rider Sport (horse) rider; (mężczyzna) horseman
jeździectw|o *n* Sport (horse GB a. horseback US) riding
jeż *m* [1] Zool. hedgehog [2] pot. (fryzura) crew cut
■ **średnio na ~a** pot. so-so, okay pot.

jeżeli książk. → **jeśli**
jeżow|iec *m* Zool. sea urchin
jeżozwierz *m* Zool. porcupine
jeż|yć *impf* **[]** *vt* to ruffle *[sierść, pióra, włosy]*
　[] **jeżyć się** ① *[sierść, grzywa]* to bristle ② pot. (przyjmować postawę obronną) to bristle
　■ **na samą myśl o tym włos się ~y** the very thought makes one's hair stand on end a. curl
jeżyn|a *f* Bot. ① (krzew) blackberry bush ② (owoc) blackberry
jeżynow|y *adi. [dżem, sok]* blackberry
jęczeć¹ → **jęknąć**
jęcz|eć² *impf vi* ① przen. (cierpieć) to groan przen. ② (domagać się) to whine, to moan
jęczmie|ń *m* ① Roln. barley ② Med. sty(e)
jędrn|y *adi. [ciało, skóra]* well-toned, supple; *[owoc, piersi]* firm; przen. *[język, styl]* robust
jędz|a *f* ① (w bajce) witch ② (złośnica) bitch pot., obraźl.
jędzowa|ty *adi. [osoba]* bitchy pot.; *[charakter, mina]* mean, nasty
jęk *m* ① groan, moan ② przen. (wiatru) wail; (piły, maszyny) whine
jękliw|y *adi [głos, dźwięk]* groaning, moaning
ję|knąć *pf* — **ję|czeć¹** *impf vi* (pod wpływem bólu) to groan, to moan; (z wysiłku) to groan
jęt|ka *f* Zool. ephemerid
język *m* ① Anat. tongue ② (mowa) language; (specjalistyczny) language, jargon; **~ ojczysty** one's native a. mother tongue; **~ programowania** a programming language ③ przen. tongue; **~i ognia** tongues of flames ④ pot. (nauka języka) language lessons a. classes; **mieć dobre stopnie z ~ów** to have good grades in languages
　■ **biegać z wywieszonym ~iem** to be run off one's feet; **ciągnąć kogoś za ~** to pump sb pot.; **mieć cięty** a. **ostry ~** to have a nasty a. (razor-)-sharp tongue; **mieć (za) długi ~** to have a big mouth pot.; **mieć coś na końcu ~a** to have sth on the tip of one's tongue; **pleść** a. **gadać, co ślina na ~ przyniesie** to say whatever comes into one's head; **strzępić (sobie) ~** to waste one's breath; **trzymać ~ za zębami** to hold one's tongue pot.; **zapomnieć ~a w gębie** to lose one's tongue; **zasięgnąć ~a** to ask around; **~ się jej plątał** she was stumbling over her words
językoznawc|a *m* linguist
językoznawstw|o *n* linguistics
jo|d *m* iodine
jodeł|ka *f* ① Bot. fir (tree) ② (wzór) herringbone (pattern); **marynarka w ~ę** a herringbone jacket
jod|ła *f* ① Bot. fir (tree) ② (drewno) fir (wood)
jodyn|a *f* iodine
jo|ga *f* yoga

jogur|t *m* yog(h)urt
jon *m* ion
jubila|t *m*, **~tka** *f person celebrating an anniversary*
jubile|r *m* (osoba) jeweller, jeweler US; pot. (sklep) jeweller's (shop)
jubileusz *m* (rocznica) jubilee, anniversary; (uroczystości) jubilee celebrations
jubileuszow|y *adi. [rok, uroczystości]* jubilee
judasz *m* ① (osoba) Judas przen. ② (w drzwiach) judas (hole), peephole
ju|ka *f* ① Bot. yucca, Adam's needle ② Włók. yucca fibre GB a. fiber US
junio|r *m* junior; **John F. Kennedy ~r** John F. Kennedy Junior
juro|r *m* juror, juryman
juror|ka *f* juror, jurywoman
jury *n inv.* jury; **zasiadać w ~** to be a. serve on a jury
jurysdykcj|a *f* książk. jurisdiction
jut|ro **[]** *n* tomorrow; **do ~ra!** see you tomorrow!; **nie myśleć o ~rze** to not think about tomorrow a. the future
　[] *adv.* tomorrow; **~ro z samego rana** first thing tomorrow
jutrzej|szy *adi. [uroczystość, wydarzenia]* tomorrow's
już **[]** *adv.* already; (w pytaniach) yet; **widziałem ~ ten film** I've already seen this film, I've seen this film before; **czy ona ~ przyjechała?** has she arrived yet?; **czy mogę ~ wejść?** can I go in now a. yet?; **noga ~ mnie nie boli** my leg has stopped aching (now); **~ miała wychodzić...** she was just about to leave a. on the point of leaving...; **~ po wszystkim** (all) over!; **~ cię tu nie ma!** (be) off with you! pot.; **ale ~!** right now!; double quick! GB pot.; **~ idę** I'm coming; **„obiad na stole" – „~, ~"** 'dinner's ready' – 'just coming!'
　[] *part.* ① (w przeszłości) already; **~ starożytni Grecy uważali, że...** (even) the ancient Greeks believed that... ② (stosunkowo późno) already; **jest ~ godzina dziesiąta** it's ten o'clock already ③ (stosunkowo wcześnie) **~ w listopadzie spadł śnieg** it was already snowing in November; **~ niedługo!** not much longer now!; **~ wkrótce się spotkamy** we'll see each other very soon ④ (więcej) **nie dostaniesz ~ ode mnie ani grosza** you won't get another penny out of me; **nie ma ~ nic w lodówce** there's nothing left in the fridge ⑤ (emfatycznie) **to ~ coś** that's something anyway; **~ ja ci pokażę!** pot. I'll show you! pot.
　■ **i ~** and that's that; **nie i ~!** I said no, and that's that!

K

K, k *n inv.* K, k

kabacz|ek *m* marrow

kaba|ła *f* [1] (wróżenie) fortune-telling *(by cards)* [2] pot. (trudna sytuacja) pickle pot.; **wpakować się** a. **wplątać się w ~łę** to get into a pickle [3] Relig. cab(b)ala

kabanos *m* Kulin. *thin, dry, smoked, pepperoni sausage*

kabare|t *m* cabaret

kab|el *m* [1] (przewód) cable; (zasilający) lead; (od drukarki, monitora) cable, lead; (od słuchawek) wire [2] pot. (o osobie) nark, fink US pot.

kabin|a *f* [1] (wydzielona część) cabin; (ciężarówki) (driver's) cab; **~a reżyserska/mikserska** Radio the director's/a mixing booth; **~a pilota** Lotn. the pilot's cabin a. cockpit; **~a kosmiczna** the crew compartment; **~a projekcyjna** Kino a projection room a. booth [2] (budka) cubicle, booth; **~a kąpielowa** a. **prysznicowa** a shower cubicle; **~a telefoniczna** a (tele)phone booth; **~a do głosowania** a voting booth

kabl|ować *impf vi* pot. to snitch, to grass GB, to fink US pot. (**na kogoś** on sb)

kablow|y *adi.* [obudowa, izolacja] cable; **telewizja ~a** cable television a. TV

kablów|ka *f* pot. cable (TV)

kabłąk *m* [1] (wygięcie w łuk) **pochylić** a. **zgiąć się w ~** to arch one's back [2] Techn. bail, bar

kabotyn *m*, **~ka** *f* książk. show-off; (aktor) ham (actor) pot.

kabriole|t *m* [1] Aut. convertible, soft top [2] przest. (powóz) cabriolet

kabu|ra *f* Wojsk. holster

kac *m* pot. hangover

kacze|niec *m* marsh marigold

kacz|ka *f* [1] Zool. duck; **~ka krzyżówka** a mallard [2] pot. (plotka) piece of gossip; canard książk. [3] (naczynie na mocz) (male) urinal

■ **puszczać ~ki** to play ducks and drakes

kaczo|r *m* drake

kacz|y *adi.* duck's; **~y chód** a waddling gait

kadencj|a *f* [1] (prezydenta, sejmu) term (of office), tenure [2] Muz. cadence

kadłub *m* Techn. body; **~ samolotu** a plane's fuselage; **~ statku** a ship's hull

kad|r *m* Kino frame; **~r ze znanego filmu** a still a. shot from a well-known film

kad|ra *f* [1] (pracownicy) personnel, staff; **~ra naukowa** research personnel; **~ra nauczycielska** (teaching) staff; **~y** pot. personnel (department), human resources (department) [2] Wojsk. corps, cadre [3] Sport team; **~ra narodowa** national team a. squad

kadzid|ło *n* incense

kafej|ka *f* pot. café

kaf|el *m* tile

kaftani|k *m* baby's top

kaga|niec *m* muzzle

kajak *m* kayak, (Alaskan) canoe; Sport canoe

kajaka|rz *m*, **~rka** *f* canoeist

kajdan|ki *plt* handcuffs

kaju|ta *f* cabin

kajzer|ka *f* kaiser roll US

kakao *n inv.* cocoa

kakaow|y *adi.* [masło, smak] cocoa; [likier, ziarno] cacao

kaktus *m* cactus

kalafio|r *m* cauliflower

kalafiorow|y [I] *adi.* [liście, zupa] cauliflower [II] **kalafiorowa** *f* (zupa) cauliflower soup

kalambu|r *m* pun

kalarep|a *f* kohlrabi

kalectw|o *n* disability, handicap

kalecz|yć *impf* [I] *vt* to cut, to injure; **druty ~yły mu ręce** the wires were cutting into his hands; **~yć francuski** przen. to speak broken French [II] **kaleczyć się** (ranić się) to cut a. injure oneself

kalejdoskop *m* kaleidoscope także przen.; **zmieniać się jak w ~ie** to chop and change

kale|ka *m, f* [1] (dotknięty kalectwem) disabled person; cripple przest. [2] pot. (niezaradny) loser pot.; lame duck

kale|ki *adi.* [osoba] disabled, crippled; [nogi] crippled; **~ka niemczyzna** broken German

kalendarz *m* calendar; (notes) diary

kalendarzyk *m* pocket diary; **~ małżeński** the rhythm method

kaleson|y *plt* underpants, undershorts US; **długie ~y** long johns

kaletni|k *m*, **~czka** *f* leather worker

kali|a *f* calla (lily), arum lily

kalib|er *m* calibre GB, caliber US; **pistolet ~ru 7,6 a** 7.6 calibre pistol

kaligrafi|a *f* calligraphy

kalin|a *f* viburnum

kal|ka *f* [1] (papier) carbon (paper); **~ka maszynowa** carbon paper; **~ka techniczna** tracing paper [2] (powtórzenie) carbon copy [3] Jęz. loan translation, calque

kalkomani|a *f* transfer GB, decal US

kalk|ować *impf vt* to trace *[rysunek, napis]*

kalkulacj|a *f* calculation także przen.

kalkulato|r *m* calculator

kalkul|ować *impf* **[]** *vt* (ustalać) to calculate, to compute *[zysk, cenę, koszt]*

[] ** *vi* (rozważać) to calculate, to estimate; **~owali, czy warto otworzyć ten interes they were working out whether it would be profitable to set up the business

[]] kalkulować się pot. [1] (wynikać z obliczeń) to work out; **ta książka ~uje się drogo** the book works out rather expensive [2] (opłacać się) to pay (off); **kupno tego samochodu nie ~uje się** buying this car won't pay

kalma|r *m* squid

kalori|a *f* Miary [1] (w pokarmach) (small) calorie [2] (kilokaloria) (large) calorie

kaloryczn|y *adi. [posiłek, potrawa]* high-calorie, calorific GB; *[wartość]* calorific GB

kaloryfe|r *m* radiator; **~r olejowy** an oil heater

kalosz *m* [1] (gumowiec) wellington (boot) GB, rubber boot; **~e** rubbers US [2] (wierzchni but gumowy) galosh, overshoe

ka|ł *m* faeces GB, feces US, excrement

kałuż|a *f* puddle, pool **~a krwi** a pool of blood

kameleon *m* chameleon także przen.

kameli|a *f* camellia

kame|ra *f* camera; **~ra wideo** a video camera, a camcorder; **ukryta ~ra** candid camera

kameraln|y *adi.* [1] *[kawiarnia, atmosfera]* cosy, cozy US; **spotkanie w ~ym gronie** a small get-together [2] *[muzyka, orkiestra]* chamber

kamerdyne|r *m* butler

kamerzy|sta *m* cameraman

kamfo|ra *f* camphor; **zniknąć jak ~ra** pot. to vanish into thin air

kamieniarz *m* [1] (obrabiający kamienie) (stone)mason, stoneworker [2] (wykonujący nagrobki) monumental mason, gravestone a. tombstone carver

kamienic|a *f* tenement (house a. building)

kamieni|eć *impf vi* [1] (twardnieć) *[glina, beton]* to harden; *[drewno, żywica]* to petrify [2] przen. (nieruchomieć) to become petrified przen. [3] książk. (obojętnieć) to become hardened a. callous

kamieniołom *m* quarry

kamienn|y *adi.* rocky, stony

kamienn|y *adi.* [1] (z kamienia) *[krąg, most]* stone; **~a płyta chodnikowa** a flag(stone) [2] przen. (nieruchomy, niewzruszony) **~a twarz** a. **~y wyraz twarzy** a stony face a. expression; **~e serce** a heart of stone [3] przen. (głęboki, zupełny) **~a cisza** dead a. stone

silence; **~y sen** a deep sleep; **zachować ~y spokój** to keep a stiff upper lip

kamie|ń *m* [1] (bryła skalna) stone; (duży) rock; **~ń młyński** a millstone [2] (klejnot) stone, gem(stone) [3] Med. stone; **~nie nerkowe** kidney stones; **~ń żółciowy** a gallstone; **~ń nazębny** tartar [4] (osad) (lime)scale, fur GB

□ **~ń nagrobny** gravestone, tombstone; **~ń węgielny** (narożny) cornerstone; (pierwszy) foundation stone także przen.

■ **~ń spadł mu/mi z serca** it was a load a. weight off his/my mind; **spać jak ~ń** to sleep like a log; **przepaść a. zniknąć jak ~ń w wodę** to vanish into thin air

kamizel|ka *f* waistcoat, vest US; **~ka ratunkowa** life jacket

kampani|a *f* campaign; **prowadzić ~ę na rzecz kogoś/czegoś** to campaign for sb/sth

kamufl|ować *impf* **[]** *vt* (maskować) to camouflage, to disguise

[] **kamuflować się** [1] (maskować się) to hide (**z czymś** sth) [2] pot., żart. (chować się) to hide out pot.

kamy|k *m* pebble

kanali|a *m*, *f* bastard pot.

kanalizacj|a *f* sewer a. sewage system; **~a burzowa** a storm drain system; **~a magistralna** a sewage main

kanalizacyjn|y *adi.* **system ~y** (w budynku) plumbing; (w mieście) sewer a. sewage system

kana|ł *m* [1] (naturalny) channel; (sztuczny) canal; **~ł nawadniający/osuszający** an irrigation/a drainage canal; **Kanał La Manche** the English Channel [2] (ściek) sewer; **~ł deszczowy** an underground drainpipe [3] Budow., Techn. duct; **~ł odpływowy/spływowy** an outlet/outflow duct; **~ł wentylacyjny** an air duct a. shaft [4] Anat. (w zębie) root canal [5] Radio, TV, Telekom. channel [6] Techn. (do serwisu podwozia) service a. inspection pit [7] Teatr orchestra pit [8] przen. (droga) channel; **~ły dyplomatyczne** diplomatic channels

kanap|a *f* couch, sofa; (rozkładana) sofa bed

kanap|ka *f* (z jednej kromki) open sandwich, canapé; (z dwóch kromek) sandwich

kanar|ek *m* canary

kanarkow|y *adi. [piórka, trele]* canary, canary's; *[kolor]* canary yellow

kance|ra *f* damaged stamp

kanciarz *m* pot. con man a. artist, grifter US pot.

kancia|sty *adi.* [1] (mający kanty) *[kontur, sylwetka]* angular [2] przen. (niezgrabny) *[ruchy]* awkward, clumsy

kanclerz *m* chancellor

kandyda|t *m* candidate; **~ci do Nagrody Nobla** candidates for the Nobel Prize; **~t na posła** a parliamentary candidate; **~ci na uniwersytet** university applicants; **~t do (czyjejś) ręki** książk. a suitor

kandydatu|ra f candidacy; **zgłosić swoją/czy-jąś ~rę** to announce one's/sb's candidacy

kandyd|ować impf vi to run, to stand GB; **~ować na prezydenta** to run for president

kandyz|ować impf vt to candy *[śliwki, morele]*

kangu|r m kangaroo

ka|nia f [1] Zool. kite [2] Bot. parasol mushroom

kanibal m cannibal

kanion m canyon

kanist|er m can(ister); **~er na paliwo** a petrol can

kanon m [1] książk. (zasada) canon książk.; principle [2] (zbiór książek, filmów) canon [3] Relig. canon; **~ Pisma Świętego** the canon of Holy Scripture [4] Muz. canon, round; **śpiewać ~em** to sing a canon

kanonizacj|a f canonization

kanoniz|ować pf, impf vt to canonize

kan|t m [1] (krawędź) edge; **~t stołu** the edge of the table [2] (na nogawce) crease; **prasować spodnie w ~t** to iron a. press a crease into (one's) trousers [3] pot. (oszustwo) con (trick), scam pot.

kanto|r m currency exchange (bureau), bureau de change GB

kantyn|a f canteen

kap|a f bedspread

kapać impf → **kapnąć**

kap|ać² impf vi [1] (o deszczu) to drizzle [2] (ociekać) **~ać czymś** a. **od czegoś** to be dripping with sth; **mundury ~iące od złota** przen. uniforms dripping with gold braid przen. [3] pot. (przepuszczać wodę) to leak, to drip; **z kranu znów ~ie** the tap is dripping again

kap|eć m [1] (domowy pantofel) slipper [2] pot. (opona) flat pot.; (piłka) deflated ball; **jechać na ~ciu** to drive with a flat

kapel|a f [1] (ludowa) folk band [2] pot. (zespół rockowy) rock band a. group

kapelan m chaplain

kapelusz m [1] (nakrycie głowy) hat [2] (część grzyba) (mushroom) cap

kapiszon m [1] (do pistoletów-zabawek) cap; **strzelać z ~ów** to shoot caps [2] (kaptur) hood

kapitali|sta m, **~stka** f capitalist

kapitalistyczn|y adi. *[system, przedsiębiorstwo]* capitalist

kapitalizm m capitalism

kapitaln|y adi. [1] *[znaczenie, warunek]* primary, fundamental; *[odkrycie]* major; **remont ~y** complete refurbishing [2] pot. *[pomysł, zabawa]* terrific pot.

kapita|ł [] m [1] (pieniądze) capital; **żyć z procentów od ~łu** to live on the interest from one's investments; **zbić na czymś ~ł** to make a fortune on sth a. out of sth; **~ł akcyjny** equity; **~ł obrotowy** working capital; **~ł trwały** fixed a. permanent capital [2] (dorobek) wealth; **ogromny ~ł wiedzy** an enormous wealth of knowledge

[] **kapitały** plt Fin. funds

kapitan m captain; **~ portu** harbour master GB, harbormaster US

kapitulacj|a f capitulation; **~a wobec trudności** surrender in the face of difficulties

kapitul|ować pf, impf vi [1] (poddać się) to capitulate; **~ować przed czymś** to surrender to sth [2] przen. (ustępować) to capitulate, to give in a. up

kaplic|a f chapel

kaplicz|ka f (przy drodze) shrine

kapłan m priest

kapłan|ka f priestess

kapłaństw|o n priesthood; **obchodzi czterdziestolecie ~a** it's the fortieth anniversary of his ordination

kap|nąć pf — **kap|ać¹** impf vi [1] (spływać kroplami) *[woda, łzy]* to drip [2] pot. (o pieniądzach) **latem zawsze mi ~nie parę groszy** I can always count on a bit of extra money during the summer

kapok m life jacket

kapral m corporal

kaprys m [1] (zachcianka) whim, caprice; **przelotny ~** a passing fancy; **zrobić coś dla ~u** to do sth on a whim; **~y pogody** the vagaries of the weather; **~y losu** a. **fortuny** the whims of fate a. fortune [2] Muz. capriccio, caprice

kapry|sić impf vi to be fussy pot.; **~sić przy jedzeniu** to be fussy about one's food

kapryśn|y adi. grad. [1] (mający kaprysy) *[osoba, dziecko]* petulant, sulky; *[charakter]* fussy [2] (zmienny) *[moda, pogoda]* changeable, fickle

kaps|el m bottle cap a. top

kapsl|ować impf vt to cap *[butelki]*

kapsuł|ka f capsule

kaptu|r m hood

kapu|sta f cabbage; **kiszona ~sta** sauerkraut; **~sta włoska** savoy cabbage

kapustnik m Zool. bielinek **~** a cabbage white (butterfly)

kapu|ś m pot. (pracujący dla policji) grass GB, rat US pot.; (w szkole) sneak GB pot.

kapuśnia|k m [1] (zupa) cabbage soup [2] (deszcz) drizzle

ka|ra f [1] (konsekwencje złego czynu) punishment (**za coś** for sth); **kara śmierci** capital punishment, the death penalty; **kara pozbawienia wolności** imprisonment, a prison sentence a. term; **kara cielesna** corporal punishment; **skazać kogoś na karę grzywny** to impose a fine on sb; **zasłużyć na karę** to get a. receive one's just deserts; **pod karą czegoś** on a. under pain a. penalty of sth [2] Sport penalty

karabin m rifle, gun; (ciężki) **~ maszynowy** a (heavy) machine gun; **ręczny ~ maszynowy** a light automatic rifle, a carbine

ka|rać impf vt to punish (**kogoś za coś** sb for sth); Sport to penalize (**kogoś za coś** sb for sth); **karać kogoś grzywną/mandatem** to fine/ticket sb;

karać kogoś więzieniem/śmiercią to impose a prison sentence/the death sentence on sb

karaf|ka f carafe, decanter

karaln|y adi. [czyn] punishable

karaluch m cockroach

karambol m [1] pot. (kraksa) pile-up pot. [2] Gry (rodzaj bilardu) (English) billiards GB, (carom) billiards US; (uderzenie) cannon (shot) GB, carom (shot) US; (czerwona kula) red

kara|ś m crucian (carp)

kara|t m carat

karawan m hearse

karawan|a f caravan

karce|r m [1] (cela) punishment cell [2] (kara) solitary confinement

karcia|rz m, ~**rka** f pot. card player

kar|cić impf vt to reprimand, to rebuke (**kogoś za coś** sb for sth)

karcz|ma f inn

karczma|rz m, ~**rka** f innkeeper

karczoch m (globe) artichoke

karcz|ować impf vt to fell [drzewa]; to clear [teren]

kardiochirurgi|a f cardiac a. heart surgery

kardiolo|g m cardiologist

kardiologi|a f cardiology

kardiologiczn|y adi. [klinika, leczenie] cardiological, cardiology

kardynaln|y adi. książk. [zasada, błąd] cardinal, fundamental

kardyna|ł m Relig. cardinal

kare|ta f carriage

karet|ka f [1] (samochód) van; ~**ka pogotowia** an ambulance [2] (w maszynie do pisania) carriage; **klawisz powrotu** ~**ki** Komput. the carriage return key

karie|ra f career

karierowicz m, ~**ka** f careerist

karima|ta f foam mattress GB, foam rubber mattress US

kark m nape (of one's neck); (szyja) neck

■ **mieć coś na** ~**u** pot. to have sth on one's hands; **mieć** a. **dźwigać sześćdziesiątkę na** ~**u** to be in one's sixties; **mieć kogoś na** ~**u** pot. (być ściganym) to have sb breathing down one's neck pot.; (zajmować się) to have sb on one's hands pot.; **nadstawiać** ~**u za kogoś** to stick one's neck out for sb; **pędzić** a. **lecieć na złamanie** ~**u** pot. to rush at breakneck speed; **złamać** a. **skręcić** ~ to break one's neck; **złamania** ~**u!** pot. break a leg!

karków|ka f Kulin. ~**ka wieprzowa/cielęca** neck of pork/veal

karłowa|ty adi. [1] [osoba] (very) short, of (very) short stature; dwarfish daw. [2] [roślina, zwierzę] (specjalnie hodowany) dwarf, pigmy; (z powodu niesprzyjających warunków) stunted [3] przen. [gospodarstwo, poletko] (greatly) diminished

karm|a f feed; ~**a dla ptaków** birdseed

karm|ić impf [] vt [1] (podawać jedzenie) to feed [osobę, zwierzę]; ~**ić kogoś łyżeczką/butelką** to spoon-feed/bottle-feed sb; **świnie** ~**ione kartoflami** pigs fed on potatoes [2] (własnym mlekiem) [kobieta, matka] to breastfeed, to nurse [dziecko]; [kotka, suka] to suckle [małe] [3] przen. to feed; ~**ić kogoś propagandą** to feed sb propaganda

[] **karmić się** przen. to feed przen. (**czymś** on a. off sth); ~**ić się nadzieją** to feed on hope

karmnik m feeder; ~ **dla ptaków** a bird feeder

karnacj|a f complexion

karnawa|ł m carnival

karnawałow|y adi. [bal, strój] carnival

karne|t m (karta wstępu) pass, ticket; (na cały cykl) season ticket; ~**t na festiwal filmowy/wyciągi** a film festival/ski lift pass

karnisz m curtain rod/rail

karnoś|ć f discipline; **był wychowywany w** ~**ci** he was brought up strictly

karn|y [] adi. [1] (będący karą) [zwolnienie, przeniesienie] disciplinary; [obóz, kolonia] penal; [sankcje] punitive; [punkt] penalty; **zostać pociągniętym do odpowiedzialności** ~**ej** to be brought to justice [2] Prawo [kodeks] penal; [system] criminal justice [3] Sport [rzut] penalty [4] (zdyscyplinowany) [żołnierz, pies] (well-)disciplined

[] m pot., Sport penalty; **strzelać** ~**ego** to take a penalty; **strzelić/nie strzelić** ~**ego** to score/miss a penalty

kar|o n, n inv [1] Gry diamond(s) [2] (dekolt) **suknia wycięta w** ~**o** a dress with a square neckline

karoseri|a f (car) body

karp m carp

kar|ta f [1] (do gry) card; **przełożyć** ~**ty** to cut the cards; **rozdać po pięć** ~**t** to deal five cards to each player; **mieć dobre/słabe** ~**ty** to have a good/poor hand; **mocna** ~**ta** a strong suit także przen. [2] (kartonik) card; ~**ta katalogowa** an index a. a file card; ~**ta do głosowania** a ballot (card) [3] (z plastiku) card; ~**ta kredytowa** a credit card; ~**ta płatnicza** a charge/debit card; ~**ta do bankomatu** a cash card GB; ~**ta telefoniczna** a telephone card, a phonecard [4] (dokument) card; (pozwolenie) licence; ~**ta wstępu** an entrance a. admission ticket, a pass; ~**ta członkowska** a membership card; ~**ta łowiecka** a hunting licence [5] (spis potraw) menu; ~**ta win** a wine list [6] przen. page, leaf; **wspaniałe** ~**ty w naszej historii** glorious pages of a. in our history [7] (akt prawny) charter; ~**ta nauczyciela/pacjenta** the teacher's/patient's charter [8] Komput. card

■ **grać z kimś w otwarte** ~**ty** to play straight with sb; **postawić wszystko na jedną** ~**tę** to stake everything on one card a. one roll of the dice

kartel m cartel

kart|ka f [1] (kawałek papieru) piece of paper; (arkusz) sheet (of paper); (w zeszycie, książce) page, leaf;

mówić z ~**ki** to read a speech; **mówić bez** ~**ki** to speak without notes ② (kupon) ration coupon ❑ ~**ka świąteczna** (na Boże Narodzenie) Christmas card; (na Wielkanoc) Easter card

kartk|ować *impf vt* to leaf through *[książkę, akta]*

kartków|ka *f* pot., Szkol. (short) test; **zrobić** ~**kę** to give a test

kartof|el *m* potato; **młode** ~**le** new potatoes; **tłuczone** ~**le** mashed potatoes; ~**le w mundurkach** potatoes in their jackets GB

kartoflan|ka *f* pot. potato soup

kartografi|a *f* cartography

karton *m* ① (papier) (gruby) cardboard; (cienki) Bristol board GB, construction paper US ② (pudło) carton, cardboard box; ~ **mleka** a carton of milk

kartote|ka *f* card index; ~**ka przestępców** criminal records; ~**ka policyjna** police files; **figurować w** ~**ce** to be on file

karuzel|a *f* merry-go-round, roundabout GB, carousel US

karygodn|y *adi. [zaniedbanie, czyn]* criminal; *[błąd, grzech]* unforgivable; *[postępek]* reprehensible

karykatu|ra *f* caricature

karykaturzy|sta *m*, ~**stka** *f* caricaturist

ka|rzeł *m* ① (bardzo niska osoba) midget, dwarf ② (krasnal) dwarf

kas|a *f* ① (sejf) strongbox; ~**a pancerna** a (metal) strongbox; ~**a ogniotrwała** a fireproof safe ② pot. (budżet) budget; ~**a rodzinna** the family budget a. finances ③ (fundusze) **obliczać** ~**ę** to count the takings; **sprawdzać stan** ~**y** to check the till; **prowadzić** ~**ę** to do the accounts ④ (pokój) cashier's office; (okienko) cashier's window a. counter; (w sklepie) cash desk GB; (na dworcu) (okienko) ticket window; (pokój) ticket office; (w kinie, teatrze) box office ⑤ (urządzenie liczące) cash register, till; ~**a fiskalna** a cash register ⑥ (instytucja) (w nazwach banków) bank; ~**a zapomogowo-pożyczkowa** a mutual assistance fund GB, a savings and loan association US ⑦ pot. (pieniądze) cash; **nie mam** ~**y** I'm short of cash; **zrobić** ~**ę** to make loads of money

kase|ta *f* cassette

kaset|ka *f* case, casket GB; ~**ka z biżuterią/pieniędzmi** a jewel(lery)/cash box

kasiarz *m* pot. safe-breaker, safe-cracker

kasje|r *m*, ~**rka** *f* cashier; (w supermarkecie) checkout assistant, checker US; (w kinie) ticket seller; ~**r biletowy** a ticket clerk; ~**r w banku** a bank teller a. cashier

kask *m* helmet

kaskade|r *m* stunt performer, stuntman

kasłać → **kaszlnąć**

kas|ować *impf* **❙** *vt* ① (jako opłata) to validate *[bilet]*; (stemplować) to stamp; (dziurkować) to punch ② Audio, Komput. to erase *[nagranie, piosenkę]*; to erase, to delete *[dane, plik]* ③ Prawo (uchylić) to revoke, to annul *[wyrok]* ④ Aut. to scrap, to write off *[samochód,*

pojazd] ⑤ pot., przen. (brać pieniądze) to rake in pot.; **za każdą naprawę** ~**ował 100 złotych** he raked in 100 zlotys for each repair job

❙❙ kasować się (likwidować się wzajemnie) to cancel each other out

kasownik *m* (w autobusie, tramwaju) validating machine; (dziurkujący) ticket punch, ticket-punching machine; (stemplujący) stamping machine

kasow|y *adi.* ① *[obroty]* cash; **wpływy** ~**e** (w sklepie) takings; (w kinie, teatrze) box office takings a. receipts; **okienko** ~**e** (na dworcu) a ticket office a. window; (w kinie, teatrze) the box office ② (dochodowy) money-making, commercially successful; *[sztuka, płyta]* hit pot.; *[aktor, pisarz]* bankable; **przebój** ~**y** (commercial) hit; (film, książka) a blockbuster

kastaniet|y *plt* castanets

kasyn|o *n* ① (miejsce hazardu) casino ② Wojsk. mess

kasz|a *f* Kulin. groats, kasha; ~**a krakowska** ≈ buckwheat grits; ~**a gryczana/jęczmienna/jaglana** buckwheat/barley/millet (groats); ~**a kukurydziana** grits; ~**a manna** semolina; ~**a perłowa** pearl barley

kaszan|ka *f* Kulin. black a. blood pudding, blood sausage *(with buckwheat)*

kasz|el *m* cough

ka|szlnąć *pf* — **ka|słać, ka|szlać, ka|szleć** *impf vi* to cough; **on bardzo kaszle** he has a bad cough

kasztan *m* ① (koń) chestnut (horse) ② Bot. (drzewo) (horse) chestnut (tree); (jadalny) (sweet) chestnut (tree); (owoc) conker GB pot.; chestnut; (jadalny) (sweet) chestnut

kasztanow|iec *m* Bot. (horse) chestnut, (horse) chestnut tree

kasztanow|y *adi.* ① *[liść, drewno]*; ~**a aleja** a chestnut-lined road ② (rudobrązowy) *[włosy]* auburn, chestnut

ka|t *m* ① executioner; (wieszający skazanych) hangman ② przen. butcher przen.

kataklizm *m* cataclysm także przen.

katalog *m* ① (spis) catalogue, catalog US; ~ **biblioteczny** a library catalogue a. index ② (broszura) catalogue, catalog US ③ Komput. directory

katalog|ować *impf vt* to catalogue, to catalog US *[książki, zbiory]*

katapul|ta *f* ① Hist. catapult ② Lotn. (wyrzutnia) catapult; (w czasie awarii) ejector seat

kata|r *m* catarrh; runny nose pot.; (zatkany nos) nasal congestion; stuffy nose pot.; **mieć** ~**r** to have a runny/stuffy nose; ~**r sienny** hay fever

kataryn|ka *f* barrel organ

katastrof|a *f* disaster, catastrophe; ~**a budowlana** a building a. construction disaster; ~**a ekologiczna** an ecological disaster a. catastrophe; ~**a lotnicza/kolejowa** a plane/rail crash; **ulec** ~**ie** *[samolot, pociąg]* to crash; *[statek]* to sink, to go down

katastrofaln|y *adi.* disastrous *także przen.*

katechizm *m* catechism

kated|ra *f* [1] Archit., Relig. cathedral [2] Uniw. department; (stanowisko) chair; **objął ~rę fizyki teoretycznej** he took (over) the chair of theoretical physics [3] Szkol., Uniw. (stół) teacher's desk, lecturer's bench; (pulpit) lectern; (podium) podium

kategori|a *f* category; **~a wiekowa** an age category; **restauracja pierwszej ~i** a first-class restaurant; **obywatel drugiej ~i** a second-class citizen; **myśleć w ~ach opłacalności** to think in terms of profit

kategoryczn|y *adi. [żądanie, rozkaz]* categorical; *[sądy, oceny]* uncompromising; **obowiązuje ~y zakaz palenia** smoking is strictly prohibited

katolic|ki *adi.* (Roman) Catholic

katolicyzm *m* (Roman) Catholicism

katoli|k *m*, **~czka** *f* (Roman) Catholic

kat|ować *impf* [] *vt* (bić) to beat; (torturować) to torture

[] **katować się** to torment oneself (**czymś** with sth)

kaucj|a *f* [1] Prawo bail [2] (zastaw) deposit; **~a za butelki** a bottle deposit

kauczuk *m* rubber

kaw|a *f* coffee

■ **~a na ławę** *pot.* without mincing words, without beating about the bush; **wyłożyć ~ę na ławę** to not mince words

kawale|r *m* [1] (nieżonaty) bachelor; **stary ~r** a confirmed bachelor [2] przest., żart. fellow *pot.* [3] (osoba odznaczona orderem) knight

kawaleri|a *f* cavalry

kawaler|ka *f* (mieszkanie) a bachelor a. one-room flat GB, one-room apartment US

kawalerzy|sta *m* cavalryman

kawa|ł *m* [1] (porcja) large piece; (mięsa, tynku) chunk; (ziemi, gliny) lump [2] *pot.* (duża część) a lot, a good deal; **~ł drogi/czasu** a long way/time; **zwiedził ~ł świata** he saw a good deal of the world [3] *pot.* (dowcip) joke; **zrobić komuś ~ł** to play a joke on sb; **dla ~łu** for a laugh *pot.*

■ **~ł drania/chama/świni** *pot.* a right a. real bastard/swine/pig *pot.*; **~ł grosza** *pot.* quite a packet *pot.*; **~ł chłopa** *pot.* a strapping lad

kawał|ek *m* [1] (część) piece, bit; (chleba, ciasta) piece, slice; (papieru) bit, scrap; (drewna) piece, chunk [2] *pot.* (odrobina) bit; **~ek dalej** a bit further [3] *pot.* (utwór) piece; **puścił niezły ~ek** he played a good track

kawiar|nia *f* café, coffee house

kawio|r *m* caviar

kaw|ka *f* jackdaw

kawon *m* watermelon

ka|zać *pf, impf vi* [1] (polecić) to order; **kazać komuś coś zrobić** to tell sb to do sth; **rób, co ci każą** do as you're told [2] (zmuszać) to force, to make; **kazał na siebie czekać** he kept me/us waiting [3] (wy-

magać) to demand, to require [4] *pot.* (zamówić) to order; **kazał sobie podać dużą kawę** he ordered a large cup of coffee

■ **kazał ci się kłaniać** he asked me to remember him to you

kaza|nie *n* [1] Relig. sermon, homily [2] przen. sermon; **prawić ~nia** to sermonize, to preach

■ **czuć się/siedzieć jak na tureckim ~niu** *pot.* to not have a clue about what is going on (around one) *pot.*

kazirodztw|o *n* incest

kaznodziej|a *m* Relig. preacher

każdorazow|y *adi. [trudność, dyskusja]* each, every

każd|y [] *pron.* [1] (bez wyjątku) every; (z określonej grupy) each; **~y z nich/nas** each of them/us, every one of them/us; **~y dzień/rok** each day/year; **~ego dnia/roku** every day/year; **z ~ym dniem/rokiem** with each passing day/year; **to dotyczy ~ego z was** that applies to each (and every) one of you a. all of you; **za ~ym razem, kiedy ją widzę** each a. every time I see her; **przychodził na ~e wezwanie** he came whenever he was called; **na ~ym kroku** (wszędzie) everywhere; (ciągle) at every turn, every step of the way [2] (dowolny) any; **w ~ej chwili** at any time a. moment; **o ~ej porze** (at) any time (of the day); **~y nauczyciel powie ci to samo** every a. any teacher will tell you the same

[] **każd|y** *m*, **~a** *f*, **~e** *n* (bez wyjątku) every; (z określonej grupy) each; **~y o tym dobrze wie** everybody knows that full well; **dla ~ego wystarczy** there's enough for everybody a. everyone; **~y, kto przyjdzie, będzie mile widziany** whoever comes will be most welcome; **równie dobry jak ~y inny** as good as any other

kącik *m* corner; **~i oczu/ust** the corners of the eyes/mouth; **~ filatelistyczny/sportowy** a stamp collecting/sports column **~ zabaw** a play area

kąkol *m* corncockle

kąp|ać *impf* [] *vt* (myć) to bath, to bathe

[] **kąpać się** to bathe; **~ać się w wannie** to have GB a. take a bath; **~ać się w jeziorze/morzu** to swim in the lake/sea

kąpiel *f* bath; **przygotować komuś ~** to run a bath for sb

kąpielisk|o *n* [1] (miejscowość) bathing resort [2] (miejsce nad wodą) bathing beach

kąpielow|y *adi. [kostium, spodenki]* bathing, swimming; **płaszcz ~y** a bathrobe; **ręcznik ~y** a bath towel

kąpielów|ki *plt* bathing a. swimming trunks

kąs|ać *impf vt* to bite, to nip; *[owad]* to sting

kąs|ek *m* titbit, nibble

kąśliw|y *adi. [uwaga, recenzja]* biting

ką|t *m* [1] Mat. angle [2] (między ścianami) corner; **chodzić z kąta w kąt** to walk back and forth; **zajrzeć w każdy kąt** to look into every nook and cranny; **płakać po kątach** to snivel in corners

3 pot. (mieszkanie) place pot.; **wycierać cudze/obce kąty** s own; **mieć swój kąt** to have one's own place 4 pot. (miejscowość) spot; **odwiedzić stare kąty** to revisit old haunts
■ **cztery kąty** digs GB pot.

kątomierz *m* protractor

kątownik *m* try square, bevel

kciuk *m* thumb; **trzymać ~i za kogoś** to keep one's fingers crossed for sb

keczup *m* ketchup

kefi|r *m* kefir

keks *m* fruit cake

kelne|r *m* waiter

kelner|ka *f* waitress

kemping *m* camping site GB, campsite GB, campground US

kempingow|y *adi.* *[urządzenia, teren]* camping; **domek ~y** a holiday chalet GB, a tourist cabin US; **pole ~e** a campsite

kergulen|a *f* icefish

kęp|a *f* 1 (drzew) clump, cluster; (trawy) tussock, tuft 2 (wyniosłość) hillock, hurst 3 (wysepka) islet 4 (włosów) tuft

kęs *m* (kawałek) mouthful, bite

kibic *m* 1 supporter GB, fan 2 przen. (obserwator) observer, onlooker

kibic|ować *impf vi* 1 to support (**komuś** sb); to root pot. (**komuś** for sb) 2 przen. (obserwować) to observe, to watch; **~ować przy pokerze** to watch a poker game

kica|ć *impf vi [królik, wiewiórka]* to hop

kich|nąć *pf* — **kich|ać** *impf vi* to sneeze

kicz *m* kitsch

kiczowa|ty *adi.* *[obraz, film]* kitschy, kitsch

kiedy I *pron.* 1 (pytajny) when; **~ wrócisz?** when will you be back?; **~ jest koncert?** when is the concert?; **od ~** since when, (for) how long; **od ~ się znacie?** how long have you known each other?; „**biorę urlop" – „od ~ do ~?"** 'I'm taking some leave' – 'from when until when?'; **na ~ to ma być gotowe?** when does it have to be ready (by)?; **nie wiem, na ~ są te bilety** I don't know when a. which day these tickets are for 2 (względny) (w trakcie) as, while; (po) when; **~ oglądali mecz, ktoś zadzwonił do drzwi** while they were watching the match, someone rang the bell; **przyjdę po ciebie, ~ skończę pracę** I'll call for you after a. when I finish work; **wtedy, ~** when; **w dniu, ~...** on the day when...; **~ tylko** (zaraz jak) as soon as; (kiedykolwiek) whenever; **~ tylko przyszedł, zabrał się do sprzątania** as soon as he came, he started cleaning up; **~ tylko mam czas, chodzę na spacery** whenever I have (the) time, I go for walks 3 pot. (nieokreślony) some time, one day
II *coni.* 1 (tymczasem) when, whereas; (jednak) when, if 2 pot. (skoro) if, when; **~ jesteś taki ciekawy, to...** if you really want to know...

■ **~ indziej** some other time; **mało** a. **rzadko ~** rarely, hardly ever; **(on) rzadko ~ pisze** he hardly ever writes

kiedykolwiek *pron.* 1 (nieokreślony) (w dowolnym czasie) (at) any time; (w ogóle) ever; **gdybyś ~ potrzebował pomocy...** if you ever need any help... 2 (względny) whenever; **~ prosiłem ją o pomoc, zawsze odmawiała** whenever I asked her for help, she always refused

kiedyś *pron.* 1 (w przeszłości) once, at one time; **była ~ piękną kobietą** at one time she was a beautiful woman; **~ paliłem** I used to smoke; **tak jak ~** like in the old days; **żył sobie ~ dobry król** once upon a time there lived a good king 2 (w przyszłości) some time, some day; **odwiedź nas ~** come and see us some time a. day

kielich *m* 1 (naczynie) goblet, glass; **~ mszalny** a chalice 2 pot. (porcja alkoholu) drink; (wódki) shot pot.; **pójść na ~a** to go and have a drink 3 Bot. calyx

kielisz|ek *m* 1 (naczynie) glass; (do wina) wine glass; (do szampana) (wysoki) champagne flute; (płaski) champagne a. cocktail glass; (do wódki) shot glass US, jigger; (do koniaku) brandy snifter; (do likieru) liqueur glass; (do jajek) egg cup 2 (porcja alkoholu) drink; **zwierzać się przy ~ku** to bare one's soul over a drink

kielni|a *f* trowel

k|ieł *m* (ząb) fang; (słonia, dzika) tusk

kiełbas|a *f* (continental) sausage; **biała ~a** ≈ raw sausage; **~a sucha** ≈ dried smoked sausage

kieł|ek *m* shoot, sprout

kiełk|ować *impf vi* 1 *[rośliny, nasiona]* to sprout 2 przen. (rodzić się) *[myśl, pomysł]* to germinate; **w jej sercu zaczęła ~ować nadzieja** hope was kindled in her heart

kieps|ki *adi.* pot. *[książka, aktor]* crummy, lousy pot.

kiepsko *adv.* pot. poorly; **uczył się ~** he was a lousy a. crummy student pot.; **czuć się ~** to feel lousy a. crummy pot.; **z nim jest już ~** he's on his last legs pot.

kie|r *m* Gry heart

kiermasz *m* sale, fair; **~ artykułów szkolnych** a back-to-school sale; **~ dobroczynny** a bring-and-buy a. charity sale

kier|ować *impf* I *vt* 1 (ustawiać) to point *[reflektor, lunetę]*; to aim *[ciosy, broń]* 2 (wysłać) to dispatch, to send *[towary]*; to refer *[pacjenta, ustawę]*; to direct, to (re)route *[ruch]*; **~ować sprawę do sądu** to bring a. take a case to court 3 (zwracać się) to direct, to aim *[słowa, myśli]* 4 (prowadzić) to steer, to drive *[samochodem, motocyklem]*; to navigate, to steer *[statkiem, samolotem]* 5 (zarządzać) to manage, to run (**czymś** sth); **~ował budową mostu** he was in charge of the construction of a bridge 6 (wpływać) to control (**kimś** sb) 7 (działać pod wpływem) **~owała nim ambicja** he was driven by ambition
II **kierować się** 1 (ustawiać się) to be pointed a.

directed ②(iść) to head, to aim; **~ować się do wyjścia** to head for the exit ③ (być adresowanym) *[słowa, myśli]* to be directed ④ (powodować się) **~ować się czymś** to be guided a. governed by sth *[logiką, instynktem]*; to be driven by sth *[ambicją, nienawiścią]*

kierowc|a m driver

kierownic|a f (w samochodzie) (steering) wheel; (w rowerze, motocyklu) handlebars; **stracić panowanie nad ~ą** to lose control of the car

kierownictw|o n management; **objął ~o redakcji** he took over as editor

kierownicz|y adi. ① *[stanowisko, zdolności]* managerial; **wyższa kadra ~a** senior management ② *[układ, przekładnia]* steering

kierowni|k m, **~czka** f manager, director; **~k artystyczny teatru** the artistic director of a theatre; **~k działu** a department manager; **~k budowy** a site manager

kierun|ek m ① (strona) direction; **iść w ~ku centrum** to walk in the direction of the town centre; **spojrzał w moim ~ku** he looked towards me a. in my direction; **idź w ~ku południowym** go south; **droga biegnie dalej w ~ku północnym** the road continues in a northerly direction; **jedziemy w przeciwnym ~ku** (niż inni) we're going the other way; (niewłaściwym) we're going the wrong way a. in the opposite direction; **w ~ku ruchu wskazówek zegara** clockwise, in a clockwise direction; **w ~ku przeciwnym do ruchu wskazówek zegara** anticlockwise GB, in an anticlockwise direction GB, counterclockwise US, in a counterclockwise direction US; **na tej drodze obowiązuje jeden ~ek ruchu** this is a one-way street; **ruch w ~ku Wrocławia** Wrocław-bound traffic ② (postępowanie) trend, direction; **~ki polityki zagranicznej** trends in foreign policy ③ (w sztuce, muzyce, literaturze) movement, trend; (w nauce) trend, direction; **~ek studiów** Uniw. subject, field of study, major US ④ Wojsk. line; **~ek ataku** a line of attack

kierunkowskaz m ① (w samochodzie) indicator, turn signal US ② (znak drogowy) signpost, guidepost

kierunkow|y adi. ① (wskazujący kierunek) *[tablica, ruch]* directional ② (celowy) *[założenia]* guiding, operational; **przedmioty ~e** Szkol. the principal subjects, the core curriculum; **przedmiot ~y** Uniw. field of study, major US

Ⅱ m Telekom. (numer) telephone a. dialling code GB, area code US

❑ **numer ~y** Telekom. telephone a. dialling code GB, area code US

kiesze|ń f pocket; **tylna ~ń spodni** a hip pocket; **wyłożył na to z własnej ~ni** przen. he paid for it out of his own pocket

■ **bić** a. **uderzać kogoś po ~ni** pot. to be hard on the pocket pot.; **zwycięstwo mają w ~ni** they're

certain to win; **mieć węża w ~ni** pot. to be tight-fisted a. close-fisted; **znać kogoś/coś jak własną ~ń** to know sb/sth like the back of one's hand, to know sb/sth inside out

kieszonkow|iec m pot. pickpocket

kieszonkow|y ① adi. *[słownik, wydanie]* pocket **Ⅱ** **kieszonkowe** n pocket money GB, allowance US

kij m ① (patyk) stick; (trzonek) handle; **~ od miotły** a broomstick ② Sport (hokejowy) stick; (baseballowy) bat; (golfowy) club; (bilardowy) cue

■ **jakby ~ połknął** pot. (as) stiff as a poker a. ramrod; **metoda ~a i marchewki** the carrot and stick approach; **nie ~em go to pałką** there's more than one way to skin a cat przysł.; **(to) nie w ~ dmuchał** pot. it is/was no mean feat; **wetknąć** a. **wsadzić** a. **włożyć ~ w mrowisko** to stir up a hornets' nest

kijan|ka f Zool. tadpole

kiku|t m ① (część kończyny) stump ② (pozostały fragment) stump, stub; **~ty spalonych drzew** stumps of burnt trees

kilk|a pron. some; (niewiele) a few; (więcej) several; **daj mi ~a śliwek** give me some/a few plums; **dziecko urodzi się za ~a miesięcy** the baby's due in a few months; **~a osób już mi to mówiło** I've heard from several (other) people

kilk|adziesiąt pron. several dozen

kilkakrotn|y adi. *[próby, ostrzeżenia]* repeated; *[zysk, obrót]* multiple; **~y medalista** a multiple medallist

kilk|anaście pron. a dozen or so, between ten and twenty

kilkanaścior|o pron. a dozen or so, between ten and twenty

kilk|aset pron. several hundred, a few hundred

kilkor|o pron. several, a few

kilkunastoletni adi. *[chłopiec, dziewczyna]* teenage(d); **~e doświadczenie w kierowaniu biurem** over a decade of experience in office management

kilkuosobow|y adi. **~y zespół** a team of several people; **~y pokój** a multiple-occupancy room

kilo n inv. pot. kilo

kilof m pick(axe)

kilogramow|y adi. *[odważnik, opakowanie]* one-kilo(gramme) GB, one-kilo(gram) US

kilomet|r m ① (jednostka długości) kilometre GB, kilometer US; **na piątym ~rze** at five kilometres; **jechać 100 ~rów na godzinę** to go 100 kilometres per hour ② przen. **~rami** *[ciągnąć się]* for miles; **na ~r** *[słychać, czuć]* miles away a. off pot.

kinematografi|a f cinematography

kineskop m picture tube

kineskopow|y adi. **lampa ~a** a (cathode ray) tube

kinkie|t m wall lamp; (ze świecą) sconce

kin|o *n* [1] (budynek) cinema, movie theater US; **co grają w ~ie?** what's on at the cinema? [2] (gatunek filmowy) cinema; **~o grozy** horror films; **~o prawdy** cinéma vérité [3] (seans filmowy) film, movie US; **pieniądze na ~o** money for a cinema ticket

kinoman *m*, **~ka** *f* cinema-goer, movie-goer US

kiosk *m* stand, kiosk; **~ biletowy** a ticket booth; **~ z gazetami** a newsagent's stand GB, a newspaper stand, a news-stand; **~ z książkami** a bookstall

kioska|rz *m*, **~rka** *f* ≈ newsagent GB, stall a. booth keeper

kipi|eć *impf vi* [1] (przelewać się) *[garnek, mleko]* to boil over [2] książk. (burzyć się) to churn, to seethe; **~ąca rzeka** a churning river [3] przen. *[osoba]* to be seething a. boiling; **~eć gniewem** a. **z gniewu** to be seething with anger; **~eć energią** to be bursting with energy; **miasto ~ało życiem** the city teemed a. throbbed with life

ki|sić *impf* [] *vt* (marynować) to pickle; **kiszona kapusta** sauerkraut

[] **kisić się** [1] (marynować się) to marinate [2] pot., pejor. (siedzieć bezczynnie) to vegetate

kisiel *m* Kulin. a type of blancmange

■ **dziesiąta woda po ~u** ≈ a very distant relative

ki|snąć *impf vi* [1] pot. (ulegać fermentacji) to ferment [2] pot. (siedzieć bezczynnie) to vegetate; **kisnąć z nudów** to be bored to death a. to tears

kisz|ka *f* [1] (jelito) intestine, bowel; **głód skręca mi ~ki** I'm starving; **ślepa ~ka** pot. appendix; **~ka stolcowa** rectum [2] Kulin. (kaszanka) black a. blood pudding; (pasztetowa) liver sausage [3] (pomieszczenie) narrow room

■ **~ki mi marsza grają** my tummy's a. stomach's rumbling pot.

ki|t *m* putty

■ **do kitu** pot. crummy, lousy pot.; **wciskać komuś kit** pot. to bullshit sb posp.

ki|ta *f* [1] pot. (ogon) bushy tail; **lisia kita** a brush (of a fox) [2] (pęk piór lub włosia) crest; (pióropusz) plume

■ **odwalić kitę** pot. to kick the bucket, to snuff it GB pot.

kit|el *m* (ochronny) coverall(s), protective gown; (lekarski) (doctor's) lab coat; (chirurga) surgical gown, scrubs; **~el laboratoryjny** a lab coat

kiwa|ć¹ *impf vt* pot. (oszukiwać) to double-cross; to con pot.

kiwać² *impf* → **kiwnąć**

kiwi *m inv.* Zool. kiwi; Bot. kiwi (fruit)

kiw|nąć *pf* — **kiw|ać²** *impf* [] *vi* [1] (poruszyć w dwóch kierunkach) **~nąć głową** to nod; **~nąć ręką** to wave one's hand; **~ać głową nad kimś/czymś** to shake one's head (in dismay) over sb/sth; **~ać na kogoś** pot. (ręką) to wave at a. to sb; (palcem) to beckon to sb; **nie ~nąć palcem** pot. to not lift a finger [2] Sport to dribble; **~nął bramkarza** he dribbled past the goalkeeper

[] **kiwnąć się** — **kiwać się** [1] (huśtać się) to swing, to sway; **~ać się na krześle** to rock back in one's chair; **głowa mu się ~a** he's nodding off [2] (chwiać się) *[stół, krzesło]* to wobble [3] Sport to dribble

klacz *f* mare

klakson *m* horn przest.; **nacisnąć ~** to beep, to sound the horn

klam|ka *f* door handle; (kulista) doorknob

■ **pocałować ~kę** pot. ≈ to find no one at home; **~ka zapadła** the die is cast

klam|ra *f* [1] (zapięcie) buckle ; **zapiąć/rozpiąć ~rę** to do/undo the buckle [2] Sport (przy wspinaczce) step iron; (w boksie) clinch [3] Med. staple

klan *m* clan

klap|a *f* [1] (pokrywa) flap, lid; **~a bagażnika** boot lid GB, trunk lid US; **~a ciężarówki** (lorry) tailgate; **~a do piwnicy** cellar trapdoor [2] (marynarki) lapel [3] pot. (klęska) flop, disaster pot; **sztuka zrobiła ~ę** the play flopped a. was a flop

klap|ać *impf* → **klapnąć¹**

klap|ek *m* (domowy) mule; (plażowy) flip-flop

klap|ka *f* flap; (końska) blinker, blinder US

klap|nąć¹ *pf* — **kla|pać** *impf vi* to slap; **~nąć kogoś po ramieniu** to clap sb on the shoulder

klapn|ąć² *pf vi* pot. to flop, to plop pot.; **~nął na kanapę** he flopped down on the sofa; **~ij sobie** sit yourself down, take the load off your feet pot.

klaps *m* [1] (uderzenie) spank, smack; **dać dziecku ~a** to spank a child [2] Kino (przedmiot) clapperboard; (ujęcie) take

klarne|t *m* clarinet

klarown|y *adi. grad.* [1] (czysty) clear; (przezroczysty) transparent; **~e niebo** a cloudless sky; **~a woda** crystalline water [2] (zrozumiały) *[wyjaśnienia]* clear, lucid

klas|a [] *f* [1] (kategoria) class, category; **zabytek ~y zerowej** a Grade 1 listed monument [2] (w społeczeństwie) class; **~a średnia** the middle class; **~a robotnicza** the working class; **~a rządząca** the ruling class [3] (oddział w szkole) year, form GB, grade US; **~a maturalna** the final year of secondary school; **w której jesteś ~ie?** which year are you in? [4] (uczniowie) class; **to zdolna ~a** they're a clever class [5] (sala) classroom [6] (wysoka jakość) class; **światowej ~y specjalista** a world-class specialist [7] (w środkach komunikacji) class; **podróżować pierwszą ~ą** to travel first class; **bilet ~y turystycznej** an economy class ticket

[] **klasy** *plt* Gry hopscotch

■ **mieć ~ę** pot. to have class; **robić wszystko z ~ą** to do everthing in a. with style

klase|r *m* (na znaczki) stamp album; (na monety) coin album

kla|snąć *pf* — **kla|skać** *impf vi* [1] (dłonią o dłoń) to clap; **długo ~skano artystom** the performers received lengthy applause; **~skać w rytm muzyki** to clap along to the music [2] (uderzać) to slap

klasow|y *adi.* [1] Socjol. *[świadomość]* class [2] Szkol. *[dziennik]* class; **zadanie ~e** a. **praca ~a** a (class) test

klasów|ka *f* Szkol. test; **~ka z matematyki** a maths test

klasycyzm *m* Literat., Szt. neo-classicism; Muz. classicism

klasyczn|y *adi.* *[sztuka, mitologia, medycyna, muzyka]* classical; *[przykład, objaw, sukienka, garnitur]* classic

klasyfikacj|a *f* [1] *(podział)* classification [2] *(sportowców, drużyn)* ranking

klasyfik|ować *impf vt* [1] *(dzielić na grupy)* to classify, to categorize *[uczestników, dzieła]* [2] *(przypisywać cechy)* to classify; **~ować coś jako dzieło sztuki** to classify sth as a work of art [3] *(w konkursie, zawodach)* to rank [4] *(oceniać)* *[nauczyciel]* to give marks GB, to grade US

klasy|ka *f* classics; **~ka kina światowego** world cinema classics

klaszto|r *m* [1] *(budynek)* (dla zakonników) monastery; *(dla zakonnic)* convent, nunnery [2] *(zakon)* *(monastic)* order

klat|ka *f* [1] *(dla zwierząt)* cage; **~ka dla ptaków** a birdcage; **~ka na króliki** a rabbit hutch [2] *(w budynku)* staircase, (stair)well, stairs [3] Fot., Kino frame

klauzul|a *f* clause

klawiatu|ra *f* keyboard

klawisz *m* key; **~ spacji** the space bar

kl|ąć *impf* [] *vi* [1] *(złorzeczyć)* to swear, to curse; **kląć na pogodę** to curse the weather [2] *(rzucać klątwę)* to curse (**na kogoś** sb) [] **kląć się** *(przysięgać)* to swear

klątw|a *f* [1] Relig. anathema, excommunication [2] *(przekleństwo)* curse; **rzucić ~ę na kogoś** to put a curse on sb

kle|ić *impf* [] *vt* to glue (together); **~ić modele samolotów** to make model planes [] **kleić się** [1] *(lepić się)* to be sticky; **powieki** a. **oczy jej się ~ją** her eyelids are drooping [2] *(przywierać)* to stick; **błoto ~iło się do butów** the mud stuck to his/her shoes [3] pot. *(przytulać się)* to cling (**do kogoś** to sb)

klei|k *m* pap, gruel

klej *m* glue; **ten ~ dobrze trzyma** this glue sticks well

klejno|t *m* [1] *(kamień szlachetny)* jewel, gem; *(wyrób jubilerski)* piece of jewellery [2] książk. *(herb)* coat of arms

kleko|t *m* [1] *(głos bociana)* clatter(ing) [2] *(turkot)* clatter, rattle [3] pot. *(stary pojazd)* banger, jalopy pot.

kleko|tać *impf vi* [1] *[bocian]* to clatter [2] *[samochód, kołatka]* to clatter, to rattle [3] *(trajkotać)* to chatter, to rattle

kleks *m* (ink) blot

klepać[1] *impf* → **klepnąć**

klep|ać[2] *impf vt* [1] to hammer *[blachę, kosę]*; to beat *[len, konopie]* [2] pot. *(paplać)* to prattle
■ **~ać biedę** pot. to live from hand to mouth

klep|ka *f* [1] *(podłogowa)* woodblock; *(w beczce, łodzi)* stave [2] pot. *(podłoga)* woodblock floor, parquet

klep|nąć *pf* — **klep|ać**[1] *impf vt* to pat; **~nąć kogoś w ramię/po plecach** to pat sb on the shoulder/back

klepsyd|ra *f* [1] *(piaskowa)* hourglass, sandglass; *(wodna)* water clock [2] *(ogłoszenie o śmierci)* obituary

kleptoman *m*, **~ka** *f* kleptomaniac

kleptomani|a *f* kleptomania

kle|r *m* clergy

klerykaln|y *adi.* clerical

kleszcz *m* Zool. tick

kleszcz|e *plt* [1] *(raka, skorpiona)* pincers, nippers [2] Techn. nippers, pliers [3] Med. forceps

klęcz|eć *impf vi* to kneel

klęcz|ki *plt* **paść na ~ki** to go down on one's knees; **błagać kogoś na ~kach** to beg sb on one's knees

klęcznik *m* prie-dieu

klęk|nąć *pf* — **klęk|ać** *impf vi* to kneel (down); **~ać do modlitwy** to kneel (down) to pray

klęs|ka *f* [1] *(niepomyślny wynik)* defeat; **sromotna ~ka** a resounding a. an ignominious defeat [2] *(niepowodzenie)* defeat, misfortune [3] *(żywioł)* disaster, calamity; **~ka żywiołowa** a natural disaster; **~ka nieurodzaju** (a) harvest a. crop failure; **~ka głodu** famine; **~ka urodzaju** a glut

klien|t *m*, **~tka** *f* customer, client; **stały ~t** regular customer;

klientel|a *f* clientele

kli|ka *f* clique

klimakterium *n inv.* Med. climacteric

klima|t *m* [1] Meteo. climate; **w ~cie pustynnym** in desert climates [2] przen. *(nastrój)* atmosphere, climate; **odpowiedni ~t do pracy** the right atmosphere for work

klimatyzacj|a *f* air-conditioning

klimatyz|ować *impf vt* to air-condition *[dom, halę fabryczną]*

klin *m* [1] *(narzędzie do łupania)* splitting wedge [2] *(do blokowania)* wedge [3] *(bryt)* gore; *(wstawka)* gusset; **spódnica z ~ów** a. **w ~y** a gored skirt [4] Meteo. ridge, wedge; **~ wysokiego ciśnienia** a ridge of high pressure [5] pot. *(porcja alkoholu na kaca)* a hair of the dog (that bit you)
■ **~ ~em** pot. one nail drives out another przysł.

kliniczn|y *adi.* *[badania, testy]* clinical; **szpital ~y** a teaching hospital; **~y przykład bezmyślności** a clinical a. textbook case of thoughtlessness

klini|ka *f* *(szpital)* (teaching) hospital; *(oddział szpitalny)* ward, clinic

klinow|y *adi.* [1] *(w kształcie klina)* wedge-shaped [2] *[pismo, tabliczki]* cuneiform

klips *m* clip-on (earring)

klisz|a *f* [1] Fot. plate [2] (film) roll of film [3] książk., przen. cliché; **~e propagandowe** propaganda clichés

klit|ka *f* pot. cubbyhole

kloc *m* [1] (pień ściętego drzewa) log; (kawał drewna) chunk of wood [2] (o osobie) lump (of lard), klutz US pot.

kloc|ek *m* [1] (kawałek drewna) block [2] (zabawka) (building) block

klomb *m* flower bed; **~ róż** a rose bed

klon[1] *m* Bot. maple

klon[2] *m* Biol., Komput. clone *także przen.*

klon|ować *impf vt* Biol. to clone

klops *m* [1] Kulin. (kotlet) meatball; (pieczeń rzymska) meat loaf [2] przen. (kłopot) bummer pot.; **no to ~!** **skończyła się benzyna** that's a bummer! we've run out of petrol

klosz *m* [1] (osłona żarówki) (lamp)shade [2] (osłona do przykrywania) glass dome [3] (szklane naczynie) bowl; **~ z owocami** a bowl of fruit [4] Moda flare
■ **trzymać** a. **chować kogoś pod ~em** to mollycoddle sb

klown *m* clown

kloze|t *m* [1] pot. (ubikacja) loo GB, lav pot. [2] (sedes) toilet

klub *m* [1] (organizacja) club; **witaj w ~ie!** pot., przen. welcome to a. join the club! pot., przen. [2] Polit. grouping; **~ parlamentarny** a. **poselski** a parliamentary grouping

klubow|y *adi. [spotkanie, składka]* club

klucz *m* [1] (do zamka) key; **~ do piwnicy** the key to the cellar; **~ od garażu** the key to the garage; **~ od drzwi wejściowych** a front-door key a. latchkey; **zamknąć drzwi ~em** a. **na klucz/ otworzyć drzwi ~em** a. **z klucza** to lock/unlock the door; **trzymać coś pod ~em** to keep sth locked up a. under lock and key; **dostać się pod ~** a. **znaleźć się pod ~em** to be put away a. locked up; **dom/mieszkanie pod ~** pot. a house/a flat ready to move into [2] Techn. spanner GB, wrench; **~ francuski** an adjustable spanner GB, a monkey wrench [3] przen. (metoda) key; **~ do sukcesu** the key to success [4] (zasada) principle, formula; (szyfru) key; **złamać ~ (szyfrowy)** to break a. crack a code [5] (rozwiązania zadań, ćwiczeń) key [6] (ptaków, samolotów) V-formation [7] Muz. clef; **~ wiolinowy** the treble clef

kluczow|y *adi.* książk. *[problem, znaczenie]* crucial; *[pozycja, stanowisko]* key

klucz|yć *impf vi* to wander around a. about; przen. to fudge, to pussyfoot around pot.

kluć się *impf v refl.* [1] (wylęgać się) *[pisklęta, żółwie]* to hatch [2] przen. (rodzić się) *[miłość, nienawiść]* to be born; *[plan, pomysł]* to be hatched, to germinate

klus|ka *f* dumpling; **~ki francuskie** French noodles; **~ki kładzione** drop dumplings; **lane ~ki** batter dumplings a. noodles

kład|ka *f* [1] (mostek) makeshift wooden bridge [2] (nad ulicą) footbridge, pedestrian bridge

kłam|ać *impf vi* to lie (**komuś** to sb); **~ać jak najęty** a. **jak z nut** to tell bare-faced lies/a bare-faced lie; **~ać w żywe oczy** a. **bez zmrużenia powiek** to lie through one's teeth pot.

kłamczuch *m*, **~a** *f* pot. liar

kłamstw|o *n* lie

kłania|ć się *impf v refl.* [1] (składać ukłon) (niski) to bow (**komuś** to sb); (samą głową) to nod (**komuś** to sb); (dygając) to curts(e)y (**komuś** to sb); **nie ~ć komuś** to snub sb [2] (w formach grzecznościowych) to send one's regards; **halo, dzień dobry, ~ się Marek Adamski** hello, this is Marek Adamski; **~j się ode mnie ojcu** remember me to your father; **nie będę się ~ł władzy** I'm not going to kowtow to the authorities

kłap|nąć *pf* — **kłap|ać** *impf vi* pot. [1] (otwierać szczęki i zamykać) to snap; **~ać zębami/dziobem** to snap one's teeth/beak [2] (uderzać miarowo) **pies ~ał uszami** the dog flapped its ears; **wiatr ~ał okiennicami** the shutters were banging in the wind

kła|ść *impf* [I] *vt* [1] (umieszczać) to put; **~ść coś na półkę** a. **na półce** to put sth on the shelf; **~ść coś na miejsce** to put sth away; **~ść podpis na dokumencie** to put one's signature to a document [2] (układać) to lay; **~ść fundamenty** to lay the foundations; **~ść pasjansa** to play solitaire [3] (umieszczać w pozycji leżącej) to lay, to put (down); **~ść dziecko spać** to put the baby to bed [4] (zakładać) to put on; **~dź szybko płaszcz** put your coat on quickly
[II] **kłaść się** [1] (przybrać pozycję leżącą) to lie down; **~ść się na łóżku** to lie down on the bed; **~ść się do łóżka** to go to bed [2] (iść spać) to go to bed; to turn in pot.

kłęb|ek *m* (nici, sznurka) ball; (dymu, pary) puff, wisp
■ **~ek nerwów** pot. a bundle of nerves

kłęb|ić się *impf v refl. [dym, chmury]* to billow; *[ludzie, rzeczy]* to teem

kłębowisk|o *n* [1] (rzeczy) jumble; (zwierząt, osób) swarm; **~o ludzi** a teeming mass of people; **~o żmij** a nest of vipers [2] (natłok uczuć, wrażeń) whirl

kł|oda *f* log; **rzucać (komuś) kłody pod nogi** to put stumbling blocks in sb's way

kłopo|t *m* [1] (trudna sytuacja) problem, trouble; **mieć ~t z kimś** (zmartwienie) to worry about sb; (niewygodę) to have trouble a. a problem with sb; (nieprzyjemności) to be in trouble with sb; **mieć ~ty w pracy** (trudności) to have trouble a. problems at work; (nieprzyjemności) to be in trouble at work; **~t w tym, że...** the trouble a. problem is that...; **w czym ~t?** what seems to be the trouble a. problem?; **sprawić komuś ~t** to cause sb trouble, to inconvenience sb; **wpaść w ~ty** to get in(to) trouble; **wplątać a. wpakować kogoś w ~ty** to get sb in(to) trouble; **nie rób sobie ~tu** don't put yourself out; **to żaden ~t** it's no trouble at all; **no i po ~cie!** and that takes care of that! ② (zmartwienie) problem, trouble; ~**ty finansowe** financial trouble(s) a. problems

kłopo|tać *impf* **Ⅰ** *vt* książk. (sprawiać kłopot) to bother, to trouble; ~**tać kogoś swymi sprawami** to bother sb with one's problems

Ⅱ kłopotać się (martwić się) to worry; ~**tać się o dzieci** to worry about one's children

kłopotliw|y *adi.* ① (uciążliwy) *[sąsiad, zadanie]* troublesome ② (wprawiający w zakłopotanie) *[milczenie, pytanie]* embarrassing, awkward

kłos *m* spike; (zboża) ear

kłó|cić się *impf v refl.* ① (spierać się) to quarrel, to argue (**z kimś** with sb); ~**cić się o coś** to quarrel a. argue about a. over sth ② (nie pasować) to be at odds, to clash (**z czymś** with sth); ~**cić się ze zdrowym rozsądkiem** to not make sense; **te kolory się** ~**cą** these colours clash

kłód|ka *f* padlock; ~**ka do roweru** a bicycle lock

kłótliw|y *adi. grad.* quarrelsome; **mieć** ~**e usposobienie** to be (very) argumentative

kłótni|a *f* quarrel, argument; ~**a brata z siostrą** a quarrel between brother and sister; ~**a z sąsiadami** a quarrel with the a. one's neighbours; ~**a między pracownikami** a disagreement among employees

k|łuć *impf* **Ⅰ** *vt* (kaleczyć) *[osoba, ciernie]* to prick; **kłuć kogoś/coś bagnetem** to stab sb/sth with a bayonet; **krzaki kłuły mnie w nogi** the bushes scratched my legs

Ⅱ *v imp.* **kłuje mnie w boku** I can feel a stabbing pain in my side

■ **kłuć kogoś w oczy** *[światło]* to blind a. sting sb's eyes; *[bogactwo]* to make sb jealous

kłus **Ⅰ** *m* trot

Ⅱ kłusem *adv. [biec, jechać]* at a trot

kłus|ować¹ *impf vi* (polować) to poach; **przyłapać kogoś na** ~**owaniu** to catch sb poaching

kłus|ować² *impf vi [koń, jeździec]* to trot

kłusowni|k *m* poacher

kmin|ek *m* Bot. caraway; Kulin. caraway (seed)

knajp|a *f* pot. (bar) (cheap) bar, pub GB; (restauracja) eatery pot.; **jadać w** ~**ach** to eat out

kneb|el *m* gag także przen.

knebl|ować *impf vt* to gag także przen.

kned|el *m* Kulin. potato dumpling

knu|ć *impf vt* to plot; ~**ć spisek przeciwko komuś** to hatch a plot against sb

koal|a *m* koala; **miś** ~**a** a koala bear

koalicj|a *f* coalition

koalicjan|t *m* coalition partner

koalicyjn|y *adi. [rząd, wojska]* coalition

kobieciarz *m* pot. womanizer

kobiecoś|ć *f* femininity

kobiec|y *adi. [stroje, czasopismo]* women's; *[uroda, wrażliwość]* feminine; **po** ~**emu** *[zachowywać się]* in a feminine way, like a woman

kobie|ta *f* woman; **wiejska** ~**ta** a. ~**ta ze wsi** a countrywoman; ~**ta szpieg/menedżer** a woman spy/manager

kob|ra *f* cobra

kobuz *m* (northern) hobby

koby|ła *f* ① (klacz) (old) mare ② pot. (książka) monster of a book

koc *m* blanket

kocha|ć *impf* **Ⅰ** *vt* to love *[osobę, zwierzę, kraj, pieniądze]*; **bardzo kogoś** ~**ć** to love sb dearly a. very much; ~**ć kogoś do szaleństwa a. nad życie** to be deeply a. madly in love with sb

Ⅱ kochać się ① (siebie samego) to love oneself ② (jeden drugiego) to love each other; ~**jąca się rodzina** a loving family ③ (być zakochanym) to be in love (**w kimś** with sb) ④ (odbywać stosunek seksualny) to make love (**z kimś** to sb)

kochan|ek *m* lover

kochani|e *n* darling, sweetheart

kochan|ka *f* lover, mistress

kochan|y **Ⅰ** *adi.* ① (drogi) *[mąż, żona, dzieci]* darling, beloved; **prezent dla** ~**ej osoby** a gift for a loved one; **dziękuję, jesteś** ~**y** thank you, you're so sweet; **mój** ~**y stary samochód** my dear old car ② (w poufałych zwrotach) dear; ~**a Mamo!** (w liście) Dear Mum,...; **nie mam czasu,** ~**a pani** I don't have time, dear a. love GB pot.

Ⅱ kochan|y *m*, ~**a** *f* ① sweetheart ② (w poufałych zwrotach) **chodźmy, moi** ~**i** let's go, my dears; ~**a, ty lepiej uważaj** you'd better watch out, dearie pot.

koche|r *m* (kuchenka) spirit stove

kochliw|y *adi. [młodzieniec, panna]* amorous, impressionable

koci *adi.* ① (mający związek z kotem) *[ogon, oczy]* cat's; *[choroba, zwyczaje]* feline ② (taki jak u kota) catlike; ~**a zwinność** catlike agility

■ ~**a mama** żart. a cat lady pot., żart.; ~**a muzyka** (hałas) racket; (muzyka) charivari US; ~**e łby** cobblestones

kocia|k *m* ① (kotek) kitten ② pot. (dziewczyna) chick pot.

ko|cić się *impf v refl. [kocica]* to kitten, to have kittens; *[owca]* to lamb; *[koza]* to kid

kocię *n* kitten

ko|cioł *m* ① (garnek) pot; (zawieszany nad ogniem) cauldron; **kocioł na bieliznę** a laundry copper; **dwa kotły zupy** two pots a. potfuls of soup ② Techn. boiler ③ Geol. cirque ④ Muz. kettledrum ⑤ (zasadzka) trap

kocioł|ek *m* (garnek) pot; (wieszany nad ogniem) cauldron

kocu|r *m* tomcat

kocz|ować *impf vi* ① (być koczownikiem) to live as a nomad, to lead a nomadic life ② przen. (przebywać tymczasowo) **uchodźcy** ~**ujący pod gołym niebem** refugees camping out in the open air; ~**ować na lotnisku** to be stranded at the airport

koczowni|k *m*, ~**czka** *f* nomad

ko|d *m* code; **złamać kod** to break a. crack a code; **kod dostępu** Komput. password, access code; **kod kreskowy** bar code; **kod pocztowy** postal code a. postcode GB, zip code US; **kod telekomunikacyjny** dialling a. STD code GB, area code US

kodeks *m* ① (zbiór norm) code; ~ **drogowy** the Highway Code GB; ~ **pracy** employment regulations; ~ **honorowy** a code of honour ② (księga) codex

kod|ować *impf vt* ① (szyfrować) to encode *[dane, wiadomość]*; to scramble *[program telewizyjny, rozmowę telefoniczną]*; ~**ować coś alfabetem Morse'a** to put sth into Morse code ② (oznaczać) to code; ~**owanie kreskowe produktów** bar coding of goods

kodowan|y *adi. [wiadomość, list]* (en)coded; *[program telewizyjny]* scrambled

kofein|a *f* caffeine

kogu|t *m* ① (samiec kury) cock, rooster ② (samiec bażanta, cietrzewia) cock ③ (na dachu samochodu) roof light

ko|ić *impf vt* to soothe *[ból, cierpienie]*

ko|ja *f* bunk

kojarz|yć *impf* [] *vt* ① (zauważać związek) to associate; ~**yć fakty** to put two and two together ② (łączyć w związki) to match (up) *[ludzi]*; to mate *[zwierzęta]* ③ (jednoczyć) to combine, to blend (**coś z czymś** sth with sth) ④ pot. (rozpoznawać) **nie** ~**ę go** I don't remember him ⑤ pot. (rozumieć) **czegoś tu nie** ~**ę** I don't quite get it pot.

[] **kojarzyć się** ① (nasuwać myśl) to be associated (**z kimś/czymś** with sb/sth); **to mi się** ~**y z dzieciństwem** it reminds me of my childhood; **to mi się źle/dobrze** ~**y** it has bad/good associations for me ② (łączyć się w związki) *[ludzie]* to form a relationship

koj|ec *m* ① (dla zwierząt) pen; ~**ec dla świń** a pigsty, a pigpen US ② (dla dziecka) playpen

kojo|t *m* coyote

kok *m* bun, chignon; **włosy upięte w** ~ hair tied in a bun a. roll

kokain|a *f* cocaine

kokar|da *f* bow

kokieteri|a *f* ① (zalotność) flirtatiousness, coquetry ② (udawana skromność) coyness

kokiet|ka *f* coquette

kokiet|ować *impf vt* ① *[kobieta]* to flirt (**kogoś** with sb); ~**ować kogoś uśmiechem/spojrzeniem** to smile/look at sb coquettishly ② (udawać skromność) to be coy ③ (schlebiać) to make (friendly/romantic) overtures (**kogoś** to sb); to try and win [sb] over

koklusz *m* Med. whooping cough

kokon *m* cocoon także przen.

kokos [] *m* (orzech) coconut; (palma) coconut palm

[] **kokosy** *plt* pot. **zarabiać** a. **robić** ~**y (na czymś)** to make piles a. heaps of money (on sth) pot.

koks *m* ① (opał) coke ② pot. (doping) dope pot.

kolaboracj|a *f* collaboration

kolaboran|t *m*, ~**tka** *f* collaborator

kolabor|ować *impf vi* to collaborate (**z kimś** with sb)

kolacj|a *f* (lekka) supper; (duży posiłek) dinner

kolan|ko [] *n* ① (część ciała) knee ② Bot. node ③ Techn. (w rurze) elbow, knee

[] **kolanka** *plt* Kulin. macaroni, elbow-shaped pasta

kolan|o [] *n* knee; **woda/śnieg do** ~ a. **po** ~**a** knee-deep water/snow; **spódnica do** ~ a knee-length skirt; **buty do** ~ knee-high boots, knee boots

[] **kolana** *plt* lap; **usiąść komuś na** ~**ach** to sit on sb's lap a. knee

■ **łysy jak** ~**o** as bald as a coot; **napisać coś na** ~**ie** to scrawl sth hastily

kolarstw|o *n* cycling

kolarz *m* cyclist

kolaż *m* (obraz) collage; (technika) collage, montage

kolb|a *f* ① Wojsk. butt; ~**a karabinu** a rifle butt ② Bot. (kukurydzy) (z ziarnami) head of maize, ear (of corn) US; (bez ziaren) corn cob; (gotowana) corn on the cob ③ (naczynie laboratoryjne) flask ④ Techn. ~**a lutownicza** a soldering iron

kolczat|ka *f* ① (obroża) spiked collar ② (rozkładana na drodze) road spikes, stinger® US ③ Zool. spiny anteater

kolczyk *m* ① (ozdoba) (pierced) earring ② (u zwierzęcia) ring

koleb|ka *f* cradle także przen. ~**ka cywilizacji** the cradle of civilization

kol|ec [] *m* ① Bot. thorn ② Zool. (jeża, jeżowca) spine, quill ③ (ostra część przedmiotu) spike; **śnieżne opony z** ~**cami** snow tyres with spikes

[] **kolce** *plt* Sport spikes

kole|ga *m* ① (znajomy) friend; pal, mate GB pot.; ~**ga ze szkoły** a school friend, a schoolmate; ~**ga z klasy** a classmate; ~**ga z pracy** a friend from work, a workmate GB ② (współpracownik) colleague; ~**ga Nowak** (Mr) Nowak ③ (pracujący w tym samym zawodzie) ~**ga po fachu** a fellow lawyer/teacher/doctor; ~**ga po piórze** a fellow writer

kolegi|um *n* ① (zespół) body; ~**um sędziowskie** a body of judges; ~**um elektorów** an electoral college ② (zebranie) ~**um redakcyjne** an editorial meeting ③ pot. (sąd) ≈ magistrates' court GB, ≈ misdemeanor court US ④ (uczelnia) college

koleg|ować się *impf v refl.* pot. to be friends (**z kimś** with sb)

kolein|a *f* ① (ślad kół) rut; „~**y**" (znak drogowy) 'caution: (deep) ruts ahead' ② przen. rut, groove; **życie toczy się utartymi** ~**ami** life follows the same old pattern

kole|j [] *f* ① (system transportu) railway(s) GB, railroad(s) US ② (pociąg) train; **jechać** ~**ją** to go a. travel by train a. rail ③ (następstwo) turn; (pora) time; **czekać na swoją** ~**j** to wait one's turn; ~**j na**

egzaminy (it's) time for the exams; **po ∼i** one after the other a. after another, in turn; **wszystko po ∼i!** one thing at a time! 4 (bieg rzeczy) course; **zwykła ∼j rzeczy** the normal course of events; **∼je życia/losu** the ups and downs of life; **obraz przechodził różne ∼je** this painting has an interesting history attached to it

II **z kolei** *adv.* 1 (z rzędu) in a row; **to już czwarty z ∼i telefon w tej sprawie** that's the fourth call in a row about it 2 (następnie) next, then; (jako reakcja) in turn 3 (nawiązujące) on the other hand; (przeciwstawiające) by contrast

■ **mieć nie (wszystko) po ∼i (w głowie)** to be not all there, to have something missing pot.

koleja|rz *m* railwayman GB, railroad man US, railman

kolej|ka *f* 1 (środek transportu) narrow-gauge railway 2 (rząd ludzi) queue GB, line US; **∼ka po bilety** a queue for tickets; **∼ka do kina** a queue outside the cinema; **stanąć w ∼ce** to join a queue GB, to get into line US; **ustawiać się w ∼ce** to form a queue GB a. line US, to queue up GB, to line up US; **czekać w ∼ce do dentysty** to wait for one's turn at the dentist's 3 (wyznaczone miejsce) place, turn; **jego ∼ka przepadła** he lost his place in the queue; **wejść bez ∼ki** a. **poza ∼ką do lekarza** to get in to see the doctor without taking one's turn in the queue 4 pot. round; **dzisiaj ja stawiam ∼kę** today the drinks are on me pot.

kolejno *adv.* (jeden za drugim) one by one, one after the other; (nie naraz) in turn

kolejnoś|ć *f* order; **w odwrotnej ∼ci** in reverse order; **∼ć zdarzeń** the sequence of events; **zamówienia są realizowane w ∼ci zgłoszeń** orders are fulfilled on a first-come, first-served basis; **wpuścić kogoś poza ∼cią** to admit sb out of turn

kolejn|y *adi.* (następny) next, subsequent; (jeszcze jeden) another; (jeden po drugim) *[set]* consecutive, successive; **∼a pozycja na liście** the next item on the list; **∼e wydanie książki** another a. a subsequent edition of the book; **to już ∼a pomyłka** this is not the first mistake; **po raz ∼y** once a. yet again

kolekcj|a *f* collection

kolekcjone|r *m*, **∼rka** *f* collector

kolekcjon|ować *impf vt* to collect *[znaczki, monety]*

kolend|ra *f* coriander

kole|ś *m* pot. pal, mate GB, buddy US pot.; **jakiś ∼ś na ciebie czeka** there's some guy waiting for you

koleżan|ka *f* 1 (znajoma) (girl)friend; **szkolna ∼ka** a school friend, a schoolmate; **∼ka z klasy** a classmate 2 (współpracownica) colleague

koleżeńs|ki *adi.* 1 (dotyczący kolegów) **∼a pomoc** help from (one's) friends/a friend; **∼ka przysługa**

a favour from a friend; **∼kie stosunki** team spirit, friendly relations; **spotkanie ∼kie** a friendly get-together; **dyskusja ∼ka** a friendly discussion, a discussion among friends 2 (przyjacielski) *[postawa, zachowanie]* friendly; **po ∼ku** in a friendly way

kolę|da *f* (Christmas) carol; **chodzić po ∼dzie** *[ksiądz]* to make a round of house calls on one's parishioners

kolędni|k *m* carol singer, (Christmas) caroller GB a. caroler US

kolęd|ować *impf vi* (śpiewać kolędy) to sing (Christmas) carols

koli|a *f* necklace

kolib|er *m* hummingbird

kolid|ować *impf vi* to collide, to clash (**z czymś** with sth); **czyn ∼ujący z prawem** an illegal act

koli|sty *adi. [kształt, klomb]* round, circular; **∼ste ruchy** circular movements

kolizj|a *f* 1 (zderzenie) collision, crash 2 (konflikt) conflict, clash; **wejść w ∼ę z prawem** to fall foul of the law GB, to run afoul of the law US

kol|ka *f* Med. colic; (od biegania) stitch; **mieć ∼kę** to have a colic attack

kolokwi|um *n* Uniw. test; **∼um z matematyki** a maths test

koloni|a I *f* 1 Polit., Biol. colony 2 (emigranci) (immigrant) community, colony 3 (osiedle) settlement 4 (grupa dzieci) summer camp group

II **kolonie** *plt* summer camp (*for young children*)

kolonizacj|a *f* 1 (podporządkowanie) colonization 2 (zagospodarowanie) settlement

koloniz|ować *impf vt* 1 (przekształcać w kolonię) to colonize *[kraj]* 2 (zasiedlać) to settle *[teren]*

kolo|r I *m* 1 (barwa) colour GB, color US; **∼r czerwony/niebieski** (the colour) red/blue; **∼r ochronny** protective colouring; **∼r oczu/włosów** eye/hair colour; **szminka pod ∼r sukienki** lipstick to match a. matching the dress; **nabrać czerwonego ∼ru** to turn red, to take on a red colour; **w jakim ∼rze** a. **jakiego ∼ru jest twój samochód?** what colour is your car? 2 (rasa) colour GB, color US; **∼r skóry** skin colour, the colour of one's skin 3 (barwnik) colour GB, color US; **∼r puszcza w praniu** the colour runs in the wash 4 (w kartach) suit; **zgłosić ∼r** to declare a suit

II **kolory** *plt* 1 (rumieńce) colour GB, color US; **odzyskał ∼ry** he regained his colour 2 (kolorowe ubrania) colours GB, colors US; **∼ry należy prać oddzielnie** colours should be washed separately

koloratu|ra *f* coloratura

kolorow|y *adi.* 1 (barwny) coloured GB, colored US 2 (wielobarwny) colourful GB, colorful US; **∼y tłum** a colourful crowd 3 *[fotografia, film, telewizor]* colour GB, color US 4 (o rasie) *[osoba]* non-white; coloured GB, colored US obraźl. 5 przen. (ciekawy) *[życie, przeszłość]* colourful GB, colorful US

kolory|t *m* 1 (dominujące barwy) colour(s) GB, color(s) US, colouring GB, coloring US; ~**t jesieni** a. **jesienny** ~**t** the colours of autumn 2 (miejsca, okresu) flavour GB, flavor US, atmosphere; ~**t lokalny** local colour; **oddać** ~**t epoki** to capture the atmosphere a. flavour of the period

koloryz|ować *impf vt* 1 (upiększać) to embroider, to embellish *[historię]*; to colour GB, to color US *[fakty]* 2 (malować) *[szampon]* to colour GB, to color US *[włosy]*; **szampon** ~**ujący** colour shampoo

kolos *m* colossus; ~ **na glinianych nogach** a giant a. colossus with feet of clay

kolosaln|y *adi. [suma, budowla]* colossal

kolportaż *m* (newspaper) distribution

kolporte|r *m*, ~**rka** *f* distributor

kolport|ować *impf vt* to distribute *[gazety, ulotki]*

kolumn|a *f* 1 Archit., Wojsk. column 2 pot. (zespół ludzi) unit; ~**a sanitarna/dezynfekcyjna** a sanitation/disinfection unit 3 Druk. (strona) page; (szpalta) column; ~**a rozkładowa** a two-page spread 4 (liczb, cyfr, słów) column 5 pot. (głośnik) (loud)-speaker

kolumna|da *f* Archit. colonnade

koła|tać *impf vi* 1 (stukać) to knock; ~**tać do drzwi** to knock at a. on the door; **wiatr** ~**cze w okna** the wind is rattling the windows 2 (o sercu, pulsie) to pound, to palpitate 3 przen. (prosić) to appeal, to turn (**do kogoś** to sb); to request (**o coś** sth); to apply (**o coś** for sth)

kołat|ka *f* 1 (u drzwi, bramy) knocker 2 Muz. rattle, clapper

kołd|ra *f* duvet GB, quilt; **puchowa** ~**ra** an eiderdown

koł|ek *m* 1 (palik) stake, peg; ~**ki do namiotu** tent pegs; ~**k osinowy** an aspen stake 2 (wieszak) peg 3 pot. (do łączenia) dowel 4 (do śruby) Rawlplug® GB, wall anchor a. plug 5 Muz. tuning peg

■ **stać** a. **siedzieć** ~**kiem** a. **jak** ~**ek** pot. to stand a. sit stock-still

kołnierz *m* 1 (część ubrania) collar 2 (u zwierząt) ruff 3 Techn. flange, collar; ~ **masztu** a mast coat; ~ **stalowy do rur** a steel pipe flange

■ **nie wylewać za** ~ pot. to like a drop of the hard stuff pot.

kołnierzyk *m* collar; **numer** ~**ka** a collar size

k|oło¹ *n* 1 (pojazdu) wheel; **koło wozu** a cartwheel; **dostać się pod koła** to be run over 2 (okrąg) circle; **zatoczyć koło** to come full circle 3 (zrzeszenie) association, circle; **koło łowieckie** a hunters' association; **koło teatralne** a theatre club a. group 4 (grono) circle; **koło rodzinne** one's family circle 5 (w zabawach) circle, ring; **stanąć w kole** to form a circle a. ring

II koła *plt* (kręgi) circles; **koła polityczne** the political world

III kołem *adv.* (dookoła) in a circle; **obstąpili go kołem** they surrounded him

IV w koło *adv.* 1 (okrążając) (a)round (in circles); round and round 2 (na wszystkie strony) around; **rozglądać się w koło** to look around 3 (ciągle) over and over

❏ **błędne koło** vicious circle a. cycle; **koło ratunkowe** lifebelt, life ring GB, life preserver US; **koło zębate** gear

■ **potrzebne mi te kłopoty jak piąte koło u wozu** I need these problems like I need a hole in my head pot.

koło² *praep.* 1 (obok) by, next to; ~ **domu rosła brzoza** there was a birch tree by the house; **siedział** ~ **mnie** he was sitting next to me 2 pot. (przy) **majstrować** ~ **radia** to tinker with the radio; **krzątać się** ~ **czegoś** to busy oneself with sth; **skakać** ~ **kogoś** przen. to dance attendance on sb 3 (około) about, around; **mieć** ~ **pięćdziesiątki** to be about a. around fifty; **było** ~ **północy** it was around midnight

koł|ować *impf* **I** *vt* pot. (oszukiwać) to con pot.

II *vi* 1 (zataczać koła) to circle; **orzeł** ~**uje wysoko** an eagle is circling high above 2 *[samolot]* to taxi; **samolot** ~**ował po pasie** the plane was taxiing on the runway

III kołować się (kręcić się) to spin; ~**uje mi się w głowie** pot. my head is spinning

kołowr|ót *m* 1 (przy wejściu) turnstile 2 przen. whirl; **codzienny** ~**ót zajęć** the daily grind pot.

kołow|y *adi.* 1 (na kołach) wheeled; **pojazd** ~**y** a wheeled vehicle; **ruch** ~**y** road traffic 2 (w kształcie koła) *[orbita, tor]* circular

kołtun *m* 1 (osoba) blimp GB, reactionary 2 Med. plica (polonica) 3 (plątanina) tangle; ~**y** matted hair

koły|sać *impf* **I** *vt* to swing; ~**sać niemowlę w ramionach** to rock the baby in one's arms; **wiatr** ~**sał gałęziami drzew** the wind was swaying the trees; ~**sać biodrami** to swing a. sway one's hips

II kołysać się (bujać się) ~**sać się w tańcu** to sway in a dance; ~**sać się w fotelu na biegunach** to rock in a rocking chair; **statek** ~**sał się na falach** the ship was rolling on the waves

kołysan|ka *f* lullaby

kołys|ka *f* cradle

komandos *m* Wojsk. (do zadań specjalnych) commando; (w jednostce powietrzno-desantowej) paratrooper

koma|r *m* gnat, mosquito

kombajn *m* combine (harvester)

kombatan|t *m*, ~**tka** *f* veteran

kombi *n inv.* estate car GB, station wagon US

kombinacj|a *f* 1 (połączenie) combination 2 (podstępne działanie) underhandedness 3 Sport (konkurencja narciarska) combined event; (szachowa) combination; ~**a alpejska/klasyczna** a. **norweska** Alpine/Nordic combined

kombinato|r *m*, ~**rka** *f* pot. sharp operator pot.

kombiner|ki *plt* (a pair of) pliers, (a pair of) pincers

kombinezon *m* overalls GB, coveralls US; ~ **lotniczy/narciarski** a flight a. flying/ski suit

kombin|ować *impf* **[]** *vt* (zestawiać) to combine *[dodatki, stroje]*

[] *vi* pot. [] (głowić się) to ponder, to mull over; **tak sobie ~uję, że...** I'm thinking maybe... pot.; **źle ~ujesz** you're barking up the wrong tree pot. [] pejor. (knuć) **co ty znów ~ujesz?** what are you up to now? pot. [] (mieć romans) to carry on pot. (**z kimś** with sb)

komedi|a **[]** *f* [] (utwór, film) comedy [] pot. (obłuda) play-acting; **grać przed kimś ~ę** to put on a show for sb's benefit

[] *inter.* pot. (wyraz rozbawienia) what a comedy! pot.; (wyraz dezaprobaty) what a farce a. joke! pot.

komediopisa|rz *m*, **~rka** *f* comedy writer

komediow|y *adi. [repertuar]* comedy; *[element, talent]* comic; *[scena, zachowanie]* comic, funny

komen|da *f* [] (rozkaz) command; **na moją ~dę...** on my command... [] (dowodzenie) command; **pod czyjąś ~dą** under sb's command [] (siedziba) (command) headquarters

■ **jak na ~dę** in unison, all at once a. at the same instant

komendan|t *m* [] (zwierzchnik) chief; **~t policji** the chief of police, the police chief; **~t straży pożarnej/żandarmerii** a fire (brigade)/military police chief [] Wojsk. (dowódca) commanding officer

komender|ować *impf vi* [] Wojsk. (wydawać rozkazy) to give orders (**kimś** to sb); to order (**kimś** sb); przest. (dowodzić) to be in command (**czymś** of sth) [] pot. (rządzić) to push [sb] around a. about

komentarz *m* [] (objaśnienie) commentary; ~ **do czegoś** a commentary on sth [] (artykuł publicystyczny) commentary, editorial; ~ **z meczu** a commentary on a match [] pot. (uwaga) comment; **bez ~a!** no comment

komentato|r *m*, **~rka** *f* commentator

koment|ować *impf vt* [] (oceniać) to comment on a. about *[wydarzenia]* [] (interpretować) to interpret, to analyse GB, to analyze US *[dzieło, utwór]* [] (krytykować) to make comments on a. about [] Sport (relacjonować) to commentate on

komercyjn|y *adi.* commercial

kome|ta *f* comet

komet|ka *f* [] (gra) badminton [] (lotka) shuttlecock

komfor|t *m* [] (wygoda) luxury, comfort; **żyć w ~cie** to live in comfort [] (spokój ducha) comfort

komfortow|y *adi. [mieszkanie, samochód]* luxury, luxurious; *[sytuacja, warunki, życie]* comfortable

komiczn|y *adi. grad. [mina, sytuacja, osoba]* comical, funny; *[opera]* comic

komi|k *m* (aktor) comic a. comedy actor; (w kabarecie) comedian, comic

komiks *m* (historyjka) comic strip, cartoon (strip); (wydawnictwo) comic

komin *m* (budynku) chimney; (statku, lokomotywy) funnel, smokestack; **fabryczne ~y** factory chimneys; **kopcić** a. **palić jak ~** pot. to smoke like a chimney

komin|ek *m* [] (palenisko) fireplace [] przen. (spotkanie) soireé

kominiar|ka *f* balaclava (helmet)

kominiarz *m* chimney sweep

komis *m* [] pot. (sklep) second-hand shop [] (pośrednictwo) commission sale

komisaria|t *m* (posterunek) police station; (obszar) police district

komisarz *m* [] (w policji) (police) commissioner GB, (police) superintendent GB [] (urzędnik) officer; **wysoki ~** high commissioner

komisj|a *f* [] committee, commission; (lekarska, egzaminacyjna) board; **~a rewizyjna** a review board a. body; **~a sędziowska** a panel of judges; **zasiadać w ~i** to sit on a committee [] pot. (posiedzenie) committee meeting [] (urząd) commission, department; **Komisja Europejska** European Commission

komisyjn|y *adi. [zebranie]* committee, board; **zdawać egzamin ~y** to take an exam before a board

komite|t *m* committee

komizm *m* humour GB, humor US, comedy; ~ **tej sytuacji** the funny side of the situation

komna|ta *f* chamber

kom|oda *f* chest of drawers GB, bureau US

kom|ora *f* [] (pomieszczenie) chamber [] Anat. ventricle

❏ **~ora celna** customs (house); **~ora gazowa** gas chamber

komorn|e *n* rent

komorni|k *m* debt collector, bailiff

komór|ka *f* [] (schowek) cubbyhole; **~ka na węgiel** a coal-hole [] Biol. cell; **~ka jajowa** an egg (cell) [] (w organizacji) section [] pot. (telefon) mobile (phone) GB, cellphone US

■ **szare ~ki** pot. grey matter pot.

kompak|t *m* pot. [] (płyta) CD, compact disc [] (odtwarzacz) CD player

kompaktow|y *adi. [lampa, świetlówka]* compact; **płyta ~a** a compact disc, a CD; **odtwarzacz ~y** a compact disc a. CD player

kompan *m* pot. (kolega) mate GB, buddy US pot.

kompani|a *f* Wojsk. company; **~a reprezentacyjna** a guard of honour

kompas *m* compass

kompetencj|a *f* książk. [] (uprawnienia) authority, competence; **przekroczyć swoje ~e** to act outside one's authority, to overstep one's authority; **ta sprawa nie leży w ich ~ach** this matter falls outside their competence a. jurisdiction ② (facho-wość) competence

kompetentn|y *adi.* książk. *[lekarz]* competent, qualified; *[źródła, informacje]* reliable

kompleks *m* ① (poczucie niepewności) complex; **mieć ~ na punkcie czegoś** to have a complex about sth; **wpaść w ~y** to develop a complex; **robić coś bez ~ów** to have no inhibitions about doing sth; **~ niższości** inferiority complex ② (budynków, witamin, leśny) complex; **~ sportowy** a sports centre

kompleksow|y *adi.* książk. *[badania, rozwój]* comprehensive, extensive

komplemen|t *m* compliment; **powiedzieć komuś ~t** to pay sb a compliment; **prawić komuś ~ty** to compliment sb

komplement|ować *impf vt* to compliment

komple|t *m* ① (zestaw) set; **~t mebli** a furniture suite; **~t do kawy/herbaty** a coffee/tea service; **~t sędziowski** Prawo the bench ② (całość) full complement; **jesteśmy w ~cie** everybody's here; **na widowni był ~t widzów** the auditorium was filled to capacity a. completely full

kompletn|y *adi.* ① (pełny) *[wyposażenie, lista]* complete ② pot. *[pomyłka, ciemność]* complete

komplet|ować *impf vt* (zbierać) to assemble *[pracowników, zespół]*; **~ować listę gości** to draw up a list of guests; **~ować księgozbiór** to add to a book collection

komplikacj|a *f* complication

komplik|ować *impf* Ⅰ *vt* to complicate

Ⅱ **komplikować się** *[sprawa, problem]* to become complicated

kompon|ować *impf* Ⅰ *vt* ① Muz. to compose *[muzykę, melodię]* ② (tworzyć) to arrange *[bukiet]*; **~ować barwy** to match colours

Ⅱ **komponować się** (pasować) to match (**z czymś** sth)

kompo|st *m* compost

kompo|t *m* ① Kulin. compote; **~t z wiśni** cherry compote ② pot. (narkotyk) Polish heroin pot. *(poppy straw extract)*

kompozycj|a *f* composition; **~a kwiatowa** a flower arrangement

kompozyto|r *m*, **~rka** *f* composer

kompres *m* compress

kompromis *m* compromise; **pójść na ~ w sprawie czegoś** to compromise on sth

kompromit|ować *impf* Ⅰ *vt* ① (ośmieszać) to expose [sb] to ridicule, to embarrass ② (demaskować) to compromise; **~ujące dokumenty** compromising documents

Ⅱ **kompromitować się** (ośmieszać się) to compromise oneself

kompute|r *m* computer

komputerow|iec *m* pot. computer expert; computer man pot.

komputerow|y *adi. [program, gra]* computer; **~e badanie wzroku** a computerized eye examination

komunaln|y *adi. [mieszkanie, budownictwo]* council; **cmentarz ~y** a municipal cemetery

komuni|a *f* (Holy) Communion

komunikacj|a *f* ① (transport) transport, communication(s); **~a miejska** public transport ② książk. (łączność) communications ③ książk. (porozumiewanie się) communication; **~a wzrokowa** eye contact

komunikacyjn|y *adi. [linia, sieć, węzeł]* communications; *[satelita, pasma]* communication(s)

komunika|t *m* announcement, communiqué; **~t prasowy** a press announcement

komunik|ować *impf* Ⅰ *vt* książk. to announce, to communicate

Ⅱ **komunikować się** to communicate (**z kimś** with sb)

komuni|sta *m*, **~stka** *f* communist

komunistyczn|y *adi.* communist

komunizm *m* communism

kom|ża *f* surplice

kona|ć *impf vi* książk. to die także przen.; **~ć ze zmęczenia/śmiechu** przen. to die of fatigue/laughter

kona|r *m* limb, bough

koncentracyjn|y *adi.* **obóz ~y** a concentration camp

koncentra|t *m* concentrate; **~t pomidorowy** tomato concentrate

koncentr|ować *impf* Ⅰ *vt* książk. to concentrate *[wysiłki]*; **~ować uwagę na czymś** to fix a. focus one's attention on sth

Ⅱ **koncentrować się** ① (skupiać uwagę) *[osoba]* to concentrate (**na czymś** on sth); (dotyczyć) *[dyskusja]* to centre GB, to center US, (**na czymś** around a. on sth); to concentrate (**na czymś** on sth) ② (gromadzić się) *[wojsko, ludność]* to concentrate ③ (być skupionym) *[handel, przemysł]* to be concentrated

koncepcj|a *f* conception, concept; **mieć ~ę czegoś** to have a conception of sth

koncern *m* concern

koncer|t *m* ① (impreza) concert ② (utwór) concerto ③ przen. (popis) virtuoso a. bravura performance ❑ **~t życzeń** pot. listeners' choice

koncert|ować *impf vi [orkiestra, artysta]* to give concerts/a concert

koncertow|y *adi.* ① *[skrzypce, fortepian]* concert ② *[suita]* concerto ③ przen. *[gra, interpretacja]* virtuoso

koncesj|a *f* ① (zezwolenie) concession; **mieć ~ę na sprzedaż alkoholu** to be licensed to sell alcohol ② książk. (ustępstwo) concession; **czynić ~e na rzecz kogoś/czegoś** to make concessions to sb/sth

kondensato|r *m* ① Elektr. capacitor ② Chem., Techn. condenser

kondens|ować *impf* Ⅰ *vt* ① książk. (czynić zwięzłym) to condense *[treść, tekst]* ② (zagęszczać) to condense

[mleko, przetwory] ③ to condense, to precipitate *[gaz, parę]*
Ⅱ **kondensować się** *[gaz, para]* to condense, to precipitate
kondolencj|e *plt* condolences
kondo|r *m* Zool. condor
konduk|t *m* cortège, funeral procession
kondukto|r *m* conductor, guard
konduktor|ka *f* ① conductress ② (torebka) accordion bag
kondycj|a *f* ① (stan fizyczny) condition, form; **utrzymywać ∼ę** to keep fit ② (stan ekonomiczny) position, situation
konese|r *m*, **∼rka** *f* connoisseur
konew|ka *f* watering can
konfekcj|a *f* (odzież) (ready-to-wear) clothing; **∼a damska/męska** women's/men's wear
konferansje|r *m* master of ceremonies, MC; emcee US pot.
konferencj|a *f* conference
konfesjona|ł *m* confessional
konfiska|ta *f* confiscation
konfisk|ować *impf vt* to confiscate *[majątek, pisma]*
konfitu|ra *f* preserve; **smażyć ∼ry** to make preserves
konflik|t *m* conflict; **∼t zbrojny** an armed conflict; **∼t charakterów** a personality clash; **∼t pokoleń** the generation gap
konfliktow|y *adi. [osoba]* confrontational, contentious; *[sprawa, sytuacja]* contentious, controversial
konfrontacj|a *f* książk. confrontation; **w ∼i z kimś/czymś** in comparison with sb/sth
kongres *m* congress
koniak *m* cognac
koniczyn|a *f* clover
ko|niec *m* ① (finał) end; **koniec świata** the end of the world; **dobiec końca** to come to an end; **mieć się ku końcowi** to be drawing to an end a. a close; **bez końca** endlessly; **i tak bez końca** and so on ad infinitum; **trwać bez końca** to last a. take forever; **do końca roku/miesiąca** by the end of the year/month; **zostać do samego końca** to stay to the very end; **doprowadzić coś do końca** to bring sth to a (successful) conclusion; **nie do końca rozumiem** I don't quite understand; **do końca świata** until a. till the end of time; **do końca życia** a. **swoich dni** to a. until one's dying day, to the end of one's days; **i (na tym) koniec** (and) that's final; (and) that's that a. flat GB; **koniec (i) kropka** that's the end of it, full stop GB; period US pot.; **koniec końców** pot. (wreszcie) in the end; (ostatecznie) after all; **na koniec** (wreszcie) in the end, finally; (na zakończenie) finally, lastly; **na samym końcu** at the very end, last of all; **pod koniec maja/roku** toward(s) the end of May/the year; **w końcu**

(wreszcie) in the end, finally; (ostatecznie) after all; **z końcem maja/roku** at the end of May/the year; **na dzisiaj koniec** that's it a. all for today; **od dziś koniec z paleniem!** as from today, no more smoking! a. it's goodbye to smoking! ② (zakończenie) ending; **zaskakujący koniec filmu** the film's surprise ending a. surprising conclusion ③ (najdalszy punkt) end; **drugi koniec miasta** the other a. far end of town; **na samym końcu ogrodu** at the very end of the garden; **na końcu książki** at the back of the book; **na końcu listy** at the end a. bottom of the list; **pojechać na koniec świata** to go to the ends of the earth; **od końca do końca** from end to end ④ (czubek) (języka, palca) tip, end; (noża, igły) point; (ołówka) tip, point ⑤ (końcówka) end; **to koniec zapasów** that's the end of the supplies ⑥ książk. (śmierć) end; **czuł, że jego koniec jest bliski** he felt the end was near
koniecznoś|ć *f* necessity, need; **w razie ∼ci** if the need arises, in case of necessity; **z ∼ci** (z przymusu) from a. out of necessity
konieczn|y *adi. grad.* necessary; **∼e jest, żeby...** it is necessary that...; **jeżeli okaże się to ∼e** if it proves a. should it prove necessary
konik *m* ① pot. (o osobie) (ticket) tout GB; scalper US pot. ② pot. (ulubione zajęcie) hobby; (ulubiony temat) hobby horse, pet subject
❑ **∼ morski** sea horse; **∼ polny** grasshopper
koniugacj|a *f* conjugation
koniunktu|ra *f* economic situation; **zła/dobra ∼ra** a slump/a boom in the economy; **∼ra na coś** the demand for sth; **przy obecnej ∼rze** in the present a. current economic climate
konklud|ować *impf vi* książk. to conclude; **∼ując...** to conclude a. in conclusion...
konkluzj|a *f* książk. conclusion
konkre|t *m* concrete fact; **przejdźmy do ∼tów** (do faktów) let's get down to facts; (do szczegółów) let's get down to business a. specifics
konkretn|y *adi. grad.* ① (rzeczowy) *[osoba]* matter-of-fact, businesslike, nononsense ② (precyzyjny) *[wskazówki]* precise, exact ③ pot. (znaczny) considerable; **zjeść coś ∼ego** to eat something solid a. substantial ④ (określony) specific; **w tym ∼ym przypadku** in this particular case a. instance ⑤ (realny) *[zagrożenie]* real; *[dowody, pomoc]* concrete
konkretyz|ować *impf* książk. Ⅰ *vt* ① (uszczegółowić) to specify ② (realizować) to carry out, to realize *[plany]* Ⅱ **konkretyzować się** *[plany]* to take shape, to materialize; *[marzenia]* to be realized, to come true
konkub|ent, **∼in** *m* common-law husband
konkubin|a *f* common-law wife
konkubina|t *m* common-law marriage; **żyć w ∼cie** to cohabit książk.; to live together as husband and wife
konkurencj|a *f* ① (rywalizacja) competition; **∼a firm krajowych i zagranicznych** competition

between domestic and foreign companies ② (konkurenci) competitors, competition; **być ~ą dla kogoś/czegoś** to compete with sb/sth ③ Sport event
konkurencyjn|y adi. [firma] rival, competing; [oferta] competitive; [cena] competitive, keen GB
konkur|ować impf vi to compete (**z kimś/czymś** against a. with sb/sth); **~ować o coś** to compete for sth
konkurs m (pianistyczny, krzyżówkowy) competition; (tańca, literacki) competition, contest; (piosenki) contest; **~ piękności** a beauty contest a. pageant US; **~ skoków narciarskich** a ski jump event; **poza ~em** (brać udział) without competing, as an unofficial competitor; hors concours książk.
konkursow|y adi. competition; **prace ~e** (competition) entries; **komisja ~a** a judging panel
konno adv. [jechać] (on) horseback
konn|y adi. horse GB, horseback US; **~a przejażdżka** a horse ride GB, a horseback ride US; **jazda ~a** horse riding GB, horseback riding US; **policja ~a** mounted police; **~y wóz** a horse-drawn cart; **wyścigi ~e** horse racing
konsekwencj|a f ① (następstwo) consequence; **mieć poważne ~e** to have serious consequences ② (logiczna ciągłość) ramification ③ (w działaniu) consistency
■ **wyciągnąć ~e** (ukarać) to take appropriate measures (**wobec kogoś** against sb)
konsekwentn|y adi. [postępowanie, polityka] consistent
konserw|a f① Kulin. tinned food GB, canned food US; **~a mięsna/rybna** tinned meat/fish ② (puszka) tin GB, can US ③ pot. (konserwatyści) diehards
konserwacj|a f (dzieł sztuki, zabytków) conservation, restoration; (sprzętu, urządzeń) maintenance
konserwato|r m (dzieł sztuki) conservator, restorer; (sprzętu) maintenance person, technician
konserwatori|um n (music) conservatoire GB, (music) conservatory US
konserwaty|sta m, **~stka** f conservative
konserwatywn|y adi. conservative
konserw|ować impf ① vt ① (zabezpieczać) to conserve, to restore [zabytki, dzieła sztuki]; to maintain [maszyny, broń] ② (przetwarzać) to preserve [mięso, warzywa]
Ⅱ **konserwować się** (o żywności) to keep (well)
konserwowan|y adi. tinned GB, canned US; [śledzie, ogórki] pickled
konserwow|y adi. [mięso, warzywa, owoce] tinned GB, canned US
konsol|a f① (stolik) console table ② Techn. console, control desk a. panel
konsorcj|um n consortium
konspek|t m summary, synopsis
konspiracj|a f ① (tajna działalność) underground activity, clandestine activity ② (ruch) the resistance (movement) ③ przen. secrecy

konspiracyjn|y adi. [ruch, działacz] underground; [działanie, zebranie] clandestine; [walka] resistance; [szept] conspiratorial
konspirato|r m, **~rka** f (spiskowiec) conspirator; (podziemny) underground activist
konspir|ować impf ① vi (spiskować) to conspire (**przeciw komuś/czemuś** against sb/sth)
Ⅱ **konspirować się** to hide out; przen. to put on a false front, to hide one's true colours
konsternacj|a f książk. consternation, dismay
konstrukcj|a f① (struktura) structure; **~a budynku** the structure of a building ② (przedmiot) construction, structure ③ (tworzenie) construction, building
konstrukto|r m, **~rka** f designer
konstru|ować impf vt ① (budować) to construct [most, maszynę] ② (tworzyć) to formulate [tekst, teorię]; to put together, to form [koalicję]; to draw up [umowę, budżet]
konstytucj|a f constitution
konsul m consul
konsula|t m consulate
konsultacj|a f① (porada, opinia) counsel, advice ② (naradzanie się) consultation; **prowadzić ~e wśród...** to hold consultations among...
konsultan|t m, **~tka** f consultant
konsult|ować impf ① vt ① (zasięgać opinii) to consult; **~ować coś z kimś** to consult (with) sb about sth ② (wydawać opinię) to act as (a) consultant on [projekt, scenariusz]
Ⅱ **konsultować się** (naradzać się) to consult (**z kimś** with sb)
konsumen|t m książk. ① (nabywca) consumer, customer; (w restauracji) patron, customer ② (użytkownik) consumer, user; **~ci literatury** the public for literature
konsum|ować impf vt książk. ① (jeść) to consume, to eat [żywność]; to consume, to drink [napoje] ② (zużywać) to consume, to use (up) [węgiel, energię]
konsumpcj|a f książk. (spożycie) consumption
konsyli|um n Med. case (management) conference
konsystencj|a f książk. consistency
kontak|t m ① (styczność) contact; **mieć ~t z kimś** to be in contact a. touch with sb; **nawiązać ~t z kimś** to get in touch with sb; **ożywione ~ty towarzyskie** an active social life ② (przełącznik) (light) switch ③ (gniazdko) socket
kontakt|ować impf ① vt (pośredniczyć) to put [sb] in touch (**z kimś** with sb)
Ⅱ vi pot. ① [urządzenie elektryczne] to be connected; **żarówka nie ~uje** the bulb is loose ② pot. (rozumieć) **nie ~ować** to be completely out of it pot.
Ⅲ **kontaktować się** (nawiązywać kontakt) to get in touch (**z kimś** with sb); (utrzymywać kontakty) to be in touch (**z kimś** with sb)
kontek|st m context
kontemplacj|a f książk. contemplation

kontempl|ować *impf vt* [1] (oglądać) to contemplate *[obraz, krajobraz]* [2] (rozmyślać) to ponder, to reflect on

kontene|r *m* container; (zawartość) container(ful)

kontenerow|iec *m* container ship

kontest|ować *impf vt* książk. to rebel against

kon|to *n* account; **na ~cie** in one's account; **wyciąg z ~ta** a bank statement; **sprawdzić stan ~ta** to check the balance of one's account
■ **mieć coś na (swoim) ~cie** to have sth to one's credit; **zapisać coś na czyjeś ~to** to give sb the credit for sth

kont|ra [] *f* [1] (riposta) objection (**przeciw czemuś** to a. against sth); opposition (**przeciw czemuś** to sth) [2] Sport (w boksie) counter(punch); (w grach zespołowych) counter-attack [3] (w brydżu) double
[II] *praef.* versus; **rozum ~ra uczucie** thought versus feeling

kontrabas *m* double bass

kontrafał|da *f* box pleat

kontrahen|t *m* contracting party; (wykonawca, dostawca) contractor; (klient) client

kontrak|t *m* (umowa) contract; **~t na dostawę czegoś** a contract for the supply of sth; **zawrzeć z kimś ~t** to enter into a contract with sb; **być zatrudnionym na ~cie** to be a contract worker; **być na ~cie** pot. to work abroad

kontrakt|ować *impf vt* to contract for the supply of a. to supply *[zboże, ziemniaki, owoce]*

kontraktow|y *adi.* *[cena, warunki]* contractual; **pracownik ~y** a contract worker

kontrapunk|t *m* counterpoint

kontrargumen|t *m* counter-argument

kontra|st *m* contrast (**między czymś a czymś** between sth and sth); **stanowić ~st z czymś** to stand in contrast to sth

kontrast|ować *impf* [] *vt* (przeciwstawiać) to contrast, to juxtapose *[kolory, cechy]*
[II] *vi* (odróżniać się) to contrast (**z czymś** with sth); **~ujące kolory** contrasting colours

kontrastow|y *adi.* *[kolory, postawy]* contrasting; *[film, zdjęcie]* high-contrast

kontratak *m* counter-attack

kontrol|a *f* [1] (sprawdzanie) inspection, check; **~a biletów** ticket inspection; **~a antydopingowa** a drug test; **~a osobista** a body search; **~a radarowa** a speed a. radar trap; **~a paszportowa** passport control [2] (władza) control (**nad czymś** over sth)

kontrole|r *m*, **~rka** *f* inspector, controller; **~r biletów** a ticket inspector; **~r ruchu lotniczego** an air traffic controller

kontrol|ka *f* pot. [1] (lampka) indicator light [2] (notatnik) record book

kontroln|y *adi.* *[przyrząd, urządzenie]* testing, monitoring; *[jazda, lot]* test; *[pakiet, udział]* controlling

kontrol|ować *impf* [] *vt* [1] (sprawdzać) to inspect, to check; (stale) to monitor; **~ować stan pacjenta** to monitor a patient's condition [2] (kierować) to control *[rynek, firmę]*; **poślizg ~owany** a controlled slide a. skid [3] (panować) to control *[reakcje, emocje]*; **~ować sytuację** to be in control of the situation
[II] **kontrolować się** [1] (panować nad sobą) to control oneself [2] (sprawdzać się wzajemnie) to check on one another

kontrwywia|d *m* counterintelligence, counterespionage

kontu|r *m* outline, contour

kontuzj|a *f* injury; **doznać ~i** to receive a. sustain an injury

kontuzj|ować *pf, impf vt* to injure

kontynen|t *m* [1] (część świata) continent [2] (Europa) the Continent

kontynentaln|y *adi.* [1] *[klimat, powietrze, fauna]* continental [2] (europejski) Continental

kontynu|ować *impf* [] *vt* [1] (wznawiać) to continue *[pracę, dyskusję]* [2] (rozwijać) to carry on *[tradycję, obrzędy]*
[II] *vi* (mówić dalej) to continue; **proszę, niech pan ~uje** please continue

konwali|a *f* lily of the valley

konwencj|a *f* convention

konwencjonaln|y *adi.* *[uśmiech, gest]* polite, formal; *[symbole, pismo]* conventional

konwersacj|a *f* książk. conversation

konwersatori|um *n* Uniw. seminar

konwojen|t *m* (armed) guard, (armed) escort

konwoj|ować *impf vt* to escort *[statki]*; to convoy *[skazanych]*

konw|ój *m* convoy; **~ój z pomocą humanitarną** a humanitarian aid convoy

konwulsj|e *plt* convulsions; **dostać ~i** to go into convulsions

ko|ń *m* [1] Zool. horse; **koń pociągowy** a carthorse, a draught horse GB, a draft horse US; **koń wierzchowy** a. **pod wierzch** a riding horse, a saddle horse US; **jechać na koniu** to ride a horse; **wsiąść na a. dosiąść konia** to get on a. mount a horse; **zsiąść z konia** to dismount; **na koń!** to horse!; **być zdrowym jak koń** to have the constitution of a horse [2] Gry knight [3] Sport (vaulting) horse
❑ **koń mechaniczny** horsepower
■ **znać się jak łyse konie** pot. to know each other inside out pot.; **zrobić kogoś w konia** pot. to take sb for a ride, to con sb pot.; **koń by się uśmiał** it's enough to make a cat laugh; **darowanemu koniowi nie zagląda się w zęby** przysł. don't a. never look a gift horse in the mouth przysł.

końców|ka *f* [1] (zakończenie) end(ing) [2] (czubek) tip; (wymienna) attachment [3] (reszta) remainder, remnant [4] Sport finish [5] Jęz. ending

kończ|yć *impf* **▯** *vt* ▯ (doprowadzać do końca) to finish *[rozmowę, obiad]*; **już ~ę** I've almost finished ▢ (zamykać) to end, to close *[przemówienie, list]* (**czymś** with sth); **poczynając od..., a ~ąc na...** beginning with..., and ending with... ▣ Szkol. to finish, to complete *[szkołę, kurs]* ▤ (osiągać wiek) **w tym roku ~y 18 lat** he'll be 18 this year

▯▯ *vi* ▯ pot. (zrywać) to give up (**z kimś/czymś** sb/ sth) ▢ pot. (znaleźć się) to end up; **tacy jak on zwykle ~ą w więzieniu** his sort usually ends a. winds up in prison

▯▯▯ **kończyć się** ▯ *[wakacje, rok]* to end; **~yć się czymś** *[film, książka, zebranie]* to end with sth; **~yć się zwycięstwem** to end in victory ▢ (ograniczać się) to be limited; **jej rola ~y się na...** her role is limited to... ▣ (wyczerpywać się) *[zapasy, pieniądze]* to run out, to give out ▤ pot. (tracić umiejętności) to have had it, to be washed up a. finished pot.; **~yć się jako trener** to be washed up a. finished as a coach

kończyn|a *f* ▯ (człowieka) limb; **~y górne/dolne** the upper/lower limbs ▢ (zwierzęcia) leg; **~y przednie/tylne** the front/hind legs

koordynacj|a *f* coordination

koordynato|r *m*, **~rka** *f* coordinator

koordyn|ować *impf vt* to coordinate *[działania, pracę]*

kop|ać¹ *impf vt* ▯ (spulchniać) to dig *[ziemię]*; **~ać ogródek** to dig over a. up the garden ▢ (drążyć) to dig *[dół, studnię]* ▣ (wydobywać) to dig for, to mine for *[węgiel, rudę]*; to dig up *[ziemniaki, buraki]*

kop|ać² *impf* → **kopnąć**

kopal|nia *f* mine także przen.; **~nia węgla/soli** coal/salt mine; **~nia kredy/gliny** a chalk/clay pit; **~nia odkrywkowa** an opencast mine GB, a strip mine US; **~nia wiedzy/informacji** a mine of knowledge/information

kopar|ka *f* digger, excavator

kop|cić *impf* **▯** *vt* pot. to smoke *[papierosa, fajkę]* **▯▯** *vi* (dymić) *[świeca, komin]* to smoke **▯▯▯** **kopcić się** ▯ (dymić) *[świeca, lampa]* to smoke, to smoulder GB, to smolder US ▢ (palić się) to burn

kopciusz|ek *m* Cinderella

koper|ek *m* dill (weed)

koper|ta *f* ▯ (na list) envelope ▢ (w zegarku) watch case ▣ (torebka) clutch (bag) ▤ (poszwa) duvet cover *(with a square opening)*

kopi|a *f* copy; **jest wierną ~ą swojej matki** przen. she's the (very) image of her mother

kopiar|ka *f* ▯ (kserokopiarka) photocopier ▢ Fot. copying a. printing frame ▣ Audio, Kino copier

kop|iec *m* ▯ (usypisko) mound ▢ (do przechowywania warzyw) (storage) clamp

kopiej|ka *f* kope(c)k

kopi|ować *impf vt* ▯ (reprodukować) to copy *[obraz, rzeźbę]*; to copy, to duplicate *[testament, dokumenty]*; **~ować nagranie/płytę kompaktową** to make a copy of a recording/CD ▢ (naśladować) to copy, to

imitate *[osobę, zachowanie]* ▣ Fot. to make a print of *[odbitki, zdjęcia]*

kop|nąć *pf* — **kop|ać²** *impf vt* ▯ (uderzyć nogą) to kick *[osobę, piłkę]* ▢ pot. **~nął go prąd** he got a shock ▣ pot. *[karabin]* to kick pot.

kopniak *m* pot. kick; **dać komuś ~a** to give sb a kick; **dostać ~a** to get a kick

kopnię|ty *adi.* pot. *[osoba]* loony, batty pot.

kopulacj|a *f* copulation

kopul|ować *impf vi* to copulate

kopu|ła *f* dome, cupola

kopyt|ka *plt* Kulin. *dumplings made of mashed potatoes, eggs and flour*

kopy|to *n* ▯ (u zwierząt) hoof ▢ (szewskie) shoemaker's last ▣ pot. (stopa) trotter GB pot.; dog US **■ na jedno ~to** from the same mould; **ruszyć z ~ta** to take off like a shot pot.

ko|ra *f* ▯ (drzew) bark ▢ Anat. cortex ▣ Włók. seersucker

koral ▯ *m* ▯ (ozdoba) bead; **bursztynowe ~e** amber beads ▢ Zool. coral ▣ (kolor) coral **▯▯** **korale** *plt* (u indyka) wattle, dewlap

korb|a *f* Techn. crank

kor|cić *impf vi* **~ciło go, żeby powiedzieć prawdę** he was itching to tell the truth

kordon *m* ▯ (szpaler) cordon; **otoczyć coś ~em** to cordon sth off ▢ (na granicy) border posts

kordon|ek *m* (embroidery) floss, floss (silk), filoselle GB

kor|ek *m* ▯ (butelki) stopper, cork; **~ek od butelki** a bottle stopper; **zatkać butelkę ~kiem** to cork a bottle; **wyciągnąć ~ek** to uncork a bottle ▢ (surowiec) cork ▣ (but) cork-soled shoe ▤ (obcas) cork wedge heel ▥ pot. (uliczny) traffic jam ▦ pot. (bezpiecznik) fuse; **przepaliły się** a. **wysiadły ~ki** the fuses blew

korek|ta *f* ▯ (poprawianie) proofreading; **~ta autorska** an author's revision; **robić ~tę czegoś** to proofread sth; **oddać tekst do ~ty** to have a text proofread ▢ (poprawka) correction ▣ pot. (odbitka) proof; **czytać ~tę** to read proofs

korekto|r *m* ▯ (osoba) proofreader ▢ (do poprawiania błędów) white-out, correction fluid ▣ Kosmet. concealer

korektor|ka *f* proofreader

korepetycj|e *plt* (private) tuition GB, private lessons; **~e z matematyki** (private) tuition a. private lessons in maths

korepetyto|r *m*, **~rka** *f* (private) tutor, coach

korespondencj|a *f* ▯ (pisanie listów) correspondence ▢ (zbiór listów) correspondence; (porcja listów) post GB, mail; **przejrzeć ~ę** to go through one's post a. mail

koresponden|t *m*, **~tka** *f* correspondent

korespond|ować *impf vi* to correspond (**z kimś** with sb)

korkociąg *m* 1 (do butelek) corkscrew 2 Lotn. (w dół) spin, spiral dive; (w górę) corkscrew manoeuvre GB, corkscrew maneuver US

kormoran *m* cormorant

kornik *m* bark beetle, woodworm; **przeżarty przez** ~**i** worm-eaten

korniszon *m* cocktail gherkin

korod|ować *impf vt, vi* to corrode

koron|a *f* 1 (na głowie) crown; (diadem) tiara 2 (władza) crown; **zdobyć/stracić** ~**ę** to win/lose the crown 3 Stomat. cap; **wstawić sobie** ~**ę** to have a tooth crowned

koronacj|a *f* coronation

koron|ka *f* lace; ~**ki brukselskie** Brussels lace

koronn|y *adi.* 1 [*insygnia, ziemie*] crown 2 Prawo **być świadkiem** ~**ym** to turn Queen's/King's evidence GB, to turn state's evidence US

koron|ować *pf impf* 1 *vt* to crown [*władcę*]

1 **koronować się** 1 (zostać ukoronowanym) to be crowned 2 (dokonać własnej koronacji) to crown oneself

korow|ód 1 *m* procession

1 **korowody** *plt* (zabiegi) manoeuvring GB, maneuvering US; (ceregiele) fuss; **po długich** ~**odach** after a lot of fuss; **prawnicze** ~**ody** legal manoeuvring

korozj|a *f* corrosion; **odporny/podatny na** ~**ę** corrosion-proof/corrosion-prone

korporacj|a *f* corporation

korpulentn|y *adi.* książk. [*osoba*] corpulent książk.

korpus *m* 1 (tułów) trunk, torso 2 (główna część) (statku) hull, (main) body; (silnika, budynku) (main) body 3 Wojsk. corps 4 Jęz. corpus

□ ~ **dyplomatyczny** the diplomatic corps

kor|t *m* Sport court

korump|ować *impf vt* to corrupt [*polityka, urzędnika*]

korupcj|a *f* corruption

koryg|ować *impf vt* to correct [*błąd, harmonogram*]

korytarz *m* 1 (w budynku) corridor, hall(way) US; **na** ~**u** in the corridor a. hall(way) 2 (tunel) corridor, tunnel; (w kopalni) gallery

kory|to *n* 1 (dla zwierząt) trough 2 (rzeki) (river) bed

korzenn|y *adi. [aromat, sos]* spice; **przyprawy** ~**e** spices

korze|ń 1 *m* root; **zapuścić** ~**nie** [*roślina*] to establish roots, to take root; przen. [*osoba, rodzina*] to put down roots

1 **korzenie** *plt* 1 Kulin. (przyprawy) spices 2 (pochodzenie) roots

korz|yć się *impf v refl.* książk. to humble oneself (**przed kimś** before sb)

korzysta|ć *impf vi* 1 (używać) to use; ~**ć z czegoś** to use sth; ~**ć z czyichś rad** to take sb's advice; ~**ć z czyichś usług** to make use of sb's services 2 (wykorzystywać) to take advantage (**z czegoś** of sth); ~**ć z okazji** to make the most of an opportunity; **robić karierę,** ~**jąc ze znajomości** to build one's career thanks to one's connections 3 (mieć prawo)

~**ć z przywileju/prawa** to exercise a privilege/right; ~**ć ze stypendium** to receive a grant 4 (odnosić korzyści) to benefit (**na czymś** from sth)

korzystn|y *adi. grad. [oferta]* attractive, tempting; [*położenie, sytuacja*] beneficial, favourable GB, favorable US; [*wrażenie*] favourable GB, favorable US

korzyś|ć *f* 1 (pożytek) benefit; ~**ci płynące z czegoś** the benefits of a. accruing from sth; **wyjść komuś na** ~**ć** to work to sb's advantage a. benefit; **ograniczyć coś na** ~**ć czegoś** to reduce sth in favour of sth; **przemawiać na czyjąś** ~**ć** to reflect well on a. to speak well of sb; **zmienić się na** ~**ć** [*osoba*] to change for the better; **porówna-nie wypadło na naszą** ~**ć** the comparison was in our favour 2 (zysk) profit, benefit; **czerpać** ~**ci z czegoś** to profit a. benefit from sth; **sprzedać coś z** ~**cią** to sell sth at a profit

kos *m* Zool. blackbird

kos|a *f* (narzędzie) scythe

kosa|ciec *m* Bot. iris, flag

kosiar|ka *f* 1 (maszyna rolnicza) mower, reaper 2 (do trawników) lawn mower

ko|sić *impf vt* (ścinać) to reap [*zboże*]; (kosą) to scythe; (maszyną) to mow [*trawę, trawnik*]

kosma|ty *adi.* [*gąsienica, zwierzę*] hairy; [*zwierzę, włosy*] shaggy; [*materiał, ręcznik*] fleecy; ~**te myśli** pot. naughty thoughts pot.

kosmetycz|ka *f* 1 (osoba) beautician, cosmetician US 2 (torebka) vanity case a. bag

kosmetyczn|y *adi.* 1 [*artykuł, preparat*] cosmetic; **zabieg/gabinet** ~**y** a beauty treatment/parlour 2 przen. [*prace, zmiana*] cosmetic

kosmetyk *m* cosmetic; ~**i** (do mycia) toiletries; ~**i do pielęgnacji włosów** hair-care products

kosmiczn|y *adi.* 1 (pozaziemski) [*promieniowanie, materia*] cosmic; [*podróż, statek*] space 2 (nie do ogarnięcia) [*problem, dramat*] tremendous

kosmi|ta *m,* ~**tka** *f* alien

kosmonau|ta *m,* ~**tka** *f* astronaut; (rosyjski) cosmonaut

kosmopoli|ta *m,* ~**tka** *f* cosmopolitan, cosmopolite

kosmos *m* 1 (przestrzeń pozaziemska) outer space; **lot w** ~ a space flight 2 (wszechświat) universe, cosmos

kosmyk *m* lock a. strand of hair

kos|odrzewina, ~**ówka** *f* dwarf mountain pine

kostium *m* 1 (ubranie) (skirt) suit 2 (przebranie) costume 3 Sport kit GB; ~ **gimnastyczny** gym kit; ~ **kąpielowy** a swimming costume

kostiumow|y *adi.* Teatr costume; **próba** ~**a** a dress rehearsal

kost|ka *f* 1 (w szkielecie) (small) bone 2 (w nodze) ankle bone; (nad nadgarstkiem) wrist bone; (w zaciśniętej pięści) knuckle; **sukienka do** ~**ek** an ankle-length dress 3 Gry dice; ~**ki domina** dominoes 4 (kształt) cube; ~**ka masła** a packet of butter; **złożyć coś**

w ~**kę** to fold sth (up) neatly 5 Budow. (do brukowania) sett (stone), paving block

kostnic|a *f* mortuary, morgue

kostni|eć *impf vi* 1 (marznąć) *[osoba, część ciała]* to go numb, to freeze 2 (nie ulegać zmianom) to become ossified książk. 3 Anat. *[tkanka]* to ossify

kostn|y *adi. [szpik, układ]* bone; **mączka** ~**a** bonemeal

kosz *m* 1 (pojemnik) basket; (zawartość) basket(ful) 2 (na śmieci) waste-paper basket GB, wastebasket US, waste a. rubbish bin GB 3 (plażowy) (roofed wicker) beach chair 4 (przy motocyklu) sidecar 5 Sport (obręcz, celny rzut) basket 6 pot. (koszykówka) basketball

■ **dać komuś** ~**a** to turn sb down; **dostać** ~**a** to be a. get turned down

koszar|y *plt* barracks

koszma|r *m* (zły sen) nightmare także przen.

kosz|t *m* cost, expense; **na czyjś** ~**t** at sb's expense; ~**tem wyrzeczeń** with a certain amount of sacrifice; ~**tem zdrowia** at the expense a. cost of one's health; **małym** a. **tanim** ~**tem** (za niewielką cenę) at little cost; (bez trudu) with little effort

kosztorys *m* (cost) estimate

koszt|ować *impf vt* 1 (stanowić wartość) to cost; **ile to** ~**uje?** how much does it cost a. is it? 2 (wymagać) to cost; **to mnie** ~**owało wiele zdrowia** it was a nerve-racking experience; **uprzejmość nic nie** ~**uje** it doesn't cost anything to be polite 3 książk. (próbować) to sample, to taste (**coś** a. **czegoś** sth)

kosztowności *plt* valuables

kosztown|y *adi. grad. [naszyjnik, pierścionek]* expensive, costly; *[błąd, pomyłka]* costly, expensive

koszul|a *f* shirt; ~**a nocna** nightdress

koszul|ka *f* 1 (bez rękawów) sleeveless top, vest; (z krótkim rękawem) T-shirt 2 (osłona) cover, wrapper; **plastikowe** ~**ki na dokumenty** plastic sleeves for holding documents

koszyk *m* (pojemnik) basket; (zawartość) basket(ful)

koszyka|rz *m*, ~**rka** *f* 1 Sport basketball player 2 (rzemieślnik) basket-maker, basket-weaver

koszyków|ka *f* basketball

kościeln|y 1 *adi. [dzwon, ślub]* church 2 *m* sexton

kościotrup *m* 1 pot., żart. (o osobie) walking skeleton pot. 2 (szkielet) skeleton

kości|ół *m* 1 (świątynia) church 2 (instytucja) **Kościół** the Church

kości|sty *adi.* bony

koś|ć 1 *f* Anat. bone 2 **kości** *plt* Gry dice

❑ ~**ć słoniowa** ivory

■ **kobieta/mężczyzna przy** ~**ci** a stout woman/man; ~**ć niezgody** książk. a bone of contention; **psia** ~**ć!** pot. damn it! pot.; **dać komuś w** ~**ć** (zmusić do wysiłku) to give sb a hard time pot.; (pokonać) to walk all over sb pot.; **dostać w** ~**ć** pot. (przegrać) to get clobbered pot.; (doświadczyć boleśnie) to have a hard

time (of it) pot.; **rozejść się po** ~**ciach** pot. *[sprawa]* to die a natural death; to blow over pot.; **zmarznąć na** ~**ć** pot. to be frozen a. chilled to the bone; ~**ci zostały rzucone** the die is cast

koślaw|y *adi.* 1 (krzywy) *[buty]* misshapen; *[litery]* crooked, lopsided 2 pot. (nieudolny) *[styl, polszczyzna]* sloppy, slovenly

ko|t 1 *m* cat

2 **koty** *plt* pot. (kurz) balls of dust

■ **bawić się z kimś jak kot z myszką** to play cat and mouse with sb; **drzeć z kimś koty** to be at loggerheads a. at daggers drawn with sb; **mieć kota na punkcie czegoś** pot. to be mad about sth pot.; **tyle, co kot napłakał** next to nothing

kota|ra *f* (heavy) curtain, drape US

kot|ka 1 *f* (samica kota) (female) cat, she-cat

2 **kotki** *plt* (bazie) (willow) catkins

kotle|t *m* cutlet, chop; ~**t schabowy** a pork cutlet a. chop; ~**t mielony** a rissole

kotlin|a *f* valley, basin

kotłowni|a *f* (pomieszczenie) boiler room; (budynek) boiler house

kotwic|a *f* anchor

kowad|ło *n* anvil

kowal *m* (black)smith; (kujący konia) farrier

kowboj *m* cowboy

kowboj|ka *f* cowboy boot

k|oza *f* 1 Zool. goat 2 pot. (piecyk) ≈ pot-bellied stove 3 pot. (więzienie) the clink pot. 4 pot. (z nosa) bog(e)y GB, booger US pot. 5 (dziewczyna) young girl; **głupia koza** a silly goose pot. 6 Muz. bagpipe(s)

■ **przyszła koza do woza** so you want my help now, do you? iron.; **raz kozie śmierć!** pot. you (can) only die once, right? pot.

koza|k *m* 1 Hist. (żołnierz) Cossack 2 (ryzykant) daredevil, swashbuckler 3 (taniec) Cossack dance 4 (but) (knee-high) boot 5 Bot. birch bolete (mushroom)

kozet|ka *f* couch

kozic|a *f* chamois

ko|zioł *m* 1 Zool. (samiec kozy) (billy) goat; (samiec sarny) buck 2 (dla woźnicy) (coachman's) box, coachman's seat 3 (przyrząd gimnastyczny) horse, (vault) buck

■ **fiknąć kozła** pot. (zrobić przewrót) to turn a. do a somersault; (wywrócić się) to come a cropper GB pot.; to take a tumble a. spill

kozioł|ek *m* (przewrót) somersault; **fikać** a. **wywracać** ~**ki** to turn a. do somersaults

koziołk|ować *impf vi [kaskader, sportowiec]* to somersault; (bezwładnie) *[osoba]* to take a tumble a. spill; *[zwierzę]* to tumble; *[samochód]* to roll over, to somersault

Kozioroż|ec *m* Capricorn

kozioroż|ec *m* ibex

kozł|ować *impf* Sport 1 *vt* to dribble *[piłkę]*

2 *vi* 1 *[zawodnik]* to dribble 2 *[piłka]* to bounce

koźl|ę *n* kid
kożuch *m* [1] (skóra) sheepskin; (ubranie) sheepskin coat; (krótki) sheepskin jacket [2] (na powierzchni) film, coat(ing); (w mleku) skin
kół|ko [] *n* [1] (w pojeździe, maszynie) wheel; ~**ko zębate** a cogwheel [2] (figura geometryczna) circle, ring; **w** ~**ko** (po okręgu) *[jeździć, chodzić]* in circles; (wokół własnej osi) *[kręcić się, obracać się]* (around and) around; (ciągle) *[powtarzać, robić]* over and over, all the time; **wziąć coś w** ~**ko** to circle sth; **ustawić się w** ~**ko** to form a circle [3] (pierścień) ring; ~**ko od kluczy** a key ring [4] Szkol. club, circle; ~**ka zainteresowań** activity clubs, special-interest groups
[] **kółka** *plt* Sport rings
■ **cztery** ~**ka** pot. (samochód) wheels pot.; ~**ko i krzyżyk** noughts and crosses GB, tic-tac-toe US; **siedzieć za** ~**kiem** pot. to be behind the wheel
kpiarz *m* mocker, scoffer
kpi|ć *impf vi* to jeer (**z kogoś** at sb); to mock (**z kogoś** sb); ~**ć sobie z przepisów** to thumb one's nose at the regulations
kpin|a *f* mockery, ridicule; **robić sobie z kogoś/czegoś** ~**y** to mock (at) a. jibe at sb/sth; **to były** ~**y, a nie proces** the trial was a mockery a. a farce
k|ra *f* (ice) floe
krab *m* crab
krach *m* (na giełdzie) crash; (firmy, gospodarki) crash, collapse
kracia|sty *adi.* *[materiał, ubranie, koc]* checked, chequered GB, checkered US
kradzież *f* theft; **towary pochodzące z** ~**y** stolen goods
kraj *m* [1] (państwo) country; **wiadomości z** ~**u i zagranicy** domestic and foreign news [2] (obszar) region
■ **co** ~, **to obyczaj** przysł. every country has its own customs
kraj|ać *impf vt* [1] (ciąć) to cut *[mięso, warzywa, blache]*; (na plasterki) to slice, to cut (into slices); ~**ać coś w kostkę** to cut sth into cubes, to dice a. cube sth [2] pot. *[chirurg]* to cut open pot. *[pacjenta]*
krajobraz *m* [1] (widok) landscape, scenery [2] Szt. (pejzaż) landscape
krajow|iec *m* indigenous a. native(-born) inhabitant; native pejor.
krajow|y *adi.* *[lot, rynek, sprawy]* domestic; *[konferencja, konkurs]* national
krajoznawcz|y *adi.* *[wycieczka]* tourist
kra|kać *impf vi* [1] *[kruk, wrona]* to caw [2] pot. (przepowiadać) **ciągle** ~**kał, że będzie wojna** he kept prophesying war
krakers *m* cracker
kraks|a *f* smash-up pot.; crash
kram *m* [1] (stragan) stall, stand [2] pot. (bałagan) clutter, mess [3] pot. (zamieszanie) bother; **było z tym sporo** ~**u** it was a right old to-do pot.

kran *m* [1] (z wodą) tap, faucet US; **umyć coś pod** ~**em** to wash sth under the tap [2] Techn. tap
kra|niec *m* (skraj) end; (miasta, pola) edge
krasnolud|ek *m* dwarf
kra|ść *impf vt* to steal
kra|ta *f* [1] (zabezpieczenie) grating, bars; (przegroda) grill(e), lattice [2] (wzór) check; **sukienka w** ~**tę** a check a. checked dress
■ **za** ~**tami** pot. behind bars pot.; **trafić za** ~**ty** pot. to end up a. wind up behind bars pot.
krate|r *m* crater
krat|ka *f* [1] (konstrukcja) screen, (small) grill(e); (w ogrodzie) trellis [2] (wzór) (na materiale) check; (na papierze) square ruling, grid; **spódnica w** ~**kę** a check a. checked skirt; **zeszyt w** ~**kę** a square-ruled exercise book [3] (w krzyżówce, formularzu) square
■ **w** ~**kę** pot. off and on, on and off pot.; **pogoda w** ~**kę** changeable weather, spotty weather US; **siedzieć za** ~**kami** pot. to be behind bars pot.; **trafić za** ~**ki** pot. to end up a. wind up behind bars pot.
kraul *m* (front) crawl (stroke)
krawa|t *m* tie, necktie US
krawcow|a *f* dressmaker, seamstress
krawę|dź *f* [1] (dachu, narty) edge; (przepaści) brink [2] przen. brink, verge
krawężnik *m* kerb GB, curb US
kraw|iec *m* [1] (rzemieślnik) tailor; ~**iec damski** a dressmaker, a ladies' a. women's tailor; ~**iec męski** a men's tailor [2] (projektant mody) designer, couturier
krawiectw|o *n* sewing, tailoring; ~**o damskie** women's tailoring, dressmaking; ~**o męskie** men's tailoring; ~**o miarowe** bespoke tailoring GB, custom tailoring
kr|ąg [] *m* [1] (koło) circle, ring; **samolot zatoczył krąg nad lotniskiem** the plane circled over the airport [2] (kształt) **krąg słoneczny** the Sun's disc [3] (obszar) sphere, range; **czyjś krąg zainteresowań** sb's sphere of interests; **literatura hiszpańskiego kręgu językowego** literature of the Spanish-speaking countries a. world [4] przen. (grono) circle, sphere; **krąg przyjaciół** sb's circle of friends; **krąg rodzinny** the family, the family circle [5] Anat. vertebra
[] **kręgiem** *adv.* (w koło) *[stanąć]* in a circle a. ring
[] **w krąg** *adv.* (dookoła) *[biegać, zasiąść]* (all) around
■ **zaczarowany** a. **zaklęty krąg** (w bajkach) a magic circle; (sytuacja) a vicious circle; **zataczać szerokie kręgi** to have wide-ranging effects, to spread far and wide
krąż|ek *m* [1] (kółko) (small) circle; ~**ki cebuli** onion rings; ~**ek kiełbasy** a slice of sausage; **pokroić coś w** ~**ki** to cut sth into slices [2] pot. (płyta) disc [3] Sport (hockey) puck
krążownik *m* cruiser

krąż|yć *impf vi* [1] (zataczać kręgi) to circle, to revolve; **planety ~ą wokół Słońca** the planets revolve around a. orbit (around) the Sun; **ptaki ~yły w powietrzu** birds were circling in the air [2] (przemieszczać się) **po mieście ~yły patrole policji** police patrols were cruising around town; **gospodyni ~yła wśród gości** the hostess circulated among the guests [3] (być podawanym) *[półmiski, zdjęcia]* to be passed a. handed round [4] (rozprzestrzeniać się) *[plotka, wiadomość]* to circulate, to go (a)round; to make the rounds pot. [5] (obiegać) *[krew, woda]* to circulate, to flow [6] (nie mówić wprost) to beat about the bush GB, to beat around the bush US pot.

kreacj|a *f* [1] (suknia) dress, gown; (z dodatkami) outfit; [2] Kino, Teatr performance, acting; **stworzył wybitną ~ę jako Hamlet** he was brilliant in the role of Hamlet [3] książk. (akt tworzenia) creation

kreato|r *m*, ~**rka** *f* książk. (baletu, sztuki) creator; (idei, teorii) originator; ~**r mody** a fashion designer

kreatu|ra *f* pot. louse pot.

kreatywn|y *adi.* książk. *[osoba, myślenie, umysł]* creative

kre|da *f* chalk

kredens *m* dresser, sideboard

kred|ka *f* [1] (do rysowania) coloured pencil GB, colored pencil US; ~**ki woskowe** a. **świecowe** (wax) crayons [2] Kosmet. (do ust) lipstick; (do oczu) eye pencil, eyeliner; (do brwi) eyebrow pencil

kredy|t *m* credit, loan; ~**t mieszkaniowy** a mortgage, a home loan; **wziąć** a. **zaciągnąć/spłacić ~t** to take out/pay off a loan; **kupić coś na ~t** to buy sth on credit

■ **uwierzyć komuś na ~t** to give sb the benefit of the doubt

kredytobiorc|a *m* borrower

kredytodawc|a *m* creditor, lender

krem *m* [1] Kulin. (deser) cream; (zupa) cream soup [2] Kosmet. cream

krematori|um *n* crematorium, crematory US

kremow|y *adi* [1] *[ciastko]* cream; **śmietana ~a** double a. whipping cream [2] *[bluzka]* cream, cream-coloured GB, cream-colored US

kre|ować *pf, impf* [] *vt* książk. [1] (tworzyć) to create *[dzieło, styl]* [2] (grać) *[aktor]* to play, to act *[rolę]*
[] **kreować się** to pose (**na coś** as sth); to fancy oneself pot. (**na coś** as sth)

krep|a *f* crêpe

kres|ka *f* [1] (linia) line, stroke; **oddzielić przeszłość grubą ~ką** przen. to put the past behind one [2] (znak graficzny) (myślnik) dash; (łącznik) hyphen; (nad literą) diacritic, (acute) accent [3] (w alfabecie Morse'a) dash [4] (na skali) degree

■ **być pod ~ką** pot. to be broke pot.; **kupować na ~kę** pot. to buy sth on tick a. on the cuff US pot.; **mieć u kogoś ~kę** pot. to be in the doghouse with sb pot.

kresków|ka *f* pot. cartoon

kreślarz *m* draughtsman, drafter US

kreśl|ić *impf vt* [1] (rysować) to draw *[mapę, wykres]* [2] (przekreślać) to cross out [3] (bazgrać) to scribble, to doodle [4] książk. (formułować) to envision *[plany, wizje]*

kre|t *m* mole

kreton *m* patterned cotton, cretonne, calico US

kretyn *m* pot. cretin pot.

kretyńs|ki *adi.* pot. *[pomysł, uśmiech]* moronic, idiotic pot.; *[fryzura, strój]* idiotic pot.

kr|ew *f* blood; **leci mi krew z nosa** my nose is bleeding; **krew odpłynęła jej z twarzy** the colour left her face; **w jego żyłach płynie kozacka krew** he has Cossack blood in his veins; **klacz czystej krwi arabskiej** a pure-bred Arabian a. Arab mare

■ **postać z krwi i kości** a full-blooded a. larger-than-life character; **aktor z krwi i kości** an actor to the core a. through and through; **krew z mlekiem** peaches and cream; **mieć gorącą krew** to be hot-tempered; **napsuć komuś krwi** to get on sb's nerves; **mrożący krew w żyłach** blood-curdling, blood-chilling; **wejść komuś w krew** to become second nature to sb; **krew się we mnie burzy** a. **krew mnie zalewa, kiedy...** it makes my blood boil a. it gets my blood up when...; **krew w nim zawrzała** it made his blood boil; **to mi idzie jak krew z nosa** pot. it's a real slog a. uphill struggle

krewet|ka *f* shrimp; (duża) prawn

krewnia|k *m*, ~**czka** *f* pot. relative, relation

krewn|y *m*, ~**a** *f* relative, relation; ~**y ze strony ojca/matki** a relative on one's father's/mother's side; ~**y po mieczu/po kądzieli** przest. a relative on the spear/distaff side przest.

krę|cić *impf* [] *vt* [1] Kulin. to mix, to beat *[ciasto, krem]*; to grind *[mak]* [2] (układać w loki) to curl *[włosy]* [3] Kino to shoot *[film]* [4] (zwijać) to twist *[linę, sznur]*; ~**cić papierosa** to roll a cigarette
[] *vi* [1] (obracać) to turn *[korbką]*; to twist *[gałką]*; to work *[pedałami]*; ~**cić głową nad czymś** to shake one's head (in dismay) over sth [2] (kołysać) ~**cić biodrami** to wiggle one's hips [3] pot. (flirtować) to carry on pot. (**z kimś** with sb) [4] pot. (kierować) **ona tu wszystkim ~ci** she runs the whole show pot. [5] pot. (oszukiwać) to hoodwink pot.
[] **kręcić się** [1] (obracać się) *[osoba]* to spin, to whirl; *[karuzela, wiatrak]* to spin, to turn; *[świat]* to turn; (wokół osi) to rotate; (wokół Słońca) to revolve [2] (wiercić się) to squirm [3] (przemieszczać się) to hang around a. about pot. [4] *[włosy]* to curl; **włosy jej się same ~cą** her hair is naturally curly [5] pot. (zabiegać o względy) ~**cić się koło** a. **wokół kogoś** to hang around sb pot. [6] pot. (dbać) ~**cić się koło czegoś** to see to sth [7] pot. (dotyczyć) *[rozmowa, życie]* to revolve (**wokół kogoś/czegoś** around sb/sth)

kręg *m* Anat. vertebra

kręg|iel [] *m* skittle
[] **kręgle** *plt* (gra) bowling; (w dziewięć kręgli) ninepins,

skittles GB; (w dziesięć kręgli) (tenpin) bowling, tenpins US

kręgielni|a *f* bowling alley

kręgosłup *m* ① Anat. spine, backbone ② przen. (charakter) backbone, spine; **przetrącić komuś** ~ to destroy sb's moral fibre

kręgow|iec *m* vertebrate

kręp|ować *impf* **[]** *vt* ① (żenować) *[osoba, sytuacja]* to make [sb] (feel) uncomfortable ② (ograniczać swobodę ruchów) *[gorset, spodnie]* to restrict; **ubranie mnie** ~**uje** my clothes are too tight ③ (związywać) to tie up *[osobę]*; to tie *[nogi, ręce]* ④ (ograniczać wolność) to hinder *[osobę, rozwój]*

[] **krępować się** to feel embarrassed a. uncomfortable; ~**ować się coś zrobić** to feel shy about doing sth; **nie** ~**uj się mną** don't mind me; **nie** ~**uj się, jedz!** don't be shy, tuck in! pot.

kręp|y *adi. [osoba, sylwetka]* chunky, stocky

krętacz *m*, ~**ka** *f* cheat, cheater US

krę|ty *adi. [droga, schody]* winding

krnąbrn|y *adi. grad. [dziecko, uczeń]* unruly, wayward

krochmal *m* starch

krochmal|ić *impf vt* to starch *[koszule, pościel]*

kroci|e *plt* książk. ① (majątek) fortune; **zarobić** ~**e (na czymś)** to make a fortune (on sth); **wydawać** ~**e (na coś)** to spend vast sums (on sth) ② (masa) multitudes

krocz|e *n* crotch

krocz|yć *impf vi* (stąpać) to stride; (maszerować) to march; ~**yć po raz obranej drodze** przen. to follow one's chosen path

krogul|ec *m* Zool. sparrowhawk

kr|oić *impf* **[]** *vi* ① (ciąć) to cut *[mięso, warzywa, deski]*; (na plasterki) to slice *[chleb, wędlinę]*; **kroić coś drobno** to chop sth finely ② *[krawiec]* to cut *[materiał, ubranie]* ③ pot. *[chirurg]* to cut open pot. *[pacjenta]*

[] **kroić się** pot. *[awantura]* to be about to happen; **kroi ci się długa podróż** you're in for a long journey

krok *m* ① (stąpnięcie) step; (odgłos) footstep; **iść** ~ **za** ~**iem** to go step by step a. one step at a time; ~ **po** ~**u zdobyłem jej zaufanie** little by little, I won her trust; **iść za kimś** ~ **w** ~ to be dogging sb a. sb's footsteps; **na każdym** ~**u** a. **co** ~ **widać było ślady wojny** the traces of war were visible at every turn; **ani** ~**u (dalej)!** don't move! ② (sposób chodzenia) walk, step; (tempo chodzenia) pace; ~ **defiladowy** the goose-step; **dotrzymywać komuś/czemuś** ~**u** to keep up with sb/sth także przen.; **równaj** ~**!** (rozkaz) get in step! ③ (w tańcu) step ④ (posunięcie) step, move ⑤ przen. (odległość) **mieszkać o parę** ~**ów od czegoś** to live (just) a stone's throw (away) from sth; **to dwa** ~**i stąd** it's just around the corner; it's just a hop, skip, and (a) jump from here pot.; **jesteśmy o** ~ **od zwycię-**

stwa victory is just around the corner; **on nie ustąpi ani na** ~ he won't budge an inch ⑥ (część ciała, spodni) crotch

krokie|t *m* ① Kulin. (w bułce tartej) croquette; (w naleśniku) pancake roll ② Sport croquet

krokodyl *m* crocodile

krokus *m* crocus

krom|ka *f* slice (of bread)

kroni|ka *f* chronicle; ~**ka filmowa** a newsreel

kronika|rz *m*, ~**rka** *f* chronicler

krop|ić[1] *impf* **[]** *vt* to sprinkle

[] *vi* ~**i deszcz** it's spitting GB a. sprinkling US

kropić[2] *impf* → **kropnąć**[2]

kropid|ło *n* aspergillum

krop|ka *f* ① (plamka) spot, dot; (na tkaninie) polka dot ② (znak interpunkcyjny) full stop, period US ③ (znak diakrytyczny) dot; „**z**" **z** ~**ką** a dotted 'z'; **ćwierćnuta z** ~**ką** a dotted crotchet GB, a dotted quarter note US ④ (w alfabecie Morse'a) dot

■ ~**ka w** ~**kę taka sama sukienka** pot. exactly the same dress; **być** ~**ka w** ~**kę jak ktoś** pot. to be the spitting image of sb pot.; **postawić** ~**kę nad i** (wyjaśnić) to dot the i's and cross the t's; (rozstrzygnąć wynik) *[drużyna, zawodnik]* to seal one's victory; **znalazłem się w** ~**ce** I am/was in a fix a. spot; **i** ~**ka!** a. **koniec (i)** ~**ka!** full stop! GB, period! US

krop|la *f* **[]** ① (płynu) drop; ~**la deszczu** a drop of rain, a raindrop; ~**le potu** drops a. beads of sweat ② (mała ilość) drop; **wypić coś do ostatniej** ~**li** to drink sth to the last drop

[] **krople** *plt* Med. drops; ~**le żołądkowe** stomach bitters

■ **byli podobni jak dwie** ~**le wody** they were like two peas in a pod

kroplomierz *m* dropper

kroplów|ka *f* Med. (intravenous a. IV) drip

kro|sta *f* pimple; spot GB pot.; (z ropą) pustule; (z płynem) blister

kr|owa *f* cow; **mleczna krowa** a dairy cow

kr|ój *m* ① (fason) cut; (robienie wykrojów) cutting; **kursy kroju i szycia** dressmaking courses ② Druk. **krój (czcionki)** a typeface

król *m* king także przen.; ~ **strzelców** the top scorer □ **Trzech Króli** (święto) Epiphany, Twelfth Night; **Trzej Królowie** the Three Wise Men, the Magi

królestw|o *n* ① (państwo) kingdom ② (dziedzina) domain; **ten pokój to moje** ~**o** this room is my territory

□ ~**o Boże** the Kingdom of God; ~**o niebieskie** the Kingdom of Heaven

królewicz *m* prince, king's son; ~ **z bajki** a fairy-tale prince

królew|na *f* princess, king's daughter

■ **Śpiąca Królewna** Sleeping Beauty; **śpiąca** ~**na** sleepyhead

królews|ki *adi. [klejnoty, zamek]* royal; *[dar, przyjęcie]* splendid; **po** ~**ku** *[mieszkać, żyć]* like a king; *[potraktować, przywitać]* royally; **mieć ~ki gest** to be very generous

królicz|y *adi. [futerko, nora]* rabbit

królik *m* rabbit; ~ **doświadczalny** a guinea pig

królow|a *f* queen także przen.

król|ować *impf vi* ① książk. (rządzić) to reign (**nad kimś/czymś** over sb/sth) ② przen. (dominować) *[mebel, osoba]* to reign supreme, to dominate ③ (górować) *[wieża, zamek]* to rise (**nad czymś** over sth); to dominate (**nad czymś** sth)

krót|ki *adi. grad. [spódnica, włosy]* short; *[list, opis, pobyt]* short, brief; **pójść gdzieś najkrótszą drogą** to go somewhere by the shortest route

król|tko *adv. grad.* ① (o długości, rozmiarze) ~**tko obcięte włosy** hair cut short, short hair; **ostrzyc się** ~**tko** to have one's hair cut short; **nosić się** ~**tko** to wear short skirts/dresses; **trzymać psa** ~**tko** to hold one's dog on a short leash a. lead ② (w niewielu słowach) *[opisać, opowiedzieć]* briefly; ~**tko mówiąc** in short a. brief ③ (o czasie) *[trwać]* a short time; *[grać, rozmawiać]* for a short time; **(na)** ~**tko przed wojną** shortly before the war; **przyjechać na** ~**tko** to come for a short stay ■ ~**tko kogoś trzymać** to keep sb in line

krótkofalów|ka *f* pot. short-wave radio; (przenośna) walkie-talkie pot.

krótkometrażow|y *adi.* **film** ~**y** a short film

krótkowidz *m* **być** ~**em** to be short-sighted a. myopic

krótkowzroczn|y *adi.* short-sighted, myopic także przen.

krta|ń *f* voice box

krucho *adv.* pot. ~ **u nas z pieniędzmi** we're short of money; ~ **u nich z czasem** they're pressed for time; ~ **z nim** (jest chory) he's in a bad way pot.; (ma kłopot) he's in trouble

kru|chy *adi. [kości, lód]* brittle; *[chleb, ciasto]* crumbly; *[mięso]* tender; *[staruszka, zdrowie]* frail; *[konstrukcja]* fragile; *[nadzieja]* slender; ~**che ciasto** shortcrust (pastry)

krucyfiks *m* crucifix

krucz|ek *m* (wybieg) trick; (niejasność przepisów) loophole; (trudność) catch; ~**ki prawne** legal tricks

kruk *m* raven; **biały** ~ a rare book

krupie|r *m*, ~**rka** *f* croupier

krupni|k *m* (zupa) barley soup; (napój alkoholowy) *spirits with honey and spices*

krusz|ec *m* (metal szlachetny) precious metal; (ruda) precious metal ore

krusz|eć *impf vi* ① *[skała, tynk]* to crumble ② Kulin. *[dziczyzna]* to age

kruszon|ka *f* crumble (topping)

krusz|yć *impf* **[]** *vt* to crumble *[chleb, grudkę ziemi]*; to crush *[kamienie, skałę]*; przen. to break *[opór, upór]* **[]** *vi* (śmiecić) ~**yć na dywan** to make a. drop crumbs on the carpet **[]]** **kruszyć się** (rozpadać się) *[cegła, ser]* to crumble

krwaw|ić *impf* **[]** *vt [ciernie]* to make [sth] bleed *[nogi, ręce]*

[] *vi [osoba, rana]* to bleed; **serce mi** ~**i** a. **moje serce** ~**i, kiedy tak się dzieje** książk. it breaks my heart to see it happen

krwaw|y **[]** *adi. grad.* (okrutny) *[bitwa, tyran]* bloody **[]** *adi. [ochłap, ślad]* bloody; *[trud, znój]* back-breaking; *[zachód słońca]* blood-red; ~**a plama** a bloodstain

krwiak *m* haematoma GB, hematoma US

krwin|ka *f* blood cell

krwiobieg *m* ① (układ krwionośny) blood circulation system; (krążenie krwi) (blood) circulation, blood flow ② przen. bloodstream przen.

krwiodaw|ca *m*, ~**czyni** *f* blood donor

krwiodawstw|o *n* blood donation

krwionośn|y *adi.* **układ** ~**y** the vascular system; **naczynia** ~**e** blood vessels

krwiopij|ca *m* bloodsucker pot.

krwiożercz|y *adi. [bestia]* ferocious, bloodthirsty; *[osoba, rządy]* bloodthirsty, murderous

krwi|sty *adi.* ① *[obrzęk, poty]* bloody ② *[befsztyk, pieczeń]* underdone, rare ③ (nabiegły krwią) *[cera, policzki]* ruddy, florid ④ (energiczny) *[osoba]* red-blooded, vigorous ⑤ przen. *[inscenizacja, postać]* vibrant, vivid

krwotok *m* bleeding; haemorrhage GB, hemorrhage US; ~ **z nosa** a nosebleed

kry|ć *impf* **[]** *vt* ① (chować) to hide, to conceal (**coś przed kimś** sth from sb) ② (zasłaniać) to hide; **mgła** ~**ła pola i lasy** fog hid the fields and woods ③ (pokrywać) to cover; **dom** ~**ty gontem** a house with a shingle(d) roof ④ (zawierać) **archiwum** ~**je ważne dokumenty** there are important documents buried in the archives ⑤ pot. (osłaniać) to cover pot. *[osobę]* ⑥ pot. (usprawiedliwiać) to cover (up) (**kogoś for sb**) ⑦ Sport to cover, to mark GB *[zawodnika]* ⑧ *[buhaj, ogier]* to cover *[samicę]*

[] *vi* (w zabawie w chowanego) to be 'it'

[]] **kryć się** ① (chować się) to hide (**przed kimś/czymś from sb/sth**) ② (nie ujawniać) to hide, to conceal (**z czymś sth**) ③ (nie być widocznym) *[dom, słońce]* to be hidden; **w tej prostej opowiastce** ~**je się głęboki sens** this simple story has a profound meaning ④ Sport *[bokser]* to cover up

kryjów|ka *f* (schronienie) hiding place, hideaway; (przestępców) hideout

krykie|t *m* Sport cricket

kryminali|sta *m*, ~**stka** *f* criminal

kryminalisty|ka *f* criminology

kryminaln|y **[]** *adi. [policja, kartoteka, przeszłość]* criminal; *[wydział]* crime, criminal; *[powieść]* crime, detective

[] *m* pot. (więzień) con pot.

kryminał *m* ① (powieść) crime a. detective novel; whodunnit GB pot., whodunit US pot.; (film) detective film [2] pot. (więzienie) jug, stir US pot. [3] pot. (zbrodnia) crime

kryp|ta f crypt, vault

kryptonim m cryptonym, code name

kryptoreklam|a f surreptitious advertising

krystaliz|ować pf, impf [I] vt książk. to formulate, to crystallize [plany, poglądy]
[II] vi to crystallize
[III] krystalizować się [roztwór] to crystallize także przen.

kryszta|ł m [1] (szkło) crystal (glass); **czysty jak ~ł** [powietrze, woda] crystal-clear; [osoba] (as) honest as the day is long; **ten człowiek to ~ł** he's (the) salt of the earth [2] (wyrób) crystal piece [3] (cukier) granulated sugar [4] Chem., Miner. crystal

kryształow|y adi. [1] (ze szkła kryształowego) crystal (glass) [2] (przezroczysty) crystal clear [3] przen. [osoba] honest; [charakter] impeccable

kryteri|um n [1] (miernik) criterion [2] Sport circuit (cycle) race

kry|ty adi. [1] (pokryty) covered (**czymś** with sth); [budynek] roofed (**czymś** with sth); **chata ~ta strzechą** a thatched cottage; **~te zapięcie** (koszuli, bluzki) a fly front; (spódnicy) a concealed fastening [2] (pod dachem) [basen, stadion] indoor
■ **być ~tym** pot. to be covered; **podejrzany jest ~ty** the suspect has an alibi

krytyczn|y adi. [1] [myślenie, uwaga] critical [2] [moment, sytuacja] critical, crucial [3] [masa, stan, temperatura] critical

kryty|k m critic

kryty|ka f [1] (surowa ocena) criticism [2] (analiza) criticism [3] (ogół krytyków) critics
■ **być poniżej (wszelkiej) ~ki** [postępowanie, zachowanie] to be beneath (all) criticism

krytyk|ować impf vt to criticize [osobę, zachowanie]; **~ować kogoś za coś** to criticize sb for sth

kryzys m crisis

krzak m bush, shrub

krząta|ć się impf v refl. [1] (zajmować się pracą) to bustle about a. around [2] (zabiegać) to busy oneself (**wokół** a. **koło kogoś/czegoś** with sb/sth)

krzem m silicon

krzep|a f pot. brawn, muscle; **mieć ~ę w rękach** to have strong hands

krzep|ki adi. [dziewczyna, staruszek] robust, vigorous; [uścisk, uderzenie] powerful, strong; [dłonie, ramiona] burly, brawny; [nalewka] strong; [sen] refreshing; [powietrze] refreshing, bracing

krzepliwość|ć f coagulability

krzep|nąć impf vi [1] (zastygać) [krew] to clot, to coagulate; [galareta] to set; [woda] to freeze; [wosk] to solidify [2] książk. (stawać się silnym) to grow strong; [uczucie, władza] to be reinforced

krze|sło n chair; **~sło elektryczne** the electric chair

krzew m bush, shrub

krzew|ić impf [I] vt książk. to disseminate, to propagate książk. [idee, obyczaje, wiedzę]
[II] **krzewić się** [1] [rośliny] to propagate [2] książk. (szerzyć się) [idee, kult] to spread

krztu|sić się impf v refl. [1] (dusić się) to choke [2] (zachłystywać się) to choke, to be choked; **~sić się ze śmiechu** to be choking with laughter [3] przen. [silnik] to cough

krzyczeć[1] impf → **krzyknąć**

krzycz|eć[2] impf vi [1] (domagać się) to shout, to cry out (**o coś** for sth) [2] (głośno płakać) to cry, to scream

krzyk m [1] (głośne mówienie) shout, yell; **wracam do domu, a ona do mnie z ~iem** I come home and she starts yelling a. shouting at me [2] (ze strachu, bólu, emocji) scream, cry; **obudzić się z ~iem** to wake up screaming [3] (głos ptaków) cry [4] pot. (sprzeciw) kerfuffle GB, to-do pot.; **~ protestu** a cry of protest; **tyle ~u i po co?** what was all the fuss a. uproar about?; **podnieść ~** (upominać się) to kick up a fuss pot.; (ganić) to raise Cain pot.; (zaprotestować) to raise a hue and cry, to raise an outcry
■ (ostatni) **~ mody** all the rage; **i po ~u** pot. it's (all) over (and done with)

krzy|knąć pf — **krzy|czeć**[1] impf [I] vt (mówić głośno) to shout (**do kogoś** at sb)
[II] vi [1] (pod wpływem emocji) to shout, to cry out; **~czeć z radości** to shout for joy; **~czeć z bólu/przerażenia** to scream in pain/fear [2] (strofować) to yell, to shout (**na kogoś** at sb) [3] (o ptakach) to cry (out)

krzyw|da f (niesprawiedliwość) injustice, wrong; (psychologiczna) (psychological a. emotional) damage; (fizyczna) injury, harm; **nikomu nie stanie się ~da** no one will get hurt; **naprawić ~dę** to make amends

krzyw|dzić impf vt [1] (wyrządzać szkodę moralną) to be unfair a. unjust (**kogoś** to sb); to wrong (**kogoś** sb); (wyrządzać szkodę fizyczną) to hurt, to harm; **~dzisz go tymi podejrzeniami** your suspicions do him an injustice; **~dzące zarzuty** damaging allegations [2] [decyzja, ocena] to be unjust a. unfair (**kogoś** to sb); to wrong (**kogoś** sb); **~dzący wyrok** an unjust verdict

krzywic|a f Med. rickets

krzyw|ić impf [I] vt to bend, to twist [gwoździe, pręty]; **~ić twarz z bólu** to grimace with pain; **~ić usta wzgardliwie** to sneer (in disdain)
[II] **krzywić się** [1] (wyginać się) [drut] to be bent a. twisted; [blacha] to be warped a. bent [2] (robić grymasy) to pull a face GB, to make a face; **~ić się z bólu** to wince a. grimace in pain

krzyw|o adv. grad. crookedly, askew
■ **patrzeć ~o na kogoś/coś** to look askance at sb/sth; **uśmiechać się do kogoś ~o** to smile wryly at sb

krzywoprzysięstw|o n książk. perjury

krzyw|y [] *adi. [drzewo, zęby]* crooked; *[podłoga, stół]* uneven; ~**e nogi** bandy legs; ~**y uśmiech** przen. a wry smile; ~**e spojrzenie** przen. a frown

[] **krzywa** *f* Mat. curve

■ **patrzeć na kogoś/coś** ~**ym okiem** to look askance at sb/sth

krzyż *m* [] Relig. cross [] (kształt) cross; **w kształcie** ~**a** cross-shaped; **na** ~ crosswise; **okna zabito na** ~ **deskami** the window was nailed up with crossed boards [] (order) cross [] przen. (cierpienie) cross; **dźwigać swój** ~ to have one's own cross to bear [] (część kręgosłupa) lower back [] pot. (kręgosłup) spine, back

■ **leżeć** ~**em** to lie prostrate; **mieć z kimś** ~ **pański** to go through a. endure the trials of Job with sb; **w pokoju stało kilka mebli na** ~ pot. there was hardly any furniture in the room

krzyżak *m* [] (pająk) garden a. cross spider [] (część konstrukcji) trestle; ~ **do choinki** a Christmas tree stand

krzyż|ować *impf* [] *vt* [] (układać na krzyż) to cross; ~**ować ręce na piersiach** to cross one's arms on a. over one's chest [] (psuć celowo) to thwart; (stanowić przeszkodę) to stand in the way of; ~**ować komuś plany** to stand in the way of a. thwart sb's plans [] to crucify *[osobę]* [] Biol. to cross(-breed) *[zwierzęta]*; to cross(-fertilize) *[rośliny]*

[] **krzyżować się** [] (przecinać się) *[szlaki, ślady]* to cross, to intersect [] przen. *[idee, wpływy]* to merge, to blend [] Biol. *[zwierzęta]* to interbreed; (rośliny) to be cross-fertilized

krzyżow|y [] *adi.* [] (z różnych stron) ~**y ogień** crossfire; **dostać się w** ~**y ogień pytań** przen. to be caught in a crossfire of questions [] Hist. **wyprawa** ~**a** a crusade [] Anat. sacral; **kość** ~**a** the sacrum

[] **krzyżowa** *f* Kulin. round (steak)

krzyżów|ka *f* [] (w gazecie) crossword (puzzle) [] Biol. (roślina, zwierzę) cross(-breed), hybrid [] (kaczka) mallard [] pot. (skrzyżowanie) crossroads

krzyżyk [] *m* [] Relig. (small) cross [] (znak) X, cross; **przy wybranej odpowiedzi należy postawić** ~ mark your answer with an X; **podpisywać się** ~**ami** a. ~**iem** to make one's cross [] Muz. sharp [] przen. (dziesiątek lat) **mieć na karku piąty** ~ to be in one's fifties

[] **krzyżyki** *plt* (ściег) cross-stitch

■ **postawić na kimś** ~ to give up on sb

ksero [] *n inv.* [] (maszyna) Xerox®, (photo)copier [] (kserokopia) Xerox®(copy), (photo)copy [] (punkt usługowy) photocopying place a. point

[] *adi. inv.* **odbitka** a. **kopia** ~ a Xerox® (copy), a (photo)copy

kserokopi|a *f* Xerox® (copy), (photo)copy

kserokopiar|ka *f* Xerox® (machine), (photo)copier

kser|ować *impf vt* to xerox, to (photo)copy

ksi|ądz *m* priest; ~**ądz Krzysztof Kowalski** Father a. the Reverend Krzysztof Kowalski; **tak, proszę** ~**ędza** yes, Father

książecz|ka *f* [] (mała książka) (small) book; (w miękkiej okładce) booklet; ~**ka do nabożeństwa** a prayer book [] (dokument) book; ~**ka oszczędnościowa** a bank book, a passbook; ~**ka mieszkaniowa** ≈ a building society book; ~**ka czekowa** a cheque-book GB, a checkbook US; ~**ka zdrowia** a health record; ~**ka wojskowa** service papers [] (rachunek w banku) savings account

ksi|ążę *m* duke; (potomek króla) prince

książ|ka *f* [] (do czytania) book; ~**ka o czymś** a book on a. about sth; ~**ka kucharska** a cookbook, a cookery book; ~**ka telefoniczna** a phone book, a telephone directory [] (dokument) book; ~**ka rachunkowa** an account book; ~**ka skarg i zażaleń** a complaint(s) book [] pot. (podręcznik szkolny) (text)book

książkow|y *adi.* [] *[bohater, dorobek]* literary; *[wydanie, zbiory]* book [] *[słowo, styl]* bookish

ksi|ęga *f* [] (duża książka) book [] (rozdział) book [] (dokument) book, register; ~**ęga wieczysta** Prawo land register

księgar|nia *f* bookshop GB, bookstore US; ~**nia wysyłkowa** a mail-order book company

księgarz *m* bookseller, book dealer

księg|ować *impf vt* to enter, to post *[wydatki, wpływy]*

księgowoś|ć *f* [] (prowadzenie ksiąg) bookkeeping, accountancy [] (dział) accounts

księgow|y *m*, ~**a** *f* accountant, bookkeeper; **dyplomowany** ~**y** a chartered accountant; **główny** ~**y** the chief accountant

księgozbi|ór *m* book collection, library

księstw|o *n* duchy, principality

księżn|a *f* princess, duchess

księżnicz|ka *f* princess

księżyc *m* moon; (satelita Ziemi) the moon; ~ **w pełni/w nowiu** a full/new moon; **blask/światło** ~**a** moonlight; **przy** ~**u** pot. in the moonlight, by moonlight

■ **wyglądać jak** ~ **w pełni** to be moon-faced a. full-faced

księżycow|y *adi. [orbita, pojazd]* lunar; ~**a noc** a moonlit night; **poświata** ~**a** moonlight; ~**y krajobraz** a moonscape

kształ|cić *impf* [] *vt* [] (uczyć) to educate, to train *[dzieci, młodzież]* [] (doskonalić) to train *[głos, pamięć]*; ~**cić czyjś charakter** to mould sb's character

[] *vi* (dostarczać informacji) **podróże** ~**cą** travel broadens the mind

[] **kształcić się** (uczyć się) to study; ~**cić się na uniwersytecie** to study at university

kształ|t [] *m* shape; **w** a. **o** ~**cie czegoś** in the shape a. form of sth; **pudełko w** ~**cie serca** a heart-shaped box; **chmury przybierały**

rozmaite ∼ty the clouds took on various shapes
II **kształty** *plt* (kobiece) curves; **rubensowskie** ∼ty
ample curves

■ **przybierać realne** ∼ty to take on real shape
kształt|ować *impf* **I** *vt* **1** (formować) to shape
[metal, teren] **2** przen. (nadawać cechy) to shape, to
mould GB, to mold US *[charakter, opinię]*
II **kształtować się** **1** (wykształcać się) to develop, to
be shaped **2** książk. (osiągać wartość) **ceny biletów**
∼**ują się w okolicach 300 złotych** the tickets are
going for around 300 zlotys; **wzrost produkcji**
∼**uje się w granicach 5 procent** production
growth is running at about 5 per cent

kszyk *m* common snipe

k|to *pron.* **1** (pytajny) who; **kto to (jest)?** (wskazując)
who's that?; **kto to** a. **tam?** (u drzwi) who is it?, who's
there?; **kto mówi?** who's speaking?; **kto ci o tym**
powiedział? who told you about it?; „**mam**
mnóstwo kłopotów" – „a kto ich nie ma?"
'I've got so many problems' – 'who hasn't?'; **dla**
kogo to kupiłeś? who did you buy this for?; **komu**
dałeś te kwiaty? who did you give those flowers
to?; **kogo zaprosiłeś?** who(m) did you invite?;
z kim ona była? who was she with?; **o kim**
mówicie? who are you talking about?; **zgadnij,**
kogo wczoraj spotkałam guess who I met
yesterday; **kto jest kto** a. **kim** who's who
2 (względny) (właśnie ten) who; (każdy) whoever; **ten,**
kto zgubił klucze the person who lost their keys;
zapytaj o to kogoś, kto się na tym zna ask
someone who knows something about it; **kto zda**
egzamin, zostanie przyjęty whoever passes the
exam will be accepted; **kto żyw** everyone, everybody, one and all **3** (nieokreślony) someone, somebody; (w pytaniach) anyone, anybody; **nie ma kto** a.
komu herbaty zaparzyć there's no one to make
the tea; **mało** a. **rzadko kto** hardly anyone a.
anybody; **(a) kogo to obchodzi?** who cares? a.
gives a damn? pot.

k|tokolwiek *pron.* **1** (obojętnie kto) anyone, any-
body; **lepiej niż ktokolwiek inny** better than
anyone a. anybody (else); **daj te książki komu-**
kolwiek give the books to anyone you like;
gdybym miał kogokolwiek podejrzewać... if I
were to suspect anyone... **2** (ten, kto) whoever;
wychodź, kimkolwiek jesteś come out, whoever
you are

k|toś **I** *pron.* somebody, someone; (w pytaniach)
anybody, anyone; **ktoś wszedł do pokoju** someone a. somebody entered the room; **czy spotkałeś**
kogoś w parku? did you see anyone in the park?;
ktoś inny somebody else, someone else; **był kimś,**
komu mogła zaufać he was someone she could
trust

II *m* **1** somebody, someone; **on jest kimś w**
przemyśle filmowym he's somebody in the film

industry **2** pot. **czy ja znam tego ktosia?** do I
know this someone?

któr|ędy *pron.* which way; ∼ **przebiega granica?**
which way a. where does the border run?

któ|ry *pron.* **1** (przymiotny) which; ∼**ry plecak jest**
twój? which rucksack is yours?; **z** ∼**rymi**
kolegami utrzymujesz kontakty? which (of
your) friends are you in touch with?; „**wzięłam**
twoją bransoletkę?" – „∼rą?" 'I've taken your
bracelet' – 'which one?'; **zgadnij, na** ∼**rym**
piętrze mieszkam guess which floor I'm on; **nie**
wiem, ∼**ry kolor wybrać** I don't know which a.
what colour to choose; ∼**ra godzina?** what time is
it?, what's the time?; **o** ∼**rej masz samolot?** what
time is your plane?; ∼**ry dzisiaj** a. ∼**rego dziś**
mamy? what's the date today?; ∼**ry to raz**
obiecujesz poprawę? how many times have you
promised to mend your ways? książk. **2** (względny)
(osobowy) who; (w przypadkach zależnych) whom; (nieoso-
bowy) which; (w użyciu dzierżawczym) whose; **chłopcy,**
∼**rych spotkałem** the boys (whom a. that) I met;
samochód, ∼**ry wynająłem** the car (which a.
that) I hired; **wiersz, z** ∼**rego pochodzą te słowa**
the poem (that) these words come from; **autor,**
∼**rego książka jest na liście bestsellerów** an
author whose book is on the bestseller list; **kraj,**
w ∼**rym mieszkam** the country I live in; **dzień,**
w ∼**rym popełniono zbrodnię** the day (on
which) the crime was committed **3** (nieokreślony)
any; **niech no mi się** ∼**ry spóźni, to pożałuje!** if
any of you are late, you'll be sorry!; ∼**rą drogę**
wybierzesz, dojedziesz do wybrzeża whichever
road you choose, it'll take you to the coast; **mało** a.
rzadko ∼**ry** hardly any; **obojętnie** ∼**ry** whichever (one), no matter which (one)

któ|rykolwiek *pron.* **1** (nieokreślony) any (one),
whichever (one); (z dwóch) either; **pożycz mi**
∼**rąkolwiek książkę** lend me a book – any book;
jest kilka możliwości, a ∼**rąkolwiek wybie-**
rzesz... there are several options, and whichever
(one) you choose...; „**którą z tych dwóch**
koszulek chcesz?" – „∼rąkolwiek 'which of
the two shirts would you like?' – 'either';
∼**rykolwiek z nas/z nich** any (one) of us/them;
(z dwóch) either (one) of us/them **2** (względny)
∼**rykolwiek z nich wygra, znajdzie się**
w drużynie olimpijskiej whoever wins will get a
place in the Olympic squad

któr|yś *pron.* (bliżej nieokreślony) some; (z grupy, ze
zbioru) one; **widziałem go w** ∼**ymś programie**
telewizyjnym I saw him on some television
programme (or other); ∼**yś z nas/z nich** one of
us/them; ∼**egoś dnia** (w przeszłości) one day;
(w przyszłości) one a. some day; **po raz** ∼**yś**
z rzędu a. ∼**yś tam raz** for the nth time (in a
row); **w roku tysiąc dziewięćset sześćdziesią-**
tym ∼**ymś** in nineteen-sixty-something; **trzy-**

dziesta ∼aś tam **książka z tego cyklu** the thirtieth-odd a. thirtieth or so book in the series

ku *praep.* książk. [1] (kierunek) to, towards (**komuś/ czemuś** sb/sth); **ku górze** up(wards); **ku dołowi** down(wards); **słońce chyliło się ku zachodowi** the sun was sinking in the west [2] (skutek) to, towards; **ku mojemu zaskoczeniu** to my surprise; **ku jej zgorszeniu** to her horror; **tablica ku czci** a. **pamięci ofiar stalinizmu** a plaque a. in memory of the victims of Stalinism; **wiersz ku pokrzepieniu serc** a heart-warming poem; **zbliżać się ku końcowi** to be drawing to an end a. a close

■ **mieć się ku sobie** przest. to be (very) fond of each other

kub|ek *m* (naczynie) mug, cup; (zawartość) mugful, cupful

■ ∼**ek w** ∼**ek** pot. exactly the same; **ona jest podobna do matki** ∼**ek w** ∼**ek** she's the living a. spitting image of her mother

kub|eł *m* (wiadro) bucket, pail; (zawartość) bucketful, pailful; ∼**eł na śmieci** a waste a. rubbish bin

kucać *impf* → **kucnąć**

kuchar|ka *f* cook; **gdzie** ∼**ek sześć, tam nie ma co jeść** przysł. too many cooks spoil the broth przysł.

kuchars|ki *adi.* [szkoła] culinary; [kurs] cookery; [uczeń, pomocnik] cook's; [talent, umiejętności] cooking, culinary; **sztuka** ∼**ka** the art of cooking

kucharz *m* cook; (mistrz) chef

kuchenn|y *adi.* [meble, naczynia] kitchen; **blacha** ∼**a** an oven tray

kuch|nia *f* [1] (pomieszczenie) kitchen [2] (elektryczna, gazowa) ∼**nia węglowa** a coal-burning stove [3] (potrawy) cooking, cuisine; ∼**nia domowa** home cooking; **smakuje mi jej** ∼**nia** I like her cooking [4] (gotowanie) cooking; **znać się na** ∼**ni** to be a good cook [5] pot. (szczegóły pracy) tricks of the trade; **znać coś od** ∼**ni** to know sth from the inside

❏ ∼**nia polowa** field kitchen

kuc|nąć *pf* — **kuc|ać** *impf vi* [osoba, zwierzę] to squat, to sit on one's haunches

kucyk *m* (koń) pony; (uczesanie) pigtail

ku|ć *impf* [**I**] *vt* [1] (obrabiać) to forge, to hammer [żelazo] [2] (w kamieniu) (rozkruszać) to hew [skałę]; (wyrąbywać) to bore [tunel]; to carve [nagrobek, pomnik]; to carve, to chisel [napis] [3] to shoe [konia] [4] pot. (uczyć się) to grind away at, to swot up (on) GB pot. [fizykę]

[**II**] *vi* pot. (uczyć się) to cram, to swot (up) GB pot.; **kuć do egzaminu** to swot (up) a. cram for an exam

kudła|ty *adi.* [osoba] tousle-haired; [zwierzę] shaggy

kuf|el *m* (naczynie) (beer) mug; (zawartość) ≈ pint (of beer)

kuf|er *m* [1] (skrzynia) trunk, chest [2] pot. (bagażnik) (samochodowy) boot GB, trunk US; (motocyklowy, rowerowy) pannier

kujon *m* pot. swot GB, grind US pot.

kukieł|ka *f* puppet

kukuł|ka *f* cuckoo

kukurydz|a *f* maize, corn US; (kolba) (corn)cob; ∼**a (gotowana) w kolbach** corn on the cob

kul|a¹ *f* [1] (bryła) sphere; ∼**a ziemska** the globe [2] (kształt) ball; ∼**a śnieżna** a snowball [3] Gry ball; (bilardowa) (billiard) ball; (w kręglach) bowl, bowling ball [4] Sport shot; **pchnięcie** ∼**ą** the shot-put, putting the shot [5] (pocisk, nabój) bullet; ∼**a w łeb** pot. a bullet through the head

■ ∼**a u nogi** ball and chain

kul|a² *f* (inwalidzka) crutch

kulaw|y *adi.* [1] [osoba, zwierzę] lame; **być** ∼**ym** to have a limp, to be lame [2] [krzesło, stół] wobbly, rickety [3] (kiepski) [prawo, system] defective; [rym] clumsy; [wymówka] lame, feeble

kul|eć *impf vi* [1] (utykać) to limp, to walk with a limp [2] przen. (szwankować) [firma, gospodarka] to flounder; [rozmowa] to flag, to falter

kul|ić *impf* [**I**] *vi* to hunch [plecy, ramiona]; ∼**ić głowę w ramionach** to bury one's head in one's shoulders

[**II**] **kulić się** (ze strachu) to cower, to cringe; (z zimna) to huddle (up), to hunch (up); (w łóżku) to curl up, to snuggle down; ∼**ić się z przerażenia** to cringe in terror

kulig *m* sleigh ride

kulik *m* curlew

kulinarn|y *adi.* [gusty, sztuka] culinary

kuloodporn|y *adi.* bulletproof

kul|t *m* worship, cult także przen.; ∼**t świętych** veneration of the saints; ∼**t jednostki** personality cult

kultow|y *adi.* [1] [czynności, ofiara] cultic; [naczynia, obrazy] cult [2] przen. [film, zespół] cult

kultu|ra *f* [1] (dorobek) culture [2] (społeczeństwo) culture, civilization [3] (muzyczna, literacka) education [4] (ogłada) culture, refinement; **mieć** ∼**rę** to be well-bred; ∼**ra jazdy** road manners; ∼**ra współżycia społecznego** social norms a. customs [5] Biol. culture

kulturaln|y [**I**] *adi.* grad. [osoba, towarzystwo] cultured, well-bred; [rozmowa, zachowanie] cultured

[**II**] *adi.* [instytucje, współpraca] cultural

kultury|sta *m* bodybuilder

kuluar|y *plt* back room(s); (do spotkań z wyborcami) lobby GB; **w** ∼**ach** przen. unofficially, behind the scenes

kumk|ać *impf vi* to croak

kump|el *m* pot. pal, mate GB, buddy US pot.; ∼**el z pracy/ze szkoły** a workmate/a schoolmate; ∼**el z wojska** a mate from the army

kun|a *f* marten

kund|el *m* pot. mongrel; mutt pot.

kunsztown|y *adi. grad.* (mistrzowski) *[dzieło, wykonanie]* masterful; (misterny) *[fryzura, wzór]* elaborate, intricate

kup|a *f* pot. ① (sterta) (kamieni, śmieci) heap; (gazet, gruzu) pile; ~**a gnoju** a dungheap, a dunghill; **zebrać coś na** ~**ę** to pile sth (up) in a heap ② (grupa) ~**a ludzi** a load of people pot.; **trzymać się w** ~**ie** to stick together; ~**ą pojechaliśmy na wycieczkę** a whole gang of us went on a trip pot. ③ (mnóstwo, masa) load pot.; ~**a czegoś** loads a. heaps of sth. *[czasu, pieniędzy, roboty]*; ~**a śmiechu** a good laugh; **mieć** ~**ę rzeczy do zrobienia** to have heaps of things to do; **mieć** ~**ę kłopotów** to be in a load of trouble; ~**a złomu** pot. (stara rzecz) a rustheap pot.; (rzecz zepsuta) a write-off pot. ④ pot. (stolec) pooh GB, poop US pot.; (psia) dog pooh a. turd wulg.; **zrobić** ~**ę** to (have a) pooh GB, to take a dump US pot.
■ **nie trzymać się** ~**y** pot. *[argument, teoria]* to not hold water, to not stand a. hold up; *[film, relacja]* to not hold a. hang together pot.; **wziąć się w** ~**ę** a. **pozbierać się do** ~**y** pot. to pull oneself together pot.

kup|ić *pf* — **kup|ować** *impf vt* ① (nabyć) to buy, to purchase; **co ci** ~**ić na urodziny?** what shall I get you for your birthday?; ~**ić coś za pół darmo** a. **za bezcen** to get sth for a song a. for next to nothing pot.; ~**ić coś na kredyt/na raty** to buy sth on credit/on hire purchase GB a. on the installment plan US; ~**ić coś za gotówkę** to pay cash for sth; ~**ić coś hurtem** to buy sth wholesale; ~**ić coś na wagę** to buy sth by weight ② przen. (zyskać) to buy *[osobę, sympatię]* ③ przen. (przekupić) to buy (off), to pay off *[polityka, urzędnika]*; **każdego można** ~**ić** everyone has their price ④ pot. (uwierzyć) to buy pot.; **ludzie wszystko** ~**ią** people will buy anything ⑤ pot. (zaakceptować) to go for pot. *[pomysł, propozycję]*

kup|iec *m* ① (nabywca) buyer (**na coś** for sth) ② (handlowiec) trader, dealer; (hurtownik) wholesaler; Hist. merchant

kupn|o *n* purchase; ~**o na kredyt** credit purchase; ~**o na raty** hire purchase GB, purchase on the installment plan US

kupon *m* ① (blankiet) coupon, voucher ② (odcinek biletu) (ticket) stub ③ (kawałek tkaniny) length
■ **odcinać** ~**y od czegoś** to cash in on a. capitalize on sth

kupować *impf* → **kupić**

kupując|y *m*, ~**a** *f* buyer; (w sklepie) shopper

ku|ra *f* ① (ptak domowy) hen, domestic fowl ② Kulin. chicken ③ (samica ptaków łownych) hen
■ **kura domowa** pot. hausfrau pot.; **chodzić spać z kurami** to turn in early, to go to bed with the chickens; **wyglądać jak zmokła kura** pot. (przemoknięty) to look like a drowned rat pot.; **znać się na czymś jak kura na pieprzu** pot. to not know a bean GB a. beans US about sth pot.

kuracj|a *f* (leczenie) treatment, therapy; (seria zabiegów, środków) course of treatment; **przechodzić** ~**ę** to undertake a course of treatment (**na coś** for sth); (w sanatorium) to take a cure

kuracjusz *m*, ~**ka** *f* (w sanatorium) patient; (w uzdrowisku) client

kuratel|a *f* ① (kontrola) (close a. strict) supervision (**nad kimś/czymś** of sb/sth); **pod czyjąś** ~**ą** under sb's supervision; **wyzwolić się spod** ~**i rodziców** to free oneself from parental control ② Prawo (nad osobą) (legal) custody, guardianship; (nad majątkiem) custody; **być pod czyjąś** ~**ą** *[osoba]* to be in sb's custody; *[nieletni]* to be sb's ward; **być pod** ~**ą sądową** *[nieletni]* to be a ward of court

kurato|r *m*, ~**rka** *f* ① Prawo (opiekun) guardian; (nad skazanym) probation officer ② (w oświacie) chief education officer, schools superintendent ③ (wystawy) curator

kuratori|um *n* (oświatowe) ≈ education office, ≈ board of education US

kurcz *m* (w nodze) cramp; (mięśni) spasm

kurczak *m* chicken

kurcz|ę *n* chicken, chick

kurcz|yć się *impf v refl.* ① *[tkanina]* to shrink; *[mięsień]* to contract ② przen. *[liczba, zasoby]* to shrink

kur|ek *m* ① (pokrętło) tap GB, faucet US; (w beczce) spigot; Techn. stopcock ② (pistoletu) cock, hammer ③ (cel do strzelania) rooster-shaped target; (na dachu) weathercock, weathervane

kurie|r *m* ① (o osobie) courier, messenger; (na motocyklu, konny) dispatch rider ② (gazeta) courier, herald

kurnik *m* (dla drobiu) henhouse, poultry house

kuropatw|a *f* Zool. partridge

kuror|t *m* health resort, spa

kur|ować *impf* ① *vt* to treat, to nurse *[pacjenta]*; to heal *[rany]*; ~**ować kogoś czymś** to treat sb with sth
Ⅱ **kurować się** to be treated, to undergo treatment (**z czegoś** for sth); (w uzdrowisku) to take a cure

kurs *m* ① (szkolenie) course ② (cena) rate; ~ **dolara** the dollar (exchange) rate; ~ **wymiany** exchange rate, conversion rate ③ (przejazd) trip, journey; (trasa) run; (wyznaczona drogą) route; **trafił mu się daleki** ~ (o taksówce) he got a long fare; (o ciężarówce, autobusie) he got a long-distance run ④ (kierunek polityki) course, direction; **nowy** ~ **w polityce** a change in policy ⑤ (obieg) circulation; **puścić coś w** ~ to put sth into circulation, to circulate sth
■ **wypaść z** ~**u** pot. to lose touch, to be out of touch

kurso|r *m* Komput. cursor

kurs|ować *impf vi* ① *[autobus, pociąg]* to run; *[statek]* to sail (regularly); *[samolot]* to fly (regularly); ~**ować co dwie godziny** to run every two hours ② przen. *[osoba]* to (go) to and fro pot. (**pomiędzy czymś a czymś** from sth to sth, between somewhere and somewhere) ③ przen. (być w obiegu) *[banknoty, plotki]* to be in circulation

kurt|ka *f* jacket, coat

kurtyn|a *f* curtain; ~**a siedem razy szła w górę** there were seven curtain calls

❑ **żelazna** ~**a** Teatr safety a. fireproof curtain; Polit. the Iron Curtain

■ **przy otwartej** a. **podniesionej** a. **odsłoniętej** ~**ie** *[obradować, odbywać się]* (out) in the open

kurz *m* dust

kurz|yć *impf* **▯** *vt* pot. ~**yć fajkę/papierosa** to puff on one's pipe/cigarette

▯ *vi* to raise a cloud a. clouds of dust

▯▯▯ **kurzyć się** ① (pokrywać się kurzem) *[książki, meble]* to be getting dusty ② (wznosić się) **na drodze** ~**yło się** the road was dusty ③ (o dymie) ~**y się z komina** smoke is billowing from the chimney

■ **kłamać** a. **łgać, aż się** ~**y** pot. to lie through one's teeth pot.; **uciekać** a. **wiać, aż się** ~**y** to run for one's life

ku|sić *impf vt* ① (wabić) to lure, to entice; **wystawy kusiły atrakcyjnymi towarami** attractive wares beckoned alluringly from the shop windows ② (namawiać) to entice, to tempt (**kogoś czymś** sb with sth); **nie kuś mnie do złego** don't tempt me (to do wrong)

■ **kusić los** to tempt fate a. providence

kustosz *m* custodian, curator

kuszący *adi. [spojrzenie, uśmiech]* alluring, seductive; *[perspektywa]* tempting, enticing

kuśnierz *m* furrier

kut|er *m* (jacht) cutter; (rybacki) (fishing) cutter, smack; (do przewożenia załogi) (ship's) launch

kuwe|ta *f* ① Fot. (photo) processing tray ② (do farby) paint a. roller tray ③ (dla kota, chomika) litter tray a. box

kuzyn *m*, ~**ka** *f* cousin

kuźni|a *f* (warsztat rzemieślniczy) smithy, blacksmith's shop; (dział huty) forge; ~**a talentów** a breeding ground for new a. fresh talent

kwadrans *m* fifteen minutes, quarter of an hour; **za** ~ **druga** (a) quarter to two GB, (a) quarter of two US

kwadra|t *m* ① (kształt) square ② Mat. square; **trzy do** ~**tu równa się dziewięć** three squared equals nine

■ **głupota do** ~**tu** pot. the ultimate in stupidity

kwadratow|y *adi. [centymetr, okno, twarz, szczęka]* square; *[sylwetka]* stocky

kwa|knąć *pf* — **kwa|kać** *impf vi* to quack

kwalifik|ować *impf* **▯** *vt* to classify *[osoby, zjawiska]*; ~**ować zboże** to grade and certify grain

▯▯ **kwalifikować się** ① (nadawać się) to qualify; ~**ować się na ministra** to have the makings of a minister; **sprawa** ~**uje się do sądu** the case should go to court ② Sport to qualify (**do czegoś** for sth)

kwap|ić się *impf v refl.* **nie** ~**ić się do pracy** to not be too keen on working, to not feel like working; **nie** ~**ić się z wyjaśnieniem** to be in no hurry to explain

kwartał *m* ① (część roku) quarter (of a year), three months ② (część miasta) quarter, district

kwas **▯** *m* acid

▯▯ **kwasy** *plt* pot. grudges; **rodzinne** ~**y** family squabbles

kwas|ek *m* ~**ek cytrynowy** citric acid

kwa|sić *impf* **▯** *vt* ① to pickle *[warzywa]* ② pot., przen. to spoil *[humor, nastrój]*

▯▯ **kwasić się** to sour, to ferment

kwaskow|aty, ~**y** *adi. [smak, zapach]* slightly tart a. acid

kwaśni|eć *impf vi* ① (żywność) to ferment, to sour ② przen. to sour, to turn sour

kwaśn|y **▯** *adi. grad.* ① *[smak]* sour, tart; *[zapach, śmietana]* sour; **mleko jest już** ~**e** (zepsute) the milk's gone off; (zsiadłe) the milk's turned sour ② przen. *[mina, uśmiech, uwaga]* sour

▯▯ *adi.* Chem. acid

■ **zbić** a. **stłuc kogoś na** ~**e jabłko** to beat sb black and blue,

kwate|ra *f* ① (dla wojska) billet, quarters; (do wynajęcia) lodgings ② (czworoboczna płaszczyzna) plot ③ (na cmentarzu) (pojedyncza) plot; (obszar) section

❑ ~**ra główna** Wojsk. headquarters; ~**ra prywatna** private rooms, private accommodation GB, private accommodations US

kwaterun|ek *m* pot. ≈ housing office a. department; **mieszkanie w a. z** ~**ku** ≈ a council flat

kwe|sta *f* collection

kwesti|a *f* ① (zagadnienie) issue, question; **w tej** ~**i nie mam nic do powiedzenia** I have nothing to say on the matter ② Teatr line

■ **robić** ~**ę z czegoś** to make an issue (out) of sth

kwestionariusz *m* (ankieta) questionnaire (form); (formularz) form

kwestion|ować *impf vt* książk. (podawać w wątpliwość) to question, to query; (zaprzeczać) to dispute, to challenge

kwest|ować *impf vi* to collect; ~**ować na rzecz PCK** to collect for the Polish Red Cross

kwiaciar|ka *f* florist

kwiaciar|nia *f* florist's, flower shop

kwi|at *m* ① (część rośliny) flower ② pot. (roślina ozdobna, doniczkowa) pot a. house plant ③ przen. flower, cream; ~**at młodzieży** the flower of youth ④ (motyw dekoracyjny) flower; **materiał w** ~**aty** flowered a. flower-patterned fabric

■ **w** ~**ecie wieku** in the prime of life

kwiczoł *m* Zool. fieldfare

kwie|cień *m* April

kwieci|sty *adi. [przemówienie, styl]* flowery; *[styl]* ornate; *[materiał]* flowered, flowery; *[łąka]* flowery

kwietnik *m* [1] (klomb) flower bed [2] (mebel) flower a. plant stand

kwi|t *m* [1] (dowód otrzymania) receipt, ticket; ~**t bagażowy** a luggage ticket a. receipt GB, a baggage check US; ~**t celny** a docket [2] (pokwitowanie) receipt, voucher [3] pot. **mieć ~ty na kogoś** to have the goods on sb pot.

kwit|ek *m* (small) ticket
■ **odejść z ~kiem** to go empty-handed

kwit|nąć *impf vi* [1] to flower, to (be in) bloom [2] *[osoba]* to bloom, to flower [3] *[handel, przemysł]* to thrive, to flourish

kwit|ować *impf vt* [1] (potwierdzać podpisem) to sign for; ~**ować odbiór czegoś** to sign for sth, to confirm receipt of sth [2] (odpowiadać) to respond; ~**ować coś śmiechem/wzruszeniem ramion** to laugh/shrug sth off

kwo|ka *f* mother hen także przen.

kwo|ta *f* [1] (suma pieniędzy) amount, sum [2] (kontyngent) quota

L

L, l *n inv.* L, l

labiryn|t *m* labyrinth, maze także przen.

laboran|t *m*, **~tka** *f* lab(oratory) technician

laboratori|um *n* laboratory

l|ać *impf* **I** *vt* [1] (wylewać) to pour *[wodę, mleko, sos]* (**na coś** on sth); [2] pot. (bić) to beat [3] (odlewać) to cast *[kule, dzwony]*

II *vi [deszcz]* to pour; **lało przez cały tydzień** it rained the whole week

III lać się [1] (płynąć) *[woda]* to pour; **leje mu się z nosa** his nose is running; **leje się ze mnie** pot. (jestem spocony) I'm dripping with sweat; **żar leje się z nieba** przen. it's boiling hot pot. [2] pot. (bić się) to pummel each other

la|da¹ *f* counter

lada² *part.* [1] (byle) **tancerz nie ~** a first-rate dancer; **nie ~ sukces** a considerable success; **~ jaki** (just) any [2] (o czasie) any; **~ dzień** any day (now); **~ chwila** any moment a. time (now)

lagun|a *f* lagoon

laic|ki *adi.* [1] (świecki) *[wychowanie, państwo]* secular, lay [2] (niefachowy) *[podejście]* amateur, layperson's

lai|k *m* layperson; **kompletny ~k** a complete amateur

lak *m* sealing wax; **z braku ~u** for want of anything better

la|ka *f* lacquer

lakie|r *m* (do malowania) varnish; (na samochodzie) paint; **~r do paznokci** nail polish; **~r do włosów** hairspray

lakier|ek *m* patent leather shoe

lakierni|k *m* (car) sprayer

lakier|ować *impf vt* to varnish *[drewno, metal]*; to spray *[karoserię]*; to paint *[paznokcie]*

lakonicznie *adv. grad.* laconically książk.

lakoniczność *n* brevity

lakoniczn|y *adi. grad.* laconic książk.

lal|a *f* doll

■ **malowana ~a** pot. ≈ a Barbie doll pot.; **jak ta ~a** pot. *[samochód, kucharz]* top-notch pot.; *[działać, pracować]* like a dream

lal|ka *f* [1] (zabawka) doll; **bawić się ~kami** to play with one's dolls [2] (w teatrze) puppet

lalka|rz *m*, **~rka** *f* [1] (aktor, aktorka) puppeteer [2] (wytwórca) puppet-maker

lalu|ś *m* pansy pot.

lam|a *f* Zool. llama

lamen|t *m* lament książk.

lamów|ka *f* trim(ming)

lamp|a *f* [1] (do oświetlania) lamp [2] Elektron. valve GB, (vacuum) tube US

lampar|t *m* leopard

lampas *m* [1] (pasek materiału) (side) stripe [2] (na ścianie) trim

lamperi|a *f* dado

lampion *m* lantern

lamp|ka *f* [1] (do oświetlania) lamp; **~ka sygnaliza-cyjna/kontrolna** an indicator/control light; **~ka nocna** bedside lamp; **~ki choinkowe** fairy lights GB [2] (zawartość kieliszka) glass

lamus *m* książk. junk room; **odejść do ~a** to go out of date; **odłożyć coś do ~a** to mothball sth

lance|t *m* lancet

landryn|ka *f* fruit drop

landrynkow|y *adi. [smak]* artificial; *[kolor]* sweet

langu|sta *f* crayfish

la|nie *n* pot. hiding pot.; **spuścić komuś lanie** to give sb a hiding

lans|ować *impf vt* to promote *[talent, modę]*; **on ~uje opinię, że...** he endorses the opinion that...

lapidarnie *adv. grad.* książk. succinctly

lapidarn|y *adi. grad.* książk. succinct

lapsus *m* książk. lapsus linguae książk.

larw|a *f* larva

laryngolo|g *m* ear, nose, and throat specialist a. ENT specialist

laryngologi|a *f* [1] Med. *the branch of medicine dealing with ear, nose and throat diseases* [2] pot. (oddział w szpitalu) ENT (ward)

l|as *m* (skupisko drzew) forest; (mniejszy) wood(s); **las rąk** a forest of hands

■ **być z czymś (jeszcze) w lesie** pot. to not be ready with sth

lase|r *m* laser

las|ka *f* [1] (do podpierania) walking stick; **chodzić o ~ce** to use a walking stick [2] (wanilii, cynamonu, dynamitu) stick [3] pot. (atrakcyjna dziewczyna) (great-looking) chick pot.; **niezła ~ka!** a real looker! a. stunner! pot.

lastr|yko, **~iko** *n, n inv.* terrazzo

lata|ć *impf vi* [1] (poruszać się w powietrzu) *[ptak, owad, samolot]* to fly (**nad czymś** over sth) *[ziemią, wodą]* [2] (podróżować, sterować) **~ć samolotem** (jako pasażer) to travel by air; (jako pilot) to fly; **~ć helikopterem**

to fly a helicopter ③ (drżeć) *[powieka]* to flutter; *[głowa, ręce]* to shake ④ pot. (biegać) to dash; **~ać za kimś** pot. to run after sb pot.

latar|ka *f* torch; **~ka kieszonkowa** a penlight

latar|nia *f* lamp post; **~nia morska** a lighthouse

latarni|k *m* lighthouse keeper

lataw|iec *m* kite

l|ato *n* summer; **w lecie** a. **latem** in (the) summer; **babie lato** (dni) Indian summer; (nitki pajęczyny) gossamer

latorośl *f* ① (winorośl) vine; **winna ~** grapevine ② żart. (dziecko) offspring żart.; progeny

latryn|a *f* latrine

lau|r *m* ① (wieniec) laurel wreath ② przen. laurels; **spocząć na ~rach** to rest on one's laurels; **zbierać ~ry** to win a. reap laurels

laurea|t *m*, **~tka** *f* prizewinner; **~t Nagrody Nobla** a Nobel prizewinner a. laureate

laur|ka *f* ① (powinszowania) greetings card *(handmade by a child)* ② przen. (przesadna pochwała) puff pot.; **wystawić komuś ~kę** to give sb a good write-up

laurow|y *adi. [gałązki]* laurel; **wieniec ~y** a laurel wreath także przen.

law|a *f* lava

lawen|da *f* lavender

lawendow|y *adi. [zapach, mydło]* lavender

lawe|ta *f* ① Wojsk. gun carriage ② Techn. platform trailer

lawin|a *f* avalanche także przen.

lawinowo *adv. [narastać]* dramatically

lawinow|y *adi* ① *[zagrożenie]* avalanche ② (gwałtowny, szybki) dramatic; **sprawa miała ~y przebieg** the whole thing snowballed

lawiran|t *m*, **~tka** *f* pot. smooth a. slick operator pot.

lawir|ować *impf vi* ① (uciekać się do wykrętów) to manoeuvre GB, to maneuver US ② (omijać przeszkody) to dodge

lazu|r *m* książk. azure książk.

lą|d *m* land; **stały ląd** mainland

ląd|ować *impf vi* to land; **~ować w szpitalu** pot. to land a. end up in hospital

lądowisk|o *n* landing field a. strip; **~o dla helikopterów** a landing a. helicopter pad

lądow|y *adi. [granica]* land; **transport ~y** overland transportation

le|c, le|gnąć *pf vi* książk. ① (położyć się) to lie down (**na czymś** on sth) ② (polec) to be killed; **lec w boju** to fall in battle ③ (ulec zniszczeniu) **miasto legło w gruzach** the town was reduced to a heap of rubble

le|cieć *impf vi* ① (w powietrzu) *[ptak, samolot, pocisk]* to fly ② (spadać) *[kamień]* to plunge; *[akcje, ceny]* to go down ③ (spływać) *[łzy, woda]* to run a. flow down; **krew leciała mu z nosa** his nose was bleeding ④ pot. (biec) to dash; **lecieć za kimś** to run after a. chase (after) sb; **muszę lecieć** I must dash a. fly

⑤ pot. (o czasie) to fly ⑥ pot. (być granym) to be on pot. *[film, piosenka]*

■ **brać/kupować coś jak leci** pot. to take/buy things as fast as they come; **w telewizji ogląda wszystko, jak leci** she/he watches whatever comes on; **jak leci?** pot. how's it going? pot.; **lecieć na kogoś** pot. to be after sb; **lecieć na łeb, na szyję** to run at breakneck speed; **wszystko leci mi z rąk** pot. I'm all fingers and thumbs

lecz *coni.* książk. ① (ale) but; yet książk.; **mogła zaprotestować, ~ milczała** she could have protested, but a. yet she kept quiet ② (tylko) but; **nie mówiła po polsku, ~ po rosyjsku** she didn't speak Polish, but Russian

lecznic|a *f* ① (przychodnia) clinic; **~a dla zwierząt** an animal a. a veterinary clinic ② (szpital) (private) hospital

lecznictw|o *n* health care a. services

lecznicz|y *adi. [kąpiele]* curative; *[środki, zioła]* medicinal; *[działanie]* healing

leczo Kulin. *n inv.* letcho

lecz|yć *impf* **Ⅰ** *vt* ① *[lekarz, weterynarz]* to treat *[osobę, zwierzę, dolegliwości]*; *[lekarstwo]* to help cure *[chorobę]*; **~yć kogoś na coś** to treat sb for sth **~yć kogoś czymś** to treat sb with sth ② przen. (łagodzić) to help cure *[nieśmiałość, smutek]*

Ⅱ leczyć się to be treated (**na coś** for sth); **~yć się ziołami** to treat oneself with herbs

ledw|o, ~ie **Ⅰ** *adv.* ① (prawie nie, z trudem) hardly; **~słyszalny/widoczny** barely audible/visible ② (dopiero co) only just

Ⅱ *coni.* **~o wyszli, zaczęło padać** they had only just left a. hardly got outside when it started to rain; **~o zabrał się do pracy, zadzwonił telefon** he had scarcely got down to (some) work when the phone rang; **~o ..., a już** as soon as...

legalizacj|a *f* legalization

legaliz|ować *impf vt* ① (stwierdzać zgodność z normą) to (officially) approve *[urządzenie]* ② (znosić sankcję karną) *[ustawa]* to legalize *[eutanazję, narkotyk]*

legalnie *adv. grad. [działać, pracować]* legally; *[postąpić]* lawfully

legaln|y *adi. [działalność, praca, sposób]* lawful

legen|da *f* ① (opowieść) legend; **~da głosi, że...** legend has it that... ② (objaśnienie) legend

legendarn|y *adi.* legendary

legi|a *f* legion; **~a cudzoziemska** the (French) Foreign Legion

legitymacj|a *f* card; **~a szkolna/studencka** a student card; **~a członkowska** a membership card

legitym|ować *impf vt* ① (sprawdzać tożsamość) **~ować kogoś** to check sb's ID ② książk. (uprawniać) **~ować kogoś do czegoś** to give sb the right a. authorize sb to do sth

legnąć → lec

legowisk|o *n* (ludzi) makeshift bed; (zwierząt) lair

legumin|a *f* flummery
legwan *m* iguana
lej *m* crater
lejc|e *plt* reins
lej|ek *m* funnel
lekarstw|o *n* ① medicine; **jak na** ~**o** pot. a tiny bit/drop ② przen. cure (**na coś** for sth)
leka|rz *m*, ~**rka** *f* doctor; ~ **rodzinny** a family doctor
lekceważąc|y *adi. [stosunek]* dismissive; *[uśmiech]* disdainful; *[ton]* disrespectful; *[głos]* supercilious
lekceważ|yć *impf vt* ① (traktować bez szacunku) to show disrespect to; (traktować pogardliwie) to treat [sb] with contempt a. disdain; ~**yć kolegów** to snub a. slight one's colleagues ② (bagatelizować) ~**yć przepisy** to disregard a. flout the rules; ~**yć (swoje) obowiązki** to neglect one's duties
lekcj|a *f* ① (zajęcia szkolne) lesson; (godzina lekcyjna) period; **po** ~**ach** after school ② (partia materiału w podręczniku) unit ③ (zadanie do odrobienia) homework; **odrabiać** ~**e** to do one's homework
l|ekki *adi. grad. [osoba, rzecz, mróz, posiłek]* light; *[uśmiech, zapach]* faint; **mieć lekką śmierć** to have a. die a painless death
■ **mieć lekką rękę do czegoś** to make light work of sth; **mieć lekką rękę** (być rozrzutnym) to be a big spender; **z lekkim sercem** with a light heart
l|ekko *adv. grad.* ① (nie ciężko) **wyjmij słownik z plecaka, będzie ci lżej** take the dictionary out of your bag, it'll be lighter ② (bez trudu) **klucz w zamku przekręcił się lekko** the key turned easily in the lock ③ (beztrosko) *[czuć się]* carefree; **lekko mu było na sercu** he felt light-hearted ④ (nieznacznie) *[dotknąć, umalować się]* lightly; **miała lekko falujące włosy** she had soft wavy hair ⑤ (przewiewnie) *[ubrany]* lightly ⑥ (lekkostrawnie) *[gotować, jeść]* lightly ⑦ (lekceważąco) *[traktować]* lightly
■ **lekko licząc** at a conservative estimate; **nie ma lekko!** pot. there's always something! pot.
lekkoatle|ta *m*, ~**tka** *f* athlete GB
lekkoatlety|ka *f* athletics GB, track and field US
lekkoduch *m* good-for-nothing
lekkomyślnoś|ć *f* recklessness
lekkomyśln|y *adi.* reckless
lekkostrawn|y *adi.* light
lekoman *m*, ~**ka** *f* pill-popper pot.
lekomani|a /ˌleko'maɲja/ *f* drug dependence
leksykon *m* (informator) lexicon; (tematyczny) companion (guide)
lekto|r *m*, ~**rka** *f* ① (czytający głośno) reader; ~**r radiowy/telewizyjny** a radio/television announcer; **komentarz** ~**ra** a voice-over commentary ② (nauczyciel) foreign language teacher
lektora|t *m* foreign language course
lektu|ra *f* ① (czytanie) reading ② (książka, zbiór książek) reading matter; ~**ra szkolna** a set text; **lista** ~**r** a reading list

lekty|ka *f* sedan chair
lemonia|da *f* lemonade
lemu|r *m* lemur
l|en *m* ① (roślina) flax; (nasiona) linseed ② (tkanina) linen (fabric)
le|nić się *impf v refl.* to laze about a. around
lenistw|o *n* laziness
leniuch *m* pot. lazybones pot.
leniuch|ować *impf vi* pot. to lounge about a. around
leniw|iec *m* sloth
leniw|y Ⅰ *adi. grad.* ① *[osoba]* lazy; **jest strasznie** ~**y** he's bone idle pot. ② *[chód, ruch]* lazy; *[rozmowa]* leisurely; *[poza]* languid
Ⅱ **leniwe** *plt* Kulin. cottage cheese dumplings
le|ń *m* lazybones pot.
leopar|d *m* leopard
lep *m* ~ **na muchy** flypaper
lep|ić *impf* Ⅰ *vt* ① (formować) to mould GB, to mold US *[figurkę, garnek]* (**z czegoś** from a. out of sth); to build *[gniazdo]* (**z czegoś** of a. out of sth); ~**ić bałwana** to make a snowman ② (sklejać) to glue a. stick [sth] together *[skorupy]* (**czymś** with sth)
Ⅱ **lepić się** to be sticky; ~**ić się do czegoś** to stick a. cling to sth; **ręce** ~**ią mi się od miodu** my hands are sticky with honey; **ciało** ~**iło mu się od potu** he felt hot and sticky
■ ~**ić się do kogoś** pot. to cling a. stick to sb like a leech; ~**ić się od** a. **z brudu** to be grimy a. filthy; **wszystko mu się** ~**i do rąk** pot. he's got sticky a. itchy fingers pot.
lep|ki *adi. [błoto, powierzchnia]* sticky; *[sok]* syrupy; *[substancja]* viscous; **ręce** ~**kie od potu** clammy hands
lesbij|ka *f* lesbian
leszcz *m* bream
leszczyn|a *f* hazel
leśniczów|ka *f* forester's lodge
leśnicz|y *m* forester; (w lesie prywatnym) gamekeeper
leśni|k *m* forester
leśn|y *adi.* ① *[droga, gospodarka, zwierzyna]* forest; **robotnik** ~**y** a forestry worker ② *[teren, wzgórza]* woody a. wooded
letarg *m* lethargy także przen.
letni *adi.* ① *[obóz, ubiór, wakacje]* summer ② *[herbata, uczucie]* lukewarm
letni|k *m*, ~**czka** *f* pot. (summer) holidaymaker
letnisk|o *n* summer resort
leukocy|t *m* leucocyte, leukocyte
L|ew *m* Astron., Astrol. Leo
l|ew *m* lion; **lew morski** sea lion; **odważny jak lew** (as) bold a. brave as a lion; **walczyć jak lew** to fight like a tiger
lewa|r *m* Techn. jack
lewatyw|a *f* enema
lewic|a *f* Polit. the Left; **obóz** ~**y** the left wing

lewicow|y *adi. [działacz, polityk]* left-wing; *[gazety, poglądy]* leftist

lew|o *adv.* left; **na ~o od czegoś** on a. to the left of sth; **iść/patrzeć w ~o** a. **na ~o** to go/look left; **pierwsze drzwi na ~o** the first door on the left; **skręcić w ~o** to turn (to the) left; **w ~o zwrot!** left turn!; **z ~a na prawo** from left to right
■ **robić coś na ~o** pot. to do sth on the side pot.

leworęcznoś|ć *f* left-handedness

leworęczn|y *adi.* left-handed

lewostronn|y *adi. [paraliż]* left-side; **w tym kraju obowiązuje ruch ~y** in this country one drives on the left (side of the road)

lew|y [] ** *adi.* ① *[but, noga, strona]* left; **po (czyjejś) ~ej ręce on sb's left ② *(odwrotny)* **włożył koszulę na ~ą stronę** he put on his shirt inside out a. the wrong side out ③ Polit. *[odłam, skrzydło]* left ④ pot. *[dokument]* phoney pot.; *[interes]* shady pot.; *[towar]* hot pot.; *[urządzenie]* clumsy
[] *m* Sport left
■ **mieć dwie ~e ręce** pot. to be all fingers and thumbs GB pot.; **wstać ~ą nogą (z łóżka)** pot. to get out of bed on the wrong side

l|eźć *impf vi* pot. ① (wlec się) to shamble; (z trudem) to trudge ② (pchać się) **gdzie leziesz, baranie!?** where do you think you're going, you clown? pot.

leża|k *m* deckchair

leżak|ować *impf vi* ① *[osoba]* to rest ② *[koniak, wino]* to mature

leżan|ka *f* couch

leż|eć *impf vi* ① *[osoba, rzecz]* to lie (**na czymś** on sth); **~eć w szpitalu** to be in hospital ② (pasować) *[ubranie]* to fit; **garnitur ~y na nim jak ulał** the suit fits him like a glove ③ (znajdować się) **miasto ~y nad rzeką** the town lies on a river ④ pot. (być w niekorzystnej sytuacji) **robota ~y** we're behind with the work; **jeśli nie oddam pieniędzy, to ~ę (i kwiczę)** if I don't give the money back, I'm done for pot.
■ **~eć do góry brzuchem** pot., pejor. to lie about a. around; **~eć na pieniądzach** pot. to be rolling in money pot.

l|ęgnąć się *impf v refl. [pisklęta]* to hatch; *[pasożyty]* to breed; przen. *[podejrzenia]* to be bred; *[plotki]* to be hatched

lęk *m* ① (strach) fear (**przed kimś/czymś** of sb/sth) ② Psych. anxiety; **~ przed szkołą** anxiety about a. over school; **~ przestrzeni** (a) fear of open spaces; **~ wysokości** (a) fear of heights

lęka|ć się *impf v refl.* książk. to fear (**czegoś** sth); **~ć się o bezpieczeństwo dziecka** to fear for one's child's safety

lękliw|y *adi. grad. [mina, uśmiech]* anxious

lgn|ąć *impf vi* ① (przylepiać się) *[glina, śnieg]* to stick (**do czegoś** to sth) ② przen. (odczuwać sympatię) **~ąć do kogoś** to feel drawn towards sb

libacj|a *f* carousal

liberi|a *f* livery

liceali|sta *m*, **~stka** *f* ≈ secondary-school pupil GB, ≈ high-school student US

licencj|a *f* licence GB, license US; **na ~i japońskiej** under Japanese licence

licencja|t *m* (stopień) ≈ bachelor's degree; **~t nauk humanistycznych/ścisłych** Bachelor of Arts/Science

lice|um *n* ≈ secondary school GB, ≈ high school US

lich|o *n* pot. evil spirit; **po kiego ~a się wtrącasz?** why the hell don't you stay out of this a. it? pot.
■ **do ~a (i trochę)** pot. a heck a. hell of a lot pot.; **~o nie śpi** przysł. you never know what might happen

lichtarz *m* candlestick

lichwia|rz *m*, **~rka** *f* usurer

li|chy *adi. grad.* pot. *[zdrowie, ziemia, poeta]* poor; *[dom, warunki]* miserable; *[posiłek]* frugal; *[zarobek]* paltry

licytacj|a *f* ① (publiczna sprzedaż) auction; (licytowanie) bidding ② Gry bidding

**licyt|ować [] ** *vt* ① (sprzedawać) to sell [sth] by auction *[majątek]* ② Gry to bid
[] **licytować się** pot. (przechwalać się) to have a bragging contest a. match pot.

liczb|a *f* ① Mat. number ② (ilość) number; **~a białych ciałek we krwi** the white blood cell count; **zespół w ~ie dwudziestu ludzi** a team of twenty (people) ③ Jęz. number; **~a pojedyncza/mnoga** the singular/plural

liczbow|y *adi. [dane, wartość]* numerical; **stosunek ~y** a ratio

liczebnik *m* numeral

liczebnoś|ć *f* (członków, gatunków) number; (armii, floty) numerical strength; (grupy, populacji) size

liczebn|y *adi.* numerical; **mieć nad kimś przewagę ~ą** to outnumber sb

licznie *adv. grad. [przybyć, występować]* in large a. great numbers; *[reprezentowany]* strongly

licznik *m* ① Techn. meter; (w taksówce) (taxi)meter ② Mat. numerator

liczn|y *adi. grad. [obowiązki, przykłady]* numerous; *[grupa, rodzina]* large; *[naśladowcy]* countless

licz|yć *impf* **[]** *vt* ① (rachować, dodawać) to count *[osoby, rzeczy]*; **nie ~ąc** not including ② (mierzyć) to calculate *[czas, odległość]* ③ Sport to count out *[boksera]*
[] *vi* ① (wymieniać liczby w kolejności) to count; **~yć od 1 do 10** to count from 1 to 10 ② (mieć) to have; **dom ~y sześć pięter** the house has six storeys a. is six storeys high; **grupa ~yła 20 osób** there were twenty people in the group ③ (spodziewać się) **~yć na kogoś/na coś** to count a. rely a. depend on sb/sth
[] **liczyć się** ① (być liczonym) to count; **urlop ~y mi się od środy** my leave runs from Wednesday

2 (mieć znaczenie) to matter; **~ące się firmy** major companies; **~y się to, że...** what matters a. counts is that... 3 (brać pod uwagę) to take into account; **musisz ~yć to z tym, że...** you have to take into account that...; **nie ~yć się z czyimś zdaniem** to ignore sb's opinion; **nie ~yć się z innymi** to show no consideration for others

■ **~ się ze słowami!** watch your tongue!

lide|r m leader; (w zespole muzycznym) frontman

li|ga f 1 Sport (grupa drużyn) league; (system rozgrywek) league (competition) 2 (organizacja) league; **Liga Narodów** the League of Nations

lignin|a f cellulose wadding

likie|r m liqueur

likwidacj|a f 1 (patologii, zjawiska) eradication; (odpadów) disposal; (sklepu) closing down; (przedsiębiorstwa) liquidation 2 euf. (zgładzenie) elimination

likwid|ować impf vt 1 (usuwać) to eliminate [ból, patologię]; to close down [organizację, przedsiębiorstwo]; to abolish [monopol]; to close [konto] 2 euf. (zabijać) to liquidate [świadka, wroga]

lila n inv., adi. inv. lilac

lili|a f lily

lilij|ka f (harcerska) scout's badge

liliow|y[1] adi. (o kolorze) lilac(-coloured a. colored US)

liliow|y[2] adi. [bukiet, wieniec] lily

lilipu|t m dwarf

limf|a f lymph

limi|t m limit

limit|ować impf vt książk. to limit [dostawy, produkcję]; **seria ~owana** a limited edition

limuzyn|a f limousine

lin|a f rope; (gruba, mocna) cable

lincz m lynching

lincz|ować impf vt to lynch

lini|a /'linja/ f 1 (znak graficzny) line; **~a przerywana** (na papierze) a dotted line; (na jezdni) a broken line; **~e papilarne** lines on the palm, fingers, and thumb 2 (granica) line; **~a horyzontu** the line of the horizon; **~a brzegowa** a shoreline 3 (szereg) line; **ustawić coś w jednej ~i** to arrange sth in a line 4 (kształt) (samochodu) shape; (spodni) cut 5 (figura) figure; **dbać o ~ę** to watch one's figure 6 Elektr., Telekom. line 7 (trasa) **~a tramwajowa** a tram line a. route; **~a autobusowa** a bus route a. service; **~a kolejowa Warszawa-Kraków** the Warsaw-Cracow (railway) line; **~a lotnicza** an airline 8 Przem. line; **~a produkcyjna/montażowa** the production/assembly line 9 Wojsk. **~a frontu** the front line 10 (ród) line; **pochodzić w prostej ~i od kogoś** to be a direct descendant of sb

lini|eć impf vi 1 Zool. to moult 2 pot. [kot, pies] to shed hair(s) a. a coat

linij|ka f 1 (do mierzenia) ruler 2 (wiersz, wers) line, verse

liniow|iec /lin'jovjets/ m 1 (osoba) front-line soldier 2 (statek) liner; (okręt wojenny) battleship

lin|ka f cord

linoskocz|ek m tightrope walker

lip|a f 1 Bot. lime a. linden (tree) 2 pot. (kłamstwo) utter a. downright lie 3 pot. (tandeta) (piece of) junk

■ **na ~ę** (niestarannie) sloppily, carelessly; (nieuczciwie) dishonestly, unfairly

lip|iec m July

lipn|y adi. pot. [adres, dokument] phoney; [robota] botched

liry|ka f (rodzaj literacki) lyric (genre); (utwory) lyric poetry a. verse

lis m fox także przen.; **farbowany ~** pot. double-dealer

lisic|a f vixen

li|st m letter; **list polecony** registered a. certified US letter; **list gończy** a warrant for sb's arrest

li|sta f list; **lista obecności** the roll; **lista płac** the payroll; **lista przebojów** the (hit) charts; **lista wyborcza** the electoral register

list|ek m 1 (celofanu, papieru) (small) sheet 2 (płaskie opakowanie) sachet GB, packet

❏ **~ek figowy** fig leaf

listonosz m postman, mailman US

listopa|d m November

listown|y adi. [kontakt, zawiadomienie] by mail a. letter a. post

list|wa f 1 (z drewna) (wooden) slat; **~wa przypodłogowa** skirting (board) GB, baseboard US 2 Moda (z materiału) binding

lisza|j m 1 Med. lichen 2 (skaza) blemish; **~je zacieków na ścianie** patches of water stains on the wall

liścia|sty adi. [herbata, warzywo] leaf; [drzewo, las] broadleaved

liś|ć m leaf

litani|a /li'tanja/ f litany także przen.

lite|ra f letter; **wielka ~ra** a capital letter; **~ry drukowane** block letters

literac|ki adi. [dzieło, gatunek] literary

literalnie adv. książk. literally

literaln|y adi. książk. literal; **~y przekład** a literal a. word-for-word translation

litera|t m writer

literat|ka f 1 (pisarka) (woman) writer 2 (szklaneczka) vodka glass

literatu|ra f literature; **~ra piękna** belles-lettres książk.; **~ra faktu** non-fiction; **~ra fachowa** specialist literature

liter|ować impf vt to spell

literów|ka f typo pot.

litościw|y adi. grad. [osoba] merciful; [gest, uczynek] compassionate; [słowa, spojrzenia] pitying

litoś|ć f (łaska) mercy; (współczucie) compassion; (pożałowanie) pity; **bez ~ci** without mercy; **z ~ci** out of pity

lit|ować się impf v refl. 1 (współczuć) to feel sorry (**nad kimś/czymś** for sb); (z pożałowaniem) to pity (**nad kimś** sb) ☐ (okazywać łaskę) to have mercy (**nad kimś/czymś** on sb/sth)

lit|r *m* litre GB, liter US

liturgi|a *f* liturgy

liturgiczn|y *adi.* liturgical

li|ty *adi. [drewno, skała]* solid; *[posąg, złoto]* cast

lizać → **liznąć**[1]

lizak *m* lollipop

li|znąć[1] *pf* — **li|zać** *impf vi* to lick także przen.

■ **lizać rany** to lick one's wounds; **palce lizać** finger-licking good US pot.

li|znąć[2] *pf vt* ☐ pot. (spróbować) **liznęła tylko zupę** she barely touched the soup ☐ pot. (poznać powierz-chownie) to learn a smattering of *[łaciny]*

lizus *m*, **~ka** *f* pot. crawler pot., pejor.

loch *m* dungeon

lo|cha *f* sow

lodołamacz *m* ice-breaker

lodowato *adv.* ☐ (o temperaturze) icy; **woda była ~ zimna** the water was ice-cold; **w pokoju jest ~** the room's freezing ☐ przen. *[zachować się, spojrzeć]* icily

lodowa|ty *adi. [woda, nogi]* ice-cold; *[ton, wzrok]* icy

lodowcow|y *adi. [osady, erozja]* glacial; **epoka ~a** ice age

lodow|iec *m* glacier

lodowisk|o *n* skating a. ice rink

lodow|y *adi.* ☐ (z lodu) ice; **wierzchołek góry ~ej** the tip of the iceberg także przen. ☐ Kulin. ice-cream; **tort ~y** an ice-cream gateau

lodów|ka *f* (chłodziarka) refrigerator; fridge pot.; (turystyczna) cooler

lodziarz *m* ice-cream vendor

logarytm *m* logarithm

loggi|a /'lodʒja/ *f* ☐ (kryty balkon) (recessed) balcony ☐ Archit. loggia

logicznie ☐ *adv. [uzasadniony, powiązany]* logically; **~ rzecz biorąc** logically speaking ☐ *adv. grad. [myśleć, mówić]* logically

logiczn|y ☐ *adi. [błąd, umysł, myślenie]* logical ☐ *adi. grad. [rozwiązanie, posunięcie]* logical

logi|ka *f* logic; **to wbrew ~ce** it's illogical

logope|da *m* speech therapist

log|ować się *impf v refl.* to log on a. in

lojalnie *adv. grad. [postępować]* loyally; **~ cię uprzedzam, że...** I must warn you that...

lojalnoś|ć *f* loyalty (**wobec kogoś** to sb)

lojaln|y *adi. grad.* loyal

lok *m* (pukiel włosów) lock; (wijący się) curl

lokal *m* ☐ książk. (mieszkanie) flat GB, apartment US; **~ zastępczy** temporary accommodation ☐ książk. (pomieszczenie) place; **~ handlowy/użytkowy** com-mercial/business premises ☐ (restauracja) restaurant; (kawiarnia) café; **nocny ~** a nightclub

lokalizacj|a *f* location

lokaliz|ować *impf vt* to locate *[budynek, obiekt]*; to localize *[problem, pożar]*

lokalnie *adv.* locally; **~ gęste mgły** dense fog patches

lokaln|y *adi. [przymrozki, tradycja]* local; **władze ~e** the local authority, local government

loka|ta *f* ☐ (kapitału) investment; (oszczędności) deposit ☐ (miejsce) place; **zająć drugą ~tę** to finish second a. to come in second place

lokato|r *m*, **~rka** *f* ☐ (kamienicy, budynku) resident; (mieszkania) occupant ☐ (najemca) tenant; **dziki ~r** a squatter

lokomotyw|a *f* ☐ (railway) engine, locomotive ☐ przen. motive a. driving force przen.; **~a uprze-mysłowienia** the motive a. driving force behind industrialization

lok|ować *impf* ☐ *vt* książk. ☐ (umieszczać w banku) to deposit *[pieniądze, oszczędności]*; (inwestować) to invest *[pieniądze, oszczędności]*; **~ować pieniądze w nie-ruchomościach** to invest in property a. real estate US ☐ (rozmieszczać) to accommodate *[gościa]*; (sadzać) to seat *[osobę]* ☐ (umieszczać) to place *[przedmiot]*; to locate *[siedzibę, przedstawicielstwo]*

loków|ka *f* (elektryczna) electric curler a. roller; (wałeczek) curler

lombar|d *m* pawnshop

lon|t *m* fuse

lornet|ka *f* (pair of) binoculars; **~ka teatralna** opera glasses

los *m* ☐ (koleje życia) lot ☐ (przeznaczenie) fate; **zdać się na ~ szczęścia** to take pot luck ☐ (na loterii) ticket; **szczęśliwy ~** a winning ticket; **wygrać ~ na loterii** przen. to hit the jackpot pot.

■ **masz ci ~!** pot. bad luck!

los|ować *impf vt* to draw *[numer, zwycięzcę]*

losowa|nie *n* draw

losowo *adv. [wybierać, pojawiać się]* randomly

losow|y *adi. [wybór, zdarzenie]* random; **gry ~e** games of chance

lo|t *m* flight; **robić coś w locie** *[ptak, owad]* to do sth in flight; przen. to do sth on the run; **patrzeć na coś z lotu ptaka** to have a bird's-eye view of sth

■ **obniżyć loty** to lower one's standards; **w lot** *[pojąć, zrozumieć]* at once

loteri|a *f* lottery także przen.; **~a fantowa** a tombola; **~a pieniężna** a cash lottery

lot|ka *f* ☐ (pióro) flight feather ☐ Lotn. aileron, flap ☐ (w badmintonie) shuttlecock

lotni|a *f* hang-glider

lotniarz *m* hang-glider (pilot)

lotnictw|o *n* (dziedzina) aviation; (transport) air transport; (siły zbrojne) air force

lotnicz|y *adi. [katastrofa, baza]* air; *[przemysł, paliwo]* aviation; *[fotografia]* aerial; *[inżynieria, technika]* aeronautical; **linia ~a** an airline; **poczta ~a** airmail; **port ~y** an airport

lotni|k *m* pilot

lotnisk|o n airfield; (port lotniczy) airport
lotniskow|iec m aircraft carrier
lotn|y [] adi. [1] Fiz. (gazowy) gaseous; (łatwo parujący) volatile [2] (zwiewny) airborne [3] (zmieniający miejsce pobytu) ~**a brygada** a flying squad
[] adi. grad. [osoba] bright; [umysł] sharp
lotos m [1] Bot. lotus [2] (pozycja) lotus (position a. posture)
l|oża f [1] (w teatrze, parlamencie) box; **loża prasowa** the press gallery [2] (w masonerii) lodge
l|ód [] m (zamarznięta woda) ice; **whisky z lodem** whisky on the rocks
[] **lody** plt ice cream; **lody na patyku/w waflu** an ice lolly/a wafer
■ **budować** a. **stawiać zamki na lodzie** to build castles in the air; **mieć forsy jak lodu** pot. to have loads of money pot.; **zostać na lodzie** to be left out in the cold; **zostawić kogoś na lodzie** to leave sb in the lurch
lśniąc|y adi. [włosy] glossy; [oczy] shining; [parkiet] shiny
lśni|ć impf vi [1] [brylant, włosy] to gleam [2] (być czystym) to shine
lub coni. or; ~ **też** or (else); ~ **też nie** or not (as the case may be)
lubczyk m lovage
lubi|ć impf vt to like [osobę, mleko, książki]; ~**ć kogoś za coś** to like sb for sth; **był** ~**any w szkole** he was well-liked at school
luboś|ć f książk. **z** ~**cią** [przeciągać się, wygrzewać się] luxuriously
lu|d m [1] (klasa społeczna) people; **wywodzić się z ludu** to come from the lower classes of society [2] pot. (tłum) crowd; **kupa luda** a crowd of people [3] (plemię, szczep) people
ludnoś|ć f population
ludn|y adi. grad. [okolica, teren] populous; [ulica, plac] crowded
ludobójcz|y adi. [wojna, walki] genocidal
ludobójstw|o n książk. genocide
ludoja|d m maneater; **tygrys/rekin** ~**d** a man-eating tiger/shark
ludow|y adi. [1] [muzyka, stroje, festyn] folk; **kuchnia** ~**a** a regional cuisine [2] [ruch] popular; **działacz** ~**y** a peasant activist; **republika** ~**a** a people's republic
ludożerc|a m cannibal
ludzik m figurine; ~**i z żołędzi** figures made from acorns
❏ **zielone** ~**i** pot. little green men żart.
ludz|ki [] adi. [1] [czaszka, natura, mowa] human; **zrobić wszystko, co w** ~**kiej mocy** to do everything humanly possible [2] (życzliwy, dobry) humane
[] **po ludzku** adv. (przychylnie) kindly; (jak należy) [ubierać się, mieszkać] decently; [wyglądać] decent
ludzkoś|ć f humankind

luf|a f (część broni palnej) barrel
lufcik m ≈ window vent
luf|t m **być do** ~**tu** pot. to be good for nothing
luk m Żegl. [1] (otwór) hatch(way); ~ **wentylacyjny** a ventilation hatch [2] (ładownia) hold
lu|ka f [1] (puste miejsce) gap [2] przen. blank; **luki w pamięci** a mental blank; **luka prawna** a legal loophole
luk|ier m icing
lukr|ować impf vt to ice [tort, pączki]
luksus m luxury
luksusowo adv. luxuriously; **żyć** ~ to live in luxury
luksusow|y adi. [auto, hotel] luxury; [ubrania, jacht] luxurious; [prezent] extravagant
lula|ć impf vt pot. ~**ć dziecko do snu** to lull a baby to sleep
lump m pot. layabout pot.
lunaty|k m, ~**czka** f sleepwalker
lu|nąć pf vi [deszcz] to start pouring down
lune|ta f telescope
lup|a f magnifying glass; **wziąć coś pod** ~**ę** pot. to place sth under the microscope
lu|ra f pot. dishwater przen.
luster|ko n mirror; ~**ko kieszonkowe** a pocket mirror; ~**ko boczne/wsteczne** a wing/rear-view a. driving mirror
lustracj|a f [1] książk. (przegląd) inspection, survey [2] Polit. ≈ vetting
lust|ro n [1] (zwierciadło) mirror; ~**ro weneckie** (do obserwowania) two-way mirror [2] przen. (powierzchnia wody) surface
lustr|ować impf vt [1] (dokonywać przeglądu) to inspect [teren robót, plac budowy] [2] Polit. to vet [urzędnika, polityka] [3] (przyglądać się) to scrutinize
lustrzan|ka f Fot. reflex camera
luteran|in m, ~**ka** f Lutheran
luteranizm m Lutheranism
lutni|a f lute
lutnictw|o n violin-making
lutni|k m violin-maker
lutni|sta m, ~**stka** f lutenist
lut|ować impf vt to solder; (mosiądzem) to braze
lutownic|a f soldering iron
lut|y m February
luz [] m [1] (wolna przestrzeń) room [2] (wolny czas) free time [3] pot. (odprężenie psychiczne) ease; (swoboda zachowania) ease of manner; **to facet na** ~**ie** he's a laid-back kind of guy pot.; **podejdź do tego na** ~**ie** take it easy [4] Techn. (odstęp) clearance; (nadmierny) backlash [5] Aut. (pozycja) neutral; **na** ~**ie** (o trybach, biegach) in neutral; (o maszynie, silniku) idling
[] **luzem** adv. [1] (bez opakowania) loose [2] (bez opieki) **puszczać dzieci** ~**em** to let children out a. off on their own; **biegać** ~**em** [zwierzę] to run loose
luzac|ki adi. pot. [zachowanie, sposób bycia] laid-back pot.

luzacko *adv.* pot. *[ubierać się]* casually; *[wyglądać, zachowywać się]* laid-back pot.

luza|k *m* 1 (o osobie) pot. cool guy pot. 2 spare horse *(led along unsaddled and/or unbridled)*

luz|ować *impf vt* 1 (zastępować) to relieve *[wachtę, brygadę]* 2 (zmniejszać naprężenie) to loosen *[linę, uprząż]*

luźn|o [] *adv. grad.* loosely; **w pociągu zrobiło się** ~**iej** the train became less crowded

[] *adv.* 1 (swobodnie) **pies biegający** ~**o bez smyczy** a dog running (around) loose a. free 2 przen. ~**o wtrącone uwagi** asides; ~**o połączone epizody powieści** the loosely-linked episodes of the novel

luźn|y [] *adi. grad.* 1 *[płaszcz, spodnie]* loose-(-fitting), baggy; *[obuwie]* roomy; **ta spódnica jest na mnie za** ~**a** this skirt is too big for me 2 (niezwarty) **osiedla o** ~**ej zabudowie** a well-spaced a. well-laid-out housing estate 3 pot. (wolny) free; **jutro będę** ~**iejsza** I'll have more free time tomorrow

[] *adi.* 1 (niezwiązany) loose; *[fabuła]* loose(ly)-knit; **kilka** ~**ych uwag** a few miscellaneous remarks 2 przen. (niezobowiązujący) casual; ~**a rozmowa** a casual conversation 3 pot. (o autobusie, tramwaju) not crowded

lwi *adi. [grzywa, paszcza]* lion's; ~**a część** the lion's share

lwic|a *f* lioness

lyc|ra /'lajkra/ *f* Lycra®

Ł

łabę|dź *m* swan; (samiec) cob
łach *m* pot. old rag
ła|cha *f* sandbank
łachman *m* pot. shabby old clothes
łachmy|ta *m, f* pot. scruff GB pot.
łacia|ty *adi. [krowa, pies]* spotted; *[koń]* piebald
łacin|a *f* ① (język łaciński) Latin ② pot. (język wulgarny) bad a. vulgar language
łacińs|ki *adi.* Latin
ła|d *m* order; **dojść z czymś do ładu** to get to grips with sth; **dojść z kimś do ładu** to come to terms with sb; **bez ładu (i składu)** chaotically
ładnie **Ⅰ** *adv. grad.* nicely; **jest ∼** it's nice (weather); **∼j ci w niebieskim** blue suits you better; **to bardzo ∼ z twojej strony** that's very kind a. nice of you
Ⅱ *adv.* pot. ① (podkreślając wielkość) **∼ zarabiać** to earn a. make good money ② pot., iron. **∼ mnie urządziłeś!** (this is) a fine a. nice mess you've got me into!
ładni|eć *impf vi* to grow prettier
ładn|y **Ⅰ** *adi. grad. [osoba, oczy, miasto]* pretty; *[piosenka, pogoda]* nice; *[charakter pisma]* neat
Ⅱ *adi.* pot. ① (znaczny) considerable; **∼a sumka** a tidy sum; **znamy się ∼ych parę lat** we've known each other for a good many a. a good few years ② pot., iron. fine iron.; **∼y z ciebie przyjaciel!** a fine friend you are!; **∼e kwiatki!** how nice!
ład|ować *impf* **Ⅰ** *vt* ① (pakować, napełniać) to load *[ciężarówkę, statek, pistolet]* ② Fiz. to charge *[akumulator, baterię]* ③ pot. (inwestować) to invest; **∼ować w coś forsę** to pour money into sth
Ⅱ ładować się pot. (wchodzić) to get in; **∼ować się do autobusu** to clamber onto a bus; *[wiele osób]* to pile onto a bus; (rozpychając się) to push a. shove one's way onto a bus; **∼ować się do środka** to pile in; (bez pozwolenia) to barge in
ładowni|a *f* Lotn., Żegl. (cargo) hold
ładowność *f* capacity
ładun|ek *m* ① (towar) cargo ② (materiał wybuchowy) (explosive) charge ③ przen. (emocji, uczuć) charge, build-up ④ Fiz. charge
łagodnie *adv. grad. [patrzeć]* kindly; *[uśmiechać się, wznosić się, zahamować]* gently; *[traktować]* leniently
łagodni|eć *impf vi [osoba, głos, rysy twarzy]* to soften; *[upał]* to ease off; *[wiatr]* to abate książk.; *[ból]* to ease

łagodn|y *adi. grad. [głos, usposobienie]* gentle; *[wyrok]* lenient; *[dźwięk, światło]* soft; *[klimat, przyprawa]* mild; *[lądowanie, zakręt]* gentle
łag|odzić *impf vt* to ease *[ból, napięcia]*; to alleviate książk.; to relieve *[cierpienia]*; to mitigate *[karę, objawy choroby]*; to cushion *[uderzenie]*; **∼odzić konflikt** to tone down a conflict
łaj|ać *impf vt* książk. to reprimand (**kogoś za coś** sb for sth)
łajb|a *f* pot. (old) tub pot.
łajdacz|yć się *impf v refl.* pot. to lead a dissolute a. debauched life
łajda|k *m* nasty piece of work pejor.
łajn|o *n* dung
łakn|ąć *impf vi* książk. ① (odczuwać głód) to be a. feel hungry ② (pragnąć) to crave (**czegoś** sth); to thirst (**czegoś** after a. for sth); **∼ąć miłości** to long a. yearn for love
łaknieni|e *n* książk. craving
łakoci|e *plt* sweets
łakomczuch *m*, **∼a** *f* gourmand
łakom|ić się *impf v refl.* to covet (**na coś** sth)
łakomstw|o *n* greed(iness)
łakom|y *adi.* greedy także przen.; **patrzyć ∼ym wzrokiem na coś** to eye sth greedily; **∼y kąsek** a tasty morsel
łam *m* Druk. column; **na ∼ach gazet** a. prasy in the papers; **trafić na ∼y gazet** to get into a. make the papers
łam|ać *impf* **Ⅰ** *vt* ① (kruszyć) to break *[gałąź, kość]*; **∼ać komuś karierę** przen. to ruin a. wreck sb's career ② (pokonywać) to break *[opór, szyfr]* ③ (naruszać) to break *[prawo, przepisy]* ④ Druk. to make up *[tekst]*
Ⅱ łamać się ① (pękać) to break ② (zniechęcać się) *[osoba]* to give up ③ pot. (wahać się) to dither; to dilly-dally pot.
■ **∼ać sobie głowę (nad czymś)** pot. to rack one's brains a. to puzzle (over sth); **∼ać sobie język** pot. to twist one's tongue; **∼ie mnie w kościach** pot. my bones are aching
łama|ga *m, f* pot. (clumsy) oaf
łaman|y *adi. [linia]* broken; **mówić ∼ą polszczyzną** to speak (in) broken Polish; **pięć ∼e przez siedem** five stroke seven
łamigłów|ka *f* (układanka) jigsaw (puzzle); (zagadka) puzzle także przen.

łamistrajk *m* pot. strike-breaker; blackleg GB pot., pejor.

łamliw|y *adi. [włosy, paznokcie]* brittle

łan *m* książk. cornfield

ła|nia *f* (samica jelenia) hind; (samica daniela) doe

łańcuch *m* chain także przen.; ~ **górski** a (mountain) range a. chain

łańcusz|ek *m* (haft, wzór szydełkowy) chain stitch

łap|a *f* 1 (zwierzęcia) paw; (ptaka) foot 2 pot. (ręka) mitt pot.
■ **dać komuś w ~ę** pot. to give sb a backhander GB, to grease sb's palm pot.; **dostać a. oberwać po ~ach** pot. to get a rap on a. over the knuckles; **położyć na czymś ~ę** pot. to get a. lay one's hands on sth

łap|ać *impf* 1 *vt* 1 (chwytać) to catch *[osobę, rzecz]*; to pick up *[falę, stację]*; ~**ać kogoś za ramię** to grab a. catch sb by the arm; ~**ać oddech** to gasp (for breath a. air); ~**ać złodzieja!** stop thief!; (czuję, że) ~**ie mnie grypa** (I feel like) I'm coming down with (the) flu 2 pot. (rozumieć) to get; **zaczął już ~ać angielski** he's getting the hang of English now
2 **łapać się** to grab hold (**czegoś** of sth); ~**ać się za serce** to put one's hand on one's heart; ~**ać się na czymś** pot. to catch oneself doing sth; ~**ać się za coś** pot. to get down to sth *[zmywanie, sprzątanie]*
■ ~**ać kogoś za słowa** pot. to trip sb up (on his/ her words)

łapan|ka *f* pot. **ministrowie z ~ki** hastily a. hurriedly recruited ministers

łapczywie *adv. grad. [jeść]* hungrily; *[pić]* greedily

łapczyw|y *adi.* greedy

łap|ka *f* 1 pot. (do garnków) pot holder; (do piekarnika) oven glove a. mitt 2 (pułapka) trap; ~ **ka na myszy** a mousetrap
❏ ~**ka na muchy** fly swatter a. swat

łapów|ka *f* pot. backhander pot.

łapówkarz *m* pot. bribe-taker

łasic|a *f* weasel

ła|sić się *impf v refl.* to fawn także przen. (**do kogoś** on a. over sb)

łas|ka *f* 1 (przychylność) favour GB, favor US; **wkraść się w czyjeś ~ki** to ingratiate oneself with sb, to curry favour with sb; **zaskarbić sobie czyjeś ~ki** to win sb's favour 2 (uwolnienie od kary) reprieve; **prawo ~ki** (royal) prerogative of mercy GB, (executive) clemency power US 3 Relig. grace
■ **bez ~ki!** pot. don't do me any (big) favours! iron.; **a podziękować nie ~ka?** iron. shouldn't you say thank you?; **artysta z bożej ~ki** iron. a piteous a. pathetic artist; **podaj mi gazetę, z ~ki swojej** could you please hand me the paper?; **być na czyjejś ~ce** to be at sb's mercy; **zostawić kogoś na ~ce losu** to leave sb to their fate; **wrócić do ~k** *[osoba]* to be back in grace; *[getry, kapelusze]* to be back in style a. fashion

łaskawie *adv. grad. [uśmiechnąć się, wysłuchać]* kindly

łaskaw|y 1 *adi. grad. [spojrzenie, uśmiech]* kind; *[los]* favourable
2 *adi.* książk. (w formach grzecznościowych) ~**y panie/ ~a pani** dear sir/madam

łasko|tać *impf vt* to tickle

łaskot|ki *plt* **bać się ~ek** to hate being tickled; **mieć ~ki** to be ticklish

łas|ować *impf vi* pot. to filch titbits pot.

łasuch *m* pot. gourmand

łas|y *adi.* książk. greedy także przen. (**na coś** for sth); **być ~ym na słodycze** to have a sweet tooth

łaszczy|ć się *impf v refl.* pot. ~**ć się na coś** to be lured by sth

ła|ta *f* 1 (w ubraniu, bucie) patch pot. 2 (na sierści, upierzeniu) patch; **krowa w łaty** a piebald cow

łata|ć *impf vt* to patch *[ubranie]*; ~**ć budżet** pot. to patch (up) gaps in the budget

łat|ka *f* (small) patch; **przypiąć komuś ~kę** to have a. take a dig at sb

łatwi|zna *f* pot. cinch, doss GB pot.; **to ~zna** it's a piece of cake pot.; **iść na ~znę** to take the easy way out

łatw|o *adv. grad. [przekonać, nudzić się]* easily; ~**o powiedzieć** it's all very well to say, it's easy to say; **nie jest mu ~o** he doesn't have it easy; **ta melodia ~o wpada w ucho** it's a catchy tune

łatwopaln|y *adi.* inflammable GB, flammable

łatwoś|ć *f* 1 (brak trudności) easiness, ease; **zrobić coś z ~cią** to do sth with ease; **wygrać z ~cią** to win hands down 2 (umiejętność) ~**ć uczenia się** aptitude for learning

łatwowiern|y *adi.* gullible

łatw|y *adi. grad.* 1 (prosty) *[egzamin]* easy; ~**y do konserwacji** *[ubranie]* easy-care; ~**y do przewidzenia** predictable; ~**y w montażu** quick-assembly, easy to assemble; ~**y w obsłudze** user-friendly, easy to use 2 (bezkonfliktowy) **była ~a w obejściu** she was easy-going; **nie miała z nim ~ego życia** she didn't have an easy life with him 3 (zdobyty bez wysiłku) *[pieniądze, powodzenie]* easy 4 (popularny) *[rozrywka]* light; **muzyka lekka, ~a i przyjemna** easy listening

ław|a *f* (do siedzenia) bench; (niski stół) coffee table; ~**a oskarżonych** the dock GB; ~**a przysięgłych** the jury

ławic|a *f* 1 (ryb) school 2 (mielizna) shoal

ław|ka *f* 1 (do siedzenia) bench; ~**ka kościelna** a pew 2 (w szkole) desk; **siedzieć w ~ce** to sit at a desk

ławni|k *m* Prawo ≈ juror

ła|zić *impf vi* pot. to traipse pot.; to trudge; **łazić po sklepach** to traipse a. tramp (a)round the shops; **ledwo łaził** he could barely walk
■ **łazić za czymś** pot. to go looking for sth; **łazić za kimś** pot. to pursue sb

łazien|ka f ① (do mycia) bathroom ② euf. loo GB pot., euf.; bathroom US euf.

łaźni|a f bathhouse; **parno jak w ~i** as humid as a steam bath

łącz|e n ① Telekom. connection; (internetowe) link ② Techn. connector, joint

łącz|ka f (wzór) pattern of tiny flowers (on cotton, silk)

łącznicz|ka f liaison; Wojsk. liaison officer

łącznie adv. (razem) including; (w sumie) in all, altogether; **pisać coś ~** to write sth as one word

łączni|k m ① (osoba) liaison; Wojsk. liaison officer ② Sport midfielder ③ (więź) link ④ Jęz. (dywiz) hyphen; (spójka) linking verb ⑤ Budow. passage; (na wysokości) elevated walkway ⑥ Techn. connector, fastener

łącznoś|ć f ① (kontakt) contact (**z kimś** with sb); **utrzymywać ~ć z kimś** to be in contact with sb ② (dział komunikacji) communication(s)

łączn|y adi. ① (połączony) [suma, zysk] total; **~a wartość** combined value; **pisownia ~a** un-hyphenated spelling ② (spajający) connective; **tkan-ka ~a** connective tissue

łącz|yć impf ❚ vt ① (spajać) to join [elementy]; **~ą nas wspólne zainteresowania** we have common interests ② (umożliwiać komunikację) to connect; **kanał ~y morze z jeziorem** the canal connects the lake with the sea ③ (tworzyć całość) to match [kolory, części ubrania] ④ (godzić) to combine [funkcje, obowiązki] ⑤ (kojarzyć) to link (**z czymś** with sth); **czy należy ~yć tę chorobę z otyłością?** is there a link between this illness and obesity? ⑥ Telekom. to connect

❚❚ **łączyć się** ① (stykać się) [elementy] to be joined; [ręce] to join; [gałęzie, drogi] to meet ② Telekom. to get through (**z kimś** to sb); Radio to go over (**z czymś** to sth); **~ymy się z Krakowem** we're going over to Cracow ③ (kojarzyć się) to be associated (**z czymś** with sth) ④ Chem. to combine (**z czymś** with sth)

łą|ka f meadow

ł|eb m ① (zwierzęcia) head ② pot. (człowieka) noggin pot. ■ **zakuty łeb** a blockhead pot.; **łeb w łeb (z kimś)** neck and neck (with sb); **na łeb, na szyję** pot. [pędzić, spadać] headlong, head first; **patrzeć spode łba** to scowl, to glower; **ukręcić czemuś łeb** pot. to hush sth up; **wziąć w łeb** pot. [plany] to fall through; **wziąć kogoś za łeb** pot. to take sb (well a. firmly) in hand

łeb|ek m ① pot. (osoba) **od ~ka** per head; **jechać na ~ka** to get a lift a. ride (for payment) ② (gwoździa, zapałki) head; **~ek szpilki** pinhead ■ **po ~kach** pot. cursorily; **przejrzeć coś po ~kach** to skim over a. through sth

łebs|ki adi. pot. brainy pot.

łechtacz|ka f Anat. clitoris

łech|tać impf vt to tickle także przen.

łepek → **łebek**

łez|ka f ① (dekolt) keyhole neckline ② (wisiorek) teardrop pendant; (kolczyki) **~ki** eardrops ■ **film/opowieść z ~ką** a tear jerker pot.; **wspominać coś z ~ką w oku** to tearfully reminisce about sth

ł|gać impf vi pot. to lie

łgarstw|o n książk. lie

łgarz m książk. liar

łka|ć impf vi to sob, to whine

łobuz m pot. (urwis) rascal żart.; (chuligan) roughneck pot.

łobuzers|ki adi. [mina, uśmiech] roguish; [wybryk] low(-down) pot.

łody|ga f stem

łojotok m seborrh(o)ea

łok|ieć m elbow; **trącić kogoś ~ciem** to nudge sb

łom m (pręt) crowbar; (złodziejski) jemmy GB, jimmy US

łomo|t m (głuchy odgłos) thud; (dudnienie) rumble; (huk) bang

łomo|tać impf vi to thud; [serce] to pound; **~tać do drzwi** to bang a. hammer on the door

łon|o n ① Anat. womb ② książk., przen. bosom książk., przen.; **na ~ie natury** in the bosom of nature; **rozłam w ~ie partii** a split within the ranks of the party

łopa|ta f (do przerzucania) shovel; (do kopania) spade; **kłaść coś komuś ~tą do głowy** pot. to try to get sth across to sb

łopat|ka f ① (zabawka) toy shovel; (do smażenia) spatula ② Techn. paddle ③ Anat. shoulder blade; **rozłożyć kogoś na (obie) ~ki** Sport to pin sb down; pot., przen. to knock sb into a cocked hat; **leżymy na obie ~ki** pot. we're done for pot. ④ Kulin. blade (bone), shoulder

łopian m burdock

łopo|t m flap, flapping

łopo|tać impf vi [flaga, skrzydła, żagiel] to flap; **~tać na wietrze** to flap in the wind; **~tać skrzydłami** to flap its wings

łosko|t m (pociągu) clatter; (dział, gromu) rumble; **brama zamknęła się z ~tem** the gate banged shut

łosko|tać impf vi [pociąg, kopyta] to clatter; [grzmot] to rumble

łososiow|y adi. [kolor] salmon-pink

łoso|ś m salmon

łosz|a f elk cow, moose cow US

ło|ś m elk, moose US

łot|r m książk. scoundrel

łowc|a m książk. hunter także przen.; **~y głów** headhunters; **~a posągów** a fortune hunter; **~a talentów** a talent scout

ł|owić impf vt ① [osoba] to catch [homary, motyle]; **łowić ryby** to fish ② [drapieżnik] to hunt [myszy, owady]

łowiectw|o n hunting

łowisk|o *n* Ryboł. fishing ground; Myślis. hunting ground

ł|ożyć *impf vi* łożyć **na kogoś/coś** to provide for sb/sth

łożysk|o *n* ① (rzeki) (river) bed ② Techn. bearing ③ Anat. placenta

łód|ka *f* ① Żegl. boat ② (dekolt) bateau neck

ł|ódź *f* boat; **łódź podwodna** submarine

ł|ój *m* ① Kulin. suet ② Fizj. sebum

łóżecz|ko *n* cot GB, crib US

łóż|ko *n* ① (mebel) bed; **~ko piętrowe** a bunk bed, bunks; **~ko polowe** a camp bed; **położyć się do ~ka** (pójść spać) to get into bed; (zachorować) to take to one's bed ② pot. (seks) **pójść z kimś do ~ka** to go to bed with sb pot.; **być dobrym w ~ku** to be good in bed pot.

łubian|ka *f* punnet

łubin *m* lupin(e)

łucznictw|o *n* archery

łuczni|k *m*, **~czka** *f* archer

łu|dzić się *impf v refl.* to delude oneself; **nie łudź się** don't fool yourself

łuk *m* ① (broń) bow; **strzelać z ~u (do czegoś)** to shoot with a bow and arrow (at sth) ② Anat., Archit. arch ③ Mat. arc

■ **omijać kogoś/coś szerokim ~iem** to give sb/ sth a wide berth

łun|a *f* glow

łup *m* loot; **~y wojenne** spoils of war

łupać[1] *impf →* **łupnąć**[1]

łup|ać[2] *impf vt* to split [drewno]; to crack [orzechy]

łupież *m* dandruff

łupin|a *f* (orzecha) shell; (owoców, warzyw) peel; (grochu, fasoli) pod; (cebuli) skin

łup|nąć[1] *pf —* **łup|ać**[1] *impf vi* pot. (zaboleć) **~ie mnie w kościach** my bones ache; **~ie mnie w głowie** my head is splitting

łupn|ąć[2] *pf* pot. **Ⅰ** *vt* ① (uderzyć) to whack pot.; **~ąć kogoś w głowę** to whack sb on the head ② (kazać zapłacić) **~ąć komuś mandat** to slap a fine on sb pot.

Ⅱ *vi* ① (trzasnąć) to bang, to slam (**czymś** sth) ② (upaść) to bang; **~ąć na podłogę** to fall bang on the floor ③ (huknąć) to boom

łus|ka *f* ① Zool. scale; **pokryty ~ką** covered with scales ② Bot. scale; (zboża, słonecznika) husk ③ Wojsk. cartridge case

łuska|ć *impf vt* to shell

łuskan|y *adi.* [orzechy, migdały, groch] shelled

łuszczyc|a *f* psoriasis

łuszcz|yć się *impf v refl.* [skóra, farba, kora] to peel

łu|t *m* łut szczęścia a bit of luck

łuz|a *f* Gry pocket; **wbić bilę do ~y** to pocket a ball

łyd|ka *f* calf; **spódnica do połowy ~ki** a mid-calf-length skirt

łyk *m* swallow; (duży) gulp; (mały) sip; (powietrza) gulp; **daj ~a!** pot. give me a swig! pot.

łyk|nąć *pf —* **łyk|ać** *impf vt* to swallow [jedzenie, napój, pigułkę]; to gulp [powietrze]

łykowa|ty *adi.* [mięso, warzywo] stringy

łyp|nąć *pf —* **łyp|ać** *impf vi* pot. (gniewnie) to glower (**na kogoś** at sb); (ukradkiem) to peer (**na kogoś** at sb)

łysaw|y *adi.* [osoba, głowa] baldish

łysi|eć *impf vi* to go bald

łysin|a *f* ① (łyse miejsce) bald patch a. spot ② pot. (łysa głowa) bald head

łys|ka *f* Zool. coot

łyso *adv.* ① (bez włosów) **ostrzyc się na ~** to shave one's head; (u fryzjera) to have one's head shaved ② pot. (głupio) **było mi ~** I felt stupid

łys|y *adi.* bald

łyżecz|ka *f* teaspoon; (zawartość) teaspoon(ful) (**czegoś** of sth); **~ka do kawy** a coffee spoon; **~ka deserowa** a dessertspoon

łyż|ka *f* ① (kuchenna) spoon; (zawartość) spoon(ful); **~ka stołowa** a (table)spoon; **~ka cedzakowa** a strainer; **~ka wazowa** a ladle ② (w koparce) bucket ❑ **~ka do butów** shoehorn

■ **chętnie utopiłby mnie w ~ce wody** he would happily strangle me

łyż|wa *f* (ice) skate; **jeździć na ~wach** to skate

łyżwiars|ki *adi.* [wyścig, tor] skating

łyżwiarstw|o *n* (ice) skating; **~o szybkie/ figurowe** speed/figure-skating

łyżwia|rz *m*, **~rka** *f* (ice) skater

łyżworol|ka *f* in-line skate, Rollerblade®

ł|za *f* tear(drop); **uśmiać się do łez** to laugh until one cries; **rozbawić kogoś do łez** to give sb a good laugh; **wzruszyć się do łez** to be moved to tears; **mówić coś przez łzy** to say sth tearfully; **śmiech przez łzy** laughter through tears; **łza się w oku kręci, kiedy o tym myślę** it brings tears to my eyes to think about it

■ **(czysty) jak łza** [obrus] pristine; [osoba] (as) pure as the driven snow; **na otarcie łez** as a consolation

łzaw|ić *impf vi* [oczy] to water; **oczy mi ~ią od cebuli** onion makes my eyes water

łzaw|y *adi.* tearful

M

M, m *n inv.* M, m
maca|ć *impf vt* (dotykać) to feel; (lubieżnie) to grope pot.
machać *impf* → **machnąć**
machin|a *f* ① (wielka maszyna) (huge) machine
② (państwa) machinery
machinaln|y *adi. [gest, ruch]* mechanical
mach|nąć *pf* — **mach|ać** *impf vi* ① (poruszyć wahadłowo) to wave *[chorągiewką, ręką]*; to swing *[nogami]*; to brandish *[laską]*; *[pies]* to wag *[ogonem]*; *[ptak]* to flap *[skrzydłami]* ② pot. (zrobić szybko) to knock off pot. *[artykuł, list]*
■ ~nąć ręką na coś to give sth up
macic|a *f* uterus
macierzan|ka *f* thyme
macierzyńs|ki *adi. [uczucia]* motherly; *[instynkt]* maternal; **po ~ku** in a motherly way; **urlop ~ki** maternity leave
macierzyństw|o *n* maternity; **świadome ~o** planned parenthood a. pregnancy
macierzy|sty *adi.* **~sty port** a home port; **firma ~sta** the parent company; **komórka ~sta** Biol. a stem cell
macio|ra *f* sow
mac|ka *f* tentacle
maco|cha *f* stepmother
macza|ć *impf vt* to dip (**coś w czymś** sth in sth); **~ć bułkę w mleku** to dunk a roll in milk
■ ~ć palce w czymś to have a hand in sth
maczu|ga *f* Sport (Indian) club
mafi|a *f* mafia; **~a sycylijska** the (Sicilian) Mafia
magazyn *m* ① (budynek) storehouse; **~ zbożowy** a granary ② (zapas) store ③ (program telewizyjny, radiowy) magazine (programme); **~ kulturalny/informacyjny** a cultural/news magazine ④ (czasopismo) magazine; **~ ilustrowany** an illustrated magazine
magazyn|ek *m* ① (na naboje) magazine ② (składzik) storage room
magazyn|ować *impf vt* ① (przechowywać) to store *[towary, zboże]* ② (odkładać) *[organizm]* to store (up) *[substancje]*
magi|a *f* magic; **biała/czarna ~a** white/black magic
■ to dla mnie czarna ~a it's a closed book to me
magiczn|y *adi. [napój, zaklęcie]* magic; *[moc, wiedza, właściwości]* magical; **~e sztuki** magic

mag|iel *m* ① (maszyna) mangle; **oddawać pościel do ~la** to have one's sheets pressed ② pot., przen. (tłok) crush ③ pot., przen. (zamieszanie) bustle
magi|k *m* ① (iluzjonista) magician ② pot., żart. (spec) handyman; Mr Fix it żart.
magist|er *m* ① (osoba) *person holding a master's degree*; (tytuł) master's (degree); **~er nauk humanistycznych/ścisłych** Master of Arts/Science ② pot. (farmaceuta) *title used to address a pharmacist*
magistral|a *f* ① Transp. trunk route; **~a kolejowa** a main railway line ② Techn. (cieplna, wodociągowa) main
magl|ować *impf vt* ① (wygładzać) to mangle *[obrusy, pościel]* ② pot. (przepytywać) to grill *[ucznia]* ③ pot. (omawiać) to go on (**o coś** about sth); **~ować w kółko ten sam temat** to keep harping upon the same thing
magna|t *m* ① Hist. magnate ② przen. baron, tycoon US
magnes *m* magnet także przen.
magnetofon *m* (tape) recorder; **~ kasetowy** a cassette recorder
magnetowi|d *m* video (cassette recorder)
magnez *m* magnesium
magnoli|a *f* magnolia
mahometan|in *m*, **~ka** *f* Muslim
maho|ń *m* ① (drzewo) mahogany ② (drewno) mahogany ③ (kolor) mahogany
maj *m* May
majacz|yć *impf* **Ⅰ** *vi* ① (być słabo widocznym) to show faintly ② (bredzić) to be delirious
Ⅱ majaczyć się ① (zarysowywać się) to show faintly ② (zwidywać się) to appear
majak *m* phantom
mają|tek *m* ① (ogół dóbr) wealth ② (posiadłość ziemska) estate ③ (bogactwo) fortune
majątkow|y *adi. [ubezpieczenia]* property; *[sytuacja]* material; **nabyć prawa ~e** to acquire property rights
majeran|ek *m* marjoram
majesta|t *m* książk. majesty; **obraza ~tu** lese-majesty; także przen.; **w ~cie prawa** with the (full) sanction of the law
majestatyczn|y *adi. grad.* książk. *[postać, ruchy]* majestic
majonez *m* mayonnaise
majo|r *m* (osoba, stopień, tytuł) major; (lotnictwa) major, squadron leader GB

majów|ka f (spring/summer) picnic

majst|er m [1] (rzemieślnik) master craftsman [2] (nadzorujący) foreman [3] pot. (fachowiec) expert

majsterklep|ka m pot. jack of all trades

majsterk|ować impf vi (konstruować) to do DIY; (naprawiać) to do odd repairs

majsterkowicz m pot. DIY enthusiast

majstersztyk m (arcydzieło) masterpiece; (mistrzowskie posunięcie) master stroke

majstr|ować impf pot. [I] vt to knock together [zabawki]

[II] vi (manipulować) to fiddle (around) (**przy czymś** with sth); (przy samochodzie) to tinker

majt|ki plt [1] (damskie) panties, knickers GB [2] pot. (męskie) underpants, pants GB

■ **robić w ∼ki ze strachu** pot. to wet one's pants pot.

mak m (kwiat) poppy (flower); (nasiona) poppy seed(s)

■ **cicho** a. **cisza jak ∼iem zasiał** deathly silence a. hush; **rozbić się** a. **rozpaść się w drobny ∼** to smash to bits

makaron m pasta; (do zupy) noodles; (nitki) spaghetti; (rurki) macaroni

makie|ta f [1] (budynku, osiedla) (scale) model [2] Film, Teatr mock-up [3] Druk. paste-up; **∼ta książki** a dummy

makijaż m [1] Kosmet. make-up [2] (czynność) making up

makle|r m broker; **∼r giełdowy** a stockbroker

makow|iec m poppy-seed cake

makrel|a f mackerel

maksim|um [I] n maximum; **to ∼um tego, co można zrobić** it's all a. the most one can do; **ustawić ogrzewanie na ∼um** to turn the heating up full

[II] part. at (the) most; **ona ma ∼um dwadzieścia lat** she's twenty at the most; **to zajmie ∼um dziesięć minut** it'll take ten minutes at (the) most

maksym|a f książk. maxim

maksymaln|y adi. [prędkość, temperatura] maximum; [wygoda, wysiłek] utmost

makulatu|ra f [1] (niepotrzebne papiery) waste paper; **z ∼ry** made from recycled paper [2] pejor. (książki) trash; (czasopisma) pulp magazines

malari|a f malaria

malarstw|o n painting; **wystawa ∼a** an exhibition of paintings

malarz m [1] (artysta) painter [2] (rzemieślnik) (house) painter

mal|eć impf vi [liczba, wartość] to diminish; [odległość, produkcja] to decrease; [szanse, zapasy] to dwindle; [popularność, popyt] to decline

malin|a f (owoc) raspberry; (krzak) raspberry cane a. bush

■ **dziewczyna jak ∼a** pot. a peach of a girl pot.;

wpuścić kogoś w ∼y pot. to lead sb up the garden path

malkonten|t m, **∼tka** f malcontent

mal|ować impf [I] vt [1] (pokrywać farbą) to paint [ścianę, mieszkanie, przedmiot]; **∼ować coś na biało** to paint sth white; „**świeżo ∼owane**" 'wet paint' [2] (upiększać) to paint [paznokcie]; **∼ować sobie usta szminką** to put on one's lipstick [3] Szt. to paint [obraz, martwą naturę, pejzaż]; **∼ować farbami olejnymi** to paint a. work in oils; **∼ować z natury** to paint from nature [4] książk., przen. to portray [postać, sytuację]; **∼ować coś w ciemnych barwach** to paint a black a. gloomy picture of sth; **∼ować coś w jasnych barwach** to paint a rosy picture of sth

[II] **malować się** [1] (upiększać się) to make (oneself) up, to put on (one's) make-up; **czy ona się ∼uje?** does she wear make-up? [2] książk. (być widocznym) to show; **w oddali ∼owała się wieża kościoła** the church tower showed in the distance; **w jej oczach ∼ował się smutek** there was a sad look in her eyes; **∼ować się w ciemnych barwach** to look black a. bleak; **∼ować się w jasnych barwach** to look bright a. rosy

malowid|ło n painting; **∼ło ścienne** a mural

malownicz|y adi. [1] [widok, wieś, dolina] picturesque; **niezwykle ∼a kraina** an area of great scenic beauty [2] przen. [opis, opowiadanie] vivid; [postać] colourful

maltret|ować impf vt to maltreat [osobę, zwierzę]; **∼owanie (fizyczne) żony/dziecka** wife/child battering

maluch m pot. (dziecko) kiddy pot.; (uczący się chodzić) toddler

malwersacj|a f embezzlement, misappropriation of funds; **dopuścić się ∼i** to embezzle a. misappropriate funds

m|ało [I] adv. grad. **mało inteligentny** not very intelligent; **mało popularny** rather unpopular; **mało jeść/czytać/wiedzieć** to not eat/read/know much; **za mało zarabiać** to earn too little; **mniej palić** to smoke less; **mało prawdopodobny** unlikely; **mało znany** little known; **z mniejszym lub większym zainteresowaniem** with varying degrees of interest

[II] pron. [1] (niewiele) (z policzalnymi) not many; (z niepoliczalnymi) not much; **mieć mało książek** to not have many books; **mieć mało czasu** to not have much time; **mieć za mało czasu** to have too little time; **mieć za mało lat** to be too young; **jakich mało** like no other [2] (rzadko) hardly; **mało co** hardly anything; **mało kto** hardly anyone; **mało kto o tym wie** (very) few people know that; **jest skąpy jak mało kto** he's as greedy as they come

[III] part. **on jest wysoki, mało wysoki – olbrzymi** he's tall – no, tall isn't the word – he's gigantic

IV mniej *adv. comp.* Szkol. **trzy/cztery mniej** C/B minus

V najmniej *part.* at least; **najmniej trzy tysiące** at least three thousand; **co najmniej** (przynajmniej) at least; (emfatycznie) to say the least

■ **mało tego...** (and) what's more...; **jakby tego było mało** as if that weren't enough!; **jeszcze mu mało** he's still not satisfied; **mało ci tego, że dostałaś dom i samochód?** you got the house and the car, what more do you want?; **mniej więcej** more or less; **o mało co** very nearly

małola|t *m*, ∼**ta** *f* pot. teenager

małoletni [] *adi.* ∼ **przestępca** a young offender; **jest** ∼**a** she's under-age

[] **małoletn|i** *m*, ∼**a** *f* Prawo minor

małomiasteczkow|y *adi. [mentalność, atmosfera]* small-town

małomówn|y *adi.* taciturn

małostkow|y *adi. [osoba]* petty(-minded); *[zachowanie, postępowanie]* mean

małp|a *f* [] Zool. monkey; (bez ogona) ape; ∼**a człekokształtna** anthropoid a. great ape; **zręczny jak** ∼**a** (as) agile as a monkey [] pot., obraźl. nasty character [] pot., Komput. 'at' sign

małpiat|ka *f* prosimian

małp|ować *impf vt* (naśladować) to ape; (przedrzeźniać) to mimic

m|ały [] *adi. grad.* [] (niewielki) *[dawka, kwota, rozmiar]* small; *[domek, piesek]* little; **mały wybór** a limited selection; **z małymi wyjątkami** with few exceptions [] (nieistotny) *[problem, błąd]* minor; *[prośba]* small; *[znaczenie]* little; *[wypadek, różnica]* slight; **mam mały problem** I've got a bit of a problem [] (młody) small; **dwójka małych dzieci** two small children; **kiedy byłem mały** when I was little a. a child [] (niski) *[osoba]* short; **mały jak na swój wiek** small for one's age [] (krótki) *[przejażdżka, spacer, wycieczka]* short [] (z określeniem czasu) just under; **mała godzinka** just under an hour

[] **mały** *m*, **mała** *f* (dziecko) kid; (zwierzę) offspring; **od małego** from an early age; **znam ją od małego** I've known her since she was a child

[] **mniejsza** *part.* **mniejsza z tym** it doesn't matter; **mniejsza o to, co myślisz** what you think is neither here nor there

małż *m* bivalve; ∼ **jadalny** a mussel

małżeńs|ki *adi. [problemy, obowiązki, wierność]* marital; *[miłość]* married; conjugal książk.; *[umowa, więzy]* marriage; **para** ∼**ka** a married couple; **przysięga** ∼**ka** marriage a. wedding vows

małżeństw|o *n* [] (związek) marriage; matrimony książk.; ∼**o z miłości** a love match; ∼**o dla pieniędzy** (a) marriage for money; ∼**o z rozsądku** a marriage of convenience; **zawrzeć** ∼**o (z kimś)** to enter into (a) marriage; **jej syn z pierwszego** ∼**a** her son from a. by her first marriage [] (para) (married) couple; **bezdzietne**

∼**o** a childless couple; ∼**o Kowalskich** Mr and Mrs Kowalski

małżon|ek *m* [] książk. (mąż) husband; spouse książk. [] Prawo (mąż albo żona) spouse książk.; ∼**kowie** a married couple

małżon|ka *f* książk. wife; spouse książk.; **moja prawowita** ∼**ka** my lawful wedded wife

małżowin|a *f* ∼**a uszna** Anat. auricle

mam|a *f* pot. mum GB, mom US pot.

mam|ić *impf vt* książk. [] (łudzić) to beguile książk. [] (wabić) to lure

mamid|ło *n* delusion

maminsyn|ek *m* pejor. mummy's boy GB, mama's boy US pot., pejor.

mamin|y *adi.* mum's GB, mom's US pot.

mammografi|a *f* [] Med. (zabieg) mammography [] pot. (zdjęcie) mammogram

mamro|tać *impf vt* to mutter

manat|ki *plt* pot. (bagaż) traps GB pot.; (rzeczy) stuff pot.

mandaryn|ka *f* (drzewo) mandarin; (owoc) mandarin

mandarynkow|y *adi. [sok, gaj]* mandarin

manda|t *m* [] (kara) fine; (druczek) (traffic/parking) ticket; ∼**t za przekroczenie prędkości** a speeding ticket; ∼**t za złe parkowanie** a parking ticket; **dostać** ∼**t** to get a ticket; **ukarać kogoś** ∼**tem** to give sb a ticket [] (pełnomocnictwo) mandate Polit. (w parlamencie) seat; **stracić** ∼**t** to lose one's seat

mandatariusz *m* książk. mandatary

mandatow|y *adi. [terytorium]* mandated; *[system, władze]* mandatory

mandolin|a *f* mandolin

manekin *m* (u krawca) dummy; (na wystawie) mannequin; przen., pejor. automaton pejor.

manew|r *m* manoeuvre GB, maneuver US

manewr|ować *impf* to manoeuvre GB, to maneuver US (**czymś** sth)

mango *n inv.* (drzewo) mango (tree); (owoc) mango

mani|a *f* 'manja/ *f* [] (upodobanie) mania; **ludzie ogarnięci** ∼**ą podróżowania** people obsessed with travelling [] Med., Psych. (obsesja) complex; (zaburzenia nastroju) mania; ∼**a prześladowcza** a persecution complex a. mania; ∼**a wielkości** a superiority complex

mania|k *m*, ∼**czka** *f* maniac; **z uporem** ∼**ka** like a man obsessed

manie|ra [] *f* [] (zachowanie) mannerism pejor. [] (styl artystyczny) style; ∼**ra stylistyczna pisarza** a writer's style

[] **maniery** *plt* (ogłada) manners; **mieć dobre/złe** ∼**ry** to have good/bad manners

manier|ka *f* canteen

manife|st *m* manifesto także przen.; **ogłosić** ∼**st** to issue a manifesto

manifestacj|a *f* ① (demonstracja) demonstration; **~a przeciwko czemuś** a demonstration against sth ② przen. (okazywanie uczuć) manifestation

manifest|ować *impf* **Ⅰ** *vt* (okazywać) to display *[uczucia, pogardę]* **Ⅱ** *vi* (demonstrować) *[tłum]* to demonstrate

manipulacj|a *f* ① (precyzyjna czynność) (manual) adjustment ② pejor. manipulation; **łatwo ulegać ~i** to be easily manipulated

manipulacyjn|y *adi. [sprawność, zręczność]* manual; *[opłaty, koszty]* handling; *[zachowanie]* manipulative

manipul|ować *impf vt, vi* to manipulate *[ludźmi, danymi]*; **~ować przy czymś** to fiddle with sth

mankamen|t *m* (wada) shortcoming; (defekt) flaw

mankie|t *m* ① (rękawa) cuff; **~t u koszuli** a shirt cuff ② (spodni) turn-up GB, cuff US

mank|o *n* deficit

mann|a *f* ① (kasza) semolina ② Bot. (trawa) manna grass
■ **~a z nieba** manna from heaven

manualn|y *adi.* książk. *[zdolności, zręczność]* manual

mańku|t *m* pot. left-hander; lefty pot.; **być ~tem** to be left-handed

map|a *f* map; (nawigacyjna) chart; **~a samochodowa/turystyczna** a road/tourist map

maraton *m* ① Sport marathon (race); **biec w ~ie** to run (in) a marathon ② przen. marathon; **~ filmowy/rockowy** a film/rock marathon

maratończy|k *m* Sport marathon runner

marazm *m* książk. apathy; **otrząsnąć się z ~u** to shake off one's apathy; **pogrążyć się w ~ie** to sink into a state of apathy a. lethargy

marcepan *m* marzipan

march|ew *f* carrot; **pęczek ~wi** a bunch of carrots

margaryn|a *f* margarine

margeryt|ka *f* (ox-eye) daisy

marginaln|y *adi.* książk. *[sprawa, zjawisko, znaczenie]* marginal

margines *m* ① (brzeg) margin; **uwagi na ~ie** notes in the margin ② przen. margin; periphery książk.; **żyć na ~ie społeczeństwa** to live on the fringe(s) a. margins of society ③ Socjol. underclass
■ **to tylko tak na ~ie** that's just by the way; **zepchnąć kogoś na ~to** push sb on to the sidelines

marginesow|y *adi. [uwagi, sprawa, zjawisko]* marginal

marihuan|a *f* marijuana, marihuana

marines /ˌmaˈrins/ *plt inv.* Wojsk. Marines, Marine Corps

marionet|ka *f* puppet; **być ~ką w czyichś rękach** to be a puppet in sb's hands

mar|ka *f* ① (znak firmowy) (papierosów, kosmetyków) brand; (telewizorów, komputerów) make; **samochód ~ki Fiat** a Fiat (car); **jakiej ~ki jest twój sa-**

mochód? what make is your car? ② (jakość) quality; **wino przedniej ~ki** superior a. premium quality wine ③ książk. (opinia) reputation

markotni|eć *impf vi* to become a. grow morose

markotn|y *adi. grad. [osoba]* glum, morose; *[spojrzenie]* glum; **być ~ym** to feel down(hearted)

mark|ować *impf vt* ① (pozorować) *[osoba]* to feign *[chorobę, obojętność]*; **~ować śpiewanie** to pretend one is singing ② Sport to feint *[cios, strzał]*; **~owany cios** a feint

marksizm *m* Marxism

marmola|da *f* (fruit) preserve
■ **zrobić z kogoś ~dę** pot. to beat a. smash sb to a pulp

marmu|r *m* marble; **nagrobek z ~ru** a marble tombstone

marni|eć *impf vi [osoba]* to waste away; *[rośliny]* to wilt

marnotrawstw|o *n [pieniędzy]* waste; *[materiałów, surowców]* wastage

marn|ować *impf* **Ⅰ** *vt* to waste *[prąd, surowce, siły]*; to squander *[pieniądze]*; **~ować czas na coś** to waste (one's) time on sth
Ⅱ marnować się ① (nie wykorzystywać możliwości) to be wasted; **~ujesz się w tej pracy** you're wasted in this job ② (niszczeć) *[żywność]* to go to waste

marn|y *adi. grad.* pot. *[zdrowie, jedzenie, perspektywy, pracownik]* poor; *[obiad]* meagre GB, meager US; *[płaca]* paltry; *[wymówka]* flimsy; *[życie]* miserable; *[literatura]* second-rate; **towar ~ej jakości** poor-quality goods
Ⅱ *adi.* książk. (bezcelowy) *[trud]* wasted
■ **pójść na ~e** to go down the drain pot.; **za ~e pieniądze** for peanuts pot.; **czeka go ~y koniec** he'll come to a sticky end; **~y twój los** you're in for some real trouble pot.

marsz *m* **Ⅰ** *m* ① (ruch) march; **w ~u** on the march; **godzina ~u stąd** an hour's march from here ② (demonstracja) march; **~ protestacyjny** a protest march ③ Muz. march; **~ pogrzebowy/weselny** a funeral/wedding march
Ⅱ *inter.* ① pot. off you go!; **~ do łóżka!** off to bed (with you)! ② Wojsk. march!; **biegiem ~!** at the double!; **naprzód ~!** forward march!
■ **z ~u** right a. straight away

marszał|ek *m* ① Wojsk. marshal; **~ek polny** a field marshal ② Polit. Speaker; **~ek sejmu/senatu** the Speaker of the Sejm/Senate

marszcz|yć *impf* **Ⅰ** *vt* ① (kurczyć) to wrinkle *[czoło, nos, twarz]*; **~yć brwi** to frown ② (fałdować) to ruffle *[taflę wody]*; to gather *[materiał, zasłony]*; **suknia ~ona w talii** a dress gathered at the waist
Ⅱ marszczyć się *[czoło, twarz, skóra]* to become wrinkled a. lined; *[materiał, spódnica]* to ruck up; *[woda]* to ripple

martwic|a *f* Med. necrosis

martw|ić *impf* **[I]** *vt* (niepokoić) to worry; (smucić) to sadden; **nie chcę cię ~ić, ale...** I don't want to worry a. upset you, but...

[II] martwić się to worry (oneself) (**czymś** a. **o coś** about sth); **nie ~ się** don't (you) worry; **nie ma czym się ~ić** there's nothing to worry about

martw|y *adi.* ① *[osoba, zwierzę, drzewo, tkanka]* dead; **powstać z ~ych** to rise from the dead ② (nieruchomy) *[oczy, twarz]* lifeless ③ (nieaktualny) *[prawo, przepis, idea]* defunct ④ (nieożywiony) *[cisza]* dead, dead(ly); *[świat, okolica]* desolate

marude|r *m* latecomer

marudn|y *adi. grad.* pot. ① (leniwy) *[robotnik, uczeń]* sluggish ② (żmudny) *[praca, czynność]* tedious ③ (zrzędliwy) grumpy

maru|dzić *impf vi* pot. ① (zrzędzić) to gripe (**na coś** about sth); to whinge GB pot. (**na coś** about sth) ② (grzebać się) to dawdle; to dilly-dally pot.; **~dzić z robotą** to dawdle over one's work ③ (nudzić) to go on (and on) pot. (**o czymś** about sth)

marynar|ka *f* ① Moda jacket; **chodzić w ~ce/bez ~ki** to wear/to not wear a jacket ② (flota) navy; **~ka handlowa** the merchant navy; **~ka wojenna** the navy

marynarz *m* sailor, seaman

■ **grać w ~a** pot. ≈ to draw a. cast lots

maryna|ta *f* ① (potrawa) pickle ② (zalewa) marinade

maryn|ować *impf* **[I]** *vt* to marinate *[mięso, warzywa]*

[II] marynować się to be pickled a. marinated

ma|rzec *m* March

■ **w marcu jak w garncu** przysł. ≈ March comes in like a lion and goes out like a lamb przysł.

marze|nie *n* ① (nadzieja) dream; (mrzonka) daydream; **~nia senne** Psych. dreams; **pogrążyć się w ~niach** to be lost in thought; **oddawać się ~niom** to daydream; **spełnienie ~ń** a dream come true; **w najśmielszych ~niach** in one's wildest dreams; **żyć w świecie ~ń** to live in a dreamworld ② (przedmiot pragnień) dream; **piękny jak ~nie** as pretty as a picture

■ **~nie ściętej głowy** pot. pie in the sky pot.; **senne ~nie** książk. nothing but a dream

marz|nąć /'marznonte/ *impf vi* ① (przemarzać) *[nogi, rośliny]* to freeze; **~ną mi ręce** my hands are freezing ② (zamarzać) to freeze; **~nąca mżawka** freezing drizzle; **zimą jezioro ~nie** in winter the lake freezes over

marzyciel *m*, **~ka** *f* dreamer

marzyciels|ki *adi. [uśmiech, spojrzenie]* dreamy; **mieć ~kie usposobienie** to be a dreamer

marz|yć *impf* **[I]** *vi* ① (wyobrażać sobie) to daydream ② (pragnąć) to dream (**o czymś** of sth)

[II] marzyć się (być upragnionym) **~y mi się dom na wsi** I dream of (having) a house in the country

marż|a *f* Ekon., Handl. mark-up; **~a detaliczna** a retail margin; **~a hurtowa** a wholesale margin; **~a zysku** a profit margin

mas|a *f* ① (substancja) mass; **~a papiernicza** paper pulp ② (wiele) a mass; masses pot.; **~a ludzi** loads of people pot. ③ (ciężar) mass ④ Prawo estate

masak|ra *f* massacre także przen.

masakr|ować *impf vt* ① (zabijać) to massacre *[ludzi]* ② (bić) to batter *[ofiarę]*

masaż *m* massage

masaży|sta *m*, **~tka** *f* massage therapist

maseczka|ka *f* ① Kosmet. face mask a. pack ② (balowa) mask

maselnicz|ka *f* butter dish

mas|ka *f* ① (osłona) mask; (ochronna) face guard a. mask ② przen. (poza) mask przen.; veneer książk.; **zrzucić ~kę** to drop one's mask ③ Kosmet. face mask a. pack ④ (samochodu) bonnet GB, hood US; (samolotu, czołgu) engine cover

maskot|ka *f* ① (na szczęście) mascot ② (zabawka) stuffed toy

mask|ować *impf* **[I]** *vt* ① (zasłaniać) to camouflage *[osobę, rzecz]* ② (ukrywać) to hide *[uczucia]*; to conceal książk. *[strach, niepokój]*

[II] maskować się to maintain a front a. façade (**przed kimś** in front of sb)

ma|sło *n* butter; **masło roślinne** butter substitute

■ **iść jak po maśle** to go swimmingly; **(to) bułka z masłem** pot. (it's a) piece of cake; **masło maślane** pot. tautology

mas|ować *impf vt* to massage *[część ciała, osobę]*

masow|y *adi. [produkcja, protest]* mass

masturbacj|a *f* masturbation

masyw *m* ① Geol. massif ② (bryła) bulk

masywn|y *adi. grad. [gmach, postać]* massive

maszer|ować *impf vi* to march

masz|t *m* ① (słup) flagpole; **~t antenowy** Radio, TV an aerial mast; **opuścić flagę do połowy ~tu** to lower a flag to half mast ② Żegl. mast

maszyn|a *f* machine także przen.; **~a do szycia** a sewing machine; **~a parowa** a steam engine; **~a do pisania** a typewriter

maszyneri|a *f* ① (mechanizm wewnętrzny) machinery; (maszyny, samochodu) workings; (zegara) moving parts ② Teatr stage machinery a. equipment ③ przen. machinery; **~a władzy** the machinery a. mechanics of power

maszyni|sta *m* Kolej. engine driver

maszynist|ka *f* typist

maszyn|ka *f* ① (przyrząd) machine; **~ka do golenia** a shaver; **~ka do mięsa** a meat mincer GB, a meat grinder ② (kuchenka) portable cooker GB, portable stove

maszynopis *m* typescript

maszynowni|a *f* (okrętu) engine room

maś|ć f [1] (lekarstwo) ointment [2] (ubarwienie) (coat) colour GB, (coat) color US

■ **różnej** ~**ci** iron. of all descriptions

maśla|k m boletus

maślan|ka f buttermilk

maślan|y adi. butter

■ ~**e oczy** pot. bleary eyes

ma|t¹ m (stopień) ≈ leading seaman GB, ≈ seaman US

ma|t² m Gry (check)mate

ma|t³ m (brak połysku) matt(e)

ma|ta f mat

matactw|o n chicanery

matado|r m matador

matematyczn|y adi. [równanie, wzór] mathematical; [zadanie] maths GB, math US pot.; **z** ~**ą dokładnością** with mathematical precision

matematy|k m, ~**czka** f [1] (naukowiec) mathematician [2] pot. (nauczyciel) maths GB a. math US teacher pot.

matematy|ka f mathematics

materac m mattress; (nadmuchiwany) air bed GB, air mattress; ~ **wodny** a waterbed

materiali|sta m, ~**stka** f materialist

materializm m materialism

materializ|ować impf [] vt książk. to carry out [plany]

[] **materializować się** [projekt] to materialize; **jego marzenia wreszcie się** ~**ują** his dreams are finally coming true

materialn|y adi. [1] (finansowy) [korzyść, pomoc, sytuacja] financial [2] (fizyczny) [postać, świat] material

materia|ł m [1] (tworzywo) material; ~**ły wybuchowe** Chem. explosives [2] (wyposażenie) supplies; ~**ły piśmienne** stationery (supplies) [3] (zbiór wiadomości) material; ~**ł dowodowy** Prawo evidence; **zbierać** ~**ły do książki** to do research for a book [4] (tkanina) material

■ **być dobrym** ~**łem na męża/żonę** to be good husband/wife material

mat|ka f [1] (rodzicielka) mother; ~**ka biologiczna** one's biological mother; ~**ka zastępcza** a surrogate mother; **samotne** ~**ki** single mothers; ~**ka chrzestna** a godmother; ~**ka natura** książk. Mother Nature; ~**ka Ziemia** książk. Mother Earth; **Matka Boga** a. **Matka Boska** Relig. Mother of God [2] Zool. (samica) mother; (u owadów) queen [3] (w zakonie) Mother; ~**ka przełożona** Mother Superior

■ **taki jak go** ~**ka urodziła** (as) naked as the day he was born; ~**ko święta!** pot. good Lord! a. heavens! iron.; **potrzeba jest** ~**ką wynalazku** przysł. necessity is the mother of invention przysł.

matk|ować impf vi to mother [dziecku, rodzeństwu]

matni|a f (trudna sytuacja) predicament; (zawiła sytuacja) tangle przen.; imbroglio książk.

mato|ł m pot., obraźl. thickhead; moron pot., obraźl.

matowi|eć impf vi [cera, włosy] to (become) dull; [lustro, metal] to tarnish

matow|y adi. [cera, lakier] matt(e); [szkło] frosted; [dźwięk, głos] mellow; ~**e włosy** dull a. lifeless hair; ~**a żarówka** a pearl a. frosted lightbulb

matryc|a f [1] Druk., Komput. matrix [2] Techn. matrix; (do metalu) die [3] (szablon) stencil [4] Biol. template; ~**a genetyczna** a genetic template

matrymonialn|y adi. książk. [zamiary] matrimonial; [biuro] marriage; **ogłoszenia** ~**e** singles ads

matu|ra f [1] (egzamin) (secondary) school-leaving exam(s) [2] (świadectwo) ≈ A-level certificate GB, ≈ high school diploma US

maturzy|sta m, ~**stka** f recent secondary-school leaver

mazak m [1] (flamaster) marker (pen) [2] (pędzel) broad paintbrush

mazga|j m pot. cry baby pot., pejor.

ma|ź f pot. gunk pot.

mą|cić impf [] vt [1] (poruszać) to ruffle [powierzchnię wody]; to cloud [ciecz] [2] (zakłócać) to disturb [ciszę, spokój]; to disrupt [harmonię]; to ruffle [humor]

[] **mącić się** [1] (mętnieć) [ciecz] to become cloudy a. turbid [2] (stawać się chaotycznym) [myśli, wątki] to become confused

■ **mącić komuś w głowie** to confuse sb

mącz|ka f fine powder; (paszowa) meal; ~**ka kostna/rybna** bonemeal/fishmeal

mądral|a m, f pot. smart alec(k), wise guy US, clever Dick GB pot.

mądroś|ć f [1] (rozum) wisdom; ~**ć książkowa** book learning; ~**ć życiowa** practical wisdom [2] (decyzji, postępowania) wisdom [3] (spryt) sagacity książk.; ~**ć polityczna** political sagacity [4] pot. (powiedzenie, stwierdzenie) word a. piece of wisdom; **oszczędź mi tych swoich** ~**ci** keep your pearls of wisdom to yourself iron.

mąd|ry adi. grad. [1] (rozumny) [nauczyciel, ojciec] wise [2] (sensowny) [decyzja] wise; [rada, wypowiedź] sage książk.; [plan] clever [3] iron. (uczony) [cytat, wykład] clever [4] (inteligentny) [osoba] shrewd; [zwierzę] clever; **nie bądź taki** ~**ry** iron. don't be so clever!

■ **bądź tu** ~**ry** (człowieku) ~**ry** pot. (and) try to be wise now!; ~**ry Polak po szkodzie** przysł. it is easy to be wise after the event

mądrz|eć impf vi to become a. grow wiser

mądrz|yć się impf v refl. pot., pejor. to mouth off pot., pejor.; ~**yć się na temat czegoś** to mouth off about sth

mą|ka f flour; (grubiej mielona) meal; **mąka razowa** (pszenna) wholemeal flour GB, wholewheat a. graham flour US; (żytnia) wholemeal rye flour

m|ąż m [1] (poślubiony partner) husband [2] książk. (mężczyzna) man; **mąż opatrznościowy** a saviour; **mąż stanu** an statesman; **mąż zaufania** an intermediary

■ **złapać męża** pot. to catch a husband; **jak ona**

nazywa się po mężu a. z męża? what's her married name?; **wydać córkę za mąż** to give one's daughter in marriage; **wyjść** a. **wydać się za mąż** *[kobieta]* to get married

mdl|eć *impf vi* [1] (tracić przytomność) to faint ~eć ze zmęczenia to faint a. be weak from fatigue; ~eć z zachwytu nad kimś/czymś to swoon (with delight) over sb/sth [2] *[noga, ręka]* to grow numb

mdl|ić *impf* [] *vt [potrawa, zapach]* to make [sb] sick [] *v imp.* (wywoływać mdłości) ~i mnie I feel sick a. nauseous; ~i mnie na samą myśl o tym I feel sick at the very thought of it

mdłości *plt* nausea; **czuć** ~ to feel sick a. nauseous

mdł|y *adi.* [1] (wywołujący odruch wymiotny) nauseous [2] (bez smaku) bland [3] (rozproszony) *[światło]* faint [4] (nijaki) *[dzieło, interpretacja, styl]* insipid; *[wygląd]* nondescript; *[osobowość, utwór]* vapid [5] (blady) *[kolor]* dull

meb|el *m* piece a. item of furniture; **komplet ~li do sypialni** a bedroom suite

mebl|ować *impf vt* to furnish *[biuro, dom, pokój]*

mecenas *m* [1] (patron) patron [2] Prawo lawyer; ~ **Kowalski prowadzi moją sprawę** Mr Kowalski is conducting my case

mecena|t *m* patronage; ~**t nad sztuką** patronage of the arts

m|ech *m* moss

mechanicznie *adv.* [1] (maszynowo) mechanically [2] (automatycznie) mechanically

mechaniczn|y *adi.* [1] (napędzany silnikiem) *[urządzenie, zabawka]* mechanical; *[napęd, pojazd]* motor; *[piła, pompa]* motor-driven [2] (dotyczący mechanizmu) *[część, uszkodzenie]* mechanical [3] (maszynowy) *[czyszczenie, obróbka]* mechanical [4] Fiz. *[energia, ruch]* mechanical [5] (bezwiedny) *[czynność, gest, ruch]* mechanical

mechani|k *m* [1] (rzemieślnik) mechanic; ~**k samochodowy** a car mechanic [2] (inżynier) engineer; **inżynier ~k** a mechanical engineer

mechanizacj|a *f* mechanization

mechanizm *m* mechanism *także przen.*; ~ **zegarowy** a clockwork mechanism

mecz *m* Sport match

mecz|eć *impf vi [koza, owca]* to bleat

medal *m* medal; **zdobyć** ~ to win a medal; **otrzymać** ~ **za odwagę** to receive a. be awarded a medal for bravery

■ **być na** ~ pot. to come a. turn trumps GB pot.; **zrobić coś na** ~ to do a first-class job of sth

medalik *m* (religious) medallion

medali|sta *m*, ~**stka** *f* [1] Sport medallist GB, medalist US; **(złoty/brązowy)** ~**sta olimpijski** an Olympic (gold/bronze) medallist [2] (zwierzę) champion

mediacj|a *f* książk. mediation

mediato|r *m*, ~**rka** *f* książk. mediator

meduz|a *f* jellyfish

medycyn|a *f* medicine; **student** ~**y** a medical student

medyczn|y *adi. [opieka, personel, terminologia]* medical; **akademia** ~**a** a medical school

medytacj|a *f* książk. meditation; ~**e o** a. **nad czymś** meditation(s) on sth;

medyt|ować *impf vi* to meditate (**nad czymś** (up)on sth)

megafon *m* megaphone, loudhailer GB

megalomani|a /ˌmegaloˈmaɲja/ *f* książk. megalomania

melancholi|a *f* melancholy

melancholijn|y *adi. [muzyka, nastrój, usposobienie]* melancholy

meld|ować *impf* [] *vt* [1] (informować) to report (**komuś o czymś** sth to sb); to inform (**kogoś o czymś** sb of a. about sth); ~**ować o czyimś przybyciu** to announce sb's arrival; ~**ować o czyimś zaginięciu** to report sb missing [2] (w hotelu) to check a. book in *[gościa]*; (w mieszkaniu) to register *[lokatora]*

[] **meldować się** [1] (zgłaszać się) *[podwładny]* to report (**komuś** to sb); **raz w tygodniu** ~**ował się na policji** he reported to the police once a week [2] (w hotelu) *[gość]* to check a. sign in; (w mieszkaniu) *[lokator]* to register; ~**ować się na pobyt stały/czasowy** to register for permanent/temporary residence

meldun|ek *m* [1] (doniesienie) report; ~**ek o zaginięciu dziecka** a report of a missing child [2] (zgłoszenie pobytu) registration; ~**ek stały/czasowy** a permanent/temporary residence [3] Wojsk. dispatch; ~**ek z pola walki** a battle dispatch

melin|a *f* pot. [1] (kryjówka) hideout [2] (z narkotykami) den; (z alkoholem) illegal drinking place [3] (spelunka) dive, honky-tonk US pot.

melioracj|a *f* Roln. land improvement; (osuszanie) land reclamation; (nawadnianie) irrigation

melodi|a *f* (linia melodyczna) melody; (utwór) tune

melodrama|t *m* melodrama; **robić z czegoś** ~**t** to be melodramatic about sth

melodyjn|y *adi. [głos, śpiew]* melodious; *[utwór]* tuneful; *[śmiech]* musical; *[język]* melodious

meloman *m*, ~**ka** *f* music lover

melon *m* melon

melonik *m* bowler (hat)

membran|a *f* (w głośniku, mikrofonie) diaphragm; (w instrumentach muzycznych) membrane

menażeri|a *f* książk., żart. menagerie

menaż|ka *f* [1] (wojskowa) mess tin; (turystyczna) pot, dixie [2] (do przenoszenia posiłków) food carrier

menedże|r *m* [1] (zarządzający) manager; (kobieta) manageress [2] (agent) manager

menedżers|ki *adi. [doświadczenie, zdolności]* managerial; *[techniki, zespół, studia]* management

mennic|a *f* mint

menstruacj|a *f* Med. menstruation
mentalnoś|ć *f* mentality
mentors|ki *adi.* książk. *[ton]* moralizing
menu /'me'ny/ *n inv.* [1] (zestaw posiłków) menu; ~ **na obiad** a dinner menu [2] (karta dań) menu [3] Komput., TV, Video menu
menzur|ka *f* measuring cylinder
merda|ć *impf vi* to wag; **pies** ~**ł ogonem** the dog wagged its tail
meritum *n inv.* książk. essence; **przejść do** ~ **(sprawy)** to go to the heart of the matter
merytoryczn|y *adi.* książk. concerning the merits a. (essential) facts; substantive książk.; **błędy** ~**e (w tekście)** factual errors (in a text)
mesz|ek *m* down
me|ta *f* [1] Sport finishing line [2] przen. (zakończenie działalności) finish [3] pot. (kryjówka) hideout; (miejsce spotkań) haunt; hang-out pot. [4] pot. (melina) illegal drinking place
■ **na dłuższą** a. **dalszą/krótką metę** in the long/short run; **z mety** pot. right a. straight away
metabolizm *m* metabolism
metafo|ra *f* metaphor
metal *m* metal; ~**e kolorowe** non-ferrous metals; ~**e szlachetne** noble metals
metaliczn|y *adi.* metallic
metalik *m* [1] (lakier) metallic paint [2] pot. (samochód) metallic car
metalow|y *adi.* [1] *[przemysł]* metallurgical [2] *[części, okucia]* metal [3] Muz. metal
metamorfoz|a *f* książk. metamorphosis
meteo|r *m* meteor
meteorologi|a *f* meteorology
meteory|t *m* meteorite
met|ka *f* label; ~**ka z ceną** a price tag
metk|ować *impf vt* to label *[towary, ubrania]*
meto|da *f* method
■ **w tym szaleństwie jest** ~**da** there is method in this madness
metody|ka *f* methodology
met|r *m* [1] Miary metre, meter US; ~**r bieżący** a linear metre; ~**r kwadratowy** a square metre; ~**r sześcienny** a cubic metre [2] (miarka) rule; ~**r stolarski** a folding rule; ~**r krawiecki** a tape measure [3] pot. (zboża, ziemniaków) hundred kilograms ■ **od** ~**ra** pot. a lot
met|ro *n* underground (railway) GB, subway US
metry|ka *f* [1] Admin., Relig. certificate; ~**ka urodzenia/zgonu** a birth/death certificate [2] (zwierzęcia) pedigree (certificate)
mew|a *f* seagull; ~**a śmieszka** a black-headed gull
mezalians *m* książk. mésalliance
męczar|nia *f* [1] (cierpienie) torment [2] pot. hard time
męczenni|k, *m*, ~**ca** *f* [1] Relig. martyr [2] pot. sufferer, martyr

męcz|yć *impf* [**I**] *vt* [1] (zadawać ból) to torture [2] (wyczerpywać) to tire out; ~**yć sobie wzrok** to strain one's eyes [3] (denerwować) to pester (**kogoś czymś** sb with sth) [4] pot. (robić niechętnie) to toil (**coś** over sth)
[**II**] **męczyć się** [1] (cierpieć) to suffer [2] (szybko tracić siły) to tire [3] (robić z trudem) to toil (**nad** a. **z czymś** at sth); to sweat (**nad** a. **z czymś** over sth)
męd|rzec *m* sage
m|ęka *f* książk. [1] (cierpienia) agony [2] (tortury) torture także przen.
męs|ki *adi.* [1] (dotyczący mężczyzn) *[populacja, zachowania]* male; *[imię, zawód, obuwie, ubranie]* man's; **fryzjer** ~**ki** a barber; ~**kie towarzystwo** male company [2] (typowy dla mężczyzny) *[uroda]* masculine; (jurny) virile; *[odwaga, stanowczość]* manly; ~**ka decyzja** a snap decision; **po** ~**ku** like a man [3] Biol. *[narządy, osobniki]* male [4] Jęz. *[końcówka, rodzaj]* masculine
■ **wiek** ~**ki** a. **lata** ~**kie** manhood
męskoś|ć *f* [1] (bycie mężczyzną) maleness; (cechy męskie) manliness [2] euf. (narządy płciowe) manhood [3] (potencja) virility
męstw|o *n* książk. [1] (odwaga) valour [2] (hart ducha) fortitude; **znosić coś z** ~**em** to bear sth with fortitude
mętlik *m* pot. [1] (intelektualny) muddle; **mieć** ~ **w głowie** to be in a muddle [2] (bałagan, chaos) mess
mętni|eć *impf vi* [1] (stawać się nieprzejrzystym) to cloud [2] (być słabo widocznym) to become dim a. indistinct [3] (tracić blask) to cloud (over)
mętn|y *adi. grad.* [1] (nieprzejrzysty) *[kawa, piwo, woda]* cloudy; *[szkło]* opaque; *[rzeka]* turbid [2] (przytłumiony) *[światło]* dim [3] (niewyraźny) *[kontur]* fuzzy [4] (zamglony) *[oczy, spojrzenie, wzrok]* dull [5] przen. (zagmatwany) *[tok rozumowania]* woolly; *[opowieść]* muddled; *[plan]* muddle-headed; *[komentarz]* obscure [6] (podejrzany) *[interesy]* shady; *[wyjaśnienie]* fishy
mężat|ka *f* married woman; **to panna czy** ~**ka?** is she single or married?; **młoda** ~**ka** a young wife
mężczy|zna *m* man
mężni|eć *impf vi* (nabierać sił) to grow stronger; (dojrzewać) to become a man
mężn|y *adi. grad.* [1] (odważny) *[osoba, obrona]* gallant; *[czyn]* courageous; *[bohater, żołnierz]* valiant [2] (obdarzony hartem ducha) *[osoba]* stout-hearted książk.
mgli|sty *adi.* *[dzień, pogoda]* hazy; *[horyzont, kontury, światło]* misty; *[idee, nadzieje, obietnice]* vague; *[przeszłość]* misty; *[pamięć, wspomnienia]* hazy
mg|ła *f* mist; (gęsta) fog; **jak przez mgłę** *[widzieć, słyszeć]* as if through a haze; *[pamiętać]* vaguely
mgławic|a *f* Astron. nebula
mgnie|nie *n* [1] (mrugnięcie) blink; **w** ~**niu oka** in the blink a. twinkling of an eye [2] przen. (chwila) instant
mia|ł *m* dust; ~**ł węglowy** coal dust

miał|ki *adi.* [1] (drobny) *[cukier, piasek]* fine(-grained); *[kreda]* powdery [2] (nijaki) *[charakter, opis, styl]* bland; *[osoba]* insipid; *[idee, koncepcje]* superficial

mian|ować *pf, impf vt* to appoint; ~**ować kogoś na stanowisko dyrektora** to appoint sb director; **z** ~**owania** by nomination

mianowicie *coni.* książk. namely

mianownik *m* Mat. denominator; **sprowadzać coś do wspólnego** ~**a** to reduce sth to the lowest common denominator

mi|ara *f* [1] (wielkość) measure, measurement; **wagi i miary** weights and measures; **jednostki miary** units of measure [2] (przyrząd) measure; (krawiecka) measuring tape; (kuchenna) measuring cup a. jug [3] (rozmiar) measurement; **wziąć miarę z kogoś (na garnitur)** to take sb's measurements a. measure sb (for a suit); **szyty na miarę** made to measure [4] (kryterium) measure; **bogactwo nie jest miarą szczęścia** wealth isn't a measure of happiness [5] książk. (umiar) moderation; **zachować miarę (w jedzeniu)** to exercise moderation (in eating) [6] (przymiarka) fitting; **przyjść do miary** to come for a fitting [7] (stopień) measure książk.; degree; **chwalić i ganić w równej mierze** to distribute praise and blame in equal measure; **w jakiejś mierze** in some measure a. degree; **w znacznej mierze** in large measure a. degree [8] (jakość) stature; **artysta wielkiej miary** an artist of great stature; **dzieło na miarę epoki** a work worthy of the age

■ **bez miary** beyond measure książk.; **(po)nad miarę** to excess; **w tej mierze** książk. in this respect; **ze wszech miar** in every respect; **w miarę dobry/tani** good/cheap fairly; **w miarę potrzeb** as the need arises; **w miarę upływu czasu** with the passage of time; **w miarę jak słuchali...** as they listened...

miar|ka *f* [1] (przyrząd) measure; (krawiecka) tape measure; (kuchenna) measuring cup a. jug [2] (porcja) measure; ~**ka zboża/whisky** a measure of grain/whisky

■ **mierzyć wszystkich jedną** ~**ką** to tar everyone with the same brush; **przebrać** ~**kę** to overstep the mark a. the line; **przebrała się** ~**ka** the worm has turned

miarow|y *adi.* [1] *[stukot]* steady; *[kroki, ruchy]* measured; *[oddech]* even [2] *[obuwie, krawiectwo]* made-to-measure

miastecz|ko *n* (small) town; **wesołe** ~**ko** a funfair GB, an amusement park US

mi|asto *n* [1] town; (wielkie) city; (centrum) the city; **rodzinne miasto** one's home town; **pojechać do miasta** to go (in)to town a. the city; **iść na miasto** pot. to go shopping; **spotkać się na mieście** to meet in town; **wyjechać za miasto** to go to the country(side); **iść** a. **ruszyć w miasto** pot. to go out on the town [2] pot. (mieszkańcy) town; **na mieście mówią, że...** there are rumours that...

miau|knąć /ˈmjawknɔɲtɕ/ *pf* — **miau|czeć** /ˈmjawtʃɛtɕ/ *impf vi* to miaow GB, to meow US

miaz|ga *f* [1] (masa) pulp; **rozbić coś na** ~**gę** to crush sth to a pulp [2] Stomat. (dental) pulp [3] Bot. cambium

■ **zetrzeć kogoś na** ~**gę** to wipe the floor with sb pot.

miażdżyc|a *f* Med. atherosclerosis

miażdż|yć *impf vt* to crush; ~**yć przeciwnika** przen. to crush an opponent; ~**yć kogoś wzrokiem** a. **spojrzeniem** przen. to give sb a withering look

m|iąć *impf* [] *vt* to crumple

[] **miąć się** to crumple

miąższ *m* [1] (miękisz) pulp; (chleba) (the) inside [2] Anat., Bot. parenchyma

miecz *m* [1] (broń) sword; **dobyć** ~**a** to draw a sword; **ogniem i** ~**em** with fire and sword [2] Żegl. centreboard GB, centerboard US

■ **kto** ~**em wojuje, (ten) od** ~**a ginie** przysł. he who lives by the sword dies by the sword przysł.

m|ieć *impf* [] *vt* [1] (posiadać) (na własność) to have (got) *[dom, samochód, mikrofalówkę]*; (do dyspozycji) to have (got) (prowadzić) to run *[firmę, warsztat]*; **gdzie masz rower?** where's your bike? pot.; **mieć na coś** to have money for sth; **jak masz na imię?** what's your name?; **mieć coś na sobie** to be wearing sth; **mieć kogoś u siebie** to have sb staying with one; **masz!/macie!** (weź/weźcie) here!; **masz, włóż to na siebie!** here, put this on!; **(a) masz!** (zadając razy) take that!; **masz za swoje!** (dobrze ci tak) serves you right! [2] (liczyć sobie) to be; **mieć dwadzieścia lat** to be twenty (years old); **mieć sześć metrów głębokości/szerokości** to be six metres deep/wide; **kilometr ma tysiąc metrów** one kilometre is a thousand metres [3] (posiadać jako cechę) to have (got); **mieć niebieskie oczy/siwe włosy** to have blue eyes/grey hair; **miała męża Włocha/inżyniera** her husband was Italian/an engineer; **mieć talent** to have talent; **nie mieć cierpliwości/odwagi** to lack patience/courage; **mieć kształt prostokąta** a. **prostokątny** to be rectangular (in shape); **urodę miała po matce** her looks came from her mother; **mieć w sobie coś** (być interesującym) to have a certain something; **on ma w sobie coś z dziecka** there is something of the child in a. about him [4] (o stanie fizycznym i psychicznym) to have *[boleści, grypę, trudności]*; to feel *[żal]*; to bear *[urazę]*; **mieć temperaturę** to have a. be running a temperature; **mieć pragnienie** to be thirsty [5] (o relacjach między ludźmi) to have *[córkę, przyjaciół]*; **nie mieć matki/ojca** to have no mother/father; **miała z nim dwóch synów** she had two sons by him; **mieć w kimś rywala/sojusznika** to have a rival/an ally in sb; **mieć kogoś** pot. (być związanym z kimś) to have somebody; **mieć kogoś/coś przeciwko sobie** to have sb/sth against one; **mieć coś do kogoś** pot. to have something against sb;

mieć coś na kogoś to have the goods a. the dope on sb pot.; **niczego na mnie nie mają** they've got nothing on me pot.; **mieć kogoś pod sobą** to be in charge of sb; **mieć kogoś za sobą** (być popieranym) to have sb behind one; **za kogo pan mnie ma!** what do you take me for! 6 (znajdować się w jakiejś sytuacji) to have (got) *[długi, posadę, połączenie]*; **mieć słuszność** a. **rację** to be right; **mieć coś przed sobą** (w perspektywie) to have sth ahead of a. before one; **mieć coś (po)za sobą** to have sth behind one; **nie mieć gdzie mieszkać/spać** to have nowhere to live/sleep; **nie masz co narzekać** you've got nothing to complain about; **nie masz czego** a. **co żałować** you didn't miss much; **w domu nie masz co się pokazywać** you'd better not show your face at home pot. 7 (brać udział) to have *[zebranie, koncert, egzamin, próbę]*; **mieć sprawę** a. **proces** to be on trial 8 (ukończyć etap nauki) to have *[dyplom, tytuł]*; **mieć studia** a. **wyższe wykształcenie** to have completed higher education 9 (znaleźć się w określonym miejscu lub czasie) **mieć kogoś po prawej/lewej stronie** to have sb on one's right/left; **którego dziś mamy?** what's the date today?; **którą mamy godzinę?** what time do you make it? pot.; **wreszcie mamy stację** here's the station at last

II *v aux.* 1 (dla wyrażenia powinności) **mieć coś do zrobienia** to have sth to do; **masz to zrobić natychmiast!** you're to do it right now!; **co mam jej powiedzieć?** what am I (supposed) to tell her?; **mam sprawę do załatwienia** I've got something to sort out 2 (zamiar, przewidywanie) **ona ma przyjść o drugiej** she's expected (to come) at two; **samolot miał wylądować w Warszawie, ale...** the plane was supposed to land in Warsaw, but...; **i co ja mam z tym zrobić?** what am I (supposed) to do with it?; **jeśli mielibyśmy się nie zobaczyć przed twoim wyjazdem...** in case we don't see each other before you leave...; **właśnie miałem wyjść, kiedy...** I was just about to leave a. just on the point of leaving when...; **czy mam przez to rozumieć, że...** am I to understand (by that) that...; **choćby** a. **żeby nie wiem co się miało stać, (to)...** no matter what happens a. might happen... 3 (rezultat) **mieć coś zrobione** to have sth done; **czy macie załatwione bilety?** have you booked/got the tickets?; **mam obiecaną podwyżkę** I've been promised a rise 4 (zdziwienie, rozczarowanie) **ja miałbym to powiedzieć?** I said that?!; **to ma być hotel czterogwiazdkowy?** (z dezaprobatą) and this is supposed to be a four-star hotel?!; **ten grubas to miałbym być ja!?** (z niedowierzaniem) is this/that fatso really me? pot.

III mieć się 1 (być w stanie, położeniu) to be; (czuć się) to feel; **mieć się dobrze** to be doing well; **jak się mają twoi rodzice?** how are your parents?; **jak się masz!** (powitanie) how's it going? pot.; **mam się**

dzisiaj lepiej I feel better today; **sprawy mają się nieźle** things are working out (quite) well; **jak się rzeczy mają?** how do things stand?; **rzecz ma się tak, że...** the thing is that...; **teoria nijak się miała do praktyki** the theory was completely divorced from practice 2 (uważać się za) **mieć się za artystę** to consider oneself (to be) an artist 3 (być bliskim) **mieć się ku końcowi** to be drawing to a close a. an end; **ma się na deszcz** it looks like rain; **miało się na burzę** there was thunder in the air

IV ma Fin. (zapis księgowy) credit; **winien i ma** debit and credit; **zapisać coś po stronie „ma"** to enter sth on the credit side

V mam! inter. (przypomniałem sobie) I've got it!; **mam cię!** a. **tu cię mam!** (złapałem cię, przyłapałem cię) got you! pot.

VI nie ma → być

■ **ma się rozumieć** a. **wiedzieć!** it a. that goes without saying!; **ma się rozumieć, że przyjdę** of course I'll come; **mieć kogoś/coś w nosie** pot. a. **gdzieś** euf. to not care a damn about sb/sth pot.; to not give a monkey's about sb/sth posp.; **mam to wszystko gdzieś!** pot. to hell with it all! pot.; **sie masz!** pot. (powitanie) hi! pot.

miedz|a f 1 (na polu) baulk GB, balk US 2 przen. (granica) border; **graniczyć** a. **sąsiadować o ~ę** to be neighbours (z kimś with sb); **sąsiad zza ~ą** one's next-door neighbour

mie|dź f copper

miejsc|e n 1 (wolna przestrzeń) room (na coś a. dla czegoś for sth); **dużo wolnego ~a** plenty of room; **zrobić komuś ~e** to make room for sb; **zabierać dużo ~a** to take up a lot of space 2 (lokalizacja, punkt) place; **czyjeś ~e pracy/zamieszkania** sb's place of work/residence; **czyjeś ~e urodzenia** sb's birthplace; **~e kultu** a place of worship; **w ~ach publicznych** in public places; **w którym ~u pana boli?** tell me where it hurts; **przeczytaj od tego ~a** start reading from here; **w którym ~u skończyliśmy?** where did we stop?; **kierowca poniósł śmierć na ~u** the driver died on the spot; **zapakować, czy zje pani na ~u?** to eat here or take away? 3 (dla jednej osoby) seat; **~e przy oknie** a window seat; **~e stojące** standing room; **czy to ~e jest wolne?** is this seat free?; **zajmij mi ~e!** save me a place!; **zamienić się z kimś ~ami** to change places with sb 4 (lokata) place; **zająć drugie ~e w konkursie** to take second place in a contest; **zajmować jedno z czołowych ~** to rank high on the list 5 (stanowisko) job; (mandat) seat; **tworzyć nowe ~a pracy** to create new jobs; **partia zdobyła 35 ~ w parlamencie** the party won 35 seats in Parliament 6 Mat. place; **do pięciu ~ po przecinku** to five decimal places

II miejscami *adv.* in places a. parts

III z miejsca *adv.* pot. right away; right off pot.

■ **na** ~**a!** Sport on your marks! GB, on your mark! US; **na** ~**e** a. **w** ~**e czegoś** książk. in place of sth; **nie zagrzać (długo)** ~**a** to not stay long; **ruszyć z** ~**a** to get off the ground; **zająć** ~**e kogoś/ czegoś** to take the place of sb/sth; **znać swoje** ~**e** to know one's place; **na twoim** ~**u postąpiłbym tak samo** I'd do the same in your shoes

miejscowoś|ć f town; ~**ć wypoczynkowa** a holiday town a. resort; **turystyczna** ~**ć nad morzem** a seaside resort

miejscow|y adi. ① (tutejszy) *[prasa, władze, obyczaj]* local; **godzina 8 czasu** ~**ego** 8 o'clock local time ② Med. *[wysypka, znieczulenie]* local

miejsców|ka f (bilet) seat reservation; (miejsce) reserved seat; **pociąg z** ~**kami** a train with reserved seats only

miejs|ki adi. *[komunikacja, życie]* urban; *[straż, rada]* municipal; **ludność** ~**ka** townspeople

mieli|zna f ① shoal; **osiąść na** ~**źnie** to run aground ② przen. (w książce, filmie) weakness

mie|nić się impf v refl. ① (iskrzyć się) to shimmer ② (na twarzy) to flush

mieni|e n książk. property; ~**e państwowe** public property; **utracić całe swoje** ~**e** to lose all one's possessions

miernik m ① (kryterium) yardstick ② (wskaźnik) gauge; ~ **szybkości** a speedometer

miern|y ① adi. *[uczeń, malarz, utwór]* mediocre; *[wzrost, dochody]* average
Ⅱ m Szkol. ≈ D

mierze|ja f sandbar

mierzw|ić impf **Ⅰ** vt to ruffle *[włosy, sierść, trawę]*
Ⅱ mierzwić się *[włosy, sierść]* to be ruffled

mierz|yć impf **Ⅰ** vt ① (sprawdzać, oceniać) to measure (up) *[materiał, długość, osobę]*; ~**yć komuś temperaturę/puls** to take sb's temperature/pulse; ~**yć czas zawodników** to time the competitors ② (przymierzać) to try on *[ubranie, buty]*
Ⅱ vi ① (liczyć sobie) to measure; ~**yć dwadzieścia metrów (wysokości)** to be twenty metres high ② (celować) to aim; ~**yć z karabinu** to aim a gun; ~**yć w coś palcem** to point (a finger) at sth
Ⅲ mierzyć się ① (samego siebie) to measure one's height; (jeden drugiego) to measure each another ② książk. (zmagać się) to square up (**z czymś** to sth) ③ (dorównywać) **nie móc się** ~**yć z kimś/czymś** to be no match for sb/sth
■ ~**yć kogoś spojrzeniem** a. **wzrokiem** (badaw-czo) to eye sb up and down; (groźnie) to glare at sb

miesi|ąc m month

miesiącz|ka f period; **mieć/dostać** ~**kę** to have/ get one's period

miesiączk|ować impf vi to menstruate

miesiączkow|y adi. *[bóle]* period

miesięcznik m monthly

miesięczn|y adi. ① *[pensja]* monthly; **bilet** ~**y** a monthly ticket ② *[niemowlę]* (one-)month-old

miesza|ć impf **Ⅰ** vt ① (łączyć) to mix (up); (bełtać) to stir *[herbatę, sos]*; ~**ć mąkę z cukrem** to mix flour with sugar; ~**ać rzeczywistość z fantazją** to blend fact and fiction ② (mylić) to mix up *[fakty, nazwiska, pojęcia]* ③ (wciągać) to involve (**kogoś w coś** sb in sth); **mnie do tego nie** ~**j!** I don't want (to have) anything to do with it! ④ (wprawiać w zakłopotanie) to disconcert
Ⅱ vi pot. (mącić) to interfere; ~**ć komuś w głowie** to confuse sb
Ⅲ mieszać się ① (łączyć się) to blend (**z czymś** with sth) ② (wtrącać się) to interfere (**w coś** in sth); ~**ć się do cudzej rozmowy** to interrupt sb's conversation; **nie** ~**j się w nie swoje sprawy** mind your own business ③ (mylić się) **starszym ludziom** ~**ją się fakty** elderly people mix things up; **wszystko mi się** ~ I'm getting everything mixed up ④ (peszyć się) to be disconcerted

mieszanin|a f ① (substancja) mixture ② przen. (zlepek) blend

mieszan|ka f ① (produkt) blend ② przen. (zlepek) blend

mieszan|y adi. *[las, chór, towarzystwo, reakcja]* mixed; **cera** ~**a** mixed skin; **gra** ~**a** Sport mixed doubles; **z** ~**ymi uczuciami** with mixed feelings

mieszczańs|ki adi. *[pochodzenie, mentalność, smak]* bourgeois

mieszczuch m townie pot.

mieszka|ć impf vi ① (stale przebywać) to live; ~**ć z rodzicami** to live with one's parents; ~**ć z kimś przez ścianę** to live next door to sb; ~**ć w mieście/na wsi** to live in town/in the country ② (nocować) to stay; ~**ć w hotelu Savoy** to stay at the Savoy Hotel; ~**ć u przyjaciela** to stay with a friend

mieszka|nie n flat GB, apartment US

mieszka|niec m (miasta, wsi) inhabitant; (kraju) resident; (mieszkania, domu) occupant; ~**niec miasta/wsi** a city/country dweller; **wspólnota** ~**ńców** a (local) resident's association

mie|ścić impf **Ⅰ** vi ① *[budynek]* to house; *[naczynie, kosz]* to hold; **sala** ~**ści sto osób** the hall holds a. seats a hundred people ② (zawierać) to contain
Ⅱ mieścić się ① (znajdować się) to be located ② (znajdować dość miejsca) to fit; **z łatwością** ~**ścić się w kieszeni** to fit easily in(to) one's pocket ③ (zawierać się) to fall into; ~**ścić się w granicach normy** to be within normal limits

miewa|ć impf **Ⅰ** vi to have (occasionally); ~**ć dziwne pomysły** to have strange ideas
Ⅱ miewać się (czuć się) ~**ć się dobrze** to be fine a. well; ~**ć się źle** to not be (very) well; **jak się** ~**sz?** how are you?

mięczak m ① Zool. mollusc GB, mollusk US ② pot. (o osobie) wimp pot., pejor.

między praep. ① (w przestrzeni) (pośrodku) between; (w otoczeniu) among; **pociąg kursuje** ~ **Krakowem**

a Berlinem the train runs from Cracow to Berlin; **wejść** ~ **tłum** to mingle with the crowd [2] (w czasie) between; ~ **(godziną) drugą a trzecią** between two and three; ~ **posiłkami** between meals [3] (zależność) (dwóch) between; (kilku) among; **współpraca** ~ **członkami organizacji** cooperation among the members of an organization [4] (podział, wybór) (dwóch) between; (kilku) among; **wybierać** ~ **dwoma kandydatami** to choose between two candidates [5] (o wspólnych cechach) between; **coś pośredniego** ~ **powieścią a autobiografią** something between a novel and an autobiography [6] książk. (spośród, ze) (from) among

■ **mówiąc** ~ **nami** a. ~ **nami mówiąc** (just) between you and me

międzylądowa|nie n Lotn. stopover; (dla uzupełnienia paliwa) refuelling stop; **rejs bez** ~**nia** a nonstop flight

międzyludz|ki adi. [stosunki, konflikty] interpersonal

międzymiastow|y adi. [komunikacja] intercity; **rozmowa** ~**a** a long-distance call

międzynarodow|y adi. [współpraca, rynki, nagroda] international

mięk|ki adi. grad. [1] (nietwardy, niesztywny) [materac, ziemia, włosy] soft; [mięso, warzywa] tender; **książka w** ~**kiej oprawie** a paperback, a softback US; ~**ka woda** soft water [2] (łagodny, harmonijny) [głos, linie, rysy, krok, światło] soft [3] (mało stanowczy) [osoba, charakter] soft; **mieć** ~**kie serce** to be soft- a. tender-hearted [4] Jęz. [spółgłoska, wymowa] soft

mięk|ko adv. grad. [1] [układać się] softly; **na kanapie będzie ci** ~**ko** you'll be comfortable on the couch; **gotować jajko na** ~**ko** to soft-boil an egg [2] (harmonijnie) [stąpać, chodzić] softly [3] (nieostro) [świecić] softly [4] (czule) [mówić, spojrzeć] tenderly

mięk|nąć impf vi (tracić twardość) to soften [2] przen. (łagodnieć) [głos, rysy, spojrzenie] to soften; [osoba, serce] to melt [3] pot. (ustępować) to yield

mię|sień m muscle

mięsi|sty adi. [wargi, nos, liście] fleshy; [tkanina] thick

mię|sny adi. [przemysł, przetwórstwo, danie] meat; **sklep** ~**sny** butcher's (shop); **konserwa** ~**sna** tinned meat

mięs|o n [1] Kulin. meat; ~**o wieprzowe** pork; ~**o wołowe** beef [2] (ciało) flesh

■ ~**o armatnie** cannon fodder

mię|ta f [1] Bot. mint; ~**ta pieprzowa** peppermint [2] (napar) mint tea [3] Kulin. mint (leaves)

mięto|sić impf vt pot. to crumple

miętow|y adi. [smak] mint; [lody, czekolada] mint-flavoured GB, mint-flavored US; **cukierek** ~**y** a mint

mig [] m [1] pot. (sygnał) sign; **porozumiewać się na** ~**i (z kimś)** to signal a. sign (to sb) [2] (głuchoniemych)

(hand) sign; **uczyć się** ~**ów** to learn sign language

[II] **migiem** a. **w mig** adv. pot. in a flash

migacz m Aut. indicator GB, turn signal US

migać¹ impf → **mignąć**

miga|ć² impf vi [głuchoniemy] to sign

migaw|ka f [1] (scena, zdjęcie) shot; (reportaż) clip [2] Fot. shutter

migda|ł m almond; **gorzkie** ~**ły** bitter almonds

■ **myśleć o niebieskich** ~**łach** pot. to daydream

migdałow|y adi. [ciasto, krem, oczy] almond

mig|nąć pf — **migać¹** impf [] vi [1] (świecić nierówno) to blink; (błysnąć) to flash [2] (pojawić się i zniknąć) to flash (by); **w tłumie** ~**nęła mu jej twarz** he glimpsed her face in the crowd

[II] **migać się** pot. to skive GB pot.; ~**ać się od czegoś** to dodge a. shirk sth

migo|tać impf vi [1] (błyskać) [lampa] to blink; [świeca] to flicker; [gwiazdy, światła] to twinkle [2] (połyskiwać) to shimmer

migow|y adi. [1] (wykonywany za pomocą gestów) **znaki** ~**e** hand signs; **język** ~**y** sign language [2] Techn. **światła** ~**e** signal lights

migracj|a f Biol., Geol., Socjol., Zool. migration

migren|a f migraine

migr|ować impf vi Socjol., Zool. to migrate

mijać impf → **minąć**

mikołaj|ki plt St. Nicholas' Day

mikrofal|a f [1] Fiz. microwave [2] pot. (kuchenka) microwave

mikrofilm m microfilm

mikrofon m microphone; ~ **butonierkowy** a lapel a. clip-on microphone; ~ **kierunkowy** a directional microphone; **mówić do** ~**u/przez** ~ to talk into/through a microphone; **próba** ~**u!** testing microphone!

mikroskop m microscope; **badać coś pod** ~**em** to examine sth under a microscope

mikse|r m [1] Kulin. (stojący) liquidizer GB, blender; (ręczny) mixer [2] Radio, TV mixer

mil|a f Miary mile; ~**a angielska** a (land) mile; ~**a morska** a nautical mile

milcząc|y adi. [1] (małomówny) taciturn [2] przen. [oburzenie, protest] silent; **przy czyjejś** ~**ej aprobacie** with sb's tacit approval

milcz|eć impf vi [1] (nie mówić) to be silent; ~**eć!** be quiet! [2] (nie protestować) to remain silent [3] (dochować tajemnicy) to keep silent; ~**eć jak głaz** a. **grób** to be (as) silent as the grave

milczeni|e n silence; **zapłata za** ~**e** hush money pot.

mile adv. grad. [1] [uśmiechnąć się, witać] nicely; ~ **kogoś wspominać** to remember sb fondly; **być** ~ **widzianym gościem** to be a welcome guest [2] [chłodzić, spędzać czas] pleasantly; **być** ~ **zaskoczonym** to be pleasantly surprised

miliar|d num. billion; ~**dy** (mnóstwo) billions pot.

milimet|r *m* millimetre GB, millimeter US
milion *num.* million
milione|r *m*, ~**rka** *f* millionaire
militarn|y *adi. [potencjał, konflikt]* military
milk|nąć *impf vi [osoba]* to fall silent; *[oklaski, łkanie]* to cease; (stopniowo) *[głos, gwar]* to trail away a. off
mi|ło *adv. grad.* [1] *[uśmiechać się, gawędzić]* pleasantly; **miło spędzać czas** to have a nice time [2] (w zwrotach grzecznościowych) **miło mi panią poznać** nice to meet you; **to miło z pana strony** that's nice of you
miłosierdzi|e *n* książk. mercy; **bez** ~**a** *[potraktować]* mercilessly
miłosn|y *adi. [list, poezja]* love; *[spojrzenie]* amorous; **zawód** ~**y** a disappointment in love
miłoś|ć *f* [1] (uczucie) love (**do kogoś** for sb); ~**ć bez wzajemności** unrequited love; ~**ć od pierwszego wejrzenia** love at first sight; **wyznał jej** ~**ć** he said he loved her [2] pot. (zamiłowanie) love (**do czegoś** of sth); passion (**do czegoś** for sth) [3] (obiekt uczucia) love; ~**ć jego życia** the love of his life [4] książk. (seks) sex; **uprawiać** ~**ć (z kimś)** to have sex (with sb)
■ **stara** ~**ć nie rdzewieje** przysł. old love never dies
miłośni|k *m*, ~**czka** *f* (amator) enthusiast; (wielbiciel) admirer; ~**k wyścigów konnych** a horse-racing enthusiast; ~**k kina** a film lover
mi|ły [1] *adi. grad.* [1] (sprawiający przyjemność) *[niespodzianka, wrażenia]* pleasant; *[słowa, dźwięki]* pleasing; (sympatyczny) *[osoba, uśmiech]* nice; *[nastrój]* agreeable; *[wspomnienia]* fond; **miły dla oka/ucha** pleasing to the eye/ear [2] (uprzejmy) nice; **być miłym dla kogoś** to be nice to sb [3] (bliski) dear; **nasz najmilszy przyjaciel** our dearest friend; **być miłym czyjemuś sercu** to be close a. dear to sb's heart [4] (w zwrotach grzecznościowych) *[czytelnicy, goście]* dear; **bądź tak miły i otwórz okno** would you be so kind as to open the window?; **do miłego zobaczenia** książk. see you soon
[2] **miły** *m*, **miła** *f* książk. beloved
mim *m* mime (artist)
mimi|ka *f* facial expressions
mimo *praep.* in spite of, despite; ~ **trudności** in spite of difficulties; ~ **wszystko** in spite of a. despite everything; ~ **wszystko ich lubię** I (still) like them all the same; ~ **to** yet, still; ~ **że...** even though...
mimochodem *adv. [wspomnieć, napomknąć]* in passing; *[zauważyć]* parenthetically
mimowoln|y *adi.* [1] (bezwiedny) *[błąd]* unintentional; *[odruch]* involuntary [2] (przypadkowy) *[sprawca, bohater]* unwitting
mimoz|a *f* mimosa
min|a¹ *f* (wyraz twarzy) face; **robić** a. **stroić** ~**y** to make faces; **mieć urażoną** ~**ę** to have a hurt look

on one's face; **mieć** ~**ę niewiniątka** to look as if butter wouldn't melt in one's mouth pot.
■ **nadrabiać** ~**ą** to put on a brave front; **robić dobrą** ~**ę (do złej gry)** to put a brave a. bold face on it
min|a² *f* (materiał wybuchowy) mine; ~**a lądowa** a landmine; ~**a przeciwpiechotna/przeciwczołgowa** an anti-personnel/anti-tank mine; **podłożyć** ~**ę** to lay a mine
mi|nąć *pf* — **mi|jać** *impf* [1] *vt* [1] (przemieścić się obok) to go past; **minąć kogoś/coś w pędzie** to rush a. flash past sb/sth [2] (nie przypaść) **minęła go okazja** he missed out on an opportunity; **nie minie cię kara/nagroda** you shan't go unpunished/unrewarded; **minął go awans** he's been passed over for promotion
[2] *vi* [1] (upłynąć) *[czas, okres]* to pass, to elapse; **minęła godzina, odkąd wyszedł** it's been an hour since he left; „**która godzina?**" – „**minęła ósma**" 'what's the time?' – 'it's (just) past a. gone eight o'clock'; **nie mija moda na kapelusze** hats are still in; **było, minęło** pot. it's over and done with pot.; **weekend minął nam na sprzątaniu** we spent the weekend cleaning up [2] (ustąpić) *[ból, napięcie]* to pass; *[smutek, wstrząs]* to wear off; **minął jej dobry humor** her good mood had gone a. vanished; **niebezpieczeństwo minęło** the danger was over
[3] **minąć się** – **mijać się** [1] (przejść, przejechać obok siebie) to pass each other; **mijam się z nim** a. **mijamy się codziennie na ulicy** I pass him a. we pass each other in the street every day [2] (nie zetknąć się) *[osoby]* to fail to meet; **nasze listy minęły się po drodze** our letters crossed [3] (być niezgodnym) *[teorie, opinie]* to diverge; *[osoby, charaktery]* to differ
mineraln|y *adi. [woda, oleje, złoża]* mineral
minera|ł *m* mineral
miniatu|ra *f* [1] (model) miniature; ~**ra samolotu** a miniature aeroplane; **w** ~**rze** in miniature; **pudel/jamnik** ~**ra** a toy poodle/dachshund [2] Szt. miniature [3] Literat., Muz., Teatr short piece
miniaturow|y *adi. [model, wersja, portret]* miniature; ~**y aparat fotograficzny** a mini a. miniature camera
minim|um [1] *n* minimum; **ograniczyć wydatki do** ~**um** to keep costs to a minimum; **zarabiać poniżej** ~**um** to earn less than the minimum wage
[2] *adv.* at least; ~**um dwa tysiące** at least two thousand
minion|y *adi.* książk. [1] (ubiegły) past; **w** ~**ych latach** in past years; ~**ej nocy** last night [2] (dawny) *[pokolenia, epoka]* bygone; *[przeżycia, urazy]* past; **w dawno** ~**ych stuleciach** in centuries past
minist|er *m* (government) minister GB, secretary US; ~**er spraw zagranicznych** the Minister of Foreign Affairs; (w Wielkiej Brytanii) the Foreign

Secretary; (w USA) the Secretary of State; **~er pełnomocny** minister plenipotentiary

ministerstw|o n ① (urząd) ministry GB, (government) department; **Ministerstwo Obrony Narodowej** the Ministry of Defence; (w USA) the Department of Defense ② (budynek) ministry (building)

ministrant m (altar) server; (chłopiec) altar boy

min|ować impf vt Wojsk. to mine

mintaj m walleye pollack

minus Ⅰ m ① Mat. minus (sign) ② Szkol. (obniżenie oceny) minus; (kara) order mark GB; **trójka z ~em** three minus ③ pot. (wada) minus; **plusy i ~y mieszkania na wsi** the pros and cons of living in the country

Ⅱ adi. inv. minus; **~ pięć stopni** minus five degrees

Ⅲ coni. ① Mat. minus; **siedem ~ cztery** seven minus four ② pot. (pomijając) minus pot.; **cała pensja ~ spłata kredytu** the full salary minus a. less the credit repayment

■ **być na ~ie** pot. to be in debt; **mieć u kogoś ~** pot. to be in sb's bad books; **policzyć** a. **zapisać coś komuś na ~** pot. to chalk sth up against sb; **zmienić się na ~** to change for the worse

minu|ta f ① (jednostka czasu) minute; **~ta ciszy** a minute's silence; **za ~tę piąta** one minute to five ② pot. (chwila) minute pot.; **za ~tę** in a minute; **z ~ty na ~tę** a. **z każdą ~tą** by the minute ③ Geog., Mat. (arc) minute

■ **jeszcze nie nadeszło moje pięć ~t** pot. my day is still to come

miodow|y adi. ① [piernik, cukierek] honey ② [bluzka] honey-coloured GB, honey-colored US ③ przen. [słówka] honeyed

■ **~y miesiąc** honeymoon

mio|t m Zool. litter

miotacz m ① (sportowiec) **~ dyskiem/młotem/oszczepem** a discus-/hammer-/javelin-thrower; **~ kulą** a shot-putter ② (broń) **~ ognia** a flame-thrower

miotacz|ka f Sport thrower

miota|ć impf Ⅰ vt książk. ① (rzucać) to throw (**czymś w kogoś** sth at sb); **~ć dyskiem/młotem** to throw the discus/hammer; **~ć kulą** to put the shot ② (wypowiadać) to hurl (**coś** sth); **~ć obelgi na kogoś** to hurl a. throw insults at sb ③ przen. [uczucia, gniew] to seize; **~ła nim zazdrość** he was seized with jealousy; **~ły nim sprzeczne uczucia** he was torn between conflicting emotions ④ (trząść, szarpać) [wiatr, burza] to toss (**czymś** sth)

Ⅱ **miotać się** ① (szarpać się) to thrash about a. around; **~ć się po pokoju** to pace about a. around the room ② (być niezdecydowanym) to vacillate ③ (czynić daremne wysiłki) to run (a)round in circles

mio|tła f broom; (z chrustu) besom

■ **nowa ~ła** pot. a new broom

mi|ód m ① honey; **miód płynny** liquid honey; **chleb na miodzie** honey bread ② (alkohol) mead

mirabel|ka f mirabelle plum

misecz|ka f ① (naczynie) bowl ② (kształt) cup; **~ki biustonosza** the cups of a bra; **rozmiar ~ki (stanika)** cup size ③ Bot. cup

misj|a f ① (zadanie) mission; **wysłać kogoś z ~ą** to send a. dispatch sb on a mission ② (placówka) mission; **~a gospodarcza/wojskowa** a trade/military mission ③ Relig. mission; **prowadzić ~ę** to run a mission

misjona|rz m, **~rka** f missionary

mis|ka f (naczynie) bowl; (zawartość) bowl(ful)

❑ **~ka klozetowa** (toilet) bowl; **~ka olejowa** Techn. sump GB, oil pan US

■ **sprzedać coś za ~kę soczewicy** książk. to sell sth for a mess of pottage

mistern|y adi. grad. [haft, plan, intryga] elaborate; [wzór] intricate

mistrz m ① (znawca) master; **~ pędzla** a master of painting; **~ ceremonii** the master of ceremonies; **~ kierownicy** an expert driver ② Sport champion; (w szachach) master; **~ świata** a world champion ③ (rzemieślnik) master; **~ stolarski** a master carpenter ④ przen. (nauczyciel) master ⑤ (loży, zakonu) master; **Wielki Mistrz** a Grand Master

mistrzostw|o n ① (biegłość) expertise; (w sztuce) artistry; **z ~em** with mastery ② Sport (tytuł) championship (title); **~o ligi tenisowej** the tennis league championship

mistrzows|ki adi. ① (doskonały) masterly; **po ~ku** in (a) masterly fashion ② Sport **tytuł ~ki** championship (title) ③ (w rzemiośle) [egzamin, tytuł] master's

mistrzy|ni f ① (znawczyni) mistress ② Sport champion

mi|ś m ① (zabawka) teddy (bear) ② pot. (tkanina) fake fur

mi|t m ① myth; **mity greckie** the Greek myths; **mit o Syzyfie** the myth of Sisyphus ② przen. myth; **obalić mit** to debunk a. explode a myth; **rozwiać mit** to dispel a myth

mitologi|a f mythology także przen.; **~a rzymska** Roman mythology

mityczn|y adi. mythic(al) także przen.

mityg|ować impf książk. Ⅰ vt (powściągać) to placate [osobę]; (uspokajać) to pacify [osobę]; **~ować czyjś gniew** to appease a. soothe sb's anger

Ⅱ **mitygować się** to restrain oneself

mityng m ① (wiec) rally; **~ przedwyborczy** a pre-election rally ② Sport meeting, meet US

mizeri|a f ① Kulin. cucumber salad ② książk. (bieda) deprivation; **~a finansowa** financial hardship

mizerni|eć impf vi to waste away

mizern|y adi. grad. ① (wychudły) [dziecko, twarz] haggard ② (nędzny) [brawa] feeble; [zarobki, emerytura] meagre GB, meager US; [jedzenie, mieszkanie] wretched

mkn|ąć *impf vi [osoba, zwierzę]* to scurry; *[pojazd]* to speed; *[chmury]* to scud; *[czas, lata, życie]* to fly by

mla|snąć *pf* — **mla|skać** *impf vi* ① *[osoba]* to smack one's lips; ~**skać przy jedzeniu** to make smacking noises when eating ② *[błoto, bagno]* to squelch

mlecz *m* ① Bot. dandelion ② Zool. milt

mleczar|nia *f* ① (zakład) dairy, creamery ② (na farmie) dairy

mleczarz *m* ① (w mleczarni) dairyman ② (roznosiciel) milkman

mlecz|ko *n* Kosmet. (do pielęgnacji) cleansing milk; (nawilżające) moisturizing lotion

mleczn|y *adi.* ① *[czekolada, napój, dieta]* milk; **gospodarstwo** ~**e** a dairy farm; **produkty** ~**e** dairy produce ② *[bydło, rasa]* dairy ③ *[mgła, światło]* milky; **szkło** ~**e** milk-glass; **żarówka** ~**a** a pearl (light) bulb

m|leć *impf vt* to grind *[kawę, mąkę, pieprz, zboże]*; to mince GB, to grind US *[mięso]*

■ **mleć te same problemy** pot. to keep harping on the same issues

mlek|o *n* ① milk; ~**o chude/półtłuste** skimmed/semi-skimmed milk; ~**o pełne** a. **pełnotłuste** whole a. full-cream milk; ~**o skondensowane** condensed a. evaporated milk; ~**o w proszku** powdered a. dried milk ② Fizj., Bot. milk; ~**o kokosowe/palmowe** coconut/palm milk

■ **mieć** ~**o pod nosem** pot. to be (still) wet behind the ears; **kraina** ~**iem i miodem płynąca** a land flowing with milk and honey; **nie ma co płakać nad rozlanym** ~**iem** it's no use a. no good crying over spilt milk

młodni|eć *impf vi* to get younger

mło|do *adv. grad. [czuć się, umrzeć, wyglądać]* young; **ona wygląda** ~**dziej niż ty** she looks younger than you

młodocian|y *adi. [bohater, czytelnik]* young; *[twórczość]* juvenile; ~**y przestępca** a juvenile offender

młodoś|ć *f* ① (okres w życiu) youth; **szaleństwa** ~**ci** the follies of youth; **druga** ~**ć** second youth; **być nie pierwszej** ~**ci** *[osoba]* to be past one's prime; *[ubranie, samochód]* to have seen better days ② (początki) early days

mło|dy **[I]** *adi. grad.* ① (niestary) young; ~**dy Kowalski** Kowalski junior; ~**da krew** przen. young blood przen.; **za** ~**du** early on in life ② (młodzieńczy) *[głos, wygląd]* youthful; ~**dy wiek** a tender age ③ Bot., Kulin. *[liście, pędy, warzywa]* young; ~**de ziemniaki** new potatoes ④ (nowy) young; ~**da demokracja** a young democracy

[II] **młodszy** *adi. comp.* (rangą) *[asystent, partner]* junior; ~**dszy stopniem** lower in rank

[III] **młode** *n* Zool. young

młodzież *f* young people; ~ **szkolna** secondary school children; ~ **uniwersytecka** university students

młodzieżow|y *adi. [obóz, organizacja]* youth; *[literatura]* juvenile; **muzyka** ~**a** teenage music

mło|t *m* ① hammer; ~**t drewniany** a maul; ~**t dwuręczny** a. **oburęczny** a sledgehammer ② Techn. hammer; ~**t pneumatyczny** a pneumatic drill ③ Sport hammer; **rzucać** ~**tem** to throw the hammer; **rzut** ~**tem** the hammer (throw) ④ pot. (o osobie) blockhead pot.

■ **znaleźć się między** ~**tem a kowadłem** to be caught between the devil and the deep blue sea; **serce bije** a. **wali mi (jak)** ~**tem** a. **jak** ~**t** my heart is pounding

młot|ek *m* ① (narzędzie) hammer; (drewniany) mallet; **wbić gwóźdź** ~**kiem** to hammer in a nail; ~**ek licytacyjny** a gavel ② Techn. hammer ③ (do gry w krokieta) mallet ④ Muz. hammer

■ **pójść pod** ~**ek** pot. to come a. go under the hammer

młó|cić *impf vt* ① to thresh *[zboże]* ② pot. (powtarzać) ~**ić wciąż to samo** to keep on about the same thing pot. ③ pot. (bić) to batter; ~**cić powietrze** to flail about a. around; ~**cić w drzwi** to pound on the door

młyn *m* ① (budynek) mill; ~ **wiatrowy/wodny** a windmill/watermill ② Techn. (maszyna) grinder; **węglowy** a coal pulverizer ③ pot. (zamęt) carry-on GB pot.; **mam w głowie** ~ my head's (all) spinning ④ Sport (w rugby) scrum(mage)

młynarz *m* miller

młyn|ek *m* grinder; ~**ek do kawy** a coffee grinder; ~**ek do pieprzu** a pepper mill; ~**ek do mielenia odpadków** a garbage a. refuse disposal unit

mni|ch *m* monk

mniejszoś|ć *f* minority; ~**ć parlamentarna/narodowa** a parliamentary/national minority

mniema|ć *impf vi* książk. to believe; **jak** ~**m** as I see it

mniema|nie *n* książk. belief, opinion; **mieć o kimś dobre/wysokie** ~**nie** to think well/the world of sb; **mieć o sobie wygórowane** ~**nie** to be too big for one's boots a. breeches; **w czyimś** ~**niu** in sb's belief a. opinion

mnisz|ek *m* dandelion

mnisz|ka *f* nun

mno|gi *adi.* ① książk. *[korzyści]* numerous ② Jęz. **liczba** ~**ga** the plural

mnoże|nie *n* multiplication

mn|ożyć *impf* **[I]** *vt* ① Mat. to multiply; **mnożyć 2 przez 3** to multiply 2 by 3 ② (rozmnażać, rozplenić) to breed *[rośliny, zwierzęta]* ③ (zwiększać) to increase *[kapitał, trudności]*

[II] **mnożyć się** ① (zwiększać liczbę) *[kluby, partie]* to multiply, to proliferate; **mnożą się rozboje** mugging is on the increase ② (rozmnażać się) *[bakterie, rośliny, zwierzęta]* to reproduce

mnóstw|o *n* multitude

mobilizacj|a f ⊥ Wojsk. mobilization ② książk. (grupy, sił) activation; ∼**a do pracy** motivation to work
mobiliz|ować impf **[]** vt ⊥ Wojsk. to mobilize [armię, flotę]; to call up [rezerwistów] ② książk. (uaktywniać) to motivate; ∼**ować kogoś do działania** to motivate a. encourage sb to act; ∼**ować wszystkie siły** to summon all one's strength
[] mobilizować się książk. to pull oneself together; ∼**ować się do czegoś** to summon up the strength to do sth

moc [] f ⊥ (siła psychiczna, fizyczna) power; **z (całą)** ∼**ą** [podkreślać] strongly, wholeheartedly; **z całej** ∼**y** [szarpać] with all one's might; **zrobić wszystko, co w czyjejś** a. **ludzkiej** ∼**y** to do everything in one's power a. everything humanly possible ② (sztormu, wybuchu) force ③ (zdolność wywierania wpływu) power; **dobre/złe** ∼**e** the powers of good/evil; **lecznicza** ∼ **ziół** the therapeutic power of herbs ④ Prawo force; ∼ **prawna** (dekretu, dokumentu) legal force; **dekret z** ∼**ą ustawy** a decree having the force of law; **pozostawać w** ∼**y** to remain in force ⑤ Przem. capabilities; ∼**e przerobowe** processing capacity ⑥ (alkoholu, herbaty, kawy) strength ⑦ Techn. strength ⑧ Fiz. power; **silnik o znacznej** ∼**y** a powerful engine
[] pron. książk. (dużo) a (whole) host książk.
■ **być** a. **leżeć w czyjejś** ∼**y** książk. to be in sb's power; **na** a. **z** ∼**y czegoś** książk. on the strength of sth

mocarstw|o n (world) power; ∼**o atomowe** a nuclear power
mocn|o adv. grad. ⊥ (silnie, energicznie) firmly; **uścisnęli sobie** ∼**o dłonie** they shook hands firmly ② pot. (bardzo) really; ∼**o spóźniony** really a. terribly late; ∼**o podejrzany** highly suspicious; **ta opinia jest** ∼**o przesadzona** that's a highly exaggerated view a. opinion; **najmocniej dziękuję** thank you (ever) so much; **najmocniej przepraszam** I'm ever so a. I'm awfully sorry ③ (intensywnie) intensely; ∼**o niebieski** intensely blue; **kochać kogoś** ∼**o** to love sb intensely; **słońce prażyło** ∼**o** the sun was beating down ④ (głęboko, silnie) deeply; ∼**o wierzyć w coś** to believe deeply a. strongly in sth; ∼**o spać** to sleep soundly ⑤ (w sposób pewny) strong(ly); **dolar trzyma się** ∼**o** the dollar remains strong ⑥ (dobitnie) strongly; ∼**o coś podkreślić** to emphasize sth strongly; ∼**o coś wyrazić** to express sth forcibly ⑦ (trwale) securely; **klej trzymał** ∼**o** the glue held fast

mocn|y adi. grad. ⊥ (silny) strong; ∼**y głos** a strong a. powerful voice; ∼**e uderzenie** a heavy a. strong blow; ∼**y uścisk dłoni** a firm a. strong handshake; ∼**a budowa ciała** a strong build ② (wytrzymały, zdrowy) [nerwy, serce, zęby] strong ③ (solidny, trwały) [buty] sturdy; [fundamenty] solid; ∼**y sen** a deep a. sound sleep ④ Techn. [silnik, żarówka] powerful ⑤ (intensywny) [kolor, zapach] intense; (esencjonalny)

[herbata, kawa, roztwór] strong ⑥ (wpływowy) [organizacja] influential; [państwo] powerful. ⑦ (silny w rywalizacji) [kandydat, zespół] strong ⑧ (o ustabilizowanej pozycji) strong; ∼**y złoty** a strong zloty; ∼**a pozycja zawodowa** a secure employment position ⑨ (nieugięty) [charakter, wiara] unbending; ∼**e postanowienie** a firm resolution ⑩ (trwały) [więź, związek] lasting ⑪ (nie do odparcia) [argument, dowód] firm ⑫ (intensywnie przeżywany) strong; **amatorzy** ∼**ych wrażeń** sensation seekers ⑬ (dosadny, wyrazisty) [film, scena] graphic; ∼**e słowa** harsh words; (przekleństwa) swear words ⑭ (biegły) good; **być** ∼**ym w czymś** to be good at a. strong in sth
■ **być** ∼**ym w gębie** pot. to be all mouth (and no trousers); **na niego/na to nie ma** ∼**ych** he's/it's a hopeless case

moc|ować impf vt to fasten (**coś do czegoś** sth to sth); to mount (**coś na czymś** sth on sth)
moc|ować się impf v refl. ⊥ (walczyć) to wrestle (**z kimś** with sb) ② (siłować się) to struggle (**z czymś** with sth) ③ przen. (przezwyciężać) to fight (**z czymś** against sth); to struggle (**z czymś** with a. against sth); ∼**ować się ze sobą** to wrestle with oneself

mocz m urine
moczopędn|y adi. [działanie] diuretic; **środek** ∼**y** a diuretic
mocz|yć impf ⊥ vt (czynić mokrym) to wet [ręcznik, obrusy] ② (trzymać w płynie) to soak [nogi, pranie]
mocz|yć się impf v refl. ⊥ (stawać się wilgotnym) [nogawka, rękaw] to get wet ② (być trzymanym w wodzie) [pranie, śledzie] to soak; ∼**yć się w wannie** pot., żart. to soak in the bath ③ Med. to wet the bed

m|oda f ⊥ (trend) fashion; **moda na coś** the fashion for sth; **być/nie być w modzie** to be in/out of fashion; **wchodzić w modę/wyjść z mody** to come into/go out of fashion; **ostatni krzyk mody** all the rage pot. ② (popularność) fashion; (chwilowa) fad; **być w modzie** to be in vogue

model m ⊥ Szt. model ② Moda (male) model ③ (maszyny, ubrania) design, model; **tradycyjny** ∼ **rodziny** the traditional family model
modelarstw|o n model-making; ∼**o lotnicze** aeromodelling
model|ka f model
model|ować impf vt ⊥ (nadawać kształt) to model [kapelusz, naczynia gliniane]; to shape [włosy]; ∼**ować coś w glinie** to model sth in clay ② przen. to mould GB, to mold US, to shape [postawy, zachowania]

modernizacj|a f modernization
moderniz|ować impf **[]** vt to modernize [fabrykę, metody produkcji]
[] modernizować się [armia, przemysł] to undergo modernization

m|odlić się impf v refl. to pray (**o coś** for sth); **modlić się za czyjąś duszę** to pray for sb's soul;

modlę się, żeby jak najszybciej przyjechał
I hope to goodness he comes as quickly as possible
modlitewnik *m* prayer book
modlitw|a *f* prayer; ~**a za zmarłych/o pokój**
a prayer for the deceased/for peace
modn|y *adi.* fashionable
modrzew *m* ① (drzewo) larch ② (drewno) larch
(wood)
modyfikacj|a *f* alteration
modyfik|ować *impf* Ⅰ *vt* to modify *[metody pracy,
przepisy]*
Ⅱ **modyfikować się** *[obyczaje, poglądy]* to change
modyst|ka *f* milliner
mogi|ła *f* książk. (grób) grave; (kopiec na grobie) mound
mohe|r *m* Włók. mohair
mokasyn *m* ① (indiański) moccasin ② (rodzaj półbuta)
loafer
m|oknąć *impf vi* to get wet
mokrad|ło *n* bog
mokro *adv.* **dziecko ma** ~ the baby's wet
mok|ry *adi.* ① (wilgotny) *[gleba, ubranie, włosy]*
wet; **poduszka** ~**ra od łez** a tear-stained pillow
② (spocony) sweating; ~**ry ze strachu** sweating
with fear ③ (deszczowy) *[lato]* wet ④ (świeży) *[farba,
zaprawa]* wet
molest|ować *impf vt* ① (natrętnie prosić) to badger;
~**ować kogoś o coś** to pester a. badger sb for sth
② (seksualnie) to molest; ~**owanie seksualne**
sexual harassment
mol|o *n* pier
moloch *m* książk. behemoth
momen|t *m* ① (chwila) moment; **wrócę za** ~**t** I'll
be back in a moment; **lada** ~**t** any moment now;
w pewnym ~**cie** at one point; ~**t kulminacyjny**
the climax; **decydujący** ~**t** the crunch; ~**ty** pot.
juicy moments ② Fiz. moment
monar|cha *m* monarch
monarchi|a *f* monarchy
mone|ta *f* coin; ~**ta pięciozłotowa** a 5-zloty coin
■ **brzęcząca** ~**ta** książk. hard cash, cold cash US;
przyjąć a. **wziąć coś za dobrą** ~**tę** to take sth at
face value
monito|r *m* ① (komputera, ultrasonografu) monitor
② (czasopismo urzędowe) gazette
monitoring *m* (obserwacja) monitoring; (nadzór)
video surveillance
monitor|ować *impf vt* to monitor *[pracę, proces]*
monogami|a *f* monogamy
monogram *m* monogram
monolog *m* monologue, monolog US; ~ **wewnętrzny** an interior monologue
monopol *m* ① (wyłączność) monopoly także przen.;
mieć ~ **na coś** to have a. hold a monopoly on sth
② (zrzeszenie) monopoly ③ pot. (sklep) off-licence GB,
liquor store US ④ pot. (napoje alkoholowe) booze pot.
monopoli|sta *m* monopolist

monopolow|y *adi.* ① *[ceny, restrykcje]* monopoly
② *[napoje]* alcoholic; **sklep** ~**y** an off-licence GB, a
liquor store US
monoteizm *m* monotheism
monotoni|a /ˌmonoˈtoɲja/ *f* monotony
monotonn|y *adi.* ① (jednostajny) *[warkot]* monot-
onous; *[recytacja]* monotone ② (nieurozmaicony) *[praca,
życie]* humdrum; *[krajobraz, styl]* monochromatic
monstrualn|y *adi.* książk. ① (olbrzymi) *[gmach]*
enormous ② (potworny) *[postać, wygląd]* monstrous
monstr|um *n* książk. monster
monsun *m* monsoon
montaż *m* ① (składanie) assembly; (instalowanie) installation; **meble do samodzielnego** ~**u** self-
assembly furniture ② Kino, Radio, TV montage; ~
reżyserski the director's cut
monte|r *m* (składający) assembler; (montujący) fitter;
(naprawiający) repairman
mont|ować *impf vt* ① (składać) to assemble *[mebel,
urządzenie]*; (instalować) to instal(l) *[alarm]*; to fit
[część] ② Kino, Radio, TV to edit *[film, program]* ③ pot.
(organizować) to put together pot. *[zespół]*; to form
[koalicję]
monumen|t *m* monument
mops *m* pug *[dog]*
■ **nudzić się jak** ~ pot. to be bored stiff pot.
morali|sta *m*, ~**stka** *f* książk. moralist; sermonizer
pejor.
moraliz|ować *impf vi* to moralize
moralnoś|ć *f* morality; **podwójna** ~**ć** double
standards
moraln|y *adi. [norma, problem, wsparcie]* moral
mora|ł Ⅰ *m* moral; **jaki z tego wynika** ~**ł?** what's
the moral of it?
Ⅱ **morały** *plt* pot. moralizing
mor|d *m* murder; (masowy) massacre
mor|da *f* ① (u psa, krowy) muzzle; (u świni) snout
② pot. (twarz, usta) kisser pot.; **drzeć** ~**dę** posp. to
scream a. yell blue murder pot.; **wyjechać z** ~**dą** a.
rozedrzeć ~**dę** posp. to start mouthing off pot.;
dostać po ~**dzie** pot. to get a facer GB pot.;
zamknij ~**dę!** posp. shut your gob a. trap! pot.
■ **o w** ~**dę!** pot. bloody hell! pot.; **trzymać/wziąć
kogoś za** ~**dę** pot. to have/get sb by the short and
curlies a. by the short hairs pot.
morderc|a *m* murderer; **seryjny** ~**a** a serial
killer
mordercz|y *adi. [instynkt]* murderous; *[skłonności]*
homicidal; *[cios, strzał]* fatal; *[praca, upał, wysiłek]*
gruelling; *[tempo]* breakneck
morderczy|ni *f* murderess
morderstw|o *n* murder, homicide US; (polityczne)
assassination; ~**o w afekcie** a crime of passion;
~**o z premedytacją** premeditated murder; ~**o na
tle rabunkowym** robbery and murder
mordę|ga *f* pot. grind pot.

mord|ować impf **I** vt ① (zabijać) to murder; (masowo) to slaughter; (z pobudek politycznych) to assassinate ② pot. (męczyć, nużyć) to pester; to hassle pot. ③ (psuć) to murder *[piosenkę]*; to hammer pot. *[silnik]*
II mordować się ① (zabijać jeden drugiego) to kill each other ② pot., przen. (męczyć się) to kill oneself pot.
morel|a f (drzewo) apricot (tree); (owoc) apricot
mors[1] m Zool. walrus
mors[2] m pot. (alfabet) Morse (code)
mors|ki adi. ① *[brzeg, choroba, podróż, sól, szlak]* sea; *[granica, klimat, kodeks, przemysł]* maritime; *[fauna, flora]* marine ② *[baza, bitwa, szkoła]* naval ③ *[kolor]* sea green
morszczuk m hake
morw|a f (drzewo) mulberry (tree a. bush); (owoc) mulberry
m|orze n ① sea; **wypłynąć w morze** to put (out) a. go to sea; **jechać nad morze** to go to the seaside a. coast ② przen. (mnóstwo) sea przen.; ocean pot.; **morze głów** a sea of faces; **morze łez** oceans a. an ocean of tears; **on może wypić morze kawy** he can drink gallons of coffee pot.

■ **kropla w morzu (potrzeb)** pot. a drop in the ocean a. in a bucket
mosiądz m (stop miedzi i cynku) brass; (stop miedzi, cynku i cyny) ormolu; **wyroby z ∼u** brassware; **w kolorze ∼u** brass-coloured
mo|st m ① (konstrukcja) bridge ② przen. (trasa) route; **most powietrzny** a. **lotniczy** an airlift route ③ przen. (łącznik) bridge; **budować most między pokoleniami** to bridge the gap between the generations ④ Stomat. bridge ⑤ Techn. (napędowy) axle; (suwnicy) bridge

■ **mieszkać pod mostem** pot. to live on the streets; **palić za sobą mosty** to burn one's bridges a. boats; **prosto z mostu** *[mówić]* straight from the shoulder pot.; *[oświadczać]* straight out
most|ek m ① (kładka) (small) bridge ② Anat. sternum ③ Żegl. (kapitański, nawigacyjny) bridge; (trap) gangway ④ Sport (w gimnastyce, zapasach) bridge ⑤ Kulin. brisket ⑥ Stomat. bridge
mo|ścić impf **I** vt to line *[gniazdo, legowisko]*
II mościć się to snuggle down, to snug down US
mota|ć impf **I** vt ① (nawijać) to wind *[nici, sznurek]* ② (plątać) *[wiatr]* to tangle *[włosy]*; to toss *[gałęzie]* ③ pot. (utrudniać zrozumienie) to confuse *[opowieść]* ④ pot. (intrygować) to scheme, to plot (**przeciwko komuś** against sb)
II motać się ① (plątać się) *[nici, włosy]* to become tangled ② pot. (mieszać się) to get mixed up pot. (**w coś** in sth)
mot|ek m ① (zwinięty luźno) hank; (na szpulce) skein ② (szpulka) reel; (w maszynie, krośnie) bobbin
motel m motel
motłoch m ① (tłum) mob ② (pospólstwo) riff-raff
motocykl m motorbike

motocykli|sta m, **∼stka** f motorcyclist
moto|r m ① (elektryczny) motor; (parowy, spalinowy) engine ② pot. (motocykl) (motor)bike ③ przen. driving force
motornicz|y m, **∼a** f tram driver
motorów|ka f motor boat
motoryzacj|a f motorization
mot|to n ① (cytat) epigraph ② (dewiza) motto
moty|ka f hoe
motyl m ① Zool. butterfly ② (kokarda) bow ③ Żegl. spinnaker
motyl|ek m Sport butterfly (stroke)
motyw m ① (powód) motive (**czegoś** for sth) ② Literat., Muz., Szt. motif; **∼ przewodni** leitmotif; **film na ∼ach powieści** a film based on a novel
motywacj|a f książk. ① (zachęta) motivation (**do czegoś** for sth); **mieć ∼ę do pracy** to be motivated to work ② (uzasadnienie) justification (**czegoś** for sth)
motyw|ować impf vt książk. ① (uzasadniać) *[osoba]* to justify *[odmowę, postępowanie]*; to give reasons a. a reason (**coś** for sth) ② (zachęcać) to motivate
m|owa f ① (zdolność mówienia) speech; **narządy mowy** speech organs ② (wymowa) diction; **wyraźna/ śpiewna mowa** clear/melodious diction ③ (język) language; **mowa dziecka** baby talk a. language; **mowa ojczysta** one's native a. mother tongue; **mowa potoczna** a. **codzienna** colloquial language a. speech; **części mowy** parts of speech ④ (przemówienie) speech; **mowa powitalna** a welcoming speech; **wygłosić mowę** to deliver a. make a speech ⑤ przen. (gestów, kolorów, zwierząt) language; **mowa ciała** body language

■ **drętwa mowa** pot. stodgy a. dry speech; **mowa-trawa** pot. claptrap pot.; **nie ma mowy** that's out of the question; **wzruszenie** a. **ze wzruszenia odjęło mu mowę** he was speechless a. choked with emotion; **mowę ci odjęło?** pot. has the cat got your tongue? pot.; **właśnie była mowa o tobie** we were just talking about you; **po co** a. **do kogo ta mowa?** pot. you're wasting your breath pot.
mozai|ka f mosaic także przen.
moz|olić się impf v refl. książk. to labour away GB, to labor away US (**nad czymś** at sth); to toil (away) (**nad czymś** at sth); **∼olić się nad zadaniem z matematyki** to rack one's brains over a maths problem
mozoln|y adi. grad. (czasochłonny) *[ćwiczenia]* laborious; (męczący) *[praca, wspinaczka]* arduous
moździerz m ① (naczynie) mortar ② Wojsk. mortar
może part. ① (przypuszczenie) maybe; **∼ już nie pada** maybe it's stopped raining; **(być) ∼ masz rację** maybe a. perhaps you're right; **spotkaliśmy się ∼ trzykrotnie** we've met maybe three times; **∼ źle ją oceniam, ale...** I may be wrong about her, but... ② (propozycja) perhaps; **∼ byś coś zjadł?** perhaps a.

maybe you'd like something to eat?; ~ **kieliszek koniaku?** how about a glass of brandy?

możliwie *adv.* [1] (w miarę możliwości) ~ **najwcześniej** as early as possible; ~ **najwyższa cena** the highest possible price [2] pot. (dość dobrze) *[zagrany, wykonany]* fairly well; *[wyglądać]* good enough; **nawet** ~ **napisałeś ten test** you didn't do at all badly in the test

możliwoś|ć [] *f* [1] (zdolność, ewentualność) possibility; **nie widzę** ~**ci przełożenia terminu** I can see no possibility a. chance of postponing the deadline; **miałem** ~**ć przyjrzeć się temu** I was able to have a look at it [2] (sposobność) opportunity; **mieć** ~**ć zrobienia czegoś** to have an opportunity a. a chance to do sth; **nie dano mu** ~**ci obrony** he was given no opportunity a. chance to defend himself [3] (wybór) option; **mieć ograniczone** ~**ci** to have a limited number of options; **wyczerpać wszystkie** a. **wszelkie** ~**ci** to have no options left

[] **możliwości** *plt* [1] (umiejętności) abilities; (zakres zdolności) capabilities; **być u szczytu swoich** ~**ci** to be at the peak of one's abilities; **leżeć w zasięgu czyichś** ~**ci** to be within sb's capabilities; **przekraczać** a. **przerastać czyjeś** ~**ci** to be beyond sb's capabilities [2] (potencjał) potential; ~**ci rozwojowe firmy** the company's potential for development

możliw|y *adi. grad.* [1] (realny) *[kompromis, rozwój]* possible; **zrobienie tego jest** ~**e** it is possible to do that; **metody** ~**e do zastosowania** practicable a. feasible methods; **przeszkody** ~**e do pokonania** negotiable a. surmountable obstacles [2] (dostępny) *[rozwiązanie, sposób, źródło]* available [3] (mogący się zdarzyć) *[niebezpieczeństwo, skutek]* possible; **(bardzo)** ~**e, że przegramy** it's (quite) possible that we'll lose [4] pot. (niezły) *[uczeń, stan]* passable

można *praed.* [1] (możliwość) **ten zegar** ~ **jeszcze naprawić** this clock can still be repaired; **na to nie** ~ **liczyć** you can't count on that; ~ **się było tego spodziewać** one could a. might have expected that; **łatwiejszy, niż** ~ **by przypuszczać** easier than one might have supposed; ~ **śmiało powiedzieć, że...** it's safe to say a. we can safely say that...; **nie** ~ **powiedzieć, żeby film nas rozczarował** I can't a. wouldn't say the film disappointed us; **nie** ~ **zaprzeczyć temu, że...** there's no denying the fact that...; **nie** ~ **z tobą wytrzymać** you're (absolutely) impossible! pot.; ~ **wytrzymać** pot. (z powątpiewaniem) it's all right a. okay; **cholery** ~ **dostać!** pot. it's enough to drive you up the wall! pot.; **gdzie/kiedy tylko** ~ wherever/whenever possible; **jeżeli tylko** ~ if it's (at all) possible [2] (przyzwolenie) **nie** ~ **tego dotykać** you mustn't touch it; **czy** ~**?** can I?; may I? książk.; **czy** ~ **wejść?** can a. may I come in?; **czy** ~ **otworzyć okno?** do you mind if I open the window?; **jeśli** ~ if I may książk.; **jeśli** ~ **tak powiedzieć** if I may

say so [3] (propozycja, prośba) ~ **ci w czymś pomóc?** can I help you in any way?; ~ **pana prosić o otwarcie drzwi?** could you open the door, please?; **czy** ~ **panią prosić do tańca?** would you like to dance?; may I have this dance? książk.; ~ **by zaprosić kilka osób** I/we could invite one or two people over

możn|y *adi. grad. [protektor, ród]* (high and) mighty; *[władca]* powerful

m|óc *impf vi* [1] (być w stanie) to be able; **móc coś zrobić** to be able to do sth; **jeśli będę mogła, zadzwonię** I'll call you if I can a. if I'm able to; **w nocy nie mogłam spać** I couldn't sleep during the night; **staram się, jak mogę** (w tej chwili) I'm doing my best; (w ogóle) I do what I can; **cóż mogą zrobić?** what can they do?; **nie mogę się nadziwić, jak on to zrobił** I just can't imagine how he did it; **zawsze mogłam na niego liczyć** I could always count on him; **możemy przypuszczać, że...** it's fair a. reasonable to assume that...; **dziękuję, już (więcej) nie mogę** no thanks, I'm full up [2] (mieć prawo) **„mamo, mogę iść na podwórko?" – „możesz"** 'Mum, can I go outside?' – 'yes, you can'; **policja nie może dokonać rewizji bez nakazu** the police can't carry out a search without a warrant [3] (w przypuszczeniach) **może być deszcz albo śnieg** it might a. may rain or snow; **mogli mieć po szesnaście, siedemnaście lat** they could have been sixteen or seventeen [4] (w prośbach) **możesz mi podać widelec?** could a. can you pass me a fork?; **czy mógłbym prosić do telefonu Janka?** could a. can I speak to Janek, please?; **czy może pan przymknąć okno?** can a. could you close the window, please? [5] (w pytaniach) **kto/co to może być?** who/what can a. could that be?; **gdzie mogą być moje okulary?** where can my glasses be?; **jak to się mogło stać?** how could it have happened?; **w czym mogę panu pomóc?** what can I do for you? [6] (w propozycjach, życzeniach) **zawsze możesz przecież pójść tam i poprosić** you can always go there and ask; **mógł pan przyjść po pożyczkę do mnie** you could have come to me for the money; **mogłeś mu o tym nie mówić** you didn't have to tell him about it; **mógłby już spaść śnieg** it's about time it snowed [7] (wyrażając irytację) **jak możesz** a. **jak mogłeś!** how can a. could you!; **jak on mógł tak postąpić?** how could he do such a thing?; **tak dalej być nie może!** things can't go on like this! [8] (wyrażając lekceważenie) **możesz sobie krzyczeć i tak nie zmienię zdania** you can shout as much as you like, but I still won't change my mind; **co ty możesz wiedzieć?** what do you know (about it)?

■ **co ja mogę?** what can I do (about it)?; **pogoda jak cię mogę** pot. passable a. tolerable weather; **(ja) nie mogę!** (ze zniecierpliwieniem) (God) give me strength!; (z zachwytem) (oh) wow! pot.; **ja już tak**

dłużej nie mogę! I just can't go on like this!; **może być!** pot. fine; **nie może być!** that's impossible!

m|ój [] *pron.* (przed rzeczownikiem) my; (bez rzeczownika) mine; **mój samochód** my car; **ten ołówek jest mój** this pencil is mine; **to moja przyjaciółka** this is a friend of mine; **co u ciebie, mój drogi?** how are things (with you), my friend? książk., żart.; **moja droga Anno** (w liście) dear Anna; **usiądź sobie, moje dziecko** sit down, (my) dear; **mój Boże** my God!

II mój *m*, **moja** *f* pot. my other half pot., żart.

III moi *plt* pot. (rodzina) my family; (znajomi) my friends

IV moje *n* pot. **wara ci od mojego** keep away from my things; **wyszło na moje** it turned out that I was right

V po mojemu pot. [] (według mnie) to my mind; **po mojemu to się nie uda** in my view it won't work [] (tak, jak chcę) my way; **wszystko ma być po mojemu** everything has to be done my way

m|ól *m* moth; **zjedzony** a. **zniszczony przez mole** moth-eaten

■ **mól książkowy** pot. bookworm pot.; **każdy ma swojego mola, co go gryzie** pot. we all have our problems

mów|ca *m*, **~czyni** *f* speaker

mów|ić *impf* [] *vt* [] (przekazywać) to tell (**coś komuś** sb sth a. sth to sb); to say (**coś komuś** sth to sb); **~ić z pamięci** to speak from memory; **on zawsze ~i mi dzień dobry** he always says hello to me; **halo, kto ~i?** (przez telefon) hallo, who's there a. speaking?; **dzień dobry, ~i Jacek** hello, Jacek speaking; **(tu) ~i Warszawa** (w radio) this is Warsaw [] (plotkować) to say; **~ić coś na kogoś** a. **o kimś** to say sth about sb; **cała wieś o nich ~i** the whole village is talking about them; **~ią, że miał dwie żony** he's said to have had two wives [] (informować) [przepisy] to say; [wygląd, znak] to mean; (podpowiadać) [intuicja, rozum, serce] to tell; **jego mina ~i, że...** you can tell from his face that...; **~i ci to coś?** does it mean anything to you?; **przeczucie** a. **coś mi ~i, że nam się uda** something tells me a. I have a feeling that we'll succeed; **fakty ~ią (nam) co innego** the facts tell (us) a different story; **fakty ~ią same za siebie** the facts speak for themselves

[] *vi* [] (posługiwać się mową) to speak; **~ić po niemiecku** (znać język) to speak German; (używać języka) to speak a. talk in German; **kiedy dziecko zaczyna ~ić?** when do children start to talk a. speak? [] (rozmawiać) to talk; **~ić (z kimś) o kimś/czymś** to talk (to a. with US sb) about sb/sth; **czy mogę ~ić z Janem?** (przez telefon) can I speak to Jan, please?; **~ić do kogoś** to talk to sb; **jak śmiesz tak do mnie ~ić!** how dare you talk a. speak to me like that!; **~ić o kimś dobrze/źle** to

speak well/ill of sb [] (zwracać się, nazywać) to call; **~ił do niej po imieniu** he called her by her first name [] pot. (podczas śledztwa, przesłuchania) to talk

■ **a nie ~iłem?** I told you so!; **co ja ~ię** pot. what am I saying? pot.; **czy ja coś ~ię?** did I say anything? żart.; **dobrze** a. **łatwo ci ~ić** it's easy for you to say; **jak to ~ią** a. **jak to się ~i** pot. as they say; **~ co chcesz** pot. say what you like; **~ za siebie!** speak for yourself!; **~ić do kogoś jak do kogoś dobrego** a. **~ić komuś jak komu dobremu** to try to make sb understand; **~ić z kimś wspólnym** a. **tym samym językiem** to speak the same language as sb; **~ię ci!** I (can) tell you!; **nie ma co ~ić** pot. no two ways about it; **nie ma o czym ~ić** (odpowiedź na podziękowanie) my pleasure; (odpowiedź na przeprosiny) don't mention it; (odmowa) it's out of the question; **nie ~!** you don't say (so)! pot.; **nie ~iąc o...** książk. not to mention...

mównic|a *f* (podwyższenie) rostrum; (pulpit) lectern

mózg *m* [] Anat. brain; [] (umysł) brain; **być ~iem czegoś** to be the brains behind sth

■ **padło** a. **rzuciło mu się na ~** pot. he's off his rocker pot.; **~ staje** pot. it's mind-boggling pot.

mózgow|y *adi.* [kora] cerebral; [tkanka] brain; **opony ~e** meninges

móżdż|ek *m* [] Anat. cerebellum [] Kulin. brains

■ **kurzy** a. **ptasi ~ek** pot. birdbrain pot.

mroczn|y *adi. grad.* książk. [] [niebo] lowering książk.; [pokój, światło] dim; [ulica] gloomy; [las, piwnica] dark [] (ponury) [prognozy] gloomy; [lata, myśli, spojrzenie] dark; **~e zakamarki czyjejś duszy** the dark recesses of sb's mind; **~a strona ludzkiej natury** the dark side of human nature

mrok *m* [] (ciemność) gloom; (w pomieszczeniu) darkness; **~ gęstniał** the gloom deepened [] przen. mist; **w ~ach dziejów** a. **historii** in the mists of time; **tonąć w ~ach niepamięci** to sink into oblivion

mrowisk|o *n* anthill

mro|zić *impf* [] *vt* [] (ziębić) [wiatr] to chill [ręce, twarz] [] (ścinać mrozem) [przymrozek] to freeze [rośliny] [] (zamrażać) to freeze [żywność]

[] **mrozić się** [deser] to chill

mroźn|y *adi. grad.* [pogoda, ranek] frosty; [temperatura] freezing; [powietrze, wiatr] icy (cold)

mrożon|ka *f* frozen food

mrówcz|y *adi.* [] [jaja, kolonia] ant [] przen. [praca, wysiłek] laborious

mrów|ka [] *f* [] ant; **być pracowitym jak ~ka** a. **pracować jak ~ka** to work like a beaver [] przen. busy bee pot.

[] **mrówki** *plt* pot. (ciarki) pins and needles

mrówkoja|d *m* anteater

mr|óz *m* [] (zimno) frost; **sześć stopni mrozu** six degrees of frost GB a. below zero; **odporny na mróz** frost-resistant [] (szron) hoar a. white frost; **siwy mróz** freezing fog

■ **poczuł, że mróz przechodzi mu po plecach** he felt a chill a. shiver run down his spine

mruczeć *impf* → **mruknąć**

mrug|nąć *pf* — **mrug|ać¹** *impf vi [osoba]* (powiekami) to blink; (jednym okiem) to wink; *[lampa, żarówka]* to flicker; *[gwiazdy]* to twinkle; ~**nąć do kogoś porozumiewawczo** to wink at sb knowingly

■ **zrobić coś bez** ~**nięcia (okiem)** to do sth without batting an eye(lid)

mrukliw|y *adi. grad. [osoba, usposobienie]* uncommunicative; *[odpowiedź]* terse

mru|knąć *pf* — **mru|czeć** *impf* **[]** *vt* (powiedzieć) to mutter

[] *vi [kot]* to purr; *[drapieżnik]* to growl

mruż|yć *impf* **[]** *vt* to screw up *[oczy]*; to narrow *[powieki]*

[] **mrużyć się** (zamykać się) **oczy mu się** ~**ą ze zmęczenia** he's so tired he can't keep his eyes open

mrzon|ka *f* książk. chimera książk.; pipe dream

msz|a *f* Relig., Muz. Mass; ~**a święta** Holy Mass; ~**a w czyjejś intencji** a Mass for sb; ~**a za czyjąś duszę** a Mass for sb's soul

■ **czarna** ~**a** black mass

mszyc|a *f* aphid

mściciel *m*, ~**ka** *f* książk. avenger

m|ścić się *impf v refl.* [] (brać odwet) *[osoba]* to avenge oneself (**na kimś za coś** on sb for sth) [] (mieć przykre następstwa) *[błąd]* to rebound (**na kimś** on sb); (odnosić odwrotny skutek) to backfire (**na kimś** on sb)

mściw|y *adi. [osoba, zamiar]* vindictive

mu|cha *f* [] Zool. fly [] Moda bow tie; dicky bow pot. [] pot. (traszka) piece of cake pot.

■ **nawet muchy by nie zabił** a. skrzywdził he wouldn't hurt a. harm a fly; **mieć muchy w nosie** pot. to have the hump pot.; **chyba go mucha ugryzła** pot. he's like a bear with a sore head

muchomo|r *m* toadstool

Mula|t *m*, ~**tka** *f* mulatto przest.

mu|ł¹ *m* Zool. mule także pot., przen.

mu|ł² *m* (jeziorny) ooze; (rzeczny, morski) silt

mumi|a *f* mummy

mundial *m* Sport the World Cup

mundu|r *m* uniform

mundur|ek *m* uniform

■ **ziemniaki** a. **kartofle w** ~**kach** Kulin. jacket potatoes

mu|r [] *m* Budow., Sport wall

[] **mury** *plt* walls; **za murami miasta** beyond the city walls; **w murach szkoły** within the confines of the school

■ **przyprzeć** a. **przycisnąć kogoś do muru** to pin sb down; **być przypartym** a. **przyciśniętym do muru** to be up against the wall pot.; **głową muru nie przebijesz** pot. there's no point in a. it's no use banging your head against a brick wall; **stać**

murem za kimś/czymś pot. to be a. stand firmly behind sb/sth; **przyjdę na mur** a. **mur beton** pot. I'll be there, don't worry pot.

murarz *m* bricklayer

muraw|a *f* [] (trawa) grass [] Sport turf; **sztuczna** ~**a** artificial turf

mur|ować *impf vt* to build *[dom, ściany]*

murowan|y *adi.* [] *[dom, ogrodzenie]* (z cegły) brick; (z kamienia) stone [] pot. (pewny) *[awans, wygrana]* sure; *[waluta]* rock-solid pot.; **pogoda jest** ~**a** the weather's bound to be good; ~**e, że będzie padać** you can bet your life it's going to rain pot.; ~**e!** it's in the bag a. bank pot.

Murzyn *m* black (man); Negro obraźl.

Murzyn|ka *f* black (woman); Negro obraźl.

mus¹ *m* Kulin. mousse

mus² *m* pot. (konieczność) necessity; (przymus) compulsion; **robić coś z** ~**u** to do sth out of necessity; **jak** ~**, to** ~ a man's got to do what a man's got to do pot., żart.

mu|sieć *impf vi* [] (podlegać przymusowi) **musisz to zrobić** you have to a. you've got to do it; **zostanę, jeśli będę musiał** I'll stay if I have to; **czy muszę iść na przyjęcie?** do I have to go to the party?; **wszyscy musimy kiedyś umrzeć** we all have to die some day; **tak musi być** this is how it's got to be [] (uznawać za potrzebne) **musisz to zrobić** you must a. you have to do it; **nie musiałeś tego robić** you didn't have to a. need to do that; **muszę już iść** I have to a. I've got to go now; **musisz mi wszystko opowiedzieć** you must tell me everything; **muszę powiedzieć, że zachował się bardzo szlachetnie** I must say he behaved very nobly [] (bardzo chcieć) **muszę mieć tę sukienkę!** I must have this dress!; **muszę z nim pomówić** I must speak to him [] (prawdopodobieństwo) **musiałeś o tym słyszeć** you must have heard about it; **w tym musi coś być** there must be something in a. to it [] (pewność) **musiało tu padać, bo ulice są mokre** it must have rained here, the streets are wet; **musiałem cię już gdzieś widzieć** I'm sure I've seen you somewhere before [] (konieczność, zachęta) **musisz zobaczyć ten film** you must see a. you've got to see this film; **musicie koniecznie spróbować mojego ciasta** you simply must try my cake [] (nie móc się powstrzymać) **on zawsze musi postawić na swoim** he always has to have his own way; **dlaczego ty zawsze musisz się spóźniać?** why do you always have to be late? [] (nieuchronność) **to musiało się stać** this (just) had to happen

muskać *impf* → **musnąć**

muskularn|y *adi. grad. [zapaśnik, ciało]* muscular

musku|ł *m* muscle

mu|snąć *pf* — **mu|skać** *impf vt* to brush; **kula musnęła go w ramię**; the bullet grazed his arm; **wiatr muskał jej twarz** przen.; the wind caressed a. kissed her face

mus|ować *impf vi* to fizz (up); **wino** ~**ujące** sparkling wine; **napój** ~**ujący** a fizzy drink; **tabletki** ~**ujące** effervescent tablets

musz|ka *f* [1] Zool. fly [2] Moda bow tie [3] (w celowniku) bead; **trzymać kogoś na** ~**ce** to have sb in one's sights [4] Kosmet. beauty spot

musz|la *f* [1] Zool. shell [2] (sedes) ~**la (klozetowa)** toilet bowl [3] (kształt) shell; ~**la koncertowa** a concert shell; ~**la stadionu** the shell of a stadium

musztar|da *f* mustard

muszt|ra *f* drill

musztr|ować *impf vt* to drill *[żołnierzy, uczniów]*

muślin *m* muslin

mutacj|a *f* [1] (głosu) breaking (of the voice); **przechodzi** ~**ę** his voice is breaking [2] Biol. mutation także przen.

muze|um *n* museum

muzułman|in *m*, ~**ka** *f* Muslim

muzyczn|y *adi. [instrument, utwór]* musical; *[krytyk, festiwal, szkoła]* music

muzy|k *m* musician

muzy|ka *f* music

muzykaln|y *adi. [osoba, rodzina]* musical

muzykan|t *m* musician

muzyk|ować *impf vi* to make music; (grać) to play; (śpiewać) to sing

my *pron.* (jako podmiot) we; (w pozostałych przypadkach) us; **było nas trzech** there were three of us; **kupili nam radio** they bought us a radio; **z nami/bez nas** with/without us

my|ć *impf* [1] *vt* to wash *[ręce, twarz, okna, owoce];* to brush *[zęby]*

[2] **myć się** to wash oneself; **myć się w wannie/ pod prysznicem** to have a bath/to take a. have a shower

mydelnicz|ka *f* (pudełko) soapbox; (podstawka) soap dish

mydl|ić *impf* [1] *vt* to soap

[2] **mydlić się** [1] (siebie samego) to soap a. lather oneself [2] (pienić się) to lather

■ ~**ić komuś oczy** pot. to pull the wool over sb's eyes

mydlin|y *plt* (woda z mydłem) (soap) suds; (piana) lather

mydł|ło *n* [1] (do mycia, prania) soap; **kostka** ~**ła** a bar of soap [2] (krawieckie) tailor's a. French chalk

■ ~**ło i powidło** iron. a bit of everything

myj|ka *f* (do mycia się) flannel; (do twarzy) facecloth; (rękawica) washing glove

myjni|a *f* [1] (w fabryce) washing station [2] (samochodowa) car wash

myl|ić *impf* [1] *vt* [1] (mieszać) to mix up *[fakty, kierunki, osoby]* [2] (brać jedną rzecz za drugą) to confuse *(coś z czymś* sth with sth); **wszyscy** ~**ili bliźniaków** everyone got the twins mixed up; ~**isz mnie z moją siostrą** you're mistaking me for my sister [3] (wprowadzić w błąd) to mislead; **słuch**

mnie jeszcze nie ~**i** I'm not deaf yet; **o ile mnie pamięć nie** ~**i** if my memory serves me well; **pozory** ~**ą** appearances can be deceptive

[2] **mylić się** [1] (popełniać błąd) to make a mistake (**w czymś** about sth); ~**ą mi się daty i fakty historyczne** I get historical dates and facts mixed up [2] (nie mieć racji) to be mistaken (**w czymś** in sth); ~**iłam się co do niego** I was wrong about him

mysz *f* [1] Zool. (house) mouse [2] Komput. mouse

■ ~**y tańcują, gdy kota nie czują** przysł. while the cat's away, the mice will play przysł.; **biedny jak** ~ **kościelna** przysł. as poor as a church mouse przysł.; **siedzieć (cicho) jak** ~ **pod miotłą** pot. to be as quiet as a mouse; **być spoconym jak** ~ to be bathed in sweat

myszk|ować *impf vi* to ferret a. poke around

myszołów *m* (common) buzzard

myśl *f* [1] thought; **być zatopionym** a. **pogrążonym w** ~**ach** to be deep in thought; **zebrać** ~**i** to collect one's thoughts; **uciec** ~**ą od czegoś** książk. (to try) to put sth out of one's mind; **zwrócić się** ~**ą** a. ~**ami ku czemuś/komuś** to turn one's thoughts to sth/sb; **ogarnąć coś** ~**ą** to grasp sth (mentally); ~**ami byłem z rodziną** my thoughts were with my family; **był nieobecny** ~**ami** his thoughts were elsewhere; **na samą** ~ **o tym robi mi się słabo** I feel faint at the mere thought of it; **to zdjęcie przywodzi mi na** ~ **wakacje w Grecji** this photo reminds me of my holidays in Greece; **wcale tego nie miałem na** ~**i** I didn't mean that at all; **podzielić się z kimś** ~**ami** to share one's thoughts with sb; **być z kimś jednej** ~**i** to be of the same mind a. opinion as sb; **być dobrej/złej** ~ to be optimistic/pessimistic; **przyszło mi na** ~, **że...** it crossed my mind that...; **ani** a. **nawet mi to przez** ~ **nie przeszło, żeby...** it never even crossed my mind to... [2] (pomysł) idea; **to jest** ~**!** that's an idea a. a thought; **porzucić** ~ **o czymś** to give up the idea of sth; **strzeliła mi do głowy** ~ I had a sudden idea; **nosił się z** ~**ą o zakupie samochodu** he was thinking about buying a car [3] (intencja) intention; **wszystko idzie po mojej** ~**i** everything is going as I intended; **w** ~ **czegoś** in accordance with sth

■ **mieć kosmate** a. **włochate** ~**i** pot. to have a dirty mind

myśląc|y *adi. [osoba]* thinking; *[oczy, twarz]* intelligent

myśl|eć *impf vi* [1] (rozumować, rozważać) to think; **często** ~**ała o przeszłości** she often thought about the past; ~**eli, jak rozwiązać tę sprawę** they were thinking (about) how to solve the problem; **co on sobie** ~**i!** who does he think he is!; **niewiele** ~**ąc** without thinking a. (sądzić) to think; ~**ę, że nie masz racji** I think you're wrong; ~**ałem, że przyjedziesz** I thought you'd come; **mówię to, co** ~**ę** I say what I think [3] (troszczyć się) to think; **muszę ~eć o rodzinie** I must think about my family ④ (mieć zamiar) to think (**o czymś** about sth); to intend (**o czymś** to do sth); **~ę o budowie domu** I'm thinking of building a house; **ani ~ę pożyczać mu pieniądze** I've no intention of lending him money ■ **(ja) ~ę!** I should think so!; **głośno ~eć** to think aloud

myśliciel *m,* **~ka** *f* thinker
myśliw|iec *m* Lotn., Wojsk. fighter (plane)
myśliw|y *m* hunter
myślnik *m* dash
myślow|y *adi. [proces, skojarzenia]* mental; **schematy ~e** set patterns of thinking
mżaw|ka *f* drizzle
mż|yć *impf vi [deszcz]* to drizzle

N

N, n *n inv.* N, n

na *praep.* [1] (wskazuje na kontakt z powierzchnią) *[znajdować się]* on; **na niebie** in the sky; **na morzu** at sea; **na zdjęciu/obrazie** in a photo/picture; **na środku czegoś** in the middle of sth; **na początku/końcu czegoś** at the beginning/end of sth [2] (wskazuje na pomieszczenie, miejsce) at, in; **na stadionie** at the stadium; **na korytarzu** in the corridor; **na ulicy** in the street; **na ulicy Klonowej** in a. on Klonowa Street; **na dworcu/przystanku autobusowym** at the station/bus stop; **na wschodzie** in the East; **na Węgrzech** in Hungary; **na wsi** in the country; **na uniwersytecie** at (the) a. in the university; **na górze/dole** at the top/bottom; (w budynku) upstairs/downstairs [3] (wskazuje na kierunek) *[pójść, prowadzić]* to; **iść na północ** to go north; **na górę/dół** (wyżej/niżej) up/down; (w budynku) upstairs/downstairs; **patrzeć na kogoś** to look at sb [4] (wskazuje na odcinek czasu) for; **na zawsze** forever, for ever [5] (wskazuje na termin) **na środę** for Wednesday; **przesunąć coś na jutro** to postpone sth till tomorrow [6] (wskazuje na okazję) for; **na śniadanie** for breakfast; **zaprosić kogoś na wesele** invite sb to a wedding [7] (z nazwami środków lokomocji) on; **jechać na rowerze** to ride a bike; **jeździć na łyżwach/nartach** to skate/to ski [8] (wskazujące na podporę) on; **fotel/koń na biegunach** a rocking chair/horse; **spodnie na szelkach** trousers with braces [9] (wskazuje na narzędzie) on; **na komputerze** on a computer; **grać na skrzypcach** to play (on) the violin [10] (wskazuje na sposób) **usmażyć coś na maśle** to fry sth in butter; **pomalować coś na niebiesko** to paint sth blue; **ubierać się na biało** to dress in white [11] (wskazuje na przeznaczenie) for; **dom na sprzedaż** a house for sale; **butelka na mleko** a milk bottle [12] (wskazuje na cel) on; **pójść na zakupy** to go shopping [13] (wskazuje na skutek) to, into; **na strzępy/kawałki** to shreds/pieces [14] (wskazuje na przyczynę) at; **na czyjąś prośbę** at sb's request [15] (w pomiarach, obliczeniach) **100 kilometrów na godzinę** a hundred kilometres per a. an hour; **dwa razy na rok** twice a year; **jeden na dziesięciu** one in ten a. out of ten; **długi na sześć metrów** six metres deep

nabia|ł *m* eggs and dairy produce

nabi|ć *pf* — **nabi|jać** *impf* **I** *vt* [1] (wypełnić) to fill *[fajkę, materac]* (**czymś** with sth); (to load *[pistolet,*

działo] [2] (nadziać) to spear *[kiełbasę]* (**na coś** on sth)

II nabijać się *pot.* to make fun (**z kogoś** of sb)

nabierać *impf* → **nabrać**

nabi|ty *adi. pot. [autobus, sala]* packed; *[osoba]* sturdy

nabożeństw|o *n* [1] (obrzęd) church service; **książeczka do ~a** a prayer book [2] książk. (szacunek) reverence; **nie mieć do czegoś ~a** to not be particularly keen on sth

nab|ój *m* cartridge; (do syfonu) refill; **ślepy ~ój** a blank (cartridge); **~ój ostry** a live cartridge

nab|rać *pf* — **nab|ierać** *impf* **I** *vt* [1] (zaczerpnąć) to scoop (up) *[mąki, lodów]*; (podnieść) to pick up *[siana, ziemi]*; **~rać powietrza w płuca** to fill one's lungs with air [2] *pot.* (oszukać) to con *pot.* [3] (zyskać) to gain *[prędkości, wysokości]*

II nabrać się — **nabierać się** *pot.* (dać się oszukać) **dać się ~rać na coś** to fall for sth *pot.*

nabrzeż|e *n* wharf, quay

nab|yć *pf* — **nab|ywać** *impf* książk. *vt* [1] (kupić) to purchase [2] (zyskać) to acquire książk.

nabyt|ek *m* książk. (zakup) purchase; (muzeum, galerii) acquisition

nabywać *impf* → **nabyć**

nabyw|ca *m*, **~czyni** *f* książk. purchaser

nachaln|y *adi. grad. pot. [dziennikarz]* pushy *pot.*; *[propaganda]* aggressive

nachodzić *impf* → **najść**

nachyl|ić *pf* — **nachyl|ać** *impf* **I** *vt* (pochylić) to tilt; (nagiąć) to bend

II nachylić się — **nachylać się** to lean (forward)

naciągacz *m pot.* con man *pot.*

naciąg|nąć *pf* — **naciąg|ać** *impf* **I** *vt* [1] (naprężyć) to tighten *[linę, strunę]* [2] (nasunąć, nałożyć) to pull *[sth]* on *[rękawiczki, pokrowiec]* [3] Med. to strain *[mięsień, ścięgno]* [4] *pot.* (przedstawić nierzetelnie) to make *[sth]* up *[dowody]*; **~any argument** a tenuous argument [5] *pot.* (namówić) to trick (**kogoś na coś** sb into sth)

II *vi* (zaparzyć się) *[herbata, kawa]* to draw

III naciągnąć się — **naciągać się** *[lina]* to tighten

nacierać *impf* → **natrzeć**

nacię|cie *n* [1] (rowek, wgłębienie) cut; (na drzewie) notch; (na tkaninie) slit [2] Med. incision

nacisk *m* [1] pressure; **pod czyimś ~iem** under pressure from sb [2] (akcent) emphasis

naci|snąć *pf* — **naci|skać** *impf vt* 1 (przycisnąć) to press *[przycisk]* 2 (wywrzeć presję) to put pressure on (**kogoś** a. **na kogoś** sb)

nacjonalizm *m* nationalism

naczelni|k *m* (kierownik) head; (przywódca) commander; ~**k** **więzienia** a prison governor a. warden US

naczeln|y [] *adi.* 1 (główny) *[cel]* principal; *[idea, temat]* leading 2 (zarządzający) *[dyrektor, redaktor]* chief; (w tytułach) general

[] **naczeln|y** *m*, ~**a** *f* pot. boss pot.

[]] **naczelne** *plt* Zool. primates

naczy|nie *n* 1 vessel; (stołowe) dish; (pojemnik) container; **zmywać** ~**nia** to do the dishes 2 Anat. vessel

❑ ~**nia połączone** communicating tubes; przen. ≈ self-regulating system

na|ć *f* (marchwi, rzodkiewek) tops; (selera) top, leaf stalks; (pietruszki, kopru) leaves

naćpan|y *adi.* pot. stoned pot.

naćpa|ć się *pf v refl.* pot. 1 (odurzyć się) to get stoned pot. (**czymś** on sth) 2 (najeść się) to stuff oneself pot. (**czegoś** with sth)

nad *praep.* 1 (powyżej) over, above 2 (w pobliżu) ~ **Wisłą** on the Vistula; ~ **rzeką** by the river; ~ **morze/jezioro** to the seaside/the lake 3 (wskazuje na podporządkowanie) over 4 (wskazuje na temat) on, about; **praca** ~ **czymś** work on a. at sth; **rozmyślać** ~ **czymś** to ponder on a. over sth 5 (z określeniami wyrażającymi uczucia) at, over; **użalać się** ~ **kimś** to feel sorry for sb 6 (tuż przed) (just) before; ~ **ranem** (just) before dawn 7 książk. (bardziej niż) than; **kochać kogoś** ~ **życie** to love sb more than life itself; **łotr** ~ **łotrami** an arch-villain książk.; ~**e wszystko** above all (else)

nada|ć *pf* — **nada|wać** *impf* [] *vt* 1 (wysłać) to send; (pocztą) to post GB, to mail *[list, paczkę]*; ~**ć coś na bagaż** (do samolotu) to check sth in 2 Radio, TV to broadcast *[program, audycję]*; to send *[komunikat, sygnał]* 3 (zmienić charakter) to give *[kształt, formę, prędkość]*; to lend *[sens, urok, wygląd]*; ~**ć czemuś rozgłos** to publicize sth 4 (przyznać) to grant *[dobra, przywilej]* (**komuś** sb a. to sb); to confer *[tytuł, stopień]* (**komuś** on sb); to award *[odznaczenie, order]* (**komuś** sb a. to sb) 5 pot. (polecić) ~**ć komuś robotę** to fix sb up with a job

[] **nadać się** — **nadawać się** to be fit a. suitable (**do czegoś** for sth); **ona się nie** ~**je na aktorkę** she's not cut out to be an actress

nadajnik *m* transmitter

nadal *adv.* still

nadaremnie *adv.* książk. in vain

nadaremn|y *adi.* książk. *[działania, wysiłki]* futile

nadawać *impf* → **nadać**

nadaw|ca *m*, ~**czyni** *f* (listu) sender; (ładunku) forwarder

nadarz|yć się *pf* — **nadarz|ać się** *impf v refl.* *[okazja, szansa]* to present itself

nad|ąć *pf* — **nad|ymać** *impf* [] *vt* (nadmuchać) to inflate *[balon]*; to puff out a. up *[policzki]*

[] **nadąć się** — **nadymać się** 1 *[osoba]* to take a deep breath; *[policzki]* to puff out a. up; *[żagle]* to swell 2 pot. (nadąsać się) to go into a sulk

nadąsan|y *adi.* *[dziecko, mina]* sulky

nadąż|yć *pf* — **nadąż|ać** *impf vi* 1 (dotrzymać kroku) to keep up (**za kimś** with sb) 2 (zdążyć) to be on time (**z czymś** with sth) 3 (zrozumieć) to follow (**za czymś** sth)

nadbagaż *m* excess baggage

nadbrzeż|e *n* waterside, shore

nadchodzić *impf* → **nadejść**

nadciąg|nąć *pf* — **nadciąg|ać** *impf vi* (przybyć) *[tłum]* to arrive; (zbliżać się) *[wojsko, burza]* to approach; *[noc, upały]* to close in; *[wiosna, czas]* to draw near

nadciśnie|nie *n* Med. hypertension; Fiz. highpressure

nadczynnoś|ć *f* hyperactivity

nad|ejść *pf* — **nad|chodzić** *impf vi* *[osoba, paczka, wiosna, burza]* to come; *[pociąg]* to arrive

nad|erwać *pf* — **nad|rywać** *impf* [] *vt* to strain *[mięsień, ścięgno]*; to tear *[sth]* partly away a. off *[ucho, kołnierzyk]*

[] **naderwać się** — **nadrywać się** *[uchwyt]* to become loose

nadę|ty *adi.* pot. 1 (nadąsany) *[osoba]* huffy; *[mina]* sulky 2 (wyniosły) *[osoba]* stuck-up pot.; *[styl]* pompous

nadganiać *impf* → **nadgonić**

nadgarst|ek *m* wrist

nadgodzin|a [] *f* hour of overtime

[] **nadgodziny** *plt* pot. overtime; **brać** ~**y** to do overtime

nadg|onić *pf* — **nadg|aniać** *impf vt* pot. to make up (for) *[czas, zaległości]*

nadgorliw|y *adi.* overzealous

nadgraniczn|y *adi.* *[strefa, miasto]* border

nadkładać *impf* → **nadłożyć**

nadl|ecieć *pf* — **nadl|atywać** *impf vi* 1 (przylecieć) *[pocisk, owad]* to come (flying); *[samolot]* to arrive; *[dźwięk]* to come 2 pot. (przybiec) *[osoba]* to come flying

nadludz|ki *adi.* superhuman

nad|łożyć *pf* — **nad|kładać** *impf vt* ~**łożyć drogi** to take a roundabout way; ~**łożyć dziesięć kilometrów** to go ten kilometers out of one's way

nadmia|r *m* excess; **w** ~**rze** in excess

nadmieni|ć *pf* — **nadmieni|ać** *impf vi* książk. to mention

nadmiern|y *adi.* excessive

nadmors|ki *adi.* *[ptaki, prowincja]* coastal; *[miasto]* seaside

nadmuch|ać *pf* — **nadmuch|iwać** *impf vt* to blow *[sth]* up *[materac, balon]*

nadobowiązkow|y *adi.* optional

nadopiekuńcz|y *adi.* overprotective (**wobec kogoś** of a. towards sb)

nadpła|cić *pf* — **nadpła|cać** *impf vt* to overpay

nadpła|ta *f* overpayment

nadpobudliw|y *adi.* overly excitable; *[dziecko]* hyperactive

nadprogramow|y *adi.* additional; (poza programem szkolnym) extra-curricular

nadr|obić *pf* — **nadr|abiać** *impf vt* to make up for

■ ~**abiać miną** to put on a brave face

nadruk *m* printed inscription

nadrywać *impf* → **naderwać**

nadrzędn|y *adi.* książk. superior (**wobec czegoś** to sth)

nadskak|iwać *impf vi* to dance attendance (**komuś** on sb)

nadsłuch|iwać *impf vi* to listen out (**czegoś** for sth)

nadstaw|ić *pf* — **nadstaw|iać** *impf vt* to hold out *[naczynie, ręce]*; to offer, to present *[policzek, usta]*; ~**iać karku** przen. to stick one's neck out

naduży|cie *n* abuse; (przestępstwo finansowe) misappropriation of funds

naduży|ć *pf* — **naduży|wać** *impf vt* książk. to abuse *[alkoholu]*; ~**ć czyjegoś zaufania** to betray sb's trust

nadwa|ga *f* overweight; **mieć** ~**gę** to be overweight

nadweręż|yć *pf* — **nadweręż|ać** *impf* **[] *vt*** książk. to strain *[rękę, mięsień]*

[]] nadwerężyć się — **nadwerężać się** to overstrain oneself

nadwozi|e *n* body(work)

nadwrażliw|y *adi.* oversensitive; Med. hypersensitive (**na coś** to sth)

nadwyż|ka *f* surplus

nadzi|ać *pf* — **nadzi|ewać** *impf* **[] *vt*** [] (wypełnić farszem) to stuff *[mięso]*; to fill *[ciasto]* [2] (wbić) to impale

[]] nadziać się — **nadziewać się** [] (wbić się) to impale oneself (**na coś** on sth) [2] pot. (natknąć się) ~**ać się na kogoś** to bump into sb pot.

nadzie|ja *f* hope; **mieć** ~**ję** to hope; **pokładać** ~**ję w kimś** książk. to pin one's hopes on sb; **robić sobie/komuś** ~**ję** to delude oneself/sb; **z** ~**ją** a. **w** ~**i, że...** in hope of...

nadzie|nie *n* (ciasta) filling; (mięsa) stuffing

nadziewać *impf* → **nadziać**

nadzor|ować /ˌnadzo'rɔvatɕ/ *pf vt* to supervise

nadz|ór /'nadzur/ *m* supervision; **sprawować** ~**ór nad czymś** to supervise sth; **pozostawiać kogoś bez** ~**oru** to leave sb unattended

nadzwyczajnie /ˌnadzvɨ'tʃajɲe/ *adv.* remarkably a. exceptionally well

nadzwyczajn|y /ˌnadzvɨ'tʃajnɨ/ *adi.* [] (niezwykły) exceptional [2] (specjalny) special

naelektryz|ować *pf* **[] *vt*** to charge

[]] naelektryzować się to become electrically charged

nafaszer|ować *pf* **[] *vt*** [] Kulin. to stuff [2] pot., przen. to stuff pot. *[osobę]* (**czymś** with sth); to pack *[tekst]* (**czymś** with sth)

[]] nafaszerować się to pump oneself full (**czymś** of sth)

naf|ta *f* [] Chem. liquid paraffin, kerosene [2] pot. (ropa naftowa) oil

naftalin|a *f* naphthalene

naftow|y *adi.* [] *[szyb, przemysł]* oil; **ropa** ~**a** oil [2] *[lampa]* paraffin GB , kerosene

nagada|ć *pf* pot. **[] *vt*** to tell *[bzdur, głupot]*

[]] *vi* [] (obmówić) to blab pot. (**na kogoś** about sth) [2] (nawymyślać) ~**ć komuś** to give sb an earful pot.

nagan|a *f* reprimand; **udzielić komuś** ~**y** to reprimand sb

nagann|y *adi.* reprehensible

na|gi *adi.* [] (nieubrany) naked [2] *[drzewa, ziemia, ściany]* bare [3] (bez upiększeń) bare, unadorned

nag|iąć *pf* — **nag|inać** *impf* **[] *vt*** to bend także przen.

[]] nagiąć się — **naginać się** [] (zgiąć się) to bend [2] (zgodzić się) *[osoba]* to give in (**do czegoś** to sth)

nagiet|ek *m* marigold

nagląc|y *adi. [sprawa, gest]* urgent

nagle *adv.* suddenly

nagł|ośnić *pf* — **nagł|aśniać** *impf vt* [] (nadać rozgłos) to publicize *[sprawę, skandal]* [2] Techn. to have a PA system installed in *[salę, budynek]*

nagłów|ek *m* (w gazecie) headline; (nad tekstem) heading

nag|ły *adi.* (niespodziewany) sudden; (pilny) urgent; ~**ły wypadek** an emergency

nagniot|ek *m [na stopie]* corn

nag|o *adv.* naked; **rozebrać się do** ~**a** to strip naked

nagon|ka *f* [] (na polowaniu) battue [2] przen. (na osobę) smear campaign (**na kogoś** against sb)

nagoś|ć *f* nudity

nagr|ać *pf* — **nagr|ywać** *impf* **[] *vt*** [] (zarejestrować) to record *[audycję, płytę]* [2] Komput. (zapisać) to copy [3] pot. (załatwić) to arrange *[spotkanie, pracę]*

[]] nagrać się — **nagrywać się** (własny głos) to record oneself; ~**ać się na sekretarkę** pot. to leave a message on the answering machine

nagradzać *impf* → **nagrodzić**

nagra|nie *n* recording

nagrob|ek *m* gravestone; (pionowy) headstone

nagr|oda *f* (wyróżnienie) prize; (wynagrodzenie) reward; ~**oda Nobla** the Nobel Prize; ~**oda pocieszenia** a consolation prize; ~**oda za coś** an award a. a prize for sth; **w** ~**odę za coś** as a reward for sth

nagr|odzić *pf* — **nagr|adzać** *impf vt* [] (wyróżnić) to award [2] (zrekompensować) to compensate

nagrywać *impf* → **nagrać**

nagrz|ać *pf* — **nagrz|ewać** *impf* **I** *vt* to heat (up) *[pokój]*; to heat up *[wody]*

II nagrzać się — nagrzewać się *[pokój]* to warm up

naiwnia|k *m*, **~czka** *f* pot. simpleton

naiwnoś|ć *f* naivety

naiwn|y *adi. grad. [osoba]* gullible, naive; *[wiara, pomysł]* artless, naive

■ pierwsza ~a ingénue

najadać się *impf* → **najeść się**

naj|azd *m* ① invasion; (mniejszy) raid ② przen. (tłumne przybycie) descent, onslaught

naj|ąć *pf* — **naj|mować** *impf* **I** *vt* to rent *[dom, mieszkanie]*; to hire *[osobę]*

II nająć się — najmować się to hire oneself out

■ gadać jak ~ęty to chatter on

naj|echać *pf* — **naj|eżdżać** *impf* *vi* ① (potrącić) ~echać na drzewo to run into a tree ② (skierować) ~echać na coś kamerą to focus the camera on sth ③ pot. (skrytykować) ~echać na kogoś to pitch into sb pot.

najedz|ony *adi. [osoba]* full (up)

naj|em *m* rental; wziąć coś w ~em to rent sth

najem|ca *m*, **~czyni** *f* tenant

najemn|y *adi. [pracownik]* hired

najemni|k *m* mercenary; przen. hireling

naj|eść się *pf* — **naj|adać się** *impf* *vi* to eat one's fill (czegoś of sth)

najeźdźc|a *m* książk. invader

najeżdżać *impf* → **najechać**

najeż|yć *pf* — **najeż|ać** *impf* **I** *vt* (nastroszyć) ~yć sierść to bristle (up)

II najeżyć się — najeżać się ① *[zwierzę, sierść]* to bristle (up) ② pot., przen. *[osoba]* to bristle

najmować *impf* → **nająć**

najpierw *adv.* (at) first

na|jść *pf* — **na|chodzić** *impf* *vt* ① (odwiedzić) nachodzić kogoś to intrude (up)on sb ② (ogarnąć) naszła go chęć do wyjazdu he felt like going away

nakarm|ić *pf vt* to feed

nakaz *m* ① (zarządzenie) order; ~ aresztowania a warrant for sb's arrest ② (wymóg) dictate; ~y mody dictates of fashion

naka|zać *pf* — **naka|zywać** *impf vt* ① (rozkazać) to order; ~zać komuś coś zrobić to order sb to do sth ② (wymagać) *[sytuacja]* to require *[ostrożność]*

nakle|ić *pf* — **nakle|jać** *impf vt* to stick *[plakat, znaczek]*

naklej|ka *f* sticker; (etykieta) (sticky) label

nakła|d *m* ① (koszt) expenditure; olbrzymim ~dem sił with a tremendous amount of effort ② Druk. (książki) edition; (gazety) circulation

nakładać *impf* → **nałożyć**

nakład|ka *f* (osłona) cover

nakł|onić *pf* — **nakł|aniać** *impf vt* ~onić kogoś do zrobienia czegoś to make sb do sth

nakłu|ć *pf* — **nakłu|wać** *impf vt* to pierce

nakreśl|ić *pf* — **nakreśl|ać** *impf vt* to sketch także przen.

nakrę|cić *pf* — **nakrę|cać** *impf* **I** *vt* ① (wprawić w ruch) to wind (up) *[zegarek, zabawkę]*; przen. to fuel *[inflację, koniunkturę]* ② (nawinąć) to wind *[sznurek]* (na coś on a. onto sth); ~cić włosy na lokówki to put one's hair in curlers ③ (zarejestrować) to shoot *[film, scenę]*

II *vi* pot. (nakłamać) to tell (a pack of) lies

nakręt|ka *f* ① (mutra) nut ② (słoika, butelki) (screw) top; (tubki) (screw) cap

nakrusz|yć *pf vt* ~yć gdzieś chlebem to spill breadcrumbs on sth

nakry|cie *n* ① (przykrycie) ~cie głowy a headdress ② (zastawa stołowa) place setting; przygotować ~cie na sześć osób to lay a. set the table for six

nakry|ć *pf* — **nakry|wać** *impf* **I** *vt* ① (przykryć) to cover ② pot. to nail pot. *[złodzieja]*

II nakryć się — nakrywać się to cover oneself

■ ~ć do stołu to lay a. set the table

nal|ać *pf* — **nal|ewać** *impf vt* ① (napełnić płynem) to pour; ~ać zupę do talerzy to ladle (out) soup into plates ② (rozlać) to spill

nalan|y *adi. [twarz]* bloated

nal|ecieć *pf* — **nal|atywać** *impf vi* ① *[ptaki, owady]* to fly in ② *[dym, gaz]* to come flying in ③ pot. (skrytykować) ~atywać na kogoś to lash out at sb pot.

nalega|ć *impf vi* to insist (na coś on (doing) sth)

nalepi|ć *pf* — **nalepi|ać** *impf vt* to stick (on) *[etykietkę]*; to paste (up) *[ogłoszenie]*

nalep|ka *f* sticker

naleśnik *m* pancake, crêpe

nalewać *impf* → **nalać**

należ|eć *impf* **I** *vi* ① (być własnością, członkiem) to belong (do kogoś/czegoś to sb/sth); ~eć do spisku to be involved in a conspiracy; wilki ~ą do drapieżników wolves are predators; to nie ~y do przyjemności it's not exactly pleasant ② (być obowiązkiem) ~eć do kogoś to be sb's responsibility; ~eć do czyichś obowiązków to be one of sb's duties; decyzja ~y do ciebie it's up to you to decide

II *v imp.* (trzeba) ~y coś zrobić sth should be done

III należeć się (przysługiwać) to mu się ~y (zasłużył) he deserves it; (jest uprawniony) he's entitled to it; ~y mi się 20 zł I'm owed 20 zlotys; ile się ~y? how much a. what do I owe you?

należnoś|ć *f* książk. amount due

należn|y *adi.* książk. *[suma, szacunek]* due

należy|ty *adi. [wyjaśnienie, higiena]* proper; *[staranność]* due

nalicz|yć *pf* — **nalicz|ać** *impf vt* ① książk. to calculate *[karę, premię]* ② (znaleźć) to count

nalo|t *m* [1] (warstewka) coating; (na metalu) tarnish [2] przen. (wpływ) influence [3] Wojsk. air raid [4] pot. (kontrola) raid; **zrobić ~t na coś** to raid sth

nałogow|iec *m* addict

nałogowo *adv.* **palić ~** to be a compulsive smoker

nałogow|y *adi.* compulsive; **~y palacz** a heavy smoker

na|łożyć *pf* — **na|kładać** *impf* [I] *vt* [1] (umieścić) to put; (założyć) to put [sth] on [płaszcz, kapelusz]; (rozsmarować) to apply [makijaż, krem] [2] (obciążyć) to impose [embargo, cło] (**na kogoś** on sb)
[II] **nałożyć się — nakładać się** [linie, terminy] to overlap

nał|óg *m* addiction; **wejść komuś w ~óg** przen. to become a habit with sb

nałyka|ć się *pf v refl.* to swallow [tabletek]
■ **~ać się strachu** to get a fright

namacaln|y *adi.* książk. [dowód, korzyść] tangible

namal|ować *pf vt* to paint

namawiać *impf* → **namówić**

namia|r [I] *m* (położenie) bearing; (określenie położenia) direction finding
[II] **namiary** *plt* pot. (adres) details

namiast|ka *f* (poor) substitute (**czegoś** for sth)

namierz|yć *pf* — **namierz|ać** *impf vt* to get a fix on [okręt, satelitę]; pot. to locate [osobę]

namiętnoś|ć *f* passion

namiętn|y *adi.* książk. [1] [pocałunek, kochanek] passionate [2] [spór, dyskusja] heated [3] (zapalony) [gracz] avid, passionate

namio|t *m* tent; **rozbić ~t** to put up a tent; **zwinąć ~t** to take down a tent

namocz|yć *pf* [I] *vt* to soak [ubranie, fasolę]
[II] **namoczyć się** to soak

namota|ć *pf vi* pot. (narobić intryg) to muddle things up

nam|owa *f* persuasion; **za czyjąś ~ową** at sb's prompting

nam|ówić *pf* — **nam|awiać** *impf* [I] *vt* (nakłonić) to persuade
[II] **namówić się — namawiać się** pot. (zmówić się) to plot (**z kimś** with sb)

namy|sł *m* thought; **po głębokim ~śle** after much thought; **zgodził się bez ~słu** he agreed straight away

namyśl|ić się *pf* — **namyśl|ać się** *impf v refl.* [1] (rozważyć) to think deeply (**nad czymś** about sth) [2] (podjąć decyzję) to make up one's mind

nan|ieść *pf* — **nan|osić** *impf vt* (zaznaczyć) to mark

naoczn|y *adi.* [dowód] clear; **~y świadek** an eyewitness

naokoło [I] *adv.* [1] (ze wszystkich stron) (all) around [2] (wzdłuż obwodu) around, round GB
[II] *praep.* around, round GB

naoliw|ić *pf* — **naoliw|iać** *impf vt* to oil

naostrz|yć *pf vt* to sharpen

nap|a *f* press stud GB, snap fastener US

napa|d *m* [1] (napaść) assault; **~d na bank** a bank robbery [2] pot. (gwałtowna reakcja) fit; (przypływ emocji) surge; **~d złości** an outburst of anger; **~d kaszlu** a coughing fit [3] Sport attack

napadać¹ *pf* → **napaść¹**

napada|ć² *pf v imp.* [deszcz] to fall

napal|ić *pf* — **napal|ać** *impf* [I] *vi* [1] (rozpalić ogień) to light the fire [2] (zadymić papierosami) to fill a place with tobacco smoke
[II] **napalić się — napalać się** pot. to have a yen pot.; **~ić się na kogoś** to have the hots for sb pot.

napa|r *m* infusion

naparst|ek *m* thimble; (porcja płynu) thimbleful

naparz|yć *pf* — **naparz|ać** *impf* [I] *vt* to infuse [ziół]; **~yć kawy/herbaty** to brew coffee/tea
[II] **naparzyć się — naparzać się** [zioła] to infuse; [kawa, herbata] to brew
[III] **naparzać się** pot. to have a dust-up pot.

napastliw|y *adi. grad.* książk. [osoba, ton] aggressive; [artykuł, uwaga] hostile

napastni|k *m* [1] (osoba) assailant, attacker [2] Wojsk. aggressor [3] Sport forward

napast|ować *pf vt* książk. (zaczepiać) to bully; (naprzykrzać się) to harass

napa|ść¹ *pf* — **napa|dać¹** *impf vt* to attack; **~ść (na) kogoś** to attack sb; **~dła go złość** he suddenly got really angry

napaś|ć² *f* książk. assault

napatrz|yć się, napatrz|eć się *pf v refl.* **nie mógł się ~yć na...** he couldn't take his eyes off...

napeł|nić *pf* — **napeł|niać** *impf* [I] *vt* to fill (**coś czymś** sth with sth); **~nić kogoś niepokojem** przen. to make sb anxious
[II] **napełnić się — napełniać się** to fill (**czymś** with sth)

napęczni|eć *pf vi* to swell

napę|d *m* drive także przen.

napędow|y *adi.* propelling; **olej ~y** diesel (fuel a. oil)

napędza|ć *impf* [1] Techn. to drive; **~ny energią słoneczną** solar powered [2] (przyspieszać) to accelerate [inflację]

nap|iąć *pf* — **nap|inać** *impf* [I] *vt* to stretch [płótno]; to tense [mięśnie]; to tighten [cięciwę]
[II] **napiąć się — napinać się** [lina] to tighten; [mięśnie] to tense (up)

napi|ć się *pf v refl.* [1] (ugasić pragnienie) to drink [wody, mleka] [2] (wypić alkohol) to have a drink

napierać *impf* → **naprzeć**

napię|cie *n* [1] (podenerwowanie, konflikt) tension (**między kimś a kimś** between sb and sb) [2] (elektryczne) voltage, tension; **przewód pod ~ciem** live wire

napiętn|ować *pf vt* książk. (potępić) to stigmatize; **godny ~owania** deplorable

napię|ty adi. [nerwy, mięśnie, sytuacja] tense; [lina, materiał] stretched; [harmonogram] tight

napinać impf → **napiąć**

napis m inscription; (informacja) notice; ∼y (z nazwiskami) credits; (tłumaczenie) subtitles

napi|sać pf vt to write [artykuł, powieść]; ∼sać coś na maszynie/komputerze to type sth on a typewriter/computer

napiw|ek m tip

naplu|ć pf vi to spit

napły|nąć pf — **napły|wać** impf ① [woda] to flow in ② (przypłynąć) [statki] to come ③ książk. (przybyć) [osoby, zapach, informacje] to come in; **twarz** ∼nęła **mu krwią** the blood rushed to his face

napływ m ① (napływanie) inflow ② (o uczuciach) surge

napływać impf → **napłynąć**

napocz|ąć pf — **napocz|ynać** impf to start [opakowanie]

nap|oić pf vt to water [zwierzę]; to give something to drink to [gości]

napom|knąć pf — **napom|ykać** impf vi książk. to mention (**o czymś** sth)

napomp|ować pf vt ① (nadmuchać) to inflate; (pompką) to pump up ② (przemieścić) to pump [cieczy, gazu]

napotn|y adi. sweat-inducing

nap|ój m drink, beverage

nap|ór m ① (nacisk) pressure; **ustąpić pod** ∼**orem** to yield to pressure ② (w fizyce) thrust

napraw|a f ① (reperacja) repair; **oddać coś do** ∼y to take sth to be repaired ② (rekompensata) recompense ③ (poprawa) improvement

napraw|ić pf — **napraw|iać** impf vt ① (zreperować) to repair [samochód, drogę]; to fix [kran, półkę] ② (poprawić) to repair [stosunki]; to remedy [sytuację, wady]; to rectify [błąd] ③ (zrekompensować) to repair [szkodę]; to redress [zło, krzywdę]

naprawdę Ⅰ part. really; **tak** ∼ actually Ⅱ adv. [wydarzyć się] really

naprędce adv. książk. (w pośpiechu) [zbudować, zmontować] hastily; (na poczekaniu) [wygłosić, skomponować] ad lib; [wymyślić] impromptu

napręż|yć pf — **napręż|ać** impf Ⅰ vt to tense; (na pokaz) to flex [mięśnie]; to tighten [linę, cięciwę, strunę] Ⅱ **naprężyć się** — **naprężać się** ① [osoba] to tense up ② [mięśnie, lina] to tighten

naprowadz|ić pf — **naprowadz|ać** impf vt to guide [statek, pocisk] (**na coś** to sth); ∼**ić kogoś na właściwy trop** przen. to put sb on the right track

naprzeciw, ∼**ko** Ⅰ praep. opposite, across from; **wyjść komuś** ∼ to go out to meet sb (on their way); przen. to meet sb halfway Ⅱ adv. opposite
■ **mieć coś** ∼ to have objections (**czemuś** to sth)

nap|rzeć pf — **nap|ierać** impf Ⅰ vi to push (**na coś** against sth); [tłum] to press forward; [wojsko] to advance; ∼**ierać na kogoś, żeby coś zrobił** przen. to push sb to do a. into doing sth Ⅱ **naprzeć się** — **napierać się** pot. to insist

naprzód adv. ① (przed siebie) [ruszyć, posunąć się] forward(s); [biec, iść] ahead ② (na czele) **idź** ∼ go first ③ (wcześniej) ahead, in advance

naprzykrza|ć się impf v refl. to pester (**komuś o coś** sb for sth)

napuszon|y adi. [osoba, styl] pompous

napu|ścić pf — **napu|szczać** impf vt ① (napełnić) to let [sth] in [dymu, kurzu]; to run [wody, deszczówki] ② pot. (nasłać) to set (**kogoś na kogoś** sb (up)on sb)

nara|da f meeting, council

nara|dzić się pf — **nara|dzać się** impf v refl. książk. to confer (**z kimś** with sb)

naraz adv. ① (nagle) all of a sudden ② (jednocześnie) at the same time

nara|zić pf — **nara|żać** impf Ⅰ vt to expose (**kogoś na coś** sb to sth); ∼**żać swoje zdrowie** to risk one's life Ⅱ **narazić się** — **narażać się** ① (siebie samego) to expose oneself (**na coś** to sth) ② (rozgniewać) to fall into disfavour GB a. disfavor US (**komuś** with sb)

narąb|ać pf Ⅰ vt to chop [drewna] Ⅱ **narąbać się** posp. (upić się) to get smashed pot.

narciar|ka Ⅰ f ① (osoba) skier ② pot. (czapka) woollen ski hat Ⅱ **narciarki** plt pot. (spodnie) ski pants

narciarstw|o n skiing

narciarz m skier

narcyz m ① Bot. narcissus ② (o osobie) narcissist książk.

nareszcie Ⅰ adv. at (long) last, finally Ⅱ inter. at last!

narkoman m, ∼**ka** f drug addict

narkomani|a /ˌnarkoˈmanja/ f drug abuse a. addiction

narkotyk m ① Med. narcotic ② (nielegalny) drug

narkotyz|ować się pf v refl. to take drugs

narkoz|a f (general) anaesthesia a. anesthesia US; **być pod** ∼**ą** to be anaesthetized

nar|obić pf Ⅰ vt to make [błędów, ciastek]; to cause [zamieszania, szkód]; **coś ty** ∼**obił?** what on earth have you done? Ⅱ vi posp. (wydalić mocz) to pee pot.; (wydalić kał) to do one's business pot.

narodowoś|ć f (ethnic) nationality

narodow|y adi. ① [kultura, hymn, tradycja] national ② Polit. [polityk, partia] nationalist

narodzin|y plt książk. birth także przen.

narośl f growth

narożnik m ① (róg) corner ② (kanapa) corner sofa

nar|ód m nation

narracj|a f narration

narrato|r m, ∼**rka** f narrator

nar|ta f ski; **jeździć na** ∼**tach** to ski

nartostra|da f ski run

narusz|yć *pf* — **narusz|ać** *impf vt* ① (napocząć) to break into *[fundusze, oszczędności]* ② (uszkodzić) to disturb *[korzenie]*; to damage *[kość]*; to weaken *[konstrukcję]* ③ (zakłócić) to disturb *[równowagę]* ④ (pogwałcić) to violate *[prawo, prywatność, umowę]*

narw|ać *pf vt* to pick *[kwiatów, owoców]*

narwa|niec *m* pot. madcap pot.

narwan|y *adi.* pot. madcap pot.

naryb|ek *m* fry; przen. new a. young blood

narys|ować *pf vt* to draw *[portret, linię, postać]*

narząd *m* organ

narzeczon|a *f* fiancée

narzeczon|y *m* fiancé

narzeka|ć *impf vi* to complain (**na coś** about sth); **nie mógł** ~**ć na brak pieniędzy** he did not want for money

narzędzi|e *n* ① (proste) tool; (precyzyjne) instrument ② (środek, metoda) tool, device

narzu|cić *pf* — **narzu|cać** *impf* **[I** *vt* ① (nałożyć) to throw; ~**cić płaszcz** to fling a. throw a coat on ② (zmusić) to impose *[decyzję, opinię]* (**komuś** upon sb)

[II narzucić się — narzucać się** to impose oneself (**komuś** on sb)

[III narzucać się** to suggest itself; **takie porównanie samo się** ~**ca** there's no escaping the comparison

narzu|t *m* (marża) profit margin

narzu|ta *f* (na łóżko) bedspread, coverlet; (na inne meble) throw

nasa|da *f* ① (trzon) *[kciuka, pnia, liścia]* base; *[kości]* head; *[dłoni]* heel; *[języka, skrzydła, włosów]* root ② (uchwyt) *[noża, młotka]* handle; *[pilnika]* shaft (pokrywa, nakładka) cap, cover

nasad|ka *f* (końcówka) attachment

nasącz|yć *pf* — **nasącz|ać** *impf* **[I** *vt* (nawilżyć) to soak *[bandaże, szmaty]*; to moisten *[ciasto, wacik]*; to impregnate *[materiał]*

[II nasączyć się — nasączać się** to become soaked

nasenn|y *adi.* soporific; **tabletka** ~**a** a sleeping pill

nasiadów|ka *f* ① (kąpiel, wanna) sitz bath ② pot. (zebranie) talk(ing) shop GB, confab US pot.

nasiąk|nąć *pf* — **nasiąk|ać** *impf vi* to become soaked; (zapachem) to become permeated

nasi|enie *n* ① Bot. seed ② (sperma) semen, sperm

nasileni|e *n* ① (intensywność) intensity ② (wzmożenie) (konfliktu, wojny) escalation; (emocji, prac, tempa) build-up; (opadów, wiatru, wysiłków) increase

nasil|ić *pf* — **nasil|ać** *impf* **[I** *vt* to intensify *[wysiłki]*

[II nasilić się — nasilać się** *[ból]* to grow worse; *[emocje, wysiłki]* to intensify; *[deszcz, hałas]* to increase

nasi|ono *n* seed

naskarż|yć *pf vi* pot. to tell (tales) pot. (**na kogoś** on sb)

naskór|ek *m* epidermis

na|słać *pf* — **na|syłać** *impf vt* (napuścić) to set *[policję, kontrolę]* (**na kogoś** on sb)

nasłuch *m* (kontrola audycji) monitoring; (radarowy, radiowy) watch

nasłucha|ć się *pf v refl.* to hear *[plotek, kłamstw]*

nasłuch|iwać *impf vi* to listen out

nasta|ć *pf* — **nasta|wać** *impf vi* ① (nastąpić) *[dzień]* to break; *[milczenie]* to ensue; *[mróz, zima, zła pogoda]* to set in; *[nowa era]* to dawn ② (objąć stanowisko) to come to a. into office

nastaw|ić *pf* — **nastaw|iać** *impf* **[I** *vt* ① (skierować) to turn *[łódź, twarz]*; to hold out *[nogę, rękę]* ② (do ugotowania) to put [sth] on *[zupę]* ③ (naregulować) to adjust *[ostrość, zegarek]*; to set *[budzik]*; to tune *[radio, telewizor]*; to put [sth] on *[płytę]* ④ (przystosować) to gear ⑤ (usposobić) to predispose (**kogoś do czegoś** sb to a. towards sth); **być krytycznie do czegoś** ~**ionym** to have a critical attitude towards sth ⑥ Med. to set *[nogę, rękę]*

[II nastawić się — nastawiać się** (oczekiwać) ~**ić się na coś** to anticipate sth

nastawie|nie *n* (stosunek) attitude (**do czegoś** towards sth); **przyszedł z** ~**niem, że...** he came expecting that...

nast|ąpić *pf* — **nast|ępować** *impf vi* ① (nadepnąć) to step (**na coś** on sth) ② (pojawić się po kolei) ~**ępować po czymś** to follow sth ③ (zdarzyć się) to happen; ~**ąpił rozłam w partii** there was a break within the party

następc|a *m* successor; ~**a tronu** the heir to the throne

następnie [I *adv.* (potem) next, then

[II *part.* (poza tym) then

następn|y *adi.* (kolejny) next; (jeszcze jeden) another

następować *impf* → **nastąpić**

następstw|o *n* ① (wynik) result; **w** ~**ie czegoś** as a result of sth ② (kolejność) sequence

następując|y *adi.* (przy wymienianiu) the following

nastolat|ek *m,* ~**ka** *f* teenager; **problemy** ~**ków** teenage problems

nastr|oić *pf* — **nastr|ajać** *impf vt* ① (nastawić) to tune in *[radio, telewizor]* ② (usposobić) to predispose *[osobę]*

nastrojow|y *adi.* książk. romantic, atmospheric

nastrosz|yć [I *vt* (najeżyć) to bristle (up) *[sierść]*; to ruffle *[pióra]*; to rough up *[włosy]*

[II nastroszyć się** ① *[sierść]* to bristle (up); *[pióra]* to puff up; *[włosy]* to stand on end ② przen. *[osoba]* to bristle

nastr|ój *m* ① (samopoczucie) mood; **nie mieć** ~**oju** to be out of sorts; ~**oje społeczne** public feeling ② (atmosfera) mood

nasturcj|a *f* nasturtium

nasu|nąć *pf* — **nasu|wać** *impf* **[I]** *vt* (naciągnąć) to draw *[kołdrę]*; to put on *[pantofle, buty]*

[II] nasunąć się — **nasuwać się** *[podejrzenie]* to arise

nasy|cić *pf* — **nasy|cać** *impf* **[I]** *vt* [1] (zaspokoić) to satisfy *[głód, ciekawość]* [2] (przeniknąć) *[płyn, zapach]* to permeate [3] (wypełnić) to saturate *[substancję, rynek]*

[II] nasycić się — **nasycać się** [1] (najeść się) to eat one's fill; ~**cić się czymś** przen. to enjoy [sth] to the full [2] (przesiąknąć) to become permeated [3] *[substancja, rynek]* to become saturated

nasyłać *impf* → **nasłać**

nasyp *m* embankment

nasyp|ać *pf* — **nasyp|ywać** *impf* **[I]** *vt* (wsypać) to put *[cukier, piasek]*

[II] nasypać się — **nasypywać się** *[piasek, mąka]* to get

naszpik|ować *pf vt* to lard także przen. *[pieczeń, przemówienie]*; ~**ować kogoś lekarstwami** to stuff sb with drugs

naświetl|ić *pf* — **naświetl|ać** *impf* **[I]** *vt* [1] (napromieniować) to irradiate, to expose *[kliszę]* [2] (wyjaśnić) to elucidate *[sprawę]*

[II] naświetlić się — **naświetlać się** (kwarcówką) to take sunlamp treatment

na|sz [I] *pron.* (przed rzeczownikiem) our; (bez rzeczownika) ours

[II] nasi *plt* pot. (sportowcy) our side

[III] nasze *n* pot. what is ours; **wyszło na nasze** we were proved right in the end

[IV] po naszemu (swoim językiem) in our language; (swoim zwyczajem) our (own) way

naszkic|ować *pf vt* [1] (narysować) to sketch *[portret]* [2] (przedstawić) to outline *[teorię, sytuację]*

naszy|ć *pf* — **naszy|wać** *impf vt* to sew [sth] on *[kieszeń, łatę]*

naszyjnik *m* necklace

naszywać *impf* → **naszyć**

naszyw|ka *f* tab; Wojsk. stripe

naślad|ować *pf vt* [1] (wzorować się) to imitate; **postawa godna ~owania** exemplary behaviour [2] (udawać) to take off *[osobę]*; to mimic *[ruchy, miny]*

naśladownictw|o *n* imitation

natar|cie *n* attack, offensive

natarczyw|y *adi. grad.* [1] (natrętny) *[akwizytor, adorator]* importunate; *[pytania, żądania]* persistent [2] (drażniący) *[dźwięk]* *[ból]* nagging

natchn|ąć *pf vt* to inspire

natchnie|nie *n* inspiration

natęże|nie *n* [1] (barwy, światła) intensity; (dźwięku) volume; ~**nie prądu** amperage [2] (koncentracja) concentration; **w ~niu** intently

natęż|yć *pf* — **natęż|ać** *impf* **[I]** *vt* to strain *[słuch, wzrok]*

[II] natężyć się — **natężać się** (zrobić wysiłek) to make an effort

nat|ka *f* [1] (liście, łodyga) (vegetable) tops a. leaves [2] (pietruszka) parsley

natłok *m* [1] (tłok) crowd [2] (ogrom) multitude

natomiast *coni.* książk. [1] (podczas gdy) while, whereas [2] (ale) however, but

natrę|t *m* nuisance

natrętn|y *adi. grad.* [1] (naprzykrzający się) *[gość, sąsiad]* bothersome; *[dziecko]* pestering; *[podrywacz]* importunate; *[mucha, komar]* annoying [2] (uporczywy) *[zaczepki]* persistent; *[myśli]* obsessive

natrysk *m* [1] (prysznic) shower [2] Techn. spray shower

na|trzeć *pf* — **na|cierać** *impf* **[I]** *vt* natrzeć coś czymś to rub sth into sth

[II] *vi* (zaatakować) to attack (**na kogoś** sb)

[III] natrzeć się — nacierać się (posmarować się) natrzeć się czymś to rub sth into one's body

natu|ra *f* [1] (przyroda) nature [2] (cechy wrodzone, istota) nature; **z ~ry** by nature; **trudności ~ry technicznej** difficulties of a technical nature

naturalnie [I] *adv. grad.* (normalnie) *[zachowywać się]* naturally

[II] *adv.* (z natury) naturally

[III] *part.* (oczywiście) obviously

[IV] *inter.* of course

naturaln|y [I] *adi. grad.* (szczery) *[sposób bycia]* natural, unaffected

[II] *adi.* natural; **rzeźba ~ej wielkości** a full-size(d) a. full-scale sculpture

natury|sta *m*, ~**stka** *f* naturist

naturyzm *m* naturism

natychmiast *adv.* immediately

natychmiastow|y *adi.* immediate

nauczać *impf* → **nauczyć**

naucz|ka *f* lesson; **dostać (dobrą) ~kę** to learn one's lesson; **dać komuś ~kę** to teach sb a lesson

nauczyciel *m*, ~**ka** *f* teacher; ~ **historii/matematyki** a history/maths teacher

naucz|yć *pf* — **naucz|ać** *impf* **[I]** *vt* (przekazać wiedzę) to teach; ~**yć kogoś czytać** to teach sb (how) to read; ~**ony doświadczeniem** having learnt the lesson of experience

[II] nauczyć się to learn

nau|ka *f* [1] (wiedza) learning; (ścisła) science; (badania) research [2] (dziedzina) science; ~**ki medyczne** medical sciences [3] (edukacja) learning; (odrabianie lekcji) study; **mieć trudności w ~ce** to have learning difficulties; **robić postępy w ~ce** to make good progress with one's studies [4] (morał) lesson

naukow|iec *m* (badacz) researcher; (w naukach ścisłych i przyrodniczych) scientist

naukowo *adv. [zbadać, opisać]* scientifically; **pracować ~** (w naukach ścisłych) to work as a scientist a. researcher; (na uczelni) to be an academic

naukow|y *adi.* [1] *[dyscyplina, eksperyment]* scientific; **pracownik ~y** a researcher, a research worker;

stopień ~**y** a university a. an academic degree [2] (edukacyjny) **pomoce** ~**e** study aids

naumyślnie *adv.* deliberately

nausznik [] *m* (część czapki) ear flap [II] **nauszniki** *plt* (ear)muffs; (dźwiękoszczelne) noise muffs

naw|a *f* (główna) (central) nave; (boczna) (side) aisle

nawal|ić *pf* — **nawal|ać** *impf* pot. [] *vi* [1] (zawieść) to blow it pot. [2] (zepsuć się) *[urządzenie, samochód, wątroba]* to pack in a. up pot.; *[komputer]* to crash, to play up pot. [II] **nawalić się** — **nawalać się** (alkoholem, narkotykami) to get stoned pot.

nawa|ł *m* multitude; **mam** ~**ł pracy** I'm up to my eyes in work

nawałnic|a *f* książk. squall

nawet *part.* [1] (aż, choćby) even [2] (dosyć) rather; ~**, ~** pot. not bad

nawias *m* bracket; ~ **okrągły** parenthesis; **wziąć coś w** ~ to put sth in brackets; **wyciągnąć coś przed** ~ to take sth outside the brackets; **wyłączyć kogoś poza** ~ przen. to put sb on the sidelines ■ ~**em mówiąc** pot. by the way, incidentally

nawią|zać *pf* — **nawią|zywać** *impf* [] *vt* książk. to establish *[kontakt, współpracę]* (**z kimś** with sb); ~**zać z kimś znajomość** to make friends with sb [II] *vi* (odwołać się) to refer (**do czegoś** to sth) [III] **nawiązać się** — **nawiązywać się** *[przyjaźń, porozumienie]* to develop

nawiedz|ony *adi.* [1] (zwariowany) crazy pot. [2] *[dom]* haunted

nawierzchni|a *f* (road) surface

naw|ieźć *pf* — **naw|ozić** *impf vt* to fertilize *[ziemię]*

nawigacj|a *f* navigation

nawigato|r *m* navigator

nawijać *impf* → **nawinąć**

nawilżacz *m* (do powietrza) humidifier; **żelazko z** ~**em** a steam iron

nawilż|yć *pf* — **nawilż|ać** *impf vt* to dampen *[ubranie]*; to moisturize *[naskórek]*

nawi|nąć *pf* — **nawi|jać** *imp* [] *vt* to roll up *[sznur]*; ~**nąć nić na szpulkę** to spool a. reel (in) thread [II] **nawinąć się** — **nawijać się** pot. (trafić się) ~**nęła się okazja** an opportunity presented itself

nawl|ec *pf* — **nawl|ekać** *impf vt* (nanizać) to thread *[igłę, sznurowadła]*; ~**ec paciorki na nitkę** to string beads (on a thread)

naw|odnić *pf* — **naw|adniać** *impf vt* to water *[pola, uprawy]*; **kanały** ~**adniające** irrigation channels

nawoł|ywać *impf vt* to call także przen. *[osobę]* (**do czegoś** for sth)

nawozić *impf* → **nawieźć**

naw|óz *m* fertilizer; (zwierzęcy) manure

nawr|ócić *pf* — **nawr|acać** *impf* [] *vt* (zmienić wiarę) to convert także przen. (**kogoś na coś** sb to sth) [II] *vi* (powrócić) *[zima, objawy]* to return [III] **nawrócić się** — **nawracać się** (zmienić wiarę) to convert także przen. (**na coś** to sth)

nawr|ót *m* [1] (powrócenie) return; (choroby) recurrence [2] (zmiana kierunku) reversal

nawyk *m* habit; **z** ~**u** out of habit; **wejść komuś w** ~ to become a habit with sb

na wynos *[zamówić]* to take away GB, to go US

na wyrost [1] (przesadnie) **martwić się** ~ to worry beforehand [2] (za duży) **ubranie** ~ clothes with room to grow into

na wyrywki pot. (nie po kolei) at random

nawzajem [] *adv.* (wzajemnie) *[wspierać się, potrzebować się]* each other, one another; **wykluczać się** ~ to be mutually exclusive [II] *inter.* (the) same to you [III] **i nawzajem** *part.* **nie lubię jej i** ~ I don't like her and it's mutual

nazajutrz *adv.* książk. (on) the next a. following day

nazbiera|ć *pf* [] *vt* to pick a. pick up US *[grzybów, jagód]*; to round up *[ochotników]* [II] **nazbierać się** *[ludzie]* to gather; *[woda, kurz]* to collect

nazębn|y *adi.* **kamień** ~**y** tartar; **płytka** ~**a** (dental) plaque

naziemn|y *adi.* [1] *[personel, obsługa]* ground [2] Bot., Zool. terrestrial

nazw|a *f* name; **nadawać czemuś** ~**ę** to name sth; **tylko z** ~**y** in name only

naz|wać *pf* — **naz|ywać** *impf* [] *vt* [1] (nadać imię, określić) to call [2] (zwracać się) to call; ~**wać kogoś po imieniu** to call sb by their name [II] **nazywać się** [1] (mieć nazwę) to be called [2] (nosić imię, nazwisko) ~**ywam się Jan Kowalski** my name is Jan Kowalski; **jak się** ~**ywasz?** what's your name?

nazwisk|o *n* [1] (nazwa rodziny) surname, last name; ~**o panieńskie** the maiden name; ~**o po mężu** the married name; **moje** ~**o Kowalski** my name is Kowalski; **zwracać się do kogoś po** ~**u** to call sb by their surname [2] (znana osoba, sława) name; **wielkie** ~**a** great a. big names

nazywać *impf* → **nazwać**

negatyw *m* [1] (zdjęcie) negative [2] książk. (minus) disadvantage, negative

negatywn|y *adi.* negative

negliż *m* **w** ~**u** in a state of déshabillé a. undress

negocjacj|e *plt* negotiations

negocjato|r *m*, ~**rka** *f* negotiator

negocj|ować *impf vt* to negotiate

neg|ować *impf vt* książk. to negate, to deny

nekrolog *m* obituary (notice)

nekta|r *m* nectar także przen.

nektaryn|ka *f* nectarine

neon *m* ⟦1⟧ (reklama) neon light, neon sign ⟦2⟧ (gaz) neon

ner|ka *f* ⟦1⟧ Anat., Kulin. kidney ⟦2⟧ (naczynie) kidney dish

nerw ⟦I⟧ *m* ⟦1⟧ Anat. nerve ⟦2⟧ (zdolności) bent; **robić coś z ~em** to do sth with gusto a. verve ⟦3⟧ Bot. nerve, vein

⟦II⟧ **nerwy** *plt* nerves; **mieć mocne/słabe ~y** to have strong/weak nerves; **działać komuś na ~y** pot. to get on sb's nerves pot.; **~y mu puściły** pot. he lost his temper; **był (cały) w ~ach** pot. he was all nerves

nerwic|a *f* neurosis

nerwoból *m* neuralgia

nerwus *m* pot. bundle of nerves pot.

nesese|r *m* dressing case

netto ⟦I⟧ *adi. inv.* *[dochód, cena, waga]* net, nett GB

⟦II⟧ *adv. inv.* **zarobić dwa tysiące ~** to net two thousand

neurolo|g /new'rrolog/ *m* neurologist

neurologi|a /ˌnewro'logja/ *f* neurology

neuron /'newron/ *m* nerve cell

neutraliz|ować /ˌneutrali'zovatɕ/ *impf* ⟦I⟧ *vt* ⟦1⟧ (poddawać reakcji) to neutralize *[zasadę, kwas]* ⟦2⟧ (oczyszczać) to treat *[ścieki, odpady]* ⟦3⟧ (osłabiać) to neutralize *[wpływy, smak, osobę]*

⟦II⟧ **neutralizować się** ⟦1⟧ *[kwas, zasada]* to become neutral ⟦2⟧ (wzajemnie) *[wpływy, stanowiska]* to counteract each other

neutralnoś|ć /ˌneu'tralnoɕtɕ/ *f* neutrality

neutraln|y /ˌneu'tralnɨ/ *adi.* ⟦1⟧ (bezstronny) *[państwo, postawa]* neutral; *[obserwator]* impartial ⟦2⟧ (obojętny) *[substancja, kolor, słownictwo]* neutral

nę|cić *impf vt* (przyciągać) to entice (**kogoś czymś** sb with sth); **to go nie nęci** it holds no allure for him

nędz|a *f* ⟦1⟧ (materialna) poverty; **skrajna ~a** destitution ⟦2⟧ książk. (marność) misery ⟦3⟧ pot. (tandeta) trash

nędza|rz *m*, **~rka** *f* pauper

nędzn|y *adi. grad.* ⟦1⟧ (biedny) *[ubranie, meble]* poor ⟦2⟧ pot. (słaby, chory) *[postura, zwierzę]* meagre GB, meager US; *[roślina, kwiat]* sorry-looking ⟦3⟧ pot. (marny) *[jakość, ilość]* measly pot.; *[towar, film]* lousy pot.; *[hotel, kino]* seedy ⟦4⟧ pot. (mały) *[suma, porcja]* meagre GB, meager US; *[płaca, stawka]* measly pot.

nęka|ć *impf vt* to harass *[wroga, obywateli]*; *[prasa, dziennikarze]* to hound; *[niepewność, strach]* to gnaw at; *[problemy, wątpliwości]* to beset; *[choroby, kłopoty]* to plague

niańcz|yć *impf vt* ⟦1⟧ (opiekować się) to look after *[dziecko]* ⟦2⟧ pot., przen. to wet-nurse pot.

nia|ńka *f* nanny także przen.

niby ⟦I⟧ *praep.* (jak) like

⟦II⟧ *coni.* (jakby) as if, as though

⟦III⟧ *part.* ⟦1⟧ (jakoby) supposedly; (na pozór) apparently, seemingly; **~ racja** I guess it's true ⟦2⟧ (w pytaniach) **~ dlaczego?** why would that be?

⟦IV⟧ **na niby** (nie naprawdę) **bitwa na ~** a pretend battle; **robić coś na ~** to pretend to be doing sth

ni|c ⟦I⟧ *pron.* nothing; (w pytaniu) anything; **nic podobnego** nothing of the kind a. sort; **nic dziwnego, że...** it's no wonder that...; **szukaliśmy cały dzień, i nic** we were searching all day, all for nothing; **nic tu po tobie** you have no business being here; **nic takiego** nothing important; **to nic** never mind; **mieć kogoś za nic** to not care about sb; **z niczym** *[przyjść, odejść]* empty-handed; **być do niczego** pot. to be hopeless; **nic z tego** (nie uda się) it's no use; (nie ma mowy) no way! pot.; **nic, tylko płakać** it's enough to make you weep

⟦II⟧ *part.* (wcale) not a bit; **łzy nic tu nie pomogą** it's no use crying

⟦III⟧ *n* (o osobie) nobody; (o rzeczy) nothing

nicoś|ć *f* książk. nothingness

nicpoń *m* książk. ne'er-do-well

niczy|j *pron.* nobody's, no one's

ni|ć *f* thread; **nici chirurgiczne** (surgical) suture; **nici dentystyczne** dental floss

■ **grubymi nićmi szyte oskarżenia** pot. trumped-up charges; **z wycieczki wyszły nici** pot. nothing came of the trip

nie ⟦I⟧ *part.* ⟦1⟧ (z czasownikiem) not; **~ znam jej** I don't know her; **obawiam się, że ~** I'm afraid not; **wyszedł ~ płacąc** he left without paying; **~ to, że...** pot. (it's) not that... ⟦2⟧ (z rzeczownikiem) no, not; **to ~ żart** it's no joke, it's not a joke; **~ do pomyślenia** unthinkable; **to ~ do wiary** it's unbelievable ⟦3⟧ (z przymiotnikiem, przysłówkiem) not; **~ mniej niż 50 osób** no fewer than 50 people; **jeszcze ~** not yet; **już ~** no longer; **~ wiadomo kiedy/jak** no one knows when/how; **~ później niż we wtorek** on Tuesday at the latest

⟦II⟧ *inter.* ⟦1⟧ (odmowa, zaprzeczenie) no ⟦2⟧ pot. (szukanie potwierdzenia) **cieszysz się, (co) ~?** you're glad, aren't you? ⟦3⟧ (zakaz) no!, don't!; **~ i już** pot. 'no' means 'no'; **co to, to ~** pot. no way pot.

⟦III⟧ *coni.* (niezdecydowanie) or not; **jechać ~ jechać, sam nie wiem** should I stay or should I go? – I can't make up my mind

nieagresj|a *f* non-aggression

nieaktualn|y *adi.* *[dane, mapa, paszport]* out-of-date

nieapetyczn|y *adi.* *[potrawa, jedzenie]* unappetizing; *[zapach, wrażenie]* unsavoury; *[wygląd]* unappealing

nieatrakcyjn|y *adi.* unattractive

niebanaln|y *adi.* *[wygląd, cechy]* remarkable

niebezpieczeństw|o *n* (groźna sytuacja) danger; (ryzyko) hazard; **stanowić ~o dla kogoś** to pose a danger to sb

niebezpieczn|y *adi. grad.* ⟦1⟧ (zagrażający bezpieczeństwu) dangerous; **~y dla zdrowia** hazardous to health ⟦2⟧ (drażliwy) *[kwestia, temat]* sensitive

niebies|ki *adi.* [1] (błękitny) blue [2] *[ciało]* heavenly; *[południk]* celestial [3] (rajski) *[chóry, chwała]* heavenly

nieb|o *n* [1] (nad ziemią) sky; **na** ~**ie** in the sky [2] (raj) heaven

■ **być w siódmym** ~**ie** *pot.* to be in seventh heaven; **być o** ~**o lepszym od czegoś** to be worlds better than sth; **poruszyć** ~**o i ziemię** to move heaven and earth

nieboszcz|yk *m,* ~**ka** *f* corpse

niebrzyd|ki *adi. grad. [osoba]* not bad-looking; *[przedmiot]* rather nice

nieby|t *m* non-existence; **pogrążyć się w** ~**cie** *przen.* to sink into oblivion

niebywa|ły *adi.* książk. exceptional

nieca|ły *adi.* **za** ~**ły miesiąc** in less than a month; ~**ły kilometr** just under a kilometre

niecelny *adi. [strzał, podanie]* inaccurate

niecenzuralny *adi.* obscene

niech [I] *part.* [1] (w poleceniach, życzeniach) ~ **pomyślę** let me think; ~ **tylko spróbuje!** just let him try!; ~ **pani spocznie** please take a seat; ~ **będzie** oh, all right; ~ **się dzieje, co chce** come what may; **(a)** ~ **go!** *pot.* damn him! *pot.* [2] (oby) ~ **będą szczęśliwi!** may they be happy! [3] książk. (przypuśćmy) ~ **x = 45** let x equal 45

[II] *coni.* ~ **tylko zrobi się ciepło, to...** let's just wait till it gets warmer, then...

niechcący *adv.* accidentally

niechę|ć *f* [1] (brak ochoty) reluctance [2] (nieżyczliwość) dislike (**do kogoś** for sb)

niechętn|y *adi.* [1] (opieszały) reluctant [2] (nieprzyjazny) unfriendly

niechluj *m* pot. slob pot.

niechlujn|y *adi.* [1] (zaniedbany) *[osoba, ubranie]* slovenly; *[mieszkanie, biuro]* messy [2] (niestaranny) sloppy; *[praca, wykonanie]* shoddy

nieciekaw|y *adi.* [1] (nieinteresujący) *[książka, film]* boring [2] pot. (nieprzyjemny) *[sytuacja]* tough pot. [3] pot. (podejrzany) *[towarzystwo, przeszłość]* shady pot.

niecierpliw|ić się *impf v refl.* to be impatient

niecierpliwoś|ć *f* impatience

niecierpliw|y *adi.* impatient

nieco *adv., pron. inv.* (trochę) a (little) bit

niecodzienny *adi.* unusual

nieczu|ły *adi. [osoba]* unfeeling; **być** ~**łym na coś** to be unmoved by sth

nieczynn|y *adi. [telefon, winda]* out of order; *[bank, restauracja]* closed; *[wulkan]* inactive

nieczy|sty *adi.* [1] (nieuczciwy) *[interesy]* dirty; *[zamiary]* dubious; *[zagranie]* foul; **mieć** ~**ste sumienie** to have a guilty conscience [2] (niemoralny) unchaste [3] *[ton, dźwięk]* off-key

■ **siła** ~**sta** książk. sinister a. dark force

nieczyteln|y *adi.* książk. *[napis]* illegible; *[artykuł]* unintelligible

niedale|ki *adi.* [1] (bliski) *[miasto, błyskawice]* nearby [2] (krótki) *[podróż, droga]* short [3] (niedawny) *[wyda-*

rzenia] recent; (nadchodzący) *[termin, wybory]* (up)coming

niedaleko [I] *adv.* [1] (w przestrzeni) not far [2] (w czasie) not far off

[II] *praep.* [1] (w przestrzeni) near, not far from [2] (w czasie) near, close on

niedawn|o *adv.* recently; **do** ~**a** until recently; **od** ~**a** not for long

niedawn|y *adi.* [1] *[wydarzenie, znajomość]* recent [2] (byly) former

niedba|ły *adi. [osoba, strój, praca]* careless; *[gest, krok]* casual

niedelikatn|y *adi. [osoba, uwaga]* tactless

niedługo *adv.* [1] (krótko) briefly [2] (wkrótce) soon

niedob|ór *m* (substancji) deficiency; *[materiałów, ludzi]* shortage; ~**ory w kasie** a cash deficit

niedobran|y *adi. [małżeństwo]* mismatched

niedob|ry *adi. [wiadomość, pomysł]* bad; *[spojrzenie]* hostile

niedobrze *adv.* [1] (niewłaściwie) badly; **to** ~**, że...** it's bad that... [2] (niezdrowo) *[czuć się]* not well; ~ **mi** I feel sick; ~ **mi się robi** przen. it makes me sick; ~ **z nim** he's not doing well [3] (niewygodnie) *[czuć się]* uncomfortable [4] (nieefektownie) ~ **ci w niebieskim** blue doesn't suit you

niedojrzałoś|ć *f* immaturity

niedojrza|ły *adi.* [1] (biologicznie, emocjonalnie) *[osoba, zachowanie]* immature [2] *[owoc]* un(der)ripe, unripened [3] *[ser]* unmatured, unripe(ned)

niedokładn|y *adi.* [1] (niestaranny) *[wykonanie]* careless; *[osoba]* inaccurate [2] (przybliżony) *[obliczenie, pomiar]* approximate

niedol|a *f* książk. misery

niedołę|ga *m, f* pot. loser pot.

niedołężni|eć *impf vi* to become infirm

niedołężn|y *adi. grad.* [1] (niesprawny) *[osoba]* infirm [2] (nieudolny) *[styl, usiłowania]* clumsy

niedomaga|ć *impf vi* książk. (chorować) to be in poor health; przen. *[gospodarka]* to be ailing

niedomówie|nie *n* unclear situation; **mówić bez** ~**ń** to speak plainly

niedomyśln|y *adi. [osoba]* unperceptive

niedopał|ek *m* butt(-end)

niedopatrze|nie *n* (przeoczenie) oversight; (niedbałość) negligence

niedopowiedze|nie *n* pełno było ~**ń** a lot remained unsaid

niedopuszczaln|y *adi.* unacceptable

niedoraj|da *m, f* pot. (niezręczny) clodhopper pot.; (niezaradny) loser pot.

niedoro|sły *adi. [zachowanie, osobnik]* immature

niedorozwinię|ty *adi.* [1] (upośledzony) retarded [2] (niewykształcony) *[narząd]* underdeveloped

niedorzeczn|y *adi.* preposterous

niedoskona|ły *adi.* imperfect

niedosłyszaln|y *adi.* inaudible

niedosłysz|eć *impf vi* to be hard of hearing

niedostatecznie *adv.* insufficiently
niedostateczn|y [] *adi.* [] *[ilość]* insufficient
[2] *(stopień)* **ocena** ~**a** a fail
[] *m (stopień)* fail
niedostat|ek *m* [] (bieda) privation; **żyć w** ~**ku** to
live in want [2] (niedociągnięcie) deficiency [3] (niedobór)
scarcity
niedostępn|y *adi.* [] (trudny do zdobycia) *[towar,
usługa]* unavailable; (zbyt kosztowny) unaffordable
[2] (nieosiągalny) *[szczyt, region]* inaccessible [3] (nieprzystępny) *[osoba]* unapproachable
niedostrzegaln|y *adi.* imperceptible
niedosz|ły *adi.* [] (odwołany) cancelled; ~**ły wyjazd**
a trip that never happened [2] (niespełniony) *[artysta,
bohater]* would-be
niedoświadcz|ony *adi.* inexperienced
niedotlenieni|e *n* hypoxia
niedoucz|ony *adi.* poorly educated
niedowiar|ek *m* pot. doubter
niedowi|dzieć *impf vi* to have poor a. bad
eyesight
niedozwol|ony *adi.* (zabroniony przez prawo) *[działa-
nia, działalność]* unlawful; (zakazany przepisami) *[chwyt,
środki]* prohibited
niedożywi|ony *adi.* malnourished
niedro|gi *adi.* inexpensive
niedrożn|y *adi.* blocked
niedużo [] *adv.* not much
[] *pron.* (z policzalnymi) not many; (z niepoliczalnymi) not
much
niedu|ży *adi. [pensja, dom]* rather small; *[osoba,
postura]* rather short
niedyskretn|y *adi.* indiscreet
niedysponowan|y *adi.* indisposed
niedyspozycj|a *f* indisposition
niedziel|a *f* Sunday
niedźwiedzic|a *f* Zool. female bear
❑ **Mała Niedźwiedzica** the Little Bear, Ursa
Minor; **Wielka Niedźwiedzica** the Great Bear,
Ursa Major
niedźwie|dź *m* bear
nieefektown|y *adi.* unattractive
nieekonomiczn|y *adi.* uneconomical
nieeleganc|ki *adi. [osoba, strój, zachowanie]* inele-
gant
niefachow|y *adi.* [] (niespecjalistyczny) nonspecialist
[2] (niewykwalifikowany) *[pracownik]* unqualified [3] (źle
wykonany) amateurish
nieformaln|y *adi.* informal
niegłupi *adi.* pot. (quite) smart pot.
niego|dny *adi.* książk. [] (niewart) unworthy (**czegoś**
of sth); ~**dny uwagi** undeserving of attention;
~**dzien mężczyzny** unmanly [2] (nikczemny) despicable
niegrzeczn|y *adi.* grad. *[osoba, uwaga]* impolite;
[dziecko, zachowanie] naughty
nieistotn|y *adi.* książk. irrelevant

niejadaln|y *adi.* inedible
niejad|ek *m* pot. poor eater
nieja|ki *pron.* książk. [] (bliżej nieznany) a (certain);
~**ki pan Kowalski** a Mr Kowalski [2] (pewien)
certain
nieja|sny *adi.* vague
niejawn|y *adi. [obrady]* secret
niejed|en *pron.* more than one; ~**en raz** more
than once
niejednoznaczn|y *adi.* ambiguous
niekiedy *adv.* sometimes
niekompetentn|y *adi.* incompetent
niekompletn|y *adi.* incomplete
niekonsekwentn|y *adi.* inconsistent
niekorzystn|y *adi.* grad. *[transakcja, umowa]*
disadvantageous; *[położenie, decyzja, wrażenie]* unfavourable GB, unfavorable US
niektó|ry [] *pron.* some; **w** ~**rych przypadkach**
in some cases
[] **niektórzy** *plt* some; ~**rzy mówią, że...** some
(people) say that...
nielegaln|y *adi.* illegal
nieletni [] *adi.* under age
[] **nieletni** *m,* ~**a** *f* minor; **przestępczość** ~**ch**
juvenile delinquency
nieliczn|y [] *adi. [grupa, oddział]* small; *[znajomi,
przechodnie]* few; *[przypadki]* rare
[] **nieliczni** *plt* few; **jeden z** ~**ych, którzy...** one
of the few who...
nielojaln|y *adi.* disloyal
nieludz|ki *adi.* [] (okrutny) inhumane [2] (ogromny)
[wysiłek] superhuman
nieładn|y *adi.* [] (brzydki) ugly [2] (niedobry) *[czyn,
postępek, zachowanie]* nasty
niełatw|y *adi. [zadanie]* rather hard; **być** ~**ym we
współżyciu** *[osoba]* to not be easy to get along with
nie|mal, ~**omal** *part.* almost
niemało [] *pron.* quite a lot (**czegoś** of sth)
[] *adv.* a good deal
niema|ły *adi. [ogród, mieszkanie]* quite big; *[zyski,
koszty]* considerable; *[problem, błąd]* serious
niemi|ły *adi. [osoba, sytuacja]* disagreeable; *[głos,
uczucie]* unpleasant
niemo *adv.* silently
niemoc *f* (bezsilność) impotence; ~ **twórcza**
artist's block
niemodn|y *adi. [strój]* unfashionable; *[poglądy]*
outmoded
niemoraln|y *adi.* immoral
niem|owa *m, f* [] (niemy) mute [2] pot., żart. (osoba
małomówna) taciturn person
niemowl|ę *n* infant; **odżywki dla** ~**ąt** baby food
niemożliw|y [] *adi.* [] (nierealny) impossible [2] pot.
(nieznośny) *[osoba]* impossible
[] **niemożliwe** *adi.* praed. impossible; **to** ~, **żeby
był złodziejem** he can't possibly be a thief

niem|y *adi.* [1] (niemówiący) mute; ~**y z oburzenia** przen. speechless with indignation [2] (niewyrażony słowami) *[gest, rozpacz]* silent

nienagann|y *adi.* *[wymowa, postawa]* impeccable

nienasyc|ony *adi.* [1] *[osoba, głód]* insatiable [2] *[tłuszcz, roztwór]* unsaturated

nienaturaln|y *adi.* unnatural

nienawi|dzić *impf* [1] *vt* to hate
[1] **nienawidzić się** [1] (samego siebie) to hate oneself [2] (siebie nawzajem) to hate each other

nienawiś|ć *f* hate, hatred

nieobecnoś|ć *f* absence; **podczas mojej** ~**ci** during a. in my absence

nieobecn|y [1] *adi.* *[uczeń, pracownik]* absent; **być** ~**ym w szkole/pracy** to be absent from school/ work [2] (zamyślony) *[osoba]* remote; *[uśmiech]* absent; *[spojrzenie]* distant
[1] **nieobecn|y** *m*, ~**a** *f* (na zebraniu) absentee; (na zajęciach) absent student

nieobliczaln|y *adi.* [1] *[osoba, konsekwencje]* unpredictable [2] *[straty]* incalculable

nieoby|ty *adi.* [1] (niewyrobiony) *[osoba]* gauche [2] (nieobeznany) unfamiliar (**z czymś** with sth)

nieoceni|ony *adi.* *[przyjaciel, pomoc]* invaluable; *[korzyść, wkład]* inestimable

nieoczekiwan|y *adi.* unexpected

nieodmienn|y *adi.* [1] (niezmienny) invariable [2] Jęz. uninflected, invariable

nieodpowiedzialn|y *adi.* irresponsible

nieodwołaln|y *adi.* *[wyrok, decyzja]* irrevocable; *[konsekwencja, wpływ]* irreversible; *[katastrofa]* inevitable

nieodwracaln|y *adi.* *[uszkodzenie]* irreparable; *[proces]* irreversible

nieoficjaln|y *adi.* [1] (nieurzędowy) *[spotkanie, wiadomość]* unofficial [2] (prywatny) *[strój, wizyta]* informal

nieograniczon|y *adi.* *[władza, ilość]* unlimited; *[zapas, rezerwy]* limitless; *[energia, zapał]* boundless

nieokreśl|ony *adi.* [1] (niewyraźny) *[uczucie, tęsknota]* vague; *[kształt, dźwięk]* indefinable; **bliżej** ~**ony** undetermined [2] (nieustalony) *[wartość, długość, stopień]* unspecified; *[status, okres, czas]* indefinite; **umowa na czas** ~**ony** an open-ended contract

nieomyln|y *adi.* infallible; *[sygnał, znak]* sure

nieopanowan|y *adi.* *[osoba, charakter]* quick-tempered; *[śmiech, gniew]* uncontrollable

nieopłacaln|y *adi.* unprofitable

nieosiągaln|y *adi.* [1] (niedostępny) *[cel, ideał]* unattainable; *[towar]* unobtainable [2] (nieobecny) *[szef, wierzyciel]* unavailable

nieost|ry *adi.* [1] (tępy) blunt [2] (niewyraźny) *[fotografia, obraz]* fuzzy [3] (niejasny) *[kryteria, granice]* vague

niepaląc|y [1] *adi.* non-smoking
[1] **niepaląc|y** *m*, ~**a** *f* non-smoker

nieparzy|sty *adi.* [1] (niepodzielny przez dwa) *[liczba, dni]* odd [2] (nie w parze) *[gracz, chromosom]* unpaired

niepełnoletni [1] *adi.* under-age
[1] **niepełnoletni** *m*, ~**a** *f* minor

niepełnosprawn|y [1] *adi.* *[osoba]* disabled
[1] **niepełnosprawn|y** *m*, ~**a** *f* disabled person; ~**i** the disabled

niepełn|y *adi.* *[szklanka, zbiornik]* partially filled; *[dane, adres]* incomplete; ~**y miesiąc** not quite a month

niepewnie *adv.* *[chodzić, stać]* unsteadily; *[spoglądać, uśmiechać się]* uncertainly; **czuć się** ~ to feel insecure

niepew|ny *adi.* [1] *[przyszłość, pogoda, zysk]* uncertain; *[posada]* insecure; *[dane, metoda, sojusznik]* unreliable, uncertain [2] (niespokojny) *[osoba]* unsure; ~**ny siebie** unsure of oneself; **być** ~**nym jutra** to be unsure of tomorrow [3] (nieśmiały, niezdecydowany) *[krok, głos]* hesitant; *[mina]* uncertain

niepijąc|y [1] *adi.* non-drinking, teetotal
[1] **niepijąc|y** *m*, ~**a** *f* non-drinker, teetotaller GB, teetotaler US

niepłodn|y *adi.* *[kobieta, mężczyzna, zwierzę, gleba]* infertile; **okres** ~**y** the safe period

niepoczytaln|y *adi.* *[osoba]* insane, non compos (mentis)

niepodległoś|ć *f* independence

niepodleg|ły *adi.* *[kraj]* independent

niepodobn|y *adi.* dissimilar, unalike; **są zupełnie** ~**i do siebie** they're totally unlike each other a. totally unlike
■ **to do niej** ~**e** pot. that's unlike her

niepodważaln|y *adi.* *[fakt, prawda]* indisputable; *[argument]* irrefutable; *[zaleta, autorytet]* unquestionable

niepodzieln|y *adi.* *[wyraz, część]* indivisible; *[władza]* undivided

niepogo|da *f* bad weather; przen. bad climate

niepohamowan|y *adi.* *[śmiech, chęć]* uncontrollable; *[ciekawość]* unbridled

niepoję|ty *adi.* incomprehensible

niepok|oić *impf* [1] *vt* [1] (wywoływać niepokój) to worry [2] (zakłócać spokój) to bother
[1] **niepokoić się** to worry (**o coś** about a. over sth); to be worried (**o kogoś** about sb)

niepokojąc|y *adi.* *[objawy, wieści]* worrying; *[cisza, urok]* disturbing

niepokonan|y *adi.* *[zawodnik]* undefeated; *[armia]* invincible; *[strach]* unconquerable; *[przeszkoda]* insurmountable

niepok|ój *m* [1] (obawa) anxiety; **dawać powody do** ~**oju** to give cause for concern [2] (niezadowolenie) unrest; ~**oje społeczne** social unrest

niepoprawn|y *adi.* [1] *[odpowiedź, nazwa]* incorrect [2] *[romantyk, optymista]* incurable

nieporadn|y *adi.* *[osoba]* inept; *[ruchy]* awkward

nieporozumie|nie *n* [1] misunderstanding; ~**nia rodzinne** domestic misunderstandings [2] pot. (błąd) (big) mistake

nieporząd|ek *m* mess

nieporządn|y *adi. grad. [dziecko, pismo]* messy; *[pracownik]* careless; *[praca]* slipshod

niepoważnie *adv. [zachowywać się]* frivolously; *[postępować]* irresponsibly

niepoważn|y *adi. [osoba, zachowanie]* flippant

niepowodze|nie *n* failure; **zakończyć się** ~**niem** to end in failure

niepowołan|y *adi. [osoba, użycie]* unauthorized

niepozorn|y *adi.* inconspicuous

niepraktyczn|y *adi.* impractical

niepraw|da [] *f* untruth; **to** ~**da, że...** it's untrue a. not true that...

[] *inter.* [] (sprzeciw) that's not true! [] (w pytaniach) **mam rację,** ~**da(ż)?** I'm right, aren't I?

nieprawdopodobn|y *adi.* [] *[historia, wiadomość]* unlikely, improbable [] *(niezwykły) [bogactwo, szczęście]* incredible

nieprawdziw|y *adi.* [] *(zmyślony) [zarzut, adres]* false [] *(sztuczny) [biżuteria, banknot]* fake

nieprawidłow|y *adi. [odpowiedź, decyzja]* incorrect; *[kolejność, dieta]* wrong; *[gen, przemiana materii]* abnormal

nieprędko *adv.* [] (za długi czas) not soon [] (wolno) slowly

nieprosz|ony *adi.* uninvited; **przyszedł** ~**ony** he came uninvited

nieprzemakaln|y *adi.* waterproof; przen. *[osoba]* impervious to argument

nieprzerwan|y *adi.* [] (nieustanny) incessant [] (jednolity) uninterrupted

nieprzyjaci|el *m* enemy

nieprzyjaciels|ki *adi. [obóz, armia]* enemy

nieprzyja|zny *adi. [osoba, stosunek]* unfriendly; *[warunki, klimat]* unfavourable GB, unfavorable US

nieprzyjemn|y *adi. grad.* unpleasant

nieprzytomn|y *adi.* [] (nieświadomy) *[osoba]* unconscious; *[wyraz twarzy]* vacant; ~**y ze strachu** przen. numb(ed) with fear; ~**y z radości** przen. delirious with joy [] przen. (gwałtowny) *[hałas, pęd]* mad

nieprzyzwoi|ty *adi.* indecent

niepunktualn|y *adi.* unpunctual

nierad *adi. praed.* książk. displeased

nieraz *adv.* [] (często) a number of times [] (czasem) once in a while

nierdzewn|y *adi.* stainless

nierealn|y *adi. [świat, postać]* unreal; *[plan, marzenie]* unrealistic

nierówn|y *adi.* [] (niegładki) *[ściana, teren, pismo]* uneven; ~**a droga** a bumpy road [] (różny jakościowo) erratic [] (nierytmiczny) *[tempo, rytm, oddech]* uneven, irregular [] (niejednakowy) *[podział, odstępy]* uneven, unequal

nieruchom|y *adi.* [] (nieporuszający się) *[tłum]* motionless; *[twarz]* unmoved [] (umocowany na stałe) fixed

niesamodzieln|y *adi.* [] (niezaradny) *[osoba]* dependent [] (podległy) *[państwo]* dependent

niesamowi|ty *adi.* [] (niezwykły) *[sen, widok, historia]* amazing [] (budzący podziw) *[kobieta, pamięć, wieczór]* remarkable

niesforn|y *adi. [dziecko, włosy]* unruly

nieskomplikowan|y *adi.* uncomplicated

nieskończonoś|ć *f* infinity; **w** ~**ć** ad infinitum, endlessly

nieskończ|ony *adi. [przestrzeń, pustynia]* endless; *[nędza, bogactwo]* infinite

niesmaczn|y *adi.* tasteless także przen.

niespodzian|ka *f* surprise; **zrobić komuś** ~**kę** to spring a surprise on sb

niespokojn|y *adi. grad.* [] (ruchliwy) *[osoba, wzrok, ruchy]* restless [] (zmartwiony) *[osoba]* worried [] (gwałtowny) *[czasy]* turbulent

niesprawiedliwoś|ć *f* injustice

niesprawiedliw|y *adi. grad.* unfair

niesprawn|y *adi. [osoba]* disabled; *[noga, ręka]* crippled; *[organ]* malfunctioning; *[urządzenie]* faulty

niestety *part.* unfortunately

niestrawnoś|ć *f* indigestion

niestrawn|y *adi.* [] Med. indigestible [] przen. *[styl, film]* unpalatable

nieswojo *adv.* **czuć się** ~ to feel uncomfortable

nieszczer|y *adi.* insincere

nieszczęś|cie *n* [] (tragedia) tragedy [] (pech) bad luck; **na** ~**cie** unfortunately

nieszczęśliw|y [] *adi. grad.* [] *[osoba]* (cierpiący) unhappy; (godny współczucia) poor; *[mina]* miserable [] (niepomyślny) *[dzieciństwo, miłość]* unhappy [] *adi.* (przynoszący niepowodzenie) *[lot, wypadek]* illfated; (pechowy) unlucky

nieszkodliw|y *adi.* harmless także przen.

nieścisłoś|ć *f* inaccuracy

ni|eść *impf* [] *vt* [] *[osoba, rzeka, wiatr]* to carry *[przedmiot, osobę]* [] książk. (ofiarowywać) to bring *[pociechę, pomoc, ulgę]* [] (zawierać) to carry *[ryzyko]* [] pot. *[kura]* to lay *[jaja]* [] *vi* Wojsk. *[działo, karabin, łuk]* to carry [] **nieść się** książk. [] (rozprzestrzeniać się) *[zapach, dźwięk]* to spread [] (przemieszczać się) *[chmury, łódź]* to drift [] *[kura]* to lay eggs

nieślubn|y *adi. [dziecko]* illegitimate

nieśmia|ły *adi. [osoba, uśmiech, głos]* shy

nieśmierteln|y *adi.* [] (wieczny) immortal [] przen. *[spór, temat]* everlasting; *[parasol, kapelusz]* inevitable żart.

nieświadomoś|ć *f* unawareness; **utrzymywać kogoś w** ~**ci** to keep sb ignorant

nieświadom|y *adi.* [] *[osoba]* unaware (**czegoś** of sth) [] (podświadomy) *[ruchy, motywy]* subconscious

nieśwież|y *adi.* [] *[mięso, ryba, jajka]* bad; *[mleko]* sour; *[masło]* rancid; *[chleb, ciastka]* stale; *[sałata, kapusta]* tired [] *[pościel, bielizna, ubranie]* dirty, soiled [3] *[osoba]* untidy [4] (nieoryginalny) *[pomysł, temat]* unoriginal; *[dowcip, frazes, zwrot]* stale [5] pot. (nieaktualny) *[informacje, wiadomości]* stale

nietak|t *m* gaffe; **to był ~t** it was tactless

nietaktown|y *adi.* tactless

nietknię|ty *adi. [budowla, posiłek, suma]* intact, untouched; *[praca]* untouched

nietoperz *m* bat

nietowarzys|ki *adi.* unsociable

nietrwa|ły *adi. [sojusz, kolor, struktura]* impermanent; *[związek, romans]* passing; *[towar]* perishable

nietrzeźw|y **I** *adi. [osoba]* intoxicated

II **nietrzeźw|y** *m*, **~a** *f* intoxicated person

nietykaln|y *adi.* **być ~ym** *[osoba]* to have immunity

nietypow|y *adi. [składnik, objaw]* untypical; *[zachowanie, reakcja]* uncharacteristic; *[przedstawiciel, egzemplarz]* atypical

nieuchronn|y *adi.* inevitable

nieuchwytn|y *adi.* [1] *[zbieg, szczęście, cel]* elusive [2] (nieokreślony) *[wpływ, wdzięk]* indefinable; *[różnice]* indiscernible; *[kształt, pojęcie]* vague; *[dźwięk, zapach]* imperceptible

nieuczciwoś|ć *f* dishonesty

nieuczciw|y *adi. [osoba, zachowanie, interes]* dishonest; **~a konkurencja** unfair competition

nieudaczni|k *m* pot. loser pot.

nieudoln|y *adi. [zarządzanie, wiersz]* inept; *[amator, debiutant]* bungling; *[urzędnik, rząd]* ineffectual

nieufn|y *adi.* (podejrzliwy) mistrustful; (niedowierzający) distrustful (**wobec kogoś/czegoś** of sb/sth)

nieugię|ty *adi. [przeciwnik, opór]* staunch; *[polityk, upór]* pertinacious książk.; *[wiara, postawa]* unyielding; *[charakter, wola]* indomitable

nieuk *m* (głupiec) ignoramus; (w szkole) dunce

nieuleczaln|y *adi. [choroba, schorzenie]* incurable; pot. *[głupota, lenistwo]* hopeless

nieumyśln|y *adi.* unintentional

nieurodzaj *m* crop failure, poor harvest

nieurodzajn|y *adi. [gleba, region]* infertile

nieustając|y *adi. [pomoc]* incessant; *[ból, presja]* unrelenting; *[stres, walka]* constant

nieustann|y *adi. [zmiany, opady]* ceaseless; *[stres, walka]* constant

nieuwa|ga *f* inattention; **przez ~gę** accidentally

nieuważnie *adv. [słuchać, czytać]* inattentively; *[pracować]* carelessly

nieuważn|y *adi. [uczeń, słuchacz]* inattentive; *[ruch, krok]* careless

nieużyt|ek *m* (teren) wasteland

niewar|t *adi. praed.* [1] (o mniejszej wartości) not worthy; **nic ~t** worthless [2] (niegodny) unworthy (**czegoś** of sth)

niewdzięczn|y *adi. [osoba]* ungrateful; *[zadanie]* thankless

niewiadom|a *f* unknown (quantity)

niewiarygodn|y *adi.* [1] *[świadek]* unreliable [2] (nieprawdopodobny) incredible

niewidom|y **I** *adi.* blind

II **niewidom|y** *m*, **~a** *f* blind person

niewidzialn|y *adi.* invisible

niewiedz|a *f* ignorance

niewiel|e **I** *pron.* (z niepoliczalnymi) not much; (z policzalnymi) not many

II *adv.* (trochę) not much

niewiel|ki *adi. [grupa, miejscowość]* rather small; *[majątek, szansa]* little

niewiern|y **I** *adi.* [1] *[mąż, żona]* unfaithful [2] *[przekład, relacja]* inaccurate

II **niewiern|y** *m*, **~a** *f* infidel

niewierząc|y **I** *adi.* non-believing

II **niewierząc|y** *m*, **~a** *f* non-believer

niewinn|y **I** *adi.* [1] (bez winy) *[osoba, mina]* innocent [2] (nieszkodliwy) *[żart, rozrywka]* inoffensive

II **niewinn|y** *m*, **~a** *f* innocent person

niewłaściw|y *adi.* wrong

niewol|a *f* [1] (brak wolności) bondage [2] (uwięzienie) captivity; **dostać się do ~i** to be captured a. taken prisoner; **wziąć kogoś do ~i** to capture sb, to take sb prisoner

niewolnictw|o *n* slavery

niewolni|k *m*, **~ca** *f* slave także przen.

niewybredn|y *adi.* [1] (niewymagający) *[osoba]* undiscriminating [2] (pospolity) *[gust]* unrefined; *[słowa, ataki]* vulgar

niewychowan|y *adi. [osoba]* ill-mannered

niewyczerpan|y *adi.* inexhaustible

niewydarz|ony *adi.* pot. *[osoba]* inept; *[pomysł]* half-baked

niewyg|oda *f* discomfort

niewygodn|y *adi. [ubranie, łóżko]* uncomfortable; *[dojazd, termin, fakty]* inconvenient

niewykształc|ony *adi.* uneducated

niewymusz|ony *adi. [wesołość, styl]* unaffected; *[wdzięk]* unforced

niewypa|ł *m* [1] Wojsk. unexploded shell [2] pot. (fiasko) washout

niewypłacaln|y *adi.* insolvent

niewyraźnie *adv.* (słabo) indistinctly; **czuć się ~** (o zdrowiu) to feel unwell; (niepewnie) to feel ill at ease

niewyraźn|y *adi.* [1] *[zarys, postać, głos]* indistinct [2] pot. *[osoba]* (chory) out of sorts; (nieswój) uneasy [3] pot. (podejrzany) *[typ, przeszłość]* fishy pot.

niewyrobi|ony *adi. [osoba]* inexperienced; *[ręka]* untrained

niewyży|ty *adi. [ambicja]* insatiable; *[osoba]* indefatigable

niewzrusz|ony *adi.* [1] (nieugięty) *[osoba]* unmoved; *[twarz, spojrzenie]* stony [2] (niezmienny) *[przyjaźń]* steadfast; *[wiara, zaufanie]* unshaken

niezależnie *adv.* [1] (samodzielnie) *[żyć, myśleć]* independently; **~ od siebie** independently of each other [2] (bez względu) regardless (**od czegoś** of sth)

niezależn|y adi. [1] [kraj, osoba] independent; (materialnie) [osoba] self-supporting [2] (niepowiązany) [zjawiska, procesy] independent (**od czegoś** of sth)

niezamężn|y adi. [kobieta] unmarried

niezapominaj|ka f forget-me-not

niezapomnian|y adi. unforgettable

niezastąpi|ony adi. [część, narzędzie] irreplaceable; [asystent, pomoc] indispensable

niezawodn|y adi. [1] [urządzenie, system, przyjaciel] reliable; [instynkt, umiejętność] unfailing; [metoda, plan] foolproof; [pamięć, lekarstwo] infallible [2] (pewny) [oznaka, zapowiedź] sure

niezbadan|y adi. [przyczyny, tajemnica] unfathomable; [początki, przyszłość] obscure

niezbędn|y adi. grad. indispensable

niezbi|ty adi. [dowód] irrefutable

niezbyt adv. [dobry, bogaty, ciekawy] not very; [wysilić się, kwapić się] not too much

niezda|ra m, f pot. butterfingers pot.

niezdarn|y adi. [osoba, ruch] clumsy; [rysunek, rzeźba] artless

niezdecydowa|nie n indecision

niezdecydowan|y adi. [1] [osoba] (zwlekający z decyzją) undecided; (niezdolny do decydowania) indecisive; [odpowiedź, mina] irresolute; [ruch, krok] hesitant [2] (nieokreślony) [kolor] indeterminate; [pogoda] unsettled

niezdolnoś|ć f inability

niezdoln|y adi. [1] (niemogący) incapable (**do czegoś** of sth); (niezdatny) unfit (**do czegoś** for sth) [2] (tępy) [uczeń] slow(-witted)

niezdr|owy adi. [osoba, cera, jedzenie] unhealthy; [podniecenie, ciekawość] unwholesome, unhealthy

niezgo|da f [1] (konflikt) disagreement; **siać** ~**dę** to sow discord; **stać w** ~**dzie z czymś** przen. to be at odds a. variance with sth; **być kością** ~**dy** to be a bone of contention [2] (brak aprobaty) disagreement (**na coś** with sth)

niezgrabn|y adi. [1] (nieproporcjonalny) [dziewczyna, figura] unshapely; [budynek, meble] heavy; [przedmiot, model] clumsy; [płaszcz, futro] cumbersome; [bluzka, sweter] shapeless [2] (niezdarny) [ruch, krok, gest] awkward

niezlicz|ony adi. innumerable

nie|zły adi. pot. [1] (dość dobry) [uczeń, film, pomysł] pretty good pot. [2] (oceniany pozytywnie) [samochód, obiad] great pot. [3] (spory) [porcja, ilość] decent

niezmienn|y adi. [uczucia, tradycja, przekonania] unchanging

nieznaczn|y adi. [wzrost, spadek] slight; [rola] minor

**nieznajom|y [] adi. [osoba] strange; [zapach, okolica] unfamiliar

[] nieznajom|y m, ~**a** f stranger

nieznan|y [] adi. unknown

[] nieznane n the unknown; **jechać w** ~**e** to go into unknown

nieznośn|y adi. [1] [ból, upał] unbearable [2] [dziecko, uczeń] troublesome

niezręczn|y adi. [1] (niezdarny) [osoba, ruchy, ukłon] clumsy [2] (nieudolny) [polityk, mediator] inept [3] (niestosowny) [żart, pytanie] inappropriate; [milczenie, sytuacja] awkward

niezrozumia|ły adi. [wykład, słowa] incomprehensible; [zachowanie, lęk] inexplicable

niezupełnie [] adv. not quite

[] inter. not really

niezupełn|y adi. [sukces] incomplete

niezwykle adv. (dziwnie) unusually; (bardzo) extremely

niezwyk|ły adi. [osoba, czyn] unusual; [upór, dobroć, siła] extraordinary

nieźle adv. pot. [1] (dość dobrze) quite well, not bad [2] (świetnie) very well [3] (bardzo) pretty pot.; ~ **się upił** he got pretty drunk

nieżona|ty [] adi. [mężczyzna] unmarried

[] m bachelor

nieży|t m catarrh; ~**t żołądka** gastritis

nieżyw|y adi. dead

nigdy pron. never; (w pytaniu) ever; ~ **więcej** never again; ~ **przenigdy** never ever; **jak gdyby** ~ **nic** (beztrosko) as if nothing had happened; (bez wysiłku) with the greatest of ease

nigdzie pron. nowhere; (w pytaniu) anywhere; **jak** ~ **indziej** unlike anywhere else

nihilizm m nihilism

nija|ki adi. pot. [osoba, życie, styl] unremarkable; [smak, jedzenie] insipid

nijako adv. pot. [1] (bezbarwnie) dully [2] (niezręcznie) **jakoś** ~ **było wyjść** it didn't feel right to leave

nik|iel m nickel

nik|ły adi. grad. [dźwięk, uśmiech] faint

nik|nąć impf vi to disappear

nikotyn|a f nicotine

nik|t [] pron. nobody, no one; (po przeczeniu, w pytaniu) anybody, anyone; ~**t z nas** none of us; **jak** ~**t** like no one a. nobody (else);

[] m a nobody

nimf|a f nymph

nios|ka f laying hen

ni|ski adi. grad. [1] (nieduży) [budynek, cena, temperatura] low; [wzrost, osoba] short [2] książk. (mało znaczący) [stanowisko, ranga] low; [pochodzenie, status] humble [3] [dźwięk] low, deep [4] książk. (niemoralny) [pobudka, motyw] low, base

ni|sko adv. grad. [1] [schylić się, ukłonić się] low [2] [brzmieć] low; **śpiewać za nisko** to sing flat [3] (słabo) **nisko oprocentowany** low-interest; **nisko coś oceniać** to have a low opinion of sth

niszcz|eć impf vi [budynek, urządzenia] to deteriorate; [gleba, środowisko] to decay

niszcz|yć impf **I** vt **1** (likwidować) to destroy *[dowody, budynek]* **2** (zużywać) to wear out *[sprzęt, narzędzia, buty]* **3** (osłabiać) *[choroba, alkohol]* to ruin *[osobę, zdrowie, życie]*

II niszczyć się *[budynek, samochód, rower]* to deteriorate; *[ubrania, buty]* to wear out

ni|t m rivet

nit|ka f **1** (nić) thread **2** Bot. filament

■ **nie zostawić na kimś suchej ~ki** pot. to tear sb to pieces a. shreds

niuans m nuance

nizin|a f lowland, lowlands

niż¹ m **1** Meteo. depression, low **2** (nizina) lowland, lowlands

❏ **~ demograficzny** Stat. population decline

niż² **I** coni. **1** (w wyższym stopniu) than **2** (raczej) (rather) than

II praep. than

no pot. inter. **1** (w odpowiedzi) (jako twierdzenie) yep! pot.; (jako pytanie) yeah? pot.; **no pewnie!** you bet! pot. **2** (ponaglenie) come on! **3** (nawiązujące) well; **no, muszę już iść** well, I've got to go; **no nie!** (wyraz zaskoczenia) (no,) I don't believe it!; **no nie?** eh?; **no tak** (wyraz niezadowolenia) that figures pot., iron.; **no proszę** (wyraz zaskoczenia) well, well; **no, no** (wyrażające ostrzeżenie) now, now; (wyrażające zdziwienie) well, well

II part. **no to do widzenia** bye, then pot.; **no to co?** so what? pot.

nobli|sta m, **~stka** f Noble prizewinner

noc f **1** (część doby) night; **w ~y** at night(-time); **wczoraj w ~y** last night; **od świtu a. rana do ~y** from dawn to dusk **2** pot. (nocna zmiana) night shift

❏ **~ poślubna** wedding night

nocleg m **1** (noc) night; **przyjąć kogoś na ~** to put sb up for the night **2** (kwatera) accommodation; **szukać ~u** to look for a place to stay the night

noclegow|y adi. *[dom]* lodging

nocnik m chamber pot; potty pot.

nocn|y adi. **1** *[przymrozek, niebo]* night **2** (działający nocą) *[tramwaj, pociąg, lot]* night; *[zwierzę, modlitwa, spacer]* nocturnal; *[patrol, uroczystość, wizyta]* night-time; **~y sklep** an all-night shop GB, a convenience store US **3** (do użytku nocą) **~a lampka** a bedside lamp; **~a koszula** a nightgown, a night-dress

noc|ować impf vi to stay overnight

no|ga f **1** (kończyna) leg; **założyć nogę na nogę** to cross one's legs; **chwiać się na nogach** to stagger; **trzymać się na nogach** to keep one's balance; **nogi ugięły się pode mną** I went weak at the knees **2** (stopa) foot; **palce u nóg** toes **3** (część stołu, krzesła, przyrządu) leg **4** pot. (tępak) turkey pot.

■ **do góry nogami** upside down; **na jednej nodze** *[pójść, pobiec]* on a. at the double; **być cały dzień na nogach** to be on one's feet all day; **dać nogę** pot. to leg it pot.; **stanąć na własnych nogach** to stand on one's own (two) feet; **wziąć**

nogi za pas to take to one's heels; **zerwać się na równe nogi** to jump to one's feet; **w nogi!** run for it!

nogaw|ka f leg

nokau|t /ˈnokawt/ m knockout

nokaut|ować /ˌnokawˈtovate/ impf vt to knock out

nominacj|a f nomination

nomina|ł m face a. nominal value; **banknot o ~le 100 zł** a 100-zloty banknote

nonsens m nonsense; **mówić ~y** to talk nonsense

nonsensown|y adi. nonsensical

no|ra f **1** (kryjówka zwierząt) burrow, hole; **lisia nora** a fox earth **2** pot. (mieszkanie) hovel; (lokal) hole pot.

nor|ka f Zool. mink

norm|a f **1** (zasada) norm; **odbiegający od ~y** deviating from the norm; **wrócić do ~y** to go back to normal **2** (przydział) standard, norm; **dzienna ~a** (żywności) the daily intake; (pracy) the daily workload

normaliz|ować impf **I** vt **1** (regulować) to normalize *[stosunki, oddech]* **2** (standaryzować) to standardize *[wymiary, kształt]*

II normalizować się *[stosunki]* to normalize

normalnie I adv. grad. (prawidłowo) normally

II adv. **1** (zwykle) normally **2** pot. (zwyczajnie) simply

normaln|y I adi. grad. **1** *[objaw, poziom, ceny]* normal **2** pot. (typowy, zwykły) *[oszust, kradzież]* plain

II adi. **1** (zdrowy) *[osoba]* normal **2** (bez zniżki) *[cena, opłata]* standard, normal; *[bilet]* full fare, ordinary

III m pot. (bilet) ≈ full fare

nos m **1** (część twarzy) nose; **mieć zatkany ~** to have a blocked nose; **wytrzeć ~** to wipe one's nose; **chustka do ~a** a tissue; **pociągać ~em** to sniff, to sniffle; **leci mi z ~a** I have a runny nose **2** (czubek) nose, tip

■ **(tuż) pod czyimś ~em** pot. (right) under sb's nose; **kręcić ~em na coś** pot. to turn one's nose up at sth; **mamrotać pod ~em** to mumble under one's breath; **mieć kogoś w ~ie** pot. to not give a hoot about sb pot.; **pilnować swojego ~a** pot. to mind one's own business; **podsuwać komuś coś pod ~** pot. to shove sth right in front of sb's face; **utrzeć komuś ~a** pot. to cut sb down to size; **wtykać ~ w nie swoje sprawy** pot. to poke one's nose into other people's business; **zadzierać ~a** pot. to put on airs; **zagrać komuś na ~ie** pot. to thumb one's nose at sb

nosiciel m, **~ka** f (choroby, wirusa) carrier

no|sić impf **I** vt **1** (mieć na sobie) to wear *[buty, skarpety, okulary]* **2** (mieć) to wear, to have *[wąsy, brodę]* **3** (dźwigać) to carry *[bagaże, walizki, paczki]* **4** (mieć w sobie) to carry *[chorobę, ryzyko]*; to bear *[ślady, imię]*

II nosić się 1 (ubierać się) to dress **2** (zachowywać się) to carry oneself **3** (planować) **nosić się z zamiarem czegoś** to intend doing sth

nosoroż|ec m rhinoceros

nosz|e *plt* stretcher
nośnik *m* carrier; ~ **informacji** an information medium
nośn|y *adi.* [1] *[ściana, konstrukcja]* load-bearing; **siła** ~**a** carrying capacity; **rakieta** ~**a** a booster (rocket) [2] *[kura, gęś, kaczka]* egg-laying
no|ta *f* [1] (pismo urzędowe, objaśnienie) note [2] (ocena) mark GB, grade US
notarialn|y *adi. [czynności, aplikant]* notarial; **akt** ~**y** a notarial deed; **kancelaria** ~**a** a notary's office
notariusz *m* notary (public)
notat|ka *f* [1] (zapisek) note; **robić** ~**ki** to make a. take notes; ~**ka służbowa** a memo [2] (w prasie) paragraph
notatnik *m* notebook, scratch pad US
notes *m* notebook
notorycznie *adv.* notoriously
notoryczn|y *adi. [kłamca, pijak]* notorious
not|ować *impf* [1] *vt* [1] (zapisywać) to take down *[adres, telefon]* [2] (rejestrować) to register; ~**ujemy wyraźny spadek produkcji** there has been a marked fall in production
[1] *vi* to take notes
nowalij|ka *f* spring vegetable
nowatorstw|o *n* inventiveness
nowicjusz *m*, ~**ka** *f* novice
nowin|a *f* news; **dla mnie to nie** ~**a** it's no news to me
now|o *adv.* newly; ~**o zbudowany most** a newly-constructed bridge; **od** ~**a** (od początku) anew
nowobogac|ki *m*, ~**ka** *f* upstart, nouveau riche
nowocze|sny *adi.* modern
nowofundland, ~**czyk** *m* Newfoundland (dog)
noworoczn|y *adi. [życzenia, kartka]* New Year
noworod|ek *m* infant
nowoś|ć *f* [1] (innowacja) novelty, innovation; ~**ci wydawnicze** the latest publications [2] (bycie nowym) newness [3] (nowa wiadomość) news
nowotw|ór *m* tumour GB, tumor US; ~**ór złośliwy** cancer; ~**ór niezłośliwy** a benign tumour
nowożeńc|y *plt* newly-weds, honeymooners
now|y [1] *adi. grad. [hotel, samochód, uczeń]* new; **najnowsze wiadomości** the latest news
[1] **now|y** *m*, ~**a** *f* newcomer; (uczeń) new student
[1] **nowe** *n* the new; **idzie** ~**e!** it's time for some changes!
[1] **po nowemu** *adv* pot. (nowocześnie) **myśleć po** ~**emu** to be on the ball pot.
nozdrz|e *n* nostril
nożyc|e *plt* [1] (duże nożyczki) scissors, shears; ~**e ogrodnicze** garden shears; ~**e do cięcia blachy** snips [2] przen. (rozpiętość między wartościami) differential; ~**e cen/płac** price/pay differentials [3] Sport scissor(s) jump

nożycz|ki *plt* scissors; ~**ki do paznokci** nail scissors
n|ów *m* new moon; **księżyc w nowiu** the new moon
n|óż *m* [1] (narzędzie) knife; **nóż kuchenny** a kitchen knife; **nóż sprężynowy** a flick knife [2] (ostrze) blade ■ **być z kimś na noże** pot. to be at daggers drawn with sb; **mieć nóż na gardle** to be in a tight spot a. corner
nu|cić *impf vt* to hum *[piosenkę, melodię]*
nu|da *f* [1] (bezczynność) boredom; **umierać z nudów** to be bored to death [2] (rzecz nudna) bore; yawn pot.
nudn|o, ~**ie** *adv. grad.* boringly; ~**o mi** I'm bored
nudności *plt* nausea; **mieć** ~ to feel nauseous
nudn|y *adi. grad.* boring
nudy|sta *m*, ~**stka** *f* nudist
nudzia|rz *m*, ~**ra** *f* pot. bore
nu|dzić *impf* [1] *vt* [1] (wywoływać uczucie nudy) to bore *[osobę]* [2] (naprzykrzać się) to nag (**o coś** for sth)
[1] *vi* [1] (mówić) to harp on [2] (kaprysić) to moan
[1] *v imp.* **nudzi mnie od tego** it makes me feel sick
[1] **nudzić się** [1] *[osoba]* to be bored; **nudzi mi się** I'm bored [2] *[zabawa, przedmiot]* to become boring
nume|r *m* [1] (liczba) number; ~**r telefonu** a telephone number; ~**r wewnętrzny** an extension (number); **autobus** ~**r sześć** a number 6 (bus) [2] (rozmiar) size; **o dwa** ~**ry za duży** two sizes too big [3] (egzemplarz) issue [4] (część widowiska) number, act [5] pot. (zaskakujący postępek) stunt; **wyciąć komuś** ~**r** to pull a fast one on sb pot.; **nie ze mną takie** ~**ry** you won't fool me like that pot. [6] pot. (stosunek płciowy) trick pot. [7] pot. (o osobie) he's a right card! pot., żart.
numeracj|a *f* numbering; ~**a stron** page numbers
numer|ować *impf vi* to number
numizmaty|ka *f* numismatics
nur|ek *m* [1] (osoba) diver; (w kombinezonie) frogman [2] (skok do wody) dive; **dać** ~**ka** (do wody) to dive in; (skryć się) to dive
nurk|ować *impf vi* [1] (zanurzać się) to dive; ~**ować w krzakach** to dive into the bushes [2] *[samolot]* to dive (down)
nur|t *m* [1] (strumień) current; (skłębiona woda) rapids [2] (bieg) course [3] (styl) trend
nu|ta [1] *f* [1] Muz. note; **cała nuta** a semibreve GB, a whole note US [2] (brzmienie) note; **nuta smutku w czyimś głosie** a note a. touch of sadness in sb's voice [3] (odcień zapachu, smaku) flavour GB, flavor US
[1] **nuty** *plt* (partytura) score, music; **czytać nuty** to read music
■ **kłamać jak z nut** to lie through one's teeth
nutri|a *f* Zool. nutria, coypu
nużąc|y *adi. [praca, rozmowa]* tiresome
nuż|yć *impf vt* to tire *[osobę]*
nygus *m* pot. skiver pot.

O

O, o *n inv.* o

o *praep.* [1] (wskazujące na temat) *[rozmowa, informacja, pogłoski]* about; *[mówić, myśleć]* about, of; **książka o czymś** a book about a. on sth; **o czym jest ten film?** what's the film about? [2] (wskazujące na cel) for; **prosić o coś** to ask for sth [3] (wskazujące na kontakt fizyczny) on, against; **uderzyć głową o coś** to hit a. bang one's head on a. against sth; **oparł drabinę o ścianę** he leant the ladder against the wall [4] (z określeniami czasu) at [5] (z określeniami ilości, liczby) by; **wzrosnąć/obniżyć się o 10%** to rise/fall by 10 per cent; **o połowę krótszy/tańszy** half the length/price; **o dwa numery za duży** two sizes too big [6] książk. (określające cechę) with; **dziewczyna o niebieskich oczach** a girl with blue eyes; **mydło o zapachu cytryny** lemon-scented soap [7] (posługując się) **chodzić o lasce** to walk with a stick; **poruszać się o kulach** to walk on crutches

oaz|a *f* oasis także przen.

ob|aj, ob|ydwaj *pron.* both

obal|ić *pf* — **obal|ać** *impf vt* [1] (przewrócić) to knock down [2] (unieważnić) to invalidate *[teorię, twierdzenie]*; to debunk *[mit, pogląd]*; to refute *[oskarżenie, zarzuty]*; to nullify *[testament]*; to overthrow *[rząd, władcę]*

obandaż|ować *pf vt* to bandage *[rannego, rękę]*

obaw|a *f* anxiety, fear; **w ~ie** a. **z ~y przed czymś** in fear of sth; **nie ma ~** a. **bez ~!** pot. never fear!; no fear! GB pot.

obawia|ć się *impf v refl.* to be afraid **(czegoś** of sth), to fear **(czegoś** sth); **~ć się o kogoś** to fear for a. to be anxious about sb

obcas *m* heel; **buty na wysokim ~ie** high-heeled shoes

obcęg|i *plt* (a pair of) pincers; (płaskie) (a pair of) pliers

obchodzić *impf* → **obejść**

obch|ód [I] *m* (szpitalny) round; (policyjny) beat
[II] **obchody** *plt* celebration

ob|ciąć *pf* — **ob|cinać** *impf* [I] *vt* [1] (uciąć) to cut off *[gałąź, materiał, nogawki]*; (skrócić) to cut *[włosy]*; to clip *[paznokcie, żywopłot]* [2] (uszczuplić) to cut *[koszty, wydatki]*
[II] **obciąć się** — **obcinać się** pot. (ostrzyc się) to get a haircut

obciążać *impf* → **obciążyć**

obciąże|nie *n* [1] (ciężar) load [2] (obowiązek) responsibility [3] przen. strain; **~nie psychiczne** mental strain a. stress; **~nie dziedziczne** genetic predisposition; **~nie pracą** one's workload [4] Elektr., Techn. load

obciąż|yć *pf* — **obciąż|ać** *impf vt* [1] (objuczyć) to burden **(kogoś czymś** sb with sth) [2] (zlecić) to charge **(kogoś czymś** sb with sth); **~yć kogoś kosztami (czegoś)** to charge sb (for sth); **~yć kogoś podatkiem** to tax sb [3] (obwinić) to put the blame on; (w sądzie) to incriminate; **~ać kogoś winą za coś** to blame sb for sth; **~ać kogoś odpowiedzialnością za coś** to hold sb responsible for sth; **dowody ~ające** incriminating evidence [4] (przeciążyć) to overload *[linię, sieć]*; to strain *[kręgosłup, stawy]*; **~ać sobie pamięć datami** to clutter one's memory with dates

obcie|knąć, obcie|c *pf* — **obcie|kać** *impf vi* *[ciecz]* to trickle; *[parasol, płaszcz]* to drip

obcierać *impf* → **obetrzeć**

obcinać *impf* → **obciąć**

obci|sły *adi. grad. [spodnie, sweter]* close-fitting

obcojęzyczn|y *adi. [książka, napis]* foreign-language

obcokrajow|iec *m* foreigner

obc|y [I] *adi.* [1] (zagraniczny) *[język, waluta]* foreign [2] (nieznany) strange; **zupełnie ~y człowiek** a perfect stranger; **w ~ym mieście** in an unfamiliar town
[II] *m* [1] (nieznajomy) stranger; „**~ym wstęp wzbroniony**" 'no trespassing' [2] (w science fiction) alien

obecnie *adv.* at present

obecnoś|ć *f* presence; **~ć na lekcjach** attendance in class

obecn|y *adi.* [1] (uczestniczący) present; **~y!** present!, here! [2] (teraźniejszy) current; **w ~ej chwili** at this moment in time książk.

obejmować *impf* → **objąć**

o|bejrzeć *pf* — **o|glądać**[1] *impf* [I] *vt* [1] (przypatrzeć się) to examine [2] (zapoznać się) to see *[film, wystawę]*; to watch *[telewizję]*
[II] **obejrzeć się** — **oglądać się** [1] (siebie samego) to look at oneself; **oglądać się w lustrze** to examine oneself in a mirror [2] (do tyłu) to look back; **oglądać się na boki** to look around

ob|ejść *pf* — **ob|chodzić** *impf* [I] *vt* [1] (zrobić obchód) to make a round **(coś** of sth) [2] (okrążyć) to go

a. walk (a)round *[dom, biurko]*; **obejść prawo** przen. to evade the law ③ (zainteresować) to concern; **co cię to obchodzi!** what's it got to do with you?! pot.; **to mnie mało obchodzi** I couldn't care less ④ (uczcić) to celebrate *[jubileusz, urodziny]*

II obejść się — obchodzić się ① (potraktować) **obejść się z kimś dobrze/źle** to treat sb well/badly ② (posługiwać się) to use (**z czymś** sth) ③ (obyć się) to do without; **obejdę się bez twojej pomocy** I can do without your help; **obejdzie się!** iron. thanks a lot! iron. ④ (zadowolić się) to make do (**czymś** with sth)

obel|ga *f* insult; **obrzucić kogoś ~gami** to hurl abuse a. insults at sb

ob|erwać *pf* — **ob|rywać** *impf* **I** *vt* (urwać) to tear off *[falbankę, guzik]*; to pick *[owoce]*; to pluck *[listki]*; **oberwanie chmury** przen. a cloudburst

II *vi* pot. (dostać lanie) to get a. take a beating; **oberwie ci się za to!** you're in for it now! pot.

III oberwać się — obrywać się to come off; **guzik mi się oberwał** my button came off

oberżyn|a *f* aubergine GB, eggplant US

ob|eschnąć *pf* — **ob|sychać** *impf* *vi* to dry, to become dry

ob|etrzeć *pf* — **ob|cierać** *impf* *vt* ① (wytrzeć) to wipe *[czoło]*; to wipe (away) *[łzy]* ② (skaleczyć) to graze *[piętę, skórę]*

obezwładni|ć *pf* — **obezwładni|ać** *impf vt* to overpower *[przeciwnika]*; **~ająca nieśmiałość** crippling shyness; **~ający strach** paralysing fear

obficie *adv. grad.* *[pocić się, pienić się]* profusely; *[posypać, podlać]* generously

obfi|ty *adi. grad.* *[krwawienie]* heavy; *[plony, opady]* abundant; *[posiłek]* lavish; *[korespondencja]* voluminous

obgad|ać *pf* — **obgad|ywać** *impf vt* pot. to run down *[osobę]*; to kick *[sth]* around pot. *[sprawę, plan]*

obgry|źć *pf* — **obgry|zać** *impf vt* to gnaw (**coś** at a. on sth); **~zać paznokcie** to bite one's nails

obi|ad *m* dinner; (wczesnym popołudniem) lunch; **~ad z trzech dań** a three-course dinner; **jeść ~ad** to have lunch/dinner

obiadow|y *adi.* *[danie, stół, serwis]* dinner; **w porze ~ej** at lunchtime/dinner time; **przerwa ~a** a lunch break

obi|cie *n* (na meblach) upholstery; (na drzwiach) padding

obi|ć *pf* — **obi|jać** *impf* **I** *vt* ① (obtłuc) to chip *[dzbanek, filiżankę]*; to bruise *[jabłko]* ② (pokryć materiałem) to upholster *[kanapę, krzesło]* (**czymś** with sth); to pad *[drzwi]* (**czymś** with sth) ③ (uderzyć się) to bump *[głowę]*; to knock *[rękę]* (**o coś** on sth)

II obijać się pot. (nie pracować) to loaf around a. about

obiec|ać *pf* — **obiec|ywać** *impf vt* to promise (**komuś coś** sb sth a. sth to sb); **wiele sobie ~ywać po czymś** to expect a great deal from sth

obieg *m* ① (planet) revolution ② (dokumentów, krwi, towarów) circulation; **być w ~u** *[banknot, znaczek]* to be in circulation; **wyjść z ~u** *[moneta, banknot]* to go a. drop out of circulation

obiek|t *m* ① (rzecz, przedmiot zainteresowań) object; **~t na mapie** a feature on a map; **być ~tem czyichś żartów** to be the butt of sb's jokes ② (budynek) building; (zespół budynków) complex; **~t przemysłowy** an industrial works a. plant; **~t wojskowy** military installations

obiektyw *m* lens

obiektywi|zm *m* objectivity

obiektywn|y *adi.* *[obserwator, prawda]* objective

obierać *impf* → **obrać**

obier|ek *m*, **~ka** *f* piece of peel

obietnic|a *f* promise; **złożyć komuś ~ę** to make a promise to sb; **dotrzymać ~y** to keep a promise

obijać *impf* → **obić**

objadać *impf* → **objeść**

objaśni|ć *pf* — **objaśni|ać** *impf vt* to explain (**coś komuś** sth to sb)

objaśnie|nie *n* explanation; (do tekstu) commentary; (w tekście) (explanatory) note

objaw *m* (oznaka) sign; (choroby) symptom

obj|azd *m* (omijanie) diversion; (boczna droga) detour

obj|ąć *pf* — **ob|ejmować** *impf vt* ① (przytulić) to embrace; **objąć kogoś wpół** to put one's arm around sb's waist ② (przejąć) to assume *[urząd, władzę]*; **objąć prowadzenie** to go into a. take the lead ③ (rozszerzyć się) to spread; **płomienie objęły dach** flames enveloped a. engulfed the roof ④ (zawrzeć) to include, to cover; **cena nie obejmuje posiłków** the price does not include meals ⑤ (dotyczyć) to involve; **te towary nie są objęte podatkiem VAT** these goods are not subject to VAT; **gatunki objęte ochroną** protected species

obj|echać *pf* — **obj|eżdżać** *impf vt* ① (okrążyć) to go a. drive round *[rynek, skwer]* ② (odwiedzić) to travel (a)round, to visit *[miasta, kraje]* ③ pot. (zwymyślać) to tell *[sb]* off, to give *[sb]* a tongue-lashing

obj|eść się *pf* — **obj|adać się** *impf v refl.* to stuff oneself pot. (**czymś** with sth a. full of sth)

objeżdżać *impf* → **objechać**

objętoś|ć *f* volume; (naczynia, bagażnika) capacity; (książki, dokumentu) size; **miara ~ci** a measure of volume

obkładać *impf* → **obłożyć**

obkroić → **okroić**

obl|ać *pf* — **obl|ewać** *impf* **I** *vt* ① (polać) to pour; **~ać spodnie kawą** to spill coffee over one's trousers ② (pokryć) to cover; **pierniki ~ewane czekoladą** chocolate-covered gingerbread; **~ewać coś lukrem** to ice a. frost sth ③ (otaczać) *[morze]* to surround *[wyspę]*; *[światło]* to bathe *[dom, ogród]* ④ Uniw. to fail; to flunk US pot. *[egzamin, studenta]* ⑤ pot. (uczcić) to drink to *[awans, kontrakt]*; **~ewać nowe mieszkanie** to have a house-warming (party); **musimy to ~ać** that calls for a drink a. celebration

oblepi|ć *pf* — **oblepi|ać** *impf vt* [1] (zalepić) to smear [2] (szczelnie pokryć) to cover; (obcisnąć) to cling (tightly); **buty ~one błotem** shoes caked with mud

oblewać *impf* → **oblać**

ob|leźć *pf* — **ob|łazić** *impf* [I] *vt [insekty, robaki]* to crawl (all) over
[II] *vi [farba, tynk]* to peel a. flake off

oblęże|nie *n* siege

obliczać *impf* → **obliczyć**

blicz|e *n* książk. countenance książk.; **w ~u niebezpieczeństwa** in the face of danger; **w ~u prawa** under the law, in the eyes of the law; **odsłonił swoje prawdziwe ~e** he showed his true colours, he revealed his true self

oblicze|nie *n* (działanie) counting; (wynik) calculation

blicz|yć *pf* — **oblicz|ać** *impf vt* [1] (wykonać działania arytmetyczne) to calculate *[cenę, ilość, prędkość]*; to count *[głosy]*; **źle coś ~yć** to miscalculate sth [2] (ocenić) to estimate [3] (zaplanować) to design; **przyjęcie ~one na dwadzieścia osób** a party for twenty people

obli|zać *pf* — **obli|zywać** *impf* [I] *vt* to lick
[II] **oblizać się** — **oblizywać się** to lick one's lips; **~zywać się na samą myśl o czymś** to lick one's lips at the thought of sth

obładow|ać *pf* — **obładow|ywać** *impf vt* to load **(kogoś czymś** sb with sth)

obław|a *f* [1] (polowanie) (battue) hunt; (naganiacze) battue, beaters [2] (na człowieka) manhunt **(na kogoś** for sb); **~a na złodziei samochodów** a crackdown on car thieves

obłazić *impf* → **obleźć**

obłąkan|y *adi. [osoba]* demented; *[spojrzenie, idea]* mad

obłę|d *m* [1] Med. paranoia [2] pot., przen. madness; **istny ~d** sheer lunacy a. madness; **doprowadzić kogoś do ~du** to drive sb mad

obłędn|y *adi.* [1] (szalony) *[spojrzenie, śmiech]* demented; *[oczy, taniec]* wild [2] pot. *[suma]* staggering; *[szybkość, tempo]* breakneck; *[film, impreza]* wicked pot.

obłok *m* cloud; **~ spalin** a cloud of exhaust (fumes)
■ **bujać w ~ach** pot. to have one's head in the clouds

ob|łożyć *pf* — **ob|kładać** *impf vt* [1] (otoczyć) to surround **(czymś** with sth); (pokryć) to cover **(coś czymś** sth with sth); **obłożyć kogoś poduszkami** to prop sb up with pillows [2] (założyć okładkę) **obłożyć książkę** to put a cover on a book; **obłożyła zeszyt w brązowy papier** she covered the exercise book in brown paper [3] (obciążyć) to load, to saddle **(kogoś czymś** sb with sth); **jestem obłożona pracą** I'm bogged down a. swamped with work pot.;

obłożyć coś podatkiem to impose a. put a tax on sth

obłu|da *f* hypocrisy

obłudni|k *m*, **~ca** *f* hypocrite

obłudn|y *adi. grad. [osoba, polityk]* hypocritical; *[uśmiech, zachowanie]* insincere; *[moralność, współczucie]* feigned

obmawiać *impf* → **obmówić**

obm|ówić *pf* — **obm|awiać** *impf vt* **~ówić kogoś przed kimś** to badmouth sb to sb; **~awiać kogoś za jego plecami** to talk about sb behind their back pot.

obmur|ować *pf* — **obmur|owywać** *impf vt* [1] (obłożyć) (cegłą) to face [sth] with brick; (kamieniami) to face [sth] with stone [2] (ogrodzić) to wall (in) *[ogród]*

obmy|ć *pf* — **obmy|wać** *impf vt* [1] (usunąć brud) to wash *[ciało]*; to cleanse *[ranę]*; **~ć (sobie) twarz z kurzu** to wash the dirt off one's face [2] (oblać) *[fale]* to wash *[plażę, skały, brzeg]*

obmyśl|ić *pf* — **obmyśl|ać** *impf vt* to work out *[szczegóły]*; to conceive, to devise *[plan, taktykę]*; **dobrze ~ony plan** a well-thought-out plan

obmywać *impf* → **obmyć**

obnaż|yć *pf* — **obnaż|ać** *impf* [I] *vt* to bare *[ramiona, tors, kły]*; to expose *[głupotę, hipokryzję]*
[II] **obnażyć się** — **obnażać się** to strip (off); *[ekshibicjonista]* to expose oneself **(przed kimś** to sb)

obniżać *impf* → **obniżyć**

obniż|ka *f* reduction; **posezonowe ~ki cen** post-season markdowns a. discounts

obniż|yć *pf* — **obniż|ać** *impf* [I] *vt* [1] (umieścić niżej) to lower *[sufit, poprzeczkę, poziom wody]*; **~enie terenu** depression [2] (zmniejszyć) to reduce *[cenę, koszt, ciśnienie krwi]*; to cut *[podatki]*; to bring down *[gorączkę]*; **kupić coś po ~onej cenie** to buy sth at a reduced price a. a discount
[II] **obniżyć się** — **obniżać się** (zmniejszyć się) *[ceny, poziom wody, temperatura]* to go down; *[ciśnienie]* to drop; *[stopa życiowa, liczba, zużycie paliwa]* to decrease

obojczyk *m* collarbone

oboj|e *num. mult.* both

obojętnie [I] *adv. grad. [patrzeć, słuchać]* with indifference
[II] *part.* **~ kto** whoever, no matter who; **~ dokąd** wherever, no matter where; **pożycz mi książkę, ~ jaką** lend me a book, any book

obojętn|y *adi.* [1] (nieczuły) indifferent **(na coś** a. **wobec czegoś** to sth) [2] (nieistotny) *[sprawa, temat]* unimportant; **jest mi ~e, co się z nim stanie** I don't care what happens to him; **jako mężczyzna był jej ~y** she had no romantic interest in him [3] (nijaki) *[mina, wzrok, twarz]* blank [4] (nieszkodliwy) harmless **(dla czegoś** to sth) [5] *[cząsteczka, substancja]* neutral

obok **Ⅰ** *praep.* by, next to; **siedzieli ~ siebie** they were sitting next to each other a. side by side
Ⅱ *adv.* **mieszkamy ~** we live next door; **tuż ~ czegoś** right next to sth
ob|ora *f* cowshed
obornik *m* manure
obostrz|yć *pf* — **obostrz|ać** *impf vt* to tighten up *[przepisy, zasady]*
obowiąz|ek *m* duty, responsibility; **poczucie ~ku** a sense of duty a. responsibility; **czuć się w ~ku coś zrobić** to feel obliged a. duty-bound to do sth; **zakres ~ków** a job description
obowiązkow|y *adi.* **Ⅰ** *[lektura, szkolenie]* obligatory, compulsory; **obecność ~a** attendance required **Ⅱ** *[uczeń, pracownik]* dutiful, conscientious
obowiąz|ywać *impf vi* (mieć moc prawną) *[przepis]* to be in effect a. force; (dotyczyć) to apply (**kogoś** to sb); **~uje strój wieczorowy** evening dress is de rigueur
oboz|ować *impf vi* to camp
obozowisk|o *n* campsite GB, campground US
ob|ój *m* oboe
ob|óz *m* camp; **obóz harcerski** a scout camp; **obóz narciarski/żeglarski** a ski/sailing camp; **rozbić obóz** to make a. pitch camp; **zwinąć obóz** to break a. strike camp
obrabiać *impf* → **obrobić**
obrabiar|ka *f* machine tool
obrab|ować *pf vt* to rob *[osobę, bank, sklep]*
obracać¹ *impf* → **obrócić**
obraca|ć² *impf vt* **~ć dużymi kwotami** to deal in large sums
obraca|ć się *impf v refl.* (bywać) **~ć się w kołach artystycznych** to move in artistic circles; **~ć się wśród gwiazd filmowych** to socialize with film stars, to rub shoulders GB a. elbows US with film stars
ob|rać *pf* — **ob|ierać** *impf vt* to peel *[jabłka, ziemniaki]*; to shell *[jajko, groch, orzechy]*; to skin *[brzoskwinię, pomidora]*; **obrać rybę z ości** to bone a fish
obrad|ować *impf vi* to debate (**nad czymś** sth); **Sejm w tym tygodniu nie ~uje** the Sejm isn't sitting a. in session this week
obrad|y *plt* (komisji, jury) deliberations; **~y Sejmu** a parliamentary session
obradzać *impf* → **obrodzić**
obrastać *impf* → **obrosnąć**
obraz *m* **Ⅰ** (malowidło) painting, picture; **~ pędzla Picassa** a painting by Picasso **Ⅱ** (widok) sight, scene; (w pamięci, wyobraźni) picture, image; **~ kontrolny** a. **testowy** (w TV) test card
■ **patrzeć w kogoś jak w ~** to think the world of sb
obraz|ek *m* picture; **książka z ~kami** a picture book

obra|zić *pf* — **obra|żać** *impf* **Ⅰ** *vt* to offend, to insult; **~żać czyjeś uczucia/czyjąś dumę** to hurt sb's feelings/pride
Ⅱ **obrazić się** — **obrażać się** to be offended, to take offence GB a. offense US (**na kogoś** at sb); **~zić się o coś** to take offence at sth
obrazkow|y *adi.* **historyjka ~a** a comic strip; **pismo ~e** picture a. pictographic writing
obraźliw|y *adi. grad.* *[wypowiedź, aluzja]* offensive, insulting
obrażać *impf* → **obrazić**
obrażals|ki *m*, **~ka** *f* pot. Mr/Ms Hypersensitive pot., żart.
obraże|nie *n* injury; **wyszedł z wypadku bez ~ń** he escaped the accident uninjured
obraż|ony *adi.* *[osoba, głos]* offended; **mieć ~oną minę** to look offended
obrącz|ka *f* **Ⅰ** (ślubna) wedding ring a. band **Ⅱ** (na nodze ptaka) ring, band
obręb|ić *pf* — **obręb|iać** *impf vt* to hem *[obrus, materiał]*
obręcz *f* **Ⅰ** (obejma) hoop, band **Ⅱ** Aut. (wheel) rim **Ⅲ** Sport hoop
obr|obić *pf* — **obr|abiać** *impf* **Ⅰ** *vt* **Ⅰ** (ukształtować) to work *[kamień, brąz]*; (maszynowo) to machine *[kamień, szkło]* **Ⅱ** (obrębić) to hem *[brzeg, chusteczkę]* **Ⅲ** pot. (opracować) to process *[dane]*; to edit *[tekst]* **Ⅳ** pot. (okraść) to clean out pot. *[osobę, mieszkanie]*; **~obić bank** to do a bank pot.
Ⅱ **obrobić się** pot. to get everything done pot.
obr|odzić *pf* — **obr|adzać** *impf* *[zboże, drzewo, warzywa]* to crop well, to yield a plentiful crop; *[owoce, grzyby]* to be plentiful, to be abundant
obron|a *f* **Ⅰ** (odpieranie ataku, zarzutów) defence GB, defense US; **~a pracy doktorskiej/magisterskiej** Uniw. doctoral/master's defence **Ⅱ** (ochrona) protection
obro|nić *pf* **Ⅰ** *vt* **Ⅰ** (odeprzeć atak) to defend (**kogoś przed kimś/czymś** sb against a. from sb/sth) **Ⅱ** (ustrzec) to defend, to save **Ⅲ** (udowodnić słuszność) to defend *[tezę, stanowisko]* **Ⅳ** Uniw. to defend *[pracę magisterską, doktorską]* **Ⅴ** Sport *[bramkarz]* to save *[strzał]*; *[zawodnik]* to defend *[tytuł]*
Ⅱ **obronić się** Uniw. **~nił się dwa lata temu** he did his MA/PhD two years ago
obronn|y *adi.* *[pozycja, akcja]* defensive; **pies ~y** a guard dog
■ **wyjść z czegoś ~ą ręką** to get through sth a. emerge from sth unscathed
obrońc|a *m* **Ⅰ** (występujący w obronie) defender; (w sądzie) defence counsel GB, defense attorney US; **~a z urzędu** a court-appointed defence lawyer GB, a public defender US **Ⅱ** (gracz) defender, defensive player; **~a tytułu mistrzowskiego** a defending champion
obrotn|y *adi. grad.* pot. *[osoba]* resourceful
obrotomierz *m* tachometer, revolution counter

obrotow|y *adi. [ruch]* rotational, rotary; *[drzwi, scena]* revolving; **krzesło** ~**e** a swivel chair; **taca** ~**a** a lazy Susan

obr|oża *f* (dog) collar

obrób|ka *f* (drewna, metalu, danych) processing; ~**ka skrawaniem** machining

obr|ócić *pf* — **obr|acać**[1] *impf* **[I]** *vt* [1] (przekręcić) to turn; (wokół osi) to rotate; **stał** ~**ócony tyłem do okna** he stood with his back to the window [2] książk. (zamienić) to change, to turn (**coś w coś** sth into sth); ~**ócić coś w żart** to make a joke (out) of sth **[II]** *vi* pot. (tam i z powrotem) to go back and forth a. to and fro; (w górę i w dół) to go up and down **[III] obrócić się** — **obracać się** [1] (zakręcić się) to turn; (wokół osi) to rotate, to revolve; ~**acać się wokół Słońca** to revolve around the sun; ~**ócić się do kogoś tyłem** to turn one's back on sb [2] książk. (zmienić się) to turn; ~**ócić się na lepsze/gorsze** to take a turn for the better/worse

obr|ót *m* [1] (dokoła osi) rotation; ~**ót o 180°** a 180-degree turn [2] (kierunek) turn; **przybrać pomyślny** ~**ót** to take a turn for the better [3] Ekon. turnover ■ **pracować na najwyższych** ~**otach** *[silnik]* to be in top gear; *[fabryka]* to work at full capacity a. at full steam; *[osoba]* to work flat out pot.; **brać kogoś w** ~**oty** pot. to put the screws on sb pot.

obrus *m* tablecloth

obrys|ować *pf* — **obrys|owywać** *impf vt* to outline

obrywać *impf* → **oberwać**

obrząd|ek *m* [1] (ceremonia) rite [2] (prace gospodarskie) farmyard chores; ~**ek inwentarza** tending of farm animals

obrzeż|e *n* edge; **na** ~**ach miasta** on the outskirts of town

obrzę|d *m* ceremony, rite

obrzęk *m* swelling; ~**płuc** pulmonary oedema

obrzęk|nąć *pf* — **obrzęk|ać** *impf vi [noga, palec]* to swell (up); *[twarz]* to puff up

obrzu|cić *pf* — **obrzu|cać** *impf vt* [1] (obsypać) to shower (**kogoś czymś** sb with sth), to throw (**kogoś czymś** sth at sb) [2] (obszyć) to overcast, to whip(stitch) *[brzegi, szew]*

obrzydliw|y *adi. grad. [smak, zapach, widok]* disgusting; *[postępek]* detestable

obrzyd|nąć *pf vi* to become abhorrent (**komuś** to sb); ~**ły mi twoje ciągłe narzekania** I'm sick and tired of your constant carping

obrzydzać *impf* → **obrzydzić**

obrzydzeni|e *n* disgust; **z** ~**em** in disgust

obrzy|dzić *pf* — **obrzy|dzać** *impf vt* to put [sb] off; ~**dzić komuś życie** to make sb's life unbearable

obsa|da *f* [1] (personel) personnel, staff [2] (w filmie, sztuce) cast, line-up; **zmienić** ~**dę sztuki** to recast a play

obsa|dzić *pf* — **obsa|dzać** *impf vt* [1] (zasadzić) to plant [2] (umocować) to mount *[drzwi, kołek, koło]* [3] (powierzyć) to fill *[etat, stanowisko]*; to cast *[rolę, sztukę]*; ~**dzić kogoś w roli Ofelii** to cast sb in the role of Ophelia a. as Ophelia

obserwacj|a *f* (przyglądanie się) observation; (policyjna) surveillance

obserwacyjn|y *adi. [balon, satelita]* observation; *[misja]* observer; *[sprzęt, system, urządzenie]* monitoring, tracking; **punkt** ~**y** a lookout, a vantage point; **zmysł** ~**y** one's powers of observation

obserwato|r *m*, ~**rka** *f* książk. observer, watcher; (świadek) bystander, onlooker

obserwatori|um *n* observatory

obserw|ować *impf vt* to monitor *[chorego, stan pacjenta]*; to observe *[zjawiska]*; to watch *[podejrzanego, ptaki]*; to sight *[UFO, samolot]*

obsesj|a *f* obsession; **mieć** ~**ę na punkcie czegoś/kogoś** to be obsessed with a. by sth/sb

obsłu|ga *f* [1] (gości, klientów) service; (konta, transakcji) handling, servicing; (urządzeń) operation [2] (personel, załoga) personnel, staff; ~**ga naziemna** the ground crew; ~**ga techniczna** support services; ~**ga hotelowa** the hotel staff

obsłu|żyć *pf* — **obsłu|giwać** *impf* **[I]** *vt* [1] (w restauracji) to wait on, to serve; (w sklepie, urzędzie) to attend to [2] (używać, zajmować się) to operate *[komputer, maszynę]*; to man *[centralę telefoniczną, pompy]*; to handle *[konta, rachunki]*; to service *[zadłużenie, pożyczki]* **[II] obsłużyć się** — **obsługiwać się** to help a. serve oneself

obstaw|a *f* bodyguards

obsta|wać *impf vi* to stick (**przy czymś** to sth); **uparcie** ~**wali, że...** they insisted that...; ~**wać przy swoim** to stick to one's guns pot.

obstaw|ić *pf* — **obstaw|iać** *impf vt* [1] (otoczyć) to surround; ~**ili wszystkie wyjścia** they covered all the exits [2] (w grach hazardowych) to bet on *[kolory, liczby, gonitwę]*; to call *[orła, reszkę]* [3] Sport to mark *[przeciwnika]*

obst|ąpić *pf* — **obst|ępować** *impf vt* to surround

obstrukcj|a *f* [1] Med. constipation; **mieć** ~**ę** to be constipated [2] (utrudnianie) obstruction

obsusz|yć *pf* — **obsusz|ać** *impf vt* (częściowo) to let [sth] dry a bit; (powierzchownie) to dry

obsuwać się *impf* → **obsunąć się**

obsychać *impf* → **obeschnąć**

obsyp|ać *pf* — **obsyp|ywać** *impf* **[I]** *vt* [1] (opróżnić) ~**ać coś czymś** to sprinkle sth with sth *[serem, orzechami]*; to dust a. dredge sth with sth *[mąką, bułką tartą]*; ~**ać kogoś piaskiem** to cover sb with sand; ~**ać kogoś czymś** przen. to shower sb with sth *[pocałunkami, prezentami, wyzwiskami]*; to shower sth on sb *[pochwałami, nagrodami]* [2] (wystąpić w dużej ilości) *[piegi, plamy]* to speckle

Ⅱ obsypać się — obsypywać się [1] (siebie samego) [drzewa, gałęzie] to be/become covered with sth [kwieciem]; ~**ać się wypryskami** [osoba, skóra] to break out a. to come out GB in spots [2] (odpaść) [kwiaty, płatki, śnieg] to fall (**z czegoś** from sth) [3] (obdarzać się) ~**ać się czymś** to shower each other with sth [pocałunkami, obelgami]

obsza|r m area; **na całym** ~**rze** all over

obszczek|ać pf — **obszczek|iwać** impf vt [pies] to bark (**kogoś** at sb)

obszernie adv. grad. [opisać, komentować] extensively, at (great) length

obszern|y adi. grad. [dom, pokój] spacious; [kieszenie, torba, samochód] roomy; [sweter, szorty] loose-fitting; [spódnica, rękaw] full; [tematyka, wybór] extensive

obszuk|ać pf — **obszuk|iwać** impf vt to frisk [osobę]; to search [osobę, dom, kieszenie]

obszy|ć pf — **obszy|wać** impf vt [1] (oblamować) to trim, to edge (**coś czymś** sth with sth); **rękawy** ~**te koronką** lace-trimmed a. lace-edged cuffs [2] (obrębić) to bind [dziurki od guzików] [3] (pokryć) to cover; ~**ć coś skórą/płótnem** to cover sth with leather/canvas

obtaczać impf → **obtoczyć**

obtar|cie n graze

obtłu|c pf — **obtłu|kiwać** impf vt to chip [dzbanek, talerz]; to bruise [kolano, owoc]

obt|oczyć pf — **obt|aczać** impf vt [1] (oblepić) ~**oczyć coś w czymś** to coat sth in a. with sth [2] (wygładzić) to turn, to lathe [gałkę, tralkę]

obud|owa f [1] (turbiny, komputera) casing; (silnika, łożyska) housing; (kompasu, zegarka) case [2] (wyposażenie wnętrza) fixtures and fittings; ~**owa kuchni** the kitchen fixtures; **umywalka w** ~**owie** a sink unit

obud|owywać pf — **obud|owywać** impf vt to line [sth] with buildings [plac, ulicę]; to encase [kaloryfer]; to fit [kuchnię]

obu|dzić pf **Ⅱ** vt [1] (przerwać sen) to wake (up), to awake [2] (wywołać) to stir (up), to rouse [uczucie, zainteresowanie]; ~**dzić wspomnienia** to bring back memories

Ⅱ obudzić się [1] (przestać spać) to wake (up), to awake(n) [2] (powstawać) [wspomnienia, współczucie] to be (a)roused

obum|rzeć pf — **obum|ierać** impf vi [1] [tkanki, roślina] to die; [zwierzęta] to die off; [gatunek] to die out [2] książk. [uczucia] to die; [tradycja, instytucja] to die out

oburzać impf → **oburzyć**

oburzeni|e n indignation; (silne) outrage; **święte** ~**e** righteous indignation

oburz|ony adi. [osoba, spojrzenie] indignant (**czymś** over a. about sth); (silnie) outraged (**czymś** at sth)

oburz|yć pf — **oburz|ać** impf **Ⅱ** vt to incense; (silnie) to outrage; ~**yło nas, że...** we were outraged that...

Ⅱ oburzyć się — oburzać się to be incensed (**na coś** at sth); (silnie) to be outraged (**na coś** at sth)

obustronn|y adi. [1] [ruch] two-way; [plakat] double-sided, two-sided; ~**e zapalenie płuc** double pneumonia [2] [korzyść, porozumienie] mutual; [kontrola, układ, pomoc] bilateral

obuwi|e n książk. footwear; **sklep z** ~**em** a shoe shop; **zmienić** ~**e** to change one's shoes

obwąch|ać pf — **obwąch|iwać** impf vt to sniff

obwią|zać pf — **obwią|zywać** impf vt to tie, to bind; ~**zać pudełko sznurkiem** to tie a string around a box

obwieszczać impf → **obwieścić**

obwieszcze|nie n announcement

obwie|ścić pf — **obwie|szczać** impf vt to announce

obw|ieść pf — **obw|odzić** impf vt (otoczyć) to encircle, to surround; **tekst** ~**iedziony ramką** a boxed text

obwi|nić pf — **obwi|niać** impf vt (oskarżać) to accuse (**kogoś o coś** sb of sth); (zarzucać) to blame (**kogoś za coś** sb for sth)

obwodnic|a f ring road GB, beltway US

obwodzić impf → **obwieść**

obwolu|ta f dust jacket

obw|ód m [1] (wieloboku) perimeter; (koła) circumference [2] (rozmiar) ~**ód pasa/bioder** waist/hip size [3] (okręg) district [4] (elektryczny) circuit

obwód|ka f [1] (szlaczek) edge, rim; (ozdobna) border; **kartka z czarną** ~**ką** a page edged in black [2] (lamówka) trim, edging

oby part. ~ **się nie rozmyśliła** let's hope she doesn't change her mind; ~ **tak dalej** let's keep it that way

obyci|e n [1] (ogłada) good manners, polish [2] (oswojenie się) familiarity (**z czymś** with sth); experience (**z czymś** in a. with sth); ~**e z komputerem** computer literacy

obyczaj m [1] (zwyczaj) custom [2] (przyzwyczajenie) habit; **dobre** ~**e** (mere) decency

obyczajow|y adi. [1] (w kinie, literaturze) **powieść/komedia** ~**a** a novel/comedy of manners; **film** ~**y** a (contemporary) film drama [2] (dotyczący moralności) **skandal** ~**y** a sex scandal; **swoboda** ~**a** sexual freedom

ob|yć się pf — **ob|ywać się** impf v refl. [1] (obejść się) **obyć się bez czegoś** to go a. do without sth; **obyło się bez wypadku** an accident was avoided; **nie obędzie się bez kłótni** there's bound to be an argument [2] (zadowolić się) **obyć się czymś** to make do with sth

obywatel m, ~**ka** f citizen; ~ **świata** a citizen of the world

obywatelstw|o n citizenship

obżarstw|o n pot. gluttony

obżartuch m pot. glutton

ocalać impf → **ocalić**

ocal|eć *pf vi* to survive; ~**eć z wypadku** to survive an accident; ~**eć od śmierci** to escape death

ocal|ić *pf* — **ocal|ać** *impf vt* to rescue, to save (**kogoś/coś od czegoś** sb/sth from sth); ~**ić coś od zapomnienia** to preserve sth for posterity

ocean *m* ocean

ocen|a *f* ① (osąd) assessment; ~**a pracownika** a job appraisal ② (wycena) evaluation ③ Szkol. mark GB, grade US (**z czegoś** in sth)

oce|nić *pf* — **oce|niać** *impf vt* ① (wydać opinię) to judge *[osobę, dzieło]*; to assess *[czyn, postępowanie]* ② (oszacować) to assess *[szkody]*; to estimate *[szanse, wartość]* ③ (postawić ocenę) *[nauczyciel]* to assess *[pracę, ucznia]*

ocenzur|ować *pf vt* to censor *[tekst]*

oc|et *m* vinegar

ochlap|ać *pf* — **ochlap|ywać** *impf* **[]** *vt* ① (zmoczyć) to splash ② pot. (pomalować niestarannie) to slap

[] **ochlapać się** pot. (szybko się umyć) to have a quick wash

ochładzać *impf* → **ochłodzić**

ochłodze|nie *n* ① (spadek temperatury) cooler weather; **nagłe** ~**nie** a cold snap ② przen. cooling; ~**nie stosunków międzynarodowych** a cooling in international relations

ochł|odzić *pf* — **ochł|adzać** *impf* **[]** *vt* ① *[osoba]* to cool (down) *[deser, napój]*; *[kąpiel, wiatr]* to refresh *[osobę]* ② przen. *[kłótnia, rozłąka]* to cause [sth] to cool off *[stosunki]*

[] **ochłodzić się** — **ochładzać się** ① (o pogodzie) to get cooler/colder ② przen. *[kontakty, stosunki]* to cool (off)

ochło|nąć *pf vi* (z emocji) to cool down; to simmer down pot.; (z wysiłku) to cool off a. down

ocho|ta *f* willingness; **mieć** ~**tę na coś** to feel like (doing) sth; **czy macie** ~**tę na coś słodkiego?** would you care for something sweet?; **pracować z** ~**tą** to work enthusiastically

ochotnicz|y *adi. [praca, służba]* voluntary

ochotni|k *m*, ~**czka** *f* volunteer; **zgłosić się na** ~**ka (do czegoś)** to volunteer (for sth)

ochraniacz *m* ~**e na kolana/łokcie** knee/elbow pads

ochraniać *impf* → **ochronić**

ochron|a *f* ① (zabytków) preservation; (danych, praw) protection; ~**a przyrody** wildlife conservation; ~**a środowiska** environmental preservation a. protection; **rośliny/zwierzęta pod** ~**ą** protected plants/animals; ~**a zdrowia** health care ② (zabezpieczenie) protection (**przed czymś** against a. from sth); safeguard (**przed czymś** against sth) ③ (budynku, lotniska) security; (osoby) bodyguard(s)

ochroniarz *m* pot. (osoby) bodyguard; (budynku) security guard

ochr|onić *pf* — **ochr|aniać** *impf vt* to protect

ochronn|y *adi. [barwy, ubranie, warstwa]* protective; **szczepienia** ~**e** immunization, vaccination; **krem** ~**y** a barrier cream

ochryp|nąć *pf vi [osoba]* to make oneself hoarse; *[głos]* to become hoarse a. husky; ~**ł od krzyku** he shouted himself hoarse

ochrz|cić *pf* **[]** *vt* ① *[ksiądz]* to baptize *[dziecko]* ② (nadać imię, nazwę) to christen ③ pot. (rozcieńczyć) to water down *[wino, zupę]*

[] **ochrzcić się** to be baptized

ociąga|ć się *impf v refl.* ① (robić powoli) to linger, to dally (**z czymś** over sth) ② (zwlekać) ~**ć się z czymś** to delay (doing) sth, to be reluctant to do sth

ocie|knąć *pf* — **ocie|kać** *impf vi [woda]* to drip; *[naczynia]* to drain

ociel|ić się *pf v refl.* to calve

ocieplacz *m* ① (materiał) insulation (material); (wszyty w ubranie) lining; (część odzieży) warmer; **kurtka z** ~**em** a quilted a. padded jacket ② (pokrowiec) casing; ~ **na dzbanek z herbatą** a tea cosy

ocieplać *impf* → **ocieplić**

ociep|le|nie *n* ① (wzrost temperatury) warm spell; **globalne** ~**nie** global warming ② przen. thaw; ~**nie stosunków międzynarodowych** a thaw in international relations

ociep|lić *pf* — **ociep|lać** *impf* **[]** *vt* ① (materiałem) to insulate *[dom, ściany]*; **rękawiczki** ~**one futerkiem** fur-lined gloves ② przen. to warm up *[atmosferę]*

[] **ocieplić się** — **ocieplać się** ① *[klimat]* to warm (up) ② przen. *[atmosfera, kontakty]* to thaw (out)

ocierać *impf* → **otrzeć**

ocio|sać *pf* — **ocio|sywać** *impf vt* to hew *[drewno, kamień]*

ockn|ąć się *pf v refl.* (ze snu) to wake up; (z omdlenia, uśpienia) to come to a. round; (z zamyślenia) to rouse oneself

ocl|ić *pf vt* to impose a. levy a customs duty on; **czy ma pan coś do** ~**enia?** have you got anything to declare?

ocu|cić *pf* — **ocu|cać** *impf vt* to revive, to bring [sb] to, to bring [sb] round GB a. around US

oczek|iwać *impf vt* ① (czekać) to wait (**kogoś/czegoś** for sb/sth); ~**ują ich poważne zadania** they have serious business ahead of them ② (spodziewać się) to expect; ~**iwałem po tobie więcej rozsądku** I expected you to have more common sense; **moja siostra** ~**uje dziecka** my sister is expecting a baby

oczekiwa|nie *n* expectation (**czegoś** a. **na coś** of sth); **spełnić czyjeś** ~**nia** to measure a. live up to sb's expectations

oczer|nić *pf* — **oczer|niać** *impf* książk. *vt* to defame książk.; to smear przen.

ocz|ko *n* ① (w pierścionku) gem, stone ② (w sieci, sitku) mesh; (w tarce) hole ③ (w dzianinie) stitch; (rozprucie)

run, ladder GB; **w prawej pończosze poszło ci**
~**ko** you've got a run a. ladder in your right
stocking ④ Gry (hazardowa gra) blackjack; (21 punktów)
pontoon
■ **być (czymś)** ~**kiem w głowie** to be the apple
of sb's eye
oczyszczać *impf* → **oczyścić**
oczyszczalni|a *f* ~**a ścieków** sewage treatment
plant
oczy|ścić *pf* — **oczy|szczać** *impf vt* ① (usunąć
brud) to clean *[ranę, skórę]*; to purify *[płyn]*; ~**ścić**
buty z błota to clean the mud off one's shoes;
~**ścić organizm z toksyn** to cleanse the body of
toxins ② (zrehabilitować) to clear; **sąd** ~**ścił go**
z zarzutów the court cleared him of the charges
oczywi|sty *adi. [fakt, pomyłka]* obvious; **było**
~**ste, że...** it was obvious a. clear that...
oczywiście *part.* of course, certainly; **nie mógł** ~
tego przewidzieć of course, he couldn't have
foreseen that; **„mogę pożyczyć twoje pióro?"** –
„~**"** 'can I borrow your pen?' - 'of course',
'certainly'
od, **ode** *praep.* ① (z miejsca, z kierunku) from; **od**
zachodu from the west; **odległość od drzwi do**
okna the distance from the door to the window;
chodzić od sklepu do sklepu to go from shop to
shop; **właśnie wracałam od dentysty** I was just
on my way back from the dentist; **goście wstali od**
stołu the guests got up from the table ② (określające
położenie) from; **od wewnątrz/zewnątrz** from the
inside/outside; **druga półka od dołu/góry** the
second shelf from the bottom/top; **piąty wagon od**
końca the fifth carriage from the end; **okna od**
ulicy/podwórza the front/back windows; **na**
południe od Krakowa (to the) south of Cracow
③ (wskazujące na oddzielenie) from; **oddzielić coś od**
czegoś to separate sth from sth; **stronić od kogoś/**
czegoś to avoid a. shun sb/sth; **nie mógł oderwać**
się od książki he couldn't tear himself away from
the book; **odejmij pięć od trzynastu** subtract five
from thirteen ④ (określające pochodzenie) from; **list od**
brata a letter from one's brother; **dostała ode**
mnie książkę she got a book from me; **zaraził się**
odrą ode mnie he caught the measles from me
⑤ (określające moment początkowy) from; (w przeszłości)
since; **od tej chwili** from that moment on; **od jutra**
from tomorrow, as of a. from tomorrow; **od**
poniedziałku/marca since (last) Monday/March;
od jak dawna tu mieszkasz? how long have you
lived a. been living here? ⑥ (określające czas trwania)
for; **od roku/trzech tygodni** for a year/three
weeks; **od dawna** for a long time; **od jakiegoś**
czasu for some time ⑦ (określające dolną granicę) from;
od drugiej do piątej po południu from two p.m.
till five p.m.; **od poniedziałku do środy** from
Monday to Wednesday; **zaprosimy od 50 do 60**
osób we'll invite (from) 50 to 60 people; **od 1000**

złotych w górę from 1,000 zlotys up a. upwards;
można tu kupić wszystko: od śrubek po
komputery you can buy everything here – from
screws to computers ⑧ (określające przyczynę) from,
with; **oczy czerwone od płaczu** eyes red from
crying a. tears; **jego twarz rozpalona od gorączki**
his face flushed with fever; **ochrypł od krzyku** he
grew hoarse from a. with shouting; **rury popękały**
od mrozu the pipes had burst from the cold; **dom**
zapalił się od pioruna the house was set on fire by
lightning ⑨ (przeciwko) from; **chronić coś od**
słońca/chłodu to protect sth from (the) sun-
light/cold; **oganiać się od komarów** to fight off
the gnats; **być ubezpieczonym od pożaru/**
kradzieży to be insured against fire/theft; **uchylać**
się od czegoś to shirk sth ⑩ (określające przeznaczenie) **dziurka od klucza** a keyhole; **kluczyki od**
samochodu car keys; **okulary od słońca** sunglasses; **pasek od zegarka** a watch strap; **tabletki**
od bólu głowy headache pills a. tablets; **syrop od**
kaszlu cough mixture a. syrup; **od czego jest ta**
śrubka? where does this screw come from?
⑪ (określające specjalizację) **pan od matematyki/**
angielskiego the maths/English teacher; **ekspert**
od informatyki an expert in computer science;
policja jest od tego, żeby zaprowadzić
w mieście porządek it's the job of the police to
restore order in the city; **nie jestem od tego, żeby**
was pouczać it's not up to me to lecture you
⑫ (niż) than; **to mieszkanie jest mniejsze od**
waszego this flat is smaller than yours; **ona jest**
starsza od brata o dwa lata she's two years older
than her brother; **wyszedł wcześniej ode mnie**
he left earlier than I did ⑬ (podstawa obliczenia) by,
per; **płatny od wiersza/godziny** paid by the line/
hour; **50 złotych od metra** 50 zlotys a metre
oda *f* ode
odbarw|ić *pf* — **odbarw|iać** *impf* Ⅰ *vt* to
bleach *[włosy, tkaninę]*
Ⅱ **odbarwić się** — **odbarwiać się** *[tkanina]* to
fade
odbezpiecz|yć *pf* — **odbezpiecz|ać** *impf vt* to
release the safety catch of *[broń]*; to arm *[granat]*
odbi|ć *pf* — **odbi|jać**¹ *impf* Ⅰ *vt* ① (w fizyce) to
reflect *[dźwięk, światło]* ② (ukazać) *[lustro, woda]* to
reflect, to mirror *[obraz]* ③ Sport (zmienić kierunek) to
deflect *[strzał, piłkę]*; (w tenisie, badmintonie) to return
[lotkę, piłkę] ④ (nanieść maszynowo) to print; (powielić) to
copy, to make a copy of; (odcisnąć) to impress; ~**ć**
coś na ksero(kopiarce) to xerox a. photocopy sth
⑤ (uwolnić) to retake, to recapture *[miasto]*; to rescue
[zakładników] ⑥ pot. (uwieść) to take away *[chłopaka,*
dziewczynę]; (w tańcu) to cut in
Ⅱ *vi* ① (oddalić się od brzegu) *[łódź]* to push off; *[statek,*
załoga] to set sail ② (skręcić) *[kierowca, pojazd]* to turn
off (**od czegoś** sth); *[droga]* to diverge, to branch off
(**od czegoś** from sth)

III odbić się — odbijać się ① Fiz. *[dźwięk, fale, promieniowanie]* to reflect (**od czegoś** off sth) ② *[postać, twarz]* to be mirrored a. reflected (**w czymś** in sth) ③ *[uczucia]* to be mirrored przen.; **na jej twarzy ~ło się zdumienie** her face expressed amazement ④ *[piłka, strzał]* to rebound (**od czegoś** from sth); to bounce, to bound (**od czegoś** off sth) ⑤ *[ślad]* to be impressed ⑥ *[przeżycia, sytuacja]* to affect ⑦ (po posiłku) **dziecku ~ło się** the child belched a. burped pot.

IV odbić sobie — odbijać sobie to make up for *[straty]*; **straciliśmy mnóstwo czasu, ale ~jemy to sobie** we've lost a lot of time, but we'll make up for it

odbie|c *pf* — **odbie|gać** *impf vi* to run away (**od kogoś/czegoś** from sb/sth); **~c od tematu** przen. to digress a. stray from the subject

odbierać[1] *impf* → **odebrać**

odbiera|ć[2] *impf vt [radio, telewizor]* to pick up, to receive; *[słuchacz, widz]* to receive; **to radio nie ~ fal długich** you can't get long wave on this radio

odbijać[1] *impf* → **odbić**

odbija|ć[2] *impf* **[I]** *vi* książk. (wyróżniać się korzystnie) to stand out (**od kogoś/czegoś** from sb/sth); (odróżniać się) to differ, to be different (**od kogoś/czegoś** from sb/sth)

II odbijać się (wyróżniać się na tle) to stand out

odbiorc|a *m* (nagrody, przesyłki) receiver; (gazu, prądu, towaru) consumer; (programu) (telewizyjnego) (TV)viewer; (radiowego) listener; (filmu, muzyki) member of an audience; **masowy ~a** a mass audience

odbiornik *m* receiver; **~ telewizyjny** a TV set

odbi|ór *m* ① (nagrody) receipt; (przesyłki) collection; **~ór bagażu** (na lotnisku) baggage reclaim ② (pracy) acceptance; **~ór techniczny** technical acceptance ③ książk. (dzieła artystycznego) reception ④ (fal, sygnału) reception; „~ór!” 'over!'; „bez ~oru!” 'over and out!'

odbit|ka *f* (tekstu) copy; (zdjęcia) print

odblask *m* (odbite światło) reflected light; (refleks światła) gleam

odblok|ować *pf* — **odblok|owywać** *impf vt* ① (usunąć przeszkodę) to clear *[drogę]*; (znieść blokadę) to lift a blockade ② (umożliwić działanie) to unblock *[przewód]* ③ (udostępnić) to unfreeze *[ceny, płace]*; to unblock *[konto]* ④ pot. (uwolnić) to release *[uczucia]*; to unleash *[energię]*

odbudow|a *f* reconstruction

odbud|ować *pf* — **odbud|owywać** *impf vt* to rebuild *[miasto, przemysł, karierę]*; to restore *[zaufanie, gospodarkę]*

odbur|knąć *pf* — **odbur|kiwać** *impf vi* to snap (out) (**komuś** at sb)

odb|yć *pf* — **odb|ywać** *impf* **[I]** *pf* ① (zostać poddanym) to undergo *[kurację, szkolenie]*; to serve *[karę, staż]*; **~yć służbę wojskową** to do military service ② (wziąć udział) to hold *[konsultacje, rozmowę]*;

to make *[tournée]*; **~yć podróż po Europie** to go on a tour of Europe

II odbyć się — odbywać się *[konferencja, zawody sportowe]* to take place; *[egzamin, operacja, pogrzeb]* to be held

odby|t *m* Anat. anus

odbytnic|a *f* Anat. rectum

odbywać *impf* → **odbyć**

odce|dzić *pf* — **odce|dzać** *impf vt* to drain (off), to strain *[makaron, ziemniaki]*

odchod|y *plt* faeces, feces US; (ptaków, gryzoni, owiec) droppings; (bydła, koni) dung

odchodzić[1] *impf* → **odejść**

odcho|dzić[2] *impf vi [kabel, ulica]* to diverge, to branch off (**od czegoś** from sth)

odchu|dzić *pf* — **odchu|dzać** *impf* **[I]** *vt* to slim [sb/sth] down *[osobę, zwierzę]*; to streamline *[instytucję]*; to reduce *[budżet]*

II odchudzić się — odchudzać się to lose weight

odchyl|ić *pf* — **odchyl|ać** *impf vt* (na krótko odsunąć) to draw a. pull aside *[zasłonę]*; (przechylić) to tilt *[głowę, krzesło]*

od|ciąć *pf* — **od|cinać** *impf* **[I]** *vt* ① (nożem, nożyczkami) to cut away a. off; (zbędne części) to trim away a. off ② (przerwać dopływ) to cut a. shut off *[gaz, prąd, wodę, telefon]* ③ (odizolować) to cut off (**od kogoś/czegoś** from sb/sth); (zablokować) to cut off, to block *[dostęp, drogę ucieczki]*; **lawina odcięła nam drogę** we were cut off by an avalanche

II odciąć się — odcinać się pot. ① (zająć odrębne stanowisko) to dissociate oneself (**od kogoś/czegoś** from sb/sth); to cut oneself off (**od czegoś** from sth) ② (odpowiedzieć) to answer [sb] back, to talk back (**komuś** to sb)

III odcinać się (kontrastować) to show up, to stand out (**od czegoś** against sth)

odciąż|yć *pf* — **odciąż|ać** *impf vt* ① (zmniejszyć obciążenie) to lighten *[bagażnik, przyczepę]*; to relieve *[nacisk]*; to unweight *[nartę]* ② (ulżyć) to relieve, to disburden; **~yć kogoś od czegoś** to relieve sb of sth

odcie|c, odcie|knąć *pf* — **odcie|kać** *impf vi [sałata, ser]* to drain

odcie|ń *m* ① (odmiana koloru) shade, hue; (zabarwienie) tint, tinge ② (różnica) (w brzmieniu) tone; (w nastroju) shade

odcinać *impf* → **odciąć**

odcin|ek *m* ① (fragment) section; (podróży, wyścigu) stage; (czasu) stretch, length ② (serialu) episode, part; (filmu, programu) instalment GB, installment US ③ (kwit kontrolny) counterfoil; **~ek czeku** a cheque stub ④ (część prostej) segment

odcisk *m* ① (zgrubienie naskórka) call(o)us; (na stopie) corn; **nadepnąć komuś na ~** to tread a. step on sb's toes ② (odciśnięty zarys) impression, imprint; (znak pieczęci, stempla) impress; **~ stopy** a. **buta**

a footprint; ~ **palca** a. **linii papilarnych** a fingerprint

odci|snąć *pf* — **odci|skać** *impf vt* [1] (zostawić ślad) to impress, to imprint *[wzór, znak]*; to leave *[ślad]* (**na czymś** on sth) [2] (wycisnąć płyn) to squeeze *[sok]*

odcyfr|ować *pf* — **odcyfr|owywać** *impf vt* to decipher *[niewyraźne pismo, szyfr]*; to decode, to decrypt *[symbole]*

odczep|ić *pf* — **odczep|iać** *impf* [] *vt* (odłączyć) to uncouple *[wagon]*; to unfasten *[linę]*; (wypiąć z haka) to unhook *[linę]*

[] **odczepić się** pot. to rid oneself (**od kogoś/czegoś** of sb/sth); (przestać się zajmować) to leave alone; ~ **się wreszcie!** just leave me alone! pot.

odczu|cie *n* (wrażenie, reakcja) impression, feeling; (stosunek, opinia) sentiment; (wrażenie zmysłowe) sensation

odczu|ć *pf* — **odczu|wać** *impf vt* [1] to feel *[ból, głód, samotność]* [2] (instynktownie wyczuć) to sense; (intuicyjnie zrozumieć, ocenić) to feel

odczyn *m* reaction

odczynnik *m* reagent

odczy|t *m* [1] (prelekcja) lecture (**na temat czegoś** on sth) [2] Komput., Techn. reading; **plik tylko do** ~**tu** a read-only file

odczyt|ać *pf* — **odczyt|ywać** *impf vt* [1] (odszyfrować) to decipher *[bazgroły]*; to decode, to decrypt *[szyfr]* [2] (zinterpretować) to decipher, to interpret *[intencje, zachowanie]* [3] (głośno przeczytać) to read out; ~**ać listę obecności** to call the register [4] Komput. to read *[dane, plik]* [5] (sprawdzić) to read *[licznik, pomiar]*

odda|ć *pf* — **odda|wać** *impf* [] *vt* [1] (zwrócić) to give back, to return *[pożyczony przedmiot]*; to pay back *[dług]* [2] (ofiarować) to give, to hand over *[majątek]*; to donate *[dary, sumę pieniędzy]*; ~**ć krew** to give a. donate blood; ~**ć życie za kogoś/coś** to lay down one's life for sb/sth [3] (przekazać na jakiś czas) to deposit *[pieniądze, obraz]* [4] (zlecić usługę) ~**ć coś do pralni** a. **prania** to take sth to the laundry; ~**ć coś do naprawy** to have sth repaired [5] (zakończyć pracę) to hand a. give in *[pracę, projekt]* [6] (ulokować) to put; **musieli** ~**ć ją do domu opieki** they had to put her in a nursing home [7] (wyrazić) to convey, to render *[nastrój, uczucie]*

[] **oddać się** — **oddawać się** [1] (poddać się) **terrorysta** ~**ł się w ręce policji** the terrorist turned himself in to the police; ~**ję się do pana dyspozycji** I place myself at your disposal książk. [2] (zająć się) to devote oneself, to give oneself over (**komuś/czemuś** to sb/sth); (poddać się uczuciowo) to abandon oneself, to give oneself over (**czemuś** to sth) [3] książk. (seksualnie) to surrender a. give oneself (**komuś** to sb)

oddal|ić *pf* — **oddal|ać** *impf* [] *vt* [1] (w sądzie) to dismiss *[sprawę, wniosek]* [2] (odsunąć) to put off *[rozstanie, rozmowę]*; to avert *[niebezpieczeństwo, podejrzenia]*

[] **oddalić się** — **oddalać się** *[osoba, zwierzę]* to walk a. go away, to wander off (**od kogoś/czegoś** from sb/sth); *[pojazd, światło, cel]* to recede; *[szanse, wspomnienia]* to fade

oddan|y *adi.* [1] (przywiązany) *[przyjaciel]* devoted (**komuś** to sb); (gorliwy) *[pracownik]* committed (**czemuś** to sth); **szczerze** ~**y** książk. (w korespondencji) yours truly [2] (pochłonięty) devoted (**czemuś** to sth); immersed (**czemuś** in sth)

oddawać *impf* → **oddać**

oddech *m* [1] (oddychanie) breathing; (wdech i wydech) breath; **nieświeży** ~ bad breath; **wziąć** ~ to take a breath, to breathe in; **z trudem łapał** ~ he was gasping for breath a. air [2] przen. (odpoczynek) respite książk.; breather pot.

oddycha|ć *impf* → **odetchnąć**[1]

oddzia|ł *m* [1] (jednostka wojska, policji) unit; (desantowy, zwiadowczy) party; (interwencyjny, specjalny) squad [2] (dział instytucji, biura) department; (filia) branch; (część fabryki) shop [3] Med. ward; ~**ł intensywnej opieki medycznej** an intensive care unit

oddział|ać *pf* — **oddział|ywać** *impf vi* [1] (wywrzeć wpływ) *[osoba, sytuacja]* to have an influence a. impact (**na kogoś/coś** on sb/sth); (wywołać skutki) *[kryzys]* to affect (**na coś** sth); to have an effect (**na coś** on sth) [2] (chemicznie) *[substancja]* to interact (**na coś** with sth)

oddziałow|a *f* pot. ward sister GB

oddziaływać *impf* → **oddziałać**

oddziel|ić *pf* — **oddziel|ać** *impf vt* to separate (**coś od czegoś** sth from sth)

oddzielnie *adv.* *[prać]* separately; *[rozpatrywać]* individually; **mieszkamy** ~ we live separately a. apart; „**nie ma**" **piszemy** ~ 'nie ma' is written as two separate words

oddzieln|y *adi.* *[grupa, pokój, wejście]* separate; *[opis]* individual

oddzierać *impf* → **odedrzeć**

oddzw|onić *pf* — **oddzw|aniać** *impf vi* to call a. ring *[sb]* back, to return a call

oddźwięk *m* response

ode → **od**

od|ebrać *pf* — **od|bierać**[1] *impf vt* [1] (odzyskać własność) to take back; **odebrać od kogoś książkę** to take one's book back from sb [2] (zabrać z przechowania, z naprawy) to collect *[bagaż, pranie, zegarek]*; to reclaim *[depozyt]*; **odebrać dziecko ze szkoły** to collect one's child from school [3] (przyjąć) to collect, to pick up *[przesyłkę]*; to receive, to pick up *[nagrodę]* [4] (pozbawić, skonfiskować) to take (away) *[broń, tytuł]*; to seize, to confiscate *[narkotyki]*; to deprive *[sb]* of *[nadzieję, prawo]*; to divest *[sb]* of *[władzę]*; to snatch *[przywództwo]*; **odebrać sobie życie** he took his own life [5] (drogą radiową, satelitarną) to pick up, to receive *[sygnał, program]*; **odebrać telefon** to answer a. get the telephone [6] (zrozumieć, zinterpretować) to construe *[wypowiedź,* *zachowanie]*; to interpret *[film, przedstawienie]* [7] (w tenisie) to return *[piłkę, zagrywkę]* [8] Med. to deliver *[dziecko]*; **odebrać poród** to assist in a birth

odechc|ieć się *pf* — **odechc|iewać się** *impf v imp.* pot. ~**iało mi się spać** I don't feel like sleeping any more; **wszystkiego mi się** ~**iewa** I just want to curl up and die

od|egrać *pf* — **od|grywać** *impf* **[]** *vt* [1] Muz. to play *[utwór]*; to perform *[solo, wariacje]* [2] (w filmie, teatrze) *[aktor]* to play, to act *[rolę]*; to portray *[postać]*; *[zespół]* to perform, to act *[sztukę]*; to enact *[scenę]* [3] (udawać) to play *[bohatera]*; to act *[głupiego]*; to act (out) *[rolę pocieszyciela]*

[] **odegrać się** — **odgrywać się** [1] (w grze) to win back [2] pot. (zemścić się) to get even pot. (**na kimś** with sb); to get one's own back pot. (**na kimś** on sb)

odejmować *impf* → **odjąć**

odejmowa|nie *n* subtraction

od|ejść *pf* — **od|chodzić¹** *impf vi* [1] (oddalić się) to walk away; (opuścić) to leave, to abandon (**od kogoś** sb); *[autobus, pociąg]* to leave, to depart [2] (zrezygnować) to resign (**z czegoś** from sth); **odejść na emeryturę** to retire [3] (oderwać się) *[podeszwa, tapeta]* to come off; *[farba, lakier]* to peel off, to come away (**od czegoś** from sth) [4] książk. (umrzeć) to pass away książk.

od|epchnąć *pf* — **od|pychać¹** *impf* **[]** *vt* [1] (odsunąć) to push, to shove; (od siebie) to push away, to shove [sb/sth] out of the way [2] (odtrącić) to reject, to spurn *[osobę, przyjaźń]*

[] **odepchnąć się** — **odpychać się** to push off (**od czegoś** from sth)

od|eprzeć¹ *pf* — **od|pierać** *impf vt* [1] (zmusić do odwrotu) to drive back *[wroga]*; to repel *[atak]*; to repulse *[nieprzyjaciela, szturm]* [2] (kontrować) to parry *[atak, cios, pytania]*; to refute *[argumenty, oskarżenie, zarzuty]*

odeprzeć² *pf vi* książk. (odpowiedzieć) to reply

od|erwać *pf* — **od|rywać** *impf* **[]** *vt* [1] (oddzielić) to tear out; (gwałtownie urwać) to tear away a. off [2] (przerwać czynność) to drag a. tear [sb] away (**od czegoś** from sth); **nie mógł od niej oderwać oczu** przen. he couldn't tear his eyes away from her

[] **oderwać się** — **odrywać się** [1] (odpaść) *[guzik, rączka, tapeta]* to come off; *[gałąź, sopel]* to break off [2] (stracić kontakt) *[osoba, grupa]* to break away (**od czegoś** from sth); **samolot oderwał się od ziemi** the aeroplane took off [3] (zrobić przerwę) to stop; **oderwać się od pracy** to stop working; **książka, od której nie można się oderwać** a book you cannot put down; an unputdownable book pot.

od|esłać *pf* — **od|syłać** *impf vt* [1] (zwrócić) to send (back) *[przesyłkę]* [2] (skierować) to send, to refer; **odsyłano mnie od urzędu do urzędu** I was sent from one office to another [3] (wskazać źródło informacji) to refer

od|espać *pf* — **od|sypiać** *impf vt* to sleep off *[dyżur, podróż]*

od|etchnąć¹ *pf* — **od|dychać** *impf vi* to breathe; **oddychać czymś** to breathe in sth

odetchn|ąć² *pf vi* [1] (uspokoić się) to breathe again; **zatrzymał się, żeby trochę** ~**ąć** he stopped for a breather pot.; ~**ął z ulgą** he heaved a sigh of relief [2] (wypocząć) to have a break, to relax

od|etkać *pf* — **od|tykać** *impf vt* [1] (odblokować) to unclog, to unblock *[wannę, zlew]* [2] (otworzyć) to uncork *[butelkę]*

odezw|a *f* (apel) appeal; (plakat) public notice

od|ezwać się *pf* — **od|zywać się** *impf v refl.* [1] (powiedzieć) to speak, to say [2] (zadzwonić) to call; (napisać list) to drop a line [3] (zabrzmieć) *[echo, głos]* to be heard, to sound; **odezwał się dzwonek u drzwi** there was a ring at the door [4] pot. (ujawnić się) *[choroba]* to return; **odezwał się w nim pedagog** the teacher in him came out

odgad|nąć *pf* — **odgad|ywać** *impf vt* [1] (znaleźć rozwiązanie) to guess *[hasło, odpowiedź]*; ~**nąć zagadkę** to solve a riddle [2] (domyślić się) to guess, to puzzle out *[cel, myśli, zamiar]*; ~**nąć przyszłość** to foretell the future

odgałęzie|nie *n* branch, turn-off

odganiać *impf* → **odegnać**

odgarn|ąć *pf* — **odgarn|iać** *impf vt* to sweep a. brush aside *[liście, śnieg]*; ~**ąć włosy z czoła** to brush one's hair off one's forehead

odgłos *m* sound

odgonić → **odegnać**

odgradzać *impf* → **odgrodzić**

odgraża|ć się *impf v refl.* to threaten

odgr|odzić *pf* — **odgr|adzać** *impf* **[]** *vt* to separate (**coś od czegoś** sth from sth); ~**odzić coś murem/płotem** to wall/fence sth off

[] **odgrodzić się** — **odgradzać się** to isolate oneself, to shut oneself off (**od czegoś/kogoś** from sth/sb)

odgrywać *impf* → **odegrać**

odgry|źć *pf* — **odgry|zać** *impf* **[]** *vt* to bite off

[] **odgryźć się** — **odgryzać się** pot. to strike a. snap back (**komuś** at sb)

odgrz|ać *pf* — **odgrz|ewać** *impf vt* [1] Kulin. to heat a. warm up *[obiad]* [2] pejor. (przypomnieć sobie) to rehash, to dredge up *[wspomnienia]*; ~**ewane dowcipy** rehashed jokes

odhacz|yć *pf* — **odhacz|ać** *impf vt* pot. [1] (zaznaczyć) to tick GB a. check US off [2] (odczepić) to take [sth] off the hook *[rybę]*

odhol|ować *pf vt* [1] (odciągnąć) to tow a. haul away *[łódź, samochód]* [2] pot. (odprowadzić) to escort *[kolegę]*

odj|azd *m* (osoby, autobusu, pociągu) departure; ~**azd!** go!

od|jąć *pf* — **od|ejmować** *impf vt* [1] (odłączyć) to take off *[część]* [2] (zmniejszyć wartość) to subtract, to take (away); **sześć odjąć dwa równa się cztery**

six minus two equals four ③ (pozbawić) **odjęło jej mowę** she was (left) speechless pot.

odj|echać *pf* — **odj|eżdżać** *impf vi* to go away, to leave; **pociąg** ~**eżdża z peronu siódmego** the train leaves a. departs from platform seven; ~**echać na rowerze** to ride off on one's bike

odjemn|a *f* minuend

odjemnik *m* subtrahend

odjeżdżać *impf* → odjechać

odka|zić *pf* — **odka|żać** *impf vt* to disinfect *[narzędzia, ranę]*; to decontaminate *[teren, wodę]*

odkąd *pron.* ① (pytajny) (od jakiego czasu) since when; (jak długo) how long ② (względny) (od czasu gdy) since; **już trzy miesiące,** ~ **rzuciłem palenie** it's three months since I gave up smoking; ~ **pamiętam...** for as long as I can remember... ③ (pytajny) (od jakiego miejsca) where from; ~ **mam zacząć?** where shall a. should I begin?

odkle|ić *pf* — **odkle|jać** *impf* **❶** *vt* to unstick **❷ odkleić się** — **odklejać się** *[tapeta, znaczek]* to peel off

odkładać *impf* → odłożyć

odkoch|ać się *pf* — **odkoch|iwać się** *impf v refl.* pot. to fall out of love

odkop|ać *pf* — **odkop|ywać** *impf vt* to dig up a. out *[skarby]*; to dig out *[osobę]*

odkrawać *impf* → odkroić

odkrę|cić *pf* — **odkrę|cać** *impf vt* ① (zdjąć śruby) to unscrew *[pokrywę]*; (zdjąć nakrętkę) to undo, to twist off *[słoik]* ② (umożliwić przepływ) to turn a. switch on *[gaz, wodę]*; to open *[zawór]*

odkr|oić *pf* — **odkr|awać** *impf vt* to cut off

odkry|cie *n* discovery

odkry|ć *pf* — **odkry|wać** *impf vt* ① (odsłonić) to unveil *[pojemnik]*; ~**ć twarz** to uncover a. show one's face ② (poznać) to discover *[nowy ląd, pierwiastek chemiczny, zdolności]*; ~**ć prawdę** to find out a. discover the truth ③ (pomóc w karierze) to discover *[aktora, sportowca]* ④ (ujawnić) to reveal ■ ~**ć Amerykę** iron. to reinvent the wheel

odkry|ty *adi. [pojazd]* open; *[basen]* outdoor; *[głowa, ramiona]* bare

odkrywać *impf* → odkryć

odkryw|ca *m*, ~**czyni** *f* discoverer

odkup|ić *pf* — **odkup|ywać** *impf vt* ① (kupić od kogoś) to purchase, to buy; (odzyskać) to buy back, to repurchase ② przen. to expiate, to atone for *[grzechy]*

odkurzacz *m* vacuum cleaner, Hoover GB

odkurz|yć *pf* — **odkurz|ać** *impf vt* ① (oczyścić) (odkurzaczem) to vacuum(-clean), to hoover GB *[dywan]*; (szmatką) to dust *[meble]* ② przen. (przypomnieć) to dust off, to revisit *[hipotezę, pomysł]*

odl|ać *pf* — **odl|ewać** *impf vt* ① (zlać) to pour out ② (odcedzić) to drain, to strain *[makaron, ziemniaki]* ③ (zrobić odlew) to cast *[posąg]*

odl|ecieć *pf* — **odl|atywać** *impf vi* ① *[ptak]* to fly away a. off; *[samolot]* to take off, to depart ② pot. *[guzik, obcas]* to come off

odległoś|ć *f* distance (**od czegoś do czegoś** from sth to sth); **porozumiewać się na** ~**ć** to communicate from a. over a distance; **na** ~**ć kroku** within a step

odległ|y *adi. grad. [głosy, sprawy]* distant; *[miejsce]* remote

odlep|ić *pf* — **odlep|iać** *impf* **❶** *vt* to unstick *[etykietę, znaczek]* **❷ odlepić się** — **odlepiać się** *[tapeta, znaczek]* to peel off, to come unstuck a. off

odlew *m* cast

odlewać *impf* → odlać

odleżyn|a *f* bedsore

odliczać *impf* → odliczyć

odlicz|yć *pf* — **odlicz|ać** *impf* **❶** *vt* ① (odmierzyć) to count out; **przygotuj** ~**oną kwotę** prepare the exact amount ② (odjąć) to deduct *[koszty]* **❷** *vi* (stojąc w szeregu) to number off; ~**yć do dwóch** to number off to two

odlo|t *m* ① (samolotu) departure, take-off; ~**t ptaków (do ciepłych krajów)** the migration of birds (to warmer climates) ② pot. (po zażyciu narkotyku) trip pot.

odlud|ek *m* recluse

odludzi|e *n* mieszkać na ~**u** to live in the middle of nowhere

odłam *m* faction

odłam|ać *pf* — **odłam|ywać** *impf vt* to break off *[gałąź]*

odłam|ek *m* ① Wojsk. shrapnel ② (szkła) chip

odłamywać *impf* → odłamać

odłącz|yć *pf* — **odłącz|ać** *impf* **❶** *vt* ① (oddzielić) to uncouple *[lokomotywę, wagon]*; to separate *[ziemię]* (**od czegoś** from sth); to detach *[ogniwo]* (**od czegoś** from sth) ② (uniemożliwić korzystanie) to disconnect, to cut off *[gaz, prąd, wodę, telefon]* ③ Med. to disconnect; ~**yć kogoś od respiratora** to take sb off the respirator **❷ odłączyć się** — **odłączać się** *[osoba, zwierzę]* to wander off, to separate oneself/itself (**od czegoś** from sth)

od|łożyć *pf* — **od|kładać** *impf* **❶** *vt* ① (położyć na miejsce) to put back; **odłożyć słuchawkę** to hang up (the receiver); **odłożyć coś na bok** to put sth aside także przen. ② (przełożyć na inny termin) to put off *[egzamin, wyjazd]* ③ (zostawić na później) to put aside a. away; **odłóż dla mnie kawałek ciasta** save some cake for me ④ (oszczędzić) to put a. set aside, to save ⑤ (zgromadzić) to accumulate, to deposit *[sole mineralne, tłuszcze]* **❷ odłożyć się** — **odkładać się** *[cholesterol, tłuszcz]* to be deposited, to accumulate

odmaczać *impf* → odmoczyć

odmawiać *impf* → odmówić

odmian|a *f* [1] (przemiana) change; **dla** ~**y** for a change [2] (w biologii) variety [3] (wyrazów) inflection

odmie|nić *pf* — **odmie|niać** *impf vt* [1] to change, to alter *[obyczaje, wygląd, życie]* [2] to inflect *[wyraz]*

odmienn|y *adi.* [1] (inny) *[przyzwyczajenia, zapatrywania]* different [2] Jęz. *[część mowy]* inflected

odmierz|yć *pf* — **odmierz|ać** *impf vt* (ilość) to measure out; (długość) to measure off

odmładzać *impf* → **odmłodzić**

odmłodni|eć *pf vi [osoba]* to be rejuvenated

odmł|odzić *pf* — **odmł|adzać** *impf vt* to rejuvenate *[osobę, skórę]*; to inject new blood into *[zespół]*

odm|oczyć *pf* — **odm|aczać** *impf vt* to soak off *[etykietę, opatrunek]*

odm|owa *f* refusal

odm|ówić *pf* — **odm|awiać** *impf* **[I]** *vt* [1] (wypowiedzieć) to say *[modlitwę]* [2] pot. (odwołać) to cancel *[wizytę]* [3] pot. (wyperswadować) ~**ówić kogoś od czegoś** to talk sb out of sth **[II]** *vi* [1] (nie zgodzić się) to refuse, to decline; ~**ówić komuś pomocy** to refuse to help sb [2] (nie przyznać) to refuse to acknowledge, to deny; **nie można mu** ~**ówić talentu** there's no denying his talent

odmr|ozić *pf* — **odmr|ażać** *impf vt* [1] (uszkodzić) to injure [sth] by frostbite *[ręce, uszy]* [2] (spowodować odtajanie) to defrost *[szybę]*; to thaw (out) *[rury, zamek]* [3] Ekon. to unfreeze *[ceny, płace]*

odmroże|nie *n* frostbite

odmykać *impf* → **odemknąć**

odnajdywać *impf* → **odnaleźć**

odna|leźć *pf* — **odna|jdywać** *impf* **[I]** *vt* to find *[drogę, zgubiony przedmiot]*; to track down *[osobę, zwierzę]*; to trace *[skradziony samochód, świadka]*; to discover *[skarb]* **[II] odnaleźć się** — **odnajdywać się** [1] (wrócić) *[osoba, zwierzę]* to turn up [2] przen. (znaleźć swoje miejsce) to pull oneself together, to be oneself again

odnawiać *impf* → **odnowić**

odn|ieść *pf* — **odn|osić** *impf* **[I]** *vt* [1] (zwrócić) to take a. carry back [2] (zanieść) to take [3] (osiągnąć) to achieve *[sukces, zwycięstwo]* [4] (doświadczyć) to sustain *[obrażenia]*; ~**iosłem wrażenie, że...** I got the impression that... [5] (przypisać) to relate; ~**ieść wydarzenie do kogoś** to relate an event to sb **[II] odnieść się** — **odnosić się** [1] (zachowywać się) to treat; ~**osić się do kogoś życzliwie** to treat sb kindly [2] (dotyczyć) to concern, to relate to

odn|oga *f* branch

odnosić *impf* → **odnieść**

odnośnik *m* (znak) reference; (przypis) note; (u dołu strony) footnote; (na końcu tekstu) endnote

odnow|a *f* (tkanki) regeneration; (zabytku) restoration; (gospodarki) revival

odn|owić *pf* — **odn|awiać** *impf vt* to renovate *[budynek, mebel]*; to revive *[znajomość]*; to resume *[działalność]*

odnóż|e *n* limb

odosobnie|nie *n* seclusion; **miejsce** ~**nia** euf. a penal institution

od|ór *m* odour, stench

odpa|d *m* waste

odpadać *impf* → **odpaść**

odpad|ek *m* [1] (resztka) scraps [2] (surowiec wtórny) refuse, waste

odpal|ić *pf* — **odpal|ać** *impf vt* [1] (wystrzelić) to fire *[torpedę]*; to let off *[bombę, fajerwerk]* [2] pot. (uruchomić) to launch *[rakietę]*; to start *[samochód]*

odpar|ować[1] *pf* — **odpar|owywać**[1] *impf vt, vi* (pozbawić wody) to evaporate

odpar|ować[2] *pf* — **odpar|owywać**[2] *impf vt* [1] (odeprzeć cios, zarzut) to parry [2] (odpowiedzieć zaczepnie) to retort, to riposte

odparze|nie *n* chafe, irritation

odpa|ść *pf* — **odpa|dać** *impf vi* [1] *[obcas, tynk]* to come off (**od czegoś** sth); *[tapeta]* to peel off (**od czegoś** sth) [2] *[część terytorium]* to be a. get separated, to be severed (**od czegoś** from sth) [3] pot. *[kandydat, zawodnik]* to drop out (**z czegoś** from sth); *[osoba, wyjazd]* to be out of the question; **zmywanie ci** ~**da** you're relieved of washing up żart.

odpę|dzić *pf* — **odpę|dzać** *impf vt* to drive away, to force back *[gapiów]*; to chase off *[komary, muchy]*

od|piąć *pf* — **od|pinać** *impf* **[I]** *vt* to unfasten, to undo *[guzik, pas]*; to unpin *[broszkę]*; to detach *[kaptur, podpinkę]* **[II] odpiąć się** — **odpinać się** *[agrafka, klamerka]* to come undone

odpierać *impf* → **odeprzeć**[1]

odpinać *impf* → **odpiąć**

odpis *m* [1] (kopia) copy [2] (w księgowości) deduction (**z czegoś** from sth)

odpi|sać *pf* — **odpi|sywać** *impf vt* [1] (odpowiedzieć pisemnie) to write back; ~**sać na list** to answer a letter [2] (ściągnąć) to copy; to crib pot. [3] (odliczyć sumę) to deduct

odplamiacz *m* spot a. stain remover

odpła|cić *pf* — **odpła|cać** *impf vi* to repay, to pay back (**za coś** for sth); ~**cić dobrem za zło** to return good for evil; ~**cić pięknym za nadobne** to give tit for tat

odpłatn|y *adi. [badania, usługa]* payable, paid

odpły|nąć *pf* — **odpły|wać** *impf vi [osoba, zwierzę]* to swim away; *[statek]* to sail away; *[woda]* to run a. drain off; ~**nąć gdzieś myślami** przen. to let one's thoughts wander

odpływ *m* [1] (morza) low tide [2] Techn. (obniżenie się poziomu cieczy) outflow; (otwór) drain hole, outlet [3] przen. (gotówki, informacji) outflow

odpływać *impf* → **odpłynąć**

odpocz|ąć *pf* — **odpocz|ywać** *impf vi* to rest, to take a. have a rest

odpoczyn|ek *m* (przerwa) break; (odpoczywanie) rest

odpoczywać *impf* → **odpocząć**

odporność *f* [1] (wytrzymałość) resistance (**na coś** to sth) [2] Med. resistance, immunity

odporn|y *adi. grad. [osoba]* immune, resistant (**na coś** to sth); *[materiał]* resistant, proof; ~**y na wilgoć** damp-proof; ~**y na wstrząsy** shock-resistant

odpowiadać[1] *impf* → **odpowiedzieć**

odpowiada|ć[2] *impf vi* [1] (zadowalać) *[praca, termin]* to suit (**komuś** sb) [2] (zgadzać się) to answer (**czemuś** sth); to correspond (**czemuś** to sth); to match (**czemuś** sth)

odpowiedni *adi. grad. [okazja, osoba]* suitable; *[czas, kolejność, temperatura]* right; *[prezent, strój]* appropriate

odpowiedzialnoś|ć *f* responsibility (**za coś** for sth); **pociągnąć kogoś do** ~**ci** to call sb to account

odpowiedzialn|y *adi. grad. [osoba, stanowisko, zadanie]* responsible; **być** ~**ym za kogoś/coś** to be responsible for sb/sth, to have charge of sb/sth; **być** ~**ym za coś** to be responsible for sth

odpowi|edzieć *pf* — **odpowi|adać**[1] *impf vi* [1] (udzielić odpowiedzi) to answer; ~**edzieć na pytanie** to reply to a. answer a question [2] (zareagować) to respond (**na coś** to sth); to answer (**na coś** sth); **telefon nie** ~**adał** nobody answered the phone [3] Szkol. to be tested/examined (**z czegoś** on sth); ~**adać pisemnie/ustnie** to have a written/an oral test/exam [4] (odwzajemnić się) to return; ~**adać na ukłon/na pozdrowienie** to return a nod/a greeting [5] (ponosić odpowiedzialność) to be responsible, to answer (**za kogoś/coś** for sb/sth); ~**adać przed sądem** to be brought to trial, to be tried (**za coś** for sth); ~**ecie mi za to!** you'll answer a. pay for this!

odpowie|dź *f* (na pytanie) answer (**na coś** to sth); (reakcja) response (**na coś** to sth); **wywoływać ucznia do** ~**dzi** to call a pupil to the blackboard

odpraw|a *f* [1] (narada) briefing [2] (na lotnisku) check-in; (celna) customs clearance [3] (ostra replika) rebuff [4] (jednorazowe wynagrodzenie) gratuity GB

odpraw|ić *pf* — **odpraw|iać** *impf vt* [1] (pozbyć się) to send (away) *[osobę]*; ~**ić kogoś z niczym a. z kwitkiem** to turn sb down [2] (zwolnić) to dismiss *[pracownika]* [3] (wyekspediować) to clear *[pociąg, samolot]*; **czy celnicy już was** ~**ili?** have you been through customs yet? [4] (w kościele) to celebrate, to say *[mszę, nabożeństwo]*

odpręż|yć *pf* — **odpręż|ać** *impf* [I] *vt* to relax *[mięśnie]*

[II] **odprężyć się** — **odprężać się** *[osoba]* to relax, to unwind

odprowa|dzić *pf* — **odprowa|dzać** *impf vt* [1] (towarzyszyć) to accompany, to see off; ~**dzić kogoś do domu** to walk sb home [2] (usunąć) to carry, to channel *[ścieki, wodę]* [3] (przeznaczyć) to allocate *[pieniądze, środki]* (**na coś** to sth)

odpru|ć *pf* — **odpru|wać** *impf* [I] *vt* to unstitch *[kołnierz, rękaw]*; to unpick *[obrębek]*; ~**łem plakietkę z rękawa** I removed the badge from the sleeve

[II] **odpruć się** — **odpruwać się** *[guzik, mankiet, rękaw]* to come unstitched, to come off

odprysk *m* [1] (odłamek) chip, splinter [2] (ślad) chip; ~**i na ścianie** chips in the wall

odpry|snąć *pf* — **odpry|skiwać** *impf vi [lakier, tynk]* to chip a. flake off

odpu|ścić *pf* — **odpu|szczać** *impf vt* [1] książk. (darować) to forgive *[winy]*; ~**ścić komuś grzechy** Relig. to absolve sb's sins [2] pot. (zrezygnować) ~**ścić sobie** to ease up a. off; ~**ścić sobie egzamin** (nie zdawać) to miss an exam; (nie przygotować się) to not study enough for an exam

odpychać[1] *impf* → **odepchnąć**

odpycha|ć[2] *impf* [I] *vt* (razić) *[cecha, zjawisko]* to repel, to repulse

[II] **odpychać się** *[ciała, ładunki elektryczne]* to repel each other

odpychając|y *adi. [mina, osoba, wygląd]* repulsive

odpyt|ać *pf* — **odpyt|ywać** *impf vt [nauczyciel]* to test *[ucznia]*; *[policjant, urzędnik]* to question, to examine *[świadka]*

od|ra *f* measles

odrabiać *impf* → **odrobić**

odraczać *impf* → **odroczyć**

odra|dzić *pf* — **odra|dzać** *impf vt* ~**dzić komuś coś** to advise sb against (doing) sth

odrastać *impf* → **odrosnąć**

odrat|ować *pf* — **odrat|owywać** *impf vt* to bring [sb] back to life

odraz|a *f* disgust, aversion

odreag|ować *pf* — **odreag|owywać** *impf vt* to abreact *[napięcie, stres]*; ~**ować coś na kimś** to take it out on sb

odrębn|y *adi. [przepis, temat]* distinct; *[teren]* separate

odręczn|y *adi.* [1] *[notatka, rysunek]* handwritten [2] *[działania, pożyczka]* instant; ~**e naprawy** on-the-spot repairs

odr|obić *pf* — **odr|abiać** *impf vt* to do *[lekcje]*

odrobin|a *f* bit, drop; ~**a chleba/mięsa** a morsel of bread/meat; **przy** ~**ie szczęścia** przen. with a bit of luck; ~**ę bolało** it hurt a just bit

odr|oczyć *pf* — **odr|aczać** *impf vt* to postpone *[spotkanie]*; to adjourn *[posiedzenie]*

odr|odzić się *pf* — **odr|adzać się** *impf v refl. [przyroda]* to revive; *[tkanka]* to regenerate

odr|osnąć *pf* — **odr|astać** *impf vi [trawa, włosy]* to grow again, to regenerate

odróżni|ć *pf* — **odróżni|ać** *impf* **I** *vt* to distinguish (**coś od czegoś** sth from sth); **on nie ~a kolorów** he's colour-blind

II odróżnić się — odróżniać się to differ (**od kogoś/czegoś** from sb/sth)

odróżnie|nie *n* distinction; **dla ~nia** to differentiate; **w ~niu** in contrast (**od kogoś/czegoś** to sb/sth); as opposed (**od kogoś/czegoś** to sb/sth)

odruch *m* [1] (mimowolna reakcja) reflex [2] (nawyk) reaction, impulse; **ludzkie ~y** human feelings a. impulses

odruchow|y *adi.* [gest] involuntary; [zachowanie, sprzeciw] impulsive

odrywać *impf* → **oderwać**

odrzu|cić *pf* — **odrzu|cać** *impf vt* [1] (nie akceptować) to reject [osobę, pomysł, przeszczep]; **~ca mnie od tych powieści** these novels really put me off [2] (rzucić dalej) to throw off [kamień]; (oddać rzucając) to throw back [piłkę]

odrzu|t *m* [1] (broni) recoil [2] pot. (niepełnowartościowy towar) reject [3] Med. rejection

odrzutow|iec *m* jet (aircraft)

odset|ek **I** *m* percentage, proportion

II odsetki *plt* Ekon. interest (**od czegoś** on sth)

odsi|edzieć *pf* — **odsi|adywać** *impf vt* pot. (odbyć karę) to serve one's time; **~adywać wyrok** to do time a. bird GB pot.

odskoczni|a *f* [1] Sport springboard [2] przen. (punkt wyjścia) stepping stone (**do czegoś** in sth) [3] przen. (oderwanie się) (form of) escape (**od czegoś** from sth)

odsł|onić *pf* — **odsł|aniać** *impf* **I** *vt* [1] (pokazać) to bare [szyję, ramiona]; **~onić głowę** to take off one's hat; **~onić pomnik** to unveil a monument [2] (odsunąć) **~onić firanki** to draw back a. open the curtains; **~onić żaluzje** to pull up a. open the (Venetian) blinds [3] (pozbawić zabezpieczenia) to expose, to leave [sth] open to attack [skrzydło]; to uncover [figurę szachową] [4] przen. (ujawnić) to reveal [prawdę, plany]

II odsłonić się — odsłaniać się [1] (stać się widocznym) to emerge, to appear; [widok] to unfold, to open out [2] (pozbawić się osłony) to expose oneself; [bokser] to leave oneself open, to lower one's guard

odsta|ć się *pf* — **odsta|wać się** *impf v refl.* [ciecz] to settle; [wino] to mature

■ **co się stało, to się nie ~nie** what's done cannot be undone

odsta|wać *impf vi* [1] (odłączyć się) [tynk, fornir] to come off a. loose; **~jące uszy** protruding a. bat ears [2] (różnić się) to diverge (**od czegoś** from sth) [3] (zostawać w tyle) to fall a. lag behind

odstaw|ić *pf* — **odstaw|iać** *impf vt* [1] (odłożyć) (na bok) to put [sth] away; (na miejsce) to put [sth] back [krzesło, talerz]; **~ić lek** to stop taking a. medicine [2] (dostarczyć) **~ić zboże do magazynu** to deliver grain to a store; **~ić złodzieja na policję** to take a thief to the police (station) [3] pot. (udawać)

to play, to act; **~iać bohatera** to play a. act the hero

odstaw|ka *f* pot. **pójść w ~kę** to be put out to grass pot.

odst|ąpić *pf* — **odst|ępować** *impf* **I** *vt* (zrzec się) to give (**coś komuś** sth to sb); **~ąpić komuś mieszkanie** (użyczyć) to let sb have the use of one's flat; (odsprzedać) to sell one's flat to sb

II *vi* [1] (na bok) to move a. step aside; (cofnąć się) to move a. stand back; **nie ~ępować kogoś (ani) na krok** to dog sb [2] (zrezygnować) **~ąpić od czegoś** to withdraw from sth [umowy, kontraktu]

odstęp *m* (odległość) distance; (w czasie) interval; (między literami, wyrazami) space

odstępować *impf* → **odstąpić**

odstrasz|yć *pf* — **odstrasz|ać** *impf vt* to scare [sb] off, to drive [sb] away [klientów, inwestorów]

odsu|nąć *pf* — **odsu|wać** *impf* **I** *vt* [1] (odstawić) to move away a. back [krzesło, szafę]; **~nąć coś na bok** to move sth aside a. to the side [2] przen. to turn away; **~nąć kogoś od władzy** to remove sb from power; **~wać od siebie przykre myśli** to drive away a. put aside unpleasant thoughts [3] (odciągnąć) to open, to draw [zasłonę]; **~nąć zasuwkę** to slide the bolt open

II odsunąć się — odsuwać się [1] (zostać odsuniętym) [rygiel] to slide open [2] (oddalić się) to move away; **~nąć się na bok** to move aside [3] przen. (zerwać stosunki) to turn away (**od kogoś** from sb); **~nąć się od życia towarzyskiego** to withdraw from social life; **wszyscy się od niego ~nęli** everyone deserted him [4] (zostać odłożonym w czasie) to be postponed a. put off

odsyłacz *m* [1] (znak graficzny) reference (mark) [2] (przypis) note; (u dołu strony) footnote; (na końcu strony) endnote [3] (odesłanie) cross reference (**do czegoś** to sth)

odsyłać *impf* → **odesłać**

odsyp|ać *pf* — **odsyp|ywać** *impf vt* to pour [sth] out [cukru, mąki]

odsypiać *impf* → **odespać**

odsypywać *impf* → **odsypać**

odszkodowa|nie *n* compensation, damages; (od ubezpieczyciela) indemnity, compensation

odszuk|ać *pf* — **odszuk|iwać** *impf vt* to seek a. search [sb] out; **nie mógł ~ać swojej rodziny** he's been unable to trace his family

odszyfr|ować *pf* — **odszyfr|owywać** *impf vt* to decode, to decipher [kod, wiadomość]; to decipher [receptę]; to guess (at) [motywy, intencje]

odśnież|yć *pf* — **odśnież|ać** *impf vt* to clear [sth] of snow [chodnik, ulicę]; **~anie** snow clearance

odświeżacz *m* **~ powietrza** an air-freshener; **~ do ust** a breath freshener

odśwież|yć *pf* — **odśwież|ać** *impf* **I** *vt* książk. to freshen up [meble, ubranie]; to renew [znajomość]

II **odświeżyć się — odświeżać się** [1] *[osoba]* to freshen (oneself) up [2] *[powietrze]* to freshen

odświętn|y *adi. [nastrój, charakter]* festive; **w ~ym ubraniu** in one's (Sunday) best

odtąd *pron.* [1] (od teraz) from now on; (od wtedy) from then on; **~ nie rozmawiają ze sobą** since then they haven't spoken a. been speaking to each other; **~, odkąd** since; **~, odkąd się poznaliśmy** ever since we met [2] (od tego miejsca) from here; (od tamtego miejsca) from there; **przeczytaj ~ dotąd** read it from here to here

odtrą|cić *pf* — **odtrą|cać** *impf vt* to push away; **~cić czyjąś pomoc** to reject a. spurn sb's help

odtru|ć *pf* — **odtru|wać** *impf vt* to detoxicate, to detoxify *[organizm, atmosferę]*

odtrut|ka *f* antidote *także przen.* (**na coś** to sth)

odtruwać *impf* → **odtruć**

odtwarzacz *m* player

odtw|orzyć *pf* — **odtw|arzać** *impf vt* [1] (zregenerować) to regenerate *[tkankę]* [2] (zrekonstruować) to reconstruct *[ornamenty, rękopisy]* [3] Techn. to play (back) *[koncert, piosenkę]*

odtwór|ca *m,* **~czyni** *f* książk. performer; **~a/ ~czyni głównej roli** the lead(ing) man/the lead(ing) lady

odtykać *impf* → **odetkać**

odurz|yć *pf* — **odurz|ać** *impf vt* to daze (**kogoś czymś** sb with sth); **był ~ony szczęściem** he was dizzy with happiness

odwadniać *impf* → **odwodnić**

odwa|ga *f* courage; **~ga cywilna** moral courage; **zebrać się na ~gę, żeby coś zrobić** to pluck up one's courage to do sth; **~gi!** take heart!

odwal|ić *pf* — **odwal|ać** *impf* **II** *vt* [1] to remove *[przeszkodę]* [2] pot. (niedbale wykonać) to bash out; **~ić robotę byle jak** to bash out a job [3] pot. (dobrze wykonać) to do; **~ić kawał dobrej roboty** to do a whole lot of work [4] pot. (wyeliminować) to reject, to eliminate; **~ili mnie na egzaminie** they failed me at the exam

II **odwalić się — odwalać się** pot. **~ się!** get lost! pot.; **~ się od mojej dziewczyny!** leave my girl alone!

odwa|r *m* decoction

odważnik *m* weight

odważn|y *adi. grad. [żołnierz]* brave

odważ|yć się *pf* — **odważ|ać się** *impf vt* to dare; **~yć się podejść do kogoś** to dare (to) approach sb

odwdzięcz|yć się *pf* — **odwdzięcz|ać się** *impf v refl.* to repay (**za coś** sth)

odwe|t *m* revenge; **wziąć na kimś ~t** to take revenge on sb

odwią|zać *pf* — **odwią|zywać** *impf vt* to undo, to untie *[sznurek, węzeł]*

odwiedza|ć¹ *impf vt* to frequent *[nocne kluby]*

odwie|dzić *pf* — **odwie|dzać²** *impf vt* to visit *[rodzinę, przyjaciół]*

odwiedzin|y *plt* visit; **przyjść do kogoś w ~y** to pay sb a visit; **pora ~** (w szpitalu) visiting hours

odw|ieźć *pf* — **odw|ozić** *impf vt* to take (back); **~ieźć kogoś na lotnisko** to take sb to the airport

odwilż *f* thaw *także przen.*

odwi|nąć *pf* — **odwi|jać** *impf vt* [1] (zdjąć osłonę) to unwrap [2] (rozwinąć) to unreel, to unwind *[linę]* [3] (odchylać) to unroll *[rękawy]*

odwir|ować *pf* — **odwir|owywać** *impf vt* to spin; **~ować pranie** to spin-dry the washing

odwl|ec *pf* — **odwl|ekać** *impf vt* [1] (odsunąć) to drag away [2] (opóźnić) to delay, to put off *[ślub]*; to put off *[decyzję]*

■ **co się ~ecze, to nie uciecze** pot. there's luck in leisure

odwoł|ać *pf* — **odwoł|ywać** *impf* **II** *vt* [1] (skłonić do odejścia) to call; **~ać kogoś na stronę** to call sb aside [2] (zwolnić) to dismiss; **ambasador został ~any** the ambassador was recalled [3] (anulować) to cancel *[lot, wykład]*; to call off *[alarm]*; to withdraw *[zeznania]*; **~aj to, co powiedziałeś** take back what you said

II **odwołać się — odwoływać się** [1] (zaapelować) to appeal, to refer; **~ać się do czyjegoś rozsądku** to appeal to sb's reason [2] (powołać się) to appeal, to invoke; **~am się do przykładu...** I will refer to the example of...

odwoła|nie *n* [1] (ze stanowiska) dismissal [2] Prawo appeal; **do ~nia** until further notice

odwoływać *impf* → **odwołać**

odwozić *impf* → **odwieźć**

odwracać *impf* → **odwrócić**

odwrotnie *adv.* [1] (przeciwnie, inaczej) the other way round; **i ~** and vice versa; **zawsze zrobi ~, niż mu powiem** he always does the opposite of what I tell him [2] (do góry nogami) upside down

odwrotn|y *adi.* opposite; **wszystkie moje działania miały ~y skutek** all my endeavours backfired; **na ~ej stronie kartki** on the reverse

■ **~a strona medalu** the other side of the coin; **~ą pocztą** pot. by return post

odwr|ócić *pf* — **odwr|acać** *impf* **II** *vt* [1] (skierować w inną stronę) to turn [sth] away; **~ócić czyjąś uwagę** to distract a. divert sb's attention [2] (zmienić położenie) to turn; **~acać kartki książki** to turn over the pages of a book; **~ócić koszulę na lewą stronę** to turn a shirt inside out

II **odwrócić się — odwracać się** [1] (skierować się w inną stronę) to turn; **nie patrz, ~óć się** don't look, turn away [2] książk., przen. (odsunąć się) to turn one's back (**od kogoś** on sb); **szczęście się od nich ~óciło** luck deserted them

odwr|ót **II** *m* (wojska) retreat, withdrawal; przen. move away

II **na odwrót** *adv.* (przeciwnie) on the contrary;

(spodem na wierzch) inside out; (tył na przód) back to front

odwyk *m* pot. detox pot.; (od alkoholu) drying-out (treatment); **być na ~u** to be in detox/to undergo drying-out treatment

odwyk|nąć *pf* — **odwyk|ać** *impf vi* to get out of the habit (of), to lose the habit (of)

odwzajemni|ć *pf* — **odwzajemni|ać** *pf* **[]** *vt* to reciprocate *[uczucia]*; to return *[uśmiech]*

[II] odwzajemnić się — **odwzajemniać się** to repay (**komuś za coś** sb for sth)

odzież *f* książk. clothes; clothing; **~ damska** womenswear; **~ męska** menswear; **~ ochronna** protective clothing; **~ używana** used a. second-hand clothes

odznaczać *impf* → **odznaczyć**

odznacze|nie /ˌodznaˈtʃɛɲe/ *n* decoration

odznacz|yć /odˈznatʃɨtɕ/ *pf* — **odznacz|ać** /odˈznatʃatɕ/ *impf* **[]** *vt* to decorate; **~ony medalami za waleczność** decorated with medals for bravery

[II] odznaczyć się **[]** (wyróżnić się) to distinguish oneself **[]** (zostawić ślad) to show up, to leave a mark **[III] odznaczać się** to be characterized (**czymś** by sth)

odzna|ka /odˈznaka/ *f* badge

odzwycza|ić /ˌodzvɨˈtʃaitɕ/ *pf* — **odzwycza|jać** /ˌodzvɨˈtʃajatɕ/ *impf* **[]** *vt* to disaccustom; to wean [sb] away (**od czegoś** from sth); **~jać dziecko od smoczka** to wean a baby off a dummy

[II] odzwyczaić się — **odzwyczajać się** to disaccustom oneself, to break a. kick a habit; **~jać się od palenia** to give up smoking

odzysk|ać /odˈzɨskatɕ/ *pf* — **odzysk|iwać** /ˌodzɨsˈkivatɕ/ *impf vt* to recover *[dom, pieniądze]*; to regain *[niepodległość, przytomność]*; to retrieve *[dane, plik]*

odzywać się *impf* → **odezwać się**

odżywcz|y /odˈʒɨftʃɨ/ *adi. [pokarmy, produkty]* nutritious; *[walory, wartość]* nutritional; *[krem]* nourishing; *[balsam, szampon]* conditioning

odżywia|ć /odˈʒɨvjatɕ/ *impf* **[]** *vt* **[]** (karmić) to feed; **chorego trzeba ~ć dożylnie** the patient needs to be drip-fed **[]** (w kosmetyce) to nourish

[II] odżywiać się to eat, to feed; **~ć się jarzynami** to eat only vegetables; **dobrze się ~ć** to eat properly

odżyw|ka /odˈʒɨfka/ *f* **[]** (środek odżywczy) **~ka dla dzieci** baby food **[]** (do włosów) conditioner

ofensyw|a *f* **[]** Sport, Wojsk. offensive **[]** pot. (nadmiar) barrage przen.

oferm|a *m, f* pot. (niezaradny) loser; wimp pot.; (niezdarny) moron pot.

ofer|ta *f* offer

ofi|ara *f* **[]** (ranny, zabity) victim, casualty; **~ara śmiertelna** fatality **[]** (poszkodowany) victim **[]** Relig. offering, sacrifice **[]** (datek) donation; **~ara na tacę**

collection (money) **[]** (wyrzeczenie) sacrifice **[]** pot. sucker, dupe pot.; **~ara losu** a born loser

■ paść ~arą kogoś/czegoś to fall victim to sb/sth; **robić z siebie ~arę** to play the martyr, to make a martyr of oneself

office|r *m* officer

oficjalnie *adv. grad. [ogłosić, zatwierdzić]* officially; *[przyjąć, potraktować]* formally

oficjaln|y *adi. grad. [komunikat, wersja]* official; *[ton, strój]* formal

oga|r *m* hound

ogarn|ąć *pf* — **ogarn|iać** *impf* **[]** *vt* **[]** (objąć rękami) to embrace; (objąć zasięgiem) to spread a. sweep through; (objąć wzrokiem) to take in **[]** (zrozumieć) to grasp, to comprehend *[problem]* **[]** *[mgła, ciemności]* to engulf **[]** *[niepokój, strach]* to seize, to grip **[]** pot. to tidy up *[dom, mieszkanie]*

[II] ogarnąć się — **ogarniać się** pot. to tidy a. spruce oneself up

og|ień *m* **[]** (płomień, pożar) fire; **dołożyć** a. **dorzucić do ognia** to fuel/stoke a fire; **zimne ognie** sparklers; **ognia!** (komenda) fire! **[]** przen. heat, passion

■ dać komuś ognia to give sb a light; **dolać oliwy do ognia** to add fuel to the fire a. flame, to make things worse; **posłać kogoś/iść na pierwszy ogień** to send sb/to go to the front line; **pójść** a. **skoczyć za kimś w ogień** to go through fire and water for sb; **wziąć kogoś w krzyżowy ogień pytań** to cross-examine sb

ogie|r *m* stallion

oglądać¹ *impf* → **obejrzeć**

oglądа|ć² *impf* **[]** *vt* to watch; **nie chcę cię tu więcej ~ć!** I don't want to see you here again!

[II] oglądać się to look (**na kogoś** to sb); to count (**na kogoś** on sb); **mieli się nie ~ć na koszty** they were told to ignore a. not to mind the costs

oglądalnoś|ć *f* audience; **pora największej ~ci telewizji** prime time

ogła|da *f* refinement, polish

ogł|osić *pf* — **ogł|aszać** *impf* **[]** *vt* **[]** (obwieścić) to announce *[zaręczyny]*; to proclaim *[zwycięstwo]*; (opublikować) to publish *[rozprawę, artykuł]* **[]** (mianować) to pronounce, to proclaim; **~oszono go królem** he was proclaimed king

[II] ogłosić się — **ogłaszać się** (dać ogłoszenie) to advertise

ogłosze|nie *n* **[]** (wiadomość) advertisement; **~nie drobne** a classified advertisement; **~nie matrymonialne** a personal ad **[]** (oznajmienie) announcement; **~nie niepodległości** a declaration of independence; **~nie wyników egzaminu** the announcement of exam results

ogłoszeniow|y *adi.* rubryka **~a** an advertisement column; **słup ~y** a noticeboard; **tablica ~a** hoarding GB, billboard US

ogłuch|nąć *pf vi* to become a. to go deaf

ogłusz|yć *pf* — **ogłusz|ać** *impf vt* ① (pozbawić słuchu) to deafen ② (uderzyć) to knock out

ogniotrwa|ły *adi. [cegła, szkło]* fireproof; *[ubranie]* fire-retardant

ognisk|o *n* ① (palący się stos drewna) bonfire; **palić ~o** to build a bonfire ② (spotkanie towarzyskie) bonfire ③ przen. (ośrodek) centre, center US; (choroby, zarazy) hotbed; **~o domowe** (hearth and) home ④ Fiz., Mat., Med. focus

ogniw|o *n* ① (spojenie) link ② przen. (więź) bond; (w organizacji) link

og|olić *pf* [] *vt* to shave (off) *[brodę, wąsy, włosy]*
[] ogolić się to shave

ogon *m* tail
■ **odwrócić** a. **wykręcić kota ~em** to twist everything round pot.; **wlec się** a. **zostawać w ~ie** pot. to fall behind

ogon|ek *m* ① Bot. stalk ② Jęz. hook, tail ③ pot. (kolejka) queue GB, line US

ogólniak *m* pot. ≈ grammar school

ogólnik *m* generality; **mówić ~ami** to talk in generalities

ogólnikow|y *adi. [komentarz, obietnica]* vague; **~e stwierdzenie** a generalization

ogóln|y [] *adi. grad.* ① (dotyczący ogółu osób) *[dobro, stół]* common ② (bez szczegółów) *[wrażenie, pojęcie]* vague; *[wykształcenie, wniosek]* general; *[teoria, zasada]* broad
**[] *adi.* (łączny) *[koszt, suma]* total

ogó|ł [] *m* ① (całość) the whole, the body; **~ł społeczeństwa** the whole of society, the general public ② (społeczność) the community, the population
[] ogółem (w sumie) altogether, all in all
[] na ogół (zazwyczaj) in general, on the whole; **na ~ł się nie mylę** I'm usually right, I'm not usually wrong
[] w ogóle ① (w sumie) generally speaking, in general ② (wcale) (not) at all, (not) whatsoever

ogór|ek *m* cucumber; **~ek konserwowy/kiszony** a gherkin/dill pickle; **~ek małosolny** a semi-pickled cucumber

ogradzać *impf* → ogrodzić

ograniczać *impf* → ograniczyć

ogranicze|nie *n* ① (zakaz, limit) restriction; **~nie szybkości do 30 km/godz.** a speed limit of 30 km/h ② (tępota) narrow-mindedness

graniczon|y *adi.* ① (niewielki) *[możliwości, zasięg]* limited ② (nieinteligentny) *[osoba]* dull, thick; **~ony umysłowo** Med. mentally retarded

granicz|yć *pf* — **granicz|ać** *impf* [] *vt* ① (wyznaczyć) to enclose *[teren]* ② (zmniejszyć) to limit *[zużycie, wydatki]*; to cut down on *[palenie, alkohol]*; to curb *[wpływy, inflację]*; to cut *[koszty, budżet]*; to moderate *[żądania, ambicje]*
[] ograniczyć się — ograniczać się ① (zadowolić się) to limit a. restrict oneself (**do czegoś** to sth)

② (okazać się mniejszym) to be limited a. restricted (**do czegoś** to sth); **szkody ~yły się do kilku wybitych szyb** the damage amounted to a few broken windows

ogrodni|k *m*, **~czka** *f* gardener

ogrodze|nie *n* ① (zabezpieczenie) (płot, parkan) fence; (murowane) wall; (żywopłot) hedge; (z prętów) railing ② (ogrodzona przestrzeń) enclosure; (dla zwierząt) pen

ogr|odzić *pf* — **ogr|adzać** *impf vt* ① (otoczyć) to surround, to enclose; (płotem) to fence (in); (murem) to wall (in); (prętami) to rail (in); (żywopłotem) to hedge (in) ② (oddzielić) to shut off

ogromn|y *adi. grad. [budynek, zwierzę, zysk]* huge; *[powierzchnia, doświadczenie]* vast; *[smutek, entuzjazm]* great, tremendous; *[ulga, wysiłek]* immense

ogr|ód *m* (kwietnik) (flower) garden; (warzywnik) kitchen a. vegetable garden

ogród|ek *m* (część kawiarni) pavement café, tea garden

ogryzać *impf* → ogryźć

ogryz|ek *m* (owocu) core; (ołówka) stub

ogry|źć *pf* — **ogry|zać** *impf vt* to chew at *[ołówek, długopis]*; to bite *[jabłko]*; **pies ~zał kości** the dog was gnawing a. chewing on some bones

ogrz|ać *pf* — **ogrz|ewać** *impf vt* to warm *[dłonie, stopy]*; to heat (up) *[wodę, gaz]*; to heat *[mieszkanie, budynek]*

ogrzewacz *m* heater

ogrzewać *impf* → ogrzać

ogrzewani|e *n* heating; **centralne ~e** central heating

ohydn|y *adi. grad. [zapach, postępek]* atrocious

oj|ciec *m* ① (mężczyzna mający dziecko) father; **ojciec nieznany** paternity unknown ② Zool. father; (w hodowli koni, bydła) sire ③ Relig. (duchowny) Father; **Bóg Ojciec** God the Father; **Ojciec Święty** Holy Father

ojcostw|o *n* fatherhood, paternity; **sprawa o ustalenie ~a** a paternity case

ojczym *m* stepfather

ojczy|sty *adi.* ① (dotyczący ojczyzny) *[mowa, historia]* native ② (dotyczący miejsca urodzenia) home, mother; **kraj ~sty** one's mother country

ojczy|zna *f* home country, homeland

okaleczać *impf* → okaleczyć

okalecze|nie *n* (bodily) injury; (celowe) mutilation

okalecz|yć *pf* — **okalecz|ać** *impf vt* ① (zranić) to cripple, to mutilate; **~one stopy** mutilated feet ② przen. (zniszczyć) to mutilate *[mebel, pomnik]*

okap *m* ① (część dachu) eaves ② (w kuchni) ventilation hood

okaz *m* ① (egzemplarz) specimen; **~ muzealny** an antique także przen. ② (wzór) **~ głupoty** a perfect fool; **~ zdrowia** picture of health

oka|zać *pf* — **oka|zywać** *impf* [] *vt* ① (pokazać) to present, to show *[paszport, dokumenty]* ② (uzewnętrznić) to show *[wstyd, odwagę]*; **~zać komuś wdzięcz-**

ność to express one's gratitude to sb; **~zać komuś pomoc** to be of help to sb **Ⅱ okazać się — okazywać się** to turn out; **film ~zał się arcydziełem** the film turned out to be a masterpiece; **jak się ~zało...** as it turned out...; **to się jeszcze ~że** it is yet to be seen

okaza|ły adi. grad. [budynek, wzrost] impressive; [zamek, mury, bankiet] magnificent; [wesele] lavish

okaziciel m, **~ka** f bearer; **czek/obligacja na ~a** a bearer cheque/bond

okazj|a **Ⅱ** f ① (możliwość) chance, opportunity; **stracić ~ę** to miss a chance; **ten dom to była prawdziwa ~a** this house was a real bargain ② (powód) occasion; **wszystkiego najlepszego z ~i urodzin!** happy birthday! Many happy returns!; **życzenia z ~i ślubu** congratulations on (the occasion of) sb's wedding ③ pot. (samochód) lift; **podróżować ~ą** to hitch pot.; to hitch-hike **Ⅱ przy okazji** ① (w odpowiedniej chwili) when the opportunity arises a. occurs ② (w czasie) during; **przy ~i badań okresowych wyszły na jaw jego problemy z sercem** his heart problems were revealed during (the course of) a routine medical check-up ③ (korzystając ze sposobnej chwili) by the way, while we're on the subject; **a przy ~i, co z twoją ostatnią książką?** by the way, what about your latest book?

okazywać impf → okazać

okien|ko n ① (stanowisko) counter, window; **~ko kasowe** a cash desk ② (otwór) window; **koperta z ~kiem** a window envelope ③ (rubryka) blank (space), box ④ pot. (przerwa) free (period) ⑤ Komput. window; (z komunikatem) dialog box; **~ka** pot. Windows®

okiennic|a f shutter

oklask|i plt applause; **~i dla naszego gościa!** let's give our guest a big hand!

oklask|iwać impf vt to applaud [występ, mówcę]

okle|ić pf — **okle|jać** impf vt to cover; (taśmą) to tape; (fornirem) to veneer

oklein|a f veneer

oklejać impf → okleić

oklepan|y adi. pot. **~a melodia** a tired old melody; **~e morały/słowa** trite morals/words; **~y zwrot** a well-worn phrase

okła|d **Ⅱ** m- (kompres) compress; (z rośliny) poultice **Ⅱ z okładem** part. more than, over

okład|ka f ① (książki, czasopisma) cover; **książka w miękkiej/twardej ~ce** a paperback/hardback; **jej zdjęcie trafiło na ~kę „Newsweeka"** she made the cover of 'Newsweek' ② (osłona) cover; **~ka na książkę** a book cover

okładzin|a f facing

okłam|ać pf — **okłam|ywać** impf vt to lie (kogoś to sb); **~ywać siebie samego** to deceive a. to delude oneself

ok|no n ① (otwór, szyba) window ② Komput. box; (aplikacji) window

o|ko n ① (narząd) eye ② (kółko) dot; **oka na a. w rosole** drops of fat in the broth ③ (sieci) mesh ❏ **oko cyklonu** eye of the storm, storm centre ■ **bez zmrużenia oka** without batting an eye(lid); **dobrze/źle mu/jej z oczu patrzy** he/she has a kind/a forbidding look in his/her eyes; **dwoi a. troi mu się w oczach** he sees double/triple; **jak a. gdzie okiem sięgnąć** as far as the eye can see; **zrobiło mu się ciemno przed oczami** he saw spots before his eyes; **mieć kogoś/coś na oku** a. **mieć oko na kogoś/coś** to keep an eye a. a sharp eye on sb/sth; **mieć oczy (szeroko) otwarte** to keep one's eyes open a. skinned, to keep one's weather eye (on sth); **powiedzieć a. wygarnąć komuś coś prosto w oczy** to say sth in sb's face; **na oko** more or less; **pilnować a. strzec kogoś/ czegoś jak oka w głowie** to guard sth/sb with one's life; **rozmawiać/spotkać się z kimś w cztery oczy** to talk/to meet with sb face to face a. tête-à-tête; **spotkać się a. znaleźć się a. stanąć z kimś/z czymś oko w oko** to be eyeball to eyeball with sb/sth; **w żywe oczy** blatantly; **kłamać w żywe oczy** to lie through one's teeth, to tell brazen lies; **widoczny gołym okiem** visible to the naked eye; **widzieć a. zobaczyć coś a. przekonać się o czymś na własne oczy** to see sth with one's own eyes; **wpaść komuś w oko** to catch one's fancy; (zwrócić uwagę) to catch sb's eye; **z zamkniętymi a. zawiązanymi oczami** with one hand (tied) behind one's back; **przymykać na coś oczy** to turn a blind eye to sth; **zejść komuś z oczu** to get out of sb's sight

oko|cić się pf v refl. (o kotce) to kitten; (o owcy) to lamb

okolic|a f ① (obszar) surroundings, vicinity; (na ciele) area ② pot. (sąsiedzi) neighbourhood; **cała ~a się z ciebie śmieje** the whole neighbourhood is laughing at you ③ (region) region

okolicznościow|y adi. occasional; **kartka ~a** a notelet; **urlop ~y** compassionate leave

okoliczność f circumstance; **w tych ~ciach** in a. under circumstances; **zbieg ~ci** coincidence; **~ci łagodzące** Prawo extenuations; **~ci obciążające** Prawo aggravating a. incriminating circumstances

około praep. (round) about; **~ stu osób** about a. around a hundred people; **~ szóstej/północy** about a. around six/midnight; **~ 1990 roku** around 1990

oko|ń m perch ■ **stawać ~niem (komuś/czemuś)** książk. to make a. to take a stand against sb/sth

okop m trench

okra|ść pf — **okra|dać** impf vt to rob

okr|ąg m ① Mat. circle; **obwód ~ęgu** a circumference ② książk. (krąg) circle, ring

okrąg|ły *adi. grad.* rotund; ~**łe kształty (kobiety)** curves; ~**ła twarz** a chubby a. round face; ~**łe litery** rounded letters; ~**ła rocznica** a round anniversary

okrążać *impf* → **okrążyć**

okrąże|nie *n* ① Wojsk. encirclement, envelopment; **znaleźć się w** ~**niu** to find oneself encircled ② Sport lap

okrąż|yć — okrąż|ać *impf vt* ① (zatoczyć krąg) to go (a)round; **ptak** ~**ył dolinę** a bird made a circle over the valley ② (ominąć) to skirt (**coś** sth) ③ (obstąpić) to encircle, to surround *[nieprzyjaciela]*

okres *m* ① (czas trwania) period, season; ~ **świąteczny** the holiday season; ~ **przydatności produktu do spożycia** a product's lifetime; ~ **próbny** a trial period, probation ② (epoka) period, era ③ (semestr) term ④ pot. (menstruacja) period ⑤ (cykl) period, cycle

okresow|y *adi. [deszcze, susze]* periodic; *[moda, trudności]* temporary; *[plan, oceny]* term

określać *impf* → **określić**

określe|nie *n* (epitet) epithet; (termin) term

określ|ić — określ|ać *impf vt* ① (wyznaczyć, ustalić) to determine ② (wyrazić) to describe ③ (zdeterminować) to define; **pieniądz** ~**a kondycję człowieka** money defines a person's condition

określ|ony *adi.* definite, specific

okrę|cić — okrę|cać *impf* **I** *vt* ① (owinąć) to wrap ② (obrócić) to twist, to twirl **II okręcić się — okręcać się** ① (otulić się) to wrap ② (obrócić się) to turn round; ~**cić się na pięcie** to turn (around) on one's heel

okręg *m* district; ~ **wyborczy** Polit. constituency

okrę|t *m* (w marynarce wojennej) warship; (duży statek) ship

okręt|ka *f* running stitch; **zszyć coś na** ~**kę** to oversew sth

okręż|ny *adi.* ① *[ulica, ruch]* circular, roundabout; **droga** ~**a** a roundabout route ② przen. *[pytania, sposób]* indirect

okropnie *adv. grad.* ① (przerażająco) horribly ② (źle, brzydko) *[śpiewać, wyglądać]* dreadfully, terribly ③ pot. (bardzo) *[zmęczyć się, zmoknąć]* awfully

okropn|y *adi. grad.* ① (przerażający) *[zbrodnia, widok]* horrible, dreadful; *[scena, wypadek]* ghastly; *[warunki, poziom]* abominable ② (brzydki) *[akcent, pogoda]* atrocious, horrible ③ pot. (intensywny) *[strach, mróz]* terrible, dreadful

okruch *m* (pieczywa, ciasta) crumb; (szkła, sera) sliver; przen. (prawdy) scrap, shred

okrucieństw|o *n* (skłonność) cruelty; (czyn) atrocities

okrutn|y *adi. grad. [morderca]* brutal; *[kara, sędzia, postępowanie]* cruel; *[bitwa, wzrok]* fierce; *[tyran, reżim]* pitiless; **być** ~**ym dla kogoś** to be cruel towards sb

okry|cie *n* (przykrycie) cover; (ubranie) overcoat

okrzyk *m* shout; ~ **bólu** a cry of pain; **wznosić** ~**i na czyjąś cześć** to cheer somebody

oku|cie *n* ① (laski, słupka) ferrule ② (w budownictwie) fitting

okula|r **I** *m* (część przyrządu optycznego) eyepiece **II** **okulary** *plt* glasses; ~**ry przeciwsłoneczne** sunglasses; ~**ry pływackie** swimming goggles

okul|eć *pf vi* to get a limp, to go a. become lame

okuli|sta *m* ophthalmologist, (ophthalmic) optician

okulisty|ka *f* ① (dział medycyny) ophthalmology ② pot. (oddział szpitala) ophthalmological unit (ward)

okup *m* ransom

okupacj|a *f* occupation

okup|ić — okup|ywać *impf vt* ① (opłacić) to pay (**coś** for sth) ② (wynagrodzić) to atone (**coś** for sth)

okup|ować *impf vt* to occupy *[fabrykę, kraj]*; ~**ować telefon** pot. to occupy the phone

okupywać *impf* → **okupić**

olbrzym *m* giant także przen.

olbrzymi *adi. [budynek, teren]* huge; *[znaczenie, możliwości]* enormous

ol|cha *f* (drzewo) alder (tree); (drewno) alder

ole|j *m* (tłuszcz) oil ② pot. (obraz olejny) an oil painting
  ■ **nie mieć** ~**ju w głowie** pot. to be out of one's mind

olej|ek *m* Farm., Kosmet. oil

olimpia|da *f* ① Sport the Olympic Games a. the Olympics ② Szkol. (konkurs) contest

olimpijczy|k *m* ① Sport Olympian, Olympic athlete ② Szkol. school-contest prize-winner

olimpijs|ki *adi. [komitet, laur]* Olympic; ~**ki spokój** Olympian calm

oliw|a *f* olive oil
  ■ ~**a sprawiedliwa (zawsze) na wierzch wypływa** przysł. (the) truth will out

oliwi|ć *impf vt* to oil *[zamek, zawiasy]*

oliw|ka *f* ① (owoc) olive; (drzewo) olive (tree) ② (olejek) baby oil

oliwkow|y *adi. [drzewo, gaj, skóra]* olive; *[oczy, spodnie]* olive green

olśni|ć — olśni|ewać *impf vt* to dazzle przen.; ~**ła nas jej uroda** we were dazzled by her beauty
  ■ ~**ło mnie/go** I/he saw daylight a. the light; I/he had a brainwave GB pot.

olśnie|nie *n* inspiration, enlightenment, illumination; **doznać** ~**nia** to have inspiration, to have a moment of enlightenment; **w nagłym** ~**niu** in a flash of inspiration

olśniewać *impf* → **olśnić**

oł|ów *m* Chem. lead

ołów|ek *m* pencil; **z** ~**kiem w ręku** *[planować, gospodarować]* economizing where one can

ołtarz *m* altar; **pójść z kimś do** ~**a** książk. to marry sb

omam *m* mieć ~y wzrokowe/słuchowe to have visual/auditory hallucinations, to be seeing/hearing things

omawiać *impf* → **omówić**

omdl|eć *pf* — **omdl|ewać** *impf vi* [1] (stracić przytomność) to faint; to swoon książk. [2] (osłabnąć) [palce, kończyny] to weaken, to grow weary

omdle|nie *n* faint; swoon książk.; **ocknąć się z ~nia** to come to a. round

omdlewać *impf* → **omdleć**

omi|eść *pf* — **omi|atać** *impf vt* to sweep out [mieszkanie]; to sweep [kurz, pajęczyny]; **~otła wzrokiem pokój** przen. her eyes swept the room

omi|jać[1] *impf vt* (unikać) to avoid, to evade [osobę, dom, temat]; **~jać kogoś z daleka** to steer clear of sb

omi|nąć *pf* — **omi|jać**[2] *impf vt* [1] (zatoczyć łuk) [droga, linia kolejowa] to bypass [miasto, przeszkodę]; [osoba] to walk (a)round [kałużę]; [samochód, kierowca] to drive (a)round [dziurę, przeszkodę] [2] (nie stać się udziałem) [przygody, doświadczenia] to pass by; [pocisk, odłamek] to miss; [nagroda, sukces] to elude; **kara ich nie ~nie** they won't go unpunished [3] (nie uwzględnić) to pass over [kandydata, temat] [4] (zignorować) to evade [prawo, obowiązki]; to circumwent [zakaz, przepis]

omle|t *m* omelette GB, omelet US

om|ówić *pf* — **om|awiać** *impf vt* [1] (zreferować) to discuss [sytuacje, teorie]; (rozwinąć) to elaborate [temat] [2] (przedyskutować) to discuss, to talk over a. through [problem, pomysł, plan]; **omówmy tę sprawę jutro** let's talk it a. the matter over tomorrow

omówie|nie *n* (wydarzenia artystycznego, książki) write-up, review; (zagadnienia, problemu) elaboration, discussion

omyln|y *adi.* [osoba, pamięć] fallible; **człowiek jest ~y** we all make mistakes

on *pron.* [1] (o osobie) (jako podmiot) he; (w pozostałych przypadkach) him; **on tego nie zrobił** he didn't do it; **daj mu to** give it to him; **to on!** that's/it's him! [2] (o zwierzęciu) he, it; (o przedmiocie, pojęciu) it

ona *pron.* [1] (o osobie) (jako podmiot) she; (w pozostałych przypadkach) her; **ona ma już dwa lata** she's two years old now; **nic jej nie mów o tym** don't tell her anything about it [2] (o zwierzęciu) she, it; (o przedmiocie, pojęciu) it

onaniz|ować się *impf v refl.* to masturbate

ondulacj|a *f* trwała ~a a perm, a permanent wave

one *pron.* (jako podmiot) they; (w pozostałych przypadkach) them

oni *pron.* (jako podmiot) they; (w pozostałych przypadkach) them

oniemi|eć *pf vi* to be (left) speechless; **~ała z przerażenia/zachwytu** she was speechless with horror/wonder

onieśmiel|ić *pf* — **onieśmiel|ać** *impf vt* to make [sb] shy

onkolo|g *m* oncologist

onkologi|a *f* [1] Med. oncology [2] pot. (oddział) cancer ward

ono *pron.* it

opa|d *m* [1] Meteo. precipitation; **~dy deszczu** rainfall; **~dy śniegu** snowfall [2] (radioaktywny) fallout [3] Med. erythrocyte sedimentation rate, ESR

opadać *impf* → **opaść**[1]

opakowa|nie *n* [1] (papier, torebka) wrapping; (pudełko) packaging; (plastikowe, szklane) container [2] (porcja) packet, pack

opalacz *m* beachwear

opalać *impf* → **opalić**

opaleni|zna *f* (sun)tan

opal|ić *pf* — **opal|ać** *impf* [I] *vt* [1] (ogrzać) to heat [2] (osmalić) to char [drewno]; to singe [kurczaka] [3] (wystawić na słońce) to tan [twarz, plecy]
[II] **opalić się** — **opalać się** to get a tan; **~ać się** (zażywać kąpieli słonecznych) to sunbathe

opal|ony *adi.* [twarz, nogi] (sun)tanned; **była ~ona** she had a tan

opa|ł *m* fuel; **drzewo na ~ł** firewood

opamięta|ć się *pf v refl.* to come to one's senses

opan|ować *pf* — **opan|owywać** *impf* [I] *vt* [1] (zdobyć) to take control of [kraj, miasto] [2] (pojawić się licznie) to overrun [okolicę, dzielnicę] [3] (stłumić) to bring a. get under control; **nie móc ~ować radości** to be unable to contain one's joy [4] (ogarnąć) [zazdrość, złość, smutek] to overcome, to overtake [5] (posiąść umiejętność) to master, to learn [obcy język, grę na fortepianie]
[II] **opanować się** — **opanowywać się** to control oneself
■ **~ować sytuację** to bring the situation under control; **sytuacja została ~owana** everything's under control

opanowan|y *adi.* [osoba] composed; [ton, głos] steady; [gesty, zachowanie] controlled

opanowywać *impf* → **opanować**

opa|r *m* (para) mist; (wyziew) odour

opar|cie *n* [1] (podpora) support także przen.; **nie mieć w nikim oparcia** to be out on a limb [2] (krzesła, kanapy) back(rest); (na rękę) armrest; (dla głowy) headrest; **krzesło z wysokim ~ciem** an upright chair

oparze|nie *n* burn

oparz|yć *pf* [I] *vt* [płomień] to burn; [gorący płyn, para] to scald; [pokrzywa] to sting
[II] **oparzyć się** to get burnt

opas|ka *f* band; (wchłaniająca pot) sweatband; (na ramię) armband; **~ka na włosy** a hairband; **~ka żałobna** a mourning a. black band; **~ka uciskowa** Med. tourniquet; **zasłonić komuś oczy ~ką** to blindfold sb

opasywać *impf* → **opasać**

opa|ść *pf* — **opa|dać** *impf vi* [1] (osunąć się) to drop [2] (odpaść) *[liście, owoce]* to fall (**z czegoś** off sth) [3] (obniżyć się) *[woda, poziom]* to go down; **teren łagodnie** ~**da** the land descends gently [4] (osłabnąć) *[emocje, gorączka]* to subside [5] (osaczyć) *[psy, wierzyciele]* to assail [6] przen. (dręczyć) *[wyrzuty sumienia, wątpliwości]* to torment (**kogoś** sb)
■ ~**ść z sił** to weaken, to grow faint; **ręce** ~**dają!** I give up!

opatent|ować *pf vt* to patent *[wynalazek, model]*

opatrun|ek *m* dressing

opatrywać *impf* → **opatrzyć**

opatrznoś|ć *f* providence

opat|rzyć *pf* — **opat|rywać** *impf vt* [1] (założyć opatrunek) to dress *[ranę]*; to tend to *[rannego]* [2] (uszczelnić) to draughtproof *[okna, drzwi]* [3] (wyposażyć) to provide; ~**rzyć artykuł przypisami** to write footnotes to an article; ~**rzyć dokument pieczęcią** to affix a seal to a document

opatrz|yć się *pf v refl.* to lose one's attraction a. appeal; **te buty już mi się** ~**yły** I can't look at these shoes any more

opcj|a *f* książk. option; **przyjąć jakąś** ~**ę** to choose an option

ope|ra *f* opera

operacj|a *f* [1] Med. operation, surgery [2] Ekon., Komput., Wojsk. operation

operato|r *m* [1] (kamerzysta) cameraman [2] Techn. operator

operet|ka *f* operetta; przen. farce

oper|ować *impf* **[]** *vt* Med. to operate (**kogoś** on sb); ~**ować komuś nerkę** to perform a kidney operation on sb
[] *vi* [1] (działać) to operate; **słońce najsilniej** ~**uje między dwunastą a piętnastą** the sun is (at its) hottest between noon and three p.m. [2] (posługiwać się) to use *[głosem, metaforą]*; to trade in *[pieniędzmi, akcjami]*

opęt|ać *pf* — **opęt|ywać** *impf vt* [1] (omotać) *[osoba]* to beguile; **diabeł go** ~**ał** he's possessed by the devil a. an evil spirit [2] (ogarnąć) *[uczucie, żądza]* to possess; *[myśli, chciwość]* to obsess

opętan|y *adi.* książk. frenzied

opętywać *impf* → **opętać**

op|iąć *pf* — **op|inać** *impf vt [suknia]* to hug; **spodnie opięte na biodrach** a pair of trousers hugging the hips

opi|ć *pf* — **opi|jać** *impf* pot. **[]** *vt* (uczcić) to celebrate, to drink to *[egzamin, sukces]*; **to trzeba** ~**ć** this calls for a drink
[] **opić się** — **opijać się** (wypić za dużo) to overindulge (**czegoś** in sth); (upić się) to overdrink

opie|c *pf* — **opie|kać** *impf* **[]** *vt* Kulin. (nad ogniem, na grillu) to grill, to broil US; (w tosterze) to toast; (w tłuszczu) to fry *[mięso, rybę]*; ~**c kurczaka na rożnie** to spit-roast a chicken

opieczęt|ować *pf* — **opieczęt|owywać** *impf vt* [1] (ostemplować) to stamp *[dokument, paszport]*; to date-stamp *[list, paczkę]* [2] (zabezpieczyć) to seal *[kontener, kopertę, mieszkanie]*

opie|ka *f* [1] (dbanie) care; ~**ka lekarska** medical attention; ~**ka społeczna** (instytucja) social welfare; (działalność) welfare services; **towarzystwo** ~**ki nad zwierzętami** an animal welfare organization; **powierzyć komuś** ~**kę nad dzieckiem** to entrust a child to sb's care [2] (nadzór) keeping; **pod czyjąś** ~**ką** in sb's keeping a. charge; **zostawiać kogoś bez** ~**ki** to leave sb unattended [3] (kuratela) custody; (prawny nadzór) guardianship

opiekacz *m* toaster

opiekać *impf* → **opiec**

opiek|ować się *impf v refl.* to look after *[chorym, kwiatami, kotem]*

opiekun *m* [1] (chorego, inwalidy, dziecka) carer GB, caregiver US; ~ **roku** Uniw. a tutor GB; ~ **społeczny** a social worker, a caseworker [2] Prawo guardian, conservator US

opiekun|ka *f* (chorego, inwalidy, dziecka) carer GB, caregiver US

opierać[1] *impf* → **oprzeć**

opierać[2] *impf* → **oprać**

opię|ty *adi.* close-fitting

opijać *impf* → **opić**

opił|ek *m* filing

opił|ować *pf* — **opił|owywać** *impf vt* to file *[paznokcie, krawędzie]*

opini|a /o'pinja/ *f* [1] (pogląd) opinion (**o kimś/czymś** about sb/sth); ~**a publiczna** public opinion [2] (renoma) reputation; **cieszyć się dobrą** ~**ą** to have a good reputation; **psuć komuś** ~**ę** to destroy a. tarnish sb's reputation [3] (ekspertyza) opinion (**na temat czegoś** on sth); (ocena) testimonial

opini|ować *impf vt* to give one's opinion on

opis *m* [1] (wyglądu, przebiegu) description; (relacja) account [2] (do rysunku, mapy, wykresu) legend, key; ~ **techniczny** specification

opi|sać *pf* — **opi|sywać** *impf vt* [1] (przedstawić) to describe *[wygląd, cechy]*; **scena nie do** ~**sania** a scene defying description; **upał nie do** ~**sania** indescribable heat [2] (objaśniać) to provide a legend a. key to *[mapę, wykres]* [3] Mat. to circumscribe *[figurę geometryczną]*

opisywać *impf* → **opisać**

oplatać *impf* → **opleść**

opl|eść *pf* — **opl|atać** *impf* **[]** *vt* [1] (owinąć) to wind, to twist; ~**eść kogoś ramionami** to wrap a. twine one's arms around sb [2] (owinąć się) *[liany, łodygi]* to entwine around *[pień, kolumnę]*; (pokryć) *[winorośl, róże]* to cover *[altanę, płot]*
[] **opleść się** — **oplatać się** *[winorośl, bluszcz]* to twine, to wind (**wokół czegoś** (a)round sth); ~**etli**

się ramionami they wrapped a. twined their arms around each other

oplotk|ować *pf* — **oplotk|owywać** *impf vt* to gossip (**kogoś przed kimś** about sb to sb)

oplu|ć *pf* — **oplu|wać** *impf* **[]** *vt* [] to spit (**kogoś/ coś** at a. on sb/sth) [] *przen.* to sling mud (**kogoś** at sb)

opłacać *impf* → **opłacić**[1]

opłacaln|y *adi. [produkcja, praca]* profitable; *[inwestycja, metody]* cost-effective

opła|cić[1] *pf* — **opła|cać** *impf* [] *vt* [] (zapłacić) to cover *[koszty, należność]*; to pay *[abonament, czynsz]*; ~**cić coś z góry** to prepay sth [] (wynagrodzić) to pay *[korepetytora, gosposię]*

[] opłacić się — **opłacać się** [] (przynieść) (zysk) to be profitable; (korzyść) to pay; **to się nie** ~**ca** it's not worth the trouble; ~**ca się być uczciwym** it pays to be honest [] (przekupić) to bribe (**komuś** sb); ~**cać się mafii** to pay protection money to the mafia

opła|cić[2] *pf vi* (ponieść konsekwencje) to pay; ~**cić coś bólem głowy** to pay with a headache for sth

opła|kać *pf* — **opła|kiwać** *impf vt* to bemoan, to lament *[zmarłych, stratę]*

opłakan|y *adi. [sytuacja, warunki]* lamentable; *[skutki, stan]* pitiful

opłakiwać *impf* → **opłakać**

opła|ta *f* [] (należność) charge; (za przejazd) fare; (za transport) freight; (za naukę, usługę) fee; ~**ta celna** a customs duty [] (opłacanie) payment

opłat|ek *m* wafer; **łamać się z kimś** ~**kiem** to exchange Christmas greetings with sb

opłu|kać *pf* — **opłu|kiwać** *impf vt* to rinse *[owoce, talerze]*

opły|nąć *pf* — **opły|wać**[1] *impf vt [żeglarz, statek]* to circumnavigate *[świat, wyspę]*; to sail around *[kontynent, jezioro]*; to round *[przylądek, półwysep]*; *[pływak, zwierzę]* to swim around *[wyspę, jezioro, półwysep]*

opły|wać[2] *impf vi* ~**wać w coś** to enjoy sth *[zaszczyty, przywileje]*; ~**ywać w dostatki** to be a. live in clover

opływow|y *adi. [model, kształt]* streamlined, aerodynamic

opodatk|ować *pf* — **opodatk|owywać** *impf* [] *vt* Prawo to tax; to impose a tax on *[transakcję, dochody]*; **dochody przed** ~**owaniem** pre-tax income

[] opodatkować się — **opodatkowywać się** to subscribe (**na coś** to sth)

opon|a *f* [] (ogumienie) tyre GB, tire US [] Med. (mózgowa, rdzeniowa) meninx; **zapalenie** ~ **mózgowych** meningitis

opon|ować *impf vi* książk. (przeczyć) to oppose (**komuś** sb); (sprzeciwiać się) to object (**przeciw czemuś** to sth); to oppose (**przeciw czemuś** sth)

opornik *m* [] (w obwodzie elektrycznym) resistor [] Wojsk. (mechaniczny) recoil spring; (hydrauliczny) recoil cylinder

oporn|y *adi. grad.* [] (uparty) *[uczeń, dziecko, zwierzę]* wilful, willful US; (niechętny) *[współpracownik, partner]* obstructive [] (wytrzymały) *[skała, tkaniny, metal]* resistant (**na coś** to sth) [] (stawiający opór) *[śruba, plama]* stubborn

oportuni|sta *m*, ~**stka** *f* książk. opportunist, time-server

opowiadać[1] *impf* → **opowiedzieć**

opowiad|ać[2] *impf* [] *vt* pot. (nie mówić prawdy) to tell stories; ~**asz!** you're kidding!; ~**ać bzdury** a. **głupstwa** pot. to talk nonsense a. rubbish

[] *vi [film, książka]* to tell (**o czymś** about sth)

opowiada|nie *n* [] (relacja) story, tale [] (utwór) short story

opowi|edzieć *pf* — **opowi|adać**[1] *impf* [] *vt* to tell *[anegdotę, kawał]*; to tell (**komuś o czymś** sb about sth); **długo by** ~**adać** it's a long story

[] opowiedzieć się — **opowiadać się** książk. [] (poinformować) to tell, to inform (**komuś** sb); **bez** ~**edzenia się** without telling anyone [] (poprzeć) to be in favour (**za kimś/czymś** of sb/sth); ~**adać się przeciwko komuś/czemuś** to be against sb/sth

opowieś|ć *f* story, tale (**o czymś** about sth)

opozycj|a *f* opposition (**wobec czegoś** to a. against sth)

opozycjoni|sta *m*, ~**stka** *f* Polit. oppositionist

op|ór *m* [] (przeciwstawienie się) resistance (**wobec czegoś** to sth); **stawiać komuś opór** to resist sb; **nie stawiać oporu** to put up a. offer no resistance [] (sprzeciw) qualm (**przed czymś** about sth); **mieć opory** to have qualms; **z oporami** pot. (z trudnością) with difficulty; (niechętnie) reluctantly [] (elektryczny) resistance

■ do oporu pot. *[pracować, spać, czytać]* to the limit; **iść po linii najmniejszego oporu** to take the line a. path of least resistance

opóźni|ć *pf* — **opóźni|ać** *impf* [] *vt* (odwlec) to delay; (przełożyć) to postpone; **pociąg jest** ~**ony o piętnaście minut** the train is fifteen minutes behind schedule

[] opóźnić się — **opóźniać się** [] (zwlekać) to lag behind (**z czymś** with sth); ~**amy się z wykonaniem planu** we're behind schedule [] (nastąpić po terminie) to be delayed, to be late [] *[zegarek]* to be slow

opóźnie|nie *n* delay; **masz pół godziny** ~**nia** you're half an hour late

opóźni|ony *adi. [pociąg, samolot]* delayed; *[kolacja, zebranie]* late; ~**ony w rozwoju** Psych. retarded

oprac|ować *pf* — **oprac|owywać** *impf vt* to draw up *[projekt, ustawę, przepisy]*

opracowa|nie *n* study; ~**nie monograficzne** a monograph

opracowywać *impf* → **opracować**

opraw|a *f* [1] (książki) cover, binding; **w twardej/ miękkiej ~ie** in hardback/paperback [2] (obrazu, zdjęcia) frame; (klejnotu) setting; (okularów) rim(s) [3] (muzyczna, plastyczna) setting

oprawi|ć *pf* — **oprawi|ać** *impf vt* to bind *[książkę, rękopis]*; to frame *[obraz, fotografię]*; to set *[klejnot]*; to flay *[kurę, rybę]*

opraw|ka *f* (żarówki) socket; (okularów) rims, frame

opresj|a *f* książk. trouble; **wybawić kogoś z ~i** to get sb out of trouble

oprocentowa|nie *n* interest

oprogramowa|nie *n* Komput. software

oprowa|dzić *pf* — **oprowa|dzać** *impf vt* to show [sb] around; **~dzić kogoś po mieście** to show sb around town

oprócz *praep.* [1] (z wyjątkiem) apart a. aside from, except (for) **(kogoś/czegoś** sb/sth) [2] (obok, niezależnie) besides, apart a. aside from **(kogoś/czegoś** sb/sth); **~ tego** (ponadto) apart from that, besides that

opróżni|ć *pf* — **opróżni|ać** *impf vt* to empty *[butelkę, kieszenie, szufladę]*; to unload *[wagon]*; to vacate *[pokój, dom]*

oprysk|ać *pf* — **oprysk|iwać** *impf vt* [1] (zmoczyć) to spatter, to splash [2] (środkami chemicznymi) to spray

opryskliw|y *adi. grad.* książk. *[osoba]* brusque; *[odpowiedź]* brusque, abrupt; *[głos, ton]* brusque, curt

opryszcz|ka *f* herpes; **~ka na wardze** a cold sore

oprysz|ek *m* pot. pejor. thug, hoodlum

op|rzeć *pf* — **op|ierać** *impf* **[I]** *vt* [1] (przystawić) to lean, to prop *[drabinę, rower]* **(o coś** against sth); (postawić) to rest *[paczkę, walizkę]* **(o coś** a. **na czymś** against a. on sth); **oprzeć głowę na czyimś ramieniu** to lean a. rest one's head on sb's shoulder [2] (wziąć za podstawę) to base **(coś na czymś** sth on sth); **teza oparta na szczegółowych badaniach** a theory grounded in a. founded on thorough research

[II] oprzeć się — **opierać się** [1] (wesprzeć się) to lean **(na czymś/o coś** on/against sth); **oprzyj się o mnie** lean on me [2] (wziąć za podstawę) **oprzeć się na czymś** to base one's ideas/theories on sth [3] (polegać) to rely **(na kimś** on sb) [4] (stawić opór) to resist *[osobie, namowom, pokusie]*

[III] oprzeć się (zostać skierowanym) **oprzeć się o sąd** to go a. to be brought to court

oprzytomni|eć *pf vi* (odzyskać przytomność) to regain a. recover consciousness, to come round a. to; (obudzić się) to fully awaken; przen. to come to one's senses, to sober up

opty|k *m* optician, dispensing optician GB

optymi|sta *m*, **~stka** *f* optimist

optymistyczn|y *adi.* optimistic; **zbyt ~e prognozy** over-optimistic forecasts

optymizm *m* optimism

opublik|ować *pf vt* to publish *[artykuł, dane]*

opuchli|zna *f* swelling

opuch|nąć *pf vi [powieki, oczy]* to puff up; *[palec, noga]* to swell (up)

opuchnię|ty *adi. [ręce, nogi]* swollen; *[twarz]* puffy

opuk|ać *pf* — **opuk|iwać** *impf vt* [1] (ostukać) to tap **(coś** (on) sth) [2] Med. to tap *[pacjenta, plecy]*

opustosza|ły *adi.* książk. *[ulice, domy]* desolate, deserted

opustosz|eć *pf vi* książk. *[plaża, kościół, plac]* to empty, to become deserted

opuszczać *impf* → **opuścić**

opuszcz|ony *adi. [osoba, ogród]* abandoned

opusz|ka *f* (u człowieka) fingertip; (u zwierząt) pad

opu|ścić *pf* — **opu|szczać** *impf* **[I]** *vt* [1] (obniżyć) to lower *[flagę, cenę]*; **~ścić szybę (w samochodzie)** to wind down a window; **~ść ręce, powoli!** put your hands down slowly! [2] (pominąć) to skip *[wyraz, stronę]*; to miss, to skip *[lekcję, zajęcia]* [3] (porzucić) to leave *[żonę, kraj]*; **~ścić rodzinę** to walk out on one's family; **~ściła mnie odwaga** przen. my courage left a. failed me

[II] opuścić się — **opuszczać się** [1] (zniżyć się) to go a. move down; **winda ~szczała się w głąb szybu** the lift moved down the shaft [2] pot. (zaniedbać się) to neglect **(w czymś** sth); to slack off

o|rać *impf* **[I]** *vt* to plough, to plow US *[ziemię]* **[II]** *vi* pot. (pracować) to drudge, to slave ■ **orać kimś** a. **w kogoś** pot. to make sb work their guts out; **każdy orze, jak może** przysł. you do your best a. what you can

orangutan *m* orangutan(g)

oranża|da *f* orangeade

oratori|um *n* oratorio

oraz *coni.* książk. and, as well as

orbi|ta *f* orbit także przen.

orchide|a *f* orchid

orde|r *m* order; **przyznać komuś ~r za coś** to award sb an order for sth

ordynarnie *adv. grad. [odezwać się, zachowywać się]* rudely; *[ubierać się, malować]* vulgarly

ordynarn|y *adi. grad. [osoba, zachowanie, słowa, makijaż]* vulgar; **~y dowcip** a crude a. vulgar joke

ordynato|r *m* ≈ senior registrar

orędzi|e *n* address

organ *m* [1] (narząd) organ [2] (urząd) body, authority [3] (gazeta) organ

organizacj|a *f* [1] (stowarzyszenie) organization; **Organizacja Narodów Zjednoczonych** the United Nations (Organization) [2] (urządzenie) organization, organizing; **zająć się ~ą wycieczki** to organize a trip

organizato|r *m*, **~rka** *f* organizer

organizm *m* organism także przen.; (człowieka) body, system

organiz|ować *impf* **[I]** *vt* [1] (urządzać) to organize *[wycieczkę, pracę]* [2] (zakładać) to establish *[spółkę,* *firmę]* ③ pot. (zdobywać) to procure *[bilety, żywność]*

II organizować się (zrzeszać się) ~**ować się w związki** to organize into trade unions

organk|i *plt* mouth organ, harmonica

organ|y *plt* (pipe) organ

orgazm *m* orgasm

orgi|a *f* ① (rozwiązła zabawa) orgy ② przen. riot; ~**a kolorów** a riot of colours

orientacj|a *f* ① (w terenie) sense of direction ② (rozeznanie) knowledge, grasp (**w czymś** of sth) ③ (poglądy) orientation; ~**a polityczna/seksualna** political/sexual orientation

orientacyjn|y *adi.* ① (rozpoznawczy) **punkt** ~**y** a landmark; **mapa** ~**a** an orienteering map; **zmysł** ~**y** a sense of direction ② (przybliżony) *[dane, pomiary, ceny]* approximate

orientali|sta *m,* ~**stka** *f* orientalist

orientalisty|ka *f* Oriental studies

orient|ować się *impf v refl.* ① (rozeznawać się) to be familiar (**w czymś** with sth); to be knowledgeable (**w czymś** about sth); (rozumieć) to realize; **o ile się** ~**uję...** as far as I know... ② (w terenie) to get one's bearings *także przen.*; to orient(ate) oneself; ~**ować się na coś** *także przen.* to head for sth *także przen.*

or|ka¹ *f* ① (w rolnictwie) ploughing GB, plowing US ② pot., przen. graft pot.; **orka na ugorze** hard graft

or|ka² *f* Zool. killer whale

orkiest|ra *f* orchestra, band; ~**ra dęta** a brass band

ornamen|t *m* ① (zdobienie) ornament, design; **ozdabiać coś** ~**tami** to ornament sth ② Muz. ornament

ornitolo|g *m* ornithologist

ornitologi|a *f* ornithology

orszak *m* (pochód) procession; (świta) retinue

ortalion *m* Włók. ≈ polyamide

ortografi|a *f* Jęz. (zasady) orthography; (pisownia) spelling

ortograficznie *adv.* **pisać** ~ to have no problem with spelling

ortograficzn|y *adi. [zasady, słownik]* orthographic(al); **błąd** ~**y** a spelling mistake, a misspelling

ortope|da *m* ① Med. orthopaedist GB, orthopedist US ② (protetyk) orthopaedic technician GB, orthopedic technician US

ortopedi|a *f* Med. orthopaedics GB, orthopedics US

oryginalnie *adv. grad. [ubierać się]* originally, in an original way

oryginaln|y *adi. grad.* ① (autentyczny) *[dokument, podpis, obraz]* genuine, authentic ② (pierwotny) original; **film w wersji** ~**ej** a film in the original language version ③ (samodzielny) *[styl, pomysł, artysta]* original ④ (niebanalny) *[uroda, strój]* remarkable, unique

orygina|ł *m* ① (autentyk) original ② (osoba) original, eccentric

orzech *m* ① (owoc) nut; (drzewo) walnut (tree) ② (kolor) walnut, hazel

■ **twardy** ~ **do zgryzienia** a tough a. hard nut (to crack)

orzechow|y *adi. [smak, czekolada, tort]* nutty, nut *[meble, boazeria]* walnut; *[oczy, włosy]* hazel, nut-brown; **lody** ~**e** walnut ice cream

orzecze|nie *n* ① Prawo (wyrok) ruling, adjudication ② książk. (opinia) statement; ~**nie lekarskie** a medical certificate ③ Jęz. predicate

orzekać *impf* → **orzec**

o|rzeł *m* ① Zool. eagle ② (godło) eagle; (na monecie) heads; **orzeł czy reszka?** heads or tails?; **zagramy w orła i reszkę?** let's toss a. flip a coin, let's toss for it ③ (o osobie) wizard (**w czymś** at sth)

■ **wywinąć orła** pot., żart. to come a cropper pot.

orzeźwiać *impf* → **orzeźwić**

orzeźwiająco|y *adi. [kąpiel, bryza, działanie]* refreshing, invigorating; **napoje** ~**e** refreshing drinks, liquid refreshment

orzeźw|ić *pf* — **orzeźw|iać** *impf* **I** *vt* to refresh, to invigorate

II orzeźwić się — **orzeźwiać się** to refresh oneself

os|a *f* ① Zool. wasp; **cienka jak osa** wasp-waisted ② przen. (osoba dokuczliwa) gadfly przen.

osacz|yć *pf* — **osacz|ać** *impf vt* to corner *[przestępcę]*; to surround *[wroga]*; *[problemy, trudności]* to assault, to bombard; ~**yć zwierzynę** to bring the quarry to bay

osa|d *m* deposit, residue

osa|da *f* ① (miejscowość) settlement, hamlet ② Sport crew

osa|dzić *pf* — **osa|dzać** *impf* **I** *vt* ① (umocować) to fix *[bagnet, łopatę]*; **głęboko** ~**dzone oczy** deep-set eyes ② (umiejscowić) *[autor, reżyser]* to set *[powieść, sztukę, film]*; ~**dzić kogoś w więzieniu** to put sb in prison ③ (zatrzymać) ~**dzić konia** to bring up a. rein in a horse ④ przen. (pohamować) to put [sb] in place; **próbował coś powiedzieć, ale z miejsca go** ~**dzono** he tried to say something, but he was immediately cut short

II osadzić się — **osadzać się** (zgromadzić się) to settle

osącz|yć *pf* — **osącz|ać** *impf vt* to drain *[makaron, warzywa]*

osą|d *m* książk. judg(e)ment

osą|dzić *pf* — **osą|dzać** *impf vt* ① (ocenić) to judge, to assess; **trudno** ~**dzić, jak naprawdę było** it's difficult to say how it really was ② (wydać wyrok) to judge; ~**dzić kogoś za morderstwo** to judge sb guilty of murder

oschle *adv. grad. [przywitać się, odpowiedzieć]* coldly, drily

oschł|y *adi. [osoba]* hard-faced; *[powitanie, głos]* cold, dry

oses|ek *m* suckling, nursling

o|set *m* thistle

osiadać *impf* → **osiąść**

osiąg|nąć *pf* — **osiąg|ać** *impf vt* ① (zdobyć) to achieve, to attain *[sukces, cel]* ② (dojść do kresu) to attain, to reach; **ten samochód ~a prędkość ponad 200 km/godz.** this car can reach speeds of over 200 kph ③ (dotrzeć do celu) to reach

osiągnię|cie *n* achievement, accomplishment

osi|ąść *pf* — **osi|adać** *impf vi* ① (osiedlić się) to settle; **~ąść na stałe w Stanach** to settle permanently in the US ② (opaść) *[kurz, śnieg]* to settle; (zapaść się) *[budynek, fundamenty]* to subside, to sink ③ (wylądować) *[balon, pojazd kosmiczny]* to land

osiedlać *impf* → **osiedlić**

osiedl|e *n* estate; **~e mieszkaniowe** a housing estate a. development

osiedl|ić się *pf* — **osiedl|ać się** *impf v refl.* to settle

o|siem *num.* eight

osiemdziesi|ąt *num.* eighty

osiemdziesiąt|ka *f* eighty

osiemdziesią|ty *num. ord.* eightieth

osiemnast|ka *f* eighteen

osiemnastolat|ek *m,* **~ka** *f* eighteen-year-old

osiemnastoletni *adi. [osoba]* eighteen-year-old; *[okres, staż]* eighteen-year

osiemnastowieczn|y *adi. [pałacyk, muzyka]* eighteenth-century

osiemna|sty *num. ord.* eighteenth

osiemna|ście *num.* eighteen

o|siemset *num.* eight hundred

osiero|cić *pf* — **osiero|cać** *impf vt* to orphan *[dzieci, syna]*

osiodła|ć *pf vt* to saddle (up) *[konia, wielbłąda]*

o|sioł *m* ① (zwierzę) donkey, ass; (samiec) jackass ② pot. (o osobie) ass GB, jackass US, donkey pot.

■ **głupi jak osioł** (as) thick as a plank pot.; **uparty jak osioł** (as) stubborn as a mule

osiwi|eć *pf vi [osoba, włosy]* to (go) grey, to (go) gray US

oskarżać[1] *impf* → **oskarżyć**

oskarża|ć[2] *impf vi* Prawo (jako oskarżyciel) to prosecute

oskarże|nie *n* ① (skarga) accusation; (zarzut) charge (**o coś** of sth); (o poważne przestępstwo) indictment (**o coś** for sth) ② (strona oskarżająca) prosecution; **świadek ~nia** a witness for the prosecution

oskarż|ony *m,* **~ona** *f* Prawo the accused, defendant

oskarżyciel *m,* **~ka** *f* Prawo prosecutor

oskarż|yć *pf* — **oskarż|ać**[1] *impf vt* (obwinić) to accuse (**kogoś o coś** sb of sth); (postawić w stan oskarżenia) *[policja, prokurator]* to charge; **został ~ony o morderstwo** he has been charged with murder

oskrob|ać *pf* — **oskrob|ywać** *impf vt* to scale *[rybę]*; to peel *[warzywa, ziemniaki]*

oskrzel|e *n* Anat. bronchus; (bliższe tchawicy) bronchial tube

oskub|ać *pf* — **obskub|ywać** *impf vt* ① (oczyścić z piór) to pluck *[kurę, kaczkę]* ② (oderwać) to pick (off) *[listki, płatki]* ③ pot., żart. (pozbawić pieniędzy) to fleece pot. *[klienta, turystów]*

osłab|ić *pf* — **osłab|iać** *impf vt* ① (uczynić słabszym) *[gorączka, choroba]* to weaken, to debilitate *[osobę]*; *[hałas, stres]* to impair *[słuch, wzrok]* ② (uczynić mniej intensywnym) to blunt *[apetyt, wrażliwość]*; to abate *[zapał, ferwor]*; to cushion *[upadek, wstrząs]*; to ease *[ból, napięcie]*; to weaken *[gospodarkę, pozycję]*; to enfeeble *[kraj]*

osłabieni|e *n* (fizyczna słabość) weakness; (słabość organizmu) debility; (gorszy, słabszy stan) feebleness, impairment

osłab|nąć *pf vi* ① (opaść z sił) *[osoba, zwierzę]* to weaken, to grow weak a. feeble ② (zmniejszyć się) *[zapał, aktywność]* to flag, to die down; *[burza, storm]* to abate; *[napięcie, presja]* to ease (off), to let up

osładzać *impf* → **osłodzić**

osłaniać *impf* → **osłonić**

osł|odzić *pf* — **osładzać** *impf vt* ① (dodać cukier) to sweeten *[kawę, herbatę]* ② przen. to sweeten *[starość, życie]*; to make *[sth]* more palatable *[porażkę, niepowodzenia]*

osłon|a *f* ① (zabezpieczenie) protection (**przed czymś** against a. from sth); (schronienie) cover, shelter (**przed czymś** from sth); **pod ~ą ciemności** under (the) cover of darkness ② Wojsk. (akcja) cover

osł|onić *pf* — **osł|aniać** *impf vt* ① (uczynić niewidocznym) to cover, to screen; (okryć) **~onić kogoś/coś przed czymś** to shield a. protect sb/ sth from sth *[słońcem, blaskiem]*; to shelter sb/sth from sth *[niepogodą]* ② (zabezpieczać) **~onić coś przed czymś** to protect sth from sth *[ryzykiem, niebezpieczeństwem]*; to screen sth from sth *[promieniowaniem]*; **~onił ją przed ciosem** he shielded her from the blow ③ przen. (chronić, ukrywać) to shelter *[osobę]*

osłon|ka *f* (na wędlinie) casing

■ **bez ~ek** *[powiedzieć, napisać]* openly, outright

osłupieni|e *n* ① (oszołomienie) stupefaction; **ten widok wprawił go w ~e** he was dumbfounded at the sight ② Med. stupor

os|oba *f* person; **osoby dorosłe** adults; **przybył mistrz we własnej osobie** the master himself arrived; **malarz i poeta w jednej osobie** a painter and poet rolled into one

osobistoś|ć *f* (ważna, znana) personage; (popularna) personality; (wysoko postawiona) grandee

osobi|sty *adi. [rzeczy, pytanie]* personal; *[opinia, potrzeby]* individual

osobiście *adv. [dziękować, odebrać]* in person, personally; *[odpowiedzialny, dotknięty]* personally; **ta sprawa dotyczy mnie ~** the matter is of personal concern to me; **zjawić się ~** to make a personal appearance; ~ **sądzę, że...** personally, I think that...

osobliwoś|ć *f* ① (przedmiot, zjawisko) curiosity, oddity; (bibelot) curio; **gabinet ~ci** (z dziwami natury) a freak show; (z rzadkimi przedmiotami) a curio cabinet ② (dziwaczność) peculiarity, oddness

osobliw|y *adi. [reakcja, pomysł]* curious; *[język, styl]* peculiar; *[odczucie, podejrzenie]* queer; *[osoba, zachowanie]* odd

osobni|k *m* ① (indywiduum) individual, character; (typ) type ② Biol. specimen

osobno *adv.* (pojedynczo) *[pakowany, oceniany]* individually; (oddzielnie) *[gotować, przyjść]* separately; **jej rodzice mieszkają ~** her parents live apart; **płacili ~, każdy za siebie** each (of them) paid their own bill; **pytałem każdego z osobna** I asked each of them individually

osobn|y *adi. [wejście, konto]* separate; *[badania, programy]* independent; *[problem, sprawa]* another

osobowoś|ć *f* ① (wybitna osoba) personality ② (zespół cech) personality; **zaburzenia ~ci** personality disorders

osobow|y *adi.* ① (dotyczący osób) *[akta, cechy]* personal; *[winda, wagon]* passenger; **dane ~e** personal details; **pociąg ~y** a stopping train GB, a slow train US; **samochód ~y** a (motor) car GB, an automobile US, a passenger car US ② Jęz. *[zaimek, forma]* personal

osocz|e *n* plasma

os|olić *pf vt* to salt *[ziemniaki, wodę]*

osowia|ły *adi. [osoba]* dejected, dispirited; *[mina, twarz]* glum

osp|a *f* pox; **czarna ~a** smallpox; **~a wietrzna** chickenpox

ospale *adv. grad. [płynąć, reagować]* sluggishly; *[poruszać się]* listlessly; *[mówić, snuć się]* drowsily, sleepily

ospa|ły *adi. grad. [osoba, gospodarka]* sluggish, listless; *[okolica, miasteczko]* drowsy; *[osoba, wyraz twarzy]* drowsy, sleepy

osprzę|t *m* ① Techn. (dodatkowe wyposażenie) accessories; (do urządzeń gazowych, grzewczych) fittings ② Żegl. rigging

ostatecznie ❑ *adv. książk.* ① (całkowicie) *[rozwiązać, załatwić]* definitively; *[udowodnić, zidentyfikować]* conclusively; *[zamknąć, zlikwidować]* permanently ② (w końcu) finally; (w ostatecznym rachunku) ultimately; (z konieczności) as a last resort

❑ *part.* ① (przecież) after all; **~ to jego pieniądze, może je wydać na co chce** it's his money after all: he can spend it on whatever he wants ② (w zniecierpliwieniu) in the end; **więc ~ o co w tym wszystkim chodzi?** so what's it all about actually?

ostatecznoś|ć *f* ① (konieczność) necessity; (konieczne działania) last resort; **w ~ci** (w razie potrzeby) if it comes to the push a. pinch, as a last a. in the last resort

② (skrajność) extremity, extreme; **rozwścieczony do ~ci** absolutely furious

ostateczn|y *adi. książk. [argument, dowód]* conclusive; *[decyzja, odpowiedź]* definitive, final; *[porażka]* eventual; *[próba, wysiłek]* last-ditch; *[warunki]* nonnegotiable; *[rezultat, zwycięstwo]* ultimate; **~y termin** deadline, cut-off a. closing date

■ **w ~ym rachunku** a. **rozrachunku** in the final analysis, at the end of the day

ostat|ek ❑ *m książk.* (resztka) remains; **~kiem sił wczołgał się do pokoju** he managed to drag himself into the room with his last breath

❑ **ostatki** *plt pot.* Pancake Day, Shrove Tuesday

❑ **na ostatku** *adv.* (na samym końcu) at the very end

ostatni ❑ *adi.* ① (w kolejności) *[miejsce, pacjent]* last; (końcowy) *[minuty, słowa]* closing; *[wagon]* end; *[rata, spotkanie]* final, last; *[egzemplarz, seans]* last; **wyszła jako ~a** she was the last to leave; **do ~ch granic** to the utmost (limit) ② (poprzedni) last; **w ~ czwartek** last Thursday ③ (najgorszy) lowest; **był ~m uczniem w klasie** he was bottom of the class ④ (całkowity) utter; **postąpił jak ~ głupek** he acted like an utter fool ⑤ (najmniej prawdopodobny) last; **to ~ a rzecz, jaka przyszłaby mi na myśl** that's the last thing I'd think of

❑ **ostatni** *m*, **~a** *f* ① (jedyny) the last (one); **to jeden z ~ch, którzy nadal podtrzymują tę tradycję** he's one of the last to maintain the tradition ② (z wymienionych) the latter; **lubi psy i koty, szczególnie te ~e** he likes dogs and cats, especially the latter ③ (najgorszy, niegodny) good-fornothing; **~ z ~ch** the lowest of the low; **traktuje mnie jak jakąś ~ą** he treats me like dirt; **zwymyślać kogoś od ~ch** to call sb vile/the vilest (of) names

ostatnio *adv.* ① (niedawno) recently, lately; of late *książk.*; **~ nie czuję się zbyt dobrze** I haven't been feeling too well lately a. of late; **~ się dowiedziałem, że...** I heard recently that... ② (ostatnim razem) last (time); **kiedy ~ byłam w Paryżu...** (the) last time I was in Paris...

ostempl|ować *pf vt* ① (oznaczyć stemplem) to frank, to postmark *[znaczek]*; to postmark *[kartkę, kopertę]*; to stamp *[dokument, książkę]*; to validate *[bilet, paszport]* ② Techn. (podeprzeć) to prop (up) *[strop, ścianę]*; to shore up *[budynek]*

ostentacyjn|y *adi. książk. [elegancja, uprzejmość]* ostentatious

ost|ro *adv. grad.* ① (spiczasto) sharp, sharply; **~ro zakończony patyk** a sharp-pointed stick ② (intensywnie) *[świecić]* harshly; *[pachnieć]* sharp; *[zaboleć]* acutely, severely; *[pić, trenować]* hard ③ (surowo) *[oceniać, upominać]* severely, harshly; *[krytykować, odpowiedzieć]* sharply ④ (energicznie) *[skręcić, zahamować]* sharp, sharply; **wziąć się ~ro do nauki** to get down to some real studying

ostr|oga *f* spur *także przen.*

ostrosłup *m* Mat. pyramid

ostroś|ć *f* książk. ① (krawędzi, ostrza) keenness, sharpness ② (surowość) severity, strictness; (krytyki) harshness ③ (zapachu) sharpness, pungency; (światła, kolorów) harshness; (klimatu, zimy) severity; (słuchu, wzroku, węchu) keenness ④ (obrazu) clarity, sharpness; **głębia ~ci** Fot. depth of focus

ostrożnie *adv. grad. [działać, poruszać się]* cautiously; *[obchodzić się, jechać]* carefully; *[dotykać, posuwać się]* gingerly; „**~, szkło!**" 'glass – handle with care'

ostrożnoś|ć *f* care, caution; **zaleca się (wielką) ~ć** (great) caution should be exercised; **zachować środki ~ci** to take precautions

ostrożn|y *adi. grad.* ① (przezorny) careful, cautious; (nieufny) chary, wary ② (pełen rozwagi) *[jazda]* careful; *[nastawienie]* cautious, conservative; *[sformułowanie]* circumspect książk.

ostrug|ać *pf* — **ostrug|iwać** *impf vt* (wygładzić) to whittle; (heblem) to plane

ostrużyn|y *plt* shavings; (ziemniaków) peelings

ost|ry *adi. grad.* ① (naostrzony) sharp ② (stromy, ukośny) *[podejście, zejście]* steep; *[kąt, zakręt]* sharp ③ (surowy, bezwzględny) *[przepis, zakaz]* stringent, strict; *[krytyka]* harsh, strong; *[ton]* abrasive, sharp ④ (intensywny) *[ból]* acute, sharp; *[dźwięk, głos, kolor]* harsh; *[mróz]* hard; *[danie, sos]* spicy, hot ⑤ (wyrazisty) *[zdjęcie]* sharp

ostry|ga *f* oyster

ostrzał *m* (gun)fire; **~ł artyleryjski** shellfire

ostrz|e *n* ① (część narzędzia) blade; (krawędź tnąca) edge; (krawędź łyżwy) runner; (obrzeże krzywej) cusp; (grot) head; **~e strzały/włóczni** an arrowhead/a spearhead ② książk., przen. (krytyki) edge; (satyry) barb; (ironii) shaft, sting

■ **stawiać** a. **postawić sprawę na ~u noża** książk. to bring matters to a head

ostrze|c *pf* — **ostrze|gać** *impf vt* to alert, to warn; **~c kogoś przed niebezpieczeństwem** to alert sb to (a) danger

ostrzegawcz|y *adi.* książk. *[gest, spojrzenie]* admonitory książk.; cautionary, warning; *[sygnał, znak]* warning danger; *[światło, wystrzał]* warning

ostrzeże|nie *n* (przestroga) admonition książk.; warning; (napomnienie) admonition książk.; warning, caution; **~nie sztormowe/powodziowe** a gale/flood warning

ostrzy|c *pf* ① *vt* to cut *[włosy]*; to clip *[sierść psa]*; to shear *[runo owcy]*; to cut, to mow *[trawnik]*; to cut, to prune *[żywopłot]*; **~c na zero** to skin; **mieć dobrze ~żone włosy** to have a good haircut

② **ostrzyc się** (samodzielnie) to cut one's (own) hair; (zostać ostrzyżonym) to have one's hair cut, to have a haircut

ostrz|yć *impf vt* to grind, to hone *[nóż, siekierę]*; to strop *[brzytwę]*; to whet *[narzędzia]*; to sharpen *[ołówek, pal]*

■ **~ć sobie zęby na kogoś/coś** pot. to have one's eye on sb/sth, to have sb/sth in one's sights; **~yć sobie zęby na kimś** pot. to bad-mouth sb pot.; to run sb down

ostu|dzić *pf* — **ostudz|ać** *impf* ① *vt* ① (ochłodzić) to cool; (w lodówce) to chill; **~dzić coś do temperatury pokojowej** to cool sth to room temperature ② przen. (hamować) to abate książk. *[zapał]*; to cool *[nastroje]*; to dampen *[entuzjazm, optymizm]*; to temper *[radość]*

② **ostudzić się** — **ostudzać się** pot. ① (ostygnąć) *[zupa, mleko]* to cool ② przen. (ograniczyć zaangażowanie) to cool; **~dził się w swym zapale do nauki** his zeal for studying abated

ostyg|nąć *pf* — **ostyg|ać** *impf vi* ① (stać się zimnym) *[zupa, obiad]* to cool ② przen. (zmaleć) *[entuzjazm, gniew]* to cool

osu|nąć się *pf* — **osu|wać się** *impf v refl.* książk. ① (opaść, ześlizgnąć się) *[błoto, kamienie]* to slide, to slip; *[grunt, skarpa]* to subside; *[ściana]* to collapse ② (upaść) to sink, to slump

osusz|yć *pf* — **osusz|ać** *impf* ① *vt* ① (odwodnić, wysuszyć) to drain *[bagno, łąkę]*; to dehumidify *[gaz, powietrze]*; to dry *[naczynia, oczy]*; to blot *[atrament]* ② pot., żart. (opróżnić) to drain *[butelkę, kufel]*

② **osuszyć się** — **osuszać się** ① (wytrzeć się) to dry oneself (off) ② *[dach, ręcznik]* to dry (off)

osuwać się *impf* → **osunąć się**

osw|oić *pf* — **osw|ajać** *impf vt* ① (przyzwyczaić) to accustom, to adapt (**z czymś** to sth) ② (zaznajomić) to become familiar (**z czymś** with sth); **starał się ~oić rodziców z komputerami** he tried to familiarize his parents with computers ③ (obłaskawić) to tame *[lwa]*; to domesticate *[lisa, ptaka]*

oszac|ować *pf vt* to adjust *[roszczenia]*; to appraise, to assess *[wartość]*; to assess, to evaluate *[straty, szkody]*; to estimate *[rozmiary, wielkość]*; to judge, to reckon *[odległość, wiek]*; to price *[towar]*; to value *[antyk, nieruchomość]*

oszal|eć *pf vi* książk. ① (stracić panowanie nad sobą) to go berserk; to go mad a. wild pot.; **~eć z bólu/rozpaczy** to go mad with pain/grief ② (zwariować) to go insane a. mad ③ przen. (wielbić) to go crazy a. mad pot. (**na punkcie czegoś** over sth)

oszałamiać *impf* → **oszołomić**

oszcze|nić się *pf v refl. [suka, wilczyca, lisica]* to litter, to pup

oszczep *m* Sport (przyrząd) javelin; (konkurencja) javelin

oszczerstw|o *n* książk. defamation książk.; slander; **rzucać na kogoś ~a** to spread slanders about sb, to malign sb; **kampania ~ (przeciwko komuś)** a smear campaign (against sb)

oszczędnie *adi. grad. [gospodarować]* economically; *[żyć]* frugally, thriftily; *[chwalić, nagradzać]* sparingly; *[pisać, wyrażać się]* economically

oszczędnoś|ć [] *f* [1] (cecha) frugality, thrift(iness) [2] (oszczędzanie) economy, saving

[] **oszczędności** *plt* (pieniądze) savings; (zapasy) reserves

oszczędn|y *adi. grad. [gospodyni, tryb życia]* frugal; *[gospodarka, technologia]* economical; **być ~ym w słowach** to be economical with one's words; **jest ~y w pochwałach** he's sparing in his praise

oszczędza|ć[1] *impf* [] *vt* [1] (gospodarować oszczędnie) to conserve *[energię, surowce]*; to be sparing with *[paliwo, wodę]* [2] przen. (dbać, pielęgnować) to conserve *[siły]*; to save *[głos, czas]*; to spare *[oczy, wzrok]*

[] **oszczędzać się** (dbać o siebie) to save a. spare oneself

oszczę|dzić *pf* — **oszczę|dzać**[2] *impf vt* [1] (żyć oszczędnie) to economize *vi*, to save; (odkładać) to put away, to save (up); **~dzać każdy grosz** to save every penny; **~dzać na emeryturę** to save towards one's retirement; **~dzić na czymś** to economize a. save on sth [2] (uchronić) to save, to spare; (darować życie) to spare *[dziecko, jeńca]*; **~dzić komuś kłopotów** to spare sb the trouble; **~dzić sobie trudu robienia czegoś** to save oneself the bother of doing sth; **~dzę ci szczegółów** I'll spare you the details

oszlif|ować *pf vt* [1] (wygładzić) to cut *[diamenty]*; to polish *[sztućce, zderzak]*; (papierem ściernym) to sand (down) *[biurko, blat]* [2] przen. (poprawić, ulepszyć) to polish (up) *[styl]*

oszoł|omić *pf* — **oszoł|amiać** *impf vt* [1] (odurzyć) to intoxicate, to stupefy; **potężny cios go ~omił** the powerful blow left him stupefied; **znaleźli go związanego i ~omionego narkotykami** they found him tied up and drugged [2] (zdumieć) to stun, to stupefy; **jej reakcja go ~omiła** her reaction stunned him

oszpe|cić *pf* — **oszpe|cać** *impf vt* to disfigure, to scar; **twarz ~cona bliznami po ospie** a face disfigured by smallpox

oszuk|ać *pf* — **oszuk|iwać** *impf* [] *vt* (potraktować nieuczciwie) to deceive, to cheat *[męża, żonę]*; **~ali go na dużą sumę** they cheated a. swindled him out of a large sum of money

[] *vi* (wprowadzać w błąd) to be deceptive a. misleading; **lusterko nie ~uje** a mirror tells no lies

[] **oszukać się** — **oszukiwać się** [1] (okłamywać się) **~iwali się w grze w karty** they cheated each other at cards; **nie ~uj samego siebie** stop deluding yourself [2] (zawieść się) **~ali się na nim** they were disappointed in him

■ **~ać głód/żołądek** to stave off hunger; **~ać pragnienie** to stave off thirst

oszu|st *m*, **~stka** *f* swindler, fraudster

oszustw|o *n* deception, fraud

o|ś *f* [1] (linia) axis; **oś liczbowa** the (numerical) axis; **obracać się wokół własnej osi** to rotate a. revolve

around one's (own) axis [2] przen. (punkt centralny) pivot [3] Techn. pivot; (w samochodzie) axle

oś|ć *f* bone; **rybie ości** fishbones

oślepiać *impf* → **oślepić**

oślepiając|y *adi. [blask, światło]* blinding, dazzling

oślep|ić *pf* — **oślep|iać** *impf vt* [1] (pozbawić wzroku) to blind [2] (razić blaskiem) *[słońce, światło]* to blind, to dazzle [3] przen. (pozbawić rozsądku) to blind; **~ia cię miłość** love makes you blind

oślep|nąć *pf vi* (stracić wzrok) to go blind; (chwilowo przestać widzieć) to be blinded a. dazzled

ośli|zły *adi.* [1] (śliski) *[stopnie, kamienie]* slimy, slippery [2] pejor. (obrzydliwy) *[osoba, uśmieszek]* slimy pejor. [3] (nieświeży) *[szynka, mięso]* slimy

ośmiel|ić *pf* — **ośmiel|ać** *impf* książk. [] *vt* to encourage, to embolden

[] **ośmielać się** — **ośmielić się** [1] (mieć odwagę) to dare; **nie ~ił się odezwać** he didn't dare say a word [2] (nabrać odwagi) **~ić się i zacząć mówić** to gain confidence and start to talk

ośmiesz|yć *pf* — **ośmiesz|ać** *impf* [] *vt* to ridicule, to humiliate

[] **ośmieszyć się** — **ośmieszać się** to make a fool of oneself, to humiliate oneself

ośmioką|t *m* octagon

ośmiorni|ca *f* octopus

ośmior|o *num. mult.* eight

ośrod|ek *m* [1] (instytucja) centre GB, center US; **~ek zdrowia** a health centre [2] (centrum) centre GB, center US; **~ek handlu** a commercial centre; **~ek władzy** a power centre; **być ~kiem zainteresowania** to be the centre a. focus of attention

oświadczać *impf* → **oświadczyć**

oświadcze|nie *n* książk. announcement, statement; **~nie podatkowe** a tax return

oświadcz|yć *pf* — **oświadcz|ać** *impf* [] *vi* książk. to announce, to declare

[] **oświadczyć się** — **oświadczać się** to propose (**komuś** to sb)

oświadczyn|y *plt* (marriage) proposal

oświa|ta *f* [1] (podnoszenie stanu wykształcenia) education; **~ta dorosłych** adult education [2] (instytucja) education; **pracować w ~cie** to work in education

oświe|cić *pf* — **oświe|cać** *impf vt* [1] książk. (uświadomić, nauczyć) to enlighten [2] książk. (oświetlić) to illuminate, to light; **~cę wam drogę** I'll light the way for you

■ (nagle) **go/mnie ~ciło** pot. I/he had a (sudden) brainwave

oświetlać *impf* → **oświetlić**

oświetleni|e *n* (światło) light(ing), illumination; (instalacja) lighting

oświetl|ić *pf* — **oświetl|ać** *impf vt* to light, to illuminate

otaczać[1] *impf* → **otoczyć**[1]

otaczać[2] *impf* → **otoczyć**[2]

otar|cie *n* graze, scrape; **~cia na łokciu/twarzy** grazes on the elbow/face

otchła|ń *f* książk. abyss także przen.; **~ń rozpaczy** the depths of despair

otępieni|e *n* torpor, stupor; **wpaść w ~e** to sink into a state of torpor; **~e lekami** a drug-induced stupor; **~e starcze** senile dementia

oto książk. **[] *pron.*** here; **~ jestem** here I am; **~ mój paszport** here's a. this is my passport **II** *part.* **[1]** (przed zaimkiem pytajnym) **~ co/dlaczego** that's what/why **[2]** (wzmacniające) **w taki ~ sposób** (in) this way; **kupiłam ci tę ~ koszulę** I bought you this shirt

otoczeni|e *n* **[1]** (okolica) surroundings; **~e szkoły/kościoła** the school/church precincts a. grounds **[2]** (środowisko) environment, neighbourhood GB, neighborhood US; **obojętność ~a** the indifference of the people around one; **politycy z najbliższego ~a premiera** politicians from the prime minister's closest circle

ot|oczyć¹ *pf* — **ot|aczać¹** *impf* **[] *vt*** **[1]** (okolić) to surround, to enclose; **dom otoczony murem** a house surrounded by a wall **[2]** (okrążyć) to surround; **otoczono ich kordonem wojska** they were cordoned off by soldiers **[3]** przen. (stanowić towarzystwo) to surround; **otaczają mnie życzliwi ludzie** I'm surrounded by kind people; **otaczająca nas rzeczywistość** the world we live in **[4]** (obdarzyć) to surround; **otaczać kogoś czcią** to worship sb; **otaczać chorego opieką** to bestow care on a patient **II** otoczyć się — **otaczać się** książk. (mieć wokół siebie) **otaczać się kimś/czymś** to surround oneself with sb/sth [pisarzami, dziełami sztuki]

ot|oczyć² *pf* — **ot|aczać²** *impf vt* (oblepić) to coat (**coś w czymś** sth with a. in sth) **otoczyć mięso w mące** to coat the meat in flour

otóż *part.* so; **„zgadzasz się ze mną?" – „~ nie"** 'do you agree with me?' – 'no, (in fact) I don't'; **~ to!** exactly!, that's it (precisely)!; quite so! GB książk.

otr|ęby *plt* bran

otru|ć *pf* **[] *vt*** to poison (**kogoś czymś** sb with sth) **II** otruć się to poison oneself; **~ła się gazem** she gassed herself

otrz|ąsnąć, otrz|ąść *pf* — **otrz|ąsać** *impf* **[] *vt*** to shake off; **~ąsnąć śnieg z butów** to shake the snow off one's boots **II** otrząsnąć się — **otrząsać się** **[1]** (otrzepać się) to shake oneself off; **pies ~ąsał się z wody** the dog was shaking the water off his coat **[2]** przen. (dojść do siebie) to pull oneself together; to get over; **~ąsnęła się z przygnębienia** she shook off her depression **[3]** (wzdrygnąć się) to flinch

o|trzeć *pf* — **o|cierać** *impf* **[] *vt*** **[1]** (wytrzeć) to wipe [usta, pot]; **otrzeć łzy** to wipe away one's tears **[2]** (zetrzeć naskórek) to rub, to chafe; (zetrzeć skórkę owocu) to grate **II** otrzeć się — **ocierać się** **[1]** (osuszyć się) to wipe;

ocierać się ręcznikiem to dry oneself with a towel **[2]** (zetknąć się) to come into contact with; **otarł się o śmierć** he had a brush with death; **kot ocierał jej się o nogi** the cat was rubbing against her legs **[3]** otrzeć się pot. (nabrać ogłady) **otarła się o wielkich tego świata** she rubbed shoulders with some of the great celebrities of this world

otrzeźw|ić *pf* — **otrzeźw|iać** *impf vt* to sober up [pijanego]; to bring round [nieprzytomnego]; **jedna rozmowa z szefem wystarczyła, aby go ~ić** przen. one conversation with the boss was enough to disillusion him

otrzeźwi|eć *pf vi* **[1]** (stać się trzeźwym) to become sober, to sober up **[2]** (zacząć myśleć logicznie) to wake up to sth, to come to one's senses

otrzęsin|y *plt* Szkol., Uniw. initiation ceremonies a. rites, hazing US

otrzym|ać *pf* — **otrzym|ywać** *impf vt* książk. **[1]** (dostać) to receive [list, kwiaty]; **~ać stopień magistra chemii** to graduate from university with a degree in chemistry **[2]** (wytworzyć) to obtain; **azot ~ujemy z powietrza** nitrogen is obtained from the air

otu|cha *f* uplift, encouragement; **dodawać komuś ~chy** to encourage sb, to cheer sb up; **nabrać ~chy** to take heart

otwar|ty *adi.* open **■** **sprawa jest ~ta** the matter is open; **grać w ~te karty** pot. to lay one's cards on the table; **na ~tym powietrzu** a. **pod ~tym niebem** in the open air, outdoors

otwieracz *m* opener; **~ do konserw/butelek** a tin/bottle opener

otw|orzyć *pf* — **otw|ierać** *impf* **[] *vt*** **[1]** (odemknąć) to open [drzwi, butelkę]; **~orzyć siłą** to force open; **~orzyć komuś drzwi** to let sb in **[2]** (rozłożyć) to open [książkę, parasol] **[3]** (założyć, uruchomić) to open [konto, sklep]; **~orzyć własny interes** to go into business, to open up one's own business **[4]** (rozpocząć) to open [dyskusję]; **~orzyć ogień** Wojsk. to open fire (**do kogoś** on sb) **II** otworzyć się — **otwierać się** [furtka, okno] to open; [rana] to open (up); [widok, perspektywa] to open out a. up **■** **mieć oczy (i uszy) ~arte** to keep one's eyes open a. peeled a. skinned

otw|ór *m* **[1]** (dziura) hole, opening; **~ór okienny** a window opening; **~ór wentylacyjny** an air vent **[2]** (tunelu, butelki) mouth; (kanału, rury) inlet; (karabinu, lufy) muzzle **[3]** Anat. orifice, opening; **~ór gębowy** mouth, mouth opening **■** **drzwi stały (przed nimi) ~orem** the door(s) stood open before them; **świat stoi przed tobą ~orem** the world is your oyster

otyłoś|ć *f* obesity

oty|ły *adi.* obese

otynk|ować *pf vt* to plaster *[ścianę, budynek]*

owacj|a *f* ovation, applause; ~**a na stojąco** a standing ovation

owa|d *m* insect

owal *m* oval

owaln|y *adi. [stół, twarz]* oval

ow|ca *f* sheep; **stado owiec** a flock of sheep
■ **czarna owca** black sheep, rotten apple

owczar|ek *m* sheepdog

owdowi|eć *pf vi [kobieta]* to become a widow; *[mężczyzna]* to become a widower

ow|ies *m* oat

owi|nąć *pf* — **owi|jać** *impf* **[]** *vt* to wrap (up)
[] **owinąć się** — **owijać się** [1] (otulić się) to wrap (up); ~**jać się kocem** to wrap oneself (up) in a blanket [2] (wić się) to wind, to coil; **wąż** ~**nął się wokół gałęzi** the snake coiled itself round the branch

owłosieni|e *n* [1] (włosy, sierść) (body) hair [2] Bot. hair, pubescence

owłosi|ony *adi. [tors, nogi]* hairy

owoc *m* fruit także przen.; ~**e morza** Kulin. seafood

owoc|ować *impf vi* to bear fruit także przen.

owsian|ka *f* ≈ porridge GB, ≈ oatmeal US

owsik *m* pinworm, threadworm

owulacj|a *f* ovulation

ozdabiać *impf* → **ozdobić**

ozd|oba *f* książk. [1] (upiększenie) ornament, decoration [2] przen. pride

ozdobn|y *adi. grad. [rama, falbana]* decorative; *[język, styl]* ornate; *[szkło, krzew]* ornamental

ozięb|ić *pf* — **ozięb|iać** *impf* **[]** *vt* to chill, to cool *[koktail, sos]*
[] **oziębić się** — **oziębiać się** to cool; ~**iało się z dnia na dzień** it got cooler by the day; **nasze kontakty** ~**iły się od zeszłego roku** our relations have cooled since last year

ozięble *adv. grad. [potraktować, przywitać]* coldly, coolly

oziębłoś|ć *f* coolness, coldness; ~**ć płciowa** Med. frigidity

ozięb|ły *adi. grad. [ton, stosunki]* cool, cold; (seksualnie) frigid

ozi|ębnąć *pf vi [stosunki]* to cool

oznaczać[1] *impf* → **oznaczyć**

oznacz|ać[2] *impf vt* to mean; **co** ~**ają litery BBC?** what do the letters BBC stand for?; **katar nie musi** ~**ać choroby** a runny nose doesn't necessarily point to a. indicate illness

oznacze|nie *n* symbol, sign

oznacz|yć *pf* — **oznacz|ać**[1] *impf vt* [1] (oznakować) to mark [2] (określić) to denote [3] (wyznaczyć) to fix, to determine

oznajmi|ć *pf* — **oznajmi|ać** *impf vt* książk. to announce, to declare

ozna|ka *f* [1] (objaw) indication, symptom; ~**ki gniewu/radości** signs of anger/joy [2] (znak, symbol) badge, symbol

ozon *m* ozone

oz|ór *m* (język zwierzęcia) tongue

oźreb|ić się *pf v refl.* to foal

ożaglowani|e *n* Żegl. rig, rigging

ożen|ek *m* pot. marriage

ożen|ić *pf* **[]** *vt* to marry off *[mężczyznę]*
[] **ożenić się** *[mężczyzna]* to marry, to get married (**z kimś** to sb)

oż|yć *pf* — **oż|ywać** *impf vi [przyroda, wspomnienia]* to revive

ożyw|ić *pf* — **ożyw|iać** *impf* **[]** *vt* [1] (wskrzesić) to revive [2] (pobudzić) to cheer up [3] (urozmaicić) to enliven; **kolorowe zasłony** ~**iły pokój** the colourful curtains added life to the room [4] (animować) to animate *[kukiełki, lalki]*
[] **ożywić się** — **ożywiać się** [1] (stać się weselszym) to cheer up; (stać się żywszym) to liven up [2] przen. (wzmacniać się) to revive, to recover

ożywieni|e *n* [1] (podniecenie) animation, excitement [2] (intensyfikacja) revival; ~**e handlu** a revival in trade

ożywi|ony *adi. [dyskusja]* animated, lively; *[debata]* heated, energetic; *[działalność]* intense, heightened; *[handel]* booming, brisk; *[osoba, dziecko]* excited; *[głos, gesty]* animated

Ó

ósem|ka *f* [1] (cyfra) eight [2] Sport (ewolucja) figure of eight GB, figure eight US [3] Sport (łódź, załoga) eight; **wyścigi** ~**ek** eights [4] Muz. quaver GB, eighth note US

ósm|y *num. ord.* eighth

ów *pron.* książk. (ten) that; (inny) another; **ten i ów** some, one or two

ówcze|sny *adi.* *[źródła, dokumenty]* contemporary; (o obyczajach, strojach) of the time; **zgodnie z** ~**sną modą** in accordance with the fashion of the time a. day; ~**sny minister zdrowia** the then minister of health

ówdzie *pron.* książk. **tu i** ~ (gdzieniegdzie) here and there

P

n inv. P, p

pa|cha *f* [1] Anat. armpit; **ogolić się pod pachami** to shave one's armpits; **trzymać coś pod pachą** to have sth under one's arm [2] (w ubraniu) armhole

pachn|ieć *impf vi* [1] (wydzielać woń) to smell; **ładnie ~ieć** to smell nice; **~ieć jaśminem** to smell of jasmine [2] przen. **ta sprawa niedobrze ~ie** the whole affair reeks; **to ~ie kryminałem** pot. they can put you behind bars for that pot.; **wiesz, czym to ~ie!** you know what that means!

pachoł|ek *m* (słupek ostrzegawczy) bollard; (przenośny) cone; **odgrodzić coś ~kami** to cone off sth GB

pachwin|a *f* Anat. groin

pacierz *m* prayer; **zmówić ~** to say one's prayers; **znać a. umieć coś jak ~** to know sth by heart

pacjen|t *m*, **~tka** *f* patient; **~t hospitalizowany/leczony ambulatoryjnie** an inpatient/an outpatient

pac|nąć *pf* — **pac|ać** *impf* pot. **I** *vt* (uderzyć) to swat *[muchę]*; to pat *[osobę]* **II** *vi* (upaść) *[kamień]* to plop

pacyfik|ować *impf vt* to pacify *[miasto, kraj]*

pacyfi|sta *m*, **~stka** *f* pacifist

pacz|ka *f* [1] (pakunek) parcel; **~ka książek** a parcel of books; **obwiązać ~kę sznurkiem** to tie up a parcel with string [2] (zbiór) packet; **~ka banknotów/gazet** a batch of newspapers/a wad of banknotes [3] (opakowanie) packet, package US; **~ka papierosów/herbaty** a packet a. pack of cigarettes/a packet of tea [4] (przesyłka pocztowa) parcel, package US; **~ka żywnościowa** a food parcel; **wysłać/nadać ~kę** to send a parcel [5] pot. (grupa) gang pot.; **~ka przyjaciół** a gang of friends; **~ka z pracy** the crowd from work; **należeć do ~ki** to be one of the gang

paczk|ować *impf vt* to pack

padacz|ka *f* Med. epilepsy; **atak ~ki** an epileptic fit

padać¹ *impf* → **paść²**

pada|ć² *impf* **I** *vi* **deszcz/śnieg ~** it's raining/snowing **II** *v imp.* **wczoraj ~ło cały dzień** it was raining all day yesterday

padal|ec *m* slow-worm

padlin|a *f* carrion

pagór|ek *m* hill

pagórkowa|ty *adi.* *[teren, droga]* hilly

pajac *m* [1] (zabawka) puppet clown [2] pot. (o osobie) clown pejor.; **nie rób z siebie ~a** stop making a fool of yourself

pająk *m* spider

pajęczyn|a *f* spider's web; **~a intryg** przen. a web of intrigue

pakie|t *m* [1] (książek, ulotek) bundle; (towaru) batch [2] (reform, propozycji) package; **~t świadczeń socjalnych/ubezpieczeń** a benefits/an insurance package; **~t programowy** Komput. a software package [3] Fin. **~t akcji** a. **udziałów** a block a. a lot of shares; **~t mniejszościowy/większościowy** a minority/a majority interest a. shareholding

pak|ować *impf* **I** *vt* [1] (wkładać) to pack *[ubrania, książki]*; **~ować manatki** pot., przen. to pack one's bags przen. [2] (wypełniać) to pack *[plecak, torbę]* [3] (robić paczkę) to pack; (paczkować) to parcel up; **~ować coś w papier** to wrap sth in paper; **~ować coś w papier ozdobny** to gift-wrap sth [4] pot. to cram; **~ować pieniądze w coś** to sink a. pour money into sth *[projekt]* to spend money on sth *[mieszkanie]*; **~ować kogoś do więzienia** to put sb in prison; **~ować kogoś do łóżka** to pack sb off to bed; **~ować kogoś w kłopoty** to land a. get sb into trouble **II pakować się** [1] (zbierać rzeczy) to pack one's things; **jeszcze się nie zacząłem ~ować** I haven't started packing yet [2] pot. (wciskać się) to squeeze in; (tłoczyć się) to crowd in; **wszędzie ~uje się nieproszony** he always barges in uninvited [3] pot. (narażać się) **~ować się w kłopoty** a. **tarapaty** to get into hot water; **wiesz, w co się ~ujesz?** do you know what you're getting into a. doing?

pakown|y *adi.* *[torba, szafa]* capacious

pak|t *m* Polit. pact; **~t o nieagresji** a non-aggression pact

pakt|ować *impf vi* to parley

pakun|ek *m* [1] (paczka) parcel [2] Techn. packing

pal *m* pile, stake; **wbić kogoś na ~** to impale sb

palacz *m* [1] (pracownik) stoker [2] (osoba paląca) smoker; **nałogowy ~** a chain-smoker

palacz|ka *f* smoker

palan|t *m* [1] Gry ≈ rounders [2] pot., obraźl. prat pot.

palarni|a *f* [1] (dla palących) smoking room [2] Przem. roasting plant

palą|cy **I** *adi.* [1] (gorący) *[słońce]* scorching [2] (piekący) *[przyprawa]* fiery hot [3] książk., przen. *[sprawa,* *problem]* urgent; *[wstyd, tęsknota]* acute

II **palą|cy** *m*, ~**a** *f* smoker; **przedział dla** ~**ych** a smoking compartment

pal|ec *m* [1] Anat. digit [2] (u ręki) finger; (kciuk) thumb; **mały** ~**ec** the little finger; ~**ec wskazujący** the index finger; ~**ec serdeczny** the ring finger; **grozić (komuś)** ~**cem** to shake one's finger at sb; **wskazywać coś** ~**cem** to point (one's finger) at sth [3] (u nogi) toe; **wielki** ~**ec u nogi** the big toe; **stanąć na** ~**cach** to stand on tiptoe; **iść/chodzić na** ~**cach** to tiptoe

■ ~**ec boży** the hand of God; **nie kiwnąć** ~**cem w bucie** to not (even) lift a finger; **maczać w czymś** ~**ce** to have a hand in sth; **mieć coś w małym** ~**cu** to have sth at one's fingertips; **nie kłaść** ~**ca między drzwi** don't get your fingers burned; **publiczność stała – nie było gdzie** ~**ca wetknąć** the audience stood jam-packed; **nie tknąć kogoś** ~**cem** to not even lay a finger on sb; **owinąć sobie kogoś dokoła (małego)** ~**ca** to twist a. wrap sb around one's little finger; **patrzeć na coś przez** ~**ce** to turn a blind eye to sth

palenisk|o *n* hearth

pale|ta *f* [1] Szt. palette także przen. [2] Techn. pallet

pal|ić *impf* [] *vt* [1] (podtrzymywać ogień) to have a fire going; ~**ić (w piecu) drzewem/węglem** to use wood/coal for the stove [2] (oświetlać) ~**ić światło/ świecę** to have a light on/candle burning [3] (niszczyć ogniem) to cremate *[zwłoki]*; **czarownice niegdyś** ~**ono na stosach** witches were once burned at the stake [4] to smoke *[papierosy, fajkę]* [5] (parzyć) **słońce** ~**iło nas w plecy** the sun was burning down on our backs

II *vi* [1] (ogrzewać, opalać) ~**ić w piecu** to light the stove [2] (o urządzeniu, silniku) **moje auto** ~**i pięć litrów na sto kilometrów** my car does 100 kilometres to five litres (of petrol) [3] (wywoływać uczucie pieczenia) to burn; **wódka** ~**iła mnie w gardle** the vodka burned my throat [4] przen. ~**iła go zazdrość** he was consumed with envy; ~**ił ją wstyd** she burned with embarrassment; ~**iło nas pragnienie** we were dying of thirst

III **palić się** [1] (płonąć) „~**i się!**" 'fire!' [2] (świecić) **światło się** ~**i** there's a light on; **świeca się** ~**i** a candle is burning

■ ~**ić za sobą mosty** to burn one's boats a. bridges; **nie** ~**i się** pot. there's no rush; **niech się** ~**i, niech się wali** pot. come hell or high water; ~ **(to) diabli a. licho** to hell with it pot.; **robota** ~**i się jej w rękach** she's a demon for work pot.

palik *m* stake

palisa|da *f* palisade

paliw|o *n* fuel; ~**o stałe/ciekłe** solid/liquid fuel; ~**o jądrowe** nuclear fuel

palm|a *f* Bot. palm (tree); ~**a daktylowa** a date palm; ~**a kokosowa** a coconut palm a. tree

■ ~**a mu odbiła** pot. he's off his nut pot.

paln|ąć *pf* pot. [] *vt* (powiedzieć bez namysłu) to blurt (out)

II *vi* [1] (strzelić) to shoot [2] (uderzyć) to hit *[osobę]*; ~**ąć pięścią w stół** to bang the table with one's fist

III **palnąć się** (uderzyć się) to bang oneself (**w coś** on sth)

■ ~**ąć głupstwo** to put one's foot in it pot.; ~**ąć mówkę/kazanie** to launch into a tirade

palnik *m* burner; ~ **gazowy** a gas ring a. burner

pal|to *n* (over)coat; ~**to na zimę** a winter coat

paluch *m* Anat. big toe

palusz|ek *m* [1] (u ręki) finger; (u nogi) toe [2] (bateria) pencil battery; ~**ki rybne** Kulin. fish fingers

■ ~**ki lizać** yum-yum! pot.; finger-licking good US

pa|ła *f* [1] (gruby kij) club [2] pot. (u policjanta) truncheon [3] pot., Szkol. ≈ F [4] pot. (o głowie) nut pot.; **tępa pała** obraźl. (o osobie) thickhead pot.

■ **na pałę** pot. (bez przygotowania) *[odpowiedzieć, zapytać]* off the top of one's head; **ostrzyc się na pałę** pot. to have one's head shaved; **w pale się nie mieści** pot. (it's) unbelievable

pałac *m* [1] (królewski) palace [2] (reprezentacyjny budynek) mansion

pałąk *m* (uchwyt) bow-shaped handle; **zgiąć się w** ~ to bend double

pałecz|ka *f* [1] (dyrygenta) baton; (czarnoksiężnika) wand [2] (do jedzenia) chopstick [3] (do gry na perkusji) drumstick [4] Sport baton [5] Biol. bacillus

■ **przejąć** ~**kę** to step into the breach

pał|ka *f* (gruby kij) club; (policjanta) truncheon

pamiąt|ka *f* souvenir; ~**ki rodzinne** family mementoes; **przyjąć coś na** ~**kę** to accept sth as a keepsake

pamiątkow|y *adi.* commemorative; **tablica** ~**a** a memorial plaque

pamię|ć *f* [1] (zdolność) memory; ~**ć wzrokowa** visual memory; ~**ć absolutna** Psych. total recall; ~**ć długotrwała** Psych. long-term memory; ~**ć fotograficzna** a photographic memory [2] (pamiętanie) remembrance książk.; **składać hołd czyjejś** ~**ci** to pay tribute to sb's memory; **zostawić po sobie dobrą** ~**ć** to be well remembered [3] Komput. memory

■ **za mojej** ~**ci** within my memory; **błogosławionej** ~**ci** of blessed memory; **mój nieodżałowanej pamięci ojciec** my late (and much) lamented father; **cofać się** a. **sięgać** ~**cią do czegoś** to cast one's mind back to sth; **mieć dobrą/ złą** ~**ć do czegoś** to have a good memory for sth/ to have no memory for sth; **recytować z** ~**ci** to recite from memory; **uczyć się na** ~**ć** to learn sth by heart; **umieć** a. **znać coś na** ~**ć** to know sth by heart; **wyjść** a. **wypaść komuś z** ~**ci** to slip sb's memory; **zakochać się bez** ~**ci** to fall head over heels in love; **jeżeli mnie** ~**ć nie myli** a. **nie zawodzi** if my memory serves me correctly;

próbował wydobyć z ~ci jakieś nazwiska he searched his memory for some names; **żył w naszej ~ci** he lived on in our memory

pamięta|ć *impf* [] *vt* [1] (nie zapominać) to remember; **~ć coś dokładnie** to remember sth exactly [2] (brać pod uwagę) to not forget

[II] *vi* [1] (troszczyć się) to remember; **~j o swoim zdrowiu** you have to take care about your health [2] (nie zapomnieć) to remember; **~j, żeby podlać kwiaty** remember a. don't forget to water the plants

pamiętliw|y *adi.* unforgiving; **nie jestem ~y** I don't hold grudges

pamiętnik *m* (wspomnienia) memoir; (pisany na bieżąco) journal

pamiętn|y *adi.* memorable

pampers *m* disposable nappy; **~y dla dorosłych** incontinence pads

pan *m* [1] (mężczyzna) man; **starszy ~** an elderly gentleman; **dzwonił do ciebie jakiś ~** some man rang you (on the phone) [2] (z imieniem, nazwiskiem, tytułem naukowym) **nagrodę wylosował ~ Marek Brzoza** and the prize goes to (Mr) Marek Brzoza; **a teraz ~ profesor Zasławski będzie mówił o...** and now Professor Zasławski will speak about... [3] (do kogoś) (oficjalnie) sir; (mniej oficjalnie) you; **proszę ~a! czy to pański parasol?** excuse me, sir! is this your umbrella?; **przepraszam, czy ma ~ zegarek?** excuse me, have you got the time?; **~owie, sytuacja jest poważna** gentlemen, the situation is serious; **Szanowny Panie!** (w korespondencji) Dear Sir; **~ie Janku, dyrektor ~a wzywa** Janek, the boss is calling you; **widzi ~** pot. you see [4] (właściciel psa) master; **chodź do ~a!** come here! [5] (ten, kto ma władzę) master [6] (zatrudniający służbę) master [7] Hist. (możnowładca) lord [8] (nauczyciel) master; **~ od matematyki** the maths master [9] (Bóg) **Pan** Lord; **nasz Pan** (Chrystus) Our Lord

■ **~ domu** (głowa rodziny) the master of the house; (wobec gości) the host; **~ młody** the bridegroom; **~ i władca** lord and master; **być ~em siebie** to be one's own master; **być ~em u siebie** to be independent; **jestem z nim na ~** a. **mówię mu (per) ~** I'm not on first-name terms with him; **być z kimś za ~ a ~ brat** to be on friendly terms with sb

pancernik *m* [1] Zool. armadillo [2] Wojsk. battleship

pancerz *m* [1] (część zbroi) armour (plate) [2] (żółwia, skorupiaka) shell

pan|da *f* panda

panel *m* [1] (dyskusja publiczna) panel discussion; (uczestnicy dyskusji) (discussion) panel; **wziąć udział w ~u** to take part in a panel discussion [2] (część) panel; **~e podłogowe** floor panels a. panelling; **~e boazeryjne** wall panels

pa|ni *f* [1] (kobieta) woman; **starsza pani** an elderly lady; **„potrzebna pani do dziecka"** 'childminder needed'; **zdrowie pań!** to the ladies! [2] (z imieniem, nazwiskiem, tytułem naukowym) (kobieta zamężna) Mrs;

(kobieta niezamężna) Miss; (bez zaznaczenia stanu cywilnego) Ms; **spotkałem panią Marię** I met Maria; **pani Joanna Strzelecka jest naszą stałą czytelniczką** (Ms) Joanna Strzelecka is a regular reader of ours; **wywiad z panią profesor Anną Kozub** an interview with Professor Anna Kozub [3] (do kogoś) (oficjalnie) madam; (mniej oficjalnie) you; **proszę pani! proszę zaczekać!** please wait, madam!; **co pani sądzi o...?** what do you think of...?; **dzwoni pani mąż** your husband is calling; **Szanowna Pani!** (w korespondencji) Dear Madam; **patrz pani, ile to już lat minęło** pot. just see how time flies! [4] (właścicielka psa, kota) mistress; **Lulu nie odstępowała swojej pani** Lulu never left her mistress' side [5] (władczyni) mistress [6] (kobieta zatrudniająca służbę) mistress [7] (nauczycielka) mistress; **pani od polskiego** the Polish teacher

■ **pani domu** (żona gospodarza) the lady of the house; (wobec gości) the hostess; **pani czyjegoś serca** one's sweetheart; **być panią siebie** to be one's own mistress; **być panią sytuacji** to be in control; **mówimy sobie (per) pani** we aren't on first-name terms

paniczn|y *adi.* panic; **ogarnięty ~ym strachem** panic-stricken

panieńs|ki *adi. [pamiętnik, suknia]* young girl's; **nazwisko ~kie** sb's maiden name

panier|ować *impf vt* Kulin. to coat [sth] with breadcrumbs

pani|ka *f* [1] (popłoch) panic; **szerzyć ~kę** to spread panic; **uciekać w ~ce** to flee in panic; **wpaść w ~kę** to get into a panic [2] pot. (nerwowy pośpiech) panic; **bez ~ki** don't panic

panika|rz *m,* **~ra** *f* scaremonger

pan|na *f* [1] (młoda dziewczyna) young girl [2] (kobieta niezamężna) spinster; maiden przest., poet. [3] (tytuł grzecznościowy) Miss; **~na Nowakówna** Miss Nowak

■ **~na młoda** the bride; **stara ~na** an old maid

panoram|a *f* panorama; **Panorama Firm** ≈ Yellow Pages®

panoramiczn|y *adi. [widok, zdjęcie]* panoramic; **film ~y** a widescreen film; **lusterko ~e** Aut. a wide-angled mirror

panosz|yć się *impf v refl.* [1] (rządzić się) to lord it over; **zwycięzcy ~yli się w mieście** the victors tyrannized the town; **mam dość ~enia się bratowej w moim domu** I'm tired of my sister-in-law throwing her weight around in my own house [2] przen. (szerzyć się, grasować) to be rife; **w szopie ~yły się szczury** the shed was overrun by rats

pan|ować *impf vi* [1] (władać) to rule; (królować) to reign; **dynastia ~ująca** the ruling dynasty; **religia ~ująca** the dominant religion [2] (podporządkowywać sobie) to have control; **~ować nad uwagą słuchaczy** to have a. hold the attention of the audience; **~ować nad sytuacją** to be in (full) control of the situation; **nie** ~**ować nad nerwami** to not be able to control one's temper ③ (trwać) to prevail; **powszechnie** ~**uje opinia, że...** the prevailing opinion is that...; **w obozie** ~**ował tyfus** the camp was in the grip of a typhoid epidemic ④ (górować nad okolicą) to dominate

pantof|el *m* ① (lekki but) court shoe GB, pump US; (męski) (lightweight) shoe; ~**le gimnastyczne** plimsolls ② (kapeć) slipper; **ranne** ~**le** bedroom slippers

■ **wziąć kogoś pod** ~**el** to dominate sb; **być pod** ~**lem** to be henpecked pot.

pantofel|ek *m* Zool. paramecium

pantoflarz *m* henpecked husband pot.

pantomim|a *f* mime

pańs|ki *adi.* ① (pana) your; **czy to** ~**ka książka?** is this your book?; **nie** ~**ka sprawa!** it's none of your business! ② (odnoszący się do Boga) **Grób Pański** the Holy Sepulchre; **Męka Pańska** the Passion (of Christ)

państw|o[1] *n* Polit. ① (kraj) state; ~**o opiekuńcze** Polit. a welfare state; ~**o policyjne** Polit. a police state; ~**o w** ~**ie** a state within a state; **Austria i sąsiadujące** ~**a** Austria and the countries surrounding it ② (urzędy sprawujące władzę) the state

państw|o[2] *plt* ① (para) (married) couple ② (przed nazwiskiem) Mr and Mrs; **(Szanowni) Państwo Nowakowie** (na kopercie) Mr and Mrs Nowak ③ (grupa ludzi) people ④ (forma grzecznościowa) Ladies and Gentlemen; **czy Państwo się znacie** pot. a. **znają?** do you know each other?; **czy to** ~**a pies?** is this your dog?

■ ~**o młodzi** the bride and groom

państwow|y *adi.* ① *[flaga, hymn]* national ② *[przedsiębiorstwo, koleje]* state(-owned); **urzędnik** ~**y** a civil servant

papeteri|a *f* (matching) notepaper and envelopes

papie|r *m* ① paper; ~**r firmowy** letterhead paper; ~**r gazetowy** newsprint; ~**r toaletowy** toilet paper; ~**r do pisania** writing paper; ~**r do pakowania** wrapping paper; **arkusz** ~**ru** a sheet of paper; **opakować coś w** ~**r** to wrap sth up in paper ② pot. (dokument) document; **przedstawić swoje** ~**ry** to show one's papers; ~**ry wartościowe** Fin. securities

■ **na wariackich** ~**rach** pot. (spontanicznie) on the spur of the moment

papier|ek *m* ① (skrawek papieru) piece of paper; ~**ki od cukierków** sweet wrappers ② pot. (dokumenty urzędowe) paper; **przekładać** ~**ki** pot. to shuffle papers pot.

papieros *m* cigarette

papierośnic|a *f* cigarette case

papierow|y *adi.* ① (z papieru) paper ② (bardzo blady) paper-white ③ (sztuczny) *[bohater]* cardboard; *[sytuacja]* artificial

papież *m* the Pope; **być świętszym od** ~**a** iron. to be holier than the Pope

pap|ka *f* (masa) pulp; (do jedzenia) pap pejor.; **rozetrzeć coś na** ~**kę** to grind sth to a pulp

papl|a *f, m* pot. (gaduła) gasbag pot.; (niepotrafiąca dochować tajemnicy) blabbermouth

papl|ać *impf vi* pot. (dużo mówić) to prattle (on) pot.; (zdradzać sekrety) to blab pot.

paplanin|a *f* pot. babble; prattle pejor.

pap|rać *impf* pot. **[]** *vt* ① (brudzić) to get [sth] messy pot. ② (psuć) to mess up *[robotę, zadanie]*

[] **paprać się** ① (brudzić się) to get oneself messy pot.; ~**rać się błotem** to get oneself muddy; ~**rać ubranie farbą** to get paint (all) over one's clothes ② pot. *[rana]* to weep

papro|ch *m* speck of dirt; (kłaczek) piece of fluff; (okruszek) crumb

papro|ć *f* fern

paprot|ka *f* polypody

papry|ka *f* ① Bot. capsicum; (słodkawa, jedzona na surowo) pepper; (ostra) chilli (pepper); **sałatka jarzynowa z czerwoną** ~**ką** a vegetable salad with red peppers ② Kulin. (przyprawa) paprika

papu|ga *f* ① Zool. parrot ② (naśladowca) copycat pot.

pa|ra[1] *f* ① steam; **para wodna** steam, (water) vapour; **kłęby pary** clouds of steam; **gotować coś na parze** to steam sth; **odklejać/otwierać coś nad parą** to steam sth off/open; **zajść parą** *[okulary, lustro]* to steam up; **pełną parą** at full steam także przen. ② Fiz. vapour GB, vapor US

■ **nie puścić pary z ust** to not breathe a word; **uszła z niego para** he's run out of steam

pa|ra[2] *f* ① (komplet, zespół) pair; **para butów** a pair of shoes/boots; **para spodni** a pair of trousers; **pracować w parach** to work in pairs; **iść parami** to walk in pairs; **masz skarpetki nie do pary** your socks don't match; **zgubić rękawiczkę od pary** to lose one glove ② (osoby związane uczuciowo) couple; **para małżeńska** a married couple; **być dobraną/niedobraną parą** to be a well-matched/an ill-matched couple; **oni są parą** they're living together/going out together ③ (pozostały element kompletu) one of a pair; **być bez** a. **nie mieć pary** *[osoba]* to have no partner

■ **młoda para** (nowożeńcy) the young couple; **iść w parze z czymś** to go hand in hand with sth; **nieszczęścia chodzą parami** it never rains but it pours; **to inna para kaloszy** pot. (to nie to samo) that's a different kettle of fish pot.; (to inna sprawa) that's another a. different story

parabol|a *f* ① Mat. parabola ② Literat. parable

para|da *f* (pokaz) parade; (defilada) a dress parade

■ **mieć głowę nie od** ~**dy** to have brains; **wchodzić komuś w** ~**dę** pot. to get in sb's way

paradoks *m* paradox

parafi|a *f* parish
■ **każdy z innej ~i** all completely different a. unalike

parafian|in *m*, **~ka** *f* parishioner

parafin|a *f* paraffin

paraf|ować *pf, impf vt* to initial *[układ, dokument]*

paragon *m* (till) receipt

paragraf *m* ① Prawo article ② (akapit) paragraph

paraliż *m* Med. paralysis; **dotknięty ~em** paralysed

paraliż|ować *impf vt* ① *[strach]* to paralyse ② (uniemożliwiać, utrudniać funkcjonowanie) to cripple *[wysiłki, próby, system]*; to paralyse *[miasto, kraj]*; **~ować transport nieprzyjaciela** to cripple the enemy's transportation system ③ Med. (unieruchomić) to paralyse *[osobę, kończynę]*

paralotni|a *f* paraglider; **latać na ~** to paraglide

paramet|r *m* Mat., Techn. parameter

parano|ja *f* paranoia *także przen.*

parape|t *m* window sill a. ledge

parasol *m* ① (przeciwdeszczowy) umbrella; (przeciwsłoneczny) parasol; (stojący) (sun) umbrella; **~ plażowy/ogrodowy** a beach/garden umbrella ② przen. umbrella; **~ ochronny** a protective umbrella; **~ nuklearny** a nuclear umbrella

parasol|ka *f* (przeciwdeszczowa) (ladies') umbrella; (przeciwsłoneczna) parasol

parawan *m* (zasłona) screen; (na plaży) windbreak; **oddzielić coś ~em** to screen sth off; **łóżko osłonięte przenośnym ~em** a bed screened off by a movable partition

parcel|a *f* plot (of land); **~a budowlana** a building plot; **podzielić grunt na małe ~e** to parcel out land into small plots

parci|e *n* ① Fiz. hydrostatic pressure ② Med. **~e na mocz** an urge to urinate

parci|eć *impf vi* ① *[skóra, tkanina, pasek]* to rot ② *[owoc, rzodkiewka]* to become spongy

par|ę *pron.* several; a couple pot.; **~ę groszy** pot. a bit of cash

park *m* ① (zadrzewiony obszar) park; **~ narodowy** a national park; **spacerować po ~u** to have a walk in the park ② (urządzenia) **~ maszynowy** machines; **~ samochodowy** (pojazdy) a car fleet; (parking) a car park

parkan *m* fence

parkie|t *m* ① (podłoga) parquet (floor) ② (klepki) parquet (flooring) blocks ③ (do tańca) dance floor ④ Sport (boisko do siatkówki, koszykówki) court; **opuścić ~t** to leave the game ⑤ (na giełdzie) trading floor

parking *m* car park GB, parking lot US

parkom|etr, **~at** *m* parking meter

park|ować *impf* Ⅰ *vt* to park *[samochód]*
Ⅱ *vi [samochód]* to park; **samochody ~ujące przed szkołą** cars parking in front of the school

parlamen|t *m* ① Polit. (ciało ustawodawcze) parliament; **Parlament Europejski** the European Par-

liament; **wybory do ~tu** parliamentary elections; **poseł do ~tu** a member of parliament; (europejskiego) a deputy (of the European parliament); **~t obraduje** parliament is sitting ② (budynek) parliament building

parlamentarzy|sta *m*, **~stka** *f* (poseł) member of parliament; (doświadczony) parliamentarian

parn|y *adi. [powietrze, dzień]* muggy; (intensywniej) steamy

parodi|a *f* parody *także przen.*; **~a procesu** a travesty of justice

parodi|ować *impf vt* to parody

par|ować¹ *impf* Ⅰ *vt* (gotować na parze) to steam
Ⅱ *vi* ① (zmieniać stan skupienia) *[woda, benzyna]* to evaporate ② (wydzielać parę) *[potrawa, wrzątek]* to steam; **talerz ~ującej zupy** a bowl of steaming soup ③ (o roślinach) **rośliny ~ują** water evaporates from the plants

par|ować² *impf vt* ① (w szermierce, boksie) to parry ② przen. to counter *[ataki, zarzuty]*

parow|iec *m* steamer

parów|ka *f* ① Kulin. sausage ② pot. (inhalacja) steam inhalation; **~ka ziołowa** a herbal inhalation ③ pot. (łaźnia parowa) steam bath ④ pot. (kąpiel) sweat bath ⑤ pot. (zabieg kosmetyczny) steam treatment ⑥ pot. (gorące pomieszczenie) **ale tu ~ka!** the place is like a sauna!

parsk|nąć *pf* — **parsk|ać** *impf vi [osoba, koń]* to snort; *[maszyna, silnik]* to splutter; **~nąć śmiechem** to snort with laughter

partactw|o *n* pot., pejor. botch-up pot., pejor.

partacz *m* pot., pejor. botcher pot., pejor.

partacz|yć *impf vt* pot., pejor. to botch (up) pot., pejor. *[robotę]*

parte|r *m* ① (w budynku) ground floor GB, first floor US; **mieszkać na ~rze** to live on the ground floor ② Teatr (część sali) ground floor, parterre US; (widownia) stalls; **miejsca na ~rze** (seats in) the stalls ③ Sport **sprowadzenie przeciwnika do ~ru** a takedown US

parterow|y *adi. [budynek]* one-storey; *[mieszkanie, okno]* ground-floor GB, first-floor US

parti|a *f* ① Polit. party; **~a polityczna** a political party; **być członkiem ~i** to be a party member ② (część) (książki, gór) part; (towarów) batch; (ludzi) group; **wychodzić małymi ~ami** to leave in small groups ③ (w grze) round; (w brydżu) game; **~a szachów** a game of chess; **wygrać/przegrać trzy ~e** to win/lose three rounds a. games ④ Muz., Teatr part; **~a solowa** a solo part ⑤ (kandydat do małżeństwa) match

partne|r *m*, **~rka** *f* ① (współuczestnik) partner ② (osoba o równorzędnym statusie) equal; **to nie jest dla ciebie ~r do rozmowy** he's not on the same level as you

partyku|ła *f* Jęz. particle

partytu|ra *f* ① Muz. score ② Teatr director's script

partyzan|t *m* partisan; **oddział** ~**tów** a guerrilla a. partisan unit

parz|yć *impf* **[]** *vt* [1] *(od gorąca) [asfalt, kwas]* to burn; *[wrzątek, zupa]* to scald [2] *(jadem)* to sting; **pokrzywy** ~**yły go w nogi** the nettles stung his legs [3] *(zaparzać)* to brew *[herbatę, zioła]*; to make *[kawę]* **[]** **parzyć się** [1] *(od gorąca)* ~**yć się w ręce/język** to burn one's hands/tongue [2] *[herbata, zioła]* to be brewing

parz|yć się *impf v refl.* Myślis. *[zwierzę]* to mate

parzy|sty *adi. [liczba]* even; *[dzień]* even-number; *[liście, narządy]* paired

pas¹ **[]** *m* [1] *(noszony)* belt; **zbić kogoś** ~**em** to give sb the belt [2] *(część bielizny)* ~ **do pończoch** a suspender GB a. garter US belt; ~ **elastyczny** a girdle [3] Aut., Lotn. belt; ~**y bezpieczeństwa** a seat a. safety belt; **zapiąć/rozpiąć** ~**y** to fasten/unfasten one's seat belt [4] *(podłużny kawałek)* strip; ~ **ziemi** a strip of land; (szeroki) a belt of land; ~ **startowy** Lotn. a runway [5] Aut. *(część jezdni)* lane; ~ **ruchu** a traffic lane; **zmienić** ~ to change lanes [6] *(wzór)* stripe; **materiał w** ~**y** striped fabric [7] *(talia)* waist; **(czyjś) obwód** ~**a** sb's waist measurement; **włosy do** ~**a** hair down to the waist; **woda do** ~**a** a. **po** ~ waist-deep water; **rozebrać się do** ~**a** to strip to the waist; **cios poniżej** ~**a** Sport a punch below the belt; **to był chwyt poniżej** ~**a** przen. that was below the belt [8] Anat. girdle; ~ **barkowy/miednicowy** the pectoral/pelvic girdle **[]** **pasy** *plt* (przejście dla pieszych) zebra crossing ■ **być za** ~**em** *[zima, wakacje]* to be just around the corner; **kłaniać się** a. **zginać się w** ~ to bow; **popuszczać** ~**a** to live like a king; **zaciskać** ~**a** to tighten one's belt

pas² *inter.* (w brydżu) I pass!

pasa|t *m* Meteo. trade wind

pasaż *m* [1] *(przejście)* covered passage(way); ~ **handlowy** a shopping arcade [2] Muz. passage work

pasaże|r *m*, ~**rka** *f* passenger; (w taksówce) fare

pas|ek *m* [1] *(do ubrania)* belt; ~**ek do spodni/ sukienki** a trouser/dress belt; **zapiąć/rozpiąć** ~**ek** to do up/undo one's belt [2] *(do łączenia)* strap; ~**ek od zegarka** a watch strap GB, a watchband US [3] *(wąski kawałek)* strip; ~**ek papieru** a strip of paper; **pociąć coś na** ~**ki** to cut sth into strips [4] *(wzór)* stripe; **koszula w** ~**ki** a striped shirt [5] Wojsk. *(na mundurze)* stripe [6] *(podsumowanie zarobków)* payslip [7] Aut. ~**ek klinowy** a fan belt

pase|r *m*, ~**rka** *f* receiver GB; fence pot.

pasie|ka *f* apiary

pasierb *m* [1] *(przybrane dziecko)* stepson; ~**owie** (obojga płci) stepchildren [2] Bot. side shoot

pasierbic|a *f* stepdaughter

pasikonik *m* Zool. grasshopper

pasj|a *f* [1] *(zamiłowanie)* passion; ~**a do brydża** a passion for bridge; **lubić coś** ~**ami** to have a

passion for sth [2] *(wściekłość)* passion; **szewska** ~**a** a blind rage; **doprowadzać kogoś do (szewskiej)** ~**i** to make sb furious

pasjans *m* patience; **stawiać** a. **układać** ~**a** to play patience a. solitaire

pasjona|t *m* pot. (entuzjasta) fiend pot.; **być** ~**tem czegoś** to have a passion for sth

pasjon|ować *impf* **[]** *vt* (interesować) to fascinate **[]** **pasjonować się** (interesować się) ~**ować się czymś** to be fascinated by sth

pasjonując|y *adi. [film, mecz]* exciting

paskudn|y *adi. grad.* [1] (brzydki) *[wygląd, budynek]* awful; *[zapach, pogoda]* foul; ~**a rana** a nasty a. nasty-looking cut [2] *(zły) [zwyczaj, chłopak]* nasty; ~**a historia!** that's awful! [3] pot. (kiepski) rotten pot.; **być w** ~**ym humorze** to be in a rotten a. foul mood [4] (okropny) terrible pot.; awful; ~**a zupa** yucky soup pot.

pasmanteri|a *f* (wyroby, sklep) haberdashery

pa|smo *n* [1] *(wody, lądu, lasu)* strip; (ludzi, samochodów) stream; (włosów) streak; (wełny) wisp; **pasmo górskie** a mountain range [2] *(seria)* streak; **pasmo sukcesów** a streak a. run of success [3] Fiz., Radio (wave)band

pas|ować¹ *impf* **[]** *vt* (dopasowywać) to fit *[okna, ramy]* **[]** *vi* [1] (być odpowiednim) to suit **(do czegoś** sth); (harmonizować) to match **(do czegoś** sth); **ta bluzka nie** ~**uje mi do spódnicy** the blouse doesn't match my skirt; **do mięsa** ~**uje czerwone wino** red wine goes well with meat; **oni świetnie do siebie** ~**ują** they're a perfect match [2] (odpowiadać rozmiarem) *[ubranie, but]* to fit **(na kogoś/coś** sb/sth); **płaszcz** ~**ował jak ulał** the coat was a perfect fit; **te kawałki do siebie nie** ~**ują** these pieces don't fit together [3] pot. (być typowym) **to mi do niego nie** ~**uje!** it's not like him (at all)! [4] pot. (zadowalać) to suit; **poniedziałek mi** ~**uje** Monday suits me; **to mi** ~**uje** it's okay with me pot. ■ **coś mi tu nie** ~**uje** pot. something's not right here; ~**ować do czegoś jak wół do karety** a. **jak pięść do nosa** pot. to stick out like a sore thumb

pas|ować² *impf vi* [1] (w brydżu) to pass [2] pot., przen. (rezygnować) to pass pot.; **ja** ~**uję!** count me out! pot.

pasoży|t *m* parasite także przen.

pa|sta *f* [1] *(do czyszczenia)* polish; **pasta do butów/ do podłogi/do mebli** shoe/floor/furniture polish; **pasta do zębów** toothpaste [2] Kulin. paste; **pasta pomidorowa** tomato paste; **pasta jajeczna** egg spread

pastel *m* Szt. [1] (kredka) pastel (crayon); **malować** ~**ami** to work in pastel(s) [2] (technika) pastel [3] (obraz) pastel (drawing)

pastelow|y *adi.* [1] Szt. *[rysunek]* pastel [2] (o delikatnych kolorach) *[barwa, zieleń]* pastel; *[sweter, zasłony]* pastel-coloured

pasteryz|ować *impf vt* to pasteurize; ~**owane mleko** pasteurized milk

pasterz *m* [1] (bydła) cowherd; (owiec) shepherd [2] Relig. shepherd książk., przen.

pasto|r *m* Relig. pastor

past|ować *impf vt* to polish *[buty, podłogę]*

pastw|ić się *impf v refl.* ~ić się nad kimś/czymś to torment a. torture sb/sth *[ofiarą, zwierzęciem]*; przen. to tear sb/sth apart *[autorem, filmem]*

pastwisk|o *n* pasture

pastyl|ka *f* [1] (cukierek) pastille; ~ki owocowe fruit drops; ~ki miętowe peppermints [2] (lekarstwo) tablet; ~ki do ssania pastilles; ~ki na kaszel a. na gardło cough drops

pasyw|a *plt* Ekon. liabilities

pasz|a *f* Roln. fodder; (dla koni, bydła) forage; ~a dla świń pig feed

paszcz|a *f* [1] (u zwierząt) jaws; **lwia** ~**a** Bot. a snapdragon [2] pot. trap posp.

paszkwil *m* lampoon

paszpor|t *m* passport; ~t dyplomatyczny/konsularny a diplomatic/consular passport

pasztecik *m* Kulin. (bułeczka) patty; **barszcz z** ~**ami** borscht with (meat) patties

paszte|t *m* [1] Kulin. pâté; ~t z wątróbek liver pâté a. paste [2] pot. (kłopotliwa sytuacja) mess; **wpakować się w niezły** ~**t** to get oneself into a right old mess pot.

pa|ść¹ *impf* [] *vt* [1] (pilnować) to mind *[zwierzęta]*; to graze *[bydło, owce]* [2] (karmić) to feed *[zwierzęta]*; (tuczyć) to fatten up *[zwierzęta]* [3] pot., żart. (przekarmiać) to feed (**kogoś czymś** sb with sth) [4] przen. (sycić) **paść czymś oczy** to feast one's eyes on sth [] **paść się** [1] (na pastwisku) *[krowy, owce]* to graze [2] (karmić się) to feed (**czymś** on sth) [3] pot., żart. (objadać się) to stuff oneself pot. (**czymś** with sth)

pa|ść² ** *pf* — **pa|dać¹ *impf vi* [1] (przewrócić się, zwalić się) to fall (down); **paść komuś w objęcia** a. **ramiona** to fall into sb's arms; **padać ze zmęczenia** a. **wyczerpania** to be dead tired; **padam z nóg** I'm dead beat pot.; **padnij!** Wojsk. down! [2] (przemieścić się w dół) to drop [3] (zatrzymać się) *[spojrzenie, światło, cień]* to fall (**na kogoś/coś** on sb/sth) [4] (zginąć) *[żołnierz]* to fall; *[zwierzę]* to die; **paść w boju/na posterunku** to fall in battle/in the line of duty [5] (być zdobytym) *[miasto, twierdza]* to fall [6] (ponieść klęskę) *[firma]* to go under; *[przedstawienie]* to flop pot.; *[gospodarka, system]* to collapse [7] (ogarnąć) **padł na nich strach** they were seized with fear książk. [8] (przypaść w udziale) *[podejrzenie, wybór]* to fall (**na kogoś** on sb); *[głosy]* to be cast (**na kogoś/coś** for a. in favour of sb/sth); **padło 10 głosów za i 10 przeciw** there were 10 votes for and 10 against [9] (być słyszalnym) *[słowo]* to be said; *[rozkaz]* to be issued; *[propozycja, wniosek]* to be put forward; *[strzał]* to be fired; **padają głosy, że...** there is talk that... [10] Sport *[bramka]* to be scored; *[rekord]* to be set; **w meczu padł wynik bezbramkowy** the match ended in a goalless draw

■ **chyba ci na mózg padło!** you must be out of your mind! pot.

pa|t *m* [1] Gry stalemate [2] przen. deadlock

patel|nia *f* frying pan GB, skillet US; **ależ tu dzisiaj** ~**nia!** przen. it's boiling hot here today!

paten|t *m* [1] (dla wynalazcy) patent; **mieć** ~**t** to hold a patent (**na coś** for a. on sth); **być chronionym** ~**tami** to be protected by patent [2] pot. (sposób) recipe przen.; **mieć** ~**t na coś/robienie czegoś** to have a recipe for sth/for doing sth [3] pot. (drobne usprawnienie) invention [4] (dokument nominacyjny) certificate; ~**t żeglarski** a sailing licence

patent|ować *impf vt* (wydawać patent) to issue a patent (**coś** for sth); (uzyskać patent) to patent *[wyrób, wynalazek]*

pate|ra *f* (na ciasta) cake stand; (na owoce) fruit bowl

patetyczn|y *adi.* [1] (podniosły) exalted książk.; (uroczysty) solemn [2] (przesadny) *[zachowanie]* pompous pejor.; bombastic książk.; *[gest, ton]* grandiloquent książk., pejor.

patologi|a *f* [1] Med. (nauka) pathology; (zaburzenia) pathological changes a. abnormalities [2] pot. (oddział szpitalny) high-risk pregnancy unit [3] Socjol. social pathology

patologiczn|y *adi.* pathological także przen.

patos *m* [1] (podniosłość) loftiness; (powaga) solemnity [2] pejor. (przesada) grandiloquence książk., pejor.; pomposity pejor.; **mówić z** ~**em** to speak in lofty tones

patrio|ta *m*, ~**tka** *f* patriot

patriotyczn|y *adi.* patriotic

patriotyzm *m* patriotism

patrol *m* [1] (grupa) patrol; ~ **zwiadowczy** a reconaissance group; ~ **policji** a police patrol [2] (obchód) patrol; **być na** ~**u/pójść na** ~ to be (out)/go (out) on patrol

patrol|ować *impf vt* to patrol

patron *m* [1] (opiekun) patron; ~**em szkoły jest Kopernik** przen. the school is named after Copernicus; **święto** ~**a szkoły** a school fête in honour of the founder [2] Relig. patron (saint)

patrona|t *m* patronage; **pod** ~**tem ONZ/prezydenta** under UN auspices/under the patronage of the president

patron|ować *impf vi* to act as patron *[organizacji, działalności]*

patrosz|yć *impf vt* to gut *[kurczaka, rybę]*

patrz|eć, patrz|yć *impf* [] *vi* [1] (spoglądać) to look (**na kogoś/coś** at sb/sth); (obserwować) to watch; ~**eć na zegarek/w lustro** to look at one's watch/in the mirror; ~**eć komuś w oczy** to look sb in the eyes; ~**ył, jak dzieci bawiły się w ogrodzie** he was watching the children playing in the garden; **nie mogę już na to** ~**eć** I can't bear to look at it (any more); ~ **pod nogi!** watch your step!; ~, **jak idziesz!** look where you're going!; ~**cie**, ~**cie, kto to idzie!** well, well look who's coming!; ~**eć**

w przeszłość a. **wstecz** przen. to look back; ~**eć**
w przyszłość przen. to look ahead a. to the future
[2] (rozpatrywać, oceniać) to look; ~**eć na coś realnie**
to look at sth realistically; **optymistycznie** ~**eć**
na życie to have an optimistic outlook on life
[3] (zwracać uwagę) **nie** ~**ąc na to, że...** ignoring the
fact that...; ~**, żeby komuś nie zrobić krzywdy**
be careful not to hurt anybody [4] pot. (dbać) **każdy**
tylko ~**y, jak tu się dorobić** everyone's on the
make pot.

III **patrzeć się, patrzyć się** pot. to stare (**na**
kogoś/coś at sb/sth)

■ ~**eć komuś na ręce** to keep an eye on sb; ~**eć**
na kogoś z góry to look down on sb; ~**eć na**
kogoś/coś życzliwym okiem to look favourably
on sb/sth; **jak się** ~**y** first rate

patyczk|ować się impf v refl. pot. **nie** ~**ować się**
z kimś to take a tough line with sb

patyk m stick; **chudy jak** ~ as thin as a rake

patyn|a f [1] (na brązie) patina; (na miedzi) verdigris
[2] przen. **nabrać** ~**y** to take on a patina przen.

pauz|a f [1] (przerwa) pause [2] Szkol. break GB, recess
US [3] (w pisowni) dash [4] Muz. rest

paw m [1] Zool. (samiec) peacock; (samica) peahen;
dumny jak ~ as proud as a peacock [2] pot. puke
pot.; **puścić** ~**ia** to do the a. have a technicolour
yawn pot.

pawian m Zool. baboon

pawilon m [1] (sklep) ~ **meblowy** a furniture shop
[2] (część zespołu architektonicznego) pavilion; ~ **wy-**
stawowy an exhibition pavilion [3] (w ogrodzie)
pavilion

pawlacz m overhead cupboard

pazern|y adi. rapacious; **jest** ~**y na pieniądze**
he's greedy for money

paznok|ieć m nail; ~**ieć u ręki/nogi** a finger-
nail/toenail; **nożyczki/cążki do** ~**ci** nail scissors/
clippers; **lakier/zmywacz do** ~**ci** nail polish/nail
polish remover; **obgryzać** ~**cie** to bite one's nails;
mieć brud za a. **pod** ~**ciami** to have dirty
fingernails

pazu|r m [1] Zool claw; **pokazać** ~**ry** przen. [osoba] to
show one's claws [2] przen. (temperament) grit; **robić**
coś z ~**rem** to do sth with verve; **pokazać (lwi)**
~**r** to show one's true mettle

■ **ostrzyć sobie** ~**ry na coś** to have one's mind
set on (getting) sth

październik m October

pącz|ek m [1] Bot. bud; **na drzewach pokazały się**
~**ki** the trees are in bud [2] Kulin. doughnut,
donut US

pącz|kować impf vi [1] Biol., Bot. to bud [2] [firmy,
instytucje] (powstawać licznie) to mushroom; (dzielić się)
to multiply

pąk m bud; ~**i róż** rosebuds

pchać impf → **pchnąć¹**

pcha|ć się impf v refl. [1] (rozpychać się) to push; **nie**
~**j się na mnie!** stop shoving me! [2] (zmierzać, dążyć)
~**ć się na stołki** to jostle for top positions

pcheł|ki plt Gry tiddlywinks GB, tiddledywinks US

pch|ła f Zool. flea; **mieć** ~**ły** to have fleas

pch|nąć¹ pf — **pch|ać** impf vt [1] (puścić w ruch) to
push; ~**nąć kogoś na ścianę** to push sb against
the wall [2] przen. (skłonić) to drive; ~**nąć kogoś do**
przestępstwa [bieda] to drive sb to crime

pch|nąć² pf vt [1] (wysłać) to dispatch [depeszę,
posłańca] [2] (ugodzić) to stab; ~**nąć kogoś nożem** to
stab sb with a knife

pech m bad luck; **a to** ~**!** what a shame! a. pity!

pechow|iec m pot. loser

pechow|y adi. pot. [osoba, dzień, liczba] unlucky

pedago|g m [1] (nauczyciel) teacher [2] (teoretyk naucza-
nia) education(al)ist

pedagogiczn|y adi. [doświadczenie, praktyka]
teaching; pedagogic(al) książk.; [cel] educational; **to**
mało a. **niezbyt** ~**e** it doesn't set a very good
example

■ **ciało** a. **grono** ~**e** książk. the (teaching) staff

peda|ł m [1] (w maszynie, instrumencie) pedal; ~**ł gazu**
the accelerator (pedal) [2] (w rowerze) pedal; **kręcić**
~**łami** to work the pedals

pedał|ować impf vi (na rowerze) to pedal

pedan|t m, ~**tka** f pedant; **być** ~**tem/**~**tką** to
be pedantic

pediat|ra m paediatrician GB, pediatrician US

pediatri|a f paediatrics GB, pediatrics US

pedofil m paedophile GB, pedophile US

pejcz m whip

pejoratywn|y adi. pejorative

pejzaż m landscape także przen.

pekińczy|k m (pies) Pekin(g)ese

pekl|ować impf vt to pickle [sth] in brine, to corn
US [mięso]

pelargoni|a f Bot. geranium

peleryn|a f [1] (strój) cloak; ~**a przeciwdeszczo-**
wa a waterproof cape [2] (część płaszcza) cape

peleton m Sport pack; **oderwać się od** ~**u** to
break away from the pack

pelikan m Zool. pelican

pełni|a f [1] Astron. full moon [2] (szczyt) ~**a czegoś**
the height of sth [lata, sezonu, władzy]; ~**a**
zrozumienia complete understanding; **być w** ~
zdrowia to be in the best of health

III w pełni adv. (całkowicie) completely; **w** ~ **się**
z tobą zgadzam I completely a. fully agree with
you; **w** ~ **mi to odpowiada** that suits me down to
the ground a. perfectly

peł|nić impf vt [1] [osoba] to perform [funkcję, rolę];
~**nić służbę** to be on duty; ~**nić wartę** to be on
guard [2] (służyć) ~**nić funkcję** [przedmiot, pomiesz-
czenie] to serve (**jako coś** as sth)

pełn|o adv. grad. [1] (ile się zmieści) **nalać** ~**o wody**
do szklanki to fill a glass with water; **do** ~**a**

[nalać, nasypać] to the brim ② (bardzo wiele) ∼o **czegoś** a lot of sth, plenty of sth; **w sali było** ∼o **ludzi** the hall was full a. filled to capacity; **wszędzie go** ∼o he's here, there, and everywhere
pełnoletni *adi.* adult; **być** ∼**m** to be of age
pełnoletnoś|ć *f* majority; **osiągnąć** ∼**ć** to come of age
pełnometrażow|y *adi. [film]* full-length
pełnomocnictw|o *n* ① (upoważnienie) authorization; Prawo power of attorney ② (dokument) letter of attorney
pełnomocni|k *m*, ∼**czka** *f* ① (upoważniony) plenipotentiary; **występować jako** ∼**k kogoś** to act as sb's proxy ② Prawo attorney ③ (stanowisko) plenipotentiary; ∼**k rządu do spraw rodziny** the minister for family affairs
peł|ny *adi. grad.* ① (wypełniony) *[naczynie, autobus]* full; ∼**ny zapału** full of enthusiasm; **grać przy** ∼**nej sali** to play to a full house; **uzdrowisko jest** ∼**ne turystów** the resort is full of tourists; **artykuł jest** ∼**en błędów** the article is full of errors; **nie mów z** ∼**nymi ustami** don't speak a. talk with your mouth full ② (niczym nieograniczony) *[odpowiedzialność, poparcie]* full; *[zrozumienie, szczęście]* complete; *[władza]* absolute; **ma pan** ∼**ne prawo odmówić** you have every right to refuse; **darzę go** ∼**nym zaufaniem** I have absolute confidence in him ③ (całkowity, kompletny) *[zestaw, nazwisko, dane]* full; *[wydanie]* complete; *[tekst]* unabridged; *[miesiąc]* whole; **podpisać się** ∼**nym imieniem i nazwiskiem** to sign one's name in full; **w** ∼**nym składzie** at full strength; ∼**ne dwie godziny** two solid hours ④ (całkowicie rozwinięty) *[kłus, galop]* full; ∼**ną parą** *przen.* at full speed ⑤ (pulchny) *[twarz, sylwetka]* full; **mieć** ∼**ną twarz** to be full in the face
peł|zać, peł|znąć *impf vi* ① *[gad, owad, osoba]* to crawl; *[wąż]* to slither ② *przen. [roślina, mgła]* to creep; ∼**zająca inflacja** Ekon. creeping inflation
penetr|ować *impf vt* to penetrate *[teren, okolicę]*; to search through *[bibliotekę, archiwa]*; ∼**ować środowiska opozycyjne** to infiltrate opposition groups
penis *m* penis
penitencjarn|y *adi.* Prawo *[system, reforma]* prison; *[prawo]* penal; **zakład** ∼**y** a penal institution, a penitentiary US
pensj|a *f* (wynagrodzenie) wage(s); (urzędnika państwowego, menedżera) salary; ∼**a nauczycielska** a teacher's salary; **rodzina żyjąca z jednej** ∼**i** a single-income family
pensjona|t *m* boarding house
peoni|a *f* Bot. peony
pepi|tka, ∼**ta** *f* ① (wzór) dog-tooth check; (czarno-biała) shepherd's plaid ② (materiał) check (fabric)

perfekcj|a *f* perfection; **doprowadzić coś do** ∼**i** to bring sth to perfection; **dojść w czymś do** ∼**i** to become expert at sth
perfidn|y *adi. grad.* deceitful, perfidious
perfumeri|a *f* perfume shop
perfum|ować *impf* **❙** *vt* to perfume **❙❙** **perfumować się** to perfume oneself; **(ona) nigdy się nie** ∼**uje** she never wears perfume
perfum|y *plt* perfume; **flakonik** ∼ a bottle of perfume a. scent
pergamin *m* ① (papier) (do pakowania) greaseproof paper; (do pieczenia) baking parchment; (do rysowania) tracing paper ② (skóra, dokument) parchment
perka|ty *adi. [nos]* snub
perkoz *m* grebe; ∼ **dwuczuby** a great-crested grebe
perkusi|sta *m*, ∼**stka** *f* percussionist
perkusj|a *f* percussion; **grać na** ∼**i** to play percussion (instruments)
perli|czka, ∼**ca** *f* guineafowl
per|ła *f* ① (biżuteria) pearl ② przen. gem; ∼**ła kolekcji** the jewel (in the crown) of the collection
■ **rzucać** ∼**ły przed wieprze** to cast pearls before swine
perłow|y *adi. [naszyjnik, lakier, guziki]* pearl
peron *m* platform
personali|a *plt* książk. personal details; **poproszę o** ∼**a** your name and address, please; **ustalić czyjeś** ∼**a** to establish sb's identity
personaln|y *adi.* książk. personal; **dane/akta** ∼**e** personal details/files; **biuro** ∼**e/dział** ∼**y** personnel office/human resources department
personel *m* staff; ∼ **administracyjny** administrative staff a. personnel; ∼ **szpitala** the hospital staff a. personnel
perspektyw|a *f* ① Szt. perspective; **teoria** ∼**y** the theory of perspective ② (panorama) prospect ③ przen. (widoki na przyszłość) prospect; **kiepska/ponura** ∼**a** a bleak/gloomy prospect ④ przen. (odległość w czasie) perspective; **oceniać coś z** ∼**y lat** to look back on sth (some) years later
perspektywiczn|y *adi.* ① Szt. perspective ② (przyszłościowy) prospective; **plany** ∼**e** long-term plans
perswad|ować *impf vt* książk. to reason (**komuś** with sb); ∼**ować komuś, żeby coś zrobił** to try to persuade sb to do sth
perswazj|a *f* książk. persuasion; **siła** ∼**i** powers of persuasion
pertrakt|ować *impf vi* to negotiate (**o coś/o czymś** sth)
peru|ka *f* wig
perwersj|a *f* książk. perversion
perwersyjn|y *adi.* książk. *[myśli, obrazy]* perverse
peryferi|e *plt* (przedmieście) outskirts; **mieszkać na** ∼**ach Warszawy** to live on the outskirts of Warsaw
peryskop *m* periscope

perz *m* Bot. couch (grass)

pest|ka *f* ① (jabłek) pip; (winogron, truskawek, słonecznika) seed; (brzoskwiń) stone; ~**ki wiśni** cherry stones; ~**ki dyni** pumpkin seeds ② pot., przen. (drobnostka) piece of cake pot.

pesymi|sta *m*, ~**stka** *f* pessimist

pesymistyczn|y *adi. [nastrój, myśli]* pessimistic

pesymizm *m* pessimism

pesz|yć *impf* **[]** *vt* to make [sb] uneasy a. uncomfortable

[]] peszyć się to get embarrassed

petar|da *f* banger

petuni|a *f* Bot. petunia

petycj|a *f* petition; **wystosować** ~**ę do kogoś** to petition sb

pewien[1] *adi. praed.* → **pewny** ⑥

pew|ien[2] *pron.* certain; ~**ien mój znajomy** a certain acquaintance of mine; ~**nego dnia** one day; ~**nego razu** once; **przez** ~**ien czas** for some time; **w** ~**nej chwili** (określonej) at a certain a. at one point; **w** ~**nym momencie** (nieokreślonym) at some point; **w** ~**nym sensie** in a sense

pewnia|k *m* pot. ① (o osobie) (dead) cert GB, shoo-in US pot.; **iść na egzamin na** ~**ka** to be sure one will pass the exam ② (o koniu) sure bet pot.

pewnie **[]** *adv. grad.* ① (bez wahania) *[iść, odpowiadać]* confidently; **no** ~! of course! ② (bez niepokoju) **czuć się** ~ (bezpiecznie) to feel safe; (być pewnym siebie) to feel confident ③ (prawdopodobnie) (most) probably; ~ **jeszcze śpi** he's probably still asleep; **firma najpewniej upadnie** the company will most likely collapse

[]] inter. sure!

pewnik *m* ① (oczywistość) certainty; **traktować coś jako** ~ to take sth for granted ② Log. axiom

pewno *part.* (prawdopodobnie) probably; **na** ~ (z pewnością) certainly, definitely; **na** ~ **będzie padało** I'm sure it's going to rain; „**przyjadą?**" – „**na** ~" 'will they come?' – 'of course they will'

pewnoś|ć *f* ① (przekonanie) certainty; **z (całą)** ~**cią** (na pewno) certainly; **mieć** ~ **ć, że...** to be certain a. sure that...; **zrobić coś dla** ~**ci** to do sth just to be sure ② (zdecydowanie) confidence; ~**ć siebie** self-confidence

pew|ny *adi. grad.* ① (nieuchronny) *[sukces, zwycięstwo]* certain ② (niezaprzeczalny) *[informacja, dowód]* reliable; **jedno jest** ~**ne** one thing is certain; **to** ~**na** książk. that's certain ③ (niezawodny) *[przyjaciel, metoda]* reliable; **mieć** ~**ną rękę** to have a sure touch; **wiedzieć coś z** ~**nego źródła** to know sth from a reliable source ④ (zdecydowany) *[ruch, głos]* sure; **iść** ~**nym krokiem** to walk with a sure step ⑤ (bezpieczny) safe; **czuć się** ~**nym** to feel safe a. secure ⑥ (przekonany) sure; **być czegoś** ~**nym** to be sure of sth; **być** ~**nym kogoś** to have confidence in sb; **być** ~**nym siebie** to be sure of oneself; **jestem**

~**ien, że...** I'm sure that...; **jest** ~**na swego** she's (very) sure of her opinions

pęcherz *m* ① (na skórze) blister ② Anat. ~ (**moczowy**) the bladder

pęcherzyk *m* ① (na skórze) ~ **ropny** a pustule ② Anat. sac ③ (bąbelek) bubble; ~ **powietrza** an air bubble

pęczak *m* Kulin. pearl barley

pęcz|ek *m* bunch; **sprzedawać coś na** ~**ki** to sell sth in bunches a. by the bunch

■ **na** ~**ki** pot. loads of pot.

pęczni|eć *impf vi [groch, kasza]* to swell; *[żyły]* to bulge; *[balon]* to expand; ~**eć z dumy** przen. to swell with pride

pę|d[1] *m* ① (szybki ruch) rush; **pęd powietrza** a rush of air; **minąć kogoś/coś w (szalonym) pędzie** to rush past sb/sth pot. ② (skłonność) hunger; **pęd do wiedzy/władzy** a thirst for knowledge/power

■ **pobiec gdzieś w te pędy** pot. to hotfoot it somewhere pot.

pę|d[2] *m* Bot. shoot; **puścić pędy** *[roślina]* to sprout

pędz|el *m* ① (narzędzie) brush; (do malowania) (paint)brush; ~**el do golenia** a shaving brush; **chwycić za** ~**el** przen. to take up painting ② (twórczość malarska, sposób malowania) **obraz** ~**la Rubensa** a painting by Rubens

pę|dzić *impf* **[]** *vt* ① (gnać) to drive *[bydło]* ② (produkować) to distil *[spirytus]*

[] *vi [osoba, pojazd]* to rush; **nie pędź tak!** slow down!

pęk *m* (wiązka) bunch; ~ **kluczy** a bunch of keys

pękać *impf* → **pęknąć**

pęka|ty *adi.* ① (gruby) *[kieliszek]* barrel-shaped; *[butelka]* round-bellied; *[mężczyzna]* pot-bellied; *[kobieta]* plump ② (ciasno wypełniony) *[portfel, brulion]* thick

pęk|nąć *pf* — **pęk|ać** *impf vi* ① (nadłamać się) *[lód, szkło, ściana]* to crack; *[kość]* to fracture ② (przerwać się) *[gumka, sznurek]* to break; ~**ła mi struna** I broke a string ③ (podrzeć się) *[papierowa torba]* to tear; *[spodnie]* to rip; *[skóra, warga]* to crack ④ (rozerwać się) *[balon, pocisk, wrzód]* to burst; *[narząd, tętnica]* to rupture; ~**ło jej naczynko** she burst a blood vessel ⑤ (załamywać się) **struktura społeczna zaczyna** ~**ać** the social fabric is beginning to show cracks a. crumble ⑥ pot. (tchórzyć) *[osoba]* to crack przen.

■ ~**ać z dumy/radości** to be bursting with pride/joy; ~**ną z zazdrości, kiedy to zobaczą** they'll turn green with envy when they see it; ~**ać ze śmiechu** to crack up pot.; **zaraz** ~**nę** żart. (z przejedzenia) I'm fit a. ready to burst

pęknię|cie *n* ① (rysa) crack; (w ziemi, skale) fissure; (kości) fracture; (narządu, tętnicy) rupture ② Moda (rozcięcie) slit; **spódnica z** ~**ciem** a slit skirt

pęp|ek *m* navel

■ ~**ek świata** (kraj, miasto) the hub of the universe;

uważa się za ~**ek świata** pot. he thinks the whole world revolves around him; **widzieć tylko własny** ~**ek** (skupiać się na sobie) to contemplate one's navel
pępowin|a f umbilical cord także przen.

pęseta → **pinceta**

pęta|ć impf vt to bind [osobę, ręce]; to tether [zwierzę]; **długa suknia** ~**ła jej nogi** the long skirt hampered her movements

II pętać się pot. to hang a. wander around pot.; ~**ł się po kraju** he roved a. roamed about the country; ~**ć się komuś pod nogami** to get under sb's feet pot.

pętl|a f ① (na sznurze, drucie) loop; (zaciskająca się) noose; **założyć komuś** ~**ę na szyję** to put a noose round sb's neck także przen. ② (kształt) loop; **zrobić** ~**ę** (wrócić w to samo miejsce) [turysta, podróżnik] to make a round trip ③ (przystanek) terminus GB, terminal US; (odcinek torów) loop (line); ~**a tramwajowa/autobusowa** a tram/bus terminus ④ Lotn. (akrobacja) loop; **wykonać** ~**ę** to loop the loop ⑤ (o czasie) loop; **znaleźć się w** ~**i czasu** to be stuck in a time loop; **moje życie zatoczyło** ~**ę** my life has come full circle

pę|to ▯ n ① (do pętania zwierząt) tether ② Kulin. ring; **pęto kiełbasy** a ring of sausages

II pęta plt ① (do wiązania więźnia) restraints; **oswobodzić kogoś z pęt** to untie sb ② przen. chains przen.; fetters książk.; **pęta miłości** the chains of love

pi|ać impf ▯ vt **piać hymny/peany na cześć kogoś/czegoś** to sing peans to sb/sth

II vi ① [kogut] to crow ② [osoba] to talk/sing in a shrill voice ③ (wychwalać) to wax lyrical; **piać z zachwytu nad kimś/czymś** to wax lyrical a. go into raptures about sb/sth

pian|a f ① (pęcherzykowata masa) froth; **ubić** ~**ę z białek** to whisk a. beat egg whites to a froth; ~**a z mydła** soap bubbles ② (na ustach) foam; (na pysku, skórze) froth

■ **bić** ~**ę** pot. to blow sth out of proportion; **mieć** ~**ę na ustach** pot. to foam at the mouth

pianin|o n Muz. (upright) piano

piani|sta m, ~**stka** f pianist

pian|ka f ① (kosmetyk) foam; ~**ka do golenia** shaving foam; ~**ka do włosów** hair mousse ② (tworzywo) foam; **materac z** ~**ki** a foam mattress ③ Kulin. mousse; (gumowata) marshmallow

pias|ek m ① (substancja) sand; ~**ek moczowy** Med. gravel ② (piaszczysty teren) sandy area; ~**ki pustyni** desert sands; **ruchome** ~**ki** (przemieszczające się) shifting sands; (wciągające) quicksands

■ **chować głowę w** ~**ek** to stick a. bury one's head in the sand

piaskow|iec m Geol. sandstone

piaskownic|a f sandpit GB, sandbox US

piaskow|y adi. ① (cypel, ziemia) sandy ② (bezowy) sand-coloured GB, sand-colored US

piast|ować impf vt książk. (sprawować) to hold [stanowisko, urząd]; ~**ować godność senatora** to serve as senator

piaszczy|sty adi. sandy

p|iąć się impf v refl. ① (wspinać się) [osoba, samochód] to climb; **piąć się pod** a. **w górę** to climb up; **piąć się po szczeblach kariery** to work one's way up the (career) ladder ② (rosnąć) [roślina] to climb ③ przen. (wznosić się, wzrastać) [droga] to climb (up); **kurs dolara piął się w górę** the (exchange rate of the) dollar was climbing

piąt|ek m Friday

piąt|ka f ① (cyfra) five ② (ocena) ≈ A; **film/chłopak na** ~**kę** przen. a great film/guy; **spisać się na** ~**kę** przen. to do a great job ③ pot. (pięć) (złotych) five zlotys; (dolarów) five dollars; fiver US pot. ④ pot. (bieg w samochodzie) fifth; **jechać** ~**ką** to be in fifth (gear)

piątkow|y adi. ① [zebranie, wieczór] Friday ② Szkol. [uczeń, praca] excellent

pią|ty num. ord. fifth

■ ~**te przez dziesiąte** [rozumieć] vaguely; **słuchać** ~**te przez dziesiąte** to listen with half an ear

pich|cić impf vt pot. ① (gotować) to rustle up [obiad, zupę]; to fix US pot. ② przen. to grind out pot. [list, pismo]

pi|ć¹ impf vt, vi ① [osoba, zwierzę] to drink; **pić coś małymi łyczkami** to sip sth; **chce mi się pić** I'm thirsty ② [roślina] to drink too. ③ (spożywać alkohol) to drink; **pić z rozpaczy** to drink out of despair; **pić za coś** to drink to sth; **nikt nie wiedział, że on pije** nobody knew he had a drinking problem

pi|ć² impf vi (uwierać) **buty mnie piją (w palce)** these shoes pinch (my toes)

piec¹ m ① (urządzenie ogrzewcze) stove; ~ **kaflowy** a tiled stove; **napalić** a. **rozpalić w** ~**u** to light the stove; **chleb prosto z** ~**a** freshly baked bread ② Techn. (piekarski) oven; (ceramiczny) kiln; (hutniczy, odlewniczy) furnace

■ **żyje się tu** a. **jest nam tu jak u Pana Boga za** ~**em** we're as snug as a bug in a rug here żart.

pie|c² impf ▯ vt to bake [chleb, ziemniaki]; to roast [mięso, drób]; ~**c na ruszcie** to grill; ~**c na rożnie** to barbecue

II vi ① [słońce] to beat down ② (sprawiać ból) [oczy, rana] to sting; [policzki, skóra] to burn; **uszy go** ~**kły ze wstydu** his ears were burning with shame

III piec się ① (odczuwać gorąco) to bake; ~**kła się w wełnianej sukience** she was baking a. sweltering in her woollen dress ② (być pieczonym) [ciasto, chleb] to bake; [mięso, drób] to roast

piecho|ta f Wojsk. infantry; ~**ta morska** the marines

■ **iść** ~**tą** a. **na** ~**tę** to go on foot; **to dziesięć minut** ~**tą** it's a ten-minute walk

piechu|r m ① (wędrowiec) walker ② Wojsk. infantryman

piecyk *m* ① (do wody) water heater; ~ **gazowy** a gas water heater ② (piekarnik) oven

piecza|ra *f* (grota) cave

pieczar|ka *f* mushroom

pieczą t|ka *f* ① (przyrząd) stamp; ~**ka z datą** a date stamp; **przybić** ~**kę na dokumencie** to stamp a document ② (odbity znak) stamp

piecze|ń *f* Kulin. roast (meat); ~**ń wołowa/ wieprzowa** roast beef/pork; ~**ń z dzika** roast boar; **sos do** ~**ni** gravy

■ **upiec dwie** ~**nie przy** a. **na jednym ogniu** to kill two birds with one stone

pieczę|ć *f* ① (przyrząd) seal ② (znak na papierze) stamp; **dokument z** a. **opatrzony** ~**cią** a stamped document ③ (znak w laku albo wosku) seal; (pasek papieru) seal; **zerwać** ~**ć** to break a seal

pieczęt|ować *impf vt* ① (dla zabezpieczenia przed otwarciem) to seal *[kopertę]* ② (dla nadania ważności) to stamp (with a seal) *[dokument]* ③ książk., przen. (potwierdzać, przesądzać) to seal

pieczyw|o *n* bread; ~**o białe/ciemne** white/ brown bread; ~**o chrupkie** crispbread

pieg *m* freckle; **twarz pokryta** ~**ami** a freckled face

piegowa|ty *adi.* *[cera]* freckly; *[nos, twarz]* freckled; *[osoba]* freckle-faced

piekar|nia *f* ① (zakład) bakery ② (sklep przy zakładzie) the baker's (shop)

■ **spokojnie, to** a. **tu nie** ~**nia!** pot. calm down, there's no rush!

piekarnik *m* oven; ~ **elektryczny/gazowy** a gas/ an electric oven

piekarz *m* baker

piekąc|y *adi.* *[słońce, żar, skwar]* baking; *[upał]* blistering; *[ból, łzy]* burning; ~**e buty** shoes that pinch one's feet

piekieln|y *adi.* ① (taki jak w piekle) *[czeluści]* infernal; *[moce]* hellish; **ogień** ~**y** hellfire ② pot. (trudny do zniesienia) *[ból]* hellish; *[hałas]* infernal; **zrobić komuś** ~**ą awanturę** to give sb merry hell pot. ③ pot. (zły) *[pogoda, dziecko]* dreadful; *[dzień]* hellish

piek|ło *m* ① Relig. hell; **iść do** ~**ła** to go to hell; **smażyć się w** ~**le** to roast in hell ② przen. hell; ~**ło na ziemi** hell on earth; **zmienić czyjeś życie w** ~**ło** to make sb's life hell

■ **niech go** ~**ło pochłonie** przest. may he rot in hell!; **do** ~**ła by za nią poszedł** he'd go through hell and high water a. fire and water for her; **pomysł/baba z** ~**ła rodem** a hellish idea/woman

pielęgniar|ka *f* nurse

pielęgniarz *m* male nurse

pielęgn|ować *impf vt* ① to nurse *[chorego]*; to look after *[dziecko]* ② (dbać o rośliny) to nurture ③ (dbać o skórę, zęby, włosy) to take care of ④ (zachowywać) to cultivate *[obyczaje, tradycję]*; to cherish *[pamięć, wspomnienia]*; to nurture *[uczucia]*

pielgrzym *m* Relig. pilgrim

pielgrzym|ka *f* ① (wędrówka) pilgrimage także przen.; ~**ka po księgarniach** a tour of the bookshops ② (grupa pielgrzymów) a group of pilgrims

pielgrzym|ować *impf vi* to go on a. to make a pilgrimage

pielić → **pleć**

pielu|cha *f* nappy GB, diaper US

pieni|ądz ① *m* (środek płatniczy) coin; ~**ądze na drobne wydatki** pin money; ~**ądze z podatków** tax revenue; **płacić** ~**ędzmi** to pay (in) cash; **mieć/zarabiać dużo** ~**ędzy** to have/earn a lot of money; **masz przy sobie** ~**ądze?** have you got any money on you?; **ciężkie** a. **grube** ~**ądze** big money pot.; **marne** ~**ądze** very little money

■ **być przy** ~**ądzach** to be in the money pot.; **leżeć** a. **siedzieć** a. **spać na** ~**ądzach** to be rolling in money pot.; ~**ądze leżą na ulicy** the money's there for the taking; **nie zrobię tego za żadne** ~**ądze** I wouldn't do it for love or money

pie|nić się *impf v refl.* ① (wytwarzać pianę) *[mydło, szampon]* to lather ② (pokrywać się pianą) *[morze, rzeka, woda]* to foam; *[piwo]* to froth ③ pot. *[osoba]* to foam a. froth at the mouth

p|ień *m* ① (część drzewa) trunk ② (pniak) (tree) stump

pieprz *m* Bot., Kulin. pepper; ~ **czarny/zmielony** black/ground pepper; ~ **ziołowy** ersatz pepper *(a mixture of herbs used as seasoning)*; **ziarnko** ~**u** a grain of pepper

■ **suche jak** a. **wyschnięte na** ~ as dry as a bone a. bone dry; **uciekać, gdzie** ~ **rośnie** pot. to run like hell pot.

pieprznicz|ka *f* pepper pot GB, pepper shaker US

pieprzn|y *adi.* *[potrawa]* peppery; pot. *[dowcip, kawał]* spicy

pieprz|yć *impf vt* to pepper *[potrawę]*

pieprzyk *m* ① (znamię) mole; (do przyklejania) beauty spot ② przen. (szczegół dodający pikanterii) a bit of spice

piernik *m* ① (ciasto) ≈ gingerbread cake ② pot., obraźl. (o osobie) old fogey

■ **co ma** ~ **do wiatraka?** pot. what's that got to do with anything?

pier|óg *m* ① Kulin. ≈ dumpling; ~**ogi ruskie** dumplings with potato and cheese stuffing ② Kulin. (pieczony) pie; ~**óg z mięsem** a meat pie

pier|ś *f* ① (u człowieka) chest; breast książk.; (u kobiety) breast; **wyprężyć** a. **wypiąć** ~**ś** to throw out one's chest; **karmić dziecko** ~**sią** to breast-feed a. nurse a baby ② (u zwierzęcia) chest; (u ptaka) Kulin. breast; ~**ś czy udko?** breast or leg?

■ **bić się** a. **uderzać się w** ~**si** to beat one's breast

pierście|ń *m* ① (klejnot) ring; ~**ń z brylantem** a diamond ring ② (krąg) circle ③ Techn. ring

pierścion|ek *m* ① (klejnot) ring; ~**ek zaręczyno-wy** an engagement ring ② (włosów) ringlet

pierwiast|ek *m* ① (czynnik) element ② Chem. element; ~**ek chemiczny** a chemical element; ~**ki promieniotwórcze** radioactive elements;

~**ki śladowe** trace elements; **układ okresowy** ~**ków** the periodic table ③ Mat. root; ~**ek kwadratowy/sześcienny** the square/cube root (**z czegoś** of sth)

pierwiosn|ek m primrose

pierworodn|y adi. [syn, córka] first-born

pierwotn|y adi. ① (odległy w czasie) [kultura] prim(a)eval, primordial; [człowiek, wspólnota] primitive ② (w pierwszym stadium rozwoju) [narzędzia, społeczeństwo] primitive; [stan] prim(a)eval; **las** ~**y** a. **puszcza** ~**a** primeval a. virgin forest ③ (początkowy) [plan, znaczenie] original ④ (wcześniejszy, ważniejszy) primal

pierwowz|ór m ① (model) prototype, precursor ② (oryginał) original

pierwszeństw|o n ① (prawo przed innymi) priority; **mieć** ~**o przed kimś/czymś** to have priority a. precedence over sb/sth; **panie mają** ~**o!** ladies first! ② Aut. ~**o przejazdu** (the) right of way; **kto ma** ~**o na tym skrzyżowaniu?** who has the right of way at this junction?; **dać komuś** ~**o przejazdu** to give (right of) way to sb GB, to yield to sb US; **wymusić** ~**o przejazdu (na kimś)** to not give way (to sb)

■ **dzierżyć palmę** ~**a** to bear the palm; **walczyć o palmę** ~**a** to vie for the palm

pierwszorzędn|y adi. ① (doskonały) first-rate; **obuwie** ~**ej jakości** top-quality shoes ② pot. great pot.

pierwsz|y **I** num ord. [klasa, rocznica, strona] first; ~**y tom** the first volume, volume one; ~**a osoba liczby pojedynczej/mnogiej** Jęz. (the) first person singular/plural; **student** ~**ego roku** a first-year student; **kto skończył** ~**y?** who finished first?; **przyszła jako jedna z** ~**ych** she was one of the first to arrive; **idź** ~**y!** you go first!; ~**y raz tu jestem** I've never been here before; ~**a z brzegu książka** (najbliższa) the first book to hand; **wszedł do** ~**ej z brzegu kawiarni** he walked into the first café he saw a. came across; **to może zrobić** ~**y lepszy** anybody can do that

II adi. ① (początkowy) [śnieg, oznaka, wrażenie] first; ~**e truskawki** the first strawberries; **w** ~**ej chwili** at first; **od** ~**ej chwili** from the (very) first moment ② (główny) [nagroda, oficer] first; ~**a dama** the first lady; **na** ~**ym planie** in the foreground; **stawiać kogoś/coś na** ~**ym miejscu** to put sb/sth first; **wysunąć się na** ~**y plan** to come to the fore ③ (najlepszy) [gatunek, liga] first; [specjalista, znawca] leading; ~**ej klasy** a. ~**ej wody aktor** a first-class a. first-rate actor; **chce być we wszystkim** ~**y** he wants to be the best at everything; **samochód** ~**a klasa** pot. a really ace car pot.

III **pierwsze** n (danie) first course; **na** ~**e** for the first course

■ ~**y raz słyszę!** a. ~**e słyszę!** pot. it's news to

me!, it's a. that's the first I've heard of it!; **na** ~**y rzut oka** at first glance a. sight; **miłość od** ~**ego wejrzenia** love at first sight; **po** ~**e** in the first place; **kto** ~**y, ten lepszy** przysł. first come, first served przysł.

pierzch|nąć[1] pf — **pierzch|ać** impf vi ① [osoba, zwierzę] to flee; [myszy, króliki] to scamper away a. off ② przen. [dobry nastrój] to vanish; **mgła** ~**ła** the fog dispersed a. cleared

pierzch|nąć[2] impf vi [skóra, ręce, usta] to get chapped

pierz|e n ① (pióra) feathers; (upierzenie) plumage ② (do wypychania poduszek) feathers; ~**e gęsie** goose feathers; **poduszka z** ~**a** a feather pillow

pierzyn|a f feather quilt

p|ies m dog; **psy myśliwskie** hunting dogs; **psy obronne** watchdogs; **pies przewodnik** a guide dog; **„uwaga, zły pies!"** 'beware of the dog'; **łgać jak pies** książk. to lie through one's teeth; **traktować kogoś jak psa** to treat sb like a dog

☐ **zejść/schodzić na psy** (podupaść) to go to the dogs pot.; (moralnie) to go down; **a ja to pies?** and what about me?; **pies ogrodnika** a dog in the manger; **żyją ze sobą jak pies z kotem** they fight like cat and dog; **pogoda była pod psem** the weather was foul; **pogoda taka, że psa by z domu nie wygnał** weather so bad you wouldn't put a dog out; **moja cała praca (zdała się) psu na budę** (I did) all that work for nothing!; **ni pies, ni wydra** neither fish nor fowl; **tu jest pies pogrzebany!** that's the (whole) point a. thing!; **całuj psa w nos!** get stuffed! pot.; **nie dla psa kiełbasa** it's too good for you/him/them; **pies z nim tańcował!** a. **pies go trącał!** a. **pies mu mordę lizał!** posp., obraźl. to hell with him! pot.

pieszczo|ch m, ~**cha** f pet

pieszczo|ta f caress; **obsypywać kogoś** ~**tami** to fondle a. caress sb

pieszczotliw|y adi. grad. [głos, spojrzenie] tender; ~**e imię** a pet name

pieszo adv. on foot; **chodzić do pracy** ~ to walk to work

pie|szy **I** adi. ① [orszak] walking; [ruch] pedestrian; **turyści** ~**si** hikers; **pójść na** ~**szą wycieczkę** to go on a. for a hike; **zamknięty dla ruchu** ~**szego** closed to pedestrians a. pedestrian traffic ② Wojsk. [kompania, dywizja] infantry; [patrol] foot

II m (osoba) pedestrian; ~**si** pedestrians; **przejście dla** ~**szych** a pedestrian crossing

pie|ścić impf **I** vt ① (okazywać czułość) to caress [osobę]; to fondle [piersi] ② przen. (sprawiać przyjemność) ~**ścić wzrok** a. **oczy/ucho** to be pleasing to the eye/the ear

II **pieścić się** ① (okazywać czułość) to fondle each other ② pot. (postępować łagodnie) ~**ścić się z kimś** to mollycoddle sb ③ pot. (oszczędzać się) **nic ci nie jest, nie** ~**ść się!** you're fine, stop fussing!

pieśnia|rz *m*, ~**rka** *f* songster

pieś|ń *f* ① Muz. song; ~**ń ludowa** a folk song; ~**ni biesiadne/weselne** drinking/wedding songs; **zespół** ~**ni i tańca** a song and dance company ② Literat. (wiersz) song; (część poematu) canto ■ **koniec** a. **cześć** ~**ni!** pot. the party's over pot.

pietrusz|ka *f* Bot., Kulin. ① (roślina, korzeń) parsnip ② (liście) parsley; **natka** ~**ki** parsley (leaves)

pięcioboi|sta *m*, ~**stka** *f* Sport pentathlete

pięciobok *m* pentagon

pięciob|ój *m* Sport pentathlon

pięcioką|t *m* pentagon

pięciolini|a /ˌpjɛntɕɔˈliɲja/ *f* Muz. staff, stave GB

pię|ć [] *num.* five

II *n inv.* Szkol. (ocena) ≈ A
■ **wyskoczyć z czymś ni w** ~**ć, ni w dziewięć** to say something a propos of nothing a. out of nowhere

pięćdziesi|ąt *num.* fifty

pięćdziesiąt|ka *f* ① (cyfra) fifty ② pot. (wiek) fifty; **miał około** ~**ki** he was around fifty ③ pot. (banknot) fifty-zloty (bank)note ④ pot. (szybkość) fifty; **jechał** ~**ką** he was doing fifty pot.

pięćdziesią|ty *num. ord.* fiftieth

pięćdziesięciolecі|e *n* ① (rocznica) fiftieth anniversary ② (okres) fifty-year period

pię|ćset *num.* five hundred

pięćset|ka *f* ① (cyfra) five hundred ② pot. (banknot) five-hundred-zloty (bank)note; (głośnik) 500 watt-loudspeaker

pięćsetn|y *num. ord.* five hundredth

pięknie *adv. grad.* ① (bardzo ładnie) beautifully; ~ **wyglądać** to look beautiful a. lovely; **robi się** ~ (o pogodzie) it's turning out lovely; **wszystko to (bardzo)** ~**, ale...** that's all very fine a. well, but... ② (emfatycznie) ~ **dziękuję!** thanks a lot! także iron. ③ (doskonale) *[zbudowany, wykonany]* finely; ~ **ci poszło** you did very well

pięknie|ć *impf vi [kobieta]* to grow pretty a. lovely; *[mężczyzna]* to grow handsome

piękn|o *n* beauty; **poczucie** ~**a** a sense of beauty

pięknoś|ć *f* ① (cecha) beauty; **konkurs/salon** ~**ci** a beauty contest/salon ② (kobieta) beauty

piękn|y *adi.* ① (bardzo ładny) *[kobieta, ogród, suknia]* beautiful; **była** ~**a pogoda** the weather was beautiful ② (pokazowy) *[czyn, tradycje]* fine; *[zbiory, wyniki]* excellent; **to była** ~**a bramka** that was a beautiful goal ③ iron. fine iron.; ~**e rzeczy słyszę o tobie!** I've been hearing some very fine things about you!
■ **pewnego** ~**ego dnia** one fine day; ~**e słowa** a. **słówka** iron. fine words iron.; **płeć** ~**a** the fair a. fairer sex przest., żart.

pięściarz *m* boxer

pięś|ć *f* ① (dłoń) fist; **walka na** ~**ci** a fist fight; **wygrażać komuś** ~**cią** to shake one's fist at sb; **poczęstować kogoś** ~**cią** pot. to give sb a bunch of fives GB pot. a. a knuckle sandwich US pot. ② przen. (brutalna siła) iron fist a. hand; **prawo** ~**ci** the law of the jungle

pię|ta *f* ① (część stopy) heel; **przysiąść na** ~**tach** to squat on one's heels; **obrócić się na** ~**cie** to turn on one's heel ② (w skarpecie, bucie) heel(-piece)
■ ~**ta Achillesa** Achilles' heel; **deptać komuś po** ~**tach** to breathe down sb's neck

pięt|ka *f* ① (część stopy) heel ② (chleba) heel

piętnast|ka *f* fifteen

piętna|sty *num. ord.* fifteenth

piętna|ście *num.* fifteen

piętn|o *n* ① (znak) brand; **wypalić** ~**o na zwierzęciu** to brand an animal ② przen. mark przen.; imprint książk., przen.; (hańbiące) stigma ③ (znamię) birthmark

piętn|ować *impf* [] *vt* ① książk. (potępiać) to condemn; to stigmatize książk. *[zakłamanie, zakupstwo]* ② (znakować) to brand *[bydło, przestępcę]*
II piętnować się (jeden drugiego) to denounce each other

pięt|ro *n* ① (w budynku) floor; **na trzecim** ~**rze** on the third floor a. storey GB, on the fourth floor a. story US ② (w domu jednopiętrowym) upstairs ③ przen. (poziom) tier

piętrow|y *adi. [dom]* multi-storey; ~**y autobus** a double-decker (bus); ~**e łóżko** a bunk bed

piętrz|yć *impf* [] *vt* ① (gromadzić) to stack (up) *[pudła]*; to swell *[fale]*; to bank up *[śnieg]* ② przen. to pile up *[trudności]*
II piętrzyć się ① (gromadzić się) *[zaspy, śmieci]* to accumulate ② (wznosić się) *[woda, fale]* to swell; *[góry, gmachy]* to rise up ③ przen. *[przeszkody, kłopoty]* to pile up

piguł|ka *f* (tabletka) pill (**od czegoś** a. **na coś** for sth); (antykoncepcyjna) the Pill; **wziąć** a. **zażyć** ~**kę** to take a pill a. tablet; ~**ka na ból głowy/na sen** a headache/sleeping pill; **brać** ~**ki antykoncepcyjne** to be on the Pill

pigw|a *f* quince

pijac|ki *adi. [awantura, towarzystwo]* drunken; ~**ka melina** pot. a drinking den pot.

pija|ć *impf vt* to drink; **chętnie** ~**m wino** I like (to drink) wine

pija|k *m* drunk

pijan|y *adi. [osoba]* drunk(en); *[bełkot, wzrok]* drunken; ~**y kierowca** a drink-driver GB, a drunk-driver US; **prowadzenie samochodu po** ~**emu** drink-driving GB, drunk-driving US; ~**y ze szczęścia** drunk with happiness

pijaństw|o *n* ① (nałóg) drunkenness ② pot. (libacja) drunken party

pijaw|ka *f* ① Zool. leech ② przen., pejor. leech pejor.; bloodsucker pot., pejor.

pik *m* Gry spade

pikantn|y *adi.* ① *[potrawa]* spicy ② *[żart, film]* spicy; **oszczędź nam ~ych szczegółów** spare us the juicy details

piknik *m* picnic

pik|ować *impf* Ⅰ *vt* (przeszywać) to quilt *[kołdrę, kurtkę]* Ⅱ *vi* Lotn. to dive

pilnik *m* Techn. file; **~ do metalu** a metal file; **~ do paznokci** a nail file

piln|ować *impf* Ⅰ *vt* ① (strzec) to guard *[wejścia]*; to take care of *[dzieci]* ② (przestrzegać) **~ować porządku** to keep order; **~ować przepisów** to observe the rules Ⅱ **pilnować się** (uważać) to be on one's guard

piln|y *adi. grad.* ① (wymagający pośpiechu) urgent; **~a sprawa** a matter of urgency; **~e interesy** pressing business; **nic ~ego** nothing urgent ② (gorliwy, pracowity) *[student]* diligent; *[czytelnik]* ardent

pilo|t *m* ① (samolotu, holownika) pilot; **~t automatyczny** autopilot ② (wycieczki) courier ③ (urządzenie) remote control ④ (fragment programu) pilot

pilot|ka *f* ① (samolotu) pilot ② (wycieczki) courier ③ (czapka) flying cap

pilot|ować *impf vt* ① (kierować) to pilot *[helikopter, samolot]* ② (eskortować) to pilot *[statki]* ③ (wskazywać trasę) to pilot *[kolumnę transporterów, kolarzy]* ④ (oprowadzać) to guide *[wycieczkę zagraniczną]* ⑤ (nadzorować) to pilot *[program szkoleniowy]*

pi|ła *f* ① (narzędzie) saw; **piła ręczna** a handsaw; **ciąć drewno piłą** to saw wood ② Zool. sawfish ③ pot., przen. (męcząca osoba) pain pot.

pił|ka *f* Sport ① (przedmiot) ball; **~ka futbolowa** a football GB, a soccer ball; **grać w ~kę** (o dzieciach) to play ball; (o piłce nożnej) to play football GB a. soccer ② (rzut) ball; **długa/dobra ~ka** a long/good ball ③ (dyscyplina) **~ka koszykowa** basketball; **~ka nożna** (association) football GB, soccer; **~ka ręczna** handball; **~ka wodna** water polo

piłkars|ki *adi.* football GB, soccer

piłkarz *m* Sport footballer GB, soccer player; **~ ręczny** handball player

pił|ować *impf* Ⅰ *vt* ① (przecinać piłą) to saw *[deski, belki]* ② (ścierać, wygładzać) to file; **~ować paznokcie** to file one's nails ③ pot. (źle grać) **~ować skrzypce** to saw away on a. at a violin pot., żart. Ⅱ *vi* (nudzić) to harp on

pince|ta /pę'seta/ *f* tweezers

pine|zka, ~ska *f* drawing pin GB, thumbtack US

ping-pong *m* pot. ping-pong pot.

pingwin *m* penguin

pion¹ *m* ① (kierunek) the perpendicular; **ustawić coś w ~ie** to stand sth upright ② (przyrząd) plumb line; **odchylać się od ~u** to be off a. out of plumb ③ (w budynku) riser ④ (dział, resort) department

pion² *m* Gry pawn; **wykonać ruch ~em** to move a pawn

pion|ek *m* Gry (w szachach) pawn także przen.; (w warcabach) draught GB, checker US

pionie|r *m* ① (twórca nowych prądów) pioneer ② (osadnik) pioneer

pionow|y *adi. [start, lądowanie]* vertical; **~a postawa** vertical posture

piorun *m* lightning; **burza z ~ami** a thunderstorm ■ **stanął/zamilkł jak rażony** a. **trafiony ~em** he was thunderstruck; **zrobić coś ~em** to do sth double quick a. in a flash pot.

piorunochron *m* lightning conductor a. rod US

piosen|ka *f* song

piosenka|rz *m*, **~rka** *f* singer

piórni|k *m* pencil box/case

pió|ro *n* ① (ptasie) feather; **~ro wycieraczki** Techn. wiper blade ② (do pisania) pen; **gęsie ~ro** a quill (pen); **~ro kulkowe** a ball pen; **wieczne ~ro** a fountain pen; **kolega po ~rze** przen. a fellow writer

pióropusz *m* ① (pęk piór) (przy kapeluszu) plume; (przy hełmie) crest; (indiański) headdress ② przen. plume

pirac|ki *adi. [statek, radiostacja, oprogramowanie]* pirate; **~ka kaseta** a pirated cassette

piractw|o *n* piracy; **~o drogowe** road-hogging pot.; **~o komputerowe** software piracy

pirami|da *f* pyramid

pirani|a /pi'rania/ *f* Zool. piranha

pira|t *m* pirate; **~t drogowy** road hog; **~t powietrzny** hijacker

pirotechni|k *m* ① Techn. firework maker ② (w policji) **oddział ~ków** a bomb disposal unit a. squad

pirotechni|ka *f* pyrotechnics

pirue|t *m* Jeźdz., Sport, Taniec pirouette

pi|sać *impf* Ⅰ *vt* ① (zapisywać) to write; (na maszynie) to type; **pisać na komputerze** to write a. type on a computer; **coś do pisania** (długopis) something to write with; (kartka) something to write on ② (tworzyć) to write *[wiersze, piosenki]*; **żyć z pisania** to make a living from writing ③ (korespondować) to write; **pisać list do kogoś** to write a letter to sb; **pisać podanie o coś** to apply for sth ④ (informować) to report; **prasa pisze, że...** newspapers report that...; **piszą o tym wszystkie gazety** it's in all the papers Ⅱ *vi* ① (być piśmiennym) to (be able to) write; **jeszcze nie umie pisać** s/he can't write yet ② *[pióro]* to write; **ten długopis nie pisze** this pen doesn't write Ⅲ **pisać się** ① *[słowo, wyrażenie]* to be spelt; **jak się pisze?** how do you spell it?; **to się pisze rozłącznie** it's written as two words; **oni piszą się z niemiecka** they spell their name the German way ② pot. (decydować się) **pisać się na coś** to be up for sth pot.; **ja się na to nie piszę!** count me out! pot.

pisak *m* ① (flamaster) felt-tip (pen) ② Techn. (w echosondzie, sejsmografie) recorder

pisan|ka f (jajko) painted egg (at Easter)

pisarz m (literat) writer

pisemn|y adi. [egzamin, zgoda] written

pisk m squeal; ~ **opon/hamulców** a squeal of tyres/brakes

piskl|ę n Zool. chick; (nieopuszczające gniazda) nestling; (świeżo opierzone) fledg(e)ling

piskliw|y adi. grad. [głos, śmiech] shrill; **być ~ym** [osoba] to have a shrill voice

piskorz m Zool. weatherfish; **wić się jak ~** to wriggle like an eel; przen. (unikać odpowiedzi) to dodge a question

pi|smo ▯ n ▯ (pisanie) writing; **umowa zawarta na piśmie** a written contract; **przedstawić coś na piśmie** to put sth in writing; **mam to na piśmie** I have it in writing ▯ (alfabet) script; **pismo Braille'a** Braille; **pismo nutowe** Muz. musical notation ▯ (wygląd liter) writing; **czyjś charakter pisma** sb's (hand)writing; **napisany drobnym/równym pismem** written in a small/neat hand ▯ (dokument) letter; **pismo urzędowe** an official letter a. document; **Pismo Święte** the Holy Bible ▯ (czasopismo) magazine

▐▐ **pisma** plt (dzieła) writings; **pisma wszystkie Conrada** the complete works of Conrad

pi|snąć[1] pf — **pi|szczeć** impf vi (wydać wysoki dźwięk) [mysz, zabawka, dziecko] to squeak; [osoba, opony, hamulce] to squeal; [pisklę] to peep; **piszczą-ca zabawka** a squeaky toy; **pisnąć/piszczeć z zachwytu** to squeal with delight

pi|snąć[2] pf vt (wspomnieć) **nie pisnąć ani słówka o czymś** to not breathe a word of a. about sth; **nikomu nawet o tym nie pisnął** he didn't breathe a word to anybody

pisowni|a f spelling

pistacj|a f ▯ Bot. (drzewo) pistachio ▯ Bot., Kulin. (orzeszek) pistachio (nut)

pistole|t m ▯ (broń) gun; ~**t maszynowy** a submachine gun; **wyciągnąć ~t** to draw a gun; **przystawić komuś ~t do skroni** to hold a gun to sb's head także przen. ▯ Techn. gun; ~**t natryskowy** a spray gun; ~**t do farby** a paint gun

pisua|r m urinal

piszczeć impf → **pisnąć**[1]

piszczel m, f Anat. tibia

piśmienn|y adi. ▯ (umiejący pisać) [osoba] literate ▯ (papierniczy) **artykuły ~e** stationery

pitn|y adi. [woda, czekolada] drinking

pitra|sić impf vt pot. to rustle up pot. [obiad, zupę]; to fix US

piwiar|nia f beer cellar

piwnic|a f ▯ (kondygnacja) basement; (pomieszczenie) cellar ▯ (z winem) (wine) cellar; **dobrze zaopatrzona ~a** a well-stocked cellar ▯ (kawiarnia) basement café; (klub) basement club

piwn|y adi. [zapach, smak] beery; [szampon] beer; [oczy] dark brown

piw|o n (napój) beer; **grzane ~o** mulled beer; ~**o jasne** lager; **trzy ~a** three beers; **typ spod budki z ~em** przen., pejor. an unsavoury character

■ **nawarzyć (sobie)** ~**a** to make trouble for oneself; **wypić ~o, którego się nawarzyło** to face the music; **to małe ~o!** it's a piece of cake!

piwoni|a /pi'vɔɲa/ f Bot. peony

pizz|a /'pitstsa/ f Kulin. pizza

pizzeri|a /pits'tserja/ f pizza restaurant a. place

piżam|a f pyjamas GB, pajamas US; **spodnie od ~y** pyjama trousers

piżmak m Zool. muskrat

plac m ▯ (u zbiegu ulic) square; (okrągły) circus ▯ (teren) yard; ~ **załadunkowy** a freight yard; ~ **targowy** a marketplace; ~ **boju** battlefield także przen. ▯ (działka) plot (of land); ~ **budowy** a construction site; ~ **zabaw** a playground

plac|ek ▯ m ▯ Kulin. (ciasto) pie; (z kruchym spodem) tart; ~**ek ze śliwkami** a plum tart ▯ Kulin. (smażony) cake; ~**ki ziemniaczane** potato cakes; ~**ki z jabłkami** apple fritters ▯ (płaski kawałek) patch; ~**ki błota** patches of mud; **krowie ~ki** cowpats ▯ (plama) patch; ~**ki łysiny** bald patches

▐▐ **plackiem** adv. [leżeć] flat; **paść ~kiem na ziemię** to fall flat on the ground

placów|ka f ▯ (przedstawicielstwo) post; ~**ka dyplomatyczna** a diplomatic post; **wyjechać na ~kę** to be posted abroad ▯ (instytucja) centre GB, center US; ~**ki służby zdrowia** medical centres; ~**ka handlowa/usługowa** a retail/service outlet ▯ Wojsk. (miejsce do obrony) outpost; (oddział) patrol

pla|ga f plague także przen.; ~**ga myszy** a plague of mice

plagia|t m (czyn, utwór) plagiarism

plaj|ta f pot. ▯ (bankructwo) failure; **zrobić ~tę** to go bust a. to the wall pot. ▯ (niepowodzenie) washout; flop pot.

plajt|ować impf vi pot. [fabryka, firma] to go bust a. to the wall pot.; [właściciel, producent] to go broke pot.

plaka|t m poster

plakiet|ka f ▯ Szt. (metalowa) plaque; (z tkaniny) badge; (pamiątkowa) badge ▯ (identyfikator) identification a. identity badge; (z nazwą firmy) nameplate; (w wojsku) (identity) disc; dog tag US pot.

plam|a f ▯ (zabrudzenie) stain; (rozmazana) smear; ~**a z krwi** a bloodstain; ~**a po kawie** a coffee stain; **po winie zostanie ~a** wine will leave a stain; **wywabiacz ~** spot a. stain remover; ~**a ropy naftowej** an oil slick ▯ (na skórze) blotch; ~**y na twarzy/szyi** blotches on sb's face/neck; **po truskawkach dostaję ~ na twarzy** strawberries bring me out in spots; **pokryty ~ami** blotchy ▯ (miejsce wyodrębniające się z tła) patch; **rozmyta ~a zieleni** a blurred patch of green; **przed oczami migotały a. latały jej czerwone ~y** she saw red spots before her eyes ▯ przen. (hańba) blot;

~**a na honorze** a blot on one's escutcheon
■ **dać** ~**ę** pot. (skompromitować się) to blot one's
copybook pot.; (popełnić gafę) to drop a brick a. clanger
pot.

plam|ić *impf* **[I]** *vt* [1] (brudzić) to stain; ~**ić sobie
koszulę winem** to stain one's shirt with wine
[2] książk. (zniesławiać) to tarnish *[dobre imię, honor,
nazwisko]*; to sully książk.
[II] plamić się [1] (brudzić się) to get stained (**czymś**
with sth) [2] książk. (okrywać się hańbą) to stain one's
reputation

plan *m* [1] (program działania) plan; (rozkład zajęć)
schedule; (godzinowy) timetable; ~ **dyżurów** a duty
roster; ~ **lekcji** Szkol. a (school) timetable; ~
ucieczki an escape plan; **sporządzić** ~ to draw
up a. work out a plan; **trzymać się** ~**u** to keep to
a. stick to a plan; **odbyć się zgodnie z** ~**em** to go
according to plan a. as planned [2] (zamiar) plan;
zmienić ~**y** to change one's plans; **jakie masz
~y na ten weekend?** what are your plans for the
weekend?; **mieć** ~**y co do swoich dzieci** to have
plans for one's children; **mieć coś w** ~**ie** to be
planning sth; **w** ~**ie jest budowa nowej
autostrady** there are plans to build a new motorway [3] (konspekt) plan; ~ **wypracowania/opowia-
dania** an essay/a story outline [4] (miasta, marszruty)
map; (pomieszczeń, ogrodu) plan [5] Kino, Szt., Teatr **na
pierwszym/drugim** ~**ie** in the foreground/back-
ground; **na** ~**ie (filmowym)** on set; **wysunąć się
na pierwszy** ~ przen. to come to the fore; **zejść na
dalszy** a. **drugi** ~ przen. to recede into the
background

plande|ka *f* tarpaulin

plane|ta *f* planet; ~**ta Ziemia** Planet Earth
■ **nie z tej** ~**ty** pot. (like something) out of this
world pot.; **samochód nie z tej** ~**ty** a terrific car
pot.

planetari|um *n* planetarium

planetarn|y *adi.* planetary; **układ** a. **system** ~**y**
a planetary system

plan|ować *impf vt* [1] (zamierzać) to make plans for
[urlop, dzień, wycieczkę]; (określać termin) to schedule
[emisję, zakończenie projektu]; ~**owany poziom
produkcji** production target, the target level of
production; ~**owany przyjazd pociągu godzina
14.00** scheduled time of arrival is 2 p.m.; ~**ować
coś zrobić** to plan to do sth [2] (ustalać) to plan (out)
[trasę, podróż, strategię, pracę]; **menu było** ~**owane
przez szefa kuchni** the menu was prepared by the
chef [3] Archit. (projektować) to plan *[dom, osiedle]*

plansz|a *f* [1] (tablica informacyjna) display board; (do
powieszenia na ścianie) wall chart; (pomoc naukowa) flash
card [2] Gry board; ~**a do gry w szachy/w warcaby**
a chessboard/a draughtboard GB a. checkerboard US

plantacj|a *f* [1] (pole uprawne) field; ~**a buraków**
a beet field [2] (farma) plantation; ~**a herbaty** a tea
plantation

plantato|r *m* planter

plas|ować się *impf v refl.* książk. *[sportowiec, polityk,
kraj]* to come; ~**ować się na pierwszym miejscu
w rankingach** to be ranked a. to come first

plastelin|a *f* plasticine®

plast|er *m* [1] Kulin. (mięsa, sera) slice; (bekonu) rasher;
pokroić żółty ser w ~**ry** a. **na** ~**ry** to cut cheese
into slices [2] Med. (opatrunek) (sticking) plaster GB,
Band-Aid® US; ~**er na odciski** a corn plaster;
przykleić ~**er (na skaleczenie)** to put a plaster
over a cut [3] przen. (pociecha) balm przen. [4] (miodu)
(honey)comb

plastik *m* [1] (tworzywo sztuczne) plastic; **kubki z** ~**u**
plastic cups [2] Techn., Wojsk. plastic; **ładunek** ~**u**
a plastic bomb

plastyczn|y [I] *adi. grad.* [1] (dający się modelować)
[materiał] plastic [2] (obrazowy) *[opis, narracja]* vivid
[II] *adi.* [1] Szt. *[dekoracje, prace]* artistic; **szkoła** ~**a**
an art school a. college [2] (wypukły, bryłowaty) *[makieta]*
three-dimensional; **mapa** ~**a** a relief map [3] Med.,
Techn. plastic

plasty|k *m*, ~**czka** *f* (visual) artist

plasty|ka *f* [1] Szt. the fine a. visual arts
[2] (obrazowość) vividness [3] Szkol. arts and crafts;
lekcje ~**ki** art classes

platan *m* Bot. plane (tree)

platform|a *f* [1] Transp. (nadwozie) (loading) platform;
(samochód) lorry GB, truck; (wagon kolejowy) truck GB,
flatcar US; ~**a do przewożenia samochodów**
a car transporter [2] (pomost) platform [3] Techn. ~**a
wiertnicza** a drilling platform; **pracować na** ~**ie
wiertniczej** to work on an oil rig [4] przen. (płaszczyzna) platform; ~**a porozumienia** common
ground [5] pot. (but) platform (shoe); (podeszwa)
platform sole

platfus *m* pot. flat-foot; **mieć** ~**a** to be flat-footed

platyn|a *f* Chem. (metal, pierwiastek) platinum

playback /'plejbek/ *m* playback; **śpiewać z** ~**u**
to mime; **koncert z** ~**u** a pre-recorded concert

plaż|a *f* beach; **dzika** ~**a** a beach without a
lifeguard

plażow|y *adi. [piłka, kosz]* beach; **kostium** ~**y**
a sunsuit

plądr|ować *impf* **[I]** *vt* (rabować) to plunder *[miasto,
teren]*; to ransack *[mieszkanie, szafy]*
[II] *vi* (szukać) to rummage (around)

plą|tać *impf* **[I]** *vt* [1] (motać, suplać) to tangle (up) *[nici,
sznurek]* [2] (mylić) to mix up *[fakty, daty]*
[II] plątać się [1] (motać się, suplać się) *[nici, sznur]* to
get tangled [2] (mylić się, gmatwać się) *[fakty, daty]* to get
mixed up [3] (wikłać się) *[osoba]* to get confused
[4] (przeszkadzać) to get in the way; **pies** ~**tał mu się
pod nogami** the dog was getting under his feet
[5] *[obrazy, uczucia]* **w głowie** ~**tały mi się różne
myśli** various thoughts kept going through my
head [6] (krążyć, kręcić się) to mill around a. about;

~**tać się po domu** to potter around the house
7 (wdawać się, mieszać) to get mixed up (**w coś** in sth)
plątanin|a f 1 (drutu, włosów) tangle; (ulic) maze
2 (chaos) confusion
plebani|a /ple'baɲja/ f presbytery
pleca|k m rucksack GB, (back)pack; ~**k na
stelażu** a frame backpack a. rucksack; **wędrówka
z** ~**kiem** backpacking
plec|y plt 1 Anat. back; **leżeć na** ~**ach** to lie on
one's back; **zarzucić na** ~**y chustkę** to put a scarf
round one's shoulders; **odwrócić się do kogoś**
~**ami** to turn one's back on sb także przen.; **bolą
mnie** ~**y** my back's aching 2 (palta, sukienki) back;
sukienka bez ~**ów** a backless dress 3 (tył szafy,
lustra) back
■ **cios w** ~**y** a stab in the back; **nie mieć** ~**ów**
pot. to have no backing a. support; **robić coś za
czyimiś** ~**ami** to do sth behind sb's back
ple|d m blanket
plemi|ę n (szczep) tribe; ~**ę Zulusów/Siuksów**
the Zulus/Sioux
plemnik m Biol. spermatozoon, sperm
plene|r m 1 (otwarta przestrzeń) the open air; **kręcić
film w** ~**rze** to shoot a film on location; **przyjęcie
w** ~**rze** a fête champêtre; **pojechać w** ~**r** to go to
the country 2 (obraz) plein-air painting; (scena)
outdoor scene 3 Szt. (sesja malarska) plein-air workshop
ple|nić się impf v refl. 1 [rośliny] (rozrastać się) to
spread; (występować w dużych ilościach) to grow rank
2 [myszy, szczury] (rozmnażać się) to proliferate;
(występować w dużych ilościach) to be rampant; **wszędzie** ~**ni się robactwo** there are insects everywhere 3 [korupcja, narkomania] (rozszerzać się) to
spread; (być obecnym) to be rife
pl|eść impf 1 vt to plait [linę, pasek]; to weave
[koszyk, wianek]; **pleść komuś warkocze** to plait
sb's hair; **plecenie koszy** basket weaving
II vi pot. (mówić bez sensu) to drivel (on) pejor. (**o
czymś** about sth); **pleść bzdury** to talk rubbish
III **pleść się** [roślina] to wind (**wokół czegoś**
around sth)
pleśni|eć impf vi [chleb, ser] to go mouldy GB a.
moldy US; [namiot, ubranie] to become mildewed
pleś|ń 1 f (na żywności) mould GB, mold US; (na ścianie,
materiale) mildew
II **pleśnie** plt Bot. mould GB, mold US
plew|a f chaff
■ **nabrać** a. **łapać kogoś na** ~**y** to take sb in;
oddzielić a. **odsiać ziarno od** ~ książk. to separate
the wheat from the chaff
plew|ić impf vt to weed [grządki]
plik m 1 (stos) wad; ~ **dokumentów/banknotów**
a wad of documents/banknotes 2 Komput. file; ~
tekstowy a text file
plis|a f Moda 1 (fałda) pleat; **spódnica w** ~**y** a
pleated skirt 2 (naszyta) (decorative) band

plis|ować impf vt Moda to pleat [materiał]
plisz|ka f Zool. wagtail
plomb|a f 1 Stomat. filling; **założyć** ~**ę** to put in a
filling 2 Budow. infill 3 (pieczęć) (lead) seal
plomb|ować impf vt 1 (zamykać) to seal [drzwi,
pomieszczenia] 2 Stomat. to fill [ząb] 3 Techn. (wypełniać
ubytki) to fill [dziurę, dziuplę] (**czymś** with sth)
plon m 1 (zbiór) crop; (wydajność) yield; **wydać
obfity** ~ to yield a good crop; **dawać wysokie** ~**y**
[ziemia, roślina] to have a high yield 2 przen. fruit;
przynieść ~ to bear fruit
plot|ka f rumour GB, rumor US; ~**ki z życia
wyższych sfer** society gossip; **roznosić** a. **roz-
powiadać** ~**ki o kimś/czymś** to spread rumours
a. gossip about sb/sth; **krążą** a. **chodzą** ~**ki, że...**
rumour has it that...; **spędzać czas na** ~**kach** to
spend one's time gossiping
plotka|rz m, ~**rka** f gossip pejor.
plotk|ować impf vi to gossip (**o kimś/czymś**
about sb/sth)
plu|cha f foul weather; **jesienna** ~**cha** foul
autumn weather
plu|nąć pf — **plu|ć** impf vi to spit; ~**nąć na
podłogę** to spit on the floor; ~**nąć komuś
w twarz** to spit in sb's face także przen.; ~**ć na
kogoś/coś** przen. to not give a damn about sb/sth
pot.; ~**ć krwią** to spit (up) blood
■ ~**ć sobie w brodę** pot. to kick oneself pot.
plus 1 m 1 Mat. plus; **znak** ~ the plus sign 2 Szkol.
(podwyższenie oceny) plus; (oddzielna nagroda) star; **cztery**
~ a. **z** ~**em** ≈ a B plus 3 pot. (dobra strona) plus;
znajomość języka to ogromny ~ knowing the
language is a definite plus; ~**y i minusy życia
w mieście** the advantages and disadvantages of
living in a city
II adi. inv. (dodatni) plus; ~ **cztery** plus four
III coni. plus; **dwa** ~ **dwa równa się cztery** two
plus a. and two is four; **dwa plecaki** ~ **walizka** pot.
two rucksacks plus a suitcase
■ ~ **minus** more or less; **być na** ~**ie** Fin. to be in
the black; **mieć u kogoś** ~ to be in somebody's
good books; **zmienić się na** ~ to change for the
better
pluskać impf → **plusnąć**
pluskiew|ka f pot. drawing pin GB, thumbtack US
plusk|wa f 1 Zool. bedbug 2 pot., obraźl. (osoba) louse
pot., obraźl. 3 pot. (podsłuch) bug; **w mieszkaniu
założono** ~**wy** the room was bugged
plu|snąć pf — **plu|skać** impf 1 vi 1 [woda,
deszcz] to splash; [fale] to wash 2 (uderzyć, upaść
z pluskiem) to splash; **kamień** ~**snął w wodę** the
stone splashed into the water
II **pluskać się** [ludzie, kaczki] to splash (around)
plusz m Włók. plush
pluton[1] m Wojsk. platoon; ~ **piechoty** an infantry
platoon; ~ **egzekucyjny** a firing squad
pluton[2] m Chem. plutonium

płac|a f (wynagrodzenie) pay; **tygodniowa/miesięcz-na** ~**a** weekly wages/a monthly salary; ~**a minimalna** a minimum wage; ~**a zasadnicza** basic pay

płach|ta f sheet; ~**ta foliowa** a plastic sheet; ~**ta namiotowa** a groundsheet

pła|cić impf **[]** vt **[1]** (opłacać) to pay; ~**cić komuś za coś** to pay sb for sth; ~**cić za światło/gaz** to pay for the electricity/gas; ~**cić rachunki** to pay the bills; ~**cić gotówką/kartą/czekiem** to pay in cash/with a credit card/by cheque; **ile** ~**cę?** how much (is that)?; **ja** ~**cę!** it's on me! pot. **[2]** przen. to pay; **to cena, jaką** ~**cimy** a. ~**ci się za postęp techniczny** that's the price we pay for techno-logical progress

[] vi przen. to pay; ~**cić za własne błędy** to pay for one's mistakes

płacz m **[1]** (łzy) crying; **wybuch** ~**u** a flood of tears; **wybuchnąć** ~**em** to burst out crying; **powstrzy-mać się od** ~**u** to choke back a. hold back one's tears; **być bliskim** ~**u** to be on the verge of tears; **skończyć się** ~**em** [zabawa, gra] to end in tears **[2]** przen. (narzekanie) lament; **podnieść** ~ **z powodu czegoś** to start lamenting sth

płaczliw|y adi. grad. **[1]** [dziecko] tearful; weepy pot. **[2]** przen. [głos, ton] tearful; [melodia, pieśń] plaintive; [dźwięk] wailing

pła|kać impf vi **[1]** (wylewać łzy) to cry; to weep książk.; ~**kać z rozpaczy/radości** to cry out of despair/ weep for joy; ~**kać ze wzruszenia** to be moved to tears; ~**kać nad kimś/czymś** to cry over sb/sth; **dziecko** ~**kało za matką** the baby was crying for his/her mother; ~**kać mi się chce na myśl** a. **gdy pomyślę o tym** it makes me want to cry just thinking about it; **sytuacja jest taka, że tylko (u)siąść i** ~**kać** the situation's enough to make you weep **[2]** przen. (narzekać) to whine; to bemoan książk.

płas|ki adi. **[1]** (niewypukły) [powierzchnia, teren, talerz] flat; ~**ki jak stół** as flat as a pancake **[2]** [biust, brzuch] flat; pot. [kobieta] flat-chested **[3]** Moda **buty na** ~**kim obcasie** a. ~**kie buty** flat-heeled shoes; flats US pot. **[4]** Sport [piłka, podanie] through **[5]** (po-wierzchowny) [interpretacja, film] shallow; [dowcip, pochlebstwo] cheap **[6]** Mat. [figura geometryczna] plane

płaskorzeźb|a f Szt. **[1]** (rodzaj rzeźby) bas-relief **[2]** (sztuka rzeźbienia) low relief carving

płaskostopi|e n Med. flat foot; **mieć** ~**e** to be flat-footed

płaskowyż m plateau

płaszcz m **[1]** Moda (over)coat; ~ **przeciwdeszczo-wy** a raincoat **[2]** przen. (pozór) **pod** ~**em czegoś** under cover of sth

■ **powieść** ~**a i szpady** książk. a cloak-and-dagger story

płaszcz|ka f Zool. ray

płaszcz|yć się impf v refl. **[1]** (stawać się płaskim) to be flattened **[2]** (poniżać się) to bow and scrape pejor. (**przed kimś/czymś** to sb/sth)

płaszczy|zna f **[1]** (teren) plain; **porosła trawą** ~**zna** a grassy plain **[2]** (powierzchnia) surface; ~**zna ściany** the surface of a wall **[3]** Mat. plane; **punkty leżące na jednej** ~**źnie** points on the same plane **[4]** (sfera) plane; **znaleźć** ~**znę porozumienia** to find common ground

pła|t m **[1]** (materiału) piece; (papy) sheet; ~**t mięsa** (duży, nieregularny) a cut of meat; (plaster) a slice of meat; ~**ty łososia** salmon fillets; **schodzić** ~**tami** [skóra, farba] to peel off; **tynk odpadał** ~**tami ze ścian** plaster was peeling off the walls **[2]** (ziemi) patch; **gdzieniegdzie leżały** ~**ty śniegu** there were patches of snow here and there; **śnieg padał wielkimi** ~**tami** large snowflakes were falling **[3]** Anat. lobe

płat|ek m **[1]** (kwiatu) petal; ~**ki róży** rose petals **[2]** (ściślek materiału) scrap; ~**ek gazy** a layer of gauze **[3]** (kawałeczek) flake; (mięsa, wędliny) slice; ~**ki kukurydziane** cornflakes; ~**ki owsiane** porridge oats; ~**ki mydlane** soap flakes **[4]** (śniegu) flake; ~**ki śniegu** snowflakes

■ **pójść jak z** ~**ka** pot. to run like clockwork

płatnicz|y adi. **bilans** ~**y** the balance of pay-ments; **zobowiązanie** ~**e** a financial obligation

płatni|k m **[1]** (płacący należności) payer; ~**cy podatków** taxpayers **[2]** (wypłacający pieniądze) pay-master

płatnoś|ć f **[1]** (płacenie należności) payment; ~**ć gotówką** a cash payment **[2]** (należność) liability

płatn|y adi. **[1]** (otrzymujący wynagrodzenie) [informator, pracownik] paid; ~**y zabójca** a contract killer **[2]** (opłacany) [praca, usługa, urlop, wstęp] paid **[3]** (do zapłacenia) payable; ~**e gotówką** payable in cash; ~**e z góry** payable a. paid in advance; ~**e w ratach** payable in instalments; ~**e do końca miesiąca** due by the end of the month

płaz m amphibian

płciow|y adi. [cechy, organ, stosunek] sexual; [akt, popęd] sex; **choroby przenoszone drogą** ~**ą** sexually transmitted diseases; **dojrzałość** ~**a** sexual maturity

pł|eć f **[1]** (różnica) gender; **nierówne traktowanie** a. **dyskryminacja ze względu na płeć** gender bias a. discrimination; **zmiana płci** a sex change **[2]** (osoby) sex; **płeć męska/żeńska** the male/female sex; **płeć odmienna** a. **przeciwna** the other a. opposite sex; **słaba płeć** the weaker sex; **płeć brzydka** żart. the sterner sex

płetw|a f **[1]** Zool. fin; ~**a grzbietowa** a dorsal fin **[2]** Sport flipper

płetwonur|ek m (nurkujący bez kombinezonu) skin diver; (nurkujący w kombinezonie) frogman; (nurkujący z akwalungiem) scuba diver

płochliw|y adi. grad. [osoba, spojrzenie] timid

płodn|y *adi. grad.* [1] (zdolny do rozrodu) *[kobieta, samica]* fertile; **dni** ~**e** fertile days [2] (dający obfite plony) *[roślina]* prolific; *[gleba, ziemia]* fertile; fecund książk. [3] (tworzący wiele dzieł) *[pisarz, muzyk]* prolific; ~**a wyobraźnia** a fertile imagination

pł|odzić *impf vt* [1] książk. *[mężczyzna]* to father *[syna, córkę]*; *[mężczyzna i kobieta]* to produce *[dzieci, potomstwo]*; *[samiec]* to sire *[młode, potomstwo]* [2] przen., żart. to produce *[artykuły, wiersze]*

płomienn|y *adi.* [1] (żarliwy) *[bojownik]* ardent; *[kazanie]* fiery [2] (namiętny) *[miłość]* ardent; *[pocału- nek, spojrzenie]* passionate [3] (koloru ognia) flaming

płomie|ń *m* [1] (język ognia) flame [2] (żywioł) **morze** ~**ni** a sea of flames; **stanąć w** ~**niach** to burst into flames; ~**nie strawiły cały ich dobytek** everything they had went up in flames [3] książk. (silne uczucie) flame; ~**ń namiętności** a flame of passion [4] (dramatyczne wydarzenia) ~**nie wojny** the flames of war

pło|nąć *impf vi* [1] (palić się) *[dom, las, miasto, statek]* to be on fire; *[świeca, węgiel, ognisko]* to burn; **stodoła** ~**nęła jak pochodnia** the barn was ablaze [2] *[głowa, policzki]* to burn [3] przen. (doznawać intensywnych uczuć) ~**nąć ciekawością/gniewem** to be burning with curiosity/rage; ~**nąć miłością** a. **uczuciem ku komuś** to be burning with love for sb

płosz|yć *impf* **[]** *vt* [1] (budzić popłoch) to frighten away [2] (wprawiać w zakłopotanie) to disconcert [3] książk. przen. to interrupt *[myśli, ciszę]*

[]] płoszyć się [1] (wpadać w popłoch) to take fright [2] (odczuwać zakłopotanie) to feel disconcerted

pło|t *m* fence; ~**t z desek** a wooden fence; **odgrodzić teren** ~**tem** to fence off an area

płot|ek *m* Sport hurdle; **bieg przez** ~**ki** the hurdles

płot|ka *f* [1] Zool. roach [2] przen. small fry

płotka|rz *m*, ~**rka** *f* Sport hurdler

płowi|eć *impf vi* [1] (blaknąć) to fade [2] (żółknąć) *[trawa, zboże]* to turn yellow

pł|oza *f* [1] (sań) runner; (samolotu) skid [2] (ślizg narty) bottom face; (stalowa część łyżwy) runner

płócienn|y *adi. [bielizna, koszula, obrus]* linen; *[torba]* cloth; *[worek]* canvas; **książka w** ~**ej oprawie** a cloth-bound book

pł|ód [] *m* [1] Med. f(o)etus [2] książk., iron., żart. product; **płody wyobraźni** products of the imagination; **płody ludzkiej pracy** the fruits of human labour **[]] płody** *plt* (bogactwa natury) fruits; **płody rolne** agricultural produce; **płody ziemi** the fruits of the earth

płó|tno *n* [1] (tkanina bieliźniana) linen; (na żagle, namioty) canvas; **obrus z lnianego** ~**tna** a linen tablecloth; **twarz blada** a. **biała jak** ~**tno** a face as white as a sheet [2] Szt. (obraz) canvas

płuc|o *n* [1] Anat. lung; **rak** ~ lung cancer; **zapalenie** ~ pneumonia; **zrywać sobie** ~**a** to

shout at the top of one's voice a. lungs [2] przen. **zielone** ~**a** lungs przen.

pług *m* [1] Roln. plough GB, plow US; **chodzić za** ~**iem** to plough [2] Aut. (do odśnieżania) snowplough GB, snowplow US [3] Sport snowplough GB, snow- plow US

płu|kać *impf vt* to rinse *[bieliznę, naczynia, warzy- wa, włosy]*; ~**kać gardło** to gargle

płukan|ka *f* [1] (płyn) (do włosów) rinse; (do ust) mouthwash [2] (płukanie) rinse

płyn *m* [1] (ciecz) liquid; ~ **do mycia naczyń/ płukania tkanin** a dishwashing liquid/fabric conditioner; ~ **do płukania ust** mouthwash; ~ **przeciw komarom** mosquito repellent; ~ **ha- mulcowy** Aut. brake fluid; ~**y ustrojowe** Med. bodily fluids [2] Fiz. (ciecz lub gaz) fluid

pły|nąć *impf vi* [1] *[osoba, zwierzę]* to swim; ~**nąć żabką/kraulem/na wznak** to do the breast stroke/ the crawl/the backstroke [2] (być przewożonym) *[osoba]* ~**nąć łodzią** to go by boat; ~**nąć tratwą** to float on a raft [3] *[łódź, statek]* to sail [4] *[rzeka, płyn, gaz]* to flow; **krew** ~**nęła z rany** blood ran a. flowed from the wound [5] *[obłoki, księżyc]* to float [6] *[dźwięk, ciepło, zapach]* (docierać) to float [7] *[czas, życie]* to go by [8] (wynikać) *[wniosek]* to emerge; **jaka stąd** ~**nie nauka?** what lesson can we learn from this?

płynn|y [] *adi. grad. [ruch, granice, sytuacja]* fluid; *[montaż, wymiana]* smooth; *[czytanie, mówienie]* fluent; *[wiersz, styl]* flowing; *[kontur, linia]* smooth **[]] adi. *[mydło, paliwo]* liquid; *[metal, szkło]* molten

pły|ta *f* [1] (metalu) sheet; (plastiku, szkła) plate; (drewna) board; (kamienia) slab; ~**ty chodnikowe** flagstones, paving; ~**ta pilśniowa/wiórowa** hardboard/chip- board; **domy z wielkiej** ~**ty** houses built of prefabricated concrete [2] (blacha) plate; ~**ta kuchenna** a hotplate; **rozpalić ogień pod** ~**tą** to light a fire in the stove [3] Muz. (zapis dźwięku) record; ~**ta gramofonowa** a gramophone record; ~**ta kompaktowa** a compact disc; **nastawić** a. **puścić** ~**tę** to put on a record; **zmień** ~**tę** pot., przen. change the record; **złota** ~**ta** a gold disc [4] (teren) surface; ~**ta boiska/stadionu** the field; ~**ta lotniska** the apron (area) [5] (rodzaj pomnika) plaque; ~**ta pamiątkowa** a commemorative plaque; ~**ta nagrobkowa** a tombstone [6] (element konstrukcyjny urządzenia) board; ~**ta główna kompu- tera** the motherboard

płyt|ka *f* [1] (metalu, plastiku, szkła) tile; ~**ki pod- łogowe/ścienne** floor/wall tiles [2] (część maszynki elektrycznej) hotplate [3] Biol. ~**ki krwi** platelets

płyt|ki *adi. grad.* [1] *[rzeka, dół]* shallow; ~**kie pantofle** low-cut shoes; ~**ki sen** light sleep [2] pejor. *[film, sąd, utwór]* superficial pejor.

pływa|ć *impf vi* [1] *[osoba, zwierzę]* to swim; **lekcja** ~**nia** a swimming lesson [2] *[statek]* to sail [3] (unosić się) to float; *[korek, oliwa]* to float [4] (być zatrudnionym na statku) to serve; ~**ł na wielu statkach** he served on many ships

pływa|k *m* [1] Sport swimmer [2] Zool. diving beetle [3] Lotn., Ryboł., Techn. (pława) float [4] Żegl. buoy

pływalni|a *f* swimming pool; ~**a kryta/otwarta** an indoor/open-air swimming pool; **pójść na** ~**ę** to go swimming

pnącz|e *n* creeper

pniak *m* [1] (część drzewa pozostała po ścięciu) stump [2] (część pnia ściętego drzewa) block; ~ **do rąbania drzewa** a chopping block

po *praep.* [1] (później niż) after; **po śniadaniu/wojnie** after breakfast/the war; **po godzinie** an hour later; **po południu** in the afternoon; **pięć po czwartej** five past four; **po ukończeniu studiów** after a. on graduating; **po czym** after which; **pięć dni po czasie** five days late; **po pięćdziesiątce musisz zacząć dbać o siebie** when you're over fifty you need to take care of yourself [2] (w przestrzeni) **po całym mieście/kraju/domu** all over (the) town/ the country/the house; **ubrania porozrzucane po pokoju** clothes scattered around the room; **porozlewać wodę po podłodze** to spill water all over the floor; **biegać po sklepach** to run round the shops pot.; **chodzić po korytarzu** to walk up and down the corridor; **chodzić po lesie** to walk in the forest [3] (na powierzchni) (na) on; (wzdłuż) along; **jechać na rowerze po ścieżce** to cycle along a. on a path; **wchodzić po schodach** to walk up the stairs; **zjeżdżać po poręczy** to slide down the banisters; **przechodzić przez jezdnię po pasach** to cross the street at a zebra crossing; **głaskać kogoś po włosach** to stroke sb's hair [4] (o stronie) on; **po drugiej stronie ulicy** on the other side of the street; **po prawej stronie drogi** to the right of the road; **po wierzchu** on top [5] (do górnej granicy) (przestrzennej) (up/down) to; (czasowej) up to; **od Bałkanów po Skandynawię** from the Balkans up to Scandinavia; **po szyję** up to the neck; **woda była po po kolana** the water was knee-deep; **talerz pełen po brzegi** a plate full to the brim; **od profesora po sekretarkę** from the professor down to the secretary [6] (w kolejności) after; **jeden po drugim** one after the other a. another; **dzień po dniu** day after day; **krok po kroku** step by step; **nosić imię po dziadku** to be named after one's grandfather; **odziedziczyć coś po kimś** to inherit sth from sb [7] (następstwo) (sprzątać, zmywać) after (kimś sb); **obiecywać sobie coś** a. **oczekiwać czegoś po kimś/czymś** to expect sth from sb/sth; **butelka po mleku** a milk bottle [8] (na podstawie) by; **poznać kogoś po głosie** to recognize sb by their voice; **widać po twoich oczach, że...** I can see a. tell by your eyes that...; **sądząc po akcencie, (on) pochodzi z Dublina** judging by a. from his accent, he comes from Dublin [9] (cel) for; **zadzwonić po lekarza** to phone for the doctor; **pójść do sklepu**

po chleb to go to the shop for some bread; **po to, aby...** (in order) to...; **po co** what for?; **po co ci to?** what do you need that for?; **nic tu po mnie** I'm not needed here [10] (ilościowo) **po trzy z każdej strony** three on each side; **po 2 złote za sztukę** (at) 2 zlotys each a. apiece; **po ile te pomidory?** how much are these tomatoes?; **wchodziły po jednej** they went in one by one a. one at a time; **podchodzić po dwóch** to come up in twos; **dostali po dwa jabłka** they each got two apples [11] (w wyrażeniach przysłówkowych) **po ojcowsku** like a father; **zrób to po swojemu** do it your own way ■ **to nie miejsce i czas po temu** this is not the (right) time or place for it; **mam po temu powody** I have my reasons

pobi|ć *pf* **I** *vt* [1] (poturbować) to beat up; ~**li go do nieprzytomności** he was beaten unconscious [2] (zwyciężyć) to defeat; ~**ć nieprzyjaciela** a. **wroga** to defeat the enemy; ~**ć rekord** to beat a. break a record; ~**ć kogoś jego własną bronią** to beat sb at their own game
II pobić się to have a fight

pobie|c, **pobie|gnąć** *pf vi* [1] (osoba) to run; ~**c do sklepu** to run to the shop; ~**c w biegu na 100 metrów** to run in the 100 metres (race) [2] (droga, linia kolejowa) to run [3] (skierować się) **nasze myśli** ~**gły ku przyszłości** our thoughts turned to the future; ~**gła wzrokiem** a. **jej wzrok** ~**gł ku matce** she directed her gaze to her mother

pobieżn|y *adi. grad.* książk. [analiza, obserwacja, ocena] superficial; **już z** ~**ej lektury wynika, że...** even a cursory reading reveals that...

poblis|ki *adi.* [budynek, teren] nearby

pobłaża|ć *impf vi* ~**ć komuś** to be tolerant towards sb; ~**ć czyimś wybrykom** to turn a blind eye to sb's excesses; ~**ć czyjemuś lenistwu** to tolerate sb's laziness

pobłażliw|y *adi.* [uśmiech, wzrok] forgiving; [osoba] lenient; **być** ~**ym wobec kogoś** to be lenient towards a. with sb

pobłogosław|ić *pf* **I** *vt* [1] (udzielić błogosławieństwa) [kapłan] to bless [2] (zaaprobować) to give one's blessing to [plan, zamiar]
II *vi* [Bóg] to bless; ~**ić komuś** to bless sb

pobocz|e *n* (hard) shoulder; **na** ~**u** on the (hard) shoulder; **zjechać na** ~**e** to pull over

poborc|a *m* collector

poborow|y I *adi.* [karta, komisja] conscription GB, draft US
II *m* national serviceman

pobożn|y *adi. grad.* [rodzina, życie] devout; [bractwo] religious; [rozmyślania, hymn] pious

pob|ór **I** *m* [1] Wojsk. conscription; **obowiązkowy** ~**ór do wojska** conscription, the draft US [2] (czerpanie) drawing; (zużycie) consumption; ~**ór mocy** power consumption [3] (podatków, ceł) collection
II pobory *plt* książk. salary

pob|rać *pf* — **pob|ierać** *impf* **[]** *vt* [] książk. (wziąć) to charge *[opłatę, prowizję]*; to receive *[pensję, emeryturę]*; ~**rać pieniądze z konta** to withdraw a. draw money from an account; **prowiant prosimy** ~**ierać w stołówce** please pick up your lunch bags in the canteen [2] (czerpać) *[roślina, korzenie]* to take up; *[urządzenie]* to draw *[energię]*; **urządzenie** ~**iera zbyt dużo prądu** the device uses too much electricity [3] (do badań, przeszczepu) to take *[próbkę]*; **miałem** ~**ieraną krew** I had a blood sample taken

[] **pobrać się** — **pobierać się** to get married (**z kimś** to sb)

pobru|dzić *pf* **[]** *vt* to soil; (poplamić) to stain; (wysmarować) to smear; ~**dzić sobie ubranie** to soil a. dirty one's clothes; ~**dzić coś tłuszczem** to smear sth with grease; ~**dzić coś błotem** to get sth muddy

[] **pobrudzić się** to get dirty; ~**dzić się błotem** to get muddy; ~**dzić się na twarzy** to get one's face dirty

pobud|ka *f* [] (sygnał) reveille; **zagrać** ~**kę** to sound the reveille; ~**ka jest o szóstej** the wake-up time is at 6 a.m.; ~**ka!** rise and shine! pot. [2] książk. (powód) reason; (bodziec) incentive

pobudliw|y *adi. [osoba]* excitable

pobu|dzić *pf* — **pobu|dzać** *impf vt* [] (zwiększyć) to stimulate *[zainteresowanie, apetyt]*; ~**dzać czyjąś aktywność umysłową** to stimulate sb intellectually; **opisy** ~**dzające wyobraźnię** descriptions that fire the imagination [2] (zmobilizować) to prompt *[osobę]* [3] *[alkohol]* to stimulate; **kawa** ~**dza (organizm)** coffee is a stimulant; **być (nadmiernie)** ~**dzonym** to be (over-)excited [4] (seksualnie) to arouse

poby|t *m* stay; ~**t w szpitalu** a stay in hospital; **czyjeś miejsce** ~**tu** sb's whereabouts; (adres) sb's place of abode książk.; **zameldować się na** ~**t stały** to register for permanent residence

pocał|ować *pf vt* to kiss; ~**ować kogoś w usta** to kiss sb on the lips; ~**ować kogoś na dobranoc** to kiss sb goodnight; ~**uj mamusię!** give mummy a kiss!

■ **zrobi to z** ~**owaniem ręki** he'll be delighted to do it; ~**uj mnie w dupę** a. **gdzieś!** posp. kiss my arse GB a. ass US! posp.

pocałun|ek *m* kiss; ~**ek w policzek** a kiss on the cheek; **oddać** ~**ek** to return a kiss; **okryć** a. **obsypać kogoś** ~**kami** książk. to smother sb with kisses; **przesłać komuś** ~**ek** to blow sb a kiss

pochlebc|a *m* flatterer; sycophant książk., pejor.

pochleb|ić *pf* — **pochleb|iać** *impf vi* to flatter; ~**iać czyjejś próżności** to flatter sb's vanity; ~**iam sobie, że...** I flatter myself that...; ~**ia mi, że...** I'm flattered that...

pochlebstw|o *n* flattery

pochł|onąć *pf* — **pochł|aniać** *impf vt* [] (zniszczyć) *[wojna, katastrofa]* to claim *[ofiary]*; *[ogień]* to consume [2] (zużyć) to eat up *[pieniądze]*; to take *[czas, siły]* [3] (zaabsorbować) to absorb; ~**aniać czyjąś uwagę** to absorb sb's attention; **być** ~**oniętym pracą** to be absorbed a. engrossed in one's work [4] (wessać) *[lodowiec, morze]* to engulf [5] (zjeść) to devour *[posiłek]* [6] (przeczytać) to devour [7] (wciągnąć) to absorb *[kurz, zapach, dźwięk]*

pochmurn|y *adi. grad.* [] Meteo. *[niebo, dzień]* cloudy [2] (posępny) *[osoba, milczenie]* gloomy

pochodni|a *f* torch

pochodn|y **[]** *adi. [forma, produkt]* derivative; **kolory** ~**e** Szt. secondary colours

[] **pochodna** *f* [] (konsekwencja) consequence; (odbicie) reflection [2] Chem., Mat. derivative

pochodzeni|e *n* [] (społeczne) background; **był chłopem z** ~**a** he came from peasant stock [2] (narodowe) descent; **osoba polskiego** ~**a** a person of Polish descent a. origin; **był z** ~**a Niemcem** he was a) German by descent [3] (miejsce, sposób powstania) origin; **kraj** ~**a** country of origin; **skały** ~**a wulkanicznego** rocks of volcanic origin

pocho|dzić *impf vi* [] (wywodzić się) *[osoba]* to come (**z czegoś** from sth); ~**dzić z rodziny robotniczej** to come from a working-class family; **człowiek** ~**dzi od małpy** humans are descended from apes [2] (mieć źródło) *[słowo]* to derive (**od czegoś** from sth); *[ból]* to originate (**z czegoś** in sth); ~**dzić z XV wieku** to date from a. back to the 15th century; **informacja** ~**dzi z pewnego źródła** the information comes from a reliable source

pochopn|y *adi. grad. [decyzja]* hasty; *[osoba]* rash

pochowa|ć *pf* **[]** *vt* [] (pogrzebać) to bury [2] (ukryć) hide; (powkładać) to put away; ~**ć talerze do szafki** to put the plates away in the cupboard; **domy** ~**ne między drzewami** houses hidden among the trees

[] **pochować się** [] (ukryć się) *[osoby]* to hide [2] (zniknąć) *[chmury]* to disappear

poch|ód *m* [] (demonstracja) march; ~**ód pierwszomajowy** a May Day parade [2] (maszerujący ludzie) procession; **zamykać** ~**ód** to bring up the rear of a procession [3] książk. (posuwanie się) march

poch|wa *f* [] Anat. vagina [2] (pokrowiec) scabbard; **schować szablę do** ~**wy** to sheathe one's sword

pochwal|ić¹ *pf* — **pochwal|ać** *impf vt* to approve; ~**ać kogoś/coś** to approve of sb/sth

pochwal|ić² *pf* **[]** *vt* to praise; ~**ić kogoś za coś** to praise sb/sth for sth; **niech będzie** ~**ony (Jezus Chrystus)!** praise be to God!; ~**ony!** Praise the Lord!

[] **pochwalić się** [] (powiedzieć) ~**iła mi się, że...** she proudly told me that... [2] (popisać się) to show off; (chlubić się) to boast; ~**ić się czymś przed kimś** to show sth off to sb

pochwa|ła *f* praise; (oficjalna) commendation; **obsypywać kogoś** ~**łami** to heap praise(s) on sb; **otrzymywać** a. **zbierać same** ~**ły** to receive nothing but praise; **godny** ~**ły** commendable

pochyl|ić *pf* — **pochyl|ać** *impf* **[]** *vt* **[1]** (opuścić) to lower; (z szacunkiem) to bow *[głowę]*; to dip *[sztandar]*; **stać z** ~**oną głową** to stand with head bowed a. bent; ~**ić głowę przed kimś/czymś** przen. to take one's hat off to sb/sth przen.; **byli** ~**eni nad mapą** they were bent a. leaning over a map **[2]** (przekrzywić) to bend *[słup, drzewo]*

[] **pochylić się** — **pochylać się** **[1]** (zgiąć się) to bend; ~**ić się do przodu** to bend forward; ~**ić się nad kimś/czymś** to bend a. lean over sb/sth **[2]** (przekrzywić się) to tilt

pochy|ły *adi.* sloping

po|ciąć *pf* **[]** *vt* **[1]** (podzielić) to cut; **pociąć coś na kawałki** to cut sth up; **pociąć coś na plasterki** to slice sth (up); **pociąć coś na paski** to cut sth into strips **[2]** (rozciąć) to slash *[obraz]*; (porysować) to scratch *[blat]*, **czoło pocięte zmarszczkami** przen. a brow furrowed with wrinkles **[3]** pot. *[komary, mrówki]* to bite; *[osy]* to sting; *[mole]* to eat

[] **pociąć się** pot. to slash each other

pociąg *m* **[1]** Kolej. train; ~ **do Krakowa** the train to Cracow; **w** ~**u** on a. in the train; **wsiąść do/ wysiąść z** ~**u** to get on/off a train; **podróżować** ~**iem** to travel by train; **pojechać** ~**iem do Paryża** to take a train to Paris; **przyjechać** ~**iem o piątej** to arrive on the five o'clock train **[2]** (skłonność) fondness (**do kogoś/czegoś** for sb/ sth); ~ **seksualny** sexual attraction; **mieć** ~ **do wódki** to be fond of a drink

pociągać *impf* → **pociągnąć**[1]

pociągając|y *adi.* **[1]** (atrakcyjny) *[uśmiech, wygląd]* appealing **[2]** (erotycznie) *[osoba]* desirable

pociąg|ły *adi. [twarz]* elongated

pociąg|nąć[1] *pf* — **pociąg|ać** *impf vt* **[1]** (szarpnąć) to pull; ~**nąć kogoś za rękaw** to pull sb's sleeve **[2]** (nęcić) to draw; (wydawać się atrakcyjnym) to attract; **nie** ~**a mnie polityka** I don't feel drawn to politics; **ona go** ~**a** he feels attracted to her; ~**a go przygoda** he longs for adventure **[3]** (spowodować) to entail; ~**nąć za sobą poważne skutki** to entail serious consequences; ~**nąć za sobą spore straty** to entail a. result in considerable losses **[4]** (przesunąć) to draw; ~**nąć ręką po twarzy** to draw one's hand across one's face; ~**nąć smyczkiem po strunach** to draw a bow across the strings **[5]** (pokryć) to cover; ~**nąć coś warstwą farby** to go over sth with a coat of paint **[6]** (zachęcić) ~**nęła za sobą wielu ludzi** she had a large following **[7]** pot. (wypić) to take a sip of; ~**nąć wódki** to knock back some vodka pot.

■ ~**nąć kogoś do odpowiedzialności** to bring sb to justice

pociągn|ąć[2] *pf* **[]** *vt* **[1]** (w terenie) to run *[linię kolejową, rurociąg]*; ~**ąć drogę wzdłuż rzeki** to build a road along a river **[2]** (kontynuować) to carry on

with; ~**ąć sprawę do przodu** pot. to push an issue forward

[] *vi* **[1]** (przemieścić się) to head; **od rzeki** ~**ęło chłodem** there was a cool breeze off the river **[2]** pot. (pożyć) **on już długo nie** ~**ie** he won't be around much longer pot.

pociągow|y *adi. [zwierzę]* draught; *[siła]* tractive; **koń** ~**y** a carthorse

po|cić się *impf v refl.* **[1]** (z gorąca, wysiłku) to sweat; to perspire książk.; **pocić się ze strachu** to sweat with fear; **pocę się w tym swetrze** this pullover makes me sweat **[2]** (męczyć się) to sweat (**nad czymś** over sth) **[3]** pot. *[szyba, okulary]* to mist over a. up

pocie|cha *f* **[1]** (pocieszenie) solace; **słowa** ~**chy** words of comfort; **szukać** ~**chy w czymś/u kogoś** to seek solace in sth/from sb; **znajdować** ~**chę w czymś** to find solace in sth; **to marna** ~**cha, że...** (it's) cold comfort that...; **miała z niego** ~**chę** pot. (oparcie) he was a great comfort to her; (pomoc) he was a great help to her **[2]** pot. (dziecko) kiddie pot.

pocierać *impf* → **potrzeć**

pociesz|yć *pf* — **pociesz|ać** *impf* **[]** *vt* to comfort, to console; ~**yło mnie, że...** I found it consoling a. comforting that...; **jeżeli cię to** ~**y...** if it's any comfort (to you)...

[] **pocieszyć się** — **pocieszać się** to console oneself

pocisk *m* missile; (artyleryjski) shell; (z pistoletu, karabinu) bullet; ~ **przeciwpancerny** an anti-tank shell; ~ **zapalający** an incendiary bomb

począt|ek **[]** *m* beginning; **już na samym** ~**ku** a. **zaraz na** ~**ku** at the very beginning; **od** ~**ku do końca** from beginning to end; **od** ~**ku świata** since the beginning of time; **zacząć od** ~**ku** to start from the beginning; **brać** ~**ek od** a. **z czegoś** to have its beginnings a. origin in sth; **zrobić dobry** ~**ek** to make a good start; **na** a. **z** ~**ku** at first; **na** ~**ek zastanówmy się, czy...** to begin with, let's consider whether...

[] **początki** *plt* **[1]** (pierwszy okres) beginnings; ~**ki kina** the early days of cinema; ~**ki choroby** the early stages of a disease **[2]** (podstawy) basics

początkow|y *adi. [sukcesy]* initial; *[rozdziały]* early

początkując|y **[]** *adi. [kierowca]* novice

[] **początkując|y** *m*, ~**a** *f* beginner; **kurs dla** ~**ych** a beginners' course

poczciw|y *adi. grad. [osoba, twarz]* good-natured; ~**y Robert!** good old Robert!

poczeka|ć *pf vi* to wait (**na kogoś/coś** for sb/sth); ~**jmy do jutra** let's wait till tomorrow; ~**jcie, nie wszyscy naraz!** hold on, one at a time!; ~**j no, jeszcze cię dopadnę** pot. just wait till I get my hands on you! pot.; ~**j, jeszcze się przekonasz!** pot. just you wait and see! pot.

poczekalni|a *f* waiting room

poczerwieni|eć *pf vi* ① *[niebo, oczy]* to redden; *[nos, uszy]* to go red (**od czegoś** with sth); *[jabłka]* to turn red ② (zarumienić się) to redden; ~**eć jak burak** to turn as red as a beetroot

poczęst|ować *pf* **II** *vt* ① (dać) to offer (**kogoś czymś** sb sth); to treat (**kogoś czymś** sb to sth); ~**ować kogoś herbatą** to offer sb tea; ~**ować kogoś obiadem** to give sb dinner ② (potraktować) ~**ować kogoś wrogim spojrzeniem** to give sb a hostile look; ~**ować kogoś wyzwiskami** to heap a. shower abuse on sb

II poczęstować się to help oneself (**czymś** to sth)

poczęstun|ek *m* (małe przyjęcie) snack; (jedzenie) snacks

pocz|ta *f* ① (usługa) mail, post GB; (instytucja) postal service; ~**ta lądowa/lotnicza** surface mail/airmail; **wysłać coś** ~**tą** to send sth by post; **otrzymać coś** ~**tą** to receive sth through the post; **odpisać odwrotną** ~**tą** to reply by return (of post) ② (placówka) post office; **pójść na** ~**tę** to go to the post office; **pracować na** ~**cie** to work at the post office ③ (korespondencja) post GB, mail; **czy jest dla mnie jakaś** ~**ta** is there any post a. mail for me? ④ Komput. mail; ~**ta elektroniczna** (electronic) mail; **sprawdzić** ~**tę** to check one's mail

■ ~**ta pantoflowa** the grapevine pot.

pocztow|y *adi.* *[usługi]* postal; *[znaczek]* postage; *[pociąg]* mail; **przekaz** ~**y** ≈ a postal order; **worek** ~**y** a mailbag; **wolny od opłaty** ~**ej** post-free GB

pocztów|ka *f* postcard

poczuci|e *n* ① (odczucie) feeling; ~**e bezpieczeństwa** a feeling of security; **dręczy go** ~**e winy** he's tormented with guilt; **żyć z** ~**em ciągłego zagrożenia** to live in constant fear; **mam** ~**e, że jestem potrzebny** I feel needed ② (świadomość) sense; ~**e taktu** a sense of tact; **zrobić coś z** ~**a obowiązku** to do sth out of a sense of duty; **stracić** ~**e rzeczywistości** to lose one's sense of reality; **stracić** ~**e czasu** to lose all track of time; **mieć** ~**e humoru** to have a sense of humour

poczu|ć *pf* **II** *vt* ① (zmysłami) to feel; (węchem) to smell ② (doświadczyć) to feel; ~**ć radość/ulgę** to feel happy/relieved; ~**ł, że jest głodny** he felt hungry; ~**ła na sobie czyjś wzrok** she felt someone's eyes on her

II poczuć się to feel; ~**ć się niezręcznie** to feel ill at ease; ~**łem się bezradny** I felt helpless; ~**ć się w obowiązku coś zrobić** to feel obliged to do sth; ~**ł się artystą** he came to think of himself as an artist

poczytalnoś|ć *f* sanity

pod *praep.* ① (poniżej) under(neath); ~ **parasolem** under an umbrella; ~ **powierzchnią** below a. under(neath) the surface; **mieszkanie** ~**e mną** the flat below a. beneath mine; **włóż jakiś sweter** ~ **płaszcz** put a jumper on under your coat; **zginął** ~ **kołami ciężarówki** he died under the

wheels of a lorry; **jego córka wpadła** ~ **samochód** his daughter was run over a. hit by a car; **złożyć podpis** ~ **petycją** to sign a petition ② (obok) by; (z nazwą geograficzną) near; ~ **ścianą** by the wall; ~ **samym szczytem** just below a. right beneath the summit; ~ **basztą** at the foot of the tower; ~ **lasem** at the edge of the forest; **spotkajmy się** ~ **kinem** let's meet outside the cinema; **podwiózł mnie** ~ **dom** he drove me home; **podkradł się** ~ **bramę** he crept up to the gate; **miejscowość** ~ **Krakowem** a place near Cracow ③ (przeciwnie do) against; ~ **wiatr** against the wind; ~ **światło** against the light; **patrzeć na coś** ~ **słońce** to look at sth with the sun in one's eyes; **zrobić zdjęcie** ~ **słońce** to take a photo against the sun; ~ **górę** uphill; ~ **prąd** upstream; **płynąć** ~ **prąd** to go against the current także przen. ④ (wskazując podporządkowanie) under; ~ **czyimś dowództwem** under sb's command; ~ **eskortą policji** under police escort; **tereny** (znajdujące się) ~ **okupacją niemiecką** areas under German occupation; **uczniowie** ~ **moją opieką** pupils in my care; **poddać coś** ~ **głosowanie** to put sth to the vote ⑤ (wskazując na okoliczności) under; ~ **narkozą** under a general anaesthetic; ~ **moją nieobecność** in my absence; ~ (czyjąś) **presją** under pressure (from sb); ~ **przymusem** under duress a. coercion książk.; ~ **wpływem kogoś/czegoś** under the influence of sb/sth; ~ **pretekstem czegoś** under a. on the pretext of sth; **ugiąć się** ~ **ciężarem czegoś** to buckle under the weight of sth także przen.; **zeznawać** ~ **przysięgą** to testify under a. on GB oath; **znaleźć się** ~ **obstrzałem wroga** to come under enemy fire; **został aresztowany** ~ **zarzutem kradzieży** he was arrested on a theft charge a. on a charge of theft ⑥ (wskazując na konsekwencje) under; ~ **groźbą eksmisji** under threat of eviction; ~ **karą grzywny** under a. on penalty of a fine; ~ **karą śmierci** under a. on penalty of death; ~ **odpowiedzialnością karną** under penalty of law ⑦ (z nazwą, tytułem) under; ~ **pseudonimem** under a pseudonym; ~ **nazwiskiem panieńskim** under her maiden name; **wiersz** ~ **tytułem „Kot"** a poem entitled 'Cat'; **operacja** ~ **kryptonimem „Arka Noego"** an operation code-named a. under the code name 'Noah's Ark'; **kościół** ~ **wezwaniem św. Augustyna** a church dedicated to a. under the patronage of St Augustine; **urodzić się** ~ **znakiem Lwa/Raka** to be born under the sign of Leo/Cancer; **co rozumiesz** ~ **pojęciem feminizmu?** what do you understand by the concept of feminism? ⑧ (z adresem, numerem) at; **mieścić się** ~ **numerem piątym** to be located at number five; **zanieś te bagaże** ~ **ósemkę** take this luggage to (room) number eight; **więcej informacji uzyskać można** ~ **numerem 913** to find out more ring a. dial 913; **zostaw dla mnie wiadomość ~ tym numerem** leave a message for me at this number ⑨ (wskazując na dopasowanie) **kapelusz ~ kolor płaszcza** a hat to match the colour of the coat; **podkładać słowa ~ melodię** to put words to some music ⑩ (w stylu) in the style of; **obrazy malowane ~ Picassa** pictures in the style a. in imitation of Picasso; **napisał wypracowanie ~ swoją polonistkę** he wrote his essay the way his Polish teacher would like it ⑪ (blisko) towards, toward US; **~ wieczór** towards (the) evening; **~ koniec wieku** towards the end of the century; **mieć ~ pięćdziesiątkę** to be getting on for a. approaching fifty ⑫ (z okazji) to; **~ nasze spotkanie!** here's to our little get-together! pot.

poda|ć pf — **poda|wać** impf **[]** vt ① (wręczyć) to hand; (podsunąć) to pass; **~ć komuś długopis** to hand sb a pen; **~ć komuś płaszcz** (pomóc włożyć) to help sb into his/her coat; **~ć komuś krzesło** to give sb a chair; **~ć komuś rękę** (wyciągnąć) to hold out one's hand to sb; (uścisnąć) to shake sb's hand; przen. to reach out to sb; **~li sobie ręce** they shook hands; **~ł jej ramię** he offered her his arm; **czy mógłbyś mi ~ć sól?** could you pass me the salt, please? ② (zaserwować) to serve [obiad, potrawę]; **~ć do stołu** to wait on a. at table; **~no do stołu!** dinner is served! ③ (zakomunikować) to give [adres, przykład]; to provide [wiadomości, dane]; **~ć poprawną odpowiedź** to give the right answer; **~ć coś do wiadomości** to announce sth; **kroniki ~ją, że...** the chronicles record a. report that...; **jak ~ją statystyki...** according to statistics...; **~ję wyniki** here are the results ④ (złożyć) to file [skargę, zażalenie]; **~ć sprawę do sądu** to take a case to court; **~ć kogoś do sądu** to sue sb ⑤ Sport to pass [piłkę]

[] **podać się — podawać się** (udać) **~ć się za kogoś** to pass oneself off as sb

■ **~ć się do dymisji** to hand in one's resignation a. notice

poda|nie n ① (pismo) (letter of) application; **~nie o pracę** a job application; **~nie o urlop** a request for leave ② Sport pass ③ (legenda) tale (**o kimś/czymś** of sb/sth); **ludowe ~nia** folk tales

podar|ować pf vt ① (dać) to give (**coś komuś** sb sth a. sth to sb); (oficjalnie) to present (**komuś coś** sb with sth); (charytatywnie) to donate (**coś komuś** sth to sb) ② pot. (zrezygnować) to skip pot.; **~ować sobie sprzątanie** to skip the cleaning

podarun|ek m książk. gift; **obsypywać kogoś ~kami** to shower sb with gifts

podat|ek m Fin. tax; **~ek dochodowy** income tax; **~ek od nieruchomości** property tax; **~ek od wartości dodanej** value added tax; **zapłacić ~ek od czegoś** to pay tax on sth; **nakładać ~ek na kogoś/coś** to levy a. impose a tax on sb/sth; **być wolnym od ~ku** to be tax-free; **być obłożonym**

18% ~kiem to be taxed at a rate of 18 per cent; **zapłacić tysiąc złotych ~ku** to pay a thousand zlotys in tax; **można to sobie odpisać od ~ku** it's tax-deductible

podatkow|y adi. [prawo, obciążenie] tax; **deklaracja ~a** a. **zeznanie ~e** a tax return; **luka ~a** a tax loophole; **zaległości ~e** tax arrears

podatni|k m taxpayer

podaż f Ekon. supply; **~ pieniądza** money supply

podbia|ł m coltsfoot

podbi|cie n ① Anat. instep ② (płaszcza, kołdry) lining

podbi|ć pf — **podbi|jać** impf vt ① (zdobyć) to conquer [naród, państwo] ② (zyskać przychylność) to win; **~ć czyjeś serce** to win sb's heart; **~ć kogoś poczuciem humoru** to win sb over with one's sense of humour ③ (uderzyć od dołu) to flick up [piłkę] ④ pot. (podnieść) to push up [cenę, stawkę] ⑤ (podszyć) to line [płaszcz, zasłony]; **~ć kurtkę futrem** to line a jacket with fur

■ **~ć komuś oko** to give sb a black eye

podbie|c, podbie|gnąć pf — **podbie|gać** impf vi ① (zbliżyć się) to run up (**do kogoś/czegoś** to sb/sth) ② (przebiec) to run; **~c (kilka metrów) do przystanku** to run (the few metres) to the bus stop ③ (podejść płynem) to fill (**czymś** with sth); **rana ~gła ropą** a wound filled with puss; **oczy ~głe krwią** bloodshot eyes

podbiegunow|y adi. [fauna, wyprawa] polar

podbija|ć impf → **podbić**

podb|ój m ① (zdobycie) conquest także przen.; **dokonać ~oju ziem wschodnich** to conquer territories in the East; **~ój kosmosu** the conquest of space ② (uwodzenie) philandering przest.; (osoba) a conquest

podbród|ek m ① (część twarzy) chin; **cofnięty ~ek** a receding chin; **podwójny ~ek** a double chin ② (na skrzypcach) chin rest

podbrzusz|e n ① (u człowieka) abdomen; (u zwierzęcia) underbelly

podburz|yć pf — **podburz|ać** impf vt to incite; **~ać tłumy** to stir up the crowds

podchod|y plt ① (zbliżanie się) stalking ② (zabiegi) subterfuge ③ (zabawa) hare and hounds

podchodzić impf → **podejść**

podchorąż|y m Wojsk. (officer) cadet

podchwytliw|y adi. grad. **~e pytanie** a trick question

pod|ciąć pf — **pod|cinać** impf vt ① (skrócić) to cut [łodygi]; to clip [żywopłot]; to trim [włosy, trawę] ② pot. (przewrócić) to trip up ③ pot. (pozbawić energii) to dishearten

■ **~ciąć sobie żyły** to cut one's wrists

podciąg|nąć pf — **podciąg|ać** impf vt ① (do góry) to pull up [pończochy, spodnie]; **~nąć kolana pod brodę** to pull one's knees up under one's chin ② (przesunąć) to pull; **~nąć stół do okna** to pull the table over to the window; **~nąć koc pod szyję** to pull a blanket up to one's neck ③ pot. (ulepszyć) to improve *[stopień]*; ~**nąć kogoś w matematyce** a. **z matematyki** to help sb improve their maths

podczas książk. **[]** *praep.* during; ~ **jego nieobecności** during a. in his absence; ~ **robienia czegoś** while doing sth

[] **podczas gdy, podczas kiedy** *coni.* ① (w czasie) while; ~ **kiedy brałem kąpiel...** while I was having a bath... ② (natomiast) whereas; **lubię koty,** ~ **gdy on woli psy** I like cats, whereas he prefers dogs

podda|ć *pf* — **podda|wać** *impf* **[]** *vt* ① (uznać klęskę) to surrender *[miasto]* (**komuś** to sb) ② (wystawić na działanie) to subject; ~**ć kogoś kontroli** to check sb; ~**ć kogoś badaniu** to put sb through an examination ③ (skierować) to submit; ~**ć coś pod dyskusję** to submit sth for discussion ④ (podpowiedzieć) to suggest *[temat]*; to put forward *[pomysł]*

[] **poddać się** — **poddawać się** ① (uznać klęskę) to surrender (**komuś** to sb); to give in ② (zrezygnować) to give up ③ (ulec) to give in; ~**ć się rozpaczy** to give in to despair; ~**ć się czyjejś woli** to submit a. succumb to sb's will ④ (jako pacjent) to undergo *[leczeniu, operacji]*

poddasz|e *n* attic

podejmować *impf* → **podjąć**

podejrzan|y **[]** *adi.* ① (posądzony) suspected (**o coś** of sth) ② (nie budzący zaufania) *[wygląd, zachowanie]* suspicious; *[intencje, sposób]* dubious; *[okolica, towarzystwo]* disreputable; ~**y osobnik** a suspicious a. dubious character ③ (nieuczciwy) *[interes, firma]* dubious ④ (dziwny) *[szmer]* suspicious ⑤ (wątpliwy) *[elegancja, styl]* dubious

[] **podejrzan|y** *m*, ~**a** *f* Prawo suspect

pod|ejrzeć, pod|glądnąć *pf* — **pod|glądać** *impf vt* to peep (**kogoś/coś** at sb/sth); **scenki uliczne** ~**ejrzane przez fotoreportera** street scenes caught by a press photographer

podejrze|nie *n* suspicion; **być poza** ~**niem** to be above suspicion; ~**nie raka wątroby** suspected liver cancer

podejrzewa|ć *impf vt* to suspect; ~**ć kogoś o kradzież** to suspect sb of theft; **lekarz** ~ **zapalenie płuc** the doctor suspects pneumonia

podejrzliw|y *adi.* ① (nieufny) suspicious; **być** ~**ym wobec** a. **w stosunku do obcych** to be mistrustful of strangers ② (świadczący o nieufności) *[spojrzenie]* suspicious

podejś|cie *n* ① (pod górę) climb ② (stosunek) approach ③ pot. (próba) try; **za trzecim** ~**ciem** at the third attempt

pod|ejść *pf* — **pod|chodzić** *impf* **[]** *vt* ① (tropić) to stalk ② (oszukać) to trick

[] *vi* ① (zbliżyć się) to come up (**do kogoś/czegoś** to sb/sth) ② (wspiąć się) to climb ③ (wypełnić się od spodu cieczą) **mleko** ~**eszło serwatką** the curds separated from the whey; **piwnice** ~**eszły wodą** the

cellars have been flooded ④ (potraktować) to approach (**do kogoś/czegoś** sb/sth); ~**ejść do sprawy z rezerwą** to approach a matter with reserve ⑤ Lotn. ~**chodzić do lądowania** to come in to land ⑥ pot. ~**ejść do egzaminu** to take an exam

pod|eprzeć *pf* — **pod|pierać** *impf* **[]** *vt* ① (podtrzymać) to prop; ~**eprzeć głowę rękami** to prop a. support one's head on one's hands; **kolumna** ~**pierająca sklepienie** a column supporting a vault ② (wspomóc) to support; ~**eprzeć kogoś finansowo** to give sb financial support ③ (wzmocnić) to support; ~**pierać oskarżenie dowodami** to support an accusation with evidence

[] **podpierać się** — **podeprzeć się** ① (wesprzeć się) to lean; ~**pierać się laską** to lean on a walking stick; ~**eprzeć się ręką** to use one's hand for support ② (wspomóc się) ~**eprzeć się czyimś autorytetem** to back oneself up with sb's authority ■ ~**pierać ściany** to be a wallflower

podep|tać *pf vt* ① (nogami) to trample *[klomb, trawę]* ② (zniważyć) to trample upon *[prawa, uczucia, zasady]*; ~**tać czyjąś godność** to trample on sb's dignity ③ (zabrudzić) ~**tać świeżo umytą podłogę** to leave (dirty) footprints on a freshly washed floor

pod|erwać *pf* — **pod|rywać** *impf* **[]** *vt* ① (unieść) to raise ② (uaktywnić) to rouse; ~**erwać kogoś ze snu** to rouse sb from sleep ③ (osłabić) to weaken *[autorytet, wiarygodność]* ④ pot. to pick up *[dziewczynę, chłopaka]*

[] **poderwać się** — **podrywać się** ① to rise; ~**erwać się z miejsca** to jump up suddenly; ~**erwać się na równe nogi** to jump to one's feet

pode|st *m* ① (schodów) landing ② (podium) podium; (dla chóru) choir stand

podesz|ły *adi. [wiek]* advanced; **człowiek** ~**ły w latach** a man of advanced years

podesz|wa *f* (stopy) sole; **to mięso jest twarde jak** ~**wa** this meat is as tough as old boots

podglą|d *m* ① (czynności) monitoring; **być na** ~**dzie** *[obiekt]* to be monitored; *[urządzenie]* monitoring equipment a. device ③ Komput. preview; ~**d strony** page display a. preview; ~**d wydruku** print preview; **przełączyć się na** ~**d** a. **włączyć** ~**d** to switch over to preview

podglądać *impf* → **podejrzeć**

podgłów|ek *m* (łóżka, tapczanu) bolster; (fotela) head rest

podgorączkow|y *adi.* **mieć stan** ~**y** to have a slight temperature

podgórs|ki *adi.* foothill

podgrz|ać *pf* — **podgrz|ewać** *impf vt* ① (podwyższyć temperaturę) to heat a. warm up *[wodę, zupę]*; (zagrzać powtórnie) to reheat *[potrawę, obiad]*; ~**ać mleko do temperatury wrzenia** to bring milk to the boil; **basen z** ~**ewaną wodą** a heated swimming pool ② przen. to warm up *[atmosferę]*; to whip up *[emocje]*; ~**ać dyskusję** to add fuel to the debate

podi|um *n* platform; (małe) podium; ~**um dla zwycięzców** Sport the winner's podium

podj|azd *m* ① (do budynku) drive(way); (przed budynkiem) forecourt ② (ułatwiający dostęp) ramp; ~**azd dla wózków inwalidzkich** a wheelchair ramp ③ (pod górę) uphill stretch; **stromy/łagodny** ~**azd** a steep/gentle incline ④ Wojsk. (wypad) foray; **robić** ~**azdy na terytorium wroga** to make forays a. inroads into enemy territory

podj|ąć *pf* — **pod|ejmować** *impf* 🛽 *vt* ① (rozpocząć) to take up *[pracę, walkę]*; to take *[działania, kroki]*; to undertake *[badania, zadanie]*; to make *[starania]*; to enter into *[dyskusję, negocjacje]*; ~**jąć decyzję** to take a decision; ~**jąć uchwałę** to adopt a. pass a resolution; ~**jąć ryzyko** to take a risk; ~**jąć zobowiązanie** to take on an obligation ② (zainteresować się) to take up *[temat, sprawę]*; to accept *[pomysł, hasło]*; ~**jąć wyzwanie** to respond to a. take up a challenge ③ (przyłączyć się) to take up *[melodię]*; ~**jąć dyskusję** to join in a discussion ④ (kontynuować) to resume *[opowieść]* ⑤ Fin. to withdraw *[pieniądze]* ⑥ (gościć) to entertain *[gości]* (**czymś** to sth); to serve *[gości]* (**czymś** with sth); ~**jąć kogoś gościnnie** to receive sb hospitably; **często** ~**ejmują gości** they do a lot of entertaining ⑦ książk. (podnieść) to pick up

🎚 **podjąć się** — **podejmować się** (zobowiązać się) to undertake (**zrobienia czegoś** to do sth); ~**jąć się czegoś** to take on sth *[zadania, obowiązków]*; to accept sth *[funkcji]*; ~**jąć się czyjejś obrony** Prawo to take up sb's case

podj|echać *pf* — **podj|eżdżać** *impf vi* ① (zbliżyć się) (samochodem) to drive up (**do kogoś/czegoś** to sb/sth); (konno, na rowerze) to ride up (**do kogoś/ czegoś** to sb/sth); **samochód** ~**echał pod dom i zatrzymał się** the car drew up in front of the house ② (zajechać) to drive round; ~**echać do pralni** to drive round to the cleaners'; **po drodze** ~**edziemy po Marię** we'll pick up Maria on the way ③ (przebyć) to ride; ~**echać czymś** to go by sth *[tramwajem, taksówką]*; ~**echać okazją** to hitch a ride a. lift pot. ④ (pod górę) (samochodem) to drive up(hill); (konno, na rowerze) to ride up(hill) ⑤ pot. (podnosić się) *[winda]* to go up; *[spódnica, nogawki]* to ride up

podju|dzić *pf* — **podju|dzać** *impf vt* ① (zwilżyć) to incite; ~**dzać do buntu** to incite a revolt; ~**dzać kogoś przeciwko komuś** to set sb against sb

podkła|d *m* ① Techn., Budow. ground beam; ~**d podłogowy** subfloor; ~**d nawierzchni** base course ② (pierwsza warstwa) undercoat; Szt. ground; ~**d pod farbę/lakier** a primer ③ Kosmet. (krem) foundation (cream); (w płynie) foundation fluid ④ Kolej. sleeper GB, (cross)tie US ⑤ Muz. background a. incidental music; ~**d wokalny** backing vocals; ~**d muzyczny do filmu** the film's soundtrack

podkładać *impf* → **podłożyć**

podkolanów|ka *f* knee(-length) sock; (cienka) popsock

podkop *m* tunnel

podkop|ać *pf* — **podkop|ywać** *impf* 🛽 *vt* ① (usunąć ziemię) to dig (**coś** around sth); to undermine *[fundamenty]* ② (osłabić) to undermine *[autorytet]*; to erode *[zaufanie]*

🎚 **podkopać się** — **podkopywać się** to dig a tunnel

podkoszul|ek *m*, ~**ka** *f* (under)vest, undershirt US; (z rękawami) T-shirt

podk|owa *f* ① (końska) (horse)shoe; **przybić koniowi** ~**owę/**~**owy** to shoe a horse ② (kształt) horseshoe shape

podkra|ść *pf* — **podkra|dać** *impf* 🛽 *vt* to pilfer *[rzeczy]* (**komuś** from sb); to steal *[pomysły]* (**komuś** from sb)

🎚 **podkraść się** — **podkradać się** to steal a. creep up (**do kogoś** on sb); ~**dła się pod drzwi** she crept up to the door

podkreśle|nie *n* underline

podkreśl|ić *pf* — **podkreśl|ać** *impf vt* ① (narysować kreskę) to underline *[wyraz]*; ~**ony czerwoną linią** underlined in red; ~**iła oczy brązowym ołówkiem** she outlined her eyes with a brown pencil ② (zaakcentować) to emphasize *[znaczenie]*; **fakt ten zasługuje na** ~**enie** this fact needs to be stressed a. emphasized ③ (uwydatnić) to highlight *[cechę]*; to pick out *[kształt]*

podkrę|cić *pf* — **podkrę|cać** *impf vt* ① (wzmocnić) to turn up *[gałkę]*; ~**cić gaz/radio** pot. to turn up the gas/radio; ~**cić tempo** to step up the tempo ② (podwinąć) to twirl *[wąsy]*; to curl *[rzęsy]*; to curl up *[włosy]* ③ Sport to spin *[piłkę]*

podku|ć *pf* — **podku|wać** *impf vt* ① to shoe *[konia]*; to hobnail *[buty]* ② Szkol. (poduczyć się) to bone up on pot. *[przedmiot]*

podkul|ić *pf* — **podkul|ać** *impf vt* to draw a. pull up *[nogi]*; **pies** ~**ił ogon** the dog tucked its tail between its legs

podkup|ić *pf* — **podkup|ywać** *impf vt* pot. ① (dać wyższą cenę) to outbid (**komuś coś** sb for sth) ② (przekupić) to buy *[osobę]*

podku|sić *pf vt* to tempt; **nie wiem, co mnie** ~**siło** I don't know what possessed me

podl|ać *pf* — **podl|ewać** *impf vt* ① (zwilżyć) to water *[rośliny, grządkę]* ② Kulin. to baste *[pieczeń]*; ~**ać jarzyny wodą** to add a drop of water to the vegetables

podlega|ć *impf vi* ① (być zależnym) to come under (**komuś** sb); to be subordinate a. responsible (**komuś/czemuś** to sb/sth); ~**ć czyjejś władzy** to be a. come under sb's authority; ~**ć bezpośrednio dyrekcji** to be directly responsible to the management ② (być wystawionym) to be subject a. liable (**czemuś** to sth); ~**ć obowiązkowi służby wojskowej** to be liable for military service; ~**jący**

opodatkowaniu taxable; **wykroczenia** ~**jące karze** punishable offences ③ (być pod działaniem) to be subject (**czemuś** to sth); ~**ć prawu polskiemu** to be subject to Polish law; **gatunek** ~**jący ochronie** a protected species ④ (ulegać) to succumb (**czemuś** to sth)

podlicz|yć pf — **podlicz|ać** impf vt to count (up) [punkty]; to reckon up [wydatki, straty]; to add up [sumy]; ~**yć utarg** to cash up

podli|zać się pf — **podli|zywać się** impf v refl. to crawl pot., przen.

podłącz|yć pf — **podłącz|ać** impf vt to connect (up) [urządzenie, gaz]; ~**yć światło** to connect up the electricity supply; ~**yć kogoś/coś do sieci (wodnej, gazowej, elektrycznej)** to connect sb/ sth to the mains; **telewizor jest** ~**ony do głośników** the TV is connected to the speakers; ~**yć komuś kroplówkę** Med. to put sb on a drip

podło|ga f floor

podłoś|ć f ① (cecha) baseness ② (czyn) nasty act; **popełnić** ~**ć** to do something mean a. nasty

podłoż|e n ① (spodnia warstwa, podkład) base; Szt. ground ② (źródło) basis; **leżeć u** ~**a czegoś** to be a. lie at the bottom of sth ③ (powierzchnia) ground; (ziemia) soil; **skaliste** ~**e** bedrock; **kwaśne** ~**e** acid soil

pod|łożyć pf — **pod|kładać** impf [] vt ① (podsunąć) to put a. place [sth] under ② (podwinąć) to take up [spódnicę] ③ (umieścić) to plant [bombę]; ~**kładać prezenty pod choinkę** to put presents under the Christmas tree ④ ~**łożyć słowa** a. **tekst pod muzykę** to set lyrics to music

[] **podłożyć się** — **podkładać się** pot. to lay oneself wide open

■ ~**łożyć do pieca/na ogień** to stoke up the fire

podłużać impf → **podłużyć**

podłużn|y adi. ① (wzdłuż) [przekrój, pasy] longitudinal; [pęknięcie, otwór] lengthwise ② (długi i wąski) [przedmiot] oblong; [twarz] elongated

podłuż|yć pf — **podłuż|ać** impf vt to lengthen; (zmniejszyć zakład) to let down; ~**yć coś o 5 cm** to let sth down by five centimetres

pod|ły adi. grad. ① (nikczemny) [czyn] nasty; base [książk; [traktowanie] shabby; ~**łe kłamstwo!** a filthy lie! pot. ② (marny) [warunki, życie, pensja] wretched; [jedzenie, obsługa, pogoda] lousy pot.

podmiejs|ki adi. ① (położony w pobliżu miasta) [osiedle, tereny] suburban; [supermarket] out-of-town; **dzielnica** ~**ka** a suburb ② (o komunikacji) suburban; **pociąg** ~**ki** a suburban a. commuter train

podmio|t m subject

podmok|ły adi. [teren] marshy

podm|oknąć pf — **podm|akać** impf vi to become soaked

podmuch m ① (wiatru) gust; (lekki) breeze; (śniegu, liści) flurry; (spowodowany wybuchem) blast ② przen. foretaste; ~ **wiosny** a foretaste of spring

podmur|ować pf — **podmur|owywać** impf vt to underpin; ~**owany ganek/płot** a porch/ fence underpinned with masonry

podmurów|ka f underpinning

podmy|ć pf — **podmy|wać** impf [] vt ① [fale, morze] to undercut ② (umyć) to wash [sb's] private parts

[] **podmywać się** — **podmyć się** to wash one's private parts

podniebie|nie n palate także przen.; **wybredne** ~**nie** a discerning a. sophisticated palate

podnieceni|e n ① (ożywienie) excitement; **radosne** ~**e** exhilaration; **czuć** a. **odczuwać** ~**e** to feel excited ② (seksualne) (sexual) arousal, excitement; (erotyczne) titillation

podnie|cić pf — **podnie|cać** impf [] vt ① (ożywić) to excite ② (podsycić) to stimulate [wyobraźnię] ③ (seksualnie) to arouse ④ (zachęcić) to stir

[] **podniecić się** — **podniecać się** to become excited

podn|ieść pf — **podn|osić** impf [] vt ① (w górę) to lift; ~**ieść kogoś/coś do góry** to lift sb/sth up; ~**ieść słuchawkę telefonu** to pick up the receiver; ~**ieść coś z ziemi** to pick sth up from the ground; ~**ieść kołnierz** to raise one's collar; ~**ieść kurtynę** to raise the curtain ② (postawić) ~**ieść przewrócone krzesło** to pick up a chair; ~**ieść chorego na łóżku** to raise a patient up in his/her bed ③ (przybliżyć) to raise; ~**ieść coś do ust** to raise sth to one's lips; **samochód** ~**iósł tumany pyłu** the car raised clouds of dust; ~**iósł lornetkę do oczu** he lifted the binoculars to his eyes ④ (podwyższyć) to raise [poziom, ceny]; ~**ieść kwalifikacje** to improve one's qualifications ⑤ (wszcząć) to raise [alarm, bunt, protest]; ~**ieść krzyk** to start to yell; ~**ieść wrzawę** to make a din ⑥ książk. (uwydatnić) ~**ieść znaczenie czegoś** to raise the importance of sth; ~**ieść sprawę** to bring up a. raise an issue ⑦ Mat. ~**ieść liczbę do potęgi** to raise a number to a given power

[] **podnieść się** — **podnosić się** ① (wstać) to get up; ~**ieść się z krzesła** to get up from a chair; ~**ieść się na palce** to stand on tiptoe ② (zostać uniesionym) [ręce] to go up ③ (wzlecieć) [kurz, dym] to rise ④ (podwyższyć się) [poziom wody] to rise ⑤ (stać się większym) [dochody, place, ceny] to rise ⑥ przen. (otrząsnąć się) ~**ieść się z nędzy** to rise out of poverty; ~**ieść się (z łóżka)** to recover from an illness ⑦ (dać się słyszeć) [krzyki, protesty] to rise

■ ~**ieść głos (na kogoś)** to raise one's voice (to sb); ~**ieść rękę na kogoś** to raise one's hand to sb; ~**ieść kotwicę** Żegl. to weigh a. raise anchor; ~**ieść żagle** Żegl. to set sail; **iść** a. **kroczyć z** ~**iesionym czołem** to walk with (one's) head held high

podnio|sły *adi. grad. [nastrój, muzyka]* solemn; *[plan]* grandiose; *[uczucia, idea]* lofty; *[utwór, styl]* turgid

podnośnik *m* Techn. jack; ~ **hydrauliczny** a hydraulic ramp; ~ **widłowy** a forklift

podnóż|e *n* foot; **u** ~**a zamku** at the foot of the castle

podoba|ć się *impf v refl.* to appeal (**komuś** to sb); **czy ten pomysł ci się** ~? does the idea appeal to you?; **film** ~ł **się wszystkim** everybody liked the film; **chciały się** ~ć **chłopcom** they wanted to impress the boys; **rób, jak ci się** ~ do as you like a. please

■ **co/gdzie/jak się komu** (*żywnie*) ~ *pot.* whatever/wherever/however one likes

podobieństw|o *n* likeness, similarity; **rodzinne** ~**o** a family resemblance a. likeness; **uderzające** ~**o tych dwojga dzieci** a striking resemblance between the two children

podobi|zna *f* [1] *(obraz, rysunek, zdjęcie)* image; *(rzeźba)* effigy; **narysować czyjąś** ~**znę** to draw sb's likeness; **wszędzie wisiały** ~**zny cesarza** portraits of the emperor hung everywhere [2] *(wyobrażenie)* image

podobnie *adv.* [1] *(prawie identycznie)* similarly; **wyglądać** ~ to look alike; **wyglądali** ~ they resembled each other; **myślę** ~ **jak ty** I think the same way as you do [2] *(w równej mierze)* **nie widział nic** ~ **pięknego** he'd never seen anything so beautiful

podobno *part.* apparently; *(o czymś zasłyszanym)* reportedly

podobn|y *adi.* [1] *(przypominający)* similar; **bracia byli do siebie bardzo** ~**i** the brothers were very much alike [2] *(tego rodzaju)* similar; **i temu** ~**e** a. **i tym** ~**e** and so on a. forth

■ **coś** ~**ego!** imagine that!; **do czego to** ~**e?** whoever heard of such a thing?; **nic** ~**ego!** not at all!, nothing of the kind!; **to do niego/niej zupełnie** ~**e** that's just like him/her

podofice|r *m* ≈ non-commissioned officer

podom|ka *f* housecoat

podopieczn|y *m*, ~**a** *f* charge

podpadać *impf* → **podpaść**

podpalacz *m*, ~**ka** *f* arsonist, fire-raiser GB

podpalać *impf* → **podpalić**

podpale|nie *n* arson, fire-raising GB; **dopuścić się celowego** ~**nia** to commit arson

podpal|ić *pf* — **podpal|ać** *impf vt* [1] *(wzniecić pożar)* to set fire to; to torch *pot.* [2] *(spowodować zapalenie się)* to kindle *[ogień]*

podpał|ka *f* kindling, firelighter GB

podpas|ka *f* sanitary towel

podpa|ść *pf* — **podpa|dać** *impf vt* [1] *(podlegać)* ~**dać pod jakąś kategorię** to fall within a category; **oni nie** ~**dają pod amnestię** the

amnesty doesn't apply to them [2] *pot.* ~**ść komuś** *(rozgniewać)* to get into sb's bad books *pot.*

podpat|rzyć, podpat|rzeć *pf* — **podpat|rywać** *impf vt* (*zauważyć*) to see; (*obserwować*) to watch *[ptaki]*; to observe *[zachowanie]*; **niechcący** ~**rzyłem...** I accidentally saw...; **miny i gesty** ~**rzone u rodziców** expressions and gestures copied from one's parents

podpierać *impf* → **podeprzeć**

podpin|ka *f* [1] Moda (detachable) lining [2] *(poszwa)* duvet cover

podpis *m* [1] *(imię i nazwisko)* signature; **stwierdzić własnoręczność** ~**u** to authenticate a signature; **na dokumencie widnieje jego** ~ the document bears his signature [2] *(pod ilustracją)* caption (**pod czymś** under sth)

podpi|sać *pf* — **podpi|sywać** *impf* **[I]** *vt* to sign *[dokument, petycję]*; to write one's name on *[kartkę]*; ~**sać listę obecności** to sign the attendance list; ~**sać na siebie wyrok śmierci** *przen.* to sign one's own death warrant

[II] podpisać się — **podpisywać się** to sign; ~**sać się na dokumencie** to sign a document; ~**sać się pełnym imieniem i nazwiskiem** to sign one's full name; ~**sać się pod propozycją** *przen.* to agree with a. to a proposal; ~**suję się pod tym obiema rękami** *przen.* I wholeheartedly agree

podpły|nąć *pf* — **podpły|wać** *impf vi* [1] *[pływak, ryba]* to swim up; ~**nąć bliżej do kogoś/czegoś** to swim closer to sb/sth [2] *[łódź, pasażer, sternik]* to come up; **woda** ~**nęła już do drzwi** the water is already up to the door

podp|ora *f* [1] *(wzmocnienie)* support; *(w moście)* abutment [2] *przen. (oparcie)* support; **być czyjąś** ~**orą** to be sb's support [3] *przen. (najważniejsza postać)* mainstay

podporządk|ować *pf* — **podporządk|owywać** *impf vt* [1] *(opanować)* to subdue *[kraj, naród]*; to gain control over *[instytucję, organizację]*; ~**owywać sobie partię** to gain control over a party [2] *(uzależnić)* to subordinate *[procedury]* (**czemuś** to sth); ~**owywać prawo czyimś interesom** to bend the law to suit sb's interests; ~**ować wojsko władzy cywilnej** to bring the army under civilian control; **teraz wszystko jest** ~**owane dziecku** now everything revolves around the baby

[II] podporządkować się — **podporządkowywać się** to submit (**komuś/czemuś** to sb/sth); ~**owywać się czyjejś woli/decyzji** to submit a. yield to sb's will/decision; **ona nie** ~**owuje się modom** she's no fashion slave

podpowi|edzieć *pf* — **podpowi|adać** *impf vt* [1] Szkol. to feed answers (**komuś** to sb) [2] Teatr to prompt (**komuś** sb) [3] *(zasugerować)* [*osoba*] to suggest; *[instynkt, rozsądek]* to tell

podpowie|dź *f* hint

podpór|ka *f* 1 (podpora) support; (tyczka) prop; (oparcie) rest; ~**ki pod pomidory** tomato stakes; ~**ka karabinu** a gun rest 2 pot., przen. (pomoc) aid; **zrobić coś bez żadnych** ~**ek** to do sth without any help

podrabiać *impf* → **podrobić**

podrap|ać *pf* 1 *vt* to scratch; ~**ać kogoś po plecach** to scratch sb's back; **byłem cały** ~**any** I was covered in scratches; **samochód miał** ~**any lakier** the car was scratched 1 **podrapać się** to scratch oneself; ~**ać się w głowę** a. **po głowie** to scratch one's head

podrastać *impf* → **podrosnąć**

podraż|nić *pf* — **podraż|niać** *impf vt* 1 (uczulić) to irritate *[oczy, śluzówki]* 2 (zdenerwować) to annoy *[osobę]*

podręcznik *n* textbook; ~ **do angielskiego** an English textbook; ~ **użytkownika** a user's manual

podręczn|y *adi.* **bagaż** ~**y** hand luggage; **apteczka** ~**a** a first-aid kit

podr|obić *pf* — **podr|abiać** *impf vt* to forge *[podpis, banknot]*; to counterfeit *[pieniądze]*; ~**obione antyki** fake antiques; **styl nie do** ~**obienia** an inimitable style

podr|osnąć *pf* — **podr|astać** *impf vi* (stać się większym) *[osoba, drzewo]* to grow; *[włosy]* to grow longer; *[ciasto]* to rise; (wydorośleć) *[osoba]* to grow up

podroż|eć *pf vi* to increase a. go up in price; **benzyna** ~**ała o 0,5%** petrol has gone up (in price) by 0.5 per cent

podróż *f* (wyjazd) trip; (wyprawa) journey; (morska) voyage; (podróżowanie) travel; ~**e zagraniczne** foreign travel; ~ **poślubna** a honeymoon; **pojechać w** ~ **służbową** to go on a business trip; **wybrać się w** ~ **do Egiptu** to go on a trip to Egypt; **w trakcie swoich** ~**y...** in the course of his travels...; ~**e kształcą** travel broadens the mind; **jak** ~? how was your journey?; (samolotem) how was your flight?; **szczęśliwej** ~**y!** (have a) safe journey

podróżni|k *m*, ~**czka** *f* traveller GB, traveler US

podróżn|y 1 *adi. [ubranie, torba]* travelling GB, traveling US; **czeki** ~**e** traveller's cheques GB, traveler's checks US 1 **podróżn|y** *m*, ~**a** *f* passenger

podróż|ować *impf vi* to travel; ~**ować samochodem** to travel by car; ~**ować po całej Europie** to travel all around Europe

podryw *m* pot. pick-up pot.

podrywacz *m* pot. skirt-chaser pot.

podrywać *impf* → **poderwać**

pod|rzeć *pf* 1 *vt* 1 (na kawałki) to tear up *[papier]*; ~**rzeć coś w strzępy** to tear sth to shreds 2 (rozedrzeć) to rip; ~**rzeć sobie spodnie** to rip one's trousers 3 (zużyć) to wear out *[płaszcz, buty]*; ~**arte ubranie** worn-out clothes 1 **podrzeć się** *[koszula, książka]* to tear

podrzędn|y 1 *adi. grad.* (pośledni) *[pisarz, literatura]* second-rate; *[znaczenie]* secondary; *[stanowisko]* minor; **spełniać** ~**ą rolę** to play a minor role 1 *adi.* 1 (podporządkowany) *[organ, stanowisko]* subordinate (**wobec** a. **w stosunku do czegoś** to sth) 2 (mniej ważny) inferior (**wobec** a. **w stosunku do czegoś** to sth) 3 Jęz. subordinate; **zdanie** ~**e** a subordinate a. dependent clause

podrzu|cić *pf* — **podrzu|cać** *impf vt* 1 (do góry) to throw (up); ~**cić coś w górę** to toss a. throw sth into the air 2 (potrząsnąć) to toss 3 (umieścić ukradkiem) to plant *[broń, dowód]* (**komuś** on sb); ~**cić coś komuś do torebki** to plant sth in sb's handbag; ~**cić komuś dziecko** (na stałe) to leave a baby on sb's doorstep; (na czas nieobecności) to leave a child with sb 4 (dołożyć) ~**cić do ognia** to stoke the fire 5 pot. (dostarczyć) to drop [sth] round; ~**cić coś komuś do biura** to drop sth off at sb's office 6 pot. (podsunąć) to suggest *[pomysł, kandydaturę]* 7 pot. (podwieźć) to give [sb] a lift a. ride US; ~**cić kogoś samochodem** to give sb a lift in one's car; ~**cić kogoś na dworzec** to give sb a lift to the station

podrzut|ek *m* pot. foundling

podsa|dzić *pf* — **podsa|dzać** *impf vt* (podnieść) to give [sb] a leg up

podsk|oczyć *pf* — **podsk|akiwać** *impf vi* 1 (do góry) to jump up; ~**oczyć z radości** to jump for joy; ~**akiwać na jednej nodze** to hop on one leg; **szedł,** ~**akując** he was skipping along 2 (ze zdziwienia) to jump 3 (przybliżyć się) to leap (**do czegoś** to a. towards sth) 4 pot. (udać się) ~**ocz do sklepu po chleb** hop round to the shop and get some bread pot.; ~**oczę do ciebie wieczorem** I'll pop in a. drop by tonight 5 (wzrosnąć) *[cena, temperatura]* to shoot up; *[tętno]* to quicken 6 pot. (postawić się) ~**oczyć komuś** to give sb cheek

podskok *m* leap; **wbiegła do pokoju w** ~**ach** she bounced into the room; **w** ~**ach** pot. (natychmiast) like a shot

podsłuch *m* 1 (podsłuchiwanie) ~ **telefoniczny** phone tapping; **jesteśmy na** ~**u** our phones are tapped 2 (aparatura) bug; **założyć** ~ **w czyimś telefonie** to bug sb's phone

podsłuch|ać *pf* — **podsłuch|iwać** *impf vt* (celowo, podstępnie) to eavesdrop on; (przypadkiem) to overhear; ~**iwać pod drzwiami** to eavesdrop at the door

podstaw|a *f* 1 (dolna część) base; ~**a czaszki** Anat. the base of the skull 2 (zasadniczy element) base, basis; ~**y naukowe** a scientific basis; ~**y matematyki** the rudiments of maths; **stanowić** ~**ę czegoś** to form the basis for sth; **mieć** ~**ę** a. ~**y do czegoś** to have grounds for sth; **film na** ~**ie powieści Dumasa** a film based on a novel by Dumas

podstaw|ić *pf* — **podstaw|iać** *impf vt* 1 (podsunąć) to place; ~**ić komuś coś** to place sth in front of sb; ~**ić komuś nogę** to trip sb (up) 2 (przyprowadzić) to provide *[samochód]*; **pociąg do Krakowa będzie** ~**iony na peron pierwszy** the train for Cracow will be leaving from platform one ③ (zastąpić) to replace; **w miejsce X** ~ **dowolną liczbę** replace X with any number

podstaw|ka *f* (podkładka) mat; (stojak) stand; ~**ka pod kufel** a beer mat

podstawow|y *adi.* *[surowce, wiadomości, pojęcia]* basic; *[problem, zasada]* fundamental

podstawów|ka *f* pot. primary school, elementary school US

podstempl|ować *pf* — **podstempl|owywać** *impf vt* ① to underpin *[strop, ścianę]* ② to stamp *[dokument, legitymację]*

podstęp *m* (intryga) deceit; (oszustwo) trick; Wojsk. stratagem; **zdobyć coś** ~**em** to gain sth under false pretences; **za tym kryje się jakiś** ~ there must be something behind this

podstępn|y *adi.* *[osoba]* devious; *[gra, zamiary]* treacherous; ~**e pytanie** a trick(y) question

podsum|ować *pf* — **podsum|owywać** *impf vt* ① (podliczyć) to add up *[rachunki, wydatki]* ② (streścić) to sum up *[dyskusję, obrady]* ③ pot., iron. (ocenić negatywnie) to sum up *[osobę, zjawisko]*

podsu|nąć *pf* — **podsu|wać** *impf vt* ① (przysunąć) to draw up *[fotel, krzesło]*; ~**nąć komuś coś do podpisu** to give sb sth to sign ② (zaproponować) to suggest *[pomysł, radę]*

podszew|ka *f* (tkanina) lining fabric; (podszycie) lining

■ **znać coś od** ~**ki** ≈ to know sth from the inside

podszy|ć *pf* — **podszy|wać** *impf* ❙ *vt* ① (podbić) to line *[kurtkę, zasłony]* (**czymś** with sth); **płaszcz wiatrem** ~**ty** przen. a thin coat ② (wykończyć) to hem *[spódnicę, rękaw]*

❙❙ **podszyć się** — **podszywać się** (udać) ~**wać się pod kogoś** to impersonate sb

podświadomoś|ć *f* subconscious

podświadom|y *adi.* subconscious; ~**y odruch** a reflex

podtek|st *m* (ukryte znaczenie) (utworu, wypowiedzi) subtext; (sytuacji) undercurrent; ~**st seksualny** sexual innuendo

podtrzym|ać *pf* — **podtrzym|ywać** *impf vt* ① (podpierać) to support *[regał, strop, chorego]* ② (uniemożliwić opadnięcie) *[szelki, podwiązki]* to hold up *[spodnie, pończochy]* ③ (obstawać) to sustain *[żądanie, stwierdzenie]*; to abide by *[opinię]* ④ (nie dopuścić do ustania) to sustain *[życie, ciążę]*; to keep *[sth]* going *[rozmowę]*; to maintain *[przyjaźń, tradycję]*; ~**ywać kogoś na duchu** to keep up sb's spirits; ~**ywać ogień** to keep the fire going

podudzi|e *n* Anat. shank

podupa|ść *pf* — **podupa|dać** *impf vi* *[przedsiębiorstwo]* to fall into decline; ~**ść finansowo** to become impoverished; **nie** ~**daj na duchu!** don't give up!

podusz|ka *f* ① (do spania) pillow; (ozdobna) cushion; ~**ka powietrzna** Aut. an air bag; **walka na** ~**ki** a pillow fight; **czytać do** ~**ki** to read in bed ② (część mebla) squab GB ③ Anat. pad ④ Moda shoulder pad ⑤ (z tuszem) ~**ka do stempli** an ink-pad

podwajać *impf* → **podwoić**

podważ|yć *pf* — **podważ|ać** *impf vt* ① (wypchnąć) to prise GB a. pry US off *[wieczko]*; to prise GB a. pry US open *[drzwi, klapę]*; (dźwignią) to lever ② (podać w wątpliwość) to undermine *[zaufanie, autorytet]*; ~**ać czyjąś teorię** to challenge sb's theory; ~**ać czyjąś wiarygodność** to question sb's credibility

podwieczor|ek *m* (high) tea GB, afternoon snack; **proszony** ~**ek** a tea party; **w porze** ~**ku** at teatime; **zaprosić kogoś na** ~**ek** to invite sb to tea

podw|ieźć *pf* — **podw|ozić** *impf vt* (jako pasażera) to give [sb] a lift; (jako towar) to bring; ~**ieźć kogoś do domu** to give sb a lift home; ~**ieź mnie do najbliższej stacji metra** drop me at the nearest underground station

podwi|nąć *pf* — **podwi|jać** *impf* ❙ *vt* ① (wielokrotnie) to roll up *[rękawy]*; (raz) to turn back *[rękawy]*; ~**nął nogawki do kolan** he rolled his trousers up to his knees ② (schować) to draw a. pull up *[nogi]*; **siedział z** ~**niętymi po turecku nogami** he was sitting cross-legged

❙❙ **podwinąć się** — **podwijać się** *[brzeg]* to turn up; *[spódnica]* to ride up

podwładn|y ❙ *adi.* subordinate (**komuś** to sb)

❙❙ **podwładn|y** *m*, ~**a** *f* subordinate

podw|oić *pf* — **podw|ajać** *impf vt* ① (zwiększyć) to double *[zyski, liczbę]*; ~**oić swoją wartość** to double in value ② przen. to redouble *[wysiłki, starania]*

podwozić *impf* → **podwieźć**

podwozi|e *n* ① Techn. chassis ② Lotn. undercarriage; ~**e przednie** a nose wheel; **wypuścić/schować** ~**e** to lower/retract the undercarriage a. landing gear

podwójn|y *adi.* ① (dwa razy większy) *[dawka, zapłata]* double; *[wzrost]* twofold; **zachować** ~**ą ostrożność** to be doubly careful ② (złożony z dwóch części) *[album, okno]* double; ~**e kliknięcie** Komput. a double-click; ~**y obraz** (na ekranie) a ghost (image); ~**y podbródek** a double chin; ~**e szyby** double glazing; ~**a włóczka** two-ply wool; ~**y zakręt** a double bend; **napisać tekst na maszynie z** ~**ym odstępem** to type a text with double spacing ③ (dla dwojga) *[tapczan, pokój]* double; ~**e zaproszenie** an invitation for two; ~**a gra** Sport doubles ④ (istniejący w dwóch postaciach) *[korzyść, rola, sens]* double; **stosować** ~**e miary moralne** to apply double standards; **prowadzić** ~**e życie** to lead a double life; ~**y agent** a double agent; ~**e obywatelstwo** dual nationality

podwór|ko n (court)yard; (za domem) backyard; **idź się pobawić na ~ku** go and play outside
■ **własne** a. **swoje/cudze ~ko** one's own/sb else's patch a. backyard US pot.

podwyż|ka f 1 (podniesienie pensji) (pay) rise GB, (pay) raise US 2 (wzrost) increase (**czegoś** in sth); **~ka cen** a price increase

podwyższ|yć pf — **podwyższ|ać** impf 🔲 vt 1 to make [sth] higher [ogrodzenie, dom]; **~yć dom o jedno piętro** to add a storey to a house; **buty na ~onym obcasie** built-up shoes 2 (zwiększyć) to raise [cenę, podatek, wartość]; to put up [czynsz, cenę]; to raise [kwalifikacje, poziom, ofertę]; **~yć karę za rozboje** to introduce harsher penalties for robbery 3 Muz. to sharpen [dźwięk]
🔲 **podwyższyć się** — **podwyższać się** 1 [osoba] to make oneself look taller 2 [ceny, ciśnienie, temperatura] to rise

podykt|ować pf vt 1 (przeczytać) to dictate [tekst] (**komuś** to sb) 2 (narzucić) to dictate [warunki] (**komuś** to sb); **sędzia ~ował rzut karny** the referee awarded a penalty (kick) 3 (pociągnąć za sobą) **jego decyzja była ~owana koniecznością** his decision was dictated by necessity; **~owany zdrowym rozsądkiem** dictated by common sense; **rób to, co** a. **rób, jak ci serce ~uje** do what your heart tells you (to do)

podzi|ać pf — **podzi|ewać** impf 🔲 vt pot. (zgubić) to lose; **gdzie ~ałeś klucze?** what have you done with the keys?
🔲 **podziać się** — **podziewać się** 1 (przebywać) **gdzie się wszyscy ~ali?** where has everyone gone?; **gdzie to się ~ewałeś?** where did you get to? 2 (znaleźć schronienie) **gdzie ja się teraz ~eję?** where am I to go now? 3 (zgubić się) to get lost; **moja torebka gdzieś się ~ała** I can't find my handbag; **gdzie się ~ał twój optymizm?** przen. whatever happened to your optimism?

podzia|ł m 1 (rozdzielenie) (na części) division; (między osoby) distribution; (rozłam) split; **~ł administracyjny** a. **terytorialny** administrative a. territorial division; **~ł majątku między spadkobierców** division of the estate among the heirs; **dokonać ~łu czegoś** to divide sth up; **~ł dziesiętny** Mat. decimal division 2 (klasyfikacja) division 3 (różnica) division; **~ły społeczne/polityczne** social/political divisions 4 Biol. division; **~ł komórkowy** cell division
❑ **~ł dochodu narodowego** Ekon. the distribution of the national income

podział|ka f 1 (skala) scale; **~ka rysunku** the scale of a drawing; **~ka 1:1** full scale; **linijka z ~ką** a graduated ruler 2 Techn. pitch; **~ka koła zębatego** a gear pitch

podziel|ić¹ pf — **podziel|ać** impf vt to share [radość, obawy] (**z kimś** with sb); **~ić z kimś los** to share sb's fate; **~ać czyjś pogląd** to share sb's view

podziel|ić² pf 🔲 vt 1 (na części) to divide; **~ić coś na dwie części** to divide sth in two 2 (rozdzielić) to share (out) 3 (sklasyfikować) to divide; **~ił ludzi na kilka typów** he divided people into several types 4 (rozgraniczyć) to divide; **ścianka ~iła pokój na dwie części** a partition divided the room in two 5 (poróżnić) to divide [sojuszników, naród] 6 Mat. to divide
🔲 **podzielić się** 1 (rozdzielić się) to split; **~ić się na dwa obozy** to split into two camps 2 (rozdać) to divide (**czymś** sth); to share (**czymś z kimś** sth with sb) 3 (poinformować) to communicate (**czymś z kimś** sth to sb); **~ić się z kimś nowinami** to tell sb the news; **~ić się z kimś doświadczeniem** to give sb the benefit of one's experience 4 Mat. to divide

podziemi|e /pod'zemje/ n 1 (część budowli) basement; (kościoła, zamku) vault 2 (przejście) underpass, subway GB 3 Polit. (organizacja) the underground 4 Polit. (działalność) underground activity; **zejść do ~a** to go underground; **książki wydawane w ~u** books published illegally; **~e aborcyjne** przen. the backstreet abortion industry

podziewać impf → **podziać**

podzięk|ować pf vi 1 (wyrazić wdzięczność) to thank (**komuś za coś** sb for sth) 2 (odmawiając) to decline; **zatrzymywali go na obiedzie, ale ~ował** they asked him to stay to dinner but he declined 3 euf., iron. (zwolnić z pracy) to let [sb] go euf.; (zrezygnować z pracy) to hand in one's notice; **~ować za posadę** to resign from one's job

podziękowa|nie n thanks; **wyrazić komuś serdeczne ~nia** to thank sb cordially; **list z ~niem** a letter of thanks; **„~nia"** (w książce) 'acknowledgements'

podziuraw|ić pf vt **~ić coś** [osoba] to wear holes in sth [ubranie, buty]; [kule] to riddle sth with holes [mur, blachę]; **~ić coś nożem** to make holes in sth with a knife; **~ione skarpetki** socks with holes in them

podziw m admiration (**dla kogoś/czegoś** for sb/sth); **godny** a. **godzien ~u** admirable; **w sposób godny ~u** admirably; **być pełnym ~u** to be full of admiration; **patrzeć na kogoś/coś z ~em** to look at sb/sth admiringly; **nie móc wyjść z ~u** to be overawed; **nad ~** remarkably

podziwia|ć impf vt to admire [osobę, cechę, widok]; **~m twoją odwagę** a. **~m cię za odwagę** I admire your courage

poe|ta m poet

poet|ka f poet; poetess przest.

poetyc|ki adi. [talent, wyobraźnia, wizja] poetic; [utwór] poetic(al); **wieczorek ~ki** a poetry reading

poezj|a [] *f* poetry; ~**a śpiewana** poetry set to music

[] **poezje** *plt* poetry; ~**e Mickiewicza** the poetry of Mickiewicz; **zbiór** ~**i** a collection of poetry a. poems

pofru|nąć *pf vi* (polecieć) to fly; (odlecieć) to fly away a. off

pogada|ć *pf vi* pot. (porozmawiać) to have a word (**z kimś** with sb); (dla przyjemności) to (have a) chat (**z kimś** with sb); **muszę z tobą** ~**ć** I need a word with you; ~**m o tym z szefem** I'll talk to the boss about it; ~ **i przestanie** he'll say his piece and that will be it

pogadan|ka *f* talk (**o czymś** on a. about sth)

poganiać *impf* → **pogonić[1]**

pogan|in *m*, ~**ka** *f* pagan, heathen

pogar|da *f* contempt, disdain; **godny** ~**dy** contemptible; **odnosić się do kogoś z** ~**dą** to be disdainful a. contemptuous of sb

pogardliw|y *adi.* [*spojrzenie, uśmiech*] contemptuous, scornful

pogardz|ać[1] *impf vt* ~**ać kimś/czymś** to despise sb/sth

pogar|dzić *pf* — **pogar|dzać[2]** *impf vt* to spurn; **on nie** ~**dzi piwem** he won't say no to beer

■ **coś nie do** ~**dzenia** sth not to be despised, sth not to be sneezed at

pogarszać *impf* → **pogorszyć**

pogawęd|ka *f* chat

poglą|d *m* view (**na coś** on a. about sth); ~**d na świat** an outlook on life

pogłęb|ić *pf* — **pogłęb|iać** *impf* [] *vt* to deepen [*dół, studnię*]; to dredge [*dno*]; to deepen, to increase [*kryzys, świadomość*]; to deepen, to broaden [*zainteresowania, wiedzę*]

[] **pogłębić się** — **pogłębiać się** to deepen; ~**ia się przepaść między bogatymi i biednymi** there is a growing gap between the rich and the poor; **krótkowzroczność** ~**ia się z wiekiem** myopia increases with age

pogłos|ka *f* rumour GB, rumor US; **szerzyć** ~**ki** to spread rumours

pogna|ć *pf* [] *vt* to drive [*bydło*]

[] *vi* [*osoba*] to race; ~**ć do szkoły** to race off to school

pogniewa|ć się *pf v refl.* [1] (obrazić się) to get cross; ~**ć się na kogoś o coś** to get cross with sb about sth [2] (pokłócić się) to fall out (**z kimś** with sb)

pogo|da *f* [1] Meteo. weather; **oglądać** ~**dę** (**w telewizji**) pot. to watch a weather forecast (on TV); **jaka dziś** ~**da?** what's the weather like today? [2] (pora bez opadów) good weather; **nie mieliśmy** ~**dy** we had rather poor weather; **jeżeli będzie** ~**da** if the weather is good [3] (spokój wewnętrzny) cheerfulness; **odznaczać się** ~**dą ducha** to be cheerful [4] (koniunktura) good period (**dla kogoś/czegoś** for sb/sth)

pogodn|y *adi. grad.* [*niebo*] clear; [*dzień*] bright, sunny; [*nastrój, osoba*] cheerful

pog|odzić *pf* [] *vt* [1] (pojednać) to reconcile (**kogoś z kimś** sb with sb) [2] (połączyć) to combine (**coś z czymś** sth with sth); ~**odzić teorię z praktyką** to bring together theory and practice

[] **pogodzić się** [1] (pojednać się) to be reconciled (**z kimś** with sb); to make up (**z kimś** with sb) [2] (zaakceptować) to resign oneself (**z czymś** to sth)

pog|onić[1] *pf* — **pog|aniać** *impf vt* [1] (pośpieszyć) to urge [*zwierzę*]; (batem) to whip [sth] up [*konia*]; (ostrogami) to spur [sth] on [*konia*]; to rush [*osobę*] [2] pot. (odpędzić) to chase [sb] off

pogo|nić[2] *pf vi* pot. (pobiec) to rush (**za kimś** after sb); ~**nić do domu** to rush off home

pogo|ń *f* pursuit (**za kimś/czymś** of sb/sth)

pog|orszyć *pf* — **pog|arszać** *impf* [] *vt* to worsen [*położenie, warunki*]; **to tylko** ~**arsza naszą sytuację** it only makes our situation worse

[] **pogorszyć się** — **pogarszać się** [*sytuacja, zdrowie*] to deteriorate

pogorzelisk|o *n* (miejsce) site of the fire; (dom) burnt-down house

pogotowi|e *n* [1] (stan gotowości) alert; **być w** ~**u** to be on (the) alert; **postawić kogoś/coś w stan** ~**a** to place sb/sth on alert; **mieć coś w** ~**u** to have sth at the ready [2] (instytucja) emergency service; **górskie** ~**e ratunkowe** the mountain rescue service [3] Med. (instytucja) emergency ambulance service; (część szpitala) casualty GB, emergency US; (karetka) ambulance; **wezwać** ~**e** to call an ambulance

pogranicz|e *n* [1] (obszar) borderland(s) [2] przen. borderland przen.; **książka z** ~**a historii i antropologii** a book which combines the disciplines of history and anthropology

pogrąż|yć *pf* — **pogrąż|ać** *impf* [] *vt* [1] (doprowadzić) to plunge; ~**yć kraj w chaosie** to plunge a country into chaos [2] (zanurzyć) to immerse [3] (zalać) to flood [4] (pogorszyć sytuację) to incriminate [*podejrzanego*]; to destroy [*przedsiębiorstwo*]

[] **pogrążyć się** — **pogrążać się** [1] (oddać się) to lose oneself (**w czymś** in sth) [2] (wpaść) to plunge; ~**yć się w anarchii** to plunge into anarchy [3] (zanurzyć się) to sink; ~**yć się w mroku** to be plunged into darkness [4] (obciążyć się) to incriminate oneself; (doprowadzić się do zguby) to destroy oneself

pogr|ozić *pf vi* [1] (postraszyć gestem) ~**ozić komuś palcem** to wag one's finger at sb; ~**ozić komuś pięścią** to shake one's fist at sb; ~**ozić komuś kijem** to wave a stick at sb; ~**ozić komuś rewolwerem** to point a gun at sb, to threaten sb with a gun [2] (postraszyć) to threaten

pogróż|ka *f* threat

pogry|źć *pf* [] *vt* [1] [*owad, zwierzę*] to bite [2] (rozdrobnić) to chew [*jedzenie*]

[] **pogryźć się** [*psy*] to fight

pogrzeb *m* (ceremonia) funeral; (kondukt) funeral procession

pogrzebacz *m* poker

pogrzeb|ać *pf* **I** *vt* ① (pochować) to bury, to inter ② (zasypać) *[budowla, lawina]* to bury ③ przen. (zniweczyć) to ruin *[nadzieje]*
II *vi* ① (w piasku, ziemi) to dig (around) (**w czymś** in sth); (w śmieciach, szufladzie) to rummage (around) (**w czymś** through a. in sth); (narzędziem) to poke around (**w czymś** in sth) ② (w książkach) to poke around (**w czymś** in sth)

poham|ować *pf* **I** *vt* (powstrzymać) to restrain *[osobę, złość]*; to hold [sth] back *[łzy]*
II pohamować się to restrain oneself

p|oić *impf* **I** *vt* ① (dawać pić) to water *[zwierzę]*; to give [sb] a drink *[osobę]*; **poić kogoś wodą** to give water to sb ② (upijać) **poić kogoś winem** to ply sb with wine

poinform|ować *pf* **I** *vt* to inform (**kogoś o czymś** sb of a. about sth)
II poinformować się to enquire (**o coś** about sth)

pojaw|ić się *pf* — **pojaw|iać się** *impf v refl.* ① (stać się widocznym) to appear, to come out; **na ulicy ~iły się plakaty** posters went up in the streets; **jej nazwisko stale ~ia się w gazetach** she's always cropping up in the papers; **jeśli ~i się taka szansa** if the chance ever comes up ② (przybyć) *[osoba]* to turn a. show up; **w okolicy ~iły się wilki** wolves have appeared a. made an appearance in the area ③ (w sprzedaży) to come in, to appear on the market

poj|azd *m* vehicle; **~azd dwuśladowy** a four-wheeled vehicle; **~azd jednośladowy** a two-wheeled vehicle; **~azd kosmiczny** a spacecraft; **~azd samochodowy** a motor a. motorized vehicle

poj|ąć *pf* — **poj|mować** *impf vt* książk. to understand, to comprehend
■ ~ąć kogoś za żonę książk. to make sb one's wife książk.

poj|echać *pf vi* to go; **~echać autobusem/ rowerem** to go by bus/bicycle; **~echać do miasta** to go to town; **~echać w góry** to go to the mountains; **~echać nad morze** to go to the seaside; **~echać za granicę** to go abroad; **~echać na wycieczkę** to go on a trip a. an excursion

pojedn|ać *pf* — **pojedn|ywać** *impf* **I** *vt* książk. to conciliate, to reconcile
II pojednać się — **pojednywać się** to make (one's) peace (**z kimś** with sb); to reconcile a. be reconciled (**z kimś** with sb)

pojedna|nie *n* reconciliation

pojednawcz|y *adi. [gest, ton]* conciliatory

pojedynczo *adv.* (oddzielnie) one by one, individually; (samotnie) singly; **zwierzęta żyjące ~** lone animals; **domy stojące ~** detached houses

pojedyncz|y *adi. [przypadek]* isolated; *[pokój, drzwi]* single

pojedyn|ek *m* duel; **~ek na słowa** verbal duelling; a shouting match pot.

pojemnik *m* container; **~ na śmieci** a dustbin GB, trash can US; **~ na wodę** a water container, a water carrier; **~ na chleb** a bread box, a bread bin GB

pojemnoś|ć *f* capacity

pojemn|y *adi. grad. [zbiornik, bagażnik]* capacious; *[termin, umysł]* broad(-ranging), wide(-ranging)

pojezierz|e *n* lake district

poję|cie *n* ① (koncept) notion ② (pogląd) view, opinion; **w moim ~ciu...** in my opinion...; **nie miał zbyt dobrego ~cia o jej talentach** he didn't think much of her talents
■ dla mnie/niego to nie do ~cia it's beyond my/his comprehension; **nie mieć o czymś zielonego ~cia** pot. to not have the foggiest a. faintest (idea) about sth pot.

pojętn|y *adi. grad. [dziecko, pies]* clever; **jest ~ym uczniem** he's quick to learn

pojmować *impf* → **pojąć**

pojutrz|e **I** *adv.* on the day after tomorrow
II *n* the day after tomorrow

pokarm *m* ① (pożywienie) food; **~ dla kotów** cat food; **~y mączne** cereals; **~y stałe** solids; **~ dla ducha** diet przen. ② (mleko matki) breast milk

pokaz *m* display, demonstration; (impreza) show; **~ gotowania** a cookery demonstration; **~ mody** a fashion show; **~ przedpremierowy** a preview; **~ sztucznych ogni** a fireworks display

poka|zać *pf* — **poka|zywać** *impf* **I** *vt* ① (dać zobaczyć) to show; **~zać komuś drogę do wyjścia** to show sb the way out ② (nauczyć) to demonstrate; **~zać komuś, jak się gotuje rosół** to show sb how to cook broth ③ (o przyrządach pomiarowych) to show, to indicate ④ (dać dowód) to prove, to show; **czas ~że, czy...** time will tell whether...
II pokazać się — **pokazywać się** ① (stać się widocznym) to appear ② (przyjść) to show up pot.; to put in an appearance; **czemu się u nas nie ~ujesz?** why don't you ever come to see us? ③ (dać się poznać) to show oneself; **~zać się z najlepszej strony** to show oneself to one's best advantage
■ ~zać figę ≈ to thumb one's nose; **~zać komuś język** to stick out one's tongue at sb

pokaźn|y *adi.* książk. *[kolekcja]* impressive; *[pakunek]* largish, large; *[suma]* handsome, considerable; *[grzywna]* hefty; *[budowla]* substantial; *[ilość]* copious

pokątn|y *adi. [handel]* illicit; *[interes]* shady pot.

pokier|ować *pf vt* to lead *[zespołem]*; to manage *[sprawami]*

pokła|d **I** *m* ① (na statku) deck; **wszyscy na ~d!** (do pasażerów) all aboard!; (do załogi statku) all hands on deck!; **na ~dzie statku/samolotu** on board a ship/plane; **witamy na** ∼**dzie!** welcome aboard! [2] (warstwa) layer [3] Geol. seam, deposit(s)

[II] **pokłady** *plt* (energii, cierpliwości) hidden reserves

pokłó|cić *pf* [I] *vt* to sow dissent (**kogoś z kimś** between sb and sb); ∼**cił ze sobą siostry** he set the sisters at loggerheads; ∼**ciły ich interesy** they fell out over business; **rozstali się** ∼**ceni** they parted in discord

[II] **pokłócić się** to quarrel; ∼**cić się z kimś o coś** to quarrel with sb over a. about sth

pokocha|ć *pf* [I] *vt* to fall in love (**kogoś/coś** with sb/sth)

[II] **pokochać się** to fall in love with each other

pokojów|ka *f* maid; (w hotelu) chambermaid

pokole|nie *n* generation

pokon|ać *pf* — **pokon|ywać** *impf vt* to defeat *[wroga, przeciwnika]*; to overcome, to surmount *[trudności]*; to get the better of, to overcome *[nieśmiałość, strach]*; to cover *[odległość]*; to clear *[przeszkodę]*; ∼**ać rywali w biegu na 100 m** to defeat a. best one's opponents in the 100 m

poko|ra *f* humbleness, humility; **z** ∼**rą** *[patrzeć, prosić]* humbly; **znosić coś z** ∼**rą** to suffer sth meekly

pokorn|y *adi. grad. [ukłon, prośba]* humble; *[ton, mina]* meek

pok|ój[1] *m* (pomieszczenie) room; ∼**ój stołowy** a. **jadalny** a dining room; ∼**ój sypialny** a bedroom; ∼**ój dzienny** a living a. day room; ∼**ój dziecinny** (dla niemowlęcia) a nursery; (dla starszego dziecka) a children's room; ∼**ój gościnny** a guest room; ∼**ój nauczycielski** Szkol. a staffroom; ∼**ój z kuchnią** a one-roomed flat with a kitchen; ∼**ój z łazienką** a room with an en suite (bathroom); „**wolne** ∼**oje (do wynajęcia)"** 'Rooms to let', 'Vacancies'; „**wolnych** ∼**oi brak"** 'No Vacancies'

pok|ój[2] *m* [1] (stan bez wojny) peace; **w czasie** ∼**ju** in peacetime, in time of peace [2] Polit., Wojsk. (układ) peace (agreement) [3] książk. (spokój) peace; „**niech spoczywa w** ∼**oju"** a. „∼**ój jego/jej duszy"** 'may his/her soul rest in peace', 'may God rest his/her soul'

pokpi|ć *pf* [I] *vt* ∼**ić sprawę** to mess up everything, to let things slide

[II] *vi* to jeer, to jibe (**z kogoś/czegoś** at sb/sth)

pokpiwa|ć *impf vi* to jeer, to jibe (**z kogoś/czegoś** at sb/sth)

pokrajać → **pokroić**

pokrewieństw|o *n* [1] (między ludźmi) (blood) relationship; **jakie jest między nimi** ∼**o?** how are they related?; **więzy** ∼**a** blood ties [2] (wśród zwierząt) relationship, kinship [3] (podobieństwo) affinity, similarity (**z kimś/czymś** to a. with sb/sth); ∼**o charakterów** a similarity of character

pokrewn|y *adi.* [1] (podobny) related, similar; **medycyna i nauki** ∼**e** medicine and related

sciences; ∼**e dusze** kindred spirits [2] Jęz. cognate (**czemuś** with sth) [3] Biol., Chem. *[gatunek, związek]* related, allied (**czemuś** to sth)

pokrę|cić[1] *pf* — **pokrę|cać** *impf* [I] *vt* [1] (obrócić) to turn *[kurek, korbkę]* [2] (zakręcić) to curl *[włosy]*; ∼**cać wąsa** to twirl one's moustache

[II] *vi* (poruszyć) to turn, to spin; ∼**cić czymś** to turn a. spin sth *[korbką]*; to twiddle a. twist sth *[gałką, kurkiem]*; ∼**cić głową z niedowierzaniem** to shake one's head in disbelief

pokrę|cić[2] *pf* [I] *vt* [1] (zniekształcić) **palce** ∼**cone reumatyzmem** fingers misshapen a. gnarled with rheumatism [2] pot. (pomylić) to muddle up; **chyba coś** ∼**ciłam z jego nazwiskiem** I seem to have got his name muddled up a. wrong

[II] **pokręcić się** pot. [1] (powyginać się) *[gałęzie, korzenie]* to get twisted [2] (pogmatwać się) *[plany, rozkład]* to be thrown into disarray; **wszystko się** ∼**ciło** everything became a muddle; **coś ci się** ∼**ciło** you've got it all wrong a. mixed up [3] (po-obracać się) *[koło, wiatrak]* to turn (around), to spin [4] (potańczyć) to strut one's stuff pot. [5] (pochodzić) to walk around; (pokrząctać się) to potter GB a. putter US around a. about; ∼**cić się po mieście** to wander around the town [6] (poczynić starania) to try; **musisz się koło niego trochę** ∼**cić** you must work on him

pokręt|ło *n* knob, dial

pokr|oić, pokr|ajać *pf vt* [1] (pociąć) to cut [sth] up *[ciasto, materiał]*; to carve *[pieczeń, indyka]*; ∼**oić coś na kawałki** to cut sth up into pieces; ∼**oić coś w plasterki** to cut sth into slices, to slice sth up; ∼**oić coś w kostkę** to cut sth into cubes, to cube sth *[mięso]*, to dice sth *[marchewkę]*; ∼**oić drobno cebulę** chop onions finely [2] pot. (poranić) to cut [sb] up [3] pot. (dokonać operacji) to cut [sb] open

pokrow|iec *m* cover; ∼**iec na meble** a dust cover a. sheet

pokry|ć *pf* — **pokry|wać** *impf* [I] *vt* [1] (obić) to cover, to upholster *[fotel, kanapę]* (**czymś** with sth) [2] Budow. to roof (in) *[dom]* (**czymś** with sth); ∼**ć dom dachówką/gontem** to tile/shingle the roof of a house; **stodoła** ∼**ta słomą** a thatched barn [3] (powlec) ∼**ć coś farbą** to apply a coat of paint to sth; ∼**ć coś lakierem/szkliwem** to varnish/glaze sth; ∼**ć ulicę nawierzchnią/nową nawierzchnią** to surface/resurface a street; ∼**ć ściany tynkiem** to plaster the walls [4] (zakryć) *[kurz]* to cover, to coat; *[śnieg]* to cover; *[szron]* to coat; *[błona]* to line; **rzekę** ∼**wał lód** the river was ice-bound [5] (spłacić) to cover *[koszty, wydatki]*; to cover, to settle make good *[deficyt, straty]*; to discharge, to settle *[dług]* [6] (zaspokoić) to meet, to satisfy *[zapotrzebowanie]*; (uzupełnić) to make good *[braki]* [7] (zatarić) to cover, to hide *[zmieszanie, zdumienie]* [8] Zool. to cover *[samicę]*

[II] **pokryć się** — **pokrywać się** [1] (stać się pokrytym) to become covered; **niebo ~ło się chmurami** the sky clouded over ② (być zbieżnym) *[pogląd, zeznanie]* to agree, to coincide (**z czymś** with sth); *[linia, granica]* to coincide (**z czymś** with sth); **zeznania świadków nie ~wają się** the witnesses' depositions do not tally a. concur

III pokryć się (ukryć się) to hide

pokryw|a *f* ① (do nakrywania) (garnka, kotła) lid; (studzienki, włazu) cover; (silnika, chłodnicy) bonnet GB, hood US; **~a bagażnika** a boot lid GB, a trunk lid US ② (warstwa) cover; **~a lodu** an ice cap

pokrywać *impf* → **pokryć**

pokryw|ka *f* lid, cover; **przykryć (garnek) ~ką** to put on the lid

pokrzyw|a *f* (stinging) nettle

pokrzywdz|ony **[I** *adi.* (poszkodowany) aggrieved; **ludzie ~eni przez los** the disadvantaged (people) **II pokrzywdz|ony** *m*, **~ona** *f* the aggrieved a. injured party

pokrzyż|ować *pf* **[I** *vt* ① (udaremnić) to foil, to thwart *[plany, zamiary]*; **~ować komuś życie/karierę** to mar sb's life/career ② Biol. to cross, to cross-breed *[gatunki]*

II pokrzyżować się *[plany, zamiary]* to become foiled a. thwarted a. frustrated; *[linie, drogi]* to criss-cross

pokus|a *f* temptation

poku|ta *f* penance, atonement

pokut|ować *impf vi* ① Relig. to do a. perform penance (**za coś** for sth); **dusze ~ujące** souls in purgatory ② (cierpieć) to suffer, to pay (**za coś** for sth) ③ przen. (pozostawać) *[przesąd, pogląd]* to linger on, to persist

pokwitani|e *n* puberty, pubescence; **w okresie ~a** at puberty

pokwit|ować *pf vt* to receipt *[przesyłkę]*; **~ować odbiór paczki** to sign for a parcel

pokwitowa|nie *n* (wpłaconych pieniędzy) receipt; (potwierdzenie) chit

polakier|ować *pf vt* to lacquer, to enamel *[metal, drewno]*; to varnish *[drewno]*; to enamel, to varnish *[paznokcie]*

polan|a *f* forest clearing, glade; **na ~ie** in a clearing a. glade

polan|o *n* log, billet

polarn|y *adi. [flora, noc]* polar; **lis/zając ~y** an arctic fox/hare

p|ole *n* ① (teren upraw) field; **pola uprawne** farmland, ploughland; **pole pszenicy** a wheat field ② (obszar) field; **pole golfowe** a golf course; **pole lodowe** an ice field; **pole minowe** Wojsk. a minefield; **pole namiotowe** a. **kempingowe** a campsite, a camping site a. ground; **pole rażenia** Wojsk. the field of fire Wojsk. **pole wyścigowe** a racecourse, a racetrack; **w szczerym** a. **głuchym polu** in the middle of nowhere ③ (dziedzina) field, area; **pole badań** an area of research ④ (sposobność)

opportunity, chance; **pole działania** a. **do działania** scope for activity; **pole manewru** room for manoeuvre, leeway ⑤ (powierzchnia) surface, field; **biały orzeł na czerwonym polu** a white eagle on a red background ⑥ Sport (część boiska) field; **piłka znalazła się w polu przeciwnika** the ball was in the opponent's half; **drużyny zmieniły pola** the teams changed ends ⑦ Gry (w szachach) square ⑧ Fiz., Komput. field ⑨ Mat. (surface) area

❏ **martwe pole** Wojsk. dead ground; Aut. blind spot**pole bitwy** a. **walki** battlefield, battleground, the field of battle

■ **zniknąć (komuś) z pola widzenia** to disappear from view; **tracić coś z pola widzenia** to lose sight of sth; **wywieść** a. **wyprowadzić kogoś w pole** to lead sb up GB a. down US the garden path; **zginąć** a. **polec na polu chwały** to die a. be killed in battle, to fall a. be killed in action

pole|c *pf vi* książk. to fall euf.; **~c na wojnie** to be killed in war; **~c od kul** to die from bullet wounds; **~c w walce o wolność** to fall fighting for freedom

polecać *impf* → **polecić**

polece|nie *n* ① (rozkaz) order ② Komput. command ③ (zaprotegowanie) recommendation

pole|cić *pf* — **pole|cać** *impf* **[I** *vt* ① (nakazać) to tell, to order; **~cić komuś coś zrobić** to tell a. order sb to do sth ② (powierzyć) to commend, to entrust; **~cił syna opiece przyjaciół** he commended his son to his friends' care ③ (rekomendować) to recommend; **szef kuchni ~ca dziś pomidorową** today the chef recommends the tomato soup, today's special is tomato soup

II polecić się — **polecać się** to commend oneself; **~cam się waszej pamięci** I commend myself to your memory

pole|cieć *pf vi* ① *[ptak, samolot, osoba]* to fly; **~cieć rannym samolotem do Rzymu** to take the morning flight to Rome ② (wzbić się) *[latawiec]* to soar up ③ (wylecieć w górę) *[iskry]* to shoot (up) ④ pot. (wypłynąć) to run; **krew ~ciała mu z nosa** blood ran from his nose ⑤ pot. (przemieścić się) to be thrown, to be pushed ⑥ pot. (pobiec) to dash; **~ciał do sklepu** he dashed to the shop; **znów gdzieś ~ciała** she's gone a. off somewhere again ⑦ pot. (zostać zwolnionym) to be fired pot. ⑧ pot. (złakomić się) to be tempted; **~ciała na jego forsę** she was after his money ⑨ (zacząć się pruć) *[szew]* to rip; **~ciało mi oczko w rajstopach** I've got a ladder in my tights

■ **~cieć komuś po premii** pot. to reduce/retract sb's bonus

polec|ony **[I** *adi.* Poczta *[list, przesyłka]* recorded delivery, registered GB, certified US

II *m* pot. (list polecony) registered a. recorded delivery letter GB, certified letter US

polega|ć *impf vi* ① (ufać) to rely (**na kimś/czymś** on sb/sth); **czy można na nich ~ć?** are they reliable? [2] (mieć przyczynę) to consist (**na czymś** in sth); **problem** ~ **na tym, że...** the problem is that...; **różnica** ~ **na tym, że...** the difference lies in...

poległ|y *m* killed; **lista** ~**łych** a roll of honour; **pamięć** ~**łych uczczono minutą ciszy** those killed in action were honoured with a minute of silence

polemi|ka *f* polemics

polepsz|yć *pf* — **polepsz|ać** *impf* [I] *vt* to improve *[jakość, smak, warunki pracy]*

[II] **polepszyć się** — **polepszać się** *[pogoda, zdrowie]* to improve; **czy mu się** ~**yło?** has his health improved?

poler|ować *impf vt* to polish, to shine *[buty]*; to buff, to burnish *[metal]*

polew|a *f* [I] Techn. glaze, glazing [2] Kulin. (do deserów) sauce; (do ciast) coating glaze

polewać *impf* → **polać**

polędwic|a *f* [I] Anat. loin [2] Kulin. (mięso) sirloin, tenderloin; (wędlina) smoked sirloin; **befsztyki z** ~**y** porterhouse steaks

policj|a *f* [I] (organ państwowy) police; ~**a drogowa** traffic police; ~**a kryminalna** crime squad [2] (funkcjonariusze) police; **patrol** ~**i konnej** a mounted police patrol [3] (posterunek) police station; **zostać wezwanym na** ~**ę** to be summoned to the police station

policjan|t *m* policeman, (police) officer

policjant|ka *f* policewoman, (police) officer

policz|ek *m* [I] Anat. cheek [2] (uderzenie w twarz) slap across the cheek [3] przen. (zniewaga) slap in the face

policzk|ować *impf vt* to slap [sb's] face także przen.

policz|yć *pf* [I] *vt* [I] (porachować) to count *[osoby, rzeczy]*; [2] (w rachunku) to charge; ~**yć mało/dużo za robotę** to charge little/a lot for the job [3] (przy ocenie) to count; ~**yć coś komuś za zasługę** to regard sth to sb's credit; **będzie ci to** ~**one w niebie** you'll be rewarded for this in heaven

[II] *vi* to count; ~**yć do stu** to count up to a hundred

[III] **policzyć się** (rozliczyć się) to square accounts (**z kimś** with sb); ~**yć się z kimś** przen. to get even with sb

poligon *m* [I] Wojsk. training ground; ~ **artyleryjski** artillery range [2] przen. ~ **doświadczalny** testing ground

poliklini|ka *f* Med. polyclinic

polini|ować *pf vt* to line *[kartkę, zeszyt]*

polis|a *f* (insurance) policy; **wykupić** ~**ę ubezpieczeniową** to take out an insurance policy

politechni|ka *f* technical university

politowani|e *n* pitifulness; **godny** ~**a** pitiful, pathetic

politu|ra *f* French polish

polityczn|y *adi.* political

polity|k *m* politician

polity|ka *f* [I] (rządzenie państwem) politics; **poświęcić się** ~**ce** to go into politics [2] (strategia postępowania) policy; ~**ka wewnętrzna** internal policy; ~**ka nieangażowania się** the a. a policy of neutrality

poli|zać *pf vt* to lick

poln|y *adi.* **kamień** ~**y** fieldstone; **kwiaty** ~**e** wild flowers; ~**a droga** a dirt road; **mysz** ~**a** a field mouse; **konik** ~**y** a grasshopper

polo Moda [I] *adi. inv. [bluzka, koszulka]* polo [II] *n inv.* polo shirt

polonez *m* Muz., Taniec polonaise

poloni|sta *m*, ~**stka** *f* [I] (specjalista) specialist in Polish studies [2] Szkol. (nauczyciel) Polish (studies) teacher

polonisty|ka *f* (nauka, studia) Polish studies; (wydział) Polish studies department

polopiryn|a *f* ≈ aspirin

polo|t *m* imaginativeness, panache; **z** ~**tem** *[pisać, grać]* with panache, imaginatively; *[wykonawca, występ]* imaginative; **bez** ~**tu** *[pisać, grać]* unimaginatively; *[wykonawca]* unimaginative, lacklustre GB, lackluster US

pol|ować *impf vi* [I] (tropić i zabijać) *[osoba]* to hunt (**na coś** sth); (z bronią palną) to shoot GB (**na coś** sth); (jako sport) to go hunting, to go shooting GB [2] (zdobywać pożywienie) *[zwierzę]* to hunt (**na coś** sth); to prey (**na coś** on sth) [3] pot. (starać się zdobyć) ~**ować na coś** to hunt for sth *[informacje, zaproszenie]*; ~**ować na męża** to hunt for a husband; **on tylko** ~**uje na posag** he's only a fortune-hunter

polow|y *adi.* [I] Roln. *[prace]* field [2] Wojsk. *[kuchnia, szpital]* field; **ćwiczenia** ~**e** manoeuvres GB, maneuvers US; **mundur** ~**y** battledress GB, (battle) fatigues

polszczy|zna *f* the Polish language

polub|ić *pf* [I] *vt* to grow fond of, to take (a liking) to; ~**ić dalekie spacery** to grow fond of long walks

[II] **polubić się** to grow fond of each other, to take to each other

poła|mać *pf* [I] *vt* to break (up) *[gałęzie, patyk]*; ~**ać sobie ręce** to break one's arms; **czuję się a. jestem** ~**ana** pot. I'm aching all over

[II] *v imp.* pot. **stał w przeciągu i go** ~**ało** he'd been standing in a draught and now he can hardly move a. he feels all achy

[III] **połamać się** *[krzesło, drzewo]* to break (up) ■ ~ **ręce/nogi!** a. ~**ania rąk/nóg!** pot. break a leg! pot.

połącze|nie *n* [I] Techn. joint [2] Elektr. connection [3] (zestawienie) combination; ~**nie tragedii z farsą** a combination a. blend of tragedy and farce, a cross between a tragedy and a farce; **w** ~**niu z czymś** in combination with sth, combined with sth [4] Transp. connection, link (**z czymś** with sth); ~**nia**

kolejowe/lotnicze rail/air links a. connections 5 Telekom. (łączność) link; (rozmowa) connection, call; ~**nie miejscowe** a local area call; ~**nie międzymiastowe** a. **zamiejscowe** a trunk call; STD GB; **międzynarodowe** ~**nie automatyczne** international direct dialling GB, IDD GB; **bezpośrednie** ~**nie satelitarne** a direct link by satellite; **prosić o** ~**nie z kimś** to ask to be connected to sb; ~**nie zostało przerwane** the line went dead 6 Ekon., Polit. merger, fusion

połącz|yć pf **I** vt 1 (zespolić) to connect, to join [końce, przewody] (**z czymś** to sth); to amalgamate [organizację, spółkę] (**z czymś** with sth); to integrate [organizację, spółkę] (**z czymś** into sth); ~**yć dwie listwy klejem** to glue together two slats; ~**yć różne kolory wełny** to combine wool of different colours 2 Transp. to connect, to link; ~**yć mostem brzegi rzeki** to bridge a river; ~**yć dwa jeziora kanałem** to link two lakes with a canal 3 Telekom. to connect; ~**yć kogoś z kimś/czymś** to connect sb to sb/sth; **czy może mnie pani** ~**yć z numerem 2567** could you get me 2567, please? 4 przen. to combine; ~**yć siły** a. **wysiłki** to combine forces, to join forces; **luźno** ~**one ze sobą epizody** loosely-connected episodes; **wszystkich ich** ~**ył ten sam los** they were all united by the same fate

II połączyć się 1 (zespolić się) [rzeki, drogi] to meet; [instytucje] to fuse, to merge 2 Telekom. to get through (**z kimś/czymś** to sb/sth); **nie mógł się** ~**yć z centralą** he couldn't get through to the operator 3 książk. (spotkać się) to be a. become reunited (**z kimś** with sb) 4 przen. (zacząć działać wspólnie) to join forces (**z kimś** with sb)

■ ~**yć się ślubem** a. **węzłem małżeńskim** książk. [para] to tie the knot; ~**yć kogoś ślubem** a. **węzłem małżeńskim** to declare sb man and wife

poł|knąć pf — **poł|ykać** impf vt 1 to swallow (down) [jedzenie, napój, pigułkę]; ~**ykać coś z apetytem** to gulp sth down hungrily; ~**ykał ślinkę na widok tortu** his mouth watered at the sight of the cake pot.; ~**knąć żeton/monetę** pot., przen. [automat] to swallow a token/coin 2 (opuścić) to swallow, to slur [głoskę, wyraz] 3 (przyswoić sobie) to devour przen. [książkę, wiedzę] 4 (pochłonąć) to swallow [sth] up pot. [mniejszą firmę, obszar] 5 (przyjąć) to swallow [docinki, obelgę]

poł|owa f 1 (część) half; ~**owa ludzi/jabłek** half (of) the people/apples; **w drugiej** ~**owie XX wieku** in the second a. latter half of the 20th century; **podzielić/przeciąć coś na** ~**owę** to divide/cut sth in half; **mniejszy/większy o** ~**owę** half the size/half as big again; **pomysł jest w** ~**owie mój** the idea is partly mine 2 (punkt, moment) middle, mid-; **do** ~**owy miesiąca** till a. until the middle of the month; **w** ~**owie kwietnia/XIX wieku** in mid-June/in the mid-

19th century; **rok szkolny dobiegał** ~**owy** the school year was halfway through a. over; **zatrzymać się w** ~**owie drogi** to stop halfway; **w** ~**owie strony** halfway down the page; **wszystkie flagi opuszczono do** ~**owy masztu** all flags were at half mast 3 Sport (część meczu, boiska) half

■ **brzydsza** ~**owa rodzaju** a. **rodu ludzkiego** żart. the male sex; **piękniejsza** a. **ładniejsza** ~**owa rodzaju** a. **rodu ludzkiego** żart. the fair sex; **jego/ jej lepsza** a. **druga** ~**owa** żart. his/her better a. other half

położe|nie n 1 (miejsce) location, situation; ~**nie gwiazd na niebie** the position of the stars in the sky 2 (sytuacja) situation, position; **ciężkie** ~**nie** a grave situation; **ich** ~**nie materialne** their circumstances; **stawiać kogoś w kłopotliwym** ~**niu** to put sb in an awkward situation

położn|a f midwife

położnictw|o n 1 (dział medycyny) obstetrics, midwifery 2 (oddział szpitalny) obstetrics

położni|k m obstetrician

poł|ożyć pf **I** vt 1 (umieścić) to put, to place; ~**óż to!** put it down!; ~**óż to na miejsce!** put it back!; ~**ożyć coś na półce** to put a. place sth on a shelf; ~**ożyć dłonie na klawiszach** to rest one's hands on the keyboard; ~**ożył mi rękę na czole** he laid his hand on my forehead; ~**ożyć palec na ustach** to put one's finger to one's lips 2 (ułożyć poziomo) to lay (down); ~**óżmy go na plecach** let's lay him on his back; **grad** ~**ożył całe zboże** the hail beat down a. flattened all the corn; **huragan** ~**ożył pokotem wiele drzew** the hurricane blew down a. felled many trees; ~**ożyć kogoś na obie łopatki** Sport to pin sb down; przen. to knock sb into a cocked hat pot. 3 (przenocować) to put up (**for the night**); (ułożyć do snu) to put [sb] to bed 4 (ułożyć) to lay [kafelki, tory]; ~**ożyć tynki** to plaster walls 5 pot. (zepsuć) to make a dog's breakfast a. dinner (out) of sth pot. [rolę, sztukę]; to blow pot. [dowcip]

II położyć się 1 (w leżącej pozycji) to lie down 2 (pójść spać) to go to bed; to turn in pot. 3 (przechylić się) [samolot] to bank; [łódź, statek] to careen, to list; (przewrócić się) [łódź, statek] to keel over

■ ~**ożyć akcent** a. **nacisk na coś** to lay a. put stress on sth, to place a. put the emphasis on sth; ~**ożyć kres czemuś** to put a stop a. an end to sth; ~**ożyć pieczęć na czymś** to put a. set the seal on sth

poł|ów m Ryboł. 1 (łowienie) fishing (**czegoś** for sth); catching (**czegoś** of sth); ~**ów** a. ~**owy dorsza** cod fishing; ~**owy przybrzeżne/dalekomorskie** coastal/deep-sea fishing; **wyruszyć** a. **wypłynąć na** ~**ów** to set sail to the fishing grounds; **prowadzić** ~**owy na Oceanie Atlantyckim** to fish in the Atlantic 2 (zdobycz) catch, haul

połów|ka *f* ① (połowa) half; **wypalił** ~**kę papie-rosa** he smoked half a cigarette ② pot. (butelka) half-litre GB a. liter US bottle of vodka

południ|e *n* ① (godzina dwunasta) noon; (środek dnia) midday; **w samo** ~**e** at high noon; **o dwunastej w** ~**e** at twelve noon; **przed** ~**em** in the morning; **po** ~**u** in the afternoon; **dziś przed** ~**em** this morning; **wczoraj po** ~**u** yesterday afternoon; **jest czwarta po** ~**u** it's 4 p.m. ② (strona świata) south; **droga skręca na** ~**e** a. **ku** ~**owi** the road turns south a. southward(s); **okna wychodzą na** ~**e** the windows face south; **wieś leży na** ~**e od Warszawy** the village lies south a. to the south of Warsaw; **autostrada omija miasto od** ~**a** the motorway goes south of the town; **wiatr wieje z** ~**a** the wind is blowing from the south; **droga prowadząca na** ~**e** a southbound road; **najdalej na** ~**e wysunięty punkt** the most southerly point; **najdalej na** ~**e położone miasto** the southernmost town; ~**e Polski** the south of Poland, southern Poland; **przelotne deszcze na** ~**u** scattered showers in the south ③ (region geograficzny) the South; **spędził zimę na** ~**u** he spent the winter in the South

południk *m* Geog. meridian, line of longitude; ~ **zerowy** prime a. Greenwich meridian

południowo-wschodni *adi.* [strona, ściana] south-east; [region, wybrzeże] south-eastern; [wiatr] south-east, south-easterly

południowo-zachodni *adi.* [strona, ściana] south-west; [region, wybrzeże] south-western; [wiatr] south-west, south-westerly

południow|y *adi.* ① (w środku dnia) [skwar, słońce] noon, midday; **przerwa** ~**a w pracy** a midday break ② (o stronie świata) [ściana, wybrzeże] south, southern; [region, akcent] southern; [wiatr] south, southerly

połykać *impf* → **połknąć**

połysk *m* (drewna, materiału) sheen; (metalu, włosów) sheen, lustre GB, luster US; (wody) shimmer; **wytrzeć coś do** ~**u** to give sth a shine; **nadać czemuś** ~ to give sth polish a. a shine; **bez** ~**u** matt, lustreless GB; **z** ~**iem** [zdjęcie, meble] with a gloss finish; [papier] glossy, satiny; **meble na wysoki** ~ highly-polished furniture; **wszystko zorganizowali na wysoki** ~ pot., przen. they arranged everything in great detail

pomad|ka *f* ① Kosmet. lipstick ② Kulin. chocolate; **pudełko** ~**ek** a box of chocolates

pomagać *impf* → **pomóc**

pomału ① *adv.* ① (powoli) [posuwać się] slowly, without haste ② (stopniowo) gradually, bit by bit ② *inter.* pot. hold on!, slow down!

pomarańcz|a *f* (owoc) orange; (drzewo) orange tree

pomarańczow|y *adi.* ① (z pomarańczy) [dżem, gaj, zapach] orange; **o smaku** ~**ym** orange-flavoured ② (kolor) [farba, sukienka] orange

pomarszcz|ony *adi.* [twarz, skóra] wrinkled, creased; [staruszek, ręce] shrivelled, wizened; [owoc, liście] shrivelled, dried up

pomawiać *impf* → **pomówić**[1]

poma|zać *pf* ① *vt* ① (pobrudzić) to smudge [ręce, ubranie] ② (pokryć gryzmołami) to scribble; ~**zać ścianę napisami** to cover the wall with graffitti ③ książk. (uroczyście namaścić) to anoint

② **pomazać się** to get smeared

pomia|r *m* ① (mierzenie) measurement; **przeprowa-dzać** ~**ry** to take measurements ② (wynik) measure-ment; ~**ry kartograficzne** surveying

pomiata|ć *impf vt* pot. to kick [sb] around a. about; ~**ć ludźmi** to treat people like dirt

pomido|r *m* tomato

pomidorow|y ① *adi.* Kulin. [sok, zupa] tomato

② **pomidorowa** *f* pot. tomato soup

pomiesza|ć *pf* ① *vt* ① (połączyć) to mix; ~**ć dokładnie wszystkie składniki** to mix all the ingredients together well ② (przez pewien czas) to stir; ~**ć zupę w garnku** to stir the soup in the pot ③ (pomylić) to confuse, to mix up; ~**ć komuś w głowie** to confuse sb ④ (wprowadzić bałagan) to shuffle [karty, listy]

② **pomieszać się** ① (przeniknąć się) [dźwięki, smaki] to mingle ② (pomylić się) [fakty, słowa] to get mixed up; **wszystko mi się** ~**ło** I got completely confused a. mixed up pot. ③ (znaleźć się w nieładzie) [przedmioty] to get mixed up

pomieszcze|nie *n* room; ~**nie gospodarcze** a utility room; ~**nia biurowe** office space; ~**nia mieszkalne** living quarters

pomie|ścić *pf* ① *vt* (zmieścić) to hold [rzeczy]; to house [urzędy, firmy]; to accommodate [ludzi, zwierzęta]; **teatr może** ~**ścić ośmiuset widzów** the theatre has a capacity of eight hundred; **jak ja** ~**szczę tylu gości?** how shall I find room for so many people?

② **pomieścić się** [przedmioty, ludzie, zwierzęta] to fit, to go into

pomiędzy → **między**

pomijać *impf* → **pominąć**

pomimo książk. → **mimo**

pomi|nąć *pf* — **pomi|jać** *impf vt* ① (opuścić) to omit, to pass over [fakt, informację]; to skip [zdanie, akapit]; ~**nąć coś milczeniem** to pass over sth in silence ② (nie uwzględnić) to pass [sb] over; ~**nąwszy** a. ~**jając płacę, praca była doskonała** except for a. apart from the pay, the job was great

pomnażać *impf* → **pomnożyć**

pomniejsz|yć *pf* — **pomniejsz|ać** *impf* ① *vt* ① (zmniejszyć) to reduce in size [obraz]; to reduce [ilość, koszty] ② (umniejszyć) to diminish [odpowie-dzialność, straty]; to belittle [osiągnięcia, zasługi]; to play down [znaczenie, powagę]

② **pomniejszyć się** — **pomniejszać się** (zmniej-szyć się) [obszar, suma] to decrease

pomnik m ① (znanej osoby) monument, memorial; ~ **Chopina** a monument to Chopin; ~ **ku czci obrońców Westerplatte** a memorial to a. a monument commemorating the defenders of Westerplatte ② (nagrobek) gravestone, tombstone ③ (zabytek) monument; ~ **polskiej literatury** a classic of Polish literature

pomn|ożyć pf — **pomn|ażać** impf ▯ vt ① (powiększać) to accumulate *[majątek]*; to enlarge *[zbiory]*; to increase *[dochód, wartość]* ② Mat. to multiply; ~ożyć **2 przez 4** to multiply 2 by 4

▯ **pomnożyć się** — **pomnażać się** *[dochody, zyski]* to grow, to increase

pomoc f ① (pomaganie) help, assistance; (wsparcie) aid; (ratunek) rescue; ~ **lekarska/finansowa** medical/financial assistance; ~ **państwa** state aid; **wołać o** ~ a. **wzywać** ~y to call for help; ~y! a. **na** ~! help!; **przy czyjejś** ~y a. **z czyjąś** ~ą with sb's help; **za** ~**ą czegoś** a. **przy** ~y **czegoś** with the use of sth ② (pomocnik) help, aid; ~ **biurowa** an office junior; ~ **kuchenna** a kitchen maid; ~ **domowa** a domestic (help) ③ Sport fullbacks

❑ **pierwsza** ~ first aid; ~ **drogowa** breakdown service; ~**e szkolne** Szkol. teaching aids

pomocni|k m ① (osoba) helper, assistant ② Sport halfback ③ (mebel) occasional table

pomo|st m ① (nad jeziorem, rzeką) pier, jetty ② (na rusztowaniu) catwalk; (w tramwaju) platform ③ (łączący statek z nabrzeżem) gangway; (między burtami) bridge ④ przen. bridge

pom|óc pf — **pom|agać** impf vi ① (ułatwić) to help; ~óc **komuś w sprzątaniu** to help sb clean; ~óc **komuś przy myciu okien** to help sb with cleaning the windows; ~**agać dziecku w nauce** to help a child with school work; ~**agać w domu** to help with the housework; ~**agać komuś finansowo** to help sb financially, to give financial assistance to sb ② (poskutkować) to help; **krzyk ci nie** ~**oże** shouting won't help you; **żadne perswazje nie** ~**ogły** persuasion was of no avail

pomp|a¹ f ① Techn. pump; ~**a uliczna** a hydrant ② pot. (ulewa) downpour

pomp|a² f ① (uroczysta oprawa) pomp; **z wielką** ~**ą i paradą** with great pomp and ceremony ② (uroczyste wydarzenie) ceremony

pomp|ka f ① (do roweru, piłki) (small) pump ② Sport press-up GB, push-up US

pompon m pompom, pompon

pomp|ować impf vt ① (tłoczyć) to pump *[ciecz, gaz]* ② (napełniać) to pump up *[materac, dętkę]* ③ pot. to pump *[pieniądze, środki]* (**w coś** into sth)

pomruk m ① (gardłowy dźwięk) growl; ~ **niezadowolenia** a rumble of discontent ② przen. rumble; ~ **burzy** the rumble of thunder

pom|ścić pf vt to avenge *[krzywdę, upokorzenie]*

pomyl|ić pf ▯ vt to confuse *[daty, nazwiska]*; ~ić **osoby** to mistake one person for another

▯ **pomylić się** to make a mistake a. an error; ~ić **się w obliczeniach** to make a mistake in one's calculations; ~**iłam się co do niego** I was mistaken about him; **wszystko mi się** ~**iło** I got utterly confused a. totally mixed up

pomył|ka f ① (błąd) mistake, error; **popełnić/ naprawić** ~**kę** to make/correct a mistake; **przez** ~**kę** by mistake ② Telekom. wrong number; „**czy mogę mówić z Julią?" – „** ~**ka**" 'may I speak to Julia, please?' – 'wrong number'

pomy|sł m idea; **mieć głowę pełną** ~**słów** to be full of ideas; **wpaść na** ~**sł** to hit (up)on an idea ■ **dom urządzone z** ~**słem/bez** ~**słu** a house decorated imaginatively/unimaginatively; **ty masz** ~**sły!** pot. you and your ideas!

pomysłodawc|a m originator

pomysłowoś|ć f ingeniousness, inventiveness

pomysłow|y adi. *[osoba]* inventive, full of ideas; *[urządzenie]* ingenious, clever

pomyśl|eć pf vi ① (zastanowić się) to think; ~, **zanim coś powiesz** think before you say; **muszę chwilę** ~**eć** a. **daj mi** ~**eć** let me think; ~ **o czymś miłym** think about sth nice; **gotów ktoś** ~**eć, że...** somebody might think (that)... ② (wyobrazić sobie) to think; ~, **co by było, gdyby...** think what would have happened if...; **kto by** ~**ał, że...** who would have thought (that)...; **i** ~**eć, że jeszcze rano byłam w Nowym Jorku!** imagine that this morning I was still in New York!

■ **być nie do** ~**enia** to be unthinkable; **czy takie rozwiązanie jest w ogóle do** ~**enia?** is such a solution at all thinkable?

ponad ▯ praep. ① (wyżej niż) over, above; ~ **miastem** above a. over the city ② (w porównaniach) over, above; **przedkładać szczęście** ~ **bogactwo** to value happiness over wealth; **stawiać jakość** ~ **ilość** to put quality before quantity; **kochać kogoś** ~ **wszystko** to love sb more than anything else in the world ③ (przekroczyć poziom) beyond, above; ~ **przeciętną** above average; **dojrzały** ~ **wiek** mature beyond his age; **praca** ~ **siły** superhuman work

▯ part. over, more than; ~ **godzinę** over a. more than an hour; ~ **pięciokrotny wzrost** a more than fivefold increase, over a fivefold increase; **ona ma** ~ **sześćdziesiąt lat** she's over sixty (years old) a. more than sixty years old

ponaddźwiękow|y adi. *[prędkość, samolot]* supersonic

ponadto part. książk. moreover, furthermore; **był zdolny, a** ~ **pracowity** he was clever and hard-working besides

ponaglać impf → **ponaglić**

ponawiać impf → **ponowić**

poncz m Kulin. punch

poniedział|ek m Monday; **lany** ~**ek** Easter Monday

pon|ieść¹ *pf* — **pon|osić¹** *impf vt* ① (doświadczyć) to incur *[koszty]*; to suffer *[klęskę, konsekwencje]*; ~**ieść śmierć** to die; ~**ieść odpowiedzialność za coś** to be held responsible for sth; ~**osić winę za coś** to be to blame for sth; ~**ieść zasłużoną karę za coś** to be rightly punished for sth ② (o emocjach) **nerwy go** ~**iosły** he lost his temper; **trochę mnie** ~**iosło** I got a bit carried away

poni|eść² *pf vt* ① (nieść) to carry; ~**eść komuś walizkę** to carry a suitcase for sb ② *[koń]* to bolt ③ (zaprowadzić) **gdzie go znowu** ~**osło?** pot. where has he gone this time?; **szedł, gdzie oczy** ~**osą** he walked ahead without looking back

ponieważ *conj.* because, as, since; ~ **padało, zostałem w domu** as it was raining I stayed at home; ~ **był najmłodszy, wszyscy go lekceważyli** because a. as he was the youngest, everybody ignored him

poniewiera|ć się *impf v refl.* (być rozrzuconym) *[przedmioty, ubrania]* to kick around pot.; (tułać się) to knock about

poniżej ❚ *praep.* ① (niżej niż) below, beneath; ~ **domu** below the house; ~ **poziomu morza** below sea level; **zwykle wędkują** ~ **mostu** they usually fish downstream from the bridge ② (mniej niż) below, under; **poniżej przeciętnej** below average; **20 stopni** ~ **zera** 20 degrees below (freezing); **temperatury** ~ **zera** sub-zero temperatures; **dla dzieci** ~ **lat dwunastu** for children up to (the age of) twelve ③ przen. ~ **normy** below (the) norm; **być** ~ **oczekiwań** to fall short of expectations; **to było** ~ **jego godności** this was beneath his dignity a. beneath him

❚❚ *adv.* ① (w przestrzeni) lower down; **zamek nad płynącym** ~ **Sanem** a castle with the San river flowing down below ② (w tekście) below; **na zdjęciu** ~ in the photograph below

poniż|enie *n* indignity, humiliation

poniż|yć *pf* — **poniż|ać** *impf* ❚ *vt* to humiliate

❚❚ **poniżyć się** — **poniżać się** to debase a. demean oneself (**przed kimś** before sb); ~**ać się prośbami o pieniądze** to stoop to asking for money

ponosić¹ *impf* → **ponieść¹**

pono|sić² *pf vt* ① (transportować) to carry *[niemowlę, plecak]* ② (używać) to wear *[buty, ubranie]*

pon|owić *pf* — **pon|awiać** *impf* ❚ *vt* to repeat *[prośbę, ostrzeżenie]*; ~**owili atak o świcie** they attacked again at dawn

❚❚ **ponowić się** — **ponawiać się** *[krwotok, atak]* to recur; ~**awiające się pytania** repeated questions

ponton *m* ① (łódka) (rubber) dinghy; **nadmuchać a. napompować** ~ to inflate a rubber dinghy ② Budow. pontoon

ponura|k *m* pot. sourpuss pot.

ponu|ry *adi.* ① (przygnębiony) gloomy, grim ② (przygnębiający) *[zamczysko]* dreary; *[miasto, dzień, pejzaż]* gloomy, bleak; *[wiadomość]* grim

pończo|cha *f* stocking

popamięta|ć *pf vt* ① (zapamiętać) to remember; **on** ~ **to na całe życie** he won't forget it till the end of his days ② pot. (pożałować) **jeszcze** ~**sz!** I'll get you one day!

poparci|e *n* ① (wsparcie) support (**dla kogoś/czegoś** for sb/sth); **na znak** ~**a dla kogoś** in support of sb ② (potwierdzenie) support; **argument na** ~**e teorii** an argument in support of a theory

poparze|nie *n* burn; (od gorącej wody, pary) scald; ~**nie pierwszego stopnia** Med. a first-degree burn

poparz|yć *pf* ❚ *vt [żelazko, kwas]* to burn; *[ukrop, para]* to scald; **twarz** ~**ona kwasem** an acid-burnt face

❚❚ **poparzyć się** to burn oneself (**czymś** with sth); (gorącą cieczą, parą) to scald oneself (**czymś** with sth)

popatrz|eć, popatrz|yć *pf* ❚ *vi* ① (spojrzeć) to look (**na kogoś/coś** at sb/sth); ~**eć przez lunetę** to have a look through a telescope; **chcesz** ~**eć?** do you want a look?; ~**ył, czy nikt nie idzie** he made sure nobody was coming; **aż przyjemnie było** ~**eć, jak sobie pomagają** it was a pleasure to watch them help each other; **było na co** ~**eć!** you should've seen it!; ~, (~), **jaki mądry!** iron. look how smart he is! iron. ② (rozważyć) to look (**na kogoś/coś** at sb/sth)

❚❚ **popatrzyć się** pot. to look (**na kogoś/coś** at sb/sth)

pop|chnąć *pf* — **pop|ychać** *impf vt* ① (posunąć) to push; **czy mógłby mnie pan** ~**chnąć?** (o samochodzie) could you give me a push? ② (skłonić) to drive *[osobę]*; ~**chnąć kogoś do samobójstwa** to drive sb to suicide ③ (zbliżyć do końca) to move *[sth]* forward *[sprawę]*

popeł|nić *pf* — **popeł|niać** *impf vt* ① (dopuścić się) to commit *[przestępstwo, grzech, samobójstwo]*; to make *[gafę, błąd]*; ~**niła mezalians** she married below her station przest. ② żart. (stworzyć) to put together *[powieść, wiersz]*

popę|d *m* ① Biol., Psych. drive; ~**d (płciowy)** sex drive ② (skłonność) urge; ~**d do hazardu** an urge to gamble

popędza|ć *impf vt* (ponaglać) to push *[osobę]*; to urge *[osobę]*; to urge [sth] on *[konia]*; „**szybciej, szybciej**" ~**ł** 'hurry up,' he urged

popę|dzić *pf* ❚ *vt* to drive *[gęsi, owce]*

❚❚ *vi* to dash (**za kimś/czymś** after sb/sth); ~**dził do pracy** he dashed off to work

popi|ć¹ *pf* — **popi|jać¹** *impf vt* to wash [sth] down (**czymś** with sth)

popi|ć² *pf* ❚ *vt* ① (napić się) to drink ② pot. (alkoholu) to drink; **on lubi sobie** ~**ć** he likes a drink

❚❚ **popić się** pot. to get drunk

popiela|ty *adi. [strój]* light grey; *[twarz, cera]* ashen

popielnicz|ka *f* ashtray

popierać *impf* → **poprzeć**

popiersi|e *n* Szt. bust

popijać¹ *impf* → **popić¹**

popija|ć² *impf vt* ① (pić po trochu) to sip *[herbatę, wino]* ② pot. (pić nałogowo) to drink

popi|ół ① *m* ash(es), cinder(s); ~**ół z papierosa** cigarette ash; **spalić się na ~iół** to burn to ashes a. to a cinder a. to cinders

Ⅱ **popioły** *plt* ashes; ~**oły przodków** ancestors' ashes

■ **powstać** a. **odrodzić się (jak feniks) z ~ołów** to rise a. emerge (like a phoenix) from the ashes; **posypać (sobie) głowę ~ołem** to wear sackcloth and ashes

popis *m* show, display; ~ **gimnastyczny** a gymnastics display; ~ **deklamatorski** (konkurs) a recitation contest; ~ **odwagi** a show of courage; ~ **ekwilibrystyczny** a balancing act; ~ **sztuki aktorskiej** a brilliant piece of acting

■ **mieć/znaleźć pole do ~u** to have/get a chance to show what one can do

popi|sać się *pf v refl.* to display *vt* (**czymś** sth) *[odwagą, siłą]*; **nie ~sałeś się** iron. you didn't exactly distinguish yourself iron.; **ale się ~sał!** iron. he really blew it! iron.

popi|sywać się *impf v refl.* to show off (**kimś/czymś** sb/sth); to show off (**przed kimś/czymś** to a. in front of sb/sth); **lubiła ~sywać się swoim bogactwem** she liked to flaunt her wealth

poplam|ić *pf* ① *vt* to stain *[obrus, podłogę]*; **ręcznik ~iony krwią** a blood-stained towel

Ⅱ **poplamić się** *[obrus]* to get stained; ~**ić się krwią** to be stained with blood

poploch *m* scare, panic; **uciec w ~u** to flee in (a) panic

popły|nąć *pf vi [płyn, energia]* to (start to) flow; *[osoba]* to swim; *[statek]* to sail; przen. **znana melodia ~nęła z głośnika** a popular tune floated from the loudspeakers; **z całej Polski ~nęły dary na powodzian** donations for flood victims started to flow in from all over Poland

popołudni|e *n* afternoon; ~**em/~ami** in the afternoon/in the afternoons

popołudniow|y *adi. [spacer, sjesta]* afternoon; *[koncert, seans]* matinee; **pracuję na ~ej zmianie** I work afternoon a. evening shifts

popraw|a *f* ① (polepszenie) improvement; ~**a pogody** an improvement in the weather (conditions); ~**a gospodarki** an upturn in the economy, an upswing in economic activity; **nastąpiła ~a jej zdrowia** her health improved ② (w zachowaniu) betterment; **obiecywać ~ę** to promise to mend one's ways

poprawczak *m* pot. community home GB, young offenders' home, detention centre

popraw|ić *pf* — **popraw|iać** *impf* ① *vt* ① (doprowadzić do porządku) to tidy up; ~**ić makijaż** to touch up one's make-up; ~**ić strój i włosy** to

smarten a. tidy oneself up; ~**ić krawat** to straighten one's tie ② (udoskonalić) to improve on *[wyniki]*; to amend *[ustawę]*; **to ~iło nam humory** it raised our spirits; ~**ić czyjś nastrój** to cheer sb up; ~**ić rekord** Sport to set a (new) record ③ (zreperować) to mend, to repair; ~**ić źle uszytą suknię** to make alterations to a. alter a badly-made dress ④ (wprowadzić poprawki) to correct; ~**ić dyktando** *[nauczyciel]* to mark a. correct mistakes in a dictation; *[uczeń]* to correct one's dictation; ~**ić błędy w korekcie** to make corrections on the (galley) proofs ⑤ (zwrócić uwagę) to correct; ~**ić błędnie wymówione nazwisko** to correct a mispronounced name ⑥ (powtórzyć cios) to hit (again); **uderzył go mocno i jeszcze ~ił** he hit him hard and added another blow for good measure

Ⅱ **poprawić się** — **poprawiać się** ① (wygodniej usiąść) ~**ić się na krześle** to settle oneself more comfortably in one's chair ② (inaczej się wyrazić) to correct oneself ③ (polepszyć się) *[pogoda, stan zdrowia]* to improve ④ (przytyć) to put on weight ⑤ (zmienić się na lepsze) ~**ić się w nauce** to make better progress at school

popraw|ka *f* ① (zmiana) alteration, amendment ② pot. (powtórny egzamin) retake, resit GB; **mieć ~kę z geografii** (zdawać) to resit a. retake (one's) geography; (mieć ocenę niedostateczną) to have to resit a. retake (one's) geography

poprawn|y *adi. grad.* ① (prawidłowy) correct; ~**a forma gramatyczna** grammatically correct form ② (zgodny z konwenansem) suitable; ~**e maniery** good manners; ~**e zachowanie** appropriate behaviour

popro|sić *pf vt* ① (mieć prośbę) to ask (**o coś** for sth); ~**sił, żebym usiadł** he invited me to sit down ② (zaprosić) ~**sił ją do tańca** he asked her to dance with him; ~**sić kogoś do telefonu** to call sb to the phone

■ ~**sić o głos** to request the right to speak, to ask for the floor; ~**sił ją o rękę** he asked her to marry him

poprzecz|ka *f* ① (listwa w poprzek) crosspiece ② Sport crossbar; **podnieść/obniżyć ~kę** przen. to raise/ lower standards

pop|rzeć *pf* — **pop|ierać** *impf* ① *vt* ① (wspomóc) to support, to back (up) *[prośbę, kandydaturę]*; ~**ierać rozwój czegoś** to promote the development of sth ② (uzasadnić, potwierdzić) to justify, to back up; ~**rzeć swoje słowa dowodami** to back one's words with proof a. evidence

Ⅱ **poprzeć się** — **popierać się** (jeden drugiego) to support each other; **solidarnie się ~ierać** to stand together

poprzedni *adi. [rozdział, strona]* preceding, previous; *[właściciel, praca]* previous; ~ **prezydent** the former president; **namoczyć fasolę ~ego dnia** (w przepisach) soak the beans the day before

poprzedni|k *m* predecessor

poprzednio *adv.* previously, formerly; **lepiej niż** ∼ better than before

poprze|dzić *pf* — **poprze|dzać** *impf vt* ① (być na przedzie) to precede ② (umieścić na przedzie) to precede, to preface (**coś czymś** sth with sth); **wykład** ∼**dzony klasycznym cytatem** a lecture prefaced with a classic quotation

popsu|ć *pf* **[]** *vt* ① (zniszczyć) to break *[maszynę, zabawki]*; to ruin *[żołądek, zęby]* ② (zakłócić) to spoil *[zabawę, popołudnie]*; **sprzeczka** ∼**ła stosunki między nami** the dispute soured our relationship ③ (rozpieścić) to spoil *[dziecko]*
II popsuć się *[samochód, telewizor]* to break down; *[jedzenie]* to spoil, to go bad a. off; *[pogoda]* to deteriorate

populacj|a *f* population

popularnonaukow|y *adi.* **przegląd/odczyt** ∼**y** a review/lecture for the general public

popularnoś|ć *f* popularity

popularn|y *adi.* grad. *[broszurka, odczyt]* nonspecialist, popular; *[napój, rozrywka, sportowiec]* popular

popu|ścić *pf* — **popu|szczać** *impf* **[]** *vt* to relax; ∼**cić cugli koniowi** to give a horse its head; ∼**szczać pasa** to loosen the belt
II *vi* pot. ① (ustąpić) to give way; **nie** ∼**szczać nikomu** not to budge for anybody; ∼**ścił uczniom** he relaxed classroom discipline ② (nie trzymać moczu, kału) ∼**szczać** to be incontinent, to lack bladder/bowel control; ∼**ścić** to have an accident pot.

popychać *impf* → **popchnąć**

popy|t *m* demand (**na coś** for sth); **wzrost/spadek** ∼**tu** an increase/a fall a. slump in demand; **cieszyć się** ∼**tem** to be in demand

po|r *m* leek

p|ora [] *f* ① (część dnia, roku) time; (okres) season; **pora dnia** a time of the day; **pora roku** (jedna z czterech) season; (moment w roku) a time of the year; **o każdej porze dnia i nocy** at any time of the day or night; **w porze obiadowej** at lunchtime; **pora deszczowa** the rainy season; **o tej porze** (dnia) at this hour; (roku) at this time of the year; **od tej pory** (od teraz) from now on; (od tamtego czasu) since then; **do tej pory** (do teraz) so far; (do wtedy) till that time ② (moment) time; **pora spać!** it's time for bed a. it's bedtime!; **na mnie już pora** I must be off now; **przyszliście w samą porę** you're just in time; **w samą porę!** a. **najwyższa pora!** about time too!
II *praed.* **pora zaczynać** it's time to start

porabia|ć *impf vi* pot. to do; **co** ∼**łeś** what have you been up to?

porachun|ek *m* ∼**ki mafijne** gang warfare; **załatwić** ∼**ki z kimś** to settle a score with sb

pora|da *f* advice; ∼**dy dla młodych matek** advice a. counselling for young mothers; **zasięgnąć** ∼**dy lekarza** to consult a physician; **za czyjąś** ∼**dą** on sb's advice

poradni|a *f* ① Med. (przychodnia) clinic ② (instytucja udzielająca porad) advice bureau, counselling service

poradnik *m* (z instrukcjami) guide; (z poradami) how-to book pot.; ∼ **budowlany** a builder's guide a. handbook

pora|dzić *pf* **[]** *vi* ① (udzielić rady) to advise; ∼**dził mi czekać** he advised me to wait; **co ci lekarz** ∼**dził?** what did the doctor say? ② (pomóc) **nic na to nie** ∼**dzę** I can't help it; **co ja (na to)** ∼**dzę, że ją lubię?** I can't help liking her
II poradzić się (zasięgnąć rady) ∼**dzić się kogoś** to ask sb's advice
III poradzić sobie to manage; ∼**dzi sobie sama** she can manage on her own

poran|ek *m* ① (rano) morning; **o** ∼**ku** książk. in the morning ② (film) a morning screening; (koncert) a morning concert

porann|y *adi. [gazeta, spacer]* morning

pora|zić *pf* — **pora|żać** *impf vt* ① (obezwładnić) to paralyse GB, to paralyze US *[nerwy, mięśnie]*; to dazzle *[oczy, wzrok]*; ∼**zić kogoś prądem** to give sb an electric shock ② (zachwycić, przerazić) to transfix; (zdumieć) to shock; (sparaliżować) to paralyse GB, to paralyze US ③ (zaatakować) to affect; **rośliny** ∼**żone chorobą** plants affected by a disease

poraże|nie *n* Med. ∼**nie dziecięce** infantile paralysis; ∼**nie nerwu twarzowego** facial palsy; ∼**nie mózgowe** cerebral palsy; ∼**nie słoneczne** sunstroke

poraż|ka *f* ① (klęska) defeat; ∼**ka w wyborach** an election defeat ② (niepowodzenie) failure; ∼**ka miłosna** a failed romance

porąb|ać *pf vt* ① (połupać) to chop *[drewno]*; ∼**ać coś na kawałki** to chop sth into pieces ② (poranić) to hack; ∼**ali go mieczami** they hacked him with their swords; **dałby się za nią** ∼**ać** przen. he would go through fire and water for her

porcelan|a *f* china, porcelain; **jadać na** ∼**ie** to use china tableware

porcj|a *f* ① (jedzenia) portion; (towarów, dokumentów) batch; **wziąć drugą** ∼**ę czegoś** to take a second helping of sth ② przen. series; ∼**a komplementów/narzekań** a series of compliments/complaints

poręcz [] *f* ① (balustrada) railing; (na schodach) banister; (góra balustrady) handrail ② (część krzesła, fotela) arm; (wyściełana) armrest
II **poręcze** *plt* Sport (symetryczne) parallel bars; (asymetryczne) asymmetric bars, uneven bars US

poręczać *impf* → **poręczyć**

poręczn|y *adi.* grad. *[walizka, książka]* handy pot.; *[sposób]* convenient; handy pot.

poręcz|yć *pf* — **poręcz|ać** *impf vt* Fin., Prawo to guarantee; ∼**yć za kogoś przy zaciąganiu pożyczki** to guarantee sb for a loan; ∼**yć weksel** to back a. guarantee a bill

pornografi|a *f* pornography; **~a twarda/miękka** hard(-core)/soft(-core) porn(ography)

pornograficzn|y *adi.* pornographic

porodow|y *adi. [skurcze, bóle]* labour GB, labor US

porodów|ka *f pot.* labour ward GB, labor ward US

poro|nić *pf vt* Med., Wet. to abort, to miscarry *[płód, dziecko]*

poronie|nie *n* Med., Wet. miscarriage; **sztuczne ~nie** euf. (an) abortion

por|osnąć *pf* — **por|astać** *impf* **[]** *vt* (pokryć) mech **~astał pnie drzew** trees were covered with moss

[] *vi* (pokryć się) **wzgórze ~osło trawą** grass has grown over the hill

poro|st *m* ① (przyrost) growth; **środek na ~st włosów** a hair restorer ② Bot. lichen

porozum|ieć się *pf* — **porozum|iewać się** *impf v refl.* ① (przekazać informację) to communicate (**z kimś** with sb); **~ieć się z kimś telefonicznie** to contact sb by phone ② (dojść do zgody) to come to a. to reach an agreement (**co do czegoś** on sth)

porozumie|nie *n* ① (wspólna zgoda) agreement; **zrobić coś w ~niu z kimś** to do sth with sb's approval; **zrobić coś bez ~nia z kimś** to do sth without consulting sb; **odejść z pracy za ~niem stron** to terminate an employment contract by mutual agreement ② Polit. (układ) agreement; **~nie o zawieszeniu broni** a ceasefire agreement

por|ód *m* (urodzenie dziecka) childbirth; (proces) labour GB, labor US; (ostatnia faza) delivery

porówn|ać *pf* — **porówn|ywać** *impf* **[]** *vt* to compare; **tych zjawisk nie da się ~ać** a. **nie można ~ywać** these phenomena cannot be compared

[] **porównać się** — **porównywać się** to compare oneself (**z kimś** a. **do kogoś** to a. with sb)

porówna|nie *n* ① (ocena podobieństwa) comparison; **w ~niu z kimś/czymś** compared a. in comparison with sb/sth; **dla ~nia** for comparison; **bez ~nia lepszy/trudniejszy** immeasurably better/harder ② Literat. simile

porównywać *impf* → **porównać**

por|t *m* ① port, harbour GB, harbor US; **~t morski** seaport; **~t lotniczy** airport; **zawinąć do ~tu** to put into port ② Komput. port; **~t wejścia/wyjścia** input/output port

portal *m* portal

portfel *m* ① wallet, billfold US, pocketbook US; **mieć gruby** a. **pełny ~** przen. to have wads of money pot. ② Ekon. portfolio

portie|r *m*, **~ka** *f* ① (odźwierny) doorkeeper, porter GB, janitor US ② (recepcjonista) receptionist

portier|nia *f* porter's lodge a. box

port|ki *plt pot.* trews GB, pants US pot.; **chodzić bez ~ek** pot. to not have two pennies to rub together pot.; **robić w ~ki** posp., przen. to be shit-scared posp.;

trząść ~kami pot., przen. to be shaking in one's shoes

portmonet|ka *f* purse

portre|t *m* ① (podobizna) portrait; **~t pamięciowy** identikit (portrait) ② (gatunek malarstwa) portraiture ③ przen. portrait, portrayal

portret|ować *impf vt* to portray także przen.

portyk *m* portico

poruczni|k *m* lieutenant

porusz|yć *pf* — **porusz|ać** *impf* **[]** *vt* ① (omówić) to bring up, to raise *[kwestię]* ② (wstrząsać) to move; **być do głębi ~onym czymś** to be deeply moved by sth

[] *vi* (wprawić w ruch) to move (**czymś** sth)

[] **poruszyć się** — **poruszać się** to move; **nie ~ać się** to keep still, to remain motionless

por|wać¹ *pf* — **por|ywać** *impf* **[]** *vt* ① (uprowadzić) to kidnap, to abduct *[osobę]*; to hijack *[autobus, samolot]* ② (unieść) *[wiatr, rzeka]* to carry away a. off ③ (chwycić) to grab, to seize ④ (wywrzeć wrażenie) *[artysta, muzyka]* to inspire, to rouse

[] **porwać się** — **porywać się** ① (rzucić się) to lunge; **~wał się na nich z nożem** he lunged at them with a knife ② (podjąć się) to attempt, to tackle (**na coś** sth)

porw|ać² *pf* **[]** *vt* (podrzeć) to tear *[list, gazetę]*; **~ać coś na strzępy** to tear sth to shreds a. pieces; **~ana koszula** a ragged shirt

[] **porwać się** (podrzeć się) to get torn

porwa|nie *n* (osoby) kidnapping, abduction; (pojazdu) hijacking

poryw **[]** *m* ① (wiatru) gust ② (emocji) surge, outburst; **w ~ie gniewu** in the heat of anger; **w pierwszym ~ie** on the spur of the moment

[] **w porywach** *part.* pot. (maksymalnie) at (the) most

porywacz *m*, **~ka** *f* (osoby) kidnapper, abductor; (pojazdu) hijacker

porywać *impf* → **porwać¹**

porywcz|y *adi.* impetuous, quick-tempered

porząd|ek **[]** *m* ① (ład) order, tidiness; **zrobić ~ek w czymś** to put sth in order; **doprowadzić coś do ~ku** to tidy up sth; **doprowadzić się do ~ku** to tidy oneself up; **~ek publiczny** public order ② (kolejność) order; **w ~ku alfabetycznym** in alphabetical order; **~ek dzienny** a. **dnia** the agenda, the order of the day

[] **porządki** *plt* (sprzątanie) cleaning

■ w ~ku! all right!; **on jest w ~ku** pot. he's OK pot.; **coś tu nie jest w ~ku** pot. something's not (quite) right here; **wszystko było w ~ku** pot. everything was fine a. all right; **dla ~ku** for form's sake; **być na ~ku dziennym** to be the order of the day; **przejść nad czymś do ~ku dziennego** to wave sth aside

porządk|ować *impf vt* ① (sprzątać) to clean, to tidy up ② (układać) to put [sth] in order *[rzeczy, książki]*

porządkow|y [] *adi. [liczebnik]* ordinal; *[numer]* serial

[] **porządkow|y** *m*, ~a *f* marshal

porządnie [] *adv.* grad. [1] (starannie) neatly; **wyglądać** ~ to look neat [2] (przyzwoicie) decently [] *adv.* pot. **wyspać się/odpocząć** ~ to get a good sleep/rest; ~ **nauczyć się czegoś** to really learn sth; **zmarzli** ~ they froze half to death pot.

porządn|y [] *adi.* grad. [1] (zadbany) neat [2] (lubiący porządek) tidy [3] (uczciwy) decent; ~**a rodzina** a respectable family

[] *adi.* pot. (potężny) *[mróz]* solid; *[ulewa]* heavy; *[posiłek]* substantial; **ojciec sprawił mu** ~**e lanie** his father gave him a good thrashing pot.

porzecz|ka *f* currant; **białe** ~**ki** white currants; **czerwone/czarne** ~**ki** redcurrants/blackcurrants

porzu|cić *pf* — **porzu|cać** *impf vt* to abandon *[dziecko]*; to leave *[kraj, żonę]*; to give up *[pracę, nadzieję]*

posa|da *f* job, position; ~**da secretarza** a secretarial position; **dobrze/źle płatna** ~**da** a well/poorly paid job; **wolna** ~**da** vacancy

■ **chwiać się** a. **drżeć w** ~**dach** to be shaken to the foundations

posa|dzić *pf vt* [1] (podnieść do pozycji siedzącej) to sit [sb] up; (pomóc usiąść) to sit [sb] down *[chorego, dziecko]*; (wskazać miejsce) to seat *[gości, słuchaczy]*; ~**dzić sobie dziecko na kolanach** to take a child on one's lap [2] (zasadzić) to plant *[roślinę]*; ~**dzić kwiaty w doniczkach** to pot the plants [3] pot. (umieścić w więzieniu) to put [sb] away pot.

posadz|ka *f* floor; **na gołej** ~**ce** on the bare floor

posag *m* dowry; **wnieść coś w** ~**u** to be dowered with sth

posą|dzić *pf* — **posą|dzać** *impf vt* (zarzucić) to accuse (**kogoś o coś** sb of sth); (podejrzewać) to suspect (**kogoś o coś** sb of sth)

posąg *m* statue

posąż|ek *m* statuette, figurine

poselstw|o *n* [1] (placówka) legation [2] (misja) mission

po|seł *m* [1] (członek parlamentu) Member of Parliament, MP [2] (wysłannik) envoy

posępn|y *adi.* grad. sombre GB, somber US

posiadacz *m*, ~**ka** *f* (samochodu, nieruchomości) owner; (konta, polisy) holder

posiada|ć *impf vt* książk. [1] (mieć) to own *[majątek]*; to have *[rodzinę, przyjaciół]*; **stan** ~**nia** assets; **objąć** a. **wziąć coś w** ~**nie** to take possession of sth; **wejść w** ~**nie czegoś** to come into (the) possession of sth; **znaleźć się w** ~**niu czegoś** to be in possession of sth [2] (charakteryzować się) to have *[cechę, dar, władzę]*; to have, to possess *[wiedzę, wykształcenie]*

■ **nie** ~**ć się z radości** to be beside oneself with joy

posiadłoś|ć [] *f* estate

[] **posiadłości** *plt* (państwa) dominions

posiedze|nie *n* sitting, session

posieka|ć *pf vt* to chop up *[mięso, warzywa]*; **drobno** ~**ne migdały** finely chopped almonds

■ **dałby się** ~**ć za kolegów** he'd go through hell for his mates; **dałaby się** ~**ć za rower górski** she'd give her eyeteeth for a mountain bike

posił|ek [] *m* meal

[] **posiłki** *plt* reinforcements; **ściągnąć** ~**ki** to call in reinforcements

posiłkow|y *adi. [czasownik]* auxiliary

poskarż|yć [] *vi* to tell (**na kogoś** on sb); *[dziecko]* to tattle (**na kogoś** on sb)

[] **poskarżyć się** [1] (obwinić) to complain (**na kogoś** about sb) [2] (narzekać) to complain (**na coś** of sth); ~**yć się komuś** to complain to sb

po|słać[1] *pf* — **po|syłać** *impf vt* to send *[list, paczkę]*; **posłać kogoś po lekarza** to send sb for the doctor; **posłać dziecko do szkoły** to send a child to school; **posłać kogoś na emeryturę** to retire sb; **posłać piłkę do bramki** to send the ball into the net; **posłać komuś całusa** to blow sb a kiss

po|słać[2], **po|ścielić** *pf vt* (przygotować spanie) to make up a bed; (złożyć pościel) to make the bed

■ **jak sobie pościelesz, tak się wyśpisz** przysł. you've made your bed, so you must lie in it przysł.

posła|nie[1] *n* książk. (przesłanie) message; (apel) appeal

posła|nie[2] *n* (spanie) bed

posła|niec *m* (z wiadomością) messenger; (z przesyłką) courier; **przez** ~**ńca** by messenger a. courier

posłan|ka *f* Member of Parliament, MP

posłannictw|o *n* mission

posł|odzić *pf vt* to sweeten *[herbatę, kompot]*

posłowi|e *n* afterword

posłuch *m* [1] (autorytet) respect; **budzić** ~ **u kogoś** a. **mieć u kogoś** ~ to command sb's respect [2] (posłuszeństwo) obedience; **zmusić kogoś do** ~**u** to make sb obey

■ **dać czemuś** ~ (uwierzyć) to believe sth *[plotkom]*; (usłuchać) to heed sth *[radom]*

posłucha|ć *pf* [] *vi* [1] (wysłuchać) to listen (**kogoś** to sb); ~**ć pod drzwiami** to listen in at the door; ~**j, jak pada deszcz** listen to the rain [2] (usłuchać) to obey (**kogoś** sb); ~**ł mojej rady** he did what I suggested

[] **posłuchać się** to obey (**kogoś** sb)

posługiwać się *impf* → **posłużyć się**

posłuszeństw|o *n* obedience (**komuś** a. **wobec kogoś** to sb); **głos odmówił mi** ~**a** przen. my voice failed me; **silnik odmówił** ~**a** przen. the engine wouldn't work

posłuszn|y *adi.* grad. obedient (**komuś** to sb)

posłuż|yć *pf vi* [1] (zostać użytym) ~**yć** (**komuś**) **za coś** to serve (sb) as sth; **te informacje** ~**yły mu do napisania książki** he used this information to write a book [2] (dobrze zrobić) ~**yć komuś** to do sb good; **ta pizza mi nie** ~**yła** the pizza didn't agree with me

posłu|żyć się *pf —* **posłu|giwać się** *impf v refl.* ~**żyć się czymś** to use sth; **umiesz się tym** ~**giwać?** do you know how to use it?; ~**giwać się angielskim** to speak English

pos|olić *pf vt* to salt, to add salt to *[wodę, potrawę]*; to put salt on *[kanapkę]*; ~**olona woda** salted water

pospoli|ty [] *adi. grad.* [] (powszechny) *[odmiana, imię, roślina]* common [] (przeciętny) *[rysy, twarz]* plain; ~**ty złodziej** a common thief [] (prostacki) *[osoba]* common

[] *adi. [nazwa, rzeczownik]* common

posprzątą|ć *pf vt* [] (zrobić porządek) to clean, to tidy up *[salę, pokój]*; ~**ć w łazience** to clean the bathroom; ~**ć na biurku** to tidy a desk [] (pozbierać) to clear [sth] away *[gruz, klocki]*; ~**j ze stołu** clear the table

posprzecza|ć się *pf v refl.* to quarrel (**z kimś** with sb); ~**ć się o coś** to quarrel over a. about sth

po|st *m* fast; **Wielki Post** Lent

posta|ć[1] *f* [] (forma) form; **w** ~**ci** a. **pod postacią czegoś** in the form of sth; **przyjąć** a. **przybrać** ~**ć łabędzia** to take a. assume the form of a swan; **to zmienia** ~**ć rzeczy** that changes everything [] (sylwetka) figure; **czyjaś szczupła** ~**ć** sb's slim figure [] (osobistość) figure; **kontrowersyjna** ~**ć** a controversial figure [] (bohater) character; **pierwszoplanowa** ~**ć** the leading character

post|ać[2] *pf vi* to stand; ~**ać parę godzin na warcie** to stand on guard for a couple of hours ■ **to mi nawet w głowie nie** ~**ało** it never entered my mind a. head; **moja noga już tu więcej nie** ~**anie** I'll never set foot in this place again

postan|owić *pf —* **postan|awiać** *impf vt* to decide; ~**owić coś zrobić** to decide to do sth; ~**owić czegoś nie robić** to decide against doing sth; ~**owiono, że...** it was decided that...; **sąd** ~**owił, że...** the court ruled that...; ~**owić sobie** to resolve

postanowie|nie *n* [] (zamiar) resolution; **powziąć** ~**nie, żeby...** to make a resolution to...; **trwać w** ~**niu** to be firm in one's resolution; **wyszedł z domu z** ~**niem, że nigdy nie wróci** he left home, resolved never to come back [] (decyzja) ruling, decision; ~**nie sądu** the court's ruling; ~**nie rządu o obniżeniu podatków** the government's decision to cut taxes

postara|ć się *pf v refl.* to try (**coś zrobić** to do sth); ~**ć się o coś** to try to get sth; ~**ł się, żeby wszyscy byli zadowoleni** he saw to it that everybody was happy

postarz|eć się *pf v refl.* to age

postaw|a *f* [] (stosunek) attitude (**wobec czegoś** towards sth); (zachowanie) conduct [] (pozycja) posture, stance; **w** ~**ie stojącej/siedzącej** in a standing/sitting position; **przyjąć** ~**ę zasadniczą** to stand

to attention [] (sylwetka) posture; (sposób noszenia się) bearing; **prawidłowa/nieprawidłowa** ~**a** good/bad posture

postaw|ić *pf* [] *vt* [] (umieścić) to put, to stand *[osobę, kieliszek]*; to put *[telewizor, mebel]*; **gdzie mogę** ~**ić samochód?** where can I park my car?; ~**ić wodę na herbatę** to put the kettle on [] (w pionowej pozycji) to set [sth] upright *[krzesło]*; to turn [sth] up *[kołnierz]*; ~**ić uszy** to prick (up) one's ears; ~**ić kogoś na nogi** to stand sb on their feet; przen. to have sb back on their feet [] (zbudować) to erect *[pomnik]*; to put [sth] up *[mur, namiot]* [] (wyznaczyć funkcję) to post *[straże]*; ~**ić kogoś na czele armii** to place sb in command of an army; **wysoko** ~**iona osoba** a highly-placed person [] (doprowadzić) to put; ~**ić kogoś w trudnej sytuacji** to put sb in a difficult situation; ~**ić kogoś przed sądem** to bring sb to court [] (napisać) to put *[krzyżyk, przecinek]* [] Szkol. to give *[ocenę]* [] (sformułować) to put [sth] forward *[tezę, wniosek, kandydaturę]*; to pose *[pytanie]*; to make *[diagnozę, warunek]*; ~**ić komuś zarzuty** to bring charges against sb; ~**ić sobie ambitne cele** to set oneself ambitious goals; ~**ić sobie za cel zrobienie czegoś** to make doing sth one's goal; ~**my sprawę jasno** let's make things clear [] (ułożyć) to play *[pasjansa]*; ~**ić komuś horoskop** to read sb's horoscope [] pot. (zafundować) ~**ić coś komuś** to stand sb sth pot. *[obiad, piwo]* [] (w hazardzie) to bet, to gamble; ~**ić na konia** to place a bet on a horse; ~**ić 100 złotych na konia** to bet 100 zlotys on a horse; ~**ić wszystko na jedną kartę** przen. to stake everything on one card; ~**ić na niewłaściwego konia** przen. to back the wrong horse

[] *vi* (wybrać) to pick (**na kogoś** sb); (zaufać) to be counting (**na kogoś** on sb); (skupić się) to focus (**na coś** on sth)

[] **postawić się** pot. (popisać się) to show off

■ ~**ić na swoim** to get one's own way; ~**ić się komuś** to stand up to sb; ~**ić się w czyimś położeniu** to put oneself in sb's shoes

post|ąpić *pf —* **post|ępować** *impf vi* [] (zachować się) to act; ~**ąpiłeś uczciwie** this was an honest thing to do; **nie wiedział, jak ma** ~**ąpić** he didn't know what to do [] (do przodu) to advance; ~**ąpić naprzód** to move forward; ~**ępować za kimś** to follow sb [] (rozwinąć się) *[choroba, badania]* to progress; **reforma** ~**ępuje bardzo powoli** the reform is proceeding very slowly

posterun|ek *m* [] (stanowisko) post; ~**ek graniczny** a frontier post; ~**ek policji** a police station; **trwać na** ~**ku** to remain at one's post [] (straż) guard; (patrol) patrol; **wystawić** ~**ki** to post guards

postęp *m* [] progress; ~ **techniczny** technological progress; **robić** ~**y w jeździe na nartach** to make progress in skiing [] (w matematyce) progression; **zwiększać się w ~ie geometrycznym** przen. to increase at an exponential rate

postęp|ek *m* deed; (zły) misdeed

postępować *impf* → **postąpić**

postępowa|nie *n* 1 (zachowanie) conduct 2 (process) proceedings; **wszcząć ~nie przeciwko komuś** to institute proceedings against sb

postępow|y *adi.* progressive

postkomunistyczn|y *adi.* post-Communist

postn|y *adi. [dzień]* fast; *[posiłek, danie]* fasting; (wielkopostny) Lenten

post|ój *m* 1 (przerwa w podróży) stop, stopover; **miejsce ~oju** a stopping place; **zrobić sobie ~ój** to make a stop 2 (przystanek) **~ój taksówek** a taxi rank, a taxi stand US; **"zakaz ~oju„** 'no waiting'

postrach *m* terror; **budzić w kimś ~** to scare sb; **strzelać na ~** to fire warning shots; **być ~em szkoły** to be the terror of a school

postrza|ł *m* 1 (rana) gunshot wound; **dostać ~ł w brzuch** to be shot in the stomach 2 Med. lumbago

postrzel|ić *pf* 1 *vt* to shoot; **~ić kogoś w nogę** to shoot sb in the leg

2 **postrzelić się** to shoot oneself; **~ić się w nogę** to shoot oneself in the leg

postrzel|ony *adi.* pot. nutty pot.

postula|t *m* demand; **~t podniesienia płac** a demand for a pay rise; **wysuwać a. stawiać ~ty** to make demands

postul|ować *impf vt* książk. to call for

postumen|t *m* plinth, pedestal

posu|nąć *pf* — **posu|wać** *impf* 1 *vt* 1 (przemieścić) to move (on) 2 (doprowadzić) **~nąć pracę naprzód** to make progress with one's work; **~nął żart za daleko** he carried the joke too far

2 **posunąć się** — **posuwać się** 1 (przemieścić się) to move, to advance; (zrobić miejsce) to move over; **~wać się krok za krokiem** a. **noga za nogą** to trudge wearily step by step, to drag one's feet 2 (rozwinąć się) to move on; **praca ~wała się pełną parą** the work was in full swing 3 (przekroczyć pewną granicę) **~nąć się do rękoczynów** to resort to fisticuffs; **~nęła się do twierdzenia, że... she** went as far as to assert that...; **~nąć się za daleko** to go too far

■ **~nąć się (w latach)** to grow old, to age

posunię|cie *n* move; **mistrzowskie ~cie** a masterful move

posuwać *impf* → **posunąć**

posyłać *impf* → **posłać**[1]

posył|ka *f* **chłopiec na ~ki** an errand-boy; **być na ~ki** to do errands

posyp|ać *pf* — **posyp|ywać** *impf vt* to sprinkle (**coś czymś** sth with sth)

2 **posypać się** *[liście]* to fall; *[tynk]* to fall off;

[pociski, razy] to rain down; *[brawa]* to break out; *[oferty]* to come pouring in

poszczególn|y *adi.* individual, separate

poszczęści|ć się *pf v imp.* **~ło się jej** she was lucky

poszczu|ć *pf vt* **~ć kogoś psami** to set dogs loose on sb

poszerz|yć *pf* — **poszerz|ać** *impf* 1 *vt* to widen, to broaden *[ulicę]*; to ream, to widen *[otwór]*; to let out *[ubranie]*; przen. to broaden *[wiedzę]*

2 **poszerzyć się** — **poszerzać się** *[droga]* to become wider; *[zespół]* to widen, to expand

poszew|ka *f* pillowcase, pillowslip GB

poszkodowan|y 1 *adi.* (fizycznie) injured; (moralnie, materialnie) harmed

2 **poszkodowan|y** *m*, **~a** *f* the aggrieved party

poszla|ka *f* circumstantial evidence

poszuka|ć *pf vi* to look for; **~j tego w słowniku** look it up in the dictionary; **~ć kogoś wzrokiem** a. **oczami** to look around for sb; **~ć czegoś w pamięci** to search one's memory for sth

poszukiwacz *m*, **~ka** *f* searcher, prospector; **~ przygód** adventurer; **~ skarbów** treasure hunter; **~e złota** gold prospectors; gold-diggers przest.

poszuk|iwać *impf vt* to seek, to try to find; **~iwać ropy naftowej** to prospect for oil; **~iwać pracy** to job-hunt pot.; **policja ~uje sprawcy wypadku** the police are on the lookout for the perpetrator of the accident; **być ~iwanym przez policję** to be on a wanted list

posz|wa *f* duvet a. quilt cover

po|ścić *impf vi* to fast

pościel *f* 1 (koce, poduszki, kołdry) bedding, bed covering 2 (prześcieradła, poszwy) bedclothes, bedlinen 3 (posłanie) bed; **zerwać się z ~i** to jump out of bed

pościelić → **posłać**[2]

pościg *m* chase, pursuit; **ruszyć w ~ za kimś** to give chase to sb, to go in pursuit of sb; **wymknąć się ~owi** to evade one's pursuers, to give one's pursuers the slip; **~ za nowościami** the pursuit a. quest for novelty

poślad|ek *m* buttock

poślizg *m* 1 Aut. skid; **wpaść w ~** to go a. get into a skid; **wyjść z ~u** to get out of a. correct a skid 2 pot., przen. slippage pot.; **bez ~ów** on deadline, as scheduled

poślizgn|ąć się *pf v refl.* to slip; **~ąć się na oblodzonej jezdni** to slip on the icy road

poślub|ić *pf* — **poślub|iać** *impf vt* to marry; to wed daw.

pośmiewisk|o *n* 1 (drwiny) ridicule; **narazić kogoś na ~o** to subject a. expose sb to ridicule 2 (przedmiot kpin) laughing stock; **zrobić z siebie ~** to make a laughing stock of oneself

pośpiech *m* hurry, haste; **w ~u** in haste; **po co ten ~?** why the rush?; **nie ma ~u** there's no rush

pośpieszać *impf* → **pośpieszyć**

pośpieszn|y [] *adi. [kroki, decyzja, wyjazd]* hurried, hasty; *[winda, pociąg]* fast

[] II *m (pociąg)* fast train; *(autobus)* fast bus

pośpiesz|yć *pf* — **pośpiesz|ać** *impf* **[]** *vi* to hurry, to hasten; ~**yć na ratunek** to hasten to the rescue; ~**yć do domu** to hurry home; ~**ył dodać, że...** he hastened to add that...

[] II pośpieszyć się to hurry up; **trzeba się** ~**yć z robotą** we must get on with our work; ~**yli się z gratulacjami** their congratulations were premature

pośredni *adi.* [] *(niebezpośredni) [wpływ, związek, koszty]* indirect; **głosowanie** ~**e** indirect voting [] *(przejściowy)* intermediate; **coś** ~**ego między farsą a komedią** something in between a farce and a comedy

pośredniak *m* pot. jobcentre GB, employment agency

pośrednictw|o *n* [] *(występowanie w roli łącznika)* agency, mediation; **za** ~**em czegoś** via sth, through (the agency of) sth [] *(kojarzenie)* agency; ~**o w obrocie nieruchomościami** an estate agency GB, a real estate agency US

pośrednicz|yć *impf vi* [] *(jako rozjemca)* to mediate; ~**yć w sporze pracowniczym** to mediate in an industrial dispute [] *(załatwiać transakcje)* to act as a go-between a. middleman

pośredni|k *m*, ~**czka** *f* [] *(rozjemca)* intermediary, go-between, mediator [] *(w transakcjach)* broker

pośrednio *adv.* indirectly

pośrodku [] *praep.* in the middle of, in the centre GB a. center US of; **przedziałek** ~ **głowy** a centre parting

[] II *adv.* in the middle, in the centre GB a. center US

poświadcz|yć *pf* — **poświadcz|ać** *impf vt* to authenticate *[podpis, dokument]*

poświęcać *impf* → **poświęcić**

poświęce|nie *n* [] *(ofiara)* sacrifice; **najwyższe** ~**nie** the utmost sacrifice [] *(oddanie)* dedication; **z** ~**niem** with dedication

poświę|cić *pf* — **poświę|cać** *impf* **[]** *vt* [] to consecrate *[kaplicę, cmentarz]*; to bless *[medalik, szpital]* [] *(złożyć w ofierze)* to sacrifice *[życie, karierę]* [] *(zająć się)* to devote, to dedicate *[czas, uwagę]* **(komuś** to sb); **monografia** ~**cona kubizmowi** a monograph on cubism

[] II poświęcić się — **poświęcać się** [] *(ponieść ofiarę)* to sacrifice oneself **(dla czegoś** for sth) [] *(obrać cel życia)* to devote oneself **(czemuś** to sth)

po|t *m* sweat, perspiration; **oblać się potem** to break out in a sweat; **w pocie czoła** in the sweat of one's brow; **wziąć coś na poty** to take a diaphoretic

potajemn|y *adi. [plan, spotkanie]* secret

potak|nąć *pf* — **potak|iwać** *impf vi* to assent; *(ruchem głowy)* to nod assent; ~**iwać komuś** to agree with sb

potarga|ć *pf* **[]** *vt* [] *(zwichrzyć)* to ruffle; ~**na broda** a dishevelled GB a. disheveled US beard [] *(podrzeć)* to tear up

[] II potargać się *[fryzura, osoba]* to get tousled

potas *m* potassium

potąd *pron.* pot. up to here; **mam tego** ~**!** I've had it up to here! pot.; **mam go** ~**!** I've had just about enough of him! pot.

potem *adv. (następnie)* then, next; *(później)* later, afterwards; **na** ~ for later; **nie odkładaj roboty na** ~ don't leave your work until a. till later

potencj|a *f* potency; ~**a twórcza** creative power

potencjaln|y *adi.* potential

potencja|ł *m* potential

potenta|t *m*, ~**tka** *f* tycoon; ~**t prasowy** a newspaper mogul

potę|ga [] *f* [] *(moc)* power, might; **wzrastać w** ~**gę** to grow more powerful; **stanąć u szczytu** ~**gi** to reach the height of (one's) power [] *(państwo)* power [] *(w matematyce)* power; **podnieść liczbę do czwartej** ~**gi** to raise a number to the fourth power

[] II na potęgę *adv.* pot. *(bardzo)* mightily; **pić na** ~**gę** to drink heavily

potęg|ować *impf* **[]** *vt* to heighten, to enhance *[wrażenie]*; to compound *[niepokój]*

[] II potęgować się *[agresja]* to escalate; *[hałas, napięcie]* to intensify

potęp|ić *pf* — **potęp|iać** *impf vt* to condemn *[wojnę, zbrodnię]*; ~**ić kogoś za coś** to condemn sb for sth

potępie|nie *n* [] *(ocena)* condemnation [] Relig. damnation

potężn|y *adi.* grad. *[mężczyzna, zwierzę, cios]* mighty; *[drzewo, budowla]* huge; *[władca, państwo]* mighty, powerful

pot|knąć się *pf* — **pot|ykać się** *impf v refl.* [] *(zaczepić nogą)* to stumble; ~**knąć się o coś** to stumble over sth [] przen. to slip up

potknię|cie *n* slip-up pot.

potłu|c [] *pf* **[]** *vt* [] *(rozbić)* to break, to shatter *[szybę, okulary]*; ~**czone szkło** broken glass [] *(uderzyć)* to bruise *[kolano, rękę]*

[] II potłuc się [] *(naczynia, szyba)* to break [] *(osoba)* to get bruised

potoczn|y *adi.* [] *[wiedza, opinia]* popular; ~**e sprawy** everyday matters; **w** ~**ym rozumieniu słowa** as the word is popularly understood [] Jęz. *[mowa, nazwa]* colloquial

potok *m* [] *(strumień)* stream, brook [] *(deszczu)* torrent; *(lawy)* stream; *(łez)* flood; **wino lało się** ~**ami** wine was flowing [] przen. flood przen.; ~ **wyzwisk** a volley of abuse

potom|ek *m*, ~**kini** *f* descendant; **być** ~**kiem rodziny szlacheckiej** to come from noble stock; **umrzeć bez męskiego** ~**ka** to die without male issue

potomnoś|ć f książk. posterity, future generations
potomn|y książk. **I** adi. [pokolenie] descendant
II **potomni** plt posterity
potomstw|o n książk. offspring, progeny
potop m 1 (biblijny) the Flood 2 przen. deluge także przen.
potraf|ić pf, impf vi 1 (umieć) ~**ić coś zrobić** to be able to do sth, to be capable of doing sth; **ona** ~**i świetnie gotować** she can cook very well 2 (mieć zwyczaj) **on** ~**i spać do południa** he's capable of sleeping until noon
potrakt|ować pf vt 1 (odnieść się) to treat; ~**ować kogoś źle** to treat sb badly; ~**ować kogoś z góry** to patronize sb 2 (uderzyć) ~**ować kogoś kijem** to give sb a thrashing with a stick; ~**ować kogoś kulą z pistoletu** to put a bullet through sb
potraw|a f dish; ~**y z jarzyn/drobiu** vegetable/poultry dishes
potraw|ka f fricassee
potrą|cić pf — **potrą|cać** impf **I** vt 1 (szturchnąć) to jostle [osobę]; to knock [krzesło, stolik] 2 (jadąc uderzyć) to knock down, to run down [pieszego] 3 (odliczyć) to deduct [sumę]
II **potrącić się** — **potrą|cać się** (nawzajem) to jostle
potrwa|ć pf vi to last; **to nie** ~ **długo** it won't be long
potrzask m trap także przen.; **zastawiać** ~**i na coś** to set traps for sth; **wpaść w** ~ to fall into a trap
potrzą|snąć pf — **potrzą|sać** impf vt to shake; ~**snąć przecząco głową** to shake one's head; ~**snąć kogoś za ramię** to shake sb by the arm
potrzeb|a f **I** f 1 (konieczność) need; **w miarę** ~**y** as the need arise; **w razie** ~**y** if need be, if necessary; **bez** ~**y** unnecessarily; **nie ma** ~**y się śpieszyć** there's no need to hurry 2 (rzecz niezbędna) need; ~**y mieszkaniowe** housing needs; **zaspokajać elementarne** ~**y** to meet the basic needs; **artykuły pierwszej** ~**y** necessities 3 (ciężkie położenie) **być w** ~**ie** to be in need; **przyjść komuś z pomocą w** ~**ie** to come to sb's help in need
II praed. ~**a nam czasu** we need time; **czego ci** ~**a?** what do you need?
■ ~**y fizjologiczne** euf. need to relieve oneself; **wyjść za własną** ~**ą** euf. to go and see a man about a dog euf.
potrzebn|y adi. grad. [osoba] needed, wanted; [przedmiot, czynność] necessary; **chorym** ~**y jest spokój** the sick need calm
potrzeb|ować impf vi ~**ować czegoś** to need sth; **nie** ~**ujesz się tłumaczyć** you don't need to explain yourself
potrzyma|ć pf vt to hold [torbę, parasol, psa]; ~**j tabletkę pod językiem** keep the tablet under your tongue; **dać komuś coś do** ~**nia** to give sb sth to hold
potuln|y adi. grad. docile, meek
poturb|ować pf vt to batter, to maul

potwarz f książk. calumny, slander
potwier|dzić pf — **potwier|dzać** impf **I** vt to confirm [fakt, wersję]; ~**dzić czyjąś tożsamość** to prove sb's identity; ~**dzić odbiór przesyłki** to acknowledge the receipt of a parcel; **wyjątek** ~**dza regułę** the exception proves the rule
II **potwierdzić się** — **potwierdzać się** [hipoteza] to prove correct; [wiadomość] to be confirmed; **ich obawy się nie** ~**dziły** their fears proved to be unfounded
potworn|y adi. grad. 1 (budzący grozę) [zbrodnia, wypadek] horrendous; [krzyk, wrzask] fearsome 2 (brzydki) [twarz, wygląd] horrible 3 (wielki) [ból, upał] horrible; [bałagan, nudziarz] frightful pot.
potw|ór m monster także przen.
potykać się impf — **potknąć się**
pouczać impf — **pouczyć**
pouczając|y adi. [książka] instructive, enlightening; [przygoda] salutary
poucze|nie n caution; **udzielić komuś** ~**nia** to caution sb
poucz|yć pf — **poucz|ać** impf vt 1 (upomnieć) to admonish; [policjant] to caution; **nikt mnie nie będzie** ~**ał** I'm not going to have anybody tell me what to do 2 (poinformować) to advise, to instruct; ~**yć kogoś, co ma robić** to instruct sb what to do 3 (nauczyć) [doświadczenie, eksperyment] to teach
poufal|ić się impf v refl. to be too familiar (**z kimś** with sb)
poufałoś|ć f familiarity; **pozwalać sobie na** ~**ci wobec kogoś** to be overfamiliar with sb
poufa|ły adi. grad. [rozmowa, pogawędka] familiar; [gest, klepnięcie] friendly; [osoba] too familiar, overfamiliar
poufn|y adi. [informacje, dokument] confidential, classified; [narada] secret; ~**a sprawa** a confidential matter
pourazow|y adi. post-traumatic
powa|ga f 1 (sposób bycia) seriousness, solemnity; **zachować** ~**gę** to keep a straight face; **z** ~**gą** seriously 2 (ważność) seriousness, gravity; ~**ga chwili** the solemnity of the situation 3 (autorytet) dignity; **użyć swojej** ~**gi** to use one's authority
powal|ić pf — **powal|ać** impf vt [osoba, wiatr] to fell; [choroba] to strike [sb]; down; ~**ić kogoś na kolana** to bring sb to their knees
poważani|e n esteem, respect; **cieszyć się czyimś** ~**em** a. **mieć** ~**e u kogoś** to be held in high regard by sb; **z** ~**em...** (do osoby nieznanej) yours faithfully...; (do osoby znanej z nazwiska) yours sincerely...; **mieć kogoś w głębokim** ~**u** iron. to not give a damn about sb pot.
poważnie adv. grad. seriously; ~ **z kimś porozmawiać** to have a serious talk with sb; **myśleć o kimś** ~ to be serious about sb; ~**?** really?; **mówię** ~**!** I mean it!; **chyba nie mówisz** ~**!** you

can't be serious!; **wyglądał nad wiek** ~ he looked older than his years

poważn|y *adi. grad. [propozycja, rozmowa, różnica]* serious; *[spojrzenie, atmosfera]* grave, solemn; *[choroba, wykroczenie]* serious, grave; **~ym głosem** in a solemn a. grave voice; **odgrywać ~ą rolę w czymś** to play a major role in sth; **mieć wobec kogoś ~e zamiary** to intend to marry sb; **być w ~ym stanie** książk. to be in a delicate condition przest.

powącha|ć *pf vt* to smell, to sniff *[kwiatek, perfumy, jedzenie]*

powesel|eć *pf vi* to cheer up

powiad|omić *pf* — **powiad|amiać** *impf vt* książk. to notify (**kogoś o czymś** sb about sth)

powi|at *m* ≈ county *(second level of local administration in Poland)*

powią|zać *pf vt* 1 *(połączyć)* to tie [sth] together *[sznurki, nitki]*; *(obwiązać)* to tie [sth] around *[walizki, paczki]*; **~zać coś w pęczki** to tie sth into bunches 2 *(znaleźć podobieństwa)* to connect *[informacje]*; **~zać ze sobą fakty** to connect facts

powid|ła *plt* plum jam

powiedze|nie *n* saying

powie|dzieć *pf vt, vi* to say *[prawdę, słowo]*; to tell *[dowcip]*; **~dzieć, że...** to say (that)...; **~dzieć coś komuś** to tell sb sth; **~dzieć komuś o czymś** to tell sb about sth; **~dzieć komuś, żeby coś zrobił** to tell sb to do sth; **~dziano nam, że...** we were told that...; **~dzieć na kogoś „głupek"** to call sb a fool; **jak już wcześniej ~działem...** as I said before...; **~dzmy, że...** let's say that...; **że tak ~m** so to speak a. say; **~dzmy sobie szczerze...** let's face it...; **trzeba sobie jasno ~dzieć, że...** we have to admit that...; **~dzieć swoje** to say one's piece; **nie ~m, żebym był zachwycony** I'm not exactly happy; **nie ~m, było całkiem przyjemnie** I must say it was quite nice; **prawdę ~dziawszy...** frankly speaking..., to be honest...; **niezbyt rozgarnięty, żeby nie ~dzieć głupi** rather simpleminded not to say stupid; **co chcesz przez to ~dzieć?** what do you mean?; **dobrze ~dziane** well said; **to (za) mało ~dziane** it's an understatement; **to za wiele** a. **dużo ~dziane** that would be saying too much; **co to ja chciałem ~dzieć?** what was I to say?; **co ty ~sz?** (ze zdumieniem) are you serious?; (ironicznie) oh, really?; **mieć wiele do ~dzenia** (mieć wpływy) to have a lot of say; (dużo wiedzieć) to have a lot to say; **wcale nie jest ~dziane, że...** no one says (that)...; **kto by ~dział, że...** who would've guessed (that)...; **co to ja chciałem ~dzieć?** what was I to say?; **jak to ~dzieć?** how shall I put it?; **co ~sz na lody?** what would you say to an ice cream?

powie|ka *f* eyelid; **dolna/górna ~ka** the lower/upper eyelid; **~ki mi się kleiły** przen. my eyelids

were heavy; **spędzać komuś sen z ~k** przen. to keep sb awake

powiel|ić *pf* — **powiel|ać** *impf vt* 1 to duplicate *[dokument]*; **~ić coś w stu egzemplarzach** to make a hundred copies of sth 2 przen. to repeat *[motyw, schemat]*

powierni|ca, **~czka** *f* confidante

powierni|k *m* 1 *(zaufany)* confidant 2 *(pełnomocnik)* trustee

powierzać *impf* → **powierzyć**

powierzchni|a *f* 1 *(wierzch)* surface także przen.; **wypłynąć na ~ę** *[łódź podwodna, nurek]* to come a. rise to the surface; **utrzymywać się na ~** to stay on the surface, to stay afloat; przen. to keep one's head above water; **zniknąć z ~ ziemi** to be wiped off the surface of the earth 2 *(przestrzeń)* space; **~a biurowa** office space 3 *(wielkość)* *(surface)* area; **mieć ~ę tysiąca metrów kwadratowych** to be a thousand square metres in area

powierzchown|y *adi.* superficial

powierz|yć *pf* — **powierz|ać** *impf vt* 1 *(zlecić)* **~yć komuś coś** to entrust sb with sth; **~yć komuś zrobienie czegoś** to entrust sb with doing sth; **~yć komuś główną rolę** to give sb a leading role 2 *(przekazać)* **~yć komuś coś** to entrust sth to sb; **~yć komuś swój sekret** to confide one's secret to sb; **~yć kogoś czyjejś opiece** to entrust sb to sb's care

powie|sić *pf* 1 *vt* 1 *(zawiesić)* to hang *[lustro, zasłony]* 2 *(zabić)* to hang *[osobę]*; **~sić kogoś na gałęzi** to hang sb from a tree; **~szono go za zdradę** he was hanged for treason

11 **powiesić się** to hang oneself; **~sił się na pasku** he hanged himself with a belt

powieściopisa|rz *m*, **~rka** *f* novelist

powieś|ć¹ *f* novel; **~ć w odcinkach** a serialized novel

powi|eść² *pf* książk. 1 *vt* (poprowadzić) to lead

11 *vi* (przesunąć) **~eść ręką po czymś** to run one's hand over sth; **~odła wzrokiem po pokoju** her eyes swept the room

111 **powieść się** *[zamiar, misja]* to succeed; **nie ~eść się** *[plan, misja]* to fail; **~odło nam się w życiu** we were successful in life; **może tym razem ci się ~edzie** maybe you'll have better luck this time

powietrz|e *n* air; **unosić się w ~u** to float in the air; **fiknąć kozła w ~u** to turn a somersault in mid-air; **wyjść na (świeże) ~e** to go outside; **na wolnym** a. **otwartym ~u** in the open air, outdoors; **coś wisi w ~u** something's rain in the air; **traktować kogoś jak ~e** to ignore sb; **to jest mi potrzebne jak ~e** I can't live without it; **zepsuć ~e** euf. to break wind

powiew *m* 1 waft, puff; **~ wiatru** a puff of wind 2 przen. hint; **~ świeżości** a breath of fresh air przen.

powiewa|ć *impf vi [flaga, wstążka]* to wave, to flutter; ~**ć na wietrze** to blow in the breeze; ~**ć chusteczką** to wave one's handkerchief

powiększać *impf →* **powiększyć**

powiększe|nie *n* [1] *(odbitka)* blow-up [2] *(skala)* magnification, enlargement; **w** ~**niu** on a larger scale

powiększ|yć *pf —* **powiększ|ać** *impf* [] *vt* to enlarge *[budynek, fotografię]*; to increase *[deficyt, dostawy, ilość]*; to extend *[fabrykę, obszar, parking]*; to magnify *[obraz, skalę]*
[] **powiększyć się —** **powiększać się** *[długi, rodzina, liczba]* to grow, to increase; *[obszar, zasięg]* to expand

powin|ien *impf vi* should, ought to; ~**naś mu to oddać** you should a. you ought to give it back to him; ~**nieneś był mu powiedzieć** you should have told him

powinsz|ować *pf vi* to congratulate *(komuś* sb*)*; ~**ował jej z okazji ślubu** he congratulated her on her marriage

powinszowa|nia *plt* congratulations; **z** ~**niem urodzin** congratulations on your birthday; **przesłać komuś** ~**nia** to send one's good wishes a. congratulations to sb

powita|ć *pf vt* to greet, to welcome; ~**ć kogoś skinieniem głowy** to greet sb with a nod

powitaln|y *adi.* welcoming

powita|nie *n* welcome; **na** ~**nie** by way of greeting

powl|ec[1] *pf —* **powl|ekać** *impf* [] *vt (pokryć)* to coat, to cover *(coś czymś* sth with sth*)*; ~**ec poduszki** to put pillows into pillowcases; ~**ec kołdry** to put on duvet covers
[] **powlec się —** **powlekać się** to cover

powl|ec[2] *pf* [] *vt (zaciągnąć)* to drag
[] **powlec się** to drag oneself

powłocz|ka *f* pillowcase, pillowslip GB

powod|ować *impf vt* [1] *(być powodem)* to cause, to bring about a. on [2] *książk. (kierować)* **nie dał sobą** ~**ować** he wouldn't have a. let anybody tell him what to do; ~**owało nią pragnienie zemsty** she was driven by a desire for revenge

powodzeni|e *n* [1] *(sukces)* success; ~**a!** good luck, best of luck!; **jego trud został uwieńczony** ~**em** his toil was rewarded with success; *(pomyślnie)* **z** ~**em** successfully; *(śmiało)* easily; **można to z** ~**em określić jako...** it can very well be described as... [2] *(popularność)* popularity; ~**e u kobiet** popularity a. success with women; **mieć** ~**e** to be popular

powodzian|in *m,* ~**ka** *f* flood victim

powodzi|ć się *impf v imp.* ~ **mu się dobrze/źle** he's faring a. doing well/badly; *(finansowo)* he's well/badly off; **jak ci się** ~**?** how are you doing?; **nieźle jej się** ~ she's not doing badly at all

powojenn|y *adi.* post-war

powoli *adv.* slowly; ~**! przemyśl to jeszcze** pot. hang on! think it over
■ **śpiesz się** ~ przysł. make haste slowly; more haste, less speed przysł.

powoln|y *adi. grad.* slow

powoł|ać *pf —* **powoł|ywać** *impf* [] *vt* [1] *(wyznaczyć)* to appoint; ~**ać rząd** to appoint a. form a government; ~**ać kogoś na stanowisko dyrektora** to appoint sb as director, to appoint sb to the position of director; ~**ać kogoś na świadka** to call sb as a witness; ~**ać do życia komisję** to set up a committee [2] *(do wojska)* ~**ać kogoś** to call up sb *(into the army)*, to enlist sb
[] **powołać się —** **powoływać się** to cite *(na kogoś/coś* sb/sth*)*; to quote *(na kogoś/coś* sb/sth*)*; ~**ując się na Pański list** in reference to your letter

powoła|nie *n* [1] *(zamiłowanie)* vocation, calling; **mieć** ~**nie do zawodu nauczycielskiego** to have a vocation to be a teacher; **minąć się z** ~**niem** to miss one's vocation a. calling; **z** ~**nia** by vocation [2] *(do wojska)* call-up, the draft US

powoływać *impf →* **powołać**

powonieni|e *n* (sense of) smell; **zmysł** ~**a** sense of smell

pow|ozić *pf vt* ~**oził kogoś samochodem po mieście** to drive sb around the town

pow|ód *m* [1] Prawo *(osoba)* plaintiff, complainant, petitioner [2] *(przyczyna)* reason, cause; ~**ód do narzekań** cause for complaint; **z** ~**odu kogoś/ czegoś** because of sb/sth; **bez** ~**odu** for no reason; **z sobie tylko znanych** ~**odów wołała...** for reasons known only to herself she preferred...; **była zła i miała** ~**ody** she was angry, and with good reason

powód|ka *f* Prawo plaintiff, complainant, petitioner

pow|ódź *f* flood także przen.; **tereny dotknięte** ~**odzią** flooded areas; ~**ódź świateł/słów** a flood of light/words

pow|ój *m* bindweed

pow|óz *m* carriage

powracać *impf →* **powrócić**

powrotn|y *adi. [droga, lot]* return; **bilet** ~**y** return ticket, return GB

powr|ócić *pf —* **powr|acać** *impf vi* [1] *(przybyć ponownie)* to return, to get back [2] *(zająć się ponownie)* to return, to get back; ~**ócić do władzy** to return to power, to come back into power; ~**ócić do rozmowy** to resume one's conversation; ~**ócić do starego nawyku** to revert to one's old habit; ~**acać myślami do czasów, kiedy...** to think back to the time when... [3] *(odzyskać)* ~**ócić do sił** to regain one's strength; ~**acać do zdrowia** to recover, to be on the mend

powr|ót *m* return; ~**ót do domu** return home, homecoming; **po** ~**ocie** on a. after one's return;

~**ót do zdrowia** recuperation, recovery; ~**ót do władzy** return to power; **z** ~**otem** a. **na** ~**ót** back; **być z** ~**otem** to be back; **schować coś z** ~**otem do szuflady** to put sth back into a drawer; **pojechał z** ~**otem do miasta** he drove back to the town; **chodzić tam i z** ~**otem** to be toing and froing; **ile ci zajmie droga tam i z** ~**otem?** how long will it take you to go there and back?

powr|óz *m* rope

powsta|ć *pf* — **powsta|wać** *impf vi* ⌐1⌐ (pojawić się) to come into being a. existence; ~**ł problem** a problem arose; **między nimi** ~**ł spór** they had an argument ⌐2⌐ książk. (podnieść się) to rise; ~**ł z krzesła/klęczek** he arose from his chair/knees; **wszyscy** ~**li** everyone rose to their feet; ~**ń! on your feet!** ⌐3⌐ książk. (zbuntować się) to rise (up) (**przeciw komuś** against sb)

powsta|nie *n* uprising, insurrection; **wybuch** ~**nia** the outbreak of an uprising; **wzniecać/ tłumić** ~**nie** to start/suppress an uprising

powsta|niec *m* insurgent, insurrectionist, insurrectionary

powstawać *impf* → **powstać**

powstrzym|ać *pf* — **powstrzym|ywać** *impf* ⌐**I**⌐ *vt* to hold back; ~**ać łzy** to hold back one's tears; ~**ać śmiech** to suppress laughter; ~**ać oddech** to hold one's breath; **nic jej nie** ~**a** nothing will stop her

⌐**II**⌐ **powstrzymać się** — **powstrzymywać się** to refrain (**od czegoś** from sth); ~**ać się od spożywania mięsa/alkoholu** to abstain from meat/alcohol; **z trudem** ~**ała się od płaczu** she could hardly contain the tears; **nie mógł** ~**ać się od śmiechu** he couldn't stop himself from laughing; ~**aj się od uwag** keep your comments to yourself

powszechnie *adi. grad.* universally; **był** ~ **lubiany** he was very popular, he was well liked; ~ **wiadomo, że...** it's a well-known fact that...

powszechn|y *adi. grad.* ⌐1⌐ (ogólny) universal, general; **historia** ~**a** general history; **głosowanie** ~**e** universal suffrage, general election; **zwrócić na siebie** ~**ą uwagę** to attract general attention ⌐2⌐ (popularny) common, widespread

powszedni *adi.* ordinary, common(place); **dzień** ~ a weekday

powszedni|eć *impf vi* to go stale; **zabawy nigdy jej nie** ~**ały** for her fun never lost its charm

powściągać *impf* → **powściągnąć**

powściągliw|y *adi. grad.* cautious, reserved; ~**y w wyrażaniu opinii** reticent in expressing his views; ~**y w okazywaniu uczuć** reserved about showing his emotions

powtarzać *impf* → **powtórzyć**

powtór|ka *f* pot. ⌐1⌐ Szkol. repetition, revision; **zrobić** ~**kę przed egzaminem** to revise the material before an exam ⌐2⌐ Radio, TV (emisja) rerun

⌐3⌐ Sport (ponowna próba) repeat attempt; Sport, TV (odtworzenie) replay

powtórn|y *adi. [wezwanie, szczepienie]* repeat; *[próba]* second

powt|órzyć *pf* — **powt|arzać** *impf* ⌐**I**⌐ *vt* ⌐1⌐ (zrobić to samo) to repeat *[czynność, słowo]*; to rerun *[serial]*; to replay *[sekwencję, scenę]*; ~**órzyć dawny błąd** to make the same mistake again; ~**arzać coś w myśli** to repeat sth to oneself; ~**arzać czyjeś gesty** to copy sb's gestures ⌐2⌐ Szkol., Uniw. to revise *[materiał, lekcję]*; to repeat *[klasę]*; to resit, to retake *[egzamin]* ⌐3⌐ (przekazywać) to repeat *[plotkę, sekret]*

⌐**II**⌐ **powtórzyć się** — **powtarzać się** ⌐1⌐ (zdarzać się ponownie) to repeat itself, to recur; ~**arzające się ataki** recurring attacks; ~**arzające się wybuchy** repeated explosions; **żeby mi się to więcej nie** ~**órzyło!** don't ever let this happen again! ⌐2⌐ pejor. (mówić to samo) to repeat oneself

powyżej ⌐**I**⌐ *praep.* ⌐1⌐ (wyżej niż) above; ~ **poziomu morza** above sea level ⌐2⌐ (więcej niż) over, above; ~ **50 procent** over 50 per cent, upwards of 50 per cent; ~ **przeciętnej** above (the) average; **temperatury** ~ **zera** above-zero temperatures

⌐**II**⌐ *adv.* ⌐1⌐ (w przestrzeni) higher up ⌐2⌐ (w tekście) above; **patrz** ~ see above; **jak wspomniano** ~ as mentioned above

powyższ|y *adi.* książk. above, above-mentioned; **w związku z** ~**ym** that being so

pow|ziąć *pf vt* książk. to come to *[decyzję]*; to adopt *[plan, uchwałę]*; to take *[działania, kroki]*; ~**ziął postanowienie, że...** he resolved to...; ~**ziął podejrzenie, że...** the suspicion grew in his mind that...

p|oza[1] *f* pose; **stanąć w niedbałej pozie** to assume a casual pose; **przybrać pozę** przen. to strike a pose a. an attitude

poza[2] ⌐**I**⌐ *praep.* ⌐1⌐ (na zewnątrz) outside; (dalej niż) beyond; ~ **granicami kraju** outside the country; **nikomu nie wolno wychodzić** ~ **bramę** no one is allowed outside a. beyond the gate; **cały dzień przebywa** ~ **domem** he's out all day long ⌐2⌐ (do tyłu, z tyłu) behind; **oglądać się** ~ **siebie** to look back a. behind (one) ⌐3⌐ (w innym czasie lub środowisku) outside; ~ **godzinami pracy** outside working hours; ~ **sezonem** out of season; **wykraczać** ~ **zakres czyichś obowiązków** to be beyond sb's responsibilities ⌐4⌐ (oprócz, wyłączając) apart a. aside from, except (for); ~ **tym niewiele się zmieniło** apart from that nothing much has changed ⌐5⌐ (obok, włączając) apart a. aside from, besides; ~ **mną było jeszcze dwóch chłopaków** apart from a. besides me there were two boys

⌐**II**⌐ **poza tym** *part.* (ponadto) besides, apart from that

pozbaw|ić *pf* — **pozbaw|iać** *impf* ⌐**I**⌐ *vt* to deprive (**kogoś czegoś** sb of sth); ~**ić kogoś złudzeń** to shatter a. dispel sb's illusions; ~**ić kogoś życia** książk. to take sb's life; ~**ić kogoś**

praw obywatelskich to disenfranchise sb; **choroba** ~iła go sił the illness drained all his strength **II** pozbawić się — pozbawiać się to deprive oneself (**czegoś** of sth); ~ić się życia to take one's life

pozbiera|ć *pf* **I** *vt* **1** (zgromadzić) to gather, to collect *[chrust, informacje]*; to gather [sb] together *[osoby]*; to pick *[owoce, warzywa]* **2** (popodnosić) to pick [sth] up; (posprzątać) to clear [sth] away; ~ć **talerze ze stołu** to clear the plates (away) **II** pozbierać się pot. ~ć się (do kupy) to pull oneself together

pozb|yć się *pf* — **pozb|ywać się** *impf v refl.* to get rid of *[świadków, rzeczy, kłopotów]*; ~yć się **złudzeń** to rid oneself of all illusions

pozdr|owić *pf* — **pozdr|awiać** *impf vt* **1** (powitać) to greet; ~owić **kogoś skinieniem głowy** to greet sb with a nod **2** (przekazać pozdrowienia) ~owić **kogoś** to give sb one's greetings a. regards; ~**ów ją ode mnie** give her my greetings a. regards

pozdrowie|nie *n* (powitanie) greeting; ~**nia** (wyrazy pamięci) regards (**dla/od kogoś** to/from sb); **przekazać komuś** ~**nia** to give sb one's regards

poze|r *m* poser, poseur

poz|ew *m* (skarga) (law)suit; (wniosek) petition; (roszczenie) claim; ~**ew rozwodowy** a divorce petition; ~**ew przeciwko komuś** a lawsuit against sb; ~**ew o obrazę** a libel lawsuit; ~**ew o odszkodowanie** a claim for compensation

poziom *m* level; **tysiąc metrów nad** ~**em morza** a thousand metres above sea level; **niski** ~ **cukru we krwi** low blood sugar level; ~ **życia** standard of living; **kursy na wszystkich** ~**ach zaawansowania** courses for all levels; **wysoki/niski** ~ **nauczania** a high standard of teaching; **człowiek na** ~**ie** pot. a man who's got class pot.; **żarty nie na** ~**ie** pot. cheap jokes

poziomic|a *f* **1** Geog. contour (line) **2** Techn. level **poziom|ka** *f* wild strawberry **poziomo** *adv.* horizontally; (w krzyżówkach) across **poziom|y** *adi.* horizontal

pozna|ć *pf* — **pozna|wać** *impf* **I** *vt* **1** (posiąść wiedzę) to get to know *[osobę, kraj]*; to learn *[obyczaje, język]* **2** (odkryć) to find *[powód, przyczynę, zasadę]*; ~ć **prawdę** to find the truth; ~**łem, że płakała** I could tell that she'd been crying; **od razu można było** ~ć**, że...** it was immediately obvious that... **3** (doświadczyć) to know, to experience *[nędzę, poniżenie]* **4** (rozpoznać) to recognize; ~ć **kogoś po chodzie** to recognize sb by their walk; **udawał, że mnie nie** ~**je** he pretended he didn't know me **5** (zawrzeć znajomość) to meet; **miło mi było pana** ~ć it was nice a. a pleasure to meet you; **nowo** ~**ni koledzy** new friends **6** (przedstawić) to introduce (**kogoś z kimś** sb to sb); ~**ła ich ze sobą** she introduced them **II** poznać się — poznawać się **1** (zawrzeć

znajomość) to meet (**z kimś** sb); ~**li się na balu** they first met at a ball **2** (zacieśnić znajomość) to get to know each other **3** (ocenić) ~ć **się na kimś** (docenić zalety) to appreciate sb; (zauważyć wady) to see through sb **4** (rozpoznać się) to recognize each other

pozna|nie *n* **1** Filoz. cognition **2** (zaznajomienie się) ~**e kogoś/czegoś** getting to know sb/sth; **zyskiwać przy bliższym** ~**u** to improve on closer acquaintance **3** (rozpoznanie) recognition; **zmienić się nie do** ~**a** to change beyond recognition **4** (zrozumienie) **dać komuś do** ~**a, że...** to give sb to understand that...

poznawać *impf* → **poznać**
pozornie *adv.* seemingly
pozorn|y *adi.* apparent
pozor|ować *impf vt* to fake *[samobójstwo, włamanie]*

pozosta|ć *pf* — **pozosta|wać** *impf vi* książk. **1** (nie odejść) to stay; (trwać) to remain; **niech to** ~**nie między nami** this is just between me and you; ~ć **przy swoim zdaniu** to not change one's mind; ~ć **przy starej metodzie** to stick to an old method; **moje pytanie** ~**ło bez odpowiedzi** my question remained unanswered; **nie** ~**wać bez wpływu na coś** to have its impact on sth **2** (stanowić resztę) to remain, to be left; ~**ła jeszcze minuta** there's one more minute left; ~**je jeszcze jedna kwestia** one issue remains to be settled; ~**je faktem, że...** the fact remains that...; **nie** ~**ło mi nic innego jak ucieczka** the only thing I could do was (to) run away

pozostałoś|ć *f* remains; ~**ci po dawnym systemie** a hungover from the old system; **ostatnie** ~**ci kolonializmu** the last vestiges of colonialism

pozosta|ły *adi.* remaining; **osoby** ~**łe na pokładzie** people who remained on board; ~**li przy życiu pasażerowie** the surviving passengers; ~**li domownicy** the other members of the household

pozostawać *impf* → **pozostać**

pozostaw|ić *pf* — **pozostaw|iać** *impf vt* to leave; ~ić **kogoś pod czyjąś opieką** to leave sb in sb's care; ~ić **kogoś na łasce losu** to leave sb to their fate; ~ić **kogoś w tyle** a. **za sobą** to leave sb behind także przen.; ~ić **coś komuś** to leave sth to sb; **nie** ~ić **nikogo przy życiu** to spare no one; ~ić **coś czyjejś domyślności** to leave it to sb to guess; ~**iać wiele do życzenia** to leave a lot to be desired; ~ić **komuś decyzję** to leave it to sb to decide; ~ić **komuś wolny wybór** to leave the choice up to sb; **nie** ~**iać wątpliwości, że...** to leave no doubt that...

poz|ować *impf vi* **1** (być modelem) to pose (**komuś** for sb); ~**ować do portretu** to pose for one's portrait **2** (udawać) to pose; ~**ować na kogoś** to pose as sb

poz|ór *m* appearance; **sądzić po** ~**orach** to judge a. go by appearances; **dla zachowania** ~**orów** a. **dla** ~**oru** for the sake of appearances, for appearances' sake; ~**ory mylą** appearances can be deceptive; **robić coś pod byle** ~**orem** to do sth on any pretext; **pod żadnym** ~**orem** under no circumstances; **na** ~**ór** a. **z** ~**oru** seemingly; **wbrew** ~**orom** contrary to a. in spite of appearances

poz|wać *pf* — **poz|ywać** *impf vt* to sue (**za coś** for sth)

pozwalać *impf* → **pozwolić**

pozwan|y *m*, ~**a** *f* defendant

pozwole|nie *n* [1] (zgoda) permission; **pytać kogoś o** ~**nie** to ask sb's permission; **zrobić coś bez** ~**nia** to do sth without permission; **za** ~**niem** by a. with your leave [2] (dokument) permit, licence, license US; ~**nie na pracę** a work permit; ~**nie na broń** a gun a. firearms licence; ~**nie na budowę** a planning permission

pozw|olić *pf* — **pozw|alać** *impf* **[]** *vi* [1] (zgodzić się) to let, to allow; ~**olić komuś coś zrobić** a. **na zrobienie czegoś** to let sb do sth, to allow sb to do sth; ~**ólcie mu mówić** let him speak; ~**olono mi wejść** I was allowed (to go) inside; **nie** ~**olę, żeby mnie wykorzystywali!** I won't have them exploit me!; ~**oli pan, że o coś zapytam** książk. let me ask you something; ~**oli pan, że się przedstawię** książk. allow me to a. let me introduce myself książk. [2] (umożliwić) *[warunki, zdrowie]* to permit, to allow; **jeżeli pogoda** ~**oli** if the weather permits, weather permitting; **wzruszenie nie** ~**alało mu mówić** he was so moved that he couldn't utter a word [3] książk. (zaproponować pójście) **pan** ~**oli ze mną do gabinetu** would you please follow me to my office?

[] **pozwolić sobie** — **pozwalać sobie** [1] (mieć możliwość) **mogę sobie** ~**olić na wyjazd na narty** I can afford a skiing holiday [2] pejor. (zachować się niewłaściwie) ~**olić sobie na zrobienie czegoś** to take the liberty of doing sth; **za dużo sobie** ~**alać (w stosunku do kogoś)** to take liberties (with sb) [3] książk. (w zwrotach grzecznościowych) ~**oliłem sobie otworzyć okno** I took the liberty of opening the window; ~**alam** a. ~**olę sobie przypomnieć, że...** let me remind you that...

pozycj|a *f* [1] (położenie) position; **z** ~**i siły** from a position of strength [2] (postawa) position; **w** ~**i stojącej** in a standing position; **przyjąć** ~**ę obronną** to assume a defensive position [3] (ranga) position; **mieć mocną** ~**ę** to be in a strong position [4] Sport (lokata) position; **zajmować pierwszą/ostatnią** ~**ę** to be in first/last place; **awansować o trzy** ~**e** to climb three positions a. places [5] Sport (miejsce na boisku) position; **grać na** ~**i bramkarza/obrońcy** to be a goalkeeper/defender; **idealna** ~**a strzelecka** a perfect scoring position

[6] (punkt w spisie) item, entry; ~**a druga** item two [7] (książka) title; (film, przedstawienie) production; **ciekawe** ~**e filmowe** interesting films [8] Wojsk. position; **zająć** ~**ę** to get into position; **stać na straconej** a. **przegranej** ~**i** przen. to be in a hopeless situation; **bronić straconych** ~**i** przen. to defend a lost cause

pozysk|ać *pf* — **pozysk|iwać** *impf vt* książk. [1] to recruit *[współpracowników, agentów]*; to win [sb] over *[zwolenników]*; ~**ać kogoś dla sprawy** to win sb over to a cause; ~**ać kogoś do współpracy** to enlist sb's cooperation [2] (zdobyć) to win *[sympatię, poparcie]* [3] (zgromadzić) to raise *[fundusze]*; to acquire *[energię]*

pozytywi|sta *m*, ~**stka** *f* positivist

pozytywizm *m* positivism

pozytyw|ka *f* (zabawka) musical toy; (pudełeczko) music(al) box; **zegar z** ~**ką** a musical clock

pozytywn|y *adi.* [1] (dobry) *[bohater, wpływ, cecha]* positive; **uzyskać** ~**y wynik na egzaminie** to pass an exam [2] Med. positive; **miał** ~**y wynik kontroli antydopingowej** he was tested positive for drugs

pozywać *impf* → **pozwać**

pożał|ować *pf* **[]** *vt* to take pity (**kogoś** on sb)

[] *vi* [1] (poczuć żal) to regret (**czegoś** sth); **wyjdź stąd, bo** ~**ujesz!** get out of here or you'll be sorry! [2] (poskąpić) ~**ować komuś jedzenia** to refuse sb food; **nie** ~**ować pieniędzy** to be generous with money; **nie** ~**ować wysiłków** a. **starań, żeby coś zrobić** to make every effort to do sth

pożałowani|e *n* **godny** ~**a incydent** a regrettable incident; **być w** ~**a godnym stanie** to be in a pitiful condition

poża|r *m* fire; (wielki) blaze; ~**r lasu** a forest fire; **wybuchł** ~**r** a fire broke out; **spowodować** ~**r** to start a fire

pożarn|y *adi.* **straż** ~**a** fire brigade

pożąda|ć *impf vt* [1] (pragnąć) to crave (**czegoś** sth); **bardzo** ~**na praca** a much-desired job [2] (czuć pociąg fizyczny) to desire *[kobiety, mężczyzny]*

pożąda|nie *n* [1] (pragnienie) desire (**czegoś** for sth); **przedmiot** ~**nia** an object of desire [2] (pociąg fizyczny) desire; (żądza) lust

pożądan|y *adi.* (odpowiedni) *[cecha, wynik]* desirable; (zamierzony) *[skutek]* desired

pożegna|ć *pf* **[]** *vt* to say goodbye (**kogoś** to sb); ~**ć kogoś na stacji** to see sb off at the station

[] **pożegnać się** to say goodbye (**z kimś** with sb); ~**ć się ze światem** książk. to depart from this world; ~**ć się z awansem** pot. to say a. kiss goodbye to the promotion pot.

pożegnaln|y *adi. [pocałunek, prezent]* parting; *[list]* farewell; **przyjęcie** ~**e** farewell party

pożegna|nie *n* [1] (pozdrowienie) goodbye, leave taking; **wyjechać bez** ~**nia** to leave without saying goodbye; **pocałować kogoś/pomachać**

komuś na ~nie to kiss/wave sb goodbye [2] (roz-stanie) parting; **nadszedł czas ~nia** the time has come to part

poż|reć *pf* — **poż|erać** *impf* **[]** *vt* to devour **[]] pożreć się** pot. to have a row pot. (**z kimś o coś** with sb over sth)

pożyci|e *n* [1] (wspólne życie) life together; **być trudnym w ~u** to be hard to live with [2] (płciowe) sex life

pożycz|ać *impf* → **pożyczyć**

pożycz|ka *f* loan; **zaciągnąć u kogoś ~kę** to borrow money from sb; **udzielić komuś ~ki** *[osoba]* to lend sb money; *[bank]* to grant sb a loan; **wziąć ~kę z banku** to take out a. raise a bank loan

pożycz|yć *pf* — **pożycz|ać** *impf* **[]** *vt* **~yć coś komuś** to lend sb sth a. sth to sb; **~yć coś od kogoś** to borrow sth from sb

[]] pożyczyć sobie — **pożyczać sobie** to borrow

pożyteczn|y *adi. grad.* *[zajęcie, praca]* useful; *[gatunek, roślina]* beneficial

pożyt|ek *m* benefit; **przynosić komuś ~ek** to be of benefit to sb; **mieć ~ek z czegoś** to find sth useful; **nie było z niego żadnego ~ku** he was of no use to anybody; **robić coś z ~kiem dla innych** to do sth for the benefit of others

pożywieni|e *n* food

p|ójść *pf* **[]** *vi* [1] (przemieścić się) to go; **pójść do domu** to go home; **pójść do kina** to go to the cinema; **pójść do lekarza** to go to the doctor's; **pójść na spacer** to go for a walk; **pójść na zakupy** to go shopping; **pójść na koncert** to go to a concert; **pójść na ryby** to go fishing; **pójść na dno** *[statek]* to go down; **pójść spać** to go to bed; **pójść popływać** to go swimming; **już (sobie) poszedł** he's already gone; **krew poszła mu z nosa** his nose started to bleed; **pójść w górę/dół** *[ceny]* to go up/down [2] (rozpocząć nowy okres w życiu) to go; **pójść do szpitala** to go to hospital; **pójść na operację** to go for an operation; **pójść na wojnę** to go to war; **pójść do wojska** (dobrowolnie) to join the army; (z poboru) to be called up (to the army); **pójść na studia/do szkoły** to go to college/school; **pójść na prawo** to go to study law; **pójść na emeryturę** to retire; **pójść na zwolnienie** to take sick leave; **pójść do niewoli** to be taken prisoner; **pójść na wygnanie** to go into exile [3] (odbyć się) to go; **jak ci poszło?** how did it go?; **wszystko poszło dobrze** everything went well; **nie poszło jej na egzami-nie** she didn't do too well in the exam; **jak tak dalej pójdzie...** the way things are going...; **a jeżeli coś pójdzie nie tak?** what if something goes wrong? [4] pot. (zostać sprzedanym) to go, to be sold [5] (zostać wykorzystanym) *[pieniądze]* to go (**na coś** on sth; **poszło na to bardzo dużo cukru** a lot of sugar was put into it [6] (zostać opublikowanym) **pójść na antenie** *[reklama, rozmowa]* to be put on the air; **artykuł poszedł w całości** the article was printed

in full [7] (zgodzić się) **pójść na coś** to agree to sth; **pójść na kompromis w sprawie czegoś** to compromise on sth; **pójść na ustępstwa wobec kogoś** to make concessions to sb; **pójść na współpracę** to agree to cooperate [8] pot. (zepsuć się) *[żarówka, pasek, bezpiecznik]* to go; **poszło jej oczko w pończosze** her stocking has laddered **[]]** *v imp.* (być powodem kłótni) **o co im poszło?** why did they fall out?

■ **pójść za czyimś przykładem/czyjąć radą** to follow sb's example/advice; **pójść w czyjeś ślady** to follow in sb's footsteps

póki *coni.* (do czasu kiedy) as long as, while; **~ jesteś młody** while you're young; **~ nie** (jak długo nie) until, till; **czekaj tu na mnie, ~ nie wrócę** wait here for me until I return

pół [] ** *num.* half; **~ jabłka/litra/godziny half an apple/a metre/an hour; **za ~ ceny** at half price **[]]** *pron.* half; **~ miasta** half (of) the town; **~ do drugiej** half past one; **do ~ uda** halfway up/down one's thighs; **przerwać komuś w ~ zdania** a. **słowa** to interrupt sb in mid-sentence **[]]]** *part.* half; **~ kobieta, ~ ryba** half woman, half fish **[]V]** **na pół** *adv.* [1] *[podzielić, złożyć]* in half [2] (nie całkiem) half-, semi-; **na ~ ugotowany** half-cooked; **na ~ przytomny** half-conscious, semi-conscious; **~ na ~** *[dzielić się, zmieszać]* half-and-half

■ **w ~ drogi** halfway, midway

półbu|t *m* shoe, brogue

półciężarów|ka *f* pickup (truck)

półetatow|y *adi.* *[pracownik, posada]* part-time

półfabryka|t *m* semi-finished product

półfinali|sta *m*, **~stka** *f* semi-finalist

półfina|ł *m* semi-final

półgł|ówek, ~upek *m* pot. halfwit, dimwit, nitwit GB pot.

półgodzinn|y *adi.* half an hour, half-hour

półgolf *m* (wykończenie) turtleneck, mock turtleneck US; (sweter) round-neck(ed) sweater

pół|ka *f* shelf; (na bagaż) rack; (w skale) ledge; **~ka na książki** a bookshelf; **pojawić się na ~kach księgarskich** to appear in bookshops

półkol|e *n* semicircle; **stać ~em** to stand in (a) semicircle

półksiężyc *m* crescent, half-moon

półkul|a *f* [1] (bryły) half-globe [2] Geog. hemisphere; **~a północna/południowa** the Northern/South-ern hemisphere

półmet|ek *m* halfway point

półmis|ek *m* platter, serving plate a. dish

półmrok *m* semi-darkness, twilight

północ *f* [1] (godzina) midnight; **o ~y** at midnight [2] (kierunek) north; **skręcać na ~** to turn north a. northward(s); **na ~ od Warszawy** north a. to the north of Warsaw; **na ~y** in the north; **najdalej na ~ wysunięty punkt** the most northerly point;

najdalej na ~ **położone miasto** the northernmost town; ~ **Polski** the north of Poland, northern Poland ③ (region geograficzny) the North
północno-wschodni adi. [strona, ściana] northeast; [region, granica] north-eastern; [wiatr] northeast, north-easterly
północno-zachodni adi. [strona, ściana] northwest; [region, granica] north-western; [wiatr] northwest, north-westerly
północn|y adi. [ściana, granica] north, northern; [wiatr, zbocze] north, northerly; ~**y wschód/zachód** north-east/north-west; **w kierunku** ~**ym** in a northerly direction
półnu|ta f Muz. minim GB, half note US
półpa|siec m shingles
półpięt|ro n (podest) landing; (piętro) mezzanine
półproduk|t m half-finished product
półrocz|e n ① (okres) half year ② Szkol. semester; **pierwsze/drugie** ~**e** the winter/summer semester a. term
półśrod|ek m half measure
półświat|ek m demi-monde, underworld
półton m ① (odcień) halftone ② Muz. semitone, halftone US
półtor|a num. one and a half
półwys|ep m peninsula
półżartem adv. half jokingly
półżyw|y adi. half dead
późni|ć się impf v refl. [zegar] to be late; ~**ć się o pięć minut** to be five minutes slow
późn|o [] adv. grad. late; **jest już** ~**o** it's late; **robi się** ~**o** it's getting late; ~**o po południu** late in the afternoon; ~**o się ożenił** he married late (in life); **za** a. **zbyt** ~**o** too late; **o pięć minut za** ~**o** five minutes too late
[] **później** adv. comp. later (on), afterwards GB, afterward US, then; **tydzień** ~**iej** the following week, a week later; **najpierw lekcje,** ~**iej zabawa** first your homework, and then you can play; **nie** ~**iej niż**... not a. no later than...; **odłożyć coś na** ~**iej** to put sth off until a. till later; **zostawić sobie coś na** ~**iej** to leave sth for later
[] **najpóźniej** part. at the latest; **jak najpóźniej** as late as possible
[] **do późna** adv. till late; **pracować do** ~**a w nocy** to work late into the night
■ **prędzej** a. **wcześniej czy** ~**iej** sooner or later; **lepiej** ~**o niż wcale** przysł. better late than never przysł.
późn|y [] adi. grad. late; ~**ym wieczorem** late at night; ~**a starość** advanced years, a ripe old age; **w** ~**ym wieku** late in life; **w** ~**iejszym terminie** at a later date
[] adi. [jarzyny, owoce, kolacja, gość] late; [decyzja] belated
[] **późniejszy** adi. comp. ① (kolejny) later, subse-

quent ② (przyszły) later; **jego** ~**iejsza żona** his future wife, his wife to be
prabab|cia f great-grandmother
prabab|ka f książk. great-grandmother
prac|a f / ① (działalność) work; (fizyczna) labour; **mieć dużo** ~**y** to have a lot of work (to do); **wziąć się do** ~**y** to get down to work; ~**a fizyczna** physical work, manual labour; ~**a umysłowa** (urzędnicza) white-collar work; ~**a społeczna** voluntary a. community work ② (zarobkowanie) work, job; **mieć** ~**ę** to have a job; **nie mieć** ~**y** to be out of work; **dostać/stracić** ~**ę** to get/lose a job; **zwolnić kogoś z** ~**y** to give sb (their) notice; ~**a w pełnym/niepełnym wymiarze godzin** a fulltime/part-time job; **staż** ~**y** seniority, length of service; **czas** ~**y** working time a. hours; **dzień wolny od** ~**y** a holiday; **godziny** ~**y** (pracownika) working hours; (biura, sklepu) business hours; **miejsce** ~**y** work(place) ③ (miejsce zatrudnienia) work; **w** ~**y** at work; **koledzy z** ~**y** fellow workers, workmates ④ (dzieło) work ⑤ Szkol., Uniw. paper, project; ~**a domowa** homework; **odrabiać** ~**ę domową** to do homework; ~**a klasowa** a class test; ~**a magisterska** a master's thesis; ~**a doktorska** a doctoral dissertation ⑥ Komput. job ⑦ Fiz. work
[] **prace** plt work; ~**e remontowe** repair work
◻ ~**e domowe** houseworksrednik; ~**e ręczne** Szkol. handicrafts
■ **bez** ~**y nie ma kołaczy** przysł. no work, no pay przysł.
pracochłonn|y adi. [czynność, zajęcie] laborious
pracodaw|ca m, ~**czyni** f employer
prac|ować impf vi ① (trudnić się, zarobkować) to work; (ciężko) to labour, to toil; (być zajętym) to be busy; ~**ować fizycznie/umysłowo** to do physical/ intellectual work; ~**ować zawodowo** to have a career; ~**ować społecznie** to do voluntary work; ~**ować jak wół** to work like a Trojan; ~**ować nad kimś** to work on sb; ~**ować nad czymś** to work at a. on sth; ~**ować w reklamie** to work in advertising; ~**ować na komputerze** to work at the computer ② (funkcjonować) [organ, biuro] to work; [maszyna] to work, to operate, to run; **poczta dzisiaj nie** ~**uje** the post office is closed today; **sklepy** ~**ują do dwudziestej** shops stay open till 8 p.m.
■ **czas** ~**uje dla niego/przeciw niemu** time is on his side/against him
pracowi|ty adi. grad. [uczeń, student] diligent, hard-working; [pracownik] diligent, industrious; [dzień, życie] arduous, busy
pracowni|a f ① (artysty) studio, atelier; (pisarza) study ② (naukowa, doświadczalna) laboratory; lab pot. ③ (zakład) (work)shop; ~**a złotnicza** a goldsmith's (work)shop; ~**a fotograficzna** a photographic studio ④ Szkol. ~**a plastyczna** an art room; ~**a**

biologiczna/fizyczna a biology/physics laboratory; **~a komputerowa** a computer room

pracowni|k *m*, **~ca** *f* worker, employee; **~k biurowy** an office worker; **~k poczty** a post office employee; **~k niższego szczebla/szczebla kierowniczego** a junior/an executive; **~cy sklepu** the shop staff

pracu|ś *m* pot., żart. busy bee, eager beaver pot.

pracz *m* szop ~ raccoon

pracz|ka *f* laundress, washerwoman

p|rać *impf* **[]** *vt* **[]** (w wodzie) to wash, to launder *[koszulę, bieliznę]*; (chemicznie) to clean; **prać coś ręcznie** to wash sth by hand; **płaszcz był prany chemicznie** the coat was dry-cleaned; **proszek do prania** washing powder **[2]** pot. (bić) to wallop pot.

[]] prać się [1] (być pranym) to be washed, to wash; **ta sukienka dobrze się pierze** this dress washes easily **[2]** pot. (bić się) to have a dust-up pot.

pradzia|d *m* **[1]** (pradziadek) great-grandfather **[2]** (przodek) grandfather, forefather

pradziad|ek [] m [1] (ojciec dziadka lub babci) great-grandfather **[2]** (przodek) grandfather, forefather

[]] pradziadkowie *plt* great-grandparents

pragn|ąć *impf vi* **[1]** książk. (bardzo chcieć) to desire (**czegoś** sth); to wish (**czegoś** for sth); **~ąć coś zrobić** to wish a. desire to do sth; **~ę wyjaśnić, że...** I want a. wish to make it clear that... **[2]** (pożądać) to desire (**kogoś** sb); to lust (**kogoś** for sb)

pragnie|nie *n* **[1]** (chęć) desire (**czegoś** for sth); **budzić czyjeś ~nia** to arouse sb's desire; **wyrazić ~nie zrobienia czegoś** to express one's desire to do sth **[2]** (w ustach) thirst; **mieć ~nie** to be thirsty; **ugasić ~nie** to quench a. slake one's thirst

praktycznie [] *adv. grad. [myśleć, działać]* practically, in a practical way

[]] *adv. [wykorzystać, zastosować]* in practice

[]]] *part.* practically, virtually; **~ (rzecz) biorąc...** to all intents and purposes...

praktyczn|y [] *adi. grad. [osoba, metoda, umiejętność]* practical; *[rada, wskazówka]* sensible; *[ubranie]* practical, sensible

[]] *adi. [szkolenie, wiedza, umiejętności]* practical

prakty|ka [] f [1] (doświadczenie) practice (**w czymś** at a. in sth); **z ~ki wiedział, że...** experience had taught him that...; **w ~ce** in practice; **sprawdzić się w ~ce** to be effective (in practice); **zastosować coś w ~ce** to put sth into practice **[2]** (staż) (w firmie) training period; (u rzemieślnika) apprenticeship; (w szkole) teaching practice; **~ki studenckie** student training; **odbywać ~kę u fryzjera** to be apprenticed to a hairdresser; **odbywać ~kę w fabryce** to work as a trainee in a factory **[3]** (wykonywanie zawodu) practice; **~ka lekarska/adwokacka** medical/legal practice; **mieć prywatną ~kę** to work a. be in private practice

[]] praktyki *plt* observance, ritual; **~ki religijne** religious observances

praktykan|t *m*, **~tka** *f* (w firmie) trainee, probationer; (u rzemieślnika) apprentice; (w szkole) student teacher

praktyk|ować *impf* **[]** *vt* to practise GB, to practice US *[metodę, magię, zwyczaj]*

[] *vi* **[1]** (wyznawać wiarę) to follow religious observances; **jest ~ującym katolikiem** he's a practising Catholic **[2]** (pracować) to be in practice; **~ować jako lekarz** to practise GB a. practice US as a doctor; **~ował w prywatnym gabinecie** he worked in private practice **[3]** (być na stażu) to be in training; **~ować u krawca** to be apprenticed to a tailor

pral|ka *f* washing machine

pralni|a *f* laundry; **~a chemiczna** (dry-)cleaner, (dry-)cleaner's; **oddać bieliznę do ~** to take linen to the laundry; **odebrać płaszcz z ~** to get a coat from the cleaner's

pra|nie *n* **[1]** (bielizna) washing, laundry; **powiesić ~nie** to hang the washing; **twoja koszula jest w ~niu** your shirt is in the wash a. with the washing **[2]** (proces) washing; **oddać palto do ~nia** to take a coat to the cleaner's; **zrobić ~nie** to do the washing

■ ~nie mózgu a. **mózgów** pot. brainwashing; **wyjdzie** a. **okaże się w ~niu** pot. it will all come out in the wash

pras|a *f* **[1]** (gazety, dziennikarze) the press; **~a codzienna/tygodniowa** the daily/weekly press; **przeglądać ~ę** to look through the papers; **w ~ie** a. **na łamach ~y** in the press; **zamieścić ogłoszenie w ~ie** to put an ad in a newspaper; **pisano o tym w ~ie** the papers wrote about it; **mieć dobrą/złą ~ę** to have a good/bad press **[2]** Druk., Techn. press

pras|ować *impf vt* **[1]** to iron *[sukienkę, koszulę]*; **deska do ~owania** an ironing board **[2]** Techn. to press *[ziarna, wióry]*; to mould GB, to mold US *[tworzywa sztuczne]*

prasow|y *adi. [artykuł, zdjęcie, wydawnictwo]* press; *[ogłoszenie]* newspaper; **agencja ~a** a press a. news agency; **rzecznik ~y** a press officer a. secretary; **wycinek ~y** a cutting GB, a clipping

praw|da [] f [1] (zgodność z rzeczywistością) the truth (**o czymś** about sth); **dowiedzieć się ~dy** to learn the truth; **ujawnić ~dę** to reveal the truth; **spojrzeć ~dzie w oczy** to face the truth; **powiedzieć ~dę** to tell the truth; **mijać się z ~dą** euf. to be economical with the truth euf.; **być dalekim od ~dy** to be far from the truth; **czy to ~da?** is it true?; **to ~da, ale...** (it's) true, but...; **~da jest taka, że...** the truth is that... **[2]** (obiegowy pogląd) truth; **stara ~da** an old truth; **~dy życiowe** common truths

[]] *inter.* [1] (w zdaniu twierdzącym) true!, that's right!; **święta ~da!** how very true! **[2]** (w pytaniu) **rok temu byłeś we Francji, ~da?** you were in France last year, weren't you?; **nigdy go nie poznałeś,** ∼**da?** you've never met him, have you?; ∼**da, jaka ona ładna?** isn't she pretty?

■ ∼**dę mówiąc** a. ∼**dę powiedziawszy** a. **po** ∼**dzie** pot. if truth be told, to tell you the truth; **Bogiem a** ∼**dą** książk. as a matter of fact; **co** ∼**da** pot. admittedly, to be sure

prawdomówn|y *adi. [osoba]* truthful; *[twarz]* honest

prawdopodobieństw|o *n* probability, likelihood; *(teorii, hipotezy)* plausibility; **nikłe** a. **znikome** ∼**o** unlikelihood, improbability; **według wszelkiego** ∼**a** in all probability; **teoria** ∼**a** the theory of probability, probability theory

prawdopodobnie *adv. grad.* probably

prawdopodobn|y *adi. grad.* ① *[wiadomość, fakt]* probable; **mało** ∼**y** unlikely, improbable ② *[termin, wydatki]* likely; *[winowajca]* presumed; **jest mało** ∼**e, żeby...** it's unlikely that...

prawdziw|ek *m* boletus, cep

prawdziwie *adv.* truly

prawdziw|y *adi. [fakty, powód]* true, real; *[perły, jedwab]* real, genuine; *[miłość, talent]* true; *[odwaga, przyjemność]* real; ∼**y Rembrandt** a genuine a. an authentic Rembrandt; **najprawdziwsza prawda** pot. the honest truth

■ **z** ∼**ego zdarzenia** real, genuine

prawic|a *f* ① *(polityczna)* the Right, the right wing ② książk. *(ręka)* right hand; **po** a. **na** ∼**y** on a. to the right

prawicow|y *adi.* right-wing, rightist

prawid|ło *n (do butów)* shoe tree, stretcher

prawidłow|y *adi. grad. [diagnoza, myślenie]* correct; *[zgryz, rozwój]* normal; ∼**a dieta** a well-balanced diet

prawie *adv.* almost, nearly; *(z przeczeniem)* hardly, scarcely; ∼ **każdy/wszystko** almost a. nearly everyone/all; ∼ **zawsze** almost a. nearly always; ∼ **nikt/nic** hardly a. scarcely anyone/anything; ∼ **nigdy** hardly a. scarcely ever, seldom if ever; ∼ **płakała** she was nearly crying; ∼ **za darmo** for next to a. for practically nothing; ∼ **go nie znam** I hardly know him; **to** ∼ **że pewne** it's almost a. practically certain

prawni|k *m,* ∼**czka** *f* lawyer

prawnucz|ek *m* great-grandson

prawnucz|ka *f* great-granddaughter

prawnuk *m* great-grandson; ∼**i** *(chłopcy)* great-grandsons; *(obojga płci)* great-grandchildren

prawn|y *adi. [akt]* legislative; *[porada, formalności, kodeks]* legal; *[kancelaria, wydział]* law, legal; *[właściciel]* lawful, rightful; **osoba** ∼**a** a legal entity; **kruczek** ∼**y** a (legal) loophole

praw|o ① *n* ① *(ogół przepisów)* law; **zgodnie z** ∼**em** in accordance with a. according to the law; **zgodnie z polskim** ∼**em** under Polish law; **wbrew** ∼**u** against the law, contrary to the law; **złamać** ∼**o** to

break the law; **być niezgodnym z** ∼**em** to be against the law; **działać w granicach** ∼**a/ niezgodnie z** ∼**em** to operate within/outside the law; **wejść w konflikt z** ∼**em** to fall foul of the law, to come into conflict with the law ② *(norma, ustawa)* law; *(zapisana)* statute; **zbiór** ∼ a legal code, a code of laws; **uchwalać** a. **stanowić** ∼**a** to enact a. make laws; **uchwalić** ∼**o** to pass a. adopt a law; **uchylić** ∼**o** to revoke a. rescind a law; ∼**o o środkach masowego przekazu** a law on the mass media ③ *(nauka)* law; **wydział** ∼**a** a law faculty; **student/studentka** ∼**a** a law student ④ *(uprawnienie)* right *(do czegoś* to sth); entitlement *(do czegoś* to sth); ∼**a człowieka** human rights; ∼**o własności** proprietorship, ownership; ∼**a miejskie** a town charter; ∼**o pierwszeństwa przejazdu** the right of way; ∼**o do emerytury** pension rights; **mieć** ∼**o do czegoś** to be entitled to sth; **mieć** ∼**o coś zrobić** to have the right a. to be entitled to do sth; **pozbawić kogoś** ∼**a wykonywania zawodu** to deprive sb of the right to practise their profession, to ban sb from practising a profession; **jakim** ∼**em?** by what right?; **jakim** ∼**em wtrącasz się w moje sprawy?** who gave you the right to interfere in my affairs?; **wszelkie** ∼**a zastrzeżone** all rights reserved; **wywiad publikowany na** ∼**ach wyłączności** an exclusive interview; **na równych** ∼**ach** on equal terms; **ona jest tu na** ∼**ach domownika** she's treated here as one of the family ⑤ Aut. ∼**o jazdy** driving licence GB, driver's license US; **egzamin na** ∼**o jazdy** a driving test; **chodzić na kurs** ∼**a jazdy** to take driving lessons ⑥ *(zasada)* law, principle; ∼**a fizyczne/natury** the laws of physics/nature

Ⅱ *adv.* ① **na** a. **w** ∼**o** *(w prawą stronę)* to the right; *(po prawej stronie)* on a. to the right; **skręcić w** ∼**o** a. **na** ∼**o** to turn right; **na** ∼**o patrz!** eyes right!; **na** ∼**o i (na) lewo** *(wszędzie)* left, right and centre pot. ② pot. *(w polityce)* **pójść na** ∼**o** to veer to the right; **być na** ∼**o od centrum** to be right of centre

Ⅲ z prawa pot. *(po prawej stronie)* from the right; **z** ∼**a i z lewa** from all sides

❑ ∼**o budowlane** building codesrednik; ∼**o ciążenia Newtona** Newton's law of gravitation; ∼**o drogowe** the rules of the road, the Highway Code GB; ∼**o wyborcze** electoral a. election law; **bierne** ∼**o wyborcze** eligibility to stand for election, right to be elected; **czynne** ∼**o wyborcze** voting rights, suffrage, franchise; **powszechne** ∼**o wyborcze** universal suffrage, universal franchise

■ ∼**o dżungli** a. **pięści** the law of the jungle

prawodawstw|o *n* legislation

prawomocn|y *adi. [wybory]* legally valid; *[akt]* legally binding, effective; *[władza]* legal, lawful; **wyrok jest** ∼**y** the (judge's) decision is final and binding; **wyrok nie jest** ~y the sentence is not legally valid

praworęczn|y [] *adi. [osoba]* right-handed
[] praworęczn|y *m,* ~a *f* right-hander

prawosławi|e *n* Relig. the Orthodox Church, the Orthodox faith

prawosławn|y *adi.* Orthodox; **kościół** ~y (budynek) an Orthodox church; (wyznanie) the Orthodox Church; **krzyż** ~y Russian cross

prawostronn|y *adi.* right(-hand); ~y **ruch pojazdów** right-hand traffic a. driving

praw|y [] *adi.* [] *[ręka, rękaw, but]* right; *[strona, róg]* right, right-hand; **oczko** ~e plain; **po** ~ej **stronie** on the right-hand side; **po jej** ~ej **ręce** on a. to her right; **z** ~ej **strony** from the right [] (wierzchni) *[strona]* right, front; **na** ~ej **stronie** (ubrania) outside; (papieru) on the front; (materiału) on the right side; **przewrócić bluzkę na** ~ą **stronę** to turn a blouse right side out [] *[odłam]* right-wing; ~e **skrzydło partii** the right wing of the party [] książk. (szlachetny) righteous, upright; (uczciwy) honest; *[charakter]* virtuous

[] *m* ~y **prosty** a straight right, a right jab; ~y **sierpowy** a right hook

praż|yć *impf* [] *vt* to roast *[migdały]*
[] *vi [słońce]* to beat a. blaze down
[] **prażyć się** to roast

prąci|e *n* penis

prą|d *m* [] Elektr. current, electricity; ~d **elektryczny** electric current; ~d **stały** direct current, DC; ~d **zmienny** alternating current, AC; **został porażony** ~dem a. **złapał go** ~d pot. he got a. was given an electric shock; **włączyć/wyłączyć** ~d to switch on/off the electricity a. the power; **przerwa w dostawie** ~du a power cut, a blackout; **natężenie/napięcie** ~du amperage/voltage [] (w rzece) current, flow, stream; (morski) current, tide, drift; **płynąć pod** ~d/z ~dem *[pływak]* to swim upstream/downstream a. against/with the current; **iść** a. **płynąć z** ~dem/**pod** ~d przen. to go a. swim with/against the tide przen.; **jechał pod** ~d przen. he was driving the wrong way up a one-way street [] (powietrza) airstream, airflow [] (tendencja) current

prądnic|a *f* generator; (w rowerze) dynamo

prąż|ek *m* (pasek) stripe; (na ciemnej tkaninie) pinstripe; (wypukły) cord, rib; **garnitur w** ~ki a pinstripe (suit)

prążkowan|y *adi. [liść, materiał, sierść]* striped, stripy; *[ciemna tkanina]* pinstripe; (w wypukłe prążki) ribbed, corded

preambu|ła *f* preamble (czegoś a. do czegoś to sth)

precedens *m* precedent; **bez** ~u without precedent, unprecedented; **stworzyć** ~ to set a precedent

prec|el *m* pretzel

precyzj|a *f* [] (dokładność) precision, accuracy; **z aptekarską** a. **jubilerską** ~ą with surgical precision [] (jasność) (wypowiedzi) preciseness; (myślenia) clarity

precyz|ować *impf vt* (uściślać) to specify, to set down *[cele, warunki]*; to pin down *[pojęcia, reguły]*; (wyjaśniać) to clarify

precyzyjn|y [] *adi.* grad. *[instrument, pomiar]* precise; *[odpowiedź]* accurate, exact; **mało** ~a **definicja** an imprecise definition
[] *adi. [przemysł, przyrząd]* precision

precz [] *adv.* away, out; **poszedł sobie** ~ he went off a. away; **cisnąć coś** ~ to throw sth away
[] *inter.* ~ **(stąd)!** get out (of it! a. here!); ~ **mi z oczu!** (get) out of my sight!; ~ **z tyranią!** down with tyranny!; ~ **z rękami!** a. **ręce** ~! hands off!

prefabryka|t *m* prefabricated element; **dom z** ~tów a prefab pot.

prefabrykowan|y *adi. [części, element]* prefabricated; **budynek** ~y a. **z elementów** ~ych a prefab pot.

prekurso|r *m,* ~rka *f* książk. forerunner, precursor

prekursors|ki *adi.* książk. *[metody, dzieło]* pioneering

preludi|um *n* prelude także przen. (**do czegoś** to sth)

premedytacj|a *f* deliberation; (w prawie) premeditation, criminal intent; **z** ~ą with deliberation; **morderstwo z** ~ą premeditated a. first degree US murder, murder with malice aforethought

premi|a *f* [] (dodatek do pensji) bonus; ~a **motywacyjna** an incentive bonus; **przyznać komuś** ~ę to give sb a bonus [] (nagroda) prize, premium

premie|r *m* premier, Prime Minister

premie|ra *f* first a. opening night, premiere; ~ra **światowa** the world premiere; ~ra **prasowa** press night; ~ra **filmu odbyła się w Cannes** the film was premiered in Cannes

prenumera|ta *f* [] (przedpłata) subscription (fee) [] (zamówienie) subscription; **wykupić** ~tę **czegoś** to take out a subscription to sth

prenumer|ować *impf vt* to subscribe to *[gazetę, czasopismo]*

prepara|t *m* preparation; ~t **ziołowy** a herbal preparation; ~ty **owadobójcze/bakteriobójcze** insecticides/germicides; ~ty **owadów/roślin** insect/plant specimens

preri|a *f* prairie

presj|a *f* książk. pressure; **pod czyjąś** ~ą under pressure from sb; **być pod** ~ą to be under pressure; **wywierać** ~ę **na kogoś** to bring pressure to bear on sb

prestiż *m* prestige; **mieć** ~ to have prestige; **podważyć czyjś** ~ to undermine sb's prestige

prestiżow|y *adi.* prestigious

pretek|st *m* pretext, excuse (**do czegoś** for sth); **szukać ~stu do kłótni** to look for a pretext for a quarrel; **pod ~stem czegoś** under a. on the pretext of sth

pretensj|a *f* 1 (uraza) grudge, grievance (**do kogoś** against sb); **mieć do kogoś ~e o coś** to bear a grudge against sb for sth; **możesz mieć ~e do samego siebie** you have only yourself to blame 2 książk. (roszczenie) claim (**do czegoś** to sth); **rościć sobie ~e do czegoś** to lay claims to sth

pretensjonaln|y *adi. grad.* pretentious

prezbiteri|um *n* chancel

prezen|t *m* present, gift; **dać komuś ~t** to give sb a present; **w ~cie** as a present; **dostać coś w ~cie (od kogoś)** to receive sth as a present (from sb)

prezente|r *m*, **~rka** *f* presenter; **~r wiadomości** a newscaster, a newsreader GB; **~r pogody** a weather forecaster

prezent|ować *impf* książk. **I** *vt* 1 (pokazywać) to present [*książki, sztukę, balet*] (**komuś** to sb); to demonstrate [*towary, wyroby*] (**komuś** to sb); **~uj broń!** present arms! 2 (wyrażać) to present [*poglądy, opinie*] 3 (przedstawiać) to introduce [*osobę*] (**komuś** to sb)

II prezentować się 1 (wyglądać) **dobrze się ~ować** to look presentable 2 (występować) [*aktor, zespół*] to appear, to make an appearance

prezerwatyw|a *f* condom, sheath

prezes *m* president, chairman; **Prezes Sądu Najwyższego** Chief Justice; **Prezes Rady Ministrów** Prime Minister

prezydenc|ki *adi.* presidential

prezyden|t *m* (państwa) president; (miasta) mayor

prezydentu|ra *f* presidency

prezydi|um *n* presidium, praesidium

pręd|ki *adi. grad.* 1 (szybki) [*ruch, kroki, decyzja*] quick; [*oddech, puls*] rapid; **do ~kiego zobaczenia!** see you soon! 2 pot. (porywczy) quick-tempered, short-tempered; **mieć ~ki charakter** to have a quick a. hot temper; **być ~kim do bijatyki** to be spoiling for a fight

pręd|ko **I** *adv. grad.* 1 (szybko) [*biec, iść, jeść*] quickly; [*mówić*] rapidly; **nie tak ~dko!** hold on a bit! pot. 2 (wkrótce) [*przyjść, przyjechać*] soon; [*odpisać*] promptly; **czym ~dzej** pot. as soon as possible; **im ~dzej, tym lepiej** the sooner the better; **~dzej czy później** sooner or later

II prędzej *part.* pot. rather; **tobie ~dzej uwierzy niż mnie** s/he's more likely to believe you than me

III *inter.* pot. quick!

prędkoś|ć *f* speed; (w fizyce) velocity; **~ć wiatru** wind speed; **jechać z prędkością 100 kilometrów na godzinę** to do 100 kilometres an hour; **mandat za jazdę z niedozwoloną ~cią** a speeding ticket

prę|ga *f* (smuga) mark

prę|t *m* (drążek) bar; **~ty balustrady** railings

prima aprilis *m, m inv.* April Fools' Day; 'April Fool!'

prioryte|t *m* książk. priority

problem *m* problem (**z czymś** with sth); **nastręczać a. sprawiać ~y** to present problems; **zrobić coś bez ~u** to have no trouble doing sth; **robić z czegoś ~** to make a fuss about sth; **~ w tym a. ~ polega na tym, że...** the trouble is that...; **w czym ~?** what's the problem?; **nie ma ~u!** a. **to żaden ~!** (it's) no problem!

problematyczn|y *adi.* [*decyzja, sprawa*] problematic; [*sukces*] questionable

problematy|ka *f* issues; **~ka powieści** the issues addressed in the novel

proboszcz *m* parish priest

probów|ka *f* test tube; **dziecko z ~ki** a test-tube baby

proc|a *f* (w kształcie widełek) catapult GB, slingshot US; (rzemienna) sling; **strzelać z ~y do czegoś** to fire a catapult at sth; **wylecieć** a. **wyskoczyć skądś jak z ~y** pot. to bolt out of somewhere

procedu|ra *f* procedure; **~ra ubiegania się o wizę** the procedure of applying for a visa

procen|t *m* 1 (setna część) per cent; **ludność jest w dziewięćdziesięciu ~tach polska** the population is ninety per cent Polish; **na sto ~t** pot. for sure; **być czegoś w stu ~tach pewnym** pot. to be (a) hundred per cent certain of sth 2 (część) percentage; **mały/duży ~t** a low/high percentage 3 (odsetki) interest; **~t** a. **~ty od kapitału** interest on capital; **pożyczać pieniądze na ~t** to lend money at interest; **oddać coś z ~tem** przen. to return sth with interest

procent|ować *impf vi* [*kapitał*] to earn interest; przen. [*praca, wysiłki*] to pay off

procentow|y *adi.* 1 [*wzrost, punkt*] percentage; **sześcioprocentowy roztwór** a six per cent solution 2 [*lokata*] interest-bearing; **stopa ~a** interest rate

proces *m* 1 (ciąg wydarzeń) process; **~y chemiczne** chemical processes; **ulegać ~owi starzenia się** to be subject to the ageing process; **przechodzić ~ fermentacji** to undergo fermentation 2 (sprawa) (law)suit (**przeciwko komuś** against sb); (rozprawa) trial; **wytoczyć komuś ~** to bring a. file a suit against sb, to sue sb; **wygrać/przegrać ~** to win/lose a lawsuit; **~ o zniesławienie** a trial for libel

procesj|a *f* procession

proceso|r *m* Komput. central processing unit, processor; **~r tekstu** word processor

proces|ować się *impf v refl.* to have a lawsuit (**z kimś o coś** with sb over sth)

proch **I** *m* 1 (materiał wybuchowy) (gun)powder; **nigdy nie wąchał ~u** przen. he's never seen battle; **~u to on nie wymyśli** przen. he won't set the world on fire 2 (pył) dust

▣ **prochy** plt ① (szczątki) ashes; dust książk.; **tu spoczywają jego** ~y his ashes rest here ② pot. (lekarstwa, narkotyki) drugs; **być na** ~**ach** to be on drugs

■ **beczka** ~**u** powder keg; **rozsypać się w** ~ książk. to turn to dust; **zetrzeć kogoś na** a. **w** ~ książk. to annihilate sb; **z** ~**u jesteś** a. **powstałeś i w** ~ **się obrócisz** Bibl. for dust thou art, and unto dust shalt thou return

prochow|iec m trench coat

prodiż m electric cake pan

producen|t m producer; ~**t wina** wine producer; ~**t rowerów** bicycle producer a. manufacturer; ~**t filmowy** (film) producer

produkcj|a f ① (proces) production; (wyroby) output; **film** ~**i polskiej** a Polish-made film; **towary krajowej** ~**i** domestic goods; **zostać wycofanym z** ~**i** to go out of production ② (film) production

produkcyjn|y adi. [proces, linia] production; **wiek** ~**y** productive age; **moc** ~**a fabryki** a factory's capacity

produk|ować impf ▣ vt to produce, to manufacture [towary]; to produce [energię, żywność, przeciwciała]; **towary** ~**owane masowo** mass-produced goods

▣ **produkować się** pot., iron. to perform

produk|t m ① (artykuł) product; ~**ty rolne** agricultural products a. produce ② (efekt) product; ~**t uboczny** a by-product

produktywn|y adi. [gospodarka, robotnik] productive; ~**y pisarz** a prolific a. productive writer

profeso|r m ① (tytuł naukowy) professor ② (w liceum) (secondary school) teacher; ~**r od matematyki** a maths teacher

profesor|ka f pot. (secondary school) teacher

profil m ① (twarzy) profile; **z** ~**u** in profile ② (zarys) outline, profile; **klasa o** ~**u matematyczno-fizycznym** a science-oriented class

profilaktyczn|y adi. prophylactic, preventive; **obuwie** ~**e** supportive shoes

profilakty|ka f prevention, prophylaxis

prognoz|a f forecast, prognosis; ~**a pogody** a weather forecast; **jaka jest na jutro** ~**a?** what's the forecast for tomorrow?; ~**y na przyszłość** predictions for the future

prognoz|ować impf vt to forecast

program m ① (plan) programme GB, program US; (harmonogram) schedule; **zgodnie z** ~**em** as scheduled; **co mamy dzisiaj w** ~**ie?** what have we got planned for today?; ~ **wyborczy** an electoral programme ② (repertuar) programme GB, program US; **gazeta z** ~**em telewizyjnym** a newspaper with a TV guide ③ (koncertu, występu) programme GB, program US ④ (audycja) programme GB, program US (**o czymś** on a. about sth); (kanał) channel; ~ **informacyjny** a news programme; **wystąpić w** ~**ie** to appear in/on a programme; **na drugim**

~**ie** on channel 2 ⑤ (nauczania) syllabus, curriculum; **w** ~**ie** on the syllabus ⑥ (w urządzeniu) programme GB, program US; ~ **prania/płukania** wash/rinse programme ⑦ (komputerowy) program; **uruchomić** ~ to run a program

programato|r m program selector

programi|sta m, ~**stka** f programmer GB, programer US

program|ować impf ▣ vt ① to programme GB, program US, to preset [kuchenkę, magnetowid] ② książk. (planować) to programme GB, to program US [uroczystość, osobę]

▣ vi Komput. to program

prohibicj|a f prohibition

projek|t m ① (zamiar) plan; ~**t podróży do Włoch** a plan to visit Italy; **zrealizować** ~**t** to carry out a plan ② (kostiumu, pomnika, urządzenia) design (**czegoś** o a. for sth); (umowy) draft; ~**t ustawy** a bill; **wykonać** ~**t czegoś** to design sth; **zbudować coś zgodnie z** ~**tem** to build sth to specification ③ (przedsięwzięcie) project

projektan|t m, ~**tka** f designer; ~**t mody/wnętrz** fashion/an interior designer

projektodaw|ca m, ~**czyni** f (ustawy, uchwały) drafter; (budynku, osiedla) designer

projekto|r m ~**r filmowy** a film projector

projekt|ować impf vt to design [budynek, maszynę]; to plan [wycieczkę, remont]

proklamacj|a f książk. proclamation; ~**a niepodległości** declaration of independence; **wydać** ~**ę** to issue a proclamation

proklam|ować pf, impf vt książk. to proclaim [niepodległość, republikę]

prokurato|r m Prawo public prosecutor; ~ **generalny** Attorney-General

prokuratu|ra f public prosecutor's office

proletaria|t m the proletariat

prolog m prologue GB, prolog US (**czegoś** to sth)

prom m ferry; **przepłynąć rzekę** ~**em** to cross a river by ferry; **wsiąść na** ~ to board a ferry

❑ ~ **kosmiczny** space shuttle

promena|da f promenade

promieniotwórcz|y adi. [pierwiastek, skażenie] radioactive

promieni|ować impf vi ① [ciepło, energia] to emanate, to radiate ② przen. to radiate; **jej twarz** ~**owała radością** a. **z jej twarzy** ~**owała radość** her face radiated delight a. was radiant with delight ③ [ból] to radiate (**na coś** to sth)

promieniowani|e n radiation

promie|ń m ① (smuga światła) ray, beam; ~**nie słoneczne** sunbeams, rays of sunlight; ~**ń radości** przen. a ray of joy a. sunshine; **ostatni** ~**ń nadziei** przen. the last ray of hope ② (w fizyce) ray; ~**nie gamma** gamma rays; ~**nie rentgenowskie** a. **Roentgena** X-rays ③ (okręgu) radius; **w** ~**niu**

dwóch metrów od czegoś within a two-metre radius from sth

prominen|t *m* książk. VIP; worthy pejor.

promocj|a *f* [1] (akcja) promotion; **kupić coś w** ∼**i** to buy sth on special offer; ∼**a książki** (spotkanie z autorem) book launch a. promotion [2] Szkol. promotion; **uzyskać** ∼**ę do następnej klasy** to move up to the next class, to be promoted to the next grade US

promoto|r *m*, ∼**rka** *f* Uniw. thesis supervisor

prom|ować [] *pf, impf vt* [1] Szkol. **zostać** ∼**owanym do następnej klasy** to move up to the next class, to be promoted to the next grade US [2] Wojsk. to promote; **zostać** ∼**owanym na oficera** to be promoted to officer rank [3] Uniw. **nowo** ∼**owani doktorzy** newly graduated doctors

[]] *impf vt* (reklamować) to promote

propagan|da *f* propaganda

propagandow|y *adi. [hasła, akcja, ulotka]* propaganda

propag|ować *impf vt* książk. to propagate; ∼**ować polską kulturę za granicą** to promote Polish culture abroad

propon|ować *impf vt* [1] (oferować) to offer (**coś komuś** sth to sb) [2] (doradzać) to suggest (**coś komuś** sth to sb); ∼**ować, żeby ktoś coś zrobił** to suggest that sb do a. should do sth; ∼**uję czekać** I suggest waiting [3] (zgłaszać) to propose; ∼**ować kogoś na przewodniczącego** to propose sb as chairman

proporcj|a *f* [1] (stosunek) proportion, ratio; **w** ∼**i** a. ∼**ach dwa do jednego** in a ratio a. proportion of two to one [2] (harmonia) proportion

proporcjonaln|y [] *adi. grad.* (harmonijny) well-proportioned; **być** ∼**ym** *[budowla]* to have good proportions

[]] *adi.* (współmierny) proportional, proportionate; **wprost/odwrotnie** ∼**y do czegoś** directly/inversely proportional to sth; **kara** ∼**a do winy** punishment commensurate with the crime

propo|rzec *m* pennant; Żegl. jack

propozycj|a *f* [1] (oferta) proposal, proposition; ∼**a kupna czegoś** a proposal to purchase sth; **zrobić komuś** ∼**ę nie do odrzucenia** żart. to make sb an offer they can't refuse [2] (rada) suggestion; **padła** ∼**a, żeby przełożyć zebranie** it was proposed that the meeting be adjourned

proroctw|o *n* prophecy

prorocz|y *adi. [sen, dar]* prophetic

proro|k *m* prophet także przen.; **nie chcę być złym** ∼**kiem, ale...** I don't want to be a prophet of doom but...; **obym był złym** ∼**kiem** I hope I'm proved wrong

■ **co rok** ∼**k** przysł. they have a new baby every year; **nikt nie jest** ∼**kiem we własnym kraju** przysł. a prophet is not without honour, save in his own country przysł.

prosektori|um *n* mortuary; (w akademii medycznej) anatomy laboratory

pro|sić *impf* [] *vt* [1] (zwracać się z prośbą) to ask (**kogoś o coś** sb for sth); ∼**sić kogoś, żeby coś zrobił** to ask sb to do sth; ∼**szę o uwagę!** may I have your attention, please?; ∼**szę o spokój!** quiet please!; ∼**szę dwa bilety** two tickets, please; **ja** ∼**siłem kawę nie herbatę** I asked for coffee, not tea; **bardzo bym** ∼**sił, żeby pan to poprawił** I'd be very grateful if you could correct it; **pan Kowalski jest** ∼**szony o zgłoszenie się do informacji** could Mr Kowalski please report to the information desk [2] (zapraszać) to ask; ∼**sić kogoś do środka** to ask sb in; ∼**szę usiąść** a. **siadać** would you like a seat?; **szef cię** ∼**si** the boss wants to see you; **przyszła nieproszona** she came uninvited [3] (do tańca) to ask; ∼**sić kogoś do tańca** to ask sb to dance; **czy mogę panią** ∼**sić?** would you like to dance?; **panie** ∼**szą panów!** ladies' invitation! [4] (przez telefon) **czy mogę** ∼**sić Adama?** can a. may I speak to Adam, please?; **wewnętrzny 125,** ∼**szę** extension 125, please

[]] **prosić się** (zachęcać) **aż się** ∼**si, żeby tu posprzątać** the place needs a good clean-up; **nie dał się dwa razy** ∼**sić** he didn't have to be asked twice

[]]] **proszę** *inter.* [1] (przy podawaniu) ∼**szę (bardzo)** here you are [2] (zaproszenie) ∼**szę (bardzo)** (do wejścia) please (do) come in; (żeby usiąść) please (do) take a seat; (żeby się poczęstować) please, help yourself [3] (jako zgoda) please; ∼**mogę przyjść jutro?** – „(bardzo) ∼**szę"** 'may I come tomorrow?' – 'yes, please do' [4] (w odpowiedzi na podziękowanie) „**dziękuję za pomoc"** – „∼**szę (bardzo)"** 'thanks for your help' – 'you're welcome' [5] (w odpowiedzi na pukanie) come in [6] (prośba o powtórzenie) ∼**szę?** pardon?, sorry? [7] (w zwrotach grzecznościowych) ∼**szę pana/pani!** sir!/madam!; ∼**szę państwa!** ladies and gentlemen! [8] (dla wyrażenia zdziwienia) ∼**szę,** ∼**szę!** a. **no** ∼**szę!** well, well, well!

■ **co** ∼**szę?** pot. what was that? pot.

prosię| *n* [1] piglet [2] pot., żart. (o osobie) pig pot., żart.

pros|o *n* millet

prospek|t *m* brochure, prospectus

prostac|ki *adi.* pot. crude; **zachowywać się po** ∼**ku** to act like a boor

prosta|k *m*, ∼**czka** *f* pot. boor

prosta|ta *f* prostate (gland)

pro|sto [] *adv. grad.* [1] (nie skręcając) *[jechać, prowadzić]* straight; **spojrzała mu** ∼**sto w oczy** she looked straight into his eyes [2] (pionowo) upright, straight; **stój** ∼**sto** stand up straight [3] (łatwo) *[tłumaczyć, mówić]* simply, plainly

[]] *adv.* (bezpośrednio) straight; **idź** ∼**sto do biura** go straight to the office; **mleko** ∼**sto od krowy** milk fresh from the cow

[]]] **po prostu** *part.* just, simply; **po** ∼**stu powiedz im prawdę** just tell them the truth;

innego wyjścia po ~**stu nie ma** there's simply no other way out

■ ~**sto z mostu** straight from the shoulder

prostoduszn|y *adi. grad.* artless, ingenuous

prostoką|t *m* rectangle

prostokątn|y *adi. [plac, stół]* rectangular; **trójkąt** ~**y** right-angled triangle

prostolinijn|y *adi. grad.* straightforward

prostopadłościan *m* cuboid

prostopad|ły *adi.* perpendicular, at right angles (**do czegoś** to sth)

prosto|ta *f* simplicity; **powiedzieć coś z** ~**tą** to say sth simply

prost|ować *impf* **[]** *vt* 1 to straighten out *[drut, blachę, fałdę]*; ~**ować plecy** to straighten one's back 2 to correct *[wypowiedź, błąd]*; to rectify *[omyłkę]*

[] **prostować się** *[osoba]* to straighten up

prostownik *m* (prądu) rectifier

pro|sty **[]** *adi.* 1 *[droga, włosy, nogi]* straight 2 (niewyszukany) *[suknia, jedzenie]* plain, simple; ~**ści ludzie** the common people 3 (nieskomplikowany) *[metoda, objaśnienie]* simple; **to dziecinnie** ~**ste** it's child's play

[] *m* (cios) straight punch

[] **prosta** *f* 1 (linia) straight line 2 (odcinek toru) straight

■ **zejść z** ~**stej drogi** to stray from the paths of righteousness książk.; **wyjść na** ~**stą** to be out of the wood(s)

prostytucj|a *f* prostitution

prostytut|ka *f* prostitute; **męska** ~**ka** a male prostitute

prosz|ek *m* 1 (substancja) powder; **mleko w** ~**ku** powdered milk; ~**ek do pieczenia** baking powder; ~**ek do prania** washing powder 2 pot. (lekarstwo) pill; **zażyć kilka** ~**ków nasennych** to take a few sleeping pills

■ **być w** ~**ku** pot. to not be ready

pr|ośba *f* request (**o coś** for sth); **mam prośbę** I would like to ask a favour; **zwrócić się do kogoś z prośbą o pomoc** to come to sb for help; **na czyjąś prośbę** at sb's request

■ **prośby i groźby** threats and entreaties; **chodzić po prośbie** to go begging

protein|a *f* protein

protekcj|a *f* książk. patronage, protection; **szukać u kogoś** ~**i** to seek sb's protection; **dzięki** ~**i** thanks to friends in high places

prote|st *m* protest (**przeciwko czemuś** against sth); **na znak** ~**stu** in protest; **bez** ~**stu** without protest

protestacyjn|y *adi. [akcja, marsz]* protest

protestanc|ki *adi.* Protestant

protestan|t *m*, ~**tka** *f* Protestant

protestantyzm *m* Protestantism

protest|ować *impf vi* to protest (**przeciwko czemuś** against sth)

protety|k *m*, ~**czka** *f* prosthodontist

protety|ka *f* prosthodontics

protez|a *f* prosthesis; ~**a dentystyczna** denture, false teeth; ~**a ortopedyczna** an artificial limb; ~**a stawu biodrowego** a hip replacement, a replacement hip

protokolan|t *m*, ~**tka** *f* minutes secretary; ~**t sądowy** court reporter

protokoł|ować *impf vt* to minute, to record

protok|ół *m* 1 (sprawozdanie) minute(s); ~**ół posiedzenia** minutes of a meeting; ~**ół rozprawy sądowej** a transcript a. record of court proceedings 2 (akt) record; ~**ół rozbieżności** record of differences 3 (zasady postępowania) protocol; ~**ół dyplomatyczny** (diplomatic) protocol; **w myśl** ~**ołu** in accordance with diplomatic protocol

prototyp *m* prototype

prowadzeni|e *n* 1 Sport the lead; **objąć** ~**e** to take the lead 2 (sposób życia) conduct; **kobieta lekkiego** ~**a** a woman of loose morals a. easy virtue przest.

prowa|dzić *impf* **[]** *vt* 1 (wieść) to lead *[dziecko, zwierzę]*; ~**dzić kogoś za rękę** to lead sb by the hand także przen.; ~**dzić kogoś na spacer** to take sb for a walk 2 (przesuwać) ~**dzić pióro/ołówek** to guide a pen/pencil; ~**dzić smyczek** to draw a bow, to bow; ~**dzić piłkę/krążek** to dribble a ball/ puck; ~**dzić ręką po czymś** to run one's hand over sth 3 (kierować) to drive *[samochód, motocykl]*; to fly *[samolot]*; **dobrze** ~**dzić** to be a good driver 4 (doprowadzać) to carry; **żyły** ~**dzą krew do serca** the veins carry blood to the heart 5 (sprawować nadzór) to run *[dom, firmę, sklep]*; to preside over, to chair *[spotkanie, obrady]*; ~**dzić orkiestrę** to conduct an orchestra 6 (realizować) to conduct *[badania]*; to carry on, to have *[rozmowę]*; to do *[interesy]*; ~**dzić spór** to have an argument; ~**dzić korespondencję** to carry on a. conduct (a) correspondence; ~**dzić dziennik** to keep a diary; ~**dzić dochodzenie** to carry out a. conduct an investigation; ~**dzić lekcję** to conduct a. hold (a) class

[] *vi* 1 (wskazywać drogę) to lead; ~**dzić do piwnicy** to lead to the cellar 2 (przodować) to lead, to be in the lead; ~**dzić o 5 sekund** to lead by 5 seconds; ~**dzić trzema punktami** to have a lead of three points 3 (powodować) to cause (**do czegoś** sth); to lead (**do czegoś** to sth)

[] **prowadzić się** (postępować) **dobrze/źle się** ~**dzić** to conduct oneself well/badly

prowian|t *m* provisions

prowincj|a *f* 1 (peryferie) the provinces; **głęboka** a. **zapadła** ~**a** the back of beyond 2 (region) province

prowizj|a *f* commission; **pobierać** ~**ę** to charge a commission

prowizor|ka *f* pot. improvised arrangement; lash-up GB pot.

prowizoryczn|y *adi.* makeshift

prowokacj|a *f* provocation; ~**a policyjna** an entrapment, a set-up

prowokacyjn|y *adi.* provocative

prowokato|r *m* (szpieg) agent provocateur; (podburzacz) agitator, inciter

prowok|ować *impf vt* ① to provoke [osobę] ② to provoke, to stir up [niepokoje społeczne, dyskusję]

proz|a *f* prose; **napisać coś** ~**ą** to write sth in prose; **poemat** ~**ą** a prose poem; **zbiór** ~**y autora** a collection of the author's prose works; ~**a życia** the prosaic aspects of life

prozaiczn|y *adi. grad.* ① [zajęcie, powód] prosaic ② [utwór] prose

prozai|k *m,* ~**czka** *f* prose writer

prób|a *f* ① (usiłowanie) attempt; **podjąć** ~**ę zrobienia czegoś** to make an attempt to do sth a. at doing sth; ~**a samobójcza** a suicide attempt; ~**a morderstwa** an attempted murder ② (sprawdzian) test, trial; **podziemne** ~**y jądrowe** underground nuclear tests; ~**a sił** a test of strength; **poddać coś** ~**ie** to test sth; **poddać kogoś** ~**ie** to put sb to the test; **na** ~**ę** as an experiment; **metodą** ~ **i błędów** by trial and error ③ przen. (trudności) trial, test; ~**a charakteru** a test of character; **ciężka** ~**a** an ordeal; **w godzinie** ~**y** at the critical a. crucial moment; **wystawić coś na ciężką** ~**ę** to put sth to the test; **wytrzymać** ~**ę czasu** to stand the test of time ④ (wynik wysiłków) attempt, effort; **jej pierwsze malarskie** ~**y** her first attempts at painting; **ta książka była jego pierwszą** ~**ą pisarską** this book was his first literary effort ⑤ (niewielka ilość) sample; ~**a losowa** a random sample ⑥ (metalu szlachetnego) purity; (stempel probierczy) hallmark; **złoto pierwszej** ~**y** ≈ 24-carat gold; **oznaczyć** ~**ę czegoś** to assay sth; **dokonania najwyższej** ~**y** przen. achievements of the highest order ⑦ Muz., Teatr rehearsal, practice; ~**a chóru/orkiestry** a choir/an orchestra rehearsal; ~**a generalna** a dress rehearsal; ~**a nowej sztuki** a rehearsal of a. for a new play; **trwają** ~**y nowej sztuki** a new play is in rehearsal ⑧ Sport trial (run); ~**a górska** a mountain trial ❑ ~**a ciążowa** pregnancy test; ~**a głosu** audition

prób|ka *f* ① (do badania) sample, specimen ② (towaru) sample; (tkaniny, tapety) sample, swatch; (kosmetyku w drogerii) tester ③ (przykład) example, sample

próbnik *m* (do pobierania próbek) probe; (do testowania) tester; ~ **kosmiczny** space probe

próbn|y *adi.* test, trial; ~**y alarm pożarowy** a fire drill; **jazda** ~**a** a test drive; **lot** ~**y** a test flight; ~**e odbitki** proofs, pulls; **egzaminy** ~**e** mock exams; **okres** ~**y** a trial a. probationary period; **zdjęcia** ~**e** (przy obsadzaniu ról) a screen test

prób|ować *impf* ❶ *vt* ① (sprawdzać smak) to try, to taste [potrawę, wino]; ~**ować wszystkiego po trochu** to sample a bit of everything ② Teatr to rehearse [scenę] ③ (poddawać próbie) to try (out), to test [metod, sposobów] ④ (poznawać) to try, to experiment with [narkotyków]; to try one's hand at [wspinaczki, dziennikarstwa] ⑤ (starać się) to try, to attempt; ~**ować ucieczki** to attempt an escape

❷ *vi* (usiłować) to try, to attempt (**coś zrobić** to do sth); ~**ować popełnić samobójstwo** to attempt suicide

próbówka → **probówka**

próchnic|a *f* ① Med. (tooth) decay, dental caries ② Roln. humus

próchni|eć *impf vi* to decay, to rot

próch|no *n* ① (w drewnie) rot, rotten a. rotting wood; **rozsypywać się w** ~**no** (to turn to) rot ② przen. (stare) ~**no** pot., obraźl. (mężczyzna) (doddering) old fool pot., obraźl.; (kobieta) (doddering) old cow a. bag pot., obraźl.

pr|óg *m* ① (wejście) threshold; (listwa) threshold, doorsill US; (stopień) doorstep; **nie ruszać się za próg** to not set (a) foot outside the door przen. ② przen. (granica) threshold, verge; **próg podatkowy** income tax threshold; **próg rentowności** break-even point; **znaleźć się na progu bankructwa** to be on the verge a. brink of bankruptcy ③ Sport take-off board ④ Muz. fret ❑ **próg zwalniający** road a. speed hump; sleeping policeman GB pot.

■ **to za wysokie progi na moje nogi** that's out of my league

prósz|yć *impf vi* ~**yło** a. **śnieg** ~**ył całą noc** it was snowing all night

próżni|a *f* vacuum; ~**a kosmiczna** the cosmic vacuum a. void; **trafiać w** ~**ę** [słowa, argumenty] to fall on deaf ears

próżniactw|o *n* idleness

próżnia|k *m* pot. layabout pot.

próżniow|y *adi.* [opakowanie, pompa] vacuum; **skafander** ~**y** a pressure suit

próżno *adv.* książk. (it's) no use; ~ **teraz się zastanawiać** no use wondering now; **na** ~ in vain, to no avail; **wszystko było na** ~ it was all in vain; **próbowali go przekonać, ale na** ~ they tried to reason with him, but to no avail

próżnoś|ć *f* vanity; **łechtać czyjąś** ~**ć** to tickle sb's vanity

próżn|ować *impf vi* to idle the time away

próżn|y *adi.* ① (pyszałkowaty) [osoba] vain ② (daremny) [obietnica, słowa] empty, idle; [nadzieja, starania] vain, futile; [obawy] groundless ③ (pusty) [słoik, butelka] empty

pru|ć *impf* ❶ *vt* ① to unravel [dzianinę, szalik, oczka] ② to unpick [szew, sukienkę] ③ to cut through [fale, chmury, powietrze]

❷ *vi* pot. ① (gnać) to scorch along GB, to burn

rubber pot. [2] (strzelać seriami) to fire a. blast away
III pruć się [1] [dzianina] to unravel; [brzeg tkaniny, rękaw] to fray [2] [sukienka, szew] to fall apart, to come apart
prusa|k m German cockroach
prych|nąć pf — **prych|ać** impf vi [1] (parskać) [osoba, koń] to snort; [kot] to spit, to hiss; ~**nąć ze złości** to give an angry snort [2] (odezwać się oprys-kliwie) to snap, to snarl (**na kogoś** at sb) [3] [maszyna, silnik] to sputter, to cough
prycz|a f pallet, plank bed
prymas m primate
pryma|t m książk. primacy (**nad czymś** over sth); **rywalizować o ~t w czymś** to compete for first place in sth
prymitywn|y adi. grad. [1] (pierwotny) primitive, primordial [2] (nienowoczesny) [narzędzia, metody] primitive, crude [3] (prostacki) crude pejor.
prymul|a f primrose, primula
prymus m [1] (uczeń) top student; **być ~em z chemii** to be top of the class in chemistry [2] (do gotowania) Primus® (stove)
prymus|ka f top student
pryska|ć¹ impf vt (zraszać) to spray [rośliny] (**czymś** with sth)
pry|snąć pf — **pry|skać²** impf vi [1] (zrosić) to spray, to sprinkle (**na kogoś** sb); (oblać) to splash, to splatter (**na kogoś** sb) [2] (rozpryskać się) [tłuszcz, błoto] to splatter; [iskry] to fly [3] (pęknąć) [szkło] to shatter, to splinter; [bańka mydlana] to burst [4] pot. (uciec) to run for it, to do a bunk a. runner GB pot.; ~**snął za granicę** he fled the country [5] przen. (zniknąć) [nastrój, humor, nadzieja] to evaporate; to go up in smoke przen.
pryszcz m [1] (na skórze) pimple, spot GB; zit pot.; **wycisnąć ~** to squeeze a pimple [2] pot. (drobnostka) cinch, piece of cake pot.
pryszcza|ty adi. pimply, spotty GB
prysznic m [1] (urządzenie) shower; **wejść pod ~** to step under the shower [2] (kąpiel) shower; **wziąć ~** to have a. take a shower, to shower [3] (pomieszczenie) shower room
prywa|ta f książk. self-interest, self-serving
prywat|ka f pot. party
prywatn|y adi. [1] (niepubliczny) [firma, kolekcja, posesja] private; „**teren ~y, wstęp wzbroniony!**" 'private property, no trespassing!'; **szkoła ~a** a private school, a public school GB [2] (osobisty) [list, rozmowa, dochody] private, personal; ~**y adres** sb's home address; **kontakty urzędowe i ~e** business and personal contacts; **do (czyjegoś) ~ego użytku** for (sb's) private a. personal use; **udać się z ~ą wizytą na Węgry** to go on a private visit to Hungary; **występować jako osoba ~a** to act in a private capacity a. as a private person
prywatyzacj|a f privatization

prywatyz|ować impf Ekon. **I** vt to privatize
II prywatyzować się to be a. become privatized
pryzm|a f (piasku, śniegu) heap; (buraków, ziemniaków) pile
prz|ąść impf vt to spin [nici, len, pajęczynę]
■ **cienko ~ąść** pot. to live from hand to mouth, to lead a hand-to-mouth existence
przebacz|yć pf — **przebacz|ać** impf vt to forgive (**komuś coś** sb sth); **prosić (kogoś) o ~enie** to ask for (sb's) forgiveness
przebi|ć pf — **przebi|jać** impf **I** vt [1] (przekłuć) to puncture [skórę, oponę]; to pierce [pancerz, ścianę]; ~**ć kogoś nożem** to stub sb with a knife [2] (przekopać) to drill [tunel] [3] (w licytacji) to outbid [rywala]; (atutem) to trump; ~**ć cenę** to offer a higher price
II przebić się — przebijać się (przeniknąć) ~**ć się przez coś** to fight one's way through sth [gąszcz, linie wroga]; to elbow one's way through sth [tłum]; [światło, dźwięk] to break through sth, to penetrate sth
przebie|c, przebie|gnąć pf — **przebie|gać¹** impf **I** vt (przebyć drogę) to run [dystans]; (na drugą stronę) to run across [drogę, tory]; ~**gł całą drogę do szkoły** he ran all the way to school; ~**c komuś drogę** to cross sb's path; ~**c coś wzrokiem** a. **oczami** to run one's eyes over sth
II vi [1] (z miejsca na miejsce) to run (**przez coś/obok czegoś** across/past sth) [2] (przemknąć) [dreszcz] to run; [uśmiech] to flash; [myśl, pomysł] to flit, to flash [3] (dokonać się) [operacja, działania] to go, to proceed
III przebiec się, przebiegnąć się — przebiegać się pot. to do some jogging
przebieg m [1] (tok) course; ~ **wydarzeń** the course of events [2] (trasa) route [3] Aut. mileage
przebiegać² impf → przebiec
przebiega|ć² impf vi (ciągnąć się) [droga, linia kolejowa] to run
przebieg|ły adi. crafty, cunning
przebiegnąć → przebiec
przebierać¹ impf → przebrać
przebiera|ć² impf vi [1] (poruszać) ~**ć palcami po stole** to tap one's fingers on the table; ~**ć palcami po klawiaturze** to run one's fingers over the keys; **szybko ~ć nogami** to take quick strides; ~**ć nogami w miejscu** to mark time [2] (nie móc się zdecydować) to pick and choose; **nie ~ć w słowach** to not mince one's words
przebieral|nia f changing room
przebijać¹ impf → przebić
przebija|ć² impf vi (przeświecać) to show (through)
przebiśnieg m snowdrop
przebojow|y adi. [1] [piosenka, film] hit; [książka] best-selling [2] [osoba] go-getting pot.
przeb|ój **I** m (piosenka) hit; (książka, produkt) best-seller; **lista ~ojów** pop charts

Ⅱ **przebojem** *adv.* by storm; ~**ojem iść przez życie** to be a go-getter pot.

przeb|rać *pf* — **przeb|ierać**[1] *impf* **Ⅰ** *vt* [1] (zmienić ubranie) to change (**kogoś w coś** sb into sth) [2] (ubrać w kostium) to dress up; ~**rać kogoś za kogoś** (dla zabawy)to dress sb up as sb; (dla zmiany wyglądu) to disguise sb as sb [3] (dokonać selekcji) to sift out

Ⅱ **przebrać się** — **przebierać się** [1] (zmienić ubranie) to change; ~**ierz się w czystą koszulę** change your shirt [2] (zmienić wygląd) (dla zabawy) to dress up; (dla ukrycia tożsamości) to disguise oneself

■ ~**rać miarę** a. **miarkę** to go too far, to overstep the mark; ~**rała się miara** a. **miarka** that's the last straw

przebra|nie *n* disguise; **w** ~**niu** in disguise

przebud|owa *f* [1] (domu) alteration, conversion; (ulicy, dzielnicy) redevelopment [2] (systemu, organizacji) restructuring

przebud|ować *pf* — **przebud|owywać** *impf vt* [1] to convert *[dom]*; ~**owana stajnia** a converted barn [2] to restructure *[system, organizacje]*

przeb|yć *pf* — **przeb|ywać**[1] *impf vt* [1] (pokonać dystans) to travel *[drogę]*; to cover *[odległość]* [2] (doświadczyć) to go through *[chorobę, trudny okres]*; to undergo *[operację]*

przebywa|ć[2] *impf vi* to stay; ~**ć z kimś** to spend time with sb; ~**ć za granicą** to be abroad; ~**ć z oficjalną wizytą w Niemczech** to pay an official visit to Germany

przecen|a *f* (obniżenie ceny) price reduction; (wyprzedaż) sale; **towary z** ~**y** cut-price goods

przece|nić *pf* — **przece|niać** *impf vt* [1] (ocenić zbyt wysoko) to overestimate, to overrate [2] (obniżyć cenę) to mark down, to reduce the price of; **towary** ~**nione** cut-price goods

przechadza|ć się *impf v refl.* to stroll, to take a stroll

przechadz|ka *f* stroll; **pójść na** ~**kę** to go for a stroll

przechodni *adi.* *[pokój]* connecting; *[puchar, sztandar]* challenge; *[czasownik]* transitive

przechodzić[1] *impf* → **przejść**

przecho|dzień *m* passer-by

przechow|ać *pf* — **przechow|ywać** *impf* **Ⅰ** *vt* [1] (zmagazynować) to keep *[drewno, żywność]*; to store *[informacje, meble]*; **czy możesz mi to** ~**ać?** can you look after this for me?; **oddać bagaż na** ~**anie** to leave one's luggage at the left-luggage office [2] (zachować) to preserve *[wspomnienia, zwyczaje]* [3] (ukryć) to give shelter (**kogoś** to sb)

Ⅱ **przechować się** — **przechowywać się** [1] *[żywność, towary]* to keep [2] *[zwyczaj, wspomnienie]* to be preserved

przechowalni|a *f* (bagażu) left luggage (office), checkroom US

przechowywać *impf* → **przechować**

przechwal|ać się *impf v refl.* to boast, to brag

przechwał|ka *f* bragging, boast

przechyl|ić *pf* — **przechyl|ać** *impf* **Ⅰ** *vt* to tip, to tilt; **z** ~**oną głową** with one's head cocked to one side

Ⅱ **przechylić się** — **przechylać się** [1] (przekrzywić się) to tilt; ~**ić się na prawą stronę** to tilt to the right; **szala zwycięstwa** ~**iła się na czyjąś stronę** the scales were tipped in sb's favour [2] (wychylić się) to lean (**przez coś** over sth)

przechytrz|yć *pf* — **przechytrz|ać** *impf vt* to outsmart, to outfox

prze|ciąć *pf* — **prze|cinać** *impf* **Ⅰ** *vt* [1] (podzielić) to cut *[sznurek, papier]*; ~**ciąć pępowinę** książk. to cut the (umbilical) cord [2] (przejść, przejechać) to cross *[ulicę, tory]*; to cut across *[plac, polanę]* [3] (przerwać) to cut short *[dyskusję, cierpienia]*; to break *[ciszę]*

Ⅱ **przeciąć się** — **przecinać się** *[linie, drogi]* (krzyżować się) to cross; (tworzyć siatkę) to criss-cross

przeciąg *m* [1] (ruch powietrza) draught GB, draft US [2] (odcinek czasu) **w** ~**u kilku godzin** within a few hours; **na** ~ **tygodnia** for a week; **na** ~ **wakacji** for the duration of the holidays

przeciągać *impf* → **przeciągnąć**

przeciąg|nąć się *pf* — **przeciąg|ać się** *impf v refl.* [1] *[obrady, pobyt]* to protract; **obiad** ~**nął się do późna** dinner stretched out until late [2] (rozprostować się) to stretch

przeciąż|yć *pf* — **przeciąż|ać** *impf vt* [1] (ładunkiem) to overload *[pojazd, statek]* [2] (obowiązkami) to overburden; ~**yć kogoś pracą** to overburden sb with work

przecie|c, przecie|knąć *pf* — **przecie|kać** *impf vi* [1] *[garnek, dach, łódź]* to leak [2] *[woda, krew]* to leak (**przez coś** through sth) [3] pot. *[informacje, tajemnice]* to leak out

■ **życie** ~**ka jej przez palce** life slips through her fingers; **pieniądze** ~**kają mu przez palce** he spends money like water

przeciek *m* [1] (wody, cieczy, gazu) leakage; (miejsce awarii) leak [2] przen. (informacji) leak; **z przecieków wiadomo, że...** it has leaked out that...

przeciekać *impf* → **przeciec**

przecie|r *m* purée, paste; ~**r pomidorowy** tomato paste; **zrobić** ~**r z warzyw** to purée a. liquidize vegetables

przecierać *impf* → **przetrzeć**

przecież *part.* [1] (uzasadniające) after all; ~ **to twoja siostra** after all, she's your sister [2] (polemiczne) but; ~ **to oczywiste!** but that's obvious!; ~ **ci mówiłem!** I told you, didn't I? [3] (wyrażające zdziwienie) but; why przest.; ~ **to Robert?** but that's Robert!, that's Robert, isn't it?

przeciętnia|k *m* pot. nonentity, mediocrity

przeciętnie **Ⅰ** *adv. grad.* unremarkably, moderately

Ⅱ *part.* (średnio) *[zarabiać, wynosić]* on average

przeciętn|y [] *adi. grad. [uczeń, film]* mediocre, run-of-the-mill

[] *adi.* average; ~**y zjadacz chleba** Mr Average, the man in the street

[] **przeciętna** *f* average; **powyżej/poniżej** ~**ej** above/below (the) average; ~**a wieku dojrzewania** the average age of puberty

przecinać *impf* → **przeciąć**

przecin|ek *m* [] (w tekście) comma [] (w matematyce) (decimal) point; **do dwóch miejsc po** ~**ku** to two decimal places; **jeden** ~**ek 25** one point twenty-five

przeci|snąć *pf* — **przeci|skać** *impf* [] *vt* to push, to force

[] **przecisnąć się** — **przeciskać się** to get through, to squeeze through (**przez coś** sth); ~**skać się przez tłum** to make one's way through the crowd

przeciw *praep., adv.* against (**komuś/czemuś** sb/sth); Prawo, Sport versus; **być** ~**ko czemuś** to be against sth; **mieć coś/nie mieć nic** ~**ko czemuś** to have something/nothing against sth; **jeśli nie masz nic** ~**ko temu** if you don't mind; **mieć kogoś/coś** ~ **sobie** to have sb/sth against one; **100 głosów za i 20** ~ 100 votes for and 20 against; **dwunastu posłów było** ~ twelve deputies were against

■ **argumenty za i** ~ arguments for and against, pros and cons; **wyważyć wszystkie za i** ~ to weigh up (all) the pros and cons

przeciwbólow|y *adi. [lek, zastrzyk]* painkilling, analgesic

przeciwci|ało *n* antibody

przeciwdziała|ć *impf vi* to counteract, to prevent (**czemuś** sth)

przeciwieństw|o *n* [] (odwrotność) opposite; **w** ~**ie do kogoś** unlike sb, in contrast to a. with sb [] (sprzeczność) contrast, conflict; ~**o poglądów** conflicting views [] (niepowodzenie) adversity; **borykać się z** ~**ami losu** to weather adversities

przeciwko [] *praep.* → **przeciw**

[] **z przeciwka** [] *[nadjeżdżać, nadchodzić]* from the opposite direction [] (z innego domu) from across the street; (z innego mieszkania) from across the landing

przeciwległ|ły *adi. [brzegi, końce]* opposite; *[brzeg, koniec]* the other

przeciwnicz|ka *f* [] (oponentka) opponent (**czegoś** of sth); objector (**czegoś** to sth) [] (rywalka) opponent, adversary

przeciwnie [] *adv.* [] (inaczej) otherwise; **jest wręcz** ~ it's just the opposite; ~ **do kogoś** a. **niż ktoś** unlike sb/sth, in contrast to sb/sth [] (w odwrotną stronę) in the opposite direction; **dwie siły skierowane** ~ two opposing forces; ~ **do ruchu wskazówek zegara** anticlockwise

[] *part.* on the contrary; **wprost** a. **wręcz** ~ just a. quite the opposite

przeciwni|k *m* [] (oponent) opponent (**czegoś** of sth); objector (**czegoś** to sth); **być** ~**kiem czegoś** to be against sth [] (rywal) opponent, adversary [] (w wojnie) enemy

przeciwnoś|ć *f* adversity; **zmagać się z** ~**ciami losu** to weather adversities; **nie zrażać się** ~**ciami** to not lose heart in (the face of) adversity

przeciwn|y *adi.* [] (odmienny) *[zdanie, twierdzenie]* opposite; **płeć** ~**a** the opposite a. other sex; **skutki** ~**e do zamierzonych** counter-productive results; **w** ~**ym razie** otherwise, or else [] (sprzeciwiający się) against (**czemuś** sth); opposed (**czemuś** to sth); **być** ~**ym czemuś** to be against sth, to oppose sth [] (przeciwległy) *[strona, koniec]* opposite, the other; **iść w** ~**ym kierunku** to go in the opposite a. other direction

przeciwprostokątn|a *f* hypotenuse

przeciwsłoneczn|y *adi. [kapelusz, osłona]* sun; **okulary** ~**e** sunglasses, dark glasses; **filtr** ~**y** (fotograficzny) sunscreen; **krem z filtrem** ~**ym** sunblock, sunscreen

przeciwstaw|ić *pf* — **przeciwstawi|ać** *impf* [] *vt* to juxtapose, to contrast (**coś czemuś** sth with sth)

[] **przeciwstawić się** — **przeciwstawiać się** to oppose, to defy (**komuś** sb); to stand up (**komuś** sb)

przeciwwa|ga *f* counterbalance, counterpoise (**dla czegoś** to sth); **stanowić** ~**gę dla czegoś** to counterbalance a. counterpoise sth

przeciwwskaza|nie *n* contraindication (**do czegoś** against a. for sth)

przeczą|cy *adi. [gest, odpowiedź, zdanie]* negative

przeczek|ać *pf* — **przeczek|iwać** *impf vt* to wait for the end of *[burzę, kryzys, wojnę]*; **trzeba** ~**ać, aż się ściemni** we must wait until a. till it gets dark; **polityka obliczona na** ~**anie** a wait-and-see policy

przecze|nie *n* negative; **podwójne** ~**nie** double negative

przecznic|a *f* side street, cross street US; ~**a Krakowskiego Przedmieścia** a street off Krakowskie Przedmieście; **druga** ~**a w lewo** the second street (to the) left; **hotel jest dwie** ~**e stąd** the hotel is two streets a. two blocks US down from here

przeczu|cie *n* premonition, presentiment; **złe** ~**cia** forebodings, misgivings; **mam** ~**cie, że...** I have a feeling that...; **tknięty złym** ~**ciem** with a feeling of apprehension

przeczu|ć *pf* — **przeczu|wać** *impf vt* to sense, to have an inkling of *[nieszczęście, śmierć]*; ~**ł grożące mu niebezpieczeństwo** he felt he was in danger

przecz|yć *impf vi* [] (negować) to contradict *[osobie, słowom, faktom]*; **wszystkiemu** ~**ył** he denied everything; ~**yła sama sobie** she contradicted herself; **nie** ~**ę, że...** I don't deny that... ② (być w sprzeczności) to contradict, to contravene *[przepisom]*; to belie *[faktom]*; **jego słowa** ~**yły czynom** his words belied his deeds; **fakty temu** ~**ą** it's contradicted by the facts

przeczyszczać *impf* → **przeczyścić**

przeczyszczeni|e *n* purge, purgation; **środek na** ~**e** laxative, purgative

przeczy|ścić *pf* — **przeczy|szczać** *impf* **Ⅰ** *vt* ① (usunąć brud) to wipe *[szybę, okulary]*; to sweep *[komin]*; to clean *[fajkę, karabin, rurę]* ② Med. to purge *[osobę]*; **środek** ~**szczający** laxative, purgative

Ⅱ *v imp.* ~**ściło go po suszonych śliwkach** he evacuated his bowels after eating prunes

przeczyta|ć *pf vt* ① to read *[książkę, list]*; ~**ć coś głośno** a. **na głos** to read sth aloud a. out loud; ~**ć coś komuś** to read sth to sb, to read sb sth; ~**j, co tu jest napisane** read out what it says for me ② (odcyfrować) to read, to decipher *[napis, bazgroły]*

p|rzeć *impf vi* ① (posuwać się) to push; **przeć naprzód/przed siebie** to push forward/ahead; **przeć na wroga** to bear down on the enemy ② (naciskać) **przeć na coś** to push against sth *[drzwi, bramę]*; (w dół) to push down ③ (forsować) **przeć do czegoś** to push for sth *[reform, ugody, walki]* ④ Med. (przy porodzie) to push, to bear down; **bóle parte** bearing down pains; **skurcze parte** pushing contractions

przed *praep.* ① (w przestrzeni) in front of, before (**czymś** sth); ~ **lustrem/telewizorem** in front of a mirror/the TV; **iść/patrzeć** ~ **siebie** to walk/look straight ahead; **skręć w lewo** ~ **rondem** turn left before the roundabout ② (wcześniej niż) before; ~ **śniadaniem/wojną** before breakfast/the war; ~ **południem** in the morning; **V wiek** ~ **naszą erą** the fifth century before Christ a. BC; **przyszła** ~ **dwunastą** she came before twelve; **najgorsze jest jeszcze** ~ **nami** the worst is yet a. still to come a. still before us; ~ **czasem** ahead of time a. schedule ③ (jakiś czas temu) before, earlier; ~ **godziną** an hour before a. earlier a. ago; ~ **laty** years ago ④ (obrona) against, from; **ochrona** ~ **zimnem** protection against (the) cold; **strach** ~ **kimś** fear of sb; **ukryć coś** ~ **kimś** to hide sth from sb ⑤ (wobec) **popisywać się** ~ **gośćmi** to show off in front of guests; **wystąpić** ~ **pełną salą** to appear in front of a. before a full house; **niczego** ~**e mną nie ukryjesz** you can't hide anything from me; **został postawiony** ~ **Trybunałem Stanu** he was brought before the State Tribunal

przedawk|ować *pf* — **przedawk|owywać** *impf vt* to take an overdose of *[leki, narkotyki]*

przedawni|ć *pf* — **przedawni|ać** *impf* **Ⅰ** *vt* to apply the statute of limitations to *[zbrodnie, roszczenia]*

Ⅱ **przedawnić się** — **przedawniać się** *[przestępstwo, roszczenia]* to fall under the statute of limitations

przedawnie|nie *n* statute of limitations; **sprawa uległa** ~**niu** the case fell under the statute of limitations; **podlegać** ~**niu** to be subject to the statute of limitations

przedbieg *m* qualifying round a. heat; **odpaść w** ~**ach** przen. to not pass muster, to not come up to scratch

przed|dzień *m* the day before; **w** ~**dzień (jego) wyjazdu** the day before his departure; **w** ~**dzień a.** ~**edniu wybuchu wojny** przen. on the eve of the outbreak of war

przede → **przed**

przedim|ek *m* article; ~**ek określony/nieokreślony** the definite/the indefinite article

przedłużacz *m* extension lead a. cable GB, extension cord US

przedłuż|yć *pf* — **przedłuż|ać** *impf* **Ⅰ** *vt* to lengthen, to extend *[ulicę, linię]*; to prolong, to extend *[pobyt]*; to prolong *[rozmowę, urlop, zebranie]*; to protract, to draw out *[dyskusję]*; to renew *[paszport, wizę]*; to extend *[termin]*

Ⅱ **przedłużyć się** — **przedłużać się** *[cisza, wizyta]* to lengthen; *[dyskusja]* to be prolonged a. protracted; *[wykład, program]* to overrun; **zebranie** ~**yło się do późnego wieczoru** the meeting didn't end until late at night; **jego pobyt w naszym domu** ~**ył się** he stayed with us longer than expected

przedmieś|cie *n* suburb, (city) outskirts

przedmio|t *m* ① (rzecz) object, article; **wartościowe** ~**ty** objects of value, valuables; ~**ty codziennego użytku** everyday articles a. items; ~**ty osobiste** personal effects, belongings; ~**t o wartości muzealnej** a museum piece; **traktować kogoś jak** ~**t** to treat sb like an object ② (temat) (filmu, książki) subject; (rozmowy, dyskusji) topic, subject; **stać się** ~**tem rozmów** to become a talking point; **odbiegać od** ~**tu** to deviate from the subject; **znawcy** ~**tu** experts on the subject ③ Szkol., Uniw. subject; ~**ty ścisłe** the sciences; ~**ty kierunkowe/dodatkowe** main/subsidiary subjects GB, majors/minors US; ~**ty obowiązkowe/fakultatywne** compulsory/optional courses GB, compulsory/elective subjects a. courses US, requirements/ electives US

przedm|owa *f* preface, foreword (**do czegoś** to sth); **opatrzyć książkę** ~**ową** to preface a book

przedmów|ca *m,* ~**czyni** *f* previous a. preceding speaker

przedmuch|ać *pf* — **przedmuch|iwać** *impf vt* to blow through *[fajkę, ustnik, gaźnik]*

przedni **Ⅰ** *adi. grad.* (znakomity) *[wino, cygaro]* delectable, exquisite; *[pomysł, rada]* excellent; *[towarzystwo, nauczyciel]* excellent, outstanding

II *adi.* (znajdujący się z przodu) *[siedzenie, koła, zęby]* front; ~**a noga** foreleg, forefoot; ~**a szyba** Aut. windscreen; **samogłoska** ~**a** front vowel; **straż** ~**a** advance guard, vanguard

przedosta|ć się *pf* — **przedosta|wać się** *impf v refl.* [1] (dotrzeć) to get; ~**ć się na drugi brzeg** to get across to the other bank; ~**ć się do środka** to get in [2] (przeniknąć) *[dźwięk, zapach]* to penetrate; *[ciecz]* to penetrate, to seep in; **woda** ~**wała się do wnętrza łodzi** water was leaking into the boat [3] (zostać ujawnionym) *[informacja, fakty]* to leak out

przedostatni *adi.* the last but one, the next to last; *[sylaba]* penultimate

przedostawać się *impf* → **przedostać się**

przedpok|ój *m* (entrance) hall, hallway

przedpołudni|e *n* (late) morning; **wczesnym** ~**em** in the morning

przedrami|ę *n* forearm

przedrost|ek *m* prefix

przedruk *m* reprint

przedrukow|ać *pf* — **przedrukow|ywać** *impf vt* to (re)print *[artykuł, wiersz]*

prze|drzeć *pf* — **prze|dzierać** *impf* **I** *vt* (rozerwać) to tear *[materiał, papier]*; ~**drzeć coś na pół** to tear sth in half

II przedrzeć się — **przedzierać się** [1] (rozerwać się) to tear, to get torn [2] (przedostać się) to force one's way through; ~**drzeć się przez obronę wroga** to break through the enemy defences; ~**drzeć się przez gąszcz przepisów** przen. to wade through a maze of regulations

przedrzeźnia|ć *impf vt* to mimic, to mock

przedsiębiorc|a *m* entrepreneur, businessman; ~**a budowlany** building contractor; ~**a pogrzebowy** undertaker, mortician US

przedsiębiorcz|y *adi.* enterprising, resourceful

przedsiębiorstw|o *n* enterprise, company; ~**o handlu zagranicznego** import-export company; ~**o pogrzebowe** funeral parlour GB a. parlor US; ~**o usług komunalnych** a public service corporation; ~**a użyteczności publicznej** public utilities

przedsięwzię|cie *n* undertaking, venture

przedsion|ek *m* [1] (sień) vestibule [2] (przybudówka) porch [3] Anat. (serca) atrium, auricle; (ucha) vestibule

przedsmak *m* foretaste; **mieć** ~ **czegoś** to have a foretaste of sth

przedsprzedaż *f* advance booking; **kupić bilety w** ~**y** to buy tickets in advance

przedstawiać[1] *impf* → **przedstawić**

przedstawia|ć[2] *impf vt* [1] (ukazywać) *[obraz, utwór]* to show, to depict *[postać, widok]* [2] (stanowić) to present *[widok, obraz]*; ~**ć znikomą wartość** to be of negligible value; **nie** ~**ć (dla kogoś) żadnej trudności** to present no problem (for sb)

przedstawiciel *m*, ~**ka** *f* [1] (reprezentant) representative (**kogoś** of sb); **najwybitniejszy** ~

polskiego romantyzmu the finest exponent of Polish Romanticism; **występować jako czyjś** ~ to appear on behalf of sb; **mieć swoich** ~**i w parlamencie** to be represented in parliament [2] (pełnomocnik) proxy, plenipotentiary

przedstawiciels|ki *adi. [organ, instytucja]* representative; *[demokracja]* representative, representational

przedstawicielstw|o *n* [1] (zespół) representation [2] (placówka) agency [3] (pełnomocnictwo) plenipotentiary powers

przedstaw|ić *pf* — **przedstaw|iać**[1] *impf* **I** *vt* [1] (zapoznać) to introduce (**komuś kogoś** sb to sb); **pan pozwoli, że** ~**ię mego syna** książk. allow me to introduce my son książk. [2] (przedłożyć) to put forward *[dokument, pogląd]*; to present *[projekt]*; to advance *[hipotezę]*; to produce *[dowody]*; ~**ić swoje warunki** to state one's conditions; ~**ić zwolnienie lekarskie** to show a doctor's note [3] (ukazać) to show, to depict *[bohatera, widok]*; ~**ić kogoś w dobrym/złym świetle** to show sb in a good/ bad a. favourable/an unfavourable light [4] (zarekomendować) to put forward *[osobę]*; ~**ić kogoś do awansu/nagrody** to put sb forward for promotion/ a prize [5] (wyobrażać sobie) ~**iać sobie coś** to visualize a. imagine sth

II przedstawić się — **przedstawiać się** [1] (wymienić nazwisko) to introduce oneself (**komuś** to sb) [2] (zaprezentować się) to present a. show oneself; ~**ić się z najlepszej strony** to show oneself at one's best

przedstawie|nie *n* [1] (widowisko) performance; **trzy** ~**nia „Hamleta"** three performances of 'Hamlet' [2] przen. spectacle; **robić z siebie** ~**nie** to make a spectacle of oneself; **skończ już to** ~**nie!** cut out the dramatics!

przedszkola|k *m* kindergarten a. nursery school pupil, pre-school pupil US, pre-schooler US

przedszkolan|ka *f* nursery school a. kindergarten teacher, pre-school teacher US

przedszkol|e *n* nursery school, kindergarten, pre-school US

przedtem *adv.* earlier, before (that); **krótko** ~ shortly before (that); **jak nigdy** ~ like never before; **nigdy go** ~ **nie widziałem** I'd never seen him before; ~ **pracowała w telewizji** previously a. before that she had worked in television

przedwcze|sny *adi. [opinie, decyzja, optymizm]* premature; *[koniec, śmierć]* premature, untimely

przedwczoraj *adv., n inv. [wrócić, wydarzyć się]* the day before yesterday; **od** ~ since the day before yesterday, for two days; **do** ~ until the day before yesterday, until two days ago; **to musi być gotowe na** ~ pot. it's really urgent

przedwiośni|e *n* early spring

przedwojenn|y *adi.* prewar

przedzia|ł *m* ☐ (kolejowy) compartment; ~**ł sypialny** sleeping compartment; ~**ł dla palących** smoking compartment; ~**ł dla niepalących** non-smoking compartment; non-smoker GB pot. ② (zakres) bracket, range; **w** ~**le wiekowym od 15 do 20 lat** in the 15-to-20 age bracket; **w tym** ~**le cenowym** in this price range

przedział|ek *m* parting GB, part US; ~**ek po lewej stronie/na środku** a left/centre parting

przedziel|ić *pf* — **przedziel|ać** *impf vt* ☐ (rozgraniczać) to divide *[kartkę, pokój, miasto]*; ~**ić coś na pół** a. **na dwie połowy** to divide sth in half a. into two halves ② (odgraniczać) to separate; **byliśmy** ~**eni cienką ścianką** we were separated by a thin wall

przedzierać *impf* → **przedrzeć**

przedziuraw|ić *pf* — **przedziuraw|iać** *impf* **[]** *vt* to make a hole in *[papier, materiał, blachę, deskę]*; to punch (a hole in); ~**iona opona** punctured tyre

[] **przedziurawić się** — **przedziurawiać się** *[buty, sweter]* to wear through; *[dach, pojemnik, łódź]* to spring a leak

przegap|ić *pf* — **przegap|iać** *impf vt* pot. to miss *[moment, osobę, miejsce]*; to overlook *[błąd, szczegół]*; **takiej okazji nie można było** ~**ić** the chance was too good to miss

przeg|iąć *pf* — **przeg|inać** *impf* **[]** *vt* ☐ to bend *[drzewo, maszt]*; to incline *[głowę]* ② pot. (przesadzić) to go over the top; **nie** ~**inaj (pały)!** (groźba) don't push your luck! pot.

[] **przegiąć się** — **przeginać się** *[osoba, drzewo]* to bend

przeglą|d *m* ☐ (kontrola) inspection; (medyczny) check-up; **dokonać** ~**du czegoś** to check sth *[wagon, pomieszczenie]*; to review sth *[prace]* ② Techn. servicing; Aut. MOT test a. inspection GB; **przeprowadzić** ~**d czegoś** to service a. overhaul sth *[urządzenia, instalacji, maszyny]*; **oddałem samochód do** ~**du** I've taken the car in for a service a. for servicing ③ (zestawienie) review; ~**d prasy** a review of the press; ~**d wydarzeń tygodnia** the week in review; ~**d naukowy/literacki** (publikacja) a scientific/literary review ④ (pokaz) review ⑤ Wojsk. inspection

przeglądać *impf* → **przejrzeć**[1]

przeglądar|ka *f* ☐ Fot. viewer ② Komput. browser

przeglądnąć → **przejrzeć**[1]

przegł|odzić *pf* — **przegł|adzać** *impf* **[]** *vt* to starve

[] **przegłodzić się** — **przegładzać się** to starve oneself

przegłos|ować *pf* — **przegłos|owywać** *impf vt* (zatwierdzić) to vote through *[wniosek, projekt, ustawę]*; (pokonać większością głosów) to outvote

przeg|onić *pf* — **przeg|aniać** *impf vt* ☐ (przepędzić) to chase out a. away ② (zmusić do zmiany miejsca)

to drive *[krowy, owce]*; **wiatr** ~**onił chmury** przen. the wind chased away the clouds ③ pot. (zmusić do pośpiechu) to hurry; ~**oniła mnie po całym mieście** she ran me all over town pot. ④ pot. (wyprzedzić) to overtake ⑤ pot. (być lepszym) to outdo

przegot|ować *pf* — **przegot|owywać** *impf* **[]** *vt* ☐ to bring [sth] to the boil *[mleko, wodę]* ② (zbyt długo) to overcook *[ziemniaki, makaron, mięso]* ③ (powtórnie) to recook

[] **przegotować się** — **przegotowywać się** ☐ (zagotować się) to boil ② (rozgotować się) to be overdone a. overcooked

przegr|ać *pf* — **przegr|ywać** *impf vt* ☐ (zostać pokonanym) to lose *[mecz, partię]* ② (stracić) to lose *[pieniądze]*; ~**ać na giełdzie/na loterii** to lose money on the stock exchange/in the lottery ③ (ponieść klęskę) to lose; ~**aliśmy proces** we lost the case ④ (odtworzyć) to play *[płytę, nagranie]* ⑤ (skopiować) to record

przegradzać *impf* → **przegrodzić**

przegran|a *f* ☐ (porażka) defeat ② (kwota) loss

przegran|y *adi.* ☐ (zrezygnowany) downhearted ② (skompromitowany) finished ③ (stracony) *[sprawa, pozycja]* lost

przegr|oda *f* ☐ (przedzielenie) barrier; (w pomieszczeniu, pojeździe) partition ② (miejsce oddzielone) compartment

przegr|odzić *pf* — **przegr|adzać** *impf vt* to partition *[pokój, pomieszczenie]*; to fence a. wall off *[teren]*; ~**odzili rzekę tamą** they built a dam across the river; ~**odził ich ocean** they were separated by the ocean

przegród|ka *f* (w portfelu, torbie, szufladzie) compartment; (na karty, klucze) pigeonhole

przegrywać *impf* → **przegrać**

przegub *m* ☐ Anat. wrist ② Techn. articulated joint

przegubow|iec *m* pot. articulated bus

przegubow|y *adi. [autobus, połączenie]* articulated; **lampa** ~**a** an anglepoise®(lamp)

przehol|ować *pf* — **przehol|owywać** *impf* **[]** *vt* (przemieścić) to tow *[pojazd, szybowiec]*; **statek** ~**owano na głębsze wody** the ship was towed into deeper waters

[] *vi* (przesadzić) to overshoot the mark; **on zawsze musi** ~**ować w żartach** his jokes are always over the top; **nie** ~**uj z piciem** don't overdo the drink

przeinacz|yć *pf* — **przeinacz|ać** *impf vt* to misrepresent *[fakt, słowa]*; ~**ona wersja wydarzeń** a twisted a. contorted version of events

przejadać *impf* → **przejeść**

przejaśni|ć się *pf* — **przejaśni|ać się** *impf v refl.* to clear (up); **na horyzoncie zaczęło się** ~**ać** the horizon started to brighten (up)

przejaśnie|nie *n* sunny spell; **zachmurzenie z** ~**niami** cloudy with bright a. sunny spells

przejaw *m* sign; (oznaka) indication; (objaw) manifestation; (wyraz) expression; **różne** ~**y życia publicznego** various aspects of public life

przejaw|ić *pf* — **przejaw|iać** *impf* **[]** *vt* (okazywać) to display *[energię, entuzjazm]*; ~**iać talent muzyczny** to reveal a talent for music

[II] przejawić się — **przejawiać się** to reveal oneself

przej|azd *m* **[1]** (samochodem) drive; (statkiem) passage; ~**azd taksówką** a taxi ride; ~**azd pociągiem** a ride on a train; ~**azd z lotniska/na lotnisko** an airport transfer; **opłata za** ~**azd autobusem/ koleją** a bus/railway fare; **jestem tu** ~**azdem** I'm just passing through **[2]** (miejsce) level crossing GB, grade crossing US; ~**azd dołem** an underpass; ~**azd górą** an overpass, a flyover GB

przejażdż|ka *f* ride; **konna** ~**ka** a horse ride; **wybrać się na** ~**kę samochodową** to go for a drive

przej|ąć *pf* — **przej|mować** *impf* **[]** *vt* **[1]** (wziąć) to take over; ~**ął w spadku po ojcu gospodarstwo rolne** he inherited a farm from his father **[2]** (przechwycić) to intercept *[list, korespondencję]*; to seize *[dostawę, agenta]* **[3]** (zastąpić) to take over *[obowiązki, funkcję, dyżur]*; to assume *[kontrolę, odpowiedzialność]*; ~**ąć władzę** to seize power **[4]** (przyswoić sobie) to adopt *[tradycje, zwyczaj]* **[5]** (przeniknąć) to overcome; ~**ął ją smutek** she was overcome by sadness; **zimno** ~**mowało go do szpiku kości** he was frozen to the marrow **[6]** (poruszyć) to distress

[II] przejąć się — **przejmować się** to become upset; ~**ąć się czymś do żywego** to take sth to heart; **nie** ~**muj się!** don't worry!; **wcale się tym nie** ~**muję** it doesn't bother me in the least

przej|echać *pf* — **przej|eżdżać** *impf* **[]** *vt* **[1]** (przemieścić się) to travel **[2]** (przekroczyć) to pass through *[skrzyżowanie, tunel]*; to go across *[most]*; ~**echać granicę państwa** to cross the border a. frontier **[3]** (minąć) to pass by **[4]** (rozjechać) to run over *[osobę, zwierzę]*

[II] *vi* (przesunąć) to run (**czymś po czymś** sth over sth); ~**echać grzebieniem po włosach** to run a comb through one's hair; ~**echać wzrokiem po kimś/po czymś** to run one's eye over sb/sth

[III] przejechać się — **przejeżdżać się** (przemieścić się) to go for a ride

■ ~**echać się na tamten świat** a. **na cmentarz** pot. to kick the bucket pot.; ~**echać się po kimś/ czymś** pot. to give sb/sth a bashing pot.; ~**echać stację/przystanek** to miss one's station/stop

przejedzeni|e *n* overeating

przej|eść *pf* — **przej|adać** *impf* **[]** *vt* to fritter away *[oszczędności, kosztowności, kredyt]*

[II] przejeść się — **przejadać się** **[1]** (zjeść za dużo) to overeat **[2]** (znudzić się) to be fed up (**czymś** with sth); to have had enough (**czymś** of sth)

przejeżdżać *impf* → **przejechać**

przejęci|e *n* excitement; **patrzyła na niego z ogromnym** ~**em** she looked at him intently;

słuchali z ~**em opowiadania** they listened to the story with rapt attention

przeję|ty *adi. [osoba, twarz]* excited

przeżyczać się *impf* → **przeżyczyć się**

przeżyczenie *n* slip of the tongue

przeżyczyć się *pf* — **przeżyczać się** *impf v refl.* to make a slip of the tongue

przejmować *impf* → **przejąć**

przejmując|y *adi. [głos, krzyk]* piercing; *[zimno]* bitter; *[ból]* searing; *[tęsknota]* acute; ~**a historia ich rodziny** the heartbreaking story of their family

prze|jrzeć¹, prze|glądnąć *pf* — **prze|glądać** *impf* **[]** *vt* **[1]** (rozszyfrować) to see through *[osobę, tajemnice, zamiary]*; ~**jrzałem go na wylot** I've got his number pot. **[2]** (przewertować) to look a. browse through; ~**glądać pocztę** to go through one's mail **[3]** to check *[samochód, broń, stan techniczny]* **[4]** przen. (przeszukać) to look through *[pokój]*; to comb through *[szuflady]*; to comb *[teren]*

[II] przejrzeć się — **przeglądać się** to look at oneself in the mirror

przejrz|eć² *pf* — **przejrze|wać** *impf vi [owoce, nasiona]* to become overripen

przejrz|eć³ *pf vi* **[1]** książk. (odzyskać wzrok) to regain one's sight **[2]** (zrozumieć) **i wtedy** ~**ałem na oczy** and then the scales fell from my eyes; **zanim** ~**ał, popełnił wiele błędów** he made a lot of mistakes before he realized what was going on

przejś|cie *n* **[1]** (miejsce) passage(way); ~**cie dla pieszych** a pedestrian crossing, a crosswalk US; ~**cie podziemne** an underpass, a subway GB an alley; ~**cie między rzędami krzeseł** an aisle; **stanąć w** ~**ciu** to stand in the way; **zrobić komuś** ~**cie** to make way for sb **[2]** (faza pośrednia) transition **[3]** (przeżycie) (trying) experience; **kobieta po** ~**ciach** a woman who's been through a lot pot.

przejściow|y *adi.* **[1]** (chwilowy) *[trudność, przepis, ochłodzenie]* temporary **[2]** (przechodni) *[pokój]* connecting **[3]** (pośredni) transition(al); **okres** ~**y między socjalizmem a kapitalizmem** the transitional period between socialism and capitalism **[4]** (tymczasowy) *[cela, więzienie]* temporary

prze|jść *pf* — **prze|chodzić** *impf* **[]** *vt* **[1]** (doświadczyć) to go through; **wiele** ~**szli podczas wojny** they had gone through a lot during the war; ~**jść twardą szkołę (życia)** to go through the school of hard knocks **[2]** (zostać poddanym badaniom) to pass *[testy]*

[II] *vi* **[1]** (przemieścić się) ~**jść piętnaście kilometrów** to cover fifteen kilometres; ~**jdźmy do mojego biura** let's go through to my office **[2]** (przesunąć się) to pass; **burza** ~**szła bokiem** the storm passed us/them by; **zaraza** ~**szła przez cały kraj** a plague swept through the entire country **[3]** (idąc minąć) to pass by *[dom, ulicę]* **[4]** (przedostać się) ~**jść przez coś** to cross *[jezdnię, most]* to climb a. get over *[płot, mur]* to go a. pass through *[bramę, punkt kontrolny]*; ~**jście wzbronione** no trespassing ⑤ (przeciąć) (o liniach, szlakach, drogach) to go a. run through ⑥ (zostać przyjętym) to be passed a. approved; **wniosek** ~**szedł 150 głosami przeciw 96** the motion was passed a. carried by 150 votes to 96; **ustawa nie** ~**szła** the bill was rejected ⑦ (minąć) to pass; **ból** ~**szedł po godzinie** the pain went away a. eased off after an hour ⑧ (zacząć coś nowego) ~**jść do cywila** to return to civilian life; ~**jść na nowe stanowisko** to take up a new post; ~**jść na dietę** to go on a diet; ~**jść do innego tematu** to change the subject; ~**jść na inną wiarę** to change one's faith; ~**jść na katolicyzm** to convert to Catholicism; ~**jść do wyższej/następnej klasy** to go up to the next year ⑨ (przekształcić się) to turn (**w coś** into sth); **energia chemiczna** ~**chodzi w elektryczną** chemical energy is converted into electrical energy ⑩ (przesiąknąć) to become permeated; **cały dom** ~**szedł zapachem smażonej ryby** the smell of fried fish filled the entire house

III przejść się to take a walk (**po czymś** around a. about sth)

■ ~**jść do historii/do potomności** książk. to go down in history/to be handed down to posterity; ~**jść do tematu** to get down to the subject; ~**jść na angielski** to switch to English; **to** ~**chodzi ludzkie** a. **wszelkie pojęcie** it's (just) beyond comprehension; ~**jść bez echa** to pass unnoticed; **ta decyzja musi jeszcze** ~**jść przez zarząd** pot. the decision still has to go through the board; ~**jść (czyjeś) najśmielsze oczekiwania** to exceed one's wildest expectations; ~**jść samego siebie** to surpass oneself

przekaz *m* ① (blankiet) form ② (pieniądze) money order; ~ **pocztowy** a postal order; **wysłać/ otrzymać pieniądze** ~**em** to send/receive a money order ③ (informacja) ~ **źródłowy** a source; **legendy zachowane w** ~**ach ustnych** legends preserved in oral tradition ④ Techn. medium; **środki (masowego)** ~**u** the mass media

przeka|zać *pf* — **przeka|zywać** *impf vt* ① (dać) to hand over *[przedmiot]*; to transfer *[pieniądze]*; to make over książk. *[akt własności]*; (w testamencie) to hand down także przen.; to bequeath książk. ② (oddać do dyspozycji) to hand over ③ (podać do wiadomości) to transmit *[informacje, spostrzeżenia]*; **prosił mnie, żebym** ~**zał ci pozdrowienia** he asked me to give you his regards ④ (przesłać) to send *[bodziec, impuls, sygnał]* ⑤ (transmitować) to broadcast *[koncert, zawody sportowe]*

przekaźnik *m* (radiowy, telewizyjny) transmitter; (elektryczny) relay

przekąs|ka *f* (między posiłkami) snack; (przed posiłkiem) hors d'oeuvre

przekątn|a *f* diagonal

przekl|ąć *pf* — **przekl|inać** *impf* **I** *vt* ① (złorzeczyć) to curse *[los]* ② (rzucić klątwę) to curse; ~**ąć wrogów** he curse one's enemies

II *vi* (wypowiedzieć przekleństwo) to swear

przekleństw|o *n* (obelga) curse; **miotać** ~**a** to curse and swear

przeklinać *impf* → **przekląć**

przekła|d *m* ① (tłumaczenie) translation; **powieść w polskim** ~**dzie** a novel in Polish translation ② (tekst przetłumaczony) translation

przekładać *impf* → **przełożyć**

przekładni|a *f* Techn. transmission (gear); ~**a ślimakowa** a worm gear

przekłu|ć *pf* — **przekłu|wać** *impf vt* ① to pierce *[uszy, nos]*; to puncture *[oponę, pęcherz, ropień]*; to prick *[balonik, pęcherz]*; „~**wanie uszu**" (w ogłoszeniu) 'ear-piercing'

przekon|ać *pf* — **przekon|ywać** *impf* **I** *vt* ① (zmienić czyjeś zdanie) to (try to) convince (**kogoś o czymś** sb of sth); (namówić) to (try to) persuade (**kogoś do zrobienia czegoś** sb to do sth); (wpłynąć na opinię) to (try to) win over; **twoje słowa nikogo nie** ~**ują** your words aren't convincing anybody

II przekonać się — **przekonywać się** ① (uwierzyć) to become convinced ② (zmienić zdanie na korzyść) to revise one's opinion

przekona|nie *n* (przeświadczenie) conviction; **w moim** ~**niu...** it's my conviction that...; **panuje** ~**nie, że...** it is generally believed that...; **w końcu doszliśmy do** ~**nia, że...** eventually we came to believe that...; **mieć** ~**nie do kogoś/czegoś** to have faith in sb/sth; **bez** ~**nia** half-heartedly

III przekonania *plt* (poglądy) beliefs

przekonując|y *adi. [alibi, argument]* convincing

przekonywać *impf* → **przekonać**

przeko|ra *f* perversity youthful perversity; **zrobić/ powiedzieć coś z (czystej)** ~**ry** to do/say sth out of (sheer) perversity

przekorn|y *adi. [osoba]* perverse; *[uśmiech, mina]* teasing

przekór *m* **robić coś na** ~ to do sth from a. out of spite

przekraczać *impf* → **przekroczyć**

przekrawać *impf* → **przekroić**

przekreśl|ić *pf* — **przekreśl|ać** *impf vt* ① (usunąć) to cross out a. through *[słowo, zdanie]* ② (zniweczyć) to shatter *[plany, nadzieje, marzenia]*; to blight *[karierę, szanse]* ③ (puścić w niepamięć) to erase *[przeżycie]*; ~**iła całą swą przeszłość** she drew a line through her entire past

■ ~**ić kogoś** to write sb off

przekrę|cić *pf* — **przekrę|cać** *impf* **I** *vt* ① (obrócić) to turn; ~**cić klucz w zamku** to turn the key in the lock; **czapka** ~**cona daszkiem do tyłu** a (peaked) cap turned back to front; **pielęgniarka** ~**ciła pacjenta na bok** the nurse turned the patient over onto his side ② (przechylić) to cock *[głowę, czapkę]* ③ (zepsuć) to overwind *[sprężynę zegarka]*; to strip *[gwint]* ④ (niedokładnie powtórzyć) to mispronounce *[słowo, nazwisko]*; (przeinaczyć) to twist *[słowa]*; to mispresent *[fakty, opinie]* ⑤ pot. (zatelefonować) to buzz pot. (**do kogoś** sb)

Ⅱ przekręcić się — przekręcać się *[osoba, zwierzę, pojazd]* to turn; *[krawat, okulary]* to become crooked; ~**cił się na drugi bok** he turned over

przekrocze|nie *n* (prawa, przepisów) contravention; **drobne** ~**nia** minor offences; ~**nie szybkości** exceeding the speed limit; **popełnić** ~**nie** to commit an offence

przekr|oczyć *pf* — **przekr|aczać** *impf vt* ① (przejść) to cross *[granicę, próg, rzekę]* ② (przewyższyć) to exceed *[normę, poziom, wiek]*; ~**oczyć dozwoloną prędkość** to exceed the speed limit; ~**oczyć stan konta** to be overdrawn ③ (naruszyć) to overstep *[normy, zasady]*; **burmistrz** ~**oczył swoje kompetencje** the mayor has overstepped a. exceeded his authority

przekr|oić *pf* — **przekr|awać** *impf vt* to cut [sth] in two; ~**oić coś na pół** to cut sth in half

przekr|ój *m* ① (obraz) section; **narysować coś w** ~**oju** to draw a section of sth ② (średnica) diameter ③ przen. cross section; ~**ój społeczny ludności** a cross section of society

przekrwi|ony *adi. [oczy]* bloodshot; *[arteria, wątroba]* congested

przekształcać *impf* → **przekształcić**

przekształce|nie *n* transformation; ~**nia gospodarcze** economic changes; ~**nia własnościowe** privatization

przekształ|cić *pf* — **przekształ|cać** *impf* **Ⅱ** *vt* ① (przeobrazić) to transform ② (zmienić funkcję) to convert *[budynek, pomieszczenie]*; ~**cić strych w** a. **na mieszkanie** to convert an attic into a flat

Ⅱ przekształcić się — przekształcać się to metamorphose (**w kogoś/coś** into sb/sth)

przekup|ić *pf* — **przekup|ywać** *impf vt* to bribe *[sędziego, urzędnika]* (**czymś** with sth)

przekupn|y *adi.* corruptible; venal książk.

przekupstw|o *n* bribery

przekupywać *impf* → **przekupić**

przekwalifik|ować *pf* — **przekwalifik|o-wywać** *impf* **Ⅱ** *vt* ① (do nowego zawodu) to reskill *[bezrobotnego]*; to retrain *[robotnika, urzędnika]* ② (do innej kategorii) to reclassify *[przestępstwo]*

Ⅱ przekwalifikować się — przekwalifikowywać się to retrain

przekwitać *impf* → **przekwitnąć**

przekwitani|e *n* menopause

przekwit|nąć *pf* — **przekwit|ać** *impf vt* ① (skończyć kwitnienie) to shed blossom ② książk. (przeminąć) to fade (away); ~**ająca sława/uroda** fading fame/beauty

przel|ać *pf* — **przel|ewać** *impf* **Ⅰ** *vt* ① (z jednego naczynia do drugiego) to pour ② pot. (spłukać) to rinse *[jarzyny, owoce]* ③ (przekazać) to transfer *[prawa, majątek]*; ~**ać pieniądze na konto bankowe** to transfer money to a bank account ④ (przenieść uczucie) to transfer *[miłość, irytację]*

Ⅱ *vi* (przepełnić) to fill to overflowing

Ⅲ przelać się — przelewać się ① *[płyn]* to brim a. spill over; *[naczynie]* to overflow; **woda** ~**ewa się z wanny** the bath is overflowing ② (przetoczyć się) to slosh; **fale** ~**ewały się przez pokład statku** waves washed the deck of the ship

■ ~**ać myśli/uczucia/wrażenia na papier** książk. to commit one's thoughts/feelings/impressions to paper; ~**ewać z pustego w próżne** to indulge in idle chatter; **mnie/im się nie** ~**ewa** I/they can hardly make ends meet

przelew *m* ① (bankowy) transfer; **dokonać** ~**u na konto** to transfer money to a bank account ② (cesja) transfer ③ Techn. (zbiornika) overflow (spillway); (wanny, umywalki) overflow (pipe)

przelewać *impf* → **przelać**

przeliczać *impf* → **przeliczyć**

przelicznik *m* conversion factor; **stosować** ~ **dolarowy do czegoś** to express sth in dollars

przelicz|yć *pf* — **przelicz|ać** *impf* **Ⅰ** *vt* ① (policzyć) to count *[pieniądze, resztę, ludzi, zwierzęta]* ② (zamienić) to convert; ~**yć złotówki na euro** to convert zlotys into euros

Ⅱ przeliczyć się — przeliczać się to miscalculate także przen.; ~**yć się z siłami** to miscalculate one's abilities

przeliter|ować *pf vt* to spell (out) *[nazwę, słowo]*

przelo|t *m* ① (lot samolotu) flight; (wędrówka ptaków) passage; ~**ty pasażerskie** passenger flights ② (rury, kanału) passage ③ (między zabudowaniami) passage(way)

■ jestem tu tylko ~**tem** I've only dropped in for a moment; **widział się/rozmawiał z nią tylko w** ~**cie** he only saw her in passing

przelotn|y *adi. [deszcz, obłoki, wiatr]* occasional; *[spojrzenie]* fleeting; *[zainteresowanie]* passing; *[romans, znajomość]* short-lived

przeludnieni|e *n* overpopulation

przeład|ować *pf* — **przeład|owywać** *impf vt* ① (przenieść) to transfer *[bagaż, ładunek, towar]* ② (obciążyć) to overload *[samochód, statek]* ③ (przeciążyć) to overload *[pamięć, żołądek]*; ~**owane programy nauczania** overloaded syllabuses; **pokój** ~**owany meblami** a room crammed with furniture

przeładun|ek *m* trans-shipment

przełam|ać *pf* — **przełam|ywać** *impf* **Ⅰ** *vt* ① to break *[bułkę, czekoladę]*; ~**ać coś na pół/dwie części** to break sth in half/two ② (przezwyciężyć) to overcome *[niechęć, nieśmiałość, trudności]*; to break down *[opór, upór]*; ~**ać linię obrony nieprzyja-**

ciela to break through the enemy's defences ③ Druk. to impose *[kolumny, tekst]*

Ⅱ przełamać się — przełamywać się ① (złamać się) *[kij, pręt]* to break ② (przemóc się) to overcome one's feelings; ~**ał się i przeprosił go pierwszy** he swallowed his pride and apologized to him ■ ~**ać (pierwsze) lody** to break the ice

przełączać *impf* → **przełączyć**

przełącznik *m* switch; Elektr. commutator

przełącz|yć *pf* — **przełącz|ać** *impf* ❒ *vt* ① Elektr. to change over; ~**yć telewizor na inną antenę** to connect the TV set to another aerial ② (zmienić tryb pracy) to switch; ~**yć radio na inną stację/ telewizor na inny kanał** to switch over to another radio station/TV channel ③ (w telekomunikacji) to transfer *[rozmówcę]*; to divert *[połączenie]*

Ⅱ przełączyć się — przełączać się to switch over

przełęcz *f* (mountain) pass

przeł|knąć *pf* — **przeł|ykać** *impf vt* ① to swallow *[kęs, łyk, ślinę]*; **nie móc niczego ~knąć** to be unable to eat anything ② (zaakceptować) to swallow *[krytykę, obelgę, przykrość]*; **rada trudna do ~knięcia** an unpalatable piece of advice

przełom *m* ① (zmiana) turning point; (sukces) breakthrough; **dokonać ~u w leczeniu raka** to make a breakthrough in the treatment of cancer ② (granica) turn; **na ~ie XIX i XX wieku** at the turn of the twentieth century; ~ **maja i czerwca** the end of May and the beginning of June

przełomow|y *adi.* *[moment, znaczenie]* crucial; ~**e wydarzenie w życiu człowieka** a turning point in one's life; ~**y okres/wynalazek** a watershed period/invention; ~**a decyzja** a landmark decision

przełożon|y ❒ *adi.* superior; **siostra** ~**a** (zakonnica) a Mother Superior; (pielęgniarka) head nurse, senior nursing officer GB

Ⅱ przełożon|y *m*, ~**a** *f* superior

prze|łożyć *pf* — **prze|kładać** *impf* ❒ *vt* ① (na inne miejsce) to transfer; ~**łożyć walizkę z jednej ręki do drugiej** to transfer one's suitcase from one hand to the other; ~**łożyć papiery do innej szuflady** to put some papers into another drawer; ~**kładać książki na biurku** to rearrange the books on a desk ② (przenieść górą) to put [sth] over; ~**łożyła rękę przez płot** she reached (her hand) over the fence; ~**łóż linę nad poprzeczką** put the rope over the bar ③ (między warstwy) to interleave; **bułka** ~**łożona szynką/serem** a ham/cheese roll ④ (zmienić termin) to postpone *[urlop, wizytę]*; to adjourn *[debatę, rozprawę]* ⑤ (przetłumaczyć) to translate; ~**łożyć powieść z polskiego na angielski** to translate a novel from Polish into English

Ⅱ przełożyć się — przekładać się *[poglądy, idee]* to translate (**na coś** into sth)

przełyk *m* Anat. gullet, oesophagus GB, esophagus US

przełykać *impf* → **przełknąć**

przemakać *impf* → **przemoknąć**

przemarsz *m* march

przemarz|nąć /pʃeˈmarznɔntɕ/ *pf* — **przemarz|ać** /pʃeˈmarzatɕ/ *impf vi* ① (bardzo zmarznąć) to freeze; ~**znąć do szpiku kości** to get chilled to the bone ② (ulec zniszczeniu) to freeze; **jabłka/ziemniaki** ~**zły** the apples/potatoes froze

przemawiać *impf* → **przemówić**

przemądrza|ły *adi.* know-all pot.; *[nastolatek, mina]* cocky pot.

przemęczać *impf* → **przemęczyć**

przemęcze|nie *n* exhaustion

przemęcz|ony *adi.* *[osoba]* exhausted; *[oczy, twarz]* strained

przemęcz|yć *pf* — **przemęcz|ać** *impf* ❒ *vt* (przeciążyć pracą, wysiłkiem) to tire out; ~**yć sobie oczy** to strain one's eyes

Ⅱ przemęczyć się — przemęczać się (wyczerpać się) to overexert oneself (**czymś** with sth); **nie** ~**ała się zbytnio nauką** iron. she didn't exactly exert herself studying iron.

przemian|a *f* książk. transformation; ~**y ekonomiczne/polityczne** economic/political changes; **ulec** ~**ie** to undergo a transformation; ~**a materii** metabolism; **produkt** ~**y materii** a waste product

przemięk|nąć *pf* — **przemięk|ać** *impf vi [buty, ubranie, opatrunek]* to become soaked (through); ~**ły mi buty** my shoes are drenched

przemijać *impf* → **przeminąć**

przemilcz|eć *pf* — **przemilcz|ać** *impf vt* ① (zataić) to pass over *[epizod, fakt]* ② (zignorować) to turn a deaf ear to *[zaczepki, uwagi, krytykę]*

przemi|nąć *pf* — **przemi|jać** *impf vi [czas]* to elapse; *[życie]* to go by; *[smutek]* to pass away; *[noc]* to slip away a. by; ~**jająca moda** a passing fashion; ~**jająca uroda** fading beauty

przemoc *f* violence; ~ **fizyczna** physical violence; ~ **psychiczna** emotional abuse a. violence; **akt** ~**y** an act of violence; ~**ą** *[robić, zabrać]* by force

przem|oknąć *pf* — **przem|akać** *impf vi* ① (zmoknąć) to get soaked a. drenched; ~**okliśmy doszczętnie** a. **do suchej nitki** we got soaked through a. to the skin ② (przemięknąć) *[ubranie, buty]* to get soaked; **namiot** ~**akał** the tent was leaking

przemoknię|ty *adi.* *[osoba]* soaked to the skin; *[ubranie]* dripping wet; *[ziemia]* saturated

przem|ówić *pf* — **przem|awiać** *impf vi* ① (wygłosić mowę) to make a speech; **na zebraniu** ~**awiały cztery osoby** four speakers addressed the meeting ② (przerwać milczenie) to speak; **czekała, aż** ~**ówi pierwszy** she was waiting for him to speak first

■ ~ówić komuś do rozumu a. rozsądku to talk sense into sb; **twoje argumenty do mnie nie ~awiają** I'm not convinced by your arguments; **zazdrość/gniew ~awia przez niego** he's consumed by jealousy/anger

przemówie|nie *n* speech; **wygłosić ~nie** to deliver a. give a speech

przemy|cić *pf* — **przemy|cać** *impf vt* to smuggle *[narkotyki, broń, gryps]*; **w swoich książkach autor ~cał dydaktyczne treści** the author slipped didactic elements into his books

przemy|ć *pf* — **przemy|wać** *impf vt* to bathe *[ranę, kolano]*; to wash *[oczy]*

przemy|sł *m* industry

przemysłow|y *adi.* industrial

przemyślan|y *adi. [projekt, plan, decyzja]* well-thought-out

przemyśl|eć *pf vt (rozważyć)* to think over; *(dokładnie)* to think through; *(ponownie)* to rethink

przemy|t *m* smuggling

przemytni|k *m* smuggler

przemywać *impf* → **przemyć**

przen|ieść *pf* — **przen|osić** *impf* ▯ *vt* ① *(umieścić gdzie indziej)* to carry *[książki, stół, bagaż]*; to move *[stolicę, szkołę]*; ~**iósł ją przez próg** he carried her across the threshold; ~**osili meble do innego pokoju** they were moving the furniture to another room; ~**osiła ciężar ciała z jednej nogi na drugą** she shifted her weight from one leg to the other ② *(rozprzestrzenić)* to spread *[choroby, zarazki]*; to transplant *[modę, zwyczaje]*; **choroby ~oszone drogą płciową** sexually transmitted diseases ③ *(zmienić sytuację)* to transfer; ~**ieść kogoś na inne stanowisko** to transfer a. move sb to a different post; ~**ieść coś na ekran/scenę** książk. to adapt sth for a. to transfer sth to the screen/stage; **film ~iósł nas w lata 70.** the film took a. transported us back to the seventies ④ *(przelać)* to transfer *[uczucia, prawa]* ⑤ to divide *[wyraz]*

▯ **przenieść się – przenosić się** to move; ~**ieść się do innego miasta** to move to a different town; **ogień ~osił się na inne domy** the fire was spreading to other buildings

■ ~**ieść się myślą** a. **myślami do kogoś/czegoś** książk. to turn one's thoughts to sb/sth

przenikać *impf* → **przeniknąć**

przenikliw|y *adi. grad. [krzyk, gwizd, wiatr, ból, wzrok]* piercing; *[woń]* powerful; *[chłód]* biting; *[umysł, analiza]* penetrating

przenik|nąć *pf* — **przenik|ać** *impf* ▯ *vt* ① *(przepełnić)* to pervade; **jego muzykę ~a smutek** an air of sadness pervades his music ② *(zgłębić)* to fathom (out); *(odgadnąć)* to penetrate; to divine książk.; ~**nąć kogoś** to make a. fathom sb out; ~**nąć czyjeś myśli** to penetrate a. divine sb's thoughts

▯ *vi* ① *[dźwięki, woń, ciepło]* to penetrate ② *[zjawiska]* to spread ③ *(niepostrzeżenie, nielegalnie) [osoba]* to penetrate; *[szpieg]* to infiltrate

przenoc|ować *pf* ▯ *vt (dać nocleg)* to put up (for the night)

▯ *vi (zanocować)* to stay the night a. overnight (**u kogoś** at sb)

przenosić *impf* → **przenieść**

przenośni|a *f* metaphor; **w ~i** metaphorically speaking; **dosłownie i w ~i** literally and figuratively

przenośn|y *adi. [radio, telefon, komputer]* portable; *[użycie, zwrot]* metaphoric(al)

przeoczać *impf* → **przeoczyć**

przeocze|nie *n (luka)* omission; *(niedopatrzenie)* oversight; **przez ~nie** due to an oversight

przeocz|yć *pf* — **przeocz|ać** *impf vt* to overlook *[błąd, fakt]*; to miss *[wydarzenie, osobę, szansę]*; ~**ył termin wizyty u dentysty** he missed his dental appointment

przepada|ć¹ *impf vi (lubić)* to be very fond (**za kimś/czymś** of sb/sth); to be very keen (**za kimś/czymś** on sb/sth); **nie ~m za kotami** I'm not very fond of cats

przepadać² *impf* → **przepaść²**

przepas|ka *f* band; ~**ka na oczy** a blindfold; ~**ka na oko** an eyepatch; ~**ka na włosy** a hairband; ~**ka na biodra** a loincloth

przepaś|ć¹ *f* ① *(urwisko)* precipice ② *(różnica)* gap; chasm książk.; ~**ć między pokoleniami** the generation gap; **rośnie ~ć między bogatymi a biednymi** the gulf between rich and poor is widening

■ **balansować na krawędzi** a. **skraju ~ci** to teeter on the brink a. edge of disaster

przepa|ść² *pf* — **przepa|dać²** *impf vi* ① *(zaginąć)* to vanish; ~**ść bez wieści** to vanish without trace; **gdzie on ~da na całe dnie?** where does he disappear to for days on end? ② *(nie dojść do skutku)* to fall through; **wszystko ~dło** all is lost

przep|chać, **przep|chnąć** *pf* — **przepy|chać** *impf* ▯ *vt* ① *(przesunąć)* to push (through) ② *(przeczyścić)* to unblock *[rurę, zlew]* ③ pot. *(przeforsować)* to push a. force through *[projekt]*; ~**chnąć sprawę** to force the issue

▯ **przepchać się, przepchnąć się** — **przepychać się** to shove (one's way); ~**ychać się do przodu** to elbow a. jostle forward; ~**ychać się przez tłum** to push a. force one's way through a crowd

przepę|dzić *pf* — **przepę|dzać** *impf vt* ① *(wypędzić)* to chase away *[intruza]*; to fight off *[napastnika]* ② *(przegnać)* to drive *[owce, gęsi]*

przepierka *f* pot. *(quick)* wash

przepierze|nie *n* partition (wall); ~**nie z dykty** a plywood partition

przepiór|ka *f* quail

przepis *m* ① Kulin. recipe; ~ **na gulasz** a recipe for goulash ② (obowiązujące zarządzenie) regulation; ~**y ruchu drogowego/bezpieczeństwa** traffic/safety regulations; ~ **prawny** a legal article; **luka w** ~**ach** a loophole in the regulations; **zgodnie z nowymi** ~**ami** under the new regulations; **przestrzegać** ~**ów** to observe a. follow the rules a. regulations

przepi|sać *pf* — **przepi|sywać** *impf vt* ① (napisać to samo) to copy; ~**sał wypracowanie na czysto** he made a fair a. clean copy of his composition ② (odpisać) *[uczeń]* to copy ③ (zalecić) to prescribe *[lekarstwo, zastrzyki, kąpiele]*; ~**sali mi specjalną dietę** I was put on a special diet ④ (przekazać) to transfer *[ziemię, dom]* (**na kogoś** to sb)

przepisow|y *adi.* regulation; ~**y mundur** a regulation uniform; ~**e godziny pracy** regular a. prescribed working hours

przepisywać *impf* → przepisać

przepła|cić *pf* — **przepła|cać** *impf vt* to overpay (**coś** a. **za coś** for sth)

przepły|nąć *pf* — **przepły|wać** *impf* ❚ *vt* (wpław) to swim across *[rzekę, jezioro]*; (statkiem, łodzią) to cross *[jezioro, morze, ocean]*
❚❚ *vi* ① (o cieczach, gazach, elektryczności) to flow; **przez miasto** ~**wa spora rzeka** a major river flows through the town ② (przemieścić się) *[tłumy]* to pass through

przepon|a *f* ① Anat. diaphragm ② Techn. membrane

przepowiadać *impf* → przepowiedzieć

przepowiedni|a *f* (proroctwo) prophecy; (prognoza) prediction

przepowi|edzieć *pf* — **przepowi|adać** *impf vt* ① to foretell *[przyszłość]*; to predict *[sytuację]*; to forecast *[pogodę, inflację]* ② pot. (powtórzyć tekst) ~**edzieć lekcję/wiersz** to say one's lessons/a poem

przeprac|ować *pf* — **przeprac|owywać** *impf* ❚ *vt* ① (spędzić czas pracując) to work ② (opracować powtórnie) to rework *[plan, projekt]*; to go through *[zagadnienie]*
❚❚ **przepracować się** — **przepracowywać się** (pracować ponad siły) to overwork

przepracowan|y *adi. [osoba]* overworked

przepracowywać *impf* → przepracować

przepraszać *impf* → przeprosić

przepraszając|y *adi. [ton, gest, wzrok]* apologetic

przepraw|a *f* ① (przejście, miejsce przejścia) crossing; ~**a przez góry/pustynię** an expedition across the mountains/desert; **szukać** ~**y przez rzekę** to look for a suitable place to cross the river ② pot. (trudności) a hard time; **miałem z szefem ciężką** ~**ę** my boss gave me a hard time a. a lot of aggro pot.

przepraw|ić *pf* — **przepraw|iać** *impf* ❚ *vt* to get [sb/sth] across
❚❚ **przeprawić się** — **przeprawiać się** to cross;

~**ić się przez góry/granicę** to cross the mountains/border; ~**ić się przez rzekę** *[osoba, pojazd]* to ford a river

przepr|osić *pf* — **przepr|aszać** *impf* ❚ *vt* to apologize; ~**osiła nas za spóźnienie** she apologized to us for being late; **chcę cię** ~**osić** I want to say I'm sorry a. to apologize
❚❚ *vi* ~**aszam** (formuła grzecznościowa) excuse me; I beg your pardon książk.; ~**aszam, która godzina?** excuse me, what time is it?; ~**aszam (chciałabym przejść)** excuse me (please, I'd like to pass); ~**aszam** (potrąciwszy kogoś) I'm sorry; (kichnąwszy) excuse me; ~**aszam, że przeszkadzam, ale...** sorry to disturb you, but...; ~**aszam na moment, muszę odebrać telefon** excuse me (for) a moment, I must answer the phone
❚❚❚ **przeprosić się** — **przepraszać się** ① (pogodzić się) to make up (with each other) ② żart. (zacząć znowu używać) ~**osić się ze starym kapeluszem** to start wearing an old hat again

przeprosin|y *plt* apology; **przyjąć** ~**y** to accept sb's apology; **przysłać bukiet kwiatów na** ~**y** to send a bouquet of flowers as an apology; **winna ci jestem** ~**y** I owe you an apology

przeprowa|dzić *pf* — **przeprowa|dzać** *impf* ❚ *vt* ① (z miejsca na miejsce) to take *[osobę, zwierzę, pojazd]* ② pot. (z mieszkania do mieszkania) to move; ~**dzić rodziców do nowego mieszkania** to move one's parents to a new flat ③ (zbudować) to build *[drogę]*; (przeciągnąć) to carry *[linię telefoniczną]* ④ (wykonać) to carry out *[badania, remont, kontrolę]*; ~**dzić wywiad/ankietę** to conduct an interview/a survey
❚❚ **przeprowadzić się** — **przeprowadzać się** to move

przeprowadz|ka *f* move

przepuklin|a *f* Anat. hernia

przepust|ka *f* ① (upoważnienie do wejścia) pass; ~**ka stała/jednorazowa** a multiple entry/single entry pass; **wydać komuś** ~**kę** to issue a pass to sb ② Techn. sluice gate

przepu|ścić *pf* — **przepu|szczać** *impf* ❚ *vt* ① (wpuścić) to let in *[osobę]*; to allow through *[samochody]* ② (ustąpić z drogi) to make way; **proszę mnie** ~**ścić!** please let me through! ③ Szkol. to allow [sb] to move up to the next form GB a. grade US *[ucznia]* ④ (poddać działaniu) ~**ścić mięso przez maszynkę** to put meat through a mincer; ~**ścić kandydatów przez szereg badań i testów** to put candidates through a series of tests ⑤ (umożliwić przedostanie się) to let in *[wodę, powietrze, światło]* ⑥ (przeoczyć) to overlook *[błąd]*; to miss *[okazję]* ⑦ pot. (roztrwonić) to blow pot. *[pieniądze, majątek]* ⑧ pot. (świadomie pominąć) ~**ścić autobus/tramwaj** to let a bus/tram go
❚❚ *vi* pot. (szukać znajomości) **to kokietka, żadnemu**

chłopakowi nie ~**ści** she's a flirt, she'll go for anything in trousers pot.

przepych *m* [1] (wystawność) splendour GB, splendor US [2] przen. (obfitość) lavishness

przepychać *impf* → **przepchać**

przerabiać *impf* → **przerobić**[1]

przerastać *impf* → **przerosnąć**

przeraźliw|y *adi. grad.* [1] (budzący strach) *[widok]* dreadful; *[krzyk]* piercing; *[blask]* blinding [2] (intensywny) *[ból, cisza]* terrible

przerażać *impf* → **przerazić**

przerażając|y *adi. [widok, wiadomość, krzyk]* terrifying; *[błąd]* terrible

przerażeni|e *n* terror; **ogarnęło go** ~**e** he was overcome with terror

przeraż|ony *adi. [głos, wzrok]* terrified

przeręb|el *m*, ~**la** *f* blowhole

przer|obić *pf* — **przer|abiać** *impf vt* [1] (na lepsze) to alter *[kapelusz, sukienkę]*; to rewrite *[powieść, sztukę]*; to redecorate *[kuchnię, łazienkę]*; (na coś innego) to convert *[piwnice, stajnie]* (**na coś** into sth); to adapt *[nowelę, sztukę]*; **kurtka** ~**obiona z płaszcza** a jacket made out of an overcoat [2] (przetworzyć) to process; ~**abiać ropę naftową na benzynę** to refine crude oil into petrol [3] Szkol. to go through; **nie** ~**abialiśmy jeszcze funkcji** we haven't done functions yet [4] (na drutach) to knit; (na prawo) to knit; (na lewo) to purl

■ ~**obić kogoś** pot. (oszukać) to do sb pot.; **dać się** ~**obić** pot. to be taken in

przer|osnąć *pf* — **przer|astać** *impf* [] *vt* [1] (stać się wyższym) to outgrow; ~**astać czyjeś siły/ możliwości** przen. to be beyond sb's strength/ capabilities [2] (prześcignąć) to surpass książk.; **sukces** ~**ósł nasze oczekiwania** the success exceeded our expectations

[]] *vi* to overgrow; ~**ośnięte ziemniaki** overgrown potatoes

przerób|ka *f* (odzieży) alteration; (tekstu) adaptation; „~**ki krawieckie**" (w ogłoszeniu) 'alterations'; **oddać kostium do** ~**ki** to have a suit altered

przerw|a *f* [1] (wstrzymanie) break; (w obradach, rozprawie) adjournment, recess US; (w dostawie, transmisji) cut; ~**a w pracy** a (work) stoppage; ~**a w rozmowie** a break a. pause in the conversation; ~**a w dopływie prądu** an electricity a. a power cut a. failure; ~**a w dostawie gazu** a gas cut; ~**a w komunikacji** disruption of transport services; **sąd zarządza teraz** ~**ę** the court will now adjourn; **z** ~**ami** at intervals; (nieregularnie) off and on; **mówić z** ~**ami** to speak in fits and starts; **bez** ~**y** *[pracować, padać]* continuously; **on bez** ~**y gada** he goes on and on pot. [2] (między lekcjami) break GB, recess US; (ferie) break; (w pracy) break; ~**a wakacyjna** the holiday break; ~**a obiadowa** a lunch break; ~**a śniadaniowa** a morning break; **dzwonek na** ~**ę** the bell for break [3] (w przedsta-

wieniu, koncercie) interval, intermission US; (w meczu) half-time [4] (puste miejsce) gap; (między wersami, stolikami) space

przer|wać *pf* — **przer|ywać** *impf* [] *vt* [1] (rozerwać) to break *[nitkę, sznurek]* [2] (zrobić wyrwę) to break through *[tamę, linię frontu]*; ~**wać blokadę** to break a blockade [3] (zrezygnować) to give up *[pracę, naukę]* [4] (zakłócić ciągłość) to stop *[czytanie, gotowanie]*; to discontinue *[dostawy, produkcję, budowę]*; ~**wać w pół słowa** a. **zdania** to stop in mid-sentence; ~**wać ciążę** *[lekarz]* to perform an abortion a. a termination; *[ciężarna]* to have an abortion; ~**wana łączność telefoniczna** disrupted telephone services; **proszę mi nie** ~**ywać** please don't interrupt (me); „**za dużo mówisz**", ~**wał Robert** 'you talk too much,' Robert broke a. cut in

[]] **przerwać się** — **przerywać się** [1] *[korale, sznurek, łańcuch]* to break [2] *[dyskusja, łączność]* to break off

przerzu|cić *pf* — **przerzu|cać** *impf* [] *vt* [1] (rzucić z jednego miejsca w inne) to throw; ~**cić kamień przez płot** to throw a stone over a fence; ~**cić piłkę ponad siatką** to send the ball over the net; **sweter** ~**cony przez oparcie krzesła** a sweater thrown over the back of a chair [2] (przetransportować) to transport *[żołnierzy, sprzęt]*; (nielegalnie) to smuggle *[broń, narkotyki, emigrantów]* [3] pot. (przetrząsnąć) to go a. rummage through; ~**cił wszystko w biurku, szukając rachunku** he went a. rummaged through his desk looking for the bill [4] (przejrzeć) to flip a. flick through *[czasopismo, gazetę, książkę]* [5] (obarczyć) to offload *[koszty, zmartwienia]* (**na kogoś** onto sb); to shift *[odpowiedzialność, pracę, winę]* (**na kogoś** onto sb)

[]] **przerzucić się** — **przerzucać się** [1] (zmienić miejsce pobytu, pracę, zajęcie) to switch; **autor** ~**cił się z prozy na poezję** the writer switched from prose to poetry; **rolnik** ~**cił się na hodowlę zwierząt** the farmer switched to breeding livestock [2] *[choroba, ogień, rdza]* to spread

przerzu|t *m* [1] (ludzi, towarów) transportation; (przemyt) smuggling; (narkotyków) trafficking [2] Med. metastasis [3] Sport (w grach piłkarskich) cross; (w zapasach, dżudo) throw; (w gimnastyce akrobatycznej, skokach do wody) somersault; (w skoku wzwyż) flop; ~**t bokiem** a cartwheel

przerzut|ka *f* gear(s)

przesa|da *f* exaggeration; **uprzejmy aż do** ~**dy** kind to a fault; **wpaść** a. **popaść w** ~**dę** to go to extremes

przesa|dzić *pf* — **przesa|dzać** *impf* [] *vt* [1] to replant *[flance, rośliny]*; (o roślinach doniczkowych) to repot [2] (przemieścić) ~**dzić ucznia do innej ławki** to move a pupil to another desk; ~**dzić kogoś przez płot** to heave sb over a fence [3] (przeskoczyć) to jump over *[ogrodzenie, rów]*

II *vi* (nie zachować umiaru) to exaggerate; ~**dził w pochwałach** he was fulsome in his praise; **starał się nie** ~**dzać w ocenie sytuacji** he tried not to exaggerate the situation

przesą|d *m* (zabobon) superstition; (uprzedzenie) prejudice

przesądn|y *adi.* superstitious

przesiadać się *impf* → **przesiąść się**

przesiad|ka *f* lot bez ~**ki** a direct flight; **mieć dwie** ~**ki w podróży** to have to change twice on the journey; **będziesz miał** ~**kę w Krakowie** you'll have to change trains in Cracow

przesiąk|nąć *pf* — **przesiąk|ać** *impf vi* ① *[krew, woda, wilgoć]* to soak (**przez coś** through sth) ② (zostać przepojonym) to become saturated (**czymś** with sth); **ubranie** ~**nęło mu dymem papierosowym** his clothes reeked of cigarette smoke ③ przen. to soak in (**czymś** sth); to imbibe przen. (**czymś** sth); ~**nąć niechęcią do wszystkiego, co obce** to develop a deep aversion to anything foreign

przesi|ąść się *pf* — **przesi|adać się** *impf v refl.* ① (usiąść gdzie indziej) to change seats; ~**ąść się z kanapy na fotel** to move from the sofa to an armchair ② (zmienić środek lokomocji) to change; ~**ąść się do innego tramwaju** to change trams; ~**ąść się z autobusu do pociągu** to change a. transfer from bus to train; ~**ąść się na pociąg do Żywca** to change for Żywiec

przesk|oczyć *pf* — **przesk|akiwać** *impf* **I** *vt* ① (pokonać przeszkodę) to jump a. leap over *[rów, przeszkodę]*; ~**akiwać po dwa stopnie naraz** to bound up the stairs two at a time ② (przekroczyć) to go beyond a. over *[poziom, próg]*; **czterdziestkę to on już dawno** ~**oczył** he's well over a. past forty; ~**oczyć kogoś** (wzrostem) to outgrow sb; (umiejętnościami) to outstrip sb ③ (pominąć) to skip (over) *[rozdział, temat, fragment]*; **takie są przepisy i ja ich nie** ~**oczę** pot. those are the regulations, there's nothing I can do; **pewnych spraw nie da się** ~**oczyć** there are certain things you can't do anything about

II *vi* ① (przemieszczać się) to jump; ~**oczyć przez coś** to jump a. leap over sth *[rów, płot, kałużę]*; to vault (over) sth *[poprzeczkę, barierę]*; ~**akiwał z kamienia na kamień** he was hopping from stone to stone; **iskra elektryczna** ~**akuje między elektrodami** a spark passes between the electrodes ② (w rozmowie, utworze) to skip; ~**akiwać z tematu na temat** to skip from one topic to another; ~**akiwać od tragizmu do komizmu** to switch from the tragic to the comic

prze|słać *pf* — **prze|syłać** *impf vt* ① (dostarczyć) to send; to forward *[list, raport, dokumentację]* (**komuś** to sb); *[urządzenie]* to transmit *[dane, obraz]* (**do czegoś** to sth); *[antena, satelita]* to beam *[obraz, sygnał]* (**do czegoś** to sth); ~**słać coś komuś**

pocztą to send sb sth a. sth to sb by post a. mail; ~**słać coś komuś telegraficznie** to cable sth to sb; ~**słać coś komuś pocztą elektroniczną** to e-mail sth to sb; ~**słać komuś depeszę/faks/e-mail** to cable/fax/e-mail sb; ~**słać paczkę przez kolegę** to get a friend to deliver a parcel; ~**ślij mu moje serdeczne życzenia** please give him my very best wishes ② (przekazać) to give *[znak, spojrzenie]* (**komuś** sb); ~**słać komuś pocałunek** to blow sb a kiss; ~**słała mu uroczy uśmiech** she flashed a charming smile at him ③ Techn. to transmit *[prąd]*; ~**syłać ropę/gaz rurociągiem** to pipe oil/gas

przesłaniać *impf* → **przesłonić**

przesła|nie *n* message; **film z** ~**niem** a film with a message; **odczytał** ~**nie papieskie** książk. he read out the Pope's message

przesłon|a *f* ① (drzew, tkaniny) screen; (dymu, mgły, chmur) veil ② (w aparacie fotograficznym) diaphragm; **szeroko otwarta/przymknięta** ~**a** a wide/narrow aperture

przesłuch|ać *pf* — **przesłuch|iwać** *impf vt* ① (na policji) to question *[podejrzanego]*; (w sądzie) to examine *[oskarżonego, świadka]* ② (sprawdzić kwalifikacje) *[komisja, jury]* to audition *[aktora, muzyka, spikera]* (**do czegoś** for sth) ③ (posłuchać) to play *[płytę, taśmę]*

przesłucha|nie *n* ① (na policji) interrogation; **przyznać się do czegoś podczas** ~**nia** to confess to sth under interrogation; **przyprowadzić podejrzanego na** ~**nie** to bring in a suspect for questioning ② (sprawdzian umiejętności) audition

przesłuchiwać *impf* → **przesłuchać**

przesłysz|eć się *pf v refl.* to mishear; **chyba się** ~**ałem!** (oburzenie) I must be hearing things!

przesmyk *m* ① (wąskie przejście) pass; (w górach) gorge ② (pas lądu) isthmus; (pas wody) inlet

prze|spać *pf* — **prze|sypiać** *impf* **I** *vt* ① (spędzić na spaniu) to sleep (for) *[godzinę]*; to sleep through *[noc, dzień]*; ~**spałem pół filmu** I slept through half the film; **być zmęczonym po źle** ~**spanej nocy** to be tired after a poor night's sleep ② (śpiąc przetrwać) to sleep off *[kaca]* ③ (śpiąc przepuścić) ~**spać godzinę odjazdu pociągu** to oversleep and miss one's train ④ przen. (przegapić) to miss *[okazję, szansę, możliwość]*

II **przespać się** — **przesypiać się** ① (zażyć trochę snu) to have a. take a nap ② pot. ~**spać się z kimś** to sleep a. go to bed with sb pot.

przesta|ć *pf* — **przesta|wać** *impf vi* ① (przerwać) to stop; to quit US pot.; ~**ć palić** to give up a. stop smoking; ~**ń!** stop it!; give it a rest! pot. ② (utracić zdolność) to stop (**coś robić** doing sth); ~**ć słyszeć na jedno ucho** to lose one's hearing in one ear ③ (ustać) to stop (**coś robić** doing sth); **deszcz** ~**ł padać** it stopped raining

przestarza|ły adi. *[zasady, styl, wyraz]* (out)dated; *[urządzenie, system]* obsolete

przestawać impf → **przestać**

przestawi|ć pf — **przestawi|ać** impf **I** vt ① (na inne miejsce) to move *[przedmiot, mebel, samochód]*; to rearrange *[przedmioty, meble]*; ~**ać coś z miejsca na miejsce** to move sth about ② (zmienić kolejność) to transpose *[litery, wyrazy]* ③ (zmienić ustawienie) to reset *[zegarek, pokrętło]*; to switch *[radio]*; ~**ć regulator w lodówce na najniższą temperaturę** to switch the fridge to the lowest temperature setting ④ (zmienić kierunek) to gear *[produkcję, przemysł]* (**na coś** to sth); ~**ł swój sposób myślenia** he changed his way of thinking ⑤ (zbudować w innym miejscu) to shift *[piec, płot]*

II przestawić się — **przestawiać się** ① (zmienić położenie) *[programator]* to move ② (zmienić sposób działania) to switch (**z czegoś na coś** from sth to sth)

przestęp|ca m, ~**czyni** f criminal; **drobny** ~**ca** a petty criminal; **młodociany** ~**ca** a young a. juvenile offender

przestępczoś|ć f crime; ~**ć gospodarcza** white-collar crime; **walka z** ~**cią** a. **zapobieganie** ~**ci** crime prevention

przestępstw|o n crime; ~**o karne** a criminal offence; ~**o gospodarcze** white-collar crime; **ciężkie** ~**o** a felony; ~**o na tle seksualnym** a sex crime a. offence; **popełnić** ~**o** a. **dopuścić się** ~**a** to commit a crime a. an offence; **organ do ścigania** ~ a law enforcement agency

przest|ój m (przerwa w pracy) stoppage

przestrasz|ony adi. *[osoba, głos, wzrok]* frightened; (nagle) startled (**czymś** by sth); *[wołanie]* fearful; **patrzyła na ojca** ~**ona** she looked at her father in fright

przestrasz|yć pf — **przestrasz|ać** impf **I** vt to frighten; (nagle) to startle; **niełatwo mnie** ~**yć** I'm not easily frightened; **ale mnie** ~**yłeś!** you gave me a fright!; ~**yłaś mnie tą wiadomością** I was alarmed by your news

II przestraszyć się — **przestraszać się** to get a fright; to take fright (**czegoś** at sth)

przestr|oga f warning (**przed czymś** against sth); **ku** ~**odze** as a warning; **opowiastka ku** ~**odze** a cautionary tale

przestronn|y adi. grad. *[dom, pokój]* spacious; commodious książk.;

przestrze|c pf — **przestrze|gać**[1] impf vt (upomnieć) to warn; ~**gał ją, żeby nie wychodziła z domu** he warned her not to go out a. against going out

przestrzega|ć[2] impf vt (stosować się do) to obey *[przepisów, prawa]*; to observe *[zwyczajów, postu]*; to abide by *[umowy, traktatu]*; to keep a. stick to *[diety]*; ~**jący prawa obywatel** a law-abiding citizen

przestrze|ń f space; **otwarta** ~**ń** an open space; ~**ń kosmiczna** (outer a. deep) space; ~**ń**

powietrzna airspace; ~**ń życiowa** przen. (living) space; **na** ~**ni wieków** over the centuries; **na** ~**ni dziejów** throughout history

przesu|nąć pf — **przesu|wać** impf **I** vt ① (przemieścić) to move *[mebel, skrzynię]*; ~**nął czapkę na tył głowy** he pushed his hat to the back of his head ② (zmienić ustawienie) to (re)set *[zegarek]*; to shift *[dźwignię]*; ~**nąć zegar do przodu/do tyłu** to put a clock forward/back; ~**nąć taśmę do przodu/do tyłu** to wind on/rewind a tape ③ (zmienić termin) to reschedule *[zebranie, wykład]* ④ (przenieść) to transfer *[pracownika]*; to reallocate *[fundusze, środki]*; to shift *[akcent]* **II** vi (lekko dotknąć) to pass (**czymś** sth); ~**nął dłonią po klawiszach** he passed a. ran his hand over the keyboard

III przesunąć się — **przesuwać się** ① (przenieść się) to move; ~**nąć się do tyłu autobusu** to move to the back of the bus; ~**ń się!** move over a. up! ② (ulec zmianie) *[termin]* (na późniejszy) to be put back; (na wcześniejszy) to be brought forward ③ (przecisnąć się) to squeeze (**przez coś** through sth)

przesyłać impf → **przesłać**[1]

przesył|ka f ① (paczka) parcel; (list) letter; (depesza) telegram; ~**ka pieniężna** a money order; ~**ka polecona** a registered letter/parcel; **nadać na poczcie** ~**kę** to post a letter/parcel ② (wysyłka) dispatch; **koszt** ~**ki** postage

przeszczep m Med. ① (operacja) transplant; ~ **serca/szpiku kostnego** a heart/bone marrow transplant; ~ **skóry** a skin graft ② (przeszczepiona tkanka) graft; (przeszczepiony narząd) transplant; ~ **przyjął się/nie przyjął się** the transplant took/was rejected

przeszczep|ić pf — **przeszczep|iać** impf vt to transplant *[serce, wątrobę, szpik kostny]*; to graft *[skórę]*

przeszkadzać impf → **przeszkodzić**

przeszkalać impf → **przeszkolić**

przeszk|oda f obstacle; **bieg z** ~**odami** Sport an obstacle race; (w jeździectwie, lekkoatletyce) a steeplechase; **nic nie stoi na** ~**odzie, aby realizować ten plan** there's no reason why the plan shouldn't be carried out

przeszk|odzić pf — **przeszk|adzać** impf vi ① (utrudnić) to disturb; „**nie** ~**adzać**" 'do not disturb'; **nie** ~**adzaj sobie** a. **proszę sobie nie** ~**adzać** don't let me disturb you; **burza** ~**odziła nam w dotarciu na szczyt** the storm prevented us from reaching the summit ② (zahamować) to hinder; **brak funduszy** ~**odził w realizacji projektu** the project was hampered a. hindered by lack of funds

przeszkole|nie n training

przeszk|olić pf — **przeszk|alać** impf vt to train

przeszło part. over; **czekałem** ~ **godzinę** I waited (for) over an hour; **od** ~ **trzech lat** for over a.

more than three years; ~ **pięciokrotny wzrost** a more than fivefold increase

przeszłoś|ć *f* past; **w** ~**ci** in the past; **żyć** ~**cią** to live in the past

■ **należeć do** ~**ci** a. **odejść w** ~**ć** to be a thing of the past; **to już należy do** ~**ci** that's all in the past; **kobieta z** ~**cią** a woman with a past

przeszuk|ać *pf* — **przeszuk|iwać** *impf vt* to search *[osobę, samochód]*; to go through *[kieszenie]*

prześcierad|ło *n* sheet; ~**ło z gumką** a fitted sheet; ~**ło kąpielowe** a bath sheet

prześlad|ować *pf vt* [1] (gnębić) to persecute [2] (nudzić) to pester [3] (nie dawać spokoju) to torment; ~**owały ją myśli samobójcze** she was obsessed with thoughts of suicide; **los** a. **pech go** ~**uje** he's dogged by misfortune

prześladowa|nie *n* persecution

prześladow|ca *m*, ~**czyni** *f* persecutor

prześwietlać *impf* → **prześwietlić**

prześwietle|nie *n* Med. X-ray; **iść na** ~**nie** to go for an X-ray; **zrobić sobie** ~**nie klatki piersiowej** to have a chest X-ray

prześwietl|ić *pf* — **prześwietl|ać** *impf* **[I]** *vt* [1] (przeniknąć) to illuminate [2] Med. to X-ray; ~**ić (sobie) płuca** to have a lung X-ray [3] (zbadać) to vet, to screen; ~**ać kandydatów startujących w wyborach** to vet a. screen election candidates [4] to overexpose *[film, klisz]*

[II] prześwietlić się — **prześwietlać się** [1] Med. to have an X-ray [2] *[film, klisza]* to be overexposed

prześwit|ywać *impf vi* *[słońce, światło]* to show through

przetaczać *impf* → **przetoczyć**

przetarg *m* [1] (licytacja) auction; **wystawić coś na** ~ to put sth up for auction; **kupił samochód na** ~**u** he bought a car at an auction [2] (konkurs ofert) tender; **ogłosić** ~ **na coś** to put sth out to tender; **wygrać/przegrać** ~ to win/lose a tender

przeterminowan|y *adi. [żywność, kosmetyk]* past the a. its sell-by date

przetłumacz|yć *pf vt* [1] (przełożyć) to translate [2] pot. (wytłumaczyć) to explain (**komuś** sb)

przetłuszcz|ony *adi. [cera, włosy]* greasy

przet|oczyć *pf* — **przet|aczać** *impf vt* [1] (przesunąć tocząc) to roll; ~**aczać pociąg na boczny tor** to shunt a train into a siding [2] (przelać, przepompować) to transfer [3] Med. to transfuse *[krew]*

przetrwa|ć *pf* **[I]** *vt* (przeżyć) to survive *[zimę, wojnę]*; to weather *[recesję, kryzys]*

[II] *vi* (wytrzymać dłużej) to outlast; **ich przyjaźń** ~**ła próbę czasu** their friendship has stood the test of time

przetrzą|snąć *pf* — **przetrzą|sać** *impf vt* [1] (przeszukać) to search *[dom, bagaże]*; ~**snąć kieszenie** to go a. rake through one's pockets [2] (zmieszać) to ted *[siano, słomę]*

prze|trzeć *pf* — **prze|cierać** *impf* **[I]** *vt* [1] (wytrzeć) to wipe *[okna, okulary, czoło]* [2] (podziurawić) to wear through *[spodnie, rękawy]*; **być** ~**tartym na łokciach** to be worn through at the elbows [3] (przepuścić przez sito) to pass [sth] through a sieve *[jarzyny, owoce]*

[II] przetrzeć się — **przecierać się** [1] (zniszczyć się) *[materiał, spodnie]* to wear through [2] (przejaśnić się) *[niebo]* to clear (up)

■ ~**trzeć drogę** (oczyścić) to clear the way; ~**trzeć szlak** (wyznaczyć) to blaze a trail; ~**cierać drogę komuś/czemuś** to pave a. smooth the way for sb/sth; ~**cierać oczy** to not believe one's eyes

przetrzym|ać *pf* — **przetrzym|ywać** *impf vt* [1] (zatrzymać dłużej) to keep (longer); ~**ać książkę z wypożyczalni** to keep an overdue library book; ~**ać uczniów po lekcjach** to keep a class in after school [2] (przechować) to store [3] (przeżyć) to survive *[suszę]*; to endure *[ból]* [4] (wytrzymać dłużej) to last out *[okres czasu]* [5] (nie puścić) to hold on (**coś** to sth)

przetw|orzyć *pf* — **przetw|arzać** *impf vt* [1] (przerobić) to process *[surowiec, substancję]*; ~**orzone mleko** processed milk [2] (przemienić) to convert [3] (przekształcić) to transform *[rzeczywistość]* [4] Komput. to process *[dane]*

przetw|ór *m* preserve; ~**ory owocowe** fruit preserves

przetwórni|a *f* food-processing plant; ~**a owoców** a fruit-processing plant; **statek-przetwórnia** a factory ship

przetykać *impf* → **przetkać**

przewa|ga *f* [1] (większa liczebność) majority; **mieć** ~**gę liczebną nad wrogiem** to outnumber the enemy; **las mieszany z** ~**gą drzew iglastych** mixed forest with a predominance of conifers [2] (wyższość) advantage (**nad kimś** over sb); **mamy tę** ~**gę, że znamy angielski** we have the advantage of knowing English; **mieć 13 sekund** ~**gi nad kimś** to be 13 seconds ahead of sb; **wygrać z** ~**gą trzech metrów** to win by three metres

przeważ|ać¹ *impf vi* (być w większości) to predominate; **wady** ~**ały nad zaletami** the disadvantages outweighed the advantages

przeważać² *impf* → **przeważyć**

przeważnie *adv.* chiefly

przeważ|yć *pf* — **przeważ|ać²** *impf* **[I]** *vt* (przechylić) to overbalance; **walizka** ~**yła wózek** the suitcase overturned the trolley

[II] *vi* (zadecydować) to prevail; **chciwość** ~**yła w nim nad rozwagą** greed got the better of his common sense

przewidując|y *adi. [gospodarz, właściciel]* prudent

przewidywać *impf* → **przewidzieć**

przewidze|nie *n* **to było do** ~**nia** that was to be expected

przewi|dzieć *pf* — **przewi|dywać** *impf vt* 1 (odgadnąć) to predict *[skutek, katastrofę, zwycięstwo]*; to forecast *[pogodę, deszcz]*; (spodziewać się) to expect; **nie mogłem ~dzieć, jakie będą tego konsekwencje** I could not have foreseen the consequences; **~duje się, że budowa potrwa rok** construction is expected to take a year 2 (zaplanować) to anticipate 3 *[kodeks, ustawa]* to provide for *[karę, rozwiązanie]*; *[program]* to include; **regulamin ~duje, że...** the regulations provide for...

przewietrz|yć *pf* — **przewietrz|ać** *impf* 1 *vt* to air *[pokój, ubranie, pościel]*; **nowy minister będzie chciał ~yć ministerstwo** pot., przen. the new minister will want to make a clean sweep of the department

1 **przewietrzyć się** — **przewietrzać się** to get some fresh air

przewiew *m* air circulation

przewiewn|y *adi. grad. [ubranie]* light; *[pomieszczenie]* airy

przew|ieźć *pf* — **przew|ozić** *impf vt* 1 (przetransportować) to transport; (statkiem) to ship; (samolotem) to fly; **samochód/pociąg ~ożący materiały wybuchowe** a lorry/train carrying explosives; **~ieziono ich helikopterem do szpitala** they were taken to a hospital by helicopter 2 pot. (wziąć na przejażdżkę) to take [sb] for a ride

przewi|nąć *pf* — **przewi|jać** *impf* 1 *vt* 1 (zmienić opatrunek) to re-bandage *[ranę, rękę]* 2 (zmienić pieluchę) to change *[dziecko]*; **trzeba ją ~nąć** she needs changing 3 (ponownie nawinąć) to rewind *[wełnę, nitkę]* 4 (do przodu) to wind on *[kliszę, taśmę]*; (szybko) to fast-forward *[taśmę, kasetę]*; (do tyłu) to rewind *[kliszę, taśmę]*

1 **przewinąć się** — **przewijać się** 1 (do przodu) *[klisza, taśma]* to wind on; (szybko) *[taśma, kaseta]* to fast-forward; (do tyłu) *[klisza, taśma]* to rewind 2 (pojawić się) **~jać się przez coś** *[temat, nuta]* to run through sth; **przez firmę ~nęło się mnóstwo osób** lots of people have worked for the company

przewinie|nie *n* offence; Sport foul; **popełnić ~nie** to commit an offence/a foul

przewl|ec *pf* — **przewl|ekać** *impf* 1 *vt* 1 (przeciągnąć) to thread *[sznur, linę]* 2 (zmienić) **~ec poduszkę** to change a pillowcase; **~ec pościel** to change the sheets 3 (przedłużać) to stall *[rozmowy, proces]*

1 **przewlec się** — **przewlekać się** to drag out

przewlek|ły *adi. [dyskusja, proces]* lengthy; *[choroba, zapalenie]* chronic

przewodni *adi.* 1 (główny) *[temat, motyw, myśl]* central 2 (przywódczy) *[rola]* leading

przewodnictw|o *n* (przewodniczenie) chairmanship; (kierowanie) leadership; **komisja/delegacja pod ~em profesora Nowaka** a committee

chaired by/delegation led by Professor Nowak; **objąć ~o zebrania** to take the chair at a meeting

przewodnicząc|y *m* 1 (zebrania, komisji) chair(person); (mężczyzna) chairman 2 Szkol. captain; **~y samorządu szkolnego** the head boy (of the school)

przewodnicz|yć *impf vi* (być przewodniczącym) to chair; (kierować) to lead; **~yć zebraniu** to chair a meeting; **~yć wyprawie** to lead an expedition

przewodni|k *m* 1 (prowadzący) guide; (wycieczki) (tour) guide; **„wstęp tylko z ~kiem"** 'guided tours only'; **służyć komuś za ~ka** to act as a guide for sb; **~k stada** the pack leader; **pies ~k** a guide dog 2 (informator turystyczny) guide(book); **~k po Polsce** a guide to Poland 3 (prądu, ciepła) conductor

przew|odzić *impf* 1 *vt* to conduct *[ciepło, prąd, sole mineralne]*; to transmit *[bodźce, impulsy]*

1 *vi* to lead; **~odzić grupie/wyprawie** to lead a group/an expedition

przewozić *impf* → **przewieźć**

przewoźni|k *m* 1 (osoba) (na promie) ferryman; (kierowca ciężarówki) haulier GB 2 (przedsiębiorstwo) carrier; **~k lotniczy** an air carrier

przew|ód *m* 1 (drut) wire; (przy żelazku, telefonie) cord; **~ody elektryczne/telefoniczne** electric/telephone wires; **~ody wysokiego napięcia** a high voltage power line; **ciągnąć a. kłaść ~ody** to lay cables 2 (kanał) duct; (rura) pipe; **~ód gazowy** a gas pipe; **~ód kanalizacyjny** a sewer; **~ód kominowy** a chimney flue; **główny ~ód gazowy** a gas main 3 Anat. canal; **~ód pokarmowy** the alimentary canal 4 (sądowy) proceedings

przew|óz *m* transport; **~ozy kolejowe/samochodowe** rail/road transport a. haulage; **~óz pasażerów** passenger transport; **opłata za ~óz bagażu** a luggage charge

przewracać *impf* → **przewrócić**

przewrażliwi|ony *adi. [osoba]* oversensitive (**na punkcie czegoś** about sth)

przewrotn|y *adi. grad. [osoba, pytanie, tytuł]* perverse; **robić coś z ~ą przyjemnością** to take a perverse pleasure in doing sth

przewr|ócić *pf* — **przewr|acać** *impf* 1 *vt* 1 (spowodować upadek) *[osoba]* to knock over *[osobę, szklankę]*; *[wiatr]* to blow down *[drzewo]* 2 (odwrócić) to turn over; **~ócić coś do góry nogami/na drugą stronę** to turn sth upside down/over; **~ócić coś na lewą stronę** to turn sth inside out; **~ócić stronę w książce** to turn (over) a page in a book 3 (przetrząsnąć) **~acać rzeczy w szafie** to rummage a. go through the contents of a wardrobe

1 **przewrócić się** — **przewracać się** 1 (upaść) to fall down; **~ócić się o wystający korzeń** to trip over a protruding root 2 (odwrócić się) to turn over; **~ócić się do góry nogami** to turn upside down;

~**acać się z boku na bok** to toss and turn; **łódka** ~**óciła się do góry dnem** the boat capsized

przewr|ót m [1] (polityczny) coup; **dokonać** ~**otu** to stage a coup [2] (przełom) revolution; **dokonać** ~**otu w nauce** to revolutionize scholarship [3] Sport (ćwiczenie) roll; **zrobić** ~**ót w przód/tył** to do a forward/backward roll

przewyższ|yć pf — **przewyższ|ać** impf vt [1] (wysokością, wzrostem) [osoba] to be taller than; [budynek, drzewo] to be higher than; ~**ał ojca o głowę** he was a head taller than his father [2] (wartością) to exceed; **wysokość szkody** ~**a 500 złotych** the cost of the damage is in excess of 500 zlotys [3] (być lepszym) to be ahead of; ~**ać kogoś wiedzą** to be more knowledgeable than sb; ~**ać kogoś o głowę pod względem doświadczenia** to have a lot more experience than sb

przez praep. [1] (na drugą stronę) across [park, pustynię]; over [przeszkodę, płot, barierę]; (na wylot) through [ścianę, chmury]; **przejść** ~ **jezdnię** to cross the street; **przeskoczyć** ~ **strumyk** to jump over a. across a stream; **wejść** ~ **okno** to come in through the window; **przeciskać się** ~ **tłum** to push one's way through the crowd; **brnąć** ~ **śnieg** to plough through the snow; **most** ~ **Wisłę** a bridge across a. over the Vistula; **pociąg do Kolonii** ~ **Hanower** a train to Cologne via Hanover; **torba z paskiem** ~ **ramię** a bag with a shoulder strap [2] (po drugiej stronie) across; **mieszkali** ~ **podwórko** they lived across the courtyard; **nocowaliśmy** ~ **ścianę** we slept in adjacent rooms [3] (o doświadczeniu) through [fazę, okres, życie]; **przejść pomyślnie** ~ **egzamin** to get through a. pass an exam; **przejść** ~ **piekło** przen. to go through hell [4] (czas trwania) for; ~ **dwa dni** for two days; ~ **chwilę** for a moment; ~ **cały czas** all the time; **pracować** ~ **całą noc** to work all through the night a. the whole night (through) [5] (w stronie biernej) by (**kogoś/coś** sb/sth); **dom zniszczony** ~ **pożar** a house destroyed by fire; **zakazany** ~ **prawo** forbidden by law [6] (za pomocą) ~ **lunetę/szkło powiększające** through a telescope/magnifying glass; ~ **telefon** [rozmawiać] on the phone; [poinformować] over the phone; **pić sok** ~ **słomkę** to drink juice through a. with a straw; **napisać coś** ~ **kalkę** to make a carbon copy of sth; **uczcili pamięć zmarłych** ~ **powstanie z miejsc** they paid tribute to the dead by rising from their seats; **głosowali** ~ **podniesienie ręki** they voted by a show of hands [7] (z powodu) through; ~ **niedopatrzenie/nieuwagę** through a. out of negligence/carelessness; ~ **złośliwość** out of malice; ~ **pomyłkę/przypadek** by mistake/accident; ~ **kogoś** because of a. through sb; **to wszystko** ~ **ciebie** it's all your fault; ~ **to** because of that [8] (za pośrednictwem) through; **rozmawiać** ~ **tłumacza** to speak through an interpreter; **zarezerwować hotel** ~ **biuro po-**

dróży to book a hotel through a travel agent; **list wysłano** ~ **gońca** the letter was sent by messenger [9] (wskazujące na interpretację) by; **co** ~ **to rozumiesz?** what do you understand by that?; **co chcesz** ~ **to powiedzieć** what do you mean by (saying) that? [10] Mat. by; **podziel/pomnóż sumę** ~ **2** divide/multiply the sum by 2

przezięb|ić pf — **przezięb|iać** impf [] vt ~**ić dziecko** to let a baby catch cold; ~**ić gardło/pęcherz** to get a throat/bladder infection
[] **przeziębić się** — **przeziębiać się** to catch a cold

przeziębie|nie n cold

przezięb|iony adi. **być** ~**onym** to have a cold

przezim|ować pf vi [1] (spędzić zimę) [osoba, zwierzę] to winter; (przetrwać zimę) [roślina, owad] to overwinter [2] pot., Szkol. to retake a year; ~**ował w trzeciej klasie** he repeated the third year

przeznaczać impf → **przeznaczyć**

przeznaczeni|e n [1] (los) destiny; **wierzyć w** ~**e** to believe in destiny; **jej** ~**em był teatr** she was destined for the stage [2] (zastosowanie, cel) purpose; **używać czegoś zgodnie/niezgodnie z** ~**em** to use/not use sth for the purpose for which it was intended; **dotrzeć do miejsca** ~**a** to reach one's destination

przeznacz|yć pf — **przeznacz|ać** impf vt [1] (wygospodarować) to allot [pieniądze, miejsce]; to allow a. set aside [czas]; (ofiarować) to donate [majątek, kwotę]; **musisz na to** ~**yć dwa dni** you'll have to allow a. to set aside two days for the job [2] (wyznaczyć cel, odbiorcę) to intend; **utwory** ~**one do druku** works intended for publication; **dom** ~**ony do rozbiórki** a house earmarked for demolition

przezorn|y adi. grad. (ostrożny) [osoba, rada, polityka] cautious; (przewidujący) [osoba] prudent
■ ~**y zawsze ubezpieczony** better safe than sorry

przezrocz|e n slide

przezroczy|sty adi. [1] (przejrzysty) transparent; [strumień, powierzchnia] clear [2] (prześwitujący) [sukienka, materiał] see-through [3] (delikatny) [skóra] translucent

przez|wać pf vt to call [osobę, przedmiot]; to nickname [osobę]

przezwisk|o n nickname; **nadać komuś** ~**o „Żyrafa"** to nickname sb 'Giraffe'

przezwycięż|yć pf — **przezwycięż|ać** impf [] vt to overcome [przeszkodę, trudność, strach, senność]
[] **przezwyciężyć się – przezwyciężać się** (przemóc się) **musisz się** ~**yć i powiedzieć prawdę** you must overcome your fear and tell the truth; **chciał zapalić, ale się** ~**ył** he overcame his desire to smoke

przezywa|ć impf vt pot. ~**ć kogoś** to call sb names

przeźrocze → przezrocze
przeźroczysty → przezroczysty
przeżegna|ć *pf* **[I]** *vt* to bless [sb/sth] with the sign of the cross *[wiernych, chleb]*
[II] przeżegnać się to cross oneself
przeżu|ć *pf* — **przeżu|wać**[1] *impf vt* **[1]** (rozdrobnić) *[osoba, zwierzę]* to chew; (głośno, dokładnie) to munch **[2]** pot. (rozważyć) to chew over pot.
■ ~**ć (w ustach) przekleństwo** pot. to curse under one's breath
przeżuwacz *m* ruminant
przeżuwać[1] *impf* → przeżuć
przeżuwa|ć[2] *impf vt* Zool. to ruminate; **zwierzęta** ~**jące** ruminant animals
przeży|cie *n* experience
przeży|ć *pf* — **przeży|wać** *impf* **[I]** *vt* **[1]** (nie umrzeć) to survive *[operację, wypadek, upadek]*; **jakoś to** ~**ję** przen. I'll get over it; **on tego nie** ~**je!** przen. he'll be devastated!; **ledwie udaje im się** ~**ć do pierwszego** przen. they can hardly make ends meet; **walczyć o** ~**cie** to struggle for survival **[2]** (doświadczyć) to go through *[kryzys, załamanie]*; to experience *[szok, wstrząs]*; to live through *[wojnę, powódź]* **[3]** (być zasmuconym) to be affected by; (być podnieconym) to be excited about **[4]** (spędzić) to spend; **dzieciństwo** ~**ła na wsi** she spent her childhood in the country; ~**yć życie spokojnie i bez kłopotów** to live a quiet and trouble-free life **[5]** (być na świecie) to live; ~**ł 90 lat** he lived to the age of 90 **[6]** (umrzeć później) to outlive; ~**ć kogoś o pięć lat** to outlive a. survive sb by five years
[II] przeżyć się — przeżywać się *[moda, tendencja]* to have had its day
przeżyt|ek *m* relic
przeżywać *impf* → przeżyć
przędz|a *f* yarn; ~**a jedwabna** spun silk
przę|sło *n* span
przod|ek *m* ancestor
przod|ować *impf vi* to lead (**w czymś** in sth)
prz|ód *m* **[1]** (przednia część) front; **mieć plamę z** ~**odu** a. **na** ~**odzie** to have a stain on the front; **usiąść z** ~**odu** (w samochodzie) to sit in the front; (w teatrze, w klasie) to sit at the front; **iść na** ~**odzie** a. ~**edzie pochodu** to walk at the head of a procession; **stać** ~**odem do kogoś** to stand facing sb; **włożyć coś tyłem na** ~**ód** to put sth on back to front **[2]** (przestrzeń przed czymś) **z** ~**odu budynku** in front of the building; **na** ~**ód** a. **do** ~**odu** forward; **przepychać się do** ~**odu** to push to the front; **pochylić się do** ~**odu** a. **ku** ~**odowi** to lean forward; **zrobić krok w** ~**ód** a. **do** ~**odu** to take a step forward także przen.; **pójść** ~**odem** to go on ahead; **przepuścić kogoś** ~**odem** to let sb in front of one **[3]** (o czasie) **przestawić zegarki o godzinę do** ~**odu** to put the clock forward an hour; **wybiegać myślami w** ~**ód** to look ahead
■ być do ~**odu z robotą** pot. to be ahead of

schedule; **być sto złotych do** ~**odu** pot. to be a hundred zlotys ahead pot.
prztycz|ek *m* pot. flick; **dać komuś** ~**ka w ucho** to flick sb's ear
przy *praep.* **[1]** (w pobliżu) by; ~ **oknie** by the window; ~ **biurku** at a desk; **usiądź** ~ **mnie** sit next to me; **zaraz** ~ **kwiaciarni** right by the flower shop; **pociąg zatrzymuje się** ~ **peronie trzecim** the train stops at platform three; **nie mam** ~ **sobie pieniędzy** I don't have any money on me; ~ **głównej ulicy** on the main road; **mieszkam przy ulicy Klonowej 20** I live at 20 Klonowa Street; **głowa** ~ **głowie, ramię** ~ **ramieniu** head to head, shoulder to shoulder **[2]** (w obecności) in front of; ~ **gościach** in front of a. in the presence of guests; **nie** ~ **ludziach!** not in front of other people!; **byłem** ~ **tym, jak to powiedział** I was (right) there when he said it **[3]** (podczas, w czasie) ~ **śniadaniu** at a. over breakfast; **grali w karty** ~ **piwie** they were playing cards and drinking beer; **wypadki** ~ **pracy** accidents at work; **kolacja** ~ **świecach** a candlelit supper; ~ **dwudziestostopniowym mrozie** at a temperature of minus twenty; ~ **tym tempie/tej prędkości** at this rate/speed; **spać** ~ **otwartym oknie** to sleep with the window open; ~ **odrobinie szczęścia** with a bit of luck; ~ **tym** a. **czym** in addition to (which), moreover; **jest przystojny,** ~ **tym niegłupi** he's good-looking and he's not stupid either **[4]** (w porównaniu do) alongside; ~ **mężu wydawała się niska** alongside her husband she appeared short; ~ **całym swoim bogactwie był skąpy** for all his wealth he was tight-fisted **[5]** (wskazuje na przyporządkowanie) **tłumacz** ~ **ONZ** a translator/an interpreter at the UN; **szkoła średnia** ~ **Akademii Rolniczej** a secondary school attached to the Agricultural Academy **[6]** (wskazuje na uzupełnienie) **pasek** ~ **spodniach** a trouser belt; **miała broszkę** ~ **sukni** she had a brooch pinned to her dress **[7]** (wskazuje na obiekt działań) **majstrować** ~ **czymś** to fiddle around with sth; **pracować** ~ **koniach** to work with horses; **przez dwie noce czuwał** ~ **chorej matce** he spent two nights watching over his ailing mother **[8]** pot. (wskazuje na posiadanie) **być** ~ **władzy** to be in power; **być** ~ **piłce** to have the ball
przybi|ć *pf* — **przybi|jać** *impf* **[I]** *vt* **[1]** (młotkiem) to nail; ~**jać coś do czegoś** to nail sth to sth **[2]** (odcisnąć) ~**ć stempel w paszporcie** to stamp a passport; ~**ć na czymś pieczątkę z datą** to date-stamp sth **[3]** (zasmucić) to distress; **był wyraźnie** ~**ty** he was clearly distressed
[II] *vi* (przypłynąć) *[łódź, statek]* to draw up; ~**ć do brzegu** to reach the shore
przybie|c, przybie|gnąć *pf* — **przybie|gać** *impf vi* to come running; ~**gł, jak tylko nas zobaczył** he ran up as soon as he saw us

przybierać *impf* → **przybrać**
przybijać *impf* → **przybić**
przybliżać *impf* → **przybliżyć**
przybliże|nie *n* approximation; **duże** ~**nie** a rough approximation; **podać** ~**nie jakiejś liczby** to give an approximate figure; **w** ~**niu** approximately; **to jest w** ~**niu to, o co nam chodzi** that's more or less what we're after
przybliż|ony *adi.* *[wartość, liczba, odległość]* approximate; *[obliczenie, tłumaczenie, ocena]* rough
przybliż|yć *pf* — **przybliż|ać** *impf* **[]** *vt* **1** (przysunąć) to move [sth] close/closer (**do czegoś** to sth) **2** (posunąć, przyśpieszyć) to bring [sb/sth] close/closer (**do czegoś** to sth); **to** ~**a rozwiązanie problemu** this brings the problem nearer to a solution **3** (upodobnić) to make [sth] similar (**do czegoś** to sth) **4** (wytworzyć więź) to bring [sb] close/closer (**do kogoś** to sb); **to nieszczęście bardzo ich do siebie** ~**yło** the tragedy brought them closer together **5** (wyjaśnić) to introduce; **chciałbym państwu** ~**yć jego osiągnięcia** let me briefly outline his achievements **6** (podać w przybliżeniu) to give an approximation of *[wartość, liczbę]* **7** (optycznie) **kamera** ~**yła ich twarze** the camera showed their faces in close-up
[] **przybliżyć się** — **przybliżać się** **1** (zmniejszyć odległość) to get close/closer (**do kogoś/czegoś** to sb/sth); (przysunąć się) to move closer (**do kogoś/czegoś** to sb/sth); (podejść) to come closer (**do kogoś/czegoś** to sb/sth); **kroki** ~**yły się** the footsteps came closer **2** (do celu) to come close/closer (**do czegoś** to sth) **3** (nadchodzić) *[pora, burza]* to approach **4** (upodobnić się) to be similar (**do czegoś** to sth) **5** (zaprzyjaźnić się) to become close/closer (**do kogoś** to sb)
przybłąka|ć się *pf v refl.* to wander up; **jakiś pies** ~**ł się na nasze podwórko** a dog strayed into our yard
przybłę|da *m, f* (zwierzę) stray; (osoba) stranger
przybornik *m* kit; ~ **rysunkowy** a drawing set
przybor|y *plt* items; ~**y toaletowe** toilet articles; ~**y kreślarskie** drawing instruments; ~**y szkolne** school gear a. things
przyb|rać *pf* — **przyb|ierać** *impf* **[]** *vt* **1** (przyjąć) to take on, to assume *[pozę, kształt, rozmiar]*; **pod** ~**ranym nazwiskiem** under an assumed name; **zjawisko** ~**rało niepokojące rozmiary** the phenomenon took on alarming proportions; **sprawy** ~**rały poważny obrót** things took a serious turn **2** (przystroić) to decorate *[pokój]*; to garnish *[potrawę]*
[] *vi* to rise; **rzeka wciąż** ~**iera** the river is still rising
■ ~**ierać na sile** *[wiatr, protesty]* to grow a. get stronger; ~**ierać na wadze** a. **ciele** pot. to put on weight
przybra|nie *n* (potrawy) garnish; (stroju) trimming

przybran|y *adi.* *[ojczyzna]* adopted; *[rodzina]* adoptive; ~**e dziecko** an adopted child; ~**i rodzice** adoptive parents
przybudów|ka *f* (część budynku) annexe GB, extension; (z jednospadowym dachem) lean-to; **dom z późniejszymi** ~**kami** a house with later additions
przyb|yć *pf* — **przyb|ywać** *impf vi* **1** (dotrzeć) to arrive; ~**yć na dworzec** to arrive at the station; ~**yć do Warszawy** to arrive in Warsaw; ~**yć z Berlina** to arrive from Berlin; **witać** ~**ywających gości** to greet the arriving guests; **dziękuję państwu za** ~**ycie** ladies and gentlemen, thank you for coming **2** (zwiększyć swoją liczebność) **we wsi** ~**yły nowe domy** new houses were built in the village; **co roku** ~**ywa nam konkurentów** the competition increases every year; ~**yło mu dziesięć centymetrów** he's grown ten centimetres; ~**yło mu lat** he's grown older; **dnia** ~**ywa** the days are getting longer
przybysz *m* (nieznajomy) stranger; ~ **z kosmosu** an alien
przybyt|ek *m* książk., żart. temple przen.; ~**ek sztuki/nauki** a temple to art/learning; ~**ek hazardu** a gambling den
■ od ~**ku głowa nie boli** you can't have too much of a good thing
przybywać *impf* → **przybyć**
przychodni|a *f* clinic; ~**a okulistyczna** an eye clinic; ~**a rejonowa** a local clinic
przychodzić *impf* → **przyjść**
przych|ód *m* income; **opodatkowanie** ~**odów** income tax
przychyl|ić *pf* — **przychyl|ać** *impf* **[]** *vt* (nachylić) to tilt *[kieliszek, filiżankę]*; **wiatr** ~**ał drzewa** the wind bent the trees
[] **przychylić się** — **przychylać się** **1** (wyrazić zgodę) ~**ić się do czyjejś prośby** to accede to sb's request **2** (być tego samego zdania) ~**ać się do czyjegoś zdania** to concur with sb's opinion; ~**iłabym się do tego, co powiedział pan minister** I'm inclined to agree with the minister
■ nieba bym jej ~**ił** I'd do anything for her
przychylnoś|ć *f* favour GB, favor US; **zdobyć sobie czyjąś** ~**ć** to win favour with sb; **spotkać się z** ~**cią** to get a sympathetic response
przychyln|y *adi.* grad. *[osoba, widownia]* sympathetic; *[opinia, odpowiedź]* favourable GB, favorable US; **patrzyć na kogoś/coś** ~**ym okiem** to be favourably disposed a. inclined towards sb/sth
przyciąg|ać¹ *impf* **[]** *vt [planeta, magnes]* to attract
[] **przyciągać się** *[planety, ciała]* to attract each other
przyciągać² *impf* → **przyciągnąć**
przyciągani|e *n* attraction; ~**e ziemskie** (the Earth's) gravity; **wzajemne** ~**e** mutual attraction

przyciąg|nąć *pf* — **przyciąg|ać²** *impf vt*
boxed-1 (fizycznie) to pull; ~**nąć kogoś do siebie** to pull
a. draw sb to oneself boxed-2 przen. to attract *[klientów,
widzów]*; ~**ać czyjąś uwagę** to draw sb's attention; ~**ać czyjś wzrok** to catch sb's eye

przycin|ek *m* snide; **robić** ~**ki do czegoś** to
make snide remarks about sth

przycisk *m* boxed-1 (przełącznik) button boxed-2 (do papierów)
paperweight boxed-3 (akcent) stress

przyci|snąć *pf* — **przyci|skać** *impf vt*
boxed-1 (przygnieść) to press; ~**snąć czoło do szyby** to
press one's forehead against the window; ~**snąć
kogoś do ziemi** to pin sb to the ground; ~**snąć
coś ciężkim przedmiotem** to weigh sth down
boxed-2 (nacisnąć) to press boxed-3 pot. (wywrzeć presję) to put the
screws on pot.

przycisz|yć *pf* — **przycisz|ać** *impf vt* to turn
down *[telewizor, muzykę]*; ~ **trochę to radio!** turn
the radio down, will you!

przyczep|a *f* trailer; (motocyklowa) sidecar; ~**a
kempingowa** a caravan GB, a trailer US

przyczep|ić *pf* — **przyczep|iać** *impf* boxed-I *vt*
(przyłączyć) to attach; ~**ić do czegoś etykietkę** to
label a. tag sth; ~**ić komuś etykietkę buntownika** przen. to label sb a rebel
boxed-II **przyczepić się** — **przyczepiać się** boxed-1 (przykleić
się) to stick (**do czegoś** to sth); **coś ci się** ~**iło do
rękawa** something's stuck to your sleeve boxed-2 (utkwić
w pamięci) ~**iła się do mnie ta melodia** I can't get
that tune out of my head boxed-3 pot. (narzucać się) to latch
on pot. (**do kogoś** to sb); ~**ił się do nas jak rzep
do psiego ogona** he stuck to us like glue pot. boxed-4 pot.
(mieć zastrzeżenia) to find fault (**do czegoś** with sth);
~**ić się do kogoś** (uwziąć się) to pick on sb; **zawsze
się do czegoś** ~**ią** they always find fault with
something

przyczyn|a *f* reason (**czegoś** for sth); cause
(**czegoś** of sth); **z niewiadomych** ~ for some
unknown reason; **gniewać się bez** ~**y** to be angry
for no reason; ~**a zgonu** (the) cause of death; **nie
będę wnikać a. wchodzić w** ~**y, dlaczego tak
się stało** I won't go into the reasons why it
happened

przyczy|nić *pf* — **przyczy|niać** *impf* boxed-I *vi* to
cause; ~**nić komuś kłopotów** to cause sb trouble
boxed-II **przyczyniać się** — **przyczynić się** to contribute (**do czegoś** to sth)

przyda|ć się *pf* — **przyda|wać się** *impf v refl.*
to be useful; **to mi się na nic nie** ~ it's of no use
to me; **może się na coś** ~**m?** can I help with
anything?; ~**łby się deszcz** we could use some
rain pot.; ~**łby mi się nowy samochód** I could
do with a new car pot.

przydarz|yć się *pf* — **przydarz|ać się** *impf
v refl.* to happen; **coś mu się** ~**yło** something's
happened to him

przydatn|y *adi. [osoba]* useful; *[narzędzie, książka]*
handy

przydawać się *impf* → **przydać się**

przydom|ek *m* nickname

przydzia|ł *m* boxed-1 (przydzielanie) allotment; (zadań)
assignment; (w wojsku) posting GB boxed-2 (przydzielone
rzeczy) ration

przydziel|ić *pf* — **przydziel|ać** *impf vt* boxed-1 (przy-
znać) to allot; ~**ić komuś mieszkanie** to assign sb
a flat boxed-2 (skierować) to assign; ~**ić kogoś do zadania**
to assign sb to a task; ~**ić komuś zadanie** to
assign sb a task

przyglądać się *impf* → **przyjrzeć się**

przyglądnąć się → **przyjrzeć się**

przygnębiać *impf* → **przygnębić**

przygnębiając|y *adi.* depressing

przygnębi|ć *pf* — **przygnębi|ać** *impf* to
depress

przygnębieni|e *n* depression; **wpaść w** ~**e** to
sink into depression

przygnębi|ony *adi.* depressed; **być czymś**
~**onym** to be depressed about a. over sth

przygni|eść *pf* — **przygni|atać** *impf vt* boxed-1 (przy-
cisnąć) to crush; (unieruchomić) to pin boxed-2 przen.
(przytłoczyć) to crush

przyg|oda *f* boxed-1 (wydarzenie) adventure; **zabawna**
~**oda** an amusing incident; **podróż minęła bez**
~**ód** the journey was uneventful; **poszukiwacz**
~**ód** an adventurer boxed-2 (przelotny romans) fling pot.
boxed-3 przen. (doświadczenia, przeżycia) exciting experience

przygodn|y *adi.* boxed-1 *[znajomość]* passing; (nieistotny)
chance; ~**e miłostki** fleeting a. casual romances
boxed-2 (spotkany przypadkiem) casual

przygot|ować *pf* — **przygot|owywać** *impf*
boxed-I *vt* boxed-1 (przyszykować) to prepare boxed-2 (uprzedzić) to
prepare *[osobę]*; **nie jestem** ~**owany na takie
ryzyko** I'm not prepared to take such a risk
boxed-3 (nauczyć) to prepare *[osobę]*; ~**ować kogoś do
egzaminu** to prepare sb for an exam
boxed-II **przygotować się** — **przygotowywać się**
boxed-1 (szykować się) to get ready; ~**owywać się do
podróży** to get ready for a journey boxed-2 (oswoić się
z myślą) to prepare oneself; ~**uj się na najgorsze**
prepare yourself for the worst boxed-3 (nauczyć się) to
prepare

przygotowa|nie *n* preparation; ~**nia wojenne**
preparations for war; ~**nia do wesela** preparations for a wedding reception

przygotowawcz|y *adi.* preparatory; **kurs** ~**y**
a foundation course; **postępowanie** ~**e** preparatory proceedings

przygotowywać *impf* → **przygotować**

przygryw|ka *f* boxed-1 (wstęp instrumentalny) prelude;
(podkład muzyczny) accompaniment; ~**ka do tańca**
a dance tune boxed-2 przen. (zapowiedź) prelude

przygry|źć *pf* — **przygry|zać** *impf* boxed-I *vt* to bite
[wargi, usta]; to chew *[wąsy]*

II *vi* pot. (dokuczyć docinkami) to make jibes (**komuś** at sb)

przyim|ek *m* preposition

przyjaci|el *m* friend

■ **prawdziwych** ~**ół poznajemy** a. **poznaje się w biedzie** przysł. a friend in need is a friend indeed przysł.

przyjaciels|ki *adi.* friendly; **być z kimś w** ~**kich stosunkach** to be on friendly terms with sb

przyjaciół|ka *f* (girl)friend

przyj|azd *m* arrival; „**Przyjazdy**" (w rozkładzie jazdy) 'Arrivals'

przyja|zny *adi. grad.* ① (życzliwy) friendly ② (korzystny) *[klimat, okolica]* pleasant; ~**zny dla środowiska** environmentally friendly; ~**zny dla użytkownika** user-friendly

przyjaź|nić się *impf v refl.* to be friends (**z kimś** with sb)

przyjaź|ń *f* friendship; **bliska** ~**ń** close friendship; ~**ń do grobowej deski** friendship to the grave; **być z kimś w** ~**ni** to be sb's friend; **więzi** ~**ni** bonds a. ties of friendship

przyj|ąć *pf* — **przyj|mować** *impf* **I** *vt* ① (wziąć) to accept *[prezent, napiwek, nagrodę]*; to take *[czek, łapówkę]* ② (zaakceptować) to accept; ~**ąć czyjąś rezygnację** to accept sb's resignation; ~**ąć uchwałę/ustawę** to pass a resolution/bill; **nie** ~**ąć oferty** to turn down an offer ③ (zażyć, zjeść) to take *[lekarstwo, pokarm]* ④ (zgodzić się wykonać) to take on *[posadę, pracę, stanowisko]*; ~**ąć zobowiązanie** to take on an obligation; **kelner** ~**ął od nas zamówienie** the waiter took our order ⑤ (wysłuchać) to accept *[raport, gratulacje]* ⑥ (zapożyczyć) to adopt *[poglądy, zwyczaje]* (**od kogoś** from sb) ⑦ (zareagować) to receive; **aktora** ~**ęto oklaskami** the actor was greeted with applause ⑧ (wziąć na siebie) to take on *[obowiązek, odpowiedzialność]* ⑨ (uczynić członkiem społeczności) to enrol, to enroll US *[uczniów, studentów]*; to admit *[pacjentów]*; ~**ąć kogoś do rodziny** to receive sb as a member of the family ⑩ (zatrudnić) to take in *[pracownika]*; **starać się o** ~**ęcie do pracy** to apply for a job ⑪ (ugościć) to receive *[gościa]* ⑫ (zgodzić się na rozmowę) to see *[interesanta]*; to receive *[delegację]*; ~**ąć kogoś lodowato** to give sb an icy welcome ⑬ *[lekarz, dentysta]* to see *[pacjenta]* ⑭ (zgodzić się zostać żoną) ~**ąć oświadczyny** to accept sb's proposal ⑮ (dać schronienie) to take in *[pogorzelców, uciekinierów]*; ~**ąć kogoś na nocleg** to put sb up ⑯ (założyć) to assume; **powszechnie** ~**muje się, że...** it is generally assumed that... ⑰ to receive *[komunię]*; ~**ąć chrzest** to be baptized; ~**ąć święcenia kapłańskie** to be ordained ⑱ Sport to catch *[podanie, piłkę]* ⑲ (przybrać) *[organizacja, osoba]* to take on *[nazwę, pseudonim]* ⑳ (zmienić) to assume *[kształt, barwę, formę]*

II przyjąć się — **przyjmować się** ① *[drzewo, roślina]* to take root ② (rozpowszechnić się) *[powiedzenie, moda, zwyczaj]* to catch on ③ *[przeszczep]* to take; **przeszczep nerki się nie** ~**ął** the kidney transplant was rejected

przy|jechać *pf* — **przy|jeżdżać** *impf vi* ① (przybyć) *[osoba, środek lokomocji]* to arrive; ~**jechać autobusem/pociągiem** to come a. arrive by bus/train; ~**jechać do Polski** to come to Poland; ~**jechać na dworzec** to arrive at the station; ~**jechać do kogoś w odwiedziny** a. **z wizytą** to come to see sb ② (stawić się) to come; ~**jeżdżaj natychmiast** come at once a. immediately

przyjemnie *adv. grad.* pleasantly; ~ **urządzone mieszkanie** a pleasantly furnished flat; ~ **spędzić urlop** to have a nice holiday

przyjemnoś|ć *f* pleasure; **sprawić komuś** ~**ć** to give sb pleasure; **robić coś dla** ~**ci** to do sth for pleasure; **z** ~**cią** with pleasure; **znajdować** ~**ć w czymś** to find pleasure in sth; **mieć** ~**ć znać/poznać kogoś** to have the pleasure of knowing/meeting sb; **cała** ~**ć po mojej stronie** the pleasure's all mine; **średnia** a. **wątpliwa** ~**ć** pot. a dubious pleasure

przyjemn|y *adi. grad.* pleasant; ~**y dla oka/ucha** pleasing to the eye/ear; **materiał** ~**y w dotyku** a material pleasant to the touch

■ **łączyć** ~**e z pożytecznym** to combine business with pleasure

przyjeżdżać *impf* → **przyjechać**

przyję|cie *n* ① (spotkanie towarzyskie) reception; **oficjalne** ~**cie** an official reception; **kameralne** ~**cie** a small party; ~**cie urodzinowe** a birthday party; ~**cie weselne** a wedding reception; **zaprosić kogoś na** ~**cie** to invite sb to a party a. reception ② (reakcja) reception; **spotkać się z gorącym** ~**ciem** *[osoba]* to get a warm welcome; *[film, przedstawienie, książka]* to receive a warm reception

przyjmować *impf* → **przyjąć**

przy|jrzeć się, **przy|glądnąć się** *pf* — **przy|glądać się** *impf v refl.* to observe; ~**jrzyj się uważnie, jak ja to robię** observe closely how I do it; ~**glądać sobie w lustrze** to examine oneself in the mirror

przy|jść *pf* — **przy|chodzić** *impf vi* ① (idąc przybyć) to come; ~**jść do domu** to come home; ~**jść (do kogoś) w odwiedziny** to come to see sb; ~**jść na spotkanie** to come to a meeting ② pot. (jadąc przybyć) to arrive; **pociąg** ~**szedł o czasie** the train arrived a. came in on time ③ pot. *[list, pieniądze]* to come ④ pot. (nastąpić) *[lato, chwila, termin]* to come; ~**szła noc** night came; ~**jdzie kolej na ciebie** your turn will come; ~**szła moda na kapelusze** hats came into fashion ⑤ pot. (powstać w umyśle) ~**szedł mi do głowy pewien pomysł** an idea came to my mind, I had

an idea; ~szła jej ochota na tańce suddenly she
felt like dancing 6 (o umiejętnościach, czynnościach) to
come; nauka ~chodzi mu łatwo studying comes
easy to him pot. 7 (osiągnąć korzyść) co ci z tego
~jdzie? what good will it do you?
■ ~jść na gotowe to come when everything is
ready; ~jść do siebie a. sił a. zdrowia to recover;
łatwo ~szło, łatwo poszło przysł. easy come,
easy go
przykaza|nie n commandment; **dziesięcioro
~ń** the Ten Commandments
przykle|ić pf — **przykle|jać** impf [] vt 1 (klejem)
to stick; ~ić znaczek na kopertę to stick a stamp
on an envelope; ~ić ogłoszenie/plakat to stick
up a notice/poster; ~ić obtłuczone uszko do
filiżanki to glue a broken handle to a cup 2 pot.
~ił czoło do szyby he pressed his forehead
against the window pane; uciekinierzy leżeli
~jeni do ziemi the fugitives lay flat on the
ground
[] **przykleić się** — **przyklejać się** [] (przywrzeć) to
stick 2 pot. to cling; ~ił się do niej na cały
wieczór he clung to her the whole evening
przykła|d [] m example; być dla kogoś ~dem to
be an example to sb; brać z kogoś ~d to follow
sb's example; dawać dobry ~d to set a good
example; ukarać kogoś dla ~du to make an
example of sb; ~d architektury gotyckiej an
example of Gothic architecture; przytoczyć ~d
na coś to quote an example of sth
[] **na przykład** part. for example, for instance
przykładać impf → **przyłożyć**[1]
przykładow|y adi. 1 (ilustracyjny) demonstration
2 (wzorowy) model
przykrę|cić pf — **przykrę|cać** impf vt 1 (przy-
mocować) to screw [półkę, tabliczkę] (do czegoś to
sth); ~cić zamek do drzwi to screw a lock onto a
door 2 (zmniejszyć dopływ) to turn down [wodę, gaz]
przyk|ro [] adv. grad. unpleasantly; ~ro mu było,
że... he felt hurt that...
[] adv. ~ro mi z powodu twojej choroby I'm
sorry about your illness; zrobiło mi się ~ro, że ją
uraziłem I felt sorry that I had hurt her; tak mi
~ro I'm so sorry
przykroś|ć f 1 (niemiłe uczucie) distress; sprawić a.
zrobić komuś ~ć to hurt sb; z ~cią muszę
powiedzieć, że... I regret to say that... 2 (nieprzyjemny fakt, zdarzenie) unpleasantness; narazić kogoś
na ~ci to get sb into trouble; spotkała mnie ~ć
I had an unpleasant experience
przyk|ry adi. grad. unpleasant
przykry|ć pf — **przykry|wać** impf [] vt to cover;
~ć kogoś kocem to cover sb with a blanket
[] **przykryć się** — **przykrywać się** to cover
oneself; ~ć się ciepło to cover oneself up warmly
przykryw|ka f 1 (pokrywa) lid 2 przen. cover;
sklepik był tylko ~ką dla jego innej działal-

ności the shop was just a cover for his other
activities
przylaszcz|ka f Bot. hepatica
przylatywać impf → **przylecieć**
przyląd|ek m cape; (wydłużony) headland; (wysoki)
promontory; **Przylądek Horn** Cape Horn
przyl|ecieć pf — **przyl|atywać** impf vi 1 (przy-
być) [ptak] to fly in; [samolot] to arrive 2 (przybyć
samolotem) [osoba] to arrive (by plane) 3 pot. (przybiec)
to come running
przylega|ć impf vi 1 (przywierać) [części] to fit tight;
[włosy] to cling 2 (stykać się) to adjoin; **pokój
jadalny ~ł do kuchni** the dining room adjoined
the kitchen
przyleg|ły adi. [pokój, teren] adjoining
przylep|ić pf — **przylep|iać** impf [] vt 1 (klejem)
to stick [znaczek, naklejkę] 2 pot., przen. ~ić nos do
szyby to press one's nose to the pane
[] **przylepić się** — **przylepiać się** 1 (przykleić się)
to stick 2 (tulić się) to cling; **dziecko ~ło się do
matki** the child clung to his/her mother
przylep|iec m sticking plaster
przylo|t m arrival; **hala ~tów** the arrival(s) hall
przyłap|ać pf — **przyłap|ywać** impf [] vt to
catch [sb] out; ~ać kogoś na kłamstwie to catch
sb lying; ~ać kogoś na gorącym uczynku to
catch sb red-handed a. in the act
[] **przyłapać się** — **przyłapywać się** to find
oneself (na czymś doing sth)
przyłącz|yć pf — **przyłącz|ać** impf [] vt to hitch
[wagon] (do czegoś to sth); to incorporate [teryto-
rium, organizację] (do czegoś into sth); to connect
[dom, dzielnicę] (do czegoś to sth); to link
[computer, urządzenie] (do czegoś to a. up with sth)
[] **przyłączyć się** — **przyłączać się** (dołączyć) to
join (do kogoś/czegoś sb/sth); to attach oneself
(do kogoś/czegoś to sb/sth); ~yć się do
towarzystwa to join the company; ~yć się do
rozmowy to join in a conversation
przy|łożyć[1] pf — **przy|kładać** impf [] vt
1 (umieścić) to apply [kompres] (na coś to sth); to
put [nóż] (do czegoś to sth); ~łożyć ucho do
drzwi to put an ear to the door 2 (obciążyć, przygnieść)
to weigh down
[] **przyłożyć się** — **przykładać się** 1 (włożyć dużo
wysiłku) to apply oneself (do czegoś to sth);
~kładać się do nauki/pracy to study/work hard
2 pot. (przespać się) to get one's head down pot.
■ **ja do tego ręki nie ~łożę!** I don't want to
have anything to do with it!; ~kładać do czegoś
wagę to attach importance to sth
przył|ożyć[2] impf vi pot. ~ożyć komuś (uderzyć) to
lay into sb pot.; **ostro ~ożył miejscowej władzy**
he came down on the local authorities like a ton of
bricks pot.
przymiar|ka f 1 fitting; **mieć ~kę u krawca** to
have a fitting (at the tailor's/dressmaker's) 2 przen.

dress rehearsal przen. (**przed czymś** for a. before sth); ~**ka przed rozruchem nowej linii produkcyjnej** a trial run of a new production line
przymierzać *impf* → **przymierzyć**
przymierzal|nia *f* fitting room, changing room US
przymierz|e *n* (sojusz) alliance (**z kimś/czymś** with sb/sth); **wejść w ~e z kimś** to enter into an alliance with sb
przymierz|yć *pf* — **przymierz|ać** *impf* ⊓ *vt* (włożyć) to try on *[buty, palto]*
⊔ **przymierzyć się** — **przymierzać się** ⊡ (przygotować się) to get ready (**do zrobienia czegoś** to do sth) ⊡ pot. (rozważyć) to think (**do czegoś/do zrobienia czegoś** of a. about sth/doing sth)
przymiotnik *m* adjective
przym|knąć *pf* — **przym|ykać** *impf* ⊓ *vt* ⊡ to push [sth] to *[drzwi, okno]*; ~**knąć powieki** a. **oczy** to close one's eyes ⊡ pot. (uwięzić) to put [sb] behind bars pot.
⊔ **przymknąć się** — **przymykać się** (zamknąć się lekko) *[drzwi, okno]* to close; **oczy mu się ~ykały ze zmęczenia** he was so tired that he couldn't keep his eyes open
⊒ **przymknąć się** pot. (zamilknąć) to pipe down pot.
■ ~**ykać na coś oczy** a. **oko** to turn a blind eye to sth
przymoc|ować *pf* — **przymoc|owywać** *impf vt* to attach; (gwoździami) to nail *[tablicę, listwę]* (**do czegoś** to sth); (kołkami) to peg down *[linkę, namiot]*; ~**ować coś sznurkiem** to fasten sth with a piece of string
przymroz|ek *m* slight frost
przymruż|yć *pf* — **przymruż|ać** *impf vt* ~**yć oczy** a. **powieki** to squint; ~**ył porozumiewawczo jedno oko** he winked conspiratorially
■ **z** ~**eniem oka** (pobłażliwie) indulgently; (żartobliwie) (with) tongue in cheek; (z powątpiewaniem) with a pinch of salt
przymus *m* ⊡ (presja) compulsion (**robienia czegoś** to do sth); (konieczność) obligation (**robienia czegoś** to do sth); ~ **wewnętrzny** an inner compulsion; **pod** ~**em** under duress; **zrobić coś bez** ~**u** to do sth of one's own free will; **stosować wobec kogoś** ~ to bring pressure to bear on sb; **nie ma** ~**u!** it's a free country! ⊡ (prawny) constraints; **środki** ~**u** coercive measures
przymusow|y *adi.* (en)forced; ~**e lądowanie** a forced landing; ~**e roboty** forced labour
przymykać *impf* → **przymknąć**
przynajmniej *part.* at least; ~ **raz na tydzień** at least once a week; **mogliby** ~ **zadzwonić** they could at least phone; ~ **tyle mogę zrobić** it's the least I can do
przynę|ta *f* bait także przen.; **na** ~**tę** as (a) bait

przyn|ieść *pf* — **przyn|osić** *impf vt* ⊡ (dostarczyć) to bring; (pójść po coś i wrócić) to fetch *[rzecz]*; ~**ieść coś komuś** to bring/fetch sb sth; ~**ieś!** (do psa) fetch (it)!; **więcej szczegółów** ~**iosły gazety** more details were provided by the press ⊡ (spowodować) to bring *[korzyść, ulgę]*; to bring about *[straty]*; (dawać) to yield *[zysk]*; to give *[satisfaction]*; ~**ieść komuś pecha** to bring sb bad luck; **każdy dzień** ~**osi nowe zmiany** each day brings new changes
przypadać *impf* → **przypaść**
przypad|ek ⊓ *m* ⊡ (traf) coincidence; (los) chance; **przez** ~**ek** by chance, by accident; **dzięki** ~**kowi** by a lucky chance a. coincidence; **pozostawić wszystko** ~**kowi** a. **zdać się na** ~**ek** to leave everything to chance; ~**ek zrządził** a. **chciał, że...** as chance would have it... ⊡ (zdarzenie, sytuacja) case; **w jego** ~**ku** in his case; **w większości** ~**ków** in most cases a. instances; **w przeciwnym** ~**ku** otherwise; **w** ~**ku pożaru** in case of fire ⊒ (osoba) case; **ona jest ciężkim** ~**kiem** she's a difficult case ⊓ Med. case; **ciężki** ~**ek anoreksji** a serious case of anorexia ⊓ (gramatyczny) case; **odmiana przez** ~**ki** declension
⊔ **przypadkiem** *adv.* ⊡ (niespodziewanie) by chance, by accident; **natknąć się na kogoś/coś** ~**kiem** to stumble upon a. across sb/sth by chance; **spotkać kogoś** ~**kiem** to chance to meet sb; **znaleźć się gdzieś** ~**kiem** to happen to be somewhere ⊡ pot. (może, czasem) by any chance
przypadkow|y *adi.* *[śmierć]* accidental; *[odkrycie, znajomość]* chance; *[znajomy]* casual; *[miejsce, wybór]* random; *[charakter]* incidental; ~**e kontakty seksualne** casual a. promiscuous sex
przypal|ić *pf* — **przypal|ać** *impf vt* ⊡ (spalić) to burn *[obiad, patelnię]*; to scorch *[materiał, koszulę]*; to cauterize *[ranę]* (**czymś** with sth) ⊡ (zapalić) to light *[papierosa]*
przypa|ść *pf* — **przypa|dać** *impf vi* ⊡ (przywrzeć) to press oneself (**do czegoś** against sth); ~**ść do ziemi** to throw oneself to the ground ⊡ (rzucić się, doskoczyć) to throw oneself (**do kogoś** at sb) ⊒ (zdarzyć się, wypaść) to fall; **rok temu Wigilia** ~**dła w sobotę** last year Christmas Eve fell on a Saturday ⊓ (należeć się) *[nagroda, tytuł, zwycięstwo]* to fall (**komuś** to sb); ~**dł mu w spadku dom z ogrodem** he inherited a house with a garden
■ **od razu** ~**dli sobie do gustu** they took an immediate liking to each other
przypat|rzyć się, przypat|rzeć się *pf* — **przypat|rywać się** *impf v refl.* ⊡ (przyjrzeć się) to eye; ~**rywać się komuś/czemuś badawczo** a. **pilnie** to scrutinize sb/sth; **odsunęła się, żeby mu się lepiej** ~**rzeć** she drew back to get a better look at him ⊡ (zbadać) to scrutinize *[dokumentowi, planom]*; to look at *[życiu, sytuacji, problemowi]*

przyp|iąć *pf* — **przyp|inać** *impf* **I** *vt* to attach; (szpilką, pinezką) to pin; (paskiem) to strap; ~**iąć komuś etykietkę złodzieja** przen. to label sb a thief

II **przypiąć się** — **przypinać się** [1] (zapiąć pasy) to fasten one's seat belt [2] pot. (przyczepić się) ~**iąć się do kogoś** to latch on to sb; **ona, jak się do czegoś** ~**nie, to łatwo nie zrezygnuje** once she sets her mind on sth, she doesn't give up easily

■ **wyglądać ni** ~**iął, ni przyłatał** to look completely out of place

przypie|c *pf* — **przypie|kać** *impf* **I** *vt* [1] (upiec) to toast *[chleb, ser]*; **za bardzo** ~**kłeś to mięso** you've overcooked the meat [2] (oparzyć) to burn; (o słońcu) to scorch

II *vi* (grzać) *[słońce]* to blaze (down)

przypinać *impf* → **przypiąć**

przypis *m* note; (na dole strony) footnote; (na końcu tekstu) endnote; **antologia zaopatrzona w** ~**y** an annotated anthology

przypły|nąć *pf* — **przypły|wać** *impf vi* [1] *[statek, pasażer]* to arrive; ~**nąć do brzegu** to reach the shore; ~**nąć do kogoś** *[pływak, delfin]* to swim up to sb; **statek** ~**nął do portu** the ship put in to port [2] przen. *[dźwięk, dym]* to waft a. drift up

przypływ *m* [1] (przybór wody) rising tide; (szczytowy moment) high tide; **w czasie** ~**u** at high tide; **był** ~ the tide was in [2] (napłynięcie) surge także przen.; **zrobić coś w** ~**ie wściekłości** to do sth in a fit of rage

przypływać *impf* → **przypłynąć**

przypomina|ć[1] *impf vt* (być podobnym) to resemble; (z wyglądu) to look like; **z profilu** ~**ł ojca** in profile he looked like his father; **on mi** ~ **mojego brata** he reminds me of my brother; **czy to ci coś** ~? does it remind you of anything? pot.; **w niczym nie** ~**ć czegoś** to bear no resemblance to sth

przypom|nieć *pf* — **przypom|inać** *impf* **I** *vt* to remind; ~**nieć komuś coś** to remind sb of sth; ~**nieć komuś, że...** to remind sb (that)...; ~**nij mi, żebym kupił gazetę** remind me to buy a newspaper; **to mi** ~**ina moją młodość** it brings back my childhood (days); ~**inam o jutrzejszej klasówce** don't forget about tomorrow's test

II **przypomnieć sobie** — **przypominać sobie** to remember; ~**niał sobie, że nie zamknął drzwi** he realized he'd forgotten to lock the door; **nie mogłem sobie** ~**nieć, jak ma na imię** I couldn't recollect his/her name; ~**nij sobie, jak to było** try to remember how it happened; **nie** ~**inam sobie** I don't a. can't remember

III **przypomnieć się** — **przypominać się** pot. **nagle mu się coś** ~**niało** he suddenly remembered something; **właśnie mi się** ~**niało, że...** I've just remembered that...

przypowieś|ć *f* parable

przypraw|a *f* Kulin. seasoning; ~**y korzenne** spices; ~**y ziołowe** herbs

przypraw|ić *pf* — **przypraw|iać** *impf vt* [1] Kulin. to season; ~**ić zupę** to season the soup; ~**ić coś na ostro** to make sth spicy; **delikatnie** ~**ione** lightly seasoned [2] (przyczepić) ~**ić sobie brodę** to put on a false beard [3] (powodować) ~**iać kogoś o niestrawność** to give sb indigestion; ~**iać kogoś o zawrót głowy** to make sb's head spin; **to mnie** ~**ia o mdłości** it makes me sick także przen.

przyprowa|dzić *pf* — **przyprowa|dzać** *impf vt* to bring *[osobę, samochód]*; ~**dź (ze sobą) znajomych** bring your friends along

przypuszczać *impf* → **przypuścić**

przypuszcze|nie *n* conjecture; **to tylko** ~**nia** it's sheer conjecture; **wyraził** ~**nie, że...** he speculated that...

przypu|ścić *pf* — **przypu|szczać** *impf* **I** *vt* [1] (dopuścić) to let [sb] (come) near [2] (przeprowadzić) ~**ścić atak** to launch an attack także przen.

II *vi* to suppose; **kto by** ~**szczał, że...** who would've supposed a. expected (that)...; ~**śćmy, że się nie zgodzi** suppose he refuses; ~**szczam, że...** I imagine (that)...; **jest gorzej, niż** ~**szczałem** it's worse than I imagined a. expected; ~**szcza się, że...** it is believed that...

przyro|da *f* [1] (natura) nature; ~**da żywa** flora and fauna; **zjawiska** ~**dy** natural phenomena; **ochrona** ~**dy** nature conservation [2] Szkol. natural science

przyrodni *adi.* ~ **brat/**~**a siostra** a stepbrother/stepsister

przyrodnicz|y *adi. [nauki]* natural; *[książka, film]* nature; *[muzeum]* natural history

przyrodni|k *m*, ~**czka** *f* (specjalista) naturalist; (nauczyciel) biology teacher

przyro|st *m* growth; ~**st ludności** population growth; ~**st produkcji** an increase in production; ~**st naturalny** the birth rate

przyrzą|d *m* appliance, device; (pomiarowy) instrument

przyrzą|dzić *pf* — **przyrzą|dzać** *impf vt* to prepare *[posiłek, napój]*

przyrze|c *pf* — **przyrzek|ać** *impf vt* to promise; (uroczyście) to pledge; ~**kł zająć się tą sprawą** he promised to see to the matter; ~**knij (mi), że więcej tam nie pójdziesz** promise (me) you won't go there again; ~**kła sobie, że już nigdy nie zaufa żadnemu mężczyźnie** she swore she'd never trust a man again

przyrzecze|nie *n* pledge; **dotrzymać** ~**nia** to keep one's pledge a. promise

przyrzekać *impf* → **przyrzec**

przysia|d *m* knee bend; **wstać z** ~**du** to rise from a squatting position

przysiadać *impf* → **przysiąść**

przysi|ąc *pf* — **przysi|ęgać** *impf vt* [1] (obiecać) to promise; (uroczyście) to swear; ~**ęgam, że nikomu nie powiem** I swear I won't tell anybody; ~**ągł jej opiekować się dziećmi** he promised her that he'd take care of the children [2] (zapewnić) to swear; ~**ęgać na Biblię** to swear on the Bible; **gotów był** ~**ąc, że kiedyś już tu był** he could have sworn he'd been there before

przysi|ąść *pf* — **przysi|adać** *impf* [I] *vt* (siadając przygnieść) to sit on

[II] *vi* [1] (usiąść) *[osoba]* to sit down; *[ptak]* to perch; *[motyl, ważka]* to land; ~**adł na brzegu ławeczki** he perched (himself) on the edge of the bench [2] (przykucnąć) *[osoba]* to squat (on one's haunches); *[zwierzę]* to sit (on one's haunches); ~**ąść z wrażenia** przen. to be dumbfounded

[III] **przysiąść się** — **przysiadać się** (przyłączyć się) ~**ąść się do kogoś** to join sb (at the table); **czy mogę się** ~**ąść?** can I join you?

przysi|ęga *f* oath; (w wojsku) swearing-in (ceremony); ~**ęga małżeńska** marriage a. wedding vows; ~**ęga na wierność** an oath of allegiance; **złamać** ~**ęgę** to break one's oath; **zeznawać pod** ~**ęgą** to testify under oath

przysięgać *impf* → **przysiąc**

przysięg|ły *adi.* **sędzia** ~**ły** a member of the jury; **tłumacz** ~**ły** a certified translator; **ława** ~**łych** the jury

przy|słać *pf* — **przy|syłać** *impf vt* to send (in) *[paczkę, pieniądze]*; ~**słać komuś pocztówkę** to send sb a postcard; ~**ślij go, jak tylko się zjawi** send him in as soon as he comes

przysłon|a *f* (otwór) aperture; (urządzenie) diaphragm; **ustawić** ~**ę** to adjust the aperture

przysł|owie *n* proverb

przysłów|ek *m* adverb

przysłu|ga *f* favour GB, favor US; **wyświadczyć komuś** ~**gę** to do sb a favour; **poprosić kogoś o** ~**gę** to ask sb for a favour

■ **wyświadczyć komuś niedźwiedzią** ~**gę** to do sb more harm than good

przysług|iwać *impf vi* ~**uje nam dzień urlopu** we are entitled to a day off; ~**uje mu prawo mianowania ambasadorów** he has the right to appoint ambassadors; **skorzystać z** ~**ującego komuś prawa** to exercise one's right; **to jej w pełni** ~**uje** she fully deserves it

przysłuż|yć się *pf v refl.* to render a service (**komuś/czemuś** to sb/sth)

przysmak *m* delicacy

przysparzać *impf* → **przysporzyć**

przyspieszać → **przyśpieszyć**

przyspiesze|nie *n* [1] (w fizyce) acceleration; **jednostka** ~**nia** a unit of acceleration [2] (szybsze tempo) acceleration; **nabrać** ~**nia** *[narracja, akcja]* to gain momentum

przyspieszony → **przyśpieszony**

przysta|ć¹ *pf* — **przysta|wać¹** *impf vi* [1] (zgodzić się) to agree; ~**ć na coś** to agree a. consent to sth; ~**ć na czyjeś warunki** to agree to sb's conditions; ~**ć na czyjąś propozycję** to accept sb's offer [2] (przystąpić) to join (**do czegoś** sth)

przyst|ać² *pf v imp.* książk. [1] (należy) **jak na sportowca** ~**ało** as befits a sportsman [2] (wypada) **to nie** ~**oi księżniczce** it's unbecoming of a princess; **nie** ~**oi ci kłamstwo** it ill befits you to lie książk.

przysta|nąć *pf* — **przysta|wać²** *impf vi* (zatrzymać się) to stop; **autobus często** ~**wał** the bus made frequent stops

przystan|ek *m* [1] (stacja) stop; ~**ek autobusowy** a bus stop; ~**ek końcowy** a terminus; ~**ek na żądanie** a request stop [2] (przerwa) stop; **po drodze robili częste** ~**ki** they made frequent stops along the way

przysta|ń *f* [1] harbour, harbor US; (dla jachtów) marina; ~**ń rybacka** a fishing harbour [2] przen. (safe) haven

przystawać¹ *impf* → **przystać¹**

przystawać² *impf* → **przystanąć**

przysta|wać³ *impf vi* (odpowiadać) to fit in; **nie** ~**wać do kogoś/czegoś** not fit in with sb/sth

przystaw|ić *pf* — **przystaw|iać** *impf vt* [1] (przysunąć) ~**ić drabinę do okna** to put a ladder up to a window; ~**ić bliżej krzesło** to draw up a chair [2] (przytknąć) to put; ~**ić komuś pistolet do skroni** to put a gun to sb's head; ~**ić pieczątkę na czymś** to stamp sth

przystaw|ka *f* [1] Kulin. appetizer [2] (końcówka) attachment

przyst|ąpić *pf* — **przyst|ępować** *impf vi* [1] (zabrać się) to set about; ~**ąpić do pracy nad czymś** to set about working on sth [2] (wziąć udział) to enter; ~**ąpić do konkursu** to enter a contest; ~**ąpić do rozmów** to enter into talks

przystępn|y *adi. grad.* [1] *[książka, język]* accessible; **przedstawić coś w** ~**y sposób** to present sth in an accessible way [2] *[osoba]* approachable [3] *[cena]* affordable

przystępować *impf* → **przystąpić**

przystojnia|k *m* pot. dish pot.

przystojn|y *adi. grad.* handsome

przystos|ować *pf* — **przystos|owywać** *impf* [I] *vt* to adapt; ~**owywać coś do czegoś** to adapt sth to sth; ~**ować coś do czyichś potrzeb** to adapt sth to suit sb's needs

[II] **przystosować się** — **przystosowywać się** *[osoba, zwierzę]* to adapt (**do czegoś** to sth); *[oczy]* to adjust (**do czegoś** to sth); **łatwo się** ~**owywać** to be adaptable

przystosowani|e *n* adaptation

przystosowywać *impf* → **przystosować**

przysu|nąć *pf* — **przysu|wać** *impf* [I] *vt* to move; ~**nąć sobie krzesło** to pull up a chair

II przysunąć się — przysuwać się to move close/closer (**do kogoś/czegoś** to sb/sth)

przysyłać *impf* → przysłać

przyszłoś|ć *f* [1] (okres) future; **w najbliższej/ niedalekiej** ~ci in the immediate/not too distant future; **plany na** ~ć plans for the future; **na** ~ć **bądź bardziej uprzejmy** be more polite in future; **samochód/komputer** ~ci the car/computer of the future; **przepowiadać komuś** ~ć to tell sb's fortune [2] (przyszłe powodzenie) future; **mieć przed sobą** ~ć to have a future; **wróżyć komuś wspaniałą** ~ć to predict a bright future for sb; **ludzie bez** ~ci people with no prospects; **ten zawód nie ma** ~ci there's no future in this kind of work

przysz|ły *adi.* [1] *[zięć, sukces, zarobki, czas]* future [2] (najbliższy) next; **w** ~**ły poniedziałek** next Monday; **w** ~**łym roku** next year

przyszy|ć *pf* — **przyszy|wać** *impf vt* to sew; ~ć **coś do czegoś** to sew sth on (to) sth

przyszyk|ować *pf* — **przyszyk|owywać** *impf* **I** *vt* to prepare; ~**ować coś do wysłania** to get sth ready for posting **II** przyszykować się — przyszykowywać się to get ready

przyszywać *impf* → przyszyć

przyśni|ć się *pf v refl.* ~ł **mi się wąż** I had a dream about a snake; ~**ło mi się, że...** I dreamt that...; **coś ci się** ~**ło!** *przen.* you're imagining things!

przyśpieszać *impf* → przyśpieszyć

przyśpieszenie → przyspieszenie

przyśpiesz|yć *pf* — **przyśpiesz|ać** *impf* **I** *vt* to speed up *[proces, rozwój]*; to precipitate *[kryzys, klęskę]*; to hasten *[rozstanie, moment]*; to bring forward *[ślub, wybory]*; ~**yć tempo reform** to increase the pace of reforms **II** *vi* [osoba, samochód] to speed up; [samochód] to accelerate; ~**yć kroku** to quicken one's pace

przytak|nąć *pf* — **przytak|iwać** *impf vi* to say yes; ~**nąć głową** to nod in assent; ~**nąć komuś** to agree with sb; **on zawsze wszystkim** ~**uje** he's a yes-man *pot.*

przytęp|ić *pf* — **przytęp|iać** *impf* **I** *vt* [1] (przytłumić) to dull *[słuch, pamięć]* [2] (stępić) to blunt *[nóż]* **II** przytępić się — przytępiać się [1] *[nóż]* to go blunt [2] *przen.* *[umysł]* to become dull; *[wzrok, pamięć]* to get worse

przytomnoś|ć *f* [1] (świadomość) consciousness; **stracić/odzyskać** ~ć to lose/regain consciousness [2] (bystrość) presence of mind; **miał na tyle** ~**ci umysłu, żeby...** he had sufficient presence of mind to...

przytomn|y *adi. grad.* [1] (trzeźwo myślący) clear-headed; (opanowany, czujny) alert; *[uwaga, komentarz]* astute [2] (świadomy) *[osoba]* conscious

przytraf|ić się *pf* — **przytraf|iać się** *impf v refl.* *[przygoda]* to happen (**komuś** to sb)

przytrza|snąć *pf* — **przytrza|skiwać** *impf vt* (przyciąć) to get [sth] caught *[płaszcz, sukienkę]*; ~**snąć komuś palce w drzwiach** to shut a. trap sb's fingers in the door

przytrzym|ać *pf* — **przytrzym|ywać** *impf vt* [1] (nie pozwolić odejść) to hold; ~**ać kogoś za rękaw** to hold sb by the sleeve [2] (zapobiec upadkowi, otwarciu, przesunięciu) to hold; ~**ać komuś drzwi** to hold the door open for sb [3] (przymocować) *[śruba, pręt]* to hold [4] (potrzymać) to hold; **możesz mi** ~**ać płaszcz?** can you hold my coat for me?

przytul|ić *pf* — **przytul|ać** *impf* **I** *vt* [1] (objąć) to hug; ~**ić kogoś mocno** to hug sb close; ~**iła dziecko mocno do piersi** she cuddled the baby close to her [2] (przyłożyć) to snuggle *[głowę, policzek]* **II** przytulić się — przytulać się to cuddle; ~**ić się do kogoś** to cuddle up to sb

przytuln|y *adi. grad.* *[mieszkanie, pokój]* cosy GB, cozy US

przytwier|dzić *pf* — **przytwier|dzać** *impf vt* [1] (przyczepić) to attach [2] *książk.* (potwierdzić) to confirm *[słowa, wersję]*; (zgodzić się) to agree; ~**dzić skinieniem głowy** to nod in assent

przytyć *pf vi* to put on weight

przytyk *m* taunt; **pozwalać sobie na złośliwe** ~**i pod czyimś adresem** to make hurtful remarks about sb

przywa|ra *f* vice

przywią|zać *pf* — **przywią|zywać**[1] *impf* **I** *vt* [1] (przymocować) to tie; ~**zać coś do czegoś** to tie sth (on) to sth [2] (emocjonalnie) ~**zał ją do siebie** she grew attached to him **II** przywiązać się — przywiązywać się [1] (przymocować się) to tie oneself (**do czegoś** to sth) [2] (emocjonalnie) to grow attached (**do kogoś/czegoś** to sb/sth)

przywiązani|e *n* attachment (**do kogoś/czegoś** to a. for sb/sth)

przywiązan|y *adi.* (emocjonalnie) attached; **być do kogoś/czegoś** ~**ym** to be attached to sb/sth

przywiązywać[1] *impf* → przywiązać

przywiąz|ywać[2] *impf vt* (przykładać) to attach *[wagę, rolę]* (**do czegoś** to sth)

przywidze|nie *n* delusion; **mieć** ~**nia** to be seeing things

przywierać *impf* → przywrzeć

przyw|ieźć *pf* — **przyw|ozić** *impf vt* to bring *[osobę, nowinę]*

przywilej *m* privilege; ~ **dyplomatyczny** diplomatic privilege; **nadać komuś** ~ to grant sb a privilege

przywita|ć *pf* **I** *vt* to greet *[osobę, wiadomość]*; ~**ć kogoś w progu** to greet sb at the door **II** przywitać się to say hello; ~**ć się z kimś** to say hello to sb; (oficjalnie) to greet sb; **~li się serdecznie** they greeted each other warmly

przywita|nie n greeting; **uśmiechnąć się do kogoś na ~nie** to greet sb with a smile

przywłaszcz|yć pf — **przywłaszcz|ać** impf vt **~yć sobie coś** to appropriate sth; (ukraść) to misappropriate sth

przywoł|ać pf — **przywoł|ywać** impf vt ☐ (zawołać) to summon ☐ (przypomnieć) to bring [sth] back *[dzieciństwo, czas]*; to evoke *[wspomnienia]* ☐ (powołać się) to refer to *[osobę]*; to quote *[przykład]* ■ **~ać kogoś do porządku** to take sb to task

przywozić impf → **przywieźć**

przywód|ca m, **~czyni** f leader; **duchowy ~ca** a spiritual leader

przywództw|o n leadership

przywr|ócić pf — **przywr|acać** impf vt ☐ (doprowadzić do poprzedniego stanu) to restore *[pokój, porządek, równowagę]*; to reintroduce *[prawo, przepis]*; **~ócić komuś wzrok/wiarę w siebie** to restore sb's sight/confidence; **~ócić coś do pierwotnego stanu** to restore sth to its original state ☐ (ponownie powołać) to restore; **~ócić kogoś do władzy** to restore sb to power; **~ócić kogoś do pracy** to give sb his/her job back

przyw|rzeć pf — **przyw|ierać** impf vi ☐ (przycisnąć się) *[osoba]* to cling; **~rzeć do kogoś/czegoś** to cling (on) to sb/sth; **~arł mocno do ściany** he pressed himself flat against the wall ☐ (przylepić się) *[ubranie, kasza]* to stick (**do czegoś** to sth)

przywyk|nąć pf — **przywyk|ać** impf vi to become accustomed (**do czegoś** to sth)

przyzna|ć pf — **przyzna|wać** impf **[]** vt ☐ (uznać za słuszne) to admit; **~ć komuś rację** to admit that sb is right; **~ł, że zawinił** he acknowledged that he was at fault; **~ję, że to wspaniały pomysł** I admit it's a great idea ☐ (udzielić) to award; **~ć komuś nagrodę/stypendium** to award sb a prize/scholarship; **~ć komuś zasiłek** to grant sb an allowance

[] **przyznać się** — **przyznawać się** to admit; **~m się, że jestem zmęczony** I'm tired, I admit; **pisał wiersze, ale się do tego nie ~wał** he wrote poetry, but he never admitted (to) it; **~ć/nie ~ć się do winy** to plead guilty/not guilty; **~ć się do popełnienia kradzieży** to own up to the theft

przyzwoi|ty adi. grad. ☐ (moralny) *[osoba, postępowanie]* decent; *[towarzystwo, zachowanie]* respectable ☐ (dostatni) *[mieszkanie, wynagrodzenie]* decent; *[ubranie]* proper

przyzwycza|ić pf — **przyzwycza|jać** impf **[]** vt to accustom; **~ić kogoś do czegoś/robienia czegoś** to accustom sb to sth/doing sth

[] **przyzwyczaić się** — **przyzwyczajać się** to get a. become used (**do czegoś** to sth); to grow a. become accustomed (**do czegoś** to sth); **~ić się do kogoś** to get used to sb

przyzwyczaje|nie n habit; **siła ~nia** force of habit; **robić coś z ~nia** to do sth out of a. from habit

pseudonim /psew'dɔɲim/ m pseudonym; **~ literacki** a pen name; **~ sceniczny** a stage name

psikus m prank

pso|cić impf vi to be up to mischief

pso|ta f prank

pstrąg m trout

pstryk|nąć pf — **pstryk|ać** impf pot. **[]** vt to snap; **~ać zdjęcia** to take photos

[] vi ☐ (nacisnąć) to flick *[przycisk]* ☐ (wydać dźwięk) *[zapalniczka, zamek]* to click ☐ (przytknąć) to flick *[pestką, grochem]*; **~kać palcami** to snap one's fingers

psu|ć impf **[]** vt ☐ (niszczyć) to damage *[maszynę, urządzenie]* ☐ (uszkadzać) to ruin *[oczy, zdrowie]* ☐ (pogarszać) to spoil *[przyjemność, zabawę]*; **~ć komuś opinię** to ruin sb's reputation ☐ (rozpieszczać) to spoil *[dziecko]*

[] **psuć się** ☐ (niszczyć się) *[samochód, urządzenie]* to break down ☐ (gnić) *[owoce]* to rot; *[mięso]* to go bad ☐ (uszkadzać się) *[wzrok, zdrowie]* to deteriorate; *[zęby]* to decay ☐ (pogarszać się) *[pogoda, stosunki]* to deteriorate

psychiat|ra m psychiatrist

psychiatri|a f psychiatry

psychiatryczn|y adi. psychiatric

psychiczn|y [] adi. ☐ *[rozwój, stan]* psychological; *[blokada, zdrowie]* mental; **uraz ~y** a trauma ☐ pot. (o osobie) mental pot.

[] **psychiczn|y** m, **~a** f pot. head case pot.

psychi|ka f psyche; **~ka ludzka** the human psyche; **~ka dziecka/przestępcy** the mentality of a child/criminal

psychoanality|k m, **~czka** f psychoanalyst

psychoanaliz|a f psychoanalysis

psycholo|g m psychologist

psychologi|a f psychology

psychologiczn|y adi. psychological; **wojna ~a** psychological warfare

psychoz|a f ☐ Med. psychosis ☐ przen. scare; **~a strachu** mass fear

pszczelarstw|o n bee-keeping

pszczelarz m bee-keeper

pszcz|oła f bee; **~oła miodna** a honey bee; **~oła robotnica** a worker bee; **rój ~ół** a swarm of bees

pszenic|a f wheat; **~a jara/ozima** spring/winter wheat

ptactw|o n fowl; (stado ptaków) birds; **~o domowe** domestic fowl; **~o łowne** game birds

ptak m bird; **~i dzikie/hodowlane** a. **domowe** wild/domestic birds; **ostoja/rezerwat ~ów** a bird sanctuary; **sezonowe wędrówki ~ów** seasonal bird migration; **wolny jak ~** (as) free as a bird; **~i drapieżne** birds of prey; **~i przelotne** a. **węd-**

rowne migratory birds, birds of passage; **rajski** ~ bird of paradise

ptasz|ek *m* (znak w kształcie litery V) tick, check US

■ **ranny** ~**ek** *żart.* an early bird a. riser

ptysiow|y *adi.* **ciasto** ~**e** puff a. choux pastry

pty|ś *m* pastry puff; ~**ś z kremem** a cream puff

publicy|sta *m*, ~**stka** *f* columnist

publicystyczn|y *adi.* current affairs

publicysty|ka *f* journalism; ~**ka społeczna/ polityczna** (piśmiennictwo) articles on social/political topics; (w radiu, telewizji) programmes on social/ political topics

publicznie *adv.* [ogłosić, oświadczyć, pochwalić] publicly; [pokazywać się, występować] in public

publicznoś|ć *f* the public; (w kinie, teatrze) audience; ~**ć teatralna** the theatre-going public; **żywo reagująca** ~**ć** a lively audience; ~**ć zgroma-dzona w studiu** a studio audience; **galeria dla** ~**ci** a public gallery

publiczn|y *adi.* ① (dotyczący ogółu) [interes, sektor, własność, biblioteka, toaleta] public; **dobro** ~**e** the common good; **miejsce** ~**e** a public place; **zakłócenie porządku** ~**ego** a breach a. disturb-ance of the peace; **roboty** ~**e** public works; **tajemnica** ~**a** an open secret; **wydatki na cele** ~**e** public expenditure; **oddać budynek do użytku** ~**ego** to open a building to the general public ② (jawny) [wystąpienie, egzekucja, spowiedź] public; **wystawić obraz na widok** ~**y** to show a painting to the public

publikacj|a *f* ① publication; **przygotować coś do** ~**i** to prepare sth for publication ② (tekst) publication; ~**a naukowa** an academic publi-cation

publik|ować *impf vt* to publish

puch *m* ① (pióra) down; **miękki jak** ~ (as) soft as down ② (meszek) down; ~ **na policzkach** down on sb's cheeks; ~ **ostu** thistledown ③ (śnieg) powdery snow

puchacz *m* eagle owl

pucha|r *m* ① (naczynie) cup; **spełnić** a. **wypić** ~**r za młodą parę** to drink a toast to the bride and groom ② (nagroda) cup; ~**r przechodni** a challenge cup; **zdobyć** ~**r w pływaniu** to win a cup for swimming ③ (zawody) cup competition a. contest; **Puchar Europejski** the European Cup

puch|nąć *impf vi* [noga, twarz] to swell (up); [powieki, oczy] to puff up

■ **głowa mi od tego wszystkiego** ~**nie** (z powodu kłopotów) I'm at my wit's end

puchow|y *adi.* down; **kołdra** ~**a** an eiderdown

pucołowa|ty *adi.* chubby

pud|el *m* poodle

pudeł|ko *n* (pojemnik) box; (blaszany) tin; (kartonowy) carton; (plastikowy) tub; (okrągły) pot; ~**ko czekola-dek** a box of chocolates; ~**ko na lekarstwa**

a pillbox; ~**ko po butach** an old shoebox; ~**ko zapałek** a matchbox

pud|er *m* powder; ~**er kosmetyczny** face pow-der; ~**er w kremie** foundation cream

pudernicz|ka *f* (powder) compact

pud|ło[1] *n* ① (pojemnik) box; (metalowe) tin; (kartonowe) carton ② (obudowa) case; ~**ło rezonansowe** sound-box ③ pot. (więzienie) slammer pot.

pud|ło[2] *n* pot. ① (niecelny strzał) miss ② pot. (niepowodzenie) boob pot.

■ **bez** ~**ła** pot. (bezbłędnie) [zgadnąć] spot on pot.; (bez. zakłóceń) [pracować, funkcjonować] without a hitch

pudł|ować *impf vi* pot. to miss (the target), to be (way) off the mark

pudr|ować *impf vt* to powder; ~**ować (sobie) nos** to powder one's nose

puenta → **pointa**

puk|nąć *pf* — **puk|ać** *impf vi* ① (uderzyć) to knock; (mocniej) to rap; ~**ać do drzwi** to knock on the door ② pot. (strzelać) to fire (**do kogoś/czegoś** at sb/sth); (niecelnie, dla zabawy) to take a potshot (**do kogoś/ czegoś** at sb/sth) ③ pot. (zderzyć się) [samochód] to hit (**w coś** sth)

■ ~**nij się w czoło** a. **głowę** a. **łeb** pot.! you must be mad! pot.

pul|a *f* ① (mieszkań, środków finansowych, nagród) pool; (materiałów, towarów) quota ② (stawka) stakes; **podwoić** ~**ę** to double the stakes ③ (w grze w karty) hand; **rozegrać** ~**ę** (w bilard) to play a game

pulchn|y *adi. grad.* ① [ciasto] spongy; [gleba] light ② [osoba, palce] podgy; [twarz] chubby

pulowe|r *m* pullover

pulpe|t *m* ① kulin. meatball ② pot. (o osobie) roly-poly pot.

pulpi|t *m* ① (do nut) music stand; ~**t dyrygencki** the conductor's podium ② (do pisania) desktop; (do czytania) bookrest; (w sali wykładowej, kościele) lectern; ~**t sterowniczy** a control panel

puls *m* ① (tętno) pulse; **zbadać komuś** ~ to take a. check sb's pulse ② przen. tempo

■ **trzymać rękę na** ~**ie** to have one's finger on the pulse (**czegoś** of sth)

puls|ować *impf vi* ① Med. to pulse; **krew** ~**owała mu w skroniach** the blood was pounding in his temples; ~**ujący ból** a throbbing pain ② przen. to throb; **miasto** ~**owało życiem** the town was throbbing with life ③ [gwiazda, światło] to pulsate

pułap *m* ceiling także przen.; ~ **płac** the wage ceiling

pułap|ka *f* trap także przen.; **zakładać** a. **zastawiać** ~**kę na coś** to set a. lay a trap for sth; **wpaść w** ~**kę** to fall into a trap; **pytanie okazało się** ~**ką** it proved to be a trick question

pułk *m* regiment

pułkownik *m* colonel

pum|a *f* puma

pumeks *m* pumice (stone)

pumpernik|iel *m* pumpernickel

punk|t [] *m* [1] (kropka) dot; **ciemny** ~t **na horyzoncie** a dark spot on the horizon [2] (miejsce) point; **najdalej położony** ~t the furthest point; ~t, **z którego nie ma powrotu** a point of no return; **mieszkamy w dobrym** ~cie we live in a good spot [3] (placówka) post; ~t **sanitarny** a first-aid post; ~t **apteczny** a dispensary; ~t **graniczny** a border post a. point; ~t **usługowy** a repair shop [4] (pozycja) post; ~t **obserwacyjny** an observation-post a. point; ~t **dowodzenia** a command post [5] (część tekstu) paragraph; (w wyliczeniach) item; (w aktach prawnych) clause [6] (element) point; **najważniejsze** ~ty **zagadnienia** the main points of the problem; ~t **kulminacyjny** the climax [7] (programu) item [8] (jednostka w grach) point; ~t **karny** a penalty point; **wygrać na** ~ty to win on points [] *part.* pot. (punktualnie) on the dot pot.
■ ~t **widzenia** a point of view; ~t **wyjścia czegoś** the point of departure for sth; ~t **zwrotny** a turning point; **czyjś mocny/słaby** ~t sb's strong/weak point; **utknąć w martwym** ~cie to come to a standstill a. an impasse

punktacj|a *f* [1] (zasady kwalifikowania) scoring [2] (suma uzyskanych punktów) score; ~a **zespołowa** the team score

punkt|ować *impf vt* [1] (przyznawać punkty) to award points to *[zawodników]* [2] (przedstawiać w punktach) to itemize *[zagadnienia]* [3] (podkreślać) to highlight

punktualnie *adv.* punctually; **pociąg przyjechał** ~ the train arrived on time; ~ **o szóstej** at precisely six o'clock

punktualnoś|ć *f* punctuality

punktualn|y *adi. grad.* punctual

pup|a *f* pot. bottom; behind pot.

pupil *m* favourite

purpu|ra *f* crimson

purpurow|y *adi. grad.* purple

pustak *m* hollow brick

pustelni|a *f* hermitage

pustelni|k *m* hermit

pust|ka *f* emptiness także przen.; **mieć** ~ki **w szafie/spiżarni** to have nothing to wear/to eat; **mam kompletną** ~kę **w głowie** my mind is a total blank; **świecić** ~kami to be practically deserted

pustkowi|e *n* wilderness

pu|sto *adv. grad.* empty; **w mieszkaniu było pusto** the flat was empty; **mieć pusto w głowie** to be empty-headed a. frivolous

pustuł|ka *f* kestrel

pu|sty *adi.* [1] (nienapełniony) empty; (niezajęty) vacant; *[przestrzeń, kartka]* blank [2] (niepoważny) *[chłopak, dziewczyna]* empty-headed; **pusta ciekawość** idle curiosity
■ **z pustego i Salomon nie naleje** przysł. ≈ you cannot get blood from a stone

pusty|nia *f* desert; ~nia **kulturalna** przen. a cultural backwater

puszcz|a *f* forest
■ **głos wołającego na** ~y a voice crying in the wilderness

puszczać *impf* → **puścić**

puszczyk *m* tawny a. brown owl

pusz|ek *m* [1] (u niemowląt, ptaków, ssaków) fluff [2] (do pudrowania) (powder) puff

pusz|ka *f* [1] (opakowanie) can, tin GB; ~ka **piwa** a can of beer; **owoce w** ~ce tinned a. canned fruit; ~ka **na herbatę** a tea caddy; ~ka **na datki** a collection box [2] (w ścianie) cable box
■ ~ka **Pandory** Pandora's box

puszy|sty *adi.* [1] *[futro, włosy]* fluffy; ~sty **ogon** a bushy tail; ~sty **kotek** a furry kitten [2] (tęgi) plump; **sklep dla** ~stych an outsize shop

pu|ścić *pf* — **pu|szczać** *impf* [] *vt* [1] (przestać trzymać) to let go; **puścić drzwi** to let go of the door [2] (spowodować przemieszczenie) **puszczać fajerwerki** to let off fireworks; **puszczać bańki mydlane** to blow soap bubbles; **puszczać latawca** to fly a kite [3] (pozwolić wyjść) **puszczać kogoś przodem** to let sb go first; **puścić kogoś na wolność** to set sb free; **puszczono go za kaucją** he was released on bail; **puszczać w obieg** to circulate; **puszczać plotki** przen. to spread gossip [4] (pozwolić wejść) to let in; **nie puszczał nikogo za próg** he didn't let anybody in [5] (wydzielać) to release; **drzewa puszczają listki** the trees are sprouting new leaves; **puścić bąka** posp. to fart posp. [6] (uruchomić) to put on; **puść tę nową płytę** put that new record on
[] *vi* [1] (ustąpić pod naciskiem) **drzwi puściły** the door gave; **oczko puściło ci w pończosze** your stocking has laddered; **szwy puściły w spódnicy** the skirt came apart at the seams [2] (tracić barwę) to run; **farba puściła w praniu** the dye ran in the wash
[] **puścić się** — **puszczać się** [1] (wyruszyć) to set out; **puścić się pędem po schodach** to rush up/down the stairs [2] (zacząć ciec) to start to run a. running; **krew puściła mu się z nosa** his nose started to bleed
■ **puścić kogoś kantem** a. **w trąbę** pot. to dump a. ditch sb pot.; **puścić coś w niepamięć** to forgive and forget sth

puzon *m* trombone

py|cha[1] *f* pride; **wpaść** a. **popaść w pychę** to become big-headed

pycha[2] *adi. inv.* pot. (o jedzeniu) delicious; scrumptious pot.

py|ł *m* dust; **pył kosmiczny** cosmic dust
■ **rozbić** a. **zetrzeć coś w pył** to annihilate sth

pył|ek *m* speck; ~ek **kwiatowy** pollen

pysk *m* [1] (zwierzęcia) muzzle; (rybi) mouth [2] posp. (twarz lub usta) trap, gob GB pot.; **wylecieć na**

(zbity) ~ to be out on one's ear pot.; **dała mu po ~u** she gave him a smack across the face
pyska|ty *adi.* pot. loud-mouthed pot.
pysk|ować *impf vi* pot. to mouth off pot.; **nie ~uj mi!** don't answer back!
pyszni|ć się *impf v refl.* to put on airs and graces; **lubił ~ć się przed kolegami** he liked to show off in front of his friends
pyszn|y[1] *adi. grad.* (wyniosły) haughty
pyszn|y[2] *adi. grad.* [1] (smakowity) delicious [2] (doskonały) great pot.
pyta|ć *impf vt* [1] (zadawać pytanie) to ask; **~ć o drogę/ godzinę** to ask the way/time; **~ć o radę** to ask for

advice; **policja ~ła o ciebie** the police were asking about you [2] (egzaminować) to test; **byłeś dziś ~ny z historii?** were you tested on history today? ■ **kpisz, czy o drogę ~sz** are you joking, or what?; **kto ~, nie błądzi** przysł. it's always best to ask
pytajnik *m* question mark
pyta|nie *n* question; **podchwytliwe ~nie** a trick question; **~nie o kogoś/coś** a question about sb/ sth; **zadawać ~nia** to ask questions; **odpowiedzieć na ~nie** to answer a question
pyton *m* python
pyz|a *f* (kluska) ≈ potato dumpling

R

R, r *n inv.* R, r
rabarba|r *m* rhubarb
raba|t *m* discount; **kupić coś z** ~**tem** to buy sth at a discount
raba|ta *f* (flower) bed
rab|ować *impf vt* to rob *[mieszkania, banki]*; to loot *[sklepy]*
rabun|ek *m* robbery
rabunkow|y *adi.* **napad** ~**y** assault and robbery; ~**a eksploatacja złóż** wasteful exploitation of resources
rabu|ś *m* robber
rac|a *f* flare
rachityczn|y *adi. [krzesła, stoły]* rickety; *[rośliny]* puny
rach|ować *impf przest.* **[] *vt*** to count **[] rachować się** (rozliczać się) to settle one's accounts
rachun|ek [] *m* [] (liczenie) calculation [] (konto bankowe) account; **na czyimś** ~**ku** in sb's account [] (do zapłacenia) bill; **wystawić** ~**ek** to make out a bill
[] rachunki *plt* [] pot. arithmetic [] (stan majątku, kapitału) accounts
❏ ~**ek prawdopodobieństwa** theory of probability; ~**ek sumienia** examination of conscience
rachunkow|y *adi.* [] (dotyczący działań na liczbach) arithmetic; **błędy** ~**e** mistakes in arithmetic [] *[sprawozdanie, zestawienie]* bookkeeping
racic|a *f* hoof
racj|a[1] *f* [] (słuszność) rightness; **mieć** ~**ę** to be right; **nie mieć** ~**i** to be wrong; **przyznać komuś** ~**ę** to agree with sb [] (argument) argument [] (powód) reason; **z** ~**i czegoś** because of sth; **z** ~**i jej wieku** by virtue of her age; **bez dania** ~**i** for no apparent reason
racj|a[2] *f* (przydział) ration
racjonalizacj|a *f* [] (usprawnienie) streamlining [] (mechanizm obronny) rationalization
racjonaln|y *adi.* [] (skuteczny) efficient [] (logiczny) rational
racjon|ować *impf vt* to ration
racu|ch *m* ≈ drop scone
raczej *part.* [] (właściwie) rather; **była** ~ **nieduża** she was a bit on the small side pot. [] (bardziej) rather; ~ **zdziwiony niż zły** more surprised than angry;

~ **wypadek niż działanie umyślne** an accident rather than intentional wrongdoing
raczk|ować *impf vi* [] *[niemowlę]* to crawl [] przen. to be a novice
ra|d[1] *adi. praed.* glad; **rad by ją poznać** he'd love to meet her; **rad nierad** willy-nilly
ra|d[2] *m* (pierwiastek) radium
ra|da *f* [] (porada) advice; **zasięgać rady u kogoś** to get advice from sb; **pójść za czyjąś radą** to follow sb's advice; **zrobić coś za czyjąś radą** to do sth on sb's advice [] (zgromadzenie) council
❏ **Rada Bezpieczeństwa ONZ** UN Security Council
■ **dać radę (coś zrobić)** to manage (to do sth); **nie ma innej rady** there's no other way; **trudna rada** there's nothing to be done
rada|r *m* radar
radc|a *m* counsellor; ~**a prawny** a legal adviser; (w firmie) a company lawyer
radieste|ta *m*, ~**tka** *f* dowser, water diviner GB
radi|o *n* [] (urządzenie) radio; **w** ~**u** on the radio; **przez** ~**o** over a. by radio [] (instytucja) radio station
radioaktywn|y *adi.* radioactive
radiofoni|a /ˌradjoˈfɔɲa/ *f* radio broadcasting
radiomagnetofon *m* radio-cassette (recorder)
radioodbiornik *m* radio set
radiosłuchacz *m*, ~**ka** *f* radio listener
radiostacj|a *f* radio station
radiowę|zeł *m* radio broadcasting system
radiow|óz *m* police car
radn|y *m* councillor, councilman US
rado|sny *adi. [osoba]* happy; *[wiadomość, nastrój]* cheerful; *[uśmiech, mina, okrzyk]* joyful
rado|ść *f* joy; **z** ~**cią zawiadamiamy, że...** it is with great pleasure that we inform you that...
radykaln|y *adi. grad.* radical
ra|dzić *impf* **[] *vi*** [] (udzielać rad) to advise (**komuś** sb) [] (naradzać się) to debate **[] radzić się** to seek advice
■ **radzić sobie z czymś** to manage sth
raf|a *f* reef; ~**a koralowa** a coral reef
raj *m* paradise także przen.; ~ **podatkowy** przen. a tax haven
raj|d *m* [] (zawody sportowe) rally [] (wycieczka) trip
rajdow|iec *m* rally driver
rajstop|y *plt* tights GB, pantyhose US
rajtuz|y *plt* tights, leggings

Rak *m* Cancer

rak *m* [1] Zool. crayfish [2] (nowotwór) cancer [3] (metalowy zaczep) crampon

rakie|ta *f* [1] (pojazd) rocket [2] (pocisk) missile, rocket; **~ta sygnalizacyjna** a flare [3] Sport (do odbijania piłki) (tennis) racket

rakiet|ka *f* (do badmintona) racket; (do tenisa stołowego) (table-tennis) bat

rakotwórcz|y *adi.* carcinogenic

ram|a [] *f* [1] (oprawa) frame; **oprawić obraz w ~y** to frame a picture [2] Techn. frame; **~a roweru** a crossbar

[] **ramy** *plt* (konstrukcja) framework; (zakres) extent; **robić coś w ~ach czegoś** to do sth as part of sth

ramiącz|ko *n* [1] (pasek) (shoulder) strap [2] (wieszak) coat hanger

rami|ę *n* [1] (bark) shoulder; **wzruszyć ~onami** to shrug one's shoulders [2] (ręka) arm; **paść sobie w ~ona** to fall into one another's arms; **przyjąć kogoś z otwartymi ~onami** przen. to receive sb with open arms

■ **działać z czyjegoś ~enia** to act on behalf of sb

ramów|ka *f* programme format

ramp|a *f* [1] (platforma) loading ramp [2] (w teatrze) footlights

ran|a *f* wound

■ **~y Julek!** pot. gosh pot.

rand|ka *f* pot. date pot.

ran|ek [] *m* morning

[] **rankiem** *adv.* in the morning

ran|ga *f* [1] (stopień służbowy) rank; **wysoki/niski ~gą** of high/low rank [2] przen. (znaczenie) **pisarz światowej ~gi** a writer of world renown; **specjaliści najwyższej ~gi** top specialists

ra|nić [] *pf, impf vt* to wound; (kaleczyć) [kolce] to cut; [kamienie] to stab

[] *impf vt* przen. (sprawić przykrość, urażać) to hurt [osobę]; to wound [dumę]

rann|y¹ [] *adi.* wounded

[] *m* wounded man; **~i** the wounded

[] **ranna** *f* wounded woman

rann|y² *adi.* morning

ran|o [] *n* morning; **nad ~em** at dawn

[] *adv.* in the morning

rapor|t *m* report; **złożyć ~t** to submit a report; **stanąć do ~tu** to be put on report

raptem *adv.* [1] (nagle) suddenly [2] (zaledwie) only; **miał ~ dwadzieścia lat** he was only twenty

ras|a *f* [1] (ludzka) race [2] Zool. breed

rasizm *m* racism

rasowy *adi.* [1] [konflikt, dyskryminacja] racial [2] Zool. (czystej krwi) pure-bred [3] przen. (prawdziwy) [pisarz, aktor] proper

ra|ta *f* instalment, installment US; **płacić za coś w ratach** to pay for sth in instalments; **kupić coś na raty** to buy sth on hire purchase GB a. on an installment plan US; **zrobić coś na raty** przen. to do sth in stages

ratle|r, ~rek *m* miniature pinscher

rat|ować *impf vt* to save; (w niebezpieczeństwie, katastrofie) to rescue; **~ować kogoś przed kimś/czymś** to save sb from sb/sth; **~ować kogoś z kłopotów** to help sb out of trouble; **~ować sytuację** to save the day a. situation

ratownik *m* rescuer; (na plaży, basenie) lifeguard

ratun|ek *m* rescue; **przyjść komuś na ~ek** to come to sb's rescue; **~ku!** help!

ratusz *m* town hall

ratyfik|ować *impf, pf vt* to ratify [układ, traktat]

rau|t *m* banquet

raz¹ [] *m* [1] (ilość wystąpień) time; **tylko ~** only once; **zrobić coś ~/dwa ~y/trzy ~y** to do sth once/twice/three times; **dwa ~y większy** twice as big; **dwa ~y więcej osób/czasu** twice as many people/as much time; **ile ~y go widzę...** every time I see him...; **po ~ pierwszy** for the first time; **po ~ kolejny** once again; **po ~ ostatni widziałem go w...** I last saw him in...; **~ czy dwa** once or twice; **ani ~u** not (even) once; **~/dwa ~y/trzy ~y na godzinę** once/twice/three times an hour; **~ na zawsze** once and for all; **było ~ ciepło, ~ zimno** it was first warm and then cold; **~ po ~** (bez przerwy) over and over (again); (co jakiś czas) every now and then; **tym ~em** this time [2] (zdarzenie) case; **w ~ie pożaru** in case of fire; **w ~ie potrzeby** if need be; **w ~ie, gdyby coś się stało** in case something happens; **w ~ie czego** if anything happens; **innym ~em** some other time; **pewnego ~u** one day; **w każdym (bądź) ~ie** in any case, anyway; **w przeciwnym ~ie** otherwise; **w takim ~ie** in that case [3] (przy liczeniu) one; **~, dwa, trzy** one, two, three

[] *adv.* [1] (kiedyś) once [2] (wreszcie) at last; **jak już zaczniesz...** once you start... [3] (po pierwsze) first; **~, że..., a dwa, że...** for one thing because..., and for another...

[] **razy** *coni.* times; **jeden ~y dwa** one times two

[] **na razie** *adv.* (w tej chwili) at the moment; (do tej pory) so far; **na ~ie!** (pożegnanie) see you later!

[] **od razu** *adv.* at once

■ **zrobić coś ~, dwa** to do sth in no time; **w sam ~ dla kogoś** perfect for sb

raz² *m* (cios) blow

razem *adv.* [1] (wspólnie) together; **mieszkać ~** to live together; **pisać coś ~** (łącznie) to write sth as one word; **~ z kimś/czymś** together with sb/sth [2] (w sumie) altogether [3] (w jednym czasie) together, at once; **nie wszyscy ~!** one at a time, please!; **a teraz wszyscy ~!** all together now!

ra|zić¹ *pf, impf vt* [piorun] to strike [osobę]

ra|zić² *impf vt* [1] (przeszkadzać) to offend [osobę] [2] (oślepiać) to dazzle [osobę]

razow|iec *m* pot. wholemeal bread

rażąc|y *adi.* ① *[niesprawiedliwość, błąd]* gross; *[kontrast, sprzeczność]* glaring; **w sposób ~y** *[nadużyć, zaniedbać]* grossly ② *[światło, kolory]* glaring

rąbać¹ *impf* → **rąbnąć**

rąb|ać² *impf vt* ① to chop *[drewno]*; to chop [sth] down *[drzewa, las]*; to hew *[węgiel]*; to hack *[mięso]*; (wycinać) to cut *[otwór, przejście]* ② pot. (zjadać) to nosh pot.

rąb|ek *m* ① (w sukni) hem ② książk. (słońca, księżyca) rim; **uchylić przed kimś ~ka tajemnicy** to let sb in on the secret

■ **złej tanecznicy przeszkadza ~ek u spódnicy** przysł. a bad workman always blames his tools przysł.

rąb|nąć *pf* — **rąb|ać**¹ *impf* pot. ❶ *vt* ① (uderzyć) to bang pot. ② (strzelić) to blast away pot.; (zabić) to do [sb] in pot. ③ (powiedzieć) to blurt out; **~nąć komuś prawdę w oczy** to give it to sb straight (from the shoulder) ④ (ukraść) to swipe pot. ⑤ (oszukać) to shaft pot.; **~nąć kogoś na sto złotych** to shaft sb out of a hundred zlotys ⑥ (wypić) **~nąć sobie kielicha** to knock one back pot.

❷ *vi* ① (upaść) **~nąć na ziemię** *[osoba]* to take a header pot.; *[przedmiot]* to go flying to the ground ② (huknąć) to bang; **nagle coś ~nęło** there was a sudden bang

❸ **rąbnąć się** — **rąbać się** ① (uderzyć się) **~nąć się w kolano** to bang one's knee ② (pomylić się) **~nąć się w obliczeniach** to get one's calculations wrong

rącz|ka *f* (uchwyt) handle

■ **złota ~ka** pot. handyman

rdz|a *f* rust

rdze|ń *m* ① Techn. core także przen. ② Anat., Bot. medulla; **~ń (kręgowy)** the spinal cord ③ (wyrazu) root

rdzewi|eć *impf vi* to rust także przen.

reag|ować *impf vi* ① *[osoba, rynek]* to react, to respond (**na coś** to sth); **po prostu nie ~uj na ich zaczepki** just ignore their jeers ② *[substancja]* to react

reakcj|a *f* ① (zareagowanie) reaction, response (**na coś** to sth) ② (sprzeciw) reaction (**przeciw czemuś** against sth) ③ (chemiczna, biologiczna) reaction

reakto|r *m* reactor

reaktyw|ować *impf, pf vt* to re-establish *[partię, katedrę]*; to revive *[idee, wartości]*; to reactivate *[oficera]*

reali|a *plt* książk. reality; **takie były wtedy ~a** that was what things were like then

reali|sta *m*, **~stka** *f* realist; **bądź ~stą!** get real! pot.

realizacj|a *f* ① (pragnień, projektów) realization; (planów) accomplishment ② (wykonanie) completion; **termin ~i** the completion date ③ (film, sztuka) production ④ (wykupienie) (czeku) cashing

realizato|r *m*, **~rka** *f* (wykonawca) **~r inwestycji** a contractor

realizm *m* realism

realiz|ować *impf* ❶ *vt* ① to realize *[marzenia]*; to accomplish *[cele, zamiary]*; to carry out *[projekt, obietnicę]*; to make *[film]*; to complete *[zamówienie]* ② (wykupywać) to cash *[czek]*; to pick up *[receptę]*

❷ **realizować się** ① *[osoba]* to fulfil oneself, to fulfill oneself US; **~ować się w czymś** to find fulfilment in sth ② *[obawy, marzenia]* to come true

realn|y ❶ *adi. grad.* ① (prawdopodobny) real ② *[ocena, pogląd]* realistic

❷ *adi.* (prawdziwy) *[świat, postać, skutek]* real

reanimacj|a *f* resuscitation

reanim|ować *pf, impf vt* to resuscitate także przen.

rebus *m* rebus

recenzj|a *f* review

recenz|ować *impf vt* to review

recepcj|a *f* ① (w hotelu) reception (area/desk) ② książk. (przyswajanie) reception

recepcjoni|sta *m*, **~stka** *f* receptionist, desk a. room clerk US

recep|ta *f* ① (zlecenie lekarskie) prescription; **lekarstwo na ~tę** a prescription medicine; **kupisz ten lek bez ~ty** you'll buy this medicine over the counter ② przen. (niezawodny sposób) recipe

recesj|a *f* recession

recho|t *m* ① (żaby) croak ② (śmiech) guffaw

recho|tać *impf vi* ① *[żaba]* to croak ② (śmiać się) to cackle

recydywi|sta *m*, **~stka** *f* reoffender

recyt|ować *impf vt* to recite

re|da *f* roadstead; **stać na redzie** to lie off

redag|ować *impf vt* to edit *[tekst, książkę]*

redakcj|a *f* ① (opracowanie) editing; **pod ~ą...** edited by... ② (wersja) version ③ (dział) editorial section; (zespół pracowników) editorial staff a. team; (lokal) editorial office

redakto|r *m* ① (w wydawnictwie) editor; **~r naczelny** the editor-in-chief ② (w radiu, telewizji) journalist

redaktor|ka *f* editor; (dziennikarka) journalist

redukcj|a *f* ① (zmniejszenie) reduction; **~a zatrudnienia** lay-offs ② (reakcja chemiczna) reduction

reduk|ować *impf vt* to reduce

refera|t *m* ① (sprawozdanie) report ② (dział) department

refer|ować *impf vt* to report

refleks *m* ① (szybkość reakcji) reflexes; **spóźniony ~** slow reflexes ② (błysk) reflection

refleksj|a *f* reflection; **dzielić się ~ami** to share one's thoughts

reflekto|r *m* (lampa) floodlight; **~r samochodowy** a headlight; **~r punktowy** (w teatrze) a spotlight; (na dworze) a searchlight

reform|a *f* reform

reformacj|a *f* the Reformation

reformato|r *m*, **~rka** *f* reformer

reform|ować *impf vt* to reform

refren *m* chorus; **powracać jak** ~ to keep recurring

rega|ł *m* bookshelf

regeneracj|a *f* [1] Biol. regeneration [2] (odzyskanie sił) recuperation [3] (naprawa) repair; (silników, urządzeń) renovation

regener|ować *impf* [] *vt* [1] *[organizm, zwierzę]* to regenerate *[komórki, tkanki]* [2] (odnawiać) ~**ować siły** to recuperate [3] (naprawiać) to renovate *[silnik]*; to retread *[oponę]*; to re-ink *[taśmę do drukarki]*

[] **regenerować się** [1] *[tkanka, komórka, narząd]* to regenerate [2] *[osoba, organizm]* to recuperate

region *m* region także przen.

regres *m* książk. (cofnięcie się) regression; (spadek) slump

regulacj|a *f* [1] (ustawianie) adjustment; (dostosowywanie) control; (naprawa) tuning; ~**a temperatury** temperature control; ~**a rzek** river regulation; ~**a urodzeń** birth control; **mieć ~ę wysokości** *[mebel]* to be height adjustable [2] (prawo) regulation

regulamin *m* rules

regularnie [] *adv. grad.* regularly

[] *adv.* [1] (stale) *[kursować, odbywać się]* on a regular basis [2] (zgodnie z regułami) *[odmieniać się]* regularly

regularn|y *adi. grad.* [1] (systematyczny) *[oddech, trening, tryb życia]* regular; *[krok]* even [2] (foremny) *[twarz, kształty, linie, pismo]* regular [3] pot. (prawdziwy) *[złodziej, lanie]* regular pot.

regul|ować *impf vt* [1] to adjust *[zegarek, sprzęgło, głośność, ostrość]*; to tune *[silnik]*; to regulate *[ciśnienie, wysokość]* [2] (określać) to regulate *[stosunki]*; to resolve *[sporne kwestie]* [3] książk. (zapłacić) to square *[należność]* [4] to regulate *[rzekę]*

regu|ła *f* [1] (zasada) rule; ~**ły gry** the rules of the game także przen.; **nie ma na to** ~**ły** there are no rules for that; **z** ~**ły** as a (general) rule [2] (zakonna) rule

rehabilitacj|a *f* [1] Med. rehabilitation [2] (skazanego) rehabilitation [3] *[osoby, idei]* vindication

rehabilit|ować *pf, impf* [] *vt* [1] to rehabilitate *[chorego, pacjenta, skazanego, ideę]*

[] **rehabilitować się** to restore one's reputation

rejest|r *m* [1] (spis) register; **wpisać coś do** ~**ru** to enter sth in a register [2] Muz. register

rejestracj|a *f* [1] (ewidencja) registration [2] (w przychodni, szpitalu) reception desk [3] (zapis) recording [4] (numer rejestracyjny) registration number [5] Muz. registration

rejestr|ować *impf* [] *vt* [1] (oficjalnie) to register *[samochody, pacjentów]* [2] Techn. to record *[temperaturę, wstrząsy]* [3] *[wzrok, słuch]* to register *[obrazy, dźwięki]*

[] **rejestrować się** to register

rejon *m* [1] (obszar) area; **w** ~**ie Warszawy** in the Warsaw area [2] (administracyjny) district; (w służbie zdrowia, szkolnictwie) (catchment) area; (dla policjanta) beat

rejs *m* [1] Żegl. voyage; (wycieczkowy) cruise [2] (lotniczy) flight

rekin *m* [1] Zool. shark [2] (bogacz) tycoon; (wyzyskiwacz) shark pot.

reklam|a *f* [1] (reklamowanie) advertising; (rozgłos) publicity; **specjalista do spraw** ~**y** a publicity agent; **zrobić czemuś** ~**ę** to give sth publicity [2] (materiał reklamowy) advertisement; (w radiu, telewizji) commercial

reklamacj|a *f* complaint

reklam|ować *impf vt* [1] (promować) to advertise *[towary, usługi, imprezę]* [2] (zgłaszać wady) to complain (**coś** about sth)

reklamów|ka *f* [1] (ulotka) advertising leaflet; (film) commercial [2] (torba) carrier bag

rekolekcj|e *plt* retreat

rekomendacj|a *f* książk. recommendation

rekomend|ować *impf vt* książk. to recommend

rekompensa|ta *f* compensation (**za coś** for sth)

rekompens|ować *impf vt* to compensate; ~**ować komuś coś** to compensate sb for sth

rekonstrukcj|a *f* reconstruction

rekonstru|ować *impf vt* to reconstruct *[budynek, rzeźbę, wydarzenia]*

rekonwalescencj|a *f* convalescence; **przechodzić** ~**ę** to be convalescing

rekonwalescen|t *m*, ~**tka** *f* convalescent

rekor|d *m* record; ~**d świata** the world record; ~**d życiowy** a personal best; **ustanowić** ~**d** to set a record

rekordzi|sta *m*, ~**stka** *f* record holder

rekru|t *m* recruit

rekrutacj|a *f* (do pracy, wojska) recruitment; (do szkół) enrolment, enrollment US

rekto|r *m* vice-chancellor GB, president US

rekwizy|t *m* (stage) prop

relacj|a *f* [1] (sprawozdanie) account; **zdać** ~**ę z czegoś** to give an account of sth [2] książk. (stosunek, zależność) relationship [3] (trasa) **pociąg** ~**i Warszawa-Kraków** the Warsaw-Cracow train

relaks *m* relaxation

relaks|ować się *impf v refl.* to relax

relatywn|y *adi.* relative

religi|a *f* religion także przen.; (przedmiot szkolny) religious instruction; (lekcja) religion (class)

reli|k|t *m* relic

remanen|t *m* stocktake, stocktaking także przen.

remis *m* draw, tie

remis|ować *impf vi* to draw, to tie

remon|t *m* (budynku) renovation; (dachu, jezdni) repair

remont|ować *impf vt* to renovate *[budynek, mieszkanie]*; to repair *[dach, maszynę]*

renci|sta *m*, ~**stka** *f* pensioner

renife|r *m* reindeer

renom|a *f* książk. renown

renomowan|y *adi.* książk. *[firma, instytucja]* reputable; *[szkoła, uczelnia]* prestigious

renowacj|a *f* książk. (budynków, zabytków) renovation; (dzieł sztuki, mebli, budynków) restoration; (futer, dywanów) repair

ren|ta *f* (świadczenia pieniężne) pension; **być na ∼cie** to draw a pension a. an allowance

rentgen *m* pot. (badanie, zdjęcie) X-ray; (aparat) X-ray machine

reperacj|a *f* repair

reper|ować *impf vt* to repair

repertua|r *m* repertoire

repet|ować *impf vt* to repeat *[klasę, rok]*

repli|ka *f* książk. [1] (na zarzuty) rejoinder; **cięta ∼ka** a cutting rejoinder [2] (kopia) replica

reportaż *m* (gatunek prozy) reportage; (telewizyjny, filmowy) documentary

reporte|r *m*, **∼ka** *f* reporter

represj|a *f* reprisal

reprezentacj|a *f* [1] Sport (szkolna, narodowa) team [2] (przedstawiciele) representatives

reprezentacyjn|y *adi.* *[strój]* formal; *[sala, gmach]* fine; *[dzielnica]* elegant; *[limuzyna]* sleek; **kompania ∼a** the guard of honour

reprezentan|t *m*, **∼tka** *f* representative

reprezent|ować *impf vt* to represent *[kraj, instytucję]*; **∼ować swój kraj** Sport to compete for one's country

reprodukcj|a *f* reproduction

republi|ka *f* republic

reputacj|a *f* reputation

resocjalizacj|a *f* rehabilitation, resocialization

resocjaliz|ować *impf vt* to rehabilitate, to socialize

reso|r *m* coil spring

resor|t *m* (government) department

respek|t *m* respect; **wzbudzać ∼t** to command respect

respekt|ować *impf vt* to respect *[prawo, przepisy]*

restauracj|a *f* [1] (lokal) restaurant [2] (budynku, ogrodu) restoration [3] (monarchy) restoration

resz|ka *f* tails; **orzeł czy ∼ka?** heads or tails?

resz|ta *f* [1] (pozostałość) rest (**czegoś** of sth); **bez ∼ty** (bez zastrzeżeń) *[poświęcić się, oddać się]* unreservedly; (całkowicie) *[zaabsorbowany, zajęty]* wholly; **do ∼ty** completely [2] (pieniądze) change; **wydać komuś ∼tę** to give sb (their) change [3] (w dzieleniu) remainder

reszt|ka [] *f* [1] (pozostałość) remains [2] (kawałek materiału) remnant

[] **resztki** *plt* (jedzenie) leftovers

retransmisj|a *f* rebroadcast

reumatyzm *m* rheumatism

rewaloryzacj|a *f* książk. [1] (odnawianie) restoration [2] (podwyższenie świadczeń) uprating; **∼a świadczeń** the index-linking of benefits

rewaloryz|ować *pf impf vt* książk. [1] (odnawiać) to restore *[zabytki, dzieła sztuki]* [2] (podwyższać) to uprate *[emerytury, świadczenia]*

rewanż *m* [1] (zemsta) revenge (**za coś** for sth) [2] (odwzajemnienie) return of a favour; **w ∼u za coś** in return for sth [3] Sport (okazja do odegrania) rematch; (drugi mecz w rundzie) second leg

rewanż|ować się *impf v refl.* [1] (brać odwet) to get one's revenge (**komuś** on sth) [2] (odwzajemniać) **∼ować się komuś** to return sb's favour

rewelacj|a *f* sensation

rewers *m* [1] (monety, medalu) reverse [2] (kwit) IOU [3] (w bibliotece) order slip

rewid|ować *impf vt* [1] (przeszukiwać) to search *[osobę, pomieszczenie]* [2] (zmieniać) to revise *[poglądy, opinię]*

rewizj|a *f* [1] (przeszukanie) search [2] (zmiana) revision; (przegląd) review [3] (wyroku) appeal

rewolucj|a *f* revolution; **mieć ∼e żołądkowe** żart. to have an upset stomach

rewolucjoni|sta *m*, **∼stka** *f* revolutionary

rewolwe|r *m* revolver

rezerw|a *f* [1] (zapas) reserve; **mieć coś w ∼ie** to keep sth in reserve [2] Sport substitutes; **∼y** (drużyna) the reserves [3] Wojsk. reserve [4] (powściągliwość) reserve

rezerwacj|a *f* booking, reservation

rezerwa|t *m* [1] (przyrodniczy) reserve [2] (Indian) reservation

rezerw|ować *impf vt* [1] (zamawiać) to book, to reserve *[stolik, pokój, miejsce]* [2] (pozostawiać) to set [sth] aside *[czas, pieniądze]*

rezerwow|y [] *adi.* (zapasowy) *[fundusze, oddział]* reserve; *[zawodnik]* substitute

[] **rezerwow|y** *m*, **∼a** *f* Sport substitute

rezolutn|y *adi. [odpowiedź]* quick-witted; *[mina]* determined; *[uczeń]* smart

rezonans *m* resonance

rezulta|t *m* result; **w ∼cie** as a result

rezydencj|a *f* residence

rezygnacj|a *f* resignation (**z czegoś** from sth); **z ∼ą** resignedly

rezygn|ować *impf vi* to give up (**z czegoś** sth)

reżim *m* [1] (dyscyplina) regime, regimen [2] Polit. regime

reżyse|r *m* director

reżyseri|a *f* direction

reżyser|ować *impf vt* to direct *[film, dramat]*

ręcznik *m* towel

ręczn|y *adi.* [1] (wykonywany ręką) *[haft]* handmade; *[notatka]* handwritten [2] (nieautomatyczny) manual; **hamulec ∼y** a handbrake

ręcz|yć *impf vi* [1] (gwarantować) to vouch; **∼yć za czyjąś uczciwość** to vouch for sb's honesty [2] (być pewnym) to be sure

■ **nie ∼ę za siebie** I won't be answerable for my actions

rę|ka [] *f* [1] (dłoń) hand; **wziąć kogoś za rękę** to take sb by the hand; **uścisnąć komuś rękę** to shake sb's hand; **załamywać ręce** to wring one's hands; **fachowa ręka** przen. the hand of an expert; **brak rąk do pracy** lack of manpower; **na rękę** pot. (gotówką) in cash; (netto) clear [2] (ramię) arm; **wykręcić komuś rękę** to twist sb's arm; **rozkładać bezradnie ręce** to spread one's arms helplessly; **wziąć kogoś pod rękę** to link one's arm through sb's

II od ręki adv. on the spot

■ **na własną rękę** on one's own initiative; **wiadomości z pierwszej ręki** first-hand information; **kupić coś z drugiej ręki** to buy sth second-hand; **być komuś na rękę** to suit sb; **być pod ręką** to be within reach; **pójść komuś na rękę** to accommodate sb, to meet sb half-way; **prosić o czyjąś rękę** to ask sb's hand in marriage; **ręce (mi) opadają (na myśl o...)** my heart fails (at the thought of...)

rękaw m [1] (w ubraniu) sleeve [2] (na lotnisku) air sock, wind sock

rękawic|a f glove; **~a kuchenna** an oven glove GB, a pot holder US; **~e bokserskie** boxing gloves; **rzucić komuś ~ę** przen. to throw down the gauntlet to sb

rękawicz|ka f glove

rękoczyn m fisticuffs; **obeszło się bez ~ów** they managed to avoid coming to blows

rękodzie|ło n handicraft

rękopis m manuscript

ring m (boxing) ring

robactw|o n vermin

robaczyw|y adi. worm-eaten

robak m worm

■ **zalewać ~a** to drown one's sorrows

r|obić impf **II** vt [1] (wytwarzać) to make [meble, herbatę, obiad]; **robić z kogoś durnia** to make a fool of sb [2] (wykonywać czynność) to do [pranie, zakupy, porządki]; to make [notatki, przygotowania]; **robić komuś prezenty** to give sb presents; **robić komuś kawały** to play tricks on sb; **co ja robię (najlepszego)?** what the heck am I doing?; **cóż (było) robić?** what was there to do?; **wiek robi swoje** age takes its toll; **niewiele sobie robić z czegoś** to not care much about sth; **robić swoje** to do one's job; **już się robi!** pot. right oh! [3] (powodować) to make [awanturę, obietnice, zamieszanie, wyjątek]; to do [krzywdę, przysługę]

II vi pot. (pracować zarobkowo) to work

III robić się [1] (być przygotowywanym) to be made [2] (stawać się) **robi się ciemno/zimno** it's getting dark/cold; **robi się z niego prawdziwy mężczyzna** he's growing into a real man

roboci|zna f labour

robocz|y adi. [ubranie, dzień, tytuł, konferencja] working; [brygada] work; **siła ~a** the workforce

robo|t m robot; **~t kuchenny** a food processor

rob|ota f [1] (praca) work; **wziąć się do ~oty** to get down to work; **mieć coś do ~oty** to have sth to do;

tort własnej ~oty a home-made cake [2] (rezultat pracy) job; **robić dobrą ~otę** to do a good job; **to twoja ~ota!** that's your doing!

robotni|k m, **~ca** f worker

roczni|ca f anniversary; **~a ślubu** a wedding anniversary; **okrągła ~a** a round anniversary

rocznik m [1] (urodzeni w tym samym roku) **z którego jesteś ~a** a. **który jesteś ~?** which year were you born in? [2] (wina) vintage [3] (czasopisma) annual bound volume [4] (wydawnictwo) yearbook

roczn|y adi. [1] [dziecko, zwierzę, wino] one-year-old [2] [urlop, pobyt, kontrakt] one-year [3] [dochód, prenumerata] annual

rodacz|ka f (fellow) countrywoman, compatriot

roda|k m (fellow) countryman, compatriot

rodowi|ty adi. [Polak, warszawianin] native

rodow|ód m [1] (pochodzenie) (dzieła, wyrazu) origin(s) [2] (historia rodu) lineage [3] Zool. pedigree

rodza|j m [1] (typ) kind, sort; **coś w ~ju hełmu** something resembling a helmet; **czy coś w tym ~ju** or something like that; **jedyny w swoim ~ju** one of its kind [2] Biol. genus [3] (gramatyczny) gender

rodzeństw|o n siblings; **czy masz ~o?** do you have any brothers or sisters?; **cioteczne ~o** cousins

rodzic|e plt parents; **~e chrzestni** godparents

ro|dzić impf **II** vt [1] (kobieta, samica) to give birth to [syna, córkę] [2] (roślina) to bear [owoce, plony] [3] (wywoływać) to give rise to [pogardę, tęsknotę]

II rodzić się [1] (osoba, zwierzę) to be born [2] (rośliny, owoce) to grow [marzenia, uczucia, potrzeby] to arise

rodzin|a f family także przen.; **zakładać ~ę** to start up a family; **~a języków** a language family

rodzinn|y adi. [tradycja, więzi, życie] family; [miasto, strony] home

rodzyn|ek m Kulin. raisin

rogacz m [1] (jeleń) stag [2] pot., żart. cuckold

rogalik m (z ciasta drożdżowego) (small) crescent roll; (z ciasta francuskiego) croissant

rogów|ka f cornea

rok [] m [1] (jednostka) year; **rok urodzenia** the year of birth; **w roku 1965** in 1965; **w tym/zeszłym roku** this/last year; **co roku** every year; **raz w roku** once a year; **z roku na rok** by the year; **lata trzydzieste** the thirties; **ile masz lat?** how old are you?; **wyglądać na swoje lata** to look one's age [2] (na uczelni) year; **być na trzecim roku** to be in one's third year

II lata plt (długi czas) years; **od lat** for years; **po latach** years later; **ostatnimi laty** in recent years

❑ **rok przestępny** leap year

■ **Nowy Rok** the New Year; **mieć swoje lata** to be no spring chicken pot.; **Sto lat!** many happy returns (of the day)!

rok|ować impf vi [1] (pertraktować) to negotiate [2] książk. (wróżyć) to prognosticate; **dobrze/źle**

~ować na przyszłość to portend well/badly for the future

rokowa|nie n ① Polit. negotiations ② Med. prognosis

r|ola¹ f 1 ① (odtwarzana postać) part, role; **rola pierwszoplanowa/drugoplanowa** the leading/ supporting part; **grać rolę** to play a part; **zapomnieć roli** to forget one's lines ② (zadanie) role; **odgrywać rolę** (mieć znaczenie) to play a part; **pieniądze nie grają roli** money is no object **r|ola**² f (ziemia) farmland; **pracować na roli** to work on the land

rola|da f roll, roulade

role|ta f roller-blind

rol|ka [] f ① (papieru, blachy, tapety) roll ② (szpulka) spool ③ (ruchomy wałek) roller

[] **rolki** plt Sport roller blades

rolnictw|o n (dział gospodarki) agriculture; (zajęcie) farming

rolni|k m, **~czka** f farmer

rol|ować impf vt to roll [dywan, koc, śpiwór]

romanisty|ka f Romance studies

romans m ① (przygoda miłosna) love-affair ② (utwór epicki) romance; (powieść) love story

romantyczn|y adi. romantic

romanty|k m, **~czka** f romantic

romb m rhombus

rond|el m saucepan; (zawartość) saucepan(ful)

ron|do n ① (na ulicy) roundabout GB, rotary US ② (w kapeluszu) brim ③ (utwór) (literacki) rondeau; (muzyczny) rondo

rop|a f ① Med. pus ② (naftowa) petroleum, oil; **silnik na ~ę** a diesel engine

ropi|eć impf vi to suppurate, to fester

rop|ień m abscess

ropu|cha f ① Zool. toad ② obraźl. old hag obraźl.

ros|a f dew

r|osnąć impf vi ① (wzrastać) [dziecko, roślina, włosy, paznokcie] to grow; (dorastać) [dziecko] to grow up ② (zwiększać się) [odległość, bezrobocie, inflacja, przestępczość] to increase; [ceny, stawki] to rise; [majątek, niepokój, sława] to grow ③ Kulin. [ciasto] to rise

ros|ół m soup stock; (potrawa) broth; (czysty) consommé

roszcze|nie n (legal) claim

ro|ścić impf vt **rościć sobie prawo do czegoś** to claim the right to sth

roślin|a f plant; **~y cebulkowe** bulbous plants; **~y doniczkowe** pot plants

roślinnoś|ć f flora, vegetation

roślinn|y adi. ① [komórka, włókno, świat] plant ② [olej, masło] vegetable

rottweile|r /ro'dvajler/ m, **~rka** /,rodvaj'lerka/ f Rottweiler

row|ek m groove; (w ziemi) furrow

rowe|r m bicycle; bike pot.; **jechać na ~rze** to cycle; **wsiąść na ~r** to mount a bike

rowerzy|sta m, **~stka** f cyclist

rozbaw|ić pf — **rozbaw|iać** impf [] vt to amuse [towarzystwo, publiczność]

[] **rozbawić się** — **rozbawiać się** to begin to enjoy oneself

rozbawi|ony adi. amused

rozbeł|tać pf — **rozbeł|tywać** impf vt to beat [zsiadłe mleko, jajka]

rozbi|ć pf — **rozbi|jać** impf [] vt ① (potłuc) to smash; (przypadkowo) to break; **~ć jajko** to break an egg ② (roztłuc) to pound [mięso] ③ (zniszczyć) to crash, to smash [samochód, samolot] ④ (zranić) to hurt; **~ć sobie kolano** to hurt one's knee; **~ć komuś nos** to smash sb's nose ⑤ (wyróżnić części) to divide; **~ć coś na grupy** to divide sth into groups ⑥ (rozgromić) to defeat [nieprzyjaciela, wojsko]; to break up [gang] ⑦ przen. to wreck [nadzieje, plany]; **~ć małżeństwo** to break up a marriage; **~te rodziny** broken families ⑧ (rozstawić) to put [sth] up [namiot]; **~ć obóz** to pitch camp

[] **rozbić się** — **rozbijać się** ① (rozdzielić się) [towarzystwo] to split ② (rozłożyć obóz) to pitch camp ③ pot. (nie powieść się) [plan] to founder

[] **rozbić się** ① (rozpaść się) [filiżanka, wazon] to break ② (zostać zniszczonym) [samochód, osoba] to crash

[] **rozbijać się** pot. (jeździć) **~jać się po mieście** to cruise around the town

rozbie|c się, rozbie|gnąć się pf — **rozbie|gać się** impf v refl. ① (uciec) to disperse ② przen. [drogi, ulice, ścieżki] to diverge

rozbieg m ① (samolotu) take-off run ② Sport run-up; **wziąć ~** to take a run-up

rozbiegać się impf → **rozbiec się**

rozbiegan|y adi. ① [ludzie] bustling ② [myśli] feverish; [oczy] restless

rozbiegnąć się → **rozbiec się**

rozbierać impf → **rozebrać**

rozbieralni|a f changing room

rozbijać impf → **rozbić**

rozbi|ór m ① (analiza) analysis ② Polit. partition

rozbiór|ka f (budynków) demolition

rozbit|ek m shipwrecked person; (wyrzucony na brzeg) castaway; **~kowie życiowi** przen. flotsam

rozbły|snąć pf — **rozbły|skiwać** impf vi [świeczka, lampy, oczy] to light up; [petarda, raca] to flare up

rozbol|eć impf vi **~ała mnie głowa** I had a headache; **~ał mnie od tego brzuch** it gave me a stomach-ache

rozb|ój m armed robbery

rozbójni|k m robber; (napadający na podróżnych) highwayman

rozbr|oić pf — **rozbr|ajać** impf [] vt to disarm [wroga, minę, krytyków]

[] **rozbroić się** — **rozbrajać się** [kraj, armia] to disarm

rozbrojeni|e n disarmament

rozbry|zgać *pf* — **rozbry|zgiwać** *impf* **I** *vt* [osoba, samochód] to splash [wodę, błoto]

II rozbryzgać się — **rozbryzgiwać się** to be splashed

rozbrzmi|eć *impf vi* książk. [1] [rozmowy, muzyka] to resound [2] [pokój, budynek] to resound (**czymś** with sth)

rozbudow|a *f* expansion

rozbud|ować *pf* — **rozbud|owywać** *impf* **I** *vt* to extend [budynek, parking, program]

II rozbudować się — **rozbudowywać się** [miasto, firma] to grow

rozbu|dzić *pf* — **rozbu|dzać** *impf* **I** *vt* [1] (obudzić) to wake [osobę] [2] (pobudzić) to arouse [ciekawość, zazdrość, wyobraźnię]; to incite [nienawiść]

II rozbudzić się — **rozbudzać się** [1] [osoba] to wake up [2] [namiętności] to be aroused

rozbuja|ć *impf* **I** *vt* to give [sb] a swing [osobę]; to set [sth] rocking [łódkę, kołyskę]; to set [sth] swinging [huśtawkę, dzwon]

II rozbujać się [osoba] to start swinging

rozchlap|ać *pf* — **rozchlap|ywać** *impf* **I** *vt* to splash (around) [wodę, błoto]

II rozchlapać się — **rozchlapywać się** [woda, błoto] to splash (around)

rozchmurz|yć *pf* — **rozchmurz|ać** *impf* **I** *vt* ~**ył twarz** his face brightened up

II rozchmurzyć się — **rozchmurzać się** [1] [niebo] to clear [2] [osoba, twarz] to brighten up

rozcho|dzić *pf* **I** *vt* [1] (rozruszać) ~**dzić zesztywniałe kolano** to walk off a stiffness in one's knee [2] (powiększyć) to wear [sth] in [buty]

II rozchodzić się [1] [osoba] to walk off a stiffness in one's legs [2] [buty] to get worn in

rozchodzić się *impf* → **rozejść się**

rozchyl|ić *pf* — **rozchyl|ać** *impf* **I** *vt* to part [zasłony, usta]; to open [koszulę, okiennice, płatki]

II rozchylić się — **rozchylać się** [zasłony, wargi] to part; [pąk, płatki] to open

roz|ciąć *pf* — **roz|cinać** *impf vt* [1] (zrobić otwór) to slit [nogawkę, namiot, płótno]; (zniszczyć) to slash [materiał, pokrowiec, obicie] [2] (skaleczyć) to cut [rękę]

rozciągać *impf* → **rozciągnąć**

rozciągliw|y *adi.* stretchy

rozciąg|nąć *pf* — **rozciąg|ać** *impf* **I** *vt* [1] (wydłużyć) to stretch [gumę, sprężynę, sweter] [2] (rozpiąć) to stretch [linę, sieć]; to run [kabel]; to spread [płachtę] [3] (rozszerzyć) to extend [zakres, władzę] [4] pot. (porozrzucać) to scatter [sth] around [przedmioty]

II rozciągnąć się — **rozciągać się** [1] (wydłużyć się) [sweter, mięśnie, guma] to stretch; ~**nąć się w czasie** to stretch in time [2] (położyć się) to stretch out

rozcieńcz|yć *pf* — **rozcieńcz|ać** *impf vt* to dilute [roztwór]; to thin [farbę, lakier]

rozcierać *impf* → **rozetrzeć**

rozcię|cie *n* [1] (skaleczenie) gash [2] (rozdarcie) rip [3] (w sukience) slit

rozcinać *impf* → **rozciąć**

rozczar|ować *pf* — **rozczar|owywać** *impf* **I** *vt* to disappoint [osobę]

II rozczarować się — **rozczarowywać się** to be disappointed (**do kogoś** with sb)

rozczarowa|nie *n* disappointment

rozczarowywać *impf* → **rozczarować**

rozcze|sać *pf* — **rozcze|sywać** *impf vt* to comb [sth] out [włosy, wełnę]

rozczochra|ć *pf* **I** *vt* to mess [sth] up [włosy]; (ręką) to ruffle [włosy]

II rozczochrać się [osoba] to mess up one's hair; [włosy] to get messed up

rozda|ć *pf* — **rozda|wać** *impf vt* [1] (dawać) to hand [sth] out [formularze, ulotki, jedzenie]; ~**wać autografy** to sign autographs [2] (w grach) to deal [karty]

rozdar|cie *n* [1] (uszkodzenie) tear [2] (niepewność) dilemma

rozdawać *impf* → **rozdać**

roz|dąć *pf* — **roz|dymać** *impf* **I** *vt* [1] (napompować) to distend [brzuch, żołądek]; to dilate [nozdrza, chrapy]; to fill [żagiel] [2] (wyolbrzymić) to hype [sth] up pot. [historię, problem]

II *vi* [jedzenie] to cause flatulence

III *v imp.* ~**dęło mnie** I feel bloated

IV rozdąć się — **rozdymać się** [policzki, zwierzę] to puff up; [brzuch, żołądek] to distend

rozdep|tać *pf* — **rozdep|tywać** *impf* **I** *vt* [1] (nadepnąć) to tread on; (celowo zmiażdżyć) to crush [owada, żuka]; to stamp [sth] out [niedopałek] [2] (zniszczyć) to wear [sth] down [buty]

II rozdeptać się — **rozdeptywać się** [buty] to get worn down

rozdmuch|ać *pf* — **rozdmuch|iwać** *impf vt* [1] (podsycić) to fan [płomień, ogień] [2] (wyolbrzymić) to blow [sth] up [problem]

rozdrabniać *impf* → **rozdrobnić**

rozdrap|ać *pf* — **rozdrap|ywać** *impf vt* [1] [osoba] to pick at [krostę, strup]; [kura] to scratch [sth] away [ziemię, grządki] [2] pot. to snap [sth] up pot. [towary]

rozdrażni|ć *pf* — **rozdrażni|ać** *impf vt* to irritate [osobę]; to provoke [zwierzę]

rozdrażni|ony *adi.* [osoba, ton] irritated

rozdr|obnić *pf* — **rozdr|abniać** *impf* **I** *vt* (rozkruszyć) to grind [sth] down [produkty, skały, kamienie]

II rozdrobnić się — **rozdrabniać się** [kraj, struktura] to become fragmented

III rozdrabniać się pot. [osoba] to get sidetracked (**na coś** into sth)

rozdymać *impf* → **rozdąć**

rozdzia|ł *m* [1] (książki) chapter także przen. [2] (środków, żywności) distribution; (kompetencji) apportionment [3] (rozgraniczenie) separation [4] (niezgoda) split

rozdziel|ić pf — **rozdziel|ać** impf **I** vt ① (podzielić) to divide *[przedmiot, grupę]*; to separate *[walczących]* ② (rozdać) to distribute ③ (rozgraniczyć) to separate ④ (przegrodzić) to divide

II rozdzielić się — rozdzielać się ① (rozpaść się) to split ② (rozgałęzić się) *[droga, rzeka, korytarz]* (na dwie odnogi) to fork; (na więcej odnóg) to branch

rozdzierać impf → **rozedrzeć**

rozdzierając|y adi. ① (przeraźliwy) *[krzyk]* ear-splitting ② (rozpaczliwy) *[jęk, płacz, szloch]* heart-rending; *[scena, widok, ból]* excruciating

rozdźwięk m rift; ~ **między teorią a praktyką** the rift between theory and practice

roz|ebrać pf — **roz|bierać** impf **I** vt ① (zdjąć ubranie) to undress *[osobę]* ② (rozłożyć) to cut [sth] up *[maszynę, radio, zegarek]*; to cut [sth] up *[tusze, mięso]*; to pull [sth] down *[budynek]*

II rozebrać się — rozbierać się to undress, to take off one's clothes; ~**ebrać się do naga/pasa** to strip naked/to the waist; ~**ebrać się do bielizny** to strip down to one's underwear

roz|edrzeć pf — **roz|dzierać** impf **I** vt (rozerwać) to tear *[papier, materiał, ubranie]*

II rozedrzeć się — rozdzierać się ① (pęknąć) *[materiał, ubranie]* to tear apart ② pot. (wrzasnąć) to yell

rozegnać pf → **rozgonić**

roz|egrać pf — **roz|grywać** impf **I** vt to play *[mecz, turniej, spotkanie]*

II rozegrać się — rozgrywać się ① książk. *[zajście, bitwa]* to take place ② *[osoba]* to get into one's stride

rozejm m truce także przen.

roz|ejrzeć się pf — **roz|glądać się** impf v refl. to look around także przen.; ~**ejrzeć się w sytuacji** to get acquainted with the situation; ~**glądać się za czymś** to look for sth

roz|ejść się pf — **roz|chodzić się** impf v refl. ① (udać się w różne strony) *[ludzie, uczniowie]* to go separate ways; *[grupa]* to break up; *[tłum]* to disperse ② *[małżeństwo]* to split up; (rozwieść się) to divorce ③ (rozprzestrzenić się) *[głos, światło]* to travel; *[woń, ciepło]* to permeate ④ *[plotka, wiadomość]* to spread ⑤ *[drogi, szlaki]* to branch ⑥ pot. *[pieniądze]* to be spent; *[nakład książki, płyty, akcje]* to sell ⑦ *[deski, klepki, szwy]* to split apart

roz|epchać, roz|epchnąć pf — **roz|pychać** impf **I** vt ① (rozciągnąć) to stretch *[buty, spodnie]* ② (roztrącać) to push and shove *[ludzi]*

II rozepchać się, rozepchnąć się — rozpychać się *[buty, sweter]* to stretch

III rozpychać się *[osoba]* to jostle; ~**pychać się do wyjścia** to elbow one's way towards the exit

roz|erwać[1] pf — **roz|rywać** impf **I** vt (rozedrzeć) to tear *[materiał, ubranie, papier]*

II rozerwać się — rozrywać się ① (pęknąć) *[sznur, łańcuch]* to break; *[materiał, ubranie, papier]* to tear ② (eksplodować) *[pocisk, granat]* to burst

rozerw|ać[2] pf **I** vt (rozweselić) to amuse

II rozerwać się (zabawić się) to entertain oneself

roz|esłać pf — **roz|syłać** impf vt to send [sth] out *[listy, zaproszenia]*

roześmi|ać się pf v refl. to burst out laughing

roz|etrzeć pf — **roz|cierać** impf vt ① (rozmasować) to chafe *[ramiona, kark]*; to rub *[dłonie]* ② (rozgnieść) to pound *[zioła, masło, żółtka]* ③ (rozprowadzić) to rub *[maść]*

rozgad|ać pf — **rozgad|ywać** impf pot. **I** vt to blab *[tajemnicę, informację]*

II rozgadać się — rozgadywać się to go on

rozgałę|ziacz, ~źnik m extension cord; (bez kabla) adapter

rozgałęzie|nie n ① (miejsce) fork; ~**nie dróg** a fork in the road ② (odnoga) branch

rozganiać impf → **rozgonić**

rozgarn|ąć pf — **rozgarn|iać** impf vt to rake [sth] up *[śnieg, piasek]*; to part *[włosy, gałęzie]*

rozgarnię|ty adi. pot. *[osoba]* sharp-witted

rozglądać się impf → **rozejrzeć się**

rozgłaszać impf → **rozgłosić**

rozgłos m renown; **robić coś bez ~u** to do sth on the quiet pot.

rozgł|osić pf — **rozgł|aszać** impf vt to make [sth] public *[wiadomość, nowinę]*

rozgłośni|a f broadcasting station

rozgni|eść pf — **rozgni|atać** impf vt to mash *[owoce, ziemniaki]*; to grind *[pieprz]*; to crush *[czosnek, robaka]*

rozgniewa|ć pf **I** vt to anger *[osobę]*

II rozgniewać się to get angry

roz|gonić, roz|egnać pf — **roz|ganiać** impf vt to disperse *[demonstrantów, gapiów]*

rozgot|ować pf — **rozgot|owywać** impf **I** vt to overcook *[kartofle, ryż]*

II rozgotować się — rozgotowywać się to overcook

rozgramiać impf → **rozgromić**

rozgranicz|yć pf — **rozgranicz|ać** impf vt ① (podzielić) to demarcate *[posiadłości]* ② (rozróżnić) to distinguish

rozgr|omić pf — **rozgr|amiać** impf vt ① (pokonać) to crush *[wroga]* ② Sport to thrash pot. *[przeciwników]*

rozgrywać impf → **rozegrać**

rozgryw|ka **I** f ① (walka) conflict ② Sport game

II rozgrywki plt Sport tournament

rozgry|źć pf — **rozgry|zać** impf vt ① (otworzyć) to bite [sth] open; (zmiażdżyć) to bite into *[tabletkę, cukierek]* ② pot. (zrozumieć) to work [sth] out

rozgrz|ać pf — **rozgrz|ewać** impf **I** vt ① (podnieść temperaturę) to heat [sth] up *[metal, asfalt]*; to warm *[ręce, nogi]* ② (wprawić w podniecenie) to warm [sb] up *[publiczność, kibiców]*

II rozgrzać się — rozgrzewać się *[osoba, silnik]* to warm up; *[piec]* to heat up

rozgrzesz|yć *pf* — **rozgrzesz|ać** *impf* **[]** *vt* to absolve (**kogoś z czegoś** sb for sth)
[] **rozgrzeszyć się** — **rozgrzeszać się** to justify oneself
rozgrzewać *impf* → **rozgrzać**
rozgrzew|ka *f* warm-up; **na ~kę** to warm oneself up
rozgwi|azda *f* starfish
rozjaśni|ć *pf* — **rozjaśni|ać** *impf* **[]** *vt* to light [sth] up; **~ć (sobie) włosy** to bleach one's hair
[] **rozjaśnić się** — **rozjaśniać się** to brighten up
**rozj|azd [] ** *m* (rozstaje) junction
[] **rozjazdy** *plt* **być w ~azdach** to be away
rozj|echać *pf* — **rozj|eżdżać** *impf* **[]** *vt* to run over a. down *[osobę, psa]*
[] **rozjechać się** — **rozjeżdżać się** **[]** (odjechać) to part **[]** (rozsunąć się) *[narty]* to go apart
rozjemc|a *m* mediator
rozjeżdżać *impf* → **rozjechać**
rozkaz *m* order; **wydawać ~y** to give orders; **być pod czyimiś ~ami** to be under sb's command; **być na czyjeś ~y** to be at sb's command
rozka|zać *pf* — **rozka|zywać** *impf vt* to order; **~zać komuś, żeby coś zrobił** to order sb to do sth
rozkazując|y *adi.* **[]** *[głos, ton]* commanding **[]** *[tryb, forma]* imperative
rozkazywać *impf* → **rozkazać**
rozkła|d *m* **[]** (plan) schedule; **~d jazdy** a timetable **[]** (rozplanowanie) layout **[]** (rozprzężenie) disintegration **[]** (gnicie) decomposition
rozkładać *impf* → **rozłożyć**
rozkładan|y *adi.* *[łóżko, fotel, stół]* fold-out; *[kanapa]* convertible
rozkojarz|ony *adi.* absent-minded
rozkoły|sać *pf* **[]** *vt* to swing *[huśtawkę, łódź]*
[] **rozkołysać się** to start to rock
rozkop|ać *pf* — **rozkop|ywać** *impf vt* to dig (up) *[ogród, ulicę]*; **~ać pościel** pot. to kick one's bedclothes off
rozkosz *f* **[]** (uczucie) bliss; (zmysłowa) pleasure **[]** (rzecz przyjemna) delight
rozkoszn|y *adi. grad.* *[smak, widok]* delicious; *[ciepło, uczucie]* pleasurable; *[niemowlę, kotek]* cute
rozkrę|cić *pf* — **rozkrę|cać** *impf* **[]** *vt* **[]** (rozprostować) to uncoil *[spiralę]* **[]** (rozłożyć na części) to take [sth] to pieces **[]** pot. (uaktywnić) to get [sth] going *[produkcję, robotę]*
[] **rozkręcić się** — **rozkręcać się** pot. *[osoba]* to warm up
rozkrok *m* straddle position; **stanąć w ~u** to stand with one's legs apart
rozkrusz|yć *pf* — **rozkrusz|ać** *impf* **[]** *vt* to crush *[tabletkę, lód]*; to crumble *[ser, chleb]*
[] **rozkruszyć się** — **rozkruszać się** to crumble
rozkwi|t *m* **[]** (rozwój) full bloom; **~t gospodarczy** economic boom; **przeżywać ~t** to be in its heyday **[]** Bot. blossom

rozkwit|nąć *pf* — **rozkwit|ać** *impf vi* **[]** (zakwitnąć) *[kwiat]* to bloom; *[drzewo]* to blossom; *[pąk]* to flower **[]** (rozwinąć się) *[osoba]* to blossom; *[cywilizacja, sztuka, handel]* to flourish
rozl|ać *pf* — **rozl|ewać** *impf* **[]** *vt* **[]** (niechcący) to spill *[wodę, mleko]* **[]** (do kilku naczyń) to pour
[] **rozlać się** — **rozlewać się** **[]** *[woda, sok]* to spill **[]** *[rzeka]* to flood
rozl|ecieć się *pf* — **rozl|atywać się** *impf v refl.* pot. (rozpaść się) *[but, mebel, książka, małżeństwo]* to fall apart
rozle|c się, **rozle|gnąć się** *pf* — **rozle|gać się**[1] *impf v refl. [dźwięk, huk, trzask]* to sound; *[echo, kroki, wołanie]* to reverberate
rozleg|ły *adi. grad. [widok, pole, wiedza]* extensive
rozlegnąć się *impf* → rozlec się
rozleniw|ić *pf* — **rozleniw|iać** *impf* **[]** *vt* to make [sb] indolent
[] **rozleniwić się** — **rozleniwiać się** to become indolent
rozlewać *impf* → rozlać
roz|leźć się *pf* — **roz|łazić się** *impf v refl.* pot. **[]** (porozchodzić się) *[osoby, zwierzęta]* to disperse; *[karaluchy, mrówki]* to sprawl **[]** (zniszczyć się) *[materiał]* to be torn
rozliczać *impf* → rozliczyć
rozlicze|nie *n* settlement; **~nie z przeszłością** przen. settling accounts with the past
rozlicz|yć *pf* — **rozlicz|ać** *impf* **[]** *vt* to account for *[koszty]*; to square *[należności]*
[] **rozliczyć się** — **rozliczać się** (uregulować rachunki) **~yć się z kimś** to settle accounts with sb; **~yć się z czegoś** to account for sth
rozluźni|ć *pf* — **rozluźni|ać** *impf* **[]** *vt* **[]** (odprężyć) to relax *[mięśnie, uchwyt]* **[]** (poluzować) to loosen *[krawat, kołnierzyk]* **[]** przen. (zrelaksować) to relax *[osobę]*
[] **rozluźnić się** — **rozluźniać się** **[]** *[sznurowadło, opatrunek, więzi]* to loosen **[]** *[autobus, pociąg]* to become less crowded **[]** (pozbyć się skrępowania) *[osoba]* to relax
rozład|ować *pf* — **rozład|owywać** *impf* **[]** *vt* **[]** to unload *[pociąg, towar]* **[]** to discharge *[baterię, akumulator]* **[]** przen. to relieve *[napięcie, stres, złość]*
[] **rozładować się** — **rozładowywać się** **[]** *[bateria, akumulator]* to go flat **[]** przen. *[napięcie, konflikt]* to be defused; *[tłok, korek uliczny]* to get relieved; *[osoba]* to let off steam
rozładun|ek *m* unloading
rozłam *m* split; (religijny) schism
rozłazić się *impf* → rozleźć się
rozłącz|yć *pf* — **rozłącz|ać** *impf* **[]** *vt* **[]** (odłączyć) to disconnect *[kable, przewody]*; **coś nas ~yło** (przez telefon) we were cut off **[]** (oddzielić) to separate *[rodzinę, przyjaciół]*
[] **rozłączyć się** — **rozłączać się** **[]** *[przewody]* to

disconnect [2] (odłożyć słuchawkę) to hang up; **nie ~aj się** hold on

rozłą|ka f separation

roz|łożyć pf — **roz|kładać** impf **[]** vt [1] (rozprostować) to unfold *[gazetę, prześcieradło]*; (rozpostrzeć) to spread *[obrus, koc]*; **~kładane łóżko** a folding bed; **~łożyć ręce** to spread one's arms [2] (położyć) to lay [sth] out *[książki, sprawunki]* [3] (rozdzielić) to divide *[prace, zadania]* [4] (rozmontować) to take [sth] to pieces *[maszynę, zegar]* [5] (doprowadzić do rozkładu) to decompose *[odpadki]*

[] **rozłożyć się** — **rozkładać się** [1] (położyć się) *[osoba]* to stretch out; **~łożyć się z towarem** to display one's goods for sale [2] (otworzyć się) *[parasol]* to unfold [3] (w czasie) to be spread out [4] (ulec rozkładowi) to decompose

rozłup|ać pf — **rozłup|ywać** impf **[]** vt to split *[orzech]*

[] **rozłupać się** — **rozłupywać się** *[orzech]* to split

rozmach m [1] (zamach) swing; **wziąć ~** to take a swing [2] (tempo, skala) **nabierać ~u** to gather momentum

rozmaitoś|ć [] f variety

[] **rozmaitości** plt sundries

rozmai|ty adi. various

rozmarzać¹ /ro'zmarzatɕ/ impf → **rozmarznąć**

rozmarzać² impf → **rozmarzyć**

rozmarz|nąć /ro'zmarznɔntɕ/ pf — **rozmarz-z|ać** /ro'zmarzatɕ/ impf vi *[mięso, ziemia]* to thaw

rozmarz|yć pf — **rozmarz|ać** impf **[]** vt to make [sb] dreamy

[] **rozmarzyć się** — **rozmarzać się** to be lost in daydreaming

rozmas|ować pf — **rozmas|owywać** impf vt to rub *[ramię, mięsień]*

rozmawia|ć impf vi to talk (**z kimś** to a. with sb); **nie ~jmy o pracy** let's not talk shop; **nie ~ją ze sobą** they are not on speaking terms

rozma|zać pf — **rozma|zywać** impf **[]** vt [1] (rozsmarować) to smear; (zabrudzić) to smudge *[tusz, atrament]* [2] (rozmyć) to blur *[obraz, różnice]*

[] **rozmazać się** — **rozmazywać się** [1] (rozsmarować się) *[szminka, makijaż, atrament]* to smudge [2] (rozmyć się) *[kształty, różnice]* to blur [3] pot. (rozpłakać się) to start blubbering pot.

rozmia|r m size; **przedmiot pokaźnych ~rów** a sizeable object; **przedmiot ~rów piłki tenisowej** an object the size of a tennis ball; **~r buta** shoe size; **jaki ~r pan nosi?** what size are you a. do you take?

rozmie|nić pf — **rozmie|niać** impf vt to change *[banknot, sumę]*

rozmie|ścić pf — **rozmie|szczać** impf vt (ustawić, ułożyć) to arrange *[przedmioty]*; to lay [sth] out *[tekst, ilustrację]*; to post *[strażników]*; to deploy

[jednostki, oddziały]; (zakwaterować) to quarter *[żołnierzy]*

rozmiękać impf → **rozmięknąć**

rozmiękcz|yć pf — **rozmiękcz|ać** impf vt [1] (zmiękczyć) to soften *[skórę]*; (namoczyć) to soak *[podłoże, glebę]* [2] (złamać opór) to soften [sb] up *[przeciwnika, świadka]*

rozmięk|nąć pf — **rozmięk|ać** impf vi *[ziemia, substancja]* to soften także przen.

rozmin|ować pf — **rozmin|owywać** impf vt to clear [sth] of mines

rozmn|ożyć pf — **rozmn|ażać** impf **[]** vt to multiply także przen. *[rośliny, zyski]*

[] **rozmnożyć się** — **rozmnażać się** (mieć potomstwo) to reproduce; (zwiększyć populację) to multiply

rozm|owa [] f [1] (wymiana zdań) conversation; **~owa przez telefon** a telephone conversation; **podtrzymywać ~owę** to keep a conversation going; **~owa kwalifikacyjna** a job interview [2] (połączenie telefoniczne) call

[] **rozmowy** plt talks; **~owy pokojowe** peace talks

rozmown|y adi. grad. (chętny do rozmowy) forthcoming; (gadatliwy) talkative

rozmów|ca m, **~czyni** f (partner w rozmowie) interlocutor książk.; (podczas wywiadu) interviewed person

rozmów|ki plt phrasebook

rozmr|ozić pf — **rozmr|ażać** impf **[]** vt to thaw, to defrost *[mięso]*; to defrost *[lodówkę, szyby]*

[] **rozmrozić się** — **rozmrażać się** *[mięso]* to thaw; *[lody]* to melt; *[lodówka]* to defrost

rozmy|ć pf — **rozmy|wać** impf **[]** vt [1] *[deszcz, rzeka]* to wash [sth] away *[ślady, brzeg, drogę]* [2] przen. to blur *[kształty, zarysy]*

[] **rozmyć się** — **rozmywać się** [1] *[ślady]* to be washed away [2] przen. *[obraz, kształty]* to blur

rozmyśla|ć impf vi to ponder (**nad czymś** over sth)

rozmyśl|ić się pf — **rozmyśl|ać się** impf v refl. to change one's mind

rozmywać impf → **rozmyć**

roznie|cić pf — **roznie|cać** impf **[]** vt to kindle także przen.

[] **rozniecić się** — **rozniecać się** *[ogień]* to kindle

rozn|ieść pf — **rozn|osić** impf **[]** vt [1] (dostarczyć) to hand [sth] around *[zeszyty]*; *[listonosz]* to deliver *[paczki, listy]*; *[kelner]* to serve *[napoje, kanapki]* [2] (przetransportować) *[krew, wiatr]* to carry [sth] around *[składniki, liście, popiół]*; *[zwierzę]* to spread *[choroby, wirusy]* [3] przen. (rozbić) to demolish *[przeciwnika, drużynę]* [4] (przepełniać) **~osiła go energia/radość** he was bouncing with energy/joy

[] **roznieść się** — **roznosić się** *[informacja, plotka]* to spread

roznosiciel *m* delivery man; ~ **gazet** a newsboy; ~ **mleka** a milkman

roznosić *impf* → **roznieść**

rozpacz *f* despair; **być pogrążonym w** ~**y** to be in despair

rozpacza|ć *impf vt* to despair; ~**ć z powodu czegoś** to be in despair at sth

rozpacżliw|y *adi. [spojrzenie, ton, list]* despairing; *[sytuacja, warunki, próba]* desperate

rozpa|d *m* ① (podział) disintegration; ~**d imperium** the demise of the empire; ~**d ich małżeństwa** the breakdown of their marriage ② (atomu, substancji) breakdown

rozpadać się[1] *impf* → **rozpaść się**

rozpada|ć się[2] *pf v refl.* to start to rain steadily

rozpadlin|a *f* cleft, crevice

rozpak|ować *pf* — **rozpak|owywać** *impf* Ⅰ *vt* to unpack *[walizkę, plecak]*

Ⅱ **rozpakować się** — **rozpakowywać się** to unpack

rozpal|ić *pf* — **rozpal|ać** *impf* Ⅰ *vt* ① (rozniecić) to light *[ogień]*; ~**ić w piecu** to light the fire in the stove ② (silnie rozgrzać) to heat; ~**ić metal do czerwoności** to heat metal red hot ③ przen. to kindle *[wyobraźnię]*

Ⅱ **rozpalić się** — **rozpalać się** to flame up

rozpał|ka *f* tinder, kindling

rozpa|ść się *pf* — **rozpa|dać się**[1] *impf v refl.* ① (zniszczyć się) *[buty, urządzenie, małżeństwo, system]* to fall apart; *[budynek]* to crumble away ② (podzielić się) *[organizacja]* to split

rozpat|rzyć, rozpat|rzeć *pf* — **rozpat|rywać** *impf* Ⅰ *vt* to examine *[możliwości, warianty]*; to investigate *[skargi, zażalenia]*; to hear *[sprawę]*

Ⅱ **rozpatrzyć się, rozpatrzeć się** — **rozpatrywać się** to acquaint oneself (**w czymś** with sth)

rozpę|d *m* momentum; **nabrać** ~**du** to gain momentum; **wziąć** ~**d** to take a run-up

rozpę|dzić *pf* — **rozpę|dzać** *impf* Ⅰ *vt* ① (rozgonić) to disperse *[demonstrantów, gapiów]* ② (przyspieszyć) to accelerate

Ⅱ **rozpędzić się** — **rozpędzać się** *[pojazd]* to gather speed; *[skoczek]* to take a run-up

roz|piąć *pf* — **roz|pinać** *impf* Ⅰ *vt* ① (otworzyć z zapięcia) to unbutton *[marynarkę, płaszcz]*; to undo *[guziki, zamek]*; to unzip *[spodnie]*; to unbuckle *[pasek, klamrę]* ② (rozciągnąć) to spread *[sieci, skrzydła]*

Ⅱ **rozpiąć się** — **rozpinać się** ① (rozpiąć guzik) ~**piąć się pod szyją** *[osoba]* to undo a button at one's neck ② *[guzik, suwak]* to become undone

rozpie|ścić *pf* — **rozpie|szczać** *impf vt* to spoil *[dziecko, psa]*

rozpinać *impf* → **rozpiąć**

rozpi|sać *pf* — **rozpi|sywać** *impf* Ⅰ *vt* ① (ogłosić) to call *[wybory]*; to send out *[ankietę]*; ~**sać konkurs (na coś)** to invite entries (for sth) ② (przepisać) to write [sth] out

Ⅱ **rozpisać się** — **rozpisywać się** (napisać rozwlekle) to write at length (**o czymś** about sth)

rozplan|ować *pf* — **rozplan|owywać** *impf vt* to lay out *[ulice]*; to plan out *[dzień, pracę]*

rozplą|tać *pf* — **rozplą|tywać** *impf vt* to untwist *[nici, sznurek]*; to undo *[węzeł]*; to untangle także przen. *[sieć, tajemnicę]*

rozpła|kać się *pf* to burst out crying

rozpocz|ąć *pf* — **rozpocz|ynać** *impf* Ⅰ *vt* to begin, to start; ~**ąć dzień od gimnastyki** to start one's day by doing exercises

Ⅱ **rozpocząć się** — **rozpoczynać się** to start, to begin

rozpog|odzić się *pf* — **rozpog|adzać się** *impf v refl.* ① *[niebo]* to clear up; ~**odziło się** it cleared up ② *[osoba]* to cheer up

rozpor|ek *m* ① (w spodniach) fly; **zapiąć/rozpiąć** ~**ek** to do up/undo one's fly ② (w spódnicy) slit

rozpowszechni|ć *pf* — **rozpowszechni|ać** *impf* Ⅰ *vt* ① (opublikować) to circulate *[plotki, pogłoski]*; to distribute *[film, materiały]* ② (upowszechnić) to spread *[zwyczaj]*

Ⅱ **rozpowszechnić się** — **rozpowszechniać się** *[tradycja, zwyczaj]* to spread; *[urządzenie, metoda]* to become commonly used

rozpozna|ć *pf* — **rozpozna|wać** *impf vt* ① (zidentyfikować) to recognize *[osobę]*; to diagnose *[chorobę]*; to identify *[potrzeby, zagrożenia]* ② *[sąd]* to hear *[sprawę, wniosek]*

rozpozna|nie *n* ① Med. diagnosis ② Wojsk. reconnaissance

rozpoznawać *impf* → **rozpoznać**

rozpras|ować *pf* — **rozpras|owywać** *impf vt* *[osoba]* to iron [sth] out *[kant, szew, zakładkę]*

rozpraszać *impf* → **rozproszyć**

rozpraw|a *f* ① (bitwa) battle także przen.; ~**a z przestępczością** a crackdown on crime ② (praca naukowa) treatise (**na temat czegoś** on sth); (na stopień naukowy) dissertation ③ (proces) trial

rozpraw|ić się *pf* — **rozpraw|iać się** *impf vt* ~**ić się z opozycją** to crush the opposition; ~**ić się z przestępczością** to crack down on crime

rozprost|ować *pf* — **rozprost|owywać** *impf* Ⅰ *vt* ① (wygładzić) to smooth [sth] out *[papier, materiał, zmarszczki]* ② (wyciągnąć) to stretch *[ramiona, nogi]*; (po zgięciu) to unbend *[palce, kolana]*

Ⅱ **rozprostować się** — **rozprostowywać się** (przeciągnąć się) *[osoba]* to stretch; (wyprostować się) *[osoba, palce]* to unbend

rozpr|oszyć *impf* — **rozpr|aszać** *pf* Ⅰ *vt* ① (rozgonić) to disperse *[tłum, mgłę, mrok]* ② (rozdrobnić) to fragment *[system, organizację]*; to split *[fundusze, wysiłki]*; to diffuse *[światło]* ③ (zdekoncentrować) to distract *[osobę]* ④ (rozwiać) to dispel *[wątpliwości, obawy, nieufność]*

Ⅱ **rozproszyć się** — **rozpraszać się** ① (rozejść się) *[tłum, chmury]* to disperse ② (rozdrobnić się) *[system,* *organizacja]* to become fragmented; *[odpowiedzialność]* to be dispersed [3] (zdekoncentrować się) *[osoba]* to be distracted

rozprowa|dzić *impf* — **rozprowa|dzać** *impf vt* [1] (rozmieść) to carry *[krew]*; to distribute *[prąd, wodę]* [2] (sprzedać) to distribute *[narkotyki]*; to pass [sth] out *[ulotki]* [3] (rozsmarować) to spread *[klej, lakier]* [4] (rozcieńczyć) to thin *[farbę]*; (rozpuścić) to dissolve *[proszek]*

rozpru|ć *pf* — **rozpru|wać** *impf* **[]** *vt* [1] (usunąć szwy) to unstitch *[szew, rękaw]*; (podrzeć) to split [2] pot. (rozciąć) to open *[sejf]*; to rip *[łódź, kadłub]*; to split [sth] open *[brzuch]*

[] **rozpruć się** — **rozpruwać się** (rozedrzeć się) to split open

rozprysk|ać *pf* — **rozprysk|iwać** *impf* **[]** *vt* (rozchlapać) to spray *[wodę, błoto]*

[] **rozpryskać się** — **rozpryskiwać się** *[olej]* to spatter

rozprzestrze|nić się *pf* — **rozprzestrze|niać się** *impf v refl. [ogień, epidemia, moda]* to spread

rozpuszczać *impf* → **rozpuścić**

rozpuszczalnik *m* solvent; ~ **do farb** paint thinner

rozpuszczaln|y *adi.* soluble; **kawa** ~**a** instant coffee

rozpu|ścić *pf* — **rozpu|szczać** *impf* **[]** *vt* [1] (utworzyć roztwór) to dissolve; (rozcieńczyć) to thin *[farbę]* [2] (roztopić) to melt *[lód, masło]* [3] (rozpiąć) to let [sth] down *[włosy]*; **z** ~**szczonymi włosami** with one's hair loose [4] (pozwolić odejść) to send [sb] home *[żołnierzy, pracowników]* [5] (rozpowszechnić) to set [sth] about *[pogłoski, wiadomości]* [6] pot. (zdemoralizować) to spoil *[dziecko]*

[] **rozpuścić się** — **rozpuszczać się** [1] (zmieszać się) *[cukier, tabletka]* to dissolve [2] *[lody, masło]* to melt [3] pot. (zdemoralizować się) to be spoilt

rozpychać *impf* → **rozepchać**

rozpylacz *m* [1] (urządzenie) sprayer; (do lekarstw) vaporizer [2] pot. machine gun

rozpyl|ić *pf* — **rozpyl|ać** *impf* **[]** *vt* to spray *[perfumy, wodę]*

[] **rozpylić się** — **rozpylać się** *[ciecz]* to break up into a fine spray

rozrabiać[1] *impf* → **rozrobić**

rozrabia|ć[2] *impf vi* pot. (robić burdy) to brawl; (wywoływać zamieszanie) *[osoba]* to stir up trouble; *[dziecko]* to be up to some mischief

rozrachun|ek *m* account; **być na własnym** ~**ku** *[organizacja]* to be self-financing; *[pracownik]* to be self-employed; **przeprowadzić** ~**ek z przeszłością** przen. to come to terms with one's past

rozrastać się *impf* → **rozrosnąć się**

rozregul|ować *pf* — **rozregul|owywać** *impf* **[]** *vt* to upset *[mechanizm]*

[] **rozregulować się** — **rozregulowywać się** to go wrong

rozr|obić *pf* — **rozr|abiać**[1] *impf vt* to mix

rozrodcz|y *adi. [komórki, gruczoły]* reproductive

rozr|osnąć się *pf* — **rozr|astać się** *impf v refl.* to grow

rozróżni|ć *pf* — **rozróżni|ać** *impf vt* to distinguish

rozruch **[]** *m* start(ing)-up, warm(ing)-up; ~ **próbny** a test run; ~ **zakładu** the start-up of a plant

[] **rozruchy** *plt* riot(s)

rozrusza|ć *pf* **[]** *vt* [1] (przywrócić sprawność) to loosen up *[nogi, stawy]* [2] (wprawić w ruch) to set [sth] in motion *[urządzenie techniczne, silnik]* [3] (ożywić) to liven up *[towarzystwo]*

[] **rozruszać się** (nabrać energii) to liven up

rozrusznik *m* starter

❑ ~ **serca** Med. (artificial) pacemaker

rozrywać *impf* → **rozerwać**[1]

rozryw|ka *f* entertainment; **robić coś dla** ~**ki** to do sth for fun

rozrywkow|y *adi. [muzyka, program]* light; **przemysł** ~**y** show business

rozrze|dzić *pf* — **rozrze|dzać** *impf* **[]** *vt* to thin (down) *[farbę]*; ~**dzone powietrze** rarefied air

[] **rozrzedzić się** — **rozrzedzić się** *[tłum, las]* to thin (out)

rozrzu|cić *pf* — **rozrzu|cać** *impf vt* to scatter *[nasiona, nawóz, zabawki]*

rozrzutnoś|ć *f* prodigality

rozrzutn|y *adi. grad.* [1] (nieliczący się z pieniędzmi) overspending [2] (marnotrawny) wasteful

rozsa|dzić *pf* — **rozsa|dzać** *impf vt* [1] (usadowić) ~**dzić gości przy stole** to seat guests around a table [2] (rozdzielić) to split [sb] up *[uczniów, dzieci]* [3] (rozrzedzić) to plant [sth] out *[rośliny, flance]* [4] (rozbić) to blast (out) *[skałę]*

rozsąd|ek *m* reason; **zdrowy** ~**ek** common sense; **w granicach** ~**ku** within reason

rozsądn|y *adi. grad. [rada]* sound; *[decyzja]* wise; *[pomysł, plan, wybór]* sensible; *[cena, propozycja, osoba]* reasonable

rozsą|dzić *pf* — **rozsą|dzać** *impf vt* to arbitrate *[spór, kwestię sporną]*

rozsi|ąść się *pf* — **rozsi|adać się** *impf v refl.* to lounge

rozsmar|ować *pf* — **rozsmar|owywać** *impf* **[]** *vt* to spread *[dżem, klej]*

[] **rozsmarować się** — **rozsmarowywać się** *[masło, margaryna]* to spread

rozsta|ć się *pf* — **rozsta|wać się** *impf v refl.* to part; ~**ć się z mężem/z żoną** to split up with one's husband/wife; **nie** ~**wał się z teczką ani na chwilę** he wouldn't be parted from his briefcase even for a moment

rozsta|nie n (pożegnanie) parting; (zerwanie) split-up; (rozłąka) separation

rozstawać się impf → rozstać się

rozstaw|ić pf — **rozstaw|iać** impf **I** vt 1 (w pewnym porządku) to deploy [straże, warty]; to set out [talerze, kieliszki]; **był** ~**iony z numerem szóstym** Sport he was seeded sixth; ~**ione w odległości 100 metrów od siebie** spaced 100 metres apart 2 (rozłożyć) to unfold [leżak, fotel] **II** **rozstawić się** — **rozstawiać się** to position a. place oneself

rozst|ąpić się pf — **rozst|ępować się** impf v refl. [tłum] to part; [skała] to split; [ziemia] to open

rozstr|oić pf — **rozstr|ajać** impf **I** vt 1 (rozdrażnić) to upset [osobę] 2 Muz. to put [sth] out of tune [instrument] **II** **rozstroić się** — **rozstrajać się** to be out of tune

rozstrzel|ać pf — **rozstrzel|iwać** impf vt to execute [sb] by firing squad

rozstrzyg|nąć pf — **rozstrzyg|ać** impf **I** vt to decide [spór, sprawę, konflikt]; to adjudicate [konkurs]; to negotiate [problem] **II** **rozstrzygnąć się** — **rozstrzygać się** to be decided

rozsu|nąć pf — **rozsu|wać** impf **I** vt 1 (odsuwając rozdzielić) to draw [sth] aside a. back [kurtynę, zasłony]; to space [sth] widely [stoliki, krzesła]; to unzip [suwak] 2 (rozstawić) to unfold [stół] **II** **rozsunąć się** — **rozsuwać się** [kurtyna, zasłona, osoby] to part

rozsyłać impf → rozesłać

rozsyp|ać pf — **rozsyp|ywać** impf **I** vt (rozrzucić) to scatter [sól, ziarno]; to strew [papiery, fotografie] **II** **rozsypać się** — **rozsypywać się** 1 (wysypać się) [cukier, sól] to spill 2 (rozpaść się) [szopa, książka] to fall apart 3 (rozejść się) [grupa osób, stado zwierząt] to disperse

rozszerz|yć pf — **rozszerz|ać** impf **I** vt to ream [otwór]; to widen [szczelinę, wiedzę]; to broaden [doświadczenie]; to expand [przywileje, wpływy]; to extend [ofertę, repertuar] **II** **rozszerzyć się** — **rozszerzać się** [droga, ulica] to widen; [spódnica, spodnie, rękawy] to flare; [ogień, pożar, epidemia] to spread; [wiedza, znaczenie wyrazu] to broaden; [ciecz, metal] to expand

rozsznur|ować pf — **rozsznur|owywać** impf **I** vt to unlace [buty, gorset, namiot] **II** **rozsznurować się** — **rozsznurowywać się** [but] to come unlaced

rozszyfr|ować pf — **rozszyfr|owywać** impf vt to decipher [tekst]; to decode [skrót, pseudonim]; to unravel [aluzję, zagadkę]

rozśmiesz|yć pf — **rozśmiesz|ać** impf vt to amuse [osobę, widownię]

roztaczać impf → roztoczyć

roztapiać impf → roztopić

roztargnieni|e n absent-mindedness

roztargni|ony adi. [osoba] absent-minded; [spojrzenie, wzrok] distracted

rozter|ka f quandary; **być w** ~**ce** to be in a quandary

rozt|oczyć pf — **rozt|aczać** impf **I** vt to unfold [perspektywy, wizję, plany]; to exude [blask, zapach]; to ooze [urok]; ~**oczyć opiekę nad czymś** to take sth under one's care **II** **roztaczać się** [widok] to stretch, to unfold

roztop m wiosenne ~**y** the spring melt a. thaw

rozt|opić pf — **rozt|apiać** impf **I** vt to melt [tłuszcz, metal, śnieg] **II** **roztopić się** — **roztapiać się** [lód, śnieg, lody, kontury] to melt

roztrw|onić pf — **roztrw|aniać** impf vt to squander [majątek, pieniądze]

roztrzask|ać pf — **roztrzask|iwać** impf **I** vt to smash; ~**ać coś na kawałki** to smash sth to pieces **II** **roztrzaskać się** — **roztrzaskiwać się** [figurka, statek] to smash

roztrzep|ać pf — **roztrzep|ywać** impf **I** vt (wymieszać) to stir and shake [zsiadłe mleko, śmietanę] **II** **roztrzepać się** — **roztrzepywać się** [włosy] to become tousled

roztrzepan|y adi. scatterbrained

roztrzepywać impf → roztrzepać

roztrzęsi|ony adi. [osoba] jittery; [głos, ręka] shaking

roztw|ór m solution

rozum m 1 (umysł) mind, intellect; **objąć coś** ~**em** to understand sth; **być niespełna** ~**u** to be out of one's mind 2 (rozsądek) reason; **miejże** ~**!** have some sense!; **brać coś na** ~ to use one's common sense

rozumi|eć impf **I** vt to understand [sens, tekst, instrukcję]; ~**eć czyjąś sytuację** to understand the situation sb is in; **nie** ~**esz po polsku?** iron. don't you understand plain Polish?; **źle** ~**ane poczucie lojalności** an ill-conceived sense of loyalty **II** **rozumieć się** 1 (wzajemnie) to understand one another 2 pot. (znać się na czymś) ~**eć się na interesach** to be well up on business 3 (jest rozumiane) **potocznie** ~**e się demokrację jako...** democracy is popularly understood as... ■ **to się samo przez się** ~**e** pot. it goes without saying; **ma się** ~**eć** pot. naturally; **to** ~**em!** pot. now you're talking!

rozwa|ga f prudence; **brać coś pod** ~**gę** to take sth into consideration

rozwal|ić pf — **rozwal|ać** impf pot. **I** vt 1 (rozbić na kawałki) to knock [sth] down [mur, ścianę, dom]; to smash [sth] up [bryłę węgla] 2 przen. to destroy [małżeństwo]; to smash [organizację, zespół] 3 (rozrzucić) to scatter [książki, ubrania] 4 (zranić) to cut [nogę, rękę]; ~**ić komuś gębę** to bash sb's mug **II** **rozwalić się** — **rozwalać się** 1 (rozpaść się) to crash [2] przen. *[rodzina, robota]* to crumble [3] (rozsiąść się) to sprawl

rozwałk|ować *pf* — **rozwałk|owywać** *impf* *vt* to roll [sth] up *[ciasto]*

rozważać *impf* → **rozważyć**

rozważn|y *adi. grad.* prudent

rozważ|yć *pf* — **rozważ|ać** *impf vt* to consider *[propozycję, możliwość]*; to ponder *[problem, zagadnienie]*; to weigh *[argumenty, dowody, czynniki]*; ~**yć zrobienie czegoś** to consider doing sth; ~**yć wszystkie za i przeciw** to weigh the pros and cons

rozwesel|ić *pf* — **rozwesel|ać** *impf* **[]** *vt* to cheer [sb] up

[] **rozweselić się** — **rozweselać się** (rozchmurzyć się) to cheer up

rozwi|ać *pf* — **rozwi|ewać** *impf* **[]** *vt* [1] *[wiatr]* to disperse *[chmury]*; to blow *[płaszcz]*; **koń z ~aną grzywą** a horse with its mane flowing in the wind [2] przen. to dispel *[obawy, wątpliwości, złudzenia]*; to disappoint *[nadzieje]*

[] **rozwiać się** — **rozwiewać się** [1] *[chmura, mgła]* to disperse; *[włosy, grzywa, sukienka]* to be blowing [2] (zniknąć) *[sny, obawy, złudzenia]* to be dispelled; *[mit]* to be shattered; *[nadzieje, marzenia]* to evaporate

rozwią|zać *pf* — **rozwiąz|ywać** *impf* **[]** *vt* [1] (odpiąć) to untie *[węzeł, sznurowadło, krawat, ręce, osobę]* [2] (znaleźć rozwiązanie) to solve *[problem, krzyżówkę, równanie, zagadkę]* [3] (unieważnić) to dissolve *[układ, małżeństwo, parlament]*; to cancel *[umowę, kontrakt]*; to disband *[organizację, partię]*

[] **rozwiązać się** — **rozwiązywać się** [1] (rozplątać się) *[węzeł, kokarda]* to come untied; *[osoba]* to untie oneself; **but ci się ~zał** your lace is undone [2] *[problem]* to solve itself [3] (przestać działać) *[sejm, parlament]* to dissolve itself; *[organizacja, partia]* to disband; *[demonstracja]* to disperse

rozwiąza|nie *n* [1] (wyjście, odpowiedź) solution; (w teście, quizie) answer [2] (parlamentu) dissolution [3] Med. delivery

rozwiązywać *impf* → **rozwiązać**

rozwidl|ić się *pf* — **rozwidl|ać się** *impf v refl.* *[rzeka, droga]* to fork

rozwiedz|iony **[]** *adi.* divorced

[] **rozwiedz|iony** *m*, ~**iona** *f* divorcee

rozw|ieść się — **rozw|odzić się** *impf v refl.* to get divorced; ~**ieść się z kimś** to divorce sb

rozwiewać *impf* → **rozwiać**

rozw|ieźć *pf* — **rozw|ozić** *impf vt* to deliver *[pocztę]*; ~**ieźć gości do hoteli** to drive the guests to their hotels

rozwi|nąć *pf* — **rozwi|jać** *impf* **[]** *vt* [1] (rozprostować) to unfurl *[żagiel, transparent, sztandar]*; to unwind *[linę, bandaż, kłębek]*; to uncoil *[drut]*; to unroll *[dywan, śpiwór, belę]*; to unreel *[kliszę, wąż ogrodowy]*; to reel [sth] off *[nitkę]* [2] (rozpakować) to unwrap *[paczkę, pakunek]* [3] (rozchylić) *[kwiat]* to

open *[płatki]* [4] (ukształtować) to develop *[cechę, umiejętności, styl, mięśnie, przemysł]* [5] (omówić) to elaborate on *[temat, plan]* [6] (osiągnąć) *[pojazd]* to reach *[prędkość]*

[] **rozwinąć się** — **rozwijać się** [1] (rozprostować się) *[drut, wąż]* to uncoil; *[taśma, lina]* to unwind; *[klisza, rolka, szpulka]* to unroll; *[spadochron]* to open [2] (rozchylić się) *[kwiat, pąk]* to open [3] (urosnąć, ukształtować się) *[osoba, organ, cecha, kraj, przemysł]* to develop [4] *[wydarzenia, sytuacja]* to unfold

rozwinię|ty *adi.* developed; **kraje wysoko ~te** the developed countries; **nadmiernie ~ty** *[mięśnie, osoba]* overdeveloped; **słabo ~ty** *[organ, mózg, zmysł]* underdeveloped

rozwl|ec *pf* — **rozwl|ekać** *impf vt* [1] (porozność) to drag [sth] around [2] (przeciągnąć) to pad [sth] out *[przemówienie, artykuł]*

rozwlek|ły *adi. grad.* *[opis, książka]* lengthy; *[styl, narracja, wywód]* diffuse; *[sposób mówienia]* slow

rozwodzić się *impf* → **rozwieść się**

rozwolnie|nie *n* diarrhoea, diarrhea US

rozwozić *impf* → **rozwieźć**

rozw|ód *m* divorce; **wziąć ~ód** to get divorced

rozw|ój *m* [1] (wzrost, kształtowanie się) development; **być opóźnionym w ~oju** to be developmentally delayed [2] (przebieg) course; ~**ój wypadków** a course of events

rozzło|ścić *pf* **[]** *vt* to make [sb] angry

[] **rozzłościć się** to get angry

rozzuchwal|ić *pf* — **rozzuchwal|ać** *impf* **[]** *vt* to encourage *[przestępcę]*

[] **rozzuchwalić się** — **rozzuchwalać się** *[dzieci]* to become unruly; *[przestępcy]* to become audacious

rozżarz|yć *pf* — **rozżarz|ać** *impf* **[]** *vt* to heat [sth] up; ~**one węgle** red-hot coals

[] **rozżarzyć się** — **rozżarzać się** *[drut]* to heat up; *[węgle]* to start glowing

roż|ek *m* [1] Kulin. (rogalik) crescent roll; (z ciasta francuskiego) croissant [2] Kulin. (wafel) cone; **lody w ~ku** an ice-cream cone [3] Muz. horn

roż|en *m* (szpikulec) spit; (urządzenie) spit-roaster

r|ód *m* family; **zwaśnione rody** feuding families; **być rodem z Warszawy** to be born in Warsaw

r|óg *m* [1] Zool. horn; **rogi jelenia** deer antlers; **wystawić rogi** *[ślimak]* to put out one's horns; **pokazać rogi** przen. to show temper [2] Muz. horn [3] (u zbiegu krawędzi) corner; **róg kartki** a corner of a page; **w rogu pokoju** in the corner of a room; **róg Hożej i Marszałkowskiej** the corner of Hoża and Marszałkowska streets; **skręcić za róg** to turn around the corner [4] Sport (miejsce, rzut rożny) corner

■ **przyprawić komuś rogi** to cuckold sb

r|ój *m* swarm także przen.

r|ów *m* ditch

rówieśni|k *m*, ~**ca** *f* peer; **być czyimś ~kiem** to be sb's age

równa|ć impf **[I]** vt ① (wyrównywać) to level *[ziemię, powierzchnię]* ② (zrównywać) ~**ć kogoś z kimś** to put sb on the same level as sb

[II] równać się ① ~**ć się czemuś** (mieć taką samą wartość) to equal sth; (oznaczać) to mean sth ② (dorównywać) ~**ć się z kimś/czymś pod względem czegoś** to equal sb/sth in sth

równa|nie n equation

równie adv. equally; ~ **szybko, jak...** as quickly as...; ~ **dobrze możemy...** we can equally well a. just as well...

również adv. also, as well; **muszę ~ powiedzieć, że...** I also have to say that...; **nie tylko ładna, ale ~ inteligentna** not only pretty but also intelligent

równik m equator

równin|a f plain

równinn|y adi. *[krajobraz]* flat; **teren ~y** flatland(s)

równ|o [I] adv. grad. ① *[rozłożyć, pomalować, przyszyć, uciąć]* evenly; ~**o wisieć** (poziomo) to be level; **książki były ~o poustawiane** the books were neatly lined up ② (miarowo) *[oddychać]* evenly; *[iść, biec]* at a steady pace ③ (stale tak samo) *[grać, pracować]* consistently

[II] adv. ① (jednakowo) *[podzielić]* evenly; **podzielić coś ~o** to divide sth evenly; **było po ~o chłopaków i dziewczyn** there was an equal number of boys and girls ② (dokładnie) exactly; ~**o o dziewiątej** at nine o'clock sharp ③ (równocześnie) ~**o z kimś** at the same time as sb

równocze|sny adi. *[czynności, działania]* simultaneous

równocześnie adv. *[występować, odbywać się]* at the same time; **chciał tego i bał się ~** he wanted it and at the same time was scared

równolat|ek m, ~**ka** f peer; **być czyimś ~kiem** to be sb's age

równoległobok m parallelogram

równoległ|y adi. *[odcinki, proste, klasy, rozwój]* parallel (**do czegoś** to a. with sth)

równoleżnik m parallel

równomiern|y adi. *[podział, oddech]* even

równorzędn|y adi. *[partner, rywal]* equal; *[stanowisko, produkt]* equivalent

równoś|ć f ① (równy status) equality; ~**ć wobec prawa** equal rights ② (równa wartość) **znak ~ci** the equal(s) sign; **stawiać znak ~ci między czymś a czymś** przen. to treat sth and sth as one

równouprawnieni|e n (równe prawa) equal rights; (zrównanie wobec prawa) granting equal rights

równowa|ga f ① (stała postawa) balance; **stracić ~gę** to lose one's balance ② (spokój) balance, equilibrium; **wytrącić kogoś z ~gi** to throw sb off balance przen.; **wyprowadzić kogoś z ~gi** to make sb angry ③ (stabilizacja) balance; ~**ga sił** the balance of power; **naruszyć ~gę** to upset the balance ④ Sport deuce

równowartoś|ć f equivalent

równoważni|a f (balance) beam

równoważ|yć impf **[I]** vt to balance *[wydatki]*; to even [sth] up *[ciężar]*; to counterbalance *[siły]*

[II] równoważyć się *[siły]* to counteract each other; *[zalety, straty]* to balance out

równoznaczn|y adi. synonymous; **być ~ym z czymś** (oznaczać coś) to be tantamount to sth

rów|ny [I] adi. grad. ① (bez wypukłości) *[powierzchnia, deska]* even; (poziomy) level ② (bez skrzywień) *[linia, zęby]* even; *[pismo]* neat; **stać w ~ej linii** to be lined up ③ (przewidywalny) *[gra, zawodnik]* consistent ④ (miarowy) *[oddech, puls, rytm]* even

[II] adi. ① (taki sam) *[odcinki, prawa, pensje, przeciwnicy]* equal ② (cały) ~**y miesiąc później** exactly a month later ③ pot. (sympatyczny) ~**y z niego gość** he's a good guy ④ (w gramatyce) **stopień ~y** the positive degree

[III] m (równorzędny partner) equal; **traktować kogoś jak ~ego** to treat sb as one's equal; **rozmawiać jak ~y z ~ym** to talk on equal terms

[IV] równe n **iść po ~ym** to walk on the level

róz|ga [I] f (do bicia) rod

[II] rózgi plt (chłosta) the birch

róż m ① (kolor) pink ② (kosmetyk) rouge

róż|a f ① Bot. rose; **dzika ~a** the wild rose; **syrop z dzikiej ~y** rosehip syrup ② Med. erysipelas

■ **nie ma ~y bez kolców** przysł. there's no rose without a thorn przysł.

róża|niec m rosary

różdż|ka f ① (magiczna) wand ② (do wykrywania wody) dowsing rod

różnic|a f difference; **z tą ~ą, że...** with the difference that...; ~**a polega na tym, że...** the difference is that...; **nie robić ~ między swoimi dziećmi** to treat all one's children fairly; **to mi nie robi ~y** it makes no difference to me; **co za ~a?** what's the difference?; **to bez ~y** same difference pot.

różnic|ować impf **[I]** vt to diversify *[społeczeństwo]*

[II] różnicować się *[gatunki, języki]* to diversify

różni|ć impf **[I]** vt (odróżniać) to make [sb/sth] different (**od czegoś** from sth); ~ **ich bardzo wiele** they are very different

[II] różnić się ① (być innym) to differ, to be different (**od czegoś** from sth); ~**ć się czymś** to differ in sth ② (sprzeczać się) ~**ć się w wielu sprawach** to have different opinions on many things; ~**ć się w ocenie czegoś** to view sth differently

różnie adv. (inaczej) differently; (na wiele sposobów) variously; ~ **w życiu bywa** life has its ups and downs

różnorodn|y adi. diverse

róż|ny adi. ① (różnorodny) different, various ② (nie ten sam) different; **liczba ~a od zera** a number other than zero ③ pot. (jakiś) all sorts; ~**i ludzie** all sorts of people

różow|y adi. ① [kolor] pink; [cera, skóra] rosy ② przen. (optymistyczny) [przyszłość] rosy

różycz|ka f Med. German measles, rubella

rtę|ć f (pierwiastek) mercury; (metal) mercury, quicksilver; **słupek** ~**ci podnosi się** the mercury rises

rub|el m rouble, ruble

rubin m ruby

rubry|ka f ① (tabela) table; (kolumna) column; (rząd) row; (puste miejsce do wypełnienia) space, blank ② (w gazecie) column

ruch m ① (zmienianie położenia) movement, motion; **być w** ~**u** to be in motion; **wprawić coś w** ~ to set sth in motion; **zgodnie z** ~**em/przeciwnie do** ~**u wskazówek zegara** clockwise/anticlockwise ② (poruszanie się) movement; (poruszenie się) move; (gest) gesture; **ociężałe** ~**y** heavy movements; ~**y wojsk** the movement of troops; **zrobić** ~ **ręką** to make a gesture with one's hand; **czytać z** ~**u warg** to lip-read; **krępować** ~**y** to restrict movement; **stać bez** ~**u** to be standing motionless ③ (aktywność fizyczna) exercise; **zażywać dużo** ~**u** to take a lot of exercise ④ (krzątanina) flurry of activity; (zamieszanie) commotion; (tłok) rush; **być w ciągłym** ~**u** to be always on the go; **mamy** ~ **w interesie** business is brisk ⑤ (drogowy) traffic; ~ **uliczny** the road traffic; **przepisy** ~**u drogowego** traffic regulations; **droga szybkiego** ~**u** a throughway ⑥ (organizacja) movement; ~ **oporu** the resistance movement ⑦ (posunięcie) move; **dobry/zły** ~ a good/bad move

ruchliw|y adi. ① [ulica, dzielnica, port] busy ② [życie] active ③ [osoba] (żywy) lively; (wiercący się) fidgety; (energiczny) energetic

ruchom|y adi. ① (będący w ruchu) [cel, kra] moving ② (zdolny do ruchu) [element, ściana, koła] mov(e)able, mobile; **schody** ~**e** an escalator, a moving staircase GB ③ (zmienny) [święto] mov(e)able; [czas pracy] flexible

ru|da f ore

rude|ra f ruin of a building pot.

ru|dy ① adi. [liść, glina, sierść] reddish-brown; [włosy, broda] red; [osoba] red-haired ② **rudy** m, **ruda** f pot. ginger pot.

ruf|a f stern

ruin|a f ① ruin; ~**a człowieka** przen. a wreck of a man; **popaść w** ~**ę** to fall into ruin; **podnieść się z** ~ to rise from the ruins

ru|ja f heat; (u łań, saren) rut; **mieć ruję** to be in heat

rujn|ować impf ① vt to devastate [budynek, miasto]; to ruin [osobę, firmę, życie, zdrowie] ② **rujnować się** (wydawać pieniądze) ~**ować się na coś** to splash out on sth

rulet|ka f (gra) roulette; (urządzenie) roulette wheel; **to zawsze** ~**ka** przen. it's always a lottery

rulon m (papieru) roll; (banknotów) wad

rumian|ek m camomile; (napar) camomile tea

rumie|nić impf ① vt Kulin. to brown [cebulę, masło] ② **rumienić się** [osoba] to blush; ~**nić się za kogoś** to blush for sb

rumie|niec m (oznaka zdrowia) colour GB, color US; (oznaka gniewu) flush; (oznaka wstydu) blush; **nabrać** ~**ńców** [osoba] to get back one's colour; przen. [mecz, dyskusja] to warm up

rumowisk|o n (gruz) rubble; ~**o skalne** rock debris

ru|nąć pf vi ① (przewrócić się, spaść) [osoba] to tumble (down); [budynek, wieża, samolot] to come down ② (rzucić się) **tłum runął do drzwi** the crowd rushed at the door ③ przen. (ponieść klęskę) [plany] to fall through; [mocarstwo, imperium] to fall

run|da f ① (etap) round ② (okrążenie) lap

run|o n ① (wełna) fleece ② (w lesie) undergrowth; **owoce** ~**a leśnego** fruits of the forest

rupie|ć m piece of junk pot.

ru|ra f tube, pipe; **rura kanalizacyjna** a drainpipe; **rura wydechowa** an exhaust pipe

rur|ka ① f tube; (do picia) straw; **karmić kogoś przez** ~**kę** to tube-feed sb; **nurkować z** ~**ką** to snorkel; ~**ka z kremem** a cream roll ② **rurki** plt ① (makaron) macaroni ② (spodnie) drainpipes

rurociąg m pipeline

rusza|ć impf → **ruszyć**

rusz|t m ① (część paleniska) grate ② Kulin. gridiron; **opiekać coś na** ~**cie** to grill sth

■ **wrzucić coś na** ~**t** pot. to have a snack

rusztowa|nie n scaffolding

rusz|yć pf — **rusz|ać** impf ① vt ① (zmienić położenie) to move; ~**yć ręką** to move one's arm; ~**yć głową** przen. to put one's thinking cap on ② (użwać) to touch; **nie** ~**aj moich rzeczy!** don't touch my things! ③ pot. (poruszyć problem) to touch on; **lepiej nie** ~**aj tej sprawy** you'd better not bring up this problem ④ pot. (wywołać emocje) **to mnie nie** ~**a** it leaves me cold ② vi ① (wyruszyć) [osoba] to set off; [samochód] to start ② (zacząć funkcjonować) [budowa, kampania] to start; [fabryka] to start operating ③ **ruszyć się — ruszać się** to move; **ledwo się** ~**ał** he could hardly move about; **ząb mi się** ~**a** one of my teeth is loose

■ **ani** ~ **nie mogę się w tym połapać** pot. I can't make head nor tail of it; **co (i)** ~ every now and then

rutyn|a f ① (wprawa) practice ② (schemat) rut, groove; **popaść w** ~**ę** to settle into a groove ③ (monotonia) routine

rw|ać impf ① vt ① (drzeć) to tear [ubranie] ② (zbierać) to pick [owoce, kwiaty] ③ (wyrywać) to pull (out) [zęby, włosy] ④ (sprawiać silny ból) [ząb, kolano] to cause [sb] shooting pain ② **rwać się** ① [lina, sznur] to break ② przen. (tracić płynność) to become broken ③ przen. (pragnąć) **rwać się**

do pracy to be raring to work; **rwać się do walki** to be spoiling for a fight

Ryb|a *f* Pisces

ryb|a *f* fish; ~a w galarecie fish in aspic; iść na ~y to go fishing; łowić ~y to fish; ~a dziś nie bierze the fish aren't biting today
■ czuć się jak ~a w wodzie to be in one's element

ryba|k *m* fisherman

rybitw|a *f* tern

rybołówstw|o *n* fishery, fishing

rycerz *m* knight także przen.

rycyn|a *f* castor oil

ryczał|t *m* (globalna suma) lump sum; (kwota podatku) flat rate; ~t na benzynę a car allowance; płacić ~tem to pay a flat rate

ryczeć *impf* → ryknąć

ry|ć *impf* **I** *vt* [1] (kopać) to dig *[rów]* [2] (wyrzynać) to engrave *[ornament, napis]*
II *vi* pot. (uczyć się) to grind away

rydz *m* saffron milk cap
■ lepszy ~ niż nic przysł. half a loaf is better than no bread przysł.

rygo|r *m* strict discipline

ryj *m* [1] (zwierzęcia) snout [2] posp. (twarz) chops pot.; oberwać po ~u to get one across the chops

ryk *m* (niedźwiedzia, lwa, silnika, tłumu) roar; (krowy) moo; (osła) bray; (dziecka) howl; (kibiców) yell; (syreny, radia) blare

ry|knąć *pf* — **ry|czeć** *impf vi [lew, niedźwiedź, morze]* to roar; *[krowa]* to moo; *[osioł]* to bray; *[syrena]* to blare; **ryczeć ze śmiechu** to roar with laughter

rym *m* rhyme

rym|ować *impf* **I** *vt* to rhyme *[słowa]*
II rymować się *[słowo]* to rhyme

ryn|ek *m* [1] (plac) market square, marketplace [2] (handel) market; wolny ~ek free market; ~ek zbytu na coś a market for sth; wprowadzić coś na ~ek to put sth on the market

ryn|na *f* [1] (do wody deszczowej) gutter, drainpipe [2] (niecka) trough

rynsztok *m* gutter; skończyć w ~u przen. to end up in the gutter

rynsztun|ek *m* gear; w pełnym ~ku in full gear

rys *m* **I** *m* [1] (właściwość) trait; ~y czyjegoś charakteru the traits of sb's character [2] (krótki opis) outline
II rysy *plt* (twarzy) features; wyraziste ~y twarzy very distinctive features

rys|a *f* (zadrapanie) scratch; (pęknięcie) crack

rysopis *m* description

rys|ować *impf* **I** *vt* [1] (kreślić kontury) to draw *[karykatury, zwierzęta]* [2] (zostawiać zadrapanie) to scratch
II rysować się [1] (stawać się widocznym) to show [2] (pokrywać się rysami) to have cracks

rysowni|k *m* graphic artist

rysun|ek *m* [1] (obraz) drawing; ~ek techniczny technical drawing [2] (kształt) shape

ry|ś *m* lynx

rytm *m* rhythm

rytua|ł *m* ritual

rywal *m*, ~ka *f* rival

rywalizacj|a *f* rivalry

rywaliz|ować *impf vi* to compete (z kimś with sb)

ryzykan|t *m*, ~tka *f* chancer

ryzyk|o *n* risk; podjąć ~o to take a risk

ryzyk|ować *impf vt* to risk

ryzykown|y *adi. grad. [krok, jazda, decyzja]* risky

ryż *m* rice; ~ dmuchany puffed rice

rzad|ki *adi. grad.* [1] *[zupa, tkanina, las, włosy]* thin [2] (nieczęsty) rare

rza|dko **I** *adv. grad.* [1] (w dużych odległościach) sparsely [2] (niecodziennie) rarely, seldom; coraz ~dziej się uśmiechała she smiled less and less often; ~dko jej się zdarza, żeby... it's rare for her to...
II *part.* (ledwie) hardly; ~dko kto hardly anybody
III z rzadka *adv.* [1] (daleko od siebie) sparsely [2] (nieczęsto) rarely

rzą|d¹ *m* Polit. government; ~dy demokratyczne democratic government; ~dy silnej ręki a strong-arm régime; utworzyć ~d to form a government

rzą|d² *m* [1] (ciąg, szereg) row; stać rzędem obok siebie to stand in a line; pięć razy z rzędu five times in a row [2] (kategoria) order; urzędnik niższego rzędu an official of a lower order [3] (w systematyce) order
■ konia z rzędem temu, kto... a king's ransom to whoever...

rządow|y *adi. [urzędnik, instytucja]* government

rzą|dzić *impf* **I** *vt* to rule (czymś sth); ~dzić państwem to govern the state
II rządzić się (gospodarować) ~dzić się u kogoś jak we własnym domu to act as though one owned the place; nie umieć się ~dzić to be incapable of managing one's (own) affairs

rzecz *f* [1] (przedmiot, zagadnienie) thing; ~y osobiste personal belongings; to dwie różne ~y these are two different things; ...i takie ~y pot. ...and stuff like that pot.; mówił o niej nieprzyjemne ~y he said unpleasant things about her; to ~ naturalna, że... it's a natural thing that... [2] (sprawa) matter; to nie twoja ~ it's none of your business
■ (cała) ~ w tym, że... the thing is (that)...; ~ prosta of course; kolej ~y a course of events; co to ma do ~y? what's that got to do with it?; być do ~y to be all right pot.; mówić do ~y to talk sense; mówić od ~y to talk nonsense; ogólnie biorąc generally speaking; stan ~y state of affairs

rzecznicz|ka *f* [1] (przedstawicielka) spokeswoman [2] (zwolenniczka) advocate

rzeczni|k *m* [1] (przedstawiciel) spokesman; ~**k praw obywatelskich** an ombudsman [2] (zwolennik) advocate

rzeczownik *m* noun

rzeczow|y *adi.* [1] *[dar, nagroda]* non-cash; **dowód** ~**y** material evidence [2] *[sposób bycia, ton]* nononsense; *[dyskusja, ocena, informacja]* matter-offact [3] **indeks** ~**y** a subject index

rzeczoznawc|a *m* expert

rzecz|pospolita *f* Rzeczpospolita Polska the Republic of Poland

rzeczywistoś|ć *f* reality; **w** ~**ci** in fact; **być niezgodnym z** ~**cią** to not correspond with the facts

rzeczywi|sty *adi. [wydarzenia, postać]* real; **członek** ~**y** a full member

rzeczywiście *adv* really, indeed

rzed|nąć *impf vi [las, tłum, włosy]* to thin (out)
■ **mina jej** ~**nie** she loses her countenance

rze|ka *f* river także przen.; ~**ka Wisła** the River Vistula; ~**ka łez** a river of tears; **miasto nad** ~**ką** a town on the river

rzekom|y *adi.* alleged

rzemieślni|k *m* craftsman, artisan

rzemio|sło *n* craft; ~**sło artystyczne** handicraft; **wystawa** ~**sła** a craft exhibition; **znać swoje** ~**sło** to know one's trade

rzemy|k *m* thong

rzep *m* [1] pot. (z łopianu, ostu) bur(r); **przyczepić się do kogoś jak** ~ **do psiego ogona** to stick to sb like a leech [2] (do zapinania) Velcro; **buty na** ~**y** Velcro shoes

rzep|a *f* turnip; **na jego szyi można by** ~**ę siać** żart. his neck is/was filthy dirty

rzepak *m* rape, colza

rzep|ka *f* Anat. kneecap, patella
■ **każdy sobie** ~**kę skrobie** everybody looks after their own

rzesz|a *f* [1] książk. mass; (tłum) crowd [2] (Niemcy) **Trzecia Rzesza** the Third Reich

rześ|ki *adi. [osoba]* fresh; *[powietrze, wiatr]* brisk

rzeteln|y *adi. grad. [osoba, pracownik]* (godny zaufania) reliable; (sumienny) diligent; *[praca, wiedza, aktorstwo]* solid; *[relacja, opis]* honest

rze|ź *f* slaughter także przen.; ~**ź niewiniątek** the Massacre of the Innocents

rzeźb|a *f* [1] (figura) sculpture; ~**a w drewnie** a wooden sculpture, a woodcarving [2] (ukształtowanie) ~**a terenu** the lie of the land

rzeźbiar|ka *f* sculptress

rzeźbiarz *m* sculptor

rzeźb|ić *impf vt* [1] (formować) *[osoba]* to sculpt [2] (ryć) *[osoba]* to carve [3] *[woda, lodowiec]* to carve *[doliny, wąwozy]*

rzeźni|a *f* slaughterhouse, abattoir

rzeźni|k *m* [1] (zajmujący się ubojem) butcher, slaughterer; (sprzedający mięso) butcher; (sklep) the butcher's (shop) [2] pot. (morderca) butcher

rzeżu|cha *f* cress

rzęs|a *f* (eye)lash

rzodkiew|ka *f* radish; **pęczek** ~**ek** a bunch of radishes

rzu|cić *impf* — **rzu|cać** *pf* **[]** *vt* [1] (cisnąć) to throw; ~**cić w kogoś kamieniem** to throw a stone at sb; ~**cić coś w kąt** to throw sth aside; ~**cić kotwicę** to drop anchor; ~**ć broń!** drop the gun!; ~**cić monetą** to toss a coin [2] (powalić) *[cios, wybuch, osoba]* to throw; ~**cić przeciwnika na deski** to throw one's opponent to the ground [3] (poruszyć gwałtownie) to toss *[głową, łódką]* [4] (wysłać) to send *[wojska, piechotę]*; *[lampa, drzewo]* to cast, to throw *[światło, cień]*; ~**cać na rynek nowy produkt** to launch a new product; ~**cić nowe światło na coś** przen. *[dowód, odkrycie]* to shed new light on sth [5] (skierować) to cast *[czar, zaklęcie, oskarżenie, spojrzenie]*; ~**cić na coś okiem** to have a look at sth [6] (powiedzieć) ~**cać uwagi** to make remarks; ~**cić pomysł, żeby...** to come up with an idea to...; ~**cić hasło do odmarszu** to give an order to depart [7] pot. (porzucić) to leave *[żonę, męża]*; **chłopak ją** ~**cił** her boyfriend dumped her pot. [8] (zrezygnować) to give [sth] up *[palenie, pracę, szkołę]*

[II] rzucić się — **rzucać się** [1] (paść) to throw oneself [2] (pobiec) to rush; (skoczyć) to lunge; ~**cić się do drzwi** to rush towards the door; ~**cić się do przodu** to lunge forward; ~**cić się do ucieczki** to dart away; ~**cić się na kogoś** to throw oneself at sb; ~**cić się w wir pracy** to throw oneself into work [3] (miotać się) to thrash about; (we śnie) to toss about

[III] rzucać się pot. (wykłócać się) to argue; (sprawiać kłopot) to cause trouble

rzu|t *m* [1] (rzucenie) throw; ~**t monetą** a toss-up; **o** ~**t kamieniem od czegoś** a stone's throw from somewhere; ~**t przez bark/biodro** Sport a shoulder/hip throw [2] Sport (w piłce nożnej) kick; (w koszykówce, piłce ręcznej) throw; **wykonać** ~**t karny/wolny/rożny** to take a penalty/free/corner kick; ~**ty osobiste** free throws [3] Sport (dyscyplina) ~**t młotem/dyskiem/oszczepem** the hammer/the discus/the javelin [4] (skok) lunge [5] (etap) stage; (część) part; (grupa osób) group; **robić coś w dwóch** ~**tach** to do sth in two stages [6] (odwzorowanie) projection; ~**t pionowy budynku** an elevation of a building; ~**t poziomy budynku** a plan of a building

rzutnik *m* (slide) projector

rzyg|nąć *impf* — **rzyg|ać** *pf vi* [1] pot. (wymiotować) to throw up, to puke pot.; ~**ać mi się chce, kiedy o tym pomyślę** it makes me want to puke thinking of it [2] (bluzgać) *[wulkan, armata]* to spit; ~**ać lawą/ogniem** to spit lava/fire

rzymskokatolic|ki *adi.* Roman Catholic

rż|eć *impf vi* ① *[koń]* to neigh, to whinny ② pot. *[osoba]* to chuckle

rżn|ąć *impf vt* ① (ciąć) to saw *[drewno]* ② (rzeźbić) to carve *[wzory]*; to cut *[kamienie, szkło]* ③ (zabijać) to slaughter *[zwierzęta]* ④ pot. (grać) to play; ~ąć w pokera/brydża to play poker/bridge; ~ąć głupa posp. to play dumb pot.

rżysk|o *n* stubble

S

S, s *n inv.* S, s
sabotaż *m* sabotage
sa|d *m* orchard
sad|ło *n* fat
sady|sta *m*, **~stka** *f* sadist
sadz|a *f* soot
sadza|ć *impf vt* to seat; **~ć gości do stołu** to seat the guests at the table; **~ć dziecko do lekcji** to make a child do homework
sadzaw|ka *f* pot. pool
sa|dzić *impf* **I** *vt* to plant *[kwiaty, drzewa, pomidory]* **II** *vi* pot. (biec) to lope
III sadzić się (silić się) to go out of one's way
sadzon|ka *f* (flanca) seedling; (odnóżka) cutting; (drzewko) sapling
sakraln|y *adi.* książk. *[architektura, muzyka]* sacred
sakramen|t *m* sacrament; **ostatni ~t** the last rites
saksofon *m* saxophone
sal|a *f* (pomieszczenie) room; **~a koncertowa/muzealna** a concert/an exhibition hall; **~a sądowa** a courtroom; **~a gimnastyczna** a gymnasium
salamand|ra *f* Zool. salamander
salami *n inv.* ① (kiełbasa) salami ② (ser) salami cheese
salater|ka *f* (naczynie) bowl; (zawartość) bowl(ful)
salceson *m* brawn GB, head cheese US
sal|do *n* balance
salon *m* ① (bawialnia) living room ② **~ literacki** a literary salon ③ (zakład usługowy) salon; **~ mody** a fashion house; **~ samochodowy** a car showroom; **~ gier** an amusement arcade GB
salow|y *m*, **~a** *f* orderly
sal|to *n* Sport somersault; **~to mortale** double somersault
salu|t *m* salute
salut|ować *impf vi* to salute (**komuś** sb)
salw|a *f* ① (wystrzał) salvo; (na cześć) salute ② przen. (śmiechu) peal; (braw) thunder
sała|ta *f* lettuce; **główka ~ty** a head of lettuce
sałat|ka *f* salad
sam¹ **I** *adi.* ① (bez pomocy) (by) oneself; **~ to zrobiłeś?** did you do it (by) yourself?; **drzwi ~e się zamknęły** the door closed on its own; **~o się nie zrobi** it won't get done by itself; **musicie ~i zdecydować** you have to decide for yourselves; **~ z siebie** of one's own accord; **nic nie dzieje się**

~o z siebie nothing happens by itself a. without a reason; **wszystko zawdzięczam ~emu sobie** I owe everything to my own efforts; **włosy jej się ~e kręcą** her hair curls naturally ② (samotny) alone; **był ~ w domu** he was alone at home; **nie wolno jej ~ej wychodzić na ulicę** she is not allowed to go out by herself; **trudno jest żyć człowiekowi ~emu** it's hard living alone; **~ jeden** all alone; **słowo „bohater" pisze się przez ~o h** the word 'bohater' is spelt with an h ③ (tylko) only; **mieli ~e córki** they had only daughters; **~e nieszczęścia nas spotykają** we've had nothing but trouble; **~e zdolności nie wystarczą** talent alone is not enough; **mówić prawdę, ~ą prawdę i tylko prawdę** to tell the truth, the whole truth, and nothing but the truth ④ (jako uściślenie) very; **w ~ym środku** in the very centre; **dom nad ~ym morzem** a house right on the sea; **do ~ego rana** right through to the morning ⑤ (jako podkreślenie) oneself; **~ sobie przeczysz** you're contradicting yourself; **~a tak powiedziała** she said so herself; **~i sobie są winni** they've only got themselves to blame; **~a widzisz, że to nie takie proste** see, it's not that easy; **~ zobacz** see a. look for yourself; **widziałem ~ego prezydenta** I saw the president himself ⑥ (wskazuje na przyczynę) mere; **na ~ą myśl o tym chce mi się płakać** the mere a. very thought of it makes me want to cry
II *pron.* **taki ~** the same; **wszyscy mężczyźni są tacy ~i** all men are alike a. the same; **ten ~** the same; **byli w tym ~ym wieku** they were the same age; **to ~o dotyczy ciebie** the same applies to you; **to jedna i ta ~a osoba** they are one and the same person; **są tak ~o winni** they are equally guilty; **zniknął tak ~o nagle, jak się pojawił** he vanished just as unexpectedly as he had appeared; **„muszę już iść" – „ja tak ~o"** 'I've got to go' – 'me too'; **mają tyle ~o lat** they're (of) the same age ■ **porozmawiać z kimś ~ na ~** to talk to sb one-on-one; **to się rozumie ~o przez się!** it goes without saying!; **tym ~ym** thus, thereby
sam² *m* pot. supermarket
samic|a *f* female
sam|iec *m* male; **stuprocentowy ~iec** pot., przen. a real macho man pot.
samobój|ca *m*, **~czyni** *f* suicide; **pilot ~ca** a suicide a. kamikaze pilot

samobójcz|y *adi.* suicidal także przen.; **próba ~a** a suicide attempt; **~a bramka** a. **~y gol** Sport an own goal

samobójstw|o *n* suicide także przen.

samochodow|y *adi.* car; *[olej]* motor; *[atlas, mapa]* road; **części ~e** car a. automotive parts; **kino ~e** a drive-in (cinema) US

samoch|ód *m* car; **~ód ciężarowy** a lorry GB, a truck; **~ód dostawczy** a delivery truck, a (delivery) van; **~ód służbowy** a company car; **prowadzić ~ód** to drive (a car); **nie piję, jestem ~odem** no thanks, I'm driving

samochwa|ła *m, f* pot. boaster

samodzielnie *adv.* ① (niezależnie) *[pracować, rządzić]* independently; **~ odrabiać lekcje** to do homework on one's own a. by oneself ② (odrębnie, oddzielnie) *[istnieć, występować]* separately

samodzieln|y *adi.* ① (zaradny) self-reliant; **stawiać pierwsze ~e kroki** to take one's first independent steps; **zestaw do ~ego montażu** a self-assembly kit ② (niezależny) *[myślenie, stanowisko, pracownik]* independent; **zachęcać dzieci do ~ego myślenia** to encourage children to think for themselves ③ (odrębny) separate; **~e mieszkanie** a self-contained flat

samogłos|ka *f* vowel

samokryty|ka *f* self-criticism

samokształceni|e *n* self-education

samolo|t *m* plane; **~t sanitarny** an air ambulance; **lecieć ~tem** to go by plane a. air; **spóźnić się na ~t** to miss one's plane a. flight

samolub *m* egoist

samolubn|y *adi.* *[osoba, zachowanie]* selfish

samoobron|a *f* ① (obrona siebie) self-defence GB, self-defense US; **działać w ~ie** to act in self-defence ② Wojsk. civil defence GB, civil defense US

samoobsługow|y *adi.* *[sklep, bar, stacja benzynowa]* self-service; **pralnia ~a** a launderette

samopoczuci|e *n* (general) physical and mental state; **mieć dobre/złe ~e** to feel well/bad

samorzą|d *m* ① (system zarządzania) self-government; **~d lokalny** local government; **~d pracowniczy** workers' self-management a. control; **~d szkolny/studencki** student government ② (grupa ludzi) self-government body

samotnie *adv.* **żyć ~** to live alone; **matka ~ wychowująca dziecko/dzieci** a single mother

samotni|k *m* recluse; **być ~kiem** to be a loner

samotnoś|ć *f* (bycie samotnym) solitude; (poczucie osamotnienia) loneliness; **żyć/umrzeć w ~ci** to live/die in solitude; **~ć we dwoje** shared solitude

samotn|y *adi.* ① (żyjący samotnie) lonely; **był zupełnie ~y** he was all a. quite alone ② (bez towarzystwa) *[spacer, życie]* solitary, lonely; *[wycieczka]* solo ③ (odosobniony) *[dom, drzewo, wyspa]* solitary ④ (nieżonaty, niezamężna) single

② *m* **samotn|y, ~a** *f* single person; **bar dla ~ych** a singles bar

samoucz|ek *m* teach-yourself book a. manual

samou|k *m* self-taught person; **malarz ~k** a self-taught painter

samowol|a *f* lawlessness

samowoln|y *adi.* *[osoba]* wilful GB, willful US; *[postępek, decyzja]* arbitrary

samozaparci|e *n* perseverance

sanatori|um *n* sanatorium

sandacz *m* pikeperch, zander

sanda|ł *m* sandal

saneczkarstw|o *n* Sport tobogganing

saneczka|rz *m,* **~rka** *f* Sport tobogganist, tobogganer

sa|nie *plt* sleigh, sledge

sanitariusz *m* ① (na wojnie) (medical) orderly, stretcher-bearer ② (w pogotowiu) ≈ paramedic

sanitariusz|ka *f* (medical) orderly, nurse

sanitar|ka *f* pot. ambulance

sanitarn|y *adi.* *[urządzenia, warunki, inspektor]* sanitary; **punkt ~y** a first-aid post

sankcj|a *f* książk. ① (kara, represja) sanction; **~e prawne** legal sanctions; **~e dyscyplinarne** disciplinary action; **~e gospodarcze** economic sanctions ② (zatwierdzenie) sanction

san|ki *plt* toboggan

sapać *impf* → **sapnąć**

sape|r *m* sapper

sap|nąć *pf* — **sap|ać** *impf vi* ① (oddychać z trudem) to pant; **~ać z wysiłku** to pant with fatigue ② przen. *[parowóz, parostatek]* to chug

sardyn|ka *f* sardine; **gnieść się** a. **tłoczyć się jak ~ki w puszce** to be packed a. crammed like sardines pot.

sarkofag *m* sarcophagus

sar|na *f* roe deer

sasan|ka *f* pasque flower

saszet|ka *f* ① (torebka) ≈ clutch bag ② (opakowanie) sachet GB, packet US; **herbata w ~kach** tea bags

sateli|ta *m* satellite; przen. (osoba) satellite, follower; (państwo) satellite (state)

saty|ra *f* satire także przen.

satysfakcj|a *f* satisfaction; **~a seksualna** sexual gratification

saun|a /'sawna/ *f* sauna

sącz|ek *m* ① (filtr) filter ② Med., Roln. drain

sącz|yć *impf* **②** *vt* ① (popijać) to sip; **~yć napój przez słomkę** to drink through a straw; **~yła wino z kieliszka** she sipped (at) her wine ② (wlewać) to trickle ③ (wydzielać) *[drzewo, roślina]* to exude *[żywicę, sok]; [rana]* to ooze ④ (cedzić) to filter *[sok, ocet]*

② **sączyć się** ① (wydzielać się) *[ropa]* to ooze; (płynąć) *[potok, woda]* to trickle ② (przenikać) *[wilgoć, światło, dym]* to seep

są|d *m* [1] (instytucja) court (of law a. justice); **sąd cywilny/karny** a civil/criminal court; **wyrok sądu** a court sentence; **oddać sprawę do sądu** to go to court; **podać** a. **zaskarżyć kogoś do sądu za coś** to sue sb for sth; **pozwać kogoś do sądu** to take sb to court; **wygrać/przegrać sprawę w sądzie** to win/lose one's court case [2] Prawo (zespół sędziów) court; **posiedzenie sądu** court sitting; **Wysoki Sądzie!** Your Lordship! GB, Your Honor! US [3] (proces) trial; **ukarać kogoś bez sądu** to punish sb without trial [4] (siedziba) court; (budynek) courthouse [5] (opinia) judgement, judgment (**o kimś/czymś** a. **na temat kogoś/czegoś** of sb/sth); **wydać sąd o kimś/czymś** to pronounce judgement on sb/sth; **wstrzymać się z wydawaniem sądów o czymś** to reserve judgement on sth ❑ **sąd doraźny** summary proceedings; **sąd kapturowy** kangaroo court; **Sąd Najwyższy** Supreme Court; **Sąd Ostateczny** the Last a. Final Judgement; **sąd polowy** court-martial; **sąd przysięgłych** jury; **sąd wojenny** court-martial; **sąd wojskowy** military tribunal

sądn|y *adi.* ~**y dzień** (katastrofa) a doomsday; pot. (zamęt) a madhouse przen.; **do** ~**ego dnia** pot. till a. until doomsday pot.

sądownictw|o *n* [1] (ogół sądów) judiciary [2] (władza sądów) judicature

są|dzić¹ *impf vt* [1] (stawiać przed sądem) to try; **być sądzonym za zdradę** to be tried for treason [2] (osądzać) to judge *[osobę, sprawę]*; **sądzić ludzi po wyglądzie/zachowaniu** to judge other people by their appearance/behaviour
■ **jest mu to sądzone** książk. he's destined for it; (negatywnie) he's doomed to it

są|dzić² *impf vi* [1] (uważać) to think; **sądzę, że masz rację** I think you're right; **nie sądzę, by to się mogło udać** I don't think it'll work; **co sądzisz o tej wystawie?** what do you think of the exhibition?; **powszechnie sądzi się, że...** it is commonly believed that... [2] (wnioskować) to judge; **sądząc z jego opisu/listów...** judging by a. from his description/letters...

sąsi|ad *m*, ~**adka** *f* neighbour GB, neighbor US; **nasi** ~**edzi zza ściany/z góry** our next-door/upstairs neighbours

sąsiad|ować *impf vi* [1] (mieszkać obok) *[osoba, rodzina]* to live next door (**z kimś** to sb) [2] (siedzieć obok) to sit next (**z kimś** to sb) [3] (graniczyć) *[państwo, wieś, szkoła]* to neighbour GB, to neighbor US (**z czymś** sth a. on sth); *[kraj, region, teren]* to border (**z czymś** sth a. on sth); ~**ujące ze sobą państwa** neighbouring countries

sąsiedni *adi.* *[kraj, wyspa, stolik]* neighbouring GB, neighboring US; *[teren, część]* adjacent; **zajmuję** ~ **pokój** I'm staying next door

sąsiedz|ki *adi.* *[pomoc, przysługa, wizyta]* neighbourly GB, neighborly US; **mieszkamy po** ~**ku** we live next door to each other

sąsiedztw|o *n* [1] (bliskość) proximity; **domy w najbliższym** ~**ie stadionu piłkarskiego** houses in the immediate vicinity of a football stadium [2] (osoby mieszkające obok) neighbours GB, neighbors US; (okolica) neighbourhood GB, neighborhood US

scal|ić *pf* — **scal|ać** *impf vt* to merge *[firmy, procesy]*; to blend *[grupy, fragmenty utworu]*; to join *[grunty, działki]*; to unite *[państwo, zespół]*

scen|a *f* [1] (podium) stage; **grać na** ~**ie** to act on stage; **wyjść na** ~**ę** to go on stage; **zejść ze** ~**y** przen. *[aktor]* to leave the stage; *[sztuka, przedstawienie]* to be performed no longer [2] (działalność teatralna) the stage; (konkretny teatr) theatre GB, theater US; **zrobić karierę na** ~**ie** to have a successful stage career [3] (część aktu) scene; **akt II,** ~**a 3** Act Two, Scene Three [4] (epizod) scene; ~**y batalistyczne** battle scenes [5] (widok) scene; **cóż za czuła** ~**a!** what a display of tenderness! [6] pot. (scysja) scene; **zrobić** a. **urządzić** ~**ę** to make a scene

scenariusz *m* [1] (tekst) script; (opis) scenario; (opis i tekst do filmu) screenplay [2] (przebieg) scenario; **katastroficzny** ~ a worst-case a. nightmare scenario; **zgodnie ze** ~**em** according to schedule

scenarzy|sta *m*, ~**stka** *f* (autor dialogów) scriptwriter; (autor opisu filmu i dialogów) screenwriter

sceneri|a *f* [1] (oprawa plastyczna) setting; **film w** ~**i dużego miasta** a film in a. with an urban setting [2] (tło) setting; (krajobraz) scenery

scenograf *m*, ~**ka** *f* (teatralny) stage designer; (filmowy) film set designer

scenografi|a *f* [1] (filmowa) film set; (teatralna) stage design; (do pojedynczej sceny) stage set [2] (sztuka, wykonanie) scenography

sceptycyzm *m* scepticism GB, skepticism US

schab *m* Kulin. loin of pork; ~ **karkowy** neck of pork

scharakteryz|ować *pf vt* to characterize *[osobę, styl, wygląd]*

schema|t *m* [1] (uproszczony szkic) diagram; (ogólny plan) outline [2] (wzorzec) formula; ~**ty myślowe** patterns of thought

schizofreni|a /sxizo'frenja/ *f* schizophrenia także przen.

schlebia|ć *impf vi* ~**ć komuś/czemuś** to flatter sb/sth *[szefowi, czyjejś próżności, ambicji]*; to pander to sth pejor. *[oczekiwaniom, gustom, poglądom]*

schludnie *adv. grad.* książk. *[ubierać się, ubrany]* neatly; *[wyglądać]* neat

schludn|y *adi. grad.* książk. *[osoba, wygląd, pomieszczenie]* tidy

s|chnąć *impf vi* [1] (suszyć się) *[włosy, pranie, glina, chleb]* to dry [2] (więdnąć) to wither [3] pot. (chudnąć) to waste away; **schnąć z miłości/żalu** przen. to pine away from love/grief

schod|y plt 1 (stopnie) (wewnątrz budynku) staircase; (na zewnątrz) steps; ~**y ewakuacyjne** (na zewnątrz budynku) fire escape; (wewnątrz budynku) emergency stairway; ~**y kuchenne** backstairs; **ruchome** ~**y** escalator; **wchodzić/schodzić** ~**ami** a. **po** ~**ach** to go up/down the stairs a. steps 2 (klatka schodowa) stairwell ■ **zaczęły się** ~**y** pot. now the hard part begins

scho|dzić impf 1 vi 1 (w dół) to descend; [łódź podwodna] to dive; ~**dzić po schodach** a. **ze schodów** to go down the stairs; **promenada** ~**dząca na plażę** a promenade leading down to the beach 2 (opuszczać miejsce) ~**dzić z roweru/motocykla** to dismount from a bicycle/motor-cycle; ~**dzić z drogi** a. **na bok** to get out of the way; **skóra** ~**dzi mi z nosa** (the skin on) my nose is peeling; **plamy z czerwonego wina ciężko** ~**dzą** red wine stains are especially stubborn a. especially hard to remove; ~**dzić na inny temat** przen. [rozmowa] to get off the subject; **samochody/telewizory** ~**dzące z taśmy produkcyjnej** cars/TV sets leaving the production line 3 (mijać) [ranek, życie] to pass; **popołudnia** ~**dzą mu na nauce** he passes the afternoons studying

II **schodzić się** 1 (gromadzić się) [ludzie, grupy] to gather 2 (łączyć się) [ścieżki, linie, trasy] to come together 3 (występować jednocześnie) [wydarzenia, daty] to coincide (**z czymś** with sth)

schowa|ć pf 1 vt 1 (umieścić, włożyć) to put (away); ~**ć chustkę do kieszeni** to put a handkerchief in one's pocket; ~**ć coś na pamiątkę** to keep sth as a memento; ~**ć chleb na drogę/na jutro** to put aside some bread for the journey/for tomorrow 2 (ukryć) to hide [sth] (away); ~**ć cukierki przed dziećmi** to hide the sweets from the children; ~**ć głowę pod poduszkę** to bury one's head under a pillow 3 (wciągnąć) to draw a. pull [sth] in [czułki, macki]; to sheathe [pazury]; to retract [podwozie]

II **schować się** 1 (zniknąć) to disappear; [księżyc, słońce] to hide 2 (schronić się) to hide out; ~**ć się przed policją** to hide from the police; ~**ć się pod drzewem/przed burzą** to find shelter under a tree/from the storm 3 (wsunąć się) to retract

■ ~**j się ze swoimi radami/pomysłami** pot. keep your advice/ideas to yourself; **inne ogrody przy twoim mogą się** ~**ć** pot. your garden puts others to shame

schow|ek m 1 (skrytka) hiding place; (pomieszczenie) cubbyhole, storeroom; (na przybory do sprzątania) broom cupboard; (pojemnik na bagaż) locker; (w samochodzie) glovebox; (w samolocie) overhead locker 2 Komput. clipboard

schron m (fortyfikacja) bunker; (dla okrętów podwodnych) submarine pen; (dla ludności cywilnej) shelter

schronić się pf v refl. to take cover a. shelter; ~**nić się przed deszczem pod drzewo** a. **pod**

drzewem to take cover a. shelter from the rain under a tree; ~**nić się w górach/lesie** to take to the hills/forest

schronie|nie n refuge; **szukać** ~**nia przed prześladowcami** to seek refuge from one's perse-cutors

schronisk|o n hostel; (dla ofiar przemocy domowej) refuge; (dla zwierząt) (animal) shelter

schud|nąć pf vi to lose weight

schwy|cić pf 1 vt 1 (złapać) to grab, to grasp; ~**cić kogoś za ramię/nogę** to seize sb's arm/leg; ~**cić kogoś za klapy marynarki** to grab sb by the lapel(s) 2 przen. **po drodze** ~**cił nas deszcz** we got caught in the rain on the way; ~**cił go strach** he was gripped with fear

II **schwycić się** to grab, to grasp (**czegoś** sth); ~**cić się za brzuch/głowę z bólu** to clutch one's stomach/head in pain; **walczący** ~**cili się za bary** the fighters grappled with each other

schwy|tać pf vt (złapać) to catch [ptaka, rybę, zająca]; (w siatkę lub sieć) to net; (w sidła) to snare; (w pułapkę) to trap; ~**tać zbiega** to capture a fugitive

schyl|ić pf — **schyl|ać** impf 1 vt to bow, to bend [głowę]

II **schylić się** — **schylać się** to bend, to lean (down); ~**ić się w ukłonie** to bow; ~**ił się, żeby podnieść monetę** he stooped to pick up a coin

schył|ek m książk. (koniec) (roku, wieku) close; (kariery) decline; ~**ek imperium** the decline of the empire; **u** ~**ku dnia** at the end of the day; **u** ~**ku życia** in the evening of one's life

scyzoryk m pocket knife

szczep|ić pf — **szczep|iać** impf 1 vt to fasten [sth] together

II **sczepić się** — **sczepiać się** to get locked together

seans m showing; ~ **popołudniowy** a matinee; ~ **spirytystyczny** seance

sedes m toilet

sedn|o n crux; **dotrzeć do** ~**a sprawy** to get to the heart of the matter; **przejdę od razu do** ~**a sprawy** I'll come straight to the point; **trafić** a. **utrafić w (samo)** ~**o** to hit the nail on the head

segmen|t m 1 (wyodrębniony element) segment; (re-gału) unit 2 (komplet mebli) unit furniture 3 (budynek) terrace(d) house

segregacj|a f segregation; (dokumentów) filing; (książek, przesyłek, zbiorów) sorting

segregato|r m (szafa) filing cabinet; (teczka) (loose-leaf a. ring) binder

segreg|ować impf vt to file [dokumenty]; to sort [książki, przesyłki, zbiory]

sejf m (szafa) safe; (skrzynka) strongbox

sejm m Polit. the Sejm, the Seym (the lower chamber of the Polish parliament)

sekato|r m clippers

sekcj|a f ① (organizacji) section; (stowarzyszenia, związku) chapter ② Med. autopsy; **przeprowadzić** a. **zrobić ~ę** to perform an autopsy a. a post-mortem ③ Techn. section

❑ **~a rytmiczna** Muz. rhythm section

sekre|t m secret; **~ty natury/ludzkiej psychiki** the mysteries of nature/the human mind; **robić z czegoś ~t** to be secretive about sth; **utrzymywać** a. **trzymać coś w ~cie** to keep sth secret a. under wraps; **cały ~t polega na...** the whole secret is a. lies in...

sekretaria|t m ① (firmy, szkoły) front office; (w rządzie, organizacji) secretariat ② (pomieszczenie) front office, secretariat

sekretar|ka f secretary; **kurs dla ~ek** a secretarial course

❑ **automatyczna ~ka** (telephone) answering machine, answerphone GB

sekretarz m secretary; **~ ambasady** (diplomatic) secretary; **~ redakcji** secretary; **~ generalny ONZ** Secretary-General of the UN; **~ stanu** secretary of state

seks m sex; **bezpieczny ~** safe sex; **uprawiać z kimś ~** to have sex with sb; **ta dziewczyna jest pełna ~u** that girl has a lot of sex appeal

seksown|y adi. grad. [dziewczyna, ruchy, bielizna] sexy

seksualn|y adi. sex; **molestowanie ~e** sexual harassment

sekto|r m ① (miasta, kraju) sector; (samolotu, basenu, widowni) section; (oceanu, regionu) area ② (dziedzina) sector; **~r państwowy/prywatny** the public/private sector

sekularyzacj|a f książk. secularization

sekularyz|ować pf, impf książk. **❚** vt to secularize [majątki, prawo, społeczeństwo, kulturę]

❚❚ sekularyzować się [społeczeństwo, kultura, szkoła] to become secularized

sekun|da f ① (miara czasu) second; **z prędkością kilku metrów na ~dę** at a speed of several metres per second ② (chwila) instant; **w kilka ~d wszystko zniknęło** everything vanished within seconds; **na ~dę zgasło światło** the light went out for an instant; **~dę!** pot. just a second pot.; **na ułamek ~dy zawahał się** he hesitated for a split second; **podjął decyzję w ciągu ~dy** a. **w jednej ~dzie** he made an instantaneous decision ③ Mat. (miara kąta) (arc) second ④ Muz. (interwał) second, supertonic

sekundnik m (wskazówka) second hand; (tarcza) second face

seledynow|y adi. [odcień, materiał] celadon, willow green

selekcj|a f selection; **kandydatów poddano starannej ~i** the candidates were hand-picked

sele|r m (korzeń) celeriac; (łodyga) celery; **~r naciowy** celery

semafo|r m semaphore

semest|r m semester; **~r zimowy/letni** the autumn/spring semester

seminari|um n ① Uniw. seminar; **~a z ekonomii/literatury** economics/literature seminars; **~um magisterskie** a graduate seminar ② Szkol. ≈ college; **~um duchowne** seminary

s|en m ① (spanie) sleep; **sen zimowy** hibernation; **obudzić kogoś ze snu** to wake sb up; **ułożyć dzieci do snu** to put the children to bed; **zapadać w sen** to go to sleep; **mówić przez sen** to talk in one's sleep ② (marzenie senne) dream (**o kimś/czymś** about sb/sth)

■ jak we śnie [poruszać się, mówić] (nieprzytomnie) in a dream; (w rozmarzeniu) dreamily; **jak zły sen** like a bad dream; **dziewczyna/suknia piękna jak sen** a dream of a girl/dress; **pamiętać** a. **przypominać sobie kogoś/coś jak przez sen** to have (only) a hazy memory of sb/sth; **przemijać jak sen** to pass too quickly; **spędzać komuś sen z oczu** a. **z powiek** to rob sb of their sleep

sena|t m Polit., Uniw. senate

senato|r m Polit., Uniw. senator

senio|r m ① (najstarszy w rodzinie) patriarch; (starszy krewny) senior ② (nestor) doyen; (starsza osoba) senior (citizen); **dom ~ra** retirement home; **klub ~ra** club for senior citizens ③ Sport senior

senior|ka f ① (w rodzinie) the eldest woman ② (nestorka) doyenne; (starsza osoba) senior (citizen) ③ Sport senior

sennoś|ć f ① (potrzeba snu) sleepiness, drowsiness; **po posiłku zawsze ogarnia go ~ć** he always becomes drowsy after a meal ② (ospałość) sleepiness; (spokój) somnolence

senn|y adi. ① [dziecko, zwierzę] sleepy, drowsy; [oczy, ruch, głos] sleepy; **popadł w ~e odrętwienie** he became torpid ② [skwar, bezruch, nastrój] sleepy; [głos, rytm] soporific ③ [majaki, wizje] seen in a dream; **~y koszmar** a nightmare; **marzenie ~e** a dream ④ (ospały) [wioska, przedmieścia] sleepy; (spokojny) [tempo, firma] drowsy

sens m ① (znaczenie) meaning; **ekologia w ~ie potocznym** ecology in the popular meaning (of the word) ② (celowość) sense; **działalność pozbawiona ~u** a. **bez ~u** a senseless a. pointless activity; **w tym, co mówisz, jest ~** a. **to, co mówisz, ma ~** what you say makes sense

■ w pewnym ~ie (niejako) in a way; (pod jednym względem) in one way; (do pewnego stopnia) in some ways; **chłopcy są do siebie podobni w ~ie fizycznym** the boys are physically similar; **coś w tym ~ie** pot. something to that effect; **mówić z ~em** to talk sense; **nareszcie mówisz z ~em** now you're talking pot.

sensacj|a ❚ f sensation; **wiadomość miała posmak ~i** the news bordered on the sensational; **zrobił z tego ~ę** he made an issue of it

II **sensacje** *plt* (niedomagania) trouble; **mieć ~e żołądkowe** to have an upset stomach a. a stomach upset

sensacyjn|y *adi.* ① (rewelcyjny) *[wiadomość, odkrycie, fakty]* sensational ② (kryminalny) **powieść ~a/film~y** a thriller

sensown|y *adi. grad.* ① (rozsądny) *[opinia, argumenty]* sensible ② *pot.* (roztropny) *[osoba]* clever *pot.*

sentymen|t *m* ① (sympatia) fondness (**do kogoś/czegoś** for sb/sth); (przywiązanie) (sentimental) attachment (**do kogoś/czegoś** to sb/sth); **czuć ~t do kogoś/czegoś** to be fond of sb/sth; **wspominać kogoś/coś z ~tem** to have fond memories of sb/sth ② (uczuciowość) sentiment; **w polityce nie ma ~tów** politics has no time for sentiment

sentymentaln|y *adi.* sentimental

separacj|a *f* separation; **żyć w ~i** *[małżonkowie]* to be separated

seple|nić *impf vi* to lisp

se|r *m* Kulin. cheese; **krowi/kozi ser** cow's/goat's milk cheese; **chudy/tłusty ser** low-fat/whole-milk a. cream cheese; **biały ser** ≈ cottage cheese; **ser topiony** processed cheese; **żółty ser** hard cheese

serc|e *n* ① (narząd) heart; **atak ~a** a heart attack; **operacja na otwartym ~u** open-heart surgery; **mieć słabe ~e** to have a weak heart; **umrzeć na ~e** to die of heart failure ② (pierś) heart ③ przen. (emocje) heart; **człowiek wielkiego ~a** a. **o wielkim ~u** a big-hearted a. generous-hearted person; **mieć dobre/miękkie ~e** to have a good/soft heart; **kochać/nienawidzić kogoś całym ~em** a. **z całego ~a** to love/hate sb with all one's heart; **zawsze okazywał nam ~e** he was always kind-hearted towards us; **oddać komuś ~e** to give one's heart to sb; **złamać komuś ~e** to break sb's heart ④ (przedmiot, symbol) heart; **~e z piernika** heart-shaped gingerbread; **wisiorek w kształcie ~a** a pendant in the shape of a heart ⑤ (środek) heart; **w ~u dżungli/miasta** in the heart of a jungle/city ⑥ (w dzwonie) clapper, tongue ■ **do głębi ~a** *[przejąć się, wzruszyć]* deeply; **w głębi ~a** *[zazdrościć, myśleć, odczuwać]* in one's heart of hearts; **z głębi ~a** *[uczucia, życzenia]* from the bottom of one's heart; **jak a. co ~e** (komuś) **dyktuje** *[mówić, pisać]* from the a. one's heart; **od ~a** *[rozmowa, wyznanie, słowa]* heart-to-heart; *[bić brawo, pomagać]* wholeheartedly; **przyjaciel od ~a** a bosom friend; **w ~u** *[uważać, czuć]* privately; **z biciem** a. **drżeniem ~a** a. **z bijącym ~em** (z niepokojem, niepewnością) with one's heart in one's mouth; (ze wzruszeniem) with a lump in one's throat; **z bólem ~a** with an aching heart; **z ciężkim ~em** with a heavy heart; **z dobrego** a. **z dobroci ~a** out of the goodness of one's heart; **ze szczerego ~a** kind-heartedly; **z lekkim ~em** (radośnie) with a light heart; (nie bacząc na konsekwencje) light-heartedly; **brać (sobie) coś do ~a** to take

sth to heart; **być bez ~a** a. **nie mieć ~a** to have no heart; **chwytać kogoś za ~e** to tug at sb's heartstrings; **czytać w czyimś ~u** to read sb's thoughts; **kamień spadł mi z ~a** that is a weight off my mind; **leży mi na ~u twoje zdrowie/szczęście** I have your health/happiness at heart; **mieć ~e dla kogoś/do czegoś** to be fond of sb/sth; **mieć ~e na dłoni** to have one's heart in the right place; **nie mieć ~a czegoś zrobić** to not have the heart to do sth; **nie mieć ~a dla** a. **do kogoś** to dislike sb; **nie mieć ~a do czegoś** (nie mieć ochoty) to be lukewarm about sth; **pójść za głosem ~a** to follow one's heart; **~e kraje się** a. **pęka mi na widok...** it breaks my heart to see...; **~e stanęło mu w gardle** a. **podeszło mu do gardła** (z niepokoju, obawy) his heart was in his mouth; (z podniecenia, wzruszenia) his heart leapt; **trafić** a. **przemówić do czyjegoś ~a** to touch sb's heart; **ująć kogoś za ~e** a. **poruszyć czyjeś ~e** (wzruszyć) to touch sb's heart; **wkładać w coś (całe) ~e** to put one's heart and soul into sth; **zdjąć komuś kamień z ~a** to take a load off sb's mind

sercow|y *adi.* ① Med. *[atak, bóle, mięsień]* heart; *[schorzenie, arytmia]* cardiac ② (uczuciowy) *[tajemnice, kłopoty]* romantic; **sprawy ~e** affairs of the heart

serdecznie *adv. grad.* ① (życzliwie) cordially; **~ uściskał go na powitanie** he greeted him warmly with a hug; **zajął się nią ~** he took good care of her; **zapraszamy was ~ na weekend** you are cordially invited for the weekend; **~ was pozdrawiam, Anna** (w liście) love a. kind regards, Anna ② (bardzo) whole-heartedly; **uśmiał się ~** he had a good laugh; **był ~ znudzony przyjęciem** he was thoroughly bored with the party; **nie znoszę go ~** I can't stand him

serdecznoś|ć *f* warmth; **przyjąć kogoś z wielką ~cią** to give sb a very warm welcome; **~ci** (słowa) endearments; (gesty) cordialities; (pozdrowienia) love

serdeczn|y *adi. grad.* *[przyjaciel]* bosom; *[osoba]* friendly; *[list, uśmiech, podziękowania]* cordial; **~y uścisk dłoni** a warm handshake; **palec ~y** ring finger

serdel|ek *m* sausage

seri|a *f* ① (ciąg wydarzeń) series; **~a zastrzyków** a course of injections; **~a zbiegów okoliczności** a series of coincidences; **~a niepowodzeń** a string of misfortunes ② (zbiór przedmiotów) series; (wyroby jednego wzoru) batch; **~a znaczków pocztowych** a series of stamps; **~a wydawnicza** book series ③ (strzałów) burst; (wybuchów) series

serial *m* series

serio **I** *adv.* seriously; **nie traktował jej ~** he didn't take her seriously; **rozgniewała się na niego na ~** she got really angry with him; **mówię całkiem ~** I (do) mean it

II *adi. inv.* serious; **był człowiekiem ~** he was a serious person

sernik m (ciasto) cheesecake

serpentyn|a f 1 (spiralna wstęga) streamer 2 (kręta droga) switchback

serw m Sport serve, service

serwe|ta f (obrus) tablecloth

serwet|ka f 1 (dla ochrony ubrania) (table) napkin, serviette GB 2 (mały obrus) doily

serwis[1] m 1 (komplet naczyń) service; ~ **do kawy** a coffee set a. service; ~ **na 24 osoby** a 24-place service a. set 2 (materiały prasowe) bulletin; ~ **informacyjny** a news bulletin 3 Techn. (obsługa techniczna) service; (punkt obsługi) (urządzeń) service centre GB, service center US; (pojazdów) garage, service station

serwis[2] m Sport serve, service

serw|ować impf vt 1 Sport to serve [piłkę] 2 książk. (podawać do stołu) to serve [obiad]

serwus inter. pot. (na powitanie) hi pot.; (na pożegnanie) bye pot.

seryjnie adv. **produkować coś** ~ to mass-produce sth

sesj|a f 1 (obrady) session; ~**a parlamentarna/ sejmowa** a parliamentary session; **zorganizować** ~**ę naukową** to organize a symposium 2 (na giełdzie) trading session 3 Uniw. (examination) session

sete|r m setter; ~**r irlandzki** an Irish setter

set|ka ❲ f pot. 1 hundred; ~**ka uczniów/żołnierzy** a hundred students/soldiers; **płacić** ~**kami** to pay in hundreds 2 (w numeracji) **mieszkam pod** ~**ką** I live at No. 100 3 (prędkość) **jechać** ~**ką** to do 100 kph 4 (porcja alkoholu) ≈ jigger (100 ml); **zamówił dwie** ~**ki wódki** he ordered two large vodkas 5 (sto lat) **dożyć** ~**ki** to live to be a hundred (years old) 6 Sport (dystans) hundred metres GB, hundred meters US 7 (wełna) pure wool
❲❲ plt (bardzo dużo) hundreds; ~**ki razy** hundreds of times

setn|y num. ord. [przedstawienie, numer, rocznica] hundredth

sezon m season; ~ **letni** the summer season; ~ **urlopowy** the holiday season; **pełnia** a. **szczyt** ~**u** the height of the season; ~ **truskawek** the strawberry season; ~ **piłkarski/narciarski** the football/ski season; ~ **ogórkowy** pot. silly season, close season; **martwy** ~ pot. off season, dead season

sędzi|a m 1 judge także przen.; ~**a przysięgły** member of the jury 2 Sport (w boksie, futbolu) referee; (w tenisie, krykiecie) umpire; ~**a liniowy** (w tenisie) linesman; ~**a punktowy** scorer

sędzi|ować impf ❲ vt Sport to umpire
❲❲ vi Prawo to judge

sęk m (na pniu) snag; (w desce) knot
■ **w tym** ~ pot. that's the problem, there's the rub

sęp m Zool. vulture także przen.

sfałsz|ować pf vt 1 (podrobić) to forge [pieniądze, dokumenty]; to falsify [miód, wino] 2 (zniekształcić) to falsify [przeszłość, dane statystyczne] 3 Muz. to sing/ play [sth] out of tune

sfaul|ować pf vt Sport to foul

sfe|ra f 1 książk. (zakres) sphere; ~**ra wpływów** the sphere of influence; ~**ra budżetowa** the public sector 2 książk. (środowisko) class; ~**ry kulturalne/ towarzyskie/naukowe** cultural/social/scientific circles; **wyższe** ~**ry** high society, upper classes 3 (niebieska) firmament, the vault of the sky

sferment|ować pf vi to ferment; (zepsuć się) to go off

sfilm|ować pf vt to film; (na taśmie video) to video; ~**ować powieść** to film a novel

sf|ora f pack także przen.

sformuł|ować pf vt to formulate [teorię, myśl, plan]; to express [opinię, wniosek]; to word [list, pytanie]; to delineate [warunki, zasady]; **starannie** ~**owane przepisy** carefully worded a. phrased regulations; **ostro** ~**owany list** a strongly-worded letter

sfotograf|ować pf vt to photograph

si|ać impf vt 1 to sow [nasiona, rośliny, wątpliwości, zamęt]; to spread [panikę, grozę]; to cause [śmierć, zgorszenie]; **siać nienawiść** to stir up hatred; **siać spustoszenie** to cause a. wreak havoc; **ciągle sieje długopisy/klucze** przen. he keeps losing his pens/ mislaying his keys

siadać impf → **siąść**

sian|o n hay; **dać koniom** ~**a** to hay horses
■ **daj sobie z tym** ~**a** pot. forget it; **mieć** ~**o w głowie** to be feather-brained a. feather-headed

siar|ka f sulphur GB, sulfur US

siat|ka f 1 (plecionka) net; (materiał) mesh; **druciana** ~**ka** wire netting; ~**ka z cienkiego drutu** chicken wire; ~**ka ze sznurka** a. **sznurowa** rope mesh; ~**ka maskująca** Wojsk. camouflage netting; ~**ka na motyle** a butterfly net; ~**ka na włosy** a hairnet; ~**ka na zakupy** (ze sznurka) a string bag; (z folii plastikowej) a shopping bag; ~**ka ochronna** a. **asekuracyjna** a safety net; ~**ka od komarów** a. **owadów** (nad łóżkiem) a mosquito net; (w oknie, drzwiach) a screen 2 (układ linii, ulic, przewodów) grid; ~**ka zajęć** Szkol., Uniw. a timetable GB, a schedule US; ~**ka organizacyjna** the structure of an organization 3 (zorganizowana grupa) ring; ~**ka szpiegowska** a spy ring 4 pot. (siatkówka) volleyball 5 Sport (w tenisie, siatkówce, badmintonie) net; (w futbolu) (goal) net; (w hokeju) cage

siatkar|ka f Sport volleyball player

siatkarz m 1 Sport volleyball player 2 Techn. netter

siatków|ka f 1 Sport volleyball; **grać w** ~**kę** to play volleyball 2 Anat. retina; **zapalenie** ~**ki** Med. retinitis

siąp|ić impf vi ~**i deszcz** a. **mżawka** it's drizzling; **zaczęło** ~**ić** it started to drizzle

si|ąść *pf* — **si|adać** *impf vi* 1 *[osoba]* to sit (down); *[zwierzę]* to sit; *[ptak]* to perch 2 pot. (nie funkcjonować) *[lodówka, silnik]* to break down; *[komputer, program]* to crash; *[firma, teatr, klub]* to go under 3 *[samolot]* to land 4 pot. (do samochodu, ciężarówki) to get in; (do autobusu, samolotu, pociągu, na konia) to get on 5 pot. (obniżyć się) *[poziom, wyniki]* to go down; *[fundament, ściany, grunt]* to subside

sid|ło *n* snare; **chwytać zwierzynę w ~ła** to snare game
■ **wpaść we własne ~ła** to be hoist with a. by one's own petard

siebie *pron.* oneself; (wzajemnie) each other, one another; **kupiłem to dla ~** I bought it for myself; **jestem zła na ~** I'm angry at a. with myself; **czuć się jak u ~** to feel at home; **nie mogą bez ~ żyć** they can't live without each other

siecz|ka *f* chaff
■ **mieć ~kę w głowie** pot. (być głupim) to be a cloth head pot.; (być zdezorientowanym) to be addled a. befuddled

sie|ć *f* 1 (do łapanie zwierząt, ryb) net; **złowić** a. **schwytać rybę/ptaka w ~ć** to catch a fish/bird in a net 2 (pułapka) net przen.; **omotany ~cią intrygi** caught in a web of intrigue; **zastawiać na kogoś ~ci** to lay a trap for sb 3 (pajęczyna) (spider's) web 4 (system rozgałęzień) network; **~ć rur kanalizacyjnych** a network of sewage pipes; **~ć ciemnych uliczek** a labyrinth of dark streets 5 (przedsiębiorstwo) chain; (system instytucji, zakładów) network 6 Komput. network; (Internet) the Web; **być w ~ci** a. **być podłączonym do ~ci** to be online; **surfować po ~ci** to surf the Web

sied|em *num.* seven
siedemdziesi|ąt *num.* seventy
siedemdziesiąt|ka *f* seventy
siedemdziesią|ty *num. ord.* seventieth
siedemnast|ka *f* seventeen
siedemnast|y *num. ord.* seventeenth
siedemna|ście *num.* seventeen
sied|emset *num.* seven hundred
siedze|nie *n* 1 (krzesła, stołka, w samochodzie) seat 2 (ubrania) seat; **spodnie mają plamę na ~niu** there's a stain on the seat of the trousers 3 pot., euf. (pośladki) rear pot.
siedzib|a *f* (miejsce urzędowania) seat; **~a główna** headquarters
sie|dzieć *impf vi* 1 to sit; **~dzieć za stołem** a. **przy stole** to sit at the table; **~dź cicho!** be quiet!; **~dzieć całymi dniami przed telewizorem** to be a couch potato 2 pot. (w więzieniu) to do time pot.
■ **~dzieć nad czymś** pot. to work on a. at sth; **~dzieć na tyłku** posp. to sit around a. about; **~dzieć na wysokim/intratnym stanowisku** to be highly placed/to have a lucrative job; **~dzieć w czymś** pot. (zajmować się) to know sth inside out pot.; **~dzieć w długach (po uszy)** pot. to be up to

one's ears in debt; **~dzieć w nocy** a. **do późna** to sit up (late); **~dzieć z założonymi rękami** to sit by; **~dź, jak ci dobrze** pot. keep your nose out of it; **~dzieć drugi rok w tej samej klasie** pot. to repeat the class a. year; **mieć na czym ~dzieć** pot. to be broad in the beam pot.

siekacz *m* Anat. incisor
sieka|ć *impf vt* to chop (up) *[mięso, jarzyny]*
siekie|ra *f* axe GB, ax US
■ **~rę można powiesić** pot. you can cut the air with a knife
sielan|ka *f* idyll; **~ka małżeńska/rodzinna** marital/family bliss
siennik *m* pallet, palliasse GB, paillasse US
si|eń *f* entrance hall, hall(way)
siepacz *m* książk. hired assassin
siero|ta *m, f* 1 (dziecko) orphan; **zostać ~tą** to be orphaned 2 pot. (niezdara) wimp pot., pejor.
sierp *m* 1 (narzędzie) sickle; **~ księżyca** a crescent moon 2 Sport hook, sidewinder US
sierp|ień *m* August
sierś|ć *f* hair; (psa, wilka) coat; (kota) fur; **sweter z wielbłądziej ~ci** a camel-hair cardigan; **gubić/zmieniać ~ć** to moult GB, to molt US
sierżan|t *m* Wojsk. sergeant
się *pron.* 1 (siebie samego) oneself; **zobaczył ~ w lustrze** he saw himself in the mirror; **zatrzymał taksówkę i kazał ~ wieźć na dworzec** he waved down a taxi and told the driver to take him to the station 2 (wzajemnie) each other, one another; **znają ~ od dwóch lat** they've known each other for two years 3 (w konstrukcjach bezosobowych) **ryż uprawia ~ w Azji** rice is grown in Asia; **powinno ~ jeść dużo warzyw** one should eat a lot of vegetables; **jak to ~ pisze?** how do you spell it?; **mówi ~, że...** they say that...; **nigdy ~ nie wie** one never knows; **jak wam ~ mieszka w nowym domu?** how's the new house?; **wygodnie ci ~ siedzi?** are you comfortable?; **tak mi ~ jakoś powiedziało** it just came out (like that) pot.; **słyszało ~ to i owo** I've heard a thing or two; **tutaj posadzi ~ żonkile** I'll/we'll plant some daffodils here 4 (w konstrukcjach biernych) **kolacja już ~ robi** dinner's almost ready; **już ~ robi!** pot. I'll be right on it! pot.
sięg|nąć *pf* — **sięg|ać** *impf vi* 1 (wyciągnąć rękę) to reach (**po coś** for sth); **~nąć do kieszeni po chusteczkę** to reach into one's pocket for a handkerchief 2 (korzystać z informacji) to refer (**do czegoś** to sth); **~ać do archiwów/słownika** to refer to the archives/a dictionary 3 przen. (starać się zdobyć) to aspire (**po coś** to sth) 4 (używać) to use (**po coś** sth); **w chwilach rozpaczy ~ała po alkohol** when she was depressed she turned to drink; **~nąć po pióro/pędzel** przen. to start writing/painting 5 (dochodzić) to reach (**czegoś** sth); **broda ~ała mu (do) pasa** his beard came down to his waist; **sukienka ~ająca kolan** a. **do kolan** a knee-

length skirt; **bezrobocie** ~**nęło 13 procent** the unemployment rate reached 13 per cent; **straty firmy** ~**ają milionów** the company's losses run into millions

■ ~**ać do kieszeni** a. **portfela** to loosen the purse strings; ~**ać po cudze** a. **po cudzą własność** to steal; ~**ać prawą ręką do lewego ucha** a. **lewą ręką do prawego ucha** to do things ass-backwards pot.

sik|nąć *pf* — **sik|ać** *impf vi* pot. ① (oddać mocz) to piss pot. ② *[woda, krew]* to gush

sikor|ka *f* ① Zool. tit, titmouse ② przen., żart. (dziewczyna) bird, chick pot.

sil|ić się *impf v refl.* to go out of one's way; ~**ić się na uprzejmość/dowcip** to try to be polite/funny

silnie *adv. grad.* ① (mocno) *[uderzyć, szarpnąć]* strongly; **wiatr wiał coraz** ~**j** the wind was getting stronger and stronger; ~ **zbudowany mężczyzna** a strongly-built a. powerfully-built man ② (intensywnie) *[przeżywać, nienawidzić]* intense-ly; ~ **działające lekarstwo** a strong a. potent drug

silnik *m* engine

silnikow|y *adi. [olej, smar, paliwo]* engine

siln|y *adi. grad.* ① (mocny) *[osoba, ręce, serce, wola]* strong; **być** ~**ym duchem** to have inner strength ② (działający z dużą siłą) *[wiatr, uderzenie, wstrząs]* strong, heavy; ~**y lek** a strong a. potent medicine; **nosić** ~**e szkła** to wear strong glasses ③ (wpływowy) *[grupa, lobby, państwo, władza]* strong, powerful; ~**a waluta** a strong currency; **mieć** ~**ą pozycję** to be in a strong position ④ (przekonujący) *[argument, wpływ]* strong; *[perswazja]* forceful ⑤ (liczny) *[eskorta, oddział, grupa]* strong ⑥ (intensywny) *[zapach, światło, akcent]* strong; ~**y ból** an intense pain; ~**y mróz** a hard frost; ~**a gorączka** a high fever ⑦ (trwały) *[uczucie, więzi, wrażenie]* strong

si|ła ❚ *f* ① (fizyczna) strength; **tracić siły** to lose one's strength; **być u kresu sił** to be absolutely exhausted; **harował ponad siły** he worked like a horse ② (możliwości) power; **przeliczyć się ze swoimi siłami** to overestimate one's ability; **wierzyć we własne siły** to have confidence in oneself; **to przerasta moje siły** it's beyond my power ③ (moc) strength; **siła argumentów** the force of argument; **siła wiatru** the force of the wind; **hałas przybierał na sile** the noise was getting louder; **siła napędowa** a. **sprawcza czegoś** przen. the driving force of sth ④ (przemoc) force ⑤ (atut) strength ⑥ (tajemnicze zjawisko) power; **siły nieczyste** the powers of darkness; **niewi-dzialna siła** an invisible force ⑦ (pracownicy) labour GB, labor US; **tania siła robocza** cheap labour (force) ⑧ (grupa ludzi) force; **siły demokratyczne/ postępowe** forces of democracy/progress ⑨ Fiz. force

❚❚ **siły** *plt* ① (możliwości) power; **połączyć siły** to

join forces; **robić coś wspólnymi siłami** to make a joint effort to do sth ② (oddziały) forces; **siły porządkowe** the forces of law and order; **siły zbrojne** the (armed) forces

❚❚❚ **siłą** *adv.* ① (przemocą) by force ② (z trudem) with difficulty

❚❙❚ **na siłę** *adv.* pot. ① (przemocą) by force; **karmić dziecko na siłę** to force-feed a child; **nie można uszczęśliwiać ludzi na siłę** you can take a horse to water but you can't make it drink przysł. ② (jeżeli nie można inaczej) at a push pot.; **na siłę zdążę na piątek** I could do it by Friday, but at a push

❑ **siła nabywcza** Ekon. purchasing power; **siła pociągowa** Techn. tractive force; **siły wytwórcze** Ekon. production forces

■ **być skazanym na własne siły** to be left to one's own devices; **być w sile wieku** to be in one's prime; **co sił w nogach** at full pelt; **co sił** a. **z całej siły** a. **z całych sił** a. **ze wszystkich sił** a. **ile sił** with all one's strength a. might; **to nie jest na moje siły** it's too much for me; **nie czuć się na siłach coś zrobić** to not feel up to doing sth; **mieć siłę przebicia** pot. to push oneself forward; **nie ma na niego/na to siły** there's nothing you can do with him/with it; **nie mieć siły** a. **sił do kogoś/ czegoś** to not put up with sb/sth any longer; **opadać z sił** to run out of steam; **próbować swoich sił w czymś** to try one's hand at sth; **robić coś o własnych siłach** a. **własnymi siłami** to do sth on one's own; **siła wyższa** circumstances beyond one's control; **siła złego na jednego** przysł. ≈ it never rains but it pours przysł.; **siłą rzeczy** perforce książk.; **trwać** a. **odbywać się siłą roz-pędu** to carry under its own steam przen.; **nie ma takiej siły, żebym tam poszedł** wild horses couldn't drag me there; **żadna siła mnie stąd nie ruszy** wild horses wouldn't drag me away from here

siłacz *m* strongman

siłacz|ka *f* strongwoman; przen. paragon of moral strength

sił|ować się *impf v refl.* to wrestle (**z kimś** with sb); ~**ować się z kimś na rękę** to arm-wrestle with sb

siłowni|a *f* ① Sport gymnasium ② Techn. power plant; ~**a wodna** a hydropower plant

singiel /'singjel/ *m* ① (płyta) single ② Sport singles

siniak *m* bruise; **nabić sobie** ~**a** to bruise oneself; ~ **pod okiem** a black eye

si|niec *m* bruise; **sińce pod oczami** shadows under sb's eyes

sini|eć *impf vi [osoba, twarz, nos]* to turn blue

sin|y *adi. [dym, mgiełka, twarz]* blue; **był** ~**y z zimna** he was blue with cold; ~**e cienie pod oczami** shadows under sb's eyes

siodeł|ko *n* (w rowerze, motocyklu) saddle; (w wyciągu) chair

siodł|ać *impf vt* to saddle (up) *[konia]*

siod|ło *n* ① (do jazdy konnej) saddle; (damskie) a side-saddle ② pot., przen. **siedzieć (mocno) w ~le** to be (firmly) in the saddle; **wysadzić kogoś z ~ła** to knock sb off their perch

siorb|nąć *pf* — **siorb|ać** *impf vt* pot. to slurp

si|ostra *f* ① (krewna) sister; **to moja starsza siostra** she's my elder sister; **byłyśmy jak siostry** we were like sisters ② (pielęgniarka) sister GB, nurse US; **siostra przełożona** head nurse ③ (zakonnica) sister; **siostry zakonne** nuns

siostrzenic|a *f* niece

siostrze|niec *m* nephew

siódem|ka *f* seven

siódm|y *num. ord.* seventh

sit|ko *n* (small) sieve, (small) strainer; **~ko do herbaty** a tea strainer

si|to *n* ① (kuchenne) sieve, strainer; **przesiać mąkę przez sito** to sieve the flour; **być dziurawym jak sito** to leak like a sieve ② przen. **przejść przez sito eliminacyjne** to pass through the qualifying round; **przejść przez sito kontroli jakości** to pass the quality control

sitowi|e *n* Bot. bulrush

siusia|ć *impf vi* pot. to pee, to wee pot.

siwi|eć *impf vi [osoba]* to go a. turn grey GB, to go a. turn gray US; *[włosy]* to grey GB, to gray US; **~eć na skroniach** to go grey at the sides

siwi|zna *f* grey GB, gray US; **włosy przyprószone ~zną** hair streaked with grey

siw|y *adi. [osoba, włosy, koń, dym]* grey GB, gray US; **starzec z ~ą brodą** a grey-bearded old man; **być ~ym jak gołąb** a. **gołąbek** to be silver-grey

skafand|er *m* ① (kurtka) anorak ② (ochronny) suit; **~er kosmiczny** a spacesuit; **~er nurka** a diving suit

skaj *m* leatherette

skakać *impf* → **skoczyć**

skakan|ka *f* skipping rope GB, jump rope US; **skakać przez ~kę** to skip GB, to skip rope US

skal|a *f* ① (zbiór liczb) scale; **~a Fahrenheita** the Fahrenheit scale; **zero stopni w ~i Celsjusza** zero degrees Celsius a. centigrade ② (w urządzeniu) scale, dial ③ (uporządkowany zbiór) scale; **~a wartości** a set of values; **~a ocen** a marking scale a. scheme; **~a porównawcza** standards for comparison ④ (zasięg) range, scale; **szeroka ~a zainteresowań** a wide range of interests; **~a barw** a range of colour; **~a głosu** the compass of a singer's voice; **~a uczuć** a gamut of emotions ⑤ (pomniejszenie) scale; **mapa w ~i 1:500 000** a map at a scale of 1:500,000; **makieta w ~i 1:5** a model on a scale of 1:5

■ **na wielką/małą ~ę** on a large/small scale; **żyć na wielką ~ę** to live it up, to live life to the full

skalecze|nie *n* (rana) cut

skalecz|yć *pf* ① *vt* to cut; **~yć rękę odłamkiem szkła** to cut one's hand on a piece of glass; **~yć nogę o kamień** to hurt one's leg on a stone; **~yć kogoś nożem** to cut sb with a knife

② **skaleczyć się** to cut oneself; **~yć się w palec** to cut one's finger; **~yć się nożem** to cut oneself with a knife

skalpel *m* Med. scalpel

ska|ła *f* rock; **twardy jak ~ła** (as) hard as a rock

skamielin|a *f* fossil także przen.

skandal *m* scandal; **rubryka ~i towarzyskich** a gossip column; **wywołać ~** to cause a. create a scandal; **to ~, że/żeby...** it's a scandal a. scandalous that...

skandaliczn|y *adi.* scandalous; *[warunki, jakość]* outrageous

skand|ować *impf vt* to chant *[pieśni, hasła]*

skane|r *m* scanner

skan|ować *impf vt* to scan *[dokumenty, powierzchnię]*

skarb *m* ① treasure; **szukać ~u** to search for buried treasure; **~y sztuki** art treasures ② przen. treasure, gem; **taki pracownik to ~** such an employee is a real gem; **jej talent to prawdziwy ~** her talent is a real treasure; **(mój) ~ie!** pot., pieszcz. darling!, sweetheart!

❑ **Skarb Państwa** State Treasury

■ **za (żadne) ~y (świata)** not for (all) the world, not for love nor a. or money

skarbni|k *m* ① (w organizacji) treasurer, collector ② (duch podziemi) kobold

skarbon|ka *f* money box GB, piggy bank

skar|cić *pf vt* to scold *[dziecko, ucznia]*; **~cić kogoś wzrokiem** to give sb a scolding look

skar|ga *f* complaint (**na kogoś/coś** about sb/sth); (w sądzie) plaint (**przeciwko komuś/czemuś** against sb/sth)

skarp|a *f* (urwiska, wykopu) escarpment, bluff; (rzeki) bank, enbankment

skarpe|ta, **~tka** *f* sock

■ **trzymać oszczędności w ~cie** a. **odkładać oszczędności do ~ty** pot. to keep one's savings under the mattress

skarż|yć *impf* ① *vt* Prawo to sue

② *vi* (donosić) to tell tales; **~yć na kogoś** to tell on sb

③ **skarżyć się** (narzekać) to complain; **~yć się na bóle** to complain of the pain; **~yć się na sąsiadów** to complain about the neighbours

skarżypy|ta *m*, *f* pot. telltale

skas|ować *pf vt* ① (przedziurkować, ostemplować) to punch *[bilet]* ② (zlikwidować) to erase *[nagranie]*; to delete *[plik]*; to cancel *[zarządzenie]*; to close down *[instytucję, urząd, sklep]* ③ Admin. to write off *[maszynę, pojazd, urządzenie]* ④ pot. (zniszczyć) to crash *[samochód, rower]*

skaz|a f [1] (usterka) flaw; ~**a w a. na materiale** a flaw in the fabric; **brylant bez** ~**y** a flawless diamond [2] przen. flaw, blemish; ~**a na honorze** a blemish on sb's honour; **człowiek bez** ~**y** an unblemished man

ska|zać pf — **ska|zywać** impf [] vt [1] (wydać wyrok) to sentence, to condemn; ~**zać kogoś na rok więzienia** to sentence sb to a year's imprisonment [2] (przesądzić o losie) to condemn; ~**zany na samotność** condemned to loneliness; **sprawa z góry** ~**zana na przegraną** an issue doomed to failure from the start

[] **skazać się** — **skazywać się** to condemn oneself (**na coś** to sth)

skaza|niec m Prawo convict; (na śmierć) condemned man

ska|zić pf — **ska|żać** impf vt to contaminate [środowisko naturalne, wodę, mięso]; to pollute [powietrze]; **teren** ~**żony** a contaminated area

skazywać impf → **skazać**

skażać impf → **skazić**

skąd [] pron. [1] (w pytaniu) where from?; ~ **masz ten zegarek?** where did you get this watch (from)?; ~ **wiesz?** how do you know?; ~ **ci to przyszło do głowy?** what gave you that idea?; ~ **ta pewność?** what makes you so sure?; **pojawił się nie wiadomo** ~ he appeared out of a. from nowhere [2] (względny) **odłóż nożyczki tam,** ~ **je wziąłeś** put the scissors back where you found them

[] inter. not at all!, why, no!; „**powiedziałeś mu?**" – „**ależ** ~" a. „~ **znowu**" 'did you tell him?' – 'of course not!'

skąp|ić impf vt [1] (nadmiernie oszczędzać) to stint (**czegoś** on sth); ~**ić grosza** to tighten the purse strings [2] przen. to spare; **nie** ~**ić wysiłków** to spare no pains a. trouble; **nie** ~**ić komuś pochwał** to spare no praise for sb

skąp|iec m miser

skąp|o adv. [1] (niewystarczająco) poorly; ~**o oświetlony pokój** a poorly lit room; ~**o odziana dziewczyna** a scantily dressed girl [2] (oszczędnie) stingily

skąpstw|o n miserliness

skąp|y adi. [1] (nadmiernie oszczędny) [osoba] mean [2] (niewystarczający) [informacje] skimpy; [posiłek, światło, strój] scanty

skier|ować pf — **skier|owywać** impf [] vt [1] (zwrócić w jakąś stronę) to direct [lunetę, strumień wody]; ~**ować broń w stronę przeciwnika** to aim at the enemy; ~**ować wzrok na kogoś/coś** to turn one's eyes towards sb/sth; ~**ować rozmowę na inne tory** to divert the conversation towards another topic [2] (posłać) to dispatch [pismo]; ~**ować sprawę do sądu** to bring a case to court [3] (kazać iść) to direct; ~**ować pacjenta do lekarza specjalisty** to refer a patient to a specialist; ~**ować kogoś w złą stronę** to misdirect sb [4] (adresować) to direct;

~**ować pytanie do kogoś** to direct a question to sb; ~**ować myśli ku komuś/czemuś** to direct one's thoughts towards a. towards sb/sth

[] **skierować się** — **skierowywać się** (zwrócić się) [osoba] to head; [oczy, pojazd] to turn

skierowa|nie n request; ~**nie na badania** a laboratory order a. request; ~**nie do szpitala** a referral to hospital

skierowywać impf → **skierować**

ski|nąć pf vi (głową) to nod; (ręką) to beckon

skinie|nie n (głową) nod; (ręką) wave

■ **być gotowym na czyjeś każde** ~**nie** to be at sb's beck and call

skle|ić pf — **skle|jać** impf [] vt [1] (połączyć) to glue [sth] together [deski, kartki, porcelanę]; **pot** ~**ił mu włosy** his hair was glued together with sweat [2] przen. (utworzyć) to put [sth] together [zdanie]; to cobble [sth] together [zespół, rząd]

[] **skleić się** — **sklejać się** [1] (zlepić się) [kartki, znaczki] to get glued together [2] (przywrzeć) [strony] to get stuck together

sklej|ka f [1] Techn. plywood [2] (w fotografii) splice

sklep m shop GB, store US; ~ **spożywczy** a grocery; ~ **warzywny** a greengrocery; ~ **obuwniczy** a shoe shop; ~ **samoobsługowy** a self-service shop; ~ **z zabawkami** a toy shop

sklepie|nie n vault; ~**nie czaszki** the cranial vault; ~**nie niebieskie** a. **nieba** the heavenly vault, the vault of heaven

skleroz|a f [1] Med. sclerosis [2] pot. **mieć** ~**ę** to be gaga pot.

skła|d m [1] (drużyny, zespołu) line-up; (komisji, zarządu) make-up; ~**d rządu** the composition of the Cabinet; ~**d narodowościowy kraju** the ethnic composition of a country; **orkiestra w pełnym** ~**dzie** a full orchestra; **drużyna w pełnym/ niepełnym** ~**dzie** the team at full strength/below strength; **wchodzić w** ~**d delegacji** to be a member of the delegation; ~**d pociągu** Kolej. number of carriages in a train [2] (substancji, kolekcji) composition; ~**d leku** the composition of a drug; „**Skład**" (na opakowaniu) 'Ingredients' [3] (magazyn) (zboża, żywności) warehouse; (drzewa, węgla) yard; (amunicji, broni) depot; **mieć coś na** ~**dzie** to have sth in stock [4] Druk. composition

składa|ć impf → **złożyć**

składak m [1] (rower) folding bike; (kajak) folding canoe [2] (samochód) kit car; **komputer** ~ a self-assembled computer

składan|ka f (muzyczna) medley; (estradowa, kabaretowa) variety act

składan|y adi. [fotel, rower, stołek] folding; **nóż** ~**y** a jackknife; **łóżko** ~**e** a foldaway bed; **program** ~**y** a variety programme

skład|ka f [1] (darowizna) subscription [2] (wpłata obowiązkowa) fee; ~**ka członkowska** a membership fee; ~**ka na fundusz emerytalny** a pension (fund) contribution ③ (zbiórka) collection; **zrobiliś-my** ~**kę na prezent dla koleżanki** we clubbed together to buy our colleague a gift

składni|a *f* Jęz. syntax

składnik *m* element, component; (potrawy) ingredient; ~**i stopu/perfum** alloy/perfume components; ~**i pokarmowe** nutrients

skłam|ać *pf vi* to tell a lie; ~**ać komuś, że...** to lie to sb that...; **żeby nie** ~**ać** *pot.* to tell the truth

skłonnoś|ć *f* tendency; **mieć** ~**ć do przesady** to be prone to exaggeration; ~**ć do tycia** a tendency to put on weight; ~**ci sadystyczne** sadistic tendencies

skłonn|y *adi.* prone (**do czegoś** to sth); **jest** ~**y do przeziębień** he's prone to (catch) colds; ~**y do przesady** prone to exaggeration; **był** ~**y się z nią pogodzić** he was inclined to make up with her

skne|ra *m, f* *pot.* miser

skno|cić *pf vt* *pot.* to botch *pot.*

skocz|ek *m* ① Sport jumper; ~**ek do wody** a diver; ~**ek narciarski** a ski jumper; ~**ek w dal** a long jumper; ~**ek wzwyż** a high jumper; ~**ek spadochronowy** a parachutist ② Gry knight

skoczni|a *f* Sport ski jump

sk|oczyć *pf* — **sk|akać** *impf vi* to jump; **skoczyć przez płot** to jump over the fence; **skakać przez skakankę** to skip; **skoczyć z dachu/z okna** to jump off the roof/out of the window; **akcje skaczą (w górę)** *pot.* stocks are shooting up a. soaring; **ceny skoczyły w górę** *pot.* prices went up ■ **skakać koło kogoś** *pot.* to be all over sb *pot.*; **skakać z radości** to jump up and down (for joy), to hop up and down with delight; **skakać z tematu na temat** to jump from one topic to another; **skoczyć komuś do gardła** to jump down sb's throat *przen.*; **skoczyć do sklepu** to dash a. rush off to a shop

skojarze|nie *n* association; **budzić określone** ~**nia** to have certain associations a. connotations

skojarz|yć *pf* **Ⅰ** *vt* ① to bring together [*parę*] ② (w umyśle) to associate (**coś z czymś** sth with sth); ~**yć fakty** to put two and two together **Ⅱ** **skojarzyć się** to become associated (**z czymś** with sth)

skok *m* ① (odbicie się od ziemi) jump ② (nagła zmiana) jump; ~ **temperatury** a temperature jump; ~ **cen** a jump in prices ③ *pot.* (zorganizowana kradzież) robbery, hold-up; **na bank** a bank raid a. robbery ④ Sport jump; ~ **w dal** the long jump GB, the broad jump US; ~ **wzwyż** the high jump; ~ **o tyczce** the pole vault; **konkurs** ~**ów narciar-skich** a ski jumping competition ■ ~ **w bok** *pot.* hanky-panky *pot.*; **jednym** ~**iem** in a bound, with one bound

skoment|ować *pf vt* to comment (**coś** on a. about sth); (skrytykować) to make comments (**coś** on sth)

skoml|eć, ~**ić** *impf vi* to whimper; ~**eć o litość** *przen.* to beg for pity

skomplet|ować *pf vt* to complete [*kolekcję*]; to assemble [*drużynę*]

skomplik|ować *pf* **Ⅰ** *vt* to complicate **Ⅱ** **skomplikować się** [*sprawa, sytuacja*] to become complicated

skomplikowan|y *adi.* complicated; [*mechanizm*] intricate; [*sytuacja*] complex

skompon|ować *pf vt* to compose

skompromit|ować *pf* **Ⅰ** *vt* ① (wystawić na wstyd) to disgrace ② (narazić na krytykę) to compromise **Ⅱ** **skompromitować się** to disgrace oneself (**czymś** with sth)

skomunik|ować się *pf v refl.* *książk.* to get in touch (**z kimś** with sb); ~**ować się z policją** to make contact with the police ■ **niech (ja)** ~**m!** *posp.* cross my heart and hope to die!

skonan|y *adi.* *pot.* dead beat *pot.*

skoncentr|ować *pf* **Ⅰ** *vt* to concentrate [*wojska*]; ~**ować uwagę na czymś** to fix a. focus one's attention on sth; ~**owany sok pomarańczowy** concentrated orange juice **Ⅱ** **skoncentrować się** to concentrate (**na czymś** on sth)

skonfisk|ować *pf vt* to confiscate [*majątek, towary*] (**komuś** from sb)

skonsum|ować *pf vt* *książk.* to consume [*posiłek, napój, energię, paliwo*]

skontakt|ować *pf* **Ⅰ** *vt* to put [sb] in touch (**z kimś** with sb) **Ⅱ** **skontaktować się** to get in touch (**z kimś** with sb); **nie można się było z nim** ~**ować** he couldn't be contacted

skontrol|ować *pf vt* to check; ~**ować stan techniczny samochodu** to have a check-up done on a car

skończ|ony *adi.* ① (całkowity) [*uroda*] consummate; [*głupiec, drań*] utter ② (przegrany) finished; **człowiek** ~**ony jako polityk** a political has-been; **jestem** ~**ony!** I'm done for

skończ|yć *pf* **Ⅰ** *vt* ① (doprowadzić do końca) to finish [*pracę, rozmowę*] ② Szkol., Uniw. to complete [*kurs, uniwersytet*]; **studia** ~**ył rok temu** he graduated a year ago ③ (osiągnąć wiek) ~**yć pięćdziesiąt lat** to be fifty **Ⅱ** *vi* ① (zaprzestać) to be through (**z czymś** with sth) ② *pot.* (zerwać) to be through *pot.* (**z kimś** with sb); **wczoraj definitywnie** ~**li ze sobą** they broke up with each other yesterday ③ *pot.* (zabić) to finish [sb] off *pot.*; ~**yć ze sobą** to take one's own life ④ *pot.* (trafić) to wind up *pot.* **Ⅲ** **skończyć się** ① (przestać trwać) to end; **wakacje się** ~**yły** the holidays are over ② (zamknąć się) to end (**czymś** with sth); ~**yć się łzami** to end in tears

③ (wyczerpać się) *[zapasy, paliwo]* to run out; **pieniądze mi się** ~**yły** I've run out of money ④ pot. (wyczerpać się twórczo) to be washed up pot. ■ ~**yło się na strachu** they/I/he got off with nothing worse than a bad fright; ~**y się na tym, że będzie musiała pożyczyć od kogoś pieniądze** she's going to have to borrow money from somebody in the end; ~**yć się na niczym** to come to naught; ~**yć z dotychczasowym życiem** to turn over a new leaf; **wszystko dobrze się** ~**yło** everything turned out well; **źle** ~**yć** to come to a sticky end

skor|ek *m* Zool. earwig

skoro *coni.* książk. since; ~ **tu jesteś, pomóż mi przesunąć stół** since you're here, you can help me move the table; ~ **tak mówisz** if you say so; ~ **tak, to sobie idę** well in that case I'll be going; ~ **już musisz to robić, to...** if you really have to do it...; ~ **już o tym mowa** since we're on the subject

skoroszy|t *m* ring binder

skorowidz *m* ① (spis) index ② (zeszyt) thumb-indexed notebook

Skorpion *m* Scorpio

skorpion *m* Zool. scorpion

skorump|ować *pf vt* to corrupt *[polityka, urzędnika]*; ~**owany policjant** the corrupt policeman

skorup|a *f* ① Zool. shell, carapace; **schować się w** ~**ie** to withdraw into its shell ② Bot. shell ③ (twarda powłoka) crust; ~**a ziemska** the earth's crust ④ (potłuczony kawałek) ~**y (z) rozbitego dzbanka** pieces of a broken jug

skorupiak *m* Zool. crustacean

sko|ry *adi.* (gotowy) willing (**do zrobienia czegoś** to do sth); (chętny) game (**do czegoś** for sth); **być** ~**rym do gniewu** to be short-tempered; **jest zawsze** ~**ry do śmiechu** he's always game for a laugh; **nie jest zbyt** ~**ry do pisania** he's not very keen on writing

skoryg|ować *pf vt* książk. to correct *[postępowanie, błędy]*; to adjust *[projekt, harmonogram]*

skorzysta|ć *pf vi* ① (posłużyć się) to use (**z czegoś** sth); ~**ć z toalety** to use the toilet; ~**ć z czyjejś rady** to take sb's advice; **skwapliwie** ~**ć z czyjegoś zaproszenia** to eagerly accept sb's invitation ② (wykorzystać) to take advantage (**z czegoś** of sth); ~**ć z okazji** to seize an opportunity ③ (użyć) ~**ć z prawa/przywileju** to exercise one's right/privilege; ~**ć z ulgi podatkowej** to take advantage of the tax relief ④ (odnieść korzyść) to benefit (**na czymś** from sth); ~**ją na tym najbiedniejsi** this will benefit the poorest

skos *m* ① (pochylenie) angle; (w pionie) slant; **przejść na** ~ a. ~**em przez pole** to cut diagonally across a field; **złożyć coś na** ~ to fold sth diagonally; **połączyć coś na** ~ to join sth at an angle ② (krój)

bias; **spódnica (skrojona) ze** ~**u** a skirt cut on the bias

sko|sić *pf vt* ① (ściąć) to reap *[zboże]*; (kosą) to scythe *[trawę, łąkę]*; (maszyną) to mow *[trawę, trawnik]*; **świeżo** ~**szony trawnik** a newly mown lawn ② pot. (zarobić) to rake in pot. *[forsę]* ③ pot. (na egzaminie) to flunk pot. *[osobę]* ④ pot. (zastrzelić) to mow [sb] down pot.

skośn|y *adi.* *[promienie]* oblique; *[sufit, ściana]* sloping; *[oczy]* slanting

skowron|ek *m* skylark, lark ■ **być całym w** ~**kach** to be happy as a lark

skó|ra *f* ① Anat. skin; ~**ra głowy** the scalp; **kolor** ~**ry** (rasa) the colour of one's/sb's skin; ~**ra schodzi mu z nosa** his nose is peeling; **zrzucić** ~**rę** Zool. to shed its skin; **ostrzyc kogoś do gołej** ~**ry** to shave sb's head; **obedrzeć kogoś żywcem ze** ~**ry** to skin sb alive także przen.; **złupić kogoś ze** ~**ry** a. **zedrzeć z kogoś** ~**rę** przen. to rip sb off pot.; **darł się** a. **krzyczał** a. **wrzeszczał, jakby go ze** ~**ry obdzierali** he was screaming his head off; ~**ra mi cierpnie na myśl, że...** przen. it gives me the creeps to think that... pot.; **została z niego** ~**ra i kości** przen. he's nothing but skin and bones; **dostać w** ~**rę** to get a licking także przen.; **są podobni, jakby** ~**rę zdjął** they are the spitting image of each other; **wejść w czyjąś** ~**rę** przen. to put oneself in sb's position; **nie chciałbym być w twojej** ~**rze** przen. I wouldn't like to be in your shoes; **ratować własną** ~**rę** przen. to save one's own skin; **bać się o własną** ~**rę** przen. (o życie) to fear for one's life; (o stanowisko) to fear for one's job; **każdy dba o własną** ~**rę** przen. it's every man for himself ② (materiał) leather; (wyprawiona) hide; (z futrem) skin; **świńska** ~**ra** pigskin skin; **sztuczna** ~**ra** imitation leather; **przedmioty ze** ~**ry** leather articles ③ pot. (skórzane ubranie) leathers; **motocykliści w** ~**rach** leather-clad bikers ■ **czuć przez** ~**rę, że...** to feel in one's bones that...; **omal ze** ~**ry nie wyskoczył z ciekawości** he was dying to find out; **przekonać się na własnej** ~**rze, że...** to personally find out that...; **wyłazić ze** ~**ry, żeby coś zrobić** to fall over oneself to do sth; **zaleźć komuś za** ~**rę** to be a nuisance to sb

skór|ka *f* ① (przy paznokciu) cuticle; (zadarta) hangnail ② (materiał) skin; ~**ki królicze** rabbit skins ③ (banana, kiełbasy) skin; (sera, cytryny) rind; (ziemniaka, jabłka) peel; (chleba) crust; ~**ka pomarańczowa** orange peel ■ **nie warta** ~**ka wyprawki** a. **nie opłaci się** ~**ka za wyprawkę** the game is not worth the candle

skracać *impf* → **skrócić**

skrada|ć się *impf v refl.* to creep

skrajać → **skroić**

skrajnie *adv.* ⊡ (niezwykle) extremely ⊡ (zupełnie) completely

skrajn|y *adi.* ⊡ *[bieda, poglądy, prawica, rozwiązania]* extreme; **mieć ~e poglądy** to be extreme in one's views ⊡ (najbardziej wysunięty) outermost

skrapiać *impf* → **skropić**

skraplać *impf* → **skroplić**

skrawać *impf* → **skroić**

skraw|ek *m* (materiału, papieru, mięsa) scrap; (ziemi, ogrodu, nieba) patch

skreśl|ić *pf* — **skreśl|ać** *impf vt* ⊡ (wykreślić) to cross off *[imię, osobę, punkt]*; to cross [sth] out *[zdanie, słowo]*; **~ić kogoś/coś z listy** to cross sb/ sth off a list; **~ić kogoś** przen. to give up on sb ⊡ (napisać) to put [sth] down *[słowa, zdanie]*; to write *[list, podpis]*

skrę|cić *pf* — **skrę|cać** *impf* **▯** *vt* ⊡ (połączyć) (wkrętami) to screw [sth] together; (śrubami) to bolt [sth] together; **meble do samodzielnego ~cenia** self-assembly a. kit furniture ⊡ (zrobić) to twist *[sznur]*; to roll *[papierosa]*; **~cić linę z prześcieradła** to twist a sheet up into a rope ⊡ (uszkodzić) to sprain *[nogę]*; **~cić sobie nogę w kostce** to twist a. sprain one's ankle; **~cić kark** to break one's neck ⊡ (obrócić) to turn *[głowę, tułów]* ⊡ pot. (denerwować) **zazdrość go ~ca** he's green with envy pot.; **aż mnie ~ca, kiedy tego słucham** it sickens me when I listen to this pot.

▯ *vi* (zmienić kierunek) *[osoba, pojazd, droga]* to turn; **~cić w prawo** to turn right; **~ć w pierwszą ulicę w lewo** to take the first turn(ing) left; **samochód ~cił gwałtownie** the car swerved abruptly

▯ **skręcić się — skręcać się** ⊡ (zwinąć się) *[włosy, liście]* to curl ⊡ (wić się) to writhe; **~cać się z bólu** to writhe in pain; **~cać się ze śmiechu** pot., przen. to be convulsed with laughter

skrępowani|e *n* self-consciousness

skrępowan|y *adi.* self-conscious; **czuć się ~ym czyjąś obecnością** to feel awkward in sb's presence

skrę|t *m* ⊡ (zmiana kierunku) turn; **~t o 90°** a 90° turn; **~t równoległy** Sport a parallel turn ⊡ (łuk) curve; **droga prowadziła łagodnymi ~tami** the road curved gently ⊡ (przekręcenie) twist; (obrót) turn; **~t kiszek** pot. intestinal torsion ⊡ pot. (papieros) roll-up GB, roll-your-own US pot.; (z marihuaną) joint pot.

skrobacz|ka *f* ⊡ (skrobak) scraper ⊡ (do obierania) peeler

skrob|ać *impf vt* to peel *[kartofle, marchew]*; to scale *[rybę]*

■ ~ać komuś marchewkę a. **marchewki** pot., żart. to tread on sb's heels

skroban|ka *f* pot. abortion

skrobi|a *f* starch; **bogaty w ~ę** starchy

skr|oić, skr|ajać *pf* — **skr|awać** *impf · vt* ⊡ (odkroić) to cut off *[skórkę, spaleniznę]* ⊡ (pokroić)

to cut *[kiełbasę, chleb]*; to shred *[kapustę]* ⊡ (wyciąć) to cut *[buty, sukienkę]*; **dobrze/źle ~ojony garnitur** a well-cut/badly-cut suit ⊡ pot. (zbić) **~oić komuś skórę** a. **tyłek** to whip sb's hide pot.

skromnie *adv. grad.* modestly

skromnoś|ć *f* modesty; **fałszywa ~ć** false modesty; **nie grzeszyć ~cią** to be rather conceited

skromn|y *adi. grad.* modest; *[ślub]* quiet; *[urzędnik, posada]* humble; **przybrać ~ą minkę** iron. to put on a demure face

skro|ń *f* Anat. temple

skr|opić *pf* — **skr|apiać** *impf* **▯** *vt* to sprinkle; **~opić koszulę przed prasowaniem** to dampen a shirt for ironing; **~opić roślinę środkiem owadobójczym** to spray a plant with a pesticide

▯ **skropić się — skrapiać się** (popryskać się) **~opić się wodą kolońską** to spray oneself with cologne

skr|oplić *impf* — **skr|aplać** *pf* **▯** *vt* to liquefy *[gaz]*; to condense *[parę wodną]*

▯ **skroplić się — skraplać się** *[gaz]* to liquefy; *[para wodna]* to condense

skr|ócić *pf* — **skr|acać** *impf* **▯** *vt* ⊡ (zmniejszyć) to shorten *[sznurek, spódnicę, okres, tekst]*; to abbreviate *[wyraz]*; **~ócić sobie drogę** to take a short-cut; **~ócić coś o połowę** to shorten sth by half; **poprzeczne paski ~acają** horizontal stripes make you look shorter; **domagać się ~ócenia czasu pracy** to demand shorter hours ⊡ Mat. to reduce *[ułamek]*

▯ **skrócić się — skracać się** to shorten; *[dzień]* to grow shorter; **~acaj się!** pot. get to the point!

skró|t *m* ⊡ (książki) abridgement; (artykułu, referatu) abstract; **~t wiadomości** news headlines; **~t meczu w telewizji** the highlights of a game on TV ⊡ (pominięcie) cut; **~t myślowy** a mental shortcut; **przedstawić coś w telegraficznym ~cie** to outline sth briefly ⊡ (skrócona nazwa) abbreviation (**od czegoś** for sth); (akronim) acronym; **od czego to jest ~t?** what is it short for? ⊡ (krótsza droga) shortcut także przen.; **pójść na ~ty** a. **~tem** a. **~tami** to take a shortcut ⊡ Komput. (desktop) shortcut

skru|cha *f* remorse; **odczuwać ~chę za coś** to repent of sth; **powiedzieć coś ze ~chą** to say sth remorsefully

skrupulatn|y *adi.* meticulous

skrupu|ł *m* scruple; **człowiek bez** a. **pozbawiony ~łów** an unscrupulous man; **robić coś bez ~łów** to have no scruples a. qualms about doing sth

skrusz|ony *adi.* *[osoba]* repentant; *[spojrzenie, mina]* remorseful

skrusz|yć *pf* **▯** *vt* ⊡ (rozdrobnić) to crush *[kamienie, bryłę]*; to break *[pieczęć]*; **~yć skałę/ściany** *[deszcz, czas]* to wear away the rock/walls ⊡ przen. to break *[opór, upór]*

II skruszyć się 1 *[ściana, skała]* to crumble 2 (poczuć skruchę) *[osoba]* to repent

skryt|ka f 1 (schowek) hiding place; **biurko ze ~ką** a desk with a secret drawer 2 **~ka pocztowa** a post office box; **~ka pocztowa 135** (w adresie) PO box 135

skry|ty adi. 1 (zamknięty w sobie) reserved; (tajemniczy) secretive 2 (ukryty) secret; **spełnić czyjeś najskrytsze marzenia** to fulfil sb's innermost dreams

skrzecz|eć impf vi *[papuga]* to squawk; *[żaba, wrona]* to croak; *[małpa]* to chatter; *[osoba, radio]* to squawk

skrzek m 1 Zool. (frog)spawn; **składać ~** *[żaba]* to spawn 2 (głos) (papugi, osoby) squawk; (żaby, wrony) croak; (małpy) chatter

skrzel|e n 1 (narząd) gill; (pokrywa) gill cover 2 Techn. slat

skrzep m Med. (blood) clot

skrzep|nąć pf vi *[krew]* to clot; *[galareta]* to set; *[tłuszcz]* to solidify

skrzętnie adv. grad. (pilnie) *[zanotować, pozbierać]* busily; (starannie) *[ułożyć, zapisać]* meticulously; **~ gospodarować pieniędzmi** to manage money economically; **~ coś omijać** to carefully avoid sth; **~ coś ukrywać** to thoroughly hide sth; **~ wykonywać rozkazy** to scrupulously carry out orders

skrzycz|eć pf vt to scold (**kogoś za coś** sb for sth)

skrzyd|ło n 1 Zool. wing; **pobiec/przylecieć jak na ~łach** przen. to run/come as if on wings 2 (część samolotu) wing 3 (otwierana część) wing; **~ło drzwi/lustra** a door/mirror leaf; **~ło ołtarza** the leaf of an altar 4 (w turbinie, wiatraku) blade 5 (fragment budynku) wing 6 Sport wing 7 Wojsk. flank; **atak na ~le** a flank(ing) attack, an attack on the flank 8 Lotn., Wojsk. (oddział) wing 9 (frakcja) wing ■ **dodać komuś ~eł** to give sb a boost; **podciąć komuś ~ła** to clip sb's wings; **rozwinąć ~ła** to spread one's wings; **wziąć kogoś pod swoje ~ła** to take sb under one's wing

skrzy|nia f 1 (pojemnik) box; (zawartość) box, boxful; (z wiekiem na zawiasach) trunk; (na owoce) crate; (kufer) chest; **~nia na narzędzia** a tool chest 2 (część wersalki) storage box; (wysuwana) storage drawer 3 (przyrząd gimnastyczny) vaulting box 4 (nadwozie ciężarówki) platform 5 Aut. **~nia biegów** a gearbox; **automatyczna ~nia biegów** automatic transmission

skrzyn|ka f 1 (pojemnik) box; (zawartość) box, boxful; (na owoce, warzywa) crate; **~ka na kwiaty** a window box; **~ka na narzędzia** a toolbox 2 (do korespondencji) box; **~ka pocztowa** (do wrzucania listów) a postbox GB, a mailbox US; Komput. a mailbox; **~ka na listy** (na drzwiach) a letter box; (przed posesją) a mailbox US; **wrzucić list do ~ki** to post a letter 3 (obudowa) casing

Q ~ka kontaktowa contact point; **czarna ~ka** black box

skrzyp|ce plt violin; **grać pierwsze ~ce** przen. to play the leading role

skrzyp|ek m violinist; (ludowy) fiddler

skrzyp|nąć pf — **skrzyp|ieć** impf vi *[podłoga, drzwi, schody]* to creak; *[pióro]* to scratch; *[śnieg]* to crunch

skrzyw|dzić pf vt (zrobić krzywdę) to harm, to wrong; **~dzić kogoś niesłusznym oskarżeniem** to unfairly accuse sb; **muchy by nie ~dził** he wouldn't hurt a fly; **ludzie ~dzeni przez los** the disadvantaged; **czuć się ~dzonym przez los** to feel ill-used

skrzyw|ić pf — **skrzyw|iać** impf **I** vt to bend *[gwóźdź, koło]*; **~ić usta w uśmiechu** to twist one's mouth into a smile

II skrzywić się — skrzywiać się 1 (wygiąć się) *[gwóźdź, drut]* to bend; *[kręgosłup]* to curve; (przechylić się) *[słup, latarnia]* to bend down 2 (zrobić minę) to grimace; **~ić się z bólu** to give a grimace of pain; **~ić się na widok kogoś/czegoś** to wince at the sight of sb/sth

skrzyż|ować pf **I** vt 1 (ułożyć na krzyż) to cross *[patyki, widelce]*; **~ować ręce na piersi** to cross one's arms on one's chest; **~ować nogi** to cross one's legs 2 Biol. to cross(breed) (**z czymś** with sth) 3 przen. (połączyć) to combine; **lotnia ~owana ze spadochronem** a combination of a hang-glider and a parachute

II skrzyżować się 1 (przeciąć się) *[linie, drogi]* to cross; **nasze spojrzenia ~owały się** our eyes met 2 Biol. *[gatunki]* to crossbreed 3 przen. (połączyć się) *[cechy]* to be combined 4 (popaść w konflikt) *[cele, zamiary]* to clash

skrzyżowa|nie n 1 (przecięcie dróg) intersection, crossroads; **~nie bezkolizyjne** (z wiaduktem) a flyover; (z tunelem) an underpass 2 Biol. cross; **~nie konia z osłem** a cross between a horse and a donkey 3 przen. (połączenie) combination

skser|ować pf vt to xerox *[dokument]*

skub|ać¹ impf vt 1 *[ges, kaczkę, pierze]*; to tease *[len, wełnę]* 2 pot. (oszukiwać) to rip off; (wyciągać pieniądze) to milk; **~ać kogoś z pieniędzy** to milk sb for money

skub|nąć pf — **skub|ać²** impf **I** vt 1 (pociągnąć) to tug at *[brodę, wąsy]*; (dłubać) to pick at *[zarost, pryszcze, chleb]* 2 (wyrwać) to pluck *[liście]* 3 (zjeść) to nibble, to pick at *[jedzenie]* 4 (uszczypnąć) to pinch 5 pot. (ukraść) to pinch pot.

II skubnąć się — skubać się (pociągnąć się) **~ać się za brodę/wąsy** to tug at one's beard/moustache

sku|ć pf — **sku|wać** impf vt 1 (usunąć) to hack [sth] off *[tynk, kafelki]* 2 (połączyć) to forge [sth] together *[pręty]* 3 (łańcuchami) to chain [sb] (up)

[więźnia, nogi]; (kajdankami) to handcuff [4] książk.
rzeka ~**ta lodem** an ice-bound river

skul|ić *pf* [I] *vt* to hunch *[ramiona, plecy]*; to draw up *[nogi]*; ~**ić głowę** to bury one's head in one's shoulders

[II] **skulić się** (ze strachu) to cower; (z zimna) to huddle (up); (w łóżku) to curl up

skunks *m* skunk także przen.

skup *m* (skupowanie) purchase; (miejsce) collection point; ~ **butelek** a bottle exchange; ~ **makulatury** a paper recycling centre

skup|ić¹ *pf* — **skup|iać** *impf* [I] *vt* [1] (skoncentrować) to focus *[uwagę, myśli]* (**na czymś** on sth); ~**iać na sobie uwagę** to be the focus of attention; ~**ić wzrok na czymś** to gaze at sth [2] (zebrać) to concentrate *[władzę, kapitał]*; ~**ić władzę w swoich rękach** to gather power in one's hands; **organizacja** ~**iająca ludzi o różnych poglądach** an organization embracing people of different opinions [3] Fiz. to focus *[światło, promienie]*

[II] **skupić się** — **skupiać się** [1] (skoncentrować się) *[osoba, działania]* to concentrate (**na czymś** on sth) [2] (zgromadzić się) *[osoby, budynki, wyniki]* to cluster (**wokół kogoś/czegoś** around sb/sth) [3] Fiz. *[światło]* to focus

skup|ić² *pf* — **skup|ować** *impf vt* to buy *[zboże, mleko, owoce leśne]* (**od kogoś** from sb); to buy [sth] in *[akcje]* (**od kogoś** from sb)

skupieni|e *n* [1] (koncentracja) concentration; **słuchać ze** ~**em** a. **w** ~**u** to be listening with concentration [2] (zagęszczenie) concentration [3] (skupisko) concentration; (grupka) cluster

skupi|ony *adi.* [1] (uważny) *[osoba, twarz]* attentive; (zmobilizowany) *[osoba]* focused; **być** ~**onym na czymś** to be focused on sth; **słuchał** ~**ony** he was listening with concentration [2] (zwarty) *[zabudowa, populacja]* dense [3] (otaczający) **stali** ~**eni wokół stołu** they clustered around the table; **politycy** ~**ieni wokół prezydenta** the politicians centred (a)round the president

skupisk|o *n* [1] (miejsce nagromadzenia) centre GB, center US; ~**ka przemysłowe** industrial centres; ~**ko miejskie** an urban agglomeration [2] (rud, minerałów) deposit; (domów, drzew, gwiazd) cluster

skupować *impf* → **skupić²**

skurcz *m* [1] Med. contraction; ~**e porodowe** contractions [2] (ból) cramp; ~**e żołądka** stomach cramps; **złapał mnie** ~ **w nodze** I've got cramp GB a. a cramp US in my leg

skurcz|yć *pf* [I] *vt [osoba]* to hunch *[ramiona]*; to clench *[palce]*; to pull [sth] up *[nogi]*

[II] **skurczyć się** [1] (skulić się) to huddle; ~**yć się z zimna** to huddle for warmth; ~**yć się ze strachu** to cower in terror [2] *[materiał, ubranie]* to shrink; ~**yć się na starość** *[osoba]* to shrink with age [3] *[naczynie krwionośne, mięsień]* to contract; *[twarz]* to contort [4] przen. *[dochód, ludność]* to shrink

sku|sić *pf* [I] *vt* (przyciągnąć) *[osoba, perspektywa]* to lure; (namówić) to tempt *[osobę]*; **już prawie dał się** ~**sić** he was half tempted; **co was** ~**siło, żeby to zrobić?** what on earth made you do that?

[II] *vi* pot. (w grze) to miss; (na skakance) to trip

[III] **skusić się** (skosztować) **może się** ~**sisz na kieliszek wina?** can I tempt you to a glass of wine?; **kto się** ~**si na kawę?** would anyone like some coffee?

skuteczn|y *adi. grad. [lekarstwo, ochrona, osoba]* effective; *[próba]* successful

skut|ek *m* effect; **zabezpieczyć coś przed** ~**kami powodzi** to protect sth against the effects of a flood; **przynieść pożądane** ~**ki** to have the desired effect; **wywołać odwrotny** ~**ek** to have the opposite effect; **odnieść** ~**ek** *[starania, zabiegi]* to be successful; **doprowadzić coś do** ~**ku** to carry out sth *[plan]*; to bring about sth *[porozumienie, reformę]*; **dojść do** ~**ku** *[spotkanie, uroczystość]* to take place; **nie dojść do** ~**ku** to not come off; **bez** ~**ku** to no effect; ~**kiem a. na** ~**ek czegoś** as a result of sth; **próbuj aż do** ~**ku** try until you succeed; **fatalna w** ~**kach decyzja** a decision with fatal consequences; **brzemienna w** ~**ki decyzja** a fateful decision

skute|r *m* (motor) scooter; ~**r wodny** a jet ski; ~**r śnieżny** a snow scooter

skuwać *impf* → **skuć**

skwa|r *m* scorching heat; **ale** ~**r!** it's scorching!

skwar|ek *m*, ~**ka** *f* ~**ki** pork scratchings

skwarn|y *adi. [dzień, popołudnie]* scorching hot

skwaśni|eć *pf vi* [1] *[mleko]* to sour; *[zupa]* to go bad [2] przen. *[osoba]* to grow bitter; **mina mu** ~**ała** his expression soured

skwe|r *m* (placyk) square; (zieleniec) green

skwiercz|eć *impf vi [tłuszcz]* to sizzle

skwit|ować *pf vt* to acknowledge; ~**ować coś śmiechem/wzruszeniem ramion** to laugh/shrug sth off

slaj|d *m* slide

slalom *m* Sport slalom; ~ **gigant** the giant slalom

slip|y, ~**ki** *plt* briefs

slogan *m* [1] (frazes) platitude [2] (hasło) slogan; (reklamowy, wyborczy) catchword

słabn|ąć *impf vi* [1] (tracić siły) to grow weaker; **wzrok mi** ~**ie** my eysight is getting weak [2] (zmniejszać się) *[ruch, wiatr]* to die down; *[zainteresowanie]* to diminish; *[ból, deszcz]* to ease off; *[tempo]* to slacken

słab|o *adv. grad.* [1] (lekko) *[uderzyć, nacisnąć]* weakly; **jest mi** a. **robi mi się** ~**o** I feel faint [2] (ledwie) barely; ~**o go pamiętam** I can hardly remember him; ~**o zaludniona okolica** a sparsely populated area; ~**o rozwinięty przemysł** a poorly developed industry [3] (źle) poorly; ~**o napisane dialogi** badly written dialogue; **bardzo** ~**o mówił po polsku** he spoke very poor Polish; ~**o zdała**

egzamin she didn't do too well in the exam; ~**o widzę/słyszę** my sight/hearing is poor

słabost|ka f weakness, foible

słaboś|ć f ① (osłabienie) weakness ② (brak silnej woli) weakness; ~**ć charakteru** weakness of character; **chwila** ~**ci** a moment of weakness ③ (brak trwałości) flimsiness ④ (wada) failing; **znać czyjeś** ~**ci** to know sb's failings ⑤ (upodobanie) weakness; **mieć** ~**ć do kogoś/czegoś** to have a weakness for sb/sth

słab|y adi. grad. ① (wątły) weak ② (uległy) weak; **człowiek** ~**ego ducha** a person weak in spirit ③ (nieznaczny) *[dźwięk, puls, światło]* faint; *[ból, podmuch]* slight; *[herbata, kawa]* weak ④ (nietrwały) *[budulec, materiał]* flimsy ⑤ (niedysponujący siłą) *[państwo, armia]* weak ⑥ (marny) *[uczeń, pamięć, wzrok, utwór, mecz]* poor; **mieć** ~**e serce** to have a weak heart

■ **mój** ~**y punkt** a. **moja** ~**a strona** my weak point

sław|a f ① (rozgłos) fame; **zdobyć** a. **zyskać** ~**ę** to achieve fame; **zdobył** ~**ę doskonałego chirurga** he gained a reputation as a splendid surgeon; **naukowiec światowej** ~**y** a scientist of world renown; **śpiewaczka u szczytu** ~**y** a singer at the peak of her fame ② (reputacja) reputation; **ten lokal cieszy się dobrą** ~**ą** this place has a good reputation ③ (osoba) celebrity; **obsada złożona z samych** ~ a cast consisting entirely of big names; ~**a w dziedzinie medycyny/archeologii** a big name in medicine/archeology

sławn|y adi. famous; **dzięki swojemu wynalazkowi stał się** ~**y** he made a name for himself with his invention

słod|ki adi. grad. ① (o smaku) *[potrawa, zapach]* sweet ② przen. *[dźwięk, głos, melodia, wspomnienia]* sweet; *[buzia, dziecko, sukienka]* cute; ~**kie słówka** sweet talk

sło|dko ① adv. grad. *[smakować, pachnieć, brzmieć, wyglądać]* sweet; *[uśmiechać się, spać]* sweetly ② **na słodko** Kulin. *[potrawa]* sweet; **ryż na** ~**dko** sweet rice

słodycz f ① (smaku, woni, dźwięku, charakteru) sweetness ② (rozkosz) (sweet) joy; ~ **zwycięstwa** the sweet joy of victory

słodycz|e plt sweets; **sklep ze** ~**ami** a sweet shop; **być łasym na** ~**e** to have a sweet tooth

sł|odzić impf vt to sweeten *[herbatę, kompot]*; **słodzisz (herbatę)?** do you take sugar (in your tea)?; **dziękuję, nie słodzę** no sugar, thanks

słodzik m sweetener

słoik m (naczynie) jar; (pojemność) jar(ful)

słom|a f straw; ~**a makowa** poppy straw; **siennik wypchany** ~**ą** a straw mattress; **chata kryta** ~**ą** a thatched cottage; **włosy koloru** ~**y** flaxen a. straw-coloured hair

■ ~**a mu wyłazi z butów** pot., iron. he's just a country bumpkin GB pejor. a. country hick US pot., pejor.

słomian|ka f doormat; (słomiana) straw doormat

słomian|y adi. ① (wykonany ze słomy) straw; ~**y dach** a thatched roof ② (koloru słomy) straw-coloured GB, straw-colored US

■ ~**a wdowa** żart. a grass widow; ~**y wdowiec** żart. a grass widower; ~**y ogień** a. **zapał** a flash in the pan

słom|ka f straw; **pić coś przez** ~**kę** to sip a. drink sth through a straw; **kapelusz ze** ~**ki** a straw hat

słonecznik m sunflower; (głowa słonecznika) sunflower head; Kulin. sunflower seeds; **skubać** ~ to pick sunflower seeds

słoneczn|y adi. *[energia, orbita]* solar; *[dzień, pogoda, pokój]* sunny; **tarcza** ~**a** the sun's disc

słono ① adv. ① *[smakować]* salty; **jadać** ~ to use a lot of salt ② pot. ~ **kosztować** to cost a pretty penny; ~ **zapłacić** to pay through the nose; ~ **sobie policzyć** to charge a steep price ② **na słono** Kulin. **twarożek na** ~ ≈ salted cottage cheese

słon|y adi. ① *[potrawa, napój]* salty; *[zapach]* somewhat salty ② pot. *[ceny, opłaty]* steep ③ pot. *[dowcip]* spicy

sło|ń m elephant; ~**ń morski** elephant seal, sea elephant

■ ~**ń w składzie porcelany** a bull in a china shop; ~**ń mu na ucho nadepnął** pot. he's tone-deaf

słońc|e n sun; **Słońce** the Sun, the sun; **ulice zalane** ~**em** sun-flooded streets; **pod** ~**e** *[patrzeć]* with the sun in one's eyes; *[robić zdjęcia]* against the sun

■ **to jasne jak** ~**e** it's (as) clear as day; **nie ma nic łatwiejszego pod** ~**em** there's nothing easier under the sun; **on jest najuczciwszym człowiekiem pod** ~**em** he's the most honest man alive; **to nic nowego pod** ~**em** that's nothing new

sło|ta f rainy weather

słowik m nightingale

słownictw|o n vocabulary; **często posługuje się dosadnym** ~**em** he often uses crude language

słownie adv. *[napisać]* in words

słownik m ① (publikacja) dictionary; ~ **języka polskiego** a dictionary of the Polish language; ~ **polsko-angielski** a Polish-English dictionary; ~ **ortograficzny** a spelling dictionary; ~ **obrazkowy** a pictorial a. visual dictionary; ~ **wyrazów bliskoznacznych** a thesaurus; **muszę sprawdzić to słowo w** ~**u** I must look that word up in a dictionary ② (słownictwo) vocabulary, lexicon

słown|y ① adi. grad. *[osoba]* dependable; **to człowiek** ~**y** he's a man of his word ② adi. *[obietnica, utarczka]* verbal; **dowcip** ~**y** a pun

sł|owo ∏ *n* ① (wyraz) word; **nie przebierać w słowach** to not mince one's words; **powiedzieć komuś kilka** a. **parę słów prawdy** to tell sb a few home truths; **powiedzieć komuś kilka słów do słuchu** to give sb a piece of one's mind; **brak mi słów** I'm at a loss for words; **chwytać** a. **łapać kogoś za słowa** to trip sb up; **wpaść komuś w słowo** to interrupt sb in mid-sentence; **od słowa do słowa zgadało się, że...** one thing led to another and it turned out that...; **skończyło się na słowach** it was just talk; **nie lubię wielkich słów** I don't like big talk; **wyszedł bez słowa** he left without saying a word ② (krótka rozmowa) word; **czy mogę zamienić z tobą kilka słów?** can I have a word with you?; **mam do ciebie słowo** there's something I'd like to tell you ③ (mowa) word; **słowo mówione/drukowane** the spoken/printed word; **mieć dar słowa** to have the gift of the gab ④ (przyrzeczenie) word; **dać/złamać słowo** to give/break one's word; **dotrzymać słowa** to keep one's word; **ręczyć za coś słowem** to swear by sth; **uwierzyć komuś na słowo** to trust sb's word; „**nikomu nie powiesz, słowo?**" – „**słowo**" 'you won't tell anybody, promise?' – 'promise'; **słowo honoru!** I swear!, I give you my word (of honour)!; **ten guzik trzyma się tylko na słowo honoru** pot. this button's hanging on by a prayer pot.; **wierzę ci na słowo** I'll take your word for it; **słowo daję, widziałam na własne oczy** believe me, I saw him with my very own eyes

∏ **słowa** *plt* ① (uwaga) remark; **masz rację, święte słowa** you're right, never was a truer word spoken książk., żart.; **moje słowa puszczał mimo uszu** he turned a deaf ear to what I said; **wspomnisz moje słowa** you mark my words! ② (tekst utworu) lyrics; **muzyka do słów znanej poetki** music to words by a well-known poet; **w połowie piosenki zapomniałam słów** in the middle of the song I forgot the words a. lyrics

❑ **słowo boże** Relig. the word of God; **słowo wstępne** preface, foreword

■ **nie można złego słowa o nim powiedzieć** I can't find a bad word to say about him; **jednym słowem** in a word; **ostatnie słowo skazańca** a convict's last words; **czy to twoje ostatnie słowo (w tej sprawie)?** is that your final word (on the matter)?; **powtórzyć coś słowo w słowo** to repeat sth word for word a. verbatim; **słowo się rzekło, kobyłka u płotu** przysł. you can't go back on your word now

sł|ój *m* ① (naczynie) large jar; (zawartość) jar(ful) ② (w drzewie) (tree) ring

słuch ∏ *m* ① (zmysł) hearing; **mieć słaby** ~ to be hard of hearing; **stracić** ~ to lose one's hearing ② Muz. ear for music; ~ **absolutny** absolute pitch; **nie mam** ~**u** I have no ear for music ③ (ucho zwierzęcia) ear

∏ **słuchy** *plt* pot. rumours; ~**y chodzą, że..** rumour has it that...; **doszły (do) nas** ~**y o twoich zaręczynach** we heard something about you getting engaged

■ **powiedzieć komuś kilka słów do** ~**u** to give sb a piece of one's mind; **od tamtej pory** ~ **po nim/niej zaginął** he/she was never heard of again after that; **zamienić się w** ~ to be all ears; **grać ze** ~**u** to play by ear

słuchacz *m*, ~**ka** *f* ① (radia, koncertu) listener ② (student) student; **wolny** ~ unenrolled student, auditor US

słucha|ć *impf* ∏ *vt* to listen (**czegoś** to sth); ~**ł, czy ktoś nie idzie** he listened in case somebody was coming; ~**j! gdzie jest najbliższy bankomat?** listen! where's the nearest cash dispenser?; ~**j, kiedy do ciebie mówię!** listen when I'm talking to you!; ~**m?** (przez telefon) hello?; ~**m? proszę powtórzyć** pardon? a. sorry? could you repeat that (please)?

∏ *vi* to obey *[rodziców, nauczyciela]*

∏∏ **słuchać się** to obey *[rodziców, nauczyciela]*

słuchaw|ka *f* ① (telefoniczna) receiver; ~**ki** radiowe headphones; **podnieść** ~**kę** to pick up the receiver; **odłożyć** ~**kę** to hang up; **proszę nie odkładać** ~**ki** hold on, please ② Med. stethoscope

słuchowisk|o *n* radio drama

słup *m* ① (telefoniczny) pole; (wysokiego napięcia) pylon; (latarni) post; (mostu) pier, pillar; ~ **graniczny** a border post; ~ **ogłoszeniowy** a poster pillar ② (dymu, ognia) column

■ **stać jak** ~ pot. to stand petrified

słup|ek *m* ① pillar; **daszek wsparty na** ~**kach** a roof supported by pillars ② (cieczy) column ③ (forma) matchstick ④ (ścieg) bar ⑤ (obcas) Cuban heel ⑥ Bot. pistil

❑ ~**ek startowy** Sport starting post

słusznie ∏ *adv. grad.* ① (trafnie) *[zauważyć, nazwać]* aptly ② (sprawiedliwie) *[ukarać, domagać się]* rightly

∏ *inter.* that's right

słuszn|y ∏ *adi. grad.* ① (trafny) *[ocena, wniosek]* right ② (uzasadniony) *[zarzut, wyrok]* just; *[zarzut]* legitimate

∏ *adi.* książk. (okazały) impressive

służąc|y ∏ *m* (man)servant

∏ **służąca** *f* (house)maid, domestic

służb|a *f* ① (instytucja) service; ~**a meteorologiczna** meteorological service ② (praca w instytucji) service; **odbywać** ~**ę w wojsku** to serve in the army ③ (pracownicy) service; ~**y specjalne** the secret service; ~**y komunalne** municipal services ④ (godziny pracy) duty; **być na/po** ~**ie** to be on/off duty ⑤ (misja) service ⑥ (praca służącego) domestic service ⑦ (ogół służących) the servants

służbowo *adv. [podróżować]* on business; **być zależnym** ~ **od kogoś** to be subordinate to sb (at work)

służbow|y *adi. [funkcje, obowiązki, kontakty]* offi-cial; *[samochód, telefon]* company ; **mieszkanie** ~e tied accommodation; **tajemnica** ~a confidential information; **wyjazd** ~y a business trip

służ|yć *impf vi* ① (poświęcać się) to serve; ~yć **krajowi** to serve one's country; **to źle** ~y **sprawie** that doesn't help our cause; ~yć **komuś pomocą** to offer help to sb; **czym mogę** ~yć? what can I do for you? ② *[pies]* to beg ③ (pełnić funkcję) to serve; ~yć **za wzór** a. **przykład** to serve as a model ④ (wpływać datnio) ~yć **komuś** *[klimat]* to do sb good ⑤ (pracować) to serve; ~yć **w wojsku** to serve in the army
■ **zdrowie mu** ~y he enjoys good health; **pamięć/ wzrok już mu nie** ~y **jak dawniej** his memory/ eyesight is failing

słychać *impf v imp.* ① (być słyszalnym) to be heard; **przez ścianę było** ~ **muzykę** I/they could hear music through the wall ② (być wiadomym) to be heard of; **wyjechał i nic nie było o nim** ~ he left and hasn't been heard of since; **co (u ciebie)** ~? how are things?; **co** ~ **z waszą przeprowadzką?** any news about your move? ③ (być wyczuwalnym) to be heard a. detected; **w jej głosie** ~ **było nutę histerii** a note of hysteria could be detected in her voice

sły|nąć *impf vi* to be famous (**z czegoś** for sth); ~nąć **z poczucia humoru** to be famous for one's sense of humour; ~nąć **na cały świat** to be world famous

słynn|y *adi. grad. [osoba, obraz]* famous; **artysta** ~y **na cały świat** a world-famous artist; **miasto** ~e **z koronek** a city famous for its lace

słysz|eć *impf vt* to hear *[muzykę, rozmowę, hałas]*; **dobrze/źle** ~eć to hear well/badly; **mówię do ciebie,** ~ysz? I'm speaking to you, do you hear?; ~ę, **że wybierasz się w podróż** I hear you're going away; **nie chciała o nim/tym** ~eć she wouldn't hear about him/it
■ **znać kogoś/coś ze** ~enia to have heard of sb/sth

smaczn|y ⫿ *adi. grad.* ① *[potrawa, napój]* tasty ② przen. *[temat, szczegół, cytat]* spicy
⫿ **smacznego!** *inter.* bon appétit!

smak *m* ① (zmysł) taste; **rozpoznać coś** ~**iem** a. **po** ~**u** to recognize sth by its taste ② (potrawy, napoju) taste; **łagodny/ostry w** ~**u** mild/harsh to the taste; **lody o** ~**u waniliowym** vanilla-flavoured ice cream; **przyprawić coś do** ~**u** to season sth to taste; **te jabłka przypominają w** ~**u ananasa** these apples taste a bit like pineapple ③ (apetyt) relish; **jeść coś ze** ~**iem** to eat sth with relish ④ (gust) taste; **ubierać się ze** ~**iem** to dress with taste; **dom urządzony ze** ~**iem** a tastefully furnished house ⑤ przen. (życia, przygody) taste; **gorzki** ~ **porażki** the bitter taste of defeat ⑥ (wywar) stock
■ **jego słowa były jej nie w** ~ his words were not to her liking a. taste; **bilety na koncert były**

wyprzedane i musieliśmy obejść się a. **obyć się** ~**iem** pot. the concert was sold out and we just had to grin and bear it

smakołyk *m* titbit GB, tidbit US; ~**i** goodies pot.

smak|ować *impf vt* ① (próbować) to taste *[potrawę, napój]* ② (rozkoszować się smakiem) to savour GB, to savor US *[potrawę, wino]* ③ *[potrawa, napój, papieros]* to taste; **naleśniki** ~**owały doskonale** the pancakes tasted delicious; ~**uje ci ta kawa?** do you like this coffee? ④ przen. (znać) to taste; **wiem, jak** ~**uje bieda/porażka** I know what poverty/defeat tastes like

smal|ec *m* Kulin. lard

smar *m* grease; ~**r grafitowy** blacklead; ~**r do nart** ski wax

smarkacz *m* pot. brat pot.

smarkul|a *f* pot. teenybopper pot.

smar|ować *impf* ⫿ *vt* ① (powlekać) (smarem) to grease; (kremem) to smear; (pastą) to spread; ~**ować chleb masłem** to butter some bread; ~**ować zawiasy smarem** to grease some hinges; ~**ować twarz kremem** to apply cream to one's face; ~**ować narty smarem** to wax skis ② pot. (mazać, pisać) to smear
⫿ **smarować się** (rozprowadzać na skórze) ~**ować się kremem** to put on some cream

smaż|yć *impf* ⫿ *vt* to fry; ~**yć coś na maśle** to fry sth in butter; ~**yć coś na patelni** to pan-fry sth; ~**yć coś w cukrze** to candy sth; ~**yć konfitury** to make fruit preserves
⫿ **smażyć się** ① *[kotlety, ryba]* to fry ② pot. *[osoba]* to roast pot.; ~**yć się na słońcu** to roast in the sun; ~**yć się w piekle** to burn in hell

smocz|ek *m* ① (do karmienia) teat GB, nipple US; **karmić dziecko** ~**kiem** a. **przez** ~**ek** to bottle-feed a baby ② (do ssania) dummy GB, pacifier US

smok *m* (potwór) dragon; ~ **ziejący ogniem** a fire-breathing dragon; **pić jak** ~ (łapczywie) to drink greedily

smoking *m* dinner jacket, tuxedo US

smoł|a *f* tar, pitch; **czarny jak** ~**a** pitch-black

smr|ód *m* ① (zapach) stench ② pot., przen. stink; **ciągnie się za nim jakiś** ~**ód** there's something fishy about him

smu|cić *impf* ⫿ *vt* to sadden *[osobę]*; **najbardziej** ~**ci mnie to, że...** what saddens me most is that...
⫿ **smucić się** to be sad

smu|ga *f* (brudu, koloru, światła) streak; (dymu, zapachu) trail

smuk|ły *adi. grad. [osoba]* slim; *[palce, sylwetka]* slender

smut|ek *m* ① (uczucie) sadness; **patrzeć na coś/ powiedzieć coś ze** ~**kiem** to look at sth/say sth sadly; **pogrążyć się w** ~**ku** to be overcome with sadness ② (troska) sorrow; **ukoić czyjeś** ~**ki** to soothe sb's sorrows; **topić** ~**ki w alkoholu** to drown one's sorrows

smutni|eć *impf vi [osoba, twarz]* to become sad

smutn|y *adi. grad.* sad; **powiedzieć coś ~ym głosem** to say sth in a sad voice; **to ~e, że...** it's sad that...; **najsmutniejsze jest to, że...** the saddest thing (of all) is that...

smycz *f* lead, leash; **założyć psu ~** to put a dog on its lead; **spuścić psa ze ~y** to unleash a dog; **trzymać kogoś na krótkiej ~y** *przen.* to keep sb on a short a. tight leash

smycz|ek *m* Muz. bow; **~ki** pot. strings

smyczkow|y *adi. [orkiestra, kwartet]* string; *[instrument]* stringed

smykał|ka *f* pot. flair

snobizm *m* snobbery; **~ na coś** a vogue for sth

snop *m* ① *(słomy, zboża)* sheaf; **wiązać coś w ~y** to sheaf ② *przen.* **~ iskier** a stream of sparks; **rzucić na coś ~ światła** to direct a shaft of light on sth

snu|ć *impf* **[]** *vt* ① *(prząść)* to spin *[przędzę, wełnę]* ② *przen.* to spin *[opowieść]*; **~ć wspomnienia** to take a trip down memory lane; **~ć domysły** a. **przypuszczenia na temat czegoś** to conjecture about sth; **~ć plany na przyszłość** to make one's plans for the future ③ *[pająk, gąsienica]* to spin *[sieć, oprzęd]*

[] **snuć się** ① *(przesuwać się) [mgła, dym, zapach]* to drift; **różne myśli ~ły mi się po głowie** all sorts of thoughts went through my head ② *(wałęsać się) [osoba, psy]* to wander a. drift about; **~ć się za kimś jak cień** to follow sb around like a shadow

sob|ek *m* egotist; **nie bądź takim ~kiem** don't be so selfish

sobie [] *pron.* → **się**

[] *part.* **zwykły ~ człowiek** quite an ordinary man; **posiedzimy, pogadamy ~** we'll sit down and have a chat (together); **idę ~ ulicą, a tu nagle...** I was calmly walking down the street when all of a sudden...; **podjadłeś ~?** have you had enough (to eat)?; **chyba ~ żartujesz** you're joking of course; **co ty ~ właściwie myślisz?** who do you think you are exactly?; **dawno, dawno temu był ~ król** once upon a time there was a king

sob|ota *f* Saturday

sobowtó|r *m* double

socjologi|a *f* sociology

soczew|ka *f* ① *(okular)* lens; **~ki kontaktowe** contact lenses; **okulary o grubych ~kach** glasses with thick lenses ② Anat. (crystalline) lens

soczy|sty *adi. grad. [owoc, mięso]* juicy; *[kolor, opis, relacja]* vivid; *[głos, dźwięk]* rich; *[język]* ripe; *[dowcip]* broad; *[przekleństwo]* earthy

so|da *f* soda; **soda oczyszczona** baking soda

sof|a *f* sofa

soja *f (roślina)* soya, soy; *(nasiona)* soya beans

sojusz *m* alliance

sojusznicz|y *adi. [wojska, kraje]* allied; **układ ~y** a treaty of alliance

sojuszni|k *m*, **~czka** *f* ally

sok *m* ① *(do picia)* juice; (syrop) squash; **~ z cytryny** lemon juice; **~ pomarańczowy** orange juice; **puścić ~** *[owoc]* to release its juice ② Bot. sap

sokowirów|ka *f* juice extractor, juicer

sok|ół *m* falcon; **~ół łowny** a hawk; **polować z ~ołami** to hawk

solenizan|t *m* (obchodzący urodziny) birthday boy; **być ~tem** (obchodzić imieniny) to have one's name day

solenizant|ka *f* (obchodząca urodziny) birthday girl; **być ~ką** (obchodzić imieniny) to have one's name day

s|olić *impf vt* (dodać soli) to add salt to *[zupę, mięso]*; (posypać solą) to sprinkle salt over *[ogórki, pomidory]*; (konserwować) to salt *[ryby]*

solidarnoś|ć *f* ① *(współodpowiedzialność)* solidarity (**z kimś** with sb); **męska/kobieca ~ć** a male/female solidarity ② Prawo joint and several obligation

solidn|y *adi.* ① *(rzetelny)* reliable; **to ~y pracownik** he's a good solid worker; **~a robota** a solid piece of work ② *(mocny) [konstrukcja, buty, meble]* solid; *[budowa ciała, osoba]* sturdy; *[kij]* heavy ③ *(gruntowny) [wiedza, wykształcenie]* solid, sound ④ pot. (duży) *[lanie]* thorough; *[guz, porcja]* good

soli|sta *m*, **~stka** *f* ① *(artysta)* soloist ② Sport singles skater

solnicz|ka *f* salt cellar a. shaker

son|da *f* ① Techn. probe; (transmitująca dane) sonde; **~da głębinowa** a plumb; **~da akustyczna** a sonic depth finder; **~da kosmiczna** a space probe ② Med. (surgical) probe; **~da żołądka** gastroscopy ③ (sondaż) survey; **~da uliczna** a street survey

sondaż *m* (badanie opinii) survey; Polit. poll; **~ opinii publicznej** a public opinion poll; **~e przedwyborcze** pre-election polls

sond|ować *impf vt* ① Techn. to sound, to plumb *[głębokość]*; to probe *[atmosferę]* ② (badać opinię) to sound out; **~ował, co wiem na ten temat** he was trying to sound me out about it ③ Med. to sound *[żołądek]*; to probe *[ranę]*

sop|el *m* icicle; **zamienić się w ~el** a. **zmarznąć na ~el** to freeze to the marrow a. to death

sort|ować *impf vt* to sort *[listy, paczki]*; to grade *[owoce, ziemniaki]*

sos *m* Kulin. sauce; **~ do pieczeni** gravy; **~ do sałatek** (salad) dressing

■ **być** a. **czuć się nie w ~ie** pot. to feel out of sorts

so|sna *f* ① Bot. pine ② (drewno) pinewood

s|owa *f* owl

só|jka *f* ① Zool. jay ② pot. (kuksaniec) poke; **dać komuś ~kę w bok** to poke sb in the ribs

■ **wybierać się jak ~ka za morze** to take one's time leaving

s|ól *f* ① Kulin. salt; **sól kuchenna** a. **jadalna** table salt; **sól gruboziarnista** coarse salt; **sól jodowana** iodized table salt ② Chem. salt; **sole mineralne** mineral salts; **sole do kąpieli** bath salts

■ **być komuś solą w oku** to be a thorn in sb's side a. flesh; **sól ziemi** książk. the salt of the earth

space|r *m* walk, stroll; **pójść na** ~**r** to go for a walk a. stroll; **wyprowadzać psa na** ~**r** to take the dog for a walk

spacer|ować *impf vi* to stroll; ~**ować po parku** to stroll about the park

spać *impf vi* to sleep; **spać głęboko** to sleep soundly; **czy oni śpią?** are they asleep?; **iść spać** to go to bed; **chce mi się spać** I'm sleepy; **ta sprawa nie daje mi spać** przen. the thing's giving me sleepless nights przen.

■ **spać z kimś** (współżyć) to sleep with sb

spadać[1] *impf* → **spaść**

spada|ć[2] *impf vi* [1] *(droga, teren)* (ostro) to drop; (łagodnie) to slope (down) [2] *[włosy]* to fall; **grzywka** ~**ła jej na oczy** her fringe fell over her eyes [3] pot. ~**j!** get lost! pot.; **no to ja** ~**m** so I'm taking off

spad|ek *m* [1] (góry, terenu) slope, gradient [2] (cen, dochodów) fall, drop; (temperatury, ciśnienia, napięcia) drop; (popularności, wartości) fall [3] (upadek) fall [4] Prawo (spuścizna) inheritance; legacy także przen.; **otrzymać** a. **dostać** ~**ek** to come into an inheritance; **otrzymać** a. **dostać coś w** ~**ku** to inherit sth; **zostawić komuś** ~**ek** to leave sb a legacy a. bequest; ~**ek po komunizmie** a legacy of Communism

spadkobierc|a *m* Prawo heir także przen.; **jedyny** ~**a** the sole beneficiary; ~**a majątku** the heir to the property

spadkobierczy|ni *f* Prawo heiress także przen.

spadochron *m* parachute; **skoczyć ze** ~**em** a. **na** ~**ie** to make a parachute jump

spadochroniarz *m* Wojsk. paratrooper; Sport parachutist, skydiver

spak|ować *pf* [I] *vt* to pack *[walizkę, rzeczy]* [II] **spakować się** to pack one's things

spalać *impf* → **spalić**[1]

spaleni|zna *f* burning; **czuję swąd** ~**zny** I can smell burning

spal|ić[1] *pf* — **spal|ać** *impf* [I] *vt* [1] (zniszczyć ogniem) to burn *[dom, listy, gałęzie, śmieci]* [2] (na ogniu) to burn *[pieczeń, garnek]*; (żelazkiem) to scorch *[ubranie]*; **twarz** ~**ona słońcem** a. **od słońca** a sunburnt face [3] (zniszczyć) to blow *[bezpiecznik]*; to burn out *[silnik, żarówkę]* [4] (zużywać) *[silnik, piec]* to consume *[benzynę, ropę, węgiel]* [5] Biol. *[organizm]* to metabolize *[substancje pokarmowe]*

[II] **spalić się** — **spalać się** (wyżyć się) to give one's all

[III] **spalić się** [1] (spłonąć) *[budynek, las]* to be burnt [2] (przepalić się) *[bezpiecznik]* to blow; *[silnik]* to burn out [3] (zostać wysuszonym) *[potrawa]* to be scorched

■ ~**ić się ze wstydu** to burn with shame; ~**ić dowcip** a. **kawał** to kill a joke

spal|ić[2] *pf vt* Sport to be a. go over the line; ~**ony** offside

spalinow|y *adi. [silnik, gazy]* combustion; **lokomotywa** ~**a** a diesel locomotive

spalin|y *plt* (exhaust) fumes

spa|nie *n* bed

sparz|yć *pf* [I] *vt* [1] (oparzyć) *[osoba, kwas, żelazko]* to burn *[osobę]*; *[zupa, wrzątek]* to scald; *[pokrzywa, meduza]* to sting *[osobę, część ciała]* [2] (polać wrzątkiem) to scald *[owoce]*

[II] **sparzyć się** [1] (oparzyć się) to burn oneself; (cieczą) to scald oneself; ~**ył się w język herbatą** the tea scalded his tongue [2] (jadem) ~**ył się pokrzywą w nogę** a nettle stung his leg [3] przen. (mieć złe doświadczenia) to get one's fingers burnt przen. (**na czymś** on sth)

spa|ść *pf* — **spa|dać** *impf vi* [1] (upaść) to fall (down); ~**ść z drzewa/roweru** to fall from a tree/ off a bike; ~**ść ze schodów** to fall down the stairs; ~**ść w przepaść** to fall down a cliff; ~**ść dziesięć metrów w dół** to fall ten metres; ~**dają mu spodnie** his trousers are falling down; ~**dały mu buty** his shoes were falling off his feet; **w nocy** ~**dł śnieg** it snowed in the night; **wreszcie** ~**dło trochę deszczu** we got some rain at last [2] (uderzyć) *[bat, kij, cios]* to fall; ~**ść na kogoś/coś** *[katastrofa, głód]* to strike sb/sth; ~**ść na kogoś** *[tragedia, nieszczęście]* to befall sb książk.; **na kraj** ~**dła klęska suszy** the country was struck by a drought; ~**dł na nas duży kłopot** we were faced with a serious problem [3] (obciążyć) *[obowiązek, zadanie]* to fall (**na kogoś/coś** to sb/sth); **wina** ~**dnie na niego** he'll get the blame [4] (zaatakować) *[drapieżnik, wojsko]* to fall (**na kogoś/coś** on sb/sth) [5] (zmniejszyć się) *[produkcja, cena, ciśnienie, dolar, akcje]* to fall; ~**ść dwukrotnie** to drop by half; ~**ść o 10%/o dwa stopnie** to fall (by) 10 per cent/two degrees; ~**ść w rankingu** to slip down the rankings; ~**ść na trzecie miejsce** to fall a. drop to third place

spawacz *m* welder

spawa|ć *impf vt* to weld

spec *m* pot. whizz, boffin GB pot.

specjali|sta *m*, ~**stka** *f* [1] (ekspert) specialist; **być** ~**stą od czegoś** to specialize in sth; ~**sta od reklamy** an advertising expert [2] Med. specialist; (ze specjalizacją) consultant; **lekarz** ~**sta** a medical specialist; ~**sta pediatra** a consultant paediatrician

specjalistyczn|y *adi. [wiedza, szpital, sklep, sprzęt]* specialist

specjaliz|ować się *impf v refl. [osoba, firma, sklep]* to specialize (**w czymś** in sth)

specjalnie *adv.* [1] (celowo) on purpose [2] (w konkretnym celu) specially, specifically; **zrobić coś** ~ **dla kogoś** to make/do sth specially for sb; **zaprojektowany** ~ **do jazdy w trudnym terenie** designed specifically for rough terrain [3] pot.

(szczególnie) particularly; **nic mu się** ~ **nie stało** nothing really happened to him; **ja się** ~ **nie dziwię** I'm not particularly surprised

specjalnoś|ć *f* [1] (specjalizacja) speciality, specialty US; **lekarze różnych** ~**ci** doctors of different specialities; **jego** ~**cią jest historia starożytna** he specializes in ancient history [2] (mocna strona) speciality, specialty US; ~**ć regionu** the speciality of a region

specjaln|y *adi.* [1] (o szczególnym przeznaczeniu, nadzwyczajny) special; **służby** ~**e** the security services; **dzieci** ~**ej troski** children with special needs; **do zadań** ~**ych** for special assignments; **na** ~**e życzenie** by special request; **ubranie na** ~**e okazje** clothes for special occasions [2] (szczególnie ważny, duży, dobry) special, particular; **to nic** ~**ego** it's nothing special; **nie mam** ~**ych zastrzeżeń** I have no particular objection; **bez** ~**ego powodu** for no special a. particular reason

spektakl *m* [1] (przedstawienie) performance; **wystąpić w** ~**u** *[aktor]* to appear in a show [2] (widowisko) spectacle; ~ **polityczny** a political spectacle

spekulacj|a *f* [1] (handel) profiteering [2] Fin. (transakcja) speculation (**czymś** in sth); ~**e giełdowe** stock exchange speculation; ~**e walutami** currency speculation [3] książk. (przypuszczenie) speculation; **snuć** ~**e** to speculate; **to tylko** ~**e** it's a. this is only speculation

spekulan|t *m*, ~**tka** *f* pejor. profiteer pejor.

spekul|ować *impf vi* [1] (handlować) to speculate (**czymś** in sth); ~**ować na giełdzie** to speculate on the Stock Exchange [2] książk. (rozważać) to speculate (**na temat czegoś** on a. about sth)

spe|łnić *pf* — **spe|łniać** *impf* [] *vt* [1] to fulfil GB, to fulfill US *[wolę, marzenie, obowiązek]*; to keep *[obietnicę, przyrzeczenie]*; to carry out *[rozkaz, groźbę]*; to grant *[prośbę, życzenie]*; to meet *[kryteria, warunki]*; to accomplish *[misję, cel]*; ~**niać funkcję czegoś** to act as sth; ~**nić czyjeś marzenia** to make sb's dreams come true; ~**niać czyjeś nadzieje** a. **oczekiwania** to measure up to sb's expectations; **nie** ~**nia pokładanych w nim nadziei** he's been a great disappointment; ~**nić toast** książk. to drink a toast

[] **spełnić się** — **spełniać się** *[marzenie, wróżba, przepowiednia]* to come true; *[nadzieje, oczekiwania]* to be fulfilled

spełnieni|e *n* fulfilment GB, fulfillment US

sperm|a *f* Biol. semen; sperm pot.

spesz|yć *pf* [] *vt [osoba, sytuacja]* to make [sb] feel uneasy

[] **speszyć się** *[osoba]* to be disconcerted (**czymś** by sth)

spę|dzić *pf* — **spę|dzać** *impf vt* [1] (przeżyć) to spend *[rok, urlop, dzieciństwo]*; ~**dzać czas na robieniu czegoś** to spend time doing sth; **przyjemnie** ~**dzać czas** to spend a pleasant time;

ulubione sposoby ~**dzania wolnego czasu** favourite pastimes [2] (przegonić) to chase off *[osobę, zwierzę]*; ~**dzić muchę ze stołu** to flick a fly off the table [3] (zgromadzić) to round up *[ludzi, więźniów]*

spi|ąć *pf* — **spi|nać** *impf* [] *vt* [1] (połączyć) to fasten together; (spinaczem) to clip together *[kartki, dokumenty]*; (zszywaczem) to staple together *[kartki, dokumenty]*; (paskiem) to strap [sth] together *[książki]*; (szpilkami) to pin [sth] together *[materiał]*; **spiąć włosy w kok** to tie one's hair up into a bun; **most spina oba brzegi rzeki** przen. the bridge joins the two banks of the river [2] (ścisnąć) to tie; **spodnie spięte pod kolanem** trousers tied under the knee [3] Jeźdz. to spur; ~**ął konia ostrogami** he spurred his horse

[] **spiąć się** — **spinać się** pot. to buck up pot.

spichlerz *m* granary

spicza|sty *adi. [bródka, nos]* pointed

spi|ć *pf* — **spi|jać** *impf* [] *vt* [1] *(osoba, zwierzę)* to drink [2] pot. to make [sb] drunk (**czymś** on sth)

[] **spić się** pot. to get drunk; ~**ć się do nieprzytomności** a. **na umór** to drink oneself senseless

spie|c *pf* — **spie|kać** *impf* [] *vt* [1] pot. (zbyt mocno opalić) to burn *[twarz, plecy]* [2] (przypalić) to scorch *[potrawę]*; ~**czona skórka od chleba** a well-done bread crust [3] (wysuszyć) to parch; **wargi** ~**czone gorączką** lips parched with fever

[] **spiec się** — **spiekać się** pot. *[osoba]* to get sunburnt

spienięż|yć *pf* — **spienięż|ać** *impf vt* książk. to redeem *[akcje, udziały]*; to sell *[pamiątki rodzinne, dom]*

spieni|ony *adi.* [1] *[fale, potok]* foaming, bubbling [2] *[koń]* foaming [3] pot. (wściekły) *[osoba]* foaming at the mouth pot.

spierać *impf* → **sprać**[1]

spiera|ć się *impf v refl.* to dispute; ~**ć się o coś** a. **na temat czegoś** to wrangle over a. about sth

spię|cie *n* [1] Elektr. (zwarcie) short circuit [2] przen. (sprzeczka) clash; **między nimi często dochodzi do** ~**ć** they're often at loggerheads with each other

spiętrz|yć *pf* — **spiętrz|ać** *impf* [] *vt* to pile up *[siano, słomę]*

[] **spiętrzyć się** — **spiętrzać się** to accumulate także przen.

spijać *impf* → **spić**

spike|r *m*, ~**rka** *f* announcer

spinacz *m* (paper)clip

spinać *impf* → **spiąć**

spin|ka *f* (do włosów) hairpin; (do krawata) tiepin; (do mankietu) cufflink; (do kołnierzyka) collar stud

spiral|a *f* [1] spiral [2] Techn. (zwój) coil; ~**a grzejna** heating coil [3] Med. (wkładka) coil, IUD

spirytus *m* spirit, alcohol

spis *m* [1] (wykaz) list; ~ **abonentów** list of subscribers; ~ **ludności** census; ~ **rzeczy** a.

treści (table of) contents ② (sporządzanie wykazu) registration

spi|sać *pf* — **spi|sywać** *impf* ❚ *vt* ① (sporządzić spis) to make a list of ② (ułożyć tekst) to write down *[wspomnienia, kronikę]*; to draw up *[umowę, testament]*

❚❚ **spisać się** — **spisywać się** książk. (postąpić) to acquit oneself; **jak się ~sujesz w szkole?** how are you doing at school?

spis|ek *m* plot; **~ek na czyjeś życie** a plot to assassinate sb

spisk|ować *impf vi* to plot, to conspire; **~ować przeciwko królowi** to plot against the king; **~ować z wrogiem** to conspire with the enemy

spiskow|iec *m* conspirator

spiskow|y *adi. [organizacja, siatka, grupa]* conspiratorial; **~a teoria dziejów** (a) conspiracy theory

spisywać *impf* → spisać

spiż *m* bronze, gunmetal

spiżarni|a *f* larder, pantry

splajt|ować *pf vi* pot. *[firma]* to go belly up pot., to go bust pot.; *[osoba]* to go bankrupt

splam|ić *pf* ❚ *vt* ① (zabrudzić) to soil, to stain *[ubranie, obrus]* ② przen. (zhańbić) to tarnish, to sully *[honor, dobre imię, reputację]*

❚❚ **splamić się** to tarnish one's reputation; **nie ~ić się pracą** to not soil one's hands with work

splatać *impf* → spleść

splą|tać *pf* ❚ *vt* to tangle up *[nici, sznurki, kable]*; przen. to muddle (up) *[wątki, akcję utworu]*

❚❚ **splątać się** *[nici, przewody, sieci, włosy]* to get tangled; przen. *[życie, losy]* to get (very) complicated

spl|eść *pf* — **spl|atać** *impf* ❚ *vt* to wreathe *[wieniec, girlandę]*; to plait *[włosy]*; to intertwine *[pasma]*; to interlace *[gałęzie]*; to lock *[palce]*

❚❚ **spleść się** — **splatać się** to intertwine także przen.

spleśni|eć *pf vi [chleb]* to go mouldy GB, to go moldy US; *[ubranie]* to go mildewy

splo|t *m* ① (gałęzi, korzeni) tangle; (włosów, liny) plait ② Włók. weave ③ Anat. plexus; **~t słoneczny** solar plexus ④ przen. coincidence; **~t wydarzeń** a series of events

splu|nąć *pf* — **splu|wać** *impf vi* to spit

spła|cić *pf* — **spła|cać** *impf vt* to pay off *[pożyczkę, odsetki]*; **~cić dług wdzięczności** to repay an obligation

spła|ta *f* repayment

spław|ić *pf* — **spław|iać** *impf vt* ① (przewieźć drogą wodną) to float *[drzewo]* ② pot. to fob off *[interesanta, klienta]*; to get rid of *[gości, natręta]*

spł|odzić *pf vt* ① książk. to beget *[dziecko]* ② przen., żart. to perpetrate żart. *[wiersz, artykuł]*

spłon|ąć *pf vi* ① *[dom, las]* to burn down ② przen. *[osoba]* to blush

spłosz|yć *pf* ~*vt* ① (spowodować ucieczkę) to scare away *[zwierzę, ptaka, złodzieja]* ② (onieśmielić) to disconcert *[osobę]*

❚❚ **spłoszyć się** ① (przestraszyć się) *[zwierzę, ptak, złodziej]* to bolt away; **konie się ~yły** the horses shied ② (zmieszać się) *[osoba]* to become disconcerted

spłu|kać *pf* — **spłu|kiwać** *impf* ❚ *vt* ① (obmyć) to rinse *[twarz, ręce]* ② (zgarnąć) *[deszcz, woda]* to wash away *[błoto, śnieg]*

❚❚ **spłukać się** — **spłukiwać się** ① (obmyć się) to wash oneself down ② pot. (finansowo) to blow all one's money pot.

spłukan|y *adi.* pot. broke, skint GB pot.; **być kompletnie ~ym** to be stony broke

spłukiwać *impf* → spłukać

spły|nąć *pf* — **spły|wać** *impf vi* ① (ściec) to flow (down); **krople deszczu ~wają po szybie** raindrops dribble down the pane; **pot ~wał mu z czoła** sweat streamed down his forehead; **łzy ~wały jej po policzkach** tears flowed down her cheeks ② książk., przen. *[mgła, mrok, światło]* to fall; **włosy ~wały jej na ramiona** her hair fell over her shoulders ③ pot. **~waj, bo oberwiesz!** shove off a. take a hike US pot., or you'll be in for it!

■ **~wać krwią/potem** to be bathed in blood/sweat

spływ *m* Sport (tratwami) rafting; (kajakami) canoeing

spo|cić się *pf v refl.* ① *[osoba]* to sweat; **~cić się z wysiłku/emocji** to break out in a sweat from exertion/excitement ② pot. *[szyba, mur]* to steam up

spoczyn|ek *m* książk. ① (odpoczynek) repose książk. ② (sen) sleep; **pora ~ku** bedtime; **udać się na ~ek** to retire (for the night) książk.

■ **generał w stanie ~ku** a retired general; **zostać przeniesionym w stan ~ku** to be retired

spod *praep.* ① (z dołu) from under; **~ stołu/kołdry** from under the table/duvet; **wyjść ~ prysznica** to come out of the shower ② (z określeniem miejsca) **pochodził ~ Krakowa** he came from somewhere around Cracow; **policja zabrała ją ~ domu** the police took her from outside a. from in front of her house ③ (poza) from; **wyzwolić się ~ czyjegoś wpływu** to free oneself from sb's influence ④ Astrol. **być ~ znaku Lwa** to be a Leo

■ **wyjść ~ czyjegoś pióra/dłuta** to have been written/sculpted by sb

spod|ek *m* (talerzyk) saucer; (zawartość) saucerful

spodni *adi. [warstwa, pokład]* bottom; **~a strona liścia** the underside of a leaf

spodni|e *plt* trousers GB, pants US; **chodzić w ~ach** to wear trousers

spodoba|ć się *pf v refl.* **~ła mi się ta sukienka** I like/liked that dress; **nie ~ł mi się ten pomysł** that idea didn't appeal to me

spodziewa|ć się *impf v refl.* ① (oczekiwać) to expect *[listu, nagrody]*; **po nim można się wszystkiego ~ć** he's capable of anything; **nie ~łam się tego**

po tobie I didn't expect that of you; **kto by się ∼ł?** who'd have expected it? ② (oczekiwać przybycia) to expect *[gości];* ∼ **się dziecka** she's expecting pot.; ∼**ją się dziecka** they're going to have a. they're expecting a baby

spoglądać *impf* → **spojrzeć**

spojów|ka *f* Anat. conjunctiva; **zapalenie** ∼**ek** conjunctivitis

sp|ojrzeć *pf* — **sp|oglądać** *impf* **[]** *vi* ① (popatrzyć) to look (**na kogoś/coś** at sb/sth); (przelotnie) to glance (**na kogoś/coś** at sb/sth); **spojrzeć w lustro** to look at oneself in the mirror; **spojrzeć spod oka** to look out of a. from the corner of one's eye; **spojrzeć po sobie** to look at one another ② (rozważyć) to look; **spojrzeć na coś obiektywnie** to look at sth objectively; **spojrzeć w przeszłość** to look back; **spojrzeć w przyszłość** to look ahead **[]** **spojrzeć się** — **spoglądać się** pot. to look (**na kogoś/coś** at sb/sth)

spojrze|nie *n* ① (wzrok) look, glance; **pytające** ∼**nie** a questioning look; **ukradkowe** ∼**nie** a sidelong glance; **nasze** ∼**nia skrzyżowały się** our eyes met; **wymieniliśmy** ∼**nia** we exchanged glances ② (sposób widzenia) look; **nowe** ∼**nie na coś** a new look at sth

spokojnie [] *adi.* grad. ① (bez emocji) *[mówić, patrzeć, zachowywać się]* calmly ② (bez incydentów) uneventfully; **w mieście było** ∼ the town was calm **[]** *adv.* (na pewno) easily; ∼ **zdążysz na pociąg** you've got plenty of time to catch your train **[]** *part.* pot. **czekam już tu** ∼ **2 godziny** I've been waiting here a good two hours **[]** *inter.* pot. **tylko** ∼**!** just calm down!, take it easy! pot.

spokojn|y *adi.* grad. ① *[osoba, twarz, głos, ton]* calm; *[charakter, usposobienie]* placid; **być** ∼**ym o coś** to be confident of sth; **mieć** ∼**ą głowę** to have an easy mind; ∼**a głowa! damy sobie radę** don't worry! we'll manage ② (bez trosk) *[czasy]* peaceful; **dom** ∼**ej starości** an old people's home; **wiedli** ∼**y żywot** they led a quiet life ③ (bez incydentów) *[dyskusja, manifestacja]* peaceful ④ (zaciszny) *[ulica, okolica]* quiet; ∼**e morze** a quiet sea ⑤ (stonowany) *[kolor, elegancja]* quiet

spok|ój *m* ① (równowaga psychiczna) calmness; (opanowanie) composure; ∼**ój ducha/sumienia** peace of mind/ease of conscience; **zachować** ∼**ój** to remain calm ② (spokojne życie) peace; **burzyć** ∼**ój** to disturb sb's peaceful life ③ (ład publiczny) peace; **demonstracje przebiegały w** ∼**oju** the demonstrations were peaceful ④ (wsi, miasteczka) tranquillity

■ **dać sobie** ∼**ój z kimś/czymś** to give up on sb/ sth; **dać komuś (święty)** ∼**ój** to leave sb alone; **modlić się za** ∼**ój czyjejś duszy** Relig. to pray for sb's soul; **niech spoczywa w** ∼**oju** Relig. may she/ he rest in peace; **zrobić coś dla świętego** ∼**oju** to

do sth for the sake of peace and quiet; ∼**ój!** a. **proszę o** ∼**ój!** silence, please!; **tylko** ∼**ój może nas uratować** the most important thing is to keep calm

spokrewni|ony *adi.* related (**z kimś/czymś** to sb/sth)

spoliczk|ować *pf vt* to slap [sb's] face

społeczeństw|o *n* society; ∼**o polskie** the Polish people, Polish society; **ogół** ∼**a** the general public

społecznie *adv.* ① *[szkodliwy, nieprzystosowany]* socially ② **pracować** ∼ (dla społeczności) to do community work a. service; (bez wynagrodzenia) to work on a voluntary basis

społeczność|ć *f* community

społeczn|y *adi.* ① *[awans, reformy, ustrój]* social; **świadomość** ∼**a** social awareness; **zasady życia** ∼**ego** the principles of social life ② *[mienie, fundusz, własność]* public ③ *[instytucja]* social; **opieka** ∼**a** (social) welfare ④ *[opinia, wysiłek, zaufanie]* public; **czyn** ∼**y** community action; **zapotrzebowanie** ∼**e** public demand ⑤ *[organizacja, szkoła]* charter, community; **inicjatywa** ∼**a** a grassroots initiative; **ruch** ∼**y** a grassroots movement

spontaniczn|y *adi.* *[osoba, zachowanie, oklaski]* spontaneous

sporn|y *adi.* *[definicja, kryterium, rola]* arguable; **kwestia** ∼**a** a controversial a. contentious issue; **punkt** ∼**y** a moot point

sporo [] *pron.* (z policzalnymi) quite a lot, a good many; (z niepoliczalnymi) quite a lot, a good deal; **mają** ∼ **racji, ale...** there's a good deal a. quite a lot (of truth/sense) in what they say, but... **[]** *adv.* quite a lot, a good deal; ∼ **podróżował** he did a fair amount of travelling

spor|t *m* sport; ∼**ty wodne/zimowe** water/winter sports; ∼**ty ekstremalne** extreme sports; **uprawiać** ∼**t** to practise GB a. practice US sport ■ **robić coś dla** ∼**tu** pot. to do sth for the fun of it pot. a. for sport

sportow|iec *m* athlete, sportsperson; (mężczyzna) sportsman; (kobieta) sportswoman

sportow|y *adi.* ① *[klub, boisko, samochód, dziennikarz]* sports; **komentator** ∼**y** a sports commentator, a sportscaster US; **strój** ∼**y** sportswear; **duch** ∼**y** sportsmanship ② *[ubranie]* casual

spo|ry *adi.* *[zainteresowanie, ilość]* considerable; *[drzewo, ogród, sypialnia]* fair-sized; **zaoszczędził** ∼**rą sumkę** he saved up a tidy sum; **miała** ∼**rą pensję** she earned a respectable salary; **do nich jest** ∼**ry kawał drogi** they live quite a long way away

spos|ób *m* ① (metoda, styl) way; ∼**ób ubierania się** a way. style of dressing; ∼**ób mówienia** a way a. manner of speaking; ∼**ób odżywiania się** eating habits; ∼**ób myślenia** a. **rozumowania** a way of thinking; ~**ób działania** a modus operandi; ~**ób bycia** manner; **swobodny** ~**ób bycia** an easy manner; **w dziwny** ~**ób** in a strange way a. manner; **zrób to w ten** ~**ób** do it this way; **na swój** ~**ób to mili ludzie** they're nice people in their own way 2 (możliwość, środek) remedy ■ **wziąć się na** ~**ób** to resort to a trick; **chwytać się wszelkich** ~**obów** to grasp at straws; **zrobiony domowym** ~**obem** home-made; **jakim** ~**obem?** how come?; **znaleźć** ~**ób (na kogoś/coś)** to find a way to deal with sb/sth; **takim czy innym** ~**obem** one way or another a. the other; **w jakiś** ~**ób** a. **jakimś** ~**obem** somehow or other; **w żaden** ~**ób** a. **żadnym** ~**obem** in no way

spostrze|c pf — **spostrze|gać** impf ▯ vt 1 (zauważyć) to spot, to catch sight (**kogoś/coś** of sb/sth) 2 (zorientować się) to realize; ~**c, że...** to become aware of the fact that...; ~**gła, że zrobiła mu przykrość** she realized that she had been unkind to him

▯ **spostrzec się — spostrzegać się** (zorientować się) to realize; **zanim się człowiek** ~**że** before you know where you are

spostrzegawcz|y adi. perceptive; **jesteś mało** ~**y** you're not very observant

spośród praep. from among, out of; **trzech** ~ **wymienionych wyżej pisarzy** three of the above-mentioned writers; ~ **drzew** out of a. from among the trees

spot|kać pf — **spot|ykać** impf ▯ vt to meet; ~**kać znajomego/kolegę** to meet a friend/colleague; ~**kać kogoś na ulicy** to chance (up)on sb in the street; ~**kała w swoim życiu wielu interesujących ludzi** in the course of her life she met many interesting people; ~**kało go nieszczęście** he met with misfortune; ~**kała go kara** he was punished; ~**kał ich afront** they were slighted; ~**kało ich dobre przyjęcie** they were well received; ~**kało ich złe przyjęcie** they got a cool reception

▯ **spotkać się — spotykać się** 1 (zejść się) to meet (**z kimś** with sb); **komitet** ~**ka się jutro** the committee will meet tomorrow 2 (być obiektem reakcji) to meet (**z czymś** with sth); ~**kać się z odmową ze strony kogoś** to meet with a refusal from sb; ~**kać się z dobrym przyjęciem** to be well received 3 przen. (schodzić się) to meet; **w tym miejscu szlak** ~**yka się z główną drogą** here the trail joins a. meets the main road; **nasze ręce się** ~**kały** our hands met

▯ **spotykać się** to see each other; ~**ykają się już od roku** they've been going out (together) for a year

■ **nasze oczy** a. **spojrzenia** ~**kały się** our eyes met; ~**kać się z kimś twarzą w twarz** a. **oko w oko** to come face to face a. eye to eye with sb

spotka|nie n 1 (kontakt) meeting; **przypadkowe** ~**nie** a chance encounter; **wyjść komuś na** ~**nie** to go out to meet sb; **mam umówione** ~**nie** I have an appointment; **mieliśmy małe** ~**nie** we had a bit of a get-together; **nie lubię** ~**ń towarzyskich** I don't like social gatherings 2 Sport match, meeting

spotykać impf → **spotkać**

spowiada|ć impf ▯ vt 1 (ksiądz) to hear [sb's] confession 2 (żądać wyjaśnienia) to grill

▯ **spowiadać się** 1 (z grzechów) to confess (to a priest) 2 (zwierzać się) to confide (**komuś** to a. in sb)

spowie|dź f confession; **tajemnica** ~**dzi** the seal of confession

■ **wyznać coś jak (księdzu) na (świętej) spowiedzi** to make a clean breast of sth

spowod|ować pf vt to cause [wypadek, zamieszanie]; to provoke [kryzys, skargi]; to bring about [zmiany, śmierć]; to occasion książk. [wizytę, telefon]; to produce [reakcję, radość, złość]; to trigger off [ból głowy, areszt]

spożyci|e n consumption, intake; **dzienne** ~**e kalorii** one's daily intake of calories; **data przydatności do** ~**a** a use-by date, an expiry date; ~**e energii elektrycznej** energy consumption; **ograniczać** ~**e alkoholu** to reduce one's alcohol consumption

spożywcz|y ▯ adi. food; **artykuły** ~**e** foodstuffs; **przemysł** ~**y** the food industry

▯ m pot. (sklep) grocery (shop a. store)

sp|ód m 1 (dno) base, bottom; **na spodzie** at the bottom; **spod spodu** from underneath; **pod spodem** (najniżej) at the bottom; (na ciele) underneath 2 (dolna część) bottom; **spód bezowy** a meringue shell 3 (część bielizny damskiej) petticoat; **koronkowa suknia na atłasowym spodzie** a lace dress lined with satin, a lace dress with a satin lining

spódnic|a f skirt

■ **policjant** a. **żandarm w** ~**y** a female despot; **trzymać się czyjejś** ~**y** to be tied to sb's apron strings

spójnik m Jęz. conjunction

spój|ny adi. grad. [powierzchnia, substancja] cohesive; [rozumowanie, teoria] consistent

spółdzielni|a f cooperative

spółgłos|ka f Jęz. consonant

spół|ka f company; ~**ka akcyjna** a joint-stock company; ~**ka z ograniczoną odpowiedzialnością** a limited liability a. public company; **wejść do** ~**ki** to enter a partnership, to go into partnership ■ **do** ~**ki (z kimś)** together (with sb); **na** ~**kę** jointly, together

sp|ór m dispute; **spór pracowniczy** an industrial dispute; **spory graniczne** border disputes; **być przedmiotem sporu** Prawo to be the subject of litigation

spóźniać się[1] impf → **spóźnić się**

spóźnia|ć się² *impf v refl. [zegar]* to be slow; **mój budzik ~ się o 10 minut** my alarm clock is 10 minutes slow

spóźnials|ki *m*, **~ka** *f pot.* latecomer

spóźni|ć *pf* — **spóźni|ać się¹** *impf v refl.* to be late; **~ać się do pracy** to be late for work; **~ć się na pociąg** to miss the a. one's train; **~ł się z płatnościami** he got behind with his payments

spóźnie|nie *n* [1] (niepunktualne przybycie) lateness; **przepraszam za ~nie** I'm sorry I'm late; **nasz pociąg ma ponad dwugodzinne ~nie** our train is running two hours late [2] (niewykonanie w porę) delay

spóźni|ony *adi.* [1] (przybyły za późno) late; **jestem już ~ony na ważne spotkanie** I'm already late for an important meeting [2] (wykonany z opóźnieniem) *[życzenia]* belated

sp|rać¹ *pf* — **sp|ierać** *impf* [I] *vt* to wash out/off; **stary, sprany fartuszek** an old, washed-out apron [II] **sprać się** — **spierać się** [1] *[brud]* to wash off; **ta plama nie chce się sprać** the stain won't wash off [2] *[kolor]* to wash out

sp|rać² *pf vt pot.* (zbić) to thrash; **sprać komuś pysk** a. **gębę** to smash sb in the gob GB pot.

spragni|ony *adi.* [1] (odczuwający pragnienie) thirsty [2] (żądny) craving (**czegoś** for sth); yearning (**czegoś** for sth); **~ony wiedzy** thirsty a. craving for knowledge

spraw|a *f* [1] (fakt, wydarzenie) matter; **nie wtrącać się do nieswoich ~** to mind one's own business; **mieszać się** a. **wtrącać się do cudzych ~** a. **nie swoich ~** to interfere in other people's affairs; **posunąć ~ę naprzód** to get things moving; **zapomnieć o ~ie** to let the matter drop; **ruszyć ~ę z miejsca** to get things going; **~ą zajmuje się policja** the police are dealing with the matter; **to zupełnie inna ~a** that's an entirely different matter [2] (rzecz do załatwienia) matter; **~a służbowa** a business matter; **~a niecierpiąca zwłoki** a matter of great urgency; **mieć kilka ~ do załatwienia** to have some things to see to; **wyjechał w ważnych ~ach** he's away on important business; **zająć się swoimi ~ami** to go about one's business; **uporządkować swoje ~y** to put one's affairs in order [3] książk. (wzniosły cel) cause; **w słusznej ~ie** for a. in a good cause [4] Prawo case; **~a rozwodowa** a divorce case; **~a o ustalenie ojcostwa** a paternity suit; **głośna ~a** a cause célèbre
❏ **~a honorowa** matter a. affair of honour
■ **~a otwarta** an open question; **~a sumienia** a matter of conscience; **~y sercowe** affairs of the heart; **brudna** a. **ciemna** a. **nieczysta ~a** shady business; **gorsza ~a, że...** what makes things a. the matter worse is...; **~a skończona** a. **załatwiona** end of story; **na dobrą ~ę** in point of fact, to all intents and purposes; **to przesądza ~ę** that settles it a. the matter; **śliska ~a** a risky business; **śmierdząca ~a** a can of worms; **to ~a dwóch,**

trzech dni/kilku tygodni it's a matter of two or three days/of a few weeks; **to moja ~a** that's my business; **to nie twoja ~a** that's none of your business; **trudna** a. **niełatwa z nim ~a** he's quite a problem; **wziąć ~ę w swoje ręce** to take the matter into one's own hands; **zdawać sobie ~ę, że...** to realize that...

spraw|ca *m*, **~czyni** *f* perpetrator; **~ca wykroczenia** an offender

sprawdzać *impf* → **sprawdzić**

sprawdzian *m* [1] (sposób skontrolowania) test, trial [2] środ., Szkol. (klasówka) (class) test; **~ z matematyki** a maths test

spraw|dzić *pf* — **spraw|dzać** *impf* [I] *vt* to test *[poziom, znajomość języka]*; to check *[bilety, mechanizm, urządzenie]*; **~dzili, czy w hotelu nie ma bomby** they checked the hotel for bombs; **kandydat do tej pracy został ~dzony przez służby specjalne** the job applicant was screened a. vetted GB by the security service(s); **warto by ~dzić, czy...** it's worth investigating whether... [II] **sprawdzić się** — **sprawdzać się** [1] (spełnić się) *[przepowiednie]* to come true; *[oczekiwania, nadzieje]* to be fulfilled [2] (okazać się przydatnym) **~dzić się jako nauczyciel** to turn out to be a good teacher [3] (okazać się sprawnym) *[urządzenie, samochód]* to perform well; **ta metoda/hipoteza ~dza się** the method/hypothesis works

spraw|ić *pf* — **spraw|iać** *impf* [I] *vt* [1] (być przyczyną) to cause; **~ić komuś ból** to cause sb pain a. distress; **~ić komuś radość** to please sb; **~ić komuś kłopot** to inconvenience sb; **nie ~i mi to żadnego kłopotu** it's no trouble at all [2] książk. (kupić) to buy; **~ić sobie futro** to get oneself a fur coat [II] **sprawić się** — **sprawiać się** (działać, funkcjonować) **jak się ~ia ten nowy goniec?** how is the new messenger boy doing?; **~ się dobrze!** do your best!; **samochód ~iał się dobrze od samego początku** the car did well from the very beginning ■ **los** a. **przypadek ~ił, że...** by coincidence...; **~iał wrażenie zmęczonego** he gave the impression of being tired

sprawiedliwoś|ć *f* [1] (prawość w osądzaniu) justice; **domagać się** a. **dochodzić** a. **szukać ~ci** to seek justice [2] (sądownictwo) justice
❏ **~ć społeczna** social justice
■ **~ci stało się zadość** justice has been done; **oddać komuś/czemuś ~ć** to do sb/sth justice; **po ~ci** pot. in all justice a. fairness; **ręka** a. **ramię ~ci** the long arm of the law; **~ć nakazuje** a. **wymaga, żeby...** the proper thing would be to...

sprawiedliw|y *adi. grad.* just
■ **spać snem ~ego** to sleep the sleep of the just

sprawn|y *adi. grad. [żołnierz, sportowiec]* fit; *[ręce, ruchy]* skilful GB, skillful US; *[administracja, orga-*

nizacja] efficient; ~**y silnik** an engine in (good) working order

spraw|ować *impf* [] *vt* to exercise *[władzę, kontrolę, nadzór]*; to hold *[urząd, godność, mandat]*; ~**ować opiekę nad kimś** książk. to take care of sb [] **sprawować się** książk. *[osoba]* to conduct oneself książk.; **dobrze się** ~**ować** to be well-behaved

sprawowani|e *n* Szkol. conduct

sprawozda|nie *n* [] report (**z czegoś** on sth); ~**nie roczne** an annual report [2] (transmisja) broadcast; ~**nie z meczu** a broadcast of a game

spręż|yć *pf* — **spręż|ać** *impf* [] *vt* Fiz. to compress *[gaz]*
[] **sprężyć się** — **sprężać się** [] (napiąć się) *[mięśnie]* to tense up; *[osoba]* to tense oneself a. one's body [2] pot. (zmobilizować się) to get oneself together pot.

sprężyn|a *f* [] (elastyczny element) spring; ~**y w łóżku** bedsprings; ~**a w zegarku** a mainspring; **zerwać się jak** ~**a** to spring to one's feet [2] przen. (osoba) prime mover; (siła napędowa) mainspring
■ **nacisnąć** a. **poruszyć wszystkie** ~**y, żeby coś zrobić** to pull every string in order to do sth

sprosta|ć *pf vi* [] (podołać) ~**ć czemuś** to face up to. sth *[obowiązkom, trudnościom]*; to meet sth *[wymaganiom]*; ~**ć zadaniu** to manage a task; ~**ć oczekiwaniom rodziców** to live up to one's parents' expectations; **nie** ~**ć czyimś oczekiwaniom** to fall short of sb's expectations [2] (dorównać) ~**ć komuś** to rival sb; **nie** ~**ć komuś** (przegrać) to be beaten by sb

sprost|ować *pf vt* to put right *[błąd, nieścisłość]*; **muszę** ~**ować pana informację** I must put a. set you right on that

sprostowa|nie *n* (poprawka) correction; (w gazecie) disclaimer

sprowa|dzić *pf* — **sprowa|dzać** *impf* [] *vt* [] (spowodować przybycie) to call *[lekarza]*; to bring in *[policję, posiłki]*; to import *[produkt]*; ~**dzić pomoc** to get help; **co pana do nas** ~**dza?** what brings you here? [2] (wywołać) to bring about *[katastrofę, wojnę]*; ~**dzić na kogoś nieszczęście** to bring bad luck on sb [3] (skierować) to direct; ~**dzić kogoś na złą drogę** przen. to lead sb astray; ~**dzić rozmowę na jakiś temat** to direct a conversation to sth [4] (pomóc zejść) to lead down [5] (ograniczyć) ~**dzał wychowanie do zakazów i nakazów** he reduced the raising of children to a set of dos and don'ts
[] **sprowadzić się** — **sprowadzać się** (wprowadzić się) to move in; ~**dzić się do kogoś** to move in with sb
[] **sprowadzać się** (ograniczać się) ~**dzać się do czegoś** *[problem, zagadnienie]* to come down to sth; **dokument** ~**dzał się do samych frazesów** the document was nothing but empty platitudes; **jego**

życie ~**dzało się do pracy** his life consisted of nothing but work

sprowok|ować *pf vt* to provoke *[reakcję, dyskusję]*; ~**ować kogoś do zrobienia czegoś** to goad sb into doing sth; **nie daj się** ~**ować** don't let yourself be provoked

sprób|ować *pf* [] *vt* [] (skosztować) to try, to taste *[potrawy, napoju]* [2] (poznać na próbę) to try; ~**ować czegoś** to try sth; ~**ować własnych sił w czymś** to try one's hand at sth
[] *vi* [] (usiłować) to try; ~**ować coś zrobić** to try to do sth; **chociaż** ~**uj!** give it a try!; **warto** ~**ować** it's worth a try; ~**uj tylko!** (groźba) just you try! [2] (upewnić się) to see; ~**uj, czy umiesz to zrobić** see if you can do it

spryciarz *m* pot. crafty bugger pot.; **być** ~**em** to be crafty; **stary** ~ an old fox

sprysk|ać *pf* — **sprysk|iwać** *impf* [] *vt* to spray *[rośliny, włosy]*; ~**ać koszulę przed prasowaniem** to dampen a shirt for ironing
[] **spryskać się** — **spryskiwać się** to spray oneself; ~**ać się wodą kolońską** to spray oneself with cologne

spry|t *m* (bystrość) smartness; (przebiegłość, zaradność) cunning; **brak mu** ~**tu** he's not cunning enough; **do tego potrzeba** ~**tu** you have to be smart to do that

sprytn|y *adi. grad.* *[osoba]* (bystry) clever; (przebiegły, zaradny) cunning; *[urządzenie, plan, intryga]* clever

sprywatyz|ować *pf* [] *vt* to privatize *[przemysł, przedsiębiorstwo]*
[] **sprywatyzować się** *[przemysł, przedsiębiorstwo]* to be privatized

sprzątacz|ka *f* cleaning lady, cleaner, charlady GB

sprzą|tnąć *pf* — **sprzą|tać** *impf vt* [] (zrobić porządek) to tidy up *[salę, pokój]*; ~**tnąć w szufladzie/na biurku** to clear out a drawer/desk; ~**tnąć po kimś** to tidy up a. clean up after sb [2] (usunąć) to clear away *[gruz, klocki]*; ~**tnąć papiery z biurka** to clear a desk of papers

sprzeciw *m* [] (brak zgody) opposition (**wobec kogoś/czegoś** to sb/sth); **powiedzieć coś tonem nieznoszącym** ~**u** to say sth in a voice that brooks no argument [2] Prawo objection; ~, **wysoki sądzie!** objection, your honour!; **podtrzymać/oddalić** ~ to sustain/overrule an objection

sprzeciw|ić się *pf* — **sprzeciw|iać się** *impf v refl.* (nie zgodzić się) to oppose *[osobie, pomysłowi]*; (zaprotestować) to object (**komuś/czemuś** to sb/sth); ~**ić się czyimś rozkazom** to go against sb's orders; „**nieprawda**" – ~**ił się** 'that's not true,' he protested

sprzecza|ć się *impf v refl.* to argue; (o drobiazgi) to bicker (**z kimś** with sb); ~**ć się o coś** to argue over sth

sprzecz|ka *f* argument; **wdać się w** ~**kę z kimś** to get into an argument with sb

sprzecznoś|ć *f* contradiction (**między czymś a czymś** between sth and sth); ~**ć interesów** a conflict of interests

sprzeczn|y *adi. [cechy, zeznania]* contradictory; ~**y z czymś** contrary to sth; **być ~ym z czymś charakterem** to be against sb's nature

sprzed *praep.* [1] (z okresu) **znam go ~ wojny** I know him from before the war; **to moje zdjęcie ~ dziesięciu lat** this is a photo of me taken ten years ago; **wydarzenia ~ roku** events from one a. a year ago; **gazeta ~ tygodnia** a week-old newspaper [2] (z miejsca) from in front of; **samochód odjechał ~ domu** the car drove off from outside a. from in front of the house

sprzeda|ć *pf* — **sprzeda|wać** *impf* **[I]** *vt* [1] (odstąpić za pieniądze) to sell; ~**ć coś komuś** to sell sth to sb, to sell sb sth; ~**ć coś za sto złotych** to sell sth for a hundred zlotys; **tanio skóry nie ~dzą** pot. they won't lie down easily [2] (zdradzić) to sell (out) *[ojczyznę, przyjaciela]* [3] (zaprezentować) ~**ć swoją wiedzę na egzaminie** to make a good impression in an exam

[II] **sprzedać się** — **sprzedawać się** [1] (pójść na współpracę) to sell out (**komuś** to sb); ~**ć się konkurencji** to sell out to the competition [2] (uprawiać nierząd) to sell oneself (**komuś** to sb) [3] pot. (zaprezentować się) to sell oneself pot.; **on umie się ~ć** he knows how to sell himself [4] *[towar]* to sell; **dobrze się ~wać** to be selling well; **~wać się jak świeże bułeczki** to be selling like hot cakes; **książka ~ła się w tysiącach egzemplarzy** the book has sold thousands of copies

sprzedaw|ca *m*, ~**czyni** *f* seller; (w sklepie) shop assistant; ~**ca gazet** a news vendor; ~**ca lodów** an ice-cream seller

sprzedaż *f* (sprzedanie) sale; (sprzedawanie) selling; (sprzedane towary) sales; ~ **hurtowa** wholesale (trading); ~ **detaliczna** retail (trading); ~ **ratalna** hire purchase; **na ~** for sale; **wystawić coś na ~** to put sth up for sale; **pójść na ~** to go on sale; **być w ~y** to be on sale; **dział ~y** a sales department; **dyrektor do spraw ~y** a sales director; ~ **wzrosła/spadła** sales are up/down

sprzęgł|o *n* clutch; **wcisnąć ~o** to press the clutch (pedal) down

sprzę|t *m* [1] (urządzenie) appliance; ~**ty domowe** (meble) furniture; ~**t gospodarstwa domowego** domestic appliances [2] (wyposażenie) equipment; ~**t medyczny/sportowy** medical/sports equipment; ~**t do wspinaczki** climbing equipment a. gear; ~**t wędkarski** fishing tackle; ~**t komputerowy** computer hardware

sprzyja|ć *impf vi* [1] (być korzystnym) ~**ć komuś** *[warunki, wiatr]* to be in sb's favour; ~**ć rozprzestrzenianiu się chorób** *[klimat]* to be conducive to the spread of disease; ~**ć powstawaniu konfliktów** to give rise to conflict; **pogoda/szczęście**

nam ~ło the weather/luck was on our side [2] (popierać) ~**ć komuś/czemuś** to support sb/sth; (być przychylnym) to be well disposed towards sb/sth

sprzykrz|yć się *pf v refl.* ~**yło mu się to robić** he got tired of doing it; ~**yło mu się samotne życie** he grew weary of living on his own

sprzymierz|yć się *pf* — **sprzymierz|ać się** *impf v refl.* to ally oneself (**z kimś** with sb)

sprzysi|ąc się, sprzysi|ęgnąć się *pf* — **sprzysi|ęgać się** *impf v refl.* [1] książk. (zawiązać spisek) to form a conspiracy (**przeciw komuś** against sb) [2] przen. *[pogoda, okoliczności]* to conspire (**przeciw komuś** against sb)

spuch|nąć *pf vi* [1] *[noga, palec, twarz]* to swell (up); *[oczy]* to puff up [2] pot. (osłabnąć) *[biegacz, piechur]* to run out of strength

spuchnię|ty *adi. [kolano, kostka]* swollen

spu|st *m* [1] (w broni palnej) trigger; **pociągnąć za a. nacisnąć ~st** to pull the trigger [2] Techn. release; ~**st migawki** a shutter release; ~**st wody** (łańcuszek) a flush chain; (przycisk) a flush button ▪ **mieć ~st** pot. to be a big eater; **zamknąć coś na cztery ~sty** to lock and bolt sth *[drzwi, pomieszczenie]*

spu|ścić *pf* — **spu|szczać** *impf* **[I]** *vt* [1] (zniżyć, zrzucić) to lower *[głowę, rolety]*; (let down) to lower *[kubeł, linę]*; to drop *[bomby]*; ~**ścić szalupę na wodę** to launch a lifeboat; ~**ścić wzrok z zakłopotaniem** to lower a. drop one's eyes in embarrassment; **nie ~szczać z kogoś wzroku** (ciągle patrzeć) to not take one's eyes off sb; **nie ~szczać kogoś/czegoś z oka** a. **oczu** (pilnować) to not let sb out of one's sight; ~**ścić cenę** a. **z ceny** pot. to lower the price; ~**ścić na coś kurtynę** a. **zasłonę** książk. to forget about sth [2] (uwolnić) to release *[psa]*; ~**ścić psa z łańcucha/ze smyczy** to let a dog off the chain/lead [3] (wylać, opróżnić) ~**ścić powietrze z materaca** to deflate a mattress; ~**ścić komuś powietrze z kół** to let down the tyres on sb's car/bike; ~**ścić wodę z basenu** to drain a pool; ~**ścić wodę (w sedesie)** to flush the toilet; ~**szczać ścieki do rzeki** *[osoba, fabryka]* to discharge a. dump sewage into a river

[II] **spuścić się** — **spuszczać się** (zniżyć się) to lower oneself; ~**ścić się na linie** to lower oneself down a rope

spychacz *m* bulldozer

spychać *impf* → **zepchnąć**

spyta|ć *pf* **[I]** *vt* to ask; ~**ć kogoś o coś** to ask sb about sth; ~**ć kogoś o drogę/godzinę** to ask sb the way/time; ~**ł mnie o rodziców/o zdrowie** he asked me how my parents were/how I was; ~**ć kogoś z matematyki** Szkol. to test sb (orally) in maths

[II] **spytać się** pot. to ask

srebrn|y *adi.* ☐ (zrobiony ze srebra) silver ☐ (w kolorze srebra) silver, silvery ☐ Sport *[medal, medalista]* silver ☐ książk. *[dźwięk, ton]* silvery

sreb|ro [] *n* ☐ (pierwiastek, materiał) silver; **bransoleta ze ~ra** a silver bracelet; **oprawić coś w ~ro** to set sth in silver ☐ Sport (medal) silver

Ⅱ srebra *plt* silverware

■ **żywe ~ro** (rtęć) quicksilver; **być żywym ~rem** *[osoba]* to be a live wire

sro|gi *adi. grad.* książk. *[władca]* ruthless; *[nauczyciel, głos]* stern; *[mróz, ból]* severe

sro|ka *f* Zool. magpie; **gapić się na kogoś/coś jak ~ka w gnat** a. **kość** to gawk at sb/sth

■ **trzymać** a. **łapać kilka ~k za ogon** to have many irons in the fire

ss|ać *impf vt* to suck; **ssać pierś** to suck at the breast; **ssie mnie w dołku** a. **żołądku** I'm terribly hungry

ssak *m* mammal

stabiln|y *adi. grad.* *[sytuacja, konstrukcja, pojazd]* stable

stacj|a *f* ☐ (dworzec, przystanek) station; **~a kolejowa** a railway station; **~a metra** an underground GB a. subway US station; **na ~i** in a. at the station; **odprowadzić kogoś na ~ę** to see sb off to the station; **pociąg wjechał na ~ę** the train pulled into the station ☐ (placówka) station; **~a doświadczalna** a research station ☐ Aut. station; **~a benzynowa** a petrol a. filling station GB, a gas station US ☐ Radio, TV station

❏ **~a dysków** Komput. disk drive; **~a kosmiczna** a. **orbitalna** space station; **~a krwiodawstwa** blood transfusion centre; **~e drogi krzyżowej** Relig. the Stations of the Cross

stacjonarn|y *adi.* ☐ (nieruchomy) stationary; **orbita ~a** a geostationary orbit ☐ Uniw. full-time

stacjon|ować *impf vi* Wojsk. to be stationed

stacyj|ka *f* Aut. ignition; **kluczyk do ~ki** an ignition key

staczać *impf* → **stoczyć**

st|ać¹ *impf vi* ☐ (w pozycji pionowej) to stand; **stać na palcach** to stand on tiptoe; **stać na rękach** to stand on one's hands; **nie może stać o własnych siłach** he's too weak to stand up on his own ☐ (trwać bez ruchu) to stand; **stać w miejscu** *[osoba]* to stand still; **stoimy w miejscu** a. **projekt stoi w miejscu** we're not making any headway a. progress; **stać w korku** to be stuck in a traffic jam; **winda stoi między piętrami** the lift is stuck between floors; **stój!** a. **stać!** (komenda wojskowa) halt!; (do uciekającego przestępcy) freeze!; **powietrze stoi** the air is still ☐ (być umiejscowionym) to stand; **stać w szeregu** to stand in a row; **na półce stały książki** there were some books on the shelf; **dom stoi na wzgórzu** the house stands on a hill; **gdzie stoisz?** (samochodem) where are you parked?; **na ulicy stoi woda** the streets are flooded with water; **stać wysoko na niebie** *[księżyc, słońce]* to be high in the sky ☐ (wykonywać czynność) **stać przy kuchni** to stand over a stove; **stać za ladą** to stand behind the counter; **stać na czele partii** to be the leader of a party; **stać na bramce** to be in goal; **stać przy maszynie** to operate a machine ☐ (znajdować się w położeniu) **stać u progu kariery** to be on the threshold of one's career; **stać wysoko w hierarchii** to be high up in the pecking order pot.; **stać wysoko w sondażach** to be riding high in the polls; **stać ponad prawem** to be above the law; **stać za czymś** przen. (być sprawcą) to be behind sth; **stać nad kimś** przen. (pilnować) to stand over sb; **stać po czyjejś stronie** (popierać) to be on sb's side; **stać z boku** to stand to one side; **stać komuś na drodze** przen. to stand in sb's way przen.; **stać w ogniu** *[budynek, miasto]* to be in flames; **dom stoi pusty** the house stands empty; **dobrze stać finansowo** *[osoba, przedsiębiorstwo]* to be doing well; **jak stoimy z czasem?** pot. how are we (doing) for time?; **stać przed problemem/wyzwaniem** to be faced with a problem/challenge; **stać wobec groźby czegoś** to face the threat of sth; **stać w obliczu konieczności zrobienia czegoś** to be confronted with the necessity of doing sth; **stać w sprzeczności z czymś** to be at odds with sth; **stać w sprzeczności ze zdrowym rozsądkiem** to go against common sense; **nic nie stoi na przeszkodzie, żebyśmy...** there's no reason why we/you shouldn't...; **chcę wiedzieć, na czym stoję.** pot. I want to know where I stand ☐ (sterczeć do góry) to stand; **stojące uszy psa** a dog's pricked-up ears ☐ (nie działać) *[fabryka]* (z powodu strajku) to be on strike; (wstrzymać produkcję) to not work; **mój zegarek stoi** my watch has stopped; **produkcja stoi** production is on hold; **cały kraj stoi** the entire country is on strike a. has come to a standstill

■ **umowa stoi!** it's a deal; **wybiegł, jak stał** he stormed out without stopping to think

stać² *praed.* ☐ (finansowo) **~/nie ~ mnie na to** I can/can't afford it ☐ (moralnie) **nie każdego byłoby ~ na coś takiego** (miałby odwagę) not everyone would have the courage to do something like that; **nie każdego stać na przebaczenie** not everyone is capable of forgiving; **~ć go było na to, żeby przyznać się do winy** he had the guts to admit his guilt

sta|ć się *pf* — **sta|wać się** *impf v refl.* ☐ (wydarzyć się) to happen; **~ało się nieszczęście** disaster struck; **co się ~ło?** what happened?, what's the matter?; **co się z nim ~ło?** what happened to him?; **nic się nikomu nie ~ło** nobody was hurt; **dobrze/niedobrze się ~ło, że...** it was lucky/unlucky that...; **jak to się ~ło, że została pani aktorką?** how did you become an actress?; **~ło się!** what's done is done!; **nic się nie ~ło!** it's all right! [2] (zostać) to become; **wszystko ~ło się jasne** everything became clear

■ **co się ~ło, to się nie odstanie** what's done cannot be undone

stadion *m* Sport stadium; **korona ~u** the rim of a stadium

stadnin|a *f* (hodowla, stado) stud

sta|do *n* [1] (bydła, bizonów, słoni) herd; (wilków) pack; (lwów) pride; (wielorybów, delfinów) school; (ptaków) flock; **~do owiec** a flock of sheep; **lecące ~do dzikich gęsi** a flight of wild geese [2] pejor. (tłum) herd; **~da turystów** herds a. flocks of tourists

staj|nia *f* [1] (pomieszczenie) stable; **~nie** mews [2] (stado koni) stable, stud; **~nia wyścigowa** a racing stable [3] pot. (zespół) stable; **kierowcy ze ~ni McLarena** drivers from the McLaren stable

■ **~nia Augiasza** the Augean stables

stal *f* steel; **nóż/szabla ze ~i** a steel knife/sword

■ **być twardym jak ~** to be as hard as steel; **mieć nerwy ze ~i** to have nerves of steel; **mieć wzrok zimny jak ~** to have steely eyes

stale *adv.* constantly, permanently

stalow|y *adi.* [konstrukcja, gwóźdź] steel; [oczy, niebo] steel blue, steely; [wola, charakter] unbending

stałoś|ć *f* (uczuć, przekonań) constancy; (charakteru) stability

sta|ły [] *adi.* [1] (o substancjach) solid; **ciało ~łe** a solid (body) [2] (niezmienny) [adres, element] permanent; **~ła kolumna w gazecie** a regular column in the paper; **~ła klientela** regular customers [3] (określony) [wielkość, cena] fixed; **opłata ~ła** a standing charge [4] (ciągły) [wystawa, zatrudnienie, opieka] permanent [5] (wytrwały) [miłość, przyjaźń] constant, lasting; [charakter] steady; **być ~łym w uczuciach** to be constant in one's feelings

[] **stała** *f* constant

[] **na stałe** *adv.* [wyjechać, osiedlić się, mieszkać] permanently; **to jest przymocowane na ~łe** it's permanently fixed; **on jest tu zameldowany na ~łe** he's permanently registered at this address

stamtąd *pron.* from there; **pojechali do Paryża, a ~ do Londynu** they went to Paris and from there a. thence to London

stan¹ *m* [1] (sytuacja) state; (kondycja) condition; **~ faktyczny czegoś** the actual state of sth; **~ liczbowy czegoś** the number of sth; **czyjś ~ majątkowy** sb's assets a. property; **czyjś ~ umysłowy/zdrowotny** sb's state of mind/health; **~ techniczny maszyny** the technical condition of a machine; **przedsiębiorstwo w ~ie likwidacji** a company in liquidation; **przywrócić coś do ~u pierwotnego** to restore sth to its original condition; **doprowadzić coś do ~u używalności** to restore sth to a usable condition; **dom był w opłakanym ~ie** the house was in a pitiful condition [2] (nastrój) state; **~ duchowy** a. **ducha** (a) state of mind

□ **~ nieważkości** zero-gravity state; **~ wojenny** Polit. martial law; **~ wyjątkowy** Polit. state of emergency

■ **być w ~ie pomóc komuś** to be able a. in a position to help sb; **nie być w ~ie dokończyć/ nauczyć się czegoś** to be unable to complete/ learn sth; **postawić kogoś w ~ oskarżenia** to bring charges against sb

stan² [] *m* [1] (część państwa) state; **Stany Zjednoczone Ameryki Północnej** the United States of America [2] Hist. (warstwa społeczna) class; **~ chłopski** the peasantry; **~ ziemiański** the gentry; **~ średni** (mieszczaństwo) the middle class; **~ trzeci** the third estate; **~ duchowny** the clergy; **~ rycerski** the knightly order; **człowiek niskiego/wysokiego ~u** a person of low/high rank; **żyć ponad ~** to live beyond one's means

[] **Stany** *plt* pot. (USA) the States pot.

stan³ *m* [1] (talia) waist, middle [2] (część tułowia) trunk; **mieć krótki/długi ~** to have a high/low waist [3] (góra sukni) bodice

sta|nąć¹ *pf* — **sta|wać** *impf vi* [1] (przybrać pozycję pionową) to stand up; **~nąć na baczność** to stand to attention; **~nąć na rękach** to do a handstand [2] (zostać ustawionym pionowo) to be placed (upright); **książki ~nęły na półkach** the books were placed on the shelves [3] (zatrzymać się w ruchu) to stop; **pociąg ~nął na stacji** the train stopped at the station; **samochód ~nął przed posterunkiem policji** the car pulled up in front of the police station [4] (przestać funkcjonować) to stop; **zegar ~nął** the clock has stopped; **fabryki ~nęły** the factories have stopped operating; **ruch uliczny ~nął** traffic was brought to a standstill [5] (zgłosić się) to appear; **~nąć przed sądem/komisją lekarską** to appear before a court/the medical board; **~nąć do konkursu** to enter a competition; **~nąć do walki z kimś** to square up to sb [6] (pojawić się) to appear, to turn up; **goście ~nęli w drzwiach naszego domu** some visitors turned up at our door

stan|ąć² *pf vi* [1] (zamarznąć) to freeze [2] (zakrzepnąć) [galaretka] to set [3] (zostać zbudowanym) [budynek, pomnik] to be raised a. erected [4] pot. (dojść do skutku) to be settled; **w końcu ~ęło na tym, że...** eventually it was decided that...

standar|d *m* standard; **~d życia** a. **życiowy** the standard of living; **~dy jazzowe** jazz standards; **samochód w wersji ~d** the standard model of a car

stani|eć *pf vi* [1] [towary, usługi] to become cheaper [2] przen. [uczciwość, odwaga, życie] to be cheapened

stanik *m* [1] (biustonosz) bra [2] (góra sukni) bodice

stanowczo *adv.* [oświadczyć, żądać] firmly; [odmówić, sprzeciwić się] categorically

stanowcz|y *adi.* [osoba] resolute; [ton, odmowa, protest] firm

stan|owić *impf* **[]** *vt* [1] (tworzyć) to make; ~**owili dobraną parę** they made a perfect couple [2] (rozstrzygać) to decide; ~**owić o swoim losie** to decide about one's future; ~**owić prawa** to establish laws; **prawo** ~**owi, że...** the law says that...
[] *vi* (być czynnikiem decydującym) to determine; **łagodny klimat** ~**owi o atrakcyjności tego miejsca** the pleasant climate makes the place attractive to visitors

stanowisk|o *n* [1] (miejsce wykonywania czynności) post, stand; ~**o archeologiczne** an archeological excavation site; ~**o pracy** a workstation; ~**o obserwacyjne** an observation post; ~**o sprzedaży biletów** a ticket-sales point [2] (miejsce postoju) **autobus odjeżdża ze** ~**a drugiego** the coach is departing from Bay Two; **samolot do Paryża kołuje na** ~**o startowe** the plane for Paris is taxiing into take-off position [3] (pozycja w hierarchii) post, position; ~**o w rządzie** a government post; **zajmować** ~**o kierownicze** to hold a managerial position [4] (punkt widzenia) position; **jakie jest twoje** ~**o w tej sprawie?** what's your position on this matter?; **wypracować wspólne** ~**o** to work out a common position a. stance; **on stoi na** ~**u, że...** he takes the view that... [5] Wojsk. position

stapiać *impf* → **stopić**

stara|ć się *impf v refl.* [1] to try; ~**ć się o posadę** to try to get a job; ~**ć się kogoś przekonać** to try to persuade sb; ~**ła się być dobrą uczennicą** she did her best to be a good pupil; ~**łam się, jak mogłam** I tried my best

starann|y *adi. grad. [pismo]* neat; *[poszukiwania]* careful; *[osoba]* diligent, meticulous

star|cie *n* [1] (potyczka) clash; ~**cie zbrojne** an armed clash; ~**cia demonstrantów z policją** clashes between demonstrators and police [2] Sport round [3] przen. (wymiana zdań) squabble

starcz|yć *pf* — **starcz|ać** *impf vi* to be enough; **żywności** ~**yło dla wszystkich** there was enough food for everyone; **pieniędzy** ~**y do końca miesiąca** the money should last until the end of the month; ~**y!** that's enough!, that'll do!

sta|ro *adv. grad. [wyglądać, czuć się]* old

staroś|ć *f* [1] (okres życia) old age [2] (dawność) antiquity; **papier pożółkły ze** ~**ci** paper yellowed with age
■ ~**ć nie radość** przysł. age is a heavy burden

staroświec|ki *adi. [człowiek, mebel, ubranie, pogląd]* old-fashioned

star|t *m* [1] Sport (początek biegu, wyścigu) start; (udział w zawodach) participation; **stanąć na linii** ~**tu** to take one's starting position; ~**t!** go! [2] (samolotu) take-off [3] przen. start; **mieć gładki** ~**t w życiu** to get off to a flying start in life; **zapewnić wszystkim równy** ~**t** to give everyone an equal start

start|ować *impf vi* [1] (stawać do zawodów) to enter a race/competition [2] (o samolocie) to take off [3] pot. (rozpoczynać działalność) to make a start; ~**ować w filmie** to make one's film debut; ~**ować w wyborach** to stand for election, to run in an election; ~**ować od zera** to start from scratch

startow|y *adi.* [1] Sport *[sygnał, blok, linia]* starting [2] Lotn. take-off; **pas** ~**y** a runway

sta|ry **[]** *adi. grad.* [1] (liczący wiele lat) old; ~**rszy syn/brat** one's elder son/brother [2] (podniszczony) old; ~**ry, zardzewiały grat** a rusty old wreck [3] (dawny) old; ~**ry numer Newsweeka** a back issue a. back copy of Newsweek; ~**rzy mistrzowie** the old masters [4] (nietracący na aktualności) *[przyjaźń, znajomość]* old; **po** ~**remu** as of old; **narzekał po** ~**remu** he was complaining as usual; **u nas wszystko po** ~**remu** things are the same as usual with us [5] (o produktach żywnościowych) stale
[] *adi.* [1] (mający doświadczenie) *[fachowiec]* old [2] *[przyjaciel, znajomy]* old
[] **starszy** *adi. comp.* [1] (niemłody) elderly [2] (stojący wyżej w hierarchii) *[redaktor, wykładowca, wspólnik]* senior; *[oficer]* superior, senior; **uczniowie (ze)** ~**rszych klas** students from the upper forms [3] (z nazwiskiem) ~**rszy Kowalski** Kowalski Senior; **Pliniusz Starszy** Pliny the Elder
[] **sta|ry** *m,* ~**ra** *f* pot. [1] (przełożony) boss [2] (ojciec) old man; (matka) old woman; (mąż) old man pot.; (żona) old lady pot.
[] **stare** *n* the old
[] **starsi** *plt* elders
[] *inter.* pot. **cześć,** ~**ry!** hello, mate! a. old son! GB, hello, old buddy! US pot.

starz|eć się *impf v refl.* [1] *[osoba]* to grow old; ~**ejące się społeczeństwo** an ageing society [2] przen. *[utwór, opinia, pogląd]* to become outdated; **niestarzejący się szlagier** an evergreen hit [3] *[olej, ser]* to go off a. bad

stat|ek *m* ship; ~**ek przetwórnia** a factory ship; ~**ek spacerowy** a pleasure boat; **podróżować** ~**kiem** to travel by ship
❑ ~**ek kosmiczny** spaceship, spacecraft; ~**ek powietrzny** airship

statuet|ka *f* statuette, figurine

statu|t *m* statute

statutow|y *adi. [zmiany, przepisy]* statutory

staty|sta *m,* ~**stka** *f* supernumerary, extra

statysty|ka *f* statistics

statyw *m* stand; ~ **trójnożny** a tripod stand

staw¹ *m* (zbiornik wodny) pond; ~ **rybny** a fish pond; ~ **górski** a tarn

staw² *m* Anat. joint

stawać *impf* → **stanąć¹**

stawać się *impf* → **stać się**

stawia|ć *impf* **[]** *vt* [1] (umieszczać) to put; ~**ć filiżanki na stole** to put cups on the table; ~**ć sidła** to lay a. set a snare [2] (podnosić do góry) to turn up;

~ć **kołnierz** to turn up a. raise one's collar; ~ć **żagle** to set sail ③ (nadawać pozycję pionową) to set [sth] upright *[kieliszek, wazon]* ④ (budować) to build *[dom, piec]*; to erect *[rusztowanie, pomnik]*; to put up *[namiot, płot]* ⑤ (przedstawiać) ~ć **komuś ultimatum** to issue an ultimatum to sb; ~ć **diagnozę** to make a diagnosis ⑥ (grać) ~ć **na konia na wyścigach** to (put a) bet on a horse at the races ⑦ pot. (fundować) to stand po.; ~ć **komuś drinka** to stand sb a drink **Ⅱ stawiać się** pot. (przeciwstawiać się) to rebel (**komuś** a. **wobec kogoś** against sb)

■ ~ć **kogoś w złym/dobrym świetle** to place sb in an unfavourable/a favourable light; ~ć **kogoś przed faktem dokonanym** to present sb with a fait accompli; ~ć **kogoś w trudnej/przykrej sytuacji** to place sb in a difficult/an unpleasant situation; ~ć **na kogoś/coś** to count on sb/sth; ~ć **pierwsze kroki** to take one's first steps; ~ć **się na równi z kimś** to consider oneself sb's equal; ~ć **kogoś/coś za wzór** a. **za przykład** to put sb/ sth forward as a model

staw|ić się *pf* — **staw|iać się** *impf v refl.* to turn up; ~**ić się na rozprawę/na egzamin** to turn up for the trial/exam; ~**iać się na czyjeś każde wezwanie** a. **zawołanie** to be at sb's beck and call

staw|ka f ① (kwota) rate; **minimalna** ~**ka godzinowa** a minimum hourly rate of pay; ~**ka za nadgodziny** the overtime rate ② (w grach hazardowych) stake; **grać o wysokie** ~**ki** to play a. gamble for high stakes; **podnieść** ~**kę** to raise the bidding a. stakes ③ przen. stake; ~**ką jest życie dziecka** the child's life is at stake ④ (konie, zawodnicy) the starters *(in a race)*

staż m ① (okres próbny) traineeship; **być na** ~**u** a. **odbywać** ~ to be on placement, to serve one's internship US ② (czas od podjęcia pracy, funkcji) seniority; **pracownik z długim** ~**em** a long-serving employee; **mam za sobą dwudziestoletni** ~ **pracy** I have twenty-years' work experience

staży|sta m, ~**stka** f trainee

stąd Ⅰ *pron.* ① (wskazuje na miejsce) from here; **dwa kilometry** ~ two kilometres from here a. away; **to dziesięć minut** ~ it's ten minutes' walk away; **blisko** ~ near here; **to kawał drogi** ~ it's a long way off a. from here; **ja nie jestem** ~ I'm not from around here a. from these parts; **zabierz to** ~ take it away (from here); **wynoś się** a. **zjeżdżaj** ~! pot. clear off! pot.; ~ **dotąd** from here to here/there; ~, **gdzie teraz stoję, widać ocean** from where I'm standing now I can see the ocean ② (wskazuje na przyczynę) **pomysł wziął się** ~, **że...** the whole idea arose because...; ~ **biorą się nasze obecne trudności** that's the source a. cause of our present difficulties **Ⅱ** *part.* hence; **był niskiego wzrostu,** ~ **jego przydomek** he was short, hence the a. his nickname ■ **ni** ~, **ni zowąd** all of a sudden; out of the blue pot.

stek m ① Kulin. steak; **krwisty** ~ a rare steak ② (nagromadzenie) ~ **głupstw** a load of rubbish; ~ **kłamstw** a pack of lies; ~ **wyzwisk** a torrent a. shower of abuse

stelaż m frame; (do nut) music stand; ~ **pod materac** a bedstead

stemp|el m ① (pieczątka) stamp ② (w kopalni) pit prop ③ Techn. die

stempl|ować *impf vt* ① (znaczyć stemplem) to postmark *[kopertę, kartkę]*; to frank, to postmark *[znaczek]*; to stamp *[paszport, bilet]* ② Techn. (podpierać) to prop (up) *[strop, ścianę, tunel]*; to shore up *[budynek]*

stenografi|a f shorthand (writing) GB, stenography US

ste|r m ① (łodzi, statku) helm; **stać za** ~**rem** to stand at the helm; **przejąć** ~**r(y)** to take over the helm ② (samolotu) rudder; ~**r wysokości** an elevator ③ przen. (władza) helm, reins przen.; **stanąć u** ~**ru rządu** to assume the reins of government

stercz|eć *impf vi* ① (wystawać) to project; ~**ące uszy** protruding ears ② pot. (tkwić) to hang around pot.; ~**ała całymi dniami przy oknie** she hung around the window for days on end

sterni|k m steersman; (na okręcie) helmsman; (w łodzi wiosłowej) coxswain; **czwórka ze** ~**kiem/bez** ~**ka** Sport a coxed/coxless four; ~**k automatyczny** autopilot

ster|ować *impf vt* ① *[osoba]* to steer; ~**ować łodzią** to steer a boat ② Techn. to control; **być** ~**owanym automatycznie** to be automatically controlled; **zdalne** ~**owanie** remote control ③ przen. ~**ować kimś** to manipulate sb

ster|ta f ① (stos) pile; ~**ta śmieci** a pile of rubbish; **ułożyć coś w** ~**tę** to pile sth up ② (zboża, siana) stack

steryliz|ować *impf vt* ① (wyjaławiać) to sterilize ② (kastrować) to sterilize

sterylizowan|y *adi.* sterilized

steryln|y *adi.* ① *[opatrunek, strzykawka]* sterile ② przen. (czysty) immaculately clean

stetoskop m stethoscope

stęch|ły *adi.* musty

stęk|ać¹ *impf vi* pot. (narzekać) to moan (**na coś** about sth)

stęk|nąć *pf* — **stęk|ać²** *impf vi* ① (z wysiłku, bólu) to grunt ② przen. *[deska, ciężki przedmiot]* to groan

stęskni|ć się *pf v refl.* ~ć **się za kimś** to miss sb greatly a. badly; ~**łem się już za zimą** I really wish it was winter again

stłu|c *pf* **Ⅰ** *vt* ① (rozbić) to break *[szybę, szklankę]* ② (uderzyć się) to bang *[łokieć, nos]*; ~ć **sobie kolano** to bang one's knee; ~**czone ramię** an injured shoulder ③ pot. (pobić) to beat up **Ⅱ stłuc się** *[talerz, lustro, wazon]* (pęknąć) to break; (zostać rozbitym) to get broken

stłucz|ka *f* pot. ① (kolizja) bump ② (przedmiot stłuczony) breakage

stłum|ić *pf vt* ① (wyciszyć) to muffle *[odgłos, kroki, okrzyki]* ② (pokonać) to put down *[bunt, powstanie]* ③ (opanować) to suppress *[uczucie]*; to stifle *[westchnie, pragnienie, śmiech]*; **~ić w sobie gniew** to hold back one's anger ④ (ograniczyć) to bring down *[inflację]*; to stifle *[rozwój]* ⑤ (zgasić) to smother *[ogień]*

st|o *num.* hundred; **już ci sto razy mówiłem** I've told you a hundred times; **już ze sto lat tam nie byłem** it's ages since I went there; **ten jest sto razy lepszy** this one's a hundred times better; **zabawa była na sto dwa** pot. we had a hell of a good time pot.

stoczni|a *f* shipyard, dockyard; **~a remontowa** a ship repair yard

st|oczyć *pf* — **st|aczać** *impf* ① *vt* ① (zepchnąć) to roll *[beczkę, pojazd]* ② (rozegrać) to fight *[bitwę]*; **stoczyć z kimś potyczkę** to skirmish with sb ② **stoczyć się** — **staczać się** ① (sturlać się) *[pojazd, beczka]* to roll; (spaść) *[osoba]* to tumble ② (zejść zataczając się) to stumble; **stoczyć się ze schodów** to stumble down the stairs ③ pot. (upaść moralnie) to end up in the gutter

stod|oła *f* barn; **dom wielki jak ~oła** a barn of a house

stoisk|o *n* ① (w domu towarowym) department ② (na ulicy, targach) stall, stand; (budka) booth; **uliczne ~o** a street stall; **~o z książkami** a bookstall

stojak *m* (podpórka) stand; (z przegródkami, prętami) rack; **~ na rowery** a bicycle rack; **~ na parasole** an umbrella stand; **~ na płyty kompaktowe** a CD rack a. stand

stojąco *adv.* **robić coś na ~** to do sth standing up; **owacja na ~** a standing ovation; **praca na ~** work involving standing

stojąc|y *adi.* ① (pionowy) upright; **w pozycji ~ej** in standing position; **zegar ~y** a grandfather clock; **lampa ~a** a standard a. floor lamp; **miejsca ~e** standing places ② *[woda, zbiornik]* stagnant

stok *m* slope; **~ narciarski** a ski slope

stokrot|ka *f* daisy

stolarz *m* carpenter; (robiący elementy budowlane) joiner; (robiący meble) cabinetmaker

stol|ec *m* stool; **wolny ~ec** loose stools

stolic|a *f* capital (city); **~a światowej mody** the fashion capital of the world

stolik *m* (small) table; **~ karciany** a card table; **~ nocny** a bedside table; **~ na kółkach** a tea trolley

stoł|ek *m* ① (mebel) stool; **~ek barowy** a bar stool ② pot. (stanowisko) job; **walka o ~ki** the struggle for power; **dba tylko o swój ~ek** all he cares about is his job; **trzymać się ~ka** to hold on to one's post

stołów|ka *f* canteen; (samoobsługowa) cafeteria

stomatolo|g *m* dental surgeon, dentist

stomatologi|a *f* dentistry

stop¹ *m* alloy; **~ drukarski** type metal

stop² ① *m* pot. ① (światło hamowania) brake a. stop light ② pot. (autostop) hitching pot.; **podróżować ~em** to hitch ② *inter.* ① (nakaz przerwania) stop, halt ② (w telegramie) stop

st|opa *f* ① (część nogi) foot; **ślady stóp** footprints; **nietknięty ludzką stopą** (dziewiczy) untrodden, unexplored ② (część pończochy, skarpety) foot ③ (w wierszu) foot ④ (jednostka długości) foot ⑤ Techn. base ⑥ (poziom) standard; **niska/wysoka stopa życiowa** a low/high standard of living ■ **być** a. **żyć z kimś na dobrej stopie** to be on friendly terms with sb; **mieć świat u swych stóp** to have the world at one's feet; **od stóp do głów** from head to foot a. toe

stope|r *m* ① Sport (piłkarz) centre back, stopper; ② (zegarek) stopwatch ③ (zatyczka) earplug

st|opić *pf* — **st|apiać** *impf* ① *vt* to melt; **stopione masło** melted butter; **stopiony ołów** molten lead ② **stopić się** — **stapiać się** *[masło, ser, śnieg]* to melt

stop|ień *m* ① (schodów) step, stair; **uwaga ~ień!** mind the step! ② (w hierarchii) rank; **urzędnik wyższego ~nia** a senior official; **~ień doktora** a doctor's degree ③ (w klasyfikacji) grade; **nagroda pierwszego ~nia** a first class award; **oparzenie I/II/III ~nia** a first/second/third degree burn ④ Szkol. mark, grade US ⑤ (jednostka) degree ⑥ (poziom, intensywność) degree, extent; **w znacznym ~niu** to a considerable degree, to a large extent; **w wysokim/najwyższym ~niu niepokojący** extremely worrying

stopni|eć *pf vi* ① *[lód, śnieg]* to melt ② przen. (zmaleć) *[kapitał, majątek]* to dwindle away

stopniowo *adv.* (powoli) gradually, little by little

stos *m* ① (rzeczy jedna na drugiej) stack, pile; **~ książek** a stack of books; **ułożyć talerze/cegły w ~** to stack up plates/bricks ② (sterta drewna) log pile; **~ pogrzebowy** a funeral pyre ③ (kara śmierci) the stake

stos|ować *impf* ① *vt* to take *[leki, środki nasenne]*; to apply *[zasady, reguły, przepisy]*; to practice *[metody, tortury]* ② **stosować się** ① (podporządkowywać się) to obey (**do czegoś** sth); to abide (**do czegoś** by sth) ② (dotyczyć) to apply (**do kogoś/czegoś** to sb/sth)

stosown|y *adi. grad. [chwila, czas]* appropriate, suitable; **niezbyt ~e żarty** inappropriate jokes; **uznać** a. **uważać za ~e przeprosić kogoś** to think it fit to apologize to sb

stosun|ek ① *m* ① (relacja) relation, relationship; **w ~ku 5:8** in a. by a ratio of 5:8; **w ~ku do kogoś/czegoś** in relation a. comparison with sb/sth ② (odnoszenie się) attitude (**do kogoś** to sb); **być uprzejmym w ~ku do obcych** to be polite to strangers ③ (seksualny) (sexual) intercourse

▣ stosunki *plt* ① (łączność) relations; ~**ki dyplo-matyczne/handlowe** diplomatic/trade relations; ~**ki międzyludzkie** human intercourse; **pozo-stajemy od wielu lat w dobrych** ~**ach** we've been on good terms for many years ② (znajomości) connections, contacts ③ (położenie, sytuacja) conditions; **nowe** ~**ki społeczne** new social conditions
stosunkowo *adv.* relatively, comparatively; **czu-ję się** ~ **dobrze** I'm feeling tolerably well
stowarzyszać *impf* → **stowarzyszyć**
stowarzysze|nie *n* association
stowarzysz|yć *pf* — **stowarzysz|ać** *impf* ▣ *vt* to affiliate
▣ stowarzyszyć się — **stowarzyszać się** *[firma, grupa]* to affiliate (**z czymś** with sth)
stoż|ek *m* cone; ~**ek wzrostu** Bot. apex
st|ół *m* table; **nakryć do stołu** to lay a. set the table; **siąść do stołu** to sit down to table; **siedzieć przy stole** to sit at the table; **sprzątać ze stołu** to clear the table; **podano do stołu!** dinner/supper is served!
❑ **szwedzki stół** buffet (meal), smorgasbord
strach ▣ *m* fear, dread; **żyć w** ~**u przed kimś/czymś** to live in dread a. fear of sb/sth; **nie móc mówić ze** ~**u** to be unable to speak for a. from fear **▣** *praed.* ~ **tak po ciemku łazić** one's afraid to go out at night; ~ **pomyśleć, że...** it's awful a. terrible to think that...; **ciemno tu, że aż** ~ it's so dark here, it's scary; **najadłem się, że aż** ~ I've eaten so much, it's awful
❑ ~ **na wróble** scarecrow
■ **mieć** ~**a** pot. to be scared; **najeść się** ~**u** to get the fright of one's life; **napędzić komuś** ~**u** a. ~**a** to scare sb out of his/her wits; **nie ma** ~**u** pot. never fear!, don't worry!; **nie znać** ~**u** to know no fear; **umierać ze** ~**u** to be dead scared
stra|cić *pf vt* ① to lose *[posadę, ząb, przyjaciół, pamięć]*; ~**cić władzę w nogach** to lose the use of one's legs; ~**cić okazję** to miss an opportunity; **okolica wiele** ~**ciła** the place lost a lot (of its beauty/attraction) ② (wykonać wyrok śmierci) to execute
■ ~**cić na wadze** to lose weight; ~**cić panowa-nie nad pojazdem** to lose control of a vehicle; ~**cić panowanie nad sobą** to lose one's compos-ure; ~**cić poczucie rzeczywistości** to lose one's grip on reality; ~**cić rozum** to lose one's mind; ~**cić w czyichś oczach** to go down in sb's estimation; **niech** ~**cę** easy come, easy go!
strac|ony *adi. [energia, czas]* wasted; ~**one złudzenia** shattered illusions; **stać na** ~**onej pozycji** to be fighting a losing battle; **to** ~**ona sprawa** it's a lost cause; **jeszcze (nie ma) nic** ~**onego** all is not yet lost
stragan *m* stall, stand; ~ **z kwiatami** a flower stall

strajk *m* strike; ~ **głodowy** hunger strike; ~ **okupacyjny** sit-in; ~ **włoski** work-to-rule, go-slow GB; **wyłamywać się ze** ~**u** to blackleg GB
strajk|ować *impf vi* to strike
strasznie *adv. grad.* ① (okropnie) *[wyglądać]* terrible, horrible; *[zachowywać się, traktować]* terribly, ap-pallingly; *[nieuprzejmy]* terribly ② pot. (bardzo) terribly, awfully; **miał** ~ **dużo szczęścia** he was terribly lucky; ~ **się o niego martwię** I'm awfully worried about him
straszn|y *adi. grad.* ① (budzący strach) terrible, dreadful; **umarł** ~**ą śmiercią** he died a terrible death ② (bardzo zły) *[warunki, pogoda]* terrible, awful ③ pot. (bardzo intensywny) *[ból, smutek, burza]* fearful; ~**y z niego drań** he's a real bastard pot.; **zarabia na tym** ~**e pieniądze** he makes a hell of a lot of money out of it pot.
strasz|yć *impf* ▣ *vt* ① (wzbudzać strach) to frighten ② (grozić) to threaten (**kogoś czymś** sb with sth); ~**yli, że go zabiją** they threatened to kill him
▣ *vi* (o duchach) to haunt; **w ich domu** ~**yło** their house was haunted; **mieszkanie** ~**yło pustką** przen. the flat was eerily empty
stra|ta *f* ① (utrata, ubytek) loss; ~**ta czasu i pieniędzy** a waste of time and money; **ponieść** ~**ty (w ludziach)** to suffer losses (in men); ~**ty w ludziach były duże** there were heavy casualties ② Ekon. loss; **sprzedać coś ze** ~**tą** to sell sth at a loss
■ **spisać coś na** ~**ty** to write sth off
strategi|a *f* Wojsk. strategy także przen.
straw|ić *pf vt* ① (o jedzeniu) to digest ② (zniszczyć) to consume, to destroy; **rdza** ~**iła metal** rust had eaten through the metal
■ **nie mógł/mogli** ~**ić jej zachowania** pot. he/they couldn't bear her conduct
strawn|y *adi. grad.* ① (łatwy do strawienia) digestible ② przen. (łatwy do zrozumienia) palatable
straż *f* guard; **zdwoić** ~**e** to double the guards; **pełnić** ~ to be on guard; **stać na** ~**y pokoju** to guard the peace
❑ ~ **ogniowa** a. **pożarna** fire brigade
straża|cki *adi.* **wóz** ~**ki** a fire engine, a firetruck US; **hełm** ~**ki** a fireman's helmet; **pompa** ~**ka** a firefighting pump; **remiza** ~**ka** a fire station, a firehouse
straża|k *m* firefighter, fireman
strażnic|a *f* watchtower
strażnicz|ka *f* guard; ~**ka więzienna** a warder a. prison officer; ~**ki moralności publicznej** przen. guardians of public morality
strażni|k *m* guard, watchman; (strzegący tradycji) guardian
strą|cić *pf* — **strą|cać** *impf vt* ① (spowodować upadek) to knock off *[jeźdźca, wazon]* ② (zestrzelić) to shoot down *[samolot]*

strąk *m* pod; **wyłuskiwać groch/fasolę ze** ~**ów** to pod peas/beans
stref|a *f* zone, area; ~**a przygraniczna** a border zone; ~**a ograniczonego parkowania** a tow-away zone; **podział świata na** ~**y wpływów** the division of the world into areas of influence
■ **szara** ~**a** Ekon. a grey area
stres *m* stress; **żyć w** ~**ie** to live under stress
stres|ować *impf* **I** *vt [sytuacja, osoba]* to stress
II stresować się to become stressed
streszczać¹ *impf* → **streścić**
streszcza|ć² *impf* **I** *vt* (zawierać) to embrace; ~**ł w sobie wady i zalety całej rodziny** he embodied the vices and virtues of the entire family
II streszczać się **I** (zawierać się) to be embraced; **żądania** ~**ły się w kilku punktach** the demands were summed up a. embraced in a few points **2** pot. (mówić krótko) to be brief
streszcze|nie *n* summary
stre|ścić *pf* — **stre|szczać¹** *impf vt* to summarize *[film, powieść]*
str|oić¹ *impf* **I** *vt* **I** (ubierać) to dress up **2** (ozdabiać) to decorate *[choinkę, stół]* **3** *[koronka, biżuteria, kwiaty]* to grace
II stroić się to dress up
str|oić² *impf vt* to tune *[instrument, odbiornik]*
stromo *adv. [wznosić się, piąć się]* steeply
strom|y *adi.* steep
stron|a *f* **I** **I** (w książce, zeszycie, gazecie) page; ~**a tytułowa (książki)** a title page; **pierwsza** ~**a (gazety)** the front page **2** (bok, ściana, brzeg) side; **parzysta/nieparzysta** ~**a ulicy** the even/odd side of the street; **przejść na drugą** ~**ę ulicy** to cross (to the other side of) the street; **oglądać coś ze wszystkich** ~ to examine sth from all sides **3** (cecha) side; **dobre/ujemne** ~**y mieszkania na wsi** the positive/negative sides of living in the country; **patrzeć na coś tylko z jednej** ~**y** to look at sth from one side only także przen.; **poznać kogoś z** a. **od dobrej** ~**y** to get to know sb's good side; **utwór ma mocne i słabe** ~**y** the piece has its strong and weak points **4** (kierunek) direction, way; **widok Warszawy od** ~**y Pragi** a view of Warsaw from Praga; **bilet w jedną** ~**ę** a single ticket GB, a one-way ticket; **bilet w obie** ~**y** a return ticket GB, a round-trip ticket US; **pójść w tę/tamtą** ~**ę** to go this/that way; **rozglądać się na wszystkie** ~**y** to look in all directions **5** (każdy z uczestników zatargu) side; **zwaśnione** ~**y** the conflicting sides; **brać czyjąś** ~**ę** to side with sb, to take sides with sb; **przejść na czyjąś** ~**ę** to go over to sb's side **6** Jęz. (forma czasownika) voice **7** Komput. web page **8** Prawo party
II strony *plt* (kraj, okolica) parts; **w moich** ~**ach...** where I come from...; **po raz pierwszy jestem w tych** ~**ach** I'm a stranger to these parts
❏ ~**y świata** the points of the compass

■ **na stronie** on the side; **porozmawiać z kimś na** ~**ie** to have a quiet word with sb; **pójść na** ~**ę** euf. to answer the call of nature; **krewny ze** ~**y matki/ojca** a relation on one's mother's/father's side; **to ładnie z twojej** ~**y, że przyszedłeś** it was nice of you to come; **z drugiej** ~**y...** on the other hand...; **z jednej** ~**y to piekielnie trudne, z drugiej (**~**y) bardzo ciekawe** on the one hand it's hellishly difficult, on the other (hand) it's very interesting; **ja ze swej** a. **swojej** ~**y zrobię, co mogę** I for my part will do my best
stronnictw|o *n* (ugrupowanie) party; (odłam) faction
stronni|k *m*, ~**czka** *f* suporter, backer
strop *m* **I** (budynku) ceiling **2** Geol., Górn. roof
str|ój¹ *m* (ubiór) dress, attire; ~**ój ludowy** national costume a. dress; ~**ój wieczorowy/uroczysty** evening/formal dress; ~**ój sportowy/roboczy** sportswear/workwear a. working clothes
str|ój² *m* Muz. **I** (nastrojenie) tuning **2** (system dźwiękowy) key
stróż *m* **I** (dozorca) caretaker, janitor US; **nocny** ~ a night watchman; ~ **porządku publicznego** a. **prawa** (policjant) a keeper of the peace, a guardian of the law; **ten pies jest wspaniałym** ~**em** this is an excellent guard dog **2** przen. (opiekun) guardian; ~ **moralności** a custodian of morals
struktu|ra *f* **I** (budowa) structure; ~**ra społeczna** the social structure **2** (zespół) structure, organization; ~**ry podziemne** underground organizations; ~**ry związkowe** trade union structures
strumie|ń *m* stream także przen.; **deszcz lał się** ~**niami** the rain came down in torrents
strun|a *f* Muz., Sport string
■ **przeciągnąć** ~**ę** pot. to overstep the mark; **trafić** a. **uderzyć w czyjąś czułą** ~**ę** to touch a raw nerve with sb; **wyprężyć** a. **wyprostować się jak** ~**a** to stand as stiff as a poker
strup *m* scab, crust; **twarz pokryta** ~**ami** a scabby face
stru|ś *m* ostrich
strych *m* attic, loft; **na** ~**u** in the attic a. loft
stryj *m* (paternal) uncle
strza|ł *m* **I** (wystrzał) shot; ~**ł z pistoletu/karabinu** a gunshot/rifle shot; **oddać** ~**ł do kogoś/czegoś** to take a shot a. to fire at sb/sth; **być poza zasięgiem** ~**łu** to be out of gunshot; **broń gotowa do** ~**łu** a gun at the ready; **bez jednego** ~**łu** without a single shot being fired **2** (w futbolu) shot
■ ~**ł w ciemno** a shot in the dark; **książka okazała się** ~**łem w dziesiątkę** the book turned out to be a great success
strza|ła *f* arrow; **mknąć** a. **pędzić jak** ~**ła** to run like the wind
strzał|ka *f* **I** (symbol) arrow; **oznaczyć coś** ~**kami** to mark sth with an arrow; **zielona** ~**ka** (na skrzyżowaniu) ≈ a filter (light) **2** (element urządzenia)

needle; ~**ka barometru** a barometer needle ③ (do rzucania) dart; **grać w** ~**ki** to play darts ④ (na czole konia) blaze ⑤ Anat. fibula

strze|c *impf* **Ⅰ** *vt* (troszczyć się) to watch over; *[poddanych, stada]*; (pilnować) to guard *[wejścia, zamku, prezydenta]*; ~**c kogoś/czegoś przed czymś** to guard sb/sth from a. against sth; ~**c tajemnicy** to guard a. keep a secret

Ⅱ strzec się (wystrzegać się) ~**c się czegoś** to guard against sth

strzelać[1] *impf* → **strzelić**

strzel|ać[2] *impf vi [wieża, drzewo]* to soar

strzelanin|a *f* (odgłos wystrzałów) gunfire; (wymiana ognia) shooting; **wywiązała się** ~**a** shots were fired

strzelb|a *f* shotgun

Strzel|ec *m* Sagittarius; the Archer

strzel|ec *m* ① (strzelający) shooter, shot ② Wojsk. rifleman; **pułk** ~**ców** a rifle regiment; ~**ec wyborowy** (expert) marksman, sharpshooter ③ Sport (uprawiający strzelanie) shooter, marksman; (w futbolu) scorer ④ (w szachach) long-range piece

strzel|ić *pf* → **strzel|ać** *impf* **Ⅰ** *vt* Sport to score *[gola]*; ~**ić/nie** ~**ić karnego** to score/miss a penalty

Ⅱ *vi* ① (wystrzelić) to fire; (posługiwać się bronią) to shoot; **dobrze** ~**ać** to shoot well; ~**ić z pistoletu** to fire a gun; ~**ić do kogoś z łuku** to shoot an arrow at sb; ~**ić sobie w łeb** pot. to blow one's brains out pot.; ~**ić w powietrze** to fire in the air; ~**ać na wiwat** to fire guns in salute ② (trzasnąć) *[piorun, patyk]* to crack; ~**ić palcami** to snap one's fingers; ~**ać z bata** to crack a whip; **coś** ~**iło w gaźniku** the engine backfired; **coś mi** ~**iło w krzyżu/kolanie** I felt a twinge in my back/knee; ~**iła mi dętka** one of my tyres blew (out) ③ (wznieść się, trysnąć) *[płomienie, strumień]* to shoot up; ~**ić w górę** *[osoba, drzewo]* to shoot up ④ Sport to shoot

■ ~**ić gafę** pot. to put one's foot in it pot.; ~**ić byka** pot. to make a blunder; ~**ić kogoś w pysk** pot. to crack sb on the jaw pot.; **prosto jak (w mordę)** ~**ił** pot. straight ahead

strzelnic|a *f* ① (do ćwiczeń) (shooting) range ② (otwór w murze) arrow slit

strzy|c *impf* **Ⅰ** *vt* to cut *[włosy, żywopłot]*; to shear *[owcę, wełnę]*; to mow *[trawnik]*; ~**c kogoś** to cut sb's hair

Ⅱ strzyc się (samego siebie) to cut one's hair; (u fryzjera) to get one's hair cut

strzykaw|ka *f* syringe; ~**ka jednorazowa** a disposable syringe

studen|t *m*, ~**tka** *f* student; ~**t biologii/ medycyny** a biology/medical student

studi|a *plt* ① (nauka) studies; (uczelnia) college; **dostać się na** ~**a** to get into university a. college; **pójść na** ~**a** to go to university a. college; **skończyć** ~**a** to finish university a. college; **w czasie** ~**ów** at university/college ② (badania) study

studi|o *n, n inv.* studio

studi|ować *impf vt* ① Uniw. to study; ~**ować prawo/medycynę** to study law/medicine; ~**ować na uniwersytecie** to study at university ② (badać, oglądać) to study

studi|um *n* ① (szkoła) school ② (rozprawa) study także przen. ③ Szt. study

studni|a *f* ① (z wodą) well; ~**a abisyńska** a driven well ② (podwórko) narrow courtyard

studniów|ka *f* Szkol. *a formal dance held a hundred days before school-leaving exams*

stu|dzić *impf* **Ⅰ** *vt* ① (chłodzić) to cool (down) *[zupę, napój]* ② przen. to cool *[gniew, zapał, entuzjazm]*

Ⅱ studzić się *[zupa, napój]* to cool (down)

studzien|ka *f* Techn. manhole; ~**ka kablowa** a cable manhole; ~**ka ściekowa** a drain; ~**ka rewizyjna** an inspection chamber

stuk|nąć *pf* — **stuk|ać** *impf* **Ⅰ** *vt* (uderzyć) to knock, to rap *[osobę]*; (szturchnąć) to poke; ~**nąć kogoś łokciem w bok** to poke a. dig sb in the ribs

Ⅱ *vi* (wydawać odgłos) *[osoba]* to tap; (do drzwi) to knock; *[buty, kopyta]* to clatter; *[drzwi]* to click; *[koła]* to rattle; *[krople]* to patter; pot. *[serce]* to tick pot.; ~**nąć ołówkiem w stół** to tap a pencil on the table

Ⅲ stuknąć się — **stukać się** ① (uderzyć się) ~**nąć się głową o coś** to knock one's head against sth ② (popukać się) ~**nąć się w głowę** a. **czoło** to tap one's forehead; ~**nij się (w głowę** a. **łeb)!** pot. are you out of your mind? pot.

■ ~**ęła mu sześćdziesiątka/siedemdziesiątka** pot. he has already turned sixty/seventy

stuleci|e *n* ① (sto lat) century; **zima** ~**a** the hardest winter of the century; **po upływie** ~**a** a century later ② (rocznica) centenary; **w** ~**e jego urodzin** on the centenary of his birth

stwardni|eć *pf vi* ① (skóra, gleba, śnieg) to harden; **ręce mu** ~**ały od pracy** his hands got calloused from hard work ② przen. *[osoba, charakter, głos]* to harden

stwarzać *impf* → **stworzyć**[1]

stwier|dzić *pf* — **stwier|dzać** *impf vt* ① (skonstatować) to find; ~**dzić autentyczność podpisu** to certify that the signature is genuine; **lekarz** ~**dził zgon** the doctor pronounced him/her dead ② (oświadczyć) to declare; ~**dzam, że głosowanie jest ważne** I declare the vote to be valid

stworze|nie *n* ① (istota żywa) creature ② książk. (wszystko co żyje) Creation

■ wyglądał jak nieboskie ~**nie** pot. he looked horrible; **ubrudził się jak nieboskie** ~**nie** he got terribly filthy pot.

stw|orzyć[1] *pf* — **stw|arzać** *impf vt* ① (powołać do życia) to create *[instytucję, sieć sklepów]*; **okolica jakby** ~**orzona do wypoczynku** an ideal recreation area; **ona jest** ~**orzona do roli matki** she was made to be a mother; **oni są jakby** ~**orzeni**

dla siebie it's as if they were created for each other; ~**orzenie świata** the Creation ② (spowodować) *[osoba]* to create *[warunki, możliwości, atmosferę]*; to generate *[napięcie, konflikt]*

stw|orzyć² *pf vt* ① (stać się autorem) to create *[dzieło]*; ② (zorganizować) to form *[zespół]* ③ (nadać cechy) to create *[wizerunek]*

stw|ór *m* creature; **niesamowity** ~**ór** an unearthly creature

Stwórc|a *m* the Creator, the Maker

stycz|eń *m* January

styg|nąć *impf vi* ① *[obiad, herbata]* to be getting cold ② przen. *[zapał, miłość]* to cool off

styk [] *m* ① (zetknięcie) junction ② (pogranicze) meeting, contact; ~ **kultur** the meeting of cultures ③ Techn. contact

[] **na styk** *adv.* przen. **mieć jedzenia/pieniędzy na** ~ to have barely enough food/money; **zdążyłam do pracy na** ~ I just managed to get to work on time

stykać *impf* → **zetknąć**

styl *m* style; **meble w** ~**u Ludwika XVI** Louis XVI (style) furniture; **ogród w** ~**u angielskim** an English-style garden; ~ **dziennikarski** journalistic style; **czyjś** ~ **ubierania się** sb's style of dressing; ~ **życia** a lifestyle, a way of life; **taka uwaga nie jest w jego** ~**u** that kind of remark is unlike him; **wróciła na scenę w wielkim** ~**u** she returned to the stage in style; ~ **sportowy** casual style; ~ **klasyczny** Sport (the) breaststroke

styli|sta *m*, ~**stka** *f* ① (pisarz) stylist ② (wizażysta) stylist ③ (projektant) designer

styp|a *f* funeral reception, wake

stypendi|um *n* grant, scholarship; ~**um naukowe** a scholarship; ~**um socjalne** a maintenance grant

subiektywn|y *adi.* *[doznanie, odczucie, pojęcie]* subjective

subskrypcj|a *f* subscription (**na coś** to sth); **cena w** ~**i** subscription price

substancj|a *f* substance

subteln|y *adi. grad.* ① (taktowny) *[osoba, zachowanie]* tactful ② (delikatny) *[uroda, zapach]* delicate ③ (nieznaczny) *[różnica]* subtle ④ (wnikliwy) *[obserwator, analiza]* subtle ⑤ (wyszukany) *[aluzja, ironia]* subtle, understated

sucha|r *m* hard tack daw.

suchar|ek *m* rusk

su|cho [] *adv. grad.* ① (bez wilgoci) dry; **mam sucho w ustach** my mouth is dry; **tego lata było zbyt sucho** summer has been too dry this year ② (oziębłe) drily, dryly ③ (mało efektownie) **wykładał sucho, nieciekawie** his lectures were dry and uninteresting; **przedstawił sucho same liczby** he just presented dry statistics ④ (o głosie, dźwięku) drily, dryly

[] **na sucho** (nie używając wody) **jeść na sucho** to eat

without a drink; **prać/czyścić na sucho** to dry-clean

[] **do sucha** dry; **wytrzeć się do sucha** to wipe oneself dry; **wytrzeć coś do sucha** to wipe sth dry

su|chy *adi. grad.* dry także przen.

■ **przejść coś suchą nogą** a. **stopą** to cross sth dry-shod

sufi|t *m* ceiling

■ **wziąć coś z** ~**tu** pot. to produce sth out of thin air; **mieć nierówno pod** ~**tem** pot. not to be right in the head

sufle|r *m* prompter; **budka** ~**ra** a prompt box

sufler|ka *f* (kobieta sufler) prompter

suger|ować *impf* [] *vt* ① (podsuwać myśl) to suggest; ~**ować komuś odpowiedź** to ask a leading question ② (dawać do zrozumienia) to imply; **dane te** ~**ują, że...** these data imply that...

[] **sugerować się** to be influenced (**czymś** by sth)

sugesti|a *f* suggestion; **zbiorowa** ~**a** Psych. collective delusion

su|ka *f* (samica psa, lisa, wilka) bitch

sukces *m* success; **odnieść** ~ to be a success; **pisarz, który odniósł** ~ a successful writer; **odniósł** ~ **jako polityk** he was a success as a politician

■ ~ **rodzi** ~ nothing succeeds like success

sukien|ka *f* dress

suk|nia *f* dress, gown; ~**nia balowa** a ball gown; ~**nia ślubna** a wedding dress

sum|a [] *f* ① (wynik, zbiór, kwota) sum; ~**a częściowa** a subtotal; **łączna** ~**a** sum total; ~**a informacji** the sum of information; **przekazać dużą** ~**ę w gotówce** to hand over a large sum of money in cash; **szybko zarobić dużą** ~**ę** to make a quick penny ② (msza) High Mass

[] **w sumie** *adv.* ① (w istocie) essentially, in essence ② (łącznie) in total, altogether; **rachunek wyniósł w** ~**ie 200 funtów** the bill totted up GB a. came to 200 pounds; **w** ~**ie spędzili w Londynie pięć lat** they spent a total of five years in London

sumie|nie *n* conscience; **z czystym** ~**niem** with a clear conscience; **ze spokojnym** ~**niem** in all conscience; **zgodnie z (własnym)** ~**niem** according to the dictates of one's conscience; **mieć wyrzuty** ~**nia** to have a guilty a. bad conscience; **nie czuł wyrzutów** ~**nia za popełnioną zbrodnię** he felt no remorse for his crime

■ ~**nie go ruszyło** he felt guilty; **być bez** ~**nia** a. **nie mieć** ~**nia** to have no scruples; **mieć coś na** ~**niu** to be guilty of sth; **mieć kogoś na** ~**niu** to have sb on one's conscience; **nie mieć** ~**nia czegoś zrobić** not to have the heart to do sth; ~**nie ją gryzie** she suffers pangs of conscience

sumienn|y *adi. grad.* conscientious, diligent

sum|ować *impf vt* ① (dodawać) to add up *[dochody, wydatki]*; to aggregate *[wyniki, punkty]* ② (uogólniać) to sum up *[doświadczenia, wrażenia]* ③ (kumulować) to sum up

suplemen|t *m* supplement (**do czegoś** to sth)

surowic|a *f* serum

surow|iec *m* (materiał naturalny) (raw) material; ~**ce mineralne** natural resources; ~**ce energetyczne** fuels; ~**ce wtórne** recyclable waste

surow|o Ⅰ *adv. grad.* ① (bez pobłażania) *[ukarać, potępić]* severely; *[spojrzeć, powiedzieć]* sternly; *[wychowywać]* strictly; **wstęp ~o wzbroniony** admittance strictly prohibited ② (bez ozdób) *[umeblowany, ubrany]* austerely

Ⅱ **na surowo** in the raw (state); **jeść jarzyny na ~o** to eat raw vegetables

surow|y Ⅰ *adi. grad.* ① *[owoce, jarzyny, mięso, jajka]* raw; ~**e mleko** unboiled milk; ~**y boczek** green a. unsmoked bacon ② *[osoba]* strict; *[mina, wzrok]* stern; *[regulamin, wyrok]* severe; *[krytyka]* heavy; *[dyscyplina]* rigorous; **jesteś zbyt ~y dla niej** you're too hard on her ③ *[wnętrze, warunki]* austere ④ *[zima, klimat]* severe

Ⅱ *adi.* ① (o surowcach, półfabrykatach) ~**e bloki kamienne** undressed stone; ~**e drewno** green a. unseasoned timber ② pot. (początkujący) raw; **jest jeszcze ~y w tym zawodzie** he's still a raw beginner in this job

surów|ka *f* Kulin. salad; ~**ka z białej kapusty** coleslaw

sus|eł *m* Zool. gopher; **spać jak ~eł** to sleep like a log

susz|a *f* drought

suszar|ka *f* ① (urządzenie) drier, dryer; ~**ka do włosów** a hairdryer; ~**ka bębnowa** a tumble dryer GB, a tumbler US ② (do naczyń) drainer GB; (do bielizny) clothes airer a. dryer

susz|yć *impf* Ⅰ *vt* to dry

Ⅱ *v imp.* pot. (po wypiciu alkoholu) ~**y mnie po wczorajszym przyjęciu** I feel dehydrated after yesterday's party

Ⅲ **suszyć się** *[pranie, siano]* to dry

sut|ek *m* (gruczoł mleczny) teat; (brodawka) nipple

suwak *m* ① (zapięcie) zip (fastener) GB, zipper US ② (w urządzeniu) slider ③ Muz. slide

❑ ~ **logarytmiczny** Mat. slide rule

sw|ąd *m* smell of burning

swet|er *m* sweater; ~**er rozpinany** a cardigan; ~**er z golfem** a polo neck sweater; ~**er zrobiony na drutach** a (hand-)knitted jumper

swę|dzić, swę|dzieć *impf vt* to itch; ~**działo mnie całe ciało** I was itching all over; ~**dzą mnie plecy** my back is itching; ~**dzi mnie kark** I've got an itch on the back of my neck; ~**dząca wysypka** an itchy rash

swob|oda Ⅰ *f* freedom; ~**oda wyboru** freedom of choice; ~**oda twórcza** artistic licence; ~**oda seksualna** (sexual) promiscuity; ~**oda ruchów** freedom of movement; **mieć pełną ~odę ruchów**

to be allowed (a) complete freedom of action; **pozostawić komuś ~odę w czymś** to allow sb latitude in sth; **rodzice dają mi dużą ~odę** my parents allow me a great deal of freedom; **mam dużą ~odę działania** I'm allowed a lot of leeway; **w puszczy wilki żyją na ~odzie** wolves live in the wild in forests

Ⅱ **swobody** *plt* liberties; ~**ody obywatelskie** civil liberties

swobodnie Ⅰ *adv. grad.* *[decydować, poruszać się]* freely; *[czuć się]* at ease, comfortable; **oddychać ~** to breathe easily

Ⅱ *adv. pot.* (bez trudu) easily; ~ **zdążę na czas** I'll make it easily

swobodn|y *adi.* *[wybór]* free; ~**y oddech** easy breath; ~**y przekład** a loose translation; ~**a atmosfera** casual atmosphere; ~**y strój** a. **ubiór** casual clothes

swojs|ki *adi.* ① (miejscowy) *[kraj, obrzęd, widok]* native ② (zwykły) *[sprawy, zapach]* familiar ③ (domowego wyrobu) home-made

sw|ój Ⅰ *pron.* ① (przed rzeczownikiem) one's (own); (mój) my; (twój) your; (jego) his; (jej) her; (o zwierzęciu, przedmiocie) its; (nasz) our; (wasz) your; (ich) their; **jak na swój wiek** for his/her age ② (bez rzeczownika) one's own; (mój) mine; (twój) yours; (jego) his; (jej) hers; (nasz) ours; (wasz) yours; (ich) theirs ③ (nieobcy) **z niego jest swój chłop** a. **gość** he's one of us

Ⅱ **swój** *m*, **swoja** *f* (rodak) fellow countryman; (przyjaciel) friend; (członek rodziny) family; **swoi** (rodzina) family ; „**kto tam?**" – „**swój**" 'who is it?' – 'it's me'; **przyjdź jutro do nas, będą sami swoi** come round and see us tomorrow, it'll be the usual crowd pot.

Ⅲ **swoje** *n* (własność) one's own property; (interes) one's own business; **gospodarować na swoim** to own one's own farm; **pilnować swojego** to look after one's own affairs; **musimy walczyć o swoje** we must fight for what's ours

■ **mieć swoją wagę** (znaczenie) to carry a certain amount of a. a good deal of weight; **mieć swoje lata** to be no spring chicken pot.; **na swój sposób** (w pewnym sensie) in a way; (po swojemu) (in) one's own way; **dostać** a. **oberwać za swoje** pot. to get one's just deserts; **postawić na swoim** to get a. have one's own way; **swój do swego ciągnie** birds of a feather flock together przysł.; **trafił swój na swego** he/she has met his/her match; **wyjść na swoje** to break even; **zrobić coś po swojemu** to do sth (in) one's own way

sy|cić *impf* książk. *vt* *[potrawa]* to fill [sb] up; **sycić głód czegoś** to sate one's appetite for sth także przen.; **sycić wzrok czymś** to feast one's eyes on sth

syczeć *impf* → **syknąć**

syfon *m* ① (butla) soda siphon ② (zagięcie rury) S bend; (zamknięcie wodne) trap

sygnalizacj|a f [1] (wysyłanie sygnałów) signalling; ~**a świetlna** light signals [2] (urządzenia) signalling system; ~**a alarmowa** the alarm system; ~**a uliczna** traffic lights

sygnalizato|r m signalling device; ~**r świetlny na skrzyżowaniu** traffic lights at a road junction; ~**r odblaskowy** a reflector

sygnaliz|ować impf vt [1] (wskazywać) [światełko, urządzenie] to indicate [awarię, zużycie]; ~**ować coś komuś ruchami rąk** to signal sth to sb; ~**ować niebezpieczeństwo** to warn of a danger [2] przen. (informować) to signal

sygna|ł m [1] (znak) signal; ~**ł ostrzegawczy** a danger a. an alarm signal; **dać komuś ~ł, że.../ żeby...** to give sb a signal, that.../to...; **dawać komuś ~ły latarką** to flash signals to sb; **karetka/radiowóz na ~le** an ambulance/a police car with the siren on; **wysyłać do kogoś sprzeczne ~ły** przen. to send conflicting signals to sb [2] (w telefonie) tone; **nie ma ~łu** the phone is dead [3] (w radiu, TV) signal

sygne|t m (pierścień) signet ring; (z pieczęcią) signet, seal ring

syk m hiss

sy|knąć pf — **sy|czeć** impf vt [osoba, wąż, gęś, gaz] to hiss; **syknąć z bólu** to hiss with pain

sylwest|er m (dzień) New Year's Eve; (zabawa) New Year's Eve party

sylwet|ka f [1] (kształt) silhouette; **widziałem tylko jego ~kę** I could only see him in silhouette [2] (charakterystyka) profile; **przedstawić czyjąś ~kę** (napisać artykuł) to write a profile of sb; **kreślić czyjąś ~kę** to sketch a portrait of sb przen. [3] (postawa) figure; **mieć zgrabną ~kę** to have a good figure; **mieć ~kę atlety** to have an athletic frame

symetri|a f symmetry także przen.

symetryczn|y adi. [budowa, kompozycja] symmetric(al)

symfoni|a /sɪmˈfɔnja/ f symphony także przen.

sympati|a [] f [1] (przychylność) liking; **darzyć kogoś ~ą** to have a liking for sb; **odnosić się do kogoś z ~ą** to be friendly towards sb; **wzbudzać ~ę** to be likeable [2] (dziewczyna) girlfriend; (chłopak) boyfriend

[]] **sympatie** plt sympathies

sympatyczn|y adi. [osoba, film, książka, wspomnienia] nice; [twarz, uśmiech, wygląd] amiable; [atmosfera] friendly

symptom m symptom także przen.

symulacj|a f simulation

symulan|t m, ~**tka** f malingerer

symul|ować impf vt to simulate

syn m son; **jedyny ~** an only son; ~ **chrzestny** godson; **Syn Boży** Relig. Son of God; **jest dla mnie jak ~** he's like a son to me; **to nieodrodny ~ swojego ojca** he's his father's son

synago|ga f synagogue

synchroniczn|y adi. książk. synchronous; **pływanie ~e** Sport synchronized swimming

synonim m synonym także przen.

synow|a f daughter-in-law

syntez|a f synthesis

sypać[1] impf → **sypnąć**

syp|ać[2] impf vt to build [kopiec, okopy, wały]

sypia|ć impf vi to sleep; **źle ~ć** to sleep badly; ~**ć po obiedzie** to have a nap after lunch; ~**ć z kimś** pot. to sleep with sb

sypial|nia f [1] (pokój) bedroom [2] (osiedle mieszkaniowe) dormitory town a. suburb, bedroom suburb US

syp|ki adi. [cukier, sól, śnieg, puder] loose; [włosy] wispy

syp|nąć pf — **syp|ać**[1] impf [] vt [1] [osoba] to pour [mąkę, ziarno]; **wiatr ~ał piaskiem** the wind blew sand [2] pot. (zdradzić) to inform on, to grass on [kolegów]

[]] vi [1] (obdarzyć) to shower; ~**nąć złotem/pieniędzmi** to shower gold/money [2] (o śniegu) **nad ranem przestało ~ać** at dawn it stopped snowing

[]]] **sypać się** [1] [cukier, mąka, piasek] to spill [2] (odpaść) [tynk] to come off [3] (rozpaść się) [mur] to crumble; pot. [osoba, samochód, firma] to be falling apart [4] (wystąpić w obfitości) [pochwały, nagrody, zamówienia] to rain down; **zewsząd ~ią się skargi** we've been inundated with complaints [5] (wystrzelić) [iskry] to shoot [6] pot. (zdradzić się) to confess [7] pot. (pomylić się) [aktor, spiker] to fluff

■ ~**nął mu się wąs** he started to sprout a moustache

syren|a f [1] (alarmowa, fabryczna) alarm, siren; (okrętowa) siren, horn; ~**a mgłowa** foghorn [2] (w mitologii) siren, mermaid

syrop m syrup, sirup US

system m system; ~ **wartości** a system of values; ~ **zarządzania przedsiębiorstwem** a company management system; ~ **dwuzmianowy** a two-shift system (of work); ~ **polityczny** the political system

systematyczn|y adi. [1] [nauka, praca] systematic; ~**y tryb życia** a regular lifestyle [2] [uczeń, pracownik] methodical [3] [wzrost, spadek] consistent [4] Biol. [układ, cecha, jednostka] systematic

sytuacj|a f situation; ~**a bez wyjścia** a dead-end situation; **znaleźć się w trudnej ~i** to find oneself in a difficult situation; **panować nad ~ą** to be in control of the situation; **zbadać ~ę** to see how the land lies przen.; **uratować ~ę** to save the situation; **co byś zrobiła w mojej ~i?** what would you do in my position?

■ **znaleźć się w ~i podbramkowej** pot. to find oneself in a tight corner a. spot

sytu|ować impf [] vt książk. (lokalizować) to locate [budynek, kuchnię, pralnię]; **akcję powieści autor ~uje w średniowieczu** the author sets his novel in the Middle Ages

II sytuować się (umiejscawiać się) to place oneself; **∼ować się ponad prawem** to place oneself above the law

sy|ty II adi. [1] [osoba] replete [2] [posiłek] filling

II syt adi. praed. przen. sated; **syty** a. **syt wrażeń** sated with adventures

III do syta adv. **najeść się do syta** to eat one's fill; **napatrzyć się na coś do syta** to look one's fill at sth

szab|la f sabre

szablon m [1] (forma) template; (wzornik) stencil; (wykrój) pattern [2] (wzorzec postępowania) convention, stereotype

szachi|sta m, **∼stka** f chess player

szach|ować impf vt to check także przen.

szachownic|a f [1] Gry chessboard [2] (wzór) chequer(board)

szach|y plt [1] (gra) chess [2] (komplet figur) chess pieces, chessmen; (razem z planszą) chess set

szac|ować impf vt to estimate [wielkość, ilość, wartość]

szacun|ek m [1] (poważanie) respect; **budzić ∼ek** to command respect; **cieszyć się powszechnym ∼kiem** to be held in high esteem by everyone; **zasługiwać na ∼ek** to deserve respect; **z wyrazami ∼ku** (w zakończeniu listu) with kind regards; **z całym ∼kiem** with due respect [2] (oszacowanie) estimate, estimation

szacunkow|y adi. [wartość, dane] approximate

szaf|a f (na ubrania) wardrobe; (na akta, dokumenty) cabinet; (biblioteczna) bookcase; **∼a wnękowa** a built-in wardrobe

❑ **∼a grająca** jukebox; **∼a pancerna** safe

■ **∼a gra** pot. (everything's) OK

szafi|r m [1] (kamień) sapphire [2] (kolor) sapphire blue

szafirow|y adi. [kolia, spinka] sapphire; [morze, niebo, oczy] sapphire blue

szaf|ka f (kuchenna, łazienkowa) cupboard; (kuchenna do zabudowy) unit; (zamykana na klucz) locker; **∼ka wisząca** a wall cupboard; **∼ka nocna** a bedside table

szaj|ka f pot. gang; **∼ka złodziei** a. **złodziejska** a gang of thieves

szal|a f scale pan

■ **∼a zwycięstwa przechyliła się na naszą stronę** the scales turned in our favour; **położyć/ rzucić coś na ∼ę** he put sth on the line

szal|eć impf vi [1] (wariować) to be mad, to be frantic; **∼eć z gniewu** to be frantic with anger; **∼eć z miłości** to be mad with love; **∼eć z radości** to be transported with joy [2] (hulać) to revel [3] przen. [burza, inflacja] to rage [4] pot. (uwielbiać) to be crazy (**za kimś/czymś** a. **na punkcie kogoś/czegoś** about sb/sth); **∼eć z zakupami** to shop like crazy

■ **jak ∼eć, to ∼eć** we might as well go the whole hog

szalenie adv. extremely; **∼ kogoś/coś lubić** to be extremely fond of sb/sth; **jestem ci ∼ wdzięczna** I'm awfully grateful to you

szale|niec m [1] (wariat) madman [2] przen. (ryzykant) daredevil; (narwaniec) madcap

szaleństw|o n madness; **doprowadzać kogoś do ∼a** to drive sb mad; **być do ∼a zazdrosnym/ zakochanym** to be madly jealous/in love; **∼o przedświątecznych zakupów** Christmas shopping splurge

szalik m scarf

szal|ony II adi. [1] (narwany) [osoba] crazy [2] (obłąkany) [osoba, zamiar, czyn] mad, insane [3] (intensywny) [taniec, życie] frantic; [wakacje] crazy; [jazda] reckless [4] (niepohamowany) [namiętność] mad; [gniew] wild; [radość] frantic [5] pot. (ogromny) [upał, apetyt, szczęście] tremendous

II szal|ony m, **∼ona** f lunatic

szalup|a f launch, ship's boat; **∼a ratunkowa** a lifeboat

sza|ł m [1] Med. frenzy; **dostać ataku** a. **napadu ∼łu** to go into a frenzy [2] książk. (szaleństwo) rage; **doprowadzić kogoś do ∼łu** to drive sb mad [3] (porządków, zakupów) mania, madness

szałas m (z gałęzi) shelter; (domek) shack; (myśliwski) cabin; (pasterski) chalet

szałwi|a f salvia; **∼a lekarska** sage

szamb|o n [1] (zbiornik na ścieki) septic tank [2] pot. (niemoralna sytuacja) cesspit, cesspool

szamo|tać II vi [wiatr] to tear [żaglami]; to sway [drzewami]

II szamotać się [osoba, zwierzę] to struggle, to tussle

szampan m (wino z Szampanii) champagne; pot. (wino musujące) sparkling wine

szampon m shampoo; **nałożyć ∼ na włosy** to shampoo one's hair

szan|ować impf II vt [1] (otaczać szacunkiem) to respect (**kogoś za coś** sb for sth); **osoba powszechnie ∼owana** a well-respected person [2] (respektować) to respect [prawo, zwyczaje]; **∼ować czyjąś tajemnicę** to keep sb's secret; **∼uj pracę innych** respect the work of others [3] (chronić przed zniszczeniem) to take care of, to look after [ubranie, książki]; **„Szanuj zieleń"** 'Keep off the Grass'

II szanować się [1] (mieć poczucie godności) to have self-respect [2] (dbać o swoje dobre imię) [dziennikarz, polityk, pismo, ugrupowanie] to know one's own worth; **każda ∼ująca się gazeta zamieszcza program kin** every decent newspaper has a cinema listing [3] (jeden drugiego) to respect one another [4] (oszczędzać się) to look after one's health

szanown|y adi. [gość, jubilat] honourable, distinguished; **Szanowny Panie!** (w liście) Dear Sir,; **Szanowna Pani!** (w liście) Dear Madam,; **Witam Szanownych Państwa!** Welcome, Ladies and Gentlemen

szans|a *f* [1] (możliwość) chance; **życiowa** ~**a** the chance of a lifetime; **dać komuś** ~**ę** to give sb a chance; **mieć** ~**e u dziewczyny/chłopaka** pot. to stand a chance with a girl/boy [2] (prawdopodobieństwo sukcesu) odds (**na coś** on sth); ~**e, że coś się wydarzy/nie wydarzy** the odds in favour of/ against sth happening

szantaż *m* blackmail; ~ **emocjonalny** emotional blackmail; **zmusić kogoś** ~**em do (zrobienia) czegoś** to blackmail sb into (doing) sth

szantaż|ować *impf vt* to blackmail [osobę]

szantaży|sta *m*, ~**stka** *f* blackmailer

szarańcz|a *f* [1] Zool. locust [2] przen. swarm

szarlot|ka *f* Kulin. ≈ apple pie

szaro *adv.* [1] [pomalowany, otynkowany] grey [2] (monotonnie) dully; ~ **upływają dni** the days pass dully [3] (mroczno) dim, grey

■ **zrobić kogoś na** ~ pot. to leave sb in the lurch

szarów|ka *f* twilight; (przedświt) dawn; (zmierzch) dusk

szarp|nąć *pf* — **szarp|ać** *impf* [1] *vt* [1] (pociągnąć) to jerk, to pull; ~**nąć za klamkę** to yank the door handle; ~**ać kogoś za włosy** to pull sb's hair [2] przen. (dokuczać) [skurcz, ból] to rack [ciało]

[1] *vi* [samochód, tramwaj, pociąg] to jerk

[1] **szarpnąć się** — **szarpać się** [1] [osoba, zwierzę] to pull [2] (tarmosić) ~**ać się za brodę/wąsy** to pluck one's beard/moustache

[1] **szarpać się** [1] przen. (zamartwiać się) [osoba] to fret [2] pot. (bić się) [chłopcy, dzieci] to fight [3] (czynić wysiłki) [osoba] to struggle (**z czymś** with sth)

sza|ry *adi.* [1] [oczy, niebo, kurtka] grey; [dni, świt, zmrok] dim; **o** ~**rej godzinie** at dusk [2] przen. [osoba, tłum] ordinary; ~**ry człowiek** a. **obywatel** man in the street [3] przen. [życie, dni, lata] dull, monotonous

szarz|eć *impf vi* [1] [ściana, obrus] to become grey; [niebo] (o świcie) to become light; (o zmierzchu) to become dusk; ~**eje** (dnieje) it's getting light; (zmierzcha się) it's growing dusk [2] (odróżniać się od tła) [las, dom] to loom

szaszły|k *m* Kulin. (shish) kebab

sza|ta *f* [1] książk. (strój) robe; **królewskie** ~**ty** the king's robes; ~**ty liturgiczne** (liturgical) vestments; **góry w zimowej** ~**cie** przen. mountains covered in snow [2] (wygląd) ~**ta graficzna książki** a book's (graphic) layout

szatan *m* [1] (diabeł) Satan [2] żart. (nieposłuszne dziecko) little fiend

szatni|a *f* (w teatrze, instytucji) cloakroom, coatroom US; (przebieralnia) dressing room; (dla uczniów, sportowców) locker room; „~**a obowiązkowa**" 'please use the cloakroom'; **numerek do** ~ a cloakroom ticket

szatnia|rz *m*, ~**rka** *f* cloakroom attendant

szatyn *m* dark a. brown-haired man; **być** ~**em** to have dark hair

szatyn|ka *f* dark a. brown-haired woman; **być** ~**ką** to have dark hair

szczaw *m* sorrel

szczeb|el *m* [1] (w drabinie) rung [2] przen. (etap) stage; **osiągnąć wyższy** ~**el rozwoju** to reach a higher stage of development [3] przen. (ranga) rank; (poziom) level; (pozycja) rung; **urzędnik wysokiego** ~**la** a high-ranking official; **współpraca na** ~**lu rządowym** cooperation at government level; **piąć się po** ~**lach kariery** to work one's way up the ladder

szczebio|tać *impf vi* [ptak, dziecko] to twitter

szczególnie [1] *part.* particularly; **cała rodzina,** ~ **jego brat** the whole family, particularly his brother

[1] *adv.* (dziwnie) peculiarly, strangely

szczególn|y *adi.* [1] (wyjątkowy) special; **mieć** ~**e znaczenie** to be of special importance; **zachować** ~**ą ostrożność** to be particularly careful; **zwracać na coś** ~**ą uwagę** to pay special attention to sth [2] (konkretny) particular; **w tym** ~**ym przypadku** in this particular case [3] (osobliwy) peculiar

szczegó|ł *m* detail; **opowiedzieć coś ze** ~**łami** to recount sth in detail; **to** ~**ł** it doesn't matter

szczegółow|o *adv. grad.* [opowiedzieć, opisać] in detail

szczek|nąć *impf* — **szczek|ać** *pf vi* [1] [pies] to bark, to woof [2] przen. [karabin maszynowy] to rattle, to crackle

szczelin|a *f* (o równych brzegach) slit; (pęknięcie) crack; ~**a skalna** a rock crevice; ~**a lodowa** a crevasse

szczelnie *adv. grad.* [zatkać, wypełnić, zawinąć] tightly; **zamknąć coś** ~ (dokładnie) to close sth tightly; (hermetycznie) to seal sth

szczeln|y *adi. grad.* [1] [zamknięcie, pojemnik, pokrywka] tight; (nieprzepuszczający powietrza) airtight; (nieprzepuszczający wody) watertight; [sieć, moskitiera] tight, impenetrable [2] przen. [system, kontrola, granica] tight

szczeniak *m* [1] (zwierzę) pup, puppy [2] (dziecko) snot-nosed kid pot., obraźl.; (wyrostek) youth

szczeni|ę *n* (psa) pup; (lisa, wilka) cub

szczep *m* [1] (o ludziach) tribe; (w harcerstwie) group of several scout troops operating in one school [2] Biol. strain

szczep|ić *impf* [1] *vt* to vaccinate, to inoculate [osobę, zwierzę] (**na coś** a. **przeciwko czemuś** against sth);

[1] **szczepić się** Med. to get oneself vaccinated (**na coś** a. **przeciwko czemuś** against sth)

szczepie|nie *n* vaccination (**przeciwko czemuś** against sth); **punkt** ~**ń** a vaccination centre

szczepion|ka *f* Med. vaccine (**na coś** a. **przeciwko czemuś** against sth); ~**ka doustna** an oral vaccine

szczerb|a *f* (w filiżance, talerzu) chip; (w murze) hole; (w uzębieniu) teeth missing

szcze|ry *adi. grad.* [1] *[osoba]* (prawdomówny) sincere; (otwarty) frank; *[odpowiedź, wyznanie]* (zgodny z prawdą) truthful; (uczciwy) honest, frank; **być wobec kogoś ~rym** to be frank with sb; **jeśli mam być ~ry,...** to be honest...; **być ~rym aż do bólu** pot. to be painfully direct a. blunt [2] (autentyczny) *[podziękowanie, przekonanie, radość, oddanie]* heartfelt; **mieć ~ry zamiar coś zrobić** to have a good mind to do sth; **mimo najszczerszych chęci** despite my/his/their best efforts; **~re złoto** pure gold; **w ~rym polu** in the middle of nowhere

szczerze *adv. grad.* [1] (zgodnie z prawdą) *[przyznać, powiedzieć]* frankly; **~ mówiąc** a. **powiedziawszy** frankly speaking [2] (bez udawania) *[nienawidzić, pragnąć, wierzyć]* genuinely

szczę|ka *f* [1] Anat. jaw; **sztuczna ~ka** false teeth, dentures; **aż mu ~ka opadła, kiedy...** pot. his jaw dropped when... pot. [2] Techn. jaws; **~ki hamulcowe** brake shoes

szczęściarz *m* pot. lucky devil pot.; **~ z ciebie!** lucky you!

szczęści|e *n* [1] (zadowolenie) happiness; **promienieć ~em** to beam with happiness; **nic jej do ~a nie brakuje** she has everything she could wish for; **jeszcze nam tylko tego do ~a brakowało!** iron. that's all we needed! iron. [2] (zrządzenie losu) luck; (pomyślność) fortune; **mieć ~e** to be lucky; **mieć ~e do współpracowników** to be fortunate in one's colleagues; **mam ~e do złodziei** iron. I seem to attract thieves; **masz ~e, że ich nie było** you were lucky they were out; **ten to ma zawsze ~e!** he's a lucky bastard! pot.; **masz więcej ~a niż rozumu!** the devil looks after his own!; **próbować ~a w czymś** to try one's luck at sth; **~e do nas uśmiechnęło** fortune smiled on us; **~e nam sprzyjało** luck was on our side; **odważnym ~e sprzyja** fortune favours the brave; **nosić coś na ~e** to wear sth as a good luck charm; **przynieść komuś ~e** to bring sb good luck; **przy odrobinie ~a** with a bit of luck; **takie to już moje ~e!** iron. my luck!; **na ~e** luckily, fortunately; **i całe ~e!** and just as well!; **(całe) ~e, że...** it was just as well that...; **~em udało mu się uciec** książk. fortunately he managed to run away; **~e w nieszczęściu, że...** it was just as well that...

szczęśliwie *adi. grad.* [1] (pomyślnie) happily; **żyli długo i ~** they lived happily ever after [2] (trafnie, korzystnie) fortunately; **niezbyt ~ dobrany tytuł** not a very felicitous title

szczęśliw|y *adi. grad.* [1] *[osoba, uśmiech, twarz]* happy; **być ~ym w małżeństwie** to be happily married; **być ~ym posiadaczem czegoś** to be the proud owner of sth [2] *[dzieciństwo, zakończenie, życie]* happy; **~y powrót do domu** a safe return home; **~ym zbiegiem okoliczności** by a happy coincidence; **~ej drogi** a. **podróży!** have a good trip!; **Szczęśliwego Nowego Roku!** Happy New Year! [3] (przynoszący szczęście) *[kamień, numer, gwiazda]* lucky [4] (trafny, korzystny) fortunate, felicitous

szczotecz|ka *f* small brush; **~ka do paznokci** a nail brush; **~ka do zębów** a toothbrush; **~ka do tuszu** a mascara brush

szczot|ka *f* brush; **~ka do butów/włosów** a shoe brush/hairbrush; **~ka do zamiatania** a broom

szczotk|ować *impf vt* to brush *[włosy, tkaninę]*; to groom *[konia, psa]*

szczud|ła *plt* stilts; **chodzić na ~łach** to walk on stilts

szczupak *m* pike

■ **dać ~a** a. **skoczyć ~iem do wody** to dive headlong into the water

szczupl|eć *impf vi* [1] (chudnąć) *[osoba]* to become thinner US [2] książk. przen. (maleć) *[zapasy, zasoby]* to dwindle

szczup|ły *adi. grad.* *[osoba, figura]* slim; przen. *[dochody, środki, zapasy]* meagre; *[przestrzeń]* small; *[grono ludzi, personel]* sparse

szczu|r *m* Zool. rat; **~r lądowy** pot., przen. landlubber pot.

szczygi|eł *m* goldfinch

szczypać¹ *impf* → **szczypnąć**

szczypa|ć² *impf vt* (podrażniać) to sting *[oczy, skórę, język]*; **dym ~ie mnie w oczy** smoke is making my eyes sting; **oczy/uszy mnie ~ią** my eyes/ears are stinging

szczyp|ce *plt* [1] (cęgi) pliers, tongs; **~ce do węgla** coal tongs; **~ce do cukru** sugar tongs [2] pot. (chrząszcza, kraba, raka) claws, pincers

szczypior|ek *m* chives

szczyp|nąć *pf* — **szczyp|ać¹** *impf vt* [1] *[osoba, zwierzę]* to pinch [2] *[zwierzę]* to nibble *[trawę, listki]*

szczyp|ta *f* [1] (soli, pieprzu, cukru) pinch [2] przen. (rozumu, szczęścia, wyobraźni) dash; (prawdy, humoru) grain

szczy|t *m* [1] (góry) peak; **wspiąć się na ~t** to climb to the top a. summit [2] (drzewa, masztu, wieży, schodów) top; (łóżka, stołu) head [3] (punkt kulminacyjny) peak, apex; **~t czyichś możliwości** the height of sb's abilities; **~t głupoty** the ultimate in stupidity; **to już jest ~t wszystkiego!** that's the limit! [4] (konferencja) summit; **~t NATO** the NATO summit; **rozmowy na ~cie** summit talks [5] (okres największego obciążenia) peak hours; **rozmowy poza ~tem są tańsze** during off-peak hours telephone calls are cheaper

szef *m* [1] (kierownik) the head, the chief; **~ kuchni** the head chef; **~ rządu** a. **gabinetu** the Prime Minister; **~ sztabu** Wojsk. the Chief of Staff [2] pot. (poufale do mężczyzny) guv pot.

szele|st *m* rustle; **poruszać się bez ~stu** to move noiselessly

szele|ścić *impf vi* *[osoba]* to rustle *[gazetą, banknotami]*; **liście ~szczą** leaves rustle

szel|ka *f* [1] (spódnicy, fartucha) shoulder strap; ~**ki** (spodni) braces GB, suspenders US; **spódnica na** ~**kach** a skirt with straps [2] (do transportu) strap [3] (dla psa, kota) ~**ki** harness; ~**ki do wózka (dziecinnego)** a safety harness for a pram

szelm|a *m, f* pot. rascal

szelmows|ki *adi.* pot. [1] *[spryt, wybryk]* roguish [2] (kokieteryjny) skittish; (urwisowski) impish; ~**ki uśmiech** a puckish smile

szep|nąć *pf* — **szep|tać** *impf vt* to whisper; ~**tać komuś do ucha** a. **na ucho** to whisper in sb's ear; ~**nąć komuś słówko za kimś/w jakiejś sprawie** to put in a good word for sb for sb/sth; ~**tać po kątach o czymś** to whisper in dark corners about sth

szep|t *m* [1] (bezdźwięczna mowa) whisper; **rozmawiać** ~**tem** to talk in a whisper; **sceniczny** a. **teatralny** ~**t** stage a. theatrical whisper [2] książk. (strumyka, fal, wiatru) murmur

szeptać *impf* → **szepnąć**

szereg [] *m* [1] (osób, rzeczy) row, line; **stać** ~**iem** a. **w** ~**u** to stand in a line; **stanąć w** ~**u** to line up; **wystąpić z** ~**u** to step out of line; **stanąć** a. **znaleźć się z kimś w jednym** ~**u** (poprzeć kogoś) to back sb up; (dorównać komuś) to get next to sb przen. [2] książk. (uporządkowany zbiór) sequence [] **szeregi** *plt* [1] Wojsk. ranks; **wstąpić w** ~**i armii** to join the ranks [2] (zbiorowość) ranks; ~**i partyjne** party ranks; **wykluczyć kogoś z** ~**ów (organizacji)** to expel sb from the ranks of an organization; **zwierać** ~**i** to close ranks

szeregow|iec *m* [1] Wojsk. private; **starszy** ~**iec** lance corporal GB, private 1st class US [2] pot. (dom) terrace(d) house GB, row house US

szermier|ka *f* [1] Sport fencing; (walka) swordplay, fencing; (umiejętność) swordsmanship; ~**ka słowna** przen. a verbal duel

szermierz *m* [1] Sport fencer [2] (władający białą bronią) swordsman [3] przen. champion; ~ **demokracji** a champion of democracy

szer|oki *adi. grad.* [1] *[rzeka, droga, ulica]* broad, wide; **mężczyzna** ~**oki w barach** a broad-shouldered man; **kapelusz z** ~**okim rondem** a wide-brimmed hat; **jezdnia** ~**oka na 5 metrów** a five metre wide road [2] (rozległy) *[panorama]* wide, vast; *[widok]* full; ~**oki otwór** a wide opening [3] (luźny) *[ubranie]* loose [4] przen. (wszechstronny) *[zainteresowania]* broad; *[plany]* extended; **badania zakrojone na** ~**oką skalę** broadly conceived research; **mieć** ~**okie uprawnienia** to have wide privileges

sze|roko *adv. grad.* [1] (na szerokość) wide; ~**roko rozstawić nogi** to spread one's legs; ~**roko otworzyć drzwi/okno** to open the door/window wide; **tu jest na pół metra** ~**roko** it's 50 centimetres wide here; **mieć oczy** ~**roko otwarte** to have one's eyes wide open; **uśmiechnąć się**

~**roko** to smile/yawn widely; ~**roko! (otwórz buzię)** open wide! [2] przen. (na dużą skalę) *[znany, reklamowany]* widely [3] przen. (rozwlekle) *[opisywać, opowiadać]* at length

szerokoś|ć *f* breadth, width; **rów** ~**ci (jednego) metra** a. **metrowej** ~**ci** a ditch one metre wide; **otworzyć okno na całą** ~**ć** to open a window wide ❑ ~**ć geograficzna** latitude ■ **pod każdą** ~**cią geograficzną** *[istnieć, być znanym]* worldwide

szersze|ń *m* hornet

szerz|yć *impf* [] *vt* [1] (propagować) to promote *[ideologię, zasady, hasła]* [2] (rozpowszechniać) to spread *[strach, demoralizację, plotki]* [] **szerzyć się** [1] (rozpowszechniać się) *[idea, poglądy]* to spread [2] (nasilać się) *[panika, terror, pożar]* to spread

szesnast|ka *f* [1] (liczba) sixteen [2] Muz. semiquaver GB, sixteenth note US

szesna|sty *num. ord.* sixteenth

szesna|ście *num.* sixteen

sześcian *m* [1] (bryła) cube [2] (trzecia potęga) cube; **pięć do** ~**u** five cubed; **podnieść dwa do** ~**u** to cube two

sześciokąt *m* hexagon

sześ|ć *num.* six

sześćdziesi|ąt *num.* sixty

sześćdziesiąt|ka *f* sixty

sześćdziesią|ty *num. ord.* sixtieth

sześćdziesięciolat|ek *m*, ~**ka** *f* sixty-year-old

sześ|ćset *num.* six hundred

sześćsetleci|e *n* [1] (rocznica) six-hundredth anniversary [2] (okres) six hundred years

sześćsetn|y *num. ord.* six hundredth

sz|ew *m* [1] (miejsce zszycia) seam; **pończochy ze szwem** stockings with seams [2] Med. stitch; **założyć komuś szew** to stitch up sb [3] Anat. suture, raphe [4] Techn. joint ■ **ubranie pęka (na nim) w szwach** his suit is too tight; **poczekalnia pękała w szwach** the waiting room was bursting at the seams

szew|c *m* (szyjący buty) shoemaker; (naprawiający buty) cobbler ■ **kląć jak** ~**c** to swear like a bargee a. trooper; ~**c bez butów chodzi** przysł. ≈ the shoemaker's children are ill-shod przysł.

szkarlatyn|a *f* scarlet fever

szkic *m* [1] (rysunek) sketch, rough drawing; ~ **do portretu** a sketch for the portrait [2] (zarys większej pracy) draft; **wstępny** ~ a rough sketch [3] (esej) sketch

szkic|ować *impf vt* [1] (rysować) to sketch *[kontury, plan budowli]*; ~**ować węglem** to sketch in charcoal; ~**ować z pamięci** to make sketches from memory [2] (przedstawiać pobieżnie) to chalk out *[projekt, plan]*

szkiele|t *m* ① (układ kostny) skeleton ② Techn. carcass, frame ③ (podstawa) outline ④ (pozostałość po zniszczeniu) skeleton, shell

szkieł|ko *n* glass; ~**ko od zegarka** a watch glass, a crystal

szklan|ka *f* ① (naczynie) glass; (zawartość) glass(ful) ② Bot. (drzewo) sour cherry (tree); (owoc) sour cherry ③ pot. (gołoledź) black ice, glaze US

szklan|y *adi.* ① [*dzbanek, tafla, paciorki*] glass ② przen. [*woda, połysk, dźwięk*] glassy; ~**y wzrok** glassy eyes

szklar|nia *f* greenhouse

szklarz *m* (wstawiający szyby) glazier

szkl|ić *impf* ▯ *vt* ① to glaze [*okno, drzwi*] ② Kulin. (lekko podsmażać) fry [sth] until transparent [*cebulę, czosnek*]
▯▯ **szklić się** to shine, to gleam; **jej oczy ~iły się od łez** her eyes shone with tears; **rosa ~iła się w słońcu** the dew sparkled in the sun
■ ~**ić komuś oczy** ≈ to pull the wool over sb's eyes

szkliw|o *n* ① (polewa, glazura) glaze ② (na zębach) enamel

szk|ło ▯ *n* ① (substancja) glass; **obrazki na ~le** pictures painted on glass; **pojemnik na ~ło** a bottle bank; **wyhodowali tę sałatę pod ~łem** they grew this lettuce in a frame; **rodzice wychowywali ją pod ~łem** przen. her parents gave her a sheltered upbringing ② (wyroby) glassware ③ (odłamek) piece of (broken) glass; **skaleczył się ~łem** he cut himself with a piece of glass ④ (soczewka) lens; ~**ła kontaktowe** contact lenses; ~**ło powiększające** a magnifying glass
▯▯ **szkła** *plt* pot. glasses

szk|oda ▯ *f* ① (strata) loss; ~**ody w ludziach** loss of life; **bez ~ody dla zdrowia** without detriment to sb's health; **wyrządzić** a. **spowodować ~odę** to do a. cause damage; ~**ody spowodowane przez burzę/mróz** storm/frost damage; **działać** a. ~**odę państwa** to act to the detriment of the state ② (w polu) **wygnać krowę ze ~ody** to chase away a stray cow
▯▯ *praed.* **jaka ~oda!** what a pity!; ~**oda zachodu** it's not worth the trouble; ~**oda wysiłku** it's a waste of effort; ~**oda mi jego matki** I feel sorry for his mother; ~**oda marnować czas na wyjaśnianie** it's a waste of time trying to explain it; ~**oda pieniędzy na...** it's no use wasting money on...; ~**oda gadać!** what can I say!; ~**oda łez!** nothing doing!; ~**oda słów** waste of breath a. words; ~**oda, że nie możesz zostać do jutra** I wish you could stay till tomorrow; ~**oda, że już się kończą wakacje** it's a pity a. it's a shame that the holidays are nearly over; **wielka ~oda, że...** it's too bad that...; **chodźmy już, bo ~oda każdej chwili** let's go now, let's not waste a single moment

szkodliw|y *adi.* harmful

szkodni|k *m* pest także przen.; ~**ki** vermin także przen.

szko|dzić *impf* *vi* to harm; ~**dzić ludzkiemu zdrowiu** to be harmful to humans; ~**dzić na wątrobę/nerki** to be bad for your liver/kidneys; **cebula mu ~dzi** onion disagrees with him; „**palenie ~dzi zdrowiu**" 'smoking can seriously damage your health'; **(nic) nie ~dzi!** never mind!, not at all!

szk|olić *impf* ▯ *vt* (uczyć) to train [*osoby, zwierzęta, głos*]; **pies ~olony na przewodnika** a trained guide dog
▯▯ **szkolić się** [*osoba*] to train, to undergo training

szkolnictw|o *n* education

szkoln|y *adi.* [*rok, boisko, podręcznik*] school; **kolega ~y** a schoolmate; **pomoce ~e** teaching aids

szk|oła *f* school także przen.; ~**oła podstawowa** primary school GB, elementary school US; ~**oła średnia** secondary school GB, high school US; ~**oła zawodowa** a vocational school; ~**oła językowa** a. **języków obcych** a language school; ~**oła tańca** a dance school; **chodzić do ~oły** to go to school; ~**oła flamandzka** (w sztuce) the Flemish school; ~**oła charakteru** a school of character; ~**oła życia** a school of hard knocks; ~**oła rodzenia** Med. antenatal classes
■ **dać komuś ~ołę** pot. to put sb through the mill; **dostać ~ołę** pot. to go through the mill

szlaban *m* ① (kolejowy, graniczny) barrier; **otworzyć** a. **podnieść ~** to raise the barrier; **opuścić** a. **zamknąć ~** to lower the barrier ② pot. (kara) **mieć ~ (na wychodzenie z domu)** to be grounded pot.

szlachcian|ka *f* Hist. ≈ gentlewoman

szlachcic *m* Hist. ≈ country gentleman, nobleman

szlachetnie ▯ *adv. grad.* ① [*postępować*] nobly; [*zachowywać się*] gentlemanly ② [*wyglądać, brzmieć*] refined
▯▯ *adv.* ~ **urodzony** of noble birth

szlachetn|y ▯ *adi. grad.* ① [*osoba, czyn, idea*] noble ② [*prostota, elegancja, linia*] refined; ~**e rysy twarzy** nobly chiseled features
▯▯ *adi.* (wysokogatunkowy) [*wino*] vintage; [*odmiana owoców, kwiatów*] noble

szlach|ta *f* (stan) (the) gentry; (grupa) the gentry

szlafrok *m* dressing gown, wrapper US

szlak *m* ① (droga naturalna) way, route ② (wytyczona trasa) trail; ~ **turystyczny/górski** a tourist/mountain trail; ~ **bojowy** książk. the combat trail; **nie zbaczajcie ze ~u!** don't stray off the trail! ③ przen. (sposób postępowania) course ④ (motyw dekoracyjny) border ⑤ Zool. migratory pattern

szlam *m* ① (muł) slime ② (osad) sludge, silt

szlif|ować *impf* *vt* ① Techn. to grind [*metal*]; to sand [*drewno*]; to cut [*kamienie szlachetne, szkło*] ② przen. to polish [*formę, język obcy, dzieło*]

szloch *m* sobbing; **tłumić** ∼ to choke back one's sobs

szmal *m* pot. dough pot.; **to będzie kosztowało kupę** ∼**u** it'll cost a bomb

szmarag|d *m* emerald

szma|ta *f* ① (gałgan) rag; ∼**ty** pot. (o ubraniu) rags ② pot., pejor. (o osobie) scumbag pot.; (o gazecie) rag pot., pejor

szmelc *m* pot. ① (złom) scrap (metal) ② (rupieć) junk; **to radio nadaje się tylko na** ∼ this radio is only fit for the scrap heap

szme|r *m* ① (liści) rustle; (deszczu) patter; (strumyka, rozmów) murmur; ∼**r niezadowolenia** a murmur of dissatisfaction ② Med. (w płucach, w sercu) murmur

szmin|ka *f* lipstick; (do charakteryzacji) greasepaint

szmi|ra *f* pot., pejor. (film, obraz) rubbish; (powieść) pulp

sznu|r *m* ① (powróz) string; (lina) rope; ∼**r do bielizny** a washing a. clothes line; ∼**r pereł** a string of pearls ② przen. (szereg) string, line; ∼**r samochodów** a string of cars; ∼**r żurawi** a string of cranes ③ (przewód do urządzeń elektrycznych) cord, flex GB; ∼**r od żelazka** iron cord

sznur|ek *m* string

sznur|ować *impf vt* to lace up *[buty]*
■ ∼**ować usta** (zaciskać) to purse one's lips; (mówić mało) to be taciturn

sznurowad|ło *n* (shoe)lace, shoestring US

sznurowan|y *adi. [buty, kamizelka, gorset]* laced

szofe|r *m* chauffeur

szofer|ka *f* (kabina) cab

szok *m* shock

szok|ować *impf vt* to shock

szop *m* Zool. raccoon, coon US; ∼ **pracz** common raccoon

szop|a *f* ① (niewielki budynek) shed; ∼**a na narzędzia** a tool shed ② (czupryna) a shock of hair

szop|ka *f* ① (betlejemska) nativity scene, crib GB, crèche US ② (jasełka) nativity play; (satyryczna) satirical puppet show *(presented on New Year's day)* ③ pot. (niepoważna sytuacja) farce

szor|ować *impf* ❶ *vt* (myć) to scrub *[garnki, podłogę]*; to scour *[zlew, kuchenkę]*
❷ *vi* (trzeć) to scrape
❸ **szorować się** (myć się) to scrub oneself
■ ∼**uj stąd!** beat it!

szorst|ki *adi. [skóra, ręka, materiał, papier]* rough; *[faktura, wełna, płótno]* coarse; *[osoba, odpowiedź, głos]* gruff

szorstko *adv.* ① (chropawo) roughly, coarsely; ∼ **wyprawiona skóra** rough (tanned) hide ② (niedelikatnie) *[odpowiadać, traktować]* brusquely, harshly

szort|y *plt* shorts

szos|a *f* highway

szowinizm *m* chauvinism; jingoism pejor.

szóst|ka *f* ① (cyfra) six ② (ocena szkolna) ≈ starred A

szó|sty *num. ord.* sixth

szpach|la *f* (do wygładzania) spatula; (do uszczelniania) putty knife

szpa|da *f* sword; Sport épée

szpad|el *m* spade

szpadzi|sta *m*, ∼**stka** *f* épéist, épée fencer

szpaga|t *m* ① (sznurek) cord, string ② Sport splits

szpak *m* starling

szpale|r *m* lane; ∼**r dębów** an avenue of oak trees; ∼**r wojska** a double file of soldiers; **utworzyć** a. **uformować** ∼**r** to form two rows

szpan *m* pot. swank pot.

szpa|ra *f* slit, gap; **mieć** ∼**rę między zębami** to have a gap between one's teeth; **zostaw** ∼**rę w drzwiach** leave the door open a crack; **zajrzał przez** ∼**rę w firankach** he peeped through a slit in the curtains; **przecisnął się przez** ∼**rę między deskami** he squeezed through a gap between the planks

szparag *m* Bot., Kulin. asparagus

szparga|ł *m* ① (skrawek papieru) scrap of paper ② (rzecz niepotrzebna) junk, rubbish

szpera|ć *impf vi* to poke around, to browse (**w czymś/po czymś** through sth); to rummage (**w czymś/po czymś** in sth); ∼**ła w torbie w poszukiwaniu chusteczki** she rummaged in her bag for a handkerchief

szpic[1] *m* ① (buta, noża) tip; **dekolt w** ∼ a V-neck ② (ozdoba choinkowa) Christmas tree spire

szpic[2] *m* (pies) spitz, Pomeranian

szpicel *m* pot. snooper pot.

szpicl|ować *impf vt* pot. to snoop pot. (**kogoś** on sb)

szpie|g *m* spy

szpieg|ować *impf vt* to spy (**kogoś/coś** on sb/ sth); ∼**ować na rzecz kogoś** to spy for sb

szpik *m* ∼ **(kostny)** (bone) marrow
■ **do** ∼**u kości** *[przemarznięty]* to the marrow; *[uczciwy, zły]* to the core

szpil|ka *f* ① (do przypinania) pin; **spiąć coś** ∼**kami** to pin sth (together); **przypiąć coś** ∼**ką do czegoś** to pin sth to sth; **ścisk w pokoju był taki, że** ∼**ki by nie wetknął** the room was jam-packed with people pot.; **książka nie** ∼**ka, nie mogła tak po prostu zginąć** the book can't have just disappeared ② (ozdoba) pin; ∼**ka do włosów** a hairpin; ∼**ka do krawata** a stick pin ③ Bot. needle ④ (w namiocie) tent hook ⑤ (obcas) spike a. stiletto heel; ∼**ki** (buty) stilettos pot.; **nosić** ∼**ki** to wear high heels
■ **siedzieć jak na** ∼**kach** to be on tenterhooks; **wbijać** a. **wsadzać komuś** ∼**ki** to needle sb

szpinak *m* spinach

szpital *m* hospital; **być w** ∼**u** to be in hospital

szpon *m* talon; **wpaść w czyjeś** ∼**y** przen. to fall into sb's clutches; **być w** ∼**ach nałogu** przen. to be in the grip of addiction

szprot|ka *f* Zool. sprat; ∼**ki w oleju** sprats in oil

szpry|cha f spoke
szpul|ka f ~ka nici a reel of cotton
szram|a f scar; ~a po ranie a scar from a wound
szron m (lodowy osad) (hoar) frost; **pokryć się** ~em to frost up; **trawa pokryta** ~em frosty grass
sztab m ① Wojsk. staff; ~ **generalny** the general staff; **szef** ~u the Chief of Staff ② (zespół) team; ~ **doradców** a team of advisors; ~ **wyborczy** a campaign team
sztab|a f ① (do drzwi, bramy) bar; **zamknąć drzwi na** ~ę to bar a door ② (złota, srebra) bar, ingot; **złoto w** ~ach gold bullion
sztache|ta f (drewniana) board; (metalowa) rail
sztafe|ta f Sport ① (wyścig) relay (race) ② (drużyna) relay team
sztalu|ga f easel
sztanda|r m flag, banner; **pod** ~rem międzynarodowej solidarności przen. under the banner of international solidarity
sztan|ga f ① Sport barbell; **podnieść** ~gę to lift a weight ② (sztaba) bar
sztangi|sta m, ~**stka** f Sport weightlifter
sztorm m storm; **wiatr o sile** ~u a storm
sztormiak m oilskins
sztruks m corduroy, cord; ~y (spodnie) corduroys, cords
sztućc|e plt cutlery, flatware US; ~**óce do sałatek** salad servers
sztucz|ka f ① (popis) trick; **karciana** ~ka a card trick; ~**ki magiczne** magic; **robić/pokazywać** ~ki to do a. perform/show tricks ② (podstęp) trick; **prawnicze** ~ki legal tricks
sztucznie [] adv. grad. [uśmiechać się] falsely; **zachowywać się** ~ to behave in an unnatural way; **jego akcent brzmi** ~ his accent sounds fake [] adv. artificially; ~ **barwiony** artificially coloured; ~ **karmić dzieci** to bottle-feed children
sztuczn|y [] adi. grad. [osoba, zachowanie, atmosfera] artificial; [postać, bohater] artificial, cardboard; [uśmiech, wesołość] false, fake [] adi. [kwiat, śnieg, futro, złoto] imitation; [jezioro, zapłodnienie, nawozy] artificial; [wąsy, oko, ząb] false, fake; ~**e oddychanie** artificial respiration; **robić** ~y tłok wokół kogoś [złodzieje] to crowd around sb
sztu|ka f ① (twórczość artystyczna) art, the arts; ~**ka ludowa** folk art; ~**ki piękne** the fine arts; ~**ka filmowa** film-making; ~**ka użytkowa** applied art ② (umiejętność) art; ~**ki walki** martial arts; **błąd w** ~**ce** a malpractice; **cała** ~**ka polega na tym, żeby...** the trick is to... ③ (wyczyn) feat; **to była nie lada** ~**ka** it was no mean feat; **to nie** a. **żadna** ~**ka stać z boku i krytykować** it's easy to stand by and criticize; **wielka mi** ~**ka!** iron. big deal! ④ Teatr. play ⑤ (egzemplarz) piece; **dwanaście** ~k **talerzy** twelve plates; **dziesięć** ~k **bydła** ten head of cattle; **sześć** ~k **bagażu/bielizny** six pieces of

luggage/underwear; ~**ka mięsa** Kulin. piece of boiled beef; **sprzedawać coś na** ~ki to sell sth per item; **dwa złote za** ~kę two zlotys apiece; **to twarda** ~ka pot. (o osobie) he/she is a tough one
szturch|nąć pf — **szturch|ać** impf vt to prod [osobę]; (dla zwrócenia uwagi) to nudge [osobę]; ~**nąć kogoś w bok** to poke a. dig sb in the ribs
szturm m storm także przen.; ~ **na pałac** the storming of the palace; **przypuścić** ~ **na pozycje nieprzyjaciela** to storm the enemy defences; ~**em** by storm; **wedrzeć się** ~**em dokądś** to storm one's way into sth; **ruszyli** ~**em do drzwi** przen. they rushed towards the door
szturm|ować impf vt to storm także przen.; ~**ować bramy stadionu** to storm one's way into a stadium; ~**ować do drzwi** to rush at the door
sztyf|t m (gwóźdź) sparable; (drewniany) pin; **klej w** ~**cie** a glue stick
sztyle|t m (broń) dagger, poniard
sztywni|eć impf vi ① [ręce, nogi] to become stiff ② przen. (stawać się chłodnym, oschłym) to stiffen
sztywn|o adv. grad. stiffly
sztywn|y adi. grad. stiff także przen.; **białka należy ubić na** ~**ą pianę** whip the egg whites until stiff; **być** ~**ym z przerażenia** to be scared stiff; ~**e przepisy** stiff regulations; **moi sąsiedzi są trochę** ~**i** my neighbours are a bit starchy ■ **aleja** a. **park** ~**ych** pot., żart. cemetery
szufel|ka f (do węgla) shovel; (do śmieci) dustpan; (do cukru, kasz) scoop
szufla|da f drawer ■ **pisać do** ~**dy** (dla siebie) to write for one's own pleasure; (nie mogąc publikować) to write without hope of publication
szufladk|ować impf vt to tag, to pigeonhole; ~**ować ludzi na dobrych i złych** to divide people into good and bad
szuj|a m, f pot. scumbag pot.
szuka|ć impf vt ① (starać się znaleźć) to look for; ~**ć czegoś w kieszeniach** a. **po kieszeniach** to search (one's) pockets for sth; ~**ć czegoś po omacku** to grope for sth; ~**ć czegoś w słowniku** to look sth up in the dictionary; ~**ć słów/ odpowiedzi** przen. to grope for words/an answer ② (chcieć) to seek [sławy, pomocy, pocieszenia]
szule|r m cheat
szum m ① (odgłos) swoosh; ~ **morskich fal** the swoosh of surf; ~ **deszczu** the beating down of rain; ~ **taśmy** the hiss of the tape; ~ **kamer** the whirr of cameras; ~ **głosów** the murmur of voices; ~ **rozmów** the hum a. buzz of conversation; ~ **samochodów** the drone of traffic; ~ **silnika** the drone of the car engine; **dokuczliwy** ~ **w skroniach** an annoying buzzing noise in one's head ② (rozgłos) fuss; **narobić** ~u to make a fuss; **o co tyle** ~u? what's all the fuss a. noise about? ■ ~ **informacyjny** Dzien. information noise

szum|ieć *impf vi* [1] *[czajnik, odkurzacz, wentylator]* to hum; ~**iało mu w głowie/w uszach** there was a buzzing noise in his head/ears; **w klasie** ~**iało jak w ulu** the class was buzzing with activity [2] (o winie, piwie) to bubble, to sparkle

szur|nąć *pf* — **szur|ać** *impf vi* [1] (przesunąć) to shuffle; ~**ać butami** to shuffle one's feet [2] (zaszeleścić) to scrape; ~**ały odsuwane krzesła** the chairs scraped across the floor

szuwar|y *plt* rush

szwag|ier *m* brother-in-law

szwagier|ka *f* sister-in-law

szwenda|ć się *impf v refl.* pot. to loiter

szwind|el *m* pot. swindle

szyb *m* mineshaft; ~ **naftowy** oil well; ~ **wentylacyjny** air shaft

szyb|a *f* (window)pane; **przednia** ~**a samochodu** the windscreen GB, the windshield US; **tylna** ~**a samochodu** the rear window; ~**a pancerna** armoured a. bulletproof glass

szyb|ki *adi. grad.* [1] *[samochód, pociąg, winda]* fast; *[posiłek, obiad]* hurried; *[drukarka, faks]* high-speed; *[puls, oddech, wzrost]* rapid, fast; ~**kie czytanie** speed-reading; ~**ki rozwój** a mushroom growth [2] *[odpowiedź, koniec]* quick; **życzyć komuś** ~**kiego powrotu do zdrowia** to wish sb a speedy recovery

szyb|ko *adv. grad.* [1] (prędko) *[mówić, pisać, biec]* fast; ~**ko się uczy** he's a quick learner [2] (zaraz) *[odpisać, odpowiedzieć, zdecydować się]* quickly; **jak najszybciej** as quickly as possible; ~**ko zorientował się w sytuacji** he swiftly got a grasp of the situation [3] (z małymi przerwami) *[oddychać]* rapidly

szybkoś|ć *f* speed; velocity książk.; **z** ~**cią 100 km na godzinę** at a rate of a 100 km an hour; ~**ć decyzji jest tu konieczna** a speedy decision is vital in this case

szybkowa|r *m* pressure cooker; **gotować w** ~**rze** to pressure-cook

szyb|ować *impf vi* (o szybowcu, ptakach) to glide, to soar; **obłoki** ~**ują po niebie** książk. clouds are floating across the sky

szybow|iec *m* glider

szy|ć *impf vt* [1] (łączyć nićmi) to sew; **nie lubię** ~**ć** I don't like sewing; ~**ć garnitur na miarę** to tailor a suit [2] pot. (zlecić uszycie) to have [sth] made [3] Med. to sew, to stitch *[ranę, przetokę]*

szydeł|ko *n* a crochet hook; **robić** ~**kiem szalik** to crochet a scarf

szyderc|a *m* scoffer, jeerer

szyderstw|o *n* sneer

szy|dzić *impf vi* to sneer (**z kogoś/czegoś** at sb/sth); to jeer (**z kogoś/czegoś** at sb/sth); ~**dzić z kogoś w żywe oczy** to deride sb openly

szyf|r *m* code, cipher; **złamać** ~**r** to break a. crack a code; **podali tę wiadomość** ~**rem** they sent this message in code a. cipher

szyfr|ować *impf vt* to encode *[wiadomość, informacje]*; ~**owanie danych** data encryption

szy|ja *f* [1] (część ciała) neck; **nosić coś na** ~**i** to wear sth round one's neck; **rzucić się komuś na** ~**ję** to fling a. throw one's arms around sb's neck; **wyciągać** ~**ję** to crane one's neck [2] (butelki, karafki) neck

■ **dawać sobie w** ~**ję** pot. to have a drop of the hard stuff; **mieć nogi (aż) po samą** ~**ję** to be all legs

szyj|ka *f* [1] (butelki, karafki) neck [2] Anat. ~**ka macicy** cervix; **rak** ~**ki macicy** cervical cancer [3] Stomat. the neck of a tooth

szyk[1] *m* (elegancja) chic; **mieć** ~ to have chic; **zadać** ~**u** pot. to cut a fine figure; **lubi czasem zadać** ~**u** she likes to dress up a bit from time to time

szyk[2] *m* [1] Wojsk. formation, array; ~ **bojowy** battle order; **stać w zwartym** ~**u** to stand in close a. compact formation; **w** ~**u defiladowym** in parade formation [2] Jęz. word order; ~ **przestawny** inversion

■ **pokrzyżować** a. **pomieszać komuś** ~**i** to throw a spanner in the works of sb, to put a spoke in sb's wheel

szykan|ować *impf vt* to persecute

szyk|ować *impf* **I** *vt* pot. [1] (planować) to plan *[napad na bank, niespodziankę]* [2] (robić) to knock up pot. *[śniadanie, obiad, kolację]* [3] (przygotowywać) to groom (**kogoś do czegoś** sb for sth); ~**ować pannę młodą do ślubu** to dress the bride for the wedding; ~**ują ją do olimpiady** they've been training her for the Olympic Games

II szykować się [1] (przygotowywać się) to gear up (**do czegoś** for sth); ~**ować się do wyjścia** to groom oneself carefully; ~**ować się na wyprawę** to be getting ready for an expedition; ~**uje się obława na kieszonkowców** they're planning a raid on the pickpockets; **już się na ciebie** ~**ują, podpadłeś im** your name's in the mud, they're going a. they're out to get you [2] (zapowiadać się) to be in prospect; **nie** ~**ują się żadne zmiany** there're no changes in the pipeline

szyl|d *m* sign; ~**d sklepu** the shop-sign; **działać pod** ~**dem czegoś** przen. to act under the aegis of sth

szympans *m* chimpanzee

szyn|a *f* [1] (część toru) track, rail [2] (do firanek) rail, runner [3] Med. splint [4] Stomat. braces

szyn|ka *f* Kulin. ham

szysz|ka *f* [1] Bot. cone; ~**ka chmielowa** hop [2] pot. (o osobie) bigwig, big cheese pot.

Ś

ścian|a *f* [1] (budowli) wall; ~**a działowa/nośna** a partition/load-bearing wall; ~**a szczytowa** a gable end; **ślepa** ~**a** a blank wall [2] (bok) side, wall [3] przen. (ognia, milczenia) wall [4] (część skały) face
■ **w czterech** ~**ach** within four walls; **postawić kogoś pod** ~**ą** (nie dać wyboru) to not give sb a choice; **zblednąć jak** ~**a** pot. to become a. go as white as a sheet

ściąć *pf* — **ścinać** *impf* [] *vt* [1] to cut *[kwiaty, włosy]*; to cut down *[drzewo]*; to mow *[trawę]*; pot. to knock down *[znak drogowy, słup]* [2] to coagulate *[krew, sos]*; to clot *[krew]*; to curdle *[mleko, białko]*; *[mróz]* to freeze over *[rzekę]* [3] (zabić) to behead, to decapitate [4] Sport (w piłce siatkowej) to spike; (w tenisie) to smash
[] **ściąć się** — **ścinać się** [1] *[krew]* to clot; *[galaretka, beton]* to set; *[krew, sos]* to coagulate; *[mleko, jajko]* to curdle; *[rzeka]* to freeze over [2] pot. (pokłócić się) to have a tiff pot.
■ **krew ścina się w żyłach na ten widok** the sight makes your blood curdle a. run cold

ścią|ga *f* pot. crib pot.

ściągacz *m* (ścieg) ribbing; **rękaw ze** ~**em** a cuff knitted in rib

ściągać *impf* → **ściągnąć**

ściągaw|ka *f* pot. crib pot.

ściąg|nąć *pf* — **ściąg|ać** *impf* [] *vt* [1] (zabrać) to whip away *[obrus]*; to pull down *[flagę]* [2] (zdjąć) to pull off *[buty, rękawiczki]* [3] (ścisnąć) to tighten (**coś czymś** sth with sth) [4] (przyciągnąć) to attract; **wystawa** ~**nęła tłumy** the exhibition drew crowds [5] (zmarszczyć) to contract; ~**nąć brwi** to knit one's brow; **twarz** ~**nięta z bólu** a face tightened from pain [6] pot. (odpisać) to crib pot. (**od kogoś** from sb)
[] *vi* [1] (zejść się) to gather [2] (dotrzeć) to make it
[] **ściągać się** — **ściągnąć się** [1] (ścisnąć się) to tighten (**czymś** with sth) [2] (skurczyć się) to contract
■ ~**nąć na siebie czyjś gniew** to incur sb's anger; ~**ać na siebie kłopoty** to get into trouble; ~**nąć kogoś z łóżka** pot. to pull sb out of bed

ścieg *m* stitch

ściek [] *m* sewer; ~ **uliczny** street gutter
[] **ścieki** *plt* sewage, waste

ście|knąć *pf* — **ście|kać** *impf vi [płyn]* to dribble

ścielić *impf* → **słać²**

ściemni|ć *pf* — **ściemni|ać** *impf* [] *vt* to dim *[światło]*
[] **ściemnić się** — **ściemniać się** *[scena]* to darken; ~**a się** it's getting dark

ściemni|eć *pf vi* to darken, to blacken; ~**ało** it got dark

ścienn|y *adi. [zegar, kalendarz, płytki]* wall; **malowidło** ~**e** a mural

ścierać *impf* → **zetrzeć**

ścier|ka *f* (do naczyń) cloth, tea towel; (do podłogi) floor cloth; (do kurzu) duster

ściernisk|o *n* stubble field

ściern|y *adi. [materiał]* abrasive

ścierp|ieć *pf vt* to bear *[osobę, zachowanie]*; **nie mogę tego** ~**ieć** I can't stand a. bear it

ścierp|nąć *pf vi* to go numb; ~**nąć na myśl o czymś** przen. to go numb at the thought of sth; **skóra mi** ~**ła na ten widok** przen. that sight made my flesh creep

ścieśni|ć *pf* — **ścieśni|ać** *impf vt [grupa]* to close up *[szeregi]*

ścież|ka *f* [1] (dróżka) path; (leśna) track; (parkowa) alley; ~**ka rowerowa** a bicycle lane; ~**ka zdrowia** Sport fitness trail [2] książk. (sposób postępowania) path; ~**ki życia** paths of life [3] (taśmy filmowej) track [4] Komput. path; ~**ka dostępu** (access) path

ścięg|no *n* sinew, tendon

ścię|ty *adi. [czubek, róg]* truncated

ściga|ć *impf* [] *vt* [1] (gonić) to chase [2] Prawo to prosecute *[przestępstwo]*; ~**ć kogoś listami gończymi** to have a warrant out for sb
[] **ścigać się** [1] (gonić) to race (**z kimś** sb) [2] pot. (współzawodniczyć) to compete (**z kimś o coś** against sb for sth)
■ ~**ć kogoś/coś oczami** a. **wzrokiem** to follow sb/sth with one's eyes; **zły los mnie** ~ bad luck follows me

ścinać *impf* → **ściąć**

ścin|ek *m* (materiału) snip; (papieru) trimming

ścisk *m* press; **w sali panuje straszny** ~ there's a crush in the hall

ściskać¹ *impf* → **ścisnąć¹**

ściska|ć² *impf* [] *vt* to hug; ~**m was mocno** (w liście) love and kisses
[] **ściskać się** to hug each other
■ ~**ć czyjąś rękę** a. **dłoń** to clasp sb's hand

ści|sły [] *adi. grad.* [1] *[stosunki, współpraca]* close; *[związek, zależność]* direct [2] *[dane]* accurate [3] *[czołówka, elita]* narrow; ~**słe grono** a select group

[] *adi.* [1] *[myślenie, umysł]* scientific; **nauki** ~**słe** science [2] *[dyscyplina, tajemnica]* rigorous; *[dieta]* strict

ści|snąć[1] *pf* — **ści|skać**[1] *impf vt* [1] (zgnieść) to press (**coś czymś** sth with sth) [2] (opasać) to bind (**czymś** with sth) [3] (uchwycić) to grip
■ ~**ska mnie za gardło** a. **w gardle** I have a lump in my throat; ~**ska ją w żołądku** a. **w dołku** a. **w środku** she has a twinge of anxiety/fear; **mróz** ~**ska** it's freezing; **serce mi się** ~**ska** my heart bleeds

ści|snąć[2] *pf vt* to squeeze; ~**snąć książki na półce** to squeeze books on a shelf

ścisz|yć *pf* — **ścisz|ać** *impf vt* to turn [sth] down *[radio]*; to lower *[głos]*; to muffle *[śmiech]*

ściśle [] *adv. grad.* [1] (blisko) closely także przen. [2] (dokładnie) exactly, precisely; ~ **mówiąc** strictly speaking

[] *adv.* [1] *[rozumować, wyrażać się]* precisely [2] *[przestrzegać, wypełniać]* strictly; ~ **tajne** strictly confidential

śla|d *m* [1] (odcisk) track (**w** a. **na czymś** on sth); (stopy) footprint, footmark [2] (pozostałość) (po ugryzieniu, oparzeniu) mark; (budowli) remains; ~**d po trądziku/ ospie** a pockmark; ~**d po uderzeniu** a weal [3] przen. (cywilizacji, uczucia) vestige [4] (odrobina) trace
■ **ani** ~**du kogoś/czegoś** not a sign of sb/sth; **iść** a. **podążać w** ~**d za kimś** to follow sb's tracks; **iść** ~**dem** a. **w** ~**dy kogoś** a. **wstępować w czyjeś** ~**dy** to follow in sb's footsteps; **naprowadzić kogoś na** ~**d** to give sb a clue; **przepaść** a. **zaginąć** a. **zniknąć bez** ~**du** to vanish into the blue

ślaz *m* mallow

ślazow|y *adi.* marshmallow

śledcz|y [] *adi.* *[oficer]* investigating; *[areszt, postępowanie]* investigative

[] **śledcz|y** *m*, ~**a** *f* examining magistrate

śle|dzić *impf vt* [1] (tropić) *[przestępcę]* to stalk *[ofiarę]*; to track *[osobę, zwierzę]*; *[wywiadowca]* to follow *[przestępcę]* [2] (obserwować) to track *[tor samolotu, komety]*; to follow through *[teorię, argumenty]*; to check on *[postępy]*; to keep up with *[modę, nowinki]*

śledzion|a *f* spleen

śledztw|o *n* investigation; inquiry (**przeciwko komuś/czemuś** against sb/sth); **wszcząć/umorzyć** ~**o** to open/close an inquiry

śle|dź *m* [1] Zool. herring [2] pot. (przy namiocie) tent peg
■ **gnieść się** a. **tłoczyć się jak** ~**dzie w beczce** pot. to be packed a. crammed in like sardines

ślepi|e *n* eye; **błysnąć** ~**ami** to leer (**na kogoś/ coś** at sb/sth); **wybałuszać na kogoś/coś** ~**a** to gape at sb/sth

ślep|iec *m* blind man

ślep|nąć *impf vi* to go blind

ślepo [] *adv.* przen. blindly

[] **na ślepo** pot. [1] **iść na** ~ to grope one's way [2] *[strzelać]* randomly

ślepo|ta *f* blindness także przen.; **kurza** ~**ta** night blindness

ślep|y [] *adi.* [1] (niewidzący) blind; ~**y na jedno oko** blind in one eye; **być** ~**ym na coś** przen. to be blind to sth [2] przen. *[miłość, posłuszeństwo]* blind; **być** ~**ym naśladowcą kogoś** to imitate sb blindly [3] przen. *[przypadek, przeznaczenie]* pure [4] *[ulica, szyb]* blind; ~**y zaułek** a blind alley [5] *[ściana, mur]* blank

[] **ślep|y** *m*, ~**a** *f* blind person
■ **znaleźć się w** ~**ym zaułku** a. **w** ~**ej uliczce** to reach a deadlock a. an impasse a. a dead end

ślęcz|eć *impf vi* pot. to pore (**nad czymś** over sth)

śliczn|y *adv. grad.* lovely

ślimak *m* [1] Zool. snail; (bez skorupy) slug [2] (motyw dekoracyjny) volute [3] (droga) spiral ramp

ślin|a *f* saliva

ślinia|k *m* bib

śli|nić *impf* [] *vt* to lick, to moisten [sth] with saliva
[] **ślinić się** *[niemowlę]* to slobber; *[zwierzę]* to salivate; *[chory]* to dribble saliva

ślis|ki *adi.* [1] *[powierzchnia]* slippery [2] pot., przen. *[sprawa, interes]* fishy; *[osoba]* slippery; *[dowcip]* slimy; *[temat]* tricky

śliw|a *f* (drzewo) plum tree

śliw|ka *f* [1] (drzewo) plum tree; (owoc) plum; **suszone** ~**ki** prunes [2] pot. (siniak) bruise, bump
■ **wpaść jak** ~**ka w kompot** pot. to get into hot water

ślizga|ć się *impf v refl.* [1] (po śliskiej powierzchni) *[osoba]* to slither, to slide; *[pojazd, koła]* to skid [2] (po lodzie) *[osoba]* to skate; *[bojer]* to plane

ślizgaw|ka *f* (lodowisko) skating rink, ice rink; **jezdnia zamieniła się w** ~**kę** the road turned into an ice rink

ślub [] *m* (małżeństwo) marriage a. wedding (ceremony); ~ **kościelny** a church wedding; ~ **cywilny** a civil marriage; **dać komuś** ~ to marry sb; **wziąć** ~ **z kimś** to marry sb

[] **śluby** *plt* vows; ~**y czystości/posłuszeństwa** the vows of chastity/obedience; ~**y zakonne** monastic vows; **złożyć** ~**y** to make a. take vows
■ ~**u z tobą nie brałem** pot. there is nothing to bind us

ślub|ować *pf, impf vt* to vow

ślubowa|nie *n* oath, pledge

ślusarz *m* locksmith

śluz *m* mucus

śluz|a *f* lock, sluice

śluzów|ka *f* mucous membrane

śmi|ać się *impf v refl.* [1] (okazywać wesołość) to laugh (**z kogoś/czegoś** at sb/sth) [2] (szydzić) to mock

(z kogoś/czegoś at sb/sth) ③ (lekceważyć) to laugh **(z czegoś** at sth)

■ **dobrze** a. **łatwo ci się** ~**ać** it's all very well for you to laugh; **ten się** ~**eje, kto się śmieje ostatni** przysł. he who laughs last laughs longest przysł.

śmiał|ek *m* daredevil

śmi|ało ▯ *adv. grad.* confidently, boldly

▯▯ *adv.* (very) well, easily; **w tym pokoju** ~**ało zmieści się piętnaście osób** this room can easily accommodate fifteen people

▯▯▯ *inter.* **proszę wejść,** ~**ało!** go ahead, come in!

śmi|ały *adi. grad.* ① *[osoba]* bold ② *[spojrzenie, zachowanie]* confident ③ *[pomysł]* daring; ~**ałe przedsięwzięcie** an enterprising venture ④ *[dekolt, zdjęcie]* bold ⑤ *[ruch]* bold

śmiech *m* ① (wyrażanie radości) laugh, laughter; **wybuch** a. **salwa** ~**u** a burst a. peal of laughter; **dusić się ze** ~**u** a. **od** ~**u** to choke with laughter; **pękać ze** ~**u** to laugh till one's sides ache; **konać** a. **umierać ze** ~**u** to die laughing a. of laughter; **ryczeć ze** ~**u** to roar with laughter; **wybuchnąć** ~**em** to burst out laughing; **zwijać** a. **skręcać się ze** ~**u** to be in convulsions; **wzbudzić** a. **wywołać** ~ to get a. raise a laugh; **moje uwagi zbyła** ~**em** she laughed off my remarks; **nie mogłem się powstrzymać od** ~**u** I couldn't keep a straight face ② (drwina) mockery, ridicule; **narazić się na czyjś** ~ to be held up to ridicule

■ ~**u warte!** that's ridiculous!

śmieciar|ka *f* pot. dustcart GB, garbage truck US

śmieciarz *m* pot. ① (pracownik) dustman, refuse collector GB, garbage man US ② pejor. scavenger

śmie|cić *impf vi* to make a mess; **nie** ~**ćcie na podłogę!** don't litter the floor!

śmie|ć[1] *m* ① (odpadek) (a piece of) rubbish; ~**cie** rubbish GB, garbage US; **wyrzucić coś do** ~**ci** to throw out sth with the rubbish ② pot., pejor. (rzecz bez wartości) (a piece of) rubbish

■ **być** a. **znaleźć się na własnych** ~**ciach** pot. to be at home a. under one's own roof; **wrócić na stare** ~**ci** pot. to return to one's humble abode a. old stamping ground

śmi|eć[2] *impf vi* książk. to dare; ~**eć coś zrobić** to dare (to) do sth; **jak** ~**esz!** how dare you!

śmier|ć *f* death; **blady jak** ~**ć** as white as a sheet; **przyjaźń na** ~**ć i życie** przen. a lifelong friendship; **walka na** ~**ć i życie** mortal combat; **aż do** ~**ci** for the rest of one's life; **na** ~**ć zapomniałam!** pot. I clean forgot!; **skazać kogoś na** ~**ć** to sentence sb to death; **zapić się na** ~**ć** to drink oneself to death

■ **iść** a. **pójść na** ~**ć** to go to one's (almost certain) death

śmierdząc|y *adi.* pot., pejor. ~**y leń** a lazy bum pot.; ~**y tchórz** a stinking coward

śmier|dzieć *impf vi* pot. ① (cuchnąć) to stink **(czymś** of sth); **w tym pokoju** ~**dzi** this room stinks

② przen. *[przedsięwzięcie, sprawa]* to smell, to stink; **coś mi tu** ~**dzi** I smell a rat here pot.

śmiertelnie *adv. [ranny]* fatally, mortally; *[chory]* terminally; *[przerażony, poważny]* dead; *[blady]* deathly; *[obrażony]* mortally; ~ **kogoś przestraszyć** to frighten sb to death; **on mnie** ~ **nudzi** he bores me stiff a. rigid; **on jest w niej** ~ **zakochany** he's madly in love with her

śmiertelni|k *m* książk. mortal; **zwykły** ~**k** przen. everyman

śmiertelnoś|ć *f* mortality (rate), death rate

śmierteln|y *adi. [choroba]* fatal; *[trucizna]* lethal; *[drgawki, ofiara, niebezpieczeństwo, wróg]* mortal; *[zmęczenie, powaga, strach]* deadly

śmiesznie *adv. grad.* ① (zabawnie) *[wyglądać]* funny; *[zachowywać się]* amusingly; (niepoważnie) ridiculously ② pot. (absurdalnie) ludicrously; ~ **niska cena** a ludicrously low price; ~ **łatwe zadanie** a ridiculously easy task a. problem; **zarabiał tam** ~ **małe pieniądze** he worked there for a pittance a. for pennies

śmieszn|y *adi. grad. [mina, zdarzenie]* funny; *[wygląd, zachowanie]* silly; *[suma, wyrok]* laughable; **nie bądź** ~**y** don't be ridiculous

śmiesz|yć *impf vi [osoba, sytuacja]* to amuse; **te mnie nie** ~**y** I'm not amused; **te dowcipy rysunkowe zawsze mnie** ~**ą** these cartoons always make me laugh

śmietan|a *f* cream

śmietan|ka *f* ① Kulin. cream ② (kosmetyk) facial lotion ③ przen. (elita) cream; ~**ka towarzyska** the cream of society

■ **spijać** ~**kę** to take the credit

śmietnicz|ka *f* dustpan

śmietnik *m* ① (pojemnik na śmieci) dustbin GB, garbage can US; (miejsce) rubbish tip GB ② pot., przen. (bałagan) mess

■ **znaleźć się na** ~**u** to end up on the waste heap; **wyrzucić coś na** ~ to get rid of sth

śmietnisk|o *n* ① (wysypisko śmieci) rubbish GB a. garbage US dump ② (sterta śmieci) rubbish GB a. garbage US heap pile

śmig|ło *n* propeller

śmigłow|iec *m* helicopter; chopper pot.

śmig|nąć *pf* — **śmig|ać** *impf vi* ① pot. (machnąć) to swish; ~**ać batem** to swish a whip ② przen. *[ptak, zwierzę]* to flit; **dziewczynka** ~**nęła przez ulicę** the little girl dashed across the road

śniada|nie *n* breakfast; **drugie** ~**nie** elevenses GB; (kanapki do szkoły, pracy) bag lunch

śnia|dy *adi.* swarthy

śni|ć *impf* ▯ *vi* ① (mieć sen) to have a dream; ~**ć o kimś/czymś** to dream about sb/sth ② (marzyć) to dream; ~**ć o sławie** to dream of fame; ~**ć na jawie** to daydream

▯▯ **śnić się** ① (ukazywać się we śnie) **wczoraj** ~**ł jej się ojciec** she dreamed about her father last night

2 (marzyć się) ~**ą mi się dalekie podróże** I dream about travelling to distant countries
■ **ani mi się** ~ pot. I haven't the slightest intention of doing it!; **nawet mi się nie** ~**ło, że...** I never dreamed (that)...

śnie|dź f patina

śnieg m snow; **pada** ~ it's snowing; **biały jak** ~ snow-white
■ **tyle mnie to obchodzi, co zeszłoroczny** ~ pot. I don't care a jot a. damn about it

śnież|ka f snowball

śnieżn|y adi. 1 [dzień, zima] snowy; **zaspa** ~**a** a snowdrift 2 przen. [bluzka, koszula] snow-white

śnieżyc|a f blizzard

śnieżyn|ka f snowflake

śpiąc|y adi. sleepy, drowsy

śpiącz|ka f coma; **zapaść w** ~**kę** to fall a. go into a coma

śpiesz|yć impf 1 vi książk. to hurry; ~**yć do domu/pracy** to hurry home/to work; ~**yć komuś z pomocą** to hurry a. rush to sb's aid; ~**yć na ratunek tonącym** to go a. rush to the rescue of those drowning; ~**ę wyjaśnić, że...** I hasten to explain that...
2 **śpieszyć się** 1 [osoba] to be in a hurry a. rush; ~**yć się do pracy** to be in a hurry a. rush to get to work; ~**yć się na pociąg/zebranie** to be in a hurry to catch a train/to get to a meeting; ~**yli się z budową domu** they were in a hurry to get the house finished; **dokąd się tak** ~**ysz?** where are you dashing off to?; **nie** ~**y mu się do powrotu** he's not in a hurry to come back 2 [zegar] to be fast; **zegar** ~**y się o pół godziny** the clock's half an hour fast

śpiew m singing; (ptaków) song, trill(ing)

śpiew|ać impf 1 vt to sing; ~**ać czysto/fałszywie** to sing in tune/out of tune
2 vi [ptaki] to sing
■ **cieniej a. inaczej** ~**ać** pot. to sing a different tune a. song; **cienko** ~**ać** pot. to have a hard a. thin time of it pot.

śpiewająco adv. pot. with flying colours

śpiewa|k m, ~**czka** f singer

śpiewnik m songbook

śpio|ch m pot. sleepyhead pot.

śpio|chy, śpio|szki plt rompers

śpiw|ór m sleeping bag

średni 1 adi. 1 (środkowy) [wzrost] medium; [syn, córka] middle; [porcja, rozmiar] medium; ~**ej wielkości** [miasto, przedsiębiorstwo] of average a. medium size; [owoc] medium-sized; **w** ~**m wieku** middle-aged 2 (niewybijający się) [student] average 3 (wyliczony) [głębokość, wysokość, długość] average, mean; ~**a emerytura/pensja** the average pension/earnings 4 pot. (nieszczególny) run-of-the-mill 5 (ponadpodstawowy) [szkoła] secondary GB, high US; ~**e wykształcenie** secondary education

średnia f average, mean
■ ~**a przyjemność** dubious pleasure

średnic|a f diameter

średnik m semicolon

średnio adv. 1 (szacunkowo) on average; ~ **na osobę wypada po 100 zł** it works out at a. comes to 100 zlotys per person 2 (przeciętnie) **uczył się** ~ he was an average pupil/student; **ta propozycja** ~ **mi się podoba** iron. I can't say I'm too keen on the idea iron.

śr|oda f Wednesday

środ|ek 1 m 1 (miejsce) centre GB, center US, middle; **sam** ~**ek** the very centre; **postawić coś na** ~**ku pokoju** to put sth in the middle a. centre of the room; **trafić dokładnie w sam** ~**ek tarczy** to hit the bullseye; ~**ek ciężkości** Fiz. centre of gravity; przen. main focus 2 (moment) middle; **w** ~**ku nocy/lekcji** in the middle of the night/lesson 3 (wnętrze) inside; **proszę wejść do** ~**ka** please come in 4 książk. (sposób) means; ~**ki komunikacji** means of communication; ~**ki płatnicze** means a. forms of payment; ~**ki przymusu** means of force; ~**ki wychowawcze** educative measures; **chwytać się różnych** ~**ków** to resort to various measures a. means 5 (lekarstwo) remedy; (preparat chemiczny) agent; ~**ki przeciwbólowe** painkillers; ~**ki chwastobójcze** weedkillers, herbicides
2 **środki** plt means, resources; **został bez** ~**ków (do życia)** he was left with nothing to live on
3 **środkiem** adv. along the middle

środkow|y adi. 1 (centralny) middle 2 Sport centre

środowisk|o n 1 (grupa ludzi) community 2 Biol. environment

śródlądow|y adi. inland

śródmieś|cie n city/town centre, downtown US

śrub|a f 1 Techn. screw; (urządzenie napędowe) screw (propeller); ~**a napędowa** a power screw 2 pot. (wkręt) bolt 3 Sport (skok do wody) twist
■ **dokręcić a. przykręcić (komuś)** ~**ę** pot. to put the screws on sb

śrubokrę|t m screwdriver

śru|t m shot, pellets

śrutow|y adi. shot; **broń** ~**a** a shotgun

świadcze|nie n service, benefit; ~**nia socjalne** social security benefits

świadcz|yć impf vi 1 (dowodzić) to show, to prove; **dobrze o kimś/czymś** ~**yć** to reflect well on sb/sth; **źle o kimś/czymś** ~**yć** to reflect badly on sb/sth; ~**yć za kimś/przeciwko komuś** to speak in sb's favour/against sb 2 (w sądzie) to testify (**za kimś/przeciw komuś** for/against sb)

świadectw|o n 1 (dokument) certificate; (szkolne) (school) report; ~**o maturalne** a. **dojrzałości** Polish school-leaving examination certificate 2 (dowód) evidence; **dawać** ~**o prawdzie** to bear witness a. testimony to the truth

świad|ek *m* witness (**czegoś** to sth); **naoczny** ~**ek** an eyewitness; **porozmawiajmy bez** ~**ków** let's talk in private

świadomie *adv. grad.* consciously; ~ **wprowadził nas w błąd** he deliberately misled us

świadomoś|ć *f* consciousness; ~**ć klasowa/ społeczna** class/social consciousness; **stracić** ~**ć** to lose consciousness; **odzyskać** ~**ć** to come round a. to; **z całą** a. **pełną** ~**cią** in full consciousness; **mieć** ~**ć czegoś** to be aware a. conscious of sth

świadom|y *adi. [osoba]* conscious (**czegoś** of sth); *[decyzja, wybór]* conscious

świ|at *m* the world; **podróż dookoła** ~**ata** a journey round a. around the world; **najwyższy na** ~**ecie** the highest in the world; **stary jak** ~**at** as old as the hills; **jest taka mgła, że** ~**ata nie widać** it's so foggy a. misty (that) you can't see anything; **szeroki** ~**at** the world at large; **iść w** ~**at** to go out into the world; **wiadomości ze** ~**ata** world news; **podwodny** ~**at** the submarine world; **cały** ~**at ją podziwiał** the entire world admired her; ~**at artystyczny/naukowy** the world of art/science; ~**at przestępczy** the criminal world

■ **do końca** ~**ta** till the end of time, forever; **wielki** ~**at** the rich and (the) famous; **zejść z tego** ~**ata** książk. to depart this life euf.; **tamten** ~**at** the next world; **przenieść się na tamten** ~**at** to go to meet one's Maker żart.; to go the way of all flesh; **dwa** ~**aty** (odrębne środowiska) two different worlds; (o osobach) completely different characters; **jak** ~**at** ~**em** (zawsze) since time immemorial; (nigdy) never; **za nic w** ~**ecie** not for all the world; **podbić** ~**at** to conquer the world; ~**ata nie widzieć poza kimś** to think all the world of sb; **przyjść na** ~**at** książk. to be born; **zapomnieć o całym** a. **bożym** ~**ecie** to be oblivious to the whole a. entire world

świ|atło *n* ① (jasność) light; ~**atło dzienne** daylight; ~**atło księżyca** moonlight; ~**atło słoneczne** sunlight ② (oświetlenie) lighting; **górne/boczne** ~**atło** overhead a. direct/side lighting; **zapalić** ~**atło** to put a. switch the light on; **zgasić** ~**atło** to turn the light(s) out, to switch the light off ③ pot. (elektryczność) electricity; **awaria** ~**atła** an electricity a. a power cut a. failure ④ (pojazdu) light; ~**atła mijania** a. **krótkie** dipped headlights GB, low beams US ⑤ (regulujące ruch) traffic light(s); **zatrzymać się na** ~**atłach** to stop at the lights

■ **w pełnym** ~**etle** in full daylight; **dać komuś zielone** ~**atło** to give sb the green light; **przedstawiać kogoś/coś w dobrym/złym/innym** ~**etle** to present sb/sth in a favourable/ bad/different light; **rzucić na coś** ~**atło** to cast a. shed a. throw light on sth

światłocie|ń *m* chiaroscuro

światłomierz *m* light meter

światłowodow|y *adi.* fibre-optic GB, fiber-optic US; **włókna** ~**e** optical fibres

światłow|ód *m* fibre-optic GB a. fiber-optic US cable

światopoglą|d *m* outlook on life

świąteczn|y *adi.* ① *[nastrój]* festive; **nieczynne w dni** ~**e** closed on Sundays and holidays ② (bożonarodzeniowy) Christmas; (wielkanocny) Easter ③ (uroczysty) solemn

świąty|nia *f* ① (kościół) church ② (budowla) temple ③ książk., przen. shrine, sanctuary

świd|er *m* bit; (ręczny) gimlet; (maszyna do wiercenia skał) drill

świdr|ować *impf* **[]** *vt* to drill

[] *vi* to pierce, to penetrate; ~**ujący ból** a piercing pain

■ ~**ować kogoś wzrokiem** pot. to look piercingly at sb

świec|a *f* ① (źródło światła) candle; **prosty jak** ~**a** straight as a rod ② (w silniku) spark plug ③ Sport (ćwiczenie gimnastyczne) shoulder stand; (lot piłki) skyer ④ (raca) flare; ~**a dymna** smoke (bomb)

■ **takiego specjalisty ze** ~**ą** (**trzeba**) **szukać** such specialists are hard to find a. few and far between

świe|cić *impf* **[]** *vi [słońce, księżyc]* to shine; ~**cić latarką/zapałkami** to shine one's torch/to light one's way with matches

[] **świecić się** to shine; **czoło** ~**ciło mu się od potu** his forehead was shining with sweat

[] *v imp.* **w jego domu** ~**ciło się do późna** the lights stayed on late in his house

■ ~**cić przykładem** to be a. provide an example; ~**cić pustkami** to be half empty; ~**cić oczami za kogoś** to be ashamed on sb's account

świecideł|ko *n* bauble, trinket

świec|ki *adi. [szkoła, muzyka]* secular; *[osoba]* lay

świecz|ka *f* small candle; (bardzo cienka) taper

świecznik *m* candlestick; (na małe, płaskie świeczki) tealight holder

■ **stać** a. **być na** ~**u** to hold a prominent position, to be in the spotlight

świergo|t *m* ① (głosy ptaków) chirp(ing) ② przen. (głosy ludzi) twitter, chatter

świergo|tać *impf vi* ① *[ptak]* to chirp, to twitter ② przen. *[dzieci, dziewczęta]* to chirp przen.

świerk *m* (drzewo) spruce; (drewno) spruce (timber)

świerszcz *m* cricket

świerzb|ić, świerzb|ieć *impf vi* to itch

świetlic|a *f* ① (w szpitalu, więzieniu) day a. television room ② (w szkole) after-school club, day-care room ③ (klub) youth club

świetlik *m* ① (w budynku) skylight; (iluminator) porthole; (otwierany ku górze) hatch ② Bot. eyebright ③ Zool. glow-worm

świetnoś|ć *f* splendour GB, splendor US; **świadectwo minionej** ~**ci miasta** a remnant of the past glory of the town

świetn|y *adi. grad. [interes, pomysł]* splendid; ~**y specjalista** an excellent specialist; **czeka cię** ~**a przyszłość** you have a great future ahead of you

świeżo *adv.* ① *[czuć się, pachnieć]* fresh; **wyglądać** ~ to look young a. healthy ② *przen. [brzmieć]* original ③ (niedawno) newly; ~ **malowane drzwi** a freshly-painted door; „~ **malowane**" 'wet paint'; ~ **otwarty sklep** a newly-opened shop; ~ **przybyli goście** newly-arrived guests; **być** ~ **po wypłacie** to have just received one's wages; **mieć coś** ~ **w pamięci** to have sth fresh in one's mind

świeżoś|ć *f* freshness także przen.; **długo utrzymywać** ~**ć** to stay fresh for a long time; ~**ć pomysłu/tematu** the novelty of an idea/a subject

śwież|y Ⅰ *adi. grad.* ① *[żywność]* fresh ② *[poranek, powietrze]* cool, fresh; **na** ~**ym powietrzu** outdoors ③ *[kolor, barwa]* bright ④ *przen. [cera, wygląd]* healthy looking, fresh; *[osoba]* refreshed, rested; **zachować** ~**y umysł** to maintain a keen mind ⑤ *przen. [pomysł, spojrzenie]* original, fresh ⑥ *pot. [ręcznik, pościel]* fresh; (nowy) *[bateria]* new ⑦ *pot. [wiadomość, wspomnienie]* recent; ~**a żałoba** new grief

Ⅱ *adi. [żywność]* fresh; *[pąki, liście, ślady]* new

świę|cić *impf* Ⅰ *vt* ① (nadawać charakter sakralny) to consecrate *[kościół]* ② książk. (świętować) to celebrate *[jubileusz]*

Ⅱ **święcić się** (dziać się) to be in the wind pot.; **co tu się** ~**ci?** what's cooking? pot.; **czuła, że** ~**ci się coś złego** she felt there was something bad afoot

■ ~**cić triumfy** a. **sukcesy** to enjoy great success

świę|to Ⅰ *n* holiday także przen.

Ⅱ **święta** *plt* (Boże Narodzenie) Christmas; (Wielkanoc) Easter; **Wesołych Świąt!** Merry Christmas!/ Happy Easter!; **obchodzić** ~**ęta** to celebrate a holiday

■ **od (wielkiego)** ~**ęta** once in a blue moon

świę|tować *impf vt* to celebrate *[wydarzenie]*

świę|ty Ⅰ *adi. grad. [msza, komunia, miejsce, ogień]* holy; pot. *[obrazek]* religious; książk., przen. *[osoba]* holy, saintly; *[sprawa]* sacred; ~**ty Franciszek** Saint Francis; **Najświętsza (Maria) Panna** the Blessed Virgin Mary

Ⅱ **święty** *m,* ~**ta** *f* saint

■ ~**ty obowiązek** bounden duty; ~**ty spokój** peace and quiet; ~**ta racja** a. **prawda** a. ~**te słowa** how very true; **masz** ~**tą rację** you're absolutely right; **mieć** ~**tą cierpliwość do kogoś/czegoś** pot. to have the patience of a saint with sb/sth; **płonąć** ~**tym oburzeniem** to be filled with righteous indignation; **zrobić coś dla** ~**tego spokoju** to do sth for one's peace of mind; **co ona powie, to (jest)** ~**te** whatever she says is (holy) gospel

świ|nia *f* ① (zwierzę domowe) pig; (samica) sow; (wieprz) hog; (knur) boar; **schlać się** a. **urżnąć się jak** ~**nia** posp., obraźl. to get pissed (out of one's mind a. head) posp.; **jeść jak** ~**nia** pejor. to eat like a pig; **nażreć się** a. **obeżreć się jak** ~**nia** posp., obraźl. to stuff oneself a. one's face like a pig, to make a pig of oneself pot. ② pot., obraźl. (wyzwisko) swine pot., obraźl.; **ty** ~**nio!** you swine!

■ **podłożyć komuś** ~**nię** pot. to do the dirty on sb pot.

świn|ka *f* ① (świnia) piggy, little pig ② (choroba) mumps ③ pot. (skarbonka) piggy bank

❑ ~**ka morska** Zool. guinea pig

świntuch *m* pot. ① (rozpustnik) lecher ② (niechluj) dirty pig pot.

świntusz|yć *impf vi* pot. ① (robić rzeczy nieprzyzwoite) to be obscene; (w mowie) to talk dirty pot. ② (brudzić, śmiecić) to make a mess

świńs|ki Ⅰ *adi.* ① *[ogon, ryj]* pig('s), hog('s); (jak u świni) *[rysy]* hoglike, porcine ② pot. (zły) swinish; ~**kie zachowanie** snide behaviour ③ pot. *[film, dowcip, uwaga]* blue pot.

Ⅱ **po świńsku** *adv.* pot. *[zachować się, postąpić]* like a swine, meanly; *[wyrażać się]* dirty

świństw|o *n* pot. ① (czyn nieetyczny) vileness; **zrobić komuś** ~**o** to do the dirty on sb pot. ② (niesmaczna potrawa) muck pot. ③ (nieprzyzwoite słowa) filthy joke

świ|st *m* (ptaka, wiatru) whistle; (pocisku) swish; (w oddechu chorego) wheezing, wheeze

świstak *m* marmot

świst|ek *m* pot. (kawałek papieru) scrap of paper; (dokument) piece of paper przen.

świ|t *m* dawn, daybreak; **od** ~**tu do nocy** from dawn till dusk; **skoro** ~**t** as soon as dawn broke

świta|ć *impf vi* to dawn także przen.

T

T, t *n inv.* T, t

tabel|a *f* table, chart; Sport (league) table; ~a wyników a scoresheet

tablet|ka *f* pill, tablet

tablic|a *f* ① (płyta z napisem) tablet; (pamiątkowa) (commemorative) plaque; (informacyjna) (notice)-board ② (w szkole) board; (do pisania kredą) blackboard, chalkboard US; (do pisania mazakami) whiteboard ③ (w książce) plate ④ (plansza) wallchart ⑤ (zestawienie liczb) table ⑥ Sport (w koszykówce) backboard ❑ ~a rejestracyjna registration a. number plate GB, license plate US

tablicz|ka *f* ① (z napisem) plate ② (do pisania) tablet; (kamienna) slate ❑ ~ka czekolady bar of chocolate; ~ka mnożenia Mat. multiplication table(s); (times) table(s) pot.

tabore|t *m* stool; (niski) tabouret, taboret US

tabu *n inv., adi. inv.* taboo, tabu

tabun *m* herd; przen. pack pot.

tac|a *f* (serving) tray; (srebrna) salver; (podczas nabożeństwa) offertory; (zebrane pieniądze) the collection

tacz|ka *f* wheelbarrow

taf|ta *f* taffeta

ta|ić *impf* książk. **[]** *vt* to hide *[uczucia, zamiary]*; to conceal *[fakty, prawdę]*; **nigdy nie taił swojego zdania** he never made a secret of his views **[]] taić się** książk. *[niepewność, złość]* to lurk (**w kimś/czymś** in sb/sth)

taj|ać *impf vi* ① (rozmarzać) *[gleba, lód, rzeka]* to thaw; *[palce, stopy]* to thaw out ② książk., przen. *[osoba]* to melt

tajemnic|a *f* ① (sekret) secret; **powiedzieć coś komuś w ~y** to tell sb sth in confidence ② (tajność) confidentiality; ~a lekarska doctor-patient privilege; ~a państwowa a state secret; ~a służbowa ≈ confidential information; ~a spowiedzi the seal of confession ③ (zagadka) mystery; ~e natury the mysteries of nature ■ ~a poliszynela a. publiczna ~a książk. open secret

tajemnicz|y *adi.* ① (otoczony tajemnicą) secret ② (zagadkowy) *[znak]* mysterious; *[uśmiech]* enigmatic ③ (skryty) secretive

tajfun *m* typhoon

taj|ga *f* taiga

tajnia|k *m* pot. (policjant) plain-clothes police officer; (pracownik wywiadu) undercover agent

tajnik|i *plt* arcana; ~i duszy ludzkiej the innermost recesses of man's soul

tajn|y *adi. grad.* ① (niejawny) *[narada, pakt]* secret; *[dokument, informacja]* classified; *[funkcjonariusz, służby]* secret ② (nielegalny) *[drukarnia, organizacja]* underground ③ (utajony) *[przejście]* secret; *[myśli, uczucia]* innermost

tak¹ *inter.* ① (potwierdzenie) yes; ~ czy nie? yes or no?; „byłeś u dentysty?" – „~" 'did you go to the dentist?' – 'yes (I did)'; **nie lubię kotów, ale psy ~** I don't like cats, but I (do) like dogs; ~ **jest!** that's right!; (w wojsku) yes, sir!; (w marynarce) aye, aye, sir! ② pot. (około) **to kosztowało ~ ze 100 złotych** it cost something like a. somewhere around 100 zlotys pot.

tak² **[]** *pron.* ① (intensywność) (przed przymiotnikiem, przysłówkiem) so; (przed czasownikiem) so much; ~ **dobry** so good; ~ **blisko/często/późno/~** so close/often/late; ~ **bardzo** so much; **bądź ~ dobry i otwórz okno** książk. would you mind opening the window?; ~ **się za tobą stęskniłem** I missed you so (much); ~ **bym chciała gdzieś wyjechać** how I wish I could (just) go away somewhere; **nie mieli ~ dużego rozmiaru** they didn't have such a large size ② (w ten sposób) **to było ~** it was like this; ~ **wyglądał twój dziadek, kiedy był młody** this is what your grandad looked like when he was young; **zrobił ~, jak mu radzono** he did as he was advised; **nic już nie będzie ~ jak dawniej** nothing's (ever) going to be like it used to be; **zrób to ~, żeby cię nie zauważył** do it so that a. in such a way that he doesn't notice you ③ (emfatyczne) **chcesz mu to dać ~ za darmo?** you want to just give it to him free?; **nie da się ~ po prostu zapomnieć** you can't just (go and) forget **[]] tak..., jak i...** *coni.* (zarówno) both... and...; **jego dzieła, ~ dramaty, jak i powieści...** his works – both the dramas and the novels...

[]]] tak że *coni.* so; **wszystko załatwiłem, ~ że się nie martw** I've arranged everything, so don't worry

■ ~ **czy inaczej** anyway; ~ **czy owak** a. **siak** in any case; ~ **sobie** pot. (nie najlepiej) so-so; (bez specjalnego powodu) for no particular reason; **nic się nie dzieje ~ sobie** there's a reason for everything;

i ~ **dalej** and so on a. forth; **i ~ dalej, i ~ dalej**
and so on and so forth; **ot ~** (bez powodu) for no
particular reason

ta|ki *pron.* ① (z rzeczownikiem lub zamiast rzeczownika)
such; **taki samochód** such a car; **taka pogoda**
such weather; **dziewczyna taka jak ty** a girl like
you; **on nie jest taki, jak myślisz** he's not the
kind of person you take him for; **z ciebie taki sam
znawca jak ze mnie** iron. you're no more of an
expert than I am; **naucz się akceptować świat
takim, jaki on jest** you must learn to accept the
world as it is; **jest taki mróz, że nie chce się
wychodzić z domu** it's so cold that one doesn't
even want to go out; **tacy to zawsze mają
szczęście** people like that are always lucky; **w
taki sposób** this way; **w taki sposób, że...** in such
a way a. manner that...; **w taki czy inny sposób**
somehow or other; **coś takiego** something like
that; **coś takiego!** well, well! ② (przed przymiotnikiem)
so; **taki miły/piękny** so nice/beautiful; **taki
wspaniały widok** such a magnificent view; **dwie
kobiety w takich samych sukienkach** two
women wearing the same dress; **taki sam samochód jak mój** the same car as mine ③ (niedoo-
kreślony) **zwyczajna torba, taka papierowa** an
ordinary bag, a paper one; **jakiś taki** a. **taki jakiś**
pot. (nieswój) out of sorts GB
■ **pani taka a taka** Ms so-and-so; **takiego a
takiego dnia, o takiej a takiej godzinie** on such
and such a day at such and such an hour; **takie
czy inne książki** books of one sort or another;
taki owaki euf. so-and-so euf.; **ty taki owaki!** you
so-and-so!; **taki sobie** pot. so-so, fair-to-middling

taksów|ka *f* taxi, taxicab

taksówkarz *m* taxi driver, cab-driver

tak|t¹ *m* (umiar) tact

tak|t² *m* (jednostka metryczna) bar, measure US; (rytm)
time, measure US; **wybijać ~t** to beat time;
klaskać do ~tu to clap in time

taktown|y *adi. grad.* tactful

taktyczn|y *adi.* tactical także przen.

takty|ka *f* tactics

także *part.* as well, also; **on ~ lubi szachy** he likes
chess as well; **to dotyczy wszystkich, ~ ciebie**
that applies to everybody, you included a. as well;
znam ją, i ty ~ I know her, and so do you; **a ~...**
and also..., as well as...

talen|t *m* talent (**do czegoś** for sth)

talerz *m* ① (do potraw) plate; **głęboki/płytki** a.
płaski ~ a soup/dinner plate ② (porcja) plateful
③ (płaski przedmiot) **~ anteny satelitarnej** a satellite
dish ④ (instrument) hi-hat, high-hat

tali|a¹ *f* ① (pas) waist; **mieć ~ę osy** to be wasp-
waisted ② (część ubrania) waist(line)

tali|a² *f* (kart) pack GB, deck (of cards) US

talizman *m* talisman, charm

talk *m* talcum powder

talon *m* coupon, voucher; **~ na benzynę** a petrol
coupon; **~ do domu towarowego** a discount
voucher for a department store

tam [] *pron.* there; (z towarzyszącym gestem) over there;
zatrzymaj się ~ stop (over) there; **połóż to ~** put
it there; **kto ~?** who is it?; **~ w górze/dole** up/
down there; **~, gdzie kończy się miasto** where
the town comes to an end
[] *part.* **co ~ u was słychać?** pot. how are things?;
co mi ~! pot. who cares? pot.; **gdzieś ~** somewhere
(or other); **kiedyś ~** some day (or other); **gdzież
mu ~ do ciebie** he's no match for you; **hej ~!**
hey, you! pot.
■ **~ i z powrotem** there and back; **chodzić ~
i z powrotem** to pace back and forth a. to and fro;
bilet ~ i z powrotem a return GB a. round-trip US
ticket; **a ~!** a. **e ~!** pot. (niedowierzanie) you're kidding! pot.

tam|a *f* ① (zapora) dam ② przen. barrier, obstacle;
położyć a. **postawić ~ę czemuś** to put a stop
to sth

tamburyn *m* tambourine

tam|ować *impf vt* ① (blokować) to block *[przejście]*
② (powstrzymywać) to stem, to staunch GB, to stanch US
[krew]

tampon *m* (do tamowania krwi) compress; (do oczy-
szczania ran) wipe, swab; (higieniczny) tampon

tam|ten *pron.* (z rzeczownikiem) that; (zamiast rzeczowni-
ka) that one; (z towarzyszącym gestem) the one over
there; **~ci** those; **pogadaliśmy o tym i ~tym** we
chatted about this and that

tamtędy *pron.* that way

tance|rz *m*, **~rka** *f* dancer

tandem *m* ① (rower) tandem (bicycle) ② (zespół)
tandem, team

tande|ta *f* pot. ① (o towarach) junk; **sklep z ~tą** a
junk shop ② (o książkach, filmach) rubbish pot.

tandetn|y *adi.* pot. *[materiał, ubranie]* shoddy;
[rozrywka] trashy

tang|o *n* tango
■ **pójść** a. **ruszyć w ~o** pot. (pić) to go on a
drinking spree; (łajdaczyć się) to sleep around

ta|ni [] *adi. grad.* cheap; **tani kredyt** cheap a. low-
interest credit
[] *adi.* przen. *[dowcip, komplement]* cheap; **tani
chwyt** a cheap trick

ta|niec [] *m* dance
[] *taniec* plt pot. dance; **zaprosić kogoś na tańce**
to invite sb to a dance

tani|eć *impf vi [produkt]* to get cheaper

tank|ować *impf* [] *vt* to fuel (up) *[pojazd]*; **~ować
paliwo** to fill up with fuel
[] *vi* pot. to booze pot.

tankow|iec *m* (oil) tanker, oiler

tantiem|a *f* royalty; **~y z płyty/za książkę**
royalties from a record/book

tańcz|yć *impf* **I** *vt* to dance (**z kimś** with sb) **II** *vi* to dance także przen.; **dobrze ~yć** to be a good dancer

■ **~yć, jak ktoś zagra** pot. to dance to sb's tune; **~yć koło kogoś** pot. to dance attendance on sb

tapczan *m* divan (bed)

tape|ta *f* ① (ścienna) (wall)paper ② pot. (makijaż) warpaint pot.

■ **wziąć coś na ~tę** pot. to get down to sth

tapet|ować *impf* **I** *vt* to (wall)paper [*pokój, ściany*] **II tapetować się** pot. to paint one's face (thickly)

tapice|r *m* upholsterer

tapicer|ka *f* upholstery

taran|ować *impf vt* to ram (**coś** into sth)

tarapat|y *plt* książk. trouble

taras *m* terrace; **~ widokowy** an observation deck

taras|ować *impf vt* to block [*ulicę, wejście*]

tarcic|a *f* ① (drewno) timber GB, lumber US ② (belka) timber; (deska) plank

tar|cie *n* friction także przen.

tarcz|a *f* ① (rycerska) shield; (policyjna) (riot) shield ② (urządzenia pomiarowego) dial; **~a zegarka** (na rękę) the dial of a. on the watch; (stojącego) the face of the clock ③ (w maszynie) disc GB, disk US; **~a szlifierska** a grinding wheel ④ Sport target; **trafić w środek ~y** to hit the bullseye ⑤ (herbowa) shield, escutcheon

❑ **~a słoneczna** the sun's disc; **~a Księżyca** the face of the moon

tarczyc|a *f* thyroid (gland)

targ **I** *m* ① (rynek) market ② pot. (o cenę) haggling; **dobić ~u** to strike a bargain a. deal; **~i** przen. (spory) bargaining **II targi** *plt* (wystawa) fair

■ **krakowskim ~iem** by way of compromise

targ|nąć *pf* — **targ|ać** *impf vt* ① (ciągnąć) to pull; **~ać kogoś za uszy/włosy** to pull sb's ears/hair; **~nął za lejce** he jerked the reins ② [*fale, wicher*] to toss [*okrętem*]; [*wiatr*] to tousle [*włosy*]

■ **~ nąć się na coś** książk. to attempt to seize sth; **~nąć się na kogoś** książk. to assault sb; **~nąć się na życie** książk. to take one's (own) life

targ|ować się *impf v refl.* ① pot. (przy kupnie) to bargain; **~ować się o cenę** to bargain over the price ② przen. to argue (**o coś** about sth)

targowisk|o *n* market(place)

tar|ka *f* grater

tar|ło *n* (składanie ikry) spawning; (okres godowy) spawning season a. time

tarmo|sić *impf vt* pot. to pull, to tug; **~sić kogoś za uszy** to pull sb's ears

tartak *m* lumber mill, sawmill

taryf|a *f* rate; **~a kolejowa** a table of fares; **~a bagażowa/pocztowa** baggage/postal charges; **~a celna** customs tariff

tarza|ć się *impf v refl.* pot. [*dziecko, zwierzę*] roll about GB a. around (**w czymś** in sth)

■ **~ć się w rozpuście** to wallow in debauchery; **~ć się ze śmiechu** to split one's sides (laughing)

tasak *m* chopper, (meat) cleaver

tasiem|iec *m* tapeworm

tasiem|ka *f* (do obszywania) (narrow) tape; (do ściągania) drawstring; (wstążeczka) ribbon

tas|ować *impf vt* to shuffle [*talię kart*]

ta|szczyć *impf vt* pot. to lug [*zakupy, walizy*]

taśm|a *f* ① (wstęga) tape; **~a klejąca** adhesive a. sticky tape; **~a tapicerska** webbing ② (do nagrywania) tape; **~a filmowa** film; **~a magnetofonowa** audio tape; **~a magnetowidowa** videotape ③ Sport tape; **przerwać ~ę** to break the tape; **wygrać rzutem na ~ę** to win by inches ④ Techn. (część przenośnika) belt; **~a montażowa** a. **produkcyjna** assembly a. production line; **pracować przy ~ie** to work at an assembly line

■ **rzut na ~ę** the last minute attempt

tatarak *m* calamus, sweet flag

taterni|k *m*, **~czka** *f* mountaineer (*in the Tatras*)

tatuaż *m* tattoo

tatu|ować *impf vt* to tattoo

tchawic|a *f* trachea, windpipe

tchn|ąć *pf vt* książk., przen. to breathe; **~ąć w coś nowego ducha** a. **nowe życie** to breathe new life into sth; **~ąć w kogoś entuzjazm** to infuse sb with enthusiasm

tchórz *m* ① (o osobie) coward ② Zool. polecat

■ **podszyty ~em** lily-livered; **~ cię obleciał?** are you chicken? pot.

tchórzliwie *adv. grad.* [*postąpić*] in cowardly fashion

tchórzliw|y *adi. grad.* cowardly; [*postępek*] craven

tchórzostw|o *n* ① (tchórzliwość) cowardice ② (postępek) cowardly act a. behaviour

tchórz|yć *impf vi* to chicken out pot.

tchu → dech

teat|r *m* ① (dziedzina sztuki) the stage; **pisać dla ~ru** to write for the stage ② (instytucja) theatre GB, theater US; **pójść do ~ru** to go to the theatre; **co grają w ~rze?** what's on at the theatre? ③ książk., przen. (miejsce wydarzeń) theatre GB, theater US przen.; **~r wojny** the theatre of war

techniczn|y *adi.* ① [*problemy, umiejętności*] mechanical; [*literatura, terminologia, przyczyny, trudności*] technical; [*rewolucja*] technological; **dokumentacja ~a** a specification sheet; **doradca ~y** a consulting engineer; **personel ~y** the maintenance crew, technical staff; **uczelnia ~a** a technical college ② [*kalka, ołówek, rysunek*] technical

techni|k *m* technician

techni|ka *f* ① (metoda, umiejętności) technique ② (wiedza i technologia) engineering; **nauka i ~ka** science and technology

technik|um *n* ≈ technical college

technologi|a *f* technology

tecz|ka *f* ① (z rączką) briefcase; (aktówka) portfolio ② (okładka) file, folder ③ (zbiór dokumentów) dossier

tegoroczn|y *adi.* this year's

te|ka *f* ① (zbiór prac) portfolio ② (zbiór dokumentów) file ③ (urząd) portfolio; **minister bez teki** minister without portfolio

tek|st *m* (przemówienia, sztuki) text; (piosenki) lyrics

tekstyli|a *plt* textiles

tektu|ra *f* cardboard

teledysk *m* music video, video clip

telefon *m* ① (aparat) (tele)phone (set); ~ **komórkowy** a mobile phone; **przez** ~ on the phone; „**Kowalski przy** ~ie" 'Kowalski speaking'; ~ **jest zajęty** the line is engaged ② (rozmowa) (phone) call; **odebrać** ~ to answer the phone; ~ **do ciebie** there's a phone call for you ③ (numer) (tele)phone number; ~ **domowy** a home number

❑ ~ **bezpośredni** direct line; ~ **grzecznościowy** contact number; ~ **wewnętrzny** extension; ~ **zaufania** helpline

■ **głuche** ~**y** *pot.* dead calls; ~ **jest głuchy** the line's (gone) dead; **grać a. bawić się w głuchy** ~ to play Chinese whispers; ~**y się urywają** *pot.* the telephone won't stop ringing

telefonicznie *adv.* on the phone, by phone

telefoniczn|y *adi.* [budka, centrala, rozmowa] telephone; **słuchawka** ~**a** a receiver; **informacja** ~**a** a call centre GB a. center US

telefoni|sta *m,* ~**stka** *f* telephonist GB, (telephone) operator US

telefon|ować *impf vi* to (tele)phone (**do kogoś** sb); ~**ować po karetkę/policję** to call an ambulance/the police

telegaze|ta *f* teletext

telegraficzn|y *adi.* ① [linia, połączenie, słup] telegraphic; [aparat, kod] telegraph ② przen. [styl] telegraphic; **w** ~**ym skrócie** very briefly

telegram *m* telegram GB, wire US

telekomunikacj|a *f* ① Techn. telecommunications ② (instytucja) telecommunications company

teleskop *m* ① Zool. telescope fish ② Techn. (do obserwacji gwiazd) telescope ③ (amortyzator) telescopic shock absorber

teleturniej *m* (television) quiz show

telewidz *m* viewer

telewizj|a *f* ① (system, program) television, TV; **pracować w** ~**i** to work in television; **oglądać** ~**ę** to watch TV; **co dziś jest w** ~**i?** what's on TV today? ② *pot.* (odbiornik) television, TV set

telewizo|r *m* television, TV set

tema|t *m* ① (treść) subject; ~**t lekcji/konferencji** the subject of a lesson/conference; ~**t rozmowy** the subject a. topic of a conversation; **artykuł na** ~**t wojny** an article on (the subject of) war; **mówić/pisać (nie) na** ~**t** to speak/write (not) to the point; **przeskakiwać z** ~**tu na** ~**t** to be

jumping about from one topic to another; **zmienić** ~**t** to change a. drop the subject; **zbaczać z** ~**tu** to be getting off the subject ② (w odmianie wyrazów) stem ③ Muz. theme (music), subject

tematy|ka *f* subject (matter)

temblak *m* sling; **mieć rękę na** ~**u** to have one's arm in a sling

temperamen|t *m* ① (usposobienie) temperament; **miał wybuchowy** ~**t** he was short-tempered; **osoba pełna** ~**tu** a person with temperament; **osoba pozbawiona** ~**tu** a person lacking character ② przen. (predyspozycja) disposition; **(jego)** ~**t pisarski** his disposition for writing

temperatu|ra *f* ① (ciepło) temperature; ~**ra pokojowa** room temperature ② (ciepłota) temperature; **dostać (wysokiej)** ~**ry** to run a. have a (high) temperature; **zmierzyć komuś** ~**rę** to take sb's temperature ③ przen. excitement; **debata podniosła** ~**rę na sali** the debate became heated

temper|ować *impf vt* ① (ostrzyć) to sharpen [ołówek] ② (powściągać) to tame [osobę]

temperów|ka *f* (pencil) sharpener

temp|o ❑ *n* ① (szybkość) pace, speed; **nadawać** ~**o** to set the pace; **zwolnić** ~**o** to slow down także przen.; **jej powieści mają znakomite** ~**o** her novels are very pacy ② Muz. tempo

❑ *inter.* ~**o!** ~**o!** move (it)!

■ **robić coś na** ~**o** to do sth in haste

temu *praep.* ago; **godzinę/rok** ~ an hour/a year ago; **dawno** ~ a long time ago, long ago

ten *pron.* ① (z rzeczownikiem) this; (wcześniej wspomniany, odleglejszy) that; **ci/te** these; (wcześniej wspomniani, odleglejsi) those; **ten mężczyzna/ta kobieta/to dziecko** this man/woman/child; **ci ludzie/te dzieci** these people/children; **w tym tygodniu** this week; **w tę środę** this Wednesday; **w tej chwili** (obecnie) at the moment; **tego dnia** that day; **ten sam/ta sama/to samo** the same ② (zamiast rzeczownika) this/that one; „**którą chcesz książkę?**" – „**tę**" 'which book do you want?' – 'this/that one'; **ten niebieski** the a. this/that blue one; **te czerwone** the a. these/those red ones; **opowiedziałam o tym Robertowi, a ten Annie** I told Robert about it and Robert a. he told Anna; **ten albo tamten** one or the other; **dnia tego a tego** on such-and-such a day ③ (w zdaniach złożonych) **ten, który...** the one who/which...; **ci, którzy...** those who...; **ten, który zwycięży** the one who wins; **te, które widzieliśmy** those (that) we saw; **ten, kto...** he who...; **kto szuka, ten znajdzie** he who seeks shall find; **nie ten, co trzeba** the wrong one

■ **te rzeczy** euf. ≈ the birds and the bees pot., euf.; **ten tego** pot. you know, like pot.; **być nie tego** (nie w porządku) pot. [osoba] to be not all a. quite there pot.

tendencj|a f ① (kierunek) tendency, trend ② (skłonność) tendency; **mieć ~ę do tycia** to have a tendency to put on weight

tendencyjn|y adi. grad. [osoba] biased; [opinia] tendentious

tenis m ① Sport tennis ② (tkanina) pinstripe

tenisi|sta m, **~stka** f tennis player

tenisów|ka f plimsoll GB, gym shoe US

teoretycznie adv. [udowodnić, uzasadnić] theoretically; **rozważać coś ~** to speculate on a. about sth; **~ masz rację** theoretically speaking you're right

teoretyczn|y adi. theoretical

teorety|k m theoretician, theorist

teoretyz|ować impf vi to theorize (**na temat czegoś** on a. about sth)

teori|a f theory; **~a poznania** epistemology

terako|ta f terracotta

terapeu|ta /ˌteraˈpewta/ m, **~tka** /ˌteraˈpewtka/ f therapist

terapi|a f therapy; **~a grupowa** group therapy; **intensywna ~a** intensive care

❑ **~a wstrząsowa** a. **szokowa** shock therapy a. treatment

teraz adv. ① (w tej chwili) at present; **rano padało, ale ~ już się rozpogodziło** it was raining in the morning but now it's sunny; **dopiero ~ zrozumiał, że postępował źle** he has only just understood that he did wrong; **(jak) na ~** pot. for now; **to tyle jak na ~** that's all for now ② (natychmiast) now; **musisz ~ wyjechać** you must leave now; **~ albo nigdy** (it's) now or never

teraźniejszoś|ć f the present (time), (the) here and now

teraźniej|szy adi. present; **czas ~szy** the present (tense)

teren m ① (obszar) land; **~y roponośne** oilfields; **~ budowy** a building a. construction site; **~ szkoły/szpitala** school/hospital premises; **~y zielone** the green areas ② przen. (miejsce wydarzeń) area, place

terie|r m terrier

terko|t m (karabinu maszynowego, kół, silnika) clatter; (budzika) jangle; **traktor przejechał z ~tem** a tractor rattled by

terko|tać impf vi [maszyna, motor] to clatter; [budzik] to jangle

term|a f ① Techn. (elektryczna) water heater; (gazowa) gas heater ② (źródło) thermal spring

termin m ① (odcinek czasu) time (limit); **napięty ~** a tight deadline; **~ gwarancyjny** a guarantee period; **wyznaczyć ~ wykonania czegoś** to set a time limit a. deadline for doing sth; **skończyć coś w ~ie** to finish sth on time; **~ upływa a. wygasa jutro** the deadline expires tomorrow; **wykonujemy projekty w ~ie pięciu dni** we execute designs within 5 days ② (konkretna data) date; **~ ważności** a sell-by date ③ (naukowy, literacki) term

terminarz m ① (rozkład) timetable, schedule; **~ dostaw** a delivery schedule; **~ rozgrywek** a match timetable ② (kalendarz) diary

terminologi|a f terminology

terminow|y adi. ① (punktualny) prompt ② (pilny) urgent

termi|t m termite, white ant

termomet|r m thermometer

termos m Thermos® flask GB, Thermos® bottle US

terpentyn|a f turpentine

terro|r m terror; **~r psychiczny** mental pressure

terrory|sta m, **~stka** f terrorist

terroryz|ować impf vt to terrorize

terytorialn|y adi. [ekspansja, roszczenia, wody] territorial; **samorząd ~y** local authority a. government

terytori|um n territory

te|st m test

testamen|t m (last) will; testament także przen.; **spisać a. sporządzić ~t** to make a will; **zapisać coś komuś w ~cie** to will sth to sb

test|ować impf vt to test

teściow|a f mother-in-law

teści|owie plt parents-in-law; in-laws pot.

teś|ć m father-in-law

tez|a f ① (pogląd) thesis ② (w matematyce) proposition

też part. ① (również) too, also; **ona ~ ma taką torbę** she's got a bag like that, too; **ja ~ cię kocham** I love you too; **„widziałem ją wczoraj" – „i ja ~"** 'I saw her yesterday' – 'and so did I'; **nie jem mięsa, i mój brat ~ (nie)** I don't eat meat and my brother doesn't either; **„nie mogę spać" – „ja ~"** 'I can't sleep' – 'me neither'; **albo** a. **bądź ~** or (else); **dlaczego ~** that's why ② (lekceważąco) some pot.; **~ (mi) samochód!** some car that is! pot., iron.; **~ coś!** fiddlesticks! przest., pot. ③ (z oburzeniem, zdziwieniem) **co ~ pan mówi?** what are you saying?

tęcz|a f rainbow

■ **patrzeć** a. **wpatrywać się w kogoś jak w ~ę** to look up to sb

tęczow|y adi. iridescent

tęczów|ka f iris

tędy pron. this way; **chodźmy ~** let's go this way; **~ kiedyś płynęła rzeka** a river flowed by here at one time; **~ i owędy** here and there

tę|gi adi. grad. ① (gruby) stout ② (mocny) large; **oberwać tęgie lanie** to get a good hiding a. a sound trashing ③ (zdolny) good; **to tęga głowa** he has a good head on his shoulders ④ (silnie odczuwany) [mróz, zima] bitter

tępak m pot., obraźl. blockhead pot.

tęp|ić impf **Ⅰ** vt ① (niszczyć) to destroy [chwasty, szkodniki] ② (prześladować) to fight [przeciwników] ③ (czynić nieostrym) to blunt [nóż, nożyczki] ④ (osłabić) to dull [słuch, wzrok] ⑤ pot. (szkodzić) to persecute [osobę]

Ⅱ tępić się (stawać się nieostrym) [nóż, kosa] to blunt

tępo *adv.* [1] (nieostro) *[zakończony]* bluntly [2] (bezmyślnie) *[patrzeć]* blankly [3] pot. (głucho) *[dudnić]* dully

tępo|ta *f* pejor. [1] (umysłu) dullness [2] (zobojętnienie) numbness

tęp|y *adi.* [1] (nieostry) *[nóż, nożyczki, ołówek]* blunt; *[cios, uderzenie, ból, odgłos, słuch, wzrok]* dull [2] pot., obraźl. *[osoba]* dull; ~y uczeń a slow learner [3] (apatyczny) *[spojrzenie, zamyślenie]* blank; *[osoba]* numb

tęskni|ć *impf vi* [1] (odczuwać smutek) to miss (**za kimś/czymś** sb/sth); ~ć **za domem** to be homesick [2] (pragnąć) to long (**do kogoś/czegoś** for sb/sth)

tęskno|ta *f* [1] (smutek) longing (**za kimś/czymś** for sb/sth); **umierać z** ~**ty** to pine away [2] (pragnienie) yearning (**za czymś** for sth)

tęten|t *m* hoofbeat

tętniak *m* aneurysm, aneurism

tętnic|a *f* artery

tętni|ć *impf vi* [1] (dudnić) to thump [2] (pulsować) to pulsate; **ulica/szkoła** ~**ąca życiem** przen. a street/school vibrant with life

tętn|o *n* pulse; **zmierzyć komuś** ~**o** to take a. feel sb's pulse

tęż|ec *m* tetanus

tęż|eć *impf vi* [1] (zastygać) *[galareta]* to set [2] książk. (wzmagać się) *[mróz, wicher]* to increase

tik *m* twitch, tic

tk|ać *impf vt* to weave; **ręcznie tkany** hand-woven

tkanin|a *f* fabric, cloth

tkan|ka *f* tissue także przen.

t|knąć¹ *pf* — **t|ykać¹** *impf vi* [1] (dotknąć) to touch także przen.; **ani się waż mnie tknąć!** don't you dare touch me!; **nawet nie tknęła jedzenia** she didn't even touch food [2] (zacząć coś robić) **nie tknąć roboty** to not do a stroke of work

t|knąć² *pf vt* (opanować) *[myśl, podejrzenie]* to seize; **tknęło mnie złe przeczucie** I had an odd feeling about it; **tknięty trwogą** horror-struck, terror-stricken
■ **coś mnie tknęło** pot. I had a premonition; **coś mnie tknęło** a. **tknęło mnie, żeby...** something prompted a. induced me to...

tkwi|ć *impf vi* [1] (być głęboko osadzonym) to stick (**w czymś** in sth); ~ć **w jakimś układzie** przen. to be mixed up in sth [2] przen. (mieć źródło) to lie (**w czymś** sth); **przyczyna konfliktu** ~ **w nietolerancji** intolerance underlies the conflict; **zło** ~ **w nas samych** evil lies within ourselves [3] pot. (trwać nieruchomo) to be stuck

tlen *m* oxygen

tlen|ek *m* oxide; ~**ek węgla** carbon monoxide

tle|nić *impf* [I] *vt* pot. to bleach *[włosy]*; ~**niona blondynka** a peroxide blonde
⬎ **tlenić się** pot. to bleach one's hair

tl|ić się *impf v refl.* [1] (żarzyć się) *[ognisko, szmaty]* to smoulder GB, to smolder US [2] przen. *[uczucie]* to flicker

t|ło *n* background także przen.; **na tle czegoś** against a background of sth; **choroba na tle nerwowym** a psychosomatic disorder
❏ **tło muzyczne** background a. incidental music
■ **być** a. **pozostawać w tle** *[osoba]* to take a back seat; **na tle kogoś/czegoś** compared to sb/sth

tłocz|yć *impf* [I] *vt* [1] (wyciskać) to press *[olej, sok]* [2] (napełniać) to pump *[paliwo]* [3] Techn. to press *[płyty]* [4] (ozdabiać) to emboss
[II] **tłoczyć się** to crowd, to throng

tłok *m* [1] (ścisk) crowd, throng [2] Techn. piston

tłu|c *impf* [I] *vt* [1] (rozbijać) to break, to smash *[naczynia]* [2] (miażdżyć) to crush *[przedmiot]*; to grind *[cynamon, pieprz]*; to mash *[kartofle]*; to crack *[orzechy]* [3] pot. (bić) to beat *[dziecko]*; ~**kł brata pięściami po głowie** he was pummelling his brother's head
[II] *vi* (łomotać) to bang; **fale** ~**kły o skały** the waves battered against the rocks; ~**kł pięściami w drzwi** he banged the door with his fists; **w złości** ~**kła głową o ścianę** she beat her head against the wall in anger
[III] **tłuc się** [1] (rozbijać się) *[naczynia, szkło]* to break [2] (uderzać) *[fale]* to bang (**o coś** against sth)

tłucz|ek *m* (do mięsa) mallet; (do kartofli) potato masher; (w moździerzu) pestle

tłum *m* crowd

tłumacz *m*, ~**ka** *f* (pisma) translator; (mowy) interpreter; **rozmawiać przez** ~**a** to speak through an interpreter; ~ **przysięgły** sworn translator

tłumacze|nie *n* [1] (przekład) translation [2] (usprawiedliwienie) excuse [3] (komentarz) explanation

tłumacz|yć *impf* [I] *vt* [1] (objaśniać) to explain *[zadanie, zagadnienie]* [2] (uzasadniać) to justify *[decyzję]*; **jak** ~**yć jej zachowanie?** how would you account for her behaviour? [3] (przekładać) to translate *[tekst]*; to interpret *[wypowiedź]*; ~**yć z polskiego na angielski** to translate from Polish into English; ~**yć coś słowo w słowo** to translate sth word for word
[II] **tłumaczyć się** [1] (usprawiedliwiać się) to excuse oneself [2] (znajdować uzasadnienie) to explain; **to się** ~**y samo przez się** this goes without saying

tłum|ić *impf vt* to put out *[ogień]*; to muffle *[hałas]*; to dampen *[drgania]*; to suppress *[bunt, powstanie]*; to contain *[uczucia]*

tłumik *m* [1] Techn. silencer [2] Muz. mute, damper

tłu|sty *adi. grad.* [1] (zawierający tłuszcz) fatty; ~**ste mleko** unskimmed a. full-cream GB milk [2] *[naczynie, palce, plama]* greasy; *[cera, włosy]* oily [3] *[osoba, część ciała]* (otyły) fat; (okrągły) *[policzki]* chubby [4] *[czcionka, druk]* bold

tłuszcz m [1] Kulin. fat, grease [2] (składnik) fat; (w nabiale) butterfat; **fałdy ~u na brzuchu** rolls of fat round sb's waist

to [I] *pron.* [1] (zamiast podmiotu, dopełnienia) it; (nie tamto) this; „co to jest?" – „(to jest) książka" 'what's this/that?' – 'it's a book'; **kto to?** who's this/that?; **i co ty na to?** (and) what do you say to that?; **to mi się nie podoba** I don't like it; **to ma być małżeństwo?** you call this a marriage?; **co to ma znaczyć?** what's that supposed to mean?; **to są poważne sprawy** these are serious issues; **było to w piątek** it was on a Friday; **to, co się później działo, trudno wyjaśnić** what happened next is hard to explain; **nie troszczy się o to, czy będzie miał za co utrzymać rodzinę** he doesn't care about whether he'll be able to provide for his family [2] (zamiast czasownika) **oglądanie telewizji to strata czasu** watching television is a waste of time; **to miło z pana strony** that's (very) nice of you; **to fajnie, że przyszedłeś** pot. it's great to see you a. that you made it pot.

[II] *part.* (ekspresywne) **a to (dopiero) pech!** what bad a. rotten luck!; **a to z jakiej racji?** and why is that exactly?; **kogo to ja widzę?** well, well, what a surprise!; **no to co z tego?** well, what of it?; **to Stefan dostał nagrodę, nie Maria** it was Stefan who got the prize, not Maria

[III] *coni.* [1] (w konstrukcjach współrzędnych) **poszukaj, to znajdziesz** look for it and you'll find it; **to jest** a. **znaczy** that is; **to bladł, to czerwieniał** he went white and red by turns [2] (w zdaniach warunkowych) **gdybyś czegoś potrzebował, to napisz** write if you need anything; **skoro tak mówię, to wiem** I (should) know what I'm saying

■ **ni to, ni sio** a. **owo** neither one thing nor the other; **ni z tego, ni z owego** all of a sudden; **gawędzić o tym i owym** to talk about this and that; **to jest to!** that's it!

toale|ta f [1] (ubikacja) toilet; **~ta publiczna** public convenience a. toilet; **~ta damska/męska** the Ladies/Gents GB, ladies'/men's room US; **czy mogę skorzystać z ~ty?** could I use the toilet? [2] (zabiegi higieniczne) toilet [3] (suknia) gown

toa|st m toast

tob|ół m bundle

tocz|yć *impf* [I] *vt* [1] (turlać) to roll *[beczkę, kamień, koło]* [2] (prowadzić) to conduct *[debatę, kampanię, rokowania]*; **~yć wojnę z kimś** to fight a war with sb [3] (lać) to draw *[piwo, wino]* [4] (niszczyć) *[korniki, robaki]* to eat *[drewno, padlinę]*; książk. *[choroba]* to eat *[sb]* away; książk. *[smutek, tęsknota]* to eat away at [5] Techn. (na tokarce) to lathe, to turn *[części, śruby]*

[II] **toczyć się** [1] *[kamień, piłka, pojazd]* to roll [2] pot., żart. to trundle; **~ył się ścieżką** he was trundling along a path [3] *[działania, narada, śledztwo]* to be under way; *[bitwa, wydarzenia]* to take place; *[prace]* to proceed; **życie ~y się dalej** life goes on

■ **~yć wzrokiem po sali** to rove one's eyes around the room

t|oga f [1] (adwokata, profesora) gown [2] (rzymska) toga

tok m [1] (przebieg) course; **być w ~u** *[prace, przygotowania]* to be under way, to be in progress; **w ~u czegoś** in the course of sth; **w ~u śledztwa ustalono, że...** during the investigation it has been established that... [2] (kierunek) line; **~ myśli** the train of thought

tokar|ka f lathe

tokarz m turner

tolerancj|a f [1] (poszanowanie) tolerance (**dla** a. **wobec kogoś/czegoś** for a. towards sb/sth); **brak ~i** intolerance [2] (pobłażanie) tolerance (**dla** a. **wobec kogoś/czegoś** for a. of sb/sth); **zero ~i dla kogoś/czegoś** zero tolerance for sb/sth [3] Biol., Med. (wytrzymałość) tolerance (**na coś** for a. to sth) [4] Techn. (dopuszczalne odchylenie) tolerance; **z ~ą do...** to tolerance of...

tolerancyjn|y *adi.* tolerant (**dla** a. **wobec kogoś/czegoś** of sb/sth); *[prawo]* lenient (**dla** a. **wobec kogoś/czegoś** with sb/towards sth)

toler|ować *impf vt* [1] (znosić) to bear *[osobę, zachowanie]*; **nie ~ował krytyki** he (just) couldn't take a. accept criticism [2] (pobłażać) to allow *[zachowanie]* [3] Biol., Med. to tolerate *[leki, mleko]*

tom m book, volume; **encyklopedia w dwunastu ~ach** a twelve-volume encyclopaedia

ton m [1] Muz. (dźwięk) (musical) tone, (musical) note; (miara) (whole) tone, (whole) step US; (tonacja) (concert) pitch; **cały ~** a whole tone; **pół ~u** a semitone a. half-tone US; **śpiewać/grać o pół ~u wyżej/niżej** to go up/down a semitone [2] (sposób wypowiadania się) tone, tenor; **nie mów do mnie takim ~em!** don't speak to me in that tone of voice! [3] (odcień) tint

■ **spuścić z ~u** pot. to come down a peg (or two); **w dobrym ~ie jest** a. **do dobrego ~u należy...** it's the done thing to...

ton|a f (metric) ton, tonne

tonacj|a f [1] (kolorystyka) colour a. color US scheme; **w pastelowej ~i** in pastel shades [2] Muz. key; **w ~i e-moll/G-dur** in E minor/G major [3] (barwa głosu) pitch

to|nąć *impf vi* [1] (iść na dno) *[przedmiot]* to go under; *[okręt]* to founder; (topić się) *[osoba, zwierzę]* to drown [2] (zapadać się) *[osoba]* to sink; **tonąć po kostki w błocie** to sink up to one's ankles in mud [3] przen. to drown przen.; **tonąć (po uszy) w długach** to be up to one's ears in debt; **miasto tonęło w ciemnościach** the town was in total darkness

■ **tonąć we łzach** to dissolve into floods of tears

tonik m [1] (water) tonic [2] (kosmetyk) skin tonic

ton|ować *impf vt* (łagodzić) to tone down *[dyskusję, głos]*

topaz m topaz

top|ić *impf* **[I]** *vt* [1] (w wodzie) to drown *[osobę, zwierzę]*; to sink *[statek]*; przen. to sink; ~**ić pieniądze w czymś** to sink money in(to) sth [2] (roztapiać) to melt *[masło, śnieg]*

[II] topić się [1] (tonąć) *[osoba, zwierzę]* to drown; (samobójczo) to drown oneself [2] (zanurzać się) to sink (**w czymś** into sth) [3] (rozpuszczać się) to melt

■ ~**ić smutek w alkoholu** to drown one's sorrows (in drink)

topiel|ec *m*, ~**ica** *f* drowned body

topni|eć *impf vi* [1] (tajać) to melt [2] książk., przen. (łagodnieć) *[osoba, serce]* to melt; *[gniew, niepokój, opór]* to melt away [3] (zmniejszać się) *[wątpliwości]* to diminish; *[poparcie, zapał]* to ebb (away); *[oszczędności, zapasy]* to dwindle (away)

topografi|a *f* (dział geodezji) (geodetic) land surveying; (rzeźba terenu) topography

top|ola *f* poplar

toporn|y *adi. grad.* pot. *[dom, most, postać]* graceless; *[rysy, twarz]* coarse; *[ruch, styl, wykonanie]* clumsy

top|ór *m* [1] (broń) battleaxe, poleaxe GB, poleax US; (mniejszych rozmiarów) hatchet [2] (strażacki, do rąbania drewna) axe GB, ax US, chopper GB; ~**ór rzeźnicki** a (meat) chopper

■ **pójść pod** ~**ór** (o zwierzętach) to be slaughtered; (o lesie, drzewie) to be felled; **wykopać/zakopać** ~**ór wojenny** to take up/to bury the hatchet

to|r *m* [1] (szyny) track, railway; **tory kolejowe/ tramwajowe** railway track/tram line; **pociąg wjedzie na tor drugi** the train comes in on track number two; **boczny tor** side track, siding; **ślepy tor** stub track; przen. (sytuacja bez wyjścia) dead end, deadlock [2] (trajektoria) path; **tor pocisku** trajectory; **tor planetoidy** asteroid a. planetoid circuit [3] Sport (kajakowy, slalomowy) course; (bobslejowy, saneczkowy) run; (kręglarski) alley, rink; (kolarski, motocyklowy) (race)track; (łyżwiarski) rink

tor|ba *f* [1] (opakowanie) bag; (zawartość) bag, bagful [2] (do noszenia) bag; (na zakupy) carrier bag; **damska** ~**ba** a handbag; ~**ba podręczna** a holdall; ~**ba podróżna** a travel bag; ~**ba na ramię** a shoulder bag [3] Zool. pouch

■ **pójść z** ~**bami** pot. to be reduced to beggary; **puścić kogoś z** ~**bami** pot. to reduce sb to beggary

torbiel *f* cyst

toreb|ka *f* [1] (opakowanie) (small) bag; (zawartość) (small) bag, packet [2] (damska) bag, handbag

torf *m* peat

tornist|er *m* school bag

tor|ować *impf vt* ~**ować drogę** to pave the way także przen. (**komuś/czemuś** for sb/sth); ~**ować sobie przejście** to clear a path for oneself; ~**ować sobie drogę łokciami** to elbow one's way; ~**ować komuś drogę do sławy** to pave sb's way to fame

torpe|da *f* torpedo

torped|ować *impf vt* to torpedo także przen.

tors *m* torso

torsj|e *plt* vomiting; **mieć** ~**e** to vomit

tor|t *m* (layer) cake

tortownic|a *f* springform pan

tortu|ra *f* [1] (fizyczna) torture [2] (moralna) torment, anguish

tortur|ować *impf vt* [1] (katować) to torture [2] (nękać) to torment

to|st *m* piece a. slice of toast

totalitaryzm *m* totalitarianism

totalizato|r *m* [1] (gra hazardowa) totalizator; ~**r piłkarski** the pools [2] (kolektura) lottery office

totem *m* totem (pole)

totolot|ek, toto-lot|ek *m* [1] (loteria) ≈ (national) lottery [2] przen., pot. lottery

tournée /turˈne/ *n inv.* tour

towa|r *m* (rzeczy) goods, merchandise; (rzecz) commodity; „**przyjęcie** ~**ru**" 'closed for deliveries'

towarow|y **[I]** *adi.* [1] *[giełda, wymiana]* goods; **bon** ~**y** a voucher; **znak** ~**y (zastrzeżony)** a (registered) trademark [2] Transp. *[winda]* service

[II] *m* freight train

towarzys|ki *adi.* [1] *[natura, osoba]* sociable, gregarious [2] *[formy, skandal]* social; *[pogawędka, zebranie]* informal; **ożywione życie** ~**kie** a busy social life

towarzystw|o *n* [1] (obecność) company; **dotrzymać komuś** ~**a** to keep sb company [2] (grupa) company; **dostać się w złe** ~**o** to fall into bad company [3] (elita) (high) society [4] (organizacja) society; ~**o naukowe** a learned society

■ **dla** ~**a** for company

towarzysz *m*, ~**ka** *f* [1] (kompan) companion; ~ **podróży** a travelling companion; ~ **broni** a comrade a. brother in arms [2] Polit. comrade

towarzysz|yć *impf vi* [1] (asystować) to accompany (**komuś** sb); to keep [sb] company; **osoba** ~**ąca** an escort; **osoby** ~**ące** entourage [2] (współwystępować) to accompany; **gorączce** ~**ył ból** the fever was accompanied by pain; **z** ~**eniem orkiestry** with the accompaniment of an orchestra

tożsamoś|ć *f* książk. identity

tra|cić *impf vt* [1] (przestawać mieć) to lose; ~**cić władzę w nodze** to lose the use of one's leg; ~**cić oddech** to get out of breath; ~**cić nadzieję** to lose a. abandon hope; ~**cić liście** to shed leaves [2] (marnować) to waste *[czas]*; ~**cić ciężko zarobione pieniądze** to fritter away hard-earned money

■ ~**cić wątek** to lose the thread; ~**cić miarę** to know no measure (**w czymś** in sth); ~**cić ducha** to lose one's spirit; ~**cić na wartości** to depreciate

tradycj|a *f* tradition

traf *m* stroke of luck; **szczęśliwy** ~ a fluke; **szczęśliwym** ~**em** as luck would have it; **dziwnym** ~**em** by a strange twist of fate; ~ **chciał, że...** as luck would have it...

traf|ić *pf* — **traf|iać** *impf* **[]** *vi* [1] (nie chybić) to hit; ~**ić do celu** to hit the target; ~**ić w dziesiątkę** to hit the bull's eye pot. [2] (znaleźć drogę) to find one's way [3] (znaleźć się w sytuacji) ~**ić do szpitala/do więzienia** to land in hospital/prison; ~**ił akurat na obiad** he came just in time for dinner; ~**ić na niespodziewany opór** to encounter unexpected resistance; ~**ić na znajomego** to come across a friend

[] **trafić się** — **trafiać się** (zdarzyć się) to come up; ~**ia się dobry kupiec** a good buyer has come up

■ ~**ić w czuły punkt** to touch a raw nerve; ~**iać komuś do przekonania** to convince sb; ~**iła kosa na kamień** przysł. ≈ he/she has met his/her match

trafnie *adv. grad.* [oceniać, scharakteryzować] accurately; [ująć] aptly; [określić] precisely

trafn|y *adi. grad.* [1] (celny) accurate [2] (właściwy) [diagnoza, prognoza] accurate; [nazwa, wybór] appropriate; [słowo] right, correct; [uwaga] pertinent

tragedi|a *f* tragedy także przen.

■ **robić** ~**ę z czegoś** to make a drama out of sth

tragiczn|y **[]** *adi. grad.* [1] [zdarzenie, wypadek] tragic [2] pot., pejor. [warunki, wygląd] terrible; **przedstawienie było na** ~**ym poziomie** the show was abysmal pot.

[] *adi.* [aktor, bohater, rola] tragic, tragical

trak|t *m* (szlak komunikacyjny) route; (droga) road; ~**t pieszy** a pedestrian walkway; ~**t wodny** a waterway

■ **w** ~**cie czegoś** in the course of sth; **jestem w** ~**cie przeprowadzki** I'm in the middle of moving (house); **w** ~**cie rozmowy powiedział, że...** in the course of the conversation he said that...

trakta|t *m* [1] (umowa) treaty [2] (rozprawa) treatise

trakto|r *m* [1] (pojazd) tractor [2] pot. (but) bovver boot GB, stogie US pot.; (podeszwa) lug sole US

trakt|ować *impf* **[]** *vt* (odnosić się) to treat; ~**uję to jako komplement** I consider it a compliment

[] *vi* książk. **książki** ~**ujące o filozofii** books treating of a. dealing with philosophy

■ ~**ować kogoś jak powietrze** to ignore sb; ~**ować kogoś z góry** to look down on sb; ~**ować życie lekko** to make light of things

tramwaj *m* tram(car) GB, streetcar US

tran *m* (wielorybi) train oil, whale oil; (rybi) fish oil; (z foki) seal oil; ~ **leczniczy** cod liver oil

transakcj|a *f* deal, transaction; ~**a bankowa** a banking transaction; ~**a wiązana** a tie-in deal także przen.

transformacj|a *f* książk. transformation

transformato|r *m* transformer

transfuzj|a *f* transfusion

transmisj|a *f* [1] (nadawanie) transmission; (program) broadcast [2] Techn. transmission

transmit|ować *impf* *vt* to broadcast [mecz, koncert, program telewizyjny]; to transmit [sygnał]

transparen|t *m* [1] (na manifestacji) banner, placard [2] (reklama) (advertising) banner

transpor|t *m* [1] (przewóz) transport GB, transportation US; ~**t sanitarny** patient transport (service); **środki** ~**tu** means of transport [2] (środki lokomocji) transport [3] (ładunek) consignment; (konwojowana grupa ludzi) transport

transport|ować *impf* *vt* to transport [towar, osoby]; to move [chorych]

tranzy|t *m* transit; **jechać** ~**tem z Polski do Włoch** to be in transit from Poland to Italy

trapez *m* [1] (figura) trapezium GB, trapezoid US [2] Sport trapeze

trap|ić *impf* książk. **[]** *vt* to trouble; **co cię** ~**i?** what's bothering you?; ~**iły go wyrzuty sumienia/wątpliwości** he was plagued by a guilty conscience/beset with doubts

[] **trapić się** to worry (oneself) (**czymś** a. **o coś** about sth); **nie** ~ **się tym tak bardzo!** don't fret about it so much!

tras|a *f* [1] (szlak komunikacyjny) route; ~**a szybkiego ruchu** ≈ an A road; **na** ~**ie Warszawa-Kraków** a. **z Warszawy do Krakowa** on the way from Warsaw to Cracow [2] (droga do przebycia) route; (marszruta) itinerary; ~**a koncertowa** a (concert) tour [3] Sport (wyścigu kolarskiego) route; (slalomu) course; ~**a narciarska** a ski run

trat|ować *impf* *vt* to trample [trawnik, uprawy]

trat|wa *f* raft

traw|a *f* [1] Bot. grass [2] pot. (marihuana) grass, weed pot.

■ **wiedzieć, co w** ~**ie piszczy** pot. to be (always) in the know

traw|ić *impf* *vt* [1] (wchłaniać) to digest [pokarm]; ~**ić dobrze/źle** to have good/poor digestion [2] [enzymy] to digest [białko, skrobię] [3] (niszczyć) to consume także przen.; **dziecko** ~**iła gorączka** the child was burning up with fever; **kraj** ~**iony korupcją** a country undermined by corruption [4] (rozpuszczać kwasem) to pickle, to etch [metal]; to etch [kliszę drukarską, szkło]

■ **nie** ~**ić czegoś** pot. to have no liking for sth; **nie** ~**ię nowoczesnej muzyki** I can't stand contemporary music

trawieni|e *n* digestion

trawnik *m* lawn; „**nie deptać** ~**ów**" 'keep off the grass'

trąb|a *f* [1] Muz. trumpet [2] Zool. trunk [3] pot. (fajtłapa) bungler; (głupiec) ass pot. [4] ~**a powietrzna** a whirlwind

■ **zrobić kogoś w** ~**ę** to make a fool of sb

trąb|ić *impf* **[]** *vt* [1] (grać na instrumencie) to play the trumpet; ~**ić na alarm** to sound the alarm; ~**ić pobudkę** to sound the reveille [2] pot. (pić) to guzzle

[] *vi* [1] [zwierzę] to trumpet [2] [kierowca] to sound the horn; „**zakaz** ~**ienia**" 'no honking' ③ pot. (rozgłaszać) ~**ić o czymś** to trumpet sth

trąb|ka f ① Muz. trumpet ② (przyrząd sygnalizacyjny) horn ③ przen. (rurka) tube; **dłoń zwinięta w** ~**kę** a cupped hand

trą|cić[1] pf — **trą|cać** impf vt (lekko uderzyć) to knock; (łokciem) to nudge; ~**cić strunę** to strike a string

■ ~**cać się kieliszkami** to clink glasses

trą|cić[2] impf vi książk. ~**cić czymś** przen. to smack of sth

trądzik m acne

trefl m club

trefn|y adi. pot. [towar] hot pot.; [osoba] fishy pot.

trem|a f nerves; (przed występem) stage fright

tren|d m książk. trend; ~**dy w modzie** fashion trends

trene|r m, ~**rka** f Sport coach

tren|ować impf [] vt ① Sport to train [zawodników]; ~**ować konie** to train horses ② (ćwiczyć) to practise GB, to practice US [dyscyplinę sportu]

[] vi Sport to train

trese|r m, ~**rka** f trainer

tres|ować impf vt to train [zwierzęta]

tresowan|y adi. [pies, koń] trained; [słoń, foka] performing

treściw|y adi. grad. ① (zwięzły) concise ② (pożywny) substantial

treś|ć f ① (wypowiedzi) content; **powiastki o** ~**ci filozoficznej** short stories with a philosophical content ② (książki, filmu) plot; ~**cią tego filmu jest...** the film is about... ③ (sens) meaning; **praca była** ~**cią jego życia** his work gave meaning to his life

tri|k m trick

triumf m triumph; ~ **dobra nad złem** the triumph of good over evil

triumfaln|y adi. [przemarsz, tournée] triumphal; [okrzyk, uśmiech] triumphant

triumf|ować impf vi ① (odnosić zwycięstwo) to triumph (**nad kimś** over sb) ② (chełpić się) to exult ③ przen. to prevail; **dobro** ~**owało nad złem** good prevailed over evil

tro|chę [] adv. ① (nieco) a bit; **wyglądało to** ~**chę inaczej** it wasn't quite like that; **ani** ~**chę** not a bit ② (jakiś czas) (for) a bit; **musisz** ~**chę poczekać** you'll have to wait a bit; **poczekaj jeszcze** ~**chę** wait a while longer

[] pron. (niewiele) (z niepoliczalnymi) a bit, a little (**czegoś** of sth); (z policzalnymi) a few; ~**chę pieprzu do smaku** a little pepper to taste; **przyszło** ~**chę ludzi** (niewiele) only a handful of a. a few people came; (sporo) quite a few people came

■ **do diabła** a. **licha i** ~**chę** a heck a. hell of a lot pot.; **po** ~**chu** (stopniowo) bit by bit; **chcę wszystkiego po** ~**chu** I want a bit of everything

trocin|y plt (wióry) sawdust

trofe|um n trophy

trojaczk|i plt triplets

troje num. mult. three

trok m strap

trolejbus m trolleybus

tron m throne; przen. (władza) the throne; **wstąpić na** ~ to ascend the throne

trop m ① (zwierzęcia) track; **pies zwęszył** ~ **dzika** the dog picked up the scent of a boar ② przen. (wskazówka) trail; **wpaść na** ~ **zbiega** to pick up the fugitive's trail; **to może naprowadzić na jej** ~ it may help find her whereabouts

■ **być na fałszywym/dobrym** ~**ie** to be on the wrong/right track

trop|ić impf vt to track [zwierzę, ślady]; to track down [przestępców]

tropik m ① (obszar) the tropics; (klimat) tropical weather; **żyć w** ~**ach** to live in the tropics ② (nakrycie namiotu) flysheet ③ (tkanina) tropical fabric

tros|ka f ① (niepokój) worry; **w jej oczach pojawiła się** ~**ka** a worried look appeared on her face; **codzienne** ~**ki** the cares of the day ② (dbałość) concern; **w** ~**ce o coś** out of concern for sth

troskliwie adv. with care

troskliw|y adi. [osoba] caring; [opieka] loving; [wzrok, spojrzenie] thoughtful

troszczy|ć się impf v refl. ① (dbać) to care (**o kogoś/coś** about a. for sb/sth); ~**ył się, żeby miała wszystko** he saw to it that she had everything; **nikt się nie** ~**ył, czy mam co jeść** nobody cared whether I had anything to eat ② (martwić się) to worry (**o kogoś/coś** about sb/sth)

trój|ka f ① (cyfra) three ② (ocena) ≈ C ③ pot. (bieg w samochodzie) third gear

trójką|t m triangle

❑ **Trójkąt Bermudzki** Bermuda Triangle; ~**t małżeński** eternal triangle; ~**t ostrzegawczy** a. **odblaskowy** warning triangle

trójkątn|y adi. triangular

truch|t m (konia) jogtrot; (osoby) jog, trot; ~**tem** at a trot

truci|zna f poison także przen.; ~**zna na szczury** rat poison

tru|ć impf [] vt to poison także przen.

[] vi pot. (mówić nieciekawie) to babble; (mówić nieprawdę) to bullshit wulg.; (zrzędzić) to nag

[] **truć się** ① (zabijać) to poison oneself także przen. ② pot. (marwić się) to worry oneself sick

tru|d m ① (wysiłek) effort; **kosztować wiele** ~**du** to be quite an effort; **zadać sobie** ~**d (zrobienia czegoś)** to take (great) pains (to do sth); **nie zadać sobie** ~**du (zrobienia czegoś)** iron. to not (even) bother (to do sth); **nie szczędzić** ~**du, żeby coś zrobić** to go to great lengths to do sth; **bez** ~**du** easily; **z** ~**dem** with (an) effort; **z** ~**dem zdążył na pociąg** he only just caught the train ② (ciężkie warunki) hardship

trudni|ć się *impf vi* książk. ~**ć się czymś** to be in(to) sth; ~**ł się handlem** he was in trade

trudno [ ] *adv. grad.* (niełatwo) hard; ~ **mi ocenić jego zachowanie** it's difficult for me to judge his behaviour; ~ **mi to zrozumieć** I can hardly understand it

[ ] *adv.* (nie można) ~ **powiedzieć** it's difficult a. hard to tell; ~ **się dziwić, że...** it's no wonder (that)...

[ ] *inter.* ~ **(i darmo)** pot. tough luck

trudnoś|ć *f* [ ] (przeszkoda) difficulty, problem; ~**ci finansowe** financial difficulties; **mieć** ~**ci z oddychaniem** to have difficulty in breathing; **matematyka nie sprawia mu** ~**ci** he has no problems with maths [ ] (cecha) difficulty; **pytania o różnym stopniu** ~**ci** questions of varying difficulty

■ **robić komuś** ~**ci** to cause difficulties for sb

trudn|y *adi. grad.* [ ] (niełatwy) *[problem, pytanie]* difficult; *[dzieciństwo, okres]* tough; ~**y do zrozumienia** difficult to understand [ ] (oporny) *[osoba, dziecko]* difficult; **jest** ~**y w pożyciu** he's difficult to deal with; **mieć** ~**y charakter** to be difficult

tru|dzić *impf* [ ] *vt* [ ] (fatygować) to trouble [ ] książk. (męczyć) to tire; ~**dzić oczy** to strain one's eyes

[ ] **trudzić się** to toil; **niepotrzebnie się pan** ~**dził** you needn't have bothered

trując|y *adi.* poisonous

trum|na *f* coffin GB, casket US

trup *m* [ ] (zwłoki) (człowieka) corpse; (zwierzęcia) carcass [ ] pot. (rupieć) piece of junk; (samochód) jalopy, old banger pot.

■ **iść po** ~**ach** to walk over everybody pot.; **położyć kogoś** ~**em** to mow sb down; **paść** ~**em** to drop dead; **po moim** ~**ie** pot. over my dead body pot.

trupi *adi.* [ ] ~**a czaszka** (symbol) a skull and crossbones [ ] przen. *[cera, skóra]* deathly pale; *[bladość]* deathly

truskaw|ka *f* strawberry

trut|ka *f* poison; ~**ka na myszy/szczury** mouse/ rat poison

trwa|ć *impf vi* [ ] (istnieć przez dłuższy czas) to last; **seans** ~**ł około godziny** the film lasted (for) about an hour; **nic nie** ~ **wiecznie** nothing lasts forever; **prace już** ~**ją** work is now in progress [ ] (pozostawać) to remain; ~**ć przy kimś** to stand by sb; ~**ć przy czymś/przy swoim** to stick to sth/to one's guns

trwa|ły [ ] *adi. grad. [związek, uczucie, wartość]* (long-)lasting; *[produkt, buty]* durable; ~**łe kalectwo** permanent disability; **na** ~**łe** permanently

[ ] **trwała** *f* perm

trwo|nić *impf vt* książk. to waste

tryb [ ] *m* [ ] (metoda) mode; ~ **postępowania** a course of action; ~ **życia** lifestyle; **zwolnić kogoś w** ~**ie natychmiastowym** książk. to dismiss sb with immediate effect; **w** ~**ie pilnym** książk. as a

matter of urgency [ ] Techn. gear(wheel) [ ] Jęz. mood

[ ] **tryby** *plt* przen. machine przen.

trybun|a *f* [ ] (dla mówcy) podium [ ] (dla władz) parade stand; ~**a honorowa** a box [ ] (dla widzów) stand; **kryta** ~**a** a grandstand; **wiwatujące** ~**y** przen. cheering spectators

trybuna|ł *m* tribunal; przen. judgement

tryko|t *m* [ ] (dzianina) tricot [ ] (kostium gimnastyczny) leotard; (bielizna) body stocking

trys|nąć *pf* — **trys|kać** *impf vi* [ ] (woda, krew) to gush (out) [ ] przen. ~**kać energią/dowcipem** to be bursting with energy/to be sparkling with wit; ~**kać zdrowiem** to be bouncing a. radiant with health

trzask *m* (gałęzi, lodu) crack; **zamknąć drzwi z** ~**iem** to bang a. slam the door

trza|snąć *pf* — **trza|skać** *impf* [ ] *vt* to bang; ~**skać drzwiami** to bang a. slam the door; ~**skać obcasami** to click one's heels

[ ] *vi (gałąź, lód)* to crack; *[drzwi]* to slam; **ogień** ~**skał w kominku** a log fire crackled in the hearth; **na dworze** ~**skający mróz** it's freezing outside

trzą|ść *impf* [ ] *vt* [ ] (gwałtownie poruszać) to shake; **gorączka go** a. **nim** ~**ęsie** he's shaking a. trembling with fever [ ] pot. (rządzić) to keep a firm grip (**kimś/czymś** on sb/sth)

[ ] *vi [samochód, wóz]* to jolt

[ ] **trząść się** (dygotać) to shake; ~**ąść się ze złości** to quiver with anger

■ ~**ąść się nad kimś/czymś** a. **o kogoś/coś** to dote (up)on sb/sth; ~**ąść się od plotek** to buzz with gossip

trzcin|a *f* [ ] Bot. reed; ~**a cukrowa** sugar cane [ ] (zarośla) reeds [ ] (do wyplatania) cane; **dach z** ~**y** a thatched roof

trzeba *praed.* [ ] (należy) ~ **pracować** it's necessary to work; ~ **mu o tym powiedzieć** he ought to a. should be told about it; ~ **być głupim, żeby tak się zachować** only a fool would behave like that; **sprawdź, czy wszystko jest jak** ~ go and check everything is all right; **pójdę tam, jeśli** ~ I'll go there, if necessary; ~ **przyznać, że...** admittedly...; ~ **dodać, że...** additionally... [ ] (potrzeba) **będzie miała wszystko, czego jej** ~ she'll have everything she needs; **do tego** ~ **dużo cierpliwości** this requires a lot of patience; „**pomóc ci?" – „nie** ~" 'do you need help?' – 'no, thanks'; ~ **czasu, aby to zrozumieć** it takes time to understand it

■ ~ **ci wiedzieć, że...** książk. you should be aware (that)...; ~ **trafu, że...** as luck would have it...

trzeci *num. ord.* third; ~ **migdał** adenoid

■ **osoby** ~**e** a. **ktoś** ~ third party; **po** ~**e** third(ly); ~ **wiek** the third age

t|rzeć *impf* [ ] *vt* [ ] (pocierać) to rub; **trzeć oczy** to rub one's eyes [ ] (na tarce) to grate *[ser, chrzan]* [ ] (rozgniatać) to grind *[mak]*

II *vi* to rub (**o coś** against a. on sth)

trzepacz|ka *f* ① (do dywanów) carpet beater ② Kulin. (egg) whisk, egg beater

trzepać¹ *impf* → **trzepnąć**

trzep|ać² *impf vt* ① (z kurzu) ~**ać dywan** to beat dust out of a carpet ② pot. (mówić szybko) to rattle off *[wiersz]*; ~**ać językiem** to prattle on

trzepak *m* hanging frame

trzep|nąć *pf* — **trzep|ać**¹ *impf* **II** *vt* pot. (uderzyć) to bop pot.; to cuff

II *vi* (potrząsnąć) to flick; ~**ać ogonem** *[ryba]* to flop its toil

trzeszcz|eć *impf vi [schody, gałęzie]* to creak

trzewi|a *plt* entrails

trzeźw|ić *impf vt* ① (cucić) to bring [sb] round GB a. around US; **sole** ~**iące** smelling salts ② przen. to sober up

trzeźwi|eć *impf vi* ① *[pijany]* to sober up ② (odzyskiwać przytomność) to come round GB a. around US

trzeźwo **II** *adv. grad. [oceniać]* soberly; **myśleć** ~ to be clear-headed

II na trzeźwo ① pot. (nie będąc pijanym) when sober ② (bez emocji) *[rozważyć, przemyśleć]* soberly

trzeźwoś|ć *f* sobriety; ~**ć umysłu** clear-headedness

trzeźw|y *adi. grad.* ① (niepijany) sober ② (rozsądny) sober; **mieć o kimś/czymś** ~**y sąd** to view sb/sth in realistic terms

trzęsie|nie *n* ~**nie ziemi** an earthquake; przen. a revolution

trzmiel *m* Zool. bumblebee, humble-bee

trz|oda *f* flock; ~**oda chlewna** pigs

trzon *m* ① (grupy, organizacji) hard core ② (grzyba) stem

trzon|ek *m* (uchwyt) handle

trzust|ka *f* pancreas

t|rzy *num.* three

■ **pracować za trzech** to work like nobody's business pot.; **jeść za trzech** to eat like a horse; **do trzech razy sztuka** przysł. third time lucky; **pleść trzy po trzy** pot. to talk nineteen to the dozen GB; **nie umieć zliczyć do trzech** to be a dunce

trzydzie|sty *num. ord.* thirtieth

trzydzie|ści *num.* thirty-

trzyma|ć *impf* **II** *vt* ① (nie wypuszczać) to hold; ~**ć dziecko na rękach** to hold a baby in one's arms; ~**ć kogoś za rękę** to hold sb by the hand ② (ograniczać) to keep; ~**ć kogoś w niewoli** to hold sb prisoner; ~**ć psa na smyczy** to lead a dog on a leash; ~**ć kogoś na diecie** to keep sb on a diet ③ (przechowywać) to keep; ~**ć pieniądze w kasie** to keep money in the till ④ pot. (hodować) to keep *[krowy, kury]*

II *vi* ① *[klej, szew]* to hold (fast) ② *[mróz, śnieg]* to hold

III trzymać się ① (chwytać się) ~**ć się czegoś** to hold on to sth *[poręczy, liny]* ② (pozostawać) ~**ć się**

razem to keep a. stick together; ~**ć się z daleka od kogoś/czegoś** to keep away from sb/sth; ~**ć się prawej strony** to keep to the right ③ (zachowywać kondycję) ~**ć się prosto** to hold oneself straight; **dobrze się** ~**ć** to be in good shape; ~**j się (ciepło)!** take care! ④ (panować nad sobą) to bear up; **nie rozpaczaj,** ~**j się!** don't give up! ⑤ (przestrzegać) ~**ć się czegoś** to adhere to sth

■ **myśl o dziecku** ~**ła ją przy życiu** the thought of her child kept her going; ~**ć kogoś krótko** to keep a tight reign on sb; ~**ć coś pod kluczem** to keep sth under lock and key; ~**ć kogoś pod pantoflem** to henpeck sb; ~**ć kogoś za słowo** to hold sb to his/her word; ~**ć się na słowo honoru** to hold together, but only just; **pieniądze się go nie** ~**ją** he never seems to have enough money; **żarty się ciebie** ~**ją** you must be joking; ~**ć z kimś** a. **trzymać czyjąś stronę** to side with sb

trzynast|ka *f* ① (liczba) thirteen ② pot. (pensja) annual bonus

trzyna|sty *num. ord.* thirteenth

trzyna|ście *num.* thirteen

trz|ysta *num.* three hundred

tu **II** *pron.* ① (wskazujący miejsce) here; (wewnątrz) in here; **jej tu nie ma** she's not here; **czy jest tu ktoś?** is anybody there?; **tu spoczywa...** (na nagrobku) here lies...; **tu mieszkam** this is where I live; **tu i tam** here and there; **tu i teraz** here and now ② (wskazujący na sytuację) here, there; **tu się mylisz** that's where you're wrong; **żal nic tu nie pomoże** it's no use grieving; **tu cię mam!** I've got you there! pot.

II *part.* ① (przedstawienie się) **tu Jan, czy mogę mówić z Adamem?** this is Jan, can a. may I speak to Adam?; **tu numer 567832** this is 567832; **tu Polskie Radio, Program I** Polish Radio, Programme 1 ② (ekspresywne) **i co tu teraz robić!** and what am I/are we (going) to do now?; **wierz tu teraz komuś!** you (just) can't trust anyone!

tub|a *f* ① (do wzmacniania głosu) speaking tube; (przedmiot w kształcie rury) tube ② przen., pejor. (głosiciel) mouthpiece ③ Muz. tuba

tubaln|y *adi. [głos, śmiech]* booming; *[głos]* stentorian

tubyl|ec *m* native także przen.

tucz|yć *impf* **II** *vt* to fatten *[drób, świnie]*; pot., żart. to feed up *[osobę]*

II *vi* to make fat; **cukier** ~**y** sugar makes you fat

■ **kradzione nie** ~**y** przysł. ill-gotten gains seldom prosper

tul|ić *impf* **II** *vt* ① (obejmować) to hug; **matka** ~**iła dziecko do piersi** the mother hugged her child (tightly) ② (dotykać) to nestle; ~**ił głowę do kolan matki** he nestled his head against his mothers knees ③ (chować) **psy** ~**iły ogony pod siebie** the dogs put their tails between their legs; **kwiat** ~**ił płatki o zmroku** the flower folded its petals at twilight

II tulić się to cuddle (up); ~**ić się do ciepłego**

pieca to nestle up against a warm stove; **dzieci ~iły się do matki** the children were cuddling up to their mother

tulipan *m* tulip

tułacz *m* książk. wanderer

tułacz|ka *f* książk. [1] (kobieta tułacz) wanderer [2] (życie bezdomne) wandering (life)

tuła|ć się *impf v refl.* [1] (wędrować) to wander; **~ć się po świecie** to wander the earth [2] (wałęsać się) to roam, to rove

tuł|ów *m* (człowieka) torso; (zwierzęcia) trunk

tuman *m* [1] (kłąb) cloud; **~ kurzu** a cloud of dust; **~ liści/śniegu** a flurry of leaves/snow [2] książk. (mgła) mist [3] pot., obraźl. (o osobie) thickhead pot., obraźl.

tunel *m* (odcinek drogi) tunnel; (pomieszczenie) passage

tuńczyk *m* tuna (fish)

tupe|t *m* [1] (śmiałość) impudence, cheek; **ale ~t!** what a cheek a. nerve! [2] (peruka) toupee

tupo|t *m* stamp(ing)

tu|ra *f* [1] (etap, runda) round [2] (grupa) group, party

turbin|a *f* turbine

turkus *m* turquoise

turl|ać *impf* **[]** *vt* to roll

[] turlać się [kulki, moneta] to roll about

turniej *m* [1] Sport championship(s); **~ szachowy** a chess championship a. tournament [2] (rycerski) tournament

tury|sta *m*, **~stka** *f* tourist

turystyczn|y *adi.* [sezon, informacja] tourist; atrakcja **~a** a showplace; **szlak ~y** a tourist route; **sprzęt ~y** camping equipment; **buty ~e** walking a. hiking boots; **przyczepa ~a** a caravan; **klasa ~a** tourist a. economy class

turysty|ka *f* tourism; **~ka piesza** hiking

tusz *m* [1] (farba) ink; **~ kreślarski** drawing ink [2] (do rzęs) mascara

tusz|a *f* [1] corpulence; **kobieta okazałej ~y** an obese woman [2] (ubite zwierzę) carcass

tutaj → **tu**

tusz|ować *impf vt* [1] (ukrywać) to cover up [przestępstwo, prawdę] [2] (maskować) to mask [braki urody, figury]

tutej|szy *adi.* [szkoła, warunki] local; **nie wiem, nie jestem ~sza** I don't know, I'm a stranger here

tuzin *m* dozen; **dwa ~y jaj** two dozen eggs

tuż *part.* [1] (w przestrzeni) **~ przed kimś/czymś** right in front of sb/sth; **~ za kimś/czymś** right behind sb/sth; **~ pod/nad oknem** just under/above the window; **~ obok kogoś/czegoś** right next to sb/ sth [2] (w czasie) **~ po/przed czymś** just after/before sth; **~ potem** shortly after(wards); **Boże Narodzenie ~, ~** Christmas is just around the corner; **zwycięstwo było ~, ~** victory was practically in our/their grasp

twardni|eć *impf vi* [1] [cement, klej] to harden [2] przen. [osoba] to harden (one's heart); [głos, rysy] to harden

twar|do *adv. grad.* [1] [udeptany, ubity] hard; **spać ~do** pot. to be sound a. fast asleep [2] przen. [wychowywać, postępować] strictly; [upierać się, żądać] firmly

twar|dy *adi. grad.* [1] (nieelastyczny) [nawierzchnia, materac] hard; [mięso] tough [2] przen. [charakter, osobowość] hard; [biznesmen, zawodnik, warunki, prawo] tough; [gra, sport] rough; [głos, słowa] harsh ■ **~dy człowiek** hard man; **~dy sen** sound sleep; **~de serce** hard heart

twar|óg *m* curd a. cottage cheese

twarz *f* face także przen.; **na zebraniu było kilka nowych ~y** there were a few new faces at the meeting ■ **do ~y jej w tym** it suits a. becomes her; **czy byłoby mi do ~y w różowym?** would I look good in pink?; **powiedzieć coś komuś (prosto) w ~** pot. to tell sb sth to their face; **leżeć/siedzieć/ stać ~ą do kogoś/czegoś** to face sb/sth; **padać na ~** pot. to be dead tired; **spotkać się a. stanąć ~ą w ~ z kimś** to come a. stand face to face with sb; **stanąć ~ą w ~ z czymś** to face sth; **stracić/ zachować ~** to lose/save face; **wyjść z czegoś z ~ą** pot. to get out of sth without losing face; **wziąć a. trzymać kogoś za ~** pot. to keep sb on a tight rein

twarzow|y *adi.* [1] (dotyczący twarzy) [nerw, mimika] facial [2] (zdobiący) becoming

twierdz|a *f* stronghold; przen. bastion przen.

twierdząco *adv.* affirmatively

twierdze|nie *n* [1] (wyrażenie opinii) statement [2] (w logice, matematyce) theorem; **~nie Pitagorasa** Pythagoras' theorem

twier|dzić *impf vi* to claim; **~dził, że jest wyleczony** he claimed he'd been cured; **~dzą, że nie jest tchórzem** they say he's not a coward; **rząd ~dzi, że cięcia w budżecie są konieczne** the government maintains budget cuts are essential

tw|orzyć *impf* **[]** *vt* to form [rząd, armię]; to build [osiedla]; to create [dzieło, powieść]; to compose [preludia, sonaty]; to form [szpaler, rozlewisko]; **tworzyli zgraną parę** they were a well-matched couple

[] tworzyć się [oddziały] to be formed; [kałuże] to form

tworzyw|o *n* material; przen. raw material; **~o sztuczne** plastic

tw|ój **[]** *pron.* (przed rzeczownikiem) your; (bez rzeczownika) yours; **twój długopis/twoje mieszkanie** your pen/flat; **pieniądze nie były twoje** the money wasn't yours; **czy to twoja książka?** is this book yours?; **to twój kolega?** is that one of your friends?

[] twój *m*, **twoja** *f* pot. your other half pot.

[] twoi *plt* (rodzina) your family; **co tam słychać u twoich?** how's the a. your family?

[] twoje *n* (własność) your property

[] po twojemu (według ciebie) according to you;

niech już będzie po twojemu okay, have it your own way

tw|ór *m* [1] (stworzenie) creature [2] (wytwór) creation

twór|ca *m*, **~czyni** *f* [1] (autor) author [2] (artysta) artist; **~cy ludowi** folk artists

twórczoś|ć *f* [1] (tworzenie) (artistic) work; **obchodził dwudziestolecie swej ~ci filmowej** he celebrated twenty years in the cinema; **dzieje życia i ~ci van Gogha** the life and works of Van Gogh [2] (dorobek) production; **jej ~ć literacka** her literary output

■ **radosna ~ć** pot., iron. messing around

twórcz|y *adi.* [1] (odkrywczy) *[działalność, koncepcja]* creative; *[dyskusja, krytyka]* constructive [2] (dotyczący twórców) *[środowisko, związki]* artistic

ty [1] *pron.* you; **ty to zrób** you do it; **czy to ty?** is this/that you?; **ty sam to napisałeś?** did you write it yourself?; **kupić ci lody?** would you like an ice cream?; **ciebie to nie dotyczy** it doesn't concern you; **dla ciebie** for you; **o tobie** about you; **z tobą/bez ciebie** with/without you; **tyś chyba zwariował!** you must be mad!; **ty idioto!** you fool!; **być na ty (z kimś)** to be on first-name terms (with sb); **przejść z kimś na ty** to get onto first-name terms with sb

[2] *inter.* pot. you; **hej ty! gdzie leziesz?** hey you! where do you think you're going! pot.

[3] *ci part.* **to ci zabawa!** what a scream a. laugh pot.; **to ci pech!** bad a. terrible luck!; **nagle jak ci nie huknie!** suddenly there was this incredible bang pot.

tycz|ka *f* [1] (palik) pole [2] Sport pole; **skok o ~ce** pole vault a. jump [3] pot. (osoba) beanpole pot.

tyczkarz *m* Sport pole-vaulter

ty|ć *impf vi* to put on weight

ty|dzień *m* week; **pada od tygodnia** it's been raining for a week; **w tygodniu jemy na mieście** during the week we eat out

tygodnik *m* weekly

tygodniowo *adv.* (co tydzień) every week; **powinienem zrobić siedem takich wzorów ~** I should do seven such designs a week

tygodniow|y *adi.* [1] *[urlop]* week's, week-long; **mamy ~e opóźnienie** we're a week late [2] *[czynsz, zarobki]* week's

tygodniów|ka *f* [1] pot. (zapłata) weekly rate [2] (kieszonkowe) (weekly) pocket money

tygrys *m* tiger

tygrysic|a *f* tigress

tykać¹ *impf* → **tknąć¹**

tykać² *impf* → **tyknąć**

tyk|nąć *pf* — **tyk|ać²** *impf vi [zegar]* to tick, to tick-tock

tyl|e *pron.* [1] (taka wielkość) (z policzalnymi) this a. that many; (z niepoliczalnymi) this a. that much; (aż tak wiele) (z policzalnymi) so many; (z niepoliczalnymi) so much; (w zdaniach porównawczych) (z policzalnymi) as many;

(z niepoliczalnymi) as much; **~e (ryżu) powinno wystarczyć** that much (rice) should be enough; **„daj mi dziesięć kopert" – „~u nie mam"** 'give me ten envelopes' – 'I don't have that many'; **(ona) mieszka w Krakowie, ~e wiem** she lives in Cracow, that's all a. that much I know; **wiem tylko ~e, że...** I only know that...; **zgłosiło się ~u ochotników, że...** so many volunteers applied that...; **~e razy go prosiłam** I've asked him so many times; **jest jeszcze ~e do zrobienia** there's so much (still) to do; **~e lat się nie widzieliśmy** we haven't seen each other for so many years; **~e wysiłku na próżno** all that effort for nothing; **~e na dziś** that's all for today; **dwa/pięć razy ~e** (z policzalnymi) twice/five times as many; (z niepoliczalnymi) twice/five times as much; **~ samo** (z policzalnymi) as many; (z niepoliczalnymi) as much; **mają ~e samo lat** they are the same age; **potrzebna nam sala na ~e duża, żeby pomieścić 100 osób** we need a room big enough to hold a hundred people; **na ~e, na ile jest to możliwe** in so far as (it is) possible; **na ~e, na ile potrafię** as much a. far as I can; **o ~e** in so far as, inasmuch as [2] (stosunkowo mało) **~e zrozumiał z tej rozmowy, że kogoś szukają** the only thing a. all he understood from the conversation was that they were looking for someone [3] (użycie spójnikowe) **nie ~e..., ile a. co...** not so much... as...; **tu chodzi nie ~e o ilość, ile o jakość** it's not so much a matter of quantity as of quality; **~e że... a. ~e tylko, że...** only, except that

■ **~e co nic** next to nothing; **~e mojego, co wyskoczę czasem do kina** the only fun I have is going to the cinema now and then; **i ~e** and that's that; **o ~e o ile** so-so

tylko [1] *part.* [1] (wyłącznie) only; **~ siostra mnie odwiedza** only my sister comes to see me; **po ~ by jadł** he could eat all day long [2] (zaledwie) only, just; **było nas ~ pięcioro** there were only a. just five of us; **uśmiechał się ~ i nic nie mówił** he merely a. just smiled and said nothing; **to ~ dziecko** she's/he's merely a. only a child [3] (prośba, groźba) just; **~ pomyśl/wyobraź sobie!** just think!/imagine!

[2] *coni.* (ale) only; **możesz tu zostać, ~ nie hałasuj** you can stay (here), only don't make any noise!; **każdy, ~ nie on!** anybody but him!; **on nie jest głupi, ~ leniwy** he's not stupid, just lazy; **rada cenna, ~ że spóźniona** valuable advice, only it comes rather late; **nie ~... lecz również** a. **także** a. **ale i...** not only... but also...

[3] *adv.* only; **co ~ zechcesz** whatever you want; **jak ~ wrócę do domu** as soon as I get back home; **odkąd ~ pamiętam** as far back as I can remember; **byle ~** as long as

■ **~ czekać** a. **patrzeć, jak tu będą** they'll be here any moment now; **jej ~ w głowie stroje** a.

ona ma ~ **stroje w głowie** the only thing she thinks about is clothes; ~ **co** (przed chwilą) only just
tyln|y *adi. [drzwi, schody]* back; *[koło, szyba]* rear; *[łapa, część]* hind; ~**a kieszeń** a back a. hip pocket
ty|ł [] I *m* [1] (tylna część) (samochodu, pochodu) the rear; (ciała, ubioru) the back; **włożyć sweter tył na przód** to put on a jumper back to front GB a. backwards US; **stać tyłem do okna** to stand with one's back to a window; **wjechać tyłem do garażu** to back a. reverse a car into a garage [2] (przestrzeń) back, rear; **ogród z tyłu domu** a garden at the back of a house; **spojrzeć do tyłu** to glance backward(s); **odrzucić do tyłu włosy** to toss one's hair; **szedł w tyle za innymi** he walked behind the others; **kiwać się w przód i w tył** to rock to and fro; **zaatakować od tyłu** to attack from behind; **zrobił krok w tył** he took a step backwards; **w tył zwrot!** about turn! GB, about face! US
II tyły *plt* [1] (zaplecze) the rear; **na tyłach fabryki/ sklepu** at the rear of a factory/store [2] Wojsk. the rear
■ **być do tyłu** pot. (mieć zaległości) to be a. get behind (**z czymś** with sth); **być w tyle** (być gorszym) to fall behind; **mieć tyły u kogoś** pot. to be in sb's black books pot.
tył|ek *m* pot. (pośladki) rear (end) pot.; **dostał w ~ek** he got a kick up the backside pot.
■ **dać komuś w ~ek** pot. (zbić, pokonać) to give sb a drubbing pot.; (zmusić do wysiłku) to drive sb hard; **dostać w ~ek** pot. (zostać zbitym, pokonanym) to get a drubbing pot.; (być zmuszonym do wysiłku) to be driven hard
tym *adv.* all the; ~ **lepiej!** all the better!; ~ **gorzej dla niej!** all the worse for her!
tymczasem [] I *adv.* [1] (natomiast) meanwhile; **czekałam na nich tutaj, a** a. **gdy ~ podjechali pod dom** I was waiting for them here, and meanwhile they drove up to the house [2] (w tym czasie) in the meantime; **rozgość się, a ja ~ się ubiorę** make yourself at home and in the meantime I'll get dressed [3] (na razie) in the meantime; ~ **musimy uzbroić się w cierpliwość** meanwhile a. in the meantime we'll just have to be patient
II *inter.* see you!
tymczasow|y *adi.* [1] (chwilowy) *[pobyt, praca]* temporary; *[dyrektor, zastępca]* acting [2] (prowizoryczny) *[rząd, granica]* provisional; *[środki, sposób]* stopgap

tymian|ek *m* thyme
tynk *m* plaster
tynk|ować *impf vt* to plaster
tynkowan|y *adi.* plastered
typ [] I *m* [1] (rodzaj) type; **broń starego ~u** a gun of the old type [2] (charakter) sort; **jakim on jest ~em człowieka?** what sort of person is he?; **jest ~em sportowca** he is a sporty type pot.; **szekspirowski ~ bohatera** a Shakespearean hero [3] pot., pejor. guy pot.
II typy *plt* pot. (w hazardzie, wyścigach) tips
■ ~ **spod ciemnej gwiazdy** a suspicious a. shady-looking individual; **być w czyimś ~ie** pot. to be sb's type pot.
typ|ować *impf vt* [1] (wybierać) to select *[kandydata, przedstawiciela]*; to single out *[jednostkę, egzemplarz]* [2] (wyznaczać) to put forward; ~**ować kogoś na sekretarza generalnego** to nominate sb as general secretary [3] (przewidywać) to predict *[wynik, kolejność, numery]*; (w wyścigach) to pick *[konia, charta]*
typow|y *adi.* typical; *[wzór, projekt]* standard; **objawy ~e dla grypy** symptoms typical of flu; **zachował się w ~y dla siebie sposób** his behaviour was typical
tyran *m* tyrant także przen.
tyrani|a *f* tyranny także przen.
tyraniz|ować *impf vt* to tyrannize (over)
tysi|ąc *num.* thousand
tyto|ń *m* tobacco; (roślina) tobacco (plant)
tytu|ł [] I *m* [1] (nazwa) title; **film pod ~łem...** a film entitled a. with the title...; **jego księgozbiór liczy kilkaset ~łów** his book collection contains several hundred titles [2] (godność) title; **nadano jej ~ł profesora** she was awarded a professorship; **nadano mu ~ł lorda** the title of Lord was conferred on him; ~**ł mistrzowski** (w sporcie) (championship) title [3] książk. (powód) ~**ł do sławy** a. **chwały** a claim to fame; **odszkodowanie z ~łu szkód** compensation for a. on account of damages; **z ~łu starszeństwa** by virtue of seniority
II tytułem *adv.* by way of; ~**łem wprowadzenia** by way of introduction
tytuł|ować *impf vt* [1] (nadawać tytuł) to title *[książkę, obraz]* [2] (zwracać się) to address; ~**ować kogoś ekscelencją** to address sb as Your Excellency
tytułow|y *adi. [strona, bohater]* title

U

U, u *n inv.* U, u

u *praep.* ① (część całości) of; **mankiet u jego koszuli** the cuff of his shirt; **zęby jak u królika** teeth like a rabbit's ② (koło) at; **u podnóża** a. **u stóp góry** at the foot of a mountain; **u źródeł rzeki** at the source of a river; **u zbiegu dwóch ulic** at the intersection of two streets; **u dołu/u góry strony** at the bottom a. foot/top of the page; **być u mety** to be at the finishing line; **być u władzy** to be in power ③ (dotyczące osoby, miejsca) **wizyta u dentysty** a visit to the dentist's; **spotkali się u Anny** they met at Anna's (place); **będę u ciebie jutro wieczorem** I'll come round a. over to your place tomorrow night; **być u siebie** (w domu) to be at home; (w pokoju) to be in one's room; **czy szef jest u siebie?** is the boss in? pot.; **czuć się jak u siebie w domu** to feel at home; **zostawię klucze u portiera** I'll leave the keys with the doorman; **leczyła się u specjalisty** she was receiving treatment from a specialist; **mam u nich konto od lat** I've had an account with them for years; **miał duże powodzenie u kobiet** he was very popular with women

uaktualni|ć *pf* — **uaktualni|ać** *impf vt* to update *[dane, podręcznik]*

uaktywni|ć *pf* — **uaktywni|ać** *impf* ① *vt* ① (pobudzić do działania) to activate *[enzym, proces]*; to mobilize *[instytucję]* ② (zachęcić) to spur a. urge (on) *[załogę]*

① **uaktywnić się** — **uaktywniać się** *[wulkan]* to become active; *[czynnik]* to come into play; *[organizacja]* to become (more) active

uatrakcyjni|ć *pf* — **uatrakcyjni|ać** *impf vt* to make *[sth]* (more) attractive *[pobyt, wygląd]*; to make *[sth]* (more) appealing *[zabawę]*

ubarwie|nie *n* colo(u)ration, colouring GB, coloring US

ubaw|ić *pf* ① *vt* to amuse (**kogoś czymś** sb with sth)

① **ubawić się** to have fun (**czymś** with sth); **~ić się setnie** to have wonderful fun

ubezpiecze|nie *n* (umowa) insurance; (składka) insurance premium; (odszkodowanie) compensation payment; **~nie od ognia/włamania** fire/burglary insurance; **~nie od (następstw) nieszczęśliwych wypadków** accident insurance; **~nie od odpowiedzialności cywilnej** liability insurance; (dla posiadaczy pojazdów) third-party insurance; **~nie** samochodu car a. auto(mobile) insurance; **wykupić ~nie** to take out insurance; **~nie zdrowotne** health insurance; **~nie na życie** life insurance; **~nie społeczne** ≈ national (health/retirement) insurance

ubezpiecz|yć *pf* — **ubezpiecz|ać** *impf* ① *vt* ① to insure *[dom, osobę, pojazd, zbiory]* (**od czegoś** against sth) ② Wojsk. to cover *[osobę, oddział, tyły]*

① **ubezpieczyć się** — **ubezpieczać się** to take out insurance a. an insurance policy; **~yć się na życie** to take out life insurance

ubi|ć *pf* — **ubi|jać** *impf vt* ① (ugnieść) to compress *[glebę, słomę, śmieci, tytoń]*; **~ty śnieg** tamped snow ② Kulin. to whip, to beat; (trzepaczką) to whisk

ubie|c *pf* — **ubie|gać** *impf vt* to anticipate *[życzenie, prośbę]*; **~c kogoś w czymś** to beat sb to sth

ubiega|ć się *impf v refl.* książk. (starać się) to apply (**o coś** for sth); (rywalizować) to vie (**o coś** for sth); **dwukrotnie ~ł się o fotel prezydenta** he ran for the presidency twice

ubieg|ły *adi. [rok, tydzień, stulecie]* last

ubikacj|a *f* (w domu, mieszkaniu) toilet; (w budynku publicznym) (public) convenience GB, restroom US

ubi|ór *m* dress

ubliż|yć *pf* — **ubliż|ać** *impf vi* to insult (**komuś** sb); to be an offence a. affront (**komuś** to sb); **to ~a ludzkiej godności** it is an affront to human dignity

ubło|cić *pf* ① *vt* to muddy *[buty, podłogę]*

① **ubłocić się** *[dywan, nogi]* to get muddy

uboczn|y *adi. [zysk]* incidental; *[wątek]* secondary; **zajęcie ~e** a sideline

ubo|gi *adi. grad.* ① (biedny) *[osoba, kraj]* poor; *[rok]* lean ② (zniszczony) shabby ③ (niedostateczny) *[roślinność]* sparse; *[dieta]* poor; *[oferta, słownictwo]* limited; **~gi w składniki odżywcze** poor in nutrients ■ **~gi krewny** poor relative; **rozrywka dla ~gich** unsophisticated entertainment

ubóstwia|ć *impf vt* to idolize *[osobę]*; to adore *[kawę, lody]*

ubóstw|o *n* poverty także przen.

ub|rać *pf* — **ub|ierać** *impf* ① *vt* ① (włożyć ubranie) to dress *[kogoś w coś* sb in sth); **ubrać coś w słowa** przen. to express sth in words ② (ozdobić) to decorate *[choinkę]*

① **ubrać się** — **ubierać się** to get dressed; **ubrać**

się w coś to put on sth; **butiki, w których ubierają się nastolatki** boutiques where teenagers buy their clothes

ubra|nie n ① (strój) clothes; (sztuka odzieży) item a. article of clothing; ~**nie gotowe** ready-made a. ready-to-wear clothes; ~**nie szyte na miarę** tailor-made a. custom-made clothes; ~**nie ochronne** protective clothing; **bez** ~**nia** with no clothes on; **w** ~**niu** fully dressed ② (garnitur) suit

ubyt|ek m (uszkodzenie zęba) cavity

ucał|ować pf vt to kiss; ~**uj ode mnie ciocię Zosię** give my love to Aunt Sophie

ucharakteryz|ować pf **[I]** vt to make up [osobę] (na kogoś as sb)
[II] ucharakteryzować się to make (oneself) up (na kogoś as sb)

u|cho n ① (narząd słuchu) ear; **być głuchym na jedno ucho** to be deaf in one ear; **prawym uchem** a. **na prawe ucho słabiej słyszę** (the hearing in) my right ear is not so good; **mówić komuś coś do ucha** a. **na ucho** to whisper sth (in)to sb's ear; **zarumieniła się po uszy** a. **po czubki uszu** her whole face turned red; **zatkał sobie uszy** he plugged his ears; **złowił uchem lekki szmer** his ear caught a faint rustle ② (przy czapce) ear flap; (przy koszu, kubku, dzbanie) handle; (z tkaniny, sznura) loop ③ (w igle) eye
■ **ciepło jak w uchu** nice and cosy GB a. cozy US; **być po uszy zakochanym** to be head over heels in love; **dzwoni mi w uszach** my ears a. eardrums are ringing; **cisza aż w uszach dzwoni** the silence is deafening; **kłaść** a. **tulić uszy po sobie** to put a. have one's tail between one's legs; **mieć kogoś/czegoś powyżej uszu** pot. to be fed up with sb/sth pot.; **mieć oczy i uszy otwarte** to keep a. have one's wits about one; **na(d)stawiać ucha** a. **uszu** (wytężać słuch) to listen closely; **obić się komuś o uszy** to ring a bell with sb pot.; **puszczać coś mimo uszu** to turn a deaf ear to sth; **słuchać jednym uchem (a drugim wypuszczać)** to listen with only half an ear; **słyszeć coś na własne uszy** to hear sth with one's own ears; **stawać na uszach, żeby...** pot. to do one's damnedest to... pot.; **strzyc uszami** a. **uchem** to prick up a. cock one's ears; **uśmiechać się od ucha do ucha** to smile a. grin from ear to ear; **wpadać w ucho** [melodia, slogan] to be catchy; **zamykać** a. **zatykać uszy na coś** to close a. shut one's ears to sth; **uczciwszy uszy** przest. (if you'll) pardon a. excuse the expression; **klął, aż wszystkim uszy więdły** his swearing made everyone's ears burn; **jadł... wcinał, aż mu się uszy trzęsły** pot. he ate ravenously; **uszy bolą** a. **pękają** a. **puchną od tego** it assaults the ear

ucho|dzić impf vi ① (być uważanym) to be regarded (za kogoś/coś as sb/sth) ② książk. to be appropriate

a. fitting; **to nie** ~**dzi, żeby...** it's not done to... ③ [rzeka, strumień] to flow (**do czegoś** into sth)

uchodź|ca m, ~**czyni** f refugee

uchro|nić pf vt ① (uratować) to save (**kogoś przed czymś** sb from sth); ~**nić kogoś od śmierci** to save sb's life ② (ustrzec) to protect (**kogoś przed czymś** sb from a. against sth)

uchwal|ić pf — **uchwal|ać** impf vt to pass [budżet, rezolucję, ustawę]

uchwa|ła f resolution

uchwy|t m (przy kubku, koszyku, urządzeniu, walizce) handle; (na urządzeniu) handgrip

uchyl|ić pf — **uchyl|ać** impf **[I]** vt ① (odemknąć) to open [sth] slightly [okno, powieki, szufladę]; **drzwi były** ~**one** the door was ajar ② (odsunąć) to draw [sth] slightly aside [zasłonę]; ~**ić kapelusza** to tip one's hat ③ (znieść) to rescind [nakaz]; to overrule [decyzję, pytanie, sprzeciw, wniosek]; to revoke [postanowienie, wyrok, zezwolenie]; to dispel [podejrzenia, wątpliwości, zarzuty]; ~**ić przepis** to repeal a regulation
[II] uchylić się — **uchylać się** ① [drzwi, okno] to open slightly ② (odchylić się) to duck (**przed czymś** sth) ③ (wymówić się) to shirk (**od czegoś** sth); ~**ać się od służby wojskowej** to dodge military service

u|ciąć pf — **u|cinać** impf vt ① (obciąć) to cut (off) [nogawkę, rękaw]; to lop off [gałąź]; **uciąć komuś głowę** to behead sb ② (przerwać) to break off [rozmowę]; to cut off a. short [dyskusję]; **uciąć w pół słowa** to break off in mid-sentence ③ pot. **uciąć sobie partyjkę szachów/pogawędkę** to have a game of chess/a chat; **uciąć sobie drzemkę** to grab forty winks pot.
■ **jak (nożem) uciął** all of a sudden

uciążliw|y adi. grad. [podróż] arduous; [obowiązki, zadanie] onerous; [milczenie, upał] oppressive; [warunki] uncomfortable; [hałas] bothersome; [osoba] tedious; [nawyk] tiresome; [narzekanie] wearisome

ucie|c pf — **ucie|kać** impf **[I]** vi ① (oddalić się) to escape (**przed kimś/czymś** from sb/sth); ~**kać w popłochu** to run for one's life; ~**c przed burzą** (schronić się) to take shelter from the storm ② (opuścić potajemnie) [osoba] to escape; [więzień] to break free a. out; (z kraju) to defect; (od rodziny) to run away; ~**c z lekcji** to skip class a. classes pot.; ~**kli przez okno** they got out through a. by the window ③ (wyjechać potajemnie) [kochankowie] to elope ④ przen. (uwolnić się) ~**c od czegoś** to escape from sth [faktów, prawdy]; to run away from sth [obowiązków, sytuacji]; ~**kać przed kimś** to avoid a. shun sb ⑤ przen. (upłynąć) [czas] to fly; [chwile, dni, życie] to slip by ⑥ pot. [gaz, powietrze, benzyna, woda] to escape ⑦ (wymknąć się) **piłka** ~**kła mi z rąk** the ball slipped out of my hands; ~**c komuś z pamięci** to slip sb's memory; ~**kł mu wątek** he lost his train of thought; **przez niego** ~**kł mi awans** I lost the promotion because of him; **taka okazja ~kła mi sprzed nosa!** what a bargain I missed! ⑧ pot. (odjechać) **~kł mu autobus/pociąg** he missed the bus/train

Ⅱ uciec się — uciekać się (posłużyć się) to fall back (**do czegoś** on sth); **bez ~kania się do czegoś** without recourse a. resort to sth

ucie|cha f (zadowolenie) delight; (zabawa) fun; (rozbawienie) amusement; **ku czyjejś ~sze** to sb's amusement; **sprawić komuś ~chę** to please sb

uciecz|ka f (uciekanie) escape także przen.; (że szkoły) absconding; (z więzienia) breakout; (z miejsca zbrodni) getaway; (z armii, kraju) defection; (z ukochanym) elopement

uciekinie|r m, **~rka** f (z obozu, więzienia) escapee; (polityczny) defector; (z domu) runaway

uciesz|yć pf **Ⅰ** vi [widok] to gladden [oczy, serce]; [reakcja, wiadomość] to gratify [osobę]; [prezent] to please [osobę]

Ⅱ ucieszyć się to be glad a. happy; **naprawdę ~yłem się z jego sukcesu** I was really happy for him

ucisk m ① (gniecenie) pressure; (w gardle, piersiach) tightness; (w żołądku) knot ② (gnębienie) oppression

ucisz|yć pf — **ucisz|ać** impf **Ⅰ** vt ① (uspokoić) to hush (up) [dziecko]; to silence [tłum] ② przen. (opanować, zagłuszyć) to silence [sumienie]; to still [głos rozsądku]; to soothe [ból, rozpacz]; to choke off [protest]; **~yć plotki** to lay rumours to rest

Ⅱ uciszyć się — uciszać się ① [osoba, ptak] to become silent; [klasa] to quiet (down); [wrzawa] to die down ② przen. [sztorm, wiatr] to moderate; [morze] to calm down

ucz|cić pf vt ① (oddać hołd) to honour GB, to honor US, to pay homage (**kogoś** to sb); **~cić pamięć zmarłego minutą ciszy** to commemorate the deceased with a minute's silence ② (świętować) to celebrate [święto, zwycięstwo]

uczciwoś|ć f honesty

uczciw|y adi. grad. ① (prawy) [osoba, spojrzenie] honest; **kryształowo ~y** (as) straight as a die ② (rzetelny) [konkurencja, oferta, rywalizacja] fair; [cena, zamiar] honest ③ (szczery) [opowieść, relacja] honest ④ pot. (solidny) [obiad, posag] decent; [lanie] sound

uczelni|a f university, college US

ucz|eń m, **~ennica** f ① (w szkole) pupil; (szkoły podstawowej) junior GB; (u prywatnego nauczyciela) tutee ② (w rzemiośle) apprentice ③ (kontynuator) disciple, follower

ucze|sać pf **Ⅰ** vt **~sać kogoś** (grzebieniem) to comb sb's hair; (zrobić fryzurę) to do sb's hair

Ⅱ uczesać się to brush/comb one's hair; (zostać uczesanym) to have one's hair done a. styled

uczesa|nie n hairstyle

uczestnictw|o n (w konferencji, zawodach) participation (**w czymś** in sth); (w kampanii, zadaniu) involvement (**w czymś** in sth)

uczestnicz|yć impf vi ① (w dyskusji, eksperymencie) to participate (**w czymś** in sth); (w ceremonii, spotkaniu) to attend (**w czymś** sth) ② (w zyskach) to share (**w czymś** in sth); (w inwestycjach) to take part (**w czymś** in sth)

uczestni|k m, **~czka** f (konferencji) participant; (zawodów) competitor; (nabożeństwa) celebrant

ucz|ony **Ⅰ** adi. [osoba] learned; [artykuł, książka] learned; [przemówienie, dyskusja] erudite

Ⅱ ucz|ony m, **~ona** f (humanista) scholar; (w naukach ścisłych) scientist

uczu|cie n ① (stan psychiczny) emotion, feeling; **apelować do czyichś ~ć** to appeal to sb's good nature ② (miłość, sympatia) affection; **darzyć kogoś głębokim ~ciem** to have a deep affection for sb ③ pot. (przejęcie) feeling; **robić coś z ~ciem** to do sth with feeling a. passion ④ (doznanie) feeling; **~cie swędzenia** an itchy a. a prickly feeling; **~cie pieczenia w gardle** a burning sensation in one's throat; **miałam nieprzyjemne ~cie, że...** I had an unpleasant feeling that...

uczule|nie n allergy (**na coś** to sth)

uczul|ić pf — **uczul|ać** impf **Ⅰ** vt to sensitize także przen. (**kogoś na coś** sb to sth)

Ⅱ uczulić się — uczulać się to become sensitized także przen. (**na coś** to sth)

ucz|yć impf **Ⅰ** vt to teach; **~yć kogoś czegoś** to teach sb sth, to teach sth to sb; **~yć w szkole** to teach at school; **doświadczenie ~y, że...** experience teaches that...

Ⅱ uczyć się to learn; (odrabiać lekcje) to study; **~yć się dobrze/źle** to be a good/poor student; **~yć się angielskiego** to learn English; **~yć się do egzaminu** to study for an exam; **~yć się czegoś na pamięć** to memorize sth, to learn sth by heart; **~yć się u mistrza** to train under a master; **~yć się na cudzych błędach** to learn from the mistakes of others; **~yć się na własnych błędach** to learn by a. from one's (own) mistakes

uczyn|ek m act; **zły ~ek** a misdeed; **dobry ~ek** an act of kindness; **spełnić dobry ~ek** to do a good deed

uczynn|y adi. grad. accommodating

uda|ć pf — **uda|wać** impf **Ⅰ** vt ① (stwarzać pozory) to dissemble [uczucia]; to fake [chorobę, podziw]; to feign [entuzjazm, zmęczenie]; to pretend [zaskoczenie, zdumienie]; to simulate [gniew, zainteresowanie]; **~wać głupka** a. **durnia** to act a. play the fool; **~wał, że...** he pretended (that)...; **~wała, że się gniewa** she put on a show of anger ② (naśladować) to act [damę]; to imitate [nauczyciela]; **złodziej ~jący policjanta** a thief pretending to be a policeman; **gips ~jący kamień** plaster made to resemble stone

Ⅱ udać się — udawać się ① (skończyć się sukcesem) *[eksperyment, żart]* to come off; *[potrawa, rysunek, zdjęcie]* to turn out well; *[plan]* to succeed; **spotkanie się** ~**ło** the meeting went well; ~**ło mi się znaleźć pracę** I managed to find a job; ~**ło mu się wszystkich przekonać** he was successful in a. at convincing everybody; **próbowała, ale jej się nie** ~**ło** she tried, but failed; **jabłka** ~**ły w tym roku** the apple crop is good this year ② książk. (pójść) to go; ~**ć się w podróż** to go on a journey; ~**ć się z wizytą do kogoś** to pay sb a visit; ~**ć się na spoczynek** to retire (to bed) **Ⅲ udać się** *[dzieci, syn]* to turn out well

udan|y *adi.* ① (dobry) *[dzień, pomysł, przyjęcie]* good; *[wakacje]* fine; *[małżeństwo]* fulfilling ② (zakończony sukcesem) *[kampania, leczenie, próba]* successful; (dobrze zrobiony) *[produkt, projekt]* well done; **przyjęcie było** ~**e** the party went well; **mają** ~**e dzieci** their children turned out well

uda|r *m* Med. stroke; ~**r słoneczny** sunstroke

udekor|ować *pf vt* ① (przystroić) to garnish *[tort]* (**czymś** with sth); to deck (out) *[budynek, stół]* (**czymś** with sth); to decorate *[ulicę]* (**czymś** with sth) ② (odznaczyć) to decorate (**kogoś czymś** sb with sth)

uderze|nie *n* ① (cios) blow; (odgłos) crash; ~**nie w plecy/twarz** a blow in the back/face; ~**nie pioruna** a stroke of lightning; ~**nia zegara/dzwonu** the striking of a clock/bell ② Wojsk. attack (**na kogoś/coś** on sb/sth)

uderz|yć *pf* — **uderz|ać** *impf* **Ⅰ** *vt* ① (zadać cios) to hit; (głową) to butt; (pięścią) to punch; (ciosem prostym) to jab; ~**yć kogoś w głowę/twarz** to strike sb on the head/to slap sb in the face ② (stuknąć) *[osoba]* to hit; ~**ył pięścią w stół** he struck the table with his fist ③ (zadziwić) to strike; ~**ające podobieństwo** striking similarity

Ⅱ *vi* ① przen. (zaszkodzić) to hit (**w kogoś/coś** at sb/ sth); **podwyżka** ~**y w najbiedniejszych** the poorest will be hit by the price rise ② *[bomba]* to hit; *[piorun]* to strike; *[fale]* to beat; **samochód** ~**ył w drzewo** the car hit a. struck the tree; ~**yć w dzwon** to sound the bell ③ *[policja, wojsko]* to assault ④ przen. (skrytykować) to attack (**w coś** sth) ⑤ (o sercu) to beat; (o krwi) to rush; **nagle** ~**yły na niego poty** suddenly he broke out into a sweat

Ⅲ uderzyć się — uderzać się to hit, to strike; ~**yłem się głową o belkę** my head struck the beam

udław|ić się *pf v refl.* to choke (**czymś** on sth)

u|do *n* thigh

udogodnie|nie *n* convenience; ~**nia dla niepełnosprawnych** facilities for the handicapped

udokument|ować *pf vt* to substantiate; ~**ować swoje prawa do spadku** to substantiate one's claim to an inheritance; **bogato** ~**owana biografia** a richly documented biography

udom|owić *pf* — **udom|awiać** *impf vt* to domesticate *[ptaka, zwierzę]*

udoskonale|nie *n* improvement

udoskonal|ić *pf* — **udoskonal|ać** *impf* **Ⅰ** *vt* to improve *[urządzenie]*; to refine *[metodę]*; to perfect *[technikę]*

Ⅱ udoskonalić się — udoskonalać się *[umiejętności]* to improve, to develop; *[osoba]* to improve oneself

udostępni|ć *pf* — **udostępni|ać** *pf vt* to make [sth] available (**komuś** to sb)

udow|odnić *pf* — **udow|adniać** *impf vt* to prove *[teorię, tezę]*; ~**adniać swoje racje** to prove one's point; ~**odnić komuś winę** to prove sb's guilt, to prove sb guilty

udrę|ka *f* torment, ordeal

udu|sić *pf* **Ⅰ** *vt* ① (za szyję) to strangle; (zatkać usta i nos) to smother ② Kulin. to stew *[jarzyny, mięso]*

Ⅱ udusić się (umrzeć) to be asphyxiated

udzia|ł *m* ① participation; (w zbrodni) complicity; **brać w czymś (czynny)** ~**ł** to take (an active) part in sth ② Ekon., Fin. share

udziałow|iec *m* shareholder

udziel|ić *pf* — **udziel|ać** *impf* **Ⅰ** *vt* to give; ~**ić komuś informacji** to give sb information; ~**ać (komuś) wyjaśnień** to provide (sb with) explanations; ~**ić komuś nagany** to reprimand sb; ~**ić komuś rady** to give sb advice; ~**ić komuś napomnienia** a. **pouczenia** to caution sb; ~**ić komuś głosu** to give sb the floor; ~**ić komuś wywiadu** to give a. grant sb an interview; ~**ać komuś lekcji** to give sb (private) lessons; ~**ać komuś swojego poparcia** to give sb one's support; ~**ić komuś schronienia** to give sb shelter; ~**ić komuś pierwszej pomocy** to give sb first aid

Ⅱ udzielić się — udzielać się *[entuzjazm]* to infect przen. (**komuś** sb)

Ⅲ udzielać się to be active; ~**ać się społecznie** a. **publicznie** to be active in community life; ~**ać się towarzysko** to have an active social life

udźwign|ąć *pf vt* ① *[osoba]* to carry; **ledwo** ~**ął walizkę** he could barely lift the suitcase; *[konstrukcja]* to bear ② przen. (poradzić sobie) to cope with

ufa|ć *impf vi* ① (polegać) to trust (**komuś/czemuś** sb/sth); ~**ć komuś bezgranicznie** to have absolute trust in sb; ~**ć we własne siły** to be self-confident; ~**ć czyimś obietnicom** to believe sb's promises ② (mieć nadzieję) to believe; ~**m, że...** I trust that...

ufarb|ować *pf vt* to dye *[materiał, włosy]*

ufnoś|ć *f* confidence

ufn|y *adi. grad.* ① (pełen zaufania) *[osoba, spojrzenie]* trustful ② (przeświadczony) confident; ~**y we własne siły** confident in his ability to cope

uform|ować *pf* **Ⅰ** *vt* to form *[kształt]* przen. to shape

Ⅱ uformować się ① (ukształtować się) to form

2 (ustawić się) to line up; **wojsko ~owało się w szyk bojowy** the army drew up in battle formation

ufund|ować *pf vt* to fund *[pomnik, tablicę]*; **~ować nagrodę** to endow a. fund a prize

ugła|skać *pf* — **ugła|skiwać** *impf vt* to mollify *[osobę]*; to soothe *[osobę, gniew]*

ugo|da *f* agreement

ugodow|y *adi.* conciliatory

ugot|ować *pf vt* to boil *[mięso, warzywa]*; to cook *[obiad, zupę]*; **~ować jajko na miękko/na twardo** to soft-boil/hard-boil an egg

ugrupowa|nie *n* (organizacja) grouping; (partia) party

ugry|źć *pf* **I** *vt* 1 (odciąć zębami) to bite into *[jabłko, bułkę]* 2 (skaleczyć) *[owad, zwierzę]* to bite 3 pot., przen. (poradzić sobie) **nie móc czegoś ~źć** to not be able to make head nor tail of sth pot.

II ugryźć się to bite; **~źć się w język** to bite one's tongue; przen. to hold one's tongue

■ **coś go ~zło** a. **giez go ~zł** a. **mucha go ~zła** something's bugging a. eating him

uhonor|ować *pf vt* 1 (uczcić) to honour GB, to honor US; **~ować kogoś medalem** to honour sb with a medal 2 (uwzględnić) to honour GB, to honor US *[umowę, warunki]*; to meet *[żądania, oczekiwania]*

ujada|ć *impf vi [pies]* to bay

ujawni|ć *pf* — **ujawni|ać** *impf* **I** *vt* 1 (podać do wiadomości) to disclose *[tajemnicę, nazwisko]*; (wyjawić) to divulge *[szczegóły, dane]*; to open up *[plany, strategię]*; to unfold *[myśli, sekrety]*; to reveal *[zamiary, opinie]* 2 (okazać) to show *[talent, umiejętność]*; to display *[uczucie, umiejętność]*

II ujawnić się — **ujawniać się** (wyjść na jaw) *[cechy, wartość]* to become apparent; *[uczucia, problemy]* to surface; *[choroba]* to manifest

uj|ąć *pf* — **uj|mować** *impf* **I** *vt* 1 (uchwycić) to take hold (**kogoś/coś** of sb/sth); **ująć coś w obie ręce** to take sth in both hands; **ujął żonę pod rękę** he linked arms with his wife 2 (przedstawić) to present *[temat, treść]*; to express *[myśl, sens]* 3 (zjednać) *[osoba]* to endear oneself (**kogoś** to sb); **ujął nas za serce** he won our hearts 4 (umniejszyć) to take (away), to detract (**czegoś** sth); **ta fryzura ujmuje ci lat** the hairstyle takes years off you; **niczego nie ujmując jego osiągnięciom...** taking nothing away a. detracting nothing from his achievements... 5 (schwytać) to capture; (zatrzymać) to apprehend *[przestępcę]* 6 (objąć) to encompass; (wymienić) to mention *[dane, zagadnienia]*

II ująć się — **ujmować się** 1 (uchwycić się) **ująć się pod boki** to stand (with) arms akimbo; **ująć się pod ręce** a. **rękę** a. **ramię** to link arms; **ujęli się za ręce** they took each other by the hand 2 (stanąć w obronie) to stand up (**za kimś** for sb)

ujemn|y *adi.* negative

uję|cie *n* 1 Kino (sekwencja) take; (jedną kamerą) shot; (w fotografii) view 2 (przedstawienie tematu) presentation; (punkt widzenia) perspective 3 (pobieranie wody) (water) intake

ujmując|y *adi.* endearing; **~y sposób bycia** an engaging manner

ujrz|eć *pf* książk. **I** *vt* to see

II ujrzeć się to see oneself także przen.

■ **~eć światło dzienne** to see the light of day

ujś|cie *n* 1 Techn. outlet 2 (rzeki, potoku) mouth 3 (uzewnętrznienie) outlet przen.; **dać ~cie** swojej **ambicji** to give vent to one's ambition

u|jść *pf* — **u|chodzić** *impf vi* 1 *[gaz, dym]* to leak (out); **powietrze uszło z dętki** the tube deflated a. ran flat 2 (nie wywołać konsekwencji) *[niedbalstwo, złe zachowanie]* to go unpunished; **wiele mu uchodziło, bo był lubiany** he could get away with a lot because they liked him 3 książk. (uniknąć) *[osoba]* to escape (**czemuś** sth)

■ **ujdzie (w tłoku)** pot. it is passable, it will do

uka|rać *pf vt* to punish *[osobę, zbrodnię]*; to penalize *[gracza, drużynę]*; **~rać kogoś grzywną** to fine sb

uka|zać *pf* — **uka|zywać** *impf* **I** *vt* 1 (przedstawić) *[autor, książka]* to portray 2 (uczynić widocznym) to show

II ukazać się — **ukazywać się** 1 (pokazać się) *[duchy, chmury]* to appear; *[słońce, księżyc]* to come out; **naszym oczom ~zał się zdumiewający widok** an amazing sight met our eyes 2 (zostać opublikowanym) to come out; **~zać się w wielkim nakładzie** to be published at a huge print run

uką|sić *pf vt [żmija, pies]* to bite; *[osa, skorpion]* to sting

ukąsze|nie *n* (zębami) bite; (żądłem) sting

ukierunk|ować *pf* — **ukierunk|owywać** *impf vt* to direct *[zainteresowania, zapał]* (**na coś** to sth); to orient *[działalność, badania]* (**na coś** to sth)

ukl|ęknąć *pf vi* to kneel (down)

ukła|d *m* 1 (uporządkowanie) order; (rozmieszczenie) arrangement; (plan) layout; **~d sił w parlamencie** the line-up of parties in the parliament; **w obecnym** a. **tym ~dzie** as things are a. stand now 2 (gwiezdny, atmosferyczny) system 3 Techn. system 4 (umowa) agreement, treaty 5 (położenie) position

układan|ka *f* Gry jigsaw (puzzle)

ukłon **I** *m* 1 (pochylenie głowy, tułowia) bow; (kiwnięcie głową) nod; **odpowiedzieć na czyjś ~** to bow back to sb 2 (okazanie sympatii, szacunku) compliment (**w stronę kogoś** to sb); tribute (**w stronę czegoś** to sth)

II ukłony *plt* (pozdrowienia) regards; (oficjalne) compliments (**dla kogoś** to sb); **proszę przekazać ~y rodzinie** please give my compliments to your family

ukło|nić się *pf vi* to bow (**komuś** to sb)

ukłu|cie n ① (ból) twinge ② (ostrym przedmiotem) prick; (przez komara) bite; (przez osy, pszczołę) sting; ~**cie zazdrości** a stab a. twinge of jealousy

ukłu|ć pf **[]** vt [osoba, szpilka] to prick; [komar] to bite; [osa, pszczoła] to sting

[] ukłuć się to prick oneself

uknu|ć pf vt to hatch (up) [plan, spisek]

ukochan|y adi. [osoba, kraj] beloved; [pisarz, potrawa] favourite GB, favorite US

[] ukochan|y m, ~a f beloved, sweetheart

ukojeni|e n książk. (ulga) relief; (pociecha) solace

ukończ|yć pf vt książk. ① (doprowadzić do końca) to finish [remont, pracę]; to complete [dzieło, wyścig] ② Szkol., Uniw. to finish [szkołę średnią]; to complete [kurs, studia]; to graduate from [uniwersytet, fakultet]; to graduate in [prawo, medycynę] ③ (osiągnąć) ~yła czterdzieści lat she is forty years of age

ukos [] m (nachylenie) slant; (pochyłość drogi, ścieżki) incline; (krawędź kamienia, drewna) bevel

[] na ukos (po przekątnej) diagonally; (skośnie) obliquely; (pod kątem, krzywo) aslant

[] z ukosa a. ukosem [patrzeć, obserwować] sidelong; patrzeć a. zerkać ~em a. z ~a (ukradkiem) to look furtively (na kogoś/coś at sb/sth); (z niechęcią, podejrzliwie) to look askance (na kogoś/coś at sb/sth)

ukośn|y adi. [linia, paski] oblique; [promienie, dach] slanting; ~e kieszenie slant pockets

ukradkiem adv. [spoglądać, obserwować] furtively; [spotykać się, wejść] surreptitiously

ukra|ść pf vt to steal; ~**ść coś komuś** to steal sth from sb, to steal sb sth

ukr|oić pf — **ukr|awać** impf vt to slice off [kawałek]; to cut [kromkę]

ukrop m boiling water

■ zwijać się a. uwijać się jak (mucha) w ~ie to be rushed off one's feet pot.

ukr|ócić pf — **ukr|acać** impf vt (ograniczyć) to curb [inflację, przekupstwo]; (przerwać) to put an end to [działalność, pogłoski]

ukry|cie n (przed niebezpieczeństwem) cover; (przed znalezieniem) concealment

ukry|ć pf — **ukry|wać**[1] impf **[]** vt ① (schować) to hide (away) [przedmiot]; to hide [osobę]; (zakryć) to conceal [broń, ciążę]; ~**ł twarz w dłoniach** he hid his face in his hands ② (zataić) to conceal [informacje, prawdę]; **nie ~wał, kim jest** he didn't conceal his identity

[] ukryć się — ukrywać się ① (schować się) [dziecko, napastnik] to hide (oneself); [zbieg] to hide out; [samotnik, zakochani] to hide away; ~**wać się pod fałszywym nazwiskiem** to live under a false name ② (stać się niewidocznym) [słońce, góry] to be hidden a. concealed

■ nic się przed nim nie ~je there's no hiding anything from him; nic się nie ~je przed ludźmi

(the) truth will out przysł.; **nie da się** ~**ć, że...** there's no denying that...

ukry|ty adi. [wada, uczucie] hidden; [przejście, zamiar] concealed; [motyw, cel] ulterior; [talent, choroba] latent; [znaczenie, krytyka] implicit; ~**ta reklama** indirect advertising

ukrywać[1] impf → ukryć

ukrywa|ć[2] impf **[]** vt ① (przysłaniać) [mur, krzaki] to conceal [widok, ogród] ② (zawierać) [dom, ściany] to hide [tajemnice, skarby]

[] ukrywać się (nie zdradzać się) ~**ł się ze swoimi uczuciami** he concealed his feelings

■ nie ma czego ~**ć** a. **co** ~**ć** to be perfectly frank, if truth be told; **co tu** ~**ć, chodziło tylko o pieniądze** truth to tell, it was all about money

ukrzyż|ować pf vt to crucify

ukształt|ować pf **[]** vt ① (uformować) to form [przedmiot]; (z plastycznej substancji) to mould GB, to mold US [obiekt] ② przen. to form [osobowość, politykę]

[] ukształtować się [osobowość, poglądy] to be formed

ukucn|ąć pf vi to squat (down)

uku|ć pf — **uku|wać** impf vt (utworzyć) to coin [termin, słowo]; to come up with [żart, aforyzm]

ul m (bee)hive

■ tu huczy a. roi się jak w ulu the place is a hive a. beehive of activity

ule|c, ule|gnąć pf — **ule|gać** impf vi ① (poddać się) to surrender (komuś to sb); (w sporcie) to be defeated (komuś by sb); nasza drużyna ~**gła zespołowi Czech 0:2** (podporządkować się) to yield (komuś/czemuś to sb/sth); ~**c czyjejś woli** to yield to sb's will; ~**c naciskom z czyjejś strony** to give in to the pressure from sb ③ (poddać się działaniu) ~**c czemuś** to surrender to sth [uczuciom]; to succumb to sth [urokom, perswazji]; to be overcome by sth [emocjom]; ~**c pokusie** to yield a. give in to temptation; ~**gać wpływom kogoś/czegoś** to be influenced by sb/sth; **łatwo** ~**gać wzruszeniu** to be easily moved ④ (poddać się przemianie, procesowi) to undergo; ~**c zagładzie** to be destroyed a. annihilated; ~**c wypadkowi** to have a. meet with an accident; **taryfy mogą ulec zmianie** rates are a. may be subject to change

■ nie ~**ga wątpliwości** a. kwestii, że... there is no doubt that..., it is beyond a. without question that...

ulecz|yć pf — **ulecz|ać** impf vt to cure [osobę, chorobę]; to heal [ranę]

uległ|y adi. grad. (posłuszny) submissive (wobec kogoś/czegoś to sb/sth); (potulny) docile; (dający sobą powodować) tractable

ulep|ić pf vt to form; ~**ić coś z gliny** to make sth from clay; **figurki** ~**ione z plasteliny** plasticine figures

ulepsze|nie n (poprawka) improvement; (zmiana) modification

ulepsz|yć pf — **ulepsz|ać** impf vt (poprawić) to improve *[metodę, system]*; to amend *[glebę]*; (unowocześnić) to upgrade *[urządzenie, sprzęt]*; (zmienić) to modify *[wersję, model]*

ulew|a f downpour (of rain)

ulewn|y adi. *[deszcz]* torrential

ul|ga f ① (odprężenie) relief; **odetchnąć z ulgą** to breathe a sigh of relief ② (niższa cena) (price) concession, reduction US; (niższa stawka) concession ③ (odliczenie) tax relief, tax deduction US; (kwota wolna od podatku) tax allowance

ulgow|y adi. ① (ze zniżką) *[stawka, opłata]* reduced ② (specjalny) *[traktowanie, warunki]* preferential; **taryfa** ~**a** przen. preferential treatment

ulic|a f street, road; **główna** ~**a miasta** the town's high street GB, the town's main street a. road; **na rogu** ~**y** on the corner (of a street); **po drugiej** a. **przeciwnej stronie** ~**y** across the street; **pokoje od** ~**y** rooms overlooking the street; **mieszkać na** a. **przy bocznej** ~**y** to live in a. on a side street ■ **leżeć na** ~**y** *[władza, praca]* to be there for the asking a. taking; *[bogactwa, pomysły]* to grow on trees pot.

uliczn|y adi. ① *[latarnia, sprzedawca]* street ② *[język, wyrażenie]* vulgar, crude

ulok|ować pf ① vt książk. ① (na nocleg) to put [sb] up; (znaleźć mieszkanie) to find lodgings a. accommodation for; **powodzian** ~**owano u krewnych** flood victims were taken in by their relatives ② (usytuować) to locate *[budynek, stadion]* ③ (zdeponować) to deposit *[oszczędności]*; (wyłożyć) to invest *[pieniądze, zyski]* ④ (związać) ~**ować w kimś swoje nadzieje** to place a. put one's hope(s) in sb ② **ulokować się** książk. (zamieszkać) to stay, to put up; (zająć miejsce) to position oneself; ~**owała się wygodnie w fotelu** she settled herself comfortably in an armchair

ulot|ka f (informacyjna, reklamowa) leaflet; (promująca produkt, imprezę) flyer, flier; (wręczana) handbill

ul|otnić się pf — **ul|atniać się** impf v refl. ① (wydobyć się) *[gaz, ciepło]* to leak; *[woń]* to waft ② (zniknąć) to evaporate także przen. ③ pot. (oddalić się) *[osoba, pojazd]* to take off pot.; (zapodziać się) *[przedmiot]* to vanish; **złodziej ulotnił się z moją torebką** a thief made off with my handbag pot.

ulotn|y adi. ① *[woń, mgła]* light ② *[publikacja, druki]* occasional ③ *[chwila, widok]* fleeting; *[związek, uczucie]* transitory; *[myśl, wspomnienie]* fleeting

ulubie|niec m, ~**nica** f (osoba) favourite GB, favorite US; (zwierzę) pet

ulubi|ony adi. grad. *[artysta, kolor]* favourite GB, favorite US; *[temat, pomysł]* pet; **to mój najulubieńszy zespół** it's my favourite band

ulż|yć pf vi ① (zmniejszyć ciężar) ~**yć komuś** to lighten sb's load; ~**ył jej, biorąc część bagażu** he

relieved her of some of the luggage she was carrying ② (złagodzić ból, niepokój) to relieve; **chciał** ~**yć doli sierot** he wanted to alleviate the plight of orphans ③ (poprawić samopoczucie) to be a relief; ~**yło mi, kiedy wyznałem prawdę** I felt better once I'd confessed

■ ~**yć sobie** euf. (załatwić się) to relieve oneself euf.; (wyrazić żale) to let off a. blow off steam pot.

ułam|ać pf — **ułam|ywać** impf ① vt to break off *[gałązkę, kawałek]* ② **ułamać się** — **ułamywać się** *[gałąź, rączka]* to break (off)

ułam|ek m fraction; **przez** ~**ek sekundy** for a fraction of a second, for a split second

ułaskaw|ić pf — **ułaskaw|iać** impf vt to pardon *[skazańca]*

ułaskawie|nie n (free) pardon

ułatw|ić pf — **ułatw|iać** impf vt to facilitate *[komunikację, zmiany]*; to expedite *[naukę, zadanie]*; ~**iać komuś pracę/życie** to make work/life easier for sb

ułatwie|nie n facilitation; **komputer to duże** ~**nie w pracy** a computer facilitates work a lot

u|łożyć pf — **u|kładać** impf ① vt ① (uporządkować) to arrange; **układać rzeczy w walizce** to arrange things in a suitcase; **ułożyć coś alfabetycznie** to alphabetize sth; **ułożyć układankę** to complete a. finish a puzzle; **układać bukiet w wazonie** to arrange flowers in a vase; **układać glazurę** to put down tiles; **układać sobie włosy** to do one's hair ② (położyć) to lay; **ułożyła dzieci do snu** she put the children to sleep ③ (stworzyć) to make up; **ułożyć wierszyk** to make up a rhyme; **ułożyć melodię do słów poety** to compose a melody to a poem ④ (uzgodnić) **układać plany na przyszłość** to make plans for the future; **cała rzecz była z góry ułożona** it was all prearranged; **układać jadłospis na przyjęcie** to plan a menu for the party ② **ułożyć się** — **układać się** ① (kłaść się) to lie down; **układać się do snu** to lie down to sleep; **ułożyć się wygodnie na leżaku** to make oneself comfortable in a deckchair ② przen. (przebiegać) **nasze stosunki z sąsiadami układały się dobrze** we got on well with the neighbours

umal|ować pf ① vt to make up *[oczy]*; ~**ować usta** to put some lipstick on ② **umalować się** to make oneself up

umar|ły adi. dead; **uznali go za** ~**łego** they gave him up for dead; **miasto wygląda jak** ~**łe** this city looks dead; **modlitwa za** ~**łych** a prayer for the dead

■ **tak głośno, że** ~**łego by obudził** a. **na nogi postawił** loud enough to wake (up) the dead

umaszczeni|e n colour GB, color US

uma|zać pf ① vt to smear; ~**zał sobie ręce atramentem** he stained his hands with ink

II **umazać się** to get soiled; **cały** ~**zał się smarem** he got all smeared with grease

umebl|ować *pf vt* to furnish *[dom, pokój]*

umeblowani|e *n* furniture; **mieszkanie z pełnym** ~**em** a fully furnished flat

umia|r *m* moderation; **pić z** ~**rem** to drink in moderation

umiarkowan|y *adi. [styl, ton wypowiedzi]* restrained; *[cena, klimat, optymizm]* moderate

umi|eć *impf vi* ① (nauczyć się) to know; ~**ał wiersz na pamięć** he knew the poem by heart ② (być w stanie) ~**esz naprawić radio?** do you know how to repair a radio?; **nie** ~**em tańczyć** I can't dance

umiejętnoś|ć *f* ability; ~**ci taneczne** dancing skills; ~**ć koncentracji** the ability to concentrate

umiejsc|owić *pf* — **umiejsc|awiać** *impf vt* ① (umieścić) to situate; **akcję powieści** ~**owiono w Paryżu** the novel is set in Paris ② (ograniczyć) to localize *[zarazę, pożar]*

umie|ścić *pf* — **umie|szczać** *impf vt* ① (ulokować) to put; ~**ścić piłkę w siatce** a. **w bramce** to net the ball ② (opublikować) to place; ~**ścił swoje ogłoszenie w Internecie** he placed a. put his ad on the Internet; ~**ścić w gazecie artykuł** to print a. run an article in the paper ③ (skierować) to place

umieśni|ony *adi. [ciało]* muscular

um|knąć *pf* — **um|ykać** *impf vi* ① (uciec) to make off; **umknąć przed napastnikami** to flee the attackers; **umknąć z łupem** to make off with one's loot ② (nie zostać zauważonym) to escape; **umknąć czyjejś uwadze** to escape sb's notice a. attention

umniejsz|yć *pf* — **umniejsz|ać** *impf vt* to belittle *[zasługi, osiągnięcia]*; **próbował** ~**yć swoją winę** he tried to play down his responsibility

um|ocnić *pf* — **um|acniać** *impf* **I** *vt* ① (wzmocnić) to strengthen *[konstrukcję, gospodarkę]* ② (ugruntować) to reinforce *[władzę, przyjaźń]* ③ (ufortyfikować) to fortify *[teren, pozycję]*
II **umocnić się** — **umacniać się** ① (wzmocnić się) *[autorytet, władza]* to consolidate ② Wojsk. to secure one's position ③ przen. **umocnić się w przekonaniu, że...** to be confirmed in one's belief that...

umoc|ować *pf* — **umoc|owywać** *impf vt* to fasten; ~**ować coś na czymś** to fasten a. secure sth to sth; ~**ować antenę na dachu** to erect an aerial on the roof; ~**ować półkę na ścianie** to put up a. hang up a shelf

um|orzyć *pf* — **um|arzać** *impf vt* to remit *[dług, podatek]*; to dismiss *[sprawę]*

um|owa *f* agreement, contract; **umowa o dzieło** a specific-task contract; **umowa o pracę** employment contract

umown|y *adi.* ① (wynikający z umowy) *[prawa, kary]* contractual ② (fikcyjny) symbolic

umożliw|ić *pf* — **umożliw|iać** *impf vt* to enable, to make [sth] possible; ~**ić przestępcom ucieczkę** to enable the criminals to escape

um|ówić *pf* — **um|awiać** *impf* **I** *vt* ① (ustalić) to agree; **umówione hasło** the agreed password ② (ustalić spotkanie) to make an appointment for; **umówiła go ze swoją przyjaciółką** she arranged a date with her friend for him
II **umówić się** ① (postanowić wspólnie) to agree; **umówić się co do ceny** to agree on a price; **umówiłem się z nią, że...** I've arranged with her that... ② (zorganizować spotkanie) to arrange to meet; **umówić się z dziewczyną** to have a date with one's girlfriend

um|rzeć *pf* — **um|ierać** *impf vi* to die także przen.; **umrzeć nagle** to die a sudden death; **umrzeć na polu walki** to die in battle; **umrzeć śmiercią naturalną** to die of natural causes; **umierać z nudów** to be dying of boredom; **umierał z ciekawości, ile ona zarabia** he was dying to know how much she earned

umundurowani|e *n* uniform

umy|ć *pf* **I** *vt* to wash *[dziecko, ręce]*; to clean *[wannę, podłogę, zęby]*; to wash up *[naczynia]*
II **umyć się** to wash (oneself)
■ ~**wam ręce od tej całej sprawy** I wash my hands of the whole affair

umy|sł *m* mind także przen.; **mieć** ~**sł zaprzątnięty różnymi sprawami** to have different things on one's mind; **najwybitniejszy** ~**sł, jaki miałem okazję spotkać** the greatest mind a. brain I've ever come across; **być zdrowym na** ~**śle** to be in one's right mind, to be of sound mind

umysłowoś|ć *f* mind

umysłow|y *adi. [rozwój, wysiłek]* intellectual; *[choroba, upośledzenie]* mental; **być w pełni władz** ~**ych** to be of sound mind

umyślnie *adv.* deliberately, intentionally

umyśln|y *adi.* deliberate, intentional

umywa|ć się *impf v refl.* **film nie** ~ **się do książki** the film is nowhere near as good as the book pot.; **nikt się do niej nie** ~ nobody can hold a candle to her pot.

umywal|ka *f* washbasin

unaoczni|ć *pf* — **unaoczni|ać** *impf vt* książk. to make [sth] evident; to reveal (**coś komuś** sth to sb)

uni|a /'unja/ *f* union

unicestwi|ć *pf* — **unicestwi|ać** *impf vt* książk. ① (zniszczyć całkowicie) to annihilate *[naród]*; to destroy *[miasto]* ② (udaremnić) to foil *[plany, zamiary]*

uniemożliw|ić *pf* — **uniemożliw|iać** *impf vt* ~**ić coś komuś** to keep a. prevent sb from doing sth; **choroba ojca** ~**iła jej wyjazd za granicę** her father's illness made it impossible for her to go abroad; **zaspy śniegu** ~**iały przejazd** snowdrifts made the road(s) impassable

unieruchom|ić *pf* — **unierucham|iać** *impf vt* to immobilize *[pojazd, nogę]*; to freeze *[kapitał, rezerwy finansowe]*; **choroba** ~**iła go w łóżku** he was bedridden because of his illness

unieszczęśliw|ić *pf* — **unieszczęśliw|iać** *impf* **[]** *vt* to make [sb] unhappy a. miserable

[] **unieszczęśliwić się — unieszczęśliwiać się** to make oneself unhappy a. miserable

unieszkodliw|ić *pf* — **unieszkodliw|iać** *impf vt* to render [sb] harmless *[osobę]*; to neutralize *[odpady radioaktywne]*; ~**ił napastnika jednym uderzeniem** he overpowered the assailant with one punch; ~**ić bombę** to defuse a bomb

un|ieść *pf* — **un|osić** *impf* **[]** *vt* **①** (podnieść, wznieść) to raise; **uniósł rękę na pożegnanie** he raised a hand in farewell; **uniosła głowę znad książki** she looked up from her book **②** (dźwignąć) to lift *[walizkę]* **③** (przemieścić) **woda uniosła za sobą most** the water swept the bridge away; **wiatr unosi tumany kurzu** the wind is raising clouds of dust

[] **unieść się — unosić się** **①** *[osoba]* to rise; **unieść się z krzesła** to rise from a chair **②** *[kurtyna]* to be raised; to go up **③** (wzbić się) to soar; **balon uniósł się wysoko** the balloon sailed high in the air **④** (stracić panowanie nad sobą) to get carried away; (zirytować się) to lose one's temper; **uniósł się ambicją** his ambition got the better of him **⑤** przen. (wisieć) (w powietrzu) to hover; (na wodzie) to float; **nad łąkami unoszą się mgły** fog hangs over the fields **⑥** przen. *[zapach]* to waft

unieważni|ć *pf* — **unieważni|ać** *impf vt* to annul *[decyzję, ustawę]*; to revoke *[umowę, dokument]*; ~**ć wybory** to declare an election null and void; **testament został** ~**ony** the will was declared invalid

uniewinni|ć *pf* — **uniewinni|ać** *impf vt* to acquit

uniezależni|ć *pf* — **uniezależni|ać** *impf* **[]** *vt* to make [sb/sth] independent

[] **uniezależnić się — uniezależniać się** to become independent

unik *m* duck; **wykonać** ~ **przed ciosem** to dodge a blow; **w dyskusji robił ciągle** ~**i** przen. he was always dodging a. sidestepping the issues

unika|t *m* **ten rękopis to** ~**t** this manuscript is unique a. one of a kind

unikatow|y *adi. [zbiór, zdjęcie]* unique, one of a kind

unik|nąć *pf* — **unik|ać** *impf vi* **①** (ustrzec się) to escape *[błędu, komplikacji]*; to avoid *[punishment]*; **cudem** ~**nęłam śmierci** I barely escaped death **②** (stronić) to avoid *[towarzystwa, alkoholu, pytania, tematu]*

■ ~**ać czyjegoś wzroku** a. **czyichś oczu** to avoid looking sb in the eye

uniwersalizm *m* **①** (w filozofii) universalism **②** książk. (powszechność) universality

uniwersaln|y *adi.* **①** (całościowy) universal **②** (nadający się do wszystkiego) all-purpose; **klucz** ~**y** a skeleton key **③** (wszechstronny) *[artysta]* versatile

uniwersyte|t *m* university

unorm|ować *pf* **[]** *vt* to normalize *[ceny]*; ~**owane godziny pracy** regular working hours

[] **unormować się** to normalize; **sytuacja już się** ~**owała** the situation returned to normal

unowocześni|ć *pf* — **unowocześni|ać** *impf vt* to update *[metody produkcji, technologię]*; to modernize *[sprzęt, kuchnię]*

uodp|ornić *pf* — **uodp|orniać**, **uodp|arniać** *impf* **[]** *vt* **①** Med. to immunize **②** (uczynić odpornym) to toughen; **medytacja** ~**arnia nas na stres** meditation increases our resistance to stress

[] **uodpornić się — uodporniać się** to become immune także przen. (**na coś** to sth)

uogólni|ć *pf* — **uogólni|ać** *impf vt* to generalize *[wnioski, zasadę]*

uogólnie|nie *n* generalization

uos|obić *pf* — **uos|abiać** *impf vt* to personify

uosobie|nie *n* personification; **ta dziewczyna to** ~**nie wdzięku** the girl is the epitome of charm

upad|ek *m* **①** (przewrócenie się) fall (**z czegoś** from sth); **niebezpieczny** ~**ek** a bad fall **②** (ruina) collapse; (częściowa) decline; **chylić się ku** ~**kowi** to be headed for collapse **③** (klęska) (down)fall; (częściowa) decline; **wzloty i** ~**ki** ups and downs pot.

upadłoś|ć *f* bankruptcy

upaln|y *adi.* hot

upa|ł *m* heat; **fala** ~**łów** a heat wave

upamiętni|ć *pf* — **upamiętni|ać** *impf vt* to commemorate *[osobę, wydarzenie]*

upar|ty *adi.* stubborn; **na** ~**tego** at a push GB pot.

upa|ść *pf* — **upa|dać** *impf vi* **①** (przewrócić się) to fall (down); ~**ść głową do przodu** to fall headlong a. head first; ~**ść na kolana** to fall a. drop to one's knees; ~**ść na plecy/twarz** to fall on one's back/face; ~**dł jak długi** he fell flat; ~**dła zemdlona** she collapsed in a faint **②** (zakończyć się niepowodzeniem) *[cywilizacja, firma, rząd, powstanie]* to collapse; *[pomysł]* to come to nothing; *[inicjatywa]* to founder; **wniosek** ~**dł** the motion was defeated **③** (stoczyć się) to decline morally; **tak nisko jeszcze nie** ~**dłem** I would never stoop a. sink so low

upat|rzyć *pf* — **upat|rywać** *impf vt* (wyszukać) to search out; (wybrać) to choose; ~**rywać stosownej okazji, żeby...** to keep an eye out for an opportunity to...; ~**ywać w czymś swoje szanse** to see one's chance of success in sth; **dążyć do** ~**rzonego celu** to work towards a set goal

up|chnąć, **up|chać** *pf* — **up|ychać** *impf* to cram; **upchnąć coś w szafie** to stuff sth into the wardrobe

upełnomocni|ć *pf* — **upełnomocni|ać** *impf vt* to empower; ~**ć kogoś do zrobienia czegoś** to authorize sb to do sth

uperfum|ować *pf* **[]** *vt* to put perfume a. scent GB on *[ramiona, szyję]*; to perfume *[chusteczkę]*

[] **uperfumować się** to spray a. dab oneself with perfume

upewni|ć *pf* — **upewni|ać** *impf* **[]** *vt* to assure (**kogoś o czymś** a. **co do czegoś** sb of sth)
[] **upewnić się** — **upewniać się** to make sure a. certain (**o czymś** a. **co do czegoś** of sth)

up|iąć *pf* — **up|inać** *impf vt* to pin (up) *[włosy]*; to swag *[materiał, zasłony]*; **upiąć włosy w kok** to gather one's hair in a bun

upi|ć *pf* — **upi|jać** *impf* **[]** *vt* **1** (nadpić) ~**ła łyk wina z kieliszka** she took a sip of wine from the glass **2** (spoić) to get [sb] drunk (**czymś** on sth)
[] **upić się** — **upijać się** to get drunk (**czymś** on sth); ~**ć się do nieprzytomności** to drink oneself into a stupor; ~**ć się szczęściem** przen. to be deliriously happy; ~**ć się sukcesem** przen. to get drunk with success przen.

upie|c *pf* **[]** *vt* to bake *[chleb, ciasto, jabłka]*; to bake, to roast *[ziemniaki]*; to roast *[mięso]*
[] **upiec się** *[chleb, ciasto, jabłka]* to bake; *[mięso]* to roast
■ **tym razem ci się** ~**kło** pot. you got away with it this time

upierzeni|e *n* plumage

upiększ|yć *pf* — **upiększ|ać** *impf vt* **1** (czynić piękniejszym) to make [sb/sth] more attractive *[mieszkanie, ogród]*; to improve the appearance of *[miasto]* **2** (idealizować) to embellish *[fakty]*

upiln|ować *pf vt* to keep an eye on *[dziecko, psa]*; ~**ować kogoś/coś przed czymś** to protect sth from a. against sth; **nie** ~**ował więźnia** he allowed the prisoner to escape

upi|ór *m* ghost; ~**ory przeszłości** the spectres of the past; **blady jak** ~**ór** (as) white a. pale as a ghost

upl|eść *pf* — **upl|atać** *impf vt* to weave *[koszyk, wianek]*; to plait GB, to braid US *[linę]*

upły|nąć *pf* — **upły|wać** *impf vi* *[czas]* to pass; *[kadencja]* to expire; **termin** ~**wa w piątek** the deadline is Friday
■ **wiele wody** ~**nie (w Wiśle) nim** a. **zanim...** a lot of water has to go under the bridge before...

upływ *m* **1** (przemijanie) passage; ~ **czasu** the passage of time; **po** ~**ie kilku lat** after several years (have passed); **przed** ~**em miesiąca** before the month is out; **w miarę** ~**u czasu** as time goes by a. on; **z** ~**em czasu** with time; **z** ~**em lat** over the years **2** (skończenie się) expiry GB, expiration US; „**nie stosować po** ~**ie terminu ważności**" 'do not use after the expiry date'

upodoba|nie *n* liking (**do czegoś** for sth); ~**nia artystyczne/kulinarne** artistic/culinary tastes; **robić coś z** ~**niem** to get a lot of pleasure out of doing sth; **znajdować w czymś** ~**nie** to enjoy sth

upodobni|ć *pf* — **upodabni|ać** *impf* **[]** *vt* to make [sth] similar (**do czegoś** to sth)
[] **upodobnić się** — **upodabniać się** to become similar (**do kogoś** to sb)

upokorze|nie *n* humiliation

upok|orzyć *pf* — **upok|arzać** *impf* **[]** *vt* to humiliate (**kogoś przed kimś** a. **wobec kogoś** sb in front of sb)
[] **upokorzyć się** — **upokarzać się** to humble oneself (**przed kimś** a. **wobec kogoś** before a. in front of sb)

upol|ować *pf vt* **1** (zabić) to shoot *[zwierzynę]* **2** przen. (zdobyć) to hunt down *[osobę, przedmiot]*; ~**ować sobie męża** to land oneself a husband pot.

upomin|ek *m* gift; **dać coś komuś w** ~**ku** to give sb sth as a gift

upom|nieć *pf* — **upom|inać** *impf* **[]** *vt* to admonish (**kogoś za coś** sb for sth); *[policja, sędzia]* to caution (**kogoś za coś** sb for sth)
[] **upomnieć się** — **upominać się** **1** (dopominać się) to demand (**o coś** sth); ~**inać się o swoje prawa** to assert one's rights; ~**nieć się u kogoś o dług** to remind sb of a debt; **mój żołądek** ~**inał się o jedzenie** przen. my stomach was demanding food **2** (brać w obronę) to stand up (**o kogoś** a. **za kimś** for sb)

upomnie|nie *n* **1** (napomnienie) admonition; (oficjalne) caution; **udzielić komuś** ~**nia** to reprimand sb **2** (monit) (letter of) reminder

uporczyw|y *adi.* *[kaszel, myśl]* persistent; *[milczenie, plama]* stubborn; ~**y dzwonek telefonu** the insistent ringing of the telephone

uporządk|ować *pf* — **uporządk|owywać** *impf vt* to straighten up *[ogród, pokój]*; to arrange *[książki, zdjęcia]*; przen. to organize *[myśli]*; ~**ować swoje papiery** to put one's papers in order; ~**ować coś alfabetycznie** to put a. arrange sth in alphabetical order; ~**ować swoje sprawy** to put one's affairs in order

uposaże|nie *n* książk. remuneration książk.; **miesięczne** ~**nie** monthly pay a. salary

upośledze|nie *n* impairment; ~**nie fizyczne/ umysłowe** a physical/mental disability; ~**nie mowy** a speech impediment

upośledz|ony *adi.* *[osoba]* handicapped; *[funkcja organizmu]* impaired

upoważni|ć *pf* — **upoważni|ać** *impf vt* to authorize; ~**ć kogoś do zrobienia czegoś** to authorize sb to do sth; **karta** ~**a do 10% zniżki** the card entitles the bearer to a 10% discount

upowszechni|ć *pf* — **upowszechni|ać** *impf* **[]** *vt* to disseminate *[informacje, wiedzę]*; to propagate *[ideę, teorię]*
[] **upowszechnić się** — **upowszechniać się** *[przekonanie, zwyczaj]* to become widespread a. popular

upozor|ować *pf* — **upozor|owywać** *impf vt* to fake *[atak serca]*; to stage *[wypadek]*

up|ór *m* obstinacy

up|rać *pf vt* to wash *[bieliznę, sukienkę]*; **uprać coś ręcznie/w pralce** to wash sth by hand/in the washing machine

upras|ować *pf vt* to iron *[koszulę, obrus]*

upraw|a *f* ① (czynności) cultivation ② (uprawiane rośliny) crop

uprawia|ć *impf vt* ① (zajmować się) to practise *[sport]*; to pursue *[zawód]* ② (hodować) to plant *[warzywa, zboże]*; to cultivate *[ziemię]*; ~**iać ogród** to garden

uprawni|ć *pf* — **uprawni|ać** *impf vt* to authorize; ~**ć kogoś do (zrobienia) czegoś** to authorize sb to (do) sth; **legitymacja ~a do darmowych przejazdów** the card entitles the bearer to free travel

uprawnie|nie ▯ *n* entitlement; ~**nie do urlopu** leave entitlement

▯▯ **uprawnienia** *plt* ① (przywileje) rights; ~**nia emerytalne/kombatanckie** retirement/veteran's rights ② (kompetencje) qualifications ③ (władza) powers; **korzystać z szerokich ~ń** to exercise wide powers; **mieć specjalne ~nia** to be vested with special powers; **przekroczyć swoje ~nia** to exceed one's authority

uprawni|ony *adi.* ① (upoważniony) entitled; **osoby ~one do głosowania** eligible voters ② (zasadny) *[działania]* justified

uprawn|y *adi. [ziemia]* cultivable; *[roślina]* cultivated

uprawomocni|ć *pf* — **uprawomocni|ać** *impf* ▯ *vt* to validate *[dokument]*; ~**ć wyrok** to render a verdict final and binding

▯▯ **uprawomocnić się** — **uprawomocniać się** *[decyzja, przepis]* to come into force

upr|osić *pf* — **upr|aszać** *impf* ▯ *vt* to beg (**kogoś o coś** sb into (doing) sth); **dać się komuś ~osić** to give in to sb's entreaties

uproszcze|nie *n* simplification; **w ~niu** to put it simply

upr|ościć *pf* — **upr|aszczać** *impf vt* ① (ułatwić) to simplify *[pracę, przepisy]* ② (ująć powierzchownie) to oversimplify *[problem]*

uprowa|dzić *pf* — **uprowa|dzać** *impf vt* to kidnap *[osobę]*; to hijack *[samolot, autobus]*

uprz|ąż *f* harness

up|rzeć się *pf* — **up|ierać się** *impf v refl.* to insist (**przy czymś** on sth); **uparł się, że zrobi to sam** he insists on doing it himself

uprzedni *adi.* książk. previous

uprzednio *adv.* książk. previously; **jak wspomniałem ~...** as I mentioned earlier...

uprzedze|nie *n* prejudice (**do kogoś/czegoś** against a. towards sb/sth); bias (**do kogoś/czegoś** against sb/sth); ~**nia klasowe/rasowe** class/racial prejudice; **być wolnym od ~ń** to be unbias(s)ed

uprze|dzić *pf* — **uprze|dzać** *impf* ▯ *vt* ① (ubiec) to forestall *[atak, dyskusję]*; ~**dzać czyjeś kaprysy** to anticipate sb's whims; **nie ~dzajmy faktów** let's wait and see what happens ② (zapowiadać z góry) to (fore)warn (**kogoś o czymś** sb about a. of sth) ③ (zniechęcić) to prejudice (**kogoś do kogoś/czegoś** sb against sb/sth); **to mnie do niego ~dziło** this put me off him

▯▯ **uprzedzić się** — **uprzedzać się** to become prejudiced (**do kogoś/czegoś** against sb/sth)

uprzejmoś|ć *f* ① (grzeczność) politeness; (życzliwość) kindness; **wyświadczyć komuś ~ć** to do sb a favour ② **~ci** courtesies; **wymienić z kimś ~ci** to exchange pleasantries with sb

uprzejm|y *adi. grad. [osoba]* (grzeczny) courteous (**dla kogoś** to sb); (usłużny) kind (**dla kogoś** to sb); *[gest, słowa, ukłon]* polite; **spotkać się z ~ym przyjęciem** to be courteously received

uprzemysłowieni|e *n* industrialization

uprzykrz|yć *pf* — **uprzykrz|ać** *impf* ▯ *vt* to spoil (**coś komuś** sth for sb)

▯▯ **uprzykrzyć się** — **uprzykrzać się** to get a. become tiresome; ~**yło mi się siedzenie w domu** I'm tired of sitting at home

uprzytomni|ć *pf* — **uprzytamni|ać** *impf vt* ~**ć komuś coś** to make sb realize sth

uprzywilejowan|y *adi. [osoba, stanowisko]* privileged; **pojazd ~y** a priority vehicle

upudr|ować *pf* ▯ *vt* to powder *[nos, twarz]*

▯▯ **upudrować się** to powder one's face

upu|st *m* (obniżenie ceny) discount

■ **dać czemuś ~st** to give vent to sth

upu|ścić *pf* — **upu|szczać** *impf vt* to drop

uran *m* uranium

urat|ować *pf* ▯ *vt* to rescue; ~**ować komuś życie** to save sb's life także przen.

▯▯ **uratować się** to save oneself; ~**ować się od śmierci** to save one's own life; ~**ować sytuację** to save the day a. situation

uraz *m* ① Med. injury; (poważny) trauma; **doznać ~u** to sustain an injury ② (psychiczny) trauma; (trwały) scar; ~ **na punkcie czegoś** a complex about sth; ~ **do czegoś** an aversion to sth

uraz|a *f* grudge (**do kogoś** against sb)

ura|zić *pf* — **ura|żać** *impf* ▯ *vt* ① (zranić) to hurt; ~**zić skaleczoną rękę** to aggravate a hand injury ② (obrazić) to hurt; ~**zić czyjąś dumę** to hurt sb's pride

▯▯ **urazić się** — **urażać się** (zranić się) ~**zić się w rękę** to hurt one's hand

uregul|ować *pf vt* ① (ująć w przepisy) to regulate ② (uporządkować, załatwić) to take care of *[sprawy]*; to settle *[dług, rachunek]*

urlop *m* leave; ~ **bezpłatny** unpaid leave; **być na ~ie** to be on holiday a. leave

urn|a *f* ① (na prochy zmarłego) urn ② (wyborcza) ballot box, voting urn

ur|obić *pf* — **ur|abiać** *impf vt* ① (uformować) to mix *[substancję]*; to work *[glinę]* ② (zmienić) to mould GB, to mold US *[charakter]*; **urobić kogoś na swoją modłę** to mould sb in one's own image; **urabiać kogoś dla jakiejś sprawy** to try to win sb over to a cause
■ **urobić sobie ręce (po łokcie)** pot. to work one's fingers to the bone

urocz|y *adi.* charming, enchanting

uroczystoś|ć *f* ① (ceremonia) celebration(s) ② (podniosłość) solemnity

uroczy|sty *adi. grad. [obiad, strój]* ceremonial; *[mina, nastrój]* solemn

uro|da *f* ① (rysy twarzy) looks ② (piękny wygląd) beauty
■ **taka już jego ∼da** pot. that's just the way he is pot., iron.

urodzaj *m* ① (żniwo) harvest ② pot., żart. (mnogość) abundance (**na coś** of sth)

urodze|nie *n* birth; **data i miejsce ∼nia** the date and place of birth; **od ∼nia** from a. since birth

ur|odzić *pf* ❶ *vt* to give birth to *[dziecko, młode]*
❷ **urodzić się** to be born

urodzin|y *plt* ① (rocznica) birthday ② (przyjęcie) birthday party ③ (narodziny dziecka) birth; **wzrasta liczba ∼** the number of births is rising

urodz|ony *adi.* ① (zawołany) *[mówca, nauczyciel, polityk]* natural(-born), born ② (rodowity) by birth; **szlachetnie ∼ony** of noble birth

ur|oić *pf vi* **uroić sobie, że...** to get it into one's head that...

uroje|nie *n* delusion także przen.; **chory z ∼nia** iron. hypochondriac

uroj|ony *adi. [historia, problem]* imaginary; *[choroba]* phantom

urok *m* ① (powab) charm; **∼i życia na wsi** the allure of the countryside; **być pod czyimś ∼iem** to be under sb's spell ② (czary) spell; **rzucić na kogoś ∼** to cast a. put a spell on sb

uro|nić *pf vt* książk. ① (przeoczyć) to miss *[gest, szczegół]*; **nie ∼nił ani słowa z przemówienia** he took in every word of the speech ② (utracić) **nie ∼nił ani kropli płynu ze szklanki** he didn't spill a drop from the glass; **∼niła kilka łez** she shed a few tears

ur|osnąć[1] *pf vi* ① (powiększyć się) to grow ② (stać się dorosłym) to grow up

ur|osnąć[2] *pf* — **ur|astać** *impf vi [autorytet, sława]* to grow; *[ciasto]* to rise; **długi urosły w sporą sumę** the debts mounted up; **na podwórzu urosła sterta śmieci** a pile of rubbish accumulated in the yard
■ **urastać do rozmiarów** a. **rangi czegoś** to assume the proportions of sth; **urosnąć w czyichś oczach** a. **w czyjejś opinii** to rise in sb's esteem

urozmaice|nie *n* variety

uruch|omić *pf* — **uruch|amiać** *impf vt* to start *[maszynę, silnik, produkcję]*; to start (up) *[fabrykę]*; to initiate *[procedurę]*

ur|wać *pf* — **ur|ywać** *impf* ❶ *vt* ① (oderwać) to tear off *[guzik, klamkę]* ② (przerwać) to stop; **urwać rozmowę** to cut a conversation short; **urwać w pół zdania** to stop (in) mid-sentence
❷ **urwać się** — **urywać się** ① *[guzik, rynna]* to come off; *[lina]* to break ② (skończyć się) to stop; *[droga]* to end; **rozmowa się urwała** the conversation broke off; **nasza korespondencja dawno się urwała** we stopped corresponding a long time ago

urwis *m* rascal, scamp

uryw|ek *m* (utworu) excerpt; (rozmowy) snatch

urząd *m* office; **∼ąd skarbowy** the tax office; **∼ąd pocztowy** the post office; **∼ąd stanu cywilnego** a registry a. register office GB; **∼ąd zatrudnienia** employment bureau; **objąć ∼ąd ministra** to take office as minister; **pełnić** a. **piastować ∼ąd prokuratora** to serve as prosecutor

urządzać *impf* → **urządzić**

urządze|nie *n* device

urzą|dzić *pf* — **urzą|dzać** *impf* ❶ *vt* ① (zorganizować) to organize *[przyjęcie, wystawę]* ② (zrobić) to make *[scenę, burdę]*; **∼dzać sobie kpiny z kogoś/czegoś** to make a mockery of sb/sth ③ (założyć) to establish *[szpital polowy]*; **w tylnym pokoiku ∼dził sobie pracownię** he turned the rear room into a studio ④ (wyposażyć) to furnish *[mieszkanie, sklep]*
❷ *vi* pot. *[termin]* to suit (**kogoś** sb); **tysiąc złotych mnie nie ∼dza** a thousand zloty doesn't do it pot.
❸ **urządzić się** — **urządzać się** (zamieszkać) to settle; **∼dzić się w nowym domu** to settle in(to) a new house

urzeczywistni|ć *pf* — **urzeczywistni|ać** *impf* ❶ *vt* to realize *[marzenie, plan]*
❷ **urzeczywistnić się** — **urzeczywistniać się** *[marzenie]* to come true; *[plan]* to be carried out

urzędnicz|y *adi. [pensja, stanowisko]* clerical

urzędni|k *m*, **∼czka** *f* (w biurze) office worker; (w organizacji, instytucji) official; **wysoki rangą ∼k** a high-ranking official; **∼k stanu cywilnego** a registrar

urzęd|ować *impf vi* to work; **w zamku ∼ują władze miejskie** the castle is the seat of the city council; **w sobotę nie ∼ujemy** pot. we're closed on Saturdays; **∼ujący** *[minister, prezydent]* incumbent

urzędow|y *adi. [druk, ceny]* official; *[ton]* formal

usamodzielni|ć się *pf* — **usamodzielni|ać się** *impf v refl.* to become independent

us|chnąć *pf* — **us|ychać** *impf vi [drzewa, kwiaty, liście]* to wither
■ **usychać z miłości** to be lovesick; **usychać z tęsknoty za kimś** to be pining away for sb

usi|ąść *pf vi* to sit (down) **(na czymś** on sth); ~**ąść przy stole** to sit (down) at the table; ~**ąść do czegoś** to sit down to do sth; ~**ąść za kierownicą** to sit behind the wheel

usił|ować *impf vi* to try; **daremnie** ~**owała zasnąć** she tried to get some sleep, but in vain

uskłada|ć *pf vt* to save (up)

uskok *m* ① (skok) dodge ② (w murze) offset ③ (tektoniczny) face, fault

usłu|ga [] *f* ① (przysługa) favour GB, favor US ② (odpłatna) service

[] usługi *plt* ① (działalność) service ② (dział gospodarki) the service industry

■ **być na czyichś** ~**gach** to work for sb

usługow|y *adi. [firma]* service; **punkt** a. **zakład** ~**y** a shop, a service centre; **prowadzić działalność** ~**ą** to be in the service sector

usłysz|eć *pf vt* to hear; ~**eć o czymś** to hear about sth; ~**eć, że...** to hear that...

■ **do** ~**enia** goodbye

usmaż|yć *pf vt* Kulin. to fry *[mięso, naleśniki]*; ~**yć omlet** to make an omelette

u|snąć *pf* — **u|sypiać¹** *impf vi* to fall asleep

uspokajając|y *adi.* soothing; **środki** ~**e** tranquillizers

uspok|oić *pf* — **uspok|ajać** *impf [] vt* ① (przywrócić spokój) to calm; ~**oić roztrzęsione nerwy** to calm a. steady one's tense nerves; ~**oić sumienie** to salve one's conscience; **daj mu coś na** ~**ojenie** give him a sedative ② (uciszyć) to quieten (down) GB, to quiet (down) US

[] uspokoić się — **uspokajać się** ① (odzyskać spokój) to cool down ② (uciszyć się) *[osoba]* to quieten down GB, to quiet (down) US; **wiatr się powoli** ~**ajał** the wind was gradually dropping; **w mieście trochę się** ~**oiło** things had calmed down a little in the city

usprawiedliw|ić *pf* — **usprawiedliw|iać** *impf [] vt* ① (wybronić) to defend *[osobę, postępowanie]* ② (uzasadnić) to justify *[zarzuty, żądania]*

[] usprawiedliwić się — **usprawiedliwiać się** to excuse oneself **(za coś** for sth); **chciał się** ~**ić przed nami** he wanted to explain himself to us

usprawiedliwie|nie *n* ① (wyjaśnienie) (ustne) excuse; (pisemne) excuse note ② (uzasadnienie) justification **(dla czegoś** for sth); **co masz na swoje** ~**nie?** what can you say to justify your behaviour?

usprawni|ć *pf* — **usprawni|ać** *impf vt* to streamline, to facilitate *[pracę, procedurę, produkcję]*

usprawnie|nie *n* improvement

ust|a *plt* mouth; (wargi) lips; **oddychać** ~**ami** to breathe through one's mouth; **pocałować kogoś w** ~**a** to kiss sb on the lips

■ **być a. znaleźć się na** ~**ach wszystkich** książk. to be on everyone's lips; **pytania cisną się mu na** ~**a** he's bursting with questions; **nabrać wody w** ~**a** to keep one's mouth shut; **nie brać czegoś**

do ~ to never touch sth; **nie ma do kogo** ~ **otworzyć** there's nobody to talk to; **nie mieć co do** ~ **włożyć** to be starving; ~**a się mu nie zamykają** he never stops talking; **z** ~ **mi to wyjąłeś** you took the words (right) out of my mouth; **zamknąć komuś** ~**a** to silence sb

ustabiliz|ować *pf [] vt* to stabilize *[ceny]*; ~**owany tryb życia** a stable life

[] ustabilizować się *[ceny, pogoda, sytuacja]* to stabilize

ust|ać¹ *pf vi* (wytrwać w jednym miejscu) to stand still; (utrzymać się na nogach) to remain standing

usta|ć² — **usta|wać** *impf vi* to stop; **deszcz** ~**ł** it's stopped raining; **kontakty pomiędzy nami nie** ~**ły** we kept in touch

ustal|ić *pf* — **ustal|ać** *impf [] vt* to establish *[fakty, normy, warunki]*; to set *[termin]*; to determine *[prawdę]*; **trzeba** ~**ić, czy...** we should decide whether...; ~**ono, że...** it was settled that...

[] ustalić się — **ustalać się** *[pogoda]* to settle

ustan|owić *pf* — **ustan|awiać** *impf vt* ① (uchwalić) to pass *[prawo, ustawę]*; ~**owić święto** to establish a holiday ② (mianować) to appoint *[dyrektora, prezesa]* ③ Sport to set *[rekord]*

ustaw|a *f* law, act; **projekt** ~**y** a bill; ~**a zasadnicza** constitution; **kiedy** ~**a wejdzie w życie?** when does the law take effect?

ustaw|ić *pf* — **ustaw|iać** *impf [] vt* ① (umieścić) to place; ~**ić stół na środku pokoju** to put a table in the middle of the room; ~**ić figury na szachownicy** to set up the pieces on the chessboard; ~**ić meble w pokoju** to arrange the furniture in a room ② (zmontować) to set up *[namiot, rusztowanie]* ③ (wyregulować) to adjust *[parametry, telewizor]*

[] ustawić się — **ustawiać się** ① (stanąć) to stand; ~**ić się w kolejce** to join the queue; ~**ić się w szeregu** to line up; ~**ić się w pary** to pair up ② pot. (urządzić się) **on to zawsze potrafi się dobrze** ~**ić** he always lands on his feet pot.

ustawodawc|a *m* legislator

ustawodawcz|y *adi.* legislative

ustawodawstw|o *n* legislation

ust|ąpić *pf* — **ust|ępować¹** *impf vi* ① (ulec) to give in **(komuś** to sb); ~**ąpić wobec czegoś** to give in to sth; **po długich perswazjach** ~**ąpiła** after a lengthy persuasion she acquiesced ② (wycofać się) to retreat; ~**ępować komuś z drogi** to make way for sb; przen. to stay out of sb's way ③ (zrezygnować) to resign; ~**ąpić ze stanowiska** to resign (from) one's position; ~**ępujący rząd** the outgoing government ④ (minąć) *[ból, gorączka]* to subside; **mgła** ~**ąpiła** the fog has lifted ⑤ (zrzec się) to give up; ~**ąpić komuś miejsca** to give up one's seat to sb ⑥ (poddać się naciskowi) *[drzwi, zamek]* to yield

uster|ka *f* Techn. defect; „przepraszamy za ∼ki" TV 'normal service will be resumed as soon as possible'

ustęp *m* [1] (w tekście) passage [2] (ubikacja) WC

ustępować[1] *impf* → **ustąpić**

ustęp|ować[2] *impf vi* to be inferior to; ∼ować komuś/czemuś to be no match for sb/sth; nie ∼ować komuś/czemuś to be the equal of sb/sth; pod względem popularności ∼ował jedynie... in terms of popularity, he was second only to...

ustępstw|o *n* concession (**na rzecz** a. **wobec** kogoś to sb); **pójść na** ∼**a** to make concessions; **zgodzić się na** ∼**a** to agree to compromise

ustnik *m* (papierosa) filter (tip); (fajki) mouthpiece

ustn|y *adi.* oral

ustr|ój *m* [1] (polityczny) system [2] Biol., Med. body

usu|nąć *pf* — **usu|wać** *impf* **I** *vt* [1] (zabrać) to remove *[gruz, meble]*; ∼**nąć śnieg z ulic** to clear the streets of snow; ∼**nąć ludzi z terenu zagrożonego powodzią** to evacuate people from the area threatened with flooding [2] (wydalić) to dismiss *[urzędnika]*; to expel *[ucznia]*; **został** ∼**nięty z boiska** Sport he was sent off [3] Med. to remove *[guz, płuco]*; to extract *[ząb]*; ∼**nąć ciążę** to have an abortion [4] (zlikwidować) to remove *[plamę, przeszkody]*; ∼**nąć awarię** to repair a breakdown **II usunąć się — usuwać się** [1] (zrobić miejsce) to move a. step aside [2] (ze stanowiska) to step down; (z życia publicznego) to withdraw
■ ∼**wać się w cień** to keep a low profile; ∼**nąć kogoś/coś w cień** a. **na drugi plan** to overshadow sb/sth

usyp|ać *pf* — **usyp|ywać** *impf vt* to build *[kopiec]*

usypiać[1] *impf* → **usnąć**

usypiać[2] *impf* → **uśpić**

usypiając|y *adi. [kołysanie]* drowsy(-making)

uszczel|ka *f* gasket

uszczelni|ć *pf* — **uszczelni|ać** *impf vt* [1] (wypełnić) to seal *[dziurę, szczelinę]*; to insulate *[okna, drzwi]* [2] przen. (zaostrzyć) to tighten up *[przepisy, system podatkowy]*; ∼**ć granice** to seal the borders

uszczęśliwi|ć *pf* — **uszczęśliwi|ać** *impf vt* to make [sb] happy

uszczypliw|y *adi. grad.* biting

uszczyp|nąć, **uszczyp|ać** *pf* **I** *vt* to pinch **II uszczypnąć się, uszczypać się** to pinch oneself

uszkadzać *impf* → **uszkodzić**

usz|ko *n* [1] (ucho) ear [2] (uchwyt) handle; (otwór w igle) eye [3] Kulin. ∼**ka** ≈ ravioli

uszkodze|nie *n* damage

uszk|odzić *pf* — **uszk|adzać** *impf* **I** *vt* [1] (popsuć) to damage *[maszynę, urządzenie]* [2] (zranić) to injure *[część ciała, organ]*
II uszkodzić się — uszkadzać się to be damaged

usztywni|ć *impf* — **usztywni|ać** *impf* **I** *vt* [1] (utwardzać) to stiffen *[kołnierzyk, mankiety]*; **pianka** ∼**ająca włosy** styling mousse [2] Med. (unieruchomić) to immobilize *[część ciała]* [3] przen. to harden *[stanowisko]*; to strengthen *[konstrukcję]*
II usztywnić się — usztywniać się to stiffen także przen.

uszy|ć *pf vt* to make *[ubranie]*

uścisk *m* hug; (mocny) grip; ∼ **dłoni** a handshake; ∼**i** (w liście) hugs (and kisses)

uści|snąć, **uści|skać** *pf vt* to hug *[osobę]*; ∼**snąć komuś dłoń** a. **rękę** to shake sb's hand; ∼**skaj ode mnie żonę** give my love to your wife

uśmi|ać się *pf v refl.* to have a good laugh

uśmiech *m* smile; **drwiący** a. **szyderczy** ∼ a sneer; **głupawy** ∼ a smirk; ∼ **od ucha do ucha** a grin from ear to ear; **szczerzyć zęby w** ∼**u** to grin; ∼ **proszę** (do fotografii) smile please; ∼ **losu** przen. a stroke of luck

uśmiech|nąć się *pf* — **uśmiech|ać się** *impf v refl.* to smile (**do kogoś/czegoś** at sb/sth)
■ ∼**ać się pod nosem** a. **wąsem** pot. to laugh up one's sleeve

uśmierz|yć *pf* — **uśmierz|ać** *impf vt* książk. [1] (koić) to relieve; **środki** ∼**ające ból** painkillers [2] (stłumić) to quell *[bunt, zamieszki]*

u|śpić *pf* — **u|sypiać**[2] *impf* [1] (ukołysać do snu) to put a. lull [sb] to sleep [2] przen. (stłumić) to dull *[czujność, podejrzenia]* [3] Med. to anaesthetize, to anesthetize US *[pacjenta]* [4] (zabić) to put down *[zwierzę]*

uświad|omić *pf* — **uświad|amiać** *impf vt* [1] (uprzytomnić) ∼**omić coś komuś** to bring sth to sb's attention; ∼**omić coś sobie** to realize sth [2] (seksualnie) to explain the facts of life to euf.

utalentowan|y *adi.* talented; **wszechstronnie** ∼**y** of many talents

utarcz|ka *f* squabble

utarg *m* takings; **mieliśmy dziś dobry** ∼ business was brisk today

utarg|ować *pf vt* [1] (kupić po niższej cenie) to beat the price down by [2] (zarobić) to make; **dzisiaj** ∼**ował sporą sumę** he made quite a lot from sales today

utar|ty *adi. [opinia]* common; ∼**te zwroty** set phrases; **podążać** ∼**tym szlakiem** to follow the beaten track także przen.

utemper|ować *pf vt* to subdue *[osobę]*

utka|ć[1] *pf vt* [1] (zrobić tkając) to weave *[materiał]* [2] książk. (przepleść) to interweave (**coś czymś** sth with sth)

ut|kać[2] *pf* — **ut|ykać**[1] *impf vt* [1] (uszczelnić) to stuff; **utkać kocem szparę pod drzwiami** to stuff a blanket in the crack under the door [2] pot. (upchać) to cram; **utykać rzeczy do walizki** to cram one's things into a suitcase

ut|knąć *pf* — **ut|ykać**[2] *impf vt* [1] (ugrzęznąć) *[pojazd]* to get bogged down (**w czymś** in sth);

statek utknął na mieliźnie the ship ran aground ② przen. (zatrzymać się) to get stuck; **utknęliśmy w korku** we got stuck in a traffic jam ③ przen. (urwać się) *[rozmowa]* to stall; **robota utknęła w miejscu** work came to a halt

utkwi|ć *pf* **[]** *vt* ~ć **w kimś/czymś oczy** a. **spojrzenie** a. **wzrok** to fix one's eyes on sb/sth; ~ić **komuś w pamięci** to be lodged a. engraved in sb's memory

[] *vi [kula, nóż, ość]* to lodge; **obcas** ~ł **mi w szparze podłogi** my heel got stuck in a crack in the floor

utłu|c *pf* — **utłu|kiwać** *impf vt* (rozkruszyć) to grind; (na papkę) to mash; ~c **coś w moździerzu** to grind sth in a mortar

utocz|yć *pf vt* ① (ulać) to draw (off) *[wina, piwa]* ② (nadać kształt) to roll *[kulę ze śniegu]*; (na tokarce) to turn (on a lathe)

uto|nąć *pf vi* ① (pójść na dno) *[osoba]* to drown; *[statek]* to sink ② przen. (zagłębić się) to sink; ~nąć **w dużym fotelu** to sink into a big armchair

utop|ić *pf* **[]** *vt* ① (pozbawić życia) to drown *[osobę, zwierzę]* ② (zanurzyć w wodzie) to sink *[beczkę, skrzynię]*

[] **utopić się** to drown (oneself)

■ ~ić **pieniądze w czymś** to sink money in(to) sth

utożsam|ić *pf* — **utożsam|iać** *impf* **[]** *vt* to equate (**kogoś/coś z kimś/czymś** sb/sth with sb/sth)

[] **utożsamić się — utożsamiać się** to identify (**z kimś/czymś** with sb/sth)

utra|cić *pf vt* książk. to lose *[majątek, zdrowie]*

utra|ta *f* loss; ~ta **pamięci** memory loss; **upił się do** ~ty **przytomności** he drank himself unconscious; **do** ~ty **tchu** pot. until one's ready to drop pot.

utrudni|ć *pf* — **utrudni|ać** *impf vt* to make [sth] hard a. difficult; ~ać **postęp** to hinder progress; **mgła** ~ała **widoczność** the fog made it hard to see

utrudnie|nie *n* impediment (**w czymś** to sth); **stwarzać** ~nia **w realizacji planu** to impede (the implementation of) a plan

utrwal|ić *pf* — **utrwal|ać** *impf* **[]** *vt* ① (umocnić) to strengthen *[pozycje, stosunki, więź]* ② (zarejestrować) to record; ~ać **na taśmie głosy ptaków** to tape bird calls ③ (zachować) to retain *[fakt]*; to consolidate *[wiadomości]*; ~ić **coś w pamięci** to retain sth in memory ④ Fot. to fix

[] **utrwalić się — utrwalać się** *[zwyczaj]* to become established

u|trzeć *pf* — **u|cierać** *impf* **[]** *vt* Kulin. (na tarce) to grate *[warzywa]*; (w misce) to blend *[składniki ciasta]*; (w moździerzu) to grind *[przyprawy]*

[] **utrzeć się** (upowszechnić się) *[zwyczaj]* to become common a. widespread

utrzym|ać *pf* — **utrzym|ywać¹** *impf* **[]** *vt* ① (nie puścić) to hold, to hold (back) *[psa]*; **pilot z trudem mógł** ~ać **ster** the pilot could barely hold on to the controls ② (podeprzeć) *[konstrukcja]* to bear, to support ③ (nie stracić) to keep *[stanowisko, przewagę]* ④ (pokrywać koszty) to support *[rodzinę]*; to keep up *[budynek]* ⑤ (zachować) to keep up *[sprawność fizyczną]*; to maintain *[kontakt, korespondencję]*

[] **utrzymać się — utrzymywać się** ① (pozostać) to stay; ~ać **się na powierzchni wody** to stay afloat; ~ać **się na stanowisku** to remain in a position; ~ać **się przy władzy** to stay in power ② (nie zmienić się) *[śnieg]* to last; **zwyczaj** ~ał **się do dziś** the custom is still popular today; **jeśli pogoda się** ~**a...** if the weather holds for a few days... ③ (zaspokoić potrzeby finansowe) to support oneself; ~uje **się z pracy jako sprzątaczka** she earns her living as a cleaning lady; **z takiej marnej pensji się nie** ~**am** I can't support myself on such a low salary

■ **dobrze/źle** ~any in good/bad condition; **udało się** ~ać **go przy życiu** they managed to keep him alive; **list był** ~any **w bardzo chłodnym tonie** his letter was very cold in tone

utrzymani|e *n* (budynku) upkeep; (osoby, rodziny) support; **koszty** ~a the cost of living; **mieszkanie z** ~em bed and board; **mieć kogoś na** ~u to support sb; **zapewnić komuś całodzienne** ~e to provide sb with full board

utrzymywać¹ *impf* → utrzymać

utrzym|ywać² *impf vt* (twierdzić) to maintain, to claim

utucz|yć *pf vt* to fatten up

utwier|dzić *pf* — **utwier|dzać** *impf* **[]** *vt* to confirm; ~dzić **kogoś w postanowieniu** to confirm sb in their decision

[] **utwierdzić się — utwierdzać się** to be confirmed; ~dzić **się w swoich podejrzeniach** to be confirmed in one's suspicions

utw|orzyć *pf* **[]** *vt* to set up *[komitet, zarząd]*; to create *[miejsca pracy]*; to form *[kałuże, sople, wydmy]*

[] **utworzyć się** to be formed

utw|ór *m* (dzieło) work; ~ory **zebrane** collected works

uty|ć *pf vi* to put on weight

utykać¹ *impf* → utkać²

utykać² *impf* → utknąć

ut|ykać³ *impf vi* (kuleć) to limp; **utykać na prawą nogę** to have a limp in the a. one's right leg; **chodził, lekko utykając** he walked with a slight limp

utylizacj|a *f* recycling; ~a **odpadów przemysłowych** industrial waste management

utyliz|ować *impf vt* to recycle *[makulaturę, złom]*; to utilize *[śmieci]*

uwa|ga [] *f* ① (koncentracja) attention; **odwracać (czyjąś)** ~gę to distract a. divert sb's attention;

przyciągać a. **zwracać** ~**gę** to attract a. draw attention; **skupiać** ~**gę na kimś/czymś** to focus one's attention on sb/sth; **w centrum** ~**gi** in the centre of attention; **słuchać z** ~**gą** to listen with attention; **proszę o** ~**gę!** attention please! ② (komentarz) remark; **wymienić** ~**gi na temat kogoś/ czegoś** to exchange comments on sb/sth ③ (pouczenie) comment ④ Szkol. (nagana) note

Ⅱ *inter.* attention!, look a. watch out!; „~**ga, zły pies"** 'beware of the dog'

■ **brać coś pod** ~**gę** to take sth into consideration a. account; **mieć kogoś/coś na** ~**dze** to have sb/sth in mind; **ujść czyjejś** ~**gi** a. ~**dze** to escape sb's notice a. attention; **zwrócić komuś** ~**gę** to reprimand sb

uwalniać *impf* → **uwolnić**

uwarunk|ować *pf* — **uwarunk|owywać** *impf vt* książk. to condition; **choroba** ~**owana genetycznie** a genetically determined illness

uważa|ć *impf* **Ⅰ** *vi* ① (koncentrować się) to pay attention; **gdybyś** ~**ł...** if you'd been paying attention...; ~**j na ten samochód!** watch out for that car!; ~**j na głowę/co mówisz!** mind your head/your tongue!; ~**j, jak idziesz!** watch your step!; ~**j!** watch it! pot. ② (strzec) ~**ć na kogoś/coś** to look after sb/sth; ~**j na siebie!** take care of yourself)! ③ (traktować) to regard, to consider; ~**ć kogoś za sprzymierzeńca** to regard sb as an ally; ~**ć czyjeś słowa za obelgę** to take sb's words as an insult ④ (sądzić) to think; ~**m, że nie masz racji** I think you're wrong; **jak** ~**sz** pot. as you wish a. like

Ⅱ uważać się to consider oneself; **on się** ~**a za geniusza** he considers himself a genius

uważnie *adv. grad.* [iść, rozglądać się] carefully; [słuchać] attentively

uważn|y *adi. grad.* [pracownik, słuchacz] attentive; [spojrzenie] sharp

uwertu|ra *f* ① Muz. overture (**do czegoś** to sth) ② przen. prelude

uwę|dzić *pf vt* Kulin. to smoke [mięso, ryby]

uwiaryg|odnić *pf* — **uwiaryg|odniać** *impf vt* to lend credence to [relacje]

uwid|ocznić *pf* — **uwid|aczniać** *impf* **Ⅰ** *vt* to reveal [niedociągnięcia, wady]

Ⅱ uwidocznić się — **uwidaczniać się** [szczegóły] to be seen a. visible

uwieczni|ć *pf* — **uwieczni|ać** *impf vt* to immortalize

uwielbia|ć *impf vt* to adore [osobę]; to love [ciastka, zwierzęta]; ~**ć coś robić** to love doing sth

uwierz|yć *pf vi* to believe (**w coś** sth); **nigdy w to nie** ~**ę** I'll never believe that; ~**yć w kogoś** to believe in sb; ~**yłem, że ona to zrobi** I trusted her to do it; ~**yli mu na słowo** they took his word for it; **to nie do** ~**enia!** that's incredible a. unbelie-

vable!; **jest nie do** ~**enia przebiegły** he's incredibly a. unbelievably cunning

uw|ieść *pf* — **uw|odzić** *impf vt* (kokietować) to flirt with; (skłonić do współżycia) to seduce; (oczarować) to delude (**kogoś czymś** sb with sth)

uwię|zić *pf vt* ① (pozbawić wolności) to confine; (osadzić w więzieniu) to imprison ② (unieruchomić) to trap

uwikła|ć *pf* **Ⅰ** *vt* to entangle; ~**ć kogoś w coś** to drag sb into sth; **kraj** ~**ny w wojnę** a country embroiled in war

Ⅱ uwikłać się to get entangled a. tangled up (**w coś** in sth)

uwodziciel *m* heartbreaker

uwodziciels|ki *adi.* seductive

uw|olnić *pf* — **uw|alniać** *impf* **Ⅰ** *vt* ① (wyzwolić) to (set) free [niewolników]; to liberate [kraj]; **uwalniać kogoś z więzów** to untie sb; **uwolnić kogoś od swojego towarzystwa** żart. to relieve sb of one's company żart. ② (wypuścić z więzienia) to release

Ⅱ uwolnić się — **uwalniać się** ① (wyzwolić się) to free oneself, to break free ② (pozbyć się) to free oneself (**od czegoś** of sth)

uwydatni|ć *pf* — **uwydatni|ać** *impf* książk. **Ⅰ** *vt* to highlight [wady, zalety, figurę, urodę]; **obcisła sukienka** ~**a jej kobiece kształty** the tight dress makes the most of her feminine curves

Ⅱ uwydatnić się — **uwydatniać się** to be highlighted

uwzględni|ć *pf* — **uwzględni|ać** *impf* ① (wziąć pod uwagę) to take into consideration a. account ② (rozpatrywać) to consider [wniosek, prośbę]

uw|ziąć się *pf v refl.* to be hell-bent pot. (**na coś** on sth); **uwziąć się na kogoś** pot. to have it in for sb pot.

uzależni|ć *pf* — **uzależni|ać** *impf* **Ⅰ** *vt* (warunkować) to make [sth] conditional (**od czegoś** on sth); ~**ł swoją zgodę od (spełnienia) kilku warunków** he agreed, subject to a few stipulations

Ⅱ uzależnić się — **uzależniać się** ① (stać się zależnym) to be(come) dependent (**od kogoś** on sb) ② (wpaść w nałóg) to get addicted (**od czegoś** to sth)

uzależnie|nie *n* ① (silne przyzwyczajenie) addiction; ~**nie od narkotyków** drug addiction ② (stan zależności) dependence

uzależni|ony **Ⅰ** *adi.* [osoba] addicted

Ⅱ uzależni|ony *m*, ~**ona** *f* addict

uzasadni|ć *pf* — **uzasadni|ać** *impf vt* to justify, to substantiate [tezę, wniosek]

uzasadni|ony *adi.* [obawy, żal] justified

uzbiera|ć *pf* **Ⅰ** *vt* to save up [pieniędzy]; to gather [grzybów, owoców, ludzi]

Ⅱ uzbierać się (o pieniądzach) to accumulate; (o ludziach) to gather

uzbr|oić *pf* — **uzbr|ajać** *impf* **Ⅰ** *vt* ① (wyposażyć w broń) to arm (**w coś** with sth) ② (uczynić gotowym do działania) to arm [bombę, pocisk] ③ (założyć instalacje) to fit (out) *[budynek]*; **teren** ~**ojony** land provided with service infrastructure

II **uzbroić się — uzbrajać się** ☐ (zaopatrzyć się w broń) to arm oneself (**w coś** with sth) ☐ (zaopatrzyć się w narzędzia) to equip a. arm oneself (**w coś** with sth)

■ ~**oić się w cierpliwość** to arm oneself with patience

uzbrojeni|e *n* Wojsk. weaponry

u|zda *f* bridle

uzdolni|ony *adi.* talented, gifted (**do czegoś** at sth)

uzdr|owić *pf* — **uzdr|awiać** *impf vt* to heal także przen.

uzdrowisk|o *n* spa, health-resort

uzewnętrzni|ć *pf* — **uzewnętrzni|ać** *impf* **I** *vt* to express *[myśli, uczucia]*

II **uzewnętrznić się — uzewnętrzniać się** to be manifested (**w czymś** in sth)

uzębieni|e *n* teeth

uzg|odnić *pf* — **uzg|adniać** *impf vt* to agree on, to set *[terminy, warunki]*

uziem|ić *pf* — **uziem|iać** *impf vt* ☐ Techn. to earth GB, to ground US ☐ pot. to put [sb] out of action

uziemie|nie *n* earthing GB, grounding US

uzna|ć *pf* — **uzna|wać** *impf vt* ☐ (zaakceptować) to acknowledge, to recognize; ~**ć dziecko** Prawo to admit paternity; ~**ć swój błąd** to admit one's mistake; ~**ć kogoś za niewinnego** to find sb innocent ☐ (poczytać) ~**ny za zmarłego** presumed dead

uznani|e *n* ☐ (akceptacja) recognition, acknow-ledgement ☐ (opinia) **według czyjegoś** ~**a** at sb's (own) discretion ☐ (poważanie) recognition; **po-**

wszechne ~**e** universal recognition; ~**e dla czyichś zasług** recognition of sb's accomplish-ments; **zyskać sobie** ~**e** to win a. gain recognition

uzupełni|ć *pf* — **uzupełni|ać** *impf* **I** *vt* to supplement *[dietę, wykształcenie]*; to replenish *[zapasy]*; to make up *[ubytek, braki]*; **szkolna lektura** ~**ająca** supplementary reading; **wybory** ~**ające** a by-election

II **uzupełnić się — uzupełniać się** to comple-ment each other

użal|ić się *pf* — **użal|ać się** *impf v refl.* ☐ (na-rzekać) to complain ☐ (litować się) to feel sorry (**nad kimś** for sb); ~**ać się nad sobą** to feel sorry for oneself

użądli|ć *pf vt [osa]* to sting

uży|cie *n* use; **łatwy w** ~**ciu** easy to use; **wstrząsnąć przed** ~**ciem** shake well before using; **wychodzić z** ~**cia** to be falling into disuse

uży|ć *pf* — **uży|wać** *impf vt* to use, to apply *[maści]*; ~**wać swobody** to enjoy one's freedom

■ ~**wać sobie** pot. to live it up pot.; ~**łem jak pies w studni** pot. it was about as much fun as a trip to the dentist pot.

użytecznoś|ć *f* usefulness; **gmachy** ~**ci pu-blicznej** public buildings

użyteczn|y *adi.* useful

użyt|ek *m* use; **zrobić z czegoś** ~**ek** to make use of sth; **na własny** ~**ek** a. **do własnego** ~**ku** for one's own (personal) use

użytkowni|k *m*, ~**czka** *f* user

użytkow|y *adi.* functional; **powierzchnia** ~**a mieszkania** usable floor space a. area; **sztuka** ~**a** applied art

używ|ka *f* substance

użyźni|ć *pf* — **użyźni|ać** *impf vt* to fertilize

W, w *n inv.* W, w

w, we *praep.* ⟦1⟧ (wskazując na miejsce) in; (o instytucji) at;
w kuchni in the kitchen; **w domu/szkole/pracy**
at home/school/work; **w górach/lesie** in the
mountains/forest; **w powietrzu/wodzie** in the
air/water; **w prasie** in the press; **w telewizji/
radiu** on television/the radio; **w drzwiach** in the
doorway ⟦2⟧ (kierunek) (in)to, in; **w stronę czegoś**
towards sth; **w góry** to the mountains; **spojrzeć
w lewo/prawo** to look (to one's) left/right;
spojrzeć w górę/dół to look up(wards)/down-
(wards); **wziąć kogoś w ramiona** he take sb in
one's arms ⟦3⟧ (wskazując na kontakt) on; **w szczękę** on
the jaw; **w usta** on the lips; **oparzyć się w rękę** to
burn one's hand ⟦4⟧ (wskazując na ubranie, opakowanie) in;
kobieta w bieli a woman (dressed) in white
⟦5⟧ (wskazując na dziedzinę) in; **nowe kierunki
w sztuce** new directions in art ⟦6⟧ (wskazując na stan)
in; (dynamicznie) into; **w nędzy** in poverty; **w
milczeniu** in silence; **wpaść w furię** to fly into a
passion ⟦7⟧ (w określeniach czasu) in; **w zimie** in (the)
winter; **w maju** in May; **we wtorek** on Tuesday; **w
ubiegły czwartek** last Thursday ⟦8⟧ (podczas) in,
during; **w rozmowie ze mną** in conversation with
me ⟦9⟧ (wskazując na formę) in; **rzeźba w marmurze** a
sculpture in marble; **w gotówce** in cash; **mapa
w skali 1:100 000** a map to a scale of 1:100,000;
mleko w proszku powdered milk; **spodnie
w jasnym kolorze** light-coloured trousers
⟦10⟧ (wzór) **sukienka w grochy** a polka-dot dress;
spódnica w kwiaty a flower-patterned skirt
⟦11⟧ (wskazując na przemianę) into; **w kostkę/plastry**
into cubes/slices; **przemienić kogoś w żabę** to
turn sb into a frog ⟦12⟧ (wskazując na ilość) in; **w dwóch
egzemplarzach** in duplicate; **poszliśmy w piątkę
do kina** the five of us went to the cinema
⟦13⟧ (odnośnie) **cierpki w smaku** bitter in taste;
szorstki w dotyku rough to the touch ⟦14⟧ (wskazując
na powód, cel) in; **w nadziei, że...** in the hope that...;
ruszyć w pogoń za kimś to set off in pursuit of sb

wab|ić *impf* ⟦I⟧ *vt* ⟦1⟧ (nęcić) to attract; (przynętą, karmą)
to lure; (naśladującym głosem) to decoy ⟦2⟧ Zool. *[samiec,
samica]* to attract ⟦3⟧ (przyciągać) (podstępem, fałszywą
obietnicą) to lure

⟦II⟧ **wabić się** (nazywać się) *[pies]* to be called

wachlarz *m* ⟦1⟧ (poruszający powietrze) fan ⟦2⟧ książk.
(zbiór) range

wachl|ować *impf* ⟦I⟧ *vt* ⟦1⟧ (ochładzać) to fan
⟦2⟧ (poruszać) to sway (**czymś** sth)
⟦II⟧ **wachlować się** to fan oneself

wach|ta *f* Żegl. (służba, załoga) watch; **pełnić ∼tę** to
keep a. stand watch

wacik *m* (płaski) swab of cotton wool; (kulisty) wad of
cotton wool

wa|da *f* ⟦1⟧ (osoby, przedmiotu) flaw; (ujemna cecha) vice;
(usterka) fault; (niekorzystna cecha) drawback ⟦2⟧ Med.
defect; **wada postawy** an abnormal curvature of
the spine

wadliw|y *adi.* *[towar]* defective; *[urządzenie]*
faulty; *[postawa, zgryz]* incorrect

waf|el *m* wafer; (do lodów) cone

Wa|ga *f* Libra

wa|ga *f* ⟦1⟧ (przyrząd) scales; (szalkowa) balance, pair of
scales; **być języczkiem u wagi** przen. to tip the
scales ⟦2⟧ (ciężar) weight; **sprzedawać coś na wagę**
to sell sth by (the) weight; **przybierać na wadze** to
put on weight ⟦3⟧ przen. (znaczenie) weight, significance; **przywiązywać (wielką) wagę do czegoś**
to attach (a lot of) weight a. significance to sth
⟦4⟧ Sport weight

wagar|ować *impf vi* to (play) truant

wagarowicz *m*, **∼ka** *f* truant (pupil)

wagar|y *plt* truancy; **chodzić na ∼y** to play
truant

wagon *m* car, carriage; **∼ dla palących** a smoking car a. carriage

waha|ć się *impf v refl.* ⟦1⟧ *[osoba]* to hesitate
⟦2⟧ (zmieniać się) *[cena, poziom]* to fluctuate; *[nastrój,
postawa]* to vacillate ⟦3⟧ (kołysać się) *[wskazówka,
wskaźnik]* to hunt; (rytmicznie) to oscillate

wahad|ło *n* pendulum

wahadłow|iec *m* (prom kosmiczny) space shuttle

wahadłow|y *adi.* ⟦1⟧ *[ruch, kołysanie]* pendulum,
pendular *[autobus, transport]* shuttle

waha|nie *n* ⟦1⟧ (niepewność) hesitation; **bez ∼nia**
without hesitation ⟦2⟧ (zmienność) (parametrów, wskaźni-
ków) fluctuation; (wokół stałej wartości) oscillation;
(nastroju, opinii) vacillation

wakacj|e *plt* holidays GB, vacation US; **jechać na
∼e** to go on holiday a. vacation

waka|t *m* ⟦1⟧ (posada) (job) vacancy ⟦2⟧ Druk. blank
page

wala|ć się *impf v refl.* pot. *[resztki, śmieci]* to lie
around a. about

walc *m* waltz

walcz|yć *impf vi* [1] (bić się) *[osoba, armia, państwo]* to fight (**przeciw czemuś** against sth) [2] (przeciwstawiać się) to oppose (**z czymś** sth); (zmagać się) to struggle (**z czymś** with sth); (rywalizować) to compete (**o coś** for sth); ~**yć** **z chorobą** to battle against an illness; ~**yć ze snem** to struggle to remain awake; ~**yć o klientów** to compete for customers; ~**yć z zamkiem błyskawicznym** to struggle a. wrestle with a zip

wal|ec *m* [1] (kształt) cylinder [2] (urządzenie) roller; ~**ec drogowy** a roadroller

waleczn|y *adi. grad.* *[osoba]* brave; *[czyn]* valiant

wale|ń *m* whale

walerian|a *f* valerian

wale|t *m* (w kartach) jack, knave

■ **na** ~**ta** pot. (nago) in the buff pot.; (naprzemianlegle) *[spać, leżeć]* head to tail; (bez zameldowania) *[mieszkać, nocować]* without being registered

walić[1] *impf* → **walnąć**

wal|ić[2] *impf* [] *vi* pot. [1] (padać) *[śnieg, deszcz, grad]* to pelt down [2] (wydobywać się) *[woda, krew]* to gush (out); *[ciecz, dym]* to pour out; *[dym, para]* to billow [3] (przemieszczać się) *[ludzie, tłum]* to flock [4] (mocno bić) *[serce, puls, tętno]* to race

[] **walić się** [1] (rozpadać się) *[szopa, płot, system, plan]* to fall apart także przen. [2] pot. (spadać) *[sufit, dach]* to collapse; *[dachówki, kamienie]* to fall down

waliz|ka *f* suitcase

wal|ka *f* [1] (starcie) fight; (na wojnie) combat; ~**ka na pięści** a fist fight [2] Sport (bokserska, zapaśnicza) match, bout [3] (zabieganie) fight, struggle; (współzawodnictwo) contest; ~**ka o pokój** the struggle for peace; ~**ka o fotel prezydencki** the presidential contest [4] (przeciwdziałanie) fight (**z czymś** against sth); ~**ka z przestępczością** the battle a. fight against crime

walkowe|r *m* wygrać ~**rem** to win by default

wal|nąć *pf* — **wal|ić**[1] *impf* [] *vt* [1] pot. (uderzyć) to bash pot. [2] pot. (rzucić) to dump [3] pot. (powiedzieć otwarcie) to say [sth] straight from the shoulder pot. [4] pot. (zrobić) ~**ić błędy ortograficzne** to make spelling mistakes

[] *vi* pot. [1] (trzasnąć) *[drzwi, okiennica]* to bang; (uderzyć) to bash [2] *[piorun, grzmot]* (uderzyć) to strike; (zagrzmieć) to boom

[] **walnąć się** — **walić się** pot. (uderzyć się) to bash pot.; ~**nąć się w głowę** to bash one's head

waln|y *adi.* [1] (istotny) *[pomoc, udział]* considerable [2] (rozstrzygający) *[zwycięstwo]* conclusive; *[bitwa]* decisive [3] (ogólny) *[zebranie]* general

walo|r [] *m* książk. (zaleta) advantage

[] **walory** *plt* [1] (papiery wartościowe) securities [2] pot. (pieniądze) money

waltorni|a *f* French horn

walu|ta *f* Fin. (jednostka pieniężna) currency; (zagraniczna) foreign exchange a. currency, valuta; **kantor**

wymiany ~**ta** a bureau de change; **twarda** ~**ta** pot. hard currency

wa|ł *m* [1] (nasyp) embankment [2] (część maszyny) shaft; (walec) roller; **wał korbowy** a crankshaft

wał|ek *m* roller; ~**ek do ciasta** a rolling pin; ~**ek do malowania ścian** a (paint) roller; **zwinąć koc w** ~**ek** to roll up a blanket

wałęsa|ć się *impf v refl.* pot. to wander around

wałk|ować *impf vt* [1] (rozpłaszczać) to roll out *[ciasto]* [2] pot. (roztrząsać) to harp on about *[problem, sprawę]*

wałów|ka *f* pot. packed lunch

wampi|r *m* vampire

wandal *m* vandal

wandalizm *m* vandalism

wanili|a *f* vanilla; (owoc) vanilla bean a. pod; **laska** ~**i** a vanilla

wan|na *f* [1] (w łazience) bath(tub) [2] Techn. tank

wapie|ń *m* limestone

wapn|o *n* [1] (budowlane) lime [2] (lekarstwo) calcium

wap|ń *m* calcium

warcab|y *plt* draughts GB, checkers US

warchla|k *m* piglet; (młody dzik) young wild boar

warczeć *impf* → **warknąć**

war|ga *f* [1] Anat. (część ust) lip; **zajęcza** ~**ga** a harelip [2] Bot., Zool. labium

wariac|ki *adi.* pot. *[pomysł, wyprawa]* crazy; *[dom, rodzinka]* wacky pot.; ~**kie tempo** a breakneck pace

warian|t *m* variant

waria|t *m* pot. [1] (umysłowo chory) madman [2] (postępujący nieobliczalnie) nutter pot.

wariat|ka *f* pot. [1] (umysłowo chora) madwoman [2] (postępująca nieobliczalnie) nutter pot.

wari|ować *impf vi* pot. to go mad także przen.; ~**ować na punkcie czegoś** to be crazy about sth

war|knąć *pf* — **war|czeć** *impf vi* [1] *[zwierzę]* to growl; *[silnik, maszyna]* to whirr [2] pot. *[osoba]* to snap (**na kogoś** at sb)

warkocz *m* [1] (splot) plait GB, braid [2] przen. (dymu, kurzu, mgły) plume

warko|t *m* (silnika, maszyny) whirr

warko|tać *impf vi* to whirr

war|ować *impf vi* [1] *[pies]* to lie down (on guard) [2] pot. *[osoba]* to stay put, to keep guard

warstw|a *f* [1] (płaszczyzna) layer; ~**a farby** a coat of paint [2] (grupa społeczna) class [3] (w geologii) stratum

warszta|t [] *m* [1] (zakład rzemieślniczy) (work)shop; ~**t samochodowy** a (repair) garage [2] (metoda pracy) technique

[] **warsztaty** *plt* [1] (dział szkoły zawodowej) workshops [2] (kurs) workshop course; ~**ty teatralne** theatre workshops

war|t *adi. praed.* [1] (mający cenę) worth [2] (godny) worth (**czegoś** sth); worthy (**czegoś** of sth); **to jest** ~**te zachodu** it's worth the trouble

war|ta *f* guard; **zmiana** ~**ty** the changing of the guard *także przen.*; **stać na** ~**cie** to be on guard duty

wart|ki *adi. [strumień, prąd]* rapid; *[akcja, narracja]* lively; *[rozmowa]* animated

warto *praed.* **to** ~ **zobaczyć** it's worth seeing; **czy to** ~**?** is it worth it?; ~ **tam być wcześniej** it's worthwhile getting there early

wartościow|y *adi. grad.* ① (kosztowny) *[przedmiot]* valuable ② (mający wiele zalet) *[pracownik]* (very) good; *[pokarm, posiłek]* nutritious; *[książka, film]* quality

wartoś|ć *f* value; **sprzęt (o)** ~**ci tysiąca funtów** a thousand pounds' worth of equipment; **spór o** ~**ci** a dispute over values

wartowni|a *f* guardroom

wartowni|k *m* guard

warun|ek ① *m* condition; **postawić** ~**ek** to make a condition; **pod** ~**kiem, że...** provided that... ② **warunki** *plt* ① (sytuacja) conditions; ~**ki życia** living conditions ② (możliwości) aptness; ~**ki zewnętrzne** appearance

warunkow|y *adi.* conditional

warz|yć *impf* ① *vt* przest., książk. to boil *[jedzenie]*; ~**yć piwo** to brew beer ② **warzyć się** ① przest. (gotować się) *[jedzenie]* to boil; *[piwo]* to brew ② (psuć się) *[mleko]* to curdle

warzywniak *m* ① (ogród) vegetable garden ② pot. (sklep) greengrocer's (shop)

warzywni|k *m* ① (rolnik) vegetable grower ② (o-gród) vegetable garden

warzyw|o *n* ① Bot. vegetable ② pot. (o osobie) vegetable pot.

wa|sz ① *pron.* (przed rzeczownikiem) your; (bez rzeczownika) yours; **Wasza Wysokość** Your Highness ② **wasi** *plt* pot. (rodzina) your family; (przyjaciele) your friends ③ **wasze** *n* pot. what's yours ④ **po waszemu** pot. (o języku) in your language; (o zwyczaju) your (own) way

wa|t *m* watt

wa|ta *f* ① (materiał opatrunkowy) cotton wool GB, (absorbent) cotton US ② (do celów technicznych) wadding; **wata szklana** glass wool ③ przen. (pustosłowie) waffle GB, padding ④ Kulin. candyfloss GB, cotton candy US

waz|a *f* ① (do zupy) (soup) tureen; (zawartość) tureenful ② (ozdobna) vase

wazelin|a *f* ① (substancja) vaseline ② pot. (pochlebianie) toadying; (pochlebca) toady

wazeliniarz *m* pot. toady

wazon *m* vase

waż|ka *f* dragonfly

ważnia|k *m* pot. ① (zarozumialec) big-head pot. ② (osoba na stanowisku) big shot pot.; **zgrywać** ~**ka** to act the big shot pot.

ważn|y *adi. grad.* ① (istotny, wpływowy) *[informacja, powód, osoba]* important ② (aktualny) *[wiza, bilet, głos]* valid ③ pot. (zarozumiały) *[osoba, mina]* self-important

waż|yć *impf* ① *vt* ① (oceniać ciężar) to weigh; ~**yć coś w dłoni** to weigh sth in one's hand ② (rozważać) to weigh *[słowa, racje]* ② *vi* ① (mieć ciężar) to weigh; **ile** ~**ysz?** how much do you weigh? ② przen. (mieć znaczenie) to have significance ③ **ważyć się** ① (sprawdzać swoją wagę) to weigh oneself ② (decydować się) *[wynik głosowania, losy]* to hang in the balance ③ (mieć odwagę) *[osoba]* to dare; **ani (mi) się** ~ **tam iść** don't you dare go there ■ **lekce sobie** ~**yć coś** książk. to disregard sth

wącha|ć *impf* *vt* ① (czuć zapach) to smell, to sniff *[kwiaty, perfumy, jedzenie]* ② pot. (węszyć) to sniff around ③ (narkotyzować się) to sniff

wąg|ier *m* ① Zool. bladder worm ② (zaskórnik) blackhead

wąs *m* ① (zarost) ~**y** moustache GB, mustache US; **podkręcać** ~**a** to twirl one's moustache ② Zool. (u kota) whisker; (u suma) barbel, whisker ③ Bot. (grochu, powoju) tendril

wąsa|ty *adi. [mężczyzna, twarz]* moustachioed, moustached; *[kot]* whiskered

w|ąski *adi. grad.* ① *[drzwi, oczy]* narrow; *[wargi, usta]* thin ② (ograniczony) *[definicja, specjalizacja]* narrow; **człowiek o wąskich horyzontach** a narrow-minded man; **wąski krąg odbiorców** a small a. limited audience

wąt|ek *m* ① (układ nici) weft ② (dyskusji, rozmowy) thread; (myśli) train; **główny** ~**ek konferencji** the main topic of the conference; **nowe** ~**ki w śledztwie** new leads in the investigation; **wrócić do przerwanego** ~**ku** to pick up the thread where one had left off ③ (powieści, filmu) motif, theme; ~**ki ludowe** folk motifs

wąt|ły *adi. grad.* ① (słaby) *[dziecko, ręce]* frail; *[konstrukcja]* fragile; *[gałązka]* delicate; *[roślinka]* weak; *[światło, płomyk]* faint ② (nieprzekonujący) *[intryga, fabuła]* flimsy

wątp|ić *impf* *vi* to doubt; ~**ię** I doubt it; ~**ię, czy... I** doubt if...

wątpliwoś|ć *f* doubt; **w razie** ~**ci** when in doubt; **budzić** ~**ci** to raise doubts; **nie ulega** ~**ci, że...** there is no doubt that...; **ponad wszelką** ~**ć** beyond (all) doubt

wątpliw|y *adi. [komplement, poczucie humoru]* dubious; *[dowód, autentyczność]* doubtful

wątr|oba *f* (the) liver; **zapalenie** ~**oby** hepatitis; **leżeć komuś na** ~**obie** pot. to be preying on sb's mind

wątrób|ka *f* Kulin. liver

wąw|óz *m* ravine

w|ąż *m* ① Zool. snake; **wić się jak wąż** *[osoba]* to wriggle like an eel a. worm ② przen. (długi szereg) snaking line ③ (rura) hose, hosepipe GB

wbi|ć *pf* — **wbi|jać** *impf* ① *vt* ① (zagłębić) to stick in *[igłę]*; to sink *[słup]*; to dig in *[paznokcie]*; ~**ć sobie drzazgę w palec** to get a splinter in one's finger;

~ć **gwóźdź młotkiem** to drive in a. hammer a nail; ~ć **komuś nóż w plecy** to stab sb in the back także przen.; ~ć **wizę do paszportu** to stamp a visa in a passport; ~ć **coś komuś do głowy** przen. to hammer sth into sb's head [2] Sport to score *[gola, bramkę]* [3] (nałożyć) to stick; ~ć **mięso na ruszt** to skewer some meat

II wbić się — wbijać się [1] *[gwóźdź, nóż]* to stick (in) [2] pot. ~ć **się w coś** to squeeze into sth *[ubranie]*

wbie|c, wbie|gnąć *pf* — **wbie|gać** *impf vi* to run; ~c **do pokoju** to run into a room; ~c **na piętro** to run upstairs

wbijać *impf* → **wbić**

wbrew *praep.* against (**czemuś** sth); in defiance of (**komuś** sb); ~ **rozsądkowi** against one's better judgment

wcale **I** *part.* (bynajmniej) ~ **nie** by no means, not at all; ~ **nie twierdzę, że...** I don't at all a. by any means claim that...

II *adv.* [1] (ani trochę) (not) at all; ~ **a** ~ not in the least [2] pot. (całkiem) quite; ~ **niemało** quite a lot

wchł|onąć *pf* — **wchł|aniać** *impf* **I** *vt* [1] (wciągnąć) to absorb *[płyn, wilgoć, lek]* [2] (zagarnąć) to absorb *[firmę]*; to swallow up *[organizację, wioskę]*

II wchłonąć się — wchłaniać się *[krem]* to absorb; *[alkohol, lek, pokarm]* to be absorbed

wchodzić *impf* → **wejść**

w|ciąć *pf* — **w|cinać** *impf* **I** *vt* [1] (w druku) to indent *[akapit, wiersz]* [2] pot. (zjeść) to polish off pot.

II *v imp.* pot. (zagubić się) **wcięło mi podręcznik** my book has disappeared

III wciąć się — wcinać się *[kanion, rzeka]* to cut (**w coś** into sth); *[półwysep, przylądek]* to jut (**w coś** into sth)

wciąg|nąć *pf* — **wciąg|ać** *impf* **I** *vt* [1] (do środka) to drag *[osobę, przedmiot]* (**do czegoś** into sth); to draw in *[pazury, brzuch]*; *[magnetofon]* to chew up *[taśmę]* [2] (do góry) to draw up *[kubeł]*; to haul a. pull up *[osobę]*; to hoist *[żagiel, flagę]* [3] (nakłonić, wmieszać) to draw in; ~**nąć kogoś w kłótnię** to draw sb into an argument [4] (zaabsorbować) *[praca]* to absorb; *[film, powieść, sztuka]* to draw in; **dyskusja tak ich** ~**nęła, że...** they were so engrossed in (the) discussion that... [5] (zapisać) to enter; ~**nąć kogoś na listę** to enter sb's name on a list [6] (o oddychaniu) to draw in *[powietrze]*; to breathe in *[dym, gaz, zapach]* [7] (wessać) *[wir]* to suck in; *[bagno]* to swallow up; ~**nąć kogoś pod wodę** to pull sb under [8] pot. (naciągnąć) to pull on *[buty, rękawiczki, spodnie]*; to roll on *[rajstopy]*

II wciągnąć się — wciągać się [1] (wejść wyżej) to pull oneself up (**po czymś** on sth) [2] pot. (przywyknąć, wprawić się) to get into the swing (**w coś** of sth)

wciąż *adv.* [1] (nadal) still [2] (ciągle) continuously

wcielać *impf* → **wcielić**

wciele|nie *n* (przybrana postać) incarnation także przen.; (uosobienie) embodiment; **może w następnym** ~**niu!** żart. maybe in my next life!; **być** ~**niem dobroci** to be kindness personified

wciel|ić *pf* — **wciel|ać** *impf* **I** *vt* [1] (przyłączyć) to incorporate (**coś do czegoś** sth into sth) [2] (powołać do wojska) to conscript [3] (urzeczywistnić) to carry out *[program, reformę]*; ~**ić słowa w czyn** to put words into action

II wcielić się — wcielać się [1] (udawać) *[dziecko, przestępca]* to impersonate (**w kogoś** sb); *[aktor]* to play (**w kogoś** sb) [2] (przyjąć ciało) *[bóstwo, dusza]* to be incarnated (**w coś** as sth)

wcierać *impf* → **wetrzeć**

wcię|cie *n* [1] (zagłębienie) incision; (w druku) indentation [2] (zwężenie) **suknia z** ~**ciem w talii** a narrow-waisted dress

wcinać *impf* → **wciąć**

wci|snąć *pf* — **wci|skać** *impf* **I** *vt* [1] (wepchnąć) to stuff (**coś w coś** sth into sth); ~**snąć kogoś do firmy** pot., przen. to get sb a job in a company; ~**skać komuś kit** pot., przen. to bullshit sb posp. [2] pot. (znaleźć czas lub miejsce) to squeeze [sb/sth] in (**do czegoś** to sth) [3] (nałożyć) to pull (down) *[czapkę]* (**na coś** over sth); to push *[obrączkę]* (**na coś** onto sth) [4] (nacisnąć) to press *[klawisz, przycisk]* [5] (wkroplić) to squeeze (**coś do czegoś** sth into sth)

II wcisnąć się — wciskać się [1] to squeeze (in) (**do czegoś** into sth); *[kurz, mróz]* to get (**do czegoś** into sth); *[wiatr, ziąb]* to penetrate (**pod coś** under sth) [2] pot. (wkręcić się) *[osoba]* to worm one's way (**do czegoś** into sth)

wczasowicz *m*, ~**ka** *f* holiday-maker GB, vacationer US

wczasow|y *adi.* *[dom, ośrodek]* holiday GB, vacation US

wczas|y *plt* holiday GB, vacation US; (lecznicze) rest-cure

wcze|sny **I** *adi. grad.* *[lato, emerytura, odmiana, utwory]* early

II wcześniejszy *adi. comp.* *[doświadczenie, okazja, próba]* previous

wcześniak *m* premature baby

wcześnie **I** *adv. grad.* early

II wcześniej *adv. comp.* (poprzednio) before, previously

III najwcześniej *adv. superl.* at the earliest

wczoraj **I** *adv.* (poprzedniego dnia) yesterday także przen.

II *n inv.* (dzień wczorajszy) yesterday także przen.

wczoraj|szy *adi.* *[wieczór]* yesterday; *[chleb, spotkanie]* yesterday's

wczu|ć się *pf* — **wczu|wać się** *impf v refl.* to empathize (**w coś** with sth); ~ć **się w problemy innych ludzi** to understand other people's problems

wda|ć się *pf* — **wda|wać się** *impf v refl.*
[1] (wplątać się) ~**ć się w coś** to get involved into sth *[konflikt, spór]*; to engage in sth książk. *[intrygi]*; to embark on sth *[dyskusję]*; to go into sth *[wyjaśnienia, szczegóły]*; ~**ć się w złe towarzystwo** to get into bad company [2] (wrodzić się) to take (**w kogoś** after sb) [3] (zaistnieć) *[bieda, gangrena, zapalenie płuc]* to set in

wdech *m* breath; **zrobić** ~ to take a breath

wdep|nąć *pf vi* [1] (wejść) to step (**w coś** in sth) [2] pot. (w nieprzyjemną sytuację) to walk (**w coś** into sth); (w aferę, sprawę) to get mixed up (**w coś** in sth) [3] pot. (wstąpić) to drop by a. in pot.

wdep|tać *pf* — **wdep|tywać** *impf vt* to tread [sth] in

wd|owa *f* widow

wdow|iec *m* widower

wdrap|ać się *pf* — **wdrap|ywać się** *impf v refl.* to climb (**na coś** sth)

wdr|ożyć *pf* — **wdr|ażać** *impf* **[]** *vt* [1] (przyzwyczaić) to accustom (**kogoś do czegoś** sb to sth) [2] (nauczyć) to drum (**coś komuś** sth into sb) [3] (rozpocząć) to institute *[postępowanie, śledztwo]* [4] (wprowadzić) to implement *[metodę, projekt]*
[] wdrożyć się — wdrażać się (przywyknąć) to get used (**do czegoś** to sth)

wdycha|ć *impf vt* to breathe in, to inhale *[dym, gaz]*

wdzierać się *impf* → **wedrzeć się**

wdzięcznoś|ć *f* gratitude; **w dowód** ~**ci** (**za coś**) in gratitude (for sth) a. appreciation (of sth); **z** ~**cią** thankfully

wdzięczn|y **[]** *adi. grad.* [1] (uroczy) *[głos, śmiech]* charming; *[postać]* graceful [2] (dający satysfakcję) *[zadanie, zawód]* rewarding; *[temat]* satisfying [3] (życzliwy) *[słuchacze, widzowie]* appreciative
[] *adi.* (zobowiązany) grateful (**komuś za coś** to sb for sth); **być komuś** ~**ym za pomoc** to appreciate sb's help

wdzięk [] m (urok) charm; (gracja) grace; **z** ~**iem** gracefully
[] wdzięki *plt* (kobiece) charms

we *praep.* → **w**

według *praep.* [1] (zgodnie z) according to; **postępować** ~ **instrukcji** to follow the instructions [2] (w opinii) according to; ~ **niego** according to him

wegetacj|a *f* [1] (rozwój roślin) growth; **okres** ~**i** the growing season [2] (egzystencja) vegetation

wegetarian|in *m*, ~**ka** *f* vegetarian

wegetarianizm *m* vegetarianism

wegetariańs|ki *adi.* vegetarian

weget|ować *impf vi* [1] *[osoba, miasto]* to vegetate [2] *[rośliny]* to grow

wejrze|nie *n* książk. (spojrzenie) gaze; **miłość od pierwszego** ~**nia** love at first sight

wejś|cie *n* [1] (drzwi) entrance (**do czegoś** to sth) [2] pot. (znajomości) connections [3] Komput. input

[4] Techn. (gniazdo, kontakt) socket; (urządzenie) input device

wejściow|y *adi.* [1] *[drzwi, otwór]* entrance [2] Komput. *[dane, urządzenia]* input [3] Techn. *[gniazdo, napięcie]* input

wejściów|ka *f* pot. standing ticket

we|jść *pf* — **w|chodzić** *impf vi* [1] (znaleźć się) to come/go; **wejść do domu** to enter a house; **wejść na orbitę** to go into orbit; **wejść pod kołdrę** to get under the bedclothes; **wejść w kałużę** to walk into a puddle; **wejść na piętro** to go upstairs; **wejść na drzewo** to climb a tree; **wejść na szczyt** to reach the summit [2] przen. to enter (**do czegoś** sth); **wejść do parlamentu** to enter parliament; **wejść w rolę** to enter a role; **wejść z kimś w konflikt** to come into conflict with sb; **wejść do finału** to reach the final; **wejść w posiadanie czegoś** książk. to come into possession of sth [3] (zmieścić się) to fit a. go into; **w skład zestawu wchodzą...** the set consists of... [4] (wdać się) to go into *[szczegóły]* [5] Komput. **wejść do czegoś** to access sth *[bazy danych]*; to open sth *[pliku, katalogu]*; **wejść na stronę** to entere a web page [6] (wcinać się) *[cypel, półwysep]* to jut (**w coś** into sth); *[zatoka]* to cut (**w coś** into sth)

wek *m* jar

wek|ować *impf vt* to pickle *[warzywa, grzyby]*; to preserve *[owoce]*

weks|el *m* bill (of exchange)

wekto|r *m* vector

welon *m* [1] (element stroju) veil [2] Zool. fringetail (goldfish)

weł|na *f* (sierść) fleece; (przędza) wool

wełnian|y *adi.* *[płaszcz, skarpety]* woollen GB, woolen US; *[przemysł]* wool

weneryczn|y *adi.* venereal

wentyl *m* valve

wentylacj|a *f* [1] (wietrzenie) ventilation [2] (system wentylatorów) air conditioning

wentylato|r *m* fan

w|epchnąć *pf* — **w|pychać** *impf* **[]** *vt* (wtłoczyć) to stuff; (popchnąć) to push; **wepchnąć coś komuś do ręki** to stuff sth into sb's hand
[] wepchnąć się — wpychać się [1] (wejść) to muscle in [2] (przeniknąć) *[dym, kurz]* to push, to force

weran|da *f* veranda(h), porch

werbaln|y *adi.* verbal

werb|ować *impf vt* to recruit

werbun|ek *m* recruitment

werdyk|t *m* verdict

wermu|t *m* vermouth

werniks *m* varnish

wernisaż *m* vernissage

wers *m* line, verse

wersal|ka *f* sofa bed

wersj|a *f* version

wertep|y *plt* bumpy terrain

wert|ować *impf vt* to leaf a. flick [sth] through

werw|a *f* książk. verve; **z** ~**ą** with verve

weryfik|ować *impf vt* książk. [1] (potwierdzać) to verify *[dokumenty, kwalifikacje]* [2] (przemyśleć) to review *[opinię, poglądy, teorię]*

wesel|e *n* [1] (przyjęcie) wedding [2] książk. (radość) merriment

wesołoś|ć *f* cheerfulness

wes|oły *adi.* *grad.* (radosny) *[osoba, dom, nastrój]* cheerful; *[śmiech, mina]* happy; ~**ołe życie** a merry life; ~**ołej zabawy!** have a good time!; **Wesołych Świąt!** (Bożego Narodzenia) Merry Christmas!; (Wielkanocnych) Happy Easter!

w|esprzeć *pf* — **w|spierać** *impf* **[]** *vt* [1] (podtrzymać) to support *[dach, konstrukcję]*; **wesprzeć głowę na rękach** to rest one's head on one's hands [2] (pomóc) to support; **wesprzeć kogoś zbrojnie** to provide military support to sb [3] (poprzeć) to support *[kandydata, projekt]*

[] **wesprzeć się** — **wspierać się** [1] (spoczywać) to rest [2] (oprzeć się) to lean (**o coś** against sth) [3] (pomóc sobie) to support each other [4] (być uzasadnionym) *[oskarżenie, podejrzenia]* to be backed up a. supported (**na czymś** by sth)

w|essać *pf* — **w|sysać** *impf* **[]** *vt* to suck [sth] in *[powietrze, ciecz]*; (odkurzaczem) to hoover [sth] up *[kurz, przedmiot]*

[] **wessać się** — **wsysać się** [1] (zostać wessanym) *[powietrze, ciecz]* to be sucked in; *[kurz, benzyna]* to be sucked up [2] (zostać wchłoniętym) *[obrzęk, krwiak]* to be absorbed

w|estchnąć *pf* — **w|zdychać**[1] *impf vi* to sigh, to (heave a) sigh

westchnie|nie *n* sigh

w|esz *f* louse

weteran *m* veteran także przen.

weterynari|a *f* veterinary medicine

weterynarz *m* veterinary surgeon GB, veterinarian US, vet GB

w|etknąć *pf* — **w|tykać** *impf vt* pot. to put; (niedbale) to shove; (do otworu) to plug

w|etrzeć *pf* — **w|cierać** *impf* **[]** *vt* to rub *[olejek, maść]* (**w coś** in(to) sth)

[] **wetrzeć się** — **wcierać się** *[olejek, maść]* to be absorbed

wewnątrz **[]** *adv.* inside; (w budynku) indoors; **zamknięty od** ~ locked from the inside; **do** ~ inwards; **poczuła** ~ **smutek** she felt sad inside a. inwardly sad

[] *praep.* (w domu, pokoju, książce) inside; (w obrębie budynku, granic, grupy) within, inside of US

wewnętrzn|y **[]** *adi.* *[organy, obrażenia, krwotok, choroby]* internal; *[kieszeń, pomieszczenie, tor]* inside; *[część, drzwi, dziedziniec]* inner; *[polityka, rynek]* domestic, home

[] *m* pot. (numer telefonu) extension number

w|ezbrać *pf* — **w|zbierać** *impf vi* [1] (przybrać) *[rzeka, potok, jezioro]* to swell; *[fala, woda]* to rise [2] książk. (wzmóc się) *[gniew, radość, uczucie, łzy]* to well up; *[protesty, śmiech]* to rise

w|ezwać *pf* — **w|zywać** *impf vt* [1] (spowodować przybycie) *[osoba, dźwięk]* to call, to summon [2] (zaapelować) to call on; **wezwać do czynu** to call for action

wezwa|nie *n* (nakaz urzędowy) summons; (przywołanie) call; ~**nie do czynu** a call a. an appeal for action

w|eżreć się *pf* — **w|żerać się** *impf v refl.* [1] *[rdza, kwas]* to eat (**w coś** into sth); *[chemikalia]* to bite (**w coś** into sth); *[dym, pył]* to penetrate (**w coś** (into) sth) [2] (uwierać) *[szew, kołnierzyk]* to bite (**w coś** into sth)

węch *m* smell; **wyczuć coś** ~**em** to detect sth by smell

węd|ka *f* fishing rod, fishing pole US

wędkarstw|o *n* angling

wędkarz *m* angler

wędk|ować *impf vi* to angle, to fish (with a fishing rod a. with a rod and line)

wędlin|a *f* cold (cooked) a. cured meat

wędr|ować *impf vi* [1] (dla przyjemności) to wander; (jako turysta) to hike; ~**ować z plecakiem** to backpack [2] (przemieszczać się) *[koczownicy, Cyganie]* to travel; *[zwierzęta, ptaki, ryby]* to migrate [3] (przesuwać się) *[niż, obłoki, ból]* to move [4] (być przekazywanym) *[listy, towary]* to be transported

wędrown|y *adi.* [1] (objazdowy) *[cyrk, teatr]* travelling, traveling US; *[aktor, handlarz]* itinerant [2] (turystyczny) *[wczasy, trasa]* walking; **obóz** ~**y** a camping trip

wędrów|ka *f* [1] (rekreacyjna) walk; (turystyczna) hike; **wybrać się na** ~**kę w góry** to go hiking in the mountains [2] (migracja) migration

wę|dzić *impf* **[]** *vt* to smoke(-dry), to cure *[ryby, mięso]*

[] **wędzić się** [1] *[żywność]* to be (dry-)smoked a. cured [2] żart. *[osoba]* to breathe in cigarette smoke

węg|iel *m* [1] (surowiec) coal; ~**iel drzewny** charcoal; **czarny jak** ~**iel** as black as coal [2] (pierwiastek) carbon; **dwutlenek** ~**la** carbon dioxide [3] (bryła żaru) coal; (wypalona) cinder; **żarzące się** ~**le** live coals a. embers; **siedzieć jak na rozżarzonych** ~**lach** to be like a cat on a hot tin roof [4] (do rysowania) (artist's) charcoal

węg|ieł *m* corner; **za** ~**łem** round the corner

węgierka *f* (owoc) purple plum; (drzewo) purple plum (tree)

węgorz *m* eel

węsz|yć *impf* **[]** *vt* [1] *[pies]* to scent *[trop]* [2] przen. (podejrzewać) to smell (out) *[podstęp, kłopoty, złodzieja]*; to sense *[ironię, kpinę]*

[] *vi* [1] (wąchać) *[zwierzę]* to sniff [2] pot. (szukać) *[osoba]* to sniff (a)round pot. (**za czymś** for sth)

wę|zeł *m* [1] (na linie, krawacie, nitce) knot; (wokół słupa, haka) hitch; **zawiązać/rozwiązać węzeł** to tie/ untie a knot [2] (kok) bun [3] (lotniczy) hub; (kolejowy) junction (point); (drogowy) interchange; (telekomunikacyjny) node [4] Żegl. (jednostka) knot [5] Techn. (ogół urządzeń) ≈ central unit

wężyk *m* [1] (na wodę) hose; (osłonka) tube [2] (falista linia) wavy line

w|giąć *pf* — **w|ginać** *impf* [] *vt* to dent *[błotnik, denko, puszkę]*

[] wgiąć się — wginać się to dent

wglą|d *m* access (**do czegoś** to sth)

wgł|ębić się *pf* — **wgł|ębiać się** *impf v refl.* [1] (wejść) *[nóż, łopata, zęby]* to sink (**w coś** in(to) sth) [2] przen. (wniknąć) to go (**w coś** into sth); ~**ębić się w szczegóły** to go into details

wgłębie|nie *n* (naturalne) hollow; (uszkodzenie) dent

wgni|eść *pf* — **wgni|atać** *impf* [] *vt* [1] (uszkodzić) to dent *[błotnik, blachę]* [2] (wcisnąć) to press (**coś w coś** sth into sth)

[] wgnieść się — wgniatać się *[blacha]* to dent; *[kanapa, łóżko]* to sag

wgramol|ić się *pf v refl.* pot. to clamber

wgry|źć się *pf* — **wzgry|zać się** *impf v refl.* [1] (przegryźć) to sink one's teeth (**w coś** into sth) [2] (wżreć się) *[brud, kwas]* to eat a. get (**w coś** into sth) [3] (przeanalizować) to get to grips (**w coś** with sth)

wi|ać *impf* [] *vt* (oddzielać ziarno) to winnow

[] *vi* [1] *[wiatr]* to blow [2] pot. (uciekać) to run away

[] *v imp.* **wieje** it's windy; **z piwnicy wieje stęchlizną** there's a musty smell wafting up from the cellar; **z ekranu wieje nudą** an air of boredom drifts from the screen

wiadomo *praed.* **jak** ~ as everybody knows; **o ile (mi)** ~ as far as I know; **nigdy nie** ~ you never know; **nie** ~ **skąd** out of nowhere; ~**, że...** it's obvious that...

wiadomoś|ć *f* (informacja) message, (piece of) news; **ostatnie** ~**ci** the latest news; **zostawić** ~**ć** to leave a message

[] **wiadomości** *plt* [1] (zasób wiedzy) knowledge [2] (serwis informacyjny) news

■ **podawać coś do publicznej** ~**ci** to make sth public; **przyjmować coś do** ~**ci** to take note of sth

wiadom|y *adi.* [1] (znany) known; **z** ~**ych powodów** for obvious reasons [2] (wspomniany) **w** ~**ym miejscu** at the usual place; ~**a osoba** you know who

wiad|ro *n* (pojemnik) bucket; (zawartość) bucket(ful)

wiaduk|t *m* flyover; (dłuższy) viaduct

wian|ek *m* [1] (z kwiatów) garland; **splatać** ~**ek** to plait a garland [2] (z przedmiotów) string

wi|ara *f* [1] (religia) faith; **wiara w Boga** faith a. belief in God [2] (przeświadczenie) belief, faith; **ślepa wiara w coś** blind faith in sth; **wiara w siebie** self-confidence [3] książk. (zaufanie) faith; **dochować**

komuś wiary to remain faithful to sb

■ **nie do wiary** pot. incredible, unbelievable; **działać w dobrej wierze** to act in good faith

wiarygodn|y *adi.* reliable

wia|ta *f* shed; ~**ta autobusowa** a bus shelter

wi|atr [] *m* (strumień powietrza) wind; **pod wiatr** against the wind, upwind; **z wiatrem** with the wind, downwind; **wiatr historii** przen. the tide of history

[] **wiatry** *plt* pot. wind; **mieć wiatry** to break wind

■ **biednemu zawsze wiatr w oczy (wieje)** przysł. the poor must pay for all; **rzucać słowa na wiatr** to make wild promises

wiatrak *m* [1] (młyn) windmill [2] (wentylator) fan

■ **walczyć z** ~**ami** to tilt at windmills; **walka z** ~**ami** a losing battle

wiatrów|ka *f* pot. [1] (kurtka) windcheater GB, windbreaker US [2] (broń) air gun

wiąz *m* elm (tree); (drewno) elm wood

wią|zać *impf* [] *vt* [1] (tworzyć węzeł) to tie *[chustkę, kokardę]* [2] (splatać) to bind *[matę, tratwę]*; to tie *[sieć]*; ~**zać coś w pęczki** to tie sth into bunches [3] (krępować) to tie [sb] up; ~**zać komuś nogi** to tie (up) a. bind sb's feet [4] przen. (jednoczyć) *[przeżycia, pokrewieństwo]* to bind [5] przen. (łączyć) to combine [6] przen. (kojarzyć) to link [7] przen. (zobowiązać) to bind; **decyzja** ~**żąca** a binding decision [8] *[zaprawa, klej]* to bond [9] (reagować) *[substancja, związek]* to bind

[] **wiązać się** [1] (przymocowywać się) to tie oneself [2] (przyłączać się) to join (**z czymś** sth); ~**zać się z kimś uczuciowo** to became involved emotionally with sb [3] (pociągać za sobą) to involve (**z czymś** sth); (zależeć) to depend (**z czymś** on sth) [4] (zobowiązywać się) to bind oneself; ~**zać się umową** to bind oneself by an agreement

■ **wiązać z czymś nadzieje** to pin one's hopes on sth

wiąza|nie *n* [1] (element łączący) truss [2] (układ cegieł lub belek) bond [3] (w cząsteczce) bond [4] (u nart) (ski) binding

wiązan|ka *f* [1] (bukiet) bouquet [2] (zbiór) pot-pourri [3] pot. (wyzwiska) **posłać komuś** ~**kę** to give sb a mouthful pot.

wiąz|ka *f* [1] (porcja) bundle [2] Techn. (kabli, przewodów) group; (elektronów, światła) beam

wibr|ować *impf vi* to vibrate

wicedyrekto|r *m*, ~**rka** *f* deputy director; (w szkole) deputy a. assistant head

wicemistrz *m*, ~**yni** *f* vice-champion

wichrz|yć *impf vt* książk. to stir up; ~**yć wśród załogi** to incite the crew to mutiny

wichu|ra *f* (strong) gale

wi|ć¹ *f* [1] (witka) twig [2] Biol. flagellum [3] Bot. runner

■ **rozesłać wici** to send out word

wi|ć² *impf* [] *vt* to build *[gniazdo]*

[] **wić się** [1] (poruszać się) *[osoba]* to writhe; *[dżdżownica, żmija]* to slither [2] *[rzeka, droga]* to meander; *[ścieżka, pochód]* to wind ③ (piąć się) to twist

widać Ⅰ *praed.* **z okna** ~ **góry** you can see the mountains from the window; **nic nie** ~ you can't see anything; **nie było cię** ~ I couldn't see you; **nie było go nigdzie** ~ he was nowhere to be seen; ~ **ci halkę** your slip is showing; **od razu** ~, **że...** you can tell immediately that...; ~ **było po nich zmęczenie** you could tell they were tired Ⅱ *part.* apparently; ~ **wypił za dużo** he must have had too much to drink; **jak** ~ as you can see, as can be seen

widel|ec *m* fork

wideł|ki *plt* ① (telefonu) cradle ② (rozwidlony przyrząd) fork(s) ③ (zakres) scale; ~**ki płacowe** wage differentials

wideo Ⅰ *n inv.* video; (odtwarzacz) video player, VCR; **nagrać coś na** ~ to record something on video; **film na** ~ a video film Ⅱ *adi. inv.* video

wideokase|ta *f* videotape

wideoklip *m* video clip

wid|ły *plt* ① (narzędzie) fork ② (rozgałęzienie) fork; **miasto leży w** ~**łach rzeki** the town lies where the river forks

widm|o *n* ① (duch) apparition; **pociąg** ~**o** przen. a ghost train ② (wizja) spectre; ~**o głodu** the spectre of famine ③ Fiz. spectrum

widnokr|ąg *m* horizon

widocznie Ⅰ *adv. grad.* (zauważalnie) noticeably Ⅱ *part.* (prawdopodobnie) evidently

widoczność|ć *f* visibility

widoczn|y *adi.* ① (widzialny) visible ② (niewątpliwy) evident

widok Ⅰ *m* ① (krajobraz) view; ~ **z boku/tyłu** a side/rear view ② (obraz) sight; **na** ~ **czegoś** at the sight of sth; **przedstawiać sobą żałosny** ~ to be a pathetic sight Ⅱ **widoki** *plt* (perspektywy) prospect(s); ~**i na przyszłość** prospects for the future

widoków|ka *f* postcard

widowisk|o *n* show; **robić (z siebie)** ~**o** to make a spectacle of oneself

widowni|a *f* ① (sala) auditorium ② (publiczność) audience ③ przen. (miejsce wydarzeń) scene przen.

wid|ywać *impf* Ⅰ *vt* to see Ⅱ **widywać się** to meet

widz *m* spectator; (oglądający telewizję) viewer; (obserwator) onlooker

widze|nie *n* ① (wizja) vision ② (w więzieniu) visit ■ **do** ~**nia** goodbye; **na do** ~**nia** on parting; **znać (kogoś) z** ~**nia** to know sb by sight

wi|dzieć *impf* Ⅰ *vt* ① (móc zobaczyć) to see; **słabo widzieć** to have poor eyesight; **widzieć coś oczami duszy** przen. to see sth in one's mind's eye ② (oglądać) to see *[film]* ③ (spotkać się) to see; **miło cię widzieć** nice to see you ④ (postrzegać) to see

[osobę, problem] ⑤ (wiedzieć) to see; **widzę, że...** I can see (that)...

Ⅱ **widzieć się** ① (swoje odbicie) to see oneself ② (jeden drugiego) to see each other ③ (spotkać się) to see (**z kimś** sb) ④ pot. (podobać się) **jak ci się widzi moja koszula?** how do you like my shirt?

wiec *m* (manifestacja) rally; (narada) assembly

wieczność|ć *f* eternity

wieczn|y *adi.* ① (nieskończony) eternal ② (nieustanny) *[kłopoty, zmartwienia]* constant

wiecz|ór *m* ① (część doby) evening; **pod** ~**ór** towards (the) evening ② (impreza) *[literacki, muzyczny]* soirée ■ **dobry** ~**ór** good evening

wiedz|a *f* ① (zasób informacji) knowledge ② (mądrość) wisdom ■ **bez czyjejś** ~**y** behind sb's back

wie|dzieć *impf vi* to know (**o czymś** about sth); ~**sz (co)?** pot. you know?; **choćby nie** ~**m jak/ co/kto** pot. no matter how/what/who; **czy ja wiem** pot. I don't really know; **jak nie wiem co** pot. like hell; **o ile** ~**m** pot. as far as I know

wiedźm|a *f* witch

wiejs|ki *adi. [droga, powietrze, szkoła]* country; *[ludność]* rural; *[chleb]* farmhouse

wiek Ⅰ *m* ① (liczba lat) age; **z** ~**iem** with age; **na swój** ~ for one's age ② (epoka) age; ~ **wielkich odkryć** the Age of Discovery ③ (stulecie) century; **w ubiegłym** ~**u** during the last century Ⅱ **wieki** *plt* (długi czas) ages; **od** ~**ów** from a. since time immemorial

wiek|o *n* lid

wiekow|y *adi.* ① (stary) *[kultura, tradycja]* ancient ② (dotyczący wieku) *[kategoria, grupa]* age

wielbiciel *m*, ~**ka** *f* ① (miłośnik) admirer, lover ② (adorator) adorer

wielb|ić *impf vt* książk. ① (uwielbiać) to adore ② (czcić) to worship

wielbłą|d *m* camel

wi|ele Ⅰ *pron.* a lot; (z policzalnymi) many; (z niepoliczalnymi) much; **pod wieloma względami** in many respects; **film jakich wiele** a film like many others; **coraz więcej ludzi** more and more people Ⅱ *adv. grad.* (skala intensywności) a lot, much; **zrobił wiele, żeby...** he did a lot to...; **o wiele więcej niż...** a good deal more than...; **o wiele młodszy** much younger; **tego już za wiele!** this is too much! pot.

Wielk|anoc *f* Easter

wiel|ki Ⅰ *adi.* ① (ogromny) *[budynek, majątek]* large; *[strach, talent]* great ② (doniosły, wybitny) *[chwila, odkrycie, osoba]* great Ⅱ *m* ~**cy (tego świata)** ≈ the good and the great

wielkoduszn|y *adi. grad.* magnanimous

wielkość|ć *f* ① (rozmiar) size; **portret naturalnej** ~**ci** a life-size portrait ② przen. (ogrom) magnitude, enormity ③ (wybitność) greatness

wielobarwn|y *adi.* multicoloured, multicolored US

wielok|t *m* polygon

wielokrop|ek *m* suspension points

wielokrotn|y *adi. [obietnice]* repeated; *[mistrz, laureat]* many times GB, many time US; *[morderca]* multiple; *[wzrost]* multiple

wieloryb *m* whale

wielościan *m* polyhedron

wieloznaczn|y *adi.* ambiguous

wielożeństw|o *n* polygamy

wie|niec *m* wreath; **złożyć** ~**niec pod pomnikiem** to lay a wreath at a memorial

wieprz *m* ① pig; (wykastrowany) hog ② (o osobie) pot., obraźl. porker pot., obraźl.

wieprzowin|a *f* pork

wier|cić *impf* ① *vt* to drill *[otwór, studnię]*
Ⅱ wiercić się to fidget
■ ~**cić komuś dziurę w brzuchu** pot. to pester sb

wiercipię|ta *m* pot. fidget

wiernie *adv. grad. [służyć, przetłumaczyć]* faithfully

wierność|ć *f* ① (oddanie) faithfulness; ~**ć małżeńska** marital fidelity; **dochować komuś** ~**ci** to remain faithful to sb ② (przekładu, relacji) faithfulness

wiern|y ① *adi. grad. [przyjaciel, mąż, tłumaczenie]* faithful
Ⅱ wierni *plt* (wyznawcy) the faithful; (zgromadzeni w) the congregation

wiersz *m* ① (utwór) poem ② (linijka) line
■ **czytać między** ~**ami** to read between the lines

wiertar|ka *f* drill

wiert|ło *n* drill bit; (dentystyczne) dental bur(r)

wierząc|y ① *adi.* **być osobą** ~**ą** to believe in God
Ⅱ wierząc|y *m*, ~**a** *f* believer

wierzb|a *f* willow; ~**a płacząca** a weeping willow

wierzch *m* ① (górna część) top; **na** ~**u** on (the) top ② (zewnętrzna strona) outside; ~ **dłoni** the back of the hand; **włożyć coś na** ~ to put sth on top
■ **zostawić coś na** ~**u** to not put sth away; **jechać** ~**em** to ride on horseback

wierzchni *adi.* outer; ~**e okrycie** outerwear

wierzchoł|ek *m* (drzewa, masztu) top; (góry) peak, summit; (trójkąta) vertex

wierzchow|iec *m* riding a. saddle horse

wierze|nia *plt* beliefs

wierzg|nąć *pf* — **wierzg|ać** *impf vi* ① (kopnąć) to kick ② pot., żart. (machnąć nogami) to waggle

wierzyciel *m* creditor

wierz|yć *impf vi* to believe (**w coś** in sth); ~**yć komuś** (ufać) to trust sb; (w czyjeś słowa) to believe sb

wiesza|ć *impf* ① *vt* ① (przyczepiać) to put [sth] up *[firany, obrazy]*; (na wieszakach) to hang [sth] up *[ubrania]* ② (zabijać) to hang *[osobę]*
Ⅱ wieszać się ① (zwieszać się) to hang down ② (odbierać sobie życie) to hang oneself

wiesza|k *m* ① (stojący) stand; (łazienkowy) (towel) rail; (kołek) peg; (haczyk) hook ② (ramiączko) (clothes) hanger ③ (pętelka) hanger loop, tab

w|ieś *f* ① (miejscowość) village; (mieszkańcy) the villagers ② (tereny poza miastem) the country; **na wsi** in the country(side)

wieś|ć¹ *f* ① (wiadomość) news; **zniknąć bez** ~**ci** to vanish without trace ② (pogłoska) rumour

wi|eść² *impf* książk. ① *vt* ① (prowadzić) *[osoba, ścieżka]* to lead; **wiedziony ciekawością** driven by curiosity ② (przeciągać) to slide (**czymś po czymś** sth over sth) ③ (odbywać) to lead *[życie]*; to have *[rozmowę]*
Ⅱ wieść się *v imp.* **wiedzie mu się całkiem nieźle** he's doing very well

wietrz|eć *impf vi* *[wino]* to go flat a. off; *[perfumy]* to lose its fragrance; przen. *[wspomnienia]* to fade away; *[skała]* to erode, to weather

wietrzn|y *adi. [pogoda, klimat]* windy

wietrz|yć *impf* ① *vt* ① (odświeżać) to air *[mieszkanie, ubranie]* ② (wyczuwać węchem) *[zwierzę]* to scent; ~**yć sensację** przen. to sniff out a scandal
Ⅱ wietrzyć się to be airing

wiewiór|ka *f* squirrel

wi|eźć *impf vt* to carry; **wieźć turystów autobusem** to take the tourists by coach

wież|a *f* ① (budowla) tower ② (w szachach) rook ③ (zestaw urządzeń) stacking hi-fi ④ (obudowa komputera) tower case ⑤ Sport (do skoków do wody) diving platform

wieżow|iec *m* (tower) block

więc ① *coni.* ① (a zatem) so ② (czyli) **a** ~ that's to say
Ⅱ *part.* ① (nawiązanie) so ② (wprowadzenie) well then

więcej *adv. comp.* → **dużo, wiele**

wi|ędnąć *impf vi [kwiaty w wazonie]* to wilt; *[roślina, osoba, uroda]* to wither także przen.

większość|ć *f* majority; ~**ć ludzi** most people

wię|zić *impf vt* to keep [sb] prisoner

więzie|nie *n* ① (budynek) prison, jail; **siedzieć dwa lata w** ~**niu** to serve two years in prison ② (wyrok, kara) prison sentence; **dożywotnie** ~**nie** a life sentence

wię|zień *m* prisoner

wię|ź *f* bond; ~**zi rodzinne** family ties

wigili|a *f* eve; (przed Bożym Narodzeniem) Christmas Eve; (kolacja) Christmas Eve supper

wigor| *m* vigour GB, vigor US; **pełen** ~**ru** vigorous

wiklin|a *f* ① (wierzba) osier, wicker ② (materiał) wicker

wikła|ć *impf* ① *vt* ① (plątać) to tangle ② (wciągać) to entangle
Ⅱ wikłać się ① (komplikować się) to become tangled ② (wplątywać się) to become embroiled a. involved (**w coś** in sth)

wik|t *m* board; **być u kogoś na** ~**cie** to board with sb

wilczu|r *m* German shepherd, Alsatian GB

wilcz|y *adi.* wolfish; **mieć ~y apetyt** to eat like a horse

wil|ga *f* oriole

wilgo|ć *f* damp(ness); (w powietrzu) humidity

wilgotn|y *adi. grad. [powietrze, klimat]* humid; *[ubranie, pokój]* damp; *[twarz, oczy]* moist

wilk *m* [1] Zool. wolf [2] pot. (owczarek alzacki) German shepherd, Alsatian GB

■ **nie wywołuj ~a z lasu** let sleeping dogs lie przysł.; **patrzeć na kogoś ~iem** to scowl at sb; **i ~ syty, i owca cała** so everyone's happy then a. now; **o ~u mowa (a ~ tu)** talk of the devil (and he's sure to appear)

will|a *f* (w mieście) villa, (detached) house; (na wsi) (country) villa

win|a *f* [1] (przewinienie) guilt; (odpowiedzialność) blame; **poczucie ~y** a sense of guilt; **przyznać się do ~y** to admit one's guilt; (w sądzie) to plead guilty; **zrzucić ~ę na kogoś** to shift the blame on sb; **poczuwać się do ~y** to feel guilty [2] (przyczyna złego) fault; **czyja to ~a?** whose fault is it?; **nie z mojej ~y** through no fault of mine

win|da *f* lift GB, elevator US; **przywołać ~dę** to call the lift; **ściągnąć ~dę na parter** to bring the lift (down) to the ground floor

winegre|t /ˌvinˈgret/ *m*, *m inv.* vinaigrette, French dressing GB

wi|nić *impf* [1] *vt* to blame (**kogoś za coś** sb for sth) [11] **winić się** [1] (samego siebie) to blame oneself (**za coś** for sth) [2] (jeden drugiego) to blame each other

win|ien [1] *adi. praed.* → **winny²**

[11] *impf vi* książk. (mieć obowiązek) should; **~ien jej okazać więcej szacunku** he should show her more respect

winie|ta *f* (w książce) vignette; (na początku rozdziału) headpiece; (na końcu rozdziału lub książki) tailpiece; (w gazecie) masthead [2] Aut. toll sticker

winnic|a *f* vineyard

winnicz|ek *m* edible a. Roman snail

winn|y¹ *adi.* [1] Bot. **krzew ~y** a vine [2] *[piwnica, handel, sos]* wine; *[smak, zapach]* wine-like

win|ny² [1] *adi.* [1] (ponoszący winę) guilty (**czegoś** of sth); **uznać kogoś ~nym** to find sb guilty; **nikt nie jest ~ien** it's nobody's fault [2] (o dłużniku) owing; **być komuś coś ~nym** to owe sb sth; **ile jestem ~ien?** how much do I owe?; **strona „~ien"** the debit side

[11] **win|ny** *m*, **~na** *f* culprit

win|o *n* [1] (napój) wine; pot. (butelka) bottle of wine; (kieliszek) glass of wine [2] pot. (winorośl) (grape)vine; **dzikie ~o** Virginia creeper, woodbine US [3] pot. (pik) spades

winobra|nie *n* grape harvest

winogron|o *n* (owoc) grape; (winorośl) (grape)vine; **kiść ~** a bunch a. cluster of grapes

winorośl *f* (grape)vine; **uprawa ~i** wine growing

winowaj|ca *m*, **~czyni** *f* culprit, wrongdoer

winsz|ować *impf* [1] *vi* [1] (składać życzenia) to wish (**komuś czegoś** sb sth) [2] (gratulować) to congratulate (**komuś czegoś** sb on sth)

[11] **winszować sobie** to congratulate oneself (**czegoś** on sth)

wiolonczel|a *f* cello

wiolonczeli|sta *m*, **~stka** *f* cellist, cello player

wio|nąć *pf, impf vi* książk. [1] (powiać) *[wiatr]* to blow [2] (być przywianym) **z otwartych drzwi ~nęło chłodem** a chill drifted through the open door

wio|sło *n* (osadzane w dulce) oar; (trzymane w ręku) paddle

wiosł|ować *impf vi* (poruszać wiosłami) (osadzonymi) to row, to oar US; (trzymanymi w ręku) to paddle

wio|sna *f* [1] (pora roku) spring [2] książk. (rok życia) summer książk.; **liczyła sobie dwadziecia ~sen** she was a girl of twenty summers

wioślarstw|o *n* rowing

wioślarz *m* rower; (członek załogi) oarsman, oar

wiot|ki *adi.* [1] (słaby) *[gałązka]* pliant; *[łodyga]* flexible; *[konstrukcja]* fragile [2] (zwiotczały) *[skóra]* slack; *[mięśnie, piersi]* flabby [3] (delikatny) *[materiał, tkanina]* fine [4] (smukły) *[kibić, postać]* slender

wió|r *m* [1] (drewniany) shaving; (metalowy, kamienny) chip; **wyschnąć na ~r** (wychudnąć) to become as thin as a rake; *[mięso]* to become bone dry [2] (do produkcji płyt) woodchip; (do wyrobu plecionek) chip GB

wiórk|ować *impf vt* [1] (czyścić) to rub [sth] with steel wool *[podłogę]* [2] Techn. to shave

wi|r *m* [1] (wodny) whirlpool; (mniejszy) eddy; (powietrzny) eddy [2] przen. whirl; **wir tańca** a swirl of dancing; **wir życia towarzyskiego** the social whirl; **w wirze walki** in the thick of the fighting; **rzucić się w wir pracy** to throw oneself into work

wiraż *m* [1] (zakręt drogi) bend, curve [2] (skręt) turn

wirnik *m* rotor; (w pralce) agitator

wir|ować *impf* [1] *vt* Techn. to centrifuge *[mleko]*; to spin a. spin-dry GB *[pranie]*

[11] *vi* (kręcić się) *[Ziemia, karuzela]* to spin; *[tancerz, śmigło, liście]* to whirl; *[woda]* to swirl

wirów|ka *f* centrifuge; (do bielizny) spin dryer; (do sałaty) salad spinner

wirtuoz *m*, **~ka** *f* virtuoso

wirus *m* [1] Biol. virus; **być nosicielem ~a HIV** to be an HIV carrier [2] Komput. virus

wi|sieć *impf vi* [1] (być zawieszonym) *[przedmiot]* to hang; *[ubranie]* to hang loosely (**na kimś** on sb); **wisieć na szubienicy** to hang on the gallows [2] (unosić się) *[mgła, chmury]* to hang; *[ptak]* to hover [3] przen. (zagrażać) *[niebezpieczeństwo, groźba]* to hang (**nad kimś** over sb) [4] pot. (być winnym pieniądze) to owe; **wisisz mi stówkę** you owe me a hundred

■ **wisieć na telefonie** pot. to be hogging the phone; **wszystko mu wisi** posp. he doesn't give a monkey's about anything posp.

wisielcz|y *adi. [nastrój]* grim; *[humor]* gallows

wisiel|ec *m* hanged man

wisior|ek *m* (na łańcuszku) lavalier(e); (przy naszyjniku, bransoletce) charm

wi|śnia *f* (owoc) sour cherry; (drzewo) sour cherry tree

wiśniow|y *adi. [dżem, sad, kolor]* cherry

wiśniów|ka *f* cherry liqueur

wita|ć *impf* **❙** *vt* 1 (pozdrawiać) to greet; (przyjmować) to meet; (w serdeczny sposób) to welcome; ~ć kogoś **w progu** to meet sb at the door; ~ć kogoś **kwiatami** to welcome sb with flowers; ~**my!** (oficjalnie) welcome! 2 (reagować) to greet *[zmiany, dymisję]*; ~ć **coś z zadowoleniem** to welcome sth **❙❙ witać się** 1 (pozdrawiać) to greet (**z kimś** sb) 2 (jeden drugiego) to greet each other

witalnoś|ć *f* książk. vitality

witaln|y *adi.* książk. *[energia, siła]* vital

witamin|a *f* 1 (związek organiczny) vitamin; **niedobór** ~ **w organizmie** vitamin deficiency 2 pot. (tabletka) vitamin tab pot.

wit|ka *f* 1 (gałązka) twig; (wierzbowa) osier 2 Biol. (wyrostek komórki) flagellum

witraż *m* (technika) stained glass; (okno) stained-glass window

witryn|a *f* 1 (wystawa sklepowa) shop window 2 (mebel) cabinet; (w muzeum, sklepie) display cabinet a. case 3 Komput. website

wiwa|t **❙** *m* cheer; **strzelić na** ~**t** to fire a salute **❙❙ wiwat!** *inter.* (niech żyje) viva(t)! **■ dać komuś do** ~**tu** pot. to give sb a hard time pot.

wiwat|ować *impf vi* to cheer; ~**ować na czyjąś cześć** to cheer sb

wiwisekcj|a *f* vivisection także przen.

wiz|a *f* visa

wizaży|sta *m*, ~**stka** *f* make-up artist

wizerun|ek *m* 1 (podobizna) image 2 przen. (wyobrażenie) image

wizj|a *f* 1 (przywidzenie) vision 2 (projekt, perspektywa) vision; **pesymistyczne** ~**e przyszłości** dark visions of the future 3 (podczas śledztwa) ~**a lokalna** a visit to the scene of the crime 4 (obraz na ekranie) vision; (ogół sygnałów wizyjnych) video signals; **być na** ~**i** to be on camera

wizje|r *m* 1 (w drzwiach wejściowych) peephole 2 (w przyrządzie optycznym, broni) sight; (w aparacie fotograficznym) (view)finder

wizualn|y *adi.* visual

wizy|ta *f* visit; ~**ta domowa** (lekarska) a home visit; ~**ta u dentysty** a dental appointment; **złożyć komuś** ~**tę** to pay sb a visit

wizytacj|a *f* 1 (kontrola) (visit of) inspection 2 (komisja) board of inspectors

wizytato|r *m*, ~**rka** *f* inspector

wizyt|ować *impf vt* to visit *[szkołę, zakład przemysłowy]*

wizytow|y *adi. [strój, suknia]* formal

wizytów|ka *f* 1 (prywatna) (visiting) card GB, calling card US; (służbowa) (business) card, calling card US 2 (tabliczka na drzwiach) (door) plate 3 przen. (typowa cecha) mark; (przedmiot dumy) showpiece

wj|azd *m* 1 (wstęp) entry; (droga w górę) way up; „**zakaz wjazdu**" 'No Entry' 2 (brama) entrance; (na autostradę) slip road GB, ramp US

wj|echać *pf* — **wj|eżdżać** *impf vi* 1 (do środka) to go/come; *[kierowca, pojazd]* to drive; (konno, na rowerze, na snowboardzie) to ride; **wjeżdżać na parking** to pull into a parking lot; **wjeżdżać samochodem na wzgórze** to drive uphill; **wjechać w kałużę** *[kierowca]* to drive into a puddle; *[rowerzysta]* to ride into a puddle; **wjechać na stół** pot., żart. *[potrawa, danie]* to be served 2 (najechać) *[kierowca, samochód]* to run (**w coś** into sth)

wkle|ić *pf* — **wkle|jać** *impf vt* to paste (in)

wkle|sły *adi. [dno, soczewka]* concave; *[policzki]* hollow

wkl|ęsnąć *pf vi [policzki]* to become hollow; *[dach, łóżko]* to sag

wkła|d *m* 1 (udział) contribution; **wnieść w coś (swój)** ~**d** to make one's contribution to sth 2 (w banku) deposit 3 (do ołówka) (pencil) lead; (do długopisu) refill; (do wiecznego pióra) (ink) cartridge

wkładać *impf* → **włożyć**

wkład|ka *f* 1 (do butów) insole; (do biustonosza) pad; (w ramionach płaszcza, marynarki) shoulder pad; ~**ka higieniczna** a panty liner 2 (do gazety, czasopisma) (luźna) insert; (do wyrwania) pull-out 3 Techn. (wypełnienie) filler 4 Kulin. **zupa z** ~**ką mięsną** soup with pieces of meat

wkłu|ć *pf* — **wkłu|wać** *impf* **❙** *vt* (wbić) to insert; (głęboko) to sink *[szpilkę, igłę]* **❙❙ wkłuć się** — **wkłuwać się** Med. ~**ć się do czegoś** to insert a needle into sth

wkraczać *impf* → **wkroczyć**

wkra|ść się *pf* — **wkra|dać się** *impf v refl.* 1 *[osoba, zwierzę]* to sneak (**do czegoś** into. sth) 2 przen. *[niepokój, wątpliwości, błąd]* to creep in

wkrę|cić *pf* — **wkrę|cać** *impf* **❙** *vt* 1 (kręcąc umocować) to screw [sth] in *[haczyk, żarówkę]* 2 (między obracające się elementy) to feed *[papier, blachę]* 3 pot. (ulokować) ~**cić kogoś na dobrą posadę** to wangle a good position for sb pot. **❙❙ wkręcić się** — **wkręcać się** 1 *[śruba, żarówka]* to go in 2 (wplątać się) *[włosy, materiał]* to become entangled 3 pot. (dostać się) to worm one's way (**do czegoś** into sth); ~**cić się na imprezę** to gate-crash a party

wkrę|t *m* screw

wkr|oczyć *pf* — **wkr|aczać** *impf vi* 1 (wejść) to enter; ~**oczyć do pokoju** to enter a room; ~**oczyć w świat polityki** to enter (the world of) politics 2 *[armia, wróg]* to invade (**do czegoś** sth) 3 przen. (pojawić się) *[zjawiska, moda]* to appear; *[pustynia, morze, roślinność]* to encroach (**do**

czegoś (up)on sth) [4] (interweniować) to step in; ~oczyć do akcji to go into action; ~aczać w czyjeś kompetencje to encroach on sb's territory

wkrótce *adv.* soon, shortly

wku|ć *pf* — **wku|wać** *impf* [] *vt* pot. (nauczyć się) to bone up on, to swot up on GB pot. *[fizykę]*; ~wać do egzaminu to swot for an exam pot.

[II] wkuć się — wkuwać się [1] (wyrąbać otwór) to chip away (w coś at sth) [2] pot. (nauczyć się) to bone up pot., to swot GB pot.

wkup|ić się *pf* — **wkup|ywać się** *impf v refl.* to buy one's way

wkuwać *impf* → wkuć

wl|ać *pf* — **wl|ewać** *impf* [] *vt* [1] (napełnić) to pour *[ciecz]*; wlać otuchę w czyjeś serce przen. to instil some hope in sb; wlać coś w siebie pot. to down sth pot. [2] pot. (zbić) wlać komuś to lay into sb pot.

[II] wlać się — wlewać się (wpłynąć) woda wlała mi się do butów the water got into my shoes

wlatywać *impf* → wlecieć

wl|ec *impf* [] *vt* to drag także przen. *[przedmiot, osobę]*

[II] wlec się [1] (ciągnąć się) to trail, to drag [2] (posuwać się opieszale) *[osoba]* to trudge; *[pociąg]* to crawl; wlec się noga za nogą to plod (along) [3] (dłużyć się) *[czas, proces]* to drag on

wl|ecieć *pf* — **wl|atywać** *impf vi* [1] *[ptak, mucha]* to fly into [2] (wpaść) *[kamień, piłka]* to fall into [3] pot. (wbiec) *[osoba]* to burst into

wlep|ić *pf* — **wlep|iać** *impf vt* [1] (wkleić) to paste [sth] in [2] pot. (ukarać) to slap pot. (komuś coś sth on sb) *[mandat]*

■ ~ić wzrok w kogoś to fix one's gaze on sb

wlewać *impf* → wlać

w|leźć *pf* — **w|łazić** *impf vi* pot. [1] (wejść) to get; wleźć pod kołdrę to get under the quilt; wleźć na drzewo to climb a tree; wleźć w błoto to step in some mud; nieproszony wlazł do pokoju he barged into the room uninvited; drzazga wlazła mi w palec I've got a splinter in my finger [2] (zmieścić się) to get; wleźć w spodnie to get into ones trousers

■ ile wlezie as much as one can

wlicz|yć *pf* — **wlicz|ać** *impf vt* to include; śniadanie jest ~one w cenę pokoju breakfast is included in the price of the room

włada|ć *impf vi* książk. [1] (panować) to rule; ~ć czymś to rule (over) sth [2] (móc poruszać) to be able to move *[nogami, palcami]* [3] (posługiwać się) to wield *[bronią, mieczem]*; ~ć angielskim to have a good command of English

władc|a *m* ruler; być czyimś panem i ~ą przen. to be sb's lord and master

władcz|y *adi. [głos, gest]* lordly, imperious

władz|a *f* [1] (rządzenie) power; przejąć ~ę to seize power; być u ~y to be in power; dojść do ~y to come to power [2] (instytucje) authority; oddać się

w ręce ~ to give oneself up to the authorities [3] (sprawność) use; ~a w nogach the use of one's legs; być w pełni ~ umysłowych to be in full possession of one's (mental) faculties

■ pan ~a (policjant) pot., żart. officer

włam|ać *pf* — **włam|ywać** *impf* [] *vt* Druk. to set

[II] włamać się — włamywać się (wedrzeć się) ~ać się do czegoś to break into sth *[domu, samochodu]*; to hack into sth *[bazy danych, komputera]*

włama|nie *n* [1] (napad) burglary [2] Komput. hacking

włamywacz *m*, ~ka *f* burglar

włamywać *impf* → włamać

własnoręczn|y *adi.* ~y podpis one's personal signature

własnoś|ć *f* [1] (majątek) property [2] (posiadanie) ownership; mieć coś na ~ć to own sth

wła|sny *adi.* (swój) *[przedmiot, pomysł, ojciec, styl]* own; ~sny kąt a place of one's own; o ~snych siłach on one's own; we ~snej osobie in person; być na ~snym utrzymaniu to be self-supporting; pracować na ~sny rachunek to be self-employed; ciasto ~snego wypieku a home-made cake

właściciel *m*, ~ka *f* owner

właściwie [] *adv. grad.* (należycie) correctly

[II] *part.* actually

właściw|y [] *adi. grad.* (odpowiedni) *[osoba, moment]* right, appropriate

[II] *adi.* [1] (typowy) characteristic (komuś/czemuś of sb/sth); z ~ą sobie energią with (his) characteristic vigour [2] (rzeczywisty) real [3] (kompetentny) *[władze, sąd]* competent

właśnie [] *part.* (dokładnie) exactly, precisely; ~ w tej chwili just at that moment; ta ~ kobieta this (very) woman; to ~ mam zamiar zrobić that's exactly what I intend to do

[II] *adv.* (akurat) just; ~ wtedy just then; ~ miałem to zrobić I was just about to do it; ~ słyszę! so I hear!

[III] *inter.* exactly!, precisely!

właz *m* (kanału) manhole; (statku, czołgu) hatch

włazić *impf* → wleźć

włączać *impf* → włączyć

włącznie *adv.* inclusive

włącz|yć *pf* — **włącz|ać** *impf* [] *vt* [1] (przyłączyć) to include *[fragment, osobę]* (do czegoś in sth) [2] (uruchomić) to turn a. switch on *[telewizor, radio, światło]*

[II] włączyć się — włączać się [1] *[światło]* to go on; *[alarm]* to go off [2] (przyłączyć się) to join (in)

włocha|ty *adi.* hairy

włos *m* [1] hair; rozpuścić ~y to let down one's hair [2] (sierść) hair [3] (w szczotce) bristles; (w kożuchu) fleece [4] Techn. (w zegarku) hairspring

■ wziąć kogoś pod ~ pot. to sweet-talk sb pot.; dzielić ~ na czworo pot. to split hairs; o mały ~ spóźniłbym się na samolot pot. I very nearly missed the plane

włoszczy|zna *f* soup vegetables
w|łożyć *pf* — **w|kładać** *impf vt* [1] (wetknąć) to put; **włożyć list do koperty** to put a letter in an envelope [2] (wdziać) to put [sth] on *[płaszcz, pierścionek]* [3] (poświęcić) to put *[pieniądze, pracę]* (**w coś** in sth)
włóczę|ga [] *m* (bezdomny) tramp [] *f* [1] pot. (wędrówka) roaming [2] (wycieczka) hike
włócz|ka *f* yarn
włóczni|a *f* spear
włócz|yć *impf* [] *vt* to drag także przen. *[przedmiot, osobę]* [] **włóczyć się** to wander, to roam; **~yć się po ulicach** to wander around the streets
włókni|sty *adi.* [1] *[warzywa, mięso]* stringy [2] Biol. *[tkanka, roślina]* fibrous
włók|no *n* fibre GB, fiber US; **~no szklane** glass fibre GB, glass fiber US
wmawiać *impf* → **wmówić**
wmiesza|ć *pf* [] *vt* [1] (dodać) to stir (**coś do czegoś** sth into sth) [2] przen. to entangle, to involve *[osobę]* [] **wmieszać się** (wtrącić się) to meddle, to butt in
wm|ówić *pf* — **wm|awiać** *impf vt* **wmówić coś komuś** to make sb believe sth
wmur|owad *pf* — **wmur|owywać** *impf vt* to set (in) *[tablicę]* (**w coś** into sth)
wmu|sić *pf* — **wmu|szać** *impf vt* **~szać w kogoś jedzenie** to force sb to eat
wnę|ka *f* alcove; **~ka kuchenna** a kitchenette
wnętrz|e *n* [1] (wewnętrzna strona) inside [2] książk. (życie duchowe) inner life [3] (pomieszczenie) interior
wnętrzności *plt* entrails
wn|ieść *pf* — **wn|osić** *impf vt* [1] (umieścić) to carry (in) [2] (mieć udział) to contribute; **wnieść opłatę** to pay a fee [3] przen. (wywołać) to bring about *[chaos, zmiany]* [4] (przedstawić do rozpatrzenia) to submit *[petycję, podanie]*; to file *[pozew]*; **wnosić o coś** to petition for sth
wnikać *impf* → **wniknąć**
wnikliwie *adv. grad.* *[zbadać]* thoroughly
wnikliw|y *adi. grad.* *[obserwator]* astute; *[pytania, spojrzenie]* penetrating; *[analiza, badanie]* thorough
wnik|nąć *pf* — **wnik|ać** *impf vi* [1] (przeniknąć) *[światło, promienie]* to penetrate (**do czegoś** sth); *[zapach]* to permeate (**do czegoś** sth); *[woda]* to get in(to) (**do czegoś** sth) [2] (zbadać) to probe (**w coś** into sth); **nie ~ając w szczegóły** without going into details [3] przen. (dostać się) to infiltrate (**do czegoś** into sth)
wnios|ek *m* [1] (propozycja) motion; **przyjąć/od-rzucić ~ek** to accept/reject a motion [2] (wynik rozumowania) conclusion; **dojść do ~ku, że...** to come to the conclusion that...; **wyciągnąć ~ek** to draw a conclusion [3] (podanie) application
wnioskodaw|ca *m*, **~czyni** *f* [1] (petent) applicant [2] (pomysłodawca) author
wniosk|ować *impf vi* (sądzić) to conclude

wnosić *impf* → **wnieść**
wnucz|ka *f* granddaughter
wnu|k *m* grandson; **~ki** (chłopcy) grandsons; (obojga płci) grandchildren
wnyk *m* snare
woal|ka *f* veil
wobec *praep.* [1] (w stosunku do) towards; **wymagania ~ kogoś** demands on sb; **być krytycznym ~ czegoś** to be critical of sth [2] (z powodu) in view of; **~ tego...** in that case... [3] (w porównaniu z) compared with [4] (w obecności) in the presence of; (w obliczu) in the face of; **~ niebezpieczeństwa** in the face of danger
w|oda [] *f* water; **woda bieżąca** running water; **nad wodą** by the water; **warzywa z wody** boiled vegetables; **wstawić wodę na herbatę** to put the kettle on; **lać wodę** pot., przen. to waffle (on) GB pot. [] **wody** *plt* przest. (uzdrowisko) the waters przest. □ **woda kolońska** (eau de) cologne; **woda święcona** holy water; **woda utleniona** hydrogen peroxide (solution); **wody płodowe** the waters ■ **cicha woda** the silent type; **iść jak woda** to sell like hot cakes
Wodnik *m* (znak zodiaku) Aquarius, the Water Bearer; (osoba) Aquarian
wodni|sty *adi.* *[zupa]* thin; *[owoce]* watery
wodn|y *adi.* *[roztwór, transport, zwierzę]* water; **elektrownia ~a** a hydroelectric (power) plant
wodociąg [] *m* (zespół urządzeń) waterworks [] **wodociągi** *plt* pot. (przedsiębiorstwo) the water board
wodogłowi|e *n* water on the brain, hydrocephalus
wodolejstw|o *n* pot. waffle pot.
wodolo|t *m* hydrofoil
wodołaz *m* Newfoundland (dog)
wodoodporn|y *adi.* *[klej, substancja]* waterproof; *[zegarek]* water-resistant
wodop|ój *m* watering place
wodoro|st *m* seaweed
wodospa|d *m* waterfall
wodoszczeln|y *adi.* watertight
wodotrysk *m* fountain
wod|ór *m* hydrogen
wodz|a *f* rein także przen. ■ **pod czyjąś ~ą** książk. under sb's command; **puścić ~e fantazji** a. **wyobraźni** to let one's imagination run free a. wild; **trzymać nerwy na ~y** to keep calm
w|odzić *impf* [] *vt* (prowadzić) to lead; **wodzić kogoś za nos** przen. to lead sb by the nose [] *vi* (przesuwać) **wodzić wzrokiem za kimś** to follow sb with one's eyes
wodzirej *m* master of ceremonies
wojenn|y *adi.* *[zbrodnia, bohater]* war; *[przeżycia, wspomnienia]* wartime
wojewo|da *m* provincial governor (in Poland)

województw|o *n* ≈ province *(in Poland)*, voivodeship

woj|na *f* ☐ (walka) war; **wypowiedzieć komuś** ~**nę** to declare war on sb ☐ (gra) *a simple card game* ❑ ~**na domowa** civil war; ~**na psychologiczna** psychological warfare

woj|ować *impf vi* to fight

wojownicz|y *adi. [naród, plemię]* warlike; *[osoba, usposobienie, ton]* aggressive, belligerent

wojowni|k *m* warrior

wojsk|o *n* ☐ (siły zbrojne) army; (oddziały armii) (military) units; (grupa żołnierzy) soldiers; **pójść do** ~**a** to go into the army ☐ pot. (obowiązkowa służba wojskowa) national service

wojskow|y ☐ *adj [wywiad, cmentarz, ćwiczenia]* military; ~**a dyscyplina** przen. almost military discipline
☐ *m* serviceman, military man

wokali|sta *m*, ~**stka** *f* vocalist, singer

wokół ☐ *praep.* around, round GB; ~ **nas/Słońca** around us/the Sun
☐ *adv.* around, round about GB; **wszędzie** ~ all around; **wszyscy** ~ everyone around; **rozglądać się** ~ to look around

wol|a ☐ *f* ☐ Psych. will (power); **silna** ~**a** (strong) will power; **słaba** ~**a** lack of will power; **z własnej** ~**i** of one's own free will ☐ (postanowienie) will; **narzucić komuś swoją** ~**ę** to impose one's will on sb
☐ **do woli** *adv.* książk. (do syta) *[jeść, pić]* one's fill
☐ **mimo woli** *adv.* książk. involuntarily
❑ **ostatnia** ~**a** książk. (życzenie) last wish; (testament) (last) will (and testament); **wolna** ~**a** free will

w|oleć *impf vt* to prefer *[coś niż coś a.* coś **od czegoś** to sth); **wolę, żebyś...** I'd rather you...

woln|o¹ *adv. grad.* (powoli) slowly

wolno² *adv.* (swobodnie) **dom** ~ **stojący** a detached house; **puścić kogoś** ~ to set sb free

wolno³ *praed.* ~ **mi to robić** I'm allowed to do it; **tu nie** ~ **palić** smoking is forbidden a. is not allowed here; **nie** ~ **ci o tym nikomu mówić** you mustn't mention this to anyone; **tak nie** ~! you can't do (a thing like) that!; **jeśli** ~ if I may książk.; **czy** ~? may I? książk.

wolnocłow|y *adi. [towar, sklep]* duty-free

wolnorynkow|y *adi. [gospodarka, ceny]* free market

wolnoś|ć ☐ *f* (swoboda) freedom; (niezależność) independence; **kara pozbawienia** ~**ci** prison sentence; **wyjść na** ~**ć** to be released from prison; **na** ~**ci** (zbiegły z niewoli) at large; (nie oswojony) in the wild
☐ **wolności** *plt* (prawa obywateli) rights, liberties
❑ ~**ć słowa** freedom of speech

woln|y¹ ☐ *adi.* ☐ (niezależny) *[osoba, zwierzę, kraj]* free ☐ (nieograniczony) *[rynek, prasa, wybory]* free; ~**e wnioski** any other business, AOB GB ☐ (niezajęty)

[miejsce, stolik] free; ~**y etat** a vacancy; ~**y czas** free a. spare time; **dzień** ~**y od pracy** a public holiday; **czy jesteś** ~**a dziś wieczorem?** are you free tonight? ☐ (nieżonaty, niezamężna) *[osoba]* single, unmarried ☐ (pozbawiony czegoś) ~**y od czegoś** free from a. of sth; **dochód** ~**y od podatku** tax-free income ☐ Sport **rzut** ~**y** a free kick
☐ *m* Sport free kick
☐ **wolne** *n* pot. time off; **wziąć** ~**e** to take some time off
■ **mieć** ~**ą rękę** to have (a) free rein a. a free hand

woln|y² *adi. grad.* (powolny) slow; **z** ~**a** slowly

wolontariusz *m*, ~**ka** *f* volunteer

wol|t *m* volt

woła|ć *impf* ☐ *vt* to call; ~**ć kogoś na obiad** to call sb in for lunch
☐ *vi* ☐ (krzyczeć) to shout; ~**ć na kogoś z daleka** to shout at sb from a distance ☐ (domagać się) to call (**o coś** for sth) ☐ (nazywać) to call; ~**li na niego Jaś** they called him Jaś

wołowin|a *f* beef

wo|ń *f* książk. fragrance

worecz|ek *m* (worek) bag; (zawartość) bag(ful)
❑ ~**ek żółciowy** Anat. gall bladder

wor|ek *m* ☐ (torba) sack, bag; (zawartość) sack(ful), bag(ful); ~**ek na śmieci** a rubbish bag, a bin liner GB ☐ (sukienka) sack (dress)
❑ ~**ek treningowy** Sport punchbag GB, punching bag US
■ ~**ki pod oczami** bags under one's eyes

wosk *m* wax; ~ **pszczeli** beeswax

wosk|ować *impf vt* to wax

woskowin|a *f* (ear)wax

w|ozić *impf vt* to carry; (samochodem) to drive *[dzieci]*

woźn|a *f* caretaker, janitor US

woźnic|a *m* coachman

woźn|y *m* ☐ (w szkole) caretaker, janitor US ☐ (w sądzie) ≈ usher, ≈ process server

wód|ka *f* vodka; **wypić dwie** ~**ki** to have two vodkas; **być po** ~**ce** to be under the influence pot.

w|ódz *m* ☐ (wojska, narodu) leader; **wódz naczelny** commander-in-chief ☐ (plemienia, szczepu) chief, chieftain

w|ół *m* ox
■ **pasować jak wół do karety** pot. to stick out like a sore thumb pot.; **pisać wołami** pot. to write in a large scrawl

w|óz *m* ☐ (furmanka) cart, wagon; (zawartość) cartful; **wóz drabiniasty** a rack wagon ☐ pot. (samochód) car ❑ **wóz policyjny** police car; **wóz strażacki** fire engine
■ **raz na wozie, raz pod wozem** you win some, you lose some; **wóz albo przewóz!** it's one or the other! pot.

wóz|ek *m* ☐ (ciągnięty przez konia) cart; (ciągnięty przez człowieka) (hand)cart; ~**ek widłowy** a forklift (truck) ☐ (w supermarkecie, na lotnisku) trolley ☐ (dzie-

cięcy) pram GB, baby carriage US; ~**ek spacerowy**
a (baby) buggy, a pushchair 4 (inwalidzki) wheelchair
wpadać *impf* → **wpaść**
wpajać *impf* → **wpoić**
wpa|ść *pf* — **wpa|dać** *impf vi* 1 (dostać się) to get;
[powietrze] to come; (upaść) *[osoba]* to fall; ~**dło mi**
coś do oka something's got in(to) my eye; ~**dł do**
domu zdyszany he rushed into the house breathless; ~**ść po uszy** przen. to fall head over heels in
love 2 (zderzyć się) to run into; ~**ść pod samochód**
to get run over by a car 3 (znaleźć się w kłopotliwej
sytuacji) ~**ść w coś** to get into sth *[kłopoty, długi]*;
~**ść w poślizg** to go into a skid; ~**ść w pułapkę**
to fall into a trap 4 (ulec emocji) ~**ść w coś** to fall
into sth *[rozpacz, panikę]* 5 pot. (odwiedzić) to drop by
a. in 6 pot. (zostać przyłapanym) to be caught 7 pot. (zajść
w ciążę) to get up the duff GB pot. 8 (uchodzić) *[rzeka,
strumień]* to flow (**do czegoś** into sth)
■ ~**ść na pomysł** to come up with an idea
wpatrywać się *impf* → **wpatrzyć się**
wpatrz|ony *adi.* być ~**onym w kogoś** to have
one's eyes fixed on sb; przen. to look up to sb
wpat|rzyć się *pf* — **wpat|rywać się** *impf vi* to
fix one's eyes (**w kogoś/coś** on sb/sth)
wpę|dzić *pf* — **wpę|dzać** *impf* 1 *vt* 1 (zmusić do
wejścia) to drive *[bydło]* 2 przen. (doprowadzić) ~**dzić**
kogoś w kłopoty to get sb into trouble; ~**dzić**
kogoś w kompleksy to give sb a complex
1 **wpędzić się** — **wpędzać się** pot. ~**dzić się**
w tarapaty to land oneself in trouble pot.
w|piąć *pf* — **w|pinać** *impf vt* to put on *[spinkę]*; to
stick *[dokument]*
wpi|ć *pf* — **wpi|jać** *impf* 1 *vt* to dig *[paznokcie]*
(**w coś** in(to) sth); to sink *[zęby]* (**w coś** in(to) sth)
1 **wpić się** — **wpijać się** 1 (ugryźć) ~**ć się w coś**
zębami to bite into sth 2 (ucisnąć) *[pasek]* to dig
(**w coś** into sth)
wpinać *impf* → **wpiąć**
wpis *m* (do pamiętnika, księgi) entry
wpi|sać *pf* — **wpi|sywać** *impf* 1 *vt* 1 (umieścić
tekst) to write (down) *[adres, numer]*; Komput. to enter
[hasło, dane] 2 (na listę) to enter
1 **wpisać się** — **wpisywać się** 1 (na listę) to put
one's name down; ~**sać się komuś do pamiętnika** to write something in sb's album 2 książk. (stać
się elementem) to become part of (**w coś** sth)
wpisow|y 1 *adi. [opłata]* registration
1 **wpisowe** *n* registration a. entrance fee
wpisywać *impf* → **wpisać**
wplatać *impf* → **wpleść**
wplą|tać *pf* — **wplą|tywać** *impf* 1 *vt* (uwikłać) to
entangle; **być w coś** ~**tanym** to be mixed up in sth
1 **wplątać się** — **wplątywać się** 1 (zaplątać się) to
get tangled (up) a. caught 2 przen. (uwikłać się) *[osoba]*
to be entangled a. embroiled (**w coś** in sth)

wpl|eść *pf* — **wpl|atać** *impf vt* to weave [sth] in
także przen.
wpła|cić *pf* — **wpła|cać** *impf vt* to pay (in)
[pieniądze, sumę]
wpła|ta *f* payment
wpły|nąć *pf* — **wpły|wać** *impf vi* 1 (dostać się) to
arrive; *[statek]* to sail (**do czegoś** (in)to sth); *[delfin,
pływak]* to swim (**do czegoś** (in) to sth) 2 (zostać
dostarczonym) *[dokumenty, pieniądze]* to come in, to be
received 3 (oddziałać) to influence (**na kogoś** sb);
~**wać ujemnie na coś** to have a negative effect on
sth 4 *[rzeka]* to flow (**do czegoś** into sth)
wpływ 1 *m* (oddziaływanie) influence; **pod** ~**em**
alkoholu under the influence of alcohol; **pod**
~**em chwili** on the spur of the moment
1 **wpływy** *plt* 1 przen. (władza) influence 2 (wpłata)
takings
wpływać *impf* → **wpłynąć**
wpływow|y *adi.* 1 *[postać, gazeta]* influential
2 pot. (ulegający wpływom) *[osoba]* easily influenced
wp|oić *pf* — **wp|ajać** *impf vt* to instil(l) (**coś**
w kogoś sth into sb)
wpół 1 *adv.* 1 (na środku) *[rozedrzeć, złamać]* in half;
zgiąć się ~ to bend double; **trzymać kogoś** ~ to
hold sb round their waist 2 (częściowo) half; **na** ~
przytomny half conscious
1 *praep.* half; ~ **do czwartej** half past three
wpraw|a *f* 1 (biegłość) skill; **nabrać** ~**y w czymś**
to become skilled at sth 2 (wprawianie się) practice;
dla ~**y** to keep in practice; **wyjść z** ~**y** to be out of
practice
wprawdzie *part.* (it's) true
wpraw|ić *pf* — **wpraw|iać** *impf* 1 *vt* 1 (umo-
cować) to set, to fix 2 (spowodować) ~**ić coś w ruch**
to set sth in motion; ~**ić kogoś w dobry nastrój**
to put sb in a good mood 3 (wdrożyć) to train (**kogoś**
do czegoś sb to sth)
1 **wprawić się** — **wprawiać się** 1 (wdrożyć się)
~**ić się w czymś** to become skilled in sth 2 (doprowadzić się) ~**ić się w dobry nastrój** to cheer
oneself up
wprost 1 *part.* 1 (bezpośrednio) directly 2 (w linii
prostej) straight; **iść** ~ **przed siebie** to walk
straight ahead 3 (wręcz) simply; ~ **przeciwnie**
just the opposite
1 *adv.* (otwarcie) *[mówić]* frankly
wprowa|dzić *pf* — **wprowa|dzać** *impf* 1 *vt*
1 (wejść z kimś) to bring [sb] in 2 (wsadzić) to insert
3 (zapoczątkować) to introduce *[zasadę, zwyczaj,
zamieszanie]*; to launch *[towar, produkt]* 4 (zaznajomić)
to familiarize *[osobę]* (**w coś** with sth) 5 (spowodować)
~**dzić kogoś w dobry nastrój** to put sb in a good
mood; ~**dzić coś w w życie** to put sth into
practice 6 (nanieść) to make *[zmiany, poprawki]*;
Komput. to enter *[dane]*
1 **wprowadzić się** — **wprowadzać się** 1 (za-

mieszkać) to move in ② (doprowadzić się) ~**dzić się w beztroski nastrój** to get into a carefree mood
wpu|ścić *pf* — **wpu|szczać** *impf vt* ① (pozwolić wejść) to let [sb/sth] in ② (umieścić) to put [sth] in *[krople]*; ~**ścić ryby do stawu** to release fish into a pond; **bluzka** ~**szczona do spodni** a blouse tucked into one's trousers
wpychać *impf* → **wepchnąć**
wrabiać *impf* → **wrobić**
wracać *impf* → **wrócić**
wradzać się *impf* → **wrodzić się**
wrak *m* wreck także przen.; ~ **człowieka** a wreck of a man
wrastać *impf* → **wrosnąć**
wraże|nie *n* ① (doznanie) sensation ② (odczucie) impression; **być pod** ~**niem** to be impressed; **zrobić na kimś** ~**nie** to make an impression on sb; **mieć** ~**nie, że...** to have a feeling a. the impression that...; **sprawiać wrażenie spokojne-go** to appear to be calm; **z** ~**nia** in all the excitement
wrażliwoś|ć *f* ① (bycie wrażliwym) sensitivity (**na coś** to sth) ② (podatność) susceptibility (**na coś** to sth)
wrażliw|y *adi. grad.* sensitive (**na coś** to sth)
wredn|y *adi. grad.* pot. *[osoba, uśmiech]* nasty; *[pogoda, nastrój]* lousy pot.
wreszcie *adv., part.* finally, at last
wręcz [] *part.* (wprost) simply; ~ **przeciwnie** just the opposite
[] *adv.* ① (otwarcie) straight out ② (bezpośrednio) **walczyć** ~ to fight hand-to-hand
wręcz|yć *pf* — **wręcz|ać** *impf vt* to present *[nagrodę, dyplom, odznaczenie]*; to give *[podarek, bukiet]*; to hand [sth] in *[wymówienie, rezygnację]*
wr|obić *pf* — **wr|abiać** *impf vt* ① (wpleść) to knit ② pot. to frame pot. *[osobę]*
wr|odzić się *pf* — **wr|adzać się** *impf vi* to take (**w kogoś** after sb)
wrodz|ony *adi. [skłonności, zdolności]* inborn, innate; *[wada]* congenital
wro|gi *adi.* ① (nieprzyjazny) *[ideologia, państwo, zamiary]* hostile ② (należący do wroga) *[armia]* enemy's; *[artyleria]* enemy
wrogo *adv. [odnosić się, patrzeć]* in a hostile manner
wrogoś|ć *f* hostility
wron|a *f* crow
wr|osnąć *pf* — **wr|astać** *impf vi [roślina]* to take root (**w coś** in sth); *[paznokieć]* to grow in
wrot|ka *f* roller skate; **jeździć na** ~**kach** to roller skate
wrób|el *m* (house) sparrow
■ **lepszy** ~**el w garści niż gołąb na dachu** przysł. a bird in the hand is worth two in the bush przysł.
wr|ócić *pf* — **wr|acać** *impf* [] *vt* przest. (przywrócić) to restore *[siły, wzrok]*; **wrócić komuś zdrowie** to restore sb's health

[] *vi* ① (przybyć z powrotem) *[osoba,]* to return, to come back; **wróćmy do pierwszego pytania** let's go back to the first question; **wrócił mu dobry humor** his good humour is back ② (zawrócić) to go back ③ (zostać zwróconym) to be returned ④ (odzyskać poprzedni stan) to return; **wracać do normy** to be getting back to normal; **wracać do siebie** (odzyskać zdrowie) to recover; (odzyskać przytomność) to regain consciousness
[] **wrócić się** — **wracać się** pot. to go a. turn back
wr|óg *m* ① (państwo, osoba) enemy ② (przeciwnik) opponent
wróżb|a *f* ① (przepowiednia) prophecy ② (zapowiedź) omen; **wziąć coś za złą** ~**ę** to take sth to be a bad omen
wróż|ka *f* ① (wróżbiarka) fortune teller, psychic ② (postać baśniowa) (dobra) good witch, fairy god-mother; (zła) (wicked) witch
wróż|yć *impf* [] *vt* to predict
[] *vi* ① (przepowiadać przyszłość) to tell fortunes; ~**yć z kart/ręki** to do card/palm readings ② (zapowiadać) to foretell; **to źle** ~**y** it's a bad sign
■ **na dwoje babka** ~**yła** pot. it could go either way
wrzask *m* ① (krzyk) scream ② pot., przen. (gwałtowna reakcja) uproar
wrz|asnąć *pf* — **wrz|eszczeć** *impf vi* ① (wydać dźwięk) to scream ② (zawołać) to shout
wrząt|ek *m* boiling water
wrzecion|o *n* spindle
w|rzeć *impf vi* ① *[woda]* to boil ② przen. (tętnić gwarem) to buzz; **w klasie wrzało jak w ulu** the class was all abuzz; **praca wre** the work is in full swing ③ książk. (kipieć z emocji) *[osoba]* to seethe; **wrzeć z gniewu** to be seething (with anger)
wrze|sień *m* September
wrzeszczeć *impf* → **wrzasnąć**
wrzos *m* heather
wrz|ód *m* Med. (ropień) sore; (żołądka, dwunastnicy) ulcer
wrzu|cić *pf* — **wrzu|cać** *impf vt* ① (rzucić do środka) to throw; ~**cić list do skrzynki** to post a. mail a letter ② Aut. to get into *[bieg]*
wsa|dzić *pf* — **wsa|dzać** *impf vt* pot. ① (wcisnąć) to put; ~**dzić kapelusz na głowę** to put one's hat on; ~**dzić kogoś do samolotu** to put sb on a plane ② pot. (uwięzić) to put [sb] away pot.
wschodni *adi. [ściana, strona, kultura]* eastern; *[wiatr]* east, easterly
wschodzić *impf* → **wzejść**
wsch|ód *m* ① (słońca) sunrise; **o** ~**odzie słońca** at sunrise ② (strona świata) east; **na** ~**ód od...** east of... ③ (kraje wschodnie) **Wschód** the East; **Bliski/Daleki** ~ the Middle/Far East
wsiadać *impf* → **wsiąść**
wsiąk|nąć *pf* — **wsiąk|ać** *impf vi* ① (wsączyć się) to soak in ② pot., przen. (zniknąć) to vanish
wsi|ąść *pf* — **wsi|adać** *impf vi* ~**ąść do czegoś** to get on sth *[autobusu]*; to get in sth *[samochodu]*;

~**aść na coś** to board *[statek]*; to get on, to mount *[konia]*

wskakiwać *impf* → **wskoczyć**

wska|zać *pf* — **wska|zywać** *impf vt* [1] (pokazać) to show; (palcem) to point at [2] (informować) *[badania, wyniki]* to indicate [3] (podać zmierzoną wartość) *[przyrząd pomiarowy]* to indicate; **zegar** ~**zywał północ** the clock said midnight [4] (wytypować) to appoint

wskazów|ka *f* [1] (zegara) hand; (wagi, szybkościomierza) indicator; (kompasu) needle [2] (pouczenie, rada) tip [3] (oznaka) sign

wskazywać *impf* → **wskazać**

wskaźnik *m* [1] (oznaka) sign [2] (dla wykładowcy) pointer [3] Techn. (przyrząd) gauge; (wskazówka, światełko kontrolne) indicator [4] (wielkość) index, rate

wsk|oczyć *pf* — **wsk|akiwać** *impf vi* [1] (dostać się) to jump; ~**oczyć do czegoś** to jump into sth *[wody]*; to hop on sth *[tramwaju, autobusu]*; ~**oczyć na coś** to jump onto sth *[rower]* [2] pot. (wpaść z wizytą) to drop in (**do kogoś** on sb)

wskrze|sić *pf* — **wskrze|szać** *impf vt* książk. [1] (ożywić) to resurrect [2] przen. (wywołać z zapomnienia) to revive *[obyczaj]*

wskutek *praep.* ~ **czegoś** as a result of sth

wsław|ić *pf* — **wsław|iać** *impf* książk. **[I]** *vt* to make *[sb/sth]* famous

[II] wsławić się — **wsławiać się** to become famous

wspak *adv.* (od tyłu) backwards GB, backward US **wszystko idzie** ~ everything's going wrong

wspaniałomyśln|y *adi. [zwycięzca, gest]* generous

wspania|ły *adi. grad.* książk. *[osoba, głos, pomysł]* wonderful; *[sukces]* tremendous; *[perspektywy]* excellent; *[bal, uroczystość]* splendid

wspar|cie *n* [1] (pomoc) support; **udzielić komuś** ~**cia** to support sb [2] Wojsk. back-up

w|spiąć się *pf* — **w|spinać się** *impf v refl.* *[osoba, roślina, ścieżka]* to climb; **wspiąć się na palce** to stand on one's toes; **wspinać się po szczeblach kariery** przen. to move up the career ladder

wspierać *impf* → **wesprzeć**

wspinacz|ka *f* climbing

wspinać się *impf* → **wspiąć się**

wspomagać *impf* → **wspomóc**

wspom|nieć *pf* — **wspom|inać** *impf vt* [1] książk. (przypomnieć sobie) to recollect; **dobrze coś** ~**inać** to have fond memories of sth; **miło** ~**inać kogoś** to remember sb fondly [2] (napomknąć) to mention; **jak** ~**niałem** as I mentioned

wspomnie|nie [I] *n* [1] (napomknięcie) mention (**o czymś** of sth) [2] (pośmiertne) posthumous tribute [3] (z jakiegoś okresu) memory; **wracać** ~**niem do czegoś** to recollect sth

[II] wspomnienia *plt* memoirs

wspom|óc *pf* — **wspom|agać** *impf vt* książk. to support

wspólni|k *m*, ~**czka** *f* [1] (w przestępstwie) accomplice [2] (w interesach) partner

wspólno|ta *f* [1] (łączność) community [2] (więź) union [3] (społeczność) community

wspóln|y *adi. [zabawa, radości, kłopoty]* shared; *[praca]* joint; *[własność, wróg]* common, joint; **mieć z kimś coś** ~**ego** to have sth in common with sb; **nie mieć z czymś nic** ~**ego** to have nothing to do with sth

współbrzmi|eć *impf vi* to harmonize także przen.

współczesnoś|ć *f* the present (time a. day)

współcze|sny [I] *adi.* contemporary

[II] *m* ~**śni (mu)** his contemporaries

współczuci|e *n* compassion; **proszę przyjąć wyrazy** ~**a** please accept my condolences

współczu|ć *impf vi* to sympathize (**komuś** with sb)

współczynnik *m* [1] (mnożnik) coefficient [2] (wielkość liczbowa) rate

współdziała|ć *impf vi* książk. *[osoby]* to cooperate; *[leki]* to have a combined effect; *[urządzenia]* to operate together

współlokato|r *m*, ~**rka** *f* (w jednym pokoju) roommate; (w jednym mieszkaniu) flatmate GB, room-mate US

współprac|a *f* cooperation; (z wywiadem, okupantem) collaboration

współprac|ować *impf vi* to cooperate; (z wywiadem, okupantem) to collaborate

współpracowni|k *m*, ~**czka** *f* [1] (partner) partner [2] (agent) collaborator

współrzędn|y [I] *adi. [spójnik, człon]* coordinate

[II] współrzędna *f* coordinate

współudzia|ł *m* participation; (w zbrodni) complicity

współzawodnictw|o *n* competition

współzawodnicz|yć *impf vi* to compete

współży|ć *impf vi* książk. [1] (obcować) to co-exist [2] (płciowo) to have (sexual) intercourse

wsta|ć *pf* — **wsta|wać** *impf vi* [1] (przyjąć pozycję stojącą) to stand up [2] (z łóżka) to get up; (z krzesła, klęczek) to rise; ~**ć od stołu** to rise from the table [3] (obudzić się) to get up [4] przen. *[słońce]* to rise

wstaw|ić *pf* — **wstaw|iać** *impf* **[I]** *vt* [1] (umieścić, włożyć) to put; ~**iać kwiaty do wazonu** to put flowers in a vase [2] (osadzić, wprawić) to put *[sth]* in *[szybę]* [3] (wpisać) to put *[sth]* in *[date]* [4] pot. (nastawić) to put *[sth]* on to boil *[ziemniaki, potrawę]*; ~**ić wodę na herbatę** to put the kettle on

[II] wstawić się — **wstawiać się** [1] (ująć się) ~**ić się za kimś** to stand up for sb [2] pot. (upić się) to get tight pot.

wstaw|ka *f* pot. [1] (dodatek) (w ubraniach) insert(ion); (w drewnie) panel [2] (przerywnik) interlude

wst|ąpić *pf* — **wst|ępować** *impf vi* [1] (odwiedzić) to stop by (**do czegoś** sth); to drop in (**do kogoś**

on sb) [2] (przystąpić) to join (**do czegoś** sth); ~**ąpić do klasztoru** to enter a monastery/convent [3] książk., przen. *[nadzieja, radość]* to fill (**w coś** sth)
wstąż|ka [] *f* ribbon

[]] **wstążki** *plt* Kulin. ≈ tagliatelle

wstecz *adv.* back; **krok** ~ a step back(wards); **działać** ~ *[prawo]* to be applied retroactively
wsteczn|y [] *adi.* [1] książk. (zacofany, reakcyjny) *[pogląd, ideologia]* reactionary [2] (kierujący w tył) *[ruch]* backward; **bieg** ~**y** reverse (gear)

[]] *m* reverse (gear)

wstęp *m* [1] (wejście, dostęp) entrance; **zakaz** ~**u** no entry [2] (część dzieła) introduction; **na** ~**ie...** to begin with... [3] (podstawy) introduction (**do czegoś** to sth)
wstępn|y *adi.* [1] (początkowy) *[badania, wyniki, rozmowy]* preliminary [2] (prowizoryczny) provisional [3] (wprowadzający) introductory
wstępować *impf* → **wstąpić**
wstrę|t *m* disgust, revulsion

■ **czynić komuś** ~**ty** książk. to place obstacles in sb's way
wstrętn|y *adi. grad.* (nieetyczny) *[osoba, postępowanie]* despicable; (wzbudzający wstręt) *[wygląd, zapach, jedzenie]* disgusting; *[pogoda]* awful; (brzydki) hideous
wstrząs *m* shock
wstrząsać *impf* → **wstrząsnąć**
wstrząsając|y *adi.* shocking
wstrząs|nąć *pf* — **wstrząs|ać** *impf* [] *vt* [1] (potrząsnąć) to shake; ~**ały nią dreszcze** she was trembling a. shaking [2] przen. (silnie wzruszyć) to shock

[]] **wstrząsnąć się** — **wstrząsać się** to shiver, to shake
wstrzemięźliw|y *adi.* książk. [1] (powściągliwy) restrained [2] (świadczący o umiarze) temperate
wstrzyk|nąć *pf* — **wstrzyk|iwać** *impf* *vt* to inject
wstrzym|ać *pf* — **wstrzym|ywać** *impf* [] *vt* [1] (zahamować, zablokować) to stop [2] (odwlec, zawiesić) to withhold *[wypłatę]*; to suspend *[prace, dostawy, produkcję]*; to hold *[oddech]*

[]] **wstrzymać się** — **wstrzymywać się** [1] (powstrzymać się) to refrain (**od czegoś** from sth) [2] (poczekać) to postpone (**z czymś** sth)
wsty|d *m* shame; (uczucie skrępowania) embarrassment; (hańba) disgrace; **przynosić komuś** ~**d** to disgrace sb; ~**d!** shame (on you)!; **co za** ~**d!** what a disgrace!
wstydliw|y *adi.* [1] (nieśmiały) *[osoba]* shy [2] (krępujący) *[sprawa, temat, milczenie]* embarrassing
wsty|dzić się *impf v refl.* [1] (odczuwać wstyd) to be ashamed (**za coś** of sth) [2] (krępować się) to be shy
wsu|nąć *pf* — **wsu|wać** *impf* [] *vt* [1] (włożyć) to slip; ~**nąć ręce do kieszeni** he put one's hands in one's pockets [2] pot. (zjeść) to scoff (down) GB pot., to scarf (down) US pot.

[]] **wsunąć się** — **wsuwać się** (wejść) to slip in; ~**nąć się pod kołdrę** to slip under the covers
wsyp|ać *pf* — **wsyp|ywać** *impf* [] *vt* [1] (nasypać) to put (**coś do czegoś** sth into sth) [2] pot. (donieść) to rat pot. (**kogoś** on sb)

[]] **wsypać się** — **wsypywać się** [1] (dostać się do wnętrza) to get (**do czegoś** into sth) [2] pot. (ujawnić się) to give oneself away
wsysać *impf* → **wessać**
wszcz|ąć *pf* — **wszcz|ynać** *impf* *vt* książk. to start *[kłótnię]*; to launch *[śledztwo]*
wszczep|ić *pf* — **wszczep|iać** *impf* *vt* [1] książk. (wpoić) to instil, to instill US [2] Med. (zarazić) to infect (**komuś coś** sb with sth) [3] Med. (przeszczepić) to implant
wszczynać *impf* → **wszcząć**
wszechstronn|y *adi. grad.* książk. [1] (uniwersalny) *[osoba]* versatile; *[wykształcenie]* comprehensive [2] (skrupulatny) *[analiza, studia]* thorough
wszechświa|t *m* universe
wszel|ki *pron.* książk. all; ~**kimi sposobami** by all possible means; **za** ~**ką cenę** at all costs
wszerz [] *praep.* across (**czegoś** sth)

[]] *adv.* in width, across; **trzy metry** ~ three metres in width a. across
wszędzie *pron.* everywhere; ~**, gdzie się pojawi** wherever he appears
wszy|ć *pf* — **wszy|wać** *impf* *vt* [1] (wstawić) to set [sth] in *[rękaw]*; to sew [sth] in *[klin, suwak]* [2] (wprowadzić do organizmu) to implant *[esperal, rozrusznik serca]*
wszys|tek [] *pron.* all; **po** ~**tkie czasy** for ever; **za** ~**tkie czasy** as never before; **ze** ~**tkich sił** with all one's might

[]] **wszyscy** everybody, all
wszystk|o *pron.* everything; **pieniądze to nie** ~**o** money is not everything; ~**o, co tylko zechcesz** anything you want; ~**o albo nic** all or nothing; **to na dzisiaj** ~**o** that's all for today; **jeszcze nie** ~**o stracone** all is not (yet) lost; **jest już po** ~**im** it's all over; **(po)mimo** ~**o** despite everything; **przede** ~**im** first of all; ~**iego najlepszego!** all the best!; ~**o jedno kto/kiedy/gdzie** it doesn't matter who/when/where
wszywać *impf* → **wszyć**
wścibs|ki *adi.* pot. (ciekawski) *[sąsiadka, pytanie]* nos(e)y pot.; *[prasa, spojrzenie]* inquisitive
wście|c *pf* — **wście|kać** *impf* [] *vi* pot. (rozgniewać) to make [sb] mad pot.

[]] **wściec się** — **wściekać się** [1] (dostać wścieklizny) *[zwierzę]* to get rabies [2] pot. (rozzłościć się) to get mad pot.
wściekli|zna *f* rabies
wściekłoś|ć *f* fury, rage; **wpaść we** ~**ć** to be furious
wściek|ły *adi.* [1] (chory na wściekliznę) *[lis, pies]* rabid [2] (gniewny, zły) *[osoba, list, tłum, spojrzenie]* furious

3 przen. (zaciekły) *[atak]* ferocious; *[zazdrość, nienawiść]* fierce 4 pot. *[sztorm, wicher, tempo]* furious; *[ból, głód, pragnienie]* intense

wśli|znąć się, wśli|zgnąć się *pf* — **wśli|zgiwać się** *impf v refl.* 1 (wpełznąć) *[wąż]* to slither (**do czegoś** into sth) 2 (wkraść się) to slip (**do czegoś/pod coś** into/under sth)

wśród *praep.* 1 (pomiędzy) among(st); ~ **drzew** among the trees 2 (podczas) in the middle of; ~ **śmiechu publiczności** amid laughter from the audience

wtajemniczać *impf* → **wtajemniczyć**

wtajemnicz|ony *m* (w sekcie) initiate; (posiadający poufne informacje) insider

wtajemnicz|yć *impf* — **wtajemnicz|ać** *impf vt* 1 (poinformować) to let [sb] in (**w coś** on sth) 2 (nauczyć, wprowadzić) to initiate (**kogoś w coś** sb into sth)

wtapiać *impf* → **wtopić**

wtarg|nąć *pf vi [osoba, woda]* to rush; ~**nąć do pokoju** to barge into a room; ~**nąć do miasta** to invade a city

wtedy *pron.* then; **dopiero** ~, **kiedy...** only when...; **co** ~? what then?

wtem *adv.* suddenly

wtłocz|yć *pf* — **wtłacz|ać** *impf* I *vt* 1 (wepchnąć) to cram *[gości, pasażerów]*; ~**yć komuś wiedzę do głowy** to cram sb's head with information 2 Techn. to pump *[gaz, powietrze]* (**do czegoś** in(to) sth); to force *[gaz, powietrze]*

II **wtłoczyć się** — **wtłaczać się** *[osoby]* to cram

wt|opić *pf* — **wt|apiać** *impf* I *vt* 1 Techn. to embed 2 przen. (wkomponować) to blend

II **wtopić się** — **wtapiać się** 1 Techn. *[elementy]* to fuse (together) 2 przen. (zespoić się, zlać się) to blend (in); **wtopić się w tłum** to melt into the crowd

wtor|ek *m* Tuesday

wtórn|y *adi.* 1 (pochodny) *[pasożyt, zmiany chorobowe]* secondary; *[choroba]* recurring; **surowce** ~**e** recyclable materials 2 (drugorzędny) *[cechy płciowe, nurt literacki]* secondary; *[technologia]* spin-off 3 (naśladujący) *[utwór, styl]* derivative

wtrą|cić *pf* — **wtrą|cać** *impf* I *vt* (wygłosić) to interject *[uwagę, spostrzeżenie]*; to throw [sth] in *[zwroty]*; **jeśli mogę coś** ~**cić...** if I could just put in a word here...

II **wtrącić się** — **wtrącać się** to butt in pot.; **przepraszam, że się** ~**cam, ale...** sorry to butt in, but...

■ ~**cić kogoś do więzienia** książk. to throw sb into prison

wtul|ić *pf* — **wtul|ać** *impf* I *vt* to nestle *[głowę]* (**w coś** in(to) sth)

II **wtulić się** — **wtulać się** (**w coś** in(to) sth)

wtycz|ka *f* 1 (do przyłączania) plug 2 pot. (informator) plant pot.

wtykać *impf* → **wetknąć**

wuj|ek *m* uncle

wulgarn|y *adi. grad. [osoba, słownictwo, rysy]* vulgar

wulgaryzm *m* vulgarism

wulkan *m* 1 (góra) volcano 2 przen. (osoba energiczna) powerhouse przen.

ww|ieźć *pf* — **ww|ozić** *impf vt* 1 (do środka) to bring (in) *[ludzi, towary]* 2 (na górę) *[kolejka, winda]* to carry

wy *pron.* you

wyartykuł|ować *pf vt* książk. to articulate książk.

wyasfalt|ować *pf vt* to surface [sth] with asphalt

wybacz|yć *pf* — **wybacz|ać** *impf vt* to forgive (**komuś coś** sb (for) sth)

wybaw|ić *pf* — **wybaw|iać** *impf vt* to save (**kogoś od** a. **z czegoś** sb from sth)

wybełko|tać *pf vt* pot. to mumble

wybi|ć *pf* — **wybi|jać** *impf* I *vt* 1 (spowodować wypadnięcie) to break *[okno, szybę]*; to dislocate *[palec, ramię]*; to knock [sth] out *[ząb]*; to poke [sth] out *[oko]* 2 przen. ~**ć kogoś ze snu** to disturb sb's sleep; ~**ć kogoś z rytmu** to put sb off (their stride) 3 (przebić) to knock [sth] out *[dziurę]* 4 (obić) to line *[ściany]* (**czymś** with sth); to cover *[krzesło, kanapę]* (**czymś** with sth) 5 Muz. to beat (out) *[rytm, takt]* 6 (wskazać) *[zegar]* to strike *[godzinę]*; *[licznik, taksometr]* to ring up *[cenę, sumę]* 7 (wycisnąć w metalu) to mint *[medal, monety]* 8 (zabić) to wipe [sth] out *[oddział, bydło]*

II *vi* (wydobyć się gwałtownie) *[źródełko, woda]* to gush out; *[studzienka ściekowa]* to overflow

III **wybić się** — **wybijać się** 1 (osiągnąć sukcesy) to make a name for oneself 2 (skoczyć) to take off

wybie|c, wybie|gnąć *pf* — **wybie|gać** *impf vi* 1 (opuścić) to run out 2 przen. (wykraczać) ~**gać poza coś** to go beyond sth

wybieg *m* 1 (dla koni) paddock; (w zoo) pen 2 (fortel) ruse 3 (dla modelek) catwalk

wybiegać *impf* → **wybiec**

wybieg|ać się *impf* pot. *[dziecko, pies]* to run oneself ragged

wybiegnąć → **wybiec**

wybielacz *m* bleach

wybiel|ić *pf* — **wybiel|ać** *impf* I *vt* 1 (rozjaśnić) to bleach *[ubrania, tkaniny, papier]*; to whiten *[zęby, cerę]*; ~**ić kogoś** przen. to whitewash sb 2 (pomalować) to whitewash *[ściany, pomieszczenie]*

II **wybielić się** — **wybielać się** 1 (stać się bielszym) to become bleached 2 przen. (usprawiedliwić się) to put on a good front

wybierać *impf* → **wybrać**

wybijać *impf* → **wybić**

wybiórcz|y *adi.* selective

wybitn|y *adi.* 1 *[uczony, postać, talent]* outstanding 2 *[poprawa, różnica]* remarkable

wyblak|nąć *pf vi [kolory, przedmiot]* to fade; *[wspomnienia]* to fade away

wyboi|sty *adi. [droga]* bumpy

wyborc|a *m* voter

wyborn|y *adi. grad. [potrawa, zapach]* delicious; *[trunek]* exquisite; *[żart, okazja]* perfect

wyb|ój *m* pothole

wyb|ór **▯** *m* ▯ (wybranie) choice; **z** ~oru by choice; **mieć coś do** ~oru to have sth to choose from ▮ (zespół, zestaw) selection; ~**ór wierszy** a selection of poems ▯ (na stanowisko) election **▮** **wybory** *plt* election(s); ~**ory do sejmu** a parliamentary election

wyb|rać *pf* — **wyb|ierać** *impf* **▯** *vt* ▯ (wyselekcjonować) to choose; (w głosowaniu) to elect ▮ (usunąć) to remove *[ziemię, piasek]*; ~**rać wodę ze studni** to take water from a well ▯ (wypłacić) to withdraw *[pieniądze]* ▯ (wyciągnąć) to haul [sth] in *[sieci]*; to weigh *[kotwicę]* **▮** **wybrać się** — **wybierać się** to go

wybredn|y *adi. grad. [osoba]* fussy; *[gust]* discriminating

wybrn|ąć *pf vi* ▯ (wyjść z trudem) to struggle (**z czegoś** out of sth) ▮ *przen.* (poradzić sobie) to get (oneself) out

wybryk *m* prank
■ ~ **natury** freak of nature

wybrzeż|e *n* (brzeg) coast; (region) seaside

wybrzusze|nie *n* bulge

wybrzydza|ć *impf vi pot.* to turn up one's nose (**na coś** at sth)

wybuch *m* ▯ (eksplozja) explosion; ~ **wulkanu** a volcanic eruption ▮ (wojny, epidemii) outbreak ▯ (złości, śmiechu) outburst

wybuch|nąć *pf* — **wybuch|ać** *impf vi* ▯ *[bomba, mina]* to explode, to go off; *[wulkan]* to erupt ▮ *przen. [wojna, pożar, panika]* to break out ▯ *[osoba]* to burst (out); ~**nąć śmiechem** to burst out laughing

wybuchow|y *adi.* ▯ *[mieszanka, ładunek]* explosive ▮ *przen. [osoba, charakter]* short-tempered

wycel|ować *pf vt* (wymierzyć) to aim *[broń]* (**w kogoś** at sb); to point *[lornetkę]* (**w coś** at sth)

wycen|a *f* valuation

wyce|nić *pf* — **wyce|niać** *impf vt* to value *[ziemię, majątek]*

wychod|ek *m pot.* privy

wychodzić *impf* → **wyjść**

wychow|ać *pf* — **wychow|ywać** *impf* **▯** *vt* ▯ (opiekować się) to bring [sb] up; **dobrze** ~**any** well-brought up; **źle** ~**any** bad-mannered ▮ (wykształcić) to educate **▮** **wychować się** — **wychowywać się** to be brought up

wychowan|ek *m* ▯ (podopieczny) foster child ▮ (absolwent) alumnus

wychowani|e *n* ▯ (opieka nad dzieckiem) upbringing ▮ (edukacja) education ▯ (ogłada) manners

wychowan|ka *f* ▯ (podopieczna) foster child ▮ (absolwentka) alumna

wychowawc|a *m*, ~**czyni** *f* ▯ (opiekun klasy) form teacher ▮ (na obozie) counsellor

wychowywać *impf* → **wychować**

wychudz|ony *adi.* emaciated

wychwy|cić, **wychwy|tać** *pf* — **wychwy|tywać** *impf vt* to detect *[błędy, wady]*

wychyl|ić *pf* — **wychyl|ać** *impf* **▯** *vt* ▯ (zmienić pozycję) to lean ▮ (wypić alkohol) to drink, to down *[kieliszek, kufel]* **▮** **wychylić się** — **wychylać się** ▯ (wyjrzeć) to lean out ▮ (przechylić się) to lean (over) ▯ *pot.* (postąpić odważnie) to stick one's neck out *pot.*

wy|ciąć *pf* — **wy|cinać** *impf vt* ▯ (wykroić) [sth] out; (wyryć) to carve (out) *[napis]* ▮ (ściąć) to cut [sth] down *[drzewa]* ▯ (usunąć) to remove *[narząd]* ▯ *pot.* (skreślić) to cut *[fragment, zdanie]* ▯ (wymordować) to slaughter

wyciąg *m* ▯ (urywek, fragment) excerpt; ~ **z konta** a bank statement ▮ (ekstrakt) extract ▯ (narciarski) ski lift ▯ (w ortopedii) traction ▯ *Techn.* (wentylator) extraction fan; (okap) ventilating hood

wyciąg|nąć *pf* — **wyciąg|ać** *impf* **▯** *vt* ▯ (wydobyć) to take a. pull [sth] out ▮ (wysunąć) to stretch [sth] out *[nogi]*; ~**nąć rękę po coś** to hold out one's hand to take sth ▯ (rozciągnąć) to stretch (out of shape) *[sweter, rękaw]* ▯ *pot.* (namówić do wyjścia) to drag [sb] out *pot.* ▯ *pot.* (wydobyć z opresji) to get [sb] out ▯ *pot.* (osiągnąć) (o zarobkach) to make; (o samochodzie) to do ▯ *pot.* (zaśpiewać) to draw out *[nutę, ton]* **▮** **wyciągnąć się** — **wyciągać się** ▯ (położyć się) to stretch out ▮ (wysunąć się do przodu) *[ręce, ramiona]* to be outstretched ▯ (ulec rozciągnięciu) *[ubranie]* to stretch ▯ *przen.* (wydłużyć się) *[cień]* to stretch; (urosnąć) *[dziecko]* to shoot up

wy|cie *n* (zwierząt) howl; (człowieka, wiatru) wail

wyciec, **wycie|knąć** *pf* — **wycie|kać** *impf vi* ▯ *[ciecz]* to leak (out) ▮ *przen. [pieniądze, towary]* to disappear

wyciecz|ka *f* ▯ (wyprawa turystyczna) trip; (piesza) hike ▮ (grupa) tour ▯ *książk.* (przytyk) critical remark

wycieczkowicz *m pot.* tripper *GB pot.*; sightseer

wyciek *m* ▯ (wypływ) leak; ~ **ropy** an oil spill ▮ (z nosa, z uszu) discharge

wyciekać *impf* → **wyciec**

wycieknąć → **wyciec**

wycieracz|ka *f* ▯ (do butów) doormat ▮ (w samochodzie) windscreen wiper *GB*, windshield wiper *US*

wycierać *impf* → **wytrzeć**

wycierpi|eć *pf vi* to suffer

wycię|cie *n* ▯ (wgłębienie) notch ▮ (dekolt) neckline

wycinać *impf* → **wyciąć**

wycinan|ka *f* paper cut-out

wycin|ek *m* [1] (fragment) section [2] (z gazety) cutting, clipping US [3] (tkanki) (tissue) sample

wyciskacz *m* squeezer; ∼ **soku** a juicer; ∼ **łez** przen. a tear jerker pot.

wycis|nąć *pf* — **wycis|kać** *impf vt* [1] (oddzielić) to squeeze *[cytrynę, pryszcz]*; to wring *[gąbkę, ścierkę]* [2] (odcisnąć ślad) to impress (**coś na czymś** sth on sth) [3] pot. (wymusić) to wring (**coś od kogoś** sth out of sb)

wycisz|yć *pf* — **wycisz|ać** *impf* **Ⅰ** *vt* [1] (wygłuszyć) to soundproof *[budynek, pokój]*; to muffle *[silnik]* [2] przen. (wytłumić) to calm *[emocje, namiętności]* [3] przen. (zatuszować) to hush *[sth] up [skandal]* **Ⅱ** **wyciszyć się** — **wyciszać się** książk. to calm (oneself) down

wycof|ać *pf* — **wycof|ywać** *impf* **Ⅰ** *vt* [1] (cofnąć) to withdraw *[rękę]*; to reverse *[samochód]* [2] (odwołać) to withdraw *[przedstawiciela, obietnicę]*; to cancel *[zaproszenie, zamówienie]*; to drop *[oskarżenia]* **Ⅱ** **wycofać się** — **wycofywać się** [1] (ustąpić z urzędu) to step down [2] (opuścić teren) *[wojska]* to retreat, to withdraw [3] (zmienić zdanie) to back out [4] (cofnąć się) *[samochód, kierowca]* to reverse

wyczerp|ać *pf* — **wyczerp|ywać** *impf* **Ⅰ** *vt* [1] (wydobyć do końca) to deplete *[złoża, zasoby]*; to use up *[zapasy]*; ∼**ać wodę ze studni** to empty a well [2] (zmęczyć) to exhaust **Ⅱ** **wyczerpać się** — **wyczerpywać się** *[zapasy, bateria]* to run out; *[towar]* to be sold out; *[nakład]* to be out of print; ∼**ać temat** to exhaust a topic

wyczerpan|y *adi.* *[osoba]* exhausted

wyczerpując|y *adi.* [1] *[odpowiedź, dane]* exhaustive [2] *[zajęcie, praca]* exhausting

wyczerpywać *impf* → **wyczerpać**

wyczuci|e *n* [1] (takt) tact [2] (odczucie) sense; **na** ∼**e** by intuition

wyczu|ć *pf* — **wyczu|wać** *impf vt* [1] (dotykiem) to feel; (węchem) to smell [2] (uświadomić sobie) to sense *[podstęp, fałsz]*

wyczyn *m* (osiągnięcie) feat

wyczynow|iec *m* competitive sportsman/sportswoman

wyczy|ścić *pf* — **wyczy|szczać** *impf* **Ⅰ** *vt* (usunąć brud) to clean; (wypolerować) to polish; ∼**ścić mieszkanie z czegoś** przen. *[złodziej]* to clear a flat of sth **Ⅱ** **wyczyścić się** — **wyczyszczać się** to be cleaned

wy|ć *impf vi* *[zwierzę]* to howl; *[osoba, wiatr]* to wail

wyćwicz|yć *pf vt* to practise

wyda|ć *pf* — **wyda|wać** *impf* **Ⅰ** *vt* [1] (zapłacić) to spend; ∼**ć komuś resztę** to give sb the change [2] (wydzielić) to give *[sth] out [obiady, narzędzia]* [3] (wystawić) to issue *[zaświadczenie, oświadczenie]*; to pronounce *[wyrok]* [4] (ujawnić) to reveal *[sekret]*; to turn *[sb] in [zbiega]* [5] (opublikować) to publish [6] (być źródłem) to make *[dźwięk]*; to give off *[zapach]* [7] (zorganizować) to hold *[przyjęcie, bankiet]*

Ⅱ **wydać się** — **wydawać się** [1] (wyglądać) to seem; ∼**je się, że...** it seems (that)... [2] (wyjść na jaw) to be revealed [3] pot. (wyjść za mąż) to marry (**za kogoś** sb)

wydajn|y *adi. grad.* *[gleba]* fertile; *[metody]* high-yield; *[urządzenie]* cost-efficient; *[pracownik]* efficient

wydal|ić *pf* — **wydal|ać** *impf vt* [1] (z pracy) to dismiss; (ze szkoły) to expel; (z kraju) to deport [2] *[organizm]* to expel *[powietrze, dwutlenek węgla]*; to excrete *[produkty przemiany materii]*

wyda|nie *n* (książki, gazety) edition

wydarzać się *impf* → **wydarzyć się**

wydarze|nie *n* event

wydarz|yć się *pf* —.**wydarz|ać się** *impf v refl.* to happen

wydat|ek *m* expense; ∼**ki publiczne** public expenditure(s)

wydawać *impf* → **wydać**

wydawc|a *m* publisher

wydawnictw|o *n* [1] (instytucja) publishing house [2] (publikacja) publication

wyd|ąć *pf* — **wyd|ymać** *impf* **Ⅰ** *vt* to fill *[żagle]*; to puff out *[policzki]*; to pout *[usta]* **Ⅱ** **wydąć się** — **wydymać się** to swell (out)

wydech *m* exhalation; **zrobić** ∼ to exhale

wydep|tać *pf* — **wydep|tywać** *impf vt* [1] (zniszczyć) to trample [sth] down *[trawę, trawnik]* [2] (utorować) to tread *[ścieżkę]*

wydę|ty *adi.* *[brzuch, policzki]* bulging; *[usta]* pouting

wydłuż|yć *pf* — **wydłuż|ać** *impf* **Ⅰ** *vt* to lengthen *[odległość]*; to extend *[drogę]*; to extend, to prolong *[gwarancję, sezon, podróż]* **Ⅱ** **wydłużyć się** — **wydłużać się** *[przedmiot, dzień]* to grow longer

wydm|a *f* (sand) dune

wydmusz|ka *f* blown egg

wydobyci|e *n* (węgla, ropy) output

wydob|yć *pf* — **wydob|ywać** *impf* **Ⅰ** *vt* [1] (wydostać) to take [sth] out; ∼**yć kogoś z kłopotów** to get sb out of trouble [2] (wykopać) to extract *[ropę]*; to mine *[węgiel, złoto, diamenty]* [3] (wydać) to make *[dźwięk]* [4] (uzyskać) to get (**coś od kogoś** sth out of a. from sb) **Ⅱ** **wydobyć się** — **wydobywać się** [1] (wydostać się) to get out także przen. [2] (ulatywać) *[dym, gaz]* to escape

wydo|ić *pf vt* [1] to milk także przen. *[krowę, kozę, osobę]* [2] pot. (wypić) to guzzle (down) *[wodę, piwo]*

wydorośl|eć *pf vi* to grow up

wydosta|ć *pf* — **wydosta|wać** *impf* **Ⅰ** *vt* to get [sth] out **Ⅱ** **wydostać się** — **wydostawać się** [1] (opuścić) to get out [2] (wydobywać się) *[dym, gaz]* to escape

wyd|ra *f* [1] Zool. otter [2] pot. (kłótliwa) vixen pot.; (wyzywająca) tart pot.

wydrąż|yć *pf vt* [1] (zrobić otwór) to bore *[otwór, tunel]*; to sink *[szyb]* [2] (usunąć środek) to hollow (out) *[pień]*

wydruk *m* printout

wydruk|ować *pf* [] *vt [osoba, gazeta]* to print *[książkę, rysunek, artykuł]*

[] **wydrukować się** to be printed (out)

wy|drzeć *pf* — **wy|dzierać** *impf* [] *vt* [1] (odedrzeć) to tear [sth] out; (zerwać) to pull [sth] out [2] (zabrać) to snatch (**coś komuś** sth from sb); **wydrzeć miasto z rąk nieprzyjaciela** to recapture a town

[] **wydrzeć się** — **wydzierać się** [1] (wydostać się) to break free [2] książk. *[krzyk, jęk]* to escape książk. [3] pot. (krzyknąć) to yell

wydymać *impf* → **wydąć**

wydzia|ł *m* (urzędu, biura) department; (uczelni) department, faculty

wydziel|ić *pf* — **wydziel|ać** *impf* [] *vt* [1] (wytwarzać) to secrete *[sok, śluz, hormony]*; to give off *[zapach, ciepło, światło]*; to generate *[energię]* [2] (oddzielić) to section a. mark off [3] (przyznać) to allot

[] **wydzielić się** — **wydzielać się** *[śluz, sok, ślina]* to be secreted; *[zapach]* to exude *[substancja, gaz]* to be liberated

wydzielin|a *f* (z gruczołu) secretion; (objaw choroby) discharge

wydzierać *impf* → **wydrzeć**

wydziwia|ć *impf vi* pot. to be fussy

wydźwięk *m* overtone

wyekspon|ować *pf vt* książk. [1] (podkreślić) to emphasize [2] (na wystawie) to exhibit *[obraz, rzeźbę]*

wyeksport|ować *pf vt* to export

wyelimin|ować *pf vt* to eliminate

wyemigr|ować *pf vi* to emigrate

wyfroter|ować *pf vt* to polish *[podłogę]*

wygada|ć *pf* pot. [] *vt* to blurt out *[sekret, prawdę]*

[] **wygadać się** [1] (zdradzić się) to give the game away; **~ć się przed kimś** to let on to sb [2] (wypowiedzieć się) to talk oneself out

wygadan|y *adi.* pot. eloquent, voluble; **być ~ym** to have the gift of the gab pot.

wygad|ywać *impf vt, vi* pot. to talk *[bzdury, głupstwa]*; **~ywać na kogoś** to speak ill of sb

wyganiać *impf* → **wygnać**

wyga|snąć *pf* — **wyga|sać** *impf vi* [1] (zgasnąć) *[ogień, płomień]* to go out [2] przen. *[epidemia]* to die out a. down; *[strajki, spory]* to end; *[entuzjazm, namiętność]* to die down; *[miłość]* to die; *[kontrakt, gwarancja]* to expire [3] przen. *[dynastia]* to die out [4] *[wulkan]* to become extinct

wyg|iąć *pf* — **wyg|inać** *impf* [] *vt* to bend *[ciało, pręt]*

[] **wygiąć się** — **wyginać się** [1] *[osoba]* to bend over a. down [2] *[drut, gałąź]* to bend

wygię|cie *n* bend

wyginać *impf* → **wygiąć**

wygin|ąć *pf vi [zwierzęta, rośliny]* to become extinct; *[osoby]* to die out

wyglą|d *m* appearance; **sądząc z ~du...** by the look(s) of him/her...; **z ~du przypominał...** he looked like...

wyglądać[1] *impf* → **wyjrzeć**

wygląda|ć[2] *impf vi* [1] (prezentować się) *[osoba, sprawy, przyszłość]* to look; **~ć źle/dobrze** to look bad/good; **~ć jak ktoś/coś** to look like sb/sth; **~ na to, że...** it looks like...; **na to ~ so it seems** [2] (wyczekiwać) **~ć (na) kogoś** to eagerly await sb

wygła|dzić *pf* — **wygła|dzać** *impf* [] *vt* [1] to smooth away a. out *[zmarszczki]*; to smooth (down) *[tkaninę]*; to round off *[krawędzie, brzegi]*; to rub down *[drewno, gips]* [2] przen. (uczynić poprawnym) to polish *[styl, tekst]*

[] **wygładzić się** — **wygładzać się** [1] *[powierzchnia, morze]* to smooth (out); *[zmarszczki]* to smooth away a. out [2] przen. *[styl]* to become polished

wygł|osić *pf* — **wygł|aszać** *impf vt* to give *[wykład, przemówienie, kazanie]*; to recite *[wiersz]*; **~aszać niepopularne opinie** to voice unpopular opinions

wygłupia|ć się *impf v refl.* pot. to fool (about a. around) pot.; **nie ~j się!** don't be silly!

wyg|nać, wyg|onić *pf* — **wyg|aniać** *impf vt* to drive [sb] out; **~onić kogoś z kuchni** to chase sb out of the kitchen

wygnani|e *n* exile; **na ~u** in exile

wygna|niec *m* exile

wygni|eść *pf* — **wygni|atać** *impf* [] *vt* [1] (wycisnąć) to press [sth] out *[sok]*; to squeeze *[pryszcz]* [2] (wyrobić) to knead *[ciasto, glinę]* [3] (zmiąć) to crumple *[spodnie, suknię]* [4] (zniszczyć) to wear [sth] out *[kanapę]*

[] **wygnieść się** — **wygniatać się** *[ubranie]* to crease

wyg|oda *f* [1] (komfort) comfort; **dla ~ody** for (the sake of) convenience [2] (urządzenie) amenity; **bez ~ód** with no modern conveniences a. amenities

wygodnictw|o *n* looking after number one pot.

wygodnie *adv. grad. [podróżować]* comfortably; **~ ci?** are you comfortable?; **kiedy im ~** whenever it suits them

wygodn|y *adi. grad.* [1] *[fotel, łóżko, buty]* comfortable [2] *[dostęp, wymówka, termin]* convenient; *[życie, posada]* comfortable [3] *[osoba]* comfort-loving

wygonić → **wygnać**

wygot|ować *pf* — **wygot|owywać** *impf* [] *vt* to boil *[słoiki, bieliznę]*

[] **wygotować się** — **wygotowywać się** [1] *[strzykawka]* to be boiled a. sterilized [2] *[zupa, mleko]* to boil away a. off

wygórowan|y *adi. [ambicje, kwota, żądania]* excessive; *[oczekiwania]* unreasonable; *[opinia]* inflated

wygr|ać pf — **wygr|ywać** impf vt, vi ① (odnieść sukces) to win [mecz, konkurs, proces, zakład, wojnę]; ~**ać z kimś** to beat sb; **doświadczenie** ~**ało z młodością** przen. experience won out over youth ② (zdobyć wygraną) [osoba, los] to win [samochód, wycieczkę]; ~**ać na czymś** przen. (skorzystać) to benefit from sth ③ (zagrać) [osoba, radio, zegar] to play [melodię] ④ (wykorzystać) to exploit; ~**ywać sytuację dla własnych celów** to cash in on a situation pot.

wygran|a f ① (zwycięstwo) win, victory ② (nagroda) prize; (pieniądze) winnings; **zdobyć główną** ~**ą** to win first prize

■ **dać za** ~**ą** to give up

wygraża|ć impf vi to threaten (**komuś** sb); ~**ć komuś pięścią** to shake one's fist at sb

wygrywać impf → **wygrać**

wyhaft|ować pf vt to embroider

wyhod|ować pf vt to breed [zwierzę]; to grow [roślinę]; to cultivate [tkankę, bakterie]

wyidealiz|ować pf vt to idealize

wyjadać impf → **wyjeść**

wyjaśni|ć pf — **wyjaśni|ać** impf I vt (objaśnić) to explain [fakt, zjawisko, zagadkę]; to clarify [okoliczności, nieporozumienie]; ~**jmy sobie jedno** let's get one thing straight

II **wyjaśnić się** — **wyjaśniać się** [sytuacja] to become clear; [punkt sporny] to be clarified

wyjaśnie|nie n explanation; **nie wymagać** ~**ń** to be self-explanatory; **tytułem** ~**nia** by way of explanation; **żądam** ~**ń** I demand an explanation

wyjawi|ć pf — **wyjawi|ać** impf vt to disclose; ~**ć komuś sekret** to reveal a secret to sb

wyj|azd m ① (odjazd) departure ② (podróż) trip; ~**azd za granicę** a trip abroad ③ (brama) exit

wyj|ąć pf — **wyj|mować** impf vt ① (wydobyć) to take [sth] out; **zdanie** ~**ęte z kontekstu** a sentence taken out of context ② książk. (wykluczyć) ~**ąwszy kogoś/coś** with the exception of sb/sth

wyjąka|ć pf vt to stammer [sth] out [odpowiedź, słowo]

wyjąt|ek m ① (osoba, zdarzenie) exception; ~**ek od zasady** an exception to the rule; **w drodze** ~**ku** as an exception; **z** ~**kiem czegoś** except for sth ② (fragment) excerpt

wyjątkow|y adi. [talent, sytuacja] exceptional

wyj|echać pf — **wyj|eżdżać** impf vi ① (opuścić) to leave; ~**echać z miasta** to leave town; ~**echać z garażu** to drive out of a garage; ~**echać na szosę** to drive into a main road ② pot. (odezwać się) to come out (**z czymś** with sth)

wyj|eść pf — **wyj|adać** impf vt to eat (up)

wyjeżdżać impf → **wyjechać**

wyjmować impf → **wyjąć**

wy|jrzeć pf — **wy|glądać**¹ impf vi [osoba] to look out; (wystawać) [spódnica] to show; **wyglądać przez okno** to look through the window

wyjś|cie n ① (czynność) departure; **po jej** ~**ciu** after she had left ② (miejsce) exit ③ (rozwiązanie) way out; ~**cie z sytuacji** a way out of a situation ④ pot. (spotkanie) outing ⑤ Techn., Komput. output

wyjściow|y adi. ① (początkowy) [baza, pozycja] starting; [stan, sytuacja] initial ② (stanowiący wyjście) [brama, drzwi] exit ③ (świąteczny) [ubranie, sukienka] Sunday ④ Techn., Komput. [gniazdko, przewód] output

wy|jść pf — **wy|chodzić** impf vi ① (opuścić miejsce) to go out; **wyjść z domu** to go out; **wyjść na spacer** to go for a walk ② przen. (stać się widocznym) [słońce] to come out; [żyły] to show ③ (zakończyć pobyt) to leave; **wyjść z wojska** to leave the army ④ (uwolnić się) **wyjść z czegoś** to get oneself out of sth [tarapatów, długów] ⑤ (wziąć początek) to originate ⑥ (być skierowanym) [okno] to face (**na coś** sth) ⑦ [książka] to come out ⑧ (udać się) to come out; **nic mu w życiu nie wychodzi** nothing works out for him; **dobrze wychodzić na zdjęciach** to photograph well ⑨ pot. (wyczerpać się) **papierosy mi wyszły** I have run out of cigarettes ⑩ pot. (wyniknąć) to result (**z czegoś** from sth); **na jedno wychodzi** it's all the same; **to ci wyjdzie na zdrowie** it'll do you good; **wychodzi na to, że...** it looks that... ⑪ (wystąpić) to come out; **wyjść z propozycją** to come out with a proposal ⑫ (zagrać) to play; **wyjść w piki** to play a spade

■ **nie móc wyjść z podziwu** to be astounded; **wyjść na głupca** to make a fool of oneself; **wyjść z założenia** to make an assumption; **wyjść za mąż** to get married; **wyjść za kogoś** to marry sb

wykałacz|ka f ① (do przekąsek) skewer ② (do zębów) toothpick

wykańczać impf → **wykończyć**

wykarm|ić pf — **wykarm|iać** impf vt to feed

wykastr|ować pf vt to castrate [osobę, zwierzę]

wykaz m list, register

wyka|zać pf — **wyka|zywać** impf I vt ① (unaocznić) to point [sth] out [nieścisłości, pomyłki]; **śledztwo** ~**zało, że...** the investigation has established that... ② (uzewnętrznić) to display [energię, inicjatywę]

II **wykazać się** — **wykazywać się** ① (pokazać) ~**zać się czymś** to display sth [wiedzą, odpowiedzialnością] ② (popisać się) to distinguish oneself

wykąp|ać pf I vt to bath [dziecko, psa]

II **wykąpać się** to bathe, to have a bath

wykiełk|ować pf vi [roślina] to sprout

wykipi|eć pf vi to boil over

wykiwa|ć pf vt pot. to trick

wykle|ić pf — **wykle|jać** impf vt ① (wylepić) to line (**coś czymś** sth with sth) ② (zrobić obrazek) to paste together [obrazek]

wykluczon|y adi. praed. (niemożliwy) out of the question; (nieprawdopodobny) impossible; (**to**) ~**e!** it's out of the question!

wyklucz|yć *pf* — **wyklucz|ać** *impf* **[]** *vt*
[1] (usunąć z grupy) to expel [2] (wyłączyć) *[osoba]* to rule
[sth] out; *[fakty]* to make [sth] impossible; **nie**
~**am, że...** it's possible that... [3] (spowodować
wykluczenie) to eliminate

[] **wykluczyć się — wykluczać się** to exclude
each other

wyklu|ć się *pf* — **wyklu|wać się** *impf v refl.* to
hatch także przen.

wykła|d *m* lecture

wykładać[1] *impf* → **wyłożyć**

wykład|ać[2] *impf vt* to lecture on *[przedmiot]*

wykładowc|a *m* (academic) teacher; (na kursie)
instructor; (stanowisko) lecturer

wykładzin|a *f* (fitted) carpet

wykole|ić *pf* — **wykole|jać** *impf* **[]** *vt* to derail
[pociąg, tramwaj]

[] **wykoleić się — wykolejać się** [1] *[pociąg]* to
derail [2] przen. *[osoba]* to become demoralized

wykoleje|niec *m* derelict

wykolej|ony *adi.* [1] *[pociąg, tramwaj]* derailed
[2] *[osoba, młodzież]* demoralized

wykombin|ować *pf vt* pot. [1] (wywnioskować) to
work [sth] out [2] (zdobyć) to manage to get

wykon|ać *pf* — **wykon|ywać** *impf vt* [1] (zrobić)
to carry out *[zadanie, pracę]*; to execute *[plan]*;
~**ywać jakiś zawód** to work as sb [2] (wytworzyć) to
make *[napis, przedmiot]* [3] (odtworzyć) to perform
[utwór]

wykona|nie *n* [1] (robocizna) workmanship [2] (pub-
liczna prezentacja) performance

wykonawc|a *m* [1] (planu, testamentu) executor
[2] (artysta) performer [3] (wytwórca) contractor

wykonywać *impf* → **wykonać**

wykończać *impf* → **wykończyć**

wykończe|nie *n* (ozdobny brzeg) trimming

wyk|ończyć *pf* — **wyk|ańczać, wyk|oń-
czać** *impf* **[]** *vt* [1] (doprowadzić do końca) to finish; **być
na** ~**ończeniu** *[praca]* to be close to completion
[2] (zużyć) to use up *[zapasy]* [3] pot. (zabić) to finish off;
ta praca mnie ~**ańcza** przen. this work is
exhausting me

[] **wykończyć się — wykańczać się, wykończać się** pot. to run oneself into the ground

wykop *m* [1] (podkop) pit [2] (roboty ziemne) earthwork
[3] Sport kick

wykop|ać *pf* — **wykop|ywać** *impf vt* [1] (utwo-
rzyć) to dig *[rów]*; to sink *[studnię]* [2] (odkopać) to
unearth [3] pot. (wyrzucić) to boot [sb] out pot.; (z pracy)
to kick [sb] out pot.

wykopalisk|o *n* (znalezisko, teren) excavation

wykopywać *impf* → **wykopać**

wykorzyst|ać *pf* — **wykorzyst|ywać** *impf vt*
[1] (użyć) to use [2] (wyzyskać) to exploit *[osobę]*;
(seksualnie) to take advantage of

wykpi|ć *pf* — **wykpi|wać** *impf* **[]** *vt* to ridicule
[osobę, wady]

[] **wykpić się — wykpiwać się** to weasel out (**od
czegoś** of sth)

wykraczać *impf* → **wykroczyć**

wykra|ść *pf* — **wykra|dać** *impf* **[]** *vt* to steal
(away) *[dokumenty, plany]*

[] **wykraść się — wykradać się** (wyjść) to sneak a.
steal out

wykre|ować *pf* **[]** *vt* (wypromować) to package, to
promote *[aktora, zespół, produkt]*

[] **wykreować się** to create one's image (**na kogoś**
as sb)

wykres *m* graph, chart

wykreśl|ić *pf* — **wykreśl|ać** *impf vt* [1] (skreślić)
to cross [sth] off [2] (narysować) to draw (up) *[projekt]*;
to plot *[krzywą]*

wykrę|cić *pf* — **wykrę|cać** *impf vt* [1] (wyjąć) to
unscrew *[śrubę, żarówkę]* [2] (przekrzywić) to twist *[rękę,
nogę]* [3] (wykonać ewolucję) to turn *[piruet]* [4] (wycisnąć
wodę) to wring *[bieliznę, pranie]*

[] *vi [kierowca, pojazd]* to turn round

[] **wykręcić się — wykręcać się** [1] (odwrócić się)
to turn [2] pot. (wymigać się) to weasel out (**od czegoś**
of sth)

wykrę|t *m* excuse

wykrętn|y *adi. grad.* evasive

wykrocze|nie *n* offence GB, offense US

wykr|oczyć *pf* — **wykr|aczać** *impf vi* [1] (prze-
kroczyć) *[zadanie, problem]* to go beyond (**poza coś**
sth) [2] (dopuścić się przewinienia) to transgress (**przeciwko czemuś** against sth)

wykr|ój *m* [1] (oczu, ust) shape [2] (ubrania) pattern

wykrwaw|ić się *pf* — **wykrwaw|iać się**
impf v refl. [1] (stracić dużo krwi) to lose a lot of blood;
(śmiertelnie) to bleed to death [2] przen. *[pułk, oddział]* to
lose a lot of men

wykry|ć *pf* — **wykry|wać** *impf vt* [1] (ujawnić) to
uncover *[prawdę, spisek]* [2] (znaleźć) to detect
[substancję, wirusa]

wykrztu|sić *pf* — **wykrztu|szać** *impf vt*
[1] (odpluć) to expectorate *[flegmę, ślinę]* [2] pot. (powiedzieć) **nie mógł** ~**sić słowa** he couldn't utter a
word

wykrzyk|nąć *pf* — **wykrzyk|iwać** *impf vt, vi*
to shout (out)

wykrzyknik *m* [1] (znak) exclamation mark
[2] (słowo) interjection

wykrzyw|ić *pf* — **wykrzyw|iać** *impf* **[]** *vt* [1] to
twist *[obcasy, gwóźdź, twarz]* [2] przen. to distort *[sens,
obraz]*

[] **wykrzywić się — wykrzywiać się** [1] *[słup]* to
bend [2] *[twarz]* to be twisted a. contorted

wykształcać *impf* → **wykształcić**

wykształceni|e *n* education; **z** ~**a** by education

wykształ|cić *pf* — **wykształ|cać** *impf* **[]** *vt*
[1] (rozwinąć) to develop *[talent, zdolności, refleks]*
[2] (ukształtować) to form [3] (dać wykształcenie) to educate
[dzieci, młodzież]

II **wykształcić się — wykształcać się** ☐ (rozwinąć się) to develop ② (zdobyć wykształcenie) to get an education

wykształc|ony *adi. [osoba]* educated

wyku|ć *pf* — **wyku|wać** *impf* **I** *vt* ☐ (w metalu) to forge; (w kamieniu) to carve ② (wydrążyć) to cut *[otwór]* ③ (nauczyć się na pamięć) to learn [sth] by heart **II** **wykuć się — wykuwać się** (nauczyć się) to learn [sth] by heart

wykup|ić *pf* — **wykup|ywać** *impf* **I** *vt* ☐ (kupić wszystko) to buy [sth] out ② (odkupić) to buy [sth] back; (z lombardu) to pawn [sth] back ③ (kupić) to buy *[akcje]*; ~**ić polisę** to take out an insurance policy ④ (z niewoli) to ransom *[jeńców, więźniów]* **II** **wykupić się — wykupywać się** ☐ (zapłacić okup) to buy oneself out ② (odebrać fant) to pay a forfeit

wykuwać *impf* → **wykuć**

wykwalifikowan|y *adi.* qualified

wyl|ać *pf* — **wyl|ewać** *impf* **I** *vt* ☐ (opróżnić) to pour [sth] out; (rozlać) to spill; ~**ewać łzy** przen. to shed tears ② (pokryć) to cover *[drogę]* (**czymś** with sth) ③ pot. (z pracy) to fire **II** *vi [rzeka]* to flood **III** **wylać się — wylewać się** ☐ *[zupa, herbata]* to spill ② przen. *[tłum]* to overflow

wylans|ować *pf vt* to promote *[osobę, ideę, piosenkę]*

wylatywać *impf* → **wylecieć**

wyląc się → **wylęgnąć się**

wyląd|ować *pf vi* ☐ (zakończyć lot) to land ② pot. (znaleźć się) to end up

wyle|c, wyle|gnąć *pf* — **wyle|gać** *impf vi [tłum]* to pour out

wyl|ecieć *pf* — **wyl|atywać** *impf vi* ☐ *[ptak, owad]* to fly out a. off ② *[samolot]* to take off ③ (wzbić się) *[dym, para, korek]* to come out; ~**ecieć w powietrze** to explode ④ pot. (wybiec) to rush out ⑤ pot. (wypaść) to fall out ⑥ pot. (z pracy) to be sacked pot.

wylecz|yć *pf vt* to cure także przen.; ~**yć kogoś z ran** to heal sb's wounds **II** **wyleczyć się** ☐ (samego siebie) to cure oneself ② (zostać wyleczonym) to be cured

wylegać *impf* → **wylec**

wylegitym|ować *pf* **I** *vt* to check [sb's] ID **II** **wylegitymować się** to show one's ID

wylęgnąć → **wylec**

wylew *m* ☐ (rzeki) flood ② Med. (krwotok) h(a)emorrhage; (udar mózgu) stroke

wylewać *impf* → **wylać**

wylewn|y *adi. grad. [osoba, powitanie]* effusive

wy|leźć *pf* — **wy|łazić** *impf vi* pot. ☐ (wypełznąć) to scramble out; (wspiąć się) to scramble up ② (wystawać) *[koszula]* to come out (**z czegoś** from sth); *[chusteczka, halka, pistolet]* to peep out (**z czegoś** from sth); *[słoma, sprężyna]* to poke out

(**z czegoś** through sth) ③ (wypaść) *[sierść, włosy]* to come out

wyl|ęgnąć się, wyl|ąc się *pf* — **wyl|ęgać się** *impf vi* to hatch także przen.

wyliczać *impf* → **wyliczyć**

wyliczan|ka *f* (counting-out) rhyme

wylicz|yć *pf* — **wylicz|ać** *impf* **I** *vt* ☐ (wymienić) to enumerate *[wady, zasługi]*; to list *[choroby, utwory, zabytki]* ② (obliczyć) to calculate *[dystans, koszt, prędkość]*; to work out *[sumę, średnią]* **II** **wyliczyć się — wyliczać się** (zdać rachunek) to account (**z czegoś komuś** for sth to sb)

wylos|ować *pf vt* to draw (**kogoś/coś** (for) sb/ sth)

wylo|t *m* ☐ (alei, ulicy) exit; (rury) outlet; (tunelu, wąwozu) mouth ② (balonu, samolotu) take-off ■ **znać kogoś na** ~**t** to know sb inside out

wyludni|ć *pf* — **wyludni|ać** *impf* **I** *vt [epidemia, wojna]* to depopulate *[kraj]* **II** **wyludnić się — wyludniać się** (opustoszeć) *[miasto, ulice]* to become deserted; (utracić mieszkańców) *[kraj, wieś]* to become depopulated

wyładni|eć *pf vi* to become prettier

wyład|ować *pf* — **wyład|owywać** *impf* **I** *vt* ☐ (opróżnić) to unload *[towar, statek]* ② (wypełnić) to load (**coś czymś** sth with sth) ③ przen. (dać ujście) to vent *[frustrację, złość]* (**na kimś** on sb) **II** **wyładować się — wyładowywać się** (znaleźć ujście) *[energia, temperament]* to find release; *[osoba]* to let off steam ③ *[akumulator, bateria]* to run down

wyładun|ek *m* unloading

wyłam|ać *pf* — **wyłam|ywać** *impf* **I** *vt* to break *[ząb]*; to break [sth] away *[deskę, pokrywę]*; to break [sth] down *[drzwi]* **II** **wyłamać się — wyłamywać się** ☐ *[szczebel]* to break; *[deska, ząb]* to break off; *[krata, zamek, zawias]* to give way ② przen. *[członek partii, związku]* to break rank(s)

wyłaniać *impf* → **wyłonić**

wyłazić *impf* → **wyleźć**

wyłączać *impf* → **wyłączyć**

wyłącznie *part.* exclusively; **wstęp** ~ **za okazaniem biletu** admission by ticket only

wyłącznik *m* (off) switch

wyłączn|y *adi. [dystrybutor, spadkobierca]* sole; *[prawo, przywilej, własność]* exclusive

wyłącz|yć *pf* — **wyłącz|ać** *impf* **I** *vt* ☐ (unieruchomić) to cut [sth] off *[gaz, prąd]*; to disconnect *[telefon]*; to turn [sth] off *[komputer, radio, muzykę]* ② (z sieci) to unplug *[kuchenkę, żelazko]* ③ (wyeliminować) to exclude (**kogoś z czegoś** sb from sth) **II** **wyłączyć się — wyłączać się** ☐ (wykluczyć nawzajem) *[założenia, zdania]* to be (mutually) exclusive ② (wycofać się) to withdraw (**z czegoś** from sth) ③ pot. (odłożyć słuchawkę) to hang up ④ (przerwać działanie) *[ogrzewanie, światło]* to go off 5 (zamyślić się) *[osoba]* to tune out pot.

wyłom *m* 1 (wyrwa) breach 2 książk. (odstępstwo) break; ~ **w tradycji** a break with tradition

wyłonić *pf* — **wyłaniać** *impf* **I** *vt* to appoint *[delegację, komisję, zarząd]*; to determine *[zwycięzcę]* **II wyłonić się** — **wyłaniać się** 1 (ukazać się) *[pociąg, księżyc]* to emerge; *[dom, kształt, sylwetka]* to loom (into view) (**z czegoś** out of sth) 2 przen. (powstać) *[trudności]* to arise; *[kwestia, sprawa]* to come up

wyłożyć *pf* — **wykładać** *impf* **I** *vt* 1 (umieścić) to lay [sth] out *[karty, towar]*; to put [sth] down *[trutkę]*; to put [sth] out *[ręczniki]* 2 (pokryć) to cover (**coś czymś** sth with sth); **wyłożyć coś kafelkami** to tile sth 3 (zapłacić) to pay *[pieniądze, sumę]* 4 (przedstawić) to expound *[pogląd, teorię]*; to lay out *[argument, propozycję]* **II wyłożyć się** — **wykładać się** pot. 1 (przewrócić się) *[osoba]* to take a tumble 2 (na egzaminie) to fail

wyłudzić *pf* — **wyłudzać** *impf vt* to wangle (**coś od kogoś** sth out of sb)

wyłupiasty *adi.* pot. *[oczy, ślepia]* protruding

wyłysieć *pf vi* 1 *[osoba, zwierzę]* to go bald 2 przen. *[miotła, pędzel, szczotka]* to lose bristles

wymachiwać *impf vi* ~**iwać czymś** to flap sth *[skrzydłami]*; to flourish sth *[biletem, dokumentem]*; to wave (about) sth *[kapeluszem, rękami]*

wymagać *impf vt* 1 (żądać) to demand (**czegoś od kogoś** sth of sb) 2 (potrzebować) *[chory, maszyna, sytuacja]* to require

wymagający *adi.* demanding

wymaganie *n* (warunek) requirement; (żądanie) demand; **spełniać** ~**nia** to meet the requirements; **mieć (duże)** ~**nia** to be demanding

wymarły *adi. [gatunek, naród, rasa]* extinct; *[okolica, ulice]* deserted

wymarzony *adi. [dom, kandydat, praca]* dream; *[pogoda]* perfect

wymarzyć *pf vt* ~**yć coś sobie** to dream of sth

wymasować *pf vt* to massage

wymawiać *impf* → **wymówić**

wymazać *pf* — **wymazywać** *impf* **I** *vt* 1 (pobrudzić) to smear (**coś czymś** sth with sth) 2 (zetrzeć) to rub [sth] out *[literę, rysunek, słowo]*; ~**zać kogoś z pamięci** przen. to blot sb out of one's memory **II wymazać się** — **wymazywać się** (pobrudzić się) to smear oneself (**czymś** with sth)

wymeldować się *pf* — **wymeldowywać się** *impf v refl.* (z hotelu) to check out (**z czegoś** of sth)

wymiana *f* 1 (zamiana) exchange (**czegoś na coś** of sth for sth); **ostra** ~**a zdań** an angry exchange; ~**a strzałów** a shooting incident; **kurs** ~**y** the exchange rate 2 (zmiana) change, replacement; ~**a oleju** oil change 3 (wizyta) exchange (visit)

wymiar *m* 1 (rozmiar) size; **praca w niepełnym** ~**rze godzin** part-time work; **najwyższy** ~**r kary** the maximum sentence 2 (długość, szerokość) dimension 3 (znaczenie) dimension ❑ ~**r sprawiedliwości** the judiciary

wymienić *pf* — **wymieniać** *impf* **I** *vt* 1 (zrobić zamianę) to exchange *[podarunki, pozdrowienia, spojrzenia, pieniądze]* 2 (zastąpić) to change *[towar, wodę, żarówkę]*; to replace *[rury, uszczelkę]* 3 (przytoczyć) to list *[tytuły]*; to mention *[nazwiska]*; to name *[kraje, planety, rośliny]* **II wymienić się** — **wymieniać się** 1 (zmienić się) *[strażnicy]* to change 2 (dokonać wymiany) to exchange (**czymś z kimś** sth with sb)

wymienny *adi. [część, filtr]* replaceable

wymierać *impf* → **wymrzeć**

wymierny *adi.* 1 (znaczący) *[efekty, korzyści]* notable 2 (obliczalny) measurable 3 Mat. rational

wymierzyć *pf* — **wymierzać** *impf vt* 1 (zmierzyć) to measure (up) 2 (wycelować) to aim (**do kogoś** at sb) 3 (uderzyć) ~**yć komuś cios** to deliver sb a blow; ~**yć komuś policzek** to slap sb in the face 4 (określić wymiar) to mete out *[sprawiedliwość]*; ~**yć komuś grzywnę** to fine sb

wymigać się *pf* — **wymigiwać się** *impf v refl.* pot. to wriggle out (**od czegoś** of sth); ~**ał się od odpowiedzi** he dodged the question; ~**iwać się od pracy** to duck out of work

wymijać *impf* → **wyminąć**

wymijający *adi. [odpowiedź]* evasive

wyminąć *pf* — **wymijać** *impf vt* 1 (przejść, przejechać obok) to pass 2 (wyprzedzić) to overtake 3 (ominąć) to steer clear (**coś** of sth)

wymiotny *adi.* emetic

wymiotować *impf vi* to vomit

wymioty *plt* 1 (torsje) vomiting 2 (wymiociny) vomit

wymknąć się *pf* — **wymykać się** *impf v refl.* 1 (wysunąć się) *[przedmiot]* to slip out; ~**knąć się komuś spod kontroli** *[sprawa]* to get out of hand 2 (uciec) *[osoba]* to escape 3 (wyjść niepostrzeżenie) *[osoba]* to slip out ■ ~**knęło jej się, że...** pot. she let (it) slip that...

wymoczek *m* pot. (pale) weakling

wymodelować *pf vt* to model *[glinę]*; to style *[włosy]*

wymontować *pf* — **wymontowywać** *impf vt* to remove

wymowa *f* 1 (sposób mówienia) pronunciation 2 (znaczenie) meaning

wymowny *adi. grad.* 1 *[gest, spojrzenie]* meaningful 2 *[osoba]* eloquent

wymóc *pf vi* ~**óc coś na kimś** to make sb do sth

wymóg *m* requirement

wymówić *pf* — **wymawiać** *impf* **I** *vt* 1 (wypowiedzieć) to pronounce *[wyraz, słowo, dźwięk]* 2 (powiedzieć) to utter *[słowo, zdanie]* 3 (zerwać umowę) ~**ówić komuś (pracę)** to give sb notice 4 (wytknąć)

~**awiać coś komuś** to reproach sb for sth

II wymówić się — wymawiać się to excuse oneself (**od czegoś** from sth)

wymówie|nie n [1] (zwolnienie) notice [2] (okres) notice period

wymów|ka f [1] (wykręt) excuse [2] (pretensja) reproach

wym|rzeć pf — **wym|ierać** impf vi [1] (umrzeć masowo) to die out a. off; [gatunek] to become extinct [2] (opustoszeć) [miejsce] to become deserted

wymu|sić pf — **wymu|szać** impf vt to extort (**coś od kogoś** sth from sb); ~**sić na kimś zrobienie czegoś** to force sb to do sth

wymusz|ony adi. [uśmiech] forced

wymykać się impf → **wymknąć się**

wymy|sł m [1] (kaprys) whim [2] (zmyślenie) invention

wymyślać[1] impf → **wymyślić**

wymyśla|ć[2] impf vi (krzyczeć) to hurl insults (**komuś** at sb)

wymyśl|ić pf — **wymyślać**[1] impf vt [1] (wynaleźć) to invent [styl, teorię, maszynę]; to devise [metodę] [2] (stworzyć) to think [sth] up [historyjkę, wymówkę]

wymyśln|y adi. grad. [metoda, projekt, kapelusz] fancy; [maszyna] elaborate

wynagradzać impf → **wynagrodzić**

wynagrodze|nie n remuneration; **praca bez** ~**nia** unpaid work

wynagr|odzić pf — **wynagr|adzać** impf vt [1] (zapłacić) to remunerate [2] (odwdzięczyć się) to reward [3] (zrekompensować) to compensate (**komuś coś** sb for sth)

wynaj|ąć pf — **wynaj|mować** impf II vt [1] (wziąć w najem) to rent [lokal]; to hire [sprzęt] [2] (oddać w najem) to rent [sth] out [3] (przyjąć do pracy) to hire

II wynająć się — wynajmować się to hire oneself out

wynajdywać impf → **wynaleźć**

wynaj|em m [1] (komuś) renting; **na** ~**em** for rent [2] (od kogoś) rent, hire

wynajmować impf → **wynająć**

wynalaz|ca m, ~**czyni** f inventor

wynalaz|ek m invention

wyna|leźć pf — **wyna|jdywać, wyna|jdo-wać** impf vt [1] (wyszukać) to find [2] (odkryć) to invent

wynegocj|ować pf vt to negotiate [kontrakt]

wyn|ieść pf — **wyn|osić** impf II vt [1] (usunąć) to take [sth] out [2] przen. (zyskać) to gain [wiedzę] [3] książk. (chwalić) ~**sić kogoś pod niebiosa** to praise sb to the skies

II vi (dawać wynik) to amount to

III wynieść się — wynosić się pot. ~**oś się!** get out of here!

wynik m result; Sport score; (działań) outcome; **w** ~**u czegoś** as a result of sth; ~**i analizy krwi** the results of a blood test

wynik|nąć pf — **wynik|ać** impf vi [1] (powstać) [kłopot, nieporozumienie] to arise [2] (okazać się) to appear; **z tego, co mówi,** ~**a, że...** from what he/she says, it appears that...

wynio|sły adi. [1] [osoba, ton] haughty [2] książk. [góry, budowla] lofty

wyniszcz|yć pf — **wyniszcz|ać** impf II vt to destroy; **kraj** ~**ony przez wojnę** a country ravaged by war

II wyniszczyć się — wyniszczać się to ruin one's health; (nawzajem) to destroy each other

wynosić impf → **wynieść**

wynurz|yć pf — **wynurz|ać** impf II vt ~**yć głowę z wody** to raise one's head out of the water

II wynurzyć się — wynurzać się [1] (wypłynąć) to surface [2] przen. (ukazać się) to emerge

wyobra|zić pf — **wyobra|żać** impf II vt książk. [artysta, obraz] to depict

II wyobrazić sobie — wyobrażać sobie to imagine; ~**z sobie, że...** imagine (that)...; ~**żam sobie** I can imagine; **tylko sobie nie** ~**żaj, że...** but don't imagine (that)...; **co pan sobie** ~**ża?!** how dare you!

wyobraźni|a f [1] (zdolność tworzenia wyobrażeń) imagination; **wytwór** ~**a** a figment of imagination [2] (widzenie przyszłości) vision; **osoba z** ~**ą** a person of vision

wyobrażać impf → **wyobrazić**

wyobraże|nie n [1] (wiedza) idea, notion (**o czymś** of sth); **fałszywe** ~**nia na temat czegoś** misconceived notions about sth [2] (obraz) (w pamięci) image; (w literaturze, sztuce) depiction

wyodrębni|ć pf — **wyodrębni|ać** impf II vt to distinguish [element, składnik]; to isolate [substancję, pierwiastek, składnik]; [cecha, właściwość, wygląd] to mark [sth] out

II wyodrębnić się — wyodrębniać się (powstać) to emerge

wyolbrzymi|ć pf — **wyolbrzymi|ać** impf vt to exaggerate

wyostrz|yć pf — **wyostrz|ać** impf II vt [1] (naostrzyć) to sharpen [nóż, kosę] [2] (uwrażliwić) to train [spostrzegawczość]; to sharpen [zmysły]; to heighten [wrażliwość, czujność]; ~**ony wzrok** keen eyesight [3] (na ekranie) to sharpen [obraz] [4] (uczynić wyrazistym) to make [sth] more prominent [rysy, profil]

II wyostrzyć się — wyostrzać się [1] [zmysły, czujność] to sharpen; [świadomość, wrażliwość] to reach new heights przen. [2] (na ekranie) [obraz] to sharpen [3] [rysy, profil, nos] to become more prominent

wypacać impf → **wypocić**

wypacz|yć pf — **wypacz|ać** impf II vt [1] (odkształcić) to warp [drewno, plastik] [2] (zafałszować) to distort [myśl, wyniki]; to twist [słowa, sens]; to warp [charakter, system wartości]

II wypaczyć się — wypaczać się *[drewno]* to warp; *[charakter, talent]* to become warped

wypa|d *m* [1] (wycieczka) outing [2] Wojsk. raid

wypad|ać *impf v imp.* [1] (być stosownym) to be appropriate; ~**ałoby podziękować** it would be polite to say thank you; **nie ~a tak się przyglądać** it isn't seemly to stare like that [2] (być słusznym) ~**a mieć nadzieję/cieszyć się, że...** one should hope/be glad that...

wypadać² *impf* → **wypaść¹**

wypad|ek II *m* [1] (nieszczęśliwe wydarzenie) accident; ~**ek samochodowy** a car accident; **ulec ~kowi** to have an accident [2] (przypadek, sytuacja) case, occurrence; (zdarzenie) event; **w ~ku czegoś** in case of a. in the event of sth; **w ~ku, gdybym...** in case I...; **w wielu ~kach** in many cases; **w najlepszym ~ku** at best; **na wszelki ~ek** just in case; **w przeciwnym ~ku** otherwise; **w żadnym ~ku** in no case **II wypadki** *plt* events; **rozwój ~ków** developments

wypal|ić *pf* — **wypal|ać** *impf* **II** *vt* [1] (zniszczyć) *[żar, ogień]* to burn [sth] down; *[słońce, upał]* to parch *[roślinność]*; to bake *[ziemię]* [2] (zużyć) to burn *[kubeł węgla]*; to smoke *[papierosa, cygaro, fajkę]* [3] Techn. to bake *[glinę, cegłę]*; to burn *[wapno]*; to roast *[rudę]* [4] (zrobić znak) to burn *[znak, dziurę]* [5] pot. (powiedzieć) to blurt (out) **II** *vi* [1] *[broń]* to go off; ~**ić z pistoletu** to fire a gun [2] pot. *[pomysł, projekt, sprawa]* to be a success **III wypalić się — wypalać się** [1] *[świeca, zapałka]* to burn (itself) out; *[papieros]* to burn away [2] przen. (wyczerpać się) *[uczucie, żądza]* to die away; *[osoba]* to burn oneself out

wypar|ować *pf* — **wypar|owywać** *impf* **II** *vt* to evaporate **II** *vi* [1] *[ciecz]* to evaporate [2] pot. (zniknąć) *[osoba, przedmiot]* to vanish into thin air

wyparz|yć *pf* — **wyparz|ać** *impf vt* to scald

wypast|ować *pf vt* to wax *[podłogę]*; to shine *[buty, skórę]*

wypa|ść, wypa|dać² *impf vi* [1] (wylecieć) *[włosy, zęby]* to fall out; ~**ść komuś z rąk** to slip out of sb's grasp; ~**ść komuś z głowy** to slip sb's mind; ~**ść z trasy** to go off course [2] (ukazać się nagle) *[osoba, zwierzę]* to run out; *[pojazd]* to come out (at full speed) [3] (wydarzyć się) *[rocznica, święto]* to fall [4] (przytrafić się) **coś im ~dło i...** something came up and...; **ciągnęliśmy losy i ~dło na mnie** we drew lots and it fell to me [5] (okazać się) *[osoba, plan]* to come out; **dobrze ~da jako mówca** he comes out well as a speaker

wyp|chać *pf* — **wyp|ychać¹** *impf* **II** *vt* to stuff *[poduszkę, materac, ptaka]*; to cram *[bagażnik, plecak, szafę]*; **broń ~ychała mu kieszeń** the gun made his pocket bulge

II wypchać się — wypychać się *[nogawki, sweter]* to bag ■ ~**chaj się** pot. get stuffed pot.

wyp|chnąć *pf* — **wyp|ychać²** *impf vt* [1] (przesunąć) to push [2] (pozbyć się) to dispose of *[towar, produkcję]*

wypeł|nić *pf* — **wypeł|niać** *impf* **II** *vt* [1] (napełnić) to fill *[pojemnik, otwór, pomieszczenie]*; to fill [sth] in *[dziurę]* [2] (wywiązać się) to fulfil, to fulfill US *[obowiązek, żądanie]*; to carry out *[życzenia, rozkaz]*; to perform *[rolę, funkcję, zadanie]* [3] (wpisywać dane) to fill [sth] in GB a. out US *[ankietę, formularz]* **II wypełnić się — wypełniać się** [1] (zapełnić się) *[pojemnik, przestrzeń]* to fill up [2] książk. *[przepowiednia, zapowiedź]* to come true

wypę|dzić *pf* — **wypę|dzać** *impf vt* (z kraju, z miasta) to expel; (z domu) to chase [sb] out

wyp|iąć *pf* — **wyp|inać** *impf* **II** *vt* [1] (wyjąć) to take [sth] out *[spinki, kartki]*; to unfasten *[broszkę, kolczyki]* [2] (wysunąć do przodu) to stick [sth] out *[brzuch]*; ~**iąć pierś** to throw out one's chest; ~**iąć tyłek** pot. (pochylić się) to stick one's bottom in the air **II wypiąć się — wypinać się** [1] (poluzować się) *[broszka]* to unfasten [2] pot. (pochylić się) to stick one's bottom in the air pot. [3] pot. (okazać lekceważenie) to thumb one's nose pot. (**na kogoś** at sb)

wypi|ć *pf* — **wypi|jać** *impf vt* to drink *[mleko, sok, lekarstwo]*; **lubić (sobie) ~ć** pot. to like the bottle pot.

wypiek II *m* baking; **domowe ~i** home-baked cakes and pastries **II wypieki** *plt* (rumieńce) flush

wypierać¹ *impf* → **wyprzeć¹**

wypierać² *impf* → **wyprać**

wypijać *impf* → **wypić**

wypinać *impf* → **wypiąć**

wypis II *m* (fragment tekstu) extract **II wypisy** *plt* (podręcznik) reader

wypi|sać *pf* — **wypi|sywać** *impf* **II** *vt* [1] (sporządzić) to write [sth] out, to write [sth] up US *[receptę, przepustkę, czek]* [2] (przepisać) to copy *[nazwiska, tytuły, cytat]* (**z czegoś** from sth); (spisać) to make a list of [3] (ze szpitala) to discharge *[pacjenta]* [4] (zużyć) to use [sth] up *[atrament, ołówek]* **II wypisać się — wypisywać się** [1] (zrezygnować) to withdraw (**z czegoś** from sth) [2] (zużyć się) *[atrament, wkład]* to run out

wyplą|tać *pf* — **wyplą|tywać** *impf* **II** *vt* to disentangle (**coś z czegoś** sth from sth) **II wyplątać się — wyplątywać się** to disentangle oneself (**z czegoś** from sth)

wyp|leć, wyp|ielić pot. *pf* — **wyp|ielać** *impf vt* to weed *[ogródek, grządkę]*; to remove *[chwasty]*

wyple|nić *pf* — **wyple|niać** *impf vt* to root up *[perz, chwasty]*; to eradicate *[zarazki, choroby]*; przen. to root out *[korupcję, przestępczość]*

wyplu|ć, wyplu|nąć *pf* — **wyplu|wać** *impf vt* to spit [sth] out *[pestkę, gumę do życia]*; przen. *[automat]* to spew (out) *[bilet, monety]*

wypła|cić *pf* — **wypła|cać** *impf vt* (zapłacić) to pay *[kwotę, pensję]*; (wycofać) to withdraw *[pieniądze]*

wypłaszać *impf* → **wypłoszyć**

wypła|ta *f* (wypłacanie należności) payment; (z własnego konta) withdrawal; **po ~cie** after pay day

wypł|oszyć *pf* — **wypł|aszać** *impf vt* to chase [sb] out

wypłowi|eć *pf vi* to fade

wypłu|kać *pf* — **wypłu|kiwać** *impf vt* to rinse (out) *[pranie, naczynia, piasek]*; ~**kiwać złoto** to pan for gold

wypły|nąć *pf* — **wypły|wać** *impf vi* [1] (odpłynąć) *[statek]* to sail out; ~**wać w morze** to go (out) to sea [2] (wynurzyć się) *[pływak, wieloryb]* to surface; przen. *[prawda]* to come out [3] (wyciec) *[ciecz]* to flow, to run [4] (wynikać) to arise (**z czegoś** from a. out of sth) [5] pot. (osiągnąć sukces) to make it pot. [6] (mieć źródło) *[rzeka]* to have its source

wyp|ocić *pf* — **wyp|acać** *impf* [I] *vt* to sweat [sth] out *[toksyny]*

[II] **wypocić się** — **wypacać się** to sweat heavily

wypocin|y *plt* rubbishy writing pot.

wypocz|ąć *pf* — **wypocz|ywać** *impf vi* to get some rest

wypoczyn|ek *m* rest

wypoczywać *impf* → **wypocząć**

wypog|odzić *pf* — **wypog|adzać** *impf* [I] *vt* to brighten *[twarz]*

[II] **wypogodzić się** — **wypogadzać się** [1] *[niebo]* to clear up [2] przen. *[twarz]* to brighten (up)

wypom|nieć *pf* — **wypom|inać** *impf vt* ~**nieć komuś coś** to reproach sb for sth

wyposażać *impf* → **wyposażyć**

wyposaże|nie *n* (kuchni, łazienki) fittings; (warsztatu, gabinetu) equipment

wyposaż|yć *pf* — **wyposaż|ać** *impf vt* to equip (**coś w coś** sth with sth)

wypowiadać *impf* → **wypowiedzieć**

wypowiedze|nie *n* notice; **z trzymiesięcznym** ~**niem** with three months' notice

wypowi|edzieć *pf* — **wypowi|adać** *impf* [I] *vt* [1] (oznajmić) to utter *[zaklęcie]*; ~**edzieć życzenie** to make a wish [2] (wyrazić) to express *[opinię]* [3] (wymówić) ~**edzieć komuś pracę** to give sb notice [4] (ogłosić) to declare *[wojnę]* (**komuś** on sb)

[II] **wypowiedzieć się** — **wypowiadać się** to speak; ~**adać się o czymś z uznaniem** to speak favourably of sth

wypowie|dź *f* statement; **sposób** ~**dzi artystycznej** przen. a mode of artistic expression

wypożyczać *impf* → **wypożyczyć**

wypożyczalni|a *f* (książek) (lending) library; (sprzętu, samochodów) rental company

wypożycz|yć *pf* — **wypożycz|ać** *impf vt* ~**yć coś komuś** to lend sb sth; ~**yć coś od kogoś** to borrow sth from sb; ~**yć żaglówkę** to hire a boat

wypracowa|nie *n* composition

wyp|rać *pf* — **wyp|ierać²** *impf vt* to wash *[obrus, ubranie]*; ~**rany z honoru** przen. devoid of honour

wypras|ować *pf vt* to iron *[ubranie, obrus]*

wypraszać¹ *impf* → **wyprosić**

wyprasza|ć² *impf vi* ~**m to sobie!** I beg your pardon!

wypraw|a *f* expedition

wyprawiać¹ *impf* → **wyprawić**

wyprawia|ć² *impf* [I] *vi* **co ty** ~**sz?** what do you think you're doing?

[II] **wyprawiać się** to be going on; **co tu się** ~? what's going on here?

wypraw|ić *pf* — **wypraw|iać** *impf* [I] *vt* [1] (wysłać) to send *[osobę]* [2] (urządzić) to give *[przyjęcie, ucztę, bal]* [3] to tan *[skórę]*

[II] **wyprawić się** — **wyprawiać się** to set off

wypręż|yć *pf* — **wypręż|ać** *impf* [I] *vt* to throw out *[pierś]*; to throw back *[ramiona]*

[II] **wyprężyć się** — **wyprężać się** *[osoba, mięśnie]* to tense up; *[lina, sznur]* to tighten

wyproduk|ować *pf vt* *[osoba, fabryka, kraj]* to produce

wyprom|ować *pf vt* to promote *[film, towar, kulturę]*

wypr|osić *pf* — **wypr|aszać¹** *impf vt* [1] (wybłagać) to wheedle [2] (kazać wyjść) to turn [sb] out; ~**osić kogoś za drzwi** to show sb the door

wyprost|ować *pf* — **wyprost|owywać** *impf* [I] *vt* [1] (rozprostować, poprawić) to straighten *[plecy, drut]* [2] (wyrównać) to smooth (out) *[papier, fałdy]* [3] pot. (wyjaśnić) to straighten out *[sprawę]*; to put [sth] right *[sytuację, błędy]*

[II] **wyprostować się** — **wyprostowywać się** [1] *[papier, fałdy]* to smooth out [2] *[osoba]* to straighten up

wyprowa|dzić *pf* — **wyprowa|dzać** *impf* [I] *vt* [1] (pomóc wyjść) to lead [sb/sth] out; ~**dzić psa na spacer** to walk the dog; ~**dzić samochód z garażu** to take the car out of the garage; ~**dzić kraj z kryzysu** przen. to pull the country out of recession [2] (wywnioskować) to deduce *[wniosek, twierdzenie]*; to derive *[wzór]*

[II] **wyprowadzić się** — **wyprowadzać się** to move (out)

wyprób|ować *pf* — **wyprób|owywać** *impf vt* [1] (sprawdzić) to try [sth] out [2] (doświadczyć) to put [sb/sth] to the test *[osobę, uczciwość, cierpliwość]*

wypróbowan|y *adi.* *[metoda, przepis]* tried-and-tested; *[osoba]* reliable

wypróżni|ć *pf* — **wypróżni|ać** *impf* [I] *vt* to empty *[kieszenie, szuflady]*

[II] **wypróżnić się** — **wypróżniać się** to have a bowel movement

wypróżnie|nie *n* bowel movement
wypru|ć *pf* — **wypru|wać** *impf* **[]** *vt* to unpick *[fastrygę]*
 [II] wypruć się — wypruwać się *[podszewka, kieszeń]* to come undone a. unstitched
 ■ ~wać z siebie żyły pot. to slog one's guts out pot.
wyprysk *m* pimple
wyp|rzeć *pf* — **wyp|ierać**[1] *impf* **[]** *vt* to drive *[nieprzyjaciela, konkurencję]*; **pergamin został** ~**arty przez papier** parchment was supplanted by paper
 [II] wyprzeć się — wypierać się [1] (zaprzeczyć) to deny (**czegoś** sth) [2] (wyrzec się) to disown *[krewnego]*; to renounce *[wiary, własnych korzeni]*
wyprzedaż *f* sale; **letnia** ~ the summer sales; **na** ~**y** at the sales GB, on sale US
wyprze|dzić *pf* — **wyprze|dzać** *impf* *vt* to overtake *[samochód, pieszego]*; to outdistance *[rywala, konkurencję]*
wypuk|ły *adi.* *[tarcza, kształt]* convex; *[oczy, czoło, brzuch]* bulging
wypunkt|ować *pf* — **wypunkt|owywać** *impf* *vt* to enumerate *[zadania, wnioski]*
wypu|ścić *pf* — **wypu|szczać** *impf* **[]** *vt* [1] (upuścić) to let go (**coś** of sth) [2] (uwolnić) to release *[więźnia]*; to let [sth] out *[powietrze]*; ~**ścić strzałę z łuku** to shoot an arrow [3] (wprowadzić do obiegu) to issue *[znaczki, banknoty]* [4] (wydać) *[roślina]* to put out *[korzenie, liście]*
 [II] wypuścić się — wypuszczać się pot. to set out
wypychać *impf* → **wypchnąć**
wyrabiać[1] *impf* → **wyrobić**
wyrabia|ć[2] *impf* **[]** *vt* [1] (produkować) to manufacture [2] pot. (dokazywać) **co ty** ~**sz?** what do you think you're doing?
 [II] wyrabiać się *v imp.* to be going on; **co tu się** ~**?** what's going on here?
wyrachowan|y *adi.* *[osoba]* calculating; *[postępowanie]* calculated
wyrastać *impf* → **wyrosnąć**
wyraz **[]** *m* [1] (słowo) word; **przekazać komuś** ~**y szacunku** książk. to give one's regards to sb [2] (przejaw, objaw) expression; ~ **twarzy** a facial expression; **dać** ~ **czemuś** to express sth
 [II] nad wyraz *adv.* książk. exceptionally
 ■ być bez ~u to be bland
wyra|zić *pf* — **wyra|żać** *impf* **[]** *vt* to express *[opinię, życzenie, uczucia]*
 [II] wyrazić się — wyrażać się [1] (mówić) to speak; **że się tak** ~**żę** so to speak [2] (objawić się) to manifest itself
wyraźnie *adv. grad.* clearly; **najwyraźniej...** obviously..., clearly...
wyraźn|y *adi. grad.* *[smak, zapach]* distinct; *[aluzja, groźba]* clear
wyrażać *impf* → **wyrazić**
wyraże|nie *n* expression

wyrecyt|ować *pf* *vt* to recite
wyregul|ować *pf* — **wyregul|owywać** *impf* *vt* to set *[temperaturę]*; to adjust *[zegarek, wagę]*
wyrejestr|ować *pf* — **wyrejestr|owywać** *impf* *vt* to sign [sth] off *[firmę, samochód]*
wyremont|ować *pf* *vt* to renovate *[dom, mieszkanie]*; to repair *[dach, maszynę]*
wyreżyser|ować *pf* *vt* [1] to direct *[film, sztukę]* [2] (zaplanować) to stage *[rozmowę]*
wyręcz|yć *pf* — **wyręcz|ać** *impf* **[]** *vt* to help; ~**yć kogoś w robieniu czegoś** to do sth for sb
 [II] wyręczyć się — wyręczać się (skorzystać z pomocy) ~**ać się kimś w robieniu czegoś** to make sb do sth for one
wyr|obić *pf* — **wyr|abiać**[1] *impf* **[]** *vt* [1] pot. to develop; ~**obić coś sobie** to develop sth *[styl, gust]*; to build sth *[mięśnie]* [2] pot. (uzyskać) to get; ~**obić komuś posadę** to get sb a job [3] to knead *[ciasto]*
 [II] wyrobić się — wyrabiać się [1] (ukształtować się) *[cecha, nawyk]* to form [2] pot. (zniszczyć się) *[łożysko, śruba]* to wear out [3] pot. *[osoba]* to become sophisticated; *[styl, smak, gust]* to improve [4] pot. (nadążyć) to make it
wyroczni|a *f* oracle; przen. authority
wyrod|ek *m* black sheep pot.
wyrodn|y *adi.* *[syn, matka]* uncaring
wyrok *m* [1] (kara) sentence; **odsiedzieć** ~ pot. to do time pot. [2] (orzeczenie sądu) verdict; ~**i losu** przen. decree of fate
wyr|osnąć *pf* — **wyr|astać** *impf vi* [1] (urosnąć) to grow; (wydorośleć) to grow up; ~**osnąć z czegoś** to grow out of sth; ~**osnąć na kogoś** to grow up to be sb [2] *[ciasto]* to rise [3] przen. (pojawić się) to materialize; *[budynek]* to spring up; ~**osnąć jak spod ziemi** to come out of nowhere [4] przen. (przerastać) to rise; ~**astać ponad otoczenie** to rise above a. to eclipse those around one [5] przen. (wywodzić się) to originate
wyrost|ek *m* [1] pot. (chłopiec) youngster [2] Anat. process; ~**ek robaczkowy** appendix
wyrozumia|ły *adi.* understanding
wyr|ób *m* [1] (produkt) product [2] (produkcja) production
wyrówn|ać *pf* — **wyrówn|ywać** *impf* **[]** *vt* [1] (wygładzić) to smooth *[powierzchnię]* [2] (ustawić w linii) to align [3] (ujednolicić) to level; ~**ywać szanse** to give equal opportunity [4] (zrekompensować) to compensate; ~**ać dług** to settle a debt [5] Sport (zremisować) to equalize
 [II] wyrównać się — wyrównywać się *[puls, ciśnienie]* to become even
wyróżni|ć *pf* — **wyróżni|ać** *impf* *vt* [1] (faworyzować) to favour GB, to favor US [2] (odróżnić) to distinguish [3] (nagrodzić) to award
 [II] wyróżnić się — wyróżniać się to stand out
wyróżnie|nie *n* distinction

wyrusz|yć *pf* — **wyrusz|ać** *impf vi* to set off

wyr|wać *pf* — **wyr|ywać** *impf* **[]** *vt* [1] (wyszarpnąć) to tear [sth] out *[kartkę]*; to root [sth] out *[roślinę]*; to pull [sth] out *[ząb]*; ~**wać komuś torebkę** to snatch sb's bag [2] przen. (obudzić) to shake [sb] out (**z czegoś** of sth) [3] przen. (uwolnić) to free (**kogoś z czegoś** sb from sth)

[] *vi* pot. (pobiec) to run

[] **wyrwać się** — **wyrywać się** [1] (wydostać się) to break out; **okrzyk** ~**wał mu się z gardła** a scream escaped his lips [2] pot. (wybrać się) to get away [3] pot. (powiedzieć) to come out (**z czymś** with sth)

wyr|yć *pf* **[]** *vt* [1] (wyżłobić) to dig *[rów, tunel, wykop]* [2] (wyrzeźbić) to engrave (**coś w czymś** sth into sth)

[] **wyryć się** książk. (pozostawić ślad) to be engraved

wyrywać *impf* → **wyrwać**

wyryw|ki *plt* **na** ~**ki** at random

wyrzą|dzić *pf* — **wyrzą|dzać** *impf vt* to cause *[przykrość]*

wyrze|c *pf* — **wyrze|kać** *impf* **[]** *vt* książk. to utter *[słowo]*

[] **wyrzec się** — **wyrzekać się** to renounce *[wiary, ideałów, przyjemności]*; to disown *[syna, córki]*

wyrzecze|nie *n* sacrifice

wyrzeźb|ić *pf vt* to sculpt; (w drewnie) to carve

wyrzu|cać *impf vi* książk. to reproach (**coś komuś** sb for sth)

wyrzu|cić *pf* — **wyrzu|cać²** *impf vt* [1] (pozbyć się) to throw [sth] away a. out [2] pot. (wysadzić) to drop [sb] off *[pasażera]* [3] przen. (wypędzić) to throw [sb] out; ~**cić kogoś z pracy** to fire sb

wyrzu|t *m* [1] (głowy, ręki) thrust [2] (wymówka) reproach; **z** ~**tem** reproachfully; ~**ty sumienia** pricks of conscience

wyrzut|ek *m* outcast

wyrzutni|a *f* launcher

wysa|dzić *pf* — **wysa|dzać** *impf vt* [1] (z samochodu) to drop [sth] off; (ze statku) to put [sb] down [2] (wystawić) to put [sth] out *[głowę, rękę]* [3] (zburzyć) to blow [sth] up [4] (obsadzić) to plant *[sadzonki]* [5] (ozdobić) to set; ~**dzany drogimi kamieniami** set with precious stones

wys|chnąć *pf* — **wys|ychać** *impf vi [woda, ciasto]* to dry; *[farba, lakier]* to set; *[źródło]* to run dry; *[osoba]* to shrivel

wysiadać *impf* → **wysiąść**

wysiad|ywać¹ *impf vi* to sit (about)

wysiad|ywać² *impf* → **wysiedzieć**

wysi|ąść *pf* — **wysi|adać** *impf vi* [1] (z autobusu) to get off; (z samochodu) to get out (of) [2] pot. (zepsuć się) *[samochód, urządzenie]* to conk out pot.

wysiedl|ić *pf* — **wysiedl|ać** *impf vt* to displace *[ludność]*; to relocate *[lokatora]*

wysi|edzieć *pf* — **wysi|adywać²** *impf* **[]** *vt [ptak]* to hatch *[jajka]*

[] *vi* (usiedzieć) ~**edzieć na filmie** to sit through a film

wysika|ć się *pf v refl.* pot. to pee pot.

wysil|ić *pf* — **wysil|ać** *impf* **[]** *vt* to strain *[wzrok, słuch, wyobraźnię]*; ~**ić umysł** to (w)rack one's brain(s)

[] **wysilić się** — **wysilać się** to make an effort

wysił|ek *m* effort

wysk|oczyć *pf* — **wysk|akiwać** *impf vi* [1] (wydostać się) to jump; ~**oczyć przez okno** to jump out (of) the window [2] pot. (pojawić się) *[pojazd]* to come; ~**oczyła mu wysypka** he came out in a rash [3] pot. (przydarzyć się) to come up [4] pot. (wyjść na chwilę) to pop out pot. [5] pot. (powiedzieć) ~**oczyć z czymś** to blurt sth (out)

wyskok *m* [1] (skok) jump [2] pot. (wybryk) excess [3] pot. (wyjazd) jaunt

wys|łać¹ *pf* — **wys|yłać** *impf vt* [1] (przekazać) to send *[list, pieniądze, osobę]* [2] (emitować) to emit *[sygnał]*

wy|słać², **wy|ścielić** *pf* — **wy|ściełać**, **wy|ścielać** *impf vt* (pokryć) to line; **wyściełane meble** upholstered furniture

wysł|owić się *pf* — **wysł|awiać** *impf v refl.* to express oneself

wysłuch|ać *pf* — **wysłuch|iwać** *impf vt* [1] (do końca) to hear [sb/sth] out *[osoby, prośby]*; to listen to *[koncertu]* [2] (spełnić) to answer *[prośby, apelu]*

wysłuż|ony *adi. [obuwie, ubranie]* worn-out; *[samochód]* run-down

wysmark|ać *pf* — **wysmark|iwać** *impf* pot.

[] *vt* ~**ać nos** to blow one's nose

[] **wysmarkać się** — **wysmarkiwać się** to blow one's nose

wysmuk|ły *adi. grad. [dziewczyna, sylwetka, kolumna]* slender

wysoce *adv.* książk. highly

wy|soki **[]** *adi.* [1] (duży) *[wieża, budynek, lot, półka]* high; *[osoba]* tall [2] (znaczny) *[ceny, stawki, temperatura, jakość]* high; **wysokiej klasy specjalista** a top-ranking specialist; **stworzony do wyższych celów** made for better things; **Sąd Najwyższy** the Supreme Court [3] *[dźwięk, głos]* high, high-pitched [4] (w gramatyce) **stopień wyższy** the comparative; **stopień najwyższy** the superlative

[] **z wysoka** *adv. [patrzeć, zejść, spadać]* from a height; **traktować kogoś z wysoka** przen. to look down on sb

wy|soko **[]** *adv. grad.* [1] (w górze) *[skoczyć, rzucić, latać]* high [2] (dużo) highly; **wysoko oprocentowany** high-interest; **(co) najwyżej** at (the) most [3] (w hierarchii) **wysoko urodzony** highborn; **wysoko postawione osoby** people in high places; **wysoko mierzyć** to aim high [4] *[śpiewać]* high

[] **wyżej** *adv. comp.* (w tekście) above

wysokogórs|ki *adi. [klimat, roślinność]* alpine, mountain; *[sprzęt, klub]* mountaineering

wysokościow|iec *m* skyscraper

wysokoś|ć *f* [1] (osoby, budynku, drzewa) height; **na ~ci 5000 m n.p.m.** at 5000 m above sea level; **na ~ci czwartego piętra** at fourth floor level [2] (temperatury, ciśnienia) level; (zarobków, mandatu) amount; (odsetek, bezrobocia) rate [3] (dźwięku) pitch

wysp|a *f* island

wys|pać się *pf* — **wys|ypiać się** *impf v refl.* to get enough sleep

wysportowan|y *adi.* fit

wyspowiada|ć *pf* [] *vt* to hear [sb's] confession [] **wyspowiadać się** to make one's confession

wystarczać *impf* → **wystarczyć**

wystarczając|y *adi.* sufficient

wystarcz|yć *pf* — **wystarcz|ać** *impf vi* to be enough; **nie ~yło mi pieniędzy** I didn't have enough money

wystart|ować *pf vi* [1] (samolot, rakieta) to take off; (biegacz, kolarz) to start [2] (wziąć udział) to take part (**w czymś** in sth)

wystaw|a *f* [1] (sztuki) exhibition; (psów, kotów, kwiatów) show [2] (w sklepie) display; **~a sklepowa** a shop window; **na ~ie** in the window

wystaw|ić *pf* — **wystaw|iać** *impf* [] *vt* [1] (wynieść na zewnątrz) to put [sth] out [2] (wysunąć) to stick [sth] out [3] (teatr, reżyser) to stage (sztukę, komedię, rewię) [4] (na wystawie) to exhibit (dzieła sztuki); to display (towary) [5] (skierować) to expose; **~ić kogoś na próbę** to put sb to the test [6] (zgłosić) to enter (konia, drużynę) [7] (wybudować) to erect (pomnik) [8] (sporządzić) to make [sth] out (czek, rachunek); to issue (dokument) [9] (nauczyciel) to give (ocenę) [] **wystawić się** — **wystawiać się** to expose oneself (**na coś** to sth)

wyst|ąpić *pf* — **wyst|ępować** *impf vi* [1] (wyjść) to step out; **~ąpić z brzegów** (rzeka) to overflow [2] (podjąć działanie) to take action; (odegrać rolę) to act; **~ąpić o podwyżkę** to ask for a rise; **~ąpić w charakterze gospodyni** to act as a hostess [3] (zabrać głos) to speak; **~ąpić z wnioskiem** to put forward a motion [4] (zagrać) (w filmie) to act; (z koncertem, w cyrku) to perform; **~ąpić na przyjęciu w nowej sukni** to appear at a party wearing a new dress [5] (z organizacji) to step out (**z czegoś** of sth) [6] (pojawić się) (objawy) to appear [7] (żyć, rosnąć) (gatunek, roślina) to occur

wystąpie|nie *n* [1] (przemowa) speech [2] (rozruchy) riot; **zbrojne ~nia** armed riots

wysteryliz|ować *pf vt* to sterilize (gazę, strzykawkę); to sterilize a. neuter (psa, kota)

występ *m* [1] (popis) performance; **~ publiczny** a public appearance [2] (wystająca część) projection

występ|ek *m* offence GB, offense US

występować *impf* → **wystąpić**

wystrasz|yć *pf* [] *vt* [1] (przestraszyć) to scare [2] (przepłoszyć) to scare [sb] away [] **wystraszyć się** to get scared (**kogoś/czegoś** of sb/sth)

wystr|oić się *pf v refl.* to dress up

wystr|ój *m* decor

wystrza|ł *m* (strzał) shot; (huk) bang

wystrzega|ć się *impf v refl.* to avoid (**czegoś** sth); **~ć się, żeby nie...** to be careful not to...

wystrzel|ić *pf* — **wystrzel|iwać** *impf vt, vi* [1] (osoba, broń) to fire; (pocisk) to shoot out; (rakieta) to shoot up; **~ić z łuku** to shoot a bow [2] (wysłać) to launch (rakietę, satelitę) [3] pot. (powiedzieć) to blurt out; (wymyślić) to come up (**z czymś** with sth)

wystrzęp|ić *pf* [] *vt* to fray (tkaninę) [] **wystrzępić się** (brzeg, tkanina) to fray

wystyg|nąć *pf vi* to cool off; (nadmiernie) to go cold

wysu|nąć *pf* — **wysu|wać** *impf* [] *vt* [1] (przestawić) to move; **~nąć skrzynkę za drzwi** to move the chest to outside the door [2] (wyciągnąć) to pull [sth] out (szufladę); to stretch [sth] out (pazury); to stick [sth] out (nogę, rękę) [3] (przedstawić) to put forward (wniosek) [] **wysunąć się** — **wysuwać się** [1] (przemieścić się) to come out; **~nąć się na prowadzenie** to take the lead [2] (wypaść, wyjść) to slip out

wysusz|yć *pf* — **wysusz|ać** *impf* [] *vt* [1] (uczynić suchym) to dry off (pranie, drzewo); to dry (włosy); to dry up (glebę) [2] pot. (wypić) to drain (butelkę) [] **wysuszyć się** — **wysuszać się** (pranie, siano) to dry (off); (skóra) to dry up; (osoba) to dry oneself (off)

wysuwać *impf* → **wysunąć**

wyswob|odzić *pf* — **wyswob|adzać** *impf* książk. [] *vt* to free [] **wyswobodzić się — wyswobadzać się** to free oneself (**z czegoś** from sth)

wysychać *impf* → **wyschnąć**

wysyłać *impf* → **wysłać**

wysyp|ać *pf* — **wysyp|ywać** *impf* [] *vt* [1] (usunąć) to pour (piasek, mąkę) [2] (posypać) to sprinkle (blachę); **~ać podjazd żwirem** to gravel a drive(way) [] **wysypać się — wysypywać się** [1] (wypaść) (cukier, mąka, sól) to pour out; (przedmioty) to fall out [2] (wyjść) (tłum) to pile out

wysypiać się *impf* → **wyspać się**

wysypisk|o *n* dump

wysyp|ka *f* Med. rash

wysypywać *impf* → **wysypać**

wyszal|eć się *pf v refl.* pot. (osoba) to blow off steam pot.

wyszczególni|ć *pf* — **wyszczególni|ać** *impf vt* to detail

wyszczególnie|nie *n* detailed list

wyszczerb|ić *pf* — **wyszczerb|iać** *impf* [] *vt* to chip (ostrze, ząb, talerz) [] **wyszczerbić się — wyszczerbiać się** (nóż, ząb, talerz) to get chipped

wyszczerz|yć *pf* — **wyszczerz|ać** *impf* [] *vt* to bare (zęby, kły); **~yć zęby w uśmiechu** to grin

II **wyszczerzyć się** — **wyszczerzać się** pot. to grin

wyszep|tać pf — **wyszep|tywać** impf vt to whisper

wyszk|olić pf **I** vt to train [osobę, zwierzę]

II **wyszkolić się** [osoba] to get training

wyszlif|ować pf vt **1** (nadać kształt) to cut [kryształ]; (wypolerować) to polish [kamień szlachetny] **2** przen. (udoskonalić) to polish (up) [styl]

wyszor|ować pf **I** vt to scrub [podłogę, garnek]

II **wyszorować się** to scrub oneself

wyszuk|ać pf — **wyszuk|iwać** impf vt to seek [sth] out

wyszukan|y adi. [potrawa, strój] elaborate; [komplement, słownictwo] sophisticated

wyszukiwać impf → wyszukać

wyszy|ć pf — **wyszy|wać** impf vt to embroider

wyścielić pf → wysłać²

wyściełać impf → wysłać²

wyścig **I** m race także przen.; **na** ~**i** vying with each other

II **wyścigi** plt (teren) race course

wyścigow|y adi. [rower, samochód, tor] racing

wyściół|ka f padding

wyśle|dzić pf vt to track (down) [osobę, zwierzę]; to detect [błędy]

wyśliz|gnąć się, **wyśliz|nąć się** pf — **wy-śliz|giwać się** impf v refl. to slip

wyśmi|ać pf — **wyśmi|ewać** impf vt to laugh (coś at sth); to ridicule [osobę]

wyśmieni|ty adi. grad. [potrawa, posiłek] delicious; [humor, zabawa] excellent

wyśmiewać impf → wyśmiać

wyśmiewa|ć się impf v refl. to laugh (z czegoś at sth)

wyświadcz|yć pf — **wyświadcz|ać** impf vt to do [przysługę]

wyświechtan|y adi. pot. [marynarka] worn out; [słowa, zwroty, frazesy] hackneyed

wyświetl|ić pf — **wyświetl|ać** impf vt **1** (pokazać) to project [slajdy, przezrocza]; to show [film] **2** (wyjaśnić) to clarify [fakty, okoliczności]

wytaczać impf → wytoczyć

wytapet|ować pf **I** vt to wallpaper [ściany]

II **wytapetować się** pot., żart. to plaster one's face with make-up

wytarg|ować pf vt ~**ować parę złotych** to talk the price down by a few zlotys

wytar|ty adi. [zwrot, hasło] hackneyed

wytęp|ić pf vt to wipe out [ludność]; to kill off [zwierzynę, ptactwo]; to eradicate [zło, przesądy]

wytęż|yć pf — **wytęż|ać** impf vt ~**yć wzrok** to look hard; ~**yć siły** to summon up one's strength

wyt|knąć pf — **wyt|ykać** impf vt **1** (wysunąć) to stick [sth] out [głowę, ogon] **2** (zwrócić uwagę) to point [sth] out [błędy]

wytłumacze|nie n explanation; (usprawiedliwienie) excuse

wytłumacz|yć pf **I** vt **1** (wyjaśnić) to explain; ~**yć komuś, żeby coś zrobił** to talk sb into doing sth **2** (usprawiedliwić) to excuse

II **wytłumaczyć się** to excuse oneself (z czegoś for (doing) sth)

wyt|oczyć pf — **wyt|aczać** impf **I** vt **1** to roll [beczkę, piłkę] **2** (przedstawić) to put [sth] forward [argumenty, żale, racje]

II **wytoczyć się** — **wytaczać się** **1** [pojazd] to roll **2** pot. (wyjść) [osoba] to roll out pot.

wytrawn|y adi. grad. **1** [gracz, znawca] expert **2** [wino] dry

wytrą|cić pf — **wytrą|cać** impf **I** vt **1** (z ręki) to knock [sth] out **2** (wyrwać) ~**cić kogoś z czegoś** to throw sb off sth [snu, równowagi] **3** (podczas reakcji) to precipitate

II **wytrącić się** — **wytrącać się** [substancja] to precipitate

wytren|ować pf vt to train [osobę, zwierzę]

wytres|ować pf vt to train [zwierzę]

wytrop|ić pf vt [myśliwy, pies] to track [zwierzynę]; to track [sb] down [osobę]

wytrwa|ć pf vi to persevere, to hang on

wytrwa|ły adi. [osoba, starania] persistent

wytrych m **1** (narzędzie) skeleton key **2** przen. buzzword pot.

wytrysk m **1** (wytryśnięcie) spurt **2** Fizjol. (nasienia) ejaculation

wytry|snąć pf — **wytry|skać**, **wytry|ski-wać** impf vi to spurt

wy|trzeć pf — **wy|cierać** impf **I** vt **1** (otrzeć) to wipe [oczy, ręce, buty] **2** (zetrzeć) wipe [sth] off; (z kurzu) to dust; (gumką) to rub [sth] out **3** (zniszczyć) to wear [sth] thin [ubranie]

II **wytrzeć się** — **wycierać się** **1** (samego siebie) to dry oneself **2** (zniszczyć się) [ubranie, mebel] to wear out

wytrzep|ać pf — **wytrzep|ywać** impf vt to beat [dywan, kanapę]

wytrzeszcz|yć pf — **wytrzeszcz|ać** impf vt pot. ~**yć oczy** to goggle

wytrzeźwi|eć pf vi to sober up

wytrzym|ać pf — **wytrzym|ywać** impf vt to withstand [obciążenie, napięcie, uderzenie]; (przetrzymać psychicznie) to hold on; ~**ać tempo** to stand the pace; ~**ać z kimś** to put up with sb

wytrzymałoś|ć f **1** (kondycja fizyczna) stamina; (odporność) resistance (**na coś** to sth); **przechodzić ludzką** ~**ć** to be unbearable **2** Techn. (na zniszczenie, zużycie) durability

wytrzyma|ły adi. grad. **1** (wytrwały) [biegacz, zwierzę] resilient **2** (odporny) [materiał, tworzywo] durable

wytrzymywać impf → wytrzymać

wytw|orzyć *pf* — **wytw|arzać** *impf* **I** *vt* to manufacture *[samochody, żywność]*; to generate *[prąd, energię]*; to induce *[pole magnetyczne, prąd]*; to create *[atmosferę, więź]*; *[organizm, gruczoł]* to produce *[substancję]*

II wytworzyć się — wytwarzać się *[więź, nastrój]* to be created

wytw|ór *m* product

wytwórc|a *m* producer

wytwórni|a *f* manufacturing company; **~a filmowa** a film studio

wytycz|yć *pf* — **wytycz|ać** *impf vt* to mark [sth] out *[ścieżkę, szlak]*; to delineate *[granice]*; to chart *[trasę, kierunki działania]*

wytykać *impf* → **wytknąć**

wytyp|ować *pf vt* 1 (wybrać) to single out *[delegata, zagadnienie]* 2 (przewidzieć) to name *[zwycięzcę]*; to guess *[wynik, kolejność]*

wywab|ić *pf* — **wywab|iać** *impf vt* 1 (skłonić do wyjścia) to lure [sb] out 2 (usunąć) to remove *[plamy]*; **trudne do ~ienia plamy** stubborn stains

wywalać *impf* → **wywalić**

wywalcz|yć *pf* — **wywalcz|ać** *impf vt* to win *[pozycję, medal]*

wywal|ić *pf* — **wywal|ać** *impf* pot. **I** *vt* to chuck [sth] out a. away pot. *[śmieci, papiery]*; to sack pot. *[pracownika]*

II wywalić się — wywalać się (przewrócić się) to fall over a. down

wywa|r *m* Kulin. stock

wyważ|yć *pf* — **wyważ|ać** *impf vt* 1 (wyłamać) to force [sth] open *[drzwi]* 2 (przemyśleć) to weigh *[słowa]* 3 to balance *[konstrukcję, elementy]*

wywęsz|yć *pf vt* 1 *[pies]* to smell [sth] out *[zające, zbiega]* 2 pot., przen. to nose (out) *[prawdę, szczegóły, informacje]*

wywia|d *m* 1 (rozmowa) interview; **przeprowadzić z kimś ~d** to interview sb 2 Wojsk. intelligence 3 Med. (medical) story

wywiadów|ka *f* Szkol. parents' evening

wywią|zać się *pf* — **wywią|zywać się** *impf v refl.* 1 (wyniknąć) *[dyskusja, kłótnia, walka]* to ensue; *[komplikacje, trudności]* to arise 2 (wypełnić) **~zać się z czegoś** to carry out sth *[zadania, obowiązków]*; to keep sth *[obietnicy]*

wywierać *impf* → **wywrzeć**

wywie|sić *pf* — **wywie|szać** *impf vt* to fly *[flagę, sztandar]*; to put [sth] up *[ogłoszenie, plakat]*; to hang [sth] out *[pranie]*

wywietrznik *m* ventilator

wywietrz|yć *pf* **I** *vt* to air *[pokój, ubranie]*

II wywietrzyć się *[pokój, ubranie]* to be aired

wyw|ieźć *pf* — **wyw|ozić** *impf vt* to carry [sth] away; *[osoba]* to take [sth] away; **~ieźć coś za granicę** to take sth out of the country

wywijać¹ *impf* → **wywinąć**

wywi|jać² *impf* **I** *vt* pot. (tańczyć) to dance [sth] in lively fashion *[oberka, polkę]*

II *vi* (wymachiwać) to wave [sth] around *[kijem, nożem]*

wywi|nąć *pf* — **wywijać¹** *impf* **I** *vt* 1 (odwinąć) to turn [sth] up *[mankiet, rękaw]*; to turn [sth] down *[kołnierz, skarpetki]* 2 (wykonać obrót) to turn *[salto, kozła]*

II wywinąć się — wywijać się 1 *[brzeg, mankiet]* to turn up 2 pot. (uciec) to escape; **~nąć się od odpowiedzialności** to shirk one's responsibility; **~nąć się policji** to give the police the slip pot.

wywl|ec *pf* — **wywl|ekać** *impf vt* 1 (wyciągnąć) to drag [sb/sth] out *[osobę, przedmiot]* 2 pot. (przypomnieć) to drag [sth] up pot. *[niemiłe przeżycia, stare dzieje]*; **~ec coś na światło dzienne** to bring sth to light

wywnętrz|yć się *pf* — **wywnętrz|ać się** *impf v refl.* to pour out one's feelings (**przed kimś** to sb)

wywniosk|ować *pf vi* to conclude

wyw|odzić się *impf v refl. [osoba, ród]* to come (**z czegoś** from sth); *[słowo, pojęcie, zjawisko]* to derive (**z czegoś** from sth)

wywoł|ać *pf* — **wywoł|ywać** *impf vt* 1 (wezwać) to call *[osobę]*; **~ywać duchy** to raise ghosts 2 (przypomnieć) to bring [sth] back *[wspomnienia]* 3 (spowodować) to trigger (off) *[reakcję, alergię]*; to provoke *[protesty, awanturę]*; to cause *[skandal, niepokój]* 4 (na kliszy) to develop *[film]*

wywozić *impf* → **wywieźć**

wyw|ód *m* argument

wyw|óz *m* (wywiezienie) transportation; (usuwanie odpadów) disposal; (eksport) export

wywracać *impf* → **wywrócić**

wywrot|ka *f* 1 (ciężarówka) dumper (truck) GB, dump truck US 2 (łodzi, jachtu) capsizing; (pojazdu) overturning; (narciarza, biegacza) fall

wywr|ócić *pf* — **wywr|acać** *impf* **I** *vt* 1 (przewrócić) to topple (over) *[osobę, drzewo]*; to overturn *[samochód, łódź]*; to upset także przen. *[skrzynkę, wazę, porządek]* 2 (na lewą stronę) to turn [sth] inside out; (do góry dnem) to turn [sth] upside down

II wywrócić się — wywracać się *[osoba, drzewo]* to fall; *[łódź, pojazd]* to overturn; *[butelka, krzesło]* to tip over

wywróż|yć *pf vt* to foretell *[przyszłość]*

wywr|zeć *pf* — **wyw|ierać** *impf vt* to exert *[nacisk, presję]*; to make *[wrażenie]*; to produce *[skutek]*

wywyższ|yć *pf* — **wywyższ|ać** *impf* **I** *vt* książk. to elevate

II wywyższać się to give oneself airs, to put on airs

wyzdrowi|eć *pf vi* to recover

wyziew *m* (gaz) fume; (woń) reek

wyznacz|yć *pf* — **wyznacz|ać** *impf vt* 1 (wytyczyć) to map out *[trasę, miejsce, teren]* 2 (ustalić) to set *[cenę, nagrodę]*; to appoint *[spotkanie, termin, kandata]*

wyzna|ć *pf* — **wyzna|wać**[1] *impf vt* ① (przyznać się) to confess ② (wyjawić) to reveal

wyzna|nie *n* ① (religia) denomination ② (zwierzenie) confession

wyznawać[1] *impf* → wyznać

wyzna|wać[2] *impf vt* (wierzyć) to profess *[religię]*

wyz|wać *pf* — **wyz|ywać** *impf vt* ① (do walki) to challenge *[osobę]* ② pot. (zwymyślać) to call [sb] names

wyzwalać *impf* → wyzwolić

wyzwa|nie *n* challenge; **podjąć** ~**nie** to take up a challenge

wyzwisk|o *n* insult

wyzw|olić *pf* — **wyzw|alać** *impf* ① *vt* ① (przywrócić wolność) to free *[więźniów, niewolników]*; to liberate *[terytorium, kraj]* ② (spowodować wystąpienie) to trigger *[reakcję]*

Ⅱ wyzwolić się — **wyzwalać się** to free oneself

wyzysk *m* exploitation

wyzywać *impf* → wyzwać

wyzywając|y *adi. [zachowanie]* arrogant; *[spojrzenie]* defiant; *[makijaż, strój]* provocative

wyż *m* (ciśnienie) high

❑ ~ **demograficzny** baby boom

wyż|ąć *pf* — **wyż|ymać** *impf vt* to wring *[bieliznę, gąbkę]*

wyż|eł *m* pointer

wyż|obić *pf* — **wyżł|abiać** *impf vt* to carve

wyższoś|ć *f* ① (bycie lepszym) superiority ② (przewaga) dominance

wyżymać *impf* → wyżąć

wyżyn|a *f* upland

Ⅱ wyżyny *plt* (najwyższy poziom) height

wyżyw|ić *pf* ① *vt* to maintain, to feed *[osobę, zwierzę]*

Ⅱ wyżywić się to (manage to) feed oneself

wyżywieni|e *n* food

wzajemnie ① *adv.* mutually

Ⅱ inter. (w życzeniach) the same to you

wzajemn|y *adi.* mutual

wzbi|ć *pf* — **wzbi|jać** *impf* ① *vt* to raise *[kurz]*

Ⅱ wzbić się — **wzbijać się** *[samolot, ptak, mgła]* to rise

wzbierać *impf impf* → wezbrać

wzbijać *impf* → wzbić

wzboga|cić *pf* — **wzboga|cać** *impf* ① *vt* ① (uczynić bogatym) to make [sb] rich ② (powiększyć) to expand *[słownictwo]*; to increase *[wiedzę]*

Ⅱ wzbogacić się — **wzbogacać się** ① *[osoba]* to become rich ② *[zbiór]* to be expanded, to be enriched

wzbr|onić *pf* — **wzbr|aniać** *impf* ① *vt* książk. to forbid (**komuś czegoś** sb sth); **wstęp** ~**oniony** no entry; **palenie** ~**onione** no smoking

Ⅱ wzbraniać się to shy away (**przed czymś** from sth)

wzbu|dzić *pf* — **wzbu|dzać** *impf vt* ① (wywołać) to cause *[strach]*; to inspire *[miłość]*; to arouse *[ciekawość, podejrzenia]* ② Electr. to induce *[prąd]*

wzburz|yć *pf* — **wzburz|ać** *impf* ① *vt* ① (zmącić) to churn [sth] up *[jezioro, fale]* ② (rozzłościć) to infuriate *[osobę]*

Ⅱ wzburzyć się — **wzburzać się** ① (morze, fale) to churn up ② (oburzyć się) to become appalled

w|zdąć *pf* — **w|zdymać** *impf vt [wiatr, podmuch]* to swell *[żagiel, firankę]*; **wzdęty brzuch** bloated stomach

wzdę|cie *n* Med. flatulence

wzdłuż ① *praep.* along

Ⅱ adv. in length; **mieć pięć metrów** ~ to be five metres long

wzdraga|ć się *impf v refl.* to shy away (**przed czymś** from sth)

wzdryg|nąć się *pf* — **wzdryg|ać się** *impf v refl.* to flinch, to shudder

wzdychać *impf* → westchnąć

wzdymać *impf* → wzdąć

w|zejść *pf* — **w|schodzić** *impf vi* ① *[słońce, księżyc]* to rise ② *[roślina]* to sprout

wzgar|dzić *pf vt* książk. to scorn *[propozycją, radą]*; to snub *[ofertą]*; to spurn *[podarunkiem, zaproszeniem]*

wzgl|ąd ① *m* ① (branie pod uwagę) account; **mieć** ~**ąd na coś** to take sth into account; **ze** ~**ędu na coś** on account of sth; **bez** ~**ędu na coś** regardless of sth ② (powód) reason; **ze** ~**ędów bezpieczeństwa** for security reasons ③ (aspekt, właściwość) respect; **pod pewnymi** ~**ędami** in some respects; **pod** ~**ędem wieku** in terms of age

Ⅱ względy *plt* (życzliwość) favour GB, favor US; **zabiegać o czyjeś** ~**ędy** to try to win sb's favour

Ⅲ względem *praep.* ① (wobec) towards; (w stosunku do) relative to ② pot. (jeśli chodzi o) with regard to

względnie ① *adv.* ① (dość) *[cichy, dobry, spokojny]* relatively ② pot. (nieźle) fairly well

Ⅱ conj. książk. or (alternatively)

względn|y *adi.* ① (relatywny) relative ② (umiarkowany) *[spokój, wygoda]* comparative; *[sukces]* qualified; *[ciemność, cisza]* relative

wzgórz|e *n* hill

wziąć *pf* — **brać** *impf* ① *vt* ① (chwycić) to take *[przedmiot, osobę, urlop, kredyt, zakładnika, lekarstwo, stanowisko, twierdzę, kąpiel]*; **wziąć dziecko na ręce** to pick up a child; **wziąć kogoś na spacer** to take sb for a walk; **wziąć coś w dzierżawę** to take out a lease on sth; **wziąć coś do siebie** to take sth personally; **wziąć kogoś za kogoś innego** to mistake sb for someone else; **wziąć ślub** to get married; **weź nogi z kanapy!** pot. take your legs off the sofa!; **wziąć na siebie winę** to take the blame; **weźmy...** let's take...; **niż wy wszyscy razem wzięci** than all of you put together pot. ② (otrzymać) to get *[pensję, napiwek, zapłatę]* ③ (zatrudnić) to employ *[korepetytora, niankę]* [4] przen., książk. (odziedziczyc) to get (**coś po kimś** sth from sb) [5] pot. (pokonać) *[koń]* to clear *[przeszkodę]*; *[samochód]* to take *[zakręt]* [6] pot. (wyprzedzić) to overtake

II wziąć się [1] (chwycić się) to hold; **wziąć się za głowę/pod boki** to hold one's head/sides; **wziąć się za ręce** to take each other's hands [2] (zająć się) to get down (**do czegoś** to sth); to do something (**za kogoś** about sb) [3] (pojawić się) to appear; *[nieufność, problem]* to stem (**z czegoś** from sth)

wzię|ty *adi.* *[pisarz]* popular; *[specjalista]* sought-after

wzl|ecieć *pf* — **wzl|atywać** *impf vi [owad, ptak, kurz, piłka]* to fly (up); *[balon, samolot]* to ascend

wzlo|t *m* (ducha, myśli) flight; ~**ty i upadki** the ups and downs

wzmacniacz *m* amplifier

wzmacniać *impf* → **wzmocnić**

wzmagać *impf* → **wzmóc**

wzmian|ka *f* mention

wzm|ocnić *pf* — **wzm|acniać** *impf* **I** *vt* [1] to strengthen *[ciało, mięśnie, maszynę, mebel, pozycję]*; to reinforce *[konstrukcję, straż, załogę]*; to prop up *[walutę]* [2] (wzmóc) to enhance *[działanie leku]*; to heighten *[doznania]*; to increase *[czujność, ochronę]*; to intensify *[emocje, kolor]*

II wzmocnić się — **wzmacniać się** [1] (nabrać sił) *[ciało, osoba]* to become stronger; *[armia, załoga]* to become reinforced; *[gospodarka, rząd, władca, więź]* to strengthen [2] (stać się intensywniejszym) *[doznania]* to heighten; *[czujność, opór]* to increase; *[emocje, kolory]* to intensify

wzm|óc *pf* — **wzm|agać** *impf* **I** *vt* to increase *[czujność, odporność, pragnienie]*

II wzmóc się — **wzmagać się** *[bezład, gniew]* to grow; *[ból, wiatr]* to increase

wznawiać *impf* → **wznowić**

wzn|ieść *pf* — **wzn|osić** *impf* **I** *vt* [1] (unieść) to lift *[głowę, rękę, szablę]*; ~**ieść toast** to propose a toast [2] (postawić) to erect *[barykadę, budynek]* [3] (wzniecić) to raise *[dym, kurz, pył]* [4] (wydać) to raise *[okrzyk]*

II wznieść się — **wznosić się** [1] (wzlecieć) *[balon, ptak, samolot]* to ascend; *[dym, para]* to rise (up) [2] (rozlec się) *[jęk, krzyk]* to arise, to go up [3] przen. (przezwyciężyć) to rise (**ponad coś** above sth)

III wznosić się [1] (piąć się w górę) *[droga]* to climb; *[grunt, wybrzeże]* to rise [2] (wystawać) *[budynek, łańcuch górski]* to rise (up)

wznio|sły *adi. grad.* [1] (szlachetny) *[charakter, umysł]* noble; *[uczucia, zasady]* lofty [2] (górnolotny) *[myśl, styl, ton]* elevated

wznosić *impf* → **wznieść**

---

wzn|owić *pf* — **wzn|awiać** *impf vt* [1] (podjąć na nowo) to resume *[działalność, produkcję]*; to restart *[grę, usługę]* [2] (wydać) to reissue *[książkę]*

wzornictw|o *n* design

wzor|ować *impf* **I** *vt* to model (**coś na czymś** sth after sth)

II wzorować się to follow the example (**na kimś** of sb)

wzorow|y I *adi.* *[ojciec, zachowanie]* exemplary; *[mąż, pracownik, uczeń]* model

II *m* Szkol. (ocena) very good conduct grade

wzo|rzec *m* [1] (model) model, pattern [2] (zespół cech ludzkich) standard; ~**rzec postępowania** a standard of behaviour [3] Techn. standard

wz|ór *m* [1] (deseń) pattern [2] (do kopiowania) model; **wzór podpisu** a specimen signature [3] (przykład) example; **brać wzór z kogoś** to follow sb's example [4] (ideał) (role) model; **stawiać kogoś za wzór (komuś)** to hold sb up as a model (for sb) [5] (zapis matematyczny) formula

wzrastać *impf* → **wzrosnąć**

wzrok *m* [1] (zmysł) (eye)sight; **w zasięgu** ~**u** in view; **na wysokości** ~**u** at eye level; **mieć krótki** ~ to be short-sighted [2] (spojrzenie) eye(s), gaze; **podnieść** ~ to raise one's eyes; **przyciągać** ~ to attract sb's eyes

wzrokow|iec *m* visualizer

wzrokowo *adv.* visually

wzrokow|y *adi.* *[nerw]* optic; *[układ, zaburzenia]* optical; *[halucynacje, pamięć]* visual

wzr|osnąć *pf* — **wzr|astać** *impf vi [deficyt, popyt, wydatki, gniew]* to grow; *[dochody, inflacja, apetyt, hałas]* to increase; *[bezrobocie, ceny]* to rise

wzro|st *m* [1] (wysokość) height; **mieć dwa metry** ~**stu** to be two metres tall; **ile masz** ~**stu?** what is your height? [2] (żywego organizmu) growth [3] (wydatków, populacji) increase

wzruszać *impf* → **wzruszyć**

wzruszając|y *adi.* moving, touching

wzrusze|nie *n* emotion; **ogarnęło go** ~**nie** he was overcome by emotion

wzrusz|ony *adi.* moved, touched

wzrusz|yć *pf* — **wzrusz|ać** *impf* **I** *vt* [1] (spulchnić) to loosen *[ziemię]* [2] (rozczulić) to move, to touch *[osobę]*

II wzruszyć się — **wzruszać się** to be moved a. touched

wzw|ód *m* erection

wzwyż *adv., part.* up, upwards; **skok** ~ the high jump; **od 30 lat** ~ from 30 up

wzywać *impf* → **wezwać**

wżerać się *impf* → **weżreć się**

Z

Z, z *n inv.* Z, z

z, ze [] *praep.* [1] (przed określeniami miejsca) from; (o pomieszczeniu, pojemniku) from, out of; (o powierzchni) off; **wyjść z domu** to leave home; **wystawać z czegoś** to sticking out of sth; **zdjąć coś ze ściany** to take sth off the wall; **podnieść coś z podłogi** to pick something up off the floor [2] (określający kierunek, stronę) from; **z prawej strony** *[znajdować się]* on a. to the right; *[zbliżać się]* from the right; **z mojej lewej strony** (tuż obok) by my left side; (nieco dalej) to my left; **z przodu/tyłu** at the front/back [3] (określający źródło, pochodzenie) from; **z doświadczenia** from experience [4] (z określeniami czasu) from, of; **zamek z XV wieku** a castle (dating) from the 15th century; **jego list z 12 maja** his letter of 12 May [5] (wskazuje na surowiec) of, from; **sok z wiśni** cherry juice [6] (wskazuje na zbiór) of; **któryś z nich** one of them [7] (wskazuje na przyczynę) out of, from; **z radości** out of joy; **z wyczerpania** from exhaustion; **z braku powietrza** through lack of air [8] (wskazuje na cechę) **znany z czegoś** well-known for sth [9] (wskazuje na natężenie) **z całego serca/ze wszystkich sił** with all one's heart/might [10] (wskazuje na element całości) with; **sklep z używaną odzieżą** a second-hand clothes shop [11] (wskazuje na sposób) with; **z trzaskiem** with a bang [12] (wskazuje na cel) **pośpieszyć komuś z pomocą** to go to sb's aid [13] (wskazuje na współzależność) with; **z wiekiem** with age [14] (z określeniami pory) with; **z końcem sierpnia** at the end of August [15] (eliptyczne) about; **co z artykułem?** what about the article? [16] (w przysłówkach) **ubrany z niemiecka** dressed in German style

[] *part.* around, about; **z godzinę** around an hour

za¹ [] *praep.* [1] (dalej, z tyłu) behind; **jeden za drugim** one after another; **oglądać się za kimś** to look back at sb [2] (poza) outside; **wyjechać za miasto** to go out of town [3] (po przeciwnej stronie) *[znajdować się, udać się]* behind; **za biurkiem** behind the desk; **za oceanem** beyond the ocean [4] (wskazuje na sposób) by; **za rękę** by the hand [5] (z określeniem kwoty) for; **za 100 złotych** for 100 zlotys; **za wszelką cenę** przen. at any price [6] (wskazuje na powód) for; **nagroda za coś** a reward for sth [7] (wskazuje na cel) for; **za ojczyznę** for one's country [8] (wskazuje na okoliczności) **za przepustką** on presentation of a valid pass; **za czyjąś zgodą** with sb's permission; **za czyjąś radą** on sb's advice [9] (wskazuje na powtarzające się okoliczności) at; **za pierwszym razem** (the) first time round; **za każdym razem** each a. every time [10] (w zastępstwie) for, instead of; **pracować za dwóch** to do enough work for two [11] (wskazujące na termin) in; **za trzy lata** in three years; **za pięć szósta** (at) five to six [12] (wskazuje na okres) during, in; **za jej życia** during a. in her lifetime [13] (wskazuje na właściwość) as; **uważać kogoś za coś** to regard sb as sth [14] (wskazuje na upodobania) **przepadać za czymś** to go in for sth, to be fond of sth; **tęsknić za kimś** to miss sb; **szaleć za kimś** to be mad about sb

[] *adi.* **argumenty za i przeciw** pros and cons; **20 głosów za** 20 votes for; **jestem za** I'm in favour

[] **za to** *part.* but, yet

za² *adv.* (zbyt) too; **za długi** too long; **za późno** too late

zaadapt|ować *pf* [] *vt* to adapt *[utwór]*; to convert *[budynek]* (**na coś** into sth)

[] **zaadaptować się** *vi* to adjust (**do czegoś** to sth)

zaadopt|ować *pf vt* to adopt *[dziecko]*

zaadres|ować *pf vt* to address także przen. *[list, paczkę, pytanie]* (**do kogoś** to sb)

zaaferowan|y *adi.* *[osoba, mina]* preoccupied

zaakcent|ować *pf vt* to stress *[potrzebę, znaczenie]*; to accentuate *[problemy]*

zaakcept|ować *pf vt* to accept

zaalarm|ować *pf vt* [1] (zawiadomić) to alert; (wezwać) to call *[policję, straż pożarną]* [2] (zaniepokoić) to alarm

zaangaż|ować *pf* [] *vt* [1] (do pracy) to employ [2] (wciągnąć) to involve *[osobę, instytucję]* (**w coś** in sth) [3] przen. to invest *[kapitał, pieniądze, czas]* (**w coś** in sth)

[] **zaangażować się** [1] (przyjąć pracę) to take up employment [2] (włączyć się) to become involved (**w coś** in sth)

zaapel|ować *pf vi* to appeal (**do kogoś** to sb); to call (**o coś** for sth); **~ować od wyroku** to appeal against a sentence GB, to appeal a sentence US

zaaplik|ować *pf vt* *[lekarz]* to administer *[kurację, lekarstwo]* (**komuś** to sb); (zalecić) to recommend (**coś komuś** sth to sb)

zaaranż|ować *impf vt* [1] (zorganizować) to arrange *[spotkanie]*; (potajemnie) to contrive *[spotkanie, wypadek]*; (nielegalnie) to fix pot. *[walkę, mecz]*; (zainscenizo-

wać) to pre-arrange *[walkę, spotkanie]* ② (urządzić) to design *[wnętrze, mieszkanie]* ③ Muz. to arrange
zaareszt|ować *pf vt* to arrest
zaatak|ować *pf vt [napastnik, krytyk, choroba]* to attack
zaawansowan|y *adi. [technologia, poziom, uczeń]* advanced; **poziom średnio** ∼y an intermediate level; **rozmowy są bardzo** ∼e the talks are well under way; **dla** ∼ych for advanced learners
zabandaż|ować *pf vt* to bandage *[ranę, nogę]*
zabarw|ić *pf* — **zabarw|iać** *impf* **[]** *vt* to colour GB, to color US *[szkło, ubranie]*; to dye *[tkaninę]*; ∼ić coś na zielono to dye sth green
[] **zabarwić się** to take on a colour GB a. color US; ∼ić się na czerwono to turn red
zabarwieni|e *n* ① (kolor) colouring GB, coloring US; **nabrać żółtego** ∼a to turn yellow ② przen. (głosu) tone; (wypowiedzi) tinge
zabarykad|ować *pf* **[]** *vt* to barricade *[drzwi]*; to block *[przejście, przejazd]*
[] **zabarykadować się** to barricade oneself (w czymś in a. into sth)
zabaw|a *f* **[]** ① (bawienie się) play; (przyjemność) fun; (gra) game; ∼a lalkami playing with dolls; **zepsuć komuś** ∼ę to spoil sb's fun; **dać coś komuś do** ∼y to give sb sth to play with; **to nie jest do** ∼y it's not a toy; **zrobić coś dla** ∼y to do sth for fun; **miłej** ∼y! have fun a. a good time! ② (tańce) party; ∼a taneczna a dance
zabaw|ka *f* toy; **samolot** ∼ka a toy plane; ∼ki choinkowe Christmas tree decorations; **sklep z** ∼kami a toyshop; **traktować kogoś jak** ∼kę to treat sb like a plaything
zabawnie *adv. grad.* funnily; **wyglądać** ∼ to look funny; **było** ∼ it was fun
zabawn|y *adi. grad. [osoba, film]* funny; ∼e, jak... it's funny how...
zabezpieczać *impf* → zabezpieczyć
zabezpiecze|nie *n* ① (ochrona) protection; (barierki) safety barrier; (siatka) safety net; (na banknotach, dokumentach) security feature; (przed atakiem, włamaniem) security device ② Prawo security
zabezpiecz|yć *pf* — **zabezpiecz|ać** *impf* **[]** *vt* ① (ochronić) *[osoba, urządzenie]* to protect *[ranę, dom]* (**przed czymś** against sth); *[przepis, prawo]* to safeguard (**przed czymś** against sth); (przed otwarciem, włamaniem) to secure *[drzwi, pojemnik]*; ∼yć coś przed rdzą to rustproof sth; ∼yć broń to put the safety catch on a gun ② (wzmocnić) to strengthen *[wał, konstrukcję]*; (podeprzeć) to support *[wykop]* ③ (zapewnić środki) to provide for; **być** ∼onym **materialnie** to be well provided for ④ (dać gwarancję) to secure *[kredyt]* ⑤ Prawo *[policja]* to seize *[dowody, broń, towary]*
[] **zabezpieczyć się** — **zabezpieczać się** to protect oneself (**przed czymś** against sth)

zabi|ć *pf* — **zabi|jać** *impf* **[]** *vt* ① (uśmiercić) to kill; **dałby się** ∼ć za nią przen. he would die for her; ∼ć w kimś spontaniczność przen. to stifle sb's spontaneity ② (zlikwidować) to kill *[zapach, smak]*; to appease *[głód]* ③ (zamknąć) to nail [sth] up; ∼ć okno **deskami** to board up the window ④ Gry to take
[] **zabić się** — **zabijać się** (popełnić samobójstwo) to kill oneself; (zginąć) to be killed
[] **zabijać się** pot. (starać się osiągnąć) to fall over oneself (**o coś** to get sth)
■ **dla** ∼**cia czasu** to kill time
zabi|ć² *pf vi [dzwon]* to ring; *[zegar]* to strike; *[serce]* to start beating
zabie|c, zabie|gnąć *pf* — **zabie|gać¹** *impf vt* (zablokować) ∼c komuś drogę to bar sb's way
zabieg **[]** *m* treatment; (chirurgiczny) operation; euf. (aborcja) abortion
[] **zabiegi** *plt* efforts
zabiegać¹ *impf* → zabiec
zabiega|ć² *impf vi* ∼c o coś to seek sth *[sławę, uznanie, względy]*
zabiegan|y *adi.* pot. *[osoba]* hard-pressed
zabiegow|y *adi. [gabinet]* treatment
zabierać *impf* → zabrać
zabijać *impf* → zabić¹
zabi|ty *m* było pięciu ∼tych five people were killed
zablok|ować *pf* **[]** *vt* ① to block *[drogę, przejście, podanie]* ② (utrudnić) to block *[reformę, plan]*; to blockade *[państwo, terytorium]* ③ (zepsuć) to jam *[mechanizm, drzwi]*; to block *[linię telefoniczną]*; ∼ować konto to freeze an account
[] **zablokować się** *[drzwi, okno]* to jam
zabłą|dzić *pf vt* (zgubić się) to get lost
zabłąkan|y *adi. [osoba, pies, kula]* stray
zabło|cić *pf* **[]** *vt* to muddy *[podłogę]*; ∼cić sobie **ubranie** to get one's clothes muddy
[] **zabłocić się** *[osoba]* to get oneself muddy; *[ubranie, ręce]* to get muddy
zabły|snąć *pf vi* ① *[światło, gwiazdy]* (pojawić się) to shine; (zamigotać) to glimmer; *[błyskawica, latarka]* to flash; *[oczy]* to light up ② (zapalić się) *[lampy, światła]* to go on ③ (wyróżnić się) ∼snąć przed kimś to dazzle sb; ∼snąć inteligencją to show one's intelligence; ∼snąć na egzaminie to shine in an exam
zabobon *m* superstition
zabobonn|y *adi.* superstitious
zabol|eć *pf vi* to hurt także przen.; **to mnie** ∼ało it hurt
zaborcz|y *adi.* ① *[osoba, miłość]* possessive ② *[kraj, polityka]* imperialist
zabójc|a *m* (mordercza) killer; (zamachowiec) assassin
zabójcz|y *adi.* ① *[dawka, środek, strzał]* lethal; *[klimat]* murderous; *[praca, tempo]* killing; *[tryb życia]* destructive ② żart. *[spojrzenie, uśmiech]*

seductive; *[wygląd]* smashing GB pot.; *[nuda, monotonia]* killing pot.

zabójstw|o *n* murder; *(zamach)* assassination; ~**o w afekcie** a crime of passion; **usiłowanie** ~**a** an attempted murder

zab|rać *pf* — **zab|ierać** *impf* **[I]** *vt* ① *(odebrać)* to take (away) (**coś komuś** sth from sb) ② *(wypełnić)* to take (up) *[czas, miejsce]* ③ *(wziąć ze sobą)* to take; ~**rać dzieci do parku** to take the children to the park ④ *(usunąć)* to take away; *(przenieść)* to take; ~**ierz stąd swoje rzeczy** take your things away **[II] zabrać się** — **zabierać się** ① *(zacząć robić)* ~**rać się do czegoś** to get down to sth; ~**rać się za kogoś** to take sb in hand ② pot. *(pojechać)* to come along; ~**rać się samochodem do miasta** to get a lift to town ③ pot. *(odejść)* to clear off pot.; ~**ieraj się stąd!** clear off!

zabrak|nąć *pf v imp.* ① *(wyczerpać się)* ~**ło mi pieniędzy** I've run short of money; ~**ło mi masła** I've run out of butter; ~**ło mu kilku sekund do pobicia rekordu** he was a few seconds short of breaking the record; ~**ło jej odwagi** her courage failed her ② *(nie pojawić się)* ~**ło kilku osób** several people failed to show up

zabr|onić *pf* — **zabr|aniać** *impf vt (zakazać)* to forbid (**komuś czegoś/robienia czegoś** sb sth/to do sth)

zabru|dzić *pf* **[I]** *vt* to make [sth] dirty **[II] zabrudzić się** to get dirty

zabud|ować *pf* — **zabud|owywać** *impf vt* ① to develop *[teren, działkę]*; **teren** ~**owany** a built-up area ② to wall off *[balkon]*; ~**ować wnękę** to build cupboards into an alcove

zabudowa|nia *plt* buildings

zaburzać *impf* → **zaburzyć**

zaburze|nie *n* ① Med. disorder ② *(nieprawidłowość)* disturbance

zaburz|yć *pf* — **zaburz|ać** *impf vt* to upset *[równowagę]*; to disturb *[spokój]*

zabyt|ek *m* ① *(architektoniczny)* monument; *(językowy, muzyczny)* relic ② pot., żart. museum piece

zabytkow|y *adi. [pomnik, kościół]* historic; *[mebel, przedmiot]* antique; *[samochód, aparat]* vintage

zachcian|ka *f* pot. whim; **spełniać czyjeś** ~**ki** to pander to sb's whims

zachc|ieć się — **zachc|iewać się** *v imp.* pot. **spać mi się** ~**iało** I felt a bit drowsy; ~**iało im się spaceru** they felt like going for a walk

zachę|cić *pf* — **zachę|cać** *impf* **[I]** *vt* to encourage (**kogoś do czegoś** sb to sth) **[II] zachęcić się** — **zachęcać się** *(nabrać ochoty)* ~**cić się do wyjazdu** to become keen on leaving a. to leave

zachę|ta *f* encouragement

zachłann|y *adi. grad.* greedy (**na coś** for sth)

zachły|snąć się *pf* — **zachły|stywać się** *impf v refl.* to choke (**czymś** on sth); ~**stywał się z zachwytu** przen. he was speechless with admiration

zachmurzać się *impf* → **zachmurzyć się**

zachmurze|nie *n* clouds; ~**nie całkowite** overcast

zachmurz|yć się *pf* — **zachmurz|ać się** *impf v refl.* ① *[niebo]* to become overcast ② przen. *[twarz]* to cloud over; *[osoba]* to become gloomy

zachodni *adi. [brzeg]* west; *[rejon]* western; *[cywilizacja]* Western

zachodzić *impf* → **zajść**

zachor|ować *pf vi* to fall a. be taken ill; ~**ować na grypę** to go down with flu

zachow|ać *pf* — **zachow|ywać** *impf* **[I]** *vt* ① *(przetrzymać)* to keep, to retain *[przedmiot]* ② *(utrzymać)* to keep, to retain *[młodość, pamięć, urodę]*; to preserve *[zwyczaj, wiarę]*; to observe *[post, dietę]*; to maintain *[dyscyplinę, dyskrecję]*; ~**ać ostrożność** to exercise caution; ~**ać powagę** to keep one's countenance; ~**ać milczenie** to remain silent; ~**ować umiar w jedzeniu** to eat in moderation; ~**ać coś dla siebie** to keep sth to oneself ③ Komput. to save *[dane, dokument]* **[II] zachować się** — **zachowywać się** ① *(przetrwać)* *[dzieło, pamiątka, legenda]* to survive ② *(postąpić)* to behave

zachowa|nie *n* behaviour GB, behavior US, conduct

zachowywać *impf* → **zachować**

zach|ód *m* ① *(pora, zjawisko)* sunset ② *(strona świata)* west; **na** ~**ód od...** west of... ③ *(kraje zachodnie)* **Zachód** the West ④ pot. *(trud)* trouble; **być wartym** ~**odu** to be worth the trouble

❏ **Dziki Zachód** the Wild West

zachryp|nąć *pf vi [osoba]* to become hoarse; *[głos]* to hoarsen

zachwal|ać *pf vt* to recommend *[kandydata]*; to tout *[towar]*

zachwi|ać *pf* **[I]** *vt* ① to shake *[budynkiem, krzesłem]* ② przen. *(naruszyć)* to upset *[równowagę]*; *(osłabić)* to shake *[wiarę]* **[II] zachwiać się** ① *[osoba]* to stagger; *[drabina, krzesło]* to wobble ② przen. *[pozycja, potęga]* to be weakened

zachwy|cić *pf* — **zachwy|cać** *impf* **[I]** *vt* to enrapture, to delight; ~**cić kogoś urodą** to enrapture sb with one's beauty **[II] zachwycić się** — **zachwycać się** ① *(zostać urzeczonym)* to admire *[urodą, grą]* ② *(wyrazić zachwyt)* to enthuse (**czymś** about sth)

zachwy|t *m* delight; **wpaść w** ~**t** to go into raptures

za|ciąć *pf* — **za|cinać¹** *impf* **[I]** *vt* ① *(skaleczyć)* to cut ② *(uderzyć)* **zaciąć konia (batem)** to lash a horse ③ *(zacisnąć)* to purse *[usta, wargi]*

II zaciąć się — zacinać się [1] (skaleczyć się) to cut oneself [2] (zablokować się) *[drzwi, mechanizm]* to jam [3] (uprzeć się) **zaciąć się (w sobie)** to dig in one's heels [4] (zająknąć się) to stumble

III zacinać się *[osoba]* to falter

zaciąg|nąć *pf* — **zaciąg|ać** *impf* **II** *vt* [1] (przenieść) to drag *[worek]*; ~**nąć kogoś siłą do dentysty** pot. to drag sb kicking and screaming to the dentist [2] (wziąć) to take out *[pożyczkę]* [3] (wystawić) to mount *[wartę]* [4] (zasunąć, zacisnąć) to draw *[zasłony, kotarę, pętlę]*; to tighten *[krawat]*; ~**nąć hamulec ręczny** to pull up the handbrake [5] (powlec) to cover; ~**nąć coś farbą** to paint sth [6] Kulin. to thicken *[zupę, sos]*

II *vi* (powiać) **od rzeki ~nęło chłodem** a cold draught came in from the river

III zaciągnąć się — zaciągać się [1] (wstąpić) to enlist; ~**nąć się na statek** to sign on a ship [2] (wciągnąć dym) to inhale; ~**nąć się dymem** to drag on a cigarette [3] (pokryć się) ~**nęło się** it became overcast

zaciek *m* damp patch

zaciekaw|ić *pf* — **zaciekaw|iać** *impf* **II** *vt* to interest; **to mnie ~iło** I found it interesting

II zaciekawić się — zaciekawiać się (zainteresować się) ~**ić się czymś** to find sth interesting; „**gdzie byłeś?", ~iła się** 'where have you been?' she asked curiously

zaciekł|y *adi. grad.* *[osoba]* dogged; *[wróg, nienawiść, spór]* fierce; *[ateista, antysemita]* rabid; *[dyskusja]* heated

zacierać *impf* → **zatrzeć**

zacieśni|ć *pf* — **zacieśni|ać** *impf* **II** *vt* [1] to tighten *[pętlę, uścisk]*; to narrow *[zakres]* [2] to strengthen *[przyjaźń, więzi]*; to intensify *[współpracę]*

II zacieśnić się — zacieśniać się [1] *[pętla]* to tighten; *[krąg, oblężenie]* to close; *[zakres, problematyka]* to narrow [2] *[przyjaźń, więź]* to become strengthened; *[współpraca, kontakty]* to be intensified

zacię|cie *n* [1] (nacięcie) notch [2] (skłonność) flair (**do czegoś** for sth); **pracować z ~ciem** to work fervently; **robić coś bez ~cia** to do sth without conviction

zacię|ty **II** *adi. grad.* [1] (uparty) *[osoba]* tenacious; *[twarz, spojrzenie]* determined [2] (zaciekły) *[komunista]* ardent; *[bój, konkurencja, wróg]* fierce; ~**ty mecz** a closely fought game

II *adi.* (zepsuty) *[mechanizm, drzwi]* jammed

zacinać¹ *impf* → **zaciąć**

zacina|ć² *impf vi [deszcz, śnieg]* to slant down

zacisk *m* Techn. clamp; (mały, ze sprężyną) clip; (w obwodzie elektrycznym) terminal

zaci|snąć *pf* — **zaci|skać** *impf* **II** *vt* [1] (ścisnąć) to clamp *[przewód]*; to close *[powieki]*; to tighten up *[śrubę]*; to clench *[szczęki, pięści, zęby]*; ~**snąć zęby**

to grit one's teeth także przen. [2] (zaciągnąć) to tighten *[sznur]*

II zacisnąć się — zaciskać się [1] *[klamra]* to close; *[szczęki, dłonie]* to clench [2] *[sznur]* to tighten

zaciszn|y *adi. grad.* [1] (osłonięty od wiatru) *[miejsce]* sheltered [2] (przytulny) *[pokój, mieszkanie]* snug

zacofani|e *n* backwardness

zacofan|y *adi. [obszar, region]* backward; *[osoba, lud, kraj]* benighted; *[poglądy]* stick-in-the-mud pot.

zacum|ować *pf vt, vi* to moor (**do czegoś** to sth)

zacyt|ować *pf vt* to quote

zacza|ić się *pf v refl. [napastnik, zwierzę]* to lie in wait (**na kogoś/coś** for sb/sth); ~**ć się za drzwiami** to hide behind the door

zaczar|ować *pf vt* to enchant także przen.; ~**ować kogoś w coś** to turn sb into sth

zacz|ąć *pf* — **zacz|ynać** *impf* **II** *vt, vi* [1] to start, to begin *[dzień, życie, bochenek, paczkę]*; ~**ąć coś robić** to start doing sth a. to do sth; ~**ąć od zrobienia czegoś** to start a. begin by doing sth; ~**ąć od początku** to start again [2] (rozpocząć mówienie, pisanie) *[osoba]* to begin; **nie wiem, od czego** ~**ąć** I don't know where to begin; ~**ąć z innej beczki** pot. to change the subject [3] (rozpoczynać karierę) to begin; ~**ynać od zera** to start from scratch [4] pot. (zadzierać) ~**ynać z kimś** to mess with sb

II zacząć się — zaczynać się to start, to begin; ~**ęła się wiosna** spring has come

zaczeka|ć *pf vi* to wait (**na kogoś** for sb); ~**ć z czymś** to put sth on hold; ~**jcie, nie wszyscy naraz!** hold on, one at a time!

zaczep|ić *pf* — **zaczep|iać** *impf* **II** *vt* [1] (umocować) to fasten; (hakiem) to hook; (przypiąć) to clip [2] (zagadnąć) to accost *[osobę]* [3] (sprowokować) to provoke

II *vi* [1] (zawadzić) to catch; ~**ić nogą o coś** to catch one's foot on sth [2] pot. (wstąpić) to stop over; ~**ić o Warszawę** to stop over in Warsaw

III zaczepić się — zaczepiać się [1] (złapać się) ~**ić się rękami o coś** to catch hold of sth [2] (zahaczyć się) *[latawiec, klamra]* to get caught (**o coś** in sth) [3] pot. (zamieszkać) to stay

zaczep|ka *f* taunt; **szukać ~ki z kimś** to be looking for a fight with sb

zaczepn|y *adi. [zachowanie, uwaga]* aggressive

zaczerp|nąć *pf* — **zaczerp|ywać** *impf vt* [1] (nabrać) to scoop up *[ciecz, mąkę]*; ~**nąć wody ze studni** to draw some water out of the well; ~**nąć powietrza** (zrobić wdech) to breathe in a gulp of air; (przewietrzyć się) to get some air [2] (zapożyczyć) to take *[motyw, tytuł]*

zaczerwie|nić się *pf v refl.* [1] *[osoba]* to go red; (ze złości) to flush [2] *[pomidory, bandaż]* to turn red

zaczynać *impf* → **zacząć**

zaćm|a *f* Med. cataract

zaćmie|nie *n* ☐ Astron. eclipse; ~**nie słońca/ księżyca** a solar/lunar eclipse ☐ pot. (zamroczenie) mental block

za|d *m* ☐ Zool. rump; (u konia) croup ☐ pot. (u człowieka) (large) rump pot.

zada|ć *pf* — **zada|wać** *impf* ☐ *vt* ☐ (wyznaczyć) to ask *[pytanie, zagadkę]*; to give *[pokutę, lekcję]*; **co masz na jutro ~ne?** what's your homework for tomorrow?; ~**ć sobie wiele trudu** to go to a lot of trouble; **nawet nie ~ł sobie trudu, żeby...** he didn't even bother to... ☐ (spowodować) to inflict *[ból, klęskę]* (**komuś** on sb); to deal *[cios]* (**komuś** to sb); ☐ (dać) to give *[paszę]*

☐ **zadać się** — **zadawać się** (mieć do czynienia) ~**wać się z kimś** to associate a. hang about pot. with sb

zada|nie *n* ☐ (czynność do wykonania) task; (od zwierzchnika) assignment; (cel) objective; **wywiązać się z ~nia** to carry out a task; **mieć za ~nie zrobić coś** to have the task of doing sth; **stanąć na wysokości ~nia** to make the grade ☐ (do rozwiązania) problem; **rozwiązać ~nie** to solve a problem; ~**nie z matematyki** a maths problem

zadar|ty *adi.* *[broda, czubek buta]* turned-up; ~**ty nos** a snub nose

zadat|ek ☐ *m* deposit

☐ **zadatki** *plt* (ukryte zdolności) makings; **mieć (wszelkie) ~ki na kogoś** to have (all) the makings of sb

zadawać *impf* → **zadać**

zad|ąć *pf vi* ☐ *[wiatr]* to blow ☐ (zagrać) ~**ąć w trąbkę** to blast one's trumpet

zadba|ć *pf vi* to take care (**o coś** of sth); ~**ć, żeby...** to see to it that...

zadban|y *adi.* *[osoba, zwierzę]* well-groomed; *[włosy, paznokcie]* neat; *[ogród, dom]* spruce

zadebiut|ować *pf vi* to make one's debut

zadecyd|ować *pf* ☐ *vi* *[osoba, wydarzenie]* to decide (**o czymś** sth); ~**ować, że...** to decide that...

☐ **zadecydować się** to be decided

zadedyk|ować *pf vt* to dedicate *[książkę, wiersz]* (**komuś** to sb)

zademonstr|ować *pf vt* to demonstrate

zadłuż|yć *pf* — **zadłuż|ać** *impf* ☐ *vt* ~**yć majątek** to mortgage one's assets; **być ~onym** to be in debt

☐ **zadłużyć się** — **zadłużać się** to run up a debt

zadom|owić się *pf* — **zadom|awiać się** *impf v refl.* to settle in

zadowalać *impf* → **zadowolić**

zadowalając|y *adi.* *[ocena, wyniki]* satisfactory; *[sprzedaż, postęp]* satisfying; *[dochód, środki]* comfortable; *[praca, występ]* competent

zadowoleni|e *n* pleasure; ~**e z czegoś** pleasure of sth; ~**e z pracy** job satisfaction; **czerpać ~e z czegoś** to derive satisfaction from sth; **uśmiech-**

nąć się z ~**em** to smile with contentment; **przyjąć coś z** ~**em** to welcome sth

zadow|olić *pf* — **zadow|alać** *impf* ☐ *vi* to satisfy *[gościa, potrzeby]*

☐ **zadowolić się** — **zadowalać się** to settle (**czymś** for sth)

zadowol|ony *adi.* pleased; ~**ony z siebie** self-satisfied, smug

zad|ra *f* splinter

zadrap|ać *pf* ☐ *vt* to scratch

☐ **zadrapać się** to scratch oneself

zadrapa|nie *n* scratch

zadra|snąć *pf* ☐ *vt* to scratch

☐ **zadrasnąć się** to nick oneself

zadraśnię|cie *n* graze

za|drzeć — **za|dzierać** *impf* ☐ *vt* ☐ (naderwać) to chip *[paznokieć]* ☐ (unieść) to lift *[głowę, ogon]*; to hitch up *[spódnicę]*

☐ *vi* pot. (narazić się) to cross (**z kimś** sb)

zadrż|eć *pf vi* *[osoba]* to tremble; *[dom, ziemia]* to shake; *[samolot]* to shudder; *[płomień, światło, blask]* to flicker; *[głos, dźwięk]* to waver

zaduch *m* stuffiness

zadufan|y *adi.* self-righteous; **być ~ym w sobie** to be stuck-up pot.

zadum|a *f* reverie

zadurz|ony *adi.* infatuated (**w kimś** with sb)

zadurz|yć się *pf v refl.* książk. to be infatuated (**w kimś** with sb)

zadym|a *f* pot. (zamieszki) trouble; bovver GB pot.

zadym|ka *f* (śnieżna) snowstorm

zadyszan|y *adi.* breathless

zadysz|ka *f* breathlessness; **mieć ~kę** to be short of breath

zadziała|ć *pf vi* ☐ *[lekarstwo, uwaga]* to work; *[silnik, mechanizm]* to start working; *[alarm]* to go off ☐ pot. (załatwić sprawę) to act

zadzierać *impf* → **zadrzeć**

zadzio|r *m* splinter

zadzio|ra *m, f* pot. brawler

zadziorn|y *adi.* grad. pot. *[osoba, mina]* obstreperous

zadziw|ić *pf* — **zadziw|iać** *impf vt* to astonish

zadzwo|nić *pf vi* ☐ *[dzwonek, telefon]* to ring; *[osoba]* to ring (a bell); ~**nić do drzwi** to ring the (door)bell ☐ *[klucze]* to jingle ☐ (zatelefonować) ~**nić do kogoś** to ring sb up

zafałsz|ować *pf* — **zafałsz|owywać** *impf vt* to distort *[fakty, historię]*

zafund|ować *pf vt* ~**ować coś komuś** to treat sb to sth; ~**ować sobie coś** to treat oneself to sth

zagad|ać *pf* — **zagad|ywać**[1] *impf* pot. ☐ *vt* ☐ (odwrócić uwagę) to distract; ~**ać nauczyciela** to engage a teacher in chit chat ☐ (przegadać) to out-talk *[rozmówcę]*

☐ *vi* pot. ~**ać do kogoś** to start talking to sb

III zagadać się — zagadywać się *[osoba]* to get carried away in conversation

zagad|ka *f* [1] (pytanie) riddle; **zadać komuś ~kę** to ask sb a riddle [2] (tajemnica) riddle, secret; **~ki natury** the secrets of nature

zagadkow|y *adi.* mysterious

zagad|nąć *pf* — **zagad|ywać²** *impf vt* (zaczepić) to approach; (zapytać) to ask

zagadnie|nie *n* issue

zagadywać¹ *impf* → **zagadać**

zagadywać² *impf* → **zagadnąć**

zaganiać *impf* → **zagnać**

zagap|ić się *pf vt* [1] pot. (zapatrzyć się) to stare (**na coś** at sth) [2] (nie uważać) **~iłem się** I wasn't paying attention; (idąc, jadąc) I wasn't looking

zagarn|ąć *pf* — **zagarn|iać** *impf vt* [1] (przysunąć do siebie) to scoop up *[przedmioty, ciecz]*; **~ąć ręką pieniądze leżące na stole** to sweep up the money on the table [2] (przywłaszczyć) to grab *[majątek, władzę]*

zag|iąć *pf* — **zag|inać** *impf* **[]** *vt* [1] (zgiąć) to bend *[drut, pręt]*; to fold [sth] down *[kartkę, róg]* [2] pot. to stump *[nauczyciela, eksperta]*

[] zagiąć się — zaginać się *[drut, pręt]* to bend

zagię|cie *n* (zagniecenie) crease; (fałda) fold; (na kartce) fold mark

zaginać *impf* → **zagiąć**

zagi|nąć *pf vi [osoba, przedmiot]* to go missing; **zgłosić czyjeś ~nięcie** to report sb missing

zagini|ony **[]** *adi. [osoba]* missing; *[ląd, przedmiot]* lost

[] zaginiony *m*, **~ona** *f* missing person; Wojsk. person missing in action, MIA US; **uznano go za ~onego** he was reported missing

zagips|ować *pf vt* to plaster over *[dziurę, szparę]*; to put [sth] in plaster *[rękę, nogę]*

zaglądać *impf* → **zajrzeć**

zagła|da *f* extermination; Biol. extinction

zagłęb|ić *pf* — **zagłęb|iać** *impf* **[]** *vt* **~ić ręce w kieszeniach** to plunge one's hands into one's pockets; **~ić wiosło w wodzie** to dig one's oar into the water

[] zagłębić się — zagłębiać się [1] (zanurzyć się) **~ić się w coś** *[ostrze, wiertło]* to sink into sth; **~ić się w las** *[osoba]* to go deep into the forest [2] (zająć się) to bury oneself; **~iać się w szczegóły** to go into detail

zagł|odzić *pf* **[]** *vt* to starve

[] zagłodzić się to starve oneself

zagłos|ować *pf vi* to vote

zagłusz|yć *pf* — **zagłusz|ać** *impf vt* [1] (stłumić) to deafen *[hałas]*; to drown [sth] out *[rozmowę, osobę]*; to jam *[audycję, częstotliwość]*; to obscure *[zapach]* [2] (zdławić) **~yć w sobie wyrzuty sumienia** to appease one's conscience; **~yć lęk** to keep one's mind off one's fear [3] *[chwasty]* to choke [sth] up *[roślinę]*

zag|nać, **zag|onić** *pf* — **zag|aniać** *impf vt* [1] to drive *[bydło, świnie]*; **~onić kogoś do roboty** to put sb to work; **~onić kogoś do książek** to make sb study

zag|oić *pf* **[]** *vt* to heal *[ranę]*

[] zagoić się to heal (up)

zagon *m* (pole) patch

zagonić → **zagnać**

zagorza|ły *adi. grad. [zwolennik]* keen; *[wielbiciel, fan]* fervent; *[wyznawca]* staunch; *[dyskusja]* heated

zagospodar|ować *pf* — **zagospodar|owywać** *impf* **[]** *vt* to reclaim *[pustynię, bagna]*; to develop *[teren, rzekę]*; **~ować odpadki** to recycle waste

[] zagospodarować się — zagospodarowywać się to settle in

zagot|ować *pf* — **zagot|owywać** *impf* **[]** *vt* to boil [sth] up, to bring [sth] to the boil *[wodę]*

[] zagotować się — zagotowywać się to boil; **aż się w mnie ~owało ze złości** przen. I was boiling with rage

zagra|ć *pf* **[]** *vt* [1] (rozegrać) to play *[partię, piłkę, asa, melodię]* [2] *[aktor]* to play *[rolę]*; (udać) to feign *[ból, smutek]*; **~ć w czymś filmie** to appear in sb's film; **świetnie ~na sztuka** a very well-acted play

[] *vi* [1] (brać udział w grze) to play; **~ć w piłkę nożną/karty** to play football/cards; **~ć na skrzypcach** to play the violin [2] (zabrzmieć) *[muzyka, instrument]* to play; **w jego głosie ~ła nuta ironii** przen. there was a note of irony in his voice [3] pot. (udać się) **wszystko ~ło** everything went well

zagradzać *impf* → **zagrodzić**

zagranic|a *f* foreign countries; **przyjechać z ~y** to come from abroad

zagraniczn|y *adi. [towary, turyści]* foreign; *[kontakty]* international; **podróże ~e** travels abroad

zagra|nie *n* [1] Sport play; (podanie) pass [2] pot. (posunięcie) move

zagraża|ć *impf vi* to threaten (**komuś** sb); **~ nam niebezpieczeństwo** we are in danger; **miastu ~ powódź** the town is threatened with flooding

zagr|oda *f* [1] (gospodarstwo) homestead [2] (ogrodzony teren) enclosure; (dla zwierząt) pen; (dla bydła, koni) corral US

zagr|odzić *pf* — **zagr|adzać** *impf vt* [1] (przegrodzić) *[osoba, przedmiot]* to block *[przejście, przejazd]*; to obstruct *[dostęp]*; **~odzić komuś drogę** to bar sb's way [2] (ogrodzić) to fence off *[plac, teren]*

zagro|zić *pf vi* to threaten (**komuś** sb); **~zili jej śmiercią** they threatened to kill her

zagroże|nie *n* risk, threat; **stanowić ~nie dla czegoś** to pose a threat to sth

zagryw|ka *f* [1] Sport (serwis) serve, service [2] pot. (posunięcie) trick

zagry|źć *pf* — **zagry|zać** *impf vt* [1] (zakąsić) **~zał wódkę kiełbasą** he ate a bit of sausage after downing his vodka [2] *[zwierzę]* to bite [sth] to death [3] *(gryźć)* ~**źć wargi** to bite one's lip(s)

zagrz|ać *pf* — **zagrz|ewać** *impf* **[]** *vt* [1] *(podgrzać)* to heat [sth] up *[jedzenie]* [2] *(dopingować)* ~**ewać kogoś do działania** to spur sb to action

[] **zagrzać się** — **zagrzewać się** [1] *[jedzenie]* to heat up, to warm up [2] *[osoba]* to warm (oneself) up

[]] **zagrzać się** *[silnik, maszyna]* to overheat

zagrzmi|eć *pf* **[]** *vi* [1] *[działo]* to thunder; *[organy]* to blast out; ~**ały oklaski** there was a thunderous applause [2] *(powiedzieć)* to thunder

[] *v imp.* to thunder

zagubi|ony *adi.* [1] *(niepewny) [osoba]* adrift [2] *[wyspa, wioska]* remote

zagwarant|ować *pf vt* to guarantee

zagwi|zdać *pf vt, vi* to whistle *[piosenkę]*; ~**zdać na psa** to whistle the dog over

zahacz|yć *pf* — **zahacz|ać** *impf* **[]** *vt* *(zawiesić)* to hook

[] *vi* [1] *(zawadzić)* to catch; ~**ył rękawem o gwóźdź** he caught his sleeve on a nail [2] *pot. (wstąpić)* to stop off; ~**yć w Warszawę** to stop off at Warsaw

[]] **zahaczyć się** — **zahaczać się** to catch; **latawiec** ~**ył się o gałęzie** the kite got caught in some branches

zaham|ować *pf vt, vi* [1] to brake *[samochód, pociąg]*; ~**ować ostro** to brake hard [2] *przen. (wstrzymać)* to stop *[proces]*

zahamowa|nie *n* inhibition

zahart|ować *pf* **[]** *vt* [1] to harden *[stal, żelazo]* [2] *(uodpornić fizycznie)* to harden off *[roślinę]*; to inure *[osobę]*; *(psychicznie)* to harden, to toughen up *[osobę]*

[] **zahartować się** *[osoba]* *(fizycznie)* to harden; *(psychicznie)* to toughen up

zahipnotyz|ować *pf vt* to hypnotize

zaim|ek *m* pronoun; *(określający rzeczownik)* determiner

zaimpon|ować *pf vi* to impress (**komuś** sb)

zaimprowiz|ować *pf vt* [1] *(wymyślić, zorganizować)* to improvise *[utwór, przemówienie, konferencję]* [2] *(zrobić naprędce)* to improvise, to knock together *[stół, palenisko]*; to knock up *pot. [obiad]*

zainteres|ować *pf* **[]** *vt* [1] *(zaciekawić)* to arouse *[sb's]* interest [2] *(wyrobić zainteresowanie)* to get *[sb]* interested

[] **zainteresować się** [1] *(okazać zainteresowanie)* to become interested (**czymś** in sth) [2] *(zająć się)* to take an interest (**czymś** in sth)

zainteresowa|nie *n* interest (**czymś** into sth); **z** ~**niem** *[czytać]* avidly; *[słuchać]* intently; **wzbudzić czyjeś** ~**nie** to arouse sb's interest; **okazać** ~**nie czymś** to show interest in sth; **mieć szerokie** ~**nia** to have wide interest

zainwest|ować *pf vt* to invest (**w coś** in sth)

zaistni|eć *pf vi* [1] *książk. (powstać) [życie]* to come into being; *[trudności, niebezpieczeństwo]* to arise [2] *(stać się znanym) [osoba]* to become known

zajada|ć *impf* **[]** *vt* to eat [sth] heartily

[] **zajadać się** to gorge (**czymś** on sth)

zaj|ąc *m* hare

zaj|ąć *pf* — **zaj|mować** *impf* **[]** *vt* [1] *[mebel, przedmiot]* to occupy *[miejsce, przestrzeń]*; *[tłum]* to fill *[plac]*; ~**mować zbyt dużo miejsca** to take up too much space [2] *(użytkować)* to take *[miejsce, stolik, apartament]*; to occupy *[łazienkę, piętro]*; ~**ąć dla kogoś miejsce** to keep a seat for sb [3] *(w klasyfikacji, hierarchii)* ~**ąć pierwsze miejsce** to be first; ~**mować ważne stanowisko** to have an important position; ~**ąć stanowisko** przen. to take a. adopt a stance [4] *(zawładnąć)* to occupy *[miasto, terytorium]* [5] *(wypełnić czas)* to take *[minutę, godzinę]* [6] *(zaciekawić)* to absorb; *(zabawić)* to entertain [7] *(zarekwirować)* to distrain

[] **zająć się** — **zajmować się** [1] *(zacząć coś robić)* ~**ąć się czymś** to take up sth; **czym** ~**muje się jego firma?** what does his company do? [2] *(zaopiekować się)* to take care (**kimś** of sb); ~**mować się gośćmi** to entertain guests [3] *(zapalić się)* to catch fire (**od czegoś** from sth)

zaj|echać *pf* — **zaj|eżdżać** *impf* *vi* [1] *(przyjechać)* to arrive [2] *(podjechać)* to pull up; ~**echać przed dom** to pull up in front of the house [3] *(wstąpić)* to stop off (**do czegoś** at sth); ~**echać do kuzynów** to stop off at one's cousins' [4] *(zablokować)* ~**echać komuś drogę** to cut in on sb

[] *v imp.* pot. *(cuchnąć)* to reek (**czymś** of sth)

zajezdni|a *f* depot

zajeżdżać *impf* → **zajechać**

zaję|cie **[]** *n* [1] *(źródło utrzymania)* job; **stałe** ~**cie** a permanent job [2] *(czynność)* occupation; *(obowiązek)* job; **udać się do swoich** ~**ć** to go about one's business [3] *(zainteresowanie)* interest; **słuchać z** ~**ciem** to listen with interest [4] *(konfiskata)* distraint

[] **zajęcia** *plt (kurs)* classes; *(lekcja)* class; **rozkład** ~**ć** a timetable; **dzień wolny od** ~**ć** a day off

zaję|ty *adi. [osoba]* busy; *[miejsce]* taken; *[taksówka]* hired; *[łazienka]* occupied; *[numer]* engaged; ~**te** pot. the line is busy

zajmować *impf* → **zająć**

za|jrzeć *pf* — **za|glądać** *impf vi* [1] *(popatrzeć w głąb)* to look; **zajrzeć do czegoś/pod coś/za coś** to look into/under/behind sth; **zajrzyj do słownika** look it up in a dictionary [2] *(odwiedzić)* to drop in (**do kogoś** on sb); **zajrzeć do sklepu** to pop into a shop

zajś|cie *n* incident

za|jść *pf* — **za|chodzić** *impf* **[]** *vt (podejść ukradkiem)* to steal; **zajść kogoś od tyłu** to steal up on sb from behind

[] *vi* [1] *(przybyć)* to arrive; **zajść daleko** przen. to go far [2] *[słońce, księżyc]* *(za horyzont)* to set; *(za chmury)* to hide [3] *(wstąpić)* to call (**do kogoś** (in) on sb) [4] *(zaistnieć)* to happen; *[proces, reakcja]* to occur; **zaszła pomyłka** there was a mistake [5] *(zasnuć się)* to be covered; **oczy zaszły mu łzami** his eyes misted over (with tears) 6 (nakładać się) ~**dzić na siebie** *[listwy, dachówki]* to overlap

zakal|ec *m* sad layer

zaka|ła *m, f* ~**ła rodziny** a disgrace to the family

zakańczać *impf* → **zakończyć**

zaka|sać *pf* — **zaka|sywać** *impf vt* to roll [sth] up *[rękawy, nogawki]*; to hitch [sth] up *[spódnicę]*

■ ~**sać rękawy** pot. to pitch up

zakatarz|ony *adi.* **być** ~**onym** to have a cold

zakaz *m* ban, prohibition; **uchylić** ~ **czegoś** to lift the ban on sth

zaka|zać *pf* — **zaka|zywać** *impf vt* to forbid; (formalnie) to ban; ~**zać komuś robienia czegoś** to forbid sb to do sth; ~**zać komuś wstępu do klubu** to bar a. ban sb from a club

zakazan|y *adi.* pot. *[twarz, gęba]* ugly; *[knajpa, ulica]* seedy; ~**y typ** a dodgy GB a. shady pot. character

zaka|zić *pf* — **zaka|żać** *impf* **[]** *vt* to infect *[ranę, osobę]*; to contaminate *[wodę, powietrze]*

[] zakazić się — zakażać się to become infected (**czymś** with sth)

zakazywać *impf* → **zakazać**

zakaźn|y *adi. [choroba]* contagious, infectious

zakażać *impf* → **zakazić**

zakaże|nie *n* infection

zaką|sić *pf* — **zaką|szać** *impf vt* pot. to snack pot. (**czymś** on sth)

zaką|ska *f* (przed głównym daniem) starter; (do alkoholu) snack

zakąszać *impf* → **zakąsić**

zakąt|ek *m* nook; **malowniczy** ~**ek** a beauty spot

zakl|ąć[1] *pf* — **zakl|inać** *impf* **[]** *vt* [1] (błagać) to exhort, to implore [2] (w baśniach) to charm; ~**ęty w coś** turned into sth

[] zakląć się — zaklinać się to swear; ~**inać się, że...** to swear blind that...

zakl|ąć[2] *pf vi* (powiedzieć przekleństwo) to swear

zakle|ić *pf* — **zakle|jać** *impf* **[]** *vt* (klejem) to seal; (taśmą) to tape (up)

[] zakleić się — zaklejać się to be sealed

zaklę|cie *n* (w baśniach) spell; (formułka) magic charm, incantation

zaklę|ty *adi.* enchanted

zaklinać *impf* → **zakląć**[1]

zakła|d *m* [1] (przedsiębiorstwo) factory, plant [2] (usługowy) work(shop); works; ~**d fryzjerski** the hairdresser's; ~**d pogrzebowy** an undertaker, a funeral parlour; ~**d ubezpieczeń** an insurance company [3] (instytucja ograniczająca wolność) institution; ~**d poprawczy** a correction centre; ~**d karny** a prison; **umieścić kogoś w** ~**dzie** to institutionalize sb [4] (w wyższych uczelniach) unit [5] (o ustaloną nagrodę) bet; wager książk.; ~**d o tysiąc złotych** a one thousand zloty bet; **pójść o** ~**d, że...** to

make a. lay a bet that...; **przyjmować** ~**dy** to take bets [6] (podwinięty brzeg) hem

zakładać *impf* → **założyć**

zakład|ka *f* [1] (w materiale) tuck, fold [2] (podwinięty brzeg) turn up [3] (do książki) (book)mark

zakładni|k *m*, ~**czka** *f* hostage

zakłamani|e *n* hypocrisy

zakłaman|y *adi. [osoba, świat]* hypocritical

zakłopotan|y *adi. [mina, twarz]* embarrassed

zakłócać *impf* → **zakłócić**

zakłóce|nie *n* [1] (dezorganizacja) disruption [2] (sygnału) interference

zakłó|cić *pf* — **zakłó|cać** *impf vt* to disrupt *[komunikację, proces, lekcję]*; to shatter *[szczęście, spokój]*; to disturb *[sen, spokój, pracę]*; to impede *[rozwój]*

zakoch|ać się *pf* — **zakoch|iwać się** *impf v refl.* to fall in love (**w kimś** with sb)

zakochan|y **[]** *adi.* enamoured; **być** ~**ym w kimś** to be in love with sb; ~**a dziewczyna** a girl in love

[] zakochan|y *m*, ~**a** *f* lover

zakochiwać się *impf* → **zakochać się**

zakol|e *n* (w rzece) bend; (na drodze) curve

zakompleksi|ony *adi.* full of complexes

zakomunik|ować *pf vt* książk. to announce (**o czymś** sth); to inform (**komuś o czymś** sb about sth)

zakon *m* order

zakonnic|a *f* nun, religious

zakonni|k *m* monk, religious

zakonn|y *adi.* monastic

zakończe|nie *n* conclusion; (książki, filmu) ending; ~**nia nerwowe** nerve endings; **szczęśliwe** ~**nie** a happy ending; **na** ~**nie** in conclusion

zak|ończyć *pf* — **zak|ańczać** *impf* **[]** *vt* [1] to finish *[pracę, lekcję, dyskusję]*; to end *[spory, strajki]*; to complete *[badania, prace]* [2] (nadać kształt) **ostro** ~**ończony pręt** a pointed rod; ~**ończyć rękawy mankietem** to gather sleeves into cuffs

[] zakończyć się *[wakacje, targi]* to end; ~**ończyć się czymś** *[wyprawa, spór]* to end (up) in sth

zakop|ać *pf* — **zakop|ywać** *impf* **[]** *vt* to bury *[skarb, zmarłego]*

[] zakopać się — zakopywać się to dig oneself (**w czymś** in sth)

zakorzeni|ony *adi. [zwyczaj, tradycja]* deep-rooted; ~**ony w w czymś** rooted in sth

zakotwicz|yć[2] **zakotwicz|ać** *impf vt, vi* to anchor *[statek]*

[] zakotwiczyć się — zakotwiczać się [1] *[statek]* to anchor [2] przen. ~**yć się gdzieś** *[osoba]* to stay somewhere for good

zakpi|ć *pf vi* to jibe (**z czegoś** at sth); ~**ć sobie z kogoś** to play a trick on sb

zakradać się *impf* → **zakraść się**

zakraplacz *m* dropper

zakra|ść się *pf* — **zakra|dać się** *impf v refl.*
[1] *[osoba, zwierzę]* to steal up, to sneak up [2] przen.
[błąd] to creep in

zakres *m* [1] scope, range; **szeroki** ~ **usług** a wide
range of services; **mieć wąski/szeroki** ~ to be
narrow/broad in scope; **wchodzić w** ~ **czegoś** to
fall within the scope of sth; **robić coś we
własnym** ~**ie** to do sth on one's own [2] (częstotliwości, wielkości) range

zakrę|cić *pf* — **zakrę|cać** *impf* [1] *vt* [1] (wyłączyć) to
turn [sth] off *[kran, gaz, wodę]* [2] (docisnąć) to screw
[sth] on *[zakrętkę]*; ~**cić słoik** to screw the lid on a
jar; **słoik był mocno** ~**cony** the lid was firmly on
[3] to curl *[włosy]* [4] (zawinąć) to wrap *[linę, sznurek]*
(**wokół czegoś** around sth)

   [II] *vi* [1] (obrócić) ~**cić korbą** to wind a crank; ~**cić
gałką** to twist a knob; ~**cić partnerką w tańcu** to
spin one's partner around [2] (zmienić kierunek) *[osoba,
pojazd, droga]* to turn [3] pot. (zatelefonować) ~**cić do
kogoś** to give sb a buzz pot.

   [III] **zakręcić się** [1] (obrócić się) *[tancerz]* to spin;
~**ciło mu się w głowie** he felt dizzy [2] pot.
(zakrzątnąć się) ~**cić się wokół czegoś** to see to sth

zakrę|t *m* [1] (zakrzywienie) bend; **tuż za** ~**tem** just
round the corner; **wyjechać zza** ~**tu** to come
around the bend; **zniknąć za** ~**tem** to disappear
around the bend; **znajdować się na** ~**cie** przen. to
be at the crossroads przen. [2] (skręt) turn

zakręt|ka *f* (screw) cap, (screw) top

zakrwaw|ić *pf* — **zakrwaw|iać** *impf* [1] *vt* to
get blood on *[koszulę, prześcieradło]*

   [II] **zakrwawić się** — **zakrwawiać się** *[bandaż]* to
get stained with blood

zakry|ć *pf* — **zakry|wać** *impf* [1] *vt* (przykryć) to
cover; (ukryć) to hide; (osłonić) to shelter; ~**ć twarz
rękami** to hide one's face in one's hands

   [II] **zakryć się** — **zakrywać się** *[osoba]* to cover
oneself

zakrysti|a *f* sacristy, vestry

zakrywać *impf* → **zakryć**

zakrzep|nąć *pf vi [krew]* to clot; *[galareta]* to set;
[tłuszcz] to solidify; *[wosk]* to harden

zakrztu|sić się *pf v refl. [osoba, silnik]* to choke
(**czymś** on sth)

zakrzyw|ić *pf* — **zakrzyw|iać** *impf* [1] *vt* to
bend *[gwóźdź, drut]*; ~**iony nos** a crooked nose;
~**ione szpony** hooked claws; ~**iony dziób** a
curved beak

   [II] **zakrzywić się** — **zakrzywiać się** *[gwóźdź]* to
bend

zaksięg|ować *pf vt* to enter *[wydatki, wpływy]*

zaktualiz|ować *pf* [1] *vt* to update *[dokumenty,
kurs]*; to revise *[przepisy, podręczniki]*

   [II] **zaktualizować się** *[zagadnienie, problem]* to
become topical

zaku|ć *pf* — **zaku|wać**[1] *impf vt* ~**ć kogoś
w kajdanki** to handcuff sb; ~**ć kogoś
w łańcuchy** to put sb in chains

zakup [I] *m* purchase; **pieniądze na** ~ **czegoś**
money for the purchase of sth

   [II] **zakupy** *plt* shopping; **pójść na** ~**y** to go
shopping; **robić** ~**y** to do the shopping

zakurz|ony *adi. [meble, książki]* dusty

zakurz|yć *pf* [1] *vt* pot. to smoke *[fajkę, papierosa]*

   [II] **zakurzyć się** *[przedmiot]* to get covered in dust

zaku|ty *adi.* pot. *[fanatyk]* dim-witted pot.; ~**ta pała**
a bonehead pot.

zakuwać[1] *impf* → **zakuć**

zakuwa|ć[2] *impf vi* pot. (uczyć się) to swot pot.

zakwater|ować *pf* — **zakwater|owywać**
impf [I] *vt* to lodge *[osobę]*; to accommodate
[uchodźców, turystów]; to quarter *[żołnierzy]*

   [II] **zakwaterować się** — **zakwaterowywać się**
[sztab, wojsko] to be quartered

zakwestion|ować *pf vt* to question *[prawo,
autentyczność]*; ~**ować decyzję sędziego** Sport to
dispute the referee's decision

zakwit|nąć *pf* — **zakwit|ać** *impf vi* [1] *[kwiat]* to
bloom; *[drzewo]* to blossom, to come into flower;
[rumieniec, uśmiech] to blossom [2] *[woda, staw]* to
turn green with algae

zal|ać *pf* — **zal|ewać** *impf* [1] *vt* [1] (oblać) ~**ać
ogień** to pour water over the flames; ~**ać sobie
czymś spodnie** to spill sth over one's trousers
[2] (zatopić) to flood także przen. *[miasto, podłogę, rynek]*;
pot ~**ewał mu oczy** sweat was pouring into his
eyes; **miasto** ~**ewa fala przestępczości** przen.
a crime wave sweeps through the city [3] (wypełnić) to
fill *[otwór, dziurę]* (**czymś** with sth)

   [II] **zalać się** — **zalewać się** [1] (oblać się) ~**ać się
herbatą** to spill tea over a. on oneself; ~**ać się
łzami** przen. to break down in tears [2] pot. (upić się) to
get sloshed pot.

zalatan|y *adi.* pot. *[osoba]* busy; **być wiecznie**
~**ym** to be always on the go pot.

zaląż|ek *m* [1] Bot. ovule [2] przen. germ

zale|c *pf* — **zale|gać**[1] *impf vi* [1] (pozostać) to lie;
~**gać półki sklepowe** *[towary]* to fill the shelves;
długo ~**gać w żołądku** *[jedzenie]* to lie heavy on
the stomach [2] (zapaść) *[cisza, mrok]* to fall

zalecać *impf* → **zalecić**

zaleca|ć się *impf v refl.* ~**ć się do kogoś** to make
advances to sb

zalece|nie *n* (rada) recommendation; (rozkaz) order

zale|cić *pf* — **zale|cać** *impf vt* [1] (poradzić) to
recommend; (przepisać) to prescribe *[dietę, kurację]*;
~**cił mi, żebym...** he recommended that I
(should)... [2] (nakazać) to order; ~**cić komuś,
żeby...** to order sb to...

zaledwie [I] *part.* only; ~ **dwa lata temu** only two
years ago

   [II] *coni.* as soon as

zalegać[1] *impf* → **zalec**

zalega|ć[2] *impf vi* (spóźniać się) *[osoba]* to be behind (**z
czymś** with sth)

zalegaliz|ować *pf vt* to legalize *[narkotyki, organizację]*; to (officially) approve *[urządzenie]*

zaległoś|ć *f* (dług) arrears; ~**ci podatkowe** tax arrears; **mieć** ~**ci w pracy** to be behind in one's work; **nadrobić** ~**ci w pracy** to catch up on one's work

zaległ|y *adi.* *[rata, opłata]* overdue; *[zamówienie, praca]* outstanding; ~**ły podatek** back tax

zalep|ić *pf* — **zalep|iać** *impf vt* [1] (zakryć) to cover *[ścianę, powierzchnię]*; ~**ić ranę plastrem** to put a plaster on a cut [2] (klejem) to seal; (taśmą) to tape (up) [3] (wypełnić) to fill *[dziurę]*

zale|ta *f* (osoby) virtue; (rzeczy) good point

zalew *m* [1] (jezioro) lake [2] (zatoka) bay [3] (zalanie) flooding [4] przen. (napływ) deluge

zalewać *impf* → **zalać**

zależ|eć *impf* [1] *vi* to depend (**od kogoś/czegoś** on sb/sth)

[2] *v imp.* ~**y mi na tobie** I care about you; **co ci** ~**y!** pot. what do you care?

zależnoś|ć *f* [1] (zjawisk) relation, relationship; **w** ~**ci od pogody** depending on the weather [2] (niesamodzielność) dependence (**od kogoś** on sb); ~**ć służbowa** subordination

zależn|y *adi.* dependent; ~**y od kogoś/czegoś** dependent on sb/sth

zal|ęgnąć się *pf* — **zal|ęgać się** *impf v refl.* (rozmnożyć się) *[insekty, szkodniki]* to breed; **w szafie** ~**ęgły się mole** the wardrobe became infested with moths

zaliczać *impf* → **zaliczyć**

zalicze|nie *n* Uniw. credit

■ **wysłać coś za** ~**niem pocztowym** to send sth cash on delivery a. COD

zalicz|ka *f* advance payment (**na coś** for sth)

zalicz|yć *pf* — **zalicz|ać** *impf* [1] *vt* [1] (zaklasyfikować) to count; ~**ać kogoś do bliskich przyjaciół** to count sb among one's close friends [2] (uznać) to recognize; ~**yć kwotę na poczet spłaty długu** to recognize a sum against the repayment of a debt [3] (odnieść sukces) to pass *[test, egzamin]*; ~**yć wysokość w pierwszej próbie** Sport to clear a height with one's first attempt; ~**yć kogoś** pot. to score with sb pot. [4] pot. (odbyć) ~**yliśmy tę wystawę** we did the exhibition pot.

[2] **zaliczać się** (należeć) to rank, to be numbered (**do kogoś/czegoś** among sb/sth)

zalotn|y *adi. grad.* *[dziewczyna]* coquettish; *[spojrzenie, uśmiech]* flirtatious

zalot|y *plt* advances

zaludni|ć *pf* — **zaludni|ać** *impf* [1] *vt* to populate *[teren]*

[2] **zaludnić się** — **zaludniać się** [1] *[teren, kraj]* to become populated [2] *[ulice, plaża]* to come alive with people

zaludnieni|e *n* population

załad|ować *pf* — **załad|owywać** *impf vt* [1] (umieścić ładunek) to load (**coś na coś** sth onto sth) [2] to load *[broń]*

załadun|ek *m* loading

załag|odzić *pf* — **załag|adzać** *impf* [1] *vt* to appease *[spór, konflikt]*; ~**odzić sytuację** to ease a situation

[2] **załagodzić się** *[konflikt, spór]* to be appeased

załam|ać *pf* — **załam|ywać** *impf* [1] *vt* [1] (zagiąć) to bend *[karton, okładkę]*; to refract *[światło, falę]* [2] (doprowadzić do rozpaczy) to depress

[2] **załamać się** — **załamywać się** [1] (zgiąć się) *[karton, materiał]* to bend; *[światło, fala]* to be refracted [2] (zawalić się) *[dach, sklepienie]* to cave in; *[most]* to collapse; *[lód]* to break [3] (psychicznie) *[osoba]* to break down [4] (ulec pogorszeniu) *[ofensywa, rynek]* to collapse

załama|nie *n* [1] (kartki) bend; (tkaniny) fold; (skały) recess; (linii brzegowej) twist [2] (przygnębienie) (nervous) breakdown [3] (w gospodarce) slump

załamywać *impf* → **załamać**

załatw|ić *pf* — **załatw|iać** *impf* [1] *vt* [1] (doprowadzić do skutku) to fix *[formalności, sprawy]*; ~**ić komuś pracę** to fix sb up with a job; ~**ić komuś wizytę u specjalisty** to arrange an appointment with a specialist for sb [2] (obsłużyć) to serve *[klienta, pacjenta]* [3] pot. (rozprawić się) to fix pot. *[osobę]* [4] pot. (zabić) to do away with

[2] **załatwić się** — **załatwiać się** [1] (ukończyć) to finish (**z czymś** with sth) [2] pot. (wypróżnić się) to relieve oneself

[3] **załatwić się** pot. (rozprawić się) ~**ić się z kimś** to cook sb's goose pot.

załączać *impf* → **załączyć**

załącznik *m* (do listu) enclosure; (do umowy) annex(e) (**do czegoś** to sth); Komput. attachment

załącz|yć *pf* — **załącz|ać** *impf vt* to enclose (**coś do czegoś** sth with a. in sth); **w** ~**eniu przesyłam...** enclosed is...

zał|oga *f* [1] (pociągu, samolotu, statku) crew [2] (fabryki, kopalni) staff [3] (twierdzy) garrison

założe|nie [1] *n* [1] (teza) assumption; **wychodzić z** ~**nia, że...** to assume that...; **w** ~**niu** originally [2] (parkowe, urbanistyczne) layout

[2] **założenia** *plt* (wytyczne) principles

założyciel *m*, ~**ka** *f* founder

za|łożyć *pf* — **za|kładać** *impf* [1] *vt* [1] (stworzyć) to found *[miasto, klasztor, firmę]*; **założyć gniazdo** to build a nest; **założyć rodzinę** to start a family [2] (nałożyć) to put on *[okulary, ubranie, buty]*; **założyć nogę na nogę** to cross one's legs; **siedzieć z założonymi rękami** przen. to sit idle [3] (zainstalować) to instal(l) *[gaz, elektryczność, telefon]* [4] (podwinąć) to turn up *[brzeg, rękaw]* [5] (wpłacić za kogoś) **założyć za kogoś (składkę)** to pay (the contribution) for sb [6] (przypuścić) to assume [7] (zaplanować) to intend [8] (wnieść) to lodge *[apelację, rewizję]*

II **założyć się — zakładać się** (zrobić zakład) to bet (**z kimś** with sb); **założyć się z kimś o coś** to bet sb sth; **założę się, że...** I bet (that)...

zamach m 1 (ruch ręką) backswing; **wziąć ~** to take a swing; **za jednym ~em** pot., przen. at a. in one go 2 (na życie) attempt; **~ na prezydenta** an attempt on the life of the president; **~ stanu** a coup d'état

zamachow|iec m assassin; (podkładający bombę) bomber

zamaczać impf → **zamoczyć**

zamar|znąć /za'marznɔɳtɕ/ pf — **zamar|zać** /za'marzatɕ/ impf vi [woda, rury] to freeze; [jezioro, woda] to ice over; [osoba] to freeze to death

zamarznię|ty /ˌzamar'znɛntɨ/ adi. frozen; [szyba] icy

zamask|ować pf — **zamask|owywać** impf **II** vt 1 (zasłonić) to camouflage 2 (ukryć) to mask [uczucie]

II **zamaskować się — zamaskowywać się** 1 (zasłonić się) [wojsko, partyzanci] to camouflage oneself 2 (ukryć zamiary) to disguise one's intentions

zamaskowan|y adi. [osoba] masked

zamaskowywać impf → **zamaskować**

zamaszy|sty adi. [krok] brisk; [ruch] sweeping

zamawiać impf → **zamówić**

zamazan|y adi. [zdjęcie, obraz, tekst] blurred

zamążpójści|e n marriage

zam|ek m 1 (w drzwiach, broni) lock; **centralny ~ek** central locking 2 (budowla) castle

zameld|ować pf **II** vt 1 (zawiadomić) to report (**o czymś** (on) sth) 2 (zgłosić) to register [lokatora] **II** **zameldować się** 1 (w urzędzie) to register; **~ować się w hotelu** to book a. check into a hotel 2 (stawić się) to report (**u kogoś** to sb)

zamę|t m confusion

zamężn|y adi. [kobieta] married

zamgl|ony adi. [fotografia, obraz] blurred; [wzrok, oczy] misty, filmy

zamian|a f (wymiana) exchange, swap (**czegoś na coś** of sth for sth); **zrobić ~ę** to do a swap 2 (przekształcenie) conversion (**czegoś na coś** of sth into sth)

zamia|r m intention; **mieć ~r coś zrobić** to intend to do sth, to be going to do sth; **z ~rem zrobienia czegoś** with the purpose of doing sth; **z ~rem popełnienia przestępstwa** with criminal intent; **nosić się z ~rem zrobienia czegoś** to intend to do sth

zamiast praep., coni. instead of

zamiatać impf → **zamieść**

zamie|ć f blizzard

zamiejscow|y 1 adi. [student, uczeń] non-resident; [pracownik] commuting 2 [rozmowa] long-distance

II **zamiejscowa** f pot. (rozmowa) long-distance call

zamie|nić pf — **zamie|niać** impf **II** vt 1 (zrobić wymianę) to exchange (**coś na coś** sth for sth); **~nić**

z kimś kilka słów to have a brief word with sb 2 (przeobrazić) to turn (**coś w coś** sth into sth)

II **zamienić się — zamieniać się** 1 (dokonać wymiany) to exchange (**z kimś na coś** sth with sb); **~niłbyś się ze mną?** would you like to swap with me? 2 (przeobrazić się) to turn (**w coś** into sth)

zamienn|y adi. [część, element] replacement

zamierać impf → **zamrzeć**

zamierz|yć pf — **zamierz|ać** impf vt to plan; **~ać coś zrobić** to be going to do sth

zamiesza|ć pf **II** vt 1 to stir [zupę, herbatę]; **~ć komuś w głowie** przen. to befuddle sb 2 (wplątać) **być ~nym w coś** to be involved in sth 3 pot. (wprowadzić zamęt) to cause a stir

II **zamieszać się** (dać się wciągnąć) to become involved (**w coś** in sth)

zamieszani|e n confusion, commotion; **narobić ~a** to cause commotion

zamieszczać impf → **zamieścić**

zamieszk|ać pf vi 1 (osiąść) to settle; (wprowadzić się) to move in; (zatrzymać się) to stay

zamieszka|ły adi. 1 (mieszkający) resident; **stale ~ły za granicą** resident abroad 2 (zamieszkany) inhabited

zamiesz|ki plt disturbances, riots

zamieszk|iwać impf vt to inhabit [teren, terytorium]

zamie|ścić pf — **zamie|szczać** impf vt to print [artykuł, sprostowanie]; to place [ogłoszenie, reklamę]

zami|eść pf — **zami|atać** impf vt to sweep up a. out [pokój, podłogę, ulicę]

zamilk|nąć pf vi to go quiet; przen. [radio, armaty] to fall silent

zamiłowani|e n passion (**do czegoś** for sth); **ornitolog z ~a** an ornithologist by avocation

zam|knąć pf — **zam|ykać** impf **II** vt 1 (zakryć wejście) to close, to shut [drzwi, pojemnik, książkę, oczy]; (na klucz) to lock [drzwi, kredens]; **~knąć bramę na kłódkę/zasuwę** to padlock/bolt the gate 2 (przerwać działalność) to close down [sklep, fabrykę] 3 (w pomieszczeniu) to shut [dziecko, psa] 4 pot. (uwięzić) to lock [sb] up 5 (zablokować) to close [granicę, port] 6 pot. (wyłączyć) to switch off [radio, telewizor] 7 (zakończyć) to close, to conclude [obrady, dyskusję]

II **zamknąć się — zamykać się** 1 [drzwi, okna] to close, to shut 2 (ukryć się) to shut oneself (away) 3 (złożyć się, zwinąć się) [parasol, scyzoryk] to close 4 (dojść do końca) to end

III **zamknąć się** pot. (zamilknąć) to shut up

zamknię|cie n 1 (zamek) lock 2 (pomieszczenie) confinement

zamknię|ty adi. 1 [dziedziniec, plac, teren] closed off; (murem) walled-in; (płotem) fenced-in 2 [impreza, konkurs] closed 3 [osoba] self-contained

zamocz|yć *pf* **[]** *vt* 1 (niechcący) to get [sth] wet 2 (celowo) to soak *[pranie, bieliznę]* **[]] zamoczyć się** to get wet

zamont|ować *pf* — **zamont|owywać** *impf vt* to mount *[silnik, gaźnik]*; to instal(l) *[okna, kran]*

zamord|ować *pf vt* to murder także przen.

zamożn|y *adi. grad. [osoba]* wealthy; *[społeczeństwo]* affluent; *[kupiec, lekarz, rodzina]* well-off

zam|ówić *pf* — **zam|awiać** *impf* **[]** *vt* 1 (zlecić) to order (**coś u kogoś** sth from sb) 2 (zarezerwować) to book, to reserve *[miejsce, bilet]*; to call *[taksówkę]*; ~**ówić wizytę u lekarza** to make an appointment with the doctor 3 (w restauracji) to order *[potrawę, wino, kawę]* **[]] zamówić się — zamawiać się** (zawiadomić o przyjściu) ~**ówił się do przyjaciół na obiad** he told his friends that he would come to dinner

zamówie|nie *n* 1 (polecenie dostarczenia) order; **wykonany na** ~**nie** *[meble]* custom-built; **szyty na** ~**nie** custom-made; **złożyć** ~**nie na coś** to place an order for sth 2 (formularz) order form 3 (w restauracji) order

zamrażać *impf* → **zamrozić**

zamrażalnik *m* freezer compartment

zamrażar|ka *f* freezer, deep-freeze

zamr|ozić *pf* — **zamr|ażać** *impf* **[]** *vt* to freeze także przen. *[mięso, ryby, ceny]* **[]] zamrozić się — zamrażać się** to freeze

zam|rzeć *pf* — **zam|ierać** *impf* **[]** *vi* 1 *[ruch, życie]* to die out 2 przen. (nieruchomieć) *[osoba, twarz]* to freeze; **serce w niej** ~**arło** her heart sank 3 (umilknąć) *[dźwięk, śmiech]* to tail off; **głos** ~**arł mu w gardle** words stuck in his throat

zamsz *m* suede

zamur|ować *pf* — **zamur|owywać** *impf vt* to brick in a. up *[wnękę, otwór]*; to wall in *[grobowiec, drzwi]*; ~**owało go** pot. he was momentarily speechless

zamykać *impf* → **zamknąć**

zamy|sł *m* idea, conception

zamyśl|ić się *pf* — **zamyśl|ać się** *impf v refl.* to fall into a pensive mood; to ponder (**nad czymś** on a. over sth)

zamyśl|ony *adi. [osoba]* lost in thought; *[oczy, spojrzenie]* pensive

zaneg|ować *pf vt* książk. to negate *[zasadę, fakt]*

zaniecha|ć *pf vi* to abandon (**czegoś** sth)

zanieczyszczać *impf* → **zanieczyścić**

zanieczyszcze|nie *n* 1 (substancja) pollutant 2 (stan) pollution

zanieczy|ścić *pf* — **zanieczy|szczać** *impf vt* 1 (zatruć) to pollute *[wodę, powietrze]* 2 (stanowić domieszkę) to contaminate *[substancję]* 3 (zabrudzić) to soil

zaniedb|ać *pf* — **zaniedb|ywać** *impf* **[]** *vt* to neglect *[osobę, ogród, obowiązki]* **[]] zaniedbać się — zaniedbywać się** 1 (opuścić

się) to be negligent; ~**ać się w nauce** to fall behind in school 2 (przestać o siebie dbać) to stop looking after oneself

zaniedba|nie *n* 1 (brak troski) neglect; **dopuścić się** ~**ń** to be guilty of neglect 2 (niechlujstwo) seediness

zaniedban|y *adi. [budynek, okolica]* squalid; *[osoba]* scruffy

zaniemówi|ć *pf vt* to be struck dumb, to be dumbstruck

zaniepok|oić *pf* **[]** *vt* to alarm **[]] zaniepokoić się** to become alarmed a. worried; „**naprawdę?**", ~**oiła się** 'really?', she asked worriedly

zan|ieść *pf* — **zan|osić** *impf* **[]** *vt* to take; (trzymając na rękach) to carry; ~**ieść komuś obiad** to take sb lunch; ~**ieść komuś wiadomość** to take the news to sb **[]] zanieść się — zanosić się** 1 (nie móc opanować) ~**osić się płaczem** to sob uncontrollably; ~**osić się od śmiechu** to be whooping with laughter 2 (zasnuć się) *[niebo]* to become overcast

zanik *m* disappearance; (uczuć, więzi) degeneration; (gatunków) extinction; (organów) atrophy

zanik|nąć *pf* — **zanik|ać** *impf vi* 1 (zniknąć) *[dźwięk]* to fade out 2 (przestać istnieć) *[gatunek]* to become extinct; *[zwyczaj, gwara]* to vanish; *[organ, mięśnie]* to atrophy

zanim *coni.* before, by the time; ~ **się obejrzysz** before you know it

zanoc|ować *pf vi* to stay overnight

zanosić *impf* → **zanieść**

zanosi|ć się *impf v imp.* ~ **się na deszcz** it looks like rain; ~ **się na strajk** it looks as though there's going to be a strike

zanu|dzić *pf* — **zanu|dzać** *impf* **[]** *vt* to bore *[osobę]* **[]] zanudzić się** to be bored (stiff)

zanurk|ować *pf vi [osoba, zwierzę, samolot]* to dive

zanurzać *impf* → **zanurzyć**

zanurze|nie *n* draught; **małe/duże** ~**nie** a shallow/deep draught

zanurz|yć *pf* — **zanurz|ać** *impf* **[]** *vt* (włożyć) to plunge *[dłoń]*; (zamoczyć) to dip *[palce, stopy]*; (umieścić pod wodą) to immerse *[przedmiot, rękę]* **[]] zanurzyć się — zanurzać się** *[wieloryb, łódź podwodna]* to submerge; ~**yć się w wodzie** *[osoba]* to go into water; ~**yć się w gęstwinie** to plunge into the thicket

zaobserw|ować *pf vt* to observe

zaoczn|y *adi.* 1 *[wyrok, proces]* in absentia 2 *[system, studia]* extramural, extension GB; *[student]* external

zaogni|ć *pf* — **zaogni|ać** *impf* **[]** *vt* 1 to inflame *[stosunki, konflikt, sytuację]* 2 to inflame, to irritate *[ranę]* 3 *[chłód, alkohol]* to redden *[oczy, policzki]* **[]] zaognić się — zaogniać się** 1 *[sytuacja,* *stosunki, konflikt]* to become exacerbated a. inflamed ② *[rana, skaleczenie]* to (start to) fester ③ *[policzki, twarz]* to redden

zaokrągl|ić — zaokrągl|ać *impf* **I** *vt* ① (uczynić okrągłym) to round off *[róg, brzeg]*; to round *[samogłoskę, wargi]* ② (uprościć) to round *[liczbę]*; ~**ić coś w górę/dół** to round sth up/down; ~**ić coś do pełnej złotówki** to round sth off to the nearest whole zloty

II zaokrąglić się — zaokrąglać się *[osoba, twarz]* to fill out

zaokręt|ować *pf* **I** *vt, vi* to embark *[pasażerów]*; (do pracy) to hire *[kucharza, mechanika]*

II zaokrętować się to embark

zaopatrywać *impf* → **zaopatrzyć**

zaopatrzeni|e *n* supply; **dział** ~**a** a supplies department

zaopat|rzyć *pf* — **zaopat|rywać** *impf* **I** *vt* ① (dostarczyć) to supply *[fabrykę, miasto]* (**w coś** with sth); to stock *[sklep, spiżarnię]* (**w coś** with sth); ~**rzyć kogoś w coś** to provide sb with sth ② (wyposażyć) to supply, to provide *[urządzenie, samochód]* (**w coś** with sth); ~**rzyć książkę we wstęp** to add an introduction to a book

II zaopatrzyć się — zaopatrywać się to get (**w coś** sth)

zaopiek|ować się *pf vi* to take care (**kimś** of sb)

zao|rać *pf* — **zao|rywać** *impf* **I** *vt* to plough, to plow US *[pole, ziemię]*

II zaorać się — zaorywać się *[pojazd, koło]* to get stuck

zaostrz|yć *pf* — **zaostrz|ać** *impf* **I** *vt* ① (naostrzyć) to sharpen *[patyk, ołówek]* ② (uczynić surowszym) to tighten *[kontrolę, dyscyplinę]*; to toughen *[przepisy, kary]* ③ (wzmóc) to exacerbate *[konflikt, sytuację]*; to sharpen *[ból, apetyt]*

II zaostrzyć się — zaostrzać się ① (nabrać wyrazistości) *[różnice, rysy]* to sharpen ② (wzmóc się) *[konflikt, sytuacja]* to be exacerbated; *[apetyt, ból, zmysły]* to sharpen ③ (stać się surowym) *[kontrola, ochrona]* to become tighter; *[przepisy]* to become stricter; *[kary]* to become tougher

zaoszczę|dzić *pf* — **zaoszczę|dzać** *impf* *vt* ① (mniej zapłacić) to save; (odłożyć) to put away; ~**dzić na czymś** to economize on sth ② (darować) to spare; ~**dzić komuś szczegółów** to spare sb details

zapach *m* ① (woń) smell; **poznać coś po** ~**u** to recognize sth by smell; **mydło o** ~**u bzu** lilac-scented soap ② Kulin. essence

zapadać *impf* → **zapaść**¹

zapad|ły *adi.* *[mieścina, wieś]* godforsaken

zapadni|a *f* trapdoor; (pod szubienicą) drop

zapadni|ęty *adi.* *[policzki, oczy]* sunken

zapak|ować *pf* **I** *vt* ① (włożyć) to pack (**coś do czegoś** sth into sth); ~**ować coś w papier** to wrap sth in paper ② (wypełnić) to pack *[plecak, torbę]* ③ pot. (umieścić) ~**ować kogoś do więzienia** to put

sb in prison; ~**ować kogoś do łóżka** to pack sb off to bed

II zapakować się to pack (up)

zapalać *impf* → **zapalić**

zapalczyw|y *adi. grad. [osoba]* quick-tempered; *[słowa, przemówienie]* violent

zapale|nie *n* inflammation; ~**nie opon mózgowych** meningitis; ~**nie oskrzeli** bronchitis; ~**nie płuc** pneumonia; ~**nie spojówek** ophthalmia; ~**nie ucha** otitis; ~**nie wyrostka robaczkowego** appendicitis

zapale|niec *m* enthusiast

zapal|ić *pf* — **zapal|ać** *impf* **I** *vt* ① to light *[świeczkę, ognisko]* ② to switch on, to turn on *[lampę, światło]*; **przy** ~**onym świetle** with the light on ③ to light up *[papierosa]*; **mogę** ~**ić?** do you mind if I smoke? ④ pot. to start *[samochód, silnik]*; to switch on *[radio, telewizor]*

II zapalić się — zapalać się ① *[budynek, słoma]* to catch fire; *[zapałka, ogień]* to light ② (włączyć się) *[światło]* to go on ③ (nabrać zapału) to become enthusiastic (**do czegoś** about sth) ④ (zacietrzewić się) ~**ać się w dyskusji** to grow heated in a discussion

zapalnicz|ka *f* (cigarette) lighter

zapalnik *m* fuse

zapaln|y *adi.* ① *[materiał]* inflammable ② przen. *[temat, sytuacja]* explosive ③ Med. *[proces, zmiany]* inflammatory

zapal|ony *adi. [wędkarz, kibic]* keen

zapa|ł *m* enthusiasm (**do czegoś** for sth); **z** ~**łem** enthusiastically; **ostudzić czyjś** ~**ł** to dampen sb's enthusiasm

zapał|ka *f* match; (patyczek) matchstick; **ostrzyc kogoś na** ~**kę** to crop sb's hair; **pudełko od** ~**ek** a matchbox

zapamięt|ać *pf* — **zapamięt|ywać** *impf* **I** *vt* to remember *[zdarzenie, osobę, urazę]*; (nauczyć się na pamięć) to memorize *[tekst]*

II zapamiętać się — zapamiętywać się to be engrossed, to be absorbed (**w czymś** in sth)

zapan|ować *pf* — **zapan|owywać** *impf* *vi* ① (podporządkować sobie) to take control (**nad czymś** of sth); ~**ować nad sobą** to control oneself ② (nastąpić) *[cisza, ciemność]* to fall; *[panika]* to break out

zapar|cie *n* ① (poświęcenie) determination ② Med. constipation

zaparz|yć *pf* — **zaparz|ać** *impf* **I** *vt* to brew *[herbatę, zioła]*; ~**yć kawę** to make coffee

II zaparzyć się — zaparzać się *[herbata, zioła, kawa]* to brew

zapas **I** *m* ① (żywności, wody) supply; (drewna, węgla, pieniędzy) reserve; **kupować coś na** ~ to buy sth for storing; **martwić się na** ~ przen. to worry prematurely; **świeży** ~ **energii** przen. renewed energy ② (do puderniczki, długopisu) refill

II zapasy *plt* provisions, stores; **robić ~y czegoś** to stock up with sth

zapadać *impf* → **zapaść**[1]

zapasow|y *adi.* *[koło, części]* spare; *[kopia dokumentu]* extra; *[schody, wyjście]* emergency

zapas|y *plt* wrestling; **~y z życiem** przen. grappling with life

zapa|ść[1] *pf* — **zapa|dać** *impf* **II** *vi* [1] (osunąć się) to sink; **~ść w głęboki sen** to fall into a deep sleep; **~ść komuś w pamięć** przen. to became embedded in sb's memory [2] (wklęsnąć) *[policzki, oczy]* to sink in [3] (zachorować) to fall ill (**na coś** with sth); **~ść w śpiączkę** to fall into a coma [4] (nastąpić) *[cisza, milczenie, zmierzch]* to fall; *[decyzja]* to be made; *[wyrok]* to be reached

II zapaść się — zapadać się [1] (zawalić się) *[dach, ziemia]* to fall in [2] (ugrzęznąć) *[osoba]* to sink in [3] *[policzki]* to sink in

zapaś|ć[2] *f* collapse

zapaśni|k *m* wrestler

zapatrywać się[1] *impf* → **zapatrzyć się**

zapatr|ywać się[2] *impf v refl.* książk. **~ywać się na coś entuzjastycznie** to be enthusiastic about sth; **jak się na to ~ujesz?** what do you think of this?

zapatrywa|nie *n* (pogląd) opinion, view (**na coś** on sth)

zapatrz|ony *adi.* with one's eyes fixed (**w coś** on sth); **być ~onym w kogoś** to idolize sb

zapat|rzyć się *pf* — **zapat|rywać się**[1] *impf v refl.* [1] (utkwić wzrok) to stare (**w a. na coś** at sth) [2] (brać z kogoś przykład) to look up (**w kogoś** to sb)

zap|chać *pf* — **zap|ychać** *impf* **II** *vt* [1] (zatkać) to block a. clog [sth] up *[rurę, zlew]* [2] pot. (uszczelnić) to fill *[dziurę, szparę]* [3] pot. (zatłoczyć) to clog [sth] up *[przejście, drogę]*

II zapchać się — zapychać się [1] *[rura, zlew]* to become blocked [2] pot. (najeść się) to stuff oneself (**czymś** with sth)

zapeł|nić *pf* — **zapeł|niać** *impf* **II** *vt* to fill *[pomieszczenie, czas, lukę]*

II zapełnić się — zapełniać się to fill up

zapesz|yć *pf* — **zapesz|ać** *impf . vt* pot. to jinx *[plan]*

zapewni|ć *pf* — **zapewni|ać** *impf vt* [1] (zaręczyć) to assure (**kogoś o czymś** sb of sth) [2] (zagwarantować) to gurantee *[bezpieczeństwo]*; (dostarczyć) to provide; **~ć komuś mieszkanie** to provide sb with accommodation; **mieć ~ony byt** to be provided for

zapę|dzić *pf* — **zapę|dzać** *impf* **II** *vt* [1] (zagonić) *[osoba, wiatr]* to drive *[zwierzęta, osobę, łódź]*; (**do czegoś** into sth) [2] (zmusić) to make (**kogoś do czegoś** sb do sth); **~dzić kogoś do pracy** to drive sb to work

II zapędzić się — zapędzać się [1] (zapuścić się)

~dził się w głąb lasu he ventured deep into the forest [2] przen. (przesadzić) to go too far

zap|iąć *pf* — **zap|inać** *impf* **II** *vt* to do up *[ubranie, guziki]*; to buckle *[pasek]*; to fasten *[pasy bezpieczeństwa]*; **~iąć sukienkę na guziki/zamek błyskawiczny** to button up/zip up one's dress

II zapiąć się — zapinać się to button up

III zapinać się (mieć zapięcie) (na guziki) to button; (na zamek) to zip; **żakiet ~ina się na jeden guzik** the jacket is fastened with one button

zapie|c[1] *pf* — **zapie|kać** *impf vt* to bake *[makaron, ryż, warzywa]*

zapie|c[2] *pf vi [oczy, rana, krytyka]* to sting także przen.

zapiekan|ka *f* gratin; (kanapka) ≈ French bread pizza

zapierać *impf* → **zaprzeć**

zapię|cie *n* fastening

zapinać *impf* → **zapiąć**

zapis **II** *m* [1] (system) notation [2] (na taśmie, filmie) record, recording [3] (przepis) regulation; (testamentowy) bequest

II zapisy *plt* (do szkoły, na kurs) enrolment GB, enrollment US; (na akcje) subscription

zapi|sać *pf* — **zapi|sywać** *impf* **II** *vt* [1] (zapełnić pismem) to fill [sth] with writing *[zeszyt, margines]* [2] (zanotować) to note a. write [sth] down *[adres, nazwisko, wypowiedź]*; **~sać coś w notesie** to put sth down in one's notebook [3] (do szkoły, na kurs) to enrol GB, to enroll US [4] (zrobić zapis) to bequeath; **~sać coś komuś w testamencie** to bequeath sth to sb [5] (zalecić) to prescribe *[lek, zastrzyki]* [6] (utrwalić) to record *[głos, obraz]*; Komput. to save *[plik]*

II zapisać się — zapisywać się [1] (do szkoły, na kurs) to enrol GB, to enroll US; (do organizacji) to join (**do czegoś** sth); **~sać się do lekarza** to make an appointment with the doctor [2] (wsławić się) **~sać się w pamięci potomnych** to be remembered by posterity

zapis|ek, ~ka *m, f* note

zapisywać *impf* → **zapisać**

zaplatać *impf* → **zapleść**

zaplą|tać *pf* — **zaplą|tywać** *impf* **II** *vt* to entangle *[nić, sznurek]*

II zaplątać się — zaplątywać się [1] *[nić, sznurek]* to tangle up, to get tangled [2] *[osoba, zwierzę]* to get entangled (**w czymś** in sth); **niepotrzebnie ~tałem się w tę sprawę** I shouldn't have let myself get mixed up in that affair [3] (znaleźć się przypadkiem) to happen to be

III zaplątać się pot. to get confused a. mixed up

zaplecz|e *n* [1] (sklepu) back; (sceny) backstage [2] (struktura wspomagająca) base; **~e polityczne** powerbase

zapl|eść *pf* — **zapl|atać** *impf vt* to plait *[włosy, warkocze, wstążki]*; to lace *[palce]*

zaplomb|ować *pf vt* [1] to seal *[licznik, wagon, mieszkanie]* [2] to fill *[ząb, ubytek]* [3] to stop *[dziuplę, szczelinę]*

zapła|cić *pf vt, vi* to pay także przen. *[rachunek, czynsz, dług]*; ~**cić komuś za coś** to pay sb for sth; ~**cić za coś zdrowiem** przen. to pay for sth with one's health

zapładniać *impf* → **zapłodnić**

zapłakan|y *adi. [osoba]* crying; *[twarz]* tear-stained; *[oczy]* tear-filled

zapła|ta *f* payment; **termin** ~**ty** the due payment day

zapł|odnić *pf* — **zapł|adniać** *impf vt* [1] *[samiec]* to impregnate *[samicę]*; *[plemnik]* to fertilize *[jajo]*; (sztucznie) to inseminate *[samicę, kobietę]* [2] przen. (pobudzić) to inspire *[fantazję, wyobraźnię]*

zapłodnie|nie *n* (połączenie komórek) fertilization; (wprowadzenie nasienia) insemination

zapłon *m* ignition

■ **mieć spóźniony** ~ pot. to be slow off the mark

zapobie|c, zapobie|gnąć *pf* — **zapobie|gać** *impf vi* to prevent (**czemuś** sth)

zapobiegawcz|y *adi. [działania, środki]* preventive

zapobiegliw|y *adi. grad. [osoba]* provident, foresighted

zapodzi|ać *impf* — **zapodzi|ewać** *pf* pot. [] *vt* to mislay *[przedmiot]*

[] **zapodziać się** — **zapodziewać się** (zgubić się) **gdzieś mi się** ~**ał długopis** I've mislaid my pen

zapomina|ć *impf* → **zapomnieć**

zapominals|ki pot. [] *adi. [osoba]* forgetful

[] **zapominals|ki** *m*, ~**ka** *f* forgetful person

zapom|nieć *pf* — **zapom|inać** *impf* [] *vt, vi* [1] (przestać pamiętać) to forget; ~**nieć kogoś/czegoś** to forget sb/sth; ~**nieć o kimś/czymś** to forget about sb/sth; ~**nieć coś zrobić** to forget to do sth; ~**niany poeta** a forgotten poet; ~**nieć komuś krzywdę** to forget the wrong that sb did one [2] (nie wziąć) to forget *[parasola]*

[] **zapomnieć się** — **zapominać się** to forget oneself

zapom|oga *f* aid, benefit

zapo|ra *f* [1] (przeszkoda) barrier także przen.; (przeciwpowodziowa) dyke [2] (na rzece) dam [3] (szlaban) (railway) barrier

zapotrzebowa|nie *n* demand (**na coś** for sth)

zapowi|edzieć *pf* — **zapowi|adać** *impf* [] *vt* [1] (ogłosić) to announce *[wizytę, gościa, program]*; to forecast *[pogodę]*; ~**adana na jutro wizyta prezydenta** the president's visit scheduled for tomorrow [2] (ostrzec) to warn (**komuś** sb); ~**adam wam, że...** I warn you that...

[] **zapowiedzieć się** — **zapowiadać się** (oznajmić chęć przybycia) ~**edział się na kolację** he said he would come for supper

zapowie|dź [] *f* [1] (ogłoszenie) announcement; (przewidywanie) forecast; **zgodnie z** ~**dzią** as announced; **wbrew pesymistycznym** ~**dziom** contrary to gloomy forecasts; **przyjść bez** ~**dzi** to come unannounced [2] (oznaka) harbinger; **być** ~**dzią końca czegoś** to signal the end of sth

[] **zapowiedzi** *plt* banns; **dać na** ~**dzi** to have one's banns published

zapozna|ć *pf* — **zapozna|wać** *impf* [] *vt* [1] (zaznajomić) to acquaint (**kogoś z czymś** sb with sth) [2] (przedstawić) to introduce (**kogoś z kimś** sb to sb)

[] **zapoznać się** — **zapoznawać się** [1] (zaznajomić się) to familiarize oneself (**z czymś** with sth) [2] (zawrzeć znajomość) to become acquainted (**z kimś** with sb)

zapożycz|yć *pf* — **zapożycz|ać** *impf* [] *vt* to borrow *[zwyczaj, słowo]*

[] **zapożyczyć się** — **zapożyczać się** to run into debt

zaprac|ować *pf* — **zaprac|owywać** *impf* [] *vi* ~**ować na coś** to work hard for sth

[] **zapracować się** — **zapracowywać się** to work oneself hard

zapracowan|y *adi.* [1] *[osoba]* busy [2] *[pieniądze]* earned; **ciężko** ~**e pieniądze** hard-earned money

zapracowywać *impf* → **zapracować**

zapragn|ąć *pf vi* to feel a desire (**czegoś** for sth)

zapraszać *impf* → **zaprosić**

zapraw|a *f* [1] (spoiwo) mortar; (farba) ground [2] (ćwiczenia) practice

zaprenumer|ować *pf vt* to subscribe to *[czasopismo, gazetę]*

zaprezent|ować *pf* [] *vt* [1] (pokazać) to present *[produkty, film, sztukę]*; (na targach) to exhibit *[towary, produkty]*; to launch *[nowy model, kolekcję mody]* [2] (wyrazić) to express *[opinię]* [3] (przedstawić) to present *[gościa, rezultaty]*

[] **zaprezentować się** [1] (zrobić wrażenie) **dobrze się** ~**ować** to make a good impression [2] (przedstawić się) to present oneself [3] (wystąpić) to make an appearance

zaprogram|ować *pf vt* to programme GB, to program US także przen. *[urządzenie, osobę, zachowanie]*

zaprojekt|ować *pf vt* to design *[budynek, maszynę]*

zapropon|ować *pf vt* [1] (zaoferować) to offer (**komuś coś** sth to sb) [2] (doradzić) to suggest, to propose; ~**ować zrobienie czegoś** to suggest doing sth; ~**ował, żebym...** he suggested I (should)... [3] (zgłosić) to propose *[kandydaturę]*

zapr|osić *pf* — **zapr|aszać** *impf vt* to invite; ~**osić kogoś na obiad** to invite sb to dinner; ~**osić kogoś do środka** to ask a. invite sb in

zaprosze|nie *n* invitation (**na coś** to sth); **na czyjeś** ~**nie** at sb's invitation

zaprotest|ować *pf vi* to protest (**przeciwko czemuś** against sth)

zaprowa|dzić¹ *pf* — **zaprowa|dzać** *impf vt* (wprowadzić) to establish *[porządek, dyscyplinę]*

zaprowa|dzić² *pf vt* [1] (pokazać drogę) to lead; (zabrać) to take [2] *[ścieżka, droga]* to lead także przen.

zaprz|ąc, zaprz|ęgnąć *pf* — **zaprz|ęgać** *impf* **[I]** *vt* to harness *[konia, psy]* (**do czegoś** to sth) **[II] zaprząc się** — **zaprzęgać się** to be harnessed (**do czegoś** to sth)

zaprzecz|yć *pf* — **zaprzecz|ać** *impf vi* [1] to deny; **~yć zarzutom** to deny the accusations; **nie da się ~yć, że...** there's no denying the fact that... [2] (być w sprzeczności) to contradict

zap|rzeć *pf* — **zap|ierać** *impf* **[I]** *vt* [1] (oprzeć) to brace (**coś o coś** sth against sth) [2] (podeprzeć) to block *[bramę]* [3] (zatamować) **~ierać komuś dech w piersiach** przen. to take sb's breath away; **oglądać coś z ~artym tchem** to watch sth in awe **[II] zaprzeć się** — **zapierać się** [1] (oprzeć się) **~rzeć się rękami o coś** to brace one's hands against sth [2] (zaprzeczyć) **~rzeć się czegoś** to deny sth [3] (wyrzec się) to renounce *[wiary]* [4] pot. (uprzeć się) to dig one's heels in

zaprzęg *m* (pojazd) horse and cart; (zwierzęta) team; **psi ~** a sled dog team

zaprzęgać *impf* → **zaprząc**

zaprzyjaźni|ć się *pf* — **zaprzyjaźni|ać się** *impf v refl.* to make friends (**z kimś** with sb)

zapuchnię|ty *adi.* swollen

zapuka|ć *pf vi* to knock; **~ć do drzwi** to knock at a. on the door

zaprzęgać *impf* → **zaprząc**

zapuszcz|ony *adi. [ogród, park]* neglected

zapu|ścić *pf* — **zapu|szczać** *impf* **[I]** *vt* [1] (umieścić) to cast *[sieć, sondę]*; to put *[krople]* [2] (opuścić) to let down *[żaluzje, rolety]* [3] (zaniedbać) to neglect *[dom, ogród]* [4] (pozwolić urosnąć) to grow *[brodę, włosy]* [5] (uruchomić) to start up *[silnik, motor]* **[II] zapuścić się** — **zapuszczać się** [1] (dotrzeć w głąb) to venture [2] (przestać o siebie dbać) to stop looking after oneself

zapychać *impf* → **zapchać**

zapyl|ić *pf* — **zapyl|ać** *impf* Bot. **[I]** *vt* to pollinate **[II] zapylić się** — **zapylać się** to become pollinated

zapyt|ać *pf* — **zapyt|ywać** *impf* **[I]** *vt* to ask (**kogoś o coś** sb about sth); **~ać o pozwolenie** to ask for permission **[II] zapytać się** — **zapytywać się** to ask (**o coś** sth a. about sth)

zapyta|nie *n* inquiry, enquiry; **znak ~nia** a question mark

zapytywać *impf* → **zapytać**

zarabiać *impf* → **zarobić**

zaradn|y *adi.* resourceful

zara|dzić *pf* — **zara|dzać** *impf vi* to help; to remedy (**czemuś** sth); **nie można temu ~dzić** nothing can be done about it

zarastać *impf* → **zarosnąć**

zaraz **[I]** *part.* [1] (wkrótce) **~ po** right a. straight after; **zadzwonię do ciebie ~ po powrocie** I'll phone you as soon as I get back [2] (blisko) right, just; **~ koło dworca** right a. just next to the station; **~ za rogiem** just around the corner **[II]** *adv.* (od razu) right away, straight away; **~ wracam** I'll be right back; **od ~** pot. right away **[III]** *inter.* (chwileczkę) just a minute; (wyrażając zastanowienie) hang on

zaraz|a *f* [1] (choroba) epidemic, plague; Bot. blight [2] pot. obraźl. scumbag pot., obraźl.; (o kobiecie) hag obraźl.

zaraz|ek *m* germ

zara|zić *pf* — **zara|żać** *impf* **[I]** *vt* to infect także przen. (**kogoś czymś** sb with sth) **[II] zarazić się** — **zarażać się** to become infected (**czymś** with sth); **~zić się grypą od kogoś** to pick up (the) flu from sb

zaraźliw|y *adi.* contagious, infectious także przen.

zardzewia|ły *adi.* rusty

zardzewi|eć *pf vi* to rust (up), to become rusted

zareag|ować *pf vi* to react, to respond (**na coś** to sth)

zarejestr|ować *pf* **[I]** *vt* to register **[II] zarejestrować się** to register

zareklam|ować *pf vt* [1] (zrobić reklamę) to advertise *[film, wyrób]* [2] (zgłosić reklamację) to make a complaint (**coś** about sth)

zarekwir|ować *pf vt* to requisition

zarezerw|ować *pf vt* to book, to reserve *[pokój, stolik, miejsce]*; to set aside *[czas, pieniądze]*

zaręcz|yć *pf* — **zaręcz|ać** *impf* **[I]** *vi* (zagwarantować) to vouch, to affirm; (obiecać) to promise; **~yć za kogoś** to vouch for sb **[II] zaręczyć się** — **zaręczać się** to become engaged (**z kimś** to sb)

zaręczynow|y *adi. [przyjęcie, pierścionek]* engagement

zaręczyn|y *plt* engagement (**z kimś** to sb); (uroczystość) engagement party

zarob|ek *m* [1] (wynagrodzenie) earnings; (dzienny, tygodniowy) wage; (miesięczny, roczny) salary; **dla ~ku** for money; **szukać ~ku** to look for a job [2] (zysk) profit

zar|obić *pf* — **zarabiać** *impf vt* [1] (otrzymać wynagrodzenie) to earn; **~abiać na życie jako...** to earn a living a. one's living as...; **~abiać 1000 złotych tygodniowo** to earn a. make 1,000 zlotys a week; **~obić na czymś** to make a profit of sth [2] (zagnieść) to knead *[ciasto]*

zarod|ek *m* [1] (embrion) embryo [2] Bot. germ (cell) [3] przen. (początek) embryo, germ
■ **stłumić coś w ~ku** to nip sth in the bud

zarodnik *m* spore

zar|oić się *pf v refl. [owady]* to swarm; **na ulicy ~oiło się od ludzi** the street was teeming with people

zaropi|eć *pf vi [oczy, rana]* to fester

zar|osnąć *pf* — **zar|astać** *impf vi* [1] *[rośliny]* to overgrow; *[grządka, staw]* to become overgrown (**czymś** with sth) [2] *[rana]* to heal

zaro|st *m* facial hair; **kilkudniowy ~st** a few days' stubble

zarośl|a *plt* thickets

zarozumial|ec *m* big-head pot.

zarozumia|ły *adi. [osoba, mina]* conceited

zarumie|nić *pf* [1] *vt (przysmażyć)* to brown *[bułkę, cebulę]*

[II] **zarumienić się** [1] Kulin. *[masło, mięso]* to brown [2] *(zaczerwienić się)* to blush, to flush

zar|wać *pf* — **zar|ywać** *impf* [1] *vt* pot. **~wać noc** to sit up till late at night; **~wać studia** to drop out (of university)

[II] **zarwać się** — **zarywać się** *[sufit, most]* to collapse; *[lód]* to break (up)

zarycz|eć *pf vi [lew, niedźwiedź, osoba, silnik]* to roar; *[krowa]* to moo; *[osioł, muł]* to bray, to hee-haw

zarys *m* outline także przen.; **przedstawić coś w ~ie** to outline sth

zarys|ować *pf* — **zarys|owywać** *impf* [1] *vt* [1] *(zrobić rysę)* to scratch *[posadzkę, lakier]* [2] *(uwidocznić kontury)* **mocno ~owana szczęka** a well-defined jaw

[II] **zarysować się** — **zarysowywać się** [1] *(pokryć się rysami) [podłoga, lód]* to become scratched; *[sufit, ściana]* to crack [2] *(stać się widocznym)* to show

zarywać *impf* → **zarwać**

zaryzyk|ować *pf vt* to risk

zarzą|d *m* [1] *(osoby, instytucja)* board (of directors) [2] *(kierowanie)* management; **pod czyimś ~dem** under sb's management; **przejść pod czyjś ~d** to come under sb's control

zarządzać¹ *impf* → **zarządzić**

zarządza|ć² *impf vt* to run *[firmą, gospodarstwem]*; to steward *[majątkiem, obszarem]*; to administer, to manage *[funduszami, interesami]*

zarządze|nie *n* directive

zarzą|dzić *pf* — **zarzą|dzać¹** *impf vt* to order; **~dzić postój** to call a halt

zarzu|cić *pf* — **zarzu|cać** *impf* [1] *vt* [1] *(umieścić)* to fling *[pokrowiec, kapę]*; to fling [sth] on *[płaszcz, pelerynę]*; to cast *[wędkę, sieć]*; **~cić worek na plecy** to shoulder a sack [2] *(zasypać)* to cover; **~cić stół książkami** to scatter the table with books; **~cić kogoś pytaniami** przen. to flood sb with questions [3] *(obwinić)* to accuse (**komuś coś** sb of sth); **nie można jej niczego ~cić** it's impossible to find fault with her [4] *(zaniechać)* to give up *[studia,*

zwyczaj, picie]*; to drop *[pomysł]* [5] *(zagubić)* to misplace, to mislay

[II] *vi [pojazd]* to fishtail

zarzu|t *m (oskarżenie)* accusation, charge; **narażać się na ~t, że...** to lay oneself open to the charge that...; **pod ~tem morderstwa** on a charge of murder

■ **bez ~tu** without fault a. blemish

zasa|da¹ *f* [1] *(przekonanie)* principle; *(reguła)* rule; **człowiek z ~dami** a man of (high) principles; **złamać ~dy** to break the rules; **przestrzegać ~d** to observe the rules; **mam taką ~dę, że...** I make it a rule to...; **w ~dzie** in principle [2] *(tryb postępowania)* rule, regulation [3] *(prawidłowość)* law

zasa|da² *f (substancja)* base

zasadnicz|y *adi. [argument, różnice]* fundamental; *[osoba]* principled

zasadow|y *adi.* basic, alkaline

zasa|dzić *pf* — **zasa|dzać** *impf* [1] *vt* to plant *[roślinę]*

[II] **zasadzić się** — **zasadzać się** *(zaczaić się)* to lay in ambush a. wait (**na kogoś** for sb)

zasadz|ka *f* trap; *(na przestępców, wrogów)* ambush; **zastawić ~kę na coś** to set a trap for sth; **wpaść w ~kę** to fall into a trap

zasalut|ować *pf vt* to salute (**komuś** sb)

zasapan|y *adi. [osoba]* panting; **być ~ym** to be out of breath

zasą|dzić *pf* — **zasą|dzać** *impf vt* to adjudge *[odszkodowanie]* (**na czyjąś rzecz** to sb); to sentence *[osobę]*

zas|chnąć *pf* — **zas|ychać** *impf* [1] *vi [klej]* to set; *[błoto, krew]* to cake; *[tusz, atrament, farba]* to dry

[II] *v imp.* **~chło mi w gardle** I'm thirsty a. parched pot.

zasi|ać *pf* — **zasi|ewać** *impf vt* to sow także przen. *[pole, zboże, niezgodę]*; **~ać w kimś wątpliwości** przen. to sow the seeds of doubt in sb's mind

zasi|ąść *pf* — **zasi|adać** *impf vi* książk. [1] *(usiąść)* to seat oneself książk.; to sit down [2] *(zająć stanowisko)* **~adać w radzie** to have a seat on a council; **~ąść w ławie poselskiej** to be elected to parliament; **~adać w ławie poselskiej** to sit in parliament

zasiedl|ić *pf* — **zasiedl|ać** *impf vt* to settle *[tereny, kraj]*

zasie|dzieć się *pf v refl.* to stay (too) late; **~dzieć się w biurze** to work late at the office

zasiek|i *plt* Wojsk. entanglements

zasiewać *impf* → **zasiać**

zasięg *m* [1] *(zakres)* range; **objąć coś swoim ~iem** *[katastrofa, epidemia]* to spread over sth; **w ~u wzroku** in view; **poza ~iem słuchu** out of hearing range; **znajdować się w ~u ręki** to be within (arm's) reach; **być w czyimś ~u** przen. to be within reach for sb; **być poza czyimś ~iem** przen. to be beyond sb's reach [2] *(pocisku, samolotu)* range

zasięg|nąć *pf* — **zasięg|ać** *impf vt* ~**nąć czyjejś rady** to ask sb's advice; ~**nąć czyjejś opinii** to consult sb

zasilacz *m* power pack

zasil|ić *pf* — **zasil|ać** *impf vt* ① (dostarczyć energii) to power *[urządzenie]* ② (uzupełnić) *[rzeka, przewód]* to feed *[jezioro, zbiornik]*; ~**ić fundusz** *[osoba]* to make a contribution to a fund; *[pieniądze]* to go towards a fund

zasił|ek *m* benefit; ~**ek dla bezrobotnych** unemployment benefit; **the dole** pot.; **być na** ~**ku** to be on social security GB a. welfare US; to be on the dole pot.

zaskakiwać *impf* → zaskoczyć

zaskakując|y *adi.* surprising

zaskarż|yć *pf* — **zaskarż|ać** *impf vt* to appeal against *[decyzję, wyrok]*; to sue *[osobę]*

zaskocze|nie *n* surprise, astonishment; **ku mojemu (wielkiemu)** ~**niu...** to my (great) surprise

zask|oczyć *pf* — **zask|akiwać** *impf* ① *vt [osoba, wydarzenie]* to surprise; *[atak]* to take [sb] by surprise; ~**oczyła ich burza** they were caught in a storm
② *vi* pot. ① *[element, pokrywka]* to click into place ② *[samochód, silnik]* to start ③ pot. (zrozumieć) *[osoba]* to get it

zaskórniak *m* pot. secret nest egg pot.

zaskro|niec *m* grass snake

zasłab|nąć *pf vi* to collapse

zasłać, **zaściełać** *pf* — **zaścielać**, **zaściełać** *impf vt* (nakryć) to cover; **zasłać łóżko** to make the bed

zasłaniać *impf* → zasłonić

zasłon|a *f* ① (tkanina) curtain; **zaciągnąć** ~**y** to draw the curtains; **rozsunąć** ~**y** to open the curtains ② (osłona) cover ③ Sport guard
❏ ~**a dymna** Wojsk. smokescreen także przen.

zasł|onić *pf* — **zasł|aniać** *impf* ① *vt* ① (zakryć) to cover *[oczy]*; to obscure *[księżyc, widok]*; to shut out, to block (out) *[światło]*; ~**onić okno** to draw the curtains; ~**aniasz mi!** you're blocking my view! ② (ochronić) to shield (**kogoś przed czymś** sb from sth)
② **zasłonić się** — **zasłaniać się** ① (zakryć się) to cover oneself ② (ochronić się) to shield oneself ③ przen. ~**aniać się czymś** to use sth as an excuse

zasłu|ga *f* service; **medal za** ~**gi** an order of merit; **poczytywać coś komuś za** ~**gę** to give sb credit for sth; **umniejszać czyjeś** ~**gi** to belittle sb's achievements; **to nie moja** ~**ga** I don't deserve the credit

zasługiwać *impf* → zasłużyć

zasłuż|ony *adi.* ① *[osoba]* distinguished ② *[kara, nagroda, posiłek]* well-deserved

zasłu|żyć *pf* — **zasłu|giwać** *impf vi* to deserve; ~**żyć (sobie) na coś** to deserve sth

zasły|nąć *pf vi* to become famous (**z czegoś** for sth)

zasmak|ować *pf* ① *vt* (zakosztować) to taste *[swobody, władzy]*
① *vi* ① (polubić) to develop a taste (**w czymś** for sth) ② (spodobać się) ~**owała im wolność** they enjoyed the taste of freedom

zasmu|cić *pf* — **zasmu|cać** *impf* ① to sadden *[osobę]*
① **zasmucić się** — **zasmucać się** *[osoba]* to be saddened; *[twarz]* to turn sad

zas|nąć *pf* — **zas|ypiać**[1] *impf vi [osoba]* to fall asleep; **nie mogę** ~**nąć** I can't sleep

zas|ób ① *m* (nagromadzenie) store; (źródło) source; **duży** ~**ób słów** a large vocabulary; **niewyczerpane** ~**oby energii** boundless reserves of energy
① **zasoby** *plt* (zapasy) reserves; (surowce) resources

zasp|a *f* bank; **zaspa** ~**a śnieżna** a bank of snow, a snowbank

za|spać *pf* — **za|sypiać**[2] *impf* ① *vt* (przegapić) **zaspać sprawę** to let the chance slip
① *vi [osoba]* to oversleep

zaspan|y *adi.* sleepy

zasp|okoić *pf* — **zasp|okajać**, **zasp|akajać** *impf vt* to fulfil GB, to fulfill US *[potrzeby, pragnienie, ambicje]*; to satisfy *[ciekawość, popyt]*; to sate *[apetyt]*

zasta|ć *pf* — **zasta|wać** *impf vt* to find *[rzecz, osobę]*; **nie** ~**łem go w domu** he wasn't at home; **czy** ~**łem szefa?** is the boss in?

zastan|owić *pf* — **zastan|awiać** *impf* ① *vt* to puzzle; ~**awia mnie, dlaczego...** I wonder why...
① **zastanowić się** — **zastanawiać się** to think; ~**awiać się nad czymś** to ponder over sth; ~**owić się nad czymś** to give some thought to sth; ~**awiam się, dlaczego...** I wonder why...

zastanowieni|e *n* thought; **po** ~**u** on reflection; **zrobić coś bez** ~**a** to do sth without thinking

zastaw *m* pledge; **oddać coś w** ~ to put sth in pledge; (w lombardzie) to place sth in pawn; **pożyczać pod** ~ to borrow on security

zastaw|a *f* ~**a (stołowa)** tableware; **srebrna** ~**a** silverware

zastawać *impf* → zastać

zastaw|ić *pf* — **zastaw|iać** *impf vt* ① (wypełnić) to cram *[pokój, stół]* ② (zatarasować) to block *[przejście, wjazd]*; (zabarykadować) to barricade *[drzwi]* ③ (umieścić) to set *[pułapkę, sidła]* ④ (oddać w zastaw) to pledge (**coś u kogoś** sth with sb); ~**ić coś w lombardzie** to pawn sth
① **zastawić się** — **zastawiać się** (zasłonić się) ~**ić się parawanem** to hide behind a screen

zastaw|ka *f* Anat. valve

zast|ąpić *pf* — **zast|ępować** *impf vt* ① (przejąć obowiązki) ~**ępować kogoś** to substitute a. fill in for sb; *[nauczyciel]* to sub for sb ② (zamienić) to replace (**coś czymś** sth with sth) ③ (zajść) ~**ąpić komuś drogę** to bar sb's way

zastęp *m* [1] (grupa) army przen.; (wojska) host książk. [2] (w harcerstwie) patrol

zastęp|ca *m*, ~ **czyni** *f* replacement; (w urzędzie) deputy; (w firmie) assistant; ~**ca dyrektora** (w przedsiębiorstwie) the assistant manager; (w szkole) the deputy head

zastępcz|y *adi.* substitute; **rodzina** ~**a** a foster family

zastępować *impf* → **zastąpić**

zastępstw|o *n* replacement; **mieć** ~**o za kogoś** to fill in for sb; *[nauczyciel]* to stand in for sb

zastos|ować *pf* — **zastos|owywać** *impf* [] *vt* to apply *[sprzęt, karę]*; to use *[przedmiot]*; to employ *[terapię, metodę]*; **znaleźć** ~**owanie w czymś** to find application in sth

[] **zastosować się** — **zastosowywać się** to comply (**do czegoś** with sth);

zast|ój *m* [1] stagnation; ~**ój gospodarczy** an economic slowdown [2] Med. stasis

zastrajk|ować *pf vi* to go on strike

zastrasz|yć *pf* — **zastrasz|ać** *impf vt* to intimidate

zastrze|c *pf* — **zastrze|gać** *impf* [] *vt* to reserve *[prawo]*; ~**c sobie anonimowość** to wish to remain anonymous; **wszelkie prawa** ~**żone** all rights reserved; **z góry** ~**gam, że...** I must warn you that...

[] **zastrzec się** — **zastrzegać się** (zapewnić) to make it clear; (uprzedzić) to warn

zastrzel|ić *pf* [] *vt* to shoot (to death); **a toś mnie** ~**ił!** pot. you've got me there!

[] **zastrzelić się** to shoot oneself (to death)

zastrzeże|nie *n* (krytyczna uwaga) reservation; **mieć** ~**nia do czegoś** to have reservations about sth; **z** ~**niem, że...** on the stipulation a. with the proviso that...

zastrzyk *m* injection; shot pot.; **zrobić komuś** ~ to give sb an injection; ~ **gotówki** przen. a cash injection przen.

zastuka|ć *pf vi [osoba]* to tap; *[buty, kopyta]* to clatter; *[koła]* to rattle; *[krople]* to patter; ~**ć do drzwi** to knock at a. on the door

zastyg|nąć *pf* — **zastyg|ać** *impf vi* [1] *[galareta]* to set; *[tłuszcz]* to solidify; *[wosk, lawa, żywica]* to harden [2] książk. *[osoba, twarz, uśmiech]* to freeze

zasuger|ować *pf* [] *vt* (podsunąć myśl) to suggest; (dać do zrozumienia) to imply

[] **zasugerować się** to be influenced (**czymś** by sth); (odnieść mylne wrażenie) to be misled (**czymś** by sth)

zasu|nąć *pf* — **zasu|wać**[1] *impf* [] *vt* [1] (zasłonić) to draw *[zasłonę, firanki, zasuwę]*; to do up *[suwak]*; to slide [sth] on *[klapę, pokrywę]* [2] pot. (powiedzieć) to give *[kazanie]*; to tell *[dowcip]*

[] **zasunąć się** — **zasuwać się** *[kurtyna]* to draw; *[drzwi]* to slide shut

zasusz|yć *pf* — **zasusz|ać** *impf* [] *vt* to dry *[liść, roślinę]*

[] **zasuszyć się** — **zasuszać się** *[liść, roślina]* to dry

zasuw|a *f* bolt; **zamknąć coś na** ~**ę** to bolt sth

zasuwać¹ *impf* → **zasunąć**

zasuwa|ć² *impf vi* pot. [1] (pędzić) to scorch along pot. [2] (pracować) to beaver away pot.

zasychać *impf* → **zaschnąć**

zasycz|eć *pf vi [osoba, wąż, gęś, gaz]* to hiss

zasygnaliz|ować *pf vt* [1] (wskazać) *[światełko, urządzenie]* to indicate *[awarię, niebezpieczeństwo]* [2] przen. (dać znak) to signal

zasyp|ać *pf* — **zasyp|ywać** *impf vt* [1] (zakopać) to fill [sth] in *[dół, loch, wyrwę]*; (spychaczem) to bulldoze [sth] in [2] (pokryć) *[piasek, śnieg]* to cover [3] (przysypać) *[lawina, ziemia]* to bury; ~**ywać kogoś listami** przen. to flood sb with letters

zasypiać¹ *impf* → **zasnąć**

zasypiać² *impf* → **zaspać**

zasyp|ka *f* Med. ~**ka dla niemowląt** baby powder

zasypywać *impf* → **zasypać**

zaszczep|ić *pf* — **zaszczep|iać** *impf* [] *vt* [1] Med. to vaccinate, to inoculate (**kogoś na coś** sb against sth) [2] to graft *[roślinę]* [3] przen. to instil(l) *[miłość, szacunek]* (**komuś** in sb)

[] **zaszczepić się** — **zaszczepiać się** Med. to get oneself vaccinated (**na coś** against sth)

zaszczy|t [] *m* honour GB, honor US; **dostąpić** ~**tu robienia czegoś** to have the honour of doing sth

[] **zaszczyty** *plt* honours GB, honors US

zaszczytn|y *adi. grad.* honourable GB, honorable US

zaszele|ścić *pf vi [papier, liście]* to rustle; ~**ścić czymś** to rustle sth

zaszew|ka *f* tuck

zaszko|dzić *pf vi* [1] (wyrządzić szkodę) ~**dzić komuś** to harm sb; ~**dzić komuś w karierze** to hurt sb's career; **nie** ~**dzi spróbować** it does no harm to try [2] (źle wpłynąć na zdrowie) ~**dzić komuś** *[jedzenie, picie]* to give sb indigestion; *[praca, palenie]* to harm sb

zasznur|ować *pf* — **zasznur|owywać** *impf vt* to lace [sth] up *[buty, namiot]*

zaszok|ować *pf vt* to shock

zaszy|ć *pf* — **zaszy|wać** *impf* [] *vt* to mend *[spodnie, koszulę]*; to sew [sth] up *[dziurę, ranę]*; ~**ć coś w pasku** to sew sth into one's belt

[] **zaszyć się** — **zaszywać się** (schować się) *[zwierzę, osoba]* to hide

zaścielać *impf* → **zasłać**

zaślep|ić *pf* — **zaślep|iać** *impf vt* [1] *[duma, nienawiść]* to blind *[osobę]* [2] Techn. *[osoba]* to close *[rurę, otwór]*

zaśmi|ać się *pf v refl.* to laugh (**z czegoś** at sth)

zaśmie|cić *pf* — **zaśmie|cać** *impf vt* [1] (pokryć śmieciami) to litter (**coś czymś** sth with sth) [2] przen. to spoil *[krajobraz]*; to litter *[język]*

zaśnież|ony *adi. [ulice, pola]* snow-covered; *[szczyty]* snow-capped

zaśpiewa|ć *pf vt, vi* [1] to sing *[piosenkę, melodię]* [2] pot. (zażądać) ~**ć za coś 100 złotych** to want 100 zlotys for sth

zaświadczać *impf* → **zaświadczyć**

zaświadcze|nie *n* certificate

zaświadcz|yć *pf* — **zaświadcz|ać** *impf vt* to testify (**o czymś** to sth)

zaświat|y *plt* książk. spirit world, the beyond

zaświe|cić *pf* [**I**] *vt* [1] to light *[pochodnię, znicz]*; to strike *[zapałkę]*; to turn [sth] on *[lampę, latarnie]*; ~**cić komuś w oczy latarką** to shine a torch into sb's eyes

[**II**] *vi [słońce]* to start shining; *[światło, lampa]* to go on

[**III**] **zaświecić się** *[żarówka, latarnia]* to go on

zaświta|ć *pf vi [ranek, nadzieja]* to dawn

zataczać *impf* → **zatoczyć**

zata|ić *pf* — **zata|jać** *impf vt* to withhold *[prawdę, informację]*

zatam|ować *pf vt* [1] (zahamować) to block *[ruch uliczny]* [2] (powstrzymać) to plug *[przeciek]*; to staunch, to stanch US *[krwawienie]*

zatańcz|yć *pf vt, vi* to dance

zatapiać *impf* → **zatopić**

zataras|ować *pf vt* to obstruct *[wejście, drzwi]*

zatarg *m* dispute (**o coś** over sth)

zatelefon|ować *pf vi* to (tele)phone (**do kogoś** sb)

zatemper|ować *pf vt* to sharpen *[ołówek, kredkę]*

zatęch|ły *adi. [ubranie, pościel, słoma]* musty

zatęskni|ć *pf vi* to miss (**za czymś** sth)

zat|kać *pf* — **zat|ykać**[1] *impf* [**I**] *vt* to clog *[dziurę, rurę]*; to stop *[otwór, uszy]*; **zupełnie mnie** ~**kało** pot., przen. you could've knocked me down with a feather

[**II**] **zatkać się** — **zatykać się** to clog up; *[rura, zlew]* to block up

zat|knąć *pf* — **zat|ykać**[2] *impf vt* (wsunąć) to stick; (wbić) to plant

zatłocz|ony *adi. [pociąg, dworzec, ulice]* crowded

zat|oczyć[1] *pf* — **zat|aczać** *impf* [**I**] *vt* ~**oczyć koło** to describe a circle

[**II**] **zatoczyć się** — **zataczać się** to stagger

zatocz|yć[2] *pf vt* to roll *[beczkę]*

zato|ka *f* [1] (morza) bay, gulf [2] (jezdni) parking bay, lay-by [3] Anat. antrum, sinus

zato|nąć *pf vi [statek, dobytek]* to sink

zat|opić *pf* — **zat|apiać** *impf* [**I**] *vt* [1] (spowodować zatonięcie) to sink *[statek]* [2] (zalać wodą) to flood *[miasto, pola]* [3] (wbić) to sink *[zęby, pazury]*

[**II**] **zatopić się** — **zatapiać się** to sink; ~**opić się w lekturze** przen. to bury oneself in reading

zato|r *m* [1] (na drodze) (traffic) hold-up [2] (lodowy) ice jam [3] Med. embolism

zatrąb|ić *pf vi [trębacz]* to sound the trumpet/horn; *[słoń]* to trumpet; *[kierowca, samochód]* to toot one's horn

zatroskan|y *adi. [osoba, mina]* worried

zatroszcz|yć się *pf v refl.* to take care (**o coś** of sth); ~**yć się, żeby...** to see to it that...; ~**yć się o pieniądze na samochód** to secure money for a car

zatru|cie *n* poisoning

zatru|ć *pf* — **zatru|wać** *impf* [**I**] *vt* [1] (trucizną) to poison *[jedzenie, studnię, organizm]* [2] (zanieczyścić) to contaminate *[powietrze, wodę]* [3] przen. to sour *[stosunki, atmosferę]*

[**II**] **zatruć się** — **zatruwać się** to be poisoned

zatrudni|ć *pf* — **zatrudni|ać** *impf* [**I**] *vt* to employ

[**II**] **zatrudnić się** — **zatrudniać się** książk. to get a job

zatrudnieni|e *n* employment

zatruwać *impf* → **zatruć**

zatrzask *m* [1] (do zapinania) press stud GB, snap fastener; **koszula zapinana na** ~**i** a snap-on shirt [2] (zamek sprężynowy) latch(lock)

zatrza|snąć *pf* — **zatrza|skiwać** *impf* [**I**] *vt* [1] (zamknąć z trzaskiem) to slam *[bramę, furtkę]*; to slam down *[wieko, maskę samochodu]* [2] (zamknąć w pomieszczeniu) to lock [sb/sth] in

[**II**] **zatrzasnąć się** — **zatrzaskiwać się** [1] (zamknąć się) *[drzwi, furtka]* to slam shut; *[wieko, pokrywka]* to snap shut [2] (zamknąć siebie) to become trapped

zatrz|ąść *pf* [**I**] *vi* [1] (szybko poruszyć) to shake (**czymś** sth); ~**ąść czymś w posadach** przen. to shake a. rock sth to its foundations; ~**ęsło mną, gdy się dowiedziałem, że...** przen. it shook me to find out that... [2] *[pojazd]* to sway

[**II**] **zatrząść się** *[budynek, mury, ziemia]* to shake; *[pojazd]* to lurch; ~**ąść się z oburzenia** *[osoba]* to shake with indignation

za|trzeć *pf* — **za|cierać** *impf* [**I**] *vt* [1] (zamazać) to erase; **zatarty obraz** a blurred image [2] (ukryć) to cover up *[ślady]*; to blur *[różnice]*; **zatrzeć złe wrażenie** to cover over a bad impression [3] (spowodować uszkodzenie) to seize *[silnik, mechanizm]*

[**II**] **zatrzeć się** — **zacierać się** [1] (stać się niewyraźnym) to fade away [2] *[mechanizm, silnik]* to seize up

■ **zacierać ręce** to rub one's hands

zatrzym|ać *pf* — **zatrzym|ywać** *impf* [**I**] *vt* [1] (powstrzymać w ruchu) to stop *[osobę, maszynę, zegar]* [2] (nie puścić, nie oddać) to keep *[osobę, przedmiot]*; ~**ać kogoś na kolacji** to make sb stay for dinner [3] (pozbawić wolności) to detain [4] Med. to retain; ~**anie moczu** urine retention

[**II**] **zatrzymać się** — **zatrzymywać się** [1] (stanąć w miejscu) *[osoba, pojazd, zegar]* to stop [2] (zamieszkać na jakiś czas) to stay

zatusz|ować *pf* — **zatusz|owywać** *impf vt* to cover up *[skandal]*; to whitewash *[działanie, sprawę]*

zatwardze|nie *n* constipation

zatwardzia|ły *adi. grad. [kawaler, palacz]* confirmed; *[polityk, komunista]* diehard; *[upór]* dogged; *[grzesznik]* irredeemable; *[wróg, demokrata]* inveterate

zatwier|dzić *pf* — **zatwier|dzać** *impf vt* to approve *[plan, kandydata]*; to ratify *[traktat, umowę]*

zatycz|ka *f* (w butelce) stopper; (w beczce) bung; (do wanny, zlewu) plug; (do uszu) earplug

zatykać[1] *impf* → **zatkać**

zatykać[2] *impf* → **zatknąć**

zaufa|ć *pf vi* to trust (**komuś** sb)

zaufani|e *n* trust; **godny/niegodny** ∼ trustworthy/untrustworthy; **mieć** ∼**e do kogoś** to have confidence in sb; **w** ∼**u** in confidence

zauł|ek *m* backstreet

zaurocze|nie *n* (zachwyt) fascination; (oczarowanie) infatuation

zaurocz|yć *pf vt* [1] (oczarować) to enthral GB, to enthrall US [2] (rzucić urok) to bewitch także przen.

zauważ|yć *pf* — **zauważ|ać** *impf vt* [1] (dostrzec) to notice *[zmianę, różnicę]*; ∼**yć kogoś** to catch sight of sb; ∼, **że...** mark you, ... [2] (zrobić uwagę) to remark, to observe

zawa|da *f* książk. hindrance

zawadiac|ki *adi. [wygląd, spojrzenie]* boisterous

zawadia|ka *m* swashbuckler

zawa|dzać[1] *impf vi* (przeszkadzać) to hamper (**komuś** sb); **nikomu nie** ∼**dzać** *[osoba]* to never get in anybody's way; **nie** ∼**i to zrobić** it won't do any harm to do it

zawa|dzić *pf* — **zawa|dzać**[2] *impf vi* (zaczepić) ∼**dzić o krzesło** to knock against a chair; ∼**dzić rękawem o klamkę** to catch one's sleeve on the handle

zawaha|ć się *pf v refl.* to hesitate

zawal|ić *pf* — **zawal|ać** *impf* **[I]** *vt* [1] (zatarasować) to block *[otwór, wejście]* [2] (zasypać) to cover [sth] up; **biurko** ∼**one papierami** a desk piled a. loaded with papers; ∼**ić kogoś robotą** to give sb too much work [3] pot. (zepsuć) to bungle *[plan, robotę]*; to fluff pot. *[egzamin, test]*
[II] zawalić się — **zawalać się** [1] (runąć) *[dom, sufit]* to collapse [2] przen. (nie udać się) *[plan, projekt]* to fall through

zawa|ł *m* [1] Med. infarction; ∼**ł serca** a heart attack pot. [2] (w kopalni) cave-in

zawartoś|ć *f* (naczynia, torby, szafy) contents; (książki, artykułu) content

zaważ|yć *pf vi* to have an impact (**na czymś** on sth)

zawdzięcz|ać *impf vt* to owe (**coś komuś** sth to sb)

zawiad|omić *pf* — **zawiad|amiać** *impf vt* to inform; (oficjalnie) to notify

zawiadomie|nie *n* notice, notification

zawiadowc|a *m* stationmaster

zawias *m* hinge; **wyjąć drzwi z** ∼**ów** to unhinge the door

zawią|zać *pf* — **zawią|zywać** *impf* **[I]** *vt* [1] (przepleść koniec) to tie *[węzeł, sznurowadło, paczkę]*; ∼**zać krawat** to knot one's tie; ∼**zać komuś oczy** to blindfold sb [2] (zapakować) to tie [sth] up [3] (zamknąć otwór) to rope *[worek, torbę]* [4] (utworzyć) to set up *[spółkę, koalicję]*; to organize *[spisek]* [5] Bot. to set
[II] zawiązać się — **zawiązywać się** [1] (utworzyć się) *[komitet, stowarzyszenie]* to form [2] Bot. *[zawiązki owoców, kwiatów]* to set

zawie|ja *f* snowstorm

zawierać[1] *impf* → **zawrzeć**[1]

zawiera|ć[2] *impf* **[I]** *vt [lek, film]* to contain
[II] zawierać się [1] (być składnikiem) to be included [2] (być wyrażonym) to be expressed [3] (polegać) to consist (**w czymś** in sth)

zawie|sić *pf* — **zawie|szać** *impf vt* [1] (powiesić) to hang *[lampę, obraz]*; ∼**sić ściany obrazami** to hang the walls with pictures [2] (wstrzymać) to suspend *[obrady, karę, ucznia]*; ∼**sić głos** to pause
[II] zawiesić się — **zawieszać się** Komput. *[komputer]* to hang (up), to crash

zawiesin|a *f* suspension

zawieszać[2] *impf* → **zawiesić**

zaw|ieść[1] *pf* — **zaw|odzić**[1] *impf* **[I]** *vt* [1] (sprawić zawód) to disappoint, to let [sb] down; ∼**ieść czyjeś zaufanie** to betray sb's trust [2] (okazać się nieskutecznym) *[urządzenie, system]* to fail; *[nadzieja, marzenie]* to be frustrated; *[plan]* to fall through
[II] zawieść się — **zawodzić się** (doznać zawodu) to be disappointed (**na kimś** in sb)

zaw|ieść[2] *pf* — **zaw|odzić**[2] *impf vi* książk. (zaprowadzić) *[osoba, droga]* to lead

zaw|ieźć *pf* — **zaw|ozić** *impf vt* to take; ∼**ieźć dziecko do szkoły** to drive one's child to school

zawijać *impf* → **zawinąć**

zawijas *m* flourish także przen.

zawikła|ć *pf* **[I]** *vt* to complicate *[sprawę, interesy]*
[II] zawikłać się *[sprawa, sytuacja]* to become complicated

zawil|ec *m* anemone, windflower

zawi|ły *adi. [argumentacja, rozumowanie]* convoluted; *[sprawa]* complicated; *[wyjaśnienia]* circuitous; *[akcja powieści, filmu]* intricate

zawi|nąć *pf* — **zawi|jać** *impf* **[I]** *vt* [1] (owinąć) to wrap [sth] up [2] (podwinąć) to roll [sth] up *[rękawy, nogawki]*
[II] *vi* ∼**nąć do portu** to call at a port
[III] zawinąć się — **zawijać się** [1] (owinąć się) to wrap oneself [2] (podwinąć się) *[włosy]* to curl up

zawi|nić *pf vi* to be to blame; ∼**nić wobec kogoś** to wrong sb

zawir|ować *pf vi [tancerze, liście]* to whirl
zawi|snąć *pf* — **zawi|sać** *impf vi* ⓵ *(zostać zawieszonym) [lampa, firanka]* to be hung ⓶ *(zostać powieszonym) [zdrajca, skazaniec]* to be hanged ⓷ *(znieruchomieć w powietrzu) [ptak, helikopter]* to hover; *[ręka]* to stop in mid-air ⓸ *(zacząć zagrażać) [niebezpieczeństwo]* to loom ⓹ *książk.* (zacząć zależeć) *[los, byt]* to be contingent (**od czegoś** on a. upon sth)
zawistn|y *adi. [osoba, wzrok]* envious
zawiś|ć *f* envy
zawl|ec *pf* — **zawl|ekać** *impf* ⓵ *vt* ⓵ (zaciągnąć) to drag *[osobę, worek]* ⓶ (przenieść) to bring *[bakterie, chorobę, nasiona]*
　ⓒ **zawlec się** ⓵ *pot.* (dotrzeć) to drag oneself ⓶ (zasnuć się) *[niebo]* to cloud; *[oczy]* to mist
zawlecz|ka *f* ⓵ *Techn.* split a. cotter pin ⓶ *Wojsk.* safety pin
zawlekać *impf →* **zawlec**
zawodni|k *m,* **~czka** *f* ⓵ *Sport* contestant ⓶ *pot.* number, customer
zawodn|y *adi. [sprzęt, samochód]* unreliable; *[marzenia, nadzieje]* illusive; *[pamięć]* fallible
zawodow|iec *m* professional
zawodow|y *adi. [etyka, kwalifikacje, aktor, sport]* professional; *[choroba, ryzyko]* occupational; *[dyplomata, oficer]* career; *[szkoła]* vocational; **praca ~a** a career; **żołnierz ~y** a regular soldier
zawodów|ka *f pot.* vocational school
zawod|y *plt Sport* competition, contest
zawodzić¹ *impf →* **zawieść¹**
zawodzić² *impf →* **zawieść²**
zawoła|ć *pf vt* ⓵ (krzyknąć) to cry out; **~ć coś do kogoś** to shout sth to sb ⓶ (wezwać) to call *[kelnera, taksówkę]*
zawoła|nie *n* ⓵ (wezwanie) call; **być na czyjeś każde ~nie** to be at sb's beck and call ⓶ (okrzyk bojowy) battle cry
zawozić *impf →* **zawieźć**
zaw|ód¹ *m* (po szkole wyższej) profession; (po szkole niższego stopnia) trade; **~ód lekarza** the medical profession; **z ~odu** by profession
zaw|ód² *m* (rozczarowanie) disappointment; **doznać ~odu** to be let down; **sprawić komuś ~ód** to let sb down
zaw|ór *m* valve; **~ór bezpieczeństwa** a safety valve
zawracać *impf →* **zawrócić**
zawrotn|y *adi. grad. [szybkość, wysokość]* dizzying; *[cena]* exorbitant; *[kariera]* staggering
zawr|ócić *pf* — **zawr|acać** *impf* ⓵ *vt* (skierować z powrotem) to turn *[sb/sth]* back *[osobę, konia]*
　ⓒ *vi* (wrócić) to turn back
zawr|ót *m* **~ót głowy** vertigo
zaw|rzeć¹ *pf* — **zaw|ierać¹** *impf vt* ⓵ (przedstawić) to contain *[dane, informacje]* ⓶ (ustanowić) to conclude *[umowę]*; to form *[przymierze, sojusz]*; to enter

into *[związek małżeński]*; **~rzeć z kimś znajomość** to strike up an acquaintance with sb
zaw|rzeć² *pf vi* ⓵ (zakipieć) *[woda]* to come to the boil ⓶ (wybuchnąć) *[walka, dyskusja]* to erupt; **~rzeć gniewem** *[osoba]* to boil with rage ⓸ (ożywić się) *[sala, miasto]* to buzz
zawsty|dzić *pf* — **zawsty|dzać** *impf* ⓵ *vt* (wzbudzić uczucie wstydu) to shame; (zażenować) to embarrass
　ⓒ **zawstydzić się** — **zawstydzać się** (poczuć wstyd) to feel ashamed; (poczuć zażenowanie) to feel embarrassed
zawsze ⓵ *pron.* always; **jak ~** as ever, as always; **na ~** for good; **raz na ~** once and for all; **tam, gdzie ~** at the usual place; **~, kiedy...** whenever... ⓒ *part.* (jednak) still *pot.;* **~ to coś** it's still something
zaw|ziąć się *pf v refl.* to get the bit between a. in US one's teeth; **~ziął się, że...** he was determined to...; **~ziąć się na kogoś** *pot.* to have it in for sb
zawzię|ty *adi.* ⓵ (nieustępliwy) *[osoba]* headstrong; *[wyraz twarzy]* determined ⓶ (gwałtowny) *[kłótnia, walka]* fierce ⓷ (zapamiętały) *[palacz, kobieciarz]* inveterate
zazdro|sny *adi.* envious (**o coś** of sth); jealous (**o kogoś** of sb)
zazdro|ścić *impf vi* **~ścić komuś czegoś** to envy sb sth
zazdroś|ć *f* ⓵ (o majątek, sławę) envy (**o coś** of sth) ⓶ (o kogoś) jealousy (**o kogoś** of sb)
zazdrośni|k *m pot.* jealous man
zazięb|ić *pf* — **zazięb|iać** *impf* ⓵ *vt* to give *[sb]* a cold
　ⓒ **zaziębić się** — **zaziębiać się** to catch a cold
zaziębie|nie *n Med.* cold
zazna|ć *pf* — **zazna|wać** *impf vt* to experience *[biedy, głodu]*; **nie ~ć spokoju** to know no peace
zaznacz|yć *pf* — **zaznacz|ać** *impf* ⓵ *vt* ⓵ (oznaczyć) to mark *[datę, słowo, drogę]* ⓶ (uwydatnić) to emphasize; **~yć swoją obecność** to make one's presence felt ⓷ (powiedzieć) to stress, to emphasize; **~ył, że...** he stressed that...
　ⓒ **zaznaczyć się** — **zaznaczać się** (dać się odczuć) **~yły się między nimi różnice poglądów** the differences of opinion between them were noticeable
zaznaj|omić *pf* — **zaznaj|amiać** *impf książk.*
　ⓒ *vt* (zapoznać) to familiarize (**kogoś z czymś** sb with sth)
　ⓒ **zaznajomić się** — **zaznajamiać się** ⓵ (zapoznać się) to familiarize oneself (**z czymś** with sth) ⓶ (nawiązać znajomość) to get acquainted
zaznawać *impf →* **zaznać**
zazwyczaj *adv* usually
zażale|nie *n* ⓵ (skarga) complaint; (na piśmie) letter of complaint ⓶ (w sądzie) appeal
zażar|ty *adi. [bój, spór]* fierce; *[przeciwnik]* sworn

zażąda|ć *pf vi* to demand *[przeprosin, wyjaśnień]*

zaženowan|y *adi. [osoba]* embarrassed; *[spojrzenie, uśmiech]* sheepish

zaży|ć *pf* — **zaży|wać** *impf vt* [1] (przyjąć) to take *[lekarstwo, narkotyk]* [2] (doznać) to enjoy *[bogactw, luksusu]* [3] pot. (zaskoczyć) to put [sb] on the spot pot.

zaży|ły *adi. [przyjaźń, znajomość]* intimate

zażywać *impf* → **zażyć**

z|ąb *m* [1] Anat. tooth; **ząb mleczny/stały** a milk/permanent tooth; **powiedzieć coś przez zęby** to say sth through clenched teeth; **szczerzyć zęby** to grin; **zacisnąć zęby** to clench a. grit one's teeth; **szczękałam zębami** my teeth were chattering [2] (piły, grzebienia) tooth; (widelca, wideł) prong ■ **(a)ni w ząb** not at all; **uzbrojony po zęby** armed to the teeth

ząb|ek *m* [1] Anat. tooth [2] Kulin. **~ek czosnku** a clove of garlic [3] (wykończenie brzegu) serration

zbaczać *impf* → **zboczyć**

zbada|ć *pf* [] *vt* [1] Med. to examine *[chorego, pacjenta]*; to test, to check *[wzrok, słuch, krew]* [2] (sprawdzić) to examine *[papiery, dokumenty, przyczyny]*; to search *[teren, okolicę]* [] **zbadać się** to have a check-up

zbankrut|ować *pf vi* to go bankrupt także przen.

zbaw|ić *pf* — **zbaw|iać** *impf vt* to save *[osobę, duszę]*; **to mnie nie ~i** pot. it won't make much difference

zbawienn|y *adi.* salutary

zbędn|y *adi. [formalności, meble]* unnecessary; *[drobiazgi, szczegóły]* inessential

zbi|ć *pf* — **zbi|jać** *impf* [] *vt* [1] (stłuc) to break *[talerz, szybę]* [2] (pobić) to beat (up) *[osobę]*; to bruise *[część ciała]* [3] (połączyć gwoździami) to nail [sth] together *[deski, skrzynkę]* [4] Sport to spike *[piłkę]* [5] Gry to take *[pionek, figurę]* [6] (obalić) to refute *[dowód, rację]* [7] pot. (obniżyć) to bring down *[temperaturę, gorączkę]*; to get down *[wagę]* [] **zbić się** — **zbijać się** [1] *[talerz, szyba]* to break [2] (zgromadzić się) **~ć się w gromadkę** to herd together

zbie|c, zbie|gnąć *pf* — **zbie|gać** *impf* [] *vi* [1] (na dół) to run; **~c po schodach** to run down the stairs [2] (uciec) to flee; **~c z więzienia** to escape from prison [] **zbiec się** — **zbiegać się** [1] *[ludzie]* to come running [2] *[linie]* to meet; *[wydarzenie]* to coincide (**z czymś** with sth) [3] *[ubranie]* to shrink

zbie|g *m* [1] (osoba) fugitive [2] (miejsce zetknięcia się) meeting point; **u ~gu dwóch ulic** at the junction of two streets [3] przen. **~g okoliczności** a coincidence

zbiegać *impf* → **zbiec**

zbiegowisk|o *n* crowd

zbierać *impf* → **zebrać**

zbieżn|y *adi.* [1] *[poglądy, cele, wnioski]* coincident książk. [2] *[linie, promienie]* convergent

zbijać *impf* → **zbić**

zbiorni|k *m* [1] (pojemnik) container; **~k paliwa** a fuel tank [2] (jezioro) **~k wodny** a body of water

zbiornikow|iec *m* tanker

zbiorowisk|o *n* [1] (wspólnota) community; (zbiegowisko) crowd [2] (przedmiotów) group; (bezładne) jumble

zbiorow|y *adi. [decyzja, odpowiedzialność]* collective; *[grób, mogiła]* mass; *[zdjęcie, fotografia]* group; *[scena]* crowd

zbi|ór *m* [1] (zestaw) set; (wierszy, esejów) collection; **~ór zadań z fizyki** a book of physics problems [2] (kolekcja) collection [3] Mat. set [4] (żniwa) harvest; **tegoroczne ~ory** this year's crop

zbiór|ka *f* [1] (spotkanie) meeting; **miejsce ~ki** the assembly point; (dla podróżnych) the pick-up point [2] (kwesta) collection

zbi|r *m* pot. thug

zbi|ty *adi. [masa, ziemia]* compact; *[wełna, włókna]* matted; *[tłum, grupa]* tight

zbliżać *impf* → **zbliżyć**

zbliże|nie *n* [1] (bliski kontakt) closeness [2] Polit. rapprochement [3] (stosunek płciowy) intercourse [4] (zdjęcie) close-up

zbliż|yć *impf* — **zbliż|ać** *pf* [] *vt* [1] (przysunąć) *[osoba]* to move [sth] close/closer (**do czegoś** to sth) [2] (poprawić relacje) *[sytuacja, przeżycie]* to bring [sb] closer (**do kogoś** to sb) [3] (ułatwić osiągnięcie, zrozumienie) to bring [sb] closer (**do czegoś** to sth) [] **zbliżyć się** — **zbliżać się** [1] (przybliżyć się) *[osoba, pojazd, dźwięk, temperatura]* to approach (**do czegoś** sth); **nie ~aj się!** stay back! [2] (zaprzyjaźnić się) *[osoby]* to grow (closer) together [3] (osiągnąć postęp) *[osoba]* to get close (**do czegoś** to sth) [4] (nadchodzić) *[noc, południe, lato]* to approach; **~ać się do końca** *[książka, projekt]* to near completion; **~a się szósta** it's coming up to six o'clock

zbłaźni|ć się *pf v refl.* to make a fool of oneself

zbocz|e *n* hillside; (w wysokich górach) mountainside

zbocze|nie *n* deviation

zbocze|niec *m* pervert, deviant

zb|oczyć — **zb|aczać** *impf vi [osoba]* to turn aside; *[samolot, pocisk]* to deviate

zbombard|ować *pf vt* to bomb

zb|oże *n* [1] (roślina) cereal (crop), corn GB [2] (ziarna) grain, corn GB

zbój *m* pot. brigand przest.

zb|ór *m* (świątynia) Protestant church; (wspólnota) Protestant congregation

zbrodni|a *f* crime także przen.

zbrodnia|rz *m*, **~rka** *f* criminal

zbr|oić[1] *impf* [] *vt* [1] (zaopatrywać w broń) to arm [2] (umacniać) to reinforce *[beton, słupy]* [3] (zakładać instalację) to link [sth] to the mains *[budynek, teren]* [] **zbroić się** to arm oneself

zbr|oić[2] *pf vt* to get up to mischief

zbro|ja *f* armour GB, armor US

zbroje|nie [] *n* Techn. reinforcement [] **zbrojenia** *plt* Wojsk. armaments; **wyścig ~ń** arms race

zbrojn|y *adi.* armed

zbud|ować *pf vt* [1] (stworzyć) to build *[dom, drogę, osiedle]* [2] (zorganizować) to build *[państwo, teorię]* [3] (skonstruować) to build, to construct *[komputer, silnik, urządzenie]* [4] (wpłynąć dodatnio) to uplift *[osobę]*

zbu|dzić *pf* [] *vt* to awaken, to wake up [] **zbudzić się** (przestać spać) to wake (up)

zburz|yć *pf vt* [1] (zniszczyć) to demolish *[budowlę]* [2] przen. (zakłócić) to destroy *[szczęście]*; to disturb *[spokój, ład społeczny]*

zbutwi|eć *pf vi [drewno, liście]* to decay

zb|yć *pf* — **zb|ywać**[1] *impf vt* [1] książk. (sprzedać) to sell (up), to move *[akcje]*; to sell off *[towar, nadwyżki]* [2] (zlekceważyć) to brush off a. aside *[osobę]*

zby|t[1] *m* market; **szybki ~t na coś** a ready market for sth

zbyt[2] *adv.* too; **~ długi/krótki** too long/short

zbyteczn|y *adi.* unnecessary

zbyt|ek *m* [1] (luksus) luxury [2] (nadmiar) excess

zbywać[1] *impf* → **zbyć**

zbywa|ć[2] *impf v imp.* **pieniędzy mi nie ~** I'm never short of money

zda|ć *pf* — **zda|wać** *impf* [] *vt* [1] (oddać) to hand over *[klucze, pieniądze]* [2] (przystępować) to take *[egzamin]*; (pomyślnie odbyć) to pass *[egzamin]*; **~ć do następnej klasy** to get through to the next year [3] (skazać) **być ~nym na siebie** to be left to one's own devices [] **zdać się — zdawać się** [1] (zaufać) to count (**na kogoś** on sb); **~ć się na los** to take pot luck [2] (wydać się) to seem; **~wał się spać** he seemed to be asleep [] **zdać się** pot. **na nic się ~ły wszelkie jego starania** all his efforts were in vain [] **zdawać się** *v imp.* (w przypuszczeniach) **~je się, że będzie deszcz** it looks like rain; **~je mi się, że...** I think... ■ **~ć sobie sprawę z czegoś** to realize sth

zda|nie *n* [1] (słowa) sentence [2] (opinia) view, opinion; **różnica ~ń** a difference of opinion; **liczyć się z czyimś ~niem** to value sb's opinion; **być ~nia, że...** to hold a view that...; **moim ~niem** in my view; **nie ma dwóch ~ń** no two ways about it [3] (w logice) proposition [4] Muz. phrase

zdarzać *impf* → **zdarzyć**

zdarze|nie *n* event; **przebieg ~ń** the course of events; **z prawdziwego ~nia** real

zdarz|yć *pf* — **zdarz|ać** *impf* [] *vi* książk. **przypadek ~ył, że...** chance would have it that... [] **zdarzyć się — zdarzać się** *[wypadek, cud]* to happen; **może się ~yć, że...** it may happen that...

zdawać *impf* → **zdać**

zdawkow|y *adi.* książk. *[ukłon, uśmiech]* perfunctory; *[odpowiedź, słowa]* trite

zdąż|yć *pf* — **zdąż|ać** *impf vi* [1] (nie pozostać w tyle) to keep pace (**za kimś** with sb) [2] (zdołać zrobić) **ledwie ~yć** to have just enough time; **nie ~ył tego zrobić** he didn't manage to do it [3] (przyjść na czas) to make it; **~yć do pracy** to be on time for work

zd|echnąć *pf* — **zd|ychać** *impf vi* [1] (umrzeć) *[zwierzę, roślina]* to die; obraźl. *[osoba]* to die [2] pot. (osłabnąć) to be done in pot.; **jest zupełnie zdechły po tej podróży** he's dead tired after the journey

zdecyd|ować *pf* [] *vi [osoba, zdarzenie]* to decide [] **zdecydować się** [1] *[osoba]* to make up one's mind; **~ować się na coś** to decide on sth [2] *[los, przyszłość]* to be determined, to be decided

zdecydowan|y [] *adi.* [1] (stanowczy) *[osoba]* determined; *[ruch, krok]* decisive; *[postawa, odpowiedź]* robust; *[deklaracja, odpowiedź]* unequivocal; *[akcja, środek]* positive [2] (niewątpliwy) *[przewaga, większość, zmiana]* decided; *[sukces, poprawa]* distinct; *[poparcie, opór]* explicit; *[zwycięstwo, faworyt]* outright [] *adi. praed.* **być ~ym na coś** to be set a. intent on sth

zdeform|ować *pf* [] *vt* to deform *[stopę, kręgosłup]* [] **zdeformować się** *[twarz, nos]* to become deformed a. disfigured

zdefraud|ować *pf vt* to embezzle

zdegrad|ować *pf vt* [1] (za karę) to demote [2] (zniszczyć) to degrade *[grunty, tereny]*

zdegustowan|y *adi.* disgusted

zdejmować *impf* → **zdjąć**

zdekoncentr|ować *pf* [] *vt* to distract [] **zdekoncentrować się** to become distracted

zdemask|ować *pf* [] *vt* to unmask, to expose *[spisek, przestępcę]* [] **zdemaskować się** to reveal one's true intentions

zdemol|ować *pf vt* to vandalize *[lokal, sklep]*

zdemoraliz|ować *pf* [] *vt* to deprave [] **zdemoralizować się** to become depraved

zdenerw|ować *pf* [] *vt* to irritate [] **zdenerwować się** to become irritated

zdenerwowani|e *n* [1] (rozdrażnienie) irritation [2] (niepokój) nervousness

zdenerwowan|y *adi.* [1] (niespokojny) nervous [2] (zirytowany) annoyed

zderzać *impf* → **zderzyć**

zderzak *m* bumper

zderz|yć *pf* — **zderz|ać** *impf* [] *vt* książk. (zestawić) to confront [] **zderzyć się — zderzać się** to crash

zdesperowan|y *adi.* desperate

zdeterminowan|y *adi.* determined

zdeton|ować *pf* [] *vt* [1] to detonate, to set off *[bombę]* [2] książk., przen. to disconcert *[osobę]* [] *vi [materiał wybuchowy]* to explode

zdewast|ować *pf vt* to vandalize *[wagony, ławki]*; to devastate *[lasy]*

zdezerter|ować *pf vi* Wojsk. to desert także przen.

zdezorientowan|y *adi.* confused

zdezynfek|ować *pf vt* to disinfect

zd|jąć *pf* — **zd|ejmować** *impf vt* [1] (wziąć) to take *[książkę, szklankę]*; (usunąć) to remove *[folię, osłonę]* [2] (z siebie) to take [sth] off *[płaszcz, buty, kapelusz]* [3] (uwolnić) to take [sth] off *[obowiązek, odpowiedzialność]*; **zdjąć z kogoś ciężar** to take a burden off sb [4] (unieważnić) to lift *[ograniczenia, zakaz]* [5] (odwołać) to remove *[osobę]* [6] książk. (opanować) *[strach, niepokój]* to overcome *[osobę]*

zdję|cie *n* photo(graph), picture; **~cia z wakacji** holiday pictures; **~cie (rentgenowskie)** an X-ray; **na ~ciu** in the picture; **zrobić ~cie** to take a picture

III zdjęcia *plt* [1] (sfilmowane obrazy) camerawork [2] (filmowanie) shooting

zdław|ić *pf vt* [1] to stifle *[krzyk]* [2] przen. to suppress *[powstanie, opozycję]*

zdmuch|nąć *pf* — **zdmuch|iwać** *impf vt* [1] (usunąć) to blow off *[pyłek]* [2] (zgasić) to blow out *[świeczkę, zapałkę]*

zdobi|ć *impf vt* [1] (upiększać) *[osoba]* to decorate (**coś czymś** sth with sth) [2] (być ozdobą) *[rzeźba, kwiaty, ozdoba]* to grace *[pokój, głowę]*

zdobycz *f* [1] (nabytek) acquisition; (łup) haul; **~ wojenna** the spoils of war; **najnowsze ~e techniki** przen. the latest technological developments [2] (zwierzęcia) prey; (myśliwego) take [3] przen. (uwiedziona osoba) conquest

zdob|yć *pf* — **zdob|ywać** *impf* [] *vt* [1] (wygrać) to win *[medal, głosy, nagrodę]*; to score *[punkty, gola]* [2] (zagrabić) to capture *[miasto, twierdzę, czoło]* [3] (dotrzeć) to climb *[szczyt]*; to reach *[biegun]* [4] (uzyskać) to win *[władzę]*; to acquire *[wiedzę, doświadczenie]*; to obtain *[pozwolenie, bilety]*; **~yć kobietę** to win a woman [5] (zjednać sobie) to win *[przyjaźń, poparcie, sławę]*

II zdobyć się — **zdobywać się** (mieć dość odwagi) **~yć się na odwagę, żeby coś zrobić** to muster the courage to do sth; **nie mogłem się na to ~yć** I couldn't bring myself to do it

zdobywc|a *m* [1] (twierdzy, szczytu) conqueror [2] (nagrody, medalu) winner; **~a gola** a goalscorer

zdolnoś|ć *f* ability, capability; **~ć prawna** legal capacity; **posiadać ~ć kredytową** to be creditworthy

II zdolności *plt* abilities, capabilities

zdoln|y [] *adi. grad.* (utalentowany) able

II *adi.* capable; **być ~ym do czegoś** to be capable of sth

zdomin|ować *pf vt* książk. to dominate *[osobę, organizację]*

zdra|da *f* [1] (działanie na szkodę) betrayal, treason [2] (niewierność małżeńska) infidelity [3] (ideałów) betrayal

zdradliw|y *adi. grad.* treacherous

zdra|dzić *pf* — **zdra|dzać** *impf* [] *vt* [1] (wydać wrogowi) to betray [2] (być niewiernym) to cheat on; **~dzana żona** a betrayed wife [3] (wyrzec się) to betray *[przekonania]* [4] (wyjawić) to give away *[tajemnicę]*; **~dzić komuś swoje plany** to let sb in on one's plans [5] książk. (poinformować) to disclose; **proszę nam ~dzić, kto...** could you tell us who...? [6] (przejawiać) to betray *[emocje, niezadowolenie]*; to show *[ochotę, oznaki]*

II zdradzić się — **zdradzać się** (wyjawić) **~dzić się ze swymi zamiarami** to let on about one's plans

zdradziec|ki *adi.* treacherous

zdraj|ca *m*, **~czyni** *f* traitor

zdrap|ać *pf* — **zdrap|ywać** *impf vt* to scrape off; (paznokciami) to pick off

zdrętwi|eć *pf vi* [1] *[ręka, noga]* to become a. go numb; *[kark]* to stiffen (up) [2] (wskutek emocji) *[osoba]* to be petrified

zdrobnie|nie *n* diminutive

zdrowi|e *n* health; **służba ~a** Health Service; **stan ~a pacjenta** a patient's condition; **dbać o ~e** to look after oneself; **wrócić do ~a** to recover; **wracać do ~a** to be on the mend; **być słabego ~a** to be in poor health; **pić za czyjeś ~e** to drink sb's health a. the health of sb; **(na) ~e!** (toast) cheers!; **twoje ~e!** here's to you!; **na ~e!** (po kichnięciu) bless you!; **jak ~e?** (na powitanie) how are you?; **nie wyszło mu to na ~e** it didn't do him much good; **to go kosztowało dużo ~a** it caused him a lot of worry

zdrowi|eć *impf vi* to recover

zdr|owy [] *adi. grad.* [1] (nie chory) *[osoba, zęby, włosy, cera, wygląd]* healthy; **~ów jak ryba** as fit as a fiddle; **być ~owym** to be all right; **być przy ~owych zmysłach** to be sane; **cały i ~owy** alive and well [2] (dobry dla zdrowia) *[klimat, powietrze]* healthy, wholesome; **~owa żywność** health food [3] (prawidłowy, niezepsuty) *[gospodarka, konkurencja, atmosfera, owoc]* healthy [4] (trzeźwy) *[sąd]* sound; *[krytyka]* healthy; **~owy rozsądek** the common sense [5] pot. (duży) *[kawał, porcja]* large

II zdr|owy *m*, **~owa** *f* healthy person

■ w ~owym ciele ~owy duch a healthy mind in a healthy body

zdroż|eć *pf vi* *[towar, usługi]* to become more expensive; *[akcje]* to advance; *[koszty]* to go up

zdrzemn|ąć się *pf v refl.* (zasnąć na chwilę) to doze off; (odbyć drzemkę) to take a (cat)nap

zdumi|eć *pf* — **zdumi|ewać** *impf* [] *vt* to amaze

II zdumieć się — **zdumiewać się** to be amazed

zdumieni|e *n* amazement; **ku mojemu (najwyższemu) ~u...** to my (utter) amazement...

zdumiewać *impf* → **zdumieć**

zdumiewając|y *adi.* amazing

żdun *m* stove-fitter

zdychać *impf* → **zdechnąć**

zdymisjon|ować *pf vt* to dismiss *[ministra, urzędnika]*

zdyscyplinowan|y *adi.* (self-)disciplined

zdyskwalifik|ować *pf vt [sędzia, zachowanie]* to disqualify

zdyszan|y *adi.* breathless; **być ~ym** to be out of breath

zdzicz|eć *pf vi* ① *[roślina, zwierzę, ogród]* to run wild ② przen. *[osoba]* to become a recluse

zdziecinni|eć *pf vi* to go senile; to go gaga pot.

zdziel|ić *pf vt* pot. to bash pot.

zdzierać *impf* → **zedrzeć**

zdziwacz|eć *pf vi* to become eccentric

zdziw|ić *pf* **Ⅰ** *vt* to surprise

Ⅱ **zdziwić się** to be surprised; **nie ~iłbym się, gdyby...** I wouldn't be surprised if...

zdziwieni|e *n* surprise

ze → **z**

zeb|ra *f* ① Zool. zebra ② (na jezdni) zebra crossing GB, crosswalk US

z|ebrać *pf* — **z|bierać** *impf* **Ⅰ** *vt* ① (zgromadzić) to collect *[znaczki, informacje, pieniądze]*; (oszczędzić) to save up ② (zgrupować) to gather together *[uczniów, pracowników]* ③ (złączyć) to gather *[materiał, suknię]* ④ (zgromadzić) to pick *[owoce, grzyby]*; to harvest *[zboże, rzepak]* ⑤ (sprzątnąć) to clear away *[naczynia]* ⑥ (uzyskać) to collect *[nagrody, punkty]*; **zebrać oklaski** to be applauded

Ⅱ **zebrać się** — **zbierać się** ① (zgromadzić się) *[tłum, uczniowie]* to gather ② (pojawić się) *[woda, kurz]* to collect; *[chmury]* to gather

Ⅲ **zebrać się** — **zbierać się** *v imp.* **zbiera się na deszcz** it's going to rain

Ⅳ **zbierać się** (przygotować się) **zbierać się do zrobienia czegoś** to mean to do sth; **lepiej zbierajmy się stąd** we'd better be going

zebra|nie *n* meeting; **na ~niu** in a meeting

zebran|y **Ⅰ** *adi. [dzieła, utwory]* collected

Ⅱ **zebrani** *plt* the assembled company

zece|r *m* typesetter

zechc|ieć *pf vi* to be willing to; **kiedy tylko ~esz** any time you like; **zrobisz, jak ~esz** do as you please; **~e pan spocząć** would you mind taking a seat?

z|edrzeć *pf* — **z|dzierać** *impf* **Ⅰ** *vt* ① (zerwać) to tear off *[plakat, ubranie]* ② (otrzeć) to graze *[łokieć, kolano]* ③ (zniszczyć) to wear out *[buty, ubrania]*; **zdzierać gardło** przen. to shout oneself hoarse

Ⅱ **zedrzeć się** — **zdzierać się** ① (oderwać się) *[nalepka, strup]* to tear away ② (zniszczyć się) *[ubranie, buty]* to wear out; *[opony]* to wear down

zega|r *m* clock; **nastawić/nakręcić ~r** to set/ wind a clock; **~r słoneczny** sundial

zegar|ek *m* watch; **nakręcić ~ek** to wind (up) a watch

■ **z ~kiem w ręku** on the dot pot.

zegarmistrz *m* clockmaker, watchmaker

zegaryn|ka *f* speaking clock

zejś|cie *n* ① (droga w dół) descent; **~cie do piwnicy** the stairs to the cellar ② książk. death

zejść *pf* **Ⅰ** *vi* ① (przemieścić się w dół) *[osoba, nurek]* to go down; **zejść po schodach** to go down the stairs; **zejść na ląd** to go ashore; **zejść do lądowania** *[samolot]* to descend ② (obniżyć się) *[bezrobocie, temperatura]* to go down, to fall; **zejść do 10%** to go down to 10 per cent ③ (opuścić) to go off; **zejść z boiska** to go off the pitch; **zejść komuś z drogi** to get out of sb's way; **zejść na bok** to step aside ④ (zostać zdjętym) *[pierścionek, but]* to come off; *[skóra]* to peel off ⑤ (zniknąć) *[plama, smuga]* to come off; *[siniec]* to clear up; **zejść z ekranu/afisza** to come off ⑥ (przemierzyć) to go (a)round ⑦ pot. (zostać sprzedanym) *[towar, produkty]* to go ⑧ (upłynąć) **czas zszedł mu na czytaniu** he passed the time reading

Ⅱ **zejść się** ① (zgromadzić się) *[goście, uczestnicy]* to assemble ② (zbiegać się) *[linie, ścieżki]* to meet; **ich drogi się zeszły** przen. their paths crossed ③ (odbyć się jednocześnie) to coincide (**z czymś** with sth) ④ (dojść do porozumienia) to come together

■ **rozmowa zeszła na inny temat** the conversation moved to a different topic

zelów|ka *f* sole

zelż|eć *pf vi [deszcz, upał, ból]* to ease (off)

zelż|yć *pf vt* książk. to abuse

zeł|gać *pf vt* pot. to lie

zemdl|eć *pf vi* to faint

zemdli|ć *pf* **Ⅰ** *vi* to make [sb] feel sick, to nauseate

Ⅱ *v imp.* **~ło go** he felt sick

z|emleć *pf vt* to grind *[kawę, zboże]*; to mince *[mięso]*

zem|sta *f* revenge (**za coś** for sth); **poprzysiąc komuś ~stę** to swear vengeance on sb

zem|ścić się *pf v refl.* ① (odpłacić) to take (one's) revenge, to revenge oneself ② przen. (mieć niekorzystne skutki) to backfire, to rebound (**na kimś** on sb)

zeni|t *m* zenith także przen.; **napięcie sięgnęło ~tu** the tension reached its height

zepch|nąć *pf vt* ① (zrzucić) to push; **~nąć kogoś ze schodów** to push sb down the stairs ② przen. **~nąć na kogoś odpowiedzialność** to shift the responsibility onto sb; **~nąć coś na margines** to push sth into the background ③ (zmusić do ustąpienia) to push back *[nieprzyjaciela]*

zepsu|ć *pf* **Ⅰ** *vt* ① (uszkodzić) to break *[samochód, urządzenie]* ② (pogorszyć) to spoil *[nastrój, humor]*; **~ć sobie oczy** to ruin one's eyes ③ (rozpieścić) to spoil *[dziecko]*

Ⅱ **zepsuć się** ① (uszkodzić się) *[maszyna, samochód]* to break down ② (zgnić) *[mięso]* to go bad ③ (pogorszyć się) *[pogoda, nastrój]* to get worse; *[stosunki, wzrok, zdrowie]* to deteriorate

ze|ro n [1] (liczba) zero; (cyfra) nought; (w sporcie) nil; **poniżej zera** below zero [2] (nic) zero, nil; **od zera** from scratch

zerów|ka f reception class GB, kindergarten US

z|erwać pf — **z|rywać** impf [] vt [1] (oderwać) to tear off *[dach, plaster]*; to pick *[owoc, kwiat]*; to break *[strunę]*; **zerwać most** *[rzeka]* to wash away a bridge [2] (unieważnić) to break off *[umowę, stosunki, zaręczyny]* [3] (poderwać) *[hałas, huk, wystrzał]* to start [] **zerwać się** — **zrywać się** [1] (urwać się) *[lina, sznur]* to break [2] (poderwać się) to spring up, to jump; **zerwać się o świcie** to get up early [3] (zacząć się) *[wiatr]* to get up; *[burza]* to break; *[oklaski]* to burst out [4] pot. (uciec) **zerwać się ze szkoły** to bunk off school

■ **zerwać z kimś** to break a. split up with sb; **zerwać z czymś** to give up a. quit sth

z|erżnąć pf — **z|rzynać** impf vt [1] (ściąć) to saw off [2] pot. (odpisać) to crib *[wypracowanie]* [3] pot. (zbić) **zerżnąć komuś skórę** to give sb a hiding pot.

zesk|oczyć pf — **zesk|akiwać** impf vi to jump down

z|esłać pf — **z|syłać** impf vt [1] (deportować) to exile [2] (sprawić) *[Bóg, los]* to send *[karę, deszcz]*

zesłani|e n exile; **na ~u** in exile

zesp|olić pf — **zesp|alać** impf [] vt książk. to unite *[ludzi]*; to combine *[cechy, umiejętności]*; to join *[siły, elementy]*

[] **zespolić się** — **zespalać się** książk. to team up

zespołow|y adi. team; **praca ~a** teamwork

zesp|ół m [1] (grupa ludzi) team [2] (muzyczny) band, group [3] (zbiór) complex [4] Techn. unit [5] Med. syndrome

zestarz|eć się pf v refl. [1] (stać się starszym) to age, to get old [2] przen. (zdezaktualizować się) to become dated

zestaw m [1] (zbiór) set; (mebli) suite; (narzędzi) kit [2] (dobór) combination

zestaw|ić pf — **zestaw|iać** impf vt [1] (zdjąć) to take off; (postawić niżej) to take down [2] (złożyć w całość) to put together *[meble, elementy]*; to set *[kość, kończynę]*; to juxtapose *[kolory]*; **~ić stoły w podkowę** to arrange tables in a horseshoe [3] (porównać) to compare **(coś z czymś** sth with sth) [4] (sporządzić) to draw up *[listę, wykaz]*

zestawie|nie n [1] (połączenie) combination [2] (podsumowanie) balance sheet [3] (wykaz) list

zestrzel|ić pf — **zestrzel|iwać** impf vt to shoot down

zeszczupl|eć pf vi [1] (schudnąć) to slim; **~ała na twarzy** her face got thinner [2] przen. *[wpływy, dochody, liczba]* to dwindle

zeszłoroczn|y adi. last year's

zesz|ły adi. *[rok, tydzień]* last

zesztywni|eć pf vi to stiffen, to become stiff; **~eć ze strachu** przen. to stiffen in fear

zeszy|t m [1] (do pisania) notebook; **~t do matematyki** a maths notebook [2] (broszura) book(let)

ześlizg|nąć się pf — **ześlizg|iwać się** impf v refl. to slide (down), to slip (down); (ze zbocza) to slide downhill

ześlizgnąć się → ześlizgnąć się

zetknąć pf — **stykać** impf [] vt *[osoba]* to connect **(coś z czymś** sth to sth); *[los, przypadek]* to bring [sb] together

[] **zetknąć się** [1] (połączyć się) to come into contact [2] przen. (spotkać się) to encounter **(z czymś** sth)

zetrzeć pf — **ścierać** impf [] vt [1] (usunąć) remove; (oczyścić) to wipe off *[tablicę, kurz, wodę]*; to wipe away *[łzy]*; **zetrzeć coś gumką** to rub sth out GB, to erase sth [2] (rozdrobnić) to pulverize; (na tarce) to grate [3] przen. (zniszczyć) to pulverize *[nieprzyjaciela]*

[] **zetrzeć się** — **ścierać się** [1] (zniknąć) to be worn away [2] (natrzeć na siebie) to clash **(z kimś** with sb)

zewnątrz adv. outside; **na ~** *[znajdować się, wyjść]* outside; **otwierać się na ~** to open outwards; **od ~** from (the) outside; **z ~** from (the) outside

zewnętrzn|y adi. [1] (poza czymś) outside, outer [2] (na zewnątrz, z zewnątrz) *[obrażenia, objawy, bodziec]* external; *[wygląd]* outward; *[wpływ]* outside [3] (zagraniczny) *[polityka]* foreign

zez m squint GB, cross-eyes a. crossed eyes; **mieć ~a** to have a squint; **zrobić ~a** to cross one's eyes

zezło|ścić pf [] vt to annoy

[] **zezłościć się** to get a. be angry

zezna|ć pf — **zezna|wać** impf vi to testify

zezna|nie n [1] (w sądzie) testimony; **składać ~nia** to testify [2] (na piśmie) statement; **~nie podatkowe** a tax return

zeznawać impf → zeznać

zez|ować impf vi [1] (mieć zeza) to squint, to have a squint GB [2] pot. (zerkać ukradkiem) to sneak a glance **(na coś** at sth)

zezowa|ty adi. *[osoba]* cross-eyed; *[oczy]* squinty GB, crossed

zezwalać impf → zezwolić

zezwole|nie n [1] (zgoda) permission [2] (dokument) permit; **~nie na broń** a gun permit

zezw|olić pf — **zezw|alać** impf vi to allow, to permit; **~olić komuś na coś** to allow sb to do sth

z|eżreć pf — **z|żerać** impf vi [1] pot. (zjeść) to scoff (down) GB pot., to scarf (down) US pot. [2] pot. *[rdza]* to eat away

zęba|ty adi. *[paszcza]* toothy; *[brzeg, linia]* serrated; *[nóż, piła]* serrated, toothed

zgad|nąć impf — **zgad|ywać** impf vi to guess

zgadywan|ka f pot. guessing game także przen.

zgadzać się impf → zgodzić się

zga|ga f heartburn

zga|nić pf vt to reprimand książk.

zgarb|ić się pf v refl. *[osoba]* to stoop; (siedząc) to slump

zgarn|ąć pf — **zgarn|iać** impf vt [1] (zebrać) to scoop a. sweep (up) [2] pot. (zdobyć) to rake in pot.

[pieniądze] ③ (odsunąć na bok) to push aside a. away ④ pot. (aresztować) to nick GB pot., to pick up pot.

zga|sić *pf vt* ① (stłumić) to extinguish *[ogień, pożar]*; to put out *[papierosa, fajkę]* ② (wyłączyć) to turn a. switch off *[radio, silnik]* ③ przen. to dampen *[zapał, entuzjazm]*; ~**sić kogoś** to take the wind out of sb's sails

zga|snąć *pf vi* ① *[świeca, płomień, lampa]* to go out ② *[samochód, silnik]* to stall ③ przen. *[nadzieja, zapał]* to fade

zgasz|ony *adi. [osoba]* downcast; *[kolor]* muted

zgęstni|eć *pf vi [las, mgła, zupa, tłum]* to thicken, to get thicker; *[krew]* to coagulate; *[ciemność, mrok]* to thicken, to deepen; *[atmosfera]* to become tense

z|giąć *pf* — **z|ginać** *impf* **[]** *vt* to bend *[rękę, plecy, drut]*

[] **zgiąć się** — **zginać się** *[osoba, gałąź, błotnik]* to bend

zgiełk *m* tumult; **uliczny** ~ the hubbub of the street; **medialny** ~ przen. a big hullabaloo in the media pot.

zginać *impf* → **zgiąć**

zgi|nąć *pf vt* ① (umrzeć) to die ② przen. (znaleźć się w sytuacji bez wyjścia) to be done for ③ (przestać istnieć) *[zwyczaj]* to disappear ④ (zapodziać się) *[list, dokumenty]* to get lost

zgliszcz|a *plt* (miejsce po pożarze) site of a fire; (spalone szczątki) charred remains a. ruins

zgłaszać *impf* → **zgłosić**

zgłęb|ić *pf* — **zgłęb|iać** *impf vt* książk. to penetrate *[tajemnicę]*; to get to the bottom of *[problem]*; to grasp *[przyczyny]*

zgłodni|eć *pf vi* to get hungry

zgł|osić *pf* — **zgł|aszać** *impf* **[]** *vt* ① (zaproponować) to propose *[wniosek, poprawkę, pytanie]*; to raise *[sprzeciw, zastrzeżenia]*; to come forward with *[propozycję]* ② (zaproponować udział) to enter *[zawodnika]*; ~**osić kogoś na (jakieś) stanowisko** to propose sb for a position ③ (zameldować) to report *[włamanie, awarię]*; to register *[narodziny]*

[] **zgłosić się** — **zgłaszać się** ① (stawić się) to report (**do kogoś** to sb); ~**osić się po paczkę** to come and collect the parcel ② (oznajmić chęć uczestnictwa) to come forward; ~**osić się na ochotnika** to volunteer ③ (odezwać się) *[osoba, telefonistka]* to answer

zgłupi|eć *pf vi* pot. ① (zwariować) *[osoba]* to become stupid; *[komputer]* to go haywire; **można** ~**eć** it's enough to drive you crazy ② (stracić orientację) to get confused

zgneb|ić *pf vt* to depress

zgniatać *impf* → **zgnieść**

zgni|ć *pf vi [żywność, liście, drewno]* to rot (away); ~**ć w więzieniu** pot. to rot in prison

zgni|eść *pf* — **zgni|atać** *impf* **[]** *vt* ① (zmiażdżyć) to crumple (up) *[kartkę papieru, materiał]*; to crush *[puszkę, robaka]*; to squash *[kapelusz]* ② (pomiąć) to

crumple, to crease *[ubranie, sukienkę]* ③ przen. (stłumić) to crush, to suppress *[bunt, opór]*

[] **zgnieść się** — **zgniatać się** *[ubranie]* to crumple

zgnili|zna *f* ① (zgniła substancja) rot, decay ② (rozkład) rot, putrefaction ③ przen. (demoralizacja) corruption

zgni|ły *adi.* ① (zepsuty) *[jajko, owoc, zapach]* rotten ② *[kolor]* green brown; *[zieleń]* brownish

zgo|da [] *f* ① (harmonia) harmony; **w** ~**dzie z czymś** in accordance with sth *[przepisami]*, in keeping with sth *[tradycja]*; **żyć w** ~**dzie z kimś** to live in harmony with sb ② (pojednanie) reconciliation; **wyciągnąć rękę na** ~**dę** to extend one's hand in reconciliation; **podać sobie ręce na** ~**dę** to shake hands in agreement ③ (zgodność opinii) agreement; **panuje powszechna** ~**da co do tego, że...** there is general agreement that... ④ (przyzwolenie) assent, consent (**na coś** to sth); (oficjalne zezwolenie) permission (**na coś** for sth); **wyrazić** ~**dę** to give one's assent; **wyrazić** ~**dę na coś** to agree a. consent to sth; **za obopólną** ~**dą** by mutual consent a. agreement

[] *inter.* ① (wyraża przyzwolenie, aprobatę) all right; ~**da?** (is that) agreed? ② (wyraża pojednanie) let's be friends!

■ ~**da buduje, niezgoda rujnuje** przysł. united we stand, divided we fall

zgodn|y *adi.* ① (niekłótliwy) *[osoba, usposobienie]* agreeable, accommodating; *[rodzina, współpraca]* harmonious ② (jednomyślny) *[oświadczenie, wysiłek]* unanimous; **eksperci są** ~**i, że...** experts agree that... ③ (odpowiedni) ~**y z czymś** in accordance with sth *[przepisami]*; in keeping with sth *[tradycja]*

zg|odzić się *pf* — **zg|adzać się** *impf v refl.* ① (wyrazić zgodę) to agree; **zgodzić się na czyjąś propozycję** to agree to sb's proposal; **zgodzić się, żeby ktoś coś zrobił** to agree to sb doing sth; **zgodzić się coś zrobić** to agree to do sth ② (przyznać rację) to agree (**z kimś** with sb); **nie zgadzać się z kimś/czymś** to disagree with sb/sth; **tu się z tobą zgodzę** I'll go along with you there; **zgadza się** (that's) correct a. right ③ (być zgodnym, pokrywać się) *[liczby, sumy, fakty]* to tally, to add up; *[szczegóły]* to check out; **coś mi się tu nie zgadza** something's not quite right here

zg|olić *pf vt* to shave off *[brodę, wąsy]*

zgon *m* książk. death; demise książk.; **świadectwo** ~**u** a death certificate

zgorsz|yć *pf* **[]** *vt* to scandalize

[] **zgorszyć się** to be scandalized

zgorzel *f* gangrene

zgorzknia|ły *adi. [osoba]* embittered

zgorzkni|eć *pf vi* ① *[masło]* to go a. turn rancid ② książk. *[osoba]* to become bitter a. embittered

zgot|ować *pf vt* książk. to give *[owację, niespodziankę]*

zgrabn|y *adi. grad.* ① (foremny) *[osoba, ciało]* shapely; *[samochód, pudełko]* neat, natty ② (zwinny) *[tancerz,* *skok, ruchy]* agile, nimble ③ (udany) *[przekład, porównanie]* apt; *[historyjka]* well-rounded; *[wierszyk]* elegant

zgr|ać *pf* — **zgr|ywać**[1] *impf* **▯** *vt* to fit together *[elementy]*; to coordinate *[terminy, plan lekcji]*; ∼**ać instrumenty** to put instruments in tune with each other

▯▯ zgrać się — **zgrywać się** pot. ① (utworzyć zgodny zespół) *[drużyna, zawodnicy]* to get used to playing together; *[pracownicy]* to get used to working together ② (ograć się) *[motyw, wątek]* to become hackneyed ③ (przegrać) to gamble away one's money

zgra|ja *f* ① pot. (gromada, banda) bunch ② (stado) pack

zgran|y *adi.* ① (zżyty) *[grupa]* harmonious; **tworzyć** ∼**y zespół** *[sportowcy]* to make a good team; *[pracownicy]* to get on well together ② pot. *[motyw]* hackneyed; *[płyta]* (well-)worn

zgromadzać *impf* → **zgromadzić**

zgromadze|nie *n* ① (posiedzenie) meeting ② (grupa osób) gathering ③ Polit. assembly ④ (zakon) congregation

zgroma|dzić *pf* — **zgroma|dzać** *impf* **▯** *vt* ① (zebrać) to collect *[dane, informacje, dowody]*; to assemble *[kolekcję]*; to accumulate *[fortunę]*; to raise *[fundusze]*; to store (up) *[żywność]* ② (skupić) to assemble *[osoby]*; *[konferencja, koncert, wystawa]* to attract *[uczestników, widzów]*

▯▯ zgromadzić się — **zgromadzać się** (zebrać się) to gather

zgrom|ić *pf vt* książk. to berate (**kogoś za coś** sb for sth)

zgroz|a *f* horror; **ze** ∼**ą odkryłem, że...** I discovered to my horror that...

zgrubi|eć *impf vi* ① *[palce, gałązki]* to grow thicker; *[osoba]* to get fatter; *[skóra, ręce, rysy]* to coarsen ② pot. *[głos]* to break

zgrubie|nie *n* ① (zniekształcenie) swelling ② Jęz. augmentative (form)

zgrup|ować *pf* **▯** *vt* to group (together) *[ludzi, informacje]*

▯▯ zgrupować się (zebrać się) to gather (together); (utworzyć grupę) to form a group

zgr|ywać[1] *impf* → **zgrać**

zgr|ywać[2] *impf* **▯** *vt* pot. (pozować) to act; ∼**ywać bohatera** to play a. come pot. the hero

▯▯ zgrywać się pot. ① (pozować) to play, to act (**na kogoś** sb) ② (popisywać się) to show off; (wygłupiać się) to fool around

zgryz *m* Anat. occlusion spec.; **mieć krzywy** ∼ to have a bad bite

zgry|źć *pf* — **zgry|zać** *impf vt* to crack [sth] between one's teeth

zgryźliw|y *adi. [uwaga, ton]* scathing, acrid; *[osoba]* catty

zgrz|ać *pf* — **zgrz|ewać** *impf vt* to weld

zgrz|ać się *pf v refl.* to get sweaty

zgrzewać *impf* → **zgrzać**

zgrzy|t *m* ① (zębów, hamulców) grinding; (piły) rasp; (łopaty, klucza) scrape ② przen. (rozdźwięk) friction ③ pot. (dysonans) clash

zgrzyt|nąć *pf* — **zgrzyt|ać** *impf vi [zawiasy]* to creak; *[dźwignia biegów]* to grind; ∼**ać zębami** to grind one's teeth; (ze złości) to gnash one's teeth

zgub|a *f* ① (przedmiot) lost item ② książk. (zagłada) doom

zgub|ić *pf* **▯** *vt* ① (stracić) to lose *[pieniądze, klucz, rękawiczki]*; ∼**ić pościg** to shake off one's pursuer(s); ∼**ić drogę** to lose one's way; ∼**ić wątek** to lose the thread ② książk. (narazić) to bring [sb] to ruin książk.

▯▯ zgubić się ① (zabłądzić) to get lost także przen. ② (stracić się z oczu) to lose sight of each other ③ (zapodziać się) *[przedmiot]* to get lost

zgwał|cić *pf vt* ① (zmusić do stosunku) to rape ② pot. (zmusić) to bulldoze pot., przen.

zhańb|ić *pf* książk. **▯** *vt* to disgrace *[osobę, nazwisko]*

▯▯ zhańbić się to disgrace oneself; **nigdy nie** ∼**ił się pracą** żart. he's never stooped so low as to find a job żart.

zi|ać *impf vi* ① (dyszeć) to pant ② (buchać) to breathe; **ziać ogniem** to breathe fire; **ziać gniewem** przen. to be seething with anger ③ (rozwierać się) to gape; **ziać pustką** to be empty

ziarni|sty *adi.* ① (mający ziarna) grain; *[mąka, chleb]* wholegrain ② *[struktura, budowa]* granular, grainy

ziar|no *n* ① (owoc zbóż) grain ② (nasienie) seed ③ (piasku, kwarcu) grain; ∼**no prawdy** przen. a grain of truth

zidentyfik|ować /ˌzidentɪfiˈkovatɕ/ *pf* **▯** *vt* to identify *[przestępcę, zwłoki, pismo]*

▯▯ zidentyfikować się to identify (**z kimś** with sb)

zielars|ki *adi. [sklep]* herbalist's; *[przemysł]* herbal

zielarstw|o *n* (wiedza) herbalism; (leczenie ziołami) herbal medicine

ziela|rz *m*, ∼**rka** *f* herbalist

zi|ele *n* herb; **naparzyć ziół** to make herb tea ❑ **ziele angielskie** allspice, pimento

zieleniak *m* pot. (sklep) greengrocer's GB, (fruit and) vegetable shop

zieleni|eć *impf vi* to turn green także przen.; ∼**eć z zazdrości** to be green with envy

zielenin|a *f [zielone warzywa]* greens; (włoszczyzna) soup vegetables

ziele|ń *f* ① (kolor, barwnik) green ② (roślinność) greenery; **szanuj** ∼**ń** keep off the grass

zielono *adv.* **pomalować coś na** ∼ to paint sth green

ziel|ony **▯** *adi. grad.* ① (kolor) green ② pot. (ziemisty) *[twarz, cera]* green ③ (niedojrzały) *[zboże, owoc]* green ④ (niedoświadczony) green

▯▯ *m* pot. ① (dolar) dollar; buck US pot. ② **Zielony** (działacz) Green

III **zielone** *n* pot. [1] (do bukietów) greenery [2] (nać) greens

zielsk|o *n* weed

ziem|ia *f* [1] (glob) the Earth; **nie z tej ~i** pot. out of this world pot. [2] (gleba) soil [3] (podłoże) ground; (podłoga) floor; **pod ~ią** underground; **stąpać twardo po ~i** przen. to have both feet on the ground; **zrównać coś z ~ią** to raze sth to the ground; **zapaść się pod ~ię** przen. to vanish into thin air [4] (pola) land [5] (kraina) land; **Ziemia Obiecana** the Promised Land także przen. [6] (dzielnica) region, district

ziemi|sty *adi.* [kolor, cera] sallow

ziemniaczan|y *adi.* [pole, zupa] potato

ziemniak *m* potato

ziems|ki *adi.* (kula, atmosfera, istota) terrestrial; [sprawy, troski] earthly; [majątek, własność] landed

ziew|nąć *impf* — **ziew|ać** *impf vi* to yawn

zięb|a *f* chaffinch

zięb|ić *impf vi* (chłodzić) to chill, to cool
■ **ani mnie to ~i, ani grzeje** pot. it's all the same to me

zi|ębnąć *impf vi* to get cold

zię|ć *m* son-in-law

zignor|ować /ˌziɡnoˈrovatɕ/ *pf vt* to ignore

zilustr|ować /ˌzilusˈtrovatɕ/ *pf vt* to illustrate; **~ować coś przykładem** to provide an example to illustrate sth

zim|a *f* winter

zimn|o **[]** *n* cold; **trząść się z ~a** to shiver (in the cold)
II *adv. grad.* [1] (o temperaturze) cold; **~o mi** I'm cold [2] przen. [traktować] coldly

zimn|y *adi. grad.* [wiatr, dzień, ręce, osoba] cold także przen.
■ **dmuchać na ~e** to play it safe pot.; **zachować ~ą krew** to stay calm

zimorod|ek *m* kingfisher

zim|ować *impf vi* [1] (spędzać zimę) to spend the winter [2] pot. (powtarzać klasę) to be held back (in school)

zimowisk|o *n* [1] (miejscowość) winter resort [2] (obóz sportowy) winter camp [3] (teren zimowania) (ludzi) winter quarters; (zwierząt) winter habitat

zimow|y *adi.* [dzień, płaszcz] winter; **zapaść w sen ~y** to hibernate

zintegr|ować /ˌzinteˈɡrovatɕ/ *pf* **[]** *vt* to integrate
II **zintegrować się** książk. to be(come) integrated

zinterpret|ować /ˌzinterpreˈtovatɕ/ *pf vt* (wyjaśnić) to explain; (zrozumieć) to interpret

zinwentaryz|ować /ˌzinventarɨˈzovatɕ/ *pf vt* to make an inventory of

zi|oło *n* herb

ziołolecznictw|o *n* herbal medicine

ziołow|y *adi.* herbal

ziryt|ować / zɨrɨˈtovatɕ/ *pf* **[]** *vt* to irritate
II **zirytować się** to be irritated

zjadliw|y *adi. grad.* książk. [1] (złośliwy) [słowa, żarty, ton] scathing; [krytyk] spiteful [2] (szkodliwy) [bakterie, wirusy] virulent [3] przen. (rażący) [kolor] garish [4] żart. (nadający się do jedzenia) edible

zjaw|a *f* apparition

zjaw|ić się *pf* — **zjaw|iać się** *impf v refl.* (przybyć) to turn up; (pojawić się) to appear

zjawisk|o *n* [1] (fakt) phenomenon; (zdarzenie) occurrence [2] książk. (widziadło) apparition

zj|azd *m* [1] (zjeżdżanie) **zjazd windą trwa 45 sekund** it takes 45 seconds to go down by lift [2] (pochyła powierzchnia) descent; **zjazd z autostrady** an exit, an off ramp US [3] (naukowy) convention; (rodzinny, koleżeński) reunion [4] Sport downhill (race)

zjazdow|y *adi.* [1] [materiały, dyskusja] convention [2] Sport [narty] downhill; [tereny, trasa] skiing

zj|echać *pf* — **zj|eżdżać** *impf* **[]** *vt* pot. (skrytykować) to slam (**kogoś za coś** sb for sth) [niechlujstwo, niedopatrzenie]
II *vi* [1] (pojazdem) to drive down; (na nartach) to ski downhill; (windą) to go down; **zjeżdżaj stąd!** pot. get lost! pot. [2] (z drogi) to pull over; **zjechać do zajezdni** [autobus, tramwaj] to return to the depot [3] książk. (przybyć) to arrive [4] pot. (zsunąć się) [okulary, czapka] to slip
III **zjechać się** — **zjeżdżać się** (zgromadzić się) to arrive

zjedn|ać *pf* — **zjedn|ywać** *impf vt* książk. to win [zwolenników, sympatię]

zjednocz|yć *pf* **[]** *vt* to unite
II **zjednoczyć się** to unite

zjednywać *impf* → zjednać

zjełcz|eć *pf vt* [1] (spożyć) to eat; **przecież cię nie zjem** iron. I won't eat you [2] pot., przen. (pochłonąć) [rdza] to eat away [3] przen. (opuścić) to miss out [słowo, literę]

zjeżać *impf* → zjeżyć

zjeżdżać *impf* → zjechać

zjeżdżal|nia *f* slide

zjeż|yć *pf* — **zjeż|ać** *impf* **[]** *vt* to raise [sierść]; **strach ~ył mi włosy na głowie** przen. my hair stood on end through fear
II **zjeżyć się** — **zjeżać się** [1] (nastroszyć się) [zwierzę] to bristle (up); [włosy] to stand on end [2] przen. (obruszyć się) [osoba] to bristle

zl|ać *pf* — **zl|ewać** *impf* **[]** *vt* [1] (wylać) to pour off [2] pot. (zbić) to thrash
II **zlać się** — **zlewać się** [1] (połączyć się) to merge [2] (polać się) to pour [sth] on oneself; **zlać się potem** to be bathed in sweat [3] posp. (zsiusiać się) to wet one's pants

zlatywać *impf* → zlecieć

zlecać *impf* → zlecić

zlece|nie *n* [1] (polecenie) instructions [2] (zamówienie) order [3] (umowa) freelance agreement; **pracować na ~nie** to do freelance work

zleceniobiorc|a *m* contractor

zleceniodawc|a *m* employer
zle|cić *pf* — **zle|cać** *impf vt* to commission
zl|ecieć *pf* — **zl|atywać** *impf* **[I]** *vi* [1] (sfrunąć) to fly down [2] pot. (spaść) to fall (down); **zlecieć z drabiny** to fall off a ladder [3] przen. (upłynąć) *[czas]* to fly by [4] pot. (zbiec) to run down
[II] zlecieć się — **zlatywać się** [1] (przyfrunąć) to fly in [2] pot. (przybiec) to come (in) running
zlekceważ|yć *pf vt* to disregard *[niebezpieczeństwo, polecenie]*; to underestimate *[przeciwnika]*
zlep|ek *m* pot. blend
zlep|ić *pf* — **zlep|iać** *impf* **[I]** *vt* (złączyć) to join [sth] together; (skleić) to glue [sth] together
[II] zlepić się — **zlepiać się** to stick together
zlew *m* (kitchen) sink
zlewać *impf* → **zlać**
zlew|ki *plt* slops
zlewozmywak *m* (kitchen) sink
z|leźć *pf* — **z|łazić** *impf* pot. **[I]** *vi* [1] (zejść) to climb down [2] (obleźć) *[farba, skóra]* to peel off
[II] zleźć się — **złazić się** (zejść się) to gather
zl|ęknąć się, zl|ąc się *pf v refl.* to be frightened (**czegoś** by sth)
zlicyt|ować *pf vt* to auction off
zlicz|yć *pf* — **zlicz|ać** *impf vt* to sum up *[dochody, wydatki]*; **tylu, że trudno ~yć** so many that you can hardly count them (up)
zlikwid|ować *pf* **[I]** *vt* [1] (usunąć) to close down *[przedsiębiorstwo, spółkę]*; to eradicate *[analfabetyzm, pijaństwo]* [2] pot. (uśmiercić) to liquidate
[II] zlikwidować się *[spółka]* to go into liquidation
zlit|ować się *pf v refl.* to take pity (**nad kimś** on sb)
zli|zać *pf* — **zli|zywać** *impf vt* to lick off
zlokaliz|ować *pf vt* książk. [1] (umiejscowić) to locate [2] (ograniczyć) to localize *[epidemię]* [3] (znaleźć) to localize *[przestępcę]*
zlo|t *m* rally
zluz|ować *pf* — **zluz|owywać** *impf vt* pot. [1] (zmienić) to relieve *[straże, wartownika]* [2] (obluzować) to loosen *[łańcuch, linę]*
złagadzać *impf* → **złagodzić**
złagodni|eć *pf vi [osoba, mina]* to mellow; *[sąd, opinia]* to become less harsh; *[ruchy]* to become gentler
złag|odzić *pf* — **złag|adzać** *impf vt* to soften *[przepis]*; to alleviate *[ból]*; to turn down *[światło]*; to tone down *[kolor]*
złam|ać *pf* **[I]** *vt* [1] (przełamać) to break *[kij, pieczęć, rękę]* [2] (pokonać) to break *[opór, szyfr]*; **~ać komuś serce** to break sb's heart [3] przen. to break *[prawo, słowo]* [4] Druk. to format
[II] złamać się [1] (pęknąć) to break [2] pot. (ustąpić) to break down
złama|nie *n* Med. fracture; **na ~nie karku** przen. at breakneck speed

złaman|y *adi.* [1] *[osoba]* broken [2] *[kolor]* toned down
złap|ać *pf* **[I]** *vt* [1] (chwycić, zatrzymać) to catch *[piłkę, złodzieja, rybę]*; to pick up *[falę, stację]*; **~ać kogoś za kark** to grab sb by the scruff of their neck; **~ać kogoś na czymś** to catch sb doing sth; **~ać oddech** to catch one's breath; **~ać taksówkę** to get a taxi [2] przen. *[strach]* to seize; **~ał mnie skurcz w nodze** I got cramp in my leg [3] (zaskoczyć) *[burza]* to catch
[II] złapać się [1] (położyć rękę) to clutch; **~ać się za brzuch** to clutch one's stomach; **~ać się na czymś** to catch oneself doing sth [2] (wpaść w pułapkę) *[mysz]* to be caught [3] pot. (nabrać się) to be taken in (**na coś** by sth)
złazić *pf* → **zleźć**
złączać *impf* → **złączyć**
złącz|e *n* joint
złącz|yć *pf* — **złącz|ać** *impf* **[I]** *vt* [1] (połączyć) to join [2] przen. *[przyjaźń]* to bind
[II] złączyć się — **złączać się** to join together
zł|o *n* evil, wrong; (cecha) badness; **zło konieczne** necessary evil; **walka dobra ze złem** a battle between good and evil; **wyrządzić komuś zło** to do great harm to sb; **naprawić (wyrządzone) zło** to redress a. right a wrong; **widzieć w kimś tylko zło** to see only the bad in sb; **wybrać mniejsze zło** to choose the lesser of two evils
złocie|ń *m* chrysanthemum
złoci|sty *adi. grad.* książk. golden
złoc|ony *adi.* (galwanicznie) *[sztućce, biżuteria]* gold-plated; (farbą, folią, proszkiem) gilded, gilt
złodziej *m* thief
złodziej|ka *f* [1] (przestępczyni) thief [2] pot. (rozgałęziacz) adaptor a. adapter GB
złodziejstw|o *n* (kradzież) theft; (proceder) thieving
złom *m* [1] (surowiec) scrap; (metalowy) scrap metal; **pójść na ~** to go to the scrap heap; **oddać coś na ~** to scrap sth [2] pot. (niesprawne urządzenia) junk pot.
złomowisk|o *n* scrapyard GB, junkyard US
zło|ścić *impf* **[I]** *vt* to annoy
[II] złościć się (być rozgniewanym) to be annoyed (**na kogoś/coś** with a. at sb/sth); (okazywać gniew) to fume (**na coś** over sth);
złoś|ć *f* (wzburzenie) anger; (irytacja) annoyance; **w napadzie ~ci** in a fit of anger; **ze ~cią** angrily; **wpadać w ~ć** to lose one's temper;
■ **jak na ~ć** to make matters worse; **na ~ć** out of spite
złośliwoś|ć *f* [1] (wola czynienia zła) malice; (cecha) maliciousness; (chęć dokuczenia) spite; (charakter) nastiness [2] (uwaga) malicious a. nasty remark [3] Med. (choroby, zarazków) virulence; (nowotworu) malignancy
złośliw|y **[I]** *adi. grad.* (mający niedobre intencje) *[osoba, plotki, uśmiech]* malicious; (obraźliwy) *[żart, krytyka]* spiteful

II *adi.* Med. *[zarazki, choroba]* virulent; *[nowotwór, guz]* malignant

złośnic|a *f* pot. shrew

złośni|k *m* pot. crosspatch pot.

złotni|k *m* (wyrabiający przedmioty) goldsmith; (wykonujący złocenia) gilder

zło|to **[]** *n* 1 (metal) gold; ~**to w sztabkach** gold ingots; **pięćdziesiąt rubli w** ~**cie** fifty roubles in gold; **jak** ~**to** pot. *[dziecko]* as good as gold; *[przedmiot]* first-rate; **żyła** ~**ta** a gold mine przen. 2 pot. (złoty medal) gold; **zdobyć** ~**to** to win gold 3 (kolor) gold
II *adv.* *[świecić, mienić się]* goldenly

złotów|ka *f* (jednostka monetarna) (the) zloty; (moneta) one-zloty coin

złot|y[1] *m* (jednostka monetarna) zloty

zło|ty[2] *adi.* 1 (zawierający złoto) *[piasek, żyła]* auriferous 2 (zrobiony ze złota) *[sygnet, korona, medal]* gold 3 (pozłacany) (galwanicznie) *[świecznik, sztućce, biżuteria]* gold-plated; (farbą, folią, proszkiem) *[posążek, waza, dach]* gilded, gilt 4 (w kolorze złota) *[włosy, klamra, liście]* golden 5 (doskonały) *[czasy, chwile, dni]* golden, happy; **to** ~**ty człowiek** he's got a heart of gold
■ ~**ty środek** the golden mean

zł|owić *pf vt* 1 (złapać) to catch *[lisa, królika, rybę]*; (na haczyk) to hook; (w sieć) to net 2 przen. (zarejestrować) to catch *[widok, dźwięk]*

złowieszcz|y *adi.* książk. *[cisza, dym, słowa]* ominous

złowro|gi *adi.* *[cisza, odgłosy]* ominous; *[plany, nastrój, zamiar]* malevolent; *[działalność, spisek]* sinister; *[osoba, przepowiednia]* baleful

zł|oże *n* (surowców) deposit

złoż|ony *adi.* 1 (wieloelementowy) *[mechanizm, cząsteczka, organ]* compound; **zdanie** ~**one** a compound sentence 2 (skomplikowany) *[zagadnienie, system, proces]* complex; *[struktura, układ]* intricate

złożyć *pf* — **składać** *impf* **[]** *vt* 1 (poskładać, zamknąć) to fold (up) *[gazetę, list, leżak]*; **złożyć coś na pół** to fold sth in two 2 (zmontować, połączyć) to assemble *[silnik, szafkę]*; to piece together *[układankę, fragmenty]* 3 Med. to set *[rękę, kość]* 4 (położyć) to put; **złożyć wieniec** to lay a wreath 5 (wręczyć, oddać) to hand in *[rezygnację, wymówienie]*; to submit *[sprawozdanie, dokumenty]*; to lodge *[zażalenie, protest, odwołanie]*; to pay *[okup, depozyt, kaucję]*; to proffer *[wyjaśnienia]*; to offer *[życzenia, gratulacje, kondolencje]*; to place *[zamówienie]*; **złożyć komuś wizytę** to pay sb a visit; **złożyć podpis pod czymś** to put one's signature on sth 6 Druk. to set *[tekst, czcionki]* 7 Zool. *[ptak]* to lay *[jaja]*
II **złożyć się** — **składać się** 1 (być częścią) *[elementy, punkty]* to make up (**na coś** sth) 2 (być składanym) *[leżak, łóżko, krzesło]* to fold (flat) 3 (robić składkę) to club together 4 (być przyczyną) *[wydarzenia, powody, kłopoty]* to result (**na coś** in sth) 5 (przybrać pozycję) to assume a. take a position 6 (zdarzyć się) to

happen; **tak się składa, że...** it so happens that...; **dobrze się złożyło, że...** it was fortunate that...

złu|da *f* książk. illusion

złudn|y *adi.* książk. *[wygląd, wrażenie]* deceptive; *[spokój, nadzieje]* illusory

złudze|nie *n* 1 (iluzja) illusion; ~**nie optyczne** an optical illusion 2 (mrzonka) illusion; **rozwiać czyjeś** ~**nia** to dispel sb's illusions; **nie mieć** ~**ń** to harbour no illusions; **przypominać kogoś do** ~**nia** to be the spitting image of sb

zły **[]** *adi. grad.* 1 (niemoralny) *[osoba, towarzystwo, zachowanie, przykład]* bad; *[zamiar, siła, los, duch]* evil; **zła wola** ill will; **mieć coś komuś za złe** to bear sb a grudge for sth; **nie widzę w tym nic złego** I can't see any harm in it 2 (niekompetentny, niekorzystny, niezadowalający) *[uczeń, ojciec, wrażenie, rok, towar, gust]* bad; **złe warunki mieszkaniowe** poor housing; **zły stan zdrowia** ill health; **zły sen** a nightmare; **zła strona czegoś** a disadvantage of sth; **co gorsza** what is worse; **na domiar złego** to top it all 3 (niewłaściwy) *[kierunek, wybór]* wrong
II *adi.* (rozgniewany) *[osoba]* angry; **być złym na kogoś za** a. **o coś** to be angry with sb over sth
III *m* 1 (osoba) bad person 2 (szatan) the devil
IV **złe** *n* evil; **namówić kogoś do złego** to lead sb astray
■ **siła złego na jednego** the odds are against one; **nie ma tego złego, co by na dobre nie wyszło** przysł. every cloud has a silver lining przysł.

zmaga|ć się *impf v refl.* książk. 1 (walczyć) to grapple także przen. (**z kimś/czymś** with sb/sth) 2 (w rywalizacji) *[sportowcy, zawodnicy]* to compete

zmagazyn|ować *pf vt* to store (up)

zmal|eć *pf vi* *[produkcja, wartość]* to decrease; *[poparcie, zagrożenie]* to diminish; *[ryzyko, napięcie, ból]* to lessen; *[odległość]* to shorten

zmaltret|ować *pf vt* to maltreat

zmanierowan|y *adi.* *[osoba, zachowanie]* affected

zmar|ły **[]** *adi.* *[osoba]* dead; **moja** ~**ła żona** my late wife
II **zmar|ły** *m*, ~**ła** *f* the departed; **the deceased** książk.; ~**li** the dead

zmarni|eć *pf vi* *[osoba]* to be wasted away; *[roślina]* (zwiędnąć) to wilt; (zeschnąć) to wither

zmarn|ować *pf* **[]** *vt* to squander *[środki]*; to misspend *[pieniądze, fundusze]*; to waste *[czas, życie, talent]*
II **zmarnować się** *[majątek, talent]* to be wasted; *[osoba]* to spoil one's life

zmarszcz|ka *f* (na skórze) wrinkle; (w materiale) crease; (na wodzie) ripple

zmarszcz|yć *pf* **[]** *vt [osoba]* to wrinkle *[nos, czoło]*; (zebrać w fałdy) to gather *[materiał, spódnicę]*; *[wiatr]* to ripple *[powierzchnię, wodę]*; ~**yć brwi** to knit one's (eye)brows
II **zmarszczyć się** *[płaszcz, spódnica]* to wrinkle;

[woda, powierzchnia] to ripple; *[twarz]* to crinkle (up)

zmartw|ić *pf* **I** *vt* to upset (**kogoś czymś** sb with sth)

II zmartwić się to be upset

zmartwie|nie *n* worry; **mieć ~nie z czymś** to have trouble with sth

zmartwi|ony *adi. [osoba]* upset (**czymś** about a. by sth); *[twarz]* worried

zmartwychwsta|ć *pf* — **zmartwychwsta|wać** *impf vi* to be resurrected także przen.

zmarzl|ak /z'marzlak/, **~uch** /z'marzlux/ *m* pot. **być ~akiem** a. **~uchem** to get cold easily

zmarz|nąć /z'marznɔntɕ/ *pf vi* **1** *[osoba, zwierzę]* to be cold; **~nąć na kość** to freeze to the marrow **2** (zamarznąć) *[roślina]* to freeze

zmarznię|ty /ˌzmar'znɛntɨ/ *adi.* **1** *[gleba, ziemniaki, śnieg]* frozen **2** *[osoba, ręce, stopy]* cold

zmaterializ|ować *pf* książk. **I** *vt* to realize *[pomysł, projekt]*

II zmaterializować się to materialize

zmatowi|eć *pf vi [kieliszek, lustro]* to become tarnished; *[kolor]* to fade; *[głos, oczy]* to become dull

zmawiać *impf* → **zmówić**

zmaz|a *f* flaw

❑ **~a nocna** nocturnal emission

zma|zać *pf* — **zma|zywać** *impf vt* **1** (gąbką, szmatą) to wipe off; (gumką) to erase **2** przen. to wipe out *[grzech, winę, hańbę]*

zmą|cić *pf* — **zmą|cać** *impf* **I** *vt* **1** (wzburzyć) to make [sth] cloudy *[ciecz, wodę]* **2** (zakłócić) to disturb *[spokój, ciszę]* **3** przen. to cloud *[wzrok, myśli]*

II zmącić się — **zmącać się** **1** *[woda, wino]* to become cloudy **2** przen. *[myśl, pamięć]* to cloud

zmądrz|eć *pf vi* to grow wise

zmechaniz|ować *pf* **I** *vt* to mechanize *[pracę]*

II zmechanizować się to become mechanized

zmęczeni|e *n* fatigue

zmęcz|yć *pf* **I** *vt* **1** (wyczerpać) to tire out **2** pot. (dokończyć z trudem) to wade through *[wypracowanie, książkę]*

II zmęczyć się to get tired

zmętni|eć *pf vi [wino, sok]* to become cloudy; *[oczy, spojrzenie]* to grow dull

zmężni|eć *pf vi [chłopiec]* to grow into a man

zmian|a *f* **1** (odmiana) change; **ulec ~ie** to change **2** (wymiana) **na ~ę** in turns; **~a warty** Wojsk. a change of guard **3** (czas pracy) shift; **pracować na dwie ~y** to work double shifts **4** (bielizny, pościeli) change **5** Sport substitution

zmiatać[1] *impf* → **zmieść**

zmiata|ć[2] *impf vt* pot. (uciekać) to take off pot.

zmiażdż|yć *pf vi* to crush także przen.

z|miąć *pf* **I** *vt* to crumple *[papier, banknot, pościel]*

II zmiąć się *[spódnica, sukienka]* to get creased

zmie|nić *pf* — **zmie|niać** *impf* **I** *vt* **1** (przeobrazić) to change *[poglądy, postępowanie, wygląd]* **2** (wy-

mienić) to change *[pościel, szkołę, pieniądze, opatrunek]*

II zmienić się — **zmieniać się** **1** (ulec przemianie) to change; **~nić się w coś** to turn into sth **2** (zastąpić jeden drugiego) **~niać się** to take turns; **~nić się z kimś** to change places with sb

zmienn|a *f* variable

zmienni|k *m*, **~czka** *f* substitute

zmienn|y *adi. [pogoda, klimat]* changeable; *[osoba]* volatile

zmierza|ć *impf vi* książk. **1** (iść) to make one's way **2** przen. (dążyć) to aim; **~ć do czegoś** to aim at sth; **do czego ~sz?** what are you getting at? pot.

zmierzch *m* twilight także przen.

zmierz|yć *pf* **I** *vt* **1** (określić wymiary) to measure *[wysokość, przedmiot]*; **~yć komuś ciśnienie** to take sb's blood pressure **2** (przymierzyć) to try on *[ubranie, buty]*

II zmierzyć się **1** (zmierzyć swój wzrost) to measure oneself **2** książk. (stanąć do walki) to square up (**z kimś** to sb)

zmiesza|ć *pf* **I** *vt* **1** (połączyć) to mix, to blend (**coś z czymś** sth and sth) **2** (wprawić w zakłopotanie) to confuse *[osobę]*

II zmieszać się **1** (połączyć się) to mix, to blend **2** *[osoba]* to get confused

zmieszani|e *n* confusion

zmie|ścić *pf* **I** *vt* **1** (ulokować) to (manage to) put **2** (pomieścić) *[sala, budynek]* to seat

II zmieścić się to fit; **~ścić się w czasie** to finish within the prescribed time

zmi|eść *pf* — **zmi|atać**[1] *impf vt* **1** (sprzątnąć) *[osoba]* to sweep (up) *[śmieci, kurz, okruchy]*; *[wiatr]* to sweep away *[liście, śnieg]* **2** (zniszczyć) to wipe out **3** pot. (zjeść) to put away pot.

zmiękcz|yć *pf* — **zmiękcz|ać** *impf* **I** *vt* to soften *[tkaninę, skórę, osobę]*

II zmiękczyć się — **zmiękczać się** *[tkanina, skóra]* to get soft

zmięk|nąć *pf vi* to soften także przen.

zmił|ować się *pf v refl.* to have mercy (**nad kimś** (up)on sb);

zmiot|ka *f* sweeper

zmizerni|eć *pf vi* to become haggard

zmniejsz|yć *pf* — **zmniejsz|ać** *impf* **I** *vt* to make [sth] smaller *[przedmiot]*; to reduce *[koszty, szybkość, zapasy]*

II zmniejszyć się — **zmniejszać się** *[rozmiar, odległość, liczba]* to decrease; *[wiatr, ból]* to lessen; *[przedmiot]* to become smaller

zmobiliz|ować *pf* **I** *vt* **1** Wojsk. to call up *[rezerwistów]*; to mobilize *[armię, flotę]* **2** (uaktywnić) to motivate *[osobę]*

II zmobilizować się **1** (zmusić się do działania) to focus oneself **2** Wojsk. *[kraj]* to mobilize

zmocz|yć *pf* **I** *vt* to wet *[osobę]*; to soak *[włosy, ubranie]*

II zmoczyć się to get wet

zm|oknąć *pf vi* to get wet

zmont|ować *pf vt* ① to assemble *[urządzenie, mebel]*; to edit *[film, program]* ② pot. to put together *[zespół]*

zm|ora *f* ① (sen) nightmare; (upiór) phantom ② przen. (problem) curse

zm|owa *f* conspiracy; **być z kimś w zmowie** to be in league with sb; **zmowa milczenia** a conspiracy of silence

zm|ówić *pf* — **zm|awiać** *impf* ❚ *vt* to say *[modlitwę]*

❚❚ **zmówić się** — **zmawiać się** ① (ustalić) to arrange (together) ② (uknuć spisek) to conspire (**przeciwko komuś** against sb)

zmrok *m* dusk

zmr|ozić *pf vt* ① *[wiatr, mróz]* to chill *[osobę]*; to freeze *[rośliny]*; **~ożony szampan** chilled champagne ② przen. (przerazić) *[słowa]* to make [sb] freeze; **~ozić kogoś spojrzeniem** to give sb a chilling look

zmruż|yć *pf vt* to squint *[oczy]*; **nie ~yć oka** to not sleep a wink

zmu|sić *pf* — **zmu|szać** *impf* ❚ *vt* to force (**kogoś do czegoś** sb to do sth)

❚❚ **zmusić się** — **zmuszać się** to force oneself

zmy|ć *pf* — **zmy|wać** *impf* ❚ *vt* ① (umyć) to wash *[naczynia, podłogę]*; to wash off *[makijaż]*; **~wać po obiedzie** to wash up after dinner ② (usunąć) to wash away *[plamę, winę]*

❚❚ **zmyć się** — **zmywać się** ① *[plamy]* to come out; *[brud, makijaż]* to wash off ② pot. (uciec) to scram pot.

zmyl|ić *pf vt* ① (wprowadzić w błąd) to mislead ② (pomylić) **~ić drogę** to go the wrong way

zmy|sł ❚ *m* ① (wzrok, słuch) sense ② książk. (predyspozycja) flair; **mieć ~sł do czegoś** to have a flair for sth

❚❚ **zmysły** *plt* (popęd płciowy) sexual urges a. desires

■ **być zdrowych ~słach** to be of sound mind; **odchodzić od ~słów** to be going out of one's mind

zmysłow|y *adi.* ① Psych. *[wrażenia, bodźce]* sensory, sense ② (podniecający) *[kobieta, ciało]* sensual; *[głos, muzyka]* sensuous

zmyśl|ić — **zmyśl|ać** *impf vt* to make [sth] up

zmyśln|y *adi. grad. [osoba]* smart; *[urządzenie]* ingenious

zmywacz *m* remover

zmywać *impf* → **zmyć**

zmywak *m* (szmatka) dishcloth; (szczoteczka) washing-up brush

zmywar|ka *f* dishwasher

znacho|r *m*, **~rka** *f* healer

znaczą|cy *adi. [gest, uśmiech]* meaningful; *[rola, pozycja]* significant

znacz|ek *m* ① (nalepka) stamp; **~ek pocztowy** a postage stamp; **~ek skarbowy** a duty stamp ② (odznaka) badge ③ (symbol graficzny) mark

znacze|nie *n* ① (sens) meaning ② (ważność) significance; **bez ~nia** unimportant; **o dużym ~niu** of great significance

znaczn|y *adi. [dochód, korzyści, rola]* considerable

znacz|yć *impf* ❚ *vt* to mark *[karty, teren]*

❚❚ *vi* ① (oznaczać) to mean; **to ~y** (mianowicie) that is to say ② (mieć znaczenie) to matter; **wiele dla kogoś ~yć** to be very important to sb; **nic nieznaczący** insignificant

zna|ć¹ *impf* ❚ *vt* ① (wiedzieć) to know *[osobę, adres]*; **~ć kogoś z widzenia** to know sb by sight; **~ć kogoś ze słyszenia** to have heard of sb; **być ~nym z czegoś** to be known for sth ② (umieć) to know; **~ć angielski** to speak English

❚❚ **znać się** ① (samego siebie) to know oneself ② (wzajemnie) to know each other ③ (być znawcą) to know; **~ć się na czymś** to know (a lot) about sth

■ **dać komuś ~ć** to let sb know; **dawać ~ć o sobie** *[ból, zmęczenie]* to begin to tell on sb; **~m ten ból** pot. tell me about it pot.

znać² *praed.* **nie ~, że...** you wouldn't know (that)...; **~ po niej, że...** you could tell she...

znad *praep.* ① (z powyżej) **~ kanapy** from over the sofa; **~ biurka** from behind the desk; **spojrzeć ~ okularów** to peer over one's glasses ② (z pobliża) from; **~ morza** from the coast; **~ Renu** from somewhere on the Rhine

znajdować *impf* → **znaleźć**

znajomoś|ć *f* ① (kontakty towarzyskie) acquaintance; **nawiązać ~ć z kimś** to make sb's acquaintance ② (wiedza) knowledge; **~ć ekonomii** a knowledge of economics

❚❚ **znajomości** *plt* (układy) contacts

■ **po ~ci** through personal contacts

znajom|y ❚ *adi. [melodia, nazwa]* familiar; **mój ~y aktor** an actor friend of mine

❚❚ **znajom|y** *m*, **~a** *f* friend

znak *m* ① (symbol) sign; **~ zapytania** a question mark; **~ drogowy** a traffic sign; **~ drukarski** a character; **~ wodny** a watermark; **~i szczególne** distinguishing marks ② (sygnał, oznaka) sign; **robić coś na dany ~** to do sth on a given signal; **na ~ zgody** in token of agreement; **na ~ skruchy** in a gesture of repentance

■ **dać się (komuś) we ~i** *[osoba, sytuacja]* to make sb's life a misery

znakomicie *adv.* ① (świetnie) superbly ② książk. (znacznie) considerably

znakomi|ty ❚ *adi. grad. [muzyk]* brilliant; *[książka, obraz]* superb; *[wino, jedzenie]* delicious; *[nastrój, humor]* excellent

❚❚ *adi.* książk. (wielki) considerable; **~ta większość głosowała na demokratów** a substantial majority voted for the Democrats

znak|ować *impf vt* to mark

znalaz|ca *m*, **~czyni** *f* finder

znalezisk|o *n* find

zna|leźć *pf* — **zna|jdować, zna|jdywać** *impf* **[]** *vt* [1] (odnaleźć, zdobyć) to find *[zgubę, pracę, kupca, ślady]* [2] (doświadczyć) to find *[zrozumienie, oparcie, przyjemność]*

[]] znaleźć się — **znajdować się, znajdywać się** (zostać odnalezionym) to be found

[]]] znajdować się [1] (występować) to occur [2] (być) to be

■ **być jak** ~**lazł** pot. to be perfect

znami|ę *n* [1] (na skórze) birthmark [2] (cecha, oznaka) hallmark

znan|y *adi.* [1] (sławny) *[aktor, polityk]* well-known [2] (nieobcy) *[piosenka, nazwa, język]* familiar

znawc|a *m,* ~**czyni** *f* expert

znerwicowan|y *adi.* *[osoba, wyobraźnia]* neurotic

zneutraliz|ować *pf* **[]** *vt* to neutralize

[]] zneutralizować się to cancel each other out

znęca|ć się *impf vi* to bully (**nad kimś** sb)

znę|cić *pf vt* to lure (**kogoś czymś** sb with sth)

znicz *m* candle; ~**olimpijski** the Olympic torch

zniechęcać *impf* → **zniechęcić**

zniechęceni|e *n* discouragement; **ogarnęło go** ~**e** he became discouraged

zniechę|cić *pf* — **zniechę|cać** *impf* **[]** *vt* to discourage (**kogoś do czegoś** sb from sth)

[]] zniechęcić się — **zniechęcać się** [1] (stracić chęć) to become discouraged (**do czegoś** from sth) [2] (zrazić się) to take a dislike (**do czegoś** to sth)

zniecierpliw|ić *pf* **[]** *vt* to make [sb] impatient

[]] zniecierpliwić się to become a. get impatient

zniecierpliwieni|e *n* impatience

znieczulać *impf* → **znieczulić**

znieczulic|a *f* callous indifference

znieczul|ić *pf* — **znieczul|ać** *impf* **[]** *vt* [1] Med. to anaesthetize GB, to anesthetize US *[pacjenta, część ciała]* [2] (uczynić nieczułym) to make [sb] indifferent

[]] znieczulić się — **znieczulać się** to become indifferent

zniedołężni|eć *pf vi* to become infirm

zniekształcać *impf* → **zniekształcić**

zniekształce|nie *n* distortion

zniekształ|cić *pf* — **zniekształ|cać** *impf* **[]** *vt* to distort *[obraz, figurę, wypowiedź]*

[]] zniekształcić się — **zniekształcać się** to be distorted

znienacka *adv.* all of a sudden

znienawi|dzić *pf vt* to (start to) hate (**kogoś za coś** sb for sth)

znieruchomi|eć *pf vi* *[osoba, twarz]* to freeze

zn|ieść *pf* — **zn|osić[1]** *impf* **[]** *vt* [1] (przenieść) to carry; **znieść kogoś z boiska** to carry sb off the pitch [2] (naznosić) to amass [3] (porwać) *[prąd, wiatr]* to carry off *[łódź, balon]* [4] (zniszczyć) to wipe out [5] (unieważnić) to abolish *[zakaz, cło]* [6] *[kura]* to lay *[jajko]* [7] (wytrzymać) to endure *[ból]*; (tolerować) to bear, to stand; **nie** ~**sić kogoś** to not be able to stand sb; **nie** ~**szę, kiedy...** I hate when...

[]] znieść się — **znosić się** [1] (zneutralizować się) to cancel each other out [2] (tolerować się) to tolerate each other; **nie** ~**szą się** they can't stand each other

zniewa|ga *f* insult; **czynna** ~**ga** an assault

znieważ|yć *pf* — **znieważ|ać** *impf vt* to insult

zniekształcać *impf* → **zniekształcić**

znikąd *pron.* from nowhere, out of nowhere

znik|nąć *pf* — **znik|ać** *impf vi* to disappear; ~**nąć bez śladu** to vanish without trace; ~**nąć z ekranów** to disappear from the screen; **uśmiech** ~**nął z jej twarzy** the smile left her face

zniszcz|eć *pf vi* *[zabytek, dom]* to become dilapidated

zniszcze|nie *n* [1] (strata) damage; ~**nia wojenne** war damage [2] (ruina) destruction

zniszcz|yć *pf* **[]** *vt* [1] (zburzyć, usunąć) to destroy *[miasto, dokument, dowody]* [2] (zużyć) to wear out *[buty, sprzęt]*; ~**ona książka** a well-worn book [3] przen. (zrujnować) to ruin *[małżeństwo, karierę, zdrowie]*

[]] zniszczyć się *[buty, ubranie]* to wear out

zniżać *impf* → **zniżyć**

zniż|ka *f* [1] (obniżenie) drop; ~**ka cen** a drop in prices [2] (obniżona cena) discount; **podróżować ze** ~**ką 50%** to travel (at) half fare

zniżkow|y *adi.* *[tendencje]* downward; *[ceny]* reduced, discount; **bilet** ~**y** a reduced-fare ticket

zniż|yć *pf* — **zniż|ać** *impf* **[]** *vt* to lower *[głowę, poprzeczkę, głos]*

[]] zniżyć się — **zniżać się** [1] (opaść) *[teren, ścieżka]* to descend; *[głos]* to drop [2] przen. (dostosować się) to come down; ~**ać się do czyjegoś poziomu** to come down to sb's level; ~**yć się do czegoś** to stoop to sth

znokaut|ować /ˌznokaw'tovatɕ/ *pf vt* to knock out

znormaliz|ować *pf* **[]** *vt* to standardize *[wymiary, druk]*; to normalize *[stosunki]*

[]] znormalizować się *[sytuacja, stosunki]* to normalize

znosić[1] *impf* → **znieść**

zno|sić[2] *pf vt* to wear out *[obuwie, ubranie]*

znośn|y *adi. grad. [warunki, pogoda]* tolerable

znowu [] *adv.* (jeszcze raz) again

[]] part. [1] (przeciwstawne) **... to** ~**...** ... and then again... [2] (przecież) after all [3] (właściwie) **o co jej** ~ **chodzi?** what does she want now?

[]]] inter. skąd(że) ~**!** (przeczenie) of course not!

znudzeni|e *n* boredom; **do** ~**a** ad nauseam

znu|dzić *pf* **[]** *vt* to bore

[]] znudzić się to get bored (**czymś** of sth)

znudz|ony *adi.* bored

znużeni|e *n* weariness

znuż|ony *adi. [osoba, głos, twarz]* weary

znuż|yć *pf* **[]** *vt* (zmęczyć) to tire; (znudzić) to bore

[]] znużyć się to get tired (**czymś** of sth)

zobacz|yć *pf* **▯** *vt* ▯ (zauważyć) to see *[osobę, przedmiot]* ▯ (obejrzeć) to see *[film, mecz]* ▯ (sprawdzić, przekonać się) to see; **~, która godzina** see what time it is; **~, jakie piękne kwiaty** look at those beautiful flowers; **~ysz** you'll see; **~ymy** we'll (have to) see

▯ zobaczyć się ▯ (samego siebie) to see oneself ▯ (spotkać się) to see (**z kimś** sb)

zobojętni|eć *pf vi* to become indifferent (**na coś** to sth)

zobowią|zać *pf* — **zobowią|zywać** *impf* **▯** *vt* *[osoba, sytuacja]* to oblige (**kogoś do czegoś** sb to do sth)

▯ zobowiązać się — **zobowiązywać się** to commit oneself (**do czegoś** to sth)

zobowiąza|nie *n* obligation; **dotrzymać ~nia** to meet one's obligations

zobowiązan|y *adi.* ▯ (obowiązany) obliged ▯ (wdzięczny) obliged przest.; **byłbym ~y, gdyby...** książk. I'd be obliged if...

zobowiązywać *impf* → **zobowiązać**

zodiak *m* zodiac; **znaki ~u** the signs of the zodiac

zodiakaln|y *adi.* zodiacal; **być ~ym Bykiem** to be a Taurus

zoo *n inv.* zoo

zoolo|g *m* zoologist

zoologi|a *f* zoology

zoologiczn|y *adi.* zoological; **sklep ~y** a pet shop

zoper|ować *pf vt* to operate (**kogoś** on sb)

zorganiz|ować *pf* **▯** *vt* ▯ (urządzić) to organize *[wystawę, wycieczkę]*; to arrange *[spotkanie]* ▯ (stworzyć) to establish *[komitet, teatr, firmę]* ▯ pot. (zdobyć) to come up with

▯ zorganizować się to organize (oneself)

zorganizowan|y *adi.* organized

zorient|ować *pf* **▯** *vt* ▯ (poinformować) to inform; **~ować kogoś w sytuacji** to brief sb on the situation ▯ (ustawić) to orientate GB, to orient US *[budynek]*

▯ zorientować się ▯ (rozeznać się) to realize; **~ować się w sytuacji** to get one's bearings; **~ował się, że...** he realized, that...; **nie mogę ~ować się, o co tu chodzi** I cant figure out what this is all about ▯ (w terenie) to orientate oneself GB, to orient oneself US

z|orza *f* (poranna) daybreak; (wieczorna) twilight

❑ **zorza polarna** aurora; (na północy) northern lights, aurora borealis; (na południu) southern lights, aurora australis

zosta|ć¹ *pf* — **zosta|wać** *impf* **▯** *vi* ▯ (nie wychodzić) to stay; **~ć na noc** to stay overnight ▯ (pozostać) to be left; **~ło jeszcze trochę czasu** there's still a little time left; **~ć bez grosza** to be left penniless; **~ć w tyle** to fall behind ▯ (nie zmienić się) to remain; **wszystko ~ło po staremu** everything remained unchanged

zosta|ć² *pf vi* ▯ (w stronie biernej) to be; **~ć odznaczonym** to be honoured ▯ (stać się) to become; **~ć ojcem/lekarzem** to become a father/doctor

zostaw|ić *pf* — **zostaw|iać** *impf vt* ▯ (nie zabrać, porzucić) to leave *[osobę, przedmiot]*; **~ić dla kogoś wiadomość** to leave a message for sb; **~ił żonę dla tej dziewczyny** he left his wife for that girl; **~ mnie w spokoju** leave me alone ▯ (zachować) to put a. set aside; **~ić trochę pieniędzy na czarną godzinę** to put away some money for a rainy day; **~ić odstęp** to leave a gap ▯ (w testamencie) to leave, to bequeath ▯ (spowodować) to leave *[ślady]*; **~ić po sobie dobre wrażenie** to make a good impression ▯ (zdać się na kogoś) to leave; **~ić komuś coś** to leave it up to sb to do sth; **~ to mnie** leave it to me

zoś|ka *f* Gry footbag

zrab|ować *pf vt* to rob *[biżuterię, pieniądze]*

zra|nić *pf* **▯** *vt* to wound także przen.; **~nić nogę o wystający gwóźdź** to cut one's leg on a protruding nail; **~nić czyjąś dumę** to hurt sb's pride

▯ zranić się to hurt oneself; **~nić się w palec** to hurt one's finger

zrastać się *impf* → **zrosnąć się**

zraszać *impf* → **zrosić**

zraz *m* slice of beef; **~ wołowy zawijany** beef roulade

zra|zić *pf* — **zra|żać** *impf* **▯** *vt* to put [sb] off

▯ zrazić się — **zrażać się** to be put off; **~zić się do kogoś** to take a dislike to sb

zrealiz|ować *pf* **▯** *vt* ▯ (urzeczywistnić) to carry out *[zadanie, pomysł, zlecenie]*; to fill *[zamówienie]*; to fulfil GB, to fulfill US *[ambicje, marzenie, obietnicę]*; to cash *[czek]* ▯ (stworzyć) to produce *[film, program]* ▯ *[aptekarz, apteka]* to dispense *[receptę]*; *[pacjent, klient]* to have [sth] filled a. dispensed *[receptę]*

▯ zrealizować się ▯ (urzeczywistnić się) *[marzenia]* to come true; *[oczekiwania, ambicje]* to be fulfilled; *[plany, pomysły]* to be carried out ▯ (spełnić się) *[osoba]* to find fulfilment GB, to find fulfillment US

zredag|ować *pf vt* to edit *[tekst, audycję]*; (do druku) to copy-edit *[tekst, rękopis]*

zreduk|ować *pf* **▯** *vt* ▯ (ograniczyć) to reduce *[ilość, cenę, koszty]* ▯ (zwolnić) to cut down on *[pracowników]*; to streamline *[biurokrację]* ▯ (sprowadzić) to reduce; **~ować coś do czegoś** to reduce sth to sth ▯ Aut. **~ować bieg** to reduce gear

▯ zredukować się to be reduced

zrefer|ować *pf vt* (zdać relację) to report *[przebieg wydarzeń]*; (podsumować) to summarize *[dyskusję]*; (przedstawić) to present *[zagadnienie]*

zreform|ować *pf* **▯** *vt* to reform

▯ zreformować się to be reformed

zrekompens|ować *pf vt* to make up for *[szkodę, wydatki]*; **~ować komuś coś** to compensate sb for sth

zrekonstru|ować *pf vt* to reconstruct *[budynek, wydarzenia]*

zrelaks|ować się *pf v refl.* to relax

zremis|ować *pf vt* Sport to draw, to tie (**z kimś** with sb)

zreper|ować *pf vt* to repair *[zegarek, samochód, dach]*

zresztą *part.* (nawiasem mówiąc) as a matter of fact; (poza tym) besides

zrewanż|ować się *pf v refl.* [1] (odwzajemnić się) to reciprocate; (za krzywdę, zło) to retaliate; **~ować się za przysługę** to return a favour [2] pot. (po przegranej) to get one's revenge

zrewid|ować *pf vt* [1] (przeszukać) to search *[osobę, mieszkanie]* [2] (ponownie rozważyć) to revise *[opinie, decyzję]*

zrezygn|ować *pf vi* [1] (ze stanowiska) to resign; **~ować z funkcji prezesa** to resigned as chairman [2] (odmówić sobie, porzucić) **~ować z czegoś** to give up sth; **~ować z deseru** to skip dessert; **chciał to zrobić, ale ~ował** he wanted to do it, but decided against it

zrezygnowan|y *adi.* *[osoba, mina]* resigned

zręcznościow|y *adi.* **popisy ~e** feats of agility

zręcznoś|ć *f* (zwinność) agility; (manualna) (manual) dexterity; (spryt) astuteness

zręczn|y *adi. grad.* [1] (zwinny) *[osoba, palce]* agile; (manualnie) dext(e)rous [2] (sprytny) *[dyplomata, polityk, handlarz]* astute; *[oszust, reklama]* slick; *[kłamstwo, posunięcie]* clever; **~a odpowiedź** a deft reply

zr|obić *pf* **[1]** *vt* [1] (wytworzyć) to make *[obiad, film, gest, karierę]*; to do *[zakupy, pranie, krzywdę]*; to cause *[kłopot, zamieszanie]*; **zrobić kilka kroków** to take a few steps; **zrobić komuś zastrzyk** to give sb an injection; **zrobić porządek w pokoju** to tidy up a room; **zrobić sobie twarz** pot. to do one's make-up; **zrobić z kogoś głupca** przen.to make a fool of sb; **zrobić coś dla kogoś** to do sth for sb; **trzeba coś z tym zrobić** something must be done about it; **nie mieć co ze sobą zrobić** to have nothing to do [2] (zorganizować) to have, to hold *[zabawę, zebranie, spotkanie]*

[1] *vi* [1] (postąpić) to do; **dobrze zrobiłeś** you did well; **źle zrobiła** she was wrong [2] (wpłynąć) to do; **to ci dobrze zrobi** it'll do you good

[1] **zrobić się** [1] (stać się) to become; **zrobił się z niego postawny mężczyzna** he's grown into quite a man; **ze sprzeczki zrobiła się awantura** the argument turned into a big row; **zrobiło się zimno** it got cold; **w pokoju zrobiło się cicho** the room got quiet; **zrobiło mu się smutno** he became sad; **zrobiło mi się go żal** I felt sorry for him [2] (powstać) *[skorupa, zaspa, kra]* to be formed; *[zmarszczka, kolejka]* to form; *[szpary, pęcherz]* to appear; *[problem]* to come up; *[zamieszanie, awantura]* to break out [3] pot. (zrobić makijaż) to make

(oneself) up; **zrobiła się na bóstwo** she was done up to the nines pot.

zr|odzić *pf* książk. **[1]** *vt* to give rise to *[podejrzenia, niepokój]*

[1] **zrodzić się** *[moda, nastawienie]* to be born; *[gniew, miłość]* to arise; *[projekt, plan]* to be conceived

zr|osić *pf* — **zr|aszać** *impf vt* *[osoba]* to mist *[rośliny, liście]*; to sprinkle *[trawę]*; *[deszcz]* to dampen *[trawę]*; **pot zrosił mu twarz** his face was beaded with perspiration

zr|osnąć się *pf* — **zr|astać się** *impf v refl.* [1] (złączyć się) *[kość]* to knit [2] (stworzyć całość) *[księstwa, ugrupowania]* to unite; *[dzielnice, miasta]* to merge

zrośnię|ty *adi.* **~te brwi** joined eyebrows

zrozpacz|ony *adi.* *[osoba]* desperate; *[ton, głos]* despairing; *[mina, twarz]* agonized; **być ~onym** to be in despair

zrozumia|ły [1] (jasny) *[język, teoria, informacja]* intelligible; **to jest ~łe samo przez się** that goes without saying [2] (uzasadniony) *[powody, żal, pretensje]* understandable

zrozum|ieć *pf* **[1]** *vt* [1] (pojąć) to understand *[tekst, sens, problem, powód, osobę]*; **nie ~ mnie źle** don't misunderstand me [2] (zdać sobie sprawę) to realize *[błąd, doniosłość]*; **~ieć, że...** to realize that...

[1] **zrozumieć się** (jeden drugiego) to understand each other

zrozumieni|e *n* understanding; **brak ~a pomiędzy kimś a kimś** (a) lack of understanding between sb and sb; **dać do ~a, że...** to imply that...; **dać komuś coś do ~a** to give sb to understand sth

zrówn|ać *pf* — **zrówn|ywać** *impf* **[1]** *vt* [1] (zniwelować) to level (off a. out) *[teren, plac]* [2] (potraktować tak samo) to make *[sth/sb]* equal *[prawa, przywileje, obywateli]*

[1] **zrównać się** — **zrównywać się** (dogonić) to draw level (**z kimś** with sb); (w osiągnięciach, zarobkach) to come up to the same level (**z kimś** as sb)

zrównani|e *n* equinox

zrównoważać *impf* → zrównoważyć

zrównoważ|ony *adi.* *[osoba]* well balanced

zrównoważ|yć *pf* — **zrównoważ|ać** *impf* **[1]** *vt* to balance out *[straty]*; **~yć budżet** to balance the budget

[1] **zrównoważyć się** — **zrównoważać się** to balance (out)

zrównywać *impf* → zrównać

zróżnic|ować *pf* **[1]** *vt* to diversify *[produkcję, jakość]*; **społeczeństwo ~owane etnicznie** a multi-ethnic society

[1] **zróżnicować się** to diversify

zrujn|ować *pf* **[1]** *vt* [1] (zburzyć) *[huragan, wojna]* to destroy *[budynki, miasto]* [2] (zniszczyć) to ruin *[osobę, firmę, życie, zdrowie]*

Ⅱ zrujnować się ① (finansowo) to go bankrupt ② żart. to splurge out pot. (**na coś** on sth)

zry|ć *pf vt* to rut *[ziemię, drogę]*

zryw *m* ① (poderwanie się z miejsca) dart; (przyśpieszenie) spurt; **pracować** ~**ami** to work in spurts ② (powstanie) uprising

zrywać *impf* → **zerwać**

zrze|c się *pf* — **zrze|kać się** *impf v refl.* to renounce *[tytułu, majątku, prawa]*

zrzeszać *impf* → **zrzeszyć**

zrzesze|nie *n* association

zrzesz|yć *pf* — **zrzesz|ać** *impf* **Ⅰ** *vt* **klub** ~**ający nauczycieli** a club for teachers

Ⅱ zrzeszyć się — **zrzeszać się** to form a union a. association

zrze|da *m, f* pot. grouch pot.

zrzęd|liwy, ~ny *adi. [osoba, ton]* grouchy pot.

zrzę|dzić *impf vi* to grouch pot. (**na coś** about sth)

zrzu|cić *pf* — **zrzu|cać** *impf* **Ⅰ** *vt* ① (strącić) to knock off *[wazon, kubek]*; (rzucić w dół) to throw down *[papiery]*; to drop *[paczkę, bombę]*; *[koń]* to throw *[jeźdźca]* ② (zdjąć) to take off *[ubranie]* ③ (pozbyć się) to shed *[liście, skórę, sierść]*; to lose *[wagę, kilogramy]* ④ (w grze w karty) to discard

Ⅱ zrzucić się — **zrzucać się** pot. (zrobić składkę) to club together (**na coś** for sth)

zrzu|t *m* airdrop

zrzut|ka *f* pot. (składka) whip-round GB pot.

zrzynać *impf* → **zerżnąć**

zsa|dzić *pf* — **zsa|dzać** *impf vt* to take [sb] off (**z czegoś** sth)

zsiadać *impf* → **zsiąść**

zsiad|ły *adi. [mleko]* sour

zsi|ąść *pf* — **zsi|adać** *impf* **Ⅰ** *vi* (z konia, roweru, motocykla) to get off (**z czegoś** sth)

Ⅱ zsiąść się — **zsiadać się** *[mleko, śmietana]* to sour

zsini|eć *pf vi [skóra, twarz, wargi]* to turn blue

zsum|ować *pf* — **zsum|owywać** *impf vt* to add up *[liczby, wydatki]*

zsu|nąć *pf* — **zsu|wać** *impf* **Ⅰ** *vt* ① (opuścić) to slide [sth] down; (zdjąć) to slip off ② (połączyć) to push [sth] together *[stoły, ławki]*

Ⅱ zsunąć się — **zsuwać się** (obniżyć się) *[okulary, peruka, skarpetki]* to slip down; (spaść) to slip off

zsyłać *impf* → **zesłać**

zsyp *m* ~ **na śmieci** a rubbish chute GB, a garbage chute US

zsyp|ać *pf* — **zsyp|ywać** *impf vt* to tip *[trociny, jabłka]*; to pour *[sól, cukier]*

zszarz|eć *pf vi* ① (przybrać szarą barwę) to turn grey GB a. gray US ② książk. przen. *[życie, krajobraz]* to become drab a. dreary

zszy|ć *pf* — **zszy|wać** *impf vt* ① (połączyć szwem) to sew up *[rozdarcie, dwa kawałki]*; to sew together *[brzegi, kawałki]* ② (połączyć zszywką) to staple together *[kartki]*; to saddle-stitch *[czasopismo, broszurę]*; (po-łączyć nicią) to saddle-sew *[kartki w książce]* ③ Med. to stitch (up) *[ranę]*

zszywacz *m* stapler

zszywać *impf* → **zszyć**

zszyw|ka *f* ① (zszyty komplet) ≈ binder *(with thread-sewn sheets of paper)* ② (drucik) staple

zuch *m* ① (w organizacji harcerskiej) (chłopiec) ≈ Cub (Scout); (dziewczynka) ≈ Brownie, ≈ Brownie Guide GB ② (śmiałek) **udawać** ~**a** to pretend to be brave pot.; ~ **z ciebie!** well done!; ~ **dziewczynka** a plucky little girl

zuchwalstw|o *n* ① (postępowanie) audacity ② (czyn) act of impertinence

zuchwa|ły *adi. grad.* ① (bezczelny) *[osoba, zachowanie, uśmiech]* insolent ② (odważny) *[osoba, plan, atak]* audacious

zup|a *f* ① Kulin. soup; (gęsta, przecierana) potage ② pot. (ciepła woda) soup przen.

zupełnie *adv. [zniszczony, gładki]* completely; ~ **sam** all alone; ~ **się z tobą nie zgadzam** I totally disagree with you; ~ **jakby** just as if

zupełn|y *adi. [samotność, cisza, ciemność]* complete; *[nonsens, rozpacz]* utter; **masz** ~**ą rację** you are absolutely right

zuży|ć *pf* — **zuży|wać** *impf* **Ⅰ** *vt* ① (wyczerpać) *[osoba]* to use up *[energię, prąd, ropę, gaz]*; (zniszczyć) to wear out *[odzież, buty]* ② (spożytkować) to use *[materiał, pieniądze, siły, energię]*

Ⅱ zużyć się — **zużywać się** *[maszyna, pojazd, baterie]* to run down; *[ubrania, buty, narzędzie]* to wear out

zwab|ić *pf* — **zwab|iać** *impf vt* ① (przyciągnąć) to lure *[osobę, zwierzę]*; ~**ić kogoś w zasadzkę** to draw sb into an ambush ② Zool. *[samiec, samiczka]* to attract

zwalcz|yć *pf* — **zwalcz|ać** *impf* **Ⅰ** *vt* ~**ać kogoś** to fight *[przeciwników, rywala, chorobę, trudności]*; to combat *[przestępczość, bezrobocie]*; to (try to) eradicate *[wirusa, rasizm, biedę]*; to (try to) control *[szkodniki, epidemię]*

Ⅱ zwalczyć się — **zwalczać się** (jeden drugiego) to fight each other

zwal|ić *pf* — **zwal|ać** *impf* **Ⅰ** *vt* ① (zburzyć) *[osoba]* to pull down *[budynek, ścianę]*; *[wichura]* to blow [sth] down a. over *[drzewo, płot]* ② (przewrócić) *[osoba, zwierzę]* to knock; ~**ić coś na ziemię** to knock sth to the ground ③ (zrzucić na jedno miejsce) to dump *[śmieci, makulaturę]* ④ pot. (obarczyć) to shift *[winę, odpowiedzialność]* (**na kogoś** onto sb)

Ⅱ zwalić się — **zwalać się** ① (przewrócić się) *[drzewo, ściana, most, osoba]* to fall down; (spaść) *[samolot]* to come down; ~**ić się z roweru** to fall off a bicycle; ~**ić się na łóżko** to collapse on the bed pot. ② pot. (zgromadzić się) *[tłumy, turyści]* to descend (**na kogoś/coś** (up)on sb/sth); ~**iło się na nas za dużo pracy** we're up to our ears with work

zwalniać[1,2] *impf* → **zwolnić**[1,2]

zwar|cie [] *n* (elektryczne) short circuit; **mieć** ~**cie** to short-circuit
II *adv. grad. [zabudowany, rosnący]* densely
zwari|ować *pf vi* pot. to go mad; ~**ować na punkcie czegoś** to be mad about sth
■ **nie dać się** ~**ować** pot. to keep a cool head
zwariowan|y *adi.* pot. crazy
zwar|ty *adi.* [] (skupiony) *[grupa]* tight; *[tłum, las, zabudowa]* dense [] (solidarny) *[rodzina, społeczność]* close-knit [] (spójny) *[argumentacja, fabuła]* coherent [] (nierozczłonkowany) *[forma, roślina]* compact
zwarz|ony *adi.* [] *[mleko, sos]* curdled [] przen. (niezadowolony) *[osoba, mina]* sour przen.
zwarz|yć *pf* [] *vt [mróz, zimno]* to nip; *[upał, słońce]* to shrivel *[rośliny, liście]*
II zwarzyć się [] (zepsuć się) *[mleko, śmietana]* to curdle [] (zmarnieć) *[rośliny, kwiaty]* (pod wpływem mrozu) to be frosted; (pod wpływem gorąca) to wither [] przen. *[nastrój]* to sour
zważa|ć *impf vi* to pay a. take heed książk.; **nie** ~**jąc na to, że...** heedless of the fact that...
zważ|yć *pf* [] *vt* [] (określić ciężar) to weigh *[dziecko, paczkę]* [] pot. (odważyć) to weigh out *[dwa kilo, pół funta]* [] książk. (wziąć pod uwagę) to consider; ~**ywszy, że...** bearing in mind (the fact) that...; ~**ywszy (na) późną porę** considering the late hour
II zważyć się *[osoba]* to weigh oneself
zwątp|ić *pf vi* [] (stracić nadzieję) to lose hope; (nabrać wątpliwości) to have doubts (**w coś** about sth) [] (przestać ufać) to lose faith (**w kogoś** in sb)
zwątpie|nie *n* (wątpliwości) doubt; (brak nadziei) despondency
zwerb|ować *pf vt* to recruit
zweryfik|ować *pf vt* książk. [] (potwierdzić prawdziwość) to verify *[dokument, dane, alibi]*; to validate *[teorię, wnioski, dowody]* [] (sprawdzić kwalifikacje) to vet *[kandydata, pracownika]* [] (zmienić) to revise
zwę|dzić *pf vt* pot. to snitch pot.
zwę|zić *pf* — **zwę|żać** *impf* [] *vt* to take in *[spódnicę, rękawy, spodnie]*; to narrow *[jezdnię, rzekę]*
II zwęzić się — **zwężać się** *[potok, ścieżka]* to become narrow; *[oczy]* to narrow; ~**żać się ku górze** to taper towards the top
zwi|ać *pf* — **zwi|ewać** *impf* [] *vt* (zdmuchnąć) *[wiatr]* to blow away *[śnieg, kurz, papiery]*
II *vi* pot. (uciec) *[osoba]* to split pot.; ~**ać z lekcji** to bunk off school GB pot., to ditch school US pot.
zwia|d *m* (rozpoznanie) reconnaissance; (akcja) reconnaissance mission; (oddział) reconnaissance patrol a. party
zwiadowc|a *m* Wojsk. scout
zwią|zać *pf* — **zwią|zywać** *impf* [] *vt* [] (połączyć) końce) to tie *[końce, szalik, sznurek]* [] (skrępować) to tie up *[osobę, zwierzę]*; to tie *[ręce, nogi]* [] przen. (połączyć) to bind *[małżonków, przyjaciół]*; **być** ~**zanym umową** to be bound by a contract [] (zespolić) *[klej, kit, zaprawa]* to bind

II związać się — **związywać się** [] (przyłączyć się) to join up (**z kimś** with sb) [] (wejść w związek) ~**zał się z mężatką** he became involved with a married woman
związan|y *adi.* [] (dotyczący) connected (**z czymś** with sth) [] (będący konsekwencją) ~**y z upranianiem sportu/paleniem tytoniu** sport-/tobacco-related [] (powiązany) involving (**z czymś** sth); **działania** ~**e z ryzykiem** activities involving a certain amount of risk [] (emocjonalnie) attached (**z kimś** to sb)
związ|ek *m* [] (powiązanie) connection; (zależność) relationship; ~**ek między paleniem a zachorowalnością na raka** the link between smoking and cancer; **być bez** ~**ku z czymś** to bear no relation to sth; **w** ~**ku z czymś** (z powodu) because of sth; (w wyniku) due to sth [] (więź) bond przen.; ~**ki krwi** blood ties [] (wspólnota) relationship; **żyć w wolnym** ~**ku** to live together; **zawrzeć** ~**ek małżeński** to enter into marriage [] (organizacja) union, association; ~**ek zawodowy** a trade union [] (substancja) compound
związkow|iec *m* pot. (trade) unionist
związkow|y *adi. [działacze, prawa]* (trade) union
związywać *impf* → **związać**
zwichn|ąć *pf vt* [] Med. to dislocate *[rękę, staw]* [] przen. to ruin *[życie, karierę]*
zwie|dzić *pf* — **zwie|dzać** *impf vt* to tour (around) *[miasto]*; to visit *[wystawę]*
zwierzać *impf* → **zwierzyć**
zwierzchnictw|o *n* [] (władza) control [] (przełożeni) superiors
zwierzchni|k *m*, ~**czka** *f* superior; ~**k sił zbrojnych** head of the armed forces
zwierze|nie *n* confidence; **nie być skłonnym do** ~**ń** to not be willing to open up
zwierz|ę *n* animal; **świat** ~**ąt** the animal world
zwierzęc|y *adi.* [] *[białko, świat, instynkt]* animal [] przen. (dziki) savage
zwierz|yć *pf* — **zwierz|ać** *impf* [] *vt* to confide *[sekret]* (**komuś** to sb)
II zwierzyć się — **zwierzać się** to confide; ~**ać się komuś z czegoś** to confide sth to sb
zwierzyn|a *f* game; **gruba** ~**a** a big game
zw|ieść *pf* — **zw|odzić** *impf vt* to delude; **zwieść kogoś obietnicami** to lead sb on with promises
zwietrz|eć *pf vi* [] *[perfumy, kawa]* to go stale [] *[zapach, woń]* to be gone [] *[skały]* to be weathered [] przen. *[idea, nowina]* to become stale
zwietrz|yć *pf vt* to smell out także przen.
zwiewać *impf* → **zwiać**
zwiewn|y *adi. [suknia, tkanina]* gauzy; *[postać, zjawa]* ethereal
zw|ieźć *pf* — **zw|ozić** *impf vt* [] (zgromadzić) to bring in *[zboże, siano]* [] (w dół) to take down
zwiędł|y, ~**nięty** *adi.* [] *[kwiaty, liście]* withered, wilted [] przen. *[twarz, ręce]* withered

zwi|ędnąć *pf vi [liście, kwiaty]* to wither, to wilt

zwiększ|yć *pf* — **zwiększ|ać** *impf* [ ] *vt* to increase *[liczbę, zyski, wydajność]*

[ ] zwiększyć się — zwiększać się to increase

zwię|zły *adi. grad. [tekst, styl, odpowiedź]* concise; *[gleba, skała]* compact

zwijać *impf* → **zwinąć**

zwilż|yć *pf* — **zwilż|ać** *impf vt* to moisten *[wargi]*; to wet *[twarz]*

zwi|nąć *pf* — **zwi|jać** *impf* [ ] *vt* [ ] (złożyć) to roll (up) *[linę, dywan, gazetę, żagiel]*; ~**nąć sznurek w kłębek** to coil string into a ball [ ] pot. (likwidować) to wind up *[interes, działalność]*; ~**jać obóz** to break camp [ ] pot. (aresztować) *[policja, straż]* to nab pot. [ ] pot. (ukraść) to swipe pot.

[ ] zwinąć się — zwijać się [ ] (skręcić się) to curl (up); ~**jać się z bólu** to be writhing in pain [ ] pot. (wyjechać) to take off pot. [ ] pot. (uwijać się) to get a move on pot.

zwin|ka *f* (jaszczurka) ~**ka** sand lizard

zwinn|y *adi. grad. [osoba, ruchy, palce]* nimble

zwiotcza|ły *adi.* flabby

zwiotcz|eć *pf vi* to go flabby

zwisa|ć *impf vi* to hang

■ **to mu** ~ **(i powiewa)** posp. he doesn't give a monkey's about it pot.

zwit|ek *m* wad

zwl|ec *pf* — **zwl|ekać** *impf* [ ] *vt* (ściągnąć) to drag

[ ] zwlec się — zwlekać się pot. ~**ec się z łóżka** to drag oneself out of bed pot.

zwleka|ć *impf vi* to delay; **nie** ~**jąc** without delay

zwłaszcza *part.* especially

zwło|ka *f* delay; **jeden dzień** ~**ki** an extra day; **bez** ~**ki** without delay; **grać na** ~**kę** to play for time; **niecierpiący** ~**ki** of the utmost urgency

zwłok|i *plt* corpse

zwodnicz|y *adi. [wypowiedzi, słowa]* deceptive

zwodzić *impf* → **zwieść**

zwolenni|k *m*, ~**czka** *f* (prezydenta, króla) adherent; (partii, reform) supporter

zw|olnić[1] *pf* — **zw|alniać[1]** *impf* [ ] *vt* (uczynić wolniejszym) to slow (down) *[tempo]*; **w zwolnionym tempie** in slow motion

[ ] *vi* (zmniejszyć szybkość) *[pojazd, osoba, zwierzę]* to slow (down)

zw|olnić[2] *pf* — **zw|alniać[2]** *impf* [ ] *vt* [ ] (rozluźnić) to relax *[uścisk]* [ ] (pozbawić pracy) to dismiss [ ] (wypuścić na wolność) to release *[więźnia]* [ ] (przestać zajmować) to vacate *[pokój, mieszkanie]* [ ] (od obowiązku) to exempt; **zwolnić kogoś z lekcji** to excuse sb from class

[ ] zwolnić się — zwalniać się [ ] (uzyskać zgodę na wyjście) to be excused [ ] (odejść z pracy) to quit pot. [ ] (zostać opuszczonym) *[pokój, mieszkanie]* to be vacated

zwolnie|nie *n* [ ] (z pracy) dismissal; ~**nia grupowe** group layoffs [ ] (od obowiązków) exemption;

warunkowe ~**nie z więzienia** parole [ ] (lekarskie) sick note; **być na** ~**niu** to be on sick leave

zwoł|ać *pf* — **zwoł|ywać** *impf vt* to call *[naradę, zebranie]*; to summon *[sejm, kongres]*

zwozić *impf* → **zwieźć**

zw|ód *m* Sport feint, dummy

zw|ój *m* [ ] (tkaniny, papieru) roll; (dokument) scroll [ ] (kabla, drutu, sznura) coil

zwracać *impf* → **zwrócić**

zwro|t [ ] *m* [ ] (zmiana kierunku) turn; ~**t o sto osiemdziesiąt stopni** an about-turn także przen. [ ] (przełom) turnabout [ ] (zwrócenie) return; (długu, kredytu) repayment; (kosztów, wydatków) reimbursement [ ] (wyrażenie) expression; ~**ty grzecznościowe** polite phrases

[ ] zwroty *plt* (czasopisma, towary) returns

zwrot|ka *f* verse, stanza

zwrotnic|a *f* (kolejowa) points GB, switch US

zwrotnik *m* tropic; **Zwrotnik Koziorożca** the Tropic of Capricorn; **Zwrotnik Raka** the Tropic of Cancer

zwrotn|y *adi. grad.* [ ] (sterowny) *[łódź, pojazd]* manoeuvrable GB, maneuverable US [ ] (do zwrotu) *[opakowanie, butelka]* returnable [ ] *[zaimek, czasownik]* reflexive

zwr|ócić *pf* — **zwr|acać** *impf* [ ] *vt* [ ] (oddać) to return; ~**ócić dług** to pay back a debt; ~**ócić komuś koszty podróży** to reimburse sb's travelling expenses [ ] (skierować) to turn *[wzrok, spojrzenie]* [ ] (zwymiotować) to bring up

[ ] zwrócić się — zwracać się [ ] (skierować się) to turn [ ] (przynieść zysk) *[inwestycja]* to pay for itself [ ] (wystąpić) to turn (**przeciwko komuś** against sb) [ ] (odezwać się) to address (**do kogoś** sb); ~**ócić się do kogoś z prośbą** to ask sb a favour [ ] (poprosić) to turn to; ~**ócić się do kogoś o pomoc** to turn to sb for help

zwycięs|ki *adi. [wódz, armia]* victorious; ~**ka drużyna** the winning team

zwycięstw|o *n* victory także przen.

zwycię|zca *m*, ~**żczyni** *f* winner

zwycięż|yć *pf* — **zwycięż|ać** *impf vt, vi* (wygrać) to win; **głos rozsądku** ~**ył** przen. common sense prevailed

zwyczaj *m* [ ] (obyczaj) custom; **być w** ~**u** to be customary; **jak** ~ **każe** as is customary [ ] (przyzwyczajenie) habit; **swoim** ~**em** in one's customary manner

zwyczajnie [ ] *adv. grad.* (normalnie) ordinarily

[ ] *adv.* (po prostu) simply

zwyczajn|y *adi. grad.* [ ] (zwykły, pospolity) *[rzecz, sprawa, życie]* ordinary; **zięba** ~**a** the common chaffinch [ ] (oczywisty) *[kłamca, tchórz]* common; **najzwyczajniejsza nieuczciwość** the most blatant dishonesty

zwyczajow|y *adi.* customary

zwykle *adv.* usually; **jak** ~ as usual; **wcześniej/ więcej niż** ~ earlier/more than usual

zwyk|ły *adi. grad.* ① (pospolity) *[ubiór, zachowanie]* usual; ~**ły tryb postępowania** the usual procedure ② (przeciętny) *[urzędnik, pracownik]* ordinary ③ (oczywisty) simple; ~**ły przypadek** a sheer coincidence

zwymiot|ować *pf vt* to vomit

zwymyśla|ć *pf vt* to give [sb] a dressing-down

zwyż|ka *f* (kosztów, temperatury, ciśnienia) rise

zwyżkow|y *adi. [tendencja]* upward

zygza|k *m* zigzag; **biec** ~**kiem** *[droga]* to zigzag

zysk *m* ① (zarobek) profit; **z** ~**iem** at a profit; **przynosić** ~ to bring in a profit ② (korzyść) benefit

zysk|ać *pf* — **zysk|iwać** *impf vt* ① (zarobić) to make a profit (**na czymś** on sth) ② (skorzystać) to benefit (**na czymś** from sth) ③ (zdobyć, osiągnąć) to gain *[wiedzę, doświadczenie]*; to win *[względy, zaufanie, przyjaciół]*; ~**ać na wartości** to gain in value; ~**ać na czasie** to gain time

zyskown|y *adi.* profitable

zza *praep.* ① (z drugiej strony) from behind; ~ **rzeki** from over the river; ~ **grobu** from beyond the grave; ~ **rogu** around the corner ② (poprzez) through

zziajan|y *adi.* breathless

zzieleni|eć *pf vi* to turn green; ~**eć z zazdrości** to turn green with envy

zziębnię|ty *adi.* cold

zż|ąć *pf* — **zż|ynać** *impf vt* to reap *[owies, pszenicę]*

zżerać *impf* → zeżreć

zżółk|nąć *pf vi* to (go) yellow

zży|ć się *pf* — **zży|wać się** *impf v refl.* (przywiązać się) to become intimate (**z kimś** with sb); (przyzwyczaić się) to get a. accustomed (**z czymś** to sth)

zżynać *impf* → zżąć

zży|ty *adi.* close; **byli ze sobą bardzo** ~**ci** they were very close

Ź

źdźb|ło *n* [1] (łodyga) stalk; ~**ła trawy** blades of grass [2] (odrobina) grain, particle
■ **nie ma w tym ani** ~**ła prawdy** pot. there isn't a grain of truth in it

źle *adv. grad.* [1] (nienależycie) poorly; (błędnie) wrongly; **uczyć się** ~ to be a poor student; ~ **coś zrozumieć** to misunderstand sth; ~ **wychowany** ill-bred/-mannered [2] (słabo) **czuć się** ~ to feel unwell; ~ **wyglądać** to look ill [3] (niedostatecznie) badly; ~ **płatna praca** a badly a. poorly paid job [4] (nieuczciwie) badly; ~ **się prowadzić** to conduct oneself badly [5] (negatywnie) badly; ill książk.; **mówić o kimś** ~ to speak badly a. ill of sb; **takie zachowanie** ~ **o tobie świadczy** such behaviour does you little credit [6] (nieżyczliwie) badly; **być** ~ **usposobionym do kogoś/czegoś** to be ill-disposed to(wards) sb/sth [7] (nieprzyjemnie) ~ **mu było na obczyźnie** it was hard on him living abroad; ~ **się czuła w jego towarzystwie** she felt uncomfortable in his company [8] (niepomyślnie) badly [9] (jako równoważnik zdania) ~, **że nie przyszedł od razu po pomoc** it's too bad (that) he didn't ask for help straight away
■ ~ **z nim/z nią** pot. he/she is in a bad way pot.; **i tak** ~, **i tak niedobrze** pot. ≈ if it's not one thing it's another pot.

źrebak *m* foal; (samiec) colt

źreb|ić się *impf v refl. [klacz]* to foal

źrenic|a *f* pupil; **ogniste** ~**e** książk. passionate eyes a. orbs

źród|ło *n* [1] (rzeki) source, spring; **owoce są** ~**łem witamin** przen. fruit is a source of vitamins [2] przen. (początek) origin(s), roots [3] przen. (pochodzenie) source; ~**ło dochodów** the source of one's income; **z pewnego** ~**ła** from a reliable source; **zasięgnął informacji u** ~**ła** he got it straight from the horse's mouth [4] (wiedzy) source(s); ~**ła archiwalne** archive sources

Ż

żab|a f frog

żab|ka f ⊞ (styl pływacki) breaststroke; **pływać ∼ką** to do the breaststroke ② (uchwyt) curtain hook

żad|en Ⅰ *pron.* (ani jeden) no, not any; (z dwóch) neither; **nie miał ∼nych przyjaciół** he didn't have any friends; **z podwórza nie dolatywały ∼ne dźwięki** no sound could be heard from the courtyard; **pociąg nie zatrzymuje się po drodze na ∼nej stacji** the train doesn't stop anywhere on the way; **∼en z chłopców/domów** none of the boys/houses; (z dwóch) neither of the boys/houses, neither boy/house; **czekałem na nich, ale ∼en nie przyszedł** I waited for them, but none/neither of them came; **∼nym sposobem** a. **w ∼en sposób** książk. there's no way; **w ∼nym razie** a. **wypadku** under no circumstances; **pod ∼nym pozorem** under no circumstances; **za ∼ną cenę** a. **za ∼ne pieniądze** not for (all) the world Ⅱ *adi.* no; **∼en ze mnie polityk** I'm no politician; **to ∼na pociecha** that's no consolation; **to ∼en wstyd** it's nothing to be ashamed of

żag|iel m sail; **postawić ∼le** to set sail ■ **złapać** a. **chwycić wiatr w ∼le** to get a second wind; **zwinąć ∼le** pot. to throw in the towel

żaglow|iec m sailing ship

żaglów|ka f sailing boat, sailboat US

żakie|t m (lady's) jacket

żal m ⊞ (uczucie smutku) sorrow; (uczucie zawodu) regret; **∼ po stracie kogoś/czegoś** grief at a. over the loss of sb/sth; **pogrążony w ∼u** książk. grief-stricken ② (współczucie) sorrow; **∼ mi go** I feel sorry for him ③ (skrucha) remorse (**za coś** for sth) ④ (pretensja) resentment; **czuć głęboki ∼ do kogoś** to feel deep resentment towards sb; **mieć ∼** to have a grudge ■ **mała strata** a. **szkoda – krótki ∼** przysł. ≈ (it's) no use crying over spilt milk przysł.

żal|ić się *impf v refl.* to complain (**na coś** about a. of sth); **∼ić się komuś** to complain to sb

żaluzj|a f ⊞ (roleta) blind ② (krata zabezpieczająca) shutter

żaluzjow|y *adi. [drzwiczki]* louvred

żałob|a f ⊞ (smutek) mourning, grief; **być w ∼ie po kimś** to be in mourning for sb ② (okres żalu po śmierci) mourning (period) ③ (ubranie) mourning (clothes)

żał|ować *impf vi* ⊞ (odczuwać smutek) to regret; **niczego nie ∼uję** I have no regrets ② (odczuwać skruchę) to regret (**za coś** doing sth); **bardzo ∼uję** I'm really sorry ③ (litować się, współczuć) to pity ④ (skąpić) to stint (**czegoś** on sth); **niczego sobie nie ∼ować** to do oneself proud GB pot.; **nie ∼ować pieniędzy** pot. to spare no expense

ża|r m ⊞ (drewno, węgiel) embers ② (upał) heat ③ książk., przen. (zapał) ardour GB, ardor US książk.; (patriotyczny, religijny) fervour GB, fervor US

żarci|e n pot. (dla zwierząt) food; (dla ludzi) grub pot.

żargon m jargon

żarliw|y *adi. grad.* książk. *[wielbiciel, obrońca]* zealous; *[modlitwa, miłość]* passionate

żarłoczn|y *adi. grad.* ⊞ książk., pejor. *(łapczywy) [osoba]* gluttonous; *[zwierzę]* voracious ② przen. (zachłanny) *[osoba]* greedy

żarłok m pot. glutton

żaroodporn|y *adi. [szkło, ceramika]* heatproof, heat-resistant; *[naczynie, półmisek]* ovenproof

żarów|ka f (light) bulb

żar|t m (figiel, dowcip) joke; **pół ∼tem, pół serio** half jokingly; **to nie ∼ty** it's no joke; **z nim/tym nie ma ∼tów** you don't want to fool a. mess around with him/that pot.; **znać się na ∼tach** to know how to take a joke; **mówić coś ∼tem** a. **w ∼tach** to say sth as a joke a. in jest ■ **∼ty na bok** pot. joking aside; **∼ty się skończyły** pot. the fun and games are over; **nie na ∼ty** pot. in earnest; **obrócić coś w ∼t** to make a joke of sth

żart|ować *impf vi* ⊞ (dowcipkować) to joke, to make a joke; **∼ować z kimś o czymś** to joke with sb about sth ② (nie traktować poważnie) **∼ować z kogoś/czegoś** to make fun of sb/sth; **ojciec nie ∼uje** father is serious

żarz|yć się *impf v refl.* to glow

żąda|ć *impf vt* to demand; **∼ć czegoś od kogoś** to demand sth from sb; **∼ł, żeby opublikować dane** he demanded that the data be made public

żąda|nie n request; **∼nie czegoś** a demand for sth; **na (każde) ∼nie** on demand; **odejść na własne ∼nie** to resign at one's own request

żąd|ło n sting także przen.

żadn|y *adi.* książk. *(pragnący)* avid książk. (**czegoś** for sth); *(chciwy)* greedy (**czegoś** for sth)

żądz|a f książk. ⊞ *(gwałtowne pragnienie)* craving ② *(pożądanie)* desire

żbik m wild cat

że [] *coni.* that; **powiedział, że nie przyjdzie** he said (that) he wouldn't come; **mam nadzieję, że wiesz, co robisz** I hope you know what you're doing; **był tak zmęczony, że usnął natychmiast** he was so tired (that) he fell asleep straight away **II** *part.* [1] (ubolewanie) **że ja o tym nie wiedziałem!** if only I'd known about it!; **że też musiałeś mi o tym powiedzieć!** what did you have to (go and) tell me that for? pot. [2] (zdziwienie) **że też akurat ciebie wybrali!** fancy choosing you of all people! pot.

III **-że, -ż** *w wyrazach złożonych* (wyrażające zdziwienie, zniecierpliwienie) **siadajże!** do sit down!; **kiedyż ona wreszcie przyjdzie?** when on earth will she come? ■ **że (aż) ha** a. **hej** a. **ho, ho!** (emfatyczne) wow!; **mróz, że ho ho!** wow! it's so cold! pot.; **że tak powiem** a. **że się tak wyrażę** so to speak

żebracz|ka *f* beggar (woman)

żeb|rać *impf vi* to beg także przen.

żebra|k *m* beggar

żeb|ro *n* (kość) rib; (sklepienie) ogive

■ **policzyć** a. **porachować komuś ~ra** pot. to beat sb up

żeby [] *coni.* [1] (dla wyrażenia celu, skutku) (przed bezokolicznikiem) (in order) to, so as to; (przed zdaniem) so (that); **zadzwoń do mnie, ~ uzgodnić termin** call me to fix a date; **zrobiłam ci zakupy, ~ś nie musiał wychodzić z domu** I did the shopping for you so (that) you wouldn't have to go out; **~ nie było żadnych nieporozumień** lest there should be any misunderstanding [2] (dla wyrażenia woli, sądu) to; (przed zdaniem) if; **wątpię, ~ to był przypadek** I doubt if it was an accident; **prosiłem, ~ zaśpiewała** I asked her to sing; **chcę, ~ś mi pomógł** I want you to help me [3] (wyrażające następstwo) only to; **spłacił pożyczkę, ~ na nowo się zadłużyć** he repaid the loan, only to run into debt again [4] (dla wyrażenia intensywności) to; **był zbyt dumny, ~ prosić o pomoc** he was too proud to ask for help; **nie ~ się bała** not because/that she was afraid [5] (choćby) even if; **~ ją błagał na klęczkach, nie wróci do niego** even if he were to go down on bended knees, she wouldn't go back to him; **~ nie wiem co** come hell or high water pot.; **~ś nie wiem co mówił, i tak nikt ci nie uwierzy** whatever you say, no one is going to believe you [6] (gdyby) if; **~m wiedział jak, to bym wam pomógł** I'd help you if I knew how; **~ nie ty/twoja pomoc** if it hadn't been for your/your help, but for you/your help

II *part.* [1] (wyrażające życzenie) **~ś się nie przeziębił!** mind you don't catch cold!; **~ tylko nie padało!** let's hope it doesn't rain!; **~ to szlag!** pot. damn (it)!, goddammit! US pot. [2] (wyrażające ubolewanie) **~ sobie tak zmarnować życie!** imagine wasting your life like that!; **~ też tak się upić!** to get that drunk though! [3] (obserwacja) if only; **~ś wiedział,**

co przeżyłem! if only you knew what I've been through! [4] pot. (emfatyczne) **~ mi tu było cicho!** (I want) silence!; **~ mi to było ostatni raz!** don't let it ever happen again! pot.; **a ~ś wiedział!** I'm not joking a. kidding either! pot.

żeglar|ka *f* yachtswoman, sailor

żeglarstw|o *n* Sport sailing

żeglarz *m* [1] yachtsman, sailor [2] Zool. swallowtail (butterfly)

żegl|ować *impf vi* [1] *[osoba]* to sail, to navigate [2] *[statek]* to sail

żeglu|ga *f* navigation

żegna|ć¹ *impf* [] *vt* to say goodbye to; przen. (rozstać się) to leave *[dom, kraj]*

II **żegnać się** to say goodbye

żegna|ć² *impf* [] *vi* książk. to bless

II **żegnać się** książk. to cross oneself

żel *m* gel

żelatyn|a *f* gelatin(e)

żelaz|ko *n* iron

żela|zny *adi.* [1] (z żelaza) *[pręt, brama]* iron [2] przen. (silny) iron; **mieć ~zne zdrowie** to have an iron constitution; **mieć ~zne nerwy** to have nerves of steel [3] przen. (bezwzględny) *[wola, reguła]* iron; **~zna konsekwencja** unrelenting consistency [4] (stały) *[temat, pytanie]* fundamental; **~zny repertuar** a standard repertoire

■ **~zna rezerwa** a. **porcja** an emergency supply; **~zna kurtyna** the Iron Curtain; **~zny kapitał** nest eggs pot.; **bajka o ~znym wilku** a tall story GB, a tall tale US; **rządzić ~zną ręką** to rule with an iron fist a. hand

żelaz|o *n* iron; **huta ~a** an ironworks; **rumowisko ~a i betonu** a heap of iron and concrete

że|nić *impf* [] *vt* to marry off; **żenić kogoś z kimś** to marry sb off to sb

II **żenić się** *[mężczyzna]* to get married; **żenić się bogato** to marry rich a. money pot.

żenująco *adv.* *[zachowywać się]* embarrassingly; **~ naiwna książka** a lamentably naive book

żenując|y *adi.* *[scena, cisza]* embarrassing; *[wiedza, poziom]* lamentable

żeńs|ki *adi.* [1] *[płeć, chór]* female; **szkoła ~ka** a girls' school; **zakon ~ki** a female order [2] Jęz. feminine

żeń-sze|ń *m* ginseng

że|r *m* prey; **szukać żeru** to hunt for prey

żer|dź *f* perch, pole

żer|ować *impf vi* to prey także przen.

żeton *m* [1] (do automatu) token; (w grach) chip; **~ do telefonu** a phone token [2] (metalowy znaczek) badge

żłob|ek¹ *m* (dla dzieci) crèche GB, day care center US

żłob|ek² *m* (rowek) groove

żł|obić *impf vt* [1] (drążyć) to furrow; **koła wozu żłobiły koleiny** the cartwheels made deep furrows; **zmarszczki żłobiące jej czoło** creases furrowing her brow [2] (wycinać) to carve; **żłobione kolumny** fluted columns

żmi|ja f viper także przen.

■ **wyhodować ~ję na własnej piersi** a. **na własnym łonie** to nurse a viper in one's bosom

żniw|o [] n przen. (plon) toll; **~o śmierci** the death toll

[II] żniwa plt harvest

żołąd|ek m stomach

■ **o pustym ~ku** a. **z pustym ~kiem** on an empty stomach

żoł|ądź [] m, f [1] (owoc dębu) acorn [2] pot. (trefl) club **[II]** f Anat. glans (of the penis)

żoł|d m pay; **być** a. **pozostawać na czyimś ~dzie** to be in the pay of sb także przen., pejor.

żołnierz m [1] (wojskowy) soldier; **~ piechoty** an infantryman; **~ zawodowy** a regular soldier [2] (szeregowiec) private

żon|a f wife; **wziąć** a. **pojąć kogoś za ~ę** to take sb as one's wife książk.

żona|ty [] adi. [mężczyzna] married (**z kimś** to sb) **[II]** m married man

żongle|r m juggler

żongl|ować impf vi to juggle także przen.

żonkil m daffodil

żół|ć f [1] Anat. bile także przen. [2] (kolor) yellow

żółtacz|ka f jaundice

żółt|ko n yolk

żół|to adv. grad. **dziewczyna ubrana na ~to** a girl dressed in yellow; **pomalować dom na ~to** to paint a house yellow

żół|ty adi. yellow; **mamy ~te światło** the lights are at amber; **~ty kolor** yellow (colour); **rasa ~ta** the Mongoloid race

żółw m (morski) turtle GB, sea turtle US; (lądowy) tortoise, turtle US

żrąc|y adi. [kwas, płyn, uwagi, krytyka] caustic; [dym, opary] acrid

ż|reć impf **[]** vt pot. [1] [osoba] to gobble pot.; **żreć bez opamiętania** to stuff oneself with food pot. [2] [zwierzęta] to feed (**coś** on sth)

[II] żreć się pot. to be at each other's throats pot.

żub|r m (European) bison, wisent

żuchw|a f mandible

żu|ć impf vi to chew [gumę, kęs]

■ **żuć w ustach słowa/przekleństwa** pot. to swear under one's breath

żu|k m beetle

żul m pot. hoodlum pot.

żuraw m [1] Zool. crane [2] (przy studni) sweep [3] (dźwig) crane

żurawin|a f cranberry

żurawinow|y adi. [sok, konfitury] cranberry

żur|ek m white borscht

żuż|el m [1] (do wysypywania dróg) cinder [2] Sport speedway (racing)

żwaw|y adi. grad. [ruchy, krok] jaunty, brisk; [osoba] spry, perky

żwi|r m gravel

życi|e n [1] (proces) life; **~e na ziemi** life on earth [2] (egzystencja) life; **oddać za kogoś/coś ~e** to lay down a. give one's life for sb/sth książk.; **utrzymywać pacjenta przy ~u** to keep the patient alive; **tylko praca trzyma go przy ~u** work is the only thing that keeps him going; **nieliczni pozostali przy ~u pasażerowie** the few surviving passengers [3] (od narodzin do śmierci) life, lifetime; **styl ~a** a lifestyle; **już za ~a był postacią legendarną** he was a legend in his own lifetime; **za ~a babci to było nie do pomyślenia** it was unthinkable in grandma's time; **cieszyć się ~em** to enjoy life; **używać ~a** to live life to the full; **ułożyć sobie ~e na nowo** to make a new life for oneself [4] (utrzymanie) living; **ledwo mu starcza na ~e** he barely has enough to live on; **pieniądze na ~e** housekeeping (money) [5] (rzeczywistość) (real) life; **historia z ~a wzięta** a true-life story [6] (witalność) life; **być pełnym ~a** to be full of life a. vigour [7] (ruch) life; **to miasto tętni ~em** the city pulsates with life [8] (środowisko) life; **poznać ~e mieszkańców** to learn about the life of the locals [9] (funkcjonowanie) life; **średni czas ~a samochodu** the average life of a car

■ **bój** a. **walka** a. **wojna na śmierć i ~e** a life-and-death struggle, a struggle to the death; **brać ~e lekko** to be light-hearted; **być bez ~a** to be lifeless; **być nie do ~a** (być słabym) to be half dead a. more dead than alive; (być niezaradnym) to not be cut out for this life a. world; (o mieście) to be impossible a. hard to live in; **dać znak ~a** (napisać list) to drop a line; **jeśli ci ~e miłe** książk. if you value your life; **w szkole nie miał ~a, koledzy go szykanowali** pot. he had a hard a. tough time at school, he was bullied all the time; **mężczyzna/kobieta mojego ~a** the man/woman in my life; **samo ~e** that's life, such is life; **szkoła ~a** książk. school of hard knocks; **złamać sobie/komuś ~e** to make one's/sb's life a misery

życiorys m curriculum vitae a. CV GB, resumé US

życze|nie [] n wish; **spełnić czyjeś ~nie** to fulfil sb's wish; **zrobić coś na czyjeś ~nie** to do sth at sb's request

[II] życzenia plt wishes; **złożyć komuś ~nia** to give sb one's best wishes; **kartka z ~niami urodzinowymi** a birthday card

■ **pozostawiać wiele do ~nia** to leave a lot to be desired

życzliwie adv. grad. [uśmiechać się, traktować] in a kindly a. friendly manner; **jego powieści były ~ przyjmowane przez krytykę** his novels were well received by the critics

życzliw|y [] adi. [osoba, uśmiech] kind, friendly **[II]** m iron. **jakiś ~y już mu o tym powiedział**

some obliging soul has already told him iron.

■ **patrzeć na kogoś/coś** ~**ym okiem** to look favourably on sb/sth

życz|yć *impf vi* ① (składać życzenia) to wish; ~**yć komuś dobrze/źle** to wish sb well/ill ② (chcieć) to wish; **pogrzeb był skromny, bo tak** ~**ył sobie zmarły** the funeral was simple in accordance with the wishes of the deceased; **nie** ~**ę sobie tu żadnych hałasów** I won't have anybody making any noise (in) here; **czego pan/pani sobie** ~**y?** what can I do for you?; **jak sobie** ~**ysz** a. **jak pan/ pani sobie** ~**y** as you wish a. like

ży|ć *impf vi* ① (istnieć) to live, to be alive; **czy twój dziadek jeszcze żyje?** is your grandad still alive?; **żyli długo i szczęśliwie** they lived happily ever after; **żył w latach 1632-1677** he lived from 1632 to 1677 ② (mieszkać) to live; **żyć na wsi/w mieście** to live in the country/the city ③ (bytować) to live; **żyć skromnie** to live modestly; **żyć z kimś dobrze/źle** to be on good/bad terms with sb; **żyć z myślistwa** to live by hunting ④ (trwać) *[idea, myśl]* to live (on); **te wspomnienia wciąż w nim żyją** those memories are still alive within him

■ **jak (długo) żyję** never in (all) my life; **żyje mu się dobrze/źle** pot. he has a good/bad life; **ledwie żyję** I'm more dead than alive; **nie dawać komuś żyć** to make life hell for sb pot.; **niech żyje król/ młoda para!** long live the king/newly-weds!; **żyć jutrem** a. **przyszłością** to live for tomorrow; **żyć nadzieją** to live in hope; **żyć nie umierać** this is the life!; **żyć z kimś** to live with sb

żylak *m* varicose vein

żylet|ka *f* razor blade

ży|ła *f* vein; **podciąć sobie żyły** to slash one's wrists; **dać sobie w żyłę** pot. to shoot up pot.; **żyła złota** a gold mine

żył|ka *f* ① (naczynie krwionośne) vein, veinlet ② (nić) (fishing) line ③ (pasja) bent, flair; ~**ka pisarska** a bent for writing; **mieć** ~**kę do handlu** to have a flair for business; ~**ka podróżnicza** an urge to travel, wanderlust

żyraf|a *f* giraffe

żyrandol *m* chandelier

ży|to *n* rye; **łan żyta** a field of rye

żywic|a *f* resin

żywiciel *m* ① (rodziny) breadwinner, wage-earner ② Biol. host

żyw|ić *impf* **Ⅰ** *vt* ① (karmić) to feed; ~**ienie dietetyczne** special diets ② książk. (odczuwać) to nurture *[nadzieję, nienawiść]*; to harbour *[urazę, żal]* **Ⅱ żywić się** ① (odżywiać się) *[zwierzę]* to feed (**czymś** on sth); *[osoba]* to eat (**czymś** sth) ② przen.

(zawdzięczać istnienie) to feed (**czymś** on a. off sth); **prasa brukowa** ~**i się plotkami** tabloids feed on gossip

żywio|ł *m* ① (siła przyrody) element; **walczyć z** ~**łem** to battle the elements ② (siła) upheaval; ~**ł historii** the forces a. winds of history ③ (strefa zainteresowań) element; **jego** ~**łem była polityka** politics was his (great) passion

■ **być w swoim** ~**le** to be in one's element

żywiołow|y *adi.* ① (niepohamowany) *[osoba, zacho- wanie]* impetuous; *[śmiech]* unrestrained; ~**y tem- perament** an exuberant a. effervescent personality ② (niekontrolowany) *[rozwój, sprzeciw]* spontaneous

żywnoś|ć *f* food

żywo *adv. grad.* ① (energicznie) *[poruszać się, masze- rować]* briskly; *[gestykulować, dyskutować]* ani- matedly pot.; **akcja fimu toczy się** ~ the film is well-paced ② (intensywnie) vividly; **jego słowa** ~ **zapisały się w mojej pamięci** I still vividly remember his words; **interesować się czymś** ~ to show a lively interest in sth

■ **na** ~ live; **koncert na** ~ a live concert

żywopło|t *m* hedge; ~**t z głogu** a thorn hedge

żyw|y **Ⅰ** *adi.* ① (żyjący) living; ~**e stworzenie** a living creature; **w gruzach znaleźli dwoje** ~**ych ludzi** they found two people still alive among the debris; **przyroda** ~**a świat** ~**y** living nature; ~**a tarcza** a human shield ② (realistyczny) *[postać]* realistic, lifelike; **pies na obrazku wygląda jak** ~**y** the dog in the picture looks very lifelike ③ (najprawdziwszy) real; ~**a gotówka** hard cash

Ⅱ *adi. grad.* ① (ruchliwy) *[dziecko, ruchy]* lively; ~**y umysł** a lively mind pot. ② (intensywny) *[uczucia, zainteresowanie]* intense, deep; **utrzymuje z nią** ~**e kontakty** he keeps in constant touch with her; ~**a dyskusja** an animated a. lively discussion ③ przen. (trwały) lasting; **pamięć o nim jest ciągle** ~**a** his memory lives on ④ (wyraźny) *[kolor]* vivid, lively; *[wspomnienie]* vivid ⑤ (wartki) *[styl, dialog]* lively; **film o** ~**ej akcji** a fast-paced film

Ⅲ *m* living person; **wszystkich** ~**ych wypę- dzono poza bramę** all the survivors were driven outside the gate

■ **być ledwie** a. **na pół** a. **na wpół** ~**ym** pot. to be half dead, to be more dead than alive; **nie ma** ~**ego ducha** a. ~**ej duszy** there isn't a living soul; **poruszyć kogoś do** ~**ego** to move sb deeply; **wszystko, co** ~**e** one and all, absolutely everyone; ~**a rana** a raw wound; **obetrzeć sobie ręce do** ~**ego mięsa** to rub one's hands raw

żyzn|y *adi. grad.* fertile *także* przen.

A

a, A /eɪ/ n [1] (letter) a, A n [2] **A** Mus a, A, la n
a /eɪ, ə/ *indef art.* a tree drzewo; **an apple** jabłko;
her mother is a teacher jej matka jest nauczycielką; **50 km an hour** 50 km na godzinę; **twice a
week** dwa razy na tydzień; **fifty pence a kilo** pół
funta za kilogram
aback /ə'bæk/ *adv* **to be taken ~** być or zostać
zaskoczonym
abandon /ə'bændən/ *vt* porzuc|ić, -ać *[hope,
person]*; przer|wać, -ywać *[activity]*; zaniechać (cze-
goś) *[attempt]*
abbey /'æbɪ/ n opactwo n
abbreviate /ə'briːvɪeɪt/ *vt* skr|ócić, -acać *[word,
phrase]*
abbreviation /ə,briːvɪ'eɪʃn/ n skrót m
abdomen /'æbdəmən/ n brzuch m
abduct /əb'dʌkt/ *vt* uprowadz|ić, -ać
abide /ə'baɪd/ *vi* **to ~ by** za|stosować się do
(czegoś) *[rules, decision]*
ability /ə'bɪlətɪ/ n [1] (capability) zdolność f; **to the
best of his/her ~** jak najlepiej potrafi [2] (talent)
talent m
able /'eɪbl/ *adj* [1] (having ability to) **to be ~ to do sth**
być w stanie coś zrobić, móc coś zrobić; **she was
~ to play the piano at the age of four** w wieku
czterech lat grała już na fortepianie [2] *[lawyer,
teacher]* zdolny; *[child]* uzdolniony
able-bodied /,eɪbl'bɒdɪd/ *adj* silny, krzepki
abnormal /æb'nɔːml/ *adj* (deviant) nienormalny;
(irregular) nieprawidłowy
abnormality /,æbnɔː'mælətɪ/ n anomalia f
aboard /ə'bɔːd/ **[I]** *adv* *[be]* na pokładzie; *[go]* na
pokład
[II] *prep* **to be ~ sth** być na czymś *[ship]*; być
w czymś *[plane, train]*
abolish /ə'bɒlɪʃ/ *vt* zn|ieść, -osić *[right, tax,
allowance]*; z|likwidować *[service]*
abolition /,æbə'lɪʃn/ n (of law, right) zniesienie n; (of
service) likwidacja f
abominable /ə'bɒmɪnəbl/ *adj* *[crime, practice]*
ohydny; *[food, weather, behaviour]* obrzydliwy
aborigine /,æbə'rɪdʒənɪ/ n Aborygen m, -ka f
abort /ə'bɔːt/ *vt* spędz|ić, -ać *[foetus]*; zaniechać
(czegoś) *[plan]*; wy|jść, -chodzić z (czegoś) *[program]*
abortion /ə'bɔːʃn/ n przerwanie n ciąży
abortive /ə'bɔːtɪv/ *adj* *[mission, attack]* nieudany;
[plan, effort] chybiony

about /ə'baʊt/ **[I]** *adj* **to be ~ to do sth** właśnie
mieć coś zrobić
[II] *adv* mniej więcej, około; **it's ~ the same**
prawie to samo, prawie tak samo; **at ~ 6 pm**
około szóstej wieczorem; **there was no one ~**
nikogo tam nie było; **there is a lot of food
poisoning ~** jest wiele przypadków zatrucia
pokarmowego; **to be somewhere ~** być gdzieś
tutaj or w pobliżu
[III] *prep* [1] (concerning) **a book ~ sth** książka o
czymś; **what's it ~?** (of book, film) o czym to jest?;
it's ~ my son chodzi mi o mojego syna
[2] **there's something weird ~ him** jest
w nim coś dziwnego; **what I like ~ her is her
honesty** podoba mi się w niej jej uczciwość
[3] (around) **to wander ~ the streets** błąkać się po
ulicach [4] **how** or **what ~ some tea?** może
herbaty? [5] **what ~ the transport costs?** a co
z kosztami transportu?; **what ~ you** a ty?
IDIOMS **it's ~ time (that)...** już czas or pora,
żeby...; **~ time too!** najwyższa pora!
about-face /ə,baʊt'feɪs/ n wolta f
above /ə'bʌv/ **[I]** *prep* (po)nad (czymś), powyżej
(czegoś); (on a list) przed (czymś); **~ all else** ponad
or nade wszystko; **~ the shouting** ponad wrzawą
[II] *adj* **the ~ items** wyżej wymienione artykuły
[III] *adv* [1] **the apartment ~** mieszkanie piętro
wyżej [2] (in text) (po)wyżej [3] (more) powyżej;
children of 12 and ~ dzieci w wieku lat 12
i starsze
[IV] above all *adv phr* nade wszystko, przede
wszystkim
above-mentioned /ə,bʌv'menʃnd/ *adj* wyżej
wspomniany
abrasive /ə'breɪsɪv/ *adj* *[person]* zgryźliwy; *[man-
ner]* szorstki
abreast /ə'brest/ *adv* *[walk]* ramię przy ramieniu;
to keep ~ of sth śledzić coś *[developments]*
abroad /ə'brɔːd/ *adv* *[live, work]* za granicą; *[go]* za
granicę; *[come from]* z zagranicy
abrupt /ə'brʌpt/ *adj* *[change]* nagły; *[person]* szorstki; *[manner]* obcesowy
ABS n Aut = **anti-lock braking system** ABS
abscess /'æbses/ n ropień m
abseiling /'æbseɪlɪŋ/ n GB zjazd m na linie
absence /'æbsəns/ n (of person) nieobecność f; (of
thing) brak m

absent /'æbsənt/ *adj [person]* nieobecny; *[thing]* brakujący; ~ **from school** nieobecny w szkole
absentee /ˌæbsən'ti:/ *n* nieobecn|y *m*, -a *f*
absent-minded /ˌæbsənt'maɪndɪd/ *adj* roztargniony
absolute /'æbsəlu:t/ *adj [monarch]* absolutny; *[chaos, idiot]* kompletny; *[scandal]* prawdziwy; *[fact]* niepodważalny; *[lie]* wierutny
absolutely /'æbsəlu:tlɪ/ *adv [certain, agree, believe]* całkowicie; *[mad]* kompletnie; *[refuse]* kategorycznie
absorb /əb'zɔ:b/ *vt* wchł|onąć, -aniać; zaj|ąć, -mować *[attention, person]*
absorbent /əb'zɔ:bənt/ *adj [material]* chłonny
abstain /əb'steɪn/ *vi* powstrzym|ać, -ywać się (**from sth** od czegoś)
abstract /'æbstrækt/ *adj* abstrakcyjny
absurd /əb'sɜ:d/ *adj* absurdalny, niedorzeczny
abundant /ə'bʌndənt/ *adj [rain, resources]* obfity; *[vegetation]* bujny
abuse /ə'bju:s/ **𝐈** *n* ① (maltreatment) znęcanie się *n*; (sexual) wykorzystywanie *n* seksualne ② (misuse) nadużywanie *n*; **alcohol** ~ alkoholizm; **drug** ~ narkomania ③ (insults) wyzwiska *n pl* **𝐈𝐈** /ə'bju:z/ *vt* ① (hurt) znęcać się nad (kimś); (sexually) wykorzystywać seksualnie ② (misuse) naduży|ć, -wać (czegoś) *[drug, position, power]* ③ (insult) na|ubliżać (komuś)
abusive /ə'bju:sɪv/ *adj [person]* grubiański; *[words]* obelżywy
abyss /ə'bɪs/ *n* przepaść *f*, otchłań *f* also fig
academic /ˌækə'demɪk/ **𝐈** *n* nauczyciel *m* akademicki **𝐈𝐈** *adj* ① *[career, work]* naukowy; *[year]* akademicki ② (theoretical) teoretyczny
academy /ə'kædəmɪ/ *n* (school) szkoła *f*; (learned society) akademia *f*
accelerate /ək'seləreɪt/ *vi* przyśpiesz|yć, -ać
accelerator /ək'seləreɪtə(r)/ *n* akcelerator *m*
accent /'æksent, -sənt/ *n* akcent *m*
accentuate /æk'sentʃʊeɪt/ *vt* podkreśl|ić, -ać
accept /ək'sept/ *vt* przyj|ąć, -mować; (tolerate) za|akceptować
acceptable /ək'septəbl/ *adj [idea, offer]* (możliwy) do przyjęcia; *[level]* dopuszczalny
acceptance /ək'septəns/ *n* (of offer, invitation) przyjęcie *n*; (of plan, proposal) akceptacja *f*
access /'ækses/ **𝐈** *n* dostęp *m* (**to sth** do czegoś) **𝐈𝐈** *vt* w|ejść, -chodzić do (czegoś) *[database]*; dosta|ć, -wać się do (czegoś) *[information]*
accessible /ək'sesəbl/ *adj* dostępny (**to sb/sth** dla kogoś/czegoś)
accessory /ək'sesərɪ/ *n* (of dress) dodatek *m*; (on car) wyposażenie *n* dodatkowe
accident /'æksɪdənt/ *n* wypadek *m*; **road** ~ wypadek drogowy; **by** ~ przypadkiem

accidental /ˌæksɪ'dentl/ *adj [death, mistake]* przypadkowy
accidentally /ˌæksɪ'dentəlɪ/ *adv* (by accident) przypadkiem; (by chance) niechcący
accident-prone /ˌæksɪdənt'prəʊn/ *adj* często ulegający wypadkom
accommodate /ə'kɒmədeɪt/ *vt* ① (put up) da|ć, -wać dach nad głową (komuś) ② (hold) po|mieścić ③ (adapt to) dostosow|ać, -ywać *[plan, view]* ④ (satisfy) uwzględni|ć, -ać *[need]*
accommodating /ə'kɒmədeɪtɪŋ/ *adj [person]* (willing to help) uczynny; *[attitude]* przychylny
accommodation /əˌkɒmə'deɪʃn/ *n* (also ~**s** US) czasowe mieszkanie *n*
accommodation officer *n* urzędni|k *m*, -czka *f* biura zakwaterowań
accompany /ə'kʌmpənɪ/ *vt* ① Mus akompaniować (komuś) (**on sth** na czymś) ② (escort) towarzyszyć (komuś/czemuś)
accomplice /ə'kʌmplɪs, US ə'kɒm-/ *n* wspólni|k *m*, -czka *f* (przestępstwa)
accomplish /ə'kʌmplɪʃ, US ə'kɒm-/ *vt* osiąg|nąć, -ać *[aim]*; wykon|ać, -ywać *[task]*; za|kończyć pomyślnie *[mission]*
accomplishment /ə'kʌmplɪʃmənt, US ə'kɒm-/ *n* dokonanie *n*
accord /ə'kɔ:d/ *n* porozumienie *n*; **of my own** ~ z własnej woli
accordance /ə'kɔ:dəns/: **in accordance with** *prep phr* zgodnie z (czymś); **to be in** ~ **with sth** być zgodnym z czymś
according /ə'kɔ:dɪŋ/: **according to** *prep phr* zgodnie z (czymś)
accordingly /ə'kɔ:dɪŋlɪ/ *adv* zatem
accordion /ə'kɔ:dɪən/ *n* akordeon *m*
accost /ə'kɒst/ *vt* zaczepi|ć, -ać; (sexually) nagab|nąć, -ywać
account /ə'kaʊnt/ **𝐈** *n* ① (in bank, post office, shop) rachunek *m*; **in sb's** ~ na koncie kogoś ② **to take sth into** ~, **to take** ~ **of sth** brać coś pod uwagę ③ (description) opis *m* ④ **on** ~ **of sth** z powodu czegoś; **on no** ~ w żadnym wypadku; **on my** ~ z mojego powodu **𝐈𝐈 accounts** *npl* ① (records) księgowość *f*, księgi *f pl* rachunkowe ② (department) księgowość *f* ◼ **account for:** ① (explain) wyjaśni|ć, -ać *[events, fact, behaviour]*; rozlicz|yć, -ać się z (czegoś) *[expenses]* ② (represent) stanowić *[proportion, percentage]*
accountable /ə'kaʊntəbl/ *adj* odpowiedzialny
accountancy /ə'kaʊntənsɪ/ *n* (profession) księgowość *f*; (studies) rachunkowość *f*
accountant /ə'kaʊntənt/ *n* księgow|y *m*, -a *f*
account holder *n* posiadacz *m*, -ka *f* rachunku
accumulate /ə'kju:mjʊleɪt/ **𝐈** *vt* z|ebrać, -bierać *[evidence]*; z|gromadzić *[possessions]*

II *vi [difficulties]* s|piętrzyć się; *[interest, debts]* nar|osnąć, -astać

accuracy /'ækjərəsɪ/ *n* (of description, data) ścisłość *f*; (of figures, map) dokładność *f*; (of memory, translation) wierność *f*; (of watch) precyzja *f*; (of diagnosis, forecast) trafność *f*

accurate /'ækjərət/ *adj [figures, map]* dokładny; *[watch]* precyzyjny; *[forecast]* trafny

accurately /'ækjərətlɪ/ *adv* dokładnie

accusation /ˌækjuː'zeɪʃn/ *n* oskarżenie *n*

accuse /ə'kjuːz/ *vt* ~ **sb of sth** zarzucić komuś coś; (in law) oskarż|yć, -ać kogoś o coś

accused *n* the ~ oskarżon|y *m*, -a *f*

accuser /ə'kjuːzə(r)/ *n* oskarżyciel *m*, -ka *f*

accustomed /ə'kʌstəmd/ *adj* 1 (used to) **to be ~ to sth/doing sth** być przyzwyczajonym do czegoś/ do robienia czegoś 2 *[manner, route]* zwyczajowy

ace /eɪs/ *n* as *m*

ache /eɪk/ **I** *n* ból *m* (**in sth** czegoś) **II** *vi [back]* boleć; **I ~d all over** wszystko mnie bolało

achieve /ə'tʃiːv/ *vt* osiąg|nąć, -ać *[aim]*; do|jść, -chodzić do (czegoś) *[perfection]*; z|realizować *[ambition]*

achievement /ə'tʃiːvmənt/ *n* dokonanie *n*

aching /'eɪkɪŋ/ *adj [tooth, stomach]* bolący

acid /'æsɪd/ **I** *n* kwas *m* **II** *adj* kwaśny

acid rain *n* kwaśne deszcze *m pl*

acknowledge /ək'nɒlɪdʒ/ *vt* uzna|ć, -wać *[fact, authority]*; przyzna|ć, -wać się do (czegoś) *[error]*; potwierdz|ić, -ać odbiór (czegoś) *[letter]*

acknowledgement /ək'nɒlɪdʒmənt/ **I** *n* 1 (of error, guilt) przyznanie się *n* 2 (confirmation of receipt) potwierdzenie *n* odbioru or przyjęcia **II** **acknowledgements** *npl* (in book) podziękowania *n pl*

acne /'ækni/ *n* trądzik *m*

acorn /'eɪkɔːn/ *n* żołądź *m/f*

acoustic /ə'kuːstɪk/ *adj* akustyczny; *[material]* dźwiękochłonny

acoustic guitar *n* gitara *f* akustyczna

acoustics /ə'kuːstɪks/ *npl* the ~ of the hall are good sala ma dobrą akustykę

acquaintance /ə'kweɪntəns/ *n* znajomość *f* (**with sb/sth** z kimś/czegoś)

acquainted /ə'kweɪntɪd/ *adj* **to be ~** (**with sth**) być zaznajomionym or obeznanym z czymś; **to get** or **become ~** zapoznać się (**with sth** z czymś); poznać (**with sb** kogoś)

acquiesce /ˌækwɪ'es/ *vi* przysta|ć, -wać (**in sth** na coś)

acquire /ə'kwaɪə(r)/ *vt* w|ejść, -chodzić w posiadanie (czegoś) *[possession]*; naby|ć, -wać (czegoś) *[expertise]*; uzysk|ać, -iwać *[information]*

acquit /ə'kwɪt/ (in law) uniewinni|ć, -ać

acre /'eɪkə(r)/ *n* akr *m*

acrobat /'ækrəbæt/ *n* akrobat|a *m*, -ka *f*

acrobatics /ˌækrə'bætɪks/ *npl* akrobacje *f pl*

across /ə'krɒs/ **I** *prep* 1 przez (coś); **to go/travel ~ sth** jechać/podróżować przez coś; **the bridge ~ the river** most przez rzekę; **she leaned ~ the table** sięgnęła przez stół 2 (on the other side of) na or po drugiej stronie; ~ **the desk (from me)** po przeciwnej stronie biurka **II** *adv* **to help sb ~** pomóc komuś przejść na drugą stronę; **to go ~ to sb** podejść do kogoś; **to look ~ at sb** patrzeć na kogoś **III** **across from** *prep phr* naprzeciwko (czegoś)

acrylic /ə'krɪlɪk/ *n* 1 (fibre) akryl *m* 2 (paint) farba *f* akrylowa

act /ækt/ **I** *n* 1 (deed) czyn *m*; (action) działanie *n*; ~ **of kindness** dobry uczynek 2 (in law) ustawa *f*; **Act of Parliament** ustawa parlamentarna 3 (in show) numer *m* (sceniczny); **to put on an ~** *fig* grać komedię *fig* **II** *vt* za|grać *[part, role]* **III** *vi* 1 (take action) przyst|ąpić, -ępować do działania; (operate) działać; **to ~ as sth** służyć jako coś; **to ~ as sb** pełnić rolę kogoś 2 (behave) post|ąpić, -ępować 3 *[actor]* grać; *fig* (pretend) udawać 4 (take effect) *[drug]* za|działać ■ **act out**: od|egrać, -grywać *[part, scene]*; z|realizować *[fantasy]*

acting /'æktɪŋ/ **I** *n* (performance) występ *m*; (occupation) aktorstwo *n* **II** *adj* ~ **manager** pełniący obowiązki dyrektora

action /'ækʃn/ **I** *n* 1 działanie *n*; (steps) działania *n pl*, kroki *m pl*; **to take ~** podjąć działania, poczynić kroki (**against sb/sth** przeciwko komuś/czemuś); ~ **s speak louder than words** czyny przemawiają głośniej niż słowa 2 (fighting) akcja *f*, walka *f*; **to be killed in ~** zginąć w walce 3 (in film) akcja *f*; ~**!** kamera!

action film *n* film *m* akcji

action group *n* ciało powołane do prowadzenia kampanii politycznej

action-packed /'ækʃənpækt/ *adj [film]* o wartkiej akcji; *[holiday]* pełny wrażeń

action replay *n* GB powtórka *f*, replay *m*

activate /'æktɪveɪt/ *vt* uruch|omić, -amiać *[machine, system]*; włącz|yć, -ać *[alarm, switch]*

active /'æktɪv/ *adj [person, life]* aktywny; *[volcano]* czynny

activist /'æktɪvɪst/ *n* działacz *m*, -ka *f*

activity /æk'tɪvətɪ/ *n* działanie *n*

activity holiday *n* czynny wypoczynek *m*

actor /'æktə(r)/ *n* aktor *m*

actress /'æktrɪs/ *n* aktorka *f*

actual /'æktʃʊəl/ *adj* faktyczny; **I don't remember the ~ words** nie pamiętam dokładnie słów; **in ~ fact** w rzeczywistości; **it has nothing to do with the ~ problem** nie ma to nic wspólnego z samym problemem

actually /'æktʃʊəlɪ/ *adv* 1 (in fact) w rzeczywistości; **their profits have ~ risen** w rzeczywistości ich zyski wzrosły; **~, I don't feel like it** właściwie nie mam na to ochoty 2 (really) naprawdę; **yes, it ~ happened** tak, to się naprawdę zdarzyło

acupuncture /'ækjʊpʌŋktʃə(r)/ *n* akupunktura *f*

acute /ə'kjuːt/ *adj* 1 *[anxiety]* dręczący; *[pain]* ostry; *[boredom]* nieznośny 2 *[illness]* o ostrym przebiegu 3 *[mind]* wnikliwy 4 *[angle]* ostry

ad /æd/ *n* = **advertisement** 1 (small ~) ogłoszenie *n* drobne (**for sth** o czymś) 2 (on radio, TV) reklama *f* (**for sth** czegoś)

AD *adv* = **Anno Domini** Anno Domini, roku Pańskiego

adamant /'ædəmənt/ *adj* niewzruszony (**about sth** w sprawie czegoś); **to be ~ that...** stanowczo twierdzić, że...

adapt /ə'dæpt/ 1 *vt* przystosow|ać, -ywać (**to** or **for sth** do czegoś); (for screen) z|ekranizować *[novel]* 2 *vi* przystosow|ać, -ywać się (**to sth** do czegoś)

adaptable /ə'dæptəbl/ *adj* **to be ~** potrafić się przystosować

adapter, adaptor /ə'dæptə(r)/ *n* złączka *f*, łącznik *m*

add /æd/ *vt* 1 doda|ć, -wać (**onto** or **to sth** do czegoś) 2 (also ~ **together**) doda|ć, -wać *[numbers]*; **to ~ sth to sth** dodać coś do czegoś
■ **add up:** ¶ ~ **up** *[facts, figures]* zg|odzić, -adzać się; **to ~ up to** stanowić, wynosić *[total]* ¶ ~ **[sth] up** z|sumować *[cost, numbers]*

adder /'ædə(r)/ *n* (snake) żmija *f*

addict /'ædɪkt/ *n* 1 (drug user) narkoman *m*, -ka *f* 2 (of TV, coffee) fanaty|k *m*, -czka *f*

addicted /ə'dɪktɪd/ *adj* **to be ~ to sth** być uzależnionym od czegoś; fig być fanatykiem or entuzjastą czegoś

addiction /ə'dɪkʃn/ *n* (to drugs) uzależnienie *n*; (to alcohol, cigarettes) nałóg *m*; fig (to chocolate, gambling) pociąg *m*

addictive /ə'dɪktɪv/ *adj [drug, substance]* uzależniający; fig *[power, computer games]* wciągający

addition /ə'dɪʃn/ 1 *n* 1 (to text) dopisek *m*; (to house) dobudówka *f* 2 (in mathematics) dodawanie *n* 2 **in addition** *adv phr* w dodatku, na dodatek

additional /ə'dɪʃənl/ *adj* dodatkowy

additive /'ædɪtɪv/ *n* dodatek *m*

add-on /'ædɒn/ *adj* dodatkowy

address /ə'dres, US 'ædres/ 1 *n* adres *m*; **to change (one's) ~** zmienić adres
2 *vt* 1 za|adresować *[letter, parcel]*; **to ~ sth to sb** zaadresować coś do kogoś 2 (speak to) przem|ówić, -awiać do (kogoś) *[group]* 3 (aim) zwr|ócić, -acać się z (czymś) *[remark, complaint]* (**to sb** do kogoś)

address book *n* notes *m* na adresy

adenoids /'ædɪnɔɪdz, US -dən-/ *npl* migdałki *m pl*

adept /'ædɪnɔɪdz, US -dən-/ *adj* (proficient) znakomity; (experienced) doświadczony

adequate /'ædɪkwət/ *adj* (sufficient) wystarczający; (satisfactory) zadowalający

adhere /əd'hɪə(r)/ *vi* przyw|rzeć, -ierać (**to sth** do czegoś)

adhesive /əd'hiːsɪv/ 1 *n* klej *m*
2 *adj* klejący się; ~ **tape** taśma klejąca

adjacent /ə'dʒeɪsnt/ *adj [house, room]* przyległy; *[field, territory]* graniczący (**to sth** z czymś)

adjective /'ædʒɪktɪv/ *n* przymiotnik *m*

adjourn /ə'dʒɜːn/ *vt* odr|oczyć, -aczać *[trial]*

adjudicate /ə'dʒuːdɪkeɪt/ *vt* rozstrzyg|nąć, -ać *[competition, claim]*; rozsądz|ić, -ać *[dispute]*

adjust /ə'dʒʌst/ 1 *vt* wy|regulować *[level, volume]*; s|korygować *[figures, prices]*; poprawi|ć, -ać *[clothing]* 2 *vi* *[person]* przystosow|ać, -ywać się (**to sth** do czegoś)

adjustable /ə'dʒʌstəbl/ *adj* regulowany

adjustment /ə'dʒʌstmənt/ *n* (of rates) skorygowanie *n*; (of controls, machine) wyregulowanie *n*; (mental) przystosowanie się *n* (**to sth** do czegoś)

ad-lib /ˌæd'lɪb/ 1 *vt* za|improwizować *[performance]*
2 *vi* improwizować

administer /əd'mɪnɪstə(r)/ *vt* (also **administrate**) zarządzać (czymś) *[property, affairs, business]*; sprawować władzę nad (czymś) *[territory]*

administration /əd,mɪnɪ'streɪʃn/ *n* zarządzanie *n*; (paperwork) praca *f* administracyjna

administrative /əd'mɪnɪstrətɪv, US -streɪtɪv/ *adj* administracyjny

administrator /əd'mɪnɪstreɪtə(r)/ *n* 1 zarządca *m* 2 (of school, hospital) dyrektor *m*

admirable /'ædmərəbl/ *adj* godny podziwu

admiral /'ædmərəl/ *n* admirał *m*

admiration /ˌædmə'reɪʃn/ *n* podziw *m* (**for sb/sth** dla kogoś/czegoś); (stronger) zachwyt *m* (**for sb/sth** nad kimś/czymś)

admire /əd'maɪə(r)/ *vt* podziwiać; (stronger) zachwyc|ić, -ać się (czymś)

admirer /əd'maɪərə(r)/ *n* wielbiciel *m*, -ka *f*

admission /əd'mɪʃn/ *n* 1 (entry) wstęp *m* (**to sth** do czegoś); **'no ~'** „wstęp wzbroniony" 2 (fee) opłata *f* (za wstęp) 3 (confession) przyznanie się *n*

admissions office *n* Univ ≈ biuro *n* or dział *m* rekrutacji

admit /əd'mɪt/ *vt* 1 (accept) uzna|ć, -wać *[mistake, fact]*; **to ~ that...** przyznać, że...; **to ~ to sth** przyznać się do czegoś 2 (confess) przyzna|ć, -wać się do (czegoś) *[guilt]* 3 (let in) wpu|ścić, -szczać *[person]*; **to be ~ted to hospital** zostać przyjętym do szpitala

admittance /əd'mɪtns/ *n* wstęp *m*; **no ~!** wstęp wzbroniony!

admittedly /əd'mɪtɪdlɪ/ *adv* wprawdzie

adolescent /ˌædə'lesnt/ **I** *n* (male) ≈ nastolatek *m*; (female) ≈ nastolatka *f*
II *adj* [1] *[rebellion, years]* młodzieńczy; *[problems]* okresu dojrzewania [2] (childish) szczeniacki infml

adopt /ə'dɒpt/ *vt* za|adoptować *[child]*; przyj|ąć, -mować *[custom, bill]*; przyb|rać, -ierać *[attitude, tone]*

adopted /ə'dɒptɪd/ *adj [child]* adoptowany

adoption /ə'dɒpʃn/ *n* (of child) adopcja *f*; (of bill) przyjęcie *n*

adorable /ə'dɔːrəbl/ *adj* zachwycający

adore /ə'dɔː(r)/ *vt* uwielbiać (**doing sth** coś robić)

adoring /ə'dɔːrɪŋ/ *adj* rozkochany

adrenalin(e) /ə'drenəlɪn/ *n* adrenalina *f*

Adriatic (Sea) /ˌeɪdrɪ'ætɪk/ *prn* **the ~** Adriatyk *m*, Morze *n* Adriatyckie

adrift /ə'drɪft/ *adj, adv [boat, person]* znoszony przez prąd; **to come ~** *[book]* rozlecieć się; *[pages]* rozsypać się

adult /'ædʌlt, ə'dʌlt/ **I** *n* (grown-up) osoba *f* dorosła; (of age) pełnoletni *m*, -a *f*
II *adj* dorosły; **~ film** film dla dorosłych euph

adultery /ə'dʌltəri/ *n* cudzołóstwo *n* (**with sb** z kimś)

adulthood /'ædʌlthʊd/ *n* wiek *m* dojrzały

advance /əd'vɑːns, US -'væns/ **I** *n* [1] (of troops) posuwanie się *n* naprzód; (progress) postęp *m* [2] (sum of money) zaliczka *f* (**on sth** na poczet czegoś) [3] **to make ~s to sb** zwrócić się do kogoś (z propozycją); (sexually) zalecać się do kogoś
II in advance *adv phr [pay, thank]* z góry; *[notify, know]* z wyprzedzeniem
III *vt* [1] wypłac|ić, -ać tytułem zaliczki *[sum of money]* [2] pop|rzeć, -ierać *[cause, interests]*; **to ~ sb's career** pomóc komuś zrobić karierę
IV *vi* [1] (move forward) *[person]* zbliż|yć, -ać się (**towards sb/sth** do kogoś/czegoś); *[army]* na|trzeć, -cierać (**on sb/sth** na kogoś/coś) [2] (progress) rozwi|nąć, -jać się

advanced /əd'vɑːnst, US -'vænst/ *adj [course, level]* dla zaawansowanych; *[pupil, stage]* zaawansowany; *[equipment, technology]* nowoczesny

advance warning *n* ostrzeżenie *n*

advantage /əd'vɑːntɪdʒ, US -'vænt-/ *n* [1] korzyść *f*; **it is to his ~ to do that** zrobienie tego jest dla niego korzystne [2] (asset) zaleta *f* [3] **to take ~ of sb/sth** skorzystać z czegoś *[offer, service]*; wykorzystać coś *[situation]*; wykorzystać kogoś *[person]*

advantageous /ˌædvən'teɪdʒəs/ *adj* korzystny

advent /'ædvent/ *n* pojawienie się *n* (**of sth** czegoś); **Advent** (prior to Christmas) adwent *m*

adventure /əd'ventʃə(r)/ *n* (exciting) przygoda *f*; (risky) ryzykowne przedsięwzięcie *n*

adventurous /əd'ventʃərəs/ *adj* śmiały

adverb /'ædvɜːb/ *n* przysłówek *m*

adverse /'ædvɜːs/ *adj [decision, publicity, reaction]* niekorzystny; *[consequence, effect]* niepożądany

advert /'ædvɜːt/ *n* GB infml = **advertisement**

advertise /'ædvətaɪz/ **I** *vt* za|reklamować *[product, service]*; ogłaszać *[event]*; da|ć, -wać ogłoszenie o sprzedaży (czegoś) *[car, house]*
II *vi* [1] (for publicity) za|reklamować się [2] (for staff) zamie|ścić, -szczać ofertę pracy

advertisement /əd'vɜːtɪsmənt, US ˌædvər'taɪzmənt/ *n* [1] (for product) reklama *f* (**for sth** czegoś); (for event) ogłoszenie *n* (**for sth** o czymś); **a good/bad ~ for sth** fig dobra/zła reklama czegoś fig [2] (to sell house) ogłoszenie *n*; (in small ads) anons *m*

advertising /'ædvətaɪzɪŋ/ *n* (profession) reklama *f*; (activity) reklamowanie *n*; (advertisements) reklamy *f pl*

advertising agency *n* agencja *f* reklamowa

advertising campaign *n* kampania *f* reklamowa

advice /əd'vaɪs/ *n* rada *f*, rady *f pl* (**on** or **about sth** na temat or w sprawie czegoś); **a piece of ~** rada; **it was good ~** to była dobra rada

advisable /əd'vaɪzəbl/ *adj* **is ~ to...** zaleca się...

advise /əd'vaɪz/ *vt* [1] po|radzić (komuś), doradz|ić, -ać (komuś) (**about sth** w sprawie czegoś); **to ~ sb against doing sth** odradzić komuś zrobienie czegoś [2] zalec|ić, -ać *[rest, course of action]* [3] (inform) powiad|omić, -amiać (**of sth** o czymś)

adviser, advisor /əd'vaɪzə(r)/ *n* doradca *m* (**to sb/sth** kogoś/czegoś)

advisory service *n* poradnictwo *n*

Aegean (Sea) /iː'dʒiːən/ *prn* **the ~** Morze *n* Egejskie

aerial /'eəriəl/ **I** *n* antena *f*
II *adj [attack]* z powietrza; *[survey]* lotniczy

aerobics /eə'rəʊbɪks/ *n* aerobik *m*

aeroplane /'eərəpleɪn/ *n* GB samolot *m*

aerosol /'eərəsɒl, US -sɔːl/ *n* aerozol *m*

aesthetic /iːs'θetɪk/, **esthetic** /es'θetɪk/ US *adj* estetyczny

affair /ə'feə(r)/ *n* [1] sprawa *f*; **state of ~s** sytuacja, stan rzeczy [2] (relationship) romans *m* (**with sb** z kimś)

affect /ə'fekt/ *vt* [1] (influence) *[change]* dot|knąć, -ykać *[person, region]*; *[issue]* dotyczyć (kogoś/czegoś) *[person, region]*; wpły|nąć, -wać na (coś) *[result, career]* [2] (emotionally) porusz|yć, -ać; *[news, discovery]* wstrzą|snąć, -ać (kimś) [3] Med dot|knąć, -ykać *[person]*; za|atakować *[heart, sight]*

affection /ə'fekʃn/ *n* sympatia *f* (**for sb** do kogoś); (stronger) uczucie *n* (**for sb** do kogoś)

affectionate /ə'fekʃənət/ *adj* (friendly) serdeczny; (loving) czuły; *[animal]* przywiązany

affinity /ə'fɪnəti/ *n* [1] (attraction) sympatia *f* (**with** or **for sb/sth** do kogoś/czegoś) [2] (resemblance) podobieństwo *n*

affluence /'æfluəns/ *n* dostatek *m*

afford /ə'fɔːd/ *vt* [1] (financially) **to be able to ~ sth** móc sobie pozwolić na coś [2] (spare) **to be able to ~ sth** mieć coś *[time]* [3] (risk) **to be able to ~**

sth/to do sth pozwolić sobie na coś/na zrobienie czegoś; **he can't ~ to wait** on nie bardzo może czekać

affordable /ə'fɔːdəbl/ *adj [price]* przystępny

afield /ə'fiːld/ *adv* far ~ daleko; **further** ~ dalej

afloat /ə'fləʊt/ *adj, adv* **to stay** ~ utrzymać się na wodzie

afraid /ə'freɪd/ *adj* ① (frightened) **to be** ~ bać się (**of sth/to do sth** czegoś/zrobić coś) ② (anxious) **she was** ~ **(that) there would be an accident** obawiała się, że może zdarzyć się wypadek; **I'm** ~ **it might rain** obawiam się, że będzie padać ③ **I'm** ~ **I can't come** żałuję, ale nie mogę przyjść; **I'm** ~ **not/so** obawiam się, że nie/tak

afresh /ə'freʃ/ *adv [start, do]* od nowa; *[look at]* jeszcze raz

Africa /'æfrɪkə/ *prn* Afryka *f*

African /'æfrɪkən/ **①** *n* Afrykan|in *m*, -ka *f* **②** *adj* afrykański

Afro-Caribbean /ˌæfrəʊˌkærɪ'biːən/ *adj* afro-karaibski

after /'ɑːftə(r), US 'æftər/ **①** *adv* potem, później; **soon** or **not long** ~ wkrótce potem; **the year** ~ rok później; **the day** ~ na drugi dzień **②** *prep* ① po (czymś); **shortly** ~ **10 pm** zaraz po dziesiątej (wieczorem); ~ **that** po tym; **the day** ~ **tomorrow** pojutrze; **to tidy up** ~ **sb** sprzątać po kimś; **to ask** ~ **sb** pytać o kogoś ② **that's the house they are** ~ o ten właśnie dom im chodzi; **the police are** ~ **him** szuka go policja ③ **day** ~ **day** dzień po dniu; **it was one disaster** ~ **another** to było jedno pasmo nieszczęść ④ **we called her Anna** ~ **my mother** po mojej matce daliśmy jej na imię Anna ⑤ **US it's twenty** ~ **eleven** jest dwadzieścia po jedenastej **③** *conj* ① (in the past) ~ **we had left we realized that...** po wyjściu zorientowaliśmy się, że... ② (given that) ~ **you explained the situation they didn't call the police** gdy wyjaśniłeś sytuację, nie wezwali policji ③ **why did he do that** ~ **we'd warned him of the consequences** dlaczego to zrobił mimo naszych ostrzeżeń? **Ⅳ after all** *adv, prep* w końcu

after-effect /'ɑːftərɪfekt, US 'æf-/ *n* Med następstwo *n*; fig reperkusja *f*

aftermath /'ɑːftəmæθ, -mɑːθ, US 'æf-/ *n* następstwo *n*; **in the** ~ **of sth** w następstwie czegoś *[election, scandal, war]*

afternoon /ˌɑːftə'nuːn, US ˌæf-/ *n* popołudnie *n*; **in the** ~ po południu; **Monday** ~ w poniedziałek po południu; **good** ~ **!** dzień dobry!

after-shave /'ɑːftəʃeɪv, US 'æf-/ *n* płyn *m* po goleniu

aftershock /'ɑːftəʃɒk, US 'æf-/ *n* reperkusja *f*

aftertaste /'ɑːftəteɪst, US 'æf-/ *n* posmak *m*

afterthought /'ɑːftəθɔːt, US 'æf-/ *n* **as an** ~ po namyśle

afterwards /'ɑːftəwədz, US 'æf-/ GB, **afterward** /'ɑːftəwəd, US 'æf-/ US *adv* ① (after) potem; **straight** ~ od razu potem ② (later) później

again /ə'geɪn, ə'gen/ *adv* jeszcze raz; **once** ~ jeszcze raz; **I'll never go there** ~ nigdy więcej tam nie pójdę; **when you are well** ~ kiedy powrócisz do zdrowia

against /ə'geɪnst, ə'genst/ *prep* ~ **the wall** o ścianę; **I'm** ~ **it** jestem temu przeciwny; **to be** ~ **doing sth** być przeciwnym robieniu czegoś; **the pound fell** ~ **the dollar** funt spadł w stosunku do dolara; ~ **the background of sth** na tle czegoś; ~ **the light** pod światło

age /eɪdʒ/ **①** *n* ① wiek *m*; **to come of** ~ osiągnąć pełnoletność; **to be under** ~ być niepełnoletnim ② (era) epoka *f*; **the computer** ~ epoka komputerów; **in this day and** ~ w dzisiejszych czasach ③ infml (long time) **it's** ~ **s since I've played tennis** wieki nie grałem w tenisa; **for** ~ **s** całe wieki **②** *vt [experiences, worry]* postarz|yć, -ać *[person]*; *[dress, hairstyle]* postarzać **③** *vi [person]* ze|starzeć się

aged /eɪdʒd/ *adj* ① w wieku; **to be** ~ **10** mieć 10 lat ② (old) *[person]* w podeszłym wieku

ageism /'eɪdʒɪzəm/ *n* dyskryminacja *f* z powodu wieku

agency /'eɪdʒənsɪ/ *n* ① (organization) agencja *f* ② (firm) przedstawicielstwo *n*

agenda /ə'dʒendə/ *n* porządek *m* dzienny

agent /'eɪdʒənt/ *n* ① (for artist) agent *m*, -ka *f*; (for customer) pośredni|k *m*, -czka *f*; (for firm) przedstawiciel *m*, -ka *f* ② (spy) agent *m*, -ka *f*; **enemy/foreign** ~ wrogi/obcy agent ③ (means) czynnik *m*

aggravate /'ægrəveɪt/ *vt* ① (make worse) pog|orszyć, -arszać *[situation, health]*; ② (annoy) z|irytować, z|denerwować

aggression /ə'greʃn/ *n* napaść *f*; (of person) agresja *f*

aggressive /ə'gresɪv/ *adj [behaviour]* agresywny; *[remark]* napastliwy; *[manoeuvre, tactics]* zaczepny

aggro /'ægrəʊ/ *n* infml (violence) zadyma *f*; (hostility) wrogość *f*

agile /'ædʒaɪl, US 'ædʒl/ *adj [person, fingers]* zręczny; *[movement]* zwinny; *[mind]* lotny

agitate /'ædʒɪteɪt/ *vi* agitować (**for sb/sth** za kimś/za czymś)

agitated /'ædʒɪteɪtɪd/ *adj [person]* poruszony; *[voice]* wzburzony

agnostic /æg'nɒstɪk/ **①** *n* agnostyk *m* **②** *adj* agnostyczny

ago /ə'gəʊ/ *adv* **a week** ~ tydzień temu; **long** ~ dawno temu; **how long** ~ **?** jak dawno temu?

agonize /'ægənaɪz/ *vi* zadręczać się (**over** or **about sth** czymś)

agonizing /'ægənaɪzɪŋ/ adj [pain] przejmujący; [memory, feeling] dręczący; [decision] bolesny; [death] w męczarniach

agony /'ægənɪ/ n męka f

agony aunt n redaktorka f rubryki porad osobistych

agony column n rubryka f porad osobistych

agree /ə'griː/ **I** vt ① (concur) zg|odzić, -adzać się (**that...** że...) ② (admit) przyzna|ć, -wać (**that...** że...) ③ (consent) **to ~ to do sth** zgodzić się coś zrobić ④ (settle on, arrange) uzg|odnić, -adniać [date, price]; **we ~d to get up at six** uzgodniliśmy, że wstaniemy o szóstej

II vi ① (hold same opinion) zg|adzać, -odzić się (**with sb about** or **on sth** z kimś co do czegoś) ② (reach mutual understanding) do|jść, -chodzić do porozumienia (**about** or **as to sth** w sprawie czegoś); uzg|odnić, -adniać (**on sth** coś) ③ (consent) zgo|dzić, -adzać się (**to sth** na coś) ④ (hold with, approve) **to ~ with sth** zgadzać się z czymś [belief, practice, proposal] ⑤ (tally) [figures, statements, stories] zg|odzić, -adzać się (**with sth** z czymś) ⑥ (suit) **to ~ with sb** [climate] (dobrze) służyć komuś; [food] posłużyć komuś ⑦ (in grammar) pozosta|ć, -wać w związku zgody (**with sth/in sth** z czymś/pod względem czegoś)

III agreed pp adj [date, terms] uzgodniony; [place, signal] umówiony; **is that ~d?** zgoda?

agreeable /ə'griːəbl/ adj przyjemny; [person, feeling] miły

agreement /ə'griːmənt/ n ① porozumienie n; **to reach an ~** dojść do porozumienia ② (undertaking) zobowiązanie n ③ (contract) umowa f ④ (in grammar) związek m zgody

agricultural /ˌægrɪ'kʌltʃərəl/ adj [land, college] rolniczy; [worker] rolny

agriculture /'ægrɪkʌltʃə(r)/ n rolnictwo n

aground /ə'graʊnd/ adv **to run ~** osiąść na mieliźnie

ahead /ə'hed/ **I** adv ① [run] naprzód; **to send sb on ~** wysłać kogoś przodem; **to send one's luggage on ~** wysłać wcześniej bagaż; **a few kilometres ~** kilka kilometrów dalej ② (in time) **in the months ~** w następnych miesiącach ③ (in leading position) **to be ~ in the polls** być na pierwszej pozycji w sondażach; **to be 30 points ~** mieć przewagę 30 punktów

II ahead of prep phr ① (in front of) przed (kimś/czymś) [person, vehicle]; **to be 3 metres ~ of sb** wyprzedzać kogoś o 3 metry ② (leading) **to be ~ of sb** (in polls, ratings) wyprzedzać kogoś; **to be ~ of the others** [pupil] być lepszym od pozostałych

aid /eɪd/ **I** n pomoc f (**to sb** dla kogoś); wsparcie n (**from sb to** or **for sb** od kogoś dla kogoś); **in ~ of sth** na rzecz czegoś [charity]

II adj [organization] pomocowy

III vt pom|óc, -agać (komuś) [person]; ułatwi|ć, -ać [digestion]; przyspiesz|yć, -ać [recovery]

aide /eɪd/ n bliski współpracownik m, bliska współpracownica f

AIDS, Aids /eɪdz/ n = **Acquired Immune Deficiency Syndrome** zespół m nabytego niedoboru odporności, AIDS m/n inv

aim /eɪm/ **I** n ① (purpose) cel m ② (with weapon) cel m; **to take ~ at sth/sb** wycelować w coś/kogoś

II vt ① **to be ~ed at sb** [campaign, insult, remark] być skierowanym do kogoś ② wy|celować [gun] (**at sb/sth** w kogoś/coś); rzuc|ić, -ać [ball, stone] (**at sb/sth** w kogoś/coś)

III vi **to ~ for sth, to ~ at sth** dążyć do czegoś; **to ~ at doing sth, to ~ to do sth** (try) dążyć do zrobienia czegoś; (intend) zamierzać coś zrobić

air /eə(r)/ **I** n ① powietrze n; **in the open ~** na wolnym powietrzu; **to let the ~ out of sth** wypuścić powietrze z czegoś; **he threw the ball up into the ~** podrzucił or wyrzucił piłkę w górę ② (on radio, TV) **to be on the ~** być na antenie; **to go on the ~** wejść na antenę

II vt ① wy|wietrzyć [bed, garment, room] ② (express) da|ć, -wać wyraz (czemuś) [view, grievances]

IDIOMS **to put on ~s** zadzierać nosa; **to vanish into thin ~** wyparować infml fig

air ambulance n samolot m or helikopter m sanitarny

airbag n poduszka f powietrzna

air bed n GB nadmuchiwany materac m

air-conditioned /'eəkəndɪʃnd/ adj klimatyzowany

air-conditioning /'eəkəndɪʃənɪŋ/ n klimatyzacja f

aircraft /'eəkrɑːft, US -kræft/ n ① statek m powietrzny; ② (aeroplane) samolot m

aircrew /'eəkruː/ n załoga f (samolotu)

airfare /'eəfeə(r)/ n cena f biletu lotniczego

airfield /'eəfiːld/ n lotnisko n (zwłaszcza wojskowe)

air force n siły plt powietrzne

air-freshener /'eəfreʃənə(r)/ n odświeżacz m powietrza

air gun n wiatrówka f

airhead /'eəhed/ n infml ptasi móżdżek m infml

air hostess n stewardesa f

airline /'eəlaɪn/ n linia f lotnicza

airmail /'eəmeɪl/ n poczta f lotnicza; **by ~** pocztą lotniczą

airplane /'eəpleɪn/ n US samolot m

airport /'eəpɔːt/ n lotnisko n, port m lotniczy

air raid n nalot m

air terminal n (at airport) dworzec m lotniczy; (in town) miejski dworzec m lotniczy

airtight /'eətaɪt/ adj hermetyczny

air-traffic controller /ˌeətræfɪkkən'trəʊlə(r)/ n kontroler m, -ka f ruchu lotniczego

air travel n podróż f samolotem

airwaves /'eəweɪvz/ *npl* fale *f pl* radiowe

airy /'eərɪ/ *adj* ① *[room]* przestronny i widny ② *[attitude, manner, person]* nonszalancki

aisle /aɪl/ *n* ① (in church) nawa *f* ② (passageway) (in train, plane) korytarz *m*; (in cinema, shop) przejście *n*

ajar /ə'dʒɑː(r)/ *adj, adv* uchylony

alarm /ə'lɑːm/ ① *n* ① (warning) alarm *m*; **smoke ~** czujnik przeciwpożarowy ② (fear) obawa *f*; (stronger) trwoga *f*; (uneasiness) niepokój *m*; **in ~** zaniepokojony
   ② *vt* zatrw|ożyć, -ażać *[person]*

alarm clock *n* budzik *m*

alarmed /ə'lɑːmd/ *adj* (anxious) zaniepokojony (**at** or **by sth** czymś); (afraid) zatrwożony (**at** or **by sth** czymś)

album /'ælbəm/ *n* album *m*

alcohol /'ælkəhɒl, US -hɔːl/ *n* alkohol *m*; **~-free** bezalkoholowy

alcoholic /ˌælkə'hɒlɪk, US -hɔːl-/ ① *n* alkoholi|k *m*, -czka *f*
   ② *adj* alkoholowy

alcoholism /'ælkəhɒlɪzəm, US -hɔːl-/ *n* alkoholizm *f*

alcopop /'ælkəʊpɒp/ *n* napój *m* gazowany z niewielką ilością alkoholu

alcove /'ælkəʊv/ *n* alkowa *f*; (smaller) wnęka *f*

ale /eɪl/ *n* ale *n inv*

alert /ə'lɜːt/ ① *n* pogotowie *n*
   ② *adj* ① (lively) *[child, mind]* bystry; *[adult]* sprawny umysłowo ② (attentive) *[reader, listener]* uważny; *[guard]* czujny
   ③ *vt* ① (contact) powiad|omić, -amiać *[authorities]* ② **to ~ sb to sth** ostrzec kogoś przed czymś *[danger]*; uczulić kogoś na coś fig *[fact, situation]*

A-levels /'eɪlevl/ *npl* GB Sch egzamin *m* końcowy z jednego przedmiotu w szkole średniej

algebra /'ældʒɪbrə/ *n* algebra *f*

Algeria /æl'dʒɪərɪə/ *prn* Algieria *f*

alibi /'ælɪbaɪ/ *n* ① (in law) alibi *n inv* ② (excuse) wymówka *f*

alien /'eɪlɪən/ *n* ① cudzoziem|iec *m*, -ka *f* ② (from space) przybysz *m* z kosmosu

alienate /'eɪlɪəneɪt/ *vt* zra|zić, -żać (**from sb/sth** do kogoś/czegoś); odstręcz|yć, -ać (**from sb/sth** od kogoś/czegoś)

alight /ə'laɪt/ ① *adj* **to set sth ~** zapalić coś *[candle, match]*; podpalić coś *[building, grass]*
   ② *vi [passenger]* wysiąść (**from sth** z czegoś)

alike /ə'laɪk/ ① *adj* (identical) taki sam; (similar) podobny; **to look ~** wyglądać podobnie
   ② *adv* (identically) tak samo; (similarly) podobnie

alimony /'ælɪmənɪ, US -məʊnɪ/ *n* alimenty *plt*

alive /ə'laɪv/ *adj* ① żywy; **to burn sb ~** spalić kogoś żywcem ② **to come ~** *[party, place]* ożywić się ③ **to be ~** *[tradition]* żyć; *[interest]* trwać ④ **~ with sth** rojący się od czegoś *[insects]*

alkaline /'ælkəlaɪn/ *adj* zasadowy

all /ɔːl/ ① *pron* wszystko; **that's ~ I want** to wszystko, czego chcę; **~ of our belongings** wszystkie nasze rzeczy; **I ate it ~** zjadłem wszystko (do ostatniego kęsa)
   ② *det* wszyscy, wszystkie; **~ those people who...** wszyscy ci, którzy...; **~ his life** całe swoje życie
   ③ *adv* ① zupełnie; **to be ~ wet** być zupełnie mokrym; **~ in white** cały na biało; **~ along the canal** wzdłuż całego kanału; **to be ~ for sth** gorąco popierać coś; **it's ~ about...** to wszystko ma związek z...; **tell me ~ about it!** opowiedz mi o tym! ② Sport (**they are) six ~** (wynik) jest po sześć
   ④ **all along** *adv phr [know]* od samego początku
   ⑤ **all the** *adv phr* **~ the more difficult** trudniejszy; **~ the better!** tym lepiej!
   ⑥ **all too** *adv phr [often, easy]* (na)zbyt
   ⑦ **at all** *adv phr* wcale; **not at ~!** (acknowledging thanks) nie ma za co!; (answering query) wcale nie!; **it is not at ~ certain** to wcale nie jest takie pewne; **nothing at ~** w ogóle nic
   ⑧ **of all** *prep phr* **the easiest of ~** najłatwiejszy ze wszystkiego; **first of ~** (in the first place) po pierwsze; (in order of time) najpierw

all clear *n* **to give sb the ~ to do sth** fig dać komuś wolną rękę, żeby mógł coś zrobić

allegation /ˌælɪ'geɪʃn/ *n* (niepoparte dowodami) twierdzenie *n* (**that...** że...)

allege /ə'ledʒ/ *vt* utrzymywać (**that...** że...); **it is/was ~d that...** twierdzi się/twierdzono, że...

allegedly /ə'ledʒɪdlɪ/ *adv* rzekomo

allegiance /ə'liːdʒəns/ *n* (to authority) lojalność *f*; (to parents) posłuszeństwo *n*; (to husband, wife) oddanie *n*

allergic /ə'lɜːdʒɪk/ *adj [rash]* uczuleniowy; *[person]* uczulony (**to sth** na coś)

allergist /'ælədʒɪst/ *n* alergolog *m*

allergy /'ælədʒɪ/ *n* uczulenie *n*, alergia *f* also fig (**to sth** na coś)

alleviate /ə'liːvɪeɪt/ *vt* z|łagodzić *[pain, stress]*; zmniejsz|yć, -ać *[overcrowding, unemployment]*; zaspok|oić, -ajać *[thirst]*

alley /'ælɪ/ *n* (for pedestrians) przejście *n*; (for vehicles) uliczka *f*; (in park) alejka *f*

alliance /ə'laɪəns/ *n* przymierze *n*, sojusz *m*

allied /'ælaɪd/ *adj [powers, parties]* sprzymierzony; *[states, armies]* sojuszniczy

all-important /ˌɔːlɪm'pɔːtnt/ *adj* bardzo ważny

all-inclusive /ˌɔːlɪn'kluːsɪv/ *adj [fee, price]* łączny

all-in-one /ˌɔːlɪn'wʌn/ *adj [garment]* jednoczęściowy

all-night /ˌɔːl'naɪt/ *adj [party, meeting]* całonocny; *[café]* czynny całą noc; *[radio, station]* całodobowy

allocate /'æləkeɪt/ *vt* przydziel|ić, -ać *[funds, task]* (**to** or **for sb/sth** komuś/na coś); przeznacz|yć, -ać *[time]* (**to sb/sth** dla kogoś/na coś)

allot /ə'lɒt/ *vt* po|dzielić *[money]*; przeznacz|yć, -áć *[time]* (**to sth** na coś); przydziel|ić, -áć *[task]* (**to sb** komuś); **in the ~ted time** w wyznaczonym czasie

allotment /ə'lɒtmənt/ *n* GB (garden) działka *f*

all-out /'ɔ:laʊt/ *adj [strike]* powszechny; *[attack]* zmasowany; *[effort]* zdecydowany

all over ▯ *adj* zakończony; **when it's ~** kiedy to się skończony

▯▯ *adv* wszędzie; **he was trembling ~** cały się trząsł

▯▯▯ *prep* wszędzie, na całej powierzchni; **~ China** w całych Chinach

allow /ə'laʊ/ *vt* ① (permit) pozw|olić, -alać (komuś/czemuś) (**to do sth** na zrobienie czegoś); zezw|o-lić, -alać na (coś); **she isn't ~ed alcohol** nie wolno jej pić alkoholu; **he ~ed the situation to get worse** dopuścił do pogorszenia się sytuacji ② (enable) pozw|olić, -alać (komuś/czemuś) (**to do sth** na zrobienie czegoś); umożliwi|ć, -ać (komuś/czemuś) (**to do sth** zrobić coś) ③ (allocate) przeznacz|yć, -áć; **to ~ two days for the job** przeznaczyć dwa dni na wykonanie pracy ④ *[referee, insurer]* uzna|ć, -wać *[goal, claim]* ⑤ (condone) pozw|olić, -alać na (coś) *[rudeness, swearing]*

■ **allow for**: uwzględni|ć, -áć

allowance /ə'laʊəns/ *n* ① zasiłek *m*; (from employer) dodatek *m* ② **tax ~** ulga *f* podatkowa ③ (spending money) (for child) kieszonkowe *n*; (for student) pieniądze *m pl* na życie; (from trust) zapomoga *f* ④ **your luggage ~ is 40 kg** wolno panu/pani mieć 40 kg bagażu ⑤ **to make ~(s) for sth** wziąć pod uwagę coś, wziąć poprawkę na coś; **to make ~(s) for sb** potraktować kogoś ulgowo

alloy wheel *n* koło *n* z obręczami metalowymi (ze stopów lekkich)

all right, alright /ɔ:l'raɪt/ ▯ *adj [film, place, garment]* niezły, w porządku; **is my hair ~?** jak moje włosy?

▯▯ *adv* (giving agreement) zgoda ② *[work]* jak należy; *[hear, see]* dobrze

all-round /ɔ:l'raʊnd/ *adj [athlete]* wszechstronny; *[improvement]* ogólny

all-rounder /ɔ:l'raʊndə(r)/ *n* **to be a good ~** być wszechstronnym

all-time /'ɔ:ltaɪm/ *adj [record]* wszech czasów; **the ~ greats** (people) wielkie postaci; **~ high** absolutny rekord

all told *adv* razem wziąwszy

allusion /ə'lu:ʒn/ *n* aluzja *f* (**to sth** do czegoś)

ally ▯ /'ælaɪ/ *n* sojusznik *m*

▯▯ /ə'laɪ/ *vr* **to ~ oneself** sprzymierz|yć, -áć się (**with sb** z kimś)

almond /'ɑ:mənd/ *n* ① (nut) migdał *m* ② (also **~ tree**) migdałowiec *m*

almost /'ɔ:lməʊst/ *adv* ① (practically) prawie; **we're ~ there** jesteśmy prawie na miejscu ② mało co; **he ~ died** (o) mało co nie umarł

alone /ə'ləʊn/ ▯ *adj* sam; **all ~** zupełnie sam; **to leave sb ~** zostawić kogoś samego; (in peace) zostawić kogoś w spokoju; **leave that bike ~!** zostaw ten rower w spokoju!

▯▯ *adv* ① *[work, travel]* w pojedynkę; **to live ~** żyć samemu or samotnie ② **for this reason ~** tylko z tego powodu

IDIOMS. **to go it ~** infml działać w pojedynkę

along /ə'lɒŋ/ US ə'lɔ:ŋ/ ▯ *adv* **to push sth ~** pchać coś; **to be running ~** biec; **I'll be ~ in a second** za moment do ciebie dołączę

▯▯ *prep* ① (all along) wzdłuż (czegoś); **there were chairs ~ the wall** wzdłuż ściany stały krzesła ② **to walk ~ the beach** iść plażą; **to look ~ the shelves** rozejrzeć się po półkach; **halfway ~ the path** w pół drogi

▯▯▯ **along with** *prep phr* razem z (kimś), wraz z (kimś)

alongside /ə'lɒŋsaɪd/ US əlɔ:ŋ'saɪd/ ▯ *prep* ① (all along) wzdłuż (czegoś) ② **to draw up ~ sb** *[vehicle]* zatrzymać się przy kimś or obok kogoś

▯▯ *adv* obok

aloud /ə'laʊd/ *adv [read]* na głos; *[think]* głośno

alphabet /'ælfəbet/ *n* alfabet *m*

alphabetically /ælfə'betɪklɪ/ *adv* alfabetycznie

alpine /'ælpaɪn/ *adj* (also **Alpine**) alpejski

Alps /ælps/ *prn pl* **the ~** Alpy *plt*

already /ɔ:l'redɪ/ *adv* już; **it's 10 o'clock ~** jest już dziesiąta; **he's ~ left** już wyszedł

alright /ɔ:l'raɪt/ = **all right**

Alsatian /æl'seɪʃn/ *n* GB (dog) owczarek *m* alzacki; wilczur *m* infml

also /'ɔ:lsəʊ/ *adv* również, także

alter /'ɔ:ltə(r)/ ▯ *vt* ① zmieni|ć, -áć *[document, outlook, climate, rule]*; odmieni|ć, -áć *[person]* ② prze|robić, -abiać *[dress, skirt]*

▯▯ *vi* zmieni|ć, -áć się; *[person]* odmieni|ć, -áć się

alteration /ɔ:ltə'reɪʃn/ ▯ *n* (to building) przebudowa *f*; (to text, plan, timetable) zmiana *f*

▯▯ **alterations** *npl* (building work) przeróbki *f pl* (**to sth** czegoś)

alternate ▯ /ɔ:l'tɜ:nət/ *adj* ① (successive) *[chapters, layers]* kolejny ② (every other) co drugi; **on ~ days** co drugi dzień ③ US (other) alternatywny

▯▯ /'ɔ:ltəneɪt/ *vt* zmieniać; **he ~d a grey suit and a brown suit each day** jednego dnia zakładał szary garnitur, a następnego brązowy

▯▯▯ /'ɔ:ltəneɪt/ *vi [people]* wymieni|ć, -áć się; *[colours, patterns, seasons]* zmieniać się kolejno

alternately /ɔ:l'tɜ:nətlɪ/ *adv* na przemian

alternative /ɔ:l'tɜ:nətɪv/ ▯ *n* (from two) druga możliwość *f*; (from several) inna możliwość *f*; **to have no ~** nie mieć wyboru or alternatywy

▯▯ *adj* ① *[date, flight, plan]* drugi, inny (do wyboru); *[accommodation, product]* zastępczy; *[solution]* alternatywny ② (unconventional) *[culture, theatre]* alternatywny; *[lifestyle]* niekonwencjonalny

alternatively /ɔːlˈtɜːnətɪvlɪ/ *adv* ewentualnie; ~, **you can book by phone** można też zarezerwować telefonicznie

alternative medicine *n* medycyna *f* alternatywna

although /ɔːlˈðəʊ/ *conj* (po)mimo że

altitude /ˈæltɪtjuːd, US -tuːd/ *n* wysokość *f* (nad poziomem morza)

alto /ˈæltəʊ/ *n* (voice) (female) kontralt *m*; (male) tenor *m* altowy, kontratenor *m*

altogether /ɔːltəˈɡeðə(r)/ *adv* ① (completely) całkiem, zupełnie; **not** ~ **true** nie całkiem prawdziwy ② (in total) razem, w sumie; **how much is that** ~**?** ile to jest razem?

aluminium foil *n* folia *f* aluminiowa

always /ˈɔːlweɪz/ *adv* zawsze; **he's** ~ **complaining** zawsze narzeka

Alzheimer's disease *n* choroba *f* Alzheimera

am *adv* = **ante meridiem** przed południem; **three** ~ trzecia rano or nad ranem

amalgamate /əˈmælɡəmeɪt/ ① *vt* połączyć *[companies, schools]* (**with sth** z czymś)
② *vi [company, union]* połączyć się (**with sth** z czymś)

amateur /ˈæmətə(r)/ ① *n* amator *m*, -ka *f*
② *adj [sport]* amatorski; **an** ~ **boxer/musician** bokser/muzyk amator

amaze /əˈmeɪz/ *vt* zdumie|ć, -wać

amazed /əˈmeɪzd/ *adj* zdumiony; **I'm** ~ **(that)...** dziwię się, że...

amazement /əˈmeɪzmənt/ *n* zdumienie *n*

amazing /əˈmeɪzɪŋ/ *adj [person, chance]* niezwykły; *[achievement, reaction]* zdumiewający; *[film, success]* niewiarygodny

Amazon /ˈæməzən, US -zɒn/ *prn* Amazonka *f*

ambassador /æmˈbæsədə(r)/ *n* ambasador *m*

amber /ˈæmbə(r)/ *n* ① (resin) bursztyn *m*; (colour) (kolor *m*) złocistożółty *m*, (kolor *m*) bursztynowy *m* ② GB (traffic light) żółte światło *n*

ambiguous /æmˈbɪɡjʊəs/ *adj* (with two meanings) dwuznaczny; (with more than two meanings) wieloznaczny

ambition /æmˈbɪʃn/ *n* (quality) ambicja *f* (**to do sth** żeby coś zrobić); (aim) pragnienie *n* (**to do sth** żeby coś zrobić)

ambitious /æmˈbɪʃəs/ *adj* ambitny

ambulance /ˈæmbjʊləns/ *n* karetka *f* pogotowia ratunkowego; ~ **crew** obsada karetki

ambush /ˈæmbʊʃ/ ① *n* zasadzka *f*
② *vt* z|robić zasadzkę na (kogoś/coś)

amenable /əˈmiːnəbl/ ~ **to sth** *[person]* otwarty na coś *[reason, argument]*

amend /əˈmend/ *vt* wn|ieść, -osić poprawki do (czegoś) *[law]*; wprowadz|ić, -ać zmiany do (czegoś) *[document]*

amendment /əˈmendmənt/ *n* (to law) nowelizacja *f*; (to contract) poprawka *f*

amends /əˈmendz/ *npl* **to make** ~ **for sth** wynagrodzić coś *[damage, hurt]* (**to sb** komuś)

America /əˈmerɪkə/ *prn* Ameryka *f*

American /əˈmerɪkən/ ① *n* ① (person) Amerykan|in *m*, -nka *f* ② (also ~ **English**) amerykańska odmiana *f* języka angielskiego
② *adj* amerykański

American Indian *n* Indian|in *m*, -ka *f*

amiable /ˈeɪmɪəbl/ *adj* życzliwy (**to sb** wobec kogoś)

amicable /ˈæmɪkəbl/ *adj* (friendly) przyjacielski; **an** ~ **settlement** ugoda

amiss /əˈmɪs/ ① *adj* **there is something** ~ coś nie jest w porządku
② *adv* **to take sth** ~ poczuć się urażonym czymś

ammunition /ˌæmjʊˈnɪʃn/ *n* amunicja *f*

amnesty /ˈæmnəstɪ/ *n* amnestia *f*

among /əˈmʌŋ/, **amongst** /əˈmʌŋst/ *prep* ① (amidst) wśród (kogoś/czegoś); **to be** ~ **friends** być wśród przyjaciół ② (one of) **it is** ~ **the world's poorest countries** to jeden z najbiedniejszych krajów świata; **she was** ~ **those who survived** była jedną z ocalałych; **to be** ~ **the best** być wśród najlepszych ③ (between) między (kimś)

amount /əˈmaʊnt/ *n* (of goods, food) ilość *f*; (of people, objects) liczba *f*; (of money) kwota *f*; **the full** ~ pełna kwota
■ **amount to**: ① wyn|ieść, -osić *[total]* ② (be equivalent to) być równoznacznym z czymś *[betrayal, confession]*; **it** ~**s to the same thing** to na jedno wychodzi

amp /æmp/ *n* ① = **ampere** amper *m* ② infml = **amplifier** wzmacniacz *m*

amphetamine /æmˈfetəmiːn/ *n* amfetamina *f*

ample /ˈæmpl/ *adj* ① *[provisions]* dostatecznie duży; *[resources]* obfity; **there's** ~ **room** jest dość miejsca ② *[garment]* obszerny; *[bosom]* obfity

amplifier /ˈæmplɪfaɪə(r)/ *n* wzmacniacz *m*

amputate /ˈæmpjʊteɪt/ *vt* amputować *[arm, leg]*

amuse /əˈmjuːz/ ① *vt* ① (cause laughter) rozbawi|ć, -ać, bawić; **she was** ~**d at** or **by his jokes** rozśmieszyły ją jego dowcipy ② (entertain) *[game, story]* dostarcz|yć, -ać rozrywki (komuś) ③ (occupy) *[activity, hobby]* zaj|ąć, -mować
② *vr* **to** ~ **oneself** ① (entertain) bawić się ② (occupy) zaj|ąć, -mować się

amusement /əˈmjuːzmənt/ *n* ① (mirth) rozbawienie *n* ② (diversion) rozrywka *f*

amusement arcade *n* salon *m* gier automatycznych

amusement park *n* wesołe miasteczko *n*

amusing /əˈmjuːzɪŋ/ *adj* zabawny

an /æn, ən/ *indef art.* → **a**

anachronism /əˈnækrənɪzəm/ *n* anachronizm *m*; (old-fashioned) przeżytek *m*

anaemic /əˈniːmɪk/ *adj* Med anemiczny

anaesthetic GB, **anesthetic** US /ˌænɪsˈθetɪk/ n środek m znieczulający

anaesthetize GB, **anesthetize** US /əˈniːsθətaɪz/ vt znieczul|ić, -ać

analogy /əˈnælədʒɪ/ n analogia f

analyse GB, **analyze** US /ˈænəlaɪz/ vt prze|analizować

analysis /əˈnælɪsɪs/ n analiza f

analytic(al) /ˌænəˈlɪtɪk(l)/ adj analityczny

anarchist /ˈænəkɪst/ n anarchist|a m, -ka f

anarchy /ˈænəkɪ/ n anarchia f

anatomy /əˈnætəmɪ/ n anatomia f

ancestor /ˈænsestə(r)/ n przodek m

anchor /ˈæŋkə(r)/ n kotwica f; **to drop** ~ rzucić kotwicę

anchovy /ˈæntʃəvɪ, US ˈæntʃəʊvɪ/ n Zool sardela f; Culin anchois n inv

ancient /ˈeɪnʃənt/ adj (dating from BC) starożytny; (very old) pradawny; ~ **Greek** greka klasyczna; ~ **Greece** starożytna Grecja; ~ **monument** zabytek

and /ænd, ənd, ən, n/ conj i; **cups** ~ **plates** filiżanki i spodki; **he picked up his papers** ~ **went out** pozbierał swoje papiery i wyszedł; **two hundred** ~ **sixty-two** dwieście sześćdziesiąt dwa; **faster** ~ **faster** coraz szybciej

Andorra /ænˈdɔːrə/ prn Andora f

angel /ˈeɪndʒl/ n anioł m

anger /ˈæŋɡə(r)/ [ ] n gniew m, złość f (**at sb/sth** na kogoś/coś)
[ ] vt [words, action] roz|gniewać

angle /ˈæŋɡl/ [ ] n kąt m
[ ] vi [ ] (fish) łowić na wędkę, wędkować [ ] infml **to** ~ **for sth** przymawiać się o coś [compliments, money]

Anglo-French /ˌæŋɡləʊˈfrentʃ/ adj angielsko-francuski

angrily /ˈæŋɡrɪlɪ/ adv [react, speak] gniewnie

angry /ˈæŋɡrɪ/ adj [person] rozgniewany; [expression, words] gniewny; **to be** ~ **with** or **at sb** być złym na kogoś; **to get** ~ rozgniewać się; **to make sb** ~ rozgniewać kogoś

animal /ˈænɪml/ [ ] n zwierzę n
[ ] adj zwierzęcy

animal activist n bojowni|k m, -czka f o prawa zwierząt

animal experiment n doświadczenie n na zwierzętach

animal rights npl prawa n pl zwierząt

animal testing n testowanie n na zwierzętach

animated /ˈænɪmeɪtɪd/ adj [ ] [conversation, group] ożywiony [ ] [cartoon, films] animowany

animator /ˈænɪmeɪtə(r)/ n animator m, -ka f

ankle /ˈæŋkl/ n (part of foot) kostka f

ankle chain n łańcuszek m na kostkę

ankle sock n skarpetka f do kostki

annex [ ] /ˈæneks/ n (also **annexe** GB) (to document) załącznik m; (to building) dobudówka f
[ ] /əˈneks/ vt przyłącz|yć, -ać [land] (**to sth** do czegoś)

annihilate /əˈnaɪəleɪt/ vt z|niszczyć [enemy, city]; wyniszcz|yć, -ać [population]

anniversary /ˌænɪˈvɜːsərɪ/ n rocznica f

annotate /ˈænəteɪt/ vt opat|rzyć, -rywać przypisami

announce /əˈnaʊns/ vt ogł|osić, -aszać; **to** ~ **that...** ogłosić or oznajmić, że...

announcement /əˈnaʊnsmənt/ n ogłoszenie n; (of birth, death) zawiadomienie n

announcer /əˈnaʊnsə(r)/ n spiker m, -ka f

annoy /əˈnɔɪ/ vt [ ] (irritate) z|denerwować [ ] (cause trouble) dokucz|yć, -ać (komuś)

annoyance /əˈnɔɪəns/ n irytacja f (**at sb/sth** z powodu kogoś/czegoś)

annoyed /əˈnɔɪd/ adj poirytowany (**at** or **by sth** czymś); zły (**at** or **by sth** z powodu czegoś); ~ **with sb** zdenerwowany na kogoś

annoying /əˈnɔɪŋ/ adj irytujący

annual /ˈænjʊəl/ [ ] n [ ] (book) rocznik m [ ] (plant) roślina f jednoroczna
[ ] adj [event, meeting] doroczny; [leave, holiday] coroczny; [income, budget] roczny

annually /ˈænjʊəlɪ/ adv [earn, produce] rocznie; [inspect] corocznie

anomaly /əˈnɒməlɪ/ n nieprawidłowość f, anomalia f

anonymous /əˈnɒnɪməs/ adj anonimowy

anorak /ˈænəræk/ n anorak m

anorexia /ˌænəˈreksɪə/ n Med (also ~ **nervosa**) jadłowstręt m psychiczny

another /əˈnʌðə(r)/ [ ] det [ ] (an additional) jeszcze jeden; **would you like** ~ **drink?** masz ochotę na jeszcze jednego (drinka)?; **that will cost you** ~ **£5** to cię będzie kosztować dodatkowych 5 funtów; **without** ~ **word** bez (jednego) słowa; **in** ~ **five weeks** za następne pięć tygodni [ ] (a different) inny; ~ **time** innym razem; **he has** ~ **job now** ma teraz inną pracę
[ ] pron inny, drugi; **one after** ~ jeden po or za drugim; **in one way or** ~ w taki lub inny sposób

answer /ˈɑːnsə(r), US ˈænsər/ [ ] n (reply) odpowiedź f (**to sth** na coś); (to difficulty, puzzle) rozwiązanie n (**to sth** czegoś); **there's no** ~ (to door) nikt nie otwiera; (on phone) nikt nie odbiera; **the right/wrong** ~ dobra/zła odpowiedź
[ ] vt odpowi|edzieć, -adać na (coś) [letter, question]; odpowi|edzieć, -adać (komuś) [person]; **to** ~ **the door** otworzyć drzwi; **to** ~ **the telephone** odebrać telefon
[ ] vi [ ] odpowi|edzieć, -adać; **to** ~ **to a description** odpowiadać opisowi [ ] (be accountable) **to** ~ **to sb** odpowiadać przed kimś

■ **answer back:** (defend oneself) bronić się; (impertinently) odszczekiwać się infml

■ **answer for**: odpowie|dzieć, -adać za (coś) *[action]*; **they have a lot to ~ for!** niejedno mają na sumieniu!

answerable /'ɑːnsərəbl, US 'æns-/ *adj* odpowiedzialny (**to sb/for sth** przed kimś/za coś)

answering machine *n* automatyczna sekretarka *f*

ant /ænt/ *n* mrówka *f*

antagonize /æn'tægənaɪz/ *vt* zra|zić, -żać; (stronger) z|antagonizować

Antarctic /æn'tɑːktɪk/ **I** *prn* **the ~** Antarktyka *f* **II** *adj* antarktyczny

antelope /'æntɪləʊp/ *n* antylopa *f*

antenatal /ˌæntɪ'neɪtl/ *adj* (of woman) przedporodowy; (of foetus) przedurodzeniowy

antenatal class *n* GB szkoła *f* rodzenia

antenna /æn'tenə/ *n* [1] (animal organ) czułek *m* [2] (aerial) antena *f*

anthropology /ˌænθrə'pɒlədʒɪ/ *n* antropologia *f*

anti /'æntɪ/ **I** *prep* przeciw **II** **anti+** *in combinations* anty-, przeciw-

antibacterial /ˌæntɪbæk'tɪərɪəl/ *adj* przeciwbakteryjny

antibiotic /ˌæntɪbaɪ'ɒtɪk/ *n* antybiotyk *m*; **to be on ~s** brać antybiotyki

anticipate /æn'tɪsɪpeɪt/ *vt* [1] (foresee) przewi|dzieć, -dywać *[delay, problem]*; **as ~d** jak przewidywano [2] (guess in advance) odgad|nąć, -ywać, uprzedz|ić, -ać *[needs, results]* [3] (pre-empt) uprzedz|ić, -ać *[person, act]*

anticipation /ænˌtɪsɪ'peɪʃn/ *n* [1] (excitement) niecierpliwość *f*; (pleasure in advance) niecierpliwe wyczekiwanie *n* [2] (expectation) oczekiwanie *n*

anticlimax /ˌæntɪ'klaɪmæks/ *n* rozczarowanie *n*

anticlockwise /ˌæntɪ'klɒkwaɪz/ GB **I** *adj* przeciwny do ruchu wskazówek zegara **II** *adv* przeciwnie do ruchu wskazówek zegara

antidepressant /ˌæntɪdɪ'presnt/ *n* środek *m* przeciwdepresyjny

antidote /'æntɪdəʊt/ *n* odtrutka *f*; antidotum *n* (**to** or **for sth** przeciw czemuś)

antihistamine /ˌæntɪ'hɪstəmɪn/ *n* antyhistamina *f*

antique /æn'tiːk/ **I** *n* (object) staroć *f*; (furniture) antyk *m* **II** *adj* (old) zabytkowy; (from ancient times) starożytny

antique shop *n* sklep *m* z antykami

anti-Semitism /ˌæntɪ'semɪtɪzəm/ *n* antysemityzm *m*

antiseptic /ˌæntɪ'septɪk/ **I** *n* środek *m* antyseptyczny **II** *adj* antyseptyczny

antisocial /ˌæntɪ'səʊʃl/ *adj* [1] **~ behaviour** postawa aspołeczna; (criminal behaviour) zachowanie przestępcze [2] (reclusive) nietowarzyski

anti-theft /ˌæntɪ'θeft/ *adj* *[lock, device]* przeciwwłamaniowy

antlers /'æntləz/ *npl* poroże *n*

anxiety /æŋ'zaɪətɪ/ *n* [1] (worry) niepokój *m*, obawa *f* (**about** or **for sb/sth** o kogoś/coś); **to be in a state of high ~** bardzo się niepokoić [2] (eagerness) pragnienie *n* (**to do sth** zrobienia czegoś) [3] (in psychology) lęk *m*

anxious /'æŋkʃəs/ *adj* [1] (worried) *[person, expression]* zaniepokojony (**for sb** o kogoś); *[enquiry, request]* pełen niepokoju (**about sb/sth** o kogoś/coś); **to be ~ about doing sth** bać się coś robić [2] *[moment, time]* pełen niepokoju [3] (eager) **I am ~ for him to know** bardzo mi zależy, żeby wiedział

anxiously /'æŋkʃəslɪ/ *adv* [1] (worriedly) z niepokojem [2] (eagerly) z niecierpliwością

any /'enɪ/ *det* [1] (in questions, conditional sentences) **is there ~ tea?** jest herbata?; **if you have ~ money** jeśli masz jakieś pieniądze [2] (with negative) **I don't need ~ advice** nie potrzebuję żadnych rad [3] (no matter which) każdy; **you can have ~ cup you like** możesz wziąć jakąkolwiek filiżankę; **I'm ready to help in ~ way I can** gotów jestem zrobić wszystko, żeby pomóc; **come round and see me ~ time** wpadnij do mnie, kiedy tylko zechcesz **II** *pron* [1] (in questions, conditional sentences) **have ~ of you got a car?** czy ktoś z was ma samochód? [2] (with negative) **he hasn't got ~** nie ma (wcale); **there is hardly ~ left** prawie nic nie zostało; **she doesn't like ~ of them** nie lubi żadnego/żadnej (z nich) [3] (no matter which) którykolwiek; **'which colour would you like?' – ' ~ '** „który kolor chciałbyś?" – „którykolwiek"; **~ of them could do it** każdy z nich mógł to zrobić **III** *adv* **have you got ~ more of these?** masz jeszcze takie or więcej takich?; **do you want ~ more wine?** chcesz jeszcze wina?; **he doesn't live here ~ more** (on) już tu nie mieszka

anybody /'enɪbɒdɪ/ *pron* (also **anyone**) [1] (in questions, conditional sentences) ktoś; **is there ~ in the house?** czy jest ktoś w domu?; **if ~ asks, tell them I've gone out** gdyby ktoś pytał, powiedz, że wyszedłem [2] (with negative) nikt; **there wasn't ~ in the house** w domu nie było nikogo; **I didn't have ~ to talk to** nie miałem z kim porozmawiać [3] (no matter who) każdy; **~ could do it** każdy mógłby to zrobić; **~ who wants to, can go** każdy, kto chce, może pójść; **~ but you would have given it to him** każdy, oprócz ciebie, dałby mu to; **~ can make a mistake** każdemu zdarza się zrobić błąd; **~ would think you were deaf** można by pomyśleć, że jesteś głuchy

anyhow /'enɪhaʊ/ *adv* [1] = **anyway** [2] (carelessly) byle jak

anyone /'enɪwʌn/ *pron* = **anybody**

anything /'enɪθɪŋ/ *pron* [1] (in questions, conditional sentences) coś, cokolwiek; **is there ~ to be done?**

czy można coś zrobić? ② (with negative) nic; **she didn't say** ~ nic nie powiedziała; **he didn't have** ~ **to do** nie miał nic do roboty; **don't believe** ~ **he says** nie wierz niczemu, co mówi ③ (no matter what) wszystko; ~ **is possible** wszystko jest możliwe; **he was** ~ **but happy** wcale nie był szczęśliwy

anytime /'enɪtaɪm/ *adv* (also **any time**) ~ **after 2 pm** o każdej porze po czternastej; ~ **you like** kiedy (tylko) zechcesz; **he could arrive** ~ **now** może przyjechać w każdej chwili

anyway /'enɪweɪ/ *adv* ① (in any case) (also **anyhow**) w każdym razie, i tak; (besides) poza tym ② (all the same) jednak(że), mimo to; **I don't really like hats, but I'll try it on** ~ nie lubię kapeluszy, mimo to zmierzę go; **thanks** ~ mimo wszystko dziękuję ③ (at any rate) w każdym razie; **we can't go out, not yet** ~ nie możemy wyjść, w każdym razie jeszcze nie teraz ④ (well) ~**, we arrived at the station...** więc przyjechaliśmy na stację...

anywhere /'enɪweə(r), US -hweər/ *adv* ① (in questions, conditional sentences) gdzieś; **we're going to Spain, if** ~ jeśli w ogóle gdziekolwiek pojedziemy, to do Hiszpanii ② (with negative) nigdzie; **you can't go** ~ nigdzie nie pójdziesz; **there isn't** ~ **to sit** nie ma gdzie usiąść; **they didn't go** ~ **this weekend** nigdzie nie pojechali w ten weekend; **you won't get** ~ **if you don't pass your exams** fig do niczego nie dojdziesz, jeśli nie zdasz egzaminów; **crying isn't going to get you** ~ fig płacz nic ci nie pomoże ③ (no matter where) ~ **you like** gdzie tylko or gdziekolwiek zechcesz; ~ **in England** gdziekolwiek w Anglii

apart /ə'pɑːt/ **I** *adj, adv* ① (at a distance) **trees planted 10 metres** ~ drzewa posadzone co 10 metrów; **he stood** ~ **(from the group)** stał or trzymał się z dala (od grupy) ② (separated) **we hate being** ~ nie znosimy się rozstawać; **they need to be kept** ~ należy ich trzymać z dala od siebie

II apart from *prep phr* ① (separate from) osobno; **it stands** ~ **from the other houses** stoi z dala od innych domów; **he lives** ~ **from his wife** nie mieszka razem z żoną ② (leaving aside) pomijając (kogoś/coś), poza (kimś/czymś); ~ **from being illegal, it is also dangerous** to nie tylko nielegalne, ale i niebezpieczne

apartheid /ə'pɑːtheɪt, -aɪt/ *n* apartheid *m*
apartment /ə'pɑːtmənt/ *n* mieszkanie *n*
apartment block *n* blok *m* mieszkalny
apartment house *n* US dom *m* mieszkalny
apathetic /ˌæpə'θetɪk/ *adj* apatyczny
apex /'eɪpeks/ *n* (of triangle) wierzchołek *m*; fig szczyt *m*
apologetic /əˌpɒlə'dʒetɪk/ *adj* [*gesture*] przepraszający; [*letter*] z przeprosinami; **to be** ~ **about sth** przepraszać za coś

apologize /ə'pɒlədʒaɪz/ *vi* przepr|osić, -aszać (**to sb for doing sth** kogoś za zrobienie czegoś)
apology /ə'pɒlədʒɪ/ *n* przeprosiny *plt*; **to make an** ~ **(to sb) for sth/doing sth** przeprosić (kogoś) za coś/za zrobienie czegoś
apostrophe /ə'pɒstrəfɪ/ *n* apostrof *m*
appal GB, **appall** US /ə'pɔːl/ *vt* (shock) z|bulwersować; (horrify, dismay) przera|zić, -żać
appalling /ə'pɔːlɪŋ/ *adj* ① [*crime, conditions*] przerażający ② [*headache, manners, noise, weather*] okropny, potworny
apparatus /ˌæpə'reɪtəs, US -'rætəs/ *n* sprzęt *m*; (in lab, gym) przyrząd *m*
apparent /ə'pærənt/ *adj* ① (seeming) [*contradiction, willingness*] pozorny ② (clear) oczywisty; **for no** ~ **reason** bez wyraźnego or widocznego powodu
apparently /ə'pærəntlɪ/ *adv* ① (seemingly) pozornie ② (as it appears) widocznie ③ (in fact) faktycznie
appeal /ə'piːl/ **I** *n* ① (call) apel *m* (**for sth** o coś); (in law) apelacja *f*, odwołanie *n* ② (attraction) atrakcyjność *f*, wdzięk *m*; **it holds no** ~ **for me** to mnie nie interesuje

II *vi* ① (in law) odwoł|ać, -ywać się (**against sth** od czegoś) ② Sport **to** ~ **to the referee** odwołać się do arbitra; **to** ~ **against a decision** odwołać się od decyzji ③ (call, request) za|apelować (**to sb for sth** do kogoś o coś) ④ (attract) **to** ~ **to sb** [*idea*] przemawiać do kogoś; [*person, place*] podobać się komuś

appeal fund *n* fundusz *m* pomocy
appealing /ə'piːlɪŋ/ *adj* ① (attractive) [*child, picture*] uroczy; [*plan*] interesujący; [*modesty*] czarujący ② [*look*] błagalny
appear /ə'pɪə(r)/ *vi* ① (become visible) pojawi|ć, -ać się; [*ghost*] ukaz|ać, -ywać się ② (turn up) zjawi|ć, -ać się ③ (seem) wyda|ć, -wać się; **it** ~ **s that...** wygląda na to, że... ④ [*article, book, work*] ukaz|ać, -ywać się ⑤ **to** ~ **on stage** występować na scenie; **to** ~ **on TV** występować w telewizji ⑥ (in law) **to** ~ **in court** stawić się w sądzie
appearance /ə'pɪərəns/ *n* ① (arrival) (of person, vehicle, invention) pojawienie się *n* ② (on TV, in play, film) występ *m* ③ (look) wygląd *m*; **to judge** or **go by** ~ **s** sądzić po pozorach
appendicitis /əˌpendɪ'saɪtɪs/ *n* zapalenie *n* wyrostka robaczkowego
appendix /ə'pendɪks/ *n* wyrostek *m* robaczkowy; **to have one's** ~ **removed** mieć operację wyrostka
appetite /'æpɪtaɪt/ *n* apetyt *m*
appetite suppressant *n* środek *m* zmniejszający łaknienie
appetizer /'æpɪtaɪzə(r)/ *n* (food) przystawka *f*; (drink) aperitif *m*
appetizing /'æpɪtaɪzɪŋ/ *adj* apetyczny
applaud /ə'plɔːd/ **I** *vt* oklaskiwać [*performance*]
II *vi* bić brawo or brawa

applause /ə'plɔːz/ *n* brawa *plt*, oklaski *plt*; **there was a burst of** ~ zerwała się burza oklasków

apple /'æpl/ *n* jabłko *n*

applecore *n* ogryzek *m*

apple tree *n* jabłoń *f*

appliance /ə'plaɪəns/ *n* urządzenie *n*; **household** ~**s** sprzęt gospodarstwa domowego

applicant /'æplɪkənt/ *n* (for job) kandydat *m*, -ka *f*; (for benefit, loan, passport, citizenship, membership) ubiegając|y *m*, -a *f* się

application /ˌæplɪ'keɪʃn/ *n* [1] podanie *n* (**for sth** o coś) [2] (of ointment) posmarowanie *n* [3] (of law, penalty, rule) zastosowanie *n*

application form *n* formularz *m*; (for membership) podanie *n*

apply /ə'plaɪ/ **I** *vt* za|astosować *[rule, method]* (**to sth** do czegoś, w czymś); **to** ~ **pressure** naciskać **II** *vi* [1] **to** ~ **for sth** wystąpić o coś; **to** ~ **to a college** starać się or ubiegać się o przyjęcie na uczelnię [2] (be valid) *[ban, penalty, rule]* obowiązywać; *[definition, term]* mieć zastosowanie [3] (contact) **to** ~ **to sb/sth** zwrócić się do kogoś/czegoś **III** *vr* **to** ~ **oneself** przykładać się (**to sth** do czegoś)

appoint /ə'pɔɪnt/ *vt* [1] mianować *[person]*; **to** ~ **sb as director** or **to the position of director** mianować kogoś dyrektorem or na stanowisko dyrektora [2] wyznacz|yć, -ać *[date, place]*

appointment /ə'pɔɪntmənt/ *n* [1] (meeting) spotkanie *n* (**with sb** z kimś); (with doctor) wizyta *f* (**at** or **with sb** u kogoś); **business** ~ spotkanie w sprawach zawodowych; **to make an** ~ umówić się [2] (to post) mianowanie *n*

appraisal /ə'preɪzl/ *n* ocena *f*

appreciate /ə'priːʃɪeɪt/ **I** *vt* [1] być wdzięcznym za (coś) *[kindness, help]*; doceni|ć, -ać *[effort]*; **I'd** ~ **it if you could reply soon** będę or byłbym wdzięczny za szybką odpowiedź [2] (realize) zda|ć, -wać sobie sprawę z (czegoś) [3] (enjoy) doceni|ć, -ać *[music, art, food]* **II** *vi* *[object]* zysk|ać, -iwać na wartości; *[value]* wzr|osnąć, -astać

appreciation /əˌpriːʃɪ'eɪʃn/ *n* [1] (gratitude) wdzięczność *f* (**for sth** za coś) [2] (enjoyment) upodobanie *n* (**of sth** do czegoś) [3] (increase) wzrost *m* (**of** or **in sth** czegoś)

appreciative /ə'priːʃətɪv/ *adj* [1] (grateful) pełen wdzięczności (**of sth** za coś) [2] *[look, smile]* pełen zachwytu; *[comment]* pochwalny

apprehensive /ˌæprɪ'hensɪv/ *adj* pełen obaw; **to be** ~ **about sth** (fearful) obawiać się czegoś; (worried) niepokoić się o coś; **to be** ~ **about doing sth** bać się coś zrobić

apprentice /ə'prentɪs/ *n* praktykant *m*, -ka *f*, ucze|ń *m*, -nnica *f* (**to sb** u kogoś)

apprenticeship /ə'prentɪsʃɪp/ *n* praktyka *f*; (with craftsman) nauka *f* zawodu

approach /ə'prəʊtʃ/ **I** *n* [1] (access) dojście *n*, dostęp *m*; (to town, island) dojazd *m* [2] (arrival) nadejście *n* [3] (to problem) podejście *n* [4] **to make** ~**es to sb** zwrócić się do kogoś **II** *vt* [1] (draw near to) zbliż|yć, -ać się do (kogoś/czegoś) *[person, place]*; **he is** ~**ing sixty** zbliża się do sześćdziesiątki [2] (deal with) pod|ejść, -chodzić do (czegoś) *[problem, subject]* [3] **to** ~ **sb (about sth)** zwr|ócić, -acać się do kogoś (w związku z czymś or w sprawie czegoś) **III** *vi* *[person]* pod|ejść, -chodzić; *[car]* podje|chać, -żdżać; *[event, season]* zbliż|yć, -ać się

approachable /ə'prəʊtʃəbl/ *adj* *[person]* przystępny; *[place]* dostępny

appropriate **I** /ə'prəʊprɪət/ *adj* [1] *[behaviour, place, gift, authority]* odpowiedni; *[remark]* stosowny; *[punishment]* adekwatny; ~ **for** or **to sth** odpowiedni do czegoś *[needs, situation]*; odpowiedni na coś *[occasion]* [2] *[name, choice]* trafny **II** /ə'prəʊprɪeɪt/ *vt* [1] przywłaszcz|yć, -ać sobie *[car, property]*; zawłaszcz|yć, -ać *[land]* [2] przeznacz|yć, -ać, przyzna|ć, -wać *[funds]* (**for sth** na coś)

appropriately /ə'prəʊprɪətlɪ/ *adv* [1] *[behave, speak, dress]* stosownie [2] *[chosen, designed, sited]* właściwie, trafnie

approval /ə'pruːvl/ *n* aprobata *f* (**of sth** czegoś, dla czegoś); **on** ~ na próbę (*z prawem odbiorcy do zwrotu*)

approve /ə'pruːv/ **I** *vt* zatwierdz|ić, -ać *[decision, plan]*; (accept) za|aprobować **II** *vi* **to** ~ **of sb/sth** sprzyjać komuś/czemuś; **he doesn't** ~ **of drinking** nie pochwala picia (alkoholu)

approving /ə'pruːvɪŋ/ *adj* aprobujący, pełen aprobaty

approximate /ə'prɒksɪmət/ *adj* *[date, value]* przybliżony

approximately /ə'prɒksɪmətlɪ/ *adv* [1] (about) około, w przybliżeniu; **at** ~ **7.30 am** około 7.30 rano [2] *[correct, equal]* prawie

apricot /'eɪprɪkɒt/ *n* morela *f*

April /'eɪprɪl/ *n* kwiecień *m*

April Fools' Day *n* prima aprilis *n inv*

apron /'eɪprən/ *n* fartuch *m*

apt /æpt/ *adj* *[choice, description]* trafny, stosowny (**to** or **for sth** do czegoś)

aptitude /'æptɪtjuːd, *US* -tuːd/ *n* uzdolnienie *n* (**for** or **to sth** do czegoś)

aquarium /ə'kweərɪəm/ *n* akwarium *n*

Aquarius /ə'kweərɪəs/ *n* Wodnik *m*

aquatic /ə'kwætɪk/ *adj* wodny

aqueduct /'ækwɪdʌkt/ *n* akwedukt *m*

Arab /'ærəb/ **I** *n* Arab *m*, -ka *f* **II** *adj* arabski

Arabic /'ærəbɪk/ **I** *n* (language) (język *m*) arabski *m* **II** *adj* arabski

Arab-Israeli /ˌærəbɪz'reɪlɪ/ adj arabsko-izraelski

arbitrary /'ɑ:bɪtrərɪ, US 'ɑ:rbɪtrerɪ/ adj (random) przypadkowy; (dictatorial) arbitralny

arbitration /ˌɑ:bɪ'treɪʃn/ n arbitraż m; **to go to** ~ odwołać się do arbitrażu

arcade /ɑ:'keɪd/ n arkada f; **shopping** ~ pasaż handlowy

arch /ɑ:tʃ/ **[I]** n łuk m, łęk m

[II] vt wygi|ać, -nąć w łuk or pałąk; **the cat** ~**ed its back** kot wygiął grzbiet w pałąk or łuk

archaeologist GB, **archeologist** US /ˌɑ:kɪ'ɒlədʒɪst/ n archeolog m

archaeology GB, **archeology** US /ˌɑ:kɪ'ɒlədʒɪ/ n archeologia f

archery /'ɑ:tʃərɪ/ n łucznictwo n

architect /'ɑ:kɪtekt/ n architekt m

architecture /'ɑ:kɪtektʃə(r)/ n architektura f

archive /'ɑ:kaɪv/ n archiwum n

Arctic /'ɑ:ktɪk/ **[I]** n **the** ~ Arktyka f

[II] adj [climate, animal, expedition] arktyczny; [equipment, clothes] polarny

ardent /'ɑ:dnt/ adj [revolutionary, supporter] żarliwy, gorliwy; [defence, opposition] zaciekły

area /'eərɪə/ n **[1]** (region) obszar m; (zone) rejon m; (district) dzielnica f; **residential** ~ dzielnica mieszkaniowa; **in the London** ~ w rejonie Londynu **[2]** (in building) **dining** ~ jadalnia; **this is the non-smoking** ~ tu się nie pali; **waiting** ~ poczekalnia **[3]** (of knowledge) dziedzina f; (of business) obszar m **[4]** (in geometry) pole n; (of land) powierzchnia f

area code n numer m kierunkowy

arena /ə'ri:nə/ n arena f

Argentina /ˌɑ:dʒən'ti:nə/ prn Argentyna f

argue /'ɑ:gju:/ **[I]** vt **[1]** debatować nad (czymś) **[2]** **to** ~ **that...** utrzymywać or twierdzić, że...

[II] vi **[1]** (quarrel) spierać się (**about** or **over sth** o coś) **[2]** (debate) dyskutować (**about sth** o czymś) **[3]** (put one's case) argumentować; **to** ~ **in favour of/against doing sth** przedstawić argumenty za zrobieniem/przeciw zrobieniu czegoś

argument /'ɑ:gjʊmənt/ n **[1]** (quarrel) spór m, sprzeczka f (**about sth** o coś); **to have an** ~ pokłócić się z kimś **[2]** (discussion) polemika f (**about sth** na temat czegoś) **[3]** (case) argument m (**for/against sth** za czymś/przeciwko czemuś)

argumentative /ˌɑ:gjʊ'mentətɪv/ adj kłótliwy

Aries /'eəri:z/ n Baran m

arise /ə'raɪz/ vi **[1]** [problem] pojawi|ć, -ać się; [question] nasu|nąć, -wać się; **if the need** ~**s** jeśli zajdzie potrzeba **[2]** (be the result of) wynikać (**from sth** z czegoś); być wynikiem (**from sth** czegoś)

aristocrat /'ærɪstəkræt, US ə'rɪst-/ n arystokra-t|a m, -ka f

arithmetic /ə'rɪθmətɪk/ n arytmetyka f

arm /ɑ:m/ **[I]** n ramię n, ręka f; (of chair) poręcz f; ~ **in** ~ pod rękę; **to have a towel over one's** ~

mieć ręcznik przewieszony przez rękę; **to have a book under one's** ~ mieć książkę pod pachą; **to fold one's** ~**s** skrzyżować ręce (na piersiach)

[II] **arms** npl (weapons) broń f

[III] vt Mil uzbr|oić, -ajać, zbroić

(IDIOMS) **to keep sb at** ~**'s length** trzymać kogoś na dystans

armaments npl zbrojenia plt

armband /'ɑ:mbænd/ n (for swimmer) pływaczek m (zakładany na ramię); (for mourner) czarna opaska f

armchair /'ɑ:mtʃeə(r)/ n fotel m

armed /ɑ:md/ adj uzbrojony (**with sth** w coś); [raid] zbrojny; [robbery] z bronią w ręku

armed forces, armed services npl siły plt zbrojne

armour GB, **armor** US /'ɑ:mə(r)/ n **a suit of** ~ zbroja f

armoured GB, **armored** US /'ɑ:məd/ adj [regiment] pancerny; [vehicle] opancerzony

armour-plated GB, **armor-plated** US /ˌɑ:mə'pleɪtɪd/ adj [ship] pancerny; [vehicle] opancerzony

armpit /'ɑ:mpɪt/ n pacha f

arms control n kontrola f zbrojeń

arms race n wyścig m zbrojeń

arms treaty n traktat m rozbrojeniowy

army /'ɑ:mɪ/ **[I]** n wojska n pl, armia f; (military service) wojsko n; **to join the** ~ zaciągnąć się do wojska

[II] adj wojskowy

aroma /ə'rəʊmə/ n aromat m

aromatherapy /əˌrəʊmə'θerəpɪ/ n aromaterapia f

around /ə'raʊnd/ **[I]** adv **[1]** (approximately) około; **at** ~ **3 pm** około trzeciej po południu **[2]** (in the vicinity) **to be (somewhere)** ~ być (gdzieś) tutaj; **are they** ~? czy oni są gdzieś tutaj? **[3]** (in circulation) **CDs have been** ~ **for years** płyty kompaktowe istnieją już od lat; **one of the most gifted musicians** ~ obecnie jeden z najdzielniejszych muzyków **[4]** **all** ~ wszędzie; **the only garage for miles** ~ jedyny warsztat samochodowy w promieniu wielu kilometrów **[5]** **to ask sb to come** ~ zaprosić kogoś do siebie

[II] prep **[1]** (on all sides of) wokół (czegoś) [fire, table]; **the villages** ~ **Dublin** wioski wokół Dublina; **clothes scattered** ~ **the room** ubrania porozrzucane po całym pokoju; **(all)** ~ **the world** (wszędzie) na całym świecie; **to walk** ~ **the town** przejść się po mieście; **the people** ~ **here** tutejsi ludzie **[2]** (at) ~ **midnight** około północy

arouse /ə'raʊz/ vt wzbudz|ić, -ać [anger, interest, jealousy, suspicion]; **to be** ~**d by sth** być czymś podnieconym

arrange /ə'reɪndʒ/ **[I]** vt **[1]** ustawi|ć, -ać [ornaments, furniture]; uł|ożyć, -kładać [flowers, hair]; urządz|ić, -ać [room]; popraw|ić, -ać [garment] **[2]** (organize) urządz|ić, -ać [party]; z|organizować [meeting];

ustal|ić, -ać *[date]*; um|ówić, -awiać *[appointment]*; **to ~ to do sth** postanowić zrobić coś ③ Mus za|aranżować *[piece]*

II *vi* **to ~ for sth** załatwić coś; **to ~ for sb to do sth** ustalić, że ktoś coś zrobi

arrangement /əˈreɪndʒmənt/ *n* ① (of objects) ustawienie *n*; (of flowers) kompozycja *f* ② (agreement) umowa *f*, porozumienie *n*; **to come to an ~** dojść do porozumienia ③ (preparations) plan *m*, przygotowania *plt*; **to make ~s to do sth** poczynić przygotowania do zrobienia czegoś

array /əˈreɪ/ *n* (of goods, products) wybór *m*; asortyment *m* fml; (of objects) szereg *m*

arrears /əˈrɪəz/ *npl* zaległości *plt*; **I'm in ~ with my payments** mam zaległości w płaceniu

arrest /əˈrest/ **I** *n* aresztowanie *n*; **to be under ~** być aresztowanym

II *vt* za|aresztować

arrival /əˈraɪvl/ *n* (of person) przybycie *n*; (of car, train) przyjazd *m*; (of plane) przylot *m*; (of boat) przypłynięcie *n*; (of goods, package, season) nadejście *n*; **on sb's ~** w chwili przybycia kogoś

arrival(s) lounge *n* hala *f* przylotów

arrivals board *n* (at airport) tablica *f* przylotów; (at railway station) tablica *f* przyjazdów

arrival time *n* czas *m* przybycia

arrive /əˈraɪv/ *vi* ① przyby|ć, -wać (**at** or **from sth** do czegoś/z czegoś); (by car, train) przyje|chać, -żdżać; (by plane) przyle|cieć, -atywać ② **~ at** do|jść, -chodzić do (czegoś) *[agreement, conclusion]*; pod|jąć, -ejmować *[decision]*

arrogant /ˈærəgənt/ *adj* arogancki

arrow /ˈærəʊ/ *n* ① (weapon) strzała *f* ② (symbol) strzałka *f*

arson /ˈɑːsn/ *n* podpalenie *n*

arsonist /ˈɑːsənɪst/ *n* podpalacz *m*, -ka *f*

art /ɑːt/ *n* sztuka *f*

artefact /ˈɑːtɪfækt/ *n* przedmiot *m* (kultury materialnej)

artery /ˈɑːtəri/ *n* tętnica *f*

art exhibition *n* (paintings) wystawa *f* obrazów; (sculptures) wystawa *f* rzeźby

art gallery *n* galeria *f* sztuki

arthritis /ɑːˈθraɪtɪs/ *n* artretyzm *m*, zapalenie *n* stawów

artichoke /ˈɑːtɪtʃəʊk/ *n* karczoch *m*

article /ˈɑːtɪkl/ *n* artykuł *m* (**on/about sth** na temat czegoś/o czymś)

artificial /ˌɑːtɪˈfɪʃl/ *adj* sztuczny

artificial limb *n* proteza *f*

artificial respiration *n* sztuczne oddychanie *n*

artillery /ɑːˈtɪləri/ *n* artyleria *f*

artisan /ˌɑːtɪˈzæn, US ˈɑːrtɪzn/ *n* rzemieślnik *m*

artist /ˈɑːtɪst/ *n* artyst|a *m*, -ka *f*

artistic /ɑːˈtɪstɪk/ *adj* artystyczny

arts /ɑːts/ *npl* ① (culture) **the ~** sztuka *f* ② Univ nauki *f pl* humanistyczne ③ **~ and crafts** rzemiosło artystyczne

art school *n* szkoła *f* sztuk pięknych

arts student *n* student *m*, -ka *f* wydziału nauk humanistycznych

art student *n* student *m*, -ka *f* szkoły sztuk pięknych

as /æz, əz/ **I** *conj* ① jak; **as you know** jak (sam) wiesz; **as usual** jak zwykle; **do as I say!** rób, co ci mówię!; **leave it as it is** zostaw to tak, jak jest; **as she grew older** z wiekiem; **as a child, he...** jako dziecko, ... ② (because, since) jako że; **as you were out, I left a note** ponieważ cię nie było, zostawiłem wiadomość ③ (although) choć; **strange as it may seem** choć może się to wydać dziwne; **try as he might, he could not forget it** choć bardzo się starał, nie mógł (o tym) zapomnieć ④ **the same as...** taki sam jak...; **I've got a jacket the same as yours** mam taki sam żakiet jak ty ⑤ **so as to do sth** żeby coś zrobić

II *prep* **dressed as a sailor** w marynarskim ubraniu; **he works as a pilot** pracuje jako pilot; **a job as a teacher** posada nauczyciela; **to treat sb as an equal** traktować kogoś jak równego sobie

III *adv* (in comparisons) **he is as intelligent as you** jest tak samo inteligentny jak ty; **he is just as intelligent as you** jest równie inteligentny jak ty; **as fast as you can** najszybciej jak możesz; **he is twice as strong as me** on jest dwa razy silniejszy ode mnie; **I paid as much as she did** zapłaciłem tyle samo co ona; **as much as possible** jak najwięcej; **as little as possible** jak najmniej; **as soon as possible** jak najszybciej; **they have a house in Nice as well as an apartment in Paris** mają dom w Nicei, a także mieszkanie w Paryżu

IV **as for** *prep phr* co do (kogoś/czegoś), jeśli chodzi o (kogoś/coś)

V **as from, as of** *prep phr* (począwszy) od (czegoś)

VI **as if** *conj phr* jakby, jak gdyby; **it looks as if we've got lost** wygląda na to, że zabłądziliśmy

VII **as long as** *conj phr* tak długo jak, dopóty

VIII **as such** *prep phr* jako taki

IX **as to** *prep phr* co do (kogoś/czegoś), co się tyczy (kogoś/czegoś)

asbestos /æzˈbestɒs, æs-/ *n* azbest *m*

ascend /əˈsend/ *vt* wspi|ąć, -nać się na (coś) *[hill]*; wspi|ąć, -nać się po (czymś) *[steps]*

ascent /əˈsent/ *n* (of gas, smoke) unoszenie się *n*; (of balloon, plane) wznoszenie się *n*

ascertain /ˌæsəˈteɪn/ *vt* upewni|ć, -ać się (**that...** że...)

ash /æʃ/ *n* ① popiół *m* ② (also **~ tree**) jesion *m*

ashamed /əˈʃeɪmd/ adj zawstydzony; **to be ~** wstydzić się (**to do sth** robić coś); **to be ~ that...** wstydzić się (tego), że...

ashen /ˈæʃn/ adj [complexion] ziemisty, szary

ashore /əˈʃɔː(r)/ adv **to go ~** zejść na ląd; **washed ~** wyrzucony na brzeg (przez fale)

ashtray /ˈæʃtreɪ/ n popielniczka f

Asia /ˈeɪʃə, US ˈeɪʒə/ prn Azja f

Asian /ˈeɪʃn, US ˈeɪʒn/ **❚** n Azjat|a m, -ka f
❚❚ adj azjatycki

aside /əˈsaɪd/ **❚** n **to say sth in an ~** powiedzieć coś na stronie
❚❚ adv **to stand ~** stać z boku; **to put sth ~** odłożyć coś; **to take sb ~** wziąć kogoś na stronę
❚❚❚ **aside from** adv phr poza (czymś)

ask /ɑːsk, US æsk/ **❚** vt ① za|pytać o (coś), s|pytać o (coś); **to ~ a question** zadać pytanie; **to ~ sb sth** zapytać kogoś o coś; **to ~ sb to do sth** poprosić kogoś, żeby coś zrobił ② (invite) zapr|osić, -aszać [person]; **to ~ sb to dinner** zaprosić kogoś na kolację
❚❚ vi ① (request) po|prosić ② (make enquiries) pytać (**about sb/sth** o kogoś/coś)
❚❚❚ vr **to ~ oneself** zastanowić się nad (czymś) [reason]
■ **ask after**: dopytywać się o (kogoś)
■ **ask for**: ¶ **~ for [sth]** po|prosić o (coś) ¶ **~ for [sb]** po|prosić o (przywołanie) kogoś; (on telephone) po|prosić

askance /əˈskæns/ adv **to look ~ at sb/sth** (with suspicion) patrzeć na kogoś/coś nieufnie; (with disapproval) patrzeć na kogoś/coś krzywo

askew /əˈskjuː/ **❚** adj przekrzywiony
❚❚ adv krzywo

asking price n cena f sprzedaży

asleep /əˈsliːp/ adj **to be ~** spać; **to fall ~** zasnąć, usnąć; **to be sound** or **fast ~** spać głęboko

asparagus /əˈspærəgəs/ n szparag m

aspect /ˈæspekt/ n ① aspekt m; (angle) punkt m widzenia ② (orientation) **house with the westerly ~** dom z zachodnią elewacją

asphalt /ˈæsfælt, US -fɔːlt/ n asfalt m

aspic /ˈæspɪk/ n auszpik m, galareta f

aspiration /ˌæspɪˈreɪʃn/ n aspiracje plt; dążenie n (**to sth** do czegoś)

aspire /əˈspaɪə(r)/ vi dążyć (**to sth** do czegoś); **to ~ to do sth** mieć ambicję, żeby coś zrobić

aspirin /ˈæspərɪn/ n aspiryna f

ass /æs/ n osioł m also fig

assassin /əˈsæsɪn, US -sn/ n zabój|ca m, -czyni f; (political) zamachowiec m

assassinate /əˈsæsɪneɪt, US -sən-/ vt zabi|ć, -jać; (for political reasons) dokonać zamachu na (kogoś)

assassination /əˌsæsɪˈneɪʃn, US -səˈneɪʃn/ n zabójstwo n; (political) zamach m

assault /əˈsɔːlt/ **❚** n ① (in law) napaść f (**on sb** na kogoś) ② (attack) atak m, napaść f (**on sb/sth** na kogoś/coś)
❚❚ vt ① (in law) napa|ść, -dać na (kogoś); **to be indecently ~ed** stać się ofiarą napaści połączonej z czynem nierządnym ② Mil za|atakować [enemy]; szturmować [town]

assemble /əˈsembl/ **❚** vt ① (gather) z|gromadzić ② (construct) z|montować, złożyć, składać
❚❚ vi z|ebrać, -bierać się

assembly /əˈsemblɪ/ n ① zgromadzenie n ② Sch apel m ③ (of components, machines) montaż m

assembly line n linia f montażowa

assent /əˈsent/ **❚** n zgoda f (**to sth** na coś); aprobata f
❚❚ vi fml przychyl|ić, -ać się (**to sth** do czegoś)

assert /əˈsɜːt/ vt ① (state) twierdzić (**that...** że...); **to ~ oneself** zaznaczać swój autorytet ② domagać się (czegoś) [rights]; wyst|ąpić, -ępować z (czymś) [claim]

assertion /əˈsɜːʃn/ n twierdzenie n; **to make an ~ that...** twierdzić, że...

assertive /əˈsɜːtɪv/ adj asertywny, stanowczy

assess /əˈses/ vt ① ocenić, -ać [person, pupil, damage, value] ② wymierz|yć, -ać [tax]

assessment /əˈsesmənt/ n ① ocena f ② (of damage, value) oszacowanie n ③ (for tax) ocena f należności podatkowych

asset /ˈæset/ n zaleta f; (advantage) atut m; **~s** (private) majątek m; (of company) aktywa plt

assign /əˈsaɪn/ vt ① przydziel|ić, -ać [resources, task] (**to sb** komuś) ② **to ~ a task to sb** wyznaczyć zadanie komuś ③ (attribute) przypis|ać, -ywać [role, value]; nadać, -wać [importance, name] (**to sb** komuś) ④ (appoint) mianować (**to sth** na coś)

assignment /əˈsaɪnmənt/ n ① (specific duty) misja f ② (academic) zadana praca f

assimilate /əˈsɪmɪleɪt/ **❚** vt przysw|oić, -ajać [drug, food]; przysw|oić, -ajać sobie [facts, ideas]
❚❚ vi [immigrant] z|asymilować się

assist /əˈsɪst/ **❚** vt ① (help) pom|óc, -agać (komuś), wspom|óc, -agać (**to do/in doing sth** w robieniu czegoś) ② (facilitate) ułatwi|ć, -ać [development, process]
❚❚ vi pom|óc, -agać (**in doing sth** w robieniu czegoś); **to ~ in sth** pomóc w czymś

assistance /əˈsɪstəns/ n pomoc f; **to give ~ to sb** udzielić komuś pomocy

assistant /əˈsɪstənt/ **❚** n ① (helper) pomocni|k m, -ca f; (in hierarchy) zastęp|ca m, -czyni f ② (also **shop ~**) ekspedient m, -ka f, sprzedaw|ca m, -czyni f ③ GB (also **foreign language ~**) konsultant m językowy, konsultantka f językowa; (in university) lektor m, -ka f
❚❚ adj [editor, producer] pomocniczy, zastępujący

associate ❚ /əˈsəʊʃiət/ n współpracowni|k m, -czka f; (in business) wspólni|k m, -czka f

II /ə'səʊʃɪeɪt/ *vt* [1] po|wiązać, s|kojarzyć *[facts, ideas]* (**with sb/sth** z kimś/czymś) [2] **to be ~d with sth** *[person]* być związanym z czymś *[group, movement]*; mieć powiązania z czymś *[shady business]*

III /ə'səʊʃɪeɪt/ *vi* **to ~ with sb** zada|ć, -wać się z kimś

association /əˌsəʊsɪ'eɪʃn/ *n* stowarzyszenie *n*, towarzystwo *n*

assorted /ə'sɔ:tɪd/ *adj [foodstuffs]* mieszany; *[colours, events]* różny

assortment /ə'sɔ:tmənt/ *n* (of things) rozmaitość *f*; (of people) zbieranina *f* pej; **an ~ of colours** różne kolory

assume /ə'sju:m, US ə'su:m/ *vt* [1] (suppose) za|ło-żyć, -kładać (**that...** że...) [2] obj|ąć, -ejmować *[office, post]*; przyb|rać, -ierać *[attitude, expression]*; przej|ąć, -mować *[responsibility]*; **under an ~d name** pod przybranym nazwiskiem

assumption /ə'sʌmpʃn/ *n* przypuszczenie *n*; (belief) przekonanie *n*; (in science) założenie *n*

assurance /ə'ʃɔ:rəns, US ə'ʃʊərəns/ *n* pewność *f*, zapewnienie *n*

assure /ə'ʃɔ:(r), US ə'ʃʊər/ *vt* zapewni|ć, -ać; **to ~ sb that...** zapewnić kogoś, że...

asterisk /'æstərɪsk/ *n* gwiazdka *f*, asterysk *m*

asthma /'æsmə, US 'æzmə/ *n* astma *f*

asthmatic /æs'mætɪk/ **I** *n* astmaty|k *m*, -czka *f* **II** *adj* astmatyczny

astonish /ə'stɒnɪʃ/ *vt* (amaze) zadziwi|ć, -ać; (surprise) z|dziwić

astonished /ə'stɒnɪʃt/ *adj* zdziwiony; **to be ~ by** or **at sth** dziwić się czemuś

astonishing /ə'stɒnɪʃɪŋ/ *adj [intelligence, skill]* zadziwiający; *[beauty, career, performance, profit]* nadzwyczajny; *[speed, success]* zdumiewający

astonishment /ə'stɒnɪʃmənt/ *n* (surprise) zdziwie-nie *n*; (amazement) zadziwienie *n*

astound /ə'staʊnd/ *vt* zdumie|ć, -wać

astounding /ə'staʊndɪŋ/ *adj* zdumiewający

astray /ə'streɪ/ *adv* [1] **to go ~** (go missing) za|ginąć; *[person]* za|błądzić [2] **to lead sb ~** (confuse) wpro-wadzić kogoś w błąd; (corrupt) sprowadzić kogoś na złą drogę

astride /ə'straɪd/ **I** *adv* okrakiem
II *prep* **to sit ~ sth** siedzieć na czymś okrakiem

astrologer /ə'strɒlədʒə(r)/ **astrologist** /ə'strɒlədʒɪst/ *n* astrolog *m*

astrology /ə'strɒlədʒɪ/ *n* astrologia *f*

astronaut /'æstrənɔ:t/ *n* astronauta *m*

astronomer /ə'strɒnəmə(r)/ *n* astronom *m*

astronomic /ˌæstrə'nɒmɪk/, **astronomical** /ˌæstrə'nɒmɪkl/ *adj* astronomiczny

astronomy /ə'strɒnəmɪ/ *n* astronomia *f*

astute /ə'stju:t, US ə'stu:t/ *adj* (shrewd) przebiegły; (clever) bystry

asylum /ə'saɪləm/ *n* azyl *m*; **lunatic ~** zakład dla obłąkanych

asylum-seeker /ə'saɪləmsi:kə(r)/ *n* starając|y *m*, -a *f* się o azyl

at *prep* **~ school** w szkole; **~ 4 o'clock** o czwartej; **~ Easter** na Wielkanoc; **~ night** nocą or nocy; **~ the moment** w tej chwili; **~ my house** u mnie w domu

atheist /'eɪθɪɪst/ *n* ateist|a *m*, -ka *f*

Athens /'æθɪnz/ *prn* Ateny *plt*

athlete /'æθli:t/ *n* GB lekkoatlet|a *m*, -ka *f*; US sportowiec *m*

athlete's foot *n* grzybica *f* stóp

athletic /æθ'letɪk/ *adj* lekkoatletyczny; US spor-towy

athletics /æθ'letɪks/ *n* GB lekka atletyka *f*; US sport *m*

Atlantic /ət'læntɪk/ **I** *prn* **the ~** Atlantyk *m*
II *adj* atlantycki

atlas /'ætləs/ *n* atlas *m*

ATM *n* = **automated teller machine** banko-mat *m*

atmosphere /'ætməsfɪə(r)/ *n* [1] atmosfera *f*; (air) powietrze *n* [2] (mood) nastrój *m*, atmosfera *f*; (bad) zła atmosfera *f*

atom /'ætəm/ *n* atom *m*

atom bomb *n* bomba *f* atomowa

atomic /ə'tɒmɪk/ *adj* atomowy

atrocious /ə'trəʊʃəs/ *adj* (horrifying) potworny; (bad) okropny

atrocity /ə'trɒsɪtɪ/ *n* potworność *f*, okropność *f*

attach /ə'tætʃ/ *vt* przymocow|ać, -ywać *[handle, string]*; przyczepi|ć, -ać *[note]* (**to sth** do czegoś); (to letter) dołącz|yć, -ać

attaché /ə'tæʃeɪ, US ˌætə'ʃeɪ/ *n* attaché *m*

attaché case *n* (teczka *f*) dyplomatka *f*

attached /ə'tætʃt/ *adj* [1] (fond) przywiązany (**to sb/sth** do kogoś/czegoś) [2] *[document]* dołączony

attachment /ə'tætʃmənt/ *n* [1] (affection) przywią-zanie *n* [2] (device) nasadka *f*, końcówka *f* [3] (in e-mail) załącznik *m*

attack /ə'tæk/ **I** *n* [1] atak *m* (**on sb/sth** na kogoś/ coś); (criminal) napaść *f* (**against** or **on sb/sth** na kogoś/coś) [2] (of illness) napad *m*, atak *m*
II *vt* [1] za|atakować; (criminally) napa|ść, -dać na (kogoś) [2] zabrać się do (czegoś) *[problem, task]*

attacker /ə'tækə(r)/ *n* napastni|k *m*, -czka *f*

attempt /ə'tempt/ **I** *n* próba *f*; **to make an ~ to do sth/at doing sth** spróbować coś zrobić/podjąć próbę zrobienia czegoś; **to make an ~ on sb's life** podjąć próbę zamachu na życie kogoś
II *vt* s|próbować; **to ~ to do sth** próbować coś zrobić; **~ed murder** usiłowanie zabójstwa

attend /ə'tend/ **I** *vt* być obecnym na (czymś), uczestniczyć w (czymś) *[meeting, ceremony]*; chodzić do (czegoś) *[church, school]*; uczęszczać na (coś) *[class, course]*

II *vi* być obecnym

■ **attend to**: zająć, -mować się (kimś/czymś)

attendant /ə'tendənt/ *n* (in cloakroom) szatnia|rz *m*, -rka *f*; (in museum) strażni|k *m*, -czka *f*; (at petrol station) pracowni|k *m*, -ca *f* stacji benzynowej; (at pool) ratowni|k *m*, -czka *f*

attention /ə'tenʃn/ *n* [1] uwaga *f*, zainteresowanie *n*; **to draw ~ to sth** zwrócić na coś uwagę [2] Mil **to stand to** or **at ~** stać na baczność; **~!** baczność

attentive /ə'tentɪv/ *adj* (alert) uważny; (considerate) troszczący się (**to sb/sth** o kogoś/coś)

attic /'ætɪk/ *n* strych *m*; **in the ~** na strychu

attic room *n* pokój *m* na poddaszu, mansarda *f*

attitude /'ætɪtjuːd, US -tuːd/ *n* nastawienie *n* (**to** or **towards sb/sth** do or wobec kogoś/czegoś); stosunek *m* (**to** or **towards sb/sth** do kogoś/czegoś)

attorney /ə'tɜːnɪ/ *n* US (lawyer) adwokat *m*

attract /ə'trækt/ *vt* przyciąg|nąć, -ać

attraction /ə'trækʃn/ *n* [1] (favourable feature) atrakcyjność *f* [2] (entertainment, sight) atrakcja *f* [3] (sexual) pociąg *m* (**to sb** do kogoś)

attractive /ə'træktɪv/ *adj* [person, place] atrakcyjny; [child] uroczy

attribute **II** /'ætrɪbjuːt/ *n* atrybut *m*, cecha *f* **II** /ə'trɪbjuːt/ *vt* przypis|ać, -ywać (**sth to sb/sth** coś komuś/czemuś)

aubergine /'əʊbəʒiːn/ *n* GB bakłażan *m*, oberżyna *f*

auburn /'ɔːbən/ *adj* kasztanowy

auction /'ɔːkʃn, 'ɒkʃn/ **II** *n* aukcja *f*, licytacja *f* **II** *vt* (also **~ off**) sprzeda|ć, -wać na aukcji or na licytacji

auctioneer /ˌɔːkʃə'nɪə(r)/ *n* licytator *m*

auction house *n* dom *m* aukcyjny

audacity /ɔː'dæsətɪ/ *n* śmiałość *f*, zuchwałość *f*

audible /'ɔːdəbl/ *adj* słyszalny

audience /'ɔːdɪəns/ *n* (in theatre, cinema, concert) publiczność *f*; (listeners) słuchacze *m pl*; (of radio) radiosłuchacze *m pl*; (of TV) telewidzowie *m pl*

audience ratings *npl* (of radio) wskaźnik *m* słuchalności; (of TV) wskaźnik *m* oglądalności

audio /'ɔːdɪəʊ/ *adj* audio

audiobook /'ɔːdɪəʊbʊk/ *n* książka *f* mówiona

audiovisual, AV /ˌɔːdɪəʊ'vɪʒʊəl/ *adj* audiowizualny

audit /'ɔːdɪt/ **II** *n* kontrola *f* ksiąg (rachunkowych) **II** *vt* s|kontrolować, przeprowadz|ić, -ać audyt (czegoś)

audition /ɔː'dɪʃn/ **II** *n* przesłuchanie *n* **II** *vt* przesłuch|ać, -iwać [actor, musician] (**for sth** do czegoś) **III** *vi* brać udział w przesłuchaniu (**for sth** do czegoś)

auditor /'ɔːdɪtə(r)/ *n* [1] rewident *m* księgowy, rewidentka *f* księgowa [2] US (student) ≈ wolny słuchacz *m*, wolna słuchaczka *f*

auditorium /ˌɔːdɪ'tɔːrɪəm/ *n* widownia *f*; (people) audytorium *n*

augur /'ɔːgə(r)/ *vi* **to ~ well** dobrze wróżyć

August /'ɔːgəst/ *n* sierpień *m*

aunt /ɑːnt, US ænt/ *n* ciotka *f*

au pair /ˌəʊ'peə(r)/ *n* au pair *f inv* (młoda cudzoziemka wykonująca lekkie prace domowe)

aura /'ɔːrə/ *n* (of person) aura *f*; (of place) atmosfera *f*

aural /'ɔːrəl, 'aʊrəl/ *adj* słuchowy; **~ comprehension** Sch rozumienie ze słuchu

auspicious /ɔː'spɪʃəs/ *adj* pomyślny, obiecujący

austere /ɒ'stɪə(r), ɔː'stɪə(r)/ *adj* [interior, behaviour, building] surowy; [person] srogi; [life] prosty

austerity /ɒ'sterətɪ, ɔː'sterətɪ/ *n* (severity) surowość *f*; (lack of comfort) prostota *f*

Australia /ɒ'streɪlɪə, ɔː's-/ *prn* Australia *f*

Australian /ɒ'streɪlɪən, ɔː's-/ **II** *n* Australij|czyk *m*, -ka *f* **II** *adj* australijski

Austria /'ɒstrɪə, 'ɔːstrɪə/ *prn* Austria *f*

Austrian /'ɒstrɪən, 'ɔːstrɪən/ **II** *n* Austria|k *m*, -czka *f* **II** *adj* austriacki

authentic /ɔː'θentɪk/ *adj* [document, signature] autentyczny; [painting] oryginalny

author /'ɔːθə(r)/ *n* autor *m*, -ka *f*; (by profession) literat *m*, -ka *f*

authoritarian /ɔːˌθɒrɪ'teərɪən/ *adj* [regime] despotyczny; [ruler] autorytarny; [parent, voice] apodyktyczny

authoritative /ɔː'θɒrətətɪv, US -teɪtɪv/ *adj* [1] (forceful) [person, voice] apodyktyczny; [tone] kategoryczny [2] (reliable) [report] autorytatywny; [source] dobrze poinformowany

authority /ɔː'θɒrətɪ/ *n* [1] władza *f*; (superior position) zwierzchnictwo *n* (**over sb/sth** nad kimś/czymś); **the authorities** władze [2] (permission) upoważnienie *n*

authorization /ˌɔːθəraɪ'zeɪʃn/ *n* upoważnienie *n*

authorize /'ɔːθəraɪz/ *vt* upoważni|ć, -ać (**to do sth** do zrobienia czegoś)

autism /'ɔːtɪzəm/ *n* autyzm *m*

autobiographical /ˌɔːtəʊbaɪə'græfɪkl/ *adj* autobiograficzny

autobiography /ˌɔːtəʊbaɪ'ɒɡrəfɪ/ *n* autobiografia *f*

Autocue® /'ɔːtəʊkjuː/ *n* teleprompter *m*

autograph /'ɔːtəɡrɑːf, US -ɡræf/ **II** *n* autograf *m* **II** *vt* złożyć, składać autograf na (czymś) [book]

automatic /ˌɔːtə'mætɪk/ **II** *n* [1] (washing machine) pralka *f* automatyczna [2] (car) samochód *m* z automatyczną skrzynią biegów [3] (gun) automat *m* **II** *adj* automatyczny

automatically /ˌɔːtə'mætɪklɪ/ *adv* automatycznie; [smile] odruchowo

automatic pilot *n* (device) pilot *m* automatyczny, autopilot *m*

automation /ˌɔːtəˈmeɪʃn/ *n* automatyzacja *f*

automobile /ˈɔːtəməbiːl, ˌɔːtəməˈbiːl/ *n* samochód *m*

autonomy /ɔːˈtɒnəmɪ/ *n* (of organization, person) niezależność *f*; (of country) autonomia *f*

autopsy /ˈɔːtɒpsɪ/ *n* sekcja *f* zwłok

autumn /ˈɔːtəm/ *n* jesień *f*; **in** ~ jesienią

auxiliary /ɔːgˈzɪlɪərɪ/ **I** *n* (person) pomoc *f*
II *adj* pomocniczy

availability /əˌveɪləˈbɪlətɪ/ *n* (of option, service) dostępność *f*; **subject to** ~ (of holidays, hotel rooms, theatre seats) do wyczerpania wolnych miejsc

available /əˈveɪləbl/ *adj* [credit, information, money] dostępny (**for** or **to sb** dla kogoś); [table, seat, time] wolny

avalanche /ˈævəlɑːnʃ, US -læntʃ/ *n* lawina *f*

avarice /ˈævərɪs/ *n* chciwość *f*

avenge /əˈvendʒ/ *vt* po|mścić

avenue /ˈævənjuː, US -nuː/ *n* (road, street) aleja *f*; (driveway, path) alejka *f*, podjazd *m*

average /ˈævərɪdʒ/ **I** *n* średnia *f*; **on (the)** ~ przeciętnie; **above/below (the)** ~ powyżej/poniżej średniej/przeciętnej
II *adj* średni
III *vt* osiąg|nąć, -ać średnią

averse /əˈvɜːs/ *adj* przeciwny (**to sth** czemuś); **to be** ~ **to doing sth** być przeciwnym robieniu czegoś

aversion /əˈvɜːʃn, US əˈvɜːrʒn/ *n* niechęć *f*, awersja *f* (**to sb/sth** do kogoś/czegoś)

avert /əˈvɜːt/ *vt* [1] (prevent) zapobie|c, -gać (czemuś) [2] odwr|ócić, -acać [eyes] (**from sth** od czegoś)

aviary /ˈeɪvɪərɪ, US -vɪerɪ/ *n* ptaszarnia *f*

aviation /ˌeɪvɪˈeɪʃn/ *n* lotnictwo *n*

avid /ˈævɪd/ *adj* [reader] zapalony; [collector] namiętny; **to be** ~ **for sth** być żądnym czegoś

avocado /ˌævəˈkɑːdəʊ/ *n* (also ~ **pear**) awokado *n inv*

avoid /əˈvɔɪd/ *vt* unik|nąć, -ać (czegoś) [issue, question]

await /əˈweɪt/ *vt* oczekiwać (czegoś) [decision, event, outcome]; czekać na (coś) [opportunity]

awake /əˈweɪk/ **I** *adj* **to be** ~ nie spać; **wide** ~ całkiem rozbudzony; **the noise kept me** ~ hałas nie dawał mi spać
II *vt* o|budzić [person]

III *vi* [person] o|budzić się

award /əˈwɔːd/ **I** *n* nagroda *f* (**for sth** za coś)
II *vt* przyzna|ć, -wać [grant, prize, points]

award ceremony *n* uroczystość *f* wręczenia nagród

award-winning /əˈwɔːdwɪnɪŋ/ *adj* [book, film, writer] nagrodzony

aware /əˈweə(r)/ *adj* (conscious) świadomy; (informed) poinformowany (**of sth** o czymś)

awareness /əˈweənɪs/ *n* świadomość *f*

away /əˈweɪ/ **I** *adj* Sport [goal] zdobyty na wyjeździe; [match] wyjazdowy; [win] na wyjeździe; **the** ~ **team** drużyna gości
II *adv* [1] **to be** ~ **from school** być nieobecnym w szkole; **to be** ~ **on business** wyjechać w podróż służbową; **she's** ~ **in Canada** wyjechała do Kanady; **20 miles** ~ 20 mil stąd [2] Sport **to play** ~ grać na wyjeździe

awe /ɔː/ *n* (respect) respekt *m*; (admiration, wonder) podziw *m*; (dread) obawa *f*; **to listen in** ~ słuchać z podziwem; **to be in** ~ **of sb** czuć respekt przed kimś

awe-inspiring /ˈɔːrɪnspaɪərɪŋ/ *adj* [person] budzący strach i podziw; [experience] budzący podziw

awful /ˈɔːfl/ *adj* [1] (bad) okropny; (stronger) wstrętny [2] (horrifying) straszny; **I feel** ~ (ill) okropnie się czuję; (guilty) głupio mi [3] infml **an** ~ **lot of money** okropnie or strasznie dużo pieniędzy

awfully /ˈɔːflɪ/ *adv* strasznie; [clever, good, generous, nice] bardzo

awkward /ˈɔːkwəd/ *adj* [1] [tool, shape] niewygodny [2] (clumsy) niezdarny, niezgrabny [3] [issue] skomplikowany; [choice] trudny; [moment] niedogodny [4] (embarrassing) [question, situation, silence] kłopotliwy [5] (uncooperative) [person] trudny; sprawiający kłopot (**about sth** w związku z czymś)

awning /ˈɔːnɪŋ/ *n* (on shop) markiza *f*; (over stall) dach *m*, daszek *m*; (on tent) przedsionek *m*

awry /əˈraɪ/ **I** *adj* [tie, picture] przekrzywiony; [hair] zmierzwiony
II *adv* **to go** ~ [plan] nie powieść się; [economy] iść w złą stronę

axe, ax US /æks/ **I** *n* siekiera *f*, topór *m*
II *vt* infml obci|ąć, -nać [jobs]; okr|oić, -awać [project]; z|redukować [staff]

axis /ˈæksɪs/ *n* oś *f*

axle /ˈæksl/ *n* oś *f* (koła)

B

b, B /biː/ n ① (letter) b, B n ② B Mus H, h n

BA n = **Bachelor of Arts** ≈ licencjat m
w dziedzinie nauk humanistycznych

babe /beɪb/ n infml (woman) ślicznotka f infml

baby /'beɪbɪ/ **I** n (infant) niemowlę n; (child) dziecko n

II adj [animal] malutki; [vegetable] mały; [cup] dla
niemowląt; ~ **brother/sister** braciszek/sio-
strzyczka

baby-sit /'beɪbɪsɪt/ vi zajmować się dzieckiem/
dziećmi

baby-sitter /'beɪbɪsɪtə(r)/ n opiekun m, -ka f do
dzieci

baby-sitting /'beɪbɪsɪtɪŋ/ n opiekowanie się n
dziećmi

baccalaureate /ˌbækə'lɔːrɪət/ n Sch międzyna-
rodowa matura f; **International Baccalaureate**
bakalaureat międzynarodowy

bachelor /'bætʃələ(r)/ n ① kawaler m ② Univ
Bachelor of Arts (degree) ≈ licencjat m
w dziedzinie nauk humanistycznych

back /bæk/ **I** n ① (of human) plecy plt; (of animal)
grzbiet m; (spine) kręgosłup m; **to turn one's ~ on
sb/sth** odwrócić się od kogoś/czegoś also fig;
behind sb's ~ za plecami kogoś also fig ② (of
page, cheque, card, envelope) odwrotna strona f; (of fabric)
lewa strona f; (of coin, medal) rewers m; (of knife)
grzbiet m; (of bus, plane, building) tył m; (of chair, sofa)
oparcie n; **the steps at the ~ of the building**
schody na tyłach budynku; (of cupboard, bus) **at the
~ of the drawer** głęboko w szufladzie; **the index
is at the ~ (of the book)** indeks znajduje się na
końcu (książki); **those at the ~ couldn't see** ci
z tyłu nic nie widzieli ③ Sport obrońca m; **left ~**
lewy obrońca

II adj [wheel, leg, paw] tylny; [car, gate, garden] od
tyłu; [page] końcowy

III adv ① (after absence) **to be ~** (po)wrócić; **I'll be
~ in five minutes** będę z powrotem za pięć
minut; **to come ~ from somewhere** wrócić
skądś; **he's ~ at work** wrócił do pracy ② (in return)
to call ~ oddzwonić; **to write ~ (to sb)** odpisać
(komuś); **to give/send sth ~** oddać/odesłać coś
(to sb komuś) **(backwards)** ③ (backwards) [glance,
jump, lean] do tyłu, w tył ④ (ago) temu; **25 years
~** 25 lat temu; **~ in April** w kwietniu ⑤ (return to
former location) **to travel to London and ~**
pojechać do Londynu i z powrotem

IV vt ① (support) pop|rzeć, -ierać [candidate, bill,
project]; w|esprzeć, -spierać [undertaking]; uzasad-
ni|ć, -ać [claim] **(with sth** czymś) ② (reverse)
cof|nąć, -ać [car]; **to ~ the car into the garage**
wjechać tyłem do garażu ③ (bet on) obstawi|ć, -ać
[horse]; postawić, stawiać na (coś) [favourite,
winner]

V **back and forth** adv phr **to travel ~ and forth**
[passenger] podróżować tam i z powrotem; **the bus
runs ~ and forth between the airport and
the station** autobus kursuje między lotniskiem a
dworcem

■ **back away**: cof|nąć, -ać się; **to ~ away from
sth** wycofać się z czegoś [idea, plan]; unik|nąć, -ać
(czegoś) [confrontation]

■ **back down**: ust|ąpić, -ępować **(on** or **over sth**
w sprawie czegoś)

■ **back out**: ¶ ~ **out** ① [person] wycof|ać, -ywać
się tyłem; [car, driver] wyje|chać, -żdżać tyłem
② **to ~ out of** or **from sth** wycofać się z czegoś
[deal] ¶ ~ **[sth] out**: **to ~ the car out of the
garage** wyjechać z garażu tyłem

■ **back up**: potwierdz|ić, -ać [theory]; stanowić
uzasadnienie dla (czegoś) [claims]; pop|rzeć, -ierać
[person]; Comput z|robić zapasową kopię (czegoś)

backache /'bækeɪk/ n **I have ~** bolą mnie plecy,
boli mnie krzyż

backbencher /ˌbæk'bentʃə(r)/ n GB szeregowy
deputowany m

backbone /'bækbəʊn/ n kręgosłup m

back cover n czwarta strona f okładki

backdate /'bækdeɪt/ vt antydatować [cheque,
letter]

back door n (of car) tylne drzwi plt; (of building)
drzwi plt od tyłu, tylne wejście n

backdrop /'bækdrɒp/ n (in theatre) prospekt m;
fig tło n

backer /'bækə(r)/ n ① (of project, show, company)
sponsor m; (of artist) mecenas m ② (supporter)
stronni|k m, -czka f

backfire /'bækfaɪə/ vi ① the car ~d gaźnik
samochodu strzelił ② [scheme, tactics] przyn|ieść,
-osić odwrotny skutek; **to ~ on sb** obrócić się
przeciwko komuś

backgammon /'bækgæmən/ n tryktrak m

background /'bækgraʊnd/ **[]** *n* [1] (of person) (social) środowisko *n*; (family) pochodzenie *n*; (professional) przygotowanie *n* (zawodowe) [2] (of situation) tło *n*; **these events took place against a ~ of war** te wydarzenia rozegrały się podczas wojny; **in the ~** na drugim planie; **voices in the ~** głosy w tle [3] (of painting, photo, scene) tło *n*; **in the ~** w tle **[]** *adj* [1] *[information]* ogólny [2] ~ **lighting** dyskretne oświetlenie; ~ **music** (in film) podkład muzyczny

backhand /'bækhænd/ *n* Sport backhend *m*, backhand *m*

backhander /'bækhændə(r)/. *n* infml łapówka *f*

backing /'bækɪŋ/ **[]** *n* [1] (support) poparcie *n*; (financial) wsparcie *n* [2] (reverse layer) spód *m*, dolna warstwa *f* **[]** *adj [player]* akompaniujący; ~ **vocals** podkład wokalny

backlash /'bæklæʃ/ *n* gwałtowna reakcja *f* (**against** or **to sth** na coś)

backlog /'bæklɒg/ *n* zaległości *f pl*; **I've got a huge ~ (of work)** mam wielkie zaległości w pracy

back number *n* stary numer *m* (gazety)

backpack /'bækpæk/ *n* plecak *m*

backpacker /'bækpækə(r)/ *n* turysta *m* wędrujący z plecakiem

back pay *n* zaległa wypłata *f*

back-pedal /ˌbæk'pedl/ *vi* fig wycof|ać, -ywać się (**on sth** z czegoś)

back rest *n* oparcie *n* (krzesła, kanapy)

back seat *n* siedzenie *n* z tyłu; **to take a ~** fig trzymać się w cieniu

backside /'bæksaɪd/ *n* infml tyłek *m* infml

backstage /bæksteɪdʒ/ *adv [be, work]* za kulisami

backstreet /'bækstriːt/ **[]** *n* uliczka *f* **[]** *adj [loan shark, abortionist]* pokątny

backstroke /'bækstrəʊk/ *n* styl *m* grzbietowy

back-to-back /ˌbæktə'bæk/ *adv* **to stand ~** *[two people]* stać do siebie plecami

back to front *adj, adv* tył na przód, tyłem do przodu

backtrack /'bæktræk/ *vi* cof|nąć, -ać się; fig wycof|ać, -ywać się

backup /'bækʌp/ **[]** *n* wsparcie *n* **[]** *adj [equipment]* pomocniczy; *[system]* zapasowy; Comput *[copy, file]* zapasowy

backward /'bækwəd/ **[]** *adj* [1] *[look]* za siebie; *[step]* do tyłu, w tył; *[step]* wstecz also fig [2] *[nation, economy]* zacofany **[]** *adv* US = **backwards**

backwards /'bækwədz/ GB, **backward** /'bækwəd/ US *adv* [1] *[fall, lean, step]* do tyłu, w tył; *[walk]* tyłem; **to move ~** cofać się; ~ **and forwards** tam i z powrotem [2] *[count, recite]* od końca

backwater /'bækwɔːtə(r)/ *n* fig zakątek *m*; pej zaścianek *m* fig

backyard /ˌbæk'jɑːd/ *n* GB (courtyard) podwórko *n*, podwórze *n* (za domem); US (garden) ogród(ek) *m* (za domem)

bacon /'beɪkən/ *n* bekon *m*; ~ **and eggs** jajka na bekonie

bacteria /bæk'tɪərɪə/ *npl* bakterie *f pl*

bad /bæd/ **[]** *n* zło *n*; **there is good and ~ in everyone** w każdym tkwi dobro i zło **[]** *adj* [1] (inferior) *[answer, idea]* zły; *[eyesight, memory]* słaby; *[joke]* marny; *[language]* wulgarny; **not ~ (at all)** infml nie najgorszy; **to be ~ at sth** być słabym or kiepskim w czymś *[maths]*; **too ~!** (sympathetic) a to pech!; **it's ~ to steal** to brzydko kraść; **to feel ~ (about sth)** mieć wyrzuty sumienia (z powodu czegoś) [2] (severe) *[accident, injury, mistake]* poważny; *[case, cold]* ciężki [3] (harmful) ~ **for sb** szkodliwy dla kogoś; **smoking is ~ for you** or **for your health** palenie szkodzi [4] (diseased) **to have a ~ back** cierpieć na bóle kręgosłupa; **to have a ~ heart** chorować na serce; **to be in a ~ way** być w kiepskim stanie [5] (rotten) *[fruit]* zgniły; **to go ~** zgnić/zepsuć się

badge /bædʒ/ *n* (of rank) odznaka *f*, znaczek *m*; (symbol) oznaka *f*, atrybut *m*

badly /'bædlɪ/ *adv* [1] (not well) *[begin, behave, sleep, made, worded]* źle; **to go ~** *[exam, interview]* źle pójść; *[operation, party]* nie udać się; **to take sth ~** źle coś znieść or przyjąć; **she did ~ in her exam** nie powiodło jej się na egzaminie [2] (seriously) *[suffer]* dotkliwie; *[hurt]* ciężko; *[damaged]* poważnie; *[leak]* mocno [3] **to want/need sth ~** chcieć/potrzebować czegoś bardzo

badly behaved *adj* niegrzeczny

badly off *adj* źle sytuowany

bad-mannered /ˌbæd'mænəd/ *adj* źle wychowany

badminton /'bædmɪntn/ *n* badminton *m*, kometka *f*

bad-tempered /ˌbæd'tempəd/ *adj* (habitually) wybuchowy; (temporarily) zirytowany

baffle /'bæfl/ *vt* zbi|ć, -jać z tropu

baffled /'bæfld/ *adj* skonsternowany

bag /bæg/ **[]** *n* torba *f* **[]** **bags** *npl* bagaż *m*, bagaże *m pl*; **to pack one's ~s** spakować manatki also fig IDIOMS **to have ~s under one's eyes** mieć wory or worki pod oczami

baggage /'bægɪdʒ/ *n* bagaż *m*

baggage allowance *n* dozwolona ilość *m* bagażu

baggage reclaim *n* odbiór *f* bagażu

baggy /'bægɪ/ *adj [clothes]* workowaty

bagpipes /'bægpaɪps/ *npl* duda *f*, dudy *f pl*

bail /beɪl/ *n* kaucja *f*; **to be (out) on ~** być zwolnionym za kaucją

■ **bail out**: ¶ wysk|oczyć, -akiwać z samolotu na spadochronie ¶ ~ **[sb] out** (in law) za|płacić kaucję za (kogoś); (get out of trouble) wyciąg|nąć, -ać (kogoś) z kłopotów *[person]*

bailiff /ˈbeɪlɪf/ *n* komornik *m*

bait /beɪt/ *n* przynęta *f*

bake /beɪk/ **I** *vt* u|piec *[bread, cake]*; zapie|c, -kać *[dish, vegetables]*
II *vi* ① (make bread) *[person]* piec ② *[food]* u|piec się

baked beans *npl* fasola *f* w sosie pomidorowym

baked potato *n* ziemniak *m* pieczony w łupinie

baker /ˈbeɪkə(r)/ *n* piekarz *m*

bakery /ˈbeɪkərɪ/ *n* piekarnia *f*

balance /ˈbæləns/ **I** *n* ① (steady position) równowaga *f*; **to lose one's ~** stracić równowagę; **the right ~** właściwe proporcje ②; (scales) waga *f*; **to hang in the ~** fig ważyć się (na szali) ③ (in account) saldo *n*; **to pay the ~** zapłacić pozostałą sumę
II *vt* ① (perch) utrzymywać w równowadze ② (counterbalance) stanowić przeciwwagę dla (czegoś) ③ fig (compensate for) (also ~ **out**) z|równoważyć ④ (adjust) s|korygować *[diet]* ⑤ z|bilansować *[books, budget]*
III *vi* ① *[person]* balansować (**on sth** na czymś) ② fig (also ~ **out**) z|równoważyć się ③ *[books]* z|bilansować się; *[figures]* zg|odzić, -adzać się
IV **balanced** *pp adj [person]* zrównoważony; *[article]* obiektywny; *[view]* wyważony; *[diet]* racjonalny

balance of payments *n* bilans *m* płatniczy

balance of power *n* Pol równowaga *f* sił

balance of trade *n* bilans *m* handlowy

balance sheet *n* bilans *m*, zestawienie *n* bilansowe

balcony /ˈbælkənɪ/ *n* ① (in house) balkon *m* ② (of theatre) balkon *m*

bald /bɔːld/ *adj [man]* łysy; *[head]* wyłysiały; *[tyre]* starty; łysy infml

Balkan /ˈbɔːlkən/ **I** **the ~s** Bałkany *plt*
II *adj* bałkański

ball /bɔːl/ *n* ① (in football, tennis) piłka *f*; (in table tennis) piłeczka *f*; (in snooker, pool) kula *f* ② (of dough, clay) kula *f*; (of wool, string) kłębek *m* ③ (dance) bal *m*

ballet /ˈbæleɪ/ *n* balet *m*

ball gown *n* suknia *f* balowa

balloon /bəˈluːn/ *n* balon *m*; **hot-air ~** balon napełniany gorącym powietrzem

ballot /ˈbælət/ **I** *n* ① głosowanie *n* ② (also ~ **paper**) karta *f* do głosowania
II *vt* zasięg|nąć, -ać opinii (kogoś) poprzez głosowanie

ballot box *n* urna *f* wyborcza

ballpoint (pen) /ˈbɔːlpɔɪnt(ˈpen)/ *n* długopis *m*, pióro *n* kulkowe

ballroom /ˈbɔːlrʊm/ *n* sala *f* balowa

ballroom dancing *n* taniec *m* towarzyski

Baltic /ˈbɔːltɪk/ **I** *prn* **the ~** Bałtyk *m*
II *adj* bałtycki

ban /bæn/ **I** *n* zakaz *m* (**on sth/on doing sth** czegoś/robienia czegoś)

II *vt* zakaz|ać, -ywać (czegoś); zabr|onić, -aniać (czegoś) *[activity]*; zawie|sić, -szać *[athlete]*; **to ~ sb from sth** wykluczyć kogoś z czegoś

banal /bəˈnɑːl, US ˈbeɪnl/ *adj* banalny

banana /bəˈnɑːnə/ *n* banan *m*

band /bænd/ *n* ① (of people) grupa *f*; Mus (rock) zespół *m*; (army, municipal) orkiestra *f*; (folk) kapela *f* ② (for hair, hat) wstążka *f*; (around waist) pas *m*; (around arm) opaska *f*; (around head) opaska *f*, przepaska *f* ③ GB (of age, income) grupa *f*, przedział *m*
■ **band together**: skrzyk|nąć, -iwać się

bandage /ˈbændɪdʒ/ **I** *n* bandaż *m*
II *vt* za|bandażować *[head, limb]*; opat|rzyć, -rywać *[person, wound]*

bandit /ˈbændɪt/ *n* bandyta *m*

bandwagon /ˈbændwægən/ *n*
(IDIOMS:) **to jump** or **climb on the ~** wykorzystywać koniunkturę

bang /bæŋ/ **I** *n* (of explosion) huk *m*; (of door, window) trzaśnięcie *n*
II *adv* infml ~ **in the middle** w samym środku
III *vt* ① wal|nąć, -ić (czymś), rąb|nąć, -ać (czymś); **to ~ down the receiver** z trzaskiem odłożyć słuchawkę; **to ~ one's head against the wall** uderzy głową o ścianę ② (slam) trzas|nąć, -kać (czymś) *[door, window]*
IV *vi* (strike) **to ~ on sth** walnąć w coś *[wall, door]*
■ **bang into**: ~ **into** [sb/sth] wpa|ść, -dać na (kogoś/coś)
(IDIOMS:) ~ **goes my holiday/go my plans** infml w łeb wzięły wakacje/plany

bangle /ˈbæŋgl/ *n* bransoleta *f*, kółko *n*

banish /ˈbænɪʃ/ *vt* z|esłać, -syłać (na banicję)

banister /ˈbænɪstə(r)/ *n* poręcz *f*

bank[1] /bæŋk/ *n* ① (of river, lake, canal) brzeg *m* ② (of earth, mud) wał *m*, zwał *n*; (of snow) zaspa *f*; (of flowers) kępa *f*; (of fog, mist) tuman *m*, obłok *m*

bank[2] /bæŋk/ **I** *n* bank *m*
II *vi* **to ~ with Lloyd's** mieć konto or rachunek w banku Lloyda
■ **bank on**: liczyć na (kogoś/coś); **I wouldn't ~ on him coming** nie liczyłbym na to, że przyjdzie

bank account *n* konto *n* bankowe, rachunek *m* bankowy

bank card *n* karta *f* bankowa

bank charges *npl* opłaty *f pl* manipulacyjne

bank clerk *n* urzędnik *m* bankowy, urzędniczka *f* bankowa (niższego szczebla)

banker /ˈbæŋkə(r)/ *n* (owner) bankier *m*; (executive) bankowiec *m*

banker's draft *n* przekaz *m* bankowy

banker's order *n* bankowe polecenie *n* wypłaty

bank holiday *n* GB dzień *m* wolny od pracy; US całodzienne zawieszenie *n* operacji bankowych

banking /ˈbæŋkɪŋ/ *n* bankowość *f*

banking hours *npl* godziny *f pl* otwarcia banku/ banków

bank manager *n* dyrektor *m* (oddziału) banku

banknote /'bæŋknəʊt/ *n* banknot *m*

bank robber *n* przestępca *m* napadający na bank

bank robbery *n* napad *m* na bank

bankroll /'bæŋkrəʊl/ *vt* infml w|esprzeć, -spierać finansowo

bankrupt /'bæŋkrʌpt/ *adj [person, economy]* zrujnowany; *[company]* upadły, zbankrutowany; **to go ~** zbankrutować

bankruptcy /'bæŋkrʌpsɪ/ *n* bankructwo *n*

bank statement *n* wyciąg *m* z konta or rachunku

banner /'bænə(r)/ *n* transparent *m*

baptism /'bæptɪzəm/ *n* (act) chrzest *m*; (ceremony) chrzciny *plt*

baptize /bæp'taɪz/ *vt* o|chrzcić

bar /bɑː(r)/ **I** *n* [1] (of metal) pręt *m*, sztaba *f*; (of cage, window) pręt *m* (kraty) [2] (of chocolate) tabliczka *f*; (small) baton *m*; (of soap) kostka *f* [3] (for drinking) knajpa *f* infml; (in hotel) bar *m* [4] (profession) **the ~, the Bar** adwokatura *f*, palestra *f* [5] Mus takt *m*
II *prep* z wyjątkiem (czegoś); **all ~ one** wszyscy z wyjątkiem jednego
III *vt* [1] (block) za|blokować, za|tarasować *[entrance, road]*; **he ~red my way** zastąpił mi drogę [2] (ban) **to ~ sb from sth** zakazać komuś wstępu do czegoś *[club, pub]*; **to ~ sb from doing sth** zabronić komuś coś zrobić

barbaric /bɑː'bærɪk/ *adj* barbarzyński

barbecue /'bɑːbɪkjuː/ *n* (grill) grill *m*; (party) barbecue *n inv*

barbed wire *n* drut *m* kolczasty

barber /'bɑːbə(r)/ *n* fryzjer *m* męski

Barcelona /ˌbɑːsɪ'ləʊnə/ *prn* Barcelona *f*

bar chart *n* wykres *m* kolumnowy, histogram *m*

bar code *n* kod *m* kreskowy or paskowy

bare /beə(r)/ **I** *adj* [1] *[flesh, body]* nagi; **with one's ~ hands** gołymi rękami [2] *[cupboard, room]* pusty; **the ~ minimum** absolutne minimum
II *vt* **to ~ one's chest** obnażyć klatkę piersiową

bareback /'beəbæk/ *adv [ride]* na oklep

barefoot /'beəfʊt/ **I** *adj [person]* bosy; **to be ~** być boso
II *adv [walk, run]* boso

barely /'beəlɪ/ *adv* ledwie

bargain /'bɑːgɪn/ **I** *n* [1] (deal) umowa *f*, układ *m* [2] (good buy) okazja *f*
II *vi* [1] (for deal) pertraktować [2] (over price) targować się (**with sb** z kimś)
■ **bargain for, bargain on:** ~ **for [sth]**, ~ **on [sth]** (expect) spodziewać się (czegoś); (depend on) liczyć na (coś)

bargaining /'bɑːgɪnɪŋ/ **I** *n* pertraktacje *plt*, negocjacje *plt*
II *adj [position]* przetargowy; **greater ~ power** silniejsza pozycja przetargowa

barge /bɑːdʒ/ **I** *n* (freight) barka *f*; (in navy) szalupa *f* motorowa
II *vi* **to ~ past sb** odepchnąć kogoś
■ **barge in:** (enter rudely) wparować, wtargnąć infml; (interrupt rudely) wtrącić, -ać się bezceremonialnie

bark /bɑːk/ **I** *n* [1] (of tree) kora *f* [2] (of dog) szczek *m*, szczekanie *n*
II *vi [dog]* za|szczekać (**at sb/sth** na kogoś/coś)

barley /'bɑːlɪ/ *n* jęczmień *m*

barmaid /'bɑːmeɪd/ *n* barmanka *f*

barman /'bɑːmən/ *n* barman *m*

barn /bɑːn/ *n* (for crops) stodoła *f*; (for cattle) obora *f*

baron /'bærən/ *n* (noble) baron *m*; (tycoon) potentat *m*, magnat *m*

barrage /'bærɑːʒ, US bə'rɑːʒ/ *n* zapora *f*, stopień *m* wodny; Mil ogień *m* zaporowy

barrel /'bærəl/ *n* [1] (for wine, beer) beczka *f*; (for petroleum) baryłka *f* [2] (of firearm) lufa *f*

barricade /ˌbærɪ'keɪd/ *n* barykada *f*

barrier /'bærɪə(r)/ *n* bariera *f*

barrier cream *n* krem *m* ochronny

barring /'bɑːrɪŋ/ *prep* wyjąwszy (kogoś/coś)

barrister /'bærɪstə(r)/ *n* GB obrońca *m*, adwokat *m*, -ka *f*

barter /'bɑːtə(r)/ *vi* (by exchange) prowadzić handel wymienny; (haggle) targować się

base /beɪs/ **I** *n* (of lamp, monument) podstawa *f*; (of mountain) podnóże *n*; Mil baza *f*
II *adj* nikczemny, niegodziwy
III *vt* op|rzeć, -ierać *[work of art]* (**on sth** na czymś); **to be ~d on sth** opierać się or być opartym na czymś; **to be ~d in London** *[company]* mieścić się or mieć siedzibę w Londynie

baseball /'beɪsbɔːl/ *n* baseball *m*

basement /'beɪsmənt/ *n* (for living) suterena *f*; (for storage) piwnica *f*

bash /bæʃ/ **I** *n* [1] (blow) walnięcie *n*, rąbnięcie *n* infml [2] (attempt) próba *f*; **to have a ~ at sth, to give sth a ~** popróbować or spróbować czegoś [3] (party) jubel *m* infml
II *vt* walnąć, rąbnąć *[person]*; walnąć w (coś), rąbnąć w (coś) infml *[kerb, tree, wall]*
■ **bash into:** ~ **into [sth]** walnąć w (coś), rąbnąć w (coś)

bashful /'bæʃfl/ *adj* wstydliwy, nieśmiały

basic /'beɪsɪk/ **I basics** *npl* **the ~s** (of knowledge) podstawy *f pl*; **to get down to ~s** zająć się sprawami or kwestiami zasadniczymi
II *adj* [1] (fundamental) *[aim, principle]* podstawowy, zasadniczy [2] (elementary) *[education, rule, wage, working hours]* podstawowy

basically /'beɪsɪklɪ/ *adv* zasadniczo, z gruntu

basil /'bæzl/ *n* Bot bazylia *f*

basin /'beɪsn/ *n* [1] (bowl) miska *f* [2] (for washing) umywalka; (for washing up) zlew *m*

basis /'beɪsɪs/ *n* podstawa *f* (**of sth** czegoś); (of discussion) punkt *m* wyjścia; **a ~ for sth/for doing**

sth podstawa do czegoś/do zrobienia czegoś; **on the ~ of sth** na podstawie czegoś

basket /'bɑːskɪt, US 'bæskɪt/ n kosz m, koszyk m

basketball /'bɑːskɪtbɔːl, US 'bæsk-/ n (game) koszykówka f; (ball) piłka f do koszykówki

bass /beɪs/ **[I]** n (singer, voice) bas m; (instrument) kontrabas m

[II] adj [voice, instrument] basowy

bass drum n bęben m wielki

bastard /'bɑːstəd, US 'bæs-/ n [1] vinfml pej łajdak m, kanalia m/f [2] (illegitimate child) bękart m pej

baste /beɪst/ vt podl|ać, -ewać [meat]

bastion /'bæstɪən/ n bastion m

bat /bæt/ **[I]** n [1] Zool nietoperz m [2] Sport **baseball ~** kij baseballowy; **table tennis ~** rakieta f do tenisa stołowego

[II] vi (be batsman) być „przy kiju"; (handle a bat) odbi|ć, -jać

batch /bætʃ/ n (of goods) partia f; (of text) porcja f

bated /'beɪtɪd/ adj **with ~ breath** z zapartym tchem

bath /bɑːθ, US bæθ/ **[I]** n [1] kąpiel f [2] GB (tub) wanna f

[II] baths npl [1] (swimming pool) basen m, kryta pływalnia f [2] (in spa) zakład m wodoleczniczy

[III] vt wy|kąpać

bathe /beɪð/ **[I]** vt (wash) przemy|ć, -wać [wound] (with sth czymś); (immerse) wy|moczyć [feet] (in sth w czymś); **to be ~d in sth** być zlanym czymś [sweat]; być zalanym czymś [tears]

[II] vi [1] (swim) wy|kąpać się [2] US (take bath) wziąć, brać kąpiel

bather /'beɪðə(r)/ n kąpiąc|y m, -a f się

bathing /'beɪðɪŋ/ n kąpiel f

bathing cap n czepek m kąpielowy

bathing costume n kostium m kąpielowy

bath mat n mata f łazienkowa

bathrobe /'bɑːθrəʊb, US 'bæθ-/ n płaszcz m kąpielowy

bathroom /'bɑːθruːm, -rʊm, US 'bæθ-/ n [1] łazienka f [2] US (lavatory) toaleta f, ubikacja f

bathroom cabinet n szafka f łazienkowa

bathroom scales npl waga f łazienkowa

bath towel n ręcznik m kąpielowy

bathtub /'bɑːθtʌb, US 'bæθtʌb/ n wanna f

baton /'bætn, 'bæton, US bə'tɒn/ n (conductor's) batuta f; (in relay race) pałeczka f; GB (policeman's) pałka f policyjna

batsman /'bætsmən/ n (in cricket) zawodnik m wybijający piłkę

batter /'bætə(r)/ **[I]** n Culin rzadkie ciasto n

[II] vt z|bić, poturbować [person]

battered /'bætəd/ adj [person] poturbowany; [kettle] poobijany; [car] zdezelowany

battery /'bætərɪ/ n bateria f; (for car) akumulator m

battery charger n prostownik m

battery farming n chów m bateryjny or intensywny

battery powered adj na baterie, zasilany z baterii

battle /'bætl/ **[I]** n Mil bitwa f, bój m; fig walka f, batalia f fig

[II] vi walczyć (**with sb** z kimś); **to ~ for sth** walczyć o coś

battlefield /'bætlfiːld/ n pole n bitwy

battleship /'bætlʃɪp/ n okręt m liniowy, liniowiec m

bawdy /'bɔːdɪ/ adj hum [joke, song] sprośny

bawl /bɔːl/ vi (weep) ryczeć, wyć infml; (shout) wrz|asnąć, -eszczeć

bay /beɪ/ **[I]** n [1] zatoka f [2] Bot (also ~ **tree**) drzewo n laurowe, wawrzyn m [3] stanowisko m do parkowania; **loading ~** stanowisko załadunkowe

[II] vi [dog] za|szczekać, ujadać (**at sb/sth** na kogoś/coś)

IDIOMS: **to hold sb at ~** trzymać kogoś w dystans

bay leaf n liść m or listek m laurowy or bobkowy

bayonet /'beɪənɪt/ n bagnet m

BC = **Before Christ** p.n.e.

be /biː, bɪ/ **[I]** vi [1] (exist) być; **I think, therefore I am** myślę, więc jestem [2] (take place) [party] być, odby|ć, -wać się; **the meeting will be in the hall** zebranie odbędzie się w sali [3] (be situated, present) być; **the library is in the main building** biblioteka jest or znajduje się w budynku głównym; **I've never been to India** nigdy nie byłem w Indiach

[II] linking verb [1] (followed by a noun) być (kimś/czymś); **he's a teacher/a fool** jest nauczycielem/głupcem; **'it's me!'** „to ja!" [2] (followed by an adjective) być (jakimś); **tomatoes are expensive in winter** w zimie pomidory są drogie; **Tony is married/divorced** Tony jest żonaty/rozwiedziony; **be quiet!** cicho bądź! [3] (expressing mental and physical states) czuć się; **'how are you?' – 'I'm much better, thanks'** „jak się czujesz?" – „dziękuję, dużo lepiej"; **I'm cold/hot** jest mi zimno/gorąco [4] (expressing age) mieć; **how old are you?** ile masz lat?; **I'm 25** mam 25 lat [5] (expressing measurement) mieć; (expressing weight) ważyć; **the room is 10 by 5 metres** pokój ma 10 metrów na 5; **Adam is over six feet (tall)** Adam ma ponad sześć stóp (wzrostu) [6] (expressing cost) kosztować; **how much are the eggs?** ile kosztują jajka? [7] (expressing time) być; **how long will lunch be?** za ile będzie lunch?; **don't be too long** pośpiesz się [8] (expressing supposition) **if Robert were here** gdyby tu był Robert; **if I were you** na twoim miejscu [9] (in tag questions) **she's right, isn't she?** ona ma rację, prawda?; **so that's what you think, is it?** a więc tak uważasz? [10] (in short answers) **'are you disappointed?' – 'yes, I am/**

no, I'm not' „czy jesteś rozczarowany?" – „owszem/wcale nie"

III *v impers* [1] (relating to conditions) **it's cold/hot** jest zimno/gorąco; **it was three degrees below zero** było trzy stopnie poniżej zera; **what was it like in Australia?** jak było w Australii? [2] (expressing time) **it's three (o'clock)** jest (godzina) trzecia; **it's time for lunch** czas na lunch; **it's time to go to school** czas iść do szkoły; **it was 1956** było to w 1956 roku; **hi, Joe, it's been a long time** cześć, Joe, dawno nie widzieliśmy się [3] (expressing distance) **how far is it to Brighton?** jak daleko jest (stąd) do Brighton? [4] (introducing person, object) **it was he who suggested it** to on zaproponował; **it was me that told them** to ja im powiedziałem **IV** *modal aux* [1] (expressing obligation) **to be to do sth** mieć coś zrobić; **you're to do it now!** masz to zrobić natychmiast! [2] (expressing future arrangements, destiny, supposition) **to be to do sth** mieć coś zrobić; **he's to be greeted at the airport by the Ambassador** ma zostać powitany na lotnisku przez ambasadora; **is she to be trusted?** czy można jej ufać?

V *v aux* [1] (in progressive tenses) **don't disturb me while I'm working** nie przeszkadzaj mi, kiedy pracuję; **how long have you been waiting?** jak długo czekasz?; **when are you** or **will you be seeing her?** kiedy będziesz się z nią widzieć? [2] (in passive voice) **the castle was built in the fourteenth century** zamek zbudowano or został wybudowany w czternastym wieku; **she was told that...** powiedziano jej, że...; **it is known that...** wiadomo, że...

IDIOMS **so be it** zgoda, niech więc tak będzie
beach /biːtʃ/ *n* plaża *f*
beach ball *n* piłka *f* plażowa
beach buggy *n* lekki samochód *m* terenowy *(do jazdy po piaskach)*
beacon /'biːkən/ *n* [1] (on runway) latarnia *f* lotniskowa; (lighthouse) latarnia *f* morska [2] (also **radio** ~) radiolatarnia *f*
bead /biːd/ *n* [1] koralik *m*, paciorek *m*; **(a string of)** ~**s** korale, sznur korali [2] (of sweat, dew) kropla *f*, kropelka *f*
beak /biːk/ *n* dziób *m*
beam /biːm/ **I** *n* [1] (of light) snop *m*; (of sun) promień *m*; (of lighthouse, torch, headlights) snop *m* światła; **on full** ~ GB, **on high** ~ US Aut na światłach drogowych or długich; **on low** ~ US Aut na światłach krótkich [2] (smile) promienny uśmiech *m* [3] (timber) belka *f* nośna, dźwigar *m*
II *vt* [antenna, satellite] wysłać, -yłać, przesłać, -yłać [signal]; [TV station] nadać, -wać, transmitować [programme]
III *vi* [sun, moon] świecić
bean /biːn/ *n* fasola *f*
bean sprout *n* kiełek *m* (fasoli, sojowy)

bear /beə(r)/ **I** *n* niedźwiedź *m*
II *vt* fml [1] (carry) [person] nieść, nosić; [vehicle] wieźć, wozić; **to** ~ **a resemblance to sb/sth** być podobnym do kogoś/czegoś; **to** ~ **no relation to sth** nie mieć żadnego związku z czymś; **to** ~ **sth in mind** (remember) pamiętać o czymś [information]; (take into account) **to** ~ **in mind that...** pamiętać or brać pod uwagę, że... [2] (endure) zn|ieść, -osić [illness, smell]; **I can't** ~ **to watch!** nie mogę (na to) patrzeć! [3] (stand up to) wytrzym|ać, -ywać [scrutiny, inspection] [4] (yield) u|rodzić [crops]; **to** ~ **interest** przynosić odsetki, procentować; **to** ~ **fruit** [tree] rodzić owoce
III *vi* [1] **to** ~ **right/west** [person] kierować się na prawo/na zachód [2] **to bring pressure to** ~ **on sb** fig wywrzeć nacisk or presję na kogoś
■ **bear out**: potwierdz|ić, -ać [claim, story]; przyświadczać [person]
■ **bear up**: [person] trzymać się; [branch] wytrzym|ać, -ywać
■ **bear with**: ~ **with** [sb] okaz|ać, -ywać (komuś) cierpliwość; **please** ~ **with me for a moment** proszę o chwilę cierpliwości
bearable /'beərəbl/ *adj* znośny
beard /'bɪəd/ *n* broda *f*
bearded /'bɪədɪd/ *adj* brodaty
bearer /'beərə(r)/ *n* (of news) zwiastun *m*, -ka *f*; (of letter, gift) oddaw|ca *m*, -czyni *f*; (of note, cheque) okaziciel *m*; (of passport) właściciel *m*, -ka *f*
bearing /'beərɪŋ/ **I** *n* [1] (posture) postawa *f*; (behaviour) zachowanie *n* [2] (relevance) **to have no/little** ~ **on sth** nie mieć związku/mieć niewielki związek z czymś [3] (position) położenie *n*; **to take a** ~ **of sth** określić położenie czegoś
II bearings *npl* **to get one's** ~**s** z|orientować się, rozezna|ć, -wać się
beast /biːst/ *n* [1] (animal) zwierzę *n* [2] infml (person) bestia *f*, potwór *m*
beat /biːt/ **I** *n* [1] (of drum) bicie *n* [2] (rhythm) rytm *m*, tempo *n* [3] (of heart) uderzenie *n* [4] (in police force) (area) rewir *m*; (route) obchód *m*
II *vt* [1] (strike) z|bić [person]; **to** ~ **sb with a stick** zbić kogoś kijem; **to** ~ **time** wybijać takt or rytm [2] (defeat) pobić, pokonać [opponent, team]; **it** ~**s me how/why** nie pojmuję, jak/dlaczego; **he** ~ **me to the hotel** był przede mną w hotelu; **you can't** ~ **Italian shoes** nie ma jak włoskie buty
III *vi* **to** ~ **against sth** [waves] uderzać o (coś); [rain] bębnić o (coś); **to** ~ **at** or **on sth** [person] walić w (coś); [heart] bić; [drum] brzmieć, bić; [wing] za|trzepotać
■ **beat back**: zmu|sić, -szać do odwrotu [crowd]; **she tried to** ~ **the flames back** próbowała opanować ogień
■ **beat down**: [sun] palić żarem (kogoś/coś); [rain] lać się strumieniami na (kogoś/coś)

■ **beat off**: od|eprzeć, -pierać *[attack, attackers]*
■ **beat up**: po|bić, z|bić
beating /'bi:tɪŋ/ n [1] (punishment) lanie n [2] (of drum, heart) bicie n; (of wings) trzepot m
beautician /bju:'tɪʃn/ n kosmetyczka f
beautiful /'bju:tɪfl/ adj piękny; *[holiday, feeling]* wspaniały, cudowny
beautifully /'bju:tɪfəlɪ/ adv *[play, write]* świetnie, doskonale; *[dressed, painted]* pięknie
beauty /'bju:tɪ/ n (of landscape, poem) piękno n; (of woman) uroda f
beauty parlour n salon m kosmetyczny or piękności
beauty queen n królowa f or miss f inv piękności
beauty salon n US = **beauty parlour**
beauty spot n [1] (on skin) pieprzyk m; (fake) muszka f [2] (place) malowniczy zakątek m
beaver /'bi:və(r)/ n bóbr m
because /bɪ'kɒz, US also -kɔ:z/ [1] conj ponieważ, dlatego że
[1] **because of** prep phr z powodu (kogoś/czegoś)
beckon /'bekən/ [1] vt skinąć na (kogoś); **to ~ sb in** gestem zaprosić kogoś do środka
[1] vi skinąć (**to sb** na kogoś)
become /bɪ'kʌm/ [1] vi sta|ć, -wać się; **to ~ ill** zachorować
[1] v impers **what has ~ of your brother?** co u twego brata?
becoming /bɪ'kʌmɪŋ/ adj *[behaviour]* odpowiedni; *[garment, haircut]* twarzowy
bed /bed/ n [1] łóżko n; **to go to ~** pójść spać [2] (of flowers) grządka f, rabata f; (circular, oval) klomb m [3] (of sea, lake) dno n; (of river) łożysko n
bed and breakfast, B and B n zakwaterowanie n ze śniadaniem
bedclothes /'bedkləʊðz/ npl przykrycie n (kołdry, koce)
bedraggled /bɪ'drægld/ adj przemoczony, przemoknięty
bedridden /'bedrɪdn/ adj obłożnie chory
bedroom /'bedru:m, -rʊm/ n sypialnia f
bedside /'bedsaɪd/ [1] n brzeg m łóżka
[1] adj *[lamp]* nocny
bedsit, bedsitter /'bedsɪt, ˌbed'sɪtə/ n infml GB kawalerka f (zwykle umeblowana)
bedspread /'bedspred/ n narzuta f, kapa f
bedtime /'bedtaɪm/ n **it's ~** czas or pora spać
bee /bi:/ n pszczoła f
beech /bi:tʃ/ n buk m
beef /bi:f/ n wołowina f
beefburger /'bi:fbɜ:gə(r)/ n hamburger m z wołowiny
beehive /'bi:haɪv/ n ul m
beeline /'bi:laɪn/ n
[IDIOMS] **to make a ~ for sth** ruszyć prosto w kierunku czegoś

beep /bi:p/ [1] n (of electronic device) sygnał m akustyczny; bipnięcie n infml; (of car) dźwięk m klaksonu, klakson m
[1] vi *[electronic device]* za|brzęczeć; *[car horn]* za|trąbić
beer /bɪə(r)/ n piwo n
bee sting n użądlenie n
beet /bi:t/ n burak m
beetle /'bi:tl/ n chrząszcz m, żuk m
beetroot /'bi:tru:t/ n GB burak m (ćwikłowy)
before /bɪ'fɔ:(r)/ [1] prep [1] (earlier than) przed (czymś); **the day ~ the meeting** dzień przed spotkaniem; **the day ~ yesterday** przedwczoraj [2] (in front of) przed (czymś); **he sat ~ the fire** siedział przy kominku [3] US (in time expressions) **ten ~ six** za dziesięć szósta
[1] adv (preceding) wcześniej, przedtem; **the week/year ~** tydzień/rok wcześniej; **have you been to India ~?** czy byłeś (już kiedyś przedtem) w Indiach?; **I've never been there ~** nigdy przedtem tam nie byłem; **I've never seen him ~ in my life** nigdy w życiu go przedtem nie widziałem; **long ~** dużo wcześniej, dawno temu
[1] **before long** adv phr niedługo, wkrótce
[1] conj (in time) zanim, nim; **~ he goes, I must remind him that...** zanim wyjdzie, muszę mu przypomnieć, że...
beforehand /bɪ'fɔ:hænd/ adv (in readiness) zawczasu; (in advance) wcześniej
befriend /bɪ'frend/ vt (make friends with) zaprzyjaźni|ć, -ać się z (kimś); (look after) okaz|ać, -ywać (komuś) przyjaźń
beg /beg/ [1] vt po|prosić o (coś) *[food, money]* (**from sb** kogoś); **to ~ sb for sth** błagać or prosić kogoś o coś; **stop, I ~ (of) you!** błagam, przestań!
[1] vi *[person]* żebrać; *[dog]* prosić; **to ~ for help** prosić or błagać o pomoc
beggar /'begə(r)/ n żebra|k m, -czka f
begin /bɪ'gɪn/ [1] **to begin with** adv phr (at first) najpierw, początkowo; (firstly) po pierwsze
[1] vt zacząć, -ynać, rozpocząć, -ynać *[game, journey, meal]* (**with sth** od czegoś, czymś); zapoczątkow|ać, -ywać *[campaign, debate]*; doprowadz|ić, -ać do (czegoś) *[argument, war]*; otw|orzyć, -ierać *[festival, series]*; **to ~ to do sth, to ~ doing sth** zacząć coś robić, rozpocząć robienie czegoś; **it's ~ning to rain** zaczyna padać
[1] vi *[person]* zacz|ąć, -ynać (**with sth, by doing sth** od czegoś, od zrobienia czegoś); *[meeting, play]* zacz|ąć, -ynać się, rozpocz|ąć, -ynać się (**with sth** od czegoś); **to ~ again** zacząć od nowa
beginner /bɪ'gɪnə(r)/ n początkujący m, -a f
beginning /bɪ'gɪnɪŋ/ [1] n początek m; **at the ~** na początku (**of sth** czegoś); **in the ~** początkowo; **since the ~ of March** od początku marca
[1] **beginnings** npl (origins) początki m pl

behalf /bɪ'hɑːf, US -'hæf/ **on** ~ **of sb, on sb's** ~ GB, **in** ~ **of sb** US *prep phr [act, phone]* w imieniu kogoś; *[campaign]* na rzecz kogoś

behave /bɪ'heɪv/ **[]** *vi* zachow|ać, -ywać się (**towards sb** wobec kogoś, w stosunku do kogoś) **[]]** *vr* **to** ~ **oneself** *[person]* dobrze się zachowywać or sprawować; ~ **yourself!** zachowuj się jak należy!

behaviour GB, **behavior** US /bɪ'heɪvjə(r)/ *n* zachowanie *n* (**towards sb** wobec kogoś, w stosunku do kogoś); (in given circumstances) postępowanie *n*; **for good** ~ za dobre sprawowanie IDIOMS: **to be on one's best** ~ zachowywać się nienagannie or wzorowo

behead /bɪ'hed/ *vt* ści|ać, -nać kogoś or komuś głowę

behind /bɪ'haɪnd/ **[]** *n* infml siedzenie *n* infml **[]]** *adv [follow]* z tyłu; *[glance]* do tyłu, w tył; **to be far** ~ być daleko w tyle or z tyłu; **keep an eye on the car** ~ obserwuj samochód za nami; **to be** ~ **with sth** zalegać z czymś *[payments]*; mieć zaległości w czymś *[work]* **[]]]** *prep* [1] za (kimś/czymś); ~ **our car** za naszym samochodem; ~ **sb's back** za plecami kogoś also fig [2] (in support of) za (kimś/czymś); **to be (solidly)** ~ **sb** stać za kimś (murem)

beige /beɪʒ/ **[]** *n* beż *m*, (kolor *m*) beżowy *m* **[]]** *adj* beżowy

Beijing /beɪ'dʒɪŋ/ *prn* Pekin *m*, Beijing *m*

being /'biːɪŋ/ *n* [1] (entity) istota *f*, stworzenie *n* [2] (existence) istnienie *n*; **to come into** ~ *[university]* powstać; *[law, rule]* wejść w życie

Beirut /,beɪ'ruːt/ *prn* Bejrut *m*

belch /beltʃ/ **[]** *n* beknięcie *n* infml **[]]** *vi [person]* bek|nąć, -ać infml ■ **belch out:** wyrzuc|ić, -ać (z siebie), buch|nąć, -ać (czymś) *[smoke, flames]*

belfry /'belfrɪ/ *n* dzwonnica *f*

Belgian /'beldʒən/ **[]** *n* Belg *m*, -ijka *f* **[]]** *adj* belgijski

Belgium /'beldʒəm/ *prn* Belgia *f*

belie /bɪ'laɪ/ *vt* zada|ć, -wać kłam (czemuś) *[rumours]*

belief /bɪ'liːf/ *n* [1] (opinion) przekonanie *n* (**about sth** dotyczące czegoś) [2] (confidence) wiara *f* (**in sb/ sth** w kogoś/coś); zaufanie *n* (**in sb/sth** do kogoś/ czegoś) [3] (faith) wiara *f*; (religious system) wyznanie *n*, religia *f*

believable /bɪ'liːvəbl/ *adj* wiarygodny

believe /bɪ'liːv/ **[]** *vt* [1] u|wierzyć, da|ć, -wać wiarę (komuś, czemuś) [2] (think) sądzić, uważać **[]]** *vi* [1] **to** ~ **in sth** wierzyć w coś *[promises]* [2] **to** ~ **in God** wierzyć w Boga

believer /bɪ'liːvə(r)/ *n* wierzący|y *m*, -a *f*; ~ **in sth** zwolenni|k *m*, -czka *f* czegoś

belittle /bɪ'lɪtl/ *vt* umniejsz|yć, -ać *[effort]*; z|lekceważyć *[person]*

bell /bel/ *n* (in church) dzwon *m*; (on sheep, bicycle) dzwonek *m*; **door** ~ dzwonek u drzwi IDIOMS: **that name rings a** ~ to nazwisko wydaje mi się znajome

belligerent /bɪ'lɪdʒərənt/ **[]** *n* strona *f* wojująca **[]]** *adj [person]* wojowniczy, agresywny; *[country]* (będący) w stanie wojny, walczący

bellow /'beləʊ/ *vi [bull]* za|ryczeć; *[person]* za|grzmieć; **to** ~ **at sb** wrzasnąć or ryknąć na kogoś

bellows /'beləʊz/ *npl* miech *m*, miechy *m pl*

belly /'belɪ/ *n* infml żołądek *m* infml

bellyache /'belɪeɪk/ *n* infml ból *m* brzucha or żołądka

bellybutton /'belɪbʌtn/ *n* infml pępek *m*

belong /bɪ'lɒŋ, US -lɔːŋ/ *vi* **to** ~ **to sb** należeć do kogoś; **to** ~ **to sth** należeć do czegoś *[family, party]*; **where does this plate** ~ **?** gdzie powinien stać ten talerz?

belongings /bɪ'lɒŋɪŋz, US -'lɔːŋ-/ *npl* rzeczy *f pl*, dobytek *m*; **personal** ~ rzeczy osobiste

beloved /bɪ'lʌvɪd/ **[]** *n* ukochan|y *m*, -a *f* **[]]** *adj* ukochany

below /bɪ'ləʊ/ **[]** *prep* pod (czymś), poniżej (czegoś); ~ **sea level** poniżej poziomu morza; ~ **the average** poniżej przeciętnej **[]]** *adv* **100 metres** ~ sto metrów niżej; **the village** ~ wioska leżąca niżej or w dole; **the people (down)** ~ ludzie na dole; **the apartment** ~ mieszkanie piętro niżej; **see** ~ (on page) patrz poniżej

belt /belt/ **[]** *n* [1] pasek *m* [2] Tech taśma *f* **[]]** *vt* infml (hit) wy|łoić or z|łoić skórę (komuś) infml *[person]* ■ **belt out:** ~ **[sth] out** *[person]* za|śpiewać (coś) na całe gardło ■ **belt up:** [1] GB infml (shut up) zamknąć się infml [2] Aut zapi|ąć, -nać pasy IDIOMS: **this remark was a bit below the** ~ ta uwaga była trochę poniżej pasa; **to tighten one's** ~ zacisnąć pasa

bemused /bɪ'mjuːzd/ *adj* speszony, zdeprymowany

bench /bentʃ/ *n* [1] ławka *f*; (in workshop) warsztat *m* [2] (in law) **the** ~**, the Bench** (as profession) sędziowie *m pl*; (in one case) sąd *m*, skład *m* or komplet *m* sędziowski

benchmark /'bentʃmɑːk/ *n* [1] (in surveying) wzorzec *m*, punkt *m* odniesienia [2] Comput test *m* sprawności

bend /bend/ **[]** *n* [1] (in road) zakręt *m*; (in river) zakręt *m*, zakole *n*; (of elbow, knee) zgięcie *n* [2] (action) skłon *m* **[]]** *vt* zgi|ać, -nać, ugi|ać, -nać *[arm, leg]*; schyl|ić, -ać, pochyl|ić, -ać *[head]*; gi|ać, zgi|ać, -nać, wygi|ać, -nać *[pipe, wire]* **[]]]** *vi* [1] *[road, path]* (once) zakręc|ić, -ać, skręc|ić, -ać; (several times) wić się; *[branch, nail]* wygi|ać, -nać się, zgi|ąć, -nać się [2] *[person]* pochyl|ić, -ać się, schyl|ić, -ać się; **to ~ forward** pochylić się do przodu

■ **bend down, bend over**: pochyl|ić, -ać się, nachylić się

beneath /bɪ'ni:θ/ **[I]** *prep* [1] (under) pod (czymś), poniżej (czegoś); **~ the table** pod stołem [2] (unworthy of) **it's ~ you to make such nasty comments** takie wredne komentarze są ciebie niegodne

[II] *adv* poniżej, w dole; **the apartment ~** mieszkanie piętro niżej

benefactor /'benɪfæktə(r)/ *n* dobroczyńca *m*; (donor) ofiarodawca *m*

beneficial /ˌbenɪ'fɪʃl/ *adj* *[change, effect, influence]* zbawienny

beneficiary /ˌbenɪ'fɪʃərɪ, US -'fɪʃɪerɪ/ *n* beneficjent *m*

benefit /'benɪfɪt/ **[I]** *n* [1] (helpful effect) korzyść *f* **(from sth** z czegoś) [2] (financial aid) zasiłek *m*; **to be on ~(s)** być na zasiłku

[II] *adj [concert, match]* dobroczynny, charytatywny; *[system]* socjalny

[III] *vt* przyn|ieść, -osić korzyść (komuś/czemuś) *[person, group]*

[IV] *vi* s|korzystać **(from sth** z czegoś); **to ~ by sth** skorzystać na czymś

IDIOMS: **to give sb the ~ of the doubt** uwierzyć komuś na słowo *(mimo wątpliwości)*

benevolent /bɪ'nevələnt/ *adj* dobrotliwy, życzliwy

benign /bɪ'naɪn/ *adj* [1] (mild) *[gesture, smile]* życzliwy [2] Med *[tumour]* łagodny

bent /bent/ *adj* [1] *[nail, wire]* zgięty; *[person]* pochylony, przygarbiony [2] **to be ~ on sth** być zdecydowanym na coś; **to be ~ on doing sth** zawziąć się, żeby coś zrobić

bereaved /bɪ'ri:vd/ *adj* pogrążony w smutku

bereavement /bɪ'ri:vmənt/ *n* bolesna strata *f* *(kogoś bliskiego)*

berry /'berɪ/ *n* jagoda *f*

berserk /bə'sɜ:k/ *adj* **to go ~** wpaść w szał or furię

berth /bɜ:θ/ **[I]** *n* [1] (on ship) koja *f*; (on train) kuszetka *f* [2] (for ship) miejsce *n* postoju statku

[II] *vt* dobić, -jać (czymś) do brzegu *[ship]*; przycumow|ać, -ywać, zacumow|ać, -ywać

IDIOMS: **to give sb/sth a wide ~** omijać kogoś/coś z daleka

beset /bɪ'set/ *vt* **a country ~ by strikes** kraj nękany strajkami

beside /bɪ'saɪd/ *prep* [1] (next to) obok (kogoś/czegoś), przy (kimś/czymś); **~ the sea** nad morzem [2] (in comparison with) w porównaniu z (kimś/czymś), wobec (kogoś/czegoś)

IDIOMS: **to be ~ oneself with anger/joy** nie posiadać się z gniewu/radości

besides /bɪ'saɪdz/ **[I]** *adv* ponadto, do tego

[II] *prep* (o)prócz (kogoś/czegoś), poza (kimś/czymś)

besiege /bɪ'si:dʒ/ *vt* oblegać also fig

besotted /bɪ'sɒtɪd/ *adj* zadurzony **(with sb** w kimś)

best /best/ **[I]** *n* **the ~** najlepsz|y *m*, -a *f*, -e *n*; **it's the ~ of his stories** to najlepsze z jego opowiadań; **at ~** w najlepszym razie or przypadku; **to make the ~ of sth** zrobić najlepszy użytek z czegoś; **this is modern art at its ~** to sztuka współczesna w najlepszym wydaniu; **I'll do my ~ to make her happy** zrobię wszystko, żeby była szczęśliwa; **all the ~!** (good luck) wszystkiego najlepszego!; (cheers) na zdrowie!

[II] *adj* najlepszy; **the ~ book I've ever read** najlepsza książka, jaką przeczytałem; **to look ~** najlepiej wyglądać

[III] *adv* najlepiej; **to like sth ~** najbardziej coś lubić

best friend *n* najlepszy przyjaciel *m*, najlepsza przyjaciółka *f*

best man *n* drużba *m*

bestow /bɪ'stəʊ/ *vt* obdarz|yć, -ać (czymś) **(on** or **upon sb** kogoś); nada|ć, -wać, przyzna|ć, -wać *[title]* **(on** or **upon sb** komuś)

bestseller /ˌbest'selə(r)/ *n* bestsel(l)er *m*

best-selling /ˌbest'selɪŋ/ *adj* *[product]* najlepiej sprzedający się; *[book]* bestsel(l)erowy; **the ~ novelist of the year** najpopularniejszy powieściopisarz roku

bet /bet/ **[I]** *n* (gamble) zakład *m*

[II] *vt* (gamble) postawić, stawiać *[money]*; za|łożyć, -kładać się z (kimś) *[person]*

[III] *vi* (gamble) grać; **to ~ on sb/sth** obstawiać kogoś/coś; **you ~!** no pewnie!

betray /bɪ'treɪ/ *vt* zdradz|ić, -ać

betrayal /bɪ'treɪəl/ *n* zdrada *f*

better /'betə(r)/ **[I]** *n* **the ~** lepsz|y *m*, -a *f*, -e *n*; **to deserve ~** zasługiwać na coś lepszego; **so much the ~, all the ~** tym lepiej

[II] *adj* lepszy **(than sth** od czegoś, niż coś); **to get ~** poprawić się; *[ill person]* wy|zdrowieć; **things are getting ~** sytuacja poprawia się; **to taste ~** smakować lepiej; **that's ~!** teraz (jest) dużo lepiej!; **to be** or **feel ~** *[person]* czuć się lepiej; **she felt all the ~ for her holiday** wakacje dobrze jej zrobiły; **if it makes you feel any ~** (less worried) jeśli cię to uspokoi; (less sad) jeśli cię to pocieszy; **to feel ~ about doing sth** (less nervous, worried) mniej się przejmować robieniem czegoś; (less guilty) robić coś ze spokojniejszym sumieniem; **to be a ~ swimmer than sb** lepiej pływać od kogoś or niż ktoś; **to be ~ at sth** być lepszym w czymś *[sport]*; **the faster the car the ~** im szybszy samochód, tym lepszy

III *adv* lepiej; **you had** ~ **do it, you'd** ~ **do it** lepiej to zrób; **I'd** ~ **go** lepiej już (sobie) pójdę
IV *vt* popraw|ić, -ać
IDIOMS: **for** ~ **(or) for worse** niech się dzieje, co chce; (in wedding vow) na dobre i na złe; **to get the** ~ **of sb** zdobyć przewagę nad kimś *[opponent]*; **his curiosity got the** ~ **of him** ciekawość była silniejsza od niego; **to go one** ~ **than sb** zakasować kogoś infml; **to think** ~ **of it** zmienić zdanie (po namyśle)
better off /,betər'pf/ *adj* 1 (more wealthy) zamożniejszy, lepiej sytuowany (**than sb** od kogoś, niż ktoś) 2 (in a better situation) **she'd be** ~ **without him** lepiej byłoby jej bez niego
betting /'betɪŋ/ *n* zakłady *m pl*, obstawianie *n*
betting shop *n* GB punkt *m* przyjmowania zakładów
between /bɪ'twiːn/ **I** *prep* 1 (in time, space) (po)między (czymś a czymś); ~ **now and next year** (od teraz) do przyszłego roku; **it costs** ~ **£10 and £20** to kosztuje od 10 do 20 funtów 2 (jointly) **we spent $250** ~ **us** razem or do spółki wydaliśmy 250 dolarów
II *adv* (also **in** ~) (in space) pośrodku; (in time) w tym czasie; **a house and stables with a yard in** ~ dom i stajnie z podwórzem pośrodku
IDIOMS: ~ **ourselves,** ~ **you and me...** (mówiąc) między nami...
beverage /'bevərɪdʒ/ *n* napój *m*
beware /bɪ'weə(r)/ **I** *excl* uwaga!
II *vi* uważać (**of sb/sth** na kogoś/coś); strzec się, mieć się na baczności (**of sb/sth** przed kimś/czymś); '~ **of the dog**" „uwaga! zły pies"
bewildered /bɪ'wɪldəd/ *adj* zdumiony (**at** or **by sth** czymś)
bewildering /bɪ'wɪldərɪŋ/ *adj* zdumiewający
bewitch /bɪ'wɪtʃ/ *vt* rzuc|ić, -ać czar or urok na (kogoś), zaczarować; fig oczarow|ać, -ywać (**by** or **with sth** czymś)
beyond /bɪ'jɒnd/ **I** *prep* 1 (in space, time) ~ **the city walls** za murami miasta; **children** ~ **the age of 11** dzieci powyżej jedenastu lat 2 (more than) **the level of inflation has gone** ~ **10%** poziom inflacji przekroczył 10%; **to be** ~ **one's means** przekraczać możliwości (finansowe) kogoś; **he is** ~ **help** jemu nie można już pomóc; **it's** ~ **me!** nie potrafię tego pojąć! 3 (other than) poza (czymś)
II *adv* **in the room** ~ w następnym pokoju; **we're planning for the year 2010 and** ~ robimy plany na rok 2010 i następne lata
III *conj* **there was little I could do** ~ **reassuring him that...** niewiele mogłem zrobić poza zapewnieniem go, że...
IDIOMS: **in the back of** ~ *[house, farm]* gdzieś na końcu świata fig
bias /'baɪəs/ **I** *n* 1 (prejudice) tendencyjność *f*, stronniczość *f* 2 (tendency) nastawienie *n* (**towards sb/sth** do kogoś/czegoś)

II *vt* nastawi|ć, -ać *[person]* (**against/in favour of sb/sth** negatywnie/pozytywnie do kogoś/czegoś)
bia(s)sed /'baɪəst/ *adj [decision, person]* stronniczy; **to** ~ **be against sb/sth** być uprzedzonym do kogoś/czegoś
bib /bɪb/ *n* (baby's) śliniak *m*, śliniaczek *m*; (of apron, dungarees) karczek *m*
Bible /'baɪbl/ *n* **the** ~ Biblia *f*
biblical /'bɪblɪkl/ *adj* biblijny
bibliography /,bɪblɪ'ɒɡrəfi/ *n* bibliografia *f*
bicarbonate /,baɪ'kɑːbənət/ *n* (also ~ **of soda**) soda *f* oczyszczona
bicentenary /,baɪsen'tiːnəri, US -'sentənərɪ/ *n* dwóchsetlecie *n*, dwusetlecie *n*
biceps /'baɪseps/ *n* biceps *m*
bicker /'bɪkə(r)/ *vi* sprzeczać się, kłócić się (**about sth** o coś)
bickering /'bɪkərɪŋ/ *n* sprzeczki *f pl*
bicycle /'baɪsɪkl/ **I** *n* rower *m*; **on a** ~ na rowerze; **to ride a** ~ jeździć na rowerze
II *adj [ride, tour]* rowerowy; ~ **hire** wypożyczalnia rowerów
bicycle lane *n* ścieżka *f* rowerowa
bid /bɪd/ **I** *n* 1 (at auction) oferowana cena *f*, oferta *f* (licytacyjna) (**for sth** na coś) 2 (for contract) oferta *f* *(w przetargu)* 3 (attempt) próba *f* (**to do sth** zrobienia czegoś)
II *vt* 1 (at auction) za|oferować, za|proponować *[money]* (**for sth** za coś) 2 (say) **to** ~ **sb goodbye** powiedzieć komuś do widzenia 3 (in bridge) za|licytować
III *vi* (at auction) wziąć, brać udział w licytacji (**for sth** czegoś); sta|nąć, -wać do przetargu (**for sth** na coś)
bidder /'bɪdə(r)/ *n* licytant *m*; **to go to the highest** ~ przypaść osobie oferującej najwyższą cenę
bidding /'bɪdɪŋ/ *n* licytacja *f*
bide /baɪd/ *vi*
IDIOMS: **to** ~ **one's time** czekać na właściwy moment
bidet /'biːdeɪ, US biː'deɪ/ *n* bidet *m*
bifocals /baɪ'fəʊklz/ *npl* okulary *plt* dwugniskowe
big /bɪɡ/ *adj* 1 (in size) duży; (large) wielki; **to get** ~ **ger** (taller) wyrosnąć; (fatter) przytyć, roztyć się; **a** ~ **book** (thick) gruba książka; (large-format) duża or wielka księga 2 (in age) *[sister, brother]* starszy 3 (in extent) *[family]* duży, liczny; *[meal]* duży, obfity; **to be in** ~ **trouble** mieć poważne kłopoty; **you're making a** ~ **mistake** popełniasz poważny błąd
IDIOMS: **to have** ~ **ideas, to think** ~ infml robić or mieć wielkie plany
bigamy /'bɪɡəmɪ/ *n* bigamia *f*
big business *n* (companies collectively) wielki biznes *m*; (profitable activity) dobry or świetny interes *m*
big game *n* gruba zwierzyna *f*
bigheaded /,bɪɡ'hedɪd/ *adj* infml zarozumiały

bigmouth /'bɪgmaʊθ/ n infml pej (indiscreet person) papla m/f infml; (boastful person) chwalipięta m/f

big name n (in music, art) wielkie nazwisko n; (in film, sport) gwiazda f; fig (in industry) znana marka f

bigoted /'bɪgətɪd/ adj dogmatyczny; (about religion) bigoteryjny

bigotry /'bɪgətrɪ/ n dogmatyczność f; (about religion) bigoteria f

big screen n duży ekran m

big shot n infml gruba ryba f infml

big toe n wielki palec m u nogi

big top n namiot m cyrkowy; fig cyrk m

bike /baɪk/ n (cycle) rower m; (motorbike) motocykl m, motor m

biker /'baɪkə(r)/ n infml (cyclist) rowerzyst|a m, -ka f; (motorcyclist) motocyklist|a m, -ka f

bikini /bɪ'ki:nɪ/ n bikini n inv

bilingual /ˌbaɪ'lɪŋgwəl/ adj dwujęzyczny

bill /bɪl/ **I** n ① (note of charges) rachunek m; gas ~ rachunek za gaz ② (law) projekt m ustawy ③ (poster) plakat m, afisz m ④ US banknot m ⑤ Zool dziób m **II** vt to ~ sb for sth/doing sth wystawić komuś rachunek za coś/za zrobienie czegoś

ⓘⓘⓘ to fit or fill the ~ być idealnym, doskonale się nadawać

billboard /'bɪlbɔ:d/ n billboard m

billet /'bɪlɪt/ vt za|kwaterować [soldiers] (on or with sb u kogoś)

billiards npl bilard m

billion /'bɪlɪən/ n (a thousand million) miliard m; GB (a million million) bilion m

billionaire /ˌbɪlɪə'neə(r)/ n miliarder m, -ka f

billow /'bɪləʊ/ vi [clouds, smoke] kłębić się

■ **billow out**: [sail, skirt] wyd|ąć, -ymać się; [steam] buch|nąć, -ać

billy goat n kozioł m

bimbo /'bɪmbəʊ/ n infml pej lalunia f, dzidzia f infml

bin /bɪn/ n kubeł m na śmieci

bind /baɪnd/ vt ① (tie up) związ|ać, -ywać ② (also ~ together) z|łączyć, po|łączyć [family, community] ③ (constrain) to ~ sb to sth/to do sth zobowiązywać kogoś do czegoś/do zrobienia czegoś; to be bound by sth być związanym czymś [contract, promise] ④ oprawi|ć, -ać [book] (in sth w coś)

binder /'baɪndə(r)/ n segregator m

binding /'baɪndɪŋ/ **I** n (of book) oprawa f **II** adj [contract] wiążący; [force] obowiązujący

binge /bɪndʒ/ n infml biba f, popijawa f infml; to go on a ~ (celebrating) pójść w tango

bingo /'bɪŋgəʊ/ n bingo n inv

bin liner n worek m foliowy na śmieci

binoculars /bɪ'nɒkjʊləz/ npl lornetka f

biochemist /ˌbaɪəʊ'kemɪst/ n biochemik m

biochemistry /ˌbaɪəʊ'kemɪstrɪ/ n biochemia f

biodegradable /ˌbaɪəʊdɪ'greɪdəbl/ adj ulegający biodegradacji

biodiversity /ˌbaɪəʊdɪ'vɜːsətɪ/ n zróżnicowanie n biologiczne

bioengineering /ˌbaɪəʊˌendʒɪ'nɪərɪŋ/ n bioinżynieria f

biographical /ˌbaɪə'græfɪkl/ adj biograficzny

biography /baɪ'ɒgrəfɪ/ n biografia f

biological /ˌbaɪə'lɒdʒɪkl/ adj biologiczny

biological clock n zegar m biologiczny

biological warfare n wojna f biologiczna

biologist /baɪ'ɒlədʒɪst/ n biolog m

biology /baɪ'ɒlədʒɪ/ n biologia f

biopsy /'baɪɒpsɪ/ n biopsja f

birch /bɜːtʃ/ n brzoza f

bird /bɜːd/ n ① Zool ptak m ② GB infml (girl) panienka f infml

ⓘⓘⓘ to kill two ~s with one stone upiec dwie pieczenie przy jednym ogniu

bird of prey n ptak m drapieżny

bird's eye view n widok m z lotu ptaka

birdsong /'bɜːdsɒŋ/ n ptasi śpiew m

bird-watching /'bɜːdwɒtʃɪŋ/ n ptasiarstwo n; to go ~ udać się na podglądanie ptaków

biro® /'baɪərəʊ/ n GB długopis m

birth /bɜːθ/ n ① narodziny plt also fig; to give ~ (to a boy) urodzić (chłopca) ② (delivery) poród m

birth certificate n metryka f or świadectwo n urodzenia

birth control n (in society) kontrola f or regulacja f urodzeń; (by couple) antykoncepcja f

birthday /'bɜːθdeɪ/ n urodziny plt; to wish sb (a) happy ~ życzyć komuś wszystkiego najlepszego (z okazji urodzin)

birthday party n przyjęcie n urodzinowe, urodziny plt

birthing pool n basen m do porodów

birthmark /'bɜːθmɑːk/ n znamię n

birth mother n matka f biologiczna

birthplace /'bɜːθpleɪs/ n miejsce n urodzenia

birthrate /'bɜːθreɪt/ n wskaźnik m urodzeń

birth sign n znak m zodiaku

biscuit /'bɪskɪt/ n ① GB herbatnik m, kruche ciasteczko n ② US bułeczka f

bisexual /baɪ'seksjʊəl/ **I** n biseksualist|a m, -ka f **II** adj biseksualny

bishop /'bɪʃəp/ n ① biskup m ② (in chess) goniec m, laufer m

bit¹ /bɪt/ **I** n ① kawałek m; a ~ of cheese kawałek sera ② infml a ~ (of sth) odrobina f (czegoś); a ~ of difficulty mała trudność; to do a ~ of shopping zrobić małe zakupy

II a bit adv phr trochę; a ~ deaf nieco głuchy; it's a ~ of a surprise to trochę niespodziewane

ⓘⓘⓘ ~ by ~ stopniowo; ~s and pieces (fragments) kawałki; (belongings) manatki

bit² /bɪt/ n (on horse) wędzidło n

bitch /bɪtʃ/ n ① (of dog) suka f ② infml (woman) suka f vinfml

bite /baɪt/ **❚** *n* 1 (mouthful) kęs *m* 2 (from insect, snake) ukąszenie *n*; (from dog) ugryzienie *n*
❚❚ *vt [person, animal]* ugryźć; *[insect]* ukąsić; **to ~ one's nails** obgryzać paznokcie
❚❚❚ *vi [fish]* brać
■ **bite off**: ~ **[sth] off** odgryźć, -zać
biting /'baɪtɪŋ/ *adj [cold, wind]* przenikliwy; *[comment]* zjadliwy
bitter /'bɪtə(r)/ *adj* gorzki; *[person]* rozgoryczony; *[critic]* zaciekły; *[wind]* przenikliwy
IDIOMS **to the ~ end** *[fight]* do upadłego
bitterly /'bɪtəlɪ/ *adv [weep]* gorzko; *[say]* z goryczą; *[fight]* zawzięcie; *[disappointed]* głęboko
bitterness /'bɪtənɪs/ *n* gorycz *f*
bizarre /bɪ'zɑː(r)/ *adj* dziwaczny
black /blæk/ **❚** *n* 1 (colour) czerń *f* 2 (also **Black**) czarnoskóry *m*, -a *f*, Murzyn *m*, -ka *f* 3 (in credit) **to be in the ~** mieć saldo dodatnie
❚❚ *adj* 1 czarny; *[thoughts]* ponury; *[coffee]* czarny; *[tea]* bez mleka; **to turn ~** poczernieć 2 (also **Black**) *[person]* czarnoskóry; *[culture, area]* murzyński
■ **black out**: *[person]* s|tracić przytomność
black and white **❚** *n* technika *f* czarno-biała
❚❚ *adj [photograph, film, TV]* czarno-biały; *[situation]* jednoznaczny
blackberry /'blækbrɪ, -berɪ/ *n* jeżyna *f*
blackbird /'blækbɜːd/ *n* kos *m*
blackboard /'blækbɔːd/ *n* tablica *f* (szkolna); **on the ~** na tablicy
black box *n* czarna skrzynka *f*
blackcurrant /ˌblæk'kʌrənt/ *n* czarna porzeczka *f*
blacken /'blækən/ *vt [actor]* u|czernić *[eyes]*; *[coal]* u|smolić *[face]*
black eye *n* podbite oko *n*
blackhead /'blækhed/ *n* wągier *m*, zaskórnik *m*
black ice *n* gołoledź *f*
blacklist /'blæklɪst/ **❚** *n* czarna lista *f*
❚❚ *vt* umie|ścić, -szczać na indeksie
blackmail /'blækmeɪl/ **❚** *n* szantaż *m*
❚❚ *vt* za|szantażować
blackmailer /'blækmeɪlə(r)/ *n* szantażyst|a *m*, -ka *f*
black market *n* czarny rynek *m* **on the ~** na czarnym rynku
blackout /'blækaʊt/ *n* 1 (in wartime) zaciemnienie *n* 2 (power cut) przerwa *f* w dostawie energii elektrycznej 3 (faint) omdlenie *n*
Black Sea *prn* **the ~** Morze *n* Czarne
black sheep *n* czarna owca *f*
blacksmith /'blæksmɪθ/ *n* kowal *m*
black tie *n* (on invitation) '~' „smoking"
bladder /'blædə(r)/ *n* Anat pęcherz *m*
blade /bleɪd/ *n* (of knife, axe) ostrze *n*; (of sword) klinga *f*; (of oar, windscreen wiper) pióro *n*; (of fan) łopatka *f*; (of leaf) blaszka *f*

blame /bleɪm/ **❚** *n* wina *f*, odpowiedzialność *f* (**for sth** za coś)
❚❚ *vt* obwini|ć, -ać *[system]* (**for sth** o coś); obarcz|yć, -ać winą, winić *[person]* (**for sth** za coś); **to ~ sth on sb** obarczyć kogoś winą or odpowiedzialnością za coś; **to be to ~ for sth** ponosić winę za coś
❚❚❚ *vr* **to ~ oneself** obwiniać się (**for sth** o coś)
blameless /'bleɪmlɪs/ *adj* niewinny, bez zarzutu
blancmange /blə'mɒnʒ/ *n* budyń *m*
bland /blænd/ *adj [food, taste]* mdły, nijaki; *[person]* bezbarwny
blank /blæŋk/ **❚** *n* 1 (empty space) puste miejsce *n*; **my mind is a ~** mam w głowie pustkę 2 (also ~ **cartridge**) ślepy nabój *m*
❚❚ *adj [cassette]* czysty; *[page]* pusty; *[face, look]* pozbawiony wyrazu, obojętny; **the screen went ~** obraz zniknął z ekranu; **my mind went ~** w głowie poczułem pustkę
■ **blank out**: ~ **[sth] out** wymaz|ać, -ywać z pamięci *[event]*
blank cheque GB, **blank check** US *n* czek *m* (podpisany) in blanco; fig wolna ręka *f*, carte *f inv* blanche
blanket /'blæŋkɪt/ *n* 1 (bedcover) koc *m* 2 (of snow) pokrywa *f*; (of cloud, fog) zasłona *f*
blare /bleə(r)/ *v*
■ **blare out**: ¶ ~ **out** *[music]* rozlegać się głośno; *[radio]* grać na cały regulator ¶ ~ **out [sth]** za|grzmieć (czymś) *[music]*
blasphemous /'blæsfəməs/ *adj* bluźnierczy
blasphemy /'blæsfəmɪ/ *n* bluźnierstwo *n*
blast /blɑːst, US blæst/ **❚** *n* 1 (gust) podmuch *m* 2 (explosion) wybuch *m*; **at full ~** *[radio]* na cały regulator
❚❚ *vt* (blow up) wysadz|ić, -ać (w powietrze); **to ~ a hole in a wall** wybić otwór w murze *(za pomocą ładunku wybuchowego)*
■ **blast off**: ~ **off** *[rocket]* odpal|ić, -ać
blast-off /'blɑːstɒf, US 'blæst-/ *n* odpalenie *n*, start *m*
blatant /'bleɪtnt/ *adj [lie]* bezczelny; *[abuse, disregard]* jawny, rażący
blatantly /'bleɪtntlɪ/ *adv [copy]* jawnie, otwarcie; **to be ~ obvious** rzucać się w oczy
blaze /bleɪz/ **❚** *n* (in hearth) ogień *m*, płomień *m*; (conflagration) pożar *m*; (sudden burst) wybuch *m*
❚❚ *vi* (also ~ **away**) 1 *[fire, house]* płonąć 2 *[lights]* palić się
❚❚❚ *vt* **to ~ a trail** oznakować szlak; fig przetrzeć szlaki fig
blazer /'bleɪzə(r)/ *n* marynarka *f*
blazing *adj [building]* płonący; (violent) *[argument]* gwałtowny; *[fire]* buchający
bleach /bliːtʃ/ **❚** *n* 1 wybielacz *m*; (disinfectant) środek *m* wybielający i dezynfekujący 2 (for hair) rozjaśniacz *m*

II *vt* rozjaśni|ć, -ać *[hair]*; wybieli|ć, -ać *[linen]*

bleak /bliːk/ *adj [landscape, day]* smętny; *[future]* marny; *[surroundings]* ponury

bleary /'blɪərɪ/ *adj [eyes]* zapuchnięty

bleat /bliːt/ *vi [sheep, goat]* za|beczeć

bleed /bliːd/ **II** *vt* **to** ~ **sb dry** doprowadzić kogoś do ruiny

II *vi* krwawić; **my finger's** ~**ing** leci mi krew z palca

bleep /bliːp/ **II** *n* sygnał *m* dźwiękowy

II *vt* w|ezwać, -zywać biperem *[person]*

bleeper /'bliːpə(r)/ *n* biper *m*

blemish /'blemɪʃ/ *n* skaza *f*; (pimple) krosta *f*, pryszcz *m*; (on fruit) plamka *f*

blend /blend/ **II** *n* (of colours, smells) mieszanina *f*; (of qualities) połączenie *n*; (of styles) zlepek *m*; (of teas) mieszanka *f*

II *vt* wy|mieszać *[foods]*; z|mieszać *[colours]*; prze|mieszać *[styles]*

III *vi* **to** ~ (**together**) *[colours, styles]* pasować do siebie; **to** ~ **with sth** harmonizować z czymś; *[colours, scents, styles]* mieszać się; *[sounds]* zlewać się

■ **blend in**: ¶ ~ **in** *[colour, building]* harmonizować (**with sth** z czymś) ¶ ~ **[sth]** **in** doda|ć, -wać *[paint, eggs]*

blender /'blendə(r)/ *n* mikser *m*

bless /bles/ *vt* po|błogosławić *[people]*; po|święcić *[food]*; ~ **you!** (after sneeze) na zdrowie!; **to be** ~**ed with luck/health** cieszyć się szczęściem/zdrowiem

blessing /'blesɪŋ/ *n* błogosławieństwo *n*; fig błogosławieństwo *n* (losu); **a** ~ **in disguise** błogosławione w skutkach nieszczęście

blight /blaɪt/ *n* fig (on society) plaga *f* fig; **urban** ~ problemy nękające ubogie dzielnice miasta

blind /blaɪnd/ **II** *n* ①︎ **the** ~ niewidomi *m pl*, ociemniali *m pl* ②︎ (at window) żaluzja *f*, roleta *f*

II *adj [person]* niewidomy; **to go** ~ s|tracić wzrok; **to be** ~ **in one eye** nie widzieć or być ślepym na jedno oko

III *vt* ①︎ *[injury, accident]* s|powodować utratę wzroku or ślepotę u (kogoś) ②︎ *[sun, light]* oślepi|ć, -ać ③︎ (mislead) *[pride, love]* zaślepi|ć, -ać

IDIOMS: **to turn a** ~ **eye** przymykać oczy (**to sth** na coś)

blind alley *n* ślepa uliczka *f*

blind date *n* randka *f* w ciemno

blindfold /'blaɪndfəʊld/ **II** *n* przepaska *f* na oczy

II *adj* (also ~**ed**) mający przepaskę na oczach

III *adv [find way]* z zawiązanymi oczami

IV *vt* zawiąz|ać, -ywać (komuś) oczy

blinding /'blaɪndɪŋ/ *adj [light]* oślepiający; *[headache]* nieznośny

blindly /'blaɪndlɪ/ *adv [advance]* po omacku; *[obey]* ślepo

blindness /'blaɪndnɪs/ *n* ślepota *f*; fig zaślepienie *n*

blind spot *n* ①︎ (in eye) ślepa plamka *f* ②︎ Aut martwy punkt *m*

blink /blɪŋk/ *vi [person, light]* mrug|nąć, -ać

blinker /'blɪŋkə(r)/ **II** *n* ①︎ Aut migacz *m* ②︎ (on horse) klapka *f* na oko

II blinkered *pp adj* fig *[view]* ciasny

blip /blɪp/ *n* ①︎ (on screen) pulsujący punkt *m*; (on graph line) skok *m* ②︎ (problem) zagwozdka *f* infml

bliss /blɪs/ *n* rozkosz *f*

blissfully /'blɪsfəlɪ/ *adv [smile, sigh]* błogo; **to be** ~ **happy** być bezgranicznie szczęśliwym

blister /'blɪstə(r)/ **II** *n* (on skin) pęcherz *m*

II *vi [skin]* pokry|ć, -wać się pęcherzami or bąblami; *[paint]* łuszczyć się, złuszcz|yć, -ać się

blister pack *n* blister(ek) *m*

blithely /'blaɪðlɪ/ *adv* beztrosko, niefrasobliwie

blitz /blɪts/ **II** *n* nalot *m*

II *vt* z|bombardować

blizzard /'blɪzəd/ *n* zamieć *f*; (in Arctic regions) blizzard *m*

bloated /'bləʊtɪd/ *adj [face]* nalany; *[body]* rozdęty; *[stomach]* wzdęty

blob /blɒb/ *n* ①︎ (drop) kropla *f*, plama *f* ②︎ (shape) niewyraźny zarys *m*

block /blɒk/ **II** *n* ①︎ bryła *f*, blok *m*; (for chopping) pień *m* ②︎ (building) ~ **of flats** blok mieszkalny; **office** ~ biurowiec ③︎ (space enclosed by streets) kwartał *m*; **she lives three** ~**s away** US mieszka trzy przecznice dalej

II *vt* za|blokować *[entrance]*; za|tarasować *[road]*; zat|kać, -ykać *[hole, pipe]*; **to** ~ **the light/a view** zasłaniać światło/widok; **to have a** ~**ed nose** mieć zapchany nos

■ **block out**: ~ **[sth]** **out** ①︎ (hide) zasł|onić, -aniać *[light, view]* ②︎ (suppress) zapom|nieć, -inać o (czymś) *[problem]*

blockade /blɒ'keɪd/ **II** *n* blokada *f*

II *vt* za|blokować *[road, port]*

blockage /'blɒkɪdʒ/ *n* zator *m*

blockbook /'blɒkbʊk/ *vt* z|robić rezerwację grupową (czegoś) *[seats]*

blockbuster /'blɒkbʌstə(r)/ *n* infml (book, film) hit *m* infml

block capital, block letter *n* (on form) **in** ~**s** wielkimi or drukowanymi literami

bloke /bləʊk/ *n* infml facet *m*, gość *m* infml

blonde /blɒnd/ **II** *n* blondynka *f*

II *adj [person]* jasnowłosy; *[hair]* blond

blood /blʌd/ *n* krew *f*; **to kill sb in cold** ~ zabić kogoś z zimną krwią

blood bank *n* bank *m* krwi

bloodcurdling /'blʌdkɜːdlɪŋ/ *adj* mrożący krew w żyłach

blood donor *n* krwiodaw|ca *m*, -czyni *f*

blood group *n* grupa *f* krwi

blood pressure *n* ciśnienie *n* krwi; **high** ~ nadciśnienie

blood relation n krewn|y m, -a f
bloodshed /'blʌdʃed/ n rozlew m krwi
bloodshot /'blʌdʃɒt/ adj [eyes] nabiegły krwią
blood sport n myślistwo n
bloodstained /'blʌdsteɪnd/ adj poplamiony krwią
bloodstream /'blʌdstri:m/ n krwiobieg m
blood test n badanie n krwi
bloodthirsty /'blʌdθɜ:stɪ/ adj krwiożerczy
blood type n = blood group
bloody /'blʌdɪ/ **I** adj [1] (bleeding) krwawiący; [bandages] zakrwawiony; [battle] krwawy [2] GB vinfml (expressing anger) cholerny infml; **you ~ fool!** ty cholerny durniu!
II adv infml cholernie infml
bloom /blu:m/ **I** n kwiat m; **in ~** [plant] kwitnący
II vi (be in flower) kwitnąć; (come into flower) rozkwit|nąć, -ać
blooming adj **~ with health** tryskający zdrowiem
blossom /'blɒsəm/ **I** n (flowers) kwiaty m pl; (flower) kwiat m
II vi kwitnąć; fig rozkwit|nąć, -ać
blot /blɒt/ **I** n plama f also fig; (of ink) kleks m
II vt [1] (stain) po|plamić; s|plamić [2] (dry) osusz|yć, -ać (bibułą)
■ **blot out**: przysł|onić, -aniać [view]; zapom|nieć, -inać o (czymś) [fear]
blotch /blɒtʃ/ n (on skin) wybroczyna f; (of ink) plama f, kleks m
blotchy /'blɒtʃɪ/ adj [skin] plamisty; [paper] poplamiony
blotting paper n bibuła f
blouse /blaʊz, US blaʊs/ n bluzka f
blow /bləʊ/ **I** n **to give one's nose a ~** wytrzeć nos
II vt [1] [wind] **to ~ sth out of the window** wywiać coś za okno; **to be blown off course** [ship] zostać zepchniętym z kursu/na skały [2] [person] pu|ścić, -szczać [bubbles, smoke rings]; **to ~ glass** wydmuchiwać szkło; **to ~ one's nose** wytrzeć nos; wydmuchać nos infml; **to ~ the whistle** za|gwizdać [3] [explosion] wyrwać [hole] (**in sth** w czymś); **to ~ sth to pieces** or **bits** rozerwać coś na kawałki [4] s|powodować przepalenie się (czegoś) [fuse, lightbulb]
III vi [1] [wind] po|wiać; [person] dmuch|nąć, -ać (**on/into sth** na/w coś) [2] (move with wind) **to ~ in the wind** [clothes] powiewać na wietrze; [leaves] poruszać się na wietrze [3] [fuse, bulb] przepal|ić, -ać się; [tyre] roz|erwać, -rywać się
■ **blow away**: ¶ **~ away** [paper] odfru|nąć, -wać ¶ **~ [sth] away** [wind] por|wać, -ywać [object]
■ **blow down**: [wind] powal|ić, -ać [tree]
■ **blow off**: ¶ **~ off** [hat] odfru|nąć, -wać ¶ **~ [sth] off** [wind] zdmuch|nąć, -iwać [hat]; [explosion] z|erwać, -rywać [roof]

■ **blow out**: zdmuch|nąć, -iwać [candle]; z|gasić [flames]
■ **blow over**: [storm] ucich|nąć, -ać; [scandal] przycich|nąć, -ać
■ **blow up**: ¶ **~ up** [building] wyl|ecieć, -atywać w powietrze; [bomb] wybuch|nąć, -ać ¶ **~ [sth/sb] up** [1] wysadz|ić, -ać (coś) w powietrze [building]; roz|erwać, -rywać [person]; z|detonować [bomb] [2] na|pompować [tyre] [3] (enlarge) powiększ|yć, -ać [photo]
blow-dry /'bləʊdraɪ/ **I** n suszenie n suszarką ręczną
II vt **to ~ sb's hair** modelować komuś włosy wyżerką f infml
blowout /'bləʊaʊt/ n [1] (electrical) krótkie spięcie n [2] (of tyre) rozerwanie (się) n [3] infml (meal) wyżerka f infml
blowtorch /'bləʊtɔ:tʃ/ n lampa f lutownicza
blubber /'blʌbə(r)/ n (of whale, seal) tłuszcz m
bludgeon /'blʌdʒən/ vt **to ~ sb to death** zatłuc kogoś (na śmierć)
blue /blu:/ **I** n (kolor m) niebieski m, błękit m
II **blues** npl [1] Mus **the ~s** blues m [2] infml (depression) **to have the ~s** mieć chandrę
III adj [1] (colour) niebieski; **to feel ~** być przygnębionym or smutnym [2] infml [film] erotyczny; [joke] pieprzny infml
(IDIOMS:) **out of the ~** [appear, happen] ni z tego, ni z owego
bluebell /'blu:bel/ n Bot dzwonek m
blueberry /'blu:bərɪ/ n US czarna borówka f, jagoda f amerykańska
blue cheese n ser m niebieski (typu rokpol)
blue chip adj [company, share] bezpieczny
blue collar adj **~ worker** robotnik m, pracownik m fizyczny
blue jeans npl dżinsy plt
blueprint /'blu:prɪnt/ n światłokopia f planu or projektu; (plan) plan m, strategia f (**for sth** czegoś)
bluff /blʌf/ **I** vt zw|ieść, -odzić, zmylić
II vi za|blefować
(IDIOMS:) **to call sb's ~** zmusić kogoś do pokazania kart
blunder /'blʌndə(r)/ **I** n błąd m
II vi [1] (make mistake) popełni|ć, -ać błąd [2] (move clumsily) po|ruszać się niezdarnie
blunt /blʌnt/ **I** adj [knife, scissors] tępy; [pencil] niezaostrzony; [person, manner] szczery; [refusal] kategoryczny
II vt stępi|ć, -ać [knife]
bluntly /'blʌntlɪ/ adv szczerze
blur /blɜ:(r)/ **I** n niewyraźna plama f
II vt zamaz|ać, -ywać
blurb /blɜ:b/ n notka f reklamowa; (on book cover) notka f wydawnicza
blurred /blɜ:d/ adj nieostry, niewyraźny; **to have ~ vision** widzieć nieostro

blurt /blɜːt/ *vt*
■ **blurt out**: wygadać, zdradz|ić, -ać
blush /blʌʃ/ *vi* za|rumienić się; **he** ~ed **at her words** zaczerwienił się, słysząc jej słowa
blusher /ˈblʌʃə(r)/ *n* róż *m*
blustery /ˈblʌstərɪ/ *adj [day]* wietrzny; *[wind]* porywisty
BO *n* infml = **body odour** zapach *m* potu
boar /bɔː(r)/ *n* (wild) dzik *m*; (male pig) knur *m*
board /bɔːd/ **I** *n* [1] (committee) rada *f*, komisja *f*; ~ **of directors** zarząd [2] (plank) deska *f* [3] (in darts) tarcza *f*; (for chess, draughts) plansza *f* [4] (for writing) tablica *f*; (for information) tablica *f* informacyjna [5] Comput płyta *f* [6] (accommodation) utrzymanie *n*, wyżywienie *n*; ~ **and lodging** wikt i opierunek hum; **full** ~ całodzienne utrzymanie; **half** ~ śniadanie i kolacja
II boards *npl* deski *plt* sceniczne
III on board *adv phr* na pokładzie
IV *vt* w|ejść, -chodzić na pokład (czegoś) *[plane, ship]*; wsi|ąść, -adać do (czegoś) *[bus, train]*; (in naval battle) w|edrzeć, -dzierać się na pokład (czegoś) *[vessel]*
■ **board up**: zabi|ć, -jać or pozabijać (coś) deskami *[window]*; zam|knąć, -ykać or pozamykać (coś) na głucho *[house]*
boarder /ˈbɔːdə(r)/ *n* [1] (lodger) lokator *m*, -ka *f* [2] Sch uczeń *m* mieszkający w internacie, uczennica *f* mieszkająca w internacie
board game *n* gra *f* planszowa
boarding /ˈbɔːdɪŋ/ *n* wejście *n* na pokład
boarding card *n* karta *f* pokładowa
boarding school *n* szkoła *f* z internatem
boardroom /ˈbɔːdruːm, -rʊm/ *n* sala *f* posiedzeń
boast /bəʊst/ **I** *n* przechwałka *f*
II *vt* chlubić, szczycić się (**sth** czymś)
III *vi* chwalić się (**about sth** czymś)
boastful /ˈbəʊstfl/ *adj* chełpliwy
boat /bəʊt/ *n* łódź *f*, łódka *f*; (ship) statek *m*; **sailing** ~ żaglówka
IDIOMS **to be in the same** ~ infml jechać na tym samym wózku infml
boater /ˈbəʊtə(r)/ *n* kapelusz *m* słomkowy
boathouse /ˈbəʊthaʊs/ *n* hangar *m* dla łodzi
boating /ˈbəʊtɪŋ/ **I** *n* wodniactwo *n*
II *adj [club]* wodniacki; *[accident, holiday]* na wodzie
boatyard /ˈbəʊtjɑːd/ *n* warsztat *m* szkutniczy; (on industrial scale) stocznia *f* jachtowa
bob /bɒb/ **I** *n* równo obcięte włosy *plt*
II *vi [boat, float]* podsk|oczyć, -akiwać (na wodzie)
bobsled, bobsleigh /ˈbɒbsled, ˈbɒbsleɪ/ *n* bobslej *m*
bode /bəʊd/ *vi* **to** ~ **well/ill** dobrze/źle wróżyć (**for sb/sth** komuś/czemuś)
bodily /ˈbɒdɪlɪ/ *adj [function]* fizjologiczny; *[fluid]* ustrojowy

body /ˈbɒdɪ/ *n* [1] (of person, animal) ciało *n*; Med organizm *m* [2] (also **dead** ~) zwłoki *plt*, ciało *n* [3] (of car) karoseria *f*; (of boat, aircraft) kadłub *m* [4] (of water) akwen *m*; (of laws) zbiór *m* [5] (organization) ciało *n*, organ *m* [6] (of wine) wyraźny smak *m* i bukiet *m*; (of hair) puszystość *f*
bodybuilder /ˈbɒdɪbɪldə(r)/ *n* kulturyst|a *m*, -ka *f*
body-building /ˈbɒdɪbɪldɪŋ/ *n* kulturystyka *f*
bodyguard /ˈbɒdɪgɑːd/ *n* ochroniarz *m* infml
body language *n* mowa *f* ciała
body warmer *n* ocieplana kamizelka *f*
bodywork /ˈbɒdɪwɜːk/ *n* karoseria *f*
bog /bɒg/ *n* [1] (marshy ground) bagno *n* [2] (also **peat** ~) torfowisko *n*
IDIOMS **to get** ~**ged down** *[vehicle]* ugrzęznąć, ugrząźć; *[talks]* znaleźć się w martwym punkcie
boggle /ˈbɒgl/ *vi* **the mind** ~**s!** w głowie się nie mieści!
bog-standard /ˌbɒgˈstændəd/ *adj* infml przeciętny
bogus /ˈbəʊgəs/ *adj [document]* fałszywy; *[name]* zmyślony; *[company]* fikcyjny; ~ **doctor** osoba podająca się za lekarza
boil /bɔɪl/ **I** *n* **to bring sth to the** ~ doprowadzić coś do wrzenia
II *vt* za|gotować *[liquid]*; **to** ~ **an egg** ugotować jajko
III *vi* za|gotować się; **the kettle is** ~**ing** woda się gotuje; **to make sb's blood** ~ wzburzyć w kimś krew
IV boiled *adj [ham]* gotowany; **hard-/soft-**~**ed egg** jajko *n* na twardo/na miękko
■ **boil down**: ~ **down to sth** fig sprowadzać się do czegoś
■ **boil over**: *[milk]* wy|kipieć
boiler /ˈbɔɪlə(r)/ *n* kocioł *m*; (for hot water) bojler *m*
boiler suit *n* GB kombinezon *m*
boiling /ˈbɔɪlɪŋ/ *adj [water, oil]* wrzący; **it's** ~ **(hot) in here** (gorąco tu tak, że) można się ugotować
boiling point *n* temperatura *f* wrzenia also fig
boisterous /ˈbɔɪstərəs/ *adj [person]* hałaśliwy; *[child]* niesforny; *[game]* żywiołowy
bold /bəʊld/ **I** *n* GB **in** ~ tłustym drukiem
II *adj* [1] (daring) *[person, plan]* śmiały, odważny [2] (cheeky) *[person]* zuchwały, bezczelny [3] (strong) *[colour, pattern]* śmiały, krzykliwy
bollard /ˈbɒlɑːd/ *n* słupek *m*
bolster /ˈbəʊlstə(r)/ **I** *n* wałek *m*, podgłówek *m*
II *vt* (also ~ **up**) podn|ieść, -osić *[morale]*; doda|ć, -wać (czegoś) *[confidence]*
bolt /bəʊlt/ **I** *n* [1] (lock) rygiel *m* [2] ~ **of lightning** błyskawica *f*
II bolt upright *adj phr* sztywno (jakby kij połknął)
III *vt* [1] (lock) za|ryglować [2] (also ~ **down**) (swallow) wrzuc|ić, -ać w siebie infml *[food]*

IV *vi [person]* rzuc|ić, -ać się do ucieczki; *[horse]* pon|ieść, -osić

IDIOMS **a ~ out of the blue** grom z jasnego nieba

bomb /bɒm/ **I** *n* bomba *f*

II *vt* z|bombardować *[town, house]*

bombard /bɒm'bɑːd/ *vt* z|bombardować (**with sth** czymś)

bomb blast *n* eksplozja *f*, wybuch *m* (bomby)

bomb disposal unit *n* oddział *m* saperów

bomber /'bɒmə(r)/ *n* 1 (plane) bombowiec *m* 2 (terrorist) terroryst|a *m*, -ka *f* (podkładający bomby)

bomber jacket *n* krótka kurtka *f* (zwykle skórzana)

bombing /'bɒmɪŋ/ *n* bombardowanie *n*; (by terrorists) zamach *m* bombowy

bomb scare *n* alarm *m* bombowy

bombshell /'bɒmʃel/ *n* fig bomba *f* infml fig

bombsite /'bɒmsaɪt/ *n* teren *m* zniszczony podczas bombardowania

Bomb Squad /'bɒmskwɒd/ *n* brygada *f* antyterrorystyczna

bona fide /ˌbəʊnə'faɪdɪ/ *adj [member]* faktyczny; *[contract]* zawarty w dobrej wierze; *[attempt]* szczery

bond /bɒnd/ **I** *n* 1 (link) więź *f*, więzi *f pl*; **~s of love** więzy miłości 2 (in finance) obligacja *f*; **savings ~** bon oszczędnościowy

II *vt* sp|oić, -ajać *[surfaces]*; z|wiązać *[bricks]*

III *vi* s|tworzyć silną więź (**with sb** z kimś)

bone /bəʊn/ **I** *n* kość *f*; (of fish) ość *f*

II *vt* filetować *[chicken, fish, joint]*

IDIOMS **a ~ of contention** kość niezgody; **to have a ~ to pick with sb** mieć z kimś na pieńku

bone china *n* porcelana *f* kostna or miękka

bone dry *adj* suchutki, suchuteńki

bone idle *adj* infml obrzydliwie leniwy

bone-marrow transplant *n* przeszczep *m* szpiku kostnego

bonfire /'bɒnfaɪə(r)/ *n* ognisko *n*

Bonfire Night *n* GB noc *m* 5 listopada (rocznica spisku prochowego w 1605 roku)

bonnet /'bɒnɪt/ *n* 1 (baby's) czapeczka *f* zawiązywana pod brodą 2 GB maska *f* samochodu

bonus /'bəʊnəs/ *n* 1 (payment) premia *f* 2 (advantage) (dodatkowa) zaleta *f*

bony /'bəʊnɪ/ *adj [person, figure, arm]* kościsty; *[fish]* ościsty

boo /buː/ **I** *n* okrzyk *m* niezadowolenia

II *excl* (to give sb a fright) u!; (to jeer) łuu!

III *vt* wygwizd|ać, -ywać *[actor, speaker]*

IV *vi* głośno wyra|zić, -żać dezaprobatę

booby trap /'buːbi træp/ **I** *n* 1 mina *f*, pułapka *f* 2 (joke) psikus *m*

II booby-trap *vt* Mil pod|łożyć, -kładać (gdzieś) bombę pułapkę

booing /'buːɪŋ/ *n* głośno okazywane niezadowolenie *n*

book /bʊk/ **I** *n* 1 książka *f* (**on** or **about sb/sth** o kimś/czymś, na temat kogoś/czegoś); (exercise book) zeszyt *m* 2 (of cheques) książeczka *f* czekowa; (of tickets) bloczek *m*; (of stamps) karnecik *m*; **a ~ of matches** kartonik zapałek

II books *npl* księgi *f pl*, rejestry *m pl*

III *vt* 1 za|rezerwować *[room, holiday]*; zam|ówić, -awiać *[taxi, table]*; **to be fully ~ed** mieć wszystkie miejsca zarezerwowane 2 *[policeman]* spis|ać, -ywać infml *[motorist, offender]*; US (arrest) za|aresztować 3 Sport u|karać żółtą kartką *[player]*

IV *vi* z|robić rezerwację

IDIOMS **to be in sb's good/bad ~s** być u kogoś dobrze/źle notowanym infml

bookcase /'bʊkkeɪs/ *n* biblioteczka *f*

book club *n* klub *m* książki

booking /'bʊkɪŋ/ *n* GB (reservation) rezerwacja *f*

booking form *n* kupon *m* zamówienia

booking office *n* GB kasa *f* biletowa

bookkeeping /'bʊkkiːpɪŋ/ *n* księgowość *f*

booklet /'bʊklɪt/ *n* broszura *f*

booklist /'bʊklɪst/ *n* lista *f* lektur

bookmaker /'bʊkmeɪkə(r)/ *n* bukmacher *m*

bookmark /'bʊkmɑːk/ **I** *n* (for books, website) zakładka *f*

II *vt* Comput doda|ć, -wać *[website]*

bookseller /'bʊkselə(r)/ *n* księgarz *m*

bookshelf /'bʊkʃelf/ *n* regał *m* or półka *f* na książki

bookshop /'bʊkʃɒp/ *n* księgarnia *f*

book token *n* GB bon *m* na książki

bookworm /'bʊkwɜːm/ *n* fig mól *m* książkowy fig

boom /buːm/ **I** *n* 1 (of cannon, explosion, thunder) huk *m*; (of drum) łoskot *m*; **~ !** bum! 2 Econ boom *m*; (in demand, sales) gwałtowny wzrost *m* (**in sth** czegoś)

II *vi* 1 (make a noise) *[cannon, thunder]* za|grzmieć; *[waves]* za|huczeć 2 (prosper) *[economy]* przeży|ć, -wać rozkwit; *[exports, sales]* szybko wzr|osnąć, -astać; **business is ~ing** interes kwitnie

boon /buːn/ *n* (person) skarb *m* fig; (thing) dobrodziejstwo *n*

boost /buːst/ **I** *n* **to give sth a ~** stymulować coś

II *vt* zwiększ|yć, -ać *[profit, value]*; pobudz|ić, -ać *[economy]*; stymulować *[growth]*; **to ~ sb's confidence** dodać komuś pewności siebie; **to ~ morale** podnieść morale

booster /'buːstə(r)/ *n* Med dawka *f* przypominająca

boot /buːt/ *n* 1 but *m*, botek *m*; **climbing ~s** buty do wspinaczki 2 GB Aut bagażnik *m*

■ **boot up**: Comput **~ [sth] up** za|inicjować *[computer]*

booth /buːð, US buːθ/ *n* (in language lab, for voting, telephoning) kabina *f*; (at fair) stoisko *n*

bootlace /'buːtleɪs/ *n* sznurowadło *n*

booze /buːz/ infml *n* alkohol *m*
border /'bɔːdə(r)/ **[]** *n* ⌐1⌐ (frontier) granica *f*; **to
cross the** ~ przekroczyć granicę ⌐2⌐ (edge) (of forest)
skraj *m*; (of lake) brzeg *m* ⌐3⌐ rabat(k)a *f*
[] *adj [post]* graniczny; *[town]* przygraniczny,
nadgraniczny
[] *vt* ⌐1⌐ (lie alongside) graniczyć z (czymś) *[country]*;
przylegać do (czegoś) *[land, forest]* ⌐2⌐ (surround)
ok|olić, -alać *[field]*
■ **border on**: ~ **on [sth]** ⌐1⌐ (have a frontier with)
[country] graniczyć z (czymś); *[garden, land]*
przylegać do (czegoś) ⌐2⌐ (verge on) graniczyć
z (czymś) *[madness, rudeness]*
border dispute *n* spór *m* graniczny
borderline /'bɔːdəlaɪn/ *n* granica *f*; **a ~ case**
wątpliwy przypadek
bore /bɔː(r)/ **[]** *n* ⌐1⌐ (person) nudzia|rz *m*, -ra *f* infml
pej ⌐2⌐ (situation) nudy *f pl*; **what a ~!** co za nudy!
⌐3⌐ (of gun) kaliber *m*
[] *vt* ⌐1⌐ (annoy) nudzić, zanudz|ić, -ać ⌐2⌐ (drill)
wiercić, drążyć *[hole, tunnel]*
(IDIOMS) **to ~ sb stiff** or **to tears** zanudzić kogoś
na śmierć, nudzić kogoś śmiertelnie
bored /bɔːd/ *adj [expression]* znudzony; **to be/get
~ (with sth/with doing sth)** być znudzonym,
znudzić się (czymś/robieniem czegoś)
boredom /'bɔːdəm/ *n* nuda *f*, znudzenie *n*
boring /'bɔːrɪŋ/ *adj* nudny
born /bɔːn/ *adj* urodzony; **to be ~** urodzić się
borough /'bʌrə, US -rəʊ/ *n* (in London, New York) ≈
gmina *f*
borrow /'bɒrəʊ/ *vt* pożycz|yć, -ać **(from sb** od
kogoś)
borrower /'bɒrəʊə(r)/ *n* (from bank) pożyczko-
bior|ca *m*, -czyni *f*; (from library) czytelni|k *m*, -czka
f; (from person) pożyczając|y *m*, -a *f*
borrowing /'bɒrəʊɪŋ/ *n* zaciągnięcie *n* pożyczki
bosom /'bʊzəm/ *n* pierś *f*; **to have a large ~**
mieć duży biust; **in the ~ of one's family** na
łonie rodziny
bosom friend *n* przyjaci|el *m*, -ółka *f* od serca
boss /bɒs/ *n* infml szef *m*, -owa *f*
■ **boss about, boss around** infml: dyrygować
(kimś)
bossy /'bɒsɪ/ *adj* infml apodyktyczny
botanic(al) /bə'tænɪk(l)/ *adj* botaniczny
botany /'bɒtənɪ/ *n* botanika *f*
botch /bɒtʃ/ infml *vt* (also ~ **up**) s|knocić infml
both /bəʊθ/ **[]** *adj* (males) obaj, obydwaj; (females)
obie, obydwie; (male and female) oboje, obydwoje;
(animals, things) obie, obydwie; oba, obydwa; ~ **boys
like tennis** obaj chłopcy lubią tenis; ~ **sides of
the road** obie or obydwie strony drogi
[] *pron* (of males) obaj, obydwaj; (of females) obie,
obydwie; (of couple) oboje, obydwoje; (of animals,
things) oba, obydwa; obie, obydwie; ~ **of you are
wrong** żaden/żadna/żadne z was nie ma racji

[] *conj* **both... and...** zarówno..., jak i...; i..., i...
bother /'bɒðə(r)/ **[]** *n* ⌐1⌐ (inconvenience) problem *m*;
without any ~ bez żadnych kłopotów or prob-
lemów ⌐2⌐ GB infml (trouble) kłopot *m*; **to be in a spot
of ~** mieć mały kłopot or problem
[] *vt* ⌐1⌐ (worry) martwić, niepokoić; **don't let it ~
you** nie martw się tym ⌐2⌐ (inconvenience) przeszkadzać; **stop ~ing me!** przestań zawracać mi
głowę!
[] *vi* ⌐1⌐ (take trouble) kłopotać się; **please don't ~**
proszę nie robić sobie kłopotu; **I wouldn't ~** nie
przejmowałbym się ⌐2⌐ (worry) przejmować się
(about sb/sth kimś/czymś); **it's not worth
~ing about** nie warto się tym przejmować
bottle /'bɒtl/ **[]** *n* ⌐1⌐ butelka *f*; (for medicine)
buteleczka *f*; (for perfume) flakon(ik) *m*; (for gas) butla
f ⌐2⌐ GB infml (courage) odwaga *f*
[] *vt* rozl|ać, -ewać (coś) do butelek, butelkować
[milk, wine]; GB za|wekować *[fruit]*
[] **bottled** *pp adj [wine]* butelkowany; *[beer]*
butelkowy; ~**d water** woda mineralna
■ **bottle up**: dusić (coś) w sobie *[anger, grief]*
bottle bank *n* pojemnik *m* na szkło
bottle feed *vt* na|karmić butelką
bottleneck /'bɒtlnek/ *n* ⌐1⌐ (traffic jam) korek *m* infml
⌐2⌐ (narrow part of road) zwężenie *n* (jezdni)
bottle-opener /'bɒtlˌəʊpənə(r)/ *n* otwieracz *m* do
butelek
bottle top *n* nakrętka *f*, kapsel *m*
bottom /'bɒtəm/ **[]** *n* ⌐1⌐ (of hill, slope) podnóże *n*; (of
page, ladder) dół *m*; (in body of water) dno *n* ⌐2⌐ (underside)
spód *m*; (inner surface) dno *n* ⌐3⌐ (of list) (szary) koniec
m; (of hierarchy) dół *m*; **she was ~ of the class
again** znowu była ostatnia w klasie; **at the ~ of
the pile** (socially) na dole drabiny społecznej ⌐4⌐ (of
garden, field, street) koniec *m* ⌐5⌐ infml (buttocks) tyłek *m*
infml
[] **bottoms** *npl* infml **pyjama ~s** dół or spodnie
od piżamy; **bikini ~s** majtki od bikini
[] *adj [layer, shelf]* najniższy; *[bunk, division]*
dolny; *[apartment]* na parterze
bottom line *n* (decisive factor) kwestia *f* zasadnicza; (final, position) konkluzja *f*
boulder /'bəʊldə(r)/ *n* głaz *m*
bounce /baʊns/ **[]** *n* ⌐1⌐ (rebound) odbicie (się) *n*
⌐2⌐ (of hair, mattress, material) sprężystość *f*
[] *vt* odbi|ć, -jać
[] *vi* ⌐1⌐ *[ball, bullet]* odbi|ć, -jać się **(off sth** o coś,
od czegoś); **to ~ up and down on sth**
podskakiwać na czymś ⌐2⌐ infml *[cheque]* nie mieć
pokrycia
■ **bounce back**: *[person]* dojść do siebie; *[cur-
rency]* powrócić do normy
bouncer /'baʊnsə(r)/ *n* infml wykidajło *m* infml
bound /baʊnd/ **[]** **bounds** *npl* granice *f pl*; **to be
out of ~s** stanowić strefę zakazaną

II *adj* [1] (certain) **it was** ~ **to happen** to się musiało stać [2] (obliged) zobowiązany, związany (**by sth** czymś); **to be** ~ **to do sth** mieć obowiązek coś zrobić [3] (heading for) ~ **for sth** zdążający do (czegoś); **a plane** ~ **for New York** samolot lecący do Nowego Jorku

III *vi* poruszać się energicznie; **she** ~**ed into the room** wpadła do pokoju

boundary /'baʊndrɪ/ *n* granica *f*; (in cricket) linia *f* końcowa

bouquet /bʊ'keɪ/ *n* bukiet *m*

bourgeois /'bɔːʒwɑː, US ˌbʊər'ʒwɑː/ *adj* (relating to middle class) mieszczański; (capitalist) burżuazyjny; (philistine) drobnomieszczański

bout /baʊt/ *n* [1] (of illness) atak *m*; (of depression, coughing) napad *m*; **to go on a drinking** ~ pójść w tango *or* kurs *infml* [2] Sport pojedynek *m*

boutique /buːˈtiːk/ *n* butik *m*

bow[1] /bəʊ/ *n* [1] (weapon) łuk *m* [2] Mus smyczek *m* [3] (knot) kokarda *f*

[IDIOMS:] **to have a second string to one's** ~ chować coś w zanadrzu

bow[2] /baʊ/ **II** *n* [1] (with the body) ukłon *m*; **to take a** ~ dziękować (ukłonem) za oklaski [2] (in a ship) dziób *m*

II *vt* pochyl|ić, -ać *[head]*; przygi|ąć, -nąć *[branch, tree]*

III *vi* [1] ukłonić się (**to sb** komuś) [2] **to** ~ **to sb** ugiąć się przed kimś; **to** ~ **to sth** ustąpić wobec czegoś *[pressure, threats]*

bowel /'baʊəl/ **II** *n* Med jelito *n*

II bowels *npl* fig (inner depths) wnętrze *n*

bowl /bəʊl/ **II** *n* [1] (deep dish) miska *f*; (serving dish) salaterka *f*; (for washing) miska *f*, miednica *f* [2] (of lavatory) muszla *f* klozetowa

II *vt* rzucić, ać (czymś), potoczyć *[ball]*

III *vi* rzuc|ić, -ać kulą

■ **bowl over**: (knock down) przewr|ócić, -acać *[person]* (amaze) wprawi|ć, -ać (kogoś) w osłupienie; **she was** ~ **ed over by his look** była oczarowana jego urodą

bowlegged /ˌbəʊ'legɪd/ *adj* o pałąkowatych nogach

bowler /'bəʊlə(r)/ *n* [1] (in bowling) kręglarz *m*; (in bowls) gracz *m* w bowls [2] (also ~ **hat**) melonik *m*

bowling /'bəʊlɪŋ/ *n* kręgle *plt*

bowling alley *n* kręgielnia *f*

bowling green *n* murawa *f* do gry w bowls

bowls /bəʊlz/ *n* GB *gra polegająca na toczeniu kul po murawie*

bow tie *n* muszka *f*, mucha *f*

box /bɒks/ **II** *n* [1] (cardboard) pudło *n*; (small) pudełko *n*; (metal, wooden) skrzynka *f*; **a** ~ **of matches** pudełko *or* paczka zapałek [2] (on page) ramki *f pl*, pole *n* [3] (in theatre) loża *f*; Sport trybuna *f* honorowa [4] (also **Box**) skrytka *f* pocztowa; **Box 20** Skrytka Pocztowa 20

II *vt* [1] Sport boksować *[opponent]* [2] (strike) trzepnąć (otwartą dłonią)

boxer /'bɒksə(r)/ *n* [1] Sport bokser *m* [2] (also ~ **dog**) bokser *m*

boxer shorts *npl* (spodenki *plt*) bokserki *plt*

boxing /'bɒksɪŋ/ *n* boks *m*

Boxing Day /'bɒksɪŋdeɪ/ *n* GB drugi dzień *m* Świąt Bożego Narodzenia

box number *n* numer *m* skrytki pocztowej

box office *n* kasa *f* biletowa

boy /bɔɪ/ *n* chłopiec *m*

boycott /'bɔɪkɒt/ **II** *n* bojkot *m* (**against** *or* **of** *or* **on sth** czegoś)

II *vt* z|bojkotować

boyfriend /'bɔɪfrend/ *n* (girl's) chłopak *m*; (woman's) przyjaciel *m*

bra /brɑː/ *n* biustonosz *m*

brace /breɪs/ **II** *n* [1] (for teeth) aparat *m* (korekcyjny) [2] (for broken limb) szyna *m*

II braces *npl* GB szelki *f pl*

III *vt* napi|ąć, -nać *[muscles]*; **to** ~ **one's legs against sth** zaprzeć się o coś nogami

IV *vr* **to** ~ **oneself** (physically) z|ebrać, -bierać siły (**for sth** na wypadek czegoś, przed czymś); fig przygotow|ać, -ywać się (**for sth** na coś, do czegoś)

bracelet /'breɪslɪt/ *n* bransoletka *f*

bracing /'breɪsɪŋ/ *adj* *[climate, air]* orzeźwiający, rześki

bracken /'brækən/ *n* (paproć *f*) orlica *f*

bracket /'brækɪt/ **II** *n* [1] (sign) nawias *m*; **square** ~**s** nawiasy kwadratowe; **in** ~**s** w nawiasie [2] (category) przedział *m*, kategoria *f* [3] (for shelf) wspornik *m*; (for lamp) kinkiet *m*

II *vt* [1] (put in brackets) na|pisać (coś) w nawiasie *[word, phrase]* [2] (put in category) po|traktować razem, zalicz|yć, -ać do grupy

brag /bræg/ *vi* przechwalać się (**about sth** czymś)

braid /breɪd/ *n* [1] (of hair) warkocz *m* [2] (trimming) galon *m*

brain /breɪn/ *n* [1] mózg *m* [2] umysł *m*, rozum *m*; **he's got** ~**s** infml on ma głowę infml

brainchild /'breɪntʃaɪld/ *n* pomysł *m*

brain damage *n* uszkodzenie *n* mózgu

brain dead /ˌbreɪn'ded/ *adj* w stanie śmierci mózgowej *or* osobniczej

brain drain *n* drenaż *m* mózgów

brain surgery *n* neurochirurgia *f*

brain teaser *n* infml łamigłówka *f*

brainwash /'breɪnwɒʃ/ *vt* z|robić (komuś) pranie *n* mózgu

brainwashing /'breɪnwɒʃɪŋ/ *n* pranie *n* mózgu

brainwave /'breɪnweɪv/ *n* olśnienie *n*

brainy /'breɪnɪ/ *adj* infml bystry, uzdolniony

braise /breɪz/ *vt* u|dusić *[meat]*

brake /breɪk/ **II** *n* hamulec *m*

II *vi* (slow down) przy|hamować; (stop) za|hamować

brake pad *n* płytka *f* cierna hamulca

bramble /'bræmbl/ *n* jeżyna *f*

bran /bræn/ *n* otręby *plt*

branch /brɑːntʃ, US bræntʃ/ *n* ① (of tree) gałąź *f*; (of river) odnoga *f*; (of road) odgałęzienie *n*; (of study, subject) dziedzina *f* ② (of store, bank) oddział *m*; (of company) filia *f*

■ **branch off**: *[road]* rozchodzić się; *[river]* rozwidlać się

■ **branch out**: *[business]* rozszerz|yć, -áć działalność

brand /brænd/ **Ⅰ** *n* marka *f*

Ⅱ *vt* o|znakować *[cattle]*; **to ~ sb a coward** przyczepić komuś etykietę tchórza

branded /'brændɪd/ *adj [goods]* oznakowany (marką)

brandish /'brændɪʃ/ *vt* wymachiwać (czymś)

brand leader *n* przodująca marka *f*

brand name *n* nazwa *f* firmowa

brand-new /ˌbrænd'njuː, US -'nuː/ *adj* nowiutki

brandy /'brændɪ/ *n* brandy *f inv*; (cognac) koniak *m*

brash /bræʃ/ *adj [person, manner]* arogancki

brass /brɑːs, US bræs/ *n* ① (alloy) mosiądz *m* ② Mus (also ~ **section**) instrumenty *m pl* dęte blaszane

brass band *n* orkiestra *f* dęta

brat /bræt/ *n* infml pej bachor *m* infml pej

bravado /brə'vɑːdəʊ/ *n* brawura *f*

brave /breɪv/ **Ⅰ** *n* wojownik *m* indiański

Ⅱ *adj [person]* dzielny

Ⅲ *vt* stawi|ć, -áć czoło (czemuś) *[danger]* IDIOMS: **to put on a ~ face** robić dobrą minę do złej gry

bravely /'breɪvlɪ/ *adv* dzielnie

bravery /'breɪvərɪ/ *n* męstwo *n*

brawl /brɔːl/ **Ⅰ** *n* awantura *f*

Ⅱ *vi* **to ~ with sb** wdać się w awanturę z kimś

bray /breɪ/ *vi* za|ryczeć

brazen /'breɪzn/ *adj* bezwstydny

■ **brazen out**: **to ~ it out** zachowywać się, jak gdyby nic się nie stało

Brazil /brə'zɪl/ *prn* Brazylia *f*

breach /briːtʃ/ **Ⅰ** *n* (infringement) naruszenie *n*; (violation) pogwałcenie *n*; **to be in ~ of sth** stanowić naruszenie czegoś *[agreement, law]*

Ⅱ *vt* przełam|ać, -ywać *[defence]*; pogwałc|ić, -áć *[law]*

breach of contract *n* niedotrzymanie *n* or naruszenie *n* umowy

breach of the peace *n* zakłócenie *n* porządku publicznego

bread /bred/ *n* chleb *m*

bread and butter *n* chleb *m* z masłem; fig źródło *n* utrzymania

breadbin /'bredbɪn/ *n* GB pojemnik *m* na chleb

breadboard /'bredbɔːd/ *n* deska *f* do krojenia chleba

breadcrumb /'bredkrʌm/ **Ⅰ** *n* okruszek *m* chleba

Ⅱ **breadcrumbs** *npl* Culin bułka *f* tarta

breadline /'bredlaɪn/ *n* GB (income) **to be on the ~** żyć na granicy ubóstwa

bread roll *n* bułka *f*

breadth /bretθ/ *n* szerokość *f*; fig (of knowledge, subject) rozległość *f*

breadwinner /'bredwɪnə(r)/ *n* żywiciel *m* rodziny

break /breɪk/ **Ⅰ** *n* ① (in bone) złamanie *n*; (in plate) pęknięcie *n*; (in wall) wyrwa *f*, wyłom *m*; (in row, line) luka *f*; (in circuit) przerwanie *n* ② (pause) (in conversation, match) przerwa *f*; (in play) antrakt *m*; **(commercial) ~** przerwa na reklamę ③ (rest period) przerwa *f* (na odpoczynek); (at school) przerwa *f*, pauza *f*; **let's take a ~** zróbmy sobie przerwę; **to have a ~ from working** zrobić sobie przerwę w pracy; **the Christmas ~** przerwa świąteczna; (at school) ferie świąteczne ④ fig (rift) zerwanie *n*; **a ~ with tradition** zerwanie z tradycją

Ⅱ *vt* ① (damage) rozbi|ć, -jać *[window, egg]*; połamać *[chair]*; z|łamać *[bone]*; **to ~ one's leg** złamać (sobie) nogę ② (interrupt) przer|wać, -ywać *[monotony, silence]*; z|erwać, -rywać *[ties]* **(with sb** z kimś) ③ (violate) narusz|yć, -áć *[terms]*; z|łamać *[law]*; **he broke his promise** złamał obietnicę, nie dotrzymał obietnicy ④ (exceed) przekr|oczyć, -aczać *[speed limit]*; po|bić *[record]* ⑤ (lessen) z|łagodzić *[blow, fall]* ⑥ (tame) uje|ździć, -żdżać *[horse]* ⑦ (in tennis) **to ~ sb's serve** przełamać serwis kogoś ⑧ (announce) przekaz|ać, -ywać *[news]* **(to sb** komuś)

Ⅲ *vi* ① (get damaged) *[branch, tooth]* z|łamać się; *[egg, glass]* zbić się, s|tłuc się; *[rope]* z|erwać, -rywać się; *[paper bag]* roz|erwać, -rywać się; *[waves]* rozbi|ć, -jać się ② (change) *[good weather]* zmieni|ć, -áć się *[heatwave]* s|kończyć się, ust|ąpić, -ępować ③ (begin) *[storm]* rozpęt|ać, -ywać się; (become known) *[scandal]* wy|jść, -chodzić na jaw ④ (discontinue) **to ~ with sb** zerwać z kimś; **to ~ with tradition** zerwać z tradycją ⑤ (change tone) *[boy's voice]* ule|c, -gać mutacji

■ **break away**: ① *[rock]* od|erwać, -rywać się **(from sth** od czegoś); *[person]* odłącz|yć, -áć się **(from sb/sth** od kogoś/czegoś) ② (escape) ucie|c, -kać **(from sb** komuś)

■ **break down**: ¶ **~ down** ① *[car, machine]* ze|psuć się ② *[person]* (mentally) załam|ać, -ywać się; (physically) zapa|ść, -dać na zdrowiu ③ (cry) wy-buch|nąć, -áć płaczem ¶ **~ [sth] down** ① (demolish) wyłam|ać, -ywać *[door]*; fig przełam|ać, -ywać *[barriers, resistance]* ② (analyse) po|dzielić *[plan, task]* **(into sth** na coś); rozbi|ć, -jać *[budget, statistics]* **(into sth** na coś)

■ **break even**: wy|chodzić, -jść na czysto

■ **break free**: ucie|c, -kać

■ **break in**: ¶ **~ in** ① (enter) włam|ać, -ywać się ② (interrupt) przer|wać, -ywać, wtrąc|ić, -áć (się) ¶ **~ [sth] in** uje|ździć, -żdżać *[horse]*; **to ~ new**

shoes in rozchodzić nowe buty
■ **break into:** [1] (enter) włam|ać, -ywać się do (czegoś) *[building, safe]* [2] (start to use) otw|orzyć, -ierać, napocz|ąć, -ynać *[new packet, new bottle]* [3] (begin to do) **to ~ into song/into a run** zacząć śpiewać/puścić się biegiem
■ **break off:** ¶ **~ off** [1] *[end]* odłam|ać, -ywać się; *[handle, piece]* odpa|ść, -dać [2] (stop speaking) przer|wać, -ywać ¶ **~ [sth] off** [1] odłam|ać, -ywać *[branch]*; od|erwać, -rywać *[handle]* [2] (terminate) z|erwać, -rywać *[engagement]*; przer|wać, -ywać *[conversation]*
■ **break out:** [1] *[epidemic, fire]* wybuch|nąć, -ać; *[storm]* z|erwać, -rywać się; *[fight]* rozgorzeć; **to ~ out in a rash** *[person]* pokryć się wysypką; **to ~ out in a sweat** *[person]* zlać się potem [2] *[prisoner]* ucie|c, -kać; **to ~ out of sth** uciec z czegoś *[prison]*
■ **break up:** ¶ **~ up** [1] *[couple]* z|erwać, -rywać ze sobą [2] *[crowd]* roz|ejść, -chodzić się; *[clouds]* rozpr|oszyć, -aszać się; *[meeting]* za|kończyć się [3] GB Sch **schools ~ up on Friday** szkoły kończą lekcje w piątek ¶ **~ [sth] up** rozpędz|ić, -ać *[crowd, demonstrators]*; rozbi|ć, -jać *[drugs ring]*; doprowadz|ić, -ać do rozpadu (czegoś) *[marriage, empire]*
breakaway /'breɪkəweɪ/ *adj* **~ faction/group** frakcja/odłam; **~ state** państwo, które wydorębniło się z innego
breakdown /'breɪkdaʊn/ *n* [1] Tech awaria *f* [2] (of communications, negotiations) zerwanie *n*; (of coalition) rozpad *m*; (of discipline) rozprzężenie *n* [3] Med załamanie *n* (nerwowe); **to have a (nervous) ~** załamać się psychicznie [4] (of figures, costs) analiza *f*; **a ~ of the voters according to sex** podział elektoratu pod względem płci
breakfast /'brekfəst/ *n* śniadanie *n*
breakfast television *n* telewizja *f* śniadaniowa
break-in /'breɪkɪn/ *n* włamanie *n*
breaking point *n* fig **to be at ~** *[person]* być u kresu wytrzymałości
breakneck /'breɪknek/ *adj [speed, pace]* zawrotny
breakthrough /'breɪkθruː/ *n* przełom *m*
break-up /'breɪkʌp/ *n* rozpad *m*
breakwater /'breɪkwɔːtə(r)/ *n* falochron *m*
breast /brest/ *n* pierś *f*
breast-feed /'brestfiːd/ [1] *vt* na|karmić, wykarmić piersią
[2] *vi* karmić piersią
breast stroke *n* styl *m* klasyczny, żabka *f*
breath /breθ/ *n* [1] oddech *m*; **out of ~** bez tchu; **to hold one's ~** wstrzymać oddech; **he has bad ~** ma nieświeży oddech [2] (single act) oddech *m*, wdech *m*
(IDIOMS) **to take sb's ~ away** zapierać komuś dech (w piersiach)

breathalyse GB, **breathalyze** US /'breθəlaɪz/ *vt* z|mierzyć (komuś) zawartość alkoholu w organizmie
Breathalyzer® /'breθəlaɪzə(r)/ *n* alkomat *m*
breathe /briːð/ [1] *vt* [1] od|etchnąć, -dychać (czymś) *[air]*; wdychać *[dust, oxygen]*; **to ~ one's last** wyzionąć ducha [2] rozsi|ać, -ewać *[germs]*; **don't ~ a word!** ani pary z ust!
[2] *vi* [1] od|etchnąć, -dychać; **to ~ heavily** oddychać ciężko or z trudem [2] *[wine]* oddychać
■ **breathe in:** ¶ **~ in** z|robić wdech ¶ **~ [sth] in** wdychać *[air, gas]*
■ **breathe out:** ¶ **~ out** z|robić wydech ¶ **~ [sth] out** wydychać *[air, smoke]*
breather /'briːðə(r)/ *n* chwila *f* wytchnienia; **to take a ~** zrobić sobie krótką przerwę
breathing /'briːðɪŋ/ *n* oddychanie *n*
breathing space *n* [1] (respite) chwila *f* wytchnienia [2] (postponement) czas *m* (**in which to do sth** na zrobienie czegoś)
breathless /'breθlɪs/ *adj [runner]* z(a)dyszany; *[asthmatic]* oddychający z trudem, dyszący
breathtaking /'breθteɪkɪŋ/ *adj* zapierający dech (w piersiach)
breath test [1] *n* test *m* na zawartość alkoholu w organizmie
[2] *vt* podda|ć, -wać (kogoś) testowi na zawartość alkoholu w organizmie
breed /briːd/ [1] *n* Zool rasa *f*
[2] *vt* wy|hodować *[animals, plants]*; fig z|rodzić
[3] *vi [animals]* rozmn|ożyć, -ażać się
[4] **-bred** *in combinations* **ill-/well ~** źle/dobrze wychowany
breeder /'briːdə(r)/ *n* hodowca *m*
breeding /'briːdɪŋ/ *n* [1] (of animals) hodowla *f* [2] (upbringing) wychowanie *n*
breeding ground *n* wylęgarnia *f* also fig (**for sth** czegoś)
breeze /briːz/ [1] *n* wiaterek *m*; (at a coast, at sea) bryza *f*
[2] *vi* **to ~ into sth** wejść gdzieś bezceremonialnie, iść beztrosko przez życie; **to ~ through an exam** przejść gładko przez egzamin
brevity /'brevətɪ/ *n* (short span) krótkotrwałość *f*; (of speech, reply) zwięzłość *f*
brew /bruː/ [1] *n* (beer) piwo *n*; (tea) herbata *f*
[2] *vt* warzyć *[beer]*; **freshly ~ed coffee** kawa świeżo parzona
[3] *vi* [1] *[tea]* za|parzyć się; *[beer]* warzyć się [2] fig **a storm is ~ing** zanosi się na burzę
brewer /'bruːə(r)/ *n* piwowar *m*
brewery /'bruːərɪ/ *n* browar *m*
bribe /braɪb/ [1] *n* łapówka *f*
[2] *vt* przekup|ić, -ywać *[official, witness]*
bribery /'braɪbərɪ/ *n* łapownictwo *n*
brick /brɪk/ *n* cegła *f*
bricklayer /'brɪkleɪə(r)/ *n* murarz *m*

bridal /'braɪdl/ adj [dress] ślubny; [car] do ślubu; [feast] weselny

bride /braɪd/ n panna f młoda; **the ~ and (bride)groom** państwo młodzi, młoda para

bridegroom /'braɪdgruːm, -grʊm/ n pan m młody

bridesmaid /'braɪdzmeɪd/ n druhna f

bridge /brɪdʒ/ **Ⅰ** n ① most m (**over/across sth** nad/na czymś); (small) mostek m, kładka f; fig (link) pomost m fig ② (on ship) mostek m kapitański ③ (of nose) grzbiet m; (of spectacles) mostek m ④ Mus (on violin, guitar) podstawek m, mostek m ⑤ (for teeth) mostek m ⑥ (game) brydż m

Ⅱ vt ① **to ~ a gap in sth** wypełnić lukę w czymś [budget]; wypełnić przerwę w czymś [conversation] ② (span) obljąć, -ejmować [two eras]

bridle /'braɪdl/ **Ⅰ** n uzda f

Ⅱ vt zalłożyć, -kładać uzdę (czemuś) [horse]

Ⅲ vi żachlnąć, -ać się (**at sth** na coś); **to ~ with anger** unieść się gniewem

bridle path n ścieżka f konna

brief /briːf/ **Ⅰ** n ① GB (responsibility) zakres m obowiązków; (role) zadanie n ② (in law) akta plt

Ⅱ briefs npl (man's) slipy plt; (woman's) figi plt

Ⅲ adj [period] krótki; [account] krótki, zwięzły; **in ~** krótko mówiąc

Ⅳ vt (inform) polinformować (**on sth** o czymś); (instruct) polinstruować (**on sth** o czymś)

briefcase /'briːfkeɪs/ n teczka f; (without handles) aktówka f

briefing /'briːfɪŋ/ n odprawa f (**on sth** dotycząca czegoś)

briefly /'briːflɪ/ adv ① [describe] zwięźle; [reply] krótko; [glance] przelotnie; [pause] przez chwilę ② (in short) krótko mówiąc, jednym słowem

brigade /brɪ'geɪd/ n brygada f

bright /braɪt/ adj [sun, colour] jaskrawy; [star] jasny; [room] słoneczny; [day] pogodny; [eyes, metal] błyszczący; [person] bystry; **a ~ idea** świetny or genialny pomysł; **to look on the ~ side (of things)** patrzeć (na sprawy) optymistycznie

brighten /'braɪtn/ vt, vi

■ **brighten up**: ¶ **~ up** ① [person] poweseleć; [face, expression] rozjaśnilć, -ać się, rozpromienilć, -ać się ② [weather] poprawilć, -ać się ¶ **~ [sth] up** ożywilć, -ać [room]; rozjaśnilć, -ać [sky]

brightly /'braɪtlɪ/ adv [dressed] jaskrawo; [shine, burn] jasno

brightness /'braɪtnɪs/ n (of light) blask m; (of colour) jaskrawość f, żywość f; (of metal) połysk m

bright spark n GB infml geniusz m

brilliance /'brɪlɪəns/ n (of person) błyskotliwość f; (of colour) jaskrawość f

brilliant /'brɪlɪənt/ **Ⅰ** n brylant m

Ⅱ adj ① (successful) [person, career] błyskotliwy ② (bright) [colour] jaskrawy ③ GB infml (fantastic)

brilliantly /'brɪlɪəntlɪ/ adv ① (very well) znakomicie ② (very brightly) [shine] żywym blaskiem

brim /brɪm/ n (of hat) rondo n; (of container) brzeg m

brine /braɪn/ n ① (sea water) woda f morska ② Culin zalewa f solna

bring /brɪŋ/ vt [person] przynlieść, -osić; (by vehicle) przywlieźć, -ozić; **to ~ a smile to sb's face** wywołać uśmiech na twarzy kogoś; **to ~ sb with one** przyprowadzić kogoś (ze sobą); **to ~ sth with one** przynieść or wziąć coś (ze sobą) [object]

■ **bring about**: slpowodować [change]; doprowadzlić, -ać do (czegoś) [war]; przynlieść, -osić [failure, success]

■ **bring along**: przyprowadzlić, -ać (ze sobą) [friend]; przynlieść, -osić (ze sobą), zablrać, -ierać (ze sobą) [object]

■ **bring back**: ① (return with) przywlieźć, -ozić (ze sobą); **to ~ back memories (of sth)** [souvenir] przywołać wspomnienia (czegoś) ② (restore) przywrlócić, -acać [custom]; wskrzelsić, -szać [monarchy]

■ **bring down**: ① (overthrow) doprowadzlić, -ać do upadku (czegoś) [government] ② (lower) zmniejszlyć, -ać [expenditure, inflation]; obniżlyć, -ać [costs, temperature] ③ zestrzellić, -ać, -iwać [plane]

■ **bring forward**: przyspieszlyć, -ać datę (czegoś)

■ **bring in**: przynlieść, -osić [interest, profit]; wprowadzlić, -ać [legislation, measure]; zlebrać, -bierać, zwllieść, -ozić [wheat]; (involve) sprowadzlić, -ać [army]; doprowadzlić, -ać [suspect]

■ **bring off**: dokonlać, -ywać [feat]; zawlrzeć, -ierać [deal]

■ **bring on**: ① (provoke) wywołlać, -ywać [attack, migraine] ② (introduce) wprowadzlić, -ać [substitute]

■ **bring out**: ① (introduce) wydalć, -wać [edition]; wprowadzlić, -ać (coś) na rynek [new model] ② (highlight) wydobylć, -wać [colour]; oddalć, -wać [meaning]

■ **bring round**: ① (revive) olcucić ② (convince) przekonlać, -ywać (do swoich racji)

■ **bring up**: ① (mention) podnlieść, -osić, poruszlyć, -ać [subject] ② (vomit) zwrlócić, -acać, zlwymiotować [food] ③ (good) wychowlać, -ywać [child]; **well brought up** dobrze wychowany

brink /brɪŋk/ n krawędź f; **to be on the ~ of sth** być bliskim czegoś [death]; stać u progu czegoś [war]

brisk /brɪsk/ adj ① (efficient) [person] rzutki; [tone, manner] energiczny ② (energetic) [walk] szybki; [trot] żwawy; **at a ~ pace** żwawo, energicznie ③ [trade, business] ożywiony; **business is ~** interesy idą dobrze ④ [air, wind] rześki

bristle /'brɪsl/ **Ⅰ** n włosek m; (on pig) szczecina f

Ⅱ vi ① [hairs] zjeżyć się ② [person] najeżlyć, -ać się; **he ~d with indignation** oburzył się

Britain /'brɪtn/ *prn* (also **Great** ~) Wielka Brytania *f*

British /'brɪtɪʃ/ **I** *n* the ~ Brytyjczycy *m pl* **II** *adj* brytyjski

British Isles *prn* Wyspy *f pl* Brytyjskie

Briton /'brɪtn/ *n* Brytyj|czyk *m*, -ka *f*

brittle /'brɪtl/ *adj [porcelain]* kruchy; *[hair, fingernails]* łamliwy

broach /brəʊtʃ/ *vt* porusz|yć, -ać *[subject]*

broad /brɔːd/ *adj* ① (wide) szeroki; (extensive) rozlegly; **to have a ~ back** być szerokim w ramionach ② (general) *[meaning]* szeroki; *[outline]* ogólny ③ *[accent]* silny; **in ~ daylight** w biały dzień

broad-based /ˌbrɔːd'beɪst/ *adj [approach]* globalny; *[campaign]* szeroko zakrojony; *[consensus]* powszechny; *[education]* ogólny

broad bean *n* bób *m*

broadcast /'brɔːdkɑːst, US -kæst/ **I** *n* TV program *m*; Radio audycja *f* **II** *vt* nada|ć, -wać *[programme]*; transmitować *[concert]* **III** *vi [TV, radio station]* nadawać

broadcaster /'brɔːdkɑːstə(r), US -kæst-/ *n* prezenter *m*, -ka *f*

broadcasting /'brɔːdkɑːstɪŋ, US -kæst-/ *n* media *plt* radiowo-telewizyjne; **to work in ~** pracować w radiu/telewizji

broaden /'brɔːdn/ **I** *vt* rozszerz|yć, -ać *[horizons, knowledge]*; zwiększ|yć, -ać *[appeal]*; poszerz|yć, -ać *[road]*; **travel ~s the mind** podróże kształcą **II** *vi* rozszerz|yć -ać się

broadminded /ˌbrɔːd'maɪndɪd/ *adj [person]* o otwartym umyśle; *[attitude]* liberalny

broadsheet /'brɔːdʃiːt/ *n* gazeta *f* dużego formatu *(zwykle kojarzona z wyższą jakością)*

brocade /brə'keɪd/ *n* brokat *m*

broccoli /'brɒkəlɪ/ *n* Bot brokuł *m*; Culin brokuły *m pl*

brochure /'brəʊʃə(r), US brəʊ'ʃʊər/ *n* (booklet) broszura *f*; (glossy) prospekt *m*

broil /brɔɪl/ *vt* US opie|c, -kać *[meat]*

broke /brəʊk/ *adj* infml *[person]* bez grosza infml; **to go ~** splajtować infml

broken /'brəʊkən/ *adj [glass, window]* rozbity; *[leg]* złamany; *[radio]* zepsuty; *[man, woman]* załamany; *[English]* łamany

broken-down /ˌbrəʊkən'daʊn/ *adj [machine]* zepsuty

broken-hearted /ˌbrəʊkən'hɑːtɪd/ *adj* **to be ~** mieć złamane serce

broken home *n* rozbita rodzina *f*

broken marriage *n* rozbite małżeństwo *n*

broker /'brəʊkə(r)/ *n* pośrednik *m* handlowy; (on stock exchange) makler *m* (giełdowy); (insurance) broker *m*; **real-estate ~** US pośrednik w handlu nieruchomościami

brolly /'brɒlɪ/ *n* GB infml parasol *m*

bronchitis /brɒŋ'kaɪtɪs/ *n* zapalenie *n* oskrzeli

bronze /brɒnz/ *n* (metal) brąz *m*

brooch /brəʊtʃ/ *n* broszka *f*

brood /bruːd/ **I** *n* Zool potomstwo *n*, młode *plt*; (of birds) lęg *m*; (of mammals) miot *m* **II** *vi* ① (ponder) dumać; **to ~ about sth** rozmyślać o czymś ② *[bird]* wysiadywać

brook /brʊk/ *n* potok *m*, strumyk *m*

broom /bruːm, brom/ *n* miotła *f*

broth /brɒθ, US brɔːθ/ *n* bulion *m*

brothel /'brɒθl/ *n* burdel *m* infml

brother /'brʌðə(r)/ *n* brat *m*

brother-in-law /'brʌðərɪnlɔː/ *n* szwagier *m*

brotherly /'brʌðəlɪ/ *adj* braterski

brow /braʊ/ *n* ① (forehead) czoło *n*; (eyebrow) brew *f* ② (of hill) grzbiet *m*

brown /braʊn/ **I** *n* (kolor *m*) brązowy *m*, brąz *m* **II** *adj* ① brązowy ② (tanned) *[person, skin]* opalony na brąz; **to go ~** opalić się **III** *vt* zrumieni|ć, -ać *[onion, meat, sauce]* **IV** *vi [meat, onion]* zrumieni|ć, -ać się

brown bread *n* razowy chleb *m*, razowiec *m*

brown envelope *n* szara koperta *f*

Brownie /'braʊnɪ/ *n* dziewczynka należąca do drużyny zuchów

brown paper *n* szary papier *m*

brown rice *n* ryż *m* niełuskany

brown sugar *n* brązowy cukier *m*

browse /braʊz/ **I** *n* **to have a ~ through a book** przejrzeć or przekartkować książkę **II** *vi* ① (look at goods) roz|ejrzeć, -glądać się ② (graze) paść się

bruise /bruːz/ **I** *n* (on skin) stłuczenie *n*; (on fruit) obtłuczenie *n*, obicie *n* **II** *vt* posiniaczyć *[person]*; po|obijać *[fruit]*; **to ~ one's arm** stłuc sobie rękę

brunette /bruː'net/ *n* brunetka *f*

brunt /brʌnt/ *n* **to bear the ~ of sth** najbardziej odczuć coś; **young people are bearing the ~ of unemployment** młodych ludzi szczególnie dotyka bezrobocie

brush /brʌʃ/ **I** *n* ① (for hair, clothes, shoes) szczotka *f*; (for teeth) szczoteczka *f*; (broom) miotła *f*; (small, for sweeping) zmiotka *f*; (for paint) pędzel *m* ② (encounter) kontakt *m* (**with sb** z kimś); **to have a ~ with the police** mieć zatarg z policją **II** *vt* wy|czyścić *[carpet, clothes]*; **to ~ one's hair** wy|szczotkować włosy **III** *vi* **to ~ against sb/sth** o|trzeć, -cierać się o kogoś/coś; **to ~ past sb** przejść szybko obok kogoś

■ **brush aside**: odrzuc|ić, -ać *[idea, thought]*

■ **brush up (on)**: podszlifow|ać, -ywać *[language]*; odśwież|yć, -ać *[knowledge]*

brusque /bruːsk, US brʌsk/ *adj* (in manner) szorstki

Brussels /'brʌslz/ *prn* Bruksela *f*

Brussels sprout n brukselka f
brutal /'bruːtl/ adj brutalny, okrutny
brutality /bruː'tælətɪ/ n brutalność f
brute /bruːt/ **I** n [1] (man) brutal m [2] (animal) bestia f
II adj [strength] brutalny; **by ~ force** siłą, na siłę
BSc n GB Univ = **Bachelor of Science** licencjat m w dziedzinie nauk ścisłych
BSE n = **Bovine Spongiform Encephalopathy** gąbczaste zwyrodnienie n mózgu
bubble /'bʌbl/ **I** n (in glass, liquid) pęcherzyk m; (in champagne) bąbelek m; **to blow ~s** puszczać bańki (mydlane)
II vi [fizzy drink] pienić się, musować; [boiling liquid] bulgotać; **to ~ with sth** tryskać czymś [enthusiasm, optimism]
bubble bath n płyn m do kąpieli
bubble-wrap /'bʌblræp/ n opakowanie n z plastiku pęcherzykowego
buck /bʌk/ **I** n [1] US infml (dollar) dolec m infml [2] Zool samiec m; (of deer, goat) kozioł m
II vi [horse] wierzgać
(IDIOMS) **to pass the ~** zrzucać odpowiedzialność na innych, uchylać się od odpowiedzialności
bucket /'bʌkɪt/ n wiadro n, kubeł m
buckle /'bʌkl/ **I** n klamra f; (small) klamerka f, sprzączka f
II vt [1] zapi|ąć, -nać klamrę or sprzączkę u (czegoś), zapi|ąć, -nać (coś) na klamrę or sprzączkę [belt, shoe] [2] odkształc|ić, -ać [metal]
III vi [1] [metal, surface] odkształc|ić, -ać się; [wheel] z|wichrować się [2] [shoe, belt] zapinać się na sprzączkę or klamrę; **my knees ~d** kolana się pode mną ugięły
bud /bʌd/ **I** n pąk m, pączek m
II vi [plant] wypu|ścić, -szczać pąki, pączkować; [flowers, leaves] zawiąz|ać, -ywać się w pąki
Buddha /'bʊdə/ prn **the ~** Budda m
Buddhism /'bʊdɪzəm/ n buddyzm m
Buddhist /'bʊdɪst/ **I** n buddy|sta m, -jka f
II adj buddyjski
budding /'bʌdɪŋ/ adj [artist] obiecujący; [talent] młody; [desire, romance] budzący się
buddy /'bʌdɪ/ infml n kumpel m infml
budge /bʌdʒ/ **I** vt [1] (move) porusz|yć, -ać, ruszyć [2] (persuade) nakł|onić, -aniać (kogoś) do zmiany stanowiska
II vi [1] (move) rusz|yć, -ać się [2] (change opinion) zmieni|ć, -ać zdanie (**on sth** w sprawie czegoś); **she won't ~ an inch** nie ustąpi ani o włos
■ **budge over, budge up** infml: posu|nąć, -wać się, rusz|yć, -ać się infml
budgerigar /'bʌdʒərɪɡɑː(r)/ n papużka f falista
budget /'bʌdʒɪt/ **I** n budżet m
II vi **to ~ for sth** uwzględni|ć, -ać (w budżecie) [increase, needs]

buff /bʌf/ n [1] infml (enthusiast) mania|k m, -czka f [2] (colour) (kolor m) płowożółty m
buffalo /'bʌfələʊ/ n bawół m; US bizon m
buffer /'bʌfə(r)/ n fig ochrona f, zabezpieczenie n
buffet[1] /'bʊfeɪ, US bə'feɪ/ n bufet m, bar m
buffet[2] /'bʌfɪt/ vt [wind, sea] walić o (coś)
buffoon /bə'fuːn/ n błazen m, komediant m
bug /bʌɡ/ **I** n [1] infml (insect) robak m; Zool pluskwa f [2] infml wirus m; **to have a tummy ~** chorować na żołądek infml [3] Comput (in program) błąd m; (in computer) defekt m [4] (hidden microphone) urządzenie n podsłuchowe
II vt [1] zało|żyć, -kładać podsłuch w (czymś) [room, telephone]; **the room is ~ged** w tym pokoju jest podsłuch [2] infml (annoy) wkurz|yć, -ać infml
buggy /'bʌɡɪ/ n [1] GB (pushchair) lekki składany wózek m niemowlęcy [2] US (pram) wózek m dziecinny [3] (carriage) amerykan m
bugle /'bjuːɡl/ n trąbka f (sygnałowa)
build /bɪld/ **I** n budowa f (ciała), sylwetka f
II vt [1] z|budować, wy|budować [house, ship] [2] z|montować [car]; s|tworzyć [database]; z|budować [empire, future]; z|robić [career]
III vi **to ~ on sth** bazować na czymś, op|rzeć się, -ierać się na czymś
■ **build up:** ¶ **~ up** [gas, mud] na|gromadzić się; [traffic] wzm|óc, -agać się; [tension, pressure] narastać; [business, trade] rozwi|nąć, -jać się ¶ **~ [sth] up** z|gromadzić [wealth, collection]; pogłębi|ć, -ać [confidence, trust]; s|tworzyć [business, picture]; rozbudow|ać, -ywać [army]; wyr|obić, -abiać sobie [reputation]; wyr|obić, -abiać [muscles]; **to ~ oneself up, to ~ up one's strength** wyrabiać mięśnie or muskuły
builder /'bɪldə(r)/ n (entrepreneur) przedsiębiorca m budowlany; (worker) robotnik m budowlany
building /'bɪldɪŋ/ n budynek m; **school ~** budynek szkoły
building contractor n przedsiębiorca m budowlany
building site n plac m budowy
building society n GB ≈ oszczędnościowa kasa f mieszkaniowa
build-up /'bɪldʌp/ n [1] (increase), (of tar) odkładanie się n; (of deposit) nawarstwianie się n; (of gas) gromadzenie (się) n; (of traffic, tension, pressure) nasilanie się n [2] (publicity) promocja f
built-in /bɪlt'ɪn/ adj [wardrobe] w ścianie; [guarantee] stanowiący część integralną
built-up /bɪlt'ʌp/ adj [area, region] zabudowany
bulb /bʌlb/ n [1] (of lamp) żarówka f [2] Bot cebul(k)a f
Bulgaria /bʌl'ɡeərɪə/ prn Bułgaria f
bulge /bʌldʒ/ **I** n (in carpet, plaster, vase) wybrzuszenie n; (in cheek, breast) krągłość f

II vi [surface] wybrzusz|yć, -ać się; [stomach] sterczeć; [muscles] napi|ąć, -nąć się; [cheeks] wyd|ąć, -ymać się; **his eyes ~ d** wybałuszył oczy

bulimia (nervosa) /bju:ˌlɪmɪə nɜː'vəʊsə/ n bulimia f

bulimic /bju:'lɪmɪk/ **I** n osoba f cierpiąca na bulimię

II adj bulimiczny

bulk /bʌlk/ n ① (of bag, package) wielki rozmiar m; (of building) wielka bryła f; (of correspondence, writings) ogrom m; **the ~ of sth** większość czegoś ② **in ~** [buy, sell] hurtowo; [transport] luzem

bulk-buying /'bʌlkbaɪɪŋ, ˌbʌlk'baɪɪŋ/ n zakup m hurtowy

bulky /'bʌlki/ adj [package] pokaźnych rozmiarów; [book] opasły; [person] zwalisty

bull /bʊl/ n (bovine) byk m; (male) samiec m (słonia, wieloryba)

bullbar n Aut orurowanie n (na przednim zderzaku)

bulldog /'bʊldɒg/ n buldog m

bulldozer /'bʊldəʊzə(r)/ n spychacz m, buldożer m

bullet /'bʊlɪt/ n kul(k)a f, pocisk m

bulletin /'bʊlətɪn/ n biuletyn m; **news ~** biuletyn informacyjny

bulletin board n tablica f informacyjna; Comput elektroniczna tablica f ogłoszeniowa

bulletproof /'bʊlɪtpruːf/ adj [glass, vest] kuloodporny; [vehicle] opancerzony

bullfight /'bʊlfaɪt/ n corrida f

bullfighter /'bʊlfaɪtə(r)/ n tor(r)eador m

bullfighting /'bʊlfaɪtɪŋ/ n walki f pl byków, corrida f

bullion /'bʊliən/ n kruszec m w sztabach

bullock /'bʊlək/ n wół m

bullring /'bʊlrɪŋ/ n arena f (na której odbywają się walki byków)

bull's-eye /'bʊlzaɪ/ n środek m tarczy, dziesiątka f

bully /'bʊli/ **I** n (child) łobuz m (znęcający się nad słabszymi); (adult) despota m, tyran m

II vt tyranizować, zastraszyć

bum /bʌm/ n ① GB infml (buttocks) pupa f, tyłek m infml ② US (vagrant) tramp m; menel m infml pej

bumbag /'bʌmbæg/ n piterek m (mała torebka na pasku noszonym w talii)

bumblebee /'bʌmblbiː/ n trzmiel m

bumf, bumph /bʌmf/ n GB infml (document) papierek m infml

bump /bʌmp/ **I** n ① (lump) (on body) guz m; (on road) wybój m ② (jolt) wstrząs m ③ (noise) huk m, łoskot m

II vt **to ~ one's head against** or **on sth** uderzyć głową o coś

■ **bump into**: wpa|ść, -dać na (kogoś/coś); (meet) **to ~ into sb** wpa|ść, -dać na kogoś infml

bumper /'bʌmpə(r)/ **I** n zderzak m

II adj [crop, sales] rekordowy; [year] wyjątkowo dobry; [edition] wyjątkowo duży

bumper car n samochodzik m (w wesołym miasteczku)

bumpkin /'bʌmpkɪn/ n infml pej (also **country ~**) kmiotek m

bumpy /'bʌmpi/ adj [road] wyboisty; [surface] nierówny; **we had a ~ flight** bardzo nas wytrzęsło podczas lotu

bun /bʌn/ n ① (bread roll) bułka f, bułeczka f ② (hairstyle) kok m

bunch /bʌntʃ/ n (of flowers) pęk m; (of vegetables) pęczek m; (of keys) pęk m; (of bananas, grapes) kiść f; (of people) grupa f, grono n; pej banda f

bundle /'bʌndl/ **I** n (of books) paczka f; (of papers, banknotes) plik m, pakiet m; (of clothes) tobołek m; (of straw, sticks) wiązka f; **~ of nerves** kłębek nerwów

II vt **to ~ sth into a drawer** wepchnąć coś do szuflady

bundled software n oprogramowanie n preinstalowane (dostarczone z komputera)

bungalow /'bʌŋgələʊ/ n dom m parterowy

bungee jumping /'bʌndʒiːdʒʌmpɪŋ/ n skoki m pl na bungee

bungle /'bʌŋgl/ vt s|partaczyć, s|knocić infml [job, operation]

bunion /'bʌnjən/ n haluks m

bunk /bʌŋk/ n ① (on ship) koja f; (in train) kuszetka f ② (also **~ bed**) łóżko n piętrowe

■ **bunk off** infml: **to ~ off school** pójść na wagary

bunker /'bʌŋkə(r)/ n ① (shelter) bunkier m; (beneath building) schron m ② (for storing) bunkier m ③ (in golf) bunkier m

bunny /'bʌni/ n ① (also **~ rabbit**) króliczek m ② (also **~ girl**) króliczek m (hostessa w klubie Playboya)

bunting /'bʌntɪŋ/ n chorągiewki f pl

buoy /bɔɪ/ **I** n boja f, pława f

II vt ① (also **~ up**) podn|ieść, -osić na duchu [person] ② s|powodować wzrost (czegoś) [share prices] ③ (keep afloat) utrzym|ać, -ywać na powierzchni

buoyant /'bɔɪənt/ adj ① [object] pływający ② (cheerful) [person] pełen życia; [mood, spirits] pogodny; [step] lekki ③ rosnący; [market, economy] prężny

burden /'bɜːdn/ **I** n ① fig ciężar m, brzemię n ② (load) ciężar m

II vt (also **~ down**) ① obładow|ać, -ywać [person] (**with sth** czymś) ② fig **to ~ sb with sth** obarcz|yć, -ać kogoś czymś [problems, work]; obciąż|yć, -ać kogoś czymś [debt]

bureau /'bjʊərəʊ, US -'rəʊ/ n ① (agency) urząd m ② US (government department) biuro n, urząd m ③ GB (desk) biurko n ④ US (chest of drawers) komoda f

bureaucracy /bjʊə'rɒkrəsi/ n biurokracja f

bureaucrat /'bjʊərəkræt/ n biurokrata m

bureaucratic /ˌbjʊərə'krætɪk/ adj biurokratyczny
burgeoning /'bɜːdʒənɪŋ/ adj [project, industry] rodzący się; ~ **love/talent** kiełkująca miłość/ dojrzewający talent
burger /'bɜːgə(r)/ n hamburger m
burger bar n bar m hamburgerowy
burglar /'bɜːglə(r)/ n włamywacz m, -ka f
burglar alarm n alarm m przeciwwłamaniowy
burglary /'bɜːglərɪ/ n włamanie n; (in law) kradzież m z włamaniem
burgle /'bɜːgl/ vt włam|ać, -ywać się do (czegoś)
burgundy /'bɜːgəndɪ/ n ① (wine) burgund m ② (colour) bordo n inv; (kolor m) bordowy m
burial /'berɪəl/ n pogrzeb m
burly /'bɜːlɪ/ adj [person] krzepki, przysadzisty
Burma /'bɜːmə/ prn Birma f
burn /bɜːn/ **❶** n oparzenie n
❷ vt s|palić [papers]; przypal|ić, -ać [food]; o|parzyć, s|parzyć [finger]
❸ vi ① [house] s|palić się, s|płonąć ② [meat] przypal|ić, -ać się ③ (be painful) [skin] piec
■ **burn down**: ¶ ~ **down** [house] spalić się doszczętnie, spłonąć ¶ ~ **[sth] down** pu|ścić, -szczać z dymem [house]
■ **burn up**: spal|ić, -ać [calories]; zuży|ć, -wać [energy]
burner /'bɜːnə(r)/ n palnik m
(IDIOMS:) **to put sth on the back** ~ odłożyć coś na później [issue, question]
burning /'bɜːnɪŋ/ **❶** n spalenizna f; **there's a smell of** ~ czuć swąd
❷ adj ① (on fire) [house] płonący; [fire] palący się; (alight) [candle, lamp] zapalony ② (intense) [desire, problem] palący; [faith] gorący; [pain] piekący
burnt-out /'bɜːntaʊt/ adj [car, house] spalony; fig [person] wyczerpany
burp /bɜːp/ infml **❶** n beknięcie n infml
❷ vi bek|nąć, -ać infml
burrow /'bʌrəʊ/ **❶** n nora f, jama f
❷ vi [animal] wy|kopać jamę or norę; **to** ~ **into sth** [animal, person] zagrzebać się w coś [ground]
bursary /'bɜːsərɪ/ n GB stypendium n
burst /bɜːst/ **❶** n (of bomb) wybuch m; (of pipe, dam) pęknięcie n; (of laughter) wybuch m; (of energy) przypływ m; (of gunfire) seria f; **a** ~ **of activity** zryw (aktywności); **a** ~ **of applause** burza oklasków
❷ vt przekłu|ć, -wać [bubble, balloon]; **the river** ~ **its banks** rzeka wystąpiła z brzegów
❸ vi [bomb] wybuch|nąć, -ać; [tyre] pęk|nąć, -ać; **to be** ~**ing with health/enthusiasm** tryskać zdrowiem/entuzjazmem
■ **burst into**: ① (enter) wtargnąć do (czegoś) [room] ② (start) **to** ~ **into flames** buchnąć płomieniem; **to** ~ **into tears** zalać się łzami
■ **burst out**: **to** ~ **out laughing/crying** wybuchnąć śmiechem/płaczem

■ **burst through**: przed|rzeć, -zierać się przez (coś) [barricade]; **she burst through the door out onto the street** wypadła przez drzwi na ulicę
bury /'berɪ/ vt po|chować, po|grzebać
bus /bʌs/ n autobus m; **by** ~ autobusem; **to get on the** ~ wsiąść do autobusu
bus conductor n konduktor m autobusu
bus driver n kierowca m autobusu
bush /bʊʃ/ n ① krzak m ② **the** ~ busz m
(IDIOMS:) **don't beat about the** ~ nie owijaj w bawełnę
bushfire /'bʊʃfaɪə(r)/ n pożar m buszu
bushy /'bʊʃɪ/ adj [eyebrows] krzaczasty; [beard, hair] bujny, gęsty; [tail] puszysty
business /'bɪznɪs/ **❶** n ① (commerce) interesy m pl, działalność f handlowa; **to be in** ~ prowadzić interesy; **she's gone to Brussels on** ~ wyjechała do Brukseli służbowo or w interesach; **to mix** ~ **with pleasure** łączyć przyjemne z pożytecznym; **to lose** ~ tracić klientelę; **most of our** ~ **comes from tourism** obroty mamy głównie z turystyki; **he's in the insurance** ~ działa w branży ubezpieczeniowej ② (company) przedsiębiorstwo n, firma f; (shop) sklep m; **small** ~**es** małe firmy ③ (matters) sprawy f pl (do załatwienia); **let's get down to** ~ przejdźmy do rzeczy; **to go about one's** ~ wykonywać swoje obowiązki ④ (concern) **that's her** ~ to jej sprawa; **it's none of your** ~! to nie twoja sprawa or rzecz!; **mind your own** ~! pilnuj swoich spraw!
❷ adj [transaction, correspondence] handlowy; [address, lunch] służbowy; [pages] branżowy
(IDIOMS:) **to work like nobody's** ~ infml pracować za trzech; **she means** ~! ona nie żartuje!
business associate n partner m, -ka f; (co-owner) wspólni|k m, -czka f
business card n wizytówka f
business class n (on plane) pierwsza klasa f
business hours npl (of office) godziny f pl urzędowania; (of shop) godziny f pl otwarcia
businesslike /'bɪznɪslaɪk/ adj [manner] rzeczowy; [appearance] poważny
businessman /'bɪznɪsmən/ n biznesmen m, przedsiębiorca m
business park n centrum n biurowo-przemysłowe
business plan n biznesplan m
business school n szkoła f handlowa or biznesu
business studies npl zarządzanie n
business trip n podróż f służbowa
businesswoman /'bɪznɪswʊmən/ n businesswoman f inv, kobieta f interesu
busker /n GB uliczny artysta m, uliczna artystka f
bus lane n pas m dla autobusów
bus pass n autobusowy bilet m okresowy
bus shelter n wiata f (na przystanku autobusowym)
bus station n dworzec m autobusowy

bus stop n przystanek m autobusowy

bust /bʌst/ **I** n ① (breasts) biust m ② (sculpture) popiersie n

II adj ① (broken) zepsuty ② (bankrupt) **to go ~** s|plajtować, zrobić klapę or plajtę infml

bustle /'bʌsl/ **I** n (activity) rozgardiasz m; **the hustle and ~ of city life** zgiełk i zamęt miejskiego życia

II vi [person] krzątać się, uwijać się; **to ~ in and out** wpadać i wypadać

bustling /'bʌslɪŋ/ adj [person] zaaferowany; [street, town] tętniący życiem

busy /'bɪzɪ/ **I** adj ① (person) zajęty (**with sth/ doing sth** czymś/robieniem czegoś) ② [day, week] pracowity; [airport, street] ruchliwy; [shop, office] pełen ruchu; **were the shops ~?** czy w sklepach był duży ruch? ③ (engaged) [line] zajęty

II vr **to ~ oneself** zaj|ąć, -mować się (**with sth/ doing sth** czymś/robieniem czegoś)

busybody /'bɪzɪbɒdɪ/ n infml **he's a real ~** on jest bardzo wścibski

but /bʌt, bət/ **I** adv (only, just) tylko; **one can't help ~ admire her** nie można jej nie podziwiać

II prep **anybody ~ him** wszyscy, tylko nie on; **nobody ~ me knows how to do it** tylko ja wiem, jak tu zrobić; **he's nothing ~ a coward** jest po prostu tchórzem; **the last ~ one** przedostatni, drugi od końca; **the next street ~ one** dwie przecznice dalej

III but for prep phr **~ for you, I would have died** gdyby nie ty, umarłbym; **we would have married ~ for the war** pobralibyśmy się, gdyby nie wojna

IV conj ale; lecz fml

butane /'bjuːteɪn/ n butan m

butcher /'bʊtʃə(r)/ **I** n rzeźni|k m, -czka f; **the ~'s (shop)** sklep mięsny

II vt za|rżnąć, -rzynać [animal]; z|masakrować [prisoners]

butchery /'bʊtʃərɪ/ n ① (trade) rzeźnictwo n ② (brutal killing) masakra f

butler /'bʌtlə(r)/ n kamerdyner m

butt /bʌt/ **I** n ① (of rifle) kolba f; (of cigarette) niedopałek m ② US infml (buttocks) tyłek m infml ③ (of jokes, criticism) obiekt m

II vt [animal] u|bóść; [person] uderz|yć, -ać głową

■ **butt in**: wtrąc|ić, -ać się

butter /'bʌtə(r)/ **I** n masło n

II vt po|smarować masłem [bread]

■ **butter up** infml: **~ [up] sb** podliz|ać, -ywać się (komuś) infml

buttercup /'bʌtəkʌp/ n jaskier m

butterfingers /'bʌtəfɪŋgəz/ n niezdara f/m infml

butterfly /'bʌtəflaɪ/ n motyl m

[IDIOMS] **to have butterflies (in one's stomach)** mieć tremę

butterfly stroke n styl m motylkowy

buttock /'bʌtək/ n pośladek m

button /'bʌtn/ **I** n ① (on garment) guzik m; (switch) przycisk m, guzik m ② US (badge) znaczek m, odznaka f ③ Comput przycisk m

II vi [garment] zapinać się (na guziki)

■ **button up** po|zapinać (na guziki) [coat, shirt]

buttonhole /'bʌtnhəʊl/ **I** n ① (for button) dziurka f od guzika; (for flower) butonierka f ② GB (flower) kwiat m do butonierki

II vt infml dor|wać, -ywać infml

buttress /'bʌtrɪs/ n ① przypora f, skarpa f; **flying ~** łuk odporowy or przyporowy ② fig oparcie n, fundament m

buxom /'bʌksəm/ adj [woman] piersiasta

buy /baɪ/ **I** n **a good ~** udany zakup m

II vt kup|ić, -ować [food]; **to ~ sth from sb** kupić coś od kogoś; **to ~ sth from the supermarket** kupić coś w supermarkecie; **to ~ sb sth** kupić komuś coś; **we managed to ~ some time** fig zyskaliśmy trochę na czasie

■ **buy off**: przekup|ić, -ywać [witness]

■ **buy out**: wykup|ić, -ywać udziały (kogoś)

■ **buy up**: skup|ić, -ować [shares]; wykup|ić, -ywać [land, houses]

buyer /'baɪə(r)/ n nabywca m, kupiec m

buyout /'baɪaʊt/ n wykup m (akcji)

buzz /bʌz/ **I** n ① (of insect) bzyczenie n, brzęczenie n; (of conversation) gwar m ② infml (phone call) **to give sb a ~** zadzwonić do kogoś ③ infml (thrill) **to get a ~ from sth/out of doing sth** rajcować się czymś/robieniem czegoś infml

II vt (by buzzer, intercom) w|ezwać, -zywać

III vi [insects] bzy|knąć, -czeć; [intercom, telephone] za|dzwonić, za|brzęczeć

buzzard /'bʌzəd/ n myszołów m

buzzer /'bʌzə(r)/ n brzęczyk m, dzwonek m

buzzword /'bʌzwɜːd/ n infml modne powiedzonko n infml

by /baɪ/ **I** prep ① (indicating agent) przez (kogoś/coś); **he was bitten by a snake** został ukąszony przez węża; **a novel by Virginia Woolf** powieść Virginii Woolf ② (indicating means) **made by hand** wykonane ręcznie; **to travel by car** podróżować samochodem; **by bicycle** rowerem, na rowerze; **to pay by cheque** zapłacić czekiem; **you can reach me by phone** możesz się ze mną skontaktować telefonicznie; **to dine by candlelight** jeść kolację przy świecach; **I took him by the hand** wziąłem go za rękę; **I'll begin by introducing myself** zacznę od przedstawienia się, najpierw przedstawię się ③ (owing to) **by accident/mistake** przez przypadek/pomyłkę; **by chance** przypadkiem, przypadkowo; **he is an architect by profession** or **trade** z zawodu jest architektem ④ (according to) **by my watch it is three o'clock** na moim zegarku jest trzecia; **I knew him by his walk** poznałem go po chodzie; **is it all right by you if I**

smoke? czy nie masz nic przeciwko temu, że zapalę? ⑤ (in accordance with) **to play by the rules** postępować zgodnie z regułami gry; **by western standards** według norm zachodnich ⑥ (via) przez (coś); **we entered by the back door** weszliśmy drzwiami od tyłu or tylnymi drzwiami; **we travelled to Rome by Venice** jechaliśmy do Rzymu przez Wenecję ⑦ (near) koło (kogoś/czegoś), obok (kogoś/czegoś); **by the bed** koło or obok łóżka; **by the sea** nad morzem ⑧ (past) **she walked right by me** przeszła tuż koło or obok mnie; **they passed us by in their car** minęli nas samochodem ⑨ (before) do, przed; **it must be done by four o'clock** to musi być zrobione do czwartej; **by this time next week** o tej porze w przyszłym tygodniu; **by the time he arrived, the others had left** zanim się zjawił, pozostali wyszli; **he ought to be here by now** powinien już tu być ⑩ (during) **by daylight** w dzień, za dnia ⑪ (indicating extent of difference) **prices have risen by 20%** ceny wzrosły o 20%; **he's taller than me by two centimetres** jest ode mnie wyższy o dwa centymetry ⑫ (indicating measurement) na; **a room 20 metres by 10 metres** pokój 20 metrów na 10 ⑬ (in multiplication, division) przez; **divide six by three** podziel sześć przez trzy ⑭ (indicating rate, quantity) **to be paid by the hour** dostawać zapłatę od godziny ⑮ (in successive degrees, units) **little by little** po trochu; **day by day** dzień po dniu; **one**

by one jeden po drugim ⑯ (in compass directions) **south by south-west** południe południowy zachód ⑰ (alone) **he did it all by himself** zrobił to wszystko sam

II *adv* ① (past) obok; **to walk by** przejść obok; **a lot of time has gone by since then** (od tamtej chwili) minęło wiele czasu; **as time goes by** w miarę upływu czasu ② (near) w pobliżu, niedaleko; **he lives close by** mieszka niedaleko or w pobliżu ③ (aside) **to put money by** odkładać pieniądze

bye /baɪ/ *n excl* infml do widzenia!, pa! infml

by(e)-election /ˈbaɪɪlekʃn/ *n* GB wybory *plt* uzupełniające

bygone /ˈbaɪɡɒn/ *adj [days, years]* miniony; *[generations]* dawny; **a ~ era** miniona epoka

(IDIOMS) **to let ~s be ~s** zapomnieć o urazach

bypass /ˈbaɪpɑːs, US -pæs/ **I** *n* ① Aut obwodnica *f* ② Med pomost *m* omijający, bypass *m* ③ (for gas, electricity) obejście *n*

II *vt* Aut omiǀnąć, -jać *[town, city]*

by-product /ˈbaɪprɒːdʌkt/ *n* produkt *m* uboczny; fig efekt *m* uboczny

bystander /ˈbaɪstændə(r)/ *n* bierny widz *m*, obserwator *m*

byte /baɪt/ *n* Comput bajt *m*

byword /ˈbaɪwɜːd/ *n* dewiza *f*; **our name is a ~ for quality** nasza nazwa to synonim wysokiej jakości

C

c, C /si:/ *n* 1 (letter) c, C *n* 2 C Mus c, C, do *n*

cab /kæb/ *n* 1 (taxi) taksówka *f* 2 (for driver) szofer-ka *f*

cabbage /ˈkæbɪdʒ/ *n* kapusta *f*

cab-driver /ˈkæbdraɪvə(r)/ *n* taksówkarz *m*

cabin /ˈkæbɪn/ *n* 1 (hut) chata *f*; (in holiday camp) domek *m* kempingowy 2 (in boat) kajuta *f*; (in plane) kabina *f*

cabin crew *n* personel *m* pokładowy

cabinet /ˈkæbɪnɪt/ *n* 1 (cupboard) szafka *f*; **display ~** gablota; **cocktail ~** barek 2 GB (also **Cabinet**) gabinet *m*, Rada *f* Ministrów

cabinet minister *n* GB minister *m*

cable /ˈkeɪbl/ 【I】 *n* 1 (rope) lina *f* 2 (electric, TV) kabel *m*
【II】 *adj [channel, network]* kablowy

cable car *n* wagonik *m* kolejki linowej

cable TV *n* telewizja *f* kablowa

cab-rank /ˈkæbræŋk/ *n* postój *m* taksówek

cab stand *n* = cab-rank

cackle /ˈkækl/ *vi [hen]* za|gdakać; *[person]* (talk) gdakać infml; (laugh) za|rechotać

CAD *n* → computer-aided design

CADCAM /ˈkædkæm/ *n* Comput = **computer-aided design and computer-aided manufacture**

caddy /ˈkædɪ/ *n* 1 US (shopping trolley) wózek *m* 2 GB (also **tea ~**) puszka *f* na herbatę 3 Sport (also **caddie**) osoba *f* nosząca kije za graczem

cadet /kəˈdet/ *n* Mil kadet *m*, podchorąży *m*

cadge /kædʒ/ *vt* infml **to ~ sth off** or **from sb** wyżebrać coś od kogoś *[money, cigarette]*; **to ~ a dinner** wprosić się na obiad

Caesarean, Caesarian /sɪˈzeərɪən/ *n* (also ~ **section**) cesarskie cięcie *n*

café /ˈkæfeɪ, US kæˈfeɪ/ *n* 1 tania restauracja *f* bez wyszynku; **pavement ~, sidewalk ~** kawiarnia z ogródkiem 2 US restauracja *f*

cafeteria /ˌkæfəˈtɪərɪə/ *n* bar *m* szybkiej obsługi, bufet *m*; (in school, university) stołówka *f*

caffein(e) /ˈkæfi:n/ *n* kofeina *f*

cage /keɪdʒ/ 【I】 *n* (for bird, animal) klatka *f*; (of lift) kabina *f*
【II】 *vt* zam|knąć, -ykać w klatce *[bird, animal]*; **a ~d animal** zwierzę trzymane w klatce

cagoule /kəˈgu:l/ *n* GB nieprzemakalny skafander *m* z kapturem

cahoots /kəˈhu:ts/ *npl* infml **to be in ~ with sb** być w zmowie z kimś

Cairo /ˈkaɪərəʊ/ *prn* Kair *m*

cajole /kəˈdʒəʊl/ *vt* przymil|ić, -ać się do (kogoś)

cake /keɪk/ *n* 1 Culin (large) ciasto *n*; (small) ciastko *n* 2 (of soap, wax) kostka *f*
(IDIOMS) **it's a piece of ~** infml to pestka infml

cake shop *n* ciastkarnia *f*, cukiernia *f*

calcium /ˈkælsɪəm/ *n* wapń *m*

calculate /ˈkælkjʊleɪt/ *vt* 1 (work out) oblicz|yć, -ać *[cost, distance, price, size]* 2 (estimate) oceni|ć, -ać *[probability]*; przewi|dzieć, -dywać *[effect]* 3 **to be ~d to do sth** być obliczonym na coś

calculated /ˈkælkjʊleɪtɪd/ *adj [crime]* (dokonany) z premedytacją; *[attempt, insult]* umyślny; *[risk]* wkalkulowany

calculating /ˈkælkjʊleɪtɪŋ/ *adj [manner, person]* wyrachowany

calculation /ˌkælkjʊˈleɪʃn/ *n* wyliczenie *n*

calculator /ˈkælkjʊleɪtə(r)/ *n* kalkulator *m*

calendar /ˈkælɪndə(r)/ *n* kalendarz *m*

calf /kɑ:f, US kæf/ *n* 1 (of cow, deer, buffalo) cielę *n* 2 (leather) skóra *f* cielęca 3 Anat łydka *f*

calibre GB, **caliber** US /ˈkælɪbə(r)/ *n* kaliber *m*

California /ˌkælɪˈfɔ:nɪə/ *prn* Kalifornia *f*

call /kɔ:l/ 【I】 *n* 1 (also **(tele)phone ~**) rozmowa *f* telefoniczna; **to make a ~** zadzwonić, zatelefonować 2 (cry) wołanie *n* (**for sth** o coś); (animal) głos *m* 3 (summons) wezwanie *n* 4 (visit) wizyta *f* 5 (demand) żądanie *n* 6 (need) **there's no ~ for such behaviour** nie ma powodu tak się zachowywać 7 Sport decyzja *f* sędziego 8 (duty) **to be on ~** *[doctor, engineer]* dyżurować pod telefonem
【II】 *vt* 1 (give a name) naz|wać, -ywać; **what is he ~ed?** jak on się nazywa? 2 (summon) za|wołać; **the boss ~ed me into his office** szef wezwał mnie do swojego gabinetu 3 (arrange) ogł|osić, -aszać *[strike, election]*; zwoł|ać, -ywać *[conference, meeting]* 4 (waken) o|budzić 5 (describe as) **to ~ sb stupid** nazwać kogoś głupcem; **I wouldn't ~ this house spacious** nie powiedziałabym, że ten dom jest przestronny
【III】 *vi* 1 (cry out) wołać, krzy|knąć, -czeć 2 (telephone) za|telefonować; **who's ~ing?** kto mówi? 3 (visit) **to ~ at sb's** wpaść or wstąpić do kogoś; **to ~ at a shop/bank** wstąpić do sklepu/banku;

the **London train** ~ing at **Reading** pociąg do Londynu zatrzymujący się w Reading

■ **call back**: ¶ ~ **back** [1] (on phone) oddzw|onić, -aniać [2] (return) przy|jść, -chodzić jeszcze raz ¶ ~ [sb/sth] **back** przywoł|ać, -ywać (z powrotem) [person, animal]

■ **call for**: ~ **for** [sth] [1] (shout) w|ezwać, -zywać [doctor, ambulance]; **to** ~ **for help** wzywać pomocy [2] (demand) domagać się (czegoś) [3] (require) wymagać (czegoś) [treatment, skill]

■ **call in**: ¶ ~ **in** (visit) wst|ąpić, -ępować ¶ ~ [sb] **in** po|prosić (do środka) [client, patient]; w|ezwać, -zywać [expert]

■ **call off**: wstrzym|ać, -ywać [search]; odwoł|ać, -ywać [meeting, wedding]; **to** ~ **off one's engagement** zerwać zaręczyny

■ **call on**: [1] (visit) przy|jść, -chodzić z wizytą do (kogoś) [relative, friend]; odwiedz|ić, -ać [patient, client] [2] **to** ~ **on sb to do sth** poprosić kogoś o zrobienie czegoś

■ **call out**: ¶ ~ **out** krzy|knąć, -czeć, za|wołać ¶ ~ [sb] **out** w|ezwać, -zywać [doctor, troops]; [union] w|ezwać, -zywać do strajku (kogoś) [members] ¶ ~ [sth] **out** wywoł|ać, -ywać [name, number]

■ **call up**: ¶ ~ **up** za|wołać ¶ ~ [sb/sth] **up** [1] (on phone) za|dzwonić do (kogoś) [2] Mil powoł|ać, -ywać do wojska [soldier]

call box n GB (outside) budka f telefoniczna; (inside) kabina f telefoniczna; US telefon m S.O.S. przy drodze publicznej

call centre n informacja f telefoniczna

caller /'kɔ:lə(r)/ n [1] (on the phone) dzwoniąc|y m, -a f [2] (visitor) gość m, odwiedzając|y m, -a f

callous /'kæləs/ adj bezduszny, okrutny

call-out charge n opłata f za dojazd (do klienta)

calm /kɑːm, US also kɑːlm/ **[]** n spokój m, cisza f; (in adversity) opanowanie n
[] adj cichy, spokojny; **keep** ~! zachowaj spokój!
[] vt uspok|oić, -ajać
■ **calm down**: ¶ ~ **down** uspok|oić, -ajać się; ~ **down!** uspokój się! ¶ ~ [sb/sth] **down** po|działać uspokajająco na (kogoś/coś)

calmly /'kɑːmlɪ, US also 'kɑːlmlɪ/ adv [act, speak, sleep] spokojnie

Calor gas® /'kælə gæs/ n GB butan m

calorie /'kælərɪ/ n kaloria f

camcorder /'kæmkɔːdə(r)/ n kamkorder m

camel /'kæml/ n wielbłą|d m, -dzica f

camera /'kæmərə/ n (for photos) aparat m fotograficzny; (for movies) kamera f

camera crew n ekipa f telewizyjna

cameraman /'kæmərəmæn/ n (in film) operator m; (in TV) kamerzysta m

camisole /'kæmɪsəʊl/ n krótka haleczka f na ramiączkach

camouflage /'kæməflɑːʒ/ **[]** n kamuflaż m
[] vt za|maskować [tank] (with sth czymś)

camp /kæmp/ **[]** n obóz m
[] vi rozbi|ć, -jać obóz; **to go** ~**ing** pojechać pod namiot/na kemping

campaign /kæm'peɪn/ **[]** n kampania f
[] vi prowadzić kampanię (for/against sth na rzecz czegoś/przeciwko czemuś)

campaigner /kæm'peɪnə(r)/ n [1] bojowni|k m, -czka f (for/against sth o coś/przeciwko czemuś) [2] Pol kandydat m startujący w wyborach, kandydatka f startująca w wyborach

camp bed n łóżko n polowe

camper /'kæmpə(r)/ n [1] (person) obozowicz m, -ka f, biwakowicz m, -ka f [2] (also ~ **van**) samochód m z częścią mieszkalną

campfire /'kæmpfaɪə(r)/ n ognisko n

camping /'kæmpɪŋ/ n biwakowanie n, obozowanie n; **to go** ~ wyjechać pod namiot

campsite /'kæmpsaɪt/ n (temporary) obozowisko n; (official) pole n namiotowe, kemping m

campus /'kæmpəs/ n kampus m, miasteczko n uniwersyteckie

can[1] /kæn, kən/ modal aux [1] (be able to) ~ **you come?** możesz przyjść?; **we will do all we** ~ zrobimy wszystko, co się da [2] (permission, requests, offers, suggestions) **you** ~ **turn right here** tu można skręcić w prawo; ~ **you leave us a message?** czy możesz zostawić dla nas wiadomość?; **what** ~ **I do for you?** czym mogę służyć? [3] (know how to) **she can't drive yet** jeszcze nie umie prowadzić (samochodu); ~ **he speak English?** czy on zna angielski? [4] (with verbs of perception) ~ **you see it?** widzisz to?; **I can't hear anything** nic nie słyszę [5] (expressions) **you can't** or **cannot be serious!** chyba nie mówisz poważnie; **what** ~ **she possibly want from me?** czego ona może ode mnie chcieć?; ~ **you believe it!** dasz wiarę?; **this can't be right** to musi być pomyłka; **you can't be hungry!** to niemożliwe, żebyś był głodny!

can[2] /kæn/ **[]** n (of food, drink) puszka f; (aerosol) pojemnik m; (for oil, petrol) kanister m; (for milk) bańka f
[] vt puszkować [fruit, vegetables]; ~**ned beans** fasolka z puszki or w puszce

Canada /'kænədə/ prn Kanada f

Canadian /kə'neɪdɪən/ **[]** n Kanadyj|czyk m, -ka f
[] adj kanadyjski

canal /kə'næl/ n kanał m

canal boat, canal barge n barka f, krypa f

Canaries /kə'neərɪz/ prn (also **Canary Islands**) **the** ~ Wyspy f pl Kanaryjskie; Kanary plt infml

cancel /'kænsl/ vt odwoł|ać, -ywać [event, flight]; anulować [contract, cheque]

cancellation /ˌkænsə'leɪʃn/ n anulowanie n, unieważnienie n

cancer /'kænsə(r)/ *n* Med nowotwór *m* złośliwy, rak *m*; **to have (lung/stomach)** ~ mieć raka (płuc/żołądka)

Cancer /'kænsə(r)/ *n* Rak *m*

cancer patient *n* chor|y *m*, -a *f* na raka

cancer research *n* badania *n pl* nad rakiem

candid /'kændɪd/ *adj* szczery; *[photograph]* nieupozowany

candidate /'kændɪdət, US -deɪt/ *n* kandydat *m*, -ka *f*

candle /'kændl/ *n* świeca *f*; (small) świeczka *f*

candlelight /'kændllaɪt/ *n* blask *m* świec(y)

candlelit dinner /ˌkændllɪt'dɪnə(r)/ *n* kolacja *f* przy świecach

candlestick /'kændlstɪk/ *n* świecznik *m*, lichtarz *m*

candy /'kændɪ/ *n* US (sweets) słodycze *plt*; (sweet) cukierek *m*

candyfloss /'kændɪflɒs/ *n* GB wata *f* cukrowa

cane /keɪn/ *n* [1] (material) trzcina *f*; ~ **furniture** meble bambusowe/rattanowe/wiklinowe [2] (for walking) laska; (for plant) palik *m*; GB (for punishment) trzcinka *f*

canine /'keɪnaɪn/ *n* kieł *m*

canister /'kænɪstə(r)/ *n* pojemnik *m* metalowy; **a tear gas** ~ pocisk z gazem łzawiącym

cannabis /'kænəbɪs/ *n* konopie *plt* indyjskie; (drug) haszysz *m*, marihuana *f*

cannibal /'kænɪbl/ *n* kanibal *m*

cannon /'kænən/ *n* armata *f*, działo *n*

canoe /kə'nu:/ **[I]** *n* kajak *m*; Sport kanadyjka *f*; (Indian) kanu *n inv*
[II] *vi* pły|nąć, -wać kajakiem

canoeing /kə'nu:ɪŋ/ *n* kajakarstwo *n*

can-opener /'kænəupnə(r)/ *n* otwieracz *m* do puszek or konserw

cantankerous /kæn'tæŋkərəs/ *adj* kłótliwy

canteen /kæn'ti:n/ *n* [1] GB (dining room) stołówka *f*, kantyna *f* [2] Mil (flask) manierka *f*; (mess tin) menażka *f* [3] GB **a** ~ **of cutlery** komplet sztućców (w kasecie)

canter /'kæntə(r)/ *vi [rider, horse]* cwałować

canvas /'kænvəs/ *n* [1] (fabric) grube płótno *n* [2] (for painting) płótno *n* (malarskie); (painting) płótno *n*

canvass /'kænvəs/ *vt* **to** ~ **voters** odwiedzać wyborców; **to** ~ **opinion** or **views on sth** sondować opinię publiczną na temat czegoś; **to** ~ **an area** Pol prowadzić agitację wyborczą na (jakimś) terenie; *[salesperson]* prowadzić akwizycję na (jakimś) terenie

canvasser /'kænvəsə(r)/ *n* agitator *m*, -ka *f*

canyon /'kænjən/ *n* kanion *m*

cap /kæp/ **[I]** *n* [1] (headgear) czapka *f*; **baseball** ~ bejsbolówka [2] (of pen) skuwka *f*; (of bottle) kapsel *m* [3] (for tooth) korona *f*

[II] *vt* [1] (limit) *[government]* ogranicz|yć, -ać wydatki (czegoś) *[local authorities]* [2] (cover) pokry|ć, -wać wierzchołek (czegoś)
[IDIOMS] **to** ~ **it all** na domiar wszystkiego or złego

capability /ˌkeɪpə'bɪlətɪ/ *n* [1] (capacity) zdolność *f*; ~ **to do sth** zdolność do zrobienia czegoś [2] (aptitude) zdolności *f pl*, możliwości *f pl*; **to be outside sb's capabilities** przekraczać możliwości kogoś

capable /'keɪpəbl/ *adj* [1] (competent) kompetentny [2] (able) **to be** ~ **of doing sth** potrafić or być w stanie coś zrobić

capacity /kə'pæsətɪ/ *n* [1] (of box, bottle) pojemność *f*; (of ship, vehicle) ładowność *f*; **full to** ~ wypełniony po brzegi [2] (of factory) wydajność *f* [3] (role) **in my** ~ **as a doctor** jako lekarz [4] (ability) **to have a** ~ **for sth** mieć zdolności do czegoś *[learning, maths]*

cape /keɪp/ *n* [1] (garment) peleryna *f* [2] (headland) przylądek *m*

caper /'keɪpə(r)/ *n* [1] Kulin kapar *m* [2] infml (dishonest scheme) przekręt *m* infml [3] ~**s** (antics) zabawne perypetie *plt*

Cape Town /'keɪptaʊn/ *prn* Kapsztad *m*

capital /'kæpɪtl/ **[I]** *n* [1] (letter) duża litera *f* [2] (also ~ **city**) stolica *f* [3] (money) kapitał *m*
[II] *adj* [1] *[letter]* wielki; ~ **A** duże A [2] *[offence, crime]* karany śmiercią

capital expenditure *n* nakłady *m pl* kapitałowe

capital investment *n* lokata *f* kapitału, inwestycja *f*

capitalism /'kæpɪtəlɪzəm/ *n* kapitalizm *m*

capitalist /'kæpɪtəlɪsət/ **[I]** *n* kapitalista *m*
[II] *adj* kapitalistyczny

capitalize /'kæpɪtəlaɪz/ *vi* **to** ~ **on sth** zbi|ć, -jać kapitał na czymś

capital punishment *n* kara *f* śmierci

capitulate /kə'pɪtʃʊleɪt/ *vi* s|kapitulować (**to sb** przed kimś)

Capricorn /'kæprɪkɔ:n/ *n* Koziorożec *m*

capsize /kæp'saɪz, US 'kæpsaɪz/ *vi [boat]* wywr|ócić, -acać się (dnem do góry)

captain /'kæptɪn/ **[I]** *n* kapitan *m*
[II] *vt* sprawować funkcję kapitana (czegoś)

caption /'kæpʃn/ *n* podpis *m* (**to** or **for sth** pod czymś, do czegoś)

captivate /'kæptɪveɪt/ *vt* (fascinate) zniew|olić, -alać; (enchant) urze|c, -kać

captive /'kæptɪv/ *n* jeniec *m*

captivity /kæp'tɪvətɪ/ *n* niewola *f*

captor /'kæptə(r)/ *n* (kidnapper) porywacz *m*, -ka *f*; **his** ~ ten, który go uwięził

capture /'kæptʃə(r)/ **[I]** *n* [1] (of stronghold) zdobycie *n*; (of prisoner) pojmanie *n*; (of animal, thief) schwytanie *n*
[II] *vt* [1] zdoby|ć, -wać *[stronghold]*; s|chwytać *[animal, bird]* [2] uchwycić *[likeness]*; odda|ć, -wać *[feeling]*

car /kɑː(r)/ [I] n [1] samochód m [2] (railway carriage) wagon m; **restaurant** ~ wagon restauracyjny [II] adj *[industry, accident, alarm]* samochodowy; ~ **journey** podróż samochodem

caramel /'kærəmel/ n karmel m

carat /'kærət/ n karat m; **18** ~ **gold** osiemnastokaratowe złoto

caravan /'kærəvæn/ [I] n przyczepa f turystyczna; **gypsy/circus** ~ wóz cygański/cyrkowy [II] vi **to go** ~**ning** GB pojechać na wakacje z przyczepą

caravan site n kemping m dla przyczep turystycznych

carbohydrate /ˌkɑːbə'haɪdreɪt/ n węglowodan m

car bomb n samochód-pułapka m

carbon /'kɑːbən/ n węgiel m

carbon copy n kopia f (przez kalkę); fig wierna kopia f

carbon dioxide n dwutlenek m węgla

carbon monoxide n tlenek m węgla, czad m

car boot sale n GB giełda f rzeczy używanych *(sprzedawanych z bagażnika samochodu)*

carburettor /ˌkɑːbə'retə(r)/ GB, **carburetor** /'kɑːrbəreɪtər/ US n gaźnik m

card /kɑːd/ n [1] (for correspondence) karta f, kartka f [2] (also **playing** ~) karta f
IDIOMS: **to play one's** ~**s right** dobrze to rozegrać

cardboard /'kɑːdbɔːd/ n karton m, tektura f

cardboard city n infml koczowisko n bezdomnych *(w dużych miastach)*

card game n [1] (type of game) gra f w karty [2] (as activity) partia f kart

cardiac /'kɑːdiæk/ adj sercowy; *[medicine]* nasercowy; *[patient]* chory na serce

cardiac arrest n zatrzymanie n akcji serca

cardigan /'kɑːdɪɡən/ n sweter m rozpinany

card key n karta f magnetyczna *(zastępująca klucz)*

cardphone /'kɑːdfəʊn/ n automat m telefoniczny na kartę magnetyczną

card trick n sztuczka f karciana

care /keə(r)/ [I] n [1] (attention) ostrożność f, uwaga f; **to take** ~ **to do sth** starać się coś zrobić; '**take** ~!' „uważaj!"; (expression of farewell) „trzymaj się!" infml; '**Glass. Handle with** ~' „ostrożnie, szkło" [2] (looking after) (of person, animal) opieka f (**of sb** nad kimś); (of car, house) dbałość f (**of sth** o coś); (of plant, skin) pielęgnacja f (**of sth** czegoś); **to take** ~ **of sb** (deal with) obsługiwać kogoś *[client]*; (be responsible for) zaopiekować się czymś *[cat, house, garden]*; (be careful with) ostrożnie obchodzić się z czymś *[machine, car]*; (keep in good condition) zadbać o coś *[machine, car, teeth]*; (look after) pilnować czegoś *[shop, watch]*; **to take** ~ **of oneself** (look after oneself) dbać o siebie; (cope) radzić sobie [3] Med opieka f (**of sb** nad kimś) [4] GB **to be in** ~ *[child]*

przebywać w ośrodku opiekuńczym [5] (worry) troska f
[II] vi [1] (feel concerned) **to** ~ **about sth** interesować się czymś *[art, culture]*; przejmować się czymś *[environment, injustice]*; **I don't** ~! nie obchodzi mnie to!; **he couldn't** ~ **less** nic go to nie obchodzi; **I'm past caring** przestałem się przejmować [2] (love) **I** ~ **about her** zależy mi na niej ■ **care for**: ¶ ~ **for** *[sth]* [1] (like) lubić; **would you** ~ **for a drink?** czy ma pani/pan ochotę napić się czegoś? [2] (maintain) za|dbać o (coś) *[car, garden, skin, plant]* ¶ ~ **for** *[sb]* za|opiekować się (kimś)

care assistant n ≈ pielęgniarka f środowiskowa

career /kə'rɪə(r)/ n praca f zawodowa, kariera f

career break n przerwa f w pracy zawodowej

careers adviser, careers officer n doradca m do spraw wyboru zawodu

careers office n poradnia f zawodowa

carefree /'keəfriː/ adj beztroski

careful /'keəfl/ adj *[person, driving]* ostrożny; *[planning, examination]* staranny; **to be** ~ **to do sth** or **about doing sth** uważać, żeby coś zrobić; **to be** ~ **with sth** ostrożnie obchodzić się z czymś *[knife]*; '**be** ~!' „uważaj!"

carefully /'keəfəli/ adv [1] *[drive, handle, say]* ostrożnie [2] *[choose words]* starannie; *[listen, read, look]* uważnie

careless /'keəlɪs/ adj *[person]* nieostrożny, nieuważny; *[driving]* nieostrożny; *[work]* niedbały; *[writing]* niestaranny; **a** ~ **mistake** błąd wynikający z nieuwagi

carelessness /'keəlɪsnɪs/ n nieostrożność f

carer /'keərə(r)/ n opiekun m, -ka f *(osoby starszej, chorej lub niepełnosprawnej)*

caress /kə'res/ vt po|pieścić

caretaker /'keəteɪkə(r)/ n dozor|ca m, -czyni f

care worker n pracowni|k m, -ca f opieki społecznej

car ferry n prom m samochodowy

cargo /'kɑːɡəʊ/ n ładunek m, cargo n

cargo ship n statek m towarowy

car hire n wynajem m samochodów

car hire company n firma f wynajmująca samochody

Caribbean /ˌkærɪ'biːən/ prn **the** ~ **(Sea)** Morze n Karaibskie

caricature /'kærɪkətʃʊə(r)/ n karykatura f

caring /'keərɪŋ/ adj [1] (loving) *[parent]* kochający [2] (compassionate) *[person, attitude]* troskliwy; *[society]* opiekuńczy

carjacking /'kɑːdʒækɪŋ/ n kradzież f samochodu (połączona z czynną napaścią na kierowcę)

carnage /'kɑːnɪdʒ/ n masakra f

carnation /kɑː'neɪʃn/ n goździk m

carnival /'kɑːnɪvl/ n [1] (period before Lent) karnawał m [2] US wesołe miasteczko n

carol /'kærəl/ *n* kolęda *f*
carousel /ˌkærə'sel/ *n* [1] (merry-go-round) karuzela *f*
[2] (for luggage) taśmociąg *m* bagażowy
car park *n* GB parking *m*
carpenter /'kɑːpəntə(r)/ *n* stolarz *m*
carpentry /'kɑːpəntrɪ/ *n* stolarstwo *n*
carpet /'kɑːpɪt/ *n* (loose) dywan *m*; (fitted) wykładzina *f* dywanowa
carpet sweeper *n* szczotka *f* na kiju do dywanów
car phone /'kɑːfəʊn/ *n* radiotelefon *m* samochodowy
car radio *n* radio *n* samochodowe
carriage /'kærɪdʒ/ *n* [1] (horse-drawn) powóz *m* [2] (of train) wagon *m* kolejowy [3] (of goods) przewóz *m*, transport *m*; ~ **paid** przewóz opłacony [4] (of typewriter) karetka *f*
carriageway /'kærɪdʒweɪ/ *n* jezdnia *f* (autostrady)
carrier /'kærɪə(r)/ *n* [1] (transport company) przewoźnik *m*; (of goods) spedytor *m* [2] (of disease) nosiciel *m*, -ka *f* [3] GB (also ~ **bag**) torba *f* (papierowa lub plastikowa)
carrot /'kærət/ *n* marchew *f*, marchewka *f*
carry /'kærɪ/ [I] *vt* [1] *[person, animal]* nieść; **to** ~ **sth down** znieść coś (z góry or na dół); **to** ~ **sth in** wnieść coś (do środka); **to** ~ **sth out** wynieść coś (na zewnątrz) [2] *[vehicle]* przewieźć, -ozić; *[tide, current]* (po)nieść; *[pipe, artery]* doprowadzić, -ać [3] (feature) być opatrzonym (czymś) *[warning]* [4] (entail) nieść ze sobą *[risk]*; wiązać się z (czymś) *[responsibility]*; pociągnąć, -ać za sobą *[penalty]* [5] *[bridge, road]* wytrzymać, -ywać *[weight, traffic]* [6] Pol **the motion was carried by 20 votes to 13** wniosek przeszedł dwudziestoma głosami przeciw trzynastu [7] Med *[insect]* przenieść, -osić *[disease]*; *[person]* być nosicielem (czegoś) *[virus]* [8] (hold) trzymać, nosić *[head]* [9] (in mathematics) przenieść, -osić *[one, two]*
[II] *vi [voice, sound]* nieść się, roznosić się
■ **carry forward**: przenieść, -osić na następną stronę *[balance, total]*
■ **carry off**: zdobyć, -wać *[prize, medal]*; **to** ~ **it off** infml (succeed) poradzić sobie
■ **carry on**: ¶ ~ **on** [1] (continue) kontynuować (**doing sth** robienie czegoś) [2] infml (behave) zachowywać się ¶ ~ **on [sth]** zachować, -ywać *[tradition]*; kontynuować *[activity, discussion]*
■ **carry out**: zrealizować, wprowadzić, -ać w życie *[plan]*; spełnić, -ać *[duty, promise, threat]*; przeprowadzić, -ać *[experiment, attack, investigation, campaign]*; wykonać, -ywać *[orders, repairs]*
(IDIOMS:) **to get carried away** dać się ponieść emocjom
carryall /'kærɪɔːl/ *n* US (miękka) torba *f* sportowa
carrycot /'kærɪkɒt/ *n* GB torba *f* do noszenia niemowlęcia
carry-on /'kærɪɒn/ *n* infml zamieszanie *n*

carryout /'kærɪaʊt/ *n* danie *n* na wynos
car seat *n* fotel *m* samochodowy
carsick /'kɑːsɪk/ *adj* **to be** ~ mieć nudności *(podczas jazdy samochodem)*
cart /kɑːt/ [I] *n* wóz *m*, fura *f*
[II] *vt* infml za|targać, za|taszczyć infml *[bags]*; **to** ~ **sth around** or **about** targać or taszczyć coś ze sobą
cartel /kɑː'tel/ *n* kartel *m*; **drug** ~ kartel narkotykowy
carton /'kɑːtn/ *n* US (for house removals) karton *m*, pudło *n*; (of yoghurt, cream, ice cream) kubek *m*, kubeczek *m*; (of milk, juice) karton *m*; (of cigarettes) karton *m*
cartoon /kɑː'tuːn/ *n* [1] (film) film *m* rysunkowy, kreskówka *f* [2] (drawing) dowcip *m* rysunkowy [3] (also **strip** ~) komiks *m*
cartridge /'kɑːtrɪdʒ/ *n* (for pen, gun) nabój *m*; (for video) kaseta *f*; (for camera) rolka *f* filmu w kasecie
cartwheel /'kɑːtwiːl/ *n US* -hwiːl/ *n* **to do a** ~ zrobić gwiazdę
carve /kɑːv/ [I] *vt* [1] (shape) wy|rzeźbić *[figure]* (**out of** z czegoś) [2] (inscribe) wy|ryć *[letter, name]* (**onto/ in sth** na/w czymś) [3] Culin po|kroić, po|krajać *[chicken, joint]*
[II] *vi* po|kroić mięso
■ **carve out**: [1] fig wyrobić, -abiać sobie *[name, position]*; **to** ~ **out a niche (for oneself)** znaleźć dla siebie niszę [2] *[river]* wy|drążyć *[gorge, channel]*
■ **carve up**: infml po|dzielić *[territory, spoils]*
carving /'kɑːvɪŋ/ *n* rzeźba *f*
carving knife *n* nóż *m* do mięsa
car wash *n* myjnia *f* samochodowa
case[1] /keɪs/ [I] *n* [1] (instance) przypadek *m*, wypadek *m*; **in that** ~ w takim razie; **in 7 out of 10** ~ **s** w siedmiu przypadkach na dziesięć; **a** ~ **in point** dobry przykład [2] (in law) **the** ~ **for the Crown** GB, **the** ~ **for the State** US oskarżenie *n*; **the** ~ **for the defence** stanowisko obrony [3] (convincing argument) argumenty *m pl*
[II] **in any case** *adv phr* (besides, anyway) zresztą; (at any rate) w każdym razie
[III] **in case** *conj phr* jeśli, jeżeli; **in** ~ **it rains** w razie deszczu; **just in** ~ na wszelki wypadek
[IV] **in case of** *prep phr* w razie (czegoś); **in** ~ **of emergency** w nagłym wypadku
case[2] /keɪs/ *n* [1] (suitcase) walizka *f*; (crate, chest) skrzynia *f* [2] (display cabinet) gablota *f* [3] (for spectacles, pen) etui *n inv*; (for binoculars, camera) futerał *m*; (of watch) koperta *f*
CASE /keɪs/ *n* = **computer-aided software engineering** inżynieria *f* oprogramowania wspomagana komputerowo
case study *n* studium *n* przypadku
cash /kæʃ/ [I] *n* [1] (notes and coins) gotówka *f*; **to pay in** ~ płacić gotówką; **I haven't got any** ~ **on me** nie mam przy sobie gotówki [2] (money in general)

pieniądze *m pl* [3] (payment) zapłata *f* gotówką;
discount for ~ rabat przy płatności gotówką
II *vt* **to** ~ **a cheque** z|realizować czek
■ **cash in:** ¶ **to** ~ **in on sth** wyciągnąć z czegoś
korzyść ¶ ~ **[sth] in** spienięż|yć, -áć *[bond, policy]*; US z|realizować *[cheque]*
cash-and-carry /ˌkæʃənˈkærɪ/ *n* sprzedaż *f* za
gotówkę bez dostawy
cash card *n* karta *f* do bankomatu
cash desk *n* kasa *f*, okienko *n* kasowe
cash dispenser *n* (also **cashpoint**) bankomat *m*
cashew nut /ˈkæʃuːˈnʌt/ *n* orzech *m* nerkowca
cash flow *n* przepływy *m pl* gotówkowe
cashier /kæˈʃɪə(r)/ *n* kasjer *m*, -ka *f*
cashless /ˈkæʃlɪs/ *adj* bezgotówkowy; **the** ~
society społeczeństwo bezgotówkowe
cashmere /ˌkæʃˈmɪə(r)/ *n* kaszmir *m*
cash on delivery, **COD** *n* płatność *f* gotówką
przy odbiorze
cashpoint /ˈkæʃpɔɪnt/ *n* = **cash dispenser**
cash register *n* kasa *f* (sklepowa)
casino /kəˈsiːnəʊ/ *n* kasyno *n*
cask /kɑːsk, US kæsk/ *n* beczka *f*
casserole /ˈkæsərəʊl/ *n* [1] (container) naczynie *n*
żaroodporne [2] GB (food) potrawa *f* duszona na
małym ogniu
cassette /kəˈset/ *n* kaseta *f*
cassette deck *n* magnetofon *m* kasetowy bez
wzmacniacza, deck *m*
cassette player *n* odtwarzacz *m* kasetowy
cast /kɑːst, US kæst/ **I** *n* [1] (list of actors) obsada *f*;
the members of the ~ aktorzy [2] Med (also
plaster ~) opatrunek *m* gipsowy; gips *m* infml
[3] (mould) forma *f*; (moulded object) odlew *m*
II *vt* [1] rzuc|ić, -áć *[stone]*; **to** ~ **doubt on sth**
podać coś w wątpliwość; **to** ~ **light on sth** rzucić
na coś światło; **to** ~ **a shadow** rzucać cień; **to** ~
a spell on sb/sth rzucić na kogoś/coś czary
[2] rzuc|ić, -áć *[glance]* (**at sb/sth** na kogoś/coś)
[3] obsadz|ić, -áć *[play, film]*; **she was cast as
Snow White** obsadzono ją w roli Królewny
Śnieżki [4] odl|ać, -ewać *[plaster, metal]* [5] Pol **to**
~ **one's vote** oddać głos
castaway /ˈkɑːstəweɪ, US ˈkæst-/ *n* rozbitek *m*
caste /kɑːst/ *n* kasta *f*
caster sugar *n* GB cukier puder *m*
casting /ˈkɑːstɪŋ, US ˈkæst-/ *n* casting *m*
casting vote *n* decydujący głos *m*
cast iron *n* żeliwo *n*; **a** ~ **alibi** niezbite alibi
castle /ˈkɑːsl, US ˈkæsl/ *n* [1] (building) zamek *m* [2] (in
chess) wieża *f*
cast-offs /ˈkɑːstɒfs, US ˈkæst-/ *npl* ubrania *n pl*
używane
castrate /kæˈstreɪt, US ˈkæstreɪt/ *vt* wy|kastrować
casual /ˈkæʒʊəl/ *adj* [1] (informal) *[clothes, manner]*
swobodny [2] (occasional) *[acquaintance, relationship]*
przypadkowy; ~ **sex** przypadkowe kontakty

seksualne [3] (nonchalant) *[attitude, gesture]* niedbały;
[remark] rzucony mimochodem [4] (superficial)
[glance] pobieżny [5] *[worker, labour]* (temporary)
sezonowy; (occasional) pracujący dorywczo
casually /ˈkæʒʊəlɪ/ *adv* [1] *[inquire, remark]* mimochodem [2] *[dressed]* zwyczajnie
casualty /ˈkæʒʊəltɪ/ **I** *n* [1] (person) ofiara *f* [2] (part
of hospital) oddział *m* nagłych wypadków; **in** ~ na
oddziale nagłych wypadków
II casualties *npl* (soldiers) straty *f pl* w ludziach;
(civilians) ofiary *f pl*
casual wear *n* odzież *f* codzienna or sportowa
cat /kæt/ *n* (domestic) kot *m*; (female) kotka *f*; **the big**
~**s** wielkie drapieżniki z rodziny kotów
IDIOMS: **to let the** ~ **out of the bag** puścić farbę
infml; **to rain** ~**s and dogs** lać jak z cebra
catalogue /ˈkætəlɒg, US -lɔːg/ *n* katalog *m*
catalyst /ˈkætəlɪst/ *n* katalizator *m*
catapult /ˈkætəpʌlt/ *n* proca *f*
catarrh /kəˈtɑː(r)/ *n* Med nieżyt *m*, katar *m*
catastrophe /kəˈtæstrəfɪ/ *n* katastrofa *f*
catch /kætʃ/ **I** *n* [1] (on purse) zapięcie *n*; (on door)
zatrzask *m* [2] (drawback) haczyk *m*, kruczek *m* infml
[3] (act of catching) chwyt *m*; **to play** ~ grać w piłkę
[4] (in fishing) połów *m*
II *vt* [1] *[person]* schwy|cić, -tać, z|łapać *[ball, fish]*;
dog|onić, -aniać *[person]*; **to** ~ **hold of sth** złapać
or schwycić się czegoś; **to** ~ **sb's attention** or
eye zwrócić na siebie uwagę kogoś; **to** ~ **sight of
sb/sth** zauważyć kogoś/coś [2] (take by surprise)
przyłapać; **to** ~ **sb doing sth** przyłapać kogoś
na robieniu czegoś; **we got caught in the rain**
złapał nas deszcz infml [3] (be in time for) zdążyć na
(coś) *[bus, plane]* [4] (grasp) chwyc|ić, -tać *[arm, hand,
branch, rope]*; wzbudz|ić, -áć *[interest]* [5] (hear)
dosłysz|eć [6] (trap) **to** ~ **one's fingers in the
door** przytrzasnąć sobie palce drzwiami; **to** ~
one's sleeve on a nail zahaczyć rękawem o
gwóźdź; **to get caught in sth** *[person]* zaplątać się
w coś *[thorns, barbed wire]* [7] (get) złapać infml *[virus,
disease]* [8] **to** ~ **fire** or **light** stanąć w ogniu or
w płomieniach
III *vi* [1] **to** ~ **on sth** *[shirt, sleeve]* zaczepi|ć, -áć
się o coś; *[wheel]* o|trzeć, -cierać się o coś *[frame]*
[2] *[wood, paper]* zaj|ąć, -mować się; *[fire]* rozpal|ić,
-áć się
■ **catch on:** [1] (become popular) zysk|ać, -iwać
popularność [2] (understand) z|rozumieć, poj|ąć,
-mować
■ **catch out:** [1] (take by surprise) zask|oczyć,
-akiwać; (in wrongdoing) przyłap|ać, -ywać [2] (trick)
wy|wieść, -odzić (kogoś) w pole
■ **catch up:** ¶ ~ **up** (in race) nadr|obić, -abiać
stratę (do rywala); (in work) nadr|obić, -abiać
zaległości (**on sth** w czymś); **to** ~ **up on one's
sleep** odsypiać; **to** ~ **up on the latest news**

dowiedzieć się najnowszych wiadomości ¶ ~ **[sb/ sth] up** doglonić, -aniać

catch-22 situation *n* sytuacja *f* bez wyjścia

catching /'kætʃɪŋ/ *adj* zaraźliwy

catchphrase /'kætʃfreɪz/ *n* slogan *m*, powiedzonko *n*

catchy /'kætʃɪ/ *adj [tune]* wpadający w ucho; *[title, slogan]* chwytliwy

categorical /ˌkætə'gɒrɪkl, US -'gɔːr-/ *adj* kategoryczny

categorize /'kætəgəraɪz/ *vt* klasyfikować (**by sth** według czegoś)

category /'kætəgərɪ, US -gɔːrɪ/ *n* kategoria *f*

cater /'keɪtə(r)/ *vi* [1] (provide food) organizować przyjęcia [2] **to ~ for** GB or **to** US **sb** *[organization]* adresować swoją ofertę do kogoś; **to ~ for the needs of sb** *[programme]* zaspokajać potrzeby kogoś

caterer /'keɪtərə(r)/ *n* osoba lub firma zajmująca się organizacją bankietów i przyjęć

catering /'keɪtərɪŋ/ *n* (provision) aprowizacja *f*, catering *m*; (trade, career) gastronomia *f*

caterpillar /'kætəpɪlə(r)/ *n* gąsienica *f*

cathedral /kə'θiːdrəl/ *n* katedra *f*

Catholic /'kæθəlɪk/ **I** *n* katoli|k *m*, -czka *f* **II** katolicki

Catholicism /kə'θɒlɪsɪzəm/ *n* katolicyzm *m*

catnap /'kætnæp/ *vi* zdrzemnąć się, drzemać

Catseye[R] /'kætsaɪ/ *n* GB Aut kocie oko *n*, sygnalizator *m* odblaskowy

cattle /'kætl/ *n* bydło *n*

catwalk /'kætwɔːk/ *n* (at fashion show) wybieg *m*; ~ **show** pokaz mody

cauliflower /'kɒlɪflaʊə(r), US 'kɔːlɪ-/ *n* kalafior *m*

cause /kɔːz/ **I** *n* powód *m*, przyczyna *f* (**of sth** czegoś); **there is** ~ **for concern** jest powód do niepokoju; **to have** ~ **to do sth** mieć powód do zrobienia czegoś; **with good** ~ nie bez racji **II** *vt* s|powodować *[damage, grief, problem]*; wywoł|ać, -ywać *[chaos, controversy, confusion]*; **to ~ problems** *[issue]* stwarzać problemy; *[child]* sprawiać kłopoty

caustic /'kɔːstɪk/ *adj* żrący; fig zjadliwy

caution /'kɔːʃn/ **I** *n* [1] (care) ostrożność *f*, rozwaga *f* [2] (wariness) rezerwa *f* [3] (warning) ostrzeżenie *n* **II** *vt* [1] (warn) ostrze|c, -gać [2] Sport udziel|ić, -ać upomnienia (komuś) *[player]*

[IDIOMS] **to throw** or **cast** ~ **to the wind(s)** zapomnieć o rozsądku

cautionary /'kɔːʃənərɪ/ *adj [look, gesture]* ostrzegawczy; **a** ~ **tale** powiastka umoralniająca

cautious /'kɔːʃəs/ *adj* [1] (careful) ostrożny [2] (wary) *[person]* rozważny; *[optimism]* umiarkowany; *[response]* wyważony

cave /keɪv/ *n* jaskinia *f*

■ **cave in**: [1] *[roof, tunnel]* zawal|ić, -ać się [2] *[person]* ugi|ąć, -nać się, ust|ąpić, -ępować

caveman /'keɪvmæn/ *n* człowiek *m* jaskiniowy

caviar(e) /'kævɪɑː(r), ˌkævɪ'ɑː(r)/ *n* kawior *m*

caving /'keɪvɪŋ/ *n* alpinizm *m* podziemny or jaskiniowy; **to go** ~ uprawiać alpinizm jaskiniowy

cavity /'kævətɪ/ *n* [1] (hollow) otwór *m* [2] (in tooth) ubytek *m* tkanki zęba [3] Med jama *f*

cavort /kə'vɔːt/ *vi* brykać, hasać

caw /kɔː/ *vi* za|krakać

cc *n* = **cubic centimeter** centymetr *m* sześcienny

CCTV *n* = **closed-circuit television** telewizja *f* przemysłowa

CD *n* = **compact disc** płyta *f* kompaktowa

CD player, CD system *n* odtwarzacz *m* płyt kompaktowych

CD-ROM /ˌsiːdiː'rɒm/ *n* = **compact disc read-only memory** pamięć *f* tylko do odczytu na płycie kompaktowej, CD-ROM *m*

cease /siːs/ **I** *vt* przer|wać, -ywać **II** *vi* usta|ć, -wać

cease-fire /'siːsfaɪə(r)/ *n* zawieszenie *n* broni

cedar /'siːdə(r)/ *n* cedr *m*

cede /siːd/ *vt* s|cedować (**to sb** na kogoś)

ceiling /'siːlɪŋ/ *n* sufit *m*

celebrate /'selɪbreɪt/ **I** *vt* u|czcić; (more formally) celebrować **II** *vi* świętować

celebrated /'selɪbreɪtɪd/ *adj* sławny

celebration /ˌselɪ'breɪʃn/ *n* [1] (action of celebrating) świętowanie *n* [2] (event) uroczystość *f*, obchody *plt*

celebrity /sɪ'lebrətɪ/ **I** *n* (person) sława *f*, znakomitość *f* **II** *adj [guest]* honorowy; *[panel]* z udziałem samych znakomitości

celery /'selərɪ/ *n* seler *m* naciowy

celibate /'selɪbət/ *adj [life]* w celibacie

cell /sel/ *n* komórka *f*; (of prisoner, monk) cela *f*

cellar /'selə(r)/ *n* piwnica *f*

cello /'tʃeləʊ/ *n* wiolonczela *f*

cellphone /'selfəʊn/ *n* (also **cellular phone**) telefon *m* komórkowy

cellulite /'seljʊlaɪt/ *n* cellulit *m*

Celsius /'selsɪəs/ *adj* **the** ~ **scale** skala *f* Celsjusza

Celt /kelt, US selt/ *n* Celt *m*

Celtic /'keltɪk, US 'seltɪk/ *adj* celtycki

cement /sɪ'ment/ *n* cement *m*

cement mixer *n* betoniarka *f*

cemetery /'semətrɪ, US -terɪ/ *n* cmentarz *m*

censor /'sensə(r)/ **I** *n* cenzor *m* **II** *vt* o|cenzurować *[book, film]*

censorship /'sensəʃɪp/ *n* cenzura *f*

censure /'senʃə(r)/ **I** *n* potępienie *n* **II** *vt* ostro s|krytykować, potępi|ć, -ać

census /'sensəs/ *n* spis *m* ludności

cent /sent/ *n* cent *m*

centenary /sen'tiːnərɪ/ *n* (century) stulecie *n*; (anniversary) setna rocznica *f*

center US = **centre**

centigrade /'sentɪgreɪd/ *adj* **in degrees** ~ w skali Celsjusza

centimetre GB, **centimeter** US /'sentɪmiːtə(r)/ *n* centymetr *m*

central /'sentrəl/ *adj* [1] (in the middle) centralny [2] (in the town centre) znajdujący się w centrum miasta; **in** ~ **London** w centrum Londynu [3] (key) *[argument]* główny, kluczowy

Central America *prn* Ameryka *f* Środkowa

central heating *n* centralne ogrzewanie *n*

centralize /'sentrəlaɪz/ *vt* s|centralizować

central locking *n* Aut centralny zamek *m*

central reservation *n* GB Aut pas *m* rozdzielczy

centre GB, **center** US /'sentə(r)/ ▮ *n* centrum *n*, środek *m*; **in the** ~ w centrum; **town** ~, **city** ~ centrum miasta; **to be the** ~ **of attention** być w centrum uwagi; **business/shopping** ~ centrum biznesu/handlowe

▮▮ *vt, vi* Sport dośrodkow|ać, -ywać

■ **centre around, centre on:** *[activities, industry]* s|koncentrować się wokół (czegoś); *[person, thoughts]* skupi|ć, -ać się na (czymś)

centre-forward /ˌsentə'fɔːwəd/ *n* Sport środkowy napastnik *m*

centre ground *n* centrum *n*; **to occupy the** ~ zajmować pozycje centrową

centre-half /ˌsentə'hɑːf, US -'hæf/ *n* Sport środkowy pomocnik *m*

centre-piece GB, **center-piece** US /'sentəpiːs/ *n* (of table) dekoracja *f* pośrodku stołu; (of exhibition) największa atrakcja *f*

centre-stage /ˌsentə'steɪdʒ/ *n* **to take/occupy** ~ znaleźć się/znajdować się w centrum uwagi

century /'sentʃərɪ/ *n* wiek *m*, stulecie *n*; **in the 20th** ~ w XX wieku; **at the turn of the** ~ na przełomie wieków

ceramic /sɪ'ræmɪk/ *adj* ceramiczny

ceramics /sɪ'ræmɪks/ *n* ceramika *f*

cereal /'sɪərɪəl/ *n* zboże *n*; **breakfast** ~ płatki śniadaniowe

cerebral palsy /ˌserɪbrəl'pɔːlzɪ, US sə'riːbrəl/ *n* Med porażenie *n* mózgowe

ceremony /'serɪmənɪ, US -məʊnɪ/ *n* [1] uroczystość *f* [2] **to stand on** ~ certować się, robić ceremonie

cert /sɜːt/ *n* infml **it's a (dead)** ~ to murowane infml

certain /'sɜːtn/ *adj* [1] (sure) pewny (**about** or **of sth** czegoś); **I'm** ~ **of it** jestem tego pewien; **I'm** ~ **that I checked** jestem pewny, że sprawdzałem [2] (specific) *[amount, number]* pewien; ~ **people** pewne osoby; **to a** ~ **extent** do pewnego stopnia

certainly /'sɜːtnlɪ/ *adv* na pewno, z pewnością

certainty /'sɜːtntɪ/ *n* pewność *f*; (sure thing) rzecz *f* pewna

certificate /sə'tɪfɪkət/ *n* świadectwo *n*, zaświadczenie *n*; (of birth, death, marriage) akt *m*, metryka *f*; **18-** ~ **film** film dozwolony od lat 18

certified *adj* /'sɜːtɪfaɪd/ *[nurse]* dyplomowany; US (teacher) wykwalifikowany

certified mail US przesyłka *f* polecona

certified public accountant *n* US biegły księgowy *m*, biegła księgowa *f*

certify /'sɜːtɪfaɪ/ *vt* [1] (confirm) stwierdz|ić, -ać *[death]* [2] (authenticate) uwierzytelni|ć, -ać *[document]*; poświadcz|yć, -ać *[fact]*

cervical cancer /ˌsɜːvɪkl 'kænsə(r)/ *n* rak *m* szyjki macicy

cervical smear /ˌsɜːvɪkl 'smɪə(r)/ *n* wymaz *m* z szyjki macicy

CFC *n* = **chlorofluorocarbon** freon *m*

chafe /tʃeɪf/ *vi* (rub) ocierać się (**on** or **against sth** o coś)

chain /tʃeɪn/ ▮ *n* [1] (metal links) łańcuch *m*; (fine) łańcuszek *m* [2] (on lavatory) łańcuszek *m* (od rezerwuaru) [3] (on door) łańcuch *m* [4] (of shops, hotels) sieć *f* [5] (of events) seria *f*; (of ideas) ciąg *m*

▮▮ *vt* sku|ć, -wać łańcuchem, zaku|ć, -wać w łańcuchy *[person]*; **to** ~ **a bicycle to sth** przymocować rower łańcuchem do czegoś

chain reaction *n* reakcja *f* łańcuchowa

chain saw *n* piła *f* łańcuchowa

chain-smoke /'tʃeɪnsməʊk/ *vi* palić jak komin

chain-smoker /'tʃeɪnˌsməʊkə(r)/ *n* nałogowy palacz *m*, nałogowa palaczka *f*

chain store *n* (single shop) sklep *m* należący do sieci handlowej; (retail group) sieć *f* domów towarowych

chair /tʃeə(r)/ ▮ *n* [1] (seat) krzesło *n*; (also **arm** ~) fotel *m* [2] (chairperson) przewodnicząc|y *m*, -a *f* [3] Univ katedra *f*; **to hold the** ~ **of physics** kierować katedrą fizyki

▮▮ *vt* przewodniczyć (czemuś), po|prowadzić *[meeting]*

chair lift *n* wyciąg *m* krzesełkowy

chairman /'tʃeəmən/ *n* przewodnicząc|y *m*, -a *f*; **Mr Chairman...** Panie Przewodniczący...; **Madam Chairman...** Pani Przewodnicząca...

chairperson /'tʃeəpɜːsn/ *n* (of meeting) przewodnicząc|y *m*, -a *f*; (of company) prezes *m*

chalet /'ʃæleɪ/ *n* (holiday cabin) domek *m* letniskowy; (mountain) dom *m* w stylu alpejskim; (shelter) szałas *m* pasterski

chalk /tʃɔːk/ *n* kreda *f*

challenge /'tʃælɪndʒ/ ▮ *n* wyzwanie *n*; **to take up a** ~ odpowiedzieć na wyzwanie; **to rise to the** ~ stanąć na wysokości zadania

▮▮ *vt* [1] (dare) rzuc|ić, -ać wyzwanie (komuś); **to** ~ **sb to a duel** wyzwać kogoś na pojedynek [2] (question) za|kwestionować *[statement, authority]*

challenger /'tʃælɪndʒə(r)/ *n* rywal *m*, -ka *f*; **the** ~ **for the title** kandydat do tytułu

challenging /'tʃælɪndʒɪŋ/ *adj* [1] *[task]* ambitny [2] *[look]* wyzywający

chamber /'tʃeɪmbə(r)/ **I** *n* [1] (room) sala *f*; (in castle) komnata *f* [2] Pol izba *f*; **the upper/lower ~** izba wyższa/niższa

II chambers *npl* (barrister's office) kancelaria *f* adwokacka; (judge's office) gabinet *m* sędziego

chambermaid /'tʃeɪmbəmeɪd/ *n* pokojówka *f*

chamber music *n* muzyka *f* kameralna

Chamber of Commerce *n* izba *f* handlowa

chameleon /kə'miːlɪən/ *n* kameleon *m*

champagne /ʃæm'peɪn/ *n* szampan *m*

champion /'tʃæmpɪən/ *n* mistrz *m*, -yni *f*, czempion *m*, -ka *f*

championship /'tʃæmpɪənʃɪp/ *n* (competition) mistrzostwa *plt*; (title) mistrzostwo *n*, tytuł *m* mistrzowski

chance /tʃɑːns, US tʃæns/ **I** *n* [1] (opportunity) okazja *f*; **to have** or **get a ~ to do sth** mieć okazję coś zrobić; **you've missed your ~** przegapiłeś or straciłeś okazję or szansę [2] (likelihood) prawdopodobieństwo *n*; **there is little ~ of her getting a job** jest mało prawdopodobne, żeby znalazła pracę; **she has a good ~** ona ma duże szanse [3] (luck) przypadek *m*; **by ~** przypadkiem [4] (risk) ryzyko *n*; **to take a ~** zaryzykować [5] (possibility) szansa *f*; **not to stand a ~** nie mieć żadnej szansy; **by any ~** przypadkiem

II *vt* **to ~ doing sth** za|ryzykować zrobienie czegoś; **we have to ~ it** musimy zaryzykować

(IDIOMS:) **no ~!** infml (I won't do it) nie ma mowy!; (it can't be done) nie da rady!

chancellor /'tʃɑːnsələ(r), US 'tʃæns-/ *n* [1] kanclerz *m* [2] Univ rektor *m* tytularny

Chancellor of the Exchequer *n* GB ≈ minister *m* skarbu or finansów

chandelier /ˌʃændə'lɪə(r)/ *n* żyrandol *m*

change /tʃeɪndʒ/ **I** *n* [1] (process) zmiany *f pl*; (instance) zmiana *f*; **a ~ in the schedule** zmiana w rozkładzie/programie; **a ~ of plan** zmiana planu; **a ~ for the better** zmiana na lepsze; **a ~ of clothes** ubranie na zmianę; **that makes a nice ~** to miła odmiana; **she needs a ~** jej potrzebna jest jakaś odmiana; **I need a ~ of air** fig potrzebuję zmiany otoczenia; **for a ~** dla odmiany [2] (coins) bilon *m*; (money returned) reszta *f*; **small ~** drobne; **she gave me 6p ~** wydała mi sześć pensów reszty; **have you got ~ for £10?** możesz mi rozmienić 10 funtów?

II *vt* [1] (alter) zmieni|ć, -ać; **to ~ sth into sth** zmienić coś w coś; **to ~ one's mind** zmienić zdanie; **to ~ one's mind about doing sth** zmienić zdanie w sprawie zrobienia czegoś; **to ~ colour** (turn pale) zblednąć; (turn red) zaczerwienić się [2] (exchange for sth different) zmieni|ć, -ać *[name, car]*; (in shop) wymieni|ć, -ać *[item]* (**for sth** na coś); **to ~ places** zamienić się miejscami (**with sb** z kimś); fig zamienić się rolami [3] (replace) wymie-

nil|ć, -ać *[battery, tyre]*; **to ~ a bed** zmienić pościel [4] (exchange with sb) zamieni|ć, -ać się (czymś) *[seats, clothes]* [5] (convert) wymieni|ć, -ać *[dollars, francs]* (**into** or **for sth** na coś)

III *vi* [1] (alter) zmieni|ć, -ać się; *[wind]* zmieni|ć, -ać kierunek; **the lights ~d from red to green** światło zmieniło się z czerwonego na zielone [2] (into different clothes) przeb|rać, -ierać się; **I'm going to ~ into my jeans** przebiorę się w dżinsy; **to ~ out of sth** zdjąć coś z siebie [3] (from bus, train) przesi|ąść, -adać się

IV changed *pp adj* *[man, woman]* odmieniony

■ change round GB: przestawi|ć, -ać *[objects]*; przeprowadz|ić, -ać rotację *[workers]*

changeable /'tʃeɪndʒəbl/ *adj* *[condition, weather]* zmienny; *[price]* ruchomy

changeover /'tʃeɪndʒəʊvə(r)/ *n* zmiana *f* (**to sth** na coś)

changing /'tʃeɪndʒɪŋ/ *adj* *[attitude, colours, environment, world]* zmieniający się

changing room *n* Sport szatnia *f*; US (fitting room) przymieralnia *f*

channel /'tʃænl/ **I** *n* [1] (passage for liquid) kanał *m*; (small) kanalik *m* [2] (on TV) kanał *m*, program *m* [3] (on radio) pasmo *n*, kanał *m* [4] (groove) rowek *m* [5] **to do sth through the proper ~s** załatwić coś właściwymi or zwykłymi kanałami; **to go through official ~s** pójść drogą oficjalną or urzędową

II *vt* (carry) (to, into) doprowadz|ić, -ać do (czegoś); (from) odprowadz|ić, -ać z (czegoś)

Channel /'tʃænl/ *prn* **the (English) ~** kanał *m* la Manche

channel ferry *n* prom *m* kursujący przez kanał la Manche

channel-hop /'tʃænlhɒp/ *vi* infml skakać po kanałach infml

Channel Islands *prn* **the ~** Wyspy *f pl* Normandzkie

Channel Tunnel *prn* **the ~** tunel *m* pod kanałem la Manche

chant /tʃɑːnt, US tʃænt/ **I** *n* (of crowd) monotonny śpiew *m*; (of devotees) śpiew *m* kościelny

II *vi* *[crowd]* skandować; *[choir, monks]* monotonnie śpiewać

chaos /'keɪɒs/ *n* chaos *m*; **in a state of ~** *[country, economy]* w stanie chaosu

chaotic /keɪ'ɒtɪk/ *adj* *[person]* chaotyczny; *[jumble]* bezładny

chap /tʃæp/ **I** *n* GB infml facet *m* infml

II *vt* s|powodować spierzchnięcie or spękanie (czegoś); **~ped lips** spękane or spierzchnięte wargi

chapel /'tʃæpl/ *n* kaplica *f*

chaperone /'ʃæpərəʊn/ **I** *n* przyzwoitka *f*

II *vt* służyć (komuś) za przyzwoitkę

chaplain /'tʃæplɪn/ *n* kapelan *m*

chapter /'tʃæptə(r)/ n rozdział m; **in** ~ **3** w rozdziale trzecim

character /'kærəktə(r)/ n ① (nature) charakter m ② (in book, play, film) postać f (**from sth** z czegoś) ③ **a real** ~, **quite a** ~ niezły artysta, niezła artystka infml; **a local** ~ znana postać (w okolicy)

characteristic /ˌkærəktə'rɪstɪk/ **I** n cecha f (charakterystyczna)

II adj charakterystyczny, znamienny (**of sb/sth** dla kogoś/czegoś)

characterize /'kærəktəraɪz/ vt ① (depict) s|charakteryzować (**as sb** jako kogoś) ② (typify) cechować; **to be** ~**d by sth** charakteryzować się czymś

character reference n referencje plt

charade /ʃə'rɑːd, US ʃə'reɪd/ n ① (game) szarada f mimiczna (gra towarzyska polegająca na odgrywaniu żywych obrazów) ② (pretence) farsa f, komedia f fig

charcoal /'tʃɑːkəʊl/ **I** n ① (fuel) węgiel m drzewny ② (for drawing) węgiel m

II adj (also ~ **grey**) ciemnografitowy

charge /tʃɑːdʒ/ **I** n ① (fee) opłata f; **additional** or **extra** ~ dodatkowa opłata; **to reverse the** ~**s** dzwonić na koszt rozmówcy ② (accusation) oskarżenie n (**of sth** o coś); zarzut m (**of sth** czegoś); **murder** ~ oskarżenie o morderstwo; **to press** ~**s against sb** wnieść oskarżenie przeciwko komuś ③ (attack) atak m (**against sb/sth** na kogoś/coś) ④ (control) **to be in** ~ zarządzać (**of sth** czymś); **the person in** ~ **of sth** osoba odpowiedzialna za coś; **to take** ~ wziąć sprawę w swoje ręce ⑤ (person in one's care) podopieczn|y m, -a f ⑥ (explosive, electrical) ładunek m

II vt ① (ask) po|liczyć (komuś) [customer]; pob|rać, -ierać [commission]; nalicz|yć, -ać [interest] (**on sth** od czegoś); **to** ~ **sb for sth** policzyć komuś za coś; **how much do you** ~? ile to będzie (u pana) kosztować?; **I** ~ **£20 an hour** biorę 20 funtów za godzinę ② **to** ~ **sth to sb** or **sb's account** obciąż|yć, -ać za coś rachunek kogoś ③ [police] zarzuc|ić, -ać (komuś) [suspect] (**with sth/doing sth** coś/zrobienie czegoś) ④ (rush at) [troops] na|trzeć, -cierać na (kogoś/coś); [bull] za|atakować, rzuc|ić, -cać się na (kogoś) [person] ⑤ na|ładować [battery]

III vi **to** ~ **into a room** wpaść do pokoju; **to** ~ **out of a room** wypaść z pokoju

charge account n US kredyt m, rachunek m (w sklepie lub sieci handlowej)

charge card n karta f rozliczeniowa

char-grilled /'tʃɑːgrɪld/ adj pieczony na węglu drzewnym

charisma /kə'rɪzmə/ n charyzma f

charismatic /ˌkærɪz'mætɪk/ n adj charyzmatyczny

charitable /'tʃærɪtəbl/ adj [person] (generous) hojny; (understanding) życzliwy (**to** or **towards sb**

dla or wobec kogoś); [act] miłosierny; [organization] charytatywny

charity /'tʃærəti/ n ① (virtue) miłosierdzie n ② (aid, aid organizations) dobroczynność f ③ (individual organization) organizacja f charytatywna

charity shop n sklep m z rzeczami używanymi (którego dochód przeznaczany jest na cele charytatywne)

charity work n praca f charytatywna

charm /tʃɑːm/ n ① (attractiveness) czar m, wdzięk m ② **lucky** ~ talizman or amulet na szczęście

charming /'tʃɑːmɪŋ/ adj [person, place] czarujący

chart /tʃɑːt/ **I** n ① (graph) wykres m ② (table) tabela f, tablica f ③ (map) mapa f ④ Mus **the** ~**s** lista f przebojów

II vt ① (trace) wytycz|yć, -ać [route] ② z|obrazować or przedstawi|ć, -ać na wykresie [progress]

charter /'tʃɑːtə(r)/ **I** n ① Pol karta f; (for company) statut m ② (of coach, train) wynajem m

II vt wy|czarterować [plane]

chartered accountant, AC n GB biegły księgowy m, biegła księgowa f

charter flight n GB rejs m czarterowy, czarter m

chase /tʃeɪs/ **I** n pościg m, pogoń f (**after sb/sth** za kimś/czymś)

II vt ① gonić, ścigać [person, animal]; zabiegać o (coś) [contract]; gonić za (czymś) [success] ② (also ~ **after**) uganiać się za (kimś) infml [man, girl]

■ **chase away, chase off:** odpędz|ić, -ać, odg|onić, -aniać [animal, person]

chassis /'ʃæsi/ n podwozie n

chastity /'tʃæstəti/ n czystość f

chat /tʃæt/ **I** n pogawędka f; **to have a** ~ **with sb about sb/sth** uciąć sobie z kimś pogawędkę o kimś/czymś

II vi pogadać infml (**with** or **to sb** z kimś)

■ **chat up:** podrywać GB infml [girl]

chatline /'tʃætlaɪn/ n wewnętrzna sieć f telefoniczna; (for sexual encounters) sekstelefon m GB infml

chatroom /'tʃætruːm/ n kanał m dyskusyjny; czatroom m infml

chat show n GB talk show m inv

chatter /'tʃætə(r)/ **I** n (of person) trajkot m infml; (of birds) ćwierk m, świergot m

II vi [person] trajkotać infml; [birds] ćwierkać, świergotać; **her teeth were** ~**ing** dzwoniła zębami

chatterbox /'tʃætəbɒks/ n gaduła m/f pot.; (girl, woman) trajkotka f infml

chatty /'tʃæti/ adj [person] gadatliwy; [style] gawędziarski

chauffeur /'ʃəʊfə(r), US ʃəʊ'fɜːr/ **I** n szofer m, kierowca m; **a** ~**-driven car** samochód z kierowcą

II vt być szoferem or kierowcą (kogoś)

chauvinist /'ʃəʊvɪnɪst/ **I** n szowinist|a m, -ka f

II adj szowinistyczny

cheap /tʃi:p/ *adj* ⒈ (inexpensive) *[article]* tani; *[price]* niski ⒉ (shoddy) tani ⒊ *[jibe]* tani; *[remark]* niewybredny; *[trick]* podły; *[compliment]* płaski

cheapen /'tʃi:pən/ *vt* obniż|yć, -ać koszty (czegoś)

cheaply /'tʃi:plɪ/ *adv*; **to eat** ~ jadać oszczędnie

cheap rate *n* niższa taryfa *f*

cheat /tʃi:t/ ⒈ *n* krętacz *m*, -ka *f*, oszust *m*, -ka *f* ⒉ *vt* oszuk|ać, -iwać; **to feel** ~ed czuć się oszukanym; **to** ~ **sb (out) of sth** oszustwem pozbawić kogoś czegoś ⒊ *vi* oszuk|ać, -iwać; **to** ~ **at cards** oszukiwać w kartach; **to** ~ **in an exam** ściągać na egzaminie; **to** ~ **on one's husband** zdradzać męża

Chechnya /ˌtʃetʃˈnjɑ:/ *prn* Czeczenia *f*

check /tʃek/ ⒈ *n* ⒈ (inspection) kontrola *f* (**on sb/ sth** kogoś/czegoś) ⒉ Med badanie *n* kontrolne ⒊ (restraint) ograniczenie *n* (**on sth** czegoś) ⒋ (in chess) szach *m*; **in** ~ zaszachowany ⒌ (fabric) materiał *m* w kratę; (pattern) krata *f*, kratka *f* ⒍ US (cheque) czek *m* ⒎ US (bill) rachunek *m* ⒏ US (receipt) kwit *m* ⒐ US (tick) znak *m* w kształcie litery V; ptaszek *m* infml ⒉ *adj* *[fabric, garment]* w kratę/kratkę ⒊ *vt* ⒈ (for security) sprawdz|ić, -ać, s|kontrolować *[ticket, area, mechanism]*; (for health) z|mierzyć *[temperature]*; (inspect) sprawdz|ić, -ać *[watch, map, pocket]* ⒉ (curb) powstrzym|ać, -ywać *[price rises, inflation]*; za|hamować *[growth]*; powściąg|nąć, -ać *[emotions]* ⒋ *vi* ⒈ (verify) sprawdz|ić, -ać; **to** ~ **with sb** zapytać kogoś; **to** ~ **for sth** sprawdzać pod kątem (obecności) czegoś *[problems]*; szukać czegoś *[leaks, flaws]* ⒉ (register) **to** ~ **into a hotel** zameldować się w hotelu

■ **check in**: ¶ ~ **in** (at airport) zgł|osić, -aszać się do odprawy; (at hotel) za|meldować się ¶ ~ **[sb/ sth] in** odprawi|ć, -ać *[passenger, baggage]*

■ **check off**: zaznacz|yć, -ać *[items]*

■ **check out**: ¶ ~ **out** (leave) **to** ~ **out of a hotel** wymeldować się z hotelu ¶ ~ **[sth] out** sprawdz|ić, -ać *[information, package, building]*; zasięg|nąć, -ać informacji na temat (czegoś) *[club, scheme]*

■ **check up on**: sprawdz|ić, -ać *[person, story, details]*

checkbook *n* US = **chequebook**

checkered *adj* US = **chequered**

check-in /'tʃekɪn/ *n* ⒈ (also ~ **desk**) stanowisko *n* odprawy ⒉ (procedure) odprawa *f*

checking account *n* US rachunek *m* bieżący

checklist /'tʃeklɪst/ *n* lista *f* kontrolna

checkmate /'tʃekmeɪt/ *n* szach-mat *m*

checkout /'tʃekaʊt/ *n* kasa *f*

checkout assistant *n* kasjer *m*, -ka *f*

checkpoint /'tʃekpɔɪnt/ *n* punkt *m* kontrolny

checkroom /'tʃekru:m, -rʊm/ *n* US (cloakroom) szatnia *f*; (for baggage) przechowalnia *f* bagażu

checkup /'tʃekʌp/ *n* ⒈ (at doctor's) badania *n pl* kontrolne; **to have a** ~ zrobić sobie badania kontrolne ⒉ (at dentist's) przegląd *m* kontrolny

cheek /tʃi:k/ *n* ⒈ (of face) policzek *m*; **to dance** ~ **to** ~ tańczyć, tuląc się do siebie ⒉ (impudence) tupet *m*, bezczelność *f*; **what a** ~! co za tupet!

cheekbone /'tʃi:kbəʊn/ *n* kość *f* policzkowa

cheeky /'tʃi:kɪ/ *adj* *[person]* bezczelny; *[question]* impertynencki; *[grin]* zuchwały

cheer /tʃɪə(r)/ ⒈ *n* (radosny) okrzyk *m*; **to get a big** ~ dostać owację ⒉ **cheers** *excl* ⒈ (toast) (na) zdrowie! ⒉ GB infml (goodbye) cześć! infml ⒊ GB infml (thanks) dzięki! ⒊ *vt*, *vi* wiwatować; **to** ~ **sb** wiwatować na cześć kogoś

■ **cheer up**: ¶ ~ **up** poweseleć; ~ **up!** rozchmurz się! ¶ ~ **[sb] up** poprawi|ć, -ać nastrój (komuś) ¶ ~ **[sth] up** ożyw|ić, -ać *[room]*

cheerful /'tʃɪəfl/ *adj* *[person, mood, music]* pogodny; *[colour]* wesoły

cheerleader /'tʃɪəli:də(r)/ *n* cheerleaderka *f*

cheese /tʃi:z/ *n* ser *m*; ~ **sandwich** kanapka z serem

cheeseboard /'tʃi:zbɔ:d/ *n* (object) deska *f* do krojenia i podawania serów; (selection) sery *m pl*

cheetah /'tʃi:tə/ *n* gepard *m*

chef /ʃef/ *n* (professional) mistrz *m* kucharski; (head cook) szef *m* kuchni

chemical /'kemɪkl/ ⒈ *n* substancja *f* chemiczna ⒉ *adj* chemiczny

chemist /'kemɪst/ *n* ⒈ GB (drug dispenser) apteka|rz *m*, -rka *f*; **the** ~'**s (shop)** apteka *f* ⒉ (scientist) chemik *m*

chemistry /'kemɪstrɪ/ *n* chemia *f*

chemotherapy /ˌki:məʊˈθerəpɪ/ *n* chemioterapia *f*

cheque GB, **check** US /tʃek/ *n* czek *m*; **to write** or **make out a** ~ **for £20** wypisać czek na 20 funtów

chequebook GB, **checkbook** US /'tʃekbʊk/ *n* książeczka *f* czekowa

cheque card *n* GB karta *f* czekowa

chequered GB, **checkered** US /'tʃekəd/ *adj* ⒈ *[pattern]* w kratę ⒉ *[history, past]* burzliwy

chequers GB, **checkers** US /'tʃekəz/ *n* warcaby *pl*

cherish /'tʃerɪʃ/ *vt* żywić *[hope]*; czcić *[memory]*; u|miłować *[person]*

cherry /'tʃerɪ/ ⒈ *n* ⒈ (fruit) (sweet) czereśnia *f*; (sour) wiśnia *f* ⒉ (tree, wood) czereśnia *f*; wiśnia *f* ⒉ *adj* (also ~-**red**) wiśniowy

chess /tʃes/ *n* szachy *plt*; **a game of** ~ partia szachów

chessboard /'tʃesbɔ:d/ *n* szachownica *f*

chess set *n* szachy *plt*

chest /tʃest/ *n* [1] (of person) klatka *f* piersiowa [2] (furniture) kufer *m*; ~ **of drawers** komoda [3] (container) skrzynia *f*, paka *f* (IDIOMS:) **to get sth off one's** ~ infml zrzucić coś z serca

chestnut /'tʃesnʌt/ **[]** *n* [1] (also ~ **tree**) kasztan *m* jadalny [2] (nut) kasztan *m* [3] (horse) (male) kasztan *m*; (female) kasztanka *f*

[] *adj [hair]* kasztanowy; *[horse]* kasztanowaty

chew /tʃuː/ *vt* żuć *[food, gum]*; gryźć *[pencil]*; *[animal]* obgry|źć, -zać *[bone]*

chewing gum *n* guma *f* do żucia

chewy /'tʃuːɪ/ *adj* trudny do pogryzienia

chick /tʃɪk/ *n* (young bird) pisklę *n*; (young chicken) kurczątko *n*

chicken /'tʃɪkɪn/ *n* [1] kurczak *m*; (female) kura *f* [2] (also ~ **meat**) kurczak *m* [3] infml (coward) cykor *m* infml

■ **chicken out** infml: s|tchórzyć

chicken pox *n* ospa *f* wietrzna

chicken wire *n* gęsta siatka *f* ogrodzeniowa

chickpea /'tʃɪkpiː/ *n* ciecierzyca *f* pospolita

chicory /'tʃɪkərɪ/ *n* [1] (vegetable) cykoria *f* sałatkowa [2] (in coffee) cykoria *f*

chief /tʃiːf/ **[]** *n* [1] (of tribe) wódz *m* [2] infml (boss) szef *m*

[] *adj* [1] *[reason]* główny [2] *[editor]* naczelny

chief executive *n* dyrektor *m* naczelny

chiefly /'tʃiːflɪ/ *adv* głównie

chief of police *n* komendant *m* or szef *m* policji

Chief of Staff *n* Mil szef *m* sztabu

chiffon /'ʃɪfɒn, US ʃɪ'fɒn/ *n* szyfon *m*

chilblain /'tʃɪlbleɪn/ *n* odmrożenie *n*

child /tʃaɪld/ *n* dziecko *n*; **I've known her since I was a** ~ znam ją od dziecka; **three children** troje dzieci

child abuse *n* maltretowanie *n* nieletnich; (sexual) wykorzystywanie *n* seksualne nieletnich

childbirth /'tʃaɪldbɜːθ/ *n* poród *m*

childcare /'tʃaɪldkeə(r)/ *n* (nurseries, crèches) opieka *f* przedszkolna; (bringing up children) wychowywanie *n* dziecka

childcare facilities *npl* żłobki *m pl* i przedszkola *n pl*

childhood /'tʃaɪldhʊd/ **[]** *n* dzieciństwo *n*; **in (one's) early** ~ we wczesnym dzieciństwie

[] *adj [memory]* dziecięcy; *[friend]* z dzieciństwa; *[illness]* wieku dziecięcego

childish /'tʃaɪldɪʃ/ *adj* dziecinny

childless /'tʃaɪldlɪs/ *adj* bezdzietny

childlike /'tʃaɪldlaɪk/ *adj* dziecinny

childminder /'tʃaɪldmaɪndə(r)/ *n* GB opiekun *m*, -ka *f* do dziecka

children's home /'tʃɪldrəns'həʊm/ *n* dom *m* dziecka

Chile /'tʃɪlɪ/ *prn* Chile *n inv*

chill /tʃɪl/ **[]** *n* [1] (coldness) chłód *m*; **there's a** ~ **in the air** w powietrzu czuć chłód; **to send a** ~ **down sb's spine** przyprawić kogoś o dreszcze [2] (illness) przeziębienie *n*

[] *adj* [1] *[wind]* zimny, przejmujący [2] *[reminder, words]* groźny

[] *vt* [1] (cool) o|studzić *[soup]*; oziębi|ć, -ać *[dessert]*; schł|odzić, -adzać *[wine]* [2] *[wind]* wyziębi|ć, -ać; **to be** ~ **ed to the bone** przemarznąć do szpiku kości; **to** ~ **sb's** or **the blood** zmrozić komuś krew w żyłach

[] *vi [dessert, wine]* schł|odzić, -adzać się

■ **chill out** infml: z|relaksować się; ~ **out!** wyluzuj się! infml

chilli, chili /'tʃɪlɪ/ *n* [1] (pod) czerwony pieprz *m*; (powder) chili *n inv* [2] (also ~ **con carne**) chili con carne *n*

chilly /'tʃɪlɪ/ *adj* chłodny; **it's** ~ **today** dzisiaj jest chłodno

chime /tʃaɪm/ *n* kurant *m*

chimney /'tʃɪmnɪ/ *n* komin *m*

chimpanzee /,tʃɪmpən'ziː, ,tʃɪmpæn'ziː/ *n* szympans *m*

chin /tʃɪn/ *n* broda *f*, podbródek *m*

china /'tʃaɪnə/ **[]** *n* porcelana *f*

[] *adj [cup, plate]* porcelanowy

China /'tʃaɪnə/ *prn* Chiny *plt*

Chinese /tʃaɪ'niːz/ **[]** *n* [1] (person) Chi|ńczyk *m*, -nka *f* [2] (język *m*) chiński *m*

[] *adj* chiński

chink /tʃɪŋk/ *n* [1] (in wall) szczelina *f*; (in curtain) szpara *f* [2] (sound) brzęk *m*

chip /tʃɪp/ **[]** *n* [1] (fragment) (of glass) odłamek *m*; (of wood) drzazga *f* [2] (in china, glass) szczerba *f* [3] Comput chip *m*, układ *m* scalony

[] **chips** *npl* [1] GB (fried potatoes) frytki *f pl* [2] US (crisps) chipsy *m pl*

[] *vt* wyszczerbi|ć, -ać *[glass, plate]*; odłup|ać, -ywać *[paint]*; **to** ~ **a tooth** wyszczerbić sobie ząb

■ **chip in** GB infml: dorzuc|ić, -ać się infml

(IDIOMS:) **to have a** ~ **on one's shoulder** być przewrażliwionym (**about sth** na punkcie czegoś)

chipboard /'tʃɪpbɔːd/ *n* płyta *f* wiórowa

chip shop *n* frytkarnia *f*

chiropodist /kɪ'rɒpədɪst/ *n* pedikiurzyst|a *m*, -ka *f*

chiropractor /'kaɪərəʊpræktə(r)/ *n* kręgarz *m*, chiropraktyk *m*

chirp /tʃɜːp/ *vi [birds]* za|ćwierkać, za|świergotać

chisel /'tʃɪzl/ **[]** *n* dłuto *n*

[] *vt* wy|rzeźbić

chitchat /'tʃɪtʃæt/ *n* infml pogaduszka *f* infml

chivalry /'ʃɪvəlrɪ/ *n* (courtesy) rycerskość *f*, galanteria *f*

chive /tʃaɪv/ *n* szczypiorek *m*

chlorine /'klɔːriːn/ *n* chlor *m*

choc-ice /'tʃɒkaɪs/ *n* GB lody *plt* w polewie czekoladowej

chock-a-block /ˌtʃɒkəˈblɒk/ adj nabity, zapchany

chocolate /ˈtʃɒklət/ **I** n (substance) czekolada f; (a sweet) czekoladka f

II adj (made from) czekoladowy; (coated with) oblany czekoladą

choice /tʃɔɪs/ n wybór m; **to make a** ~ dokonać wyboru; **to be spoilt for** ~ mieć zbyt wiele możliwości wyboru; **out of** or **from** ~ z wyboru

choir /ˈkwaɪə(r)/ n chór m

choirboy /ˈkwaɪəbɔɪ/ n chłopiec m śpiewający w chórze kościelnym

choke /tʃəʊk/ **I** n Aut ssanie n

II vt (throttle, impede breathing) dusić [person]

III vi dusić się; (on food) za|dławić się

■ **choke back**: powstrzym|ać, -ywać [cough, sob]; **to** ~ **back one's tears** powstrzymywać łzy

cholera /ˈkɒlərə/ n cholera f

cholesterol /kəˈlestərɒl/ n cholesterol m

choose /tʃuːz/ **I** vt [1] (select) wyb|rać, -ierać (**from sth** z or spośród czegoś) [2] (decide) postanowić (**to do sth** coś zrobić)

II vi [1] (select) wyb|rać, -ierać; **to** ~ **between sth and sth** wybierać pomiędzy czymś a czymś [2] (prefer) woleć; **to** ~ **to do sth** woleć coś zrobić

choosy /ˈtʃuːzɪ/ adj wybredny (**about sth** jeśli chodzi o coś)

chop /tʃɒp/ **I** n Culin kotlet m; **pork** ~ kotlet wieprzowy

II vt [1] (cut up) po|rąbać [wood]; po|siekać [parsley, onion]; po|kroić [vegetables, meat]; **to** ~ **sth finely** posiekać coś drobno [2] (reduce) z|redukować [deficit]

■ **chop down**: ści|ąć, -nać, zrąbać [tree]

■ **chop off**: odrąb|ać, -ywać [branch, head, hand, finger]

IDIOMS. **to** ~ **and change** [person] być jak chorągiewka na wietrze

chopping board n deska f (do krojenia)

chopping knife n nóż m kuchenny

choppy /ˈtʃɒpɪ/ adj [sea, river] lekko wzburzony

chopsticks /ˈtʃɒpstɪks/ npl chińskie pałeczki f pl

chord /kɔːd/ n akord m

chore /tʃɔː(r)/ n (uciążliwy) obowiązek m; **to do the** ~ **s** wykonywać swoje obowiązki domowe

choreograph /ˈkɒrɪəɡrɑːf, -ɡræf, US -ɡræf/ vt opracow|ać, -ywać choreografię (czegoś)

chorus /ˈkɔːrəs/ n [1] (singers) chór m [2] (piece of music) chór m, utwór m chóralny [3] (refrain) refren m

Christ /kraɪst/ prn Chrystus m

christen /ˈkrɪsn/ vt o|chrzcić

christening /ˈkrɪsnɪŋ/ n chrzest m

Christian /ˈkrɪstʃən/ **I** n chrześcijan|in m, -ka f

II adj chrześcijański

Christianity /ˌkrɪstɪˈænətɪ/ n chrześcijaństwo n

Christian name n imię n (nadane na chrzcie)

Christmas /ˈkrɪsməs/ n ~ (**day**) Boże Narodzenie n; **at** ~ na Boże Narodzenie; **Merry** ~!, **Happy** ~! Wesołych Świąt!

Christmas card n kartka f świąteczna (na Boże Narodzenie)

Christmas Eve n Wigilia f Bożego Narodzenia

Christmas tree n choinka f

chrome /krəʊm/ n chrom m

chronic /ˈkrɒnɪk/ adj [1] [illness] chroniczny, przewlekły [2] [liar] notoryczny; [shortage] chroniczny; [problem] stały

chronicle /ˈkrɒnɪkl/ n kronika f

chronological /ˌkrɒnəˈlɒdʒɪkl/ adj chronologiczny

chubby /ˈtʃʌbɪ/ adj [child, cheeks, face] pucołowaty; [fingers] pulchny

chuck /tʃʌk/ vt infml [1] (also ~ **away**) (throw) rzuc|ić, -áć, cis|nąć, -kać [2] rzuc|ić, -áć [boyfriend, girlfriend]

chuckle /ˈtʃʌkl/ vi za|chichotać; **to** ~ **at sth** chichotać z czegoś

chuffed /tʃʌft/ adj GB infml [person, expression] uradowany (**about** or **at** or **with sth** czymś, z powodu czegoś)

chum /tʃʌm/ n infml kumpel m, -ka f infml

chunk /tʃʌŋk/ n [1] (of meat, bread) kawał m; (of wood) kloc m; **pineapple** ~ **s** ananas w kawałkach [2] (of text, day) kawał m; (of population) znaczna część f

church /tʃɜːtʃ/ **I** n kościół m

II adj kościelny; [fête] parafialny

churchgoer /ˈtʃɜːtʃɡəʊə(r)/ n człowiek m religijny or praktykujący

church hall n sala f parafialna

churchyard /ˈtʃɜːtʃjɑːd/ n cmentarz m przykościelny

churn /tʃɜːn/ **I** n [1] (for butter) maselnica f [2] GB (for milk) bańka f

II vt **to** ~ **butter** ubijać masło

■ **churn out**: produkować masowo [goods]; produkować infml [novels, sitcoms]

■ **churn up**: wzburz|yć, -áć, burzyć [water]

chute /ʃuːt/ n [1] (for rubbish) zsyp m [2] (in plane) rękaw m; (in playground, swimming pool) zjeżdżalnia f [3] (for toboggan) tor m saneczkowy

cicada /sɪˈkɑːdə, US -ˈkeɪdə/ n cykada f

cider /ˈsaɪdə(r)/ n jabłecznik m, cydr m

cigar /sɪˈɡɑː(r)/ n cygaro n

cigarette /ˌsɪɡəˈret, US ˈsɪɡərət/ **I** n papieros m

II adj [ash, smoke] z papierosa; ~ **paper** bibułka papierosowa

cigarette lighter n zapalniczka f

cinder /ˈsɪndə(r)/ n (ember) rozżarzony węgielek m; (ash) popiół m

Cinderella /ˌsɪndəˈrelə/ prn Kopciuszek m

cinecamera /ˈsɪnɪˌkæmərə/ n kamera f filmowa

cine film /ˈsɪnɪ fɪlm/ n taśma f filmowa

cinema /ˈsɪnəmɑː, ˈsɪnəmə/ n kino n

cinemagoer /ˈsɪnəməgəʊə(r)/ n (regular) kinoman m, -ka f; (spectator) widz m

cinnamon /ˈsɪnəmən/ n cynamon m

circle /ˈsɜːkl/ **I** n ① (shape) koło n, okrąg m; **to go round in** ~**s** zataczać koła; fig kręcić się w kółko fig; **to have** ~**s under one's eyes** mieć podkrążone oczy ② (in theatre) balkon m; **in the** ~ na balkonie **II** vt ① *[plane]* okrąż|yć, -ać *[airport]*; *[person, animal]* ob|ejść, -chodzić dokoła; *[vehicle]* obje|chać, -żdżać dokoła *[building]* ② (encircle) wziąć w kółko **III** vi krążyć (**around sb/sth** wokół kogoś/czegoś)

circuit /ˈsɜːkɪt/ n ① (lap) okrążenie n ② Tech obwód m

circuit breaker n wyłącznik m (automatyczny)

circular /ˈsɜːkjʊlə(r)/ **I** n (newsletter) okólnik m; (advertisement) druk m reklamowy **II** adj *[object]* okrągły; *[argument]* pokrętny

circulate /ˈsɜːkjʊleɪt/ **I** vt rozpowszechni|ć, -ać **II** vi (at party) *[host, guest]* krążyć

circulation /ˌsɜːkjʊˈleɪʃn/ n ① cyrkulacja f, obieg m ② (of newspaper) nakład m

circulation figures npl nakład m

circumcision /ˌsɜːkəmˈsɪʒn/ n obrzezanie n

circumference /səˈkʌmfərəns/ n obwód m

circumstances /ˈsɜːkəmstənsəs/ npl ① okoliczności f pl; **in** or **under the** ~ w tych okolicznościach; **under no** ~ w żadnym razie, pod żadnym pozorem ② (financial position) sytuacja f materialna

circumstantial /ˌsɜːkəmˈstænʃl/ adj ~ **evidence** poszlaki

circus /ˈsɜːkəs/ n cyrk m

CIS n = **Commonwealth of Independent States** WNP f

cistern /ˈsɪstən/ n (of lavatory) spłuczka f, rezerwuar m; (in loft or underground) zbiornik m na wodę, cysterna f

citizen /ˈsɪtɪzn/ n obywatel m, -ka f

citizenship /ˈsɪtɪznʃɪp/ n obywatelstwo n

citrus fruit n owoc m cytrusowy

city /ˈsɪti/ n miasto n; **the City** GB (londyńskie) City n inv

city centre GB, **city center** US n śródmieście n

civic /ˈsɪvɪk/ adj ① *[administration]* miejski ② *[responsibility]* obywatelski

civic centre GB, **civic center** US n centrum n administracyjno-kulturalne miasta

civil /ˈsɪvl/ adj ① *[case, court]* cywilny ② (polite) grzeczny

civil engineering n inżynieria f wodno-lądowa

civilian /sɪˈvɪliən/ n cywil m

civilization /ˌsɪvəlaɪˈzeɪʃn, US -əlɪˈz-/ n cywilizacja f

civilized /ˈsɪvəlaɪzd/ adj *[society, world]* cywilizowany; *[person, conversation]* kulturalny

civil law n prawo n cywilne

civil liberty n swobody f pl obywatelskie

civil rights npl prawa n pl obywatelskie

civil servant n urzędni|k m, -czka f służby cywilnej

civil service n służba f cywilna, administracja f państwowa

civil war n wojna f domowa

claim /kleɪm/ **I** n ① (demand) roszczenie n, pretensja f ② (in insurance) (against a person) roszczenie n; (for fire, theft) żądanie n wypłaty odszkodowania ③ (for welfare benefit) **to make** or **put in a** ~ złożyć podanie o zasiłek ④ (assertion) twierdzenie n (**about** or **of sth** o czymś) **II** vt ① (assert) twierdzić, utrzymywać (**that...** że...) ② (assert right to) zgł|osić, -aszać pretensje do (czegoś) *[money, property]* ③ (apply for) ubiegać się o (coś) *[benefit]*; wyst|ąpić, -ępować o zwrot (czegoś) *[expenses]* **III** vi ① **to** ~ **for damages** wystąpić o odszkodowanie za szkody ② (apply for benefit) wyst|ąpić, -ępować o zasiłek

claimant /ˈkleɪmənt/ n ① (for benefit, grant) ubiegający m, -a f się (**to sth** o coś) ② (to title, estate) pretendent m, -ka f (**to sth** do czegoś)

claim form n formularz m zgłoszenia roszczenia ubezpieczeniowego

clairvoyant /kleəˈvɔɪənt/ n jasnowidz m

clam /klæm/ n małż m jadalny ■ **clam up**: przestać się odzywać

clammy /ˈklæmɪ/ adj *[skin, hand]* lepki; *[surface]* oślizły

clamour GB, **clamor** US /ˈklæmə(r)/ **I** n hałas m, zgiełk m **II** vi ① *[crowd]* podn|ieść, -osić krzyk or wrzawę ② (demand) głośno domagać się (**for sth** czegoś)

clamp /klæmp/ **I** n ① Tech zacisk m, klamra f ② Aut (also **wheel** ~) blokada f koła **II** vt ① zacis|nąć, -kać *[jaw, teeth]* ② Aut (also **wheel**~) za|łożyć, -kładać blokadę na koło (czegoś) *[car]* ■ **clamp down**: ~ **down on** pod|jąć, -ejmować zdecydowane kroki przeciwko *[crime]*; ukr|ócić, -acać *[extravagance]*

clampdown /ˈklæmpdaʊn/ n zdecydowane kroki m pl (**on sb/sth** podjęte przeciwko komuś/czemuś)

clan /klæn/ n klan m

clandestine /klænˈdestɪn/ adj *[organization]* tajny; *[marriage]* potajemny

clang /ˈklæŋ/ **I** n (of bells) dzwonienie n; (of metal) szczęk m **II** vi *[bell, gong]* za|dzwonić, za|dźwięczeć; *[iron gates]* (głośno) szczęk|nąć, -ać

clap /klæp/ **I** n **to get a** ~ dostać brawa; **to give sb a** ~ bić komuś brawo; **a** ~ **of thunder** grzmot **II** vt **to** ~ **one's hands** klaskać **III** vi klaskać, bić brawo

clapping /'klæpɪŋ/ *n* oklaski *plt*, brawa *plt*
claret /'klærət/ *n* [1] (wine) bordo *n inv* [2] (colour)
bordo *n inv*, bordowy *m*
clarification /ˌklærɪfɪ'keɪʃn/ *n* wyjaśnienie *n*
clarify /'klærɪfaɪ/ *vt* wyjaśni|ć, -ać
clarinet /ˌklærə'net/ *n* klarnet *m*
clarity /'klærətɪ/ *n* jasność *f*
clash /klæʃ/ [] *n* [1] (confrontation) starcie *n* [2] (contradiction) konflikt *m*; **a ~ of cultures** zderzenie
kultur; **a personality ~** niezgodność charakterów [3] (of cymbals) brzęk *m*
[] *vt* (also **~ together**) uderz|yć, -ać (o siebie) *[bin lids]*
[] *vi* [1] (meet and fight) *[armies]* zetrzeć, ścierać się
also fig [2] (be in conflict) *[interests, beliefs]* pozostawać
w sprzeczności ze sobą [3] (inconveniently) *[meetings]*
kolidować ze sobą [4] *[colours]* kłócić się *or* gryźć
się ze sobą
clasp /klɑːsp, US klæsp/ *n* (of bracelet) zameczek *m*;
(of bag, purse) zamek *m*; (of belt) klamra *f*, sprzączka *f*
class /klɑːs, US klæs/ [] *n* [1] klasa *f*; **to be in a ~**
of one's own stanowić klasę dla siebie; **to travel**
first/economy ~ podróżować pierwszą klasą/
klasą turystyczną; **a first-/second-~ degree** GB
Univ ukończenie studiów z wynikiem bardzo
dobrym/dobrym [2] (lesson) Sch lekcja *f*; Univ zajęcia
plt (**in sth** z czegoś)
[] *vt* **to ~ sb/sth as...** zaklasyfikować kogoś/coś
jako...
class conscious *adj* świadomy różnic klasowych
classic /'klæsɪk/ [] *n* klasyczne dzieło *n*
[] *adj* klasyczny
classical /'klæsɪkl/ *adj* klasyczny
classics /'klæsɪks/ *n* filologia *f* klasyczna
classification /ˌklæsɪfɪ'keɪʃn/ *n* [1] (category) kategoria *f* [2] (categorization) klasyfikacja *f*
classified /'klæsɪfaɪd/ [] *n* (also **~ ad**) ogłoszenie *n*
drobne
[] *adj* (secret) tajny
classify /'klæsɪfaɪ/ *vt* [1] (categorize) s|klasyfikować
[books, data] [2] (declare secret) opat|rzyć, -rywać
klauzulą tajności *[document]*
classmate /'klɑːsmeɪt, US 'klæs-/ *n* kole|ga *m*,
-żanka *f* z klasy
classroom /'klɑːsruːm, -rom, US 'klæs-/ *n* klasa *f*,
sala *f* lekcyjna
class system *n* system *m* klasowy
classy /'klɑːsɪ, US 'klæsɪ/ *adj* infml *[person]* z klasą;
[dress] szykowny; *[car, hotel]* luksusowy; *[actor,*
performance] wielkiej klasy
clatter /'klætə(r)/ [] *n* (of dishes, pots) brzęk *m*; (of
hooves) stukot *m*
[] *vi [typewriter]* stukać; *[dishes]* brzęczeć
clause /klɔːz/ *n* [1] (in grammar) zdanie *n* składowe
[2] (in contract, will) klauzula *f*
claustrophobia /ˌklɔːstrə'fəʊbɪə/ *n* klaustrofobia *f*

claw /klɔː/ *n* [1] (of animal) pazur *m*; (of bird of prey)
szpon *m*; **~s** (of crab, lobster) kleszcze *plt*, szczypce
plt [2] (on hammer) pazur *m* *(do wyciągania gwoździ)*
clay /kleɪ/ *n* glina *f*
clean /kliːn/ [] *adj* [1] (not dirty) czysty; **my hands**
are ~ mam czyste ręce also fig; **~ and tidy** czysto
i porządnie; **a ~ sheet of paper** czysta kartka
papieru [2] *[joke]* przyzwoity [3] *[reputation]* dobry,
nieposzlakowany [4] Sport *[player]* grający czysto;
[hit] czysty [5] (neat) *[lines, profile]* czysty
[] *vt* wy|czyścić; **to ~ one's teeth** umyć zęby
■ **clean out**: wysprzątać *[cupboard]*; wyszorować
[toilets]
■ **clean up**: ¶ **~ up** [1] (tidy) po|sprzątać [2] (wash
oneself) wy|myć się ¶ **~ [sth] up** uprząt|nąć, -ać
clean-cut /ˌkliːn'kʌt/ *adj [image]* wyrazisty; *[person]* schludny
cleaner /'kliːnə(r)/ *n* [1] (person) sprzątacz *m*, -ka *f*
[2] (detergent) środek *m* czyszczący [3] (shop) (also
cleaner's) pralnia *f* chemiczna
cleaning /'kliːnɪŋ/ *n* sprzątanie *n*
cleaning product *n* środek *m* czyszczący
cleanliness /'klenlɪnɪs/ *n* czystość *f*, schludność *f*
cleanse /klenz/ *vt* zmy|ć, -wać *[skin]*; przemy|ć,
-wać *[wound]*
cleanser /'klenzə(r)/ *n* [1] (for face) środek *m* do
demakijażu [2] (household) środek *m* czyszczący
clean-shaven /ˌkliːn'ʃeɪvn/ *adj* gładko ogolony
clear /klɪə(r)/ [] *adj* [1] (transparent) *[glass]* przezroczysty; *[liquid]* klarowny; *[blue]* czysty; *[lens,*
varnish] bezbarwny; *[honey]* płynny; **~ soup**
bulion [2] (distinct) *[image, outline, sound, voice]*
wyraźny [3] (comprehensible) *[description, instruction]*
jasny, klarowny; **I wish to make it ~ that...**
chciałbym wyraźnie zaznaczyć, że...; **is that ~?**
czy to jasne? [4] (obvious) *[need, sign, advantage,*
majority] wyraźny; **it's ~ that...** to oczywiste, że...
[5] (not confused) *[idea, memory]* żywy; *[plan]* klarowny; **to keep a ~ head** zachować jasność umysłu
[6] (empty) *[space]* wolny; *[view]* otwarty; *[table]*
uprzątnięty [7] *[conscience]* czysty, spokojny
[8] *[skin]* gładki; *[sky]* czysty; *[day, night]* bezchmurny; **on a ~ day** w bezchmurny dzień
[] *adv* **to jump ~ of sth** wyskoczyć z czegoś
[vehicle]; **to pull sb ~ of sth** wyciągnąć kogoś
z czegoś *[wreckage]*; **to stay** *or* **steer ~ of sb/sth**
trzymać się z dala od kogoś/czegoś *[troublemakers,*
town centre]
[] *vt* [1] (remove) usu|nąć, -wać *[debris, papers,*
mines]; odgarn|ąć, -iać *[snow]* [2] (free) przeczy|ścić,
-szczać, przep|chnąć, -ychać *[drains]*; uprząt|nąć,
-ać *[table, surface]*; oczy|ścić, -szczać, opróżni|ć, -ać
[desk, room]; ewakuować *[area, building]* *[site, land]*;
oczyścić *[screen]*; **to ~ one's throat** odchrząknąć; **to ~ a path through the bushes** torować
sobie drogę przez zarośla [3] (disperse) rozpędz|ić,
-ać, rozwi|ać, -ewać *[fog, smoke]*; rozpędz|ić, -ać

[crowd] 4 (pay off) spłac|ić, -ać *[debt]*; wyrówn|ać, -ywać *[account]* 5 *[bank]* rozlicz|yć, -ać *[cheque]* 6 (from blame) oczy|ścić, -szczać z zarzutów *[accused]*; **to be ~ed of suspicion** zostać oczyszczonym z podejrzeń; **to ~ one's name** oczyścić swoje imię 7 (get approval) zatwierdz|ić, -ać *[request]*; **to ~ sth with sb** uzyskać zatwierdzenie czegoś przez kogoś 8 (overcome) pokon|ać, -ywać czysto *[hurdle, wall]* 9 **to ~ customs** przejść przez odprawę celną

IV *vi* 1 *[sky]* przejaśni|ć, -ać się, rozchmurz|yć, -ać się; *[liquid]* s|klarować się 2 *[smoke, fog, cloud]* rozwi|ać, -ewać się 3 *[air]* oczy|ścić, -szczać się 4 *[rash]* ust|ąpić, -ępować 5 *[cheque]* zostać rozliczonym

■ **clear away**: ¶ ~ **away** po|sprzątać ¶ ~ **[sth] away** usu|nąć, -wać *[leaves, rubbish]*; po|sprzątać *[papers, toys]*

■ **clear up**: ¶ ~ **up** 1 (tidy up) z|robić porządek 2 (improve) *[weather]* poprawić, -ać się; *[infection]* ust|ąpić, -ępować ¶ ~ **[sth] up** 1 (tidy) po|sprzątać *[room]*; uprząt|nąć, -ać *[mess, toys, litter]* 2 (resolve) wyjaśni|ć, -ać *[problem, misunderstanding]*

clearance /'klɪərəns/ n 1 (permission) pozwolenie n 2 (of trees) wycinanie n; (of buildings) wyburzenie n; **land ~** oczyszczanie terenu 3 (also ~ **sale**) całkowita wyprzedaż f

clear-cut /ˌklɪə'kʌt/ adj *[difference, division]* wyraźny; *[rule]* jednoznaczny; *[plan]* klarowny; *[problem]* jasno postawiony

clear-headed /ˌklɪə'hedɪd/ adj *[person]* trzeźwo myślący; *[attitude]* trzeźwy

clearing /'klɪərɪŋ/ n (glade) polana f

clearly /'klɪəlɪ/ adv 1 (distinctly) *[speak, write]* wyraźnie; *[hear, see]* wyraźnie, dobrze; *[labelled]* czytelnie 2 (obviously) najwyraźniej

clear-out /'klɪəraʊt/ n infml **to have a ~** zrobić (generalne) porządki

cleavage /'kliːvɪdʒ/ n rowek m między piersiami

cleaver /'kliːvə(r)/ n tasak m rzeźniczy

clef /klef/ n Mus klucz m; **in the treble/bass ~** w kluczu wiolinowym/basowym

cleft /kleft/ adj *[chin]* z dołkiem; *[palate]* rozszczepiony

clench /klentʃ/ vt zacis|nąć, -kać

clergy /'klɜːdʒɪ/ n duchowieństwo n, kler m

clergyman /'klɜːdʒɪmən/ n duchowny m

clerical /'klerɪkl/ adj 1 (of clergy) klerykalny 2 *[staff, work]* biurowy

clerk /klɑːk, US klɜːrk/ n 1 (in office, bank) urzędni|k m, -czka f 2 GB (to lawyer) sekretarz m; (in court) pisarz m sądowy 3 US (in hotel) recepcjonist|a m, -ka f; (in shop) ekspedient m, -ka f

clever /'klevə(r)/ adj 1 (intelligent) zdolny; *[mind]* bystry 2 (ingenious) *[person, solution, gadget]* pomysłowy 3 (skilful) zręczny 4 (cunning) sprytny; **he**

was too ~ for us przechytrzył nas; **to be too ~ by half** infml wymądrzać się

cliché /'kliːʃeɪ, US kliː'ʃeɪ/ n komunał m, klisza f

clichéd /'kliːʃeɪd, US kliː'ʃeɪd/ adj (phrase) wyświechtany; (idea) oklepany; (art, music, technique) stereotypowy

click /klɪk/ **I** n 1 (of metal) brzęk m; (of mechanism) szczęk m 2 (of heels) stuk m; (of fingers) pstryknięcie n; (of tongue) mlaśnięcie n 3 Comput kliknięcie n **II** vt **to ~ one's fingers** pstryknąć palcami; **to ~ one's heels** stuknąć obcasami **III** vi *[camera]* pstryk|nąć, -ać; *[lock]* szczęk|nąć, -ać; Comput kliknąć (**on sth** coś)

client /'klaɪənt/ n klient m, -ka f

clientele /ˌkliːən'tel, US ˌklaɪən'tel/ n klientela f

cliff /klɪf/ n (by sea) klif m; (inland) urwisko n

climate /'klaɪmɪt/ n klimat m

climax /'klaɪmæks/ n moment m kulminacyjny; (of career) apogeum n

climb /klaɪm/ **I** n (up hill, tower) wejście n; (up mountain) wspinaczka f **II** vt piąć się na (coś), wspi|ąć, -nać się na (coś) *[mountain, wall, stairs]* **III** vi 1 wspi|ąć, -nać się; **to ~ down sth** zejść po czymś *[steps]*; zejść z czegoś *[rockface]*; **to ~ over sth** przejść przez coś *[fence, wall]*; przestąpić przez coś *[stile]*; **to ~ up sth** wspiąć się po czymś *[ladder]*; wspiąć się na coś *[stairs, tree]* 2 (rise) *[aircraft]* wzn|ieść, -osić się 3 *[road]* piąć się 4 (increase) podn|ieść, -osić się ■ **climb down**: wycof|ać, -ywać się

climber /'klaɪmə(r)/ n wspinacz m, alpinist|a m, -ka f

climbing /'klaɪmɪŋ/ n wspinaczka f

clinch /klɪntʃ/ vt 1 s|finalizować *[deal]* 2 rozstrzyg|nąć, -ać *[argument]*

cling /klɪŋ/ vi 1 **to ~ (on) to sb/sth** kurczowo trzymać się kogoś/czegoś; **to ~ together** przywrzeć do siebie 2 *[dress]* przyl|gnąć, -egać 3 *[smell]* utrzym|ać, -ywać się

clingfilm /'klɪŋfɪlm/ n GB folia f samoprzylegająca

clinic /'klɪnɪk/ n przychodnia f, poradnia f

clinical /'klɪnɪkl/ adj 1 *[test, medicine]* kliniczny; *[approach]* rzeczowy 2 (unfeeling) chłodny

clink /klɪŋk/ **I** vt brzęk|nąć, -ać (czymś) *[keys, glass]*; **to ~ glasses with sb** stuknąć się kieliszkami z kimś **II** vi *[glass, keys]* brzęk|nąć, -ać

clip /klɪp/ **I** n 1 (on earring) klips m; (for hair) spinka f 2 (from film) urywek m **II** vt 1 przypi|ąć, -nać *[brooch, microphone]* 2 przyci|ąć, -nać *[nails]*; przystrzy|c, -gać *[hedge, moustache]*; o|strzyc *[dog, sheep]* IDIOMS **to ~ sb's wings** podciąć komuś skrzydła

clipart /'klɪpaːt/ n Comput gotowy obraz m

clipboard /'klɪpbɔːd/ n podkładka f do pisania z klipsem; Comput schowek m

clip frame *n* antyrama *f*

clip-ons /'klɪpɒnz/ *npl* klipsy *m pl*

clippers /'klɪpə(r)z/ *npl* (for nails) cążki *plt* do paznokci; (for hedge) sekator *m*; (for hair) maszynka *f* do strzyżenia

clipping /'klɪpɪŋ/ *n* (from newspaper) wycinek *m*

cloak /kləʊk/ **[I]** *n* peleryna *f*

[II] *vt* [1] **to be** ~**ed in sth** być okrytym or spowitym czymś *[darkness]*; być okrytym aurą czegoś *[secrecy]* [2] (disguise) skry|ć, -wać

cloakroom /'kləʊkrʊm/ *n* [1] (for coats) szatnia *f* [2] GB (lavatory) toaleta *f*

clock /klɒk/ *n* zegar *m*; Sport stoper *m*; **to put the** ~**s forward/back one hour** przestawić zegary o godzinę do przodu/tyłu; **to work around the** ~ pracować dwadzieścia cztery godziny na dobę

■ **clock off** GB: odbi|ć, -jać kartę zegarową (wychodząc z pracy)

■ **clock on** GB: odbi|ć, -jać kartę zegarową (przychodząc do pracy)

clock radio *n* radio *n* z budzikiem

clock tower *n* wieża *f* zegarowa

clockwise /'klɒkwaɪz/ **[I]** *adj* zgodny z ruchem wskazówek zegara

[II] *adv* zgodnie z ruchem wskazówek zegara

clockwork /'klɒkwɜːk/ *adj [toy]* mechaniczny
(IDIOMS) **to go like** ~ pójść jak po maśle

clog /klɒg/ *n* sabot *m*

cloister /'klɔɪstə(r)/ *n* krużganek *m*

clone /kləʊn/ **[I]** *n* klon *m*

[II] *vt* s|klonować

cloning /'kləʊnɪŋ/ *n* klonowanie *n*

close[1] /kləʊs/ **[I]** *adj* [1] (near) bliski, pobliski [2] *[relative, friend, resemblance]* bliski [3] *[contest]* wyrównany; *[result]* zbliżony [4] *[scrutiny]* drobiazgowy; *[supervision]* ścisły; **to pay** ~ **attention to sth** zwracać na coś szczególną uwagę; **to keep a** ~ **watch** or **eye on sb/ sth** pilnować kogoś/czegoś [5] *[print]* gęsty; *[formation]* zwarty [6] *[weather]* duszny; **it's** ~ jest duszno

[II] *adv* blisko; **to live quite** ~ **(by)** mieszkać w pobliżu; **to bring sth closer** przybliżyć coś; **to follow** ~ **behind (sb)** podążać tuż za (kimś); **to hold sb** ~ objąć kogoś; ~ **together** blisko siebie
(IDIOMS) **it was a** ~ **call** or **shave** or **thing** infml mało brakowało

close[2] /kləʊz/ **[I]** *n* koniec *m*, zakończenie *n*

[II] *vt* [1] (shut) zam|knąć, -ykać *[door, book]* [2] (block) zam|knąć, -ykać *[border, port]*; za|blokować *[road]* [3] (end) za|kończyć *[meeting]*; zam|knąć, -ykać

[case] [4] (reduce) **to** ~ **the gap** fig zmniejsz|yć, -ać różnicę [5] s|finalizować *[deal]*

[III] *vi* [1] *[door, shop, polls]* zam|knąć, -ykać się [2] (cease to operate) *[business]* zostać zamkniętym [3] *[meeting, play]* zakończyć się, skończyć się; **to** ~ **with sth** zakończyć się czymś *[song]* [4] (in finance) **the pound** ~**d at $1.68** w chwili zamknięcia notowań kurs funta wyniósł 1,68 dolara [5] *[gap]* z|maleć, zmniejsz|yć, -ać się

[IV] closed *pp adj* zamknięty; **behind** ~**d doors** fig za zamkniętymi drzwiami

■ **close down:** ¶ ~ **down** *[shop, business]* zostać zamkniętym ¶ ~ **[sth] down** zam|knąć, -ykać

■ **close up:** ¶ ~ **up** [1] *[flower]* zam|knąć, -ykać się; *[wound]* zasklepi|ć, -ać się; *[group]* ścieśni|ć, -ać się [2] *[shopkeeper]* zam|knąć, -ykać ¶ ~ **[sth] up** zam|knąć, -ykać *[shop]*; zat|kać, -ykać *[hole]*

closed-circuit television, CCTV /ˌkləʊzdsɜːkɪt'telɪvɪʒn/ *n* telewizja *f* przemysłowa

close-fitting /ˌkləʊs'fɪtɪŋ/ *adj* dopasowany, obcisły

close-knit /ˌkləʊs'nɪt/ *adj [family, group]* zżyty

closely /'kləʊslɪ/ *adv* [1] *[follow]* blisko; *[look]* z bliska [2] *[resemble]* blisko, bardzo; **to be** ~ **related to sb** być blisko spokrewnionym z kimś

close-run /ˌkləʊs'rʌn/ *adj* zacięty

closet /'klɒzɪt/ **[I]** *n* US (cupboard) szafa *f* wnękowa; **linen** ~ bieliźniarka

[II] *adj [alcoholic]* cichy; *[homosexual]* nieujawniający się

close-up [I] /'kləʊsʌp/ *n* zbliżenie *n*; **in** ~ w zbliżeniu

[II] close up *adv* **(from)** ~ z bliska

closing /'kləʊzɪŋ/ **[I]** *n* zamknięcie *n*

[II] *adj [minutes, words]* ostatni; *[scene, stage]* speech]* zamykający

closing date *n* ostateczny termin *m*

closing-down sale /'kləʊzɪŋdaʊnseɪl/, **closing-out sale** /'kləʊzɪŋaʊtseɪl/ US *n* wyprzedaż *f* likwidacyjna

closing time *n* godzina *f* zamknięcia

closure /'kləʊʒə(r)/ *n* zamknięcie *n*

clot /klɒt/ **[I]** *n* zakrzep *m*

[II] *vt* s|powodować krzepnięcie

cloth /klɒθ, US klɔː:θ/ *n* [1] (fabric) tkanina *f*, materiał *m* [2] (for polishing) szmatka *f*; (for dusting) ściereczka *f*; (for the floor) szmata *f*, ścierka *f*; (for drying dishes) ścierka *f*; (for table) obrus *m*

clothes /kləʊðz, US kləʊz/ *npl* ubranie *n*; **to put on/take off one's** ~ ubrać się/rozebrać się

clothes brush *n* szczotka *f* do ubrania

clotheshanger /'kləʊðʒhæŋə(r), US 'kləʊz-/ *n* wieszak *m*

clothes shop *n* sklep *m* odzieżowy

clothing /'kləʊðɪŋ/ *n* odzież *f*; **an item** or **article of** ~ sztuka odzieży

cloud /klaʊd/ 🔲 *n* chmura *f*; **to cast a ~ over sth** rzucać się cieniem na coś

🔳 *vt* ① *[steam, breath, tears]* zamglić *[mirror, vision]* ② fig przesł|onić, -aniać *[judgment]*; zaćmi|ć, -ewać *[memory]*

■ **cloud over**: za|chmurzyć się

(IDIOMS:) **to be living in ~-cuckoo-land** spaść z księżyca, urwać się z choinki infml

cloudy /ˈklaʊdɪ/ *adj* ① *[weather]* pochmurny ② *[liquid]* mętny

clout /klaʊt/ *n* ① (blow) uderzenie *n*, walnięcie *n* ② (weight) siła *f*, znaczenie *n*; **~ with sb/sth** wpływ na kogoś/coś

clove /kləʊv/ *n* ① (spice) goździk *m* ② (of garlic) ząbek *m*

clover /ˈkləʊvə(r)/ *n* koniczyna *f*

clown /klaʊn/ *n* klown *m*

■ **clown around**: GB błaznować

club /klʌb/ *n* ① (society) klub *m* ② infml (nightclub) nocny klub *m* ③ (stick) pałka *f*; (weapon) maczuga *f* ④ (for golf) kij *m* golfowy ⑤ (at cards) trefl *m*

■ **club together**: złożyć, składać się (**for sth** na coś)

club car *n* US wagon *m* pierwszej klasy (z bufetem)

club class *n* (on aircraft) pierwsza klasa *f*

cluck /klʌk/ *vi* *[hen]* gdakać

clue /kluː/ *n* ① trop *m*, wskazówka *f* (**to** or **as to sth** co do czegoś); **I haven't (got) a ~** infml nie mam pojęcia ② (to crossword) hasło *n*

clued-up /ˌkluːdˈʌp/ *adj* infml oblatany infml (**about sth** w czymś)

clueless /ˈkluːlɪs/ *adj* infml ciemny infml (**about sth** jeśli chodzi o coś)

clump /klʌmp/ *n* (of flowers, grass, trees) kępa *f*; (of earth) gruda *f*

clumsiness /ˈklʌmzɪnɪs/ *n* (carelessness) nieuwaga *f*; (awkwardness) niezdarność *f*; (of system) niepraktyczność *f*

clumsy /ˈklʌmzɪ/ *adj* *[person]* niezdarny; *[attempt]* niezręczny; *[object, style]* toporny; *[tool]* nieporęczny

cluster /ˈklʌstə(r)/ 🔲 *n* (of berries) grono *n*; (of people) grupka *f*, gromadka *f*; (of trees) kępa *f*; (of flowers) kępka *f*; (of houses, islands) skupisko *n*; (of stars) gromada *f*

🔳 *vi* *[people]* skupi|ć, -ać się, z|gromadzić się (**around sth** wokół czegoś)

clutch /klʌtʃ/ 🔲 *n* Aut sprzęgło *n*

🔳 *vt* trzymać kurczowo, ściskać

■ **clutch at**: chwy|cić, -tać się (kogoś/czegoś) *[branch, rail, person]*

clutch bag *n* kopertówka *f*

clutches *npl* **to fall into the ~ of sb/sth** wpaść w szpony kogoś/czegoś

clutter /ˈklʌtə(r)/ 🔲 *n* rupiecie *m pl*; **in a ~** w nieporządku

🔳 (also **~ up**) **clutter up** zagrac|ić, -ać

c/o = **care of** na adres

Co *n* = **company** spółka *f*

coach /kəʊtʃ/ 🔲 *n* ① (long-distance) autobus *m* dalekobieżny; (tourist) autokar *m* ② GB (of train) wagon *m* ③ Sport trener *m*, -ka *f* ④ (tutor) nauczyciel *m*, -ka *f*; (for drama, voice) korepetytor *m*, -ka *f* ⑤ (horse-drawn) powóz *m*; (ceremonial) kareta *m*

🔳 *vt* ① Sport trenować *[team]* ② (teach) **to ~ sb** udzielać komuś korepetycji (**in sth** z czegoś)

coach station *n* dworzec *m* autobusowy

coal /kəʊl/ *n* (mineral) węgiel *m*

(IDIOMS:) **to haul sb over the ~s** infml zmieszać kogoś z błotem

coalfield /ˈkəʊlfiːld/ *n* zagłębie *n* węglowe

coal fire *n* kominek *m*

coalition /ˌkəʊəˈlɪʃn/ *n* koalicja *f*

coalmine /ˈkəʊlmaɪn/ *n* kopalnia *f* węgla

coalminer /ˈkəʊlmaɪnə(r)/ *n* górnik *m*

coarse /kɔːs/ *adj* ① *[texture, skin]* szorstki; *[salt, sandpaper]* gruboziarnisty ② *[manners, language, joke]* ordynarny

coast /kəʊst/ 🔲 *n* wybrzeże *n*; **off the ~** niedaleko brzegu

🔳 *vi* **to ~ downhill** *[car]* zjeżdżać z góry na luzie

coastal /ˈkəʊstl/ *adj* *[waters]* przybrzeżny; *[town, area]* nadmorski

coaster /ˈkəʊstə(r)/ *n* (mat) podkładka *f* pod szklankę

coastguard /ˈkəʊstɡɑːd/ *n* ① (organization) straż *f* przybrzeżna ② (person) (also **coastguardsman**) strażnik *m* straży przybrzeżnej

coastline /ˈkəʊstlaɪn/ *n* linia *f* brzegowa

coat /kəʊt/ 🔲 *n* ① (garment) (full-length) płaszcz *m*; (short) kurtka *f* ② (of animals) sierść *f* ③ (layer) warstwa *f*

🔳 *vt* (cover) **to ~ sth with sth** powlec coś czymś *[paint, adhesive]*; pokryć coś czymś *[dust, oil]*; **to ~ sth in** or **with sth** obtoczyć coś w czymś *[breadcrumbs, flour]*; polać coś czymś *[chocolate, sauce]*

coat hanger *n* wieszak *m*

coat of arms *n* (sign) herb *m*; (shield) tarcza *f* herbowa

coat rack *n* wieszak *m*

coax /kəʊks/ *vt* **to ~ sb into doing sth** namówić kogoś do zrobienia czegoś

cobbler /ˈkɒblə(r)/ *n* szewc *m*

cobblestones /ˈkɒblstəʊnz/ *npl* bruk *m*

cobweb /ˈkɒbweb/ *n* pajęczyna *f*

cocaine /kəʊˈkeɪn/ *n* kokaina *f*

cock /kɒk/ 🔲 *n* ① (rooster) kogut *m* ② (male bird) samiec *m*

🔳 *vt* ① **to ~ an eyebrow** unieść brew; **to ~ a leg** podnieść or zadrzeć nogę; **to ~ an ear** *[animal]* zastrzyc uchem; fig *[person]* nastawić ucha

2 (tilt) przekrzywi|ć, -ać 3 to ~ **a gun** odwieść kurek

cock-and-bull story /ˌkɒkn'bʊlstɔːrɪ/ n bajeczka f

cockatoo /ˌkɒkə'tuː/ n kakadu n inv

cockerel /'kɒkərəl/ n kogucik m

cockle /'kɒkl/ n sercówka f jadalna

cockpit /'kɒkpɪt/ n kabina f pilota, kokpit m

cockroach /'kɒkrəʊtʃ/ n karaluch m

cocktail /'kɒkteɪl/ n koktajl m

cocktail bar n bar m, koktajlbar m

cocky /'kɒkɪ/ adj pewny siebie

cocoa /'kəʊkəʊ/ n kakao n

coconut /'kəʊkənʌt/ n kokos m

cocoon /kə'kuːn/ n kokon m, oprzęd m

cod /kɒd/ n dorsz m

COD n = **cash on delivery** płatne gotówką przy odbiorze

code /kəʊd/ **I** n 1 (of laws) kodeks m 2 (of behaviour) normy f pl 3 (cipher) szyfr m, kod m 4 (also **dialling** ~) numer m kierunkowy **II** vt za|szyfrować, za|kodować

codeine /'kəʊdiːn/ n kodeina f

code name n kryptonim m

codeword /'kəʊdwɜːd/ n hasło n

coeducational /ˌkəʊedʒuːˈkeɪʃənl/ adj koedukacyjny

coerce /kəʊ'ɜːs/ vt zmu|sić, -szać; **to ~ sb into doing sth** zmusić kogoś do zrobienia czegoś

coexist /ˌkəʊɪg'zɪst/ vi współistnieć (**with sb/sth** z kimś/czymś)

coffee /'kɒfɪ, US 'kɔːfɪ/ **I** n kawa f; **a black/white** ~ czarna kawa/kawa z mlekiem **II** adj [cake, dessert] kawowy; [cup, filter, spoon] do kawy

coffee break n przerwa f na kawę

coffee pot n dzbanek m do kawy

coffee table n niski stolik m

coffin /'kɒfɪn/ n trumna f

cog /kɒg/ n (tooth) tryb m; (wheel) kółko n zębate

cohabit /kəʊ'hæbɪt/ vi żyć w konkubinacie (**with sb** z kimś)

coherent /kəʊ'hɪərənt/ adj spójny

coil /kɔɪl/ **I** n 1 (of rope, barbed wire) zwój m; (of hair) lok m, pukiel m 2 (contraceptive) spirala f **II** vt (also ~ **up**) zwi|nąć, -jać; owi|nąć, -jać (**around sth** wokół czegoś) **III** vi [road, river] wić się; [animal] zwi|nąć, -ijać się w kłębek

coin /kɔɪn/ **I** n moneta f; **a pound** ~ moneta jednofuntowa **II** vt uku|ć, -wać [word, term]

coin box n (pay phone) automat m telefoniczny (na monety)

coincide /ˌkəʊɪn'saɪd/ vi zbie|c, -gać się (**with sth** z czymś)

coincidence /kəʊ'ɪnsɪdəns/ n zbieg m okoliczności; **by** ~ przypadkowo

coincidental /kəʊˌɪnsɪ'dentl/ adj przypadkowy

coin-operated /'kɔɪnˌɒpəreɪtɪd/ adj [vending machine, ticket dispenser] na monety

coke /kəʊk/ n 1 (fuel) koks m 2 infml (cocaine) koka f infml

Coke n infml cola f infml

colander /'kʌləndə(r)/ n durszlak m, cedzak m

cold /kəʊld/ **I** n 1 (chilliness) chłód m; **to feel the** ~ marznąć 2 Med przeziębienie n; **to have a** ~ być przeziębionym **II** adj 1 (chilly) zimny; **I am** or **feel** ~ jest mi zimno; **the room was** ~ w pokoju było zimno; **it's** or **the weather is** ~ jest zimno; **to go** ~ [food, water] wystygnąć 2 [manner, logic] chłodny; **to be** ~ **to** or **towards sb** zachowywać się chłodno wobec kogoś

IDIOMS: **in** ~ **blood** z zimną krwią; **to be out** ~ być nieprzytomnym

cold-blooded /ˌkəʊld'blʌdɪd/ adj [animal] zimnokrwisty; [killer] bezlitosny

cold calling n akwizycja f przez telefon

coldness /'kəʊldnɪs/ n chłód m

cold shoulder n **to give sb the** ~ potraktować kogoś oziębie

cold sore n opryszczka f (na wardze)

cold sweat n zimny pot m; **to bring sb out in a** ~ sprawić, że ktoś oblewa się zimnym potem

cold turkey n infml 1 (treatment) leczenie uzależnienia przez raptowne odstawienie narkotyków 2 (reaction) głód m narkotyczny; **to be** ~ być na głodzie infml

Cold War n zimna wojna f

coleslaw /'kəʊlslɔː/ n surówka f z białej kapusty

colic /'kɒlɪk/ n kolka f

collaborate /kə'læbəreɪt/ vi współpracować (**with sb/sth** z kimś/czymś)

collaboration /kəˌlæbə'reɪʃn/ n współpraca f

collaborator /kə'læbəreɪtə(r)/ n współpracowni|k m, -czka f; (with enemy) kolaborant m, -ka f

collapse /kə'læps/ **I** n 1 (of building, bridge) zawalenie się n 2 (of regime) upadek m; (of economy) krach m; (of deals, talks) załamanie się n; (of marriage) rozpad m 3 Med (physical) zapaść f; (mental) załamanie n nerwowe 4 Med (of lung) zapadnięcie się n **II** vi 1 [talks, economy, deal] załam|ać, -ywać się 2 [company] upa|ść, -dać; z|bankrutować 3 (faint) ze|mdleć, zasłabnąć 4 [building, bridge] zawal|ić, -ać się, runąć 5 (fold) [bicycle, wheelchair] złożyć się 6 Med [lung] zapa|ść, -dać się

collapsible /kə'læpsəbl/ adj [chair, bike] składany

collar /'kɒlə(r)/ n 1 (of coat) kołnierz m 2 (for dog) obroża f

IDIOMS: **to get hot under the** ~ infml wściec się infml

collarbone /'kɒləbəʊn/ n obojczyk m

collar size *n* numer *m* kołnierzyka

collate /kə'leɪt/ *vt* porówn|ać, -ywać, zestawi|ć, -ać

colleague /'kɒli:g/ *n* kole|ga *m*, -żanka *f*

collect /kə'lekt/ **[] adv** US **to call sb ∼** zadzwonić do kogoś na koszt rozmówcy

[] vt [] z|ebrać, -bierać *[litter, wood, signatures]*; z|gromadzić *[information, facts]* [] (as hobby) zbierać *[stamps, coins]* [] (receive, contain) **the shelves ∼ a lot of dust** na tych półkach zbiera się mnóstwo kurzu [] (obtain) ściąg|nąć, -ać *[rent]*; pob|rać, -ierać *[pension]*; za|inkasować *[fares]*; wy|egzekwować *[debt, tax, fine]* [] (take away) wyb|rać, -ierać *[mail, post]* [] (pick up) od|ebrać, -bierać *[person, keys, book]*

[] vi [] *[dust, leaves, crowd]* z|ebrać, -bierać się [] **to ∼ for charity** kwestować na cele charytatywne

[] collected *pp adj* [] *[person]* spokojny, opanowany [] (assembled) **the ∼ed works of Dickens** dzieła zebrane Dickensa

collection /kə'lekʃn/ *n* [] (of coins, records) kolekcja *f*, zbiór *m*; (anthology) zbiór *m*; **art ∼** kolekcja obrazów [] (money) zebrane pieniądze *m pl* **(for sth** na coś) [] (of mail) wybieranie *n* poczty; **refuse ∼** wywóz śmieci

collective /kə'lektɪv/ *adj* zbiorowy

collective ownership *n* własność *f* wspólna

collector /kə'lektə(r)/ *n* [] (of antiques, butterflies) kolekcjoner *m*, -ka *f* [] (of taxes) poborca *m*; (of rates) inkasent *m*, -ka *f*; (of debt) egzekutor *m*

collector's item *n* rzadki okaz *m*, rarytas *m*

college /'kɒlɪdʒ/ *n* kolegium *n*, uczelnia *f* wyższa; (school) szkoła *f* pomaturalna; (part of university) kolegium *n*, college *m*; US fakultet *m*, wydział *m*; **to be at** or **in ∼**, **to go to ∼** US studiować (na wyższej uczelni)

collide /kə'laɪd/ *vi [vehicle]* zderz|yć, -ać się **(with sth** z czymś)

collie /'kɒlɪ/ *n* collie *m inv*, owczarek *m* szkocki

colliery /'kɒlɪərɪ/ *n* kopalnia *f*

collision /kə'lɪʒn/ *n* zderzenie *n*, kolizja *f*

colloquial /kə'ləʊkwɪəl/ *adj* potoczny

colon /'kəʊlən/ *n* [] Anat okrężnica *f* [] (punctuation) dwukropek *m*

colonel /'kɜ:nl/ *n* pułkownik *m*

colonialist /kə'ləʊnɪəlɪst/ *n* kolonialista *m*

colonization /ˌkɒlənaɪ'zeɪʃn, US -nɪ'z-/ *n* kolonizacja *f*

colonize /'kɒlənaɪz/ *vt* s|kolonizować

colonizer /'kɒlənaɪzə(r)/ *n* kolonizator *m*

colony /'kɒlənɪ/ *n* kolonia *f*

colour GB, **color** /'kʌlə(r)/ **[] *n*** [] (hue) kolor *m*, barwa *f*; **what ∼ is it?** jakiego *m* jest koloru?; **that should put a bit of ∼ into her cheeks!** to przyda jej rumieńców! [] (dye) (for food) barwnik *m*; (for hair) farba *f*

[] vt [] (with paints, crayons) po|kolorować; (with food dye) zabarwi|ć, -ać; (with hair dye) u|farbować [] (prejudice) zaważyć na (czymś) *[judgment]*

[] vi *[person]* po|czerwienieć (na twarzy)

IDIOMS **to be off ∼** być nie w formie; **to show one's true ∼s** ukazać swoje prawdziwe oblicze

colour blind *adj* **to be ∼** być daltonistą

coloured GB, **colored** US /'kʌləd/ *adj [paper, bead]* kolorowy; **∼ pencils** kredki

colour film *n* (for camera) film *m* kolorowy

colourful GB, **colorful** US /'kʌləfl/ *adj* kolorowy; barwny also fig

colouring GB, **coloring** US /'kʌlərɪŋ/ *n* [] (of plant, animal) ubarwienie *n*; (complexion) karnacja *f* [] (for food) barwnik *m*; (for hair) farba *f*

colour scheme *n* kolorystyka *f*

colour supplement *n* dodatek *m* ilustrowany

colour television *n* telewizja *f* kolorowa

colt /kəʊlt/ *n* źrebak *m*

column /'kɒləm/ *n* [] (pillar) kolumna *f*, filar *m* [] (block of print) szpalta *f*; (newspaper section) rubryka *f*, dział *m*

columnist /'kɒləmnɪst/ *n* felietonist|a *m*, -ka *f*

coma /'kəʊmə/ *n* śpiączka *f*; **in a ∼** w śpiączce

comatose /'kəʊmətəʊs/ *adj* Med w stanie śpiączki; fig otępiały, otumaniony

comb /kəʊm/ **[] *n*** (for hair) grzebień *m*; (for animals) zgrzebło *n*

[] vt to ∼ one's hair u|czesać się

combat /'kɒmbæt/ **[] *n*** walka *f*, bój *m*

[] vt walczyć z (czymś)

combat jacket *n* bluza *f* żołnierska

combination /ˌkɒmbɪ'neɪʃn/ *n* kombinacja *f*

combine **[]** /'kɒmbaɪn/ *n* kartel *m*, syndykat *m*

[] /kəm'baɪn/ *vt* [] po|łączyć *[activities, colours, items]* **(with sth** z czymś); po|wiązać *[ideas, aims]* **(with sth** z czymś); **to ∼ forces** (merge) zjednoczyć się; (cooperate) połączyć siły [] Culin wymieszać **(with sth** z czymś)

[] /kəm'baɪn/ *vi* [] *[activities, colours, firms]* po|łączyć się [] *[people, groups]* z|jednoczyć się

combined /kəm'baɪnd/ *adj* [] (joint) **∼ operation** wspólne działania; **a ∼ effort** wspólny wysiłek [] (total) *[salary, age]* łączny

combine harvester *n* kombajn *m*

come /kʌm/ *vi* [] (arrive) *[person, day, war]* przy|jść, -chodzić; *[train]* przyje|chać, -żdżać; *[spring, storm, news]* nad|ejść, -chodzić; **to ∼ down sth** zejść z czegoś *[stairs, ladder]*; **to ∼ up sth** wejść na coś *[stairs, ladder]*; **to ∼ into sth** wejść do czegoś *[room, house]*; **when the time ∼s** kiedy przyjdzie or nadejdzie czas; **(I'm) coming!** idę!; **to ∼ to sb for sth** przyjść do kogoś po coś *[advice, money]*; **to ∼ as a shock to sb** być dla kogoś szokiem; **don't ∼ any closer** nie zbliżaj się, nie podchodź; **I could see it coming** (of accident) wiedziałem, że tak będzie [] (reach) **to ∼ to** or **down to sth** *[dress,* *curtain, water]* sięgać do czegoś; **to ~ up to sth** *[water]* dochodzić do czegoś ③ (happen) **how ~?** jak to się stało?; **~ what may** niech się dzieje, co chce; **to take things as they ~** brać życie takim, jakie jest ④ (begin) **to ~ to love/hate sb/sth** pokochać/znienawidzić kogoś/coś; **to ~ to understand sb/sth** zrozumieć kogoś/coś ⑤ **to ~ from sth** *[word, legend, person]* pochodzić z czegoś; *[smell, sound]* dochodzić z czegoś ⑥ (in sequence) **to ~ after sth** nastąpić po czymś; **to ~ before sth** (in time) poprzedzać coś; (in importance) być ważniejszym niż coś or od czegoś; **to ~ first/last** (in race, competition) zająć pierwsze/ostatnie miejsce ⑦ **when it ~s to sth/to doing sth** gdy chodzi o coś/zrobienie czegoś ⑧ **to ~ true** spełnić się; **to ~ undone** *[lace]* rozwiązać się; *[button, zip]* rozpiąć się

■ **come across**: ¶ **~ across** *[meaning, message]* być jasnym or zrozumiałym; *[feelings]* uzewnętrznić, -ać się; **to ~ across as a liar** sprawić wrażenie kłamcy; **to ~ across as being honest** wydać się uczciwym ¶ **~ across [sth]** nat|knąć, -ykać się na (coś), na|trafiać na (coś)

■ **come along**: ① (arrive) *[person]* zjawi|ć, -ać się; *[bus]* przyje|chać, -żdżać; *[opportunity]* pojawi|ć, -ać się ② (hurry up) **~ along!** chodź już! ③ (attend) przy|jść, -chodzić (**to sth** na coś) ④ (make progress) *[pupil]* robić postępy; *[project, thesis, book]* posuwać się; *[studies]* iść dobrze

■ **come apart**: ① (accidentally) *[book, camera]* roz-pa|ść, -dać się ② (intentionally) *[components]* da|ć, -wać się rozdziel|ić; *[machine]* da|ć, -wać rozłożyć się na części

■ **come around** US = **come round**

■ **come away**: (leave) *[person]* od|ejść, -chodzić (**from sth** od czegoś); *[handle, shelf]* odpa|ść, -dać (**from sth** od czegoś); **to ~ away from a meeting** wyjść z zebrania

■ **come back**: ① (return) wr|ócić, -acać ② *[law, system]* zosta|ć, -wać przywróconym; *[trend]* wr|ó-cić, -acać

■ **come down**: ① *[person]* zejść, schodzić; *[lift]* zje|chać, -żdżać; *[curtain]* opa|ść, -dać ② *[price, inflation, temperature]* spa|ść, -dać; *[cost]* zmniejsz|yć, -ać się ③ *[rain, snow]* padać ④ *[plane, ceiling, wall]* runąć; *[hem]* odpru|ć, -wać się ⑤ **to ~ down with sth** zachorować na coś

■ **come forward**: ① (step forward) posu|nąć, -wać się do przodu ② (volunteer) zgł|osić, -aszać się

■ **come in**: ① (enter) w|ejść, -chodzić (**through sth** przez coś); *[tide]* nad|ejść, -chodzić ② **to ~ in handy** or **useful** przydać się ③ **to ~ in for criticism** *[person, plan]* zostać skrytykowanym

■ **come into**: ① (inherit) o|dziedziczyć *[fortune, title, money]* ② **luck doesn't ~ into it** szczęście nie ma tu nic do rzeczy

■ **come off**: ① *[button]* ur|wać, -ywać się; *[handle,*

paint, lid] odpa|ść, -dać ② *[ink, stain]* zejść, schodzić ③ *[plan, attempt]* powieść się

■ **come on**: ① **~ on!** chodź! ② (make progress) *[person]* z|robić postępy; *[patient]* po|czuć się lepiej; *[plant]* rozwijać się ③ *[light]* zapal|ić, -ać się; *[electricity, gas, heating]* włącz|yć, -ać się ④ *[actor]* wy|jść, -chodzić na scenę

■ **come out**: ① *[person, animal]* wy|jść, -chodzić (**of sth** z czegoś); *[vehicle]* wyje|chać, -żdżać (**of sth** z czegoś); *[sun, moon]* wy|jść, -chodzić; *[stars, buds]* pojawi|ć, -ać się ② (strike) za|strajkować; **to ~ out on strike** zastrajkować ③ *[contact lens, tooth, contents]* wypa|ść, -dać; *[cork]* wy|jść, -chodzić ④ *[smoke, air]* wydosta|ć, -wać się; *[blood, water]* wypły|nąć, -wać (**through sth** przez coś) ⑤ *[stain]* zejść, schodzić (**of sth** z czegoś) ⑥ *[product]* pojawi|ć, -ać się; *[book, magazine]* ukaz|ać, -ywać się; *[film]* w|ejść, -chodzić na ekrany ⑦ *[details, facts]* wy|jść, -chodzić na jaw; *[news]* roz|ejść, -chodzić się; *[results]* zosta|ć, -wać ogłoszonym ⑧ *[photo, colour]* wy|jść, -chodzić ⑨ **to ~ out with sth** zna|leźć, -jdować coś *[excuse]*; wysk|o-czyć, -akiwać z czymś infml *[nonsense]*; **to ~ straight out with it** powiedzieć wprost ⑩ *[homosexual]* ujawni|ć, -ać swoją orientację seksualną

■ **come over**: ¶ wpa|ść, -dać; **he came over to collect his bike** wpadł po swój rower ¶ **what's come over you?** co cię napadło? infml

■ **come round** GB, **come around** US ① (regain consciousness) odzysk|ać, -iwać przytomność ② (visit) wpa|ść, -dać infml ③ (change one's mind) zmieni|ć, -ać zdanie

■ **come through**: ¶ **~ through** ① (survive) przetrwać ② *[cold, light]* przenik|nąć, -ać; *[ink]* przebi|ć, -jać ¶ **~ through [sth]** przetrwać *[crisis]*; przeżyć *[operation]*

■ **come to**: ¶ **~ to** (regain consciousness) ocknąć się ¶ **~ to [sth]** (total) *[bill, total]* wyn|ieść, -osić; *[shopping]* kosztować; **that ~s to £40 altogether** to razem będzie 40 funtów; **it may not ~ to that** może do tego nie dojdzie

■ **come under**: **~ under [sth]** ① **to ~ under threat** być zagrożonym ② (be classified under) **to ~ under history/reference** znajdować się w dziale historii/encyklopedii

■ **come up**: ① *[problem, issue]* pojawi|ć, -ać się; *[name]* pa|ść, -dać ② *[opportunity]* wył|onić, -aniać się; **something urgent has come up** wynikło coś pilnego ③ *[sun, moon, daffodils]* w|zejść, -schodzić ④ *[case]* znaleźć się na wokandzie ⑤ **to ~ up against sth** sta|nąć, -wać wobec czegoś *[problem]* ⑥ **to ~ up with sth** zna|leźć, -jdować coś *[answer]*; wy|starać się o coś *[money]*

comeback /'kʌmbæk/ *n* comeback *m*; **to make a ~** *[person]* mieć swój comeback; *[style]* wracać do mody

comedian /kə'mi:dɪən/ *n* artysta *m* komediowy, artystka *f* komediowa

comedienne /kə‚mi:dɪ'en/ *n* aktorka *f* komediowa

comedy /'kɒmədɪ/ *n* komedia *f*

comet /'kɒmɪt/ *n* kometa *f*

comeuppance /kʌm'ʌpəns/ *n* infml **to get one's** ~ dostać za swoje

comfort /'kʌmfət/ **Ⅰ** *n* ⊡ (conditions) wygoda *f*, komfort *m*; **to live in** ~ mieszkać wygodnie; **home** ~**s** wygody domowe ⊡ (consolation) pociecha *f*, pocieszenie *n*
Ⅱ *vt* pociesz|yć, -ać, doda|ć, -wać otuchy (komuś)

comfortable /'kʌmftəbl, US -fərt-/ *adj* ⊡ *[car, clothes, journey]* wygodny; *[temperature]* przyjemny ⊡ *[person]* odprężony

comfortably /'kʌmftəblɪ, US -fərt-/ *adv* wygodnie; (easily) z łatwością; **to be** ~ **off** być w dobrej sytuacji materialnej

comforting /'kʌmfətɪŋ/ *adj* pocieszający

comic /'kɒmɪk/ **Ⅰ** *n* ⊡ komik *m* ⊡ (magazine) komiks *m*
Ⅱ *adj* komiczny

comical /'kɒmɪkl/ *adj* komiczny

comic strip *n* historyjka *f* obrazkowa, komiks *m*

coming /'kʌmɪŋ/ **Ⅰ** *n* przybycie *n*; ~**s and goings** ruch, krzątanina
Ⅱ *adj [election, event]* nadchodzący; *[week, month]* przyszły

comma /'kɒmə/ *n* przecinek *m*

command /kə'mɑ:nd, US -'mænd/ **Ⅰ** *n* ⊡ Mil rozkaz *f*, komenda *f* ⊡ (authority) dowództwo *n*; **to be in** ~ **(of sth)** dowodzić (czymś); **to be in** ~ **of the situation** panować nad sytuacją ⊡ (of language) znajomość *f*; **to have an excellent** ~ **of Russian** biegle władać rosyjskim ⊡ Comput polecenie *n*
Ⅱ *vt* ⊡ (order) rozkaz|ać, -ywać (komuś); **to** ~ **sb to do sth** rozkazać komuś coś zrobić ⊡ cieszyć się (czymś) *[affection]*; wzbudzać *[respect]* ⊡ Mil dowodzić (czymś) *[regiment]*

commander /kə'mɑ:ndə(r), US -mæn-/ *n* dowódca *m*

commanding /kə'mɑ:ndɪŋ, US -'mæn-/ *adj [look, manner]* władczy; *[presence]* imponujący

commanding officer, CO *n* dowódca *m*

commando /kə'mɑ:ndəʊ, US -'mæn-/ *n* jednostka *f* do zadań specjalnych

commemorate /kə'meməreɪt/ *vt* upamiętni|ć, -ać *[event]*; u|czcić pamięć (kogoś) *[person]*

commence /kə'mens/ fml **Ⅰ** *vt* rozpocz|ąć, -ynać
Ⅱ *vi* rozpocz|ąć, -ynać się

commend /kə'mend/ *vt* po|chwalić **(for** or **on sth** za coś)

comment /'kɒment/ **Ⅰ** *n* ⊡ (public) komentarz *m* **(on sb/sth** na temat kogoś/czegoś); (in conversation) uwaga *f* **(on sb/sth** na temat kogoś/czegoś); (written) adnotacja *f* ⊡ **to be a** ~ **on sth** źle świadczyć o czymś

Ⅱ *vi* **to** ~ **on sb/on sth** wypowiedzieć się o kimś/o czymś

commentary /'kɒməntrɪ, US -terɪ/ *n* komentarz *m* **(on sth** na temat czegoś)

commentator /'kɒmənteɪtə(r)/ *n* (sports) komentator *m*, sprawozdawca *m*; (current affairs) komentator *m*

commerce /'kɒmɜ:s/ *n* handel *m*

commercial /kə'mɜ:ʃl/ **Ⅰ** *n* reklama *f*
Ⅱ *adj [sector, organization]* handlowy; *[bank]* komercyjny

commercial break *n* przerwa *f* na reklamę

commercial traveller *n* komiwojażer *m*

commiserate /kə'mɪzəreɪt/ *vi* **to** ~ **with sb about** or **over sth** współczuć komuś z powodu czegoś

commission /kə'mɪʃn/ **Ⅰ** *n* ⊡ (fee) prowizja *f* ⊡ (advance order) zamówienie *n*, zlecenie *n* **(for sth** na coś) ⊡ (committee) komisja *f*
Ⅱ *vt* ⊡ (order) zam|ówić, -awiać **(from sb** u kogoś); **to** ~ **sb to do sth** zlecić komuś zrobienie czegoś ⊡ Mil mianować na stopień oficerski

commissioner /kə'mɪʃənə(r)/ *n* ⊡ członek *m* komisji; (functionary) komisarz *m* ⊡ (in the EC) komisarz *m* Komisji Europejskiej ⊡ GB (in police) komendant *m* policji

commit /kə'mɪt/ *vt* ⊡ (do) popełni|ć, -ać *[crime, error, sin, suicide]* ⊡ (assign) przeznacz|yć, -ać *[money, time]* **(to sth** na coś) ⊡ **to** ~ **oneself** zobowiąz|ać, -ywać się **(to sth/to do sth** do czegoś/do zrobienia czegoś)

commitment /kə'mɪtmənt/ *n* ⊡ (obligation) zobowiązanie *n* **(to do sth** do zrobienia czegoś) ⊡ (dedication) oddanie *n* **(to sth** czemuś); zaangażowanie *n* **(to sth** w coś)

committed /kə'mɪtɪd/ *adj [parent, teacher]* oddany; *[Christian]* wierny; *[Socialist]* zagorzały; **to be** ~ **to sth/to doing sth** być oddanym czemuś/robieniu czegoś

committee /kə'mɪtɪ/ *n* komitet *m*; (to investigate, report) komisja *f*

commodity /kə'mɒdətɪ/ *n* towar *m*, artykuł *m*; (of food) artykuł *m* spożywczy

common /'kɒmən/ **Ⅰ** *n* (public land) ≈ błonia *n pl*
Ⅱ **Commons** *npl* GB Pol **the Commons** Izba *f* Gmin
Ⅲ *adj* ⊡ (frequent) pospolity; **in** ~ **use** w powszechnym użyciu ⊡ (shared) wspólny **(to sb/ sth** dla kogoś/czegoś); **in** ~ wspólnie; **it is** ~ **knowledge** to rzecz powszechnie znana ⊡ **the** ~ **people** prości ludzie; **a** ~ **criminal** pospolity przestępca ⊡ (low-class) prostacki; **it looks/ sounds** ~ to wygląda/brzmi prostacko

common-law husband /‚kɒmənlɔ:'hʌzbənd/ *n* konkubent *m*

common-law marriage /‚kɒmənlɔ:'mærɪdʒ/ *n* konkubinat *m*

common-law wife /ˌkɒmənlɔːˈwaɪf/ *n* konkubina *f*

commonly /ˈkɒmənlɪ/ *adv* powszechnie

Common Market *n* the ~ Wspólny Rynek *m*

commonplace /ˈkɒmənpleɪs/ *adj* (widespread) powszechny, pospolity; (banal) banalny

common room *n* (in school) świetlica *f*

common sense *n* zdrowy rozsądek *m*

Commonwealth /ˈkɒmənwelθ/ *n* GB Pol the ~ (Brytyjska) Wspólnota *f* Narodów, Commonwealth *m*

Commonwealth of Independent States, CIS *n* the ~ Wspólnota *f* Niepodległych Państw, WNP

commotion /kəˈməʊʃn/ *n* [1] (noise) hałas *m*, zgiełk *m* [2] (outrage) zamieszki *plt*, rozruchy *plt*

communal /ˈkɒmjʊnl, kəˈmjuːnl/ *adj [property, area, showers, garden]* wspólny; *[life]* społeczny

commune /ˈkɒmjuːn/ *n* (group of people) komuna *f*

communicate /kəˈmjuːnɪkeɪt/ **[1]** *vt* przekaz|ać, -ywać *[ideas, feelings, information]* (**to sb** komuś) **[2]** *vi* porozumie|ć, -wać się (**with sb** z kimś)

communication /kəˌmjuːnɪˈkeɪʃn/ *n* [1] (of information, ideas) przekazywanie *n* [2] (contact) porozumienie *n*

communication cord *n* GB hamulec *m* bezpieczeństwa

communications /kəˌmjuːnɪˈkeɪʃnz/ *npl* łączność *f*

communications company *n* firma *f* telekomunikacyjna

communication studies *n* nauka *f* o komunikacji społecznej

communion /kəˈmjuːnɪən/ *n* Relig komunia *f*

communism /ˈkɒmjʊnɪzəm/ *n* komunizm *m*

communist /ˈkɒmjʊnɪst/ **[1]** *n* komunist|a *m*, -ka *f* **[2]** *adj* komunistyczny

community /kəˈmjuːnətɪ/ *n* [1] (society at large) the ~ społeczeństwo *n* [2] (large grouping) społeczność *f*; (professional) środowisko *n* [3] (**religious**) ~ wspólnota *f* wyznaniowa

community care *n* opieka *f* pozaszpitalna *(dla osób przewlekle chorych i starszych)*

community centre GB, **community center** US *n* ≈ dom *m* kultury

community service *n* praca *f* na rzecz społeczności lokalnej

commute /kəˈmjuːt/ *vi* dojeżdżać do pracy; **he ~s between Oksford and London** dojeżdża z Oxfordu do Londynu

commuter /kəˈmjuːtə(r)/ *n* dojeżdżając|y *m*, -a *f* do pracy

compact [1] /ˈkɒmpækt/ *n* (also **powder** ~) puderniczka *f (z pudrem w kamieniu)* **[2]** /kəmˈpækt/ *adj [snow]* zbity, ubity; *[style]* zwięzły; *[equipment]* niewielkich rozmiarów

companion /kəmˈpænɪən/ *n* towarzysz *m*, -ka *f*

companionship /kəmˈpænɪənʃɪp/ *n* towarzystwo *n*

company /ˈkʌmpənɪ/ *n* [1] (business enterprise) przedsiębiorstwo *n*, firma *f*; **airline** ~ towarzystwo lotnicze [2] **theatre** ~ zespół teatralny [3] Mil kompania *f* [4] (companionship) towarzystwo *n*; **to keep sb** ~ dotrzymywać komuś towarzystwa [5] (visitors) goście *m pl*

company car *n* samochód *m* służbowy

company director *n* dyrektor *m* spółki or przedsiębiorstwa

company pension scheme *n* system *m* emerytalny przedsiębiorstwa

company secretary *n* ≈ dyrektor *m* finansowy przedsiębiorstwa

comparable /ˈkɒmpərəbl/ *adj* porównywalny (**to** or **with** sth z czymś)

comparative /kəmˈpærətɪv/ *adj* [1] (in grammar) wyższy [2] (relative) względny; **in** ~ **terms** w kategoriach względnych [3] *[study]* porównawczy

comparatively /kəmˈpærətɪvlɪ/ *adv* stosunkowo

compare /kəmˈpeə(r)/ **[1]** *vt* porówn|ać, -ywać; **to ~ sb/sth with** or **to sb/sth** porównywać kogoś/coś z kimś/czymś **[2]** compared with *prep phr* ~d **with sb/sth** w porównaniu z kimś/czymś **[3]** *vi* być porównywalnym (**with sb/sth** z kimś/czymś) **[4]** *vr* **to** ~ **oneself with** or **to sb** porównywać siebie z kimś

comparison /kəmˈpærɪsn/ *n* porównanie *n*; **in** or **by** ~ **with sb/sth** w porównaniu z kimś/czymś

compartment /kəmˈpɑːtmənt/ *n* [1] (in train) przedział *m* [2] (in box) przegródka *f*

compass /ˈkʌmpəs/ *n* busola *f*, kompas *m*; **the points of the** ~ rumby, znaki rumbowe

compasses /ˈkʌmpəsez/ *npl* **a pair of** ~ cyrkiel *m*

compassion /kəmˈpæʃn/ *n* współczucie *n*, litość *f* (**for sb** dla kogoś)

compassionate /kəmˈpæʃənət/ *adj* pełen współczucia; **on** ~ **grounds** z powodów osobistych

compatible /kəmˈpætəbl/ *adj* zgodny (**with sb/ sth** z kimś/czymś); Comput *[software]* kompatybilny

compel /kəmˈpel/ *vt* **to** ~ **sb to do sth** zmu|sić, -szać kogoś do zrobienia czegoś

compelling /kəmˈpelɪŋ/ *adj [reason]* ważny; *[argument]* nie do odparcia; *[film, novel]* frapujący

compensate /ˈkɒmpenseɪt/ **[1]** *vt* (indemnify) wynagr|odzić, -adzać **[2]** *vi* **to** ~ **for sth** z|rekompensować coś

compensation /ˌkɒmpenˈseɪʃn/ *n* rekompensata *f*; (in law) odszkodowanie *n*

compete /kəmˈpiːt/ **[1]** *vi* [1] *[people]* rywalizować; **to** ~ **against** or **with sb for sth** rywalizować z kimś o coś [2] (commercially) *[companies]* konkurować; **to** ~ **against** or **with sb** konkurować z kimś (**for sth** o coś) ③ Sport rywalizować, współzawodniczyć (**with** or **against sb** z kimś); **to ~ in the Olympics** wystartować w olimpiadzie

II competing *prp adj* rywalizujący

competence /'kɒmpɪtəns/ *n* ① (ability) umiejętność *f* ② (skill) kwalifikacje *f pl*

competent /'kɒmpɪtənt/ *adj* kompetentny

competition /ˌkɒmpə'tɪʃn/ *n* konkurencja *f*, rywalizacja *f*; (contest) konkurs *m*; (race) wyścig *m*; (competitors) konkurencja *f*

competitive /kəm'petɪtɪv/ *adj* ① [*person*] ambitny; [*environment*] zmuszający do rywalizacji ② [*price, product*] konkurencyjny ③ [*sports*] wyczynowy

competitor /kəm'petɪtə(r)/ *n* rywal *m*, -ka *f*; Sport zawodni|k *m*, -czka *f*

compilation /ˌkɒmpɪ'leɪʃn/ *n* ① (on compact disc, video) wybór *m*, składanka *f* ② (act of compiling) (of reference book) kompilacja *f*, opracowanie *n*; (of report, dossier) sporządzanie *n*

compile /kəm'paɪl/ *vt* sporządz|ić, -ać [*report, list*]; opracow|ać, -ywać, s|kompilować [*catalogue*]

complacent /kəm'pleɪsnt/ *adj* zadowolony z siebie; **to be ~ about sth** być zbyt pewnym czegoś [*success, future*]

complain /kəm'pleɪn/ *vi* (informally) po|skarżyć się (**about** or **of sth** na coś); (officially) złożyć, składać skargę or zażalenie; **to ~ to sb** poskarżyć się komuś

complaint /kəm'pleɪnt/ *n* skarga *f*; (usually written) zażalenie *n*; (about faulty product) reklamacja *f*; **there have been ~s about the noise** były skargi na hałas; **to have grounds** or **cause for ~** mieć powody or podstawy do narzekań or skarg

complement /'kɒmplɪmənt/ **I** *n* uzupełnienie *n*, dopełnienie *n*

II *vt* uzupełni|ć, -ać

complementary /ˌkɒmplɪ'mentrɪ/ *adj* uzupełniający

complementary medicine *n* medycyna *f* niekonwencjonalna

complete /kəm'pliːt/ **I** *adj* kompletny, całkowity; (finished) ukończony

II *vt* ① (finish) u|kończyć, s|kończyć [*building, course, exercise, task*]; za|kończyć [*journey*] ② (make whole) s|kompletować [*collection*]; uzupełni|ć, -ać [*phrase*] ③ (fill in) wypełni|ć, -ać [*form*]

completely /kəm'pliːtlɪ/ *adv* całkowicie, zupełnie

completion /kəm'pliːʃn/ *n* ukończenie *n*

complex /'kɒmpleks, US kəm'pleks/ **I** *n* kompleks *m*; **sports ~** kompleks sportowy; **he's got a ~ about his weight** ma kompleks na punkcie swej tuszy

II *adj* skomplikowany

complexion /kəm'plekʃn/ *n* cera *f*, karnacja *f*

complexity /kəm'pleksətɪ/ *n* złożoność *f*

compliance /kəm'plaɪəns/ *n* zastosowanie się *n* (**with sth** do czegoś); **in ~ with sth** zgodnie z czymś

compliant /kəm'plaɪənt/ *adj* uległy

complicate /'kɒmplɪkeɪt/ *vt* s|komplikować

complicated /'kɒmplɪkeɪtɪd/ *adj* skomplikowany

complication /ˌkɒmplɪ'keɪʃn/ *n* problem *m*; Med powikłanie *n*

compliment /'kɒmplɪmənt/ **I** *n* komplement *m*; **to pay sb a ~** powiedzieć komuś komplement; **~s** wyrazy uznania (**to sb** dla kogoś)

II *vt* po|chwalić

complimentary /ˌkɒmplɪ'mentrɪ/ *adj* ① [*remark*] pochlebny ② (free) bezpłatny

comply /kəm'plaɪ/ *vi* za|stosować się (**with sth** do czegoś); **failure to ~ with the rules** niepodporządkowanie się przepisom

component /kəm'pəʊnənt/ *n* składnik *m*; (in car, machine) część *f*; (electrical) element *m*

compose /kəm'pəʊz/ **I** *vt* u|łożyć, -kładać [*poem, reply*]; s|komponować [*music*]; **to be ~d of sth** składać się z czegoś

II *vr* **to ~ oneself** nastr|oić, -ajać się

composed /kəm'pəʊzd/ *adj* opanowany

composer /kəm'pəʊzə(r)/ *n* kompozytor *m*, -ka *f*

composition /ˌkɒmpə'zɪʃn/ *n* ① (structure, ingredients) skład *m*, struktura *f* ② Mus kompozycja *f*, utwór *m* ③ Sch wypracowanie *n* (**about** or **on sth** na temat czegoś)

compost /'kɒmpɒst/ *n* kompost *m*

composure /kəm'pəʊʒə(r)/ *n* opanowanie *n*

compound /'kɒmpaʊnd/ **I** *n* ① (substance) związek *m* chemiczny (**of sth** czegoś) ② (word) wyraz *m* złożony ③ (enclosure) ogrodzony or zamknięty teren *m*

II *adj* złożony; **~ fracture** złamanie wieloodłamowe

comprehend /ˌkɒmprɪ'hend/ *vt* poj|ąć, -mować

comprehensible /ˌkɒmprɪ'hensəbl/ *adj* zrozumiały

comprehension /ˌkɒmprɪ'henʃn/ *n* zrozumienie *n*

comprehensive /ˌkɒmprɪ'hensɪv/ **I** *n* GB ≈ państwowa szkoła *f* średnia

II *adj* [*report*] wyczerpujący; [*list*] pełny; [*knowledge*] wszechstronny; **~ insurance policy** ubezpieczenie pełne

compress /'kɒmpres/ **I** *n* kompres *m*, okład *m*

II /kəm'pres/ *vt* s|kondensować

comprise /kəm'praɪz/ *vt* (include) obejmować; (consist of) składać się z (czegoś)

compromise /'kɒmprəmaɪz/ **I** *n* kompromis *m*

II *vt* s|kompromitować

III *vi* **to ~ on sth** pójść na kompromis w sprawie czegoś

compromising /'kɒmprəmaɪzɪŋ/ *adj* kompromitujący

compulsive /kəm'pʌlsɪv/ *adj* ① (inveterate) *[gambler]* nałogowy; (psychologically) kompulsywny ② (fascinating) fascynujący

compulsory /kəm'pʌlsərɪ/ *adj* obowiązkowy, przymusowy

computer /kəm'pju:tə(r)/ *n* komputer *m*

computer-aided design, CAD *n* projektowanie *n* wspomagane komputerowo

computer-aided learning, CAL *n* uczenie (się) *n* wspomagane komputerem

computer crime *n* piractwo *n* komputerowe

computer game *n* gra *f* komputerowa

computer graphics *n* grafika *f* komputerowa

computer hacker *n* haker *m*

computerize /kəm'pju:təraɪz/ *vt* s|komputeryzować *[records]*; przetw|orzyć, -arzać komputerowo *[list]*

computer-literate /kəm'pju:tə'lɪtərət/ *adj* to be ~ umieć posługiwać się komputerem

computer program *n* program *m* komputerowy

computer programmer *n* programist|a *m*, -ka *f*

computer science *n* informatyka *f*

computer scientist *n* informatyk *m*

computing /kəm'pju:tɪŋ/ *n* informatyka *f*

comrade /'kɒmreɪd, US -ræd/ *n* towarzysz *m*, -ka *f*

comradeship *n* braterstwo *n*

con /kɒn/ *infml* ① *n* (swindle) kant *m* infml ② *vt* (trick) o|kantować infml

conceal /kən'si:l/ *vt* ukry|ć, -wać (**from sb** przed kimś)

concede /kən'si:d/ ① *vt* przyzna|ć, -wać się do (czegoś) *[defeat]*; uzna|ć, -wać *[superiority]* ② *vi* ust|ąpić, -ępować, da|ć, -wać za wygraną

conceit /kən'si:t/ *n* zarozumialstwo *n*

conceited /kən'si:tɪd/ *adj* *[person]* zarozumiały; *[remark]* przemądrzały

conceive /kən'si:v/ ① *vt* ① począć *[child]* ② stw|orzyć, -arzać *[idea]* ② *vi* ① zaj|ść, -chodzić w ciążę ② to ~ of sth wyobra|zić, -żać sobie coś

concentrate /'kɒnsntreɪt/ ① *vt* s|koncentrować, skupi|ć, -ać *[effort, attention]* ② *vi* skupi|ć, -ać się (**on sth/on doing sth** na czymś/na robieniu czegoś)

concentration /ˌkɒnsn'treɪʃn/ *n* koncentracja *f*, skupienie *n* (**on sth** na czymś); **to lose one's ~** zdekoncentrować się

concentration camp *n* obóz *m* koncentracyjny

concept /'kɒnsept/ *n* pojęcie *n*

conception /kən'sepʃn/ *n* ① Med poczęcie *n* ② (idea) koncepcja *f*, pojęcie *n* (**of sth** czegoś)

concern /kən'sɜːn/ ① *n* ① (worry) niepokój *m*, obawa *f* (**about** or **over sth** z powodu czegoś, o coś); **there is cause for ~** istnieją powody do obaw or niepokoju ② (preoccupation) zainteresowanie *n*; **environmental ~s** względy ekologiczne

③ (company) przedsiębiorstwo *n*; **a going ~** rentowne przedsiębiorstwo ② *vt* ① (worry) z|martwić ② (affect, interest) dotyczyć (kogoś/czegoś); **'to whom it may ~'** „zaświadczenie" (*w nagłówku pisma bez określonego adresata*); **as far as the pay is ~ed** jeśli chodzi o pieniądze ③ (be about) *[book, programme]* traktować o (czymś); *[fax, letter]* dotyczyć (czegoś)

concerned /kən'sɜːnd/ *adj* ① (anxious) zaniepokojony (**about** czymś); **to be ~ for sb** niepokoić się o kogoś ② (involved) zainteresowany; **all (those) ~** wszyscy zainteresowani

concerning /kən'sɜːnɪŋ/ *prep* odnośnie do (kogoś/czegoś)

concert /'kɒnsət/ *n* koncert *m*

concerted /kən'sɜːtɪd/ *adj* *[action, campaign]* wspólny; **to make a ~ effort to do sth** podjąć wspólny trud zrobienia czegoś

concert hall *n* sala *f* koncertowa

concertina /ˌkɒnsə'ti:nə/ ① *n* concertina *f* ② *vi* *[part of vehicle]* ulec zgnieceniu

concerto /kən'tʃeətəʊ, -'tʃɜːt-/ *n* koncert *m*

concession /kən'seʃn/ *n* ① (compromise) ustępstwo *n* (**on sth** w sprawie czegoś) ② (discount) zniżka *f*, ulga *f*

conciliatory /kən'sɪlɪətərɪ, US -tɔːrɪ/ *adj* *[gesture, measures]* pojednawczy

concise /kən'saɪs/ *adj* zwięzły

conclude /kən'klu:d/ ① *vt* (finish) za|kończyć ② *vi* *[story, event]* za|kończyć się (**with sth** czymś); *[speaker]* za|kończyć (**with sth** czymś)

concluding /kən'klu:dɪŋ/ *adj* końcowy

conclusion /kən'klu:ʒn/ *n* ① (end) zakończenie *n*, koniec *m* ② (opinion, resolution) wniosek *m*

conclusive /kən'klu:sɪv/ *adj* ostateczny, rozstrzygający

concoct /kən'kɒkt/ *vt* ① Culin przyrządz|ić, -ać ② (invent) wymyśl|ić, -ać

concrete /'kɒŋkri:t/ ① *n* beton *m* ② *adj* ① *[block, base]* betonowy ② (real) konkretny

concuss /kən'kʌs/ *vt* **to be ~ed** doznać wstrząśnienia mózgu

concussion /kən'kʌʃn/ *n* wstrząśnienie *n* mózgu

condemn /kən'dem/ ① *vt* ① potępi|ć, -ać ② (declare unsafe) przeznacz|yć, -ać do rozbiórki *[building]* ② **condemned** *pp adj* ~**ed man/woman** skazany/skazana na śmierć; ~**ed cell** cela śmierci

condensation /ˌkɒndən'seɪʃn/ *n* skroplona para *f*

condense /kən'dens/ ① *vt* ① (thicken) zagęś|cić, -szczać *[soup]* ② skr|oplić, -aplać *[gas]* ② *vi* *[gas]* skr|oplić, -aplać się; *[liquids]* z|gęstnieć

condensed milk *n* mleko *n* skondensowane

condescend /ˌkɒndɪ'send/ *vt* **to ~ to do sth** raczyć coś zrobić

condescending /ˌkɒndɪ'sendɪŋ/ *adj* protekcjonalny

condition /kənˈdɪʃn/ *n* [1] warunek *m*; **on ~ that...** pod warunkiem, że... [2] (state) stan *m*; **to be in good/bad ~** *[house, car]* być w dobrym/złym stanie [3] (disease) choroba *f*

conditional /kənˈdɪʃənl/ *adj* warunkowy

conditioner /kənˈdɪʃənə(r)/ *n* (for hair) odżywka *f*; (for laundry) płyn *m* do płukania tkanin

condolences /kənˈdəʊlənsɪs/ *npl* kondolencje *plt*

condom /ˈkɒndɒm/ *n* prezerwatywa *f*

condominium /ˌkɒndəˈmɪnɪəm/ *n* US (also ~ **unit**) (apartment) ≈ mieszkanie *n* własnościowe; (building) blok *m* z mieszkaniami własnościowymi

condone /kənˈdəʊn/ *vt* przyzwolić, -alać na (coś)

conducive /kənˈdjuːsɪv, US -ˈduː-/ *adj* sprzyjający (**to sth** czemuś)

conduct [1] /ˈkɒndʌkt/ *n* zachowanie *n* (**towards sb** wobec kogoś)
[2] /kənˈdʌkt/ *vt* [1] prowadzić *[business, life]* [2] przeprowadz|ić, -ać *[experiment, research]*; odprawi|ć, -ać *[ceremony]* [3] Mus dyrygować (czymś) *[orchestra]* [4] przewodzić *[heat, electricity]*

conductor /kənˈdʌktə(r)/ *n* [1] Mus dyrygent *m*, -ka *f* [2] (on bus, train) konduktor *m*, -ka *f*

conductress /kənˈdʌktrɪs/ *n* konduktorka *f*

cone /kəʊn/ *n* [1] (shape) stożek *m* [2] (on tree) szyszka *f* [3] (also **ice-cream ~**) rożek *m* [4] (for traffic) pachołek *m*

confectioner /kənˈfekʃənə(r)/ *n* cukiernik *m*; **~'s (shop)** cukiernia

confectionery /kənˈfekʃənərɪ, US -ʃenerɪ/ *n* (sweets) słodycze *plt*; (cakes) ciastka *n pl*

confer /kənˈfɜː(r)/ [1] *vt* nada|ć, -wać, przyzna|ć, -wać (**on** or **upon sb** komuś)
[2] *vi* naradz|ić, -ać się (**about sth** o czymś)

conference /ˈkɒnfərəns/ *n* konferencja *f*, kongres *m*, zjazd *m*; **peace ~** konferencja pokojowa

confess /kənˈfes/ [1] *vt* [1] (avow) przyzna|ć, -wać się do (czegoś); **to ~ that...** wyznać, że... [2] (in religion) wyzna|ć, -wać *[sins]*
[2] *vi* przyzna|ć, -wać się; **to ~ to a crime** przyznać się do popełnienia przestępstwa

confession /kənˈfeʃn/ *n* [1] przyznanie się *n* [2] (in religion) spowiedź *f*; **to go to ~** chodzić or przystępować do spowiedzi

confetti /kənˈfetɪ/ *n* konfetti *n inv*

confide /kənˈfaɪd/ *vi* **to ~ in sb** zwierz|yć, -ać się komuś

confidence /ˈkɒnfɪdəns/ *n* [1] (faith) zaufanie *n* (**in sb/sth** do kogoś/czegoś); **to have every ~ in sb/ sth** mieć pełne zaufanie do kogoś/czegoś [2] **vote of ~** wotum zaufania; **motion of no ~** wniosek o wotum nieufności [3] (self-assurance) pewność *f* siebie [4] **to tell sb sth in (strict) ~** powiedzieć coś komuś w (głębokiej) tajemnicy

confidence trick *n* oszustwo *n*

confident /ˈkɒnfɪdənt/ *adj* [1] (sure) pewny [2] (self-assured) pewny siebie

confidential /ˌkɒnfɪˈdenʃl/ *adj* poufny

confine /kənˈfaɪn/ *vt* [1] zam|knąć, -ykać *[person]* (**in** or **to sth** w czymś) [2] ogranicz|yć, -ać *[comments, opinion]* (**to sth** do czegoś)

confined /kənˈfaɪnd/ *adj [area, space]* ograniczony

confinement /kənˈfaɪnmənt/ *n* zamknięcie *n* (**in** or **to sth** w czymś)

confirm /kənˈfɜːm/ *vt* potwierdz|ić, -ać; **to ~ receipt of sth** potwierdzić odbiór czegoś *[goods]*

confirmation /ˌkɒnfəˈmeɪʃn/ *n* potwierdzenie *n*

confirmed /kənˈfɜːmd/ *adj [liar, smoker]* notoryczny; *[bachelor]* zaprzysięgły; *[sinner]* zatwardziały

confiscate /ˈkɒnfɪskeɪt/ *vt* s|konfiskować (**from sb** komuś)

conflict [1] /ˈkɒnflɪkt/ *n* konflikt *m*
[2] /kənˈflɪkt/ *vi* być sprzecznym (**with sth** z czymś)

conflicting /kənˈflɪktɪŋ/ *adj* sprzeczny

conform /kənˈfɔːm/ [1] *vt* dopasow|ać, -ywać, dostosow|ać, -ywać (**to sth** do czegoś)
[2] *vi [person]* dostosow|ać, -ywać się (**to** or **with sth** do czegoś)

conformist /kənˈfɔːmɪst/ [1] *n* konformist|a *m*, -ka *f*
[2] *adj* konformistyczny

confront /kənˈfrʌnt/ *vt* sta|nąć, -wać twarzą w twarz z (kimś/czymś) *[danger, enemy]*; **to be ~ed by sth** stanąć wobec czegoś *[problem]*

confrontation /ˌkɒnfrʌnˈteɪʃn/ *n* starcie *n*, konfrontacja *f*

confrontational /ˌkɒnfrənˈteɪʃənəl/ *adj* konfrontacyjny

confuse /kənˈfjuːz/ *vt* [1] (bewilder) z|dezorientować [2] (fail to distinguish) po|mylić (**with sb/sth** z kimś/ czymś) [3] (complicate) po|gmatwać; **to ~ the issue** zagmatwać sprawę

confused /kənˈfjuːzd/ *adj [person]* zdezorientowany; **~ thoughts** or **mind** pomieszanie myśli; **to get ~** pogubić się

confusing /kənˈfjuːzɪŋ/ *adj* dezorientujący

confusion /kənˈfjuːʒn/ *n* [1] (chaos) zamieszanie *n*; (in sb's mind) zamęt *m* [2] (misunderstanding) nieporozumienie *n*, pomyłka *f*

congeal /kənˈdʒiːl/ *vi [blood]* s|krzepnąć; *[oil, fat]* zastyg|nąć, -ać, s|tężeć

congenial /kənˈdʒiːnɪəl/ *adj* miły, przyjemny

congenital /kənˈdʒenɪtl/ *adj* wrodzony

congested /kənˈdʒestɪd/ *adj* [1] *[road]* zatłoczony; *[district]* przeludniony [2] *[lung]* przekrwiony

congestion /kənˈdʒestʃn/ *n* [1] **traffic ~** korki infml [2] (of nose) zapchanie *n*; (of lung) przekrwienie *n*

conglomerate /kənˈglɒmərət/ *n* konglomerat *m*

congratulate /kənˈɡrætʃʊleɪt/ *vt* po|gratulować (komuś) (**on sth** z powodu czegoś)

congratulations /kənˌɡrætʃʊˈleɪʃnz/ *npl* gratulacje *plt*; **my ~ on the birth of your first baby** gratulacje z okazji narodzin pierwszego dziecka

congregate /'kɒŋgrɪgeɪt/ *vi* z|gromadzić się
congregation /ˌkɒŋgrɪ'geɪʃn/ *n* (in church) wierni *m pl*
congress /'kɒŋgres, US 'kɒŋgrəs/ *n* kongres *m* (**on sth** na temat czegoś)
Congress /'kɒŋgres, US 'kɒŋgrəs/ *n* US Kongres *m*
congressman /'kɒŋgresmən, US 'kɒŋgrəs-/ *n* US kongresman *m*
conifer /'kɒnɪfə(r), 'kəʊn-/ *n* drzewo *n* iglaste or szpilkowe
conjugal /'kɒndʒʊgl/ *adj* małżeński
conjugate /'kɒndʒʊgeɪt/ **I** *vt* odmieni|ć, -áć **II** *vi [verb]* odmieniać się
conjunctivitis /kənˌdʒʌŋktɪ'vaɪtɪs/ *n* zapalenie *n* spojówek
conjure /kən'dʒʊə(r)/ *vt* wyczarow|ać, -ywáć
■ **conjure up**: przywoł|ać, -ywáć *[memory, image]*
conjurer /'kʌndʒərə(r)/ *n* iluzjonista *m*
con man *n* oszust *m*; kanciarz *m* infml
connect /kə'nekt/ *vt* ① po|łączyć, z|łączyć *[end, hose]* (**to sth** z czymś); do|łącz|yć, -áć *[carriage, coach]* (**to sth** do czegoś) ② *[road, railway]* po|łączyć *[place, road]* (**to** or **with sth** z czymś) ③ pod|łączyć, -áć *[appliance]* (**to sth** do czegoś); pod|łącz|yć, -áć *[phone]*
connected /kə'nektɪd/ *adj* ① *[story, sentence]* logicznie powiązany (**to** or **with sth** z czymś); **everything ~ with music** wszystko, co ma związek z muzyką ② (in family) spokrewniony (**to sb** z kimś)
connecting /kə'nektɪŋ/ *adj [room]* przejściowy; **~ flight** połączenie
connection /kə'nekʃn/ *n* ① (link) związek *m*; **in ~ with sth** w związku z czymś ② **~s** (contacts) znajomości *f pl*; **to have useful ~s** mieć znajomości or kontakty ③ (to mains) podłączenie *n* ④ (in transportation) połączenie *n* ⑤ (to network) podłączenie *n* (**to sth** do czegoś); (to number) połączenie *n* (**to sb/sth** z kimś/czymś); **bad ~** zła linia, zakłócenia na linii ⑥ Comput połączenie *n*; **Internet ~** połączenie z Internetem
connive /kə'naɪv/ *vi* **to ~ at sth** tolerować coś; **to ~ (with sb) to do sth** zrobić coś w zmowie (z kimś)
connoisseur /ˌkɒnə'sɜː(r)/ *n* koneser *m*, znawca *m*
conquer /'kɒŋkə(r)/ *vt* podbi|ć, -jáć *[territory, nation]*; pokon|ać, -ywáć *[enemy]*; po|radzić sobie z (czymś) *[unemployment]*
conqueror /'kɒŋkərə(r)/ *n* zdobywca *m*
conquest /'kɒŋkwest/ *n* podbój *m*
conscience /'kɒnʃəns/ *n* sumienie *n*; **to have a guilty/clear ~** mieć nieczyste/czyste sumienie
conscientious /ˌkɒnʃɪ'enʃəs/ *adj [person, work]* sumienny
conscientious objector, CO *n* obdżektor *m*
conscious /'kɒnʃəs/ *adj* ① (aware) świadomy; **to be ~ of sth** być świadomym czegoś ② (deliberate) *[decision]* świadomy; *[irony]* zamierzony ③ (awake) przytomny
consciousness /'kɒnʃəsnɪs/ *n* **to lose/regain ~** stracić/odzyskać przytomność
conscript /'kɒnskrɪpt/ *n* poborowy *m*
conscription /kən'skrɪpʃn/ *n* pobór *m*
consecrate /'kɒnsɪkreɪt/ *vt* poświęc|lić, -áć, konsekrować
consecutive /kən'sekjʊtɪv/ *adj* kolejny
consensus /kən'sensəs/ *n* konsensus *m* (**about** or **on sth** co do czegoś); **there is no ~ among the experts** wśród ekspertów nie ma zgody
consent /kən'sent/ **I** *n* pozwolenie *n*, przyzwolenie *n*; **by common ~** za powszechną aprobatą; **by mutual ~** za obopólną zgodą; **age of ~** wiek, w którym prawo dopuszcza współżycie seksualne i zawarcie małżeństwa **II** *vi* z|godzić, -adzáć się; **to ~ to to sb doing sth** zgodzić się, żeby ktoś coś zrobił
consequence /'kɒnsɪkwəns, US -kwens/ *n* ① (result) konsekwencja *f*, następstwo *n*; **as a ~ of sth** wskutek czegoś *[change, process]*; w następstwie czegoś *[event]* ② (importance) znaczenie *n*, waga *f*
consequently /'kɒnsɪkwəntlɪ, US -kwentlɪ/ *adv* w konsekwencji
conservation /ˌkɒnsə'veɪʃn/ *n* ochrona *f*, konserwacja *f*; **energy ~** oszczędzanie energii
conservation area *n* zespół *m* zabytkowy objęty ochroną konserwatora
conservationist /ˌkɒnsə'veɪʃənɪst/ *n* działacz *m*, -ka *f* ruchu na rzecz ochrony przyrody
conservative /kən'sɜːvətɪv/ **I** *n* konserwatyst|a *m*, -ka *f* **II** *adj* ① *[party]* konserwatywny ② *[taste]* tradycyjny; *[style]* klasyczny
Conservative Party *n* GB Partia *f* Konserwatywna
conservatory /kən'sɜːvətrɪ, US -tɔːrɪ/ *n* ① (for plants) oranżeria *f* ② Mus konserwatorium *n*
conserve /kən'sɜːv/ **I** *n* konfitura *f* **II** *vt* ① (protect) chronić *[forests, wildlife, remains, ruins]* ② (save up) oszczędz|lić, -áć *[resources, energy]*
consider /kən'sɪdə(r)/ *vt* ① (give thought to, study) rozważ|yć, -áć *[options, problem]*; rozpat|rzyć, -rywáć *[evidence, facts, offer]* ② (take into account) wziąć, brać pod uwagę *[risk, cost]*; mieć wzgląd na (kogoś/coś) *[person, feelings]* ③ (envisage) **to ~ doing sth** zastanawiać się nad zrobieniem czegoś ④ (regard) uważać; **to ~ that...** uważać, że...; **to ~ oneself (to be) a genius** mieć się za geniusza
considerable /kən'sɪdərəbl/ *adj* znaczący
considerate /kən'sɪdərət/ *adj [person]* liczący się z innymi; *[behaviour, remark]* taktowny; **to be ~ towards sb** być uprzejmym wobec kogoś
consideration /kənˌsɪdə'reɪʃn/ *n* ① (regard) wzgląd *m* (**for sb/sth** na kogoś/coś); **to do sth out of ~ for sb** zrobić coś przez wzgląd na kogoś;

to give sth careful ~ gruntownie coś rozważyć; **to take sth into** ~ wziąć coś pod uwagę ☐ (fee) **for a** ~ za wynagrodzeniem

considering /kən'sɪdərɪŋ/ **[]** *prep* zważywszy **[]** *adv* mimo wszystko

consign /kən'saɪn/ *vt* wys|łać, -yłać *[goods]*

consignment /kən'saɪnmənt/ *n* (sending) wysyłka *f*, ekspedycja *f*; (goods) partia *f* towaru, przesyłka *f*

consist /kən'sɪst/ *vi* **to** ~ **of sth** składać się z czegoś; **to** ~ **in sth/doing sth** polegać na czymś/ na robieniu czegoś

consistency /kən'sɪstənsɪ/ *n* ☐ (texture) konsysten- cja *f* ☐ (coherence) konsekwencja *f*

consistent /kən'sɪstənt/ *adj* ☐ *[growth, level, quality]* stały ☐ *[attempts, demands]* uporczywy ☐ *[argument]* logiczny, spójny; ~ **with sth** *[ac- count, belief]* zgodny z czymś

consistently /kən'sɪstəntlɪ/ *adv* (invariably) kon- sekwentnie, stale; (repeatedly) systematycznie

consolation /ˌkɒnsə'leɪʃn/ *n* pociecha *f* (**to sb** dla kogoś)

console **[]** /'kɒnsəʊl/ *n* ☐ (controls) konsola *f*, konsoleta *f* ☐ (cabinet) szafka *f* **[]** *vt* pociesz|yć, -ać (**with sth** czymś)

consolidate /kən'sɒlɪdeɪt/ *vt* ☐ utrwal|ić, -ać *[knowledge]*; um|ocnić, -acniać *[position]* ☐ s|konsolidować, scal|ić, -ać *[resources]*; poł|ączyć *[companies]*

consonant /'kɒnsənənt/ *n* spółgłoska *f*

consortium /kən'sɔːtɪəm/ *n* konsorcjum *n*

conspicuous /kən'spɪkjʊəs/ *adj [feature, sign]* widoczny; *[garment]* rzucający się w oczy; **to be** ~ zwracać na siebie uwagę

conspiracy /kən'spɪrəsɪ/ *n* spisek *m*

conspirator /kən'spɪrətə(r)/ *n* konspirator *m*, -ka *f*

conspire /kən'spaɪə(r)/ *vi* spiskować (**against sb** przeciwko komuś); *[circumstances, weather]* sprzy- si|ąc, -ęgać się (**against sb** przeciwko komuś)

constable /'kʌnstəbl, US 'kɒn-/ *n* GB posterunko- wy *m*

constant /'kɒnstənt/ *adj [problem, care, tempera- ture]* stały; *[questions, attempts]* ciągły; *[threat, re- minder]* nieustanny; *[companion]* nieodłączny

constantly /'kɒnstəntlɪ/ *adv* stale

constellation /ˌkɒnstə'leɪʃn/ *n* gwiazdozbiór *m*, konstelacja *f*

constipated /'kɒnstɪpeɪtɪd/ *adj* cierpiący na zaparcie

constipation /ˌkɒnstɪ'peɪʃn/ *n* zaparcie *n*

constituency /kən'stɪtjʊənsɪ/ *n* (district) okręg *m* wyborczy; (voters) elektorat *m*

constituent /kən'stɪtjʊənt/ *n* ☐ (in politics) wy- borca *m* ☐ (element) część *f* składowa

constitute /'kɒnstɪtjuːt/ *vt* stanowić

constitution /ˌkɒnstɪ'tjuːʃn, US -'tuːʃn/ *n* kon- stytucja *f*

constitutional /ˌkɒnstɪ'tjuːʃənl, US -'tuː-/ *adj* konstytucyjny

constraint /kən'streɪnt/ *n* ograniczenie *n*

constrict /kən'strɪkt/ *vt* zwę|zić, -żać *[blood vessel]*; hamować *[flow]*; ogranicz|yć, -ać *[movement]*; utrud- ni|ć, -ać *[breathing]*

construct /kən'strʌkt/ *vt* z|budować

construction /kən'strʌkʃn/ *n* ☐ (act of building) budowa *f* ☐ (also ~ **industry**) budownictwo *n*

construction site *n* plac *m* budowy

construction worker *n* robotnik *m* budowlany

constructive /kən'strʌktɪv/ *adj* konstruktywny

consul /'kɒnsl/ *n* konsul *m*

consulate /'kɒnsjʊlət, US -səl-/ *n* konsulat *m*

consult /kən'sʌlt/ **[]** *vt* po|radzić się (kogoś) *[expert]* (**about sth** w sprawie czegoś) **[]** *vi* s|konsultować się (**about sth** w sprawie czegoś)

consultancy /kən'sʌltənsɪ/ *n* (also ~ **firm**) firma *f* konsultingowa

consultant /kən'sʌltənt/ *n* ☐ (expert) doradca *m*, konsultant *m*, -ka *f* (**in** or **on sth** do spraw czegoś) ☐ GB (doctor) ≈ lekarz *m* specjalista *(najwyższego stopnia)*

consultation /ˌkɒnsl'teɪʃn/ *n* (for advice) konsul- tacja *f*; (for discussion) narada *f* (**about sth** w sprawie czegoś)

consumables /kən'sjuːməblz, US -'suːm-/ *npl* towary *m pl* konsumpcyjne

consume /kən'sjuːm, US -'suːm-/ *vt* ☐ z|jeść, z|jadać *[food]*; wy|pić, wy|pijać *[drink]*; zuży|ć, -wać *[fuel]* ☐ *[envy]* zżerać; *[desire]* trawić *[person]*; **he was** ~ **d by** or **with guilt** dręczyły go wyrzuty sumienia

consumer /kən'sjuːmə(r), US -'suːm-/ *n* konsu- ment *m*, -ka *f*; (of electricity, gas) odbiorca *m*

consumer advice *n* porady *f pl* dla konsumen- tów

consumer goods *n* towary *m pl* konsumpcyjne

consumer protection *n* ochrona *f* konsumenta

consumer society *n* społeczeństwo *n* konsump- cyjne

consummate /'kɒnsəmeɪt/ *vt* s|konsumować *[marriage]*

consumption /kən'sʌmpʃn/ *n* (of food, alcohol) spożycie *n*; (of goods) konsumpcja *f*; (of fuel, energy) zużycie *n*

contact **[]** /'kɒntækt/ *n* ☐ (link) kontakt *m* (**with sb** z kimś); **to be in** ~ być w kontakcie; **to make** ~ nawiązać kontakt ☐ (acquaintance) znajo- m|y *m*, -a *f*; (professional) kontakt *m*, kontakty *m pl* infml **[]** /kən'tækt, 'kɒntækt/ *vt* s|kontaktować się z (kimś)

contact lens *n* soczewka *f* kontaktowa; ~ **es** szkła kontaktowe

contagious /kən'teɪdʒəs/ *adj* zaraźliwy

contain /kən'teɪn/ *vt* [1] (hold) zawierać *[amount, ingredients, mistakes, information]* [2] (curb) powstrzym|ać, -ywać *[blaze]*; zapobie|c, -gać rozprzestrzenianiu się (czegoś) *[epidemic]*; ogranicz|yć, -áć *[costs]*

container /kən'teɪnə(r)/ *n* (for food, liquid) pojemnik *m*; (for waste, for transporting) kontener *m*

contaminate /kən'tæmɪneɪt/ *vt* zanieczy|ścić, -szczać

contamination /kən,tæmɪ'neɪʃn/ *n* skażenie *n*, zanieczyszczenie *n*

contemplate /'kɒntəmpleɪt/ *vt* [1] (consider) rozważ|yć, -áć [2] (look at) podziwiać

contemporary /kən'temprərɪ, US -pərerɪ/ **I** *n* (of same age) rówieśni|k *m*, -czka *f*; (living at same time) współczesn|y *m*, -a *f*
II *adj* (present-day) współczesny; (up-to-date) nowoczesny; (of same period) *[writer]* współczesny; *[style]* z tej samej epoki

contempt /kən'tempt/ *n* pogarda *f*; **to feel ~ for sb/sth** odczuwać pogardę dla kogoś/czegoś; **to hold sb/sth in ~** gardzić *or* pogardzać kimś/czymś; **~ of court** obraza *f* sądu

contemptible /kən'temptəbl/ *adj* godny pogardy

contemptuous /kən'temptjʊəs/ *adj* pogardliwy

contend /kən'tend/ **I** *vt* utrzymywać (**that...** że...)
II *vi* [1] (deal) zmagać się (**with sth** z czymś) [2] (compete) rywalizować (**for sth** o coś)

contender /kən'tendə(r)/ *n* [1] Sport zawodni|k *m*, -czka *f* [2] (for post) kandydat *m*, -ka *f* (**for sth** na coś)

content **I** /'kɒntent/ *n* [1] (quantity) zawartość *f* [2] (meaning) treść *f*; **table** *or* **list of ~s** spis rzeczy
II *adj* zadowolony (**with sth** z czegoś)

contented /kən'tentɪd/ *adj* zadowolony (**with sth** z czegoś); **a ~ feeling** uczucie zadowolenia

contention /kən'tenʃn/ *n* [1] (opinion) twierdzenie *n* [2] (dispute) spór *m* (**about sth** o coś) [3] (competition) rywalizacja *f*

contentment /kən'tentmənt/ *n* zadowolenie *n*

contest **I** /'kɒntest/ *n* [1] (competition) konkurs *m*; Sport zawody *plt* [2] (struggle) walka *f*
II /kən'test/ *vt* [1] za|kwestionować *[decision, will]* [2] (compete for) walczyć o zwycięstwo w (czymś) *[match]*

contestant /kən'testənt/ *n* Sport zawodni|k *m*, -czka *f*; (in fight) przeciwni|k *m*, -czka *f*; (for job, in election) kandydat *m*, -ka *f*

context /'kɒntekst/ *n* kontekst *m*

continent /'kɒntɪnənt/ *n* [1] kontynent *m* [2] **the Continent** GB kontynent *m* europejski *(bez Wysp Brytyjskich)*

continental /,kɒntɪ'nentl/ [1] kontynentalny [2] GB *[philosophy, universities]* Europy kontynentalnej; **~ holiday** wakacje na kontynencie (europejskim)

continental breakfast *n* śniadanie *n* kontynentalne *(złożone z kawy, pieczywa, masła, dżemu)*

continental quilt *n* GB kołdra *f*

contingency /kən'tɪndʒənsɪ/ *n* ewentualność *f*

contingency fund *n* rezerwa *f* budżetowa

contingency plan *n* plan *m* awaryjny

continual /kən'tɪnjʊəl/ *adj* ciągły, nieustanny

continually /kən'tɪnjʊəlɪ/ *adv* ciągle, nieustannie

continuation /kən,tɪnjʊ'eɪʃn/ *n* kontynuacja *f*; (in book) ciąg *m* dalszy; (of route) przedłużenie *n*

continue /kən'tɪnjuː/ **I** *vt* kontynuować; **to ~ to do sth** *or* **doing sth** nadal robić coś
II *vi* *[noise, debate, strike]* trwać; **to ~ with sth** kontynuować coś *[treatment]*; wykonywać coś nadal *[duties]*

continuity /,kɒntɪ'njuːɪtɪ/ *n* ciągłość *f*

continuous /kən'tɪnjʊəs/ *adj* [1] *[growth, decline, care]* stały; *[noise]* nieustanny; *[line]* ciągły; **~ assessment** GB ocena na podstawie pracy przez cały okres nauki [2] *[tense]* ciągły

continuously /kən'tɪnjʊəslɪ/ *adv* ciągle

contort /kən'tɔːt/ *vt* po|wykręcać, po|wykrzywiać

contortion /kən'tɔːʃn/ *n* (of face) grymas *m*; (of muscles) skurcz *m*

contour /'kɒntʊə(r)/ *n* [1] (outline) kontur *m*, zarys *m* [2] (**also ~ line**) poziomica *f*

contraband /'kɒntrəbænd/ *n* kontrabanda *f*

contraception /,kɒntrə'sepʃn/ *n* antykoncepcja *f*

contraceptive /,kɒntrə'septɪv/ **I** *n* środek *m* antykoncepcyjny
II *adj* antykoncepcyjny

contract **I** /'kɒntrækt/ *n* kontrakt *m*, umowa *f*
II /kən'trækt/ *vt* [1] (develop) zara|zić, -żać się (czymś) *[disease, virus]* [2] **to be ~ed to do sth** być związanym umową na zrobienie czegoś
III /kən'trækt/ *vi* [1] **to ~ to do sth** zawrzeć umowę na zrobienie czegoś [2] *[muscle, wood]* s|kurczyć się

contraction /kən'trækʃn/ *n* kurczenie się *n*

contract killer *n* płatny morderca *m*

contractor /kən'træktə(r)/ *n* [1] (business) przedsiębiorca *m* *(zwykle budowlany)* [2] (worker) wykonawca *m*

contradict /,kɒntrə'dɪkt/ *vt, vi* zaprzecz|yć, -áć (komuś/czemuś)

contradiction /,kɒntrə'dɪkʃn/ *n* sprzeczność *f*

contradictory /,kɒntrə'dɪktərɪ/ *adj* sprzeczny

contraflow /'kɒntrəfləʊ/ GB *n* ruch dwukierunkowy wprowadzony czasowo na jednym pasie drogi

contraindication /,kɒntraɪndɪ'keɪʃn/ *n* przeciwwskazanie *n*

contrary /'kɒntrərɪ, US -trerɪ/ **I** *n* przeciwieństwo *n*; **on the ~** (wręcz) przeciwnie; **unless there is evidence to the ~** o ile nie pojawią się dowody świadczące przeciw temu
II *adj* [1] *[ideas, views]* sprzeczny [2] /kən'treərɪ/ *[person]* przekorny
III **contrary to** *prep phr* wbrew (czemuś)

contrast /'kɒntrɑːst, US -træst/ **[** *n* kontrast *m*; **by** or **in** ~ (however) natomiast; **in** ~ **to sb/sth, by** ~ **with sb/sth** w odróżnieniu od kogoś/czegoś, w przeciwieństwie do kogoś/czegoś **[II]** *vt* porówn|ać, -ywać *[things, persons]*; **to** ~ **sth with sth** zestawiać coś z czymś **[III]** *vi* (differ) różnić się (**with sth** od czegoś); (show contrast) kontrastować (**with sth** z czymś)

contrasting /kɒn'trɑːstɪŋ/ *adj [colour]* kontrastujący, kontrastowy; *[view]* pełen kontrastów

contribute /kən'trɪbjuːt/ **[** *vt* **1** wpłac|ić, -ać *[sum]* (**to sth** na coś); **to** ~ **£50** wnieść 50 funtów **2** (donate) ofiarow|ać, -ywać *[money, gift]* (**to** or **towards sth** na coś) **3** *[writer]* na|pisać *[article]* **[II]** *vi* **1** (be a factor in) **to** ~ **to** or **towards sth** przyczyni|ć, -ać się do czegoś *[change, downfall]* **2** (participate) **to** ~ **to sth** włączyć się w coś *[community life, research]*; (to newspaper, programme) współpracować (**to sth** z czymś) **3** (give money) **to** ~ **to sth** w|esprzeć, -spierać finansowo coś *[charity]* **4** (pay) **to** ~ **to sth** wpłac|ić, -ać (pieniądze) na coś *[pension fund]*

contribution /ˌkɒntrɪ'bjuːʃn/ *n* **1** (to tax, pension, insurance) składka *f* (**to** or **towards sth** na coś) **2** (to charity, campaign) datek *m*, dar *m* (**to** or **towards sth** na coś); **to make a** ~ ofiarować datek **3** (role played) **his/her** ~ **to sth** jego/jej udział w czymś *[success, undertaking]*; jego/jej wkład w coś *[science]* **4** (to programme) współudział *m*; (to magazine) artykuł *m*

contributor /kən'trɪbjʊtə(r)/ *n* (to charity) ofiarodaw|ca *m*, -czyni *f*; (in discussion) uczestni|k *m*, -czka *f*; (to magazine) współpracowni|k *m*, -czka *f*; (to book) współautor *m*, -ka *f*

con trick *n* kant *m*, szwindel *m* infml

contrive /kən'traɪv/ *vt* (arrange) za|aranżować; **to** ~ **to do sth** zdołać coś zrobić

contrived /kən'traɪvd/ *adj* **1** *[meeting, coincidence]* zaaranżowany **2** *[plot]* naciągany infml; *[style]* nienaturalny

control /kən'trəʊl/ **[** *n* **1** (domination) panowanie *n* (**of sb/sth** nad kimś/czymś); (of operation, project) nadzór *m* (**of sth** nad czymś); (of life, fate) wpływ *m* (**of** or **over sb/sth** na kogoś/coś); **to be in** ~ **of a territory** *[army]* mieć kontrolę na obszarze; **to be in** ~ **of an operation/a project** kierować operacją/przedsięwzięciem; **to be in** ~ **of a problem** radzić sobie z problemem; **to bring** or **get sth under** ~ opanować coś *[fire, riot]*; **to lose** ~ **of sth** stracić nad czymś panowanie or kontrolę **2** (physical mastery) panowanie *n* (nad czymś) *[vehicle, machine]* **3** (lever, switch) przełącznik *m*; **to be at the** ~ **s** *[pilot]* siedzieć za sterem **[II]** *vt* **1** (dominate) kierować (czymś) *[traffic, project]*; mieć pakiet kontrolny (czegoś) *[company]*; kontrolować *[territory]*; panować nad (czymś) *[situation]* **2** (discipline) opanow|ać, -ywać *[inflation,

fire]; za|panować nad (kimś/czymś) *[person, animal, emotion]*; zwalcz|yć, -ać *[epidemic]*; powstrzym|ać, -ywać *[laughter]*; **to** ~ **oneself** kontrolować się, panować nad sobą **3** (operate) sterować (czymś) *[machine, boat]*; kierować (czymś) *[vehicle]*; pilotować *[plane]*; panować nad (czymś) *[ball]* **4** (regulate) regulować *[speed, temperature]*; kontrolować *[immigration, trade]*

control panel *n* (for car) deska *f* rozdzielcza; (for plane) tablica *f* sterownicza; (on television) panel *m* sterowania; (on machine) pulpit *m* sterowniczy

control room *n* reżyserka *f*

control tower *n* wieża *f* kontroli lotów

controversial /ˌkɒntrə'vɜːʃl/ *adj* kontrowersyjny

controversy /'kɒntrəvɜːsɪ, kən'trɒvəsɪ/ *n* kontrowersja *f*, spór *m*

conundrum /kə'nʌndrəm/ *n* zagadka *f*

convalesce /ˌkɒnvə'les/ *vi* przychodzić do zdrowia

convene /kən'viːn/ *vt* zwoł|ać, -ywać *[meeting]*

convenience /kən'viːnɪəns/ *n* wygoda *f*; **the** ~ **of sth** zaleta or dogodność czegoś *[method]*; praktyczność *f* czegoś *[device]*; **for (the sake of)** ~ dla wygody; **at your** ~ w dogodnym dla ciebie czasie

convenience foods *npl* dania *n pl* gotowe

convenient /kən'viːnɪənt/ *adj* **1** *[time, place]* dogodny; **to be** ~ **for sb** być wygodnym dla kogoś **2** (useful, practical) praktyczny **3** *[shops]* blisko położony; *[chair]* stojący obok

convent /'kɒnvənt, US -vent/ *n* klasztor *m* żeński

convention /kən'venʃn/ *n* **1** (meeting) kongres *m*, zjazd *m* **2** (social norms) konwenanse *m pl*

conventional /kən'venʃənl/ *adj* konwencjonalny

converge /kən'vɜːdʒ/ *vi [lines, roads]* zbiegać się

conversant /kən'vɜːsnt/ *adj* **to be** ~ **with sth** doskonale coś znać

conversation /ˌkɒnvə'seɪʃn/ *n* rozmowa *f*

converse /'kɒnvɜːs/ *vi* po|rozmawiać (**about sb/ sth** o kimś/czymś)

conversion /kən'vɜːʃn, US kən'vɜːrʒn/ *n* **1** (of currency, measurement) przeliczanie *n*; ~ **from sth into sth** przeliczanie or zamiana czegoś na coś **2** (of building) adaptacja *f*, przebudowa *f* **3** (religious) nawrócenie *n*

conversion rate *n* kurs *m* wymiany

convert **[** /'kɒnvɜːt/ *n* neofit|a *m*, -ka *f* **[II]** /kən'vɜːt/ *vt* **1** (change into sth else) przer|obić, -abiać, przelicz|yć, -ać *[currency, measurement]* (**to** or **into sth** na coś); za|adaptować, przer|obić, -abiać *[barn, loft]* (**to** or **into sth** na coś) **2** (change views of) nawr|ócić, -acać *[person]* (**to sth** na coś) **[III]** /kən'vɜːt/ *vi* **1** *[sofa, device]* rozkładać się; **the sofa** ~**s into a bad** kanapa rozkłada się do spania **2** *[person]* zmieni|ć, -ać wyznanie; (in politics) zmieni|ć, -ać orientację polityczną

convertible /kən'vɜːtəbl/ *n* kabriolet *m*

convex /'kɒnveks/ *adj* wypukły

convey /kən'veɪ/ *vt* 1 *[person]* przekaz|ać, -ywać *[message, thanks, condolences]* (**to sb** komuś); wyra|zić, -żać *[feeling]*; **to** ~ **to sb that...** przekazać komuś, że... 2 *[words, images]* odda|ć, -wać, wyra|zić, -żać *[mood, impression]* 3 (transport) *[vehicle]* przew|ieźć, -ozić; *[pipes]* doprowadz|ić, -ać

conveyancing /kən'veɪənsɪŋ/ *n* przeniesienie *n* tytułu własności

conveyor belt /kən'veɪə(r) belt/ *n* przenośnik *m* taśmowy; (for luggage) taśmociąg *m* bagażowy

convict 1 /'kɒnvɪkt/ *n* (imprisoned criminal) więz|zień *m*, -źniarka *f*; (deported criminal) zesłaniec *m* 2 /kən'vɪkt/ *vt* uzna|ć, -wać za winnego (**of sth/ doing sth** czegoś/popełnienia czegoś)

conviction /kən'vɪkʃn/ *n* 1 (by jury) skazanie *n* (**for sth** za coś) 2 (belief) przekonanie *n* (**that...** że...)

convince /kən'vɪns/ *vt* 1 przekon|ać, -ywać (**of sth/that...** o czymś/że...) 2 nam|ówić, -awiać (**to do sth** do zrobienia czegoś)

convincing /kən'vɪnsɪŋ/ *adj [account, evidence]* przekonujący; *[victory, lead]* zdecydowany

convoy /'kɒnvɔɪ/ *n* konwój *m*

convulsion /kən'vʌlʃn/ *n* drgawki *plt*

coo /ku:/ *vi* gruchać

cook /kʊk/ 1 *n* kucha|rz *m*, -rka *f*
2 *vt* u|gotować *[food, meal]* (**for sb** dla kogoś)
3 *vi [person]* gotować; *[vegetable, meal]* gotować się

cook-chill foods /ˌkʊk'tʃɪlfu:dz/ *npl* dania *n pl* gotowe mrożone

cooker /'kʊkə(r)/ *n* GB kuchenka *f*

cookery book /'kʊkərɪ'bʊk/ *n* książka *f* kucharska

cookie /'kʊkɪ/ *n* 1 (biscuit) kruche ciasteczko *n*, herbatnik *m* 2 Comput cookie *n inv*

cooking /'kʊkɪŋ/ *n* gotowanie *n*

cooking apple *n* jabłko *n* do gotowania lub pieczenia

cooking chocolate *n* czekolada *f* do ciast i deserów

cool /ku:l/ 1 *adj* 1 (coldness) chłód *m* 2 *infml* (calm) spokój *m*; **to keep one's** ~ (stay calm) zachować spokój; (not get angry) nie dać się wyprowadzić z równowagi; **to lose one's** ~ (get angry) wyjść z siebie *infml*; (panic) stracić głowę *infml*
2 *adj* 1 *[day, drink, water, weather]* chłodny; *[dress]* lekki; *[colour]* zimny 2 (calm) spokojny 3 (unfriendly) chłodny, oziębły 4 (casual) na luzie *infml* 5 *infml* (trendy) *[clothes, car]* odjazdowy *infml*
3 *vt* o|studzić *[soup]*; schł|odzić, -adzać *[wine]*; ochł|odzić, -adzać *[room]*
4 *vi* 1 (get colder) *[iron, soup]* o|stygnąć 2 (subside) *[enthusiasm, friendship]* o|stygnąć
■ **cool down**: *[engine, water]* o|stygnąć; fig *[person]* ochłonąć; *[situation]* uspok|oić, -ajać się

cool bag *n* GB torba *f* z izolacją cieplną

cool box *n* GB lodówka *f* turystyczna

cooling-off period /ˌku:lɪŋ'ɒfpɪərɪəd/ *n* okres, w którym strony mogą odstąpić od umowy; (in industrial relations) przerwa *f* w negocjacjach

coop /ku:p/ *n* (also **chicken** ~) kojec *m*, klatka *f*
■ **coop up**: ~ **[sb/sth] up** u|więzić, zam|knąć, -ykać

cooperate /kəʊ'ɒpəreɪt/ *vi* współpracować (**with sb** z kimś); **to** ~ **in sth/in doing sth** współpracować w czymś/przy robieniu czegoś

cooperation /kəʊˌɒpə'reɪʃn/ *n* współpraca *f* (**on sth** w czymś)

cooperative /kəʊ'ɒpərətɪv/ 1 *n* 1 (organization) spółdzielnia *f* 2 US (apartment house) ≈ spółdzielczy blok *m* mieszkalny
2 *adj [effort]* wspólny; *[organization]* spółdzielczy; *[person]* skłonny do współpracy

coordinate /ˌkəʊ'ɔ:dɪnət/ 1 *n* współrzędna *f*
2 /ˌkəʊ'ɔ:dɪneɪt/ *vt* s|koordynować *[movements]*; uzg|odnić, -adniać *[response]* (**with sb** z kimś)

coordinates /ˌkəʊ'ɔ:dɪnəts/ *npl* (clothes) elementy *m pl* stroju (*które można dowolnie zestawiać*)

coordination /ˌkəʊˌɔ:dɪ'neɪʃn/ *n* koordynacja *f*

coordinator /ˌkəʊ'ɔ:dɪneɪtə(r)/ *n* koordynator *m*, -ka *f*

cope /kəʊp/ *vi* po|radzić sobie; **to** ~ **with sb/sth** uporać się z czymś *[work]*; sprostać czemuś *[demand]*; poradzić sobie z kimś/czymś *[person, disaster]*; zn|ieść, -osić *[death, depression]*

Copenhagen /ˌkəʊpn'heɪgən/ *prn* Kopenhaga *f*

copious /'kəʊpɪəs/ *adj* 1 (plentiful) *[crop, snow]* obfity 2 (generous) *[serving]* obfity; *[quantity]* pokaźny

cop-out /'kɒpaʊt/ *n infml* wykręt *m*

copper /'kɒpə(r)/ *n* 1 (metal) miedź *f* 2 GB infml (policeman) glina *m*, gliniarz *m* infml 3 GB infml (coin) miedziak *m*

copy /'kɒpɪ/ 1 *n* 1 (duplicate) kopia *f* 2 (of book, newspaper, record) egzemplarz *m*
2 *vt* s|kopiować *[document]*
3 *vi* odpis|ać, -ywać (**from sb** od kogoś)
■ **copy down, copy out**: przepis|ać, -ywać

copyright /'kɒpɪraɪt/ *n* prawo *n* autorskie

coral /'kɒrəl, US 'kɔ:rəl/ *n* koral *m*

cord /kɔ:d/ 1 *n* sznur *m*, sznurek *m*
2 **cords** *npl* infml (also **corduroys**) sztruksy *plt* infml

cordial /'kɔ:dɪəl, US 'kɔ:rdʒəl/ 1 *n* 1 (fruit juice) syrop *m* owocowy 2 US (liqueur) likier *m*
2 *adj* serdeczny (**to** or **with sb** wobec or w stosunku do kogoś)

cordless /'kɔ:dlɪs/ *adj [telephone, kettle]* bezprzewodowy

cordon /'kɔ:dn/ *n* kordon *m*
■ **cordon off**: zam|knąć, -ykać kordonem *[street]*; opas|ać, -ywać kordonem *[area]*

corduroy /'kɔːdərɔɪ/ n sztruks m
core /kɔː(r)/ n ⊡ (of apple) gniazdo n nasienne; (remains of apple) ogryzek m ⊡ (of problem) istota f, sedno n ⊡ **rotten to the** ~ zepsuty do szpiku kości; **English to the** ~ Anglik w każdym calu ⊡ (nuclear) rdzeń m ⊡ (small group) wąska grupa f, trzon m
Corfu /kɔː'fuː/ prn Korfu n inv
cork /kɔːk/ n korek m
corkscrew /'kɔːkskruː/ n korkociąg m
corn /kɔːn/ n ⊡ GB (wheat) pszenica f ⊡ US (maize) kukurydza f ⊡ (on foot) nagniotek m, odcisk m
cornea /'kɔːnɪə/ n rogówka f
corner /'kɔːnə(r)/ **Ⅰ** n ⊡ (in geometry) kąt m; (of street) róg m; **the house on the** ~ dom na rogu; **at the** ~ **of the street** na rogu ulicy; **to go round the** ~ skręcić za róg; **he lives just around the** ~ **from me** on mieszka dwa kroki ode mnie; **out of the** ~ **of one's eye** kątem oka ⊡ (bend) zakręt m; (sharp) wiraż m ⊡ (in boxing) narożnik m; (in football, hockey) korner m, rzut m rożny
Ⅱ vt ⊡ osacz|yć, -ać [person, animal]; przyp|rzeć, -ierać do muru [person] ⊡ z|monopolizować [market]
⟨IDIOMS⟩ **to be in a tight** ~ znaleźć się w trudnej sytuacji; **to cut** ~**s** (financially) robić oszczędności
corner shop n pobliski sklepik m
cornerstone /'kɔːnəstəʊn/ n kamień m węgielny
cornflour /'kɔːnflaʊə(r)/ n mąka f kukurydziana
cornflower /'kɔːnflaʊə(r)/ n chaber m, bława- tek m
Cornwall /'kɔːnwɔːl/ prn Kornwalia f
corny /'kɔːnɪ/ adj infml [joke] (old) oklepany infml; (feeble) kiepski; [song, film] ckliwy
coronary /'kɒrənrɪ, US 'kɔːrənerɪ/ n zawał m (serca)
coronation /ˌkɒrə'neɪʃn, US ˌkɔːr-/ n koronacja f
coroner /'kɒrənə(r), US 'kɔːr-/ n koroner m
corporal /'kɔːpərəl/ n kapral m
corporal punishment n kara f cielesna
corporate /'kɔːpərət/ adj ⊡ [accounts, funds, clients, employees] spółki ⊡ [action, decision] wspólny
corporate identity, corporate image n tożsamość f firmy
corporate raider n inwestor-drapieżca m
corporation /ˌkɔːpə'reɪʃn/ n korporacja f
corps /kɔː(r)/ n korpus m
corpse /kɔːps/ n zwłoki plt, trup m
correct /kə'rekt/ **Ⅰ** adj ⊡ [answer] poprawny; [amount, decision] właściwy; **what's the** ~ **time?** która dokładnie godzina? ⊡ [behaviour, dress] od- powiedni
Ⅱ vt poprawi|ć, -ać
correcting fluid n korektor m w płynie
correction /kə'rekʃn/ n ⊡ (act) poprawianie n ⊡ (on manuscript) poprawka f ⊡ (adjustment) korekta f

correspond /ˌkɒrɪ'spɒnd, US ˌkɔːr-/ vi ⊡ (match up) zg|odzić, -adzać się (**with sth** z czymś) ⊡ (be equivalent) odpowiadać (**to sth** czemuś) ⊡ (exchange letters) korespondować (**with sb** z kimś)
correspondence /ˌkɒrɪ'spɒndəns, US ˌkɔːr-/ n korespondencja f
correspondence course n kurs m korespon- dencyjny
correspondent /ˌkɒrɪ'spɒndənt, US ˌkɔːr-/ n korespondent m, -ka f
corresponding /ˌkɒrɪ'spɒndɪŋ, US ˌkɔːr-/ adj (matching) odpowiedni; (similar) analogiczny (**to sth** do czegoś)
corridor /'kɒrɪdɔː(r), US 'kɔːr-/ n korytarz m
corroborate /kə'rɒbəreɪt/ vt potwierdz|ić, -ać
corrode /kə'rəʊd/ **Ⅰ** vt s|korodować
Ⅱ vi ule|c, -gać korozji
corrosion /kə'rəʊʒn/ n (process) korozja f; (damage) rdza f
corrugated /'kɒrəgeɪtɪd, US 'kɔːr-/ adj pofałdo- wany
corrugated iron n blacha f stalowa falista
corrupt /kə'rʌpt/ **Ⅰ** adj ⊡ (dishonest) skorumpowa- ny ⊡ (depraved) niemoralny ⊡ Comput uszkodzony
Ⅱ vt (pervert) z|demoralizować; (through bribery) s|korumpować
corruption /kə'rʌpʃn/ n ⊡ (immorality) zepsucie n; (dishonesty) korupcja f
Corsica /'kɔːsɪkə/ prn Korsyka f
cosh /kɒʃ/ GB n pała f, pałka f
cosmetic /kɒz'metɪk/ **Ⅰ** n kosmetyk m
Ⅱ adj (superficial) kosmetyczny
cosmetic surgery n chirurgia f kosmetyczna
cosmonaut /'kɒzmənɔːt/ n kosmonaut|a m, -ka f
cosmopolitan /ˌkɒzmə'pɒlɪtn/ **Ⅰ** n kosmopoli- t|a m, -ka f
Ⅱ adj kosmopolityczny
cost /kɒst, US kɔːst/ **Ⅰ** n ⊡ (price) koszt m, cena f (**of sth** czegoś); **at no extra** ~ bez dodatkowych kosztów ⊡ fig koszt m, cena f; **at all** ~**s** za wszelką cenę; **I know to my** ~ **that...** przekonałem się na własnej skórze, że...
Ⅱ vt ⊡ kosztować; **how much does it** ~? ile to kosztuje?; **the TV will** ~ **£50 to repair** naprawa telewizora będzie kosztowała 50 funtów ⊡ (calculate cost of) s|kalkulować koszt (czegoś) [product, project]
co-star /'kəʊstɑː(r)/ **Ⅰ** n her ~ **is X** obok niej w głównej roli występuje X
Ⅱ vi **a film** ~**ring X and Y** film z udziałem X i Y
cost-cutting /'kɒstkʌtɪŋ, US 'kɔːst-/ n obniżanie n kosztów
cost-effective /ˌkɒstɪ'fektɪv, US ˌkɔːst-/ adj opła- calny
costly /'kɒstlɪ, US 'kɔːstlɪ/ adj kosztowny
cost of living n koszty m pl utrzymania
cost price n cena f po kosztach własnych

costume /ˈkɒstjuːm, US -tuːm/ n [1] (clothes) strój m [2] GB (also **swimming** ~) kostium m kąpielowy

costume jewellery GB, **costume jewelry** US n sztuczna biżuteria f

cosy, cozy US /ˈkəʊzɪ/ adj przytulny; [atmosphere] kameralny

cot /kɒt/ n [1] GB (for baby) łóżeczko n dziecinne [2] US (camp bed) łóżko n polowe

cot death n GB śmierć f łóżeczkowa

cottage /ˈkɒtɪdʒ/ n domek m; (thatched) chata f; **summer** ~ domek letniskowy

cottage cheese n ≈ twaróg m, twarożek m

cotton /ˈkɒtn/ n bawełna f

cotton bud n wacik m na patyczku

cotton wool n wata f

couch /kaʊtʃ/ n [1] (sofa) kanapa f [2] (doctor's) leżanka f; (psychoanalyst's) kozetka f

couch potato n infml leniwiec m infml fig

cough /kɒf, US kɔːf/ **I** n kaszel m; **to have a** ~ kasłać

II vi kasłać

cough mixture n syrop m na kaszel

could /kʊd, kəd/ modal aux [1] (be able to) móc; **I couldn't move** nie mogłem się ruszyć; **she couldn't come yesterday** nie mogła wczoraj przyjść [2] (know how to) potrafić; **he couldn't swim** nie umiał pływać; **she ~ speak four languages** mówiła czterema językami [3] (permission, requests, suggestions) **we ~ only go out at weekends** mogliśmy wychodzić tylko w weekendy; ~ **I speak to...?** czy mogę rozmawiać z...?; ~ **you help me?** czy mógłbyś mi pomóc? [4] (with verbs of perception) **I couldn't see a thing** nic nie widziałem; **they couldn't understand me** nie rozumieli mnie; **we ~ hear them laughing** słyszeliśmy, jak się śmieją [5] **you ~ have died** mogłeś zginąć; **they ~ have warned us** mogli nas ostrzec; **I ~ be wrong** być może się mylę; **if only I ~ start again** gdybym tylko mógł zacząć od nowa

council /ˈkaʊnsl/ n rada f; **the town** ~ rada miejska; **the Council of Europe** Rada Europy

council estate n osiedle n domów komunalnych

council house n komunalny dom m mieszkalny

council housing n budownictwo n komunalne

councillor, councilor US /ˈkaʊnsələ(r)/ n radny m, -a f

council tax n GB podatek m lokalny

counsel /ˈkaʊnsl/ **I** n adwokat m

II vt doradz|ić, -ać, radzić (komuś) (**about** or **on** sth na temat czegoś, w sprawie czegoś); (recommend) zalec|ić, -ać [caution, silence]

counselling, counseling US /ˈkaʊnsəlɪŋ/ n (psychological advice) pomoc f psychologa; (practical advice) doradztwo n, poradnictwo n; **bereavement** ~ pomoc dla osób, które straciły bliskich; **debt**

~ poradnictwo finansowe (dla osób mające problemy ze spłatą długów

counsellor, counselor US /ˈkaʊnsələ(r)/ n doradca m

count /kaʊnt/ **I** n [1] (act of counting) liczenie n; (of votes) obliczanie n; **at the last** ~ ostatecznie; **to keep (a) ~ of sth** liczyć coś; **to lose ~ of sth** stracić rachubę czegoś; **to be out for the** ~ infml zostać znokautowanym [2] (level) poziom m; **cholesterol** ~ poziom cholesterolu [3] (figure) liczba f [4] (in law) zarzut m; **she was found guilty on both** ~**s** została uznana winną obu zarzucanych jej czynów [5] (nobleman) hrabia m

II vt [1] po|liczyć, przelicz|yć, -ać [points, people]; wylicz|yć, -ać [reasons, causes]; **not** ~**ing the driver** nie licząc kierowcy [2] (consider) **to** ~ **sb as sth** uznać kogoś za coś

III vi [1] po|liczyć; **to** ~ **to 50** policzyć do pięćdziesięciu [2] (be relevant) liczyć się; **it's the thought that** ~**s** liczą się intencje

■ **count against**: działać na niekorzyść (kogoś)

■ **count on**: liczyć na (kogoś/coś) [person, event]; **don't** ~ **on it!** nie licz na to!

■ **count up**: podlicz|yć, -ać [points]; po|liczyć [money, boxes]

countdown /ˈkaʊntdaʊn/ n odliczanie n

counter /ˈkaʊntə(r)/ **I** n [1] (in shop) lada f, kontuar m; (in snack bar) bufet m, lada f; (in bank, post office) okienko n; (in bar, pub) bar m [2] (in game) żeton m

II vt odrzuc|ić, -ać [threat]; przeciwdziałać (czemuś) [effect, inflation]; odparow|ać, -ywać [blow]

III vi ripostować

IV counter to prep phr **to run** or **go to** ~ **sth** być sprzecznym z czymś

counteract /ˌkaʊntəˈrækt/ vt przeciwdziałać (czemuś) [decision, influence]; z|neutralizować [effects]

counter-attack /ˈkaʊntərətæk/ n kontratak m

counter-clockwise /ˌkaʊntəˈklɒkwaɪz/ US **I** adj przeciwny do kierunku ruchu wskazówek zegara

II adv przeciwnie do kierunku ruchu wskazówek zegara

counterfeit /ˈkaʊntəfɪt/ **I** adj [signature] sfałszowany; [note, money] fałszywy

II vt podr|obić, -abiać

counterfoil /ˈkaʊntəfɔɪl/ n odcinek m kontrolny

counterpart /ˈkaʊntəpɑːt/ n (of person, company, institution) odpowiednik m (**of** or **to** sb/sth kogoś/ czegoś)

counter-productive /ˌkaʊntəprəˈdʌktɪv/ adj przynoszący efekt przeciwny do zamierzonego

countersign /ˈkaʊntəsaɪn/ vt kontrasygnować

countess /ˈkaʊntɪs/ n hrabina f

countless /ˈkaʊntlɪs/ adj niezliczony; **on** ~ **occasions** niezliczoną ilość razy

country /'kʌntrɪ/ n ① kraj m; **developing/third world** ~ kraj rozwijający się/trzeciego świata; ~ **of birth** kraj rodzinny ② (also ~**side**) wieś f; **in the** ~ na wsi; **open** ~ otwarta przestrzeń; **across** ~ na przełaj

country club n ≈ ekskluzywny ośrodek m rekreacyjno-sportowy za miastem

country dancing n tańce m pl ludowe

country house n wiejska rezydencja f

country music n muzyka f country

countryside /'kʌntrɪsaɪd/ n wieś f

county /'kaʊntɪ/ n GB hrabstwo n; US ≈ hrabstwo n, powiat m

county council n GB władze f pl samorządowe hrabstwa

coup /kuː/ n (also ~ **d'état**) zamach m stanu; **to pull off a** ~ fig dokonać nie lada sztuki

couple /'kʌpl/ n ① para f; **young (married)** ~ młoda para ② **a** ~ **of people** (two) dwie osoby; (few) kilka or parę osób; **a** ~ **of times** parę razy

coupon /'kuːpɒn/ n ① (for goods) bon m, talon m; **petrol** ~ GB talon na benzynę ② (form) kupon m; **reply** ~ kupon zwrotny

courage /'kʌrɪdʒ/ n odwaga f

courageous /kə'reɪdʒəs/ adj odważny

courgette /kɔː'ʒet/ n cukinia f

courier /'kʊrɪə(r)/ n ① (also **travel** ~) (guide) pilot m wycieczki ② (for parcels, documents) kurier m, posłaniec m; (for drugs) kurier m

course /kɔːs/ ❶ n ① (of time) bieg m; (of event) przebieg m; **in the** ~ **of sth** w trakcie czegoś; **in the** ~ **of time** (at some future time) z czasem; (gradually) z biegiem czasu; **in due** ~ we właściwym czasie; ~ **of action** sposób or tryb postępowania ② (route) (of boat, plane) kurs m; **to be on** ~ trzymać kurs; **to go off** ~ zboczyć z kursu; **to change** ~ zmienić kierunek; [boat, plane] zmienić kurs ③ (classes) kurs m, zajęcia n pl (**in** or **of sth** z czegoś) ④ Med **a** ~ **of treatment** kuracja, leczenie ⑤ Sport (in golf) pole n golfowe; (in athletics) bieżnia f ⑥ (part of meal) danie n; **three-~ meal** posiłek trzydaniowy; **the main** ~ drugie danie ❷ **of course** adv phr oczywiście, naturalnie

course book n podręcznik m

coursework /'kɔːswɜːk/ n praca f okresowa

court /kɔːt/ ❶ n ① (of law) sąd m; **to go to** ~ (**over sth**) wystąpić na drogę sądową (w związku z czymś); **to take sb to** ~ pozwać kogoś do sądu ② (of sovereign) dwór m ③ (for tennis, squash) kort m; (for baseball) boisko n ④ (also **courty yard**) dziedziniec m ❷ vt zalecać się do (kogoś) [woman]; kokietować [voters]

court case n sprawa f sądowa, proces m

courteous /'kɜːtɪəs/ adj uprzejmy (**to** or **towards sb** wobec kogoś)

courtesy /'kɜːtəsɪ/ n uprzejmość f, grzeczność f

courthouse /'kɔːthaʊs/ n gmach m sądu

court-martial /ˌkɔːt'mɑːʃl/ vt oddać, -wać pod sąd wojskowy [soldier]

courtroom /'kɔːtruːm, -rʊm/ n sala f sądowa

courtyard /'kɔːtjɑːd/ n (of palace) dziedziniec m; (of house) podwórze n

cousin /'kʌzn/ n kuzyn m, -ka f

cove /kəʊv/ n (bay) zatoczka f

cover /'kʌvə(r)/ ❶ n ① (lid) nakrycie n, przykrycie n; (for furniture) pokrowiec m; (for cushion) poszewka f; (for duvet) poszwa f; (for typewriter) wieko n; (of book record) okładka f; ~**s** (bedclothes) przykrycie ② (shelter) schronienie n; **take** ~! kryć się!; **under** ~ pod dachem ③ (for teacher, doctor) zastępstwo n ④ (insurance) ochrona f ubezpieczeniowa (**for** or **against sth** od czegoś, na wypadek czegoś) ❷ vt ① przykryć, -wać, nakryć, -wać [table, bed] (**with sth** czymś); oblec, -kać [cushion] (**with sth** czymś); pokryć, -wać [surface, person, cake] (**with sth** czymś) ② (deal with) [author, text] objąć, -ejmować; [journalist] zająć, -mować się (czymś) ③ (in insurance) ubezpieczyć, -ać [person, property] (**for** or **against sth** od czegoś, na wypadek czegoś)

■ **cover for:** zastąpić, -ępować [employee]

■ **cover up:** ¶ ~ **to** ~ **up for sb/sth** kryć kogoś/coś infml [friend] ¶ ~ [sth] **up** zatuszować [mistake, truth]

coverage /'kʌvərɪdʒ/ n **live** ~ relacja na żywo; **newspaper** ~ relacja prasowa

cover charge n opłata f za wstęp

covering /'kʌvərɪŋ/ n ① (for wall, floor) pokrycie n ② (of snow, moss) warstwa f

covering letter n list m przewodni

cover note n (in insurance) nota f pokrycia

covert /'kʌvət, US 'kəʊvəːrt/ adj [operation] tajny; [glance] ukradkowy; [threat] zawoalowany

cover-up /'kʌvərʌp/ n próba f zatuszowania faktów

cover version n Mus nowe wykonanie n

covetous /'kʌvɪtəs/ adj chciwy

cow /kaʊ/ n krowa f

coward /'kaʊəd/ n tchórz m

cowardice /'kaʊədɪs/ n tchórzostwo n

cowardly /'kaʊədlɪ/ adj tchórzliwy

cowboy /'kaʊbɔɪ/ n ① US kowboj m ② (incompetent worker) partacz m

cower /'kaʊə(r)/ vi skulić się (ze strachu)

cox /kɒks/ ❶ n sternik m ❷ vt sterować (czymś) ❸ vi być sternikiem

coy /kɔɪ/ adj ① [smile, look] wstydliwy ② (reticent) nieskory (**about sth** do czegoś)

cozy adj US = **cosy**

crab /kræb/ n krab m

crack /kræk/ ❶ n ① (marked line) pęknięcie n, rysa f ② (in door, curtains, wall) szpara f; (in rock) pęknięcie n, szczelina f ③ (also ~ **cocaine**) crack m infml

4 (noise) trzask *m* 5 infml (attempt) próba *f*; **to have a ~ at doing sth** próbować coś zrobić

II *adj [troops, regiment]* wyborowy; *[player]* pierwszorzędny

III *vt* 1 s|powodować pęknięcie (czegoś) *[cup, bone]* 2 rozbi|ć, -jać *[egg]*; rozłup|ać, -ywać *[nut]*; **to ~ a safe** włamać się do sejfu; **let's ~ open a bottle of wine** napijmy się wina; **to ~ one's head open** infml rozwalić sobie głowę infml 3 **to ~ a code** złamać szyfr 4 trzas|nąć, -kać (czymś), strzel|ić, -ać (czymś) *[whip]*; wyłamywać (sobie) *[knuckles]*

IV *vi* 1 *[cup, wall, varnish]* pęk|nąć, -ać; *[skin, ground]* po|pękać 2 *[person]* zała|mać, -mywać się 3 *[knuckles]* za|trzeszczeć; *[twig]* trzas|nąć, -kać; *[whip]* strzel|ić, -ać 4 *[voice]* zała|mać, -ywać się

■ **crack down**: rozprawi|ć, -ać się (**on sth** z czymś)

crackdown /'krækdaʊn/ *n* rozprawa *f* (**on sth** z czymś); **the ~ on drugs** rozprawienie się z handlarzami narkotyków

cracker /'krækə(r)/ *n* 1 (biscuit) krakers *m* 2 (for Christmas) *strzelająca zabawka bożonarodzeniowa z niespodzianką*

crackle /'krækl/ **I** *n* (of fire, of radio) trzaski *m pl*

II *vi [sausages]* za|skwierczeć; *[radio]* trzeszczeć; *[twigs, fire]* trzaskać

cradle /'kreɪdl/ **I** *n* (for baby) kołyska *f*

II *vt* u|kołysać *[baby]*; **to ~ sth in one's arms** tulić coś w ramionach

craft /krɑːft, US kræft/ *n* 1 (skill) rzemiosło *n*, sztuka *f* 2 (handiwork) rękodzielnictwo *n*, rękodzieło *n*; **arts and ~s** rękodzieło artystyczne 3 (boat) statek *m*

craftsman /'krɑːftsmən, US 'kræft-/ *n* rzemieślnik *m*

crafty /'krɑːftɪ, US 'kræftɪ/ *adj* chytry, przebiegły

crag /kræg/ *n* grań *f*

cram /kræm/ **I** *vt* w|epchnąć, -pychać; **they ~med us all into one car** wepchnęli nas wszystkich do jednego samochodu; **a room ~med full of furniture** pokój zastawiony meblami

II *vi [student]* kuć, wkuwać infml (**for sth** do czegoś)

cramp /kræmp/ **I** *n* kurcz *m*, skurcz *m*

II *vt* za|hamować *[progress]*

cramped /kræmpt/ *adj* ciasny

cranberry /'krænbərɪ, US -berɪ/ *n* żurawina *f*

crane /kreɪn/ *n* żuraw *m*

crank /kræŋk/ *n* 1 infml (freak) maniak *m* 2 Tech korba *f*

crash /kræʃ/ **I** *n* 1 (noise) łoskot *m* 2 (accident) katastrofa *f*; **car ~** kraksa; **train ~** katastrofa kolejowa 3 (of stock market) krach *m*

II *vt* **she ~ed the car** rozbiła samochód

III *vi* 1 *[car, plane]* rozbi|ć, -jać się; *[vehicles, planes]* zderz|yć, -ać się (ze sobą); **to ~ into sb/sth** wpaść na kogoś/coś 2 *[company]* upa|ść, -dać, z|bankrutować; *[share prices]* spa|ść, -dać gwałtownie

■ **crash out** infml: (go to sleep) uderz|yć, -ać w kimono infml; (collapse) pa|ść, -dać

crash course *n* intensywny kurs *m*

crash diet *n* intensywna dieta *f* odchudzająca

crash helmet *n* kask *m*

crash landing *n* lądowanie *n* awaryjne

crass /kræs/ *adj [person]* prostacki; *[ignorance]* rażący

crate /kreɪt/ *n* skrzynka *f*

crater /'kreɪtə(r)/ krater *m*; (caused by explosion) lej *m*

cravat /krə'væt/ *n* fular *m*

crave /kreɪv/ *vt* (also ~ **for**) łaknąć (czegoś) *[food, affection]*

crawl /krɔːl/ **I** *n* 1 Sport kraul *m* 2 **at a ~** w żółwim tempie; **to go to a ~** *[vehicle]* wlec się

II *vi* 1 *[insect, snake]* pełz|ać, -nąć; *[person]* czołgać się 2 *[baby]* raczkować 3 *[vehicle]* wlec się 4 *[time]* wlec się 5 **to be ~ing with sth** roić się od czegoś *[insects, tourists]* 6 infml (flatter) podlizywać się (**to sb** komuś)

crayfish /'kreɪfɪʃ/ *n* 1 (freshwater) rak *m* 2 (spiny lobster) langusta *f*

crayon /'kreɪən/ *n* kredka *f*

craze /kreɪz/ *n* moda *f*; szał *m* infml; **to be the latest ~** być ostatnim krzykiem mody

crazy /'kreɪzɪ/ *adj [person, idea]* szalony, zwariowany; **to be ~ about sb** szaleć za kimś

crazy golf *n* GB minigolf *m*

creak /kriːk/ *vi [hinge]* za|skrzypieć; *[bone]* za|trzeszczeć

cream /kriːm/ **I** *n* 1 (dairy product) śmietanka *f* 2 (cosmetic) krem *m* 3 (soup) zupa-krem *f*

II *adj* 1 *[cake, bun]* z kremem 2 (colour) kremowy

■ **cream off**: **~ off [sth]**, **~ [sth] off** zagarn|ąć -iać *[profits]*; **they ~ed off the best musicians** ściągnęli najlepszych muzyków

cream cheese *n* serek *m* śmietankowy

cream soda *n* napój *m* gazowany o zapachu waniliowym

crease /kriːs/ **I** *n* (in paper) zagięcie *n*; (of trousers) kant *m*

II *vt* po|gnieść *[cloth, paper]*

III *vi [cloth]* po|gnieść się

create /kriː'eɪt/ *vt* stw|orzyć, -arzać *[interest, problem]*; s|powodować *[crisis]*; z|robić *[good impression]*

creation /kriː'eɪʃn/ *n* 1 (act) tworzenie *n* 2 (thing created) dzieło *n*

creative /kriː'eɪtɪv/ *adj* twórczy

creator /kriː'eɪtə(r)/ *n* twórca *m* (**of sth** czegoś)

creature /'kriːtʃə(r)/ *n* istota *f* żywa, stworzenie *n*

crèche /kreʃ, kreɪʃ/ n GB (nursery) żłobek m; (in shop, hotel) przechowalnia f dla dzieci

credentials /krɪ'denʃlz/ npl ☐ (qualifications) kwalifikacje plt ☐ (of competence) referencje plt; (of identity) dokument m potwierdzający tożsamość

credibility /ˌkredə'bɪlətɪ/ n wiarygodność f

credible /'kredəbl/ adj wiarygodny

credit /'kredɪt/ ▮ n ☐ (approval) uznanie n (for sth za coś); **to take the ~** przypisywać sobie zasługi; **to be a ~ to sb/sth** być chlubą kogoś/czegoś ☐ (credence) wiara f ☐ (in commerce) kredyt m; **to buy sth on ~** kupić coś na kredyt; **to be £25 in ~** mieć 25 funtów po stronie „ma"

▮▮ **credits** npl (in film) napisy m pl; (opening) czołówka f

▮▮▮ vt ☐ **to ~ sb with sth** przypisywać komuś coś ☐ uznaǀć, -wać [account]

credit card n karta f kredytowa

credit facilities npl udogodnienia n pl kredytowe

credit note n nota f kredytowa

creditor /'kredɪtə(r)/ n wierzyciel m, -ka f

creditworthy /'kredɪtwɜːðɪ/ adj mający zdolność kredytową

credulous /'kredjʊləs, US -dʒə-/ adj łatwowierny, naiwny

creed /kriːd/ n (religious persuasion) wyznanie n; (opinions) kredo n

creek /kriːk, US also krɪk/ n ☐ GB (inlet) zatoka f ☐ US (stream) strumyk m

creep /kriːp/ vi ☐ skradać się; **to ~ in/out** zakraść się/wymknąć się chyłkiem; **to ~ under sth** wczołgać się pod coś; **to ~ along** [vehicle] wlec się; [insect] pełzać; [cat] skradać się ☐ [plant] (horizontally) płożyć się; (climb) piąć się (w górę)

creeper /'kriːpə(r)/ n (in jungle) liana f; (climbing plant) pnącze n

creepy /'kriːpɪ/ adj infml [film, feeling] przyprawiający o gęsią skórkę

creepy-crawly /ˌkriːpɪ'krɔːlɪ/ n infml robal m infml

cremate /krɪ'meɪt/ vt sǀkremować

cremation /krɪ'meɪʃn/ n kremacja f

crematorium /ˌkremə'tɔːrɪəm/ n GB krematorium n

crepe, crêpe /kreɪp/ n ☐ (fabric) krepa f ☐ Culin cienki naleśnik m

crescent /'kresnt/ n półksiężyc m

crescent moon n sierp m księżyca

cress /kres/ n rzeżucha f

crest /krest/ n ☐ (of wave) grzbiet m ☐ (coat of arms) herb m

Crete /kriːt/ prn Kreta f

Creutzfeldt-Jakob disease, CJD /ˌkrɔɪtsfeld' jækəb dɪziːz/ n choroba f Creutzfeldta-Jakoba

crevice /'krevɪs/ n szczelina f, pęknięcie n

crew /kruː/ n ☐ (of ship, plane) załoga f ☐ (on film, radio) ekipa f

crewcut /'kruːkʌt/ n fryzura f na jeża

crew neck sweater n sweter m pod szyję

crib /krɪb/ ▮ n (child's bed) łóżeczko n dziecinne ▮▮ vi (in exam) ściągać infml (**from sb/sth** od kogoś/z czegoś)

crick /krɪk/ n **to get a ~ in one's neck** odczuć nagły ból w szyi

cricket /'krɪkɪt/ n ☐ (insect) świerszcz m ☐ (game) krykiet m

cricketer /'krɪkɪtə(r)/ n gracz m w krykieta

crime /kraɪm/ n ☐ (minor) przestępstwo n; (serious) zbrodnia f ☐ (criminal activity) przestępczość f

criminal /'krɪmɪnl/ ▮ n przestępǀca m, -czyni f ▮▮ adj przestępczy

criminal record n karalność f uprzednia; **to have a ~** mieć kryminalną przeszłość

crimson /'krɪmzn/ ▮ n szkarłat m ▮▮ adj szkarłatny

cringe /krɪndʒ/ vi ☐ (physically) sǀkulić się ☐ (in embarrassment) poǀczuć zażenowanie

cripple /'krɪpl/ ▮ n kaleka m/f ▮▮ vt ☐ uǀczynić (kogoś) kaleką; **to be ~d for life** zostać kaleką na całe życie ☐ sǀparaliżować [country, industry]

crisis /'kraɪsɪs/ n kryzys m; **~ over the budget** kryzys w związku z budżetem

crisp /krɪsp/ adj [biscuit, fruit] kruchy; [bacon] chrupiący; [banknote] szeleszczący; [snow] skrzypiący; [air] rześki; [manner] rzeczowy

crispbread /'krɪspbred/ n pieczywo n chrupkie

crisps /krɪsps/ npl (also **potato ~**) czipsy m pl, chipsy m pl

crisscross /'krɪskrɒs, US -krɔːs/ ▮ adj [design] kratkowany ▮▮ vt przeciǀąć, -nać (wzdłuż i wszerz)

criterion /kraɪ'tɪərɪən/ n kryterium n (**for sth** czegoś)

critic /'krɪtɪk/ n krytyk m

critical /'krɪtɪkl/ adj [stage] decydujący; [moment, point, condition] krytyczny; **to be ~ of sb/sth** być krytycznym wobec kogoś/czegoś

critically /'krɪtɪklɪ/ adv ☐ [examine] krytycznie ☐ [ill] poważnie

criticism /'krɪtɪsɪzəm/ n krytyka f

criticize /'krɪtɪsaɪz/ vt sǀkrytykować

croak /krəʊk/ vi [frog] zaǀrechotać

Croatia /krəʊ'eɪʃə/ prn Chorwacja f

crochet /'krəʊʃeɪ, US krəʊ'ʃeɪ/ vt zǀrobić szydełkiem; **a ~ed shawl** szydełkowy szal

crockery /'krɒkərɪ/ n naczynia n pl stołowe

crocodile /'krɒkədaɪl/ n krokodyl m

croissant /'krwɑːsɑːnt/ n rogalik m francuski, croissant m

crony /'krəʊnɪ/ n kumpel m infml

crook /krʊk/ n ☐ (person) oszust m, -ka f ☐ (of arm) zgięcie n łokciowe ☐ (shepherd's) zakrzywiony kij m pastuszy

IDIOMS: **by hook or by** ~ takim czy innym sposobem

crooked /'krʊkɪd/ *adj* ① *[line]* zakrzywiony; *[teeth]* krzywy; (off-centre) przekrzywiony ② infml (dishonest) nieuczciwy

crop /krɒp/ *n* ① (produce) uprawa *f*; (harvest) plon *m*, zbiory *m pl* ② (also **riding** ~) szpicruta *f*

■ **crop up**: *[matter, name, problem, opportunity]* pojawi|ć, -áć się

cross /krɒs, US krɔːs/ ▮ *n* ① krzyż *m*; **to put a** ~ **against sth** postawić krzyżyk przy czymś *[name, item]* ② (hybrid) krzyżówka *f*

▮▮ *adj* (angry) rozgniewany; **to be** ~ **with sb** być na kogoś złym; **to get** ~ **with sb** rozzłościć się na kogoś

▮▮▮ *vt* ① przekr|oczyć, -aczać *[border, line]*; **it** ~ **ed his mind that...** przyszło mu na myśl, że...; **to** ~ **one's legs/arms** skrzyżować nogi/ręce ② (intersect with) s|krzyżować się z (czymś) *[road]* ③ **to** ~ **a cheque** zakreślić or zakrosować czek

▮▼ *vi* s|krzyżować się

■ **cross off, cross out**: skreśl|ić, -áć, wykreśl|ić, -áć *[name, thing]*

cross-border /'krɒsbɔːdə(r), US 'krɔːs-/ *adj* (przy)graniczny

cross-Channel /'krɒstʃænl, US 'krɔːs-/ *adj* ~ **ferry** prom *m* (kursujący) przez kanał La Manche

cross-check /ˌkrɒs'tʃek, US ˌkrɔːs-/ *vt* z|weryfiko- wać

cross-country /ˌkrɒs'kʌntrɪ, US ˌkrɔːs-/ *n* ① (in running) bieg *m* przełajowy, kros *m* ② (in skiing) bieg *m* narciarski

cross-cultural /ˌkrɒs'kʌltʃərəl, US ˌkrɔːs-/ *adj* międzykulturowy

cross-examine /ˌkrɒsɪg'zæmɪn, US ˌkrɔːs-/ *vt* za- dawać pytania (świadkowi strony przeciwnej); fig wziąć, brać w krzyżowy ogień pytań

cross-eyed /'krɒsaɪd, US ˌkrɔːs-/ *adj* zezowaty; **she's** ~ ona ma zeza

crossfire /'krɒsfaɪə(r), US 'krɔːs-/ *n* krzyżowy ogień *m*; **to get caught in the** ~ znaleźć się pod presją

crossing /'krɒsɪŋ, US 'krɔːsɪŋ/ *n* ① (journey) (over water) przeprawa *f*; (by air) przelot *m* ② (for pedestrians) przejście *n* dla pieszych ③ **border** ~ przejście *n* graniczne

cross-legged /ˌkrɒs'legɪd, US ˌkrɔːs-/ *adv* *[sit]* po turecku

cross-purposes /ˌkrɒs'pɜːpəsɪz, US ˌkrɔːs-/ *npl* **we are at** ~ **(with each other)** (misunderstanding) nie rozumiemy się; (disagreement) nie możemy dojść (ze sobą) do porozumienia

cross-reference /ˌkrɒs'refrəns, US ˌkrɔːs-/ *n* odnośnik *m*, odsyłacz *m* (**to sth** do czegoś)

crossroads /'krɒsrəʊdz, US 'krɔːs-/ *n* skrzyżowa- nie *n* dróg

cross-section /ˌkrɒs'sekʃn, US ˌkrɔːs-/ *n* przekrój *m* poprzeczny

crossword /'krɒswɜːd, US 'krɔːs-/ *n* (also ~ **puzzle**) krzyżówka *f*

crotch /krɒtʃ/ *n* ① Anat krocze *n* ② (in trousers) krok *m*

crotchet /'krɒtʃɪt/ *n* GB Mus ćwier|cnuta *f*

crouch /kraʊtʃ/ *vi* (also ~ **down**) *[person]* przy- kuc|nąć, -áć; *[animal]* gotować się (do skoku)

crow /krəʊ/ ▮ *n* wrona *f*

▮▮ *vi* ① (exult) piać (z zachwytu) (**over** or **about sth** nad czymś) ② *[cock]* zapiać

IDIOMS: **as the** ~ **flies** w linii prostej

crowbar /'krəʊbɑː(r)/ *n* łom *m*

crowd /kraʊd/ ▮ *n* tłum *m*; (audience) publiczność *f*, widownia *f*

▮▮ *vt* ① s|tłoczyć się na (czymś) *[platform]*; wtł|oczyć, -aczać *[people, furniture]* (**into sth** do środka czegoś) ② zagrac|ić, -áć infml *[room, house]* (**with sth** czymś)

▮▮▮ *vi* s|tłoczyć się; **to** ~ **into sth** wepchnąć się do czegoś *[room, lift, vehicle]*

crowded /'kraʊdɪd/ *adj* *[train]* zatłoczony; *[area]* przeludniony; **to be** ~ **with people** być zatło- czonym or pełnym ludzi; ~ **schedule** przełado- wany plan

crowd-puller /'kraʊdpʊlə(r)/ *n* (event) (wielka) atrakcja *f*

crown /kraʊn/ ▮ *n* ① (of monarch) korona *f* ② (of head) ciemię *n*; (of hill) szczyt *m* ③ (on tooth) korona *f*

▮▮ *vt* u|koronować

Crown court *n* GB Sąd *m* Koronny

crown jewels *npl* klejnoty *m pl* koronne

crown prince *n* następca *m* tronu

crow's nest *n* (on ship) bociane gniazdo *n*

crucial /'kruːʃl/ *adj* *[role]* decydujący; *[decision]* zasadniczy

crucifix /'kruːsɪfɪks/ *n* krucyfiks *m*

crude /kruːd/ *adj* ① *[method]* prymitywny; *[esti- mate]* przybliżony ② *[joke, person]* ordynarny ③ (un- processed) surowy; ~ **oil** ropa naftowa

cruel /'kruːəl/ *adj* okrutny

cruelty /'kruːəltɪ/ *n* okrucieństwo *n*

cruise /kruːz/ ▮ *n* rejs *m* wycieczkowy; **to go on a** ~ wyruszyć w rejs

▮▮ *vt* *[driver, taxi]* krążyć po (czymś) *[street, city]*

▮▮▮ *vi* *[liner, tourist]* odby|ć, -wać rejs wycieczko- wy; *[plane]* lecieć ze stałą prędkością

cruise missile *n* pocisk *m* samosterujący dale- kiego zasięgu

cruiser /'kruːzə(r)/ *n* ① (cabin cruiser) łódź *f* motorowa z kabiną ② (ship) krążownik *m*

crumb /krʌm/ *n* okruch *m*

crumble /'krʌmbl/ ▮ *vt* (also ~ **up**) po|kruszyć *[bread]*

▮▮ *vi* ① *[cliff]* kruszyć się; *[building]* popa|ść, -dać w ruinę ② *[relationship, empire]* rozpa|lść, -dać się;

[economy] popa|ść, -dać w ruinę; *[opposition]* o|słabnąć

crummy /'krʌmɪ/ *adj* infml [1] (substandard) nędzny, lichy [2] US (unwell) **to feel** ~ czuc się podle

crumple /'krʌmpl/ *vt* zgni|eść, -atać *[piece of paper, can]*; **to** ~ **sth into a ball** zgnieść coś w kulkę

crunch /krʌntʃ/ *vt* s|chrupać *[apple, toast]*
(IDIOMS) **when** or **if it comes to the** ~ kiedy or jak przyjdzie co do czego

crunchy /'krʌntʃɪ/ *adj [vegetable]* chrupki; *[biscuit]* chrupiący

crusade /kru:'seɪd/ *n* krucjata *f*

crush /krʌʃ/ [I] *n* ścisk *m*, tłok *m*
[II] *vt* [1] fig z|dławić *[protest, uprising]*; rozn|ieść, -osić *[enemy]* [2] zgni|eść, -atać *[can]*; rozgni|eść, -atać *[fruit, vegetable]*; z|miażdżyć *[person, part of body, vehicle]* [3] po|gnieść, z|miąć *[garment, fabric]*

crushing /'krʌʃɪŋ/ *adj [weight]* przygniatający; *[defeat]* miażdżący; *[blow]* druzgocący

crust /krʌst/ *n* [1] (on bread, pie) skórka *f* [2] (of mud, ice) skorupa *f*; **the earth's** ~ skorupa ziemska

crutch /krʌtʃ/ *n* kula *f* (inwalidzka)

crux /krʌks/ *n* **the** ~ **of the matter** sedno sprawy

cry /kraɪ/ [I] *n* krzyk *m*, okrzyk *m*
[II] *vi* za|płakać *(about sth* z powodu czegoś); **to** ~ **with laughter** popłakać się ze śmiechu
■ **cry off** GB: (cancel) odwoł|ać, -ywać
■ **cry out:** [1] (with pain, grief) krzy|knąć, -czeć [2] (call) za|wołać

cryogenics /ˌkraɪə'dʒenɪks/ *n* kriogenika *f*

crypt /krɪpt/ *n* krypta *f*

cryptic /'krɪptɪk/ *adj [allusion]* tajemniczy; *[remark]* enigmatyczny

crystal /'krɪstl/ *n* kryształ *m*

crystal ball *n* kryształowa or szklana kula *f*

crystal clear *adj* [1] *[water, sound]* kryształowo czysty [2] *[explanation]* jasny, przejrzysty

CS gas *n* gaz *m* łzawiący

cub /kʌb/ *n* Zool młode *n*

Cuba /'kju:bə/ *prn* Kuba *f*

cubby-hole /'kʌbɪhəʊl/ *n* infml klitka *f*; kanciapa *f* infml

cube /kju:b/ [I] *n* [1] (in geometry) sześcian *m* [2] (of stock, sugar) kostka *f*; **ice** ~ kostka lodu
[II] *vt* po|kroić w kostkę

cubic /'kju:bɪk/ *adj* sześcienny

cubicle /'kju:bɪkl/ *n* kabina *f*

cuckoo /'kʊku:/ *n* kukułka *f*

cucumber /'kju:kʌmbə(r)/ *n* ogórek *m*

cuddle /'kʌdl/ [I] *n* **to give sb a** ~ przytulić kogoś
[II] *vt* przytul|ić, -ać, tulić

cuddly toy /'kʌdlɪ tɔɪ/ *n* GB przytulanka *f*

cue /kju:/ *n* [1] (in play) (line) końcówka *f*; (action) sygnał *m* dla aktora; (on TV, radio) sygnał *m* [2] Sport kij *m* bilardowy

cuff /kʌf/ *n* mankiet *m*
(IDIOMS) **to speak off the** ~ mówić bez

przygotowania; **to say sth off the** ~ powiedzieć coś bez zastanowienia

cuff link *n* spinka *f* do mankietu

cul-de-sac /'kʌldəsæk/ *n* ślepa uliczka *f*, ślepy zaułek *m*

culinary /'kʌlɪnərɪ, US -nerɪ/ *adj* kulinarny

cull /kʌl/ [I] *vt* ubój *m*
[II] przetrzebi|ć, -ać *[seal, whale]*

culminate /'kʌlmɪneɪt/ *vi* **to** ~ **in sth** za|kończyć się czymś

culottes /kju:'lɒts/ *n* spódnica-spodnie *f*

culprit /'kʌlprɪt/ *n* winowaj|ca *m*, -czyni *f*

cult /kʌlt/ [I] *n* kult *m*; (contemporary religion) sekta *f*
[II] *adj [figure, film]* kultowy

cultivate /'kʌltɪvert/ *vt* uprawiać; fig pielęgnować, kultywować *[friendship]*

cultural /'kʌltʃərəl/ *adj [activities]* kulturalny; *[background]* kulturowy

culture /'kʌltʃə(r)/ *n* kultura *f*

cultured /'kʌltʃəd/ *adj [person]* kulturalny; *[pearl]* hodowlany

culture shock *n* szok *m* kulturowy

culture vulture *n* infml **to be a** ~ biegać z jednej imprezy kulturalnej na drugą

cumbersome /'kʌmbəsəm/ *adj [luggage]* nieporęczny; *[phrase]* niezręczny

cumulative /'kju:mjʊlətɪv, US -leɪtɪv/ *adj [process]* narastający; *[total]* łączny

cunning /'kʌnɪŋ/ [I] *n* przebiegłość *f*
[II] *adj* [1] *[person]* przebiegły [2] *[trick]* sprytny; *[device]* zmyślny

cup /kʌp/ [I] *n* [1] (for tea, coffee) filiżanka *f* [2] Sport puchar *m*
[II] *vt* **to** ~ **sth in one's hands** trzymać coś w złączonych dłoniach

cupboard /'kʌbəd/ *n* szafka *f* (kuchenna)

curable /'kjʊərəbl/ *adj* uleczalny

curate /'kjʊərət/ *n* wikariusz *m*

curator /kjʊə'reɪtə(r), US also 'kjʊərətər/ *n* (of museum) kustosz *m*; (of exhibition) kurator *m*

curb /kɜ:b/ [I] *n* [1] (control) ograniczenie *n* (**on sth** nałożone na coś) [2] US (in street) krawężnik *m*
[II] *vt* (control) po|hamować *[desires]*; ogranicz|yć, -ać *[powers, consumption]*

curdle /'kɜ:dl/ *vi [milk]* zsi|ąść, -adać się; *[sauce]* z|warzyć się

cure /'kjʊə(r)/ [I] *n* (remedy) środek *m* zaradczy (**for sth** na coś); (drug) lekarstwo *n* (**for sth** na coś)
[II] *vt* [1] (heal) wy|leczyć *[person]*; (**of sth** z czegoś) [2] Culin (dry) wy|suszyć; (salt) za|solić; (smoke) u|wędzić

cure-all /'kjʊərɔ:l/ *n* panaceum *n* (**for sth** na coś)

curfew /'kɜ:fju:/ *n* godzina *f* policyjna; **ten o'clock** ~ godzina policyjna od dziesiątej

curio /'kjʊərɪəʊ/ *n* osobliwość *f*

curiosity /ˌkjʊərɪ'ɒsətɪ/ *n* ciekawość *f* (**about sth** czegoś); **out of** ~ z czystej ciekawości

curious /'kjʊərɪəs/ adj ciekawy

curiously /'kjʊərɪəslɪ/ adv [silent, detached] dziwnie; ~ **enough...** co ciekawe...

curl /kɜːl/ **I** n (of hair) lok m; (of smoke) kłąb m
II vt zakręc|ić, -ać [hair]
III vi [hair] kręcić się; [leaf, paper] zwi|nąć, -jać się; [edges, corners] wywi|nąć, -jać się
■ **curl up**: [person, animal] zwi|nąć, -jać się w kłębek

curler /'kɜːlə(r)/ n (roller) lokówka f, wałek m

curly /'kɜːlɪ/ adj [hair] (tight curls) kędzierzawy; (loose curls) kręcony; [tail] zakręcony; [eyelashes] podwinięty do góry

currant /'kʌrənt/ n koryntka f

currency /'kʌrənsɪ/ n waluta f, środek m płatniczy

current /'kʌrənt/ **I** n (of electricity, water) prąd m
II adj [leader, situation, policy] obecny; [year] bieżący

current account n GB rachunek m beżący

current affairs npl aktualności f pl

currently /'kʌrəntlɪ/ adv obecnie

curriculum /kə'rɪkjʊləm/ n program m nauczania; **in the** ~ w programie nauczania

curriculum vitae, CV n życiorys m

curry /'kʌrɪ/ **I** n curry m inv; **chicken** ~ curry z kurczaka
II vt **to** ~ **favour with sb** przypochlebiać się komuś

curse /kɜːs/ **I** n ⫶1⫶ (problem) przekleństwo n fig ⫶2⫶ (swearword) przekleństwo n ⫶3⫶ (spell) klątwa f
II vi kląć; **to** ~ **and swear at sth** miotać przekleństwa na coś

cursor /'kɜːsə(r)/ n Comput kursor m

curt /kɜːt/ adj [manner, tone] szorstki

curtail /kɜː'teɪl/ vtr ⫶1⫶ (restrict) ogranicz|yć, -ać [right] ⫶2⫶ (cut back) z|redukować

curtain /'kɜːtn/ n ⫶1⫶ (drape) zasłona f; (heavy) kotara f, portiera f; (of lace) firanka f ⫶2⫶ (in theatre) kurtyna f

curtsey /'kɜːtsɪ/ **I** n dygnięcie n
II vi dyg|nąć, -ać

curve /kɜːv/ **I** n (in line) krzywa f; (in road) łuk m
II vi [line] wygi|ąć, -nać się; [wall] zaokrągl|ić, -ać się; [road, railway] zakręc|ić, -ać łukiem

cushion /'kʊʃn/ **I** n poduszka f
II vt z|amortyzować

cushy /'kʊʃɪ/ adj infml [situation] komfortowy; ~ **job** ciepła posadka infml

custard /'kʌstəd/ n GB słodki sos m z mleka i jajek z dodatkiem mąki

custodian /kʌ'stəʊdɪən/ n (caretaker) dozorca m; (of collection) strażnik m; (in museum) kustosz m

custody /'kʌstədɪ/ n ⫶1⫶ (detention) areszt m; **to take sb into** ~ zaaresztować kogoś ⫶2⫶ (of child) opieka f

custom /'kʌstəm/ n ⫶1⫶ (habit) zwyczaj m ⫶2⫶ (patronage) stała klientela f

customary /'kʌstəmərɪ, US -merɪ/ adj tradycyjny, zwyczajowy

customer /'kʌstəmə(r)/ n klient m, -ka f

customer services n dział m obsługi klienta

customize /'kʌstəmaɪz/ vt wykon|ać, -ywać na zamówienie

custom-made /ˌkʌstəm'meɪd/ adj [shirt, shoes] na miarę

customs /'kʌstəmz/ n urząd m celny; **to go through** ~ przechodzić odprawę celną

customs duties npl opłaty f pl celne

customs hall n urząd m celny

customs officer, customs official n celni|k m, -czka f

cut /kʌt/ **I** n ⫶1⫶ (incision) rozcięcie n; (in surgery) nacięcie n ⫶2⫶ (wound) skaleczenie n ⫶3⫶ (hairstyle) fryzura f ⫶4⫶ infml (share) część f, udział m ⫶5⫶ (reduction) obniżka f (**in sth** czegoś); **job** ~**s** redukcje zatrudnienia; **a** ~ **in salary** obniżka pensji
II vt ⫶1⫶ (slice) po|kroić [bread]; po|ciąć [paper]; **to** ~ **oneself** skaleczyć się; **to** ~ **one's finger** skaleczyć się w palec; **to have one's hair cut** ostrzyc się, obciąć włosy ⫶2⫶ (give shape) o|szlifować [gem]; ocios|ać, -ywać [wood]; s|kroić [suit] ⫶3⫶ (edit) skr|ócić, -acać [article, film]; wyci|ąć, -nać [scene] ⫶4⫶ (reduce) zmniejsz|yć, -ać [cost, inflation]; okr|oić, -awać [budget] ⫶5⫶ **the baby's** ~**ting a tooth** dziecku wyrzyna się ząb ⫶6⫶ (record) nagr|ać, -ywać [album] ⫶7⫶ Comput wyci|ąć, -nać [paragraph]
III vi ⫶1⫶ (make an incision) ciąć; (slice) kroić; **to** ~ **into sth** rozkroić coś [cake]; rozciąć coś [fabric, paper]; zrobić nacięcie w czymś [flesh] ⫶2⫶ **to** ~ **down a side street** pojechać na skróty boczną uliczką
■ **cut back**: ¶ ~ **back** oszczędz|ić, -ać ¶ ~ **[sth] back** ⫶1⫶ ogranicz|yć, -ać [spending] ⫶2⫶ (prune) przyci|ąć, -nać [plant]
■ **cut down**: ¶ ~ **down** ogranicz|yć, -ać się; **to** ~ **down on sth** ograniczać spożycie czegoś [alcohol]; ¶ ~ **[sth] down** ⫶1⫶ ści|ąć, -nać [tree] ⫶2⫶ z|redukować [spending]
■ **cut off**: ¶ ~ **off [sth]** ⫶1⫶ odci|ąć, -nać [piece]; odkr|oić, -awać [crusts]; ści|ąć, -nać [hair, corner] ⫶2⫶ (disconnect) odci|ąć, -nać [mains service] ⫶3⫶ wstrzym|ać, -ywać [financial, aid] ¶ ~ **[sb] off** ⫶1⫶ (on the phone) rozłącz|yć, -ać ⫶2⫶ (interrupt) przer|wać, -ywać (komuś)
■ **cut out**: ¶ ~ **out** [engine, motor] z|gasnąć ¶ ~ **[sth] out** ⫶1⫶ (snip out) wyci|ąć, -nać (**from sth** z czegoś) ⫶2⫶ infml ~ **it out!** przestań!
■ **cut short**: skr|ócić, -acać [holiday, discussion]
■ **cut up**: po|ciąć [paper]; po|kroić [bread]
⌜IDIOMS⌝ **to** ~ **sb dead** zignorować kogoś

cut and paste n Comput wycinanie n i wklejanie n

cutback /'kʌtbæk/ n ~**s in sth** cięcia w wydatkach na coś [defence, health]; **government** ~**s** rządowe cięcia w budżecie

cute /kjuːt/ *adj* infml [1] (nice) milutki, uroczy [2] US (clever) rezolutny, sprytny

cutlery /'kʌtlərɪ/ *n* sztućce *m pl*

cutlet /'kʌtlɪt/ *n* kotlet *m*

cut-off /'kʌtɒf/ [I] *n* (upper limit) granica *f* [II] **cut-offs** *npl* obcięte dżinsy *plt*

cut-price /ˌkʌt'praɪs/ GB, **cut-rate** /ˌkʌt'reɪt/ US *adj* przeceniony, po obniżonej cenie

cut-throat /'kʌtθrəʊt/ *adj [competition]* zaciekły; **a ~ business** dziedzina, w której trzeba twardo walczyć o swoje

cutting /'kʌtɪŋ/ [I] *n* [1] (newspaper extract) wycinek *m* (**from sth** z czegoś) [2] (in film production) montaż *m* [II] *adj [wind]* przenikliwy; *[remark, tone]* kąśliwy, uszczypliwy

cutting edge *n* **to be at the ~ of sth** torować nowe drogi w czymś

CV, cv *n* = **curriculum vitae** życiorys *m*, CV *n inv*

cyanide /'saɪənaɪd/ *n* cyjanek *m*

cycle /'saɪkl/ [I] *n* [1] cykl *m* [2] (bicycle) rower *m* [II] *vi* jechać, jeździć na rowerze

cycle lane *n* ścieżka *f* rowerowa

cycle race *n* wyścig *m* kolarski

cycling /'saɪklɪŋ/ *n* jazda *f* na rowerze; Sport kolarstwo *n*

cycling shorts *npl* spodenki *plt* kolarskie

cyclist /'saɪklɪst/ *n* rowerzyst|a *m*, -ka *f*; Sport kolarz *m*

cyclone /'saɪkləʊn/ *n* cyklon *m*

cygnet /'sɪgnɪt/ *n* młody łabędź *m*

cylinder /'sɪlɪndə(r)/ *n* [1] walec *m* [2] (in engine) cylinder *m* [3] (of gas) butla *f* (na gaz) [4] GB (also **hot water ~**) bojler *m*

cynic /'sɪnɪk/ *n* cynik *m*

cynical /'sɪnɪkl/ *adj* cyniczny

cynicism /'sɪnɪsɪzəm/ *n* cynizm *m*

Cyprus /'saɪprəs/ *prn* Cypr *m*

cyst /sɪst/ *n* cysta *f*, torbiel *f*

Czech /tʃek/ [I] *n* [1] (person) Cze|ch *m*, -szka *f* [2] (język *m*) czeski *m* [II] *adj* czeski

Czech Republic *prn* **the ~** Republika *f* Czeska, Czechy *plt*

D

d, D /di:/ n [1] (letter) D, d n [2] **D** Mus d, D, re n
dab /dæb/ [1] n (of butter) odrobina f; (of glue) maźnięcie n
[2] vt mus|nąć, -kać [eyes, wound] (**with sth** czymś)
dabble /'dæbl/ vt
■ **dabble in**: bawić się w (coś); **to ~ in the Stock Exchange** grywać na giełdzie
dachshund /'dækshʊnd/ n jamnik m
dad, Dad /dæd/ n infml tata m
daddy, Daddy /'dædɪ/ n infml tatuś m
daffodil /'dæfədɪl/ n żonkil m
daft /dɑːft, US dæft/ adj infml głupi
dagger /'dægə(r)/ n sztylet m
[IDIOMS] **to look ~s at sb** rzucać komuś mordercze spojrzenie
daily /'deɪlɪ/ [1] n (newspaper) dziennik m
[2] adj [visit, routine] codzienny; [wage, rate] dzienny; **on a ~ basis** codziennie
[3] adv codziennie; **twice ~** dwa razy dziennie
dainty /'deɪntɪ/ adj [porcelain] delikatny; [shoe, hat] maleńki; [hand, foot] drobny
dairy /'deərɪ/ [1] n [1] (on farm) mleczarnia f; (shop) sklep m nabiałowy [2] (company) zakład m mleczarski
[2] adj [butter] śmietankowy; [cow, farm, product] mleczny
daisy /'deɪzɪ/ n (common) stokrotka f; (garden) margerytka f
[IDIOMS] **(as) fresh as a ~** świeży jak pączek róży
dam /dæm/ n zapora f (wodna)
damage /'dæmɪdʒ/ [1] n [1] (physical) uszkodzenia n pl (**to sth** czegoś) [2] (medical) uszkodzenie n; **brain ~** uszkodzenie mózgu [3] fig **to do ~ to sth** zaszkodzić czemuś; **the ~ is done** stało się
[2] **damages** npl odszkodowanie n
[3] vt [1] (physically) uszk|odzić, -adzać [building]; nara|zić, -żać na szwank [health]; z|niszczyć [environment] [2] fig za|szkodzić (czemuś) [reputation]
damaging /'dæmɪdʒɪŋ/ adj (to reputation, person) przynoszący szkodę (**to sb/sth** komuś/czemuś); [effect] szkodliwy; (to health, environment) niszczący (**to sth** kogoś/coś)
damn /dæm/ infml [1] n **not to give a ~ about sb/ sth** mieć kogoś/coś gdzieś or w nosie infml
[2] adj (also **damned**) przeklęty infml
[3] excl cholera! infml

damp /dæmp/ [1] n wilgoć f
[2] adj wilgotny
dampen /'dæmpən/ vt [1] zwilż|yć, -ać [cloth] [2] fig o|studzić [enthusiasm]; **to ~ sb's spirits** zepsuć or popsuć komuś humor
damson /'dæmzn/ n śliwka f damaszka
dance /dɑːns, US dæns/ [1] n taniec m; (social occasion) zabawa f
[2] vi za|tańczyć (**with sb** z kimś)
■ **dance about, dance up and down**: podskakiwać w miejscu
dancer /'dɑːnsə(r), US 'dænsər/ n tance|rz `m, -rka f
dancing /'dɑːnsɪŋ, US 'dænsɪŋ/ n tańce m pl
dandruff /'dændrʌf/ n łupież m
danger /'deɪndʒə(r)/ n niebezpieczeństwo n (**to sb/sth** dla kogoś/czegoś); **(to be) in ~** (być) w niebezpieczeństwie; **he's out of ~** nie zagraża mu niebezpieczeństwo; **there is no ~ in doing sth** robienie czegoś niczym nie grozi
danger list n **on the ~** Med w stanie krytycznym
dangerous /'deɪndʒərəs/ adj niebezpieczny (**for** or **to sb/sth** dla kogoś/czegoś)
[IDIOMS] **to be on ~ ground** stąpać po śliskim gruncie
dangerously /'deɪndʒərəslɪ/ adv niebezpiecznie; [ill] poważnie; **to live ~** lubić ryzyko
danger signal n sygnał m ostrzegawczy also fig
dangle /'dæŋgl/ [1] vt wymachiwać (czymś)
[2] vi dyndać (**from sth** na czymś); [puppet, keys] zwisać
Danish /'deɪnɪʃ/ [1] n (language) (język m) duński m
[2] adj duński
dare /deə(r)/ [1] n wyzwanie n
[2] modal aux [1] (to have courage to) odważ|yć, -ać się (**do sth** or **to do sth** coś zrobić); **I ~ say, I daresay** GB zapewne [2] (expressing anger) **don't (you) ~ speak to me like that!** nie waż się do mnie tak mówić!
[3] vt **to ~ sb to do sth** rzucić (komuś) wyzwanie, żeby coś zrobił; **go on, I ~ you!** no dalej, spróbuj!
daredevil /'deədevl/ [1] n śmiałek m
[2] adj [stunt] szaleńczy
daring /'deərɪŋ/ adj śmiały

dark /dɑːk/ **[]** n **in the ~** w ciemnościach; **before ~** przed zmrokiem; **after ~** po (zapadnięciu) zmroku

[] adj [1] [room, alley] ciemny; [day] ponury; **it is getting ~** robi się ciemno; **it is ~** jest ciemno [2] [colour, suit] ciemny; **~ blue** ciemnoniebieski [3] [hair, eyes] ciemny; [complexion] (swarthy) śniady; (black or brown) ciemny [4] [thoughts] czarny; [secret] mroczny

(IDIOMS) **to be in the ~** nic nie wiedzieć (**about sth** o czymś); **to leave sb in the ~** pozostawić kogoś w nieświadomości; **to keep sb in the ~ about sth** utrzymywać kogoś w nieświadomości co do czegoś

darken /'dɑːkən/ **[]** vt [1] (reduce light) przesł|onić, -aniać [sky, landscape]; zaciemni|ć, -ać [house] [2] (in colour) przyciemni|ć, -ać [complexion, colour]

[] vi [1] [sky] po|ciemnieć [2] (in colour) ś|ciemnieć

dark glasses npl ciemne okulary plt

darkness /'dɑːknɪs/ n (blackness) ciemność f; **in the ~** w ciemnościach

darkroom /'dɑːkruːm/ n ciemnia f

dark-skinned /ˌdɑːk'skɪnd/ adj ciemnoskóry

darling /'dɑːlɪŋ/ n [1] (to loved one) kochanie n; (to a child) moje maleństwo n; (to acquaintance) mój drogi m, moja droga f [2] (kind, lovable person) kochan|y m, -a f

darn /dɑːn/ vt za|cerować [socks]

dart /dɑːt/ n strzałka f; **to play ~s** grać w strzałki

dartboard /'dɑːtbɔːd/ n tarcza f do gry w strzałki

dash /dæʃ/ **[]** n [1] (rush) **to make a ~ for sth** rzucić się do czegoś; **it has been a mad ~** zwijaliśmy się jak w ukropie infml fig [2] (small amount) odrobina f; (of liquid) kropla f; (of pepper, salt) szczypta f [3] (punctuation) myślnik m

[] vt [1] (throw) roztrzask|ać, -iwać [boat, glass]; **to ~ sb/sth against sth** rzucić kimś o coś/ roztrzaskać coś o coś [2] fig z|niweczyć [hopes]

[] vi po|pędzić; **to ~ out** wpaść/wypaść

■ **dash off**: **¶ ~ off** pędem oddal|ić, -ać się **¶ ~ [sth] off** machnąć infml [note, essay]

dashboard /'dæʃbɔːd/ n deska f rozdzielcza

data /'deɪtə/ npl dane plt

database /'deɪtəbeɪs/ n baza f danych

data entry n wprowadzanie n danych

data processing n (procedure) przetwarzanie n danych; (career) informatyka f; (department) dział m informatyczny

data protection n ochrona f danych

data security n ochrona f danych

date[1] /deɪt/ **[]** n [1] data f; **~ of birth** data urodzin; **what's the ~ today?** jaki dziś mamy dzień?; **at a later ~** w późniejszym terminie [2] (on coin) data f emisji [3] (meeting) (umówione) spotkanie n; (with boyfriend, girlfriend) randka f; **to have a lunch ~** być umówionym na lunch; **to make a ~ for Monday** umówić się na poniedziałek [4] **who's your ~ for tonight?** z kim jesteś dziś umówiony?

[] **to date** adv phr do chwili obecnej

[] vt [1] [person] na|pisać datę na (czymś); [machine] datować [2] (go out with) spotykać się z (kimś)

[] vi **to ~ back to** or **from sth** [building] pochodzić z czegoś; [problem] datować się od czegoś; [friendship] sięgać czegoś

date[2] /deɪt/ n (fruit) daktyl m

dated /'deɪtɪd/ adj [clothes, style] niemodny; [ideas, custom] przestarzały; **to be ~** trącić myszką

dating agency n agencja f kojarząca pary

daughter /'dɔːtə(r)/ n córka f also fig

daughter-in-law /'dɔːtərɪnˌlɔː/ n synowa f

daunting /'dɔːntɪŋ/ adj [task, prospect] zniechęcający; [person] onieśmielający

dawdle /'dɔːdl/ vi mitrężyć czas; **he ~d along the road** wlókł się drogą

dawn /dɔːn/ **[]** n świt m; **at ~** o świcie or brzasku; **at the crack of ~** bladym świtem

[] vi [1] [day] wstać, za|świtać [2] **it ~ed on me that...** zaświtało mi (w głowie), że...; **it suddenly ~ed on him why** nagle pojął dlaczego

dawn raid n (policyjny) nalot m o świcie

day /deɪ/ **[]** n [1] (24 hours) doba f [2] (unit of time) dzień m; **what ~ is it today?** jaki dziś dzień?; **every ~** codziennie; **every other ~** co drugi dzień; **from ~ to ~** z dnia na dzień; **the ~ when...** or **that...** w dniu, w którym...; **the ~ after/before** następnego/poprzedniego dnia; **the ~ before yesterday** przedwczoraj; **the ~ after tomorrow** pojutrze [3] (until evening) dzień m; **all ~** cały dzień; **during the ~** w ciągu dnia [4] (historical period) czasy m pl; **in those ~s** w tamtych czasach; **these ~s** w tamtych czasach

(IDIOMS) **those were the ~s** to były czasy; **that'll be the ~!** to jest bardzo mało prawdopodobne; akurat! infml; **to call it a ~** zawiesić działalność also fig; **to save the ~** uratować sytuację

daybreak /'deɪbreɪk/ n świt m

day-care /'deɪkeə(r)/ n (for children) opieka f dzienna

daydream /'deɪdriːm/ **[]** n marzenia n pl

[] vi rozmarz|yć, -ać się (**about sth** o czymś)

daylight /'deɪlaɪt/ n [1] (light) dzień m; **it was still ~** było jeszcze jasno; **in (the) ~** (by day) za dnia; (in natural light) w świetle dziennym [2] (dawn) świt m

daylight robbery n infml **it's ~!** to rozbój w biały dzień

day nursery n żłobek m

day release n urlop m szkoleniowy

daytime /'deɪtaɪm/ n dzień m

day-to-day /ˌdeɪtə'deɪ/ adj [life, chores, expenditure] codzienny; [event, occurrence] zwykły; **on a ~ basis** codziennie or co dzień

day-trip /'deɪtrɪp/ n jednodniowa wycieczka f

daze /deɪz/ n **in a ~** (from blow) ogłuszony; (from drugs) otępiały; (from news) oszołomiony

dazed /deɪzd/ *adj* (by blow) ogłuszony; (by good news) oszołomiony; (by bad news) porażony

dazzle /ˈdæzl/ *vt [sun, torch]* oślepi|ć, -ać; **to ~ sb with sth** fig olśnić kogoś czymś

dazzling /ˈdæzlɪŋ/ *adj [beauty, performance]* olśniewający; *[light]* oślepiający

D-day /ˈdiːdeɪ/ *n* ① (important day) ważna data *f* ② (historical) dzień „D" *m* (lądowanie Aliantów w Normandii, 6 czerwca 1944 r.)

dead /ded/ ① *n* ① **the ~** zmarli *m pl* ② (middle) **at ~ of night** w środku nocy; **in the ~ of winter** w (samym) środku zimy

② *adj [person]* zmarły; *[animal]* zdechły; **the ~ man/woman** zmarły/zmarła; **a ~ body** zwłoki; **to drop (down) ~** paść trupem; **the phone went ~** przerwało połączenie infml

③ *adv* GB (absolutely) zupełnie; **to be ~ on time** być punktualnym co do minuty; **it's ~ easy!** infml to dziecinnie proste!; **they were ~ lucky** infml mieli piekielne szczęście! infml; **~ drunk** infml zalany w trupa infml; **~ tired** infml skonany infml; **to be ~ set on doing sth** upierać się, żeby coś zrobić; **he stopped ~** stanął jak wryty

deaden /ˈdedn/ *vt* s|tłumić *[sound]*; uśmierz|yć, -ać *[pain]*; z|łagodzić *[blow]*

dead end /ˌded'end/ ① *n* ślepa uliczka *f*

② **dead-end** /ˈdedend/ *adj [job]* bez perspektyw

dead heat *n* (in athletics) bieg *m* nierozstrzygnięty; (in horseracing) gonitwa *f* nierozstrzygnięta

deadline /ˈdedlaɪn/ *n* nieprzekraczalny termin *m*; **to meet a ~** zdążyć przed ostatecznym terminem

deadlock /ˈdedlɒk/ *n* martwy punkt *m*; **to reach (a) ~** znaleźć się w martwym punkcie

dead loss *n* infml **to be a ~** być do niczego infml

deadly /ˈdedlɪ/ ① *adj* ① *[poison, attack]* śmiertelny; *[weapon]* śmiercionośny ② **in ~ earnest** ze śmiertelną powagą

② *adv [dull, boring]* śmiertelnie

deadpan /ˈdedpæn/ *adj* **~ humour** dowcipy opowiadane z kamienną twarzą

deaf /def/ ① *n* **the ~** głusi *m pl*

② *adj* głuchy; **to go ~** ogłuchnąć, stracić słuch; **to turn a ~ ear to sth** fig puścić coś mimo uszu

deaf aid *n* GB aparat *m* słuchowy

deafening /ˈdefnɪŋ/ *adj* ogłuszający

deaf without speech *n* **the ~** głuchoniemi *m pl*

deal /diːl/ ① *n* ① (agreement) układ *m*; (in commerce) umowa *f*; **it's a ~!** umowa stoi! ② (amount) **a great** or **good ~** dużo, wiele **(of sth** czegoś)

② *vt* ① wymierz|yć, -ać *[blow]* **(with sth** czymś) ② rozda|ć, -wać *[cards]*; dal|ć, -wać *[hand]*

③ *vi* **to ~ in sth** handlować czymś

■ **deal with**: ① poradzić sobie z (czymś) *[problem, matter]* ② (discuss) zaj|ąć, -mować się (czymś) *[issue]*

dealer /ˈdiːlə(r)/ *n* ① (on a large scale) handlowiec *m*; (for a product, make of car) dealer *m* ② (on stock exchange) makler *m* ③ infml (in drugs) dealer *m*

dealing /ˈdiːlɪŋ/ ① *n* ① (trading) prowadzenie *n* działalności handlowej; (on stock exchange) obrót *m* akcjami; **foreign exchange ~** transakcje *w* handlu międzynarodowym ② (trafficking) **drug ~** handel narkotykami

② **dealings** *npl* (relations) stosunki *m pl*; (business) interesy *m pl* **(with sb** z kimś); **to have ~s with sb** kontaktować się z kimś; (do business) prowadzić interesy z kimś

dear /dɪə(r)/ ① *n* kochan|y *m*, -a *f*; (more formal) mój drogi *m*, moja droga *f*

② *adj* ① *[person]* kochany; **she's a very ~ friend of mine** jest moją serdeczną przyjaciółką; **to hold sb/sth very ~** bardzo kogoś/coś cenić ② (in letter) drogi; **Dear Sir/Madam** Szanowny Panie/Szanowna Pani; **Dear Sirs** Szanowni Państwo; **Dear Mr Jones** Szanowny Panie; **Dear Mr and Mrs Jones** Szanowni Państwo; **Dear David and Patricia** Drodzy or Kochani Dawidzie i Patrycjo

③ *excl* **oh ~!** (dismay, surprise) o Boże!; (less serious) ojejku! infml

death /deθ/ *n* śmierć *f*; Med zgon *m*; **to drink/work oneself to ~** zapić się/zapracować się na śmierć infml

IDIOMS: **to be at ~'s door** być jedną nogą w grobie infml; **to frighten sb to ~** infml śmiertelnie kogoś przerazić; **I'm sick to ~ of this!** infml mam tego serdecznie dosyć!

death camp *n* obóz *m* śmierci

death penalty *n* kara *f* śmierci

death row *n* US cele *f pl* skazańców

death sentence *n* wyrok *m* śmierci also fig

death threat *n* grożenie *n* śmiercią

death toll *n* liczba *f* ofiar śmiertelnych

death trap *n* śmiertelna pułapka *f*

debar /dɪˈbɑː(r)/ *vt* **to ~ sb from sth** wyklucz|yć, -ać kogoś z czegoś *[club]*; nie dopu|ścić, -szczać kogoś do uczestnictwa w czymś *[race]*

debatable /dɪˈbeɪtəbl/ *adj* dyskusyjny

debate /dɪˈbeɪt/ *n* (formal) debata *f* **(on** or **about sth** nad czymś); (more informal) dyskusja *f* **(about sth** o czymś); **to hold a ~ on sth** debatować nad czymś *[issue]*

debauchery /dɪˈbɔːtʃərɪ/ *n* rozpasanie *n*

debit /ˈdebɪt/ ① *n* debet *m*

② *vt* debetować *[account]*; **to ~ sb/sb's account with a sum** obciążyć kogoś/rachunek sumą

debrief /ˌdiːˈbriːf/ *vt* wysłuch|ać, -iwać sprawozdania; **to be ~ed** *[diplomat, agent]* składać sprawozdanie; *[defector, freed hostage]* być przesłuchiwanym

debris /ˈdeɪbriː, 'de-, US dəˈbriː/ *n* (of plane) szczątki *m pl*; (of building) ruiny *f pl*; (waste) gruz *m*

debt /det/ *n* dług *m* **(to sb/sth** wobec kogoś/czegoś); **to get into ~** znaleźć się w długach

debt collector n poborca m należności

debtor /'detə(r)/ n dłużni|k m, -czka f

debug /ˌdiː'bʌg/ vt usu|nąć, -wać usterki or błędy w (czymś) [program]

debut /'deɪbjuː, US dɪ'bjuː/ n debiut m; **to make one's ~ as an actor** zadebiutować jako aktor

decade /'dekeɪd, dɪ'keɪd, US dɪ'keɪd/ n dziesięciolecie n

decadent /'dekədənt/ adj dekadencki

decaffeinated /ˌdiː'kæfeɪneɪtɪd/ adj bezkofeinowy

decanter /dɪ'kæntə(r)/ n karafka f

decathlon /dɪ'kæθlɒn/ n dziesięciobój m

decay /dɪ'keɪ/ **I** n ① (of vegetable matter) gnicie n; (of wood) próchnienie n; (of building) niszczenie n; (of area) upadek m ② (dental) próchnica f ③ (of society) upadek m
II vi [food] z|gnić; [timber] s|próchnieć; [corpse] roz|łożyć, -kładać się; [tooth] ze|psuć się; [building] ule|c, -gać zniszczeniu

deceased /dɪ'siːst/ **I** n the ~ (dead person) zmarły m, -a f; (the dead collectively) zmarli m pl
II adj nieżyjący

deceit /dɪ'siːt/ n (deceitfulness) nieuczciwość f; (act) oszustwo n

deceitful /dɪ'siːtfl/ adj [person] kłamliwy; [behaviour] oszukańczy

deceive /dɪ'siːv/ **I** vt ① oszuk|ać, -iwać [friend]; **to be ~d** zostać oszukanym ② zdradz|ić, -ać [spouse, lover] (**with sb** z kimś)
II vr **to ~ oneself** oszukiwać się

December /dɪ'sembə(r)/ n grudzień m

decency /'diːsnsɪ/ n ① (good manners) dobre obyczaje m pl ② (propriety) przyzwoitość f

decent /'diːsnt/ adj ① [family, man, woman] porządny; **it's ~ of him** to miło or ładnie z jego strony ② (adequate) [wages, level] przyzwoity ③ (good) [camera, education, result] całkiem dobry; **to make a ~ living** przyzwoicie zarabiać na życie ④ (not indecent) [behaviour, clothes, language] przyzwoity

decentralize /diː'sentrəlaɪz/ vt z|decentralizować [government, company]; z|dekoncentrować [industry, population]

deception /dɪ'sepʃn/ n (deceiving) oszukiwanie n; (trick) podstęp m; **by ~** podstępem

deceptive /dɪ'septɪv/ adj zwodniczy

decide /dɪ'saɪd/ **I** vt ① **to ~ to do sth** postanowić coś zrobić ② (settle) rozstrzyg|nąć, -ać [matter]; przesądzić o (czymś) [fate, outcome]
II vi z|decydować (się); **to ~ against doing sth** zrezygnować ze zrobienia czegoś; **to ~ against sth** zarzucić coś [plan, idea]; **it's difficult to ~ between the two** trudno wybrać
■ **decide on:** ① wyb|rać, -ierać [hat, wallpaper]; ustali|ć, -ać [date] ② ustal|ić, -ać [policy, course of action, size, budget]

deciduous /dɪ'sɪdjʊəs, dɪ'sɪdʒʊəs/ adj [tree, forest] liściasty

decimal /'desɪml/ adj [system] dziesiętny; ~ **currency** dziesiętny system monetarny; ~ **point** przecinek

decipher /dɪ'saɪfə(r)/ vt rozszyfrow|ać, -ywać [message]; z|łamać [code]

decision /dɪ'sɪʒn/ n postanowienie n, decyzja f (**about sb/sth** dotyczący kogoś/czegoś); **to make** or **take a ~** podjąć decyzję

decision-making /dɪ'sɪʒnmeɪkɪŋ/ n **to be good at ~** umieć podejmować decyzję; **to be bad at ~** nie umieć podejmować decyzji

decisive /dɪ'saɪsɪv/ adj ① [manner] stanowczy; [tone] zdecydowany ② [battle, factor] decydujący

deck /dek/ n ① (on ship) pokład m; **to be on ~** być na pokładzie; **below ~(s)** pod pokładem ② US (terrace) taras m ③ **a ~ of cards** talia f kart
(IDIOMS) **to clear the ~s** przygotować grunt

deckchair /'dektʃeə(r)/ n leżak m

declaration /ˌdeklə'reɪʃn/ n oświadczenie n; **a customs ~** deklaracja celna

declare /dɪ'kleə(r)/ vt ① oświadcz|yć, -ać (**that... że...**); (state openly) oznajmi|ć, -ać [intention, decision] ② wypowi|edzieć, -adać [war]; ogł|osić, -aszać [independence] ③ za|deklarować [goods]; wykaz|ać, -ywać w deklaracji or bilansie [income]

decline /dɪ'klaɪn/ **I** n ① (waning) upadek m (**of sb/sth** kogoś/czegoś); **to be in ~** [empire, civilization] przeżywać (swój) upadek; [economy, industry] podupadać ② (decrease) spadek m (**of** or **in sth** czegoś); **to be on the** or **in ~** spadać, zmniejszać się
II vi ① (drop) spa|ść, -dać; [quality] pog|orszyć, -arszać się; [business] podupa|ść, -dać ② (wane) [empire] chylić się ku upadkowi; [influence] z|maleć; [status] obniż|yć, -ać się ③ (refuse) odm|ówić, -awiać (czegoś)

decode /ˌdiː'kəʊd/ vt rozszyfrow|ać, -ywać [message, signal]; z|łamać [code]

decompose /ˌdiːkəm'pəʊz/ vi [corpse, substance] roz|łożyć, -kładać się; [leaves, wood] z|butwieć

decor /'deɪkɔː(r), US deɪ'kɔːr/ n (of house, room) wystrój m; (in theatre) dekoracja f, dekoracje f pl

decorate /'dekəreɪt/ **I** vt ① u|dekorować [room]; przyb|rać, -ierać [cake]; ubr|ać, -ierać [Christmas tree] ② (paint and paper) odn|owić, -awiać [house, room]; (paint only) po|malować; (paper only) wy|tapetować
II vi odn|owić, -awiać; (with paint) po|malować; (with paper) wy|tapetować

decoration /ˌdekə'reɪʃn/ n (for festivitites) dekoracja f; (on garment) ozdoba f; (on cake) przybranie n

decorative /'dekərətɪv, US 'dekəreɪtɪv/ adj [border, design] ozdobny; [sculpture] dekoracyjny

decorator /'dekəreɪtə(r)/ n (painting) malarz m pokojowy; (papering) tapeciarz m

decoy /'diːkɔɪ/ **I** n przynęta f; (for hunting) wabik m
II /dɪ'kɔɪ/ vt z|wabić

decrease [] /'diːkriːs/ *n* (in price, inflation) spadek *m* (**in sth** czegoś); (controlled) redukcja *f* (**in sth** czegoś)
[] /dɪ'kriːs/ *vi* [price, inflation] spa|ść, -dać; [support, interest] o|słabnąć

decreasing /dɪ'kriːsɪŋ/ *adj* [number, population] zmniejszający się; [price] obniżający się; [enthusiasm, power] słabnący

decree /dɪ'kriː/ *n* [] (order) dekret *m* [] (judgment) wyrok *m*

decrepit /dɪ'krepɪt/ *adj* [chair, table] rozpadający się; [building] walący się; [old person, horse] niedołężny

decriminalize /diː'krɪmɪnəlaɪz/ *vt* zalegalizować

dedicate /'dedɪkeɪt/ *vt* poświęci|ć, -ać [life] (**to sth** czemuś or na coś); za|dedykować [book] (**to sb** komuś)

dedicated /'dedɪkeɪtɪd/ *adj* [teacher, fan, worker] oddany; [opponent] zagorzały; [student] gorliwy

dedication /ˌdedɪ'keɪʃn/ *n* [] (devotion) poświęcenie *n*, oddanie *n* (**to sth** czemuś); **her** ~ **to duty** jej obowiązkowość [] (in a book) dedykacja *f*

deduce /dɪ'djuːs, US -'dus/ *vt* wy|wnioskować (**from sth** z czegoś)

deduct /dɪ'dʌkt/ *vt* odlicz|yć, -ać [expenses] (**from sth** od czegoś); od|jąć, -ejmować [number] (**from sth** od czegoś); potrąc|ić, -ać [tax] (**from sth** z czegoś)

deduction /dɪ'dʌkʃn/ *n* [] (on wages) potrącenie *n*; (on bill) odliczenie *n* [] (conclusion) wniosek *m*; **to make a** ~ wysnuć wniosek (**from sth** z czegoś)

deed /diːd/ *n* [] (act) czyn *m*, uczynek *m*; **to do one's good** ~ **for the day** spełnić dobry uczynek [] (for property) akt *m* własności

deep /diːp/ [] *adj* [] (vertically) głęboki; [grass] wysoki; **a** ~**-pile carpet** dywan z długim włosem; **how** ~ **is the river?** jak głęboka jest rzeka?; **the lake is 13 m** ~ jezioro ma 13 m głębokości [] [colour] głęboki, ciemny; ~ **blue eyes** ciemnoniebieskie oczy [] ~ **in sth** pogrążony w czymś [thought, conversation]; zajęty or zaabsorbowany czymś [book]; **to be** ~ **in debt** tonąć w długach [] *adv* [] [dig, bury, cut] głęboko [] ~ **down** or **inside** w głębi duszy or serca; **to run** ~ [belief, feeling] być głęboko zakorzenionym

deepen /'diːpən/ [] *vt* [] pogłębi|ć, -ać [channel, hole] [] pogłębi|ć, -ać [knowledge, understanding]; wzm|óc, -agać [concern, interest]
[] *vi* [] [concern, love] wzm|óc, -agać się; [knowledge, mystery, silence] pogłębi|ć, -ać się [] [tone, voice] zniż|yć, -ać się [] [colour] pogłębi|ć, -ać się
[] **deepening** *prp adj* [awareness, crisis] pogłębiający się; [interest, need] wzrastający; [confusion, rift] zwiększający się

deep-(fat-)fryer /ˌdiːp'fæt'fraɪə(r)/ *n* frytkownica *f*

deep-freeze /ˌdiːp'friːz/ *n* zamrażarka *f*

deep-fry /ˌdiːp'fraɪ/ *vt* u|smażyć w głębokim tłuszczu

deeply /'diːplɪ/ *adv* [moving, think, breath, cut] głęboko; [discuss, study] dogłębnie

deep-rooted /ˌdiːp'ruːtɪd/ *adj* głęboko zakorzeniony

deep-sea /ˌdiːp'siː/ *adj* [organism, diver] głębinowy; [fishing] dalekomorski

deer /dɪə(r)/ *n* (stag) jeleń *m*; (doe) łania *f*; (fawn) jelonek *m*; **roe** ~ sarna; **fallow** ~ daniel

de-escalate /diː'eskəleɪt/ *vt* powstrzym|ać, -ywać or zahamować eskalację (czegoś) [war, violence]; za|łagodzić [conflict]; z|łagodzić [crisis]

deface /dɪ'feɪs/ *vt* z|niszczyć [wall, door]; pokry|ć, -wać napisami [monument, painting]

default /dɪ'fɔːlt/ [] *vi* **to** ~ **(on payments)** nie uiścić należności; **to** ~ **on a loan** nie spłacić pożyczki
[] **by default** *adv phr* **to win by** ~ wygrać walkowerem; **to be elected by** ~ zostać wybranym z braku innych kandydatów

defeat /dɪ'fiːt/ [] *n* porażka *f*; **to suffer a** ~ doznać porażki; **to admit** ~ przyznać się do porażki
[] *vt* [] (beat) pokon|ać, -ywać [enemy, opposition, opponent]; od|eprzeć, -pierać [argument] [] (reject) odrzuc|ić, -ać [motion, proposal] [] **it** ~**s me** nie pojmuję tego

defeatist /dɪ'fiːtɪst/ *n* defetysta *m*

defect [] /'diːfekt/ *n* (flaw) defekt *m*, wada *f*; (minor) usterka *f*; **speech** ~ wada wymowy
[] /dɪ'fekt/ *vi* przejść na stronę przeciwnika; **a spy who** ~**ed to the West** szpieg, który uciekł na Zachód

defective /dɪ'fektɪv/ *adj* [part] wadliwy

defector /dɪ'fektə(r)/ *n* zbieg *m*, uciekinier *m*, -ka *f*

defence GB, **defense** US /dɪ'fens/ *n* obrona *f* (**against sb/sth** przed kimś/czymś); **to put up a spirited** ~ [competitor, troops] stawiać zacięty opór; **in** ~ **of the right to strike** w obronie prawa do strajku

defenceless GB, **defenseless** US /dɪ'fenslɪs/ *adj* [animal, person] bezbronny; [country, town] pozbawiony obrony

defend /dɪ'fend/ *vt* o|bronić [country, person, freedom, title] (**against** or **from sb/sth** przed kimś/czymś); uzasadni|ć, -ać [behaviour, decision]

defendant /dɪ'fendənt/ *n* oskarżon|y *m*, -a *f*

defender /dɪ'fendə(r)/ *n* obrońca *m*

defensive /dɪ'fensɪv/ *adj* [behaviour, reaction] obronny; [weapon] defensywny; **to be (very)** ~ **about sth** być (bardzo) niechętnym czemuś

defer /dɪ'fɜː(r)/ [] *vt* od|roczyć, -aczać [payment]; od|łożyć, -kładać [departure]
[] *vi* **to** ~ **to sb** zda|ć, -wać się na kogoś

deference /'defərəns/ *n* szacunek *m*; **in** ~ **to sb/ sth** przez szacunek dla kogoś/czegoś

defiance /dɪˈfaɪəns/ n (noncompliance) nieposłuszeństwo n (**of sth** czemuś); (resistance) opór m (**of sth** wobec czegoś); (disregard) lekceważenie n (**of sth** czegoś); **in ~ of sb/sth** wbrew or na przekór komuś/czemuś

defiant /dɪˈfaɪənt/ adj [person] arogancki; [behaviour] wyzywający

deficiency /dɪˈfɪʃənsɪ/ n ⊡ (shortage) niedostatek m (**of** or **in sth** czegoś); (of vitamins) niedobór m (**of sth** czegoś) ⊡ (weakness) (human) niedoskonałość f; (of system, argument) mankament m

deficient /dɪˈfɪʃnt/ adj niedostateczny; **to be ~ in sth** wykazywać brak czegoś

deficit /ˈdefɪsɪt/ n deficyt m

define /dɪˈfaɪn/ vt z|definiować [word] (**as sth** jako coś); (pinpoint) s|precyzować [problem]

definite /ˈdefɪnɪt/ adj ⊡ [plan, criteria] określony; [result, amount] dokładny; **a ~ answer** wyraźna odpowiedź; **nothing is ~ yet** jeszcze nic nie jest ustalone ⊡ [person] pewny; **to be ~ about sth** być pewnym czegoś

definitely /ˈdefɪnɪtlɪ/ adv z pewnością, na pewno; **it is ~ colder today** dzisiaj jest zdecydowanie chłodniej

definition /ˌdefɪˈnɪʃn/ n definicja f

definitive /dɪˈfɪnɪtɪv/ adj ostateczny, definitywny

deflate /dɪˈfleɪt/ vt spu|ścić, -szczać powietrze z (czegoś)

deflationary /ˌdiːˈfleɪʃənərɪ, US -nerɪ/ adj deflacyjny

deflect /dɪˈflekt/ vt odchyl|ić, -ać kurs (czegoś) [missile]; fig odwr|ócić, -acać [attention]; od|eprzeć, -pierać [criticism, accusation]

defraud /dɪˈfrɔːd/ vt oszuk|ać, -iwać [client, employer]; okra|ść, -dać [person]

defrost /ˌdiːˈfrɒst/ ⓘ vt rozmr|ozić, -ażać [food, refrigerator]; odmr|ozić, -ażać [windscreen]
ⓘⓘ vi [windscreen] odmarz|nąć, -ać; [food, freezer] rozmr|ozić, -ażać się

deft /deft/ adj [movement] zwinny; [worker, mechanic] sprawny

defunct /dɪˈfʌŋkt/ adj [organization, company] nieistniejący; [custom] zapomniany

defuse /ˌdiːˈfjuːz/ vt rozbr|oić, -ajać [bomb]; rozładow|ać, -ywać fig [situation]

defy /dɪˈfaɪ/ vt ⊡ (resist) przeciwstawi|ć, -ać się (komuś/czemuś) [person, authority, law] ⊡ **to ~ sb to do sth** sprowokować kogoś do zrobienia czegoś ⊡ (elude) op|rzeć, -ierać się (czemuś) [attempt, efforts]; **to ~ description** być nie do opisania

degenerate ⓘ /dɪˈdʒenərət/ adj zdegenerowany
ⓘⓘ /dɪˈdʒenəreɪt/ vi [morals] z|degenerować się; [health, quality] pog|orszyć, -arszać się

degrade /dɪˈɡreɪd/ vt poniż|yć, -ać [person]

degrading /dɪˈɡreɪdɪŋ/ adj [conditions, film, treatment] poniżający (**to sb** dla kogoś); (stronger) [work] hańbiący

degree /dɪˈɡriː/ n ⊡ (measurement) stopień m ⊡ (from university) stopień m (naukowy); **first** or **bachelor's ~** licencjat ⊡ (amount) stopień m; **to such a ~ that...** do takiego stopnia, że...; **by ~s** stopniowo; **with varying ~s of success** ze zmiennym szczęściem ⊡ US **murder in the first ~** morderstwo z premedytacją

degree ceremony n GB Univ uroczystość f wręczania dyplomów

degree course n GB Univ studia plt dyplomowe

dehydrated /ˌdiːhaɪˈdreɪtɪd/ adj [food] liofilizowany; [person] odwodniony; **to become ~** odwodnić się

de-icer /ˌdiːˈaɪsə(r)/ n odmrażacz m

deign /deɪn/ vi **to ~ to do sth** raczyć coś zrobić iron

deity /ˈdiːɪtɪ/ n bóstwo n

dejected /dɪˈdʒektɪd/ adj przygnębiony

delay /dɪˈleɪ/ ⓘ n ⊡ (of train, flight) opóźnienie n ⊡ (slowness) **without (further) ~** (dłużej) nie zwlekając
ⓘⓘ vt ⊡ (postpone) od|łożyć, -kładać [departure, decision] ⊡ (hold up) zatrzym|ać, -ywać [person]; wstrzym|ać, -ywać [action]; **flights were ~ed by up to 12 hours** opóźnienie lotów dochodziło do 12 godzin

delayed /dɪˈleɪd/ adj opóźniony; [passenger] spóźniony

delegate ⓘ /ˈdelɪɡət/ n delegat m, -ka f
ⓘⓘ /ˈdelɪɡeɪt/ vt przekaz|ać, -ywać [power, duty] (**to sb** komuś); zlec|ić, -ać [task] (**to sb** komuś)

delegation /ˌdelɪˈɡeɪʃn/ n delegacja f

delete /dɪˈliːt/ vt (with pen) wykreśl|ić, -ać; (on computer) s|kasować

deliberate /dɪˈlɪbərət/ adj ⊡ (intentional) rozmyślny; **it was ~** to było rozmyślne ⊡ (measured) [steps, movement] miarowy

deliberately /dɪˈlɪbərətlɪ/ adv (intentionally) [do, say] rozmyślnie; [act, do] celowo

delicacy /ˈdelɪkəsɪ/ n ⊡ (of object, situation) delikatność f; (of touch) lekkość f; (of mechanism) czułość f; (of senses) wrażliwość f ⊡ (food) przysmak m

delicate /ˈdelɪkət/ adj [china, fabric, features, situation] delikatny; [mechanism] czuły

delicatessen /ˌdelɪkəˈtesn/ n ⊡ (shop) delikatesy plt ⊡ US (eating place) bar m

delicious /dɪˈlɪʃəs/ adj pyszny

delight /dɪˈlaɪt/ ⓘ n (joy) radość f; (pleasure) przyjemność f; **to take ~ in doing sth** robić coś z przyjemnością; **to take ~ in sth** czerpać radość z czegoś
ⓘⓘ vt zachwyc|ić, -ać [person] (**with sth** czymś)

delighted /dɪˈlaɪtɪd/ adj (happy) uszczęśliwiony (**with** or **by** or **about sth** czymś); (pleased) zachwycony (**with** or **by** or **about sth** czymś); (**I am**) ~ **to meet you** bardzo mi miło pana/panią poznać

delightful /dɪ'laɪtfl/ *adj* zachwycający; *[child, animal]* rozkoszny; *[meal, story]* wspaniały

delinquency /dɪ'lɪŋkwənsɪ/ *n* przestępczość *f*

delinquent /dɪ'lɪŋkwənt/ **I** *n* winny *m*, -a *f* przestępstwa

II *adj* przestępczy; **a** ~ **child** nieletni or niepełnoletni przestępca

delirious /dɪ'lɪrɪəs/ *adj [patient]* majaczący; *[condition]* deliryczny; *[crowd, fan]* rozentuzjazmowany

deliver /dɪ'lɪvə(r)/ **I** *vt* ① (take) dostarcz|yć, -ać (**to sb** komuś); (to several houses) rozn|ieść, -osić; (by vehicle) rozw|ieźć, -ozić; '~ **ed to your door**' „z dostawą do domu" ② Med od|ebrać, -bierać poród (kogoś/czegoś) *[baby, baby animal]* ③ (utter) wygł|osić, -aszać *[speech]*; ogł|osić, -aszać *[verdict]*; postawić, stawiać *[ultimatum]*

II *vi [tradesman]* dostarcz|yć, -ać; *[postman]* przynosić pocztę

delivery /dɪ'lɪvərɪ/ *n* ① (of goods) dostawa *f*; (of mail, newspapers) dostarczanie *n*; **on** ~ przy odbiorze ② (of baby) poród *m*

delude /dɪ'lu:d/ *vt* zw|ieść, -odzić (**with sth** czymś); **to** ~ **oneself** łudzić się

deluge /'delju:dʒ/ *n* potop *m*; fig zalew *m*

delusion /dɪ'lu:ʒn/ *n* urojenie *n*; ~**s of grandeur** mania wielkości

demand /dɪ'mɑ:nd, US dɪ'mænd/ **I** *n* ① żądanie *n*; **on** ~ *[divorce, access]* na żądanie; *[payable]* a vista; **to be in** ~ mieć wzięcie ② (pressure) wymóg *m* ③ (for goods) popyt *m* (**for sth** na coś)

II *vt* ① (request) domagać się (czegoś) *[reform, release]*; za|żądać (czegoś) *[attention, payment]* ② (require) wymagać *[patience, skill]* (**of sb** od kogoś)

demanding /dɪ'mɑ:ndɪŋ, US -'mænd-/ *adj [boss, teacher]* wymagający; *[work, course]* trudny; *[schedule]* napięty

demean /dɪ'mi:n/ *vr* **to** ~ **oneself** poniż|yć, -ać się

demeaning /dɪ'mi:nɪŋ/ *adj* poniżający

demented /dɪ'mentɪd/ *adj [person]* obłąkany; *[screams]* obłąkańczy

dementia /dɪ'menʃə/ *n* demencja *f*

demerara (sugar) /ˌdeməˈreərə/ *n* brązowy cukier *m* trzcinowy

demilitarize /ˌdiː'mɪlɪtəraɪz/ *vt* z|demilitaryzować

demister /ˌdiː'mɪstə(r)/ *n* GB odmgławiacz *m* szyb

demo /'deməʊ/ *n* infml = **demonstration** demonstracja *f*

demobilize /diː'məʊbɪlaɪz/ *vt* z|demobilizować

democracy /dɪ'mɒkrəsɪ/ *n* (system) demokracja *f*; (country) państwo *n* demokratyczne

democrat /'deməkræt/ *n* demokrat|a *m*, -ka *f*

democratic /ˌdemə'krætɪk/ *adj* demokratyczny

demolish /dɪ'mɒlɪʃ/ *vt* wyburz|yć, -ać *[building, wall]*; z|burzyć *[order, town]*; obal|ić, -ać *[argument, theory]*

demolition /ˌdemə'lɪʃn/ *n* (of building, wall) rozbiórka *f*; (of system, town) zburzenie *n*; (of argument, theory) obalenie *n*

demon /'diːmən/ *n* demon *m*

demonstrate /'demənstreɪt/ **I** *vt* ① (prove) dow|ieść, -odzić słuszności (czegoś) *[theory, principle]* ② (show) okaz|ać, -ywać *[concern, support]*; wyka|z|ać, -ywać się (czymś) *[skill]*; za|demonstrować *[machine, product]*

II *vi* manifestować; **to** ~ **for/against sth** demonstrować na rzecz czegoś/przeciwko czemuś

demonstration /ˌdemən'streɪʃn/ *n* ① (march) demonstracja *f*; ~ **against/for sth** demonstracja na rzecz czegoś/przeciwko czemuś ② (of machine) pokaz *m*; (of theory) pokazanie *n*; **to give a** ~ zrobić pokaz

demonstrative /dɪ'mɒnstrətɪv/ *adj* ① *[person]* wylewny ② *[pronoun]* wskazujący

demonstrator /'demənstreɪtə(r)/ *n* demonstrant *m*, -ka *f*

demoralize /dɪ'mɒrəlaɪz, US -'mɔːr-/ *vt* ① (dishearten) zniechęc|ić, -ać ② (corrupt) z|demoralizować

demote /ˌdiː'məʊt/ *vt* z|degradować *[person]*

den /den/ *n* ① (of lion) legowisko *n*; (of fox) nora *f* ② (room) pokój *m*

denial /dɪ'naɪəl/ *n* (of rumours, accusation) zaprzeczenie *n*; (of request, rights) odmowa *f*

denim /'denɪm/ **I** *n* (fabric) dżins *m*; ~**s** (trousers) dżinsy *plt*

II *adj [jacket, shirt]* dżinsowy

Denmark /'denmɑːk/ *prn* Dania *f*

denomination /dɪˌnɒmɪ'neɪʃn/ *n* ① (name) nazwa *f* ② (faith) wyznanie *n* fml ③ (value) wartość *f* nominalna, nominał *m*

denounce /dɪ'naʊns/ *vt* ① (inform on) za|denuncjować ② (criticize) potępi|ć, -ać (**for sth** za coś) ③ (accuse) otwarcie oskarż|yć, -ać (**for sth/doing sth** o coś/o zrobienie czegoś)

dense /dens/ *adj [liquid, fog, wood]* gęsty; *[crowd, housing]* zwarty

density /'densətɪ/ *n* gęstość *f*; (of housing, crowd) zwartość *f*

dent /dent/ **I** *n* (in metal) wgniecenie *n*

II *vt* wgni|eść, -atać *[metal object]*; stuknąć infml *[car]*

dental /'dentl/ *adj* dentystyczny; ~ **hygiene** higiena jamy ustnej

dental floss *n* nić *f* dentystyczna

dental surgeon *n* dentyst|a *m*, -ka *f*

dental surgery *n* GB (premises) gabinet *m* dentystyczny

dentist /'dentɪst/ *n* dentyst|a *m*, -ka *f*

dentistry /'dentɪstrɪ/ *n* dentystyka *f*

dentures /'dentʃərs/ *npl* sztuczna szczęka *f*

deny /dɪ'naɪ/ *vt* ⑴ zaprzecz|yć, -ać (czemuś) *[accusation, rumour]*; **to ~ doing/having done sth** zaprzeczyć, że się coś zrobiło ⑵ **to ~ sb sth** odmówić komuś czegoś

deodorant /di:'əʊdərənt/ *n* (personal) dezodorant *m*; (for room) odświeżacz *m* powietrza

depart /dɪ'pɑːt/ *vi* ⑴ *[person]* wy|rusz|yć, -ać; *[train, bus]* odje|chać, -żdżać; *[plane]* odl|ecieć, -atywać; *[boat]* odpły|nąć, -wać ⑵ (deviate) **to ~ from sth** odbiegać od czegoś *[position, attitude]*; **to ~ from the truth** rozminąć się z prawdą

department /dɪ'pɑːtmənt/ *n* ⑴ (of company) (wy)dział *m* ⑵ (governmental) ministerstwo *n*; (part of ministry) departament *m* ⑶ (in store) dział *m* ⑷ (in hospital) oddział *m*; **X ray ~ radiologia** ⑸ (in university) wydział *m*

departmental /ˌdiːpɑːt'mentl/ *adj* ⑴ (in politics) ministerialny ⑵ (in administration) wydziału

department store *n* dom *m* towarowy

departure /dɪ'pɑːtʃə(r)/ *n* ⑴ (of bus, train, person) odjazd *m*; (of plane) odlot *m* ⑵ (from policy, tradition) odejście *n* (**from sth** od czegoś)

departure gate *n* wyjście *n* (do samolotu), bramka *f*

departures board *n* (at airport) tablica *f* odlotów; (at train station) tablica *f* odjazdów

depend /dɪ'pend/ *vi* polegać (**on sb/sth** na kimś/czymś); liczyć (**on sb/sth** na kogoś/coś); **the temperature varies ~ing on the season** temperatura zmienia się w zależności od pory roku

dependable /dɪ'pendəbl/ *adj [person]* godny zaufania; *[machine]* niezawodny; *[news, source]* pewny

dependant /dɪ'pendənt/ *n* **to be sb's ~** być na utrzymaniu kogoś; **he has five ~s** ma pięć osób na (swoim) utrzymaniu

dependence GB, **dependance** US /dɪ'pendəns/ *n* ⑴ (reliance) zaufanie *n* (**on sth/sb** do czegoś/kogoś) ⑵ (addiction) uzależnienie *n* (**on sth** od czegoś)

dependent /dɪ'pendənt/ *adj* zależny (**on sth/sb** od czegoś/kogoś); (on drugs) uzależniony; **to be ~ on** *or* **upon sb/sth** być zależnym od kogoś/czegoś; **~ relatives** krewni na utrzymaniu

depict /dɪ'pɪkt/ *vt* (visually) na|malować; (in writing) przedstawi|ć, -ać

depiction /dɪ'pɪkʃn/ *n* przedstawienie *n*, obraz *m*

deplete /dɪ'pliːt/ *vt* (reduce) uszczupl|ić, -ać *[reserves]*; zmniejsz|yć, -ać *[number]*; (exhaust) wyczer-p|ać, -ywać *[supply, energy]*

deplorable /dɪ'plɔːrəbl/ *adj [behaviour]* godny ubolewania; *[state]* opłakany

deplore /dɪ'plɔː(r)/ *vt* ubolewać nad (czymś)

deploy /dɪ'plɔɪ/ *vt* rozlokow|ać, -ywać *[soldiers, equipment]*

depopulation /diːˌpɒpjʊ'leɪʃn/ *n* wyludnienie *n*

deport /dɪ'pɔːt/ *vt* deportować *[immigrant, criminal]*

deportation /ˌdiːpɔː'teɪʃn/ *n* deportacja *f*

depose /dɪ'pəʊz/ *vt* z|detronizować *[king]*; obal|ić, -ać *[dictator]*; z|dymisjonować *[minister]*

deposit /dɪ'pɒzɪt/ ❚ *n* ⑴ (to bank account) wpłata *f* ⑵ (on house, hire purchase goods) zaliczka *f* (**on sth** na coś) ⑶ (on holiday, hotel room) zadatek *m* ⑷ (paid by hirer, tenant) kaucja *f* ⑸ (on bottle) zastaw *m* ⑹ (of silt, mud) nanos *m*; (of oil, ore) złoże *n*
❚❚ *vt* (entrust) z|deponować *[valuables, documents]* (**with sb/sth** u kogoś/w czymś); (earning interest) wpłac|ić, -ać *[money]*

depot /'depəʊ, US 'diːpəʊ/ *n* ⑴ (for storage) skład *m* ⑵ US (bus or train station) dworzec *m*

depress /dɪ'pres/ *vt* ⑴ przygnębi|ć, -ać *[person]* ⑵ (lower) obniż|yć, -ać *[prices]*; zmniejsz|yć, -ać *[investments]*; doprowadz|ić, -ać do zastoju w (czymś) *[trading]*

depressed /dɪ'prest/ *adj* ⑴ *[person]* przygnębiony; *[mood]* smutny ⑵ *[industry, region]* dotknięty kryzysem; **~ market** osłabiony rynek

depressing /dɪ'presɪŋ/ *adj* przygnębiający

depression /dɪ'preʃn/ *n* depresja *f*

deprivation /ˌdeprɪ'veɪʃn/ *n* (poverty) nędza *f*

deprive /dɪ'praɪv/ *vt* pozbawi|ć, -ać

deprived /dɪ'praɪvd/ *adj [area]* ubogi; *[child]* z ubogiej rodziny; *[existence]* w biedzie

depth /depθ/ ❚ *n* ⑴ (of hole, water) głębokość *f*; (of layer, snow) grubość *f*; **to be out of one's ~** (in water) stracić grunt; (in situation) czuć się zagubionym ⑵ (of colour) głębia *f*; (of crisis) powaga *f*; (of ignorance) bezdenność *f*; (of emotion) bezmiar *m* ⑶ (of analysis, knowledge) dogłębność *f*; (of novel) głębia *f*; **in ~** *[examine, study]* wnikliwie
❚❚ **depths** *npl* głębia *f*; **in the ~s of winter** w pełni zimy; **to be in the ~s of despair** być na dnie rozpaczy

deputize /'depjʊtaɪz/ *vi* **to ~ for sb** zastąpić kogoś

deputy /'depjʊti/ ❚ *n* ⑴ (aide) zastęp|ca *m*, -czyni *f* (**to sb** kogoś) ⑵ (politician) deputowan|y *m*, -a *f*
❚❚ *adj* **~ minister/director** wiceminister/wice-dyrektor; **~ sheriff** zastępca szeryfa

deputy chairman *n* wiceprzewodniczący *m*

deputy president *n* wiceprezes *m*

derail /dɪ'reɪl/ *vt* s|podowodać wykolejenie się (czegoś) *[train]*

deregulate /ˌdiː'regjʊleɪt/ *vt* uw|olnić, -alniać *[prices]*; wyj|ąć, -mować spod kontroli *[market]*

derelict /'derəlɪkt/ *adj [building, land]* (abandoned) opuszczony; (ruined) w ruinie

derision /dɪ'rɪʒn/ *n* drwiny *f pl*

derive /dɪ'raɪv/ *vt* czerpać *[profit, power]* (**from sth** z czegoś); zna|leźć, -jdować *[pleasure, joy]* (**from sth** w czymś)

derogatory /dɪ'rɒgətri, US -tɔːri/ *adj [remark]* uwłaczający; *[review, article]* obraźliwy

descend /dɪ'send/ **I** vt zejść, schodzić po (czymś) or z (czegoś) [steps]; zejść, schodzić z (czegoś) [slope]; zejść, schodzić w dół (czymś) [path]

II vi [1] (go down) [person, road] zejść, schodzić; [aircraft] obniż|yć, -ać lot [2] [rain] s|padać; [mist] opa|ść, -dać; [darkness] zapa|ść, -dać [3] [tourists, visitors] zwal|lić, -ać się infml (**on sb/sth** do kogoś/czegoś) [4] (be related to) **to ~ from sb** pochodzić od kogoś

descendant /dɪ'sendənt/ n potom|ek m, -kini f (**of sb** kogoś)

descent /dɪ'sent/ n [1] (movement) zejście n, schodzenie n [2] (extraction) pochodzenie n

describe /dɪ'skraɪb/ vt opis|ać, -ywać [event, person, thing]; (characterize) określ|ić, -ać; **to ~ sb as an idiot** przedstawić kogoś jako idiotę

description /dɪ'skrɪpʃn/ n opis m (**of sb/sth** kogoś/czegoś); (for police) rysopis m (**of sb** kogoś)

descriptive /dɪ'skrɪptɪv/ adj opisowy

desecrate /'desɪkreɪt/ vt s|profanować [church, altar]

desert **I** /'dezət/ n pustynia f

II /dɪ'zɜːt/ vt opu|ścić, -szczać [person, post]

III /dɪ'zɜːt/ vi [soldier] z|dezerterować

deserted /dɪ'zɜːtɪd/ adj [street, area] opustoszały

deserter /dɪ'zɜːtə(r)/ n dezerter m (**from sth** z czegoś)

desert island n bezludna wyspa f

deserve /dɪ'zɜːv/ vt zasłu|żyć, -giwać na (coś) [success, reward]

deserving /dɪ'zɜːvɪŋ/ adj [winner] zasłużony; [cause] słuszny

design /dɪ'zaɪn/ **I** n [1] (idea, sketch) projekt m (**for sth** czegoś) [2] (planning, development) projektowanie n [3] (pattern) wzór m; (decorative) deseń m; (of room, building) wystrój m; **a leaf ~** deseń w liście

II vt [1] (conceive, plan) za|projektować [2] (intend) przeznacz|yć, -ać (**for sb/sth** dla kogoś/na coś); **these measures are ~ed to reduce pollution** te środki mają zmniejszyć zanieczyszczenie środowiska

designate /'dezɪgneɪt/ vt **to ~ sb (as) sth** wyznaczyć or desygnować kogoś na coś; **to ~ sth (as) sth** uznać coś za coś; **to ~ sth for sb/sth** przeznaczyć coś dla kogoś/do czegoś

designer /dɪ'zaɪnə(r)/ **I** n projektant m, -ka f; (of software) autor m, -ka f; (of cars, bridges) konstruktor m, -ka f; **theatre ~** (of sets) scenograf

II adj [drink, cocktail] najmodniejszy; **~ jeans/sunglasses** dżinsy/okulary słoneczne znanego domu mody; **~ label** metka domu mody

design fault n błąd m projektowy

desirable /dɪ'zaɪərəbl/ adj [1] [outcome, solution] pożądany; [job, quality] upragniony; [gift] mile widziany [2] (sexually) [man] atrakcyjny; [woman] pociągająca

desire /dɪ'zaɪə(r)/ **I** n ochota f (**for sth** na coś); pragnienie n (**for sth** czegoś); (sexual) pożądanie n; **to have no ~ to do sth** nie mieć ochoty zrobić czegoś

II vt za|pragnąć (kogoś/czegoś), mieć ochotę na (coś); (sexually) pożądać (kogoś); **to ~ to do sth** pragnąć zrobić coś; **it leaves a lot to be ~d** pozostawia wiele do życzenia

desk /desk/ n [1] biurko n [2] (pupil's) ławka f; (teacher's) stolik m [3] **reception ~** recepcja; **information ~** informacja; **cash ~** kasa

desktop /'desktɒp/ n (also **~ computer, ~ PC**) komputer m biurkowy

desolate /'desələt/ adj [1] (deserted) [landscape, place] wymarły; [building] opuszczony; (devastated) zrujnowany [2] (forlorn) beznadziejnie smutny

despair /dɪ'speə(r)/ **I** n rozpacz f; **to be in ~ about** or **over sth** zamartwiać się o coś; **to do sth in** or **out of ~** zrobić coś w or z rozpaczy

II vi tracić nadzieję (**of sth/doing sth** na coś/zrobienie czegoś); rozpaczać (**of sb/sth** nad kimś/czymś or z powodu kogoś/czegoś)

desperate /'despərət/ adj [person] zrozpaczony; [search, effort] rozpaczliwy; **to be ~ for sth** rozpaczliwie potrzebować czegoś; **to do sth ~** posunąć się do ostateczności

desperately /'despərətlɪ/ adv [1] [search, plead, need] rozpaczliwie; [look, ask] z rozpaczą [2] [ill] beznadziejnie; [poor] koszmarnie infml

desperation /,despə'reɪʃn/ n rozpacz f

despicable /dɪ'spɪkəbl, 'despɪkəbl/ adj podły

despise /dɪ'spaɪz/ vt gardzić (kimś/czymś) (**for sth** za coś, z powodu czegoś)

despite /dɪ'spaɪt/ prep (po)mimo (czegoś)

despondent /dɪ'spɒndənt/ adj [person] przygnębiony; (disheartened) zniechęcony

despot /'despɒt/ n despot|a m, -ka f

dessert /dɪ'zɜːt/ n deser m

dessertspoon /dɪ'zɜːtspuːn/ n łyżeczka f deserowa

dessert wine n wino n deserowe

destabilize /,diː'steɪbəlaɪz/ vt z|destabilizować [country, economy]; osłabi|ć, -ać pozycję (kogoś/czegoś) [government, president]

destination /,destɪ'neɪʃn/ n (of journey) cel m podróży; (of letter, parcel) miejsce n przeznaczenia; (of train) stacja f docelowa; (of ship, aircraft) port m przeznaczenia

destined /'destɪnd/ adj [1] (preordained) przeznaczony (**for sth** or **to do sth** do czegoś); **it was ~ to happen** to musiało się wydarzyć [2] (bound for) **this letter/parcel is ~ for Paris** miejscem przeznaczenia tego listu/tej paczki jest Paryż

destiny /'destɪnɪ/ n los m

destitute /'destɪtjuːt, US -tuːt/ adj bez środków do życia

destroy /dɪ'strɔɪ/ *vt* [1] z|niszczyć *[building, evidence, career]*; obal|ić, -ać *[faith, authority]* [2] (kill) wyni-szcz|yć, -ać *[population]*; rozgr|omić, -amiać *[enemy]*; zabi|ć, -jać *[animal]*; dobi|ć, -jać *[injured animal]*

destruction /dɪ'strʌkʃn/ *n* zniszczenie *n*

destructive /dɪ'strʌktɪv/ *adj [force, fire]* niszczą-cy; *[behaviour, method]* destrukcyjny

detach /dɪ'tætʃ/ *vt* odpi|ąć, -nać *[hood, lining]* (**from sth** od czegoś); od|erwać, -rywać *[sticker]*; odłącz|yć, -ać *[handle, link of chain]*; odczepi|ć, -ać *[carriage]* (**from sth** od czegoś); oddziel|ić, -ać *[group, person]* (**from sb** od kogoś)

detachable /dɪ'tætʃəbl/ *adj [collar, lining]* odpina-ny; *[coupon, section of form]* do oderwania; *[lens, handle, lever]* zdejmowany

detached /dɪ'tætʃt/ *adj* [1] (separate) osobny [2] (dis-interested) obojętny; (neutral) obiektywny

detached house *n* dom *m* (jednorodzinny) wolno stojący

detachment /dɪ'tætʃmənt/ *n* [1] (separation) oddzie-lenie (się) *n*; (by accident) oderwanie (się) *n* [2] (lack of interest) obojętność *f*; (neutrality) bezstronność *f*

detail /'diːteɪl, US dɪ'teɪl/ **I** *n* szczegół *m*; (insignifi-cant) drobiazg *m*; **in more ~** bardziej szczegółowo; **to go into ~s** wdawać się w szczegóły
II *vt* opis|ać, -ywać szczegółowo *[plans, changes]*; wyszczególni|ć, -ać *[items]*

detain /dɪ'teɪn/ *vt* [1] (delay) zatrzym|ać, -ywać [2] (keep in custody) *[police]* zatrzym|ać, -ywać (w areszcie) *[offender]*

detainee /diːteɪ'niː/ *n* zatrzymany *m*, -a *f*

detect /dɪ'tekt/ *vt* wykry|ć, -wać *[error, traces, crime]*; wyczu|ć, -wać *[gas, mood]*

detectable /dɪ'tektəbl/ *adj [trace, element]* wykry-walny; *[emotion]* (in sb's voice) wyczuwalny; (in sb's expression) dostrzegalny

detection /dɪ'tekʃn/ *n* (of disease, error) wykry|cie, -wanie *n*; **crime ~** wykrywalność przestępstw; **to escape ~** *[criminal]* wymknąć się; *[error]* nie zostać wykrytym

detective /dɪ'tektɪv/ *n* (in police) oficer *m* z wydziału dochodzeniowo-śledczego; (private) detektyw *m*; **store ~** pracownik ochrony

detective story *n* opowiadanie *n* kryminalne

detector /dɪ'tektə(r)/ *n* wykrywacz *m*

detention /dɪ'tenʃn/ *n* [1] (confinement) uwięzienie *n*; (prison sentence) pozbawienie *n* wolności; (awaiting trial) areszt *m* tymczasowy [2] (in school) **I've got an hour's ~** muszę za karę zostać godzinę po lekcjach

deter /dɪ'tɜː(r)/ *vt* (dissuade) powstrzym|ać, -ywać; (discourage) zniechęc|ić, -ać (**from (doing) sth** do (robienia) czegoś)

detergent /dɪ'tɜːdʒənt/ *n* detergent *m*

deteriorate /dɪ'tɪərɪəreɪt/ *vi [health, situation]* pog|orszyć, -arszać się; *[material, weather]* po|psuć

się; *[area]* podupa|ść, -dać; *[chemical compound]* rozłoż|yć, -kładać się

determination /dɪˌtɜːmɪ'neɪʃn/ *n* zdecydowa-nie *n*, determinacja *f*

determine /dɪ'tɜːmɪn/ *vt* ustal|ić, -ać

determined /dɪ'tɜːmɪnd/ *adj [person]* zdecydowa-ny (**to do sth** na coś, na zrobienie czegoś); *[expression, manner]* stanowczy

deterrent /dɪ'terənt, US -'tɜː-/ *n* środek *m* odstra-szający; **to be a ~ to sb** powstrzymywać kogoś

detest /dɪ'test/ *vt* nie cierpieć (kogoś/czegoś)

detonate /'detəneɪt/ *vt* z|detonować *[bomb, device]*

detour /'diːtʊə(r), US dɪ'tʊər/ *n* objazd *m*

detract /dɪ'trækt/ *vi* **to ~ from sth** pomniejsz|yć, -ać coś *[success, value]*; za|szkodzić czemuś *[harmony, image]*; ze|psuć coś *[pleasure]*

detriment /'detrɪmənt/ *n* **to the ~ of sb/sth** ze szkodą or z uszczerbkiem dla kogoś/czegoś

detrimental /ˌdetrɪ'mentl/ *adj [effect, influence]* szkodliwy (**to sb/sth** dla kogoś/czegoś); *[criticism, decision]* krzywdzący (**to sb/sth** dla kogoś/czegoś)

deuce /djuːs, US duːs/ *n* (in tennis) równowaga *f*

devaluation /ˌdiːvæljʊ'eɪʃn/ *n* (of currency) dewa-luacja *f*; (of shares) obniżenie *n* wartości

devastated /'devəsteɪtɪd/ *adj [region]* spustoszo-ny; *[person]* załamany

devastation /ˌdevə'steɪʃn/ *n* (of land, town) spusto-szenie *n*; (of building) dewastacja *f*

develop /dɪ'veləp/ **I** *vt* [1] (acquire) naby|ć, -wać *[knowledge]*; nab|rać, -ierać *[habit]*; **to ~ an awareness of sth** uświadomić sobie coś; **she ~ed the symptoms of flu** pojawiły się or wystąpiły u niej objawy grypy [2] (evolve) rozwi|nąć, -jać *[plan, story]*; u|doskonalić *[invention, technique]* [3] (expand) rozwi|nąć, -jać *[intellect, muscles, busi-ness]*; pogłęb|ić, -ać *[friendship, knowledge]* [4] (im-prove) zagospodarow|ać, -ywać *[land, site]*; rozbudo-w|ać, -ywać *[city centre]* [5] (in photography) wywoł|ać, -ywać *[photographs]*
II *vi* [1] (evolve) *[child, intelligence, skills, society, plot]* rozwi|nąć się, -jać się (**into sth** w coś) [2] (come into being) *[friendship]* na|rodzić się; *[trouble, crack]* powsta|ć, -wać; *[illness]* pojawi|ć, -ać się [3] (progress, advance) *[friendship, war, illness]* rozwi|nąć, -jać się; *[difficulty, fault]* pogłęb|ić, -ać się; *[game, story]* roz|egrać -grywać się [4] (in size, extent) *[town, business]* rozwi|nąć, -jać się

developer /dɪ'veləpə(r)/ *n* (also **property ~**) deweloper *m*, firma *f* deweloperska

developing country *n* kraj *m* rozwijający się

development /dɪ'veləpmənt/ *n* [1] (creation) (of product) stworzenie *n*; (of new industry) rozwój *m* [2] (of land) zagospodarowanie *n*; (of site, city centre) rozbudowa *f*; (of region) rozwój *m* [3] (land developed) **housing ~** osiedle domków jednorodzinnych; **commercial ~** centrum handlowo-usługowe [4] (innovation) **research and ~** prace badawczorozwojowe; (name of a department) dział badań naukowych; **major** ~**s** znaczący postęp 5 (event) rozwój *m* wydarzeń; **the latest** ~**s** ostatnie wydarzenia

deviate /'di:vɪeɪt/ *vi* 1 (from norm, subject) odbie|c, -gać; (from intentions, principles) odst|ąpić, -ępować; **to** ~ **from the truth** .mijać się z prawdą 2 (from course) zb|oczyć, -aczać (**from sth** z czegoś)

device /dɪ'vaɪs/ *n* 1 (household) urządzenie *n* (**for sth/doing sth** do czegoś/do robienia czegoś) 2 Tech przyrząd *m* 3 (also **explosive** ~, **incendiary** ~) bomba *f* 4 (means) sposób *m* (**for doing sth/to do sth** żeby coś zrobić)
IDIOMS: **to leave sb to their own** ~**s** pozostawić kogoś własnemu losowi

devil /'devl/ *n* 1 (also **Devil**) **the** ~ szatan *m* 2 (evil spirit) diabeł *m*
IDIOMS: **speak of the** ~ (**and he is bound to appear**) o wilku mowa (a wilk tu)

devious /'di:vɪəs/ *n* [means, method] pokrętny; [mind] krętacki; [person, plan] chytry

devise /dɪ'vaɪz/ *vt* opracow|ać, -ywać [plan, method]; wymyśl|ić, -ać [ending for a novel]; za|projektować [fashion, tool]; obmyśl|ić, -ać [plot, trap]

devoid /dɪ'vɔɪd/ *adj* ~ **of sth** pozbawiony czegoś [talent, common sense]

devolution /ˌdi:və'lu:ʃn, US ˌdev-/ *n* (transfer) przekazanie *n*

devote /dɪ'vəʊt/ *vt* poświęc|ić, -ać [time, effort] (**to sth/to doing sth** na coś/na zrobienie czegoś); poświęc|ić, -ać [article, novel] (**to sth** czemuś); **to** ~ **oneself** poświęc|ić, -ać się (**to sb/sth** komuś/czemuś)

devoted /dɪ'vəʊtɪd/ *adj* [person, follower] oddany (**to sb/sth** komuś/czemuś); [animal] wierny; [friendship] zażyły

devotion /dɪ'vəʊʃn/ *n* oddanie *n* (**to sth/sb** czemuś/komuś)

devour /dɪ'vaʊə(r)/ *vt* poż|reć, -erać [food, book]; z|eżreć, -żerać [resources]; pochł|onąć, -aniać [big sums of money]

devout /dɪ'vaʊt/ *adj* [prayer] żarliwy; [person, act] pobożny

dew /dju:, US du:/ *n* rosa *f*

diabetes /ˌdaɪə'bi:ti:z/ *n* cukrzyca *f*

diabetic /ˌdaɪə'betɪk/ **1** *n* diabety|k *m*, -czka *f* **11** *adj* [condition] cukrzycowy

diagnose /'daɪəɡnəʊz, US ˌdaɪəɡ'nəʊs/ *vt* z|diagnozować [patient]; rozpozna|ć, -wać [illness]

diagnosis /ˌdaɪəɡ'nəʊsɪs/ *n* rozpoznanie *n*, diagnoza *f*

diagonal /daɪ'æɡənl/ **1** *n* (line) linia *f* ukośna **11** *adj* ukośny; **our street is** ~ **to the main road** nasza ulica odchodzi ukosem od głównej drogi

diagonally /daɪ'æɡənəlɪ/ *adv* ukośnie

diagram /'daɪəɡræm/ *n* schemat *m*; (in mathematics) wykres *m*

dial /'daɪəl/ **1** *n* tarcza *f* **11** *vt* wyb|rać, -ierać [number]; **to** ~ **999** (for police, ambulance or for fire brigade) zadzwonić pod numer 999

dialect /'daɪəlekt/ *n* dialekt *m*

dialling code *n* GB numer *m* kierunkowy

dialling tone GB, **dial tone** US *n* sygnał *m* zgłoszenia

dialogue /'daɪəlɒɡ, US -lɔ:ɡ/ *n* rozmowa *f* (**with sb** z kimś)

dialysis /daɪ'æləsɪs/ *n* dializa *f*

diameter /daɪ'æmɪtə(r)/ *n* średnica *f*; **to be 2 metres in** ~ mieć 2 metry średnicy

diamond /'daɪəmənd/ *n* 1 (stone) (unpolished) diament *m*; (polished) brylant *m* 2 (shape) romb *m* 3 (in cards) karo *n*

diaper /'daɪəpə(r), US 'daɪpər/ US *n* pieluszka *f*

diaphragm /'daɪəfræm/ *n* przepona *f*

diarrhoea GB, **diarrhea** US /ˌdaɪə'rɪə/ *n* (condition) biegunka *f*

diary /'daɪərɪ/ *n* 1 (for appointments) terminarz *m*; **to put sth in one's** ~ zanotować coś w terminarzu 2 (journal) dziennik *m*

dice /daɪs/ **1** *n* (object) kostka *f*; (game) kości *plt* **11** *vt* po|kroić w kostkę

dictate 1 /dɪk'teɪt, US 'dɪkteɪt/ *vt* 1 (read aloud) po|dyktować [text] (**to sb** komuś) 2 (impose) dyktować [terms, conditions] (**to sb** komuś); narzuc|ić, -ać [behaviour] (**to sb** komuś) **11** /dɪk'teɪt, US 'dɪkteɪt/ *vi* 1 (read aloud) po|dyktować (**to sb** komuś) 2 (give orders) dyrygować (**to sb** kimś)

dictation /dɪk'teɪʃn/ *n* dyktowanie *n* (**of sth** czegoś); **to take** ~ notować pod dyktando

dictator /dɪk'teɪtə(r), US 'dɪkteɪtər/ *n* dyktator *m*, -ka *f*

dictatorship /dɪk'teɪtəʃɪp, US 'dɪkt-/ *n* dyktatura *f*

dictionary /'dɪkʃənrɪ, US -nerɪ/ *n* słownik *m*

die /daɪ/ *vi* 1 [person] um|rzeć, -ierać; [animal] zd|echnąć, -ychać; **to** ~ **of** or **from sth** umrzeć na coś [illness]; umrzeć z czegoś [starvation]; **to** ~ **for sth** umrzeć or zginąć za coś [country, beliefs]; um|rzeć, -ierać (**of sth** z czegoś) 2 (infml) (long) **to be dying for sth** marzyć o czymś [cup of tea, something to eat]; nie móc się doczekać czegoś [break, change]

■ **die down**: [storm, emotion] uspok|oić się, -ajać się; [noise, scandal] przycich|nąć, -ać; [pain] ust|ąpić, -ępować; [flames] przygas|nąć, -ać; [fighting] o|słabnąć

■ **die out**: wym|rzeć, -ierać; [tribe, dynasty] wygas|nąć, -ać

diesel /'di:zl/ *n* 1 (also ~ **fuel**, ~ **oil**) olej *m* napędowy 2 (also ~ **car**) samochód *m* z silnikiem Diesla

diesel engine *n* (in car) silnik *m* Diesla; (in train) silnik *m* wysokoprężny

diet /ˈdaɪət/ n [1] (of person) sposób m odżywiania się; (of animal) pokarm m [2] (limiting food) dieta f; **to go on a ~** przejść na dietę

dietician, dietitian /ˌdaɪəˈtɪʃn/ n dietetyk m, -czka f

differ /ˈdɪfə(r)/ vi [1] (be different) różnić się (**from sb/sth** od kogoś/czegoś); **to ~ in sth** różnić się czymś [2] (disagree) **to ~ from sb** być odmiennego zdania niż ktoś (**about** or **on sth** jeśli chodzi o coś, co do czegoś)

difference /ˈdɪfrəns/ n [1] (dissimilarity) różnica f (**in sth** w czymś); **to tell the ~ between sth and sth** odróżnić coś od czegoś; **it makes no ~ to me** to mi nie robi różnicy [2] (disagreement) nieporozumienie n (**over sth** co do czegoś); **a ~ of opinion** różnica zdań

different /ˈdɪfrənt/ adj inny (**from** or **to** GB or **than** US **sb/sth** niż ktoś/coś); **that's ~** to zupełnie co innego; **he always has to be ~** on zawsze musi się czymś wyróżniać

differentiate /ˌdɪfəˈrenʃɪeɪt/ [1] vt odróżni|ć, -ać (**from sb/sth** od kogoś/czegoś)

[2] vi [1] (tell the difference) odróżni|ć, -ać [2] (show the difference) rozróżni|ć, -ać

differently /ˈdɪfrəntlɪ/ adv inaczej (**from sb/sth** niż ktoś/coś)

difficult /ˈdɪfɪkəlt/ adj trudny; **I find it ~ to understand** trudno mi to zrozumieć; **he is ~ to get on with** trudno z nim wytrzymać

difficulty /ˈdɪfɪkəltɪ/ n trudność f; **to have ~ (in) doing sth** mieć trudności ze zrobieniem czegoś

diffident /ˈdɪfɪdənt/ adj (not self-confident) niepewny siebie; (modest) nieśmiały; **she is rather ~ about expressing her views** niechętnie wyraża swoją opinię

dig /dɪg/ [1] n [1] (with elbow) szturchaniec m; **to give sb a ~ in the ribs** szturchnąć kogoś w żebra [2] infml (jibe) przytyk m (**at sb** pod adresem kogoś); **to get in a ~ at sb** zrobić przytyk pod adresem kogoś [3] (in archaeology) wykopalisko n pl

[2] **digs** npl GB wynajęty pokój m

[3] vt [1] (excavate) wykop|ać, -ywać [ditch, grave]; (in sth w czymś); przekop|ać, -ywać [tunnel]; skopać [garden]; rozkop|ać, -ywać [site] [2] (extract) kopać [root crops] (**out of sth** z czegoś); wydoby|ć, -wać [coal] (**out of sth** z czegoś)

[4] vi kopać; **to ~ for sth** kopać w poszukiwaniu czegoś [ore, remains, treasure]

■ **dig up** odgrzeb|ać, -ywać [body]; odkop|ać, -ywać [treasure]; wykop|ać, -ywać [crop, plant]; rozkop|ać, -ywać [road]; skopać [garden]; dokop|ać, -ywać się do (czegoś) [facts, scandal]

digest /daɪˈdʒest, dɪ-/ vt s|trawić [food]; przetra-wi|ć, -ać [information]

digestion /daɪˈdʒestʃn, dɪ-/ n trawienie n

digit /ˈdɪdʒɪt/ n [1] (number) cyfra f [2] (finger, toe) palec m

digital /ˈdɪdʒɪtl/ adj [display, clock, recording] cyfrowy

dignified /ˈdɪgnɪfaɪd/ adj [person] dostojny; [manner] godny; [behaviour] pełen godności

dignity /ˈdɪgnətɪ/ n (of person) godność f; (of occasion) powaga f

digress /daɪˈgres/ vi z|robić dygresję

dilapidated /dɪˈlæpɪdeɪtɪd/ adj rozpadający się; [vehicle] zdezelowany infml; [condition] opłakany

dilate /daɪˈleɪt/ [1] vt rozszerz|yć, -ać

[2] vi [pupil, blood vessel] rozszerz|yć, -ać się

dilemma /daɪˈlemə, dɪ-/ n rozterka f; **to be in a ~ over** or **about which to choose** być w rozterce, co wybrać

diligent /ˈdɪlɪdʒənt/ adj (industrious) [person] pracowity; [pupil] pilny; (conscientious) [worker, researcher] sumienny; [efforts] usilny

dilute /daɪˈljuːt, US -ˈluːt/ vt rozcieńcz|yć, -ać [liquid] (**with sth** czymś)

dim /dɪm/ [1] adj [1] [room] ciemny [2] [light] słaby [3] [outline] niewyraźny [4] [recollection] niewyraźny; [feeling] niejasny [5] infml (stupid) [person] tępy infml; [remark] głupi

[2] vt przyga|sić, -szać [light]; US przełącz|yć, -ać [headlights]

dime /daɪm/ n US dziesięciocentówka f

[IDIOMS] **they're a ~ a dozen** infml jest ich na kopy infml

dimension /dɪˈmenʃn/ n wymiar m

-dimensional /-dɪˈmenʃənl/ in combinations **three-~** trójwymiarowy

dime store n US tani sklep m wielobranżowy

diminish /dɪˈmɪnɪʃ/ [1] vt zmniejsz|yć, -ać, osłabi|ć, -ać [authority, enthusiasm, love]; z|mącić [happiness]

[2] vi [numbers, supplies, chances] z|maleć; [value, interest rate] spa|ść, -dać; [emotion, strength] o|słabnąć

dimple /ˈdɪmpl/ n (in cheek) dołeczek m

din /dɪn/ n (of machines) łoskot m; (of people) wrzawa f

dine /daɪn/ vi (at midday) z|jeść obiad; (in the evening) z|jeść kolację

diner /ˈdaɪnə(r)/ n [1] (person) gość m [2] US (restaurant) tania restauracja f

dinghy /ˈdɪŋgɪ/ n [1] (also **sailing ~**) jolka f [2] (inflatable) ponton m

dingy /ˈdɪndʒɪ/ adj [colour] wyblakły; [place] obskurny

dining car n wagon m restauracyjny

dining room n (in house) pokój m stołowy; (in hotel) sala f restauracyjna

dinner /ˈdɪnə(r)/ n [1] (meal) (evening) kolacja f; (midday) obiad m; **to go to ~** iść na proszony obiad/proszoną kolację [2] (banquet) przyjęcie n

dinner hour n GB Sch przerwa f obiadowa

dinner party n uroczysta kolacja f

dinnertime /'dɪnətaɪm/ n (midday) pora f obiadowa; (evening) pora f kolacji

dinosaur /'daɪnəsɔː(r)/ n dinozaur m

dip /dɪp/ **[]** n [1] (bathe) krótka kąpiel f [2] (in ground) obniżenie n terenu; (in road) spadek m [3] (in prices, rates, sales) spadek m (**in sth** czegoś) [4] Culin dip m **[]** vt [1] zanurz|yć, -ać *[fingers, toes]* (**in** or **into sth** w czymś); zam|oczyć, -aczać *[garment, cloth]* [2] GB Aut przełącz|yć, -ać (światła) z długich na mijania *[headlights]*; ~**ped headlights** światła mijania **[]** vi [1] zniż|yć, -ać się; *[bird]* za|nurkować; *[plane]* pikować; **the sun** ~**ped below the horizon** słońce schowało się za horyzontem [2] *[land, level]* obniż|yć, -ać się; *[path]* opa|ść, -dać [3] *[person]* sięg|nąć, -ać (**for sth** po coś); **to** ~ **into one's savings** sięgnąć głęboko do kieszeni; **to** ~ **into sth** za|jrzeć, -glądać do czegoś *[book, report]*

diploma /dɪ'pləʊmə/ n dyplom m (**in sth** z czegoś, w dziedzinie czegoś)

diplomacy /dɪp'ləʊməsɪ/ n dyplomacja f

diplomat /'dɪpləmæt/ n dyplomata m

diplomatic /ˌdɪplə'mætɪk/ adj dyplomatyczny; (tactful) *[person, remark]* taktowny

dipstick /'dɪpstɪk/ n prętowy wskaźnik m poziomu

direct /daɪ'rekt, dɪ-/ **[]** adj [1] bezpośredni; **in** ~ **contact with sth** (touching) stykający się z czymś; (communicating) w bezpośrednim kontakcie z czymś; **to be a** ~ **descendant of sb** wywodzić się w prostej linii od kogoś [2] (straightforward) *[method]* bezpośredni; *[answer, person]* bezpośredni, szczery **[]** adv bezpośrednio; **to fly** ~ (**from Warsaw to New York**) lecieć bezpośrednio (z Warszawy do Nowego Jorku) **[]** vt [1] (address, aim) s|kierować *[appeal, criticism]* (**at sb against sb/sth** do kogoś przeciwko komuś/czemuś); skierow|ać, -ywać *[effort, resource]* (**to** or **towards sth** na coś); **to** ~ **sb's attention to sb/sth** zwrócić uwagę kogoś na kogoś/coś [2] (control) kierować (kimś/czymś) *[company, project]*; regulować *[traffic]* [3] (point, aim) s|kierować *[attack, light]* (**at sb/sth** na kogoś/coś) [4] wy|reżyserować *[film, drama, opera]*; po|prowadzić *[actor, cameraman]* [5] (show route) **to** ~ **sb to sth** skierować kogoś gdzieś **[]** vi (in cinema, radio, TV) **Lee** ~**ed** reżyserował Lee

direct debit n stałe zlecenie n płatnicze; **by** ~ na podstawie dyspozycji bankowej

direction /daɪ'rekʃn, dɪ-/ **[]** n kierunek m; **in the wrong/right/opposite** ~ w złym/dobrym/przeciwnym kierunku; **from all** ~**s** ze wszystkich stron **[]** directions npl [1] (for route) wskazówki f pl; **to ask for** ~**s** (**from sb**) pytać (kogoś) o drogę [2] (for use) instrukcja f (**as to** or **about sth** co do czegoś); ~**s for use** instrukcja użytkowania

directly /daɪ'rektlɪ, dɪ-/ adv [1] *[go, contact]* bezpośrednio; *[move]* prosto; *[aim, point, challenge]* wprost [2] (at once) tuż; ~ **after sth** tuż or zaraz po czymś; ~ **before sth** tuż przed czymś [3] (very soon) zaraz [4] (frankly) *[speak]* szczerze

direct mail n reklama f bezpośrednia

director /daɪ'rektə(r), dɪ-/ n [1] (of company, organization) kierowni|k m, -czka f; (solely in control) dyrektor m naczelny; (one of board) członek m zarządu [2] (of play, film) reżyser m, -ka f [3] (of orchestra) dyrygent m, -ka f

directory /daɪ'rektərɪ, dɪ-/ n [1] (also **telephone** ~) książka f telefoniczna [2] (for business use) branżowy katalog m firm; **street** ~ spis ulic

directory assistance n US = **directory enquiries**

directory enquiries npl GB informacja f telefoniczna

direct speech n mowa f niezależna

dirt /dɜːt/ n [1] (mess) brud m [2] (soil) ziemia f; (mud) błoto n

dirt track n tor m żużlowy

dirty /'dɜːtɪ/ **[]** adj [1] (soiled) brudny; *[nose]* zasmarkany; **to get** ~ ubrudzić się; **to get sth** ~ zabrudzić or ubrudzić coś [2] *[needle]* brudny; *[wound]* zakażony [3] infml *[book, idea]* nieprzyzwoity; *[joke]* świński infml; **to have a** ~ **mind** mieć sprośne or kosmate myśli [4] infml *[contest, player]* nieuczciwy; *[cheat, liar, lie]* podły **[]** vt u|brudzić, za|brudzić *[carpet, nappy]* [IDIOMS] **to give sb a** ~ **look** infml krzywo na kogoś spojrzeć

disability /ˌdɪsə'bɪlətɪ/ n upośledzenie n; (physical) kalectwo n

disable /dɪs'eɪbl/ vt [1] *[illness, accident]* przyprawi|ć, -ać o kalectwo; *[chronic illness]* dokucz|yć, -ać (komuś) [2] Tech unieruch|omić, -amiać *[machinery, ship]* [3] Comput za|blokować

disabled /dɪs'eɪbld/ **[]** n **the** ~ niepełnosprawni m pl **[]** adj niepełnosprawny; **mentally** ~ upośledzony umysłowo

disabled access n podjazd m dla wózków inwalidzkich

disadvantage /ˌdɪsəd'vɑːntɪdʒ, US -'væn-/ n [1] (drawback) wada f [2] (position of weakness) niekorzyść f; **to be at a** ~ być w niekorzystnej sytuacji

disadvantaged /ˌdɪsəd'vɑːntɪdʒd, US -'væn-/ adj pokrzywdzony przez los

disagree /ˌdɪsə'griː/ vi [1] *[people, person]* nie zg|odzić, -adzać się (**with sb/sth** z kimś/czymś); **to** ~ **on** or **about sth** nie zgadzać się na temat czegoś [2] *[figures, accounts]* być sprzecznym (**with sth** z czymś) [3] **to** ~ **with sb** *[food, weather]* nie służyć komuś

disagreeable /ˌdɪsəˈgriːəbl/ adj [person, mood] niemiły; [remark, experience] przykry; [smell, situation] nieprzyjemny

disagreement /ˌdɪsəˈgriːmənt/ n [1] (difference of opinion) niezgoda f (**about** or **on sth** na temat czegoś); **to be in total ~ with sb** zupełnie się z kimś nie zgadzać (**as to sth** co do czegoś) [2] (argument) sprzeczka f (**about** or **over sth** o coś)

disallow /ˌdɪsəˈlaʊ/ vt [1] Sport nie uzna|ć, -wać (czegoś) [goal] [2] (not allow) odrzuc|ić, -ać

disappear /ˌdɪsəˈpɪə(r)/ vi (vanish) znik|nąć, -ać; (get lost) zapodzi|ać, -ewać się

disappearance /ˌdɪsəˈpɪərəns/ n (from view) zniknięcie n; (getting lost) zaginięcie n

disappoint /ˌdɪsəˈpɔɪnt/ vt rozczarow|ać, -ywać [person]

disappointed /ˌdɪsəˈpɔɪntɪd/ adj rozczarowany (**about** or **with sth** czymś); **I am ~ in you** rozczarowałeś mnie

disappointing /ˌdɪsəˈpɔɪntɪŋ/ adj [book, result] słaby; [meeting, trip] niespełniający oczekiwań

disappointment /ˌdɪsəˈpɔɪntmənt/ n rozczarowanie n; **to be a ~ to sb** sprawić komuś zawód

disapproval /ˌdɪsəˈpruːvl/ n dezaprobata f (**of sb/ sth** dla kogoś/czegoś, w stosunku do kogoś/czegoś)

disapprove /ˌdɪsəˈpruːv/ vi być przeciwnym; **to ~ of sth** nie pochwalać czegoś [behaviour, lifestyle]; być przeciwnikiem czegoś [smoking, hunting]

disapproving /ˌdɪsəˈpruːvɪŋ/ adj [look, gesture] pełen dezaprobaty

disarm /dɪsˈɑːm/ [] vt rozbr|oić, -ajać, z|demilitaryzować [country]
[] vi [nation] rozbr|oić, -ajać się

disarmament /dɪsˈɑːməmənt/ n rozbrojenie n

disaster /dɪˈzɑːstə(r), US -zæs-/ n (flood, earthquake) klęska f żywiołowa; (crash, shipwreck) katastrofa f; (trouble) nieszczęście n

disaster area n obszar m klęski żywiołowej; **my room is a ~** fig mój pokój wygląda jak pobojowisko

disaster fund n fundusz m dla ofiar klęski żywiołowej

disaster victim n ofiara f katastrofy

disastrous /dɪˈzɑːstrəs, US -zæs-/ adj [error, consequences] fatalny; [flood, fire] katastrofalny; [crash, shipwreck] tragiczny

disbelief /ˌdɪsbɪˈliːf/ n niedowierzanie n

disc, disk US /dɪsk/ n [1] (flat circular plate) krążek f; (round surface) tarcza f [2] (spine) krążek m międzykręgowy [3] Mus płyta f [4] (badge) plakietka f; **an identity ~** plakietka identyfikacyjna

discard /dɪsˈkɑːd/ vt [1] (get rid of) pozby|ć, -wać się (czegoś) [clothes, possessions]; wyrzuc|ić, -ać [litter, rubbish] [2] (abandon) zaniechać (czegoś) [idea, plan]; opu|ścić, -szczać [person]

discerning /dɪˈsɜːnɪŋ/ adj [critic, buyer] wymagający; [collector, eye] wytrawny

discharge [] /ˈdɪstʃɑːdʒ/ n [1] (of prisoner, soldier) zwolnienie n; (of patient) wypisanie n (ze szpitala) [2] (of water) wyciekanie n; (of gas) emisja f; (of waste) wyrzucanie n [3] (from eye, wound) wydzielina f
[] /dɪsˈtʃɑːdʒ/ vt [1] (free) zwol|nić, -alniać [prisoner]; wypis|ać, -ywać [patient]; **to be ~d from hospital** zostać wypisanym ze szpitala [2] (fire) zwol|nić, -alniać [employee] [3] (let) wypu|ścić, -szczać [liquid, nuclear waste]; (deliberately) spu|ścić, -szczać [waste] [4] Med wydziel|ić, -ać [fluid, pus]

discipline /ˈdɪsɪplɪn/ [] n [1] (control) dyscyplina f [2] (academic subject) dyscyplina f naukowa
[] vt (control) z|dyscyplinować [children, recruits]; zapanować nad (czymś) [emotions]; (punish) u|karać

disciplined /ˈdɪsɪplɪnd/ adj [manner, person] zdyscyplinowany; [approach] metodyczny

disclaim /dɪsˈkleɪm/ vt wyp|rzeć, -ierać się (czegoś), zaprzecz|yć, -ać (czemuś)

disclaimer /dɪsˈkleɪmə(r)/ n oficjalne sprostowanie n

disclose /dɪsˈkləʊz/ vt ukaz|ać, -ywać [sight]; ujawnić, -ać [information]

disclosure /dɪsˈkləʊʒə(r)/ n ujawnienie n (**of sth** czegoś)

disco /ˈdɪskəʊ/ n (place) dyskoteka f; (music) disco n

discomfort /dɪsˈkʌmfət/ n [1] (lack of comfort) niewygoda f [2] (slight pain) dolegliwość f; **to be in some ~** odczuwać lekki ból [3] (embarrassment) zakłopotanie n

disconcerting /ˌdɪskənˈsɜːtɪŋ/ adj (worrying) niepokojący; (unnerving) denerwujący; (embarrassing) żenujący

disconnect /ˌdɪskəˈnekt/ vt odłącz|yć, -ać [electricity, telephone]; wyłącz|yć, -ać [refrigerator, lights]; rozłącz|yć, -ać [caller]; odczepi|ć, -ać [carriage] (**from sth** od czegoś)

discontent /ˌdɪskənˈtent/ n niezadowolenie n

discontented /ˌdɪskənˈtentɪd/ adj niezadowolony (**with sth** z czegoś)

discontinue /ˌdɪskənˈtɪnjuː/ vt zaprzest|ać, -awać [production]; zawie|sić, -szać [bus service]; przer|wać, -ywać [visit]

discount [] /ˈdɪskaʊnt/ n rabat m (**on sth** na coś); **to give sb a ~** udzielić komuś rabatu or zniżki
[] /dɪsˈkaʊnt, US ˈdɪskaʊnt/ vt [1] pomi|nąć, -jać [idea, possibility] [2] (reduce price) obniż|yć, -ać cenę (czegoś) [goods]

discourage /dɪsˈkʌrɪdʒ/ vt zniechęc|ić, -ać

discover /dɪsˈkʌvə(r)/ vt [1] (learn) pozna|ć, -wać [truth]; (unexpectedly) odkry|ć, -wać; **to ~ who/how/ that...** dowiedzieć się, kto/jak/że... [2] (find) zna|leźć, -jdować [treasure, artefacts]; odna|leźć, -jdować [missing object]; odkry|ć, -wać [star, new talent]

discovery /dɪsˈkʌvərɪ/ n odkrycie n

discredit /dɪsˈkredɪt/ vt z|dyskredytować [person] (**by sth** czymś); podważ|yć, -ać [theory, raport]

discreet /dɪˈskriːt/ adj [make-up] dyskretny; [colour] stonowany

discrepancy /dɪsˈkrepənsɪ/ n rozbieżność f (**in sth** w czymś)

discretion /dɪˈskreʃn/ n ① (authority) prawo n decydowania; **to use one's (own)** ~ zdecydować samemu ② (tact) dyskrecja f

discriminate /dɪˈskrɪmɪneɪt/ vi ① (act with prejudice) dyskryminować (**against sb** kogoś); **to** ~ **in favour of sb** faworyzować kogoś ② (distinguish) rozróżni|ć, -ać; **to** ~ **between X and Y** odróżnić X od Y

discrimination /dɪˌskrɪmɪˈneɪʃn/ n dyskryminacja f (**against sb** kogoś)

discus /ˈdɪskəs/ n Sport dysk m

discuss /dɪˈskʌs/ vt (talk about) prze|dyskutować; (in writing) om|ówić, -awiać

discussion /dɪˈskʌʃn/ n dyskusja f; (in text) omówienie n

disdainful /dɪsˈdeɪnfl/ adj lekceważący

disease /dɪˈziːz/ n choroba f

disembark /ˌdɪsɪmˈbɑːk/ ① vt wyładow|ać, -ywać [cargo]; wysadz|ić, -ać [passengers]

② vi [passengers] wysi|ąść, -adać (**from sth** z czegoś)

disenchanted /ˌdɪsɪnˈtʃɑːntɪd, US -ˈtʃænt-/ adj rozczarowany (**with sth** czymś)

disengage /ˌdɪsɪnˈɡeɪdʒ/ vt rozłącz|yć, -ać; **to** ~ **the clutch** zwolnić sprzęgło

disfigure /dɪsˈfɪɡə(r), US dɪsˈfɪɡjər/ vt oszpec|ić, -ać

disgrace /dɪsˈɡreɪs/ ① n wstyd m (**of sth/doing sth** z powodu czegoś/zrobienia czegoś); **to be in** ~ być w niełasce

② vt przyn|ieść, -osić wstyd (komuś/czemuś) [school, family]; **he** ~**d himself** skompromitował się

disgraceful /dɪsˈɡreɪsfl/ adj [conduct, situation] haniebny

disguise /dɪsˈɡaɪz/ ① n przebranie n; **in** ~ w przebraniu

② vt (change appearance) zmieni|ć, -ać wygląd (komuś) [person]; zmieni|ć, -ać [voice]; za|tuszować [blemish]; ukry|ć, -wać [feelings, facts]; **to** ~ **sb as sb/sth** przebrać kogoś za kogoś/coś

disgust /dɪsˈɡʌst/ ① n wstręt m, obrzydzenie n (**at sb/sth** do kogoś/czegoś)

② vt wzbudz|ić, -ać wstręt w (kimś); (physically) napawać obrzydzeniem (kogoś); (morally) budzić odrazę w (kimś)

disgusting /dɪsˈɡʌstɪŋ/ adj odrażający

dish /dɪʃ/ n ① (plate) talerz m; (for serving) półmisek m; **to do the** ~**es** zmywać naczynia ② (also **satellite** ~) antena f satelitarna

■ **dish out**: rozda|ć, -wać [money]; prawić [compliments]; udziel|ić, -ać (czegoś) [advice]; na|łożyć, -kładać [food]

dishcloth /ˈdɪʃklɒθ, US -klɔːθ/ n (for washing) zmywak m; (for drying) ścierka f do naczyń

dishevelled /dɪˈʃevld/ adj [person] wyglądający niechlujnie; [hair] potargany; [clothes] w nieładzie

dishonest /dɪsˈɒnɪst/ adj nieuczciwy

dishonesty /dɪsˈɒnɪstɪ/ n nieuczciwość f

dishonour GB, **dishonor** US /dɪsˈɒnə(r)/ n hańba f

dishtowel /ˈdɪʃtaʊəl/ n ścierka f do naczyń

dishwasher /ˈdɪʃwɒʃə(r)/ n (person) pomywacz m, -ka f; (machine) zmywarka f do naczyń

disillusioned /ˌdɪsɪˈluːʒnd/ adj pozbawiony złudzeń; **to be** ~ **with sb/sth** być rozczarowanym kimś/czymś

disinfect /ˌdɪsɪnˈfekt/ vt odka|zić, -żać

disinfectant /ˌdɪsɪnˈfektənt/ n środek m odkażający

disintegrate /dɪsˈɪntɪɡreɪt/ vi rozpa|ść, -dać się; [rock] roz|kruszyć się

disinterested /dɪsˈɪntrəstɪd/ adj ① (impartial) bezstronny ② (uninterested) niezainteresowany (**in sth** czymś)

disk /dɪsk/ n ① Comput dysk m ② US = **disc**

dislike /dɪsˈlaɪk/ ① n niechęć f fml; **to take a** ~ **to sb/sth** poczuć niechęć do kogoś/czegoś

② vt nie lubić (**doing sth** robić czegoś); **I** ~ **her intensely** nie znoszę jej

dislocate /ˈdɪsləkeɪt, US ˈdɪsləʊkeɪt/ vt zwichnąć [shoulder, hip]

dislodge /dɪsˈlɒdʒ/ vt z|erwać, -rywać [tile] (**from sth** z czegoś); usu|nąć, -wać [obstacle] (**from sth** z czegoś); obrusz|yć, -ać [stone]

disloyal /dɪsˈlɔɪəl/ adj nielojalny (**to sb/sth** wobec or w stosunku do kogoś)

dismal /ˈdɪzməl/ adj ① [mood, place] ponury ② infml [failure, performance] fatalny

dismantle /dɪsˈmæntl/ vt roz|ebrać, -bierać [construction, motor]; rozwiąz|ać, -ywać [organization]; z|likwidować [system]

dismay /dɪsˈmeɪ/ n konsternacja f (**at sth** z powodu czegoś)

dismiss /dɪsˈmɪs/ vt ① (reject) odrzuc|ić, -ać [possibility, suggestion] ② (put out of mind) zapom|nieć, -inać o (czymś) [worry, anxiety]; odsu|nąć, -wać od siebie [thought] ③ (sack) zwol|nić, -alniać [employee]; odprawi|ć, -ać [servant]; zdymisjonować [government minister] ④ (send away) odprawi|ć, -ać [subordinate]; zwol|nić, -alniać [pupils, class] ⑤ (in law) oddal|ić, -ać [case, charges]

dismissal /dɪsˈmɪsl/ n (of employee) zwolnienie n; (of servant) odprawienie n; (of government minister) zdymisjonowanie n fml

dismissive /dɪsˈmɪsɪv/ adj lekceważący

disobedient /ˌdɪsəˈbiːdɪənt/ adj nieposłuszny

disobey /ˌdɪsəˈbeɪ/ ① vt nie po|słuchać [parents, orders]; nie przestrzegać [rules, law]

② vi być nieposłusznym

disorder /dɪsˈɔːdə(r)/ n [1] (lack of order) nieład m [2] (social, political) rozruchy plt [3] (malfunction) zaburzenia n pl; (disease) choroba f

disorganized /dɪsˈɔːɡənaɪzd/ adj [household, life] zdezorganizowany; [person, group] źle zorganizowany

disorientate /dɪsˈɔːrɪənteɪt/ vt z|dezorientować

disown /dɪsˈəʊn/ vt nie przyzna|ć, -wać się do (czegoś) [article, document]; wyrze|ć, -kać się (kogoś) [child]

dispassionate /dɪsˈpæʃənət/ adj (impartial) obiektywny (**about sb/sth** co do kogoś/czegoś)

dispatch /dɪˈspætʃ/ ◨ n (report) depesza f, komunikat m

◨◨ vt wys|łać, -yłać [letter, person, troops]

dispel /dɪˈspel/ vt rozwi|ać, -ewać [doubts, fears, illusions]

dispensary /dɪˈspensərɪ/ n (in hospital) apteka f; (in chemist's) laboratorium n

dispense /dɪˈspens/ vt [1] [machine] wyda|ć, -wać [drinks, money] [2] [pharmacist] sporządz|ić, -ać [medicine]; z|realizować [prescription] [3] (exempt) uw|olnić, -alniać, zw|olnić, -alniać (**from sth** od czegoś)

■ **dispense with**: oby|ć, -wać się bez (czegoś) [luxuries, services]; z|rezygnować z (czegoś) [formalities, policy]; (make unnecessary) u|czynić zbędnym [resource, facilities]

dispenser /dɪˈspensə(r)/ n (for liquid soap) dozownik m; (for drinks, paper cups) automat m; **cash** ~ bankomat

disperse /dɪˈspɜːs/ ◨ vt rozpr|oszyć, -aszać [crowd]; rozsi|ać, -ewać [seeds]; rozwi|ać, -ewać [fumes]

◨◨ vi [crowd, mist] rozpr|oszyć, -aszać się

displaced person n wysiedleniec m

display /dɪˈspleɪ/ ◨ n [1] (in shop) (of food, small objects) wystawa f; (of furniture, equipment, vehicles) ekspozycja f; **to be on** ~ być wystawionym; **to put sth on** ~ wystawić coś [2] (demonstration) pokaz m [3] (of emotion, quality) przejaw m; (of strength) popis m; (of wealth) pokaz m [4] (device) monitor m obrazowy; (in telephone, radio) wyświetlacz m

◨◨ vt [1] (set out) wywie|sić, -szać [poster, advertisement]; wystawi|ć, -ać [goods] [2] (reveal) przejawi|ć, -ać [intelligence, interest, skill, virtue]; okaz|ać, -ywać [emotion, strength] [3] (flaunt) obnosić się z (czymś) [wealth]; popis|ać, -ywać się (czymś) [knowledge]; chwalić się (czymś) [beauty, legs, chest]

displeased /dɪsˈpliːzd/ adj niezadowolony (**with** or **at sb/sth** z kogoś/czegoś)

disposable /dɪˈspəʊzəbl/ adj [1] (throwaway) jednorazowy [2] (available) do rozporządzenia

disposal /dɪˈspəʊzl/ n [1] (of rubbish) wywóz m; (of nuclear waste, human waste) usuwanie n; (of a body, excess stock) pozbycie się n; **for** ~ do wyrzucenia [2] (of assets, securities, business) zbycie n (**of sth** czegoś)

[3] (for use, access) dysponowanie n; **to be at sb's** ~ być do dyspozycji kogoś

dispose /dɪˈspəʊz/ vt

■ **dispose of**: [1] (get rid of) pozby|ć, -wać się (kogoś/czegoś) [body, evidence]; usu|nąć, -wać [rubbish]; unieszkodliwi|ć, -ać [bomb] [2] (sell) zby|ć, -wać [shares, property]

disproportionate /ˌdɪsprəˈpɔːʃənət/ adj (size) nieproporcjonalny (**to sth** do czegoś); (amount) niewspółmierny (**to sth** do czegoś)

disprove /dɪsˈpruːv/ vt obal|ić, -ać [theory]; zada|ć, -wać kłam (czemuś) [story]

dispute /dɪˈspjuːt/ ◨ n [1] (quarrel) spór m (**over** or **about sth** o coś, w sprawie czegoś) [2] (controversy) kontrowersja f (**over** or **about sth** w związku z czymś); **it is open to** ~ to jest sprawa dyskusyjna

◨◨ vt [1] za|kwestionować [claim, figures] [2] zgł|osić, -aszać pretensje do (czegoś) [property, title]

disqualify /dɪsˈkwɒlɪfaɪ/ vt [1] (from post, career) z|dyskwalifikować; **to** ~ **sb from doing sth** pozbawić kogoś prawa robienia czegoś [2] Sport (before event) wyklucz|yć, -ać (**from sth** z czegoś); (after event) z|dyskwalifikować (**for sth** za coś) [3] GB Aut **to** ~ **sb from driving** pozbawić kogoś prawa prowadzenia pojazdów mechanicznych

disregard /ˌdɪsrɪˈɡɑːd/ ◨ n (for problem, feelings, person, law) lekceważenie n (**for sb/sth** kogoś/czegoś); (for human life) brak m poszanowania; (for danger) niezważanie n (**for sth** na coś)

◨◨ vt [1] (discount) z|lekceważyć [feelings, instructions]; nie zważać na (coś) [dangers]; z|ignorować [remark]; nie brać pod uwagę (czegoś) [human nature, evidence] [2] (disobey) okaz|ać, -ywać brak poszanowania dla or wobec (czegoś) [law, rules]

disrepair /ˌdɪsrɪˈpeə(r)/ n zły stan m; **to fall into** ~ [building] popaść w ruinę; [machinery] zniszczyć się

disreputable /dɪsˈrepjʊtəbl/ adj mający złą opinię

disrespect /ˌdɪsrɪˈspekt/ n brak m szacunku (**for sb/sth** dla kogoś/czegoś)

disrespectful /ˌdɪsrɪˈspektfl/ adj [person] nieokazujący szacunku (**to** or **towards sb** komuś); [conduct, remark] niegrzeczny (**to** or **towards sb/sth** wobec or w stosunku do kogoś/czegoś)

disrupt /dɪsˈrʌpt/ vt zakłóc|ić, -ać [traffic, meeting]; po|krzyżować [plans]; przer|wać, -ywać [proceedings]; spowodować przerwę w (czymś) [power supply]

disruption /dɪsˈrʌpʃn/ n [1] (disorder) zamęt m (**in sth** w czymś); **to cause** ~ **to sth** wprowadzić zamęt w czymś [2] (disrupting) (of meeting, schedule) zakłócenie n; (of plan) pokrzyżowanie n

disruptive /dɪsˈrʌptɪv/ adj [behaviour] zakłócający spokój; [influence, element] destrukcyjny

dissatisfaction /ˌdɪsætɪsˈfækʃn/ n niezadowolenie n (**with sb/sth** z kogoś/czegoś)

dissatisfied /dɪ'sætɪsfaɪd/ adj niezadowolony (**with sb/sth** z kogoś/czegoś)

dissect /dɪ'sekt/ vt przeprowadz|ić, -ać sekcję (czegoś) [cadaver]; s|preparowaé [animal, plant, organ]

dissertation /ˌdɪsə'teɪʃn/ n GB Univ praca f pisemna

dissident /'dɪsɪdənt/ **I** n dysydent m, -ka f **II** adj dysydencki

dissimilar /dɪ'sɪmɪlə(r)/ adj [brothers] niepodobny (**to sb** do kogoś); [lives, people, hairstyle] odmienny (**to sb/sth** od kogoś/czegoś)

dissolve /dɪ'zɒlv/ **I** vt [1] [water, acid] rozpu|ścić, -szczać [solid, grease] [2] [person] rozpu|ścić, -szczać [powder, tablet] (**in sth** w czymś) [3] (break up) rozwiąz|ać, -ywać [assembly, partnership] **II** vi [1] [tablet] rozpu|ścić, -szczać się (**in sth** w czymś) [2] [mist, hopes] rozwi|ać, -ewać się; [outline, image] znik|nąć, -ać [3] **to ~ into tears** zalać się łzami; **to ~ into laughter** roześmiać się

dissuade /dɪ'sweɪd/ vt odw|ieść, -odzić (**sb from (doing) sth** kogoś od (zrobienia) czegoś

distance /'dɪstəns/ n odległość f (**between sth and sth** między czymś a czymś); **a long/short ~ away** daleko/niedaleko (stąd); **to keep one's ~** trzymać się z daleka (**from sb/sth** od kogoś/czegoś); **it's within walking ~** można tam dojść na piechotę

distant /'dɪstənt/ adj [1] (remote) daleki [2] (faint) [association, connection] luźny; [hope, possibility] nikły; [memory] daleki [3] (cool) [person, manner] chłodny

distaste /dɪs'teɪst/ n (slight) niesmak m; (marked) wstręt m

distinct /dɪ'stɪŋkt/ adj [1] (clear) wyraźny [2] (separate) odrębny (**from sth** w stosunku do czegoś) [3] (different) różny, odmienny (**from sth** od czegoś); **as ~ from sth** w odróżnieniu od czegoś

distinction /dɪ'stɪŋkʃn/ n [1] (difference) różnica f (**between sth and sth** między czymś a czymś) [2] Univ wyróżnienie n

distinctive /dɪ'stɪŋktɪv/ adj charakterystyczny (**of sth** dla kogoś/czegoś)

distinguish /dɪ'stɪŋgwɪʃ/ vt (separate) rozróżni|ć, -ać; **to be ~ed by sth** różnić się czymś, wyróżniać się czymś

distinguished /dɪ'stɪŋgwɪʃt/ adj [1] (elegant) dystyngowany [2] (famous) wybitny

distort /dɪ'stɔːt/ vt [1] (misrepresent) zniekształc|ić, -ać [statement]; wypacz|yć, -ać [truth]; przeinacz|yć, -ać [facts, words]; zafałszow|ać, -ywać [history] [2] zniekształc|ić, -ać [sound, reflection]; z|deformo-wać [face]; odkształc|ić, -ać [metal]

distract /dɪ'strækt/ vt rozpr|oszyć, -aszać [driver, player]; **to ~ sb from (doing) sth** odrywać kogoś od (robienia) czegoś; **to ~ (sb's) attention** odwrócić uwagę kogoś (**from sth** od czegoś)

distracting /dɪ'stræktɪŋ/ adj (interrupting) rozpra-szający; (bothering) drażniący

distraction /dɪ'strækʃn/ n [1] (from concentration) zakłócenie n spokoju; **I don't want any ~s** potrzebuję spokoju [2] (diversion) odmiana f

distraught /dɪ'strɔːt/ adj [person] zrozpaczony (**at** or **over sth** czymś)

distress /dɪ'stres/ **I** n [1] (emotional) cierpienie n; **to be in (great/deep) ~** cierpieć (bardzo/dotkli-wie) [2] (physical) ból m; **to be in ~** cierpieć [3] **in ~** [ship] w niebezpieczeństwie **II** vt (upset) z|martwić; (stronger) sprawi|ć, -ać ból (komuś)

distressed /dɪ'strest/ adj (upset) zasmucony (**at** or **by sth** czymś); (stronger) zrozpaczony (**at** or **by sth** czymś)

distressing /dɪ'stresɪŋ/ adj (sad) przygnębiający; (disturbing) niepokojący

distribute /dɪ'strɪbjuːt/ vt [1] (share out) rozda|ć, -wać [food, leaflets]; rozprowadz|ić, -ać [documents, information]; rozdziel|ić, -ać [money]; **to ~ sth to sb/sth** rozdać coś komuś/czemuś; **to ~ sth among sb/sth** rozdzielić coś pomiędzy kogoś/coś [2] (spread out) rozł|ożyć, -kładać [load, weight]

distribution /ˌdɪstrɪ'bjuːʃn/ n (of funds, food) rozdział m (**to sb** wśród or pomiędzy kogoś); (of information) rozpowszechnianie n (**to sb** wśród kogoś); (of leaflets) rozprowadzanie n

distributor /dɪ'strɪbjʊtə(r)/ n dystrybutor m (**for sth** czegoś)

district /'dɪstrɪkt/ n (in country) region m, rejon m; (in city) dzielnica f; (administrative) okręg m

district attorney n US prokurator m okręgowy

distrust /dɪs'trʌst/ vt nie ufać (komuś/czemuś)

disturb /dɪ'stɜːb/ **I** vt (interrupt) zakłóc|ić, -ać [sleep, work]; przeszk|odzić, -adzać (komuś) [person] **II** vt (upset) za|niepokoić [person]

disturbance /dɪ'stɜːbəns/ n [1] (interruption, inconveni-ence) zakłócenie n [2] (riot) niepokoje m pl; (fight) zajście n

disturbed /dɪ'stɜːbd/ adj [1] (psychologically) nie-zrównoważony; **mentally ~** chory umysłowo [2] (concerned) zaniepokojony (**by sth** czymś) [3] [sleep, night] niespokojny

disturbing /dɪ'stɜːbɪŋ/ adj niepokojący; (stronger) zatrważający

disused /dɪs'juːzd/ adj [church, factory] opuszczony

ditch /dɪtʃ/ **I** n rów m **II** vt infml z|erwać, -rywać z (kimś) [friend, ally, boyfriend, girlfriend]; porzuc|ić, -ać [car]

dither /'dɪðə(r)/ vi wahać się; **to ~ about** or **over sth** nie móc się zdecydować na coś

ditto /'dɪtəʊ/ adv infml tak samo

dive /daɪv/ **I** n [1] (into water) skok m do wody; (under water) nurkowanie n [2] (of bird) spadanie n; (of plane) lot m nurkowy; (of submarine, whale) zanurzenie się n

II *vi* [1] (into water) sk|oczyć, -akać do wody; (under water) za|nurkować [2] *[bird, plane]* spa|ść, -dać lotem nurkowym; *[whale, submarine]* zanurz|yć, -ać się

diver /'daɪvə(r)/ *n* (from board) skoczek *m* do wody; (in flippers) (płetwo)nurek *m*; (deep-sea) nurek *m*

diverge /daɪ'vɜ:dʒ/ *vi* [1] *[interests, opinions]* różnić się; **to ~ from sth** odbiegać od czegoś *[belief, truth, norm]* [2] *[railway line, road]* roz|ejść, -chodzić się

diverse /daɪ'vɜ:s/ *adj* [1] (varied) wieloraki [2] (different) odmienny

diversify /daɪ'vɜ:sɪfaɪ/ *vi [business]* poszerz|yć, -ać ofertę (**into sth** o coś)

diversion /daɪ'vɜ:ʃn, US daɪ'vɜ:rʒn/ *n* [1] (of watercourse) zmiana *f* kierunku; (of money) przekazanie *n* [2] (distraction) zajście *n* odwracające uwagę (**from sth** od czegoś) [3] GB (detour) objazd *m*

divert /daɪ'vɜ:t/ *vt* [1] zmieni|ć, -ać kierunek (czegoś) *[road, stream]*; przełącz|yć, -ać *[phone call]*; obr|ócić, -acać *[funds, energy]* (**into sth** na coś); **to ~ traffic through a town** skierować ruch przez miasto [2] (distract) odwr|ócić, -acać *[attention]* (**away from sb/sth** od kogoś/czegoś)

divide /dɪ'vaɪd/ **I** *vt* [1] (also ~ **up**) po|dzielić *[house, money, work]*; (share) rozdziel|ić, -ać; **he ~s his time between home and office** dzieli czas między dom i biuro [2] (separate) oddziel|ić, -ać (**from sth** od czegoś) [3] (cause disagreement) po|dzielić *[allies, government]* [4] (in mathematics) po|dzielić *[number]*; **38 ~d by 19 is 2** 38 podzielone przez 19 daje 2

II *vi [road, river]* rozwidl|ić, -ać się; *[crowd]* rozst|ąpić, -ępować się; *[group]* rozdziel|ić, -ać się; *[cell, organism]* po|dzielić się; **the train ~s at Dover** od Dover część składu jedzie w innym kierunku

dividend /'dɪvɪdend/ *n* (share) dywidenda *f*; fig (bonus) dodatkowa korzyść *f*

dividing line *n* linia *f* podziału

diving /'daɪvɪŋ/ *n* (swimming under water) nurkowanie *n*; (from board) skoki *m pl* do wody

diving board *n* odskocznia *f*

diving suit *n* skafander *m* nurka

division /dɪ'vɪʒn/ *n* [1] podział *m* (**into sth** na coś); (in party, organization) rozłam *m*; (of several things) rozdział *m*; (in mathematics) dzielenie *n* [2] (of troops, planes) dywizja *f*; (of ships) eskadra *f* [3] (branch) oddział *m*; (department) dział *m*; (in police) wydział *m* [4] (in football) liga *f*

divisive /dɪ'vaɪsɪv/ *adj [policy]* stwarzający podziały; **to be socially ~** dzielić społeczeństwo

divorce /dɪ'vɔ:s/ **I** *n* rozwód *m* (**from sb** z kimś) **II** *vt* rozw|ieść, -odzić się z (kimś)

divorcee /dɪ,vɔ:'si:/ *n* rozw|odnik *m*, -ódka *f*

DIY *n* GB = **do-it-yourself** majsterkowanie *n*

dizzy /'dɪzɪ/ *adj* [1] *[person]* cierpiący na zawroty głowy; **to make sb ~** przyprawić kogoś o zawrót

głowy; **I feel ~** kręci mi się w głowie [2] *[height, pace]* zawrotny

DJ *n* = **disc jockey** didżej *m*, DJ

DNA *n* = **deoxyribonucleic acid** DNA *m inv*

do /du:, də/ **I** *vt* [1] z|robić *[washing up, ironing]*; wykon|ać, -ywać *[task]*; **to do sth again** zrobić coś od początku or od nowa [2] **to do sb's hair** ułożyć komuś włosy; **to do one's teeth** umyć zęby; **to do the living room in pink** urządzić salon na różowo; **it's as good as done** to jest prawie or właściwie zrobione or skończone; **what have you done to your hair?** co zrobiłeś z włosami?; **I haven't done anything with your pen!** nawet nie dotykałem twojego pióra!; **to do 60** robić 60 na godzinę [3] infml (cheat) **we've been done** zrobiono nas w konia infml; **to do sb out of sth** oskubać kogoś z czegoś *[money]*

II *vi* [1] (behave) z|robić, wykonać; **'do as you're told'** „zrób, co ci kazano" [2] (serve purpose) **that box will do** to pudełko będzie dobre [3] (be acceptable) **this really won't do!** (as reprimand) tak dłużej być nie może [4] (be sufficient) *[amount of money]* wystarcz|yć, -ać [5] (get on) *[person, business]* radzić sobie [6] (in health) **mother and baby are both doing well** matka i dziecko czują się dobrze; **the patient is doing well** stan chorego jest coraz lepszy

III *v aux* [1] (with questions, negatives) **didn't she look wonderful?** czy(ż) nie wyglądała cudownie? [2] (for emphasis) **so you do want to go after all!** więc jednak chcesz pojechać! [3] (referring back to another verb) **he said he'd help her and he did** powiedział, że jej pomoże i dotrzymał słowa; **you draw better than I do** rysujesz lepiej ode mnie [4] (in requests, imperatives) **do sit down!** (proszę) siadaj(cie)!; **don't you tell me what to do!** nie będziesz mi mówił, co mam robić! [5] (in tag questions and responses) **he lives in England, doesn't he?** on mieszka w Anglii, prawda?; **'who wrote it?' – 'I did'** „kto to napisał?" – „ja"; **'he knows the President' – 'does he?'** „on zna prezydenta" – „naprawdę?"; **so do they/you** oni/ty też; **neither does he/she** ani on/ona

■ **do away with:** zn|ieść, -osić *[rule]*; z|likwidować *[bus service]*; z|burzyć *[building]*; infml (kill) pozbyć się (kogoś)

■ **do up:** [1] (fasten) zawiąz|ać, -ywać *[laces]*; za-pi|ąć, -nać *[buttons, zip]* [2] (wrap) z|robić *[parcel]* [3] (renovate) odn|owić, -awiać *[house, furniture]*

■ **do with:** [1] (involve) **what's it (got) to do with you?** co to ma z tobą wspólnego? [2] (tolerate) tolerować; **I can't do with all these changes** nie potrafię zaakceptować tych wszystkich zmian [3] (need) **I could do with a holiday** przydałby mi się urlop [4] (finish) **it's all over and done with** wszystko skończone

■ **do without**: oby|ć, -wać się bez (kogoś/czegoś) *[person, thing]*

IDIOMS: **how do you do** bardzo mi przyjemnie or miło; **it doesn't do to be late** nie wypada się spóźniać; **it was all I could do not to...** ledwo się powstrzymałem, żeby nie...; **nothing doing!** (no way) nie ma mowy; **well done!** dobra robota!, brawo!

dock /dɒk/ **I** *n* ① (for unloading or repair) dok *m*; **to come into ~** wejść do portu ② US (wharf) nabrzeże *n* ③ GB (in law) ława *f* oskarżonych

II *vi* (arrive) *[ship]* przybi|ć, -jać

dockworker /ˈdɒkwɜːkə(r)/ *n* doker *m*, robotnik *m* portowy

dockyard /ˈdɒkjɑːd/ *n* stocznia *f*

doctor /ˈdɒktə(r)/ **I** *n* ① Med leka|rz *m*, -rka *f* ② Univ doktor *m*

II *vt* (tamper with) s|fałszować *[document, figures]*; s|fabrykować *[evidence, text]*; **to ~ sb's coffee with rat poison** dosypać komuś trutkę na szczury do kawy

doctorate /ˈdɒktərət/ *n* doktorat *m* (**in sth** z czegoś)

document /ˈdɒkjʊmənt/ *n* dokument *m*

documentary /ˌdɒkjʊˈmentrɪ, US -terɪ/ *n* program *m* dokumentalny (**on** or **about sth** na temat czegoś, o czymś)

dodge /dɒdʒ/ **I** *n* GB infml (trick) sztuczka *f*

II *vt* uchyl|ić, -ać się przed (czymś) *[bullet, blow]*; wym|knąć, -ykać się (komuś) *[pursuers]*; unik|nąć, -kać (kogoś/czegoś) *[difficulty, confrontation]*

dodgy /ˈdɒdʒɪ/ *adj* infml GB ① (untrustworthy) *[person]* podejrzany; *[business, deal]* szemrany infml ② (risky) *[plan, investment]* ryzykowny; *[situation, moment]* niepewny

dog /dɒg, US dɔːg/ *n* ① pies *m* ② (male wolf, fox) samiec *m*

IDIOMS: **to go to the ~s** infml schodzić na psy

dog collar *n* ① (for dog) obroża *f* ② infml (for clergyman) koloratka *f*

dog-eared /ˈdɒgɪəd, US ˈdɔːg-/ *adj [book, pages]* z oślimi uszami

dogged /ˈdɒgɪd, US ˈdɔːgɪd/ *adj [person, insistence, refusal]* uparty; *[persistence, determination]* zawzięty; *[resistance]* zacięty

doghouse /ˈdɒghaʊs, US ˈdɔːg-/ *n* US psia buda *f*

IDIOMS: **to be in the ~** infml być w niełasce

dogmatic /dɒgˈmætɪk, US dɔːg-/ *adj* dogmatyczny (**about sth** w sprawie czegoś)

dog paddle *n* piesek *m*; **to swim the ~** pływać pieskiem

dogsbody /ˈdɒgzbɒdɪ, US ˈdɔːgz-/ *n* GB infml (also **general ~**) chłopak *m* or chłopiec *m* na posyłki

doh /dəʊ/ *n* Mus do *n*

doing /ˈduːɪŋ/ *n* **all of this is your ~** to wszystko twoja sprawka; **it takes some ~!** to wymaga pewnego wysiłku!

dole /dəʊl/ *n* GB infml zasiłek *m* dla bezrobotnych; **to be/go on the ~** być na zasiłku/pójść na zasiłek

■ **dole out**: rozdziel|ić, -ać *[food, money]* (**to sb** między kogoś)

doll /dɒl, US dɔːl/ *n* ① (toy) lalka *f* ② infml (pretty girl) lala *f*, laleczka *f* infml

dollar /ˈdɒlə(r)/ *n* dolar *m*

dollar bill *n* US banknot *m* dolarowy

dolphin /ˈdɒlfɪn/ *n* Zool delfin *m*

domain /dəʊˈmeɪn/ *n* dziedzina *f*, domena *f*

dome /dəʊm/ *n* kopuła *f*

domestic /dəˈmestɪk/ *adj* ① *[market, flights]* krajowy; *[politics, crisis]* wewnętrzny ② *[life, harmony, arguments]* rodzinny; *[atmosphere, comforts]* domowy

domestic appliance *n* sprzęt *m* gospodarstwa domowego

domesticate /dəˈmestɪkeɪt/ *vt* udom|owić, -awiać *[animal]*; zagospodarow|ać, -ywać *[countryside]*

dominant /ˈdɒmɪnənt/ *adj [quality, role, gene]* dominujący; *[chord, key]* dominantowy

dominate /ˈdɒmɪneɪt/ **I** *vt* z|dominować *[person, region, industry]*; **an area ~d by factories** teren, na którym przeważają fabryki

II *vi* dominować (**over sb/sth** nad kimś/czymś)

domineering /ˌdɒmɪˈnɪərɪŋ/ *adj [person]* despotyczny; *[personality, tone]* władczy

domino /ˈdɒmɪnəʊ/ *n* (piece) kostka *f* domino

donate /dəʊˈneɪt/ *vt* ofiarow|ać, -ywać *[money, goods]*; odda|ć, -wać *[blood, organ]* (**to sb/sth** komuś/czemuś)

donation /dəʊˈneɪʃn/ *n* datek *m* (**to sb/sth** dla kogoś/na coś)

done /dʌn/ **I** *pp* → **do**

II *excl* (making deal) załatwione!

donkey /ˈdɒŋkɪ/ *n* osioł *m*

donor /ˈdəʊnə(r)/ *n* ① (of organ) daw|ca *m*, -czyni *f*; ② (of money) ofiarodaw|ca *m*, -czyni *f*

donor card *n* karta *f* dawcy (*dokument potwierdzający wolę oddania organów po śmierci*)

doodle /ˈduːdl/ *vi* na|bazgrać (**on sth** na czymś)

doom /duːm/ *n* (unhappy destiny) (of person) fatum *n*; (of country, group) nieuchronność *f* przeznaczenia

door /dɔː(r)/ *n* drzwi *plt*; (of cupboard, washing-machine) drzwiczki *plt*; **a few ~s down** kilka domów dalej; **behind closed ~s** za zamkniętymi drzwiami

door bell *n* dzwonek *m* u drzwi

doorman /ˈdɔːmæn/ *n* odźwierny *m*, portier *m*

doormat /ˈdɔːmæt/ *n* wycieraczka *f*

doorstep /ˈdɔːstep/ *n* (step) stopień *m*; (threshold) próg *m*; **on one's ~** (nearby) za progiem

door-to-door /ˌdɔːtəˈdɔː(r)/ *adj [selling]* obwoźny

doorway /ˈdɔːweɪ/ *n* (frame) otwór *m* drzwiowy; (entrance) **in the ~** w drzwiach; **in a shop ~** w wejściu do sklepu

dope /dəʊp/ **I** *n* infml ① (illegal drug) narkotyk *m*; (canabis) trawka *f* infml ② (fool) palant *m* infml

II vt poda|ć, -wać środki dopingujące (komuś/ czemuś) *[horse, athlete]*; poda|ć, -wać narkotyk or narkotyki (komuś)

dope test n Sport test m antydopingowy

dormant /'dɔːmənt/ adj *[emotion, sexuality, volcano]* uśpiony

dormitory /'dɔːmɪtrɪ, US -tɔːrɪ/ n ① GB sala f sypialna; (in monastery) dormitorium n ② US Univ dom m akademicki

dormouse /'dɔːmaʊs/ n orzesznica f

dose /dəʊs/ n dawka f; **to have a nasty ~ of flu** mieć paskudną grypę

dot /dɒt/ n kropka f; GB (decimal point) przecinek m; (distant tiny mark) punkt m

(IDIOMS) **since the year ~** infml od wieków; **at two o'clock on the ~** punkt druga

dote /dəʊt/ vi **to ~ on sb/sth** hołubić kogoś/coś

dotted line n linia f kropkowana

double /'dʌbl/ **II** n ① (of whisky) podwójna f infml; (of vodka, brandy) setka f infml ② (of person) sobowtór m; (in film, play) dubler m, -ka f

II **doubles** npl (in tennis) gra f podwójna

III adj ① *[portion, width]* podwójny; *[strength]* zdwojony; **to be spelt with a ~ 'g'** pisać się przez dwa 'g'; **my phone number is six four ~ three ~ five** mój numer telefonu to sześćdziesiąt cztery, trzydzieści trzy, pięćdziesiąt pięć ② (for two) *[bed, room]* dwuosobowy; *[invitation]* dla dwóch osób

IV adv ① (twice) podwójnie ② *[fold]* na dwa; *[bend]* wpół; **to see ~** widzieć podwójnie; **he began to see ~** zaczęło mu się dwoić w oczach

V vt podw|oić, -ajać *[cost, amount]*; po|mnożyć przez dwa *[number]*

VI vi ① *[cost, size, population]* podw|oić, -ajać się ② **to ~ for sb** (actor) dublować kogoś ③ **the sofa ~s as a bed** sofa pełni również funkcję łóżka

(IDIOMS) **on** or **at the ~** szybkim marszem; fig z życiem

double act n duet m

double bass n kontrabas m

double bed n podwójne łóżko n

double-breasted /ˌdʌbl'brestɪd/ adj *[jacket]* dwurzędowy

double-check vt ponownie sprawdz|ić, -ać *[date, figures]*

double chin n podwójny podbródek m

double cream n GB śmietana f kremowa

double-cross /ˌdʌbl'krɒs/ infml vt wystawi|ć, -ać kogoś do wiatru infml

double-decker /ˌdʌbl'dekə(r)/ n GB (bus) autobus m piętrowy

double Dutch n GB infml bełkot m infml; **to talk ~** gadać bez sensu

double glazing n podwójne szyby f pl

double-park /ˌdʌbl'pɑːk/ vi za|parkować na drugiego infml

double room n dwuosobowy pokój m

double standard n **to have ~s** mieć podwójną moralność

double take n **to do a ~** mieć opóźnioną reakcję

double vision n podwójne widzenie n; **to have ~** widzieć podwójnie

double yellow line(s) n(pl) GB Aut podwójna żółta linia f *(oznaczająca zakaz parkowania)*

doubt /daʊt/ **II** n wątpliwość f; **there is no ~ that...** nie ma wątpliwości, że...; **there is little ~ that...** jest prawie pewne, że...; **no ~ the police will want to speak to you** bez wątpienia policja będzie chciała z tobą porozmawiać; **to be in ~** *[outcome]* być niepewnym; *[honesty, innocence]* być wątpliwym; **when in ~** w razie wątpliwości; **without (a) ~** bez wątpienia

II vt wątpić (**if** or **whether...** czy...); wątpić w (coś) *[ability, honesty]*; mieć wątpliwości co do (czegoś) *[existence, result]*; **I ~ it (very much)!** bardzo w to wątpię!

doubtful /'daʊtfl/ adj ① (unsure) *[person, expression]* pełen wątpliwości; *[future, weather]* niepewny; **to be ~ about doing sth** wahać się, czy coś zrobić; **to be ~ about** or **as to sth** mieć wątpliwości co do czegoś *[explanation, idea, plan]*; mieć wątpliwości w związku z czymś *[job, object, purchase]* ② (questionable) *[person, activities, past]* podejrzany; *[taste, result]* wątpliwy

dough /dəʊ/ n ciasto n; **pizza ~** ciasto na pizzę

doughnut, donut US /'dəʊnʌt/ n pączek m; (ring-shaped) pączek m wiedeński

douse, dowse /daʊs/ vt obl|ać, -ewać *[person, room]*; z|gasić *[flames, light]*; **to ~ sb/sth with water** oblać kogoś/coś wodą

dove /dʌv/ n gołąb m, gołębica f

Dover /'dəʊvə(r)/ prn Dover m

dowdy /'daʊdɪ/ adj *[woman]* zaniedbana; *[clothes]* nieelegancki

down¹ /daʊn/ **II** adv ① **to go/come ~** pójść/zejść na dół; **to fall ~** spaść; **to sit ~ on the floor** usiąść na podłodze; **to pull ~ a blind** spuścić roletę; **~ below** na dole; **two floors ~** dwa piętra niżej; **the telephone lines are ~** zerwało linie telefoniczne ② **bookings are ~ by a half** zarezerwowano o połowę mniej pokoi hotelowych; **this year's profits are well ~ on last year's** zysk w tym roku jest o wiele niższy niż w ubiegłym; **to get one's weight ~** schudnąć; **to get the price ~** obniżyć cenę; **I'm ~ to my last cigarette** został mi ostatni papieros ③ Sport **to be two sets ~** *[tennis player]* przegrywać dwoma setami ④ (as deposit) **to pay 40 pounds ~** wpłacić 40 funtów zadatku

II prep ① **they came running ~ the hill** zbiegli z górki; **she's gone ~ town** pojechała do miasta or do centrum; **they live ~ the road** mieszkają kawałek dalej ② **to go ~ the street** iść ulicą; **a**

dress with buttons all ~ the front sukienka zapinana od góry do dołu

III *adj* [1] infml **to feel ~** być w dołku infml [2] *[escalator]* w or na dół [3] *[computer]* niesprawny (IDIOMS:) **it's ~ to you to decide** decyzja należy do ciebie; **~ with tyrants!** precz z tyranią!

down² /daʊn/ *n* (feathers) puch *m*; (hairs) meszek *m*

down-and-out /ˌdaʊnənˈaʊt/ *n* kloszard *m*

downbeat /ˈdaʊnbiːt/ *adj* infml [1] (pessimistic) przygaszony; *[mood]* pesymistyczny [2] (laid back) powściągliwy

downfall /ˈdaʊnfɔːl/ *n* (of person, government) upadek *m*; **she proved to be his ~** doprowadziła go do upadku

downhearted /ˌdaʊnˈhɑːtɪd/ *adj* przygnębiony

downhill /ˌdaʊnˈhɪl/ *adv* **to go ~** *[person]* (on foot) schodzić; (on skis, by vehicle) zjeżdżać; *[road]* biec w dół; *[vehicle]* zjeżdżać; **from now on it's ~ all the way** fig (easy) teraz to już z górki infml; (disastrous) dalej jest już równia pochyła infml

downhill ski(ing) *n* narciarstwo *n* zjazdowe

download /ˌdaʊnˈləʊd/ Comput *vt* przes|łać, -yłać dane z serwera

downmarket /ˌdaʊnˈmɑːkɪt/ *adj [products, hotel, restaurant]* tandetny; *[neighbourhood]* uboższy; *[newspaper, programme]* dla niewybrednych odbiorców

down payment *n* zaliczka *f*

downpour /ˈdaʊnpɔː(r)/ *n* ulewa *f*

downright /ˈdaʊnraɪt/ **I** *adj [insult]* jawny; *[refusal]* kategoryczny; *[liar]* skończony
II *adv [stupid, rude]* wręcz

downstairs /ˌdaʊnˈsteəz/ **I** *adj [room]* na dole; (on ground floor) na parterze; (one floor below) piętro niżej; **the ~ flat** GB or **apartment** US mieszkanie na parterze
II *adv [come, go]* na dół; *[live]* (on ground floor) na parterze; (on floor below) piętro niżej

downstream /ˌdaʊnˈstriːm/ **I** *adj [journey]* w dół rzeki; *[sail]* z prądem; *[town]* w dole rzeki
II *adv [drift]* z prądem; *[travel]* w dół rzeki

down-to-earth /ˌdaʊntəˈɜːθ/ *adj [approach, person]* praktyczny; *[reason]* przyziemny; **she is very ~** (ona) twardo stąpa po ziemi

downtown /ˌdaʊnˈtaʊn/ US *adj [store, streets]* śródmiejski; **~ New York** centrum Nowego Jorku

downtrodden /ˈdaʊntrɒdn/ *adj [country]* uciskany; *[person]* poniewierany

downturn /ˈdaʊntɜːn/ *n* (in career) schyłek *m*; (in economy) tendencja *f* zniżkowa (**in sth** w dziedzinie czegoś); (in profits, demand) spadek *m* (**in sth** czegoś)

down under *adv* infml **to go ~** pojechać do Australii/Nowej Zelandii

downward /ˈdaʊnwəd/ *adj [movement, glance]* w dół

downwards /ˈdaʊnwədz/ *adv* (also **downward**) *[look, gesture]* w dół; **to slope ~** *[path]* opadać; **he**

was floating face ~ unosił się w wodzie na brzuchu

doze /dəʊz/ *vi* zdrzemnąć się
■ **doze off**: (momentarily) przys|nąć, -ypiać; (sleep) zas|nąć, -ypiać

dozen /ˈdʌzn/ *n* [1] (twelve) tuzin *m*; **by the ~** na tuziny [2] (several) **~s of people/books/times** dziesiątki ludzi/książek/razy

drab /dræb/ *adj [colour]* bury; *[existence]* bezbarwny; *[day]* szary; *[building, surroundings]* ponury

draft /drɑːft, US dræft/ *n* [1] (of letter, article, speech) szkic *m*; (of contract, law) projekt *m* [2] (on bank) polecenie *n* wypłaty; **to make a ~ on a bank** wystawić tratę or weksel na bank [3] US (conscription) pobór *m* [4] US = **draught**
II *vt* [1] na|pisać roboczą wersję or brudnopis (czegoś) *[letter, article, speech]*; sporządz|ić, -ać projekt (czegoś) *[contract, law]* [2] US (conscript) powoł|ać, -ywać (**into sth** do czegoś) [3] GB (transfer) przen|ieść, -osić *[personnel]*; oddelegow|ać, -ywać *[person]*; odkomenderow|ać, -ywać *[troops]*
■ **draft in** GB: ściąg|nąć, -ać *[experts, police]*

draft dodger *n* US dekownik *m* infml

drag /dræg/ **I** *n* [1] infml (person) nudzia|rz *m*, -ra *f*; **what a ~ !** co za męka or mordęga! infml [2] (women's clothes) **in ~** w damskim przebraniu
II *adj* [1] **~ artist** aktor w damskim przebraniu [2] **~ race** wyścig bolidów
III *vt* [1] (pull) ciągnąć; (trail) wlec (za sobą); **to ~ sth along the ground** ciągnąć or wlec coś po ziemi; **to ~ sth (up) to sth** dociągnąć or dowlec coś do czegoś; **to ~ one's feet** or **heels** wlec się noga za nogą; fig ociągać się (**on sth** z czymś) [2] przeszuk|ać, -iwać *[lake, river]* [3] Comput przeciąg|nąć, -ać *[icon]*
IV *vi* [1] (go slowly) *[hours, days, story]* wlec się [2] (trail) **to ~ in sth** *[hem, belt]* wlec się po czymś [3] **to ~ on sth** zaciągnąć się czymś *[cigarette]*
■ **drag on**: *[conflict, speech]* ciągnąć się

drain /dreɪn/ **I** *n* [1] (in street) studzienka *f*; (in sink) otwór *m* odpływowy; (ditch) kanał *m* or rów *m* odwadniający [2] (of money) topnienie *n* fig; (of people) odpływ *m*; **to be a ~ on resources** pochłaniać ogromne środki
II *vt* [1] osusz|yć, -ać *[land]*; spu|ścić, -szczać wodę z (czegoś) *[lake, radiator]* [2] wyczerp|ać, -ywać *[resources]* [3] opróżni|ć, -ać, osusz|yć, -ać *[glass]*; wypi|ć, -jać do dna *[drink]* [4] Culin odsącz|yć, -ać *[pasta, vegetables]*
III *vi* [1] *[liquid]* wypły|nąć, -wać (**out of** or **from sth** z czegoś); (from pot) wy|ciec, wyciek|nąć, -ać; *[bath, sink]* opróżni|ć, -ać się; **the blood** or **colour has ~ed from her face** krew odpłynęła jej z twarzy [2] *[dishes, food]* obcie|c, -kać

drainage /ˈdreɪnɪdʒ/ *n* (of land) osuszanie *n*; (of wound) sączkowanie *n*; (system of pipes) system *m* kanalizacyjny; (system of ditches) drenaż *m*

draining board n ociekacz m

drainpipe /'dreɪnpaɪp/ n (for rain water) rynna f; (for waste water, sewage) rura f kanalizacyjna or ściekowa

drake /dreɪk/ n kaczor m

drama /'drɑːmə/ n (genre) dramat m; (acting) aktorstwo n; (directing) reżyseria f teatralna; (play) dramat m; (on TV) sztuka f telewizyjna; (on radio) słuchowisko n; **to make a** ~ **out of sth** zrobić z czegoś dramat or tragedię

dramatic /drə'mætɪk/ adj [art, effect, situation] dramatyczny; [gesture, entrance] teatralny; [change, improvement] radykalny; [goal, comeback] spektakularny; [landscape] pełen dramatyzmu

dramatist /'dræmətɪst/ n dramaturg m

dramatize /'dræmətaɪz/ vt [1] (for stage) dokon|ać, -ywać adaptacji scenicznej (czegoś); (for screen) z|ekranizować [2] (make dramatic) udramatyczni|ć, -ać; (excessively) z|robić dramat z (czegoś) [event, problem]

drape /dreɪp/ **I** n US (curtain) zasłona f

II vt **to** ~ **sth with sth, to** ~ **sth over sth** przykryć coś czymś; ~**d in sth** [person, statue] spowity w coś

drastic /'dræstɪk/ adj [reduction, step, remedy] drastyczny; [effect] daleko idący; [change] radykalny

drastically /'dræstɪklɪ/ adv drastycznie

draught GB, **draft** US /drɑːft, US dræft/ n [1] (cold air) przeciąg m [2] **on** ~ [beer] z beczki, beczkowy

draughts /drɑːfts, US dræfts/ n GB warcaby plt

draughty GB, **drafty** US /'drɑːftɪ, US 'dræftɪ/ adj [room, house] pełen przeciągów

draw /drɔː/ **I** n [1] (in lottery) loteria f [2] Sport (in match) remis m; (in race, athletics) wynik m nierozstrzygnięty

II vt [1] (on paper) na|rysować [picture, plan, face, line] [2] (pull) po|ciągnąć; **he drew the child towards him** przyciągnął dziecko do siebie; **to** ~ **a bolt/curtains** zasunąć rygiel/zasłony; **to** ~ **blood** skaleczyć [3] wyciąg|nąć, -ać [conclusion] (from sth z czegoś); czerpać [comfort, strength] (from sth z czegoś); **information drawn from many sources** informacje pochodzące z różnych źródeł [4] (attract) przyciąg|nąć, -ać [attention, crowd]; wzbudz|ić, -ać [interest]; **to** ~ **sb into sth** wciągnąć kogoś do czegoś [conversation, argument]; **they were drawn together by their common grief** zbliżyło or połączyło ich wspólne nieszczęście [5] (take out) wyj|ąć, -mować [money] (from sth z czegoś); wystawi|ć, -ać [cheque] (on sb na kogoś); (receive) pob|rać, -ierać [wages, pension] [6] (in lottery) wy|losować [name, winner]; wyciąg|nąć, -ać [straw, card] [7] (to attack) wyciąg|nąć, -ać [gun, sword] (from sth z czegoś)

III vi [1] (make picture) rysować [2] (move) **to** ~ **ahead (of sth/sb)** wyprzedzić (coś/kogoś); fig wysunąć się do przodu (przed coś/kogoś); **to** ~ **alongside sth** [boat] przybi|ć, -jać do czegoś

[quay]; **the car drew alongside the lorry** samochód podjechał obok ciężarówki; **the time/ day is** ~**ing close when...** nadchodzi or zbliża się czas/dzień, kiedy...; **to** ~ **level with sb/sth** zrównać się z kimś/czymś [3] (in match) z|remisować (**with sb/sth** z kimś/czymś)

■ **draw away**: (move off) [vehicle] odje|chać, -żdżać; [boat] odpły|nąć, -wać; [person] oddal|ić, -ać się (**from sb/sth** od kogoś/czegoś)

■ **draw in**: ¶ ~ **in** [1] [days, nights] stawać się krótszym [2] [train] wje|chać, -żdżać; [bus] podje|chać, -żdżać ¶ ~ **[sth] in** skr|ócić, -acać [rope]; wciąg|nąć, -ać [stomach]; s|chować [claws]

■ **draw out**: ¶ ~ **out** [bus, train] odje|chać, -żdżać; **a car drew out in front of me** jakiś samochód zajechał mi drogę ¶ ~ **[sth] out** [1] (take out) wyj|ąć, -mować [handkerchief, knife] (**from** or **out of sth** z czegoś); wyciąg|nąć, -ać [cork, nail] (**from** or **out of sth** z czegoś) [2] (withdraw) pod|jąć, -ejmować [money] [3] (prolong) przeciąg|nąć, -ać [meeting, speech] ¶ ~ **[sb] out** ośmiel|ić, -ać

■ **draw up**: [1] sporządz|ić, -ać [contract, list, will] [2] (pull) wciąg|nąć, -ać [bucket]; przysu|nąć, -wać [chair, stool] (**to sb/sth** do kogoś/czegoś)

IDIOMS: **to** ~ **the line** wyznaczyć granicę

drawback /'drɔːbæk/ n wada f

drawer /drɔː(r)/ n szuflada f

drawing /'drɔːɪŋ/ n rysunek m

drawing board n deska f kreślarska; **we'll have to go back to the** ~ fig musimy zacząć od początku

drawing pin n pinezka f, pineska f

drawing room n salon m

drawl /drɔːl/ n przeciąganie n samogłosek

drawn /drɔːn/ adj [1] [face, look] wymizerowany [2] [game, match] remisowy

dread /dred/ vt (fear) bać się (czegoś); **I** ~ **to think!** drżę na (samą) myśl!

dreadful /'dredfl/ adj [weather, person] okropny; [play, film] fatalny; [accident, injury] straszny

dreadfully /'dredfəlɪ/ adv [disappointed, cross] okropnie; [suffer, treat] strasznie; **I'm** ~ **sorry** bardzo mi przykro

dream /driːm/ **I** n [1] (while asleep) sen m; **I had a** ~ **about my father last night** zeszłej nocy (przy)śnił mi się ojciec [2] (hope) marzenie n; **to make sb's** ~ **come true** spełnić marzenie kogoś

II adj [car, house, holiday] wymarzony

III vt [1] (while asleep) śnić (**that...** że...) [2] (envisage) przypuszczać; **I never** ~**ed (that)...** nawet mi się nie śniło, że...

IV vi [1] (while asleep) śnić (**about** or **of sth** o czymś) [2] (daydream) marzyć (**of** or **about sth** o czymś); **I wouldn't** ~ **of it** (because impossible) nie przyszłoby mi to do głowy; (because inappropriate) nie odważyłbym się

■ **dream up**: wy|kombinować infml *[plan, excuse]*; wymyśl|ić, -ać *[invention, character]*

dreamer /'dri:mə(r)/ *n* marzyciel *m*, -ka *f*

dreary /'drɪərɪ/ *adj [weather, landscape]* ponury; *[life]* monotonny; *[person]* nudny

dredge /dredʒ/ *vt* bagrować *[river]*

dregs /dregz/ *npl* (of wine) męty *plt*; (of coffee, tea) fusy *plt*

drench /drentʃ/ *vt* (in rain, water) przèmoczyć *[person, clothes]*; (in perfume) skr|opić, -apiać obficie (**in sth** czymś)

dress /dres/ **I** *n* ① (garment) sukienka *f* ② (clothes) ubranie *n*; **his style of** ~ jego sposób ubierania się

II *vt* ① (put clothes on) ub|rać, -ierać *[person, child]*; **to get** ~**ed** ubrać się ② Culin przyprawi|ć, -ać *[salad]*; oporządz|ić, -ać *[chicken]* ③ Med opat|rzyć, -rywać *[wound]*

III *vi* ub|rać, -ierać się; **to** ~ **in a suit** włożyć garnitur

■ **dress up**: ① (smartly) wy|stroić się; **to** ~ **up for dinner** przebrać się do kolacji ② (in fancy dress) przeb|rać, -ierać się (**as sb** za kogoś)

dress circle *n* pierwszy balkon *m*

dresser /'dresə(r)/ *n* ① **to be a sloppy/stylish** ~ ubierać się niechlujnie/elegancko ② (for dishes) kredens *m* ③ US (for clothes) komoda *f*

dressing /'dresɪŋ/ *n* ① (bandage) opatrunek *m* ② (sauce) sos *m* ③ US (stuffing) nadzienie *n*

dressing gown *n* szlafrok *m*

dressing room *n* garderoba *f*; (at sports grounds) przebieralnia *f*

dressing table *n* toaletka *f*

dressmaker /'dresmeɪkə(r)/ *n* krawiec *m* damski, krawcowa *f* damska

dress rehearsal *n* próba *f* generalna

dress sense *n* **to have** ~ ubierać się gustownie or z gustem

dribble /'drɪbl/ **I** *n* strużka *f*

II *vi* ① *[liquid]* ście|c, -kać, ciec (**on** or **onto sth** na coś); *[baby, old person]* ślinić się ② Sport dryblować

dried /draɪd/ *adj [fruit, herbs, vegetables]* suszony; *[eggs, milk]* w proszku; *[flower]* zasuszony

drier /'draɪə(r)/ *n* suszarka *f*

drift /drɪft/ **I** *n* ① (flow) **the** ~ **of the current** prąd *m* ② (of snow) zaspa *f*; (of leaves, sand) zwał *m*; (of mist, smoke) smuga *f* ③ (general meaning) sens *m*; **I don't quite catch your** ~ nie całkiem rozumiem, o co ci chodzi

II *vi* ① *[boat]* po|dryfować; *[balloon, smoke]* un|ieść, -osić się; *[fog]* po|płynąć ② *[snow]* u|tworzyć zaspy; *[leaves, sand]* na|gromadzić się ③ (move aimlessly) **to** ~ **along** *[person]* wałęsać się bez celu; **to** ~ **from job to job** stale zmieniać pracę

■ **drift apart**: odsuwać or oddalać się (**from sb/ each other** od kogoś/siebie)

drill /drɪl/ **I** *n* ① (tool) wiertarka *f*; (drilling bit) wiertło *n*; (for mining, oil) świder *m*; (for teeth) wiertło *n* ② (military) musztra *f* ③ **fire** ~ próbny alarm pożarowy

II *vt* ① przewierc|ić, -ać *[wood, metal, masonry]*; borować *[teeth]* ② (in army) wy|musztrować *[soldiers]*

III *vi* ① wiercić (**into sth** w czymś); (with drilling rig) prowadzić wiercenia (**for sth** w poszukiwaniu czegoś) ② *[soldiers]* ćwiczyć musztrę

drink /drɪŋk/ **I** *n* (nonalcoholic) napój *m*; (alcoholic) napój *m* alkoholowy, drink *m*; **to have a** ~ napić się

II *vt* wy|pić; (habitually, repeatedly) wy|pijać *[liquid, glass, bottle]*; napić się (czegoś) *[liquid]*

III *vi* pić (**from** or **out of sth** z czegoś)

drinkable /'drɪŋkəbl/ *adj* (safe) zdatny do picia; (acceptable) **it's** ~ da się wypić

drink-driving /ˌdrɪŋk'draɪvɪŋ/ GB *n* jazda *f* w stanie nietrzeźwym

drinking water *n* woda *f* pitna

drip /drɪp/ **I** *n* ① (spadająca or skapująca) kropla *f*; **the** ~ **of a tap** kapanie z kranu ② GB Med kroplówka *f*; **to be on a** ~ być podłączonym do kroplówki

II *vi* ① *[liquid]* kapać; **to** ~ **from** or **off sth** skapywać z czegoś ② *[tap]* ciec; *[branches]* ociekać; *[washing]* kapać (**onto sth** na coś); *[wound]* broczyć (krwią)

drive /draɪv/ **I** *n* ① (in car) jazda *f*; (for pleasure) przejażdżka *f*; **to go for a** ~ wybrać się na przejażdżkę; **it's only five minutes'** ~ **from here** stąd to tylko pięć minut jazdy samochodem ② (campaign) (commercial) kampania *f*; (political, social) akcja *f*; **a** ~ **against/for** or **towards sth** akcja przeciw czemuś/na rzecz czegoś ③ (motivation) zapał *m*; **the** ~ **to win** wola zwycięstwa ④ Comput stacja *f* dysków ⑤ Aut napęd *m* ⑥ (private road) (short) podjazd *m*; (longer) droga *f* dojazdowa; (in names of roads) ulica *f* ⑦ Sport (in tennis, badminton, cricket) drajw *m*; (in golf) drive *m* inv

II *vt* ① kierować (czymś) *[motor vehicle]*; powozić (czymś) *[wagon, cart]*; prowadzić *[car, bus, train]*; (cover distance) przeje|żdżać, -chać infml; **to** ~ **a car into the garage** wprowadzić samochód do garażu ② (transport) (once) za|wieźć; (many times) wozić ③ (chase or herd) pędzić *[people, animals]*; **to be driven out of** or **from the country** zostać wypędzonym z kraju ④ (propel) napędzać ⑤ wbi|ć, -jać *[nail, peg]* (**into sth** w coś) ⑥ (motivate) *[jealousy, fear]* kierować (kimś); (bring to specified state) doprowadz|ić, -ać; (force) zmu|sić, -szać; **he was driven to suicide** został doprowadzony do samobójstwa

III *vi* po|jechać; jeździć; **you can't** ~ **along the High Street** High Street jest zamknięta dla ruchu; **she** ~**s to work every day** codziennie jeździ do pracy samochodem; **to** ~ **into a tree** wjechać w drzewo

■ **drive back**: ⊡ (transport back) przyw|ieźć, -ozić z powrotem *[passenger]* ⊡ (force to retreat) od|eprzeć, -pierać *[enemy, rioters]*; odg|onić, -aniać *[animals]*

driver /'draɪvə(r)/ *n* (of motor vehicle) kierowca *m*; (of train) maszynista *m*; (of tram) motorniczy *m*; (of cart) woźnica *m*

driving /'draɪvɪŋ/ ⊡ *n* prowadzenie *n*; (travelling) jeżdżenie *n*; **her ~ has improved** coraz lepiej prowadzi samochód

⊡ *adj [rain, hail]* zacinający; *[wind]* porywisty

driving force *n* fig siła *f* napędowa

driving instructor *n* instruktor *m*, -ka *f* jazdy

driving lesson *n* lekcja *f* prowadzenia samochodu

driving licence GB, **driver's license** US *n* prawo *n* jazdy

driving school *n* szkoła *f* jazdy

driving seat *n* siedzenie *n* or fotel *m* kierowcy
(IDIOMS:) **to be in the ~** być u steru fig

driving test *n* egzamin *m* na prawo jazdy

drizzle /'drɪzl/ ⊡ *n* mżawka *f*
⊡ *vi* mżyć

drone /drəʊn/ ⊡ *n* (of engine) warkot *m*; (of insects) bzyk *m*
⊡ *vi [engine]* buczeć; *[insect]* brzęczeć

drool /druːl/ *vi* ⊡ *[baby]* zaślinić się ⊡ infml fig **to ~ over sth/sb** pożerać wzrokiem coś/kogoś; **to ~ at the thought of sth/sb** oblizywać się na samą myśl o czymś/kimś

droop /druːp/ *vi [head, shoulders, feather]* opa|ść, - dać; *[flower]* z|więdnąć; *[flag, branch, moustache]* zwisać

drop /drɒp/ ⊡ *n* ⊡ (of liquid) kropla *f*; **~ by ~** kropla po kropli ⊡ (decrease) obniżenie (się) *n*, spadek *m*; **a 5% ~ in inflation** pięcioprocentowy spadek inflacji ⊡ (incline) spadek *m*; (sheer slope) urwisko *n*; **there was a steep ~ on either side of the ridge** grań opadała na obie strony stromymi urwiskami ⊡ (delivery) (from aircraft) zrzut *m*; (from lorry) dostawa *f*; (parachute jump) skok *m* spadochronowy
⊡ *vt* ⊡ (allow to fall) (accidentally) upu|ścić, -szczać (deliberately) rzuc|ić, -ać ⊡ (from aircraft) zrzuc|ić, -ać *[bomb, supplies, troops]* ⊡ (also **~ off**) *[driver]* wysadz|ić, -ać *[passenger]* ⊡ (lower) spu|ścić, -szczać *[trousers, curtain, arm, eyes]*; obniż|yć, -ać *[price]*; zmniejsz|yć, -ać *[speed]*; zniż|yć, -ać *[voice]* ⊡ **to ~ a hint about sth** zrobić aluzję do czegoś; **to ~ sb a note** napisać do kogoś list ⊡ (abandon) z|erwać, -rywać z (kimś/czymś) *[boyfriend, habit]*; porzuc|ić, -ać *[idea, work]*; zaniechać (czegoś) *[plan, claim]*; z|rezygnować z (czegoś) *[work, subject]*; odst|ąpić, -ępować od (czegoś) *[charges, accusations]*; **to ~ everything** rzucić wszystko; **can we ~ the subject, please?** zostawmy ten temat, dobrze?

■ **drop back** ⊡ *vi* (fall) *[person, animal, cup, fruit]* spa|ść, -dać; *[flower, leaf]* opa|ść, -dać; *[tears, rain]* kapać ⊡ (move downwards) *[person, animal]* pa|ść, -dać; *[sun, aircraft]* zniż|yć, -ać się; *[arm, curtain, head]* opa|ść, -dać; **they ~ped to their knees** padli or runęli na kolana; **the plane ~ped to an altitude of 1,000 m** samolot zszedł na wysokość 1 000 m ⊡ *[cliff, road]* opadać ⊡ (decrease) *[temperature, level, speed, prices]* spa|ść, -dać; *[water level]* opa|ść, -dać; *[noise, wind]* przycich|nąć, -ać; **his voice ~ped to a whisper** zniżył głos do szeptu

■ **drop in**: zaj|ść, -chodzić; **I'll ~ in (to you) later** wpadnę do ciebie później

■ **drop off**: ⊡ (fall off) *[handle, label]* odpa|ść, -dać; *[leaf, fruit]* opa|ść, -dać ⊡ **~ off (to sleep)** zas|nąć, -ypiać; (unintentionally) przys|nąć, -ypiać ⊡ (decrease) *[attendance, support]* spa|ść, -dać; *[traffic, practice]* zmniejsz|yć, -ać się

■ **drop out**: ⊡ (fall out) wypa|ść, -dać (of sth z czegoś) ⊡ (from activity, contest, race) wycof|ać, -ywać się; (from school, university) przerwać naukę

dropout /'drɒpaʊt/ *n* (from society) wyrzutek *m*; (from school, university) porzucający *m*, -a *f* naukę

droppings /'drɒpɪŋz/ *npl* (of mouse, rabbit, sheep) bobki *m pl*; (of horse) łajno *n*; (of birds) odchody *plt*

drop shot *n* dropszot *m*

drought /draʊt/ *n* susza *f*

drown /draʊn/ ⊡ *vt* u|topić *[person, animal]*
⊡ *vi* u|tonąć, u|topić się

■ **drown out**: zagłusz|yć, -ać *[sound, person]*
(IDIOMS:) **to ~ one's sorrows** zalewać robaka infml

drowning /'draʊnɪŋ/ *n* utonięcie *n*

drowsy /'draʊzɪ/ *adj* senny; **I feel ~** spać mi się chce

drug /drʌg/ ⊡ *n* ⊡ Med lek *m*, lekarstwo *n*; **to be on ~s** zażywać leki ⊡ (illegal) narkotyk *m*; **to be on** or **to take ~s** brać narkotyki; Sport brać środki dopingujące
⊡ *vt* (sedate) *[kidnapper, vet]* u|śpić, -sypiać *[victim, animal]*

drug abuse *n* zażywanie *n* narkotyków

drug addict *n* narkoman *m*, -ka *f*

drug addiction *n* narkomania *f*

drugged /drʌgd/ *adj [person]* pod wpływem środków odurzających; **~ drink** napój ze środkiem oszałamiającym

drugs raid *n* akcja *f* policyjna oddziału antynarkotykowego

drug-taking /'drʌgteɪkɪŋ/ *n* zażywanie *n* narkotyków; Sport stosowanie *n* środków dopingujących

drug test *n* Sport test *m* antydopingowy

drug user *n* narkoman *m*, -ka *f*

drum /drʌm/ ⊡ *n* ⊡ (percussion) bęben *m* ⊡ (container) (small) baryłka *f*; (larger) beczka *f*
⊡ **drums** *npl* perkusja *f*

III *vt* **to** ~ **one's fingers** bębnić palcami (**on sth** po czymś); **I managed to** ~ **a few dates into their heads** udało mi się wbić im do głowy parę dat

■ **drum up**: nakręc|lić, -ać coś *[business, trade]*; pozysk|ać, -iwać *[customers, support]*

drummer /'drʌmə(r)/ *n* perkusista *m*

drumstick /'drʌmstɪk/ *n* ☐ Mus pałka *f* do gry na perkusji ☐ (of chicken, turkey) udko *n*

drunk /drʌŋk/ **Ⅰ** *n* (also **drunkard**) pija|k *m*, -czka *f*

Ⅱ *adj* pijany; **to get** ~ upić się

drunken /'drʌŋkən/ *adj [person]* pijany; *[fury, party, stupor]* pijacki

dry /draɪ/ **Ⅰ** *adj* ☐ (not wet) suchy; *[riverbed, well, throat]* wyschnięty; *[ingredients]* sypki; **to run** ~ *[river]* wyschnąć; **to keep sth** ~ utrzymać coś suchym; **on** ~ **land** na suchym lądzie; **a** ~ **day** bezdeszczowy dzień ☐ *[wit, remark]* ironiczny; *[person, voice]* oschły; *[book, subject matter]* nieciekawy

Ⅱ *vt* wy|suszyć *[clothes, washing]*; wy|trzeć, -cierać *[surface, wet object]*; u|suszyć *[fruit]*; (after washing) wy|trzeć, -cierać do sucha *[skin, hands]*; **to** ~ **the dishes** wytrzeć *or* powycierać naczynia; **to** ~ **one's hair** wysuszyć sobie włosy

Ⅲ *vi [clothes, washing, paint, glue]* wy|schnąć

■ **dry out**: ☐ *[walk, wood]* wys|chnąć, -ychać ☐ *infml [alcoholic]* być na odwyku infml

■ **dry up**: ¶ ~ **up** ☐ *[river, well]* wys|chnąć, -ychać ☐ (run out) wyczerp|ać -ywać się ☐ (dry the dishes) po|wycierać naczynia ¶ ~ *[sth]* **up** wysuszyć *[puddles, river]*; wycierać, powycierać (do sucha) *[dishes]*

dry-clean /ˌdraɪ'kliːn/ *vt* wy|prać chemicznie *or* na sucho; **to have sth** ~**ed** oddać coś do prania na sucho

dry-cleaner's /ˌdraɪ'kliːnəz/ *n* pralnia *f* chemiczna

dryer /'draɪə(r)/ *n* = **drier**

dual /'djuːəl, US 'duːəl/ *adj* podwójny

dual carriageway *n* GB droga *f* szybkiego ruchu

dub /dʌb/ *vt* (into foreign language) z|dubbingować; (add sound track) doda|ć, -wać postsynchrony do (czegoś) *[film]*; z|miksować *[sound effect]*; **the movie was** ~**bed into Polish** film miał polską ścieżkę dźwiękową

dubious /'djuːbɪəs, US 'duː-/ *adj [point, question]* dyskusyjny; *[character, origin]* podejrzany; *[distinction]* wątpliwy; *[person]* **to be** ~ (**about sth**) mieć wątpliwości (co do czegoś)

duchess /'dʌtʃɪs/ *n* księżna *f*

duck /dʌk/ **Ⅰ** *n* kaczka *f*

Ⅱ *vt* ☐ **to** ~ **one's head** schylić głowę ☐ (dodge) uchyl|ić, -ać się przed (czymś) *[ball, blow]*; fig uchyl|ić, -ać się od (czegoś) *[responsibility]*

III *vi* z|robić unik; **to** ~ **behind sth** dać nura za coś

duct /dʌkt/ *n* ☐ Tech kanał *m*, przewód *m* ☐ Anat przewód *m*

dud /dʌd/ *infml adj [motor, engine]* felerny infml; *[battery]* wyczerpany; *[coin, banknote]* fałszywy; *[cheque]* bez pokrycia

due /djuː, US duː/ **Ⅰ** *n* **to give sb his/her/their** ~ oddać mu/jej/im sprawiedliwość

Ⅱ *adj* ☐ (payable) **when** ~ w odpowiednim terminie; **the rent is** ~ **on the 6th** termin płacenia czynszu mija szóstego; **the balance** ~ należna kwota ☐ (entitled to) **they should pay him the money that is** ~ **to him** powinni zapłacić mu pieniądze, które mu się należą; **we are** ~ (**for**) **a wage increase** należy nam się podwyżka ☐ (appropriate) *[attention, care, solemnity]* należyty; **after** ~ **consideration** po należytym zastanowieniu; **in** ~ **course it transpired that...** po pewnym czasie okazało się, że... ☐ **to be** ~ **to do sth** mieć coś zrobić; **the train is** ~ (**in**) *or* ~ **to arrive at six** pociąg przyjeżdża o szóstej; **we're** ~ (**in**) **soon** wkrótce będziemy na miejscu

III *adv* prosto; **to face** ~ **north** *[building]* stać frontem na północ; **to go** ~ **south** iść prosto na południe

Ⅳ **due to** *prep phr* z powodu (czegoś); ~ **to unforeseen circumstances** z powodu nieprzewidzianych okoliczności; **it's all** ~ **to you** to wszystko dzięki tobie

duet /djuː'et, US duː-/ *n* duet *m*

duke /djuːk, US duːk/ *n* książę *m*

dull /dʌl/ **Ⅰ** *adj* ☐ *[book, film, person]* nudny; *[life, journey, music]* monotonny; *[appearance, outfit]* nieefektowny ☐ *[eye]* zmętniały; *[colour]* zmatowiały; *[day, weather]* pochmurny; *[complexion]* ziemisty ☐ (not sharp) *[knife, pain]* tępy

Ⅱ *vt* zmatowić *[shine]*; s|tępić *[blade]*; przytępi|ć, -ać *[senses]*; uśmierz|yć, -ać *[pain]*

duly /'djuːlɪ, US 'duː-/ *adv* (in proper fashion) należycie; (as expected) jak przewidywano; (as arranged) zgodnie z planem

dumb /dʌm/ *adj* ☐ (mute) niemy; ~ **animals** nieme stworzenia; **to be struck** ~ oniemieć ☐ *infml* (stupid) *[person]* tępy; *[idea, question]* durny infml

dumbfounded /dʌm'faʊndɪd/ *adj* oniemiały

dummy /'dʌmɪ/ **Ⅰ** *n* ☐ (model) manekin *m* ☐ GB (for baby) smoczek *m*

Ⅱ *adj [flower, fruit]* sztuczny; *[document]* podrobiony; *[bullet]* ślepy

dummy run *n* (trial) próba *f*; Mil atak *m* symulowany; (of plane) lot *m* ćwiczebny

dump /dʌmp/ **Ⅰ** *n* ☐ (public) wysypisko *n*; (rubbish heap) usypisko *n* ☐ Mil **arms/munitions** ~ skład broni/amunicji ☐ *infml* (town, village) dziura *f* infml; (hotel, house) nora *f* infml

II *vt* [1] (get rid of) wyrzuc|ić, -ać *[rubbish]*; opróżni|ć, -ać *[sewage]*; pozby|ć, -wać się (czegoś) *[nuclear waste, pollutants]* [2] infml rzuc|ić, -ać *[boyfriend]*; zostawi|ć, -ać *[car, shopping]*

(IDIOMS:) **to be down in the** ~ **s** infml mieć chandrę infml

dunce /dʌns/ *n* matołek *m* infml; **to be a** ~ **at sth** być nogą z czegoś infml

dune /djuːn, US duːn/ *n* wydma *f*

dung /dʌŋ/ *n* łajno *n*; (for manure) obornik *m*

dungarees *npl* (fashionwear) ogrodniczki *plt*; (workwear) kombinezon *m*

Dunkirk /dʌn'kɜːk/ *prn* Dunkierka *f*

duo /'djuːəʊ, US 'duːəʊ/ *n* duet *m*

duplicate **I** /'djuːplɪkət, US 'duːpləkət/ *n* kopia *f*; (spare, replacement) duplikat *m*; **in** ~ w dwóch egzemplarzach

II /'djuːplɪkət, US 'duːpləkət/ *adj* [1] *[cheque, receipt]* z kopią; **a** ~ **key** zapasowy klucz [2] (in two parts) *[form, invoice]* w dwóch egzemplarzach

III /'djuːplɪkeɪt, US 'duːpləkeɪt/ *vt* [1] (copy) sporządz|ić, -ać kopię (czegoś) *[document]*; s|kopiować *[cassette, painting]* [2] (photocopy) sporządz|ić, -ać fotokopię (czegoś), powiel|ić, -ać

durable /'djʊərəbl, US 'dʊərəbl/ *adj [material]* wytrzymały; *[equipment]* solidny; *[friendship]* niezachwiany; *[tradition]* głęboko zakorzeniony

duration /djʊ'reɪʃn, US dʊ'reɪʃn/ *n* czas *m* or okres *m* (trwania); **of long/short** ~ długotrwały/ krótkotrwały

(IDIOMS:) **for the** ~ infml nie wiadomo jak długo

during /'djʊərɪŋ/ *prep* podczas (czegoś)

dusk /dʌsk/ *n* (twilight) zmierzch *m*

dust /dʌst/ **I** *n* kurz *m*

II *vt* odkurz|yć, -ać *[furniture]*; posyp|ać, -ywać *[cake]* (**with sth** czymś)

dustbin /'dʌstbɪn/ *n* GB pojemnik *m* na śmieci

dust cover *n* (on book) obwoluta *f*; (on furniture) pokrowiec *m*

duster /'dʌstə(r)/ *n* GB ścierka *f* do kurzu

dustman /'dʌstmən/ *n* GB śmieciarz *m*

dusty /'dʌstɪ/ *adj [house, road]* zakurzony; *[climb, journey]* w kurzu

Dutch /dʌtʃ/ **I** *n* [1] (language) (język *m*) holenderski *m* [2] (people) **the** ~ Holendrzy *m pl*

II *adj* holenderski

(IDIOMS:) **to go** ~ (**with sb**) infml za|płacić każdy za siebie

duty /'djuːtɪ, US 'duːtɪ/ *n* [1] (obligation) obowiązek *m* (**to sb** w stosunku do or względem kogoś); **to have a** ~ **to do sth** mieć obowiązek zrobić coś; **in the course of** ~ Mil podczas pełnienia obowiązków służbowych [2] (task) obowiązek *m*; **to take up one's duties** zacząć pełnić obowiązki [3] (work) (of soldier, policeman) służba *f*; (of doctor, teacher) dyżur *m*; **to be on** ~ być na służbie/na dyżurze [4] (on things bought) podatek *m* (**on sth** od czegoś); (on things imported) cło *n* (**on sth** za coś); **customs duties** cła *n pl*

duty-free /ˌdjuːtɪ'friː, US ˌduː-/ **I** *adj [import, store]* wolnocłowy; *[goods]* bezcłowy

II *adv [sell, import]* bez cła

duvet /'duːveɪ/ *n* GB kołdra *f*

duvet cover *n* poszwa *f*

dwarf /dwɔːf/ **I** *n* karzeł *m*

II *adj* karłowaty

dwell /dwel/ *vi*

■ **dwell on**: (talk about) rozwodzić się na temat (czegoś); (think about) rozmyślać nad (czymś)

dwindle /'dwɪndl/ *vi [numbers]* z|maleć; *[supplies]* s|kurczyć się; *[enthusiasm, interest]* o|słabnąć

dye /daɪ/ **I** *n* (for hair, cloth, shoes) farba *f*

II *vt* u|farbować; **to** ~ **sth red** ufarbować coś na czerwono

dying /'daɪɪŋ/ *adj [person]* umierający; *[animal]* zdychający; *[plant]* obumierający; *[industry, tradition]* wymierający

dyke, dike US /daɪk/ *n* (to prevent flooding) grobla *f*, wał *m* ochronny

dynamic /daɪ'næmɪk/ *adj* dynamiczny

dynamite /'daɪnəmaɪt/ *n* dynamit *m*

dynamo /'daɪnəməʊ/ *n* [1] Tech prądnica *f* [2] infml **he's a real** ~ rozpiera go energia

dysentery /'dɪsəntrɪ, US -terɪ/ *n* czerwonka *f*

dyslexia /dɪs'leksɪə, dɪs'lekʃə/ *n* dysleksja *f*

dyslexic /dɪs'leksɪk/ **I** *n* dyslekty|k *m*, -czka *f*

II *adj* dyslektyczny

E

e, E /iː/ n ⊥ (letter) e, E n ② Mus E, e n ③ **E** (point of compass) = **East** wsch.; (on map) E

each /iːtʃ/ ⊥ det *[person, group, object]* każdy; ~ **time** za każdym razem; ~ **morning** każdego ranka; **he lifted** ~ **box in turn,** ~ **one heavier than the last** podnosił kolejno pudła, jedno cięższe od drugiego

⊥⊥ *pron* każd|y, -a, -e; **they** ~ **received a book** każdy z nich dostał książkę; **they** ~ **won a car** wygrali po samochodzie; ~ **of you** każdy z was

⊥⊥⊥ *adv* **the apples are 20 pence** ~ jabłka są po 20 pensów sztuka or za sztukę

each other *pron* (also **one another**) *[like, greet]* się; *[congratulate]* sobie (wzajemnie); *[look at]* siebie; **they know** ~ oni się znają; **to help** ~ pomagać sobie wzajemnie; **to shout at** ~ krzyczeć na siebie; **they wear** ~ **'s clothes** pożyczają sobie nawzajem ubrania

eager /iːgə(r)/ *adj* (keen) chętny; (impatient) ~ **for sth** spragniony or żądny czegoś *[knowledge, revenge]*; **to be** ~ **to do sth** nie móc się doczekać, żeby coś zrobić

eagle /iːgl/ n orzeł m

ear /ɪə(r)/ n ⊥ ucho n; **to have a good** ~ **(for music)** mieć dobry słuch (muzyczny) ② (of wheat) kłos m; (of maize) kolba f

IDIOMS: **to play it by** ~ zobaczyć, jak się sytuacja rozwija

earache /ɪəreɪk/ n ból m ucha; **he has** ~ boli go ucho

eardrum /ɪədrʌm/ n błona f bębenkowa

earl /ɜːl/ n hrabia m

early /ɜːlɪ/ ⊥ *adj* ① (one of the first) *[years, model]* wczesny; *[scene, chapter]* początkowy; *[Christians, settlers]* pierwszy; ~ **man** człowiek pierwotny ② (sooner than usual) *[breakfast, harvest]* wczesny; *[death]* przedwczesny; **to have an** ~ **lunch/night** wcześnie zjeść lunch/pójść spać; **to take** ~ **retirement** przejść na wcześniejszą emeryturę ③ (near beginning of period) wczesny; **in** ~ **childhood** we wczesnym dzieciństwie; **in** ~ **January** na początku stycznia; **at an** ~ **age** w bardzo młodym wieku

⊥⊥ *adv* ① wcześnie; **it's too** ~ **to say** jest zbyt wcześnie, żeby można było coś powiedzieć; **it started as** ~ **as 1983** to się zaczęło już w 1983; ~ **in the afternoon** wczesnym popołudniem; **as**

I said earlier... jak już mówiłem (wcześniej)... ② (before expected) wcześniej; (too soon) przed czasem; **I'm sorry I'm a bit** ~ przepraszam, że przychodzę trochę za wcześnie

earmark /ɪəmɑːk/ *vt* przeznacz|yć, -ać *[money, site]* **(for sth** na coś)

earn /ɜːn/ *vt* ① *[person]* zar|obić, -abiać *[money]*; otrzym|ać, -ywać *[salary]*; **to** ~ **a living** or **one's living** zarabiać na życie ② zdoby|ć, -wać; **to** ~ **sb's respect** *[person]* zdobyć sobie szacunek kogoś; **a well-**~**ed rest** zasłużony odpoczynek

earner /ɜːnə(r)/ n **to be a low/high** ~ mało/ dobrze zarabiać; **she is the sole** ~ **in the family** jedyna w rodzinie pracuje zarobkowo

earnest /ɜːnɪst/ ⊥ n **to be in** ~ nie żartować; **to begin in** ~ zacząć się or rozpocząć się na dobre ⊥⊥ *adj [person]* poważny; *[intention]* szczery; *[plea]* gorący

earning power n zdolność f zarobkowa

earnings /ɜːnɪŋz/ *npl* (of person) zarobki m *pl*; dochody m *pl* **(from sth** z czegoś); (of company, from shares) zyski m *pl* **(from sth** z czegoś)

earphones /ɪəfəʊnz/ *npl* słuchawki f *pl*

earring /ɪərɪŋ/ n (for pierced ear) kolczyk m

earth /ɜːθ/ ⊥ n ① (also **Earth**) (planet) Ziemia f; (world) ziemia f, świat m; (soil) ziemia f ② infml **how/ where/who on** ~ **...?** jak/gdzie/kto do or u licha...?; **nothing on** ~ **would persuade me to sell it** za nic w świecie bym tego nie sprzedał ⊥⊥ *vt* GB uziemi|ć, -ać *[appliance, plug]*

earthquake /ɜːθkweɪk/ n trzęsienie n ziemi

earth tremor n wstrząs m podziemny

earwig /ɪəwɪg/ n skorek m

ease /iːz/ ⊥ n ① (lack of difficulty) łatwość f ② (freedom from anxiety) beztroska f; **at** ~ spokojny; **to be** or **feel at** ~ być spokojnym; **to be** or **feel ill at** ~ czuć się nieswojo **(about sth** z powodu czegoś); **to put sb's mind at** ~ uspokoić kogoś **(about sth** co do czegoś)

⊥⊥ *vt* ① z|łagodzić *[tension, crisis]*; zmniejsz|yć, -ać *[burden, speed]*; **to** ~ **the pain** ukoić ból ② ułatwi|ć, -ać *[communication, transition]*; polep-sz|yć, -ać *[situation]*; włożyć ostrożnie coś do czegoś; **to** ~ **sth out of sth** wyjąć ostrożnie coś z czegoś

⊥⊥⊥ *vi [pressure, pain, tension]* zelżeć; *[pace, rate]* o|słabnąć

■ **ease off**: *[demand, traffic, rain]* zmniejsz|yć, -ać
się; *[pain, tension]* ust|ąpić, -ępować; *[person]*
zwolnić

■ **ease up**: *[person]* odpręż|yć, -ać się; *[pressure,
tension]* ust|ąpić, -ępować; **to ~ up on sb/sth**
odpuścić komuś/sobie coś infml

easel /'i:zl/ *n* sztaluga *f*

easily /'i:zɪlɪ/ *adv* [1] (with no difficulty) z łatwością;
(comfortably) *[breathe, talk]* swobodnie [2] (probably)
bardzo możliwe, (że); **she could ~ die** ona może
umrzeć

east /i:st/ **[]** *n* [1] (compass direction) wschód *m* [2] **the
East** (Orient) Wschód; (of country) wschód

[] *adj [side, coast, wind]* wschodni

[] *adv [move]* na wschód; **to live/lie ~ of sth**
mieszkać/leżeć na wschód od czegoś

Easter /'i:stə(r)/ **[]** *n* Wielkanoc *f*; **at ~** na
Wielkanoc; **Happy ~** Wesołych Świąt (Wielka-
nocnych)

[] *adj [Sunday, parade]* wielkanocny; **~ egg**
(confectionery) czekoladowe jajo wielkanocne

eastern /'i:stən/ *adj* [1] *[coast, Europe]* wschodni
[2] (also **Eastern**) (oriental) wschodni

easy /'i:zɪ/ **[]** *adj* [1] *[question, job, life, victim]* łatwy;
it's not ~ to talk to him ciężko się z nim
rozmawia; **that's ~ for you to say!** łatwo ci
mówić!; **to make things** or **life easier (for sb)**
ułatwić (komuś) życie [2] (relaxed) *[smile, grace, style]*
niewymuszony; **at an ~ pace** bez pośpiechu
[3] infml (having no preference) **I'm ~** wszystko mi jedno
[] *adv* [1] spokojnie; **to take it** or **things ~** nie
przemęczać się [2] infml **go ~ on** or **with him!**
potraktuj go łagodnie!; **go ~ on** or **with the
butter!** oszczędnie z masłem!

easygoing /ˌi:zɪ'gəʊɪŋ/ *adj* wyrozumiały

easy terms *npl* dogodne warunki *m pl*

eat /i:t/ **[]** *vt* (consume) z|jeść; (regularly, occasionally)
jadać *[fruit, dinner]*

[] *vi* [1] jeść [2] (have a meal) z|jeść (posiłek); (usually,
occasionally) jadać; **I never ~ in the canteen** nie
jadam w stołówce

■ **eat out**: (once) z|jeść poza domem; (often) jadać
poza domem

eating disorder *n* Med zaburzenia *n pl* odżywiania

eating habits *npl* sposób *m* odżywiania się

eavesdrop /'i:vzdrɒp/ *vi* podsłuch|ać, -iwać (**on
sb/sth** kogoś/coś)

ebb /eb/ **[]** *n* odpływ *m*

[] *vi [tide]* ust|ąpić, -ępować; *[support]* z|maleć; **he
could feel his strength ~ing** czuł, że opusz-
czają go siły

ebony /'ebənɪ/ *n* [1] (wood) heban *m* [2] (colour) (kolor
m) hebanowy *m*

EC *n* = European Community WE *f*

eccentric /ɪk'sentrɪk/ *n* (person) ekscentry|k *m*,
-czka *f*

ECG *n* = **electrocardiogram** EKG *n*, ekg *n*

echo /'ekəʊ/ **[]** *n* echo *n*; (of footsteps, explosion)
odgłos *m*

[] *vt* [1] rozbrzmiewać echem (czegoś); (repeat)
powt|órzyć, -arzać *[words]* [2] (agree) zg|odzić,
-adzać się z (czymś) *[opinion, criticism]*

[] *vi [sound]* odbi|ć, -jać się echem; *[cave]*
rozbrzmie|ć, -wać echem

eclipse /ɪ'klɪps/ **[]** *n* zaćmienie *n* (**of sth** czegoś);
(of power, fame) zmierzch *m*

[] *vt* zasł|onić, -aniać *[moon, sun]*; (overshadow)
spychać (kogoś/coś) na drugi plan *[person, issue]*;
przyćmi|ć, -ewać *[fame, success]*

eco-friendly /ˌi:kəʊ'frendlɪ/ *adj* przyjazny dla
środowiska

ecological /ˌi:kə'lɒdʒɪkl/ *adj* ekologiczny

ecologist /i:'kɒlədʒɪst/ *n* ekolog *m*

ecology /ɪ'kɒlədʒɪ/ *n* ekologia *f*

economic /ˌi:kə'nɒmɪk, ˌek-/ *adj [crisis, policy,
change]* gospodarczy; *[science]* ekonomiczny; (profitable) *[business, production]* rentowny

economical /ˌi:kə'nɒmɪkl, ˌek-/ *adj [machine,
method]* ekonomiczny; *[person]* oszczędny; **to be
~ with sth** oszczędnie czymś gospodarować

economics /ˌi:kə'nɒmɪks, ˌek-/ *n* (science) ekonomia *f*; (financial aspects) ekonomika *f* (**of sth** czegoś);
(subject of study) nauki *f pl* ekonomiczne, ekonomia *f*

economist /ɪ'kɒnəmɪst, ˌek-/ *n* ekonomist|a *m*, -ka *f*

economize /ɪ'kɒnəmaɪz/ *vi* oszczędzać

economy /ɪ'kɒnəmɪ/ *n* (economic system) gospodarka *f*; (thrift) oszczędność *f*

economy class *n* klasa *f* turystyczna

economy drive *n* kampania *f* or polityka *f*
oszczędnościowa

ecstasy /'ekstəsɪ/ *n* [1] ekstaza *f* [2] (drug) ekstaza *f*

eczema /'eksɪmə, US ɪg'zi:mə/ *n* egzema *f*

Eden /'i:dn/ *prn* raj *m*, Eden *m*

edge /edʒ/ **[]** *n* [1] (outer limit) brzeg *m*; (of forest, town)
skraj *m*; (of table, ruler) krawędź *f*; **the film had us
on the ~ of our seats** film trzymał nas
w napięciu [2] (of coin, plank) krawędź *f* boczna; **a
book with gilt ~s** książka ze złoconymi brzega-
mi [3] (of blade) ostrze *n* [4] **to be on ~** być
podenerwowanym

[] *vt* przesu|nąć, -wać *[chair]* (**towards sth** w
kierunku czegoś); **she ~d her way along the
precipice** ostrożnie posuwała się wzdłuż prze-
paści

edgeways /'edʒweɪz/ *adv [move]* bokiem; *[lay, put]*
na bok

(IDIOMS) **I can't get a word in ~** nie mogę dojść
do słowa

edible /'edɪbl/ *adj [fruit, mushroom]* jadalny

Edinburgh /'edɪnbərə/ *prn* Edynburg *m*

edit /'edɪt/ *vt* [1] (in publishing) z|redagować *[text]*
[2] (cut down) skr|ócić, -acać [3] z|robić montaż
(czegoś) *[film, programme]*

edition 116 **either**

edition /ɪˈdɪʃn/ n wydanie n
editor /ˈedɪtə(r)/ n (of newspaper) redaktor m
naczelny (**of sth** czegoś); (of book, manuscript)
redaktor m, -ka f; (of writer, works, anthology) edytor m
fml; (of film) montażyst|a m, -ka f
editorial /ˌedɪˈtɔːrɪəl/ ▯ n artykuł m wstępny (**on
sth** na temat czegoś)
▯▯ adj ▯ (in journalism) [policy, staff] redakcyjny ▯ (in
publishing) [policy, decision] wydawniczy; [work,
comment] redakcyjny; **to do** ~ **work** zajmować
się redagowaniem
educate /ˈedʒʊkeɪt/ vt ▯ (at school, college) wy|-
kształcić [pupil, student] ▯ (inform) poucz|yć, -ać
[public, drivers] (**about** or **in** or **on sth** o czymś)
educated /ˈedʒʊkeɪtɪd/ adj [person] (having an education) wykształcony; (cultivated) kulturalny; [taste]
wyrobiony; [accent] staranny
education /ˌedʒʊˈkeɪʃn/ n ▯ (process) kształcenie
n; (acquired knowledge) wykształcenie n ▯ (system)
szkolnictwo n ▯ (field of study) pedagogika f
educational /ˌedʒʊˈkeɪʃənl/ adj ▯ [policy, system]
oświatowy; [method, experience] pedagogiczny; ~
standards poziom nauczania ▯ [film, value] edukacyjny; [toy, game] dydaktyczny; [experience, talk]
pouczający
EEC n = **European Economic Community**
EWG f
eel /iːl/ n węgorz m
eerie /ˈɪərɪ/ adj [scream, silence] upiorny; [feeling,
place] niesamowity
effect /ɪˈfekt/ ▯ n skutek m (**of sth** czegoś);
(influence) wpływ m (**on sb/sth** na kogoś/coś);
(repercussions) konsekwencje f pl (**on sb/sth** dla
kogoś/czegoś); (efficacy) skuteczność f; **to take** ~
[pills, anaesthetic] zacząć działać; **my advice was of
no** ~ moje rady nie poskutkowały; **to come into**
~ [law] wejść/wchodzić w życie; **she dresses like
that for** ~ ubiera się tak, żeby zwrócić na siebie
uwagę
▯▯ **effects** npl fml (belongings) majątek m ruchomy;
personal ~**s** rzeczy osobiste
▯▯▯ **in effect** adv phr faktycznie, w rzeczywistości
▯▯ vt wprowadz|ić, -ać [improvement]; dokon|ać,
-ywać (czegoś) [repair, payment]; doprowadz|ić, -ać
do (czegoś) [reconciliation]
effective /ɪˈfektɪv/ adj skuteczny; **to be** ~
poskutkować
effectively /ɪˈfektɪvlɪ/ adv ▯ (efficiently) skutecznie,
efektywnie ▯ (in effect) faktycznie, w rzeczywistości
effeminate /ɪˈfemɪnət/ adj zniewieściały
efficiency /ɪˈfɪʃnsɪ/ n (ability) sprawność f; (effect-
iveness) efektywność f, skuteczność f; (productivity)
wydajność f
efficient /ɪˈfɪʃnt/ adj ▯ [person, management]
sprawny; **to be** ~ **at doing sth** sprawnie coś robić
▯ [machine, engine] wydajny

effort /ˈefət/ n ▯ (exertion) wysiłek m; **to spare no**
~ nie szczędzić wysiłków or trudu; **it's a waste of
time and** ~ szkoda czasu i wysiłku; **it was
worth the** ~ wysiłek or trud się opłacił ▯ (attempt)
staranie n, próba f; **to make an** ~ postarać się,
spróbować; **to make every** ~ dokładać wszelkich
starań; **he made no** ~ **to apologize** nawet nie
próbował się usprawiedliwić
EFL n = **English as a Foreign Language**
angielski m jako język obcy
eg = **exempli gratia** np.
egalitarian /ɪˌgælɪˈteərɪən/ adj [ideas, theory]
egalitarystyczny; [society, system] egalitarny
egg /eg/ n jajko n
eggcup /ˈegkʌp/ n kieliszek m do jajek
eggplant /ˈegplɑːnt, US -plænt/ n US bakłażan m,
oberżyna f
egg white n białko n (jaja)
egg yolk n żółtko n (jaja)
ego /ˈegəʊ, ˈiːgəʊ, US ˈiːgəʊ/ n ▯ (in psychology) ego n
inv ▯ (self-esteem) własne ja; **to boost** or **bolster
sb's** ~ dodać komuś pewności siebie
egoism /ˈegəʊɪzəm, ˈiːg-, US ˈiːg-/ n egoizm m
egoist /ˈegəʊɪst, ˈiːg-, US ˈiːg-/ n egoist|a m, -ka f
egotist /ˈegəʊtɪst, ˈiːg-, US ˈiːg-/ n egotyst|a m, -ka f
Egypt /ˈiːdʒɪpt/ prn Egipt m
eiderdown /ˈaɪdədaʊn/ n (quilt) kołdra f pucho-
wa; (down) edredon m
eight /eɪt/ ▯ n (numeral) osiem; (symbol) ósemka f;
~ **o'clock** godzina ósma
▯▯ adj osiem; (male) ośmiu; (male and female) ośmioro
eighteen /eɪˈtiːn/ ▯ n (numeral) osiemnaście; (symbol) osiemnastka f
▯▯ adj osiemnaście; (male) osiemnastu, osiemna-
ścioro
eighteenth /eɪˈtiːnθ/ ▯ n ▯ (in order) osiemnast|y
m, -a f, -e n; **the** ~ **of May** osiemnasty maja
▯ (fraction) osiemnasta f (część)
▯▯ adj osiemnasty
eighth /eɪtθ/ ▯ n ▯ (in order) ósm|y m, -a f, -e n; **the**
~ **of June** ósmy czerwca ▯ (fraction) ósma f (część)
▯▯ adj ósmy
eightieth /ˈeɪtɪəθ/ ▯ n ▯ (in order) osiemdziesią-
t|y m, -a f, -e n ▯ (fraction) osiemdziesiąta f (część)
▯▯ adj osiemdziesiąty
eighty /ˈeɪtɪ/ ▯ n (numeral) osiemdziesiąt
▯▯ adj osiemdziesiąt; (male) osiemdziesięciu; (male
and female) osiemdziesięcioro
eighty-one /ˌeɪtɪˈwʌn/ n, adj osiemdziesiąt jeden
Éire /ˈeərə/ prn Republika f Irlandii
either /ˈaɪðər, US ˈiːðər/ ▯ pron ▯ (one or other) albo
jeden, albo drugi; (in the negative) ani jeden, ani
drugi; **I don't like** ~ **of those dresses** nie
podoba mi się żadna z tych sukienek; '**which
book do you want?' – '**~' „którą chcesz
książkę?" – „wszystko jedno" ▯ (both) ~ **of the**

two possibilities obie możliwości; ~ **of us could do it** każdy z nas (dwóch) może to zrobić **II** *det* 1 (one or the other) albo jeden, albo drugi; (in the negative) ani jeden, ani drugi; **you can take** ~ **route** możesz wybrać albo jedną, albo drugą trasę; **the key wasn't in** ~ **drawer** klucza nie było ani w jednej, ani w drugiej szufladzie 2 (both) ~ **one of the solutions is acceptable** oba rozwiązania są do przyjęcia; **in** ~ **case** w obu przypadkach; ~ **way, it'll be difficult** tak czy owak, to będzie trudne **III** *adv* też (nie); **I can't do it** ~ ja też nie potrafię tego zrobić **IV** ~ **... or... conj** 1 (as alternatives) albo..., albo... 2 (in the negative) ani..., ani...; **I can't speak** ~ **Spanish or Italian** nie mówię ani po hiszpańsku, ani po włosku

eject /ɪˈdʒekt/ **I** *vt* 1 (give out) *[machine, system]* wypu|ścić, -szczać *[waste]*; wyrzuc|ić, -ać *[lava]* 2 (from tape recorder) wyrzuc|ić, -ać *[cassette]* 3 infml (throw out) wyrzuc|ić, -ać *[troublemaker]* **II** *vi [pilot]* katapultować się

eject button *n* klawisz *m* kieszeni kasety

eke /iːk/ *vt* ■ **eke out**: oszczędnie gospodarować (czymś) *[income, supplies]*; **to** ~ **out a living** z trudem wiązać koniec z końcem

elaborate I /ɪˈlæbərət/ *adj [system, procedure, plan, question]* skomplikowany; *[meal]* wymyślny; *[joke]* wyrafinowany **II** /ɪˈlæbəreɪt/ *vt* rozwi|nąć, -jać *[theory, hypothesis]* **III** /ɪˈlæbəreɪt/ *vi* **to** ~ **on sth** rozwinąć coś *[proposal, remark]*

elapse /ɪˈlæps/ *vi [time, years]* upły|nąć, -wać

elastic /ɪˈlæstɪk/ **I** *n* gum(k)a *f* **II** *adj* elastyczny

elasticated /ɪˈlæstɪkeɪtɪd/ *adj* elastyczny

elastic band *n* gumka *f*

elated /ɪˈleɪtɪd/ *adj* upojony (**at** or **by sth** czymś)

elbow /ˈelbəʊ/ *n* łokieć *m*

elbow grease *n* infml wysiłek *m*

elbowroom /ˈelbəʊruːm/ *n* (room to move) (wolna) przestrzeń *f*; fig pole *n* manewru

elder[1] /ˈeldə(r)/ **I** *n* (older person) starsza osoba *f*; (in tribe, village) starszy *m* **II** *adj* starszy

elder[2] /ˈeldə(r)/ *n* (tree) czarny bez *m*

elderly /ˈeldəli/ **I** *n* **the** ~ ludzie *plt* starsi **II** *adj [person, age]* starszy

eldest /ˈeldɪst/ **I** *n* najstarsz|y *m*, -a *f* **II** *adj* najstarszy

elect /ɪˈlekt/ *vt* wyb|rać, -ierać *[president, method, system]*; **to** ~ **to do sth** postanowić coś zrobić

election /ɪˈlekʃn/ *n* wybory *plt*; **to win an** ~ wygrać wybory

election campaign *n* kampania *f* wyborcza

electoral /ɪˈlektərəl/ *adj* wyborczy

electorate /ɪˈlektərət/ *n* elektorat *m*

electric /ɪˈlektrɪk/ *adj* elektryczny

electrical /ɪˈlektrɪkl/ *adj* elektryczny

electric blanket *n* koc *m* elektryczny

electrician /ˌɪlekˈtrɪʃn/ *n* elektryk *m*

electricity /ˌɪlekˈtrɪsəti/ *n* elektryczność *f*; **to switch off/on the** ~ wyłączyć/włączyć prąd

electric shock *n* wstrząs *m* elektryczny

electrify /ɪˈlektrɪfaɪ/ *vt* z|elektryfikować; fig z|elektryzować

electrocute /ɪˈlektrəkjuːt/ *vt* (injure) pora|zić, -żać prądem; (in electric chair) stracić na krześle elektrycznym

electronic /ˌɪlekˈtrɒnɪk/ *adj* elektroniczny

electronic engineer *n* elektronik *m*

electronic organizer *n* notes *m* elektroniczny

electronic publishing *n* wydawanie *n* książek w formie elektronicznej

electronics /ˌɪlekˈtrɒnɪks/ *n* elektronika *f*

electronic tagging *n* oznaczanie *n* przestępców lokalizatorem elektronicznym

elegant /ˈelɪɡənt/ *adj [person, clothes, restaurant]* elegancki; *[gesture, manners]* wytworny

element /ˈelɪmənt/ *n* 1 (constituent) element *m* 2 (air, water) żywioł *m* 3 (substance) pierwiastek *m* 4 (of kettle, heater) element *m* grzejny

elementary /ˌelɪˈmentri/ *adj* 1 (basic) podstawowy; (simple) elementarny 2 *[school]* podstawowy; *[teacher]* szkoły podstawowej

elephant /ˈelɪfənt/ *n* słoń *m*

elevate /ˈelɪveɪt/ *vt* wyn|ieść, -osić na wyższe stanowisko *[person]*; podn|ieść, -osić rangę (czegoś) *[town, profession]*

elevated /ˈelɪveɪtɪd/ *adj [style, thought, tone]* podniosły; *[position, status]* wysoki; *[site]* wyżej położony

elevator /ˈelɪveɪtə(r)/ *n* 1 US (in building) winda *f* 2 (hoist) podnośnik *m*

eleven /ɪˈlevn/ **I** *n* jedenaście **II** *adj* jedenaście; (male) jedenastu; (male and female) jedenaścioro

eleventh /ɪˈlevnθ/ **I** *n* 1 (in order) jedenast|y *m*, -a *f*, -e *n* 2 (fraction) jedenasta *f* (część) **II** *adj* jedenasty **III** *adv [come, finish]* na jedenastym miejscu

elf /elf/ *n* elf *m*

eligible /ˈelɪdʒəbl/ *adj [applicant, candidate]* spełniający warunki; **to be** ~ **for sth** mieć prawo ubiegać się o coś *[allowance, benefit, membership]*; **to be** ~ **to do sth** mieć prawo coś zrobić

eliminate /ɪˈlɪmɪneɪt/ *vt* wy|eliminować *[candidate, team]*; wyklucz|yć, -ać *[suspect]*

elimination /ɪˌlɪmɪˈneɪʃn/ *n* eliminacja *f*; (ruling out) odrzucenie *n*; **by a process of** ~ przez eliminację

elm /elm/ *n* wiąz *m*

elongated /ˈiːlɒŋɡeɪtɪd/ *adj* wydłużony

elope /ɪˈləʊp/ *vi* ucie|c, -kać (**with sb** z kimś)

eloquent /ˈeləkwənt/ *adj* elokwentny

else /els/ **I** *adv* [1] (other than) **somebody/nobody** ~ ktoś/nikt inny; **something** ~ coś innego; **somewhere/nowhere** ~ gdzieś/nigdzie indziej [2] (in addition) jeszcze; **where** ~ **can it be?** gdzie(ż) jeszcze może to być?

II or else *conj phr* bo (inaczej)

elsewhere /ˌelsˈweə(r), US ˌelsˈhweər/ *adv* gdzie indziej

elusive /ɪˈluːsɪv/ *adj* [person, animal] nieuchwytny; [prize, victory] nieosiągalny; [dream, thought, happiness] ulotny

emaciated /ɪˈmeɪʃɪeɪtɪd/ *adj* [person, animal, body] wychudzony; [part of body] wychudły

email, e-mail /ˈiːmeɪl/ *n* (medium) poczta *f* elektroniczna, e-mail *m*; (message) wiadomość *f*, e-mail *m*

e-mail address *n* adres *m* e-mailowy

emancipate /ɪˈmænsɪpeɪt/ *vt* wyzw|olić, -alać [slaves]; wy|emancypować [women]

emancipation /ɪˌmænsɪˈpeɪʃn/ *n* emancypacja *f*

embalm /ɪmˈbɑːm, US -ˈbɑːlm/ *vt* za|balsamować

embankment /ɪmˈbæŋkmənt/ *n* [1] (for road, railway) nasyp *m* [2] (against flooding) wał *m*

embargo /ɪmˈbɑːgəʊ/ *n* embargo *n*

embark /ɪmˈbɑːk/ *vi* [1] (on ship) zaokrętow|ać, -ywać się [2] **to** ~ **on sth** wyruszyć w coś [journey, voyage]; rozpocząć coś [career, campaign]

embarkation /ˌembɑːˈkeɪʃn/ *n* (of passengers) zaokrętowanie *n*; (of cars, goods) załadunek *m*

embarrass /ɪmˈbærəs/ *vt* wprawi|ć, -ać w zakłopotanie

embarrassing /ɪmˈbærəsɪŋ/ *adj* [person, situation, mistake] żenujący; [question] wprawiający w zakłopotanie

embarrassment /ɪmˈbærəsmənt/ *n* skrępowanie *n* (**about** or **at sth** z powodu czegoś); **to my** ~ ku memu zakłopotaniu

embassy /ˈembəsɪ/ *n* ambasada *f*

embers /ˈembəz/ *n* żar *m*

embezzle /ɪmˈbezl/ *vt* z|defraudować [funds]

emblem /ˈembləm/ *n* godło *n*; (of organization) emblemat *m*

embody /ɪmˈbɒdɪ/ *vt* uos|obić, -abiać [virtue, evil, ideal]

embrace /ɪmˈbreɪs/ **I** *n* uścisk *m*, objęcia *n pl*

II *vt* [1] (hug) obj|ąć, -ejmować [2] (include) obj|ąć, -ejmować [subject, beliefs]

III *vi* obj|ąć, -ejmować się

embroider /ɪmˈbrɔɪdə(r)/ **I** *vt* [1] wy|haftować [design] [2] fig ubarwi|ć, -ać [story, truth]

II *vi* haftować

embroidery /ɪmˈbrɔɪdərɪ/ *n* haft *m*

embryo /ˈembrɪəʊ/ *n* embrion *m*

emerald /ˈemərəld/ *n* [1] (stone) szmaragd *m* [2] (colour) (kolor *m*) szmaragdowy *m*

emerge /ɪˈmɜːdʒ/ *vi* [issue, problem, ideology] pojawi|ć, -ać się; [truth, secret] wy|jść, -chodzić na jaw; [talent] objawi|ć, -ać się; **to** ~ **from sth** [person] wyjść z czegoś; [vehicle] wyjechać z czegoś [tunnel]

emergency /ɪˈmɜːdʒənsɪ/ **I** *n* nagły wypadek *m*; **in an** ~, **in case of** ~ (in urgent situation) w nagłym przypadku; (in dangerous situation) w razie niebezpieczeństwa; **in times of** ~ w sytuacjach kryzysowych

II *adj* [meeting, session] nadzwyczajny; [measures, situation] wyjątkowy; [repairs] awaryjny

emergency exit *n* wyjście *n* awaryjne

emergency landing *n* lądowanie *n* awaryjne

emergency services *npl* pomoc *f* w nagłych wypadkach

emergency worker *n* ratowni|k *m*, -czka *f*

emigrant /ˈemɪgrənt/ *n* emigrant *m*, -ka *f*

emigrate /ˈemɪgreɪt/ *vi* wy|emigrować

emission /ɪˈmɪʃn/ *n* emisja *f*

emit /ɪˈmɪt/ *vt* wy|emitować [fumes, light, radiation]; wydziel|ić, -ać [heat, smell]; wys|łać, -yłać [signal]

emoticon /ɪˈməʊtɪkɒn/ *n* emoticon *m*, uśmieszek *m*

emotion /ɪˈməʊʃn/ *n* uczucie *n*

emotional /ɪˈməʊʃənl/ *adj* [development, problems, tie] emocjonalny; [person, mood, tie] uczuciowy; [appeal, speech] wzruszający

emotionally /ɪˈməʊʃənəlɪ/ *adv* [involved, immature] emocjonalnie; [speak] z uczuciem; ~ **deprived** niekochany; ~ **disturbed** niezrównoważony emocjonalnie

emotive /ɪˈməʊtɪv/ *adj* [issue] budzący emocje; [language, word] zabarwiony emocjonalnie

empathize /ˈempəθaɪz/ *vi* **to** ~ **with sb** identyfikować się z kimś

emperor /ˈempərə(r)/ *n* cesarz *m*

emphasis /ˈemfəsɪs/ *n* nacisk *m*; **to lay** or **put the** ~ **on sth** kłaść nacisk na coś

emphasize /ˈemfəsaɪz/ *vt* podkreśl|ić, -ać [fact, point]; położyć, kłaść nacisk na (coś) [policy, need, support]

emphatic /ɪmˈfætɪk/ *adj* [statement] stanowczy; [voice] dobitny; [manner, gesture] wymowny

empire /ˈempaɪə(r)/ *n* imperium *n*; (ruled by emperor) cesarstwo *n*

employ /ɪmˈplɔɪ/ *vt* [1] (hire) zatrudni|ć, -ać [person, company] [2] (use) za|stosować [method, technique]; wykorzyst|ać, -ywać [intelligence, resources]; po-słu|żyć, -giwać się (czymś) [term, tool]

employable /ɪmˈplɔɪəbl/ *adj* [person] zdolny do pracy

employee /ˌemplɔɪˈiː, ɪmˈplɔɪiː/ *n* pracowni|k *m*, -ca *f*

employer /ɪmˈplɔɪə(r)/ *n* pracodaw|ca *m*, -czyni *f*

employment /ɪmˈplɔɪmənt/ *n* zatrudnienie *n*

employment agency *n* biuro *n* pośrednictwa pracy

empower /ɪmˈpaʊə(r)/ *vt* (legally) **to ~ sb to do sth** upoważnić kogoś do zrobienia czegoś; *[constitution]* dawać komuś prawo do zrobienia czegoś

empress /ˈemprɪs/ *n* cesarzowa *f*

empty /ˈemptɪ/ Ⅰ *adj* [1] pusty; *[page]* czysty [2] *[gesture]* pusty; *[promise, threat]* czczy

Ⅱ *vt* (also ~ **out**) opróżni|ć, -ać *[container, building]*; wyl|ać, -ewać *[liquid]*

Ⅲ *vi* (also ~ **out**) *[building]* o|pustoszeć; *[container]* opróżni|ć, -ać się

empty-handed /ˌemptɪˈhændɪd/ *adj* z pustymi rękami

emulate /ˈemjʊleɪt/ *vt* naśladować

emulsion /ɪˈmʌlʃn/ *n* emulsja *f*

enable /ɪˈneɪbl/ *vt* umożliwi|ć, -ać *[development, growth, learning]*; **to ~ sb to do sth** umożliwić komuś zrobienie czegoś

enamel /ɪˈnæml/ *n* emalia *f*; (on teeth) szkliwo *n*

enchant /ɪnˈtʃɑːnt, US -ˈtʃænt/ *vt* oczarow|ać, -ywać

enchanting /ɪnˈtʃɑːntɪŋ, US -ˈtʃænt-/ *adj* czarujący

encircle /ɪnˈsɜːkl/ *vt* *[troops, police, fence]* ot|oczyć, -aczać; *[belt, bracelet]* opas|ać, -ywać

enclose /ɪnˈkləʊz/ *vt* [1] (surround) ot|oczyć, -aczać (**with sth** czymś); *[casing, shell]* mieścić w sobie [2] (insert in letter) załącz|yć, -ać (**in** or **with sth** do czegoś); **please find ~d a cheque for...** w załączeniu czek na...

enclosure /ɪnˈkləʊʒə(r)/ *n* [1] (for animals) zagroda *f*; (at sports grounds) sektor *m* [2] (fence) ogrodzenie *n*

encompass /ɪnˈkʌmpəs/ *vt* obj|ąć, -ejmować *[range of subjects, activities, aspects]*

encore /ˈɒŋkɔː(r)/ Ⅰ *n* bis *m*; **to play an ~** zagrać na bis

Ⅱ *excl* bis!

encounter /ɪnˈkaʊntə(r)/ Ⅰ *n* spotkanie *n* (**with sb** z kimś); (of troops) potyczka *f*

Ⅱ *vt* napot|kać, -ykać *[person, difficulties, resistance]*; doświadcz|yć, -ać (czegoś) *[setback]*

encourage /ɪnˈkʌrɪdʒ/ *vt* [1] (give hope, courage) doda|ć, -wać otuchy (komuś); (reassure) po|działać zachęcająco na (kogoś); **to ~ sb to do sth** zachęcić kogoś do zrobienia czegoś [2] (support) pobudz|ić, -ać *[activity, initiative]*; sprzyjać (czemuś) *[growth, speculation, investment]*; po|działać pobudzająco na (coś) *[industry]*

encouragement /ɪnˈkʌrɪdʒmənt/ *n* zachęta *f*

encouraging /ɪnˈkʌrɪdʒɪŋ/ *adj* zachęcający

encroach /ɪnˈkrəʊtʃ/ *vi* **to ~ on sth** *[vegetation]* zarosnąć coś; *[enemy]* wedrzeć się na terytorium czegoś *[country]*

encript /enˈkrɪpt/ *vt* za|kodować

encyclop(a)edia /ɪnˌsaɪkləˈpiːdɪə/ *n* encyklopedia *f*

end /end/ Ⅰ *n* [1] (final part) koniec *m*; **'The End'** (of film, book) „Koniec"; **to put an ~ to sth** położyć kres czemuś; **to come to an ~** skończyć się; **in the ~ I went home** w końcu poszedłem do domu; **for days on ~** całymi dniami [2] (extremity) koniec *m*; **at/on the ~ of sth** przy/na końcu czegoś; **at the ~ of the garden** na końcu ogrodu; **the third from the ~** trzeci od końca; **to stand sth on (its) ~** postawić coś na sztorc [3] (aim) cel *m*; **to this ~** w tym celu; **a means to an ~** środek do osiągnięcia celu [4] Sport pole *n*; **to change ~s** zmienić pole

Ⅱ *vt* zak|ończyć, -ańczać *[strike, search]*; **he ~ed his speech with the following words...** zakończył przemówienie następującymi słowami...; **the sale to ~ all sales** wyprzedaż, jakiej jeszcze nie było

Ⅲ *vi* *[meeting, relationship]* s|kończyć się; *[agreement, contract]* wygas|nąć, -ać

■ **end up:** s|kończyć; **to ~ up (as) president** zostać prezydentem; **I ~ed up (by) doing it myself** skończyło się na tym, że sam to zrobiłem

endanger /ɪnˈdeɪndʒə(r)/ *vt* zagr|ozić, -ażać (czemuś) *[health, life]*; stanowić zagrożenie dla (czegoś) *[environment, species]*

endangered species *n* zagrożony gatunek *m*

endearing /ɪnˈdɪərɪŋ/ *adj* *[habit, personality]* ujmujący; *[remark, child]* uroczy

endeavour GB, **endeavor** US /ɪnˈdevə(r)/ Ⅰ *n* próba *f* (**to do sth** zrobienia czegoś)

Ⅱ *vt* **to ~ to do sth** (make an effort) po|starać się coś zrobić; (try hard) usiłować coś zrobić

ending /ˈendɪŋ/ *n* zakończenie *n*

endive /ˈendɪv, US -daɪv/ *n* (curly) endywia *f*; US cykoria *f*

endless /ˈendlɪs/ *adj* (unlimited) *[energy, patience]* niewyczerpany; *[attempts, possibilities]* niezliczony; *[choice]* nieograniczony; *[argument, search, job]* niekończący się

endorse /ɪnˈdɔːs/ *vt* udziel|ić, -ać poparcia (komuś/czemuś) *[person]*; podpis|ać, -ywać na odwrocie *[cheque]*

endow /ɪnˈdaʊ/ *vt* (with money) wspom|óc, -agać *[charity, hospital]*

end result *n* wynik *m* końcowy

endurance /ɪnˈdjʊərəns, US -ˈdʊə-/ *n* wytrzymałość *f*

endure /ɪnˈdjʊə(r), US -ˈdʊər/ Ⅰ *vt* zn|ieść, -osić *[hardship, person, sight, pain]*; przetrzym|ać, -ywać *[attack]*

Ⅱ *vi* prze|trwać

enemy /ˈenəmɪ/ Ⅰ *n* wróg *m*

Ⅱ *modif [forces, aircraft, territory]* nieprzyjacielski; *[propaganda]* wrogi

energetic /ˌenəˈdʒetɪk/ *adj* energiczny

energy /ˈenədʒɪ/ *n* energia *f*

energy policy *n* polityka *f* energetyczna

energy saving ∎ *n* oszczędność *f* energii
∎∎ **energy-saving** *adj* energooszczędny
enforce /ɪn'fɔːs/ *vt* wprowadz|ić, -ać w życie *[rule, policy, decision]*; wy|egzekwować *[court order, payment, discipline]*
engage /ɪn'geɪdʒ/ ∎ *vt* ① **to be** ~**d in sth** zajmować się czymś *[activity]*; **to be** ~**d in discussions** brać udział w rozmowach ② Aut włącz|yć, -ać *[clutch, gear]*
∎∎ *vi* **to** ~ **in sth** zaj|ąć, -mować się czymś *[activity, research]*; za|angażować się w coś *[campaign]*
engaged /ɪn'geɪdʒd/ *adj* ① (before marriage) zaręczony; **to be** ~ być zaręczonym (**to sb** z kimś); **to get** ~ zaręczyć się (**to sb** z kimś) ② *[taxi, toilet, phone]* zajęty
engaged tone *n* GB sygnał *m* zajęty
engagement /ɪn'geɪdʒmənt/ *n* ① (appointment) (umówione) spotkanie *n*; (of performer, artist) występ *m* ② (before marriage) zaręczyny *plt*
engagement ring *n* pierścionek *m* zaręczynowy
engine /'endʒɪn/ *n* ① (motor) silnik *m* ② (locomotive) lokomotywa *f*; **diesel** ~ lokomotywa spalinowa
engine driver *n* maszynista *m*
engineer /ˌendʒɪ'nɪə(r)/ ∎ *n* ① (graduate) inżynier *m*; (in factory) mechanik *m*, monter *m* ② (on ship) mechanik *m*
∎∎ *vt* ① (contrive) u|knuć *[plot, revolt, scheme]* ② (build) s|konstruować
engineering /ˌendʒɪ'nɪərɪŋ/ *n* inżynieria *f*; **civil** ~ inżynieria lądowa
England /'ɪŋglənd/ *prn* Anglia *f*
English /'ɪŋglɪʃ/ ∎ *n* ① (language) (język *m*) angielski *m* ② **the** ~ Anglicy *m pl*
∎∎ *adj [countryside, accent]* angielski; ~ **lesson/textbook** lekcja/podręcznik języka angielskiego
English Channel *prn* **the** ~ kanał *m* La Manche
Englishman /'ɪŋglɪʃmən/ *n* Anglik *m*
English-speaking /'ɪŋglɪʃspiːkɪŋ/ *adj* anglojęzyczny
Englishwoman /'ɪŋglɪʃwʊmən/ *n* Angielka *f*
engrave /ɪn'greɪv/ *vt* wy|grawerować
engraving /ɪn'greɪvɪŋ/ *n* sztych *m*
engrossed /ɪn'grəʊst/ *adj* **to be** ~ **in sth** być pochłoniętym czymś *[book, spectacle, work]*; być zaabsorbowanym czymś *[problem, work]*
engulf /ɪn'gʌlf/ *vt [sea, waves]* pochłon|ąć, -aniać; *[fire]* ogar|nąć, -niać
enhance /ɪn'hɑːns, US -'hæns/ *vt* zwiększ|yć, -ać *[prospects, chances]*; popraw|ić, -ać *[reputation, appearance]*; podn|ieść, -osić *[status]*
enigma /ɪ'nɪgmə/ *n* zagadka *f*
enigmatic /ˌenɪg'mætɪk/ *adj [smile]* zagadkowy; *[statement]* enigmatyczny
enjoy /ɪn'dʒɔɪ/ ∎ *vt* ① (like) lubić; **to** ~ **doing sth** lubić coś robić; **I didn't** ~ **the party** źle się

bawiłem na przyjęciu; ~ **your meal!** smacznego!
② (benefit from) korzystać z (czegoś)
∎∎ *vr* **to** ~ **oneself** dobrze się bawić; **to** ~ **oneself doing sth** z przyjemnością coś robić
enjoyable /ɪn'dʒɔɪəbl/ *adj* przyjemny
enjoyment /ɪn'dʒɔɪmənt/ *n* przyjemność *f*
enlarge /ɪn'lɑːdʒ/ ∎ *vt* powiększ|yć, -ać
∎∎ *vi [liver, muscle]* powiększ|yć, -ać się; *[pupil]* rozszerz|yć, -ać się
enlighten /ɪn'laɪtn/ *vt* oświec|ić, -ać; **to** ~ **sb on sth** objaśnić komuś coś
enlightening /ɪn'laɪtnɪŋ/ *adj* pouczający
enlightenment /ɪn'laɪtnmənt/ *n* (edification) oświecenie *n*; (clarification) wyjaśnienie *n*; **the (Age of) Enlightenment** oświecenie *n*
enlist /ɪn'lɪst/ ∎ *vt* zjedn|ać, -ywać sobie *[supporters]*; (in army) z|werbować; **to** ~ **sb's help** uzyskać pomoc od kogoś
∎∎ *vi* zaciąg|nąć, -ać się
enmity /'enmətɪ/ *n* wrogość *f* (**towards** or **for sb/sth** wobec kogoś/czegoś)
enormity /ɪ'nɔːmətɪ/ *n* ogrom *m*
enormous /ɪ'nɔːməs/ *adj* ogromny
enough /ɪ'nʌf/ ∎ *pron, det* dosyć (czegoś); **to be** ~ **for sb** wystarczyć komuś; **will 10 be** ~? czy wystarczy dziesięć?; **have you had** ~ **to eat?** najadłeś się?; **you've had more than** ~ **to drink** dość już wypiłeś; **I've had** ~ **of him** mam go dość
∎∎ *adj* dosyć (czegoś); **do we have** ~ **glasses?** czy mamy dość kieliszków?
∎∎∎ *adv* (sufficiently) dosyć, dostatecznie; **big** ~ **to hold 60 people** na tyle duży, żeby pomieścić 60 osób; **curiously/oddly** ~ co ciekawe/dziwne
enquire *vt, vi* = **inquire**
enquiring *adj* = **inquiring**
enquiry *n* = **inquiry**
enrage /ɪn'reɪdʒ/ *vt* rozwściecz|yć, -ać
enrich /ɪn'rɪtʃ/ *vt* wzbogac|ić, -ać
enrol, enroll US /ɪn'rəʊl/ ∎ *vt [parent]* zapis|ać, -ywać; *[college, school]* przyj|ąć, -mować; *[army]* z|werbować
∎∎ *vi* zapis|ać, -ywać się
enrolment, enrollment US /ɪn'rəʊlmənt/ *n* zapisy *plt*
ensuing /ɪn'sjuːɪŋ, US -'suː-/ *adj [period]* następny; **in the** ~ **fight** w walce, która się wywiązała
en suite /ˌɒn'swiːt/ *adj [bathroom]* przyległy
ensure /ɪn'ʃɔː(r), US ɪn'ʃʊər/ *vt* zapewni|ć, -ać
entail /ɪn'teɪl/ *vt* (involve) wiązać się z (czymś) *[changes, expense, risk]*; wymagać (czegoś) *[patience, discretion]*
enter /'entə(r)/ ∎ *vt* ① (go into) w|ejść, -chodzić do (czegoś) *[room, house, parliament]* ② (begin) w|ejść, -chodzić w (coś) *[phase]* ③ (join) przyst|ąpić, -ępować do (czegoś) *[organization]*; wy|startować w (czymś) *[competition]*; **to** ~ **sb's mind** or **head** przyjść komuś na myśl or do głowy ④ (put forward)

zgł|osić, -aszać *[competitor, poem]* (**for sth** do czegoś) ⑤ (record) za|notować *[appointment, fact]* (**in sth** w czymś); wpis|ać, -ywać *[figure, fact]* (**in sth** w czymś, na czymś); wprowadz|ić, -ać *[data, item]*

II *vi* ① (come in) w|ejść, -chodzić ② (enrol) zgł|osić, -aszać się (**for sth** do czegoś)

■ **enter into**: nawiąz|ać, -ywać *[correspondence, conversation]*; pod|jąć, -ejmować *[negotiations]*

enterprise /'entəpraɪz/ *n* (undertaking) przedsięwzięcie *n*; (initiative) przedsiębiorczość *f*

enterprising /'entəpraɪzɪŋ/ *adj [person]* przedsiębiorczy; *[plan, venture]* śmiały

entertain /ˌentə'teɪn/ **I** *vt* ① (keep amused) zabawi|ć, -ać; (make laugh) rozbawi|ć, -ać; (keep interested) zaj|ąć, -mować ② (play host to) przyj|ąć, -mować ③ (nourish) żywić *[belief, hope, suspicions]*; rozważać *[idea]*

II *vi* pod|jąć, -ejmować gości

entertainer /ˌentə'teɪnə(r)/ *n* artysta *m* estradowy, artystka *f* estradowa

entertaining /ˌentə'teɪnɪŋ/ **I** *n* **they do a lot of** ~ często mają gości

II *adj* zabawny

entertainment /ˌentə'teɪnmənt/ *n* ① (amusement) rozrywka *f* ② (event) widowisko *n*

entertainment industry *n* **the** ~ przemysł *m* rozrywkowy

enthusiasm /ɪn'θjuːzɪæzəm, US -'θuːz-/ *n* entuzjazm *m* (**for sth** do or dla czegoś)

enthusiast /ɪn'θjuːzɪæst, US -'θuːz-/ *n* entuzjast|a *m*, -ka *f* (**for sth** czegoś)

enthusiastic /ɪnˌθjuːzɪ'æstɪk, US -ˌθuːz-/ *adj [response, welcome]* entuzjastyczny; *[crowd, spectators]* rozentuzjazmowany; *[discussion]* gorący; *[worker]* gorliwy; *[gardener]* zapalony

entice /ɪn'taɪs/ *vt* (with offer, prospect, money) s|kusić (**with sth** czymś); (with food, charms) z|wabić (**with sth** czymś)

entire /ɪn'taɪə(r)/ *adj* cały; **an** ~ **day** cały dzień

entirely /ɪn'taɪəlɪ/ *adv [agree, destroy]* całkowicie

entirety /ɪn'taɪərətɪ/ *n* całość *f*

entitle /ɪn'taɪtl/ *vt* **to** ~ **sb to sth** upoważnić kogoś do czegoś; **to be** ~**d to sth** mieć prawo do czegoś; **to be** ~**d to do sth** mieć prawo coś robić

entitlement /ɪn'taɪtlmənt/ *n* prawo *n* (**to sth** do czegoś)

entity /'entətɪ/ *n* (institution, state) jednostka *f*

entrance[1] /'entrəns/ *n* (door) wejście *n*; (admission) wstęp *m*; **to gain** ~ **to a university/club** zostać przyjętym na uniwersytet/do klubu

entrance[2] /ɪn'trɑːns, US -'træns/ *vt* urze|c, -kać

entrance examination *n* Sch, Univ egzamin *m* wstępny; (for civil service) egzamin *m* kwalifikacyjny

entrance fee *n* (to building) opłata *f* za wstęp; (to club, for competition) wpisowe *n*

entrance hall *n* (in house) przedpokój *m*; (in public building) hall *m*

entrance requirements *npl* wymagania *n pl* dla kandydatów

entrant /'entrənt/ *n* (in competition) uczestni|k *m*, -czka *f*; (in entrance exam) kandydat *m*, -ka *f*

entreat /ɪn'triːt/ *vt* błagać

entreaty /ɪn'triːtɪ/ *n* błaganie *n*

entrepreneur /ˌɒntrəprə'nɜː(r)/ *n* przedsiębiorca *m*

entrust /ɪn'trʌst/ *vt* **to** ~ **sb with sth, to** ~ **sth to sb** powierzyć coś komuś

entry /'entrɪ/ *n* ① (act of entering) wejście *n*; (admission) wstęp *m*; **to gain** ~ **(in)to sth** dostać się do czegoś *[building, computer file]*; **'no** ~**'** (on door) „wstęp wzbroniony"; (in one-way street) „zakaz wjazdu" ② (in dictionary) hasło *n*; (in diary) wpis *m*; (in register) zapis *m* ③ (in contest) zgłoszenie *n*; (person entered) uczestni|k *m*, -czka *f*; (thing entered) praca *f* konkursowa

entry form *n* kwestionariusz *m*

entry phone *n* domofon *m*

envelope /'envələʊp, 'ɒn-/ *n* koperta *f*

envious /'envɪəs/ *adj [person]* zazdrosny; **to be** ~ **of sb** zazdrościć komuś

environment /ɪn'vaɪərənmənt/ *n* środowisko *n*

environmental /ɪnˌvaɪərən'mentl/ *adj [changes, conditions]* środowiskowy; *[issue, group, disaster]* ekologiczny; ~ **pollution/protection** zanieczyszczenie/ochrona środowiska

environmentally /ɪnˌvaɪərən'mentəlɪ/ *adv* ~ **safe** or **sound** bezpieczny dla środowiska; ~ **friendly product** produkt ekologiczny

Environmental Studies *npl* GB Sch nauka *f* o środowisku naturalnym

envisage /ɪn'vɪzɪdʒ/ *vt* (anticipate) przewi|dzieć, -dywać; (visualize) wyobra|zić, -żać sobie

envy /'envɪ/ **I** *n* zazdrość *f*; (stronger) zawiść *f*

II *vt* **to** ~ **sb sth** zazdrościć komuś czegoś

enzyme /'enzaɪm/ *n* enzym *m*

epic /'epɪk/ **I** *n* (poem) epos *m*; (film, novel) epopeja *f* also fig

II *adj* epicki

epidemic /ˌepɪ'demɪk/ **I** *n* epidemia *f*

II *adj* epidemiczny

epidural /ˌepɪ'djʊərəl/ *n* znieczulenie *n* zewnątrzoponowe

epilepsy /'epɪlepsɪ/ *n* padaczka *f*, epilepsja *f*

epileptic /ˌepɪ'leptɪk/ *n* epilepty|k *m*, -czka *f*

episode /'epɪsəʊd/ *n* (event) wydarzenie *n*; (of story, TV serial) odcinek *m*

epitome /ɪ'pɪtəmɪ/ *n* (person) uosobienie *n* (**of sth** czegoś); (thing) typowy przykład *m* (**of sth** czegoś)

epitomize /ɪ'pɪtəmaɪz/ *vt [person]* być uosobieniem (czegoś); *[thing]* być typowym przykładem (czegoś)

epoch /'iːpɒk, US 'epək/ *n* epoka *f*

equal /'iːkwəl/ [] n równ|y m, -a f
[] adj [1] [quantity] taki sam; [number] równy; ~
opportunities/rights równe szanse/prawa; on ~
terms jak równy z równym [2] to be ~ to sth
móc sprostać czemuś [job, task]
[] adv Sport [finish] równo
[] vt równać się

equality /ɪ'kwɒlətɪ/ n równość f; sexual ~
równouprawnienie płci

equalize /'iːkwəlaɪz/ [] vt zrówn|ać, -ywać [rights,
incomes]
[] vi Sport wyrówn|ać, -ywać

equally /'iːkwəlɪ/ adv [divide, share] równo; [treat]
jednakowo; ~ easy/comfortable równie łatwy/
wygodny; ~, we might say that... równie dobrze
można by powiedzieć, że...

equate /ɪ'kweɪt/ vt (identify) utożsami|ć, -ać (with
sth z czymś); (compare) porówn|ać, -ywać (with sth
z czymś)

equation /ɪ'kweɪʒn/ n równanie n

equator /ɪ'kweɪtə(r)/ n the ~ równik m

equilibrium /ˌiːkwɪ'lɪbrɪəm/ n równowaga f

equip /ɪ'kwɪp/ vt wyposaż|yć, -ać (with sth w coś);
fig przygotow|ać, -ywać [person] (for sth do czegoś)

equipment /ɪ'kwɪpmənt/ n (of office, building)
wyposażenie n; (sports, electrical) sprzęt m

equivalent /ɪ'kwɪvələnt/ [] n odpowiednik m (for
or of sth czegoś); (of sum of money) równowartość f (of
sth czegoś)
[] adj taki sam

era /'ɪərə/ n era f

eradicate /ɪ'rædɪkeɪt/ vt wykorzeni|ć, -ać [crime];
zwalcz|yć, -ać [disease]; z|likwidować [problem]

erase /ɪ'reɪz, US ɪ'reɪs/ vt [1] (from disk, tape) s|kasować
[2] (destroy) wy|eliminować [poverty, disease]

eraser /ɪ'reɪzə(r), US -sər/ n (for paper) gumka f do
wycierania

erect /ɪ'rekt/ [] adj [posture, figure] wyprostowany;
[tail] zadarty; [ears] postawiony
[] vt wzn|ieść, -osić [building]; rozbi|ć, -jać [tent];
ustawi|ć, -ać [sign, screen]

erection /ɪ'rekʃn/ n [1] (of building) wzniesienie n;
(building) gmach m [2] (of penis) erekcja f, wzwód m

ermine /'ɜːmɪn/ n gronostaj m; (fur) gronostaje plt

erode /ɪ'rəʊd/ vt s|powodować erozję (czegoś)
[rock]; podkop|ać, -ywać [confidence]

erosion /ɪ'rəʊʒn/ n erozja f

erotic /ɪ'rɒtɪk/ adj erotyczny

err /ɜː(r)/ vi [1] (make mistake) popełni|ć, -ać błąd
[2] (do wrong) z|błądzić; to ~ on the side of
caution grzeszyć nadmiarem ostrożności

errand /'erənd/ n sprawa f do załatwienia; to run
~s załatwiać sprawy

erratic /ɪ'rætɪk/ adj [person, driver, behaviour]
nieobliczalny; [moods] zmienny

error /'erə(r)/ n błąd m

erupt /ɪ'rʌpt/ vi wybuch|nąć, -ać

eruption /ɪ'rʌpʃn/ n (of volcano, violence) wybuch m

escalate /'eskəleɪt/ vi [violence, conflict] nasil|ić, -ać
się; [prices, inflation, unemployment] wzr|osnąć, -astać

escalator /'eskəleɪtə(r)/ n schody plt ruchome

escapade /'eskəpeɪd, ˌeskə'peɪd/ n wyskok m

escape /ɪ'skeɪp/ [] n ucieczka f; to have a narrow
or lucky ~ cudem ujść cało
[] vt unik|nąć, -ać (czegoś) [defeat, danger,
responsibility]; u|jść, -chodzić (czemuś) [penalty,
death]; to ~ sb's attention umknąć uwadze
kogoś
[] vi [1] [person, animal] ucie|c, -kać; to ~ from
sth uciec z czegoś [prison, army, cage]; uciec od
czegoś [boredom]; to ~ with one's life ujść
z życiem [2] (leak) [gas] ul|otnić, -atniać się; [water]
wycie|c, -kać

escape clause n klauzula f zwalniająca od
odpowiedzialności

escape key n klawisz m „escape"

escape route n (in case of fire) droga f ewakua-
cyjna; (for fugitives) trasa f ucieczki

escapism /ɪ'skeɪpɪzəm/ n eskapizm m

escort [] n /'eskɔːt/ n [1] (for security) eskorta f; police
~ eskorta policyjna [2] (companion) osoba f towarzysząca; (in agency) osoba f do towarzystwa
[] vt /ɪ'skɔːt/ vt [1] (for security) eskortować; to ~ sb
in/out wprowadzić/wyprowadzić kogoś pod
eskortą [2] (to a function) towarzyszyć (komuś); (home,
to the door) odprowadz|ić, -ać

especially /ɪ'speʃəlɪ/ adv [1] (above all) zwłaszcza;
why her ~? dlaczego właśnie ona? [2] (on purpose)
specjalnie [3] (particularly) szczególnie

espresso /e'spresəʊ/ n kawa f z ekspresu

essay /'eseɪ/ n (of school) wypracowanie n (on or
about sth na temat czegoś); (at university) praca f
(on sth na temat czegoś); (literary) esej m (on sth o
czymś)

essence /'esns/ n sedno n

essential /ɪ'senʃl/ [] n (object) rzecz f niezbędna;
(quality, element) podstawa f; the ~s (of science)
podstawy f pl (of sth czegoś); (of living) rzeczy f pl
niezbędne
[] adj [equipment, support, qualification] niezbędny; [role, question, difference] zasadniczy; [services]
podstawowy; it's ~ that we... musimy koniecznie...

essentially /ɪ'senʃəlɪ/ adv (basically) zasadniczo;
(in essence) w gruncie rzeczy; (above all) przede
wszystkim

essential oil n olejek m eteryczny

establish /ɪ'stæblɪʃ/ vt założyć, -kładać [business];
nawiąz|ać, -ywać [contact, relationship]

establishment /ɪ'stæblɪʃmənt/ n [1] (setting up) ~
of sth założenie czegoś [2] (institution, organization)
placówka f; (shop, business) firma f [3] the Establishment establishment

estate /ɪ'steɪt/ n [1] (land and buildings) posiadłość f [2] (group of buildings) **a housing** ~ osiedle mieszkaniowe [3] (assets) majątek m [4] GB (also ~ **car**) (samochód m) kombi n inv

estate agency n GB agencja f nieruchomości

estate agent n GB pośrednik m w handlu nieruchomościami

esteem /ɪ'sti:m/ n poważanie n

estimate [I] /'estɪmət/ n [1] (of quality) ocena f; (of quantity) liczba f szacunkowa; (of cost) szacunek m [2] (quote) kosztorys m
[II] /'estɪmeɪt/ vt (guess) o|szacować [size, value]; **to** ~ **that...** oceniać, że...
[III] **estimated** /'estɪmeɪtɪd/ pp adj [cost, figure] szacunkowy; **an** ~**d 300 people** około 300 osób

Estonia /ɪ'stəʊnɪə/ prn Estonia f

estranged /ɪ'streɪndʒd/ adj **to be** ~ **from sb** [spouse] pozostawać w separacji z kimś; **his** ~ **wife** żona, która od niego odeszła

etc adv = **et cetera** itd., itp.

etching /'etʃɪŋ/ n akwaforta f

eternal /ɪ't3:nl/ adj [life, love, chatter, optimist] wieczny

ethical /'eθɪkl/ adj [problem, principles] etyczny

ethics /'eθɪks/ n etyka f; **professional** ~ etyka zawodowa

ethnic /'eθnɪk/ adj etniczny

ethnic cleansing n czystka f etniczna

etiquette /'etɪket, -kət/ n (social) etykieta f; (diplomatic) protokół m

euphemism /'ju:fəmɪzəm/ n eufemizm m

euphoria /ju:'fɔ:rɪə/ n euforia f

Euro+ in combinations euro-

eurocheque /'jʊərəʊtʃek/ n euroczek m

Eurocrat /'jʊərəʊkræt/ n eurokrat|a m, -ka f

Euro-MP /ˌjʊərəʊem'pi:/ n deputowan|y m, -a f do Parlamentu Europejskiego

Europe /'jʊərəp/ prn Europa f

European /ˌjʊərə'pi:ən/ [I] n Europej|czyk m, -ka f
[II] adj europejski

European Commission n Komisja f Europejska

European Monetary System, EMS n Europejski System m Monetarny, ESW m/n inv

European Monetary Union n Europejska Unia f Monetarna, EUW f/n inv

Eurosceptic /ˌjʊərəʊ'skeptɪk/ n eurosceptyk m

euthanasia /ˌju:θə'neɪzɪə, US -'neɪʒə/ n eutanazja f

evacuate /ɪ'vækjʊeɪt/ vt ewakuować

evacuee /ɪˌvækju'i:/ n osoba f ewakuowana

evade /ɪ'veɪd/ vt uchyl|ić, -ać się od (czegoś) [responsibility, duty]; uchyl|ić, -ać się przed (czymś) [blow]; pomi|nąć, -jać (coś) milczeniem [problem, question]

evaluate /ɪ'væljʊeɪt/ vt oceni|ć, -ać

evaluation /ɪˌvælju'eɪʃn/ n ocena f; (of property, damage) wycena f

evaporate /ɪ'væpəreɪt/ vi [liquid] wy|parować

evaporated milk /ɪ'væpəreɪtɪdmɪlk/ n mleko n skondensowane

evasion /ɪ'veɪʒn/ n (of responsibility) uchylanie się n (**of sth** od czegoś); **tax** ~ uchylanie się od płacenia podatków

evasive /ɪ'veɪsɪv/ adj [answer] wymijający

eve /i:v/ n wigilia f; **on the** ~ **of sth** w przeddzień czegoś

even[1] /'i:vn/ [I] adv [1] (emphasizing point) nawet; **he didn't** ~ **try** nawet nie spróbował; **don't tell anyone, not** ~ **Adam** nie mów nikomu, nawet Adamowi [2] (with comparative) jeszcze; ~ **colder** jeszcze zimniej
[II] **even so** adv phr mimo wszystko
[III] **even though** conj phr mimo że

even[2] /'i:vn/ adj [1] (flat) [ground, surface, teeth, hemline, contest] równy; (smooth) gładki; [progress, temperature] stały; [voice] spokojny [2] [number] parzysty; **to get** ~ **with sb** wyrównać z kimś rachunki

evening /'i:vnɪŋ/ n wieczór m; **in the** ~ wieczorem; **this** ~ dziś wieczorem or wieczór; **every** ~ co wieczór; **all** ~ cały wieczór

evening class n kurs m wieczorowy

evening dress n (formal clothes) strój m wieczorowy

event /ɪ'vent/ n [1] (incident) wydarzenie n [2] (eventuality) przypadek m; **in the** ~ **of sth** w razie czegoś; **in any** ~ w każdym razie [3] (in athletics) konkurencja f

eventful /ɪ'ventfl/ adj bogaty w wydarzenia

eventually /ɪ'ventʃʊəlɪ/ adv w końcu

ever /'evə(r)/ [I] adv [1] (at any time) kiedykolwiek; (in questions) kiedyś; (with negative) nigdy; **I doubt if I'll** ~ **come back** wątpię, czy kiedykolwiek wrócę; **have you** ~ **visited London?** czy byłeś kiedyś w Londynie?; **nobody** ~ **comes to see me** nikt mnie nigdy nie odwiedza; **hardly** ~ bardzo rzadko; **more beautiful than** ~ piękniejszy niż kiedykolwiek; **these are our worst** ~ **results** to są jak dotąd nasze najgorsze wyniki; **he's happier than he's** ~ **been** jest najszczęśliwszy niż kiedykolwiek przedtem [2] (at all times, always) zawsze; **as cheerful as** ~ jak zawsze radosny; **the same as** ~ taki sam jak zawsze; **they lived happily** ~ **after** i żyli długo i szczęśliwie
[II] **ever since** conj phr odkąd

evergreen /'evəgri:n/ n roślina f zimozielona

everlasting /ˌevə'lɑ:stɪŋ, US -'læst-/ adj wieczny

every /'evrɪ/ [I] det [1] (each) każdy; ~ **time** za każdym razem; **I've read** ~ **one of her books** przeczytałem wszystkie jej książki; ~ **one of us** każdy z nas [2] (indicating frequency, recurrence) ~ **day** codziennie; ~ **Thursday** w każdy czwartek; **once** ~ **few days** co kilka dni [3] (emphatic) **they have** ~ **right to complain** mają wszelkie prawo

narzekać; **I wish you** ~ **success** życzę ci samych
sukcesów

II every other *adj phr* co drugi; ~ **other day/**
house co drugi dzień/dom
⟨IDIOMS:⟩ ~ **now and then,** ~ **so often** co jakiś
czas

everybody /'evrɪbɒdɪ/ *pron* (also **everyone**) każdy; (all) wszyscy

everyday /'evrɪdeɪ/ *adj* codzienny; **items of** ~
use przedmioty codziennego użytku

everyone /'evrɪwʌn/ *pron* = **everybody**

everything /'evrɪθɪŋ/ *pron* wszystko

everywhere /'evrɪweə(r), US -hweər/ *adv* wszędzie

evict /ɪ'vɪkt/ *vt* wy|eksmitować (**from sth** z czegoś)

eviction /ɪ'vɪkʃn/ *n* eksmisja *f*

evidence /'evɪdəns/ *n* ⟨1⟩ (proof) dowody *m pl* (**of**
sth czegoś); ~ **for** or **in favour of sth** dowody na
coś or przemawiające za czymś; ~ **against sth**
dowody (przemawiające) przeciwko czemuś
⟨2⟩ (testimony) zeznania *n pl*; **to give** ~ złożyć
zeznania (**for/against sb** na korzyść/niekorzyść
kogoś) ⟨3⟩ (trace) (of storm, struggle) ślady *m pl*; (of ill
health) oznaki *f pl*

evident /'evɪdənt/ *adj* widoczny; **it's** ~ (**to me**)
that... jest (dla mnie) oczywiste, że...

evidently /'evɪdəntlɪ/ *adv* ⟨1⟩ (apparently) widocznie
⟨2⟩ (obviously) najwyraźniej

evil /'iːvl/ **I** *n* zło *n*
II *adj* zły; *[plan]* niecny; **an** ~ **spirit** zły duch

evolution /ˌiːvə'luːʃn/ *n* ewolucja *f*

evolve /ɪ'vɒlv/ *vi* ewoluować

ewe /juː/ *n* owca *f*

ex- /eks/ *in combinations* ex

exact /ɪg'zækt/ *adj* dokładny; **to be** ~ ściśle
mówiąc

exactly /ɪg'zæktlɪ/ *adv* dokładnie

exaggerate /ɪg'zædʒəreɪt/ **I** *vt* wyolbrzymi|ć, -ać
II *vi* przesadz|ić, -ać

exaggeration /ɪgˌzædʒə'reɪʃn/ *n* przesada *f*

exam /ɪg'zæm/ *n* egzamin *m*

examination /ɪgˌzæmɪ'neɪʃn/ *n* ⟨1⟩ (at school, university) egzamin *m* (**in sth** z czegoś); **to take an** ~
zdawać egzamin; **to pass an** ~ zdać egzamin
⟨2⟩ Med badanie *n*; **to have an** ~ zostać zbadanym

examination paper *n* (to be answered) arkusz *m*
egzaminacyjny; (written answers) praca *f* egzaminacyjna

examine /ɪg'zæmɪn/ *vt* ⟨1⟩ Med z|badać *[patient,*
part of body] ⟨2⟩ (inspect, consider) przeprowadz|ić, -ać
kontrolę (czegoś) *[luggage, equipment]*; z|badać
[facts, evidence] ⟨3⟩ (at school, university) prze|egzami-
nować ⟨4⟩ (in court) przesłuch|ać, -iwać *[witness,*
suspect]; rozpat|rzyć, -rywać *[case, evidence]*

examiner /ɪg'zæmɪnə(r)/ *n* egzaminator *m*, -ka *f*

example /ɪg'zɑːmpl, US -'zæmpl/ *n* przykład *m*
(**of sth** czegoś); **for** ~ na przykład; **to set a good**
~ dawać dobry przykład

excavate /'ekskəveɪt/ **I** *vt* odkop|ać, -ywać
[ruins]; przekop|ać, -ywać *[tunnel]*
II *vi* prowadzić wykopaliska

exceed /ɪk'siːd/ *vt* przekr|oczyć, -aczać *[limit,*
quantity]

excel /ɪk'sel/ *vi* celować (**at** or **in sth, at** or **in doing**
sth w czymś, w robieniu czegoś)

excellent /'eksələnt/ *adj* znakomity

except /ɪk'sept/ **I** *prep* z wyjątkiem (kogoś/cze-
goś); **everyone** ~ (**for**) **me** wszyscy z wyjątkiem
mnie; **who could have done it** ~ **him?** któż mógł
to zrobić, jeśli nie on?
II except for *prep phr* z wyjątkiem (kogoś/
czegoś)

exception /ɪk'sepʃn/ *n* ⟨1⟩ (special case) wyjątek *m*;
with the ~ **of sb/sth** z wyjątkiem kogoś/czegoś
⟨2⟩ **to take** ~ **to sth** poczuć się urażonym czymś

exceptional /ɪk'sepʃənl/ *adj* wyjątkowy

excess **I** /ɪk'ses/ *n* nadmiar *m* (**of sth** czegoś)
II /'ekses/ *adj* ~ **speed** nadmierna prędkość; ~
weight nadwaga

excessive /ɪk'sesɪv/ *adj* nadmierny

exchange /ɪks'tʃeɪndʒ/ **I** *n* ⟨1⟩ (swap) wymiana *f*; **in**
~ (**for sth**) w zamian (za coś) ⟨2⟩ (in banking)
wymiana *f*; **the rate of** ~ kurs (walutowy) ⟨3⟩ (also
telephone ~) centrala *f* (telefoniczna)
II *vt* wymieni|ć, -ać (**for sth** na coś)

exchange control *n* kontrola *f* dewizowa

Exchange Rate Mechanism, ERM *n* mechanizm *m* kursów walutowych (*w ramach Euro-*
pejskiego Systemu Monetarnego)

Exchequer /ɪks'tʃekə(r)/ *n* GB **the** ~ Ministerstwo *n* Skarbu

excite /ɪk'saɪt/ *vt* (make excited) ekscytować; (sexually)
podnie|cić, -cać; wzbudz|ić, -ać *[admiration, curios-*
ity, envy, suspicion]

excited /ɪk'saɪtɪd/ *adj* podniecony

excitement /ɪk'saɪtmənt/ *n* radosne podniecenie *n*

exciting /ɪk'saɪtɪŋ/ *adj [film, story]* pasjonujący;
[performer] fascynujący; *[experience]* ekscytujący

exclaim /ɪk'skleɪm/ *vi* za|wołać

exclamation mark, exclamation point *n*
wykrzyknik *m*

exclude /ɪk'skluːd/ *vt* wyklucz|yć, -ać (**from sth** z
czegoś)

excluding /ɪk'skluːdɪŋ/ *prep* wyłączając

exclusion zone *n* strefa *f* zamknięta

exclusive /ɪk'skluːsɪv/ **I** *n* (report) *wywiad publiko-*
wany na prawach wyłączności
II *adj* ⟨1⟩ (select) ekskluzywny ⟨2⟩ (restricted) *[privileges,*
rights, use] wyłączny; *[story, interview]* publikowany
na prawach wyłączności

excruciating /ɪk'skruːʃieɪtɪŋ/ *adj [pain]* straszliwy

excursion /ɪk'skɜ:ʃn/ n wycieczka f

excuse ❶ /ɪk'skju:s/ n (justification) wytłumaczenie n (**for sth** czegoś); (pretext) pretekst m; (not to do sth) wymówka f; **to be an** ~ **to do sth** or **for doing sth** być pretekstem do zrobienia czegoś; **to make an** ~ znaleźć wymówkę; **a good** ~ **for not doing sth** dobra wymówka, żeby czegoś nie robić; **there's no** ~ **for cheating** nie ma usprawiedliwienia dla oszustwa
❷ /ɪk'skju:z/ vt ① (forgive) wybacz|yć, -ać (komuś) [person]; wybacz|yć, -ać (coś) [mistake]; **to** ~ **sb for doing sth** wybaczyć komuś, że coś zrobił; ~ **me!** (apologizing) bardzo przepraszam!; (not hearing properly) słucham?; (attracting attention) przepraszam! ② (exempt) zw|olnić, -alniać (**from sth** z czegoś)

ex-directory /ˌeksdaɪ'rektərɪ, -dɪ-/ adj **an** ~ **number** numer zastrzeżony

execute /'eksɪkju:t/ vt ① (kill) stracić [criminal] ② (carry out) wykon|ać, -ywać [command, task, piece of work]; z|realizować [idea]

execution /ˌeksɪ'kju:ʃn/ n ① (killing) egzekucja f ② (of order, task) wykonanie n

executioner /ˌeksɪ'kju:ʃənə(r)/ n kat m

executive /ɪg'zekjʊtɪv/ ❶ n ① (administrator) pracownik m szczebla kierowniczego; **top** ~ członek ścisłego kierownictwa; **sales** ~ dyrektor handlowy ② (committee) kierownictwo n
❷ adj [committee, power] wykonawczy

exemplify /ɪg'zemplɪfaɪ/ vt stanowić przykład (czegoś)

exempt /ɪg'zempt/ ❶ adj zwolniony (**from sth** od czegoś)
❷ vt zwolnić ~ **sb (from sth)** zwolnić kogoś (od czegoś)

exemption /ɪg'zempʃn/ n zwolnienie n; ~ **from sth** zwolnienie od czegoś [tax]; zwolnienie z czegoś [exam]

exercise /'eksəsaɪz/ ❶ n ① (physical) gimnastyka f ② (task) ćwiczenie n ③ (military) ćwiczenia n pl
❷ vt ① (exert) ćwiczyć [body, mind]; gimnastykować [limb] ② (use) zachow|ać, -ywać [caution]; wykaz|ać, -ywać się (czymś) [tolerance]; sprawować [control]; s|korzystać z (czegoś) [rights]
❸ vi gimnastykować się

exercise bike n rower m treningowy

exercise book n zeszyt m

exert /ɪg'zɜ:t/ vt wyw|rzeć, -ierać [pressure, influence] (**on sb/sth** na kogoś/coś); **to** ~ **oneself** wysilić się

exhale /eks'heɪl/ vi wypu|ścić, -szczać powietrze (z płuc)

exhaust /ɪg'zɔ:st/ ❶ n ① (also ~ **pipe**) rura f wydechowa ② (also ~ **fumes**) spaliny plt
❷ vt (tire out) wyczerp|ać, -ywać [person, animal]

exhaustion /ɪg'zɔ:stʃn/ n wyczerpanie n

exhibit /ɪg'zɪbɪt/ ❶ n ① eksponat m ② US (exhibition) wystawa f

❷ vt wystawi|ć, -ać (na pokaz) [goods, paintings]; okaz|ać, -ywać [fear, courage]

exhibition /ˌeksɪ'bɪʃn/ n wystawa f; **art** ~ wystawa sztuki; **to make an** ~ **of oneself** zrobić z siebie widowisko

exhibition centre GB, **exhibition center** US n centrum m wystawiennicze

exhilarating /ɪg'zɪləreɪtɪŋ/ adj [experience] cudowny; [contest, argument] porywający; [journey] emocjonujący

exile /'eksaɪl/ ❶ n ① (person) wygnaniec m ② (state) wygnanie n; **in** ~ na wygnaniu
❷ vt wygnać

exist /ɪg'zɪst/ vi istnieć

existence /ɪg'zɪstəns/ n istnienie n

existing /ɪg'zɪstɪŋ/ adj [laws, order] istniejący; [policy, management, leadership] obecny

exit /'eksɪt/ ❶ n wyjście n; '**no** ~' „przejścia nie ma"
❷ vi wyj|ść, -chodzić

exodus /'eksədəs/ n exodus m

exotic /ɪg'zɒtɪk/ adj egzotyczny

expand /ɪk'spænd/ ❶ vt rozwi|nąć, -jać [business, network]; powiększ|yć, -ać [workforce, empire]; rozbudow|ać, -ywać [system]; rozszerz|yć, -ać [horizons, knowledge]
❷ vi (develop) [industry, relations, flower petals] rozwi|nąć, -jać się; [knowledge, metal, universe] rozszerz|yć, -ać się; [institution, population, market] rozr|osnąć, -astać się; [possibilities, chest] powiększ|yć, -ać się

expanse /ɪk'spæns/ n połać f

expansion /ɪk'spænʃn/ n (of economic activity) rozwój m; (of output, number) wzrost m; (of product range, research) poszerzenie n

expatriate /ˌeks'pætrɪət/ n osoba f mieszkająca na obczyźnie

expect /ɪk'spekt/ ❶ vt ① (anticipate) spodziewać się (czegoś) [event, victory, defeat, trouble]; **to** ~ **the worst** spodziewać się najgorszego; **to** ~ **sb to do sth** spodziewać się, że ktoś coś zrobi; **as one might** ~ jak można było się spodziewać ② (rely on) oczekiwać (czegoś) [sympathy, help] (**from sb** ze strony kogoś) ③ (await) spodziewać się (kogoś) [baby, guest, company] ④ (require) oczekiwać (czegoś) [commitment, hard work] (**from sb** od kogoś, po kimś) ⑤ GB (suppose) sądzić; **I** ~ **so** sądzę, że tak; **I** ~ **you're tired** pewnie jesteś zmęczony
❷ vi (be pregnant) **to be** ~**ing** spodziewać się dziecka

expectant /ɪk'spektənt/ adj ① [look] pełen wyczekiwania ② ~ **mother** przyszła matka

expectation /ˌekspek'teɪʃn/ n ① (prediction) oczekiwanie n; **against all** ~(**s**) wbrew oczekiwaniom ② (hope) nadzieja f (**of sth** na coś); **to live up to sb's** ~**s** spełniać czyjeś oczekiwania

expedient /ɪk'spiːdɪənt/ adj 1 (appropriate) wskazany 2 (advantageous) korzystny

expedition /ˌekspɪ'dɪʃn/ n wyprawa f; **to go on an** ~ udać się na wyprawę

expel /ɪk'spel/ vt wydal|ić, -ać [diplomat, dissident, pupil]; wyrzuc|ić, -ać [tenant, member]

expenditure /ɪk'spendɪtʃə(r)/ n wydatki m pl

expense /ɪk'spens/ **I** n 1 (cost) koszt m; **at one's own** ~ na własny koszt; **to go to great** ~ wykosztować się (**to do sth** żeby coś zrobić); **to spare no** ~ nie szczędzić kosztów 2 **at the** ~ **of sth** kosztem czegoś [health, public, safety]; **they had a good laugh at my** ~ dobrze się bawili moim kosztem
II **expenses** npl wydatki m pl (poniesione w związku z wykonywaną pracą)

expense account n rachunek m kosztów

expensive /ɪk'spensɪv/ adj drogi

experience /ɪk'spɪərɪəns/ **I** n doświadczenie n
II vt dozna|ć, -wać (czegoś) [emotion]; doświadcz|yć, -ać (czegoś) [misfortune]; pon|ieść, -osić [loss]; mieć [problems, difficulties]

experienced /ɪk'spɪərɪənst/ adj doświadczony

experiment /ɪk'sperɪmənt/ **I** n doświadczenie n, eksperyment m
II vi przeprowadz|ić, -ać doświadczenia (**on sb/ sth** na kimś/czymś)

experimental /ɪkˌsperɪ'mentl/ adj doświadczalny

experimentation /ɪkˌsperɪmen'teɪʃn/ n doświadczenia n pl

expert /'ekspɜːt/ **I** n specjalist|a m, -ka f, ekspert m (**in sth** w zakresie czegoś)
II adj [knowledge, opinion, advice] fachowy; **an** ~ **cook** mistrz sztuki kulinarnej

expertise /ˌekspɜː'tiːz/ n (skill) kompetencje plt (**in sth** w dziedzinie czegoś); (knowledge) znajomość f (**in sth** czegoś)

expire /ɪk'spaɪə(r)/ vi [document, licence] s|tracić ważność; [deadline, term of office] upły|nąć, -wać

expiry date n (of passport, credit card) data f ważności

explain /ɪk'spleɪn/ vt wyjaśni|ć, -ać (**to sb** komuś)

explanation /ˌeksplə'neɪʃn/ n (reason) wyjaśnienie n (**of sth** czegoś)

explicit /ɪk'splɪsɪt/ adj [order] wyraźny; [denial, refutation] jednoznaczny; [criticism] jawny

explode /ɪk'spləʊd/ **I** vt z|detonować [bomb]; fig obal|ić, -ać [argument, myth, theory]
II vi [bomb, boiler, gas] wybuch|nąć, -ać; [building, vehicle] wyl|ecieć, -atywać w powietrze

exploit **I** /'eksplɔɪt/ n wyczyn m
II /ɪk'splɔɪt/ vt (use) wykorzyst|ać, -ywać [talent, energy]; wy|eksploatować [resources]; (use unfairly) wyzysk|ać, -iwać [workers]

exploitation /ˌeksplɔɪ'teɪʃn/ n (unfair) wyzysk m

explore /ɪk'splɔː(r)/ **I** vt z|badać
II vi prze|prowadzić poszukiwania

explorer /ɪk'splɔːrə(r)/ n badacz m, -ka f

explosion /ɪk'spləʊʒn/ n wybuch m, eksplozja f

explosive /ɪk'spləʊsɪv/ **I** n materiał m wybuchowy
II adj [substance] wybuchowy; [situation] zapalny

export **I** /'ekspɔːt/ n (activity) eksport m (**of sth** czegoś); (commodity) towar m eksportowy
II /ɪk'spɔːt/ vt wy|eksportować
III /ɪk'spɔːt/ vi eksportować

exporter /ɪk'spɔːtə(r)/ n eksporter m

expose /ɪk'spəʊz/ vt 1 (display) odsł|onić, -aniać [skin] 2 (make public) ujawni|ć, -ać [scandal, identity]; z|demaskować [person, lie] 3 **to** ~ **oneself** obnaż|yć, -ać się publicznie

exposure /ɪk'spəʊʒə(r)/ n 1 (of secret, crime) ujawnienie n 2 (to light, sun, radiation) ~ **to sth** wystawienie na działanie czegoś 3 **to die of** ~ umrzeć z powodu nadmiernego wyziębienia organizmu 4 (amount of light) naświetlenie n, ekspozycja f; (picture) ujęcie n

express /ɪk'spres/ **I** n (train) ekspres m
II adj (rapid) [letter, bus, train, delivery] ekspresowy
III adv **to send sth** ~ wysłać coś ekspresem
IV vt wyra|zić, -żać; **to** ~ **oneself** wyrażać się

expression /ɪk'spreʃn/ n 1 (phrase) wyrażenie n 2 (look) wyraz m twarzy 3 (manifestation) wyraz m

expressive /ɪk'spresɪv/ adj pełen wyrazu

exquisite /'ekskwɪzɪt, ɪk'skwɪzɪt/ adj [face] piękny; [beauty, charm] wyjątkowy; [politeness, taste] wyszukany

extend /ɪk'stend/ **I** vt 1 (enlarge) rozbudow|ać, -ywać [building]; przedłuż|yć, -ać [runway]; poszerz|yć, -ać [knowledge, range]; rozszerz|yć, -ać [influence, scope] 2 (prolong) przedłuż|yć, -ać [visit, visa] 3 (stretch) wyciąg|nąć, -ać [hand]; wystawi|ć [leg]
II vi 1 (stretch) [beach, desert] rozciągać się; [fence, road] ciągnąć się 2 (cover in scope) [jurisdiction, authority, influence] rozciągać się (**to sb/sth** na kogoś/coś); [knowledge, experience] obejmować (**to sth** coś)

extension /ɪk'stenʃn/ n 1 (to house) dobudówka f; (of road, cable) przedłużenie n; (of table) dodatkowy blat m 2 (phone) telefon m wewnętrzny; (number) numer m wewnętrzny 3 (of contract, visa) przedłużenie n

extension lead n przedłużacz m

extensive /ɪk'stensɪv/ adj [knowledge, network, forest, injuries] rozległy; [list] długi; [changes, damage, loss] znaczny

extent /ɪk'stent/ n 1 (of area, problem) rozmiary m pl; (of power, knowledge) zakres m 2 (of commitment, involvement) stopień m; **to a certain/great** ~ w pewnym/dużym stopniu

exterior /ɪk'stɪərɪə(r)/ **I** n zewnętrzna strona f (**of sth** czegoś)
II adj zewnętrzny

exterminate /ɪk'stɜːmɪneɪt/ *vt* wy|tępić *[pests]*; dokon|ać, -ywać eksterminacji (kogoś) *[people]*

external /ɪk'stɜːnl/ *adj* zewnętrzny

extinct /ɪk'stɪŋkt/ *adj [species, plant, animal]* wymarły; *[volcano]* wygasły; **to become** ~ *[species, animal, plant]* wymrzeć

extinguish /ɪk'stɪŋgwɪʃ/ *vt* z|gasić *[fire, light, cigarette]*

extinguisher /ɪk'stɪŋgwɪʃə(r)/ *n* (also **fire** ~) gaśnica *f*

extra /'ekstrə/ **I** *n* 1 (additional feature) dodatek *m*; **the sunroof is an** ~ rozsuwany dach należy do dodatkowych części wyposażenia 2 (actor) statyst|a *m*, -ka *f*
II *adj* (additional) dodatkowy; **it will cost an** ~ **£1,000** to będzie kosztować dodatkowo 1000 funtów
III *adv* **to be** ~ **careful** być szczególnie ostrożnym; **you have to pay** ~ trzeba dodatkowo zapłacić

extra charge *n* dopłata *f*

extract **I** /'ekstrækt/ *n* 1 (excerpt) urywek *m* (**from sth** z czegoś) 2 (concentrate) ekstrakt *m* (**from** or **of sth** z czegoś)
II /ɪk'strækt/ *vt* 1 (pull out) usu|nąć, -wać *[tooth, bullet]* 2 wydoby|ć, -wać *[minerals, oil]*

extra-curricular /ˌekstrəkə'rɪkjʊlə(r)/ *adj* ponadprogramowy

extraordinary /ɪk'strɔːdnrɪ, US -dənerɪ/ *adj* nadzwyczajny

extraterrestrial /ˌekstrətə'restrɪəl/ *adj* pozaziemski

extra time *n* Sport dogrywka *f*

extravagance /ɪk'strævəgəns/ *n* 1 (excessive spending) rozrzutność *f* 2 (of dress, behaviour) ekstrawagancja *f*

extravagant /ɪk'strævəgənt/ *adj* 1 (wasteful) rozrzutny; **to be** ~ **with sth** nie żałować czegoś 2 (exaggerated) ekstrawagancki

extreme /ɪk'striːm/ **I** *n* 1 (situation) skrajność *f*; (measure) ostateczność *f*; **to go to** ~**s** popadać w skrajność 2 (greatest degree) najwyższy stopień *m* (**of sth** czegoś)
II *adj [heat, care, difficulty]* wyjątkowy; *[case, example]* ekstremalny; *[measure, view]* skrajny

extremely /ɪk'striːmlɪ/ *adv* niezwykle

extreme sports *npl* sporty *m pl* ekstremalne

extremism /ɪk'striːmɪzəm/ *n* ekstremizm *m*

extrovert /'ekstrəvɜːt/ *n* ekstrawerty|k *m*, -czka *f*

eye /aɪ/ **I** *n* 1 (of person, animal) oko *n*; **to have blue** ~**s** mieć niebieskie oczy; **before** or **in front of my very** ~**s** na moich oczach; **to keep an** ~ **on sb/sth** mieć oko na kogoś/coś; **to catch sb's** ~ zwrócić uwagę kogoś; **to have one's** ~ **on sb/sth** mieć kogoś/coś na oku; **to have an** ~ **for sth** mieć doskonałe wyczucie czegoś *[detail, colour]*; **in the** ~**s of the law** w świetle prawa 2 (in needle) ucho *n*; (to attach hook to) oczko *n* (haftki)
II *vt* (look at) przy|jrzeć, -glądać się (komuś/czemuś)
IDIOMS: **to make** ~**s at sb** robić słodkie oczy do kogoś; **to see** ~ **to** ~ **with sb (about sth)** podzielać punkt widzenia kogoś (w sprawie czegoś)

eyeball /'aɪbɔːl/ *n* gałka *f* oczna

eyebrow /'aɪbraʊ/ *n* brew *f*

eyebrow pencil *n* kredka *f* do brwi

eye-catching /'aɪkætʃɪŋ/ *adj* przyciągający wzrok

eyedrops /'aɪdrɒps/ *n* krople *f pl* do oczu

eyelash /'aɪlæʃ/ *n* rzęsa *f*

eyelid /'aɪlɪd/ *n* powieka *f*

eye liner *n* (pencil) kredka *f* do oczu; (liquid) tusz *m* do kresek

eye shadow *n* cień *m* do powiek

eyesight /'aɪsaɪt/ *n* wzrok *m*

eye test *n* badanie *n* wzroku

eyewitness /'aɪwɪtnɪs/ *n* naoczny świadek *m*

e-zine /'iːziːn/ *n* magazyn *m* internetowy

F

f, F /ef/ *n* ① (letter) f, F *n* ② F Mus f, F *n*

fable /'feɪbl/ *n* bajka *f*

fabric /'fæbrɪk/ *n* (cloth) materiał *m*; (of building) konstrukcja *f*; fig (of society) tkanka *f* liter

fabricate /'fæbrɪkeɪt/ *vt* zmyślić, -ać *[story]*; sfabrykować *[document]*

fabric softener *n* środek *m* do zmiękczania tkanin

fabulous /'fæbjʊləs/ *adj [beast, realm]* baśniowy; infml *[party, clothes, figure]* fantastyczny

face /feɪs/ ① *n* ① (of person) twarz *f*; (of animal) pysk *m*; **to slam the door in sb's** ~ zatrzasnąć komuś drzwi przed nosem; **to laugh in sb's** ~ roześmiać się komuś w twarz or w nos; **to look sb in the** ~ spojrzeć komuś w oczy ② (expression) mina *f*; **to pull** or **make a** ~ zrobić minę ③ (dignity) twarz *f*; **to lose/save** ~ stracić/zachować twarz ④ (of clock, watch) tarcza *f*; (of solid figure, mountain) ściana *f*; (of coin) awers *m*; (of planet) powierzchnia *f*; (of playing card, document) wierzch *m*

② **in the face of** *prep phr* pomimo *[overwhelming odds]*; w obliczu *[opposition, enemy, danger]*

③ *vt* ① (look towards) **to** ~ **north** *[person]* patrzeć na północ; *[building]* wychodzić na północ; **he turned to** ~ **the door** odwrócił się przodem do drzwi ② (meet) stanąć, -wać przed *[challenge]*; stanąć, -wać w obliczu *[crisis, defeat, redundancy]*; stanąć, -wać naprzeciw *[rival, team]*; **to be** ~**d with sth** mieć przed sobą coś *[problem, task]* ③ (acknowledge) ~ **the facts!** spójrz prawdzie w oczy!; **let's** ~ **it** spójrzmy prawdzie w oczy ④ (tolerate prospect) **I can't** ~ **working today** dzisiaj nawet nie chcę słyszeć o pracy; **he couldn't** ~ **the thought of eating** nie mógł znieść samej myśli o jedzeniu ⑤ obłożyć, -kładać *[wall]*

■ **face up to**: pogodzić się z *[truth, fact]*; sprostać *[responsibility]*

faceless /'feɪsləs/ *adj* anonimowy

face-lift /'feɪslɪft/ *n* lifting *m*; fig **to give sth a** ~ odnowić coś *[building, town centre]*

facet /'fæsɪt/ *n* (of problem) aspekt *m*; (of personality) strona *f*

face-to-face /ˌfeɪstə'feɪs/ ① *adj* a ~ **conversation** bezpośrednia rozmowa

② **face to face** *adv* **to come** ~ **with sb/sth** stanąć oko w oko z kimś/czymś; **to meet sb** ~ spotkać się z kimś osobiście

face value *n* wartość *f* nominalna; fig **to take sth at** ~ zakładać prawdziwość czegoś *[claim]*; brać coś za dobrą monetę *[compliment]*; **to take sb at** ~ sądzić kogoś po pozorach

facilitate /fə'sɪlɪteɪt/ *vt* ułatwić, -ać *[negotiations, development]*

facility /fə'sɪlətɪ/ ① *n* ① (building) obiekt *m*; **manufacturing** ~ zakład wytwórczy ② (ease) łatwość *f* ③ (feature) funkcja *f*, możliwość *f*; **'fax facilities available'** „możliwość korzystania z faksu"

② **facilities** *npl* **facilities for the disabled** udogodnienia dla niepełnosprawnych; **harbour facilities** urządzenia portowe

facsimile /fæk'sɪməlɪ/ *n* (copy) faksymile *n inv*

fact /fækt/ *n* fakt *m*; **to know for a** ~ **that...** wiedzieć na pewno, że...; **due to the** ~ **that...** w związku z tym, że...; **in** ~ faktycznie; ~**s and figures** cyfry i fakty; **to be based on** ~ opierać się na faktach

IDIOMS: **to know the** ~**s of life** wiedzieć, skąd się biorą dzieci; **the** ~**s of life** smutna rzeczywistość

fact-finding /'fæktfaɪndɪŋ/ *adj [mission]* rozpoznawczy

faction /'fækʃn/ *n* (group) frakcja *f*

factor /'fæktə(r)/ *n* ① (element) czynnik *m*; **common** ~ wspólny element; **unknown** ~ niewiadoma ② (in maths) **common** ~ wspólny dzielnik

factory /'fæktərɪ/ *n* fabryka *f*

factory farming *n* chów *m* przemysłowy

factory worker *n* robotnik *m*, -ca *f*

fact sheet *n* zestawienie *n*

factual /'fæktʃʊəl/ *adj [account, description]* oparty na faktach; ~ **error** błąd rzeczowy; ~ **programme** reportaż

faculty /'fæklti/ *n* ① (ability) zdolność *f* ② GB Univ wydział *m* ③ US Univ, Sch (staff) kadra *f*

fad /fæd/ *n* (craze) chwilowa moda *f* (**for sth** na coś); (whim) fanaberia *f*

fade /feɪd/ ① *vt* **the sun has** ~**d the curtains** zasłony wyblakły od słońca

② *vi* ① *[fabric]* (in wash) sprać, -ierać się; (in sun) wyblaknąć, splowieć ② *[flowers]* zwiędnąć ③ *[good looks]* przeminąć, -jać; *[sound]* zaniknąć,

-ać; *[interest]* opa|ść, -dać; *[smile, light]* przygas|nąć, -ać; *[memory]* o|słabnąć; *[memories]* za|trzeć, -cierać się

■ **fade away**: *[sound]* stopniowo ucich|nąć, -ać; *[sick person]* z|gasnąć

faded /'feɪdɪd/ *adj [fabric, photo]* wyblakły, spłowiały; *[beauty, flowers]* przekwitły; *[jeans]* sprany

faeces GB, **feces** US /'fiːsiːz/ *npl* kał *m*

fail /feɪl/ **𝐈** *n* Sch, Univ ocena *f* niedostateczna

𝐈𝐈 *adv [play]* uczciwie, fair

𝐈𝐈𝐈 *vt* ① (not pass) nie zdać *[exam, driving test, subject]*; obl|ać, -ewać infml *[person]* (**in sth** z czegoś) ② (omit) **to ~ to do sth** nie zrobić czegoś; **it never ~s to work** to zawsze działa ③ (let down) zaw|ieść, -odzić *[friend]*; *[courage]* opu|ścić, -szczać; *[memory]* zaw|ieść, -odzić; **words ~ me!** brak mi słów!

𝐈𝐕 *vi* ① *[exam candidate]* nie zdać; *[attempt, plan]* nie powieść się; *[technique]* nie da|ć, -wać rezultatów; **if all else ~s** jeśli wszystko inne zawiedzie; **if the crops ~** jeżeli plony będą niskie ② *[eyesight, hearing]* pog|orszyć, -arszać się; *[person]* o|słabnąć; **before the light ~s** zanim się ściemni ③ *[brakes]* zaw|ieść, -wodzić; *[engine]* ze|psuć się; *[power, electricity]* ule|c, -gać awarii; *[heart]* nie wytrzymać

failing /'feɪlɪŋ/ **𝐈** *n* wada *f*

𝐈𝐈 *prep* ~ **that** jeśli się nie uda

failure /'feɪljə(r)/ *n* ① (lack of success) niepowodzenie *n* (**in sth** w czymś); **to be a ~ at sports** być kiepskim w sporcie; **I feel a ~** nic mi się w życiu nie udaje; **to be a ~** *[film]* być nieudanym; *[experiment]* nie udać się ② (of engine, machine, power) awaria *f*; Med (of organ) niewydolność *f*; **crop ~** niskie plony ③ (omission) ~ **to keep a promise** niedotrzymanie obietnicy; ~ **to comply with the rules** niezastosowanie się do przepisów; ~ **to pay** niezapłacenie

faint /feɪnt/ **𝐈** *adj* ① *[glow, smell]* słaby; *[accent, breeze]* lekki; *[markings]* niewyraźny; *[chance, resemblance]* nikły; *[memory]* mglisty; **he hadn't the ~est idea** nie miał najmniejszego pojęcia ② **he felt ~** zrobiło mu się słabo

𝐈𝐈 *vi* zasłabnąć, ze|mdleć

fainthearted /ˌfeɪnt'hɑːtɪd/ **𝐈** *n* **the ~** ludzie *plt* małego ducha liter or/MET hum

𝐈𝐈 *adj* (cowardly) bojaźliwy; *[attempt]* nieśmiały

fair[1] /feə(r)/ *n* (market) jarmark *m*; (for charity) kiermasz *m* na cele dobroczynne; (funfair) wesołe miasteczko *n*; **book ~** targi książki

fair[2] /feə(r)/ **𝐈** *adj* ① (just) *[arrangement, person, trial]* sprawiedliwy; *[wage, deal]* uczciwy; **it's only ~ that she should be first** wypada, żeby to ona była pierwsza; **it (just) isn't ~!** to niesprawiedliwe! ② (quite good) *[condition, performance]* niezły; *[chance]* spory ③ *[amount, number, size]* spory ④ *[weather]* ładny; *[wind]* sprzyjający ⑤ *[hair, skin]*

jasny ⑥ *[lady, city]* piękny; **with her own ~ hands** własnoręcznie; **the ~ sex** płeć piękna

𝐈𝐈 *adv [play]* uczciwie, fair

[IDIOMS] **to be ~ game for sb** łatwo padać ofiarą kogoś; ~ **and square** bezdyskusyjnie

fairground /'feəɡraʊnd/ *n* (for funfair) wesołe miasteczko *n*

fair-haired /ˌfeə'heəd/ *adj* jasnowłosy

fairly /'feəlɪ/ *adv* ① (quite, rather) dość, dosyć ② *[obtain]* uczciwie; *[treat]* sprawiedliwie; *[say]* słusznie

fair-minded /ˌfeə'maɪndɪd/ *adj* bezstronny

fairness /'feənɪs/ *n* ① (justness) sprawiedliwość *f*; (of election) uczciwość *f*; **in all ~** trzeba przyznać ② (of complexion, hair) jasność *f*

fair play *n* czysta gra *f*; **to have a sense of ~** przestrzegać zasad fair play

fairy /'feərɪ/ *n* duszek *m*

fairy story, fairy tale *n* bajka *f*

faith /feɪθ/ *n* ① (confidence) wiara *f*; **to have ~ in sb** ufać komuś; **I have no ~ in her** (ona) nie budzi mojego zaufania ② (belief) wiara *f*; **people of all ~s** ludzie wszystkich wyznań

faithful /'feɪθfl/ **𝐈** *n* **the ~** wierni *plt*

𝐈𝐈 *adj* wierny (**to sb/sth** komuś/czemuś)

faithfully /'feɪθfəlɪ/ *adv* wiernie; **yours ~** z wyrazami szacunku

faith healer *n* uzdrowiciel *m*, -ka *f*

faith healing *n* uzdrawianie *n* (niekonwencjonalnymi metodami)

fake /feɪk/ **𝐈** *n* ① (jewel, work of art) imitacja *f* ② (person) oszust *m*, -ka *f*

𝐈𝐈 *adj [fur, flower, smile]* sztuczny; *[passport]* fałszywy

𝐈𝐈𝐈 *vt* s|fałszować *[signature]*; uda|ć, -wać *[emotion, illness]*

falcon /'fɔːlkən, US 'fælkən/ *n* sokół *m*

Falklands /'fɔːkləndz/ *prn pl* (also **Falkland Islands**) the ~ Falklandy *plt*

fall /fɔːl/ **𝐈** *n* ① (of person) upadek *m*; (of leaves, nuts) opadanie *n*; (of rain) opady *m pl* ② (in temperature, quality, production, popularity) spadek *m* (**in sth** czegoś) ③ (of leader, regime) upadek *m*; ~ **from grace** or **favour** popadnięcie w niełaskę ④ US (autumn) jesień *f* ⑤ (in intonation) opadanie *n* ⑥ (in wrestling) położenie *n* na łopatki; (in judo) rzut *m*

𝐈𝐈 **falls** *npl* wodospad *m*

𝐈𝐈𝐈 *vi* ① spa|ść, -dać; *[person]* upa|ść, -dać; *[wardrobe]* przew|rócić, -acać się; *[building]* zawal|ić, -ać się; **to ~ 10 metres** spaść z wysokości 10 metrów; **to ~ from** or **out of sth** wypaść z czegoś *[nest, bag, hands]*; **to ~ from** or **off sth** spaść z czegoś *[table, roof, bike]*; **to ~ down a hole** wpaść do dziury; **to ~ down the stairs** spaść ze schodów; **to ~ to earth** or **the ground** spaść/upaść na ziemię; **to ~ at sb's feet** paść komuś do nóg ② *[speed, temperature, price, quality]* spa|ść, -dać;

[standard, level, morale] obniż|yć, -ać się ③ *[town, fortress]* pa|ść, -dać; *[government, regime]* upa|ść, -dać; **to ~ from power** utracić władzę; **to ~ to the enemy** wpaść w ręce wroga ④ **to ~ ill** zachorować; **to ~ silent** or **quiet** zamilknąć; **to ~ asleep** zasnąć

■ **fall apart**: *[bike, shoes]* rozpa|ść, -dać się; *[plan, system]* walić się

■ **fall back**: cof|nąć, -ać się; Mil wycof|ać, -ywać się

■ **fall back on**: sięgnąć do *[savings]*; oprzeć się na *[parents]*

■ **fall behind**: *[runner, country]* zosta|ć, -wać w tyle; *[work]* opóźni|ć, -ać się; **to ~ behind with** GB or **in** US sth mieć zaległości w czymś *[work, payments]*

■ **fall down**: ① *[book]* spa|ść, -dać; *[person]* upa|ść, -dać; *[tree]* przewr|ócić, -acać się; *[scaffolding]* zawal|ić, -ać się ② GB *[argument, case]* upa|ść, -dać

■ **fall for**: ¶ **~ for [sth]** dać się nabrać na (coś) *[trick, story]* ¶ **~ for [sb]** zakoch|ać, -iwać w (kimś)

■ **fall in**: ① *[walls, roof]* zapa|ść, -dać się ② *[soldier]* sta|nąć, -wać w szeregu

■ **fall off**: ① *[person, hat, leaf]* spa|ść, -dać; *[label]* odpa|ść, -dać ② *[attendance, sales, output]* spa|ść, -dać; *[quality]* pog|orszyć, -arszać się; *[enthusiasm]* opa|ść, -dać

■ **fall out**: ① *[page, hair, tooth]* wypa|ść, -dać ② (quarrel) po|kłócić się (**with sb over sth** z kimś o coś)

■ **fall over**: ¶ **~ over** *[person, object]* przewr|ócić, -acać się ¶ **~ over [sth]** przewr|ócić, -acać się o (coś), pot|knąć, -ykać się o (coś)

■ **fall through**: *[deal]* nie do|jść, -chodzić do skutku; *[plan]* nie uda|ć, -wać się

fallacy /ˈfæləsɪ/ n (belief) błędne przekonanie n; (argument) błędne rozumowanie n

fallible /ˈfæləbl/ adj *[person]* omylny; *[method]* zawodny; *[system]* niedoskonały

fallout /ˈfɔːlaʊt/ n opad m (promieniotwórczy); fig efekt m uboczny

false /fɔːls/ adj ① *[impression]* błędny; *[report, allegation]* nieprawdziwy; **a ~ sense of security** złudne poczucie bezpieczeństwa; **~ alarm** fałszywy alarm; **~ start** falstart ② *[banknotes, testimony]* fałszywy; *[tax returns]* niezgodny z prawdą; **~ bottom** podwójne dno; **on** or **under ~ pretences** podstępem ③ *[eyelashes, moustache]* sztuczny; **~ teeth** sztuczna szczęka

falsely /ˈfɔːlslɪ/ adv ① *[represent, state]* fałszywie; *[confident]* bezpodstawnie; *[assume]* błędnie ② *[smile, laugh]* fałszywie

falsify /ˈfɔːlsɪfaɪ/ vt s|fałszować *[documents]*; za|fałszować *[facts]*

falsity /ˈfɔːlsətɪ/ n (of statement) fałszywość f; (of beliefs) błędność f

falter /ˈfɔːltə(r)/ vi ① *[demand, economy, courage]* o|słabnąć; *[person]* za|wahać się ② (because of emotion) mówić łamiącym się głosem; (because of hesitancy) zacinać się; *[voice]* za|łam|ać, -ywać się ③ (when walking) za|chwiać się; **to walk without ~ing** iść pewnym krokiem

faltering /ˈfɔːltərɪŋ/ adj *[demand, economy]* słabnący; *[footsteps]* niepewny

fame /feɪm/ n sława f

familiar /fəˈmɪlɪə(r)/ adj *[phrase, sight, feeling]* znajomy; *[figure, story]* dobrze znany (**to sb** komuś); **her face looked ~ to me** jej twarz wydawała mi się znajoma; **to be ~ with sth** znać coś

familiarity /fəˌmɪlɪˈærətɪ/ n znajomość f (**with sb/sth** kogoś/czegoś); (informality) poufałość f

familiarize /fəˈmɪlɪəraɪz/ ❶ vt zaznaj|omić, -amiać (**with sth** z czymś); zapozna|ć, -wać (**with sb** z kimś)

❷ vr **to ~ oneself with sth** zaznaj|omić, -amiać się z czymś *[system, work]*; osw|oić, -ajać się z czymś *[place]*

family /ˈfæməlɪ/ ❶ n rodzina f; **to run in the ~** być cechą rodzinną; **to start a ~** założyć rodzinę ❷ adj *[home, life]* rodzinny; *[accommodation]* dla całej rodziny; **for ~ reasons** z przyczyn rodzinnych; **~ name** nazwisko; **~ planning** planowanie rodziny; **~ tree** drzewo genealogiczne

famine /ˈfæmɪn/ n głód m

famished /ˈfæmɪʃt/ adj infml zgłodniały infml; **I'm ~** umieram z głodu fig

famous /ˈfeɪməs/ adj słynny (**for sth** z czegoś); *[person]* sławny

fan[1] /fæn/ ❶ n (electric) wiatrak m; (hand-held) wachlarz m; Aut wentylator m; **a ~ belt** pasek klinowy (wentylatora) ❷ vt ① podsyc|ić, -ać *[fire, hatred]* ② *[breeze]* owi|ać, -ewać; **to ~ one's face** wachlować sobie twarz

■ **fan out**: ¶ **~ out** *[lines]* roz|ejść, -chodzić się promieniście ¶ **~ [sth] out** u|łożyć, -kładać w wachlarz *[cards, papers]*

fan[2] /fæn/ n (enthusiast) wielbiciel m, -ka f; (of team) kibic m

fanatic /fəˈnætɪk/ n fanaty|k m, -czka f

fanaticism /fəˈnætɪsɪzəm/ n fanatyzm m

fancy /ˈfænsɪ/ ❶ n ① (liking) upodobanie n (**for sth** do czegoś); **to take sb's fancy** *[object]* spodobać się komuś; **he had taken her ~** (sexually) wpadł jej w oko infml; (not sexually) przypadł jej do gustu ② (whim) kaprys m; **as the ~ takes me** jak or kiedy tylko przyjdzie mi ochota ③ (fantasy) urojenie n

❷ adj *[equipment]* skomplikowany; *[food]* wyszukany; *[name, food, clothes]* wymyślny

III *vt* [1] infml (want) mieć ochotę na (coś) *[food, drink, object]*; **what do you ~ for lunch?** co byś zjadł na obiad? [2] GB infml **I ~ her** ona mi się podoba [3] (expressing surprise) **~ seeing you here!** infml ty tutaj?; **~ that!** infml a to ci dopiero! infml [4] Sport uważać (kogoś/coś) za pewniaka *[athlete, horse]*

fancy dress **I** *n* przebranie *n*

II *adj* **a ~ ball** or **party** bal kostiumowy

fang /fæŋ/ *n* (of dog, wolf) kieł *m*; (of snake) ząb *m* jadowy

fan mail *n* listy *m pl* od wielbicieli

fantasize /'fæntəsaɪz/ *vi* fantazjować (**about sth** o czymś); **to ~ about doing sth** marzyć o zrobieniu czegoś

fantastic /fæn'tæstɪk/ *adj* [1] infml *[food, holiday, news]* fantastyczny infml [2] (incredible) niesamowity [3] infml (huge) *[profit, speed]* zawrotny; *[increase]* niesamowity [4] (magical) fantastyczny

fantasy /'fæntəsɪ/ *n* [1] (dream) fantazja *f*; (imagination) urojenie *n*; (untruth) wymysł *m* [2] (genre) fantasy *n inv*

FAQ *npl* = **frequently asked questions** często zadawane pytania *n pl*

far /fɑː(r)/ **I** *adv* [1] (in space) daleko; **have you come ~?** czy przyjechałeś z daleka?; **is it ~ to London?** czy daleko jest stąd do Londynu?; **~ off** or **away** daleko; **to be ~ from home** być daleko od domu; **~ beyond the city** *[be]* daleko za miastem; **go as ~ as the traffic lights** dojdź/ dojedź do świateł [2] (in time) **~ back in the past** w zamierzchłej przeszłości; **as ~ back as 1965** już w 1965 roku; **as ~ back as he can remember** tak dawno jak tylko sięga pamięcią; **the holidays are not ~ off** wakacje już niedaleko [3] (very much) dużo; **~ better** dużo or o wiele lepszy; **~ too fast** dużo or o wiele za szybko [4] (in extent) **as** or **so ~ as I know** o ile wiem [5] (in degree) **to go too ~** *[person]* posunąć się za daleko

II *adj* [1] (remote) **the ~ north** daleka północ (**of sth** czegoś) [2] (further away) **at the ~ end of the room** w drugim końcu pokoju; **on the ~ side of the wall** po drugiej stronie muru [3] (of party) **the ~ right/left** skrajna prawica/lewica

III by far *adv phr* zdecydowanie

IV far from *prep phr* **to be ~ from satisfied** wcale nie być zadowolonym

V so far *adv phr* [1] (up till now) do tej pory; **so ~**, **so good** na razie wszystko idzie dobrze [2] (up to a point) **you can only trust him so ~** możesz mu zaufać tylko do pewnego stopnia

IDIOMS **~ and wide** wszędzie; **not to be ~ off** or **out** or **wrong** być blisko; **she will go ~** ona daleko zajdzie; **this wine won't go very ~** tego wina nie jest zbyt wiele; **to be a ~ cry from sth** bynajmniej nie przypominać czegoś

faraway /ˌfɑːrə'weɪ/ *adj* odległy

farce /fɑːs/ *n* farsa *f*

farcical /'fɑːsɪkl/ *adj* farsowy

fare /feə(r)/ *n* (cost of travelling) opłata *f* za przejazd; **air ~** cena biletu lotniczego; **full ~** pełna opłata; **half ~** opłata z pięćdziesięcioprocentową zniżką; **return ~** cena biletu powrotnego

Far East *prn* **the ~** Daleki Wschód *m*

farewell /ˌfeə'wel/ **I** *n* pożegnanie *n*; **to bid sb ~** pożegnać kogoś

II *excl* żegnaj!

far-fetched /ˌfɑː'fetʃt/ *adj* naciągany

farm /fɑːm/ **I** *n* gospodarstwo *n* (rolne); (large and specialized) farma *f*

II *vt* uprawiać *[land]*

■ **farm out**: **~ out [sth]** zlec|ić, -ać *[work]* (**to sb** komuś)

farmer /'fɑːmə(r)/ *n* rolnik *m*; **sheep ~** hodowca owiec

farming /'fɑːmɪŋ/ *n* (profession) rolnictwo *n*; (of land) uprawa *f*; (of animals) hodowla *f*

farmyard /'fɑːmjɑːd/ *n* wiejskie podwórze *n*

far-off /ˌfɑː'rɒf, US -'ɔːf/ *adj* daleki, odległy

far-reaching /ˌfɑː'riːtʃɪŋ/ *adj* *[effect, change, reform]* daleko idący; *[investigation]* dogłębny; *[plan, programme]* dalekosiężny

far-sighted /ˌfɑː'saɪtɪd/ *adj* [1] *[person, policy, idea]* dalekowzroczny [2] US **to be ~** być dalekowidzem

farther /'fɑːðə(r)/ **I** *adv* → **further** **I**[1][2]

II *adj* → **further** **II**[2]

farthest /'fɑːðɪst/ *adj, adv* → **furthest**

fascinate /'fæsɪneɪt/ *vt* za|fascynować

fascinating /'fæsɪneɪtɪŋ/ *adj* *[story, person]* pasjonujący; *[conversation]* niezwykle zajmujący

fascination /ˌfæsɪ'neɪʃn/ *n* fascynacja *f* (**with** or **for sth** czymś); **they watched in ~** patrzyli zafascynowani

fascism /'fæʃɪzəm/ *n* faszyzm *m*

fascist /'fæʃɪst/ **I** *n* faszyst|a *m*, -ka *f*

II *adj* faszystowski

fashion /'fæʃn/ **I** *n* [1] (way) sposób *m*; (style) styl *m*; **in my own ~** po swojemu; **in the Chinese ~** w stylu chińskim [2] (vogue) moda *f*; **to be in ~** być modnym; **to be out of ~** być niemodnym; **to go out of ~** wychodzić z mody

II *modif [accessory]* modny; *[jewellery]* fantazyjny; **a ~ designer** projektant; **a ~ house** dom mody; **a ~ model** model/modelka

III *vt* z|robić (**out of** or **from sth** z czegoś); **to ~ clay into sth** ulepić coś z gliny

fashionable /'fæʃnəbl/ *adj* modny (**among** or **with sb** wśród kogoś)

fast[1] /fɑːst, US fæst/ **I** *adj* [1] (speedy) szybki; **a ~ train** pociąg pośpieszny; **to be a ~ walker** szybko chodzić [2] (ahead of time) **my watch is ~** mój zegarek się śpieszy; **you're five minutes ~** twój zegarek śpieszy się pięć minut

II *adv* [1] *[move, speak]* szybko; **I need help ~** natychmiast potrzebuję pomocy [2] *[hold, stuck]* mocno; *[shut]* dobrze; **to be ~ asleep** mocno spać

fast² /fɑːst, US fæst/ **I** *n* post *m*

II *vi* (abstain from food) pościć

fasten /'fɑːsn, US 'fæsn/ **I** *vt* [1] (close) zam|knąć, -ykać *[lid, case]*; zapi|ąć, -nać *[belt, coat, buckle]* [2] (fix) przymocow|ać, -ywać *[notice, shelf]* (**to sth** do czegoś) (**onto sth** na czymś)

II *vi* (close) *[box]* zam|knąć, -ykać się; *[necklace, skirt]* zapi|ąć, -nać się

fastener /'fɑːsnə(r), US 'fæsnə(r)/ *n* (for clothing) zapięcie *n*; (zip) zamek *m*; (for box, bag) zamknięcie *n*

fast food /ˌfɑːst'fuːd, US ˌfæst-/ *n* fast food *m*

fast-forward /ˌfɑːst'fɔːwəd, US ˌfæst-/ *n* przewijanie *n* do przodu

fast-growing /ˌfɑːst'grəʊɪŋ, US ˌfæst-/ *adj* szybko rozwijający się

fast lane /'fɑːstleɪn, US 'fæst-/ *n* pas *m* ruchu do wyprzedzania

fat /fæt/ **I** *n* (substance) tłuszcz *m*; **vegetable ~s** tłuszcze roślinne; **body ~** tkanka tłuszczowa

II *adj* [1] *[person, animal]* gruby; *[cheek, finger]* pulchny; **to get ~** tyć [2] *[wallet, envelope]* wypchany; *[file, magazine]* gruby [3] *[profit, cheque]* pokaźny

fatal /'feɪtl/ *adj [accident, injury, illness]* śmiertelny; *[day, hour]* fatalny; *[flaw, mistake, decision]* fatalny w skutkach; *[influence]* zgubny

fatalist /'feɪtəlɪst/ *n* fatalist|a *m*, -ka *f*

fatality /fə'tæləti/ *n* (person killed) ofiara *f* (śmiertelna)

fatally /'feɪtəlɪ/ *adv* [1] *[wounded, ill]* śmiertelnie [2] *[flawed]* nieodwracalnie

fate /feɪt/ *n* los *m*

fateful /'feɪtfl/ *adj [decision, words]* brzemienny w skutki; *[day]* pamiętny

fat-free /ˌfæt'friː/ *adj* beztłuszczowy

father /'fɑːðə(r)/ **I** *n* ojciec *m*

II *vt* s|płodzić *[child]*

Father Christmas *n* GB Święty Mikołaj *m*

father-in-law /'fɑːðərɪnlɔː/ *n* teść *m*

fatherly /'fɑːðəlɪ/ *adj* ojcowski

fathom /'fæðəm/ **I** *n* sążeń *m* anglosaski (= 1,83m)

II *vt* (also **~ out**) pojąć, -mować

fatigue /fə'tiːg/ *n* [1] (tiredness) znużenie *n* [2] **metal ~** zmęczenie *n* metalu [3] Mil służba *f* w kuchni

fatten /'fætn/ *vt* (also **~ out**) podtucz|yć, -ać

fattening /'fætnɪŋ/ *adj [food, drink]* tuczący

fatty /'fætɪ/ *adj [tissue]* tłuszczowy; *[meat, food]* tłusty

fatuous /'fætʃʊəs/ *adj [remark, smile]* głupkowaty; *[activity]* bezmyślny

faucet /'fɔːsɪt/ *n* US kran *m*

fault /fɔːlt/ **I** *n* [1] (flaw) wada *f*; **software ~** błąd oprogramowania; **he's always finding ~** ciągle się czepia infml [2] (responsibility) wina *f*; **through no**

~ of her own nie z własnej winy; **to be at ~** być winnym [3] Sport błąd *m* serwisowy [4] (in earth) uskok *m* (tektoniczny)

II *vt* **to ~ sb for sth** zarzucać komuś coś

faultless /'fɔːltlɪs/ *adj [performance, German]* bezbłędny; *[manners, taste]* nienaganny

faulty /'fɔːltɪ/ *adj* [1] *[wiring, machine]* wadliwy [2] *[logic, argument]* błędny

fauna /'fɔːnə/ *n* fauna *f*

faux pas /ˌfəʊ 'pɑː/ *n* faux pas *n inv*

favour GB, **favor** US /'feɪvə(r)/ **I** *n* [1] (approval) przychylność *f*; **to be out of ~ with sb** *[person]* być w niełasce u kogoś; **to fall** or **go out of ~** *[idea, method]* stracić zwolenników [2] (kindness) przysługa *f*; **to do sb a ~** wyświadczyć komuś przysługę; **do me a ~ and...** bądź tak miły i...; **to return a** or **the ~** odwdzięczyć się [3] (advantage) **to be in sb's ~** *[situation, financial rates]* być korzystnym dla kogoś; *[wind, tide]* sprzyjać komuś **II in favour of** *prep phr* [1] (on the side of) **to be in ~ of sb/sth** być za kimś/czymś; **to vote in ~ of sth** głosować za czymś [2] (to the advantage of) **to work in ~ of sb** działać na korzyść kogoś; **to decide in sb's ~** rozstrzygnąć na korzyść kogoś

III *vt* [1] (prefer) woleć *[colour, date]*; opowiadać się za (czymś) *[party, solution]*; **to ~ sb** faworyzować kogoś [2] (benefit) *[weather, circumstances]* sprzyjać (czemuś)

favourable GB, **favorable** US /'feɪvərəbl/ *adj [weather, circumstance]* sprzyjający; *[reaction, review]* przychylny; *[result, impression]* korzystny; *[sign]* dobry

favourably GB, **favorably** US /'feɪvərəblɪ/ *adv [speak, consider]* przychylnie; **to compare ~ with sth** wypadać lepiej w porównaniu z czymś

favourite GB, **favorite** US /'feɪvərɪt/ **I** *n* [1] (person, animal) ulubieni|ec *m*, -ca *f*; **this film is one of his ~s** to jeden z jego ulubionych filmów [2] Sport faworyt *m*, -ka *f*

II *adj [actor, restaurant]* ulubiony; *[aunt]* ukochany

favouritism GB, **favoritism** US /'feɪvərɪtɪzəm/ *n* faworyzowanie *n*

fawn¹ /fɔːn/ *n* Zool jelonek *m*

fawn² /fɔːn/ *vi* **to ~ on sb** *[dog]* łasić się do kogoś; *[person]* przymilać się do kogoś

fax /fæks/ **I** *n* faks *m*

II *vt* prze|faksować *[document]*; wys|łać, -yłać faks do (kogoś) *[person]*

faze /feɪz/ *vt* infml s|peszyć

fear /fɪə(r)/ **I** *n* [1] (fright) strach *m*; **~ of heights** lęk wysokości [2] (apprehension) obawa *f* [3] (possibility) **there's no ~ of him** or **his being late** nie ma obawy, że się spóźni

II *vt* [1] (be afraid of) bać się *[sth/sb* czegoś/kogoś]* [2] (anticipate) obawiać się (czegoś) [3] (think) **I ~ not/ so** obawiam się, że nie/tak

III *vi* bać się, obawiać się (**for sb/sth** o kogoś/coś)

fearless /'fɪəlɪs/ adj nieustraszony

feasible /'fi:zəbl/ adj [1] [plan, proposal] realny [2] [excuse, explanation] prawdopodobny

feast /fi:st/ **I** n [1] (meal) uczta f; (formal) bankiet m [2] (religious celebration) święto n **II** vi ucztować; **to ~ on** or **upon sth** zajadać się czymś

feat /fi:t/ n wyczyn m; **a ~ of technology** cud techniki

feather /'feðə(r)/ n pióro n; **~s** (for cushions) pierze n

feature /'fi:tʃə(r)/ **I** n [1] (distinctive characteristic) cecha f [2] (aspect) **good ~s of sth** zalety or dobre strony czegoś [3] (of face) rys m; **her eyes are her best ~** najładniejsze w jej twarzy są oczy [4] (of car, computer, product) element m [5] (also **~ film**) film m fabularny pełnometrażowy [6] (in newspaper) artykuł m (**on sth** o czymś) [7] (on TV) (also **~ programme**) reportaż m (**on sth** o czymś) **II** vt [magazine, issue] zamie|ścić, -szczać; [poster, magazine, author] przedstawiać; [film] ukaz|ać, -ywać **III** vi (on list, menu) figurować

February /'februəri, US -ʊri/ n luty m

federal /'fedərəl/ adj [system, country] federacyjny; [court, police, government] federalny

federation /ˌfedə'reɪʃn/ n federacja f

fed up adj infml **to be ~ with sb/sth** mieć kogoś/ czegoś dosyć

fee /fi:/ n [1] (for professional, artistic services) honorarium n; (for other services) opłata f; **school ~s** czesne [2] (for admission) opłata f za wstęp; (for membership) składka f członkowska; (for joining organization) wpisowe n

feeble /'fi:bl/ adj [light, pulse] słaby; [argument, excuse] nieprzekonujący; [joke, performance] marny; [attempt] nieudolny

feed /fi:d/ **I** n (for animal) porcja f paszy; (for baby) karmienie n **II** vt [1] wy|żywić [person, family] (**on sth** czymś); na|karmić [person, guests, animal]; **to ~ a plant** dostarczać roślinie składników odżywczych [2] zasil|ić, -ać [lake, machine]; podsyc|ić, -ać [fire]; wrzuc|ić, -ać monety do (czegoś) [meter]; dostarcz|yć, -ać [information, secrets] (**to sb/sth** komuś/ czemuś)

feedback /'fi:dbæk/ n [1] (from people) reakcja f pl; **~ from sb on sth** reakcje kogoś na coś [2] (on hi-fi) sprzężenie n

feeding bottle n GB butelka f do karmienia niemowląt

feel /fi:l/ **I** n [1] (atmosphere) nastrój m [2] (sensation) **you can tell by the ~ (that)...** można poznać dotykiem, że...; **to have an oily ~** być tłustym w dotyku [3] **to have a ~ of sth** dotknąć czegoś; **to have a ~ for language** mieć wyczucie językowe
II vt [1] po|czuć [affection, desire, pride, blow, heat, ache]; odczu|ć, -wać [effects, consequences]; **to ~ an obligation** czuć się zobowiązanym; **to ~ a sense of isolation** mieć poczucie izolacji [2] (believe) **to ~ (that)...** czuć, że... [3] (touch) po|macać [texture, cloth]; z|badać [patient]; **to ~ one's way** iść po omacku [4] (be aware of) wyczu|ć, -wać [presence, tension, irony]; być świadomym (czegoś) [importance, seriousness]
III vi [1] czuć się [sad, happy, safe]; po|czuć się [better, young, fat]; być [nervous, angry, surprised]; **to ~ afraid** odczuwać strach; **to ~ an idiot** czuć się jak idiota; **to ~ as if** or **though...** mieć wrażenie, że...; **how do you ~ about marriage?** co sądzisz o małżeństwie?; **I ~ hot/sick** jest mi gorąco/niedobrze; **I ~ hungry** chce mi się jeść; **she isn't ~ing herself today** jest dzisiaj nie w sosie infml [2] (seem) **to ~ cold** być zimnym w dotyku; **the house ~s empty** dom wydaje się pusty; **it ~s like leather** w dotyku przypomina skórę [3] (want) mieć ochotę; **I ~ like crying** chce mi się płakać [4] (grope) **to ~ in a bag** pogrzebać w torebce; **to ~ along the wall** iść po omacku wzdłuż ściany

■ **feel around** or **about**: **to ~ around in a pocket** pomacać w kieszeni; **to ~ around for sth** poszukać czegoś

■ **feel for**: ¶ **~ for [sth]** po|szukać ¶ **~ for [sb]** współczuć (komuś)

■ **feel up to**: **~ up to [sth]** czuć się na siłach; **to ~ up to doing sth** czuć się na siłach zrobić coś

feelgood /'fi:lgʊd/ adj wywołujący dobre samopoczucie

feeling /'fi:lɪŋ/ n [1] (emotion) uczucie n; **a guilty ~** poczucie winy; **to spare sb's ~s** oszczędzić komuś przykrości [2] (opinion) odczucie n; **to have strong ~s about sth** mieć zdecydowane poglądy na coś; **~s are running high** emocje rosną [3] (sensitivity) wrażliwość f; **to play with great ~** grać z wielkim uczuciem [4] (impression) wrażenie n; **I had a ~ you'd say that** czułem, że to powiesz; **I've got a bad ~ about this** mam złe przeczucia co do tego [5] (physical sensation) uczucie n; (ability to sense) czucie n; **a dizzy ~** zawroty głowy

fee-paying /'fi:peɪɪŋ/ adj [school] płatny; [parent, pupil] płacący czesne

feign /feɪn/ vt uda|ć, -wać [enthusiasm, surprise]

fell[1] /fel/ n (mountain) góra f; (hill) wzgórze n

fell[2] /fel/ vt ści|ąć, -nać [tree]; wyrąb|ać, -ywać [forest]

fellow /'feləʊ/ **I** n [1] infml gość m infml [2] (of society, association) członek m [3] GB (lecturer) ≈ nauczyciel m akademicki; (governor) członek m kolegium zarządzającego uczelnią [4] US (researcher) stypendysta m
II adj **her ~ teachers** jej koledzy nauczyciele; **a ~ Englishman** rodak (Anglik)

fellowship /ˈfeləʊʃɪp/ n 1 (social) koleżeństwo n; (religious) braterstwo n 2 (association) bractwo n

felony /ˈfeləni/ n ciężkie przestępstwo n

felt /felt/ n filc m

felt-tip (pen) /ˈfelttɪp/ n mazak m

female /ˈfiːmeɪl/ 1 n Biol samica f; (person) kobieta f; (plant) osobnik m żeński
2 adj 1 Biol żeński; ~ **rabbit** królica 2 (relating to women) kobiecy; ~ **student** studentka

feminine /ˈfemənɪn/ 1 n rodzaj m żeński
2 adj [clothes, style] kobiecy

feminist /ˈfemɪnɪst/ n feminist|a m, -ka f

fence /fens/ 1 n 1 (barrier) ogrodzenie n; (in garden) płot m 2 (in show jumping) przeszkoda f
2 vt ogr|odzić, -adzać [area, garden]
IDIOMS: **to sit on the** ~ być niezdecydowanym

fencing /ˈfensɪŋ/ n Sport szermierka f

fend /fend/ vt **to** ~ **for oneself** po|radzić sobie samemu
■ **fend off:** od|eprzeć, -pierać [attacker, blow]; zby|ć, -wać [question]

fender /ˈfendə(r)/ n 1 (for fire) osłona f paleniska 2 US błotnik m

fennel /ˈfenl/ n Bot fenkuł m włoski; Culin koper m włoski

fern /fɜːn/ n paproć f

ferocious /fəˈrəʊʃəs/ adj [animal] dziki; [argument] zażarty; [attack] brutalny; [heat] morderczy; [climate] srogi

ferret /ˈferɪt/ n Zool fretka f
■ **ferret about:** myszkować (**in sth** w czymś)

ferry /ˈferɪ/ 1 n prom m
2 vt przew|ieźć, -ozić [people, goods]

fertile /ˈfɜːtaɪl, US ˈfɜːrtl/ adj [animal, imagination] płodny; [land, soil] żyzny; [egg] zapłodniony

fertilize /ˈfɜːtɪlaɪz/ vt użyźni|ć, -ać [land]; zapł|odnić, -adniać [animal, plant, egg]

fertilizer /ˈfɜːtɪlaɪzə(r)/ n nawóz m

fervent /ˈfɜːvənt/ adj [admirer] zagorzały; [supporter] gorący

fester /ˈfestə(r)/ vi [wound, situation] zaogni|ć, -ać się; [feeling] wzm|óc, -agać się

festival /ˈfestɪvl/ n święto n; (of music, films) festiwal m

festivity /feˈstɪvəti/ n świętowanie n

fetch /fetʃ/ vt 1 (on foot) przyn|ieść, -osić [object]; przyprowadz|ić, -ać [person, animal]; (in vehicle) przyw|ieźć, -ozić; **to** ~ **sth for sb** przynieść coś komuś; ~ **him a chair, please** proszę, przynieś mu krzesło; **to** ~ **help/a doctor** sprowadzić pomoc/lekarza; ~ ! (to dog) aport! 2 (bring financially) przyn|ieść, -osić [sum, amount]; **to** ~ **a good price** sprzedać się za dobrą cenę

fetching /ˈfetʃɪŋ/ adj [child, habit] uroczy; [smile] ujmujący

fetus n US = **foetus**

feud /fjuːd/ 1 n zatarg m
2 vi toczyć spór (**with sb over sth** z kimś o coś)

feudal /ˈfjuːdl/ adj feudalny

fever /ˈfiːvə(r)/ n gorączka f; **to have a** ~ mieć gorączkę or temperaturę

feverish /ˈfiːvərɪʃ/ adj [person] rozpalony; [eyes] rozgorączkowany; [dream] dręczący; [activity, excitement] gorączkowy

fever pitch n **to bring a crowd to** ~ [music, orator] porwać tłum; **excitement reached** ~ podniecenie sięgnęło zenitu

few /fjuː/ 1 quantif 1 (not many) mało; ~ **letters** mało listów; **with** ~ **exceptions** z nielicznymi wyjątkami 2 (some) (males) kilku; (females) kilka; (male and female) kilkoro; (animals, things) kilka; **every** ~ **days** co kilka or parę dni
2 **a few** quantif (males) kilku; (females) kilka; (male and female) kilkoro; (animals, things) kilka
3 pron 1 (not many) mało; ~ **of them** niewiele; (males) niewielu; **there are four too** ~ jest o czterech/cztery za mało; **as** ~ **as four people** tylko cztery osoby 2 (some) (males) kilku; (females) kilka; (male and female) kilkoro; (animals, things) kilka; **a** ~ **of the countries** kilka or parę z tych krajów
IDIOMS: **such people are** ~ **and far between** tacy ludzie trafiają się bardzo rzadko

fewer /ˈfjuːə(r)/ 1 adj mniej; ~ **and** ~ **people** coraz mniej ludzi or osób
2 pron mniej; ~ **than** 50 **people** mniej niż 50 osób; **no** ~ **than...** aż...,

fewest /ˈfjuːɪst/ adj najmniej

fibre GB, **fiber** US /ˈfaɪbə(r)/ n 1 (of thread, wood) włókno n 2 (in diet) błonnik m

fibre optic GB, **fiber optic** US adj [link] światłowodowy; ~ **cable** światłowód

fickle /ˈfɪkl/ adj [fate, weather] nieprzewidywalny; [moods, behaviour] zmienny; [friend] niepewny

fiction /ˈfɪkʃn/ n 1 (genre) beletrystyka f 2 (delusion) fikcja f 3 (untruth) bajka f fig

fictional /ˈfɪkʃənl/ adj fikcyjny

fictionalize /ˈfɪkʃənəlaɪz/ vt z|beletryzować

fictitious /fɪkˈtɪʃəs/ adj 1 (false) [name, address] zmyślony 2 (imaginary) [character, event] fikcyjny

fiddle /ˈfɪdl/ 1 vt infml s|fałszować [tax return, figures]
2 vi 1 (fidget) **to** ~ **with sth** bawić się czymś 2 (adjust) **to** ~ **with sth** po|kręcić czymś

fidelity /fɪˈdeləti/ n wierność f (**to sb/sth** komuś/czemuś)

fidget /ˈfɪdʒɪt/ vi wiercić się

field /fiːld/ n 1 (for crops) pole n; (with grass) łąka f 2 Sport boisko n 3 (of knowledge) dziedzina f

field day n 1 (school trip) wycieczka f 2 US (sports day) dzień m sportu
IDIOMS: **to have a** ~ (have fun) mieć używanie infml

field trip n wycieczka f (edukacyjna)

fieldwork /ˈfiːldwɜːk/ n praca f w terenie

fierce /'fɪəs/ adj [person, storm, criticism] gwałtowny; [dog] ostry; [animal] groźny; [battle] zażarty; [competition] zacięty; [voice, look] wściekły; [determination] zaciekły

fiercely /'fɪəslɪ/ adv [1] [react] gwałtownie; [compete, fight] zaciekle; [stare, shout] z wściekłością [2] [critical, jealous] strasznie; [loyal] bezwzględnie; [determined] całkowicie

fifteen /ˌfɪf'tiːn/ **I** n piętnaście

II adj piętnaście; (male) piętnastu; (male and female) piętnaścioro

fifteenth /ˌfɪf'tiːnθ/ **I** n [1] (in order) piętnast|y m, -a f, -e n [2] (fraction) piętnasta f (część)

II adj piętnasty

III adv [come, finish] na piętnastym miejscu

fifth /fɪfθ/ **I** n [1] (in order) piąt|y m, -a f, -e n [2] (fraction) piąta f (część)

II adj piąty

III adv [come, finish] na piątym miejscu

fiftieth /'fɪftɪəθ/ **I** n [1] (in order) pięćdziesiąt|y m, -a f, -e n [2] (fraction) pięćdziesiąta f (część)

II adj pięćdziesiąty

III adv [come, finish] na pięćdziesiątym miejscu

fifty /'fɪftɪ/ **I** n (numeral) pięćdziesiąt

II adj pięćdziesiąt; (male) pięćdziesięciu; (male and female) pięćdziesięcioro

fifty-fifty /ˌfɪftɪ'fɪftɪ/ **I** adj to have a ~ chance of doing sth mieć pięćdziesiąt procent szansy na zrobienie czegoś

II adv to share sth ~ podzielić się czymś pół na pół or po równo; to go ~ on sth podzielić się czymś pół na pół or po równo

fig /fɪg/ n figa f

fight /faɪt/ **I** n [1] (struggle) walka f (against sb/sth z kimś/czymś) (for sth o coś) (to do sth żeby coś zrobić); to put up a ~ bronić się; (without firearms) bójka f (between sb and sb pomiędzy kimś i kimś) (over sth o coś) [2] (battle) walka f (between sb and sb pomiędzy kimś a kimś) (for sth o coś) [3] (quarrel) kłótnia f (over sth o coś) (with sb z kimś); to have a ~ with sb kłócić się z kimś

II vt walczyć z (kimś/czymś) [disease, opponent, emotion, fire]; prowadzić [campaign, war] (against sb/sth przeciw komuś/czemuś); s|toczyć [battle] (against sb/sth z kimś/czymś); to ~ one's way through sth torować sobie siłą drogę przez coś [crowd]

III vi [1] (campaign) walczyć (for sth o coś) (against sth z czymś) (to do sth żeby coś zrobić) [2] [army, wrestler] walczyć (against sb/sth przeciwko komuś/czemuś) (with sb/sth z kimś/czymś) [3] (argue) po|kłócić się (over or about sth o coś)

■ **fight back**: ¶ to ~ back against sb/sth stawiać komuś/czemuś opór ¶ ~ back [sth] przem|óc, -agać [fear, anger]; s|tłumić [tears]

■ **fight off**: ~ off [sb/sth], ~ [sb/sth] off

od|eprzeć, -pierać [troops, attack]; przepędz|ić, -ać [attacker]; przem|óc, -agać [despair]; zwalcz|yć, -ać [illness]; odrzuc|ić, -ać [challenge, criticism]

fighter /'faɪtə(r)/ n [1] (determined person) she's a ~ ona łatwo się nie poddaje [2] (~ plane) myśliwiec m [3] (boxer) bokser m

fighting /'faɪtɪŋ/ **I** n [1] (military) walki f pl [2] (in street, pub) bójka f

II prp adj [1] (military) bojowy [2] [talk, words] ostry; a ~ spirit duch walki; to have a ~ chance mieć spore szanse (of doing sth na zrobienie czegoś); to be ~ fit być w pełni sił

figment /'fɪgmənt/ n a ~ of the/of one's imagination wytwór wyobraźni

figurative /'fɪgərətɪv/ adj przenośny

figure /'fɪgə(r), US 'fɪgjər/ **I** n [1] (digit) cyfra f; a four-~ sum suma czterocyfrowa; to be good with ~s być dobrym w rachunkach [2] (amount) liczba f; (sum of money) kwota f [3] (person) postać f; a familiar ~ znajoma postać [4] (body shape) sylwetka f; to lose one's ~ stracić figurę; to watch one's ~ dbać o linię [5] (shape) figura f [6] (diagram) rysunek m

II vi (appear) występować; (in list, report) figurować

■ **figure out**: zna|leźć, -jdować [answer, reason]; to ~ out who/why... dojść do tego, kto/dlaczego...

figurehead /'fɪgəhed, US 'fɪgjər-/ n (symbolic leader) symboliczny przywódca m; (puppet) figurant m pej

figure of speech n figura f retoryczna

figure skating n łyżwiarstwo n figurowe

file[1] /faɪl/ **I** n (tool) pilnik m

II vt opiłow|ać, -ywać [wood, edge]; to ~ one's nails opiłować paznokcie

file[2] /faɪl/ **I** n [1] (for papers) teczka f (na dokumenty); (with clips) skoroszyt m; (ring binder) segregator m [2] (record) kartoteka f; (on particular subject) akta plt; a ~ on sb akta kogoś [3] Comput plik m [4] (line) rząd m; to walk in single ~ iść rządkiem or gęsiego

II vt [1] włącz|yć, -ać do dokumentacji [invoice, letter, record] [2] wn|ieść, -osić [claim, complaint]; złożyć, składać [application, request]; to ~ a lawsuit wnieść sprawę

III vi [1] to ~ for (a) divorce wnieść sprawę rozwodową [2] (walk) iść jeden za drugim or rządkiem or gęsiego

file cabinet US, **filing cabinet** n segregator m

fill /fɪl/ **I** vt [1] [person, rain] napełni|ć, -ać (with sth czymś); [water, fruit] wypełni|ć, -ać; tears ~ed his eyes jego oczy wypełniły się łzami; [crowd, sound, smoke] wypełni|ać, -ać [room, street]; zapełni|ć, -ać [page, chapter, tape] (with sth czymś) [emotion] przepełni|ć, -ać; [sunlight] zal|ać, -ewać [2] (plug) wypełni|ć, -ać [crack, hole] (with sth czymś) [3] (fulfil) spełni|ć, -ać [requirement]; zaspok|oić, -ajać [need] [4] [company, university] obsadz|ić, -ać [post,

vacancy] (**with sb** kimś); [applicant] ob|jąć,
-ejmować [post] ⑤ [wind] wyd|ąć, -ymać

II vi [bath, bucket] napełni|ć, -ać się (**with sth**
czymś); [theatre, hall, streets] zapełni|ć; -ać się
(**with sth/sb** czymś/kimś)
■ **fill in**: ¶ **to** ~ **in for sb** zastępować kogoś
¶ ~ [sth] **in** wypełni|ć, -ać [form, section];
wpis|ać, -ywać [name, address] ¶ ~ **in** [sb], ~
[sb] **in** wprowadz|ić, -ać kogoś (**on sth** w coś)
■ **fill out**: ¶ ~ **out** [person, face] zaokrągl|ić, -ać
się ¶ ~ [sth] **out** wypełni|ć, -ać [form]; wypis|ać,
-ywać [prescription]
■ **fill up**: ¶ ~ **up** [bath] napełni|ć, -ać się;
[theatre, bus] zapełni|ć, -ać się ¶ ~ [sth] **up**
napełni|ć, -ać [jug, tank]; wypełni|ć, -ać [room]
filler /'filə(r)/ n (for pores, cracks) (for wood) kit m
szpachlowy; (for car body) szpachla f; (for walls) masa f
szpachlowa
fillet /'filɪt/ **I** n filet m; (beef) polędwica f
II vt filetować [fish]
filling /'filɪŋ/ **I** n ① Culin nadzienie n; **what kind
of** ~ **have the sandwiches got?** z czym są
kanapki? ② (for tooth) plomba f
II adj [food] sycący
filling station n stacja f benzynowa
film /film/ **I** n ① (movie) film m; **a** ~ **festival**
festiwal filmowy; **the** ~ **industry** przemysł
filmowy; **a** ~ **star** gwiazda filmowa; **a** ~ **studio**
studio filmowe ② (for camera) film m ③ (layer)
warstewka f
II vt [person] s|filmować; [camera] za|rejestrować
III vi [cameraman, crew] kręcić zdjęcia
filmset /'filmset/ n plan m filmowy
filter /'filtə(r)/ **I** n filtr m; **sun** ~ filtr przeciwsłoneczny
II vt prze|filtrować [liquid, gas]
III vi **to** ~ **into sth** [light, water] sączyć się do
czegoś; [sound] przenikać do czegoś
filth /filθ/ n ① (dirt) brud m ② (vulgarity) nieprzy-
zwoitości f pl; (swearing) rynsztokowy język m
filthy /'filθɪ/ adj [floor, rag, hands] bardzo brudny;
[habit] obrzydliwy; (vulgar) [language] ordynarny;
[book] nieprzyzwoity; GB (unpleasant) [weather] paskudny; **to have a** ~ **mind** mieć brudne myśli
fin /fin/ n płetwa f
final /'faɪnl/ **I** n Sport finał m
II adj ① [day, book] ostatni ② [decision, answer]
ostateczny
finale /fi'nɑːlɪ, US -'nælɪ/ n finał m
finalist /'faɪnəlɪst/ n finalist|a m, -ka f
finalize /'faɪnəlaɪz/ vt s|finalizować [purchase,
contract]; za|kończyć [letter, report]; ustal|ić, -ać
[details, route]
finally /'faɪnəlɪ/ adv ① (eventually) w końcu; (with
relief) nareszcie ② (lastly) na koniec ③ (definitively)
ostatecznie

finals /'faɪnlz/ npl GB egzaminy m pl dyplomowe;
US egzaminy m pl semestralne
finance /'faɪnæns, fɪ'næns/ **I** n ① (banking) finanse
plt ② (funds) fundusze m pl
II finances npl (of person) sytuacja f finansowa; (of
company, country) finanse plt
III adj [director, page] finansowy; ~ **minister**
minister finansów
IV vt s|finansować [project]
financial /faɪ'nænʃl, fɪ-/ adj finansowy; ~ **year**
GB rok podatkowy
find /faɪnd/ **I** n (discovery) odkrycie n; (lucky purchase)
okazja f
II vt ① (discover) zna|leźć, -jdować [thing, person];
(come and see) zastać, -wać [thing, person]; **to leave
sth as one found it** zostawić coś w takim stanie,
w jakim się to zastało; **to** ~ **the time for sth**
znaleźć na coś czas; **I found that...** okazało się,
że... ② (after losing) odna|leźć, -jdować; **to** ~ **one's
way out of sth** znaleźć wyjście z czegoś [building,
forest] ③ (encounter) napot|kać, -ykać [word, species];
this plant is not found in Europe ta roślina nie
występuje w Europie ④ (consider) uważać; **how did
you** ~ **her?** co o niej sądzisz?; **he** ~ s **it hard to
make friends** trudno mu nawiązywać przyjaźnie
⑤ (experience) zna|leźć, -jdować [pleasure, satisfac-
tion] (**in sth** w czymś) (**in doing sth** w robieniu
czegoś) ⑥ (in law) **to** ~ **that...** orzec, że...; **to** ~ **sb
guilty/not guilty** uznać kogoś winnym/za nie-
winnego (**of sth** czegoś)
■ **find out**: ¶ ~ **out** dowi|edzieć, -adywać się
(**about sth** o czymś) ¶ ~ [sth] **out** odkry|ć, -wać
[fact, truth]; zna|leźć, -jdować [answer]; **to** ~ **out
who/why...** dowiedzieć się, kto/dlaczego...
fine¹ /faɪn/ **I** n (punishment) grzywna f; (for traffic
offence) mandat m
II vt u|karać grzywną [offender]; (for traffic offence)
na|łożyć, -kładać mandat na (kogoś) (**for sth/
doing sth** za coś/zrobienie czegoś)
fine² /faɪn/ **I** adj ① (very good) świetny; **the** ~ st
quality najwyższa jakość ② (satisfactory) [meal,
arrangement] dobry; [holiday] udany; **that's** ~ w
porządku; '~, **thanks**' „dziękuję, dobrze"; **that's
** ~ **by me** nie mam nic przeciwko temu ③ [day]
piękny; **the weather is** ~ jest ładna pogoda; **it
turned** ~ **later** później się wypogodziło ④ [hair,
fabric, layer] cienki; [feature, crystal] delikatny; [mist]
lekki; [sieve, net] gęsty; [embroidery] misterny;
[powder, soil] drobny ⑤ [adjustment, detail] drobny;
[distinction] subtelny ⑥ [lady, clothes, manners] wytworny ⑦ (commendable) wspaniały
II adv ① [get along] świetnie ② [cut] drobno; [slice]
cienko
fine art n (also **the** ~ **s**) sztuki f pl piękne
(IDIOMS) **to have sth down to a** ~ opanować coś
do perfekcji [skill]
fine-tune /ˌfaɪn'tjuːn/ vt dostr|oić, -ajać

finger /'fɪŋɡə(r)/ **I** *n* palec *m* (u ręki)
II *vt* dotykać (palcami) *[fabric, goods]*; **to ~
one's beard** gładzić brodę
(IDIOMS) **to keep one's ~s crossed** trzymać
kciuki (**for sb** za kogoś)
fingerprint /'fɪŋɡəprɪnt/ *n* odcisk *m* palca
fingertip /'fɪŋɡətɪp/ *n* koniuszek *m* palca
finicky /'fɪnɪki/ *adj [person]* wybredny (**about sth**
w czymś); *[job, task]* żmudny
finish /'fɪnɪʃ/ **I** *n* [1] (end) koniec *m* [2] Sport
końcówka *f*; (of race) finisz *m*; (finishing line) meta *f*
[3] (of clothing, wood, car) wykończenie *n*; (of fabric,
leather) apretura *f*
II *vt* [1] (complete) s|kończyć *[sentence, task]*; u|koń-
czyć *[building, novel]*; **to ~ doing sth** skończyć
robić coś [2] (leave) s|kończyć *[work, studies]*
[3] (consume) s|kończyć *[meal, sandwich]*; dopić,
-jać *[drink]*; dopal|ić, -ać *[cigarette]* [4] (put an end
to) za|kończyć *[career]*
III *vi* [1] *[conference, holidays, term]* s|kończyć się;
the film ~es on Thursday film będzie
wyświetlany do czwartku [2] (reach end of race)
u|kończyć wyścig; **to ~ last** zająć ostatnie
miejsce [3] *[speaker]* skończyć
■ **finish off**: ~ **[sth] off** skończyć *[letter, task]*
■ **finish up**: ¶ *[person]* wylądować infml; **to ~ up
as a teacher** w końcu zostać nauczycielem ¶ ~
[sth] up dokończyć *[milk, cake]*; zużyć *[paint]*
finishing line GB, **finish line** *n* linia *f* mety
finishing touch *n* ostatni szlif *m*; **to put the
~es to sth** dopieścić coś infml *[painting, speech]*
finite /'faɪnaɪt/ *adj [resources]* ograniczony
Finland /'fɪnlənd/ *prn* Finlandia *f*
Finn /fɪn/ *n* Fin *m*, -ka *f*
Finnish /'fɪnɪʃ/ **I** *n* (language) (język *m*) fiński *m*
II *adj* fiński
fir /fɜː(r)/ *n* (also **~ tree**) jodła *f*
fire /'faɪə(r)/ **I** *n* [1] ogień *m*; **to set ~ to sth, to
set sth on ~** podpalić coś; **to be on ~** płonąć; **to
catch ~** zapalić się [2] (blaze) pożar *m*; **to start a ~**
wzniecić pożar [3] (for warmth) ogień *n*; (outside)
ognisko *n*; **to sit by the ~** siedzieć przy kominku;
(outside) siedzieć przy ognisku or ogniu [4] (shots) **to
open ~ on sb** otworzyć ogień do kogoś [5] (verve)
zapał *m*
II *excl* [1] (raising alarm) pali się! [2] (order to shoot)
ognia!
III *vt* [1] wystrzelić, strzelać z (czegoś) *[gun,
weapon]*; wystrzeli|ć, -wać *[rocket, missile]*; wypu|ś-
cić, -szczać *[arrow]*; **to ~ questions at sb** za-
sypać kogoś pytaniami [2] (dismiss) wyl|ać, -ewać
infml
IV *vi* wystrzelić, strzel|ić, -ać (**at** or **on sb/sth** do
kogoś/czegoś)
fire alarm *n* alarm *m* pożarowy
firearm /'faɪərɑːm/ *n* broń *f* palna
firebomb /'faɪəbɒmb/ **I** *n* bomba *f* zapalająca

II *vt* zrzuc|ić, -ać bomby zapalające na (coś)
[building]
fire brigade *n* straż *f* pożarna
fire engine *n* wóz *m* strażacki
fire escape *n* (staircase) schody *plt* pożarowe;
(ladder) drabinka *f* pożarowa
fire exit *n* wyjście *n* ewakuacyjne
fire extinguisher *n* gaśnica *f*
firefighter /'faɪəfaɪtə(r)/ *n* strażak *m*
fireguard /'faɪəɡɑːd/ *n* ekran *m* kominkowy
fireman /'faɪəmən/ *n* strażak *m*
fireplace /'faɪəpleɪs/ *n* kominek *m*
fireproof /'faɪəpruːf/ *adj [clothing, door]* ognioodporny; *[safe, furniture]* ogniotrwały; *[casserole, dish]*
żaroodporny
fire service *n* straż *f* pożarna
fire station *n* remiza *f* strażacka
firewood /'faɪəwʊd/ *n* drewno *n* na opał
firework /'faɪəwɜːk/ *n* fajerwerk *m*
firing /'faɪərɪŋ/ *n* (of guns) kanonada *f*
firing line *n* **to be in the ~** znajdować się na linii
ognia
firing squad *n* pluton *m* egzekucyjny
firm[1] /fɜːm/ *n* (business) firma *f*; **taxi ~** przedsiębiorstwo taksówkowe
firm[2] /fɜːm/ **I** *adj* [1] *[mattress, muscle]* twardy;
[body, fruit] jędrny; *[handshake]* mocny [2] *[table,
ladder]* stabilny [3] *[foundation, basis]* solidny [4] *[offer]*
wiążący; *[commitment]* pełny; *[intention]* niewzruzo-
ny; *[refusal]* stanowczy; *[date]* ostateczny; *[evidence]*
niezbity [5] *[person, stand]* niewzruszony (**with sb**
wobec kogoś); *[leadership, response]* zdecydowany;
[purpose] wytyczony
II *adv* **to stand ~** nie ustępować; fig trwać przy
swoim zdaniu
first /fɜːst/ **I** *pron* [1] (in order) pierwsz|y *m*, -a *f*, -e *n*
[2] (beginning) **at ~** na początku; **from the (very)
~** od (samego) początku [3] GB *dyplom z bardzo
dobrą oceną*
II *adj* pierwszy; **the ~ three pages** pierwsze
trzy strony; **at ~ glance** or **sight** na pierwszy
rzut oka; **I'll ring ~ thing tomorrow** zadzwonię
jutro z samego rana; **I don't know the ~ thing
about him** kompletnie nic o nim nie wiem
III *adv* [1] *[arrive, leave]* (jako) pierwszy; **women
and children ~** najpierw kobiety i dzieci; **to
come ~** Sport zająć pierwsze miejsce; fig być na
pierwszym miejscu [2] (to begin with) najpierw; **~ of
all** po pierwsze [3] (for the first time) po raz pierwszy; **I
~ met him in Paris** poznałem go w Paryżu
(IDIOMS) **~ things ~!** wszystko po kolei!
first aid *n* pierwsza pomoc *f*
first aid kit *n* apteczka *f*
first-class *adj* [1] *[seat, ticket]* w pierwszej klasie;
[carriage] pierwszej klasy; *[accommodation, hotel]* o
najwyższym standardzie [2] *[stamp, letter]* ≈ ekspresowy [3] GB **to graduate with ~ honours in**

chemistry ukończyć chemię z wyróżnieniem 4 (excellent) pierwszorzędny

first cousin n (aunt's son) brat m cioteczny; (uncle's son) brat m stryjeczny; (aunt's daughter) siostra f cioteczna; (uncle's daughter) siostra f stryjeczna

first floor n GB pierwsze piętro n; US parter m

first form n GB Sch pierwsza klasa f

first grade n US Sch pierwsza klasa f

firsthand /ˌfɜːstˈhænd/ adj, adv z pierwszej ręki

firstly /ˈfɜːstlɪ/ adv po pierwsze

first name n imię n

first night n premiera f

first-rate /ˌfɜːstˈreɪt/ adj pierwszorzędny

first-time buyer /ˌfɜːstˈtaɪmˈbaɪə(r)/ n osoba kupująca po raz pierwszy dom lub mieszkanie

fish /fɪʃ/ **I** n ryba f
II adj [market, shop] rybny; [scale] rybi; ~ **knife** nóż do ryb; ~ **bone** ość
III vi 1 to ~ **for trout/cod** łowić pstrągi/dorsze 2 to ~ **for compliments** domagać się komplementów
■ **fish out**: ~ [sth] out 1 (from bag, pocket) wydoby|ć, -wać (of sth z czegoś) 2 (from water) wył|owić, -awiać (of sth z czegoś)

fish and chips n smażona ryba f z frytkami

fish and chip shop n GB ≈ smażalnia f ryb

fishbowl /ˈfɪʃbəʊl/ n kuliste akwarium n

fisherman /ˈfɪʃəmən/ n rybak m; (angler) wędkarz m

fishing /ˈfɪʃɪŋ/ **I** n (industry) rybołówstwo n; (job) rybactwo n; (as sport, hobby) wędkarstwo n; **to go** ~ iść na ryby
II modif [boat, fleet, village] rybacki

fishing rod n wędka f

fishmonger /ˈfɪʃmʌŋgə(r)/ n GB handlarz m ryb; ~'s (shop) sklep rybny

fishnet /ˈfɪʃnet/ adj [tights] ażurowy; ~ **stockings** kabaretki

fish tank n akwarium n

fishy /ˈfɪʃɪ/ adj 1 [smell, taste] rybi 2 infml [explanation] mętny; [situation, business] śliski infml

fist /fɪst/ n pięść f; (of a child) piąstka f

fist[1] /fɪst/ n 1 (medical) atak m 2 (of anger) napad m; (of jealousy, passion) szał m; (of enthusiasm, panic) przypływ m
IDIOMS **by** or **in** ~**s and starts** [work] zrywami

fit[2] /fɪt/ **I** n (of garment) **to be a good/poor** ~ dobrze/źle leżeć; [shoes] pasować/nie pasować
II adj 1 (athletic) wysportowany; (in good shape) w dobrej formie; **to get** ~ nabrać formy or kondycji 2 **to be** ~ **for sth** [person] nadawać się do czegoś [work, travel]; ~ **for human consumption** nadający się or zdatny do spożycia; **it's not** ~ **to eat** to się nie nadaje do jedzenia; **he is not** ~ **to drive** on nie jest w stanie prowadzić; **to see** or **think** ~ **to do sth** uznać za stosowne zrobić coś;

to be in no ~ **state to do sth** nie być w stanie czegoś zrobić 3 (worthy) godny (**for sb** kogoś)
III vt 1 [garment, shoes] pasować na (kogoś); [key] pasować do (czegoś) [keyhole]; z|mieścić się w (czymś) [envelope, space]; **to** ~ **ages 3 to 5** nadawać się dla dzieci od 3 do 5 lat 2 **to** ~ **sth in** or **into sth** zmieścić coś w czymś [car, house, room] 3 (install) za|łożyć, -kładać [lock]; za|instalować, za|montować [door, shower] 4 (correspond) pasować do (czegoś); spełniać [requirements]
IV vi 1 [garment, shoes, object] pasować 2 [toys] z|mieścić się; **will the table** ~ **in that corner?** czy stół zmieści się w tym rogu? 3 (agree with) zgadzać się (**with sth** z czymś) [facts, statement, story]
■ **fit in**: ¶ ~ **in** 1 [key] pasować; [people, objects] zmieścić się 2 [attitude, person] pasować (**with sb/ sth** do kogoś/czegoś); [statement] zgadzać się (**with sth** z czymś); **I'll** ~ **in with your plans** dostosuję się do twoich planów ¶ ~ [sth] **in** 1 (find room for) zmieścić [objects]; w|łożyć, -kładać [key] 2 (find time for) zna|leźć, -jdować czas na (coś) [break, meeting] ¶ ~ [sb] **in** zna|leźć, -jdować czas dla (kogoś) [patient, colleague]

fitness /ˈfɪtnɪs/ **I** n (physical) sprawność f fizyczna
II adj ~ **centre** centrum odnowy biologicznej; ~ **gym/room** siłownia

fitted /ˈfɪtɪd/ adj [clothes] dopasowany; [furniture] wbudowany; [kitchen] obudowany

fitting /ˈfɪtɪŋ/ **I** n 1 (electrical, gas) element m instalacji 2 (for clothing) przymiarka f; (for hearing aid) dobranie n
II adj [description, remark] trafny; [site] odpowiedni; [memorial] stosowny

fitting room n przymierzalnia f

five /faɪv/ **I** n (numeral) pięć; (symbol) piątka f
II adj pięć; (male) pięciu; (male and female) pięcioro

five-a-side /ˌfaɪvəˈsaɪd/ GB n (also ~ **football**) piłka f nożna pięcioosobowa

fix /fɪks/ **I** n infml 1 **to be in a** ~ być w kropce infml 2 (of drugs) działka f infml; (of coffee, nicotine) dawka f
II vt 1 (decide) ustal|ić, -ać [time, venue, amount] 2 (organize) z|organizować [meeting, visit]; przygotow|ać, -ywać [drink, meal]; **to** ~ **one's hair** uczesać się; **how are we** ~**ed for time?** jak stoimy z czasem? infml 3 (mend) napraw|ić, -ać [equipment]; rozwiąz|ać [problem] 4 (attach) przymocow|ać, -ywać [handle, shelf] (**on** or **to sth** do czegoś); przywiąz|ać, -ywać [rope, string] (**on** or **to sth** do czegoś); powiesić, wieszać [notice, shelf] (**on** or **to sth** na czymś) 5 (concentrate) skupi|ć, -ać [attention, thoughts] (**on sth** na czymś); z|wiązać [hopes] (**on sth** z czymś) 6 infml ustaw|ić, -ać infml [match, fight]; s|fałszować [election]; przekup|ić, -ywać [witness, juror]

III **fixed** *pp adj [income, rate, intervals]* stały; *[menu, method]* ustalony; *[rule, principle]* sztywny; *[behaviour]* niezmienny; *[smile]* przyklejony fig; *[stare]* nieruchomy

■ **fix up**: ~ **[sth]** up z|organizować *[holiday, meeting]*; ustal|ić, -ać *[date]*; **it's all** ~ **ed up** wszystko jest załatwione

fixed-term contract *n* umowa *f* (o pracę) na czas określony

fixture /'fɪkstʃə(r)/ *n* 1 stały element *m* wyposażenia; (lighting) oświetlenie *n*; ~ **s and fittings** instalacja i wyposażenie 2 Sport impreza *f* sportowa

fizzle /'fɪzl/ *vi*
■ **fizzle out**: *[interest, enthusiasm]* wygas|nąć, -ać; *[romance]* wypal|ić, -ać się; *[strike, campaign]* za|kończyć się fiaskiem; *[story]* mieć nijakie zakończenie

fizzy /'fɪzɪ/ *adj [drink]* gazowany

flabby /'flæbɪ/ *adj [skin, cheeks]* obwisły; *[muscles]* zwiotczały; *[person]* kluchowaty infml

flag¹ /flæg/ *n* 1 (national) flaga *f*; (on ship) bandera *f*; (of regiment) sztandar *m* 2 Sport chorągiewka *f*
■ **flag down**: ~ **[sth]** down zatrzym|ać, -ywać *[train, taxi]*

flag² /flæg/ *vi [interest, morale]* o|słabnąć; *[athlete]* opa|ść, -dać z sił; *[campaigner]* s|tracić zapał; *[conversation]* przesta|ć, -wać się kleić

flagpole /'flægpəʊl/ *n* maszt *m* (flagowy); (on ship) flagsztok *m*

flagrant /'fleɪɡrənt/ *adj* rażący

flair /'fleə(r)/ *n* 1 (talent) talent *m*; **to have a** ~ **for writing** mieć lekkie pióro; **a** ~ **for organizing** zmysł organizacyjny 2 (style) klasa *f*

flake /fleɪk/ 1 *n* (of snow, cereal, soap) płatek *m*; (of chocolate) wiórek *m*; (of paint, rust) płat *m*
II *vi* (also ~ **off**) *[paint, skin]* z|łuszczyć się; *[plaster]* odpa|ść, -dać; *[stone]* odłup|ać, -ywać się

flamboyant /flæm'bɔɪənt/ *adj [person, behaviour, clothes, lifestyle]* ekstrawagancki; *[colour]* krzykliwy; *[gestures]* ekspresyjny

flame /fleɪm/ *n* płomień *m*; **to be in** ~ **s** palić się; **to go up in** or **burst into** ~ **s** stanąć w płomieniach

flaming /'fleɪmɪŋ/ *adj* 1 *[vehicle, building, torch]* płonący 2 infml (emphatic) cholerny infml

flamingo /flə'mɪŋɡəʊ/ *n* flaming *m*

flammable /'flæməbl/ *adj* palny

flan /flæn/ *n* (savoury) placek *m*; (sweet) tarta *f*

flank /flæŋk/ 1 *n* 1 (of mountain) zbocze *n* 2 Mil flanka *f*
II *vt* (place on each side) ot|oczyć, -aczać (z dwóch stron) (**by** or **with sth** czymś)

flannel /'flænl/ *n* 1 (wool, cotton) flanela *f* 2 GB (also **face** ~) myjka *f* do twarzy

flap /flæp/ 1 *n* 1 (on pocket, hat, cap) klapka *f*; (of envelope, book jacket) skrzydełko *n*; (of tent) poła *f*; (on table) opuszczany blat *m* 2 (of wings, sails) łopot *m*; (of shutter) trzaśnięcie *n*

III *vt [wind]* za|łopotać (czymś); **the bird was** ~ **ping its wings** ptak trzepotał skrzydłami
III *vi [wing]* za|trzepotać; *[sail, flag]* za|łopotać; *[shutter, door]* trzas|nąć, -kać

flare /fleə(r)/ 1 *n* 1 (on runway) latarnia *f* lotniskowa; (on target). bomba *f* oświetlająca; (distress signal) raca *f* 2 (of match, lighter, fireworks) błysk *m*
II *vi* 1 *[match, firework]* rozbłys|nąć, -kiwać 2 *[skirt, nostrils]* rozszerz|yć, -ać się
■ **flare up** 1 *[fire]* zapłonąć jaśniej; *[candle, torch]* buch|nąć, -chać jasnym płomieniem 2 *[illness, pain]* nasil|ić, -ać się ponownie

flash /flæʃ/ 1 *n* 1 (of headlights, knife) błysk *m*; (of jewels) blask *m*; **a** ~ **of lightning** błyskawica 2 **in a** ~ nagle 3 (in camera) flesz *m*
II *vi* 1 infml (display) mach|nąć, -achać (czymś) *[identification card, money]*; (flaunt) **to** ~ **sth at sb** popisywać się przed kimś czymś 2 (shine) błys|nąć, -kać (czymś) *[torch, light]*; **to** ~ **one's headlights (at sb)** dać (komuś) sygnał światłami 3 (give) rzuc|ić, -ać *[smile, look]* (**at sb** komuś) 4 (transmit) przes|łać, -yłać *[pictures, news]*
III *vi [lightning, torch]* błys|nąć, -kać; **to** ~ **on and off** migać, migotać
■ **flash about, flash around**: ~ **[sth]** about obnosić się z (czymś) *[money, credit card]*
■ **flash by, flash past** *[person, bird]* przem|knąć, -ykać jak błyskawica; *[time]* mi|nąć, -jać szybko

flashback /'flæʃbæk/ *n* 1 (in movie) retrospekcja *f*; **a** ~ **to sth** powrót do czegoś 2 (memory) wspomnienie *n*

flashing /'flæʃɪŋ/ *adj [light, sign]* migający

flash light *n* latarka *f*

flashy /'flæʃɪ/ *adj* infml pej *[driver, player]* lubiący się popisywać; *[move, presentation]* efekciarski; *[car]* szpanerski infml; *[dress, jewellery]* krzyczący

flask /flɑːsk, US flæsk/ *n* (for oil, wine) butla *f*; (small) butelka *f*; (**hip**) ~ piersiówka

flat¹ /flæt/ 1 *n* **to strike sb with the** ~ **of one's hand/sword** uderzyć kogoś otwartą dłonią/płazem miecza
II *adj* 1 *[surface, landscape, nose, dish]* płaski; **to be** ~ **on one's back** leżeć na wznak; **to have a** ~ **tyre** mieć flaka infml 2 *[refusal, denial]* kategoryczny 3 *[fare, fee]* jednolity 4 *[voice, style]* bezbarwny; *[taste]* nijaki 5 *[beer]* zwietrzały 6 GB *[battery]* wyczerpany; *[car battery]* rozładowany 7 Mus **A/D** ~ as/des; **E** ~ **major** Es-dur
III *adv* 1 *[lie, lay]* płasko 2 **in 10 minutes** ~ równo w 10 minut 3 *[sing, play]* za nisko
IDIOMS: **to fall** ~ *[joke]* nie wypalić infml; *[party]* być niewypałem; *[play]* zrobić klapę infml

flat² /flæt/ *n* mieszkanie *n*

flatmate /'flætmeɪt/ *n* GB współlokator *m*, -ka *f*

flat out /ˌflæt'aʊt/ infml *adv [drive]* z maksymalną prędkością; *[work]* tak szybko, jak tylko się da

flat rate /ˌflæt'reɪt/ **▯** n stawka f jednolita or zryczałtowana

▯▯ flat-rate modif [fee, tax] jednolity

flatten /'flætn/ **▯** vt ① [rain, storm] położyć, kłaść [crops, grass]; zwal|ić, -ać [tree, fence]; [bombing] z|równać z ziemią ② (smooth out) rozpłaszcz|yć, -ać [piece of metal]; wyrówn|ać, -ywać [surface] ③ (crush) zgni|eść, -atać

▯▯ vr **to ∼ oneself** przylgnąć płasko (**against sth** do czegoś)

flatter /'flætə(r)/ vt pochlebi|ć, -ać (komuś) (**on sth** z powodu czegoś)

flattering /'flætərɪŋ/ adj [remark] pochlebny; (excessively) pochlebczy; [portrait] korzystny; [dress, hat] twarzowy

flattery /'flætərɪ/ n pochlebstwo n

flaunt /flɔːnt/ vt pej obnosić się z (czymś) [wealth]; afiszować się z (czymś/kimś) [opinions, lover]; popisywać się (czymś) [knowledge]

flavour GB, **flavor** US /'fleɪvə(r)/ **▯** n smak m; **to be full of ∼** mieć wyrazisty smak

▯▯ vt (improve taste) nada|ć, -wać smak (czemuś); (add specific taste) doprawi|ć, -ać (**with sth** czymś)

flavouring GB, **flavoring** US /'fleɪvərɪŋ/ n (for sweet taste) aromat m; (for meat, fish) przyprawa f

flaw /flɔː/ n (in textile, china) skaza f (**in sth** na czymś); (in character, machine) wada f (**in sth** czegoś)

flawed /flɔːd/ adj [diamond] ze skazą; [person, character] pełen wad

flea /fliː/ n pchła f

flea market n pchli targ m

fleck /flek/ **▯** n (of colour) ciapka f; (of light, paint) plamka f; (of foam, milk) kropelka f; (of dust, powder) drobinka f

▯▯ vt **to be ∼ed with sth** być poplamionym czymś [paint, mud]

fledg(e)ling /'fledʒlɪŋ/ n opierzone pisklę n

flee /fliː/ **▯** vt um|knąć, -ykać z (czegoś) [place]; um|knąć, -ykać przed (kimś/czymś) [danger, enemy]

▯▯ vi um|knąć, -ykać (**before/in face of sth** przed czymś/w obliczu czegoś)

fleece /fliːs/ n ① (on animal) runo n ② (for sportswear) polar m

fleet /fliːt/ n ① (of ships, planes) flota f; (of small vessels) flotylla f ② (of vehicles) (in reserve) park m; (on road) konwój m

fleeting /'fliːtɪŋ/ adj [pleasure] chwilowy; [glance, memory] przelotny; [visit, moment] krótki

Flemish /'flemɪʃ/ **▯** n ① (język m) flamandzki m ② **the ∼** Flamandowie, Flamandczycy

▯▯ adj flamandzki

flesh /fleʃ/ n ① (soft tissue) ciało n ② (meat) mięso n; (of fruit) miąższ m

fleshy /'fleʃɪ/ adj [lip, fruit] mięsisty; [breasts, buttocks] pełny; [person, arm] pulchny

flex /fleks/ **▯** n GB przewód m

▯▯ vt ① napi|ąć, -inać [muscle] ② zgi|ąć, -nać [limb]

flexibility /ˌfleksə'bɪlətɪ/ n (of wire) giętkość f; (of person) gibkość f; (of system, approach) elastyczność f

flexible /'fleksəbl/ adj ① [arrangement, plan] elastyczny; [working hours] ruchomy ② [person] (able to bend) gibki; **to be ∼ about sth** być elastycznym w kwestii czegoś ③ [wire, stem] giętki

flexitime /'fleksɪtaɪm/ n ruchomy czas m pracy

flick /flɪk/ **▯** n (of fingers) prztyczek m; (of cloth) trzepnięcie n; (of tongue) mlaśnięcie n

▯▯ vt ① (with fingers) pstryk|nąć, -ać (czymś); (with cloth) trzep|nąć, -ać (czymś); (with tail) mach|nąć, -ać (czymś); **he ∼ed his ash onto the floor** strzepnął popiół na podłogę ② (press) pstryk|nąć, -ać infml [switch]

▪ flick through: prze|kartkować [book]

flicker /'flɪkə(r)/ vi ① [fire, light, image] za|migotać; [lightning] bły|snąć, -skać ② [needle] drg|nąć, -ać; [eyelid] za|mrugać

flick knife n GB nóż m sprężynowy

flight /flaɪt/ **▯** n ① (journey) lot m (**from sth** z czegoś) (**to sth** do czegoś); **we took the next ∼ (out) to New York** polecieliśmy następnym samolotem do Nowego Jorku ② (set) **∼ of steps/ stairs** schody; **six ∼s (of stairs)** sześć pięter ③ fig (display) **a ∼ of fancy** wymysł; **his ∼s of imagination** wytwory jego wyobraźni

▯▯ adj **∼ delay** opóźnienie lotu; **∼ information** informacja o odlotach i przylotach; **∼ path** tor m lotu

flight attendant n steward m, -esa f

flight bag n torba f na ramię

flimsy /'flɪmzɪ/ adj [fabric] cienki; [structure, appliance] nietrwały; [excuse, evidence] marny

flinch /flɪntʃ/ vi wzdrygnąć, -ać się; **without ∼ing** z kamienną twarzą; **to ∼ from doing sth** wzdragać się przed zrobieniem czegoś

fling /flɪŋ/ **▯** n infml ① (spree) szaleństwo n ② (sexual) przygoda f; (intellectual) chwilowa fascynacja f

▯▯ vt cis|nąć, -kać (coś or czymś) [ball, grenade] (**at sb/sth** w kogoś/coś)

▯▯▯ vr **to ∼ oneself** rzuc|ić, -ać się (**across sth** przez coś) (**onto sth** na coś) (**off sth** z czegoś)

▪ fling away: **∼ [sth] away** wyrzuc|ić, -ać

▪ fling open: **∼ open [sth], ∼ [sth] open** otw|orzyć, -ierać gwałtownie [door, window]

flint /flɪnt/ n ① (mineral) krzemień m ② (in lighter) kamień m

flip /flɪp/ **▯** n (somersault) przewrót m

▯▯ vt ① (toss) rzuc|ić, -ać (czymś) [coin]; podrzu-c|ić, -ać [pancakes] ② (press) pstryk|nąć, -ać [switch]

▪ flip through: przerzuc|ić, -ać [magazine, book]

flipchart /'flɪptʃɑːt/ n tablica f kartkowa

flip-flop /'flɪpflɒp/ n ① (sandal) japonka f ② US (about-face) wolta f

flippant /'flɪpənt/ adj [remark, behaviour] nonszalancki; [tone, answer] niepoważny

flipper /'flɪpə(r)/ n płetwa f

flirt /flɜːt/ **▯** n flircia|rz m, -r(k)a f infml

▯ vi flirtować (**with sb** z kimś); **to ~ with sth** igrać z czymś *[danger, death]*; rozważać coś *[idea]*

flirtatious /ˌflɜːˈteɪʃəs/ adj *[glance]* kokieteryjny; *[person]* skłonny do flirtów

flit /flɪt/ vi ▯ (also ~ **about**) *[bird, bat]* śmig|nąć, -ać ▯ *[person]* pom|knąć, -ykać ▯ *[idea, expression]* przem|knąć, -ykać (**across sth** przez coś)

float /fləʊt/ **▯** n ▯ (on net) pływak m; (on line) spławik m ▯ (in plumbing) pływak m ▯ GB (swimmer's aid) deska f (do nauki pływania); US (lifejacket) kamizelka f ratunkowa ▯ (vehicle) platforma f na kołach

▯ vt ▯ *[person]* spu|ścić, -szczać na wodę *[boat]*; *[tide, current]* un|ieść, -osić *[ship]* ▯ (in finance) wypu|ścić, -szczać *[shares, securities]*; rozpis|ać, -ywać *[loan]*; wprowadz|ać, -ić na giełdę *[company]*; upłynni|ć, -ać kurs (czegoś) *[currency]*

▯ vi ▯ *[boat, oil]* unosić się na wodzie; *[person]* leżeć na wodzie; *[object]* pły|nąć, -wać; **to ~ on one's back** leżeć na plecach na wodzie; **to ~ down the river** płynąć z prądem ▯ *[smoke, mist]* un|ieść, -osić się w powietrzu ▯ *[currency]* mieć płynny kurs

■ **float off**: *[boat]* odpły|nąć, -wać; *[feather, balloon]* odl|ecieć, -atywać

floating /ˈfləʊtɪŋ/ adj *[bridge]* pontonowy; fig (unstable) zmienny; **~ voter** niezdecydowany m wyborca

flock /flɒk/ **▯** n (of sheep, goats, birds) stado n; (of people) gromada f

▯ vi *[animals, people]* z|gromadzić się; **to ~ into sth** przybyć tłumnie na coś *[exhibition]*; **to ~ together** zgromadzić się

flog /flɒg/ vt (beat) wy|chłostać

flood /flʌd/ **▯** n powódź f; **a ~ of sth** fig powódź czegoś *[light, words]*; zalew czegoś *[letters, complaints]*; **to be in ~s of tears** zalewać się łzami

▯ vt ▯ *[river, burst pipe]* zal|ać, -ewać; *[storm]* s|powodować wystąpienie z brzegów (czegoś) *[river]* ▯ **he was ~ed with joy** ogarnęła go ogromna radość; **to ~ sb with sth** zasypywać kogoś czymś *[offers]* ▯ (oversupply) zal|ać, -ewać *[shops, market]* (**with sth** czymś) ▯ Aut zal|ać, -ewać *[engine]*

▯ vi ▯ *[meadow, street]* być zalewanym; *[river]* wyl|ać, -ewać ▯ **to ~ into sth** *[light]* zal|ać, -ewać coś; *[people]* zapełni|ć, -ać coś; **to ~ over sb** *[emotion]* ogarnąć kogoś

floodgate /ˈflʌdgeɪt/ n zastawka f

floodlight /ˈflʌdlaɪt/ **▯** n reflektor m; **to play under ~s** grać przy sztucznym oświetleniu

▯ vt podświetl|ić, -ać *[building]*; oświetl|ić, -ać *[stage]*

floor /flɔː(r)/ **▯** n ▯ (of room, car, lift) podłoga f; (stone) posadzka f; **dance ~** parkiet ▯ (of sea, tunnel, valley) dno n ▯ (of stock exchange) parkiet m; (of debating

chamber) sala f (obrad); (of factory) hala f ▯ (storey) piętro n; **on the first ~** GB na pierwszym piętrze; US na parterze

▯ vt ▯ powal|ić, -ać (na ziemię) *[attacker, boxer]* ▯ *[argument]* zam|knąć, -ykać usta (komuś) *[person]*; *[question]* zbi|ć, -jać z tropu (kogoś) *[candidate]* ⟨IDIOMS⟩ **to wipe the ~ with sb** sprawić komuś tęgie lanie

floorboard /ˈflɔːbɔːd/ n deska f podłogowa

floor cloth n ścierka f do podłogi

floor show n program m rozrywkowy (w restauracji, lokalu nocnym)

flop /flɒp/ **▯** n infml (failure) klapa f infml

▯ vi ▯ **to ~ down** *[person]* klapnąć infml; **to ~ down on a bed** zwalić się na łóżko infml ▯ infml *[play, project]* zrobić klapę infml

floppy /ˈflɒpɪ/ adj *[ears]* zwisający; *[clothes]* wiszący; *[flesh, body]* obwisły

floppy disk n dyskietka f

flora /ˈflɔːrə/ n flora f

floral /ˈflɔːrəl/ adj *[fabric, dress]* kwiecisty; *[design, fragrance, arrangement]* kwiatowy

Florida /ˈflɒrɪdə/ prn Floryda f

florist /ˈflɒrɪst/ n kwiacia|rz m, -rka f; **~'s** (shop) kwiaciarnia

floss /flɒs, US flɔːs/ n nić f dentystyczna

flotsam /ˈflɒtsəm/ n **~ and jetsam** (on water) pływające szczątki; **the ~ and jetsam of society** wyrzutki społeczeństwa

flounce[1] /flaʊns/ vi **he ~d in/out** wbiegł/wybiegł wzburzony

flounce[2] /flaʊns/ n (frill) falbana f

flounder[1] /ˈflaʊndə(r)/ n Zool ▯ GB stornia f, fląderka f ▯ US płastuga f

flounder[2] /ˈflaʊndə(r)/ vi ▯ *[animal, person]* brnąć (**through sth** przez coś) ▯ (falter) *[speaker]* plątać się; *[career, economy, company]* kuleć

flour /ˈflaʊə(r)/ n mąka f

flourish /ˈflʌrɪʃ/ **▯** n ▯ (gesture) teatralny gest m ▯ (in style) ozdobnik m; **to sign sth with a ~** podpisać się pod czymś zamaszyście

▯ vi *[plant, firm, animal]* rozkwit|nąć, -ać; *[democracy, corruption, arts]* kwitnąć

flourishing /ˈflʌrɪʃɪŋ/ adj *[town, society]* w rozkwicie; *[business]* dobrze prosperujący

flout /flaʊt/ vt z|lekceważyć *[rule, convention]*

flow /fləʊ/ **▯** n ▯ (of liquid) przepływ m; (of river, stream) prąd m; (of refugees, visitors) napływ m; (of information) przepływ m; (of time) upływ m; **to stop in full ~** fig przerwać w pół słowa ▯ (of blood) krążenie n; (of electricity) przepływ m; **to impede traffic ~** zakłócać ruch uliczny ▯ (of tide) przypływ m

▯ vi ▯ *[liquid, gas]* płynąć; fig *[people, offers, money]* napły|nąć, -wać; **to ~ past sth** przepływać obok czegoś; **the river ~s into the sea** rzeka wpływa or **wpada do morza** ▯ *[words, thoughts]* płynąć;

[conversation] toczyć się wartko; *[beer, wine]* lać się strumieniami ③ *[blood, water]* krążyć (**through** or **round sth** po czymś); *[electricity]* płynąć (**through** or **round sth** w czymś) ④ *[hair, dress]* spływać

flowchart /'fləʊtʃɑːt/ *n* diagram *m* sekwencji działań

flower /'flaʊə(r)/ **I** *n* kwiat *m*; **to be in** ~ kwitnąć

II *vi [plant, tree]* kwitnąć; *[love, talent]* rozkwit|nąć, -ać

flower arranging *n* układanie *n* kompozycji kwiatowych

flowering /'flaʊərɪŋ/ **I** *n* kwitnienie *n*

II *adj [plant, shrub]* kwitnący

flowerpot /'flaʊəpɒt/ *n* doniczka *f*; (large) donica *f*

flower shop *n* kwiaciarnia *f*

flowery /'flaʊərɪ/ *adj [field]* ukwiecony; *[design, scent]* kwiatowy; *[fabric, language]* kwiecisty

flu /fluː/ *n* grypa *f*

fluctuate /'flʌktjʊeɪt/ *vi [temperature]* wahać się (**between sth and sth** między czymś a czymś); *[opinions]* zmieniać się

flue /fluː/ *n* (of chimney) przewód *m* (kominowy); (of boiler, stove) rura *f* spalinowa

fluency /'fluːənsɪ/ *n* (competence) biegłość *f*; (eloquence) płynność *f*

fluent /'fluːənt/ *adj* ① **her French is** ~ ona biegle mówi po francusku ② *[speaker]* elokwentny; *[speech]* płynny

fluff /flʌf/ **I** *n* (on clothes, carpet) kłaczki *m pl*; (under furniture) koty *m pl* infml; (on animal) puszek *m*

II *vt* ① (also ~ **up**) *[bird, cat]* na|stroszyć *[feathers, tail]*; na|stroszyć (palcami) *[hair]* ② infml s|chrzanić infml *[exam, shot]*

fluffy /'flʌfɪ/ *adj [animal, hair, cake]* puszysty; *[material]* mechaty; *[jumper]* puchaty

fluid /'fluːɪd/ **I** *n* płyn *m*; Tech ciecz *f*

II *adj* płynny; Tech ciekły

fluid ounce *n* uncja *f* objętości

fluke /fluːk/ *n* **by a (sheer)** ~ szczęśliwym or czystym trafem

fluorescent /flɔːˈresənt, US flʊəˈr-/ *adj [badge]* odblaskowy; *[light]* fluorescencyjny

fluoride /'flɔːraɪd, US 'flʊəraɪd/ *n* fluorek *m*

flurry /'flʌrɪ/ *n* ① (of wind) podmuch *m*; (of dust, snow) tuman *m* ② (bustle) poruszenie *n*; **a** ~ **of activity** nagłe ożywienie ③ (of complaints, words) lawina *f*

flush /flʌʃ/ **I** *n* ① (on cheeks) rumieniec *m*; (from fever) wypieki *m pl* ② (surge) **a** ~ **of pride** przypływ dumy; **a** ~ **of pleasure** nagłe uczucie zadowolenia ③ (toilet device) spłuczka *f*

II *vt* przepłuk|ać, -iwać *[drain, pipe]*; **to** ~ **the toilet** spuścić wodę

III *vi* ① *[person]* po|czerwienieć (**with sth** z czegoś) ② **the toilet doesn't** ~ nie można spuścić wody

▪ **flush out**: wy|płoszyć infml *[animal, spy]*

flushed /flʌʃt/ *adj [face, cheeks]* poczerwieniały; ~ **with sth** jaśniejący czymś *[happiness, pride]*

fluster /'flʌstə(r)/ **I** *n* **to be in a** ~ być podenerwowanym; **to get in a** ~ tracić głowę

II *vt* wytrąc|ić, -ać z równowagi; **to look** ~ **ed** wyglądać na podenerwowanego

flute /fluːt/ *n* ① Mus flet *m* ② (glass) (wąska) szampanka *f*

flutter /'flʌtə(r)/ **I** *n* (of wing, lashes, flag) trzepot *m*; (of paper, leaves) (lekki) szelest *m*

II *vt* za|trzepotać (czymś) *[wing, eyelashes]*; po|machać (czymś) *[handkerchief]*

III *vi* ① *[wings, flag, eyelashes]* za|trzepotać; *[fan]* poruszać się szybko; *[eyelids]* za|mrugać; *[person, hands]* dygotać ② (also ~ **down**) *[petals]* opa|ść, -dać, wirując ③ *[heart]* bić nierówno; **his pulse was** ~ **ing** miał nierówne tętno

flux /flʌks/ *n* **to be in (a state of)** ~ ciągle się zmieniać

fly /flaɪ/ **I** *n* (insect, lure) mucha *f*

II flies *npl* (of trousers) rozporek *m*

III *vt* ① latać (czymś) *[aircraft, balloon]*; pu|ścić, -szczać *[model aircraft, kite]* ② przew|ieźć, -ozić (samolotem) *[person]*; prze|transportować (samolotem) *[supplies]* ③ *[bird, aircraft]* przel|ecieć, -atywać *[distance]* ④ *[person, organization]* wy-wie|sić, -szać *[flag]*

IV *vi* ① *[bird, balloon, kite, aircraft]* po|lecieć; **to** ~ **north** polecieć na północ; **to** ~ **over** or **across sth** przelecieć nad czymś ② **to** ~ **into Gatwick** *[passenger]* przylecieć na (lotnisko) Gatwick; **to** ~ **from Okęcie** wylecieć z Okęcia; **to** ~ **from Rome to Athens** polecieć z Rzymu do Aten; **to** ~ **LOT** lecieć LOT-em ③ *[bullet, sparks, insults]* po|lecieć; (to and fro) latać; **to** ~ **open** gwałtownie się otworzyć; **to go** ~ **ing** infml *[person]* runąć jak długi; *[object, objects]* wylecieć; **to** ~ **into a rage** wpaść we wściekłość ④ (also ~ **past**, ~ **by**) *[time]* z|lecieć; *[holidays]* przel|ecieć, -atywać ⑤ *[flag, cloak, hair]* powiewać

▪ **fly away**: odl|ecieć, -atywać; *[cares]* rozwi|ać, -ewać się

fly-by-night /'flaɪbaɪnaɪt/ *adj [company, operation]* podejrzany; *[person]* nieodpowiedzialny

fly-drive /'flaɪdraɪv/ *adj* ~ **holiday** urlop obejmujący przelot samolotem i wynajem samochodu

flying /'flaɪɪŋ/ **I** *n* latanie *n*; **to be afraid of** ~ bać się latać samolotem

II *adj [insect, machine]* latający; *[object, broken glass]* lecący; **to take a** ~ **leap** dać wielkiego susa ⟨IDIOMS⟩ **with** ~ **colours** *[pass]* śpiewająco; **to win with** ~ **colours** odnieść tryumfalne zwycięstwo

fly-on-the-wall /ˌflaɪɒnðəˈwɔːl/ *adj [documentary]* kręcony na żywo

flyover /'flaɪəʊvə(r)/ *n* ① GB wiadukt *m* ② US defilada *f* lotnicza

flyspray /'flaɪspreɪ/ n spray m na muchy
FM n = **frequency modulation** FM
foal /fəʊl/ n źrebię n
foam /fəʊm/ **[I]** n ⒈ (on sea, bath, drinks) piana f
⒉ (made of rubber, plastic) pianka f
[II] vi ⒈ [beer, water, sea] s|pienić się; **to ~ at the
mouth** [animal] toczyć pianę z pyska; fig [person]
pienić się fig ⒉ [horse] pokry|ć, -wać się pianą
fob /fɒb/ n (pocket) kieszonka f na zegarek; (watch-
chain) dewizka f
■ **fob off**: zby|ć, -wać [enquirer, customer];
odrzuc|ić, -ać [enquiry]
focal point n ⒈ (in optics) ognisko n ⒉ (place)
punkt m centralny; (person) postać f centralna
⒊ (main concern) główny punkt m
focus /'fəʊkəs/ **[I]** n ⒈ (focal point) ognisko n; **to be
in/out of** ~ [image] być ostrym/nieostrym; **to go
out of** ~ [device] rozregulować się; [image] stać się
nieostrym ⒉ (device on lens) regulacja f ostrości
⒊ (centre) **the** ~ **of sb's interest** przedmiot
zainteresowania kogoś; **to be a** ~ **of sb's
attention** być w centrum uwagi kogoś ⒋ (emphasis)
nacisk m
[II] vt ⒈ (fix) skupi|ć, -ać [beam, eye, attention] (**on
sth/sb** na czymś/kimś) ⒉ (adjust) ustawi|ć, -ać
ostrość w (czymś) [lens, camera, microscope]
[III] vi ⒈ **to** ~ **on sth** [rays, attention] skupić się
na czymś; [gaze] zatrzymać się na czymś; [photog-
rapher, camera] ustawić ostrość na coś ⒉ **to** ~ **on
sth** [person, study] skupić się na czymś
[IV] focused pp adj [person] dążący do celu
fodder /'fɒdə(r)/ n pasza f
foe /fəʊ/ n wróg m
foetus GB, **fetus** US /'fiːtəs/ n płód m
fog /fɒg/ **[I]** n mgła f
[II] vt (also ~ **up**) [steam] pokry|ć, -wać parą [glass];
[light] zamglić [film]
foggy /'fɒgɪ/ adj mglisty
foghorn /'fɒghɔːn/ n syrena f mgłowa
foible /'fɔɪbl/ n dziwactwo n
foil¹ /fɔɪl/ n folia f aluminiowa; **silver** ~ (wrapping)
sreberko
foil² /fɔɪl/ n Sport floret m
foil³ /fɔɪl/ vt powstrzym|ać, -ywać [person]; udarem-
ni|ć, -ać [attempt, plot]; po|krzyżować [plan]
foist /fɔɪst/ vt **to** ~ **sth on sb** wmusić coś komuś
fold¹ /fəʊld/ **[I]** n (in fabric, skin) fałda f (**of sth** czegoś,
na czymś); (in paper, map) zagięcie n
[II] vt ⒈ złoży|ć, składać [paper, shirt, chair, wings]
⒉ s|krzyżować [arms]; spl|eść, -atać [hands]
[III] vi ⒈ [chair] złoży|ć, składać się ⒉ (fail) [play]
zostać zdjętym z afisza; [company] zwi|nąć, -jać się
infml; [project] nie wypalić infml
■ **fold back**: odchy|lić, -ać [shutter, door];
odwi|nąć, -jać [sheet, sleeve]
■ **fold in**: doda|ć, -wać [sugar, flour]

■ **fold up**: złożyć, składać [newspaper, chair,
umbrella]
fold² /fəʊld/ n (for sleep) zagroda f
⟦IDIOMS⟧ **return to the** ~ powrócić do swoich
folder /'fəʊldə(r)/ n teczka f; (soft) koszulka f
folding /'fəʊldɪŋ/ adj [bed, bicycle, table, umbrella]
składany; [door] harmonijkowy
foliage /'fəʊlɪdʒ/ n liście m pl
folk /fəʊk/ **[I]** n (people) ludzie plt
[II] adj ⒈ (traditional) [dance, tradition] ludowy
⒉ (modern) [group, song] folkowy
folklore /'fəʊklɔː(r)/ n (art) folklor m; (wisdom)
tradycja f ludowa
follow /'fɒləʊ/ **[I]** vt ⒈ (on foot) pójść, iść za (kimś/
czymś); (in car) po|jechać, jeździć za (kimś/czymś)
⒉ [spy, police] śledzić ⒊ [event, period] nast|ąpić,
-ępować po (czymś); [item on list] być po (czymś)
⒋ (be guided by) kierować się (czymś) [instinct];
post|ąpić, -ępować zgodnie z (czymś) [tradition,
instructions]; podąż|yć, -ać za (czymś) [fashion]; **to
~ sb's example** pójść za przykładem kogoś or
w ślady kogoś ⒌ (understand) nadąż|yć, -ać za
(czymś) ⒍ poświęcić się (czemuś) [career]
[II] vi ⒈ (move after) **you go first, I'll** ~ idź
pierwszy, ja pójdę za tobą; **to** ~ **in sb's
footsteps** pójść w ślady kogoś ⒉ **there's fish
to** ~ potem będzie ryba; **the results were as
~s** wyniki były następujące ⒊ (be logical conse-
quence) wynik|nąć, -ać (**from sth** z czegoś); **that
~s to** oczywiste ⒋ (understand) rozumieć
■ **follow through**: doprowadz|ić, -ać do końca
[project]; dotrzym|ać, -ywać (czegoś) [promise];
spełni|ć, -ać [threat]
■ **follow up**: pójść, iść śladem (czegoś) [story];
za|interesować się (czymś) [article, suggestion];
rozpat|rzyć, -rywać [complaint, offer]; wykorzyst|ać,
-ywać [tip, hint]
follower /'fɒləʊə(r)/ n (of religion) wyznaw|ca m,
-czyni f; (of theory, tradition) zwolenni|k m, -czka f; (of
thinker, artist) uczeń m; (of sport, team) kibic m
following /'fɒləʊɪŋ/ **[I]** n (of theorist, party) zwo-
lennicy m pl; (of religion) wyznawcy m pl; (of soap opera,
show) widzowie m pl; (of sports team) kibice m pl
[II] adj ⒈ [day, page] następny ⒉ (in enumerations)
następujący
[III] prep (after) po (czymś); (as a result) w następstwie
(czegoś)
follow-up /'fɒləʊʌp/ **[I]** n ⒈ (film, record, programme)
dalsza część f (**to sth** czegoś) ⒉ (of patient)
katamneza f
[II] adj ⒈ [work] dalszy; [inspection] kontrolny;
[article, programme] uzupełniający; [letter] potwierdzający ⒉ (of patient, ex-inmate) [visit] kontrolny
folly /'fɒlɪ/ n głupota f
fond /fɒnd/ adj ⒈ [gesture, look, person] czuły;
[memories] miły ⒉ [wish, ambition] szczery; [hope]
głęboki ⒊ **to be** ~ **of sb/sth** bardzo kogoś/coś

lubić; **to be** ~ **of doing sth** z upodobaniem robić coś

fondle /'fɒndl/ *vt* pieścić *[child, lover]*; po|głaskać *[pet]*; po|głaskać po (czymś) *[fur, hair]*

food /fuːd/ 𝐈 *n* jedzenie *n*; **cat** ~ jedzenie or pokarm dla kotów; **frozen** ~ żywność mrożona; **Japanese** ~ japońska kuchnia; **that's** ~ **for thought** to daje do myślenia

𝐈𝐈 *adj [product, industry]* spożywczy; ~ **additives** dodatki do żywności; ~ **poisoning** zatrucie pokarmowe

food processor *n* robot *m* kuchenny

foodstuff /'fuːdstʌf/ *n* artykuł *m* spożywczy

fool /fuːl/ 𝐈 *n* 𝟙 (stupid) głupiec *m*; **you stupid** ~! durniu! infml; **to act the** ~ udawać or zgrywać głupiego; **to make sb look a** ~ (ridicule) zrobić z kogoś durnia infml; (trick) wystrychnąć kogoś na dudka 𝟚 (jester) błazen *m*

𝐈𝐈 *vt* nab|rać, -ierać

foolhardy /'fuːlhɑːdɪ/ *adj [behaviour, attempt]* ryzykancki; *[person]* lekkomyślny

foolish /'fuːlɪʃ/ *adj [person]* niemądry; *[grin, look, decision, comment]* głupi; **to look** ~ mieć głupią minę; **to feel** ~ głupio się czuć

foolproof /'fuːlpruːf/ *adj* 𝟙 *[method, plan]* niezawodny 𝟚 *[machine]* łatwy w obsłudze

foot /fʊt/ 𝐈 *n* 𝟙 (of person, stocking, sock) stopa *f*; (of cat, dog) łapa *f*; (of bird, insect) noga *f*; **on** ~ pieszo, na piechotę; **under** ~ pod stopami; **from head to** ~ od stóp do głów; **to rise to one's feet** (po)wstać 𝟚 (measurement) stopa *f* (= 0,3048 m) 𝟛 (of mountain) podnóże *n*; **at the** ~ **of sth** u stóp czegoś *[mountain, stairs]*; u dołu czegoś *[page]*; w nogach czegoś *[bed]*

𝐈𝐈 *vt* **to** ~ **the bill** zapłacić rachunek (**for sth** za coś)

(IDIOMS:) **to be/get under sb's feet** plątać się komuś pod nogami; **to put one's** ~ **in it** popełnić gafę; **to stand on one's own (two) feet** stać na własnych nogach

footage /'fʊtɪdʒ/ *n* materiał *m* filmowy

foot and mouth (disease) *n* pryszczyca *f*

football /'fʊtbɔːl/ *n* 𝟙 (game) GB piłka *f* nożna; US futbol *m* amerykański; (ball) piłka *f* futbolowa

footballer /'fʊtbɔːlə(r)/ *n* piłka|rz *m*, -rka *f*

footbrake /'fʊtbreɪk/ *n* hamulec *m* nożny

footbridge /'fʊtbrɪdʒ/ *n* kładka *f* (dla pieszych)

foothold /'fʊthəʊld/ *n* oparcie *n* dla nóg; **to gain a** ~ *[ideology]* zapuścić korzenie; *[new invention, drug]* przyjąć się

footing /'fʊtɪŋ/ *n* 𝟙 (basis) podstawa *f*; **to put sth on a legal** ~ nadać czemuś podstawy prawne; **to be on a friendly** ~ **with sb** być z kimś na przyjacielskiej stopie 𝟚 (grip for feet) **to lose one's** ~ stracić równowagę

footlights /'fʊtlaɪts/ *npl* światła *n pl* rampy

footloose /'fʊtluːs/ *adj* niczym nieskrępowany

footnote /'fʊtnəʊt/ *n* przypis *m*

foot passenger *n* pasażer *m*, -ka *f* bez samochodu

footpath /'fʊtpɑːθ, US -pæθ/ *n* (in countryside) ścieżka *f*; (in town) chodnik *m*

footprint /'fʊtprɪnt/ *n* ślad *m* (stopy)

footstep /'fʊtstep/ *n* krok *m*

footstool /'fʊtstuːl/ *n* podnóżek *m*

footwear /'fʊtweə(r)/ *n* obuwie *n*

for /fɔː(r), fə(r)/ *prep* 𝟙 (intended to be used by) dla (kogoś); **to buy sth** ~ **sb** kupić coś dla kogoś or komuś 𝟚 (intended to help) dla (kogoś); **he cooked dinner** ~ **us** ugotował nam or dla nas obiad 𝟛 (indicating purpose) do (czegoś); (of medicine) na (coś); **what is it** ~? do czego to jest or służy?; ~ **sale** na sprzedaż; **bicycles** ~ **hire** wypożyczanie rowerów; **to go** ~ **a swim** iść popływać 𝟜 (as representative, employee of) **to work** ~ **a company** (be employed) pracować w (jakiejś) firmie; (render services) pracować dla (jakiejś) firmy 𝟝 (indicating cause) **the reason** ~ **sth** (direct cause) powód czegoś; (justification) powód do czegoś; **grounds** ~ **divorce** podstawy do rozwodu; **if it weren't** ~ **her...** gdyby nie ona... 𝟞 (indicating person's attitude) dla (kogoś); **to be easy** ~ **sb** być łatwym dla kogoś; **that's good enough** ~ **me** (jak) dla mnie może być 𝟟 (considering) jak na (kogoś/coś); **to be mature** ~ **one's age** być dojrzałym (jak) na swój wiek 𝟠 (towards) dla (kogoś); **I feel sorry** ~ **her** żal mi jej 𝟡 (on behalf of) **let her answer** ~ **herself** niech sama odpowie; **say hello to him** ~ **me** pozdrów go ode mnie 𝟙𝟘 (in time expressions) **he was away** ~ **a year** nie było go (przez) rok; **will he be away** ~ **long?** długo go nie będzie?; **to last** ~ **hours** ciągnąć się godzinami; **we've been together** ~ **two years** jesteśmy ze sobą od dwóch lat; **I'm going to Spain** ~ **six months** jadę na sześć miesięcy do Hiszpanii; **it will be ready** ~ **Saturday** na sobotę będzie gotowe; **I have an appointment** ~ **4 pm** jestem umówiony or zapisany na czwartą 𝟙𝟙 (indicating distance) **to drive** ~ **miles** jechać (całymi) kilometrami; **it's the last shop** ~ **30 miles** następny sklep jest dopiero 30 mil stąd 𝟙𝟚 (indicating indicating destination) **a ticket** ~ **Dublin** bilet do Dublina 𝟙𝟛 (indicating value) **it was sold** ~ **£100** sprzedano to za 100 funtów; **I wouldn't do it** ~ **anything** za nic bym tego nie zrobił; **a cheque** ~ **£20** czek na 20 funtów 𝟙𝟜 (in favour of) za (czymś); **to be** ~ **sth** być za czymś *[peace, divorce]* 𝟙𝟝 (equivalent to) **T** ~ **Tom** T jak Tom; **what's the French** ~ **'boot'?** jak jest „but" po francusku? 𝟙𝟞 (in explanations) ~ **one thing... and** ~ **another...** po pierwsze..., a po drugie...; ~ **that matter** jeżeli już o tym mówimy; ~ **example** na przykład

forbid /fə'bɪd/ *vt* 𝟙 (disallow) zakaz|ać, -ywać; **to** ~ **sb to do sth** zakazać or zabronić komuś robienia czegoś or robić coś 𝟚 (prevent) nie pozw|olić, -alać na (coś) *[action]*; **God** ~! nie daj Boże!

forbidden /fə'bɪdn/ adj [practice, place] zakazany; **smoking is** ~ obowiązuje zakaz palenia

forbidding /fə'bɪdɪŋ/ adj [landscape, expression] złowrogi; [manner] nieprzystępny

force /fɔːs/ **I** n siła f; **to do sth by** ~ zrobić coś siłą; **the police** ~ policja; **a** ~ **10 gale** sztorm o sile dziesięciu stopni w skali Beauforta

II forces npl Mil (also **armed** ~**s**) **the** ~**s** siły plt zbrojne

III in force adv phr ① [come, attend] tłumnie ② [law, prices, ban] obowiązujący; **to be in** ~ obowiązywać

IV vt zmu|sić, -szać [person]; wymu|sić, -szać [action]; **to** ~ **one's way through sth** przedzierać się przez coś

■ **force on**: ~ **[sth] on sb** narzuc|ić, -ać (coś) komuś

forced /fɔːst/ adj [conversation, smile] wymuszony; [labour, landing] przymusowy

force-feed /'fɔːsfiːd/ vt na|karmić na siłę [person, animal]

forceful /'fɔːsfl/ adj [person, behaviour] energiczny; [character] silny; [attack, defence] zaciekły; [speech] wielki

ford /fɔːd/ **I** n bród m

II vt przeprawi|ć, -ać się w bród przez (coś) [river]

fore /fɔː(r)/ n **to be to the** ~ być na pierwszym planie; **to come to the** ~ [person, issue] wysunąć się na pierwszy plan; [quality] ujawnić się; [team, party] wysunąć się na prowadzenie

forearm /'fɔːrɑːm/ n przedramię n

foreboding /fɔː'bəʊdɪŋ/ n złe przeczucie n; **to have** ~**s about sth** żywić obawy co do czegoś

forecast /'fɔːkɑːst, US -kæst/ **I** n ① (also **weather** ~) prognoza f (pogody) ② (outlook) prognoza f (**about sth** dotycząca czegoś); **profits** ~ prognozowane zyski

II vt przepowi|edzieć, -adać [weather]; prze- wi|dzieć, -dywać [profits]

forecaster /'fɔːkɑːstə(r), US -kæst-/ n ① (of weather) meteorolog m ② (in economy) prognosta m

forecourt /'fɔːkɔːt/ n (of shop) parking m; (of garage) podjazd m; (of station) plac m dworcowy

forefinger /'fɔːfɪŋɡə(r)/ n palec m wskazujący

forefront /'fɔːfrʌnt/ n **at** or **in the** ~ **of sth** na czele czegoś [campaign, changes]; na pierwszej linii w czymś [battle]

foregone /'fɔːɡɒn, US -'ɡɔːn/ adj **it is a** ~ **conclusion** to jest z góry przesądzone

foreground /'fɔːɡraʊnd/ n pierwszy plan m

forehand /'fɔːhænd/ n forehend m

forehead /'fɒrɪd, 'fɔːhed, US 'fɔːrɪd/ n czoło n

foreign /'fɒrən, US -rɪ-/ adj ① [country, language, currency] obcy; [tourist, trade, travel] zagraniczny; ~ **relations** stosunki międzynarodowe ② (alien) [characteristics, concept] obcy (**sb/sth** komuś/czemuś)

foreign affairs npl sprawy f pl zagraniczne

foreign body n Med ciało n obce

foreign correspondent n korespondent m zagraniczny, korespondentka f zagraniczna

foreigner /'fɒrənə(r)/ n cudzoziem|iec m, -ka f

foreign exchange market n rynek m walut

foreign minister n minister m spraw zagranicznych

foreman /'fɔːmən/ n ① (in factory) brygadzista m ② (of jury) przewodniczący m ławy przysięgłych

foremost /'fɔːməʊst/ **I** adj [artist, expert] czołowy; [competitor] główny

II adv **first and** ~ przede wszystkim

forename /'fɔːneɪm/ n imię n

forensic science n medycyna f sądowa

forensic scientist n specjalist|a m, -ka f w dziedzinie medycyny sądowej

forerunner /'fɔːrʌnə(r)/ n (person) prekursor m, -ka f; (invention) zapowiedź f; (institution, model) po- przedni|k m, -czka f

foresee /fɔː'siː/ vt przewi|dzieć, -dywać

foreseeable /fɔː'siːəbl/ adj **to be** ~ być do przewidzenia; **for the** ~ **future** przez jakiś (określony) czas

foreshadow /fɔː'ʃædəʊ/ vt zapowi|edzieć, -adać

foresight /'fɔːsaɪt/ n **to have the** ~ **to do sth** być na tyle przewidującym or dalekowzrocznym, żeby coś zrobić

foreskin /'fɔːskɪn/ n napletek m

forest /'fɒrɪst, US 'fɔːr-/ n las m; **fire** ~ pożar lasu

forester /'fɒrɪstə(r), US 'fɔːr-/ n leśniczy m

forestry /'fɒrɪstrɪ, US 'fɔːr-/ n leśnictwo n

foretaste /'fɔːteɪst/ n przedsmak m (**of sth** czegoś)

foretell /fɔː'tel/ vt przepowi|edzieć, -adać

forever /fə'revə(r)/ adv ① [last, live, love] wiecznie; ~ **after(wards)** na zawsze; **the pain seemed to go on** ~ wydawało się, że ból nigdy nie ustąpi ② [leave, disappear] na zawsze ③ (persistently) bez przerwy; **to be** ~ **doing sth** robić coś bez przerwy

foreword /'fɔːwɜːd/ n słowo n wstępne

forfeit /'fɔːfɪt/ **I** n (penalty paid) kara f (pieniężna); (in game) fant m

II vt u|tracić [freedom, respect]; s|tracić [deposit]

forge /fɔːdʒ/ **I** n kuźnia f

II vt ① kuć [metal]; wyku|ć, -wać [gate] ② pod- r|obić, -abiać [banknotes, signature]; **a** ~**ed passport** fałszywy or podrobiony paszport ③ u|tworzyć [alliance]; opracow|ać, -ywać [plan]

III vi **to** ~ **ahead** posuwać się do przodu; fig rozwijać się dynamicznie

forger /'fɔːdʒə(r)/ n fałszerz m

forgery /'fɔːdʒərɪ/ n ① (counterfeiting) fałszerstwo n ② (fake object) falsyfikat m

forget /fə'ɡet/ **I** vt zapom|nieć, -inać [number, poem]; zapom|nieć, -inać o (czymś) [appointment]; **to** ~ **that...** zapomnieć, że...; **to** ~ **to do sth** zapomnieć coś zrobić

II *vi* zapom|nieć, -inać

■ **forget about**: zapom|nieć, -inać o (kimś/ czymś) *[person, birthday]*

forgetful /fəˈgetfl/ *adj* roztargniony; **to become** or **grow** ~ mieć coraz gorszą pamięć; **to be** ~ **of one's duties** zapominać o swoich obowiązkach

forget-me-not /fəˈgetmɪnɒt/ *n* niezapominajka *f*

forgive /fəˈgɪv/ *vt* wybacz|yć, -ać (komuś) *[person]*; wybacz|yć, -ać *[remark, behaviour]*; przebacz|yć, -ać *[crime]*; odpu|ścić, -szczać *[sin]*; darować *[debt]*; **to** ~ **sb (for) sth** wybaczyć or przebaczyć coś komuś; **to** ~ **sb for doing sth** wybaczyć komuś, że coś zrobił

forgiveness /fəˈgɪvnɪs/ *n* ① (for action) przebaczenie *n*; (of debt) darowanie *n* ② (willingness to forgive) wielkoduszność *f*

forgo /fɔːˈgəʊ/ *vt* odm|ówić, -awiać sobie (czegoś) *[pleasure]*; z|rezygnować z (czegoś) *[chance]*

fork /fɔːk/ **II** *n* ① (for eating) widelec *m* ② (tool) widły *plt* ③ (in tree, road, river) rozwidlenie *n* (**in sth** czegoś); (on bicycle) widelec *m*

II *vi* (also ~ **off**) **to** ~ (**off**) **to the right/left** *[road, river]* odchodzić w prawo/lewo

■ **fork out**: infml za|bulić infml (**for sth** za coś)

forklift truck *n* GB wózek *m* widłowy

forlorn /fəˈlɔːn/ *adj* ① (deserted) *[person]* opuszczony; *[place]* wymarły; (pitiable) *[face, sight]* żałosny ② (desperate) *[attempt]* rozpaczliwy

form /fɔːm/ **II** *n* ① (of transport, government, protest, work) forma *f*; (of substance, disease) postać *f* ② (document) formularz *m* ③ (shape) (of object) kształt *m*; (of person) postać *f* ④ (of athlete, horse, performer) forma *f*; **to be in good/poor** ~ być w dobrej/kiepskiej formie ⑤ (etiquette) formy *f pl*; **it's bad** ~ **to do that** tak się nie robi; **purely as a matter of** ~ wyłącznie dla formy ⑥ GB Sch klasa *f*

II *vt* za|łożyć, -kładać *[club, band, union]*; u|two-rzyć *[barrier, circle]*; s|formować *[government]*; zaw|rzeć, -ierać *[alliance]*; nawiąz|ać, -ywać *[friend-ship]*; stw|orzyć, -arzać sobie *[image]*; wyr|obić, -abiać sobie *[opinion]*; odn|ieść, -osić *[impression]*; u|kształtować *[child, personality, attitudes]*

III *vi* *[puddles, ice]* u|tworzyć się; *[idea]* na|rodzić się

formal /ˈfɔːml/ *adj* ① (official) *[announcement, resi-dence]* oficjalny; (in due form) *[request, protest]* formalny ② (not casual) *[language, occasion]* oficjal-ny; *[outfit]* galowy; (on invitation) '**dress:** ~' „strój wieczorowy" ③ *[qualification, training]* formalny

formality /fɔːˈmælətɪ/ *n* ① (legal or social convention) formalność *f* ② (of occasion, language, style) oficjalność *f*; (of dress) odświętność *f*; (of room) oficjalny wy-gląd *m*

formally /ˈfɔːməlɪ/ *adv* ① *[declare, notify]* formal-nie ② *[speak, celebrate]* oficjalnie; **to dress** ~ ubrać się galowo

format /ˈfɔːmæt/ **II** *n* ① (of product, publication) kształt *m*; (of musical group) skład *m*; (of game, TV show) formuła *f* ② (size of book, magazine) format *m* ③ Comput format *m*

II *vt* Comput s|formatować

formation /fɔːˈmeɪʃn/ *n* (of government) formowa-nie *n*; (of friendship) nawiązywanie *n*; (of company, impression) tworzenie *n*; (of character) kształtowanie *n*; (of ideas) formułowanie *n*

former /ˈfɔːmə(r)/ **II** *n* **the** ~ pierwszy

II *adj* ① (earlier) dawny; (previous) poprzedni; **he's a shadow of his** ~ **self** jest cieniem dawnego siebie ② (no longer) *[employer, husband]* były; (pre-vious) poprzedni ③ (first of two) (ten) pierwszy

formerly /ˈfɔːməlɪ/ *adv* (in earlier time, no longer) niegdyś; (previously) poprzednio

formidable /ˈfɔːmɪdəbl, fɔːˈmɪd-/ *adj* ① (intimidat-ing) *[person]* onieśmielający; *[task]* ogromny; *[obstacle]* potężny ② (awe-inspiring) robiący wrażenie

formula /ˈfɔːmjʊlə/ *n* ① (legal, religious) formuła *f*; (meaningless) formułka *f* ② (in science) wzór *m* ③ (recipe) skład *m* (**for sth** czegoś); fig recepta *f* (**for sth** na coś) ④ (for babies) modyfikowane mleko *n* w proszku

fort /fɔːt/ *n* fort *m*

forte /ˈfɔːteɪ, US fɔːrt/ *n* **to be sb's** ~ być mocną stroną czegoś

forth /fɔːθ/ *adv* **from this day** ~ od dzisiaj; **from that day** ~ od tego or tamtego dnia

forthcoming /ˌfɔːθˈkʌmɪŋ/ *adj* ① *[event, season]* nadchodzący; *[book]* mający się wkrótce ukazać ② *[person]* przystępny; **to be** ~ **about sth** mówić otwarcie o czymś

forthright /ˈfɔːθraɪt/ *adj* *[person]* prostolinijny; *[manner]* bezpośredni; *[reply]* szczery

fortieth /ˈfɔːtɪəθ/ **II** *n* ① (in order) czterdziest|y *m*, -a *f*, -e *n* ② (fraction) czterdziesta *f* (część)

II *adj* czterdziesty

III *adv* *[finish]* na czterdziestym miejscu

fortify /ˈfɔːtɪfaɪ/ *vt* um|ocnić, -acniać *[place]* (**against sb/sth** przed kimś/czymś); pokrzepi|ć, -ać *[person]*

fortnight /ˈfɔːtnaɪt/ *n* GB dwa tygodnie *m pl*

fortnightly /ˈfɔːtnaɪtlɪ/ *adj* GB *[meeting, visit]* odbywający się co dwa tygodnie or raz na dwa tygodnie; *[publication]* wychodzący co dwa tygod-nie or raz na dwa tygodnie

fortunate /ˈfɔːtʃənət/ *adj* *[event]* szczęśliwy; *[cir-cumstance]* pomyślny; **to be** ~ *[person]* mieć szczęście

fortunately /ˈfɔːtʃənətlɪ/ *adv* na szczęście

fortune /ˈfɔːtʃuːn/ *n* ① (riches) fortuna *f*; **to make a** ~ zbić fortunę or majątek (**on sth** na czymś) ② **to have the good** ~ **to do sth** mieć szczęście coś robić ③ **to tell sb's** ~ powróżyć komuś

fortune-teller /ˈfɔːtʃuːntelə(r)/ *n* (man) wróż-(biarz) *m*; (woman) wróżka *f*

forty /ˈfɔːtɪ/ **[]** n (numeral) czterdzieści; (symbol) czterdziestka f

[] adj czterdzieści; (male) czterdziestu; (male and female) czterdzieścioro

forward /ˈfɔːwəd/ **[]** n Sport napastnik m

[] adj ① (bold) bezczelny ② [movement] do przodu; **to be too far** ~ [seat] być za bardzo przesuniętym do przodu ③ [season, plant] wczesny

[] adv [go, rush] do przodu; **from this day** ~ od dzisiaj

[] vt wys|łać, -yłać [goods, parcel] (**to sb** do kogoś); przes|łać, -yłać [mail]

forwarding address n (nowy) adres m do korespondencji

forward-looking /ˌfɔːwəd'lʊkɪŋ/ adj [company, person] patrzący w przyszłość

forward planning n planowanie n perspektywiczne

forwards /ˈfɔːwədz/ adv = forward **[]**

fossil /ˈfɒsl/ n skamieniałość f

fossil fuel n paliwo n kopalne

foster /ˈfɒstə(r)/ **[]** adj [parent, child] przybrany

[] vt ① (encourage) zaszczepić, -áć [understanding, attitude]; promować [image]; pop|rzeć, -ierać [development]; rozwi|nąć, -jáć [interests]; żywić [feelings, hope] ② (act as parent) wziąć, brać na wychowanie [child]

foster family n rodzina f zastępcza

foul /faʊl/ **[]** n Sport faul m (**on sb** na kimś)

[] adj ① [place, smell, taste] obrzydliwy; [air, water] cuchnący ② [weather, day] paskudny; **in a** ~ **mood** w podłym nastroju or humorze; **to have a** ~ **temper** mieć paskudne usposobienie ③ [language] plugawy

[] vt ① zanieczy|ścić, -szczać [environment, beach, pavement] ② Sport s|faulować

foul-mouthed /ˌfaʊl'maʊðd/ adj ordynarny

foul play n ① (crime) przestępstwo n ② Sport nieczysta gra f

foul-up /ˈfaʊlʌp/ n infml wpadka f infml

found /faʊnd/ vt ① (set up) za|łożyć, -kładać [town, family]; u|fundować [school, hospital] ② (base) op|rzeć, -ierać [opinion, novel] (**on sth** na czymś)

foundation /faʊn'deɪʃn/ n ① (man-made) fundament m; (natural) podłoże n ② fig podstawa f

foundation course n GB Univ ≈ kurs m przygotowawczy

founder /ˈfaʊndə(r)/ n (of company, family) założyciel m, -ka f; (donor) fundator m, -ka f

foundry /ˈfaʊndrɪ/ n odlewnia f

fountain /ˈfaʊntɪn, US -tn/ n fontanna f

fountain pen n wieczne pióro n

four /fɔː(r)/ **[]** n cztery; (symbol) czwórka f

[] adj cztery; (male) czterech; (male and female) czworo

IDIOMS: **on all** ~**s** na czworakach

four-letter word /ˌfɔːletə'wɜːd/ n niecenzuralne słowo n

four-star /ˈfɔːstɑː(r)/ **[]** n GB (also ~ **petrol**) ≈ etylina f 98

[] adj [hotel, restaurant] czterogwiazdkowy

fourteen /ˌfɔː'tiːn/ **[]** n (numeral) czternaście; (symbol) czternastka f

[] adj czternaście; (male) czternastu; (male and female) czternaścioro

fourteenth /ˌfɔː'tiːnθ/ **[]** n ① (in order) czternast|y m, -a f, -e n ② (fraction) czternasta f (część)

[] adj czternasty

[] adv [come, finish] na czternastym miejscu

fourth /fɔːθ/ **[]** n ① (in order) czwart|y m, -a f, -e n ② (fraction) czwarta f (część)

[] adj czwarty

[] adv [come, finish] na czwartym miejscu

fowl /faʊl/ n drób m

fox /fɒks/ n lis m

foxhound /ˈfɒkshaʊnd/ n foxhound m

fraction /ˈfrækʃn/ n ① (number) ułamek m ② (tiny amount) drobna część f; **a** ~ **higher** odrobinę wyżej

fracture /ˈfræktʃə(r)/ **[]** n (of bone) złamanie n; (of rock) pęknięcie n f

[] vt z|łamać [bone]; rozłup|ać, -ywać [rock]

[] vi [bone] z|łamać się; [pipe, rock] pęk|nąć, -áć; (in several places) po|pękać

fragile /ˈfrædʒaɪl, US -dʒl/ adj [glass, happiness] kruchy; [complexion, flower] delikatny; [health] słaby

fragment /ˈfrægmənt/ n (of rock, conversation) fragment m; (of glass, food) kawałek m; (of bomb) odłamek m

fragrance /ˈfreɪɡrəns/ n zapach m

fragrant /ˈfreɪɡrənt/ adj pachnący; [herbs] aromatyczny

frail /freɪl/ adj [person, health] słabowity; [hope] słaby

frame /freɪm/ **[]** n ① (of building) szkielet m; (of ship, aircraft) wręga f; (of vehicle, bed) rama f; (of rucksack) stelaż m ② (of picture, window) rama f; (of door) futryna f, framuga f ③ (body) ciało n; (build) postura f ④ (in movies) kadr m

[] frames npl (of spectacles) oprawka f

[] vt ① oprawi|ć, -áć [picture]; obramow|ać, -ywać [face, view] ② s|formułować [question]

frame of mind n nastrój m

framework /ˈfreɪmwɜːk/ n szkielet m; fig (of novel, society) struktura f; (basis) podstawa plt; (limits) ramy plt

franc /fræŋk/ n frank m

France /frɑːns, US fræns/ prn Francja f

franchise /ˈfræntʃaɪz/ n ① (in politics) prawo n wyborcze ② (in commerce) franszyza f

frank /fræŋk/ adj [person] szczery; [curiosity] nieskrywany

frankly /'fræŋklɪ/ adv [confess] szczerze; [hostile] otwarcie

frantic /'fræntɪk/ adj [excitement] szaleńczy; [weeping] niepohamowany; [person] oszalały; [struggle] rozpaczliwy; **to be ~ with worry** odchodzić od zmysłów z niepokoju

frantically /'fræntɪklɪ/ adv (excitedly) jak oszalały; (desperately) rozpaczliwie

fraternal /frə'tɜːnl/ adj braterski

fraternity /frə'tɜːnətɪ/ n braterstwo n

fraud /frɔːd/ n oszustwo n

fraudulent /'frɔːdjʊlənt/, US -dʒʊ-/ adj [intent, offer] oszukańczy; [signature] fałszywy; [earnings] nielegalny; [statement] niezgodny z prawdą

fraught /frɔːt/ adj **to be ~ with dangers/ difficulties** być najeżonym niebezpieczeństwami/ trudnościami

fray /freɪ/ **[]** vi [fabric, edge] wy|strzępić się; [rope] prze|trzeć, -cierać się
[] **frayed** pp adj [material] postrzępiony; [nerves] stargany

frazzle /'fræzl/ n infml **I'm worn to a ~** jestem na ostatnich nogach infml; **to burn sth to a ~** spalić coś na węgiel

freak /friːk/ **[]** n [1] offensive dziwoląg m offensive [2] (strange person) dziwa|k m, -czka f [3] (unusual occurrence) anomalia f; **a ~ of nature** wybryk natury [4] infml (enthusiast) mania|k m, -czka f
[] adj [accident, weather] niecodzienny
■ freak out infml: wkurz|yć, -áć się infml

freckle /'frekl/ n pieg m

free /friː/ **[]** adj [1] (not restricted) wolny; [animal] na wolności; [end] luźny; [translation, movement] swobodny; **to break ~ of** or **from sth** uwolnić się or wyzwolić się od czegoś [influence, restriction]; **to set sb/sth ~** zwolnić or wypuścić (na wolność) kogoś [2] (costing nothing) [ticket, sample] darmowy; **'admission ~'** „wstęp wolny or bezpłatny" [3] **to be ~ with sth** nie skąpić or nie żałować czegoś [food, advice, money]; nie szczędzić czegoś [compliments]
[] adv [1] [roam, run, hang] swobodnie; **to go ~** [hostage] zostać uwolnionym; [criminal] pozostawać na wolności [2] [give, repair, travel] za darmo
[] vt [1] (set at liberty) uwol|nić, -alniać [person]; oswob|odzić, -adzać [animal]; wyzw|olić, -alać [country] [2] odblokow|ać, -ywać [money, resources]
[] **-free** in combinations **smoke-~** niedymiący; **sugar-~** bez cukru; **interest-~** nieoprocentowany
[] **for free** za darmo

freedom /'friːdəm/ n wolność f; **~ of information** swobodny dostęp do informacji

freedom fighter n bojownik m o wolność, bojowniczka f o wolność

freefall /'friːfɔːl/ n spadanie n swobodne

Freefone®, **Freephone**® /'friːfəʊn/ n GB bezpłatny numer m; (for information) bezpłatna infolinia f

free-for-all /'friːfərɔːl/ n ogólna bijatyka f

freelance /'friːlɑːns, US -læns/ **[]** n (also **freelancer**) wolny strzelec m
[] adj niezależny; **to do ~ work** pracować jako wolny strzelec

freely /'friːlɪ/ adv [1] [breathe, travel, speak] swobodnie; [spend] bez ograniczeń; [give] hojnie [2] [admit, confess] chętnie; [translate, adapt] swobodnie

free market n (also **~ economy**) wolny rynek m

Freephone® = Freefone

freepost /'friːpəʊst/ n GB (on envelope) „zwolnione z opłaty pocztowej"

free-range /ˌfriː'reɪndʒ/ adj [poultry] z wolnego chowu

free speech n wolność f słowa

freestyle /'friːstaɪl/ n (in swimming) styl m dowolny; (in skiing) akrobacje f pl narciarskie; (all-in wrestling) wolnoamerykanka f

freeway /'friːweɪ/ n US autostrada f

free will n wolna wola f; **of one's own ~** z własnej woli

freeze /friːz/ **[]** n [1] (weather) mróz m [2] (in economy) zamrożenie n (**on sth** czegoś)
[] vt [1] zamr|ozić, -ażać [food]; [cold weather] s|powodować zamarznięcie (czegoś) [liquid]; przemr|ozić, -ażać [fruit, ground] [2] zamr|ozić, -ażać [prices, assets] [3] zatrzym|ać, -ywać [frame, picture]
[] vi [1] [water, river, pipes] zamarz|nąć, -áć; [food] zamr|ozić, -ażać się [2] [person] przemarznąć [3] (become motionless) zam|rzeć, -ierać; **~!** (shouted by police) stój!

freeze-dried /ˌfriːz'draɪd/ adj liofilizowany

freeze-frame /ˌfriːz'freɪm/ n stop-klatka f

freezer /'friːzə(r)/ n (for food storage) zamrażarka f; (industrial) chłodnia f

freezer compartment n zamrażalnik m

freezing /'friːzɪŋ/ **[]** n zero n (stopni); **below ~** poniżej zera
[] adj [person] przemarznięty; [weather] mroźny; **it's ~ in here** tu jest lodowato

freezing cold adj [wind] przeraźliwie zimny; [water] lodowaty

freight /freɪt/ n [1] (goods) ładunek m [2] (transport system) przewóz m towarów; **air ~** transport or fracht lotniczy [3] (cost) koszt m przewozu

freighter /'freɪtə(r)/ n [1] (ship) frachtowiec m [2] (plane) transportowiec m

French /frentʃ/ **[]** n [1] (język m) francuski m [2] **the ~** Francuzi m pl
[] adj francuski

French fries npl frytki f pl

Frenchman /'frentʃmən/ n Francuz m

French-speaking /'frentʃspiːkɪŋ/ adj francuskojęzyczny

French window n drzwi plt balkonowe

Frenchwoman /'frentʃwʊmən/ n Francuzka f

frenetic /frə'netɪk/ adj [activity, pace] szaleńczy; [lifestyle] szalony

frenzied /'frenzɪd/ adj [activity, passion] szalony; [mob] rozszalały; [attempt, effort] desperacki

frenzy /'frenzɪ/ n gorączka f; **media** ~ wrzawa w mediach

frequency /'fri:kwənsɪ/ n częstotliwość f

frequent /'fri:kwənt/ adj częsty; **to make** ~ **use of sth** często z czegoś korzystać

frequently /'fri:kwəntlɪ/ adv często

fresco /'freskəʊ/ n fresk m

fresh /freʃ/ adj [1] [food] świeży; **to look/smell** ~ wyglądać/pachnieć świeżo; ~ **orange juice** świeżo wyciśnięty sok z pomarańczy [2] [clothes, linen] czysty; [supplies] świeży; [drink, information, evidence] nowy; **to make a** ~ **start** zacząć od nowa; **to be** ~ **from a trip abroad** być świeżo po podróży zagranicznej [3] (energetic) rześki; **to feel** or **be** ~ czuć się rześko [4] [air, day] świeży; [weather] chłodny; [water] orzeźwiający

fresh air n **to get some** ~ zaczerpnąć (świeżego) powietrza

freshen /'freʃn/ vt

■ **freshen up**: odświeżyć, -ać się

freshly /'freʃlɪ/ adv świeżo

fresh water n słodka woda f

Freudian slip n freudowska pomyłka f

friction /'frɪkʃn/ n tarcie n; fig (conflict) tarcia plt (**between sb and sb** między kimś a kimś)

Friday /'fraɪdɪ/ n piątek m

fridge /frɪdʒ/ n lodówka f

friend /frend/ n (person one knows) znajomy|y m, -a f; (at work, school) kole|ga m, -żanka f; (person one likes) przyjaci|el m, -ółka f; **to make** ~**s** zaprzyjaźnić się (**with sb** z kimś)

friendly /'frendlɪ/ [1] adj [person, behaviour, smile] przyjazny; [argument, agreement] przyjacielski; [match] towarzyski; [hotel, shop] miły; **to be** ~ **with sb** żyć z kimś w przyjaźni

[2] **-friendly** in combinations **environment-**~ przyjazny dla środowiska; **user-**~ łatwy w obsłudze

friendly fire n Mil **to be killed by** ~ zginąć od ognia swoich

friendship /'frendʃɪp/ n przyjaźń f

fright /fraɪt/ n przerażenie n; **to take** ~ przerazić się (**at sth** czymś); **to give sb a** ~ przestraszyć kogoś

frighten /'fraɪtn/ vt przera|zić, -żać

frightened /'fraɪtnd/ adj **to be** ~ bać się (**of sb/ sth** kogoś/czegoś)

frightening /'fraɪtnɪŋ/ adj [story, experience] przerażający; [statistics, prospect] zatrważający

frightful /'fraɪtfl/ adj [1] (inducing horror) przerażający [2] infml [mistake, headache] potworny

frill /frɪl/ n (on dress) falbana f; (on shirt) żabot m

fringe /frɪndʒ/ n [1] (of hair) grzywka f [2] (decorative trim) frędzle m pl [3] (of forest, meadow) skraj m; (of town) obrzeża n pl; **the extremist** ~ **of the party** skrajne skrzydło partii [4] (in theatre) **the** ~ teatr m alternatywny

fringe benefits npl dodatkowe świadczenia n pl socjalne

frisk /frɪsk/ vt obszuk|ać, -iwać [person]

frivolous /'frɪvələs/ adj [person, behaviour] niepoważny; [details] błahy

frizzy /'frɪzɪ/ adj [hair] mocno kręcony

frog /frɒg/ US /frɔːg/ n żaba f

(IDIOMS) **to have a** ~ **in one's throat** mieć chrypkę

frogman /'frɒgmən/ US /'frɔːg-/ n płetwonurek m

from /frɒm, frəm/ prep [1] (starting inside) z, ze (czegoś); (starting outside) od (czegoś); **where is he** ~**?** skąd on pochodzi?; ~ **the direction of Warsaw** od (strony) Warszawy; ~ **the door to the window** od drzwi do okna; **noises** ~ **upstairs** hałasy dochodzące z góry; **to take sth** ~ **the shelf** wziąć coś z półki; ~ **under the table** spod stołu; ~ **behind the tree** zza drzewa; ~ **in front of my house** sprzed mojego domu; ~ **among the trees** spomiędzy drzew; ~ **here/ there** stąd/stamtąd; **20 km** ~ **the sea** 20 km od morza [2] (expressing time span) od (czegoś); ~ **today** od dzisiaj; ~ **day to day** z dnia na dzień [3] (using as a basis) z (czegoś); **to speak** ~ **experience** mówić z własnego doświadczenia [4] (among) spośród (czegoś); **to choose** ~ **sth** wybrać spośród czegoś [5] (in subtraction) odjąć; **10** ~ **27 leaves 17** 27 odjąć 10 równa się 17 [6] (because of) **I know** ~ **speaking to her that...** z rozmowy z nią wiem, że...; ~ **hunger** z głodu; ~ **what I saw...** (sądząc) z tego, co widziałem...

front /frʌnt/ [1] n [1] (of building) front m; (of cupboard, sweater) przód m; (of book) okładka f; (of envelope) przednia strona f; (of coin, banknote) awers m; (of fabric) prawa strona f [2] (of train, queue, car) przód m; (of auditorium) pierwsze rzędy m pl [3] (in battle) front m [4] GB (promenade) nadbrzeżna promenada f [5] (in weather) front m [6] (outer appearance) fig **to put on a brave** ~ udawać odważnego; **to present a united** ~ stanowić jednolity front

[2] adj [1] [entrance] frontowy; [window] od ulicy; [bedroom] od frontu; [garden, lawn] przed budynkiem [2] [wheel, leg, tooth] przedni [3] [view] od frontu

[3] **in front** adv phr **who's in** ~**?** kto prowadzi?; **the teacher walked in** ~ z przodu szedł nauczyciel

[4] **in front of** prep phr [1] (before) przed (kimś/ czymś) [2] (in the presence of) przy (kimś)

[5] vt [1] infml stać na czele (czegoś) [band] [2] (on TV) po|prowadzić [TV show]

VI *vi* **to** ~ **onto** GB or **on** US sth wychodzić na coś *[sea, main road]*

front bench /ˌfrʌnt'bentʃ/ *n* GB członkowie *m pl* rządu; **the opposition** ~ przywództwo opozycji

front door *n* drzwi *plt* główne

frontier /'frʌntɪə(r), US frʌn'tɪər/ *n* granica *f*

front line /'frʌntlaɪn/ *n* linia *f* frontu; fig pierwsza linia *f* fig

front page **I** *n* pierwsza strona *f*

II **front-page** *adj* *[picture, story]* z pierwszej strony

frost /frɒst/ *n* **1** (weather condition) mróz *m* **2** (icy coating) szron *m* (**on sth** na czymś)

frostbite /'frɒstbaɪt/ *n* odmrożenie *n*

frosty /'frɒstɪ/ *adj* **1** *[air]* mroźny; *[windscreen, lawn]* oszroniony **2** *[smile, reception]* lodowaty

froth /frɒθ, US frɔːθ/ *n* (on beer, champagne) piana *f*

frown /fraʊn/ *vi* z|marszczyć brwi; **to** ~ **at sb** spojrzeć na kogoś marszcząc brwi

■ **frown on, frown upon**: krzywo patrzeć na (coś) *[behaviour, activity]*

frozen /'frəʊzn/ *adj* **1** *[lake, ground, pipe]* zamarznięty; *[person, fingers]* przemarznięty; **to be** ~ **stiff** przemarznąć na kość or do szpiku kości **2** *[vegetables, meat]* mrożony

fruit /fruːt/ *n* owoc *m*; **a piece of** ~ owoc

fruit cake *n* Culin keks *m*

fruition /fruːˈɪʃn/ *n* **to come to** ~ *[hope]* ziścić się; *[plan]* zostać zrealizowanym

fruit machine *n* automat *m* do gry

fruit salad *n* sałatka *f* owocowa

fruity /'fruːtɪ/ *adj* *[fragrance, smell]* owocowy; *[wine]* owocowy w smaku; *[voice, tone]* soczysty

frustrate /frʌ'streɪt, US 'frʌstreɪt/ *vt* z|irytować *[person]*; udaremni|ć, -ać *[attempt, plot]*; zaw|ieść, -odzić *[hopes]*; po|krzyżować *[plan]*

frustrated /frʌ'streɪtɪd, US 'frʌst-/ *adj* *[person]* sfrustrowany; *[desire, urge]* niezaspokojony; *[effort, attempt]* bezskuteczny; *[plan]* nieudany

frustrating /frʌ'streɪtɪŋ, US 'frʌst-/ *adj* *[obstinacy]* denerwujący; *[experience, situation]* frustrujący

frustration /frʌ'streɪʃn/ *n* **1** (disappointment) frustracja *f* (**at** or **with sth** z powodu czegoś) **2** (of hopes, desires) niespełnienie *n*; (of plan, project) fiasko *n*

fry /fraɪ/ **I** *vt* u|smażyć

II *vi* smażyć się

III **fried** *pp* *adj* *[fish, potatoes]* smażony

frying pan *n* GB patelnia *f*

fuel /'fjuːəl/ **I** *n* (for car, plane) paliwo *n*; (for heating) opał *m*

II *vt* **1** *[oil, gas]* napędzać *[engine]* **2** za|tankować *[plane]* **3** podsyc|ić, -ać *[tension, discord]*; napędzać *[inflation]*

fuel tank *n* (of car) bak *m*

fugitive /'fjuːdʒɪtɪv/ *n* zbieg *m*; (refugee) uciekinier *m*, -ka *f*

fulfil GB, **fulfill** US /fʊl'fɪl/ *vt* **1** spełni|ć, -ać *[promise, dream]*; z|realizować *[ambition]*; zaspok|oić, -ajać *[need]*; **to feel** ~**led** mieć satysfakcję (z tego, co się robi) **2** spełniać *[function]*; spełni|ć, -ać *[conditions, terms]*; wypełni|ć, -ać *[duty]*

fulfilment GB, **fulfillment** US /fʊl'fɪlmənt/ *n* **1** (satisfaction) satysfakcja *f*; (stronger) spełnienie *n* **2** **the** ~ **of sth** spełnienie czegoś *[prophecy, promise]*; zaspokojenie czegoś *[ambition, needs]* **3** **the** ~ **of the contract** wywiązanie się z umowy

full /fʊl/ **I** *adj* **1** (completely filled) pełny; *[room, train]* przepełniony; *[suitcase, drawer]* wypchany; **the flight is** ~ nie ma wolnych miejsc na ten lot **2** (busy) *[day, week]* ciężki; **she leads a very** ~ **life** prowadzi bardzo intensywne życie **3** *[member, partner]* pełnoprawny; *[membership, right]* pełny **4** *[employment, bloom, power]* pełny; **at** ~ **speed** pełnym gazem **5** (for emphasis) cały; **a** ~ **45 degrees** całe 45 stopni **6** *[figure, face, lips]* pełny; *[sleeve, trousers]* obszerny; ~ **skirt** szeroka spódnica

II *adv* ~ **in the face** prosto w twarz; **to know** ~ **well** wiedzieć doskonale; **with the heating up** ~ przy ogrzewaniu włączonym na cały regulator

III in full *adv phr* **to write sth in** ~ napisać coś w pełnym brzmieniu; **to pay in** ~ zapłacić w całości

full blast *adv* infml **the TV was on** or **going at** ~ telewizor grał na ful infml

full-blown /fʊl'bləʊn/ *adj* **1** *[disease]* pełnoobjawowy; *[epidemic]* prawdziwy **2** *[lawyer, doctor]* w pełni wykwalifikowany **3** *[recession, crisis, war]* na wielką skalę

full board *n* zakwaterowanie *n* z pełnym wyżywieniem

full-cream milk /ˌfʊlkriːmˈmɪlk/ *n* GB mleko *n* pełnotłuste

full-length /ˌfʊl'leŋθ/ *adj* **1** *[film]* pełnometrażowy **2** *[novel]* duży; *[portrait]* stojący; *[mirror]* do podłogi; *[dress]* długi

full name *n* pełne imię *n* i nazwisko *n*

full-scale /ˌfʊl'skeɪl/ *adj* **1** *[drawing]* w skali naturalnej; *[model]* naturalnej wielkości **2** *[search]* (prowadzony) na szeroką skalę **3** (total) *[alert, panic]* ogólny; *[war, crisis]* regularny

full-size(d) /ˌfʊl'saɪz(d)/ *adj* **1** *[bicycle, bed]* duży **2** (full-scale) naturalnej wielkości

full stop *n* GB (in punctuation) kropka *f*

full time **I** *n* Sport koniec *m* meczu

II **full-time** *adj* **1** Sport *[score]* końcowy **2** *[worker]* na pełnym etacie

III *adv* *[work]* na pełnym etacie; *[study]* na studiach dziennych

fully /'fʊlɪ/ *adv* **1** *[understand, recover]* w pełni; **to be** ~ **qualified** mieć odpowiednie kwalifikacje

② *[opened]* całkowicie; ~ **booked** w całości zarezerwowany

fully-fledged /ˌfʊlɪˈfledʒd/ *adj [citizen, member]* pełnoprawny; **a** ~ **accountant** księgowy z prawem samodzielnego wykonywania zawodu

fumble /ˈfʌmbl/ *vt* wypu|ścić, -szczać *[ball]*
■ **fumble about: to** ~ **about in the dark to find sth** szukać czegoś po omacku

fume /fjuːm/ *vi* ① *infml* be angry **he is fuming with anger** gotuje się ze złości *infml* ② (produce gas) wydzielać opary; (produce smoke) dymić

fumes /fjuːmz/ *npl* wyziewy *plt*; **petrol** ~ GB, **gas** ~ US opary benzyny

fun /fʌn/ *n* zabawa *f*; **to have** ~ **doing sth** dobrze się bawić robiąc coś; **have** ~! dobrej zabawy!; **to do sth in** ~ robić coś dla zabawy; **she's great** ~ **to be with** jest świetnym kompanem
⟨IDIOMS⟩ **to make** ~ **of** or **poke** ~ **at sb/sth** nabijać się z kogoś/czegoś *infml*

function /ˈfʌŋkʃn/ ❶ *n* ① (role) funkcja *f*; **to fulfil a** ~ *[person]* pełnić funkcję ② (ceremony) uroczystość *f*; (occasion) przyjęcie *n* ③ (in computer program, maths) funkcja *f*
❷ *vi* ① (work) funkcjonować ② (operate as) **to** ~ **as sb** pełnić funkcję kogoś; **to** ~ **as sth** służyć jako coś

functional /ˈfʌŋkʃənl/ *adj* ① *[design, furniture]* funkcjonalny ② (in working order) działający

function key *n* klawisz *m* funkcyjny

fund /fʌnd/ ❶ *n* fundusz *m*; **emergency** ~ fundusz na nieprzewidziane wydatki
❷ **funds** *npl* fundusze *m pl*; **to be in** ~s mieć pieniądze
❸ *vt* s|finansować *[company, project]*

fundamental /ˌfʌndəˈmentl/ *adj* fundamentalny

fundamentalist /ˌfʌndəˈmentəlɪst/ ❶ *n* fundamentalist|a *m*, -ka *f*
❷ *adj* fundamentalistyczny

funding /ˈfʌndɪŋ/ *n* finansowanie *n*

fund-raising /ˈfʌndreɪzɪŋ/ *n* (in the street) kwestowanie *n*; (looking for sponsors) gromadzenie *n* funduszy

funeral /ˈfjuːnərəl/ *n* pogrzeb *m*

funeral home US, **funeral parlour** GB *n* zakład *m* pogrzebowy

funfair /ˈfʌnfeə(r)/ *n* wesołe miasteczko *n*

fungus /ˈfʌŋgəs/ *n* (plant, mould) grzyb *m*

fun-loving /ˈfʌnlʌvɪŋ/ *adj [person]* lubiący się bawić

funnel /ˈfʌnl/ *n* ① (for liquids) lejek *m* ② (on ship, engine) komin *m*

funny /ˈfʌnɪ/ *adj* (amusing) zabawny; (odd) dziwny; **don't try anything** ~! *infml* tylko bez żadnych numerów! *infml*; **to feel** ~ *infml* czuć się niedobrze

fur /fɜː(r)/ ❶ *n* (on big animal) futro *n*; (on small animal) futerko *n*; **she was dressed in** ~s miała na sobie futro

❷ *adj [collar, lining]* futrzany; ~ **coat** futro

furious /ˈfjʊərɪəs/ *adj* ① (angry) wściekły (**at** or **with sb** na kogoś); **he's** ~ **about it** jest wściekły z tego powodu ② *[battle, debate]* zażarty; *[effort]* nadludzki; *[speed, energy]* szalony; *[storm]* gwałtowny

furnace /ˈfɜːnɪs/ *n* (in foundry, at home) piec *m*; (to produce steam) palenisko *n*

furnish /ˈfɜːnɪʃ/ *vt* u|meblować *[room, apartment]* (**with sth** czymś)

furniture /ˈfɜːnɪtʃə(r)/ *n* meble *m pl*; **a piece of** ~ mebel

furry /ˈfɜːrɪ/ *adj [toy, animal]* futerkowy; *[kitten]* puszysty

further /ˈfɜːðə(r)/ ❶ *adv* ① (a greater distance) (also **farther**) dalej; **how much** ~ **is it?** jak to jeszcze daleko?; **to move** ~ **back** cofnąć się dalej; ~ **away** or **off** dalej; ~ **on** dalej; **nothing could be** ~ **from the truth** nic bardziej błędnego ② (in time) (also **farther**) ~ **back than 1964** przed 1964 rokiem; **a year** ~ **on** rok później ③ (even more) **prices fell (even)** ~ ceny jeszcze spadły; **I won't delay you any** ~ nie będę cię już więcej zatrzymywał ④ (in addition) ponadto
❷ *adj* ① (additional) dalszy; (next in sequence) następny; ~ **research** dalsze badania; **without** ~ **delay** bez dalszej zwłoki; **is there anything** ~? czy jeszcze coś? ② (more distant) (also **farther**) dalszy
❸ *vt* zwiększ|yć, -ać *[chances]*; posu|nąć, -wać do przodu *[career, plan]*; promować *[cause]*

further education *n* GB ≈ doskonalenie *n* zawodowe

furthest /ˈfɜːðɪst/ ❶ *adj [point, place, part]* najdalszy
❷ *adv* ① (in space) (also **the** ~) najdalej; **the** ~ **north** najdalej na północ ② (in time) **the** ~ **back I can remember is 1970** moja pamięć sięga tylko roku 1970

furtive /ˈfɜːtɪv/ *adj [glance, movement]* ukradkowy; *[meeting]* sekretny; *[behaviour]* podejrzany

fury /ˈfjʊərɪ/ *n* wściekłość *f*; fig (of storm, wind) gwałtowność *f*

fuse /fjuːz/ ❶ *n* bezpiecznik *m*; **to blow a** ~ zrobić krótkie spięcie; *infml* wpaść w szał
❷ *vt* ① GB zaopatrzyć w bezpiecznik *[plug]* ② sto|pić, -apiać *[wires, metals]*

fuse box *n* skrzynka *f* bezpiecznikowa

fuselage /ˈfjuːzəlɑːʒ, -lɪdʒ/ *n* kadłub *m*

fuse wire *n* drut *m* bezpiecznikowy

fuss /fʌs/ ❶ *n* ① (agitation) zamieszanie *n*; **to make a** ~ **(about sth)** (create excitement) robić or wprowadzać zamieszanie (wokół czegoś); (talk a lot about sth) robić mnóstwo hałasu (wokół czegoś); (exaggerate importance of sth) robić wielką sprawę (z czegoś) ② **to kick up a** ~ zrobić awanturę ③ (attention) **to make a** ~ **of** or **over sb/sth** (spoil) rozpieszczać

kogoś/coś; (be overprotective of) cackać się z kimś/
czymś infml

II *vi* ① (worry) przejmować się (**about sth** czymś)
② (show irrational concern) wydziwiać (**about sth**
z czymś); (criticize) grymasić (**about sth** przy
czymś)

fussy /ˈfʌsɪ/ *adj* (in matters of personal taste) wybredny;
(about details) pedantyczny

futile /ˈfjuːtaɪl, US -tl/ *adj* ① *[attempt, effort]*
daremny ② *[remark]* błahy; *[conversation]* jałowy

future /ˈfjuːtʃə(r)/ **I** *n* ① przyszłość *f*; **in the near**
or **not too distant** ~ w bliskiej or niezbyt odległej
przyszłości; **to have a bright** ~ mieć przed sobą
świetlaną przyszłość ② (also ~ **tense**) czas *m*
przyszły

II *adj* przyszły; **at some** ~ **date** kiedyś
w przyszłości

fuze *n* US = **fuse**

fuzzy /ˈfʌzɪ/ *adj* ① *[hair]* kędzierzawy; *[fabric]*
puszysty ② *[picture, photo]* zamazany ③ *[difference]*
niewyraźny, rozmyty; *[mind, idea]* mętny

G

g, G /dʒiː/ *n* **1** (letter) g, G *n* **2** G Mus g **3** **g** = **gram** g

gab /gæb/ *infml*
(IDIOMS:) **to have the gift of the** ~ *infml* być wygadanym *infml*

gadget /'gædʒɪt/ *n* gadżet *m*

gaffe /gæf/ *n* gafa *f*

gag /gæg/ **I** *n* **1** (on mouth) knebel *m* **2** *infml* (joke) kawał *m*
II *vt* za|kneblować *[person]*
III *vi* za|krztusić się

gage /geɪdʒ/ *n, vt* US = **gauge**

gain /geɪn/ **I** *n* **1** (profit) zysk *m*, korzyść *f* **2** (increase) przyrost *m* (**in sth** czegoś) **3** (advantage) korzyść *f*
II *vt* zdoby|ć, -wać *[experience, advantage]*; **we have nothing to** ~ nic nie zyskamy; **to** ~ **speed** nabrać prędkości; **to** ~ **weight** przybierać na wadze
III *vi* **1** (increase) **to** ~ **in popularity** zyskać na popularności **2** (profit) **she hasn't** ~**ed by it** nie zyskała na tym
■ **gain on:** dog|onić, -aniać *[person, vehicle]*

galaxy /'gæləksɪ/ *n* galaktyka *f*; fig plejada *f*

gale /geɪl/ *n* wicher *m*, wichura *f*

gallery /'gælərɪ/ *n* **1** art ~ muzeum *n*, galeria *f* **2** (part of building) galeria *f*, krużganek *m*; (in church) chór *m* **3** (in theatre) galeria *f*

Gallic /'gælɪk/ *adj* (typowo) francuski

galling /'gɔːlɪŋ/ *adj* irytujący

gallon /'gælən/ *n* galon *m* (GB = 4,546 l; US = 3,785 l)

gallop /'gæləp/ **I** *n* galop *m*; (very fast) cwał *m*
II *vi* po|galopować; (very fast) po|cwałować

galore /gə'lɔː(r)/ *adv* w bród

galvanize /'gælvənaɪz/ *vt* fig z|elektryzować fig *[person, group]*; ożywi|ć, -ać *[campaign]*

gambit /'gæmbɪt/ *n* **1** fig manewr *m*, posunięcie *n* **2** (in chess) gambit *m*

gamble /'gæmbl/ **I** *n* (risky venture) **it's a** ~ to jest ryzykowne
II *vt* postawić, stawiać also fig (**on sth** na coś)
III *vi* uprawiać hazard; (at cards) grać na pieniądze; **to** ~ **on the horses** grać na wyścigach; **to** ~ **on shares** grać na giełdzie

gambler /'gæmblə(r)/ *n* hazardzist|a *m*, -ka *f*, gracz *m*

gambling /'gæmblɪŋ/ *n* hazard *m*

game /geɪm/ **I** *n* **1** (competitive) gra *f*; (not competitive) zabawa *f*; **to have a** ~ **of cowboys** bawić się w kowbojów **2** (match) mecz *m*; (in tennis) gem *m* **3** Culin dziczyzna *f*
II **games** *npl* **1** GB Sch zajęcia *plt* sportowe **2** (also **Games**) (sporting event) igrzyska *plt*
(IDIOMS:) **to give the** ~ **away** wszystko zdradzić

gamekeeper /'geɪmkiːpə(r)/ *n* leśniczy *m*

game plan *n* strategia *f*

game reserve *n* rezerwat *m* dzikich zwierząt

games console *n* konsola *f* gier

game show *n* teleturniej *m*

games room *n* salon *m* gier

games software *n* gry *f pl* komputerowe

gammon /'gæmən/ *n* szynka *f* wędzona

gang /gæŋ/ *n* **1** (of criminals) banda *f*, gang *m*; (of friends) paczka *f infml* **2** (of workmen, prisoners) brygada *f*, ekipa *f*
■ **gang up:** zm|ówić, -awiać się (**on** or **against sb** przeciwko komuś)

gangland /'gæŋlænd/ *n* gangi *m pl* przestępcze

gang leader *n* szef *m* gangu

gang-rape /'gæŋreɪp/ *n* gwałt *m* zbiorowy

gangster /'gæŋstə(r)/ *n* gangster *m*, bandyta *m*

gangway /'gæŋweɪ/ *n* **1** GB (in bus, cinema) przejście *n* **2** (in ship) trap *m*, schodnia *f*

gap /gæp/ *n* **1** (opening) dziura *f* (**in sth** w czymś); (between planks, curtains) szpara *f*; (between cars) odstęp *m*; (in clouds) prześwit *m* **2** (of time, in conversation) przerwa *f* **3** (discrepancy) różnica *f*; (between opinions) rozbieżność *f*; **a 15-year age** ~ piętnaście lat różnicy **4** (in knowledge) luka *f* (**in sth** w czymś) **5** (in market) luka *f*

gape /geɪp/ *vi* **1** (stare) wpatrywać się (**at sb/sth** w kogoś/coś) **2** **to** ~ **open** *[chasm]* roz|ewrzeć, -wierać się; *[garment]* rozchyl|ić, -ać się

gaping /'geɪpɪŋ/ *adj* *[person]* wpatrujący się; *[wound]* ziejący

garage /'gærɑːʒ, 'gærɪdʒ, US gə'rɑːʒ/ *n* **1** (for car) garaż *m* **2** (for repair) warsztat *m* samochodowy

garbage /'gɑːbɪdʒ/ *n* **1** US (rubbish) śmieci *m pl* **2** (nonsense) bzdury *f pl infml* pej

garbage can *n* US pojemnik *m* na śmieci

garbage truck *n* US śmieciarka *f*

garbled /'gɑːbld/ *adj* *[account, message]* przekręcony

garden /'gɑːdn/ **I** *n* ogród *m*; (smaller) ogródek *m*

II *vi* uprawiać ogród or ogródek; (work as gardener) pracować jako ogrodnik

garden centre GB, **garden center** US *n* centrum *n* ogrodnicze

gardener /'gɑːdnə(r)/ *n* ogrodni|k *m*, -czka *f*

gardening /'gɑːdnɪŋ/ *n* ogrodnictwo *n*

gargle /'gɑːgl/ *vi* wy|płukać gardło (**with sth** czymś)

garish /'geərɪʃ/ *adj* [colour] jaskrawy; [clothes] krzykliwy

garland /'gɑːlənd/ *n* girlanda *f*; (on head) wianek *m*

garlic /'gɑːlɪk/ *n* czosnek *m*

garnish /'gɑːnɪʃ/ Culin **II** *n* garnirunek *m*, przybranie *n*

II *vt* u|garnirować, przyb|rać, -ierać (**with sth** czymś)

garter /'gɑːtə(r)/ *n* podwiązka *f*

gas /gæs/ **II** *n* 1 (fuel) gaz *m* 2 (anaesthetic) znieczulenie *n* 3 US (petrol) benzyna *f*

II *vt* (injure) zatru|ć, -wać gazem; (kill) o|truć gazem

gas chamber *n* komora *f* gazowa

gas cooker *n* kuchenka *f* gazowa

gas fire *n* piecyk *m* gazowy

gash /gæʃ/ **II** *n* rozcięcie *n*

II *vt* rozci|ąć, -nać [finger, knee]

gas mask *n* maska *f* przeciwgazowa

gasoline /'gæsəliːn/ *n* US benzyna *f*

gas oven *n* piekarnik *m* gazowy

gasp /gɑːsp, US gæsp/ **II** *n* gwałtowny wdech *m*

II *vi* dyszeć; **to ~ in amazement** wydać stłumiony okrzyk zdziwienia

gas pedal *n* US pedał *m* gazu

gas station *n* US stacja *f* benzynowa

gastro-enteritis /ˌgæstrəʊˌentə'raɪtɪs/ *n* nieżyt *m* żołądka i jelit

gate /geɪt/ *n* brama *f*; (for walkers) furtka *f*; (of level crossing) szlaban *m*; (in underground) bramka *f*; (at airport) wyjście *n*; **at the ~** przy wyjściu

gatecrash /'geɪtkræʃ/ infml *vt* **to ~ a party** wkręcić się na przyjęcie infml; **to ~ a concert** wejść na koncert bez biletu

gatecrasher /'geɪtkræʃə(r)/ *n* infml **even the ~s left the stadium** nawet ci, którzy wcisnęli się bez biletu, opuścili stadion

gather /'gæðə(r)/ **II** *n* (in garment) marszczenie *n*

II *vt* 1 (get) z|ebrać, -bierać; **the movement is ~ing strength** ruch rośnie w siłę; **to ~ one's courage** zebrać się na odwagę; **to ~ speed** nabierać prędkości 2 **to ~ that...** wy|wniosкować, że...; **I ~ (that) he was here** jeżeli dobrze zrozumiałem, on tu był 3 (in sewing) z|marszczyć

III *vi* z|ebrać, -bierać się, z|gromadzić się; [darkness] zapa|ść, -dać

gathering /'gæðərɪŋ/ *n* spotkanie *n*; **family ~** rodzinne spotkanie

gaudy /'gɔːdɪ/ *adj* [jewellery] jarmarczny

gauge, gage US /geɪdʒ/ **II** *n* 1 (of gun, screw) kaliber *m*; (of metal) grubość *f*; (of wire) przekrój *m* 2 (of railway) rozstaw *m* torów 3 (measuring instrument) wskaźnik *m*, miernik *m*; **fuel ~** wskaźnik paliwa

II *vt* 1 z|mierzyć [temperature, speed]; po|liczyć [number] 2 oceni|ć, -ać [mood, reaction]

gaunt /gɔːnt/ *adj* wychudły, wyniszczony

gauze /gɔːz/ *n* (fabric) gaza *f*; (wire) siatka *f*

gay /geɪ/ **II** *n* (man) homoseksualista *m*; gej *m* infml; (woman) lesbijka *f*

II *adj* 1 homoseksualny; [community] gejowski; [club] dla gejów 2 (lively) wesoły; [laughter] beztroski

Gaza strip /ˌgɑːzə 'strɪp/ *prn* strefa *f* Gazy

gaze /geɪz/ **II** *n* spojrzenie *n*

II *vi* wpatrywać się (**at sb/sth** w kogoś/coś)

GCSE *n* = **General Certificate of Secondary Education** świadectwo ukończenia szkoły średniej nieuprawniające do podjęcia studiów

gear /gɪə(r)/ *n* 1 (equipment) sprzęt *m* 2 (clothes) **football ~** strój piłkarski 3 Aut bieg *m*; **to be in third ~** być na trzecim biegu; **to put a car in ~** włączyć or wrzucić bieg; **you're not in ~** nie wrzuciłeś biegu

■ **gear up:** przy|szykować się (**for sth** do czegoś or na coś)

gearbox /'gɪəbɒks/ *n* skrzynia *f* biegów

gel /dʒel/ **II** *n* żel *m*

II *vi* Culin s|tężeć, sta|nąć, -wać; fig [ideas, plan] s|krystalizować się, nab|rać, -ierać realnych kształtów

gem /dʒem/ *n* kamień *m* szlachetny

Gemini /'dʒemɪnaɪ, -niː/ *npl* Bliźnięta *plt*

gender /'dʒendə(r)/ *n* (of word) rodzaj *m*; (of person, animal) płeć *f*

gene /dʒiːn/ *n* gen *m*

genealogy /ˌdʒiːnɪ'ælədʒɪ/ *n* genealogia *f*

gene pool *n* pula *f* genów

general /'dʒenrəl/ **II** *n* generał *m*

II *adj* powszechny, ogólny

III **in general** *adv phr* (usually) na ogół; (overall) ogólnie rzecz biorąc

general election *n* wybory *plt* powszechne

generalization /ˌdʒenrəlaɪ'zeɪʃn, US -lɪ'z-/ *n* uogólnienie *n* (**about sth** dotyczące czegoś)

generalize /'dʒenrəlaɪz/ **II** *vt* **to ~ a conclusion/principle** sformułować ogólny wniosek/ogólną zasadę

II *vi* generalizować; **to ~ about sth** dokonywać uogólnień na temat czegoś

general knowledge *n* wiedza *f* ogólna

generally /'dʒenrəlɪ/ *adv* 1 (widely) powszechnie; (usually) na ogół; **~ ... zasadniczo...** 2 (overall) ogólnie (rzecz biorąc) 3 [talk] ogólnie

general practitioner GB *m* lekarz *m* pierwszego kontaktu

general public *n* ogół *m* społeczeństwa

general-purpose /ˌdʒenrəl'pɜːpəs/ adj *[tool]* uniwersalny

general strike n strajk m generalny

generate /'dʒenəreɪt/ vt wytw|orzyć, -arzać *[income, electricity]*; przyn|ieść, -osić *[profit, publicity]*; wywoł|ać, -ywać *[interest, tension]*

generation /ˌdʒenə'reɪʃn/ n [1] pokolenie n; **the younger/older** ~ młodsze/starsze pokolenie [2] (of electricity) wytwarzanie n; (of data) generowanie n

generation gap n konflikt m pokoleń

generator /'dʒenəreɪtə(r)/ n (of electricity) generator m; (in hospital, on farm) agregat m prądotwórczy

generosity /ˌdʒenə'rɒsətɪ/ n hojność f, szczodrość f

generous /'dʒenərəs/ adj hojny, szczodry; *[size, hem]* duży

genetic /dʒɪ'netɪk/ adj genetyczny

genetically modified, GM GB adj transgeniczny

genetic engineering n inżynieria f genetyczna

genetic fingerprinting n analiza f DNA

genetics /dʒɪ'netɪks/ n genetyka f

genetic testing n badania n pl genetyczne

Geneva /dʒɪ'niːvə/ prn Genewa f

genial /'dʒiːnɪəl/ adj sympatyczny, miły

genitals /'dʒenɪtlz/ npl genitalia plt

genius /'dʒiːnɪəs/ n geniusz m

gentle /'dʒentl/ adj łagodny; *[touch, pressure, breeze, hint]* delikatny; *[exercise]* nieforsowny

gentleman /'dʒentlmən/ n (man) pan m; (well-bred) dżentelmen m

gently /'dʒentlɪ/ adv łagodnie; *[cook]* na małym ogniu; **to break the news** ~ w delikatny sposób przekazać (złą) wiadomość

gents /dʒentz/ npl toaleta f męska

genuine /'dʒenjʊɪn/ adj *[reason, motive, jewel]* prawdziwy; *[work of art]* oryginalny; *[person, effort, interest]* autentyczny; *[buyer]* poważny

genuinely /'dʒenjʊɪnlɪ/ adv rzeczywiście; *[worried, sorry]* szczerze

geography /dʒɪ'ɒgrəfɪ/ n (study) geografia f; (layout) topografia f

geology /dʒɪ'ɒlədʒɪ/ n geologia f

geometry /dʒɪ'ɒmətrɪ/ n geometria f

gerbil /'dʒɜːbɪl/ n myszoskoczek m

geriatric /ˌdʒerɪ'ætrɪk/ adj geriatryczny

germ /dʒɜːm/ n [1] (microbe) drobnoustrój m; (carrying disease) zarazek m [2] (seed) zarodek m; zalążek m

German /'dʒɜːmən/ [1] n [1] (person) Niem|iec m, -ka f [2] (language) (język m) niemiecki m [2] adj niemiecki; *[teacher, course]* niemieckiego; *[ambassador, embassy]* Niemiec

German measles n Med różyczka f

Germany /'dʒɜːmənɪ/ prn Niemcy plt

germinate /'dʒɜːmɪneɪt/ [1] vt doprowadz|ić, -ać do kiełkowania *[seeds, plants]*; fig da|ć, -wać początek (czemuś) *[idea, emotion]*

[2] vi wy|kiełkować

germ warfare n wojna f bakteriologiczna

gesticulate /dʒe'stɪkjʊleɪt/ vi gestykulować

gesture /'dʒestʃə(r)/ [1] n gest m

[2] vi skinąć, z|robić gest; ~ **at** or **towards sb/sth** skinąć w stronę kogoś/czegoś or na kogoś/coś; **he** ~ **d to me to leave** dał mi znak, żebym wyszedł

get /get/ [1] vt [1] (receive) dosta|ć, -wać *[letter, salary]*; odbierać *[channel]* [2] (inherit) **to** ~ **sth from sb** odziedziczyć coś po kimś [3] (obtain) (by applying) otrzym|ać, -ywać; (with effort, difficulty) zdoby|ć, -wać; (buy) kup|ić, -ować; **to** ~ **sb sth, to** ~ **sth for sb** kupić coś komuś [4] (acquire) zysk|ać, -iwać, zdoby|ć, -wać *[reputation]* [5] (achieve) dosta|ć, -wać, otrzym|ać, -ywać *[grade]* [6] (fetch) przyn|ieść, -osić *[object]*; sprowadz|ić, -ać *[person, help]*; **to** ~ **sb sth, to** ~ **sth for sb** przynieść komuś coś [7] (move) **to** ~ **sth/sb downstairs** zanieść coś/sprowadzić kogoś na dół [8] (help progress) **is this discussion** ~**ting us anywhere?** czy ta dyskusja ma w ogóle jakiś sens?; **where has it got me?** co mi to dało? [9] (deal with) **I'll** ~ **it** (of phone) ja odbiorę; (of doorbell) ja otworzę [10] (prepare) z|robić *[breakfast, lunch]* [11] (take hold of) z|łapać *[person]* (by **sth** za coś) [12] infml (oblige to give) **to** ~ **sth out of sb** wyciągnąć coś od kogoś infml *[money]*; wyciągnąć coś z kogoś infml *[truth]* [13] (contract) zara|zić, -żać się (czymś) *[cold, disease]* [14] (catch) z|łapać *[bus, train]* [15] (have) **to have got sth** mieć coś; **I've got a headache** boli mnie głowa; **to** ~ **the idea that...** zacząć pojmować, że... [16] **I got a surprise** spotkała mnie niespodzianka; **to** ~ **a shock** doznać szoku; **to** ~ **a bang on the head** dostać w głowę [17] (as punishment) dosta|ć, -wać *[five years, fine]* [18] (understand, hear) z|rozumieć [19] infml (annoy) ze|złościć infml; **what** ~**s me is that...** złości mnie, że... [20] (start) **to** ~ **to hear of sth** usłyszeć o czymś; **to** ~ **to know sb** poznać kogoś; **to** ~ **to like sb** polubić kogoś [21] (have opportunity) **do you** ~ **to use the computer?** czy czasem używasz tego komputera? [22] (must) **to have got to do sth** musieć coś zrobić; **it's got to be done** to musi być zrobione [23] (persuade) skł|onić, -aniać; **I got her to talk about her problems** nakłoniłem ją, żeby opowiedziała o swoich problemach [24] **to** ~ **the car repaired** oddać samochód do naprawy; **to** ~ **one's hair cut** ostrzyc się; **to** ~ **the car going** uruchomić samochód; **to** ~ **one's socks wet** zmoczyć or zamoczyć sobie skarpetki; **to** ~ **one's fingers trapped** przyciąć sobie palce

[2] vi [1] (become) sta|ć, -wać się; **it's** ~**ting late** robi się późno; **to** ~ **(oneself) killed** zginąć; **to** ~ **hurt** odnieść obrażenia [2] (become involved) **to** ~ **into sth** infml zająć się czymś; **to** ~ **into a fight** fig wdać się w bójkę [3] (arrive) **to** ~ **somewhere** dotrzeć gdzieś; (on foot) dojść gdzieś; (by vehicle) dojechać gdzieś; **to** ~ **to the airport** dostać się na lotnisko; **how did your coat** ~ **here?** skąd tu

się wziął twój płaszcz?; **how did you** ~ **here?** jak się tu dostałeś?; **where did you** ~ **to?** (on foot) dokąd doszedłeś?; (by vehicle) dokąd dojechałeś? ④ (progress) **I'm** ~ **ting nowhere with this essay** nie idzie mi to wypracowanie; **now we are** ~ **ting somewhere** wreszcie coś się ruszyło ⑤ (put on) włożyć, -kładać *[garment]*

■ **get about:** ① (move) poruszać się ② (travel) podróżować

■ **get across:** ~ **across** [sth] (prze)dostać, -wać się przez (coś) or na drugą stronę czegoś *[river, road]*; przekaz|ać, -ywać *[message]* (**to sb** komuś)

■ **get ahead:** (make progress) posu|nąć, -wać się do przodu

■ **get along:** ① **how are you** ~ting along? (in job, school) jak ci idzie? ② **to** ~ **along with sb** być z kimś w dobrych stosunkach

■ **get around:** ¶ ~ **around** ① = get about ② (manage to do) **I haven't got around to it yet** jeszcze się do tego nie zabrałem; **she'll** ~ **around to visiting us eventually** kiedyś w końcu nas odwiedzi ¶ ~ **around** [sth] obe|jść, -chodzić *[problem, law]*

■ **get at** infml: ① (reach) dob|rać, -ierać się; **to** ~ **at the truth** dowiedzieć się prawdy ② (criticize) nask|oczyć, -akiwać na (kogoś) infml fig ③ (insinuate) **what are you** ~ting **at?** co chcesz przez to powiedzieć?

■ **get away:** ① (leave) wyrwać się infml ② (escape) ucie|c, -kać ③ **to** ~ **away with a crime** uniknąć kary za przestępstwo; **you won't** ~ **away** nie ujdzie ci to na sucho

■ **get away from:** wyrwać się z (czegoś) infml *[town]*; ucie|c, -kać (komuś or przed kimś) *[person]*; **there's no** ~ting **away from it** nie uciekniesz od tego

■ **get back:** ¶ ~ **back** ① (return) (po)wr|ócić, -acać ② (move backwards) cof|nąć, -ać się ¶ ~ **back to** [sth] (po)wr|ócić, -acać do czegoś; **we got back to Belgium** wróciliśmy do Belgii; **to** ~ **back to sleep** ponownie zasnąć; **to** ~ **back to normal** powrócić do normalności ¶ ~ **back to** [sb] (po)wr|ócić, -acać do kogoś; **I'll** ~ **right back to you** (on phone) zaraz do ciebie oddzwonię

■ **get by:** ① (pass) (on foot) prze|jść, -chodzić; (by vehicle) przeje|chać, -żdżać ② (survive) przeżyć; **to** ~ **by on** or **with sth** wyżyć z czegoś

■ **get down:** ¶ ~ **down** (descend) zejść, schodzić (**from** or **out of sth** z czegoś); (on floor) położyć się, kłaść się; (crouch) kuc|nąć, -ać; **to** ~ **down to doing sth** zabrać się or wziąć się do robienia czegoś ¶ ~ **down** [sth] (on foot) zejść z (czegoś), schodzić z (czegoś) *[slope]*; (by vehicle) zje|chać, -żdżać z (czegoś) *[slope]* ¶ ~ [sth] **down** (from height) zd|jąć, -ejmować ~ [sb] **down** infml (depress) zasmu|cić, -ać

■ **get in:** ¶ ~ **in** ① (to building) w|ejść, -chodzić; (to vehicle) wsi|ąść, -adać ② (return home) w|ejść, -chodzić ③ (arrive) *[train, coach]* przyje|chać, -żdżać; *[plane]* przyl|ecieć, -atywać ④ *[water, sunlight]* dosta|ć, -wać się do środka ⑤ (in elections) *[candidate]* prze|jść, -chodzić, zostać, -wać wybranym; *[party]* wejść, wchodzić do parlamentu ⑥ (to school, university) dosta|ć, -wać się ¶ ~ [sth] **in** (buy in) kup|ić, -ować

■ **get into:** ① (enter) w|ejść, -chodzić do (czegoś) *[building]*; wsi|ąść, -adać do (czegoś) *[vehicle]* ② (be admitted) dosta|ć, -wać się do (czegoś) *[club, university]* ③ (squeeze into) w|ejść, -chodzić w (coś) *[garment]*

■ **get off:** ¶ ~ **off** ① (from bus) wysi|ąść, -adać ② (start on journey) wyrusz|yć, -ać ③ (leave work) wy|jść, -chodzić (z pracy) ④ infml (escape punishment) wy-wi|nąć, -jać się infml ⑤ **to** ~ **off to a good start** dobrze zacząć; **to** ~ **off to sleep** zasnąć ¶ ~ **off** [sth] zejść, schodzić z (czegoś) *[wall, subject]*; wysi|ąść, -adać z (czegoś) *[bus]* ¶ **get** [sth] **off** (remove) usu|nąć, -wać

■ **get on:** ¶ ~ **on** ① (climb aboard) wsi|ąść, -adać ② GB (like each other) być ze sobą w dobrych stosunkach ③ (fare) **how did you** ~ **on?** jak ci poszło?; **how are you** ~ting **on?** jak ci idzie? ④ GB (approach) **he's** ~ting **on for 40** dobiega czterdziestki; **it's** ~ting **on for midnight** zbliża się północ ¶ ~ **on** [sth] wsi|ąść, -adać do (czegoś) *[vehicle]* ¶ ~ [sth] **on** (put on) w|łożyć, -kładać *[garment]*; za|łożyć, -kładać *[tyre]*

■ **get on with:** ¶ **to** ~ **on with one's work** dalej pracować ¶ ~ **on with** [sb] GB być w dobrych stosunkach (z kimś)

■ **get out:** ¶ ~ **out** ① (exit) wy|jść, -chodzić (**through** or **by sth** czymś or przez coś); ~ **out!** wynoś się! infml ② (alight) wysi|ąść, -adać ③ *[prisoner]* wy|jść, -chodzić ④ *[news]* wycie|c, -kać na zewnątrz fig ¶ ~ [sth] **out** ① (bring out) wy|jąć, -mować *[handkerchief]*; wyciąg|nąć, -ać *[cork]* ② (remove) wywabi|ć, -ać *[stain]* ③ (borrow) wypożycz|yć, -ać *[library book]*

■ **get out of:** ① (exit) wy|jść, -chodzić z (czegoś) *[building, prison]*; wysi|ąść, -adać z (czegoś) *[vehicle]* ② **to** ~ **out of doing sth** wymigać się od robienia czegoś ③ (quit) pozby|ć, -wać się *[habit]* ④ **what will you** ~ **out of it** co ci to da?; **what do you** ~ **out of your job?** co ci daje twoja praca?

■ **get over:** ① (move) prze|jść, -chodzić przez (coś) *[stream, bridge, fence]*; (by vehicle) przeje|chać, -żdżać przez (coś) *[stream, bridge]* ② (recuperate) do|jść, -chodzić do siebie po (czymś) *[illness, shock]*; **I can't** ~ **over it** (amazed) nie mogę się nadziwić ③ (solve) rozwiąz|ać, -ywać *[problem]*

■ **get round** GB: ¶ ~ **round** = get around ¶ ~ **round** [sb] infml ur|obić, -abiać (kogoś)

■ **get through:** ¶ ~ **through** ① (squeeze) prze-

dosta|ć, -wać się, przecis|ną|ć, -kać się $\boxed{2}$ **to** ∼
through to sb (on phone) dodzwonić się do kogoś;
(communicate with) do|trzeć, -cierać do (kogoś) fig
$\boxed{3}$ *[supplies, news]* do|trzeć, -cierać $\boxed{4}$ *[examinee]*
zdać ¶ ∼ **through** *[sth]* $\boxed{1}$ (manage) prze|jść,
-chodzić przez (coś) *[exam]*; s|kończyć *[book, meal]*
$\boxed{2}$ (use) zj|eść, -adać *[food]*; wyda|ć, -wać *[money]*

■ **get together**: ¶ ∼ **together** (assemble) z|ebrać,
-bierać się (**about** or **over sth** w związku z czymś)
¶ ∼ **[sb/sth] together** z|ebrać, -bierać *[people]*;
s|tworzyć *[company]*

■ **get up**: ¶ ∼ **up** $\boxed{1}$ (from bed, chair) wsta|ć, -wać
(**from sth** z czegoś) $\boxed{2}$ (on ledge, wall) w|ejść,
-chodzić $\boxed{3}$ *[storm, wind]* wzm|óc, -agać się $\boxed{4}$ **what
what did you** ∼ **up to?** fig (enjoyment) co tam
zwojowałeś? infml; (mischief) co tam zmalowałeś? infml
¶ ∼ **up [sth]** $\boxed{1}$ (climb) w|ejść, -chodzić na (coś)
[hill, ladder] $\boxed{2}$ (increase) zwiększ|yć, -ać *[speed]*

get-together /'gettəgeðə(r)/ *n* spotkanie *n*
ghastly /'gɑːstlɪ, US 'gæstlɪ/ *adj* koszmarny;
[person, family] okropny
gherkin /'gɜːkɪn/ *n* korniszon *m*
ghetto /'getəʊ/ *n* getto *n*
ghetto blaster *n* infml (duży) przenośny radiomagnetofon *m*
ghost /gəʊst/ *n* duch *m*
giant /'dʒaɪənt/ $\boxed{I}$ *n* olbrzym *m*
$\boxed{II}$ *adj* olbrzymi
gibberish /'dʒɪbərɪʃ/ *n* jazgotanie *n*, jazgot *m*
giddy /'gɪdɪ/ *adj* $\boxed{1}$ **I feel** ∼ kręci mi się w głowie
$\boxed{2}$ *[speed]* zawrotny; *[height]* przyprawiający o zawrót głowy
gift /gɪft/ *n* $\boxed{1}$ (present) upominek *m*; **to give sb a** ∼
dać komuś prezent; **to give sb a** ∼ **of money** dać
komuś pieniądze w prezencie $\boxed{2}$ (for charity) dar *m*
$\boxed{3}$ (talent) dar *m* (**for doing sth** robienia czegoś)
gifted /'gɪftɪd/ *adj* uzdolniony
gift shop *n* sklep *m* z upominkami
gift token, gift voucher GB *n* bon *m* towarowy
(jako prezent)
gift wrap /'gɪftræp/ *n* ozdobny papier *m* do
pakowania
gig /gɪg/ *n* infml występ *m*
gigantic /dʒaɪ'gæntɪk/ *adj* gigantyczny
giggle /'gɪgl/ $\boxed{I}$ *n* (chuckle) chichot *m*; **to get the**
∼ **s** zaśmiewać się
$\boxed{II}$ *vi* za|chichotać
gilt /gɪlt/ $\boxed{I}$ *n* złocenie *n*
$\boxed{II}$ *pp adj* złocony, pozłacany
gimmick /'gɪmɪk/ *n* (trick) chwyt *m*; (object) gadżet *m*
gin /dʒɪn/ *n* (drink) gin *m*, dżin *m*
ginger /'dʒɪndʒə(r)/ *n* $\boxed{1}$ Bot, Culin imbir *m*; **root** or
fresh ∼ świeży imbir $\boxed{2}$ (colour) (kolor *m*) rudy *m*
ginger-haired /ˌdʒɪndʒə'heəd/ *adj* rudy, rudo-
włosy

girl /gɜːl/ *n* $\boxed{1}$ (child) dziewczynka *f*; (teenager, woman)
dziewczyna *f*; **baby** ∼ dziewczynka; **little** ∼
dziewczynka $\boxed{2}$ (daughter) córka *f*
girlfriend /'gɜːlfrend/ *n* (sweetheart) dziewczyna *f*,
sympatia *f*; (friend) koleżanka *f*; (close) przyjaciółka *f*
girl guide GB, **girl scout** US *n* skautka *f*
giro /'dʒaɪrəʊ/ *n* (system) system *m* przelewowy;
(cheque) *przekaz pocztowy z zasiłkiem*
gist /dʒɪst/ *n* istota *f*, sedno *n*
give /gɪv/ $\boxed{I}$ *n* rubber has a lot of ∼ guma jest
bardzo elastyczna
$\boxed{II}$ *vt* da|ć, -wać
$\boxed{III}$ *vi [mattress, branch]* ugi|ąć, -nać się

■ **give away**: ¶ ∼ **[sth] away** $\boxed{1}$ rozda|ć, -wać
[items, samples] $\boxed{2}$ (reveal) zdradz|ić, -ać *[secret]*
$\boxed{3}$ (lose carelessly) odda|ć, -wać (za darmo) *[point,
game]* (**to sb** komuś); z|marnować *[advantage]* ¶
∼ **[sb] away** wyda|ć, -wać *[person]* (**to sb**
komuś); *[expression, fingerprints]* zdradz|ić, -ać; **to**
∼ **oneself away** zdradzić się

■ **give back**: odda|ć, -wać, zwr|ócić, -acać (**to sb**
komuś)

■ **give in**: ¶ ∼ **in** $\boxed{1}$ (yield) ule|c, -gać (**to sb/sth**
komuś/czemuś) $\boxed{2}$ (stop trying) podda|ć, -wać się;
I ∼ **in** – tell me podda|ję się, powiedz mi! ¶ ∼
[sth] in odda|ć, -wać *[work, ticket]*

■ **give off**: wydziel|ić, -ać *[fumes, radiation, heat]*;
wys|łać, -yłać *[signal, light]*

■ **give out**: ¶ ∼ **out** *[strength]* wyczerp|ać, -ywać
się; *[engine]* po|psuć się ¶ ∼ **[sth] out** (distribute)
rozda|ć, -wać *[books, leaflets]* (**to sb** komuś)

■ **give up**: ¶ ∼ **up** podda|ć, -wać się; **to** ∼ **up
on sb/sth** dać sobie spokój z kimś/czymś *[diet,
crossword, pupil]*; przestać liczyć na kogoś *[partner,
friend]* ¶ ∼ **up [sth]** $\boxed{1}$ (renounce) z|rezygnować
z (czegoś) *[job, claim]*; poświęc|ić, -ać *[free time]*; **to**
∼ **up smoking/drinking** przestać palić/pić
$\boxed{2}$ (abandon) z|rezygnować z (czegoś) *[search]*; po-
rzuc|ić, -ać *[hope, struggle, idea]* $\boxed{3}$ (surrender) odda|ć,
-wać *[territory]*; ust|ąpić, -ępować *[seat]* ¶ ∼ **[sb]
up** $\boxed{1}$ (hand over) wyda|ć, -wać *[person]* (**to sb**
komuś); **to** ∼ **oneself up to sb** oddać się
w ręce kogoś $\boxed{2}$ (resign) z|erwać, -rywać z (kimś)
[lover]

■ **give way**: $\boxed{1}$ (collapse) *[bridge, ice]* załam|ać,
-ywać się; *[fence]* zawal|ić, -ać się; *[rope]* z|erwać,
-rywać się; **her legs gave way** nogi się pod nią
ugięły $\boxed{2}$ GB (when driving) ust|ąpić, -ępować pierw-
szeństwa (**to sb** komuś) $\boxed{3}$ (yield) ust|ąpić, -ępować
(**to sb/sth** komuś/czemuś)

$\boxed{\text{IDIOMS}}$ ∼ **or take an inch or two** mniej więcej;
to ∼ **and take** iść na ustępstwa; **to** ∼ **as good
as one gets** nie pozostawać dłużnym; **to** ∼ **it all
one's got** infml dać z siebie wszystko

give-and-take /ˌgɪvn'teɪk/ *n* wzajemne ustępstwa *n pl*

giveaway /'gɪvəweɪ/ *n* **the name is a** ~ sama nazwa wiele mówi

given /'gɪvn/ **Ⅰ** *adj* 1 (specified) dany; **at any** ~ **moment** w dowolnym momencie 2 **to be** ~ **to sth/doing sth** mieć skłonność do czegoś/robienia czegoś; **I'm not** ~ **to losing my temper** na ogół trudno wyprowadzić mnie z równowagi **Ⅱ** *prep* 1 (in view of) ~ **(the fact) that...** przyjmując, że... 2 (with) ~ **the right training** przy odpowiednim treningu; ~ **an opportunity I'll tell her** jeżeli nadarzy się okazja, powiem jej **given name** *n* imię *n*

glad /glæd/ *adj* zadowolony (**about sth** z czegoś); **he was only too** ~ **to help** bardzo chętnie pomógł

gladly /'glædlɪ/ *adv* (willingly) chętnie; (with pleasure) z przyjemnością

glamorize /'glæməraɪz/ *vt* upiększ|yć, -ać *[person, room]*; dodać, -wać splendoru (czemuś) *[place]*; gloryfikować *[event]*

glamorous /'glæmərəs/ *adj* *[woman, dress, look]* efektowny; *[job]* prestiżowy; *[occasion]* uroczysty

glamour GB, **glamor** US /'glæmə(r)/ *n* (of person) atrakcyjność *f*; (of travel) urok *m*; (of job) splendor *m*

glance /glɑːns, US glæns/ **Ⅰ** *n* rzut *m* oka **Ⅱ** *vi* zerk|nąć, -ać (**at sb/sth** na kogoś/coś); **to** ~ **around a room** rozejrzeć się po pokoju ■ **glance off**: *[bullet, stone]* odbić, -jać się od (czegoś)

glancing /'glɑːnsɪŋ, US 'glænsɪŋ/ *adj [kick]* po przekątnej; **a** ~ **blow** cios częściowo chybiony

gland /glænd/ *n* gruczoł *m*; (lymph node) węzeł *m* chłonny; **swollen** ~s powiększone węzły chłonne

glandular fever /ˌglændjʊlə'fiːvə(r)/ *n* mononukleoza *f* zakaźna

glare /gleə(r)/ **Ⅰ** *n* 1 (angry look) gniewne spojrzenie *n* 2 (from lights) oślepiające światło *n* **Ⅱ** *vi* s|piorunować wzrokiem (**at sb** kogoś)

glaring /'gleərɪŋ/ *adj* 1 *[error, injustice]* rażący 2 *[light]* oślepiający

glass /glɑːs, US glæs/ **Ⅰ** *n* 1 (substance) szkło *n*; (for wine) kieliszek *m*; (for beer, water) szklanka *f* 2 (mirror) lustro *n* **Ⅱ** *adj* szklany **Ⅲ** **glasses** *npl* 1 (spectacles) okulary *plt* 2 (binoculars) lornetka *f*

glass ceiling *n* bariera *f* kulturowa

glassy-eyed /ˌglɑːsɪ'aɪd, US ˌglæs-/ *adj* (from illness, drink) o szklistym spojrzeniu; (hostile) o lodowatym spojrzeniu

glaze /gleɪz/ **Ⅰ** *n* (on pottery) glazura *f*, szkliwo *n*; Culin polewa *f* **Ⅱ** *vt* glazurować *[pottery]*; Culin pol|lać, -ewać polewą *[pastry]*

glazed /gleɪzd/ *adj [door]* oszklony; **to have a** ~ **look in one's eyes** patrzeć szklistym or szklanym wzrokiem

gleam /gliːm/ **Ⅰ** *n* (of moon, stars) poświata *f*; (of polished surface) poblask *m*; (of sunshine) blask *m* **Ⅱ** *vi [light]* świecić się; *[leather, water]* lśnić; *[eyes, metal]* błyszczeć

gleaming /'gliːmɪŋ/ *adj [surface]* lśniący; *[eyes, jewel]* błyszczący; *[room]* lśniący (czystością)

glide /glaɪd/ *vi* sunąć (**on/over sth** po czymś); (in air) po|szybować

glider /'glaɪdə(r)/ *n* szybowiec *m*

gliding /'glaɪdɪŋ/ *n* szybownictwo *n*

glimpse /glɪmps/ **Ⅰ** *n* 1 (sight) mignięcie *n*; **I caught a** ~ **of him** mignął mi (przed oczami) 2 (insight) **to give a** ~ **into sth** pozwalać zrozumieć coś; **to get a** ~ **of sth** zorientować się w czymś **Ⅱ** *vt* **he** ~**d her face among the crowd** w tłumie mignęła mu jej twarz

glisten /'glɪsn/ *vi [sweat, fur, eyes]* za|lśnić

glitch /glɪtʃ/ *n* infml usterka *f*; Comput krótkotrwałe zakłócenie *n*

glitter /'glɪtə(r)/ **Ⅰ** *n* 1 (decorative) brokat *m* 2 (of diamonds, gold) blask *m*; (of frost) skrzenie się *n*; (of star) migotanie *n* **Ⅱ** *vi [star, frost, eyes]* skrzyć się; *[gold]* bły|snąć, -szczeć

gloat /gləʊt/ *vi* chełpić się (**at** or **over sth** czymś)

global /'gləʊbl/ *adj* globalny; *[market]* światowy; *[discussion, analysis]* całościowy

global warming *n* globalne ocieplenie *n* (klimatu)

globe /gləʊb/ *n* 1 **the** ~ kula *f* ziemska 2 (model) globus *m*

gloom /gluːm/ *n* 1 (darkness) mrok *m* 2 (dejection) przygnębienie *n* (**about** or **over sth** z powodu czegoś)

gloomy /'gluːmɪ/ *adj* 1 (dark) mroczny 2 *[person, face, voice, news]* ponury

glorify /'glɔːrɪfaɪ/ *vt* wysławiać, sławić

glorious /'glɔːrɪəs/ *adj* cudowny; *[victory, achievement, leader]* wielki; *[deed]* wspaniały

glory /'glɔːrɪ/ **Ⅰ** *n* 1 (honour) chwała *f* 2 (splendour) świetność *f* **Ⅱ** *vi* **to** ~ **in sth** chlubić się or szczycić się czymś

gloss /glɒs/ *n* 1 (shine) połysk *m* 2 (paint) emalia *f* ■ **gloss over**: prześliz(g)|nąć, -giwać się po (czymś) *[problem, issue]*; zatuszow|ać, -ywać *[defect, fact]*

glossary /'glɒsərɪ/ *n* słowniczek *m*

glossy /'glɒsɪ/ *adj [material, photo]* błyszczący; *[hair]* lśniący; *[brochure]* luksusowo wydany

glossy magazine *n* ilustrowany magazyn *m* (z górnej półki)

glove /glʌv/ *n* rękawiczka *f*; (in sports or very big) rękawica *f*

glove compartment *n* schowek *m* (w samochodzie)

glow /gləʊ/ **[]** *n* ① (from fire, of candle) blask *m*; (of moon) poświata *f* ② (on face) rumieńce *m pl*
Ⅱ *vi* ① *[ember, cigarette, metal]* żarzyć się; *[lamp]* świecić (się) ② **to ~ with health** *[person]* tryskać zdrowiem
glower /ˈglaʊə(r)/ *vi* po|patrzeć spode łba (**at sb/ sth** na kogoś/coś)
glowing /ˈgləʊɪŋ/ *adj* ① *[ember]* żarzący się; *[cheeks, face]* (from exercise) zaróżowiony; (from pleasure) zarumieniony ② *[account, description]* entuzjastyczny
glue /gluː/ **[]** *n* klej *m*
Ⅱ *vt* **to ~ sth down** or **on** zakleić coś *[envelope]*; przykleić coś *[lining]*
Ⅲ glued *pp adj* infm **she is ~d to the TV** siedzi przyklejona do telewizora; **~d to the spot** przykuty do miejsca fig
glue sniffer *n* wąchacz *m* kleju
glue-sniffing /ˈgluːsnɪfɪŋ/ *n* wąchanie *m* kleju
glut /glʌt/ *n* nadmiar *m*, zalew *m*
glutton /ˈglʌtn/ *n* żarłok *m*
glycerin(e) /ˈglɪsəriːn, US -rɪn/ *n* gliceryna *f*
GMT *n* = **Greenwich Mean Time** czas *m* uniwersalny or Greenwich
gnash /næʃ/ *vt* **to ~ one's teeth** zgrzytać zębami
gnaw /nɔː/ **[]** *vt* obgry|źć, -zać *[bone, wood]*
Ⅱ *vi* ① **to ~ at** or **on sth** obgry|źć, -zać coś ② **to ~ at sb** *[hunger]* dręczyć; *[pain]* nękać; *[remorse]* gryźć, dręczyć
GNP *n* = **gross national product** PNB *m/n*
GNVQ *n* = **General National Vocational Qualification** *dyplom ukończenia zawodowych kursów kwalifikacyjnych*
go /gəʊ/ **[]** *vi* ① (on foot) pójść, iść; (habitually) chodzić; (from time to time) chadzać; (by vehicle) po|jechać; (habitually) jeździć; **they went home** poszli do domu; **to go to California** pojechać do Kalifornii; **to go to town/to the country** pojechać do miasta/na wieś; **to go on holiday** pojechać na wakacje; **to go for a drink** pójść na drinka; **to go to school/work** chodzić do szkoły/ pracy; **to go to the doctor's** pójść do lekarza ② (depart) pójść, iść; (by vehicle) po|jechać ③ (become) **to go red** poczerwienieć; **to go white** zblednąć; **to go mad** oszaleć ④ (be, remain) **to go unnoticed** przejść niezauważonym; **the question went unanswered** pytanie pozostało bez odpowiedzi ⑤ (become impaired) **his memory/voice is going** traci pamięć/głos; **the battery is going** akumulator wysiada ⑥ (of time) mi|nąć, -jać ⑦ (operate, function) *[vehicle, machine, clock]* chodzić; **to set sth going** uruchomić coś; **to keep going** *[business]* iść; *[machine]* pracować; *[person]* trzymać się ⑧ (belong, be placed) pójść, iść infm; **where do these plates go?** co zrobić z tymi talerzami?; **it won't go into the box** to nie wejdzie do pudełka; **five into four won't go** cztery nie dzieli się przez pięć ⑨ (be about to) **to be going to do sth** zamierzać coś zrobić; **it's**

going to rain będzie padać ⑩ (turn out) pójść, iść infml; **the party went very well** przyjęcie było bardzo udane ⑪ (make sound, perform action or movement) zrobić; *[bell, alarm]* za|dzwonić; **she went like this with her fingers** zrobiła tak palcami ⑫ (take one's turn) **you go next** potem ty; **you go first** najpierw ty ⑬ (match) **to go together** *[colours]* pasować do siebie
Ⅱ *vt* przeby|ć, -wać *[miles, kilometers]*
Ⅲ *n* GB (turn) kolej *f*; (try) próba *f*; **whose go is it?** czyja (teraz) kolej?

■ **go about:** zab|rać, -ierać się do (czegoś) *[task]*; **to go about one's business** zajmować się swoimi sprawami
■ **go ahead:** *[event]* przebiegać; **go ahead!** proszę bardzo, słuchamy!; **go ahead and shoot!** no dalej, strzelaj!; **they are going ahead with the project** będą realizować ten projekt
■ **go along:** iść; (by vehicle) jechać; **to make sth up as one goes along** fig wymyślić coś na poczekaniu
■ **go along with:** zg|odzić, -adzać się z (kimś/ czymś) *[person, view]*; zg|odzić, -adzać się na (coś), przysta|ć, -wać na (coś) *[plan]*
■ **go around:** ① *[person]* chodzić; (by vehicle) jeździć; **they go around everywhere together** wszędzie razem chodzą ② *[rumour]* krążyć
■ **go away** wyje|chać, -żdżać; (walk away) od|ejść, -chodzić; (drive off) odje|chać, -żdżać; **go away!** idź sobie!
■ **go back:** ① (return) wr|ócić, -acać; (turn back) zawr|ócić, -acać; **to go back to sleep** zasnąć ponownie; **to go back to work** zabrać się z powrotem do pracy ② (in time) cof|nąć się, -ać się; **to go back 20 years** cofnąć się o 20 lat; **this tradition goes back a century** ta tradycja ma już sto lat ③ (revert) wr|ócić, -acać (**to sth** do czegoś)
■ **go back on:** cof|nąć, -ać *[promise, decision]*
■ **go by:** ¶ **go by** *[person]* prze|jść, -chodzić; (by vehicle) przeje|chać, -żdżać; **as time goes by** w miarę upływu czasu ¶ **go by [sth]** sądzić po (czymś) *[appearances]*; **to go by the rules** przestrzegać zasad
■ **go down:** ¶ **go down** ① (descend) zejść, schodzić; (by vehicle) zje|chać, -żdżać; *[sun]* za|jść, -chodzić ② **to go down well/badly** zostać dobrze/źle przyjętym ③ *[standard]* obniż|yć, -ać się; *[temperature, price]* spa|ść, -dać ④ *[swelling]* ust|ąpić, -ępować; **the tyre went down** z opony uszło powietrze ⑤ *[computer, system]* pa|ść, -dać infml ¶ **go down [sth]** zejść, schodzić z (czegoś); (by vehicle) zje|chać, -żdżać z (czegoś)
■ **go for:** ¶ **go for [sb/sth]** ① infml (be keen on) lubić ② (apply to) dotyczyć kogoś/czegoś ¶ **go for [sb]** ① (attack) rzuc|ić, -ać się na (kogoś); (verbally) nask|oczyć, -akiwać na (kogoś) infml ② **he has a**

lot going for him wiele za nim przemawia ¶ **go for [sth]** ① (try) s|próbować dostać *[job]*; s|próbować zdobyć *[honour]*; **to go for victory** spróbować zwyciężyć; **she's going for the world record** chce pobić rekord świata; **go for it!** infml dawaj, dawaj! infml ② (choose) z|decydować się na coś

■ **go in:** ① (enter) w|ejść, -chodzić ② *[troops]* wkr|oczyć, -aczać ③ *[sun]* s|chować się

■ **go in for:** ① (be keen on) lubić ② (participate) przyst|ąpić, -ępować do (czegoś) *[exam]*; wy|startować w (czymś) *[competition]*

■ **go into:** ① (enter) w|ejść, -chodzić do (czegoś); (take up) zająć się (czymś) *[politics, business]* ② (examine) z|badać

■ **go off:** ¶ **go off** ① *[bomb]* wybuch|nąć, -ać ② *[alarm clock]* za|dzwonić; *[fire alarm]* włącz|yć, -ać się ③ (leave) od|ejść, -chodzić; (by vehicle) odje|chać, -żdżać ④ GB *[milk, cream, meat, butter]* ze|psuć się; *[performer, athlete]* wy|jść, -chodzić z formy ⑤ *[lights]* z|gasnąć; *[heating]* wyłącz|yć, -ać się ⑥ (happen) **to go off very well** *[organized event]* bardzo się udać ¶ **go off [sb/sth]** GB **I've gone off whisky** zbrzydła mi whisky

■ **go on:** ¶ **go on** ① (happen) **how long has this been going on?** jak długo to już trwa? ② (continue on one's way) pójść, iść dalej; (by vehicle) po|jechać dalej ③ (continue) kontynuować; **the list goes on and on** lista ciągnie się w nieskończoność ④ (of time) **as time went on...** w miarę upływu czasu...; **as the evening went on...** w miarę jak upływał wieczór... ⑤ (keep talking) **to go on about sth** ciągle o czymś mówić ⑥ (proceed) **to go on to sth** przejść do czegoś; **he went on to say that...** następnie powiedział, że... ⑦ *[lights]* zapal|ić, -ać się; *[heating]* włącz|yć, -ać się ⑧ *[actor]* w|ejść, -chodzić (na scenę) ¶ **go on [sth]** op|rzeć, -ierać się na (czymś) *[evidence, information]*; **that's all we've got to go on** wiemy tylko tyle

■ **go on at:** ¶ **go on at [sb]** krytykować w kółko (kogoś) infml

■ **go out:** ① (leave) wy|jść, -chodzić; (travel) wy-je|chać, -żdżać; **to go out for a drink** pójść na drinka ② **to go out with sb** chodzić z kimś ③ **the tide is going out** jest odpływ ④ *[light, fire]* z|gasnąć

■ **go over:** ¶ **go over** (cross over) pod|ejść, -chodzić (**to sb/sth** do kogoś/czegoś) ¶ **go over [sth]** ① (check) prze|jrzeć, -glądać *[accounts, figures, article]*; sprawdz|ić, -ać *[facts, details]* ② (exceed) przekr|oczyć, -aczać

■ **go round:** GB: ¶ **go round** ① *[wheel]* obr|ócić, -acać się, kręcić się ② **to go round to see sb** wpaść do kogoś ③ *[rumour]* krążyć ④ (make detour) prze|jść, -chodzić naokoło; (by vehicle) przeje|chać, -żdżać naokoło ¶ **go round [sth]** (visit) ob|ejść, -chodzić; (by vehicle) obje|chać, -żdżać *[shops, museums]*

■ **go through:** ¶ **go through** *[law]* prze|jść, -chodzić; *[business deal]* zostać zawartym ¶ **go through [sth]** ① (experience) prze|jść, -chodzić przez (coś) *[stage, phase]*; przeży|ć, -wać *[experience]*; **she's gone through a lot** wiele przeszła ② (check) prze|jrzeć, -glądać *[documents, files]* ③ (search) przeszuk|ać, -iwać *[belongings]* ④ (perform) załatwi|ć, -ać *[formalities]* ⑤ (use up) wyda|ć, -wać *[money]*; **we went through three bottles of wine** opróżniliśmy trzy butelki wina

■ **go through with:** z|realizować, wykon|ać, -ywać *[plan]*; **I can't go through with it** nie mogę tego zrobić

■ **go under:** *[ship]* pójść, iść na dno

■ **go up:** ¶ **go up** ① *[person]* w|ejść, -chodzić; **to go up to bed** pójść się położyć ② *[price, temperature]* wz|rosnąć; *[curtain]* podn|ieść, -osić się ¶ **go up [sth]** w|ejść, -chodzić na (coś) *[mountain]*; (by vehicle) wje|chać, -żdżać na (coś)

■ **go without:** ¶ **go without** (suffer lack) **you'll just have to go without** będziesz się musiał bez tego obejść ¶ **go without [sth]** oby|ć, -wać się bez (czegoś)

⟨IDIOMS:⟩ **to make a go of sth** rozkręcić interes; **she's always on the go** jest bez przerwy w ruchu; **in one go** za jednym zamachem; **it goes without saying that...** rozumie się samo przez się, że...; **as the saying goes** jak to się mówi; **anythings goes** wszystkie chwyty dozwolone

go-ahead /'gəʊəhed/ *n* infml **to give sb the ~ to do sth** dać komuś zgodę na zrobienie czegoś; **to get the ~ from sb** uzyskać zgodę kogoś

goal /gəʊl/ *n* (enclosed space) bramka *f*; (act of scoring or score) gol *m*

goalkeeper /'gəʊl‚ki:pə(r)/ *n* bramka|rz *m*, -rka *f*

goalpost /'gəʊlpəʊst/ *n* słupek *m* (bramki)

goat /gəʊt/ *n* koza *f*; (male) kozioł *m*, cap *m*

gobble /'gɒbl/ Ⅰ *vi* (also ~ **down**, ~ **up**) poż|reć, -erać *[food]*

Ⅱ *vi [turkey]* za|gulgotać

gobbledygook /'gɒbldɪgu:k/ *n* infml bełkot *m* infml

go-between /'gəʊbɪtwi:n/ *n* pośredni|k *m*, -czka *f*

gobsmacked /'gɒbsmækt/ *adj* GB infml **he was ~** zatkało go infml

god /gɒd/ *n* bóg *m*; **God** Bóg

godchild /'gɒdtʃaɪld/ *n* chrześnia|k *m*, -czka *f*

goddaughter /'gɒdɔ:tə(r)/ *n* chrześniaczka *f*

goddess /'gɒdɪs/ *n* bogini *f*

godfather /'gɒdfɑ:ðə(r)/ *n* (ojciec *m*) chrzestny *m*

godmother /'gɒdmʌðə(r)/ *n* (matka *f*) chrzestna *f*

godparent /'gɒdpeərənt/ *n* chrzestn|y *m*, -a *f*; **the ~s** (rodzice) chrzestni

godsend /'gɒdsend/ *n* dar *m* niebios fig

godson /'gɒdsʌn/ *n* chrześniak *m*

goggles /'gɒglz/ *npl* gogle *plt*; (for swimming) okulary *plt* pływackie

going /ˈgəʊɪŋ/ **❚** n ❑ (of bus, train, car) odjazd m ❑ (progress) **that's good** ~! niezłe tempo!; **it was slow** ~ (on journey) strasznie się dłużyło; (at work) szło opornie; **the conversation was heavy** ~ to była ciężka rozmowa ❑ **when the** ~ **gets tough** kiedy zaczynają się kłopoty; **they got out while the** ~ **was good** wycofali się w dobrym momencie **❚❚** adj ❑ [price, rate] aktualny ❑ ~ **concern** prosperująca firma ❑ **it's the best model** ~ to najlepszy model na rynku

goings-on /ˌgəʊɪŋzˈɒn/ npl infml (events) sprawy f pl; (behaviour) postępowanie n

go-kart /ˈgəʊkɑːt/ n (go)kart m

gold /gəʊld/ **❚** n złoto n **❚❚** adj [jewellery, medal] złoty; [ore, ingot] złota ɪᴅɪᴏᴍs: **he is as good as** ~ to złoty człowiek; **to be worth one's weight in** ~ być nieocenionym

gold dust n złoty pył m; **to be like** ~ fig rzadko się trafiać

golden /ˈgəʊldən/ adj ❑ (made of gold) złoty ❑ (gold-coloured) złoty, złocisty ❑ [age, years] złoty; **a** ~ **opportunity** wielka szansa

golden handshake n GB hojna odprawa f

golden rule n złota zasada f

goldfish /ˈgəʊldfɪʃ/ n karaś m złocisty

gold medal n złoty medal m

gold mine n kopalnia f złota; fig żyła f złota fig

gold-plated /ˌgəʊldˈpleɪtɪd/ adj pozłacany

gold rush n gorączka f złota

goldsmith /ˈgəʊldsmɪθ/ n złotnik m

golf /gɒlf/ n Sport golf m

golf club n ❑ (place) klub m golfowy ❑ (stick) kij m golfowy

golf course n pole n golfowe

golfer /ˈgɒlfə(r)/ n golfist|a m, -ka f

gone /gɒn/ adj ❑ **he is** ~ (departed) wyjechał; (dead) odszedł euph ❑ GB (past) **it's** ~ **six o'clock** jest po szóstej

gong /gɒŋ/ n gong m

good /gʊd/ **❚** n ❑ (virtue) dobro n; **to be up to no** ~ kombinować infml ❑ (benefit) dobro n; **it didn't do my migraine any** ~ to mi nie pomogło na migrenę ❑ (use) **it's no** ~ **crying** nie ma co płakać **❚❚** adj ❑ (enjoyable, high quality, beneficial) dobry; [day, party] udany; [weather] ładny; **I don't feel too** ~ nie czuję się najlepiej; **the** ~ **thing is that...** dobrze, że...; **it tastes** ~ to jest dobre; **to smell** ~ smakowicie pachnieć; **to look** ~ smakowicie wyglądać; **we had a** ~ **laugh** serdecznie się uśmialiśmy ❑ (competent) **she's a** ~ **singer** ona ma dobry głos; **to be** ~ **at sth** być dobrym z czegoś [Latin, physics]; dobrze grać w coś [chess, badminton]; **to be** ~ **with sb/sth** dobrze sobie radzić z kimś/czymś [children, animals] ❑ (well behaved) grzeczny ❑ (fortunate) **it's a** ~ **job** or **thing**

(that)... dobrze (że)... ❑ infml **to wait for a** ~ **hour** czekać dobrą godzinę **❚❚❚** excl dobrze!; (with relief) jak dobrze!

❚Ⅴ as **good as** adv phr w zasadzie; **to be as** ~ **as new** być jak nowy

Ⅴ for good adv phr na dobre, na zawsze ɪᴅɪᴏᴍs: ~ **for you!** bardzo dobrze!; **it's too good to be true** to zbyt piękne, żeby było prawdziwe

good afternoon excl (in greeting) dzień dobry; (in farewell) do widzenia

goodbye /gʊdˈbaɪ/ excl do widzenia!

good evening excl (on meeting) dobry wieczór; (on parting) dobranoc

good-for-nothing /ˈgʊdfənʌθɪŋ/ n nicdobrego m/f inv

good-humoured GB, **good-humored** US /ˌgʊdˈhjuːməd/ adj [crowd] rozbawiony; [smile, discussion] wesoły; [remark] żartobliwy; [rivalry] przyjacielski; **to be** ~ (of mood) być w dobrym humorze; (of character) być pogodnym

good-looking /ˌgʊdˈlʊkɪŋ/ adj [man] przystojny; [woman] atrakcyjny

good morning excl (in greeting) dzień dobry; (in farewell) do widzenia

good-natured /ˌgʊdˈneɪtʃəd/ adj [person] dobroduszny; [child] pogodny; [animal] łagodny

goodness /ˈgʊdnɪs/ **❚** n ❑ (virtue, kindness) dobroć f ❑ (of food, drink) **to be full of** ~ (food, drink) być bardzo zdrowe **❚❚** excl (also ~ **gracious**) o mój Boże! ɪᴅɪᴏᴍs: **for** ~' **sake** na miłość boską!

goodnight /gʊdˈnaɪt/ excl dobranoc

goods /gʊdz/ npl towary m pl

goods train n GB pociąg m towarowy

goodwill /gʊdˈwɪl/ n ❑ (kindness) życzliwość f ❑ (of business) renoma f firmy

goose /guːs/ n gęś f

gooseberry /ˈgʊzbərɪ, US ˈguːsberɪ/ n agrest m ɪᴅɪᴏᴍs: **to be a** or **play** ~ odgrywać przyzwoitkę

goose pimples /ˈguːspɪmplz/ npl gęsia skórka f

gorge /gɔːdʒ/ **❚** n wąwóz m, parów m; (of river) przełom m **❚❚** vr **to** ~ **oneself** ob|eżreć, -żerać się infml (**on sth** czymś)

gorgeous /ˈgɔːdʒəs/ adj ❑ infml [meal] wyborny; [weather] cudowny; [woman, baby] zachwycający ❑ (magnificent) olśniewający

gorilla /gəˈrɪlə/ n goryl m

gorse /gɔːs/ n kolcolist m (zachodni)

gory /ˈgɔːrɪ/ adj [battle] krwawy; [film] pełen przemocy

gosh /gɒʃ/ excl infml o rety!

go-slow /gəʊˈsləʊ/ n GB strajk m włoski

gospel /ˈgɒspl/ n Ewangelia f

gossip /ˈgɒsɪp/ **❚** n ❑ (news) plotki f pl (**about sb/sth** o kimś/czymś, na temat kogoś/czegoś) ❑ (person) plotka|rz m, -rka f

II *vi* po|plotkować (**about sb/sth** o kimś/czymś; na temat kogoś/czegoś)

gossip column *n* rubryka *f* towarzyska

got: **to have got** *phr* [1] **to have** ~ mieć [2] **I've** ~ **to go** muszę już iść

gourd /gʊəd/ *n* tykwa *f*

gout /gaʊt/ *n* podagra *f*, dna *f*

govern /'gʌvn/ **I** *vt* [1] (rule) rządzić (czymś) *[country, state, city]*; zarządzać (czymś) *[province, colony]* [2] (control) *[law]* rządzić (czymś) [3] (determine) kierować (czymś) *[actions]*; wpły|nąć, -wać na (coś) *[decision]*

II *vi [parliament, president]* rządzić

governess /'gʌvənɪs/ *n* guwernantka *f*

governing /'gʌvənɪŋ/ *adj [party, class]* rządzący; **the ~ principle** podstawowa zasada

government /'gʌvənmənt/ **I** *n* rząd *m*; **to be in** ~ być u władzy

II *adj [minister, plan, majority]* rządowy; *[policy]* rządu; *[funds, borrowing]* państwowy; ~ **expenditure** wydatki państwa

governmental /ˌgʌvən'mentl/ *adj* rządowy

governor /'gʌvənə(r)/ *n* (of state, colony) gubernator *m*; GB (of bank) ≈ prezes *m*; (of prison) naczelnik *m*; (of school, hospital) członek *m* zarządu; (of university) członek *m* władz uniwersytetu

gown /gaʊn/ *n* (dress) suknia *f*; (of judge, academic) toga *f*; (of surgeon) fartuch *m*, kitel *m*

GP *n* = **general practitioner** lekarz *m* pierwszego kontaktu

grab /græb/ **I** *vt* (also ~ **hold of**) z|łapać, chwy|cić, -tać *[money, object]*; s|korzystać z (czegoś) *[chance, opportunity]*; **to** ~ **sb by the arm** złapać kogoś za rękę

II *vi* **to** ~ **at sth** rzucić się na coś

grace /greɪs/ *n* [1] (charm) wdzięk *m*; **sb's saving** ~ pozytywna cecha kogoś [2] (time allowance) **to give sb two days'** ~ dać komuś jeszcze dwa dni [3] (prayer) **to say** ~ odmówić modlitwę *(przed lub po posiłku)* ⟨IDIOMS:⟩ **to be full of airs and** ~**s** pej pysznić się

graceful /'greɪsfl/ *adj* [1] *[dancer, movement]* pełen wdzięku [2] *[person]* elegancki

grade /greɪd/ **I** *n* [1] (quality) klasa *f*, gatunek *m*; **high-/low-**~ **meat** wysokogatunkowe/niskogatunkowe mięso; **high-/low-**~ **paper** papier wysokiej/niskiej klasy [2] (mark) stopień *m*, ocena *f* (**in sth** z czegoś) [3] (rank) (in administration) szczebel *m*; (in army) stopień *m* [4] US (class) klasa *f*

II *vt* (by quality) po|dzielić na klasy (**according to sth** według czegoś); (by size) po|sortować (**according to sth** według czegoś)

grade school *n* US szkoła *f* podstawowa

gradient /'greɪdɪənt/ *n* [1] (slope) pochyłość *f* [2] (degree) stopień *m* nachylenia

gradual /'grædʒʊəl/ *adj* [1] *[increase, progress]* stopniowy [2] *[slope]* łagodny

gradually /'grædʒʊlɪ/ *adv* stopniowo

graduate **I** /'grædʒʊət/ *n* absolwent *m*, -ka *f*

II /'grædʒʊeɪt/ *vi* [1] u|kończyć studia wyższe; US Sch ≈ ukończyć szkołę średnią; **she** ~**d from** or **at Oxford** skończyła Oksford [2] (progress) **to** ~ **(from sth) to sth** przejść (od or z czegoś) do czegoś

graduate training scheme *n* GB kształcenie *n* podyplomowe

graduation /ˌgrædʒʊ'eɪʃn/ *n* (also ~ **ceremony**) uroczystość *f* wręczenia dyplomów

graffiti /grə'fiːtɪ/ *n* graffiti *n inv*

graffiti artist *n* grafficiarz *m*

graft /grɑːft, US græft/ **I** *n* [1] (of plant) szczep *m* [2] Med przeszczep *m*; **skin** ~ przeszczep skóry

II *vt* za|szczepić *[plant]* (**onto sth** na czymś); przeszczepi|ć, -ać *[plant]* (**sth onto sth** coś na coś); Med przeszczepi|ć, -ać *[skin, organs]*

grain /greɪn/ *n* [1] (of rice) ziarno *n*; (of sand) ziarnko *n*; (of salt) kryształek *m* [2] (crops) zboże *n*; (different kinds) zboża *n pl* [3] fig (of hope, comfort) odrobina *f*; (of humour) szczypta *f*; (of truth) ziarno *n* [4] (in wood) słoje *m pl*; (in paper, fabric) włókna *n pl*; (in stone) żyłkowanie *n*; (in leather) lico *n*

⟨IDIOMS:⟩ **it goes against the** ~ to wbrew naturze

gram(me) /græm/ *n* gram *m*

grammar /'græmə(r)/ *n* gramatyka *f*

grammar school *n* GB *szkoła średnia dla dzieci od 11 roku życia przygotowująca do egzaminów na studia*

grammatical /grə'mætɪkl/ *adj* gramatyczny

granary /'grænərɪ/ *n* spichlerz *m*

granary bread *n* chleb *m* razowy pełnoziarnisty

grand /grænd/ *adj [building]* okazały; *[people, clothes]* wytworny; *[occasion]* doniosły; *[wedding]* huczny; **on a** ~ **scale** na wielką skalę; **she's very** ~ zgrywa wielką damę infml pej

grandchild /'græntʃaɪld/ *n* wnu|k *m*, -czka *f*

granddaughter /'grændɔːtə(r)/ *n* wnuczka *f*

grandeur /'grændʒə(r)/ *n* (of scenery, building) majestatyczność *f*

grandfather /'grænfɑːðə(r)/ *n* dziadek *m*

grandfather clock *n* zegar *m* szafkowy

grandma /'grænmɑː/ *n* babcia *f*

grandmother /'grænmʌðə(r)/ *n* babka *f*, babcia *f*

grandpa /'grænpɑː/ *n* infml dziadziuś *m* infml

grandparents /'græpeərənts/ *npl* dziadkowie *m pl*

grand piano *n* fortepian *m*

grand slam *n* (in bridge) szlem *m*; (in tennis) Wielki Szlem *m*

grandson /'grænsʌn/ *n* wnuk *m*

grandstand /'grænstænd/ *n* trybuna *f* główna

grand total *n* całkowita suma *f*

granite /'grænɪt/ *n* granit *m*

granny /'grænɪ/ *n* infml babcia *f*

grant /grɑːnt, US grænt/ **I** *n* (for study) stypendium *n*; (for research) grant *m*; (for institution) dotacja *f*; (for person) pomoc *f* finansowa

II *vt* [1] przyzna|ć, -wać *[right, pension, visa]*; udziel|ić, -ać (czegoś) *[permission, loan, interview, leave]*; ofiarow|ać, -ywać, po|darować *[land, money]* [2] **to** ~ **that...** przyznać, że...

(IDIOMS:) **to take sth for** ~**ed** (assume) za|łożyć, -kładać coś; (not be surprised) uważać coś za rzecz oczywistą; **he takes his mother for** ~**ed** uważa, że ma matkę na każde zawołanie

granulated /'grænjʊleitɪd/ *adj* ~ **sugar** cukier kryształ

granule /'grænju:l/ *n* (of coffee) granulka *f*; (of salt, sugar) kryształek *m*

grape /greɪp/ *n* winogrono *n*; **a bunch of** ~**s** kiść winogron

grapefruit /'greɪpfru:t/ *n* grejpfrut *m*

grapeseed oil /'greɪpsi:dɔɪl/ *n* olej *m* z pestek winogron(owych)

grapevine /'greɪpvaɪn/ *n* winorośl *f*

(IDIOMS:) **to hear sth on the** ~ dowiedzieć się czegoś pocztą pantoflową

graph /grɑ:f, US græf/ *n* wykres *m*

graphic /'græfɪk/ *adj* [1] graficzny [2] *[account, description]* obrazowy; (of sth unpleasant) drastyczny

graphic design *n* grafika *f*

graphic designer *n* grafik *m*

graphics /'græfɪks/ *npl* [1] (on screen) grafika *f*; **computer** ~ grafika komputerowa [2] (in book) ilustracje *f pl*; (in film, TV) grafika *f*

graphics card *n* karta *f* graficzna

graphics interface *n* interfejs *m* graficzny

graph paper *n* papier *m* milimetrowy

grasp /grɑ:sp, US græsp/ **II** *n* [1] (hold, grip) chwyt *m*; (stronger) uścisk *m* [2] (understanding) **to have a good** ~ **of sth** dobrze coś rozumieć

II *vt* [1] (catch) chwy|cić, -tać *[rope, hand]*; fig s|korzystać z (czegoś) *[opportunity]* [2] (understand) poj|ąć, -mować *[subject, situation]*; zda|ć, -wać sobie sprawę z (czegoś) *[seriousness]*

III *vi* **to** ~ **at sth** chwycić za coś *[hand, rope]*; skorzystać z czegoś *[idea, luck]*

grasping /'grɑ:spɪŋ, US 'græspɪŋ/ *adj* pej pazerny pej

grass /grɑ:s, US græs/ *n* trawa *f*

(IDIOMS:) **the** ~ **is greener (on the other side of the fence)** wszędzie dobrze, gdzie nas nie ma

grass court *n* kort *m* trawiasty

grasshopper /'grɑ:shɒpə(r), US 'græs-/ *n* konik *m* polny

grassroots /ˌgrɑ:s'ru:ts, US ˌgræs-/ **II** *npl* **the** ~ szeregowi członkowie (partii/organizacji)

II *adj* *[movement]* obywatelski; *[support]* oddolny

grate /greɪt/ **II** *n* ruszt *m*

II *vt* Culin ze|trzeć, u|trzeć, -cierać *[cheese, carrot]*; **to** ~ **cheese over sth** posypać coś tartym serem

III *vi* [1] *[hinges]* za|skrzypieć, skrzyp|nąć, -ieć; *[stones]* za|zgrzytać, zgrzyt|nąć, -ać [2] (annoy) drażnić (**on sb/sth** kogoś/coś)

grateful /'greɪtfl/ *adj* wdzięczny (**to sb for sth** komuś za coś)

grater /'greɪtə(r)/ *n* tarka *f*

gratify /'grætɪfaɪ/ *vt* u|cieszyć *[person]*; spełni|ć, -ać *[wish]*; zaspok|oić, -ajać *[desire]*; **to be gratified that...** być zadowolonym, że...

grating /'greɪtɪŋ/ **II** *n* (bars) krata *f*

II *adj* *[noise]* zgrzytliwy; *[voice]* skrzypiący

gratitude /'grætɪtju:d, US -tu:d/ *n* wdzięczność *f* (**to** or **towards sb for sth** dla kogoś or wobec kogoś za coś)

gratuitous /grə'tju:ɪtəs, US -'tu:-/ *adj* bezpłatny

grave /greɪv/ **II** *n* grób *m*

II *adj* poważny

gravel /'grævl/ *n* żwir *m*

gravestone /'greɪvstəʊn/ *n* płyta *f* nagrobkowa

graveyard /'greɪvjɑ:d/ *n* cmentarz *m*

gravitate /'grævɪteɪt/ *vi* **to** ~ **to(wards) sth** skłaniać się ku czemuś

gravity /'grævəti/ *n* [1] (force) ciążenie *n*; **centre of** ~ środek ciężkości [2] (of situation) powaga *f*

gravy /'greɪvɪ/ *n* (zagęszczony) sos *m* pieczeniowy

gravy boat *n* sosjerka *f*

gray *adj n* US = **grey**

graze /greɪz/ **II** *n* obtarcie *n*, zadrapanie *n*

II *vt* [1] ob|trzeć, -cierać *[knee]* (**on sth/against sth** na czymś/o coś) [2] (touch lightly) *[lips, fingers]* mus|nąć, -kać; *[bullet]* za|drasnąć *[skin]*

III *vi* *[sheep, cow]* paść się

grease /gri:s/ **II** *n* smar *m*

II *vt* na|smarować

greasy /'gri:sɪ/ *adj* *[hair, skin]* przetłuszczający się; *[food]* tłusty; *[paper, cloth]* zatłuszczony

great /greɪt/ *adj* [1] (large) wielki; *[force]* potężny; *[number, increase]* znaczny; *[speed, majority]* ogromny; *[temperature]* bardzo wysoki; **a** ~ **deal of sth** mnóstwo czegoś; **with** ~ **difficulty** z wielkim trudem [2] infml (excellent) *[book, film, party, opportunity]* świetny; *[future]* wspaniały; **to feel** ~ czuć się świetnie

great aunt *n* (grandfather's sister) stryjeczna babka *f*; (grandmother's sister) cioteczna babka *f*

great big *adj* infml wielgachny infml

Great Britain *prn* Wielka Brytania *f*

great grandchild *n* prawnu|k *m*, -czka *f*

great grandfather *n* pradziadek *m*

great grandmother *n* prababka *f*, prababcia *f*

great-great-grandchild /ˌgreɪtgreɪt'græntʃaɪld/ *n* praprawnu|k *m*, -czka *f*

greatly /'greɪtlɪ/ *adv* *[admire, regret, surprised]* niezwykle; *[influence]* silnie; *[exceed, prefer, superior]* zdecydowanie; *[fear, love, changed]* bardzo

greatness /'greɪtnɪs/ *n* wielkość *f*

great uncle *n* (on father's side) stryjeczny dziadek *m*; (on mother's side) cioteczny dziadek *m*

Greece /gri:s/ *prn* Grecja *f*

greed /griːd/ n ⬛1 (for money, power) chciwość f ⬛2 (also **greediness**) (for food) łakomstwo n

greedy /'griːdɪ/ adj ⬛1 (for food) łakomy; **a ~ pig** infml żarłok, obżartuch ⬛2 (for money) chciwy; **~ for power** żądny władzy

Greek /griːk/ ⬛ n ⬛1 (person) Gre|k m, -czynka f ⬛2 (language) (ancient) greka f; (modern) (język m) grecki m

⬛ adj [people, language, customs] grecki; [teacher, lesson] greckiego

(IDIOMS) **it's all ~ to me** to dla mnie chińszczyzna

green /griːn/ ⬛ n ⬛1 (colour) (kolor m) zielony m, zieleń f ⬛2 (area) zieleniec m, skwer m; (plants) zieleń f ⬛3 (in bowling) murawa f (do gry w kule); (in golf) pole n golfowe; **green** m ⬛4 [person] ekolog m; **the Greens** Zieloni

⬛ **greens** npl GB (vegetables) zielone warzywa n pl

⬛ adj ⬛1 (in colour) zielony ⬛2 [fields, countryside] zielony ⬛3 infml (naive) naiwny ⬛4 (inexperienced) zielony ⬛5 [politics] proekologiczny; [politician, candidate] zielony; [product, issue] ekologiczny

green card n zielona karta f

greenery /'griːnərɪ/ n zieleń f

greenfield site /'griːnfiːldsaɪt/ n teren m niezagospodarowany

greengrocer /'griːnɡrəʊsə(r)/ n GB (person) zielenia|rz m, -rka f; **~'s (shop)** sklep owocowo--warzywny; warzywniak infml

greenhouse /'griːnhaʊs/ n szklarnia f, cieplarnia f

greenhouse effect n efekt m cieplarniany

Greenland /'griːnlənd/ prn Grenlandia f

greet /griːt/ vt ⬛1 (welcome) przy|witać się z (kimś); (officially) przy|witać ⬛2 (react to) **the announcement was ~ed with booing** komunikat powitano okrzykami dezaprobaty

greeting /'griːtɪŋ/ ⬛ n powitanie n, przywitanie n

⬛ **greetings** npl **Christmas ~s** życzenia z okazji Bożego Narodzenia; **Season's ~s** życzenia świąteczne

greetings card GB, **greeting card** US n kartka f z życzeniami

grey GB, **gray** US /greɪ/ ⬛ n (kolor m) szary m

⬛ adj ⬛1 (colour) szary ⬛2 (grey-haired) siwy; **to turn** or **go ~** posiwieć, osiwieć ⬛3 (dull) [day, life] szary; [person, town] bezbarwny

grey area n niezbadany teren m fig

grey-haired /ˌɡreɪ'heəd/ adj siwowłosy, siwy

greyhound /'ɡreɪhaʊnd/ n chart m

grid /ɡrɪd/ n ⬛1 krata f ⬛2 GB (network) sieć f

gridlock /'ɡrɪdlɒk/ n zator m; fig impas m

grief /griːf/ n żal m

(IDIOMS) **to come to ~** [person] (fall) przewrócić się; (fail) przegrać; [business] wpaść w tarapaty; **good ~!** dobry Boże!

grief-stricken /'ɡriːfstrɪkn/ adj pogrążony w żalu

grievance /'ɡriːvns/ n żal m (**against sb** do kogoś)

grieve /griːv/ vi **to ~ over** or **for sb/sth** opłakiwać kogoś/coś

grievious bodily harm, GBH /ˌɡriːvəs ˌbɒdɪlɪ 'hɑːm/ n ciężkie uszkodzenie n ciała

grill /ɡrɪl/ ⬛ n opiekacz m

⬛ vt ⬛1 u|piec na grillu ⬛2 infml (interrogate) maglować infml

grille /ɡrɪl/ n krata f; (on car) kratownica f wlotu powietrza

grim /ɡrɪm/ adj ⬛1 [person, look] ponury ⬛2 [struggle] zacięty; [resolve] twardy

grimace /ɡrɪ'meɪs, US 'ɡrɪməs/ ⬛ n grymas m

⬛ vi [person] s|krzywić się

grime /ɡraɪm/ n brud m

grimy /'ɡraɪmɪ/ adj brudny

grin /ɡrɪn/ ⬛ n uśmiech m

⬛ vi uśmiech|nąć, -ać się (**at sb** do kogoś)

grind /ɡraɪnd/ ⬛ n infml (hard work) harówka f infml; (monotonous) mordęga f infml

⬛ vt ze|mleć [coffee beans, grain, meat]; rozkrusz|yć, -ać [stone]; **to ~ one's teeth** zgrzytać zębami

⬛ vi [machine, vehicle, engine] zgrzyt|nąć, -ać

grindstone /'ɡraɪndstəʊn/ n (machine) szlifierka f; (stone) kamień m szlifierski

(IDIOMS) **to keep** or **have one's nose to the ~** tyrać jak wół infml

grip /ɡrɪp/ ⬛ n ⬛1 (hold) chwyt m; (tighter) uścisk m; **to tighten one's ~ on sth** ścisnąć coś mocniej ⬛2 **to lose one's ~ on reality** stracić poczucie rzeczywistości; **to come to ~s with sth** zmierzyć się z czymś; **get a ~ on yourself!** weź się w garść! ⬛3 (of tyre) przyczepność f

⬛ vt ⬛1 (grab) chwy|cić, -tać, z|łapać; (hold) trzymać; (firmly) ścis|nąć, -kać ⬛2 [tyres] trzymać się (czegoś) [road]; [shoes] nie ślizgać się na (czymś) [ground] ⬛3 (captivate) [speaker, film] por|wać, -ywać [audience]

gripping /'ɡrɪpɪŋ/ adj [speaker, book] porywający

grisly /'ɡrɪzlɪ/ adj makabryczny

gristle /'ɡrɪsl/ n (in meat) chrząstki f pl

grit /ɡrɪt/ ⬛ n ⬛1 (sand) piasek m; (dirt) brud m, pył m ⬛2 GB (for roads) żwir m, grys m

⬛ vt GB wy|żwirować [road]

(IDIOMS) **to ~ one's teeth** zacisnąć zęby

grizzly /'ɡrɪzlɪ/ n (also **~ bear**) grizzly m inv

groan /ɡrəʊn/ ⬛ n (of pain, despair) jęk m; (of disgust, protest) pomruk m

⬛ vi je|knąć, -czeć

grocer /'ɡrəʊsə(r)/ n właściciel m, -ka f sklepu spożywczego; **~'s (shop)** sklep spożywczy

groceries /'ɡrəʊsərɪz/ npl ⬛1 (shopping) zakupy plt spożywcze ⬛2 (foodstuffs) artykuły m pl spożywcze

grocery /'ɡrəʊsərɪ/ n (also **~ shop** GB, **~ store** US) sklep m spożywczy

groggy /'ɡrɒɡɪ/ adj półprzytomny; **to feel ~** mieć nogi jak z waty

groin /ɡrɔɪn/ n pachwina f

groom /gruːm/ **I** *n* [1] (bridegroom) **the ~ pan
młody** [2] (for horse) stajenny *m*
II *vt* [1] oporządz|ić, -ać *[horse]* [2] **to ~ sb for sth**
przygotow|ać, -ywać (**kogoś** do czegoś) *[exam,
career]*
groove /gruːv/ *n* wyżłobienie *n*; (on screw, record)
rowek *m*
grope /grəʊp/ **I** *vt* infml (sexually) obmacywać infml
II *vi* **to ~ for sth** szukać czegoś po omacku
gross /grəʊs/ **I** *n* gros *m*
II *adj* [1] *[income, price]* brutto [2] *[error, injustice]*
rażący; *[behaviour, language]* ordynarny [3] infml
(revolting) obrzydliwy [4] infml (obese) spasiony infml
III *vt* **to ~ one thousand dollars** *[business]*
przynieść tysiąc dolarów dochodu brutto
grossly /'grəʊslɪ/ *adv [exaggerate, overrate]* grubo;
[irresponsible] rażąco; *[misleading]* całkowicie; **~
underpaid** bardzo źle opłacany; **a ~ overweight
person** osoba z dużą nadwagą
gross national product, GNP *n* produkt *m*
narodowy brutto, PNB *m*
grotesque /grəʊ'tesk/ **I** *n* groteska *f*
II *adj* groteskowy
grotto /'grɒtəʊ/ *n* grota *f*, pieczara *f*
grotty /'grɒtɪ/ *adj* infml paskudny; **to feel ~** czuć
się okropnie
ground /graʊnd/ **I** *n* [1] ziemia *f*; **on the ~** na
ziemi [2] (area, territory) ziemia *f*, teren *m* [3] (sports
ground) boisko *n*
II **grounds** *npl* [1] (of house, institution) teren *m*
[2] (reasons) podstawy *f pl* (**for sth** do czegoś); **on
the ~s that...** z powodu tego, że...
III *adj [coffee, pepper]* mielony
IV *vt* [1] nie zezwol|ić, -alać na lot (czegoś)
[aircraft] [2] *[ship]* **to be ~ed** osiąść na mieliźnie
[IDIOMS:] **to gain ~** zyskać przewagę (**on** or **over
sb** nad kimś); **to hold one's ~** nie chować się;
to go to ~ zapaść się pod ziemię infml
ground floor GB *n* parter *m*; **on the ~** na
parterze
grounding /'graʊndɪŋ/ *n* podstawy *f pl* (**in sth** w
zakresie czegoś)
groundnut oil /'graʊndnʌt ˌɔɪl/ *n* olej *m*
ground rules *n* ogólne zasady *f pl*; **to change the
~** zmieniać reguły gry
groundsheet /'graʊndʃiːt/ *n* wodoodporna mata *f*
wewnątrz namiotu
ground troops *npl* wojska *plt* lądowe
groundwork /'graʊndwɜːk/ *n* prace *f pl* przy-
gotowawcze (**for sth** do czegoś)
group /gruːp/ **I** *n* grupa *f*; **in ~s** w grupach or
grupami
II *vt* z|grupować; (classify) po|grupować
III *vi* (also ~ **together**) z|grupować się, z|ebrać,
-bierać się
group booking *n* rezerwacja *f* grupowa
group therapy *n* terapia *f* grupowa

group work *n* praca *f* w grupach
grouse /graʊs/ *n* szkocka kuropatwa *f*
grove /grəʊv/ *n* (of oak, spruce) zagajnik *m*; (of lemon,
olive trees) gaj *m*; (group of trees) kępa *f* drzew
grovel /'grɒvl/ *vi* płaszczyć się (**before** or **to sb**
przed kimś)
grow /grəʊ/ **I** *vt* [1] wy|hodować *[plant]*; uprawiać
[crops] [2] zapu|ścić, -szczać *[hair, beard, nails]*; **to ~
5 cm** *[person, plant]* urosnąć 5 cm
II *vi* [1] u|rosnąć; *[queue]* wydłuż|yć, -ać się;
[cancer] rozwi|nąć, -jać się; **to ~ to a height of
4 metres** *[plant]* osiągnąć wysokość czterech
metrów [2] (increase) wzr|osnąć, -astać; *[anger, crisis,
problem]* nar|osnąć, -astać; *[company, economy]*
rozwi|nąć, -jać się; *[opposition, movement]* u|rosnąć
w siłę [3] (become) sta|ć, -wać się *[hotter, colder]*; **to
~ old** zestarzeć się; **to ~ more and more
impatient** niecierpliwić się; **I soon grew to like
him** szybko go polubiłem
■ **grow apart: ~ apart** *[people]* oddal|ić, -ać się
od siebie fig
■ **grow on: ~ on** [sb] *[habit]* zakorzeni|ć, -ać
się w (kimś)
■ **grow out of:** wyr|osnąć, -astać z (czegoś) *[suit,
habit]*
■ **grow up:** [1] *[person]* u|rosnąć [2] (become adult)
dor|osnąć, -astać; **when I ~ up** kiedy dorosnę
grower /'grəʊə(r)/ *n* (of flowers, fruit) hodowca *m*
growl /graʊl/ **I** *n* warknięcie *n*
II *vi* *[dog]* war|knąć, -czeć
grown-up **I** /'grəʊnʌp/ *n* dorosły *m*
II /ˌgrəʊn'ʌp/ *adj* dorosły
growth /grəʊθ/ *n* [1] wzrost *m*; (of hair) porost *m*; (of
movement) rozwój *m*; **~ in** or **of the economy**
wzrost gospodarczy [2] Med guz *m*
growth area *n* dynamicznie rozwijająca się
dziedzina *f*
growth industry *n* dynamicznie rozwijająca się
gałąź *f* przemysłu
growth rate *n* tempo *n* wzrostu
grubby /'grʌbɪ/ *adj* brudny; fig haniebny
grudge /grʌdʒ/ **I** *n* uraza *f*; **to bear sb a ~** mieć
coś komuś za złe
II *vt* **to ~ doing sth** wzdragać się przed
zrobieniem czegoś; **to ~ sb their success**
zazdrościć komuś sukcesu
grudgingly /'grʌdʒɪŋlɪ/ *adv* niechętnie
gruelling, grueling US /'gruːəlɪŋ/ *adj* wyczerpujący
gruesome /'gruːsəm/ *adj* (gory) makabryczny;
(horrifying) straszliwy
gruff /grʌf/ *adj [person, reply, voice]* szorstki
grumble /'grʌmbl/ *vi* narzekać (**about sb/sth** na
kogoś/coś); **to ~ at sb** mieć pretensje do kogoś
grumpy /'grʌmpɪ/ *adj* zrzędliwy, gderliwy
grunge /grʌndʒ/ *n* infml [1] (dirt) brud *m* infml [2] (style)
grunge *m* inv

grunt /grʌnt/ **I** *n* (sound) chrząknięcie *n*; (repeated) chrząkanie *n*

II *vi [pig]* chrząk|nąć, -ać

G-string /'dʒiːstrɪŋ/ *n* stringi *plt*

guarantee /ɡærən'tiː/ **I** *n* gwarancja *f*

II *vt* udziel|ić, -ać gwarancji na (coś) *[product]*; za|gwarantować *[delivery, quality]*

guard /ɡɑːd/ **I** *n* **1** (for person, place, object) straż-ni|k *m*, -czka *f*; (soldier) wartowni|k *m*, -czka *f* **2** (military, duty) straż *f*, warta *f*; **to catch sb off ~** zaskoczyć kogoś **4** GB (on train) kierownik *m* pociągu

II *vt* pilnować, strzec *[prisoner, captive]*; chronić, ochraniać *[president, official]*; **a closely ~ed secret** pilnie strzeżona tajemnica

guard dog *n* pies *m* stróżujący

guarded /'ɡɑːdɪd/ *adj [reply, remark]* powściągli-wy; *[smile]* pełen rezerwy

guardian /'ɡɑːdɪən/ *n* strażni|k *m*, -czka *f*; (of child) opiekun *m*, -ka *f*

guardian angel *n* anioł *m* stróż

Guernsey /'ɡɜːnzɪ/ *prn* Guernsey *m*

guerrilla /ɡə'rɪlə/ *n* partyzant *m*, -ka *f*

guerrilla war *n* wojna *f* partyzancka

guess /ɡes/ **I** *n* domysł *m*; **at a** (rough) **~ I would say that...** tak na oko sądząc, ... infml; **it's any-body's ~** nikt nie może (tego) przewidzieć

II *vt* **1** (get at) odgad|nąć, -ywać *[answer]*; prze-wi|dzieć, -dywać *[result]*; **~ what! I've won a prize** nie zgadniesz! zdobyłem nagrodę **2** (suppose) sądzić, myśleć; **I ~ so/not** chyba tak/nie

III *vi* zgad|nąć, -ywać; **to keep sb ~ing** trzymać kogoś w niepewności

guesswork /'ɡeswɜːk/ *n* przypuszczenia *n pl*

guest /ɡest/ *n* gość *m*; **be my ~** bardzo proszę

guesthouse /'ɡesthaʊs/ *n* pensjonat *m*

guest room /'ɡestruːm/ *n* pokój *m* gościnny or dla gości

guestworker /'ɡestwɜːkə(r)/ *n* gastarbeiter *m*

guidance /'ɡaɪdns/ *n* (advice) wskazówki *f pl* (**from sb** kogoś)

guide /ɡaɪd/ **I** *n* **1** (person) przewodni|k *m*, -czka *f*; (book) przewodnik *m* (**to sth** po czymś) **2** (hint) wskazówka *f*; **as a rough ~** jako ogólna wskazówka **3** (also **girl guide**) skautka *f*

II *vt* po|prowadzić *[person]*; (round gallery, city) oprowadz|ić, -ać

guide book *n* przewodnik *m*

guide dog *n* pies *m* przewodnik

guided tour *n* zwiedzanie *n* z przewodnikiem

guideline /'ɡaɪdlaɪn/ *n* (rough guide) wskazówka *f*; (in political, context) wytyczne *plt*; (advice) rada *f*, pomoc *f*

guild /ɡɪld/ *n* (medieval) gildia *f*; (modern) stowarzy-szenie *n*; (of craftsmen) cech *m*

guillotine /'ɡɪlətiːn/ *n* **1** (for execution) gilotyna *f* **2** (for paper) gilotyna *f*, krajarka *f*

guilt /ɡɪlt/ *n* **1** (blame) wina *f* **2** (feeling) poczucie *n* winy

guilty /'ɡɪltɪ/ *adj* winny (**of sth** czegoś); **to feel ~ about sb/sth** czuć się winnym wobec kogoś/z powodu czegoś

guinea-pig /'ɡɪnɪpɪɡ/ *n* świnka *f* morska; fig królik *m* doświadczalny fig

guitar /ɡɪ'tɑː(r)/ *n* gitara *f*

guitarist /ɡɪ'tɑːrɪst/ *n* gitarzyst|a *m*, -ka *f*

gulch /ɡʌltʃ/ *n* US wąwóz *m*, jar *m*

gulf /ɡʌlf/ *n* zatoka *f*; fig przepaść *f* fig; (within group) rozłam *m*

Gulf States *prn pl* **the ~** (in Middle East) państwa *n pl* nad Zatoką Perską

Gulf War *prn* wojna *f* w Zatoce (Perskiej)

gull /ɡʌl/ *n* mewa *f*

gullible /'ɡʌləbl/ *adj* naiwny, łatwowierny

gully /'ɡʌlɪ/ *n* żleb *m*; (small) rynna *f*

gulp /ɡʌlp/ **I** *n* (of liquid, air) łyk *m*; (big) haust *m*; (of food) kęs *m*

II *vt* (also **~ down**) połknąć, łykać *[food, drink]*

III *vi* przeł|knąć, -ykać ślinę

gum /ɡʌm/ *n* **1** (in mouth) dziąsło *n* **2** (also **chewing ~**) guma *f* (do żucia) **3** (adhesive) klej *m*; (resin) guma *f*

gun /ɡʌn/ *n* (weapon) broń *f* palna; (revolver) rewolwer *m*; (rifle) strzelba *f*; (cannon) armata *f*; **to fire a ~** wystrzelić

■ **gun down:** zastrzelić (kogoś)

IDIOMS: **to jump the ~** zrobić falstart; **to stick to one's ~s** infml upierać się przy swoim

gunfire /'ɡʌnfaɪə(r)/ *n* (from hand-held gun) strzela-nina *f*; (from artillery) ogień *m* artyleryjski

gun laws *n* ustawa *f* o broni palnej

gun licence *n* pozwolenie *n* na broń

gunman /'ɡʌnmən/ *n* uzbrojony bandyta *m*

gunpoint /'ɡʌnpɔɪnt/ *n* **to hold sb at ~** trzymać kogoś na muszce

gunpowder /'ɡʌnpaʊdə(r)/ *n* proch *m* (strzelni-czy)

gunshot /'ɡʌnʃɒt/ *n* (shot fired) wystrzał *m*; (range) zasięg *m* strzału

gunshot wound *n* rana *f* postrzałowa

gurgle /'ɡɜːɡl/ **I** *n* (of liquid) bulgotanie *n*, bulgot *m*; (of baby) gaworzenie *n*

II *vi [water]* za|bulgotać; *[baby]* gaworzyć

guru /'ɡʊruː/, US ɡə'ruː/ *n* guru *m inv* also fig

gush /ɡʌʃ/ *vi [liquid]* wytrys|nąć, -kiwać, trys|nąć, -kać

gust /ɡʌst/ *n* **1** (of air) podmuch *m*; (of wind, blizzard) poryw *m*; **a ~ of rain/snow** gwałtowna ulewa/śnieżyca **2** (of anger) poryw *m*; (of laughter) wybuch *m*; (of happiness) fala *f*

gusto /'ɡʌstəʊ/ *n* **with ~** z entuzjazmem

gut /ɡʌt/ **I** *n* infml bandzioch *m* infml

II *adj [feeling, reaction]* instynktowny; *[instinct]* pierwotny

III *vt* *[fire]* wypal|ić, -ać doszczętnie *[building]*

guts *npl* /gʌts/ infml ① (of human, animal) flaki *m pl* ② (courage) odwaga *f*

gutsy /'gʌtsɪ/ *adj* infml (spirited) waleczny; (brave) odważny

gutter /'gʌtə(r)/ *n* (on roof) rynna *f*; (in street) rynsztok *m*

gutter press *n* prasa *f* brukowa

guy /gaɪ/ *n* infml facet *m*, gość *m* infml; **a good/bad** ∼ (in film) bohater pozytywny/czarny charakter; **hey, you** ∼**s!** hej, wy tam!

guzzle /'gʌzl/ *vt* infml (eat) ze|żreć infml; (drink) wy|żłopać infml

gym /dʒɪm/ *n* ① = **gymnasium** ② = **gymnastics**

gymnasium /dʒɪm'neɪzɪəm/ *n* sala *f* gimnastyczna; (for bodybuilders) siłownia *f*

gymnast /'dʒɪmnæst/ *n* gimnasty|k *m*, -czka *f*

gymnastics /dʒɪm'næstɪks/ *npl* gimnastyka *f*

gym shoe *n* tenisówka *f*

gynaecologist GB, **gynecologist** US /ˌgaɪnə'kɒlədʒɪst/ *n* ginekolog *m*

gypsy /'dʒɪpsɪ/ *n* Cygan *m*, -ka *f*

H

h, H /eɪtʃ/ *n* h, H *n*

habit /'hæbɪt/ *n* ① (custom) zwyczaj *m*; **to get into/ out of the ~ of doing sth** przyzwyczaić się do robienia czegoś/odzwyczaić się od robienia czegoś ② (addiction) nałóg *m* ③ (of monk, nun) habit *m*

habitable /'hæbɪtəbl/ *adj* nadający się do zamieszkania

habitat /'hæbɪtæt/ *n* siedlisko *n*

habit-forming /'hæbɪtfɔːmɪŋ/ *adj* **to be ~** uzależniać

habitual /hə'bɪtʃʊəl/ *adj [behaviour, reaction]* charakterystyczny; *[drinker, smoker]* nałogowy; *[liar]* notoryczny

habitual offender *n* recydywist|a *m*, -ka *f*

hack /hæk/ ① *n* infml pismak *m* pej ② *vt* wycinać, -nać *[bushes]*; **to ~ sb/sth to pieces** porąbać kogoś/coś na kawałki ③ *vi* ① **to ~ through sth** porąbać coś ② Comput infml **to ~ into sth** włamać się do czegoś *[system]*

hacker /'hækə(r)/ *n* (computer) ~ haker *m*

hacking /'hækɪŋ/ *n* piractwo *n* komputerowe

hackles /'hækl/ *npl* (on animal) sierść *f* (na grzbiecie)

hackneyed /'hæknɪd/ *adj [phrase, joke]* wyświechtany infml; *[subject]* oklepany infml

haddock /'hædək/ *n* plamiak *m*, łupacz *m*

haemophilia GB, **hemophilia** US /ˌhiːmə'fɪlɪə/ *n* hemofilia *f*

haemophiliac GB, **hemophiliac** US /ˌhiːmə'fɪlɪæk/ ① *n* hemofilik *m* ② *adj* cierpiący na hemofilię

haemorrhage GB, **hemorrhage** US /'hemərɪdʒ/ ① *n* krwotok *m* ② *vi* krwawić

haemorrhoids GB, **hemorrhoids** US /'hemərɔɪdz/ *n* hemoroidy plt

haggard /'hægəd/ *adj* wymizerowany

haggle /'hægl/ *vi* targować się (**over sth** o coś)

Hague /heɪg/ *prn* **The ~** Haga *f*

hail /heɪl/ ① *n* grad *m* ② *vt* ① (call) zawołać do (kogoś) *[person]*; przywoł|ać, -ywać *[taxi]* ② (praise) **to ~ sb as sth** okrzyknąć kogoś czymś; **to ~ sth as sth** uznać coś za coś ③ *v impers* **it is ~ing** pada grad

hailstone /'heɪlstəʊn/ *n* ziarnko *n* gradu

hailstorm /'heɪlstɔːm/ *n* burza *f* gradowa

hair /heə(r)/ *n* ① (on head) włosy *m* pl; (on body) włoski *m* pl; (of animal) sierść *f*; **to have one's ~ cut** ostrzyc się u fryzjera; **long - ~ed** długowłosy ② (individually) (on head) włos *m*; (on body) włosek *m* IDIOMS **to split ~s** dzielić włos na czworo

hairband /'heəbænd/ *n* opaska *f* na włosy

hairbrush /'heəbrʌʃ/ *n* szczotka *f* do włosów

haircut /'heəkʌt/ *n* strzyżenie *n*

hairdo /'heəduː/ *n* infml fryzura *f*

hairdresser /'heədresə(r)/ *n* fryzjer *m*, -ka *f*

hairdrier /'heədraɪə(r)/ *n* (hand-held) suszarka *f* do włosów; (hood) aparat *m* do suszenia włosów

hair gel *n* żel *m* do włosów

hairgrip /'heəgrɪp/ *n* GB wsuwka *f*

hairpin bend *n* zakręt *m* o 180°

hair-raising /'heəreɪzɪŋ/ *adj* jeżący włosy na głowie

hair remover /'heərɪmuːvə(r)/ *n* krem *m* do depilacji

hair-slide /'heəslaɪd/ *n* GB klamra *f* do włosów

hairspray /'heəspreɪ/ *n* lakier *m* do włosów

hairstyle /'heəstaɪl/ *n* fryzura *f*

hairy /'heərɪ/ *adj [part of body, person]* owłosiony; *[animal]* włochaty

half /hɑːf, US hæf/ ① *n* ① (part) połowa *f*; **to cut sth in ~** przeciąć coś na pół ② (fraction) pół ③ GB infml (half pint) ≈ małe piwo *n* infml ② *adj* **a ~-litre, ~ a litre** pół litra; **two and a ~ cups** dwie i pół filiżanki ③ *pron* ① (part) połowa *f*; **~ of the students** połowa studentów ② (in time) pół; **an hour and a ~** półtorej godziny; **~ past four** GB (w)pół do piątej ④ *adv [full, empty]* do połowy; *[drunk, eaten]* na (w)pół; *[remembered, understood]* nie całkiem; **to ~ close the window** przymknąć okno; **it's ~ the price** to jest dwa razy tańsze; **I ~ expected it** poniekąd spodziewałem się tego IDIOMS **to go halves with sb** podzielić się z kimś po połowie

halfback /'hɑːfbæk, US 'hæf-/ *n* Sport pomocnik *m*

half-board /ˌhɑːfbɔːd, US ˌhæf-/ *n* nocleg *m* z niepełnym wyżywieniem

half-brother /ˌhɑːfbrʌðə(r)/ *n* brat *m* przyrodni

half day *n* połowa *f* dniówki

half fare *n* bilet *m* ze zniżką 50%

half-hearted /ˌhɑːˈhɑːtɪd, US ˌhæf-/ adj [attempt] mało entuzjastyczny; [smile] wymuszony

half-heartedly /ˌhɑːˈhɑːtɪdlɪ, US ˌhæf-/ adv bez przekonania

half hour n pół n inv godziny; **on the** ~ co pół godziny

half-mast /ˌhɑːˈmɑːst, US ˌhæfˈmæst/ n **at** ~ (of flag) opuszczony do połowy masztu; (of trousers) przykrótki

half-moon /ˌhɑːˈfmuːn, US ˌhæf-/ n półksiężyc m

half price adj za pół ceny

half-sister /ˌhɑːˈsɪstə(r)/ n siostra f przyrodnia

half term GB Sch n przerwa f semestralna

half-time /ˌhɑːˈftaɪm, US ˌhæf-/ n Sport przerwa f (po pierwszej połowie meczu)

halfway /ˌhɑːˈfweɪ, US ˌhæf-/ adv [1] w połowie drogi (**between sth and sth** pomiędzy czymś a czymś); ~ **up/down** w połowie czegoś [stairs, tree]; ~ **down the page** w połowie strony [2] (in time) ~ **through sth** w połowie czegoś

halfway house n (rehabilitation centre) ośrodek m resocjalizacji

hall /hɔːl/ n [1] (in house) przedpokój m; (corridor) korytarz m; (in hotel) hol m; (in airport, station) hala f; (for public events) sala f [2] (country house) dwór m

hallelujah /ˌhælɪˈluːjə/ excl alleluja!

hallmark /ˈhɔːlmɑːk/ [I] n [1] GB (on metal) cecha f, stempel m probierczy [2] (typical feature) cecha f charakterystyczna
[II] vt cechować [silver, gold]; **to be** ~**ed** mieć stempel probierczy

hall of residence n ≈ akademik m

Halloween /ˌhæləʊˈiːn/ n wigilia f Wszystkich Świętych

hallucinate /həˈluːsɪneɪt/ vi mieć halucynacje

hallucination /həˌluːsɪˈneɪʃn/ n halucynacja f

hallway /ˈhɔːlweɪ/ n (entrance) przedpokój m; (corridor) korytarz m

halo /ˈheɪləʊ/ n [1] aureola f, nimb m [2] (in astronomy) halo n inv

halt /hɔːlt/ [I] n (stop) zatrzymanie się n; **to come to a** ~ [troops, vehicle] zatrzymać się; [work] zostać przerwanym; **to call a** ~ **to sth** zakończyć coś; **shall we call a** ~? (in work) kończymy?
[II] vt zatrzym|ać, -ywać [vehicle]; przer|wać, -ywać [activity]; za|hamować [progress]
[III] vi zatrzym|ać, -ywać się

halterneck /ˈhɔːltənek/ [I] n bluzka trykotowa z odkrytymi plecami
[II] adj ~ **dress** sukienka bez pleców

halve /hɑːv, US hæv/ [I] vt zmniejsz|yć, -ać o połowę [number, rate]; po|dzielić na pół [apple, loaf]
[II] vi [number, rate] zmniejsz|yć, -ać się o połowę; [time] skr|ócić, -acać się o połowę

ham /hæm/ n szynka f

hamburger /ˈhæmbɜːgə(r)/ n [1] (burger) hamburger m [2] US (ground beef) mielona wołowina f

hammer /ˈhæmə(r)/ [I] n (tool) młotek m; (big) młot m
[II] vt [1] (pound) walić w (coś), uderzać w (coś) [metal, table]; **to** ~ **sth into** (drive) wbijać coś w (coś) [wall, fence] [2] fig **to** ~ **sth into sb** wbijać coś do głowy (komuś); **to** ~ **home a message** uparcie przypominać o przesłaniu [3] (defeat) spu|ścić, -szczać lanie or manto infml (komuś) fig
[III] vi **to** ~ **on** or **at sth** [person] walić w coś; [hailstones] bębnić w coś
■ **hammer out**: ~ [sth] **out** (negotiate) wypracow|ać, -ywać coś [solution, formula, agreement]

hamper /ˈhæmpə(r)/ [I] n (for picnic) kosz m (z przykrywką)
[II] utrudnić, -ać [progress, movement]

hamster /ˈhæmstə(r)/ n chomik m

hamstring /ˈhæmstrɪŋ/ n ścięgno n podkolanowe

hand /hænd/ [I] n [1] (body part) ręka f; **he had a pencil in his** ~ miał w ręku ołówek; **to hold sb's** ~ trzymać kogoś za rękę; fig dodawać otuchy komuś; **to make sth by** ~ robić coś ręcznie; **the letter was delivered by** ~ list został doręczony osobiście; **to give sb a (helping)** ~ pomóc komuś; **to have sth to** ~ mieć coś pod ręką; **to be on** ~ być pod ręką; **to get out of** ~ wymknąć się spod kontroli; **to take sth in** ~ zapanować nad czymś [situation]; zająć się czymś [problem]; **to take sb in** ~ wziąć kogoś w karby [2] (cards dealt) karty f pl; (game) partia f [3] (worker) robotnik m; (crew member) członek m załogi [4] (on dial, clock) wskazówka f [5] **on the one** ~..., **on the other** ~... z jednej strony..., a z drugiej...
[II] vt **to** ~ **sth to sb** poda|ć, -wać komuś coś; (officially) wręcz|yć, -ać komuś coś
[III] **hand in hand** adj phr [1] [run, walk] trzymając się za ręce; **to go** ~ **in** ~ **(with sth)** fig iść w parze z (czymś) [2] (to spare) **she finished the exam with 20 minutes in** ~ skończyła egzamin 20 minut przed czasem; **I'll do it when I have some time in** ~ zrobię to, kiedy będę miał chwilę czasu
[IV] **out of hand** adv phr [reject, dismiss] z miejsca, od razu
■ **hand back**: ~ [sth] **back** zwr|ócić, -acać [object, essay, colony] (**to sb** komuś)
■ **hand down**: ~ [sth] **down** [1] (transmit) przekaz|ać, -ywać [property, skill] (**to sb** komuś); [2] (pass) poda|ć, -wać komuś [boxes, books]; odda|ć, -wać [old clothes]
■ **hand in**: ~ [sth] **in** [1] (submit) złożyć, składać [essay, report, petition] (**to sb** komuś); odda|ć, -wać [homework] [2] (return) odda|ć, -awać [keys]
■ **hand out**: ~ [sth] **out** rozda|ć, -wać [leaflets, books, food, gifts]; wymierz|yć, -ać [punishment, fine] (**to sb** komuś); okaz|ać, -ywać [sympathy] (**to sb** komuś); **to** ~ **out advice** pej dawać dobre rady iron

■ **hand over**: ¶ ~ **over to sb** 1 *[TV presenter]*
oddaję, -wać głos komuś 2 (transfer power) przeka-
z|ać, -ywać władzę w ręce kogoś *[deputy, successor]*
3 (on telephone) **I'll ~ you over to Anna** oddaję
słuchawkę Annie ¶ ~ **[sth] over** złożyć, składać
[weapon]; odda|ć, -wać *[camera, book, microphone,
controls]*; przekaz|ać, -ywać *[collection, controls]*
¶ ~ **[sb] over** przekaz|ać, -ywać *[prisoner, ter-
rorist]* (**to sb** komuś); **to ~ a baby/patient over
to sb** oddać dziecko/pacjenta pod opiekę (komuś)
IDIOMS: **to have one's ~s full** mieć pełne ręce
roboty; **to try one's ~ at sth** spróbować swych
sił w czymś; **to know sth like the back of one's
~** znać coś jak (swoje) pięć palców
handbag /ˈhændbæg/ *n* torebka *f*
hand baggage *n* bagaż *m* (pod)ręczny
handball /ˈhændbɔːl/ *n* piłka *f* ręczna
handbook /ˈhændbʊk/ *n* podręcznik *m*; (guide)
przewodnik *m*; (technical) poradnik *m*
handbrake /ˈhændbreɪk/ *n* hamulec *m* ręczny
handcuffs /ˈhændkʌfs/ *npl* kajdanki *plt*
handful /ˈhændfʊl/ *n* 1 (fistful) garść *f* 2 (of people)
garstka *f*; (of buildings) niewielkie skupisko *n* 3 infml
to be a ~ *[child]* być urwisem; *[horse]* być
narowistym
handgun /ˈhændɡʌn/ *n* krótka broń *f* palna
hand-held /ˌhænd'held/ *adj [camera]* reportażo-
wy; *[tool]* ręczny; *[device]* podręczny; *[computer]*
kieszonkowy
handicap /ˈhændɪkæp/ **I** *n* upośledzenie *n*
II *vt* utrudni|ć, -ać życie (komuś) *[person]*;
utrudniać *[development]*
handicapped /ˈhændɪkæpt/ *adj [person]* upośledzony; **mentally ~** upośledzeni umysłowo; **physically ~** niepełnosprawni
handiwork /ˈhændɪwɜːk/ *n* rękodzieło *n*
handkerchief /ˈhæŋkətʃɪf, -tʃiːf/ *n* chustka *f* (do
nosa)
handle /ˈhændl/ **I** *n* (on door, window) klamka *f*; (on
bucket, basket) pałąk *m*; (on cup) uszko *n*; (on bag,
saucepan) rączka *f*; (on broom, spade, hammer, cutlery)
trzonek *m*; (on pump, drawer) uchwyt *m*
II *vt* 1 (touch) dot|knąć, -ykać (czegoś); manipu-
lować przy (czymś) *[explosives]*; '**~ with care**'
„ostrożnie" 2 (manage) u|łożyć, -kładać *[horse]*;
prowadzić *[car]*; **to know how to ~ children**
umieć radzić sobie z dziećmi 3 (deal with) po|radzić
sobie z (czymś) *[crisis]*; zn|ieść, -osić *[stress]*;
[department, official] załatwi|ć, -ać *[complaints,
enquiries]*; *[lawyer]* po|prowadzić *[case]*
handlebars /ˈhændlbɑːz/ *npl* kierownica *f* roweru
handling /ˈhændlɪŋ/ *n* 1 (holding, touching) (of
substance) obchodzenie się *n*; (of tool, weapon) po-
sługiwanie się *n* 2 (way of dealing) **her ~ of the
theme** jej sposób zaprezentowania tematu; **their
~ of the economy** ich sposób zarządzania
gospodarką

handling charge *n* 1 (for goods) opłata *f* prze-
ładunkowa 2 (administrative) opłata *f* manipulacyjna
hand luggage *n* bagaż *m* (pod)ręczny
handmade /ˌhænd'meɪd/ *adj* wykonany ręcznie
handout /ˈhændaʊt/ *n* 1 (charitable) datek *m*
2 (leaflet) ulotka *f*
handpick /ˌhænd'pɪk/ *vt* z|ebrać, -bierać ręcznie
[cotton]; (at shop) własnoręcznie wyb|rać, -ierać *[fruit,
vegetables]*; starannie wy|selekcjonować *[staff]*
handshake /ˈhændʃeɪk/ *n* uścisk *m* dłoni
handsome /ˈhænsəm/ *adj* przystojny
hands-on /ˌhændz'ɒn/ *adj [approach, experience]*
praktyczny; *[control, management]* bezpośredni
handstand /ˈhændstænd/ *n* Sport stójka *f* na
rękach
handwriting /ˈhændraɪtɪŋ/ *n* charakter *m* pisma,
pismo *n*
handwritten /ˌhænd'rɪtn/ *adj* odręcznie napisany
handy /ˈhændɪ/ *adj* 1 (useful) *[tool]* przydatny;
[book, skill] użyteczny 2 (convenient) *[tool, size]*
poręczny; *[shop]* dogodnie położony; **to have/
keep sth ~** mieć/trzymać coś pod ręką *[keys,
passport]*
handyman /ˈhændɪmæn/ *n* złota rączka *f* infml
hang /hæŋ/ **I** *n* **to get the ~ of sth** infml chwytać
coś/chwytać, jak się coś robi infml
II *vt* 1 (suspend) (from hook, coat-hanger) powiesić,
wieszać (**from/by/on sth** na czymś); (from string,
rope) powiesić, wieszać (**from sth** na czymś); (peg
up) powiesić *[washing]* (**on sth** na czymś) 2 (in
decorating) nakle|ić, -jać *[wallpaper]* 3 (kill) powiesić,
wieszać *[criminal]*
III *vi* 1 (on hook, washing line) wisieć; (from height)
zwisać; **my feet ~ over the edge** wystają mi
nogi 2 *[curtain]* opadać 3 *[person]* zostać powie-
szonym (**for sth** za coś)
IV *vr* **to ~ oneself** powiesić się (**from sth** na
czymś)
■ **hang around** infml: 1 (also ~ **about**) pałętać
się, pętać się infml 2 **to ~ around with sb**
trzymać się z kimś
■ **hang back**: (in fear) trzymać się na uboczu; po
ociągać się
■ **hang down**: zwisać; *[hem]* być odprutym
■ **hang on** infml: ¶ 1 (hold on) **to ~ on (to sth)**
kurczowo trzymać się (czegoś) 2 infml (wait) po|cze-
kać; **~ on a minute** (on phone) chwileczkę! 3 infml
(survive) wytrzym|ać, -ywać; **~ on in there!** infml
wytrzymaj jeszcze trochę! ¶ **~ on [sth]** (depend
on) zależeć od (czegoś)
■ **hang out**: ¶ 1 (protrude) *[handkerchief, shirt]*
wystawać 2 infml (live) mieszkać 3 infml (sit around)
spędzać czas ¶ **~ [sth] out** wywie|sić, -szać
[washing, flags]
■ **hang up**: ¶ (on phone) od|łożyć, -kładać słu-

chawkę; **to ~ up on sb** rzucić słuchawkę podczas rozmowy z kimś ¶ **~ [sth] up** powiesić, wieszać
hangar /ˈhæŋə(r)/ n hangar m
hanger-on /ˌhæŋərˈɒn/ n infml pieczeniarz m
hang-glider /ˈhæŋɡlaɪdə(r)/ n lotnia f
hanging /ˈhæŋɪŋ/ n ⒈ (of person) powieszenie n ⒉ (curtain) zasłona f; (on wall) tkanina f dekoracyjna
hangover /ˈhæŋəʊvə(r)/ n kac m infml
hang-up /ˈhæŋʌp/ n infml (deep-rooted) zahamowanie n; (specific) problem m
hanker /ˈhæŋkə(r)/ vi **to ~ after** or **for sth** marzyć o czymś
hanky, hankie /ˈhæŋkɪ/ n infml chusteczka f do nosa
haphazard /hæpˈhæzəd/ adj (unorganized) chaotyczny; (random) przypadkowy
happen /ˈhæpən/ vi ⒈ (occur) zdarz|yć, -ać się; **what's ~ing?** co się dzieje?; **whatever ~s** cokolwiek się stanie ⒉ (occur by chance) **as it ~ed, the weather that day was bad** tak się złożyło, że pogoda tego dnia była fatalna; **if you ~ to see her say hello** jeśli się z nią zobaczysz, pozdrów ją ode mnie
happily /ˈhæpɪlɪ/ adv ⒈ (cheerfully) radośnie; [live] szczęśliwie; **a ~ married man** szczęśliwy małżonek; **they lived ~ ever after** żyli długo i szczęśliwie ⒉ (willingly) [admit, agree] ochoczo ⒊ (successfully) [chosen] trafnie
happiness /ˈhæpɪnɪs/ n szczęście n
happy /ˈhæpɪ/ adj ⒈ [person] szczęśliwy (**about sth** z powodu czegoś); [atmosphere, nature] pogodny; [memory, laughter] radosny; **I'm ~ (that)...** cieszę się, że...; **to be ~ with sth** być zadowolonym z czegoś; **to keep sb ~** zadowolić kogoś; **to be ~ to do sth** zrobić coś z przyjemnością ⒉ (in greetings) **Happy birthday!** wszystkiego najlepszego z okazji urodzin!; **Happy Christmas!** Wesołych Świąt!; **Happy New Year!** Szczęśliwego Nowego Roku!
happy ending n szczęśliwe zakończenie n, happy end m
happy medium n złoty środek m
harangue /həˈræŋ/ n (political) przemowa f; (moral) kazanie n
harass /ˈhærəs, US həˈræs/ ⒈ vt nękać [enemy]; zakłócać przebieg (czegoś) [demonstration]; (sexually) napastować
⒈⒈ **harassed** adj udręczony
harbour GB, **harbor** US /ˈhɑːbə(r)/ ⒈ n port m; (for yachts) przystań f
⒈⒈ vt żywić [feeling, suspicion]; ukry|ć, -wać [criminal]
hard /hɑːd/ ⒈ adj ⒈ (firm) twardy; **to go ~** stwardnieć ⒉ (difficult) [problem, choice, task] trudny; [work, life] ciężki; **it's ~ to do sth** trudno (jest) coś zrobić; **I find it ~ to accept it** trudno mi się z tym pogodzić; **it was ~ work** to było trudne; **to be a ~ worker** [student] być pracowitym; [manual]

worker] ciężko pracować ⒊ (severe) [person, look, words] surowy; [blow] ciężki; [winter, climate] surowy; **to be ~ on sb** być dla kogoś surowym; **~ luck!** a to pech!; **no ~ feelings!** bez urazy! ⒋ [evidence, proof] niezbity ⒌ [liquor] mocny; [drugs] twardy ⒍ [water] twardy
⒈⒈ adv [push, hit] mocno; [cry] z całych sił; [study, think] intensywnie; [work] ciężko; [look, listen] uważnie; **to try ~** (mentally) bardzo się starać; (physically) wysilać się
hard and fast adj [rule] żelazny; [distinction] niezmienny
hardback (book) n książka f w twardej or sztywnej oprawie
hardboard /ˈhɑːdbɔːd/ n płyta f pilśniowa twarda
hard-boiled egg n jajko n na twardo
hard copy n Comput wydruk m
hard core ⒈ n (of group, demonstrators) trzon m
⒈⒈ **hard-core** adj ⒈ (established) [opponent, protest, supporter] zagorzały ⒉ (extreme) [pornography] twardy
hard court n twardy or utwardzony kort m
hard disk n twardy dysk m
hard-earned /ˌhɑːdˈɜːnd/ adj [cash] ciężko zarobiony
harden /ˈhɑːdn/ ⒈ vt ⒈ utwardz|ić, -ać [paint, wax] ⒉ [time, experience] za|hartować [person] (**to sth** na coś); ugruntow|ać, -ywać [attitude]; **to ~ one's heart** stać się twardym or nieczułym (**to sb** dla kogoś)
⒈⒈ vi ⒈ [glue, wax, muscle] s|twardnieć ⒉ fig [voice] s|twardnieć; [attitude, resolve] umocni|ć, -ać się
hardened /ˈhɑːdnd/ adj [criminal] zatwardziały; [drinker] nałogowy
hard hat n (helmet) kask m; (for riding) toczek m
hard-hearted /ˌhɑːdˈhɑːtɪd/ adj nieczuły
hard-hitting /ˌhɑːdˈhɪtɪŋ/ adj demaskatorski
hard labour GB, **hard labor** US n ciężkie roboty plt
hardliner /ˌhɑːdˈlaɪnə(r)/ n twardogłowy m
hardly /ˈhɑːdlɪ/ adv ⒈ (barely) [begin, know, see] ledwo, prawie; **~ had they gone out when...** ledwie wyszli... ⒉ (not really) **it's ~ likely to** mało prawdopodobne; **it's ~ surprising** nie ma się czemu dziwić; **~! nie sądzę!; I can ~ believe it!** aż mi się wierzyć nie chce! ⒊ **~ anything/anyone** prawie nic/nikt, mało co/kto; **~ ever** prawie nigdy
hard of hearing adj **to be ~** źle słyszeć
hard-pressed /ˌhɑːdˈprest/, **hard pushed** /ˌhɑːdˈpʊʃt/ adj przyciśnięty (do muru) fig; **to be ~ for time** mieć bardzo mało czasu; **to be ~ to do sth** mieć trudności ze zrobieniem czegoś
hardship /ˈhɑːdʃɪp/ n ⒈ (difficulty) trudności plt; (poverty) ubóstwo n ⒉ (ordeal) ciężka próba f fig
hard shoulder n utwardzone pobocze n
hard up adj infml spłukany infml

hardware /ˈhɑːdweə(r)/ n ① artykuły m pl żelazne ② Comput sprzęt m komputerowy ③ Mil broń f i wyposażenie n wojskowe

hardware shop, hardware store n sklep m żelazny

hard-working /ˌhɑːdˈwɜːkɪŋ/ adj pracowity

hardy /ˈhɑːdɪ/ adj [person] odporny; [plant] wytrzymały

hare /heə(r)/ n zając m

haricot /ˈhærɪkəʊ/ n GB (also ~ **bean**) (dried) fasola f; (fresh) fasolka f szparagowa

harm /hɑːm/ ① n (injury) uszkodzenie n ciała; (damage) (to person) krzywda f; (to thing) szkoda f; **to do sb** ~ wyrządzić komuś krzywdę; **out of** ~'**s way** w bezpiecznym miejscu
II vt s|krzywdzić [person]; z|niszczyć [crops]; uszk|odzić, -adzać [lungs, object]; za|szkodzić (komuś/czemuś) [population]

harmful /ˈhɑːmfl/ adj [chemical, ray] szkodliwy; [behaviour, gossip] krzywdzący (**to sb** kogoś)

harmless /ˈhɑːmlɪs/ adj ① [chemical, virus] niegroźny; [growth] łagodny ② [person] nieszkodliwy; [joke, fun] niewinny

harmonica /hɑːˈmɒnɪkə/ n harmonijka f ustna

harmonious /hɑːˈməʊnɪəs/ adj harmonijny; [voice, song] melodyjny

harmonize /ˈhɑːmənaɪz/ ① vt z|harmonizować **II** vi [law, plan] być dostosowanym (**with sth** do czegoś); [colours, feature] harmonizować (**with sth** z czymś)

harmony /ˈhɑːmənɪ/ n harmonia f

harness /ˈhɑːnɪs/ ① n (for animal) uprząż f; (for child) szelki plt
II vt ① (attach) zaprzęg|ać, -nąć [animal] (**to sth** do czegoś) ② (channel, use) wykorzyst|ać, -ywać [resources, power]

harp /hɑːp/ n Mus harfa f
■ **harp on** infml: mówić ciągle o (czymś)

harpoon /hɑːˈpuːn/ n harpun m

harrowing /ˈhærəʊɪŋ/ adj wstrząsający

harsh /hɑːʃ/ adj ① [person, punishment] srogi; [regime] twardy; [criticism] ostry ② [colour, light] ostry

harshly /ˈhɑːʃlɪ/ adv [punish, treat] surowo; [speak] szorstko

harvest /ˈhɑːvɪst/ ① n (of wheat) żniwa plt; (of fruit) zbiór m; (of grapes) winobranie n
II vt z|ebrać, -bierać [corn, fruit]

has-been /ˈhæzbiːn/ n infml pej człowiek m skończony

hassle /ˈhæsl/ infml ① n kłopot m
II vt zamęczać (**about sth** czymś)

haste /heɪst/ n pośpiech m; **to act in** ~ działać w pośpiechu

hasten /ˈheɪsn/ ① vt przy|śpiesz|yć, -ać
II vi pośpieszyć (się); **to** ~ **to do sth** spiesznie coś zrobić

hasty /ˈheɪstɪ/ adj [departure] pośpieszny; [note, plan] wykonany w pośpiechu; [decision, conclusion] pochopny

hat /hæt/ n kapelusz m; (cotton, woolly) czapka f

hatch /hætʃ/ ① n ① (on air-craft) właz m; (in boat) luk m; (in car) drzwi plt ② (also **serving** ~) okienko n (do podawania posiłków)
II vt ① [bird] wysi|edzieć, -adywać [eggs] ② (plan) u|knuć [plot, scheme]; przygotow|ać, -ywać [surprise]
III vi [chicks] wyklu|ć, -wać się

hatchback /ˈhætʃbæk/ n (car) samochód m pięciodrzwiowy; (car door) drzwi plt tylne

hatchet /ˈhætʃɪt/ n topór m

hate /heɪt/ ① n nienawiść f
II vt ① (dislike) nie znosić; (violently) nienawidzić ② (not enjoy) nie cierpieć [food, sport] ③ (in apology) **I** ~ **to do it** przykro mi, że muszę to zrobić

hate mail n obraźliwe listy m pl

hatred /ˈheɪtrɪd/ n nienawiść f (**of** or **for sb/sth** do kogoś/czegoś); (less violent) niechęć f (**of sth** do czegoś)

haughty /ˈhɔːtɪ/ adj wyniosły

haul /hɔːl/ ① n ① (taken by criminals) łup m ② (found by police, customs) **arms** ~ skonfiskowana broń f ③ **it will be a long** ~ to będzie długa droga ④ (of fish) połów m
II vt (drag) ciągnąć

haulage /ˈhɔːlɪdʒ/ n ① (transport) fracht m ② (cost) fracht m

haunch /hɔːntʃ/ n (of human, horse) pośladek m; (of animal) zad m

haunt /hɔːnt/ ① n ulubione miejsce n (spotkań)
II vt dręczyć; [ghost] straszyć [person]; nawiedz|ić, -ać [house]

haunted /ˈhɔːntɪd/ adj [house] nawiedzony; [face, look] udręczony

haunting /ˈhɔːntɪŋ/ adj zapadający w pamięć; [memory] dręczący

have /hæv, həv/ ① vt ① (possess) mieć, posiadać; **I** ~ **(got) a car** mam samochód ② (take) **to** ~ **a sandwich** zjeść kanapkę; **to** ~ **a whisky** napić się whisky; **to** ~ **a cigarette** zapalić papierosa; **to** ~ **breakfast** zjeść śniadanie; **to** ~ **a wash** umyć się ③ (receive, get) dosta|ć, -wać [letter]; **I've had no news from him** nie mam od niego żadnych wiadomości; **to let sb** ~ **sth** dać komuś coś ④ (hold) wyda|ć, -wać [party]; mieć [meeting, conversation]; z|organizować [competition, exhibition] ⑤ (exert, exhibit) wyw|rzeć, -ierać [effect, influence]; mieć [courage] (**to do sth** żeby coś zrobić) ⑥ (spend) spędz|ić, -ać; **to** ~ **a nice day** przyjemnie spędzić dzień; **to** ~ **a good time** dobrze się bawić; **to** ~ **a hard time** przeżywać trudne chwile; **to** ~ **a good vacation** mieć udane wakacje ⑦ (also ~ **got**) **to** ~ **sth to do** mieć coś do zrobienia; **I've got letters to write** muszę napisać listy ⑧ (suffer) mieć; **to** ~

(the) flu/a heart attack mieć grypę/atak serca; **she has toothache** boli ją ząb; **he had his car stolen** ukradziono mu samochód; **she has had her windows broken** ktoś wybił jej szyby w oknach ⑨ (cause to be done) **to ~ the house painted** mieć pomalowany dom; **to ~ one's hair cut** obciąć (sobie) włosy (u fryzjera); **to ~ an injection** mieć zastrzyk ⑩ (cause to become) **she had them completely baffled** wprawiła ich w stan całkowitego osłupienia; **I had it finished by 5 o'clock** skończyłem przed piątą ⑪ (allow) pozwalać na (coś); **I won't have it!** nie pozwolę na to! ⑫ (give birth to) mieć *[child, young]*; **has she had it yet?** czy już urodziła?

Ⅱ *modal aux* ① (must) **I ~ got to leave** muszę już iść ② (need to) **you don't ~ to leave so early** nie musisz tak wcześnie wychodzić; **something had to be done** coś trzeba było zrobić

Ⅲ *aux* ① **she has lost her bag** zgubiła torebkę; **she has already left** już wyszła; **she has hurt herself** skaleczyła się ② (in tags, short answers) **you've seen that film, haven't you?** widziałeś ten film, prawda?; **you haven't seen that film, ~ you?** nie widziałeś tego filmu, prawda?; **'you've never met him' – 'yes I ~!'** „nie poznałaś go"– „właśnie, że tak!" ③ **had I know I woudn't ~ bought it** gdybym wiedział, nie kupiłbym tego

■ **have on:** być ubranym w (coś) *[coat, skirt]*; **to ~ nothing on** nie mieć nic na sobie; (be busy) nie mieć nic w planie; **to ~ sb on** infml (tease) drażnić się z (kimś)

(IDIOMS:) **I've had it (up to here)** infml mam tego po dziurki w nosie infml; **to ~ it in for sb** infml uwziąć się na kogoś; **she doesn't ~ it in her to do it** (have skill) nie potrafi tego zrobić; (have courage) nie jest zdolna do zrobienia tego; **to ~ it out with sb** rozmówić się z kimś szczerze; **the ~s and the ~-nots** bogaci i biedni

haven /'heɪvn/ *n* ① (safe place) schronienie *n* (**for sb** dla kogoś) ② (harbour) przystań *f*

havoc /'hævək/ *n* ① (devastation) spustoszenie *n*; **to wreak ~ on sth** zdewastować coś *[building]*; spustoszyć coś *[landscape]* ② (confusion) zamieszanie *n*

Hawaii /hə'waɪɪ/ *prn* Hawaje *plt*

hawk /hɔːk/ *n* jastrząb *m*

hawthorn /'hɔːθɔːn/ *n* głóg *m*

hay /heɪ/ *n* siano *n*

hay fever *n* katar *m* sienny

haystack /'heɪstæk/ *n* stóg *m* siana

(IDIOMS:) **it is/was like looking for a needle in a ~** to jak szukanie igły w stogu siana

haywire /'heɪwaɪə(r)/ *adj* infml ① (faulty) **to go ~** *[plan]* wziąć w łeb; *[machinery]* sfiksować infml ② (crazy) sfiksowany infml

hazard /'hæzəd/ **Ⅰ** *n* niebezpieczeństwo *n*; (source of danger) zagrożenie *n*; **a health ~** zagrożenie dla zdrowia

Ⅱ *vt* (venture) za|ryzykować *[opinion]*; **to ~ a guess that...** zaryzykować stwierdzenie, że...

hazardous /'hæzədəs/ *adj* niebezpieczny; *[journey, enterprise]* ryzykowny

haze /heɪz/ *n* (mist) opar *m*; (light) mgiełka *f*; (of fumes, smoke) opary *m pl*

hazel /'heɪzl/ **Ⅰ** *n* leszczyna *f*

Ⅱ *adj [eyes]* orzechowy

hazelnut /'heɪzlnʌt/ *n* orzech *m* laskowy

hazy /'heɪzɪ/ *adj [weather, morning]* mglisty; *[sun]* zamglony; *[idea, recollection]* mglisty

he /hiː, hɪ/ *pron* on; **he's seen us** zobaczył nas; **there he is** jest tam; **he's a genius** to geniusz; **he and I** on i ja

head /hed/ **Ⅰ** *n* ① głowa *f*; (of animal) łeb *m*, głowa *f*; **from ~ to foot** or **toe** od stóp do głów; **to stand on one's ~** stanąć na głowie, zrobić stójkę; **10 pounds a ~** or **per ~** 10 funtów od głowy or od osoby ② (of family, church) głowa *f*; (of company, school) dyrektor *m*, -ka *f*; szef *m*, -owa *f* infml; (of organization) przywód|ca *m*, -czyni *f*; **~ of State** głowa państwa **Ⅱ** **heads** *npl* (of coin) orzeł *m*; **~s or tails?** orzeł czy reszka?

Ⅲ *adj* ① **~ injury** uraz głowy ② (chief) główny

Ⅳ *vt* ① być na początku (czegoś) *[list, queue]*; stać or być na czele (czegoś) *[firm, team]*; po|prowadzić *[expedition, enquiry]* ② **~ed writing paper** papier listowy z nagłówkiem ③ (steer) po|prowadzić *[vehicle]* ④ Sport **to ~ the ball** zagrać główką

Ⅴ *vi* **where was the train ~ed** or **~ing?** dokąd jechał ten pociąg?; **to ~ south/north** brać kurs na południe/północ; **to ~ home** wracać do domu; **he's ~ing this way!** idzie tu or w tę stronę!

■ **head for:** zmierzać or kierować do (czegoś) or ku (czemuś); **to be ~ing for a defeat** zmierzać do klęski

(IDIOMS:) **to go to sb's ~** *[alcohol, success]* uderzyć komuś do głowy; **to keep/lose one's ~** nie tracić głowy/tracić głowę; **off the top of one's ~** *[say, answer]* bez zastanowienia

headache /'hedeɪk/ *n* ból *m* głowy; **I have a ~** boli mnie głowa

headband /'hedbænd/ *n* opaska *f* (na głowę)

headbutt /'hedbʌt/ *vt* uderzyć (kogoś) głową or bykiem

head cold *n* katar *m*

headdress /'heddres/ *n* (of feathers) pióropusz *m*; (of lace) stroik *m*

header /'hedə(r)/ *n* ① infml (dive) **to take a ~** skoczyć (do wody) na głowę ② (in sport) główka *f*

headfirst /ˌhed'fɜːst/ *adv [fall, plunge]* na głowę; *[rush into]* bez zastanowienia

head-hunt /'hedhʌnt/ vt (seek to recruit) wyszuk|ać, -iwać [experts]

head-hunter /'hedhʌntə(r)/ n „łowca m głów" infml fig

heading /'hedɪŋ/ n (of article, column) tytuł m; (of subject, area, topic) dział m; (on notepaper, letter) nagłówek m

headlamp /'hedlæmp/ n (of car) reflektor m

headlight /'hedlaɪt/ n = headlamp

headline /'hedlaɪn/ n ① (in paper) nagłówek m; to hit the ~s trafić na pierwsze strony gazet; the front-page ~ nagłówek z pierwszej strony gazety ② Radio, TV the news ~s skrót najważniejszych wiadomości

headlong /'hedlɒŋ/ ① adj a ~ dash szalony pęd ② adv [fall] głową do przodu; [run, rush] na łeb, na szyję

head office n centrala f

head-on /ˌhed'ɒn/ adj [crash, collision] czołowy

headphones /'hedfəʊnz/ npl słuchawki f pl

headquarters /ˌhed'kwɔːtəz/ npl centrala f; Mil kwatera f główna

head rest n podgłówek m; (in car) zagłówek m

head start n to have a ~over sb mieć przewagę nad kimś

headstone /'hedstəʊn/ n nagrobek m

headstrong /'hedstrɒŋ/ adj [person] uparty; [attitude] nieustępliwy

head teacher n dyrektor m, -ka f szkoły

headway /'hedweɪ/ n to make ~ posuwać się do przodu; fig robić postępy

heady /'hedɪ/ adj [mixture, wine] uderzający do głowy; [perfume] mocny; [experience] podniecający

heal /hiːl/ ① vt wy|leczyć [person, injury] ② vi [wound, cut] za|goić się; [fracture] zr|osnąć, -astać się

healer /'hiːlə(r)/ n uzdrowiciel m, -ka f

healing /'hiːlɪŋ/ ① n (of person) wy|leczenie (się) n; (of wound) za|gojenie (się) n ② adj [power, effect] leczniczy

health /helθ/ n zdrowie n; in good/bad ~ w dobrym zdrowiu/w złym stanie (zdrowia); here's to your ~! (twoje) zdrowie!, na zdrowie!

health club n fitness club m

health farm n ośrodek m odnowy biologicznej

health food n zdrowa żywność f

healthily /'helθɪlɪ/ adv zdrowo

health insurance n ubezpieczenie n zdrowotne

Health Service n ① GB służba f zdrowia ② US Univ ≈ szpital m studencki

healthy /'helθɪ/ adj [person, animal, plant, lifestyle, economy] zdrowy; [appetite] dobry; [exercise] dla zdrowia; [profit] znaczny

heap /hiːp/ ① n sterta f; ~s of sth infml kupa czegoś infml ② vt ① (pile) zgarn|ąć, -iać na stertę [leaves]; u|łożyć, -kładać jeden na drugim [bodies]; u|łożyć,

-kładać kupki (czegoś) [money] ② fig to ~ sth on sb obsypać kogoś czymś [presents, praise]

heaped /hiːpt/ adj a ~ spoonful czubata łyżka

hear /hɪə(r)/ ① vt ① (perceive) u|słyszeć; he couldn't make his voice heard nie było go słychać; fig nikt go nie słuchał ② (learn) u|słyszeć [news, rumour] ③ (listen to) wy|słuchać (kogoś/czegoś) [concert, sermon]; (judge) wysłuchać (kogoś/czegoś) [evidence]; rozpozna|ć, -wać [case] ② vi słyszeć; to ~ about sth/sb usłyszeć o czymś/kimś
■ **hear from:** dostać wiadomość od (kogoś)
■ **hear of:** słyszeć o (kimś/czymś); I won't ~ of it! nie chcę nawet o tym słyszeć!
[IDIOMS] ~! ~! racja!

hearing /'hɪərɪŋ/ n ① (sense) słuch m; his ~ is not very good on niezbyt dobrze słyszy ② (of witness) przesłuchanie n

hearing aid n aparat m słuchowy

hearing-impaired /ˌhɪərɪŋɪm'peəd/ adj upośledzony słuchowo

hearsay /'hɪəseɪ/ n pogłoska f

hearse /hɜːs/ n karawan m

heart /hɑːt/ n ① serce n; by ~ [learn, know] na pamięć; to take sth to ~ brać coś sobie do serca; right in the ~ of London w samym sercu Londynu; the ~ of the matter sedno sprawy ② (in cards) kier m
[IDIOMS] to have one's ~ set on sth bardzo chcieć czegoś; to lose ~ stracić ducha or otuchę; take ~! głowa do góry!

heartache /'hɑːteɪk/ n smutek m

heart attack n atak m serca, zawał m (serca)

heartbeat /'hɑːtbiːt/ n bicie n serca

heartbreaking /'hɑːtbreɪkɪŋ/ adj rozdzierający serce

heartbroken /'hɑːtbrəʊkn/ adj załamany

heart disease n choroba f serca

heartening /'hɑːtnɪŋ/ adj dodający otuchy

heart failure n zatrzymanie n akcji serca

heartfelt /'hɑːtfelt/ adj [sympathy] szczery; [words] serdeczny; [appeal] gorący

hearth /hɑːθ/ n (of fireplace) palenisko n; ~ rug dywanik m przed kominkiem

heartless /'hɑːtlɪs/ adj [person] bez serca; [attitude, treatment] bezduszny

heart-throb /'hɑːtθrɒb/ n infml idol m

heart-to-heart /ˌhɑːttə'hɑːt/ n to have a ~ porozmawiać szczerze (with sb z kimś)

heart transplant n przeszczep m serca

hearty /'hɑːtɪ/ adj ① [welcome, greeting, laugh] serdeczny; [person] rubaszny ② [approval] całkowity; [appetite] wilczy

heat /hiːt/ ① n ① gorąco n; (in physics) ciepło n; (weather) upał m, skwar m ② Sport wyścig m eliminacyjny; (in athletics) zawody plt eliminacyjne ③ Zool to be on or in ~ być w okresie rui

II *vt* ogrz|ać, -ewać *[house, pool]*; podgrz|ać, -ewać *[food]*; rozgrz|ać, -ewać *[oven]*

■ **heat up**: podgrz|ać, -ewać *[food]*; (reheat) odgrz|ać, -ewać

heated /'hi:tɪd/ *adj* *[pool, water]* podgrzewany; fig *[debate]* gorący; *[argument]* zaciekły, zajadły

heater /'hi:tə(r)/ *n* grzejnik *m*

heathen /'hi:ðn/ **II** *n* (unbeliever) pogan|in *m*, -ka *f*; (uncivilized) barbarzyńca *m* infml pej

II *adj* (irreligious) pogański; (uncivilized) barbarzyński

heather /'heðə(r)/ *n* wrzos *m*

heating /'hi:tɪŋ/ *n* ogrzewanie *n*

heat stroke *n* udar *m* cieplny

heatwave /'hi:tweɪv/ *n* fala *f* upałów

heave /hi:v/ **II** *vt* (lift) po|dźwignąć; (pull) prze- ciąg|nąć, -ać; (throw) cis|nąć, -kać (czymś) (at sth w coś); **to ~ a sigh** westchnąć głęboko

II *vi* [1] *[sea, ground]* podnosić się i opadać [2] (pull) po|ciągnąć z całych sił [3] (retch) mieć nudności; (vomit) z|wymiotować

heaven /'hevn/ *n* niebo *n*; **thank ~(s)!** dzięki Bogu!

heavenly /'hevənlɪ/ *adj* [1] *[choir]* niebiański; *[peace]* boski [2] infml (wonderful) boski

heavily /'hevɪlɪ/ *adv* [1] *[breathe, lean, fall, sigh]* ciężko; *[sleep]* twardo; **~ underlined** podkreślony grubą kreską [2] (abundantly) *[drink, invest, smoke]* dużo; *[bleed]* silnie; *[taxed]* wysoko; *[armed]* silnie; **it rained ~** padał ulewny deszcz; **it snowed ~** sypał gęsty śnieg

heavy /'hevɪ/ *adj* ciężki; *[coat, frame, features, line]* gruby; *[shoe]* ciężki; *[traffic]* duży; *[fine, sentence]* wysoki; *[bleeding]* obfity; *[cold, accent]* silny; *[rain]* ulewny; *[snow]* gęsty; *[perfume]* mocny; **to be a ~ sleeper** mieć mocny sen; **to be a ~ drinker** dużo pić

heavy-handed /ˌhevɪ'hændɪd/ *adj* *[person]* nie- okrzesany pej; *[remark, behaviour]* niezręczny

heavyweight /'hevɪweɪt/ *n* [1] (boxer) bokser *m* wagi ciężkiej [2] infml fig grube ryby *f* infml

Hebrew /'hi:bru:/ **II** *n* [1] (person) Hebraj|czyk *m*, -ka *f* [2] (language) (język *m*) hebrajski *m*

II *adj* hebrajski

heckle /'hekl/ **II** *vt* zakrzyczeć (kogoś) *[speaker]*

II *vi* wywoł|ać, -ywać zamieszanie pej

hectic /'hektɪk/ *adj* *[activity, period]* gorączkowy; *[day]* nerwowy; *[schedule]* napięty; **to have a ~ life** żyć w szalonym tempie

hedge /hedʒ/ **II** *n* żywopłot *m*

II *vi* (equivocate) kluczyć

IDIOMS **to ~ one's bets** asekurować się

hedgehog /'hedʒhɒg/ *n* jeż *m*

hedgerow /'hedʒrəʊ/ *n* żywopłot *m*

heed /hi:d/ **II** *n* **to take ~ of sb** zważać na kogoś; **to take ~ of sth** brać coś pod rozwagę

II *vt* zważ|yć, -ać na (coś) *[advice, warning]*

heel /hi:l/ *n* pięta *f*; (of shoe) obcas *m*

IDIOMS **to fall head over ~s in love with sb** zakochać się w kimś po uszy; **to be hot on sb's ~s** deptać komuś po piętach

heel bar *n* zakład *m* szewski

hefty /'heftɪ/ *adj* *[person]* zwalisty; *[object]* ciężki; *[sum]* ogromny; *[object]* ciężki

heifer /'hefə(r)/ *n* jałówka *f*

height /haɪt/ *n* [1] (of person) wzrost *m*; (of table, tower, tree) wysokość *f* [2] (of plane) wysokość *f*; **to gain/lose ~** nabierać wysokości/tracić wysokość; **at a ~ of 200 metres** na wysokości 200 metrów; **to be scared of ~s** mieć lęk wysokości [3] fig (peak) szczyt *m*; **at the ~ of the season** w pełni sezonu; **at the ~ of sth** w kulminacyjnym momencie or w środku czegoś; **to be the ~ of fashion** być szczytem mody

heighten /'haɪtn/ **II** *vt* wzm|óc, -agać *[tension]*; zwiększ|yć, -ać *[effect]*; s|potęgować *[emotion]*

II *vi* *[tension]* wzm|óc, -agać się

heir /eə(r)/ *n* spadkobier|ca *m*, -czyni *f* (**to sth** czegoś)

heiress /'eərɪs/ *n* spadkobierczyni *f*; (to the throne) następczyni *f* tronu

heirloom /'eəlu:m/ *n* pamiątka *f*; **a family ~** pamiątka rodzinna

helicopter /'helɪkɒptə(r)/ *n* helikopter *m*

hell /hel/ *n* [1] piekło *n*; **in ~** w piekle; **to make sb's life ~** zamienić komuś życie w piekło [2] infml (as intensifier) **a ~ of a shock** potworny szok; **it's a ~ of a lot worse** to jest o wiele gorsze; **why the ~?** dlaczego do diabła? infml; **what the ~?** a niech tam! infml

IDIOMS **to do sth for the ~ of it** infml zrobić coś dla draki infml; **to raise ~** infml zrobić piekło infml (**with sb** komuś)

hello /hə'ləʊ/ *excl* [1] (greeting) cześć!; (on phone) halo! [2] (in surprise) coś takiego!, no, no!

helm /helm/ *n* ster *m*; **at the ~** przy sterze or u steru

helmet /'helmɪt/ *n* kask *m*; Mil hełm *m*

help /help/ **II** *n* pomoc *f*; (in an emergency) ratunek *m*; **with the ~ of sth** za pomocą czegoś *[knife, stick]*; **with the ~ of sb** z pomocą kogoś *[person]*; **to be of ~ to sb** *[person]* pomóc komuś; *[information, map]* być komuś pomocnym; **you are a great ~!** iron za taką pomoc bardzo dziękujemy! iron; **to cry for ~** wołać o pomoc

II *excl* pomocy!, ratunku!

III *vt* [1] (aid) pom|óc, -agać (komuś) (**to do sth** coś zrobić); (more urgently) po|ratować (kogoś); **to ~ each other** pomagać sobie (wzajemnie); **to ~ sb across** pomóc komuś przejść przez jezdnię [2] (serve) **to ~ sb to sth** poczęstować kogoś czymś *[food, wine]*; **to ~ oneself** po|częstować się [3] (prevent) **it can't be ~ed!** nic się na to nie poradzi!

IV *vi* pom|óc, -agać; **he never** ~s **with the housework** nigdy nie pomaga przy sprzątaniu; **this map doesn't** ~ **much** ta mapa nie na wiele się przydaje
■ **help out:** ¶ ~ **out** pom|óc, -agać ¶ ~ **[sb] out** pom|óc, -agać (komuś)

helper /'helpə(r)/ *n* pomocni|k *m*, -ca *f*; (for handicapped person) pracownik *m* socjalny, pracownica *f* socjalna

helpful /'helpfl/ *adj [person]* pomocny; *[tool, advice, suggestion]* przydatny

helping /'helpıŋ/ *n* porcja *f*

helpless /'helplıs/ *adj* ① (powerless) bezsilny; (incapable) bezradny ② (defenceless) *[person]* bezbronny

helpline /'helplaın/ *n* telefon *m* zaufania

hem /hem/ *n* (of dress, skirt) rąbek *m*
■ **hem in:** okrąż|yć, -ać (kogoś)

hemisphere /'hemısfıə(r)/ *n* półkula *f*

hemp /hemp/ *n* konopie *plt*

hen /hen/ *n* kura *f*

hence /hens/ *adv* fml ① (for this reason) stąd, (a) więc ② (from now) odtąd

henchman /'hentʃmən/ *n* poplecznik *m*

henna /'henə/ *n* henna *f*

hen night *n* babski wieczór *m* infml

hen-pecked /'henpekt/ *adj* ~ **husband** pantoflarz infml

hepatitis /ˌhepə'taıtıs/ *n* zapalenie *n* wątroby

her /hɜː(r), hə(r)/ **I** *pron* ① (as object) **I like** ~ lubię ją; **give it to** ~ daj to jej ② (after preposition, or to be) **it's** ~ to ona; **for** ~ dla niej
II *det* jej

herald /'herəld/ **I** *n* herold *m*; fig zwiastun *m*, -ka *f*
II *vt* (also ~ **in**) zwiastować

heraldry /'herəldrı/ *n* heraldyka *f*

herb /hɜːb/ *n* zioło *n*; **mixed** ~s zioła prowansalskie

herbal tea *n* herbata *f* ziołowa

herd /hɜːd/ **I** *n* (of animals) stado *n*; pej (of people) tłum *m*
II *vt* zag|onić, -aniać *[animals]*; **to** ~ **people into sth** zgromadzić or stłoczyć ludzi w czymś
IDIOMS: **to follow the** ~ ulegać owczemu pędowi

here /hıə(r)/ *adv* tu, tutaj; **near** ~ blisko stąd; **come over** ~ chodź or podejdź tu; ~ **and there** (in places) tu i tam, gdzieniegdzie; ~ **she comes!** a oto ona!; ~ **you are** (offering sth) proszę; **she's not** ~ **right now** w tej chwili nie ma jej tutaj; ~ **we are at last** nareszcie jesteśmy na miejscu; **we get off** ~ tutaj wysiadamy; **now that summer's** ~ teraz, kiedy nadeszło lato; ~ **'s our chance** mamy szansę or okazję
IDIOMS: ~ **'s to our success/to you!** (toast) za nasz sukces/twoje zdrowie

hereabout US, **hereabouts** GB /'hıərəbaut(s)/ *adv* gdzieś tutaj

hereafter /hıər'ɑːftə(r)/ **I** *n* the ~ życie *n* przyszłe
II *adv* od tej chwili

here and now *n* the ~ (present) chwila *f* obecna

hereby /hıə'baı/ *adv* niniejszym

hereditary /hı'redıtrı, US -terı/ *adj* dziedziczny

heresy /'herəsı/ *n* herezja *f*

heritage /'herıtıdʒ/ *n* dziedzictwo *n*

hermit /'hɜːmıt/ *n* pustelni|k *m*, -ca *f*

hernia /'hɜːnıə/ *n* przepuklina *f*

hero /'hıərəu/ *n* bohater *m*

heroic /hı'rəuık/ *adj [person, deed]* bohaterski

heroin /'herəuın/ *n* heroina *f*

heroin addict *n* heroinist|a *m*, -ka *f*

heroine /'herəuın/ *n* bohaterka *f*

heroism /'herəuızəm/ *n* bohaterstwo *n*, heroizm *m*

heron /'herən/ *n* czapla *f*

hero-worship /'hıərəuwɜː'ʃıp/ **I** *n* uwielbienie *n*
II *vt* ubóstwiać

herring /'herıŋ/ *n* śledź *m*

hers /hɜːz/ *pron* jej; **which house is** ~? który dom jest jej?; **I'm a friend of** ~ jestem jej znajomym; **it's not** ~ to nie jej

herself /hə'self/ *pron* **she's hurt** ~ uderzyła się; **for** ~ dla siebie; **(all) by** ~ (całkiem or zupełnie) sama; **she's not** ~ **today** nie jest dzisiaj w formie

hesitant /'hezıtənt/ *adj* niezdecydowany; **to be** ~ **about sth** nie móc się na coś zdecydować; (wavering) wahać się co do czegoś *[plan, scheme]*

hesitate /'hezıteıt/ *vi* za|wahać się (**over sth** co do czegoś); **to** ~ **to do sth** zawahać się, czy coś zrobić

hesitation /ˌhezı'teıʃn/ *n* wahanie *n*

heterosexual /ˌhetərə'sekʃuəl/ **I** *n* osoba *f* heteroseksualna
II *adj* heteroseksualny

hexagon /'heksəgən, US -gɒn/ *n* sześciokąt *m*

hey /heı/ *excl* infml (call for attention) hej!; (in protest) ejże!

heyday /'heıdeı/ *n* okres *m* rozkwitu; (of fame) szczyt *m*; (of youth, vigour) pełnia *f*; **to be in one's** ~ (at one's best) przeżywać najlepszy okres or najlepsze lata; (at peak of fame) być u szczytu sławy

HGV *n* GB = **heavy goods vehicle** samochód *m* ciężarowy

hi /haı/ *excl* infml cześć! infml

hibernate /'haıbəneıt/ *vi* zapa|ść, -dać w sen zimowy

hiccup /'hıkʌp/, **hiccough** /hıkʌf, US -kɔːf/ *n* ① czkawka *f*; **to have (the)** ~s mieć czkawkę ② (setback) drobny problem *m*

hidden /'hıdn/ *adj* ukryty

hide /haıd/ **I** *n* (skin, leather) skóra *f*
II *vt* ukry|ć, -wać *[person, object]* (**from sb** przed kimś); skry|ć, -wać *[emotions]* (**from sb** przed kimś)
III *vi* ukry|ć, -wać się, s|chować się

hide and seek GB, **hide-and-go-seek** US *n* zabawa *f* w chowanego

hideaway /ˈhaɪdəwəɪ/ *n* kryjówka *f*

hideous /ˈhɪdɪəs/ *adj [object]* ohydny; *[noise]* okropny

hiding /ˈhaɪdɪŋ/ *n* ☐ (concealment) **to go into ~** ukryć się; **to come out of ~** wyjść z ukrycia ☐ (beating) lanie *n*

hiding place *n* kryjówka *f*

hierarchy /ˈhaɪərɑːkɪ/ *n* hierarchia *f*

hieroglyph, hieroglyphic /ˈhaɪərəglɪf/(ɪk) *n* hieroglif *m*

hi-fi /ˈhaɪfaɪ/ *n* ☐ (set of equipment) zestaw *m* hi-fi ☐ = **high fidelity** hi-fi *n inv*

high /haɪ/ ☐ *n* ☐ (level) **to reach a new ~** osiągnąć rekordowy poziom ☐ infml **to be on a ~** być w euforii ☐ *adj* ☐ (big) wysoki; **how ~ is the cliff?** jaka jest wysokość tego klifu?; **it is 50 cm ~** to ma 50 cm wysokości ☐ *[number, price]* wysoki; *[wind]* silny; *[playing card]* mocny; **at ~ speed** z dużą prędkością; **to have a ~ temperature** mieć gorączkę; **~ in sth** bogaty w coś *[iron]*; zawierający duże ilości czegoś *[fat]* ☐ *[quality, standard, rank]* wysoki; **to have friends in ~ places** mieć wpływowych przyjaciół ☐ *[ideal, principle]* szlachetny ☐ *[pitch, voice, note]* wysoki ☐ infml (on drug) na haju infml; (happy) w stanie euforii ☐ *adv* wysoko

highbrow /ˈhaɪbraʊ/ ☐ *n* intelektualist|a *m*, -ka *f* ☐ *adj [taste, interest]* intelektualny; *[music, literature, art]* trudny w odbiorze

high chair *n* wysokie krzesełko *n* (dziecięce)

high-class /ˈhaɪˈklɑːs, US -ˈklæs/ *adj [hotel, shop, car]* luksusowy; *[goods]* pierwszego gatunku; *[area]* elegancki

high court *n* Sąd *m* Najwyższy

high-definition TV, HDTV /ˈhaɪˌdefɪˈnɪʃn tiːviː/ *n* telewizja *f* o dużej rozdzielczości

higher education *n* wyższe studia *plt*; (of person) wyższe wykształcenie *n*

high fashion *n* haute couture *n inv*

high-flier /ˈhaɪˈflaɪə(r)/ *n* młody wilk *m* fig

high-handed /ˈhaɪˈhændɪd/ *adj [decision]* arbitralny; *[person]* arogancki

high heels *npl* (heels) wysokie obcasy *m pl*; (shoes) buty *m pl* na wysokich obcasach

high jump *n* Sport skok *m* wzwyż

Highlands /ˈhaɪləndz/ *prn pl* region *m* górski i wyżynny północnej Szkocji

highlight /ˈhaɪlaɪt/ ☐ *n* ☐ (in hair) (natural) jasne pasemko *n*; (dyed) pasemko *n* ☐ (of match, event) punkt *m* kulminacyjny; (of evening, year) najważniejsze wydarzenie *n* ☐ **highlights** *npl* (on radio, TV) przegląd *m* najważniejszych wydarzeń ☐ *vt* ☐ (with pen) zakreśl|ić, -ać ☐ (emphasize) uwydatni|ć, -ać

highlighter /ˈhaɪlaɪtə(r)/ *n* (pen) marker *m*

highly /ˈhaɪlɪ/ *adv* bardzo; *[unlikely]* wysoce; *[flammable]* łatwo; *[confidential]* ściśle; *[developed]* wysoko; *[recommend]* gorąco; *[seasoned]* mocno; **to think ~ of sb** mieć o kimś wysokie mniemanie

highly-paid /ˈhaɪlɪˈpeɪd/ *adj [job]* dobrze płatny; *[employee]* wysoko opłacany

highly-strung /ˈhaɪlɪˈstrʌŋ/ *adj* bardzo nerwowy

Highness /ˈhaɪnɪs/ *n* **His** or **Her (Royal) ~** Jego/Jej Wysokość *f*

high-pitched /ˈhaɪˈpɪtʃt/ *adj [sound]* wysoki; *[voice]* cienki, piskliwy

high point *n* apogeum *n inv*, punkt *m* kulminacyjny

high-powered /ˈhaɪˈpaʊəd/ *adj [engine, car]* o dużej mocy; *[person]* dynamiczny, energiczny; *[job]* odpowiedzialny

high-profile /ˈhaɪˈprəʊfaɪl/ *adj [politician, group]* szeroko znany; *[visit]* na wysokim szczeblu

high-ranking /ˈhaɪˈræŋkɪŋ/ *adj [position, post]* wysoki

high school *n* US liceum *n*; GB ≈ szkoła *f* ogólnokształcąca

high-speed /ˈhaɪˈspiːd/ *adj [train]* szybkobieżny

high street GB (also **High Street**) *n* główna ulica *f*

high street spending *n* codzienne wydatki *m pl*

high-street shop /ˈhaɪstriːtˈʃɒp/ *n* sklep *m* należący do sieci

high tech /ˈhaɪˈtek/ *adj [industry]* stosujący najnowocześniejsze techniki; *[equipment]* nowoczesny

high tide *n* przypływ *m*

highway /ˈhaɪweɪ/ *n* GB (main road) szosa *f*; US (motorway) autostrada *f*

Highway Code *n* GB kodeks *m* drogowy

hijack /ˈhaɪdʒæk/ *vt* por|wać, -ywać *[plane]*

hijacker /ˈhaɪdʒækə(r)/ *n* (of plane) porywacz *m*, -ka *f*

hijacking /ˈhaɪdʒækɪŋ/ *n* (of plane) uprowadzenie *n*

hike /haɪk/ ☐ *n* piesza wycieczka *f*; **to go on a ~** iść na wycieczkę ☐ *vt* (also **~ up**) podn|ieść, -osić *[rate, price]*

hiker /ˈhaɪkə(r)/ *n* turyst|a *m*, -ka *f*

hiking /ˈhaɪkɪŋ/ *n* piesze wycieczki *f pl*

hilarious /hɪˈleərɪəs/ *adj [story, person]* komiczny; *[party]* wesoły

hill /hɪl/ *n* (elevation) wzgórze *n*; (mound) pagórek *m*; (incline) wzniesienie *n*

hillside /ˈhɪlsaɪd/ *n* zbocze *n*; **on the ~** na zboczu

hilltop /ˈhɪltɒp/ *n* szczyt *m* wzgórza

hilly /ˈhɪlɪ/ *adj* pagórkowaty

him /hɪm/ *pron* ☐ (as subject) **I know ~** znam go; **give it to ~** daj mu to; **we bought ~ flowers** kupiliśmy mu kwiaty ☐ (after preposition or to be) **it's ~ to** to on; **for ~** dla niego

Himalayas /ˌhɪməˈleɪəz/ *prn pl* **the ~** Himalaje *plt*

himself /hɪm'self/ *pron* (reflexive) **he's hurt** ~ skaleczył się; **for** ~ dla siebie; **(all) by** ~ (całkiem or zupełnie) sam; **he's not** ~ **today** jest dziś nie w humorze

hind /haɪnd/ *adj* ~ **legs** nogi tylne or zadnie

hinder /'hɪndə(r)/ *vt* przeszk|odzić, -adzać (czemuś) *[development, efforts]*; opóźni|ć, -ać *[progress, plan]*

hindrance /'hɪndrəns/ *n* przeszkoda *f*; **to be a** ~ **to sb/sth** być zawadą dla kogoś/czegoś

hindsight /'haɪndsaɪt/ *n* **with (the benefit of)** ~ z perspektywy czasu

Hindu /ˌhɪn'duː, US 'hɪnduː/ **[I]** *n* Hindus *m*, -ka *f*; hinduist|a *m*, -ka *f*

[II] *adj* hinduski; *[religion]* hinduistyczny

hinge /hɪndʒ/ **[I]** *n* zawias *m*

[II] *vi* **to** ~ **on sb/sth** zależeć (całkowicie) od kogoś/czegoś

hint /hɪnt/ **[I]** *n* aluzja *f* (**about sth** do czegoś); (of spices) odrobina *f*; (of colour, accent) krztyna *f*; (of smile) cień *m*; **to drop** ~**s** robić aluzje; **give me a** ~ podpowiedz mi

[II] *vt* **to** ~ **(to sb) that...** dać (komuś) do zrozumienia, że...

[III] *vi* ~ **at sth** napom|knąć, -ykać o (czymś)

hip /hɪp/ **[I]** *n* biodro *n*

[II] *adj* infml *[person]* najmodniejszy; infml

[III] *excl* ~ ~ **hurrah!** hip hip, hura!

hippie, hippy /'hɪpɪ/ **[I]** *n* hip(p)is *m*, -ka *f*

[II] *adj* hip(p)isowski

hippo /'hɪpəʊ/ *n* hipopotam *m*

hippopotamus /ˌhɪpə'pɒtəməs/ *n* → **hippo**

hire /'haɪə(r)/ **[I]** *n* (of flat, car) wynajem *m*; (of equipment) wypożyczanie *n*; **for** ~ *[flat, car]* do wynajęcia; *[equipment]* do wypożyczenia; *[taxi]* wolny

[II] *vt* **[1]** wynaj|ąć, -mować *[flat, car]*; wypożycz|yć, -ać *[equipment]* **[2]** (employ) (for particular purpose) wynaj|ąć, -mować; (for long period) zatrudni|ć, -ać *[person]*

hire purchase, HP *n* sprzedaż *f* ratalna; **on** ~ na raty

his /hɪz/ **[I]** *det* jego

[II] *pron* jego; **the car is** ~ samochód jest jego; **a friend of** ~ jego znajomy

hiss /hɪs/ **[I]** *n* (single) syk *m*; (continuous) syczenie *n*; (of tape) szum *m*

[II] *vi* *[snake, person]* za|syczeć; *[fat]* za|skwierczeć; *[cat]* prych|nąć, -ać

historian /hɪ'stɔːrɪən/ *n* historyk *m*

historic(al) /hɪ'stɒrɪk(l), US -'stɔːr-/ *adj* historyczny

history /'hɪstrɪ/ *n* historia *f*; **to have a** ~ **of heart trouble** od dawna chorować na serce; **to have a** ~ **of violence** być uprzednio karanym za akty przemocy

hit /hɪt/ **[I]** *n* **[1]** (blow, stroke) cios *m*, uderzenie *n* **[2]** (success) (play, film) sukces *m*; (record) przebój *m*, hit *m*; **to be a big** ~ odnieść olbrzymi sukces

[II] *vt* **[1]** (strike) uderz|yć, -ać *[person, ball]*; **to** ~ **one's head on sth** uderzyć głową o coś **[2]** (when shooting) trafi|ć, -ać *[victim, target]* **[3]** (collide with) uderz|yć, -ać w (coś) *[vehicle, wall]*; *[vehicle]* potrącić (kogoś) **[4]** (affect adversely) uderz|yć, -ać w (coś) **[5]** (reach) doje|chać, -żdżać do (czegoś) *[motorway]*; trafi|ć, -ać na (coś) *[traffic, bad weather]*; *[figures, weight]* osiąg|nąć, -ać *[level]*

■ **hit back:** ¶ ~ **[sb] back** odda|ć, -wać (komuś) infml ¶ ~ **[sth] back** odbi|ć, -jać *[ball]*

IDIOMS **to** ~ **it off with sb** zaprzyjaźnić się z kimś

hit-and-run /ˌhɪtən'rʌn/ *adj* ~ **accident** wypadek drogowy, którego sprawca zbiegł

hitch /hɪtʃ/ **[I]** *n* szkopuł *m* infml

[II] *vt* **[1]** (connect) doczepi|ć, -ać *[trailer]* (**to sth** do czegoś) **[2]** infml (thumb) **to** ~ **a lift** złapać okazję infml

[III] *vi* infml je|chać, -ździć stopem infml

hitchhike /'hɪtʃhaɪk/ *vi* je|chać, -ździć autostopem

hitchhiker /'hɪtʃhaɪkə(r)/ *n* autostopowicz *m*, -ka *f*

hitchhiking /'hɪtʃhaɪkɪŋ/ *n* autostop *m*

hit man *n* płatny zabójca *m*

hit parade *n* lista *f* przebojów

hit single *n* szlagier *m*

HIV *n* = **human immunodeficiency virus** wirus *m* HIV

hive /haɪv/ *n* ul *m*; **it's a** ~ **of activity** fig tu aż wrze fig

hoard /hɔːd/ **[I]** *n* (of treasure) skarb *m*; (of provisions) zapasy *m pl*; **a miser's** ~ uciułane pieniądze

[II] *vt* z|robić zapasy (czegoś) *[food]*; **to** ~ **money** pej u|ciułać pieniądze

hoarding /'hɔːdɪŋ/ *n* GB **[1]** (for advertisements) billboard *m* **[2]** (fence) parkan *m*, płot *m*

hoarse /hɔːs/ *adj* *[voice]* zachrypnięty; **to be** ~ mieć zachrypnięty głos

hoax /həʊks/ **[I]** *n* (głupi) kawał *m*

[II] *adj* *[claim, warning]* fałszywy; ~ **call** dowcip telefoniczny

hob /hɒb/ *n* (on cooker) płyta *f* grzejna

hobble /'hɒbl/ *vi* kuśtykać

hobby /'hɒbɪ/ *n* konik *m*, hobby *n inv*

hockey /'hɒkɪ/ *n* **[1]** GB hokej *m* na trawie **[2]** US hokej *m* na lodzie

hoe /həʊ/ **[I]** *n* motyka *f*

[II] *vt* spulchni|ć, -ać *[ground]*; op|leć, -ielać *[flower beds]*

hog /hɒg/ **[I]** *n* US (pig) świnia *f*, tucznik *m*

[II] *vt* infml okupować fig hum *[bathroom]*; **to** ~ **the telephone** wisieć bez przerwy na telefonie infml

IDIOMS **to go the whole** ~ infml iść na całego

hoist /hɔɪst/ *vt* w|ciąg|nąć, -ać *[flag, sail]*; dźwig|nąć, -ać *[heavy object]*

hold /həʊld/ **[I]** *n* **[1]** (grasp) uścisk *m*; **to get** ~ **of sth** chwycić *[rope, handle]* **[2]** **to get** ~ **of sth** zdoby|ć, -wać infml *[book, ticket]*; do|trzeć, -cierać do (czegoś) *[information]* ③ **to get** ~ **of sb** s|kontaktować się z kimś ④ (control) kontrola *f* (**on** or **over sb/sth** nad kimś/czymś); **to have a** ~ **on** or **over sb** trzymać kogoś w garści infml; **to get a** ~ **of oneself** wziąć się w garść infml ⑤ **to put a call on** ~ zawiesić połączenie (do czasu zakończenia poprzedniej rozmowy) ⑥ (in plane, ship) luk *m* towarowy, ładownia *f*

II *vt* ① (clasp) trzymać; **to** ~ **sth in one's hand** trzymać coś w ręce *[brush, pencil]*; trzymać or ściskać coś w dłoni *[button, coin]*; **to** ~ **sb (in one's arms)** trzymać kogoś w ramionach; **to** ~ **sth in place** przytrzymać coś w miejscu ② (arrange) odby|ć, -wać *[meeting]*; odprawi|ć, -ać *[church service]*; przeprowadz|ić, -ać *[taks, interview, enquiry]*; wyda|ć, -wać *[reception]*; z|organizować *[exhibition, competition]* ③ (contain) *[drawer, box, case]* zawierać *[objects, possessions]* ④ wyzna|ć, -wać *[opinion, belief]* ⑤ (keep against will) przetrzym|ać, -ywać *[person]*; **to** ~ **sb hostage** przetrzymywać kogoś jako zakładnika ⑥ (possess) mieć *[power, passport, position, degree]* ⑦ **to** ~ **sb responsible** obarczyć kogoś odpowiedzialnością; **to** ~ **sb's attention** przykuć uwagę kogoś ⑧ (on phone) **can you** ~ **the line, please?** proszę czekać, proszę nie odkładać słuchawki ⑨ (defend successfully) utrzym|ać, -ywać *[territory, city, title, seat]*; **to** ~ **one's own** nie poddawać się

III *vi* ① *[rope, bridge, dam]* wytrzym|ać, -ywać ② (continue) utrzym|ać, -ywać się; *[luck]* dopis|ać, -ywać ③ (on phone) czekać ④ ~ **still!** nie ruszaj się!

■ **hold against**: **to** ~ **sth against sb** mieć coś komuś za złe

■ **hold back**: ¶ ~ **back** powstrzym|ać, -ywać się (**from doing sth** od zrobienia czegoś) ¶ ~ **[sb/sth] back** zatrzym|ać, -ywać *[water, crowd]*; powstrzym|ać, -ywać *[person, tears]*; po|hamować *[anger]*; za|hamować *[development]*

■ **hold down**: ① (grip) przytrzym|ać, -ywać *[person, piece of paper]* ② (keep) nie s|tracić (czegoś) *[job]*

■ **hold on**: ① (wait) za|czekać, poczekać; ~ **on...** (on phone) „chwileczkę..." ② (grip) trzymać się; ~ **on (tight)!** trzymaj się (mocno)!

■ **hold on to**: złapać się (kogoś/czegoś), trzymać się (kogoś/czegoś) *[branch, person, rope]*; (to prevent from falling) podtrzym|ać, -ywać *[person]*; przytrzym|ać, -ywać *[object, purse]*

■ **hold out**: ¶ ~ **out** wytrzym|ać, -ywać; **to** ~ **out against sb/sth** oprzeć się komuś/czemuś *[enemy, threat]* ¶ ~ **[sth] out** poda|ć, -wać *[glass, money, ticket]* (**to sb** komuś)

■ **hold to**: domagać się od kogoś dotrzymania (czegoś) *[promise]*

■ **hold up**: ① (support) podtrzym|ać, -ywać *[shelf, trousers]* ② (raise) un|ieść, -osić ③ (delay) zatrzym|ać,

-ywać *[person, traffic, production]*; opóźni|ć, -ać *[flight]* ④ (rob) napa|ść, -dać na (kogoś/coś)

holdall /'həʊldɔːl/ *n* torba *f* podręczna

holder /'həʊldə(r)/ *n* (of ticket, licence, permit, degree) posiadacz *m*, -ka *f*; **account** ~ posiadacz konta; **record** ~ rekordzista

hold-up /'həʊldʌp/ *n* ① (delay) opóźnienie *n*; (on road) zator *m*; korek *m* infml ② (robbery) napad *m* z bronią w ręku

hole /həʊl/ *n* ① (aperture) dziura *f* ② GB (in tooth) dziura *f* ③ (of mouse) dziura *f*, norka *f*; (of fox, rabbit) nora *f*, jama *f*

hole-in-the-wall /ˌhəʊlɪnðə'wɔːl/ *n* infml bankomat *m*

holiday /'hɒlədeɪ/ *n* ① GB (vacation) wakacje *plt*; **on** ~ na wakacjach ② GB (time off work) urlop *m* ③ (public, bank) dzień *m* wolny (od pracy)

holiday home *n* letni dom *m*

holiday job *n* GB (in summer) praca *f* wakacyjna

holidaymaker /'hɒlədeɪmeɪkə(r)/ *n* GB wczasowicz *m*, -ka *f*

holiday resort *n* miejscowość *f* wypoczynkowa

Holland /'hɒlənd/ *prn* Holandia *f*

hollow /'hɒləʊ/ **I** *n* wgłębienie *n*, wklęsłość *f*; (in tree) dziupla *f*; (in ground) zagłębienie *n*

II *adj* *[container]* pusty; *[tree]* wydrążony; *[cheeks]* zapadnięty; *[words]* czczy; **to give a** ~ **laugh** zaśmiać się nieszczerze; **to sound** ~ brzmieć nieszczerze

holly /'hɒlɪ/ *n* ostrokrzew *m*

holocaust /'hɒləkɔːst/ *n* całopalenie *n*; **the Holocaust** Holocaust *m*

hologram /'hɒləgræm/ *n* hologram *m*

holster /'həʊlstə(r)/ *n* kabura *f*

holy /'həʊlɪ/ *adj* święty; *[water]* święcony

Holy Bible *n* Biblia *f*, Pismo *n* Święte

Holy Land *n* Ziemia *f* Święta

Holy Spirit *n* Duch *m* Święty

homage /'hɒmɪdʒ/ *n* hołd *m*; **to pay** ~ **to sb** złożyć komuś hołd

home /həʊm/ **I** *n* ① (dwelling) mieszkanie *n*; (house) dom *m*; **broken** ~ rozbita rodzina; **to leave** ~ opuścić (rodzinny) dom ② (institution) dom *m*; **to put sb in a** ~ umieścić kogoś w domu opieki ③ Sport **to play at** ~ grać na własnym boisku or u siebie

II *adj* ① *[life]* rodzinny; *[comforts]* domowy ② *[market, news]* krajowy; *[affairs]* wewnętrzny ③ Sport *[team]* miejscowy; *[match, win]* na własnym boisku

III *adv* ① *[come, go]* do domu, do siebie; (to country) do kraju ② **to bring sth** ~ **to sb** uświadomić komuś coś; **to strike** ~ celnie trafić

IV **at home** *adv phr* ① *[be, stay, work]* w domu ② Sport *[play]* na własnym boisku ③ (comfortable) *[feel]* jak (u siebie) or w domu; **make yourself at** ~ czuj się jak u siebie w domu

home address n (on form) miejsce n stałego zamieszkania; (personal) adres m prywatny

home cooking n kuchnia f domowa

home economics n zajęcia plt z gospodarstwa domowego

home help n GB opiekun m domowy, opiekunka f domowa

homeland /'həʊmlænd/ n kraj m rodzinny, ojczyzna f

homeless /'həʊmlɪs/ n the ~ bezdomni m pl

homely /'həʊmlɪ/ adj ① GB (cosy, welcoming) przytulny ② GB (unpretentious) bezpretensjonalny; [cooking] niewyszukany; [person] odznaczający się prostotą ③ US (plain) nieatrakcyjny

home-made /'həʊm meɪd/ adj [jam] domowej roboty; [clothes] własnej produkcji; [bomb] wykonany domowym sposobem

Home Office n Ministerstwo n Spraw Wewnętrznych

homeopathic /ˌhəʊmɪə'pæθɪk/ adj homeopatyczny

home owner n właściciel m, -ka f domu/mieszkania

home page n strona f główna (w Internecie)

home rule n autonomia f

Home Secretary n minister m spraw wewnętrznych

home shopping n zakupy m pl przez Internet

homesick /'həʊmsɪk/ adj to be ~ (for country) tęsknić za krajem

home town n miasto n rodzinne

home video n amatorski film m wideo

homeward /'həʊmwəd/ adv to travel ~(s) wracać (do domu); to be ~ bound kierować się z powrotem (do domu)

homework /'həʊmwɜ:k/ n praca f domowa; to do some ~ on sth fig zebrać informacje na temat czegoś

homeworker /'həʊmwɜ:kə(r)/ n pracujący m w domu

homeworking /'həʊmwɜ:kɪŋ/ n praca f w domu

homicidal /ˌhɒmɪ'saɪdl/ adj [instinct] morderczy; [maniac] niebezpieczny (dla otoczenia)

homicide /'hɒmɪsaɪd/ n ① (murder) zabójstwo n ② (person) morder|ca m, -czyni f

homogenous /hə'mɒdʒɪnəs/ adj jednorodny, homogeniczny

homosexual /ˌhɒmə'sekʃʊəl/ **Ⅰ** n homoseksualista m

Ⅱ adj homoseksualny

homosexuality /ˌhɒməˌsekʃʊ'æləti/ n homoseksualizm m

honest /'ɒnɪst/ adj [answer] uczciwy; [account] rzetelny; [person] (truthful) uczciwy; (trustworthy) godny zaufania; (frank) szczery; to be ~ with sb być z kimś szczerym; to be ~... szczerze mówiąc...

honestly /'ɒnɪstlɪ/ adv ① (truthfully) szczerze ② (really) naprawdę, serio ③ (sincerely) szczerze

honesty /'ɒnɪstɪ/ n uczciwość f

honey /'hʌnɪ/ n ① (substance) miód m ② infml (endearment) kochanie n

honeycomb /'hʌnɪkəʊm/ n (in hive) plaster m woskowy; (for sale) plaster m miodu

honeymoon /'hʌnɪmu:n/ n miesiąc m miodowy; to go on ~ wyjechać w podróż poślubną

honeysuckle /'hʌnɪsʌkl/ n kapryfolium n

Hong Kong /ˌhɒŋ'kɒŋ/ prn Hongkong m

honk /hɒŋk/ vt to ~ one's horn (at sb) za|trąbić (na kogoś)

honor n, vt US → honour

honorable adj US → honourable

honorary /'ɒnərərɪ, US 'ɒnəretɪ/ adj [doctorate] honoris causa; [member, position] honorowy

honour GB, **honor** US /'ɒnə(r)/ **Ⅰ** n ① (virtue, distinction) honor m; in ~ of sb/sth na cześć kogoś/czegoś, dla uhonorowania kogoś/czegoś ② (in titles) Your Honour Wysoki Sądzie **Ⅱ** vt u|honorować [person]; honorować [cheque, contract]; spełni|ć, -ać [promise, commitment]

honourable GB, **honorable** US /'ɒnərəbl/ adj ① [person, intention] honorowy ② [profession, tradition] zaszczytny

honours degree n GB dyplom m ukończenia studiów; US dyplom m ukończenia studiów z wyróżnieniem

hood /hʊd/ n ① (on coat) kaptur m; (balaclava) kominiarka f ② (cover) (above cooker) okap m ③ GB (on car) buda f; (on pram) budka f ④ US Aut (bonnet) maska f

hoof /hu:f/ n (of horse) kopyto n; (of cow, deer) racica f

hook /hʊk/ **Ⅰ** n ① (on wall) haczyk m; (for picture) hak m ② (on fishing line) haczyk m ③ (fastener) haczyk m; ~ and eye haftka f ④ to take the phone off the ~ zdjąć słuchawkę z widełek ⑤ (in boxing) sierpowy m; left ~ lewy sierpowy **Ⅱ** vt powiesić, wieszać (on or onto sth na czymś) [IDIOMS]: to get sb off the ~ wybawić kogoś z opresji

hooked /hʊkt/ adj ① [nose, beak] haczykowaty ② to be ~ on sth być uzależnionym od czegoś [drugs]; mieć bzika na punkcie czegoś infml [computer games]

hooligan /'hu:lɪgən/ n chuligan m; soccer ~s pseudokibice piłkarscy

hoop /hu:p/ n (in ring) obręcz f; (in croquet) bramka f

hooray /hʊ'reɪ/ excl hura!

hoot /hu:t/ **Ⅰ** n (of owl) pohukiwanie n; (of car) trąbienie n **Ⅱ** vt to ~ one's horn zatrąbić **Ⅲ** vi [owl] pohukiwać, hukać; [car] za|trąbić; [people, crowd] (derisively) szyderczo gwizdać; to ~ with laughter ryczeć ze śmiechu infml

hoover /'hu:və(r)/ vt GB odkurz|yć, -ać

Hoover® /'hu:və(r)/ *n* GB odkurzacz *m*

hop /hɒp/ **I** *n* (of bird, frog, rabbit) skok *m*; (of child) podskok *m*
II hops *npl* chmiel *m*, szyszki *f pl* chmielu
III *vi [person]* sk|oczyć, -akać; (on one leg) podsk|oczyć, -akiwać (na jednej nodze); *[bird]* podsk|oczyć, -akiwać; **to ~ into bed** wskoczyć do łóżka; **to ~ off a bus** wysiąść z autobusu

hope /həʊp/ **I** *n* nadzieja *f* (**of sth** na coś); **to set one's ~s on sth** wiązać nadzieje z czymś; **to be beyond (all) ~, to be without ~** nie rokować żadnych nadziei; **to keep one's ~s high** nie tracić nadziei; **to raise sb's ~s** obudzić w kimś nadzieję; **to have no ~ of sth** nie mieć szans na coś
II *vt* mieć nadzieję (**that...** że...); **I (do) ~ so/not** mam nadzieję!/mam nadzieję, że nie!
III *vi* **to ~ for sth** mieć nadzieję or liczyć na coś

hopeful /'həʊpfl/ *adj [person, expression]* pełen nadziei; *[attitude, mood]* optymistyczny; *[sign, situation]* zachęcający

hopefully /'həʊpfəli/ *adv* [1] (with luck) przy odrobinie szczęścia [2] (with hope) *[say]* z nadzieją

hopeless /'həʊplɪs/ *adj* [1] *[attempt, case, struggle]* beznadziejny; **it's ~!** to beznadzieje! infml [2] infml (incompetent) *[person, work]* beznadziejny

hopelessness /'həʊplɪsnɪs/ *n* [1] (despair) rozpacz *f* [2] (futility) bezsensowność *f* (**of doing sth** robienia czegoś)

hopscotch /'hɒpskɒtʃ/ *n* gra *f* w klasy

horizon /hə'raɪzn/ *n* horyzont *m*; **on the ~** na horyzoncie also fig

horizontal /hɒrɪ'zɒntl, US ˌhɔːr-/ *adj* poziomy

hormone /'hɔːməʊn/ *n* hormon *m*

hormone replacement theraphy *n* hormonalna terapia *f* zastępcza, HTZ

horn /hɔːn/ *n* [1] (of animal, snail) róg *m* [2] Mus róg *m* [3] (of car) klakson *m*; (of ship) syrena *f*

hornet /'hɔːnɪt/ *n* szerszeń *m*

horoscope /'hɒrəskəʊp, US 'hɔːr-/ *n* horoskop *m*

horrendous /hɒ'rendəs/ *adj [prices]* horrendalny; *[crime, conditions]* potworny; *[damage]* ogromny; *[taste]* obrzydliwy

horrible /'hɒrɪbl, US 'hɔːr-/ *adj* [1] (unpleasant) *[place, clothes, smell, weather]* okropny; *[food]* obrzydliwy; **to be ~ to sb** okropnie kogoś traktować [2] (shocking) *[crime, death]* straszny; *[scene]* makabryczny

horrid /'hɒrɪd, US 'hɔːrɪd/ *adj* obrzydliwy

horrific /hə'rɪfɪk/ *adj* przerażający

horrifying /'hɒrɪfaɪɪŋ, US 'hɔːr-/ *adj [sight, experience]* przerażający; *[behaviour]* okropny

horror /'hɒrə(r), US 'hɔːr-/ *n* przerażenie *n* (**at sth** na widok czegoś); **to have a ~ of sth/of doing sth** panicznie bać się czegoś/robienia czegoś

horror film *n* film *m* grozy, horror *m*

horror story *n* opowiadanie *n* z dreszczykiem

horse /hɔːs/ *n* koń *m*; (stallion) ogier *m*
■ **horse about, horse around** infml: wygłupiać się infml

IDIOMS: **from the ~'s mouth** z pierwszej ręki

horseback /'hɔːsbæk/ *n* **on ~** na koniu

horseback riding *n* US jazda *f* konna, jeździectwo *n*

horse chestnut *n* (tree) kasztanowiec *m*; (fruit) kasztan *m*

horsefly /'hɔːsflaɪ/ *n* giez *m*, mucha *f* końska

horsepower /'hɔːspaʊə(r)/ *n* (unit of power) koń *m* mechaniczny

horse race *n* gonitwa *f*

horseracing /'hɔːsreɪsɪŋ/ *n* wyścigi *m pl* konne

horseradish /'hɔːsrædɪʃ/ *n* chrzan *m*

horseriding /'hɔːsraɪdɪŋ/ *n* jazda *f* konna, jeździectwo *n*

horseshoe /'hɔːsʃuː/ *n* podkowa *f*

horseshow /'hɔːsʃəʊ/ *n* konkurs *m* jeździecki

horticulture /'hɔːtɪkʌltʃə(r)/ *n* ogrodnictwo *n*

hose, hosepipe /həʊz(paɪp)/ *n* GB (for garden, cleaning) wąż *m*; (fire) ~ wąż strażacki, sikawka

hospice /'hɒspɪs/ *n* hospicjum *n*

hospitable /hɒ'spɪtəbl/ *adj [person]* gościnny (**to sb** dla kogoś); *[gesture, invitation]* serdeczny; *[climate, conditions]* przyjazny

hospital /'hɒspɪtl/ *n* szpital *m*; **to be taken to ~** zostać przyjętym do szpitala

hospitality /ˌhɒspɪ'tæləti/ *n* gościnność *f*

hospitalize /'hɒspɪtəlaɪz/ *vt* hospitalizować

host /həʊst/ **I** *n* [1] gospodarz *m* [2] (on radio, TV) gospod|arz *m*, -yni *f* programu [3] (multitude) chmara *f*, mnóstwo *n* (**of sb/sth** kogoś/coś)
II *vt* (on radio, TV) być gospodarzem (czegoś) *[party, programme]*

hostage /'hɒstɪdʒ/ *n* zakładni|k *m*, -czka *f*; **to hold sb ~** przetrzymywać kogoś jako zakładnika

host country *n* kraj *m* pełniący rolę gospodarza

hostel /'hɒstl/ *n* (for homeless, refugees) schronisko *n*; (youth) ~ schronisko młodzieżowe

hostess /'həʊstɪs/ *n* gospodyni *f*, pani *f* domu

hostile /'hɒstaɪl, US -tl/ *adj [look, attitude]* nieprzyjazny, wrogi (**to sb/sth** wobec kogoś/czegoś); *[person]* wrogo nastawiony (**to sb/sth** do kogoś/ czegoś)

hostility /hɒ'stɪləti/ *n* wrogość *f* (**towards sb/sth** do kogoś/czegoś)

hot /hɒt/ *adj* [1] (very warm) gorący; *[day]* upalny, gorący; *[sun]* palący, piekący; *[hands]* gorący, rozgrzany; *[forehead]* gorący, rozpalony; **it's ~ here** gorąco tu; **I am** or **feel ~** jest mi gorąco; **to go ~ and cold** (with fever) dostać dreszczy; (with fear) spocić się ze strachu [2] Culin *[mustard, spice]* ostry [3] **to be ~ on sb's trail** być na czyimś tropie

hot air balloon *n* balon *m* napełniony ciepłym powietrzem

hotbed /'hɒtbed/ n ① (for plants) inspekt m ② fig (of evil) siedlisko n

hot dog n hot dog m

hotel /həʊ'tel/ n hotel m

hotelier /həʊ'telɪə(r)/ n hotela|rz m, -rka f

hot-headed /ˌhɒt'hedɪd/ adj [person] w gorącej wodzie kąpany

hotline /'hɒtlaɪn/ n ① (for public) linia f specjalna ② (between heads of state) gorąca linia f

hotplate /'hɒtpleɪt/ n płytka f do podgrzewania potraw

hot seat n
⌐IDIOMS¬ to be in the ~ być w trudnym położeniu

hotshot /'hɒtʃɒt/ n infml (expert) mądrala m/f infml; (important person) ważniak m infml

hot spot n infml ① (trouble, sport) punkt m zapalny ② (sunny country) ciepły kraj m

hot-tempered /ˌhɒt'tempəd/ adj [person] wybuchowy

hot water bottle n termofor m

hound /haʊnd/ **Ⅰ** n pies m gończy
Ⅱ vt nękać [person]
■ **hound out**: zmu|sić, -szać kogoś do rezygnacji or odejścia

hour /aʊə(r)/ n godzina f; £10 per ~ 10 funtów za godzinę; **to be paid by the** ~ otrzymywać wynagrodzenie od godziny; **in the early** ~s nad ranem

hourly /'aʊəlɪ/ **Ⅰ** adj cogodzinny; [rate] godzinowy
Ⅱ adv [arrive, phone] co godzinę

house /haʊs/ **Ⅰ** (pl ~s /haʊzɪz/) n ① (residence) dom m; **at my/his** ~ u mnie/u niego; **to go to sb's** ~ pójść do kogoś; **on the** ~ na koszt firmy ② (in theatre) (audience) widownia f; (auditorium) sala f; (performance) spektakl m ③ (music) muzyka f house
Ⅱ vt /haʊzɪz/ ① (temporarily) zakwaterow|ać, -ywać [homeless, refugees]; (permanently) da|ć, -wać dom (komuś) ② [building] po|mieścić [collection, exhibition]

houseboat /'haʊsbəʊt/ n barka f mieszkalna

housebound /'haʊsbaʊnd/ adj [old people, invalids] nieopuszczający domu

house call n wizyta f domowa

household /'haʊshəʊld/ **Ⅰ** n rodzina f, domownicy m pl; (in survey) gospodarstwo n domowe; **head of the** ~ głowa rodziny
Ⅱ adj [accounts] domowy

household appliance n elektryczne urządzenie n domowe

householder /'haʊshəʊldə(r)/ n (owner) właściciel m, -ka f; (tenant) najem|ca m, -czyni f, lokator m, -ka f

household name n he's a ~ wszyscy wiedzą, kim jest

house husband n mąż m zajmujący się domem

housekeeper /'haʊskiːpə(r)/ n (in house) gosposia f; (in institution) administrator m, -ka f

housekeeping /'haʊskiːpɪŋ/ n (money) pieniądze m pl na życie

House of Commons n GB Izba f Gmin

House of Lords n GB Izba f Lordów

House of Representatives n US Izba f Reprezentantów

houseplant /'haʊsplɑːnt, US -plænt/ n roślina f domowa

house-proud /'haʊspraʊd/ adj **to be** ~ pedantycznie dbać o porządek

Houses of Parliament npl GB Parlament m Brytyjski

house-to-house /ˌhaʊstə'haʊs/ adj [search] od domu do domu

house-trained /'haʊstreɪnd/ adj GB [pet] nauczony porządku

house-warming (party) /'haʊswɔːmɪŋ ('pɑːtɪ)/ n parapetówka f infml

housewife /'haʊswaɪf/ n gospodyni f domowa

housework /'haʊswɜːk/ n prace f pl domowe; **to do the** ~ zajmować się domem

housing /'haʊzɪŋ/ n (houses) domy m pl mieszkalne; (flats) mieszkania n pl; (conditions) warunki plt mieszkaniowe

housing estate n GB osiedle n mieszkaniowe

hover /'hɒvə(r)/ vi [bird, helicopter] unosić się w powietrzu; **profite are** ~ing around 15 zyski wahają się w granicach 15

hovercraft /'hɒvəkrɑːft, US -kræft/ n poduszkowiec m

how /haʊ/ **Ⅰ** adv ① jak; **to know** ~ **to do sth** wiedzieć, jak coś zrobić, umieć coś zrobić; ~ **are you?** (as greeting) jak się masz?; (about health) jak się czujesz?; ~'s **your brother?** co u twojego brata?; ~ **are things?** co słychać?; jak leci? infml; ~ **do you do!** (greeting) miło mi! ② (in number, quantity questions) ile; ~ **much is this?** ile to kosztuje?; ~ **long will it take?** ile czasu to zajmie?; ~ **tall is the tree?** jak wysokie jest to drzewo?; ~ **far is the station?** jak daleko na dworzec?; ~ **old is she?** ile ona ma lat? ③ (in exclamation) ~ **wonderful!** to wspaniale!; ~ **clever of you!** bardzo sprytnie (z twojej strony)!
Ⅱ how come adv phr infml dlaczego; ~ **come you always win?** jak to jest or jak to się dzieje, że zawsze wygrywasz?

however /haʊ'evə(r)/ **Ⅰ** conj (nevertheless) jednak(że)
Ⅱ adv choćby, żeby; ~ **hard I try, I can't** nie mogę, choćbym nie wiem jak się starał; ~ **difficult the task is...** bez względu na to, jak trudne jest to zadanie...; ~ **long it takes...** obojętnie jak długo to potrwa...; ~ **you like** jak tylko chcesz

howl /haʊl/ **Ⅰ** n wycie n
Ⅱ vi za|wyć

HQ *n* Mil → **headquarters**

HTML *n* = **Hyper Text Markup Language** język *m* znaczników hipertekstowych

hub /hʌb/ *n* (of wheel) piasta *f*; fig centrum *n*

hubcap /'hʌbkæp/ *n* (on car wheel) kołpak *m*

huddle /'hʌdl/ *vi* **to ~ around sb/sth** skupić się wokół kogoś/czegoś

hue /hju:/ *n* [1] (colour) barwa *f* [2] **~ and cry** wrzawa *f*

huff /hʌf/ infml [I] *n* **in a ~** nabzdyczony

[II] *vi* psioczyć infml (**about sth** na coś)

hug /hʌg/ [I] *n* uścisk *m*; **to give sb a ~** (affectionate) przytulić kogoś; (friendly) uściskać kogoś

[II] *vt* [1] (embrace) (affectionately) przytul|ić, -ać, tulić; (in a friendly way) uścis|nąć, -kać [2] (keep close to) trzymać się blisko (czegoś) *[coast, kerb]*

huge /hju:dʒ/ *adj* olbrzymi; *[person]* potężny; *[smile]* szeroki

hugely /'hju:dʒlɪ/ *adv* [1] (emphatic) *[enjoyable, expensive]* niezwykle [2] *[increase]* ogromnie; *[vary]* znacznie

hull /hʌl/ *n* (of ship, plane) kadłub *m*; (of tank) pancerz *m*

hum /hʌm/ [I] *n* (of insect) brzęczenie *n*, bzyk *m*; (of machinery) buczenie *n*; (of traffic) szum *m*; (of voices) szmer *m*

[II] *vi [person]* nucić; *[insect]* bzyczeć; *[aircraft, machine]* buczeć

human /'hju:mən/ [I] *n* człowiek *m*

[II] *adj [body, behaviour]* ludzki; *[characteristic, rights]* człowieka

human being *n* człowiek *m*, istota *f* ludzka

humane /hju:'meɪn/ *adj [person]* ludzki; *[act]* humanitarny

humanitarian /hju:ˌmænɪ'teərɪən/ *adj* humanitarny

humanity /hju:'mænətɪ/ *n* ludzkość *f*

human nature *n* ludzka natura *f*

human resources manager *n* kierownik *m*, -czka *f* działu personalnego

humble /'hʌmbl/ *adj [dwelling, gift]* skromny; *[person]* pokorny; *[reply, remark]* pełny pokory

humid /'hju:mɪd/ *adj* wilgotny

humidity /hju:'mɪdətɪ/ *n* (dampness) wilgoć *f*; (amount of dampness) wilgotność *f*

humiliate /hju:'mɪlɪeɪt/ *vt* upok|orzyć, -arzać

humiliating /hju:'mɪlɪeɪtɪŋ/ *adj* upokarzający

humiliation /hju:ˌmɪlɪ'eɪʃn/ *n* upokorzenie *n*

humorous /'hju:mərəs/ *adj* [1] (amusing) humorystyczny; *[anecdote, remark]* dowcipny [2] (amused) *[person]* rozbawiony; *[smile, tone]* żartobliwy

humour GB, **humor** US /'hju:mə(r)/ [I] *n* [1] (wit) humor *m*; **a good sense of ~** poczucie humoru [2] (mood) humor *m*; **to be in good ~** być w dobrym humorze

[II] *vt* ust|ąpić, -ępować (komuś) *[person]*

hump /hʌmp/ *n* garb *m*

hunch /hʌntʃ/ [I] *n* przeczucie *n*

[II] *vt* **to ~ one's shoulders** zgarbić się

hunched /hʌntʃt/ *adj* zgarbiony

hundred /'hʌndrəd/ [I] *n* sto; (symbol) setka *f*; **two ~** dwieście; **two ~ and one** dwieście jeden; **in nineteen ~** w (roku) tysiąc dziewięćsetnym; **in nineteen ~ and three** w tysiąc dziewięćset trzecim (roku); **~s of times** setki razy

[II] *adj* sto; **two ~ pounds** dwieście funtów; **four ~ and five pounds** czterysta pięć funtów; **about a ~ people** około stu osób

hundredth /'hʌndrətθ/ [I] *n* [1] (in order) setn|y *m*, -a *f* [2] (fraction) setna *f* (część)

[II] *adj* setny

hundredweight /'hʌndrədweɪt/ *n* cetnar *m* *(GB=50,80 kg; US=45,36 kg)*

Hungarian /hʌŋ'geərɪən/ [I] *n* [1] (person) Węgier *m*, -ka *f* [2] (language) (język *m*) węgierski *m*

[II] *adj* węgierski

Hungary /'hʌŋgərɪ/ *prn* Węgry *plt*

hunger /'hʌŋgə(r)/ *n* głód *m*

hunger strike *n* głodówka *f* (protestacyjna)

hung-over /ˌhʌŋ'əʊvə(r)/ *adj* infml **to be ~** mieć kaca

hungry /'hʌŋgrɪ/ *adj* głodny; **to be ~** być głodnym; **to make sb ~** pobudzić apetyt (kogoś); **~ for sth** fig spragniony czegoś fig *[power, knowledge]*

hunk /hʌŋk/ *n* [1] (of bread, cheese) kawał *m* [2] infml (man) byczek *m* fig infml

hunt /hʌnt/ [I] *n* [1] (for animals) polowanie *n* [2] (search) poszukiwania *n pl* (**for sb/sth** kogoś/czegoś)

[II] *vt* poszukiwać *[prisoner]*; polować na (coś) *[animals]*

[III] *vi* [1] (for prey) *[animal]* polować [2] (search) **to ~ for sb/sth** poszukiwać or szukać kogoś/czegoś

hunter /'hʌntə(r)/ *n* myśliwy *m*

hunting /'hʌntɪŋ/ *n* polowanie *n* (**of sth** na coś); **to go ~** iść na polowanie

hunt saboteur *n* GB infml przeciwni|k *m*, -czka *f* polowania na lisy

hurdle /'hɜ:dl/ *n* Sport płotek *m*; fig przeszkoda *f*

hurl /hɜ:l/ *vt* cis|nąć, -kać (**at sb/sth** w kogoś/coś); **to ~ insults at sb** fig obrzucić kogoś obelgami

hurrah, hurray /hʊ'rɑ:/ *n, excl* hur(r)a!

hurricane /'hʌrɪkən, US -keɪn/ *n* huragan *m*

hurry /'hʌrɪ/ [I] *n* pośpiech *m*; **to be in a ~** śpieszyć się (**to do sth** żeby coś zrobić); **to do sth in a ~** zrobić coś w pośpiechu

[II] *vt* szybko uwinąć się z (czymś) *[meal, task]*; pośpiesz|yć, -ać *[person]*

[III] *vi* po|śpieszyć się (**over doing sth** coś zrobić); **to ~ out** wyjść pośpiesznie

■ **hurry up:** po|śpieszyć się; **~ up!** pośpiesz się!

hurt /hɜ:t/ [I] *adj* zraniony; **to feel ~** poczuć się urażonym

[II] *vt* [1] (injure) **to ~ oneself** skaleczyć się; **to ~ one's back** uszkodzić sobie kręgosłup [2] (cause

pain to) sprawi|ć, -ać ból (komuś) *[person]*; (deliber-
ately) zada|ć, -wać ból (komuś); **you're ~ing my
arm!** przestań! to boli! ③ (emotionally) sprawi|ć, -ać
(komuś) przykrość; (offend) z|ranić, urazić *[person,
feelings]*
III *vi* boleć; **my foot ~s** boli mnie noga
hurtful /ˈhɜːtfl/ *adj [attitude, words]* krzywdzący;
[rejection, truth] bolesny
hurtle /ˈhɜːtl/ *vi* **to ~ along a road** pognać or
popędzić drogą; **to ~ down a hill** pędzić w dół
zbocza
husband /ˈhʌzbənd/ *n* mąż *m*
hush /hʌʃ/ **I** *n* cisza *f*
II *excl* cicho!, sza!
■ **hush up**: ¶ ~ **[sth] up** wycisz|yć, -ać *[affair]*
¶ ~ **[sb] up** ucisz|yć, -ać *[person]*
hush-hush /ˌhʌʃˈhʌʃ/ *adj* infml poufny
hustle /ˈhʌsl/ **I** *n* ~ **and bustle** krzątanina *f*,
bieganina *f*
II *vt* przynagl|ić, -ać *[person]*
hut /hʌt/ *n* (in garden) szopa *f*; (dwelling) chata *f*; (on
beach) kabina *f*
hutch /hʌtʃ/ *n* (for rabbits) klatka *f*
hydrant /ˈhaɪdrənt/ *n* (also **fire ~**) hydrant *m*
hydraulic /haɪˈdrɔːlɪk/ *adj* hydrauliczny
hydroelectricity /ˌhaɪdrəʊɪlekˈtrɪsəti/ *n* energia *f*
elektryczna z hydroelektrowni
hydrofoil /ˈhaɪdrəfɔɪl/ *n* ① (craft) wodolot *m* ② (foil)
hydropłat *m*
hydrogen /ˈhaɪdrədʒən/ *n* wodór *m*
hyena /haɪˈiːnə/ *n* hiena *f*
hygiene /ˈhaɪdʒiːn/ *n* higiena *f*

hygienic /haɪˈdʒiːnɪk/ *adj* higieniczny
hymn /hɪm/ *n* hymn *m*
hype /haɪp/ infml *n* krzykliwa reklama *f*
■ **hype up**: z|robić szum wokół (kogoś/czegoś)
infml *[book, film, star]*; rozdmuch|ać, -iwać infml
[issue, story]
hyper /ˈhaɪpə(r)/ *adj* infml podekscytowany
hyperactive /ˌhaɪpərˈæktɪv/ *n* Med nadczynny;
Psych nadpobudliwy
hypermarket /ˈhaɪpəmɑːkɪt/ *n* GB hipermarket *m*
hyperventilate /ˌhaɪpəˈventɪleɪt/ *vi* oddychać
zbyt szybko *(wdychając za dużo dwutlenku węgla)*
hyphen /ˈhaɪfn/ *n* łącznik *m*, dywiz *m*
hypnosis /hɪpˈnəʊsɪs/ *n* hipnoza *f*
hypnotherapy /ˌhɪpnəˈθerəpɪ/ *n* hipnoterapia *f*
hypnotist /ˈhɪpnətɪst/ *n* hipnotyzer *m*, -ka *f*
hypnotize /ˈhɪpnətaɪz/ *vt* za|hipnotyzować
hypoallergenic /ˌhaɪpəʊæləˈdʒenɪk/ *adj* hipo-
alergiczny
hypocrisy /hɪˈpɒkrəsɪ/ *n* hipokryzja *f*
hypocrite /ˈhɪpəkrɪt/ *n* hipokryt|a *m*, -ka *f*
hypocritical /ˌhɪpəˈkrɪtɪkl/ *adj* hipokrytyczny
hypodermic /ˌhaɪpəˈdɜːmɪk/ *adj* podskórny
hypothermia /ˌhaɪpəʊˈθɜːmɪə/ *n* hipotermia *f*
hypothesis /haɪˈpɒθəsɪs/ *n* hipoteza *f*
hysteria /hɪˈstɪərɪə/ *n* histeria *f*
hysterical /hɪˈsterɪkl/ *adj [behaviour, laughter]*
histeryczny; *[person]* rozhisteryzowany
hysterics /hɪˈsterɪks/ *n* ① (fit) atak *m* histerii; **to
have ~** dostać ataku histerii ② (laughter) **to be in
~** śmiać się do rozpuku, pękać ze śmiechu

I

i, I /aɪ/ *n* i, I *n*

I /aɪ/ *pron* ja; **I live in London** mieszkam w Londynie; **I didn't take it** ja tego nie wziąłem; **he's a student but I'm not** on jest studentem, ale ja nie

ice /aɪs/ **[I]** *n* (frozen water) lód *m*; **there's ~ on the roads** drogi są oblodzone
[II] *vt* po|lukrować *[cake]*
[III] **iced** *pp adj [water]* z lodem; *[tea, coffee]* mrożony
■ **ice over:** *[roads, windscreen]* obl|odzić, -adzać się; *[lake, river]* pokry|ć, -wać się lodem, zamarz-z|nąć, -ać

iceberg /'aɪsbɜːg/ *n* góra *f* lodowa

icebox /'aɪsbɒks/ *n* **[1]** GB (freezer compartment) zamrażalnik *m* **[2]** US (fridge) lodówka *f*

ice-cold /ˌaɪs'kəʊld/ *adj* lodowaty

ice cream /ˌaɪs'kriːm/ *n* Culin lody *plt*

ice-cube /'aɪskjuːb/ *n* kostka *f* lodu

ice hockey *n* hokej *m* (na lodzie)

Iceland /'aɪslənd/ *prn* Islandia *f*

Icelandic **[I]** *n* (język *m*) islandzki *m*
[II] *adj* islandzki

ice rink *n* lodowisko *n*

ice skate **[I]** *n* łyżwa *f*
[II] **ice-skate** *vi* Sport uprawiać łyżwiarstwo; (as a hobby) jeździć na łyżwach

ice skating *n* łyżwiarstwo *n*

icicle /'aɪsɪkl/ *n* sopel *m* (lodu)

icing /'aɪsɪŋ/ *n* lukier *m*

icing sugar *n* GB cukier puder *m*

icon /'aɪkɒn/ *n* ikona *f*

icy /'aɪsɪ/ *adj* **[1]** (cold) *[wind]* lodowaty **[2]** *[road]* oblodzony **[3]** *[look, reception]* lodowaty

ID *n* dowód *m* tożsamości

id /ɪd/ *n* **the ~** id *n inv*

idea /aɪ'dɪə/ *n* **[1]** (thought) pomysł *m*; **to be full of ~s** mieć mnóstwo pomysłów **[2]** (knowledge) wyobrażenie *n*, pojęcie *n*; **to have no ~ why/how...** nie mieć pojęcia, dlaczego/jak...; **to have no ~ of** or **about sth** nie mieć pojęcia o czymś; **you've no ~ how pleased I was!** nie wyobrażasz sobie nawet, jaki byłem zadowolony!; **I've an ~ that he might be lying** mam wrażenie, że on nie mówi prawdy

ideal /aɪ'diːəl/ **[I]** *n* ideał *m*
[II] *adj* idealny

idealism /aɪ'dɪəlɪzəm/ *n* idealizm *m*

idealist /aɪ'dɪəlɪst/ *n* idealist|a *m*, -ka *f*

idealistic /ˌaɪdɪə'lɪstɪk/ *adj* idealistyczny

idealize /aɪ'dɪəlaɪz/ *vt* wy|idealizować

ideally /aɪ'dɪəlɪ/ *adv* **[1]** (preferably) **~, the tests should be free** najlepiej byłoby, gdyby testy były bezpłatne; **~, we'd like to stay** najchętniej zostalibyśmy **[2]** (perfectly) *[located]* idealnie

identical /aɪ'dentɪkl/ *adj* identyczny; **~ to** or **with sth** (dokładnie) taki sam jak coś

identification /aɪˌdentɪfɪ'keɪʃn/ *n* **[1]** (of species, person) identyfikacja *f* **(from sth** na podstawie czegoś) **[2]** (empathy) identyfikowanie się *n* **(with sth/sb** z czymś/kimś) **[3]** (proof of identity) dowód *m* tożsamości

identify /aɪ'dentɪfaɪ/ **[I]** *vt* z|identyfikować **(as sb** jako kogoś); (recognize) rozpozna|ć, -wać; **to ~ sb/ sth with sb/sth** identyfikować or utożsamiać kogoś/coś z kimś/czymś
[II] *vi* (empathize) **to ~ with sb/sth** identyfikować się z kimś/czymś

identikit /aɪ'dentɪkɪt/ *n* (also **Identikit®**, **~ picture**) portret *m* pamięciowy

identity /aɪ'dentətɪ/ *n* (personality) tożsamość *f*

identity bracelet *n* bransoletka *f* z blaszką identyfikacyjną

identity card *n* dowód *m* tożsamości

identity parade *n* GB okazanie *n* *(podejrzanego)*

ideological /ˌaɪdɪə'lɒdʒɪkl/ *adj* ideologiczny

ideology /ˌaɪdɪ'ɒlədʒɪ/ *n* ideologia *f*

idiom /'ɪdɪəm/ *n* **[1]** (phrase) idiom *m* **[2]** (language) (of speaker) sposób *m* mówienia; (of theatre, sport) język *m*; (of music) styl *m*

idiomatic /ˌɪdɪə'mætɪk/ *adj* idiomatyczny

idiosyncrasy /ˌɪdɪə'sɪŋkrəsɪ/ *n* (of person) specyficzna cecha *f*; (of system, language) osobliwość *f*

idiosyncratic /ˌɪdɪəsɪŋ'krætɪk/ *adj* *[response]* charakterystyczny; *[quality]* specyficzny

idiot /'ɪdɪət/ *n* idiot|a *m*, -ka *f* infml

idiotic /ˌɪdɪ'ɒtɪk/ *adj* idiotyczny

idle /'aɪdl/ **[I]** *adj* **[1]** (lazy) *[person]* leniwy **[2]** (vain) *[boast, threat]* czczy; *[curiosity, chatter]* pusty **[3]** (unoccupied) *[person]* bezczynny; *[day, hour, moment]* wolny **[4]** *[dock, mine]* nieczynny
[II] *vi* *[engine]* pracować na biegu jałowym
■ **idle away:** przepróżnować *[day]*; trwonić *[time]*

idol /'aɪdl/ *n* idol *m*

idolize /'aɪdəlaɪz/ vt wielbić

idyllic /ɪ'dɪlɪk, US aɪ'd-/ adj sielankowy

ie = that is tj., to jest

if /ɪf/ **❶** conj **1** (in the event) jeśli; **I'll help you, if you pay me** pomogę ci, jeżeli mi zapłacisz; **if I were you...** ja na twoim miejscu...; **if not** jeśli nie, w przeciwnym razie **2** (supposing) gdyby; **if it were to snow...** gdyby padał śnieg...; **if asked, I would say that...** gdyby mnie zapytano, powiedziałbym, że... **3** (whether) czy; **I wonder if they will come** ciekaw jestem, czy przyjdą; **do you mind if I smoke?** czy będzie panu/pani przeszkadzać, jeżeli zapalę?; **what if I say no?** a jeżeli powiem nie? **4** **it's a good shop, if a little expensive** to dobry sklep, chociaż dość drogi

❷ **if only** conj phr **if only because (of)...** choćby dlatego, że...; **if only for a moment** choćby przez chwilę/na chwilę; **if only I had known!** gdybym to ja wiedział!

iffy /'ɪfɪ/ adj infml (dubious) podejrzany

igloo /'ɪgluː/ n igloo n inv

ignite /ɪg'naɪt/ **❶** vt zapal|ić, -ać [material, motor]; s|powodować zapłon (czegoś) [fuel];
❷ vi [methane, rubbish, timber] zapal|ić, -ać się

ignition /ɪg'nɪʃn/ n (system) zapłon m; (starting mechanism) stacyjka f

ignition key n kluczyk m do stacyjki

ignorance /'ɪgnərəns/ n (of person) niewiedza f

ignorant /'ɪgnərənt/ adj (of a subject) nieświadomy; (uneducated) niedouczony; **to be ~ about sth** nie znać się na czymś [subject]; **to be ~ of sth** nie wiedzieć o czymś [possibilities]

ignore /ɪg'nɔː(r)/ vt z|ignorować [person]; nie za|reagować na (coś) [insult]; nie przestrzegać (czegoś) [instructions]; z|lekceważyć [mistake]

ill /ɪl/ **❶** n zło n; **to wish sb ~** źle życzyć komuś
❷ adj chory; **to be ~ with sth** chorować na coś [disease]; **to be taken ~, to fall ~** zachorować
❸ adv fml **he is ~ suited to the post** nie nadaje się na to stanowisko; **to speak ~ of sb** źle mówić o kimś

ill at ease adj skrępowany, zakłopotany

illegal /ɪ'liːgl/ **❶** n US nielegalny imigrant m, nielegalna imigrantka f
❷ adj [strike, immigrant] nielegalny; [parking] niedozwolony; Sport nieprzepisowy

illegally /ɪ'liːgəlɪ/ adv nielegalnie

illegible /ɪ'ledʒəbl/ adj nieczytelny

illegitimate /ˌɪlɪ'dʒɪtɪmət/ adj [activity] nielegalny; [child] nieślubny

ill-equipped /ˌɪlɪ'kwɪpt/ adj nieodpowiednio wyposażony

ill-fitting /ˌɪl'fɪtɪŋ/ adj [shoe, garment] źle dopasowany

ill health n zły stan m zdrowia

illicit /ɪ'lɪsɪt/ adj [substance] niedozwolony; [encounter] potajemny

ill-informed /ˌɪlɪn'fɔːmd/ adj niedoinformowany

illiterate /ɪ'lɪtərət/ **❶** n analfabet|a m, -ka f
❷ adj niepiśmienny

illness /'ɪlnɪs/ n choroba f

illogical /ɪ'lɒdʒɪkl/ adj [reaction] niedorzeczny; [argument] nielogiczny

ill-treatment /ɪl'triːtmənt/ n złe traktowanie n

illuminate /ɪ'luːmɪneɪt/ vt oświetl|ić, -ać

illuminated /ɪ'luːmɪneɪtɪd/ adj [sign] podświetlony

illumination /ɪˌluːmɪ'neɪʃn/ n (lighting) oświetlenie n

illuminations npl GB dekoracje f pl świetlne

illusion /ɪ'luːʒn/ n złudzenie n; **to have ~s about sth/sb** mieć złudzenia co do kogoś/czegoś; **to be** or **labour under the ~ that...** łudzić się, że...

illustrate /'ɪləstreɪt/ vt z|ilustrować

illustration /ˌɪlə'streɪʃn/ n ilustracja f

illustrator /'ɪləstreɪtə(r)/ n ilustrator m, -ka f

ill will n uraza f

image /'ɪmɪdʒ/ n (mental picture) obraz m; (notion) wyobrażenie n; (of company, personality) wizerunek m; **she's the (spitting) ~ of you!** jest podobna do ciebie jak dwie krople wody!

image-conscious /ˌɪmɪdʒ'kɒnʃəs/ adj **to be ~** dbać o swój wizerunek publiczny

image maker n specjalista m, -ka f od kreowania wizerunku publicznego

imagery /'ɪmɪdʒərɪ/ n obrazy m pl (of sth czegoś); (in poetry) metaforyka f

imaginary /ɪ'mædʒɪnərɪ, US -ənerɪ/ adj [character] wymyślony; [illness] wyimaginowany

imagination /ɪˌmædʒɪ'neɪʃn/ n (ability) wyobraźnia f

imaginative /ɪ'mædʒɪnətɪv, US -neɪtɪv/ adj [person] obdarzony wyobraźnią; [film, design] świadczący o wyobraźni autora; [book] napisany z polotem; [device, solution] pomysłowy

imagine /ɪ'mædʒɪn/ vt **1** (visualize) wyobra|zić, -żać sobie; **it's difficult to ~ being king/rich** trudno sobie wyobrazić, że się jest królem/bogatym; **you must have ~d it** chyba ci się przywidziało **2** (suppose) przypuszczać (that... że...)

imbalance /ˌɪm'bæləns/ n brak m równowagi

imbecile /'ɪmbəsiːl, US -sl/ **❶** n debil m, -ka f
❷ adj idiotyczny

imitate /'ɪmɪteɪt/ vt naśladować [person]; imitować [sound]; podr|obić, -abiać [handwriting]

imitation /ˌɪmɪ'teɪʃn/ **❶** n (practice) naśladownictwo n; (counterfeit) imitacja f
❷ adj [plant, snow, jewellery] sztuczny; **~ fur/ leather** imitacja futra/skóry; **~ fur coat** sztuczne futro; **~ gold** imitacja złota

imitator /'ɪmɪteɪtə(r)/ n naśladow|ca m, -czyni f

immaculate /ɪ'mækjʊlət/ adj [clothes] nieskazitelnie czysty; [manners] nieskazitelny; [performance] bezbłędny

immaterial /ˌɪmə'tɪərɪəl/ adj ① (unimportant) nieistotny ② (intangible) niematerialny

immature /ˌɪmə'tjʊə(r), US -tʊər/ adj ① [animal, fruit] niedojrzały ② pej (childish) dziecinny pej

immediate /ɪ'miːdɪət/ adj ① [effect, reaction] natychmiastowy; [thought] pierwszy ② [task, problem] najpilniejszy; [goal] najbliższy ③ [future, family] najbliższy; **in the ~ vicinity** w najbliższej okolicy

immediately /ɪ'miːdɪətlɪ/ adv natychmiast; ~ **before/after sth** tuż przed/po czymś

immense /ɪ'mens/ adj ogromny

immerse /ɪ'mɜːs/ vt zanurz|yć, -áć (**in sth** w czymś)

immersion course n GB intensywny kurs m języka obcego (prowadzony wyłącznie w tym języku)

immigrant /'ɪmɪgrənt/ **Ⅰ** n imigrant m, -ka f **Ⅱ** adj [population] imigracyjny, napływowy

immigration /ˌɪmɪ'greɪʃn/ n imigracja f; (at border, airport) kontrola f paszportowa

imminent /'ɪmɪnənt/ adj [danger] nadciągający; [arrival] bliski

immobile /ɪ'məʊbaɪl, US -bl/ adj (motionless) nieruchomy; (unable to move) unieruchomiony

immobilize /ɪ'məʊbɪlaɪz/ vt s|paraliżować [traffic, market]; unieruch|omić, -amiać [engine, limb, patient]

immoral /ɪ'mɒrəl, US ɪ'mɔːrəl/ adj niemoralny

immorality /ˌɪmə'rælətɪ/ n (quality) niemoralność f; (act) czyn m niemoralny

immortal /ɪ'mɔːtl/ adj nieśmiertelny

immortality /ˌɪmɔː'tælətɪ/ n nieśmiertelność f

immortalize /ɪ'mɔːtəlaɪz/ vt uwieczni|ć, -áć, unieśmiertelni|ć, -áć

immune /ɪ'mjuːn/ adj ① Med [person] odporny (**to sth** na coś); [system] odpornościowy ② (oblivious) ~ **to sth** nieczuły na coś ③ (exempt) ~ **from sth** zabezpieczony przed czymś [attack]; chroniony przed czymś [arrest]; zwolniony z czegoś [tax]

immunity /ɪ'mjuːnətɪ/ n ① Med odporność f (**to** or **against sth** na coś) ② (privilege) nietykalność f; (parliamentary) immunitet m

immunize /'ɪmjuːnaɪz/ vt uodporni|ć, -áć (**against sth** na coś); (by inoculation) za|szczepić (**against sth** przeciw czemuś)

impact /'ɪmpækt/ n ① (of fist, club) uderzenie n; **the bomb exploded on ~** bomba wybuchła przy uderzeniu ② (effect) wpływ m; **to make an ~ on sth/sb** wywrzeć wpływ na coś/kogoś

impair /ɪm'peə(r)/ vt niekorzystnie wpły|nąć, -wać na (coś) [career, digestion]; osłabi|ć, -áć [efficiency]; nadweręż|yć, -áć [health]

impaired /ɪm'peəd/ adj [vision, hearing] osłabiony; **his speech is ~** ma zaburzenia mowy

impart /ɪm'pɑːt/ vt ① przekaz|ać, -ywać [information, knowledge] (**to sb** komuś); wywoł|ać, -ywać [enthusiasm] (**to sb** w kimś) ② nad|ać, -wać [atmosphere] (**to sb/sth** komuś/czemuś)

impartial /ɪm'pɑːʃl/ adj bezstronny

impassable /ɪm'pɑːsəbl, US -'pæs-/ adj [road] nieprzejezdny; (**to be**) ~ [barrier] (być) nie do pokonania

impassive /ɪm'pæsɪv/ adj beznamiętny

impatience /ɪm'peɪʃns/ n ① (irritation) zniecierpliwienie n (**with sth** czymś) ② (eagerness) niecierpliwość f

impatient /ɪm'peɪʃnt/ adj ① (annoyed) zniecierpliwiony; **he is ~ with children** brakuje mu cierpliwości do dzieci ② (eager) [person, movement] niecierpliwy; **he was ~ to see her** nie mógł się doczekać, kiedy ją zobaczy

impeach /ɪm'piːtʃ/ vt postawić w stan oskarżenia [president]

impeccable /ɪm'pekəbl/ adj [behaviour, appearance] nienaganny

impede /ɪm'piːd/ vt zakłóc|ić, -áć

impending /ɪm'pendɪŋ/ adj nieuchronnie zbliżający się

impenetrable /ɪm'penɪtrəbl/ adj nieprzenikniony

imperative /ɪm'perətɪv/ **Ⅰ** n ① (obligation) konieczność f ② (command) nakaz m **Ⅱ** adj [need] pilny; [tone] rozkazujący

imperceptible /ˌɪmpə'septəbl/ adj niezauważalny

imperfect /ɪm'pɜːfɪkt/ **Ⅰ** n (in grammar) czas m przeszły niedokonany **Ⅱ** adj (incomplete) niedoskonały; (defective) [goods] wybrakowany; [logic] błędny; (in grammar) niedokonany

imperial /ɪm'pɪərɪəl/ adj ① (of empire) imperialny; (of emperor) cesarski ② GB ~ **system** angielski układ miar i wag

imperious /ɪm'pɪərɪəs/ adj władczy

impersonal /ɪm'pɜːsənl/ adj bezosobowy

impersonate /ɪm'pɜːsəneɪt/ vt (imitate) wciel|ić, -áć się w postać (kogoś); (to make people laugh) s|parodiować; (pretend to be) poda|ć, -wać się za (kogoś) [police officer]

impersonator /ɪm'pɜːsəneɪtə(r)/ n aktor m imitacyjny, aktorka f imitacyjna; (entertainer) parodyst|a m, -ka f

impertinent /ɪm'pɜːtɪnənt/ adj [remark] impertynencki; [person] bezczelny

impervious /ɪm'pɜːvɪəs/ adj (to suffering) obojętny (**to sth** na coś); (to charm, demands) nieczuły (**to sth** na coś)

impetuous /ɪm'petʃʊəs/ adj [person] porywczy; [action] gwałtowny

impetus /'ɪmpɪtəs/ n (momentum) impet m; (trigger) bodziec m

impinge /ɪm'pɪndʒ/ vi **to ~ on sth** narusz|yć, -áć coś [rights]; odbi|ć, -jáć się na czymś [budget]

implacable /ɪm'plækəbl/ adj [enemy] nieprzejednany; [demands] nieustępliwy

implant **[I]** /'implɑːnt, US -plænt/ *n* implant *m*
[II] /ɪm'plɑːnt, US -'plænt/ *vt* wszczepi|ć, -ać
implausible /ɪm'plɔːzəbl/ *adj* nieprzekonujący
implement **[I]** /'implɪmənt/ *n* narzędzie *n*; **farm**
~ **s** narzędzia rolnicze
[II] /'implɪment/ *vt* wprowadz|ić, -ać w życie *[law]*;
z|realizować *[project]*; wdr|ożyć, -ażać *[process]*
implementation /ˌimplɪmen'teɪʃn/ *n* (of law)
wprowadzenie *n* (w życie); (of contract) realizacja *f*;
(of process) wdrożenie *n*; Comput implementacja *f*
implicate /'implɪkeɪt/ *vt* wpląt|ać, -ywać (**in sth** w
coś)
implication /ˌimplɪ'keɪʃn/ *n* [1] (possible consequence) konsekwencja *f* [2] (suggestion) sugestia *f*
implicit /ɪm'plɪsɪt/ *adj* [1] (tacit) *[meaning]* ukryty
(**in sth** w czymś) [2] (absolute) *[faith, trust]* bez-
graniczny
imply /ɪm'plaɪ/ *vt* [1] *[person]* da|ć, -wać do zrozu-
mienia (**that...** że...) [2] (mean) *[decision]* implikować;
[term, silence] oznaczać
impolite /ˌimpə'laɪt/ *adj* nieuprzejmy (**to sb**
wobec kogoś)
import **[I]** /'impɔːt/ *n* import *m*
[II] /ɪm'pɔːt/ *vt* importować
importance /ɪm'pɔːtns/ *n* znaczenie *n*
important /ɪm'pɔːtnt/ *adj* ważny; **it is** ~ **that...**
ważne jest, żeby...; **his children are very** ~ **to
him** dzieci znaczą dla niego bardzo wiele
importer /ɪm'pɔːtə(r)/ *n* importer *m*
impose /ɪm'pəʊz/ **[I]** *vt* na|łożyć, -kładać *[sanc-
tions, tax, fine]* (**on sb/sth** na kogoś/coś)
[II] *vi* **to** ~ **on sb** narzucać się komuś; **to** ~ **on
sb's kindness** nadużywać uprzejmości kogoś
imposing /ɪm'pəʊzɪŋ/ *adj* *[person]* imponujący;
[sight] olśniewający
impossible /ɪm'pɒsəbl/ **[I]** *n* **the** ~ rzecz *f*
niemożliwa
[II] *adj* *[task]* niewykonalny; *[request]* niemożliwy
do spełnienia; **to make it** ~ **for sb to do sth**
uniemożliwiać komuś zrobienie czegoś
impotent /'impətənt/ *adj* bezsilny
impound /ɪm'paʊnd/ *vt* s|konfiskować *[goods]*; **his
car was** ~ **ed** jego samochód został odstawiony na
parking policyjny
impractical /ɪm'præktɪkl/ *adj* *[plan]* nieprak-
tyczny; *[idea]* nierealny; **to be** ~ być pozbawionym
zmysłu praktycznego
imprecise /ˌimprɪ'saɪs/ *adj* niedokładny
impress **[I]** /ɪm'pres/ *vt* [1] z|robić wrażenie na
(kimś) (**with sth/with doing sth** czymś/robiąc
coś); **they were** ~ **ed** byli pod wrażeniem [2] **to** ~
sth (up)on sb wp|oić, -ajać komuś coś
[II] /ɪm'pres/ *vi* z|robić dobre wrażenie
impression /ɪm'preʃn/ *n* [1] wrażenie *n*; **to have
an** ~ **that...** mieć wrażenie, że...; **to be under the**
~ **that...** sądzić, że...; **to make a good/bad** ~

robić dobre/złe wrażenie (**on sb** na kimś) [2] (humorous imitation) parodiowanie *n*
impressionable /ɪm'preʃənəbl/ *adj* podatny na
wpływy
impressive /ɪm'presɪv/ *adj* robiący wrażenie;
[building, collection] imponujący
imprint **[I]** /'imprɪnt/ *n* [1] (of footstep) odcisk *m* [2] fig
piętno *n*
[II] /ɪm'prɪnt/ *vt* [1] (stamp) odcis|nąć, -kać *[seal]* (**in/
on sth** w/na czymś) [2] (fix) wyryć *[image]* (**on sth**
w. czymś)
imprison /ɪm'prɪzn/ *vt* u|więzić
imprisonment /ɪm'prɪznmənt/ *n* kara *f* więzienia
improbable /ɪm'prɒbəbl/ *adj* (unlikely to happen)
mało prawdopodobny; (unlikely to be true) mało
wiarygodny
improper /ɪm'prɒpə(r)/ *adj* *[behaviour]* niestosowny; *[remark]* nieprzyzwoity; *[practices]* niedozwolony; *[use, term]* niewłaściwy
improve /ɪm'pruːv/ **[I]** *vt* poprawi|ć, -ać *[condi-
tions]*; ulepsz|yć, -ać *[product]*; zwiększ|yć, -ać
[chances]; **to** ~ **one's mind** rozwijać się
[II] *vi* [1] poprawi|ć, -ać się [2] **to** ~ **on sth** (better)
poprawi|ć, -ać *[score]*; przebi|ć, -jać *[offer]*
improvement /ɪm'pruːvmənt/ **[I]** *n* [1] poprawa *f*
(**in sth/of sth** w czymś/czegoś); **the new edition
is an** ~ **on the old one** nowe wydanie jest lepsze
od starego [2] (alteration) ulepszenie
[II] *n* **home** ~ **s** ulepszenie w domu
improvise /'imprəvaɪz/ **[I]** *vt* za|improwizować; **an**
~ **d table** prowizoryczny stół
[II] *vi* za|improwizować
impudent /'impjʊdənt/ *adj* zuchwały
impulse /'impʌls/ *n* impuls *m*; **to have a sudden**
~ **to do sth** poczuć nagłą chęć zrobienia czegoś; **to
act on (an)** ~ działać pod wpływem impulsu
impulse buy *n* zakup *m* dokonany pod wpływem
impulsu
impulsive /ɪm'pʌlsɪv/ *adj* (rash) impulsywny;
(spontaneous) spontaniczny
impure /ɪm'pjʊə(r)/ *adj* zanieczyszczony
in /ɪn/ [1] *prep* [1] (inside) w (czymś); **in London/
Germany** w Londynie/Niemczech; **in the drawer**
w szufladzie; **in the photo** na fotografii [2] (showing
occupation, activity) w (czymś); **to be in the team**
należeć do drużyny; **to be in politics** zajmować się
polityką [3] (during) **in May/the twenties** w maju/
latach dwudziestych; **in 1990** w 1990 roku; **at four
in the morning** o czwartej rano; **in summer** w
lecie; **in the night** w nocy [4] (within) **to do sth in
10 minutes** zrobić coś w ciągu 10 minut; **I'll be
back in half an hour** wrócę za pół godziny [5] (for)
od; **it hasn't rained in weeks** nie padało od
tygodni [6] (because of) w; **in his hurry he forgot his
keys** w. pośpiechu zapomniał kluczy; **in the
confusion** w zamieszaniu [7] (present) **you see it**

in children widać to u dzieci; **I never thought she had it in her to get that far** nie sądziłem, że (ona) zajdzie tak daleko ⑧ (showing manner, medium) **in a skirt** w spódnicy; **dressed in black** ubrany na czarno; **in German** po niemiecku; **sonata in A minor** sonata a-moll; **'no,' he said in a whisper** „nie", powiedział szeptem; **in a savoury sauce** w pikantnym sosie; **in pencil/ink** ołówkiem/atramentem ⑨ (as regards) **rich in minerals** bogaty w minerały; **deaf in one ear** głuchy na jedno ucho; **it's 10 cm in length** to ma 10 cm długości ⑩ (by) **in refusing to work abroad...** odrzucając propozycję pracy za granicą...; **in doing so** czyniąc tak ⑪ (in superlatives) **the tallest tower in the world** najwyższa wieża na świecie ⑫ (in ratios) **a gradient of 1 in 4** nachylenie 25%; **a tax of 20 pence in the pound** podatek 20 pensów od funta; **to have a one in five chance** mieć jedną szansę na pięć ⑬ (in numbers) **to cut sth in three** przeciąć coś na trzy części; **she's in her twenties** ona ma dwadzieścia kilka lat; **people in their forties** ludzie po czterdziestce

Ⅱ **in and out** prep phr **to come in and out** wchodzić i wychodzić; **to weave in and out of** lawirować wśród czegoś

Ⅲ adv ① **to come/run in** wejść/wbiec; **to ask** or **invite sb in** zaprosić kogoś do środka ② (at home) **is Robert in?** czy jest Robert?; **to stay in** zostać w domu ③ (arrived) **the train is in** pociąg stoi na stacji; **the tide is in** jest przypływ ④ Sport **the ball is in** dobra piłka ⑤ (in supply) **we don't have any in** nie mamy na składzie; **to get some beer in** przynieść piwo

Ⅳ adj infml **to be in, to be the in thing** być w modzie

⟨IDIOMS⟩ **he's in for a shock/surprise** czeka go wstrząs/niespodzianka

inability /ˌɪnəˈbɪlətɪ/ n niezdolność f; **~ to help** niemożność udzielenia pomocy

inaccessible /ˌɪnækˈsesəbl/ adj [place] niedostępny; [text] niełatwy w odbiorze

inaccuracy /ɪnˈækjərəsɪ/ n ① (of calculation) niedokładność f; (of report) nieścisłość f ② (error) nieścisłość f

inaccurate /ɪnˈækjərət/ adj niedokładny

inactive /ɪnˈæktɪv/ adj [person] bezczynny; [machine] nieczynny

inadequate /ɪnˈædɪkwət/ adj niewystarczający (**for sth/to do sth** do czegoś/do zrobienia czegoś)

inadvisable /ˌɪnədˈvaɪzəbl/ adj niewskazany

inane /ɪˈneɪn/ adj [programme] bezsensowny; [person] bezmyślny; [conversation] pusty

inanimate /ɪnˈænɪmət/ adj [object] martwy; [world] nieożywiony

inappropriate /ˌɪnəˈprəʊprɪət/ adj ① [remark, behaviour] niestosowny ② [moment] nieodpowiedni; [word] niewłaściwy

inarticulate /ˌɪnɑːˈtɪkjʊlət/ adj ① **to be ~** nie móc się wysłowić ② [mumble] nieartykułowany; [speech] niewyraźny

inasmuch conj phr (insofar as) o tyle, o ile; (seeing as) jako że

inattentive /ˌɪnəˈtentɪv/ adj [student] nieuważny

inaudible /ɪnˈɔːdəbl/ adj niesłyszalny

inauguration /ɪˌnɔːgjʊˈreɪʃn/ n (of president) wprowadzenie n na urząd; (of tradition) inauguracja f

in-between /ˌɪnbɪˈtwiːn/ adj przejściowy

inbuilt /ˌɪnˈbɪlt/ adj wrodzony

incapable /ɪnˈkeɪpəbl/ adj **to be ~ of doing sth** nie potrafić robić czegoś

incapacitate /ˌɪnkəˈpæsɪteɪt/ vt [accident, illness] czynić niesprawnym

incendiary device n ładunek m wybuchowy

incense /ˈɪnsens/ n kadzidło n

incensed /ɪnˈsenst/ adj rozsierdzony (**by sth** czymś); **to be ~ at sth** być rozsierdzonym na coś

incentive /ɪnˈsentɪv/ n ① (stimulus) bodziec m; **to give sb the ~ to do sth** zachęcić kogoś do zrobienia czegoś; **there is no ~ for people to save** ludziom brak motywacji do oszczędzania ② (also **cash ~**) premia f

incessant /ɪnˈsesnt/ adj nieustanny

incessantly /ɪnˈsesntlɪ/ adv bez ustanku

incest /ˈɪnsest/ n kazirodztwo n

incestuous /ɪnˈsestjʊəs, US -tʃʊəs/ adj kazirodczy

inch /ɪntʃ/ n ① cal m (= 2,54 cm) ② **~ by ~** cal po calu; **to be within an ~ of victory** być o krok od zwycięstwa

incidence /ˈɪnsɪdəns/ n (frequency) częstość f (występowania); **the low ~ of road accidents** niewielka liczba wypadków drogowych

incident /ˈɪnsɪdənt/ n (event) wydarzenie n

incidental /ˌɪnsɪˈdentl/ adj [remark, detail] marginalny

incidentally /ˌɪnsɪˈdentlɪ/ adv (by the way) à propos; (by chance) przy okazji

incident room n GB centrum n koordynacyjne (na miejscu zdarzenia, zajścia)

incinerate /ɪnˈsɪnəreɪt/ vt spal|ić, -ać [waste]

incite /ɪnˈsaɪt/ vt podburz|yć, -ać [people] (**to sth** do czegoś) [strike, violence]

inclination /ˌɪŋklɪˈneɪʃn/ n skłonność f (**to** or **towards sth** do czegoś)

incline **Ⅰ** /ɪnˈklaɪn/ vt ① (tilt) przechyl|ić, -ać ② **to be ~d to do sth** (have tendency) mieć skłonność do robienia czegoś; **come along, if you feel so ~d** chodź, jeżeli masz ochotę **Ⅱ** /ɪnˈklaɪn/ vi ① (tend) **to ~ to** or **towards sth** skłaniać się ku czemuś [extremism, socialism] ② (lean) pochyl|ić, -ać się

include /ɪnˈkluːd/ vt obejmować; **meals are ~d in the price** koszt posiłków jest wliczony w cenę; **all of us, dog ~d** my wszyscy, łącznie z psem

including /ɪn'kluːdɪŋ/ *prep* w tym; ~ July łącznie z lipcem; **not** ~ July nie licząc lipca; ~ **service** łącznie z obsługą

inclusive /ɪn'kluːsɪv/ *adj [charge, price]* łączny; **at an all** ~ **rate of...** za łączną opłatą wynoszącą...

incoherent /ˌɪnkəʊ'hɪərənt/ *adj [account]* chaotyczny; *[policy]* niespójny

income /'ɪŋkʌm/ *n* dochód *m*, dochody *m pl*

income bracket *n* **low-/high-** ~ grupa o niskich/wysokich dochodach

income tax *n* podatek *m* dochodowy

incoming /'ɪnkʌmɪŋ/ *adj [aircraft]* przybywający; *[mail]* napływający; *[wave]* nadchodzący; *[government]* nowy; **this phone only takes** ~ **calls** przez ten telefon można jedynie odbierać rozmowy

incomparable /ɪn'kɒmprəbl/ *adj* niezrównany

incompatible /ˌɪŋkəm'pætəbl/ *adj [aims]* niezgodny; *[couple]* niedobrany; *[computer]* niekompatybilny

incompetent /ɪn'kɒmpɪtənt/ *adj [doctor, government]* niekompetentny; *[work, performance]* nieudolny

incomplete /ˌɪŋkəm'pliːt/ *adj* [1] *[work, novel]* niedokończony [2] *[set]* niekompletny

incomprehensible /ɪnˌkɒmprɪ'hensəbl/ *adj* niezrozumiały (**to sb** dla kogoś)

inconceivable /ˌɪŋkən'siːvəbl/ *adj* niewyobrażalny

inconclusive /ˌɪŋkən'kluːsɪv/ *adj [meeting]* bezowocny; *[evidence]* nieprzekonujący

incongruous /ɪn'kɒŋgrʊəs/ *adj [sight, appearance]* osobliwy

inconsiderate /ˌɪŋkən'sɪdərət/ *adj [person]* nieliczący się z innymi; *[remark]* nietaktowny; **to be** ~ **towards sb** nie liczyć się z kimś

inconsistent /ˌɪŋkən'sɪstənt/ *adj [work]* nierówny; *[attitude]* niestały; *[argument]* niespójny; *[action]* niekonsekwentny; **to be** ~ **with sth** być niezgodnym z czymś

inconspicuous /ˌɪŋkən'spɪkjʊəs/ *adj [person, object]* nierzucający się w oczy

inconvenience /ˌɪŋkən'viːnɪəns/ [1] *n* [1] (trouble) niewygoda *f*; **to put sb to great** ~ sprawić komuś wielki kłopot [2] (disadvantage) niedogodność *f* [2] *vt* przyspｏrzyć, -arzać kłopotu (komuś)

inconvenient /ˌɪŋkən'viːnɪənt/ *adj [location, arrangement]* niedogodny; **it's rather an** ~ **time to call** to chyba nieodpowiednia pora na wizyty

incorporate /ɪn'kɔːpəreɪt/ *vt* [1] (make part of sth) włączｏyć, -ać *[idea]* (**into sth** do czegoś); przyłączｏać, -yć *[territory]* (**into sth** do czegoś) [2] (contain) zawierać (w sobie) [3] **Smith and Brown Incorporated** Smith and Brown SA

incorrect /ˌɪŋkə'rekt/ *adj [address]* niewłaściwy; *[diagnosis]* błędny

incorrigible /ɪn'kɒrɪdʒəbl/, US -'kɔːr-/ *adj* niepoprawny

increase [1] /'ɪŋkriːs/ *n* wzrost *m* (**in sth** czegoś); **an** ~ **of 5%, a 5%** ~ pięcioprocentowy wzrost; **to be on the** ~ wzrastać

[2] /ɪn'kriːs/ *vt* zwiększｏyć, -ać *[sales]*; podwyższｏyć, -ać *[tax]*; **to** ~ **sth by sth** podwyższyć coś o coś; **I** ~**d my offer to £100** podniosłem ofertę do 100 funtów

[3] /ɪn'kriːs/ *vi* wzrｏsnąć, -astać; **to** ~ **by sth** wzrosnąć o coś; **to** ~ **in size** powiększyć się; **to** ~ **in value** zyskać na wartości

increased *adj [demand, risk]* zwiększony

increasingly /ɪn'kriːsɪŋlɪ/ *adv* coraz bardziej

incredible /ɪn'kredəbl/ *adj* niewiarygodny

incredulous /ɪn'kredjʊləs, US -dʒə-/ *adj* pełen niedowierzania

incriminating *adj [evidence, testimony]* obciążający

incubator /'ɪŋkjʊbeɪtə(r)/ *n* inkubator *m*

incur /ɪn'kɜː(r)/ *vt* zaciągｏnąć, -ać *[debt]*; ponｏieść, -osić *[risk, loss, expenses]*; ściągｏnąć, -ać na siebie *[anger]*

incurable /ɪn'kjʊərəbl/ *adj [disease]* nieuleczalny; *[optimist]* niepoprawny

incursion /ɪn'kɜːʃn, US -ʒn/ *n* (into territory) wtargnięcie *n*; (into privacy) ingerencja *f*

indebted /ɪn'detɪd/ *adj* [1] (grateful) **to be** ~ **to sb (for doing sth)** być komuś zobowiązanym (za zrobienie czegoś) [2] (in debt) zadłużony

indecent /ɪn'diːsnt/ *adj [behaviour]* nieprzyzwoity; *[haste]* skandaliczny

indecent assault *n* czyn *m* lubieżny

indecent exposure *n* obnażenie się *n* w miejscu publicznym

indecisive /ˌɪndɪ'saɪsɪv/ *adj [person]* niezdecydowany (**about sth** co do czegoś); *[victory]* nierozstrzygający; *[battle]* nierozstrzygnięty

indeed /ɪn'diːd/ *adv* [1] (certainly) rzeczywiście; **'are you interested?'** – **'yes** ~ **!'** „czy to cię interesuje?" – „tak, oczywiście!"; **'can you see it from there?'** – '~ **you can'** „czy widać to stamtąd?" – „oczywiście, że tak!" [2] (in fact) istotnie [3] (for emphasis) naprawdę; **that was praise** ~**!** to prawdziwa pochwała!; **thank you very much** ~ stokrotne dzięki

indefinite /ɪn'defɪnət/ *adj* [1] (vague) niejasny [2] *[number]* nieokreślony; *[strike]* nieograniczony [3] **the** ~ **article** przedimek nieokreślony

indefinitely /ɪn'defɪnətlɪ/ *adv [postpone, ban]* na czas nieokreślony; *[wait, continue]* bez końca

indelible /ɪn'deləbl/ *adj [ink, mark]* nieścieralny; *[impression]* niezatarty

independence /ˌɪndɪ'pendəns/ *n* (of person) niezależność *f*; (of country) niepodległość *f*

Independence Day *n* Święto *n* Niepodległości

independent /ˌɪndɪ'pendənt/ *adj* [1] *[person]* niezależny (**of sb/sth** od kogoś/czegoś) [2] *[country]* niepodległy

in-depth /ˌɪn'depθ/ adj [analysis, knowledge] dogłębny; [guide] szczegółowy

in depth adv [examine, study] dogłębnie

indescribable /ˌɪndɪ'skraɪbəbl/ adj nieopisany

indestructible /ˌɪndɪ'strʌktəbl/ adj niezniszczalny

index /'ɪndeks/ n [1] (in a book) indeks m [2] (catalogue) katalog m; **card** ~ kartoteka [3] (in economy) wskaźnik m

index card n karta f katalogowa

index finger n palec m wskazujący

index-linked /ˌɪndeks'lɪŋkt/ adj indeksowany

India /'ɪndɪə/ prn Indie plt

Indian /'ɪndɪən/ [1] n [1] (from India) Hindus m, -ka f [2] (American) Indian|in m, -ka f
[2] adj [1] (of India) indyjski [2] (American) indiański

Indian Ocean prn the ~ Ocean m Indyjski

Indian summer n babie lato n

indicate /'ɪndɪkeɪt/ [1] vt wskaz|ać, -ywać; **to ~ that...** oznaczać, że...
[2] vi [driver] włącz|yć, -ać kierunkowskaz; **to ~ left/right** [driver, cyclist] sygnalizować zamiar skrętu w lewo/prawo

indication /ˌɪndɪ'keɪʃn/ n oznaka f

indicative /ɪn'dɪkətɪv/ [1] n (in grammar) tryb m oznajmujący
[2] adj **to be ~ of sth** świadczyć o czymś

indicator /'ɪndɪkeɪtə(r)/ n [1] (pointer) wskazówka f [2] (in car) kierunkowskaz m [3] (at railway station, airport) tablica f informacyjna

indict /ɪn'daɪt/ vt postawić, stawiać w stan oskarżenia

indictment /ɪn'daɪtmənt/ n [1] (in law) akt m oskarżenia [2] (condemnation) potępienie n

indie /'ɪndɪ/ infml [1] n wytwórnia f niezależna
[2] adj niezależny

indifference /ɪn'dɪfrəns/ n obojętność f

indifferent /ɪn'dɪfrənt/ adj [1] (uninterested) obojętny (**to sth** na coś); **to be ~ as to sth** być obojętnym wobec czegoś [2] (mediocre) przeciętny

indigenous /ɪn'dɪdʒɪnəs/ adj [flora] rdzenny; [custom] lokalny; **kangaroos are ~ to Australia** kangury pochodzą z Australii

indigestion /ˌɪndɪ'dʒestʃn/ n niestrawność f

indignant /ɪn'dɪgnənt/ adj oburzony (**over** or **about sth** z powodu czegoś); **to become ~ at sth** oburzać się na coś

indigo /'ɪndɪgəʊ/ [1] n (colour) indygo n inv
[2] adj indygowy

indirect /ˌɪndɪ'rekt, -daɪ'r-/ adj [1] [route] okrężny [2] [answer] wymijający

indirectly /ˌɪndɪ'rektlɪ, -daɪ'r-/ adv [1] okrężną drogą [2] [criticize] pośrednio, nie wprost

indirect speech n (in grammar) mowa f zależna

indiscreet /ˌɪndɪ'skriːt/ adj niedyskretny

indiscretion /ˌɪndɪ'skreʃn/ n (lack of discretion) brak m rozwagi; (act) uchybienie n

indiscriminate /ˌɪndɪ'skrɪmɪnət/ adj [admiration] bezkrytyczny; [reader] niewybredny

indispensable /ˌɪndɪ'spensəbl/ adj niezbędny

indisputable /ˌɪndɪ'spjuːtəbl/ adj [champion] niekwestionowany; [fact] bezsporny

indistinct /ˌɪndɪ'stɪŋkt/ adj [sound, shape] niewyraźny; [photograph] nieostry; [memory] mglisty

individual /ˌɪndɪ'vɪdʒʊəl/ [1] n jednostka f; (a particular person) osoba f
[2] adj [1] [tuition] indywidualny; [attitude] osobisty; [effort] jednostkowy; [portion] oddzielny [2] popojedynczy; **each ~ copy** każdy egzemplarz z osobna [3] (distinctive) indywidualny

individuality /ˌɪndɪˌvɪdʒʊ'ælətɪ/ n indywidualność f

individually /ˌɪndɪ'vɪdʒʊəlɪ/ adv (one at a time) pojedynczo; (in person, personally) osobiście

indoctrinate /ɪn'dɒktrɪneɪt/ vt z|indoktrynować

Indonesia /ˌɪndəʊ'niːzjə/ prn Indonezja f

indoor /ˌɪn'dɔː(r)/ adj [sports] halowy; [shoes] domowy; [photography] we wnętrzach; [swimming pool] kryty; ~ **toilet** toaleta wewnątrz budynku

indoors /ˌɪn'dɔːz/ adv wewnątrz; **to go ~** wejść do środka

induce /ɪn'djuːs, US -'duːs/ vt [1] (persuade) [situation] skł|onić, -aniać (**to do sth** do zrobienia czegoś); [people] nakł|onić, -aniać (**to do sth** do zrobienia czegoś) [2] (bring about) wywoł|ać, -ywać [response]

induction course n GB kurs m wprowadzający

indulge /ɪn'dʌldʒ/ [1] vt [1] dog|odzić, -adzać (komuś) [person, child] [2] zaspok|oić, -ajać [desire, passion]
[2] vi pozwol|ić, -alać sobie (**in sth** na coś) [food]; odda|ć, -wać się (**in sth** czemuś) [nostalgia, hobby]
[3] vr **to ~ oneself** dogadzać sobie

indulgence /ɪn'dʌldʒəns/ n [1] (tolerance) pobłażliwość f (**towards sth/sb** wobec czegoś/kogoś) [2] ~ **in food** oddawanie się przyjemności jedzenia; **it's my only ~** to moja jedyna słabość

indulgent /ɪn'dʌldʒənt/ adj pobłażliwy (**to** or **towards sb/sth** dla kogoś/wobec czegoś)

industrial /ɪn'dʌstrɪəl/ adj przemysłowy; ~ **safety** bezpieczeństwo pracy; ~ **accident** wypadek w (miejscu) pracy

industrial action n GB akcja f protestacyjna; (strike) strajk m

industrial estate n GB strefa f przemysłowa

industrialize /ɪn'dʌstrɪəlaɪz/ vt uprzemysł|owić, -awiać

industrial relations npl stosunki plt pomiędzy pracodawcami i pracownikami

industrial waste n odpady m pl przemysłowe

industrious /ɪn'dʌstrɪəs/ adj pracowity

industry /'ɪndəstrɪ/ n [1] przemysł m; **the oil ~** przemysł naftowy [2] fml (diligence) pracowitość f

inedible /ɪn'edɪbl/ adj niejadalny

ineffective /ˌɪnɪˈfektɪv/ *adj* nieskuteczny

ineffectual /ˌɪnɪˈfektʃʊəl/ *adj [person]* nieudolny; *[policy]* nieskuteczny; *[attempts]* bezskuteczny

inefficiency /ˌɪnɪˈfɪʃnsɪ/ *n* (lack of organization) nieudolność *f*; (incompetence) niekompetencja *f*; (of machine) niewydolność *f*; (of method) nieskuteczność *f*

inefficient /ˌɪnɪˈfɪʃnt/ *adj [management]* nieudolny; *[system]* niewydajny; *[method]* nieskuteczny

ineligible /ɪnˈelɪdʒəbl/ *adj* to be ~ (for job) nie spełniać wymaganych warunków (for sth do czegoś); (for election) nie mieć prawa kandydować (for sth w czymś); she is ~ to receive benefit nie przysługuje jej prawo do otrzymywania zasiłku

inequality /ˌɪnɪˈkwɒlətɪ/ *n* nierówność *f*

inert /ɪˈnɜːt/ *adj [body]* bezwładny; *[person]* bierny

inertia /ɪˈnɜːʃə/ *n* (of person) bezwład *m*; (of system) inercja *f*

inevitable /ɪnˈevɪtəbl/ *adj* nieunikniony, nieuchronny; it was ~ that he should do it było do przewidzenia, że on to zrobi

inexcusable /ˌɪnɪkˈskjuːzəbl/ *adj* niewybaczalny

inexhaustible /ˌɪnɪɡˈzɔːstəbl/ *adj* niewyczerpany

inexpensive /ˌɪnɪkˈspensɪv/ *adj* niedrogi

inexperienced /ˌɪnɪkˈspɪərɪənst/ *adj* niedoświadczony

inexplicable /ˌɪnɪkˈsplɪkəbl/ *adj* niewytłumaczalny

infallible /ɪnˈfæləbl/ *adj [person]* nieomylny; *[method]* niezawodny

infamous /ˈɪnfəməs/ *adj [person]* osławiony; *[act]* niechlubny

infancy /ˈɪnfənsɪ/ *n* ① wczesne dzieciństwo *n*; (of newborn) niemowlęctwo *n* ② stadium *n* początkowe; in its ~ *[company, project]* w powijakach

infant /ˈɪnfənt/ *n* (baby) niemowlę *n*; (child) małe dziecko *n*

infantry /ˈɪnfəntrɪ/ *n* Mil piechota *f*

infant school *n* ≈ zerówka *f (szkoła dla dzieci w wieku 5-7 lat)*

infatuated *adj* to be ~ with sth być zauroczonym czymś

infatuation /ɪnˌfætʃʊˈeɪʃn/ *n* zauroczenie *n* (with sth/sb czymś/kimś)

infect /ɪnˈfekt/ *vt* zaka|zić, -żać *[blood, wound]*; fig ska|zić, -żać *[person]*

infection /ɪnˈfekʃn/ *n* zakażenie *n*

infectious /ɪnˈfekʃəs/ *adj [disease]* zakaźny; *[person]* roznoszący infekcję; *[laugh]* zaraźliwy

infer /ɪnˈfɜː(r)/ *vt* wy|wnioskować (from sth z czegoś)

inferior /ɪnˈfɪərɪə(r)/ **Ⅰ** *n* osoba *f* o niższej pozycji; (subordinate) podwładn|y *m*, -a *f*
Ⅱ *adj* ① *[goods]* niskiej jakości; *[quality]* gorszy ② *[position]* niższy; to make sb feel ~ dać komuś odczuć swoją wyższość

inferiority /ɪnˌfɪərɪˈɒrətɪ, US -ˈɔːr-/ *n* (in quality) pośledniość *f*; (in rank) niższość *f* (to sb w stosunku do kogoś)

inferiority complex *n* kompleks *m* niższości

inferno /ɪnˈfɜːnəʊ/ *n* (hell) piekło *n*

infertile /ɪnˈfɜːtaɪl, US -tl/ *adj [land]* nieurodzajny; *[person]* bezpłodny

infertility /ˌɪnfəˈtɪlətɪ/ *n* (of land) nieurodzajność *f*; (of person) bezpłodność *f*

infest /ɪnˈfest/ *vt* za|atakować; ~ed with sth rojący się od czegoś *[insects]*

infidelity /ˌɪnfɪˈdelətɪ/ *n* niewierność *f*

infighting /ˈɪnfaɪtɪŋ/ *n* konflikt *m* wewnętrzny

infiltrate /ˈɪnfɪltreɪt/ *vt* z|infiltrować *[organization]*; umie|ścić, -szczać *[informer]* (into sth w czymś)

infinite /ˈɪnfɪnət/ *adj [space]* nieskończony; *[number]* niezliczony

infinitely /ˈɪnfɪnətlɪ/ *adv* nieskończenie

infinitive /ɪnˈfɪnətɪv/ *n* bezokolicznik *m*; in the ~ w bezokoliczniku

infinity /ɪnˈfɪnətɪ/ *n* nieskończoność *f*

infirmary /ɪnˈfɜːmərɪ/ *n* szpital *m*; (in school, prison) izba *f* chorych

inflamed *adj* w stanie zapalnym

inflammable /ɪnˈflæməbl/ *adj* łatwopalny

inflammation /ˌɪnfləˈmeɪʃn/ *n* zapalenie *n*

inflatable /ɪnˈfleɪtəbl/ *adj* nadmuchiwany; (with compressed air) pneumatyczny

inflate /ɪnˈfleɪt/ *vt* na|pompować *[tyre]*; nadmuch|ać, -iwać *[balloon]*

inflation /ɪnˈfleɪʃn/ *n* inflacja *f*

inflexible /ɪnˈfleksəbl/ *adj* ① *[material]* nieelastyczny ② *[person, attitude]* nieugięty; *[rules]* sztywny

inflict /ɪnˈflɪkt/ *vt* wymierz|yć, -ać *[punishment]* (on sb komuś); zadać, -wać *[pain]* (on sb komuś); wyrządz|ić, -ać *[damage]* (on sb komuś)

influence /ˈɪnfluəns/ **Ⅰ** *n* wpływ *m*; to be or have an ~ mieć wpływ (on sb/sth na kogoś/coś); to drive while under the ~ of alcohol prowadzić (samochód) będąc pod wpływem alkoholu
Ⅱ *vt* wpły|nąć, -wać na (kogoś/coś) *[jury, decision, events]*; to be ~d by sb/sth pozostawać pod wpływem kogoś/czegoś

influential /ˌɪnfluˈenʃl/ *adj [person, friends]* wpływowy

influenza /ˌɪnfluˈenzə/ *n* grypa *f*

influx /ˈɪnflʌks/ *n* (of visitors, liquid) napływ *m*

info /ˈɪnfəʊ/ *n* infml informacje *f pl*

inform /ɪnˈfɔːm/ **Ⅰ** *vt* po|informować (of/about sth o czymś); to keep sb ~ed informować kogoś na bieżąco (as to/of sth o czymś); I am pleased to ~ you that... miło mi powiadomić Pana/Panią, że...
Ⅱ *vi* to ~ on or against sb donosić na kogoś

informal /ɪnˈfɔːml/ *adj* ① *[person, manner]* bezpośredni; *[style]* swobodny; *[language]* potoczny;

[clothes] swobodny ② *[atmosphere, discussion]* swobodny; *[visit]* nieoficjalny

information /ˌɪnfə'meɪʃn/ *n* ① informacje *f pl* (**on/about sb/sth** o kimś/czymś); **a piece of** ~ informacja ② US informacja *f*, biuro *n* numerów

information desk, information office *n* informacja *f*, punkt *m* informacyjny

information pack *n* komplet *m* informacji

information superhighway *n* Comput infostrada *f*

information technology, IT *n* technika *f* informacyjna

informative /ɪn'fɔ:mətɪv/ *adj* bogaty w informacje

informer /ɪn'fɔ:mə(r)/ *n* (to police) informator *m*, -ka *f*

infrared /ˌɪnfrə'red/ *adj* podczerwony

infrastructure /'ɪnfrəstrʌktʃə(r)/ *n* infrastruktura *f*

infringe /ɪn'frɪndʒ/ **Ⅰ** *vt* narusz|yć, -áć *[rule, rights]*; **Ⅱ** *vi* to ~ **on** or **upon rights** naruszyć prawa

infringement /ɪn'frɪndʒmənt/ *n* pogwałcenie *n*, naruszenie *n*

infuriating /ɪn'fjʊərɪeɪtɪŋ/ *adj* ogromnie irytujący

ingenious /ɪn'dʒi:nɪəs/ *adj* pomysłowy

ingenuity /ˌɪndʒɪ'nju:ətɪ, US -'nu:-/ *n* pomysłowość *f*

ingenuous /ɪn'dʒenjʊəs/ *adj* prostoduszny; (foolish) naiwny

ingot /'ɪŋgət/ *n* (gold) sztaba *f*

ingrained /ɪn'greɪnd/ *adj [habit, hatred]* zakorzeniony (**in sb/sth** w kimś/czymś) *[society]*; **the surface of the table was** ~ **with dirt** powierzchnia stołu była (dosłownie) zarośnięta brudem

ingratitude /ɪn'grætɪtju:d, US -tu:d/ *n* niewdzięczność *f*

ingredient /ɪn'gri:dɪənt/ *n* składnik *m*; fig element *m*

inhabit /ɪn'hæbɪt/ *vt* zamieszkiwać also fig

inhabitant /ɪn'hæbɪtənt/ *n* mieszkan|iec *m*, -ka *f*

inhale /ɪn'heɪl/ **Ⅰ** *vt* wdychać, zaciąg|nąć, -áć się (czymś) **Ⅱ** *vi* (breathe in) zrobić wdech; (smoke) zaciąg|nąć, -áć się

inhaler /ɪn'heɪlə(r)/ *n* inhalator *m*

inherent /ɪn'hɪərənt, ɪn'herənt/ *adj* nieodłączny

inherit /ɪn'herɪt/ *vt* o|dziedziczyć *[property, title]* (**from sb** po kimś)

inheritance /ɪn'herɪtəns/ *n* spadek *m*; **to come into an** ~ otrzymać spadek

inhibit /ɪn'hɪbɪt/ *vt* po|hamować *[person]*; za|hamować *[development]*

inhibited /ɪn'hɪbɪtɪd/ *adj [person]* skrępowany, pełen zahamowań

inhibition /ˌɪnhɪ'bɪʃn, ˌɪnɪ'b-/ *n* zahamowanie *n*; **to get rid of one's** ~**s** pozbyć się zahamowań

inhospitable /ˌɪnhɒ'spɪtəbl/ *adj* niegościnny

in-house /'ɪnhaʊs, -'haʊs/ *adj [training]* wewnątrzzakładowy; *[publication]* wewnętrzny

inhuman /ɪn'hju:mən/ *adj* nieludzki

inhumanity /ˌɪnhju:'mænətɪ/ *n* bestialstwo *n*

initial /ɪ'nɪʃl/ **Ⅰ** *n* pierwsza litera *f* **Ⅱ** *adj* początkowy; ~ **letter** pierwsza litera **Ⅲ** *vt* parafować

initially /ɪ'nɪʃəlɪ/ *adv* początkowo

initiate **Ⅰ** /ɪ'nɪʃɪət/ *n* (into group) nowo przyjęt|y *m*, -a *f* **Ⅱ** /ɪ'nɪʃɪeɪt/ *vt* ① zapoczątkow|ać, -ywać *[talks]*; za|inicjować *[project, reform]*; **to** ~ **proceedings against sb** wszcząć postępowanie przeciw komuś ② wprowadz|ić, -áć kogoś w tajniki czegoś

initiative /ɪ'nɪʃətɪv/ *n* inicjatywa *f*; **on one's own** ~ z własnej inicjatywy

inject /ɪn'dʒekt/ *vt* wstrzyk|nąć, -iwać *[drug, liquid]*; **to** ~ **sb with sth** wstrzykiwać komuś coś

injection /ɪn'dʒekʃn/ *n* Med zastrzyk *m*; Tech wtrysk *m*

injure /'ɪndʒə(r)/ *vt* ① z|ranić *[person]*; **to** ~ **one's leg** zranić się w nogę ② za|szkodzić (czemuś) *[reputation, health]*

injured /'ɪndʒəd/ **Ⅰ** *n* the ~ ranni *m pl* **Ⅱ** *adj* ① *[person]* ranny; *[limb]* zraniony ② ~ **party** (in law) strona poszkodowana

injury /'ɪndʒərɪ/ *n* (to limb) uraz *m*; (to organ) uszkodzenie *n*; **head injuries** obrażenia głowy; **to do sb an** ~ skrzywdzić kogoś

injury time *n* Sport czas *m* doliczony za przerwy w grze

injustice /ɪn'dʒʌstɪs/ *n* niesprawiedliwość *f*

ink /ɪŋk/ *n* (for writing) atrament *m*; (for drawing) tusz *m*; (to write) **in** ~ (pisać) piórem

inkjet printer /'ɪŋkdʒet'prɪntə(r)/ *n* drukarka *f* atramentowa

inkling /'ɪŋklɪŋ/ *n* **to have an** ~ **that...** mieć pewne podejrzenia, że...; **to have no** ~ **of sth** nie mieć pojęcia o czymś

inland **Ⅰ** /'ɪnlənd/ *adj* ① *[harbour]* śródlądowy; *[town]* leżący w głębi lądu ② GB (domestic) *[transport]* krajowy; *[trade]* wewnętrzny **Ⅱ** /ˌɪn'lænd/ *adv [go]* w głąb lądu; *[lie]* w głębi lądu

Inland Revenue *n* GB urząd *m* skarbowy

in-laws /'ɪnlɔ:z/ *npl* (parents) teściowie *plt*; (other relatives) powinowaci *m pl*

inmate /'ɪnmeɪt/ *n* (of prison) więźień *m*, -źniarka *f*; (of hospital) pacjent *m*, -ka *f*; (of asylum) pensjonariusz *m*, -ka *f*

inn /ɪn/ *n* ① (country) gospoda *f* ② (pub) pub *m*

inner /'ɪnə(r)/ *adj* wewnętrzny

inner city **Ⅰ** *n* the ~ podupadła część śródmieścia **Ⅱ inner-city** *adj [problems]* dotyczący podupadłej części śródmieścia

innermost /'ɪnəməʊst/ *adj [thought]* najskrytszy

innocence /'ɪnəsns/ *n* niewinność *f*
innocent /'ɪnəsnt/ **[]** *n* niewiniątko *n*
[] *adj* niewinny
innovation /ˌɪnə'veɪʃn/ *n* innowacja *f*
innovative /'ɪnəvətɪv/ *adj [idea]* nowatorski
innovator /'ɪnəveɪtə(r)/ *n* innowator *m*
innuendo /ˌɪnju:'endəʊ/ *n* (veiled slights) insynuacja *f*; (sexual references) podtekst *m* seksualny
inoculation /ɪˌnɒkjʊ'leɪʃn/ *n* szczepienie *n*
(against sth przeciw czemuś)
inoffensive /ˌɪnə'fensɪv/ *adj [remark]* nieszkodliwy
in-patient /'ɪnpeɪʃnt/ *n* pacjent *m* hospitalizowa-
ny
input /'ɪnpʊt/ *n* **[]** (of money) wkład *m*; (of energy)
dopływ *m* **[]** (contribution) wkład *m* **[]** Comput (action)
wprowadzanie *n* danych; (data) dane *plt* wejściowe
inquest /'ɪŋkwest/ *n* dochodzenie *n* (on/into sth
w sprawie czegoś)
inquire /ɪn'kwaɪə(r)/ **[]** *vt* za|pytać o (coś) *[name,*
way]
[] *vi* za|pytać (się), spytać (się) (about sth o coś);
to ~ after sb pytać o kogoś; to ~ into sth (ask for
information) wypytywać o coś; (research) badać coś;
(formally) prowadzić dochodzenie w sprawie czegoś;
' ~ within' „wiadomość na miejscu"
inquiry /ɪn'kwaɪərɪ, US 'ɪŋkwərɪ/ *n* dochodzenie *n*,
śledztwo *n* (into sth w sprawie czegoś); **murder**
~ dochodzenie w sprawie morderstwa
inquisitive /ɪn'kwɪzətɪv/ *adj [mind]* dociekliwy;
(prying) wścibski
insane /ɪn'seɪn/ *adj [person]* obłąkany; (legally)
niepoczytalny; *[idea]* szalony
insanitary /ɪn'sænɪtərɪ, US -terɪ/ *adj [conditions]*
niehigieniczny; *[surroundings]* niezdrowy
insanity /ɪn'sænətɪ/ *n* obłęd *m*; (in law) niepoczy-
talność *f*
insatiable /ɪn'seɪʃəbl/ *adj* nienasycony
inscription /ɪn'skrɪpʃn/ *n* napis *m*
insect /'ɪnsekt/ *n* owad *m*; ~ **bite** ukąszenie *n*
owada
insecticide /ɪn'sektɪsaɪd/ **[]** *n* środek *m* owadobójczy
[] *adj* owadobójczy
insect repellent *n* środek *m* odstraszający owady
insecure /ˌɪnsɪ'kjʊə(r)/ *adj* **[]** (person) niepewny;
he is ~ brakuje mu pewności siebie **[]** *[future,*
job] niepewny
insecurity /ˌɪnsɪ'kjʊərətɪ/ *n* **[]** (psychological) brak *m*
pewności siebie; **to suffer from feelings of** ~
odczuwać brak pewności siebie **[]** (of position,
situation) niepewność *f*; **job** ~ ryzyko utraty pracy
insensitive /ɪn'sensətɪv/ *adj [person]* (tactless)
nietaktowny; (unfeeling) niewrażliwy (**to sth** na
coś); *[remark]* niedelikatny
inseparable /ɪn'seprəbl/ *adj [couple]* nierozłączny;
[part] nieodłączny (**from sth** od czegoś)

insert /ɪn'sɜːt/ *vt* wstawi|ć, -ać *[word]* (**in sth** do
czegoś); włoży|ć, -kładać *[key]* (**in sth** w coś/do
czegoś)
inside **[]** /'ɪnsaɪd/ *n* wnętrze *n*; **to overtake on**
the ~ (in Europe) wyprzedzać z prawej; (in GB,
Australia) wyprzedzać z lewej; **we've got a man on**
the ~ mamy tam swojego człowieka
[] /'ɪnsaɪd/ *adj* **[]** *[pocket, surface]* wewnętrzny;
[toilet] wewnątrz budynku **[]** *[information]* (pochodzący) z pierwszej ręki **[]** **the** ~ **lane** (of road) (in
Europe, US) prawy pas *m*; (in UK, Australia) lewy pas *m*;
(of athletic track) tor *m* wewnętrzny
[] /ɪn'saɪd/ *adv* (indoors) *[be]* wewnątrz; *[go, come,*
look] do środka; **to bring sth** ~ wnieść coś do
środka
[] /ɪn'saɪd/ *prep* (also US ~ **of**) **[]** wewnątrz; ~
sth wewnątrz czegoś *[box]*; **to be** ~ (**the house**)
być w domu **[]** (within area, organization) w (czymś)
[] (under) ~ (**of**) **an hour** w ciągu godziny
[] **inside out** /'ɪnsaɪd/ *adv phr* (of clothes) na lewą
stronę; **to turn sth** ~ **out** wywrócić coś na drugą
stronę *[bag]*; **to know sth** ~ **out** znać coś na
wylot
insider dealing *n* wykorzystywanie *n* poufnych
informacji (w transakcjach)
insides *npl* infml (intestines) wnętrzności *plt*
insight /'ɪnsaɪt/ *n* **[]** (perceptiveness) przenikliwość *f*;
to have ~ **into sth** rozumieć coś dogłębnie
[] (revealing glimpse) spostrzeżenie *n*
insignificant /ˌɪnsɪg'nɪfɪkənt/ *adj [cost, difference]*
niewielki; *[person, detail]* mało znaczący
insincere /ˌɪnsɪn'sɪə(r)/ *adj* nieszczery
insinuate /ɪn'sɪnjʊeɪt/ *vt* insynuować (**that...**
że...)
insinuation /ɪnˌsɪnjʊ'eɪʃn/ *n* insynuacja *f*
insipid /ɪn'sɪpɪd/ *adj [food]* mdły; *[performance]*
bezbarwny
insist /ɪn'sɪst/ **[]** *vt* **[]** (demand) **to** ~ **that...**
nalegać, żeby... **[]** (maintain) **to** ~ **that...** upierać
się, że...
[] *vi* nalegać; **to** ~ **on sth** domagać się czegoś; **to**
~ **on doing sth** upierać się (przy tym), żeby
zrobić coś
insistent /ɪn'sɪstənt/ *adj [person]* uparty; *[demand]*
uporczywy; **to be** ~ **about sth** nalegać na coś; **she**
was most ~ **that...** uparcie twierdziła, że...
insole /'ɪnsəʊl/ *n* wkładka *f* (do butów)
insolent /'ɪnsələnt/ *adj* bezczelny
insomnia /ɪn'sɒmnɪə/ *n* bezsenność *f*
inspect /ɪn'spekt/ *vt* z|badać *[object]*; s|kontrolo-
wać *[document, luggage, accounts]*; przeprowadz|ić,
-ać inspekcję (czegoś) *[factory]*; wizytować *[school]*
inspection /ɪn'spekʃn/ *n* (of passport, ticket) kontrola *f*; (of object) zbadanie *n*; (of premises) inspekcja *f*;
on closer ~ po bliższym zbadaniu

inspector /ɪn'spektə(r)/ n ① (supervisor) inspektor m, -ka f ② GB (in police) inspektor m ③ GB (on bus) kontroler m, -ka f

inspiration /ˌɪnspə'reɪʃn/ n inspiracja f (**for sth** do czegoś)

inspire /ɪn'spaɪə(r)/ vt za|inspirować; **the revolution was** ∼**d by these ideals** te ideały były inspiracją do rewolucji; **to** ∼ **sb with sth** natchnąć kogoś czymś

inspired /ɪn'spaɪəd/ adj [person] natchniony; [idea] szczęśliwy; **he made an** ∼ **guess** coś go olśniło

inspiring /ɪn'spaɪərɪŋ/ adj [person, talk] porywający; [thought] inspirujący

instal(l) /ɪn'stɔ:l/ vt za|instalować [heating]; za|-montować [windows]; **to** ∼ **sb in office** wprowadzić kogoś na urząd

installation /ˌɪnstə'leɪʃn/ n instalacja f

instalment, installment US /ɪn'stɔ:lmənt/ n rata f; **to repay sth in** ∼**s** spłacać coś w ratach

instance /'ɪnstəns/ n (example) przykład m; **for** ∼ na przykład

instant /'ɪnstənt/ ① n chwila f; **this (very)** ∼ w tej chwili, natychmiast
② adj ① (immediate) [response, access] natychmiastowy ② Culin [soup] błyskawiczny; [coffee] rozpuszczalny

instant camera n polaroid® m

instantly /'ɪnstəntlɪ/ adv natychmiast

instead /ɪn'sted/ ① adv za to; **we didn't go home – we went to the park** ∼ nie poszliśmy do domu, za to wybraliśmy się do parku; **I don't feel like walking – let's take a taxi** ∼ nie chce mi się iść na piechotę – weźmy raczej taksówkę; **his brother came** ∼ za to przyszedł jego brat
② **instead of** prep phr ∼ **of sth/sb** zamiast czegoś/kogoś; ∼ **of doing sth** zamiast robić coś; **let's play cards** ∼ **of watching television** zagrajmy w karty zamiast oglądać telewizję; **you can go** ∼ **of me** możesz iść zamiast mnie

instep /'ɪnstep/ n podbicie n

instigate /'ɪnstɪgeɪt/ vt wszcz|ąć, -ynać [proceedings]; przyst|ąpić, -ępować do [attack]

instil GB, **instill** US vt wp|oić, -ajać [respect] (**in/into sb** komuś); napawać (czymś) [fear] (**in/into sb** kogoś); **to** ∼ **confidence (in sb)** wzbudzać zaufanie (w kimś)

instinct /'ɪnstɪŋkt/ n instynkt m; **the** ∼ **to do sth** wrodzone zdolności do robienia czegoś

instinctive /ɪn'stɪŋktɪv/ adj instynktowny

institute /'ɪnstɪtju:t, US -tu:t/ ① n (organization) instytut m
② vt ustan|owić, -awiać [rule]; zało|żyć, -kładać [society]

institution /ˌɪnstɪ'tju:ʃn, US -'tu:ʃn/ n ① (organization) instytucja f ② zakład m (opieki); **a mental** ∼ zakład dla umysłowo chorych

institutionalize /ˌɪnstɪ'tju:ʃənəlaɪz, US -'tu:-/ vt ① (place in care) umieścić, -szczać w zakładzie [elderly, insane] ② (establish officially) z|instytucjonalizować [practice, system]; ∼ **d** [violence, racism] zinstytucjonalizowany

instruct /ɪn'strʌkt/ vt ① po|instruować; **to** ∼ **sb to do sth** zlecić or kazać komuś zrobić coś; **to be** ∼**ed to do sth** otrzymać polecenie zrobienia czegoś ② (teach) uczyć; **to** ∼ **sb in sth** uczyć kogoś czegoś

instruction /ɪn'strʌkʃn/ n (teaching) nauczanie n; ∼**s for use** sposób użycia

instruction book n instrukcja f

instructor /ɪn'strʌktə(r)/ n ① (sports) instruktor m, -ka f (**in sth** czegoś); **a driving** ∼ instruktor nauki jazdy ② US (at university) wykładowca m

instrument /'ɪnstrəmənt/ n ① (tool) przyrząd m ② Mus instrument m; **to play an** ∼ grać na instrumencie

instrumental /ˌɪnstrʊ'mentl/ ① n utwór m instrumentalny
② adj ① **to be** ∼ **in (doing) sth** walnie przyczynić się do (zrobienia) czegoś ② Mus instrumentalny

instrument panel n tablica f przyrządów (pomiarowo-kontrolnych)

insufficient /ˌɪnsə'fɪʃnt/ adj niewystarczający; **there are** ∼ **copies** jest zbyt mało egzemplarzy

insulate /'ɪnsjʊleɪt, US -səl-/ vt za|izolować [cable, wall] (**from sth** przed czymś) (**with sth** czymś); **to** ∼ **sth against cold/sound** ocieplać/wytłumić coś [room] (**with sth** czymś)

insulation /ˌɪnsjʊ'leɪʃn, US -sə'l-/ n (of building, wire) izolacja f

insulin /'ɪnsjʊlɪn, US -səl-/ n insulina f

insult ① /'ɪnsʌlt/ n zniewaga f, obelga f
② /ɪn'sʌlt/ vt obra|zić, -żać, znieważ|yć, -ać

insurance /ɪn'ʃɔ:rəns, US -'ʃʊər-/ n ubezpieczenie n (**on sth** czegoś) (**against sth** od czegoś); ∼ **for the house** ubezpieczenie domu; **to take out (an)** ∼ **against sth** ubezpieczyć się od czegoś

insurance policy n polisa f ubezpieczeniowa

insure /ɪn'ʃɔ:(r), US -'ʃʊər/ vt ubezpiecz|yć, -ać (**against sth** od czegoś)

intact /ɪn'tækt/ adj nietknięty

intake /'ɪnteɪk/ n ① (consumption) (of food) spożycie n; (of oxygen) zużycie n ② (admission) nabór m ③ **an** ∼ **of breath** wdech

intangible /ɪn'tændʒəbl/ adj nieuchwytny

integral /'ɪntɪgrəl/ adj integralny; **to be** ∼ **to sth** być nierozerwalnie związanym z czymś

integrate /'ɪntɪgreɪt/ ① vt ① (incorporate) wciel|ić, -ać, włącz|yć, -ać [region, company]; z|integrować [minority] ② (combine) po|łączyć (w jedną całość)
② vi [person] z|integrować się (**into/with sth** z czymś)

integration /ˌɪntɪˈgreɪʃn/ *n* integracja *f* (**with sth** z czymś)

integrity /ɪnˈtegrəti/ *n* (of person) prawość *f*

intellect /ˈɪntəlekt/ *n* [1] (intelligence) intelekt *m* [2] (person) wielki umysł *m*

intellectual /ˌɪntəˈlektʃʊəl/ [I] *n* intelektualist|a *m*, -ka *f*
[II] *adj* intelektualny

intelligence /ɪnˈtelɪdʒəns/ *n* [1] (powers of mind) inteligencja *f* [2] (information) informacje *f pl* (wywiadu) [3] (secret service) wywiad *m*; **military** ~ wywiad wojskowy

intelligent /ɪnˈtelɪdʒənt/ *adj* inteligentny

intelligible /ɪnˈtelɪdʒəbl/ *adj* zrozumiały (**to sb** dla kogoś)

intend /ɪnˈtend/ *vt* **to** ~ **to do sth, to** ~ **doing sth** mieć zamiar coś zrobić; **it was** ~**ed as a joke** to miał być dowcip; **to be** ~**ed for sb** [bomb, flowers] być przeznaczonym dla kogoś

intense /ɪnˈtens/ *adj* [1] [heat] wielki; [pain, colour] intensywny; [cold] dotkliwy [2] [person] zasadniczy

intensify /ɪnˈtensɪfaɪ/ [I] *vt* nasil|ić, -ać [campaign]; z|intensyfikować [farming]
[II] *vi* nasil|ić, -ać się

intensive /ɪnˈtensɪv/ *adj* intensywny

intensive care *n* intensywna opieka *f* medyczna

intensive care unit *n* oddział *m* intensywnej opieki medycznej

intent /ɪnˈtent/ *adj* [1] (absorbed) **to be** ~ **on doing sth** być skupionym na robieniu czegoś [2] (determined) **to be** ~ **on doing sth** postanowić zrobić coś
[IDIOMS] **to all** ~**s and purposes** na dobrą sprawę

intention /ɪnˈtenʃn/ *n* zamiar *m* (**of doing/to do sth** zrobienia czegoś)

intentional /ɪnˈtenʃənl/ *adj* [insult] zamierzony; [action] celowy

intentionally /ɪnˈtenʃənəli/ *adv* celowo

interact /ˌɪntərˈækt/ *vi* [substances, phenomena] oddziaływać na siebie (wzajemnie); [people] nawiązywać wzajemne kontakty; Comput komunikować się

intercept *vt* przechwy|cić, -tywać [letters]; przej|ąć, -mować [ball]

interchange [I] /ˈɪntətʃeɪndʒ/ *n* [1] (exchange) wymiana *f* [2] (road junction) rozjazd *m*
[II] /ˌɪntəˈtʃeɪndʒ/ *vt* (exchange) wymieni|ć, -ać; (change places of) zamieni|ć, -ać (miejscami)

intercom /ˈɪntəkɒm/ *n* interkom *m*; (in block of flats) domofon *m*

intercourse /ˈɪntəkɔːs/ *n* (social) stosunki *m pl*; (sexual) stosunek *m* (płciowy)

interest /ˈɪntrəst/ [I] *n* [1] (enthusiasm) zainteresowanie *n* (**in sb/sth** kimś/czymś); **to hold sb's** ~ zajmować uwagę kogoś [2] (benefit) interes *m*; **it is in your (own)** ~(**s**) **to write to them** w twoim (własnym) interesie leży napisanie do nich; **to have sb's** ~**s at heart** mieć na względzie dobro kogoś [3] (hobby) zainteresowanie *n* [4] (charge for a loan) odsetki *plt* (**on sth** od czegoś); **to earn** ~ [investment] przynosić procenty
[II] *vt* zainteresować (**in sth** czymś)

interested /ˈɪntrəstɪd/ *adj* [expression, onlooker] zaciekawiony; **to be** ~ **in sb/sth** interesować się kimś/czymś [subject, person]

interest-free loan *n* pożyczka *f* nieoprocentowana

interesting /ˈɪntrəstɪŋ/ *adj* interesujący

interest rate *n* stopa *f* procentowa

interface /ˈɪntəfeɪs/ Comput [I] *n* interfejs *m*
[II] *vt* sprzęg|nąć, -ać

interfere /ˌɪntəˈfɪə(r)/ *vi* [1] **to** ~ **in sth** wtrącać się do czegoś [quarrel]; ingerować w coś [affairs, private life] [2] **to** ~ **with sth** majstrować przy czymś [machine] [3] **to** ~ **with sth** [activity] przeszkadzać w czymś [work]

interference /ˌɪntəˈfɪərəns/ *n* (on radio) zakłócenia *n pl*

interfering /ˌɪntəˈfɪərɪŋ/ *adj* pej wścibski

interim /ˈɪntərɪm/ [I] *n* **in the** ~ w tym czasie
[II] *adj* [government, report, post] tymczasowy; [arrangement] doraźny

interior /ɪnˈtɪərɪə(r)/ [I] *n* wnętrze *n*
[II] *adj* wewnętrzny

interior decorator *n* dekorator *m* wnętrz

interlink /ˌɪntəˈlɪŋk/ *vt* **to be** ~**ed** [factors] być powiązanym (**with sth** z czymś)

interlock /ˌɪntəˈlɒk/ *vi* [pipes] połączyć się; [fingers] spl|eść, -atać się; [systems] zazębi|ć, -ać się

interlude /ˈɪntəluːd/ *n* (pause) przerwa *f*; (interval) (in theatre) antrakt *m*

intermediary /ˌɪntəˈmiːdɪəri, US -dɪeri/ [I] *n* mediator *m*, -ka *f*
[II] *adj* mediacyjny

intermediate /ˌɪntəˈmiːdɪət/ *adj* [1] [form, stage, step] pośredni [2] ~ **course** kurs dla średnio zaawansowanych; [level, student] średnio zaawansowany

intermission /ˌɪntəˈmɪʃn/ *n* przerwa *f*; (in theatre) antrakt *m*

intern [I] /ˈɪntɜːn/ *n* US Med stażyst|a *m*, -ka *f*
[II] /ɪnˈtɜːn/ *vt* internować

internal /ɪnˈtɜːnl/ *adj* [1] wewnętrzny [2] (within country) [trade] wewnętrzny; [flight] krajowy

international /ˌɪntəˈnæʃnəl/ *adj* międzynarodowy

internationally /ˌɪntəˈnæʃnəli/ *adv* [known, respected] na całym świecie

internee /ˌɪntɜːˈniː/ *n* internowan|y *m*, -a *f*

Internet /ˈɪntənet/ *n* Internet *m*; **on the** ~ w Internecie

Internet access *n* dostęp *m* do Internetu

Internet service provider, ISP *n* dostawca *m* usług internetowych

Internet user *n* użytkownik *m* internetu

interpret /ɪn'tɜːprɪt/ **[]** *vt* z|interpretować (**as sth** jako coś) [2] (translate) prze|tłumaczyć (ustnie) **[]** *vi* służyć za tłumacza (**for sb** komuś)
interpreter /ɪn'tɜːprɪtə(r)/ *n* tłumacz *m*, -ka *f* (żywego słowa)
interrogate /ɪn'terəgeɪt/ *vt* przesłuch|ać, -iwać
interrogation /ɪnˌterə'geɪʃn/ *n* przesłuchanie *n*
interrogative /ˌɪntə'rɒgətɪv/ *n* forma *f* pytająca; **in the** ~ w formie pytającej
interrupt /ˌɪntə'rʌpt/ *vt, vi* przer|wać, -ywać; **stop** ~**ing!** nie przerywaj!
interruption /ˌɪntə'rʌpʃn/ *n* przerwa *f*
intersect /ˌɪntə'sekt/ **[]** *vt* przeci|ąć, -nać **[]** *vi* [roads, wires] przeci|ąć, -nać się, krzyżować się (**with sth** z czymś)
intersection /ˌɪntə'sekʃn/ *n* skrzyżowanie *n*
interstate /ˌɪntə'steɪt/ US *n* (also ~ **highway**) autostrada *f* międzystanowa
interval /'ɪntəvl/ *n* [] odstęp *m*; **at** ~**s** regularnie, w regularnych odstępach; **at** ~**s of five minutes** w odstępach pięciominutowych; **at 100-metre** ~**s** w stumetrowych odstępach [2] GB (in theatre) antrakt *m*
intervene /ˌɪntə'viːn/ *vi* interweniować (**on behalf of sb** w sprawie kogoś)
intervention /ˌɪntə'venʃn/ *n* interwencja *f*; **an** ~ **on my behalf** poparcie dla mojej sprawy
interview /'ɪntəvjuː/ **[]** *n* [] (also **job** ~) rozmowa *f* kwalifikacyjna [2] (by journalist) wywiad *m* **[]** *vt* [] (for job, post) przeprowadz|ić, -ać rozmowę kwalifikacyjną z (kimś) [candidate] [2] [journalist] przeprowadz|ić, -ać wywiad z (kimś) [celebrity] [3] [police] przesłuch|ać, -iwać [suspect]
interviewee /ˌɪntəvjuː'iː/ *n* [] (for job, place) kandydat *m*, -ka *f* [2] (on TV, radio) osoba *f* udzielająca wywiadu
interviewer /'ɪntəvjuːə(r)/ *n* [] (for job, course) przeprowadzając|y *m*, -a *f* rozmowę kwalifikacyjną [2] [journalist] dziennikarz *m* przeprowadzający wywiad, dziennikarka *f* przeprowadzająca wywiad
interwar /ˌɪntə'wɔː(r)/ *adj* międzywojenny
intestine /ɪn'testɪn/ *n* jelito *n*
intimacy /'ɪntɪməsɪ/ *n* zażyłość *f*
intimate /'ɪntɪmət/ *adj* [] serdeczny, bliski; **to be on** ~ **terms with sb** być z kimś w zażyłych stosunkach [2] [knowledge] gruntowny
intimidate /ɪn'tɪmɪdeɪt/ *vt* zastrasz|yć, -ać
intimidating /ɪn'tɪmɪdeɪtɪŋ/ *adj* [person, sight, prospect] przerażający; [manner] zastraszający
into /'ɪntuː, 'ɪntə/ *prep* [] [put, go] do (czegoś) [place]; **to disappear** ~ **sth** zniknąć w czymś; **to bang** ~ **sb/sth** wpa|ść, -dać na kogoś/coś; **to go** ~ **town/the office** iść do miasta/biura; **to get** ~ **bed** położyć się do łóżka [2] (transform) **to translate sth** ~ **Polish** przetłumaczyć coś na polski; **to change dollars** ~ **pounds** wymienić dolary na funty [3] **to last** ~ **the 18th century** trwać (aż) do XVIII

wieku; **long** ~ **the night** do późna w nocy [4] (keen on) **to be** ~ **sth** interesować się czymś [jazz]; **to be** ~ **drugs** narkotyzować się [5] (in maths) **8** ~ **24 goes 3 times** or **is 3** 24 dzielone przez 8 równa się 3
intolerable /ɪn'tɒlərəbl/ *adj* nieznośny
intolerance /ɪn'tɒlərəns/ *n* brak *m* tolerancji (**of sb/sth** dla kogoś/czegoś); Med nietolerancja *f* (**of sth, towards sth** na coś)
intolerant /ɪn'tɒlərənt/ *adj* **to be** ~ **of sb/sth** być nietolerancyjnym wobec kogoś/czegoś
intoxicated /ɪn'tɒksɪkeɪtɪd/ *adj* odurzony
intoxicating /ɪn'tɒksɪkeɪtɪŋ/ *adj* [drink] wyskokowy; [effect] odurzający
intranet /'ɪntrənet/ *n* wewnętrzna sieć *f* komputerowa
intransitive /ɪn'trænsətɪv/ *adj* nieprzechodni
intravenous /ˌɪntrə'viːnəs/ *adj* dożylny
intravenous drug user *n* przyjmując|y *m*, -a *f* narkotyki drogą dożylną
in-tray /'ɪntreɪ/ *n* tacka *f* na korespondencję przychodzącą
intrepid /ɪn'trepɪd/ *adj* nieustraszony
intricate /'ɪntrɪkət/ *adj* [problem, plot] zawiły; [mechanism] skomplikowany; [design] misterny
intrigue **[]** /'ɪntriːg, ɪn'triːg/ *n* intryga *f* **[]** /ɪn'triːg/ *vt* za|intrygować; **I'm** ~**d to know...** ciekaw jestem...
intriguing /ɪn'triːgɪŋ/ *adj* intrygujący
introduce /ˌɪntrə'djuːs, US -'duːs/ *vt* [] (present) przedstawi|ć, -ać [person] (**as sb** jako kogoś); **to** ~ **sb to sth** zaznajomić kogoś z czymś [changes]; wprowadzić kogoś w coś [subject] [2] (put into force) wprowadz|ić, -ać [law, reform, change] [3] (on TV, radio) poprzedz|ić, -ać słowem wstępnym [programme]
introduction /ˌɪntrə'dʌkʃn/ *n* [] (presentation) prezentacja *f*; **a letter of** ~ list polecający [2] (of liquid, system, law) wprowadzenie *n* (**into sth** do czegoś) [3] (to article, speech) wprowadzenie *n*, wstęp *m*
introductory /ˌɪntrə'dʌktərɪ/ *adj* [] [remarks] wstępny; [lecture] wprowadzający [2] [offer] promocyjny
introvert /'ɪntrəvɜːt/ *n* introwerty|k *m*, -czka *f*
intrude /ɪn'truːd/ *vi* **to** ~ **on sth** zakłócać coś [privacy]; **to** ~ **in(to) sb's affairs** wtrącać się w sprawy kogoś
intruder /ɪn'truːdə(r)/ *n* intruz *m*
intrusive /ɪn'truːsɪv/ *adj* [person, question] wścibski; [phone call, presence] niepożądany
intuition /ˌɪntjuː'ɪʃn, US -tuː-/ *n* (ability) intuicja *f*; (knowledge) przeczucie *n* (**about sth** czegoś)
intuitive /ɪn'tjuːətɪv, US -'tuː-/ *adj* intuicyjny
inundate /'ɪnʌndeɪt/ *vt* zal|ać, -ewać; [land] zasyp|ać, -ywać [organization, market]
invade /ɪn'veɪd/ *vt* naje|chać, -żdżać
invalid /'ɪnvəliːd, 'ɪnvəlɪd/ **[]** *n* inwalid|a *m*, -ka *f*, niepełnosprawn|y *m*, -a *f*

II adj [claim] bezpodstawny; [passport, contract] nieważny

invaluable /ɪn'væljʊəbl/ adj [assistance] nieoceniony; [jewel, painting] bezcenny

invasion /ɪn'veɪʒn/ n (of army) najazd m; (of privacy) naruszenie n

invent /ɪn'vent/ vt wynaleźć [machine]; wymyśl|ić, -ać [character]

invention /ɪn'venʃn/ n wynalazek m

inventive /ɪn'ventɪv/ adj pomysłowy

inventor /ɪn'ventə(r)/ n wynalaz|ca m, -czyni f

inventory /'ɪnvəntrɪ, US -tɔːrɪ/ n [1] (of house) inwentarz m; (of contents) spis m [2] US (stock) zapas m

inverted commas /ɪnvɜːtɪd'kɒməz/ npl GB cudzysłów m; **in** ~ w cudzysłowie

invest /ɪn'vest/ **I** vt za|inwestować [money]; w|łożyć, -kładać [effort] (**in sth** w coś)
II vi za|inwestować (**in sth** w coś) [car, shares]

investigate /ɪn'vestɪgeɪt/ vt [1] prowadzić dochodzenie w sprawie (czegoś) [crime, accident]; sprawdz|ić, -ać [person] [2] (study) z|badać [possibilities, market]

investigation /ɪnvestɪ'geɪʃn/ n [1] (inquiry) śledztwo n, dochodzenie n (**of** or **into sth** w sprawie czegoś) [2] (of accounts, reports) kontrola f (**of sth** czegoś)

investment /ɪn'vestmənt/ n [1] (in finance) inwestycja f (**in sth** w coś) [2] (of time, energy) nakłady m pl

investment manager n zarządca m papierów wartościowych

investor /ɪn'vestə(r)/ n inwestor m

invigilate /ɪn'vɪdʒɪleɪt/ vt nadzorować [examination]

invisible /ɪn'vɪzəbl/ adj [mark] niewidoczny; [fairy] niewidzialny

invisible ink n atrament m sympatyczny

invitation /ɪnvɪ'teɪʃn/ n zaproszenie n

invitation card n zaproszenie n

invite /ɪn'vaɪt/ vt zapr|osić, -aszać [person]; **to** ~ **sb for a drink** zaprosić kogoś na drinka; **to** ~ **sb in** zaprosić kogoś do środka; **to** ~ **sb over** or **round (to one's house)** zaprosić kogoś do siebie

inviting /ɪn'vaɪtɪŋ/ adj [prospect] kuszący; [meal] zachęcający

invoice /'ɪnvɔɪs/ **I** n faktura f
II vt wystaw|ić, -ać fakturę; **to** ~ **sb for sth** wystawić komuś fakturę na coś

involve /ɪn'vɒlv/ vt [1] (entail) wymagać (czegoś), pociąg|nąć, -ać za sobą [effort, travel]; wiązać się z (czymś) [problems] [2] (cause to participate) włącz|yć, -ać [person, group] (**in sth** do czegoś); **to be** ~**d in sth** (positive) brać udział w czymś [business, project]; (negative) być zamieszanym w coś [scandal, robbery] [3] (affect) [strike, reform] obj|ąć, -ejmować; [matter] dotyczyć (kogoś/czegoś) [4] (engross) **to get** ~**d in sth** wciągnąć się w coś [film, book] [5] **to get** ~**d with sb** związać się z kimś [person]

involved /ɪn'vɒlvd/ adj [1] (complicated) [explanation] zawiły [2] [person, group] (affected) zainteresowany; (implicated) zamieszany [3] (necessary) [expense, effort] nieodłączny, towarzyszący

involvement /ɪn'vɒlvmənt/ n [1] (in activity) uczestnictwo n (**in sth** w czymś); (in enterprise, politics) zaangażowanie n (**in sth** w coś) [2] (with group) powiązania n pl; (with person) związki m pl

inward /'ɪnwəd/ **I** adj (inner) [feelings] skryty; [relief] wewnętrzny
II adv (also **inwards**) [move, turn, open] do wewnątrz

inward-looking /'ɪnwədlʊkɪŋ/ adj [person] zapatrzony w siebie; [policy] partykularny

inwards = **inward**

iodine /'aɪədiːn, US -daɪn/ n (element) jod m; (antiseptic) jodyna f

IOU n = **I owe you** rewers m

IQ n = **intelligence quotient** IQ n inv

Iran /ɪ'rɑːn/ prn Iran m

Iraq /ɪ'rɑːk/ prn Irak m

irate /aɪ'reɪt/ adj zagniewany

Ireland /'aɪələnd/ prn Irlandia f

Irish /'aɪərɪʃ/ **I** n [1] (język m) irlandzki m [2] (people) **the** ~ Irlandczycy m pl
II adj irlandzki

Irishman /'aɪərɪʃmən/ n Irlandczyk m

Irish Republic n Republika f Irlandii

Irish Sea prn Morze f Irlandzkie

Irishwoman /'aɪərɪʃwʊmən/ n Irlandka f

iron /'aɪən, US 'aɪərn/ **I** n [1] (metal) żelazo n; **scrap** ~ złom żelazny [2] (for clothes) żelazko n
II vt wy|prasować [clothes]

ironic(al) /aɪ'rɒnɪk(l)/ adj ironiczny

ironing /'aɪənɪŋ, US 'aɪərn-/ n prasowanie n

ironing board n deska f do prasowania

ironmonger /'aɪənmʌŋgə(r), US 'aɪərn-/ n właściciel m, -ka f sklepu z artykułami metalowymi; ~**'s (shop)** sklep z wyrobami żelaznymi

irony /'aɪərənɪ/ n ironia f

irrational /ɪ'ræʃənl/ adj [behaviour, fear] irracjonalny; [hostility] nieuzasadniony; **he's rather** ~ jest trochę nierozsądny

irregular /ɪ'regjʊlə(r)/ adj [1] nieregularny [2] US [merchandise] wybrakowany

irregularity /ɪregjʊ'lærətɪ/ n (of pulse) nieregularność f; (in elections) nieprawidłowość f

irrelevant /ɪ'reləvnt/ adj [1] [remark, question, facts] niezwiązany z tematem [2] (unimportant) nieistotny; **the money is** ~ pieniądze nie grają roli

irreparable /ɪ'repərəbl/ adj nie do naprawienia

irreplaceable /ɪrɪ'pleɪsəbl/ adj niezastąpiony

irrepressible /ɪrɪ'presəbl/ adj [person] żywotny; [enthusiasm] żywiołowy

irresistible /ɪrɪ'zɪstəbl/ adj nieodparty

irresponsible /ɪrɪ'spɒnsəbl/ adj nieodpowiedzialny

irreversible /ˌɪrɪ'vɜːsəbl/ *adj [process]* nieodwracalny; *[disease]* nieuleczalny; *[decision]* nieodwołalny

irritable /'ɪrɪtəbl/ *adj* drażliwy

irritable bowel syndrome *n* zespół *m* nadwrażliwości jelita grubego

irritate /'ɪrɪteɪt/ *vt* roz|drażnić, z|irytować; Med podrażni|ć, -ać

irritating /'ɪrɪteɪtɪŋ/ *adj* irytujący

Islam /'ɪzlɑːm, -læm, -'lɑːm/ *n* (religion) islam *m*

Islamic /ɪz'læmɪk/ *adj* islamski

island /'aɪlənd/ *n* ⊡ (on sea, lake) wyspa *f*; (small) wysepka *f* ⊡ (also **traffic** ~) wysepka *f*

islander /'aɪləndə(r)/ *n* wyspia|rz *m*, -rka *f*, mieszkan|iec *m*, -ka *f* wyspy

Isle of Man *prn* wyspa *f* Man

isolate /'aɪsəleɪt/ *vt* odizolow|ać, -ywać (**from sb/ sth** od kogoś/czegoś)

isolation /ˌaɪsə'leɪʃn/ *n* izolacja *f*

Israel /'ɪzreɪl/ *prn* Izrael *m*

Israeli /ɪz'reɪlɪ/ **Ⅰ** *n* Izrael|czyk *m*, -ka *f*
Ⅱ *adj* izraelski

issue /'ɪʃuː, 'ɪsjuː/ **Ⅰ** *n* ⊡ (problem) kwestia *f*; **to make an ~ (out) of sth** robić z czegoś problem; **the point at ~** rozważana kwestia ⊡ (of stamps, shares) emisja *f*; (of book) wydanie *n* ⊡ (of newspaper, journal) numer *m*; **back ~** numer archiwalny
Ⅱ *vt* ⊡ (allocate) wyda|ć, -wać *[book, uniforms]* (**to sb** komuś); **to ~ sb with sth** wydać komuś coś ⊡ wyda|ć, -wać *[declaration, order]*; udziel|ić, -ać (czegoś) *[warning]* ⊡ wy|emitować *[stamps, shares]*; wyda|ć, -wać *[book]*

it /ɪt/ *pron* ⊡ (when pointing) to; (previously mentioned) on; **don't sign it** nie podpisuj tego; **stop it!** przestań!; **he, she, it** on, ona, ono; **it's all lies** to wszystko kłamstwa; **"where's my pen?" – "you left it by the phone** gdzie jest moje pióro?" – "zostawiłeś je koło telefonu"; **it's my book – give it to me** to moja książka – daj mi ją ⊡ (after a preposition) to; **from/without/to it** z/bez/do tego ⊡ (in questions) **who is it?** kto tam?; **where is it?** gdzie to jest?; **what is it?** (of object, noise) co to (jest)?; (what's happening?) co się dzieje?; (what is the matter?) o co

chodzi? ⊡ (impersonal uses) **it's good to see you** miło cię widzieć; **it's raining** pada deszcz; **it is known that...** wiadomo, że...; **it's me** to ja

IT *n* → **information technology**

Italian /ɪ'tæljən/ **Ⅰ** *n* ⊡ (person) Wło|ch *m*, -szka *f* ⊡ (język *m*) włoski *m*
Ⅱ *adj* włoski

Italy /'ɪtəlɪ/ *prn* Włochy *plt*

itch /ɪtʃ/ **Ⅰ** *n* swędzenie *n*
Ⅱ *vi* swędzi(e)ć; **I was ~ing all over** swędziało mnie całe ciało; **these socks make me ~** te skarpetki mnie drapią

itchy /'ɪtʃɪ/ *adj* infml **I feel ~ all over** wszystko mnie swędzi
ⒾⒹⒾⓄⓂⓈ **to have ~ feet** infml nie móc usiedzieć w miejscu

item /'aɪtəm/ *n* ⊡ (object) rzecz *f*; **~s of clothing** ubrania, odzież; **news ~** (on radio, TV) wiadomość ⊡ (on agenda) punkt *m*

itemize /'aɪtəmaɪz/ *vt* wyszczególni|ć, -ać

itinerary /aɪ'tɪnərərɪ, ɪ-, US -rerɪ/ *n* plan *m* podróży, marszruta *f*

its /ɪts/ *det* (replacing feminine nouns) jej; (replacing masculine and neuter nouns) jego; (referring to subject) swój; **a child showing the teacher ~ drawings** dziecko pokazujące nauczycielowi swoje rysunki; **this proposal and ~ advantages** ta propozycja i jej zalety

itself /ɪt'self/ *pron* ⊡ (reflexive) się; **the cat hurt ~** kot skaleczył się ⊡ (emphatic) sam; **the town ~ is small** samo miasto jest niewielkie; **he was kindness ~** był uosobieniem dobroci ⊡ (after prepositions) **the heating comes on by ~** ogrzewanie włącza się samo; **learning English is not difficult in ~** sama nauka angielskiego nie jest trudna

IVF *n* = **in vitro fertilization** zapłodnienie *n* in vitro

ivory /'aɪvərɪ/ **Ⅰ** *n* kość *f* słoniowa
Ⅱ *adj* **~ skin** skóra w kolorze kości słoniowej

ivy /'aɪvɪ/ *n* bluszcz *m*

J

j, J /dʒeɪ/ *n* j, J *n*

jab /dʒæb/ **I** *n* ⬝1⬝ GB (vaccination) szczepionka *f*; (injection) zastrzyk *m* podskórny ⬝2⬝ (in boxing) (cios *m*) prosty *m*
II *vt* **to ~ sth into sth** dźgnąć coś czymś

jabber /'dʒæbə(r)/ *vi* (chatter) trajkotać; **they were ~ing away in German** szwargotali po niemiecku *infml*

jack /dʒæk/ *n* ⬝1⬝ (for car) podnośnik *m* ⬝2⬝ (in cards) walet *m* ⬝3⬝ (in bowls) biała kula *f*
■ **jack in**: GB *infml*: **~ [sth] in** rzucić, -ać *[job, task]*
(IDIOMS) **a ~ of all trades** majster do wszystkiego

jackal /'dʒækl, -kɔːl/ *n* szakal *m*

jackdaw /'dʒækdɔː/ *n* Zool kawka *f*

jacket /'dʒækɪt/ *n* ⬝1⬝ (garment) (man's) marynarka *f*; (woman's) żakiet *m*; (coat) kurtka *f* ⬝2⬝ (also **dust ~**) obwoluta *f* ⬝3⬝ US (of record) koperta *f*

jacket potatoes *npl* ziemiaki *m* w mundurkach

jack-in-the-box /'dʒækɪnðəbɒks/ *n* diabeł(ek) *m* z pudełka

jackknife /'dʒæknaɪf/ *vi* złożyć się, składać się jak scyzoryk

jackpot /'dʒækpɒt/ *n* najwyższa stawka *f*; **to hit the ~** zgarnąć pulę

jade /dʒeɪd/ *n* ⬝1⬝ (stone) jadeit *m* ⬝2⬝ (colour) (also **~ green**) (kolor *m*) zielonkawy *m*

jaded /'dʒeɪdɪd/ *adj* ⬝1⬝ (exhausted) znużony ⬝2⬝ (bored) *[person]* zblazowany

jagged /'dʒægɪd/ *adj [edge]* postrzępiony; *[cliff, rock]* poszarpany; *[knife, saw]* wyszczerbiony

jail /dʒeɪl/ **I** *n* więzienie *n*
II *vt* osadzić, -ać w więzieniu (**for sth** za coś)

jam /dʒæm/ **I** *n* ⬝1⬝ Culin dżem *m* ⬝2⬝ (of vehicles) zator *m* ⬝3⬝ (of machine) zablokowanie się *n* ⬝4⬝ *infml* (difficult situation) opały *plt*; **to get into a ~** wpaść w tarapaty ⬝5⬝ Mus (also **~ session**) jam session *n inv*
II *vt* ⬝1⬝ **to ~ one's foot on the brake** wcisnąć hamulec ⬝2⬝ (wedge) wcisnąć, -kać; **the key is ~med in the lock** klucz utkwił w zamku ⬝3⬝ (crowd) zapełnić, -ać; **cars ~med (up) the road** samochody zablokowały ulicę ⬝4⬝ (jam) (block) unieruchomić *[mechanism]*; zablokować *[lock, door, system]* ⬝5⬝ (on radio) zagłuszyć, -ać *[frequency]*
III *vi* ⬝1⬝ *[mechanism, lock, door]* zaciąć, -nać się ⬝2⬝ Mus improwizować

Jamaica /dʒə'meɪkə/ *prn* Jamajka *f*

jam-packed /ˌdʒæm'pækt/ *adj* nabity; **to be ~ with sth** być napchanym czymś

jangle /'dʒæŋgl/ **I** *n* (of bells) brzęczenie *n*; (of keys, pots) pobrzękiwanie *n*
II *vi* *[bells]* zadzwonić; *[bracelets]* pobrzękiwać

janitor /'dʒænɪtə(r)/ *n* US dozorca *m*, -czyni *f*

January /'dʒænjuərɪ, US -juerɪ/ *n* styczeń *m*

Japan /dʒə'pæn/ *prn* Japonia *f*

Japanese /ˌdʒæpə'niːz/ **I** *n* ⬝1⬝ Japończyk *m*, -nka *f* ⬝2⬝ (język *m*) japoński *m*
II *adj* japoński

jar¹ /dʒɑː(r)/ *n* słoik *m*; (large) słój *m*; (earthenware) dzban *m*

jar² /dʒɑː(r)/ **I** *n* (jolt) wstrząs *m*
II *vt* ⬝1⬝ wstrząsnąć, -ać (kimś/czymś) *[structure]*; doznać urazu (czegoś) *[shoulder]* ⬝2⬝ (US) **to ~ sb into action** popchnąć kogoś do działania
III *vi* ⬝1⬝ *[music, voice]* zafałszować; **to ~ on sb's nerves** działać komuś na nerwy ⬝2⬝ (clash) *[colours]* gryźć się; *[notes]* nie współbrzmieć

jargon /'dʒɑːgən/ *n* żargon *m*

jasmine /'dʒæzmɪn, 'dʒæs-/ *n* jaśmin *m*

jaundice /'dʒɔːndɪs/ *n* żółtaczka *f*

jaundiced /'dʒɔːndɪst/ *adj* (cynical) *[person]* pełen żółci; *[attitude]* zaprawiony żółcią

javelin /'dʒævlɪn/ *n* oszczep *m*

jaw /dʒɔː/ *n* szczęka *f*

jawbone /'dʒɔːbəʊn/ *n* żuchwa *f*

jawline /'dʒɔːlaɪn/ *n* podbródek *m*

jay /dʒeɪ/ *n* sójka *f*

jazz /dʒæz/ **I** *n* Mus jazz *m*
II *adj [musician, singer]* jazzowy; **~ band** jazz band *m*
■ **jazz up**: *infml* ożywić, -ać *[dress, room]*
(IDIOMS) **and all that ~** *infml* itd., itp. *infml*

jazzy /'dʒæzɪ/ *adj* ⬝1⬝ *[colour]* krzykliwy; *[look]* ekscentryczny ⬝2⬝ (music) jazzowy

jealous /'dʒeləs/ *adj* zazdrosny (**of sb/sth** o kogoś/ coś); **to make sb ~** wzbudzić zazdrość kogoś

jealousy /'dʒeləsɪ/ *n* zazdrość *f*

jeer /dʒɪə(r)/ **I** *n* drwiny *f pl*
II *vt* wyszydzić, -ać
III *vi* szydzić, drwić (**at sb/sth** z kogoś/z czegoś); *[crowd]* wygwizdać, -ywać (**at sb/sth** kogoś/coś)

jeering /'dʒɪərɪŋ/ *n* wyśmiewanie się *n*

jellied /'dʒelɪd/ *adj* **~ eels** węgorz w galarecie

Jell-o® /'dʒeləʊ/ n US galaretka f owocowa

jelly /'dʒelı/ n ① (savoury) galareta f; (sweet) galaretka f owocowa ② US (jam) dżem m

jellyfish /'dʒelıfıʃ/ n meduza f

jeopardize /'dʒepədaız/ vt zagr|ozić, -ażać (czemuś) [career, plans]; narazić na niebezpieczeństwo [lives, troops]

jeopardy /'dʒepədı/ n **to be in** ~ być w niebezpieczeństwie

jerk /dʒɜːk/ ① n ① (jolt) szarpnięcie n; (of muscle, limb) drgnięcie n; **with a** ~ **of his head** gwałtownym ruchem głowy ② infml (stupid man) cymbał m infml pej

  ② vt szarp|nąć, -ać [object, person]

  ③ vi [person, muscle] drg|nąć, -ać

jerky /'dʒɜːkı/ ① n US suszone mięso n

  ② adj [movement] nerwowy; [style, phrase] rwący się

jersey /'dʒɜːzı/ n ① (sweater) sweter m ② (fabric) dżersej m ③ (for spotrs) **football** ~ koszulka f piłkarska

Jersey prn wyspa f Jersey

Jerusalem /dʒə'ruːsələm/ prn Jerozolima f

jest /dʒest/ ① n żart m; **in** ~ żartem

  ② vi za|żartować

jester /'dʒestə(r)/ n błazen m

Jesuit /'dʒezjʊıt, US 'dʒeʒəwət/ ① n jezuita m

  ② adj jezuicki

Jesus /'dʒiːzəs/ ① prn Jezus m; ~ **Christ** Jezus Chrystus

  ② excl vinfml ~ **(Christ)!** Jezus (Chryste)! infml

jet /dʒet/ ① n ① (plane) odrzutowiec m ② (of water, flame) (silny) strumień m ③ (on gas ring) palnik m; (of engine) dysza f ④ (stone) gagat m

  ② vi **we** ~**ted off to the Caribbean** polecieliśmy na Karaiby

jet-black /ˌdʒet'blæk/ adj [hair] kruczoczarny; [eyes] czarny jak węgiel or jak smoła

jet engine n silnik m odrzutowy

jetfoil /'dʒetfɔıl/ n wodolot m

jetlag /'dʒetlæg/ n zmęczenie n po długiej podróży samolotem

jetlagged adj **to be** ~ być zmęczonym po długiej podróży samolotem

jet setter n osoba f znana i bogata (często podróżująca po świecie)

jet-skiing /ˌdʒet'skiːıŋ/ n pływanie n skuterem wodnym

jettison /'dʒetısn/ vt (from ship) wyrzuc|ić, -ać za burtę; (from plane) wyrzuc|ić, -ać

jetty /'dʒetı/ n molo n

Jew /dʒuː/ n Żyd m

jewel /'dʒuːəl/ n ① (piece of jewellery) klejnot m; (in watch) kamień m ② (person) skarb m; (building, object) klejnot m

jeweller GB, **jeweler** US /'dʒuːələ(r)/ n (person) jubiler m; ~**'s (shop)** sklep jubilerski, jubiler

jewellery GB, **jewelry** US /'dʒuːəlrı/ n kosztowności plt; (in shop, workshop) biżuteria f; **a piece of** ~ klejnot

Jewish /'dʒuːıʃ/ adj żydowski

jib /dʒıb/ n ① (sail) kliwer m ② (of crane) ramię n

jibe /dʒaıb/ n kpina f

jiff(y) /'dʒıfı/ n **in a** ~ za sekundkę

Jiffy bag® n koperta f z warstwą folii bąbelkowej

jig /dʒıg/ n Mus giga f

jiggle /'dʒıgl/ ① vt potrząsać

  ② vi (also ~ **about,** ~ **around**) (to music) podrygiwać; (impatiently) wiercić się

jigsaw /'dʒıgsɔː/ n ① (tool) wyrzynarka f ② (also ~ **puzzle**) układanka f

jilt /dʒılt/ vt porzuc|ić, -ać [lover]

jingle /'dʒıŋgl/ ① n ① (of bells) dzwonienie n; (of keys) brzęk m ② (in advertizing) slogan m (reklamowy); (musical) melodyjka f reklamowa infml

  ② vi [keys, coins] brzęk|nąć, pobrzękiwać

jingoist /'dʒıŋgəʊıst/ ① n szowinist|a m, -ka f

  ② adj szowinistyczny

jinx /dʒıŋks/ n ① (curse) przekleństwo n; **to put a** ~ **on sb/sth** rzucić na kogoś/coś zły czar or urok; **there's a** ~ **on this car** ten samochód jest jakiś pechowy ② (unlucky person) pechowiec m; (unlucky thing) przedmiot m przynoszący pecha

jitters /'dʒıtəz/ npl infml **to have the** ~ [person] mieć tremę; **stock market had the** ~ giełda zareagowała nerwowo

job /dʒɒb/ ① n ① (employment) praca f; (post) posada f; **to get a** ~ dostać pracę; **a teaching** ~ posada nauczyciela; **what's her** ~? co ona robi? ② (role) zadanie n; **it's my** ~ **to do it** zrobienie tego należy do mnie ③ (duty) obowiązek m; **she's only doing her** ~ ona tylko wypełnia swoje obowiązki ④ (task) zajęcie n; **to find a** ~ **for sb** znaleźć komuś zajęcie ⑤ (assignment) zlecenie n ⑥ **to make a good** ~ **of doing sth** dobrze coś zrobić ⑦ infml **it's quite a** or **some** ~ to nie lada zadanie

  ② adj ~ **offer/opportunities** oferta pracy/możliwości zatrudnienia; ~ **pages** strony z ogłoszeniami o pracy

  ③ IDIOMS **that'll do the** ~ to załatwi sprawę

Job Centre n GB biuro n pośrednictwa pracy

job creation scheme n (GB) plan m tworzenia miejsc pracy

job description n zakres m obowiązków

job-hunting /'dʒɒbhʌntıŋ/ n poszukiwanie n pracy

jobless /'dʒɒblıs/ n **the** ~ bezrobotni m pl

job-share /'dʒɒbʃeə(r)/ n podział m etatu

job sharing n dzielenie n etatu

jockey /'dʒɒkı/ n dżokej m, -ka f

jockey shorts npl US bokserki plt

jockstrap /'dʒɒkstræp/ n infml (for sportsman) ochraniacz m na genitalia

jodhpurs /'dʒɒdpəz/ npl bryczesy plt

jog /dʒɒg/ **I** n ⌐1⌐ (with elbow) szturchnięcie n ⌐2⌐ (trot) trucht m ⌐3⌐ Sport **to go for a** ∼ iść pobiegać ⌐4⌐ US (in road) zakręt m

II vt trąc|ić, -ać *[table]*; **to** ∼ **sb's memory** odświeżyć pamięć komuś

III vi Sport uprawiać jogging

jogger /'dʒɒgə(r)/ n osoba f uprawiająca jogging

jogging /'dʒɒgɪŋ/ n jogging m

join /dʒɔɪn/ **I** n złącze n

II vt ⌐1⌐ (meet up with) dołącz|yć, -ać do (kogoś); **may I** ∼ **you?** czy mogę się do ciebie/do was przyłączyć? ⌐2⌐ (become a part of) dołącz|yć, -ać do (czegoś) *[queue]*; wst|ąpić, -ępować do (czegoś) *[army, organization]*; zapis|ać, -ywać się do (czegoś) *[club, library]*; (become a part of) przyłącz|yć, -ać się do (czegoś) *[crowd]*; zatrudni|ć, -ać się w (czymś) *[firm]*; **to** ∼ **a union** zapisać się do związku ⌐3⌐ (connect) zł|ączyć *[ends]*; po|łączyć, sp|oić, -ajać *[parts, pieces, points, towns]* ⌐4⌐ *[road]* łączyć się z (czymś) *[motorway]*; *[river]* wpadać do (czegoś) *[sea]*

III vi ⌐1⌐ (become a member) (of class, club) zapis|ać, -ywać się; (of party) wst|ąpić, -ępować; (of group) przyłącz|yć, -ać się ⌐2⌐ *[pieces, pipes, roads]* po|łączyć się

■ **join in:** ¶ ∼ **in** przyłącz|yć, -ać się ¶ ∼ **in [sth]** włącz|yć, -ać się do (czegoś) *[discussion]*; wziąć, brać udział w (czymś) *[game, demonstration]*; **to** ∼ **in the bidding** przystąpić do licytacji; **to** ∼ **in the fun** przyłączyć się do zabawy

■ **join up:** ¶ ∼ **up** ⌐1⌐ (enlist) wst|ąpić, -ępować or pójść do wojska ⌐2⌐ (meet up) *[people]* z|bierać, -ebrać się; *[roads, tracks]* łączyć się ¶ ∼ **[sth] up** po|łączyć *[dots]*; zł|ączyć *[letters]*

joiner /'dʒɔɪnə(r)/ n stolarz m

joint /dʒɔɪnt/ **I** n ⌐1⌐ Anat staw m; **to be out of** ∼ *[elbow, knee]* być zwichniętym ⌐2⌐ (in carpentry) połączenie n; (in metalwork) złącze n ⌐3⌐ Culin mięso n na pieczeń ⌐4⌐ infml pej (place) dziura f infml; (night club) spelun(k)a f infml ⌐5⌐ infml (cannabis cigarette) skręt m, joint m infml

II adj *[action, programme, session]* wspólny; *[measures, procedures]* łączny; *[winner]* ex aequo; *[talks]* wielostronny

joint account n wspólne konto n bankowe

joint effort n wspólny wysiłek m

joint honours npl GB Univ dyplom z więcej niż jednej dziedzin naukowych

jointly /'dʒɔɪntlɪ/ adv wspólnie

joint owner n współwłaściciel m, -ka f

joint venture n spółka f typu joint venture; fig wspólne przedsięwzięcie n

joke /dʒəʊk/ **I** n ⌐1⌐ (amusing story) dowcip m (**about sb/sth** o kimś/czymś); **to tell a** ∼ opowiedzieć dowcip; **it's no** ∼ **getting up at six in the morning** to żadna przyjemność wstawać o szóstej

rano; **to play a** ∼ **on sb** zrobić komuś kawał ⌐2⌐ (person) pośmiewisko n; (event, situation) farsa f

II vi za|żartować; **you must be joking!** chyba żartujesz!

joker /'dʒəʊkə(r)/ n ⌐1⌐ (who tells jokes) żartowni|ś m, -sia f; (who plays tricks) kawala|rz m, -rka f ⌐2⌐ (in cards) dżoker m

jolly /'dʒɒlɪ/ **I** adj *[person, tune]* radosny

II vt to ∼ **sb along** zachęcać kogoś

jolt /dʒəʊlt, dʒɒlt/ **I** n ⌐1⌐ (jerk) szarpnięcie n ⌐2⌐ (shock) wstrząs m, szok m

II vt rzucać (kimś/czymś) *[passengers, coach]*

III vi *[vehicle]* trząść się

Jordan /'dʒɔːdn/ prn (country) Jordania f

jostle /'dʒɒsl/ vi przepychać się (**for sth/to do sth** do czegoś/żeby coś zrobić)

jot /dʒɒt/ vt

■ **jot down:** za|notować *[ideas, names]*

journal /'dʒɜːnl/ n ⌐1⌐ (periodical) czasopismo n; (newspaper) gazeta f ⌐2⌐ (diary) dziennik m

journalism /'dʒɜːnəlɪzəm/ n dziennikarstwo n

journalist /'dʒɜːnəlɪst/ n dziennika|rz m -rka f

journey /'dʒɜːnɪ/ n (long) podróż f; (short or habitual) jazda f, przejazd m; **bus** ∼ przejazd autobusem; **to go on a** ∼ wybrać się w podróż

jowl /dʒaʊl/ n (jaw) żuchwa f; (fleshy fold) obwisły policzek m

joy /dʒɔɪ/ n ⌐1⌐ (delight) radość f (**at sth** z powodu czegoś) ⌐2⌐ (pleasure) przyjemność f; **the** ∼ **of doing sth** przyjemność robienia czegoś

IDIOMS: **to be full of the** ∼ **s of spring** być całym w skowronkach infml

joyrider /'dʒɔɪraɪdə(r)/ n amator m przejażdżki kradzionym samochodem

joyriding /'dʒɔɪraɪdɪŋ/ n jazda f kradzionym samochodem

joystick /'dʒɔɪstɪk/ n (in plane) drążek m sterowy; (in video games) joystick m

jubilant /'dʒuːbɪlənt/ adj *[person]* rozradowany; *[crowd]* rozentuzjazmowany; *[expression, mood]* radosny

jubilee /'dʒuːbɪliː/ n jubileusz m

Judaism /'dʒuːdeɪɪzəm, US -dɪɪzəm/ n judaizm m

judge /dʒʌdʒ/ **I** n ⌐1⌐ (in law) sędzia m ⌐2⌐ (of competition) juror m, -ka f; Sport sędzia m ⌐3⌐ fig **to be a good** ∼ **of character** dobrze znać się na ludziach

II vt ⌐1⌐ (in law) osądz|ić, -ać *[person]* ⌐2⌐ Sport sędziować w (czymś) *[show, competition]* ⌐3⌐ (estimate) oceni|ć, -ać *[distance, age]*; (in future) określ|ić, -ać *[outcome, reaction]* ⌐4⌐ (consider) uzna|ć, -wać

III vi (at competition) sędziować; (in a lawcourt) sądzić; **judging by** or **from sth** sądząc z czegoś or po czymś

judgment, judgement /'dʒʌdʒmənt/ n (sentence) wyrok m; (decision) werdykt m

judicial /dʒuː'dɪʃl/ adj ⌐1⌐ sądowy ⌐2⌐ (wise) rozsądny

judiciary /dʒuːˈdɪʃərɪ, US -ʃɪerɪ/ *n* [1] (system of courts) sądownictwo *n* [2] (judges) sędziowie *m pl*
judo /ˈdʒuːdəʊ/ *n* judo *n inv*
jug /dʒʌg/ *n* GB (large) dzban *m*; (for milk, cream) dzbanek *m*; **water** ~ dzbanek na wodę
juggernaut /ˈdʒʌgənɔːt/ *n* GB wielka ciężarówka *f*
juggle /ˈdʒʌgl/ *vi* żonglować (**with sth** czymś)
juggler /ˈdʒʌglə(r)/ *n* żongler *m*, -ka *f*
jugular /ˈdʒʌgjʊlə(r)/ *n* (also ~ **vein**) żyła *f* szyjna
juice /dʒuːs/ *n* sok *m*; (of meat) sos *m* własny; **gastric** ~ **s** soki żołądkowe or trawienne
juicy /ˈdʒuːsɪ/ *adj* [1] *[fruit]* soczysty [2] *infml [story]* pikantny
jukebox /ˈdʒuːkbɒks/ *n* szafa *f* grająca
July /dʒʊˈlaɪ/ *n* lipiec *m*
jumble /ˈdʒʌmbl/ *n* [1] (of objects) (bezładna) mieszanina *f*; (of papers) (bezładny) stos *m*; (of ideas, words) pomieszanie *n* [2] GB (items for sale) rzeczy *f pl* używane (*przeznaczone do wyprzedaży*)
■ **jumble up**: po|mieszać *[letters, shapes]*
jumble sale *n* GB wyprzedaż *f* rzeczy używanych (*na cele dobroczynne*)
jumbo /ˈdʒʌmbəʊ/ *n* (also ~ **jet**) wielki odrzutowiec *m* pasażerski
jump /dʒʌmp/ [I] *n* [1] (leap) skok *m*; **parachute** ~ skok na spadachronie [2] (in horse race) przeszkoda *f* [3] (sudden increase) skok *m* (**in sth** czegoś)
[II] *vt* przesk|oczyć, -akiwać *[obstacle, ditch]*; **to** ~ **the lights** *[motorist]* ruszyć na czerwonym świetle; **to** ~ **the queue** wepchnąć się poza kolejką; **to** ~ **the ship** *[crewman]* uciec ze statku
[III] *vi* [1] (leap) sk|oczyć, -akać; **to** ~ **across** or **over sth** przeskoczyć przez coś; **to** ~ **up and down** podskakiwać; (in anger) trząść się ze złości [2] (start, in suprise) pod|skoczyć [3] *[prices, profits]* wzr|osnąć, -astać gwałtownie [4] **to** ~ **at sth** skwapliwie skorzystać z czegoś *[opportunity]*; entuzjastycznie przyjąć coś *[offer]*
■ **jump back**: *[person]* odskoczyć do tyłu; *[lever, spring]* wr|ócić, -acać do pozycji wyjściowej
■ **jump down**: zesk|oczyć, -akiwać (**from sth** z czegoś)
■ **jump on**: ¶ ~ **on sth** (mount) wsk|oczyć, -akiwać do (czegoś) *[bus, train]*; wsk|oczyć, -akiwać na (coś) *[bicycle, horse]* ¶ ~ **on [sb]** nask|oczyć, -akiwać na (kogoś)
■ **jump out**: *[person]* wysk|oczyć, -akiwać; **to** ~ **out of sth** wyskakiwać przez (coś) *[window]*; wyskakiwć z (czegoś) *[bed, train]*
■ **jump up**: *[person]* podsk|oczyć, -akiwać
jumper /ˈdʒʌmpə(r)/ *n* [1] GB (sweater) pulower *m* [2] US (pinafore) fartuszek *m*
jump leads *npl* przewody *m pl* rozruchowe
jump-start /ˈdʒʌmpˈstɑːt/ *vt* (with jump leads) uruch|omić, -amiać samochód przez zwarcie przewodów
jump suit *n* kombinezon *m* jednoczęściowy

jumpy /ˈdʒʌmpɪ/ *adj [person]* nerwowy; *[market]* niestabilny
junction /ˈdʒʌŋkʃn/ *n* [1] (of roads) skrzyżowanie *n* [2] (of railway lines) węzeł *m* kolejowy; (station) stacja *f* węzłowa
June /dʒuːn/ *n* czerwiec *m*
jungle /ˈdʒʌŋgl/ *n* dżungla *f*
junior /ˈdʒuːnɪə(r)/ [I] *n* [1] (younger person) **to be (10 years) sb's** ~ być (o dziesięć lat) młodszym od kogoś [2] (low-ranking worker) pracownik *m* niższy rangą [3] GB Sch ucze|ń *m*, -nnica *f* szkoły podstawowej [4] US Univ student *m*, -ka *f* przedostatniego roku; (in high school) ucze|ń *m*, -nnica *f* przedostatniej klasy
[II] *adj* [1] *[colleague, worker]* (inferior) niższy rangą; *[post, rank, position]* niższy rangą [2] Sport ~ **champion/race** mistrz/wyścig juniorów; *[player]* w klasie juniorów [3] (also **Junior**) **Bob Mortimer** ~ Bob Mortimer junior
junior high school *n* US szkoła *f* średnia
junior minister *n* ≈ podsekretarz *m* stanu
junior school *n* GB szkoła *f* podstawowa
junk /dʒʌŋk/ *n* [1] (old things) rupiecie *m pl*; (merchandise) tandeta *f* [2] (second-hand) starzyzna *f* [3] (boat) dżonka *f*
junk food *n* niezdrowe, tanie jedzenie *n*
junkie /ˈdʒʌŋkɪ/ *n* infml ćpun *m* infml
junk mail *n* niezamówione przesyłki *f pl* reklamowe
junk shop *n* sklep *m* ze starzyzną
junkyard /ˈdʒʌŋkjɑːd/ *n* (for scrap) złomowisko *n*; (for old cars) cmentarzysko *n* samochodów
junta /ˈdʒʌntə/ *n* pej junta *f*
Jupiter *n* Jowisz *m*
jurisdiction /ˌdʒʊərɪsˈdɪkʃn/ *n* jurysdykcja *f*; **to come within** or **under sb's** ~ podlegać kompetencji kogoś; **to be outside sb's** ~ nie podlegać kompetencji kogoś
juror /ˈdʒʊərə(r)/ *n* sędzia *m* przysięgły; (for competition) juror *m*, -ka *f*
jury /ˈdʒʊərɪ/ *n* [1] (in law) ława *f* przysięgłych [2] (for competition) jury *n inv*
jury box *n* ława *f* przysięgłych
jury duty US, **jury service** GB *n* **to do** ~ wziąć udział w procesie jako sędzia przysięgły
just[1] /dʒʌst/ [I] *adv* [1] **to have** ~ **done sth** właśnie zrobić coś; **it's** ~ **been varnished** (to) ma świeżo położony lakier [2] (immediately) zaraz; ~ **after you left** zaraz po twoim wyjściu; ~ **before** tuż przed [3] (slightly) trochę; ~ **over 20 kg** trochę ponad 20 kg [4] (only, merely) tylko; ~ **for fun** (tylko) dla zabawy; ~ **two days ago** zaledwie dwa dni temu; **he is** ~ **a child** jest tylko dzieckiem [5] (purposely) (tylko) po to, żeby; **he did it** ~ **to annoy us** zrobił to (tylko) po to, żeby nas zdenerwować [6] (barely) ledwo, ledwie; ~ **on time** ledwo na czas; **he is** ~ **20** on ma zaledwie 20 lat; **I (only)** ~ **caught the**

train ledwo zdążyłem na pociąg [7] (simply) po prostu; ~ **tell the truth** po prostu powiedz prawdę; **she** ~ **won't listen** ona po prostu nie słucha; ~ **a moment** (when interrupting, disagreeing) chwileczkę [8] (exactly) właśnie; **that's** ~ **what I suggested** właśnie to proponowałem; **it's** ~ **right** właśnie tak; **she looks** ~ **like her father** wygląda zupełnie jak ojciec; **it's** ~ **like you to be late** to do ciebie podobne, żeby się spóźnić [9] (possibly) **it** ~ **might** or **could be true** całkiem niewykluczone, że to prawda [10] (at this or that very moment) właśnie; **to be** ~ **doing sth** właśnie coś robić; **to be** ~ **about to do sth** właśnie mieć coś zrobić; **I'm** ~ **coming** już idę [11] (positively, totally) **that was** ~ **ridiculous** to było po prostu idiotyczne [12] (with imperatives) tylko; ~ **you dare!** tylko spróbuj!; ~ **think, you could have been hurt!** pomyśl tylko, mógłeś się skaleczyć! [13] (in requests) **if I could** ~ **interrupt you** jeśli mógłbym panu/pani przerwać [14] (equally) ~ **as big as...** równie duży jak...

II just about adv phr prawie; ~ **about everything** prawie wszystko; **I can** ~ **about see it** już niemal to widzę

III just now adv phr (at the moment) w tej chwili; **I saw him** ~ **now** dopiero co go widziałem

IV just as conj phr właśnie kiedy; **he arrived** ~ **as I was leaving** zjawił się akurat w chwili, kiedy wychodziłem

just² /dʒʌst/ adj [person, decision] sprawiedliwy; [demand, claim, criticism] słuszny

justice /'dʒʌstɪs/ n [1] (fairness) sprawiedliwość f; **the portrait doesn't do her** ~ na tym portrecie nie wygląda korzystnie [2] (the law) sprawiedliwość f; **to bring sb to** ~ postawić kogoś przed sądem

Justice Department n US departament m sprawiedliwości

Justice of the Peace, JP n GB sędzia m pokoju

justifiable /'dʒʌstɪfaɪəbl/ adj (that is justified) uzasadniony; (that can be justified) dający się uzasadnić

justification /ˌdʒʌstɪfɪ'keɪʃn/ n uzasadnienie n; **to have some** ~ **for doing sth** mieć (jakieś) powody, żeby coś zrobić

justified /'dʒʌstɪfaɪd/ adj [anger] uzasadniony; [action] usprawiedliwiony; **to feel** ~ **in doing sth** czuć się uprawnionym do zrobienia czegoś

justify /'dʒʌstɪfaɪ/ vt usprawiedliwi|ć, -ać [people, actions]; uzasadni|ć, -ać [decisions]

jut /dʒʌt/ vi (also ~ **out**) [cape] wcinać się (**into sth** w coś); [balcony] wystawać (**over sth** nad czymś)

juvenile /'dʒuːvənaɪl/ n (young person) młodzieniec m; (in law) nieletni m, -a f

juvenile delinquency n przestępczość f nieletnich

juvenile delinquent n młodociany przestępca m

juvenile offender n młodociany przestępca m

K

k, K /keɪ/ *n* k, K *n*
kale /keɪl/ *n* (also **curly ~**) jarmuż *m*
kaleidoscope /kə'laɪdəskəʊp/ *n* kalejdoskop *m*
kangaroo /ˌkæŋgə'ruː/ *n* kangu|r *m*, -rzyca *f*
karaoke /ˌkærɪ'əʊkeɪ, -kɪ/ *n* karaoke *n inv*
karate /kə'rɑːtɪ/ *n* karate *n inv*
Kashmir /kæʃ'mɪə(r)/ *prn* Kaszmir *m*
kayak /'kaɪæk/ *n* kajak *m*
kebab /kɪ'bæb/ *n* (also **shish ~**) kebab *m*
kedgeree /'kedʒəriː, ˌkedʒə'riː/ *n* GB potrawka *f* z ryżu, ryby i jaj
keel /kiːl/ *n* kil *m*
■ **keel over**: *[boat]* wywr|ócić, -acać się (do góry dnem)
keen /kiːn/ *adj* [1] (eager) *[worker, sportsplayer, supporter]* zapalony; *[student]* pilny; **to be ~ on sth** palić się do czegoś *[plan, project]*; **to be ~ to do sth** or **on doing sth** infml uwielbiać coś robić [2] *[interest]* żywy; *[hearing, sight, sense of smell]* wyostrzony; *[appetite]* wilczy; *[eye]* bystry; *[intelligence]* błyskotliwy; *[competition]* ostry
keep /kiːp/ **I** *n* [1] utrzymanie *n*; **to pay for one's ~** płacić za or na swoje utrzymanie [2] (in tower) donżon *m*
II *vt* [1] (retain) zatrzym|ać, -ywać *[money]*; zachow|ać, -ywać *[letter, receipt]*; przypilnować *[seat]*; **to ~ sb/sth clean** utrzymywać kogoś/coś w czystości; **to ~ sth warm** trzymać coś w cieple; **to ~ sb talking** sprawić, żeby ktoś mówił dalej; **to ~ sb waiting** kazać komuś czekać; **to ~ an engine running** trzymać silnik na chodzie [2] (detain) zatrzym|ać, -ywać; **I won't ~ you a minute** to zajmie tylko chwilę [3] (own) prowadzić *[shop]*; trzymać *[dog]*; hodować *[chickens]* [4] (sustain) **to ~ sth going** podtrzymywać coś *[conversation, fire, tradition]*; **I'll make you a sandwich to ~ you going** zrobię ci kanapkę, żebyś nie osłabł [5] (store) trzymać; **I ~ a spare key in the cupboard** zapasowy klucz trzymam w szafie [6] (support financially) utrzym|ać, -ywać *[family]* [7] prowadzić *[accounts, diary]* [8] **to ~ sth from sb** trzymać coś w tajemnicy, ukrywać coś przed kimś [9] **to ~ sb from doing sth** powstrzymać kogoś przed zrobieniem czegoś [10] dotrzym|ać, -ywać (czegoś) *[promise, secret]*; **to keep appointment** stawić się na umówione spotkanie [11] Mus **to ~ time** podawać tempo

III *vi* [1] (continue) **to ~ doing sth** robić coś dalej; **to ~ going** iść dalej [2] (remain) **to ~ out of the rain** chronić się przed deszczem; **to ~ warm** unikać zimna; **to ~ calm** zachowywać spokój; **to ~ silent** milczeć [3] *[food]* nie psuć się [4] **'how are you ~ing?'** „jak się pani/pan miewa?"; **her father is ~ing well** jej ojciec trzyma się dobrze
IV *vr* **to ~ oneself to oneself** trzymać się na uboczu
V **for ~s** *adv phr* na zawsze
■ **keep away**: ¶ **~ away** trzymać się z daleka or z dala (**from sb/sth** od kogoś/czegoś) ¶ **~ to ~ sb away from sb/sth** nie dać się komuś zbliżyć do kogoś/czegoś
■ **keep back**: ¶ **~ back** nie zbliż|yć, -ać się ¶ **~ [sb/sth] back** [1] nie pozwol|ić, -alać się zbliżyć (**from sb/sth** do kogoś/czegoś); *[dam]* zatrzym|ać, -ywać *[water]* [2] (retain) zatrzym|ać, -ywać *[money]*; zachow|ać, -ywać *[food]*
■ **keep down**: **~ [sth] down** ogranicz|yć, -ać *[number, speed, inflation]*; utrzym|ać, -ywać na niskim poziomie *[prices, unemployment]*; **~ your voice down!** mów ciszej!
■ **keep off**: ¶ **~ off [sth]** [1] (stay away from) trzymać się z dala od (czegoś); **'~ off the grass'** „nie deptać trawników" [2] (avoid) unikać (czegoś) *[alcohol]*; nie porusz|yć, -ać (czegoś) *[subject]* ¶ **~ [sth] off** osł|onić, -aniać od (czegoś) or przed (czymś) *[sun, dust]*; ochr|onić, -aniać przed (czymś) *[insects]*
■ **keep on**: ¶ **to ~ on doing sth** nie przestawać robić czegoś; **to ~ on about sth** nudzić o czymś; **to ~ on at sb** molestować kogoś (**to do sth** żeby coś zrobił) ¶ **~ [sb] on** nie zw|olnić, -alniać (kogoś)
■ **keep out**: ¶ **~ out of [sth]** [1] (not enter) nie w|ejść, -chodzić do (czegoś) *[house]*; **'~ out!'** (on notice) „zakaz wstępu!" [2] (avoid) unikać (czegoś) *[sunshine, danger]*; nie mieszać się w (coś) *[argument]*; **to ~ out of sb's way** (not hinder) schodzić komuś z drogi; (avoid seeing) unikać kogoś ¶ **~ [sb/sth] out** nie wpuścić, -szczać (kogoś/czegoś)
■ **keep to**: **~ to [sth]** trzymać się (czegoś) *[road]*; przestrzegać (czegoś) *[law, rules]*
■ **keep up**: ¶ **~ up** *[car, runner, competitors]* nadąż|yć, -ać (**with sb/sth** za kimś/czymś) ¶ **~ [sth] up** [1] (hold) przytrzym|ać, -ywać *[trousers]*

2 (continue) kontynuować *[attack, studies]*; utrzym|ać, -ywać *[correspondence, pace]*; podtrzym|ać, -ywać *[friendship, tradition]* ¶ ~ **[sb] up** *[noise]* nie dać, -wać (komuś) zasnąć

■ **keep up with**: dotrzym|ać, -ywać kroku (komuś) *[person]*; nadąż|yć, -ać za (kimś/czymś) *[class]*; *[wages]* nadąż|yć, -ać za (czymś) *[cost of living]*; śledzić *[developments, fashion]*

keeper /'ki:pə(r)/ *n* (curator) kustosz *m*; (guard) strażni|k *m*, -czka *f*

keep fit /ˌki:p'fɪt/ *n* zajęcia *plt* gimnastyczne

keeping /'ki:pɪŋ/ *n* 1 (custody) opieka *f*; **in sb's ~** pod opieką kogoś; **to put sb/sth in sb's ~** pozostawić kogoś/coś pod opieką kogoś 2 (conformity) **to be in ~ with sth** pasować do czegoś *[surroundings, image]*; być zgodnym z czymś *[character, rules, tradition]*

keg /keg/ *n* (for beer) baryłka *f*; (for gunpowder) beczułka *f*

kennel /'kenl/ *n* GB (for dog) buda *f*; (for several dogs) psiarnia *f*

Kenya /'kenjə/ *prn* Kenia *f*

kerb /kɜ:b/ *n* GB krawężnik *m*

kernel /'kɜ:nl/ *n* (of nut, fruitstone) jądro *n*

kerosene, kerosine /'kerəsi:n/ *n* 1 US (paraffin) nafta *f* 2 (aircraft fuel) paliwo *n* lotnicze

kestrel /'kestrəl/ *n* Zool pustułka *f*

kettle /'ketl/ *n* czajnik *m*; **to put the ~ on** wstawić wodę

kettledrum /'ketldrʌm/ *n* Mus kocioł *m*

key /ki:/ **I** *n* 1 klucz *m*; **front-door ~** klucz do drzwi wejściowych; **a bunch** or **set of ~s** pęk kluczy; **under lock and ~** pod kluczem; **radiator ~** przełącznik grzejnika 2 (on piano, phone, typewriter) klawisz *m*; (on oboe, flute) klapka *f* 3 (vital clue) klucz *m* fig (**to sth** do czegoś); **the ~ to the mystery** klucz do tajemnicy 4 (on maps) legenda *f*; (for code) klucz *m*; (to abbreviations, symbols) wykaz *m* 5 (in riddles, tests) odpowiedzi *f pl*, klucz *m* 6 Mus tonacja *f*; **to sing in/off ~** śpiewać czysto/fałszować

II *adj [figure]* najważniejszy; *[problem]* kluczowy; *[factor]* zasadniczy

III *vt* 1 (also ~ **in**) wprowadz|ić, -ać *[data]* 2 (adapt) dostosow|ać, -ywać

keyboard /'ki:bɔ:d/ *n* klawiatura *f*

keyboards *npl* Mus syntetyzator *m*

keyed-up /ˌki:d'ʌp/ *adj* (excited) podekscytowany; (tense) podenerwowany

keyhole /'ki:həʊl/ *n* dziurka *f* od klucza

keyhole surgery *n* chirurgia *f* endoskopowa

keynote speech *n* przemówienie *n* programowe

key-ring /'ki:rɪŋ/ *n* kółko *n* na klucze

keyword /'ki:wɜ:d/ *n* słowo *n* kluczowe

khaki /'kɑ:kɪ/ *adj* khaki

kibbutz /kɪ'bʊts/ *n* kibuc *m*

kick /kɪk/ **I** *n* 1 (of person) kopniak *m*; (of donkey, horse) wierzgnięcie *n* 2 infml (thrill) **to get a ~ from**

doing sth mieć frajdę z robienia czegoś infml 3 (of firearm) odrzut *m*

II *vt [person, animal]* kop|nąć, -ać (**sb/sth** kogoś/coś or w coś); **to ~ sb on the leg** *[person, horse]* kopnąć kogoś w nogę

III *vi [swimmer]* pracować nogami; *[horse, mule]* wierzgać

■ **kick about, kick around**: kopać (dla zabawy) *[ball]*

■ **kick off**: 1 Sport rozpocz|ąć, -ynać mecz or grę 2 infml *[concert, meeting]* rozpocz|ąć, -ynać się

■ **kick out**: ¶ ~ **out** *[animal]* wierzg|nąć, -ać kopytami ¶ ~ **[sb] out** infml wykopać infml *[troublemaker]*; wyrzuc|ić, -ać *[employee]*

IDIOMS: **to ~ the habit** infml (of smoking, taking drugs) rzucić nałóg; **I could have ~ed myself** pluję sobie w brodę infml

kick-off /'kɪkɒf/ *n* Sport rozpoczęcie *n* meczu

kick-start /'kɪkstɑ:t/ **I** *n* (also ~**-starter**) (on motorbike) rozrusznik *m* nożny

II *vt* uruch|omić, -amiać rozrusznikiem nożnym *[motorbike]*; ożywi|ć, -ać *[economy]*

kid /kɪd/ **I** *n* 1 infml (child) dzieciak *m* infml 2 (young goat) koźlę *n* 3 (goatskin) skóra *f* koźlęca

II *vi* infml stroić sobie żarty (z kogoś) (**about sth** z powodu czegoś)

III *vi* infml żartować; **no ~ding!** słowo daję!

IV *vi* infml **to ~ oneself** łudzić się

kidnap /'kɪdnæp/ *vt* por|wać, -ywać

kidnapper /'kɪdnæpə(r)/ *n* porywacz *m*, -ka *f*

kidnapping /'kɪdnæpɪŋ/ *n* porwanie *n*

kidney /'kɪdnɪ/ *n* Anat nerka *f*; Culin cynadra *f*

kidney bean *n* fasola *f* czerwona kidney

kidney machine *n* Med sztuczna nerka *f*; **to be on a ~** być dializowanym

kill /kɪl/ **I** *n* zabicie *n*

II *vt* 1 zabi|ć, -jać *[person, animal]*; **they ~ed each other** pozabijali się; **I'll do it (even) if it ~s me!** infml zrobię to, choćby nie wiem co!; **her legs are ~ing her** strasznie bolą ją nogi 2 (end) wycof|ać, -ywać *[story]*; zaprzecz|yć, -ać (czemuś) *[rumour]* 3 (deaden) zabi|ć, -jać *[smell]*; s|tłumić *[sound]*; uśmierz|yć, -ać *[pain]* 4 **to ~ time** zabijać czas (**by doing sth** robiąc coś)

III *vi* zabi|ć, -jać

IV *vr* **to ~ oneself** zabi|ć, -jać się

killer /'kɪlə(r)/ *n* (person) zabój|ca *m*, -czyni *f*; (animal) drapieżnik *m*; **heroin is a ~** heroina jest zabójcza

killer whale *n* orka *f*

killing /'kɪlɪŋ/ *n* (of individual) zabójstwo *n*; (of animal) ubój *m*

killjoy /'kɪldʒɔɪ/ *n* **to be a ~** psuć każdą zabawę

kiln /kɪln/ *n* piec *m*

kilo /'ki:ləʊ/ *n* kilo *n inv*

kilobyte, KB /'kɪləbaɪt/ *n* kilobajt *m*

kilogram(me) /'kɪləgræm/ *n* kilogram *m*

kilometre GB, **kilometer** US /'kıləmi:tə(r), kı'lɒmıtə(r)/ n kilometr m

kilowatt /'kıləwɒt/ n kilowat m

kind /kaınd/ **I** n ① (sort, type) rodzaj m, typ m; **this ~ of book** ten rodzaj książek; **this ~ of dog** ta rasa psów; **all ~s of people** ludzie wszelkiego pokroju; **what ~ of person is she?** jakim ona jest człowiekiem?; **this is one of a ~** to jedyny okaz tego rodzaju ② (expressing vague classification) **a ~ of soup** coś w rodzaju zupy; **I heard a ~ of rattling noise** usłyszałem jakiś grzechot or klekot ③ (classified type) typ m; **I know his ~** znam takich jak on; **they stick with their own ~** tacy jak oni trzymają się razem

II adj [person] życzliwy; [gesture, act] pełen dobroci; [words] miły, uprzejmy; **to be ~ to sb** być życzliwym dla kogoś; **to be ~ to animals** być dobrym dla zwierząt; **that's very ~ of you** to bardzo miło z twojej strony; **would you be ~ enough to pass me the salt?** bądź tak uprzejmy i podaj mi sól

III **in kind** adv phr **to pay in ~** zapłacić w naturze

IV **kind of** adv phr infml **he's ~ of cute** jest całkiem miły; **I ~ of like him** ja go nawet lubię; **'is it interesting?' – '~ of'** „czy to jest ciekawe" – „niby tak"

kindergarten /'kındəgɑ:tn/ n przedszkole n

kind-hearted /ˌkaınd'hɑ:tıd/ adj [person] życzliwy

kindle /'kındl/ vt rozpal|ić, -ać [fire]; wzniec|ić, -ać [desire]; wzbudz|ić, -ać [interest]

kindly /'kaındlı/ **I** adj [person, smile] życzliwy

II adv ① (in a kind way) życzliwie; **to speak ~ of sb** wyrażać się o kimś życzliwie ② (obligingly) łaskawie; **would you ~ do it** czy byłby pan łaskaw zrobić to ③ (favourably) **to take ~ to sth/sb** odnieść się do czegoś życzliwie [idea]

kindness /'kaındnıs/ n dobroć f

kindred spirit /ˌkındrıd 'spırıt/ n bratnia dusza f

kinetics /kı'netıks/ n kinetyka f

king /kıŋ/ n ① (monarch) król m; **King Charles** król Karol ② (in chess, cards) król m; (in draughts, checkers) damka f

kingdom /'kıŋdəm/ n królestwo n; **the animal ~** królestwo zwierząt

kingfisher /'kıŋfıʃə(r)/ n zimorodek m

king-size(d) /'kıŋsaız(d)/ adj [cigarettes] długi; [packet] wielki; [portion, garden] ogromny; **a ~ bed** wielkie łoże

kink /kıŋk/ n (in rope) supeł m; (in pipe) zgięcie n; **the hosepipe has a ~ in it** wąż się zagiął

kiosk /'ki:ɒsk/ n ① (stand) kiosk m ② GB budka f telefoniczna

kipper /'kıpə(r)/ GB n solony, wędzony śledź m

kiss /kıs/ **I** n pocałunek m; całus m infml

II vt po|całować [person]; **to ~ sb on the lips/ cheek** pocałować kogoś w usta/w policzek; **to ~ (each other)** całować się

III vi po|całować się

kiss of life n GB sztuczne oddychanie n metodą usta-usta; **to give sb the ~** zrobić komuś sztuczne oddychanie

kit /kıt/ n ① (implements) komplet m ② (gear) sprzęt m; **football ~** strój do gry w piłkę nożną ③ (parts for assembly) zestaw m elementów ④ (soldier's) ekwipunek m

■ **kit out** GB: wyposaż|yć, -ać [person, interior] (in sth w coś)

kitbag /'kıtbæg/ n (for travel, sport) torba f; (soldier's) tornister m

kitchen /'kıtʃın/ n kuchnia f

kitchen foil n folia f aluminiowa

kitchen roll n ręczniki m pl jednorazowe (w rolce)

kitchen sink n zlew m (kuchenny)

kitchen unit n szafka f kuchenna

kite /kaıt/ n latawiec m; **to fly a ~** puszczać latawca

kitten /'kıtn/ n kocię n, kociak m

kitty /'kıtı/ n kicia f, kiciuś m

kiwi fruit /'ki:wi: fru:t/ n (owoc m) kiwi n

kleptomaniac /ˌkleptə'meınıæk/ n kleptoman m, -ka f

knack /næk/ n ① (dexterity) wprawa f (of doing sth w robieniu czegoś); **to get the ~** nabrać wprawy; **to lose the ~** wyjść z wprawy ② (talent) dryg m infml; **to have the ~ for doing sth** mieć dryg do robienia czegoś

knapsack /'næpsæk/ n plecak m

knave /neıv/ n (in cards) walet m

knead /ni:d/ vt zagni|eść, -atać [dough]; wy|maso-wać [flesh]

knee /ni:/ **I** n kolano n; **on (one's) hands and ~s** na czworakach

II vt kop|nąć, -ać kolanem [person]

IDIOMS **I go weak at the ~s (at the thought of sth)** uginają się pode mną nogi (na myśl o czymś)

kneecap /'ni:kæp/ n rzepka f

knee-deep /ˌni:'di:p/ adj **the snow was ~** śnieg sięgał (do) kolan

kneel /ni:l/ vi (also ~ **down**) klęk|nąć, -ać, klęczeć

knee-length /'ni:leŋθ/ adj [skirt] do kolan

knickers /'nıkəz/ npl GB majtki plt

knick-knack /'nıknæk/ n bibelot m

knife /naıf/ **I** n nóż m

II vt za|sztyletować; **he had been ~d in the back** dostał nożem w plecy

knife-edge /'naıfedʒ/ n **to be (living) on a ~** [person] balansować nad przepaścią fig

knife-point /'naıfpɔınt/ n **at ~** z nożem na gardle

knight /naıt/ **I** n ① rycerz m ② (in chess) koń m, skoczek m

II *vt* GB pasować na rycerza *[person]*

knighthood /'naɪthʊd/ *n* GB (title) tytuł *m* szlachecki

knit /nɪt/ **I** *vt* z|robić na drutach; ~**ted** zrobiony na drutach

II *vi* ① *[person]* robić na drutach ② *[broken bones]* zr|osnąć, -astać się

knitting /'nɪtɪŋ/ *n* robótka *f*; (activity) robienie *n* na drutach

knitwear /'nɪtweə(r)/ *n* dzianina *f*

knob /nɒb/ *n* gałka *f*

knobbly /'nɒblɪ/ GB, **knobby** /'nɒbɪ/ US *adj* guzłowaty

knock /nɒk/ **I** *n* ① (blow) uderzenie *n*; **a ~ at the door** pukanie do drzwi; ~! ~! puk, puk! ② (setback) **to take a ~** dostać cięgi

II *vt* ① (strike) stuk|nąć, -ać *[object]*; **to ~ one's head on sth** uderzyć głową o coś; **to ~ sb unconscious** ogłuszyć kogoś; **to ~ sth off** or **out of sth** strącić coś z czegoś ② infml (criticize) s|krytykować

III *vi* ① *[branch, object]* stuk|nąć, -ać (**on** or **against sth** o coś); *[engine]* stuk|nąć, -ać ② (collide) **to ~ into** or **against sth** wpaść na coś

■ **knock down**: ① (deliberately) powal|ić, -ać *[opponent]*; wyważ|yć, -ać *[door]*; roz|ebrać, -bierać *[building]*; (accidentally) przewr|ócić, -acać *[person, object]*; zwal|ić, -ać *[fence]* ② *[buyer]* wy|targować *[price]*; *[seller]* obniż|yć, -ać *[price]*

■ **knock off**: ¶ ~ **off** infml *[worker]* s|kończyć pracę ¶ ~ **[sb/sth] off** ① (cause to fall) strąc|ić, -ać *[object]*; przewr|ócić, -acać *[person]* ② infml (reduce) obniż|yć, -ać *[price]* ③ infml ~ **it off!** przestań!

■ **knock out**: ① wybi|ć, -jać *[tooth]* ② (make unconscious) *[person, blow]* ogłusz|yć, -ać; *[drug]* zwal|ić, -ać z nóg infml; *[boxer]* z|nokautować *[opponent]* ③ Sport (eliminate) wy|eliminować *[opponent, team]*

■ **knock over**: przewr|ócić, -acać

knockdown /'nɒkdaʊn/ *adj [price]* bardzo niski

knocker /'nɒkə(r)/ *n* (on door) kołatka *f*

knocking /'nɒkɪŋ/ *n* (at door) pukanie *n*; (in engine) stukanie *n*

knock-kneed /ˌnɒk'niːd/ *adj* koślawy

knock-on effect /ˌnɒk'ɒn ɪ'fekt/ *n* efekt *m* domina

knock-out /'nɒkaʊt/ **I** *n* (in boxing) nokaut *m* **II** *adj* ① Sport *[competition]* rozgrywany w eliminacjach ② infml *[pills]* zwalający z nóg infml

knot /nɒt/ **I** *n* ① (on rope) węzeł *m*; (on string) supeł *m*; **to tie sth in a ~** związać coś w węzeł or

na supeł ② (in wood) sęk *m* ③ (group) gromadka *f*, grupa *f*

II *vt* związ|ać, -ywać (**together** ze sobą)

know /nəʊ/ **I** *vt* znać *[person, place, way]*; wiedzieć *[everything, something]*; **to ~ why/how** wiedzieć dlaczego/jak; **to ~ sb by sight** znać kogoś z widzenia; **to ~ how to do sth** umieć coś zrobić; **to ~ that...** wiedzieć, że...; **to get to ~ sb** poznać kogoś; **he ~s all about it** wie wszystko na ten temat; **I knew it!** wiedziałem!

II *vi* wiedzieć; **as you ~** jak wiesz; **to ~ about sth** (have information) wiedzieć o czymś; (have skill) znać się na czymś; **to ~ of sth** (from experience) znać coś; (from information) wiedzieć o czymś; **to let sb ~ about** or **of sth** zawiadomić kogoś o czymś

IDIOMS **to be in the ~** infml wiedzieć, co w trawie piszczy; **to be in the ~ about sth** infml orientować się w czymś

know-all /'nəʊɔːl/ *n* GB infml mędrek *m* infml

know-how /'nəʊhaʊ/ *n* infml specjalistyczna wiedza *f*, know-how *m/n inv*

knowing /'nəʊɪŋ/ *adj [glance, smile, gesture]* znaczący

knowledge /'nɒlɪdʒ/ *n* ① (awareness) wiedza *f*; **to my ~** o ile wiem; **without sb's ~** bez wiedzy kogoś ② (factual wisdom) wiedza *f*; (of specific field) znajomość *f*; **technical ~** wiedza techniczna

knowledgeable /'nɒlɪdʒəbl/ *adj [person]* znający się na rzeczy; **to be ~ about sth** dobrze znać się na czymś

known /nəʊn/ *[authority, danger]* poznany; *[celebrity, cure]* znany

knuckle /'nʌkl/ *n* ① (of person) knykieć *m*, kłykieć *m* ② Culin (of lamb, mutton) udziec *m*; (of pork) golonka *f*

■ **knuckle down** infml: **to ~ down to sth** zabrać się na serio do czegoś

knuckle-duster /'nʌkldʌstə(r)/ *n* kastet *m*

koala (bear) /kəʊ'ɑːlə(beə)/ *n* (niedźwiadek *m*) koala *m*

Koran /kə'rɑːn/ *n* Koran *m*

Korea /kə'rɪə/ *prn* Korea *f*

kosher /'kəʊʃə(r)/ *adj* ① *[food, restaurant]* koszerny ② infml (legitimate) **it's ~** to jest w porządku

Kosovo /'kɒsəvəʊ/ *prn* Kosowo *n*

Kurd /kɜːd/ *n* Kurd *m*, -yjka *f*

Kurdish /'kɜːdɪʃ/ *adj* kurdyjski

Kurdistan /ˌkɜːdɪ'stæn/ *prn* Kurdystan *m*

Kuwait /kʊ'weɪt/ *prn* Kuwejt *m*

L

l, L /el/ *n* l, L *n*

lab /læb/ *n* laboratorium *n*

lab coat *n* biały fartuch *m*

label /'leɪbl/ **I** *n* ① (on clothing) metka *f*; (on bottle, file) nalepka *f* ② (record company) wytwórnia *f* płytowa ③ Comput etykieta *f*
II *vt* opat|rzyć, -rywać etykietą or nalepką *[bottle, luggage]*; fig za|szufladkować (**as sth** jako coś)

labor *n* US = **labour**

laboratory /lə'bɒrətrɪ, US 'læbrətɔːrɪ/ *n* (for research) laboratorium *n*; (for teaching) pracownia *f*

laborer *n* US = **labourer**

labor union *n* US związek *m* zawodowy

labour GB, **labor** US /'leɪbə(r)/ **I** *n* ① (work) praca *f*; (exertion) robota *f*; (task) trud *m*; **material and ~** materiał i robocizna ② (workforce) siła *f* robocza ③ Med poród *m*; **to go into ~** zacząć rodzić
II *vi* ① (work) pracować (**on** or **at sth** nad czymś) ② (have difficulties) wysilać się (**to do sth** żeby coś zrobić)
IDIOMS: **to ~ the point** rozwodzić się nad zagadnieniem or problemem

Labour /'leɪbə(r)/ GB **I** *n* Partia *f* Pracy
II *adj* laburzystowski

labourer GB, **laborer** US /'leɪbərə(r)/ *n* pracownik *m* fizyczny, pracownica *f* fizyczna

Labour Party *n* GB Partia *f* Pracy

labour-saving /'leɪbəseɪvɪŋ/ *adj [equipment, system]* usprawniający pracę

labyrinth /'læbərɪnθ/ *n* labirynt *m* also fig

lace /leɪs/ **I** *n* ① (fabric) koronka *f* ② (on shoe, boot) sznurowadło *n*; (on dress) sznurówka *f*
II *vt* ① zasznurow|ać, -ywać *[shoes]* ② **to ~ coffee with alcohol** zaprawić kawę alkoholem

lace-up (shoe) /ˌleɪsʌp'ʃuː/ *n* but *m* sznurowany

lack /læk/ **I** *n* **~ of sb/sth** brak *m* kogoś/czegoś; **for ~ of something** z braku czegoś
II *vt* nie mieć (czegoś) *[confidence, funds]*; **he doesn't ~ enthusiasm** nie brak mu entuzjazmu
III *vi* **they are ~ing for nothing** niczego im nie brak(uje)

lacklustre GB, **lackluster** US /'læklʌstə(r)/ *adj [person]* nijaki; *[performance]* bez wyrazu

lacquer /'lækə(r)/ *n* lakier *m*; **hair ~** lakier do włosów

lacy /'leɪsɪ/ *adj* koronkowy

lad /læd/ *n* infml (boy) chłopak *m* infml

ladder /'lædə(r)/ **I** *n* ① (for climbing) drabina *f* ② GB (in stockings) oczko *n*
II *vt* **I've ~ed my tights** poleciało or poszło mi oczko w rajstopach
III *vi* **her stocking has ~ed** poszło or poleciało jej oczko w pończosze

ladle /'leɪdl/ *n* (in kitchen) chochla *f*; (piece of cutlery) łyżka *f* wazowa

lady /'leɪdɪ/ **I** *n* ① (woman) pani *f*; **ladies and gentlemen!** Panie i Panowie!, Szanowni Państwo!; **a little old ~** staruszka; **she's a real ~** prawdziwa z niej dama ② GB (in titles) **Lady Churchill** Lady Churchill
II **ladies** *npl* toaleta *f* damska or dla pań; (on door) „dla pań"

ladybird /'leɪdɪbɜːd/ *n* biedronka *f*

ladylike /'leɪdɪlaɪk/ *adj [behaviour]* wytworny

lag /læg/ **I** *n* (interval) odstęp *m* czasu; (delay) opóźnienie *n*
II *vt* o|błożyć, -kładać warstwą izolującą *[pipe, roof]*
■ **lag behind**: ¶ **~ behind** *[person, wages]* (po)zostawać w tyle ¶ **~ behind [sb/sth]** (po)zostawać w tyle za kimś/czymś; **wages are ~ging behind inflation** wzrost zarobków nie nadąża za inflacją

lager /'lɑːgə(r)/ *n* piwo *n* pełne jasne

lager lout *n* GB chuligan *m*

lagoon /lə'guːn/ *n* laguna *f*

laidback /ˌleɪd'bæk/ *adj* infml *[attitude]* niefrasobliwy; *[atmosphere]* swobodny

lake /leɪk/ *n* jezioro *n*

lamb /læm/ *n* jagnię *n*; **leg of ~** udziec jagnięcy

lamb's wool *n* miękka wełna *f* owcza

lame /leɪm/ *adj [person]* kulejący; *[animal]* kulawy

lament /lə'ment/ **I** *n* lament *m*; (mourning) opłakiwanie *n*
II *vt* biadać nad (czymś) *[misfortune, failure]*

lamentable /'læməntəbl/ *adj [condition]* opłakany; *[incident]* godny pożałowania

laminated /'læmɪneɪtɪd/ *adj [plastic, wood]* (wielo)warstwowy; *[paper]* laminowany

lamp /læmp/ *n* lampa *f*; (in street) latarnia *f*; (on bicycle, car) światło *n*

lamppost /'læmppəʊst/ *n* słup *m* latarni

lampshade /'læmpʃeɪd/ *n* (of cloth, paper) abażur *m*; (of glass) klosz *m*

lance /lɑːns, US læns/ *vt* przecił|ąć, -nać *[boil]*

land /lænd/ **[I]** *n* [1] (ground) teren *m*; **a plot of** ~ działka [2] (farmland) ziemia *f* [3] (country) kraj *m* [4] (not sea) ląd *m*; **dry** ~ stały ląd; **to reach** ~ dotrzeć do lądu; **by** ~ drogą lądową

[II] *vt* [1] sprowadz|ić, -áć na ziemię *[aircraft]*; przeprowadz|ić, -áć lądowanie (czegoś) *[spacecraft]* [2] z|łowić *[fish]* [3] infml zała|pać, -ywać infml *[job, contract]*; z|łapáć infml *[husband]* [4] infml **to** ~ **sb with sth** zwalić na kogoś coś infml *[task]*; **to** ~ **sb in sth** wpakować kogoś w coś infml *[trouble, debt]*

[III] *vi* [1] *[aircraft, passenger]* wy|lądować; (disembark) wysi|ąść, -adáć [2] *[ship]* przybi|ć, -jáć do brzegu; *[passenger]* zejść, schodzić na ląd [3] *[sportsman]* wy|lądować (**on sth** na czymś); *[object]* upa|ść, -dáć (**on sth** na coś); *[soot]* osi|ąść, -adáć (**on sth** na czymś)

landing /'lændɪŋ/ *n* [1] (at turn of stairs) podest *m* (schodów); **his room is on the next** ~ jego pokój jest piętro wyżej [2] (of troops) desant *m*; (of supplies from aircraft) zrzut *m* [3] (of plane) lądowanie *n*; (on water) wodowanie *n*

landing card *n* karta *f* zejścia na ląd
landing gear *n* podwozie *n* (samolotu)
landing strip *n* lądowisko *n*
landlady /'lændleɪdɪ/ *n* (owner of property) właścicielka *f*; (living-in) gospodyni *f*; (pub keeper) kierowniczka *f*
landlord /'lændlɔːd/ *n* (owner) właściciel *m*; (living-in) gospodarz *m*; (pub keeper) kierownik *m*
landmark /'lændmɑːk/ *n* (serving as a guide) punkt *m* orientacyjny; (prominent object) charakterystyczny obiekt *m*; fig (marking a stage) kamień *m* milowy fig; (marking a turning point) punkt *m* zwrotny
land mine *n* mina *f* lądowa
landowner /'lændəʊnə(r)/ *n* właściciel *m* ziemski
landscape /'lændskeɪp/ *n* krajobraz *m*; (in art) pejzaż *m*
landscape gardener *n* projektant *m*, -ka *f* ogrodów
landslide /'lændslaɪd/ *n* osuwisko *n*; fig walne zwycięstwo *n*
lane /leɪn/ *n* [1] (in town) uliczka *f*; (in country) wąska droga *f*; (path) dróżka *f* [2] (of road) pas *m* (ruchu); Sport tor *m*
language /'læŋgwɪdʒ/ *n* język *m*; **legal** ~ język prawniczy; **programming** ~ Comput język programowania; **bad** or **foul** ~ ordynarne słownictwo
language barrier *n* bariera *f* językowa
language laboratory *n* laboratorium *n* językowe
languish /'læŋgwɪʃ/ *vi* *[industry, organization]* podupa|ść, -dáć; *[person]* marnieć
lank /læŋk/ *adj* *[hair]* prosty
lantern /'læntən/ *n* latarnia *f*
lap /læp/ *n* [1] kolana *n pl*; **to fold one's hands in one's** ~ złożyć ręce na podołku or na kolanach [2] Sport okrążenie *n* [3] (stage) etap *m*

■ **lap up**: wy|chłeptáć *[milk, water]*; fig wziąć, brać coś za dobrą monetę *[flattery, lies]*
IDIOMS: **to live in the** ~ **of luxury** opływać w dostatki
lap belt *n* biodrowy pas *m* bezpieczeństwa
lapel /lə'pel/ *n* klapa *f* (marynarki)
lapse /læps/ **[I]** *n* [1] (error) błąd *m*; (slip) odstępstwo *n*; **a** ~ **in concentration** chwila nieuwagi [2] (interval) okres *m*; **after a** ~ **of several years** po upływie kilku lat

[II] *vi* [1] *[policy, contract]* wygas|nąć, -áć [2] *[standard]* obniż|yć, -áć się; **to** ~ **into unconsciousness** stracić przytomność; **to** ~ **into bad habits** nabrać złych nawyków; **to** ~ **into English** przejść na angielski
laptop /'læptɒp/ *n* laptop *m*
lard /lɑːd/ *n* smalec *m*
larder /'lɑːdə(r)/ *n* spiżarnia *f*
large /lɑːdʒ/ **[I]** *adj* *[animal, area, number]* duży; *[crowd]* wielki; *[meal]* obfity; *[family, group]* liczny; *[powers]* szeroki

[II] at large *adj phr* [1] (free) na wolności [2] *[society, population]* jako całość; **the public at** ~ ogół (społeczeństwa)
IDIOMS: **by and** ~ w zasadzie
large-scale /ˌlɑːdʒ'skeɪl/ *adj* *[map]* w dużej skali; *[search]* (zakrojony) na szeroką or wielką skalę
lark /lɑːk/ *n* [1] skowronek *m* [2] infml **for a** ~ dla hecy
laryngitis /ˌlærɪn'dʒaɪtɪs/ *n* zapalenie *n* krtani
larynx /'lærɪŋks/ *n* krtań *f*
laser /'leɪzə(r)/ **[I]** *n* laser *m*
[II] *adj* laserowy
laser treatment *n* laseroterapia *f*
lash /læʃ/ **[I]** *n* [1] (eyelash) rzęsa *f* [2] (stroke of whip) smagnięcie *n*

[II] *vt* wy|chłostáć *[person, animal]*; *[rain, wind]* wy|smagáć *[windows]*
■ **lash out**: (spend freely) zaszaleć infml; **to** ~ **out at sb** zaatakować kogoś
last /lɑːst, US læst/ **[I]** *n, pron* **the** ~ ostatni; **she was the** ~ **to leave** wyszła (jako) ostatnia; **the** ~ **but one** przedostatni; **the night before** ~ (evening) przedwczoraj wieczorem; (night) przedwczoraj w nocy; **the week before** ~ dwa tygodnie temu

[II] *adj* ostatni; *[bus stop, station]* końcowy; ~ **Tuesday** w zeszły wtorek; ~ **summer** latem zeszłego roku; ~ **night** (evening) wczoraj wieczorem; (night-time) (dziś) w nocy; **over the** ~ **five years** w ciągu ostatnich pięciu lat

[III] *adv* [1] *[arrive]* na końcu; (in competition) na ostatnim miejscu; **I went in** ~ wszedłem ostatni or na końcu; **to rank** ~ *[runner]* zająć ostatnie miejsce; ~ **of all** na koniec [2] **she was** ~ **in Canada in 1976** ostatni raz or po raz ostatni była w Kanadzie w 1976 roku

IV vi [1] *[situation]* trwać; **it won't** ~! to się kiedyś musi skończyć!; **it's too good to** ~! to zbyt dobre, żeby miało trwać wiecznie! [2] *[fabric]* być trwałym; *[perishables]* zachow|ać, -ywać świeżość

V at last *adv phr* wreszcie, nareszcie, w końcu

last-ditch /'lɑːstdɪtʃ, US 'læst-/ *adj [attempt, stand]* ostatni

lasting /'lɑːstɪŋ, US 'læstɪŋ/ *adj [effect, peace]* trwały; **to leave a** ~ **impression (on sb)** wywrzeć (na kimś) niezatarte wrażenie

lastly /'lɑːstlɪ, US 'læstlɪ/ *adv* na koniec

last-minute /ˌlɑːst'mɪnɪt, US ˌlæst-/ *adj* (made very late) z ostatniej chwili; (left till very late) ostatni

last name *n* nazwisko *n*

last rites *npl* the ~ ostatnie namaszczenie *n*

latch /lætʃ/ *n* (fastening) zasuw(k)a *f*; (spring lock) zatrzask *m*

■ **latch on to** infml: uczepić się (czegoś) *[person, idea]*

late /leɪt/ **I** *adj* [1] *[arrival]* spóźniony; **to be** ~ spóźnić się **(for sth** na coś); **to be** ~ **with sth** spóźnić się z czymś; **I'm sorry I'm** ~ przepraszam za spóźnienie [2] *[hour, meal]* późny; *[show]* nocny; *[change]* (dokonany) w ostatniej chwili; **to have a** ~ **night** późno położyć się spać; **to be in one's** ~ **fifties** zbliżać się do sześćdziesiątki; **a man in his** ~ **thirties** mężczyzna pod czterdziestkę; **in the** ~ **50s** pod koniec lat 50. [3] (deceased) zmarły; **her** ~ **husband** jej zmarły mąż

II *adv* [1] *[arrive, start, finish]* z opóźnieniem; *[get up, marry]* późno; **it's getting** ~ robi się późno; **to be running** ~ *[person]* być spóźnionym; *[bus, train]* być opóźnionym; **to start three months** ~ rozpocząć się z trzymiesięcznym opóźnieniem [2] ~ **in the afternoon** późnym popołudniem; ~ **in 1941** pod koniec 1941 roku; ~ **at night** późno w nocy; ~ **into the night** do późna w nocy

latecomer /'leɪtkʌmə(r)/ *n* (to lecture, event) spóźnion|y *m*, -a *f*

late developer *n* **to be a** ~ *[child]* (in academic, technical abilities) wolniej się rozwijać; (physically) wolniej dojrzewać

lately /'leɪtlɪ/ *adv* ostatnio

late-night /'leɪtnaɪt/ *adj [film, session]* nocny; **it's** ~ **shopping on Thursdays** w czwartki sklepy są otwarte do późna

later /'leɪtə(r)/ **I** *adj* późniejszy

II *adv* później; **bring it no** ~ **than Friday** przynieś to najpóźniej w piątek; ~ **on** później; **see you** ~! na razie! infml

latest /'leɪtɪst/ **I** *adj* (last) *[train]* ostatni; *[figures, news]* najnowszy

II at the latest *adv phr* najpóźniej

latex /'leɪteks/ *n* lateks *m*

lathe /leɪð/ *n* tokarka *f*

lather /'lɑːðə(r), 'læðə(r), US 'læð-/ *n* piana *f*

Latin /'lætɪn, US 'lætn/ **I** *n* łacina *f*

II *adj* łaciński

Latin America *prn* Ameryka *f* Łacińska

Latin American *adj* latynoamerykański

latitude /'lætɪtjuːd, US -tuːd/ *n* [1] szerokość *f* geograficzna [2] (liberty) swoboda *f*

latter /'lætə(r)/ *n* the ~ (ten) drugi

Latvia /'lætvɪə/ *prn* Łotwa *f*

laugh /lɑːf, US læf/ **I** *n* śmiech *m*; **to like a good** ~ lubić się pośmiać; **to get a** ~ wzbudzać śmiech; **for a** ~ infml dla hecy infml

II *vi* śmiać się **(about** or **over sth** z czegoś); **to** ~ **at sb/sth** (be amused) śmiać się z kogoś/czegoś; (jeer) wyśmiewać się z kogoś/czegoś; **to make sb** ~ rozśmieszyć kogoś

■ **laugh off**: zbyl|ć, -wać śmiechem *[accusation, insult]*

laughable /'lɑːfəbl, US 'læf-/ *adj* śmieszny

laughing stock *n* pośmiewisko *n*

laughter /'lɑːftə(r), US 'læf-/ *n* śmiech *m*

launch /lɔːntʃ/ **I** *n* [1] (boat) łódź *f* motorowa; (carried by ship) szalupa *f* [2] (of new boat) wodowanie *n*; (of lifeboat) spuszczenie *n* na wodę; (of rocket) wystrzelenie *n*; (of campaign) rozpoczęcie *n*; (of product) wprowadzenie *n* na rynek

II *vt* [1] spul|ścić, -szczać na wodę *[lifeboat, dinghy]*; z|wodować *[new vessel]*; wystrzeli|ć, -wać *[missile]* [2] (initiate) rozpocz|ąć, -ynać *[campaign]*; wprowadz|ić, -ać *[scheme]*; wszcz|ąć, -ynać *[investigation]*; rozpocz|ąć, -ynać realizację (czegoś) *[project]*

launch(ing) pad *n* płyta *f* wyrzutni rakietowej

launder /'lɔːndə(r)/ *vt* wy|prać *[clothes]*; **to** ~ **money** prać brudne pieniądze

launderette /lɔːn'dret, ˌlɔːndə'rət/ GB, **laundromat** /'lɔːndrəmæt/ US *n* pralnia *f* samoobsługowa

laundry /'lɔːndrɪ/ *n* [1] (place) pralnia *f* [2] (linen) pranie *n*; **to do the (dirty)** ~ zrobić pranie

laurel /'lɒrəl, US 'lɔːrəl/ *n* wawrzyn *m*

lava /'lɑːvə/ *n* lawa *f*

lavatory /'lævətrɪ, US -tɔːrɪ/ *n* toaleta *f*

lavender /'lævəndə(r)/ *n* lawenda *f*

lavish /'lævɪʃ/ **I** *adj [person]* hojny; *[meal]* obfity; *[party, lifestyle]* wystawny

II *vt* **to** ~ **sth on sb/sth** nie szczędzić komuś/czemuś czegoś *[praise]*

lavishly /'lævɪʃlɪ/ *adv [decorated]* bogato; *[give, pay]* hojnie; **to spend** ~ szastać pieniędzmi

law /lɔː/ *n* prawo *n*; **to obey the** ~ przestrzegać prawa; **to break the** ~ złamać prawo; **to be against the** ~ być wbrew prawu; **permitted by** ~ prawnie dozwolony; **under Polish** ~ zgodnie z polskim prawem; **to pass a** ~ przyjąć ustawę; **to study** ~ studiować prawo

law-abiding /'lɔːəbaɪdɪŋ/ *adj* przestrzegający prawa

law and order *n* ład *m* i porządek *m* publiczny

law court *n* sąd *m*

law firm n kancelaria f adwokacka

lawful /'lɔːfl/ adj [owner, strike] legalny; [conduct] zgodny z prawem; [spouse, heir] prawowity

lawless /'lɔːlɪs/ adj ①[activity] bezprawny ②[society] zanarchizowany

lawn /lɔːn/ n trawnik m

lawnmower /'lɔːnməʊə(r)/ n kosiarka f do trawy

law school n wydział m prawa

lawsuit /'lɔːsuːt/ n proces m (sądowy)

lawyer /'lɔːjə(r)/ n (solicitor, barrister) adwokat, -ka f; (expert in law) prawni|k m, -czka f

lax /læks/ adj [discipline] rozluźniony; [person] zbyt pobłażliwy

laxative /'læksətɪv/ n środek m przeczyszczający

lay /leɪ/ ① adj ①(not expert) ~ **person** laik m ②[preacher] świecki; [education] laicki
② vt ①(place) położyć, kłaść [baby, book]; złożyć, składać [wreath]; (spread out) roz|łożyć, -kładać [rug, blanket]; (arrange) u|łożyć, -kładać [photos]; **to ~ the table** nakrywać do stołu ②(prepare) u|łożyć, -kładać [plan]; zaznacz|yć, -ać [trail]; zastawi|ć, -ać [trap]; **to ~ the foundation(s)** or **basis for sth** fig przygotować grunt dla czegoś or pod coś fig ③**to ~ eggs** [bird] zn|ieść, -osić jaja; [insect] złożyć, składać jaja
③ vi [bird] zn|ieść, -osić jaja, nieść się; [reptile] złożyć, składać jaja

■ **lay down:** ①(put) położyć, kłaść [object, patient]; roz|łożyć, -kładać [blanket, garment]; od|łożyć, -kładać [book, implement]; złożyć, składać [weapon]; **to ~ down one's life for sb/sth** oddać życie za kogoś/coś ②(fix) ustal|ić, -ać [plan]; określ|ić, -ać [policy]

■ **lay off:** (permanently) zw|olnić, -alniać (z pracy); (temporarily) wys|łać, -yłać na urlop bezpłatny

■ **lay on:** na|łożyć, -kładać [paint]; zapewni|ć, -ać [meal, transport]; z|organizować [excursion]

■ **lay out:** ①(spread out) wy|łożyć, -kładać [goods, food]; roz|łożyć, -kładać [map]; przygotow|ać, -ywać [clothes] ②(plan) rozplanow|ać, -ywać [garden]; za|projektować [advertisement]; **to be well laid out** [document, page] mieć przejrzysty układ; [flat] mieć dobry rozkład

layabout /'leɪəbaʊt/ n nierób m infml

lay-by /'leɪbaɪ/ n GB (in road) zato(cz)ka f

layer /'leɪə(r)/ ① n warstwa f
② vt ①wy|cieniować [hair] ②u|łożyć, -kładać warstwami [potatoes, cheese]

layman /'leɪmən/ n laik m

lay-off /'leɪfɒf/ n (permanent) zwolnienie n z pracy; (temporary) przymusowy urlop m bezpłatny

layout /'leɪaʊt/ n (of text, newspaper) układ m; (of building, flat) rozkład m; (of garden, room) plan m; (of advertisement, shop-window) kompozycja f

laze /leɪz/ vi (also ~ **about, ~ around**) leniuchować

lazily /'leɪzɪlɪ/ adv [move, flow] leniwie; [lie, sit] bezczynnie

laziness /'leɪzɪnɪs/ n lenistwo n

lazy /'leɪzɪ/ adj [person] leniwy; [movement, pace] (po)wolny; [day, weekend] spokojny

lead[1] /liːd/ ① n ①**to be in the ~** prowadzić; **to go into the ~** objąć prowadzenie; **to increase one's ~** zwiększyć przewagę ②**to take the ~** przejąć inicjatywę; **to follow sb's ~** pójść za przykładem kogoś ③(clue) trop m; (information) wskazówka f ④(role) główna rola f ⑤(wire) kabel m ⑥GB (for dog) smycz f
② adj [guitarist] wiodący; [part, soprano] główny
③ vt ①(guide, escort) za|prowadzić (**to sb/sth** do kogoś/czegoś); **to ~ sb into the kitchen** wprowadzić kogoś do kuchni ②(bring) [road, sign] za|prowadzić (**to sth** do czegoś) ③(be in charge) po|prowadzić [army, attack, orchestra]; po|kierować (czymś) [company]; sta|nąć, -ć na czele (czegoś) [government]; iść na czele (czegoś) [procession]; kierować (czymś) [research] ④(cause) **to ~ sb to sth** doprowadz|ić, -ać kogoś do czegoś [despair]; skł|onić, -aniać kogoś do czegoś [conclusion] ⑤(conduct) prowadzić [active life]; **to ~ a life of luxury** żyć w luksusie
④ vi ①[street] prowadzić (**to** or **into sth** do czegoś); [pipe] iść (**to sth** do czegoś, w kierunku czegoś); [door] wychodzić (**into sth** na coś) ②(result in) **to ~ to sth** doprowadz|ić, -ać do czegoś [discovery, accident] ③[runner, company, team] prowadzić; **to ~ by 9 seconds** prowadzić o 9 sekund ④(in walk, dancing) prowadzić; (in action, organization) przewodzić; (in discussion) zaga|ić, -jać

■ **lead up to:** ①(precede) poprzedz|ić, -ać ②(culminate in) do|prowadzić do (czegoś) [argument]

lead[2] /led/ n (metal) ołów m; (in pencil) grafit m

leaded petrol GB, **leaded gasoline** US n benzyna f ołowiowa

leader /'liːdə(r)/ n ①(of nation, gang, strike, movement) przywód|ca m, -czyni f; (of government, company) szef m, -owa f; (of party, trade union) lider m ②(in competition) prowadzą|cy m, -a f; (in market, field) lider m

leadership /'liːdəʃɪp/ n (of party, company) kierownictwo n; (of state) władze plt; **under the ~ of sb** pod kierownictwem kogoś

leadership contest, leadership election n wybory plt do władz partyjnych

leadership qualities npl cechy f pl przywódcze

lead-free /'ledfriː/ adj bezołowiowy

leading /'liːdɪŋ/ adj ①[lawyer, politician] czołowy; [brand, product] popularny; [company, position] przodujący ②[position] pierwszoplanowy; [influence] główny; **to play the ~ role (in sth)** [actor] zagrać główną rolę (w czymś); fig odegrać ważną rolę (w czymś) ③Sport [car, runner] prowadzący

leading edge **I** *n* to be at the ~ of technological development wieść prym w dziedzinie techniki

II **leading-edge** *adj [technology, organization]* przodujący

lead story *n* (in press) temat *m* dnia

leaf /liːf/ *n* **1** (of plant) liść *m* **2** (of book) kartka *f*

■ **leaf through**: przekartkow|ać, -ywać *[book, magazine]*

IDIOMS: **to turn over a new** ~ rozpocząć nowy rozdział (w życiu)

leaflet /'liːflɪt/ *n* ulotka *f*

league /liːg/ *n* **1** (alliance) liga *f*; **to be in** ~ **(with sb)** fig mieć (z kimś) konszachty **2** GB Sport liga *f* **3** fig poziom *m*; **they are not in the same** ~ nie ma między nimi żadnego porównania

league table *n* ranking *m*

leak /liːk/ **I** *n* pęknięcie *n*; (of liquid, gas) wyciek *m*
II *vt* ujawni|ć, -ać *[information, plan]*
III *vi* **1** *[boat, roof]* przeciekać; *[pipe]* być nieszczelnym **2** *[liquid]* wyciec, wyciek|nąć, -ać **(from sth** z czegoś); *[gas]* ul|otnić, -atniać się **(from sth** z czegoś)

leaky /'liːkɪ/ *adj [roof, boat]* cieknący; *[container, tap]* nieszczelny

lean /liːn/ **I** *adj* **1** *[face, body]* szczupły; *[meat]* chudy **2** *[time]* trudny; *[year]* chudy
II *vt* **to** ~ **sth against sth** op|rzeć, -ierać coś o coś
III *vi* *[wall, building]* pochyl|ić, -ać się; *[person]* op|rzeć, -ierać się; *[ladder, bicycle]* być opartym; **to** ~ **against sth** opierać się o coś; **to** ~ **out of the window** wychylić się przez okno

■ **lean back**: *[person]* odchyl|ić, -ać się

■ **lean forward**: pochyl|ić, -ać się do przodu

■ **lean on**: ¶ ~ **on [sb/sth]** (physically) op|rzeć, -ierać się or w|esprzeć, -spierać się na (kimś/czymś) *[person, stick, windowsill]* ¶ ~ **on [sb]** (depend on) liczyć na (kogoś); (put pressure on) naciskać na (kogoś)

■ **lean over**: ~ **over [sth]** przechyl|ić, -ać się przez (coś) *[wall, shoulder]*

leap /liːp/ **I** *n* **1** (jump) skok *m* **2** (progress) krok *m* **3** (in price) skok *m* **(in sth** czegoś)
II *vi* **1** *[person, animal]* sk|oczyć, -akać; **to** ~ **across** or **over sth** przeskoczyć (przez) coś; **to** ~ **up** podskoczyć; **to** ~ **to one's feet** zerwać się na równe nogi **2** *[heart]* zabić mocniej **3** *[price, profit]* sk|oczyć, -akać

■ **leap at**: ~ **at [sth]** fig s|korzystać skwapliwie z (czegoś) *[chance, offer]*

■ **leap up**: *[person]* skoczyć na równe nogi; *[price, rate]* sk|oczyć, -akać

leapfrog /'liːpfrɒg/ *n* zabawa, której uczestnicy kolejno przeskakują przez siebie jak przez kozioł

leap year *n* rok *m* przestępny

learn /lɜːn/ **I** *vt* na|uczyć się (czegoś) *[language]*; wyucz|yć, -ać się (czegoś) *[trade]*; zdoby|ć, -wać *[skills]*; **to** ~ **(how) to do sth** nauczyć się coś robić; **to** ~ **that...** dowiedzieć się, że...
II *vi* uczyć się **(about sth** o czymś); **to** ~ **from one's mistakes** uczyć się na własnych błędach; **to** ~ **about** or **of sth** dowiedzieć się o czymś

learned /lɜːnɪd/ *adj [person, book]* uczony; *[journal]* specjalistyczny; *[society]* naukowy

learner /'lɜːnə(r)/ *n* uczący się *m*, -a się *f*; **to be a fast** ~ szybko się uczyć; **to be a slow** ~ mieć trudności z nauką

learner driver *n* uczący *m*, -a *f* się prowadzić (samochód)

learning /'lɜːnɪŋ/ *n* **1** (knowledge) wiedza *f* **2** (gaining knowledge) uczenie się *n*

learning difficulties *npl* trudności *f pl* w nauce

lease /liːs/ **I** *n* najem *m*; (contract) umowa *f* najmu
II *vt* wynaj|ąć, -mować *[house, car]* **(to sb** komuś)

leaseholder /'liːshəʊldə(r)/ *n* najemca *m*

leash /liːʃ/ *n* (for dog) smycz *f*

leasing /'liːsɪŋ/ **I** *n* leasing *m*
II *adj [agreement, company]* leasingowy

least /liːst/ **I** *quantif* **(the)** ~ najmniej; **she has the** ~ **money** ona ma najmniej pieniędzy; **I haven't the** ~ **idea** nie mam najmniejszego pojęcia
II *pron* **the** ~ najmniej; **we have the** ~ mamy najmniej; **it was the** ~ **I could do** przynajmniej tyle mogłem zrobić; **that's the** ~ **of our worries** to nasze najmniejsze zmartwienie
III *adv* **(the)** ~ najmniej; **the** ~ **expensive of the three** najtańszy z trzech; **I like that one (the)** ~ ten mi się podoba najmniej
IV **at least** *adv phr* (not less than) co najmniej; (possibly more) przynajmniej; (qualifying statement) przynajmniej; **she's at** ~ **40** ona ma co najmniej 40 lat; **they could at** ~ **have phoned!** mogli przynajmniej zadzwonić!; **he's gone to bed – at** ~ **I think so** poszedł spać, przynajmniej tak mi się zdaje
V **in the least** *adv phr* wcale; **I'm not worried in the** ~ wcale or zupełnie się nie denerwuję
IDIOMS: **last but not** ~, **last but by no means** ~ ostatni, ale nie mniej ważny

leather /'leðə(r)/ **I** *n* (material) skóra *f*
II *adj [object, garment]* skórzany

leave /liːv/ **I** *n* urlop *m*; **three day's** ~ trzy dni urlopu
II *vt* **1** (go away from) *[person]* wyj|ść, -chodzić z (czegoś) *[house, room]*; *[train]* odje|chać, -żdżać z (czegoś) *[station]*; *[plane]* od|lecieć, -atywać z (czegoś) *[airport]*; *[ship]* wypły|nąć, -wać z (czegoś) *[port]*; **she left home at the age of 17** opuściła dom, kiedy miała 17 lat; **to** ~ **school** (having completed it) skończyć szkołę; (without completing it) przerwać naukę; **to** ~ **the table** wstać od stołu

2 (abandon) porzuc|ić, -ać *[family]*; **she left her husband for another man** rzuciła or zostawiła męża dla innego mężczyzny 3 (deposit) zostawi|ć, -ać *[object, instructions]* (**for sb** dla kogoś); **to ~ sb/sth in sb's care** powierzyć kogoś/coś opiece kogoś 4 (let remain) zostawi|ć, -ać *[food, gap]*; pozostawi|ć, -ać *[stain, scar]*; **she ~s her things all over the place** wszędzie rozrzuca swoje rzeczy; **there are** or **we have five minutes left** mamy or zostało nam jeszcze pięć minut 5 **to ~ sth to sb** pozostawić komuś wykonanie czegoś *[job, task]*; **to ~ it (up) to sb to do sth** pozostawić komuś zrobienie czegoś; **~ it to** or **with me!** pozostaw to mnie!; **to ~ sb to it** zostawić kogoś w spokoju 6 (postpone) zostawi|ć, -ać *[task, housework]*; **~ it till tomorrow** zostaw or odłóż to do jutra 7 (bequeath) **to ~ sth to sb** (po)zostawić coś komuś (w spadku)

III *vi* **to ~ for another company** odejść do innej firmy

■ **leave behind:** 1 (go faster than) zostawi|ć, -ać (kogoś/coś) w tyle; **to be/get left behind** *[country, company]* być/zostać w tyle 2 (move away from) *[traveller]* (po)zostawi|ć, -ać za sobą *[town, country]*; *[person]* zostawi|ć, -ać *[family, husband]*; fig zostawi|ć, -ać coś za sobą *[past]* 3 (accidentally) zapom|nieć, -inać (czegoś) *[object]*; zostawi|ć, -ać *[child, animal]*

■ **leave out:** 1 (omit) pomi|nąć, -jać *[word, name, fact]* 2 (exclude) wyłącz|yć, -ać *[person]*; **to ~ sb out of sth** wyłączyć kogoś z czegoś *[group]* 3 (outdoors) zostawi|ć, -ać na zewnątrz *[bicycle]*

leaving /ˈliːvɪŋ/ **I** *n* (of person) (on foot) wyjście *n*; (by car, train) wyjazd *m*

II *adj [party, present]* pożegnalny

Lebanon /ˈlebənən/ *prn* (also **the ~**) Liban *m*

lecherous /ˈletʃərəs/ *adj* lubieżny

lectern /ˈlektɜːn/ *n* (in church) pulpit *m*; (speaker's) mównica *f*; (lecturer's) katedra *f*

lecture /ˈlektʃə(r)/ **I** *n* (public talk) prelekcja *f* (**on sth** na temat czegoś); GB Univ wykład *m* (**on sth** na temat czegoś)

II *vt* 1 GB (teach) prowadzić wykład(y) dla (kogoś) *[students]* 2 (scold) palnąć (komuś) kazanie infml *[child, pupil]*

III *vi* 1 GB **to ~ in mathematics** wykładać matematykę 2 wygł|osić, -aszać prelekcję (**on sth** na temat czegoś, o czymś)

lecture notes *npl* (student's) notatki *f pl* z wykładu; (lecturer's) konspekt *m* wykładu

lecturer /ˈlektʃərə(r)/ *n* 1 (speaker) prelegent *m*, -ka *f* 2 GB Univ wykładowca *m*

lecture theatre *n* aula *f*

ledge /ledʒ/ *n* 1 (in house) występ *m*; (small shelf) półka *f* 2 (on mountain) półka *f*

ledger /ˈledʒə(r)/ *n* księga *f* główna

leech /liːtʃ/ *n* pijawka *f*

leek /liːk/ *n* por *m*

leer /lɪə(r)/ *vi* łyp|nąć, -ać okiem (**at sb/sth** na kogoś/coś)

leeway /ˈliːweɪ/ *n* pole *n* manewru

left /left/ **I** *n* lewa strona *f*; **on the ~** po lewej; (politically) na lewicy

II *adj* lewy

III *adv* w lewo, na lewo

left-hand /ˌleftˈhænd/ *adj [side]* lewy; *[turn]* w lewo

left-hand drive *n* samochód *m* z lewostronnym układem kierowniczym

left-handed /ˌleftˈhændɪd/ *adj* leworęczny

left-luggage (office) /ˌleftˈlʌgɪdʒɒfɪs, US -ɔːfɪs/ *n* GB przechowalnia *f* bagażu

leftovers /ˈleftəʊvə(r)z/ *npl* (of food) resztki *f pl*

left wing **I** *n* **the ~** lewica *f*

II **left-wing** *adj [group, view]* lewicowy

leg /leg/ *n* 1 (of person, horse) noga *f*; (of non-hoofed animal) łapa *f* 2 (of furniture) noga *f* 3 Culin (of lamb) udziec *m*; (of pork) szynka *f*; (of poultry) nóżka *f*; (of chicken) udko *n* 4 (of trousers) nogawka *f* 5 (of journey, race) etap *m*

(IDIOMS) **to pull sb's ~** nabierać kogoś infml

legacy /ˈlegəsɪ/ *n* spadek *m*; fig spuścizna *f*; **the ~ of sth** dziedzictwo czegoś *[hatred, era]*

legal /ˈliːgl/ *adj* 1 *[document, system]* prawny; *[costs]* sądowy; *[career]* prawniczy; **to take ~ advice** zasięgnąć porady prawnej 2 *[requirement, claim]* prawny; *[owner]* prawowity; *[import]* legalny

legal action *n* **to take ~ (against sb)** wystąpić na drogę sądową (przeciwko komuś)

legal aid *n* pomoc *f* prawna

legal holiday *n* US dzień *m* ustawowo wolny od pracy

legalize /ˈliːgəlaɪz/ *vt* za|legalizować

legally /ˈliːgəlɪ/ *adv* 1 *[valid, responsible]* prawnie; **this contract is ~ binding** ten kontrakt jest prawnie obowiązujący 2 *[act]* zgodnie z prawem; *[work]* legalnie

legal proceedings *npl* postępowanie *n* sądowe

legal tender *n* prawny środek *m* płatniczy

legend /ˈledʒənd/ *n* (story) legenda *f* (**of sb/sth** o kimś/czymś)

legendary /ˈledʒəndrɪ, US -derɪ/ *adj* legendarny

leggings /ˈlegɪŋz/ *npl* (for walker) getry *plt*; (for woman) legginsy *plt*; (for baby) śpioszki *plt*

legible /ˈledʒəbl/ *adj* czytelny

legislation /ˌledʒɪsˈleɪʃn/ *n* (body of laws) ustawodawstwo *n*; (process) legislacja *f*

legitimate /lɪˈdʒɪtɪmət/ *adj* 1 (justifiable) *[action, reason]* uzasadniony; *[refusal, reasoning]* zasadny 2 (lawful) *[business]* legalny; *[heir, owner, child]* prawowity

legitimize /lɪˈdʒɪtɪmaɪz/ *vt* za|legalizować *[organization]*; uzna|ć, -wać *[child]*; usprawiedliwi|ć, -ać *[action]*

leisure /'leʒə(r), US 'li:ʒə(r)/ **[I]** *n* czas *m* wolny; (relaxation) wypoczynek *m*; **to do sth at (one's)** ~ zrobić coś bez pośpiechu; (with time for thought) zrobić coś w stosownej chwili

[II] *adj [centre, facilities]* rekreacyjny

leisure time *n* czas *m* wolny

leisure wear *n* strój *m* sportowy

lemon /'lemən/ *n* (fruit) cytryna *f*

lemonade /ˌleməˈneɪd/ *n* (fizzy) lemoniada *f*; (with fresh fruit) napój *m* cytrynowy

lemon juice *n* sok *m* z cytryny; GB (drink) sok *m* cytrynowy

lemon tea *n* herbata *f* cytrynowa; (with a slice of lemon) herbata *f* z cytryną

lemon tree *n* drzewo *n* cytrynowe

lend /lend/ *vt* ① (loan) pożycz|yć, -ać *[money, object]*; **to** ~ **sb sth, to** ~ **sth to sb** pożyczyć coś komuś ② (give) przyda|ć, -wać (czegoś) *[importance, quality]* (**to sb/sth** komuś/czemuś); **to** ~ **support to sb** udzielić komuś poparcia; **to** ~ **sb a hand (with sth)** pomóc komuś (w czymś); **to** ~ **one's name to a project** firmować projekt swoim nazwiskiem

lender /'lendə(r)/ *n* pożyczkodawca *m*

lending /'lendɪŋ/ *n* (of books) wypożyczanie *n*; (in finance) udzielanie *n* pożyczek or kredytów

length /leŋθ/ **[I]** *n* ① (size) długość *f*; **what** ~ **is the plank?** jakiej długości jest ta deska?; **to be 15 cm in** ~ mieć 15 cm długości ② (of book, film, list) długość *f*; (of event) czas *m* trwania; **a film one hour in** ~ film trwający godzinę ③ (of string, carpet, wood) kawałek *m*; (of river, road) odcinek *m*; (of piping, track) fragment *m*; **a dress** ~ kupon na sukienkę ④ Sport **to swim 20** ~ **s** przepłynąć 20 długości (basenu)

[II] at length *adv phr* (for a long time) **at great** ~ *[discuss]* bardzo obszernie; *[speak]* bardzo długo; (in detail) *[discuss]* szczegółowo

⌈IDIOMS:⌉ **to go to great** ~**s to do sth** zadać sobie wiele trudu, żeby coś zrobić

lengthen /'leŋθən/ **[I]** *vt* podłuż|yć, -ać *[garment]*; przedłuż|yć, -ać *[shelf, stay]*; wydłuż|yć, -ać *[queue, list]*

[II] *vi [queue, list, days]* wydłuż|yć, -ać się; *[visit]* przedłuż|yć, -ać się

lengthy /'leŋθɪ/ *adj* dość długi; (too long) przydługi

lenient /'li:nɪənt/ *adj [person]* pobłażliwy (**with sb** dla kogoś); *[punishment]* łagodny

lens /lenz/ *n* (in optical instruments) soczewka *f*; (in glasses) szkło *n*; (in camera) obiektyw *m*; **contact** ~**es** szkła kontaktowe

lens cap *n* osłona *f* obiektywu

Lent /lent/ *n* Wielki Post *m*

lentil /'lentl/ *n* soczewica *f*

Leo /'li:əʊ/ *n* Lew *m*

leopard /'lepəd/ *n* pantera *f*

leotard /'li:ətɑ:d/ *n* trykot *m*

leper /'lepə(r)/ *n* trędowat|y *m*, -a *f*

leprosy /'leprəsɪ/ *n* trąd *m*

lesbian /'lezbɪən/ *n* lesbijka *f*

less /les/ **[I]** *quantif* mniej (czegoś); ~ **beer** mniej piwa; **I have** ~ **money than you** mam mniej pieniędzy niż ty or od ciebie

[II] *pron* mniej; **I have** ~ **than you** mam mniej niż ty or od ciebie; ~ **than 18** mniej niż 18; **a sum not** ~ **than £1,000** suma nie mniejsza niż 1 000 funtów; **it's nothing** ~ **than a scandal!** to po prostu skandal!

[III] *adv* mniej; **the more I see him, the** ~ **I like him** im częściej go widuję, tym mniej go lubię; **no** ~ **than 85%** nie mniej niż or co najmniej 85%

[IV] *prep* ~ **15% discount** minus 15% rabatu; ~ **tax** minus podatek

[V] less and less *adj phr, adv phr* coraz mniej

lessen /'lesn/ *vt* zmniejsz|yć, -ać *[risk, love, influence]*; z|łagodzić *[punishment, pain]*; obniż|yć, -ać *[cost]*

lesser /'lesə(r)/ **[I]** *adj [amount, talent]* mniejszy; *[artist]* pomniejszy; **to a** ~ **extent** w mniejszym stopniu

[II] *adv* ~ **known** mniej znany

lesson /'lesn/ *n* ① (at school) lekcja *f*; **a French** ~ lekcja francuskiego ② fig nauczka *f*; **she needs to be taught a** ~! trzeba jej dać nauczkę!

let /let/ *vt* ① (when making suggestion, expressing command) ~**'s go** chodźmy; ~**'s not talk about that!**, **don't** ~**'s talk about that!** GB nie mówmy o tym!; ~ **them think what they want!** niech sobie myślą, co chcą! ② (allow) **to** ~ **sb do sth** pozwolić komuś coś robić or na zrobienie czegoś; **she wanted to leave but they didn't** ~ **her** chciała wyjść, ale jej nie dali; **don't** ~ **it get you down** nie pozwól, żeby to cię załamało; ~ **me have a look** pozwól, że spojrzę; **to** ~ **one's hair grow** zapuścić włosy; **to** ~ **sb through** przepuścić kogoś ③ (lease) (also ~ **out** GB) wynaj|ąć, -mować; **'room to** ~' „pokój do wynajęcia"

■ **let down:** ¶ ~ **[sb] down** ① (disappoint) zaw|ieść, -odzić; **don't** ~ **me down!** nie zawiedź mnie! ② (embarrass) przyn|ieść, -osić (komuś) wstyd ¶ ~ **[sth] down** ① GB spu|ścić, -szczać or wypu|ścić, -szczać powietrze z (czegoś) *[tyre]* ② (lengthen) podłuż|yć, -ać *[dress]*

■ **let go:** ¶ ~ **go** pu|ścić, -szczać; **to** ~ **go of sb/ sth** puścić kogoś/coś ¶ ~ **[sb] go** wypu|ścić, -szczać *[prisoner]*; pu|ścić, -szczać *[person, arm]*; zw|olnić, -alniać *[employee]*; **to** ~ **oneself go** zaniedb|ać, -ywać się ¶~ **[sth] go** pu|ścić, -szczać *[rope, bar]*

■ **let in:** ¶ ~ **[sth] in** *[roof, window]* prze-pu|ścić, -szczać *[water, light]* ¶ ~ **[sb] in** ① (allow to enter) wpu|ścić, -szczać; (open the door for) otw|orzyć, -ierać (komuś) ② **to** ~ **oneself in for sth** narażać się na coś *[trouble]*

■ **let off:** ¶ ~ **off [sth]** pu|ścić, -szczać *[fire-*

works]; odpal|ić, -ać *[bomb]*; wy|strzelić z (czegoś) *[gun]* ¶ ~ **[sb] off** ① (excuse) **to ~ sb off sth** zwolnić kogoś z czegoś *[homework]* ② (leave unpunished) darow|ać, -ywać (komuś) *[culprit]*; **to ~ sb off with a reprimand/a fine** ukarać kogoś jedynie naganą/grzywną

■ **let out:** ¶ ~ **out** US *[school]* s|kończyć się ¶ ~ **out [sth]** ① wyda|ć, -wać *[cry]*; **to ~ out a roar** ryknąć ② GB (reveal) **to ~ out that...** wygadać (się) or zdradzić, że... ¶ ~ **[sth] out** ① wypu|ścić, -szczać *[animal]* ② da|ć, -wać wyraz (czemuś) *[anger]* ③ (loosen) wypu|ścić, -szczać *[waistband]* ¶ ~ **[sb] out** wypu|ścić, -szczać *[prisoner]*; zw|olnić, -alniać *[pupils, employees]*

■ **let up** *[rain]* usta|ć, -wać; *[heat, wind]* o|słabnąć; *[pressure]* zelżeć

letdown /'letdaʊn/ *n* rozczarowanie *n*

lethal /'liːθl/ *adj [dose, disease, blow]* śmiertelny; *[weapon]* śmiercionośny

lethargic /lɪ'θɑːdʒɪk/ *adj* w śnie letargicznym; (lazy) *[person]* ospały; **to feel ~** nie mieć energii

letter /'letə(r)/ *n* ① (text) list *m*; **a ~ to sb/from sb** list do kogoś/od kogoś ② (of alphabet) litera *f*

letter bomb *n* przesyłka *f* pocztowa z materiałem wybuchowym

letter box *n* (for posting) skrzynka *f* pocztowa; (for delivery) skrzynka *f* na listy

letterhead /'letəhed/ *n* nagłówek *m* *(na papierze firmowym)*

letters page *n* dział *m* listów do redakcji

lettuce /'letɪs/ *n* sałata *f*

letup /'letʌp/ *n* (in demand) spadek *m* (**in sth** czegoś); **with no ~** bez przerwy

leuk(a)emia /luː'kiːmɪə/ *n* białaczka *f*

level /'levl/ **❚** *n* ① (height) poziom *m* also fig; **at street ~** na poziomie or wysokości ulicy; **a high ~ of illiteracy** wysoki wskaźnik analfabetyzmu; **the ~ of service** poziom usług; **to be on the same ~ as sb/sth** być na tym samym poziomie co ktoś/coś ② (rank) szczebel *m*; **at national ~** na szczeblu krajowym

❚❚ *adj* ① *[floor, surface]* poziomy; *[ground]* równy; *[plain]* płaski; **a ~ teaspoon of flour** płaska łyżeczka mąki; **the picture is not ~** ten obrazek krzywo wisi ② (equally high) równy; **to be ~ (with sth)** być równo (z czymś); **to remain ~** *[figures]* utrzymywać się na tym samym poziomie

❚❚❚ *adv* **to draw ~ (with sb)** *[competitors]* zrównać się (z kimś)

❚❚❚❚ *vt* ① (destroy) zrówn|ać, -ywać z ziemią *[village]* ② **to ~ sth at sb** wycelować do kogoś z czegoś *[gun]*; skierować pod adresem kogoś *[accusation]*; wysunąć przeciwko komuś *[charges]* ③ (make even) wyrówn|ać, -ywać *[surface, score]*

■ **level off:** *[prices]* u|stabilizować się; *[curve]* wyrówn|ać, -ywać się

IDIOMS: **to be ~-pegging** iść łeb w łeb; **to ~ with sb** infml być uczciwym or szczerym wobec kogoś

level crossing *n* przejazd *m* kolejowy

level-headed /ˌlevl'hedɪd/ *adj [person]* trzeźwo myślący; *[decision]* rozsądny

lever /'liːvə(r), US 'levər/ *n* dźwignia *f*; (for lifting) lewar(ek) *m*

levy /'levɪ/ **❚** *n* podatek *m* (**on sth** od czegoś) **❚❚** *vt* na|łożyć, -kładać *[tax, duty]*; wymierz|yć, -ać *[fine]*

lewd /ljuːd, US luːd/ *adj [joke, gesture, person]* wulgarny; *[stare]* lubieżny

lexicon /'leksɪkən, US -kɒn/ *n* słownik *m* encyklopedyczny; (glossary) słowniczek *m*

liability /ˌlaɪə'bɪlətɪ/ **❚** *n* ① (in law) odpowiedzialność *f* ② (drawback) ciężar *m* fig **❚❚ liabilities** *npl* (of company) należności *f pl*; (of person) długi *m pl*

liable /'laɪəbl/ *adj* ① (subject to) **to be ~ to sth** podlegać czemuś *[fine]*; **goods ~ for** or **to duty** towary podlegające ocleniu ② (likely) **to be ~ to do sth** prawie na pewno coś zrobić; **it's ~ to rain** pewnie będzie padać

liaise /lɪ'eɪz/ *vi* współpracować (**with sb/sth** z kimś/czymś)

liaison /lɪ'eɪzn, US 'lɪəzɒn/ *n* (military) łączność *f*; (civilian) kontakt *m*

liar /'laɪə(r)/ *n* kłamca *m*

libel /'laɪbl/ **❚** *n* zniesławienie *n* **❚❚** *vt* zniesławi|ć, -ać

libellous GB, **libelous** US /'laɪbələs/ *adj* oszczerczy

liberal /'lɪbərəl/ **❚** *n* liberał *m* **❚❚** *adj* ① *[person, views]* liberalny ② (generous) *[sponsor]* hojny; *[dose]* spory

Liberal /'lɪbərəl/ *n* liberał *m*

Liberal Democrat *n* GB liberalny demokrata *m*

liberalism /'lɪbərəlɪzəm/ *n* liberalizm *m*

liberalize /'lɪbərəlaɪz/ *vt* z|liberalizować

liberate /'lɪbəreɪt/ *vt* wyzw|olić, -alać *[country]*; uw|olnić, -alniać *[prisoner]* **❚❚ liberated** *pp adj [lifestyle]* niczym nieskrępowany; *[woman]* wyzwolona **❚❚❚ liberating** *prp adj [experience]* dający poczucie swobody

liberation /ˌlɪbə'reɪʃn/ *n* (of prisoner) uwolnienie *n*; (of nation) oswobodzenie *n*; **women's ~** wyzwolenie kobiet

liberty /'lɪbətɪ/ *n* wolność *f*

Libra /'liːbrə/ *n* Waga *f*

librarian /laɪ'breərɪən/ *n* bibliotekarz *m*, -rka *f*

library /'laɪbrərɪ, US -brerɪ/ *n* (institution, room) biblioteka *f*; (book collection) księgozbiór *m*; **public ~** biblioteka publiczna

lice /laɪs/ *npl* → **louse**

licence GB, **license** US /'laɪsns/ n [1] (to produce) pozwolenie n; (to use brand name) licencja f; (to sell) koncesja f (**for sth** na coś); **driving** ~ prawo jazdy; **fishing** ~ karta wędkarska [2] (freedom) swoboda f

licence number n (of car) numer m rejestracyjny; (of driver) numer m prawa jazdy

licence plate n tablica f rejestracyjna

license /'laɪsns/ [] n US = **licence**
[] vt [1] [authority] udziel|ić, -ać zezwolenia (komuś) (**to do sth** na robienie czegoś) [2] za|rejestrować [car]

licensed /'laɪsnst/ adj [1] [pilot] licencjonowany; [dealer, taxi] koncesjonowany; [restaurant] z wyszynkiem; **to be** ~ **to carry a gun** mieć pozwolenie na broń [2] (registered) [TV, vehicle] zarejestrowany

licensing laws npl GB przepisy m pl dotyczące sprzedaży napojów alkoholowych

lick /lɪk/ [] n [1] (with tongue) liźnięcie n [2] **to give sth a** ~ **of paint** maznąć coś farbą
[] vt [1] (with tongue) liz|nąć, -ać; **to** ~ **one's lips** oblizywać wargi [2] infml da|ć, -wać (komuś) łomot infml [opponent, team]; **to get** ~**ed** (in game) dostać łomot infml
IDIOMS: **to** ~ **one's wounds** lizać rany

licorice n US = **liquorice**

lid /lɪd/ n [1] (of case) wieko n; (of large container) pokrywa f; (of pot) pokrywka f [2] (eyelid) powieka f

lie[1] /laɪ/ [] n kłamstwo n; **to tell a** ~ skłamać
[] vi (tell falsehood) s|kłamać (**about sb/sth** w sprawie kogoś/czegoś, na temat kogoś/czegoś); **to** ~ **to sb** okłam|ać, -ywać kogoś

lie[2] /laɪ/ vi [1] [person, animal, object] leżeć; (get into horizontal position) (also ~ **down**) położyć się, kłaść się; ~ **still!** leż spokojnie!; **to** ~ **on one's back** leżeć na plecach; **to** ~ **in bed all morning** wylegiwać się w łóżku przez cały ranek; **here** ~**s John Brown** tu leży or spoczywa John Brown [2] (be situated, remain) leżeć, być; **to** ~ **empty** być pustym; **to** ~ **heavy (on sb)** ciążyć (komuś); **a new life lay before them** przed nimi otwierało się nowe życie; **that's where our future** ~**s** w tym jest nasza przyszłość; **what** ~**s ahead?** co przyniesie przyszłość? [3] (can be found) tkwić, znajdować się; **their interests** ~ **elsewhere** są zainteresowani czym innym; **the decision** ~**s with him** decyzja należy do niego; **the responsibility** ~**s with them** na nich spoczywa odpowiedzialność

■ **lie around**: [person] wylegiwać się; [papers] poniewierać się; **to leave sth lying around** zostawić coś porozrzucane [books]; zostawić coś na wierzchu [document]

■ **lie down**: [person, animal] położyć, kłaść się
IDIOMS: **to** ~ **low** przyczaić się; **to take sth lying down** przyjąć coś potulnie

lie detector n wykrywacz m kłamstw

lie-in /'laɪɪn/ n **to have a** ~ poleżeć sobie (dłużej)

lieu /lju:/ [] **in lieu** adv phr **one week's holiday in** ~ tydzień wakacji tytułem rekompensaty
[] **in lieu of** prep phr zamiast (czegoś)

life /laɪf/ n [1] (of person, animal) życie n; **throughout one's** ~ przez całe życie; **the first time in my** ~ pierwszy raz w życiu; **a job/friend for** ~ praca/przyjaciel na całe życie; **for the rest of one's** ~ przez resztę życia; **to be full of** ~ być pełnym życia or werwy or energii; **to come to** ~ [person] odzyskać przytomność; fig [person, party] ożywić się; **a way of** ~ tryb życia [2] (of machine) żywotność f [3] **to sentence sb to** ~ skazać kogoś na karę dożywotniego więzienia
IDIOMS: **to have the time of one's** ~ ubawić się, jak nigdy w życiu

lifebelt /'laɪfbelt/ n pas m ratunkowy

lifeboat /'laɪfbəʊt/ n łódź f ratunkowa; (on ship) szalupa f

life drawing n rysunek m z natury

life expectancy n średnia długość f życia; (of car) przewidywana żywotność f; (of carpet) trwałość f

lifeguard /'laɪfgɑːd/ n ratowni|k m, -czka f

life imprisonment n dożywotnie więzienie n

life insurance n ubezpieczenie n na życie

life jacket n kamizelka f ratunkowa

lifeless /'laɪflɪs/ adj [body, person, voice] martwy; [performance] bez wyrazu

lifelike /'laɪflaɪk/ adj [painting] realistyczny; **to be** ~ [sculpture] wyglądać jak żywy

lifeline /'laɪflaɪn/ n lina f ratownicza; fig ostatnia deska f ratunku

lifelong /'laɪflɒŋ/ adj [ambition] życiowy; [friend] na całe życie; [love] dozgonny; **to have a** ~ **ambition to do sth** przez całe życie pragnąć zrobić coś

lifesaving /'laɪfseɪvɪŋ/ n ratowanie n życia

life sentence n wyrok m dożywotniego więzienia

life-size /'laɪfsaɪz/ adj [model] naturalnej wielkości

life span n długość f życia

life story n historia f życia

lifestyle /'laɪfstaɪl/ n (image) styl m życia; (routine) tryb m życia

life-support machine /ˌlaɪfsəpɔːtməˈʃiːn/ n respirator m

lifetime /'laɪftaɪm/ n życie n; (of object) okres m trwałości; **in her** ~ za jej życia; **the chance of a** ~ życiowa szansa; **we waited for what seemed a** ~ wydawało nam się, że czekamy już całe wieki

lift /lɪft/ [] n [1] GB (elevator) winda f; Tech dźwig m [2] (ride) **she asked me for a** ~ poprosiła mnie o podwiezienie; **can I give you a** ~? czy mogę cię dokądś podwieźć? [3] infml (boost) **to give sb a** ~ dodać komuś otuchy
[] vt [1] (pick up) podn|ieść, -osić [object, person]; (with more effort) dźwig|nąć, -ać; (raise) podn|ieść, -osić, un|ieść, -osić [arm, head]; **to** ~ **sth off a ledge** zdjąć coś z półki [2] (remove) zn|ieść, -osić [ban,

sanctions] ③ (boost) **to ~ sb's spirits** podnieść kogoś na duchu ④ infml (steal) podwędz|lić, -áć infml ▪ **III** *vi [curtain, fog]* podn|lieść, -osić się; **his spirit began to ~** nastrój zaczął mu się poprawiać ■ **lift off:** ¶ **~ off** *[rocket]* wy|startować; *[lid, top]* podn|lieść, -osić się ¶ **~ [sth] off** podn|lieść, -osić *[cover, lid]*

■ **lift up:** podn|lieść, -osić *[book, head, eyes]*; un|lieść, -osić *[veil, head, eyes]*

lift-off /'lɪftɒf/ *n* (of spacecraft) start *m*

ligament /'lɪgəmənt/ *n* wiązadło *n*

light[1] **[]** /laɪt/ *n* ① (brightness) światło *n*; **to read in a poor ~** czytać przy słabym świetle or oświetleniu ② (in building, vehicle) światło *n*; (on dashboard) światełko *n*; **the city ~s** światła miasta ③ (traffic control) światło *n*; **the ~s are red** jest czerwone światło ④ (flame) **to set ~ to sth** podpalić coś *[house]*; **have you got a ~?** czy masz ogień? ⑤ (aspect) światło *n*; **to see sth in a new ~** widzieć or postrzegać coś w nowym świetle ⑥ **to come to** or **be brought to ~** zostać wydobytym na światło dzienne ▪ **II** *adj [room]* widny; **it was getting** or **growing ~er** robiło się coraz widniej or jaśniej; **while it's still ~** dopóki jest widno ▪ **III** *vt* ① zapal|lić, -áć *[candle, cigarette, gas]*; podpal|lić, -áć *[wood, paper]*; **to ~ a fire** rozpalić ognisko ② (illuminate) oświetl|lić, -áć *[room, scene]* ▪ **IV** *vi [candle, gas]* zapal|lić, -áć się

■ **light up:** *[lamp]* zapal|lić, -áć się; *[face]* roz-jaśn|lić, -áć się; *[eyes]* rozbłysnąć

light[2] /laɪt/ *adj* ① *[colour, fabric, wood, hair]* jasny; **~ green** jasnozielony ② *[fabric, clothing, meal, wind, sleep]* lekki; *[rain]* drobny; **to be a ~ drinker** mało pić; **to be ~ sleeper** mieć lekki sen ③ *[knock, footsteps]* lekki; *[kiss]* delikatny ④ *[work]* lekki; **~ housework** lżejsze prace domowe ⑤ *[music]* lekki; **same ~ reading** coś lekkiego do czytania

light bulb *n* żarówka *f*

lighten /'laɪtn/ **[]** *vt* rozjaśn|lić, -áć *[sky, colour, hair]* ▪ **II** *vi [sky, colour, hair]* pojaśnieć

light entertainment *n* lekka rozrywka *f*

lighter /'laɪtə(r)/ *n* (for cigarettes) zapalniczka *f*; (for gas) zapalarka *f*

lighter fuel *n* (gas) gaz *m* do zapalniczki; (liquid) benzyna *f* do zapalniczki

light-hearted /ˌlaɪt'hɑːtɪd/ *adj [person]* radosny; *[approach]* niefrasobliwy; *[account]* żartobliwy

lighthouse /'laɪthaʊs/ *n* latarnia *f* morska

lighting /'laɪtɪŋ/ *n* oświetlenie *n*

lightly /'laɪtlɪ/ *adv [touch, dress, season]* lekko; *[accuse]* pochopnie; *[say]* beztrosko; **to get off ~** wykręcić się sianem

lightning /'laɪtnɪŋ/ **[]** *n* ① (in sky) błyskawice *f pl*; **a flash of ~** błyskawica ② (striking sth) pioruny *m pl*; **he was struck by ~** trafił go piorun ▪ **II** *adj [raid]* błyskawiczny; *[visit]* krótki

light switch *n* włącznik *m* or wyłącznik *m* światła

lightweight /'laɪtweɪt/ *adj [garment]* lekki; **~ champion** mistrz wagi lekkiej

light year *n* rok *m* świetlny

like[1] /laɪk/ **[]** *prep* ① (taki) jak (ktoś/coś); **what's she ~?** jaka (ona) jest?; **what does he look ~?** jak on wygląda?; **what was Spain ~?** jak było w Hiszpanii?; **she's very ~ her mother** jest bardzo podobna do matki; **you know what she's ~!** wiesz, jaka ona jest!; **it looks ~ rain** wygląda na to, że będzie padać ② (typical of) **that's not ~ her** to do niej niepodobne; **it's just ~ him to be so spiteful!** zawsze jest taki złośliwy! ▪ **II** *conj* ① (in the same way as) tak jak; **nobody can sing this song ~ he did** nikt nie potrafi zaśpiewać tej piosenki tak jak on ② infml (as if) (tak) jakby; **she acts ~ she knows everything** zachowuje się (tak) jakby wszystko wiedziała ▪ **III** *n* dukes, barons and the **~** książęta, baronowie i temu podobni (dostojnicy); **she won't even speak to the ~s of us** infml nawet nie zechce rozmawiać z takimi jak my

like[2] /laɪk/ *vt* ① (be fond of) lubić; **to ~ to do sth** or **doing sth** lubić coś robić; **I ~ beer best** najbardziej lubię piwo; **how do you ~ my new car?** jak ci się podoba mój nowy samochód?; **how do you ~ living in London?** jak ci się mieszka w Londynie?; **she doesn't ~ to be kept waiting** (now) nie podoba się jej, że musi czekać; (in general) nie lubi, kiedy każe się jej czekać ② (wish) chcieć; **I don't ~ to mention it, but...** niechętnie o tym wspominam, ale...; **I would ~ a ticket** chciałbym bilet; **would you ~ to come to dinner?** czy miałbyś ochotę przyjść na obiad?; **if you ~** jeśli chcesz; **you can do what you ~** możesz robić, co ci się podoba

likeable /'laɪkəbl/ *adj [person]* sympatyczny; *[novel, film]* przyjemny

likelihood /'laɪklɪhʊd/ *n* prawdopodobieństwo *n*; **in all ~** najprawdopodobniej

likely /'laɪklɪ/ *adj* ① *[explanation, cause]* prawdopodobny; **prices are ~ to rise** ceny prawdopodobnie pójdą w górę; **he is ~ to become president** ma duże szanse zostać prezydentem; **the man most ~ to win** prawdopodobny zwycięzca; **a ~ story!** iron akurat!, uważaj bo uwierzę! infml ② (promising) *[candidate]* obiecujący

like-minded /'laɪkmaɪndɪd/ *adj* (sharing similar opinions) podobnie myślący; (sharing similar interests) o podobnych upodobaniach

liken /'laɪkən/ *vt* **to ~ sb/sth to sb/sth** przy-równ|lać, -ywać kogoś/coś do kogoś/czegoś

likeness /'laɪknɪs/ *n* ① (resemblance) podobieństwo *n* (**to sb/sth** do kogoś/czegoś); **a family ~** rodzinne podobieństwo ② (portrait) **a good ~** wierna podobizna

likewise /'laɪkwaɪz/ *adv [act, think]* podobnie; **I'm leaving and I suggest you do** ~ wychodzę i proponuję, żebyś zrobił to samo

liking /'laɪkɪŋ/ *n* **to take a** ~ **to sb** polubić kogoś; **to be to sb's** ~ odpowiadać komuś

lilac /'laɪlək/ **∏** *n* bez *m*
∏ *adj [colour]* lila

lily /'lɪlɪ/ *n* lilia *f*

lily of the valley *n* konwalia *f*

limb /lɪm/ *n* 1 (of person, animal) kończyna *f* 2 (of tree) konar *m*

limber /'lɪmbə(r)/ *vi*
■ **limber up**: Sport rozgrz|ać, -ewać się

limbo /'lɪmbəʊ/ *n* 1 otchłań *f*; fig stan *m* zawieszenia 2 **the** ~ limbo *n inv (taniec pochodzący z Karaibów)*

lime /laɪm/ *n* 1 (calcium) wapno *n* 2 (citrus) lima *f*, limeta *f* 3 (linden) lipa *f*

lime green *adj* żółtozielony

lime juice *n* sok *m* z limy

limelight /'laɪmlaɪt/ *n* światła *n pl* rampy; **to be in the** ~ stanąć w blasku jupiterów; fig znajdować się w centrum zainteresowania

limestone /'laɪmstəʊn/ *n* wapień *m*

limit /'lɪmɪt/ **∏** *n* granica *f*; **within the city** ~ **s** w obrębie miasta; **within** ~ **s** do pewnego stopnia; **to push sb to the** ~ zmuszać kogoś do wielkiego wysiłku; **speed** ~ dopuszczalna prędkość
∏ *vt* ogranicz|yć, -ać

limitation /ˌlɪmɪ'teɪʃn/ **∏** *n* (restriction) ograniczenie *n* (**on sth** czegoś)
∏ **limitations** *npl* (shortcomings) niedoskonałość *f*; **to know one's (own)** ~ **s** znać własne możliwości

limited /'lɪmɪtɪd/ *adj* ograniczony

limited company *n* GB spółka *f* z ograniczoną odpowiedzialnością

limousine /'lɪməzi:n, ˌlɪmə'zi:n/ *n* limuzyna *f*

limp /lɪmp/ **∏** *n* **to have a** ~ kuleć
∏ *adj* wiotki, zwiotczały
∏ *vi* utykać; **she** ~ **ed along the path** szła ścieżką, utykając

linchpin /'lɪntʃpɪn/ *n* (person) filar *m* fig; (idea, principle) podstawa *f*

line /laɪn/ **∏** *n* 1 (mark) linia *f*; (shorter) kreska *f*; (on pitch, court) linia *f*; (in art) kreska *f*; **a straight** ~ linia prosta 2 (of people, objects) rząd *m*; (shoulder to shoulder) szereg *m*; **to stand/wait in** ~ stać/czekać w kolejce 3 (on skin) zmarszczka *f*; (deep) bruzda *f* 4 (rope) lina *f*; (for fishing) żyłka *f*; **to put the washing on the** ~ powiesić pranie na sznurze 5 (cable) linia *f* (elektryczna) 6 (telephone) linia *f*, połączenie *n*; **all the** ~ **s were engaged** wszystkie linie były zajęte; **the** ~ **went dead** przerwało połączenie 7 (railway route) trasa *f*; (track) tory *m pl*; (in shipping, air transport) linia *f* 8 (in genealogy) linia *f* 9 (of prose) linijka *f*; (in poetry) wers *m*; **to learn one's** ~ **s**

nauczyć sie roli 10 **to bring sb into** ~ przywołać kogoś do porządku; **her statement is out of** ~ **with their account** jej oświadczenie nie zgadza się z ich relacją; **to keep sb in** ~ trzymać kogoś w karbach 11 (stance) stanowisko *n* (on sth w sprawie czegoś); **the party** ~ linia or kurs partii; **to take a firm** ~ **with sb** zająć wobec kogoś twarde stanowisko 12 (type of trade) branża *f*; **what** ~ **(of business) is she in?** w jakiej branży pracuje? 13 (type of product) wzór *m* 14 Mil **enemy** ~ **s** linie or pozycje nieprzyjaciela
∏ **in line with** *prep phr* (in agreement with) w zgodzie z (czymś); **to be in** ~ **with sth** być zgodnym z czymś *[expectations, recommendation]*; **to increase in** ~ **with sth** wzrastać proporcjonalnie do czegoś
∏ *vt* podszy|ć, -wać *[garment]* (**with sth** czymś); wy|łożyć, -kładać *[shelf]* (**with sth** czymś); stać wzdłuż (czegoś) *[route]*
■ **line up**: ¶ ~ **up** (side by side) ustawi|ć, -ać się w szeregu; (one behind the other) ustawi|ć, -ać się jeden za drugim ¶ ~ **[sth] up** 1 (align) ustawi|ć, -ać równo (**with sth** z czymś) 2 (put together) z|montować infml *[team]*

lined /laɪnd/ *adj [face]* (permanently) pomarszczony; (temporarily) zmarszczony; *[paper]* w linie; *[curtains]* na podszewce

line manager *n* dyrektor *m* odpowiedzialny

linen /'lɪnɪn/ *n* 1 (fabric) płótno *n* (lniane) 2 (for bed) bielizna *f* pościelowa; (underwear) bielizna *f* osobista

linen basket *n* kosz *m* na brudną bieliznę

linen cupboard GB, **linen closet** US *n* bieliźniarka *f*

line of fire *n* linia *f* ognia

line of work *n* rzemiosło *n*

liner /'laɪnə(r)/ *n* liniowiec *m*

linesman /'laɪnzmən/ *n* GB sędzia *m* liniowy

line-up /'laɪnʌp/ *n* (of sports team, pop group) skład *m*; (for concert) lista *f* wykonawców; (of theatre show) obsada *f*

linger /'lɪŋgə(r)/ *vi* 1 *[person]* (delay leaving) zosta|ć, -wać (dłużej); (tarry) zwlekać (z odejściem) 2 *[smell, doubt]* pozosta|ć, -wać; *[sensation]* utrzym|ać, -ywać się; *[memory]* trwać

lingerie /'lænʒəri:, US ˌlɑ:ndʒə'reɪ/ *n* bielizna *f* damska

linguist /'lɪŋgwɪst/ *n* językoznawca *m*

linguistic /lɪŋ'gwɪstɪk/ *adj [difference]* językowy; *[analysis]* lingwistyczny

linguistics /lɪŋ'gwɪstɪks/ *n* językoznawstwo *n*

lining /'laɪnɪŋ/ *n* (of clothing) podszewka *f*; (for warmth) podbicie *n*; (detachable) podpinka *f*

link /lɪŋk/ **∏** *n* 1 (of chain) ogniwo *n* 2 **rail/air** ~ połączenie kolejowe/lotnicze 3 (between facts, events) związek *m* (**between sth and sth** pomiędzy czymś a czymś); (between people) powiązanie *n* (**with**

sb/sth z kimś/czymś 4 (trading, political) stosunki *m pl* (**with sb** z kimś); (financial) powiązania *f pl*; (cultural, historical) związki *m pl* (**with sth** z czymś) 5 Techn połączenie *n*, łączność *f*

II *vt* 1 (join) po|łączyć *[places, objects, computers]*; (by radio, TV) s|tworzyć połączenie pomiędzy (czymś) *[places]*; **to ~ arms with sb** wziąć kogoś pod rękę; **to ~ A to B, to ~ A and B** połączyć A z B 2 (relate) **to ~ sth to** or **with sth** po|wiązać or łączyć coś z czymś; (establish connection between) ustalić związek z czymś

III linked *pp adj [rings, circles]* połączony; *[issues, problems]* powiązany (ze sobą)

■ **link up**: *[firms, colleges]* połączyć się (**with sb/ sth** z kimś/czymś)

link road *n* droga *f* łącząca

link-up /'lɪŋkʌp/ *n* 1 (on radio, TV) połączenie *n* 2 (relationship) powiązania *n pl*; (partnership) fuzja *f*

lino /'laɪnəʊ/ *n* linoleum *n*

lint /lɪnt/ *n* szarpie *plt*

lion /'laɪən/ *n* lew *m*

lion cub *n* lwię *n*

lioness /'laɪənes/ *n* lwica *f*

lip /lɪp/ *n* 1 (of person) warga *f* 2 (of jug) dziobek *m*

liposuction /'laɪpəʊsʌkʃn, 'lɪpəʊ-/ *n* odsysanie *n* tłuszczu

lip-read /'lɪpriːd/ *vi* czytać z ruchu warg

lipsalve /'lɪpsælv/ *n* maść *f* do warg

lip service *n* **to pay ~ to sth** składać gołosłowne deklaracje poparcia czegoś

lipstick /'lɪpstɪk/ *n* szminka *f*

liqueur /lɪ'kjʊə(r), US -'kɜːr/ *n* likier *m*

liquid /'lɪkwɪd/ **I** *n* płyn *m*

II *adj [ammonia]* ciekły; *[wax]* płynny

liquidate /'lɪkwɪdeɪt/ *vt* z|likwidować *[company]*

liquidation /ˌlɪkwɪ'deɪʃn/ *n* likwidacja *f*

liquidizer /'lɪkwɪdaɪzə(r)/ *n* GB Culin mikser *m*

liquor /'lɪkə(r)/ *n* alkohol *m* wysokoprocentowy

liquorice, licorice US /'lɪkərɪs/ *n* (plant, substance) lukrecja *f*

liquor store *n* US sklep *m* monopolowy

Lisbon /'lɪzbən/ *prn* Lizbona *f*

lisp /lɪsp/ *n* seplenienie *n*; **to have a ~** seplenić

list[1] /lɪst/ **I** *n* (of names) lista *f*; (of figures) zestawienie *n*

II *vt* 1 spis|ać, -ywać *[names, items]*; (enter) wpis|ać, -ywać na listę; **to be ~ed in a telephone directory** figurować w książce telefonicznej 2 Comput umie|ścić, -szczać w spisie 3 (on Stock Exchange) notować (na giełdzie)

III listed *pp adj* **a ~ed building** zabytek *m*, obiekt *m* pod ochroną

list[2] /lɪst/ *vi [ship]* mieć przechył, przechyl|ić, -ać się

listen /'lɪsn/ *vi* słuchać; **to ~ to sb/sth** słuchać kogoś/czegoś; **to ~ to reason** posłuchać głosu rozsądku; **to ~ for sth** nasłuchiwać czegoś

■ **listen in**: podsłuchiwać (**on sth** coś)

listener /'lɪsnə(r)/ *n* słuchacz *m*, -ka *f*; **to be a good ~** umieć słuchać

listeria /lɪ'stɪərɪə/ *n* (bacteria) listerie *f pl*; (illness) listerioza *f*

listing /'lɪstɪŋ/ **I** *n* 1 pozycja *f* (**in sth** w czymś); **Stock Exchange ~** lista firm dopuszczonych do obrotu giełdowego 2 Comput listing *m*

II listings *npl* strony *f pl* informacyjne *(programy radiowe i telewizyjne, repertuar kin i teatrów)*

listless /'lɪstlɪs/ *adj [person]* apatyczny

list price *n* cena *f* katalogowa

literacy /'lɪtərəsɪ/ *n* umiejętność *f* czytania i pisania; **computer ~** umiejętność obsługi komputera

literal /'lɪtərəl/ *adj [translation, meaning]* dosłowny

literally /'lɪtərəlɪ/ *adv [translate]* słowo w słowo; *[mean]* dosłownie; **to take sth ~** brać coś dosłownie; **he was quite ~ starving** dosłownie głodował

literary /'lɪtərərɪ, US 'lɪtərerɪ/ *adj* literacki

literary criticism *n* krytyka *f* literacka

literate /'lɪtərət/ *adj* 1 (able to read and write) piśmienny; **to be ~** umieć czytać i pisać 2 (cultured) *[person]* (well educated) wykształcony; (well read) oczytany

literature /'lɪtrətʃə(r), US -tʃʊər/ *n* 1 literatura *f*; **a work of ~** dzieło literackie 2 (pamphlets) materiały *m pl* informacyjne

lithe /laɪð/ *adj* gietki

Lithuania /ˌlɪθjuː'eɪnɪə/ *prn* Litwa *f*; **in ~** na Litwie

litigation /ˌlɪtɪ'geɪʃn/ *n* spór *m* sądowy

litre, liter US /'liːtə(r)/ *n* litr *m*

litter /'lɪtə(r)/ **I** *n* 1 (rubbish) śmieci(e) *m pl*; **to drop ~** śmiecić 2 (of young) miot *m*; **to have a ~** urodzić młode 3 (for cat) ściółka *f*

II *vt [leaves]* za|słać, -ścielać *[ground]*

litter bin *n* pojemnik *m* na śmieci

little /'lɪtl/ **I** *adj* (small) mały; (not much) mało; **~ chance** mała szansa; **~ damage was done** szkody były niewielkie; **there's so ~ time** zostało tak mało czasu

II *pron* 1 (not much) mało; **she remembers very ~** niewiele pamięta; **~ of what he says is true** w tym, co mówi, jest mało prawdy; **there's ~ I can do** niewiele mogę zrobić; **~ or nothing** prawie nic 2 (some) **a ~** trochę; **save a ~ for me** zostaw mi trochę

III *adv* 1 (not much) mało; **he goes out very ~** rzadko gdzieś wychodzi; **his music is ~ known in Austria** jego muzyka jest mało znana w Austrii; **~ more than an hour ago** niewiele ponad godzinę temu 2 (not at all) wcale nie; **~ did she realize that...** zupełnie sobie nie zdawała sprawy z tego, że...

IV **a little (bit)** *adv phr* trochę; **a ~ (bit) anxious** trochę zdenerwowany; **a ~ less/more**

trochę mniej/więcej; **this will hurt a** ~ to będzie trochę bolało

V **as little as** *adv phr* **as** ~ **as possible** jak najmniej; **for as** ~ **as 10 dollars a day** za jedyne 10 dolarów dziennie

(IDIOMS:) ~ **by** ~ stopniowo, po trochu

little finger *n* mały palec *m* (u ręki)

(IDIOMS:) **to wrap** or **twist sb around one's** ~ owinąć sobie kogoś wokół (małego) palca

live[1] /lɪv/ *vi* [1] (dwell) *[person]* mieszkać; *[animal]* żyć; **he** ~**s at number 7** on mieszka pod siódemką; **the house isn't fit to** ~ **in** dom nie nadaje się do zamieszkania; **he's not very easy to** ~ **with** niełatwo jest z nim mieszkać pod jednym dachem [2] (be alive) żyć; (remain alive) dożyć, -wać; (survive) przeżyć, -wać; **to** ~ **to be a hundred** dożyć stu lat; **you'll** ~ **to regret it** jeszcze kiedyś tego pożałujesz; **long** ~ **democracy!** niech żyje demokracja!; **to** ~ **on** or **off sth** żyć z czegoś *[salary]*; żywić się czymś *[fruit]* [3] (put up with) **to** ~ **with sth** żyć z czymś *[disease]*; (po)godzić się z czymś *[situation]*; znosić coś *[noise]*

■ **live in:** *[servant]* mieszkać na miejscu

■ **live on:** *[tradition, memory]* być nadal żywym

■ **live up to:** *[person]* pozostać, -wać wiernym (czemuś) *[ideals]*; spełnić, -ać *[expectations]*

(IDIOMS:) **to** ~ **it up** infml cieszyć się życiem, używać życia

live[2] /laɪv/ **I** *adj* [1] (not dead) żywy [2] *[performance]* na żywo; *[broadcast]* bezpośredni; *[album]* koncertowy; **recorded before a** ~ **audience** nagrywany na żywo z udziałem publiczności [3] *[wire]* pod napięciem

II *adv [perform, appear]* na żywo; *[broadcast]* bezpośrednio

live-in /'lɪvɪn/ *adj [servant, nanny]* stały; **she has a** ~ **boyfriend** mieszka z przyjacielem

livelihood /'laɪvlɪhʊd/ *n* środki *plt* do życia

lively /'laɪvlɪ/ *adj [person]* żwawy; *[dance]* żywy; *[conversation]* ożywiony; *[pace]* dziarski; *[party]* wesoły

liven /'laɪvn/ *vt*

■ **liven up:** ¶ ~ **up** ożywić, -ać się ¶ ~ **[sth] up** ożywić, -ać *[place, atmosphere]*

liver /'lɪvə(r)/ *n* Anat wątroba *f*; Culin wątróbka *f*

livery /'lɪvərɪ/ *n* [1] (uniform) liberia *f* [2] (for horses) stajnie *f pl (wynajmowane właścicielom koni, prowadzące szkółkę jeździecką)*

livestock /'laɪvstɒk/ *n* inwentarz *m* żywy

live wire *n* **to be a real** ~ fig być jak żywe srebro

livid /'lɪvɪd/ *adj* [1] (blue) *[flesh, scar]* siny [2] (furious) wściekły

living /'lɪvɪŋ/ **I** *n* [1] (keep) **to work for a** ~ utrzymywać się z pracy; **what do you do for a** ~? czym się zajmujesz? [2] (lifestyle) życie *n*; **clean** ~ cnotliwe życie

II *adj* żywy; **within** ~ **memory** za ludzkiej pamięci

living conditions *npl* warunki *m pl* życia

living expenses *npl* koszty *m pl* utrzymania

living room *n* pokój *m* dzienny

living standards *npl* stopa *f* życiowa

living will *n* testament *m* życia

lizard /'lɪzəd/ *n* jaszczurka *f*

llama /'lɑːmə/ *n* lama *f*

load /ləʊd/ **I** *n* [1] (sth carried) (by vehicle) ładunek *m*; (by person, animal) ciężar *m*; **a bus-**~ **of children** autobus pełen dzieci; **it's a** ~ **off my mind** kamień spadł mi z serca [2] (weight) (of structure) obciążenie *n*; (of vehicle) udźwig *m*; (of bridge) nośność *f* [3] (shipment) ładunek *m*; (batch) porcja *f* [4] infml (a lot) **a whole** ~ **of people** (cała) masa ludzi; **a** ~ **of rubbish** stek bzdur

II **loads** *npl* infml **to have** ~**s of work** mieć kupę roboty infml; **I've done this** ~**s of times** robiłem to mnóstwo razy

III *vt* [1] załadow|ać, -ywać *[vehicle]* (**with sth** czymś); obładow|ać, -ywać *[person]* (**with sth** czymś); za|ładować *[gun]*; **to** ~ **a program (into a computer)** zainstalować program (w komputerze) [2] **to** ~ **sb with sth** obsypywać kogoś czymś *[presents, honours]*

loaded /'ləʊdɪd/ *adj* [1] *[animal, person]* obładowany; *[gun]* naładowany [2] *[question]* tendencyjny [3] infml (rich) nadziany infml

loaf /ləʊf/ *n* bochenek *m*; **a** ~ **of bread** bochenek chleba

■ **loaf about, loaf around:** wałkonić się infml

loafer /'ləʊfə(r)/ *n* [1] (idler) próżniak *m* [2] (shoe) mokasyn *m*

loan /ləʊn/ **I** *n* pożyczka *f*; **the book is already out on** ~ książka jest już wypożyczona

II *vt* (also ~ **out**) **to** ~ **sb sth, to** ~ **sth to sb** pożyczyć or wypożyczyć komuś coś

loan shark *n* infml lichwia|rz *m*, -rka *f*

loath /ləʊθ/ *adj* **to be** ~ **to do sth** wcale nie mieć ochoty czegoś zrobić

loathe /ləʊð/ *vt* nie cierpieć (**doing sth** robienia czegoś)

loathsome /'ləʊðsəm/ *adj* wstrętny

lobby /'lɒbɪ/ **I** *n* [1] (of hotel) hol *m*; (of theatre) foyer *n inv* [2] (also ~ **group**) lobby *n inv*

II *vi* przeprowadz|ić, -ać kampanię (**for sth** na rzecz czegoś)

lobbying /'lɒbɪɪŋ/ *n* lobbying *m*

lobe /ləʊb/ *n* Anat, Bot płat *m*

lobster /'lɒbstə(r)/ *n* homar *m*

local /'ləʊkl/ **I** *n* [1] **the** ~**s** miejscowi [2] (pub) pobliski pub *m*

II *adj [library, shop]* pobliski; *[newspaper]* lokalny; *[telephone call]* miejscowy; *[radio]* regionalny

local anaesthetic *n* znieczulenie *n* miejscowe

local authority *n* GB władze *f pl* lokalne

local election n wybory plt lokalne or do władz lokalnych

local government n samorząd m lokalny

locality /ləʊˈkælətɪ/ n ① (area) okolica f ② (place) miejscowość f

locate /ləʊˈkeɪt, US ˈləʊkeɪt/ vt ① (find) z|lokalizować [object] ② (position) u|lokować [office]; u|sytuować [building]

location /ləʊˈkeɪʃn/ n (exact site) lokalizacja f; (position) położenie n; **on** ~ [filmed] w plenerach

lock /lɒk/ ❶ n ① (with key) zamek m; (with bolt) zasuw(k)a f; **under** ~ **and key** pod kluczem ② (on canal) śluza f ③ (of hair) kosmyk m, lok m ④ Comput blokada f
❷ vt zam|knąć, -ykać na klucz
❸ vi ① [door, drawer] zam|knąć, -ykać się na klucz ② [steering wheel] za|blokować się
■ **lock in**: zam|knąć, -ykać [person]; **to** ~ **oneself in** zatrzasnąć się
■ **lock out**: **to** ~ **sb out** nie wpuścić kogoś do środka; **I've** ~ **ed myself out of my car** zatrzasnąłem kluczyki w samochodzie
■ **lock together**: [components, pieces] po|łączyć się ze sobą
■ **lock up**: ¶ ~ [sth] **up** zam|knąć, -ykać (na klucz) [house] ¶ ~ [sb] **up** u|więzić [hostage]; zam|knąć, -ykać [killer]

locker /ˈlɒkə(r)/ n szafka f; (at bus, station) schowek m na bagaż

locker room n szatnia f (przy sali gimnastycznej, basenie)

locket /ˈlɒkɪt/ n medalion m

locksmith /ˈlɒksmɪθ/ n ślusarz m

locomotive /ˌləʊkəˈməʊtɪv/ n lokomotywa f

locum /ˈləʊkəm/ n GB zastęp|ca m, -czyni f

lodge /lɒdʒ/ ❶ n (for summer) domek m letniskowy; (for gatekeeper) stróżówka f
❷ vt ① (put up) da|ć, -wać (komuś) zakwaterowanie; (for night) prze|nocować ② (present) w|nieść, -nosić [appeal]; złożyć, składać [complaint, protest]
❸ vi ① (reside) mieszkać (**with sb** u kogoś) ② [bullet] utkwić (**in sth** w czymś)

lodger /ˈlɒdʒə(r)/ n lokator m, -ka f; **to take (in)** ~ **s** wynajmować pokoje

lodgings /ˈlɒdʒɪŋz/ npl wynajmowany pokój m

loft /lɒft, US lɔːft/ n ① (for storage) strych m; (for living) poddasze n ② US (apartment) mieszkanie n w dawnych zaadaptowanych składach

loft conversion n adaptacja f strychu

log /lɒg, US lɔːg/ ❶ n ① (of wood) kłoda f; (for burning) polano n ② (of plane, ship) dziennik m pokładowy
❷ vt ① (record) za|notować ② (also ~ **up**) [car] przejechać [miles]
■ **log in, log on**: Comput za|logować się
■ **log off, log out**: Comput wylogow|ać, -ywać się
IDIOMS **to sleep like a** ~ spać jak kamień

log book n (of car) karta f drogowa; (written record) rejestr m

log cabin n chata f z bali

log fire n płonące polana n pl

loggerheads /ˈlɒgəhedz/ npl **to be at** ~ (**with sb**) drzeć koty (z kimś)

logic /ˈlɒdʒɪk/ n logika f

logical /ˈlɒdʒɪkl/ adj logiczny

logistics /ləˈdʒɪstɪks/ n logistyka f

logo /ˈləʊgəʊ/ n logo n inv

loin /lɔɪn/ n (of veal) górka f; (of lamb) comber m; (of pork) schab m

loiter /ˈlɔɪtə(r)/ vi (pleasurably) wałęsać się; (indolently) marudzić; (idly) pętać się

loll /lɒl/ vi [person] obijać się; [head] zwis|nąć, -ać; **the dog's tongue** ~ **ed out** pies wywiesił język

lollipop /ˈlɒlɪpɒp/ n (candy) lizak m

London /ˈlʌndən/ prn Londyn m

Londoner /ˈlʌndənə(r)/ n londy|ńczyk m, -nka f

lone /ləʊn/ adj [competitor] jedyny; [voice] pojedynczy

loneliness /ˈləʊnlɪnɪs/ n (of person) samotność f; (of place) ustronność f

lonely /ˈləʊnlɪ/ adj [person, life] samotny; [place] odludny

lonely hearts' column n kącik m samotnych serc

loner /ˈləʊnə(r)/ n samotni|k m, -ca f

lonesome /ˈləʊnsəm/ adj US [person] samotny

long[1] /lɒŋ, US lɔːŋ/ ❶ adj długi; [delay] duży; [grass] wysoki; **his speech was 20 minutes** ~ jego przemówienie trwało 20 minut; **the rope is 40 metres** ~ ten sznur ma 40 metrów (długości); **to get** ~ **er** [days, intervals] stawać się coraz dłuższym; **she's been away a** ~ **time** wyjechała na długo; **it's been a** ~ **time since I last saw you** dawno cię nie widziałem; **to take a** ~ **time** [task] zająć wiele czasu; [event] trwać długo; **it's a** ~ **way (from here)** to daleko (stąd); **we could hear the shooting a** ~ **way off** z daleka or z oddali słychać było strzały; **we've come a** ~ **way to be here tonight** przebyliśmy długą drogę, żeby się tu dziś spotkać; **to go a** ~ **way** [person] daleko zajść; [provisions] na długo wystarczać; **a little kindness goes a** ~ **way** uprzejmością można wiele zdziałać
❷ adv ① (a long time) długo; **I won't be** ~ (doing sth) to nie potrwa długo; (departing) niedługo wrócę; **how** ~ **will you be on the phone?** jak długo będziesz rozmawiać przez telefon?; **don't be** ~ pośpiesz się; **I haven't got** ~ nie mam wiele czasu; **before** ~ wkrótce, niebawem; **not for** ~ nie na długo; ~ **after** znacznie później; **it's** ~ **after your bedtime** już dawno powinieneś być w łóżku; **not** ~ **after** niedługo potem; ~ **ago** dawno temu; ~ **before** dużo wcześniej; ~ **before we were married** na długo przed naszym

ślubem; **he is no ~er head** nie jest już szefem; **I can't stand it any ~er** nie mogę dłużej tego znieść [2] (for a long time) od dawna; **those days are ~ gone** te czasy dawno minęły [3] (throughout) **all night ~** przez całą noc
III **as long as** *conj phr* (provided that) jeśli tylko; **as ~ as you're back by 12** pod warunkiem, że wrócisz przed 12
(IDIOMS) **~ time no see!** infml kopę lat! infml; **so ~!** infml do zobaczenia!

long² /lɒŋ, US lɔːŋ/ *vi* **to ~ for sb/sth** tęsknić za kimś/czymś or do kogoś/czegoś; (want) gorąco pragnąć kogoś/czegoś; **to ~ to do sth** marzyć o zrobieniu czegoś

long-awaited /ˌlɒŋə'weɪtəd, US ˌlɔːŋ-/ *adj* długo oczekiwany

long-distance /ˌlɒŋ'dɪstəns, US ˌlɔːŋ-/ *adj [bus]* dalekobieżny; *[telephone call]* (within the country) zamiejscowy; (abroad) międzynarodowy; **~ lorry driver** GB kierowca tira; **~ runner** długodystansowiec

long-haired /ˌlɒŋ'heəd, US ˌlɔːŋ-/ *adj* długowłosy

longhand /'lɒŋhænd, US 'lɔːŋ-/ *n* written in **~** napisany odręcznie

long-haul /'lɒŋhɔːl, US 'lɔːŋ-/ *adj [plane]* dalekiego zasięgu

longing /'lɒŋɪŋ, US 'lɔːŋɪŋ/ *n* (nostalgia) tęsknota *f* (**for sb/sth** za kimś/czymś); (desire) ochota *f* (**for sth** na coś); (stronger) pragnienie *n* (**for sth** czegoś)

longitude /'lɒndʒɪtjuːd, US -tuːd/ *n* długość *f* geograficzna

long jump *n* GB skok *m* w dal

long-life /ˌlɒŋ'laɪf, US ˌlɔːŋ-/ *adj* o przedłużonej trwałości

long-range /ˌlɒŋ'reɪndʒ, US ˌlɔːŋ-/ *adj [missile]* dalekiego zasięgu; *[forecast]* długofalowy

long-sighted /ˌlɒŋ'saɪtɪd, US ˌlɔːŋ-/ *adj* dalekowzroczny also fig; **he's ~ on** jest dalekowidzem

long-standing /ˌlɒŋ'stændɪŋ, US ˌlɔːŋ-/ *adj* długoletni

long term **[I]** *n* **in the ~** na dłuższą metę
[II] **long-term** *adj [loan]* długoterminowy

long-time /ˌlɒŋ'taɪm, US ˌlɔːŋ-/ *adj [friend]* stary; *[enemy]* odwieczny

long-wave /ˌlɒŋ'weɪv, US ˌlɔːŋ-/ *n* fale *f pl* długie

long-winded /ˌlɒŋ'wɪndɪd, US ˌlɔːŋ-/ *adj [speech]* rozwlekły; *[person]* nużąco gadatliwy

loo /luː/ *n* GB infml ubikacja *f*

look /lʊk/ **[I]** *n* [1] (glance) spojrzenie *n*; **to have** or **take a ~ (at sb/sth)** (briefly) spojrzeć (na kogoś/coś); (closely) przyjrzeć się (komuś/czemuś); **to have** or **take a good ~ at sb/sth** dobrze się przyjrzeć komuś/czemuś *[suspect]*; obejrzeć kogoś/coś *[car]*; **to have a ~ inside/behind sth** zajrzeć do (wnętrza) czegoś/za coś; **to have a ~ round** rozejrzeć się [2] (search) **to have a ~** poszukać (**for sb/sth** kogoś/czegoś [3] (expression) mina *f*; **a ~ of**

sadness wzrok pełen smutku; **from the ~ on his face...** sądząc po jego minie... [4] (appearance) wygląd *m*; **the house had a familiar ~ about it** dom wyglądał znajomo
[II] **looks** *npl* **~s aren't everything** uroda to nie wszystko; **he's loosing his ~s** już nie jest taki przystojny jak kiedyś
[III] *vt* [1] (gaze, stare) **to ~ sb in the eye** popatrzyć komuś w oczy [2] (appear) **to ~ one's age** wyglądać na swój wiek; **she's 40, but she doesn't ~ it** ma 40 lat, ale nie wygląda na tyle; **to ~ one's best** wyglądać korzystnie
[IV] *vi* [1] (gaze) po|patrzeć (**at sb/sth** na kogoś/coś); (more carefully) przy|jrzeć, -glądać się (**at sb/sth** komuś/czemuś); **to ~ away** patrzeć w drugą stronę; **to ~ out of the window** wyglądać przez okno [2] (search) po|szukać (**for sb/sth** kogoś/czegoś); **have you ~ed under the bed?** czy zajrzałeś pod łóżko? [3] (seem) wyglądać; **to ~ cold** wyglądać na zmarzniętego; **he ~s young for his age** wygląda młodo jak na swój wiek; **that dress makes you ~ younger** ta sukienka cię odmładza; **the picture will ~ good in the study** obraz będzie się dobrze prezentował w gabinecie; **things aren't ~ing too good** sprawy przedstawiają się niezbyt dobrze [4] **to ~ like sb/sth** wyglądać jak ktoś/coś; **what does he ~ like?** jak on wygląda?; **it ~s like rain** zanosi się na deszcz

■ **look after:** [1] (to take care of) zaj|ąć, -mować się (kimś/czymś) *[guests]*; doglądać (kogoś/czegoś) *[patient]*; za|dbać o (kogoś/coś) *[person]*; po|pilnować (kogoś/coś) *[child, possessions]*; **~ after my things for me** popilnuj moich rzeczy [2] (be responsible for) zaj|ąć, -mować się (czymś) *[financial matters, shop]*

■ **look around:** ¶ **~ around** [1] (glance) roz|ejrzeć, -glądać się [2] **to ~ around for sth/sb** roz|ejrzeć, -glądać się za czymś/kimś ¶ **~ around** [sth] roz|ejrzeć, -glądać się po (czymś) *[room]*; zwie|dzić, -dzać *[town]*

■ **look at:** [1] po|patrzeć na (kogoś/coś) [2] (examine) przy|jrzeć, -glądać się (czemuś) *[problem]*; o|bejrzeć, -glądać *[equipment, patient]* [3] (see, view) spojrzeć na *[life, situation]*

■ **look back:** [1] (turn around) o|bejrzeć, -glądać się (za siebie) [2] **to ~ back on sth** wracać myślami do czegoś *[past]*; zrobić bilans czegoś fig *[marriage]*; **~ing back on it, I think...** z perspektywy czasu, uważam, że...

■ **look down:** ¶ **~ down** (from height) spo|jrzeć, -glądać w dół ¶ **~ down on** [sb/sth] (despise) patrzyć z góry na (kogoś) fig *[person]*; gardzić (czymś) *[lifestyle]*

■ **look for:** po|szukać (kogoś/czegoś)

■ **look forward:** **~ forward to** [sth] cieszyć się na (coś) *[event]*; z niecierpliwością oczekiwać

(czegoś) *[letter, news]*; **I'm really** ∼**ing forward
to tomorrow** nie mogę się doczekać jutra
■ **look into:** rozpat|rzyć, -rywać *[complaint]*;
z|badać sprawę (czegoś) *[theft]*
■ **look on:** ¶ ∼ **on** (watch) przyglądać się ¶ ∼
on [sb/sth] (regard) po|patrzeć na (kogoś/coś);
they ∼ **on us as cheap labour** traktują nas jak
tanią siłę roboczą
■ **look out:** ¶ ∼ **out** (be careful) uważać (**for sb/
sth** na kogoś/coś); ∼ **out!** uważaj! ¶ ∼ **out for
[sb/sth]** roz|ejrzeć, -glądać się za (kimś/czymś)
[person, book]
■ **look round** = **look around**
■ **look through:** ¶ ∼ **through [sth]** [1] prze|j-
rzeć, -glądać *[notes, magazines]* [2] przeszuk|ać,
-iwać *[belongings]* ¶ ∼ **through [sb]** nie zauwa-
ż|yć, -ać; (pretend not to notice) po|traktować (kogoś)
jak powietrze
■ **look to:** [1] (rely on) liczyć na (kogoś/coś); **to** ∼
to sb for support liczyć na poparcie kogoś [2] (turn
to) zwr|ócić, -acać się do (kogoś/czegoś)
■ **look up:** ¶ ∼ **up** [1] (raise eyes) po|patrzyć
w górę; **he** ∼**ed up from his book** podniósł
wzrok znad książki [2] (improve) *[things]* wyglądać
(coraz) lepiej; **business is** ∼**ing up** interesy idą
coraz lepiej ¶ ∼ **[sb] up** odwiedz|ić, -ać *[friend]*
¶ ∼ **[sb/sth] up** sprawdz|ić, -ać *[word, name]*
¶ ∼ **up to [sb]** podziwiać (kogoś) (**for sth** za
coś)
look-alike /ˈlʊkəlaɪk/ n sobowtór m
look-in /ˈlʊkɪn/ n GB infml szansa f; **to give sb a** ∼
dać komuś szansę
look-out /ˈlʊkaʊt/ n [1] **to be on the** ∼ **for sb/sth**
poszukiwać kogoś/czegoś *[stolen vehicle]*; rozglądać
się za kimś/czymś *[bargain, new recruits]*; wyglądać
kogoś *[visitor]* [2] (military) punkt m obserwacyjny
loom /luːm/ **Ⅰ** n krosno n
Ⅱ [1] (also ∼ **up**) wyłon|ić, -aniać się (**out of sth** z
czegoś) [2] *[war, crisis]* wisieć w powietrzu fig; **to** ∼
over sb/sth *[threat, exam]* wisieć nad kimś/czymś
fig; **the issue will** ∼ **large at the conference** ta
sprawa zdominuje konferencję
loony /ˈluːnɪ/ n infml (eccentric) dziwa|k m, -czka f;
(crazy) pomyleniec m
loop /luːp/ **Ⅰ** n pętla f
Ⅱ vt z|robić pętlę or pętelkę na (czymś) *[string]*
Ⅲ vi *[road, path]* zakręcać
loophole /ˈluːphəʊl/ n furtka f fig
loose /luːs/ adj [1] *[blouse, knot]* luźny; *[screw]*
obluzowany; *[tooth]* ruszający się; *[thread]* nieumo-
cowany; **to hang** ∼ *[hair]* opadać; ∼ **connection**
obluzowany kabel [2] *[vegetables]* niepakowany; *[tea]*
na wagę; ∼ **change** drobne (pieniądze) [3] *[stones]*
pojedynczy; **these pages have come** ∼ te strony
wypadają [4] *[soil, earth]* sypki; *[weave]* luźny [5] (free)
to break ∼ *[animal]* (from chain) zerwać się z uwięzi;
(from cage) wydostać się na wolność; **to let sb** ∼

uwolnić kogoś [6] *[translation, wording]* luźny; *[term,
thinking]* nieprecyzyjny; *[discipline]* rozluźniony
[7] ∼ **morals** rozwiązłość
IDIOMS **to be at a** ∼ **end** GB, **to be at a** ∼ **ends**
US nie wiedzieć, co ze sobą począć
loosely /ˈluːslɪ/ adv [1] *[attach, tie]* luźno; **his
clothes hung** ∼ **on him** ubranie wisiało na nim
[2] *[connected]* słabo; ∼ **structured** o luźnej struk-
turze [3] *[interpret]* dowolnie; *[describe]* nieprecyzyj-
nie
loosely knit adj *[group, structure]* luźny
loosen /ˈluːsn/ vt poluźnić, -ać *[knot, collar]*;
popu|ścić, -szczać *[belt]*; obruszl|yć, -ać *[screw]*;
rozpu|ścić, -szczać *[hair]*; z|łagodzić *[laws]*; **to** ∼
one's grip or **hold on sth** wypuścić coś z rąk
■ **loosen up:** Sport rozgrz|ać, -ewać się; (relax)
rozluźni|ć, -ać się
loot /luːt/ **Ⅰ** n łup m
Ⅱ vt s|plądrować *[shop]*
looter /ˈluːtə(r)/ n szabrownik m
lopsided /ˌlɒpˈsaɪdɪd/ adj *[hat]* przekrzywiony;
[smile] krzywy; *[view]* jednostronny
lord /lɔːd/ n [1] (master) pan m [2] (peer) lord m; **the
(House of) Lords** Izba Lordów; **my Lord** (to noble)
milordzie
IDIOMS **to** ∼ **it over sb** infml traktować kogoś z
góry
Lord /lɔːd/ n [1] **the** ∼, **Our** ∼ (nasz) Pan m
[2] infml (in exclamations) **good** ∼! dobry Boże!
Lord Mayor n GB burmistrz m *(w największych
miastach brytyjskich)*
lordship /ˈlɔːdʃɪp/ n (also **Lordship**) **your/his** ∼
(to noble) wasza/jego lordowska mość; (to judge in court)
Wysoki Sądzie
lorry /ˈlɒrɪ, US ˈlɔːrɪ/ n GB ciężarówka f
lorry driver n GB kierowca m ciężarówki
lose /luːz/ **Ⅰ** vt [1] (not keep) z|gubić *[object]*; u|tracić
[right]; **to** ∼ **one's way** zabłądzić; **to** ∼ **interest
in sth** przestać się czymś interesować [2] (not win)
przegr|ać, -ywać *[war]* [3] (get rid of) pozbyć, -wać się
(kogoś/czegoś) *[unwanted object]*; z|gubić *[pursuer]*
Ⅱ vi [1] (not win) przegr|ać, -ywać (**to sb** z kimś)
[2] *[clock]* spóźniać się
■ **lose out:** dozna|ć, -wać niepowodzenia
loser /ˈluːzə(r)/ n (in game, contest) przegrywając|y
m, -a f
loss /lɒs, US lɔːs/ n (of possessions) strata f; (of faculties)
utrata f; **to be at a** ∼ (puzzled) być w rozterce;
(helpless) nie wiedzieć, co począć; **I was at a** ∼ **for
words** nie wiedziałem, co powiedzieć
lost /lɒst, US lɔːst/ adj [1] (missing, mislaid) *[person,
animal]* zaginiony; *[object]* zgubiony; **to get** ∼
zgubić or zagubić się; **get** ∼! infml spadaj! infml
[2] *[opportunity, time]* stracony; *[innocence]* utraco-
ny; *[civilization]* zaginiony; **good advice is** ∼ **on
her** ona nie słucha dobrych rad; **I'm** ∼ **for words**
słów mi brak; **to be** ∼ **in sth** być pochłoniętym

czymś *[book]*; pogrążyć się w czymś *[thought]*
3 *[election]* przegrany
lost and found *n* biuro *n* rzeczy znalezionych
lost property *n* GB = **lost and found**
lot¹ /lɒt/ **Ⅰ** *pron* 1 (great deal) **a** ~ dużo; **he knows
a** ~ **about sport** dużo wie o sporcie; **quite a** ~
dość dużo or wiele 2 infml **the** ~ wszystko
Ⅱ *quantif* **a** ~ **of money/energy** dużo or wiele
pieniędzy/energii; **I see a** ~ **of him** często go
widuję; **quite a** ~ **of support** spore poparcie
Ⅲ lots *quantif, pron* infml ~**s (and** ~**s) of sb/sth**
(całe) mnóstwo kogoś/czegoś; **there are** ~**s of
things to do** jest mnóstwo rzeczy do zrobienia
Ⅳ **a lot** *adv phr* dużo; **a** ~ **better/worse** dużo or
znacznie lepiej/gorzej; **this happens quite a** ~
to się zdarza dość często
lot² /lɒt/ *n* 1 (fate) los *m* 2 (piece of land) parcela *f*
3 (at auction) pozycja *f* 4 (in lottery) los *m*; **to draw**
~**s for sth** losować coś 5 (of merchandise) partia *f*
lotion /'ləʊʃn/ *n* płyn *m* (kosmetyczny)
lottery /'lɒtərɪ/ *n* loteria *f* also fig
loud /laʊd/ **Ⅰ** *adj* 1 *[noise, music]* głośny; *[person]*
hałaśliwy; *[scream]* ogłuszający 2 *[colour]* krzykliwy
fig; *[behaviour, person]* wyzywający
Ⅱ *adv [speak]* głośno; **to read sth out** ~
przeczytać coś na głos
loudly /'laʊdlɪ/ *adv [talk]* głośno; *[scream]* na cały
głos; *[play]* hałaśliwie
loudspeaker /ˌlaʊd'spiːkə(r)/ *n* głośnik *m*
lounge /laʊndʒ/ *n* 1 (in house) salon *m*; (in hotel)
hol *m*; (at airport, station) poczekalnia *f*; **departure** ~
sala odlotów 2 US (also **cocktail** ~) bar *m*
■ **lounge about, lounge around** oddawać się
lenistwu
lousy /'laʊzɪ/ *adj [film]* chałowy infml; *[meal]*
kiepski; *[weather]* podły; **a** ~ **trick** świństwo
lout /laʊt/ *n* (bad-mannered) cham *m* infml; (aggressive)
żul *m* infml
loutish /'laʊtɪʃ/ *adj [behaviour]* chamski; *[person]*
nieokrzesany
louvred GB, **louvered** US /'luːvəd/ *adj [door]*
żaluzjowy
lovable /'lʌvəbl/ *adj [child, puppy]* rozkoszny
love /lʌv/ **Ⅰ** *n* 1 (emotion) miłość *f*; **to be in** ~
with sb być zakochanym w kimś; **to fall in** ~
with sb zakochać się w kimś; **to make** ~ kochać
się (**with** or **to sb** z kimś) 2 *[idea]* **Sarah sends her** ~
Sara przesyła pozdrowienia; **with** ~ **from Adam,**
~ **Adam** (in letter) pozdrowienia, Adam 3 GB (term
of address) kochanie *n* 4 (in tennis) zero *n*
Ⅱ *vt* 1 kochać; **to** ~ **each other** kochać się
2 (like) lubić; (stronger) uwielbiać; **I** ~ **your dress**
bardzo mi się podoba ta sukienka; **to** ~ **doing** or
to do sth lubić or uwielbiać coś robić; **'can you
come?'** – **'yes, I'd** ~ **to'** „możesz przyjść?" – „z
przyjemnością"

IDIOMS: ~ **at first sight** miłość od pierwszego
wejrzenia
love affair *n* romans *m* (**with sb** z kimś)
love life *n* życie *n* intymne or erotyczne
lovely /'lʌvlɪ/ *adj* 1 (beautiful) *[woman]* śliczny;
[hair] piękny; *[garden]* uroczy; *[baby]* rozkoszny;
you look ~ wyglądasz ślicznie 2 (pleasant) *[person]*
uroczy; *[day]* śliczny; *[idea]* wspaniały; **it was** ~
to see you miło było cię widzieć
lover /'lʌvə(r)/ *n* 1 (partner) kochan|ek *m*, -ka *f*
2 (person in love) zakochan|y *m*, -a *f* 3 (enthusiast)
miłośni|k *m*, -czka *f*; **jazz** ~ miłośnik jazzu
loving /'lʌvɪŋ/ *adj [father]* kochający; *[family]*
kochający się; *[look]* pełen miłości
low /ləʊ/ **Ⅰ** *n* 1 (in weather) niż *m* 2 fig **to hit a new**
or **all-time** ~ *[prices, popularity]* spaść do rekordowo niskiego poziomu
Ⅱ *adj* 1 *[building]* niski; *[point]* nisko położony;
[sound] cichy; **in a** ~ **voice** cicho, cichym głosem
2 *[quality]* niski; *[speed, number]* niewielki; **these
products are** ~ **in calories** to są produkty są
niskokaloryczne; **we're getting** or **running** ~ **on
milk** kończy się nam mleko; **we're** ~ **on skilled
staff** mamy mało wykwalifikowanego personelu
3 **to feel** ~ (physically) źle się czuć; (emotionally)
mieć chandrę 4 *[behaviour]* podły
Ⅲ *adv* 1 *[aim, fly]* nisko 2 **it is very** ~ **(down)
on the list** fig to sprawa zupełnie drugorzędna
3 *[buy]* tanio; *[speak]* cicho; **to turn the radio
down** ~ ściszyć radio
Ⅳ *vi [cow]* zamuczeć, zaryczeć
low-alcohol /ˌləʊ'ælkəhɒl/ *adj* niskoalkoholowy
lowbrow /'ləʊbraʊ/ *adj [entertainment]* niewyszukany; *[literature, newspaper]* na niskim poziomie
low-budget /ˌləʊ'bʌdʒɪt/ *adj* niskobudżetowy
low-calorie /ˌləʊ'kælərɪ/ *adj* niskokaloryczny
low-cost /ˌləʊ'kɒst, US -'kɔːst/ *adj* tani
low-cut /ˌləʊ'kʌt/ *adj* wydekoltowany
low-down /'ləʊdaʊn/ *adj* infml *[person]* podły
lower /'ləʊə(r)/ **Ⅰ** *comp adj [price]* niższy; *[jaw]*
dolny
Ⅱ *vt* 1 (in height) spu|ścić, -szczać *[curtain]*;
opu|ścić, -szczać *[barrier, flag]*; obniż|yć, -ać
[ceiling]; **to** ~ **one's eyes** spuścić oczy 2 (reduce)
obniż|yć, -ać *[prices, standards]*; ścisz|yć, -ać *[sound
volume]*; przyga|snąć, -sać *[light]*; **to** ~ **one's
voice** zniżyć głos 3 (on ship) zrzuc|ić, -ać *[sail]*
Ⅲ *vr* **to** ~ **oneself** 1 fig poniż|yć, -ać się 2 **to** ~
oneself into a chair usiąść w fotelu
lower class *n* the ~(**es**) klasy *f pl* niższe
lower sixth *n* GB Sch *niższa z dwóch klas
przygotowujących uczniów do studiów*
low-fat /ˌləʊ'fæt/ *adj [diet]* niskotłuszczowy; *[milk]*
o obniżonej zawartości tłuszczu
low-income /ˌləʊ'ɪŋkʌm/ *adj [family]* o niskich
dochodach

low-key /ˌləʊˈkiː/ adj [approach] powściągliwy; [meeting] kameralny; [ceremony] skromny

low-level /ˌləʊˈlevl/ adj [bombing] z małej wysokości; [talks] na niższym szczeblu; [radiation] o niewielkim natężeniu

low-lying /ˌləʊˈlaɪɪŋ/ adj nisko położony

low-paid /ˌləʊˈpeɪd/ adj [job] źle płatny; [worker] nisko opłacany

low-priced /ˌləʊˈpraɪst/ adj tani

low-profile /ˌləʊˈprəʊfaɪl/ adj [operation] cichy; [approach] dyskretny

low-quality /ˌləʊˈkwɒləti/ adj niskiej jakości

low-risk /ˌləʊˈrɪsk/ adj o niewielkim stopniu ryzyka

low season n martwy sezon m

low-tech /ˌləʊˈtek/ adj wykorzystujący tradycyjne rozwiązania techniczne

low tide n odpływ m

loyal /ˈlɔɪəl/ adj [friend] lojalny (**to sb/sth** wobec kogoś/czegoś); [customer] wierny

loyalty /ˈlɔɪəlti/ n lojalność f (**to** or **towards sb/ sth** wobec kogoś/czegoś)

loyalty card n karta f stałego klienta

lozenge /ˈlɒzɪndʒ/ n pastylka f (do ssania)

LP n płyta f długogrająca

L-plate /ˈelpleɪt/ n GB Aut tablica f nauki jazdy

Ltd GB = **limited (liability)** z o.o. (z ograniczoną odpowiedzialnością)

lubricant /ˈluːbrɪkənt/ n (for machine) smar m; (for body) środek m nawilżający

lucid /ˈluːsɪd/ adj [1] (clear) przejrzysty [2] (sane) przytomny; ~ **moments** przebłyski świadomości

luck /lʌk/ n **good** ~ szczęście n; **bad** ~ pech m; **to bring (sb) good/bad** ~ przynosić (komuś) szczęście/pecha; **bad** or **hard** ~! co za pech!; **good** ~! powodzenia!; **to be in/out of** ~ mieć szczęście/nie mieć szczęścia

luckily /ˈlʌkɪli/ adv na szczęście; ~ **for him** szczęśliwie dla niego

lucky /ˈlʌki/ adj [1] (fortunate) **to be** ~ mieć szczęście [2] [charm, colour] szczęśliwy

lucrative /ˈluːkrətɪv/ adj [business] lukratywny; [job] intratny

ludicrous /ˈluːdɪkrəs/ adj [idea] niedorzeczny; [appearance] groteskowy

luggage /ˈlʌgɪdʒ/ n bagaż m

luggage rack n półka f bagażowa

lukewarm /ˌluːkˈwɔːm/ adj (not hot enough) letni; (not cold enough) ciepławy

lull /lʌl/ [I] n (in storm) chwila f ciszy; (in conversation) przerwa f; (in fighting) przejściowy spokój m
[II] vt u|śpić, -sypiać; **to** ~ **sb to sleep** ukołysać kogoś do snu; **to** ~ **sb into a false sense of security** uśpić czujność kogoś; **he** ~**ed them into thinking that they were safe** wmówił im, że są bezpieczni

lullaby /ˈlʌləbaɪ/ n kołysanka f

lumber /ˈlʌmbə(r)/ [I] n US tarcica f
[II] vt GB (burden) **to be** ~**ed with sth** [person] być or zostać czymś obarczonym [job, task]; **to be** ~**ed with sb** mieć kogoś na głowie
[III] vi US ciężko stąpać; [vehicle] toczyć się ciężko

lumberjack /ˈlʌmbədʒæk/ n drwal m

luminous /ˈluːmɪnəs/ adj świecący

lump /lʌmp/ [I] n [1] (of rock) bryła f; (of soil) gruda f; (in sauce) grudka f; (of meat) kawałek m; (of sugar) kostka f [2] (from knock) guz m (**on sth** na czymś); (tumour) guz m (**on** or **in sth** na czymś or czegoś)
[II] vt z|grupować (**with sb/sth** z kimś/czymś); **you can** ~ **all those items together under one heading** możesz dać to wszystko razem pod jednym nagłówkiem
IDIOMS: **a** ~ **in one's throat** ściśnięte gardło

lump sum n pełna kwota f (wypłacana jednorazowo); (decided in advance) ryczałt m

lunar /ˈluːnə(r)/ adj [landscape] księżycowy; ~ **eclipse** zaćmienie księżyca; ~ **landing** lądowanie na Księżycu

lunatic /ˈluːnətɪk/ n szaleniec m

lunch /lʌntʃ/ n lunch m; **to have** ~ zjeść lunch; **he took me out for** ~ zabrał mnie na lunch do restauracji

lunchbox /ˈlʌntʃbɒks/ n pojemnik m na kanapki

lunchbreak /ˈlʌntʃbreɪk/ n przerwa f obiadowa

lunch hour n przerwa f na lunch

lunchtime /ˈlʌntʃtaɪm/ n pora f lunchu

lung /lʌŋ/ n płuco n

lunge /lʌndʒ/ vi rzucić się (**at sb/sth** na kogoś/ coś); **to** ~ **forward** rzucić się do przodu

lurch /lɜːtʃ/ vi [person] iść zataczając się; [vehicle] przechyl|ić, -ać się; **to** ~ **forward** [car] szarpnąć do przodu
IDIOMS: **to leave sb in the** ~ zostawić kogoś na lodzie

lure /lʊə(r)/ [I] n [1] (attraction) powab m [2] (in hunting) wabik m; (in fishing) przynęta f
[II] vt z|wabić (**with sth** czymś); **to** ~ **sb into doing sth** nakłonić kogoś do zrobienia czegoś; **they** ~**d him out of his house** wywabili go z domu

lurid /ˈlʊərɪd/ adj [1] [details] drastyczny; [past] ciemny [2] [colour] krzykliwy

lurk /lɜːk/ vi [person, danger] czaić się; [suspicion] tlić się

luscious /ˈlʌʃəs/ adj [food] pyszny; [woman] ponętny

lush /lʌʃ/ adj [vegetation] bujny; [hotel] luksusowy; [carpet] puszysty

lust /lʌst/ [I] n (sexual) pożądanie n; (deadly sin) nieczystość f; **the** ~ **for power** żądza władzy
[II] vi **to** ~ **after** or **for sb/sth** pożądać kogoś/ czegoś

Luxembourg /ˈlʌksəmbɜːg/ prn Luksemburg m

luxurious /lʌgˈzjʊərɪəs/ *adj [apartment]* luksusowy; *[bath]* rozkoszny; **people with ~ tastes** ludzie gustujący w luksusach

luxury /ˈlʌkʃərɪ/ **▯** *n* luksus *m*
▯ *adj [hotel]* luksusowy; **~ items** przedmioty zbytku

lychee /ˈlaɪtʃiː, ˌlaɪˈtʃiː/ *n* śliwka *f* liczi

lying /ˈlaɪɪŋ/ *n* kłamstwo *n*

lynch /lɪntʃ/ *vt* z‖linczować

lynch mob *n* zgraja *f* dokonująca samosądu

lyrical /ˈlɪrɪkl/ *adj* liryczny; **to wax ~ about sb/ sth** rozpływać się nad kimś/czymś

lyrics /ˈlɪrɪks/ *npl* słowa *n pl*, tekst *m* (piosenki)

lyric-writer /ˈlɪrɪkraɪtə(r)/ *n* autor *m*, -ka *f* słów

M

m, M /em/ *n* m, M *n*

MA *n* = Master of Arts ≈ mgr

macaroni /ˌmækəˈrəʊnɪ/ *n* makaron *m* rurki

mace /meɪs/ *n* (spice) gałka *f* muszkatołowa

Macedonia /ˌmæsɪˈdəʊnɪə/ *prn* Macedonia *f*

machete /məˈʃetɪ, US məˈʃetɪ/ *n* maczeta *f*

machine /məˈʃiːn/ *n* maszyna *f*; **sewing** ~ maszyna do szycia

machine gun *n* karabin *m* maszynowy

machine-readable /məˌʃiːnˈriːdəbl/ *adj* [data] odczytywalny komputerowo; [passport] z identyfikatorem cyfrowym

machinery /məˈʃiːnərɪ/ *n* 1 (equipment) maszyny *f pl*; **a piece of** ~ urządzenie 2 (working parts) mechanizm *m* 3 fig aparat *m*

macho /ˈmætʃəʊ/ *adj* pej macho

mackerel /ˈmækrəl/ *n* makrela *f*

mackintosh, macintosh /ˈmækɪntɒʃ/ *n* płaszcz *m* przeciwdeszczowy

mad /mæd/ *adj* 1 [person] szalony; [bull] rozjuszony; [dog] rozwścieczony; **to go** ~ oszaleć, zwariować 2 [idea, scheme] szalony 3 infml (angry) wściekły infml; **to be** ~ **at** or **with sb** być wściekłym na kogoś; **to go** ~ wpaść w furię; **to drive sb** ~ doprowadzać kogoś do szału 4 infml (enthusiastic) **to be** ~ **about** or **on sb/sth** mieć bzika or fioła na punkcie kogoś/czegoś infml 5 (frantic) [panic] obłędny; **the audience went** ~ publiczność oszalała
(IDIOMS) **to run like** ~ pędzić jak szalony

madam /ˈmædəm/ *n* (as title) Pani *f*; (form of address) proszę pani; **Dear Madam** (in letter) Szanowna Pani

mad cow disease *n* choroba *f* szalonych krów

maddening /ˈmædnɪŋ/ *adj* nieznośny

made /meɪd/ 1 *adj* **to be** ~ być ustawionym infml 2 **-made** in combinations **foreign-**~ **goods** towary pochodzenia zagranicznego; **Italian-**~ produkcji włoskiej

made-to-measure /ˌmeɪdtəˈmeʒə(r)/ *adj* [garment] szyty na miarę

made-up /ˌmeɪdˈʌp/ *adj* 1 [face] umalowany 2 [story] zmyślony

madly /ˈmædlɪ/ *adv* ~ **in love** zakochany do szaleństwa

Madeira /məˈdɪərə/ *prn* Madera *f*

madman /ˈmædmən/ *n* infml wariat *m* also fig

madness /ˈmædnɪs/ *n* szaleństwo *n*

Madrid *prn* Madryt *m*

mafia, Mafia /ˈmæfɪə, US ˈmɑː-/ *n* **the Mafia** mafia *f*

magazine /ˌmægəˈziːn/ *n* 1 (newspaper) czasopismo *n*; **monthly** ~ miesięcznik 2 (on radio, TV) magazyn *m* 3 (of gun, camera) magazynek *m*

maggot /ˈmægət/ *n* robak *m*

magic /ˈmædʒɪk/ 1 *n* magia *f*; **to believe in** ~ wierzyć w czary 2 *adj* 1 magiczny 2 infml cudowny, fantastyczny

magical /ˈmædʒɪkl/ *adj* 1 (supernatural) [ritual, object] magiczny; [hat, potion] czarodziejski; ~ **carpet** latający dywan 2 (enchanting) cudowny

magician /məˈdʒɪʃn/ *n* (wizard) czarodziej *m*, -ka *f*; (entertainer) iluzjonist|a *m*, -ka *f*

magistrate /ˈmædʒɪstreɪt/ *n* sędzia *m* pokoju

magnate /ˈmægneɪt/ *n* magnat *m*; **oil** ~ potentat naftowy

magnesium /mægˈniːzɪəm/ *n* magnez *m*

magnet /ˈmægnɪt/ *n* magnes *m*

magnetic /mægˈnetɪk/ *adj* magnetyczny; fig zniewalający

magnificent /mægˈnɪfɪsnt/ *adj* wspaniały

magnify /ˈmægnɪfaɪ/ *vt* powiększ|yć, -ać; (exaggerate) wyolbrzymi|ć, -iać

magnitude /ˈmægnɪtjuːd, US -tuːd/ *n* (of problem) ranga *f*; (of epidemic) rozmiary *m pl*; (of explosion) siła *f*

magnolia /mægˈnəʊlɪə/ *n* magnolia *f*

magpie /ˈmægpaɪ/ *n* sroka *f*

mahogany /məˈhɒgənɪ/ *n* (wood, colour) mahoń *m*; (tree) mahoniowiec *m*

maid /meɪd/ *n* pokojówka *f*

maiden /ˈmeɪdn/ *adj* [voyage, flight] dziewiczy

maiden name *n* nazwisko *n* panieńskie

mail /meɪl/ 1 *n* 1 (postal service) poczta *f*; **by** ~ pocztą 2 (correspondence) poczta *f* 2 *vt* wysłać, -yłać [letter, parcel] (**to sb** do kogoś)

mailbox /ˈmeɪlbɒks/ *n* US (for posting) skrzynka *f* pocztowa; (for delivery) skrzynka *f* na listy; (for e-mail) skrzynka *f* odbiorcza

mailman /ˈmeɪlmæn/ *n* US listonosz *m*

main /meɪn/ 1 *n* 1 (for water, gas, electricity) magistrala *f*; (for sewage) główny kanał *m* ściekowy 2 **the** ~**s** (of water) sieć *f* wodociągowa; (of sewage) sieć *f* kanalizacyjna; (of gas, electricity) sieć *f*

☐ *adj* główny; **the ~ thing is...** najważniejsza rzecz to...

main course *n* danie *n* główne

mainland /ˈmeɪnlənd/ *n* **on the ~** na lądzie stałym; **the Chinese ~** Chiny kontynentalne

main line /ˌmeɪnˈlaɪn/ *n* magistrala *f* kolejowa

mainly /ˈmeɪnlɪ/ *adv* głównie

maintain /meɪnˈteɪn/ *vt* ① (keep) utrzym|ać, -ywać *[temperature, standards]*; zachow|ać, -ywać *[confidence, silence]*; podtrzym|ać, -ywać *[friendship]* ② (support) utrzym|ać, -ywać *[family, army]*; zacho-w|ać, -ywać *[lifestyle]* ③ (look after) utrzym|ać, -ywać w dobrym stanie *[car, roads]*; konserwować *[equip-ment]* ④ (assert) twierdzić

maintenance /ˈmeɪntənəns/ *n* ① (of road) utrzy-manie *n*; (of car, building) konserwacja *f* ② (of morale, standards) zachowanie *n*

maize /meɪz/ *n* kukurydza *f*

majestic /məˈdʒestɪk/ *adj* majestatyczny

majesty /ˈmædʒəstɪ/ ☐ *n* ① (of building, ceremony) majestatyczność *f* ② (royal authority) majestat *m* ☐ **Majesty** *n* (in titles) **Her/His ~** Jego/Jej Królewska Mość

major /ˈmeɪdʒə(r)/ ☐ *n* ① (in army) major *m* ② US (at university) przedmiot *m* kierunkowy ③ (in law) pełnoletni *m*, -a *f* ④ Mus tonacja *f* durowa, dur *m* ☐ *adj* ① (important) *[championship, event]* ważny; *[change, contribution]* znaczny; *[client, damage]* poważny; *[influence, significance]* olbrzymi ② (main) *[problem, difficulty]* główny ③ Mus durowy

majority /məˈdʒɒrɪtɪ, US -ˈdʒɔːr-/ *n* ① GB więk-szość *f* (**of sth** czegoś); **to be in a** or **the ~** być w większości ② (in politics) przewaga *f*; **by a ~ of 50** przewaga 50 głosów ③ (in law) pełnoletność *f*

make /meɪk/ ☐ *n* (brand) marka *f* ☐ *vt* ① (create) z|robić *[cake, film, mess]*; u|szyć *[dress, shoes]*; wy|produkować *[car, paper]*; wytwo|-rzyć, -arzać *[oil, substance]*; ustan|owić, -awiać, stanowić *[law]*; ustal|ić, -ać *[rule]*; zaw|rzeć, -ierać *[pact, treaty]*; **to ~ the bed** pościelić or posłać łóżko; **to ~ a fire** rozpalić ogień; **to ~ room for sth** zrobić miejsce dla czegoś; **to ~ the time for sth** znaleźć czas na coś; **to be made (out) of sth** być (zrobionym) z czegoś ② (cause to be or become) **to ~ friends (with sb)** zaprzyjaźnić się (z kimś); **to ~ enemies** narobić sobie wrogów; **to ~ sb happy** uszczęśliwić kogoś; **the work made me hungry** zrobiłem się głodny przy tej pracy; **to ~ sth bigger** powiększyć coś; **to ~ it possible to do sth** umożliwić zrobienie czegoś ③ (cause to do) **to ~ sb laugh** rozśmieszyć kogoś; **to ~ sb cry** doprowadzić kogoś do płaczu; **to ~ sb think** dać komuś do myślenia; **he made her lose patience** przez niego straciła cierpliwość; **to ~ sth happen** sprawić, że coś się stanie ④ (force, compel) **to ~ sb do sth** zmusić kogoś do zrobienia czegoś; **to ~ sb wait** kazać komuś czekać; **to ~**

sb **see reason** przemówić komuś do rozsądku ⑤ (turn into) **to ~ sb sth, to ~ sth of sb** zrobić z kogoś coś; **to ~ sb one's assistant** zrobić kogoś swoim asystentem; **he'll never ~ a teacher** z niego nigdy nie będzie nauczyciel; **to ~ a good shelter** okazać się dobrym schronie-niem; **it ~s pleasant reading** to się przyjemnie czyta ⑥ (amount to) **three and three ~ six** trzy dodać trzy równa się sześć; **that ~s ten altogether** w sumie będzie dziesięć ⑦ (earn) zar|obić, -abiać; **to ~ a living** zarabiać na życie; **to ~ a profit** osiągnąć zysk; **to ~ a loss** *[deal]* przynieść stratę; *[person]* ponieść stratę ⑧ (reach) **we'll never ~ it** za nic nie zdążymy; **to ~ the first team** dostać się do pierwszej drużyny; **to ~ the front page** trafić na pierwszą stronę ⑨ (es-timate) **what time do you ~ it?** którą masz godzinę? *infml*; **can we ~ it a bit later?** czy można by było trochę później?; **what do you ~ of it?** co o tym sądzisz?

■ **make do: to ~ do with sth** zadowolić się czymś; **to ~ do without sth** obywać się bez czegoś

■ **make for:** ① (head for) s|kierować się ku (cze-muś) or do (czegoś) ② (help create) sprzyjać (czemuś)

■ **make good:** ¶ **~ good** odnieść sukces ¶ **~ good** **[sth]** ① z|rekompensować *[damage]*; wyna-gr|odzić, -adzać *[loss]*; nadr|obić, -abiać *[lost time]*; pokry|ć, -wać *[deficit]* ② spełni|ć, -ać *[promise, threat]*

■ **make out:** ¶ **~ out** utrzymywać (**that...** że...) ¶ **~ [sth] out** ① (distinguish) dostrze|c, -gać *[shape]*; odcyfrow|ać, -ywać *[inscription]*; (hear) dosłyszeć ② (claim) **to ~ sth out to be sth** udawać, że coś jest czymś ③ (understand) rozszyfrow|ać, -ywać ④ (write out) wypis|ać, -ywać *[prescription]*; sporzą-dz|ić, -ać *[list]*; **to ~ out a cheque to sb** wystawić czek na kogoś

■ **make up:** ¶ **~ up** ① u|malować się ② (after quarrel) po|godzić się (**with sb** z kimś) ③ **to ~ up for sth** nadr|obić, -abiać coś *[lost time, missed meal]*; pokry|ć, -wać coś *[deficit]*; z|rekompensować coś *[personal loss]* ¶ **~ [sth] up** ① (invent) wy-myśl|ić, -ać ② za|pakować *[parcel]*; z|robić *[bundle]*; pościelić *[bed]*; **to ~ up a prescription** sporzą-dzić lek według recepty ③ **to be made up of sth** składać się z czegoś; **to ~ up 10% of sth** stanowić 10% czegoś ④ nadr|obić, -abiać *[loss, time]*; pokry|ć, -wać *[deficit]*

make-believe /ˈmeɪkbɪliːv/ *n* fantazja *f*; **to indulge in ~** fantazjować

maker /ˈmeɪkə(r)/ *n* (of clothes, food, appliance) wytwórca *m*

makeshift /ˈmeɪkʃɪft/ *adj* prowizoryczny

make-up /ˈmeɪkʌp/ *n* ① (cosmetics) makijaż *m*; (actor's) charakteryzacja *f*; **to put on ~** umalować się ② (character) charakter *m*

make-up bag n kosmetyczka f
make-up remover n preparat m do demakijażu
making /'meɪkɪŋ/ n (of film, programme) realizacja f; (of product) (by machines) produkcja f; (by hand) wyrób m; (of clothes) szycie n; **her problems are of her own** ~ sama jest sobie winna
IDIOMS: **to have all the** ~**s of sth** mieć wszelkie zadatki na coś
maladjusted /ˌmælə'dʒʌstɪd/ adj nieprzystosowany
malaria /mə'leərɪə/ n malaria f
Malaysia /mə'leɪzɪə/ prn Malezja f
male /meɪl/ **I** n [1] (animal) samiec m [2] (man) mężczyzna m
II adj [gamete, sex] męski; [instinct] samczy; [relative, child] płci męskiej; ~ **nurse** pielęgniarz; ~ **student** student
male chauvinism n męski szowinizm m
male chauvinist n męski szowinista m
male model n model m
malevolent /mə'levələnt/ adj zły
malformed /ˌmæl'fɔ:md/ adj [limb, nose] zdeformowany; [heart, leaf] wadliwie rozwinięty
malfunction /ˌmæl'fʌŋkʃn/ **I** n [1] (poor operation) wadliwe działanie n [2] (breakdown) awaria f
II vi źle funkcjonować
malice /'mælɪs/ n złośliwość f (**towards sb** w stosunku do kogoś); **out of** ~ złośliwie
malicious /mə'lɪʃəs/ adj [comment, person] złośliwy; [act, allegation] nikczemny
malign /mə'laɪn/ vt szkalować
malignant /mə'lɪgnənt/ adj złośliwy
mall /mæl, mɔ:l/ n [1] (shopping arcade) (in town) ≈ pasaż m handlowy; (in suburbs) US centrum n handlowe [2] US (street) ciąg m pieszy
malnutrition /ˌmælnjuː'trɪʃn, US -nuː-/ n niedożywienie n
malpractice /ˌmæl'præktɪs/ n [1] (in law) nadużycia n pl; **administrative** ~ malwersacje; **electoral** ~ fałszowanie wyborów [2] US Med pomyłka f lekarska
malt /mɔ:lt/ n [1] (grain) słód m [2] (whisky) whisky f słodowa
Malta /'mɔ:ltə/ prn Malta f
maltreat /ˌmæl'triːt/ vt maltretować
mammal /'mæml/ n ssak m
mammoth /'mæməθ/ **I** n mamut m
II adj [task, organization] gigantyczny
man /mæn/ **I** n [1] (adult male) mężczyzna m; **as one** ~ **to another** jak mężczyzna z mężczyzną; **a blind** ~ niewidomy; **an old** ~ starzec [2] (husband) mąż m; (partner) partner m [3] (person) człowiek m [4] (in chess) figura f; (in draughts) pionek m
II vt obsługiwać [switchboard, pumps]; stanowić załogę (czegoś) [ship, fortress]
IDIOMS: **it's every** ~ **for himself** każdy dba o własną skórę

manage /'mænɪdʒ/ **I** vt [1] (succeed) po|radzić sobie; **to** ~ **to do sth** zdołać zrobić coś; **she** ~**d a smile** zdobyła się na uśmiech [2] (administer) kierować (czymś) [project, company]; zarządzać (czymś) [finances, estate]; prowadzić [business, affairs]; być dyrektorem (czegoś) [bank, school]; gospodarować (czymś) [time, money] [3] (handle) po|kierować (czymś) [boat]; posłu|żyć, -giwać się (czymś) [tool]; ob|ejść, -chodzić się z (czymś) [animal]; post|ąpić, -ępować z (kimś) [children]
II vi da|ć, -wać sobie radę
manageable /'mænɪdʒəbl/ adj [task] wykonalny; [problem] możliwy do rozwiązania; [size, quantity] rozsądny; [machine] łatwy w obsłudze; [person, animal] posłuszny
management /'mænɪdʒmənt/ n [1] (of farm, fund) zarządzanie n; (of department, staff) kierowanie n; (of business) prowadzenie n [2] (managers) kierownictwo n; **top** ~ kierownictwo najwyższego szczebla; ~ **costs** koszty administracyjne
management consultant n konsultant m do spraw zarządzania
manager /'mænɪdʒə(r)/ n (of company, bank, theatre) dyrektor m; (of restaurant) kierownik m; (of estate, farm) zarządca m; (in show business, sport) menedżer m
manageress /ˌmænɪdʒə'res/ n (of shop, restaurant, hotel) kierowniczka f; (of company) (pani) dyrektor f
managerial /ˌmænɪ'dʒɪərɪəl/ adj [staff] kierowniczy; [decision] kierownictwa; [experience] w zarządzaniu
managing director n dyrektor m naczelny or generalny
mandarin¹ /'mændərɪn/ n (Chinese) mandaryn m
mandarin² /'mændərɪn/ n (tree, fruit) mandarynka f
mandate /'mændeɪt/ n (authority) pełnomocnictwo n; (in politics) mandat m
mane /meɪn/ n grzywa f
mangle /'mæŋgl/ vt po|gruchotać [body, vehicle]
mango /'mæŋgəʊ/ n mango n
mangrove /'mæŋgrəʊv/ n namorzyn m
mangy /'meɪndʒɪ/ adj [animal] parchaty infml
manhandle /'mænhændl/ vt poniewierać (kimś)
manhole /'mænhəʊl/ n (in road) studzienka f włazowa
manhood /'mænhʊd/ n (state) wiek m męski; (masculinity) męskość f
mania /'meɪnɪə/ n mania f
maniac /'meɪnɪæk/ n [1] mania|k m, -czka f [2] infml fanaty|k m, -czka f
manic /'mænɪk/ adj [1] (obsessive) maniakalny; (manic-depressive) maniakalno-depresyjny [2] fig [activity, pace] szaleńczy; [behaviour] rozgorączkowany
manicure /'mænɪkjʊə(r)/ **I** n manikiur m
II vt **to** ~ **one's nails** robić sobie manikiur
manifest /'mænɪfest/ **I** adj wyraźny
II vt okaz|ać, -ywać [fear, fatigue]; za|manifestować [feelings, dissatisfaction]

manifesto /ˌmænɪˈfestəʊ/ n manifest m

manipulate /məˈnɪpjʊleɪt/ vt [1] (control) manipulować (czymś) *[control, gears]* [2] pej manipulować (kimś/czymś) *[person, situation, opinion]*; oddziaływać, -ywać na (coś) *[market]*

manipulative /məˈnɪpjʊlətɪv/ adj to be ~ manipulować ludźmi

mankind /ˌmænˈkaɪnd/ n ludzkość f

manly /ˈmænlɪ/ adj męski

man-made /ˌmænˈmeɪd/ adj *[fibre, fabric, snow]* sztuczny; *[object, tool]* wytworzony przez człowieka; *[environment]* stworzony przez człowieka

manner /ˈmænə(r)/ [] n [1] (way, method) sposób m; **in this ~** w ten sposób; **in a ~ of speaking** poniekąd [2] (way of behaving) zachowanie n; **she has a bad ~** jest niesympatyczna [3] (sort, kind) rodzaj m

[] **manners** npl [1] (social behaviour) maniery f pl; **to have good/bad ~s** być dobrze/źle wychowanym; **it's bad ~s to do it** niegrzecznie jest to robić [2] (social habits) obyczaje m pl

mannerism /ˈmænərɪzəm/ n [1] (habit) nawyk m [2] pej (quirk) maniera f

manoeuvre GB, **maneuver** US /məˈnuːvə(r)/ [] n manewr m

[] vt [1] manewrować (czymś) *[vehicle, object]* [2] fig manewrować (kimś) *[person]*; pokierować (czymś) *[discussion]*

[] vi manewrować

manor /ˈmænə(r)/ n (also ~ **house**) rezydencja f ziemska

manpower /ˈmænpaʊə(r)/ n siła f robocza

mansion /ˈmænʃn/ n rezydencja f

manslaughter /ˈmænslɔːtə(r)/ n nieumyślne spowodowanie n śmierci

mantelpiece /ˈmæntlpiːs/ n gzyms m kominka; **on the ~** na kominku

manual /ˈmænjʊəl/ [] n podręcznik m

[] adj *[work, worker]* fizyczny; *[pump, gearbox]* ręczny; *[dexterity, skills]* manualny

manufacture /ˌmænjʊˈfæktʃə(r)/ [] n produkcja f

[] vt wytwłorzyć, -arzać *[goods]*

manufacturer /ˌmænjʊˈfæktʃərə(r)/ n wytwórca m

manure /məˈnjʊə(r)/ n nawóz m naturalny; (dung) obornik m

manuscript /ˈmænjʊskrɪpt/ n rękopis m

many /ˈmenɪ/ [] quantif wiele; ~ **times** wiele razy; **for ~ years** przez wiele lat; **in ~ ways** na wiele sposobów; **his ~ friends** jego liczni przyjaciele; **how ~ people?** ile osób?; **how ~ times?** ile razy?; **too ~ people** zbyt wiele osób; **I have as ~ books as you (do)** mam tyle książek co ty; **five exams in as ~ days** pięć egzaminów w ciągu pięciu dni

[] pron wiele; (of men) wielu; **not ~** niewiele/niewielu; **how ~?** ile/ilu?; **as ~ as you like**

(tyle) ile chcesz; **I didn't know there were so ~** nie wiedziałam, że jest aż tyle; **one too ~** jeden za dużo

many-sided /ˌmenɪˈsaɪdɪd/ adj *[personality]* wielowymiarowy; *[interests]* wielostronny

map /mæp/ n (of region) mapa f; (of city, underground) plan m; **road ~** mapa samochodowa; **street ~** plan miasta

■ **map out**: nakreśljić, -ać *[plan, strategy]*; zalplanować *[career, holiday]*

maple /ˈmeɪpl/ n klon m

mar /mɑː(r)/ vt zelpsuć *[holiday]*; oszpecjić, -ać *[appearance]*

marathon /ˈmærəθən, US -θɒn/ [] n maraton m

[] adj [1] Sport ~ **runner** maratończyk; **the ~ route** trasa maratonu [2] *[session, hike]* długi i wyczerpujący

marble /ˈmɑːbl/ n [1] (stone) marmur m [2] (for playing) szklana kulka f

march /mɑːtʃ/ [] n marsz m

[] vi [1] Mil maszerować; **to ~ (for) 40 km** przemaszerować 40 km; **forward ~!** naprzód marsz! [2] (in protest) demonstrować, manifestować (**against/for sth** przeciw czemuś/wyrażając poparcie dla czegoś) [3] (walk briskly) **to ~ in** wmaszerować; **to ~ out** wymaszerować; **she ~ed up to his desk** pewnym krokiem podeszła do jego biurka

March /mɑːtʃ/ n marzec m

marcher /ˈmɑːtʃə(r)/ n (in demonstration) demonstrant m, -ka f; (in procession) maszerujący m, -a f

mare /meə(r)/ n (horse) klacz f; (donkey) oślica f

margarine /ˌmɑːdʒəˈriːn/ n margaryna f

margin /ˈmɑːdʒɪn/ n [1] margines m; **in the ~** na marginesie; ~ **of** or **for error** margines błędu [2] różnica f; **to win by a narrow ~** wygrać niewielką przewagą [3] (also **profit ~**) zysk m, marża f zysku

marginal /ˈmɑːdʒɪnl/ adj *[importance]* marginesowy; *[difference]* znikomy; *[figure, role]* drugoplanowy

marginalize /ˈmɑːdʒɪnəlaɪz/ vt usuljnąć, -wać na dalszy plan

marigold /ˈmærɪɡəʊld/ n nagietek m

marijuana /ˌmærjuˈɑːnə/ n marihuana f

marinade /ˌmærɪˈneɪd/ [] n marynata f

[] vt (also **marinate**) zalmarynować

marine /məˈriːn/ [] n [1] (soldier) żołnierz m piechoty morskiej; **the Marines** piechota morska [2] (navy) **the merchant ~** marynarka handlowa

[] adj morski

marital /ˈmærɪtl/ adj małżeński; ~ **status** stan cywilny

marjoram /ˈmɑːdʒərəm/ n majeranek m

mark /mɑːk/ [] n [1] (stain) plama f; (on animal) łata f; (from injury) ślad m [2] (symbol) **as a ~ of sth** na znak czegoś *[esteem]* [3] Sch ocena f [4] (on scale) poziom m;

the high-tide ~ linia zasięgu fal pływowych
5 Sport linia f startowa; **on your** ~**s** na miejsca
II vt 1 (stain) po|plamić; (for identification) oznacz|yć,
-ać 2 (indicate) *[person]* zaznacz|yć, -ać; *[arrow, sign,*
label] wskaz|ać, -ywać 3 Sch sprawdz|ić, -ać; **to** ~
sb absent zaznaczyć komuś nieobecność 4 Sport
kryć *[player]*
III vi 1 *[teacher]* sprawdz|ić, -ać prace uczniów
2 (stain) plamić się 3 Sport kryć
IV **mark you** conj phr zauważ
(IDIOMS:) **to** ~ **time** *[soldiers]* maszerować
w miejscu; **I'm** ~**ing time working as a**
waitress żeby czymś się zająć, pracuję jako
kelnerka
marked /mɑːkt/ adj 1 (noticeable) wyraźny 2 **he's**
a ~ **man** (disturbed) to człowiek napiętnowany; (in
danger) grozi mu niebezpieczeństwo
marker /ˈmɑːkə(r)/ n 1 (pen) marker m 2 (bookmark) zakładka f (do książki)
market /ˈmɑːkɪt/ **I** n 1 (for goods) rynek m
2 (potential customers) rynek m zbytu (**for sth** na
coś) 3 (place) rynek m 4 (stock market) giełda f
II vt 1 (sell) sprzedawać 2 (promote) wprowadz|ić,
-ać na rynek
market day n dzień m targowy; (in finance) dzień m
giełdowy
market economy n gospodarka f rynkowa
market forces npl tendencje f pl rynkowe
market gardening n ogrodnictwo n, warzyw-
nictwo n
marketing /ˈmɑːkɪtɪŋ/ n 1 (process) marketing m
2 (department) dział m marketingu
marketing strategy n strategia f marketingowa
market leader n (product) produkt m wiodący;
(company) lider m na rynku
marketplace /ˈmɑːkɪtpleɪs/ n plac m targowy
market research n badania n pl rynku
market town n miasto n targowe
market trader n straiania|rz m, -rka f
market value n wartość f rynkowa
marksman /ˈmɑːksmən/ n strzelec m wyborowy
marmalade /ˈmɑːməleɪd/ n dżem m z owoców
cytrusowych
maroon[1] /məˈruːn/ n (colour) (kolor m) rdzawo-
czerwony m
maroon[2] /məˈruːn/ vt **to be** ~**ed on an island**
zostać porzuconym na wyspie; **to be** ~**ed in a**
traffic jam tkwić w korku
marquee /mɑːˈkiː/ n 1 GB (tent) duży namiot m; (of
circus) namiot m cyrkowy 2 US (canopy) markiza f
marriage /ˈmærɪdʒ/ n 1 (wedlock) małżeństwo n
(**to sb** z kimś) 2 (ceremony) ślub m
marriage certificate n akt m or metryka f ślubu
married /ˈmærɪd/ adj 1 *[man]* żonaty (**to sb** z
kimś); *[woman]* zamężna (**to sb** z kimś); ~ **couple**
małżonkowie 2 *[state, life]* małżeński

marrow /ˈmærəʊ/ n 1 (also **bone** ~) szpik m
kostny 2 GB (green) cukinia f; (white) kabaczek m
marrowbone /ˈmærəʊbəʊn/ n Culin kość f szpi-
kowa
marry /ˈmærɪ/ **I** vt *[priest, registrar]* udziel|ić, -ać
ślubu (komuś); *[man, woman]* poślubić (kogoś);
will you ~ **me?** (to woman) wyjdziesz za mnie?; (to
man) ożenisz się ze mną?
II vi *[woman]* wy|jść, -chodzić za mąż; *[man]*
o|żenić się; *[couple]* pob|rać, -ierać się
marsh /mɑːʃ/ n (also **marshland**) (terrain) bagno n;
(region) bagna n pl
marshal /ˈmɑːʃl/ **I** n 1 (title) marszałek m 2 (at
public gathering) człon|ek m, -kini f służb porządko-
wych 3 US (sheriff) urzędnik m z władzą szeryfa
4 US (in fire service) komendant m straży pożarnej
II vt ustawi|ć, -ać w szereg *[troops]*
martial /ˈmɑːʃl/ adj *[music, training]* wojskowy;
[spirit] wojowniczy; ~ **law** stan wyjątkowy
martyr /ˈmɑːtə(r)/ n męczenni|k m, -ca f
martyrdom /ˈmɑːtədəm/ n męczeństwo n
marvel /ˈmɑːvl/ **I** n cud m
II vi **to** ~ **at sb/sth** (in admiration) zachwyc|ać, -ić
się kimś/czymś; (in astonishment) zdumie|ć, -wać się
kimś/czymś
marvellous GB, **marvelous** US /ˈmɑːvələs/ adj
cudowny; **that's** ~! to cudownie!
marzipan /ˈmɑːzɪpæn, ˌmɑːzɪˈpæn/ n marcepan m
mascot /ˈmæskət, -skɒt/ n maskotka f
masculine /ˈmæskjʊlɪn/ adj męski
masculinity /ˌmæskjʊˈlɪnətɪ/ n męskość f
mash /mæʃ/ **I** n (in brewing) zacier m
II vt (also ~ **up**) u|tłuc *[potatoes]*; rozgni|eść, -atać
[fruit]; ~ **ed potatoes** purée ziemniaczane
mask /mɑːsk, US mæsk/ n maska f
masking tape n taśma f maskująca
masochist /ˈmæsəkɪst/ **I** n masochist|a m, -ka f
II adj masochistyczny
mason /ˈmeɪsn/ n 1 kamieniarz m 2 **Mason** (also
Freemason) mason m, -ka f, wolnomularz m
masonry /ˈmeɪsnrɪ/ n 1 kamieniarstwo n
2 **Masonry** (also **Freemasonry**) masoneria f,
wolnomularstwo n
masquerade /ˌmɑːskəˈreɪd, US ˌmæsk-/ **I** n mas-
karada f also fig
II vi **to** ~ **as sb** (pretend) udawać kogoś; (say one is
sb) podawać się za kogoś
mass[1] /mæs/ **I** n mnóstwo n, masa f
II **masses** npl 1 (the people) **the** ~ **es** masy m pl
2 GB infml (lots) **to have** ~**es of work** mieć masę
pracy; ~**es of time** mnóstwo czasu
III adj *[protest, unemployment]* masowy; ~
meeting wiec 2 *[culture, tourism]* masowy; *[con-*
sciousness, hysteria] zbiorowy
IV vi *[troops]* s|koncentrować się; *[bees]* zl|ecieć,
-atywać się; *[clouds]* z|gromadzić się
mass[2] /mæs/ n msza f

massacre /'mæsəkə(r)/ **❶** *n* masakra *f*
❷ *vt* dokon|ać, -ywać masakry (kogoś/czegoś) *[enemy, army]*

massage /'mæsɑːʒ, US mə'sɑːʒ/ **❶** *n* masaż *m*
❷ *vt* wy|masować *[person]*; rozmasow|ać, -ywać *[stiffness]*

mass grave *n* zbiorowa mogiła *f*

massive /'mæsɪv/ *adj [furniture]* masywny; *[animal, explosion]* potężny; *[scandal, error]* ogromny; *[victory, majority]* przytłaczający; *[heart attack]* rozległy

mass-marketing /ˌmæsˈmɑːkɪtɪŋ/ *n* działania *n pl* marketingowe nastawione na masowego odbiorcę

mass media *n* środki *m pl* masowego przekazu

mass murderer *n* zbrodniarz *m* winny ludobójstwa

mass production *n* produkcja *f* masowa

mast /mɑːst, US mæst/ *n* maszt *m*

master /'mɑːstə(r), US 'mæs-/ **❶** *n* ⨂ (in charge) pan *m*, pani *f*; **the ~ of the house** pan domu; **to be one's own ~** nie być od nikogo zależnym ② (person who excels) mistrz *m*, -yni *f*; **a ~ of the violin** wirtuoz skrzypiec ③ (at school) (primary) nauczyciel *m*; (secondary) profesor *m*; (headmaster) dyrektor *m* ④ GB (of college) ≈ dziekan *m* ⑤ (also ~ **copy**) oryginał *m* ⑥ (graduate) ≈ magister *m*; **~'s (degree)** stopień magistra
❷ *adj* ~ **carpenter/builder** mistrz stolarski/murarski; ~ **spy** as wywiadu
❸ *vt* opanow|ać, -ywać *[language, craft]*; posi|ąść, -adać *[skill]*; za|panować nad (kimś/czymś) *[emotions, situation]*; pokon|ać, -ywać *[phobia]*

master key *n* klucz *m* uniwersalny

masterly /'mɑːstəlɪ, US 'mæs-/ *adj* mistrzowski

mastermind /'mɑːstəmaɪnd, US 'mæs-/ **❶** *n* mózg *m* fig (**of** or **behind sth** czegoś)
❷ *vt* zaplanować *[crime]*; zorganizować *[event]*

Master of Arts *n* ≈ magister *m* nauk humanistycznych

master of ceremonies *n* (presenting entertainment) konferansjer *m*; (at formal occasion) mistrz *m* ceremonii

Master of Science *n* ≈ magister *m* nauk ścisłych or przyrodniczych

masterpiece /'mɑːstəpiːs, US 'mæs-/ *n* arcydzieło *n*

mastery /'mɑːstərɪ, US 'mæs-/ *n* mistrzostwo *n*; ~ **of sth** biegłe opanowanie czegoś *[technique, language]*; biegłość w posługiwaniu się czymś *[weapon]*

mat /mæt/ *n* ⨂ (small rug) dywanik *m*; (straw) mata *f*; (for wiping feet) wycieraczka *f*; (for gymnastics) mata *f* ② (on table) mata *f* stołowa

match¹ /mætʃ/ **❶** *n* ⨂ Sport mecz *m* ② (equal) **to be a ~ for sb** być dla kogoś godnym przeciwnikiem; **to be no ~ for sb** nie móc się równać z kimś
❷ *vt* ⨂ (harmonize with) *[coat, bag]* pasować do (czegoś); *[blood sample]* być zgodnym z (czymś);

[product, supply] odpowiadać (czemuś) ② (compete) dorówn|ać, -ywać (czemuś) *[achievements]*; wyrówn|ać, -ywać *[record]*
❸ *vi [colours, clothes, pieces]* pasować do siebie; **with gloves to** ~ z rękawiczkami dobranymi do całości

match² /mætʃ/ *n* zapałka *f*

matchbox /'mætʃbɒks/ *n* pudełko *n* zapałek; (when empty) pudełko *n* od zapałek

match point *n* meczbol *m*

matchstick /'mætʃstɪk/ *n* zapałka *f*

mate¹ /meɪt/ **❶** *n* ⨂ GB infml (friend) kumpel *m* infml; (at work, school) kolega *m* ② Zool (male) samiec *m*; (female) samica *f* ③ (assistant) pomocnik *m*
❷ *vt* s|kojarzyć w parę *[animals]* (**with sth** z czymś)
❸ *vi [animal]* parzyć się (**with sth** z czymś)

mate² /meɪt/ **❶** *n* (in chess) mat *m*
❷ *vt* da|ć, -wać mata (komuś)

material /mə'tɪərɪəl/ **❶** *n* ⨂ (information, data) materiały *m pl*; **teaching** ~ materiały do nauki ② (subject matter) materiał *m* ③ (substance) materiał *m*; **waste** ~ odpady ④ (fabric) materiał *m* ⑤ (potential) dobry materiał *m* fig; **she's star** ~ ma zadatki na gwiazdę
❷ **materials** *npl* (equipment) materiały *m pl*; **cleaning** ~ **s** środki czystości
❸ *adj* ⨂ (relevant) *[benefit, change, evidence]* istotny; *[damage, effect]* poważny ② *[comfort, need, success]* materialny

materialistic /məˌtɪərɪə'lɪstɪk/ *adj* materialistyczny

materialize /mə'tɪərɪəlaɪz/ *vi* ⨂ *[plan, idea]* urzeczywistni|ć, -ać się; *[hopes]* zi|ścić, -szczać się; *[event]* do|jść, -chodzić do skutku; *[situation]* zaistnieć ② hum *[person, ghost, object]* pojawi|ć, -ać się

maternal /mə'tɜːnl/ *adj [duties, influence]* matczyny; *[instinct]* macierzyński; *[ancestor]* ze strony matki

maternity /mə'tɜːnətɪ/ **❶** *n* (motherhood) macierzyństwo *n*; (motherliness) uczucia *n pl* macierzyńskie
❷ *adj [clothes]* ciążowy; *[hospital, ward]* położniczy

maternity leave *n* urlop *m* macierzyński

math /mæθ/ *n* US infml = **maths**

mathematical /ˌmæθə'mætɪkl/ *adj* matematyczny

mathematician /ˌmæθəmə'tɪʃn/ *n* matematyk *m*

mathematics /ˌmæθə'mætɪks/ *n* matematyka *f*

maths /mæθs/ *n* GB infml matma *f* infml

matinée /'mætɪneɪ, 'mætneɪ, US ˌmætn'eɪ/ *n* (in theatre) popołudniówka *f*; (in cinema) seans *m* popołudniowy

mating season *n* okres *m* godowy

matriculate /mə'trɪkjʊleɪt/ *vi* zapis|ać, -ywać się na studia

matrimony /'mætrɪmənɪ, US -məʊnɪ/ *n* związek *m* małżeński

matrix /'meɪtrɪks/ *n* [1] Tech, Comput matryca *f* [2] (in mathematics) macierz *f*

matron /'meɪtrən/ *n* [1] GB (in hospital) przełożona *f* pielęgniarek; (in school) pielęgniarka *f* [2] (of orphanage, nursing home) kierowniczka *f* [3] US (warder) strażniczka *f*

matt GB, **matte** US /mæt/ *adj [paint]* matowy; *[photograph]* na papierze matowym

matter /'mætə(r)/ **❚** *n* [1] (of specified nature) sprawa *f*; (requiring solution) problem *m*; **business** ~s sprawy handlowe; **the main** ~ **on the agenda** główny punkt porządku dnia; **this is a** ~ **for the police** tą sprawą powinna się zająć policja; **it's no small** ~ to nie błahostka; **the fact of the** ~ **is that...** sprawa wygląda tak, że... [2] (question) kwestia *f*; **a** ~ **of taste** kwestia gustu [3] **the** ~ (trouble) kłopot *m*; **is anything the** ~? czy coś się stało?; **there's nothing the** ~ wszystko jest w porządku; **what's the** ~? o co chodzi?; **there's nothing the** ~ **with me** nic mi nie jest [4] (substance) materia *f*; **vegetable** ~ substancja *f* roślinna [5] (on paper) **advertising** ~ materiały reklamowe; **printed** ~ druki; **reading** ~ lektura [6] (content of book, speech) treść *f*; **subject** ~ temat; ~ **and style** treść i styl [7] (pus) ropa *f* **❚❚** *vi* **to** ~ **to sb** *[behaviour, action]* mieć dla kogoś znaczenie; *[person]* być dla kogoś kimś ważnym; **it** ~**s to me where you go** obchodzi mnie, gdzie chodzisz; **it doesn't** ~ to nie ma znaczenia ⟨IDIOMS⟩ **as a** ~ **of course** w sposób oczywisty; **as a** ~ **of fact** właściwie; **for that** ~ jeśli o to chodzi; **no** ~! nieważne!; **no** ~ **how late it is** obojętne or bez względu na to, jak późno; **to make** ~**s worse** na domiar złego

matter-of-fact /ˌmætərəv'fækt/ *adj* (practical) rzeczowy; (unemotional) obojętny

mattress /'mætrɪs/ *n* materac *m*

mature /mə'tjʊə(r), US -'tʊər/ **❚** *adj* [1] *[plant, animal]* dorosły [2] *[person]* dorosły; *[attitude, reader]* dojrzały [3] *[wine, cheese]* dojrzały **❚❚** *vi* [1] *[person, animal, plant, attitude]* dojrzeļć, -wać [2] *[idea, plan]* s|krystalizować się [3] *[wine, whisky]* leżakować; *[cheese]* dojrzeļć, -wać

maul /mɔːl/ *vt [animal]* poturbować; (fatally) rozszarpać

mauve /məʊv/ **❚** *n* (kolor *m*) fioletoworóżowy *m* **❚❚** *adj* fioletoworóżowy

maverick /'mævərɪk/ **❚** *n* indywidualist|a *m*, -ka *f* **❚❚** *adj [behaviour]* niestereotypowy; *[person]* nieszablonowy; *[politician, writer]* niezależny

maxim /'mæksɪm/ *n* maksyma *f*

maximize /'mæksɪmaɪz/ *vt* [1] maksymalnie zwiększ|yć, -ać *[results, chances]* [2] Comput maksymalizować

maximum /'mæksɪməm/ **❚** *n* maksimum *n* **❚❚** *adj* maksymalny

maximum security prison *n* więzienie *n* o zaostrzonym rygorze

may /meɪ/ *modal aux* [1] (possibility) **it** ~ **rain** może padać; **'are you going to come?'...** – '**I** ~' „przyjdziesz?" – „może"; **he** ~ **be lazy, but he's not stupid** może i jest leniwy, ale nie głupi; **come what** ~ niech się dzieje co chce; **be that as it** ~ tak czy owak [2] (permission) ~ **I make a suggestion?** czy mogę coś zaproponować?; **I'll sit down, if I** ~ usiądę, jeśli można; **if I** ~ **say so** jeśli mi wolno tak powiedzieć; ~ **I have your name and address, please?** proszę podać nazwisko i adres [3] (indicating purpose) **a space so that you** ~ **add your comments** miejsce, żebyś mógł dopisać swoje uwagi [4] (expressing wishes) ~ **they be happy!** niech im szczęście sprzyja!

May /meɪ/ *n* maj *m*

maybe /'meɪbiː/ *adv* (być) może; ~ **three weeks ago** może trzy tygodnie temu

May Day /'meɪdeɪ/ *n* 1 Maja *m*, Święto *n* Pracy

mayday *n* wzywanie *n* pomocy

mayhem /'meɪhem/ *n* [1] (chaos) chaos *m*; (violence) awantura *f*; **to create** ~ spowodować chaos [2] US rozmyślne okaleczenie *n*

mayor /meə(r), US 'meɪər/ *n* burmistrz *m*

mayoress /'meərɪs, US 'meɪə-/ *n* (wife of mayor) burmistrzowa *f*; (lady mayor) pani *f* burmistrz

maze /meɪz/ *n* (puzzle) labirynt *m*; (of pipes) plątanina *f*, gąszcz *m*

MBA *n* Univ = **Master of Business Administration** ≈ magister *m* zarządzania

MC *n* = **Master of Ceremonies** (at banquet) mistrz *m* ceremonii; (in cabaret) konferansjer *m*

me /miː, mɪ/ *pron* [1] **for me** dla mnie; **with me** ze mną; **without me** beze mnie; **give it to me** daj to mnie, daj mi to; **she's older than me** jest ode mnie starsza [2] (emphatic) **it's me** to ja; **silly me!** głupiec ze mnie!

meadow /'medəʊ/ *n* [1] (field) łąka *f* [2] (also ~ **land**) łąki *f pl* [3] (also **water** ~) łęg *m*

meagre GB, **meager** US /'miːgə(r)/ *adj [sum, meal]* mizerny; *[living]* skromny; *[person, animal]* mizerny, wątły

meal[1] /miːl/ *n* (food) posiłek *m*; **to go out for a** ~ pójść do restauracji

meal[2] /miːl/ *n* (from grain) mączka *f*

mean[1] /miːn/ *vt* [1] *[word, symbol, phrase]* znaczyć (**that...** że...); *[sign]* oznaczać; **the name** ~**s nothing to me** ta nazwa nic mi nie mówi [2] (intend) **to** ~ **to do sth** zamierzać coś zrobić; **to be meant for sb** *[bomb]* być przeznaczonym dla kogoś; *[question]* być skierowanym do kogoś; **he** ~**s no harm to you** nie chce zrobić ci krzywdy; **to** ~ **well** chcieć dobrze; **she** ~**s business** ona nie żartuje; **I didn't** ~ **to do it** tak jakoś wyszło; **without** ~**ing to** niechcący [3] (entail) *[strike, law]* znaczyć, oznaczać *[shortages, changes]* [4] (intend to say)

what do you ~ **by that remark?** co chcesz przez to powiedzieć?; **do you** ~ **me?** mówisz o mnie?; **I know what you** ~ rozumiem, co masz na myśli ⑤ (be of value) **a promise** ~**s nothing** obietnica znaczy tyle, co nic; **she** ~**s everything to me** ona jest dla mnie wszystkim ⑥ (be destined) **you weren't meant to hear that** to nie było przeznaczone dla twoich uszu; **she was meant to become a doctor** miała zostać lekarzem; **it was meant to be** or **happen** tak było pisane ⑦ (be supposed to be) **you're meant to be impartial** masz być bezstronny

mean² /miːn/ *adj* ① (ungenerous) *[person]* skąpy; *[attitude]* małostkowy; *[examiner]* surowy; **to be** ~ **with sth** żałować czegoś *[time, water]* ② (unkind) *[person, action]* podły; **to be** ~ **to sb** być niedobrym dla kogoś; (stronger) postępować podle w stosunku do kogoś ③ (vicious) *[animal, person, expression]* złośliwy ④ infml (skilful) *[cook, shot]* doskonały, świetny; **you're no** ~ **artist** nie byle jaki z ciebie artysta

mean³ /miːn/ **❚** *n* średnia *f*
❚❚ *adj [weight, temperature]* średni

meander /mɪˈændə(r)/ **❚** *n* meander *m*
❚❚ *vi [river, path]* wić się

meaning /ˈmiːnɪŋ/ *n* ① (sense) znaczenie *n*; **what is the** ~ **of this?** co to ma znaczyć? ② (purpose) sens *m*; **full of** ~ wymowny, znaczący

meaningful /ˈmiːnɪŋfl/ *adj* ① (significant) *[word, sign]* znaczący; *[statement, comment]* istotny; *[explanation]* sensowny; *[results]* konkretny ② (profound) *[relationship, experience]* ważny; *[comment]* poważny; *[insight]* wnikliwy ③ (eloquent) *[look, gesture]* znaczący; *[pause]* wymowny

meaningless /ˈmiːnɪŋlɪs/ *adj* ① (having no sense) bez znaczenia; (incomprehensible) niezrozumiały ② (worthless) *[chatter]* pusty; *[effort]* daremny; **a** ~ **exercise** próżny trud ③ (pointless) *[act, violence]* bezsensowny

means /miːnz/ **❚** *n* (way) sposób *m*; **a** ~ **of transport** środek or środki transportu; **by** ~ **of sth** za pomocą czegoś *[tool, machine]*; **a** ~ **of doing sth** sposób zrobienia czegoś; **yes, by all** ~ ależ tak, jak najbardziej; **by no** ~, **not by any** ~ w żadnym wypadku
❚❚ *npl* (resources) środki *plt*; **of moderate** ~ średnio zamożny; **to live beyond one's** ~ żyć ponad stan

means test *n* ankieta *f* dotycząca środków utrzymania

meantime /ˈmiːntaɪm/ *adv* **(in the)** ~ w tym czasie, tymczasem

meanwhile /ˈmiːnwaɪl/ *adv* tymczasem; (since then) przez ten czas

measles /ˈmiːzlz/ *n* odra *f*

measure /ˈmeʒə(r)/ **❚** *n* ① (standard) miara *f*; (unit) jednostka *f* miary; **dry** ~ miara objętości ciał sypkich ② (container) miara *f*, miarka *f*; **he gave me short** ~ dał mi niepełną miarę ③ (size) **to make**

sth to ~ uszyć coś na miarę *[garment]*; zrobić coś na miarę *[shoes]* ④ (action) środek *m* (**against sth** przeciw czemuś); krok *m*; **to take** ~**s** podjąć kroki; **safety** or **security** ~**s** środki bezpieczeństwa; **as a temporary** ~ prowizorycznie
❚❚ *vt* ① *[person]* z|mierzyć *[length, rate, object]*; **to** ~ **sth in inches** mierzyć coś w calach; **to** ~ **sb for a suit** wziąć z kogoś miarę na garnitur ② (have measurement of) mierzyć; **to** ~ **four by five metres** mierzyć or mieć cztery metry na pięć (metrów) ③ (assess) oceni|ć, -ać *[ability, performance]*; **to** ~ **sb/sth against sth** przyrównywać kogoś/coś do czegoś

■ **measure out**: odmierz|yć, -ać *[quantity, ingredients]*; wymierz|yć, -ać *[land]*

■ **measure up**: spełni|ć, -ać oczekiwania; **to** ~ **up to sb's expectations** sprostać oczekiwaniom kogoś

IDIOMS: **for good** ~ na dodatek, na dokładkę

measurement /ˈmeʒəmənt/ *n* ① (act) pomiar *m* ② (dimension) wymiar *m*; **to take the** ~**s of sth** wymierzyć coś ③ (for garment) miara *f*; **to take sb's** ~**s** wziąć miarę z kogoś; **waist** ~ obwód talii; **arm** ~ długość rękawa

meat /miːt/ **❚** *n* mięso *n*; **cold** ~**s** wędliny
❚❚ *adj [dish, industry]* mięsny; ~ **products** wyroby mięsne

meat-eater /ˈmiːtiːtə(r)/ *n* (animal) zwierzę *n* mięsożerne; **they are not great** ~**s** nie przepadają za mięsem

meaty /ˈmiːtɪ/ *adj* ① *[stew]* z dużą ilością mięsa; ~ **flavour/smell** smak/zapach mięsa ② *[cheeks, lips]* mięsisty; *[person]* umięśniony ③ fig *[book, discussion]* treściwy

mechanic /mɪˈkænɪk/ *n* mechanik *m*

mechanical /mɪˈkænɪkl/ *adj [device, toy]* mechaniczny; *[difficulties, problems]* techniczny; *[gesture, reply]* mechaniczny

mechanical engineering *n* budowa *f* maszyn

mechanics /mɪˈkænɪks/ *n* ① (subject) mechanika *f* ② (workings) mechanizm *m*

mechanism /ˈmekənɪzəm/ *n* mechanizm *m* also fig; **legal** ~**s** mechanizmy or procedury prawne

mechanization /ˌmekənaɪˈzeɪʃn, US -nɪˈz-/ *n* mechanizacja *f*

medal /ˈmedl/ *n* medal *m*; **silver** ~ srebrny medal

medallion /mɪˈdælɪən/ *n* medalion *m*

medallist GB, **medalist** US /ˈmedəlɪst/ *n* medalist|a *m*, -ka *f*; **gold** ~ złoty medalista

meddle /ˈmedl/ *vi* **to** ~ **in sb's affairs** wtrącać się w sprawy kogoś; **to** ~ **with sb's things** ruszać rzeczy kogoś

media /ˈmiːdɪə/ **❚** *npl* **(the mass)** ~ mass media
❚❚ *adj [image, event]* medialny; ~ **advertising** reklama w mediach; ~ **attention** uwaga mediów; ~ **personality** osobowość radiowa/telewizyjna; ~ **people** pracownicy prasy, radia i telewizji

mediate /'mi:dɪeɪt/ **❚** *vt* (as negotiator) wy|negocjować *[agreement, cease-fire]*
❚❚ *vi* pośredniczyć
mediator /'mi:dɪeɪtə(r)/ *n* mediator *m*, rozjemca *m*
medical /'medɪkl/ **❚** *n* (in school, army, for job) badania *n pl*
❚❚ *adj* medyczny; **on** ~ **grounds** z przyczyn zdrowotnych
medical insurance *n* ubezpieczenie *n* zdrowotne
medical student *n* student *m*, -ka *f* medycyny
medicated /'medɪkeɪtɪd/ *adj [shampoo]* leczniczy; *[dressing]* z substancją leczniczą
medication /,medɪ'keɪʃn/ *n* ① (drug treatment) kuracja *f* (lekami); **to be on** ~ przyjmować leki; **to put sb on** ~ przepisać komuś leki; **to take sb off** ~ zalecić komuś odstawienie leków ② (medicine) lek *m*
medicinal /mɪ'dɪsɪnl/ *adj* leczniczy; ~ **drugs** leki, **I drink brandy for** ~ **purposes** hum piję brandy w celach leczniczych
medicine /'medsn, US 'medɪsn/ *n* ① (discipline) medycyna *f* ② (drug) lek *m*, lekarstwo *n* (**for sth** na coś); **the best** ~ najlepsze lekarstwo also fig
medicine cabinet *n* (also ~ **cupboard**) apteczka *f*
medicine man *n* szaman *m*
medieval /,medɪ'i:vl, US ,mi:d-, *also* mɪ'di:vl/ *adj* średniowieczny also fig; ~ **times** czasy średniowiecza
mediocre /,mi:dɪ'əʊkə(r)/ *adj* mierny
mediocrity /,mi:dɪ'ɒkrətɪ/ *n* ① (state) mierność *f* ② (person) miernota *m/f* pej
meditate /'medɪteɪt/ **❚** *vt* (consider) **to** ~ **sth/doing sth** rozważać coś/zrobienie czegoś
❚❚ *vi* medytować
Mediterranean /,medɪtə'reɪnɪən/ **❚** *prn* ① (also **the** ~ **sea**) Morze *n* Śródziemne ② (region) **the** ~ rejon *m* Morza Śródziemnego ③ (native) mieszka|niec *m*, -ka *f* kraju śródziemnomorskiego
❚❚ *adj* śródziemnomorski
medium /'mi:dɪəm/ **❚** *n* ① (radio, TV) środek *m* przekazu; **advertising** ~ nośnik reklamy; **through the** ~ **of radio/the press** za pośrednictwem radia/prasy ② (technique) środek *m* wyrazu; (material) materiał *m* ③ (midpoint) środek *m*; **to find** or **strike a happy** ~ znaleźć złoty środek ④ (spiritualist) medium *n*
❚❚ *adj* ① *[size, temperature]* średni; **of** ~ **build** średniej budowy ciała ② *[waves]* średni; **on** ~ **wave** na falach średnich
medium-dry /,mi:dɪəm'draɪ/ *adj [drink]* półwytrawny
medium-rare /,mi:dɪəm'reə(r)/ *adj [meat]* średnio wysmażony
medium-sized /,mi:dɪəm'saɪzd/ *adj [tree]* średniej wysokości; *[object]* średniej wielkości

medley /'medlɪ/ *n* ① (of songs) składanka *f* ② (in swimming) styl *m* zmienny ③ (mixture) mieszanina *f*
meek /mi:k/ *adj* potulny
meet /mi:t/ **❚** *n* Sport zawody *plt* (sportowe), mityng *m*
❚❚ *vt* ① (encounter) spot|kać, -ykać *[person]*; spot|kać, -ykać się z (kimś) *[team, opponent]* ② (make acquaintance of) pozna|ć, -wać; **'pleased to** ~ **you!'** „miło mi (panią/pana) poznać" ③ (welcome) przy|witać; (collect on arrival) wy|jść, -chodzić po (kogoś); **he came out to** ~ **me** wyszedł mi na powitanie; **to** ~ **sb off** GB or **at** US **the bus/plane** wyjść/wyjechać po kogoś na autobus/samolot ④ *[hand]* dot|knąć, -ykać (czegoś); *[line]* zetknąć, stykać się z (czymś) ⑤ spełni|ć, -ać *[condition, criteria]*; zaspok|oić, -ajać *[demand, needs]*; wypełni|ć, -ać *[obligations]*; osiąg|nąć, -ać *[goal]*; pokry|ć, -wać *[costs, loss]*; za|płacić, u|regulować *[bill]* ⑥ odpowiadać (czemuś) *[standards]*; sprostać (czemuś) *[challenge, requirements]*
❚❚❚ *vi* ① (come together) spot|kać, -ykać się ② (make acquaintance) pozna|ć, -wać się ③ *[hands, eyes]* spot|kać, -ykać się; *[lines, roads]* po|łączyć się; **the two cars met head-on** samochody zderzyły się czołowo
■ **meet up** infml: spot|kać, -ykać się (**with sb** z kimś)
■ **meet with**: ¶ ~ **with [sb]** spot|kać, -ykać się z (kimś) ¶ ~ **with [sth]** spot|kać, -ykać się z (czymś) *[approval, criticism]*; napot|kać, -ykać *[difficulties]*; zostać przyjętym z (czymś) *[praise]*; ule|c, -gać (czemuś) *[accident]*; **to** ~ **with success** odnieść sukces
meeting /'mi:tɪŋ/ *n* ① (official) zebranie *n*; **to be in a** ~ być na zebraniu ② (coming together) spotkanie *n* ③ GB Sport zawody *plt* sportowe, mityng *m*
meeting-place /'mi:tɪŋpleɪs/ *n* miejsce *n* spotkania
meeting point *n* punkt *m* zborny
megabyte /'megəbaɪt/ *n* megabajt *m*
megalomaniac /,megələ'meɪnɪæk/ **❚** *n* megaloman *m*, -ka *f*
❚❚ *adj* megalomański
megaphone /'megəfəʊn/ *n* megafon *m*
melancholy /'melənkəlɪ/ **❚** *n* melancholia *f*
❚❚ *adj [person, face]* przygnębiony; *[news]* przygnębiający; *[music, mood]* melancholijny
mellow /'meləʊ/ **❚** *adj* ① (smooth) *[taste, flavour]* łagodny; *[tone, sound]* miękki; *[voice, sound]* aksamitny; *[colour, light]* stonowany ② (calm) łagodny; (relaxed) odprężony; **to grow** ~ **with age** łagodnieć z wiekiem
❚❚ *vt [experience, time]* zmiękcz|yć, -ać *[person]*; *[person]* z|łagodzić *[view]*; *[music, wine]* odpręż|yć, -ać *[person]*
❚❚❚ *vi [person, behaviour]* z|łagodnieć
melodrama /'melədrɑ:mə/ *n* melodramat *m*

melodramatic /ˌmelədrə'mætɪk/ *adj* melodrama- tyczny

melody /'melədɪ/ *n* melodia *f*

melon /'melən/ *n* melon *m*

melt /melt/ **[]** *vt [heat, sun, person]* rozt|opić, -apiać, topić; fig zmiększ|yć, -ać fig *[heart, person]*
[] *vi [butter, ice cream]* rozt|opić, -apiać się, topić się; *[ice, snow]* s|topnieć; *[metal, plastic]* s|topić się; *[chocolate]* rozpły|nąć, -wać się; **to ~ into the crowd** wtopić się w tłum

meltdown /'meltdaʊn/ *n* topnienie *n* rdzenia reaktora nuklearnego

melting point *n* temperatura *f* topnienia

member /'membə(r)/ *n* [] człon|ek *m*, -kini *f*; **to be a ~ of sth** należeć do czegoś *[family, party]*; być członkiem czegoś *[tribe, jury, society]*; **~ of staff** pracownik; Sch nauczyciel; **~ of the public** (in the street) przechodzień; (in theatre, cinema) widz [2] (also **Member**) (of parliament) pos|eł *m*, -łanka *f* [3] (limb) **~ s** członki *plt*

membership /'membəʃɪp/ *n* [] członkostwo *n* (**of sth** w czymś); **EU ~** członkostwo w UE [2] (fee) składka *f* członkowska [3] (people belonging) członko- wie *m pl*; (number of members) liczba *f* członków

membrane /'membreɪn/ *n* [] (tissue) błona *f* [2] Tech membrana *f*

memento /mɪ'mentəʊ/ *n* pamiątka *f*

memo /'meməʊ/ *n* notatka *f* służbowa

memoirs /'memwɑː(r)/ *npl* wspomnienia *n pl*

memo pad *n* bloczek *m* do notatek

memorable /'memərəbl/ *adj [event]* pamiętny; *[person]* niezapomniany; *[tune]* wpadający w ucho

memorial /mə'mɔːrɪəl/ **[]** *n* pomnik *m* (**to sb/sth** upamiętniający kogoś/coś)
[] *adj* pamiątkowy; **~ service** nabożeństwo żałobne

memorize /'meməraɪz/ *vt* na|uczyć się na pamięć (czegoś)

memory /'memərɪ/ *n* pamięć *f*; (recollection) wspomnienie *n*; **to have a good ~ for faces** mieć dobrą pamięć do twarzy; **to have a long ~** być pamiętliwym; **from ~** z pamięci; **in (loving) ~ of sb** dla uczczenia pamięci kogoś; **to have vivid memories of sth** mieć coś żywo w pamięci

menace /'menəs/ **[]** *n* [] (threat) groźba *f* [2] (danger) zagrożenie *n* (**to sb/sth** dla kogoś/czegoś)
[] *vt* zagr|ozić, -ażać (komuś), grozić (komuś) (**with sth** czymś)

mend /mend/ **[]** *vt* napraw|ić, -ać *[car, road]*; z|reperować *[clothes, shoes]*; (stitch) zaszy|ć, -wać; (darn) za|cerować; (add patch) za|łatać
[] *vi [injury]* za|goić się; *[person]* powr|ócić, -acać do zdrowia
IDIOMS: **to be on the ~** *[person]* (po)wracać do zdrowia; *[economy, weather]* poprawiać się; *[com- pany]* stawać na nogi fig

menial /'miːnɪəl/ *adj [work]* niewdzięczny; *[atti- tude]* służalczy

meningitis /ˌmenɪn'dʒaɪtɪs/ *n* zapalenie *n* opon mózgowych

menopause /'menəpɔːz/ *n* menopauza *f*

menswear /'menzweə(r)/ *n* odzież *f* męska

mental /'mentl/ *adj* [] Med *[illness]* umysłowy; *[patient]* chory psychicznie; *[hospital]* psychia- tryczny [2] (of the mind) *[process]* myślowy; *[effort, ability]* intelektualny; *[exhaustion]* psychiczny

mentality /men'tælətɪ/ *n* mentalność *f*

mentally /'mentəlɪ/ *adv [retarded, exhausted]* umysłowo; **the ~ ill** chorzy umysłowo; **to be ~ alert** mieć jasny umysł

mentholated /'menθəleɪtɪd/ *adj* mentolowy

mention /'menʃn/ **[]** *n* (reference) wzmianka *f* (**of sb/sth** o kimś/czymś); **it got a ~ on the radio** mówiono o tym w radiu
[] *vt* [] (say) wspom|nieć, -inać o (kimś/czymś) *[person, topic, fact]*; **please don't ~ my name** proszę nie wymieniać mojego nazwiska; **to ~ sb/ sth to sb** wspomnieć komuś o kimś/o czymś; **without ~ing any names** bez nazwisk; **just ~ my name** powołaj się na mnie; **don't ~ it!** nie ma o czym mówić! [2] (acknowledge) wymieni|ć, -ać *[name]*; wspom|nieć, -inać o (czymś) *[services]*

menu /'menjuː/ *n* [] (food served) zestaw *m* potraw; (list) karta *f* (dań), jadłospis *m* [2] Comput menu *n inv*

MEP *n* = **Member of the European Parliament** poseł *m* do Parlamentu Europejskiego

mercenary /'mɜːsɪnərɪ, US -nerɪ/ **[]** *n* najemnik *m*
[] *adj* wyrachowany

merchandise /'mɜːtʃəndaɪz/ *n* towar *m*, towa- ry *m pl*

merchant /'mɜːtʃənt/ **[]** *n* Comm kupiec *m*; (selling in bulk) handlowiec *m*; (selling in small quantities) handlarz *m*; (retailer) detalista *m*
[] *adj [ship]* handlowy

merchant navy GB, **merchant marine** US *n* flota *f* handlowa

merciful /'mɜːsɪfl/ *adj* [] *[person]* litościwy (**to** or **towards sb** dla kogoś, w stosunku do kogoś); *[God, act]* miłosierny; *[sentence]* łagodny [2] *[occurrence]* szczęśliwy

merciless /'mɜːsɪlɪs/ *adj [person, attitude]* bezlitos- ny (**to** or **towards sb** dla kogoś, w stosunku do kogoś); *[rain, heat, cold]* niemiłosierny

mercury /'mɜːkjʊrɪ/ *n* rtęć *f*

mercy /'mɜːsɪ/ *n* [] (compassion) litość *f*, miłosier- dzie *n*; **to have ~ on sb** ulitować się nad kimś; **to beg for ~** błagać o litość [2] (power) łaska *f*; **to be at the ~ of sb/sth** być zdanym na łaskę kogoś/ czegoś

mercy killing *n* eutanazja *f*

mere /mɪə(r)/ *adj* [] (simple) *[formality, assistant]* zwykły; *[coincidence, nonsense]* czysty; **he's a ~ child** to tylko dziecko [2] (very) *[sight, thought]* sam;

the ~ **idea of sth** już sama myśl o czymś; **the merest noise** najmniejszy hałas ③ (bare) zaledwie; **to last a ~ 20 minutes** trwać raptem 20 minut

merely /ˈmɪəlɪ/ *adv [say, imply]* jedynie; *[weigh, measure, take]* zaledwie

merge /mɜːdʒ/ **[I]** *vt* ① (join) **to ~ sth with sth** połączyć coś z czymś; **to ~ sth into sth** połączyć coś w coś *[group]* ② (combine) poǀłączyć *[colour, design]*
[II] *vi* ① (also ~ **together**) *[companies, roads]* poǀłączyć się ② *[colour, shapes, sound]* zlǀać, -ewać się (**with sth** z czymś)

merger /ˈmɜːdʒə(r)/ *n* (of companies) połączenie *n*, fuzja *f*

merit /ˈmerɪt/ **[I]** *n* ① (worth) wartość *f*; **a man of ~** wartościowy człowiek ② (praiseworthy quality) zaleta *f*; (personal credit) zasługa *f*; **to judge sb on his/her own ~s** oceniać kogoś według zasług
[II] *vt* zasłuǀżyć, -giwać na (coś) *[prize, reply]*

mermaid /ˈmɜːmeɪd/ *n* syrena *f*

merrily /ˈmerɪlɪ/ *adv* ① (joyfully) wesoło ② (uncocernedly) beztrosko

merry /ˈmerɪ/ *adj* ① (happy) wesoły; ~ **Christmas!** Wesołych Świąt! ② infml (tipsy) podchmielony infml

merry-go-round /ˈmerɪɡəʊraʊnd/ *n* karuzela *f*

mesh /meʃ/ **[I]** *n* (netting) siatka *f*
[II] *vi* (also ~ **together**) *[ideas]* zazębiǀć, -ać się (**with sth** z czymś)

mesmerize /ˈmezməraɪz/ **[I]** *vt* zaǀhipnotyzować
[II] mesmerized *pp adj* zahipnotyzowany, zafascynowany

mess /mes/ **[I]** *n* ① (untidy state) bałagan *m*; **to make a ~** *[children]* nabałaganić; *[workers]* narobić bałaganu; **the kitchen is (in) a ~** w kuchni jest bałagan; **this report is a ~!** to sprawozdanie jest napisane bez ładu i składu!; **you got us into this ~** to przez ciebie mamy takie kłopoty; **the dog made a ~ on the carpet** pies nabrudził na dywan ② (military) kantyna *f*; **officers' ~** (in the army) kasyno oficerskie; (in the navy) mesa oficerska
[II] *vi* infml **I don't ~ with drugs** trzymam się z dala od narkotyków; **don't ~ with him** nie zadzieraj z nim

■ **mess about, mess around** infml: ¶ ~ **around** wygłupiać się; **to ~ around with sth** bawić się czymś *[knife, matches]* ¶ ~ [**sb**] **around** infml zwodzić

■ **mess up** infml: ¶ ~ **up** US naǀmieszać infml ¶ ~ [**sth**] **up** ① (get untidy) narobić bałaganu w (czymś) *[kitchen]*; pomieszać *[papers]*; zabrudzić *[napkin]* ② (ruin) spaprać infml *[plan, work]*; zmarnować *[life, chance]*; zawalić infml *[exam]* ¶ ~ [**sb**] **up** *[drugs, alcohol]* zǀniszczyć infml; *[experience]* załamać

message /ˈmesɪdʒ/ *n* ① (communication) wiadomość *f* ② (meaning) przesłanie *n*; (political) orędzie *n*

messaging /ˈmesɪdʒɪŋ/ *n* Comput przesyłanie *n* komunikatów

messenger /ˈmesɪndʒə(r)/ *n* posłaniec *m*; (for hotel, company) goniec *m*; (official courier) kurier *m*

messy /ˈmesɪ/ *adj [appearance]* niechlujny; *[hair]* w nieładzie; *[house]* zaniedbany; *[activity]* brudny; *[pen]* brudzący; *[affair]* nieprzyjemny; *[business]* brudny fig; **he is a ~ eater** brudzi się przy jedzeniu

metal /ˈmetl/ **[I]** *n* metal *m*
[II] *adj* metalowy

metallic /mɪˈtælɪk/ *adj [substance, state]* metaliczny; *[paint, finish]* o metalicznym połysku; ~ **taste** smak metalu

metaphor /ˈmetəfɔː(r)/ *n* przenośnia *f*, metafora *f*

mete /miːt/ *vt*
■ **mete out**: wymierzǀyć, -ać *[punishment, justice]*; wydaǀć, -wać *[sentence]*

meteor /ˈmiːtɪə(r)/ *n* meteor *m*

meteorite /ˈmiːtɪəraɪt/ *n* meteoryt *m*

meter /ˈmiːtə(r)/ **[I]** *n* ① licznik *m*; **gas ~** licznik gazowy; **taxi ~** taksometr ② (also **parking ~**) parkometr *m* ③ US = **metre**
[II] *vt* zǀmierzyć *[flow, pressure]*; zǀmierzyć zużycie (czegoś) *[water, electricity]*

method /ˈmeθəd/ *n* metoda *f* (**for doing sth** robienia czegoś); ~ **of payment** forma zapłaty; ~ **of transport** środek transportu; **a man of ~** człowiek metodyczny

methodical /mɪˈθɒdɪkl/ *adj* metodyczny

Methodist /ˈmeθədɪst/ **[I]** *n* metodystǀa *m*, -ka *f*
[II] *adj* metodystyczny

methylated spirit(s) *n* spirytus *m* skażony, denaturat *m*

meticulous /mɪˈtɪkjʊləs/ *adj [observation, methods]* drobiazgowy; *[person]* skrupulatny (**about sth** w czymś)

metre GB, **meter** US /ˈmiːtə(r)/ *n* metr *m*

metric /ˈmetrɪk/ *adj* metryczny

metropolitan /ˌmetrəˈpɒlɪtən/ *adj [traffic, architecture]* wielkomiejski; (of capital) *[amenities, bustle]* stołeczny; *[area, population]* miejski

mettle /ˈmetl/ *n* siła *f* charakteru; (combativeness) duch *m* walki; **they showed their ~** pokazali, na co ich stać; **to be on one's ~** dawać z siebie wszystko

Mexico /ˈmeksɪkəʊ/ *prn* Meksyk *m*

miaow /miːˈaʊ/ **[I]** *n* miauknięcie *n*
[II] *vi* miauǀknąć, -czeć, zamiauczeć

microbe /ˈmaɪkrəʊb/ *n* drobnoustrój *m*, zarazek *m*

microchip /ˈmaɪkrəʊtʃɪp/ *n* mikroukład *m*

microcosm /ˈmaɪkrəkɒzəm/ *n* mikrokosmos *m*

microfilm /ˈmaɪkrəʊfɪlm/ *n* mikrofilm *m*

microphone /ˈmaɪkrəfəʊn/ *n* mikrofon *m*

microscope /ˈmaɪkrəskəʊp/ *n* mikroskop *m*

microwave /'maɪkrəweɪv/ **[]** *n* (~ **oven**) kuchenka *f* mikrofalowa

[] *vt* podgrz|ać, -ewać w kuchence mikrofalowej

mid+ /mɪd/ *in combinations* **in the** ~**-20th century** w połowie XX wieku; ~**-afternoon** popołudnie; **in** ~**-May** w połowie maja; **he's in his** ~**-forties** (on) ma około 45 lat

midair /ˌmɪd'eə(r)/ **[]** *adj* powietrzny

[] **in midair** *adv phr* (in mid-flight) w powietrzu

midday /ˌmɪd'deɪ/ *n* południe *n*

middle /'mɪdl/ **[]** *n* **[1]** środek *m*; **in the** ~ **of the road** na środku *or* pośrodku drogi/jezdni; **in the** ~ **of the night** w środku nocy; **in the** ~ **of June** w połowie czerwca; **in the** ~ **of sth/doing sth** w trakcie czegoś/robienia czegoś; **to split (sth) down the** ~ podzielić (coś) na pół *or* połowę *[bill, work]*; podzielić *[group, opinion]* **[2]** (waist) pas *m*, talia *f*

[] *adj [door, shelf]* środkowy; *[size, height]* średni; *[price]* niewygórowany; **there must be a** ~ **way** *or* **course** fig musi istnieć jakaś droga pośrednia

middle-aged /ˌmɪdl'eɪdʒd/ *adj [person]* w średnim wieku; *[outlook, view]* typowy dla osoby w średnim wieku

Middle Ages *prn* **the** ~ średniowiecze *n*

middle class **[]** *n* klasa *f* średnia

[] *adj* ~ **person** przedstawiciel klasy średniej; ~ **attitude/view** nastawienie/pogląd właściwy klasie średniej

Middle East *prn* **the** ~ Bliski Wschód *m*

middle-eastern /ˌmɪdl'iːstən/ *adj [nation, politics]* bliskowschodni

middleman /'mɪdlmæn/ *n* pośrednik *m*; (mediator) rozjemca *m*

middle-size(d) /ˌmɪdl'saɪz(d)/ *adj [person]* średniego wzrostu; *[object]* średniej wielkości

middleweight /'mɪdlweɪt/ *n* Sport waga *f* średnia

middling /'mɪdlɪŋ/ *adj [size]* przeciętny; *[importance]* umiarkowany; *[ability]* taki sobie

midfield /ˌmɪd'fiːld/ *n* środek *m* boiska

midge /mɪdʒ/ *n* muszka *f*

midget /'mɪdʒɪt/ *n* ka|rzeł *m*, -rlica *f*

midnight /'mɪdnaɪt/ *n* północ *f*

midriff /'mɪdrɪf/ *n* brzuch *m*

midsummer /ˌmɪd'sʌmə(r)/ *n* (high summer) środek *m* lata; (solstice) przesilenie *n* letnie

midtown /'mɪdtaʊn/ *n* US środek *m* miasta

midway /ˌmɪd'weɪ/ **[]** *adj [stage, point]* środkowy; *[position, post]* w połowie drogi

[] *adv* (of distance) w połowie drogi (**between sth and sth** pomiędzy czymś i czymś); (of time, process) w połowie (**through sth** czegoś)

midweek /ˌmɪd'wiːk/ *adj, adv* w środku tygodnia

midwife /'mɪdwaɪf/ *n* położna *f*

midwinter /ˌmɪd'wɪntə(r)/ *n* (season) środek *m* zimy; (solstice) przesilenie *n* zimowe

might¹ /maɪt/ *modal aux* **[1]** (indicating possibility) **she** ~ **be right** (być) może ma rację; **they** ~ **not go**

może nie pójdą; **'will you come?' – 'I** ~**'** „przyjdziesz?" – „możliwe"; **you** ~ **have met her already** możliwe, że ją już kiedyś spotkałeś; **I** ~ **(well) lose my job** mogę stracić pracę; **try as I** ~**, I can't do it** robię, co mogę, ale nie daję rady; **however unlikely that** ~ **be** jakkolwiek nieprawdopodobne może się to wydawać **[2]** (indicating unrealized possibility) **I dread to think what** ~ **have happened** boję się pomyśleć, co mogłoby się stać; **if they had acted quickly, he** ~ **well be alive today** gdyby się wtedy pośpieszyli, bardzo możliwe, że dziś by żył **[3]** (in sequence of tenses) **I said I** ~ **go into town** powiedziałem, że może pójdę do miasta; **they thought she** ~ **have been his lover** sądzili, że mogła być jego kochanką; **I thought it** ~ **rain** sądziłem, że może będzie padać **[4]** fml (when making requests) ~ **I make a suggestion?** czy mógłbym coś zaproponować?; ~ **I ask who is calling?** czy mogę spytać, z kim rozmawiam? **[5]** (when making suggestions) **it** ~ **be a good idea to go there** może warto byłoby tam pójść; **you** ~ **try making some more enquiries** może spróbowałbyś dowiedzieć się czegoś więcej **[6]** (when making statement) **one** ~ **argue** *or* **it** ~ **be argued that...** można zaryzykować stwierdzenie, że...; **as one** *or* **you** ~ **expect** jak można (by) przypuszczać **[7]** (expressing irritation) **I** ~ **have known** *or* **guessed!** mogłem się domyślić!; **he** ~ **at least apologize!** mógłby przynajmniej przeprosić! **[8]** (in concessives) **they** ~ **not be fast but they're reliable** może nie są szybcy, ale można na nich polegać

might² /maɪt/ *n* **[1]** (power) potęga *f* **[2]** (physical strength) siła *f*; **with all his** ~ z całej siły

mighty /'maɪtɪ/ *adj* potężny

migrant /'maɪɡrənt/ **[]** *n* (person) przesiedleniec *m*; (bird) ptak *m* wędrowny; (animal) wędrowny gatunek *m* zwierząt

[] *adj* **[1]** *[labour]* napływowy; *[labourer]* sezonowy; *[tribe]* koczowniczy **[2]** Zool migrujący

migrate /maɪ'ɡreɪt, US 'maɪɡreɪt/ *vi [people]* przen|ieść, -osić się; *[bird, animal]* migrować

mike /maɪk/ *n* infml mikrofon *m*

mild /maɪld/ *adj* **[1]** *[protest, effect]* łagodny; *[interest, irritation]* lekki **[2]** *[weather]* przyjemny; *[winter, climate]* łagodny **[3]** *[character, voice]* łagodny **[4]** *[soap, detergent]* łagodny **[5]** *[symptom, infection]* łagodny **[6]** *[beer, taste]* łagodny

mildew /'mɪldjuː, US -duː/ *n* pleśń *f*

mile /maɪl/ *n* **[1]** mila *f* (= 1609 m); **it's 50** ~**s away** ≈ to około 80 kilometrów stąd **[2]** fig **for** ~**s and** ~**s** jak okiem sięgnąć; **to stretch for** ~**s** ciągnąć się kilometrami; **it's** ~ **away!** ależ to na końcu świata!; **to stand out a** ~**, to stick out a** ~ rzucać się w oczy

mileage /'maɪlɪdʒ/ *n* **[1]** (distance) odległość *f* w milach; **what's the** ~ **for the trip?** ≈ ile kilometrów przejedziemy podczas tej wycieczki?

2 (done by car) przebieg *m* 3 (miles per gallon) zużycie *n* paliwa (na milę)

milestone /'maɪlstəʊn/ *n* słupek *m* milowy; fig kamień *m* milowy fig

militant /'mɪlɪtənt/ **I** *n* bojownik *m*, -czka *f*
II *adj [pressure group]* wojujący; *[protest]* gwałtowny; *[mood]* bojowy; *[tribe]* wojowniczy

militarize /'mɪlɪtəraɪz/ *vt* z|militaryzować

military /'mɪlɪtrɪ, US -terɪ/ **I** *n* the ~ (army) wojsko *n*; (soldiers) wojsko *n*
II *adj [strength, action]* militarny; *[uniform, coup]* wojskowy; **of** ~ **age** w wieku poborowym

military service *n* służba *f* wojskowa

militia /mɪ'lɪʃə/ *n* 1 (citizen army) milicja *f* 2 US the ~ rezerwa *f*

milk /mɪlk/ **I** *n* mleko *n*; **powdered** ~ mleko w proszku; **full-cream** ~ mleko pełnotłuste
II *vt* 1 wy|doić *[cow]* 2 (exploit) wykorzyst|ać, -ywać *[company, state]*; **to** ~ **sb dry** oskubać kogoś z pieniędzy infml

milk chocolate *n* czekolada *f* mleczna

milkman /'mɪlkmən/ *n* mleczarz *m*

milky /'mɪlkɪ/ *adj* 1 *[drink, diet]* mleczny; *[tea, coffee]* z mlekiem 2 *[skin, gem]* mleczny; *[liquid]* mętny

Milky Way *n* Droga *f* Mleczna

mill /mɪl/ **I** *n* 1 (for flour) młyn *m*; (factory) zakład *m* przemysłowy; **paper** ~ papiernia *f* 2 (for pepper) młynek *m*
II *vt* 1 ze|mleć *[flour, pepper]* 2 produkować *[steel, paper]*; prząść *[cotton]*; tkać *[textiles]*

millennium /mɪ'lenɪəm/ *n* tysiąclecie *n*

milligram(me) /'mɪlɪgræm/ *n* miligram *m*

millimetre GB, **millimeter** US /'mɪlɪmi:tə(r)/ *n* milimetr *m*

million /'mɪljən/ **I** *n* milion *m*
II *adj* **a** ~ **people/pounds** milion ludzi/funtów

milometer /maɪ'lɒmɪtə(r)/ *n* GB licznik *m* mil

mime /maɪm/ **I** *n* 1 (art) pantomima *f* 2 (performer) mim *m*
II *vt* od|egrać, -grywać bez słów *[part, action]*; (communicate) pokaz|ać, -ywać na migi
III *vi* od|egrać, -grywać pantomimę

mime artist *n* mim *m*

mimic /'mɪmɪk/ **I** *n* naśladow|ca *m*, -czyni *f*; (professional) parodyst|a *m*, -ka *f*
II *vt* 1 (amuse) naśladować; (ridicule) przedrzeźniać; *[entertainer]* parodiować 2 (simulate) udawać *[ability, condition]*

mince /mɪns/ **I** *n* GB mięso *n* mielone; **beef** ~ mielona wołowina
II *vt* ze|mleć

mind /maɪnd/ **I** *n* 1 (centre of thought) umysł *m*, rozum *m*; **peace of** ~ spokój ducha; **it's all in the** ~ to urojenie; **to cross sb's** ~ przyjść komuś na myśl; **at the back of my** ~ w głębi serca; **to have sth on one's** ~ mieć umysł zaprzątnięty

czymś; **to set sb's** ~ **at rest** rozproszyć obawy kogoś; **I can't get it out of my** ~ nie mogę o tym zapomnieć; **it went right** or **completely out of my** ~ zupełnie wyleciało mi to z głowy; **my** ~**'s a blank** mam pustkę w głowie; **her** ~ **is going** traci rozum; **to drive sb out of his/her** ~ doprowadzać kogoś do szaleństwa 2 (brain) umysł *m*; **with a** ~ **of a two-year-old** o umysłowości dwuletniego dziecka; **to have a very good** ~ być bardzo inteligentnym; **to have a logical** ~ mieć logiczny umysł 3 (opinion) zdanie *n*; **to be of one** ~ być jednomyślnym; **to be in two** ~**s about sth** wahać się z czymś; **to my** ~ moim zdaniem; **to make up one's** ~ **about sth/to do sth** zdecydować się na coś/coś zrobić; **to change one's** ~ zmienić zdanie 4 (attention) uwaga *f*; **to keep one's** ~ **on sth** skupić uwagę na czymś; **to take sb's** ~ **off sth** odwrócić myśli or uwagę kogoś od czegoś
II in mind *adv phr* **I have something in** ~ **for the weekend** mam pewne plany na weekend; **with the future in** ~ z myślą o przyszłości; **with this in** ~ ... z tą myślą...
III *vt* 1 (be careful of) uważać na (coś) *[hazard]*; zwracać uwagę na (kogoś/coś) *[manners, language]*; ~ **the step!** uwaga! stopień 2 (object to) mieć coś przeciw(ko) (komuś/czemuś); **I don't** ~ **the cold** zimno mi nie przeszkadza; **'do you** ~ **if I smoke?'** „pozwolisz, że zapalę?"; **today or tomorrow?' – 'I don't** ~**'** „dziś czy jutro?" – „wszystko mi jedno"; **will they** ~ **us being late?** czy będą się gniewać, jeśli się spóźnimy?; **would you** ~ **keeping my seat for me?** czy mógłbyś przypilnować mi miejsca; **I wouldn't** ~ **a glass of wine** chętnie wypiję kieliszek wina 3 (care) przejmować się (czymś); **do you** ~**!** iron no wiesz!; **never** ~ (don't worry) mniejsza o to; (it doesn't matter) nic nie szkodzi 4 (look after) przy|pilnować *[children, animals, shop]*
(IDIOMS) **to read sb's** ~ czytać w myślach kogoś; **to see sth in one's** ~**'s eye** widzieć coś oczyma duszy

mind-blowing /'maɪndbləʊɪŋ/ *adj* infml fantastyczny infml

mind-boggling /'maɪndbɒglɪŋ/ *adj* infml niepojęty

mindless /'maɪndlɪs/ *adj [person, destruction]* bezmyślny; *[task]* niewymagający myślenia

mine[1] /maɪn/ *pron* mój; **which (glass) is** ~ ? który (kieliszek) jest mój?; **a friend of** ~ mój znajomy; **it's not** ~ to nie moje

mine[2] /maɪn/ **I** *n* 1 (in mining) kopalnia; **to work in** or **down the** ~**s** pracować pod ziemią; **a** ~ **of information** fig kopalnia informacji 2 (explosive) mina *f*

II *vt* [1] (extract) wydoby|ć, -wać *[gems, mineral]*; wy|eksploatować *[area]* [2] (lay mines in) zaminow|ać, -ywać *[area]*

minefield /'maɪnfiːld/ *n* pole *n* minowe; fig grząski grunt *m* fig

miner /'maɪnə(r)/ *n* górnik *m*

mineral /'mɪnərəl/ **II** *n* minerał *m*; (for extraction) kopalina *f*

II *adj* mineralny; ~ **ore** ruda

mineral water *n* woda *f* mineralna

mingle /'mɪŋgl/ *vi* **to** ~ **with guests** rozmawiać z gośćmi; **to** ~ **with certain people** obracać się wśród określonej grupy ludzi [2] (combine) *[sounds, feelings]* z|mieszać się

miniature /'mɪnətʃə(r), US 'mɪnɪətʃʊər/ **II** *n* miniatura *f*

II *adj [bottle, camera]* miniaturowy; *[world, version]* w miniaturze

minicab /'mɪnɪkæb/ *n* GB taksówka *f* (na telefon)

minidisc /'mɪnɪdɪsk/ *n* czysta płyta *f* kompaktowa

minimalist /'mɪnɪməlɪst/ **II** *n* minimalist|a *m*, -ka *f*

II *adj* minimalistyczny

minimum /'mɪnɪməm/ **II** *n* minimum *n inv*; **to keep sth to a** or **the** ~ ograniczać coś do minimum

II *adj* minimalny

mining /'maɪnɪŋ/ **II** *n* górnictwo *n*

II *adj [area, town, union]* górniczy; ~ **accident** wypadek *m* w kopalni; ~ **industry** przemysł wydobywczy

minister /'mɪnɪstə(r)/ **II** *n* [1] GB (politician) minister *m*; ~ **of** or **for Defence/Defence** ~ minister obrony narodowej [2] (clergyman) pastor *m*

II *vi* **to** ~ **to sb** pielęgnować kogoś; **to** ~ **to sb's needs** dbać o potrzeby kogoś

minister of state *n* GB sekretarz *m* stanu

ministry /'mɪnɪstrɪ/ *n* GB ministerstwo *n*

mink /mɪŋk/ *n* [1] (animal) norka *f* [2] (fur, coat) norki *plt*

minor /'maɪnə(r)/ **II** *n* nieletni *m*, -a *f*

II *adj* [1] (lesser) *[change, repair, defect]* drobny; *[role]* niewielki; *[position, artist]* drugorzędny [2] (not serious) *[injury, fracture, surgery]* niegroźny [3] Mus molowy

minority /maɪ'nɒrətɪ, US -'nɔːr-/ *n* mniejszość *f*; **to be in the** ~ być w mniejszości

minstrel /'mɪnstrəl/ *n* minstrel *m*

mint¹ /mɪnt/ **II** *n* [1] (plant) mięta *f* [2] (sweet) miętówka *f*

II *adj [sauce, tea]* miętowy

mint² /mɪnt/ **II** *n* mennica *f*

II *adj* nowy; **in** ~ **condition** w idealnym stanie

III *vt* wybi|ć, -jać, bić *[coin]*; fig ukuć *[word, expression]*

minuet /ˌmɪnjʊ'et/ *n* menuet *m*

minus /'maɪnəs/ **II** *n* minus *m*

II *adj* [1] *[number, value]* ujemny; *[temperature]* minusowy; ~ **sign** znak minusa [2] (disadvantageous) **a** ~ **factor/point** minus; **on the** ~ **side....** minusem jest to, że....

III *prep* [1] (in counting) minus; **what is 20** ~ **8?** ile jest 20 minus or odjąć 8?; **it is** ~ **15 (degrees)** jest minus 15 (stopni) [2] (without) bez (czegoś)

minuscule /'mɪnəskjuːl/ *adj [object]* maleńki; *[letter]* mały

minute¹ /'mɪnɪt/ **II** *n* minuta *f*; **five** ~ **s past ten** pięć (minut) po dziesiątej; **it's five** ~ **s' walk away** to stąd pięć minut piechotą; **she won't be a** ~ ona zaraz przyjdzie; **the** ~ **I heard the news** jak tylko usłyszałem wiadomość; **any** ~ **now** lada chwila; **to put sth off to the last** ~ odkładać coś na ostatnią chwilę

II minutes *npl* protokół *m*; **to take the** ~ **s** protokołować

minute² /maɪ'njuːt, US -'nuːt/ *adj [particle]* maleńki; *[quantity]* znikomy; *[risk, variation]* minimalny; *[description]* szczegółowy

minute hand *n* wskazówka *f* minutowa

miracle /'mɪrəkl/ *n* cud *m*

miraculous /mɪ'rækjʊləs/ *adj [cure, survival]* cudowny; *[success, memory]* niebywały

mirror /'mɪrə(r)/ **II** *n* lustro *n*; (in car) lusterko *n*

II *vt* odbi|ć, -jać; **to be** ~ **ed in sth** odbijać się w czymś

mirth /mɜːθ/ *n* (laughter) rozbawienie *n*; (joy) radość *f*

misapprehension /ˌmɪsæprɪ'henʃn/ *n* błędne mniemanie *n*; **to be (labouring) under a** ~ trwać w błędnym przeświadczeniu

misappropriate /ˌmɪsə'prəʊprɪeɪt/ *vt* sprzenie-wierz|yć, -ać *[funds]*

misbehave /ˌmɪsbɪ'heɪv/ *vi [child]* źle się zacho-w|ać, -ywać; *[adult]* źle się prowadzić

miscalculation /ˌmɪskælkjʊ'leɪʃn/ *n* błąd *m* w obliczeniach; fig błędna ocena *f*

miscarriage /'mɪskærɪdʒ, ˌmɪs'kærɪdʒ/ *n* [1] Med poronienie *n*; **to have a** ~ poronić [2] (in law) **a** ~ **of justice** pomyłka *f* sądowa

miscellaneous /ˌmɪsə'leɪnɪəs/ *adj* rozmaity

mischief /'mɪstʃɪf/ *n* (playfulness) figlarność *f*; (maliciousness) intrygi *f pl*; (done by children) psoty *f pl*; **to get into** ~ napsocić; **to be full of** ~ uwielbiać psocić; **it keeps them out of** ~ to daje im zajęcie

mischievous /'mɪstʃɪvəs/ *adj [child]* psotny; *[comedy]* swawolny; *[eyes, smile]* szelmowski

misconception /ˌmɪskən'sepʃn/ *n* błędne wyob-rażenie *n* or przekonanie *n*

misdemeanour GB, **misdemeanor** US /ˌmɪsdɪ'miːnə(r)/ *n* wykroczenie *n*

miser /'maɪzə(r)/ *n* skąpiec *m*

miserable /'mɪzrəbl/ *adj [person, expression]* nie-szczęśliwy; *[weather, mood]* ponury; *[quantity, sal-*

ary] nędzny; *[performance, attempts]* żałosny; *[result]* opłakany; *[life]* żałosny; *[dwelling, clothes]* nędzny

miserly /'maɪzəlɪ/ *adj [person]* skąpy; *[amount]* skromny

misery /'mɪzərɪ/ *n* [1] (unhappiness) nieszczęście *n*; (gloom) przygnębienie *n*; **to make sb's life a** ~ zmienić życie kogoś w pasmo udręki [2] (misfortune) niedola *f* [3] GB infml (adult) ponurak *m* infml; (child) maruda *m/f* infml

misfire /ˌmɪs'faɪə(r)/ *vi [gun, rocket]* nie wypal|ić, -ać; *[engine]* nie zapal|ić, -ać; fig *[plan, joke]* nie wypalić infml

misfit /'mɪsfɪt/ *n* (in a group) odmieniec *m*; **he is a social** ~ jest społecznie nieprzystosowany

misfortune /ˌmɪs'fɔːtʃuːn/ *n* (unfortunate event) nieszczęście *n*; (bad luck) pech *m*; **it's a** ~ **that...** źle się złożyło, że...

misgiving /ˌmɪs'gɪvɪŋ/ *n* złe przeczucie *n*; **to have ~s about sth** żywić obawy co do czegoś; **to have ~s about sb** mieć wątpliwości co do kogoś

misguided /ˌmɪs'gaɪdɪd/ *adj [opinion, belief]* błędny; *[strategy, attempt]* chybiony; *[politician, teacher]* niemający rozeznania

mishandle /ˌmɪs'hændl/ *vt* [1] (badly) nieudolnie przeprowadz|ić, -ać *[operation]*; źle po|prowadzić *[meeting]*; mieć niewłaściwe podejście do (kogoś/ czegoś) *[child, relationship]* [2] (roughly) nieostrożnie się obchodzić z (czymś) *[object]*; znęcać się nad (czymś) *[animal]*

mishap /'mɪshæp/ *n* niefortunny wypadek *m*

mishear /ˌmɪs'hɪə(r)/ *vt* źle usłyszeć

misinform /ˌmɪsɪn'fɔːm/ *vt* wprowadz|ić, -ać w błąd; (intentionally) dezinformować

misinterpret /ˌmɪsɪn'tɜːprɪt/ *vt* błędnie z|interpretować

misjudge /ˌmɪs'dʒʌdʒ/ *vt* błędnie oceni|ć, -ać *[distance, speed]*; źle wymierz|yć, -ać *[shot]*; źle osądz|ić, -ać *[person, motive]*

mislay /ˌmɪs'leɪ/ *vt* zapodzi|ać, -ewać *[pen, keys, document]*

mislead /ˌmɪs'liːd/ *vt* zmylić

misleading /ˌmɪs'liːdɪŋ/ *adj [title, information, advertisement]* mylący; *[impression]* złudny

mismanage /ˌmɪs'mænɪdʒ/ *vt* źle zarządzać (czymś) *[company, factory]*

misplace /ˌmɪs'pleɪs/ *vt* [1] (lose) zawieruszyć *[keys, money]* [2] (put) postawić, stawiać nie na swoje miejsce *[vase]*; od|łożyć, -kładać nie na swoje miejsce *[book]*

misprint /'mɪsprɪnt/ *n* błąd *m* zecerski

mispronounce /ˌmɪsprə'naʊns/ *vt* źle wym|ówić, -awiać *[word]*

misread /ˌmɪs'riːd/ *vt* błędnie odczyt|ać, -ywać *[word, map]*; fig błędnie z|rozumieć *[actions, intentions]*

misrepresent /ˌmɪsˌreprɪ'zent/ *vt* przedstawi|ć, -ać w nieprawdziwym świetle *[person]*; wypacz|yć, -ać *[views, intentions]*; przeinacz|yć, -ać *[facts]*

misrepresentation /ˌmɪsˌreprɪzen'teɪʃn/ *n* (of opinions, intentions) wypaczenie *n*; (of person) fałszywy obraz *m*

miss /mɪs/ **I** *n* [1] (in game) niecelny strzał *m* [2] **to give sth a** ~ infml odpu|ścić, -szczać sobie coś infml [3] (failure) porażka *f*
II *vt* [1] (fail to hit) nie trafi|ć, -ać w (coś) or do (czegoś) *[target]*; nie pobić (czegoś) *[record]* [2] (be late) nie zdąż|yć, -ać na (coś), spóźni|ć, -ać się na (coś) *[bus, plane, event]*; rozmi|nąć, -jać się z (kimś) *[person]*; przegapi|ć, -ać infml *[connection, bargain]*; przepu|ścić -szczać, s|tracić *[chance, opportunity]*; **I ~ed the train by five minutes** spóźniłem się na pociąg (o) pięć minut [3] (fail to notice) nie zauważ|yć, -ać (czegoś) *[sign, mistake, person]*; mi|nąć *[turning]* [4] (fail to hear) nie dosłyszeć (czegoś); (fail to understand) nie z|rozumieć (czegoś) *[joke, remark]*; **she doesn't ~ much** niewiele uchodzi jej uwadze [5] (omit) opu|ścić, -szczać *[line, page, meal, school]* [6] (escape) unik|nąć, -ać (czegoś); **she just ~ed getting soaked** zdołała jeszcze umknąć przed ulewą [7] (regret) za|tęsknić za (kimś/czymś) *[person, place]*; **he ~ed Paris** tęsknił za Paryżem
III *vi* [1] (fail to hit) chybi|ć, -ać [2] *[engine]* nie zapal|ić, -ać
■ **miss out:** ¶ ~ **out** być stratnym ¶ ~ **out on [sth]** przegapi|ć, -ać ¶ ~ **[sb/sth] out** opu|ścić, -szczać *[line, verse]*; pomi|nąć, -jać *[fact, point, person]*

Miss /mɪs/ *n* [1] (woman's title) panna *f* [2] (in beauty contest) miss *f inv* [3] (mode of address) pani *f*

misshapen /ˌmɪs'ʃeɪpən/ *adj* zniekształcony

missile /'mɪsaɪl, US 'mɪsl/ *n* pocisk *m*

missing /'mɪsɪŋ/ *adj [thing]* brakujący; *[person]* zaginiony; **sb/sth is** ~ kogoś/czegoś brakuje or nie ma; **to go** ~ *[person]* zaginąć; *[object]* zgubić się; **to report sb** ~ zgłosić zaginięcie kogoś

mission /'mɪʃn/ *n* misja *f*

missionary /'mɪʃənrɪ, US -nerɪ/ *n* misjona|rz *m*, -rka *f*

mist /mɪst/ *n* (thin fog) mgła *f*; (of perfume) mgiełka *f*; (from breath, on window) para *f*
■ **mist over, mist up:** *[lens, mirror]* zaparow|ać, -ywać

mistake /mɪ'steɪk/ **I** *n* (error) błąd *m*; **to make a** ~ (in decision) popełnić błąd; (in spelling, typing) zrobić błąd ortograficzny (**in sth** w czymś); (in calculation, date) pomylić się (**in sth** w czymś); **to make a** ~ **about sb/sth** pomylić się co do kogoś/czegoś; **by** ~ przez pomyłkę; **there's no** ~ pomyłka jest wykluczona; **to learn by one's ~s** uczyć się na (własnych) błędach

II *vt* [1] (confuse) **to ~ sth for sth** pomylić coś z czymś; **to ~ sb for sb else** wziąć kogoś za kogoś innego [2] (misinterpret) opacznie z|rozumieć *[meaning]*

mistaken /mɪˈsteɪkən/ *adj* [1] **to be ~** mylić się; **he was ~ in thinking it was over** mylił się sądząc, że (jest) już po wszystkim; **to do sth in the ~ belief that...** zrobić coś w błędnym przekonaniu, że... [2] *[enthusiasm, loyalty]* nieuzasadniony

mistletoe /ˈmɪsltəʊ/ *n* jemioła *f*

mistranslation /ˌmɪstrænsˈleɪʃn/ *n* błąd *m* w tłumaczeniu

mistreat /ˌmɪsˈtriːt/ *vt* znęcać się nad (kimś/czymś)

mistress /ˈmɪstrɪs/ *n* kochanka *f*

mistrust /ˌmɪsˈtrʌst/ **I** *n* nieufność *f* (**of** or **towards sb/sth** do kogoś/czegoś)

II *vt* nie ufać (komuś), nie dowierzać (komuś)

misty /ˈmɪstɪ/ *adj [conditions, morning]* mglisty; *[view, look]* zamglony; *[lens, window]* zaparowany; *[photo, TV picture]* nieostry

misunderstand /ˌmɪsˌʌndəˈstænd/ **I** *vt* źle z|rozumieć; (completely) nie z|rozumieć (kogoś/czegoś)

II misunderstood *pp adj* **to feel misunderstood** czuć się nierozumianym

misunderstanding /ˌmɪsˌʌndəˈstændɪŋ/ *n* nieporozumienie *n*

misuse **I** /ˌmɪsˈjuːs/ *n* (of equipment, word) niewłaściwe użycie *n*; (of power, authority) nadużycie *n*; (of talents, information, resources) niewłaściwe wykorzystanie *n*

II /ˌmɪsˈjuːz/ *vt* nieprawidłowo uży|ć, -wać (czegoś) *[equipment, word]*; naduży|ć, -wać (czegoś) *[power, authority]*; niewłaściwie spożytkow|ać, -ywać *[talents, information]*

mitigate /ˈmɪtɪgeɪt/ *vt* z|łagodzić *[effect, punishment, sentence]*; zmniejsz|yć, -ać *[risk, loss]*

mitre GB, **miter** US /ˈmaɪtə(r)/ *n* mitra *f*

mitten /ˈmɪtn/ *n* (covering hand) rękawiczka *f* z jednym palcem; (leaving fingers uncovered) mitenka *f*

mix /mɪks/ **I** *n* [1] (combination) mieszanina *f*; (of styles, colours) połączenie *n* [2] Mus miks *m*

II *vt* z|mieszać *[ingredients, colours]*; prze|mieszać *[people, objects]*; po|łączyć *[systems, styles, methods]* (**with sth** z czymś); rozr|obić, -abiać *[cement, paste]*; przyrządz|ić, -ać *[drink, salad]*; Mus z|miksować

III *vi* [1] (be combined) (also **~ together**) wy|mieszać się (**with sth** z czymś) [2] (socialize) **he finds it hard to ~ at parties** ma trudności z nawiązywaniem znajomości na przyjęciach

■ **mix up**: **~ [sb/sth] up** [1] (confuse) po|mylić *[dates, names, tickets]* [2] (jumble up) po|mieszać *[papers, photos, clothes]* [3] (involve) **to be ~ed up in sth** być w coś zamieszanym; **to get ~ed up in sth** wplątać się w coś

mixed /mɪkst/ *adj* [1] *[collection, programme, diet, group, community]* zróżnicowany; *[nuts, sweets]* róż-

nego rodzaju [2] *[school, sauna]* koedukacyjny; **in ~ company** w mieszanym towarzystwie [3] *[response, reaction, reception]* mieszany

mixed ability *adj [class, teaching]* bez podziału na grupy

mixed race *n* **to be of ~** być rasy mieszanej

mixer /ˈmɪksə(r)/ *n* [1] Culin mikser *m* [2] (drink) bezalkoholowy dodatek *m* do drinków [3] **to be a good/bad ~** łatwo/trudno nawiązywać znajomości

mixture /ˈmɪkstʃə(r)/ *n* mieszanka *f*; (of people) mieszanina *f*

mix-up /ˈmɪksʌp/ *n* nieporozumienie *n*

moan /məʊn/ **I** *n* [1] (of person) jęk *m*; (prolonged) zawodzenie *n* [2] infml biadolenie *n* infml (**about sth** na coś)

II *vi* [1] je|knąć, -czeć; **to ~ with pain** jęczeć z bólu [2] infml (complain) narzekać (**about sb/sth** na kogoś/coś); *[child]* marudzić

moat /məʊt/ *n* fosa *f*

mob /mɒb/ **I** tłum *m*; motłoch *m* pej

II *vt* oble|c, -gać *[person, place]*

mobile /ˈməʊbaɪl, US -bl, *also* -biːl/ **I** *n* (also **~ phone**) telefon *m* komórkowy

II *adj* [1] (movable) *[staircase, stage]* ruchomy; *[hospital, canteen]* polowy; *[population, workforce]* mobilny [2] (able to get around) **to be ~** (able to walk) móc chodzić or poruszać się; (able to travel) mieć czym jeździć

mobilize /ˈməʊbɪlaɪz/ **I** *vt* z|mobilizować *[troops, reservists]*; postawić, stawiać w stan gotowości bojowej *[tanks, aeroplanes]*; z|mobilizować *[supporters, resources]*; z|organizować *[workforce, voter support]*

II *vi* *[country, armed forces]* z|mobilizować się; *[army reserve, nation]* stanąć, stawać pod bronią

mocha /ˈmɒkə, US ˈməʊkə/ *n* [1] (coffee) mokka *f* [2] (flavouring) aromat *m* czekoladowo-kawowy

mock /mɒk/ **I** *n* GB Sch infml próbny egzamin *m*

II *adj* [1] (imitation) *[leather, ivory]* sztuczny [2] (feigned) *[innocence, solemnity]* udawany; *[accident, battle]* pozorowany; **in ~ terror** udając przerażenie

III *vt* (laugh at) wyśmi|ać, -ewać; (mimic) przedrzeźniać

IV *vi* wyśmiewać się

mockery /ˈmɒkərɪ/ *n* kpiny *f pl*, drwiny *f pl*

mode /məʊd/ *n* [1] (way) sposób *m*; **~ of transport** środek transportu [2] (of equipment) tryb *m* (pracy); (of person) nastrój *m*

model /ˈmɒdl/ **I** *n* [1] (scale representation) makieta *f*, model *m* [2] (version of car, appliance, garment) model *m* [3] (person) model *m*, -ka *f* [4] (example) wzór *m*

II *adj* [1] (miniature) **~ aeroplane** model samolotu; **~ car** model samochodu; (toy) samochodzik; **~ train** kolejka; **~ village** makieta miasteczka [2] (exemplary) *[farm, hospital, prison]* modelowy, wzorowy [3] (perfect) *[spouse, student]* wzorowy

III *vt* [1] za|prezentować *[garment, design]* [2] *[sculptor, artist]* wy|modelować; **to ~ sth in clay** modelować coś w glinie

IV *vi* [1] *[artist's model]* pozować (**for sb** komuś) [2] *[fashion model]* pracować jako model/modelka

modelling, modeling US /ˈmɒdəlɪŋ/ *n* [1] (of clothes) **to take up ~** zacząć pracować jako model/modelka [2] (for artist) pozowanie *n* [3] Comput modelowanie *n*

moderate [I] /ˈmɒdərət/ *adj* [1] *[views, demands, price]* umiarkowany (**in sth** w czymś); *[tone]* spokojny; *[person]* o umiarkowanych poglądach [2] *[ability, achievements]* przeciętny

[II] /ˈmɒdəreɪt/ *vt* z|łagodzić *[opinions]*; po-wściąg|nąć, -ać *[demands]*

[III] /ˈmɒdəreɪt/ *vi* *[person]* stać się bardziej umiarkowanym w poglądach; *[wind]* o|słabnąć; *[storm]* uciszyć się, cichnąć

moderation /ˌmɒdəˈreɪʃn/ *n* umiar *m* (**in sth** w czymś); **in ~** z umiarem

modern /ˈmɒdn/ *adj* [1] *[car, system, person]* nowoczesny [2] *[art, world]* współczesny; *[era]* nowożytny; **~ Berlin** dzisiejszy Berlin; **in ~ times** w dzisiejszych czasach

modernize /ˈmɒdənaɪz/ *vt* z|modernizować

modest /ˈmɒdɪst/ *adj* [1] *[dress, person]* skromny; **to be ~ about sth** nie chwalić się czymś [2] *[gift, aim, salary]* skromny; *[amount, improvement]* niewielki

modesty /ˈmɒdɪstɪ/ *n* (of person) poczucie *n* przyzwoitości; (of dress) przyzwoitość

modify /ˈmɒdɪfaɪ/ *vt* z|modyfikować *[design, wording]*; ulepsz|yć, -ać *[drug]*; z|łagodzić *[demand, statement]*

modular /ˈmɒdjʊlə(r), US -dʒʊ-/ *adj* *[design, construction]* modułowy; *[program]* modularny; **~ furniture** meble z segmentów

module /ˈmɒdjuːl, US -dʒʊ-/ *n* moduł *m*

mogul /ˈməʊgl/ *n* magnat *m*

Mohammed /məʊˈhæmed/ *prn* Mahomet *m*

moist /mɔɪst/ *adj* *[climate, soil, towel, cake]* wilgotny; *[skin]* dobrze nawilżony

moisten /ˈmɔɪsn/ *vt* zwilż|yć, -ać *[soil, cloth]*; Culin nasącz|yć, -ać

moisture /ˈmɔɪstʃə(r)/ *n* (of soil, in walls) wilgoć *f*; (on glass) para *f*

moisturizer /ˈmɔɪstʃəraɪzə(r)/ *n* (lotion) mleczko *n* nawilżające; (cream) krem *m* nawilżający

molar /ˈməʊlə(r)/ *n* ząb *m* trzonowy

mold *n, vt* US = **mould**

mole[1] /məʊl/ *n* (animal) kret *m*

mole[2] /məʊl/ *n* (on skin) pieprzyk *m*

molecule /ˈmɒlɪkjuːl/ *n* cząsteczka *f*

molest /məˈlest/ *vt* molestować seksualnie

mollycoddle /ˈmɒlɪkɒdl/ *vt* rozpie|ścić, -szczać

molt *n, vi* US = **moult**

molten /ˈməʊltən/ *adj* roztopiony

moment /ˈməʊmənt/ *n* [1] (instant) chwila *f*, moment *m*; **in a ~** za chwilę; **for the ~** na razie, chwilowo; **at any ~** w każdej chwili [2] (point in time) moment *m*; **at the right ~** w odpowiednim momencie; **phone me the ~ (that) he arrives** zadzwoń do mnie, jak tylko przyjedzie

momentarily /ˈməʊməntrəlɪ, US ˌməʊmənˈterəlɪ/ *adv* [1] *[stop, forget]* na moment; *[glance, hesitate]* przez chwilę [2] US (very soon) za chwilę; (at any moment) lada chwila

momentary /ˈməʊməntrɪ, US -terɪ/ *adj* chwilowy; *[impulse, indecision]* chwilowy; *[glimpse]* przelotny

momentous /məˈmentəs, məʊˈm-/ *adj* doniosły

momentum /məˈmentəm, məʊˈm-/ *n* (pace) rozmach *m*; (in physics) pęd *m*

monarch /ˈmɒnək/ *n* monarch|a *m*, -ini *f*

monarchy /ˈmɒnəkɪ/ *n* monarchia *f*

monastery /ˈmɒnəstrɪ, US -terɪ/ *n* klasztor *m* (męski)

Monday /ˈmʌndeɪ, -dɪ/ *n* poniedziałek *m*

money /ˈmʌnɪ/ *n* pieniądze *plt*; (salary) płaca *f*; **to make ~** *[person]* zarabiać; *[business, project]* przynosić zyski

[IDIOMS] **to get one's ~'s worth, to get a good run for one's ~** nie wydawać pieniędzy na darmo; **your ~ or your life!** pieniądze albo życie!

money belt *n* pas *m* na pieniądze

moneybox /ˈmʌnɪbɒks/ *n* skarbonka *f*

moneylender /ˈmʌnɪlendə(r)/ *n* pożyczkodaw-ca *m*

moneymaker /ˈmʌnɪmeɪkə(r)/ *n* *[product]* przebój *m* rynkowy; *[activity]* kokosowy or złoty interes *m*

mongrel /ˈmʌŋgrl/ *n* kundel *m*

monitor /ˈmɒnɪtə(r)/ [I] *n* monitor *m*

[II] *vt* monitorować *[traffic, pollution]*; s|kontrolować *[temperature, process]*; nadzorować *[election]*; obserwować *[patient]*; przeprowadz|ić, -ać nasłuch (czegoś) *[broadcasts]*

monk /mʌŋk/ *n* mnich *m*

monkey /ˈmʌŋkɪ/ *n* małpa *f*

monochrome /ˈmɒnəkrəʊm/ *adj* [1] *[film]* czarno--biały [2] fig bezbarwny

monogamy /məˈnɒgəmɪ/ *n* monogamia *f*

monologue, monolog US /ˈmɒnəlɒg/ *n* monolog *m*

monopolize /məˈnɒpəlaɪz/ *vt* [1] z|monopolizować *[market, supply]* [2] fig z|dominować *[conversation]*; przywłaszcz|yć, -ać sobie *[toy]*

monopoly /məˈnɒpəlɪ/ *n* monopol *m*

monotonous /məˈnɒtənəs/ *adj* jednostajny, monotonny

monotony /məˈnɒtənɪ/ *n* jednostajność *f*, monotonia *f*

monsoon /mɒnˈsuːn/ *n* monsun *m*

monster /'mɒnstə(r)/ n potwór m

monstrous /'mɒnstrəs/ adj [1] (atrocious) [creature, crime] potworny; (ugly) [building] monstrualny [2] (huge) gigantyczny

month /mʌnθ/ n miesiąc m; **in two ~s, in two ~s' time** za dwa miesiące; **every other ~** co dwa miesiące; **at the end of the ~** pod koniec miesiąca; **what day of the ~ is today?** który dzisiaj?; **a ~'s rent** miesięczny czynsz

monthly /'mʌnθlɪ/ [I] n miesięcznik m
[II] adj [meeting, visit] comiesięczny; [payment, income] miesięczny
[III] adv [pay, earn] miesięcznie; [happen, publish] co miesiąc

monument /'mɒnjʊmənt/ n pomnik m

moo /muː/ vi [cow] za|ryczeć

mood /muːd/ n [1] (frame of mind) nastrój m, humor m; **in a good/bad ~** w dobrym/złym humorze; **to be in the ~ for doing sth** mieć ochotę coś zrobić; **to be in a relaxed ~** być odprężonym [2] (bad temper) zły nastrój m; **to be in a ~** być w złym humorze [3] (of place, artwork) nastrój m; (in meeting) atmosfera f

moody /'muːdɪ/ adj [1] (unpredictable) kapryśny [2] (sad) [person, expression] markotny; [appearance] ponury, posępny

moon /muːn/ n księżyc m; **new ~** nów; **full ~** pełnia księżyca; **a crescent ~** sierp księżyca; **half ~** półksiężyc
(IDIOMS) **to be over the ~** nie posiadać się ze szczęścia; **once in a blue ~** od wielkiego dzwonu

moonlight /'muːnlaɪt/ [I] n blask m księżyca
[II] vi dorabiać na boku infml

moonlit /'muːnlɪt/ adj [evening, sky] rozświetlony księżycową poświatą; **a ~ night** księżycowa noc

moor[1] /mɔː(r), US mʊər/ n wrzosowisko n

moor[2] /mɔː(r), US mʊər/ [I] vt przy|cumować [ship]
[II] vi [ship] za|cumować

moorland /'mɔːlənd, US 'mʊər-/ n wrzosowisko n pl

moose /muːs/ n łoś m

mop /mɒp/ [I] n [1] (for floors) mop m; (for dishes) zmywak m (z rączką) [2] (hair) czupryna f
[II] vt u|myć, zmy|ć, -wać [floor]; o|trzeć, -cierać [face]; wy|trzeć, -cierać, zetrzeć, ścierać [worktop]
■ **mop up**: zetrzeć, ścierać [liquid]; uprząt|nąć, -ać, zmi|eść, -atać [mess]

mope /məʊp/ vi rozczulać się nad sobą
■ **mope about, mope around**: snuć się z kąta w kąt z nieszczęśliwą miną

moped /'məʊped/ n motorower m

moral /'mɒrəl/ [I] n morał m
[II] morals npl moralność f
[III] adj moralny

morale /mə'rɑːl, US -'ræl/ n morale n inv; (troops') duch m bojowy

morality /mə'rælətɪ/ n moralność f

morbid /'mɔːbɪd/ adj [curiosity, interest] chorobliwy; [comment, joke] makabryczny

more /mɔː(r)/ [I] adv [1] (comparative) bardziej; **it's ~ serious than we thought** to poważniejsze niż sądziliśmy; **the ~ intelligent child of the two** (to) inteligentniejsze dziecko z dwojga [2] (to a greater extent) więcej; **you must sleep ~** musisz więcej spać; **he is (all) the ~ angry because...** jest tym bardziej zły, ponieważ... [3] (longer) **I don't work there any ~** już tam nie pracuję [4] (again) **once ~** jeszcze raz [5] (rather) raczej; **~ surprised than angry** bardziej zdziwiony niż zły
[II] quantif więcej; **~ cars than expected** więcej samochodów niż się spodziewano; **some ~ books** trochę więcej książek; **there's no ~ bread** nie ma już (więcej) chleba; **have you any ~ questions?** masz jeszcze jakieś pytania?; **nothing ~** nic więcej; **something ~** coś jeszcze
[III] pron [1] (larger amount or number) więcej; **it costs ~ than the other one** to jest droższe od tamtego; **he eats ~ than you** on je więcej od ciebie [2] (additional amount or number) więcej; **I need ~ of them** potrzebuję ich więcej; **we need ~ of it** potrzebujemy tego więcej; **I have nothing ~ to say** nie mam już nic więcej do powiedzenia
[IV] **more and more** det phr, adv phr (amount) coraz więcej; (intensity) coraz bardziej
[V] **more or less** adv phr mniej więcej
[VI] **more than** adv phr, prep phr [1] (greater amount or number) więcej niż, ponad; **~ than 20 people** ponad dwudzieścia osób; **~ than half** ponad połowa; **~ than enough** za or zbyt dużo [2] (extremely) **~ than generous** więcej niż hojny

moreover /mɔː'rəʊvə(r)/ adv ponadto, poza tym

morning /'mɔːnɪŋ/ [I] n ranek m; **(on) Monday ~** w poniedziałek rano; **later this ~** dziś przed południem; **early** or **first thing in the ~** z samego rana
[II] adj [air, news] poranny; [flight, train] ranny
[III] excl (also **good ~**) dzień dobry!

morsel /'mɔːsl/ n (of food) kęs m; (of sense, self-respect) odrobina f

mortal /'mɔːtl/ [I] n śmiertelni|k m, -czka f
[II] adj śmiertelny

mortality /mɔː'tælətɪ/ n śmiertelność f

mortar /'mɔːtə(r)/ n [1] (weapon, vessel) moździerz m [2] (in building) zaprawa f murarska

mortgage /'mɔːgɪdʒ/ n hipoteka f (**on sth** na czymś)

mortuary /'mɔːtʃərɪ, US 'mɔːtʃʊerɪ/ n kostnica f

mosaic /məʊ'zeɪɪk/ n mozaika f

Moscow /'mɒskəʊ/ prn Moskwa f

Moslem /'mɒzləm/ n, adj = **Muslim**

mosque /mɒsk/ n meczet m

mosquito /məs'kiːtəʊ, mɒs-/ n komar m; (in tropics) moskit m

mosquito repellent n środek m przeciw komarom

moss /mɒs, US mɔːs/ n mech m

most /məʊst/ **I** det [1] (the majority of) większość; ~ **people** większość ludzi [2] (superlative) najwięcej; **she got the** ~ **votes** zdobyła najwięcej głosów **II** pron [1] (the greatest number) większość; ~ **of us** większość z nas; ~ **of the bread** większa część chleba; **for** ~ **of the day** przez większą część dnia [2] (the maximum) maksimum; **the** ~ **I can do is...** maksimum, co mogę zrobić, to... [3] (more than all the others) najwięcej; **Robert has got the** ~ Robert ma najwięcej **III** adv [1] (in superlatives) **the** ~ **important event in my life** najważniejsze wydarzenie mojego życia; ~ **easily** najłatwiej [2] (very) bardzo, wyjątkowo; ~ **encouraging** bardzo zachęcający; ~ **probably** najprawdopodobniej [3] (more than all the rest) najbardziej; **what** ~ **annoyed him (of all) was...** najbardziej zirytowało go to, że... **IV** **at (the) most** adv phr (co) najwyżej **V** **for the most part** adv phr (most of them) w przeważającej części; (most of the time) przez większość czasu; (basically) na ogół **VI** most of all adv phr przede wszystkim IDIOMS: **to make the** ~ **of sth** najkorzystniej spożytkować coś [abilities, space]; maksymalnie wykorzystać coś [situation, good weather]

mostly /ˈməʊstlɪ/ adv [1] (chiefly) głównie; (most of them) w większości [2] (most of the time) przeważnie

MOT /ˌeməʊˈtiː/ GB **I** = Ministry of Transport **II** n (also ~ **test,** ~ **inspection**) ≈ przegląd m techniczny (pojazdu samochodowego)

moth /mɒθ, US mɔːθ/ n ćma f; (in clothes) mól m

mother /ˈmʌðə(r)/ **I** n matka f **II** vt [1] (rear) wychowl|ać, -ywać [2] (look after) matkować (komuś)

motherhood /ˈmʌðəhʊd/ n macierzyństwo n

mother-in-law /ˈmʌðərɪnlɔː/ n teściowa f

motherly /ˈmʌðəlɪ/ adj macierzyński, matczyny

mother-of-pearl /ˌmʌðərəvˈpɜːl/ n macica f perłowa

mother tongue n język m ojczysty

motion /ˈməʊʃn/ **I** n [1] (activity) ruch m; **to set sth in** ~ wprawić w ruch coś [pendulum]; fig nadać bieg czemuś [plan]; uruchomić coś [chain of events] [2] (of hand) gest m; (of head) ruch m [3] (proposal) wniosek m **II** vt **to** ~ **sb to approach** przywołać ruchem ręki kogoś **III** vi **to** ~ **to sb** skinąć na kogoś

motionless /ˈməʊʃnlɪs/ adj nieruchomy

motivate /ˈməʊtɪveɪt/ vt motywować

motivated /ˈməʊtɪveɪtɪd/ adj [1] [person, pupil] mający motywację; **he does not seem** ~ najwyraźniej brakuje mu motywacji [2] **politically/racially** ~ [act] o podłożu politycznym/rasowym

motivation /ˌməʊtɪˈveɪʃn/ n [1] (reason) motywy m pl; **the** ~ **for sth** motywy czegoś [decision]; **the** ~(s) **behind sth** uzasadnienie czegoś [act] [2] (drive) motywacja f

motive /ˈməʊtɪv/ n motyw m, pobudka f (**for** or **behind sth** czegoś)

motley /ˈmɒtlɪ/ adj [crowd, gathering] kolorowy; ~ **collection** zbieranina also pej

motor /ˈməʊtə(r)/ **I** n silnik m **II** adj [industry, mechanic, racing] samochodowy; ~ **vehicle** pojazd mechaniczny

motorbike /ˈməʊtəbaɪk/ n motocykl m

motorboat /ˈməʊtəbəʊt/ n łódź f motorowa, motorówka f

motorcycle /ˈməʊtəsaɪkl/ n motocykl m

motorcyclist /ˈməʊtəsaɪklɪst/ n motocyklist|a m, -ka f

motor home n samochód m z częścią mieszkalną

motorist /ˈməʊtərɪst/ n kierowca m

motorway /ˈməʊtəweɪ/ n GB autostrada f

mottled /ˈmɒtld/ adj [skin] cętkowany; [pattern] w cętki; [hands] w plamy

motto /ˈmɒtəʊ/ n dewiza f, motto n

mould¹ GB, **mold** US /məʊld/ **I** n [1] (container) forma f; (small) foremka f [2] fig typ m; **in the** ~ **of sb** pokroju kogoś **II** vt [1] u|formować; **to** ~ **clay into sth** uformować coś z gliny; **to** ~ **metal into sth** odlać coś z metalu [2] u|kształtować [person, opinion]; u|formować [character]

mould² GB, **mold** US /məʊld/ n (fungi) pleśń f

mouldy GB, **moldy** US /ˈməʊldɪ/ adj [bread, cheese] spleśniały; [smell] stęchły; **to go** ~ spleśnieć

moult GB, **molt** US /məʊlt/ vi [animal] wy|linieć, lenieć; [bird] gubić pióra

mound /maʊnd/ n [1] (natural) wzgórek m; (artificial) kopiec m [2] (heap) sterta f

mount /maʊnt/ **I** vt [1] (climb) wstąpić, -epować na (coś) [platform, scaffold]; wspiąć, -nać się na (coś) [stairs]; wsi|ąść, -adać na (coś) [bicycle, horse] [2] (fix) umiel|ścić, -szczać [stamp, exhibit] (**on sth** w czymś); za|mocować [engine]; oprawil|ć, -ać [jewels] (**in** or **on sth** w coś) [3] (organize) urządzl|ić, -ać [exhibition, demonstration]; wystawil|ć, -ać [play, musical] **II** vi [1] [climber, staircase] wspiąć, -nać się (**to sth** na coś) [2] (on horse) dosi|ąść, -adać konia; (on bicycle) wsi|ąść, -adać na rower [3] [temperature, number] wzr|osnąć, -astać; [debts, excitement] nar|osnąć, -astać; [concern] nasil|ić, -ać się

mountain /ˈmaʊntɪn, US -ntn/ **I** n góra f **II** adj [road, air, stream] górski

mountain bike n rower m górski

mountaineer /ˌmaʊntɪˈnɪə(r), US -ntnˈɪər/ *n*
(climber) alpinist|a *m*, -ka *f*; (in the Tatras) taterni|k *m*,
-czka *f*

mountaineering /ˌmaʊntɪˈnɪərɪŋ, US -ntnˈɪərɪŋ/
n alpinizm *m*; (in the Tatras) taternictwo *n*

mountainous /ˈmaʊntɪnəs, US -ntənəs/ *adj*
[country, landscape] górzysty

mountain top *n* szczyt *m*, wierzchołek *m*

mourn /mɔːn/ **[I]** *vt* opłakiwać

[II] *vi* być w żałobie; **to ~ for sb/sth** opłakiwać
kogoś/coś

mourning /ˈmɔːnɪŋ/ *n* żałoba *f*; **to be in ~ (for
sb)** być w żałobie (po kimś)

mouse /maʊs/ *n* mysz *f*

moustache GB, **mustache** US /məˈstɑːʃ/ *n* wąsy *m pl*, wąs *m*

mouth /maʊθ/ **[I]** *n* [1] (of human) usta *plt*; (of child)
buzia *f*; (of mammal) pysk *m*, morda *f*; (of other animal)
otwór *m* gębowy [2] (of tunnel, cave, valley) wylot *m*; (of
geyser, volcano) krater *m*; (of river) ujście *n*; (of bag, bottle,
jar) otwór *m*

[II] *vt* powiedzieć, mówić bezgłośnie

(IDIOMS) **by word of ~** z ust do ust

mouthful /ˈmaʊθfʊl/ *n* (of food) kęs *m*; (of liquid)
łyk *m*

mouth organ *n* harmonijka *f* ustna, organki *plt*

mouth-to-mouth resuscitation *n* sztuczne
oddychanie *n* metodą usta-usta

mouthwash /ˈmaʊθwɒʃ/ *n* płyn *m* do płukania
ust

mouth-watering /ˈmaʊθwɔːtərɪŋ/ *adj* apetyczny

move /muːv/ **[I]** *n* [1] (movement) ruch *m*; (gesture) gest
m [2] (of residence) przeprowadzka *f*; **to make the ~
to London** przeprowadzić się do Londynu [3] (in
games) ruch *m*, zagranie *n* [4] (step, act) posunięcie *n*;
a good/bad ~ dobre/złe posunięcie; **to make
the first ~** zrobić pierwszy krok

[II] on the move *adj phr* **to be on the ~** *[army]*
być w marszu; *[train]* znajdować się w ruchu

[III] *vt* [1] (change place of) przen|ieść, -osić *[bus stop]*;
przesu|nąć, -wać *[cursor, furniture]*; przestawi|ć, -ać
[car]; przen|ieść, -osić *[patient]*; przerzuc|ić, -ać
[army]; przen|ieść, -osić *[staff, office]*; przew|ieźć,
-ozić *[furniture, belongings, equipment]*; **to ~ sth
upstairs** wnieść coś na górę; **to ~ house** prze-
prowadzić się [2] (set in motion) *[person]* porusz|yć, -ać
(czymś), zgi|ąć, -nać *[limb, finger]*; *[wind, water]*
porusz|yć, -ać, ruszać (czymś) *[leaf, branch]*; *[mech-
anism]* porusz|yć, -ać, wprawi|ć, -ać w ruch *[wheel,
cog]* [3] (affect) wzrusz|yć, -ać *[person]*; **to be ~d by
sth** wzruszyć się czymś

[IV] *vi* [1] *[person, branch, lips]* porusz|yć, -ać się;
[earth] za|drżeć [2] *[vehicle]* jechać; *[person]* iść;
[procession, army] posuwać się; **to ~ back** cofnąć
się; **to ~ forward** posuwać się do przodu; **to ~
away** odejść [3] (change home, location) przeprowa-

dz|ić, -ać się; **to ~ to the countryside** przenieść
się na wieś [4] (change job) przen|ieść, -osić się [5] (act)
za|działać; **to ~ to do sth** zabrać się do robienia
czegoś

■ **move about, move around**: [1] (change position)
[person] rusz|yć, -ać się; *[object]* przesu|nąć, -wać
się [2] (change residence) przeprowadz|ić, -ać się

■ **move along**: ¶ **~ along** (disperse) **~ along,
please** proszę się rozejść; '**~ along, ~ along,**'
said the constable „nie zatrzymywać się, jechać
dalej", powiedział policjant ¶ **~ [sb] along** kazać
się rozejść (komuś) *[crowd]*

■ **move away**: (by moving house) wyprowadz|ić, -ać
się; (by leaving scene) od|ejść, -chodzić

■ **move in**: [1] (to house) wprowadz|ić, -ać się; **to
~ in with sb** zamieszkać razem z kimś [2] **to ~
in on sb/sth** (come closer) zbliżyć się do kogoś/
czegoś; (surround and prepare to attack) otoczyć kogoś/
coś

■ **move on**: *[person, traveller]* wyrusz|yć, -ać;
[vehicle] odje|chać, -żdżać; *[time]* mi|nąć, -jać; **to
~ on to the next item** przejść do następnego
punktu

■ **move out**: **~ out** (of house) wyprowadz|ić, -ać
się; *[soldiers]* wymaszerować

■ **move over**: przesu|nąć, -wać się; fig ust|ąpić,
-ępować miejsca (**for sb** komuś)

■ **move up**: [1] (make room) przesu|nąć, -wać się
[2] (be promoted) awansować

movement /ˈmuːvmənt/ *n* ruch *m*; (of hand, arm)
ruch *m*, gest *m*

movie /ˈmuːvɪ/ **[I]** *n* US film *m*

[II] movies *npl* **the ~s** kino *n*

movie camera *n* kamera *f* filmowa

movie star *n* gwiazdor *m* filmowy, gwiazda *f*
filmowa

movie theater *n* US kino *n*

moving /ˈmuːvɪŋ/ *adj* [1] *[vehicle]* jadący; *[parts,
target]* ruchomy; **~ staircase** GB schody ruchome;
~ walkway chodnik ruchomy [2] fig *[scene, speech]*
wzruszający

mow /məʊ/ *vt* s|kosić, ści|ąć, -nać *[grass, hay]*

mower /ˈməʊə(r)/ *n* (machine) kosiarka *f*; (person)
kosiarz *m*

MP *n* GB = **Member of Parliament**

Mr /ˈmɪstə(r)/ *n* pan *m*

Mrs /ˈmɪsɪz/ *n* pani *f* (mężatka)

Ms /mɪz, məz/ *n* pani *f*

MSc *n* Univ = **Master of Science**

much /mʌtʃ/ **[I]** *adv* [1] (to a considerable degree)
znacznie, wiele; **~ smaller** znacznie mniejszy;
~ more interesting znacznie ciekawszy; **she
doesn't worry ~ about it** ona się tym specjalnie
nie przejmuje; **they are ~ to be pitied** należy
ich bardzo żałować; **he's not ~ good at cooking**
nie jest zbyt dobrym kucharzem; **does it hurt ~?**
bardzo boli?; **~ to my surprise** ku mojemu

wielkiemu zaskoczeniu ② (often) często; **we don't go out** ~ rzadko gdzieś bywamy; **do you go to concerts** ~? często chodzisz na koncerty? ③ (nearly) niemal, prawie; **his condition is** ~ **the same** jego stan się prawie nie zmienił; **in** ~ **the same way (as)** niemal w ten sam sposób (co) ④ (specifying degree) **too** ~ za bardzo, zbytnio; **very** ~ bardzo; **I felt very** ~ **the foreigner** czułem się prawie jak obcy; **so** ~ tak bardzo; **I like them as** ~ **as you (do)** lubię ich tak samo (bardzo) jak ty; **I thought as** ~ tak właśnie myślałem; **however** ~ obojętnie jak bardzo

II *pron* ① (a great deal) dużo, wiele; (in negative sentences) niewiele; **do you have** ~ **left?** dużo ci zostało?; **we didn't eat** ~ niewiele jedliśmy; **it leaves** ~ **to be desired** to pozostawia wiele do życzenia; ~ **of sth** znaczna część czegoś; **I don't see** ~ **of them now** nieczęsto ich teraz widuję ② (expressing a relative amount, degree) **so** ~ tyle; **we've eaten so** ~ **that...** zjedliśmy tyle, że...; **too** ~ za or zbyt wiele; **it costs too** ~ to jest za or zbyt drogie; **it's too** ~! za dużo!; (in protest) tego już za wiele!; **she was too** ~ **of an egoist to do that** była zbyt wielką egoistką, żeby to zrobić; **the heat was too** ~ **for them** nie wytrzymali upału; **twice as** ~ dwa razy tyle; **as** ~ **as possible** *[earn, learn]* jak najwięcej; *[confuse, improve]* jak najbardziej; **it can cost as** ~ **as £50** to może kosztować nawet 50 funtów; **it was as** ~ **as I could do not to laugh** robiłem co mogłem, żeby się nie roześmiać; **how** ~? ile?; **do you know how** ~ **this means to me?** wiesz, ile to dla mnie znaczy? ③ (focusing on limitations, inadequacy) **it's not** or **nothing** ~ to niewiele; **he's not** ~ **to look at** nie należy do przystojnych; **she doesn't think** ~ **of him** nie ma o nim zbyt wysokiego mniemania; **I'm not** ~ **of a reader** nie lubię czytać

III *quantif* dużo, wiele; **I haven't got (very)** ~ **time** nie mam (bardzo) wiele czasu; **she didn't speak** ~ **English** słabo mówiła po angielsku; **we paid twice as** ~ **money** zapłaciliśmy dwa razy tyle (pieniędzy); **how** ~ **time have we got left?** ile czasu nam (jeszcze) zostało?

IV **much as** *conj phr* mimo że; ~ **as we regret our decision, we have no choice** mimo że z żalem podejmujemy tę decyzję, to jednak nie mamy wyboru

V **much less** *conj phr* tym bardziej (nie); **I've never seen him** ~ **less spoken to him** nigdy go nie widziałem, a tym bardziej nie rozmawiałem z nim

VI **so much as** *adv phr* **without so** ~ **as saying goodbye/as an apology** bez słowa pożegnania/ przeprosin; **if you so** ~ **as move** jeśli tylko drgniesz

muck /mʌk/ *n* ① (dirt) brud *m*; (mud) błoto *n* ② (manure) gnój *m*, łajno *n*
■ **muck about, muck around** infml: ¶ ~ **about** (fool about) wygłupiać się; (potter about) obijać się infml; **to** ~ **about with sth** majstrować przy czymś ¶ ~ **[sb] about** robić z kogoś wariata infml
■ **muck in**: (share task) przyłączyć się (**with sb** do kogoś); (share room) dzielić pokój (**with sb** z kimś)
mud /mʌd/ *n* błoto *n*

muddle /'mʌdl/ *n* ① (mess) bałagan *m*; (of string, roots) plątanina *f*; fig (in administration) zamęt *m* ② (mix-up) zamieszanie *n* (**over sth** z czymś) ③ (mental confusion) mętlik *m*; **to be in a** ~ mieć mętlik w głowie
■ **muddle up**: ¶ ~ **[sth] up** po|mieszać *[papers]*; po|plątać *[string]*; **to get** ~ **d up** *[objects]* pomieszać się ¶ ~ **[sb] up** na|mieszać komuś w głowie; **to be** ~ **d up** mieć w głowie zamęt

muddy /'mʌdɪ/ *adj* ① *[hands]* ubrudzony błotem; *[clothes, shoes]* ubłocony, zabłocony; *[river, road]* błotnisty ② fig *[coffee, water]* mętny; *[complexion]* ziemisty; *[pink]* brudny; *[green, brown]* z brunatnym odcieniem

mudguard /'mʌdɡɑːd/ *n* błotnik *m*

muffle /'mʌfl/ *vt* s|tłumić, wytłumić *[bell, drum]*; przycisz|yć, -ać *[voice, laughter]*

mug /mʌɡ/ **[]** *n* ① (for tea, coffee) kubek *m*; (for beer) kufel *m* ② GB (fool) frajer *m*, -ka *f* infml; **it's a** ~**'s game** to dla frajerów
[] *vt* infml napa|ść, -dać na (kogoś); **to be** ~**ged** zostać napadniętym

mugger /'mʌɡə(r)/ *n* (uliczny) bandyta *m*

mugging /'mʌɡɪŋ/ *n* ① (attack) bandycki napad *m* (na ulicy) ② (crime) rozbój *m*

muggy /'mʌɡɪ/ *adj* *[weather, day]* parny; *[room]* duszny

mule¹ /mjuːl/ *n* Zool muł *m*, mulica *f*

mule² /mjuːl/ *n* (shoe) klapek *m*

mull /mʌl/ *vt* za|grzać z korzeniami *[alcohol]*
■ **mull over**: rozważ|yć, -ać; rozmyślać nad (czymś)

multicultural /ˌmʌltɪˈkʌltʃərəl/ *adj* wielokulturowy

multidisciplinary /ˌmʌltɪdɪsɪˈplɪnərɪ, US -nerɪ/ *adj* wielodyscyplinarny

multi-function /ˌmʌltɪˈfʌŋkʃn/ *adj* wielofunkcyjny

multigym /'mʌltɪdʒɪm/ *n* Sport atlas *m*

multilateral /ˌmʌltɪˈlætərəl/ *adj* *[trade]* wielostronny; *[talks, agreement]* multilateralny

multimedia /ˌmʌltɪˈmiːdɪə/ *adj* multimedialny

multinational /ˌmʌltɪˈnæʃənl/ *adj* *[society, country]* wielonarodowy; *[agreement, organization]* międzynarodowy

multiple /'mʌltɪpl/ **[]** *n* wielokrotność *f*
[] *adj* *[interests, causes, achievements]* wieloraki; ~ **collision** karambol

multiple choice adj ~ **test** test wielokrotnego wyboru

multiplex /'mʌltɪpleks/ n multikino n, multipleks m

multiply /'mʌltɪplaɪ/ **I** vt po|mnożyć; fig zwielokr|otnić, -atniać [chances, opportunities] **II** vi ① (in maths) mnożyć ② (increase) pomn|ożyć, -ażać się ③ Biol rozmn|ożyć, -ażać się

multipurpose /,mʌltɪ'pɜːpəs/ adj [tool, gadget] wieloczynnościowy; [organization] prowadzący wszechstronną działalność; [area] służący różnym celom

multistorey /,mʌltɪ'stɔːrɪ/ adj GB [carpark] wielopoziomowy; [building] wielopiętrowy

multitude /'mʌltɪtjuːd, US -tuːd/ n mnóstwo n; **for a ~ of reasons** z wielu różnych powodów

mum /mʌm/ n GB infml mama f infml

mumble /'mʌmbl/ vt, vi wy|mamrotać [apology, reply]

mumbo jumbo /,mʌmbəʊ'dʒʌmbəʊ/ n infml brednie f pl infml

mummy[1] /'mʌmɪ/ n infml mamusia f infml

mummy[2] /'mʌmɪ/ n (embalmed body) mumia f

mumps /mʌmps/ n świnka f, zapalenie n ślinianki przyusznej

munch /mʌntʃ/ vt s|chrupać [apple, biscuit]; przeżu|ć, -wać; żuć [food]

mundane /mʌn'deɪn/ adj [matter, goal] przyziemny, prozaiczny; [life] szary

municipal /mjuː'nɪsɪpl/ adj [offices] miejski; [transport] miejski

mural /'mjʊərəl/ n malowidło n ścienne; (in cave) malowidło n naskalne

murder /'mɜːdə(r)/ **I** n morderstwo n, zabójstwo n **II** vt za|mordować (**with sth** czymś) ⟨IDIOMS⟩ **to get away with ~** być bezkarnym

murderer /'mɜːdərə(r)/ n morderca m, zabójca m

murderess /'mɜːdərɪs/ n morderczyni f, zabójczyni f

murderous /'mɜːdərəs/ adj [look, attack, thoughts] morderczy; [regime, intent] zbrodniczy

murky /'mɜːkɪ/ adj ① (gloomy) [streets, hour] mroczny, ciemny; [darkness] gęsty; [weather] ponury; [liquid] mętny ② (suspect) [past, secret] mroczny

murmur /'mɜːmə(r)/ **I** n (of traffic) szum m; (of voices, stream) szmer m **II** vt wy|szeptać [words, thanks] **III** vi [person] mruczeć; [stream] szemrać; [wind] szumieć

muscle /'mʌsl/ n mięsień m
■ **muscle in**: infml w|pakować się (**on sth** do czegoś)

muscle strain n naciągnięcie n mięśnia

muscular /'mʌskjʊlə(r)/ adj [disease, tissue] mięśniowy; [person, body] umięśniony

museum /mjuː'zɪəm/ n muzeum n

mushroom /'mʌʃrʊm, -ruːm/ n ① Bot, Culin grzyb m ② (colour) (kolor m) beżowy m z odcieniem różowym

music /'mjuːzɪk/ n muzyka f

musical /'mjuːzɪkl/ **I** n (for stage) musical m; (movie) komedia f muzyczna **II** adj ① [person] muzykalny; **he's a ~ person** (interested) lubi muzykę ② [voice, laughter] melodyjny ③ [score, education] muzyczny

musical instrument n instrument m muzyczny

musician /mjuː'zɪʃn/ n muzyk m

music video n teledysk m, wideoklip m

musk /mʌsk/ n piżmo n

Muslim /'mʊzlɪm, US 'mʌzləm/ **I** n muzułman|in m, -ka f **II** adj muzułmański

mussel /'mʌsl/ n małż m; (edible) omułek m

must /mʌst, məst/ **I** modal aux ① (indicating obligation) **you mustn't mention this to anyone** nie wolno ci nikomu o tym mówić; **all visitors ~ leave the museum** wszyscy goście muszą opuścić muzeum; **the loan ~ be repaid in one year** pożyczkę należy spłacić w ciągu roku ② (indicating requirement) **candidates ~ be EU nationals** kandydaci muszą być obywatelami kraju należącego do Unii Europejskiej ③ (stressing importance) **you ~ be patient** musisz być cierpliwy; **tell her she mustn't worry** powiedz jej, żeby się nie martwiła; **you ~ never forget** nie wolno ci zapomnieć; **it ~ be said that...** trzeba or należy powiedzieć, że... ④ (expressing intention) **we ~ ask them about it soon** w niedługim czasie będziemy musieli zapytać ich o to; **we mustn't forget to let the cat out** musimy pamiętać, żeby wypuścić kota ⑤ (indicating irritation) **well, come in if you ~** cóż, wejdź, jeśli już musisz; **why ~ she always be so stubborn?** dlaczego ona zawsze musi być taka uparta?; **~ you make such a mess?** musisz robić taki bałagan? ⑥ (invitations, suggestions) **we really ~ get together soon!** koniecznie musimy się niedługo spotkać!; **you ~ meet Flora Brown** musisz koniecznie poznać Florę Brown ⑦ (expressing assumption) **it ~ be difficult living here** życie tutaj musi być trudne; **there ~ be some mistake!** musiała zajść jakaś pomyłka!; **viewers ~ have been surprised** widzowie musieli być zdziwieni ⑧ (expressing desire) **this I ~ see!** koniecznie muszę to zobaczyć!; **we simply ~ get away from here!** po prostu musimy się stąd wyrwać! infml
II n **this book is a ~ for all gardeners** tę książkę powinien mieć każdy ogrodnik; **this film is a ~** ten film trzeba koniecznie zobaczyć

mustache n US = **moustache**

mustard /'mʌstəd/ n ① (plant) gorczyca f ② (condiment) musztarda f

muster /'mʌstə(r)/ *vt* (also ~ **up**) z|ebrać, -bierać *[energy, troops]*; zdoby|ć, -wać *[support, majority]*; wykrzes|ać, -ywać *[enthusiasm]*
IDIOMS: **to pass** ~ zdać egzamin fig

musty /'mʌstɪ/ *adj [room, clothing]* o zapachu stęchlizny; *[food, smell]* stęchły

mute /mjuːt/ *adj* niemy

mutilate /'mjuːtɪleɪt/ *vt* okalecz|yć, -ać *[person]*; uszk|odzić, -adzać *[object]*

mutiny /'mjuːtɪnɪ/ *n* bunt *m*

mutter /'mʌtə(r)/ **I** *vt* wy|mamrotać *[prayer, reply]*; mru|knąć, -czeć pod nosem *[curse, insult]* **II** *vi* mamrotać, mruczeć

mutton /'mʌtn/ *n* baranina *f*

mutual /'mjuːtʃʊəl/ *adj* (reciprocal) wzajemny; (common) wspólny; **by ~ agreement** za obopólną zgodą

mutual aid *n* pomoc *f* wzajemna

my /maɪ/ **I** *det* mój; **my son/daughter/children** mój syn/moja córka/moje dzieci

II *excl* **my my!, oh my!** ojej!, ojej!

myself /maɪ'self, mə'self/ *pron* [1] (reflexive) **I hurt ~** uderzyłem się [2] (emphatic) sam; **I saw it ~** widziałem/widziałam to na własne oczy [3] (after preposition) **(all) by ~** (całkiem or zupełnie) sam/ sama; **for ~** dla siebie; **I'm not proud of ~** nie jestem z siebie dumny

mysterious /mɪ'stɪərɪəs/ *adj* [1] (puzzling) zagadkowy [2] (enigmatic) *[person, look, place, smile]* tajemniczy; **to be ~ about sth** robić wielką tajemnicę z czegoś

mystery /'mɪstərɪ/ *n* [1] (puzzle) tajemnica *f*; **it's a ~ to me why...** nie rozumiem, dlaczego... [2] (of smile, person) tajemniczość *f* [3] (book) powieść *f* kryminalna

mystify /'mɪstɪfaɪ/ *vt* zadziwi|ć, -ać; **to be mystified by sth** nie móc pojąć czegoś

myth /mɪθ/ *n* mit *m*

mythology /mɪ'θɒlədʒɪ/ *n* mitologia *f*

N

n, N /en/ *n* [1] (letter) n, N *n*; **for the nth time** po raz enty infml [2] (compass direction) **N = north** płn.

naff /næf/ *adj* GB infml do kitu infml

nag /næg/ [I] *vt* suszyć głowę (komuś) (**about sth** o coś)

[II] **nagging** *prp adj* [*pain, suspicion*] dokuczliwy, dręczący

nail /neɪl/ [I] *n* [1] (on finger, toe) paznokieć *m* [2] Tech gwóźdź *m*

[II] *vt* przybi|ć, -jać (gwoździami)

■ **nail down:** ¶ ~ [**sth**] **down** [1] (fasten) przybi|ć, -jać [2] (define) ostatecznie ustal|ić, -ać *[details, policy]* ¶ ~ [**sb**] **down** przyp|rzeć, -ierać do muru (kogoś)

nail-biting /'neɪlbaɪtɪŋ/ *adj* [*finish, match*] trzymający w napięciu; [*wait*] nerwowy

nail brush *n* szczoteczka *f* do paznokci

nail file *n* pilnik *m* do paznokci

nail varnish *n* GB = **nail polish**

naïve /naɪˈiːv/ *adj* naiwny

naked /'neɪkɪd/ *adj* [*person, body*] nagi, goły; [*light bulb*] goły; [*sword*] nagi

name /neɪm/ [I] *n* [1] (of person) (first name) imię *n*; (surname) nazwisko *n*; (of place, object) nazwa *f*; (of book, film) tytuł *m*; **my ~ is Adam** mam na imię Adam; **he goes by the ~ of Max** mówią na niego Max [2] (reputation) reputacja *f* [3] (insult) wyzwisko *n*; **to call sb ~s** obrzucić kogoś wyzwiskami

[II] *vt* [1] (call) naz|wać, -ywać; **they ~d her after her mother** dali jej imię po matce; **a boy ~d Adam** chłopiec o imieniu Adam [2] (cite) wymieni|ć, -ać; ~ **three American States** wymień trzy stany Ameryki Północnej [3] (reveal identity of) wymieni|ć, -ać *[sources]*; wskaz|ać, -ywać z nazwiska *[suspect];* **to ~ ~s** podać nazwiska; **naming no ~s** bez nazwisk; **he was ~d as a suspect** wymieniono go z nazwiska jako podejrzanego [4] (state) wyznacz|yć, -ać *[place, time];* ~ **your price** podaj swoją cenę

name-drop /'neɪmdrɒp/ *vi* wtrącać nazwiska (znanych osób)

namely /'neɪmlɪ/ *adv* (a) mianowicie

namesake /'neɪmseɪk/ *n* imienni|k *m*, -czka *f*

nanny /'nænɪ/ *n* GB niania *f*

nanny goat *n* koza *f*

nap /næp/ [I] *n* drzemka *f*; **afternoon ~** poobiednia drzemka

[II] *vi* drzemać

nape /neɪp/ *n* kark *m*; **the ~ of the neck** kark

napkin /'næpkɪn/ *n* serwetka *f*

nappy /'næpɪ/ *n* GB pielucha *f*

narcotic /nɑːˈkɒtɪk/ [I] *n* narkotyk *m*

[II] *adj* narkotyczny

narked /nɑːkt/ *adj* infml wkurzony infml

narration /nəˈreɪʃn/ *n* narracja *f*

narrative /'nærətɪv/ [I] *n* (account) relacja *f*; (story-telling) narracja *f*

[II] *adj* [*prose, poem*] narracyjny; [*skills*] narratorski

narrator /nəˈreɪtə(r)/ *n* narrator *m*, -ka *f*

narrow /'nærəʊ/ [I] *adj* [1] [*object*] wąski [2] [*range, field*] ograniczony; [*definition, interpretation*] zawężony; [*majority*] znikomy; [*margin*] wąski; **to have a ~ lead** mieć nieznaczną przewagę; **he won a ~ victory** o mały włos nie przegrał; **to have a ~ escape** [*victim of accident*] ledwo ujść cało

[II] *vt* [1] (limit) ogranicz|yć, -ać [*choice, range*] (**to sth** do czegoś); zawęż|zić, -żać [*definition*] (**to sth** do czegoś); zmniejsz|yć, -ać [*gap, margin*] (**from sth to sth** z czegoś do czegoś) [2] zwęż|zić, -żać [*road, arteries*]; **to ~ one's eyes** zmrużyć oczy

[III] *vi* [*valley, arteries, choice*] zwęż|zić, -żać się; [*gap, margin*] zmniejsz|yć, -ać się (**to sth** do czegoś)

■ **narrow down:** ~ [**sth**] **down** ogranicz|yć, -ać [*choice, research*] (**to sth** do czegoś); zawęż|zić, -żać [*investigation, list*] (**to sth** do czegoś)

narrowly /'nærəʊlɪ/ *adv* (barely) ledwie, ledwo

narrow-minded /ˌnærəʊ'maɪndɪd/ *adj* ograniczony

nasal /'neɪzl/ *adj* nosowy

nasal spray *n* krople *f pl* do nosa w sprayu

nasty /'nɑːstɪ, US 'næs-/ *adj* [1] [*person, rumour*] złośliwy; [*experience, smell, surprise, sight*] okropny; [*habit, trick*] paskudny; [*business, feeling*] nieprzyjemny; [*expression, look*] zły; **I got a ~ fright** okropnie się przestraszyłem; **a ~ piece of work** (man) wstrętny typ infml; (woman) wstrętne babsko infml [2] (serious) [*cold, bruise*] paskudny; [*accident, fall*] poważny [3] (ugly) wstrętny

nation /'neɪʃn/ *n* państwo *n*, kraj *m*; (people) naród *m*

national /'næʃənl/ [I] *n* (citizen) obywatel *m*, -ka *f*

[II] *adj* [1] (concerning country) [*event, news, channel*] krajowy; **the ~ press** or **newspapers** GB prasa krajowa; ~ **affairs** sprawy wewnętrzne [2] (particular to country) *[characteristics, costume]* narodowy; *[flag]* państwowy

national anthem *n* hymn *m* państwowy

National Curriculum *n* GB program *m* nauczania *(dla szkół podstawowych i średnich)*

National Insurance, NI *n* GB system *m* ubezpieczeń społecznych

nationalism /ˈnæʃnəlɪzəm/ *n* nacjonalizm *m*

nationality /ˌnæʃəˈnælətɪ/ *n* (national group) narodowość *f*; (citizenship) obywatelstwo *n*

nationalize /ˈnæʃnəlaɪz/ *vt* z|nacjonalizować

nationwide /ˌneɪʃnˈwaɪd/ **I** *adj [appeal, campaign, coverage, strike]* ogólnokrajowy; *[survey]* obejmujący cały kraj

II *adv* w całym kraju

native /ˈneɪtɪv/ **I** *n* mieszkan|iec *m*, -ka *f*; **to be a ~ of sth** *[person]* pochodzić z czegoś *[town, country]*; *[animal, plant]* być gatunkiem występującym gdzieś *[forest, area]*; **to speak Polish like a ~** mówić po polsku jak rodowity Polak

II *adj* [1] (original) *[land]* rodzinny; *[language]* ojczysty; **~ Londoner** rodowity londyńczyk; **he is a ~ German speaker** jego ojczystym językiem jest niemiecki [2] *[flora, fauna]* występujący naturalnie; **to be ~ to Britain** występować w Wielkiej Brytanii

Native American **I** *n* Indianin *m* północnoamerykański, Indianka *f* północnoamerykańska

II *adj* ~ **community/languages** społeczność/ języki Indian północnoamerykańskich

Nativity /nəˈtɪvətɪ/ *n* **the ~** narodzenie *n* Chrystusa

natural /ˈnætʃrəl/ *adj* [1] (not artificial) naturalny [2] *[talent, trait]* wrodzony; *[artist, storyteller]* urodzony [3] (unaffected) *[person, manner]* naturalny

naturalize /ˈnætʃrəlaɪz/ *vt* naturalizować *[person]*; **to be ~d** uzyskać obywatelstwo

naturally /ˈnætʃrəlɪ/ *adv* [1] (obviously) naturalnie, oczywiście [2] (by nature) z natury; **her hair is ~ blond** ma naturalne blond włosy; **politeness comes ~ to him** jest z natury uprzejmy [3] *[behave, speak, smile]* naturalnie

nature /ˈneɪtʃə(r)/ *n* [1] (the natural world) natura *f*, przyroda *f*; **let ~ take its course** zostawmy to naturze [2] (temperament) natura *f*; **it's not in her ~ to be aggressive** agresywność nie leży w jej naturze; **it is in the ~ of things that...** to zupełnie naturalne, że...

nature conservancy *n* ochrona *f* przyrody

nature reserve *n* rezerwat *m* przyrody

nature trail *n* szlak *m* krajobrazowy

naughty /ˈnɔːtɪ/ *adj* [1] (disobedient) nieposłuszny [2] (suggestive) *[joke, story]* nieprzyzwoity; *[gesture, picture]* dwuznaczny

nausea /ˈnɔːsɪə, ˈnɔːz-/ *n* mdłości *plt*, nudności *plt*

nauseating /ˈnɔːsɪeɪtɪŋ, ˈnɔːz-/ *adj* przyprawiający o mdłości

nauseous /ˈnɔːsɪəs, ˈnɔːʃəs/ *adj [taste, smell]* przyprawiający o mdłości or nudności; **I feel ~** niedobrze mi

nautical /ˈnɔːtɪkl/ *adj [skill, term, instrument]* żeglarski; *[theme, flavour]* morski; **~ mile** mila morska

naval /ˈneɪvl/ *adj [base, strength]* morski; *[uniform]* marynarski; **~ officer** oficer marynarki

nave /neɪv/ *n* nawa *f* główna

navel /ˈneɪvl/ *n* pępek *m*

navigate /ˈnævɪɡeɪt/ **I** *vt* żeglować po (czymś) *[ocean, river]*; (steer) pilotować *[plane]*; sterować (czymś) *[ship]*

II *vi* (in ship, plane) nawigować; (in rally) być pilotem; (on journey) *[passenger]* odnajdywać drogę

navigation /ˌnævɪˈɡeɪʃn/ *n* nawigacja *f*

navigator /ˈnævɪɡeɪtə(r)/ *n* (in ship, plane) nawigator *m*; (in car) pilot *m*

navy /ˈneɪvɪ/ **I** *n* (fleet) flota *f*; (fighting force) marynarka *f* wojenna

II *adj* [1] (also ~ **blue**) granatowy [2] *[life, uniform]* marynarski

Nazi /ˈnɑːtsɪ/ **I** *n* nazist|a *m*, -ka *f*

II *adj* nazistowski

near /nɪə(r)/ **I** *adv* [1] (close) blisko (**to sb/sth** do kogoś/czegoś); **to move** or **draw ~er** przysunąć się jeszcze bliżej (**to sb/sth** do kogoś/czegoś) [2] (nearly) prawie; **as ~ perfect as it could be** tak bliskie ideału, jak to tylko możliwe; **it's nowhere ~ finished** jeszcze daleko do końca

II **near enough** *adv phr* (sufficiently close) **that's ~ enough** (not any closer) już bliżej nie trzeba; (acceptable in quantity) to wystarczy

III *prep* blisko (kogoś/czegoś); **it's getting ~ Christmas** zbliża się Boże Narodzenie; **~ the beginning/end of the article** bliżej początku/ końca artykułu; **he's no ~er (making) a decision** nie jest wcale bliższy podjęcia decyzji

IV **near to** *prep phr* [1] (in space) blisko, (kogoś/ czegoś); **how ~ are we to Exeter?** jak daleko (mamy) jeszcze do Exeter? [2] (on point of) na krawędzi (czegoś) *[collapse]*; bliski (czegoś) *[hysteria, tears]*; **he came ~ to giving up** był bliski zrezygnowania

V *adj* bliski; **it's the ~est thing to sth** to jest najbardziej zbliżone do czegoś

VI *vt* zbliża|ć, -ć się do (czegoś); **to ~ completion** *[book, project]* zbliżać się do końca

nearby /ˈnɪəbaɪ/ **I** *adj [person]* znajdujący się obok; *[town, village]* pobliski

II /nɪəˈbaɪ/ *adv [wait, stand]* blisko; **~, there is a village** w pobliżu jest wioska

nearly /ˈnɪəlɪ/ *adv* niemal, prawie; **have you ~ finished?** kończysz już?; **I very ~ gave up** już prawie zrezygnowałem; **the exam wasn't ~ as difficult as I'd expected** egzamin wcale nie był aż tak trudny, jak się spodziewałem

near miss *n* sytuacja *f* grożąca wypadkiem; **to have a** ~ *[planes, cars]* omal nie zderzyć się

near-sighted /ˌnɪəˈsaɪtɪd/ *adj* krótkowzroczny

neat /niːt/ **Ⅰ** *adj* ① (tidy) *[person]* (in habits) staranny; (in appearance) czysty; *[desk]* uporządkowany; *[handwriting]* staranny; *[garden, room]* zadbany; **in** ~ **piles** w porządnie or równo ułożonych stosach ② *[explanation, slogan]* zgrabny; *[solution]* zręczny ③ *[figure]* zgrabny; *[features]* regularny ④ *[alcohol, spirits]* czysty **Ⅱ** *adv [drink, vodka]* bez rozcieńczania

neatly /ˈniːtlɪ/ *adv* ① (tidily) *[dress]* schludnie; *[write]* starannie ② (perfectly) *[link]* doskonale; *[illustrate]* trafnie; **the dictionary fits** ~ **into your pocket** ten słownik doskonale mieści się w kieszeni

necessarily /ˌnesəˈserəlɪ, ˈnesəsərəlɪ/ *adv* (definitely) koniecznie; (of necessity) z konieczności

necessary /ˈnesəsərɪ/ *adj* niezbędny; *[qualification]* konieczny; **if** ~ jeśli to konieczne; **as** ~ o ile to konieczne; **'no experience** ~' „doświadczenie (w zawodzie) nie jest wymagane"; **it is** ~ **for him to do it** on musi to zrobić

necessitate /nɪˈsesɪteɪt/ *vt* wymagać (czegoś); **the job would** ~ **your moving** podjęcie tej pracy oznaczałoby dla ciebie przeprowadzkę

necessity /nɪˈsesətɪ/ *n* ① (need) konieczność *f*; **from** or **out of** ~ z konieczności; **the** ~ **for sth** potrzeba czegoś ② (essential item) artykuł *m* pierwszej potrzeby; (essential measure) konieczność *f*; **the necessities of life** potrzeby życiowe; **to be a** ~ być niezbędnym

neck /nek/ *n* ① Anat szyja *f* ② (collar) kołnierz *m*; (neckline) wycięcie *n* (na głowę), dekolt *m*; **with a high** ~ wysoko pod szyję; **with a low** ~ z głębokim dekoltem ③ (narrowest part) szyjka *f*; **the** ~ **of the womb** szyjka macicy ⌐IDIOMS⌐ **to be** ~ **and** ~ **(with sb)** iść łeb w łeb (z kimś) *infml*; **to stick one's** ~ **out** *infml* nadstawiać karku

necklace /ˈneklɪs/ *n* naszyjnik *m*

neckline /ˈneklaɪn/ *n* dekolt *m*, wycięcie *n*

necktie /ˈnektaɪ/ *US* krawat *m*

nectar /ˈnektə(r)/ *n* nektar *m*

nectarine /ˈnektərɪn/ *n* nektaryna *f*

need /niːd/ **Ⅰ** *modal aux* **'I waited'** – **'you needn't have'** „czekałem" – „niepotrzebnie"; ~ **he reply?** czy on musi odpowiedzieć?; ~ **I say more?** chyba nie muszę nic dodawać **Ⅱ** *vt* ① (require) **to** ~ **sth** potrzebować czegoś; **my shoes** ~ **to be polished, my shoes** ~ **polishing** muszę wyczyścić buty; **I** ~ **you to hold the ladder** porzeby mi jesteś do potrzymania drabiny; **more money is** ~ **ed** (po)trzeba więcej pieniędzy; **everything you** ~ wszystko, czego ci tylko (po)trzeba; **they** ~ **to have the things explained to them** trzeba im to wszystko

wytłumaczyć; **you don't** ~ **to tell me that...** nie musisz mi mówić, że...; **everything you** ~ **to know about computers** wszystko, co należy wiedzieć o komputerach ② (have to) musieć; **you'll** ~ **to work hard** będziesz musiał ciężko pracować; **something** ~ **ed to be done** należało coś zrobić; **that's all I** ~! tego mi tylko potrzeba! **Ⅲ** *n* ① (necessity) konieczność *f*, potrzeba *f* (**for sth** czegoś); **I can't see the** ~ **for it** nie widzę takiej potrzeby; **to feel the** ~ **to do sth** czuć potrzebę zrobienia czegoś; **there's no** ~ **to wait** nie ma potrzeby czekać; **there's no** ~ **to worry** nie ma co się martwić; **if** ~ **be** jeśli zajdzie taka potrzeba; **if the** ~ **arises** jeśli okaże się to konieczne ② (want, requirement) potrzeba *f* (**for sth** czegoś); **to satisfy a** ~ zaspokajać potrzebę; **my** ~ **s are few** mam skromne potrzeby ③ (poverty) bieda *f*; **to be in** ~ być w biedzie

needle /ˈniːdl/ **Ⅰ** *n* ① (for sewing, injection) igła *f*; (for knitting) drut *m* **Ⅱ** *vt* dokucz|yć, -ać (komuś) ⌐IDIOMS⌐ **to have pins and** ~ **s** czuć mrowienie

needless /ˈniːdlɪs/ *adj [anxiety, suffering]* niepotrzebny; *[intrusion, intervention]* zbyteczny

needlework /ˈniːdlwɜːk/ *n* (object) robótka *f* (ręczna); (activity) robótki *f pl* ręczne

needy /ˈniːdɪ/ *adj* ubogi

negate /nɪˈgeɪt/ *vt* (cancel out) z|niweczyć *[efforts, work]*; z|marnować *[achievement, advantage]*; (deny) za|negować *[concept, fact]*; (contradict) zaprzecz|yć, -ać (czemuś) *[theory, results]*

negative /ˈnegətɪv/ **Ⅰ** *n* ① (of photo) negatyw *m* ② (in grammar) przeczenie *n*; **in the** ~ w formie przeczącej **Ⅱ** *adj [answer, attitude, effect, influence]* negatywny; *[statement]* zaprzeczający

neglect /nɪˈglekt/ **Ⅰ** *n* ① (lack of care) zaniedbanie *n*; ② (lack of interest) brak *m* zainteresowania (**of sth** czymś) **Ⅱ** *vt* zaniedb|ać, -ywać *[person, building, pet]*; zapuścić *[house, garden]*; nie dbać o (coś) *[health, appearance, plant]*; **to** ~ **to do sth** nie zrobić czegoś (przez zaniedbanie); **to** ~ **to mention sb/ sth** zapomnieć wspomnieć o kimś/czymś

neglected /nɪˈglektɪd/ *adj* zaniedbany; *[building, garden]* zapuszczony; **to feel** ~ czuć się opuszczonym

negligence /ˈneglɪdʒəns/ *n* niedbalstwo *n*

negligent /ˈneglɪdʒənt/ *adj [person]* niedbały; *[procedure]* niestaranny; *[air, manner]* nonszalancki

negligible /ˈneglɪdʒəbl/ *adj* nieistotny

negotiable /nɪˈɡəʊʃəbl/ *adj* ① *[price, rate, terms]* do negocjacji ② *[road, mountain pass]* przejezdny; *[obstacle]* (możliwy) do pokonania

negotiate /nɪˈɡəʊʃɪeɪt/ **Ⅰ** *vt* ① (discuss) wy|negocjować (**with sb** z kimś); **'to be** ~**d'** „do uzgodnienia" [2] (manoeuvre around) pokon|ać, -ywać *[bend, turn, obstacle]*

II *vi* pertraktować, negocjować; **to ~ with sb for sth** pertraktować z kimś w sprawie czegoś

III negotiated *pp adj [peace, settlement]* wynegocjowany

negotiation /nɪˌgəʊʃɪˈeɪʃn/ *n* negocjacje *plt*, pertraktacje *plt*; **under ~** będący przedmiotem negocjacji; **to be open for ~** być do uzgodnienia

negotiator /nɪˈgəʊʃɪeɪtə(r)/ *n* negocjator *m*, -ka *f*

neigh /neɪ/ *vi* za|rżeć

neighbour GB, **neighbor** US /ˈneɪbə(r)/ *n* sąsiad *m*, -ka *f*; **next-door ~** najbliższy sąsiad; **New Zealand's nearest ~ is Australia** najbliższym sąsiadem Nowej Zelandii jest Australia

neighbourhood GB, **neighborhood** US /ˈneɪbəhʊd/ *n* [1] (district) dzielnica *f* [2] (vicinity) sąsiedztwo *n*; **in the ~** w okolicy

neighbouring GB, **neighboring** US /ˈneɪbərɪŋ/ *adj* sąsiedni

neither /ˈnaɪðə(r), ˈniːð-/ **I** *conj* **neither... nor...** ani..., ani...; **I have ~ the time nor the money** nie mam ani czasu, ani pieniędzy; **you don't have to tell him, ~ should you** nie musisz mu mówić, a nawet nie powinieneś

II *det* żaden z dwóch; **~ book is suitable** żadna z tych książek nie jest odpowiednia

III *pron* ani jeden, ani drugi; **~ of them came** żaden z nich nie przyszedł

neon /ˈniːɒn/ **I** *n* neon *m*

II *adj [light, lighting]* neonowy; **~ atom** atom neonu

nephew /ˈnevjuː, ˈnef-/ *n* (brother's son) bratanek *m*; (sister's son) siostrzeniec *m*

nerve /nɜːv/ **I** *n* [1] Anat, Bot nerw *m* [2] (courage) odwaga *f*; (confidence) pewność *f* siebie; **to keep one's ~** zachować zimną krew [3] *infml* (impudence) bezczelność *f*

II nerves *npl* (nervousness) nerwy *plt*; (stage fright) trema *f*; **to calm sb's ~s** uspokoić kogoś **to get on sb's ~s** działać komuś na nerwy

nerve (w)racking *adj* stresujący

nervous /ˈnɜːvəs/ *adj* [1] *[person]* (fearful) zalękniony; (anxious) zdenerwowany; (highly strung) spięty; *[smile, laugh, habit]* nerwowy; **to be ~ of** GB or **about** US **sb/sth** obawiać się kogoś/czegoś; **to be ~ about doing sth** obawiać się robienia czegoś; **to feel ~** (apprehensive) być zdenerwowanym; (before performance) mieć tremę; (afraid) lękać się; (ill at ease) czuć się nieswojo [2] Anat, Med nerwowy

nervous breakdown *n* załamanie *n* nerwowe

nervously /ˈnɜːvəslɪ/ *adv* nerwowo

nervous wreck *n* infml kłębek *m* nerwów

nest /nest/ **I** *n* [1] (of birds, reptiles) gniazdo *n* [2] (of boxes, bowls) komplet *m*, zestaw *m*; **a ~ of tables** zestaw stolików *(wsuwanych jeden pod drugi)*

II *vi [bird]* za|gnieździć się

nest egg *n* infml sumka *f* na czarną godzinę

nestle /ˈnesl/ *vi* [1] *[person, animal]* umościć się (**under sth** pod czymś); **to ~ against sth** przytulić się do czegoś [2] *[village, house]* przycupnąć

net¹ /net/ **I** *n* (in fishing) sieć *f*; (in tennis, hunting) siatka *f*; (in football) bramka *f*

II *vt* z|łowić (w sieci) *[fish]*; z|łapać w siatkę *[butterfly, wild animal]*

net² /net/ **I** *adj* (also **nett**) *[profit, loss]* netto; *[result, increase]* na czysto

II *vt* (financially) *[person, company]* zar|obić, -abiać na czysto; *[export, sales]* przyn|ieść, -osić czysty zysk w wysokości (czegoś)

netball /ˈnetbɔːl/ *n* netball *m*

net curtain *n* firanka *f*

Netherlands /ˈneðələndz/ *prn* **the ~** Holandia *f*

netting /ˈnetɪŋ/ *n* (of rope) sieć *f*; (of metal, plastic) siatka *f*; (fabric) tiul *m*

nettle /ˈnetl/ *n* (also **stinging ~**) pokrzywa *f* zwyczajna

network /ˈnetwɜːk/ **I** *n* (of canals, contacts) sieć *f*; (of wrinkles, threads) siateczka *f*

II *vt* nada|ć, -wać w sieci *[programme]*; po|łączyć w sieć *[computers]*

III *vi* nawiąz|ać, -ywać korzystne kontakty

networking /ˈnetwɜːkɪŋ/ *n* [1] Comput podłączenie *n* (do sieci); (exchange of information) łączność *f* sieciowa [2] (establishing contacts) nawiązywanie *n* kontaktów

network television *n* US telewizja *f* krajowa

neurosis /njʊəˈrəʊsɪs, US nʊ-/ *n* nerwica *f*

neurotic /njʊəˈrɒtɪk, US nʊ-/ *adj* neurotyczny

neuter /ˈnjuːtə(r), US ˈnuː-/ **I** *n* (in grammar) rodzaj *m* nijaki

II *adj* [1] (in grammar) **~ form** forma rodzaju nijakiego [2] Bot, Zool bezpłciowy

III *vt* wy|sterylizować *[animal]*

neutral /ˈnjuːtrəl, US ˈnuː-/ **I** *n* (gear) bieg *m* jałowy; **in ~** na biegu jałowym; **into ~** na bieg jałowy

II *adj* [1] (in politics, conflict) neutralny; **to adopt a ~ policy** przyjąć politykę nieangażowania się [2] *[expression]* obojętny; *[colour]* neutralny; *[shoe polish]* bezbarwny

neutrality /njuːˈtrælətɪ, US nuː-/ *n* neutralność *f* (**towards sb/sth** względem kogoś/czegoś)

neutralize /ˈnjuːtrəlaɪz, US ˈnuː-/ *vt* z|neutralizować

never /ˈnevə(r)/ *adv* [1] (not ever) nigdy; **it is now or ~** teraz albo nigdy; **~ again** nigdy więcej; **he ~ ever drinks alcohol** nie bierze nawet kropli alkoholu do ust [2] (emphatic negative) **he ~ said a word** nawet słowa nie powiedział; **I ~ knew it** w ogóle o tym nie wiedziałem; **he ~ so much as apologized** nawet nie powiedział przepraszam

never-ending /ˌnevərˈendɪŋ/ *adj* niekończący się

nevertheless /ˌnevəðə'les/ *adv* [1] (all the same) niemniej (jednak); **thanks** ~ mimo wszystko dziękuję [2] (nonetheless) pomimo to or tego; **so strong yet** ~ **so gentle** taki silny, a przy tym bardzo delikatny

new /njuː, US nuː/ *adj* nowy; (brand new) nieużywany; **the area is** ~ **to me** nie znam tej okolicy; **the subject is** ~ **to me** nie zetknąłem się z tym tematem; **as good as** ~ jak nowy; **we're** ~ **to this area** dopiero niedawno tu się sprowadziliśmy

New Age *adj* ~ **music/ideas** muzyka/idee New Age

newborn /'njuːbɔːn, US 'nuː-/ *adj* nowo narodzony; ~ **baby** noworodek

newcomer /'njuːkʌmə(r), US 'nuː-/ *n* (in club, congregation) nowy członek *m*; (in place) nowo przybyły *m*; (in sport, theatre) nowicjusz *m*, -ka *f*

newfound /ˌnjuː'faʊnd, US ˌnuː-/ *adj* nowo odkryty

new look [I] *n* nowy styl *m*
[II] **new-look** *adj* [car] nowy; [team] odnowiony; [edition] w nowej szacie graficznej; [show] w nowej oprawie scenicznej; ~ **product** nowa wersja produktu

newly /'njuːlɪ, US 'nuː-/ *adv* [1] (recently) nowo; [washed] świeżo; [married] od niedawna [2] (differently) na nowo; [named] inaczej

newlyweds /'njuːlɪwedz, US 'nuː-/ *npl* nowożeńcy *plt*

news /njuːz, US nuːz/ *n* [1] (new political information) wiadomość *f*, wiadomości *f pl*; (personal information) wieści *f pl*, nowiny *f pl*; **a piece of** ~ wiadomość; **to be in the** ~ być tematem dla prasy/telewizji; **have you heard the** ~ słyszałeś nowinę? [2] (on radio, TV) **the** ~ wiadomości *f pl*; **to see sb/sth on the** ~ zobaczyć kogoś/coś w wiadomościach

news agency *n* agencja *f* prasowa

newsagent's /'njuːzeɪdʒənts, US 'nuːz-/ *n* GB kiosk *m* z gazetami

news bulletin *n* wiadomości *f pl*

newscaster /'njuːzkɑːstə(r), US 'nuːzkæstər/ *n* US prezenter *m*, -ka *f* wiadomości

news conference *n* konferencja *f* prasowa

newsdealer /'njuːzdiːlə(r), US 'nuːz-/ *n* US sprzedaw|ca *m*, -czyni *f* gazet

news editor *n* redaktor *m*, -ka *f* wiadomości

news headlines *npl* (on TV) skrót *m* najważniejszych wiadomości

news item *n* informacja *f*, wiadomość *f*

newsletter /'njuːzletə(r), US 'nuːz-/ *n* biuletyn *m*

newspaper /'njuːspeɪpə(r), US 'nuːz-/ *n* gazeta *f* (codzienna)

newsreader /'njuːzriːdə(r), US 'nuːz-/ *n* GB prezenter *m*, -ka *f* wiadomości

newsreel /'njuːzriːl, US 'nuːz-/ *n* kronika *f* filmowa

newsstand /'njuːzstænd, US 'nuːz-/ *n* kiosk *m* z gazetami

New Year *n* Nowy Rok *m*; **Happy** ~! Szczęśliwego Nowego Roku!; **to see in** or **bring in the** ~ przywitać Nowy Rok

New Zealand /ˌnjuː'ziːlənd, US ˌnuː-/ *prn* Nowa Zelandia *f*

next /nekst/ [I] *pron* **I hope my** ~ **will be a boy** mam nadzieję, że następny będzie chłopiec; **from one moment to the** ~ z minuty na minutę; **the** ~ **to speak was Mary** jako następna głos zabrała Mary; **the week/month after** ~ za dwa tygodnie/miesiące
[II] *adj* [1] (following) kolejny; (still to come) następny; **get the** ~ **train** pojedź następnym pociągiem; '~!' „następny!"; **'you're** ~' „teraz ty"; ~ **to last** przedostatni; **the** ~ **size (up)** rozmiar o numer większy; ~ **Thursday** przyszły or najbliższy czwartek; **he's due to come in the** ~ **10 minutes** przyjdzie w ciągu (najbliższych) 10 minut; **this time** ~ **week** za tydzień o tej samej porze; **the** ~ **day** następnego dnia [2] [room, street, house] sąsiedni
[III] *adv* [1] (afterwards) następnie, potem; **what happened** ~? i co się potem stało? [2] (on a future occasion) **when I** ~ **go there** następnym razem, kiedy tam pojadę [3] (in order) **the** ~ **tallest is Adam** Adam jest drugi pod względem wzrostu; **after champagne, sparkling white wine is the** ~ **best thing** po szampanie, najlepsze jest białe wino musujące
[IV] **next to** *adv phr* [1] (almost) prawie; ~ **to impossible** prawie niemożliwe; **to get sth for** ~ **to nothing** dostać coś prawie za darmo; **in** ~ **to no time it was over** skończyło się, zanim się na dobre zaczęło [2] (near) obok (kogoś/czegoś); **two seats** ~ **to each other** dwa miejsca obok siebie; **to wear silk** ~ **to the skin** nosić jedwabną bieliznę; ~ **to Picasso, my favourite painter is Chagall** obok Picassa moim ulubionym malarzem jest Chagall

next door [I] *adj* (also **next-door**) [garden, building] sąsiedni; **the girl** ~ dziewczyna mieszkająca po sąsiedzku or obok
[II] *adv* [live, move in] po sąsiedzku

next-door neighbour /ˌneksdɔː'neɪbə(r)/ *n* najbliższy sąsiad *m*, najbliższa sąsiadka *f*

next of kin *n* **to be sb's** ~ być najbliższym krewnym kogoś

nib /nɪb/ *n* stalówka *f*

nibble /'nɪbl/ *vi* [person, animal] skubać, pogryzać

nice /naɪs/ *adj* [1] (enjoyable) miły, przyjemny; ~ **weather, isn't it?** ładna pogoda, prawda?; **did you have a** ~ **time?** miło spędziłeś czas?; ~ **to have met you** miło mi było panią/pana poznać; **have a** ~ **day!** miłego dnia! [2] (attractive) ładny; **you look very** ~ bardzo ładnie wyglądasz

3 (tasty) smaczny; **it tastes ~ to** jest smaczne
4 (kind) miły, sympatyczny; **to be ~ to sb** być dla
kogoś miłym 5 (socially acceptable) *[neighbourhood, school]* porządny; *[manners, behaviour]* grzeczny; **it is not ~ to do it** nieładnie tak robić
IDIOMS **~ one!** (in admiration) brawo!; (ironic) pięknie, nie ma co!

nice-looking /ˌnaɪsˈlʊkɪŋ/ *adj* atrakcyjny

nicely /ˈnaɪslɪ/ *adv* 1 (kindly) miło, uprzejmie
2 (attractively) ładnie 3 (satisfactorily) dobrze; **that will do ~** to w zupełności wystarczy 4 (politely) grzecznie

niche /nɪtʃ, niːʃ/ *n* (role) miejsce *n*; (recess) nisza *f*, wnęka *f*; (in market) luka *f* rynkowa

niche market *n* rynek *m* niszowy

nick /nɪk/ **I** *n* (in plank) nacięcie *n* (**in sth** w czymś); (in skin) zadraśnięcie *n* (**in sth** czegoś)
II *vt* 1 (cut) nacijąć, -ciąć *[stick, surface]*; zaǀdrasnąć *[varnish, skin]* 2 GB infml (steal) rąbnąć infml 3 GB infml (arrest) przyskrzynijć, -ać infml
IDIOMS **in the ~ of time** infml w ostatniej chwili, w samą porę

nickel /ˈnɪkl/ *n* 1 US (coin) pięciocentówka *f*
2 (metal) nikiel *m*

nickname /ˈnɪkneɪm/ **I** *n* przezwisko *n*
II *vt* nadajć, -wać (komuś) przezwisko

nicotine /ˈnɪkətiːn/ *n* nikotyna *f*

nicotine patch *n* plaster *m* nikotynowy *(stosowany w terapii odwykowej)*

niece /niːs/ *n* (brother's daughter) bratanica *f*; (sister's daughter) siostrzenica *f*

niggle /ˈnɪgl/ infml **I** *n* (complaint) zastrzeżenie *n*;
I've got a ~ at the back of my mind coś mi nie daje spokoju
II *vt* (irritate) męczyć

niggling /ˈnɪglɪŋ/ *adj [doubt, worry]* dręczący

night /naɪt/ *n* noc *f*; (before going to bed) wieczór *m*; **at ~** (in the evening) wieczorem; (during the night) w nocy;
all ~ (long) przez całą noc; **late at ~** późno wieczorem; **he returned last ~** (during the night) wrócił dziś w nocy; (in the evening) wrócił wczoraj wieczorem; **I slept badly last ~** źle dziś spałem;
on Thursday ~s w czwartkowe wieczory; **to get an early ~** położyć się wcześnie spać; **to stay out all ~** spędzić noc poza domem

nightclub /ˈnaɪtklʌb/ *n* nocny klub *m* or lokal *m*

nightclubbing /ˈnaɪtklʌbɪŋ/ *n* **to go ~** zrobić rundę po nocnych lokalach

nightdress /ˈnaɪtdres/ *n* koszula *f* nocna

nightingale /ˈnaɪtɪŋgeɪl, US -tng-/ *n* słowik *m*

nightlife /ˈnaɪtlaɪf/ *n* nocne życie *n*

nightmare /ˈnaɪtmeə(r)/ *n* koszmar *m* senny; **to have a ~ about sth** mieć zły sen o czymś

night school *n* szkoła *f* wieczorowa

night shelter *n* noclegownia *f*

night shift *n* nocna zmiana *f*; **to be/work on the ~** być/pracować na nocnej zmianie

nightshirt /ˈnaɪtʃɜːt/ *n* męska koszula *f* nocna

night spot *n* infml nocny lokal *m*

night-time /ˈnaɪttaɪm/ *n* noc *f*; **at ~** w nocy

night watchman *n* stróż *m* nocny

nil /nɪl/ *n* 1 **to be ~** *[courage, enthusiasm]* być zerowym 2 Sport zero *n*

Nile /naɪl/ *prn* **the ~** Nil *m*

nimble /ˈnɪmbl/ *adj [person, movement]* zwinny; *[mind, wits]* bystry

nine /naɪn/ **I** *n* dziewięć
II *adj* dziewięć; (male) dziewięciu; (male and female) dziewięcioro

nineteen /ˌnaɪnˈtiːn/ **I** *n* dziewiętnaście
II *adj* dziewiętnaście; (male) dziewiętnastu; (male and female) dziewiętnaścioro
IDIOMS **to talk ~ to the dozen** pleść trzy po trzy

nineteenth /ˌnaɪnˈtiːnθ/ **I** *n* 1 (in order) dziewiętnasty *m*, -a *f*, -e *n*; **the ~ of June** dziewiętnasty czerwca 2 (fraction) dziewiętnasta *f* (część)
II *adj* dziewiętnasty
III *adv [come, finish]* na dziewiętnastym miejscu

ninetieth /ˈnaɪntɪəθ/ **I** *n* dziewięćdziesiąty *m*, -a *f*, -e *n*
II *adj* dziewięćdziesiąty
III *adv [come, finish]* na dziewięćdziesiątym miejscu

nine-to-five /ˌnaɪntəˈfaɪv/ *adj [job, routine]* biurowy

ninety /ˈnaɪntɪ/ **I** *n* dziewięćdziesiąt
II *adj* dziewięćdziesiąt; (male) dziewięćdziesięciu; (male and female) dziewięćdziesięcioro

nip /nɪp/ **I** *n* (pinch) uszczypnięcie *n*; (bite) przygryzienie *n*; **there is a ~ in the air** fig powietrze jest ostre
II *vt* (pinch) uǀszczypnąć; (bite) lekko uǀgryźć
III *vi* (bite) *[animal]* uǀgryźć

nipple /ˈnɪpl/ *n* brodawka *f* sutkowa, sutek *m*

nippy /ˈnɪpɪ/ *adj* infml 1 (cold) rześki; **it's a bit ~ today** powietrze jest dzisiaj rześkie 2 *[person]* żwawy; *[car]* szybki

nit /nɪt/ *n* (egg) gnida *f*; (larva) larwa *f* wszy

nit-pick /ˈnɪtpɪk/ *vi* czepiać się infml

nitrogen /ˈnaɪtrədʒən/ *n* azot *m*

nitty-gritty /ˌnɪtɪˈgrɪtɪ/ *n* infml **the ~** sedno *n*; **to get down to the ~** przejść do konkretów

no /nəʊ/ **I** *particle* nie
II *det* 1 (none, not any) **to have no money/shoes** nie mieć pieniędzy/butów; **no intelligent man would have done that** żaden inteligentny człowiek by tego nie zrobił; **of no importance** zupełnie nieważny; **there is no chocolate like Belgian chocolate** nie ma to jak belgijska czekolada 2 (prohibiting) **no smoking** palenie wzbronione; **no parking** zakaz parkowania; **no talking!** cisza! 3 (for emphasis) **he's no expert** żaden z niego ekspert; **this is no time to cry** nie

czas na łzy ④ (hardly any) **in no time** w okamgnieniu; **it's no distance** to bardzo blisko

Ⅲ *adv* **it's no further/easier than...** to wcale nie jest dalej/łatwiejsze niż...; **I no longer work there** już tam nie pracuję; **no later than Wednesday** nie później niż w środę; **it's no different from driving a car** to tak jak prowadzenie samochodu; **no fewer than 50 people** co najmniej 50 osób

nobility /nəʊ'bɪlətɪ/ *n* (social class) **the ~** arystokracja *f*; (of appearance, action) szlachetność *f*

noble /'nəʊbl/ **Ⅰ** *n* arystokrat|a *m*, -ka *f*

Ⅱ *adj* *[family]* szlachecki; (virtuous) *[character, act]* szlachetny

nobody /'nəʊbədɪ/ **Ⅰ** *pron* (also **no-one**) nikt; **~ saw her** nikt jej nie widział; **there was ~ in the car** w samochodzie nie było nikogo

Ⅱ *n* **to be a ~** być nikim

nocturnal /nɒk'tɜːnl/ *adj* nocny

nod /nɒd/ **Ⅰ** *n* kiwnięcie *n* głową; **she gave him a ~** dała mu znak skinieniem głowy; (as greeting) skinęła mu głową (na powitanie); (indicating assent) kiwnęła głową przytakująco

Ⅱ *vt* **to ~ one's head** skinąć głową; (to indicate assent) przytaknąć

Ⅲ *vi* kiw|nąć, -ać głową; **to ~ to sb** (in assent) przytaknąć komuś

no-go area /ˌnəʊ'gəʊ/ /ˌɑː(r)/ *n* (district) zakazana dzielnica *f*

no-hoper /ˌnəʊ'həʊpə(r)/ *n* infml nieudacznik *m* infml

noise /nɔɪz/ *n* hałas *m*; (shouting) wrzask *m*; **background ~** odgłosy w tle; **a rattling ~** grzechot

noisy /'nɔɪzɪ/ *adj* *[person]* hałaśliwy; *[city, street]* pełen zgiełku; *[protest, discussion]* głośny

nomad /'nəʊmæd/ *n* koczowni|k *m*, -czka *f*

nominal /'nɒmɪnl/ *adj* (in name only) nominalny; (small) *[fee, sum]* symboliczny; *[fine, penalty]* minimalny

nominate /'nɒmɪneɪt/ *vt* ① (propose) nominować; **to ~ sb for a prize** przedstawić kogoś do nagrody ② (appoint) mianować; **to ~ sb (as) chairman** mianować kogoś przewodniczącym

nomination /ˌnɒmɪ'neɪʃn/ *n* (as candidate) nominacja *f*, kandydatura *f*; (appointment) mianowanie *n* (**to sth** na coś); (for award) nominowanie *n* (**for sth** do czegoś)

nominative /'nɒmɪnətɪv/ **Ⅰ** *n* mianownik *m*

Ⅱ *adj* mianownikowy

nonaddictive /ˌnɒnə'dɪktɪv/ *adj* nieuzależniający

nonalcoholic /ˌnɒnælkə'hɒlɪk/ *adj* bezalkoholowy

nonbeliever /ˌnɒnbɪ'liːvə(r)/ *n* niewierząc|y *m*, -a *f*

nonchalant /'nɒnʃələnt/ *adj* nonszalancki

noncommittal /ˌnɒnkə'mɪtl/ *adj* *[reply]* niezobowiązujący; **to be ~ about sth** *[person]* unikać jednoznacznej odpowiedzi w sprawie czegoś

noncompliance /ˌnɒnkəm'plaɪəns/ *n* (with standards) niezgodność *f* (**with sth** z czymś); (with orders) niestosowanie się *n* (**with sth** do czegoś)

nonconformist /ˌnɒnkən'fɔːmɪst/ *adj* nonkonformistyczny

noncooperation /ˌnɒnkəʊˌɒpə'reɪʃn/ *n* odmowa *f* współpracy

nondenominational /ˌnɒndɪˌnɒmɪ'neɪʃənl/ *adj* *[church]* ekumeniczny; *[school]* bezwyznaniowy

nondescript /'nɒndɪskrɪpt/ *adj* *[person, object]* nijaki; *[colour]* nieokreślony; *[performance]* bez wyrazu

none /nʌn/ *pron* ① (not one) żaden, ani jeden; (no part) nic, ani trochę; **~ of them** żaden z nich; **he saw three dogs, ~ of which was black** zobaczył trzy psy, ale żaden z nich nie był czarny; **~ of the wine/milk** ani trochę wina/mleka; **~ of the bread/cheese** ani okruszyny chleba/sera; **'did you have any difficulty?' – '~ whatsoever** or **at all'** "miałeś jakieś trudności?" – "żadnych"; **there's ~ left** nic nie zostało; **~ of it was true** nie było w tym krzty prawdy ② (nobody) nikt; **there is ~ so clever as Maria** nie ma nikogo inteligentniejszego od Marii; **~ but you/him** nikt tylko ty/on

nonentity /nɒ'nentətɪ/ *n* (person) miernota *m/f*, zero *n*

nonessentials /ˌnɒnɪ'senʃlz/ *npl* (objects) rzeczy *f pl* zbędne; (details) sprawy *f pl* mniejszej wagi

nonetheless /ˌnʌnðə'les/ *adv* → **nevertheless**

nonexistent /ˌnɒnɪg'zɪstənt/ *adj* nieistniejący

nonfiction /ˌnɒn'fɪkʃn/ *n* literatura *f* faktu

no-nonsense /ˌnəʊ'nɒnsəns/ *adj* *[attitude, policy]* rozsądny; *[person, manner, tone]* rzeczowy

nonplussed /ˌnɒn'plʌst/ *adj* skonsternowany

non-profitmaking /ˌnɒn'prɒfɪtmeɪkɪŋ/ *adj* *[organization]* non profit, nienastawiony na zyski

nonresident /ˌnɒn'rezɪdənt/ *n* (of hotel) **the restaurant is open to ~s** restauracja jest otwarta również dla osób spoza hotelu

nonsense /'nɒnsns, US -sens/ *n* nonsens *m*; **it's a ~ that...** to absurd, że...; **to make (a) ~ of sth** odbierać sens czemuś

non-smoker /ˌnɒn'sməʊkə(r)/ *n* niepaląc|y *m*, -a *f*

non-smoking /ˌnɒn'sməʊkɪŋ/ *adj* dla niepalących

nonstarter /ˌnɒn'stɑːtə(r)/ *n* **to be a ~** *[person]* nie mieć szans; *[idea, plan]* być skazanym na niepowodzenie

nonstick /ˌnɒn'stɪk/ *adj* *[pan, surface]* nieprzywierający

nonstop /ˌnɒn'stɒp/ **Ⅰ** *adj* *[flight]* bez międzylądowania; *[journey]* bez przerw, non stop; *[train]*

niezatrzymujący się na stacjach pośrednich; *[talk, pressure, noise]* nieustanny

II *adv [talk, work]* bez przerwy; *[fly]* bez między-lądowania

non-taxable /ˌnɒn'tæksəbl/ *adj* niepodlegający opodatkowaniu

noodles /'nu:dlz/ *npl* kluski *f pl*

nook /nʊk/ *n* kącik *m*, zakątek *m*

IDIOMS: **every** ~ **and cranny** wszystkie zakamar-ki

noon /nu:n/ *n* południe *n*; **at 12** ~ o dwunastej w południe

no-one /'nəʊwʌn/ *pron* = **nobody** **II**

noose /nu:s/ *n* (loop) pętla *f*; (for hanging) stryczek *m*

nor /nɔ:(r), nə(r)/ *conj* ani; **you don't need to tell him,** ~ **should you** nie musisz mu mówić, i nie powinieneś; **he was not a cruel man,** ~ **a mean one** nie był okrutny ani złośliwy → **neither**

norm /nɔ:m/ *n* norma *f* **(for sth** czegoś); **it is the** ~ **among students to wear jeans** wśród studentów noszenie dżinsów jest regułą

normal /'nɔ:ml/ **II** *n* (in maths) normalna *f*; **above/below** ~ powyżej/poniżej normy

II *adj [place, time]* zwykły; *[amount, method, temperature]* normalny; **as** ~ (tak) jak zwykle or zazwyczaj

normality /nɔ:'mælətɪ/ *n* normalność *f*

normally /'nɔ:məlɪ/ *adv* (as a rule) zwykle, zazwyczaj; (in normal manner) normalnie

north /nɔ:θ/ **II** *n* (compass direction) północ *f*

II North *prn* **the North** (of world, country) północ *f*; **the far North** daleka północ or Północ

III *adj [coast, side, wind]* północny

IV *adv [lie, live]* na północy; *[go, move, sail]* na północ

North Africa *prn* Afryka *f* Północna

North America *prn* Ameryka *f* Północna

northeast /ˌnɔ:θ'i:st/ **II** *n* północny wschód *m*

II *adj [coast, side, wind]* północno-wschodni

III *adv [move]* na północny wschód; *[lie, live]* na północnym wschodzie

northern /'nɔ:ðən/ *adj [coast, boundary, hemisphere]* północny; *[town]* położony na północy; *[accent]* z północy

Northern Ireland *prn* Irlandia *f* Północna

North Pole *n* biegun *m* północny

North Sea *prn* **the** ~ Morze *n* Północne

northwest /ˌnɔ:θ'west/ **II** *n* północny zachód *m*

II *adj [coast, side, wind]* północno-zachodni

III *adv [move]* na północny zachód; *[lie, live]* na północnym zachodzie

Norway /'nɔ:weɪ/ *prn* Norwegia *f*

Norwegian /nɔ:'wi:dʒən/ **II** *n* **1** Norweg|g *m*, -żka *f* **2** (language) (język *m*) norweski *m*

II *adj* norweski

nose /nəʊz/ *n* nos *m*

■ **nose about, nose around**: węszyć (**in sth** w czymś)

IDIOMS: **to look down one's** ~ **at sb/sth** traktować kogoś/coś z góry; **to poke** or **stick one's** ~ **into sth** infml wściubiać or wtykać nos w coś infml; **to turn up one's** ~ **at sth** wzgardzić czymś

nosebleed /'nəʊzbli:d/ *n* krwotok *m* z nosa

nose-dive /'nəʊzdaɪv/ *n* lot *m* nurkowy; **to go into** or **take a** ~ *[currency, rate]* spaść na łeb na szyję infml

nostalgia /nɒ'stældʒə/ *n* nostalgia *f*

nostalgic /nɒ'stældʒɪk/ *adj* nostalgiczny; **to feel** ~ **for sth** tęsknić za czymś

nostril /'nɒstrɪl/ *n* nozdrze *n*

nosy /'nəʊzɪ/ *adj* infml wścibski

not /nɒt/ **II** *adv* nie; **she isn't at home** nie ma jej w domu; **we won't need the car** nie będzie nam potrzebny samochód; **hasn't he seen it?** nie widział tego?; **I hope** ~ mam nadzieję, że nie; **certainly** ~ na pewno nie; ~ **only** or **just** nie tylko, (ale); **whether it rains or** ~, **I'm going** idę, bez względu na to, czy pada czy nie; **why** ~? dlaczego nie?; ~ **everyone likes it** nie każdemu to się podoba; **it's** ~ **every day that...** niecodziennie się zdarza, żeby...; ~ **a sound was heard** nie słychać było żadnego dźwięku

II not at all *adv phr* wcale nie; (responding to thanks) nie ma za co

III not that *conj phr* ~ **that I know of** o ile mi wiadomo; **if she refuses,** ~ **that she will...** jeśli odmówi, chociaż nie przypuszczam, że to zrobi...

notable /'nəʊtəbl/ *adj [person, success]* wybitny; *[improvement, difference]* godny uwagi

notably /'nəʊtəblɪ/ *adv* (in particular) szczególnie; (markedly) wyraźnie; **most** ~ a w szczególności

notch /nɒtʃ/ **II** *n* (in plank, fabric) nacięcie *n*; (in belt) dziurka *f*

II *vt* (mark) naci|ąć, -nać *[surface, stick]*

■ **notch up** infml: zdoby|ć, -wać *[point, prize]*

note /nəʊt/ **II** *n* **1** (written record) notatka *f*; (short letter) liścik *m*; **to make a** ~ **of sth** zanotować coś *[date, address]* **2** (in music) nuta *f*; **the black** ~**s** (on keyboard) czarne klawisze **3** (banknote) banknot *m*

II of note *adj phr [person]* wybitny; *[development, contribution]* godny uwagi

III *vt* (observe) zauważy|ć, -ać; (pay attention to) zwr|ócić, -acać uwagę na (coś)

■ **note down**: za|notować

IDIOMS: **to compare** ~**s** wymienić wrażenia (**with sb** z kimś)

notebook /'nəʊtbʊk/ *n* notes *m*; (computer) notebook *m*

noted /'nəʊtɪd/ *adj* znany; **to be** ~ **for sth** słynąć z czegoś

notepad /'nəʊtpæd/ n (for letters) blok m listowy; (for notes) blok m biurowy

notepaper /'nəʊtpeɪpə(r)/ n papier m listowy

noteworthy /'nəʊtwɜːðɪ/ adj godny uwagi

nothing /'nʌθɪŋ/ **I** pron nic; **I knew ~ about it** nic o tym nie wiedziałem; **we can do ~ (about it)** nie możemy nic zrobić (w tej sprawie); **there's ~ much on TV** w telewizji nie ma nic ciekawego; **~ else** nic innego; **if ~ else, it will be a change for us** to będzie dla nas chociaż jakaś odmiana; **I had ~ to do with it!** nie miałem z tym nic wspólnego!; **it's ~ to do with us** to nas nie dotyczy; **to stop at ~** nie cofnąć się przed niczym fig; **he means** or **is ~ to me** on nic dla mnie nie znaczy; **the names meant ~ to him** te nazwiska nic mu nie mówiły; **there's really ~ to it!** to całkiem łatwe or proste!; **for ~** (for free) za darmo; (pointlessly) na nic

II adv **it is ~ like as difficult as...** to nie jest wcale tak trudne jak...; **she is ~ like her sister** zupełnie nie jest podobna do siostry; **it's ~ short of brilliant** to po prostu genialne

III **nothing but** adv phr **he's ~ but a coward** jest zwykłym tchórzem; **they've done ~ but moan** infml nic, tylko jęczą infml; **it's caused me ~ but trouble** miałem przez to same kłopoty

notice /'nəʊtɪs/ **I** n [1] (in newspaper) ogłoszenie n; (announcing birth, death, marriage) zawiadomienie n [2] (attention) uwaga f; **to take ~ of sb/sth** zwrócić uwagę na kogoś/coś [3] (notification) **a month's ~** zawiadomienie z miesięcznym wyprzedzeniem; **to do sth at short ~** zrobić coś bezzwłocznie; **until further ~** do odwołania; **I'm sorry it's such short ~** przepraszam, że tak w ostatniej chwili; **to give in** or **hand in one's ~** złożyć wymówienie

II vt zauważ|yć, -ać [absence, mark]; **I ~ that...** widzę, że...; **to get oneself ~d** zwrócić na siebie uwagę

noticeable /'nəʊtɪsəbl/ adj zauważalny

noticeboard /'nəʊtɪsbɔːd/ n tablica f ogłoszeń

notification /ˌnəʊtɪfɪ'keɪʃn/ n powiadomienie n; (in newspaper) ogłoszenie n; **to receive ~ that...** zostać powiadomionym, że...

notify /'nəʊtɪfaɪ/ vt zgłoś|ić, -aszać [police, authorities]; **to ~ sb of** or **about sth** powiadomić kogoś o czymś

notion /'nəʊʃn/ n [1] (idea) myśl f; **I never had any ~ of asking her** nigdy nie pomyślałem o tym, żeby ją poprosić [2] (understanding) pojęcie n

notorious /nəʊ'tɔːrɪəs/ adj [criminal, drunk] notoryczny; [organization, place] mający złą sławę; [case] głośny; **to be ~ for sth** być znanym z czegoś

notoriously /nəʊ'tɔːrɪəslɪ/ adv **he is ~ lazy/ stupid** jest znany z lenistwa/głupoty

notwithstanding /ˌnɒtwɪθ'stændɪŋ/ **I** adv jednak, mimo wszystko

II prep pomimo (czegoś)

nought /nɔːt/ n zero n

noun /naʊn/ n rzeczownik m

nourish /'nʌrɪʃ/ vt odżywi|ć, -ać [person, animal, plant, skin] (with sth czymś); naw|ieźć, -ozić [soil]

nourishment /'nʌrɪʃmənt/ n pożywienie n, pokarm m

novel[1] /'nɒvl/ n powieść f

novel[2] /'nɒvl/ adj (new) [invention] nowatorski; [experience] nowy; (original) oryginalny

novelist /'nɒvəlɪst/ n powieściopisa|rz m, -rka f

novelty /'nɒvəltɪ/ n nowość f

November /nə'vembə(r)/ n listopad m

novice /'nɒvɪs/ n nowicjusz m, -ka f

now /naʊ/ **I** conj **~ (that) I know her** skoro ją już znam

II adv [1] (at present) teraz; **I'm doing it ~** właśnie to robię; **right ~** w tej chwili; **he could arrive any time** or **moment ~** lada chwila może się zjawić; **every ~ and then** od czasu do czasu; **~ for the next question** przejdźmy do następnego pytania [2] (with preposition) **you should have phoned him before ~** powinieneś już wcześniej do niego zadzwonić; **before** or **until ~** wcześniej; **he should be finished by ~** do tej pory powinien już skończyć; **between ~ and next Friday** do przyszłego piątku; **from ~ on(wards)** od tej chwili [3] (in past) **it was ~ 4 pm** była wówczas godz. 16; **by ~ it was too late** było już wówczas za późno [4] **~ there's a man I can trust!** nareszcie człowiek, któremu mogę zaufać!; **careful ~!** uwaga! ostrożnie!; **~ let's see** co my tu mamy

nowadays /'naʊədeɪz/ adv (these days) ostatnio; (now) teraz

nowhere /'nəʊweə(r)/ **I** adv nigdzie; **I've got ~ else to go** nie mam dokąd pójść; **there's ~ to sit down** nie ma gdzie usiąść; **all this talk is getting us ~** cała ta gadanina do niczego nie prowadzi infml; **flattery will get you ~!** pochlebstwem nic nie wskórasz! infml

II **nowhere near** adv phr, prep phr **~ near sufficient** zupełnie niewystarczający

noxious /'nɒkʃəs/ adj [gas, substance] trujący; [ideas, influence] szkodliwy

nozzle /'nɒzl/ n (of hose, pipe) otwór m wylotowy; (of bellows) dysza f

nuclear /'njuːklɪə(r), US 'nuː-/ adj nuklearny

nuclear bomb n bomba f jądrowa

nuclear deterrent n środek m nuklearnego odstraszania

nuclear energy, nuclear power n energia f jądrowa or nuklearna

nuclear power station n elektrownia f jądrowa

nucleus /'njuːklɪəs, US 'nuː-/ n jądro n

nude /njuːd, US nuːd/ **I** n **in the ~** nago

II adj [person] nagi, goły

nudge /nʌdʒ/ *vt* (push) potrąc|ić, -ać, szturch|nąć, -ać; (brush against) o|trzeć, -cierać się o (kogoś)
nudist /'nju:dıst, US 'nu:-/ *n* nudyst|a *m*, -ka *f*
nugget /'nʌgıt/ *n* (of gold, silver) bryłka *f*
nuisance /'nju:sns, US 'nu:-/ *n* niedogodność *f*, uciążliwość *f*; (legal offence) zakłócenie *n* porządku;
to make a ~ **of oneself** naprzykrzać się
nuisance call *n* telefon *m* anonimowy
null /nʌl/ *adj* ~ **and void** bez mocy prawnej, nieważny
nullify /'nʌlıfaı/ *vt* unieważni|ć, -ać
numb /nʌm/ **[]** *adj* [1] *[limb, face]* (from cold) zdrętwiały; (from anaesthetic) bez czucia; ~ **with cold** skostniały; ~ **to go** ~ zdrętwieć [2] fig *[person]* otępiały; ~ **with fear** sparaliżowany strachem
[] *vt* *[cold]* s|powodować drętwienie (czegoś); *[anaesthetic]* od|ebrać, -bierać czucie w (czymś); **to** ~ **the pain** uśmierzyć ból
number /'nʌmbə(r)/ **[]** *n* [1] (amount) liczba *f*; **a four-figure** ~ liczba czterocyfrowa; **a** ~ **of people/times** (some) pewna liczba osób/razy, kilka osób/razy; **for a** ~ **of reasons** z kilku powodów; **large** ~**s of people** bardzo dużo ludzi; **on a** ~ **of occasions** dość często [2] (of bus, house, page, telephone) numer *m*; **a wrong** ~ pomyłka [3] (by performer) numer *m*; (song) piosenka *f*
[] *vt* [1] (allocate number to) po|numerować [2] (amount to) liczyć; **the regiment** ~**ed 1000 men** pułk liczył tysiąc żołnierzy [3] (include) zalicz|yć, -ać; **to** ~ **sb among one's closest friends** zaliczać kogoś do grona najbliższych przyjaciół
IDIOMS: **your** ~**'s up!** infml koniec z tobą!; **to do sth by the** ~**s** US or **by** ~**s** robić coś mechanicznie
numberplate /'nʌmbəpleıt/ *n* GB tablica *f* rejestracyjna
numeracy /'nju:mərəsı, US 'nu:-/ *n* umiejętność *f* liczenia
numeral /'nju:mərəl, US 'nu:-/ *n* cyfra *f*

numerical /nju:'merıkl, US nu:-/ *adj* liczbowy
numerous /'nju:mərəs, US 'nu:-/ *adj* liczny
nun /nʌn/ *n* zakonnica *f*
nurse /nɜːs/ **[]** *n* [1] Med pielęgniarka *f*; **male** ~ pielęgniarz [2] = **nursemaid**
[] *vt* [1] pielęgnować *[person]* [2] (suckle) karmić piersią *[baby]* [3] żywić *[grievance, hope]*
nursemaid /'nɜːsmeıd/ *n* niania *f*
nursery /'nɜːsərı/ *n* [1] (also **day** ~) żłobek *m*; (in hotel, shop) pokój *m* dla dzieci [2] (room) pokój *m* dziecinny [3] (for plants) szkółka *f*
nursery rhyme *n* rymowanka *f* infml
nursery school *n* przedszkole *n*
nursing /'nɜːsıŋ/ *n* (profession) pielęgniarstwo *n*; (care) opieka *f* pielęgniarska
nursing home *n* [1] (old people's) dom *m* spokojnej starości; (convalescent) ≈ sanatorium *n* [2] GB (private hospital) prywatna klinika *f*; (maternity) prywatna klinika *f* położnicza
nurture /'nɜːtʃə(r)/ *vt* [1] wychowywać *[child]*; pielęgnować *[plant]* [2] pielęgnować, żywić *[feeling]*; czuwać nad (czymś) *[project, talent]*
nut /nʌt/ *n* [1] orzech *m*; (almond) migdał *m* [2] Tech nakrętka *f*
nutmeg /'nʌtmeg/ *n* gałka *f* muszkatołowa
nutrition /nju:'trıʃn, US nu:-/ *n* (process) odżywianie *n*; (science) dietetyka *f*
nutritional /nju:'trıʃənl, US nu:-/ *adj* *[value]* odżywczy; *[information]* żywieniowy
nutritious /nju:'trıʃəs, US nu:-/ *adj* pożywny
nutshell /'nʌtʃel/ *n* łupina *f* orzecha; **in a** ~ fig jednym słowem
nuzzle /'nʌzl/ *vt* *[horse, dog]* trąc|ić, -ać nosem
■ **nuzzle up**: **to** ~ **up against** or **to sb** *[person]* przytul|ić, -ać się do kogoś; *[dog]* łasić się
nylon /'naılɒn/ *n* nylon *m*
nymph /nımf/ *n* nimfa *f*

O

o, O /əʊ/ *n* [1] (letter) o, O *n* [2] (spoken number) zero *n*
oaf /əʊf/ *n* (clumsy) niezdara *m/f*; (loutish) prosta|k *m*,
-czka *f*
oak /əʊk/ [1] *n* dąb *m*
[2] *adj* dębowy
OAP *n* GB = **old age pensioner** emeryt *m*, -ka *f*
oar /ɔː(r)/ *n* wiosło *n*
oasis /əʊˈeɪsɪs/ *n* oaza *f* also fig
oat /əʊt/ *n* ∼**s** owies
[IDIOMS:] **to sow one's wild** ∼**s** wyszumieć się
oath /əʊθ/ *n* [1] (declaration) przysięga *f*; **under** ∼,
on ∼ GB pod przysięgą [2] (swearword) przekleństwo *n*
oatmeal /ˈəʊtmiːl/ *n* [1] (cereal) mąka *f* owsiana
[2] US (porridge) owsianka *f*
obedience /əˈbiːdɪəns/ *n* posłuszeństwo *n* (**to sb/
sth** wobec kogoś/czegoś)
obedient /əˈbiːdɪənt/ *adj* posłuszny
obese /əʊˈbiːs/ *adj* otyły
obesity /əʊˈbiːsəti/ *n* otyłość *f*
obey /əˈbeɪ/ [1] *vt* przestrzegać (czegoś) *[rule, law]*;
być posłusznym (komuś) *[person]*; kierować się
(czymś) *[instinct]*
[2] *vi* podporządkow|ać, -ywać się
obituary /əˈbɪtʃʊəri, US -tʃʊeri/ *n* (also ∼ **notice**)
nekrolog *m*
object [1] /ˈɒbdʒɪkt/ *n* [1] (item) przedmiot *m* [2] (goal)
cel *m* [3] (of actions, feelings) przedmiot *m*, obiekt *m*
[4] (in grammar) dopełnienie *n*
[2] /əbˈdʒekt/ *vt* **to** ∼ **that...** zaprotestować,
uważając, że...
[3] /əbˈdʒekt/ *vi* sprzeciwi|ć, -ać się; **to** ∼ **to sth**
sprzeciwiać się czemuś *[plan]*; **to** ∼ **to sb** być
przeciwnym komuś *[candidate]*; **do you** ∼ **to me**
or **my smoking?** czy nie przeszkadza ci, że palę?
objection /əbˈdʒekʃn/ *n* sprzeciw *m*; **to have no**
∼(**s**) nie mieć zastrzeżeń; **I've no** ∼ **to them
coming** nie mam nic przeciwko temu, żeby
przyszli
objectionable /əbˈdʒekʃənəbl/ *adj [remark]* nie
na miejscu; *[behaviour]* niedopuszczalny; *[person]*
nieprzyjemny
objective /əbˈdʒektɪv/ [1] *n* cel *m*
[2] *adj* obiektywny
objectively /əbˈdʒektɪvli/ *adv* obiektywnie
obligation /ˌɒblɪˈɡeɪʃn/ *n* [1] (duty) obowiązek *m*
(**to** or **towards sb** wobec kogoś); **to be under (an)**

∼ **to do sth** być zobowiązanym zrobić coś
[2] (commitment) zobowiązanie *n* (**to sb** w stosunku
do kogoś) (**to do sth** żeby coś zrobić) [3] (debt)
zobowiązanie *n* finansowe; (of gratitude) dług *m*
wdzięczności
obligatory /əˈblɪɡətri, US -tɔːri/ *adj* obowiązkowy;
it is ∼ **to vote** głosowanie jest obowiązkowe
oblige /əˈblaɪdʒ/ *vt* [1] (compel) zobowiąz|ać, -ywać
(**to do sth** do zrobienia czegoś) [2] (be helpful to)
wyświadcz|yć, -ać przysługę (komuś) [3] (be grateful)
to be ∼**d to sb** być wdzięcznym or zobowiązanym
komuś (**for sth** za coś)
obliging /əˈblaɪdʒɪŋ/ *adj [person]* uczynny; *[manner]*
uprzejmy
obliterate /əˈblɪtəreɪt/ *vt* z|równać z ziemią fig
[city]; za|trzeć, -cierać *[trace]*; zamaz|ać, -ywać
[word]; wymaz|ać, -ywać z pamięci *[memory]*
oblivion /əˈblɪvɪən/ *n* zapomnienie *n*
oblivious /əˈblɪvɪəs/ *adj* (unaware) nieświadomy (**of**
or **to sth** czegoś)
oblong /ˈɒblɒŋ, US -lɔːŋ/ [1] *n* wydłużony prostokąt *m*
[2] *adj* podłużny
obnoxious /əbˈnɒkʃəs/ *adj* wstrętny, okropny
obscene /əbˈsiːn/ *adj [film, joke]* obsceniczny;
[remark] nieprzyzwoity
obscure /əbˈskjʊə(r)/ [1] *adj [motive]* niejasny;
[book, writer] mało znany
[2] *vt* zaciemni|ć, -ać *[issue]*; przesł|onić, -aniać
[view]
observant /əbˈzɜːvənt/ *adj* spostrzegawczy; *[Jew]*
religijny
observation /ˌɒbzəˈveɪʃn/ *n* [1] (scrutiny) obserwacja *f*; **to be under** ∼ być pod obserwacją;
(in hospital) być na obserwacji [2] (remark) spostrzeżenie *n*
observe /əbˈzɜːv/ *vt* [1] (see) zauważyć *[thing, person]*
[2] (watch) obserwować [3] (remark) zauważyć (**that...**
że...) [4] przestrzegać (czegoś) *[law, custom]*
observer /əbˈzɜːvə(r)/ *n* obserwator *m*, -ka *f*
obsess /əbˈses/ *vt [fears]* prześladować; **to be** ∼**ed
by** or **with sb** mieć obsesję na punkcie kogoś
obsession /əbˈseʃn/ *n* obsesja *f* (**with sth** na
punkcie czegoś)
obsessive /əbˈsesɪv/ *adj [thought]* natrętny
obsolescence /ˌɒbsəˈlesns/ *n* (of technology, word)
wychodzenie *n* z użycia; (of idea) wychodzenie *n*

z mody; **built-in** ~, **planned** ~ zakładana żywotność (urządzenia)

obsolete /ˈɒbsəliːt/ adj przestarzały

obstacle /ˈɒbstəkl/ n przeszkoda f; **to be an** ~ **to sth** stanowić przeszkodę w czymś [work]

obstacle course n tor m przeszkód

obstetrician /ˌɒbstəˈtrɪʃn/ n położnik m

obstinate /ˈɒbstənət/ adj [person] uparty (**about sth** w kwestii czegoś); [cough, silence] uporczywy

obstruct /əbˈstrʌkt/ vt [1] (block) przesł|onić, -aniać [view]; za|tarasować, za|blokować [road] [2] (hamper) utrudni|ć, -ać [progress]; **to** ~ **justice** utrudniać postępowanie sądowe

obstruction /əbˈstrʌkʃn/ n [1] (to traffic, progress) przeszkoda f; (in pipe) czop m, zator m [2] (in sport) (niedozwolone) blokowanie n

obtain /əbˈteɪn/ vt uzysk|ać, -iwać [permission]; otrzym|ać, -ywać [goods]; naby|ć, -wać (czegoś) [experience]

obtrusive /əbˈtruːsɪv/ adj [noise] nieznośny; [person] natrętny; [behaviour] męczący

obtuse /əbˈtjuːs, US -ˈtuːs/ adj [person] tępy

obvious /ˈɒbvɪəs/ adj oczywisty (**to sb** dla kogoś); **it's** ~ **that...** to oczywiste, że...; **she is the** ~ **choice for the job** jest najodpowiedniejszą osobą na to stanowisko; **for** ~ **reasons** z oczywistych względów

obviously /ˈɒbvɪəslɪ/ [1] adv wyraźnie; **she** ~ **needs help** najwyraźniej potrzebuje pomocy [2] excl oczywiście

occasion /əˈkeɪʒn/ n [1] (opportunity) sposobność f; **on that** ~ przy tej sposobności; **on** ~ od czasu do czasu; **on the** ~ **of (sth)** z okazji (czegoś); **to rise to the** ~ stanąć na wysokości zadania [2] (event, function) okazja f; **on special** ~**s** na specjalne okazje; **the wedding was quite an** ~ ten ślub to było wielkie wydarzenie

occasional /əˈkeɪʒənl/ adj [event] sporadyczny; ~ **showers** przelotne deszcze

occasionally /əˈkeɪʒənəlɪ/ adv od czasu do czasu; **very** ~ bardzo rzadko

occult [1] /ɒˈkʌlt, US əˈkʌlt/ n **the** ~ wiedza f tajemna
[2] /ɒˈkʌlt/ adj [powers] tajemny; [arts] okultystyczny

occupant /ˈɒkjʊpənt/ n (of building) lokator m, -ka f; (of office) użytkowni|k m, -czka f

occupation /ˌɒkjʊˈpeɪʃn/ n [1] (military) okupacja f; **to come under** ~ znaleźć się pod okupacją [2] (job) zawód m [3] (leisure activity) zajęcie n

occupational /ˌɒkjʊˈpeɪʃənl/ adj [activity, risk] zawodowy; ~ **accident** wypadek przy pracy

occupational hazard n ryzyko n zawodowe

occupier /ˈɒkjʊpaɪə(r)/ n (of house, flat) najemca m; (of land) dzierżawca m

occupy /ˈɒkjʊpaɪ/ vt [1] (inhabit, fill) zaj|ąć, -mować [house, seat] [2] (take over) okupować [country, build-

ing] [3] **to be occupied with sb/sth** być zajętym or zajmować się kimś/czymś

occur /əˈkɜː(r)/ vi [1] [change] nast|ąpić, -ępować; [mistake] wyst|ąpić, -ępować; [accident] zdarz|yć, -ać się [2] [disease] pojawi|ć, -ać się [3] (suggest itself) **the idea** ~**red to me that...** przyszła mi do głowy myśl, że...

occurrence /əˈkʌrəns/ n zdarzenie n; **to be a rare** ~ rzadko się zdarzać

ocean /ˈəʊʃn/ n ocean m

octagon /ˈɒktəgən, US -gɒn/ n ośmiokąt m, ośmiobok m

octave /ˈɒktɪv/ n oktawa f

October /ɒkˈtəʊbə(r)/ n październik m

octopus /ˈɒktəpəs/ n ośmiornica f

OD /ˌəʊˈdiː/ infml [1] n = **overdose**
[2] vi **to** ~ **(on sth)** przedawkować (coś) [tablets, drugs]; opchać się (czymś) infml [chocolate]

odd /ɒd/ [1] adj [1] (strange) [person, occurrence] dziwny, osobliwy; **that's** ~ (to) dziwne [2] (occasional) **I have the** ~ **drink** raz na jakiś czas wypiję drinka [3] (unmatched) [socks] nie do pary [4] (miscellaneous) **a few** ~ **coins** kilka różnych monet [5] [number] nieparzysty [6] (different) **to be the** ~ **one out** nie pasować do reszty; **to feel the** ~ **one out** czuć się obco
[2] -**odd** in combinations (approximately) **there were sixty-** ~ **people** było jakieś sześćdziesiąt osób

oddity /ˈɒdɪtɪ/ n osobliwość f

odd job n praca f dorywcza; **to do** ~**s around the house** wykonywać różne drobne prace w domu

odd-job man /ˌɒdˈdʒɒbmæn/ n majster m do wszystkiego; (skilful) złota rączka f infml

odds /ɒdz/ npl [1] (in betting) notowania n pl (u bukmacherów); **the** ~ **are 20 to 1** szanse wygranej są 20 do 1 [2] (chance, likelihood) szanse f pl; **the** ~ **are against/in favour of sth** coś jest mało/bardzo prawdopodobne; **the** ~ **are in our favour** mamy duże szanse; **to win against the** ~ wbrew oczekiwaniom wygrać
[IDIOMS] **it makes no** ~ GB to nie ma znaczenia; **to be at** ~ (in dispute) nie zgadzać się; (inconsistent) nie pasować, kłócić się

odds and ends infml n GB drobiazgi m pl

odour GB, **odor** US /ˈəʊdə(r)/ n woń f

of /ɒv, əv/ prep [1] (objective) **a lover of music** miłośnik muzyki [2] (possession) **the property of the state** własność państwa or państwowa [3] (made of) z/ze; **what is it made of?** z czego to jest zrobione? [4] **some of us** niektórzy z nas; **a friend of ours** nasz znajomy; **a loan of £20** pożyczka w wysokości 20 funtów; **the city of Rome** miasto Rzym

off /ɒf, US ɔːf/ [1] adv [1] (leaving) **to be** ~ (on foot) odejść; (by vehicle) odjechać; **it's time you were** ~ (on foot) musisz już iść; (by vehicle) musisz już jechać; **I'm** ~ wychodzę [2] (at a distance) **to be 30 metres**

~ być oddalonym o trzydzieści metrów; **some way** ~ dość daleko ③ (ahead in time) **Easter is a month** ~ za miesiąc Wielkanoc; **the exam is several months** ~ egzamin jest za kilka miesięcy

Ⅱ *adj* ① (free) **to have Monday** ~ wziąć wolne w poniedziałek infml; **Tuesday is my day** ~ wtorek to mój wolny dzień ② (turned off) **to be** ~ *[water, gas, tap]* być zakręconym; *[light, TV]* być zgaszonym ③ (cancelled) **to be** ~ *[match, party]* być odwołanym; **our engagement is** ~ zerwaliśmy zaręczyny ④ (removed) **the lid is** ~ puszka jest otwarta; **with her make-up** ~ bez makijażu; **25%** ~ 25% taniej ⑤ infml (bad) **to be** ~ *[food]* zepsuć się; *[milk]* skwaśnieć

Ⅲ *prep* ① (also **just** ~) tuż przy; **(just)** ~ **the path** tuż przy ścieżce; **in a street** ~ **the main road** na ulicy odchodzącej od głównej drogi ② **it's** ~ **the point** to zupełnie inna sprawa ③ infml **to be** ~ **one's food** nie mieć apetytu

⌐IDIOMS⌐ **to feel a bit** ~ infml kiepsko się czuć; **to have an** ~ **day** mieć zły dzień

off-centre GB, **off-center** US /ˌɒfˈsentə(r), US ˌɔːf/ *adj* **to be** ~ nie być na samym środku

off-chance /ˈɒftʃɑːns, US ˈɔːftʃæns/ *n* **(just) on the** ~ **that...** na (wszelki) wypadek, gdyby...

off-colour /ˌɒfˈkʌlə(r)/ *adv* infml **to feel** ~ kiepsko się czuć

offence GB, **offense** US /əˈfens/ *n* ① (crime) przestępstwo *n* ② (insult) obraza *f*; **to cause** ~ **to sb** obrazić kogoś; **to take** ~ **(at sb)** obrazić się (na kogoś); **to take** ~ **at sth** poczuć się urażonym czymś ③ Mil ofensywa *f*

offend /əˈfend/ **Ⅰ** *vt* obra|zić, -żać

Ⅱ *vi* (in law) z|łamać prawo, popełni|ć, -ać wykroczenie

offender /əˈfendə(r)/ *n* ① (against the law) przestęp-ca *m*; (against regulations) spraw|ca *m*, -czyni *f* wykro-czenia ② (culprit) winowaj|ca *m*, -czyni *f*

offensive /əˈfensɪv/ **Ⅰ** *n* (military) ofensywa *f*; Sport atak *m*

Ⅱ *adj [remark, behaviour]* obraźliwy (**to sb** dla kogoś); *[language]* ordynarny

offer /ˈɒfə(r), US ˈɔːf/ **Ⅰ** *n* oferta *f*, propozycja *f* (**to do sth** zrobienia czegoś); **a job** ~ oferta pracy; **to be on special** ~ być (sprzedawanym) w ofercie specjalnej

Ⅱ *vt* za|proponować *[job]* (**to sb** komuś); za|oferować *[service]* (**to sb** komuś); udziel|ić, -ać (czegoś) *[advice, information]* (**to sb** komuś); **to** ~ **sth for sale** wystawić coś na sprzedaż

Ⅲ *vi* zaofiarow|ać, -ywać się

offering /ˈɒfərɪŋ, US ˈɔːf/ *n* (what is offered) propozycja *f*; (sacrifice) ofiara *f*

offhand /ˌɒfˈhænd, US ˌɔːf/ **Ⅰ** *adj* bezceremonial-ny

Ⅱ *adv* ~, **I don't know** tak na poczekaniu, to nie wiem

office /ˈɒfɪs, US ˈɔːf/ *n* ① (place) biuro *n* ② (position) urząd *m*; **public** ~ urząd publiczny; **to hold** ~ *[person]* piastować urząd; *[political party]* sprawo-wać władzę

office block, office building *n* GB biurowiec *m*

officer /ˈɒfɪsə(r), US ˈɔːf/ *n* ① (in army, navy) oficer *m* ② (also **police** ~) policjant *m*, -ka *f*

office worker *n* urzędni|k *m*, -czka *f*

official /əˈfɪʃl/ **Ⅰ** *n* (of government, state) urzędnik *m*; (of party, police) funkcjonariusz *m*

Ⅱ *adj* oficjalny; *[certificate]* urzędowy

offing /ˈɒfɪŋ, US ˈɔːf/ *n* **to be in the** ~ *[storm, war]* nadciągać; *[business, deal]* być bliskim reali-zacji

off-key /ˌɒfˈkiː, US ˌɔːfˈkiː/ *adj* Mus fałszywy

off-licence /ˈɒflaɪsns, US ˈɔːf/ *n* GB sklep *m* monopolowy

off-limits /ˌɒfˈlɪmɪts, US ˌɔːf/ *adj* zakazany

off-line /ˈɒflaɪn, US ˈɔːf/ *adj* Comput autonomiczny

off-load /ˌɒfˈləʊd, US ˌɔːf/ *vt* (get rid of) pozby|ć, -wać się (czegoś); **to** ~ **the blame onto sb** zrzucić winę na kogoś

off-peak /ˌɒfˈpiːk, US ˌɔːf/ *adj [travel]* poza godzinami szczytu; *[electricity]* liczony według taryfy nocnej

off-putting /ˌɒfˈpʊtɪŋ, US ˌɔːf/ *adj [manner, person]* odpychający

off-road vehicle /ˌɒfrəʊdˈvɪəkl, US ˈɔːfrəʊd viːhɪkl/ *n* pojazd *m* terenowy

off-season /ˈɒfsiːzn, US ˌɔːf/ *adj* ~ **cruise** rejs poza sezonem

offset /ˈɒfset, US ˈɔːf/ *vt* z|równoważyć (**by sth** czymś); **to** ~ **sth against sth** kompensować coś czymś

offshore /ˌɒfˈʃɔː(r), US ˌɔːf/ *adj [fishing]* morski; *[island]* przybrzeżny; *[platform]* na morzu

offside /ˌɒfˈsaɪd, US ˌɔːf/ **Ⅰ** *n* GB strona *f* kierowcy

Ⅱ *adj* ① GB **the** ~ **lane** (in Britain) prawy pas; (outside Britain) lewy pas ② Sport *[position]* spalony

offspring /ˈɒfsprɪŋ, US ˈɔːf/ *n* (of animal) młode *n*; (children) potomstwo *n*

offstage /ˌɒfˈsteɪdʒ, US ˌɔːf/ **Ⅰ** *adj* zza sceny

Ⅱ *adv* poza sceną

off-the-cuff /ˌɒfðəˈkʌf, US ˌɔːf/ *adj [remark]* spontaniczny; *[speech]* zaimprowizowany

off-the-peg /ˌɒfðəˈpeg, US ˌɔːf/ *adj [garment]* gotowy

off-the-shelf /ˌɒfðəˈʃelf, US ˌɔːf/ *adj [goods]* do-stępny od ręki; ~ **software** gotowe oprogramo-wanie

off-the-wall /ˌɒfðəˈwɔːl, US ˌɔːf/ *adj* infml zwario-wany

off-white /ˌɒfˈwaɪt, US ˌɔːf/ *adj* w kolorze złamanej bieli

often /'ɒfn, 'ɒftən, US 'ɔːfn/ *adv* często; **as ~ as not, more ~ than not** najczęściej; **how ~ do you meet?** jak często się spotykacie?; **once too ~** o jeden raz za dużo; **every so ~** od czasu do czasu

oh /əʊ/ *excl* (surprise) och!; (joy) och!, ach!; **oh dear!** (sympathetic) ojej!; (dismayed, cross) a niech to!; **oh (really)?** (interested) tak?; (sceptical) ejże!

oil /ɔɪl/ **[I]** *n* ① (mineral) ropa *f* (naftowa); (for fuel, lubrication) olej *m*; **engine/heating ~** olej silnikowy/opałowy ② Culin olej *m* **[II]** *vt* naoliwi|ć, -ać, oliwić

oil change *n* wymiana *f* oleju

oilcloth /'ɔɪlklɒθ, US -klɔːθ/ *n* cerata *f*

oil field *n* pole *n* naftowe

oil painting *n* malarstwo *n* olejne; (picture) obraz *m* olejny, olej *m*

oil refinery *n* rafineria *f* (ropy naftowej)

oil rig *n* (offshore) platforma *f* wiertnicza; (on land) wiertnia *f*, szyb *m* naftowy

oilseed rape /ˌɔɪlsiːd'reɪp/ *n* rzepak *m*

oil slick *n* plama *f* ropy (*na wodzie*)

oil well *n* szyb *m* naftowy

oily /'ɔɪli/ *adj [hair]* tłusty; *[food]* ociekający tłuszczem; *[cloth]* zatłuszczony; *[substance]* oleisty

ointment /'ɔɪntmənt/ *n* maść *f*

okay, OK /əʊ'keɪ/ *infml* **[I]** *n* zgoda *f*; **to give sth the ~** zgodzić się na coś **[II]** *adj* **it's ~ by me** nie mam nic przeciwko temu; **is it ~ if I come tomorrow?** mogę przyjść jutro?; **he's ~** on jest w porządku; **to feel ~** dobrze się czuć; **'how was the meeting?' – '~'** „jak poszło zebranie?" – „w porządku" **[III]** *adv [cope, work out]* nieźle **[IV]** *particle* dobrze; dobra, okej infml

old /əʊld/ *adj* ① (not young) stary; **an ~ man** stary człowiek; **~ people** starzy ludzie; **to get ~** zestarzeć się; **how ~ are you?** ile masz lat?; **a six-year-~ boy** sześciolatek; **this bread is a week ~** ten chleb ma już tydzień; **my ~er brother** mój starszy brat; **I'm the ~est** jestem najstarszy ② (former, previous) *[address, school]* stary; *[admirer, boss]* dawny; **in the ~ days** w dawnych czasach

old age *n* starość *f*

old-age pensioner /ˌəʊldeɪdʒ'penʃənə(r)/, **OAP** *n* GB emeryt *m*, -ka *f*

old-fashioned /ˌəʊld'fæʃnd/ *adj [garment, style, device]* staromodny; *[attitude, person, idea]* staroświecki

old people's home *n* dom *m* starców *m*; dom *m* spokojnej starości fml

old wives' tale *n* przesąd *m*

olive /'ɒlɪv/ **[I]** *n* ① (fruit) oliwka *f* ② (also ~ **tree**) oliwka *f*, drzewo *n* oliwne **[II]** *adj* oliwkowy

olive green [I] *n* (kolor *m*) oliwkowy *m* **[II]** *adj* oliwkowy

olive oil *n* oliwa *f* z oliwek

Olympic /ə'lɪmpɪk/ *n* **the ~ s** (also **Olympic Games**) olimpiada *f*, igrzyska *plt* olimpijskie

ombudsman /'ɒmbʊdzmən/ *n* rzecznik *m* praw obywatelskich

omelette /'ɒmlɪt/ *n* omlet *m*

omen /'əʊmən/ *n* omen *m*, znak *m*

ominous /'ɒmɪnəs/ *adj* złowieszczy

omission /ə'mɪʃn/ *n* przeoczenie *n*

omit /ə'mɪt/ *vt* pomin|ąć, -ać, (accidentally) przeoczyć; **to ~ to do sth** nie zrobić czegoś

omnipotent /ɒm'nɪpətənt/ *adj [authority]* wszechpotężny; *[deity]* wszechmocny

on /ɒn/ **[I]** *prep* ① (position) na (czymś); **on the sea** nad morzem; **on top of the piano** na fortepianie; **on the wall** na ścianie; **there's a stain on it** na tym jest plama; **to live on Park Avenue** mieszkać na Park Avenue; **on the M4 motorway** na autostradzie M4; **to hang sth on a nail** powiesić coś na gwoździu; **on a string** na sznurku; **to punch sb on the nose** uderzyć kogoś pięścią w nos; **I've got no small change on me** nie mam przy sobie drobnych; **to have a smile on one's face** mieć uśmiech na twarzy ② (about) o (czymś), na temat (czegoś); **a programme on Africa** program o Afryce; **to be on** należeć do (czegoś) *[team]*; być członkiem (czegoś) *[committee]* ③ (in expressions of time) **on 22 May** dwudziestego drugiego maja; **on Friday** w piątek; **on or about the 23rd** około dwudziestego trzeciego; **on sunny days** w słoneczne dni ④ (immediately after) **on his arrival** (zaraz) po przyjeździe; **on hearing the truth, she...** kiedy usłyszała prawdę, ... ⑤ (taking) **to be on antibiotics** brać antybiotyki; **to be on drugs** brać narkotyki ⑥ (powered by) **to run on batteries** działać or być na baterie; **to run on electricity** być na prąd ⑦ (indicating a medium) **on TV** w telewizji; **I heard it on the news** słyszałem o tym w wiadomościach; **on video** na wideo; **on the phone** przez telefon ⑧ (earning) **to be on £20,000 a year** zarabiać 20 000 funtów rocznie; **to be on a low income** mało zarabiać ⑨ (at the expense of) **this round is on me** tym razem ja płacę ⑩ (indicating means of transport) **to travel on the bus** podróżować autobusem; **on the plane** w samolocie; **to be on one's bike** siedzieć na rowerze; **to leave on the first train** odjechać pierwszym pociągiem **[II]** *adj* ① **to be on** *[event]* mieć miejsce; **I've got nothing on tonight** nie mam żadnych planów na dzisiejszy wieczór; **I've got a lot on** jestem bardzo zajęty; **the news is on in 10 minutes** za 10 minut są wiadomości; **what's on?** (on TV) co jest w telewizji?; (at cinema, theatre) co grają?; **there's nothing on** nie ma nic ciekawego (*w kinie, teatrze, telewizji*) ② **to be on** *[dishwasher, TV, light]* być włączonym; *[tap]* być odkręconym; *[handbrake]* być zaciągniętym; **the power is back on** znowu jest prąd ③ GB (permissible) **it's just** or **simply not on** (out of the question) to po prostu wykluczone; (not the done thing) tak się nie robi ④ **the lid is on (the tin)** puszka jest zamknięta

III *adv* ① **to have a hat on** mieć kapelusz na głowie; **he has nothing on** nic na sobie nie ma; **with slippers on** w kapciach ② **20 years on** po 20 latach; **from that day on** od tamtego dnia; **to walk on** iść dalej; **to go to Paris and then on to Marseilles** pojechać do Paryża, a potem dalej, do Marsylii

IV **on and off** *adv phr* **to see sb on and off** widywać kogoś od czasu do czasu

V **on and on** *adv phr* **to go on and on** *[speaker]* mówić i mówić; *[speech]* trwać bez końca; **to go on and on about sth** bez końca opowiadać o czymś ⬚IDIOMS⬚ **you're on** zgoda; **to be always on at sb** zamęczać kogoś; **what's he on about?** GB o czym on gada? infml

once /wʌns/ **I** *n* (jeden) raz *m*; **just this ~** tylko ten jeden raz; **for ~** (this time) tym razem; (one time at least) chociaż (jeden) raz

II *adv* ① (one time) (jeden) raz; **~ and for all** raz na zawsze; **~ too often** o jeden raz za dużo; **~ a day** raz dziennie ② (formerly) kiedyś; **~ upon a time there was...** dawno, dawno temu, był/była sobie...

III **at once** *adv phr* ① (immediately) od razu; **all at ~** nagle, ni z tego ni z owego ② (simultaneously) naraz

IV *conj* jak tylko

once-over /ˈwʌnsəʊvə(r)/ *n* infml **to give sth the ~** rzucić okiem na coś; **to give sb the ~** zmierzyć kogoś wzrokiem

oncoming /ˈɒnkʌmɪŋ/ *adj [car]* nadjeżdżający (z przeciwka); *[election]* nadchodzący

one /wʌn/ **I** *n* (number) jeden; (digit) jedynka *f*; (hour) (godzina *f*) pierwsza *f*; **to arrive in ~s and twos** przyjść pojedynczo i małymi grupkami

II *adj* ① (single) jeden; **to raise ~ hand** podnieść (jedną) rękę ② (unique, sole) jedyny; **she's the ~ person who can help** jest jedyną osobą, która może pomóc; **the ~ and only Edith Piaf** jedyna i niepowtarzalna Edith Piaf ③ (same) jeden (i ten sam); **at ~ and the same time** w jednym i tym samym czasie; **it's all ~ to me** jest mi wszystko jedno

III *pron* ① (indefinite) jed|en *m*, -na *f*, -no *n*; **can you lend me ~?** pożyczysz mi?; **she's ~ of us** jest jedną z nas ② (impersonal subject or object) ~ **never knows for sure** nigdy nie ma się pewności ③ (specific) **the big ~** ten duży/ta duża/to duże; **this ~** ten/ta/to; **which ~?** który?; **that's the ~** to ten/ta/to; **he's the ~ who did it** to on to zrobił; **I'm not ~ for football** piłka nożna to nie

dla mnie ④ ~ **-fifty** (in sterling) funt pięćdziesiąt; (in dollars) dolar pięćdziesiąt

IV **one by one** *adv phr* jeden po drugim ⬚IDIOMS⬚ **to be ~ up on sb** infml mieć nad kimś przewagę; **to go ~ better than sb** przebić kogoś infml fig

one another *pron* **they love ~** kochają się; **to help ~** pomagać sobie (nawzajem); **we often use ~'s cars** często wymieniamy się samochodami; **to worry about ~** martwić się o siebie nawzajem

one-off GB /ˌwʌnˈɒf/ *adj [event, payment]* jednorazowy; *[example]* jedyny w swoim rodzaju

one-parent family /ˌwʌnpeərənt'fæməlɪ/ *n* niepełna rodzina *f*

one-piece /ˌwʌnˈpiːs/ *adj* jednoczęściowy

one's /wʌnz/ *det* swój; **to wash ~ hands** myć ręce; **when one tries to do ~ best...** kiedy się bardzo starasz...

oneself /ˌwʌnˈself/ *pron* ① (reflexive) (as direct object) się; (as indirect object) sobie; **to wash/hurt ~** umyć/zranić się ② (emphatic) samemu ③ (after preposition) siebie; **to be sure of ~** być pewnym siebie; **(all) by ~** (do sth) samodzielnie; (live) samotnie

one-sided /ˌwʌnˈsaɪdɪd/ *adj [decision, contest]* jednostronny

one-time /ˈwʌntaɪm/ *adj [politician]* były

one-to-one /ˌwʌntəˈwʌn/ *adj [tuition]* indywidualny; ~ **meeting** spotkanie w cztery oczy

one-way /ˌwʌnˈweɪ/ *adj* ① *[traffic, street]* jednokierunkowy ② ~ **ticket** bilet w jedną stronę

ongoing /ˈɒngəʊɪŋ/ *adj [process]* trwający; *[battle]* toczący się; *[situation]* istniejący

onion /ˈʌnɪən/ *n* cebula *f*

on-line /ˌɒnˈlaɪn/ *adj* Comput *[data processing]* na bieżąco, on-line; *[mode]* on-line

onlooker /ˈɒnlʊkə(r)/ *n* obserwator *m*, -ka *f*, gap *m*

only /ˈəʊnlɪ/ **I** *conj* (but) tylko; **I'd come ~ I'm working tonight** przyszedłbym, tylko że pracuję dzisiaj w nocy

II *adj* jedyny; ~ **child** jedynak/jedynaczka

III *adv* ① (exclusively) tylko, jedynie; ~ **in Italy can one...** tylko we Włoszech można...; ~ **time will tell** czas pokaże; **'men ~'** „tylko dla mężczyzn"; **I've ~ met her once** widziałem ją tylko raz ② (nothing more than) **it's ~ polite** tego wymaga uprzejmość ③ (in expressions of time) **~ yesterday** dopiero wczoraj; **I saw him ~ recently** dopiero co go widziałem; **it seems like ~ yesterday** wydaje się, jakby to było (dopiero) wczoraj

IV **only just** *adv phr* ① (recently) dopiero (co); **I've ~ just arrived** dopiero (co) przyjechałem ② (barely) **it's ~ just tolerable** to jest prawie nie do zniesienia; **I caught the bus, but ~ just** zdążyłem na autobus, ale ledwo, ledwo

Ⅴ only too *adv phr* **I** remember it ~ **too well** pamiętam to aż za dobrze; **you should be** ~ **too glad that...** powinieneś się tylko cieszyć, że...

o.n.o. GB = **or nearest offer** lub za najwyższą oferowaną cenę

on-screen /ˌɒn'skriːn/ *adj* na ekranie

onset /'ɒnset/ *n* nadejście *n*, początek *m*

onside /ˌɒn'saɪd/ **Ⅰ** *adj* Sport **an ~ position** prawidłowa pozycja

Ⅱ *adv* **to be** ~ nie być na spalonym

on-site /ˌɒn'saɪt/ *adj* dostępny na miejscu

onslaught /'ɒnslɔːt/ *n* szturm *m*; (verbal, of disease) atak *m*

on-the-job /ˌɒnðə'dʒɒb/ *adj* ~ **training** zdobywanie kwalifikacji podczas pracy

on the spot /ˌɒnðə'spɒt/ **Ⅰ** *adj [reporting]* z miejsca zdarzenia; *[advice]* natychmiastowy

Ⅱ on the spot *adv [agree]* z miejsca

onto /'ɒntuː/ *prep* (also **on to**) (on top of) na; (towards) do

(IDIOMS) **to be ~ something** infml być na tropie

onus /'əʊnəs/ *n* obowiązek *m*; **the ~ is on sb to do sth** obowiązkiem kogoś jest zrobienie czegoś

onward /'ɒnwəd/ **Ⅰ** *adj* ~ **flight to Manchester** dalszy lot do Manchesteru

Ⅱ *adv* = **onwards**

onwards /'ɒnwədz/ *adv* **from tomorrow** ~ od jutra; **from now** ~ odtąd; **from that day** ~ od tamtego dnia

ooze /uːz/ **Ⅰ** *vt* **to** ~ **blood** krwawić; **to** ~ **pus** ropieć

Ⅱ *vi* **to** ~ **with sth** roztaczać (wokół siebie) *[charm]*

opal /'əʊpl/ *n* opal *m*

opaque /əʊ'peɪk/ *adj [liquid]* nieprzejrzysty; *[glass]* matowy

open /'əʊpən/ **Ⅰ** *n* **in the** ~ (outside) na świeżym powietrzu; **to bring sth out into the** ~ fig ujawnić coś

Ⅱ *adj* ①*[door]* otwarty; *[shirt]* rozpięty; *[legs]* rozłożony; **the door was half** ~ drzwi były na wpół otwarte; **in the** ~ **air** na świeżym powietrzu; ~ **country** otwarta przestrzeń; **the** ~ **road** (main road) główna droga; **the** ~ **sea** otwarte morze ② (not covered) *[car, carriage]* odkryty ③ ~ **to the wind/to the elements** wystawiony na działanie wiatru/ czynników atmosferycznych; ~ **to attack** wystawiony na ataki; **to be** ~ **to offers** być otwartym na oferty; **to lay oneself** ~ **to criticism** narazić się na krytykę ④ (accessible) *[access]* wolny; *[contest]* otwarty; *[session]* przy drzwiach otwartych ⑤ (candid) *[person]* otwarty, szczery ⑥ (blatant) *[hostility]* jawny; *[war]* otwarty ⑦ **to leave the date** ~ kwestię daty pozostawić otwartą; **to keep an** ~ **mind about sth** nie zajmować stanowiska w sprawie czegoś; ~ **ticket** bilet otwarty

Ⅲ *vt* otwⱮorzyć, -ierać

Ⅳ *vi* ① *[door, eyes, flower]* otwⱮorzyć, -ierać się; *[curtain]* rozsuⱮnąć, -wać się; **to** ~ **onto sth** *[door, window]* wychodzić na coś ② *[shop, bar]* być czynnym or otwartym; *[meeting, play]* rozpocząć, -ynać się (**with sth** czymś) ③ *[film]* wejść, wchodzić na ekrany; *[exhibition]* zostać otwartym

■ **open up**: ¶ ~ **up** ① *[gap]* powstaⱮć, -wać ② *[person]* otwⱮorzyć, -ierać się ③ *[shop, branch]* rozpocząć, -ynać działalność ¶ ~ **[sth] up** otwⱮorzyć -ierać

open-air /ˌəʊpən'eə(r)/ *adj [pool]* odkryty; *[stage]* na wolnym or otwartym powietrzu

open day *n* dzień *m* otwarty

opener /'əʊpnə(r)/ *n* (for bottles, cans) otwieracz *m*

open-heart surgery /ˌəʊpənˌhɑːt'sɜːdʒərɪ/ *n* (operation) operacja *f* na otwartym sercu

opening /'əʊpnɪŋ/ **Ⅰ** *n* ① (of book, film) początek *m* ② (of assembly, exhibition) otwarcie *n*; (of play, film) premiera *f* ③ (in wall, fence) otwór *m* ④ (opportunity) sposobność *f* (**to do sth** do zrobienia czegoś); (in market) możliwość *f* zbytu; (for employment) wolna posada *f*

Ⅱ *adj [scene, move]* pierwszy; *[remark]* wstępny

opening hours *npl* (of shop) godziny *f pl* otwarcia; (of bank) godziny *f pl* urzędowania

open market *n* wolny rynek *m*

open-minded /ˌəʊpən'maɪndɪd/ *adj* otwarty; **to be** ~ **about sth** nie mieć uprzedzeń do czegoś

open-necked /ˌəʊpən'nekt/ *adj [shirt]* rozpięty pod szyją

open-plan /ˌəʊpən'plæn/ *adj [office]* bez ścianek działowych

Open University, OU *n* GB Univ uniwersytet *m* otwarty

opera /'ɒprə/ *n* opera *f*

opera glasses *npl* lornetka *f* teatralna

opera house *n* opera *f*

operate /'ɒpəreɪt/ **Ⅰ** *vt* ① (use) obsługiwać *[appliance]*; posługiwać się (czymś) *[tool]* ② (enforce) wprowadzⱮić, -ać *[system]*; prowadzić *[policy]* ③ (manage) prowadzić *[store]*

Ⅱ *vi* ① (do business) działać ② *[machine]* działać; *[department]* funkcjonować ③ *[factor]* działać; *[law]* obowiązywać ④ Med zⱮoperować; **to be** ~ **d on** być operowanym; **to** ~ **on sb's leg** operować komuś nogę

operating instructions *npl* zalecenia *f pl* eksploatacyjne

operating room US, **operating theatre** GB *n* sala *f* operacyjna

operating system *n* Comput system *m* operacyjny

operation /ˌɒpə'reɪʃn/ *n* ① (working) działanie *n* ② Med operacja *f*; **to have a heart** ~ mieć operację serca ③ **to be in** ~ *[plan]* być aktualnie stosowanym; *[rule]* obowiązywać; *[mine]* być eksploatowanym; *[machine]* działać

operational /ˌɒpəˈreɪʃənl/ *adj* ① (working) sprawny ② *[budget, costs]* bieżący, operacyjny

operative /ˈɒpərətɪv, US -reɪt-/ **I** *n* (worker) pracownik *m*
II *adj [law]* obowiązujący; *[system]* funkcjonujący

operator /ˈɒpəreɪtə(r)/ *n* ① (for telephone) telefonist|a *m*, -ka *f* ② (of machine, computer) operator *m* ③ **he's a smooth** ~ niezły z niego kombinator

opinion /əˈpɪnɪən/ *n* zdanie *n*, opinia *f* (**about** or **on sb/sth** o kimś/czymś); **in my** ~ moim zdaniem; **to have a high/low** ~ **of sb** mieć o kimś dobre/złe zdanie; **to have a high/low** ~ **of sth** wysoko/nisko oceniać coś

opinionated /əˈpɪnɪəneɪtɪd/ *adj [person]* zadufany w sobie; *[tone]* pewny siebie

opinion poll *n* badanie *n* opinii publicznej

opponent /əˈpəʊnənt/ *n* przeciwni|k *m*, -czka *f*; (in discussion) oponent *m*, -ka *f*

opportune /ˈɒpətjuːn, US -tuːn/ *adj [moment]* odpowiedni, dogodny

opportunist /ˌɒpəˈtjuːnɪst, US -ˈtuːn-/ **I** *n* oportunist|a *m*, -ka *f*
II *adj* oportunistyczny

opportunity /ˌɒpəˈtjuːnəti, US -ˈtuːn-/ *n* okazja *f*, sposobność *f* (**for sth** do czegoś); **to take the** ~ **to say sth** skorzystać z okazji, żeby powiedzieć coś; **training opportunities** możliwości szkolenia

oppose /əˈpəʊz/ **I** *vt* sprzeciwi|ć, -ać się (komuś/czemuś); **to be** ~**d to sth/doing sth** być przeciwnym czemuś/zrobieniu czegoś
II **opposing** *prp adj [party, team]* przeciwny; *[view, style]* przeciwstawny
III **as opposed to** *prep phr* w przeciwieństwie do

opposite /ˈɒpəzɪt/ **I** *n* przeciwieństwo *n* (**of/to sth** czegoś)
II *adj* przeciwległy; *[effect]* przeciwny; *[sex]* odmienny; ~ **building** budynek naprzeciwko; **at** ~ **ends of sth** na przeciwległych końcach czegoś
III *adv [live]* naprzeciw(ko); **directly** ~ dokładnie naprzeciwko
IV *prep* (in front of) naprzeciw(ko) (kogoś/czegoś) *[building, park, person]*

opposite number *n* (in politics, sport) odpowiedni|k *m*, -czka *f*

opposition /ˌɒpəˈzɪʃn/ *n* ① (protest) sprzeciw *m* (**to sb/sth** wobec kogoś/czegoś) ② (in politics) (also **Opposition**) opozycja *f*

oppress /əˈpres/ *vt* gnębić, ciemiężyć

oppressive /əˈpresɪv/ *adj* ① *[law]* oparty na ucisku ② *[atmosphere]* przytłaczający; *[heat]* uciążliwy, męczący

opt /ɒpt/ *vi* **to** ~ **for sth** wybierać coś; **to** ~ **to do sth** zdecydować się zrobić coś
■ **opt out:** *[person, country]* wycof|ać, -ywać się

optical /ˈɒptɪkl/ *adj* optyczny

optical illusion *n* złudzenie *n* optyczne

optician /ɒpˈtɪʃn/ *n* optyk *m*

optimism /ˈɒptɪmɪzəm/ *n* optymizm *m*

optimist /ˈɒptɪmɪst/ *n* optymist|a *m*, -ka *f*

optimistic /ˌɒptɪˈmɪstɪk/ *adj* optymistyczny; **to be** ~ **about sth** być optymistą, jeśli chodzi o coś

optimize /ˈɒptɪmaɪz/ *vt* z|optymalizować

optimum /ˈɒptɪməm/ **I** *n* optimum *n*
II *adj* optymalny

option /ˈɒpʃn/ *n* możliwość *f*; **to have the** ~ **of doing sth** mieć możliwość zrobienia czegoś; **I have little** ~ mam niewielki wybór

optional /ˈɒpʃənl/ *adj [activity]* nieobowiązkowy; *[course]* fakultatywny; ~ **extras** wyposażenie dodatkowe

or /ɔː(r)/ *conj* ① (in the positive) albo, lub; **either... or...** albo..., albo... ② (in the negative) **not today or tomorrow** ani dzisiaj, ani jutro; **she doesn't drink or smoke** ona nie pije i nie pali ③ (in questions) **with or without sugar?** z cukrem czy bez?; **whether you like it or not** czy ci się to podoba, czy nie; **in a week or so** za jakiś tydzień; **or should I say...** a właściwie... ④ (otherwise) bo; **be careful or you'll cut yourself** uważaj, bo się skaleczysz

oral /ˈɔːrəl/ **I** *n* egzamin *m* ustny
II *adj [test]* ustny; *[medicine]* doustny; ~ **hygiene** higiena jamy ustnej

orange /ˈɒrɪndʒ, US ˈɔːr-/ **I** *n* ① (fruit) pomarańcza *f* ② (colour) (kolor *m*) pomarańczowy *m*
II *adj* pomarańczowy

orange juice *n* sok *m* pomarańczowy

orbit /ˈɔːbɪt/ **I** *n* orbita *f*
II *vt* krążyć po orbicie

orchard /ˈɔːtʃəd/ *n* sad *m*

orchestra /ˈɔːkɪstrə/ *n* orkiestra *f*

orchestrate /ˈɔːkɪstreɪt/ *vt* z|orkiestrować

orchid /ˈɔːkɪd/ *n* storczyk *m*, orchidea *f*

ordain /ɔːˈdeɪn/ *vt* ① **to** ~ **that...** zarządzić, że... ② (of priest) wyświęc|ić, -ać

ordeal /ɔːˈdiːl, ˈɔːdiːl/ *n* męka *f*

order /ˈɔːdə(r)/ **I** *n* ① (arrangement) porządek *m*; **in alphabetical** ~ w kolejności alfabetycznej; **to restore** ~ przywrócić porządek ② (command) rozkaz *m* (**to do sth** zrobienia czegoś); (doctor's) zalecenie *n*; **to be under** ~**s to do sth** mieć rozkaz zrobienia czegoś ③ (in shop, restaurant) zamówienie *n* ④ (operational state) **in working** ~ na chodzie; **to be out of** ~ *[phone line]* być uszkodzonym; *[lift, machine]* być niesprawnym ⑤ (correct procedure) **your remark was way out of** ~ twoja uwaga była bardzo nie na miejscu; **I hear that congratulations are in** ~ zdaje się, że pora na gratulacje ⑥ (religious) zakon *m*
II **in order that** *conj phr* aby, żeby; **I've come in** ~ **that I might help you** przyszedłem, żeby ci pomóc

III in order to *prep phr* żeby; **in** ~ **to talk to you** żeby z tobą porozmawiać
IV *vt* ⒈ (command) zarządz|ić, -ać *[inquiry]*; **to** ~ **sb to do sth** nakazać komuś zrobić coś ⒉ (as service) zam|ówić, -awiać *[meal, goods, taxi]* (**for sb** dla kogoś)
V *vi [diner, customer]* złożyć, składać zamówienie
VI ordered /'ɔːdəd/ *pp adj* uporządkowany
■ **order about, order around**: ~ [**sb**] **about** dyrygować (kimś)
order form *n* formularz *m* zamówieniowy
orderly /'ɔːdəlɪ/ **I** *n* ≈ sanitariusz *m*, -ka *f*
II *adj [queue, society]* zdyscyplinowany; *[manner]* zorganizowany; *[pattern]* regularny; *[lifestyle]* uporządkowany; *[person]* systematyczny; *[demonstration]* spokojny
ordinary /'ɔːdənrɪ, US 'ɔːrdənerɪ/ **I** *n* **out of the** ~ niezwykły
II *adj* ⒈ (normal) zwykły, zwyczajny; **no** ~ **concert** niezwykły koncert ⒉ (average) *[consumer, family]* przeciętny ⒊ (mediocre) **very** ~ przeciętny
ore /ɔː(r)/ *n* ruda *f*; **iron** ~ ruda żelaza
organ /'ɔːgən/ *n* ⒈ (of body) narząd *m* ⒉ (instrument) organy *plt*
organ donor *n* daw|ca *m*, -czyni *f* narządu
organic /ɔː'gænɪk/ *adj* organiczny; *[produce, farming]* naturalny
organism /'ɔːgənɪzəm/ *n* organizm *m*
organization /ˌɔːgənaɪ'zeɪʃn, US -nɪ'z-/ *n* ⒈ (group) organizacja *f* ⒉ (of society, political party) organizacja *f*, struktura *f*
organize /'ɔːgənaɪz/ *vt* z|organizować *[event, meeting]*; u|porządkować *[books, papers]*; załatwi|ć -ać *[babysitter]*
organized crime *n* przestępczość *f* zorganizowana
organizer /'ɔːgənaɪzə(r)/ *n* ⒈ (person) organizator *m*, -ka *f* ⒉ (also **personal** ~) notes *m* (menedżerski); **electronic** ~ notes elektroniczny
organ transplant *n* przeszczep *m* narządu
orgy /'ɔːdʒɪ/ *n* orgia *f* also fig
orient /'ɔːrɪənt/ **I** *n* **the Orient** Orient *m*
II *vt* (also **orientate**) fig ukierunkow|ać, -ywać *[person, company]* (**at/towards sth** na coś)
oriental /ˌɔːrɪ'entl/ *adj* orientalny, wschodni
orienteering /ˌɔːrɪən'tɪərɪŋ/ *n* biegi *m pl* na orientację
origin /'ɒrɪdʒɪn/ *n* pochodzenie *n*; **the problem has its** ~(**s**) **in...** sedno problemu leży w...
original /ə'rɪdʒənl/ **I** *n* oryginał *m*
II *adj* ⒈ (initial) *[inhabitant, owner]* pierwotny; *[strategy]* początkowy ⒉ (new, authentic) oryginalny
originality /əˌrɪdʒə'nælətɪ/ *n* oryginalność *f*
originally /ə'rɪdʒənəlɪ/ *adv* ⒈ (initially) początkowo, z początku ⒉ (in the first place) pierwotnie

originate /ə'rɪdʒɪneɪt/ *vi [custom, style, tradition]* pojawi|ć, -ać się; *[fire]* zacz|ąć, -ynać się; **to** ~ **from sth** *[goods]* pochodzić z czegoś
originator /ə'rɪdʒɪneɪtə(r)/ *n* (of idea, rumour) autor *m*, -ka *f*; (of innovation, system) pomysłodawca *m*
ornament /'ɔːnəmənt/ *n* ⒈ (trinket) ozdoba *f* ⒉ (decoration) ozdoby *f pl*
ornamental /ˌɔːnə'mentl/ *adj [plant]* ozdobny; *[purpose]* dekoracyjny; *[motif]* ornamentacyjny
ornate /ɔː'neɪt/ *adj* ozdobny; *[style]* kwiecisty
ornithology /ˌɔːnɪ'θɒlədʒɪ/ *n* ornitologia *f*
orphan /'ɔːfn/ *n* sierota *m/f*
orphanage /'ɔːfənɪdʒ/ *n* sierociniec *m*, dom *m* dziecka
orthodox /'ɔːθədɒks/ *adj* ⒈ *[medicine]* konwencjonalny ⒉ *[Jew]* ortodoksyjny; **Greek Orthodox** grekokatolicki; **Russian Orthodox** prawosławny
orthopaedic, orthopedic US /ˌɔːθə'piːdɪk/ *adj* ortopedyczny
ostentatious /ˌɒsten'teɪʃəs/ *adj [behaviour]* ostentacyjny; *[dress]* pretensjonalny
osteopath /'ɒstɪəpæθ/ *n* kręgarz *m*
ostracize /'ɒstrəsaɪz/ *vt* z|bojkotować (towarzysko)
ostrich /'ɒstrɪtʃ/ *n* struś *m*
other /'ʌðə(r)/ **I** *adj* inny; **the** ~ **one** ten drugi/ ta druga/to drugie; **I was going the** ~ **way** szedłem w drugą stronę; **the** ~ **25** (of men) pozostałych dwudziestu pięciu; (of women, children, objects) pozostałe dwadzieścia pięć; **the** ~ **day** któregoś dnia; **every** ~ **year** raz na dwa lata; **every** ~ **Saturday** w co drugą sobotę
II other than *prep phr* ~ than that poza tym; **there's nobody here** ~ **than Anna** poza Anną nikogo tu nie ma; **we can't get home** ~ **than by car** nie dostaniemy się do domu inaczej niż samochodem
III *pron* **the** ~ (ten) drugi, (ta) druga, (to) drugie; **the** ~**s** (of men) pozostali; (of women, children) pozostałe; ~**s** (of men) inni; (of women, children) inne; **one after the** ~ jeden po drugim; **someone or** ~ ktoś (tam); **in some book or** ~ w jakiejś książce; **somehow or** ~ jakoś (tam), w ten czy inny sposób
otherwise /'ʌðəwaɪz/ **I** *adv* **no woman, married or** ~ żadna kobieta, zamężna lub nie; **unless we are told** ~ chyba że otrzymamy jakieś inne polecenia
II *conj* inaczej; **it's quite safe,** ~ **I wouldn't do it** to jest zupełnie bezpieczne, inaczej bym tego nie robił
otter /'ɒtə(r)/ *n* wydra *f*
ouch /aʊtʃ/ *excl* au!
ought /ɔːt/ *modal aux* **that** ~ **to be enough** to powinno wystarczyć; **oughtn't we to ask?** czy nie powinniśmy zapytać?; **you** ~ **to know that...** powinieneś wiedzieć, że...; **you** ~ **to have seen her face!** szkoda, że nie widziałeś jej twarzy!

ounce /aʊns/ n uncja f (= 28,35 g)

our /'aʊə(r), ɑ:(r)/ det nasz, -a, -e

ours /'aʊəz/ pron nasz, -a, -e; **which tickets are** ~ ? które bilety są nasze?; **a friend of** ~ nasza znajoma; ~ **hasn't been a bad marriage** nasze małżeństwo jest całkiem udane

ourselves /aʊə'selvz, ɑ:-/ pron [1] (as direct object) się; (as indirect object) siebie [2] (emphatic) same; (men) sami; **we saw it** ~ widzieliśmy to na własne oczy; **(all) by** ~ (całkiem or zupełnie) sami/same [3] (after preposition) **for** ~ dla siebie; **between** ~ między sobą

out /aʊt/ **[]** vt infml ujawni|ć, -ać, że (ktoś) jest homoseksualistą

[] adv [1] (outside) na zewnątrz; **to stand** ~ **in the rain** stać na deszczu; ~ **there** tam [2] **to go** or **walk** ~ wyjść; **to take sth** ~ wyjąć coś; **I couldn't find my way** ~ nie mogłem znaleźć wyjścia; **when the tide is** ~ w czasie odpływu; **further** ~ dalej; **to invite sb** ~ **for dinner** zaprosić kogoś do restauracji na kolację [3] (absent) **he's** ~ nie ma go [4] (published) **the results are due** ~ **next week** wyniki będą ogłoszone w przyszłym tygodniu [5] **to be** ~ [sun, moon, stars] świecić na niebie [6] (extinguished) **the fire was nearly** ~ pożar był już prawie ugaszony; **the light was** ~ światło było zgaszone [7] Sport **to be** ~ [player] zostać wyeliminowanym; **'** ~ **!'** (of ball) „aut!" [8] (over) **before the week is** ~ przed końcem tygodnia [9] infml **to be** ~ **to do sth** koniecznie chcieć coś zrobić; **to be** ~ [style] być niemodnym

[] out of prep phr [1] (from) **get** ~ **of here!** wyjdź (stąd)!; **to jump** ~ **of the window** wyskoczyć z okna; **to take sth** ~ **of a box** wyjąć coś z pudełka [2] (expressing ratio) **two** ~ **of every three people** dwie osoby na trzy [3] (beyond range of) ~ **of reach** poza zasięgiem; ~ **of sight** poza zasięgiem wzroku; ~ **of town** poza miastem; ~ **of the sun** ukryty przed słońcem [4] (lacking) **we are (right)** ~ **of coffee** nie mamy (już) kawy ⟦IDIOMS:⟧ **to be** ~ **of it** infml (after drinking alcohol) być zamroczonym

out-and-out /ˌaʊtən'aʊt/ adj [villain, fool] skończony; [failure, success] całkowity; [adherent] zdeklarowany

outback /'aʊtbæk/ n **the** ~ odludzie n; (in Australia) busz m (australijski)

outboard motor /ɔʊtbɔːd mɔʊtə(r)/ n silnik m przyczepny

outbreak /'aʊtbreɪk/ n (of war) wybuch m; (of disease) wybuch m epidemii; (of violence) gwałtowna fala f; (of fever) (nagłe) wystąpienie n

outbuilding /'aʊtbɪldɪŋ/ n ≈ budynek m gospodarczy

outburst /'aʊtbɜːst/ n (of laughter) wybuch m; (of energy) przypływ m

outcast /'aʊtkɑːst, US -kæst/ n wygnan|iec m, -ka f

outcome /'aʊtkʌm/ n wynik m, rezultat m

outcry /'aʊtkraɪ/ n głosy m pl protestu (**about sth** w sprawie czegoś) (**against sth** przeciwko czemuś)

outdated /ˌaʊt'deɪtɪd/ adj przestarzały; [clothing] niemodny

outdo /ˌaʊt'duː/ vt przewyższ|yć, -ać

outdoor /'aʊtdɔː(r)/ adj [activity] na (świeżym) powietrzu; [restaurant] na wolnym powietrzu; [swimming pool] odkryty

outdoors /ˌaʊt'dɔːz/ adv na dworze; **to go** ~ wyjść na dwór

outer /'aʊtə(r)/ adj [1] [limit] najdalszy [2] (outside) zewnętrzny

outer space n przestrzeń f kosmiczna

outfit /'aʊtfɪt/ n strój m

outgoing /'aʊtgəʊɪŋ/ adj [1] [personality] otwarty, towarzyski [2] [government] ustępujący; [mail] wychodzący

outgoings /'aʊtgəʊɪŋz/ npl GB wydatki m pl

outgrow /ˌaʊt'grəʊ/ vt [1] (grow too big or old for) wyr|osnąć, -astać z (czegoś) [clothes] [2] (grow taller than) prze|r|osnąć, -astać

outlandish /aʊt'lændɪʃ/ adj dziwaczny

outlast /ˌaʊt'lɑːst/ vt [object] przetrwać; [person] przetrzym|ać, -ywać

outlaw /'aʊtlɔː/ **[]** n człowiek m wyjęty spod prawa **[]** vt zakaz|ać, -ywać (czegoś) [practice]; z|delegalizować [organization]

outlay /'aʊtleɪ/ n wydatek m (**on sth** na coś)

outlet /'aʊtlet/ n [1] (for water, gas, air) odpływ m [2] (market) rynek m zbytu; **retail** ~ punkt sprzedaży detalicznej [3] (for energy, talent) ujście n [4] US (socket) gniazdko n

outline /'aʊtlaɪn/ **[]** n [1] (of object) zarys m, kontur m [2] (of plan, policy) zarys m, szkic m; (of essay) plan m **[]** vt przedstawi|ć, -ać w skrócie [situation, reasons]; na|szkicować [plan]

outlive /ˌaʊt'lɪv/ vt przeży|ć, -wać [person]

outlook /'aʊtlʊk/ n [1] (attitude) pogląd m [2] (prospects) perspektywy f pl

outlying /'aʊtlaɪŋ/ adj oddalony

outnumber /ˌaʊt'nʌmbə(r)/ vt przewyższ|yć, -ać liczebnie

out-of-date /ˌaʊtəv'deɪt/ adj [ticket, passport] nieważny; [concept] nieaktualny

outpatient /'aʊtpeɪʃnt/ n pacjent m leczony ambulatoryjnie; ~ **s' department** poradnia

outpost /'aʊtpəʊst/ n placówka f

output /'aʊtpʊt/ n wydajność f; (of factory) produkcja f

outrage /'aʊtreɪdʒ/ **[]** n [1] (anger) oburzenie n (**at sb/sth** na kogoś/coś) [2] (horrifying act) akt m przemocy [3] (against decency) obraza f, zniewaga f **[]** vt oburz|yć, -ać [public]

outrageous /aʊt'reɪdʒəs/ adj oburzający, skandaliczny; [remark] szokujący

outright /'aʊtraɪt/ **I** adj [ban] kategoryczny; [majority] absolutny; [winner] niekwestionowany **II** adv kategorycznie; [kill] na miejscu

outset /'aʊtset/ n at the ~ na początku; from the ~ od początku

outside /aʊt'saɪd, 'aʊtsaɪd/ **I** n 1 (of object, building) on the ~ na or z zewnątrz 2 (maximum) at the ~ maksymalnie **II** adj 1 [toilet] na zewnątrz; [world] zewnętrzny 2 ~ lane (in GB) prawy pas; (in Europe, US) lewy pas; (on athletics track) zewnętrzny tor; an ~ chance mała szansa **III** adv na zewnątrz **IV** prep (also ~ of) 1 (poza (czymś) [city]; to drugiej stronie (czegoś) [boundary]; na zewnątrz (czegoś) [prison] 2 (in front of) przed (czymś) [house, shop]

outsider /aʊt'saɪdə(r)/ n 1 (in community) obcy m, outsider m, -ka f 2 (unlikely to win) outsider m, -ka f

outsize /'aʊtsaɪz/ adj [clothing] w nietypowych dużych rozmiarach

outskirts /'aʊtskɜːts/ npl (of town) peryferie plt

outsourcing n zlecenie n wykonania usług na zewnątrz

outspoken /aʊt'spəʊkən/ adj to be ~ mówić bez ogródek

outstanding /aʊt'stændɪŋ/ adj 1 [scientist] wybitny 2 [example] znakomity 3 [problem] nierozstrzygnięty; [bill, work] zaległy; ~ debts wierzytelności

outstay /aʊt'steɪ/ vt to ~ one's welcome nadużyć gościnności

outstretched /aʊt'stretʃt/ adj [hand] wyciągnięty; [fingers] rozczapierzony; [wings] rozpostarty

outstrip /aʊt'strɪp/ vt prześcig|nąć, -ać [person]; przewyższ|yć, -ać [demand, production]

outward /'aʊtwəd/ **I** adj [appearance, calm] zewnętrzny **II** adv = outwards

outwardly /'aʊtwədlɪ/ adv (apparently) pozornie, na pozór

outwards /'aʊtwədz/ adv (also outward) [open, bend] na zewnątrz

outweigh /aʊt'weɪ/ vt przeważ|yć, -ać

outwit /aʊt'wɪt/ vt przechytrz|yć, -ać

outworker /'aʊtwɜːkə(r)/ n pracujący m w domu

oval /'əʊvl/ **I** n owal m **II** adj owalny

ovary /'əʊvərɪ/ n jajnik m

ovation /əʊ'veɪʃn/ n owacja f; to give sb a standing ~ zgotować komuś owację na stojąco

oven /ʌvn/ n piekarnik m

oven glove n rękawica f kuchenna

over /'əʊvə(r)/ **I** prep 1 to jump ~ a wall przeskoczyć przez mur; to wear a sweater ~ one's shirt nosić sweter na koszulę; a bridge ~ the Thames most na Tamizie or przez Tamizę

2 (across) it's just ~ the road to jest dosłownie po drugiej stronie ulicy; ~ here/there tu/tam; come ~ here! chodź tu!, podejdź tu! 3 (above) nad, ponad; they live ~ the shop mieszkają nad sklepem 4 (more than) przeszło, ponad; children ~ six dzieci powyżej sześciu lat; temperatures ~ 40° temperatury powyżej 40° 5 (in the course of) ~ the weekend przez cały weekend; ~ the last few days przez ostatnie kilka dni; ~ the years przez te lata; ~ Christmas w czasie świąt Bożego Narodzenia 6 to be ~ sth mieć za sobą coś [illness, operation]; to be ~ the worst mieć najgorsze za sobą 7 (by means of) ~ the phone/ the radio przez telefon/radio 8 (everywhere in) to search all ~ the house przeszukać cały dom **II** adj, adv 1 (finished) to be ~ [term, meeting] skończyć się 2 (more) children of six and ~ dzieci w wieku sześciu lat i powyżej 3 to invite or ask sb ~ zaprosić kogoś do siebie; we had them ~ on Sunday byli u nas w niedzielę 4 (on radio, TV) ~ (to you)! odbiór!; now ~ to our Paris studios a teraz przenosimy się do naszego studia w Paryżu 5 (showing repetition) five times ~ pięć razy z rzędu; to start all ~ again zacząć jeszcze raz od początku; I had to do it ~ US musiałem zrobić to jeszcze raz; I've told you ~ and ~ (again)... powtarzałem ci już setki razy...

overact /əʊvər'ækt/ vi popa|ść, -dać w przesadę

overall /'əʊvərɔːl/ **I** n GB (coat-type) kitel m, fartuch m; (child's) kombinezon m **II** overalls npl GB kombinezon m; US (with a bib front) ogrodniczki plt **III** /əʊvər'ɔːl/ adj [cost] całkowity; [improvement, effect] ogólny; [majority] absolutny **IV** /əʊvər'ɔːl/ adv 1 (in total) w sumie 2 (in general) ogólnie

overawe /əʊvər'ɔː/ vt onieśmiel|ić, -ać

overbalance /əʊvə'bæləns/ vi [person] s|tracić równowagę; [pile of objects] przewr|ócić, -acać się

overboard /'əʊvəbɔːd/ adv man ~! człowiek za burtą!

overbook /əʊvə'bʊk/ vt sprzeda|ć, -wać więcej biletów niż jest miejsc na (coś) [flight, concert]; przyjm|ować, -ać zbyt wiele rezerwacji w (czymś) [hotel]

overcast /əʊvə'kɑːst, US -'kæst/ adj pochmurny

overcharge /əʊvə'tʃɑːdʒ/ vt policzyć za dużo (komuś)

overcoat /'əʊvəkəʊt/ n płaszcz m

overcome /əʊvə'kʌm/ **I** vt pokon|ać, -ywać [opponent]; przezwycięż|yć, -ać [fear]; za|panować nad (czymś) [nerves]; ~ by or with jealousy owładnięty zazdrością **II** vi za|triumfować

overcook /əʊvə'kʊk/ vt rozgotow|ać, -ywać

overcrowded /əʊvə'kraʊdɪd/ adj [train, room, class] przepełniony; [country] przeludniony

overcrowding /ˌəʊvəˈkraʊdɪŋ/ n przepełnienie n; (in country) przeludnienie n

overdo /ˌəʊvəˈduː/ vt **to ~ it** (when describing, performing) przesadzać; (when working) przemęczać się

overdose [I] /ˈəʊvədəʊs/ n (large dose) nadmierna dawka f; (lethal dose) (of medicine) dawka f śmiertelna; (of drugs) przedawkowanie n; **to take an ~ of sth** przedawkować coś

[II] /ˌəʊvəˈdəʊs/ vi (on medicine, drugs) przedawkować

overdraft /ˈəʊvədrɑːft, US -dræft/ n debet m

overdressed /ˌəʊvəˈdres/ adj (przesadnie) wystrojony

overdrive /ˈəʊvədraɪv/ n fig **to be in ~** pracować na najwyższych obrotach fig

overdue /ˌəʊvəˈdjuː, US -ˈduː/ adj [train] opóźniony; [bill] zaległy; [cheque] przeterminowany; **the baby is two weeks ~** termin porodu upłynął dwa tygodnie temu; **this measure is long ~** już dawno należało zastosować ten środek

overeat /ˌəʊvərˈiːt/ vi przej|eść, -adać się

overestimate /ˌəʊvərˈestɪmeɪt/ vt przeceni|ć, -ać [capabilities, person]; zbyt wysoko oszacować [amount]

overexcited /ˌəʊvərɪkˈsaɪtɪd/ adj zbyt podniecony; [child] zbyt ożywiony

overflow /ˌəʊvəˈfləʊ/ [I] vt [river] zal|ać, -ewać [land]; przel|ać, -ewać się przez (coś), wyst|ąpić, -ępować z (czegoś) [banks]

[II] vi [river] wyl|ać, -ewać się (**into sth** do czegoś)

overgrown /ˌəʊvəˈɡrəʊn/ adj [garden] zarośnięty

overhaul [I] /ˈəʊvəhɔːl/ n (of machine) (examination) przegląd m; (repair) naprawa f; (major) remont m kapitalny; (of system) restrukturyzacja f

[II] /ˌəʊvəˈhɔːl/ vt (examine) przeprowadz|ić, -ać przegląd (czegoś); (make repairs to) dokon|ać, -ywać remontu kapitalnego (czegoś) [engine, car]; z|restrukturyzować [system]

overhead /ˈəʊvəhed/ [I] **overheads** npl GB koszty m pl ogólne

[II] /ˈəʊvəhed/ adj [cable, railway] napowietrzny

[III] /ˌəʊvəˈhed/ adv nad głową, w górze

overhead projector n rzutnik m

overhear /ˌəʊvəˈhɪə(r)/ vt u|słyszeć, przypadkiem podsłuchać

overheat /ˌəʊvəˈhiːt/ vi [car, equipment] przegrz|ać, -ewać się

overindulge /ˌəʊvərɪnˈdʌldʒ/ vi nadmiernie do-g|odzić, -adzać sobie

overjoyed /ˌəʊvəˈdʒɔɪd/ adj niezmiernie uradowany; **to be ~ at sth** ogromnie ucieszyć się z czegoś

overkill /ˈəʊvəkɪl/ n **in advertising ~** natarczywość reklam

overland /ˈəʊvəlænd/ [I] adj [route] lądowy; [cables] naziemny

[II] adv lądem, drogą lądową

overlap /ˌəʊvəˈlæp/ vi [theories] pokrywać się częściowo (**with sth** z czymś); [materials] zachodzić na siebie

overleaf /ˌəʊvəˈliːf/ adv na odwrocie (strony)

overload /ˌəʊvəˈləʊd/ vt przeładow|ać, -ywać [vehicle] (**with sth** czymś); przeciąż|yć, -ać [system] (**with sth** czymś)

overlook /ˌəʊvəˈlʊk/ vt [1] [window] wychodzić na (coś); [building] górować or wznosić się nad (czymś) [2] (miss) przeoczyć [detail, error]; **to ~ the fact that...** nie zauważyć, że... [3] (ignore) przym|knąć, -ykać oczy na (coś) [offence]; nie dostrze|c, -gać (czegoś) [fact]

overnight [I] /ˈəʊvənaɪt/ adj [1] [journey, train] nocny; **~ stop** nocleg [2] [success] natychmiastowy

[II] /ˌəʊvəˈnaɪt/ adv [1] **to stay ~** zostać na noc, zanocować [2] (rapidly) z dnia na dzień

overnight bag n (niewielka) torba f podróżna

overpopulated /ˌəʊvəˈpɒpjʊleɪtɪd/ adj przeludniony

overpower /ˌəʊvəˈpaʊə(r)/ vt [1] (subdue) obez-władni|ć, -ać [thief]; zwycięż|yć, -ać [army] [2] [smell, smoke] dławić

overpowering /ˌəʊvəˈpaʊərɪŋ/ adj [person] znie-walający; [personality] dominujący; [desire] prze-możny; [smell] nieznośny

overpriced /ˌəʊvəˈpraɪst/ adj [product] zbyt drogi

overqualified /ˌəʊvəˈkwɒlɪfaɪd/ adj o zbyt wysokich kwalifikacjach

overrated /ˌəʊvəˈreɪtɪd/ adj [film] przereklamowany; [poet] przeceniany

overreact /ˌəʊvərɪˈækt/ vi za|reagować zbyt mocno

override /ˌəʊvəˈraɪd/ vt być ważniejszym od (czegoś) [decision]; uchyl|ić, -ać [order]

overriding /ˌəʊvəˈraɪdɪŋ/ adj nadrzędny

overrule /ˌəʊvəˈruːl/ vt unieważni|ć, -ać, anulować [decision]

overrun /ˌəʊvəˈrʌn/ vt [1] (invade) naje|chać, -żdżać na (coś) [country]; opanow|ać, -ywać [building] [2] (exceed) przekr|oczyć, -aczać [time, budget]

overseas /ˌəʊvəˈsiːz/ [I] adj [1] [student, investor] zagraniczny [2] [trade, market] zagraniczny

[II] adv [work] za granicą; (across the sea) za morzem

overshadow /ˌəʊvəˈʃædəʊ/ vt usu|nąć, -wać w cień [achievement]

oversight /ˈəʊvəsaɪt/ n przeoczenie n; **due to an ~** przez niedopatrzenie

oversimplify /ˌəʊvəˈsɪmplɪfaɪ/ vt zbytnio upr|ość-cić, -aszczać

oversleep /ˌəʊvəˈsliːp/ vi zaspać

overspend /ˌəʊvəˈspend/ vi [person] wyda|ć, -wać zbyt dużo; [government] przekr|oczyć, -aczać budżet

overstay /ˌəʊvəˈsteɪ/ vt **to ~ one's welcome** nadużyć gościnności; **to ~ one's visa** przekroczyć termin ważności wizy

overstep /ˌəʊvəˈstep/ vt przekr|oczyć, -aczać [bounds]; **to ~ the mark** przekroczyć dopuszczalne granice

overt /ˈəʊvɜːt, US əʊˈvɜːrt/ adj [hostility] jawny; [sign] wyraźny

overtake /ˌəʊvəˈteɪk/ **[]** *vt* *[vehicle, person]* wyprzedz|ić, -ać
[] *vi* **'no overtaking'** „zakaz wyprzedzania"
over-the-top, OTT /ˌəʊvəðəˈtɒp/ *adj* infml skrajny; **to go over the top** wściec się infml; (overreact) przesadzić (**about sth** z czymś)
overthrow /ˌəʊvəˈθrəʊ/ *vt* obal|ić, -ać *[government, system]*
overtime /ˈəʊvətaɪm/ **[]** *n* nadgodziny *f pl*
[] *adv* **to work** ~ *[person]* pracować w nadgodzinach
overtone /ˈəʊvətəʊn/ *n* podtekst *m*
overture /ˈəʊvətjʊə(r)/ *n* uwertura *f*
overturn /ˌəʊvəˈtɜːn/ **[]** *vt* [1] (turn) wywr|ócić, -acać, przewr|ócić, -acać *[car, chair, boat]* [2] (make invalid) unieważni|ć, -ać *[decision, sentence]*
[] *vi* *[boat, car, chair]* wywr|ócić, -acać się
overweight /ˌəʊvəˈweɪt/ *adj* ~ **person** osoba z nadwagą; **to be** ~ mieć nadwagę
overwhelm /ˌəʊvəˈwelm/, US -ˈhwelm/ **[]** *vt* [1] *[avalanche]* zasyp|ać, -ywać; *[wave]* zal|ać, -ewać; *[enemy]* z|miażdżyć [2] *[shame]* ogarn|ąć, -iać, owładnąć (kimś); *[unhappiness]* przytł|oczyć, -aczać
[] **overwhelmed** *pp adj* (with letters, offers, phone calls) zasypany fig (**with** or **by sth** czymś); (with unhappiness, work) przytłoczony (**with** or **by sth** czymś); (by sight, experience) do głębi poruszony (**by sth** czymś)
overwhelming /ˌəʊvəˈwelmɪŋ/, US -ˈhwelm-/ *adj* *[victory, defeat]* druzgocący; *[majority]* przytłaczający; *[desire]* nieodparty, przemożny; *[sorrow, heat]* dojmujący; *[support]* entuzjastyczny
overwork /ˌəʊvəˈwɜːk/ *vi* przepracow|ać, -ywać się

overworked /ˌəʊvəˈwɜːkt/ *adj* przepracowany
owe /əʊ/ *vt* być winnym *[money]*; **to** ~ **sth to sb** zawdzięczać komuś coś *[talent]*; być komuś winnym coś *[money]*
owing /ˈəʊɪŋ/ **[]** *adj* należny, do zapłaty (**for sth** za coś)
[] **owing to** *prep phr* z powodu (czegoś); ~ **to the fact that...** ponieważ..., w związku z tym, że...
owl /aʊl/ *n* sowa *f*
own /əʊn/ **[]** *adj* własny; **his** ~ **car** jego własny samochód; **he's very nice in his** ~ **way** na swój sposób jest bardzo miły; **she does her** ~ **cooking** sama sobie gotuje
[] *pron* **my** ~ mój (własny); **his/her** ~ jego/jej (własny); **he has a room of his** ~ ma własny pokój; **a house of our (very)** ~ nasz własny dom
[] *vt* mieć, posiadać *[car, dog, house]*; **she** ~ **s three shops** ma trzy sklepy; **who** ~ **s this house?** kto jest właścicielem tego domu?
■ **own up**: przyzna|ć, -wać się
IDIOMS **to get one's** ~ **back** zemścić się (**on sb** na kimś); **on one's** ~ samodzielnie, bez niczyjej pomocy
owner /ˈəʊnə(r)/ *n* właściciel *m*, -ka *f*, posiadacz *m*, -ka *f*; **car** ~ właściciel samochodu
ownership /ˈəʊnəʃɪp/ *n* własność *f*; (right of possession) prawo *n* własności
ox /ɒks/ *n* wół *m*
oxygen /ˈɒksɪdʒən/ *n* tlen *m*
oyster /ˈɔɪstə(r)/ *n* ostryga *f*
ozone /ˈəʊzəʊn/ *n* ozon *m*
ozone layer *n* warstwa *f* ozonowa

P

p, P /piː/ *n* p, P *n*

PA *n* = **personal assistant** asystentka *f* sekretarka, asystent *m* sekretarz

pace /peɪs/ **[]** *n* (step) krok *m*; (speed) tempo *n*, szybkość *f*; **at a fast/slow** ~ szybko/wolno; **at walking** ~ spacerowym krokiem
[] *vi* **to** ~ **up and down** chodzić tam i z powrotem; **to** ~ **up and down a room** przemierzać pokój tam i z powrotem

pacemaker /ˈpeɪsmeɪkə(r)/ *n* [1] Med rozrusznik *m* or stymulator *m* serca [2] (athlete) narzucający *m* tempo

Pacific /pəˈsɪfɪk/ *prn* **the** ~ **(Ocean)** Ocean *m* Spokojny, Pacyfik *m*

pacifist /ˈpæsɪfɪst/ **[]** *n* pacyfist|a *m*, -ka *f*
[] *adj* pacyfistyczny

pacify /ˈpæsɪfaɪ/ *vt* uspok|oić, -ajać *[worried person]*; ułag|odzić, -adzać *[angry person]*

pack /pæk/ **[]** *n* [1] (box) paczka *f*; (bag) opakowanie *n* [2] (group) grupa *f*; (of dogs) sfora *f*; **a** ~ **of lies** stek kłamstw [3] (in rugby) napastnicy *m pl* [4] (of cards) talia *f* (kart) [5] (rucksack) plecak *m*
[] *vt* [1] za|pakować, spakować *[clothes, suitcase]* [2] (commercially) paczkować *[fruit, meat, goods]* [3] *[crowd]* szczelnie wypełni|ć, -ać *[church, theatre]* [4] (press firmly) ubi|ć, -jać *[snow, earth]*
[] *vi* [1] *[person]* za|pakować się, spakować się [2] (crowd) **to** ~ **into the station/theatre** cisnąć się na stację/do teatru
■ pack up: ¶ ~ **up** [1] *[person]* zwi|nąć, -jać się infml [2] infml (break down) *[TV, car]* nawal|ić, -ać, wysi|ąść, -adać infml ¶ ~ **[sth] up** spakować, zapakować

package /ˈpækɪdʒ/ **[]** *n* [1] (parcel) paczka *f*, pakunek *m* [2] (of measures, proposals) pakiet *m* [3] Comput pakiet *m*
[] *vt* za|pakować

package deal *n* umowa *f* wiązana

package holiday GB, **package tour** *n* wakacje *plt* zorganizowane

packaging /ˈpækɪdʒɪŋ/ *n* opakowanie *n*

packed /pækt/ *adj [place]* pełny, zatłoczony; **to be** ~ **with sth** być pełnym czegoś

packed lunch *n* (in school) drugie śniadanie *n*; (on a trip) suchy prowiant *m*

packet /ˈpækɪt/ *n* (for cigarettes, biscuits) paczka *f*; (bag) torba *f*, torebka *f*

packing /ˈpækɪŋ/ *n* [1] (packaging) opakowanie *n* [2] **to do one's** ~ pakować się

pact /pækt/ *n* pakt *m*, układ *m*

pad /pæd/ **[]** *n* [1] (of paper) blok *m*; (small) bloczek *m* [2] (for leg) ochraniacz *m* [3] (of paw) poduszka *f*, poduszeczka *f*; (of finger) opuszka *f* [4] (also **launch** ~) (for spaceships) wyrzutnia *f* rakietowa; (for helicopters) lądowisko *n*
[] *vt* wy|słać, -ściełać *[walls, chair]*; wywatow|ać, -ywać *[shoulders, jacket]* (**with sth** czymś)
[] *vi* **to** ~ **along/around** cicho stąpać or chodzić
■ pad out: rozwle|c, -kać *[speech, essay]*

padded envelope *n* koperta *f* wyściełana

padding /ˈpædɪŋ/ *n* (material) wyściółka *f*

paddle /ˈpædl/ **[]** *n* [1] (oar) wiosło *n* [2] **to go for a** ~ iść sobie pobrodzić
[] *vi* [1] (row) po|wiosłować [2] (wade) po|brodzić [3] *[duck, swan]* po|płynąć, po|pływać

paddling pool *n* (public) brodzik *m*; (inflatable) basen *m* nadmuchiwany

padlock /ˈpædlɒk/ **[]** *n* kłódka *f*
[] *vt* zam|knąć, -ykać na kłódkę *[door, gate]*; zabezpiecz|yć, -ać kłódką *[bicycle]*

paediatrician GB, **pediatrician** US /ˌpiːdɪəˈtrɪʃn/ *n* pediatra *m*

paedophile GB, **pedophile** US /ˈpiːdəfaɪl/ *n* pedofil *m*

pagan /ˈpeɪɡən/ **[]** *n* pogan|in *m*, -ka *f*
[] *adj* pogański

page /peɪdʒ/ **[]** *n* [1] (in book) strona *f*, stronica *f*; **on** ~ **two** na stronie drugiej [2] (attendant) boy *m*; US goniec *m*
[] *vt* przywoł|ać, -ywać, w|ezwać, -zywać

pageant /ˈpædʒənt/ *n* (procession) parada *f*; (show) widowisko *n* historyczne na świeżym powietrzu

pageboy /ˈpeɪdʒbɔɪ/ *n* (at wedding) pazik *m* *(towarzyszący pannie młodej)*

pager /ˈpeɪdʒə(r)/ *n* pager *m*, przywoływacz *m*

paid /peɪd/ *adj [job]* z wynagrodzeniem; *[holiday]* płatny; ~ **assassin** płatny morderca

pain /peɪn/ **[]** *n* [1] ból *m*; **to be in** ~ odczuwać ból, cierpieć; **period** ~**s** bóle menstruacyjne [2] infml (annoying person) zaraza *f* infml; (annoying thing) cholerstwo *n* infml; **he's a** ~ **in the neck** on jest nie do wytrzymania
[] **pains** *npl* trudy *m pl*, starania *n pl*; **to be at** ~**s to do sth** bardzo się starać coś zrobić; dokładać

starań, żeby coś zrobić; **to take great ∼s over** or **with sth** zadać sobie wiele trudu z czymś, bardzo się nad czymś namęczyć

painful /'peɪnfl/ *adj* bolesny; *[duty]* przykry; *[task, progress]* żmudny

painkiller /'peɪnkɪlə(r)/ *n* środek *m* przeciwbólowy

painless /'peɪnlɪs/ *adj* bezbolesny

painstaking /'peɪnzteɪkɪŋ/ *adj* *[worker]* skrupulatny; *[research]* drobiazgowy

paint /peɪnt/ **I** *n* farba *f*
II paints *npl* farby *f pl*
III *vt* ① po|malować *[object]*; na|malować *[person, picture]*; **to ∼ sth blue** pomalować coś na niebiesko; **to ∼ one's nails** pomalować sobie paznokcie ② (depict) odmalow|ać, -ywać
IV *vi* malować

paintbox /'peɪntbɒks/ *n* pudło *n* farb (wodnych)

paintbrush /'peɪntbrʌʃ/ *n* pędzel *m*

painter /'peɪntə(r)/ *n* mala|rz *m*, -rka *f*

painting /'peɪntɪŋ/ *n* ① (art form) malarstwo *n*; (activity) malowanie *n* ② (work of art) obraz *m*; (on canvas) płótno *n*; (of person) portret *m* ③ (decorating) malowanie *n*

pair /peə(r)/ *n* ① (two items) para *f*; **to be one of a ∼** być jednym z pary; **to work in ∼s** pracować w parach ② (couple) para *f*, dwójka *f*
■ **pair off**: **∼ off** tworzyć parę
■ **pair up**: **∼ up** *[dancers, lovers]* s|tworzyć parę; *[competitors]* dobrać się do pary

paisley /'peɪzlɪ/ *n* tkanina *f* w „tureckie" wzory

pajamas *npl* US = **pyjamas**

Pakistan /ˌpɑːkɪ'stɑːn, ˌpækɪ-/ *prn* Pakistan *m*

Pakistani /ˌpɑːkɪ'stɑːnɪ, ˌpækɪ-/ **I** *n* Pakista|ńczyk *m*, -nka *f*
II *adj* pakistański

palace /'pælɪs/ *n* pałac *m*

palatable /'pælətəbl/ *adj* *[food]* smaczny; *[solution, law]* do przyjęcia

palate /'pælət/ *n* podniebienie *n*

pale /peɪl/ **I** *adj* blady; **to go** or **turn ∼** zblednąć, poblednąć
II *vi* z|blednąć, poblednąć; **to ∼ into insignificance (beside sth)** być niczym (w porównaniu z czymś)

Palestine /'pæləstaɪn/ *prn* Palestyna *f*

Palestinian /ˌpælɪ'stɪnɪən/ **I** *n* Palesty|ńczyk *m*, -nka *f*
II *adj* palestyński

palette /'pælɪt/ *n* paleta *f*

pallet /'pælɪt/ *n* (for loading) paleta *f*

pallid /'pælɪd/ *adj* *[skin, light]* blady

palm /pɑːm/ *n* ① dłoń *f*; **in the ∼ of one's hand** w dłoni; **he read my ∼** powróżył mi z ręki ② (also **∼ tree**) palma *f* ③ (also **∼ leaf**) liść *m* palmy
■ **palm off** *infml*: **to ∼ sth off** (sell) op|chnąć,

-ychać coś *infml*; **to ∼ sth off on sb, to ∼ sb off with sth** wcisnąć coś komuś *infml*

Palm Sunday *n* Niedziela *f* Palmowa

palmtop /'pɑːmtɒp/ *n* (also **∼ computer**) komputer *m* kieszonkowy, palmtop *m*

palpable /'pælpəbl/ *adj* *[tension, relief]* wyraźny; *[lie, error, nonsense]* ewidentny

palpitate /'pælpɪteɪt/ *vi [heart]* kołatać

paltry /'pɔːltrɪ/ *adj [sum]* śmiesznie mały; *[excuse]* kiepski, marny

pamper /'pæmpə(r)/ *vt* rozpieszczać *[person, pet]*

pamphlet /'pæmflɪt/ *n* broszura *f*; (political) pamflet *m*

pan /pæn/ **I** *n* rondel *m*; (small) rondelek *m*; (with two handles) garnek *m*
II *vt infml* (criticize) zje|chać, -żdżać, schlastać *infml*
III *vi* (in photography) panoramować

pancake /'pæŋkeɪk/ *n* naleśnik *m*

pancake day *n* ostatki *plt* (ostatni dzień karnawału)

pandemonium /ˌpændɪ'məʊnɪəm/ *n* chaos *m*, pandemonium *n*

pander /'pændə(r)/ *vi* **to ∼ to sb** ulegać kaprysom kogoś, dogadzać komuś; **to ∼ to sb's whims** dogadzać or ulegać kaprysom kogoś

pane /peɪn/ *n* szyba *f*

panel /'pænl/ *n* ① (of experts) zespół *m*; (in discussion) panel *m*; (on discussion programme) uczestnicy *m pl* dyskusji; (on quiz show) jury *n inv*, komisja *f* sędziowska ② (section of wall, door) (of wood) płycina *f*; (of glass) tafla *f* ③ (of instruments, switches) pulpit *m* sterowniczy

pang /pæŋ/ *n* ściśnięcie *n* serca; **a ∼ of jealousy** ukłucie zazdrości; **∼s of hunger** skurcze głodowe or żołądka

panhandler /'pænhændlə(r)/ *n* US *infml* żebra|k *m*, -czka *f*

panic /'pænɪk/ **I** *n* panika *f*, popłoch *m*
II *vt* przestrasz|yć, -ać *[person]*; s|płoszyć *[animal]*; wywoł|ać, -ywać panikę wśród (kogoś) *[crowd]*
III *vi* wpa|ść, -dać w panikę

panic buying *n* masowe wykupywanie *n* towarów

panorama /ˌpænə'rɑːmə/ *n* panorama *f*

pansy /'pænzɪ/ *n* bratek *m*; (wild) fiołek *m*

pant /pænt/ *vi [person]* dyszeć, sapać; *[dog]* ziajać

panther /'pænθə(r)/ *n* ① (leopard) pantera *f* ② US (puma) puma *f*

pantomime /'pæntəmaɪm/ *n* GB muzyczne przedstawienie *n* gwiazdkowe *(dla dzieci)*

pantry /'pæntrɪ/ *n* spiżarnia *f*

pants /pænts/ *npl* ① US (trousers) spodnie *plt*; (short) spodenki *plt* ② GB (underwear) (woman's) majtki *plt*; (man's) slipy *plt*, kalesony *plt*

pantyhose /'pæntɪhəʊz/ *n* US rajstopy *plt*

panty-liner /'pæntɪlaɪnə(r)/ *n* wkładka *f* higieniczna

paper /'peɪpə(r)/ **I** *n* [1] papier *m* [2] (also **wall**~) tapeta *f* [3] (newspaper) gazeta *f* [4] (article) artykuł *m* (**on sth** na temat czegoś); (lecture) referat *m* (**on sth** na temat czegoś) [5] (examination) egzamin *m* pisemny **II papers** *npl* papiery *m pl*, dokumenty *m pl* **III** *adj* papierowy **IV** *vt* wy|tapetować *[room, wall]*

paperback /'peɪpəbæk/ *n* książka *f* w miękkiej or broszurowej oprawie

paperclip /'peɪpəklɪp/ *n* spinacz *m*

paper knife *n* nóż *m* do papieru

paper round *n* he does a ~ on roznosi gazety

paper shop *n* kiosk *m* z gazetami

paper towel *n* ręcznik *m* papierowy

paperweight /'peɪpəweɪt/ *n* przycisk *m* do papieru

paperwork /'peɪpəwɜːk/ *n* (administration) papierkowa robota *f* or praca *f*; (documentation) papiery *plt*

par /pɑː(r)/ *n* [1] **to be on a** ~ **with sb/sth** dorównywać komuś/czemuś, stać na równi z kimś/ czymś; **to be below** or **under** ~ być nie na poziomie [2] (in golf) norma *f*

parachute /'pærəʃuːt/ **I** *n* spadochron *m* **II** *vi* sk|oczyć, -akać na spadochronie

parachute drop *n* zrzut *m* (*na spadochronie*)

parachute jump *n* skok *m* spadochronowy

parachuting /'pærəʃuːtɪŋ/ *n* spadochroniarstwo *n*

parade /pə'reɪd/ **I** *n* [1] (procession) parada *f*; (ceremonial) pochód *m*, defilada *f* [2] Mil (march) parada *f*; (review) defilada *f*; (in barracks) apel *m* **II** *vt* (display) afiszować się (czymś) *[knowledge, wealth]*; obnosić się z (czymś) *[feelings]* **III** *vi* defilować, maszerować; **to ~ up and down** *[soldier]* maszerować tam i z powrotem; *[person, child]* paradować infml

parade ground *n* plac *m* apelowy

paradise /'pærədaɪs/ *n* raj *m*; **in** ~ w raju

paradox /'pærədɒks/ *n* paradoks *m*

paradoxical /ˌpærə'dɒksɪkl/ *adj* paradoksalny

paraffin /'pærəfɪn/ *n* [1] GB (fuel) nafta *f* [2] (also ~ **wax**) parafina *f*

paragliding /'pærəglaɪdɪŋ/ *n* paralotniarstwo *n*

paragon /'pærəgən, US -gɒn/ *n* wzór *m*, wcielenie *n* (**of sth** czegoś)

paragraph /'pærəgrɑːf, US -græf/ *n* akapit *m*, ustęp *m*

parallel /'pærəlel/ **I** *n* [1] (comparison) porównanie *n*; (similarity) podobieństwo *n* [2] (in mathematics) równoległa *f* **II** *adj* [1] równoległy [2] (similar) podobny, zbliżony (**to** or **with sth** do czegoś) **III** *adv* ~ **to** or **with sth** równolegle do czegoś or z czymś

paralyse GB, **paralyze** US /'pærəlaɪz/ *vt* s|paraliżować

paralysis /pə'ræləsɪs/ *n* paraliż *m*, porażenie *n*

paramedic /ˌpærə'medɪk/ *n* pracownik *m* paramedyczny, pracowniczka *f* paramedyczna

parameter /pə'ræmɪtə(r)/ *n* parametr *m*

paramilitary /ˌpærə'mɪlɪtrɪ, US -terɪ/ **I** *n* czło‐ n|ek *m*, -kini *f* organizacji paramilitarnej **II** *adj* paramilitarny

paramount /'pærəmaʊnt/ *adj* **to be** ~, **to be of** ~ **importance** mieć kapitalne znaczenie

paranoid /'pærənɔɪd/ *adj* paranoidalny, paranoiczny; **to be** ~ **about sth** fig reagować paranoicznie na coś

paraphernalia /ˌpærəfə'neɪlɪə/ *n* rzeczy *f pl*; (for particular activity) akcesoria *plt*, sprzęt *m*

paraphrase /'pærəfreɪz/ *vt* s|parafrazować

parascending /'pærəsendɪŋ/ *n* lotniarstwo *n* na spadochronie wynoszonym w powietrze przez samochód/motorówkę

parasite /'pærəsaɪt/ *n* pasożyt *m*

paratrooper /'pærətruːpə(r)/ *n* spadochroniarz *m*

parcel /'pɑːsl/ *n* paczka *f*, pakunek *m* ■ **parcel up:** ~ **[sth] up** za|pakować [IDIOMS] **to be part and** ~ **of sth** być nieodłączną częścią czegoś, stanowić nieodłączną część czegoś

parcel bomb *n* przesyłka *f* zawierająca ładunek wybuchowy

parched /pɑːtʃt/ *adj* [1] *[lips, skin]* spieczony; *[throat]* suchy; *[earth]* spalony, spękany [2] (thirsty) **I'm** ~ zaschło mi w gardle

parchment /'pɑːtʃmənt/ *n* pergamin *m*

pardon /'pɑːdn/ **I** *n* [1] wybaczenie *n* [2] (also **free** ~) ułaskawienie *n*, darowanie *n* kary **II** *excl* (what?) słucham?; przepraszam, nie dosły‐ szałem; (sorry) (bardzo) przepraszam **III** *vt* przebacz|yć, -ać, wybacz|yć, -ać; (in law) ułaskawi|ć, -ać, darować (komuś) winę *[offender]*

parent /'peərənt/ *n* (father) ojciec *m*; (mother) mat‐ ka *f*; ~**s** rodzice *plt*

parental /pə'rentl/ *adj* rodzicielski

parent company *m* spółka *f* or firma *f* macie‐ rzysta

parenthood /'peərənthʊd/ *n* rodzicielstwo *n*; (fatherhood) ojcostwo *n*; (motherhood) macierzyństwo *n*

parenting /'peərəntɪŋ/ *n* wychowanie *n* dzieci

parents' evening *m* zebranie *n* rodziców; wywiadówka *n* infml

Paris /'pærɪs/ *prn* Paryż *m*

parish /'pærɪʃ/ *n* [1] (area) parafia *f*; (residents) parafianie *m pl* [2] GB (administrative) ≈ gmina *f*

Parisian /pə'rɪzɪən/ **I** *n* paryżan|in *m*, -ka *f* **II** *adj* paryski

park /pɑːk/ **I** *n* [1] (public garden) park *m*, ogród *m* [2] (estate) park *m* [3] (on automatic gearbox) park *m* **II** *vt* za|parkować *[vehicle]* **III** *vi* za|parkować **IV parked** *pp adj* zaparkowany

park-and-ride /ˌpɑːkənˈraɪd/ *n system parkowania na obrzeżach miasta i dojeżdżania do centrum publicznymi środkami transportu*

parking /ˈpɑːkɪŋ/ *n* parkowanie *n*; **'no ~'** „zakaz parkowania"

parking lot *n* US parking *m*

parking meter *n* parkometr *m*, parkomat *m*

parking place, parking space *n* miejsce *n* do parkowania

parking ticket *n* (fine) mandat *m* za nieprawidłowe parkowanie

parliament /ˈpɑːləmənt/ *n* parlament *m*

parliamentary /ˌpɑːləˈmentrɪ/, US -terɪ/ *adj* parlamentarny

parlour GB, **parlor** US /ˈpɑːlə(r)/ *n* salon *m*

parody /ˈpærədɪ/ **[I]** *n* parodia *f*
[II] *vt* s|parodiować *[person, style]*

parole /pəˈrəʊl/ *n* zwolnienie *n* warunkowe; **to release sb on ~** zwolnić kogoś warunkowo

parrot /ˈpærət/ *n* papuga *f*

parry /ˈpærɪ/ *vt* [1] Sport odparow|ać, -ywać *[blow]* [2] od|eprzeć, -pierać *[attack, argument]*

parsley /ˈpɑːslɪ/ *n* pietruszka *f* naciowa; Culin natka *f* pietruszki

parsnip /ˈpɑːsnɪp/ *n* pasternak *m*

part /pɑːt/ **[I]** *n* [1] (of whole) część *f*; **for the most ~** (usually) przeważnie, na ogół; (generally) w przeważającej części; **that's the best/hardest ~** to jest najlepsze/najgorsze; **to be (a) ~ of sth** być częścią czegoś [2] Tech (component) część *f*; **spare ~s** części zamienne or zapasowe [3] (of serial, story) część *f* [4] (role) rola *f*, udział *m* (**in sth** w czymś); **to take ~ in sth** wziąć udział w czymś [5] (actor's role) rola *f* [6] (measure) część *f* [7] (behalf) **on the ~ of sb** ze strony kogoś; **for my ~** co do mnie [8] US (in hair) przedziałek *m*
[II] *adv* (partly) częściowo, trochę; **I was ~ angry, ~ relieved** byłem trochę zły, a trochę odczuwałem ulgę
[III] *vt* rozdziel|ić, -ać *[couple, friends]*; rozchyl|ić, -ać *[lips, curtains]*; rozsu|nąć, -wać *[legs]*; **to ~ one's hair** zrobić sobie przedziałek
[IV] *vi* [1] (split up) rozsta|ć, -wać się (**from sb** z kimś) [2] *[crowd]* rozstą|pić, -powć się; *[clouds]* roz|ejść, -chodzić się
■ **part with**: odda|ć, -wać *[money, object]*

part exchange *n* GB *sprzedaż połączona z oddaniem przez klienta starego sprzętu*; **to take sth in ~** wziąć coś w rozliczeniu

partial /ˈpɑːʃl/ *adj* [1] (not complete) częściowy [2] (biased) *[judge, arbiter]* stronniczy; *[attitude]* tendencyjny [3] (fond) **to be ~ to sth** mieć słabość do czegoś

partially sighted /ˈpɑːʃəlɪˈsaɪtɪd/ *n* **the ~** osoby *f pl* niedowidzące

participant /pɑːˈtɪsɪpənt/ *n* uczestni|k *m*, -czka *f* (**in sth** czegoś)

participate /pɑːˈtɪsɪpeɪt/ *vi* uczestniczyć, wziąć, brać udział (**in sth** w czymś)

participation /pɑːˌtɪsɪˈpeɪʃn/ *n* udział *m*, uczestnictwo *n* (**in sth** w czymś)

participle /ˈpɑːtɪsɪpl/ *n* imiesłów *m*

particle /ˈpɑːtɪkl/ *n* [1] (of ash, dust, metal, food) drobina *f* [2] (in physics) cząstka *f* (elementarna)

particular /pəˈtɪkjʊlə(r)/ **[I]** *adj* [1] (specific) szczególny, konkretny [2] (fussy) wymagający; **to be ~ about sth** przywiązywać dużą wagę do czegoś; być bardzo wymagającym, jeśli chodzi o coś
[II] particulars *npl* szczegółowe dane *plt* (**of sb/sth** dotyczące kogoś/czegoś)
[III] in particular *adv phr* szczególnie, w szczególności, zwłaszcza

particularly /pəˈtɪkjʊləlɪ/ *adv* (especially) szczególnie; (in particular) w szczególności

parting /ˈpɑːtɪŋ/ *n* [1] (farewell) rozstanie *n* [2] GB (in hair) przedziałek *m*

partisan /ˈpɑːtɪzæn, ˌpɑːtɪˈzæn, US ˈpɑːrtɪzn/ *n* [1] (supporter) zwolenni|k *m*, -czka *f* [2] Mil partyzant *m*, -ka *f*

partition /pɑːˈtɪʃn/ **[I]** *n* [1] (in room, house) ścianka *f* działowa, przepierzenie *n* [2] (of country) podział *m*; (in Polish history) rozbiór *m*
[II] *vt* [1] przedziel|ić, -ać ścianką *[area, room]* [2] po|dzielić *[country]*
■ **partition off**: **~ off [sth], ~ [sth] off** oddziel|ić, -ać *[space, area]*

partly /ˈpɑːtlɪ/ *adv* częściowo

partner /ˈpɑːtnə(r)/ *n* [1] wspólni|k *m*, -czka *f*, partner *m* (**in sth** w czymś, czegoś) [2] (economic, political, sporting) partner *m* [3] (unmarried) partner *m*, -ka *f*; (married) towarzysz *m*, -ka *f* życia

partnership /ˈpɑːtnəʃɪp/ *n* spółka *f* cywilna; **to go into ~ with sb** zawiązać spółkę or przystąpić do spółki z kimś

part of speech *n* część *f* mowy

part-time /ˌpɑːtˈtaɪm/ **[I]** *adj [worker]* pracujący w niepełnym wymiarze godzin; *[job]* w niepełnym wymiarze godzin
[II] *adv [work]* w niepełnym wymiarze godzin

party /ˈpɑːtɪ/ *n* [1] (social event) przyjęcie *n*, party *n inv* [2] (group) grupa *f*; Mil oddział *m*; **rescue ~** grupa ratownicza [3] (in politics) partia *f*, stronnictwo *n* [4] (in law) strona *f* (zainteresowana)

party dress *n* sukienka *f* wyjściowa

party line *n* [1] **the ~** linia *f* partii; fig linia *f* postępowania [2] (phone line) telefon *m* towarzyski

pass /pɑːs, US pæs/ **[I]** *n* [1] (permit) przepustka *f*; **a monthly ~** bilet miesięczny [2] Sch ocena *f* dostateczna, dostateczny *m* (**in sth** z czegoś); Univ zaliczenie *n* (**in sth** z czegoś); **to get a ~** zdać ocenę dostateczną/zaliczyć [3] Sport (in ball games) podanie *n*; (in fencing) wypad *m* [4] (in mountains) przełęcz *f*

II vt ⊡ mi|nąć, -jać, wymi|nąć, -jać; (overtake) wyprzedz|lić, -ać; (go to other side of) *[person]* prze|jść, -chodzić przez (coś) *[checkpoint, customs]*; *[vehicle]* przeje|chać, -żdżać przez (coś) *[checkpoint, barrier]*; **to ∼ sb in the street** minąć kogoś na ulicy ⊡ (exceed) przekr|oczyć, -aczać *[limit]*; prze|jść, -chodzić *[expectations]* ⊡ (hand over) poda|ć, -wać *[plate, ball]* ⊡ spędz|lić, -ać *[time]* ⊡ (succeed in) zdać *[exam, test]* ⊡ oceni|ć, -ać pozytywnie *[candidate]* ⊡ przyj|ąć, -mować *[bill, motion]* ⊡ wyda|ć, -wać *[judgment, verdict]*

III vi *[person]* prze|jść, -chodzić (obok); *[vehicle]* przeje|chać, -żdżać (obok); (in exam) zdać

■ **pass around, pass round**: poda|ć, -wać z ręki do ręki, pu|ścić, -szczać obiegiem *[document, photos]*; poda|ć, -wać *[food, plates]*

■ **pass away**: umrzeć; odejść euph

■ **pass by**: *[person, procession]* prze|jść, -chodzić (obok); *[vehicle]* przeje|chać, -żdżać (obok)

■ **pass down**: przekaz|ać, -ywać *[secret, knowledge, title]*

■ **pass off**: **to ∼ oneself off as a journalist** podawać się za dziennikarza

■ **pass on**: przekaz|ać, -ywać *[message, greetings]* (**to sb** komuś); odda|ć, -wać *[books, clothes]* (**to sb** komuś)

■ **pass out**: (faint) ze|mdleć; (fall drunk) spić się do nieprzytomności, stracić świadomość

■ **pass through**: prze|jść, -chodzić przez (coś) *[experience, place]*; (by vehicle) przeje|chać, -żdżać przez (coś)

(IDIOMS:) **to make a ∼ at sb** przystawiać się do kogoś infml

passable /'pɑːsəbl, US 'pæs-/ adj ⊡ (adequate) znośny, taki sobie ⊡ *[road]* przejezdny; **the river is not ∼** nie można się przeprawić przez rzekę

passage /'pæsɪdʒ/ n ⊡ (in book) fragment m, ustęp m ⊡ (also ∼ **way**) (indoors) korytarz m ⊡ (journey) podróż f

passenger /'pæsɪndʒə(r)/ n pasażer m, -ka f

passerby /,pɑːsə'baɪ, US ,pæs-/ n przechodzień m

passing /'pɑːsɪŋ, US 'pæs-/ adj ⊡ *[pedestrian]* przechodzący; *[motorist]* przejeżdżający ⊡ *[whim]* przelotny ⊡ *[reference]* pobieżny; *[resemblance]* niewielki

passion /'pæʃn/ n (love) namiętność f, żarliwe uczucie n; (enthusiasm) zamiłowanie n; (object of enthusiasm) pasja f

passionate /'pæʃənət/ adj *[kiss, lover, relationship]* namiętny; *[person, nature, belief]* gorący; *[advocate, plea]* żarliwy; *[speech]* płomienny

passive /'pæsɪv/ **I** n **the ∼** strona f bierna
II adj bierny, pasywny

passkey /'pɑːskiː, US 'pæs-/ n klucz m uniwersalny

pass mark n Sch ocena f dopuszczająca; Univ ocena f dostateczna

Passover /'pɑːsəʊvə(r), US 'pæs-/ n Pascha f

passport /'pɑːspɔːt, US 'pæs-/ n paszport m

password /'pɑːswɔːd, US 'pæs-/ n hasło n

past /pɑːst, US pæst/ **I** n przeszłość f; **in the ∼** w przeszłości

II adj ⊡ (preceding) *[week, month]* zeszły, ubiegły ⊡ (former) *[experience, life]* dawny, przeszły; *[president]* były, dawny; **in times ∼** w dawnych czasach ⊡ **summer is ∼** lato się skończyło; **that's all ∼** to już należy do przeszłości

III prep ⊡ **to walk** or **go ∼ sb/sth** przechodzić koło or obok kogoś/czegoś; **to drive ∼ sth** przejeżdżać obok or koło czegoś ⊡ (in time) **it's ∼ 6** jest po szóstej; **half ∼ seven** wpół do ósmej; **he is ∼ 70** ma ponad siedemdziesiąt lat ⊡ (beyond) za (kimś/czymś); **to be ∼ caring** przestać się przejmować

IV adv obok; **I saw her as I walked ∼** zobaczyłem ją, kiedy przechodziłem

(IDIOMS:) **to be ∼ it** infml być za starym; **to be ∼ its best** *[cheese]* być nie pierwszej świeżości; *[wine]* ledwo nadawać się do picia; **I wouldn't put it ∼ her to do it** wcale bym się nie zdziwił, gdyby to zrobiła

pasta /'pæstə/ n pasta f (wszelkie rodzaje makaronu, pierożków)

paste /peɪst/ **I** n ⊡ (glue) klej m ⊡ (mixture) masa f, papka f ⊡ Culin (fish, meat) pasta f; (vegetable) przecier m

II vt przykle|ić, -jać, nakle|ić, -jać; Comput wkle|ić, -jać, wstawi|ć, -ać

pastel /'pæstl, US pæ'stel/ **I** n pastel m
II adj pastelowy

pasteurize /'pɑːstʃəraɪz, US 'pæst-/ vt pasteryzować

pastime /'pɑːstaɪm, US 'pæs-/ n rozrywka f

pastor /'pɑːstə(r), US 'pæs-/ n (Protestant) pastor m; (Roman Catholic) proboszcz m

pastoral /'pɑːstərəl, US 'pæs-/ adj ⊡ (rural) sielski; (bucolic) sielankowy ⊡ *[role, work]* wychowawczy, opiekuńczy

pastry /'peɪstrɪ/ n ⊡ (mixture) ciasto n ⊡ (cake) ciastko n

past tense n czas m przeszły

pasture /'pɑːstʃə(r), US 'pæs-/ n pastwisko n

pat /pæt/ **I** n ⊡ (gentle tap) klepnięcie n ⊡ (of butter) kawałek m, kawałeczek m

II vt klepać, poklep|ać, -ywać *[dog]*; (affectionately) po|głaskać *[hand]*

(IDIOMS:) **to have sth off** GB or **down ∼** znać coś na wyrywki

patch /pætʃ/ **I** n ⊡ (in clothes, on tyre) łata f, łatka f; (on eye) przepaska f ⊡ (of snow, rust) płat m; (of damp, sunlight) plama f, plamka f; (of blue sky) skrawek m ⊡ (area of ground) skrawek m; (for planting) zagon m, grządka f; **a ∼ of grass** miejsce porośnięte trawą

4 GB infml (territory) (of gangster) terytorium *n*; (of policeman) rewir *m* 5 infml (period) okres *m*, passa *f*

II *vt* za|łatać, połatać *[hole, trousers]*; nakle|ić, -jać łatkę na (coś) *[tyre]*

■ **patch up**: ¶ ~ [sth] **up** za|łatać, połatać *[hole, trousers, ceiling]*; naprawi|ć, -ać, wy|reperować *[furniture, car]*; u|ratować *[marriage]* ¶ ~ **up** [sth] za|łagodzić, zażegn|ać, -ywać *[differences]*

IDIOMS **the film isn't a** ~ **on the book** film nie umywa się do książki

patchy /'pætʃɪ/ *adj [colour]* niejednolity; *[essay, quality]* nierówny; *[knowledge]* niepełny, wyrywkowy; ~ **cloud** lokalne zachmurzenia

pâté /'pæteɪ, US pɑːteɪ/ *n* pasztet *m*; **salmon** ~ pasta z łososia

patent /'pætnt, 'peɪtnt, US 'pætnt/ **I** *n* patent *m* (**for** or **on sth** na coś)

II *adj [lie, nonsense]* wierutny; *[mistake, impossibility]* oczywisty

III *vt* o|patentować

patent leather *n* skóra *f* lakierowana

paternal /pə'tɜːnl/ *adj [love, pride]* ojcowski; *[grandfather, aunt]* ze strony ojca

paternity /pə'tɜːnətɪ/ *n* ojcostwo *n*

paternity leave *n* urlop *m* przyznawany ojcu w związku z narodzinami dziecka

path /pɑːθ, US pæθ/ *n* 1 (track) (also ~ **way**) droga *f*; (narrower) ścieżka *f*, dróżka *f*; (in park) alejka *f* 2 (course) (of projectile, planet) tor *m*, trajektoria *f*; (of vehicle) tor *m* 3 (means) droga *f* fig (**to sth** do czegoś)

pathetic /pə'θetɪk/ *adj* 1 (pitiful) *[sight]* wzruszający; *[person, fate]* godny współczucia 2 (inadequate) żałosny

pathological /ˌpæθə'lɒdʒɪkl/ *adj* patologiczny

pathology /pə'θɒlədʒɪ/ *n* patologia *f*

patience /'peɪʃns/ *n* 1 cierpliwość *f* (**with sb/sth** do kogoś/czegoś) 2 (game) pasjans *m*

patient /'peɪʃnt/ **I** *n* pacjent *m*, -ka *f*

II *adj [person]* cierpliwy; *[research, investigation]* wytrwały; **to be** ~ **with sb** mieć cierpliwość do kogoś

patiently /'peɪʃntlɪ/ *adj* cierpliwie

patio /'pætɪəʊ/ *n* 1 (terrace) taras *m* 2 (courtyard) patio *n*

patio doors *npl* drzwi *plt* balkonowe

patriot /'pætrɪət, US 'peɪt-/ *n* patriot|a *m*, -ka *f*

patriotic /ˌpætrɪ'ɒtɪk, US 'peɪt-/ *adj [song, mood]* patriotyczny; *[person]* kochający ojczyznę

patriotism /'pætrɪətɪzəm, US 'peɪt-/ *n* patriotyzm *m*

patrol /pə'trəʊl/ **I** *n* patrol *m*; (of scouts) zastęp *m*

II *vt* s|patrolować *[area, town]*

III *vi* przeprowadz|ić, -ać patrol

patrol boat, **patrol vessel** *n* łódź *f* patrolowa

patrol car *n* radiowóz *m*

patron /'peɪtrən/ *n* 1 (of artist) mecenas *m*; (of charity) patron *m* 2 (of shop) (stały) klient *m*, (stała) klientka *f*; (of hotel, restaurant) gość *m*

patronage /'pætrənɪdʒ/ *n* patronat *m*, mecenat *m*

patronize /'pætrənaɪz/ *vt* 1 po|traktować protekcjonalnie *[person]* 2 często bywać w (czymś) *[cinema, restaurant]*

patronizing /'pætrənaɪzɪŋ/ *adj* protekcjonalny

patron saint *n* (święty) patron *m*, (święta) patronka *f*

patter /'pætə(r)/ **I** *n* 1 (of feet) tupot *m*; (of rain) stuk *m*, bębnienie *n* 2 (talk) gadka *f* infml

II *vi [rain]* za|stukać, za|bębnić; *[child]* za|tupotać; *[mouse]* za|chorobotać

pattern /'pætn/ *n* 1 (decoration) wzór *m*, deseń *m* 2 (of behaviour) wzór *m*, wzorzec *m*; **weather** ~ typ pogody 3 (in dressmaking) wykrój *m*, szablon *m*; (in knitting) wzór *m* 4 (model) wzór *m*, model *m*

patterned /'pætnd/ *adj [fabric]* wzorzysty

paunch /pɔːntʃ/ *n* wystający brzuch *m*; bandzioch *m* infml

pauper /'pɔːpə(r)/ *n* nędza|rz *m*, -rka *f*

pause /pɔːz/ **I** *n* 1 (silence) pauza *f* 2 (in activity) przerwa *f*

II *vi* (stop speaking) przer|wać, -ywać; (hesitate) za|wahać się; **to** ~ **in sth** przerwać coś *[activity]*; **to** ~ **for thought** zastanowić się przez chwilę

pave /peɪv/ *vt* wy|brukować (**with sth** czymś); **to** ~ **the way for sb/sth** utorować drogę komuś/czemuś

pavement /'peɪvmənt/ *n* 1 GB (footpath) chodnik *m*, trotuar *m* 2 US (roadway) jezdnia *f*; (road surface) nawierzchnia *f* (drogowa)

pavement café *n* kawiarnia *m* z ogródkiem

pavilion /pə'vɪlɪən/ *n* pawilon *m*

paving slab, **paving stone** *n* płyta *f* chodnikowa

paw /pɔː/ **I** *n* łapa *f*

II *vt* **to** ~ **the ground** *[horse, bull]* grzebać kopytem (w ziemi)

pawn /pɔːn/ **I** *n* (in chess) pion(ek) *m*; fig pionek *m*

II *vt* zastawi|ć, -ać, oddal|ć, -wać w zastaw

pawnbroker /'pɔːnbrəʊkə(r)/ *n* właściciel *m*, -ka *f* lombardu, makler *m* lombardowy

pawnshop /'pɔːnʃɒp/ *n* lombard *m*

pay /peɪ/ **I** *n* płaca *f*, stałe wynagrodzenie *n*

II *vt* 1 za|płacić (komuś) *[employee]*; za|płacić *[price]*; za|płacić, opłac|ić, -ać *[bill]*; spłac|ić, -ać *[debt]*; **to** ~ **cash** płacić gotówką; **to** ~ **a sum into an account** wpłacić sumę na konto; **all expenses paid** wszystkie koszty opłacone 2 *[account]* przyn|ieść, -osić, da|ć, -wać *[interest]* 3 (give) **to** ~ **attention to sth** zwracać na coś uwagę; **to** ~ **tribute to sb** składać hołd komuś; **to** ~ **sb a compliment** powiedzieć komuś komplement; **to** ~ **sb a visit** odwiedzić kogoś, złożyć komuś wizytę [4] (benefit) opłac|ić, -ać się (komuś) (**to do sth** coś zrobić)

III *vi* [1] *[person]* za|płacić (**for sth** za coś); **you have to ~ to get in** musisz zapłacić za wstęp; **to ~ one's own way** płacić za siebie; **this work doesn't ~ very well** to nie jest dobrze płatna praca [2] *[business, activity]* opłac|ić, -ać się; **to ~ for itself** *[business, purchase]* zwracać się

■ **pay back**: zwr|ócić, -acać (komuś) pieniądze *[person]*; zwr|ócić, -acać *[money]*

■ **pay in** GB: wpłac|ić, -ać *[sum]*

■ **pay off**: ¶ ~ **off** *[effort]* opłac|ić, -ać się ¶ ~ **[sb] off** [1] (dismiss) odprawi|ć, -ać, da|ć, -wać (komuś) odprawę *[worker]* [2] (bribe) kupl|ić, -ować milczenie (kogoś) ¶ ~ **[sth] off** spłac|ić, -ać *[debt]*

■ **pay up** infml: za|płacić, odda|ć, -wać pieniądze

payable /'peɪəbl/ *adj* płatny; **to make the cheque ~ to sb** wystawić czek na kogoś

pay cheque GB, **pay check** US *n* wypłata *f* (poborów) czekiem

payday /'peɪdeɪ/ *n* dzień *m* wypłaty

payee /peɪ'iː/ *n* (of cheque) beneficjent *m*, remitent *m*; (of postal order) odbiorca *m*

payment /'peɪmənt/ *n* zapłata *f*; (sum due) płatność *f*; (in settlement) spłata *f*; (into account) wpłata *f*; (instalment) wpłata *f*, rata *f*; **in monthly ~s** w miesięcznych ratach

pay-packet /'peɪpækɪt/ *n* koperta *f* z wypłatą

pay phone *n* automat *m* telefoniczny

payslip /'peɪslɪp/ *n* pasek *m* infml (*z wyszczególnieniem zarobków, wysokości zaliczki na podatek i innych odliczeń*)

pc, PC *n* = **personal computer** komputer *m* osobisty; pecet *m* infml

PE *n* = **physical education** WF *m*, wf *m*

pea /piː/ *n* [1] (plant) groch *m*; (seed) ziarnko *n* grochu [2] Culin (also **green ~**) groszek *m* zielony

peace /piːs/ *n* spokój *m*; (between countries) pokój *m*; **to keep the ~** (between countries) zapewnić or utrzymać pokój; (in town) *[police]* utrzymywać spokój or porządek; **I need a bit of ~ and quiet** potrzebuję trochę spokoju i ciszy; **to find ~ of mind** znaleźć spokój (duszy)

peaceful /'piːsfl/ *adj* [1] *[animal, place, day]* spokojny [2] *[protest, solution]* pokojowy

peacefully /'piːsfəlɪ/ *adv* *[sit, protest]* spokojnie

peace-keeping forces /'piːskiːpɪŋ 'fɔːsɪs/ *npl* siły *f pl* pokojowe

peacemaker /'piːsmeɪkə(r)/ *n* mediator *m*, rozjemca *m*

peace process *n* proces *m* pokojowy

peace talks *npl* rozmowy *f pl* pokojowe

peacetime /'piːstaɪm/ *n* czas *m* pokoju, pokój *m*

peach /piːtʃ/ *n* brzoskwinia *f*

peacock /'piːkɒk/ *n* paw *m*

peak /piːk/ **I** *n* [1] (of mountain) szczyt *m* [2] (of cap) daszek *m* [3] (of career, form) szczyt *m*; **in the ~ of**

condition w doskonałej formie; **to be past one's ~** mieć za sobą swój najlepszy okres [4] (of inflation, quantity, demand) najwyższa wartość *f*, maksimum *n*; (on graph) wierzchołek *m*

II *adj* *[figure, level, price]* maksymalny; *[fitness]* szczytowy

III *vi* *[demand, inflation, rate]* osiąg|nąć, -ać poziom szczytowy; *[athlete]* osiąg|nąć, -ać szczytową formę; *[career, enthusiasm]* osiąg|nąć, -ać szczyt

peaked /piːkt/ *adj* [1] *[cap, hat]* z daszkiem; *[roof]* spiczasty [2] US mizerny

peak period *n* okres *m* największego ruchu

peak rate *n* (for phone calls) taryfa *f* maksymalna

peak time *n* (on TV) godziny *f pl* największej oglądalności; (for switchboard) godziny *f pl* największego obciążenia; (for traffic) godziny *f pl* szczytu

peaky /'piːkɪ/ *adj* infml mizerny

peal /piːl/ *n* (of bells) bicie *n*; (of thunder) łoskot *m*, grzmot *m*; **~s of laughter** salwy śmiechu

peanut /'piːnʌt/ *n* (nut) orzech *m* ziemny or arachidowy; (tree) orzech *m* ziemny

peanut butter *n* masło *n* orzechowe

pear /peə(r)/ *n* (fruit) gruszka *f*; (tree) grusz(k)a *f*

pearl /pɜːl/ **I** *n* perła *f*; (of dew, sweat) kropla *f*, kropelka *f*

II *adj* *[brooch, button]* perłowy; *[necklace]* z pereł

pear tree *n* grusz(k)a *f*

peasant /'peznt/ *n* chłop *m*, -ka *f*, wieśnia|k *m*, -czka *f*

peat /piːt/ *n* torf *m*

pebble /'pebl/ *n* kamyk *m*

pecan /'piːkən, pɪ'kæn, US pɪ'kɑːn/ *n* (nut) pekan *m*

peck /pek/ **I** *n* [1] (of bird) dziobnięcie *n* [2] infml (kiss) **to give sb a ~ (on the cheek)** cmoknąć kogoś w policzek

II *vt* *[bird]* dziob|nąć, -ać

III *vi* [1] *[bird]* **to ~ at sth** dziobać or wydziobywać coś *[food]* [2] infml **to ~ at one's food** *[person]* jeść jak ptaszek, skubać (jedzenie)

pecking order *n* „porządek *m* dziobania" (*hierarchia w obrębie grupy*)

peckish /'pekɪʃ/ *adj* infml **to be ~** mieć ochotę na małe co nieco infml

pectorals /'pektərəls/ *npl* (also **pecs** infml) mięśnie *m pl* piersiowe

peculiar /pɪ'kjuːlɪə(r)/ *adj* [1] (strange) dziwny, osobliwy [2] **to be ~ to sb/sth** *[feature, trait]* być charakterystycznym or typowym dla kogoś/czegoś

peculiarity /pɪˌkjuːlɪ'ærətɪ/ *n* [1] (feature) szczególna cecha *f* [2] (strangeness) dziwaczność *f*

pedal /'pedl/ **I** *n* pedał *m*

II *vi* pedałować

pedal bin *n* GB pojemnik *m* (na odpadki) z pedałem

pedal boat *n* rower *m* wodny

pedantic /pɪ'dæntɪk/ *adj* pedantyczny, drobiazgowy

peddle /'pedl/ *vt* handlować po domach (czymś) *[wares]*; propagować *[ideas]*; **to ~ drugs** rozprowadzać narkotyki

peddler /'pedlə(r)/ *n* 1 (street vendor) handlarz *m* uliczny, handlarka *f* uliczna 2 **drug ~** handlarz narkotyków, dealer, diler

pedestal /'pedɪstl/ *n* cokół *m*, piedestał *m*; **to put sb on a ~** stawiać kogoś na piedestale; **to knock sb off their ~** strącić kogoś z piedestału

pedestrian /pɪ'destrɪən/ 1 *n* pieszy *m*
2 *adj [street, area]* dla pieszych

pedestrian crossing *n* przejście *n* dla pieszych

pedestrian precinct *n* GB strefa *f* zamknięta dla ruchu kołowego

pediatrician /ˌpiːdɪə'trɪʃn/ *n* US → **paediatrician**

pedicure /'pedɪkjʊə(r)/ *n* pedikiur *m*, pedicure *n* *inv*; **to have a ~** zrobić sobie pedikiur

pedigree /'pedɪgriː/ 1 *n* 1 (of animal) rodowód *m*; (of person) genealogia *f*, pochodzenie *n* 2 (purebred animal) zwierzę *n* rodowodowe
2 *adj [animal]* rodowodowy

pee /piː/ *n* infml siusiu *n inv* infml; **to have a ~** zrobić siusiu

peek /piːk/ *n* **to have a ~ at sb/sth** rzucić okiem or zerknąć na kogoś/coś

peel /piːl/ 1 *n* (of citrus fruit, onion) skórka *f*, łupina *f*; (peelings) obierki *f pl*, łupiny *f pl*
2 *vt* ob|rać, -ierać *[vegetable, fruit]*; o|czyścić *[prawn]*; oskrob|ać, -ywać, skrobać *[stick]*
3 *vi* (paint, skin) z|łuszczyć się, zejść, schodzić płatami
■ **peel off**: ¶ **~ off** *[label, wallpaper]* odlepi|ć, -ać się; *[paint]* z|łuszczyć się, zejść, schodzić ¶ **~ [sth] off** odkle|ić, -jać *[sticker]*; z|edrzeć, -dzierać *[paint]*; zrzuc|ić, -ać *[clothing]*

peeler /'piːlə(r)/ *n* (manual) nożyk *m* do obierania warzyw i owoców; (mechanical) obieraczka *f* do warzyw

peelings /'piːlɪŋz/ *npl* obierki *f pl*, obierzyny *f pl*

peep /piːp/ 1 *n* **to have a ~ at sb/sth** zerknąć na kogoś/coś
2 *vi* 1 (look) zerk|nąć, -ać (**at sb/sth** na kogoś/ coś); (furtively) pod|ejrzeć, -glądać (**at sb** kogoś) 2 *[bird]* za|ćwierkać, za|świergotać

peephole /'piːphəʊl/ *n* dziurka *f*, otwór *m*; (in door) wizjer *m*, judasz *m*

peer /pɪə(r)/ 1 *n* 1 (equal) równ|y *m*, -a *f*; (in profession) kolega *m* (z pracy), współpracownik *m* 2 (contemporary) rówieśni|k *m*, -czka *f* 3 GB (also ~ **of the realm**) par *m*, członek *m* Izby Lordów
2 *vi* **to ~ at sb/sth** przy|jrzeć, -glądać się (badawczo) (**at sb/sth** komuś/czemuś); spoj|rzeć, -glądać (badawczo) (**at sb/sth** na kogoś/coś)

peerage /'pɪərɪdʒ/ *n* GB **the ~** parowie *m pl* ; **to be given a ~** otrzymać tytuł para

peer group *n* 1 (of same status) grupa *f* reprezentująca ten sam status społeczny 2 (of same age) grupa *f* rówieśnicza

peer group pressure *n* presja *f* grupy rówieśniczej

peg /peg/ *n* 1 (hook) wieszak *m*, kołek *m* 2 GB (also **clothes ~**) klamerka *f* do bielizny 3 (of tent) kołek *m*, palik *m* 4 (in carpentry) kołek *m* 5 (in barrel) czop *m*, szpunt *m*

pejorative /pɪ'dʒɒrətɪv, US -'dʒɔːr-/ *adj [word, sense]* pejoratywny; *[remark]* niepochlebny

Peking /ˌpiː'kɪŋ/ *prn* Pekin *m*

pelican /'pelɪkən/ *n* pelikan *m*

pellet /'pelɪt/ *n* 1 (of paper, wax) kulka *f*; (of mud) grudka *f* 2 (of shot) śrucina *f*

pelmet /'pelmɪt/ *n* (drapery) lambrekin *m*; (board) karnisz *m*

pelt /pelt/ 1 *n* (fur) skóra *f*, skórka *f*
2 *vt* **to ~ sb with sth** obrzucić, -ać kogoś czymś *[eggs, insults]*; zasyp|ać, -ywać kogoś czymś *[questions]*
3 *vi* 1 (also **~ down**) *[rain]* lać 2 (run) po|pędzić

pelvis /'pelvɪs/ *n* Anat miednica *f*

pen /pen/ *n* 1 (for writing) pióro *n* 2 (for animals) zagroda *f*

penal /'piːnl/ *adj [law, code]* karny; *[offence]* karalny, zagrożony karą

penalize /'piːnəlaɪz/ *vt* u|karać

penalty /'penltɪ/ *n* 1 (punishment) kara *f*; (fine) grzywna *f* 2 fig cena *f* fig (**for sth** za coś) 3 (in soccer, rugby) rzut *m* karny

pence /pens/ *npl* GB → **penny**

pencil /'pensl/ *n* ołówek *m*; **in ~** ołówkiem
■ **pencil in**: **~ [sth] in** wpis|ać, -ywać ołówkiem; **let's ~ in Monday** umówmy się wstępnie na poniedziałek

pencil case *n* piórnik *m*

pencil sharpener *n* temperówka *f*

pendant /'pendənt/ *n* (on necklace) wisior *m*, wisiorek *m*

pending /'pendɪŋ/ 1 *adj* 1 *[case]* w toku, trwający; *[matter]* do załatwienia, oczekujący na załatwienie 2 (imminent) zbliżający się
2 *prep* do czasu (czegoś), w oczekiwaniu na (coś)

pendulum /'pendjʊləm, US -dʒʊləm/ *n* wahadło *n*

penetrate /'penɪtreɪt/ *vt* 1 przebi|ć, -jać *[skin, surface]*; prze|drzeć, -dzierać się przez (coś) *[cloud, defences]*; przeszy|ć, -wać *[silence]*; przedosta|ć się, -wać się przez (coś) *[wall]* 2 *[spy]* przenik|nąć, -ać do (czegoś) *[organization]*

penetrating /'penɪtreɪtɪŋ/ *adj [eyes, voice, cold]* przenikliwy

pen friend *n* korespondencyjny przyjaciel *m*, korespondencyjna przyjaciółka *f*

penguin /'peŋgwɪn/ *n* pingwin *m*

penicillin /ˌpenɪ'sɪlɪn/ *n* penicylina *f*

peninsula /pə'nɪnsjʊlə, US -nsələ/ *n* półwysep *m*

penis /'pi:nɪs/ n penis m, prącie n

penitent /'penɪtənt/ **[I]** n penitent m, -ka f, pokutni|k m, -ca f
[II] adj skruszony

penitentiary /ˌpenɪ'tenʃərɪ/ n US zakład m penitencjarny or karny

penknife /'pennaɪf/ n scyzoryk m

pennant /'penənt/ n [1] (on ship) flaga f; (for decoration) chorągiewka f; (of sports team) proporzec m, proporczyk m [2] US Sport mistrzostwo n

penniless /'penɪlɪs/ adj (pozostający) bez środków do życia; bez grosza fig

penny /'penɪ/ n [1] GB pens m; **a five pence** or **a five p piece** pięciopensówka; **a 25 p stamp** znaczek za 25 pensów [2] US cent m
(IDIOMS:) **the ~ dropped** infml dotarło do mnie infml; **to not have a ~ to one's name** nie mieć grosza przy duszy, być gołym jak święty turecki

pension /'penʃn/ n (old-age) emerytura f; (for widow, invalid) renta f

pensioner /'penʃənə(r)/ n rencist|a m, -ka f; (retired) emeryt m, -ka f

pension scheme n system m emerytalny

pentagon /'pentəgən, US -gɒn/ n [1] pięciokąt m [2] **the Pentagon** US Pentagon m

Pentecost /'pentɪkɒst, US -kɔ:st/ n Zielone Świątki plt, Dzień m Zesłania Ducha Świętego

penthouse /'penthaʊs/ n penthouse m

pent-up /ˌpent'ʌp/ adj [feeling, frustration] tłumiony, skrywany; [energy] skumulowany

penultimate /pen'ʌltɪmət/ adj przedostatni

people /'pi:pl/ **[I]** n (nation) naród m
[II] npl [1] (in general) ludzie plt; (individuals) osoby f pl; **old ~** ludzie starzy, osoby starsze; **they're nice ~** to mili ludzie; **there were a lot of ~** było dużo ludzi; **other ~'s property** cudza własność [2] (of a town) mieszkańcy m pl, obywatele m pl [3] (citizens) **the ~** obywatele m pl, społeczeństwo n

pep /pep/ n werwa f, animusz m
■ **pep up:** doda|ć, -wać (komuś) energii [person]; ożywi|ć, -ać [party]

pepper /'pepə(r)/ n [1] (spice) pieprz m [2] (vegetable) papryka f

peppercorn /'pepəkɔ:n/ n ziarnko n pieprzu

pepper mill n młynek m do pieprzu

peppermint /'pepəmɪnt/ n [1] (plant) mięta f pieprzowa [2] (sweet) miętus m, miętówka f

pepper pot, pepper shake n pieprzniczka f

pep talk n infml przemowa f zagrzewająca do wysiłku

per /pɜ:(r)/ prep na; **~ annum** rocznie, na rok; **~ head** na głowę, od osoby; **80 km ~ hour** 80 km na godzinę; **£5 ~ hour** 5 funtów za godzinę; **as ~ your instructions** zgodnie z pańskimi wskazówkami

per capita /pə'kæpɪtə/ adj, adv na głowę

perceive /pə'si:v/ vt dostrze|c, -gać, spostrze|c, -gać

per cent /pə'sent/ n procent m; **profits are up 20 ~** zyski wzrosły o 20 procent

percentage /pə'sentɪdʒ/ n procent m; (rate, part) odsetek m

perceptible /pə'septəbl/ adj [difference, effect] dostrzegalny (**to sb** dla kogoś); [sound] słyszalny

perception /pə'sepʃn/ n [1] (by senses) percepcja f, postrzeganie n [2] (view) wyobrażenie n (**of sb/sth** o kimś/czymś); pogląd m (**of sb/sth** na temat kogoś/czegoś) [3] (insight) wnikliwość f

perceptive /pə'septɪv/ adj [person] spostrzegawczy; [study] wnikliwy; [comment] trafny

perch /pɜ:tʃ/ **[I]** n [1] (for hens) grzęda f; (in birdcage) żerdź f, żerdka f [2] (fish) okoń n
[II] vi [bird] usiąść, siadać; [person] przysi|ąść, -adać (**on sth** na czymś)

percolator /'pɜ:kəleɪtə(r)/ n ekspres m do kawy

percussion /pə'kʌʃn/ n Mus perkusja f

perennial /pə'renɪəl/ adj [1] [subject, problem] stały; [charm] nieprzemijający, wieczny [2] [plant] wieloletni

perfect [I] /'pɜ:fɪkt/ n czas m przeszły dokonany
[II] /'pɜ:fɪkt/ adj doskonały; [behaviour] nieganny; [performance] perfekcyjny; [actor, candidate, husband] idealny
[III] /pə'fekt/ vt udoskonal|ić, -ać, doskonalić [technique, English]; ugruntow|ać, -ywać [knowledge]

perfection /pə'fekʃn/ n doskonałość f, perfekcja f; (of performance) perfekcyjność f

perfectionist /pə'fekʃənɪst/ n perfekcjonist|a m, -ka f ~

perfectly /'pɜ:fɪktlɪ/ adv [1] (totally) zupełnie, absolutnie [2] (very well) [fit, illustrate] doskonale

perforate /'pɜ:fəreɪt/ vt przebi|ć, -jać [eardrum, lung]; dziurkować, perforować [paper]

perform /pə'fɔ:m/ **[I]** vt [1] wykon|ać, -ywać [task]; przeprowadz|ić, -ać [operation]; wypełni|ć, -ać, pełnić [duties]; odprawi|ć, -ać [ceremony] [2] [actor] od|egrać, -grywać, odtw|orzyć, -arzać [part]; wysta|wi|ć, -ać [play]; wykon|ać, -ywać [song]; z|robić [trick]
[II] vi [1] [actor] wyst|ąpić, -ępować; [musician] za|grać [2] **to ~ well/badly** [team] spisać się dobrze/źle; [interviewee, candidate] wypaść dobrze/źle; [company] dobrze/źle sobie radzić

performance /pə'fɔ:məns/ n [1] (of concert) wykonanie n; (of role) interpretacja f [2] (show, play) przedstawienie n, spektakl m; (concert) koncert m; (by actor, musician) występ m; **to put on a ~ of 'Hamlet'** wystawić „Hamleta" [3] (of team, sportsman) wyniki m pl (**in sth** w czymś); (of machine) wydajność f; (of car) osiągi plt [4] (of duties) wypełnienie n; (of task) wykonanie n

performance artist n performer m

performance indicators *npl* wskaźniki *m pl* wydajności

performer /pəˈfɔːmə(r)/ *n* (actor) aktor *m*, -ka *f*; (entertainer) artyst|a *m*, -ka *f*

performing arts *n* sztuka *f* widowiskowa

perfume /ˈpɜːfjuːm, US pərˈfjuːm/ **[]** *n* (fluid) perfumy *plt*; (fragrance) woń *f*, aromat *m* **[]** *vt* na|perfumować

perhaps /pəˈhæps/ *adv* (być) może

peril /ˈperəl/ *n* zagrożenie *n*, niebezpieczeństwo *n*

perimeter /pəˈrɪmɪtə(r)/ *n* granica *f*, obrzeża *plt*; (in mathematics) obwód *m*

period /ˈpɪərɪəd/ **[]** *n* **1** okres *m*; (era) epoka *f* **2** US (full stop) kropka *f* **3** (menstruation) okres *m*, miesiączka *f* **4** Sch (lesson) godzina *f* lekcyjna; **to have a free** ~ mieć okienko *infml* **[]** *adj* (of a certain era) *[costume, furniture]* stylowy

periodical /ˌpɪərɪˈɒdɪkl/ **[]** *n* czasopismo *n* **[]** *adj* okresowy, periodyczny

peripheral /pəˈrɪfərəl/ *adj* *[suburb]* peryferyjny; *[issue]* marginesowy, mający drugorzędne znaczenie

periphery /pəˈrɪfərɪ/ *n* (of town) peryferie *plt*; (of site) skraj *m*; **to remain on the** ~ **of sth** pozostawać na uboczu czegoś *[events]*

periscope /ˈperɪskəʊp/ *n* peryskop *m*

perish /ˈperɪʃ/ *vi* **1** (die) z|ginąć **2** *[food]* ze|psuć się; *[rubber]* z|butwieć

perishables /ˈperɪʃəblz/ *npl* produkty *m pl* łatwo psujące się

perjure /ˈpɜːdʒə(r)/ *vr* **to** ~ **oneself** krzywoprzysią|c, -egać

perjury /ˈpɜːdʒərɪ/ *n* krzywoprzysięstwo *n*

perk /pɜːk/ *n* infml zaleta *f*, korzyść *f*

■ **perk up**: *[person, business, life]* ożywi|ć, -ać się

perky /ˈpɜːkɪ/ *adj* (cheerful) radosny; (jaunty) żwawy, dziarski

perm /pɜːm/ *n* trwała *f* (ondulacja *f*); **to have a** ~ mieć trwałą

permanent /ˈpɜːmənənt/ **[]** *n* US trwała *f* (ondulacja *f*) **[]** *adj* *[address, job]* stały; *[damage, relationship]* trwały

permanently /ˈpɜːmənəntlɪ/ *adv* *[happy, tired]* wiecznie; *[employ, emigrate, settle]* na stałe; *[disabled]* trwale

permeate /ˈpɜːmɪeɪt/ *vt* *[liquid, odour, ideas]* przenik|nąć, -ać; *[gas]* wypełni|ć, -ać

permissible /pəˈmɪsɪbl/ *adj* (permitted) dozwolony; (acceptable) dopuszczalny

permission /pəˈmɪʃn/ *n* pozwolenie *n*; (official) zezwolenie *n*, zgoda *f*; **to have** ~ **to do sth** mieć pozwolenie na zrobienie czegoś

permissive /pəˈmɪsɪv/ *adj* *[society]* permisywny; *[view, law]* liberalny; *[parent, attitude]* pobłażliwy

permit **[]** /ˈpɜːmɪt/ *n* **1** (document) zezwolenie *n*; (entrance pass) przepustka *f*; **work** ~ zezwolenie na pracę **2** US Aut prawo *n* jazdy

[] /pəˈmɪt/ *vt* pozwol|olić, -alać na (coś); (officially) zezw|olić, -alać na (coś); **smoking is not** ~ **ted** palenie zabronione or wzbronione; **to** ~ **sb to do sth** pozwolić komuś coś zrobić, zezwolić komuś na zrobienie czegoś

[] /pəˈmɪt/ *vi* pozwol|olić, -alać

pernickety /pəˈnɪkətɪ/ *adj* infml **1** (detail-conscious) przesadnie skrupulatny (**about sth** w czymś) **2** (choosy) wybredny, wymagający (**about sth** co do czegoś)

peroxide blonde /pəˈrɒksaɪdˈblɒnd/ *n* tleniona blondyna *f*

perpendicular /ˌpɜːpənˈdɪkjʊlə(r)/ *adj* prostopadły

perpetrate /ˈpɜːpɪtreɪt/ *vt* popełni|ć, -ać *[crime, deed]*; dopu|ścić, -szczać się (czegoś) *[fraud]*; **to** ~ **a hoax on sb** nabrać kogoś infml

perpetrator /ˈpɜːpɪtreɪtə(r)/ *n* spraw|ca *m*, -czyni *f*

perpetual /pəˈpetʃʊəl/ *adj* *[darkness, problem]* wieczny; *[meetings, turmoil]* nieustanny

perpetuate /pəˈpetʃʊeɪt/ *vt* zachow|ać, -ywać *[system, skills, memory]*; utrwal|ić, -ać *[divisions, poverty, ideas]*

perplexed /pəˈplekst/ *adj* *[person]* zakłopotany, skonsternowany; *[voice, look]* pełen zdumienia

persecute /ˈpɜːsɪkjuːt/ *vt* **1** (victimize) prześladować (**for sth** za coś) **2** (tease) zadręczać, nie dawać (komuś) spokoju

persecution /ˌpɜːsɪˈkjuːʃn/ *n* prześladowania *n pl*

perseverance /ˌpɜːsɪˈvɪərəns/ *n* wytrwałość *f*

persevere /ˌpɜːsɪˈvɪə(r)/ *vi* wytrwać, nie ustawać (**with** or **at sth** w czymś)

persist /pəˈsɪst/ *vi* nie ustawać (**in sth** w czymś); upierać się (**in sth** przy czymś); **to** ~ **in doing sth** uparcie coś robić

persistence /pəˈsɪstəns/ *n* (of person) wytrwałość *f*, upór *m*; (of pain, illness) uporczywość *f*; (of belief) trwanie *n*, utrzymywanie się *n*

persistent /pəˈsɪstənt/ *adj* **1** (persevering) wytrwały; (obstinate) nieustępliwy, uparty **2** *[pain, noise]* uporczywy; *[inquiries, fears]* ciągły, stały; *[denial]* uparty; *[rain]* ciągły; *[problem]* wieczny

persistent offender *n* recydywist|a *m*, -ka *f*

person /ˈpɜːsn/ *n* osoba *f*; **in** ~ osobiście; **to have sth about one's** ~ mieć coś przy sobie

personable /ˈpɜːsənəbl/ *adj* ujmujący, o ujmującej powierzchowności; *[man]* przystojny

personal /ˈpɜːsənl/ **[]** *n* US ogłoszenie *n* drobne **[]** *adj* osobisty; *[belief, experience]* własny; *[call, life]* prywatny; *[insurance]* osobowy; **to make a** ~ **appearance** zjawić się osobiście

personal ad *n* ogłoszenie *n* drobne

personal column *n* dział *m* ogłoszeń drobnych, ogłoszenia *n pl* drobne

personality /ˌpɜːsəˈnælətɪ/ *n* **1** (of person) osobowość *f*; (of house, town) charakter *m* **2** (celebrity) osobistość *f*, postać *f*

personal loan n kredyt m indywidualny
personally /'pɜːsənəlɪ/ adv osobiście
personal organizer n terminarz m
personal property n majątek m osobisty, własność f osobista
personal stereo n odtwarzacz m osobisty
personify /pə'sɒnɪfaɪ/ vt uosabiać, być wcieleniem (czegoś) [ideal]
personnel /ˌpɜːsə'nel/ n ① personel m ② (department) dział m kadr or osobowy; kadry plt infml
perspective /pə'spektɪv/ n perspektywa f, punkt m widzenia; **to keep things in** ~ zachować dystans; **to put sth into** ~ nabrać do czegoś dystansu
perspex® /'pɜːspeks/ n pleksiglas m, plexiglas m
perspiration /ˌpɜːspɪ'reɪʃn/ n ① (sweat) pot m ② (sweating) pocenie się n
perspire /pə'spaɪə(r)/ vi s|pocić się
persuade /pə'sweɪd/ vt ① (influence) przekon|ać, -ywać; **to** ~ **sb to do sth** przekonać kogoś, żeby coś zrobił ② (convince) przekon|ać, -ywać (**of sth** o czymś, co do czegoś)
persuasion /pə'sweɪʒn/ n ① (persuading) perswazja f, przekonywanie n ② (religion) wyznanie n ③ (political views) przekonanie n
persuasive /pə'sweɪsɪv/ adj [argument, excuse] przekonujący, przekonywający; [person] elokwentny, wymowny
pert /pɜːt/ adj [person] zuchwały, zadziorny; [manner] łobuzerski, szelmowski; [nose] zadarty; [hat] zawadiacki
pertinent /'pɜːtɪnənt, US -tənənt/ adj [remark] trafny, celny; [question] mający związek z tematem
perturb /pə'tɜːb/ vt (worry) za|niepokoić; (more deeply) z|denerwować
perturbing /pə'tɜːbɪŋ/ adj niepokojący; (more deeply) bulwersujący
pervade /pə'veɪd/ vt [smell, smoke] przenik|nąć, -ać; [idea, mood] przep|oić, -ajać [atmosphere, book]; owładnąć (czymś) [mind]
perverse /pə'vɜːs/ adj ① (twisted) [person, attitude] przewrotny; [desire] perwersyjny; **she takes a** ~ **pleasure in upsetting me** denerwowanie mnie sprawia jej wręcz perwersyjną przyjemność ② (contrary) [refusal, attempt] pozbawiony logiki; [effect] wręcz przeciwny
perversion /pə'vɜːʃn, US -ʒn/ n ① (deviation) perwersja f, zboczenie n ② (of facts) wypaczenie n; ~ **of justice** niesprawiedliwość w majestacie prawa
pervert **I** /'pɜːvɜːt/ n dewiant m, zboczeniec m **II** /pə'vɜːt/ vt ① (corrupt) z|demoralizować, z|deprawować ② (misrepresent) wypacz|yć, -ać, nagi|ąć, -nać [meaning, truth]; **to** ~ **the course of justice** utrudniać prawidłowe funkcjonowanie wymiaru sprawiedliwości

perverted /pə'vɜːtɪd/ adj (deviant) zboczony; (distorted) [idea] wypaczony
pessimism /'pesɪmɪzəm/ n pesymizm m
pessimist /'pesɪmɪst/ n pesymist|a m, -ka f
pessimistic /ˌpesɪ'mɪstɪk/ adj pesymistyczny
pest /pest/ n ① (animal) szkodnik m ② infml (person) zaraza f fig
pester /'pestə(r)/ vt dręczyć, zadręczać; (sexually) natrętnie narzucać się (komuś)
pesticide /'pestɪsaɪd/ n pestycyd m
pet /pet/ **I** n ① (animal) zwierzę n (chowane w domu) ② (person) ulubieni|ec m, -ca f, pupil|ek m, -ka f **II** adj [subject, theory] ulubiony; ~ **dog** pies **III** vt po|głaskać, poklep|ać, -ywać, klepać [animal] **IV** vi [people] pieścić się
petal /'petl/ n płatek m
peter /'piːtə(r)/ vi
■ **peter out**: [supplies] wyczerp|ać, -ywać się; [process, meeting] dobie|c, -gać końca
pet food n pokarm m dla psów i kotów
pet hate n GB his ~ **is...** szczególnie mierzi/mierzą go...
petition /pə'tɪʃn/ **I** n petycja f **II** vt wn|ieść, -osić petycję do (kogoś/czegoś) [person, body] **III** vi **to** ~ **for divorce** wnieść pozew o rozwód
pet name n pieszczotliwe przezwisko n
pet project n ukochane dziecko n fig
petrified /'petrɪfaɪd/ adj skamieniały
petrol /'petrəl/ n GB benzyna f; **to fill up with** ~ zatankować
petrol can n kanister m
petroleum /pə'trəʊlɪəm/ n ropa f naftowa
petrol station n GB stacja f benzynowa
pet shop GB, **pet store** US n sklep m zoologiczny
petticoat /'petɪkəʊt/ n halka f
petty /'petɪ/ adj [person, squabble] małostkowy; [detail] błahy, nieistotny
petty cash n kasa f podręczna
petty crime n drobne przestępstwo n
petty officer n mat m (w marynarce wojennej)
petty theft n drobna kradzież f
pew /pjuː/ n ławka f kościelna
pewter /'pjuːtə(r)/ n stop m cyny z ołowiem
PGCE n = **Postgraduate Certificate in Education** ≈ dyplom m magisterskich studiów pedagogicznych
pharmaceutical /ˌfɑːmə'sjuːtɪkl, US -'suː-/ adj farmaceutyczny
pharmacist /'fɑːməsɪst/ n (in shop) apteka|rz m, -rka f; (in industry) farmaceut|a m, -ka f
pharmacy /'fɑːməsɪ/ n ① (shop) apteka f ② (science) farmacja f
phase /feɪz/ **I** n etap m, faza f; (of illness, development) stadium n; **it's just a** ~ (**she's going through**) to jej minie or przejdzie

II *vt* rozłożyć, -kładać na etapy, przeprowadzłić, -ać etapami

■ **phase in**: wprowadzłić, -ać stopniowo or etapowo

■ **phase out**: wycofłać, -ywać stopniowo or etapowo

PhD *n* = Doctor of Philosophy (award) doktorat *m*; (person) doktor *m*, dr

pheasant /'feznt/ *n* bażant *m*

phenomenal /fə'nɒmɪnl/ *adj [result, growth]* wyjątkowy; *[amount]* niezwykły; *[talent, success, performance]* fenomenalny

phenomenon /fə'nɒmɪnən/ *n* [1] (event) zjawisko *n*, fenomen *m* [2] (person) fenomen *m*

phew /fjuː/ *excl* uf!

philanthropist /fɪ'lænθrəpɪst/ *n* filantrop *m*, -ka *f*

philistine /'fɪlɪstaɪn/ *n* filister *m*

philosopher /fɪ'lɒsəfə(r)/ *n* filozof *m*

philosophic(al) /ˌfɪlə'sɒfɪk(l)/ *adj* filozoficzny; **to be ~ about sth** podejść do czegoś filozoficznie

philosophy /fɪ'lɒsəfɪ/ *n* filozofia *f*

phobia /'fəʊbɪə/ *n* fobia *f*, chorobliwy lęk *m*

phone /fəʊn/ **I** *n* telefon *m*; **to be on the ~** (have telephone) mieć telefon; (be talking) rozmawiać przez telefon (**to sb** z kimś)

II *vt* (also ~ **up**) załdzwonić do (kogoś/czegoś), załtelefonować do (kogoś/czegoś)

III *vi* (also ~ **up**) załdzwonić, załtelefonować; **to ~ for a taxi** zadzwonić po taksówkę

phone book *n* książka *f* telefoniczna

phone booth, phone box GB *n* budka *f* or kabina *f* telefoniczna

phone call *n* rozmowa *f* telefoniczna; telefon *m* infml

phone card *n* karta *f* telefoniczna

phone-in /'fəʊnɪn/ *n* program *m* z telefonicznym udziałem słuchaczy/widzów

phone link *n* połączenie *n* telefoniczne

phone number *n* numer *m* telefonu or telefoniczny

phoney /'fəʊnɪ/ infml **I** *n* (affected person) pozer *m*; (impostor) oszust *m*, -ka *f*, szarlatan *m*

II *adj [jewel, address]* fałszywy; *[accent]* sztuczny; *[emotion]* udawany; *[excuse]* lipny infml; *[company]* lewy infml

phoney war *n* the ~ dziwna wojna *f* (Francji i Anglii z Niemcami na początku II wojny światowej)

phosphates *npl* fosfaty *m pl*, nawozy *m pl* fosforowe

photo /'fəʊtəʊ/ *n* → **photograph I**

photo album *n* album *m* fotograficzny

photo booth *n* automat *m* fotograficzny

photo call /'fəʊtəʊkɔːl/ *n* sesja *f* zdjęciowa

photocopier /'fəʊtəʊkɒpɪə(r)/ *n* fotokopiarka *f*

photocopy /'fəʊtəʊkɒpɪ/ **I** *n* fotokopia *f*

II *vt* złrobić fotokopię (czegoś)

photogenic /ˌfəʊtəʊ'dʒenɪk/ *adj* fotogeniczny

photograph /'fəʊtəɡrɑːf, US -ɡræf/ **I** *n* (also **photo**) zdjęcie *n*, fotografia *f*; **in the ~** na zdjęciu, na fotografii; **to take a ~ of sb/sth** zrobić komuś/czemuś zdjęcie

II *vt* słfotografować, złrobić zdjęcie (czegoś)

photographer /fə'tɒɡrəfə(r)/ *n* fotograf *m*

photography /fə'tɒɡrəfɪ/ *n* fotografika *f*

photo opportunity *n* sesja *f* zdjęciowa

photo session *n* sesja *f* zdjęciowa

phrase /freɪz/ **I** *n* zwrot *m*, wyrażenie *n*

II *vt* wyrałzić, -żać *[idea]*; słformułować *[question]*; ułożyć, -kładać *[speech]*

phrasebook /'freɪzbʊk/ *n* rozmówki *plt*

physical /'fɪzɪkl/ **I** *n* infml badanie *n* lekarskie

II *adj* fizyczny; *[injury]* cielesny

physical fitness *n* sprawność *f* fizyczna

physically handicapped /'fɪzɪklɪ'hændɪkæpt/ *adj* **to be ~** być upośledzonym fizycznie, być kaleką

physicist /'fɪzɪsɪst/ *n* fizyk *m*

physics /'fɪzɪks/ *n* fizyka *f*

physiology /ˌfɪzɪ'ɒlədʒɪ/ *n* fizjologia *f*

physiotherapy /ˌfɪzɪəʊ'θerəpɪ/ *n* fizjoterapia *f*

physique /fɪ'ziːk/ *n* budowa *f* ciała

pianist /'pɪənɪst/ *n* pianistła *m*, -ka *f*

piano /pɪ'ænəʊ/ *n* fortepian *m*; (upright) pianino *n*

pick /pɪk/ **I** *n* [1] (tool) kilof *m*, oskard *m*; (of climber) dziób *m* [2] (choice) wybór *m*; **to have one's ~ of sth** mieć możliwość wyboru spośród czegoś; **take your ~** wybieraj; **the ~ of the bunch** najlepsi ze wszystkich

II *vt* [1] (choose) wybłrać, -ierać (**from sb/sth** spośród kogoś/czegoś); **to ~ a fight (with sb)** (physically) wywołać bójkę (z kimś); (quarrel) wywołać kłótnię (z kimś) [2] infml **to ~ one's way through sth** iść wśród czegoś (ostrożnie wybierając drogę) [3] złerwać, -rywać *[fruit, flowers]* [4] zdrapłać, -ywać, rozdrapłać, -ywać *[spot, scab]*; **to ~ one's nose/teeth** dłubać w nosie/zębach

III *vi* **to ~ and choose** przebierać (**among** or **between sth** w czymś)

■ **pick at**: *[person]* dłubać w (czymś) *[food]*; rozdrapywać *[spot, scab]*; *[bird]* dziobać *[crumbs]*

■ **pick on**: (victimize) szykanować; (physically) napastować

■ **pick out**: [1] (select) wybłrać, -ierać; (single out) wyróżniłć, -ać [2] dostrzełc, -gać *[landmark, person in crowd]*; rozpoznalć, -awać *[person in photo]*

■ **pick up**: ¶ ~ **up** *[business, weather]* poprawiłć, -ać się, polepszłyć, -ać się; *[ill person]* wrłacać, -ócić do zdrowia ¶ ~ **[sb/sth] up** [1] (lift up) podnłieść, -osić; (collect to tidy) pozbierać, zebrać; **to ~ up the telephone** podnieść słuchawkę; **to ~ oneself up** podnieść się (po upadku); fig (recover) pozbierać się infml [2] zabłrać, -ierać *[passenger, cargo]*; odłebrać, -bierać *[ticket, key]*; **could you ~ me up?** czy mógłbyś po mnie przyjechać? ③ nauczyć się (czegoś) *[language]*; zdoby|ć, -wać *[knowledge, skill]*; nab|rać, -ierać (czegoś) *[accent, habit]*; zara|zić, -żać się (czymś) *[illness]*; zna|leźć, -jdować *[error]*; wykry|ć, -wać *[defect]* ④ (detect) *[radar]* wykry|ć, -wać *[aircraft, person, object]*; trafi|ć, -ać na (coś) *[trail, scent]*; *[radio receiver]* od|ebrać, -bierać *[signal]* ⑤ zysk|ać, -iwać, zdoby|ć, -wać *[point, reputation]*; **to ~ up speed** zwiększać prędkość, przyśpieszać ⑥ (resume) pod|jąć, -ejmować na nowo *[conversation, career]* ⑦ pod|erwać, -rywać infml *[prostitute, partner]*

pickaxe GB, **pickax** US /ˈpɪkæks/ n kilof m, oskard m

picket /ˈpɪkɪt/ **I** n (group) pikieta f; (one person) pikietując|y m, -a f
II vt pikietować *[factory]*

picking /ˈpɪkɪŋ/ **I** n (of fruit) zrywanie n; (of strawberries, mushrooms) zbieranie n
II pickings npl (rewards) zyski m pl, profit m

pickle /ˈpɪkl/ **I** n ① (preserves) marynata f ② (gherkin) korniszon m
II vt (in vinegar) za|marynować
(IDIOMS:) **to be in a ~** napytać sobie biedy; ładnie się urządzić infml

pick-me-up /ˈpɪkmiʌp/ n napój m orzeźwiający

pickpocket /ˈpɪkpɒkɪt/ n złodziej m kieszonkowy; kieszonkowiec m infml

pickup truck /ˈpɪkʌpˈtrʌk/ GB furgonetka f; pikap m infml

picnic /ˈpɪknɪk/ n piknik m

picture /ˈpɪktʃə(r)/ **I** n ① (painting) obraz m; (small) obrazek m; (drawing) rysunek m; (in book) rycina f ② (description) obraz m ③ (snapshot) zdjęcie n, fotografia f ④ **to put sb in the ~** wprowadzić kogoś w sytuację; **get the ~?** infml kapujesz? infml ⑤ (film) film m ⑥ (on TV screen) obraz m
II vt wyobra|zić, -żać sobie

picture card n figura f (karciana)

picture frame n rama f obrazu; (small) ramka f

picture hook n haczyk m do zawieszania obrazów

picturesque /ˌpɪktʃəˈresk/ adj *[view]* malowniczy; *[character, style]* barwny

pie /paɪ/ n ① (savoury) ≈ pieróg m; (small) pasztecik m; **meat ~** pieróg nadziewany mięsem ② (sweet) **apple ~** szarlotka

piece /piːs/ n ① (of bread, fabric, string) kawałek m; (unit) sztuka f; **a ~ of advice** rada; **a ~ of furniture** mebel; **a ~ of information** informacja; **I've had a ~ of bad luck** miałem pecha; **to fall to ~s** rozpaść się na kawałki, rozlecieć się; **to go to ~s** (from shock) załamać się; (in crisis) stracić głowę ② (part) część f; **to take sth to ~s** rozłożyć or rozebrać coś na części ③ (article) artykuł m (**on sb/sth** na temat kogoś/czegoś) ④ (coin) moneta f;

a 50p ~ pięćdziesięciopensówka ⑤ (in chess) pionek m, pion m

■ **piece together**: **~ [sth] together** po|składać *[fragments]*; u|łożyć, -kładać *[puzzle]*; po|łączyć w jedną całość *[facts]*
(IDIOMS:) **to give sb a ~ of one's mind** powiedzieć komuś kilka słów prawdy

piecemeal /ˈpiːsmiːl/ **I** adj *[reforms]* fragmentaryczny; *[story]* chaotyczny, nieuporządkowany; *[research]* wyrywkowy
II adv po trochu

pie chart n diagram m kołowy

pier /pɪə(r)/ n (at seaside) molo n; (landing stage) przystań f

pierce /pɪəs/ vt ① przedziurawi|ć, -ać *[paper]*; przekłu|ć, -wać *[ears, nose]* ② *[cold, wind]* przenik|nąć, -ać

piercing /ˈpɪəsɪŋ/ adj *[wind, scream]* przenikliwy, przeszywający; *[light]* oślepiający

pig /pɪg/ n ① (animal) świnia f ② infml (person) (nasty) świnia f infml; (greedy) żarłok m; (dirty) świntuch m, prosię n infml; **to make a ~ of oneself** objeść się, opchać się infml

■ **pig out** infml: ob|eżreć, -żerać się infml (**on sth** czegoś)

pigeon /ˈpɪdʒɪn/ n gołąb m

pigeonhole /ˈpɪdʒɪnhəʊl/ GB **I** n przegródka f
II vt po|sortować; fig za|szufladkować *[person, idea]*

pigeon-toed /ˌpɪdʒɪnˈtəʊd/ adj **to be ~** stawiać stopy palcami do środka

piggyback (ride) /ˈpɪgɪbæk (raɪd)/ n **to give sb a ~** wziąć/nieść kogoś na barana

piggy bank n świnka f *(skarbonka)*

pigheaded /ˌpɪgˈhedɪd/ adj uparty jak osioł

piglet /ˈpɪglɪt/ n prosię n, prosiak m

pigment /ˈpɪgmənt/ n pigment m, barwnik m

pigpen /ˈpɪgpen/ n US = **pigsty**

pigskin /ˈpɪgskɪn/ n świńska skóra f

pigsty /ˈpɪgstaɪ/, **pigpen** /ˈpɪgpen/ US n chlew m

pigtail /ˈpɪgteɪl/ n (hair) warkocz m

pike /paɪk/ n (fish) szczupak m

pile /paɪl/ **I** n ① (heap) kupa f, sterta f; (stack) stos m; **in a ~** na kupie ② (of fabric) meszek m; (of carpet) włos m ③ infml **~s of sth** kupa czegoś infml
II piles npl Med hemoroidy plt
III vt zwal|ić, -ać (na kupę) (**on sth** na czymś, na coś)

■ **pile up**: *[debts, problems]* nar|osnąć, -astać; *[work]* u|zbierać się

pileup /ˈpaɪlʌp/ n karambol m

pilfer /ˈpɪlfə(r)/ **I** vt podkradać (**from sb** komuś)
II vi kraść

pilgrim /ˈpɪlgrɪm/ n pielgrzym m, pątnik m

pilgrimage /ˈpɪlgrɪmɪdʒ/ n pielgrzymka f

pill /pɪl/ n tabletka f, pigułka f; **to be on the ~** brać pigułki antykoncepcyjne

pillage /'pɪlɪdʒ/ **Ⅰ** vt z|łupić, s|plądrować
Ⅱ vi grabić
pillar /'pɪlə(r)/ n filar m; (of smoke, fire, rock) słup m
pillar box n GB skrzynka f pocztowa
pillion /'pɪlɪən/ **Ⅰ** n (also ~ **seat**) tylne siodełko n (motocykla)
Ⅱ adv **to ride** ~ jechać na tylnym siodełku
pillow /'pɪləʊ/ n poduszka f; (small) jasiek m
pillowcase /'pɪləʊkeɪs/ n powłoczka f or poszew-ka f na poduszkę
pilot /'paɪlət/ **Ⅰ** n pilot m
Ⅱ adj **①** [course, project, study] pilotażowy; [pro-gramme, series] pilotowy **②** [error] pilotażowy
pilot light n (gas) płomień m pilotujący; (electric) lampka f sygnalizująca
pilot scheme n program m pilotażowy
pimp /pɪmp/ n sutener m, stręczyciel m
pimple /'pɪmpl/ n pryszcz m, krosta f
pimply /'pɪmplɪ/ adj pryszczaty, krostowaty
pin /pɪn/ **Ⅰ** n **①** (for cloth, paper) szpilka f **②** (for wood) czop m, kołek m; (for metal) sworzeń m, bolec m; **three-**~ **plug** wtyczka z trzema bolcami **③** Med gwóźdź m **④** (brooch) szpil(k)a f
Ⅱ vt **①** spi|ąć, -nąć szpilkami [dress, curtain]; podpi|ąć, -inać [hem] **②** (trap) **to** ~ **sb to the wall** przyprzeć kogoś do ściany; **to** ~ **sb to the floor** przycisnąć kogoś do podłogi **③** infml **to** ~ **a crime on sb** obarczyć kogoś winą za przestępstwo
■ **pin down:** ¶ ~ **[sb] down ①** (physically) przy-gni|eść, -atać, przydu|sić, -szać [person] **②** fig przycis|nąć, -kać, nacis|nąć, -kać na (kogoś); **to** ~ **sb down to a definite date** zmusić kogoś do podania konkretnej daty ¶ ~ **[sth] down** określ|ić, -ać, z|definiować
■ **pin up:** powiesić, wieszać [poster]; wywie|sić, -szać [notice] (**on sth** na czymś)
PIN (number) n (= **personal identification number**) PIN m inv
pinafore /'pɪnəfɔ:(r)/ n fartuch
pinball /'pɪnbɔ:l/ n flip(p)er m
pincers /'pɪnsəz/ npl (ob)cęgi plt, obcążki plt
pinch /pɪntʃ/ **Ⅰ** n **①** (u)szczypnięcie n; **to give sb a** ~ uszczypnąć kogoś **②** (of salt, pepper) szczypta f
Ⅱ vt **①** (with fingers) uszczypnąć, szczypać **②** [shoes] uwierać **③** infml (steal) zwędzić, buchnąć infml
Ⅲ vi [shoes] pić, cisnąć
(IDIOMS) **to feel the** ~ odczuwać skutki finansowe; zacząć cienko prząść infml
pine /paɪn/ **Ⅰ** n sosna f
Ⅱ adj sosnowy
Ⅲ vi usychać z tęsknoty (**for sb/sth** za kimś/czymś)
pineapple /'paɪnæpl/ n ananas m
pinecone /'paɪnkəʊn/ vt szyszka f sosnowa
ping-pong /'pɪŋpɒn/ n ping-pong
pink /pɪŋk/ **Ⅰ** vt **①** (colour) (kolor m) różowy m, róż m **②** (flower) goździk m

Ⅱ adj różowy; **to go** or **turn** ~ poróżowieć; (person) poczerwienieć (**with sth** od czegoś)
pinnacle /'pɪnəkl/ n (on building) pinakiel m, fiala m; (of rock, ambition, success) szczyt m
pinpoint /'pɪnpɔɪnt/ vt określ|ić, -ać z maksymalną dokładnością
pinstripe(d) /'pɪnstraɪpt/ adj [fabric, suit] w prążki
pint /paɪnt/ n ≈ pół n litra (GB = 0,57 l, US = 0,47 l); **a** ~ **of milk** pół litra mleka; **to go for a** ~ skoczyć na piwko infml
pinup /'pɪnʌp/ n (of star, idol) plakat m; (seminaked) gołe zdjęcie n infml
pioneer /ˌpaɪə'nɪə(r)/ **Ⅰ** n pionier m, -ka f
Ⅱ vt **to** ~ **the use of sth** zapoczątkować wykorzystywanie czegoś
pious /'paɪəs/ adj pobożny, nabożny
pip /pɪp/ n **①** (seed) pestka f (jabłka, pomarańczy, melona) **②** (on radio) **the** ~**s** sygnał czasu
(IDIOMS) **to be** ~**ped at** or **to the post** odpaść na ostatniej prostej fig
pipe /paɪp/ **Ⅰ** n **①** rura f, przewód m; (small) rurka f **②** (smoker's) fajka f
Ⅱ **pipes** npl Mus dudy plt
Ⅲ vt **to** ~ **water (in)to a house** doprowadzić wodę do domu
■ **pipe down** infml: ucisz|yć, -ać się; przym|knąć, -ykać się infml
■ **pipe up:** [voice] rozle|c, -gać się
pipe-dream /'paɪpdri:m/ n mrzonka f
pipeline /'paɪplaɪn/ n rurociąg m; **to be in the** ~ fig [changes] szykować się; [new product, book] być w przygotowaniu
piping hot adj wrzący
pique /pi:k/ n (resentment) uraza f; (annoyance) irytacja f; **in a fit of** ~ w przypływie złości
pirate /'paɪərət/ **Ⅰ** n **①** pirat m **②** (copy) kopia f piracka
Ⅱ adj piracki
Ⅲ vt nielegalnie s|kopiować [tape, video, software]
pirouette /ˌpɪrʊ'et/ n piruet m
Pisa /'pi:zə/ prn Piza f
Pisces /'paɪsi:z/ n Ryby f pl
pistol /'pɪstl/ n pistolet m
piston /'pɪstən/ n tłok m
pit /pɪt/ **Ⅰ** n **①** (in ground) dół m, jama f; (in garage) kanał m; **gravel** ~ żwirownia **②** (mine) kopalnia f **③** (in theatre) parter m; **orchestra** ~ fosa, kanał dla orkiestry **④** US (in fruit) pestka f
Ⅱ vt **to** ~ **sb against sb** wystawić kogoś do walki przeciwko komuś; **to** ~ **one's wits against sb** zmierzyć się z kimś
(IDIOMS) **it's the** ~**s!** infml to samo dno! infml
pit bull terrier n pitbulterier m
pitch /pɪtʃ/ **Ⅰ** n **①** (sportsground) boisko n; **football** ~ boisko do gry w piłkę nożną **②** (of note, voice) ton m, tonacja f **③** (highest point) szczyt m, zenit m **④** (sales talk) siła f perswazji **⑤** GB (for street seller)

stanowisko *n*, miejsce *n (ulicznego handlarza, żebraka)*

II *vt* ①︎ (throw) rzuc|ić, -ać (czymś, coś), cis|nąć, -kać (czymś, coś) *[object]* ②︎ s|kierować, adresować *[publicity, campaign]* (**at sb** do kogoś) ③︎ *[singer]* za|śpiewać *[note]* ④︎ rozbi|ć, -jać *[tent, camp]*

III *vi* ①︎ *[boat]* zakołysać się ②︎ US (in baseball) rzuc|ić, -ać (piłkę), miotać

■ **pitch in** infml: ①︎ (help) przy|jść, -chodzić z pomocą ②︎ (eat) zab|rać, -ierać się do jedzenia

pitch-black /ˌpɪtʃˈblæk/ *adj* czarny jak smoła

pitcher /ˈpɪtʃə(r)/ *n* ①︎ (jug) dzban *m* ②︎ US Sport miotacz *m*

pitchfork /ˈpɪtʃfɔːk/ *n* widły *plt*

pitfall /ˈpɪtfɔːl/ *n* problem *m*, kłopot *m*; pułapka *f* fig

pith /pɪθ/ *n* (of fruit) białe włókno *n (owoców cytrusowych)*; (of plant) miękisz *m (łodyg traw, trzcin)*

pitiful /ˈpɪtɪfl/ *adj [cry, sight, condition]* żałosny, budzący litość; *[amount]* nędzny

pitiless /ˈpɪtɪlɪs/ *adj [tyrant]* bezlitosny; *[heat]* niemiłosierny

pittance /ˈpɪtns/ *n* **to earn a** ~ zarabiać nędzne grosze; **to live on a** ~ klepać biedę

pity /ˈpɪti/ **I** *n* ①︎ (compassion) litość *f* (**for sb/sth** dla kogoś/czegoś); **out of** ~ z litości, przez litość; **to take** ~ **on sb** zlitować się nad kimś, mieć litość dla kogoś ②︎ (shame) szkoda *f*; **what a** ~! jaka szkoda!

II *vt* żałować (kogoś), współczuć (komuś)

pivot /ˈpɪvət/ **I** *vt* podn|ieść, -osić *[lever]*; obr|ócić, -acać *[lamp]*

II *vi* ①︎ *[lamp, device]* obr|ócić, -acać się (**on sth** na czymś) ②︎ fig **to** ~ **on sth** *[outcome, success]* zależeć od czegoś

pixel /ˈpɪksl/ *n* Comput piksel *f*

pizza /ˈpiːtsə/ *n* pizza *f*

placard /ˈplækɑːd/ *n* (at protest march) transparent *m*; (on wall) plakat *m*, afisz *m*

place /pleɪs/ **I** *n* ①︎ (location, position) miejsce *n*; **in** ~ **s** *[hilly, damaged, worn]* miejscami; ~ **of birth/ work/residence** miejsce urodzenia/pracy/zamieszkania; **all over the** ~ **s** (everywhere) wszędzie ②︎ (home) dom *m*; (apartment) mieszkanie *n*; **at Adam's** ~ u Adama; **your** ~ **or mine?** u ciebie czy u mnie? ③︎ (on bus, at table, in queue) miejsce *n*; (setting at table) nakrycie *n* ④︎ (on team) miejsce *n*; (with firm) posada *f*; **a** ~ **as a cook** praca kucharza; **to get a** ~ **on the physics course** dostać się na fizykę, zostać przyjętym na fizykę ⑤︎ (in competition, race) lokata *f*, miejsce *n*; **to finish in first** ~ zdobyć pierwsze miejsce; **in the first** ~ (firstly) po pierwsze, przede wszystkim ⑥︎ (correct position) właściwe or swoje miejsce *n*; **in** ~ *[system, scheme]* gotowy do wdrożenia; **everything is in its** ~ wszystko jest na swoim miejscu; **to hold sth in** ~

przytrzymywać coś (na swoim miejscu); **to put sb in his/her** ~ pokazać komuś, gdzie jego/jej miejsce ⑦︎ (personal level or position) **it's not my** ~ **to criticize** nie do mnie należy krytykowanie; **in his** ~ na jego miejscu ⑧︎ (moment) moment *m*, chwila *f*; **in** ~ **s** *[funny, boring, silly]* miejscami, chwilami

II out of place *adj phr [remark, behaviour]* nie na miejscu; *[object]* nie na swoim miejscu; **to look out of** ~ *[building]* nie pasować do otoczenia

III *vt* ①︎ umie|ścić, -szczać; **to** ~ **an order for sth** zamówić coś ②︎ (rank) s|klasyfikować ③︎ (identify) rozpozna|ć, -wać *[person, accent]*

place mat *n* podkładka *f* pod nakrycie

placement /ˈpleɪsmənt/ *n* (also **work** ~) staż *m*

place-name /ˈpleɪsneɪm/ *n* nazwa *f* geograficzna

placid /ˈplæsɪd/ *adj [person, animal, smile]* łagodny; *[sea, place]* spokojny

plagiarize /ˈpleɪdʒəraɪz/ **I** *vt* przepis|ać, -ywać (z cudzego dzieła) *[chapter]*; przywłaszcz|yć, -ać sobie *[idea, style]*

II *vi* popełni|ć, -ać plagiat

plague /pleɪɡ/ **I** *n* (disease) dżuma *f*; (epidemic) zaraza *f*; fig (of insects, rats, locusts) plaga *f*; **what a** ~ **that boy is!** dopust boży z tym chłopakiem!

II *vt* nie dawać żyć (komuś), zadręcz|yć, -ać; **to be** ~ **d by sth** być dręczonym czymś *[doubt]*; być nękanym przez coś *[difficulties]*

plaice /pleɪs/ *n* gładzica *f*

plaid /plæd/ *n* (fabric) tartan *m*; (design) wzór *m* w szkocką kratę

plain /pleɪn/ **I** *n* równina *f*

II *adj* ①︎ (simple) prosty; *[food]* niewyszukany ②︎ (of one colour) *[fabric, paper]* gładki; *[envelope]* zwyczajny ③︎ *[woman]* nieładny ④︎ (obvious) jasny, oczywisty; **it's** ~ **to see** to od razu widać ⑤︎ *[ignorance, common sense]* zwykły ⑥︎ *[bun, cake]* zwykły; *[yoghurt]* naturalny

plain chocolate *n* ≈ czekolada *f* deserowa

plain clothes *adj [policeman]* (ubrany) po cywilnemu

plainly /ˈpleɪnli/ *adv* ①︎ (obviously) najwyraźniej ②︎ *[see]* wyraźnie; *[remember]* dokładnie ③︎ *[speak]* szczerze, otwarcie ④︎ *[furnished, dressed]* skromnie

plait /plæt/ *n* (of hair) warkocz *m*

plan /plæn/ **I** *n* plan *m*, projekt *m*; (intention) zamiar *m*, zamysł *m*; **to have a** ~ **to do sth** planować coś zrobić; **to go according to** ~ pójść zgodnie z planem

II *vt* ①︎ (prepare, organize) za|planować *[future, day, crime]*; przygotow|ać, -ywać *[meeting, expedition]*; rozplanow|ać, -ywać *[timetable, essay, book]* ②︎ (intend) planować *[trip, visit]*; **to** ~ **to do sth** zamierzać coś zrobić ③︎ (design) za|projektować

III *vi* planować, robić plany; **to** ~ **for sth** (make preparations) robić przygotowania do czegoś; (expect)

spodziewać się czegoś; **to ~ on doing sth** (intend) zamierzać coś zrobić

■ **plan ahead**: robić plany na przyszłość

plane /pleɪn/ n ① (aircraft) samolot m ② (in geometry) płaszczyzna f ③ (tool) strug m, hebel m ④ (also **~ tree**) platan m

planet /'plænɪt/ n planeta f

plank /plæŋk/ n deska f

planner /'plænə(r)/ n (in economy) planista m; (of project, strategy) autor m, -ka f planu; (in town planning) urbanista m

planning /'plænɪŋ/ n ① (of industry, economy, work) planowanie n; (of holiday, party) za|planowanie n ② (in town) planowanie n przestrzenne, urbanistyka f; (of housing estate) projektowanie n

planning permission n pozwolenie n na budowę

plant /plɑːnt, US plænt/ ① n ① Bot roślina f ② (factory) zakład m przemysłowy, zakłady m pl
② vt ① za|sadzić, po|sadzić *[bulb, tree]*; za|siać, po|siać *[seeds]* ② pod|łożyć, -kładać *[bomb, explosive]*; **to ~ drugs on sb** podrzucić komuś narkotyki
③ vr **to ~ oneself in front of sth** ulokować się przed czymś

plantation /plæn'teɪʃn/ n plantacja f

plaque /plɑːk, US plæk/ n ① (on wall, monument) płyta f, tablica f ② (on teeth) kamień m nazębny, płytka f nazębna

plaster /'plɑːstə(r), US 'plæs-/ ① n ① (on wall) tynk m ② (for broken limb, sculpture) gips m ③ GB (also **sticking ~**) plaster m, przylepiec m
② vt ① o|tynkować *[wall]* ② (cover) po|oklejać (**with sth** czymś)

plaster cast n (for broken limb) gips m; (in art) odlew m gipsowy

plasterer /'plɑːstərə(r), US 'plæst-/ n tynkarz m

plastic /'plæstɪk/ ① n ① (material) plastik m, plastyk m ② (credit cards) karty f pl kredytowe, plastikowe pieniądze m pl infml
② adj ① *[bag, bucket]* plastikowy, plastykowy ② (easily formed) *[substance]* plastyczny

plastic surgeon n chirurg m plastyczny

plastic surgery n (branch of surgery) chirurgia f plastyczna; (operation) operacja f plastyczna

plate /pleɪt/ ① n ① (dish) (for eating) talerz m; (small) talerzyk m; (for serving) półmisek m ② (sheet of metal) płyta f; (thin) arkusz m (blachy) ③ (on door) tabliczka f; (on car) tablica f rejestracyjna ④ (illustration) ilustracja f *(zwykle całostronicowa)* ⑤ (in dentistry) proteza f dentystyczna ⑥ (in earth's crust) płyta f
② **-plated** in combinations **gold/silver-~d** powlekany złotem/srebrem, platerowany

plate glass n szkło n okienne

platform /'plætfɔːm/ n ① (for performance) estrada f; (at public meeting) podium n, trybuna f ② (in scaffolding) pomost m ③ (in politics) program m, platforma f

polityczna ④ (at station) peron m ⑤ Comput platforma f

platform shoes npl buty m pl na platformach; platformy f pl infml

platinum /'plætɪnəm/ n platyna f

platinum blonde n platynowa blondynka f

platonic /plə'tɒnɪk/ adj platoniczny

platoon /plə'tuːn/ n pluton m

platter /'plætə(r)/ n półmisek m

plausible /'plɔːzəbl/ adj *[story]* prawdopodobnie brzmiący; *[person]* wiarygodny, wiarogodny

play /pleɪ/ ① n ① (in theatre) sztuka f (teatralna) (**about sb/sth** o kimś/czymś, na temat kogoś/ czegoś) ② (recreation) zabawa f, rozrywka f ③ Sport (game) gra f, rozgrywka f; **the ball is out of ~/in ~** piłka jest poza boiskiem/na boisku ④ (movement, interaction) gra f; **to come into ~** dać o sobie znać, wchodzić w grę; **a ~ on words** gra słów
② vt ① za|grać w (coś) *[cards, football]*; roz|egrać, -grywać *[game]*; **to ~ hide and seek** bawić się w chowanego; **to ~ a joke on sb** zrobić komuś kawał, spłatać komuś figla ② za|grać *[symphony, chord]*; grać na (czymś) *[instrument]* ③ (in theatre) za|grać, od|egrać, -grywać *[role]* ④ pu|ścić, -szczać *[tape, video, CD]*
③ vi ① bawić się ② Sport za|grać (**at sth** w coś) ③ *[musician, orchestra]* za|grać (**for** or **to sb** dla kogoś, komuś)

■ **play along**: **to ~ along with sb** akompaniować komuś; fig iść komuś na rękę

■ **play down**: pomniejsz|yć, -áć znaczenie (czegoś), z|minimalizować

■ **play out**: od|egrać, -grywać *[fantasy]*

■ **play up** infml: *[person]* dawać się we znaki; *[computer]* nawalać infml

(IDIOMS) **to ~ for time** grać na zwłokę

play-acting /'pleɪæktɪŋ/ n udawanie n, komediantwo n

playboy /'pleɪbɔɪ/ n playboy m

player /'pleɪə(r)/ n ① (in sport) gracz m, zawodni|k m, -czka f; (in music) wykonaw|ca m, -czyni f, muzyk m; (actor) aktor m, -ka f; **tennis ~** tenisista

playful /'pleɪfl/ adj *[kitten]* swawolny; *[child]* rozdokazywany; *[remark]* żartobliwy

playground /'pleɪɡraʊnd/ n (in park, city) plac m zabaw; (in school) dziedziniec m

playgroup /'pleɪɡruːp/ n grupa f przedszkolna

playhouse /'pleɪhaʊs/ n teatr m

playing card n karta f do gry

playing field n boisko n

play-off /'pleɪɒf/ n GB spotkanie n barażowe; US decydujący mecz m

playroom /'pleɪrʊm/ n pokój m zabaw

playschool /'pleɪskuːl/ n grupa f przedszkolna

plaything /'pleɪθɪŋ/ n zabawka f, igraszka f

playtime /'pleɪtaɪm/ n (in school) długa przerwa f

playwright /'pleɪraɪt/ n dramaturg m, dramato-pisa|rz m, -rka f

plaza /'plɑːzə, US 'plæzə/ n ① (square) plac m; (market square) rynek m; **shopping** ~ centrum handlowe ② US (toll point) punkt m pobierania opłat drogo-wych

plc, PLC n GB = public limited company SA

plea /pliː/ n ① apel m, wołanie n (**for sth** o coś) ② (in law) **to enter a** ~ **of guilty/not guilty** przyznać się/nie przyznać się do winy

plead /pliːd/ ① vt (beg) błagać
Ⅱ vi ① prosić, apelować; (more fervently) błagać; **to** ~ **with sb** błagać kogoś ② (in law) **to** ~ **guilty/not guilty** przyznawać/nie przyznawać się do winy

pleasant /'pleznt/ adj przyjemny; *[weather]* ładny; *[person]* miły, sympatyczny

please /pliːz/ ① adv proszę; **'may I?'** – '~ **do'** „czy mogę?" – „bardzo proszę"
Ⅱ vt (make happy) sprawi|ć, -ać przyjemność (komuś); (satisfy) zadow|olić, -alać, dog|odzić, -adzać (komuś); **she is hard to** ~ trudno ją zadowolić or jej dogodzić
Ⅲ vi **do as you** ~ rób, jak chcesz or jak uważasz

pleased /pliːzd/ adj zadowolony (**about** or **at** or **with sb/sth** z kogoś/czegoś); **to be** ~ **that...** cieszyć się, że...; **to be** ~ **with oneself** być zadowolonym z siebie; **I am** ~ **to inform you that...** z przyjemnością zawiadamiam, że...; ~ **to meet you** miło mi pana/panią poznać

pleasing /'pliːzɪŋ/ adj miły, ujmujący; *[news]* miły; *[colour, shape]* ładny; *[effect, result]* korzystny

pleasurable /'pleʒərəbl/ adj przyjemny, miły

pleasure /'pleʒə(r)/ n przyjemność f (**of sth/doing sth** czegoś/robienia czegoś); (satisfaction) zadowolenie n (**of sth/doing sth** z czegoś/z robienia czegoś); **my** ~ **for** ~ dla przyjemności; (replying to request for help) z przyjemnością; (replying to thanks) cała przyjemność po mojej stronie

pleat /pliːt/ n fałda f, plisa f

pleated /'pliːtɪd/ adj *[skirt]* plisowany; *[trousers]* z zaprasowanymi zaszewkami

pledge /pledʒ/ ① n ① (promise) zobowiązanie n, przyrzeczenie n ② (money promised to charity) dekla-racja f wsparcia finansowego
Ⅱ vt przyrze|c, -kać *[allegiance, aid, support]* (**to sb** komuś); **to** ~ **one's word** dawać słowo (honoru)

plentiful /'plentɪfl/ adj obfity

plenty /'plentɪ/ quantif, pron mnóstwo, dużo; ~ **of time/problems** mnóstwo czasu/kłopotów

pliable /'plaɪəbl/ adj *[twig]* giętki, sprężysty; *[plastic]* miękki; *[person]* elastyczny; (too easily influ-enced) uległy, łatwo ulegający wpływom

pliers /'plaɪəz/ npl szczypce plt, cęgi plt; **a pair of** ~ para kleszczy or cęgów

plight /plaɪt/ n ① (dilemma) trudna sytuacja f, trudne położenie n ② (suffering) ciężki los m, ciężka dola f

plimsoll /'plɪmsəl/ n GB tenisówka f

plod /plɒd/ vi
■ **plod along**: wlec się
■ **plod away**: harować

plodder /'plɒdə(r)/ n maruda m/f, guzdrała m/f infml

plonk /plɒŋk/ infml ① n sikacz m, bełt n infml
Ⅱ vt (also ~ **down**) postawić, stawiać *[box, sack]* (**on sth** na czymś)

plot /plɒt/ ① n ① (conspiracy) spisek m, zmowa f ② (of novel, film, play) akcja f, fabuła f ③ (piece of land) ~ **of land** parcela f, działka f; **a vegetable** ~ grządka warzywna ④ (building site) plac m budowy
Ⅱ vt ① (plan) u|knuć *[murder]*; przygotow|ać, -ywać *[revolution, attack]* ② (chart) wykreśl|ić, -ać *[course]* ③ (on graph) wykreśl|ić, -ać *[curve]*; sporządz|ić, -ać *[graph]*
Ⅲ vi spiskować (**against sb/sth** przeciwko komuś/czemuś)

plough GB, **plow** US /plaʊ/ ① n pług m
Ⅱ vt ① za|orać *[land, field]*; wyor|ać, -ywać *[furrow]* ② (invest) **to** ~ **money into sth** za|inwestować w coś *[project, company]*
■ **plough back**: ~ [sth] **back** reinwestować *[money, profit]* (**into sth** w coś)
■ **plough through**: .brnąć przez (coś) *[snow, mud]*; przebrnąć przez (coś) *[book]*

ploy /plɔɪ/ n wybieg m, sztuczka f

pluck /plʌk/ ① n hart m ducha
Ⅱ vt ① z|erwać, -rywać *[flower, fruit]* ② o|skubać *[chicken]*; **to** ~ **one's eyebrows** wyskubać sobie brwi ③ (in music) szarp|nąć, -ać *[strings]*; brzd|ęk-nąć, -ąkać na (czymś) *[guitar]*

plucky /'plʌki/ adj dzielny

plug /plʌg/ ① n ① (on appliance) wtyczka f ② (in bath, sink) zatyczka f, korek m ③ Aut (also **spark** ~) świeca f zapłonowa ④ (in advertising) reklama f; **to give sth a** ~ reklamować coś
Ⅱ vt ① zat|kać, -ykać *[hole]* (**with sth** czymś) ② infml (promote) lansować ③ (insert) **to** ~ **sth into sth** podłącz|yć, -ać coś do czegoś
■ **plug in**: ¶ ~ **in** mieć wtyczkę ¶ ~ [sth] **in** (into socket) włącz|yć, -ać do kontaktu; (into another appliance) podłącz|yć, -ać

plug and play n Comput system m „włącz i używaj"

plughole /'plʌghəʊl/ n GB odpływ m, otwór m odpływu

plum /plʌm/ ① n (fruit) śliwka f; (tree) śliwa f
Ⅱ adj ① (colour) śliwkowy ② infml **a** ~ **job** synekura

plumb /plʌm/ ① adv ① US infml *[crazy]* zupełnie ② infml ~ **in the middle** w samym środku

II *vt* wy|sondować *[depth]*; **to ~ the depths of sth** fig znaleźć się na samym dnie czegoś *[despair, misery]*

plumber /'plʌmə(r)/ *n* hydraulik *m*

plumbing /'plʌmɪŋ/ *n* instalacja *f* wodno-kanalizacyjna

plummet /'plʌmɪt/ *vi [bird, plane]* spa|ść, -dać; fig *[prices, temperature]* gwałtownie spa|ść, -dać

plump /plʌmp/ *adj [person, cheek, arm]* pulchny

plunge /plʌndʒ/ **II** *vt* **to ~ sth into sth** zagłębi|ć, -ać coś w czymś; (in water) zanurz|yć, -ać coś w czymś

II *vi [road, cliff]* opa|ść, -dać; (dive) *[person, plane]* za|nurkować; (fall) *[person]* spa|ść, -dać; *[rate, value]* spa|ść, -dać gwałtownie

(IDIOMS) **to take the ~** zdobyć się na śmiały krok

plunger /'plʌndʒə(r)/ *n* (for sink) przepychacz *m*

plural /'plʊərəl/ **II** *n* liczba *f* mnoga; **in the ~** w liczbie mnogiej

II *adj [noun, adjective]* w liczbie mnogiej; *[form, ending]* liczby mnogiej

plus /plʌs/ **II** *n* plus *m*

II *adj* dodatni; **on the ~ side** po stronie plusów; **the 65-~ age group** grupa wiekowa od 65 lat (w górę)

III *prep* plus, dodać; **15 ~ 12** 15 plus or dodać 12

IV *conj* plus, a do tego; **bedroom ~ bathroom** sypialnia plus łazienka

plus-fours /,plʌs'fɔːz/ *npl* pumpy *plt* do kolan

plus sign *n* znak *m* plus

Pluto /'pluːtəʊ/ *prn* (planet) Pluton *m*

plutonium /pluː'təʊnɪəm/ *n* pluton *m*

ply /plaɪ/ **II** *vi* [1] sprzedawać, handlować (czymś) *[wares]*; **to ~ one's trade** wykonywać swój zawód [2] (press to take) **to ~ sb with food/drink** raczyć kogoś jedzeniem/alkoholem

II *vi [boat, bus]* kursować (**between sth** pomiędzy czymś)

plywood /'plaɪwʊd/ *n* sklejka *f*

pm *adv* = **post meridiem** po południu; **at 2 pm** o 2 po południu, o 14

pneumatic drill /njuː'mætɪk'drɪl, US nuː-/ *n* młot *m* pneumatyczny

pneumonia /njuː'məʊnɪə, US nuː-/ *n* zapalenie *n* płuc

poach /pəʊtʃ/ **II** *vt* [1] polować nielegalnie na (coś) *[game]* [2] Culin u|gotować bez skorupki *[egg]*

II *vi* (hunt) kłusować

poacher /'pəʊtʃə(r)/ *n* kłusownik *m*

PO Box *n* skr. poczt.

pocket /'pɒkɪt/ **II** *n* [1] kieszeń *f* [2] (in billiards) łuza *f*

II *adj [edition, dictionary]* kieszonkowy

III *vt* w|łożyć, -kładać do kieszeni; fig przywłaszcz|yć, -ać sobie

pocketbook /'pɒkɪtbʊk/ *n* US (wallet) portfel *m*; (handbag) torebka *f*, koperta *f*

pocketknife /'pɒkɪtnaɪf/ *n* scyzoryk *m*

pocket money *n* kieszonkowe *n*

podgy /'pɒdʒɪ/ *adj* infml *[person]* pękaty; *[arms, fingers]* pulchny

podium /'pəʊdɪəm/ *n* podium *n*

poem /'pəʊɪm/ *n* wiersz *m*; (longer) poemat *m*

poet /'pəʊɪt/ *n* poet|a *m*, -ka *f*

poetic /pəʊ'etɪk/ *adj* poetycki; fig poetyczny

poetry /'pəʊɪtrɪ/ *n* poezja *f*; **to write/read ~** pisać/czytać poezję

poignant /'pɔɪnjənt/ *adj [emotion]* przejmujący; *[moment]* wzruszający; *[look, plea]* żałosny; *[pain]* dojmujący; *[remark, taste]* cierpki; *[wit]* cięty; *[smell]* ostry

point /pɔɪnt/ **II** *n* [1] (of knife, needle) koniuszek *m*, czubek *m* [2] (place) punkt *m*; (less specific) miejsce *n* [3] (extent, degree) stopień *m*, poziom *m*; **up to a ~** do pewnego stopnia [4] (moment) moment *m*, chwila *f*; (stage) etap *m*; **at one ~** w pewnej chwili, w pewnym momencie; **at some ~ in the future** kiedyś w przyszłości; **at this ~ in her career** na tym etapie jej kariery; **to be on the ~ of doing sth** mieć właśnie coś zrobić [5] (matter) sprawa *f*, kwestia *f*; (idea) pomysł *m*; **to make the ~ that...** powiedzieć or zauważyć, że...; **you've made your ~** powiedziałeś swoje; **to make a ~ of doing sth** (deliberately) dokładać starań, żeby coś zrobić; (proudly) zrobić coś manifestacyjnie [6] (central idea) sens *m*, sedno *n*; **to come straight to the ~** przejść od razu do sedna sprawy or do rzeczy; **to keep** or **stick to the ~** trzymać się tematu; **to miss the ~** nie zrozumieć; **that's beside the ~** nie o to chodzi; **to get the ~** zrozumieć, pojąć; **that's the ~** o to chodzi, w tym rzecz [7] (purpose) cel *m*; **what's the ~ of having a car?** jaki jest sens posiadania samochodu?; **there's no ~ asking him** nie ma sensu go pytać [8] (feature, characteristic) cecha *f*; **her strong ~** jej mocna strona [9] (in scoring) punkt *m*; **match ~** (in tennis) piłka meczowa [10] (dot) kropka *f*; (decimal) przecinek *m* dziesiętny *(w języku angielskim oznaczany kropką)* [11] (headland) cypel *m*

II *vt* [1] (aim, direct) wy|celować or wy|mierzyć z (czegoś) *[gun]* (**at sb/sth** w kogoś/coś); nakierow|ać, -ywać, s|kierować *[camera]* (**at sb/sth** na kogoś/coś); **to ~ one's finger at sb** pokazać kogoś palcem [2] (show) **to ~ the way to sth** *[person, signpost]* wskazywać drogę do czegoś [3] (in ballet) **to ~ one's toes** obciąg|nąć, -ać palce

III *vi* [1] (indicate) wskaz|ać, -ywać palcem; **to ~ at sb** wskazać kogoś or na kogoś [2] *[signpost, arrow]* wskazywać (**at sth** coś); *[camera]* być skierowanym (**at sb/sth** na kogoś/coś); *[gun]* być wymierzonym or wycelowanym (**at sb/sth** w kogoś/coś)

■ **point out:** (show) wskaz|ać, -ywać, pokaz|ać, -ywać; (mention) zwr|ócić, -acać uwagę na (coś) *[error, discrepancy]*

point-blank /ˌpɔɪnt'blæŋk/ *adv* [1] *[shoot]* z bliska [2] *[refuse, deny]* kategorycznie

pointed /'pɔɪntɪd/ *adj* [1] *[nose, chin, hat]* spiczasty, szpiczasty [2] *[remark]* uszczypliwy

pointer /'pɔɪntə(r)/ *n* [1] (piece of information) wskazówka *f* [2] (on projector screen) wskaźnik *m* [3] Comput wskaźnik *m*

pointless /'pɔɪntlɪs/ *adj [request, activity]* bezcelowy; **it's ~ to argue with her** spieranie się z nią nie ma sensu

point of view *n* punkt *m* widzenia

poise /pɔɪz/ *n* [1] (confidence) pewność *f* siebie [2] (physical elegance) wytworność *f (w ruchach)*

poised /pɔɪzd/ *adj* [1] (self-possessed) opanowany [2] (elegant) wytworny [3] (on the point of) **to be ~ to do sth** być gotowym do zrobienia czegoś

poison /'pɔɪzn/ **[]** *n* trucizna *f*
[] *vt* o|truć *[person, animal]*; zatru|ć, -wać *[water, foodstuffs]*; ska|zić, -żać *[environment]*

poisoning /'pɔɪzənɪŋ/ *n* zatrucie *n*

poisonous /'pɔɪzənəs/ *adj* [1] *[chemical, fumes, mushroom, berry]* trujący; *[snake, insect]* jadowity; *[bite]* powodujący reakcję toksyczną [2] *[rumours]* obrzydliwy; *[propaganda]* szkodliwy

poke /pəʊk/ *vt* [1] (jab, prod) szturch|nąć, -ać, poszturchiwać *[person]*; grzebać w (czymś), rozgrzeb|ać, -ywać *[pile, substance]*; przegarn|ąć, -iać *[fire]* [2] (push, put) w|etknąć, -tykać, wsadz|ić, -ać **(into sth** do czegoś, w coś); **to ~ one's head out of the window** wystawić głowę przez okno
■ **poke around, poke about**: grzebać, szperać **(in sth** w czymś)
■ **poke out**: ¶ ~ **out** *[elbow, toe]* wystawać; *[blade]* sterczeć ¶ ~ **[sth] out** wysu|nąć, -wać *[head, nose, tongue]*

poker /'pəʊkə(r)/ *n* [1] (for fire) pogrzebacz *m* [2] (card game) poker *m*
◰ (IDIOMS) **(as) stiff as a ~** prosty, jakby kij połknął

poker-faced /'pəʊkəfeɪst/ *adj [person]* z kamienną twarzą

Poland /'pəʊlənd/ *prn* Polska *f*

polar /'pəʊlə(r)/ *adj [bear]* polarny; *[circle, region]* podbiegunowy

pole /pəʊl/ *n* [1] (stick) słup *m*, pal *m*; (thinner) tyka *f*, żerdź *f*; (for skiing) kijek *m* [2] (of earth's axis) biegun *m*

Pole /pəʊl/ *n* Pol|ak *m*, -ka *f*

pole star *n* gwiazda *f* przewodnia

pole vault /'pəʊlvɔːlt/ *n* skok *m* o tyczce

police /pə'liːs/ **[]** *n* [1] (force) **the ~** policja *f* [2] (policemen) policjanci *m pl*
[] *vt* patrolować *[area]*

police constable, PC *n* posterunkowy *m*

Police Department, PD *n* US wydział *m* policji

police force *n* policja *f*

policeman /pə'liːsmən/ *n* policjant *m*

police officer *n* funkcjonariusz *m*, -ka *f* policji, policjant *m*, -ka *f*

police station *n* posterunek *m* policji; (larger) komisariat *m*

policewoman /pə'liːswʊmən/ *n* policjantka *f*

policing /pə'liːsɪŋ/ *n* [1] (keeping law and order) pilnowanie *n* porządku publicznego [2] (of demonstration, match) ochrona *f* policyjna [3] (monitoring) nadzorowanie *n* przestrzegania **(of sth** czegoś)

policy /'pɒləsɪ/ *n* [1] (plan, rule) polityka *f* **(on sth** dotycząca czegoś) [2] (in insurance) polisa *f* ubezpieczeniowa

policyholder /'pɒləsɪhəʊldə(r)/ *n* posiadacz *m*, -ka *f* polisy, ubezpieczon|y *m*, -a *f*

policy unit *n* komitet *m* doradców politycznych

polio /'pəʊlɪəʊ/ *n* heinemedina *f*, polio *n*

polish /'pɒlɪʃ/ **[]** *n* [1] (for wood, floor, shoes) pasta *f*; (for brass, silver, car) środek *m* do czyszczenia [2] (shiny surface) połysk *m* [3] (of performance, style) błyskotliwość *f*
[] *vt* [1] wy|pastować *[floor, shoes]*; (make shiny) wy|froterować *[floor]*; wy|polerować *[furniture, glass]*; (clean) wy|czyścić do połysku *[shoes, leather, glass, silver]* [2] (refine) wy|szlifować, wygładz|ić, -ać *[performance, style]*; poprawi|ć, -ać *[image]*
■ **polish off** infml: s|pałaszować infml *[food]*; odwal|ić, -ać infml *[job]*

Polish /'pəʊlɪʃ/ **[]** *n* (język *m*) polski *m*
[] *adj* polski

polished /'pɒlɪʃt/ *adj* [1] *[floor]* wyfroterowany; *[shoes]* wyczyszczony do połysku; *[wood, surface]* wypolerowany [2] *[manner]* wytworny [3] *[performance]* pierwszorzędny

polite /pə'laɪt/ *adj* uprzejmy, grzeczny **(to sb** w stosunku do kogoś)

politeness /pə'laɪtnɪs/ *n* uprzejmość *f*

political /pə'lɪtɪkl/ *adj* polityczny

politically correct, PC /pə'lɪtɪklɪ kə'rekt/ *adj* politycznie poprawny

political prisoner *n* więzień *m* polityczny

politician /ˌpɒlɪ'tɪʃn/ *n* polityk *m*

politicize /pə'lɪtɪsaɪz/ *vt* upolityczni|ć, -ać

politics /'pɒlɪtɪks/ *n* [1] polityka *f* [2] (subject) nauki *f pl* polityczne [3] (views) przekonania *plt* polityczne

poll /pəʊl/ **[]** *n* [1] (vote casting) głosowanie *n*; (election) wybory *plt*; **to go to the ~s** *[voters]* pójść do urn wyborczych [2] (survey) ankieta *f*, sondaż *m* **(on sth** dotyczący czegoś)
[] *vt* [1] z|ebrać, -bierać *[votes]* [2] (canvass) ankietować *[group]*

pollen /'pɒlən/ *n* pyłek *m* kwiatowy

polling booth *n* kabina *f* do głosowania

polling day *n* dzień *m* wyborów

polling station *n* lokal *m* wyborczy

poll tax *n* GB pogłówne *n*

pollutant /pə'luːtənt/ *n* polutant *m (substancja zanieczyszczająca środowisko)*

pollute /pə'luːt/ *vt* zanieczy|ścić, -szczać, ska|zić, -żać

polluter /pə'lu:tə(r)/ *n* truciciel *m*, -ka *f* fig
pollution /pə'lu:ʃn/ *n* zanieczyszczenie *n*, skażenie *n*
polo /'pəʊləʊ/ *n* ① Sport polo *n inv* ② GB (sweater, collar) golf *m*
polo neck *n* GB golf *m*
poltergeist /'pɒltəgaɪst/ *n* złośliwy, hałaśliwy duch *m*
poly /'pɒlɪ/ ❶ *n* GB infml → **polytechnic**
❷ **poly+** *in combinations* poli-, wielo-
polystyrene /ˌpɒlɪ'staɪri:n/ *n* polistyren *m*
polytechnic /ˌpɒlɪ'teknɪk/ *n* GB (also **poly**) ≈ szkoła *f* wyższa zawodowa
polythene /'pɒlɪθi:n/ *n* GB polietylen *m*
pomegranate /'pɒmɪɡrænɪt/ *n* (fruit) granat *m*; (tree) granatowiec *m*, granat *m*
pompom /'pɒmpɒm/, **pompon** /'pɒmpɒn/ *n* pompon *m*
pompous /'pɒmpəs/ *adj* napuszony, pompatyczny
pond /pɒnd/ *n* staw *m*; (small) sadzawka *f*; (in garden) oczko *n* wodne
ponder /'pɒndə(r)/ *vi* zastanawiać się (**on sth** nad czymś)
pontiff /'pɒntɪf/ *n* papież *m*
pontoon /pɒn'tu:n/ *n* ① (pier) ponton *m* ② GB Games blackjack *m*; oczko *n* infml
pony /'pəʊnɪ/ *n* kuc(yk) *m*
ponytail /'pəʊnɪteɪl/ *n* koński ogon *m* *(fryzura)*
poodle /'pu:dl/ *n* pudel *m*
pool /pu:l/ ❶ *n* ① (pond) sadzawka *f*; (larger) staw *m* ② (also **swimming** ~) basen *m* kąpielowy ③ (of blood) kałuża *f*; (of light) krąg *m* ④ (kitty) pula *f*, bank *m* ⑤ (of money, resources) wspólna pula *f*; (of experience) zasób *m* ⑥ (billiards) pool *m*, pul *m*
❷ **pools** *npl* GB (also **football** ~s) totalizator *m* piłkarski
❸ *vt* z|ebrać, -bierać *[money, experience, information]*
pool table *n* stół *m* bilardowy do gry w pool
poor /pɔ:(r), pʊə(r)/ *adj* ① *[person, country]* biedny, ubogi ② (inferior) kiepski, marny; *[memory, visibility]* słaby; *[meal, diet]* lichy ③ (deserving pity) biedny, nieszczęsny; ~ **you!** biedactwo! ④ *[attempt, excuse]* żałosny
poorly /'pɔ:lɪ, 'pʊəlɪ/ *adv* ① (not richly) ubogo, biednie ② (badly) źle
pop /pɒp/ ❶ *n* ① (sound) (of bursting balloon) trzask *m*; (of champagne cork) wystrzał *m*; **to go** ~ trzasnąć, wystrzel|ić ② infml (drink) napój *m* gazowany ③ (music) pop *m*
❷ *adj* popowy; ~ **music** muzyka pop
❸ *vt* ① przebi|ć, -jać *[balloon, bubble]* ② wyciąg|nąć, -ać *[cork]* ③ infml (put) **to** ~ **sth in(to) sth** wrzuc|ić, -ać coś do czegoś *[oven, cupboard, mouth]*
❹ *vi* ① *[balloon]* pęk|nąć, -ać z trzaskiem; *[cork]* wystrzel|ić ② *[ears]* od|etkać, -tykać się; **her eyes**

were ~ **ping out of her head** oczy wychodziły jej z orbit ③ GB infml (go) **to** ~ **into the bank** skoczyć do banku infml
■ **pop in** GB infml: wpa|šć, -dać infml
■ **pop out** GB: wysk|oczyć, -akiwać infml
■ **pop round, pop over** GB: wpa|šć, -dać infml
pope /pəʊp/ *n* papież *m*; **Pope John Paul II** papież Jan Paweł II
poplar /'pɒplə(r)/ *n* topola *f*
poppy /'pɒpɪ/ *n* mak *m*; **wild poppies** polne maki
pop sock *n* podkolanówka *f*
popular /'pɒpjʊlə(r)/ *adj* ① (well-liked) popularny, lubiany; **to be** ~ **with** or **among sb** cieszyć się popularnością u or wśród kogoś ② (of or for the people) *[music, literature, press]* popularny; *[entertainment]* lekki; *[programme]* dla szerokiej publiczności
popularity /ˌpɒpjʊ'lærətɪ/ *n* popularność *f*, wzięcie *n* (**with sb** u or wśród kogoś)
popularize /'pɒpjʊləraɪz/ *vt* (make popular) s|popularyzować; (make accessible) upowszechni|ć, -ać
population /ˌpɒpjʊ'leɪʃn/ *n* ludność *f*, mieszkańcy *m pl*
pop-up menu /'pɒpʌp'menju:/ *n* Comput menu *n* rozwijalne
porcelain /'pɔ:səlɪn/ *n* porcelana *f*
porch /pɔ:tʃ/ *n* ① (of house) ganek *m*; (of church) przedsionek *m* ② US (veranda) weranda *f*
porcupine /'pɔ:kjʊpaɪn/ *n* jeżozwierz *m*
pore /pɔ:(r)/ *n* (hole) por *m*
■ **pore over**: ślęczeć nad (czymś) *[książką]*; studiować *[mapę]*
pork /pɔ:k/ *n* wieprzowina *f*
pornographic /ˌpɔ:nə'ɡræfik/ *adj* pornograficzny
pornography /pɔ:'nɒɡrəfi/ *n* pornografia *f*
porpoise /'pɔ:pəs/ *n* morświn *m*
porridge /'pɒrɪdʒ, US 'pɔ:r-/ *n* owsianka *f*
port /pɔ:t/ *n* ① (harbour) port *m*; **in** ~ w porcie; ~ **of call** port pośredni; fig (stop) przystanek fig ② (drink) porto *n inv* ③ Comput port *m*
portable /'pɔ:təbl/ *adj* przenośny; *[typewriter]* walizkowy
porter /'pɔ:tə(r)/ *n* ① (in station, airport) bagażowy *m*; (in hospital) sanitariusz *m* ② GB (doorman) odźwierny; (of hotel, apartment block) portier *m* ③ US (steward) steward *m* w wagonie sypialnym
portfolio /pɔ:t'fəʊlɪəʊ/ *n* ① (case) aktówka *f*; (for drawings) teczka *f* ② (sample) portfolio *n* ③ (in politics) teka *f* (ministerialna) ④ (in finance) portfel *m*
porthole /'pɔ:thəʊl/ *n* (in ship) iluminator *m*; (in plane) okienko *n*
portion /'pɔ:ʃn/ *n* część *f*; (of food) porcja *f*
portrait /'pɔ:treɪt, -trɪt/ *n* portret *m*
portray /pɔ:'treɪ/ *vt* ① (depict) przedstawi|ć, -ać; opis|ać, -ywać ② *[actor]* za|ɡrać, od|eɡrać, -ɡrywać *[character]* ③ *[artist]* s|portretować *[person]*; *[picture, artist]* ukaz|ać, -ywać *[scene]*

Portugal /'pɔːtʃʊgl/ *prn* Portugalia *f*
Portuguese /ˌpɔːtʃʊ'giːz/ **[]** *n* [1] (person) Portu-
gal|czyk *m*, -ka *f* [2] (language) (język *m*) portugal-
ski *m*
[] *adj* portugalski
pose /pəʊz/ **[]** *vt* stanowić *[problem, challenge, risk,
threat]* (**to sb/sth** dla kogoś/czegoś); postawić,
stawiać *[question]* (**about sth** w związku z czymś)
[] *vi* [1] (for artist) pozować (**for sb** komuś) [2] (pretend
to be) **to ~ as sb/sth** pozować na kogoś/coś
[3] (posture) przybierać pozę fig
poser /'pəʊzə(r)/ *n infml* [1] (person) pozer *m*, -ka *f*
[2] (puzzle) łamigłówka *f*; zagwozdka *f infml*
posh /pɒʃ/ *adj infml [person]* wytworny; *[school,
district, club]* ekskluzywny
position /pə'zɪʃn/ **[]** *n* [1] (location) położenie *n*,
usytuowanie *n*; **to be in ~** (in place) być na swoim
miejscu; (ready) być gotowym [2] (situation) położenie *n*,
pozycja *f*; **to be in a ~ to do sth** być w stanie coś
zrobić; **to be in a good ~ to do sth** być w sytuacji
umożliwiającej zrobienie czegoś [3] Sport pozycja *f*;
what ~ does he play? na jakiej gra pozycji?
[4] (job) stanowisko *n*
[] *vt* ustawi|ć, -ać *[objects]*; rozstawi|ć, -ać *[guards,
troops]*
positive /'pɒzətɪv/ *adj* [1] *[answer]* twierdzący,
pozytywny [2] (optimistic) *[attitude]* pozytywny; *[mes-
sage, tone]* optymistyczny [3] (constructive) *[contribu-
tion, help]* konkretny; *[advantage, good]* faktyczny;
[effect, influence] pozytywny [4] (sure) *[fact, proof]*
niezbity; *[identification]* jednoznaczny; **to be ~** być
pewnym (**about sth** czegoś) [5] (forceful) *[action]*
zdecydowany [6] (in mathematics, science) dodatni
[7] (extreme) *[pleasure, disgrace, outrage, fool]* prawdziwy; *[miracle]* istny
positive discrimination *n* dyskryminacja *f*
pozytywna
possess /pə'zes/ *vt* [1] posiadać *[property, weapon,
proof, charm]*; mieć *[power, advantage]* [2] (take control
of) *[rage, fury]* opanować *[person]*; *[devil]* opętać
[person]; **what ~ed you to do that?** co cię opętało,
żeby to zrobić?
possession /pə'zeʃn/ **[]** *n* [1] posiadanie *n* [2] (in
law) (illegal) (nielegalne) posiadanie *n*
[] **possessions** *npl* (belongings) dobytek *m*
possessive /pə'zesɪv/ **[]** *n* (case) dopełniacz *m*;
(pronoun) zaimek *m* dzierżawczy; (adjective) przymiotnik *m* dzierżawczy
[] *adj* zaborczy (**towards sb** w stosunku do
kogoś)
possibility /ˌpɒsə'bɪlətɪ/ *n* możliwość *f*
possible /'pɒsəbl/ *adj* możliwy; **he did as much
as ~** zrobił, ile mógł; **as far as ~** na ile to
możliwe; **as quickly as ~** jak najszybciej
possibly /'pɒsəblɪ/ *adv* [1] (maybe) być może,
możliwe (że) [2] (for emphasis) **how could they ~
have known?** skąd mogli wiedzieć?; **we can't ~**

afford it w żaden sposób nie możemy sobie na to
pozwolić
post /pəʊst/ **[]** *n* [1] (job) stanowisko *n* [2] GB (system,
letters) poczta *f*; **by return of ~** odwrotną pocztą;
the parcel was lost in the ~ paczka zaginęła
w trakcie przesyłki [3] Mil posterunek *m* [4] (pole)
słup *m*, pal *m*
[] **post-** *in combinations* post-, po-; **in ~-1992
Europe** w Europie po roku 1992
[] *vt* [1] GB (send by post) wysł|ać, -yłać; (put in letter
box) wrzuc|ić, -ać do skrzynki pocztowej; (at post
office) nada|ć, -wać [2] (stick up) nalepi|ć, -ać *[poster,
notice]*; wywie|sić, -szać *[details, results]* [3] (send
abroad) wysła|ć, -yłać [4] Mil ustawi|ć, -ać na
posterunku
postage /'pəʊstɪdʒ/ *n* opłata *f* pocztowa; **including
~ and packing** włączając koszt przesyłki
i opakowania; **~ free** wolny od opłaty pocztowej
postal /'pəʊstl/ *adj [code, charges]* pocztowy;
[application] listowny
postal order, PO *n* GB ≈ przekaz *m* pocztowy
postbox /'pəʊstbɒks/ *n* GB skrzynka *f* pocztowa or
na listy
postcard /'pəʊstkɑːd/ *n* kartka *f* pocztowa; (with
view) widokówka *f*, pocztówka *f*
post code *n* GB kod *m* pocztowy
postdate /ˌpəʊst'deɪt/ *vt* postdatować, opat|rzyć,
-rywać data późniejszą
poster /'pəʊstə(r)/ *n* plakat *m*, afisz *m*
posterity /pɒ'sterətɪ/ *n* potomność *f*
poster paint *n* farba *f* plakatowa; plakatówka *f*
infml
postgraduate /ˌpəʊst'grædʒʊət/ **[]** *n* (for master's
degree) ≈ magistrant *m*, -ka *f*; (for PhD) ≈ dokto-
rant *m*, -ka *f*
[] *adj* (for master's degree) ≈ magisterski; (for PhD) ≈
doktorancki
posthumous /'pɒstjʊməs, US 'pɒstʃəməs/ *adj*
pośmiertny
postman /'pəʊstmən/ *n* listonosz *m*
postmark /'pəʊstmɑːk/ *n* stempel *m* pocztowy
post-mortem /ˌpəʊst'mɔːtəm/ *n* sekcja *f* zwłok,
autopsja *f*
post-natal /ˌpəʊst'neɪtl/ *adj* poporodowy
post office, PO *n* poczta *f*, urząd *m* pocztowy
postpone /pə'spəʊn/ *vt* odł|ożyć, -kładać, prze|-
łożyć, -kładać
postscript /'pəʊstskrɪpt/ *n* (in letter) postscriptum
n inv (**to sth** do czegoś); (to book) posłowie *n* (**to sth**
do czegoś)
posture /'pɒstʃə(r)/ **[]** *n* (of body) postawa *f*; (pose)
poza *f*; fig postawa *f*, stanowisko *n*; **to have good/
bad ~** mieć prawidłową/nieprawidłową postawę
[] *vi* pozować, przybierać pozy
postwar /ˌpəʊst'wɔː(r)/ *adj* powojenny
pot /pɒt/ **[]** *n* [1] (for cooking) garnek *m*; (small)
garnuszek *m*; (for tea, coffee) dzbanek *m*; **~s and**

pans naczynia (kuchenne) [2] (piece of pottery) wyrób
m ceramiczny

II *vt* [1] za|wekować *[jam]* [2] (in billiards) **to ~ the
red** wbi|ć, -jać czerwoną bilę do łuzy [3] po|sadzić
w doniczce *[plant]*

III potted *pp adj* [1] *[plant]* doniczkowy [2] *[bio-
graphy, history]* krótki

IDIOMS: **to go to ~** infml zejść na psy; **to take ~
luck** zdać się na los; (for meal) GB zadowolić się tym,
co jest

potassium /pə'tæsɪəm/ *n* potas *m*

potato /pə'teɪtəʊ/ *n* ziemniak *m*, kartofel *m*

potato crisps GB, **potato chips** US *n* chipsy
m pl, czipsy *m pl*

potato peeler *n* skrobaczka *f* do warzyw

pot belly *n* (from overeating) duży brzuch *m*; (from
malnutrition) wzdęty brzuch *m*

potent /'pəʊtnt/ *adj* [1] *[drink]* mocny; *[drug]* silnie
działający; *[symbol]* silnie oddziałujący [2] (sexually)
sprawny seksualnie

potential /pə'tenʃl/ **II** *n* (capacity) potencjał *m*;
(possibilities) możliwości *f pl* (**for sth** czegoś); **to
show great ~ as a singer** zapowiadać się na
doskonałego śpiewaka; **to fulfil one's ~** osiągnąć
pełnię swoich możliwości

II *adj* potencjalny; **to be a ~ musician** mieć
zadatki na muzyka; **to be a ~ success** zapowiadać się jako sukces

pothole /'pɒthəʊl/ *n* wybój *m*

potholing /'pɒthəʊlɪŋ/ *n* GB eksploracja *f* jaskiń

pot plant *n* roślina *f* doniczkowa

potter /'pɒtə(r)/ *n* garncarz *m*

■ **potter about, potter around** GB: (do odd jobs)
majsterkować; (go about daily chores) krzątać się

pottery /'pɒtərɪ/ *n* [1] (craft) garncarstwo *n* [2] (ware)
ceramika *f*, wyroby *m pl* garncarskie

potting compost *n* podkład *m* do doniczek

potty /'pɒtɪ/ **II** *n* nocniczek *m*

II *adj* GB *[person]* stuknięty infml; *[idea]* idiotyczny;
to be ~ about sb/sth mieć bzika na punkcie
kogoś/czegoś infml

pouch /paʊtʃ/ *n* [1] (bag) woreczek *m*; (for tobacco)
kapciuch *m*; (for ammunition) ładownica *f* [2] (of
kangaroo) torba *f*

poultry /'pəʊltrɪ/ *n* (birds) drób *m*; (meat) mięso *n*
drobiowe

pounce /paʊns/ *vi* sk|oczyć, -akać; **to ~ on sb/sth**
rzucić się na kogoś/coś

pound /paʊnd/ **II** *n* [1] (weight measurement) funt *m*
(= 453,6 g); **two ~s of apples** ≈ kilogram jabłek
[2] (unit of currency) funt *m* [3] (for dogs) schronisko *n*
dla zwierząt; (for cars) parking *m* policyjny

II *vt* [1] Culin u|trzeć, -cierać, roz|etrzeć, -cierać
[spices, grain]; zbić *[meat]* [2] *[waves]* bić o (coś),
uderzać (o coś) *[shore]* [3] *[artillery]* bombardować
[city]

III *vi* *[heart]* walić, łomotać; **to ~ on sth** walić or
łomotać w coś; **to ~ up/down the stairs**
z tupotem wbiec na schody/zbiec ze schodów;
my head is ~ing głowa mi pęka z bólu

pour /pɔ:(r)/ **II** *vt* [1] lać *[liquid]*; sypać *[salt, sugar]*
[2] (also ~ **out**) (serve) nal|ać, -ewać *[drink]* [3] (supply
freely) **to ~ money into sth** inwestować dużo
w coś; (wastefully) pakować pieniądze w coś infml

II *vi* [1] *[liquid]* lać się, ciec; **to ~ into sth** *[liquid]*
wlewać się do czegoś; *[light]* zalewać coś *[room]*;
[smoke, fumes] przedostawać się do czegoś; **tears
~ed down her face** łzy spływały jej po twarzy
[2] fig **to ~ into sth** *[people]* przybywać tłumnie do
czegoś; **to ~ out of sth** *[people]* wylewać się
tłumnie z czegoś; *[cars]* wyjeżdżać jeden za drugim
z czegoś

III *v impers* **it's ~ing (with rain)** leje (deszcz)

■ **pour away** odl|ać, -ewać, zl|ać, -ewać

■ **pour in:** *[water]* wl|ać, -ewać się do środka;
[letters, money] napły|nąć, -wać; *[people]* przyby|ć,
-wać tłumnie

■ **pour out:** ¶ ~ **out** *[smoke]* wydoby|ć, -wać się;
[liquid] wyl|ać, -ewać się; *[people]* wyle|c, -gać
tłumnie ¶ ~ **[sth] out** [1] rozl|ać, -ewać, nal|ać,
-ewać (czegoś) *[coffee, wine]* [2] wypu|ścić, -szczać
[fumes, sewage]; **to ~ out one's troubles** or **heart
to sb** otworzyć przed kimś serce

pout /paʊt/ *vi* wyd|ąć, -ymać wargi, na|dąsać się

poverty /'pɒvətɪ/ *n* bieda *f*, ubóstwo *n*; (more severe)
nędza *f*

poverty line *n* minimum *n* socjalne

poverty-stricken /'pɒvətɪstrɪkn/ *adj* dotknięty
ubóstwem

POW *n* = **prisoner of war** jeniec *m* wojenny

powder /'paʊdə(r)/ **II** *n* proszek *m*; (cosmetic)
puder *m*

II *vt* **to ~ one's face** upudrować sobie twarz

powdered /'paʊdəd/ *adj* *[egg, milk]* w proszku,
sproszkowany; *[coffee]* rozpuszczalny

powdery /'paʊdərɪ/ *adj* *[snow]* sypki; *[stone]*
miałki

power /'paʊə(r)/ **II** *n* [1] (control) władza *f*; **to be in
~** być u władzy; **to come to ~** dojść do władzy;
to be in sb's ~ być zdanym na czyjąś łaskę
(i niełaskę) [2] (influence) wpływ *m* (**over sb/sth** na
kogoś/coś); kontrola *f* (**over sb/sth** nad kimś/
czymś) [3] (capability) zdolność *f*; **I did everything
in my ~** zrobiłem wszystko, co w mojej mocy
[4] (also ~**s**) (authority) uprawnienia *n pl*, kompetencje *f pl* [5] (physical force) siła *f* [6] Tech energia *f*;
(current) prąd *m*; **switch on the ~** włącz prąd [7] (of
vehicle, plane) moc *f*; **to be running at full/half ~**
pracować pełną parą/na pół mocy [8] (in mathematics)
potęga *f*; **10 to the ~ of 3** 10 do trzeciej potęgi
[9] (country) mocarstwo *n*

II *adj* *[drill, cable]* elektryczny; *[brakes]* ze wspomaganiem

III vt zasilać [engine]; napędzać [boat, plane]
IDIOMS: **to do sb a ~ of good** bardzo dobrze komuś zrobić; **the ~s that be** ludzie sprawujący władzę; góra infml

powerboat /'pauəbəut/ n motorówka f, łódź f motorowa

power cut n przerwa f w dostawie energii elektrycznej

powerful /'pauəfl/ adj potężny; [argument] mocny; [emotion] silny; [smell, voice] silny, mocny

powerless /'pauələs/ adj bezsilny (**against sb/sth** wobec kogoś/czegoś); **to be ~ to do sth** nie być w stanie czegoś zrobić

power line n linia f wysokiego napięcia

power of attorney n pełnomocnictwo n

power sharing n dzielenie się n władzą

power station, power plant US n elektrownia f

power steering n układ m kierowniczy ze wspomaganiem

power user n Comput użytkownik m zaawansowany

PR n ① = **public relations** public relations plt inv ② → **proportional representation**

practical /'præktɪkl/ **I** n (exam) egzamin m praktyczny; (lesson) zajęcia plt praktyczne
II adj praktyczny; [plan] wykonalny

practicality /,præktɪ'kæləti/ n ① (of person) praktyczność f; (of equipment) funkcjonalność f ② (of project) wykonalność f; (of idea) realność f

practical joke n psikus m, figiel m

practically /'præktɪkli/ adv ① (almost) właściwie, niemal ② [consider, think] praktycznie; [say] roztropnie

practice /'præktɪs/ **I** n ① (exercises) ćwiczenia n pl; (experience) praktyka f; **to have had ~ in** or **at sth/ in** or **at doing sth** mieć doświadczenie w czymś/w robieniu czegoś; **to be out of ~** wyjść z wprawy ② (for sport) trening m ③ (procedure) zwyczaj m; **a standard ~** przyjęty sposób postępowania; **business ~** sposób prowadzenia interesów ④ (custom) obyczaj m ⑤ (of doctor, lawyer) praktyka f ⑥ (not theory) praktyka f; **in ~** w praktyce, w rzeczywistości
II adj [exam, test, run] próbny; [flight] treningowy
III vt, vi US = **practise**
IDIOMS: **~ makes perfect** Prov ćwiczenie czyni mistrza

practise GB, **practice** US /'præktɪs/ **I** vt ① prze|ćwiczyć [song]; wprawi|ć, -ać się w (czymś) [English]; przepowi|edzieć, -adać [speech]; z|robić próbę (czegoś) [play]; **to ~ the piano** grać wprawki na fortepianie ② (use) wypraktykow|ać, -ywać, za|stosować [method]; zachow|ać, -ywać [patience, restraint] ③ wyznawać [religion]; praktykować [custom]

II vi ① (at instrument) ćwiczyć; (for sport) trenować; (for play, concert) przygotowywać się ② (work) praktykować; **to ~ as a doctor/lawyer** praktykować jako lekarz/prawnik

practising GB, **practicing** US /'præktɪsɪŋ/ adj [Christian, doctor, lawyer] praktykujący; [homosexual] aktywny

pragmatic /præg'mætɪk/ adj pragmatyczny

pragmatist /'prægmətɪst/ n pragmatyk m

prairie /'preəri/ n preria f

praise /preɪz/ **I** n pochwała f
II vt ① po|chwalić, wychwalać; **to ~ sb for sth/ for doing sth** chwalić kogoś za coś/za zrobienie czegoś ② sławić, chwalić [God]

praiseworthy /'preɪzwɜ:ðɪ/ adj [person] godny pochwały or uznania; [deed] chwalebny

pram /præm/ n GB wózek m dziecięcy

prance /prɑ:ns, US præns/ vi [horse] bryk|nąć, -ać; [person] podskakiwać

prank /præŋk/ n figiel m, psikus m

prattle /'prætl/ vi paplać; [child] szczebiotać; **to ~ on about sth** paplać bez końca o czymś

prawn /prɔ:n/ n krewetka f

pray /preɪ/ vi po|modlić się (**for sth** o coś)

prayer /'preə(r)/ n modlitwa f; **to say one's ~s** modlić się

preach /pri:tʃ/ **I** vt wygł|osić, -aszać [sermon]; propagować [tolerance]
II vi wygł|osić, -aszać kazanie (**to sb** do kogoś); fig prawić kazania (**to** or **at sb** komuś)
IDIOMS: **to practise what one ~es** być w zgodzie z własnymi przekonaniami

preacher /'pri:tʃə(r)/ n kaznodzieja m

prearrange /,pri:ə'reɪndʒ/ vt przygotow|ać, -ywać [revolt, strike]; ustal|ić, -ać [time, place]

precarious /prɪ'keərɪəs/ adj [bridge, crossing] niebezpieczny; [position, grip, peace] niepewny

precaution /prɪ'kɔ:ʃn/ n zabezpieczenie n (**against sth** na wypadek czegoś)

precautionary /prɪ'kɔ:ʃənərɪ, US -nerɪ/ adj zapobiegawczy

precede /prɪ'si:d/ vt [event] poprzedz|ić, -ać; [person] iść przed (kimś/czymś); [vehicle] jechać przed (kimś/czymś)

precedence /'presɪdəns/ n pierwszeństwo n (**over sb/sth** przed kimś/czymś)

precedent /'presɪdənt/ n precedens m; **to set a ~** stworzyć precedens

preceding /prɪ'si:dɪŋ/ adj poprzedni

precinct /'pri:sɪŋkt/ n ① GB (also **shopping ~**) pasaż m handlowy (zamknięty dla ruchu kołowego) ② GB (also **pedestrian ~**) strefa f zamknięta dla ruchu kołowego ③ US (electoral) okręg m; (police) dystrykt m

precious /'preʃəs/ adj ① (valuable) cenny, drogocenny ② (held dear) [person, memory] drogi ③ (affected) afektowany

precipice /'presɪpɪs/ n urwisko n, przepaść f

précis /'preɪsiː, US preɪ'siː/ n streszczenie n

precise /prɪ'saɪs/ adj ① (exact) dokładny; *[definition, measurements]* precyzyjny ② (meticulous) *[person]* skrupulatny, precyzyjny

precisely /prɪ'saɪslɪ/ adv ① (exactly) dokładnie; **at two o'clock** ~ dokładnie o drugiej ② *[describe]* dokładnie, szczegółowo; *[measure, define]* precyzyjnie

precision /prɪ'sɪʒn/ n precyzja f, dokładność f

preclude /prɪ'kluːd/ vt wyklucz|yć, -ać *[possibility]*; uniemożliwi|ć, -ać *[action]*

precocious /prɪ'kəʊʃəs/ adj *[ability, talent]* wcześnie rozwinięty; *[age]* młody

preconceived /ˌpriːkən'siːvd/ adj *[idea, notion]* przyjęty z góry

preconception /ˌpriːkən'sepʃn/ n z góry przyjęty osąd m

precondition /ˌpriːkən'dɪʃn/ n konieczny warunek m

precursor /prɪ'kɜːsə(r)/ n (person) prekursor m, -ka f; (sign) zwiastun m

predate /ˌpriː'deɪt/ vt ① antydatować, opat|rzyć, -rywać wcześniejszą datą *[document]* ② poprzedz|ić, -ać *[event, discovery]*

predator /'predətə(r)/ n drapieżnik m

predecessor /'priːdɪsesə(r), US 'predə-/ n poprzedni|k m, -czka f

predetermine /ˌpriːdɪ'tɜːmɪn/ vt określ|ić, -ać z góry *[costs]*; ustal|ić, -ać zawczasu *[plan, signal]*

predicament /prɪ'dɪkəmənt/ n kłopotliwe położenie n

predict /prɪ'dɪkt/ vt przewi|dzieć, -dywać, przepowi|edzieć, -adać

predictable /prɪ'dɪktəbl/ adj przewidywalny, łatwy do przewidzenia

prediction /prɪ'dɪkʃn/ n przewidywanie n, przepowiednia f

predispose /ˌpriːdɪ'spəʊz/ vt ① (to job) predysponować; (to person) uspos|obić, -abiać ② (make liable) **to be** ~**d to sth** mieć skłonności do czegoś, być podatnym na coś *[illness]*

predominant /prɪ'dɒmɪnənt/ adj dominujący, przeważający

predominantly /prɪ'dɒmɪnəntlɪ/ adv w przeważającej mierze

predominate /prɪ'dɒmɪneɪt/ vi dominować

pre-eminent /ˌpriː'emɪnənt/ adj ① (distinguished) wybitny ② (leading) przodujący

pre-empt /ˌpriː'empt/ vt ① uprzedz|ić, -ać *[question, decision, move, person]* ② (thwart) udaremni|ć, -ać *[action, plan]*

pre-emptive /ˌpriː'emptɪv/ adj *[attack]* wyprzedzający

preen /priːn/ vr **to** ~ **oneself** *[bird]* czyścić sobie piórka; *[person]* odszykow|ać, -ywać się infml

prefab /'priːfæb, US ˌpriː'fæb/ n dom m z prefabrykatów

preface /'prefɪs/ n (to speech) wstęp m; (to book) przedmowa f, wstęp m

prefect /'priːfekt/ n GB Sch uczeń starszej klasy odpowiedzialny za dyscyplinę

prefer /prɪ'fɜː(r)/ vt ① (like better) woleć, preferować; **I** ~ **reading to watching TV** wolę czytać niż oglądać telewizję; **to** ~ **it if...** woleć, żeby... ② (in law) **to** ~ **charges** wn|ieść, -osić oskarżenie

preferable /'prefrəbl/ adj (better) lepszy (**to sth** od czegoś, niż coś); (more desirable) bardziej pożądany (**to sth** od czegoś, niż coś)

preferably /'prefrəblɪ/ adv najlepiej

preference /'prefrəns/ n preferencja f; **to have a** ~ **for sth** woleć coś; **to give** ~ **to sb** (**over sb**) dawać komuś pierwszeństwo (przed kimś)

preferential /ˌprefə'renʃl/ adj preferencyjny

prefigure /ˌpriː'fɪgə(r), US -gjər/ vt ① *[event]* zapowi|edzieć, -adać, wróżyć ② *[person]* przewi|dzieć, -dywać, wyobra|zić, -żać sobie

prefix /'priːfɪks/ n przedrostek m, prefiks m

pregnancy /'pregnənsɪ/ n ciąża f

pregnant /'pregnənt/ adj w ciąży, ciężarna; **to get sb** ~ infml zrobić komuś brzuch infml

preheat /ˌpriː'hiːt/ vt rozgrz|ać, -ewać, nagrz|ać, -ewać *[oven]*

prehistoric /ˌpriːhɪ'stɒrɪk, US -tɔːrɪk/ adj prehistoryczny, przedhistoryczny

prejudice /'predʒʊdɪs/ ❶ n uprzedzenie n (**against sb/sth** do kogoś/czegoś); **racial/political** ~ uprzedzenia rasowe/polityczne
❷ vt ① (bias) uprzedzi|ć, -ać (**against sb/sth** do kogoś/czegoś); **to** ~ **sb in favour of sb/sth** usposobić kogoś przychylnie do kogoś/czegoś ② (harm) przyn|ieść, -osić uszczerbek (czemuś) *[claim, case]*; s|krzywdzić *[person]*; zmniejsz|yć, -ać *[chances]*

prejudiced /'predʒʊdɪst/ adj *[person]* uprzedzony; *[opinion]* stronniczy; *[account]* tendencyjny

preliminary /prɪ'lɪmɪnərɪ, US -nerɪ/ ❶ n ① wstęp m; (spoken first) wstępna uwaga f ② Sport eliminacje f pl
❷ **preliminaries** npl preliminaria plt (**to sth** czegoś)
❸ adj wstępny

prelude /'preljuːd/ n preludium n (**to sth** do czegoś)

premarital /ˌpriː'mærɪtl/ adj *[sex]* przedmałżeński; *[contract]* przedślubny

premature /'premətjʊə(r), US ˌpriːmə'tʊər/ adj przedwczesny; **to be two weeks** ~ *[baby]* urodzić się dwa tygodnie przed terminem

premeditate /ˌpriː'medɪteɪt/ vt za|planować

premier /'premɪə(r), US 'priːmɪər/ ❶ n premier m
❷ adj główny

première /'premɪeə(r), US 'priːmɪər/ **I** *n* premiera *f*

II *vt* za|prezentować po raz pierwszy *[film, play]*

premises /'premɪsɪz/ *npl* (site) teren *m*; (building) nieruchomość *f*; (part of building) lokal *m*; (of firm) siedziba *f*; **on the** ~ na miejscu; **off the** ~ poza terenem/lokalem; **to leave the** ~ wyjść or opuścić lokal

premium /'priːmɪəm/ *n* ① (bonus) dodatkowa zapłata *f*; (for employees) premia *f* ② (on Stock Exchange) premia *f* ③ (in insurance) składka *f* ubezpieczeniowa ④ fig **to be at a** ~ być na wagę złota; **to set a (high)** ~ **on sth** wysoko cenić coś

premium bond *n* GB obligacja *f* pożyczki premiowej

premonition /ˌpriːmə'nɪʃn, ˌpre-/ *n* przeczucie *n*

prenatal /ˌpriː'neɪtl/ *adj* prenatalny

preoccupation /ˌpriːˌɒkjʊ'peɪʃn/ *n* (worry) troska *f* (**with sth** o coś); (absorption) zaabsorbowanie *n* (**with sth** czymś)

preoccupied /ˌpriː'ɒkjʊpaɪd/ *adj* (absorbed) zaabsorbowany; (worried) zatroskany

preoccupy /ˌpriː'ɒkjʊpaɪ/ *vt* absorbować, pochłaniać

prepaid /ˌpriː'peɪd/ *adj* opłacony (z góry); ~ **envelope** koperta zwrotna *(ze znaczkiem)*

preparation /ˌprepə'reɪʃn/ *n* przygotowanie *n*; **in** ~ **for sth** w oczekiwaniu czegoś or na coś

preparatory /prɪ'pærətrɪ, US -tɔːrɪ/ *adj [training, course, meeting]* przygotowawczy; *[report, investigations]* wstępny

preparatory school *n* ① GB prywatna szkoła *f* podstawowa ② US prywatne liceum *n*

prepare /prɪ'peə(r)/ **I** *vt* przygotow|ać, -ywać sporządz|ić, -ać *[report, medicine]*; przyrządz|ić, -ać *[meal]*; **to** ~ **to do sth** przygotować się do zrobienia czegoś

II *vi* **to** ~ **for sth** przygotow|ać, -ywać się do czegoś; **to** ~ **oneself** przygotowywać się

prepared /prɪ'peəd/ *adj* ① (willing) **to be** ~ **to do sth** być gotowym coś zrobić ② (ready) **to be** ~ **for sth** być przygotowanym na coś *[event]*; **to be** ~ **for the worst** być przygotowanym na najgorsze

preposition /ˌprepə'zɪʃn/ *n* przyimek *m*

preposterous /prɪ'pɒstərəs/ *adj [idea]* niedorzeczny; *[appearance]* groteskowy

prerequisite /ˌpriː'rekwɪzɪt/ *n* warunek *m* wstępny or zasadniczy (**of** or **for sth** czegoś)

prerogative /prɪ'rɒgətɪv/ *n* (official) prerogatywa *f*; (personal) prawo *n*, przywilej *m*

preschool /'priːskuːl/ **I** *n* US przedszkole *n*

II *adj [age, years]* przedszkolny; *[child]* w wieku przedszkolnym

prescribe /prɪ'skraɪb/ *vt* ① przepis|ać, -ywać, zapis|ać, -ywać *[drug]* (**for sb for sth** komuś na coś) ② ustan|owić, -awiać *[rule]*

prescription /prɪ'skrɪpʃn/ *n* recepta *f*; **'repeat** ~' „powtórzyć"

prescription charges *npl* zryczałtowana opłata *f* za realizację recepty

presence /'prezns/ *n* obecność *f*

presence of mind *n* przytomność *f* umysłu

present **I** /'preznt/ *n* ① (gift) prezent *m*, podarunek *m*, upominek *m* ② (now) **the** ~ teraźniejszość *f*; **for the** ~ na razie ③ (also ~ **tense**) czas *m* teraźniejszy

II /'preznt/ *adj* ① (attending) obecny (**at sth** na czymś) ② (current) obecny; **up to the** ~ **day** aż do dziś, do chwili obecnej

III /prɪ'zent/ *vt* wręcz|yć, -ać *[prize, certificate]* (**to sb** komuś); da|ć, -wać *[chance, opportunity]*; **to be** ~**ed with a choice** stanąć wobec konieczności wyboru

IV /prɪ'zent/ *vr* **to** ~ **oneself** staw|ić, -ać się; **to** ~ **itself** *[thought]* pojawi|ć, -ać się; *[opportunity]* zdarz|yć, -ać się; trafi|ć, -ać się

V **at present** *adv phr* (at this moment) teraz, w tej chwili; (nowadays) zatroskie

presentable /prɪ'zentəbl/ *adj* przyzwoity, porządny

presentation /ˌprezən'teɪʃn/ *n* ① (of plan, petition) przedstawienie *n*; (of identification, cheque) okazanie *n*, przedłożenie *n* ② (talk) prezentacja *f* ③ (of gift, award) wręczenie *n*

present-day /ˌprezənt'deɪ/ *adj* obecny, współczesny

presenter /prɪ'zentə(r)/ *n* prezenter *m*, -ka *f*

presently /'prezntlɪ/ *adv* ① (currently) obecnie ② (soon, in future) niebawem, wkrótce

present perfect *n* czas *m* teraźniejszy dokonany

preservation /ˌprezə'veɪʃn/ *n* (of wildlife) ochrona *f*; (of peace) utrzymanie *n*; (of building) konserwacja *f*; (of food) konserwowanie *n*

preservative /prɪ'zɜːvətɪv/ *n* środek *m* konserwujący; (for food) konserwant *m*

preserve /prɪ'zɜːv/ **I** *n* ① Culin (jam) dżem *m*, marmolada *f*; (very sweet) konfitura *f*; (pickle) marynata *f* ② (sphere) domena *f*

II *vt* ① (save) zachow|ać, -ywać, ocal|ić, -ać *[land, building, tradition]*; zabezpiecz|yć, -ać, za|konserwować *[wood, leather]* ② (maintain) zachow|ać, -ywać *[peace, standards, health, humour]*; utrzym|ać, -ywać *[order]* ③ za|konserwować *[food]*

preset /ˌpriː'set/ *vt* włącz|yć, -ać (wcześniej) *[oven]*; nastaw|ić, -ać *[video]*

preside /prɪ'zaɪd/ *vi* przewodniczyć (**at** or **over sth** czemuś)

presidency /'prezɪdənsɪ/ *n* prezydentura *f*; (in EU) prezydencja *f*; US (of company) prezesura *f*

president /'prezɪdənt/ *n* ① prezydent *m*; **to run for** ~ ubiegać się o urząd prezydenta ② US (of company) prezes *m*; (of society) przewodnicząc|y *m*, -a *f*

presidential /ˌprezɪ'denʃl/ adj [election] prezydencki; [candidate] na prezydenta; [adviser, office]
prezydenta

press /pres/ **Ⅰ** n ① (newspapers, journals) **the ~, the
Press** prasa f; **to get a good/bad ~** mieć dobrą/
złą prasę ②; (also **printing ~**) maszyna f drukar-
ska, prasa f; **in (the) ~** w druku ③ (for flattening)
prasa f

Ⅱ vt ① (push) nacis|nąć, -kać; przycis|nąć, -kać; **to
~ sth in** wcisnąć coś; **to ~ one's nose against
the window** przycisnąć nos do szyby ② (squeeze)
wycis|nąć, -kać [lemon, orange]; ścis|nąć, -kać [arm,
hand] ③ (iron) wy|prasować, u|prasować [clothes]
④ (urge) naciskać na (kogoś) [person]; forsować
[issue]; **to ~ sb to do sth** naciskać na kogoś, żeby
coś zrobił; **to ~ a point** upierać się przy (jakiejś)
kwestii

Ⅲ vi ① (with hand, foot) **to ~ (down) on sth**
przycisnąć coś ② [crowd, person] s|tłoczyć się; **to
~ forward** przeć do przodu

Ⅳ vr **to ~ oneself against sb/sth** przylgnąć do
kogoś/czegoś

■ **press for**: domagać się (czegoś); **to be ~ed
for time/cash** mieć niewiele czasu/gotówki

■ **press on**: nie ustawać; **to ~ on with sth** posuwać do przodu coś [reform, plan]

press agency n agencja f prasowa

press conference n konferencja f prasowa

pressing /'presɪŋ/ adj ① (urgent) pilny, niecierpią-
cy zwłoki ② [invitation] natarczywy

press release n komunikat m prasowy

press-stud /'presstʌd/ n GB zatrzask m

press-up /'presʌp/ n pompka f (ćwiczenie gimnastyczne)

pressure /'preʃə(r)/ n ① ciśnienie n; fig nacisk m,
presja f; **to put ~ on sb** wywierać na kogoś presję;
to do sth under ~ zrobić coś pod presją ② (of
tourists) napór m; **~ of traffic** wzmożony ruch
drogowy

pressure cooker n szybkowar m

pressure group n grupa f nacisku

pressurize /'preʃəraɪz/ vt ① utrzym|ać, -ywać
zwiększone ciśnienie w (czymś) [cabin, suit]; sprę-
ż|yć, -ać [gas] ② wpły|nąć, -wać na (kogoś); **to ~ sb
into doing sth** wpłynąć na kogoś, żeby coś zrobił;
(stronger) zmusić kogoś do zrobienia czegoś

prestige /pre'stiːʒ/ n prestiż m

prestigious /pre'stɪdʒəs/ adj [award, job] prestiżowy; [school] renomowany; [name] znakomity

presumably /prɪ'zjuːməblɪ, US -'zuːm-/ adv przy-
puszczalnie

presume /prɪ'zjuːm, US -'zuːm/ vt ① (suppose)
sądzić, przypuszczać ② (dare) **to ~ to do sth**
ośmielić się coś zrobić

presumptuous /prɪ'zʌmptʃʊəs/ adj arogancki,
bezczelny

presuppose /ˌpriːsə'pəʊz/ vt z góry przyj|ąć,
-mować; **to ~ that...** zakładać, że...

pre-tax /ˌpriː'tæks/ adj brutto, przed opodatkowa-
niem

pretence GB, **pretense** US /prɪ'tens/ n pozory
m pl; **to make a ~ of sth** stwarzać pozory czegoś;
to make a ~ of doing sth udawać, że się coś robi

pretend /prɪ'tend/ **Ⅰ** vt uda|ć, -wać; **to ~ that...**
udawać, że...; **to ~ to do sth** udawać, że się coś
robi

Ⅱ vi udawać

pretension /prɪ'tenʃn/ n pretensja f

pretentious /prɪ'tenʃəs/ adj pretensjonalny

preterite /'pretərət/ n czas m przeszły

pretext /'priːtekst/ n pretekst m

pretty /'prɪtɪ/ **Ⅰ** adj ładny, śliczny; **it was not a
~ sight** to nie był miły widok

Ⅱ adv infml [good, clever, certain, well] całkiem;
[awful, bad, boring, stupid] dosyć, dość

prevail /prɪ'veɪl/ vi ① (win) zwycięż|yć, -ać; **to ~
against sb/sth** wziąć górę nad kimś/czymś ② (be
common) [situation, confusion, custom] panować;
(predominate) [sunshine, attitude] przeważać

■ **prevail upon**: nakł|onić, -aniać

prevailing /prɪ'veɪlɪŋ/ adj [custom, attitude] panujący; [wind] przeważający; [rate] aktualny

prevalent /'prevələnt/ adj ① (widespread) szeroko
rozpowszechniony ② (predominant) przeważający,
dominujący

prevaricate /prɪ'værɪkeɪt/ vi wykręcać się od
jasnej odpowiedzi

prevent /prɪ'vent/ vt zapobie|c, -gać (czemuś); **to
~ the marriage** [person] nie dopuścić do małżeń-
stwa; [circumstance] stanąć na przeszkodzie małżeń-
stwu; **to ~ sb (from) doing sth** uniemożliwić
komuś zrobienie czegoś

preventable /prɪ'ventəbl/ adj (możliwy) do unik-
nięcia

prevention /prɪ'venʃn/ n zapobieganie n; **crime
~** walka z przestępczością

preventive /prɪ'ventɪv/ adj zapobiegawczy, profi-
laktyczny

preview /'priːvjuː/ n (of film, play) pokaz m przedpremierowy

previous /'priːvɪəs/ adj poprzedni; (further back in
time) wcześniejszy

previously /'priːvɪəslɪ/ adv ① (formerly) poprzednio; (up until that time) przedtem ② (earlier) wcześniej

prewar /ˌpriː'wɔː(r)/ adj przedwojenny

prey /preɪ/ n (hunted) ofiara f; (captured) zdobycz f,
łup m

■ **prey on**: ① (hunt) polować na (coś) ② (worry) **to
~ on sb's mind** dręczyć kogoś, nie dawać komuś
spokoju ③ (exploit) wykorzyst|ać, -ywać [fears,
worries]

price /praɪs/ **Ⅰ** n ① (cost) cena f, koszt m; **cars
have gone up in ~** ceny samochodów wzrosły; **to**

pay a high ~ **for sth** drogo zapłacić za coś; **at any** ~ za każdą cenę; *fig* za wszelką cenę ②(value) wartość *f*; **to put a** ~ **on sth** wycenić coś *[object, antique]*

Ⅱ *vt* okreś|lić, -ać cenę (czegoś); **a dress** ~**d at £30** sukienka w cenie 30 funtów

price cut *n* obniżka *f* ceny

price freeze *n* zamrożenie *n* cen

priceless /'praɪslɪs/ *adj* ① (extremely valuable) bezcenny; *[person]* nieoceniony ② *infml* (amusing) *[joke, speech]* przepyszny *infml*

price list *n* cennik *m*

price rise *n* wzrost *m* ceny

price tag *n* metka *f* z ceną; cena *f infml*

price war *n* wojna *f* cenowa

prick /prɪk/ **Ⅰ** *n* (of needle) (pain) ukłucie *n*; (hole) nakłucie *n*

Ⅱ *vt* u|kłuć; **to** ~ **one's finger** ukłuć się w palec
Ⅲ *vi* ① (sting) szczypać ② *[bush, thorn]* kłuć
■ **prick up**: **to** ~ **up its ears** *[dog]* postawić uszy; **to** ~ **up one's ears** *[person]* nadstawić ucha or uszu

prickle /'prɪkl/ **Ⅰ** *n* (of hedgehog, plant) kolec *m*
Ⅱ *vi* **my hair** ~**d (with fear)** włosy mi się zjeżyły (ze strachu)

prickly /'prɪklɪ/ *adj* ① *[bush]* ciernisty, kolczasty; *[leaf, thorn]* kłujący; *[animal]* kolczasty ② (itchy) *[beard]* kłujący, drapiący; *[jumper]* gryzący, drapiący ③ *infml* (touchy) drażliwy

pride /praɪd/ **Ⅰ** *n* ① duma *f*, chluba *f*; **to be sb's** ~ **and joy** być czyjąś dumą i radością; **to take** ~ **in sth** być dumnym z czegoś ② (of lions) stado *n*
Ⅱ *vr* **to** ~ **oneself on sth** szczycić się or chlubić się czymś
(IDIOMS) **to have** ~ **of place** zajmować honorowe or poczesne miejsce

priest /priːst/ *n* ① kapłan *m*; (Roman Catholic) ksiądz *m*; (in Orthodox church) pop *m*; **parish** ~ proboszcz

priesthood /'priːsthʊd/ *n* kapłaństwo *n*; **to enter the** ~ wstąpić do stanu duchownego

prig /prɪg/ *n* skromni|ś *m*, -sia *f*

prim /prɪm/ *adj* (also ~ **and proper**) (prudish) *[person]* pruderyjny; (formal) *[person, manner]* sztywny; *[appearance, clothing]* wymuskany; *[voice, expression]* afektowany

primarily /'praɪmərəlɪ, US praɪ'merəlɪ/ *adv* (chiefly) głównie, przede wszystkim; (originally) pierwotnie

primary /'praɪmərɪ, US -merɪ/ **Ⅰ** *n* US (also ~ **election**) prawybory *plt*
Ⅱ *adj* ① (main) główny; *[sense, meaning]* podstawowy; **of** ~ **importance** o zasadniczym or pierwszorzędnym znaczeniu ② *[education]* podstawowy ③ *[industry, products]* podstawowy

primary colour GB, **primary color** US *n* barwa *f* podstawowa

primary school *n* ≈ szkoła *f* podstawowa

primary (school) teacher *n* GB nauczyciel *m*, -ka *f* szkoły podstawowej

primate /'praɪmeɪt/ *n* ① (mammal) naczelny *m*, ssak *m* z rzędu naczelnych ② (archbishop) prymas *m*

prime /praɪm/ **Ⅰ** *n* **in one's** ~ (professionally) u szczytu kariery; (physically) w kwiecie wieku; **in its** ~ *[organization, industry]* w rozkwicie; **to be past its** ~ mieć już za sobą okres świetności
Ⅱ *adj* ① (chief) główny; *[importance]* fundamentalny ② (good quality) *[site, meat]* pierwszorzędny, doskonały; *[foodstuffs]* wyborowy; **of** ~ **quality** najwyższej jakości ③ *[example]* klasyczny, typowy
Ⅲ *vt* ① (brief) po|instruować, przygotow|ać, -ywać; **to** ~ **sb about sth** uprzedzić kogoś o czymś ② Tech zal|ać, -ewać *[pump]* ③ Mil uzbr|oić, -ajać *[device, bomb]*; nabi|ć, -jać, załadow|ać, -ywać *[firearm]*

prime minister, PM *n* premier *m*

prime mover *n* **to be the** ~ **of sth** *[person]* być motorem czegoś

prime number *n* liczba *f* pierwsza

prime time *n* (on TV) godziny *f pl* największej oglądalności; (on radio) najlepsze godziny *f pl* antenowe

primeval /praɪ'miːvl/ *adj* *[beast, tribes, rocks]* prastary; *[condition, forest]* pierwotny; *[instinct, terror]* prymitywny

primitive /'prɪmɪtɪv/ **Ⅰ** *n* (painter) prymitywista *m*; (painting) prymityw *m*
Ⅱ *adj* prymitywny

primrose /'prɪmrəʊz/ *n* pierwiosnek *m*, pierwiosnka *f*

prince /prɪns/ *n* książę *m*

princess /prɪn'ses/ *n* (daughter) księżniczka *f*; (wife) księżna *f*

principal /'prɪnsəpl/ **Ⅰ** *n* dyrektor *m*, -ka *f* szkoły
Ⅱ *adj* główny

principle /'prɪnsəpl/ *n* zasada *f*; (scientific) prawo *n*, reguła *f*; **in** ~ w zasadzie; **on** ~ dla zasady

print /prɪnt/ **Ⅰ** *n* ① (typeface) czcionka *f*, druk *m*; **the small** or **fine** ~ *fig* drobny druk; **in** ~ (published) wydany drukiem, opublikowany; (available) dostępny (na rynku); **the book is out of** ~ nakład książki jest wyczerpany ② (engraving) grafika *f*, rycina *f*; (etching) sztych *m* ③ (of photo) odbitka *f* ④ (of foot, finger, tyre) ślad *m* ⑤ (fabric) tkanina *f* drukowana
Ⅱ *vt* ① wy|drukować *[book, banknote, design]* ② (publish) o|publikować ③ z|robić odbitkę z (czegoś) *[photos]* ④ (write) na|pisać (starannym pismem)
■ **print off**: z|robić *[copies]*
■ **print out**: wy|drukować

printer /'prɪntə(r)/ *n* (person) drukarz *m*; (firm) drukarnia *f*; (machine) drukarka *f*

printout /'prɪntaʊt/ *n* wydruk *m*

print-preview /'prɪntpriːvjuː/ n Comput podgląd m wydruku

prior /'praɪə(r)/ **❶** adj ① (previous) wcześniejszy; **to give ~ notice** powiadomić wcześniej ② (more important) mający pierwszeństwo **❷ prior to** prep phr przed (czymś)

priority /praɪ'ɒrəti, US -'ɔːr-/ n priorytet m

priory /'praɪəri/ n klasztor m

prise /praɪz/ vt
■ **prise apart**: rozdziel|ić, -ać [layers, people]
■ **prise off**: podważ|yć, -ać [lid]
■ **prise open**: otw|orzyć, -ierać (siłą)

prism /'prɪzəm/ n ① (glass) pryzmat m ② (in geometry) graniastosłup m

prison /'prɪzn/ n więzienie n; **to put sb in ~** uwięzić kogoś

prisoner /'prɪznə(r)/ n (in jail) wię|zień m, -źniarka f; (in custody) areszt|owan|y m, -a f, aresztant m

prison officer n (officially) oficer m więziennictwa; (guard) strażnik m więzienny, strażniczka f więzienna

prison sentence n kara f pozbawienia wolności, kara f więzienia

pristine /'prɪstiːn, 'prɪstaɪn/ adj [whiteness] nieskazitelny; [cloth] nieskazitelnie czysty

privacy /'prɪvəsi, 'praɪ-/ n ① (private life) prywatność f; **to invade sb's ~** zakłócać życie prywatne kogoś ② (solitude) zacisze n, odosobnienie n

private /'praɪvɪt/ **❶** n (soldier) szeregowy m **❷** adj prywatny; **room with ~ bath** pokój z łazienką **❸ in private** adv phr **she told me in ~** powiedziała mi w zaufaniu; **to talk in ~** porozmawiać bez świadków

private eye n infml prywatny detektyw m

privately /'praɪvɪtli/ adv ① (not publicly) prywatnie; **~-owned** prywatny ② (in one's own heart) w głębi serca, w głębi duszy

privatization /ˌpraɪvɪtaɪ'zeɪʃn, US -tɪ'z-/ n prywatyzacja f

privatize /'praɪvɪtaɪz/ vt s|prywatyzować

privilege /'prɪvəlɪdʒ/ n przywilej m

privileged /'prɪvəlɪdʒd/ adj ① [minority, position] uprzywilejowany ② [information] objęty tajemnicą zawodową

prize /praɪz/ **❶** n ① (award) nagroda f; (in lottery) wygrana f; **first ~** pierwsza nagroda; (in lottery) główna wygrana ② (valued object) łakomy kąsek m; (reward for effort) nagroda f **❷** adj ① [pupil] wzorowy; [vegetable, bull] (award-winning) nagrodzony ② [possession] cenny ③ [idiot] kompletny; **a ~ example of sth** klasyczny przykład czegoś

prize draw n losowanie n nagród

prize-giving /'praɪzgɪvɪŋ/ n wręczenie n or rozdanie n nagród

prize money n (for one prize) wygrana f; (total amount given out) pula f nagród

prizewinner /'praɪzwɪnə(r)/ n (in lottery) zdobyw|ca m, -czyni f nagrody; (of award) laureat m, -ka f

pro /prəʊ/ **❶** n ① infml (professional) zawodowiec m ② (advantage) **the ~s and cons** za i przeciw; **the ~s and cons of sth** wszystko, co przemawia za i przeciw czemuś; zalety i wady czegoś **❷** prep infml (in favor of) za (kimś/czymś)

proactive /prəʊ'æktɪv/ adj aktywny, czynny

probability /ˌprɒbə'bɪləti/ n ① (likelihood) prawdopodobieństwo n; ② (desirable) szansa f, widoki plt; (undesirable) niebezpieczeństwo n, ryzyko n

probable /'prɒbəbl/ adj prawdopodobny

probably /'prɒbəbli/ adv prawdopodobnie

probation /prə'beɪʃn, US prəʊ-/ n ① (in law) nadzór m kuratorski, dozór m sądowy ② (trial period) okres m próbny

probationary /prə'beɪʃnri, US prəʊ'beɪʃənəri/ adj ① (trial) [period, year] próbny ② (training) [period] przygotowawczy

probation officer n kurator m sądowy

probe /prəʊb/ **❶** n ① (investigation) śledztwo n, dochodzenie n ② (instrument) sonda f **❷** vt Med, Tech z|badać, sondować

probing /'prəʊbɪŋ/ adj [look] sondujący; [examination] dociekliwy

problem /'prɒbləm/ **❶** n ① (difficulty) problem m, kłopot m; **what's the ~?** o co chodzi? ② (in mathematics, logic) zadanie n; **to solve a ~** rozwiązać zadanie **❷** adj [child] trudny; [family] z problemami

problematic(al) /ˌprɒblə'mætɪk(l)/ adj (difficult) skomplikowany; (uncertain) problematyczny

problem page n kącik m porad

procedure /prə'siːdʒə(r)/ n sposób m postępowania, procedura f

proceed /prə'siːd, prəʊ-/ vi ① (act) post|ąpić, -ępować; (continue) kontynuować; **to ~ with sth** przystąpić do realizacji czegoś ② (be in progress) [work, interview, talks] przebie|c, -gać, odby|ć, -wać się; [trial] toczyć się ③ [person] pójść, iść dalej; [vehicle] po|jechać dalej; [road] ciągnąć się, biec

proceedings /prə'siːdɪŋz/ npl ① (meeeting, discussion) obrady plt; (ceremony) uroczystości f pl, obchody plt ② (in law) postępowanie n

proceeds /'prəʊsiːdz/ npl (of sale) dochód m; (of event) wpływy plt

process /'prəʊses, US 'prɒses/ **❶** n ① przebieg m, proces m; **to be in the ~ of doing sth** być w trakcie robienia czegoś, właśnie coś robić; **in the ~** przy okazji, równocześnie ② (method) proces m, metoda f **❷** vt ① rozpat|rzyć, -rywać [applications, complaints] ② przetw|orzyć, -arzać, przer|obić, -abiać [raw material, chemical, waste] ③ wywoł|ać, -ywać [film] ④ Culin (mix) z|miksować; (chop) po|siekać

processing /'prəʊsesɪŋ, US 'prɒ-/ n przetwarzanie n; **the food ~ industry** przetwórstwo spożywcze, przemysł przetwórczy

procession /prə'seʃn/ n (demonstration) pochód m; (carnival) parada f; (religious) procesja f

processor /'prəʊsesə(r), US 'prɒ-/ n Comput procesor m

proclaim /prə'kleɪm/ vt ogł|osić, -aszać [war, good news]; proklamować [independence, republic]

proclamation /ˌprɒklə'meɪʃn/ n proklamacja f, oświadczenie n

procrastinate /prəʊ'kræstɪneɪt/ vi zwlekać

procure /prə'kjʊə(r)/ vt wystarać się o (coś) (**for sb** dla kogoś)

prod /prɒd/ **I** n ① (poke) szturchnięcie n ② (stimulus) **to give sb a ~** zdopingować or zmobilizować kogoś

II vt (also **~ at**) szturch|nąć, -ać; (lightly) trąc|ić, -ać; (with fork) dźg|nąć, -ać

prodigy /'prɒdɪdʒɪ/ n ① (person) wyjątkowy talent m ② (wonder) cud m

produce I /'prɒdjuːs, US -duːs/ n produkty m pl rolne

II /prə'djuːs, US -'duːs/ vt ① (cause) s|powodować, wywoł|ać, -ywać [reaction]; przyn|ieść, -osić [effect, result]; doprowadz|ić, -ać do (czegoś) [change] ② wy|produkować, wytw|orzyć, -arzać [goods] ③ (present) okaz|ać, -ywać [passport, ticket]; przedstawi|ć, -ać [evidence, argument, report]; **to ~ sth from one's pocket** wyjąć coś z kieszeni ④ z|realizować [film, show]; GB wystawi|ć, -ać [play] ⑤ (put together) wyda|ć, -wać [brochure, guidebook]; opracow|ać, -ywać [timetable]; przyrządz|ić, -ać, przygotow|ać, -ywać [meal]; przedstawi|ć, -ać [solution]

producer /prə'djuːsə(r), US -'duːs-/ n ① (of food, machinery, goods) producent m ② (of film) realizator m, -ka f; (in charge of funds) producent m, -ka f; GB (of play) reżyser m

product /'prɒdʌkt/ n produkt m, wyrób m

production /prə'dʌkʃn/ n ① (of goods) produkcja f ② (of film) realizacja f; (of play) inscenizacja f

production line n linia f produkcyjna

productive /prə'dʌktɪv/ adj [factory] wydajny, produktywny; [land] urodzajny; [methods, efforts] efektywny; [discussion, period] owocny

productivity /ˌprɒdʌk'tɪvətɪ/ n (of labour) wydajność f; (of land) żyzność f

profane /prə'feɪn, US prəʊ'feɪn/ adj ① (blasphemous) bluźnierczy ② (secular) świecki

profession /prə'feʃn/ n zawód m

professional /prə'feʃənl/ **I** n profesjonalist|a m, -ka f; (in sport) zawodowiec m

II adj [duty, experience, dancer, soldier] zawodowy; [advice, help, person] fachowy

professionalism /prə'feʃənəlɪzəm/ n profesjonalizm m

professionally /prə'feʃənəlɪ/ adv ① (expertly) profesjonalnie, fachowo ② (in work situation) służbowo ③ [play sport, sing] zawodowo

professor /prə'fesə(r)/ n ① Univ (title) profesor m; (chair holder) kierownik m katedry ② US Univ (teacher) nauczyciel m akademicki

proficiency /prə'fɪʃnsɪ/ n biegłość f (**at** or **in sth** w czymś); sprawność f (**at doing sth** w robieniu czegoś)

proficient /prə'fɪʃnt/ adj biegły

profile /'prəʊfaɪl/ n (of face) profil m; (of body) sylwetka f; **in ~** z profilu; **to have** or **maintain a high ~** być bardzo widocznym, odgrywać ważną rolę

profit /'prɒfɪt/ **I** n ① zysk m, dochód m; **gross/net ~** zysk brutto/netto ② fig (benefit) korzyść f, pożytek m

II vt opłac|ić, -ać się (komuś), przyn|ieść, -osić korzyści (komuś)

III vi **to ~ by** or **from sth** odn|ieść, -osić korzyść z czegoś

profitable /'prɒfɪtəbl/ adj [company] rentowny, dochodowy; [investment] zyskowny; [deal] intratny, opłacalny; fig [meeting, negotiations] owocny; [day] pożytecznie spędzony

profit margin n marża f zysku

profit sharing n podział m zysków, udział m w zyskach

profound /prə'faʊnd/ adj [remark, contempt] głęboki; [knowledge, change] gruntowny; [thinker] wnikliwy; [silence] przenikliwy; [emotion, influence] przemożny; [ignorance] całkowity, zupełny

profuse /prə'fjuːs/ adj [growth, bleeding] obfity; [thanks] wylewny

profusely /prə'fjuːslɪ/ adv [bleed, sweat] obficie; [thank] wylewnie; **to apologize ~** przepraszać z całego serca or gorąco

prognosis /prɒg'nəʊsɪs/ n ① Med rokowanie n (**on** or **about sb/sth** co do kogoś/czegoś) ② (prediction) prognoza f

program /'prəʊgræm, US -grəm/ **I** n ① Comput program m ② US (on radio, TV) program m

II vt za|programować

III vi programować

programme GB, **program** US /'prəʊgræm, US -grəm/ **I** n ① (broadcast) program m; (on radio) audycja f ② (schedule) program m; (for the day) rozkład m zajęć or dnia ③ (for play, opera) program m

II vt nastawi|ć, -ać [machine]

programmer GB, **programer** US /'prəʊgræmə(r), US -grəm-/ n programist|a m, -ka f

progress I /'prəʊgres, US 'prɒgres/ n ① (advances) postęp m; **to make ~** robić postępy ② (of person) posuwanie się n; (of disease, career, talks) przebieg m; **to be in ~** trwać, być w toku

II /prə'gres/ vi [society, technology] rozwi|nąć, -jać się; [work] posu|nąć, -wać się do przodu; [person]

z|robić postępy; *[patient]* po|czuć się lepiej; **to ~ towards sth** zmierzać ku czemuś

progression /prə'greʃn/ *n* [1] (development) rozwój *m*; (of student, worker) postępy *m pl*; (of patient) poprawa *f* (stanu zdrowia) [2] (of hills, events) łańcuch *m*, pasmo *n*

progressive /prə'gresɪv/ *adj* [1] *[change, improvement, illness]* postępujący [2] (radical) postępowy; *[school]* nowoczesny

progress report *n* (on construction work) raport *m* o stanie robót; (on project) sprawozdanie *n* z realizacji projektu; (on patient) biuletyn *m* o stanie zdrowia

prohibit /prə'hɪbɪt, US prəʊ-/ *vt* zakaz|ać, -ywać (komuś), zabr|onić, -aniać (komuś); **to ~ sb from doing sth** zakazać or zabronić komuś coś robić

prohibition /ˌprəʊhɪ'bɪʃn, US ˌprəʊə'bɪʃn/ *n* zakaz *m* (**on** or **against sth** czegoś)

prohibitive /prə'hɪbətɪv, US prəʊ-/ *adj [cost]* ogromny; *[price]* wyśrubowany

project [I] /'prɒdʒekt/ *n* [1] (scheme) projekt *m*, plan *m*, przedsięwzięcie *n*; (construction) inwestycja *f* [2] Sch, Univ praca *f* (**on sth** na temat czegoś, dotycząca czegoś) [3] US (state housing) ≈ osiedle *n* domów komunalnych

[II] /prə'dʒekt/ *vt* [1] wystrzel|ić, -ać *[missile]*; **to ~ one's voice** mówić głośno i wyraźnie [2] (transfer) przen|ieść, -osić *[guilt, anxiety]* (**onto sb/sth** na kogoś/coś) [3] (estimate) określ|ić, -ać *[figures, rate]*; przewi|dzieć, -dywać *[results]* [4] rzuc|ić, -ać *[image]*; wyświetl|ić, -ać *[slides]*

projecting /prə'dʒektɪŋ/ *adj* sterczący, wystający

projector /prə'dʒektə(r)/ *n* projektor *m*

pro-life /ˌprəʊ'laɪf/ *adj* opowiadający się za zakazem przerywania ciąży

proliferate /prə'lɪfəreɪt, US prəʊ-/ *vi [pubs, hotels]* namnożyć się; *[nuclear weapons]* rozprzestrzeni|ć, -ać się

prolific /prə'lɪfɪk/ *adj [author, decade]* płodny; *[growth]* bujny

prologue /'prəʊlɒg, US -lɔːg/ *n* prolog *m* (**to sth** czegoś)

prolong /prə'lɒŋ, US -'lɔːŋ/ *vt* przedłuż|yć, -ać

promenade /ˌprɒmə'nɑːd, US -'neɪd/ *n* promenada *f*

prominent /'prɒmɪnənt/ *adj [person, figure, role]* znaczący; *[artist]* wybitny; *[feature]* rzucający się w oczy; *[place]* widoczny; *[nose]* wydatny; *[eye]* wyłupiasty; *[teeth, ridge]* wystający

promiscuity /ˌprɒmɪ'skjuːəti/ *n* swoboda *f* seksualna

promiscuous /prə'mɪskjʊəs/ *adj* prowadzący bogate życie seksualne

promise /'prɒmɪs/ [I] *n* obietnica *f*, przyrzeczenie *n*; **to break one's ~** złamać obietnicę or przyrzeczenie; **she shows great ~** ona zapowiada się bardzo dobrze

[II] *vt* obiec|ać, -ywać, przyrze|c, -kać; **to ~ sb sth** obiecać or przyrzec coś komuś

[III] *vi* obiec|ać, -ywać, przyrze|c, -kać; **do you ~?** obiecujesz?

promising /'prɒmɪsɪŋ/ *adj [pupil, writer]* obiecujący, dobrze się zapowiadający; *[situation, result]* rokujący nadzieje; *[sign]* dobry

promote /prə'məʊt/ *vt* [1] (in rank) awansować, przen|ieść, -osić na wyższe stanowisko [2] (advertise) promować *[product]*; propagować *[theory]* [3] (encourage) działać na rzecz (czegoś) [4] GB (in football) **to be ~d from the fourth to the third division** awansować z czwartej do trzeciej ligi

promotion /prə'məʊʃn/ *n* [1] (of employee) awans *m* [2] (of product) promocja *f*, kampania *f* promocyjna; (of research) wspieranie *n*; (of trade) pobudzanie *n*

promotional video *n* wideoklip *m*

prompt /prɒmpt/ [I] *adj* natychmiastowy, szybki; **to be ~ to do sth** zrobić coś natychmiast or bezzwłocznie

[II] *vt* [1] (cause) s|powodować, do|prowadzić do (czegoś), s|prowokować *[action, remark]*; wywoł|ać, -ywać *[feeling]*; **to ~ sb to do sth** skłonić kogoś do zrobienia czegoś [2] (remind) podpowi|edzieć, -adać (komuś) *[actor]*

prompter /'prɒmptə(r)/ *n* [1] (in theatre) sufler *m*, -ka *f* [2] US (teleprompter) teleprompter *m*

promptly /'prɒmptlɪ/ *adv* [1] (immediately) natychmiast, szybko [2] (without delay) natychmiast, bezzwłocznie [3] (punctually) punktualnie, dokładnie; **at six o'clock** punktualnie or dokładnie o szóstej

prone /prəʊn/ *adj* [1] **to be ~ to sth** mieć skłonność do czegoś *[colds, depression]*; być podatnym na coś *[disease, infection]* [2] **to lie ~** leżeć na brzuchu

pronoun /'prəʊnaʊn/ *n* zaimek *m*

pronounce /prə'naʊns/ *vt* wym|ówić, -awiać *[word, letter]*

■ **pronounce on:** wypowi|edzieć, -adać się na temat (czegoś)

pronounced /prə'naʊnst/ *adj [accent, tendency, difference]* wyraźny; *[feature]* wyrazisty

pronunciation /prəˌnʌnsɪ'eɪʃn/ *n* wymowa *f*

proof /pruːf/ *n* [1] (evidence) dowód *m*; **~ of identity** dowód tożsamości [2] (in printing) odbitka *f* korektorska; korekta *f* infml; (in photography) odbitka *f* próbna [3] (of alcohol) **to be 70% ~** mieć 40%

proofread /'pruːfriːd/ *vt* (check copy) sprawdz|ić, -ać; (check proofs) z|robić korektę (czegoś)

prop /prɒp/ [I] *n* podpora *f*

[II] **props** *npl* rekwizyty *m pl*

[III] *vt* [1] (also ~ **up**) pod|eprzeć, -pierać [2] (lean) op|rzeć, -ierać (**against sth** o coś)

propaganda /ˌprɒpə'gændə/ *n* propaganda *f*

propagate /'prɒpəgeɪt/ [I] *vt* [1] rozmn|ożyć, -ażać *[plant]* [2] propagować *[idea]*

[II] *vi [plant]* rozmnażać się

propel /prə'pel/ *vt* wprawi|ć, -ać w ruch
propeller /prə'pelə(r)/ *n* (in plane) śmigło *n*; (in ship) śruba *f* napędowa
proper /'prɒpə(r)/ *adj* ⟨1⟩ (correct) właściwy; *[spelling]* poprawny; *[clothing, tool]* odpowiedni; **everything is in the ~ place** wszystko jest na swoim miejscu ⟨2⟩ (adequate) *[training, education]* odpowiedni; *[recognition]* należny; *[care, control]* należyty, odpowiedni ⟨3⟩ (respectable) *[person]* dobrze wychowany, układny; *[upbringing]* staranny ⟨4⟩ (real, full) *[doctor, holiday]* prawdziwy; *[holiday, job]* porządny ⟨5⟩ (actual) **in the village ~** w samej wiosce
properly /'prɒpəlɪ/ *adv* ⟨1⟩ (correctly) jak należy; *[behave, dress]* stosownie, odpowiednio; *[eat]* właściwie, odpowiednio; *[write, spell]* poprawnie ⟨2⟩ (fully) dostatecznie, jak należy; **I didn't have time to thank you ~** nie miałem czasu, żeby należycie ci podziękować
proper name, proper noun *n* nazwa *f* własna
property /'prɒpətɪ/ *n* ⟨1⟩ (possessions) własność *f*, mienie *n* ⟨2⟩ (real estate) nieruchomość *f* ⟨3⟩ (house) dom *m* ⟨4⟩ (characteristic) właściwość *f*, własność *f*
property developer *n* deweloper *m*; (company) firma *f* deweloperska
property owner *n* właściciel *m*, -ka *f* nieruchomości
prophecy /'prɒfəsɪ/ *n* przepowiednia *f*, proroctwo *n*
prophet /'prɒfɪt/ *n* prorok *m*
proportion /prə'pɔ:ʃn/ ⟨I⟩ *n* ⟨1⟩ (part, quantity) (pewien) odsetek *m*, (pewna) część *f* ⟨2⟩ (ratio) stosunek *m*, proporcja *f* ⟨3⟩ (harmony) proporcja *f*, proporcjonalność *f* ⟨4⟩ (perspective) **to get sth out of ~** robić z czegoś wielki dramat; **to be out of all ~ to sth** być niewspółmiernym do czegoś ⟨II⟩ **proportions** *npl* (of building, machine) proporcje *f pl*; (of problem, project) rozmiary *m pl*
proportional /prə'pɔ:ʃənl/ *adj* proporcjonalny
proportional reprersentation, PR *n* przedstawicielstwo *n* proporcjonalne
proposal /prə'pəʊzl/ *n* ⟨1⟩ (suggestion) propozycja *f* ⟨2⟩ (of marriage) oświadczyny *plt*
propose /prə'pəʊz/ ⟨I⟩ *vt* za|proponować, wystą|pić, -epować z (czymś) *[motion]* ⟨II⟩ *vi* oświadcz|yć, -ać się (**to sb** komuś) ⟨III⟩ **proposed** *pp adj [action, reform]* proponowany
proposition /,prɒpə'zɪʃn/ ⟨I⟩ *n* ⟨1⟩ (suggestion) propozycja *f* ⟨2⟩ (assertion) twierdzenie *n* ⟨II⟩ *vt* z|robić (komuś) niestosowną propozycję
proprietor /prə'praɪətə(r)/ *n* właściciel *m*, -ka *f*
propriety /prə'praɪətɪ/ *n* ⟨1⟩ (politeness) dobre wychowanie *n*, kultura *f* osobista ⟨2⟩ (morality) przyzwoitość *f*
proscribe /prə'skraɪb, US prəʊ-/ *vt* zakaz|ać, -ywać (czegoś); wyj|ąć, -mować spod prawa *[person]*; z|delegalizować *[organization]*
prose /prəʊz/ *n* ⟨1⟩ (not verse) proza *f* ⟨2⟩ GB (translation) ćwiczenie *n* z tłumaczenia na język obcy

prosecute /'prɒsɪkju:t/ ⟨I⟩ *vt* wn|ieść, -osić oskarżenie przeciwko (komuś), ścigać sądownie ⟨II⟩ *vi* wn|ieść, -osić sprawę do sądu
prosecution /,prɒsɪ'kju:ʃn/ *n* ⟨1⟩ (accusation) wniesienie *n* oskarżenia ⟨2⟩ (party) **the ~** (private) oskarżyciel *m* prywatny; (state, Crown) oskarżyciel *m* publiczny, prokurator *m*
prosecutor /'prɒsɪkju:tə(r)/ *n* oskarżyciel *m*; (in court) oskarżyciel *m*, prokurator *m*
prospect ⟨I⟩ /'prɒspekt/ *n* ⟨1⟩ (hope) perspektywa *f*, szansa *f* ⟨2⟩ (outlook) perspektywa *f* ⟨II⟩ **prospects** *npl* perspektywy *f pl*
prospective /prə'spektɪv/ *adj [buyer, candidate]* potencjalny; *[husband, wife]* przyszły
prospectus /prə'spektəs/ *n* broszura *f*, prospekt *m*
prosper /'prɒspə(r)/ *vi* prosperować, rozwijać się pomyślnie
prosperity /prɒ'sperətɪ/ *n* (of society) dobrobyt *m*; (of company, economy) dobra koniunktura *f*; (of person) powodzenie *n*
prosperous /'prɒspərəs/ *adj [company]* dobrze prosperujący; *[person]* zamożny; *[country]* bogaty
prostate /'prɒsteɪt/ *n* (also **~ gland**) prostata *f*, gruczoł *m* krokowy
prostitute /'prɒstɪtju:t, US -tu:t/ ⟨I⟩ *n* prostytutka *f* ⟨II⟩ *vt* s|prostytuować *[person, talent]*
prostitution /,prɒstɪ'tju:ʃn, US -tu:ʃn/ *n* prostytucja *f*
prostrate /'prɒstreɪt/ *adj* **to lie ~** leżeć twarzą ku ziemi; **~ with grief** przygnieciony smutkiem
protagonist /prə'tægənɪst/ *n* (of book, film, play) bohater *m*, -ka *f*
protect /prə'tekt/ *vt* ⟨1⟩ (keep safe) chronić, ochr|onić, -aniać *[home, person]*; zabezpiecz|yć, -ać *[rights, interests]* ⟨2⟩ (defend) o|bronić *[consumer]* (**against sth** przed czymś); bronić (czegoś) *[interests]* (**against sth** przed czymś)
protection /prə'tekʃn/ *n* ochrona *f*, zabezpieczenie *n*
protection factor *n* (of sun cream) faktor *m*
protection racket *n* wymuszanie *n* pieniędzy w zamian za ochronę; rekiet *m* infml
protective /prə'tektɪv/ *adj [clothing, cover, layer]* ochronny; *[measure]* zabezpieczający
protein /'prəʊti:n/ *n* białko *n*, proteina *f*
protest ⟨I⟩ /'prəʊtest/ *n* ⟨1⟩ protest *m*; **in ~** na znak protestu, w proteście ⟨2⟩ (demonstration) akcja *f* protestacyjna ⟨II⟩ /prə'test/ *vt* ⟨1⟩ (declare) zapewni|ć, -ać o (czymś) *[loyalty, truth, innocence]* ⟨2⟩ US (complain about) za|protestować przeciwko (czemuś) ⟨III⟩ /prə'test/ *vi* ⟨1⟩ (complain) po|skarżyć się ⟨2⟩ (demonstrate) za|protestować
Protestant /'prɒtɪstənt/ ⟨I⟩ *n* protestant *m*, -ka *f* ⟨II⟩ *adj* protestancki
protester /prə'testə(r)/ *n* protestując|y *m*, -a *f*
protocol /'prəʊtəkɒl, US -kɔ:l/ *n* protokół *m*

prototype /'prəʊtətaɪp/ n prototyp m, pierwo-wzór m

protrude /prə'truːd, US prəʊ-/ vi wystawać, ster-czeć

protruding /prə'truːdɪŋ, US prəʊ-/ adj [rock, rib] wystający, sterczący; [eyes] wybałuszony; [ears] odstający, sterczący; [chin] wysunięty do przodu

proud /praʊd/ adj 1 dumny (of sb/sth z kogoś/czegoś) 2 [day, moment] szczęśliwy, wielki; [building, view] wspaniały

prove /pruːv/ ▯ vt udow|odnić, -adniać; (by demonstration) dow|ieść, -odzić (czegoś); to ~ one's point dowieść swych racji
▯ vi okaz|ać, -ywać się
▮ vr to ~ oneself sprawdzić się; to ~ oneself (to be) the best okazać się najlepszym

proverb /'prɒvɜːb/ n przysłowie n

provide /prə'vaɪd/ vt 1 (supply) zapewni|ć, -ać [accommodation, food, support] (for sb komuś); dostarczy|ć, -ać (czegoś) [opportunity, evidence] (for sb komuś); stanowić [chance, example, incentive] (for sb dla kogoś) 2 (stipulate) [will, clause, agreement] przewi|dzieć, -dywać; stanowić
■ **provide for**: (account for) uwzględni|ć, -ać, przewi|dzieć, -dywać [expenses, eventuality]; utrzym|ać, -ywać [family]; to be well ~d for być dobrze zabezpieczonym

provided /prə'vaɪdɪd/, **providing** /prə'vaɪdɪŋ/ conj (also ~ that) pod warunkiem, że; o ile

province /'prɒvɪns/ n prowincja f; in the ~s na prowincji

provincial /prə'vɪnʃl/ adj 1 [doctor, life] prowincjonalny; [newspaper] lokalny, regionalny 2 (narrow) zaściankowy

provision /prə'vɪʒn/ ▯ n 1 (of equipment, food) zaopatrywanie n, zaopatrzenie n; (of service) świadczenie n 2 (for future) zabezpieczenie n 3 (in agreement, bill, act) postanowienie n
▮ **provisions** npl (food) (for winter) zapasy m pl; (for journey) prowiant m

provisional /prə'vɪʒənl/ adj tymczasowy

provocative /prə'vɒkətɪv/ adj 1 [remark, dress] prowokacyjny 2 [book] skłaniający do refleksji

provoke /prə'vəʊk/ vt 1 (annoy) rozdrażni|ć, -ać, s|prowokować 2 (cause) wywoł|ać, -ywać [laughter, reaction]; s|powodować [crisis, complaints]

prow /praʊ/ n dziób m (okrętu, łodzi)

prowess /'praʊɪs/ n 1 (skill) sprawność f 2 (bravery) męstwo n, waleczność f

prowl /praʊl/ ▯ vt to ~ the streets krążyć po ulicach
▮ vi 1 (quietly) skradać się 2 (restlessly) chodzić tam i z powrotem

proximity /prɒk'sɪmətɪ/ n bliskość f

proxy /'prɒksɪ/ n 1 (person) pełnomocni|k m, -czka f 2 (authority) pełnomocnictwo n; by ~ per procura, z upoważnienia

prudent /'pruːdnt/ adj rozważny, roztropny

prudish /'pruːdɪʃ/ adj pruderyjny

prune /pruːn/ ▯ n Culin suszona śliwka f
▮ vt 1 (cut back) przyci|ąć, -nać [branches, rose]; przystrzy|c, -gać [hedge] 2 (thin out) okr|oić, -ajać [budget]; zmniejsz|yć, -ać [costs]; skr|ócić, -acać [article]

pry /praɪ/ vi (interfere) to ~ into sth wtrącać się w coś

PS n = postscriptum PS n

psalm /sɑːm/ n psalm m

pseudonym /'sjuːdənɪm, US 'suːd-/ n pseudonim m

psych /saɪk/ vt
■ **psych up** infml: to ~ oneself up przygotow|ać, -ywać się psychicznie (for sth na coś, do czegoś)

psychiatric /ˌsaɪkɪ'ætrɪk/ adj psychiatryczny; [illness] psychiczny; [patient] chory psychicznie

psychiatrist /saɪ'kaɪətrɪst, US sɪ-/ n psychiatra m

psychiatry /saɪ'kaɪətrɪ, US sɪ-/ n psychiatria f

psychic /'saɪkɪk/ n osoba f mająca zdolności parapsychologiczne, medium n

psychoanalysis /ˌsaɪkəʊə'næləsɪs/ n psychoanaliza f

psychological /ˌsaɪkə'lɒdʒɪkl/ adj psychologiczny; (of the mind) psychiczny

psychologist /saɪ'kɒlədʒɪst/ n psycholog m

psychology /saɪ'kɒlədʒɪ/ n psychologia f

psychopath /'saɪkəʊpæθ/ n psychopat|a m, -ka f

psychotherapist /ˌsaɪkəʊ'θerəpɪst/ n psychoterapeut|a m, -ka f

PTO = please turn over verte

pub n GB pub m

puberty /'pjuːbətɪ/ n okres m dojrzewania płciowego

public /'pʌblɪk/ ▯ n the ~ (of country) społeczeństwo n, ludzie plt; (in theatre, cinema) publiczność f; (of newspaper) odbiorcy m pl, czytelnicy m pl; (of museum) zwiedzający m pl
▮ adj publiczny; [enthusiasm, support] społeczny; [duty, spirit] obywatelski; to be in the ~ eye znaleźć się w centrum zainteresowania
▮ in public adv phr publicznie

public address (system) n urządzenia n pl nagłaśniające, nagłośnienie n

public assistance n US pomoc f socjalna

publication /ˌpʌblɪ'keɪʃn/ n publikacja f

public company n spółka f publiczna

public convenience n GB toaleta f publiczna, szalet m publiczny

public holiday n GB dzień m ustawowo wolny od pracy (poza sobotą i niedzielą)

publicity /pʌb'lɪsətɪ/ n rozgłos m; to attract ~ przyciągać uwagę

publicity campaign n kampania f reklamowa or promocyjna

publicity stunt n chwyt m reklamowy

publicize /ˈpʌblɪsaɪz/ *vt* ① nagłⅼośnić, -aśniać *[issue, event]* ② (make public) podaⅼć, -wać do wiadomości publicznej *[facts]* ③ zaⅼreklamować *[show]*

publicly /ˈpʌblɪklɪ/ *adv* publicznie

public opinion *n* opinia *f* publiczna

public prosecutor *n* oskarżyciel *m* publiczny

public relations, **PR** *npl* public relations *plt inv*

public school *n* ① GB szkoła *f* prywatna ② US szkoła *f* publiczna

public sector *n* sektor *m* publiczny

public transport *n* publiczne środki *m pl* transportu

publish /ˈpʌblɪʃ/ *vt* wydaⅼć, -wać *[book, newspaper]*; oⅼpublikować *[article, letter]*

publisher /ˈpʌblɪʃə(r)/ *n* ① wydawca *m* ② (also **publishing house**) wydawnictwo *n*

publishing /ˈpʌblɪʃɪŋ/ *n* działalność *f* wydawnicza

pudding /ˈpʊdɪŋ/ *n* ① GB (dessert) deser *m* ② (cooked) potrawa z mięsa i warzyw, gotowana na parze, często w cieście ③ GB (sausage) **black** ~ kaszanka; **white** ~ kiełbasa pasztetowa

puddle /ˈpʌdl/ *n* kałuża *f*

puff /pʌf/ **Ⅰ** *n* (of wind) podmuch *m*; (of smoke, steam) obłok *m*, obłoczek *m*; (large) kłąb *m*; (of breath) dmuchnięcie *n*

Ⅱ *vt* kurzyć *[pipe]*

Ⅲ *vi* ① to ~ at one's cigarette kurzyć papierosa *infml* ② (pant) dyszeć, sapać

■ **puff out**: ① wydⅼąć, -ymać *[cheeks]*; *[bird]* naⅼstroszyć *[feathers]* ② wypuⅼścić, -szczać *[smoke]*

■ **puff up**: ¶ ~ **up** *[feathers]* naⅼstroszyć się; *[eyes]* podpuchnąć; *[rice]* naⅼpęcznieć ¶ ~ **[sth] up** naⅼstroszyć *[feathers]*; zⅼjeżyć *[fur]*; **to be ~ed up with pride** nadąć się jak paw, być dumnym jak paw

puff pastry *n* ciasto *n* francuskie

puffy /ˈpʌfɪ/ *adj [face]* opuchnięty, obrzmiały; *[eyes]* podpuchnięty

pull /pʊl/ **Ⅰ** *n* ① (tug) pociągnięcie *n*; (sharp) szarpnięcie *n*; **to give sth a** ~ pociągnąć za coś, szarpnąć coś ② (of magnet) przyciąganie *n*; (of current, stream, water) siła *f*; *fig* przyciągająca siła *f*

Ⅱ *vt* ① poⅼciągnąć za coś, szarpⅼnąć, -ać *[rope, cord]*; **he** ~**ed her attackers off her** odciągnął od niej napastników; **to** ~ **sth out of a drawer** wyciągnąć coś z szuflady; **to** ~ **a gun on sb** zagrozić komuś pistoletem ② (operate) pociągⅼnąć, -ać za (coś) *[trigger]* ③ naciągnąć *[muscle]* ④ **to** ~ **a face** wykrzywić się

Ⅲ *vi* (tug) pociągⅼnąć, -ać, ciągⅼnąć, szarpⅼnąć, -ać (**at** or **on sth** za coś)

■ **pull apart**: ① (dismantle) rozⅼłożyć, -kładać na części ② (destroy) *[child]* rozwalⅼić, -ać *infml [toy]*; *[animal]* rozszarpⅼać, -ywać *[prey]*

■ **pull away**: ¶ ~ **away** *[car]* odjeⅼchać, -żdżać ¶ ~ **[sb/sth] away** odciągⅼnąć, -ać (**from sb/sth** od kogoś/czegoś); **to** ~ **one's hand away** cofnąć rękę; **to** ~ **sth away from sb** wyrwać coś komuś

■ **pull back**: *[troops]* wycofⅼać, -ywać się; *[car, person]* cofⅼnąć, -ać się

■ **pull down**: ① (demolish) zⅼburzyć; (piece by piece) rozⅼebrać, -bierać *[building]* ② spuⅼścić, -szczać *[blind, trousers]*

■ **pull in**: *[bus, driver]* zatrzymⅼać, -ywać się

■ **pull off**: ① ściągⅼnąć, -ać, zdⅼjąć, -ejmować *[coat, shoes]*; zⅼerwać, -rywać, odkleⅼić, -jać *[sticker]* ② zawⅼrzeć, -ierać *[deal]*; dokonⅼać, -ywać (czegoś) *[feat]*

■ **pull out**: ¶ ~ **out** ① *[bus, train]* ruszⅼyć, -ać, odjeⅼchać, -żdżać; **to** ~ **out of sth** wyjeżdżać z czegoś ② *[troops, competitor]* wycofⅼać, -ywać się ¶ ~ **[sth] out** (extract) wyciągⅼnąć, -ać *[splinter]*; wyrⅼwać, -ywać *[tooth]* ② (take out) wyciągⅼnąć, -ać *[gun, hankerchief]*

■ **pull over**: ¶ ~ **over** *[motorist, car]* zjeⅼchać, -żdżać na bok; (stop) zatrzymⅼać, -ywać się (na poboczu) ¶ ~ **[sb/sth] over** *[police]* zmuⅼsić, -szać do zjechania na bok

■ **pull through**: (from injury) przyⅼjść, -chodzić do siebie

■ **pull together**: ¶ ~ **together** działać wspólnie ¶ ~ **oneself together** wziąć się w garść

■ **pull up**: ¶ ~ **up** *[car, driver]* zatrzymⅼać, -ywać się ¶ ~ **[sth] up** ① (uproot) wyrⅼwać, -ywać ② podnⅼieść, -osić *[anchor]*; podciągⅼnąć, -ać *[trousers, socks]*; **to** ~ **up a chair** przysunąć krzesło ¶ ~ **[sb] up** ① (lift) wciągⅼnąć, -ać ② (reprimand) obⅼsztorcować *infml* ③ *[policeman]* zatrzymⅼać, -ywać *[driver]*

pull-down menu /ˌpʊldaʊnˈmenjuː/ *n* Comput menu *n* rozwijane

pulley /ˈpʊlɪ/ *n* (simple machine) blok *m*; (with driving belt) koło *n* pasowe

pullover /ˈpʊləʊvə(r)/ *n* pulower *m*

pulp /pʌlp/ **Ⅰ** *n* (of fruit, vegetable) miąższ *m*; (crushed mass) miazga *f*, papka *f*

Ⅱ *vt* rozⅼetrzeć, -cierać na miazgę *[fruit, vegetables]*; rozwłóknⅼić, -ać *[wood]*; przerⅼobić, -abiać na masę papierniczą *[newspapers, books]*

pulp fiction *n* szmatława czytadło *n infml*

pulpit /ˈpʊlpɪt/ *n* ambona *f*

pulse /pʌls/ *n* tętno *n*, puls *m*

pulse rate *n* tętno *n*

pulverize /ˈpʌlvəraɪz/ *vt* sⅼproszkować

pump /pʌmp/ **Ⅰ** *n* ① pompa *f*; **bicycle** ~ pompka rowerowa ② (plimsoll) tenisówka *f*; GB (flat shoe) balerinka *f*; US (shoe with heel) czółenko *n*

Ⅱ *vt* ① pompować *[air, blood, water]*; wypompoⅼwać, -ywać (**out of sth** z czegoś) ② *infml* (question) poⅼciągnąć za język *infml [person]* ③ Med **to** ~ **sb's stomach** zrobić komuś płukanie żołądka

Ⅲ *vi [heart]* mocno bić

■ **pump up**: naⅼpompować *[tyre]*

pumpkin /ˈpʌmpkɪn/ *n* dynia *f*

pun /pʌn/ n gra f słów, kalambur m

punch /pʌntʃ/ **I** n 1 (blow) cios m pięścią 2 (of style, performance) wyrazistość m, ostrość f 3 (drink) poncz m

II vt 1 uderzyć pięścią [person]; **to ~ sb in the face** uderzyć kogoś pięścią w twarz 2 prze|-dziurkować; Comput perforować [cards, tape]; **to ~ a ticket** kasować or dziurkować bilet

Punch-and-Judy show /ˌpʌntʃən'dʒuːdɪʃəʊ/ n tradycyjne angielskie widowisko kukiełkowe

punchbag /'pʌntʃbæg/ n GB worek m treningowy

punch line n puenta f, pointa f

punch-up /'pʌntʃʌp/ n GB infml bijatyka f, bójka f

punctual /'pʌŋktʃʊəl/ adj punktualny

punctually /'pʌŋktʃʊəlɪ/ adv punktualnie

punctuation /ˌpʌŋktʃʊ'eɪʃn/ n interpunkcja f, przestankowanie n

punctuation mark n znak m interpunkcyjny or przestankowy

puncture /'pʌŋktʃə(r)/ **I** n przebicie n; dziura f infml; **we had a ~ on the way here** po drodze złapaliśmy gumę infml

II vt przebi|ć, -jać

puncture (repair) kit n zestaw m do naprawy dętek

pundit /'pʌndɪt/ n ekspert m; spec m infml

pungent /'pʌndʒənt/ adj [taste, smell] ostry; [gas, smoke] gryzący

punish /'pʌnɪʃ/ vt u|karać

punishment /'pʌnɪʃmənt/ n kara f

punitive /'pjuːnətɪv/ adj [action, expedition] karny; [measures] odwetowy

punk /pʌŋk/ **I** n 1 (music) punk m, punk rock m 2 (punk rocker) punk m, punkowiec m 3 US infml chuligan m

II adj punkowy

punnet /'pʌnɪt/ n GB łubianka f

punt /pʌnt/ n 1 (boat) łódź f płaskodenna 2 (Irish pound) funt m irlandzki

puny /'pjuːnɪ/ adj [person] mizerny, wątły; [body] słaby; [plant, limbs] rachityczny

pup /pʌp/ n (also **puppy**) szczeniak m, szczenię n

pupil /'pjuːpɪl/ n 1 Sch ucze|ń m, -nnica f 2 (in eye) źrenica f

puppet /'pʌpɪt/ n kukiełka f; (marionette) mario-netka f; (glove puppet) pacynka f

purchase /'pɜːtʃəs/ **I** n zakup m, kupno n; (thing bought) zakup m, nabytek m

II kup|ić, -ować, zakup|ić, -ywać, naby|ć, -wać

purchasing power n (of currency) siła f nabyw-cza; (of individual) zdolność f nabywcza

pure /pjʊə(r)/ n czysty

puree /'pjʊəreɪ, US pjʊə'reɪ/ n (of vegetables) piure n inv, purée n inv; (of fruit) przecier m

purely /'pjʊəlɪ/ adv wyłącznie, jedynie

purge /pɜːdʒ/ **I** n czystka f

II vt 1 przeprowadz|ić, -ać czystkę w (czymś) [party]; przeprowadz|ić, -ać czystkę wśród (kogoś) [opponents]; wy|eliminować [opposition] 2 oczy|ś-cić, -szczać się z (czegoś) [sin]

purify /'pjʊərɪfaɪ/ vt oczy|ścić, -szczać

purist /'pjʊərɪst/ **I** n puryst|a m, -ka f

II adj purystyczny

purity /'pjʊərətɪ/ n czystość f

purple /'pɜːpl/ **I** n (kolor m) fioletowy m, fiolet m

II adj (bluish) fioletowy; (reddish) purpurowy

purpose /'pɜːpəs/ **I** n 1 (aim) cel m; (intention, reason) zamiar m; **for the ~s of this experiment** w tym doświadczeniu 2 (also **strength of ~**) wola f, determinacja f, nieziomność f

II on purpose adv phr celowo, umyślnie

purposely /'pɜːpəslɪ/ adv celowo, umyślnie

purpose-made /ˌpɜːpəs'meɪd/ adj specjalnie za-projektowany

purr /pɜː(r)/ **I** n (of cat) mruczenie n; (of engine) warkot m

II vi [cat] za|mruczeć; [engine] perkotać

purse /pɜːs/ **I** n 1 (for coins) portmonetka f; (for coins and notes) portfel m 2 US (handbag) torebka f (damska)

IDIOMS: **to hold the ~ strings** trzymać kasę infml

purser /'pɜːsə(r)/ n główny steward m

pursue /pə'sjuː, US -'suː/ vt 1 ścigać [person, animal] 2 dążyć do (czegoś) [aim, excellence]; pro-wadzić [policy, research] 3 zajmować się (czymś) [occupation]; rozwijać [interests]

pursuer /pə'sjuːə(r), US -'suː-/ n ścigający m; (persistent) prześladow|ca m, -czyni f

pursuit /pə'sjuːt, US -'suː-/ n 1 (chase) pogoń f, pościg m; **in ~ of sth** w pościgu or pogoni za czymś; **in hot ~** depcząc po piętach 2 (activity) zajęcie n; **artistic ~s** praca artystyczna

push /pʊʃ/ **I** n (shove) pchnięcie n, popchnięcie n; (press) naciśnięcie n, przyciśnięcie n; **to give sb/sth a ~** popchnąć kogoś/coś

II vt 1 (shove) pop|chnąć, -ychać, pchać; (move) odsu|nąć, -wać; (press) nacis|nąć, -kać, przycis|nąć, -kać; **to ~ sb/sth away** odepchnąć kogoś/coś; **to ~ sb down the stairs** zepchnąć kogoś ze schodów; **to ~ sb too far** fig doprowadzać kogoś do ostateczności 2 infml (promote) wy|lansować [policy, theory] 3 infml (sell) handlować (czymś), rozprowadzać [drugs]

III vi (move) pop|chnąć, -ychać, pchać; (press) nacis|nąć, -kać; **to ~ past sb** przecisnąć się obok kogoś

■ **push around** infml: (bully) dyrygować (kimś) fig

■ **push for**: przeć do (czegoś), nawoływać do (czegoś)

■ **push in**: ¶ **~ in** w|epchnąć, -pychać się ¶ [sth] **in** wcis|nąć, -kać [button]; wyłam|ać, -ywać [window, door]

■ **push over**: ¶ **~ over** infml posu|nąć, -wać się

¶ ~ [sb/sth] over przewr|ócić, -acać *[person, car, table]*; wywr|ócić, -acać *[car, table]*

■ **push through**: doprowadz|ić, -ać do przyjęcia (czegoś) *[bill, legislation]*; s|finalizować *[deal]*

⟨IDIOMS:⟩ **at a** ~ GB infml na siłę, na upartego; **to** ~ **one's luck** igrać z losem

push-button /'pʊʃˌbʌtn/ *adj [telephone]* z klawiaturą numeryczną

pushchair /'pʊʃtʃeə(r)/ *n* GB wózek *m* spacerowy, spacerówka *f*

pusher /'pʊʃə(r)/ *n* infml (also **drug** ~) dealer *m* or diler *m* narkotykowy

push-start /ˌpʊʃ'stɑːt/ *vt* zapal|ić, -ać na pych infml *[car]*

push-up /'pʊʃʌp/ *n* Sport pompka *f*

pushy /'pʊʃi/ *adj* infml bezczelny; **to be very** ~ umieć rozpychać się łokciami fig

put /pʊt/ *vt* [1] (place) położyć, kłaść *[book, flat object]*; postawić, stawiać *[plates, vase]*; **to** ~ **sugar in one's tea** posłodzić herbatę; **to** ~ **sb in the spare room** umieścić kogoś w pokoju gościnnym; **to** ~ **a letter through a letterbox** wrzucić list do skrzynki; **to** ~ **sth through a test** przetestować coś; **to** ~ **sb through college** wykształcić kogoś; **to** ~ **sb through an ordeal** poddać kogoś ciężkiej próbie [2] (devote, invest) w|łożyć, -kładać *[money, energy]* (**into sth** w coś); **I've put a lot of time into it** poświęciłem temu wiele czasu [3] (add) **to** ~ **money towards sth** dać pieniądze na coś; **to** ~ **tax on sth** nałożyć podatek na coś [4] (express) wyra|zić, -żać; **let me** ~ **it another way** ujmę to inaczej; **to** ~ **it bluntly** mówiąc bez ogródek

■ **put across**: przedstawi|ć, -ać *[idea, case]*

■ **put away**: [1] (tidy away) od|łożyć, -kładać na miejsce [2] (save) od|łożyć, -kładać *[money]* [3] infml s|pałaszować infml *[food]*; wytrąbić infml *[drink]*

■ **put back**: [1] (return) od|łożyć, -kładać, odstawi|ć, -ać; **to** ~ **sth back where it belongs** odłożyć/ odstawić coś na (swoje) miejsce [2] (postpone) przesu|nąć, -wać, prze|łożyć, -kładać *[meeting, date]* [3] (reset) cof|nąć, -ać *[clock, watch]*

■ **put down**: ¶ ~ [sth] **down** [1] położyć, kłaść *[book, spectacles]*; postawić, stawiać *[cup, chair]*; spu|ścić, -szczać *[blind]*; opu|ścić, -szczać *[hand]* [2] s|tłumić *[revolt]* [3] (write down) zapis|ać, -ywać, za|notować [4] (attribute) **to** ~ **sth down to sth** przypisywać coś czemuś; **to** ~ **the disaster down to the fact that...** przyczynę katastrofę upatrywać w tym, że... [5] (by injection) u|śpić, -sypiać *[animal]* [6] wpłac|ić, -ać *[deposit]*; **to** ~ **£50 down on sth** wpłacić na coś zadatek w wysokości 50 funtów ¶ ~ [sb] **down** [1] wysadz|ić, -ać *[passenger]* [2] infml (humiliate) upok|orzyć, -arzać

■ **put forward**: [1] (propose) wysu|nąć, -wać *[theory]*; za|proponować *[plan]*; wyst|ąpić, -ępować z (czymś) *[proposal]*; przedstawi|ć, -ać *[opinion]*

[2] (in time) przyśpiesz|yć, -ać datę (czegoś) *[meeting]* [3] (reset) przesu|nąć, -wać do przodu *[clock]*

■ **put in**: ¶ [1] *[ship]* zawi|nąć, -jać (do portu), przybi|ć, -jać [2] **to** ~ **in for sth** ubiegać się o coś *[job, transfer]* ¶ ~ [sth] **in** [1] za|łożyć, -kładać, za|instalować *[central heating, shower]* [2] (make) wyst|ąpić, -ępować z (czymś) *[request, claim]*; **to** ~ **in an appearance** pokazać się, pojawić się [3] poświęc|ić, -ać *[time]* [4] (insert) wstawi|ć, -ać

■ **put off**: ¶ ~ [sth] **off** [1] (delay, defer) prze|łożyć, -kładać, od|łożyć, -kładać [2] (switch off) wyłącz|yć, -ać *[radio]*; z|gasić *[light]* ¶ ~ [sb] **off** [1] (fob off) zniechęc|ić, -ać, zby|ć, -wać; **to be easily put off** dawać się łatwo zbyć [2] (repel) *[appearance, smell]* budzić wstręt w (kimś), odstręcz|yć, -ać; *[manner, person]* zra|zić, -żać

■ **put on**: [1] za|łożyć, -kładać, w|łożyć, -kładać *[garment]*; **to** ~ **on make-up** zrobić makijaż [2] (switch on) włącz|yć, -ać *[light, heating]*; nastawi|ć, -ać *[record, music]*; **to** ~ **the kettle on** nastawić wodę (w czajniku) [3] (gain) **I put on a few pounds** przybyło mi kilka kilogramów; **he's put a lot of weight on** bardzo przytył [4] (produce) przygotow|ać, -ywać *[exhibition]*; wystawi|ć, -ać *[play]* [5] (adopt) przyj|ąć, -mować *[expression]*; uda|ć, -wać *[accent]*; **he's** ~**ting it on** on (tylko) udaje

■ **put out**: [1] (extend) wyciąg|nąć, -ać *[hand]*; **to** ~ **out one's tongue** pokazać język [2] z|gasić *[cigarette, candle]*; u|gasić *[fire]* [3] wystawi|ć, -ać *[dustbins, rubbish]*; wypu|ścić, -szczać *[cat]* [4] ogł|osić, -aszać *[statement, warning]* [5] wy|łożyć, -kładać *[towels]*; wystawi|ć, -ać, przygotow|ać, -ywać *[dishes]* [6] (dislocate) wywichnąć *[shoulder]* [7] (inconvenience) spraw|ić, -ać or z|robić (komuś) kłopot; (upset) z|denerowować

■ **put through**: [1] (implement) przeprowadz|ić, -ać *[reform]*; wprowadz|ić, -ać w życie *[bill]* [2] (by telephone) po|łączyć *[caller]* (**to sb** z kimś)

■ **put together**: [1] (assemble) z|łożyć, składać *[pieces, parts]*; **to** ~ **sth back together** złożyć coś z powrotem [2] (place together) z|ebrać, -bierać razem [3] (make) przygotow|ać, -ywać *[list]*; z|montować *[film, video]* [4] (present) przedstawi|ć, -ać *[case, argument]*

■ **put up**: ¶ ~ **up** [sth] stawi|ć, -ać *[resistance]*; **to** ~ **up a fight** walczyć ¶ ~ [sth] **up** [1] wciąg|nąć, -ać *[flag]*; podn|ieść, -osić *[sail]*; na|stroszyć *[hair]*; **to** ~ **up one's hand** unieść rękę [2] wywie|sić, -szać, powiesi|ć *[notice, list]* [3] postawi|ć, stawiać *[tent, fence]* [4] podwyższ|yć, -ać *[rent, price, tax, temperature]* [5] (provide) wy|łożyć, -kładać *[money]* (**for sth** na coś); w|łożyć, -kładać *[money]* (**for sth** w coś) ¶ ~ [sb] **up** [1] (lodge) przyj|ąć, -mować (u siebie); (for one night) przenocować, dać (komuś) nocleg ¶ ~ (incite) **to** ~ **sb up to sth** nam|ówić, -awiać kogoś do czegoś

■ **put up with**: znosić *[person, situation]*

[IDIOMS:] **I wouldn't ~ it past him!** po nim można się wszystkiego spodziewać!
put-down /'pʊtdaʊn/ *n* upokarzająca uwaga *f*
putty /'pʌtɪ/ *n* kit *m*
puzzle /'pʌzl/ **[I]** *n* [1] (mystery) zagadka *f*, tajemnica *f* [2] (riddle) zagadka *f*; (toy) łamigłówka *f*; (jigsaw) układanka *f*
[II] *vt [question, attitude]* zastan|owić, -awiać *[person]*
puzzle book *n* książeczka *f* z rozrywkami umysłowymi

puzzled /'pʌzld/ *adj* zdziwiony, zaintrygowany
PVC *n* = **polyvinyl chloride** PCW *m/n inv*
pygmy /'pɪgmɪ/ *n* Pigmej *m*, -ka *f*
pyjamas GB, **pajamas** US /pə'dʒɑːməs/ *npl* piżama *f*; **a pair of ~** piżama
pylon /'paɪlən, -lɒn/ *n* [1] (electricity) słup *m* wysokiego napięcia [2] (of aircraft) wspornik *m*
pyramid /'pɪrəmɪd/ *n* piramida *f*
python /'paɪθn, US 'paɪθɒn/ *n* pyton *m*

Q

q, Q /kjuː/ n q, Q n

quack /kwæk/ **▯** n ⊡ (of duck) kwak m; ~, ~ kwa, kwa! ⊡ GB (doctor) medyk m; konował m infml ⊡ (impostor) szarlatan n infml
▯ vi kwaknąć, za|kwakać

quadrangle /'kwɒdræŋgl/ n ⊡ (shape) czworo-kąt m ⊡ (courtyard) czworokątny dziedziniec m

quadruple **▯** /'kwɒdrʊpl, US kwɒ'druːpl/ n czterokrotność f
▯ /'kwɒdrʊpl, US kwɒ'druːpl/ adj poczwórny; (four times) czterokrotny
▯ vt /kwɒ'druːpl/ czterokrotnie zwiększ|yć, -ać
▯ vi /kwɒ'druːpl/ czterokrotnie wzr|osnąć, -astać

quadruplet /'kwɒdrʊplət, US kwɒ'druːp-/ n jedno n z czworaczków; ~s czworaczki

quagmire /'kwɒgmaɪə(r), 'kwæg-/ n bagno n, trzęsawisko n

quail /kweɪl/ **▯** n przepiórka f; ~'s eggs prze-piórcze jaja
▯ vi s|truchleć

quaint /kweɪnt/ adj ⊡ (pretty) uroczy ⊡ (old world) staroświecki ⊡ (odd) oryginalny, osobliwy

quake /kweɪk/ vi [earth] za|trząść się; [person] za|drżeć, za|dygotać

qualification /ˌkwɒlɪfɪ'keɪʃn/ n ⊡ (diploma, degree) dyplom m (**in sth** w dziedzinie czegoś); (experience, skills) kwalifikacje f pl ⊡ (restriction) zastrzeżenie n

qualified /'kwɒlɪfaɪd/ adj ⊡ (for job) (having diploma) dyplomowany; (having experience, skills) wykwalifiko-wany ⊡ (competent) (having authority) upoważniony, uprawniony (**to do sth** do zrobienia czegoś); (having knowledge) kompetentny (**to do sth** do zrobienia czegoś) ⊡ (limited) [success] względny; [praise] umiarkowany

qualifier /'kwɒlɪfaɪə(r)/ n (contestant) zakwalifiko-wan|y m, -a f; (match) mecz m eliminacyjny

qualify /'kwɒlɪfaɪ/ **▯** vt ⊡ (modify) s|precyzować, uściśl|ić, -ać [statement, remark] ⊡ (entitle) **to ~ sb to do sth** uprawniać kogoś do zrobienia czegoś
▯ vi ⊡ (get diploma, degree) zdoby|ć, -wać dyplom ⊡ (be eligible) spełni|ć, -ać warunki; **to ~ for sth** spełniać warunki konieczne do uzyskania czegoś ⊡ Sport za|kwalifikować się

qualitative /'kwɒlɪtətɪv, US -teɪt-/ adj jakościowy

quality /'kwɒlətɪ/ **▯** n ⊡ (worth) jakość f ⊡ (attribute) przymiot m, właściwość f
▯ adj wysokiej jakości

quality control n kontrola f jakości

qualm /kwaːm/ n skrupuły plt

quandary /'kwɒndərɪ/ n rozterka f, dylemat m

quantifiable /ˌkwɒntɪ'faɪəbl/ adj wymierny

quantify /'kwɒntɪfaɪ/ vt określ|ić, -ać ilościowo

quantitative /'kwɒntɪtətɪv, US -teɪt-/ adj ilościowy

quantity /'kwɒntətɪ/ n ilość f; (in mathematics) wielkość f; **in ~** w dużych ilościach

quantity surveyor n rzeczoznawca m

quantum leap /'kwɒntəm liːp/ n przejście n kwantowe; fig olbrzymi skok m fig

quarantine /'kwɒrəntiːn, US 'kwɔːr-/ **▯** n kwa-rantanna f
▯ vt podda|ć, -wać kwarantannie

quarrel /'kwɒrəl, US 'kwɔːrəl/ **▯** n kłótnia f, sprzeczka f (**about** or **over sth** o coś); **to have a ~** pokłócić się
▯ vi ⊡ (argue) po|kłócić się, po|sprzeczać się ⊡ (dispute) **to ~ with sth** za|kwestionować coś, poda|ć, -wać coś w wątpliwość

quarrelling GB, **quarreling** US /'kwɒrəlɪŋ, US 'kwɔː-/ n kłótnie f pl, swary plt

quarrelsome /'kwɒrəlsəm, US 'kwɔː-/ adj [person] kłótliwy, swarliwy; [remark] napastliwy

quarry /'kwɒrɪ, US 'kwɔːrɪ/ **▯** n ⊡ (in ground) kamieniołom m ⊡ (prey) zdobycz f
▯ vt wydoby|ć, -wać [stone]

quarry tile n kamienna płyta f podłogowa

quart /kwɔːt/ n kwarta f (GB = 1,136 litra, US = 0,946 litra)

quarter /'kwɔːtə(r)/ **▯** n ⊡ (one fourth) ćwierć f; **in ~ of an hour** za kwadrans ⊡ (three months) kwar-tał m ⊡ (district) dzielnica f
▯ quarters npl Mil kwatery f pl
▯ pron ⊡ (25%) czwarta część f; **only a ~ passed** zdała tylko jedna czwarta kandydatów ⊡ (in time phrases) **at (a) ~ to 11** GB, **at a ~ of 11** US za kwadrans jedenasta; **an hour and a ~** godzina i piętnaście minut
▯ adj **a ~ century** ćwierć wieku
▯ adv **a ~ full** w jednej czwartej pełny
▯ vt po|kroić na ćwiartki [apple, cake]
▯ **at close quarters** adv phr [see] z bliska; [fight] wręcz

quarterfinal /ˌkwɔːtə'faɪnl/ n ćwierćfinał m

quarterly /'kwɔːtəlɪ/ **▯** n kwartalnik m
▯ adj kwartalny

quartermaster /ˈkwɔːtəmɑːstə(r), US -mæstə(r)/
n (in army) kwatermistrz *m*; (in navy) podoficer *m*
zawiadujący sterownią

quartet /kwɔːˈtet/ *n* kwartet *m*

quartz /kwɔːts/ *n* kwarc *m*

quash /kwɒʃ/ *vt* odrzuc|ić, -ać *[proposal]*; s|tłumić
[rebellion]

quasi+ /ˈkweɪzaɪ, ˈkwɑːzɪ/ *in combinations* quasi-,
niby-

quaver /ˈkweɪvə(r)/ **I** *n* 1 GB Mus ósemka *f*
2 (trembling) drżenie *n*
II *vi [voice]* drżeć

quay /kiː/ *n* nabrzeże *n*; **on the** ~ na nabrzeżu

quayside /ˈkiːsaɪd/ *n* nabrzeże *n*; **at the** ~ przy
nabrzeżu

queasiness /ˈkwiːzɪnɪs/ *n* mdłości *plt*, nudności *plt*

queasy /ˈkwiːzɪ/ *adj* **to be** ~ mieć mdłości

Quebec /kwɪˈbek/ *prn* Quebec *m*

queen /kwiːn/ *n* 1 królowa *f* 2 (in cards) dama *f*

queen bee *n* królowa *f*

queen mother *n* królowa matka *f*

Queen's Counsel, QC *n* GB *tytuł honorowy*
członka palestry

queer /kwɪə(r)/ *adj* 1 (strange) dziwny 2 (suspicious)
podejrzany

quell /kwel/ *vt* s|tłumić *[anger, rebellion]*; rozpr|o-
szyć, -aszać, rozwi|ać, -ewać *[anxiety]*

quench /kwentʃ/ *vt* u|gasić *[thirst]*; zaspok|oić,
-ajać *[desire]*

querulous /ˈkwerʊləs/ *adj [person]* kwękający;
[voice] płaczliwy

query /ˈkwɪərɪ/ **I** *n* pytanie *n* (**about sth**
odnośnie czegoś); **queries from customers** prośby klientów o informację
II *vt* za|kwestionować *[statement, right]*

quest /kwest/ *n* poszukiwanie *n* (**for sb/sth** kogoś/
czegoś)

question /ˈkwestʃən/ **I** *n* 1 (request) pytanie *n*
(**about sb/sth** o kogoś/coś); **to ask sb a** ~ zadać
pytanie komuś 2 (issue) kwestia *f*, sprawa *f*; (ethical
issue) dylemat *m* (moralny); **it's a** ~ **of doing sth**
to kwestia zrobienia czegoś; **that's another** ~ to
zupełnie inna or osobna kwestia; **there was never
any** ~ **of you paying** nigdy nie było mowy o tym,
że masz zapłacić; **the person in** ~ osoba, o którą
chodzi; **it's out of the** ~ to wykluczone 3 (doubt)
wątpliwość *f*; **to call sth into** ~ podać coś
w wątpliwość; **it's open to** ~ to kwestia otwarta
II *vt* 1 (interrogate) przesłuch|ać, -iwać *[suspect,
politician]* 2 (cast doubt upon) za|kwestionować *[tac-
tics, methods]*

questionable /ˈkwestʃənəbl/ *adj* wątpliwy; **it's**
~ **whether this is an original** nie jest pewne, czy
to oryginał

questioner /ˈkwestʃənə(r)/ *n* (interrogator) przesłu-
chujący *m*, -a *f*; (at a meeting) osoba *f* zadająca
pytanie

questioning /ˈkwestʃənɪŋ/ *n* przesłuchanie *n*; **to
bring the suspect in for** ~ doprowadzić podejrzanego na przesłuchanie

question mark *n* pytajnik *m*, znak *m* zapytania

questionnaire /ˌkwestʃəˈneə(r)/ *n* kwestionariusz *m*, ankieta *f* (**on sth** na temat czegoś)

queue /kjuː/ **I** *n* GB (of people) kolejka *f*; ogonek *m*
infml; (of vehicles) kolejka *f*; **to stand in a** ~ stać
w kolejce; **to join the** ~ dołączyć do kolejki; **to
jump the** ~ infml wepchnąć się do kolejki infml
II *vi* (also ~ **up**) ustawi|ć, -ać się w kolejce (**for
sth** po coś)

queue-jump /ˈkjuːdʒʌmp/ *vi* GB w|epchnąć,
-pychać się bez kolejki infml

quibble /ˈkwɪbl/ *vi* spierać się (**about** or **over sth**
o coś)

quick /kwɪk/ **I** *n* **to bite one's nails to the** ~
obgryzać paznokcie do żywego mięsa
II *adj* 1 (speedy) *[pace, reply, profit]* szybki; *[storm,
shower of rain]* przelotny; **to have a** ~ **coffee**
wypić kawę na stojąco or w biegu; **to have a** ~
wash szybko się umyć; **the** ~**est way to lose
your friends is...** najłatwiej stracić przyjaciół
przez...; **she's a** ~ **worker** robota pali jej się
w rękach; **to make a** ~ **recovery** szybko
powrócić do zdrowia; **be** ~ (**about it)!** pośpiesz
się! 2 (clever) *[child, student]* bystry 3 (prompt) **to be
a** ~ **learner** szybko się uczyć
III *adv* ~! szybko!; ~ **as a flash** błyskawicznie
IDIOMS: **to cut** or **sting sb to the** ~ dotknąć kogoś
do żywego

quicken /ˈkwɪkən/ **I** *vt* przyśpiesz|yć, -ać *[pace]*;
wzm|óc, -agać *[interest]*
II *vi [pulse]* przyśpiesz|yć, -ać; *[anger]* wzm|óc,
-agać się

quick-fire /ˈkwɪkfaɪə/ *adj [dialogue]* błyskotliwy

quicklime /ˈkwɪklaɪm/ *n* wapno *n* niegaszone

quickly /ˈkwɪklɪ/ *adv* (rapidly) szybko; (without delay)
natychmiast, bezzwłocznie

quick march *n* Mil szybki marsz *m*

quicksand /ˈkwɪksænd/ *n* ruchome piaski *plt*; fig
grząski grunt *m* fig

quicksilver /ˈkwɪksɪlvə(r)/ *n* rtęć *f*

quick-tempered /ˈkwɪkˈtempəd/ *adj* porywczy,
zapalczywy

quid /kwɪd/ *n* GB infml funciak *m* infml

quiet /ˈkwaɪət/ **I** *n* 1 (silence) cisza *f* 2 (peace)
spokój *m* 3 infml (secret) **on the** ~ cichcem,
cichaczem
II *adj* 1 (silent) *[room, person]* cichy; **to keep** ~
być cicho; **to go** ~ zamilknąć; **to keep sb** ~
uciszyć kogoś; **be** ~! (stop talking) ucisz się!,
zamilknij!; (make no noise) bądź cicho! 2 (not noisy)
[voice] cichy; *[cough, laugh]* dyskretny; **in a** ~
voice cichym głosem; **that should keep the
children** ~ dzięki temu dzieci będą przez jakiś
czas cicho 3 (discreet) *[diplomacy]* dyskretny; *[deal]*

prywatny; *[confidence]* ostrożny; *[despair]* tłumiony; *[colour]* spokojny; **to have a ~ word with sb** porozmawiać z kimś prywatnie 4 (calm) cichy, spokojny 5 *[meal]* kameralny; *[wedding]* cichy 6 (secret) **to keep sth ~** trzymać coś w tajemnicy

quieten /'kwaɪətn/ *vt* 1 (calm) uspok|oić, -ajać *[child, animal]* 2 (silence) ucisz|yć, -ać *[children]*; zam|knąć, -ykać usta (komuś) *[critics]*

■ **quieten down**: ¶ ~ **down** 1 (become calm) *[child, activity]* uspok|oić, -ajać się 2 (fall silent) ucisz|yć, -ać się, za|milknąć ¶ ~ **[sb/sth] down** 1 (calm) uspok|oić, -ajać 2 (silence) ucisz|yć, -ać

quietly /'kwaɪətlɪ/ *adv* 1 (not noisily) *[move]* 2 (silently) *[play, read]* po cichu 3 (calmly) spokojnie

quietness /'kwaɪətnɪs/ *n* 1 (silence) cisza *f* 2 (of voice) słabość *f* 3 (of place) spokój *m*

quiff /kwɪf/ *n* GB (hairstyle) czub *m*

quill /kwɪl/ *n* 1 (feather) pióro *n*; (stem of feather) dutka *f* 2 (on porcupine) kolec *m* 3 (also ~ **pen**) gęsie pióro *n*

quilt /kwɪlt/ **I** *n* 1 GB (duvet) kołdra *f* 2 (bed cover) kapa *f*, narzuta *f*
II *vt* przepikow|ać, -ywać

quinine /kwɪ'niːn, US 'kwaɪnaɪn/ *n* chinina *f*

quintuplet /'kwɪntjʊplɪt, kwɪn'tjuːplɪt, US kwɪn'tuːplɪt/ *n* jedno *n* z pięcioraczków; **~s** pięcioraczki

quip /kwɪp/ **I** *n* dowcipna uwaga *f*
II *vi* za|żartować

quirk /kwɜːk/ *n* (of person) dziwactwo *n*; (of fate) (dziwny) przypadek *m*; **a ~ of nature** wybryk natury

quit /kwɪt/ **I** *vt* rzuc|ić, -ać *[job]*; opu|ścić, -szczać *[place, person]*; od|ejść, -chodzić od (czegoś) *[profession]*
II *vi* 1 (give up) **to ~ doing sth** przestać robić coś 2 (resign) *[employee]* od|ejść, -chodzić; *[politician]* poda|ć, -wać się do dymisji

quite /kwaɪt/ *adv* 1 (completely) całkowicie, zupełnie; **I ~ agree** całkowicie się zgadzam; **you're ~ right** masz całkowitą or zupełną rację; **it's ~ all right** (in reply to apology) w porządku, nic nie szkodzi; **I saw it ~ clearly** widziałam to całkiem wyraźnie 2 (exactly) **not ~** nie całkiem; **not ~ so much** niezupełnie tyle; **I don't ~ know** nie jestem całkiem pewny 3 (rather) *[big, easily, often]* całkiem, dosyć, dość; **it's ~ small** to jest dość

małe; **it's ~ warm today** dzisiaj jest dość ciepło; **it's ~ likely that...** jest całkiem prawdopodobne, że...; **~ a few** or **~ a lot of examples** sporo or niemało przykładów; **~ a lot of money** sporo or niemało pieniędzy; **I've thought about it ~ a bit** sporo o tym myślałem 4 (as intensifier) **~ simply** po prostu; **~ a difference** całkiem spora różnica; **that will be ~ a change for you** to będzie dla ciebie prawdziwa odmiana; **she's ~ a woman!** co za kobieta! 5 (expressing agreement) **~ (so)** właśnie

quits /kwɪts/ *adj* infml **to be ~** być kwita (**with sb** z kimś)

quiver /'kwɪvə(r)/ **I** *n* 1 (of voice, part of body, leaves) drżenie *n*; (sound) szelest *m*, szmer *m* 2 (for arrows) kołczan *m*
II *vi* *[voice, lip, animal, leaves]* za|drżeć; *[flames]* za|migotać

quiz /kwɪz/ **I** *n* 1 (on radio) quiz *m*, kwiz *m*, zgaduj-zgadula *f*; (on TV) teleturniej *m*; (written, in magazine) quiz *m*, kwiz *m* 2 US Sch test *m*, sprawdzian *m*
II *vt* wypyt|ać, -ywać (**about sb/sth** o kogoś/coś)

quiz game, quiz show *n* quiz *m*, zgaduj-zgadula *f*; (on TV) teleturniej *m*

quizzical /'kwɪzɪkl/ *adj [look]* lekko zdziwiony; *[smile]* zagadkowy

quota /'kwəʊtə/ *n* 1 (prescribed number) kontyngent *m* (**for** or **of sth** czegoś); **export/import ~** kwota eksportowa/importowa 2 (share) udział *m*; (officially allocated) przydział *m*

quotation /kwəʊ'teɪʃn/ *n* 1 (quote) cytat *m* 2 (estimate) wycena *f*

quotation marks *npl* (also **quotes**) cudzysłów *m*; **in ~** w cudzysłowie

quote /kwəʊt/ **I** *n* 1 (quotation) cytat *m* (**from sb/sth** z kogoś/czegoś) 2 (statement to journalist) wypowiedź *f* (dla prasy) 3 (estimate) wycena *f*
II **quotes** *npl* = **quotation marks**
III *vt* 1 za|cytować *[person]*; za|cytować, przyt|o-czyć, -aczać *[passage, words]*; **she was ~d as saying that...** przytoczono jej słowa, że... 2 (state) poda|ć, -wać *[price, figure]*; **they ~d us £200 for repairing the car** wycenili naprawę samochodu na 200 funtów 3 (on stock exchange) notować *[share, price]*
IV *vi* (from text, author) cytować; **to ~ from Keats** cytować Keatsa

R

r, R /ɑ:(r)/ *n* r, R *n*
rabbi /'ræbaɪ/ *n* rabin *m*
rabbit /'ræbɪt/ *n* królik *m*
rabid /'ræbɪd, US 'reɪbɪd/ *adj* ① (with rabies) wściekły ② (fanatical) zacieкły
rabies /'reɪbi:z/ *n* wścieklizna *f*
race¹ /reɪs/ **Ⅰ** *n* Sport wyścig *m*; (of runners) bieg *m*; (of horses) gonitwa *f*; **to run a ~** ścigać się (**with sb z** kimś)
Ⅱ *vt* ścigać się z (kimś/czymś) *[person, car, horse]*
Ⅲ *vi* ① (compete) ścigać się (**to sth** do czegoś) ② (rush) po|gnać, po|pędzić; **to ~ in/out** wpaść/wypaść ③ *[heart]* bić gwałtownie; *[engine]* być na wysokich obrotach ④ (hurry) śpieszyć się; **to ~ to do sth** śpieszyć się, żeby coś zrobić
race² /reɪs/ *n* rasa *f*
racehorse /'reɪshɔ:s/ *n* koń *m* wyścigowy
racer /'reɪsə(r)/ *n* (bike) rower *m* wyścigowy
race relations *npl* stosunki *m pl* rasowe
racetrack /'reɪstræk/ *n* (for horses) tor *m* wyścigów konnych; (for cars, cycles) tor *m* wyścigowy
racial /'reɪʃl/ *adj [prejudice]* rasowy; *[violence]* na tle rasowym
racing /'reɪsɪŋ/ **Ⅰ** *n* (of cars, bikes, animals) wyścigi *m pl*; (of boats) regaty *plt*
Ⅱ *adj [drivers, car, bike]* wyścigowy; *[boat, yacht]* regatowy
racing cyclist *n* kola|rz *m*, -rka *f*
racism /'reɪsɪzəm/ *n* rasizm *m*
racist /'reɪsɪst/ **Ⅰ** *n* rasist|a *m*, -ka *f*
Ⅱ *adj* rasistowski
rack /ræk/ **Ⅰ** *n* ① (for plates) suszarka *f*; (in dishwasher) koszyk *m*; (on train) półka *f* bagażowa; (for clothes) wieszak *m*; (for bottles, magazines) stojak *m* ② (torture) **to put sb on the ~** łamać kogoś kołem
Ⅱ *vt* fig *[nightmares]* dręczyć; *[pain]* nękać
(IDIOMS:) **to ~ one's brains** łamać sobie głowę
racket¹ /'rækɪt/ *n* Sport (in tennis) rakieta *f*; (in table tennis) rakietka *f*
racket² /'rækɪt/ *n* ① infml (noise) harmider *m*; **to make a ~** robić harmider ② (swindle) przekręt *m* infml; **the drugs ~** handel narkotykami
racketeering /ˌrækə'tɪərɪŋ/ *n* wymuszanie *n* okupu
racquetball /'rækɪtbɔ:l/ *n* US ≈ squash *m*
racy /'reɪsɪ/ *adj [style]* barwny; (risqué) pikantny
radar /'reɪdɑ:(r)/ *n* radar *m*

radiant /'reɪdɪənt/ *adj [person]* rozpromieniony; *[smile]* promienny
radiate /'reɪdɪeɪt/ *vt* ① promieniować (czymś) *[happiness]*; tryskać (czymś) *[health]*; emanować (czymś) *[confidence]* ② wypromieniow|ać, -ywać *[heat]*
radiation /ˌreɪdɪ'eɪʃn/ *n* promieniowanie *n*
radiation exposure *n* napromieniowanie *n*
radiation sickness *n* choroba *f* popromienna
radiator /'reɪdɪeɪtə(r)/ *n* ① (for heat) kaloryfer *m* ② (in car) chłodnica *f*
radical /'rædɪkl/ **Ⅰ** *n* radykał *m*
Ⅱ *adj* radykalny
radio /'reɪdɪəʊ/ **Ⅰ** *n* radio *n*; **on the ~** w radiu
Ⅱ *adj* radiowy
Ⅲ *vt* **to ~ (sb) sth** przesłać (komuś) przez radio coś *[message]*; podać (komuś) przez radio coś *[position]*
Ⅳ *vi* **to ~ for help** wzywać pomocy przez radio
radioactive /ˌreɪdɪəʊ'æktɪv/ *adj* promieniotwórczy, radioaktywny
radio alarm (clock) *n* radio *n* z budzikiem
radio announcer *n* spiker *m* radiowy
radio cassette (recorder) *n* radiomagnetofon *m*
radiotherapy /ˌreɪdɪəʊ'θerəpɪ/ *n* radioterapia *f*
radio station *n* (channel) stacja *f* (radiowa); (installation) radiostacja *f*
radish /'rædɪʃ/ *n* rzodkiew *f*, rzodkiewka *f*
radius /'reɪdɪəs/ *n* promień *m*
raffle /'ræfl/ *n* loteria *f*; **in a ~** na loterii
raft /rɑ:ft, US ræft/ *n* tratwa *f*
rafter /'rɑ:ftə(r), US 'ræftə(r)/ *n* krokiew *f*
rag /ræg/ **Ⅰ** *n* ① (cloth) szmata *f* ② infml (newspaper) gazeta *f*; (tabloid) szmatławiec *m* infml pej
Ⅱ rags *npl* (old clothes) szmaty *f pl*
(IDIOMS:) **it's like a red ~ to a bull** to działa jak czerwona płachta na byka; **to feel like a wet ~** czuć się jak wyżęta szmata infml
rage /reɪdʒ/ **Ⅰ** *n* ① (anger) wściekłość *f*; (fit of anger) napad *m* szału; **to fly into a ~** wpaść w szał ② infml **to be all the ~** być ostatnim krzykiem mody
Ⅱ *vi* ① *[storm, battle]* szaleć ② **to ~ at sb/sth** wściekać się na kogoś/coś

ragged /'rægɪd/ adj ☐ *[garment]* złachmaniony; *[collar, cuff]* przetarty; *[person]* obdarty ☐ (uneven) nierówny, postrzępiony

raging /'reɪdʒɪŋ/ adj ☐ *[passion, thirst, pain]* szalony; *[argument]* zaciekły; *[pain]* wściekły; *[hatred]* dziki ☐ *[blizzard, sea]* rozszalały

raid /reɪd/ ☐ n (by troops) wypad m; (by ships) atak m (**on sth** na coś); (by aircraft) nalot m (**on sth** na coś); (on bank) napad m (**on sth** na coś); (on house) włamanie n (**on sth** do czegoś); (by police, customs) nalot m infml (**on sth** na coś) ☐ vt *[soldiers]* za|atakować; *[aircraft]* przeprowadz|ić, -ać nalot na (coś); *[robbers]* napa|ść, -dać na (coś)

raider /'reɪdə(r)/ n napastni|k m, -czka f; (soldier) komandos m

rail /reɪl/ ☐ n ☐ (for protection, support) barierka f; (on balcony) balustrada f; (handrail) poręcz f ☐ (for hanging things) drążek m; (for curtains) szyna f ☐ (track) szyna f; **by** ~ koleją

railing /'reɪlɪŋ/ n (also ~s) ogrodzenie n

railroad /'reɪlrəʊd/ n US ☐ (network, company) kolej f ☐ (also ~ **track**) tory m pl kolejowe

railroad car n US wagon m (kolejowy)

railway /'reɪlweɪ/ GB ☐ n ☐ (network, company) kolej f ☐ (also ~ **line**) linia f kolejowa ☐ (also ~ **track**) tory m pl (kolejowe) ☐ adj *[link, bridge, accident]* kolejowy

railway carriage n GB wagon m (kolejowy)

railway station n GB (small) stacja f kolejowa; (large) dworzec m kolejowy

rain /reɪn/ ☐ n deszcz m; **to walk in the** ~ chodzić po deszczu ☐ v impers padać; **it's** ~**ing** pada (deszcz)

rainbow /'reɪnbəʊ/ n tęcza f

raincoat /'reɪnkəʊt/ n płaszcz m od deszczu or przeciwdeszczowy

raindrop /'reɪndrɒp/ n kropla f deszczu

rainfall /'reɪnfɔːl/ n poziom m opadów

rainforest /'reɪnfɒrɪst, US -fɔːrɪst/ n las m deszczowy

rainy /'reɪnɪ/ adj deszczowy; **it's a** ~ **place** tu ciągle pada

raise /reɪz/ ☐ n US (pay rise) podwyżka f ☐ vt ☐ (lift) podn|ieść, -osić, un|ieść, -osić *[lid]*; **to** ~ **one's glass to sb** wypić zdrowie kogoś; **to** ~ **one's hat to sb** uchylić przed kimś kapelusza ☐ (increase) podn|ieść, -osić *[salary, price, standard]*; zwiększ|yć, -ać *[volume]*; podwyższ|yć, -ać *[limit, offer]*; **to** ~ **one's voice (at sb)** podnieść głos (na kogoś) ☐ (cause) wzbudz|ić, -ać *[doubts, fears]*; wywoł|ać, -ywać *[blush, commotion]*; przywoł|ać, -ywać *[memories]*; **to** ~ **the alarm** podnieść alarm ☐ (mention) porusz|yć, -ać *[issue, matter]*; zgł|osić, -aszać *[objection]* ☐ (bring up) wychow|ać, -ywać *[child]* ☐ (breed) wy|hodować *[livestock]* ☐ (collect) z|ebrać, -bierać *[funds, capital]*; zdoby|ć, -wać

[support] ☐ (end) za|kończyć *[siege]*; zn|ieść, -osić *[ban, embargo]*

raised /reɪzd/ adj *[platform, jetty]* podniesiony

raisin /'reɪzn/ n rodzynek m, rodzynka f

rake /reɪk/ ☐ n (tool) grabie plt ☐ vt grabić *[grass, leaves]*
■ **rake up**: ~ **[sth] up** rozgrzeb|ać, -ywać *[grievance, past]*

rally /'rælɪ/ ☐ n ☐ (meeting) wiec m ☐ (car race) rajd m (samochodowy) ☐ (in tennis) wymiana f ☐ vt z|gromadzić *[support]*; z|ebrać, -bierać *[troops]*; z|mobilizować *[public opinion]* ☐ vi ☐ *[people]* z|gromadzić się; *[troops]* z|ebrać, -bierać się ☐ (recover) *[patient]* do|jść, -chodzić do siebie; *[sportsperson]* odzysk|ać, -iwać siły

rallying call n wezwanie n

ram /ræm/ ☐ n baran m ☐ vt ☐ (crash into) s|taranować ☐ (push) wbi|ć, -jać *[post]*; wcis|nąć, -kać *[books, pipe]*

RAM /ræm/ n = **random access memory** RAM m

ramble /'ræmbl/ n wycieczka f
■ **ramble on**: rozwodzić się (**about sth** o czymś)

rambler /'ræmblə(r)/ n turysta m pieszy

rambling /'ræmblɪŋ/ adj ☐ *[house]* pełen zakamarków; *[town]* rozproszony ☐ *[speech, letter]* rozwlekły

ramification /ˌræmɪfɪ'keɪʃn/ n konsekwencja f

ramp /ræmp/ n ☐ (slope) pochylnia f; (for wheelchairs) podjazd m; GB (to slow traffic) próg m zwalniający ☐ (for plane) schodki m pl ☐ US (on highway) wjazd m; (off highway) zjazd m

rampage /'ræmpeɪdʒ/ n **to be** or **go on the** ~ demolować wszystko po drodze

rampant /'ræmpənt/ adj *[crime, disease]* szalejący

rampart /'ræmpɑːt/ n szaniec m

ramshackle /'ræmʃækl/ adj *[building]* rozpadający się; *[vehicle]* rozklekotany

ranch /rɑːntʃ, US ræntʃ/ n ranczo n

rancid /'rænsɪd/ adj zjełczały; **to go** ~ zjełczeć

random /'rændəm/ adj *[choice]* przypadkowy; *[sample]* losowy

range /reɪndʒ/ ☐ n ☐ (of products) asortyment m, wybór m ☐ (of abilities, issues) wachlarz m; (of colours) gama f; (of prices, ages) rozpiętość f ☐ (bracket) przedział m; (scope) zakres m ☐ (of radar, weapon, transmitter) zasięg m ☐ US (prairie) preria f; **on the** ~ na pastwisku ☐ (of mountains) łańcuch m; (of hills) pasmo n ☐ (stove) (wood) piec m, kuchnia f; (gas, electric) kuchenka f ☐ vi ☐ (vary) **their ages** ~ **from 12 to 20** są w wieku od 12 do 20 lat ☐ (cover) **to** ~ **over many topics** *[person]* poruszyć wiele tematów; *[conversation]* dotyczyć wiele tematów

ranger /'reɪndʒə(r)/ n strażnik m leśny

rank¹ /ræŋk/ ☐ n ☐ (in military, police) stopień m, ranga f; (in company, politics) stanowisko n; (social status) pozycja f (społeczna) ☐ (line) szereg m; **to break**

~s wyłamać się z szeregu; *[politician]* wyłamać się;
to close ~s zewrzeć szeregi ③ **taxi** ~ postój *m*
taksówek

II *vt* **I** ~ him **alongside Brahms** stawiam go
na równi z Brahmsem; **he** ~s **it among the
city's best restaurants** uważa ją za jedną
z najlepszych restauracji w mieście

III *vi* **to** ~ **as a great composer** zaliczać się do
(grona) wielkich kompozytorów; **to** ~ **alongside
sb** być równym rangą komuś

rank² /ræŋk/ *adj* ① (absolute) *[outsider, beginner]*
zupełny; *[injustice, stupidity]* kompletny ② *[odour]*
obrzydliwy ③ *[ivy, weeds]* wybujały

rank and file /ˌræŋkən'faɪl/ *n* the ~ szeregowi
członkowie *m pl*

ranking /'ræŋkɪŋ/ *n* ranking *m*

rankle /'ræŋkl/ *vi* **to** ~ **with sb** boleć kogoś fig;
his failure still ~d wciąż nie mógł się otrząsnąć
po porażce

ransack /'rænsæk, US ræn'sæk/ *vt* przetrzą|snąć,
-ać *[luggage, drawer]* (**for sth** w poszukiwaniu
czegoś); s|plądrować *[house]*

ransom /'rænsəm/ *n* okup *m*; **to hold sb to** GB or
for US ~ trzymać kogoś dla okupu; fig szantażo-
wać kogoś

rant /rænt/ *vi* **to** ~ **and rave** ciskać gromy (**at sth**
na coś); **to** ~ **on** rozprawiać (**about sth** o czymś)

rap /ræp/ **II** *n* ① (single) stuknięcie *n*; (series) stukanie *n* ② Mus rap *m*

II *vt* za|stukać w (coś) *[table]*

rape¹ /reɪp/ **II** *n* gwałt *m*

II *vt* z|gwałcić

rape² /reɪp/ *n* (plant) rzepak *m*

rapid /'ræpɪd/ *adj [pulse, pace]* szybki; *[current]*
bystry

rapidly /'ræpɪdlɪ/ *adv* szybko

rapids /'ræpɪdz/ *n* bystrza *n pl*

rapist /'reɪpɪst/ *n* gwałciciel *m*

rapper /'ræpə(r)/ *n* Mus raper *m*

rapport /ræ'pɔː(r), US -'pɔːrt/ *n* dobre stosunki *plt*

rapture /'ræptʃə(r)/ *n* zachwyt *m*; **to go into** ~s
over or **about sth** zachwycać się czymś

rapturous /'ræptʃərəs/ *adj [welcome, applause]*
entuzjastyczny; ~ **delight** najwyższy zachwyt

rare /reə(r)/ *adj* ① (uncommon) rzadki ② (steak)
krwisty

rarely /'reəlɪ/ *adv* rzadko

raring /'reərɪŋ/ *adj* **to be** ~ **to do sth** nie móc się
doczekać, by coś zrobić

rarity /'reərətɪ/ *n* rzadkość *f*

rascal /'rɑːskl, US 'ræskl/ *n* nicpoń *m*; (child) urwis *m*

rash¹ /ræʃ/ *n* ① (on skin) wysypka *f* ② fig lawina *f* fig

rash² /ræʃ/ *adj [decision, promise]* pochopny; *[person]*
lekkomyślny; *[move, plan]* nierozważny

rasher /'ræʃə(r)/ *n* plasterek *m*

raspberry /'rɑːzbrɪ, US 'ræzberɪ/ *n* malina *f*

rasping /'rɑːspɪŋ, US ræspɪŋ/ *adj [sound]* zgrzytliwy, *[voice]* chrypiący

rat /ræt/ *n* szczur *m*

rate /reɪt/ **II** *n* ① (speed) tempo *n*; **to drive at a
terrific** ~ jechać z ogromną prędkością ② (level)
the unemployment ~ poziom bezrobocia; **the
interest** ~ stopa procentowa ③ (charge) taryfa *f*;
hourly ~ stawka za godzinę ④ (in foreign exchange)
kurs *m*

II rates *npl* GB ≈ podatek *m* od nieruchomości

III *vt* ① (classify) **to** ~ **sb as a great composer**
uważać kogoś za wybitnego kompozytora; **to** ~
sb among the best zaliczać kogoś do najlepszych ② (value) cenić (sobie) *[honesty, friendship,
person]*

IDIOMS: **at any** ~ w każdym razie

ratepayer /'reɪtpeɪə(r)/ *n* GB płatnik *m* podatku od
nieruchomości

rather /'rɑːðə(r)/ *adv* ① (somewhat) raczej; **I** ~
think that... jednak wydaje mi się, że...; **it's** ~
fun to jest dosyć or dość zabawne; **it's** ~ **a pity**
trochę szkoda ② (preferably) raczej; **I would
(much)** ~ **do sth** (zdecydowanie) wolałbym
zrobić coś; **I'd** ~ **not** wolałbym nie

ratify /'rætɪfaɪ/ *vt* ratyfikować

rating /'reɪtɪŋ/ **II** *n* wskaźnik *m*; (assessment) ocena *f*

II ratings *npl* (for TV) wskaźnik *m* oglądalności; (for
radio) wskaźnik *m* słuchalności

ratio /'reɪʃɪəʊ/ *n* stosunek *m*; **the pupil to teacher**
~ liczba uczniów przypadających na jednego
nauczyciela

ration /'ræʃn/ **II** *n* przydział *m*

II *vt* racjonować

rational /'ræʃənl/ *adj [approach, argument]* racjonalny; *[person]* rozsądny

rationale /ˌræʃə'nɑːl, US -'næl/ *n* ① **the** ~ **for
doing sth** powody zrobienia czegoś ② (logic)
racjonalne przesłanki *f pl* (**behind sth** czegoś)

rationalize /'ræʃnəlaɪz/ *vt* ① (justify) usprawiedli-
wi|ć, -ać ② GB (streamline) z|racjonalizować

rationing /'ræʃnɪŋ/ *n* racjonowanie *n*

rat race *n* wyścig *m* szczurów fig pej

rat run *n* GB *boczna uliczka pozwalająca ominąć
korki*

rattle /'rætl/ **II** *n* ① (of bottles, cutlery) brzęk *m*; (of
chains) szczęk *m*; (of window) trzaskanie *n*; (of machine)
terkot *m*; (of car engine) stukanie *n* ② (toy) grzechotka *f*

II *vt [wind]* szarp|nąć, -ać (czymś) *[window]*;
[person] szarp|nąć, -ać za (coś) *[handle]*

III *vi [bottles, cutlery, chains]* za|brzęczeć; *[window]*
za|stukać

rattlesnake /'rætlsneɪk/ *n* grzechotnik *m*

raucous /'rɔːkəs/ *adj [laughter]* rechotliwy; *[person]*
hałaśliwy

raunchy /'rɔːntʃɪ/ *adj* infml *[story, song]* sprośny

ravage /'rævɪdʒ/ *vt [fire, troops]* s|pustoszyć

rave /reɪv/ **II** *n* GB infml (party) ubaw *m* infml

II adj infml ~ **reviews** entuzjastyczne recenzje
III vi [1] (enthusiastically) zachwycać się (**about sth**
czymś) [2] (when fevered) majaczyć
ravenous /'rævənəs/ adj [person, animal] wygłodniały; [appetite] wilczy
ravine /rə'vi:n/ n wąwóz m, jar m
raving /'reɪvɪŋ/ adj szaleńczy, wściekły; **a ~
lunatic** kompletny wariat infml
ravishing /'rævɪʃɪŋ/ adj uroczy
raw /rɔː/ adj [1] [cotton, data, food, sugar] surowy;
[sewage] nieoczyszczony [2] [part of body] obtarty
[3] [weather] zimny i mokry; [wind] przenikliwy
[4] [novice] surowy infml fig; [youngster] nieopierzony
hum [5] [scenery, style] surowy; [description] naturalistyczny
IDIOMS: **to get a ~ deal** infml zostać źle
potraktowanym
raw material n surowiec m
ray /reɪ/ n (beam) promień m
raze /reɪz/ vt **to ~ sth to the ground** zrównać coś
z ziemią
razor /'reɪzə(r)/ n (straight razor) brzytwa f; (safety razor)
maszynka f do golenia, golarka f
razor blade n żyletka f
re¹ /reɪ/ n Mus re n inv
re² /ri:/ prep = **with reference to** (in letter head) dot.;
(about) odnośnie do (czegoś)
reach /ri:tʃ/ **I** n zasięg m; **it's beyond** or **out of
my ~** nie dosięgnę do tego; **within easy ~ of sth**
w pobliżu czegoś
II reaches npl **the upper/lower ~es** (of river)
górny/dolny bieg
III vt [1] (arrive) do|trzeć, -cierać do (kogoś/czegoś);
(after walking) do|jść, -chodzić do (kogoś/czegoś); (by
vehicle) doje|chać, -żdżać do (kogoś/czegoś); (by boat,
after swimming) dopły|nąć, -wać do (kogoś/czegoś);
(after flying) do|lecieć, -atywać do (kogoś/czegoś)
[2] (come to) osiąg|nąć, -ać [agreement, compromise];
to ~ a conclusion dojść do wniosku; **to ~ a
decision** podjąć decyzję [3] (win) do|trzeć, -cierać
do (kogoś) [audience, public] (**with sth** z czymś);
zdoby|ć, -wać [market] [4] (in hight, length) sięgać do
(czegoś) [floor, ceiling]
IV vi [1] **to ~ up/down to do sth** wyciągnąć
rękę, żeby coś zrobić [2] (extend) **to ~ (up/down)
to sth** sięgać (do) czegoś
react /ri'ækt/ vi za|reagować (**to sth** na coś); **to ~
against sth** przeciwstawiać się czemuś
reaction /ri'ækʃn/ n reakcja f
reactionary /ri'ækʃənri, US -əneri/ **I** n reakcjonist|a m, -ka f
II adj reakcyjny
reactor /ri'æktə(r)/ n reaktor m
read /ri:d/ **I** vt [1] prze|czytać [text]; wy|czytać,
prze|czytać [information, news]; **can you ~ music?**
czy umiesz czytać nuty?; **I can ~ German** umiem
czytać po niemiecku [2] Univ studiować [3] [therm-

ometer] wskaz|ać, -ywać; **the card ~s...** na kartce
jest napisane...
II vi czytać; **to ~ to sb** czytać komuś
■ **read out:** odczyt|ać, -ywać
■ **read up: to ~ up on sb/sth** poczytać o kimś/
czymś
readable /'ri:dəbl/ adj czytelny; **a highly ~
article** artykuł, który dobrze się czyta
reader /'ri:də(r)/ n czytelni|k m, -czka f
readily /'redɪli/ adv [1] [accept, agree] chętnie
[2] [available] łatwo; [forget] szybko; [understand]
bez trudu
reading /'ri:dɪŋ/ n [1] (activity) czytanie n; **his ~ is
poor** kiepsko czyta [2] (text) lektura f; **to make
interesting ~** stanowić ciekawą lekturę; **a
woman of wide ~** bardzo oczytana kobieta
[3] (measurement) odczyt m
reading glasses npl okulary plt do czytania
reading list n lista f lektur
readjust /ˌri:ə'dʒʌst/ **I** vt (ponownie) wy|regulować [television]; przestawi|ć, -ać [watch]
II vi przystosow|ać, -ywać się (ponownie) (**to sth**
do czegoś)
readvertise /ri:'ædvətaɪz/ vt **to ~ a position**
zamieścić kolejne ogłoszenie o pracy
ready /'redi/ adj [1] (prepared) gotowy (**for sth** do
czegoś); ~ **to do sth** gotowy, żeby coś zrobić; **to
get ~** przygotować się; **to get sth ~** przygotować coś; ~, **steady, go!** do biegu, gotowi,
start! [2] (resolved) gotowy; **to be ~ for sth** być
gotowym na coś
ready-made /ˌredɪ'meɪd/ adj [clothes, answer]
gotowy
ready-to-wear /ˌredɪtə'weə(r)/ adj [garment] gotowy
real /rɪəl/ adj [1] (not imaginary) rzeczywisty, realny;
in ~ life w rzeczywistości [2] (genuine) [diamond,
flower, leather] prawdziwy [3] (proper) [holiday, altruism] prawdziwy [4] (for emphasis) [charmer, pleasure] prawdziwy; **it's a ~ shame!** wielka szkoda!
real estate n [1] (property) nieruchomość f [2] US
(profession) pośrednictwo n w handlu nieruchomościami
realism /'ri:əlɪzəm/ n realizm m
realist /'ri:əlɪst/ n realist|a m, -ka f
realistic /ˌrɪə'lɪstɪk/ adj realistyczny
reality /rɪ'æləti/ vt (real world) rzeczywistość f; (facts)
realia plt
realization /ˌrɪəlaɪ'zeɪʃn, US -lɪ'z-/ n **to come to
the ~ that...** zdać sobie sprawę, że...
realize /'rɪəlaɪz/ vt [1] (become aware of) zda|ć, -wać
sobie sprawę z (czegoś) [error, significance, fact]; **to
make sb ~ sth** uświadomić komuś coś [2] (make
real) z|realizować [idea, dream, goal, design]
really /'rɪəli/ **I** adv [1] (for emphasis) naprawdę; ~
good naprawdę dobry [2] (in actual fact) tak naprawdę; '**do you like it?' – 'not ~**' „podoba ci się?" –

„niespecjalnie" [3] (expressing disbelief) ~? naprawdę?, czyżby?; **'I'm 45' – 'are you ~?'** „mam 45 lat" – „naprawdę?"

[II] *excl* (also **well** ~) no nie!

reap /riːp/ *vt* [1] (cut) s|kosić, z|żąć *[barley, crop]* [2] fig z|ebrać, -bierać *[profits]*; **to ~ the rewards of one's efforts** zbierać owoce swoich wysiłków

reappear /ˌriːəˈpɪə(r)/ *vi* pojawi|ć, -ać się ponownie

reapply /ˌriːəˈplaɪ/ *vi [candidate, person]* zgł|osić, -aszać się ponownie

rear[1] /rɪə(r)/ [I] *n* [1] (of building, car, procession) tył *m* [2] (of person) tylna część *f* ciała euph

[II] *adj [light, seat, suspension]* tylny; ~ **garden** ogród na tyłach domu

rear[2] /rɪə(r)/ [I] *vt* wychow|ać, -ywać *[children]*; wy|hodować *[plants, animals]*

[II] *vi* (also ~ **up**) *[horse]* sta|nąć, -wać dęba; *[snake]* sta|nąć, -wać pionowo

rearmament /ˌriːˈɑːməmənt/ *n* remilitaryzacja *f*

rearrange /ˌriːəˈreɪndʒ/ *vt* przestawi|ć, -ać *[furniture]*; przemeblow|ać, -ywać *[room]*; zmieni|ć, -ać *[plans]*; przeł|ożyć, -kładać *[appointment]*

rear-view mirror /ˌrɪəvjuːˈmɪrə(r)/ *n* lusterko *n* wsteczne

reason /ˈriːzn/ [I] *n* [1] (cause) powód *m* (**for** or **behind sth** czegoś); **for no (good)** ~ bez wyraźnego powodu; **for health** ~s z przyczyn zdrowotnych; **the** ~ **why...** powód, dla którego... [2] (grounds) powód *m*; **a good/bad** ~ **for doing sth** wystarczający/niewystarczający powód, żeby coś zrobić; **to have every** ~ **to do sth** mieć wszelkie podstawy do zrobienia czegoś; **I have** ~ **to believe...** mam powody przypuszczać, że... [3] (common sense) (zdrowy) rozsądek *m*; **to lose one's** ~ stracić rozum; **to listen to** or **see** ~ posłuchać głosu rozsądku; **it stands to** ~ **that...** to zrozumiałe, że...; **within** ~ w granicach rozsądku [4] (intellect) rozum *m*; **the Age of Reason** okres oświecenia

[II] *vi* **to** ~ **with sb** przekonywać kogoś

reasonable /ˈriːznəbl/ *adj* [1] *[person]* rozsądny; **to be** ~ **about sth** podchodzić do czegoś rozsądnie [2] *[fear, suspicion]* uzasadniony; *[explanation, attitude]* sensowny; **it is** ~ **to suppose that...** można przypuszczać, że... [3] *[fee, price]* rozsądny; *[food, weather]* znośny

reasonably /ˈriːznəblɪ/ *adv* [1] *[fear, suspect]* słusznie; *[behave, conclude]* rozsądnie [2] (rather) dość; **I'm** ~ **certain of it** jestem o tym raczej przekonany

reasoning /ˈriːznɪŋ/ *n* rozumowanie *n*

reassert /ˌriːəˈsɜːt/ *vt* um|ocnić, -acniać *[authority, dominance]*

reassess /ˌriːəˈses/ *vt* oceni|ć, -ać ponownie *[problem, situation]*; wylicz|yć, -ać ponownie *[liability, taxes]*

reassurance /ˌriːəˈʃɔːrəns/, US -ˈʃʊər-/ *n* [1] (comfort) otucha *f* [2] (guarantee) zapewnienie *n*

reassure /ˌriːəˈʃɔː(r)/, US -ˈʃʊər/ *vt* uspok|oić, -ajać

reassuring /ˌriːəˈʃɔːrɪŋ/, US -ˈʃʊər-/ *adj* dodający otuchy

rebate /ˈriːbeɪt/ *n* zwrot *m*

rebel [I] /ˈrebl/ *n* buntownik *m*

[II] /rɪˈbel/ *vi* z|buntować się

rebellion /rɪˈbeliən/ *n* bunt *m*

rebellious /rɪˈbeliəs/ *adj [tribes, attitudes]* buntowniczy; *[child]* zbuntowany

rebuff /rɪˈbʌf/ [I] *n* odmowa *f*

[II] *vt* odm|ówić, -awiać (komuś) *[person]*; odrzuc|ić, -ać *[suggestion, offer]*; odtrąc|ić, -ać *[advances]*

rebuild /ˌriːˈbɪld/ *vt* odbudow|ać, -ywać *[building, confidence]*; (change) przebudow|ać, -ywać *[building, system]*

rebuke /rɪˈbjuːk/ [I] *n* nagana *f*

[II] *vt* z|ganić (**for sth/doing sth** za coś/zrobienie czegoś)

rebut /rɪˈbʌt/ *vt* od|eprzeć, -pierać *[accusation, criticism]*; obal|ić, -ać *[evidence, charge]*

recall [I] /ˈriːkɔːl/ *n* pamięć *f*; **to have total ~ of sth** pamiętać coś dokładnie

[II] /rɪˈkɔːl/ *vt* [1] (remember) przypom|nieć, -inać sobie; **I ~ what happened** pamiętam, co się stało [2] (remind of) przypom|nieć, -inać

recapitulate /ˌriːkəˈpɪtʃʊleɪt/ *vt, vi* z|rekapitulować

recapture /ˌriːˈkæptʃə(r)/ *vt* [1] (catch) ponownie uj|ąć, -mować *[prisoner, animal]* [2] (win) odbi|ć, -jać *[town, position, seat]* [3] fig odtw|orzyć, -arzać *[atmosphere, period]*

recede [I] /rɪˈsiːd/ *vi [tide]* cof|nąć, -ać się; fig *[threat]* mi|nąć, -jać; *[hopes]* z|maleć; *[memory]* za|trzeć, -cierać się

[II] **receding** /rɪˈsiːdɪŋ/ *prp adj [chin, forehead]* cofnięty; **a receding hairline** początki łysiny

receipt /rɪˈsiːt/ *n* [1] (for money) pokwitowanie *n*; (from till) paragon *m* (**for sth** na coś) [2] (on delivery) potwierdzenie *n* odbioru (**for sth** czegoś) [3] (of goods, letter) otrzymanie *n*; **payable on** ~ płatny przy odbiorze

[II] **receipts** *npl* (takings) wpływy *plt* (**from sth** z czegoś)

receive /rɪˈsiːv/ [I] *vt* [1] (get) otrzym|ać, -ywać *[letter, award, punch, education]*; spot|kać, -ykać się z (czymś) *[criticism, refusal]*; **to ~ stolen goods** zajmować się paserstwem [2] (meet) przyj|ąć, -mować *[guest, proposal, article]* [3] (on radio, TV) od|ebrać, -bierać *[channel, programme, signals]*

[II] **received** *pp adj [opinion, view]* (ogólnie) przyjęty

receiver /rɪˈsiːvə(r)/ *n* [1] (telephone) słuchawka *f* [2] (equipment) odbiornik *m*

receiving /rɪˈsiːvɪŋ/ *n* paserstwo *n*

recent /ˈriːsnt/ *adj [event, change]* niedawny; *[arrival, film]* najnowszy; *[acquaintance]* nowy;

[developments, days] ostatni; **in** ~ **years** w ostatnich latach

recently /'ri:sntlɪ/ *adv* ostatnio, niedawno; **until** ~ do niedawna

reception /rɪ'sepʃn/ *n* 1 (also ~ **desk**) recepcja *f* 2 (gathering) przyjęcie *n* (**for sb/sth** na cześć kogoś/ z okazji czegoś) 3 (public response) przyjęcie *n*; **to be given a favourable** ~ spotkać się z przychylnym przyjęciem 4 (on radio, TV) odbiór *m*

receptionist /rɪ'sepʃənɪst/ *n* recepcjonist|a *m*, -ka *f*

receptive /rɪ'septɪv/ *adj [mind]* chłonny; *[attitude]* otwarty (**to sth** na coś)

recess /rɪ'ses, US 'ri:ses/ I *n* 1 (of parliament) wakacje *plt* parlamentarne; (in court) przerwa *f* wakacyjna 2 US (in school) przerwa *f* w zajęciach; (during meeting) przerwa *f* w obradach 3 (alcove) wnęka *f*
II **recesses** *npl* **the** ~**es of sth** zakamarki czegoś *[cupboard, building, memory]*

recession /rɪ'seʃn/ *n* recesja *f*

recharge /,ri:'tʃɑːdʒ/ *vt* (ponownie) na|ładować *[battery, gun]*

rechargeable /,ri:'tʃɑːdʒəbl/ *adj* **are these batteries** ~? czy te baterie można ładować?

recipe /'resəpɪ/ *n* przepis *m* (**for sth** na coś); fig recepta *f* (**for sth** na coś)

recipient /rɪ'sɪpɪənt/ *n* (of mail, aid) odbior|ca *m*, -czyni *f*; (of award) laureat *m*, -ka *f*; (of blood, tissue) biorca *m*

reciprocal /rɪ'sɪprəkl/ *adj [relations, affection]* wzajemny; *[agreement]* dwustronny; *[reduction]* obustronny

reciprocate /rɪ'sɪprəkeɪt/ I *vt* odwzajemni|ć, -ać *[compliment, kindness, affection]*
II *vi* odwzajemni|ć, -ać się

recital /rɪ'saɪtl/ *n* 1 (of music) recital *m* 2 (of facts, events) wyliczenie *n*

recite /rɪ'saɪt/ I *vt* wy|recytować *[poem]*; wygłosić, -aszać *[speech]*; wylicz|yć, -ać *[facts]*
II *vi* recytować

reckless /'reklɪs/ *adj [person, behaviour]* lekkomyślny; *[driving]* niebezpieczny

reckon /'rekən/ *vt* 1 (judge) uważać; **he's** ~**ed to be...** uważany jest or uważa się go... 2 infml (think) myśleć; **I** ~ **we should go** myślę, że powinniśmy już iść 3 (accurately) wylicz|yć, -ać *[amount, number]*
■ **reckon on** infml: ~ **on [sb/sth]** liczyć na (kogoś/coś); ~ **on sb** or **sb's doing sth** liczyć na to, że ktoś coś zrobi
■ **reckon with**: liczyć się z (kimś/czymś)

reckoning /'rekənɪŋ/ *n* (estimation) ocena *f*; (calculation) obliczenia *n pl*

reclaim /rɪ'kleɪm/ *vt* 1 (salvage) osusz|yć, -ać *[coastal land, marsh]*; wy|karczować *[forest]*; na-w|odnić, -adniać *[desert]*; z|rekultywować *[polluted land]*; (recycle) odzysk|ać, -iwać *[glass, metal]* 2 (get back) od|ebrać, -bierać *[deposit, money]*

reclaimable /rɪ'kleɪməbl/ *adj [waste, product]* nadający się do ponownego wykorzystania

recline /rɪ'klaɪn/ *vi [person]* u|łożyć, -kładać się w pozycji półleżącej; *[seat]* odchyl|ić, -ać się

reclining /rɪ'klaɪnɪŋ/ *adj* 1 *[figure]* półleżący 2 *[chair]* z regulowanym oparciem; *[seat]* odchylany

recluse /rɪ'kluːs/ *n* samotni|k *m*, -ca *f*

recognition /,rekəg'nɪʃn/ *n* 1 (identification) rozpoznanie *n* 2 (acknowledgement) uznanie *n*; **to receive** or **win** ~ **for sth** zdobyć or zyskać uznanie czymś *[talent, work]*

recognizable /,rekəg'naɪzəbl, 'rekəgnaɪzəbl/ *adj* **very** ~ bardzo łatwy do rozpoznania; **hardly** ~ z trudem dający się rozpoznać

recognize /'rekəgnaɪz/ *vt* 1 (identity) rozpozna|ć, -wać, pozna|ć, -wać *[person]* (**by sth** po czymś) 2 (acknowledge) uzna|ć, -wać *[achievement, government]*

recoil /rɪ'kɔɪl/ *vi* (physically) cof|nąć, -ać się; (mentally) wzdryg|nąć, -ać się

recollect /,rekə'lekt/ *vt, vi* przypom|nieć, -inać sobie

recollection /,rekə'lekʃn/ *n* wspomnienie *n*

recommend /,rekə'mend/ *vt* polec|ić, -ać *[person, company, book]*; (**as sb/sth** jako kogoś/coś); zalec|ić, -ać *[investigation, treatment, policy]*

recommendation /,rekəmen'deɪʃn/ *n* 1 (favourable statement) rekomendacja *f*; **to speak in** ~ **of sb/ sth** polecać kogoś/coś; **to write sb a** ~ napisać komuś list polecający 2 (advice) zalecenie *n* (**to sb/ on sth** dla kogoś/dotyczące czegoś)

recommended reading *n* lista *f* zalecanych lektur

recompense /'rekəmpens/ *n* rekompensata *f* (**for sth** za coś); (in law) odszkodowanie *n* (**for sth** za coś)

reconcile /'rekənsaɪl/ *vt* po|godzić; **to be** or **become** ~**d** pogodzić się (**with sb** z kimś); **to become** ~**d to sth** pogodzić się z czymś

reconnaissance /rɪ'kɒnɪsns/ *n* rozpoznanie *n*, zwiad *m*, rekonesans *m*

reconnoitre GB, **reconnoiter** US /,rekə'nɔɪtə(r)/ I *vt* rozpozna|ć, -wać
II *vi* przeprowadz|ić, -ać rozpoznanie

reconsider /,ri:kən'sɪdə(r)/ I *vt* rozważ|yć, -ać ponownie
II *vi* (think further) zastanowić się jeszcze raz

reconstruct /,ri:kən'strʌkt/ *vt* 1 (restore) odbudow|ać, -ywać *[building]*; z|rekonstruować *[vase, text]* 2 *[police]* dokon|ać, -ywać rekonstrukcji (czegoś) *[crime]*

reconstruction /,ri:kən'strʌkʃn/ *n* 1 (of building, country) odbudowa *f* 2 (of party, system) przebudowa *f* 3 (of object, event, crime) rekonstrukcja *f*

record I /'rekɔːd, US 'rekərd/ *n* 1 (of facts, events) zapis *m*; (of proceedings) protokół *m*; **to keep a** ~ **of**

sth zapisywać coś; (officially) rejestrować coś; **he is on ~ as saying that...** stwierdził publicznie, że...; **to say sth off the ~** powiedzieć coś poza protokołem ②　(also ~**s**) (historical) archiwa n pl; (personal, administrative) akta plt; (register) spis m, rejestr m ③ (musical) płyta f ④ (best performance) rekord m (**for** or **in sth** w czymś) ⑤ (also **criminal ~**) kartoteka f kryminalna; **to have no ~** nie być notowanym

Ⅱ /'rekɔːd, US 'rekərd/ adj ① [company] płytowy; **~ collection** kolekcja płyt; **~ shop** sklep z płytami ② [result, sales, time] rekordowy; **at a ~ high** na rekordowo wysokim poziomie

Ⅲ /rɪ'kɔːd/ vt ① (note) zapis|ać, -ywać, za|notować [detail, idea, opinion] ② (on disc, tape) nagr|ać, -ywać ③ [equipment] za|rejestrować [temperature]; [dial] wskaz|ać, -ywać [pressure, speed]

record book n księga f rekordów

recorded /rɪ'kɔːdɪd/ adj (on tape, record) nagrany; [fact, history] udokumentowany; **~ delivery** GB list m polecony

recorder /rɪ'kɔːdə(r)/ n flet m podłużny

record-holder /'rekɔːdhəʊldə(r), US 'rekərd-/ n rekordzist|a m, -ka f

recording /rɪ'kɔːdɪŋ/ n nagranie n

record player n gramofon m, adapter m

recourse /rɪ'kɔːs/ n **to have ~ to sth** uciec się do czegoś

recover /rɪ'kʌvə(r)/ Ⅰ vt odzysk|ać, -iwać [money, vehicle, territory]; (from water) wydoby|ć, -wać [body, wreck]; **to ~ one's health** odzyskać zdrowie; **to ~ damages from sb** uzyskać odszkodowanie od kogoś

Ⅱ vi ① (from illness) wy|zdrowieć (**from sth** po czymś); (from defeat) do|jść, -chodzić do siebie (**from sth** po czymś) ② [economy, market] do|jść, -chodzić do siebie fig; [shares, currency] wr|ócić, -acać do dawnego poziomu

recovery /rɪ'kʌvərɪ/ n ① (after illness) powrót m do zdrowia ② (of economy, company, market) powrót m do normy

recovery vehicle n pomoc f drogowa

recreate /ˌriːkrɪ'eɪt/ vt odtw|orzyć, -arzać

recreation /ˌrekrɪ'eɪʃn/ n ① (leisure) rekreacja f ② (break) przerwa f rekreacyjna

recreational drug n narkotyk zażywany okazjonalnie

recreational vehicle, RV n US samochód m turystyczny

recrimination /rɪˌkrɪmɪ'neɪʃn/ n wzajemne oskarżenia n pl

recruit /rɪ'kruːt/ Ⅰ n rekrut m

Ⅱ vt z|werbować (**from sb** spośród kogoś)

recruiting officer n oficer m do spraw rekrutacji

recruitment /rɪ'kruːtmənt/ n rekrutacja f

rectangle /'rektæŋgl/ n prostokąt m

rectangular /rek'tæŋgjʊlə(r)/ adj prostokątny

rectify /'rektɪfaɪ/ vt s|prostować [error]; naprawi|ć, -ać [damage, situation]

rector /'rektə(r)/ n (in Anglican churches) proboszcz m

recuperate /rɪ'kuːpəreɪt/ vi wr|ócić, -acać do zdrowia (**from sth** po czymś)

recur /rɪ'kɜː(r)/ vi [error, event] powt|órzyć, -arzać się; [illness, pain] nawr|ócić, -acać; [thought, memory] powr|ócić, -acać

recurrence /rɪ'kʌrəns/ n (of illness) nawrót m; (of symptom, event) powtórzenie się n

recurrent /rɪ'kʌrənt/ adj [theme, feeling, problem] powracający

recycle /ˌriː'saɪkl/ vt przetw|orzyć, -arzać; **~d paper** papier z makulatury

recycling /ˌriː'saɪklɪŋ/ n recykling m

red /red/ Ⅰ n ① (kolor m) czerwony m, czerwień f ② **to be in the ~** [individual] mieć saldo debetowe na koncie; [company] mieć deficyt

Ⅱ adj [apple, face, cheek, sky] czerwony; [hair, squirrel] rudy; **to go** or **turn ~** zaczerwienić się IDIOMS: **to be caught ~-handed** zostać przyłapanym na gorącym uczynku; **to see ~** wściec się

red alert n stan m najwyższego pogotowia

Red Cross n Czerwony Krzyż m

redcurrant /ˌred'kʌrənt/ n czerwona porzeczka f

redden /'redn/ vi [face, leaves] po|czerwienieć

redecorate /ˌriː'dekəreɪt/ vt odn|owić, -awiać [house, room]

redeem /rɪ'diːm/ vt ① z|realizować [voucher]; spienięż|yć, -ać [bond, security] ② wykup|ić, -ywać [pawned goods] ③ u|ratować [situation]; z|rekompensować [fault] ④ (in religion) odkupić

redevelop /ˌriːdɪ'veləp/ vt przebudow|ać, -ywać [area, estate]

red-faced /ˌred'feɪst/ adj (embarrassed) zmieszany; (permanently) rumiany

redhead /'redhed/ n rudzielec m infml

red herring n temat m zastępczy

red-hot /ˌred'hɒt/ adj [metal, coal] rozgrzany do czerwoności

redial /ˌriː'daɪəl/ Ⅰ vt ponownie wyb|rać, -ierać [number]

Ⅱ vi ponownie wyb|rać, -ierać numer

redirect /ˌriːdɪ'rekt/ vt przesu|nąć, -wać [resources]; s|kierować w inną stronę [traffic]; przes|łać, -yłać pod inny adres [mail]

rediscover /ˌriːdɪ'skʌvə(r)/ vt odzysk|ać, -iwać [skill, enthusiasm]

red light area n dzielnica f domów publicznych

redo /ˌriː'duː/ vt ① (start from beginning) przer|obić, -abiać od początku ② (repaint) przemalow|ać, -ywać

red pepper n czerwona papryka f

redress /rɪ'dres/ vt naprawi|ć, -ać [error, situation]; zadośćuczynić za (coś) [grievances, injustice]; **to ~ the balance** przywrócić równowagę

red tape n biurokracja f

reduce /rɪ'dju:s, US -'du:s/ *vt* [1] (make smaller) obniż|yć, -ać *[costs, prices, temperature]*; zmniej-sz|yć, -ać *[inflation, pressure, impact, number, work-force]*; skr|ócić, -acać *[article, chapter]* [2] (alter the state of) **to ~ sth to shreds** podrzeć coś na strzępy; **to ~ sth to ruins** doprowadzić coś do ruiny; **~ sb to tears** doprowadzić kogoś do łez; **to be ~d to begging** zostać zmuszonym do żebrania [3] (thicken) odparow|ać, -ywać *[sauce, stock]*

reduction /rɪ'dʌkʃn/ *n* [1] (of costs) obniżenie *n*, redukcja *f*; (of volume, speed, size) zmniejszenie *n* [2] (reduced price) obniżka *f*

redundancy /rɪ'dʌndənsɪ/ *n* redukcja *f* zatrud-nienia; **400 redundancies** zwolnienie 400 pracow-ników

redundant /rɪ'dʌndənt/ *adj* [1] GB *[worker]* zredu-kowany; **to be made ~** zostać zredukowanym [2] *[information, device]* zbędny; *[land, machinery]* niewykorzystany

reed /ri:d/ *n* [1] Bot trzcina *f* [2] Mus stroik *m*

reef /ri:f/ *n* (in sea) rafa *f*

reek /ri:k/ *vi* **to ~ of sth** śmierdzieć czymś also fig

reel¹ /ri:l/ *n* [1] (for cotton, tape) szpulka *f*; (for cable) szpula *f*; (of film) szpula *f* [2] (on fishing rod) kołowro-tek *m*

■ **reel off:** wy|recytować *[list, names]*

reel² /ri:l/ *vi* (sway) *[person]* zat|oczyć, -aczać się; **the blow sent him ~ing** zatoczył się od tego ciosu; **the news sent him ~ing** fig kiedy usłyszał tę wiadomość, nogi się pod nim ugięły; **the government is still ~ing after its defeat** rząd nie pozbierał się jeszcze po porażce

re-elect /ˌri:ɪ'lekt/ *vt* ponownie wyb|rać, -ierać

re-emerge /ˌri:ɪ'mɜ:dʒ/ *vi [person, problem]* poja-wi|ć, -ać się ponownie; *[sun]* ponownie pokaz|ać, -ywać się

re-examine /ˌri:ɪg'zæmɪn/ *vt* [1] ponownie z|badać *[issue]* [2] ponownie przesłuch|ać, -iwać *[witness]*

refectory /rɪ'fektrɪ, 'refɪktrɪ/ *n* (in religious institution) refektarz *m*; (in school) sala *f* jadalna

refer /rɪ'fɜ:(r)/ **[I]** *vt* przekaz|ać, -ywać *[task, problem, enquiry]* (**to sb** komuś); **to be ~red to a specialist** zostać skierowanym do specjalisty

[II] *vi* [1] **to ~ to sb** wspomnieć o kimś; **to ~ to sth** nawiązać do czegoś *[topic, event]* [2] *[number, term]* oznaczać (**to sth** coś) [3] **to ~ to sth** sprawdzić w czymś *[notes, dictionary]*

referee /ˌrefə'ri:/ **[I]** *n* [1] Sport sędzia *m*, arbiter *m* [2] GB (giving job reference) osoba *f* udzielająca referencji

[II] *vt, vi* sędziować

reference /'refərəns/ **[I]** *n* [1] (mention) wzmianka *f*; **few ~s are made to it** rzadko się o tym mówi [2] (consultation) **to do sth without ~ to sth** zrobić coś bez sprawdzania w czymś; **for future ~** na przyszłość [3] (allusion) **to make ~ to sb/sth** zrobić

aluzję do kogoś/czegoś [4] (in book) źródło *n* [5] (testimonial) referencje *f pl*

[II] with reference to *prep phr* odnośnie do (czegoś)

reference book *n* publikacja *f* encyklopedyczna

reference number *n* numer *m* referencyjny

referendum /ˌrefə'rendəm/ *n* referendum *n*

referral /rɪ'fɜ:rəl/ *n* [1] (of person) skierowanie *n* (**to sth** na coś) [2] (of matter, problem) odesłanie *n* (**to sth** do czegoś)

refill **[I]** /'ri:fɪl/ *n* (for fountain pen) nabój *m*; (for ball-point, notebook, pencil) grafit *m*

[II] /ˌri:'fɪl/ *vt* ponownie napełni|ć, -ać *[lighter, pen, glass]*

refine /rɪ'faɪn/ *vt* [1] Tech rafinować *[oil, sugar]* [2] (improve) dopracow|ać, -ywać *[theory]*; wygładz|ić, -ać *[language]*; udoskonal|ić, -ać *[method]*

refined /rɪ'faɪnd/ *adj* wytworny

refinement /rɪ'faɪnmənt/ *n* wytworność *f*

refinery /rɪ'faɪnərɪ/ *n* rafineria *f*

reflect /rɪ'flekt/ **[I]** *vt* [1] (not absorb) odbi|ć, -jać *[light, sound, heat]*; **to be ~ed in sth** odbijać się w czymś [2] fig odzwierciedl|ić, -ać *[ideas, views, problems]*; **to be ~ed in sth** znajdować odzwier-ciedlenie w czymś [3] (think) po|myśleć

[II] *vi* [1] zastan|owić, -awiać się (**on** or **upon sth** nad czymś) [2] **to ~ well/badly on sb** dobrze/źle o kimś świadczyć

reflection /rɪ'flekʃn/ *n* [1] (image) odbicie *n* (**of sth** czegoś); odzwierciedlenie *n* (**of sth** czegoś) also fig [2] (thought) refleksja *f*; **on ~** po zastanowieniu

reflector /rɪ'flektə(r)/ *n* (on vehicle) światło *n* od-blaskowe

reflex /'ri:fleks/ **[I]** *n* odruch *m*

[II] *adj [action]* odruchowy

reflexive verb *n* czasownik *m* w stronie zwrotnej

reform /rɪ'fɔ:m/ **[I]** *n* reforma *f*

[II] *vt* z|reformować

reformation /ˌrefə'meɪʃn/ *n* (of system) reforma *f*; (of person) zmiana *f* na lepsze; **the Reformation** Reformacja

refrain¹ /rɪ'freɪn/ *n* refren *m*

refrain² /rɪ'freɪn/ *vi* powstrzym|ać, -ywać się; **to ~ from doing sth** powstrzymać się od zrobienia czegoś; **to ~ from comment** powstrzymać się od komentarza; **please, ~ from smoking** fml pro-simy o niepalenie

refresh /rɪ'freʃ/ *vt [bath]* odśwież|yć, -ać; *[cold drink]* orzeźwi|ć, -ać; **to ~ sb's memory** odświeżyć pamięć kogoś

refresher course *n* kurs *m* utrwalający wiedzę

refreshing /rɪ'freʃɪŋ/ *adj [drink, shower, breeze]* orzeźwiający; *[sleep]* krzepiący

refreshments /rɪ'freʃmənts/ *npl* (drinks) napoje *m pl*; (food) przekąski *f pl*

refrigerate /rɪ'frɪdʒəreɪt/ *vt* przechowywać w niskiej temperaturze

refrigerator /rɪ'frɪdʒəreɪtə(r)/ n (at home) lodówka f; (industrial) chłodnia f

refuel /ˌriː'fjuəl/ vi uzupełni|ć, -ać zapas paliwa

refuge /'refjuːdʒ/ n schronienie n; **to take ~ from sb/sth** schronić się przed kimś/czymś

refugee /ˌrefjʊ'dʒiː, US 'refjʊdʒiː/ **[]** n uchodźca m

[II] adj a ~ **camp** obóz dla uchodźców; ~ **status** status uchodźcy

refund **[]** /'riːfʌnd/ n zwrot m pieniędzy

[II] /'riːfʌnd/ vt zwr|ócić, -acać [cost, expenses]

refurbish /ˌriː'fɜːbɪʃ/ n odn|owić, -awiać

refusal /rɪ'fjuːzl/ n odmowa f (**to do sth** zrobienia czegoś)

refuse¹ /rɪ'fjuːz/ **[]** vt odm|ówić, -awiać (**to do sth** zrobienia czegoś)

[II] vi odm|ówić, -awiać

refuse² /'refjuːs/ GB n (household, garden) śmieci m pl, odpadki m pl; (industrial) odpady m pl

refuse collector n GB śmieciarz m infml

refute /rɪ'fjuːt/ vt obal|ić, -ać [argument]; **to ~ sb** udowodnić komuś, że się myli

regain /rɪ'geɪn/ vt odzysk|ać, -iwać [health, freedom, territory, balance, title]; wr|ócić, -acać do (czegoś) [consciousness]; nadr|obić, -abiać [time]

regal /'riːgl/ adj królewski

regale /rɪ'geɪl/ vt podejmować [guest] (**with sth** czymś)

regalia /rɪ'geɪlɪə/ npl (emblems) regalia plt; (official) uroczysty strój m

regard /rɪ'gɑːd/ **[]** n **[1]** (consideration) wzgląd m; **out of ~ for sth** przez wzgląd na coś **[2]** (esteem) szacunek m (**for sb/sth** dla kogoś/czegoś); **to hold sb/sth in high ~** wysoce sobie cenić kogoś/coś **[3]** (connection) **with** or **in ~ to...** jeśli chodzi o...

[II] regards npl pozdrowienia n pl; **give them my ~s** pozdrów ich ode mnie

[III] vt uważać; **to ~ sb/sth with contempt** gardzić kimś/czymś; **to ~ sb with suspicion** traktować kogoś podejrzliwie

regarding /rɪ'gɑːdɪŋ/ prep w związku z (czymś)

regardless /rɪ'gɑːdlɪs/ **[]** prep ~ **of cost** niezależnie od kosztów

[II] adv mimo wszystko

regatta /rɪ'gætə/ n regaty plt

regent /'riːdʒənt/ n regent m, -ka f

reggae /'regeɪ/ n inv reggae inv

regime, régime /reɪ'ʒiːm, 'reʒiːm/ n reżim m

regiment /'redʒɪmənt/ n pułk m

region /'riːdʒən/ **[]** n region m

[II] in the region of prep phr około, w granicach

regional /'riːdʒənl/ adj regionalny

register /'redʒɪstə(r)/ **[]** n rejestr m; (at shool) dziennik m

[II] vt **[1]** [person] zgł|osić, -aszać [birth, complaint]; za|rejestrować [vehicle, trademark]; nada|ć, -wać [luggage] **[2]** [official] zapis|ać, -ywać [student]; przyj|ąć, -mować zgłoszenie (czegoś) [death, mar-

riage]; za|rejestrować [company, firearm] **[3]** [instrument] wskaz|ać, -ywać [person, face] wyra|żać, -zić; [action] świadczyć o (czymś) [emotion] **[4]** (post) wys|łać, -yłać jako przesyłkę wartościową [letter]

[III] vi (for course, school) zapis|ać, -ywać się; (at hotel) za|meldować się

registered /'redʒɪstəd/ adj **[1]** [firearm, patent, voter, charity] zarejestrowany; [student] zapisany; **a ~ design** wzór zastrzeżony **[2]** [letter, post] polecony

registered trademark n znak m handlowy zastrzeżony

registrar /ˌredʒɪs'trɑː(r), 'redʒ-/ n **[1]** GB urzędnik m stanu cywilnego **[2]** (at university) ≈ kierownik m dziekanatu

registration /ˌredʒɪ'streɪʃn/ n (for course, institution) zapisanie n; (period) zapisy m pl; (of vehicle, birth, firearm, company) rejestracja f; (of complaint, birth, death) zgłoszenie n

registration number n numer m rejestracyjny

registry office n GB urząd m stanu cywilnego; **to get married in a ~** wziąć ślub cywilny

regress /rɪ'gres/ vi cof|nąć, -ać się w rozwoju; **to ~ to one's old habits** powrócić do starych przyzwyczajeń

regret /rɪ'gret/ **[]** n żal m (**about sth** z powodu czegoś); **to have no ~s about doing sth** nie żałować, że się coś zrobiło

[II] vt po|żałować (czegoś) [decision, remark]; **to ~ doing** or **having done sth** żałować, że się coś zrobiło; **we ~ to announce that...** z przykrością zawiadamiamy, że...

regretfully /rɪ'gretfəlɪ/ adv z żalem

regrettable /rɪ'gretəbl/ adj **it is ~ that...** niestety..., szkoda, że...

regular /'regjʊlə(r)/ **[]** n **[1]** (client) stały klient m, stała klientka f; (guest) stały gość m **[2]** US benzyna f zwykła

[II] adj **[1]** [habit, income, job] stały; [interval] regularny; **on a ~ basis** regularnie; **to keep ~ hours** prowadzić regularny tryb życia; **in ~ use** w ciągłym użyciu **[2]** [shape, features] regularny; [polygon] foremny **[3]** [customer, partner, time] stały; [method, procedure] zwykły; (in commerce) [price, size] normalny **[4]** [army] regularny; [officer, policeman] zawodowy; [staff] stały **[5]** [pulse, heartbeat] regularny

regularity /ˌregjʊ'lærətɪ/ n regularność f

regulate /'regjʊleɪt/ vt **[1]** u|regulować [lifestyle, activity, traffic] **[2]** wy|regulować [mechanism, temperature]

regulation /ˌregjʊ'leɪʃn/ **[]** n **[1]** (rule) przepis m; (legal requirement) uregulowanie n prawne, regulacja f prawna; **EU ~s** przepisy Unii Europejskiej; **fire ~s** przepisy przeciwpożarowe; **under the (new) ~s** zgodnie z (nowymi) przepisami; **against the ~s** wbrew przepisom **[2]** (controlling) kontrola f

[II] adj [width, length, uniform] przepisowy

regurgitate /rɪ'gɜːdʒɪteɪt/ vt [1] [animal, person] zwr|ócić, -acać [food] [2] fig bezmyślnie powt|órzyć, -arzać [facts, opinions]

rehabilitate /ˌriːə'bɪlɪteɪt/ vt [1] (medically) rehabilitować; (to society) z|resocjalizować [2] (restore) od-n|owić, -awiać [building]; przywr|ócić, -acać do dawnego stanu [area]; uzdr|owić, -awiać [environment]

rehabilitation centre GB, **rehabilitation center** US n (for the handicapped) ośrodek m integracyjny; (for addicts, ex-prisoners) ośrodek m resocjalizacji

rehearsal /rɪ'hɜːsl/ n próba f

rehearse /rɪ'hɜːs/ vt [actors] próbować [scene]; fig przygotowywać sobie [excuse]; powtarzać sobie [speech]

reheat /ˌriː'hiːt/ vt odgrz|ać, -ewać

rehouse /ˌriː'haʊz/ vt przekwaterow|ać, -ywać

reign /reɪn/ [1] n panowanie n; fig rządy plt [2] vi [monarch] panować; [chaos, silence] za|panować

reimburse /ˌriːɪm'bɜːs/ vt zwr|ócić, -acać [expenses]

rein /reɪn/ n lejce plt, cugle plt

reincarnation /ˌriːɪnkɑː'neɪʃn/ n (rebirth) reinkarnacja f; (creature) wcielenie n

reindeer /'reɪndɪə(r)/ n renifer m, ren m

reinforce /ˌriːɪn'fɔːs/ vt wzm|ocnić, -acniać; fig um|ocnić, -acniać [feeling, opinion]; ~ ed concrete żeloazobeton, żelbet

reinforcement /ˌriːɪn'fɔːsmənt/ n (action) wzmacnianie n; (support) wzmocnienie n; ~s Mil posiłki plt also fig

reinstate /ˌriːɪn'steɪt/ vt przywr|ócić, -acać na stanowisko [person]

reiterate /riː'ɪtəreɪt/ vt stale powtarzać

reject [1] /'riːdʒekt/ n odrzut m, wybrakowany produkt m [2] /rɪ'dʒekt/ vt (not accept) odrzuc|ić, -ać

rejection /rɪ'dʒekʃn/ n odrzucenie n

rejection letter n pismo n odmowne

rejoice /rɪ'dʒɔɪs/ vi u|radować się (at or over sth z czegoś or czymś)

rejuvenate /rɪ'dʒuːvɪneɪt/ vt odmłodzić, -adzać [person, skin]

rekindle /ˌriː'kɪndl/ vt na nowo rozpal|ić, -ać [fire]; na nowo rozbudz|ić, -ać [hope, interest]

relapse [1] /'riːlæps/ n pogorszenie n [2] /rɪ'læps/ vi powr|ócić, -acać (into sth do czegoś) [bad habits]; **he** ~ **d** pogorszyło mu się

relate /rɪ'leɪt/ [1] vt [1] (connect) po|wiązać fig [2] (re-count) opowi|edzieć, -adać [story] (to sb komuś) [2] vi [1] (have connection) to ~ to sb/sth dotyczyć kogoś/czegoś [2] (communicate) to ~ to sb znajdować z kimś wspólny język

related /rɪ'leɪtɪd/ adj [1] [person, language, species] spokrewniony (to sb/sth z kimś/czymś); ~ by marriage spowinowacony [2] (connected) to be ~ to

sth [matter, crime] być związanym z czymś; **work-** ~ mający związek z pracą

relation /rɪ'leɪʃn/ [1] n [1] (relative) krewn|y m, -a f [2] (connection) związek m; **with** ~ **to sth** w związku z czymś; **in** ~ **to sth** w stosunku do czegoś [2] **relations** npl (dealings) stosunki m pl, relacje f pl

relationship /rɪ'leɪʃnʃɪp/ n [1] (human) stosunki m pl; **to form a** ~ **with sb** nawiązywać stosunki z kimś; **a working** ~ stosunki na stopie zawodowej; **sexual** ~ współżycie seksualne; **we have a good** ~ między nami dobrze się układa [2] (logical) związek m (**with sth** z czymś) [3] (family bond) pokrewieństwo n (**to sb** z kimś); **family** ~ **s** związki rodzinne

relative /'relətɪv/ [1] n krewn|y m, -a f [2] adj względny

relatively /'relətɪvli/ adv stosunkowo; ~ **speaking** z zachowaniem wszelkich proporcji

relax /rɪ'læks/ [1] vt rozluźni|ć, -ać [muscle, discipline]; zwolni|ć, -ać [grip]; odprężyć, -ać [body, muscle]; z|łagodzić [restrictions, policy]; rozpu|ścić, -szczać [hair]; **to** ~ **one's attention** przestać uważać [2] vi [1] [person] odpręż|yć, -ać się, z|relaksować się [2] [grip, muscle, discipline] rozluźni|ć, -ać się; [policy, restrictions] zostać złagodzonym

relaxation /ˌriːlæk'seɪʃn/ n [1] (recreation) relaks m [2] (of muscle, jaw, discipline) rozluźnienie n; (of grip) zwolnienie n; (of efforts, concentration) osłabienie n; (of restrictions, policy) złagodzenie n

relaxed /rɪ'lækst/ n [person, muscle] rozluźniony; [manner, atmosphere, discussion] swobodny

relaxing /rɪ'læksɪŋ/ adj relaksujący

relay [1] /'riːleɪ/ n [1] (shift) zmiana f [2] (also ~ **race**) sztafeta f, bieg m sztafetowy [2] /'riːleɪ, rɪ'leɪ/ vt przekaz|ać, -ywać [message, question] (**to sb** komuś)

release /rɪ'liːs/ [1] n [1] (liberation) uwolnienie n; (from prison) zwolnienie n [2] (relief) **a feeling of** ~ uczucie ulgi [3] (announcement) komunikat m [4] (of film) wejście na ekrany; (of book) wydanie n [5] (deliverance) zwolnienie n; **the** ~ **of goods from bond** zwolnienie towarów spod sekwestru [2] vt [1] (free) zw|olnić, -alniać [prisoner]; uw|olnić, -alniać, wypu|ścić, -szczać [hostage]; wyswob|odzić, -adzać [accident victim]; wypu|ścić, -szczać [animal] [2] fig zw|olnić, -alniać (**from sth** z czegoś) [promise, obligation] [3] (disengage) zw|olnić, -alniać [shutter, handbrake, clutch] [4] (shoot) wypu|ścić, -szczać [arrow]; zrzuc|ić, -ać [bomb]; wystrzeli|ć, -wać [missile] [5] (let go) zw|olnić, -alniać [grip]; pu|ścić, -szczać [object, hand] [6] (publish) ogł|osić, -aszać [news]; o|publikować [picture] [7] [company] wprowadz|ić, -ać na ekrany [film]; wypu|ścić, -wać [record]

relegate /'relɪgeɪt/ vt [1] z|degradować [person]; przen|ieść, -osić (**to sth** do czegoś) [2] GB Sport **to be** ~ **d to the third division** spaść do trzeciej ligi

relegation /ˌrelɪ'geɪʃn/ n ① (downgrading) degradacja f ② GB Sport degradacja f, spadek m (**to sth do czegoś**)

relent /rɪ'lent/ vi [person, government] ust|ąpić, -ępować; [weather] poprawi|ć, -ać się; [storm] u|cichnąć

relentless /rɪ'lentlɪs/ adj [ambition] niepohamowany; [urge] nieopanowany; [attack, pursuit, enemy] nieustępliwy; [noise, activity] nieustający

relevant /'reləvənt/ adj ① [issue, facts, remark] istotny; [theory] mający znaczenie; [resource] użyteczny; **that's not ~ to the subject** to nie ma związku z tą sprawą ② [chapter, experience] odpowiedni; [time, period] o którym mowa

reliable /rɪ'laɪəbl/ adj [friend, machine, memory] niezawodny; [employee, firm] solidny; [witness, information] wiarygodny

reliant /rɪ'laɪənt/ adj **to be ~ on sth** być uzależnionym od czegoś

relic /'relɪk/ n ① (custom, object) relikt m; (building) pozostałość f ② (in religion) relikwia f

relief /rɪ'liːf/ n ① (from pain, distress, anxiety) ulga f ② **tax ~** ulga podatkowa; **debt ~** umorzenie długu ③ (help) pomoc f (humanitarna); **famine ~** pomoc dla ofiar głodu ④ (of garrison, troops) odsiecz f (**of sb/sth** dla kogoś/czegoś) ⑤ (in art, geography) relief m

relief agency n organizacja f humanitarna

relief fund n fundusz m pomocowy

relief supplies npl pomoc f humanitarna

relief work n pomoc f humanitarna

relief worker n pracownik m organizacji humanitarnej

relieve /rɪ'liːv/ vt ① (alleviate) z|łagodzić [pain, suffering]; rozładow|ać, -ywać [tension]; przełam|ać, -ywać [monotony]; rozpr|oszyć, -aszać [boredom]; **to be ~d at sth** z ulgą przyjąć coś [news]; odetchnąć (z ulgą) na wieść o czymś [results] ② **to ~ sb of sth** uwolnić kogoś od czegoś [burden, responsibility] ③ (help) przy|jść, -chodzić z pomocą (komuś) [population] ④ (take over from) zmieni|ć, -ać [worker, sentry]

religion /rɪ'lɪdʒən/ n religia f; **what ~ is he?** jakiego on jest wyznania?

religious /rɪ'lɪdʒəs/ adj religijny

relinquish /rɪ'lɪŋkwɪʃ/ vt zrze|c, -kać się (czegoś) [claim, privilege, title] (**to sb** na rzecz kogoś); z|rezygnować z (czegoś) [efforts, struggle]

relish /'relɪʃ/ **Ⅰ** n ① **to eat/drink with ~** jeść/pić z lubością; **with ~** [sing, perform] z wyraźną przyjemnością ② Culin dodatek m zaostrzający smak **Ⅱ** vt delektować się (czymś) [food]; cieszyć się z (czegoś) [opportunity, prospect]

relocate /ˌriːləʊ'keɪt, US ˌriː'ləʊkeɪt/ **Ⅰ** vt przen|ieść, -osić [employee, offices] (**to sth** do czegoś) **Ⅱ** vi [company, employee] przen|ieść, -osić się

reluctance /rɪ'lʌktəns/ n niechęć f

reluctant /rɪ'lʌktənt/ adj niechętny; **they were ~ to admit they had been wrong** nie chcieli przyznać się do błędu

reluctantly /rɪ'lʌktəntlɪ/ adv [agree] niechętnie; [decide] z ociąganiem

rely /rɪ'laɪ/ vi ① (be dependent) **to ~ on sth** być uzależnionym od czegoś [subsidy, aid]; [economy, system] opierać się na czymś [exports, industry, method]; [plant] stosować [technology]; [government] uciekać się do czegoś [deterrent] ② (count) **to ~ on sb/sth** liczyć na kogoś/coś

remain /rɪ'meɪn/ vi pozosta|ć, -wać; **it ~s to be seen whether...** okaże się, czy...; **to ~ silent** nie odzywać się

remainder /rɪ'meɪndə(r)/ n reszta f

remains /rɪ'meɪnz/ npl ① (of meal, fortune, building) pozostałości f pl, resztki f pl ② (corpse) szczątki m pl

remand /rɪ'mɑːnd, US rɪ'mænd/ **Ⅰ** n **to be on ~** (in custody) przebywać w areszcie śledczym; (on bail) zostać wypuszczonym na wolność za kaucją **Ⅱ** vt **to be ~ed in custody** zostać tymczasowo aresztowanym

remand centre n GB areszt m śledczy

remark /rɪ'mɑːk/ **Ⅰ** n uwaga f (**about sth** dotycząca czegoś) **Ⅱ** vt zauważyć (**that...** że...)

remarkable /rɪ'mɑːkəbl/ adj niezwykły

remarry /ˌriː'mærɪ/ vi [man] powtórnie się ożenić; [woman] powtórnie wyjść za mąż

remedial /rɪ'miːdɪəl/ adj [class] wyrównawczy

remedy /'remədɪ/ **Ⅰ** n lekarstwo n (**for sth** na coś) **Ⅱ** vt naprawi|ć, -ać

remember /rɪ'membə(r)/ **Ⅰ** vt ① (have in mind) za|pamiętać [fact, name, place, event]; **she ~s leaving her watch on the table** pamięta, że zostawiła zegarek na stole; **a night to ~** niezapomniana noc ② (not forget) **did you ~ to feed the cat?** czy pamiętałeś, żeby nakarmić kota?; **~ where you are** nie zapominaj, gdzie jesteś ③ (bring to one's mind) przypom|nieć, -inać sobie; **I can't ~ her name for the moment** nie mogę sobie chwilowo przypomnieć jej imienia ④ (convey greetings from) **to ~ sb to sb** pozdrowić kogoś od kogoś **Ⅱ** vi pamiętać

remind /rɪ'maɪnd/ vt przypom|nieć, -inać; **to ~ sb of sth** przypominać coś komuś; **to ~ sb to do sth** przypomnieć komuś, żeby coś zrobił

reminder /rɪ'maɪndə(r)/ n przypomnienie n (**of sth** o czymś); **a ~ to sb to do sth** przypomnienie dla kogoś, żeby coś zrobił

reminisce /ˌremɪ'nɪs/ vi wspominać (**about sth** coś)

reminiscent /ˌremɪ'nɪsnt/ adj **to be ~ of sb/sth** przypominać kogoś/coś

remiss /rɪ'mɪs/ adj **it was ~ of him not to reply** to niedbalstwo z jego strony, że nie odpowiedział

remission /rɪ'mɪʃn/ *n* ① (of sentence, debt) umorzenie *n* ② Med remisja *f*

remit /'ri:mɪt/ *n* **it's outside my** ~ to nie leży w mojej gestii; **to exceed one's** ~ przekroczyć swoje kompetencje

remnant /'remnənt/ *n* (of building) resztka *f*, pozostałość *f*; (of fabric) resztka *f*; (of past) pozostałość *f*

remorse /rɪ'mɔ:s/ *n* wyrzuty *m pl* sumienia; **a fit of** ~ przypływ skruchy

remote /rɪ'məʊt/ *adj* ① *[era, antiquity]* zamierzchły; *[country, planet]* odległy; *[ancestor]* daleki ② *[area, village]* oddalony; ~ **from society** poza społeczeństwem ③ (aloof) *[person]* wyniosły ④ *[chance, connection, resemblance]* niewielki

remote control *n* (gadget) pilot *m*; (technique) zdalne sterowanie *n*

remote-controlled /rɪ,məʊtkən'trəʊld/ *adj* zdalnie sterowany

remotely /rɪ'məʊtlɪ/ *adv* *[resemble]* trochę; **he's not** ~ **interested** on nie jest ani trochę zainteresowany

removal /rɪ'mu:vl/ *n* ① (of barrier, threat) usunięcie *n*; (of tax, subsidy) zniesienie *n*; **stain** ~ usuwanie plam ② Med usunięcie *n* ③ (change of home) przeprowadzka *f* (**from sth** z czegoś) (**to sth** do czegoś)

remove /rɪ'mu:v/ *vt* ① (take off) zdjąć, -wać *[object, stain, tumour, organ]*; zdjąć, -ejmować *[clothes, shoes]*; znieść, -osić *[tax, subsidy]*; **to** ~ **one's make-up** zmyć makijaż; **cousins once** ~**d** dalsi kuzyni ② (fire) zwolnić, -alniać *[employee]*; **to** ~ **sb from office** usunąć kogoś ze stanowiska ③ (take away) rozwiać, -ewać *[fears, doubt]*; usunąć, -wać *[obstacle, difficulty]*

remover /rɪ'mu:və(r)/ *n* (person) pracownik *m* firmy przeprowadzkowej

remuneration /rɪ,mju:nə'reɪʃn/ *n* fml wynagrodzenie *n*

renaissance /rɪ'neɪsns, US 'renəsɑ:ns/ *n* **the Renaissance** Odrodzenie, Renesans

render /'rendə(r)/ *vt* ① (cause to become) **to** ~ **sb homeless** pozbawić kogoś dachu nad głową; **to** ~ **sth impossible** uniemożliwić coś; **to** ~ **sth harmless** unieszkodliwić coś ② (provide) wyświadczyć *[service]* (**to sb** komuś) ③ oddać, -wać *[mood, style]*; wykonać, -ywać *[piece]*; przetłumaczyć *[text, phrase]* (**into sth** na coś)

rendezvous /'rɒndɪvu:/ **①** *n* spotkanie *n*; (of lovers) randka *f*

II *vi* spotkać, -ykać się (**with sb** z kimś)

renegade /'renɪgeɪd/ *n* zdrajca *m*, -czyni *f*, renegat *m*

renew /rɪ'nju:, US -'nu:/ *vt* odnowić, -awiać *[acquaintance, relations]*; przedłużyć, -ać *[contract]*; przedłużyć, -ać ważność (czegoś) *[passport]*; uzupełnić, -ać *[stock]*; wznowić, -awiać *[efforts, negotiations]*

renewal /rɪ'nju:əl, US -'nu:əl/ *n* (of subscription, lease) odnowienie *n*; (of passport) przedłużenie *n* ważności; (of diplomatic relations, hostilities) wznowienie *n*

renewed /rɪ'nju:, US -'nu:/ *adj [interest, energy]* nowy

renounce /rɪ'naʊns/ *vt* zrzec, -kać się (czegoś) *[title, claim, nationality]*; wyrzec, -kać się (czegoś) *[habit, faith, violence]*; porzucić, -ać *[strategy, party]*

renovate /'renəveɪt/ *vt* odnowić, -awiać *[building]*

renovation /,renə'veɪʃn/ *n* (of building) remont *m*; (of statue) renowacja *f*; ~ **s** remont

renowned /rɪ'naʊnd/ *adj* ~ **for sth** znany z czegoś

rent /rent/ **①** *n* (for accommodation) czynsz *m*; **for** ~ do wynajęcia

II *vt* ① (hire) wynająć, -mować *[house, apartment]*; wypożyczyć, -ać *[car, TV]* ② (let) = **rent out**

III *vi [tenant, landlord]* wynająć, -mować pokój/mieszkanie; **he's** ~**ing to students** wynajmuje pokoje studentom

■ **rent out:** ~ [**sth**] **out** wynająć, -mować (**to sb** komuś)

rental /'rentl/ *n* (for premises) czynsz *m*; (for car, TV) opłata *f* za wypożyczenie; **line** ~ abonament telefoniczny

reopen /,ri:'əʊpən/ **①** *vt* ponownie otworzyć, -ierać *[shop, debate]*

II *vi [school, shop]* zostać ponownie otwartym; *[talks, play]* zostać wznowionym

reorganize /,ri:'ɔ:gənaɪz/ *vt* zreorganizować

rep /rep/ *n* (in commerce) przedstawiciel *m*, -ka *f*

repair /rɪ'peə(r)/ **①** *n* naprawa *f*; **under** ~ *[building, ship]* w remoncie; **to be (damaged) beyond** ~ nie nadawać się do naprawy; **to be in good/bad** ~ być w dobrym/złym stanie

II *vt* naprawić, -ać

repairman /rɪ'peəmæn/ *n* człowiek *m* dokonujący napraw

repatriate /ri:'pætrɪeɪt, US -'peɪt-/ *vt* repatriować

repatriation /,ri:pætrɪ'eɪʃn, US -peɪt-/ *n* repatriacja *f*

repay /rɪ'peɪ/ *vt* spłacić, -ać *[person, debt]*; odwdzięczyć, -ać się za (coś) *[hospitality, favour]*

repayment /rɪ'peɪmənt/ *n* (process) spłata *f* (**on sth** czegoś); (sum) rata *f* spłaty

repeal /rɪ'pi:l/ **①** *n* (of law) uchylenie *n*

II *vt* uchylić, -ać

repeat /rɪ'pi:t/ **①** *n* powtórzenie *n*, powtórka *f*

II *vt* powtórzyć, -arzać *[word, action, programme]*; ponowić, -awiać *[offer]*; *[pupil]* powtórzyć, -arzać, repetować *[year]*

repeated /rɪ'pi:tɪd/ *adj [criticisms, difficulties]* powtarzający się; *[warnings, attempts]* wielokrotny; *[defeats, setbacks]* następujący po sobie

repeatedly /rɪ'pi:tɪdlɪ/ *adv* ciągle, wielokrotnie

repel /rɪ'pel/ *vt* ① odeprzeć, -pierać *[invader, attack]* ② (disgust) odpychać

repellent /rɪ'pelənt/ *adj [idea]* budzący odrazę; *[smell]* odrażający; *[image]* odpychający

repent /rɪ'pent/ *vi* żałować, odczuwać żal

repercussion /ˌriːpə'kʌʃn/ *n* (consequence) reperkusja *f*

repertoire /'repətwɑː(r)/ *n* repertuar *m*

repetition /ˌrepɪ'tɪʃn/ *n* (activity) powtarzanie *n*; (instance) powtórzenie *n*

repetitive /rɪ'petɪtɪv/ *adj [job, work]* monotonny; *[tune]* pełen powtórzeń

replace /rɪ'pleɪs/ *vt* [1] (put back) od|łożyć, -kładać na miejsce; **to ~ a cork** z powrotem zakorkować [2] (take place of) zast|ąpić, -ępować [3] (exchange) wymieni|ć, -ać (**with sb/sth** na kogoś/coś)

replacement /rɪ'pleɪsmənt/ *n* [1] (person) **to be a ~ for sb** zastępować kogoś [2] (instance) wymiana *f* [3] (spare part) część *f* zapasowa

replay [1] /'riːpleɪ/ *n* Sport (match) powtórzony mecz *m*; (sequence) powtórka *f*
[2] /ˌriː'pleɪ/ *vt* za|grać jeszcze raz *[piece]*; pu|ścić, -szczać jeszcze raz *[disc]*; powtórnie roz|egrać, -grywać *[match]*

replenish /rɪ'plenɪʃ/ *vt* uzupełni|ć, -ać *[stock, account]*; zaopat|rzyć, -rywać *[larder, shop]*

replica /'replɪkə/ *n* kopia *f*

reply /rɪ'plaɪ/ [1] *n* odpowiedź *f*
[2] *vt, vi* odpowi|edzieć, -adać

report /rɪ'pɔːt/ [1] *n* [1] (account) sprawozdanie *n*; (notification) zgłoszenie *n* [2] (published findings) raport *m* [3] (in press) doniesienie *n*; (longer) relacja *f* [4] GB Sch raport *m* o wynikach w nauce; (at the end of year) ≈ świadectwo *n*
[2] *vt* [1] po|informować o (czymś) *[fact, occurrence]*; **to ~ sth to sb** poinformować kogoś o czymś *[decision]*; przekazać komuś coś *[news, result]* [2] *[press]* (give account of) z|relacjonować; (inform about) don|ieść, -osić o (czymś) [3] (notify authorities about) zgł|osić, -aszać *[theft]*; po|informować or zawiad|o-mić, -amiać o (czymś) *[accident, case]*; **to ~ sb to sb** złożyć na kogoś skargę do kogoś; pej donieść na kogoś
[3] *vi* [1] **to ~ on sth** składać sprawozdanie z czegoś *[talks, progress]*; *[press, TV]* relacjonować coś *[event]* [2] *[committee, group]* przedstawi|ć, -ać raport (**on sth** na temat czegoś) [3] (present oneself) zgł|osić, -aszać się (**to sb** do kogoś); *[soldier]* za|meldować się (**to sb** u kogoś); **to ~ sick** powiadomić o chorobie [4] **to ~ to sb** podlegać bezpośrednio komuś

report card *n* US świadectwo *n* szkolne

reporter /rɪ'pɔːtə(r)/ *n* reporter *m*, -ka *f*

repose /rɪ'pəʊz/ *n* spoczynek *m*; **in ~** podczas odpoczynku

repossess /ˌriːpə'zes/ *vt* przejąć, -mować *[property, goods]*

repossession /ˌriːpə'zeʃn/ *n* przejęcie *n*

reprehensible /ˌreprɪ'hensɪbl/ *adj* naganny

represent /ˌreprɪ'zent/ *vt* [1] reprezentować; **under-~ed** niedostatecznie reprezentowany; **well ~ed** licznie reprezentowany [2] (portray) przedstawi|ć, -ać *[person, situation, event]* (**as sth** jako coś)

representation /ˌreprɪzen'teɪʃn/ *n* [1] reprezentacja *f* [2] **to make ~s to sb** (make requests) zwracać się z petycją do kogoś; (complain) składać protest na ręce kogoś

representative /ˌreprɪ'zentətɪv/ [1] *n* przedstawiciel *m*, -ka *f*
[2] *adj* [1] (typical) reprezentatywny [2] *[government, institution]* przedstawicielski

repress /rɪ'pres/ *vt* s|tłumić

reprieve /rɪ'priːv/ [1] *n* [1] (remission) ułaskawienie *n*; (delay) wstrzymanie *n* egzekucji [2] (respite) wytchnienie *n*
[2] *vt* wstrzymać egzekucję (kogoś) *[person]*

reprimand /'reprɪmɑːnd, US -mænd/ [1] *n* nagana *f*
[2] *vt* udziel|ić, -ać nagany (komuś)

reprisal /rɪ'praɪzl/ *n* odwet *m* (**for sth** za coś); **in ~ against sb** w odwecie wobec kogoś

reproach /rɪ'prəʊtʃ/ [1] *n* wyrzut *m*; **above** or **beyond ~** bez zarzutu
[2] *vt* robić wyrzuty (komuś) *[person]*; **to ~ sb with** or **for sth** robić komuś wyrzuty z powodu czegoś

reprocessing plant *n* zakład *m* utylizacji odpadów radioaktywnych

reproduce /ˌriːprə'djuːs, US -'duːs/ [1] *vt* wykon|ać, -ywać reprodukcję (czegoś), reprodukować *[picture, drawing]*; odtw|orzyć, -arzać *[sound]*; powt|ó-rzyć, -arzać *[results]*
[2] *vi* rozmn|ożyć, -ażać się

reproduction /ˌriːprə'dʌkʃn/ *n* [1] (of pictures) reprodukcja *f*; (of sounds) odtwarzanie *n* [2] Biol rozmnażanie *n*, reprodukcja *f*

reproduction furniture *n* meble *m pl* stylowe

reproductive /ˌriːprə'dʌktɪv/ *adj [organ, cycle]* rozrodczy

reproof /rɪ'pruːf/ *n* nagana *f*

reprove /rɪ'pruːv/ *vt* z|ganić (**for doing sth** za zrobienie czegoś)

reptile /'reptaɪl, US -tl/ *n* gad *m*

republic /rɪ'pʌblɪk/ *n* republika *f*; **the Republic of Poland** Rzeczpospolita *f* Polska

republican /rɪ'pʌblɪkən/ [1] *n* republikan|in *m*, -ka *f*
[2] *adj* republikański

repudiate /rɪ'pjuːdɪeɪt/ *vt* odrzuc|ić, -ać *[offer, charge]*

repugnant /rɪ'pʌgnənt/ *adj* odrażający

repulse /rɪ'pʌls/ *vt* od|eprzeć, -pierać *[attack, enemy]*

repulsion /rɪ'pʌlʃn/ *n* wstręt *m*

repulsive /rɪ'pʌlsɪv/ *adj* odrażający

reputable /'repjʊtəbl/ *adj [firm]* mający dobrą renomę; *[accountant]* ceniony; *[profession]* szanowany

reputation /ˌrepjʊ'teɪʃn/ *n* reputacja *f*; **he has a ~ for honesty** ma opinię uczciwego

repute /rɪ'pjuːt/ *n* **to be of high/low ~** mieć dobrą/złą reputację

reputed /rɪ'pjuːtɪd/ *adj* ① (well known) renomowany ② (alleged) domniemany

request /rɪ'kwest/ **Ⅰ** *n* prośba *f* (**for sth** o coś) (**to sb** do kogoś); (stronger) żądanie *n*; (order) zamówienie *n*; **on ~** na życzenie; **to play a ~ for sb** grać utwór z dedykacją dla kogoś

Ⅱ *vt* (ask) po|prosić o (coś) *[information, help, money]*; (demand) za|żądać (czegoś) *[information, help, money]*

require /rɪ'kwaɪə(r)/ *vt* ① (need) wymagać (czegoś) *[surgery]*; potrzebować (czegoś) *[help, money, staff]* ② (demand) *[job, situation]* wymagać (czegoś) *[funds, obedience, qualifications]*; **to ~ sth of** or **from sb** wymagać czegoś od kogoś

requirement /rɪ'kwaɪəmənt/ *n* ① (need) potrzeba *f* ② (condition) wymagania *n pl* ③ (obligation) wymóg *m* (**to do sth** żeby coś zrobić) ④ US (at university) przedmiot *m* obowiązkowy

requisite /'rekwɪzɪt/ *adj* wymagany

requisition /ˌrekwɪ'zɪʃn/ *vt* za|rekwirować

reschedule /ˌriː'ʃedjuːl, US -'skedʒʊl/ *vt* (change time) zmieni|ć, -ać harmonogram (czegoś); (change date of) zmieni|ć, -ać datę (czegoś)

rescue /'reskjuː/ **Ⅰ** *n* ① (aid) ratunek *m*, pomoc *f*; **to come/to go to sb's ~** przyjść/pośpieszyć komuś z pomocą; **to come/to go to the ~** przybyć/pośpieszyć na ratunek ② (operation) operacja *f* ratunkowa

Ⅱ *adj [operation, team, bid]* ratunkowy; *[helicopter, service]* ratowniczy

Ⅲ *vt* ① (save) ocal|ić, -ać *[person, wildlife, factory]* ② (aid) przy|jść, -chodzić z pomocą (komuś/czemuś) *[person, company]* ③ (release) uw|olnić, -alniać

rescue worker *n* ratownik *m*

research /rɪ'sɜːtʃ, 'riːsɜːtʃ/ **Ⅰ** *n* badania *n pl* (**into** or **on sth** nad czymś); **cancer ~** badania nad rakiem

Ⅱ *adj [institute, grant, project]* badawczy

Ⅲ *vt* prowadzić badania (na temat czegoś) *[topic]*; z|ebrać, -bierać materiały (do czegoś) *[book, article]*

researcher /rɪ'sɜːtʃə(r), 'riːsɜːtʃə(r)/ *n* pracownik *m* naukowy, badacz *m*, -ka *f*

resemblance /rɪ'zembləns/ *n* podobieństwo *n* (**between sb/sth and sb/sth** pomiędzy kimś/czymś a kimś/czymś) (**to sb/sth** do kogoś/czegoś)

resemble /rɪ'zembl/ *vt* być podobnym do (kogoś/czegoś)

resent /rɪ'zent/ *vt* **to ~ sb** żywić do kogoś urazę; **to ~ sb for doing sth** mieć komuś za złe, że coś

zrobił; **I ~ that remark** nie podoba mi się ta uwaga

resentful /rɪ'zentfl/ *adj* **to be ~ of sb** żywić do kogoś urazę; **to be ~ at sth** być niemile dotkniętym czymś

resentment /rɪ'zentmənt/ *n* uraza *f*; **to feel ~ towards sb** czuć do kogoś urazę

reservation /ˌrezə'veɪʃn/ *n* ① (doubt) zastrzeżenie *n*; **to have ~s about sth** mieć zastrzeżenia (co) do czegoś ② (booking) rezerwacja *f* ③ US (Indian land) rezerwat *m*

reservation desk *n* biuro *n* rezerwacji

reserve /rɪ'zɜːv/ **Ⅰ** *n* ① (stock) zapas *m*; (of minerals) zasoby *m pl*; **to keep sth in ~** mieć coś w rezerwie ② (reticence) rezerwa *f*; **to lose one's ~** dać się ponieść emocjom ③ Mil **the ~(s)** rezerwa *f* ④ Sport rezerwowy *m*, -a *f* ⑤ (area) rezerwat *m*; **wildlife ~** rezerwat przyrody

Ⅱ *vt* ① (set aside) zachow|ać, -ywać; **to ~ the right to do sth** zastrzec sobie prawo do zrobienia czegoś ② za|rezerwować *[room, seat]*

reserved /rɪ'zɜːvd/ *adj* ① *[person]* skryty ② *[table, room]* zarezerwowany

reservoir /'rezəvwɑː(r)/ *n* zbiornik *m*

reset /ˌriː'set/ *vt* wy|regulować *[machine]*; przesta-wi|ć, -ać *[watch]*

reshuffle /ˌriː'ʃʌfl/ *n* przetasowanie *n*

reside /rɪ'zaɪd/ *vi* mieszkać; *[official]* rezydować

residence /'rezɪdəns/ *n* ① (dwelling) rezydencja *f* ② (official address) **place of ~** miejsce zamieszkania; **to take up ~** zamieszkać; **~ permit** pozwolenie na pobyt stały

resident /'rezɪdənt/ **Ⅰ** *n* mieszkan|iec *m*, -ka *f*; (of rest home) pensjonariusz *m*, -ka *f*; (of hostel) gość *m*

Ⅱ *adj [population, work force]* stały; *[species]* miejscowy; *[staff, tutor]* mieszkający na miejscu

residential /ˌrezɪ'denʃl/ *adj* ① *[area, district]* mieszkalny ② *[staff]* mieszkający na miejscu; *[course]* z zakwaterowaniem na miejscu; **to be in ~ care** przebywać w domu opieki

residue /'rezɪdjuː; US -duː/ *n* ① (of liquid) osad *m* ② fig pozostałość *f*

resign /rɪ'zaɪn/ **Ⅰ** *vt* ust|ąpić, -ępować z (czegoś) *[post]*; z|rezygnować z (czegoś) *[job]*

Ⅱ *vi* ust|ąpić, -ępować; **to ~ as president** ustąpić ze stanowiska prezydenta

Ⅲ *vr* **to ~ oneself to sth** pogodzić się z czymś

resignation /ˌrezɪg'neɪʃn/ *n* rezygnacja *f*; **~ from a post** rezygnacja ze stanowiska; **~ as president** rezygnacja z urzędu prezydenta

resigned /rɪ'zaɪnd/ *adj* **~ to sth** skazany na coś fig

resilient /rɪ'zɪliənt/ *adj [person]* odporny (**to sth** na coś); *[market]* prężny; *[material]* sprężysty

resin /'rezɪn, US 'rezn/ *n* żywica *f*

resist /rɪ'zɪst/ **Ⅰ** *vt* sprzeciwi|ć, -ać się (czemuś) *[reform, attempt]*; stawi|ć, -ać opór (komuś) *[enemy]*; od|eprzeć, -pierać *[attack]*; wytrzym|ać, -ywać

[shock]; op|rzeć, -ierać się (czemuś) *[temptation, suggestion]*; być odpornym na (coś) *[heat, rust]*
II *vi* sprzeciwi|ć, -ać się; *[army, organization]* stawi|ć, -ać opór

resistance /rɪ'zɪstəns/ *n* [1] (military) opór *m* (**to sb/ sth** stawiany komuś/wobec czegoś) [2] (opposition) sprzeciw *m* (**to sth** wobec czegoś) [3] (to wear, disease) odporność *f* (**to sth** na coś) [4] (electric) opór *m*
Resistance /rɪ'zɪstəns/ *n* the ~ ruch *m* oporu
resistance fighter *n* bojowni|k *m*, -czka *f* ruchu oporu

resistant /rɪ'zɪstənt/ *adj* [1] *[virus]* oporny (**to sth** na coś); **heat-**~ żaroodporny; **water-**~ wodoodporny; **fire-**~ ognioodporny [2] (opposed) ~ **to sth** przeciwny czemuś *[change]*; niechętny czemuś *[innovations]*

resit /ˌriː'sɪt/ *vt* GB zdawać ponownie *[exam, test]*
resolute /'rezəluːt/ *adj [person, action]* stanowczy
resolution /ˌrezə'luːʃn/ *n* [1] (determination) zdecydowanie *n*, stanowczość *f* (**in sth** w czymś) [2] (decree) uchwała *f*, rezolucja *f* [3] (promise) postanowienie *n* [4] (in optics) rozdzielczość *f*
resolve /rɪ'zɒlv/ **I** *n* (determination) determinacja *f*; (decision) postanowienie *n*
II *vt* [1] rozwiąz|ać, -ywać *[problem, dispute]*; rozwi|ać, -ewać *[doubts]*; uzg|lodnić, -adniać *[differences]* [2] (decide) **to** ~ **that...** postanowić, że...; **to** ~ **to do sth** postanowić zrobić coś
resonant /'rezənənt/ *adj [voice]* donośny; *[sound]* wyraźny
resort /rɪ'zɔːt/ **I** *n* [1] (resource) **our only** ~ **is...** pozostaje nam tylko...; **as a last** ~ w ostateczności; **without** ~ **to sth** bez uciekania się do czegoś [2] (holiday centre) kurort *m*
II *vi* **to** ~ **to sth** uciec się do czegoś
resound /rɪ'zaʊnd/ *vi* rozbrzmiewać
resounding /rɪ'zaʊndɪŋ/ *adj* [1] *[voice]* donośny; *[cheers]* gromki; *[crash]* głośny [2] *[success]* spektakularny; *[defeat]* sromotny
resource /rɪ'sɔːs, -'zɔːs, US 'riːsɔːrs/ *n* **natural** ~**s** bogactwa naturalne; **financial** ~**s** środki finansowe; **human** ~**s** zasoby ludzkie
resource centre GB, **resource center** US *n* biblioteka *f* dydaktyczna
resourceful /rɪ'sɔːsfl, -'zɔːsfl, US 'riːsɔːrsfl/ *adj* zaradny
respect /rɪ'spekt/ **I** *n* [1] (admiration) szacunek *m*; (connected with fear) respekt *m*; **to command** ~ wzbudzać szacunek; **out of** ~ z szacunku (**for sb/ sth** dla kogoś/czegoś) [2] (regard) poszanowanie *n* (**for sth** czegoś) [3] (aspect) **in this** ~ pod tym względem
II respects *npl* wyrazy *m pl* uszanowania; **to offer** or **pay one's** ~**s to sb** złożyć komuś uszanowanie
III *vt* [1] (honour) szanować [2] (recognize) u|szanować *[privacy]*; respektować *[neutrality]*

respectable /rɪ'spektəbl/ *adj* [1] (reputable) szanowany, poważany; (deserving respect) godny szacunku [2] *[number, crowd]* pokaźny; *[performance, salary]* przyzwoity
respectful /rɪ'spektfl/ *adj* pełen szacunku (**to** or **towards sb/sth** dla kogoś/czegoś)
respective /rɪ'spektɪv/ *adj* **they went their** ~ **ways** każdy poszedł w swoją stronę; **they came with their** ~ **wives** przyszli ze swoimi żonami; **both men excel in their** ~ **fields** obaj wybijają się w swoich dziedzinach
respiration /ˌrespɪ'reɪʃn/ *n* oddychanie *n*
respirator /'respɪreɪtə(r)/ *n* respirator *m*
respiratory /rɪ'spɪrətrɪ, US -tɔːrɪ/ *adj* oddechowy
respite /'respaɪt, 'respɪt/ *n* wytchnienie *n* (**from sb/sth** od kogoś/czegoś)
respond /rɪ'spɒnd/ *vi* [1] (answer) odpowi|edzieć, -adać (**to sb/sth** komuś/na coś) [2] (react) za|reagować (**to sth** na coś)
response /rɪ'spɒns/ *n* [1] (answer) odpowiedź *f* (**to sth** na coś) [2] (reaction) reakcja *f* (**to sth** na coś); (to appeal) odzew *m* (**to sth** na coś)
responsibility /rɪˌspɒnsə'bɪlətɪ/ *n* [1] (duty) obowiązek *m*; **to have a** ~ **to sb/sth** mieć zobowiązania wobec kogoś/czegoś [2] (accountability) odpowiedzialność *f*; **to take** ~ **for sth** brać odpowiedzialność za coś
responsible /rɪ'spɒnsəbl/ *adj* odpowiedzialny; **to be** ~ **for sb/sth** być odpowiedzialnym za kogoś/ coś; **to be** ~ **to sb/sth** odpowiadać przed kimś/ czymś; **to hold sb** ~ obarczać kogoś odpowiedzialnością (**for sth** za coś)
responsive /rɪ'spɒnsɪv/ *adj [audience]* żywo reagujący; *[pupil, class]* chłonny
rest /rest/ **I** *n* (repose) odpoczynek *m*, wypoczynek *m*; **to have a** ~ odpocząć or wypocząć
II *vt* [1] (lean) op|rzeć, -ierać *[back, ladder]* (**on sth** o coś); położyć, kłaść *[cup]* (**on sth** na czymś); **she** ~ **ed her chin on her hand** podparła podbródek dłonią [2] (give rest to) da|ć, -wać odpocząć (komuś/ czemuś) *[person, horse, legs]*; oszczędzać *[injured limb]*
III *vi* [1] (relax) odpocz|ąć, -ywać (**from sth** od czegoś); (have vacation) wypocz|ąć, -ywać [2] (be supported) op|rzeć, -ierać się (**against sth** o coś); **to** ~ **on sth** opierać się na czymś
■ **rest with:** ~ **with** [sb/sth] *[decision]* należeć do kogoś/czegoś
restart /ˌriː'stɑːt/ *vt* wzn|owić, -awiać *[work, talks]*; ponownie uruch|omić, -amiać *[engine]*
restaurant /'restrɒnt, US -tərənt/ *n* restauracja *f*
restaurant car *n* GB wagon *m* restauracyjny
restful /'restfl/ *adj [sound]* kojący; *[colour]* uspokajający; *[place]* spokojny
restless /'restlɪs/ *adj* niespokojny; **to feel** ~ być zdenerwowanym

restock /ˌriːˈstɒk/ *vt* zapełni|ć, -ać na nowo *[shelf]* (**with sth** czymś); uzupełni|ć, -ać zaopatrzenie (czegoś) *[shop]* (**with sth** w coś)

restoration /ˌrestəˈreɪʃn/ *n* [1] (of property) zwrot *m* (**to sb** komuś) [2] (of custom) powrót *m* (**of sth** do czegoś); (of law) przywrócenie *n*; (of monarchy, dynasty) restauracja *f*

restore /rɪˈstɔː(r)/ *vt* [1] (give back) zwr|ócić, -acać *[property]* (**to sb** komuś); przywr|ócić, -acać *[health, faculty, right]* (**to sb** komuś); przywr|ócić, -acać *[law, peace]* (**to sth** w czymś); ożywi|ć, -ać *[custom, tradition]*; **to ~ sb to power** przywrócić kogoś do władzy [2] (renovate) od|restaurować *[building]*; odn|owić, -awiać *[painting]*

restrain /rɪˈstreɪn/ [1] *vt* powstrzym|ać, -ywać *[person, desire, tears, attacker, crowd]*

[2] *vr* **to ~ oneself** pohamować się

restrained /rɪˈstreɪnd/ *adj [person, style]* powściągliwy; *[lifestyle, dress]* skromny; *[emotion, laughter]* tłumiony

restraint /rɪˈstreɪnt/ *n* [1] (moderation) powściągliwość *f* (**in sth** w czymś) [2] (restriction) ograniczenie *n* (**on sth** czegoś); **social ~s** konwenanse

restrict /rɪˈstrɪkt/ *vt* ogranicz|yć, -ać (**to sth** do czegoś)

restricted /rɪˈstrɪktɪd/ *adj [budget, growth, movement]* ograniczony; *[hours]* wyznaczony; *[document, file]* poufny, tajny

restriction /rɪˈstrɪkʃn/ *n* ograniczenie *n*; (political) restrykcja *f*

re-string /ˌriːˈstrɪŋ/ *vt* zmieni|ć, -ać struny w (czymś) *[instrument]*; zmieni|ć, -ać naciąg w (czymś) *[racket]*

rest room *n* US toaleta *f*

result /rɪˈzʌlt/ [1] *n* [1] (consequence) skutek *m*; **as a ~** w efekcie; **as a ~ of sth** na skutek czegoś [2] (of exam, election, match) wynik *m*

[2] *vi* wynik|nąć, -ać; **to ~ in sth** (end in particular way) skończyć się czymś *[failure]*; (come about as consequence) spowodować coś *[damage]*

resume /rɪˈzjuːm, US -ˈzuːm/ [1] *vt* podj|ąć, -ejmować na nowo *[work, duties]*; wzn|owić, -awiać *[talks, service]*

[2] *vi [discussion, hostilities]* rozpocz|ąć, -ynać się na nowo

resumption /rɪˈzʌmpʃn/ *n* wznowienie *n*

resurface /ˌriːˈsɜːfɪs/ [1] *vt* pokry|ć, -wać nową nawierzchnią

[2] *vi [submarine, diver]* wynurz|yć, -ać się

resurrect /ˌrezəˈrekt/ *vt* wskrze|sić, -szać

resurrection /ˌrezəˈrekʃn/ *n* wskrzeszenie *n*; **the Resurrection** Zmartwychwstanie *n*

resuscitate /rɪˈsʌsɪteɪt/ *vt* reanimować

retail /ˈriːteɪl/ [1] *n* sprzedaż *f* detaliczna; **by ~** w detalu

[2] *adj [sector, shop, price, trade]* detaliczny

[3] *adv* detalicznie, w detalu

[4] *vi* **to ~ at 5 euros** kosztować w detalu 5 euro

retailer /ˈriːteɪlə(r)/ *n* (person) detalist|a *m*, -ka *f*; (company) detalista *m*

retain /rɪˈteɪn/ *vt* zachow|ać, -ywać *[control, dignity]*; zatrzym|ać, -ywać *[property, heat]*; utrzym|ać, -ywać *[lead, title]*; zachow|ać, -ywać w pamięci *[fact, image]*

retaliate /rɪˈtælɪeɪt/ *vi* wziąć, brać odwet

retaliation /rɪˌtælɪˈeɪʃn/ *n* odwet *m*; **in ~** w odwecie (**for sth** za coś) (**against sb** przeciwko komuś)

retarded /rɪˈtɑːdɪd/ *adj* upośledzony

retch /retʃ/ *vi* mieć odruch wymiotny

rethink /ˈriːθɪŋk/ *n* **to have a ~** zastanowić się jeszcze raz (**about sth** nad czymś)

reticent /ˈretɪsnt/ *adj* powściągliwy; **to be ~ about sth** niechętnie mówić o czymś

retina /ˈretɪnə, US ˈretənə/ *n* siatkówka *f*

retinue /ˈretɪnjuː, US ˈretənuː/ *n* świta *f*

retire /rɪˈtaɪə(r)/ [1] *vi* [1] (from work) prze|jść, -chodzić or pójść na emeryturę [2] (withdraw) **to ~ from sth** *[jury]* opuścić coś; *[person]* wycofać się z czegoś *[public life]*

[2] *retired adj* emerytowany

retirement /rɪˈtaɪəmənt/ *n* [1] (action) przejście *n* na emeryturę; **to take early ~** przejść na wcześniejszą emeryturę [2] (state) emerytura *f*

retirement age *n* wiek *m* emerytalny

retirement home *n* dom *m* emeryta

retort /rɪˈtɔːt/ [1] *n* (reply) riposta *f*

[2] *vt* za|ripostować

retrace /ˌriːˈtreɪs/ *vt* **to ~ one's steps** pójść z powrotem

retract /rɪˈtrækt/ [1] *vt* [1] cof|nąć, -ać *[statement, allegation]*; wycof|ać, -ywać *[claim]* [2] wciąg|nąć, -ać *[landing gear]*

[2] *vi [landing gear]* s|chować się

retrain /ˌriːˈtreɪn/ [1] *vt* przekwalifikow|ać, -ywać

[2] *vi* przekwalifikow|ać, -ywać się

retraining /ˌriːˈtreɪnɪŋ/ *n* przekwalifikowanie *n*

retreat /rɪˈtriːt/ [1] *n* [1] (of person, government) wycofanie się *n*; (of army) odwrót *m* [2] (quiet place) ustronie *n*; (hiding place) kryjówka *f*

[2] *vi* [1] *[person, army]* wycof|ać, -ywać się (**from sth** z czegoś) (**before sth** przed czymś); **to ~ into a dream world** uciec w świat marzeń [2] *[glacier, flood water]* wy|cofać się

retrial /ˌriːˈtraɪəl/ *n* ponowny proces *m*

retrieve /rɪˈtriːv/ *vt* [1] (get back) odzysk|ać, -iwać *[object]* [2] (save) u|ratować *[situation]*; napraw|ić, -ać *[error]* [3] Comput wyszuk|ać, -iwać *[data]*

retrograde /ˈretrəɡreɪd/ *adj* wsteczny

retrospective /ˌretrəˈspektɪv/ [1] *n* retrospektywa *f*

[2] *adj* [1] *[approach, view, exhibition]* retrospektywny [2] *[law]* działający wstecz; *[application]* z mocą wsteczną

return /rɪ'tɜːn/ **[I]** *n* [1] powrót *m*; **on my ~** po powrocie [2] (of symptoms) nawrót *m* [3] (sending back) zwrot *m* [4] (on investment) zysk *m* (**on sth** z czegoś) [5] (ticket) bilet *m* powrotny

[II] in return *adv phr* w zamian (**for sth** za coś) **[III]** *vt* [1] (give back) zwr|ócić, -acać [2] (put back) od|łożyć, -kładać z powrotem [3] (send back) od|e-słać, -syłać; **to ~ sb's call** oddzwonić do kogoś; '**~ to sender**' „zwrot do nadawcy" [4] (reciprocate) odwzajemni|ć, -ać *[love]* [5] **to ~ the favour** zrewanżować się za przysługę [6] przyn|ieść, -osić *[income]*

[IV] *vi* [1] (come back) (po)wr|ócić, -acać; (go back) wr|ócić, -acać [2] (resume) **to ~ to sth** (po)wrócić do czegoś *[activity, topic]* [3] *[symptom, doubt, time]* powr|ócić, -acać

(IDIOMS:) **many happy ~ s!** wszystkiego najlepszego w dniu urodzin!

return fare *n* cena *f* biletu powrotnego
return ticket *n* bilet *m* powrotny
return trip *n* powrót *m*

reunification /ˌriːjuːnɪfɪ'keɪʃn/ *n* ponowne zjednoczenie *n*

reunion /ˌriː'juːnɪən/ *n* spotkanie *n*; **a family ~** zjazd rodzinny

reunite /ˌriːjuː'naɪt/ *vt* ponownie po|łączyć *[family]*; ponownie z|jednoczyć *[country, party]*

reuse /ˌriː'juːz/ *vt* ponownie wykorzyst|ać, -ywać

rev /rev/ infml *vt* zwiększ|yć, -ać obroty (czegoś) *[engine]*

revalue /ˌriː'væljuː/ *vt* z|rewaluować *[currency]*; ponownie wyceni|ć, -ać *[property]*

revamp /ˌriː'væmp/ *vt* zmieni|ć, -ać *[image]*; z|reorganizować *[company]*; przer|obić, -abiać *[room, play]*

reveal /rɪ'viːl/ *vt* [1] wyjawi|ć, -ać *[truth, secret]* (**to sb** komuś); ujawni|ć, -ać *[plan]* (**to sb** komuś) [2] ukaz|ać, -ywać *[view, picture]*

revealing /rɪ'viːlɪŋ/ *adj* [1] *[interview]* wiele mówiący; *[remark]* odkrywczy [2] *[blouse]* wydekoltowany

revel /'revl/ *vi* **to ~ in sth** upajać się czymś

revelation /ˌrevə'leɪʃn/ *n* [1] (of identity) ujawnienie *n* [2] (striking disclosure) rewelacja *f*

revenge /rɪ'vendʒ/ *n* zemsta *f*; **to get one's ~** zemścić się (**on sb/for sth** na kimś/za coś)

revenue /'revənjuː, US -ənuː/ *n* dochód *m*

reverberate /rɪ'vɜːbəreɪt/ *vi* *[hills, room]* rozbrzmiewać (**with sth** czymś); *[thunder, footsteps]* rozle|c, -gać się; *[words, idea]* odbi|ć, -jać się głośnym or szerokim echem (**through sth** w czymś)

revere /rɪ'vɪə(r)/ *vt* (with respect) szanować; (with veneration) czcić

reverence /'revərəns/ *n* (respect) szacunek *m*; (veneration) cześć *f*

Reverend /'revərənd/ *n* [1] (Protestant) pastor *m* [2] (as title) **the ~ Jones** (Anglican) wielebny Jones; **~ Mother** wielebna matka

reverent /'revərənt/ *adj* nabożny

reversal /rɪ'vɜːsl/ *n* (of policy) zwrot *m* (**of sth** w czymś); (of order, trend) odwrócenie *n*

reverse /rɪ'vɜːs/ **[I]** *n* [1] (opposite) **quite the ~** wprost przeciwnie; **the truth was exactly the ~** tak naprawdę było zupełnie odwrotnie [2] (back) **the ~** (of coin) rewers *m*; (of paper) odwrotna strona *f*; (of cloth) lewa strona *f* [3] (also **~ gear**) bieg *m* wsteczny

[II] *adj* [1] (opposite) *[process]* odwrotny; *[direction, effect]* przeciwny [2] (other) **the ~ side** (of cloth) lewa strona; (of coin) rewers *m* [3] (backwards) **~ somersault** przewrót w tył; **in ~ order** od końca [4] **~ gear** bieg wsteczny

[III] in reverse *adv phr* od końca
[IV] *vt* odwr|ócić, -acać *[order, direction]*; zamieni|ć, -ać się (czymś) *[roles]*; cof|nąć, -ać *[car, mechanism]*; **to ~ the charges** dzwonić na koszt rozmówcy
[V] *vi* *[driver]* cof|nąć, -ać (się)

reverse charge call *n* rozmowa *f* na koszt rozmówcy

reversible /rɪ'vɜːsəbl/ *adj* *[trend, image]* odwracalny; *[garment]* dwustronny; *[decision]* odwołalny

revert /rɪ'vɜːt/ *vi* **to ~ to sth** powr|ócić, -acać do czegoś *[habit, name]*; zamienić się z powrotem w coś *[moorlands, wilderness]*

review /rɪ'vjuː/ **[I]** *n* [1] (of events, facts) przegląd *m*; (of policy) rewizja *f* [2] (assessment) recenzja *f* [3] (magazine) przegląd *m* [4] (of troops) przegląd *m* [5] US Sch, Univ powtórka *f*

[II] *vt* [1] prze|analizować *[situation, facts]*; z|rewidować *[policy, attitude]* [2] z|recenzować *[book, film]* [3] US Sch, Univ powt|órzyć, -arzać *[subject, lesson]*

reviewer /rɪ'vjuːə(r)/ *n* recenzent *m*, -ka *f*

revise /rɪ'vaɪz/ **[I]** *vt* [1] (modify) z|rewidować *[attitude, treaty]*; s|korygować *[figures, estimate]* [2] GB (for exam) powt|órzyć, -arzać *[subject]* [3] (correct) popra-wi|ć, -ać *[text]*
[II] *vi* GB (for exam) powtarzać (**for sth** do czegoś)

revision /rɪ'vɪʒn/ *n* (of budget, text) korekta *f*; (of schedule, plan) zmiana *f*; (for exam) powtórka *f*

revitalize /ˌriː'vaɪtəlaɪz/ *vt* ożywi|ć, -ać

revival /rɪ'vaɪvl/ *n* (of economy) ożywienie *n*; (of hope, interest) rozbudzenie *n* na nowo; (of custom, language) odrodzenie się *n*; (of fashion) powrót *m*

revive /rɪ'vaɪv/ **[I]** *vt* [1] (from faint) przywr|ócić, -acać przytomność (komuś) [2] fig wskrze|sić, -szać *[custom, language]*; rozbudz|ić, -ać (na nowo) *[hopes, interest]*; przywr|ócić, -acać *[fashion, style]*; ożywi|ć, -ać *[economy, debate]*
[II] *vi* [1] *[person]* odzysk|ać, -iwać przytomność or świadomość; *[plant]* odży|ć, -wać [2] *[hopes]* ożyć, -wać; *[enthusiasm, interest]* odży|ć, -wać; *[economy]* ożywi|ć, -ać się

revoke /rɪ'vəʊk/ *vt* unieważni|ć, -ać

revolt /rɪ'vəʊlt/ **[]** *n* (violent) rewolta *f*, bunt *m* (**against sb/sth** przeciw komuś/czemuś); (refusal to obey) sprzeciw *m* (**over sth** wobec czegoś)

[] II *vt* wz|budzić odrazę w (kimś) *[person]*

III *vi* z|buntować się (**against sb/sth** przeciw komuś/czemuś)

revolting /rɪ'vəʊltɪŋ/ *adj* [] *[cruelty, act]* odrażają-cy [2] *infml [smell, dress]* ohydny

revolution /ˌrevə'lu:ʃn/ *n* [] (revolt) rewolucja *f* (**in sth** w czymś) [2] (of wheel, record, propeller) obrót *m*

revolutionary /ˌrevə'lu:ʃənərɪ, US -nerɪ/ **[]** *n* rewolucjonist|a *m*, -ka *f*

[] II *adj [movement, leader]* rewolucyjny; *[process]* o rewolucyjnym znaczeniu

revolutionize /ˌrevə'lu:ʃənaɪz/ *vt* z|rewolucjoni-zować

revolve /rɪ'vɒlv/ *vi* obr|ócić, -acać się

revolving /rɪ'vɒlvɪŋ/ *adj [chair, door, stage]* ob-rotowy

revue /rɪ'vju:/ *n* rewia *f*

revulsion /rɪ'vʌlʃn/ *n* odraza *f*

reward /rɪ'wɔ:d/ **[]** *n* [] (recompense) nagroda *f* [2] fig satysfakcja *f*

[] II *vt* nagr|odzić, -adzać (**for sth** za coś)

rewarding /rɪ'wɔ:dɪŋ/ *adj [experience]* cenny; *[job, work]* dający satysfakcję

rewind /ˌri:'waɪnd/ *vt* przewi|nąć, -jać do tyłu, cof|nąć, -ać *[film, tape]*

rewire /ˌri:'waɪə(r)/ *vt* wymienić instalację elek-tryczną w (czymś) *[house]*

reword /ˌri:'wɜ:d/ *vt* przeredagow|ać, -ywać *[sen-tence, paragraph]*

rework /ˌri:'wɜ:k/ *vt* s|tworzyć nową wersję (cze-goś) *[classic, myth]*

rewrite /ˌri:'raɪt/ *vt* (copy) przepis|ać, -ywać; (rework) przer|obić, -abiać *[story, script]*

rhapsody /'ræpsədɪ/ *n* [] (piece of music) rapsodia *f* [2] (poem) rapsod *m*

rhetoric /'retərɪk/ *n* retoryka *f*

rhetorical /rɪ'ðmrɪkl, US -'tɔːr-/ *adj* retoryczny

rheumatism /'ru:mətɪzəm/ *n* reumatyzm *m*

Rhine /raɪn/ *prn* Ren *m*

rhinoceros /raɪ'nɒsərəs/ *n* nosorożec *m*

rhubarb /'ru:bɑ:b/ *n* rabarbar *m*

rhyme /raɪm/ **[]** *n* [] (poem) wiersz *m*; (children's) wierszyk *m* [2] (fact of rhyming) rym *m*

[] II *vi* rymować się

rhythm /'rɪðəm/ *n* rytm *m*

rhythmic(al) /'rɪðmɪk(l)/ *adj* rytmiczny

rib /rɪb/ *n* żebro *n*; Culin żeberka *n pl*; (of leaf) żyłka *f*, nerw *m*; (of umbrella) drut *m*

ribbon /'rɪbən/ *n* (for hair) wstążka *f*; (for medal) wstęga *f*; (for typewriter) taśma *f*

rib cage *n* klatka *f* piersiowa

rice /raɪs/ *n* ryż *m*

rich /rɪtʃ/ **[]** **the ~** bogaci *m pl*

[] II *adj* [] *[person, tradition]* bogaty; *[soil]* żyzny; *[profit]* znaczny; **to grow** or **get ~** wzbogacić się [2] *[gift]* hojny; *[food]* wysokokaloryczny; *[smell]* mocny; *[colour]* intensywny; *[sound]* głęboki

richness /'rɪtʃnɪs/ *n* [] (of person, experience) bogac-two *n*; (of soil) żyzność *f* [2] (of costumes) przepych *m*; (of meal) sutość *f* [3] (of colour) intensywność *f*

rickety /'rɪkətɪ/ *adj [chair]* kiwający się; *[staircase]* skrzypiący; *[car]* rozklekotany *infml*

rickshaw /'rɪkʃɔ:/ *n* riksza *f*

rid /rɪd/ **[]** *vt* **to ~ the house of mice** pozbyć się myszy z domu; **to ~ the world of famine** uwolnić świat od głodu

[] II *pp adj* **to get ~ of sth** pozbyć się czegoś

riddance /'rɪdns/ *n*
(IDIOMS) **good ~ (to bad rubbish)!** krzyżyk na drogę!

riddle[1] /'rɪdl/ *n* zagadka *f*

riddle[2] /'rɪdl/ *vt* [] (perforate) po|dziurawić [2] (under-mine) **to be ~d with disease** *[person, organ]* być wyniszczonym chorobą; **he's ~d with guilt** dręczy go poczucie winy; **to be ~d with errors** roić się od błędów; **~d with corruption** przeżarty korupcją

ride /raɪd/ **[]** *n* [] (act of going) jazda *f*; (getting from A to B) przejazd *m*; **day's ~** dzień jazdy [2] (for pleasure) przejażdżka *f*; **sleigh ~** kulig; **to go for a ~** pojechać na przejażdżkę

[] II *vt* [] (as rider) po|jechać, jeździć na (czymś) *[animal, bike, motorcycle]*; (regularly) jeździć na (czymś) *[animal, bike, motorcycle]* [2] US po|jechać (czymś) *[subway, bus]*; (regularly) jeździć (czymś) *[subway, bus]*; przemierz|yć, -ać *[prairies, range]* [3] *[surfer]* płynąć na (czymś) *[waves]*

III *vi* [] (as rider) po|jechać; (regularly) jeździć [2] (travel) **to ~ in** or **on sth** jechać czymś *[taxi, bus]*

■ **ride out**: przetrwać *[crisis, recession, storm]*

■ **ride up**: [] (approach) podje|chać, -żdżać (**to sb/sth** do kogoś/czegoś) [2] *[skirt]* podwi|nąć, -jać się
(IDIOMS) **to take sb for a ~** *infml* (swindle) wykołować kogoś *infml*

rider /'raɪdə(r)/ *n* [] (on horse) jeździec *m*, amazon-ka *f*; (on motorbike) motocyklist|a *m*, -ka *f*; (on bike) rowerzyst|a *m*, -ka *f* [2] (to document) aneks *m*

ridge /rɪdʒ/ *n* [] (of wave, mountain) grzbiet *m* [2] (mountain range) pasmo *n* (górskie) [3] (on rock) fałd *m*; (on metal surface, on fabric) fałda *f* [4] (on roof) kalenica *f*

ridicule /'rɪdɪkju:l/ **[]** *n* pośmiewisko *n*

[] II *vt* wyśmi|ać, -ewać

ridiculous /rɪ'dɪkjʊləs/ *adj* śmieszny; **a ~ price** absurdalna cena

riding /'raɪdɪŋ/ **[]** *n* jazda *f* konna; **to go ~** przejechać się konno

II *adj* ~ **clothes** strój do jazdy konnej; ~
lesson lekcja jazdy konnej
rife /raɪf/ *adj* **to be** ~ *[crime, disease]* szerzyć się
riffraff /'rɪfræf/ *n* motłoch *m*, hołota *f*
rifle[1] /'raɪfl/ *n* karabin *m*; (for hunting) strzelba *f*
rifle[2] /'raɪfl/ *vt* s|plądrować *[house]*; opróżni|ć, -ać
[drawer, safe]
■ **rifle through**: ~ **through** [**sth**] grzebać
w czymś
rift /rɪft/ *n* [1] (disagreement) rozdźwięk *m*; (permanent)
rozłam *m* [2] (in rock) rozpadlina *f*; (in clouds) szczelina *f*
rig /rɪg/ **II** *n* [1] (for oil) (on land) wieża *f* wiertnicza;
(offshore) platforma *f* wiertnicza [2] (apparatus) urządzenie *n*; (equipment) sprzęt *m*
II *vt* s|fałszować *[results, election]*; ustawi|ć, -ać
wyniki (czegoś) *[race, competition]*
■ **rig up**: sklec|ić, -ać *[equipment, shelter]*
rigging /'rɪgɪŋ/ *n* [1] (on ship) takielunek *m* [2] (of
election, result) fałszowanie *n*; (of competition, race)
ustawianie *n* wyników
right /raɪt/ **II** *n* [1] (side) prawa strona *f*; **on** or **to**
your ~ po prawej stronie; **take the second** ~
skręć w prawo w następną ulicę [2] (in politics) (also
Right) the ~ prawica *f* [3] (morally) dobro *n* [4] (just
claim) prawo *n*; **to have a** or **the** ~ **to do sth** mieć
prawo coś zrobić; **human** ~**s** prawa człowieka
II rights *npl* [1] prawa *n pl*; **sole** ~**s to sth**
wyłączne prawa do czegoś [2] (moral) **the** ~**s and**
wrongs of a matter moralne aspekty zagadnie-
nia
III *adj* [1] (not left) prawy [2] (morally) słuszny,
właściwy; **it's not** ~ **to steal** nie wolno kraść;
to do the ~ **thing** słusznie or właściwie postąpić
[3] (correct) *[choice, conditions, decision]* dobry; (accurate) *[time]* dokładny; *[word]* właściwy; **to be** ~
[person] mieć rację; **to do sth the** ~ **way** zrobić
coś, jak należy [4] (suitable) odpowiedni, właściwy;
when the time is ~ we właściwym czasie; **to be**
in the ~ **place at the** ~ **time** znaleźć się we
właściwym czasie na właściwym miejscu [5] (in good
order) **I don't feel quite** ~ **these days** nie
najlepiej się ostatnio czuję; **the engine isn't**
quite ~ z silnikiem jest coś nie w porządku; **to**
put or **set sth** ~ poprawić coś *[mistake]*;
naprawić coś *[injustice, situation, machine]* [6] (in
geometry) prosty; **at a** ~ **angle to sth** pod kątem
prostym do czegoś [7] GB infml (emphatic) **he's a** ~
idiot! jest skończonym idiotą!; **it's a** ~ **mess**
straszny tu bałagan
IV *adv* [1] (of direction) w prawo; **to turn** ~ skręcić
w prawo; **she looked neither** ~ **nor left** nie
rozglądała się na boki [2] (directly) **I'll be** ~ **back**
zaraz wracam; **go** ~ **home** idź prosto do domu;
~ **before/after sth** tuż przed/po czymś [3] (exactly) ~ **in the middle of the room** na samym
środku pokoju; ~ **now** (immediately) natychmiast;

US (at this point in time) teraz [4] (correctly) dobrze; **to do**
sth ~ zrobić coś dobrze or jak należy; **did I hear**
you ~? czy dobrze cię zrozumiałem? [5] (completely) ~ **around the garden** wokół całego ogrodu;
~ **at the bottom** na samym dole; **to turn** ~
around odwrócić się o 180 stopni; **to turn the**
central heating ~ **up** włączyć ogrzewanie na
cały regulator [6] (very well) dobrze; ~, **let's have a**
look! no dobrze, popatrzmy!
V *vt* napraw|ić, -ać *[injustice, wrong]*
IDIOMS: **by** ~**s** właściwie
right away *adv* natychmiast
righteous /'raɪtʃəs/ *adj* [1] *[person]* prawy; *[thought,*
anger] szlachetny [2] *[indignation]* słuszny
rightful /'raɪtfl/ *adj* prawowity
right-hand /,raɪt'hænd/ *adj* prawy
right-handed /,raɪt'hændɪd/ *adj [person]* prawo-
ręczny; ~ **blow** cios prawą ręką
right-hand man /,raɪthænd'mæn/ *n* prawa ręka *f* fig
rightly /'raɪtlɪ/ *adv* [1] (accurately) prawidłowo
[2] (justifiably) słusznie [3] (with certainty) **I can't** ~
say nie potrafię powiedzieć; **I don't** ~ **know**
naprawdę nie wiem
right-of-centre /,raɪtəv'sentə(r)/ *adj* centropra-
wicowy
right of way *n* [1] (in traffic) pierwszeństwo *n*
(przejazdu) [2] (over land) prawo *n* przejścia/prze-
jazdu przez teren prywatny
right-on /,raɪt'ɒn/ *adj* infml **they're very** ~
hołdują modzie na lewicowość
right-thinking /'raɪtθɪŋkɪŋ/ *adj* prawomyślny
right wing **II** *n* **the** ~ prawica *f*
II right-wing *adj* prawicowy
rigid /'rɪdʒɪd/ *adj [person, rules, material]* sztywny;
[controls, timetable] ścisły
rigidly /'rɪdʒɪdlɪ/ *adv [stand]* sztywno; *[opposed]*
zdecydowanie; *[controlled]* ściśle; *[obey]* rygorystycz-
nie
rigorous /'rɪgərəs/ *adj [law, rule]* rygorystyczny;
[discipline, regime] surowy; *[adherence, observance]*
ścisły
rigour GB, **rigor** US /'rɪgə(r)/ *n* (of discipline) ry-
gor *m*; (of law, punishment) surowość *f*
rim /rɪm/ *n* (of cup) brzeg *m*, krawędź *f*; (on wheel)
obręcz *f*; (of spectacles) oprawka *f*
rind /raɪnd/ *n* skórka *f*
ring[1] /rɪŋ/ *n* [1] (with jewel) pierścionek *m*; (large)
pierścień *m*; **a wedding** ~ obrączka; **a** ~ **in the**
nose (for person) kolczyk w nosie; (for bull) kółko
w nosie [2] (for gymnast) obręcz *f* [3] (circle) kółko *n*; (in
tree trunk) słój *m*; (of people, objects) krąg *m* [4] (in circus)
arena *f*; (for boxing) ring *m* [5] (of smugglers, dealers)
gang *m*; (of spies) siatka *f* [6] (on bird's leg) obrączka *f*
[7] (on cooker) (electric) płytka *f* grzejna; (gas) palnik *m*
ring[2] /rɪŋ/ **II** *n* [1] (sound) (at door, of phone) dzwonek *m*;
(of church bell) dźwięk *m* dzwonu; **to have a nice** ~

to it ładnie brzmieć; **that has a familiar ~ (to it)** to brzmi znajomo [2] GB (phone call) telefon *m*; **to give sb a ~** zadzwonić do kogoś

II *vt* [1] (cause to sound) za|dzwonić (czymś) *[hand bell]*; uderzyć, bić w (coś) *[church bell]*; **to ~ the doorbell** zadzwonić do drzwi [2] GB (call) za|dzwonić do (kogoś) *[person]*; za|dzwonić na (coś) *[station, airport]*; za|dzwonić pod (coś) *[number]*

III *vi* [1] (sound) *[doorbell, telephone]* za|dzwonić; *[church bell]* za|dzwonić, bić; **the doorbell rang** zadzwonił dzwonek u drzwi [2] (sound bell) *[person]* za|dzwonić; **to ~ at the door** zadzwonić do drzwi; **'please ~ for service'** „proszę dzwonić na obsługę" [3] (resonate) *[footsteps, laughter, words]* rozbrzmie|ć, -wać; **the house rang with laughter** dom rozbrzmiewał śmiechem; **that noise makes my ears ~** w uszach mi dzwoni od tego hałasu; **to ~ true/false** brzmieć wiarygodnie/fałszywie [4] GB (phone) za|dzwonić (**for sth** po coś) *[ambulance, taxi]*

■ **ring back** GB: oddzw|onić, -aniać
■ **ring in** GB: (to work) za|dzwonić do pracy
■ **ring off** GB: rozłącz|yć, -ać się
■ **ring out**: *[voice, cry]* rozle|c, -gać się; *[bells]* rozdzw|onić, -aniać się
■ **ring up** GB: ¶ ~ **up** za|dzwonić ¶ ~ **up [sth]** [1] (on phone) za|dzwonić na (coś) *[station, airport]*; za|dzwonić do (czegoś) *[information]* [2] (on cash register) wbi|ć, -jać *[figure, total]* ¶ ~ **[sb] up** za|dzwonić do (kogoś) *[friend, operator]*

(IDIOMS:) **to ~ down/up the curtain** opuścić/podnieść kurtynę; **to ~ down the curtain on an era** fig zamknąć pewną epokę; **to ~ in the New Year** witać Nowy Rok

ring binder *n* segregator *m*
ringleader /'rɪŋliːdə(r)/ *n* prowodyr *m*
ringlet /'rɪŋlɪt/ *n* pukiel *m*
ringroad /'rɪŋrəʊd/ *n* GB obwodnica *f*
rinse /rɪns/ **I** *n* płukanie *n*; (for hair) płukanka *f*

II *vt* spłuk|ać, -iwać *[soap]*; o|płukać *[dishes]*; s|płukać *[hair]*; (wash) przepłuk|ać, -iwać *[clothes, mouth]*

riot /'raɪət/ **I** *n* [1] (violence) zamieszki *plt*, rozruchy *plt*; **football ~** wybryki kibiców piłkarskich [2] **to be a ~ of colours** mienić się wszystkimi kolorami

II *vi* wziąć, brać udział w zamieszkach; *[prisoner]* z|buntować się

(IDIOMS:) **to run ~** *[person]* szaleć; fig *[inflation]* galopować; *[plant]* rosnąć jak szalony

rioter /'raɪətə(r)/ *n* uczestni|k *m*, -czka *f* zamieszek; (in prison) buntownik *m*
riot gear *n* wyposażenie *n* bojowe
rioting /'raɪətɪŋ/ *n* zamieszki *plt*
riot police *n* policyjne oddziały *m pl* prewencji

rip /rɪp/ **I** *vt* [1] (tear) roz|edrzeć, -dzierać; (cut) rozci|ąć, -nać [2] (snatch) wyr|wać, -ywać (**from sb** komuś) (**off** or **from sth** z czegoś)

II *vi* *[fabric]* po|drzeć się
■ **rip off**: ¶ ~ **[sth] off** [1] (remove) z|erwać, -rywać *[garment, roof]* [2] infml zwi|nąć, -jać infml *[goods]*; obr|obić, -abiać infml *[bank]*; z|erżnąć, -rzynać infml *[idea, design]* ¶ ~ **[sb] off** infml z|edrzeć, -dzierać z (kogoś) infml
■ **rip through**: ~ **through [sth]** *[bomb, blast]* z|dewastować *[building]*

RIP = **requiescat/requiescant in pace** niech spoczywa/spoczywają w spokoju
ripe /raɪp/ *adj [crop, fruit, cheese]* dojrzały
ripen /'raɪpən/ **I** *vt* **the sun-~ed tomatoes** dojrzałe w słońcu pomidory

II *vi [fruit, cheese]* dojrze|ć, -wać
rip-off /'rɪpɒf/ *n* infml zdzierstwo *n* infml
ripple /'rɪpl/ **I** *n* (in water) zmarszczka *f* (na powierzchni wody); (in hair) drobna fala *f*

II *vi* [1] *[water]* (make waves) po|marszczyć się; (make sound) szemrać [2] *[corn, hair]* falować; *[muscles]* prężyć się

rise /raɪz/ **I** *n* [1] (increase) wzrost *m* (**in sth** czegoś); (in standards) podniesienie się *n* (**in sth** czegoś) [2] (of person) awans *m*; (of empire, company) rozkwit *m* [3] (slope) wzniesienie *n* [4] fig **give ~ to sth** dać początek czemuś *[rumours]*; doprowadzić do czegoś *[unemployment]*; być źródłem czegoś *[happiness, problems]*

II *vi* [1] *[water]* w|ezbrać, -zbierać; przyb|rać, -ierać; *[curtain]* podn|ieść, -osić się; *[price, temperature]* wzr|osnąć, -astać [2] *[hopes]* wzr|osnąć, -astać; *[anger]* w|ezbrać, -zbierać *[pressure, tension]* nar|osnąć, -astać [3] (get up) *[person]* wsta|ć, -wać; **to ~ from the dead** (po)wstać z martwych; **to ~ to the occasion** stanąć na wysokości zadania [4] *[ground, road]* wzn|ieść, -osić się [5] *[sun, moon]* wzejść, wschodzić [6] *[dough, cake]* wy|rosnąć

rising /'raɪzɪŋ/ **I** *n* powstanie *n*

II *adj [price, unemployment]* rosnący; *[sun, moon]* wschodzący; *[ground]* wznoszący się; *[politician]* obiecujący

risk /rɪsk/ **I** *n* ryzyko *n*; **to run the ~ of being injured** narażać się na kontuzję; **to take ~s** ryzykować; **their future is at ~** ich przyszłość jest zagrożona; **at one's own ~** na własne ryzyko

II *vt* za|ryzykować; **to ~ death** narażać się na śmierć

risqué /'riːskeɪ, US rɪ'skeɪ/ *adj [story, remark]* pikantny
risky /'rɪski/ *adj* ryzykowny
rite /raɪt/ *n* (ceremony) obrzęd *m*; (in primitive religions) rytuał *m*
ritual /'rɪtʃʊəl/ **I** *n* rytuał *m*

II *adj* rytualny

rival /'raɪvl/ **I** n (in love, competition) rywal m, -ka f; (in business) konkurent m, -ka f

II adj [firm, version] konkurencyjny; [team] przeciwny

III vt **to** ~ **sb/sth** dorówn|ać, -ywać komuś/ czemuś (**in sth** czymś)

rivalry /'raɪvlrɪ/ n rywalizacja f (**between sb and sb** pomiędzy kimś a kimś)

river /'rɪvə(r)/ n rzeka f; (of mud, lava) strumień m

riverbank /'rɪvəbæŋk/ n brzeg m rzeki

riverside /'rɪvəsaɪd/ **I** n the ~ brzeg m rzeki; **to grow by the** ~ rosnąć nad rzeką

II adj [café, trees] nadrzeczny

rivet /'rɪvɪt/ **I** n nit m

II vt przyku|ć, -wać [gaze, attention]; **to be** ~**ed by sth** być pochłoniętym czymś; **to be** ~**ed to the spot** [person] nie móc się ruszyć

road /rəʊd/ **I** n ① droga f; (outside built-up area) szosa f, droga f ②; (in built-up area) ulica f; **the** ~ **home** droga do domu; **transported by** ~ przewożony transportem samochodowym ③ fig droga f; **to be on the** ~ **to success** być na dobrej drodze do sukcesu

II adj [condition, accident, traffic] drogi

roadblock /'rəʊdblɒk/ n blokada f drogi

road hump n próg m zwalniający

roadshow /'rəʊdʃəʊ/ n ① (play, show) przedstawienie n objazdowe ② (publicity tour) objazdowa akcja f reklamowa

roadside /'rəʊdsaɪd/ n pobocze n

roadsign /'rəʊdsaɪn/ n znak m drogowy

roadworks /'rəʊdwɜːks/ npl roboty f pl drogowe

roadworthy /'rəʊdwɜːðɪ/ adj [car] sprawny

roam /rəʊm/ vt przemierz|yć, -ać [countryside]; włóczyć się po (czymś) [shops]

■ **roam around**: [person] wałęsać się infml

roar /rɔː(r)/ **I** n (of lion, person, waterfall, sea) ryk m; (of wind) wycie n; (of engine, crowd) ryk m; ~ **of laughter** huragan śmiechu; **a** ~ **of applause** gromki aplauz

II vi [lion] za|ryczeć; [person] ry|knąć, -czeć; [sea] ryczeć; [engine, crowd] za|wyć

roaring /'rɔːrɪŋ/ adj ① [thunder, fire] huczący; [storm] gwałtowny; [engine] ryczący ② [success] oszałamiający

roast /rəʊst/ **I** n ① Culin (roasted) pieczeń f; (intended for roasting) mięso n na pieczeń ② US (barbecue) piknik m z grillem

II adj [meat, potatoes] pieczony; [peanuts] prażony; [coffee beans] palony; ~ **beef** pieczeń wołowa

III vt u|piec [meat, potatoes]; u|prażyć [peanuts]; palić [coffee beans]

rob /rɒb/ vt okra|ść, -dać [person, organization]; obrabow|ać, -ywać [bank, train]; **to** ~ **sb of sth** pozbawić kogoś czegoś

robber /'rɒbə(r)/ n złodziej m, rabuś m

robbery /'rɒbərɪ/ n kradzież f; (with violence) rabunek m

robe /rəʊb/ n szata f; (of judge, academic) toga f

robin /'rɒbɪn/ n Zool rudzik m

robot /'rəʊbɒt/ n robot m

robust /rəʊ'bʌst/ adj [person] zdrowy i silny; [furniture, defence] solidny; [economy] silny; [appetite] zdrowy; [plant] odporny; [humour] rubaszny; [reply, attitude] zdecydowany

rock[1] /rɒk/ n ① (substance) skała f ② (boulder) głaz m, skała f; **Scotch on the** ~**s** fig szkocka z lodem; **their marriage was on the** ~**s** fig ich małżeństwo rozpadało się

rock[2] /rɒk/ **I** n (also ~ **music**) rock m

II adj [band, concert] rockowy

III vt ① (move gently) kołysać (czymś) [cradle, boat]; u|kołysać [baby] ② (shake) [tremor, scandal] wstrząs|nąć, -ać (czymś)

IV vi ① (sway) [person, cradle, hammock] kołysać się; [ship, chair] za|kołysać się; **to** ~ **with laughter** śmiać się do rozpuku ② (shake) [ground, building] za|trząść się ③ (dance) tańczyć rock and rolla

rock and roll /ˌrɒkən'rəʊl/ n rock and roll m

rock bottom /ˌrɒk'bɒtəm/ n **to hit** ~ [price] spaść do najniższego poziomu; [person] stoczyć się na samo dno

rock climber n wspinacz m skałkowy

rock climbing n wspinaczka f (skałkowa)

rockery /'rɒkərɪ/ n GB ogródek m skalny

rocket[1] /'rɒkɪt/ **I** n (firework) rakieta f, raca f; (spacecraft, missile) rakieta f

II vi [price, profit, level] podsk|oczyć, -akiwać fig

rocket[2] /'rɒkɪt/ n (plant) rokietta f siewna

rock face n ściana f skalna

rockfall /'rɒkfɔːl/ n lawina f kamieni

rocking chair n fotel m bujany

rocking horse n koń m na biegunach

rock star n gwiazda f rocka

rocky[1] /'rɒkɪ/ adj [beach, soil, coast] skalisty

rocky[2] /'rɒkɪ/ adj [piece of furniture] chybotliwy; [person, relationship] chwiejny; [time, business] niepewny; [health] wątły

Rocky Mountains prn pl the ~ Góry f pl Skaliste

rod /rɒd/ n ① (stick) pręt m ② (for punishment) kij m ③ (for fishing) wędka f ④ (staff of office) laska f

rodent /'rəʊdnt/ n gryzoń m

roe /rəʊ/ n ① (eggs) ikra f ② (of male fish) mlecz m

roe deer /ˌrəʊ'dɪə(r)/ n sarna f

rogue /rəʊg/ n łobuz m, drań m

role /rəʊl/ n rola f (**in sth** w czymś)

role model n wzór m (do naśladowania)

role-play /'rəʊlpleɪ/ n ① (in psychology) psychodrama f ② (at school) scenka f

roll /rəʊl/ **I** n ① (of paper) rolka f, zwój m; (big) rola f, bela f; (of cloth) bela f; (of banknotes) zwitek m; **a** ~ **of film** rolka filmu ② (bread) bułka f; **cheese**

~ bułka z serem ③ (of ship, train) kołysanie *n* ④ (of dice) rzut *m* ⑤ (register) wykaz *m*; **electoral** ~ lista wyborcza

II *vt* ① (push) po|toczyć, po|turlać *[ball, log]* ② (wrap round) skręc|ić, -ać *[cigarette]*; zwi|nąć, -jąć, z|rolować *[carpet]* ③ (flatten) walcować *[metal]*; rozwałkow|ać, -ywać *[dough, pastry]*

III *vi* ① *[ball, person]* po|toczyć się, po|turlać się ② *[plane]* wykon|ać, -ywać beczkę; *[car]* prze|koziołkować ③ *[ship]* za|kołysać się ④ *[thunder]* prze|toczyć, -aczać się; *[drum]* za|warczeć ⑤ *[camera]* kręcić infml; *[press]* chodzić infml

■ **roll about** GB, **roll around**: *[animal, person]* tarzać się; *[marbles, tins]* toczyć się, turlać się

■ **roll down**: opu|ścić, -szczać *[blind]*; odwi|nąć, -jać *[sleeve]*

■ **roll over**: przewr|ócić, -acać się

■ **roll up**: zwi|nąć, -jać, z|rolować *[poster, rug]*; podwi|nąć, -jać *[sleeve]*

roller /'rəʊlə(r)/ *n* ① (in machine) wałek *m*, rolka *f*; (to crush, smooth) walec *m* ② (curler) wałek *m*

Rollerblade® /'rəʊləbleɪd/ *n* łyżworolka *f*

roller blind *n* roleta *f*

roller coaster *n* kolejka *f* górska

roller-skate /'rəʊləskeɪt/ *n* wrotka *f*

roller-skating /'rəʊləskeɪtɪŋ/ *n* jazda *f* na wrotkach, wrotkarstwo *n*

rolling pin *n* wałek *m* (do ciasta)

rollneck /'rəʊlnek/ *n* golf *m*

ROM /rɒm/ *n* = read-only memory ROM *m*

roman /'rəʊmən/ *n* antykwa *f*

Roman Catholic **I** *n* katoli|k *m*, -czka *f*
II *adj* (rzymsko)katolicki

romance /rəʊ'mæns/ *n* ① (of era, place) romantyzm *m*, romantyczność *f* ② (love affair) romans *m* ③ (novel) romans *m*; (film) film *m* o miłości

Romania /rəʊ'meɪnɪə/ *prn* Rumunia *f*

Romanian /rəʊ'meɪnɪən/ **I** *n* ① (person) Rumun *m*, -ka *f* ② (język *m*) rumuński *m*
II *adj* rumuński

romantic /rəʊ'mæntɪk/ **I** *n* romanty|k *m*, -czka *f*
II *adj* ① *[setting, story, person]* romantyczny ② (involving affair) miłosny ③ **a** ~ **film** film o miłości; **a** ~ **novel** romans

romantic fiction *n* (genre) romanse *m pl*

romanticize /rəʊ'mæntɪsaɪz/ *vt* wy|idealizować

Romany /'rɒmənɪ/ *n* Rom *m*, -ka *f*

romp /rɒmp/ **I** *n* (frolic) igraszki *f pl*
II *vi* baraszkować

rompers /'rɒmpəz/ *npl* (also **romper suit**) pajacyk *m*

roof /ruːf/ *n* ① (of building, car) dach *m*; (of cave, mine) strop *m* ② **the** ~ **of the mouth** podniebienie *n* (IDIOMS:) **to go through the** or **hit the** ~ infml *[person]* wpa|ść, -dać w szał infml; *[prices]* osiąg|nąć, -ać niebotyczny poziom

roof rack *n* bagażnik *m* dachowy

rooftop /'ruːftɒp/ *n* dach *m*

rook¹ /rʊk/ *n* Zool gawron *m*

rook² /rʊk/ *n* (in chess) wieża *f*

room /ruːm, rʊm/ **I** *n* ① pomieszczenie *n*; (for living, working) pokój *m*; (for teaching, operating) sala *f*; ~ **and board** pokój z wyżywieniem ② (space) miejsce *n*; ~ **for improvement** możliwość poprawy
II *vi* US mieszkać; **to** ~ **with sb** mieszkać u kogoś

roommate /'ruːmmeɪt/ *n* współlokator *m*, -ka *f*

room service *n* obsługa *f* (kelnerska) w pokojach (hotelowych)

room temperature *n* temperatura *f* pokojowa

roomy /'ruːmɪ/ *adj [car, house, cupboard]* przestronny; *[garment, bag]* obszerny

roost /ruːst/ **I** *n* grzęda *f*
II *vi [birds]* nocować
(IDIOMS:) **to rule the** ~ rządzić

rooster /'ruːstə(r)/ *n* kogut *m*

root /ruːt/ **I** *n* ① (of plant) korzeń *m*; **to take** ~ *[plant]* wypuścić korzenie, ukorzenić się; *[idea, system]* zakorzenić się; *[company]* zdobyć pozycję ② fig (origins) korzenie *plt*; (of problem, unhappiness) źródło *n* fig ③ (in maths) pierwiastek *m*
II *vt* **deeply-**~**ed in sth** głęboko zakorzeniony w czymś; **he was** ~**ed to the spot** stał, jakby mu nogi wrosły w ziemię

■ **root around, root about**: *[animal]* ryć (**in sth** w czymś); *[person]* grzebać (**in sth** w czymś)

■ **root out**: wykorzeni|ć, -ać *[corruption]*; zna|leźć, -jdować *[culprit]*

rootless /'ruːtlɪs/ *adj* pozbawiony korzeni

rope /rəʊp/ **I** *n* ① (cord) lina *f*; (thin) sznur *m* ② (of pearls) sznur *m*; (of hair) warkocz *m*
II *vt* (restrain) związ|ać, -ywać liną; (fasten) przywiąz|ać, -ywać liną (**to sth** do czegoś)

■ **rope in** infml: ~ **[sb] in** GB (to help with task) ściąg|nąć, -ać do pomocy
(IDIOMS:) **to know the** ~**s** wiedzieć, o co chodzi

rope ladder *n* drabinka *f* sznurowa

rosary /'rəʊzərɪ/ *n* (beads) różaniec *m*; (prayer) modlitwa *f* różańcowa

rose /rəʊz/ *n* róża *f*

rose-coloured GB, **rose-colored** US /'rəʊzkʌləd/ *adj* ① (red) różowy ② fig (optimistic) *[idea, view]* optymistyczny
(IDIOMS:) **to see the world through** ~ **spectacles** or **glasses** patrzeć na świat przez różowe okulary

rosebud /'rəʊzbʌd/ *n* pąk *m* róży

rose bush *n* krzew *m* różany

rosemary /'rəʊzmərɪ, US -merɪ/ *n* rozmaryn *m*

rose-tinted /'rəʊztɪntɪd/ *adj* = **rose-coloured**

rosette /rəʊ'zet/ *n* rozetka *f*

roster /'rɒstə(r)/ *n* (also **duty** ~) harmonogram *m* dyżurów

rostrum /'rɒstrəm/ *n* mównica *f*

rosy /'rəʊzɪ/ *adj [cheek, light, dawn]* różowy; **to look** ~ *[future, prospects]* wyglądać obiecująco; **to paint**

a ∼ **picture of sth** przedstawiać coś w jasnych kolorach

rot /rɒt/ **I** n rozkład m, gnicie n

II vt z|niszczyć [tyres]; po|psuć [teeth]; **TV** ∼**s your brain** telewizja ogłupia

III vi (also ∼ **away**) [food, vegetables] z|gnić; [leaves] z|butwieć, z|gnić

rota /'rəʊtə/ n GB grafik m; **on the** ∼ **basis** zgodnie z grafikiem

rotary /'rəʊtəri/ adj [motion] obrotowy; [pump, mower] rotacyjny

rotate /rəʊ'teɪt, US 'rəʊteɪt/ **I** vt obr|ócić, -acać [blade, handle]

II vi [blade, handle, wings] obr|ócić, -acać się

rotation /rəʊ'teɪʃn/ n **1** (turning) rotacja f, obracanie (się) n **2** (cycle) obrót m

rote /rəʊt/ n **by** ∼ [learn] na pamięć; [say] z pamięci

rotten /'rɒtn/ adj **1** [vegetation, smell] zgniły; [wood] zbutwiały; [product, teeth] zepsuty **2** [person] zdemoralizowany, zepsuty; [organization] przeżarty korupcją **3** infml (bad) [food] podły infml; [cook, driver] kiepski infml; ∼ **weather** pogoda pod psem

rouble /'ru:bl/ n rubel m

rough /rʌf/ **I** adj **1** [skin, material] szorstki; [rock] chropowaty; [road] wyboisty; [grass] nierówny **2** [treatment, person, play, sport] brutalny; [area] niebezpieczny **3** [estimate, figure] przybliżony; [copy] roboczy; [plan] ogólny; **a** ∼ **outline of sth** ogólny zarys czegoś **4** [life, period] ciężki **5** [person, behaviour] nieokrzesany; [dwelling, table] prymitywny **6** (harsh) [voice, taste] ostry; [wine] cierpki **7** [sea] wzburzony; [weather] zły; [wind] gwałtowny; [journey] ciężki; [landing] twardy

II adv (outdoors) **to sleep** ∼ spać pod gołym niebem

(IDIOMS) **to** ∼ **it** koczować

roughage /'rʌfɪdʒ/ n błonnik m

rough-and-ready /ˌrʌfən'redɪ/ adj [person, conditions] prosty; [manner] niewyszukany; [calculation] przybliżony; [equipment] prowizoryczny; [method] prymitywny

roughen /'rʌfn/ u|czynić chropowatym

roughly /'rʌflɪ/ adv **1** [calculate, sketch] z grubsza; [equal, equivalent] mniej więcej; ∼ **speaking** mniej więcej **2** [treat, hit] brutalnie; [answer, speak] ostro **3** [make] niedbale; [chop] grubo

rough paper n papier m do pisania na brudno

roulette /ru:'let/ n ruletka f

round /raʊnd/ **I** adv GB **1** all ∼ wszędzie naokoło; **whisky all** ∼! whisky dla wszystkich! **2** (in circles) naokoło; **to go** ∼ **and** ∼ [wheel, carousel] kręcić się, obracać się; [person] kręcić się w koło **3** (to specific place) **to go** ∼ **to sth** wpaść do czegoś [office, school]; **to ask sb** ∼ powiedzieć komuś, żeby wpadł **4** **all year** ∼ przez okrągły rok; **this time** ∼ tym razem

II prep GB **1** wokół (czegoś); **the wall goes right** ∼ **the house** mur biegnie wokół całego domu or otacza cały dom **2** **to go** ∼ **the corner** skręcić za róg; **to go** ∼ **an obstacle** ominąć przeszkodę **3** **to take sb** ∼ **the city** oprowadzić kogoś po mieście; **to go** ∼ **the shops** chodzić po sklepach

III **round about** adv phr **1** (approximately) około **2** (in the vicinity) **the people** ∼ **about** ludzie w okolicy

IV n **1** (series) runda f; (in golf, cards) partia f; (in boxing) runda f; (in election) tura f; (of drinks) kolejka f; **it's my** ∼! ja stawiam! **2** (bullet) nabój m; (shot) wystrzał m **3** ∼ **of applause** burza oklasków; **a** ∼ **of toast** toasty **4** (route) **to do one's** ∼**s** [doctor, security guard] robić obchód; [postman] roznosić pocztę; [refuse collector] objeżdżać domy; **to go** or **do the** ∼**s** [rumour, joke, document] krążyć **5** (shape) okrągły plaster m

V adj (circular) okrągły; (curved) zaokrąglony; **to have** ∼ **shoulders** mieć zaokrąglone plecy; **in** ∼ **figures** w zaokrągleniu; **a** ∼ **dozen** dokładnie dwanaście

VI vt omi|nąć, -jać; [ship] opły|nąć, -wać; **to** ∼ **the corner** skręcić za rogiem; **to** ∼ **a bend** wziąć zakręt

■ **round off: 1** za|kończyć [meal, evening, speech] (**with sth** czymś) **2** wygładz|ić, -ać [corner, edge] **3** zaokrągl|ić, -ać [figure]

■ **round on** GB: ∼ **on** [sb] na|trzeć, -cierać na (kogoś) [opponent, critic]

■ **round up:** z|gromadzić [protesters]; z|robić obławę na (kogoś)

roundabout /'raʊndəbaʊt/ **I** n GB **1** (in fairground) karuzela f **2** (junction) rondo n

II adj **to take a** ∼ **way** pójść naokoło or okrężną drogą; **by** ∼ **means** w okrężny sposób; **a** ∼ **way of saying sth** zawoalowany sposób powiedzenia czegoś

round-neck(ed) sweater /raʊnd'nek'swetə(r)/ n półgolf m

round-the-clock /ˌraʊndðə'klɒk/ adj całodobowy

round-the-world /ˌraʊndðə'wɜːld/ adj [trip] dookoła świata

round trip n podróż f w obie strony

roundup /'raʊndʌp/ n **1** (by police) nalot m infml **2** (herding) zgromadzenie n w jednym miejscu **3** (summary) podsumowanie n

rouse /raʊz/ vt **1** (wake) z|budzić **2** (stir) wzbudz|ić, -ać [anger, interest]; **to** ∼ **public opinion** poruszyć opinię publiczną; **to** ∼ **sb to action** pobudzić kogoś do działania

rousing /'raʊzɪŋ/ adj [welcome] gorący; [speech] porywający

rout /raʊt/ **I** n pogrom m

II vt rozgr|omić, -amiać [enemy, team]

route /ruːt/ **I** n [1] (itenerary) trasa f; (to workplace) droga f (**to sth** do czegoś); (in aviation) trasa f; (in shipping) szlak m [2] fig droga f (**to sth** do czegoś) **II** vt wys|łać, -yłać *[goods, people]* (**to sth** do czegoś)

routine /ruːˈtiːn/ **I** n [1] (procedure) ustalony porządek m; **the daily** ~ codzienne zajęcia [2] (drudgery) rutyna f [3] (act) układ m **II** adj rutynowy

routinely /ruːˈtiːnlɪ/ adv [1] (as part of routine) rutynowo [2] (commonly) stale

row[1] /rəʊ/ n [1] (of plants, seats, books) rząd m; (of stitches) rządek m; (of people) (one after another) rząd m; (one beside another) szereg m [2] (succession) **six times in a** ~ sześć razy z rzędu

row[2] /rəʊ/ **I** vt **to** ~ **a boat up the river** płynąć łodzią w górę rzeki **II** vi po|wiosłować

row[3] /raʊ/ **I** n [1] (dispute) awantura f; **to have a** ~ **with sb about** or **over sth** pokłócić się z kimś o coś [2] (loud noise) hałasy m pl; **to make a** ~ hałasować **II** vi po|kłócić się (**with sb** z kimś) (**about** or **over sth** o coś)

rowboat /ˈrəʊbəʊt/ n US łódź f wiosłowa

rowdy /ˈraʊdɪ/ adj (noisy) hałaśliwy; (violent) chuligański; *[pupil]* niesforny

rowing /ˈrəʊɪŋ/ n (activity) wiosłowanie n; (in sport) wioślarstwo n

rowing boat n GB łódź f wiosłowa

royal /ˈrɔɪəl/ adj królewski

royal blue I n (kolor m) szafirowy m **II** adj szafirowy

Royal Highness n His/Her ~ Jego/Jej Królewska Wysokość

royalty /ˈrɔɪəltɪ/ n [1] (persons) członkowie m pl rodziny królewskiej [2] (to author, musician) tantiema f (**on sth** z czegoś); (to publisher) należność f (**on sth** za coś)

rub /rʌb/ **I** n [1] (massage) **to give sth a** ~ pomasować coś *[back, elbow]* [2] (polish) **to give sth a** ~ przetrzeć coś *[spoons, table]*; zetrzeć coś *[stain]* **II** vt [1] (massage) po|trzeć, -cierać *[chin, eyes]*; **to** ~ **sth on to the skin** rozetrzeć coś na skórze; **to** ~ **sth into the skin** wetrzeć coś w skórę [2] (polish) zetrzeć, ścierać *[stain]*; wy|trzeć, -cierać *[surface]* **III** vi [1] (scrub) trzeć [2] (chafe) *[shoe]* obcierać ■ **rub in**: ~ **[sth]** in w|etrzeć, -cierać *[cream, margarine]*; **there's no need to** ~ **it in!** infml nie ma co ciągle do tego wracać! ■ **rub out**: wymaz|ać, -ywać *[word, drawing]* (IDIOMS) **to** ~ **sb up the wrong way** nadepnąć komuś na odcisk

rubber /ˈrʌbə(r)/ **I** n [1] (substance) guma f [2] GB (for erasing) gumka f (do ścierania) **II** adj gumowy

rubber band n gumka f (recepturka)

rubber plant n kauczukowiec m

rubber stamp n pieczątka f

rubber tree n kauczukowiec m brazylijski

rubbish /ˈrʌbɪʃ/ **I** n [1] (refuse) śmieci m pl; (domestic) śmieci m pl, odpadki plt; (industrial) odpady plt [2] (inferior goods) tandeta f [3] (nonsense) bzdury f pl infml pej; **this book is** ~ ! to głupia książka! **II** vt GB z|mieszać z błotem *[person, achievement]*

rubbish bin n GB pojemnik m na śmieci

rubbish dump n GB wysypisko n śmieci

rubbish heap n GB sterta f śmieci

rubble /ˈrʌbl/ n gruz m

ruby /ˈruːbɪ/ **I** n [1] (gem) rubin m [2] (also ~ **red**) (kolor m) rubinowy m **II** adj *[liquid, lips]* rubinowy; *[necklace, ring]* z rubinem; ~ **wedding** rubinowe gody

rucksack /ˈrʌksæk/ n plecak m

rudder /ˈrʌdə(r)/ n (on boat, plane) ster m

ruddy /ˈrʌdɪ/ adj *[cheeks]* rumiany

rude /ruːd/ adj [1] (impolite) niegrzeczny; **it is** ~ **to do sth** nie wypada robić czegoś [2] (indecent) nieprzyzwoity; ~ **word** brzydkie słowo

rudimentary /ˌruːdɪˈmentrɪ/ adj (primitive) pierwotny; (basic) podstawowy

rudiments /ˈruːdɪmənts/ npl podstawy f pl

rueful /ˈruːfl/ adj *[sigh]* żałosny; *[thought]* smutny

ruff /rʌf/ n kreza f, kryza f [2] (of fur, feathers) kołnierz m

ruffle /ˈrʌfl/ **I** n (at sleeve) mankiet m koronkowy; (at neck) kreza f, kryza f; (on shirt front) żabot m **II** vt [1] z|mierzwić, potargać *[hair, fur]*; na|stroszyć *[feathers]*; z|marszczyć *[water]* [2] (disconcert) zbić, -jać z tropu

rug /rʌg/ n [1] (carpet) chodnik m, dywanik m [2] GB (blanket) pled m

rugby /ˈrʌgbɪ/ n rugby n inv

rugby league n rugby n inv trzynastoosobowe

rugby union rugby n inv piętnastoosobowe

rugged /ˈrʌgɪd/ adj [1] *[terrain]* nierówny; *[path]* wyboisty; *[landscape]* surowy; *[coastline]* urwisty; *[mountains, range]* poszarpany [2] *[man, features]* surowy

ruin /ˈruːɪn/ **I** n ruina f **II** vt [1] z|rujnować *[economy, career, health]*; **to** ~ **one's eyesight** popsuć sobie wzrok [2] ze|psuć *[holiday, meal]*; z|niszczyć *[shoes, clothes]* (IDIOMS) **to go to rack and** ~ popadać w ruinę

ruined /ˈruːɪnd/ adj [1] (derelict) zrujnowany [2] (spoilt) *[career, marriage, life]* zrujnowany; *[holiday, meal]* zepsuty; *[clothes, furniture]* zniszczony [3] (financially) zrujnowany

rule /ruːl/ **I** n [1] (of game) zasada f; (of sport, language) reguła f; (of organization) przepis m; (of religion) nakaz m; ~ **s and regulations** przepisy; **to bend the** ~ s naginać przepisy; **as a (general)** ~ z reguły [2] (colonial, foreign) panowanie n; (Tory, communist) rządy plt [3] (for measure) linijka f **II** vt [1] *[ruler, party, army]* rządzić (czymś) *[country, empire]* [2] *[person, consideration]* po|kierować (czymś) *[behaviour]*; *[factor]* wyznacz|yć, -ać *[strategy]*; **to be ~d by sb** słuchać (się) kogoś *[father, parents]* ③ (draw) na|kreślić *[line]*; **~d paper** papier w linie ④ *[court, judge]* orze|c, -kać (**that...** że...)

III *vi* ① *[government]* rządzić; **anarchy ~s** panuje anarchia ② *[court, judge]* wyda|ć, -wać postanowienie; Sport *[referee, umpire]* rozstrzyg|nąć, -ać ■ **rule out:** ① wyklucz|yć, -ać *[possibility, candidate]* ② uniemożliwi|ć, -ać *[activity]*

ruler /'ru:lə(r)/ *n* ① (leader) wład|ca *m*, -czyni *f* ② (measure) linijka *f*

ruling /'ru:lɪŋ/ **I** *n* orzeczenie *n*; **to give a ~** wydać orzeczenie

II *adj* ① *[party]* rządzący; *[class]* panujący ② *[principle]* przewodni; *[passion]* główny; *[price]* obowiązujący

rum /rʌm/ *n* rum *m*

rumble /'rʌmbl/ **I** *n* (of thunder, artillery, trucks) dudnienie *n*; (of stomach) burczenie *n*; (in pipes) bulgotanie *n*

II *vi* *[thunder]* przet|oczyć, -aczać się; *[artillery, machines]* za|dudnić; *[voice]* grzmieć; *[pipes]* za|-bulgotać; **his stomach ~s** burczy mu w brzuchu

ruminate /'ru:mɪneɪt/ *vi* ① *[person]* rozmyślać (**on** or **about sth** nad czymś) ② Zool przeżu|ć, -wać

rummage /'rʌmɪdʒ/ *vi* grzebać (**through sth** w czymś)

rummy /'rʌmi/ *n* remi *m inv*

rumour GB, **rumor** US /'ru:mə(r)/ *n* pogłoska *f*, plotka *f*

rumoured GB, **rumored** US /'ru:məd/ *adj* **it is ~ that...** chodzą słuchy, że...

rump /rʌmp/ *n* ① (also **~ steak**) (cut of beef) krzyżowa *f*, krzyżówka *f*; (steak) rumsztyk *m* ② (of animal) zad *m*; (of bird) kuper *m*

rumple /'rʌmpl/ *vt* z|miąć *[clothes, paper]*; roz|czochrać *[hair]*

run /rʌn/ **I** *n* ① (act or period) bieg *m*; **to go for a ~** pójść pobiegać; **to break into a ~** zacząć biec ② (flight) **to be on the ~ from sb/sth** uciekać od kogoś/czegoś; **to make a ~ for it** rzucić się do ucieczki ③ (series) seria *f*; **a ~ of (good)/bad luck** dobra/zła passa; **a ~ of fine weather** okres pięknej pogody ④ (trend) **in the normal ~ of things...** naturalną or normalną koleją rzeczy... ⑤ (in printing) nakład *m*; (in industry) partia *f* ⑥ (trip) **to go out for a ~ in the car** wybrać się na przejażdżkę samochodem ⑦ (in cricket, baseball) punkt *m* ⑧ (for rabbit, chickens) wybieg *m* ⑨ (in tights, material) oczko *n* ⑩ (for skiing) trasa *f* ⑪ (in cards) sekwens *m*

II *vt* ① (cover) przebie|c, -gać *[distance]* ② (take part in) po|biec, bie|c, -gać w (czymś) *[race, heat, marathon]* ③ (drive) zaw|ieźć, -ozić; **to ~ sb to the station** zawieźć kogoś na dworzec ④ **to ~ one's hand over sth** przejechać ręką po czymś;

to ~ one's eye(s) over sth rzucić okiem na coś ⑤ (manage) zarządzać (czymś) *[company]*; rządzić (czymś) or w (czymś) *[country]*; prowadzić *[hotel, school, store]* ⑥ (operate) włącz|yć, -ać *[machine, engine]*; uruch|omić, -amiać *[program]*; **to ~ a film** puścić film ⑦ (conduct) przeprowadz|ić, -ać *[test, survey]* ⑧ (organize) z|organizować *[competition]*; udziel|ić, -ać *[lessons]*; po|prowadzić *[course]*; **we ~ regular buses to the airport** mamy regularną linię autobusową na lotnisko ⑨ (pass) przeciąg|nąć, -ać *[cable]* ⑩ (cause to flow) pu|ścić, -szczać *[water]*; odkręc|ić, -ać *[tap]* ⑪ (enter) wystaw|ić, -ać *[candidate]*

III *vi* ① *[person, animal]* po|biec; (regularly) biegać; **to ~ across sth** przebiec przez coś; **to ~ down sth** zbiec z czegoś; **to ~ up sth** wbiec na coś; **~ for the exit** biec do wyjścia; **she came ~ning towards me** wybiegła mi na spotkanie ② (flee) ucie|c, -kać; **to ~ for one's life** uciekać w popłochu ③ infml (rush off) wyl|ecieć, -atywać infml ④ *[machine]* pracować; **to ~ off the mains** być zasilanym z sieci elektrycznej; **to ~ fast/slow** *[clock]* śpieszyć się/późnić się ⑤ (continue, last) **the contract/lease has another month to ~** umowa/dzierżawa wygasa dopiero za miesiąc; **to ~ from... to...** *[school year, season]* trwać od... do... ⑥ *[play, musical]* być granym ⑦ *[frontier, path, line]* przebiegać ⑧ *[vehicle, sledge]* sunąć; *[curtain]* przesu|nąć, -wać się; *[stone]* toczyć się ⑨ *[buses, trains]* kursować ⑩ *[water, stream]* płynąć; **the tap is ~ning** z kranu leci woda; **my nose is ~ning** cieknie mi z nosa ⑪ *[dye, colour]* zejść, schodzić; *[ink, make-up]* spły|nąć, -wać; *[butter, cheese]* po|płynąć infml; *[garment]* farbować ⑫ (as candidate) kandydować; **to ~ for mayor** kandydować na burmistrza

■ **run about, run around:** biegać

■ **run away:** ¶ **~ away** ucie|c, -kać (**from sb** od kogoś) ¶ **~ away with [sb]** ucie|c, -kać z (kimś) ¶ **~ away with [sth]** zgarn|ąć, -iać infml *[prizes, title]*

■ **run down:** ¶ **~ down** *[battery]* rozładow|ać, -ywać się, wyczerp|ać, -ywać się; *[reserves]* zmniejsz|yć, -ać się; *[machine]* zuży|ć, -wać się; **the clock has run down** zegar wymaga nakręcenia ¶ **[sb/sth] down** ① (in vehicle) przeje|chać, -żdżać ② ogranicz|yć, -ać *[production, reserves]*; zużyć, -wać *[battery]* ③ (disparage) obgad|ać, -ywać *[person]*; s|krytykować *[ideas]*

■ **run into:** ① wje|chać, -żdżać w (coś) *[car, wall]*; wpa|ść, -dać na (coś) ② (meet) wpa|ść, -dać na (kogoś) fig *[person]*; napot|kać, -ykać *[difficulty, opposition]* ③ (amount to) **their debt ~s into millions** ich dług liczy się na miliony

■ **run off:** ucie|c, -kać

■ **run out:** ¶ **~ out** ① *[supplies, resources]* wyczerp|ać, -ywać się; **time is ~ning out** czas się kończy ② *[pen]* wypis|ać, -ywać się ③ *[lease]* s|kończyć się; *[passport]* s|tracić ważność ¶ ~ **out of [sth]** (have no more) **we have run out of petrol** skończyła nam się benzyna; **to be** ~**ning out of time** mieć już mało czasu

■ **run through**: przewi|nąć, -jać się przez (coś) *[work, history]*; być obecnym w (czymś) *[society]*

■ **run up**: (accumulate) **she's run up an enormous bill for clothes** wydała mnóstwo pieniędzy na ubrania

■ **run up against**: napot|kać, -ykać *[obstacle, difficulty]*

(IDIOMS:) **in the long** ~ na dłuższą metę; **in the short** ~ na krótszą metę

runaway /'rʌnəweɪ/ *adj [slave]* zbiegły; **a** ~ **teenager** nastolatek, który uciekł z domu; **a** ~ **husband** mąż, który porzucił żonę; **a** ~ **lorry** ciężarówka, nad którą kierowca stracił panowanie; **a** ~ **horse** koń, który poniósł

rundown /'rʌndaʊn/ *n* podsumowanie *n* (**on sth** czegoś)

run-down /ˌrʌn'daʊn/ *adj* ① (exhausted) wykończony infml ② (shabby) podupadły

rung /rʌŋ/ *n* szczebel *m* also fig

run-in /'rʌnɪn/ *n* infml starcie *n*

runner /'rʌnə(r)/ *n* ① **to be a fast** ~ szybko biegać ② (in horse-racing) koń *m* wyścigowy ③ (messenger) posłaniec *m* ④ (of sliding door, seat, drawer) prowadnica *f*; (for curtain) szyna *f*; (on sledge) płoza *f* ⑤ (of cloth, lace) bieżnik *m*; (carpet) chodnik *m*

runner bean *n* GB fasola *f* wielokwiatowa

runner-up /ˌrʌnər'ʌp/ *n* zdobyw|ca *m*, -czyni *f* drugiego miejsca (**to sb** za kimś)

running /'rʌnɪŋ/ **Ⅰ** *n* ① (sport) biegi *m pl*; (exercise) bieganie *n* ② (management) kierowanie *n*

Ⅱ *adj* ① *[water]* bieżący; *[tap]* odkręcony; *[knot]* ruchomy ② **five days** ~ pięć dni z rzędu
(IDIOMS:) **to be in the** ~ (**for sth**) mieć szansę (na coś)

running battle *n* fig nieustanna walka *f*

running commentary *n* relacja *f* na żywo

running total *n* bieżące saldo *n*

runny /'rʌnɪ/ *adj [jam, icing]* płynny; *[sauce]* rzadki; *[butter, chocolate]* roztopiony; *[omelette, scrambled eggs]* z nieściętym białkiem

run-of-the-mill /ˌrʌnəvðə'mɪl/ *adj* przeciętny

runt /rʌnt/ *n* ① (of litter) najsłabszy *m* w miocie ② (weakling) chuchro *n* pej

run-up /'rʌnʌp/ *n* ① Sport rozbieg *m*; **to take a** ~ wziąć rozbieg ② (preceding period) **the** ~ **to sth** okres poprzedzający coś

runway /'rʌnweɪ/ *n* pas *m* startowy

rupee /ruː'piː/ *n* rupia *f*

rupture /'rʌptʃə(r)/ *n* przepuklina *f*

rural /'rʊərəl/ *adj* ① *[life, community]* wiejski ② *[scene, beauty]* sielski

ruse /ruːz/ *n* podstęp *m*

rush[1] /rʌʃ/ **Ⅰ** *n* ① (of crowd) pęd *m*; **to make a** ~ **at/ for sth** *[crowd, person]* rzucić się na coś/do czegoś ② (hurry) pośpiech *m*; **to be in a** ~ śpieszyć się (**to do sth** żeby coś zrobić); **there's no** ~ nie ma pośpiechu ③ (of energy, emotion) (nagły) przypływ *m*; (of air) podmuch *m*; (of water) (silny) strumień *m*; (of complaints) lawina *f* fig

Ⅱ *vt* ① (transport) wys|łać, -yłać niezwłocznie; **to** ~ **sb to hospital** niezwłocznie odwieźć kogoś do szpitala ② (do hastily) po|śpieszyć się z (czymś) *[task, essay, speech]* ③ (hurry) pog|onić, -aniać, popędz|lić, -ać *[person]* ④ (charge at) rzuc|lić, -ać się na (kogoś) *[guard, defender]*; w|edrzeć, -dzierać się do (czegoś) *[building]*

Ⅲ *vi* ① *[person]* (make haste) po|śpieszyć się (**to do sth** żeby coś zrobić); (rush forward) po|pędzić; **they** ~**ed to help her** rzucili się, żeby jej pomóc; **to** ~ **out of the room** wypaść z pokoju ② *[train, car]* pędzić; **to** ~ **past** przemknąć

■ **rush into**: ¶ **to** ~ **into a purchase** kupić coś bez zastanowienia; **to** ~ **into a decision** pośpiesznie podjąć decyzję ¶ ~ **[sb] into doing sth** przynagl|ić, -ać do zrobienia czegoś

■ **rush out**: wypaść, wylecieć infml

■ **rush through**: ¶ ~ **through** wykon|ać, -ywać w pośpiechu *[task]* ¶ ~ **[sth] through** przyj|ąć, -mować w pośpiechu *[legislation]*; błyskawicznie zrealizować *[order]*

rush[2] /rʌʃ/ *n* Bot sitowie *n*

rushed /rʌʃt/ *adj [attempt, job]* pośpiesznie wykonany; *[letter]* napisany naprędce

rush hour *n* godzina *f* szczytu

rusk /rʌsk/ *n* sucharek *m*

russet /'rʌsɪt/ *adj [hair]* rudawy; *[leaves]* rdzawy

Russia /'rʌʃə/ *prn* Rosja *f*

Russian /'rʌʃn/ **Ⅰ** *n* ① (person) Rosjan|in *m*, -ka *f* ② (język *m*) rosyjski *m*
Ⅱ *adj* rosyjski

rust /rʌst/ **Ⅰ** *n* rdza *f*

Ⅱ *vt* s|powodować rdzewienie (czegoś)

Ⅲ *vi* za|rdzewieć

rustic /'rʌstɪk/ *adj [cottage, accent]* wiejski; *[architecture, furniture]* rustykalny; *[charm]* sielski

rustle /'rʌsl/ **Ⅰ** *n* szelest *m*

Ⅱ *vt* za|szeleścić (czymś) *[leaves, newspaper]*

rusty /'rʌstɪ/ *adj* zardzewiały

rut[1] /rʌt/ *n* ① (in ground) koleina *f* ② (routine) rutyna *f*; **to get into a** ~ popaść w rutynę

rut[2] /rʌt/ *n* (mating) **the** ~ ruja *f*

ruthless /'ruːθlɪs/ *adj [person, dictatorship]* bezwzględny; *[punishment]* bezlitosny

RV *n* US Aut → **recreational vehicle**

Rwanda /rʊ'ændə/ *prn* Rwanda *f*, Ruanda *f*

rye /raɪ/ **Ⅰ** *n* ① żyto *n* ② US (also ~ **whiskey**) żytnia whisky *f inv*

Ⅱ *adj [bread, flour]* żytni; ~ **field** pole żyta

S

s, S /es/ *n* s, S *n*

sabbath /'sæbəθ/ *n* (also **Sabbath**) (Jewish) szabas *m*; (Christian) dzień *m* pański

sabbatical /sə'bætɪkl/ *n* urlop *m* naukowy

sabotage /'sæbətɑːʒ/ **I** *n* sabotaż *m*
II *vt* sabotować

saboteur /ˌsæbə'tɜː(r)/ *n* sabotażyst|a *m*, -ka *f*

sabre, saber US /'seɪbə(r)/ *n* szabla *f*

sachet /'sæʃeɪ, US sæ'ʃeɪ/ *n* torebka *f*, saszetka *f*

sack /sæk/ **I** *n* ① (bag) worek *m* ② infml **to get the ~** zostać wylanym z pracy infml
II *vt* ① infml wyl|ać, -ewać infml *[employee]* ② (loot) o|grabić, s|plądrować

sacrament /'sækrəmənt/ *n* sakrament *m*

sacred /'seɪkrɪd/ *adj* święty (**to sb** dla kogoś)

sacrifice /'sækrɪfaɪs/ **I** *n* ofiara *f*; fig poświęcenie *n*
II *vt* złożyć, składać w ofierze (**to sb** komuś); fig poświęc|ić, -ać
III *vr* **to ~ oneself** poświęc|ić, -ać się (**for sb/sth** dla kogoś/czegoś)

sacrilege /'sækrɪlɪdʒ/ *n* świętokradztwo *n*

sacrosanct /'sækrəʊsæŋkt/ *adj* święty

sad /sæd/ *adj* smutny; **it makes me ~** to mnie zasmuca

sadden /'sædn/ *vt* zasmuc|ić, -ać

saddle /'sædl/ **I** *n* (on horse) siodło *n*; (on bike) siodełko *n*
II *vt* ① o|siodłać *[horse]* ② fig **to ~ sb with sth** obciążyć kogoś czymś *[responsibility]*; obarczyć kogoś czymś *[task]*

saddle bag *n* sakwa *f*

sadist /'seɪdɪst/ *n* sadyst|a *m*, -ka *f*

sadistic /sə'dɪstɪk/ *adj* sadystyczny

sadness /'sædnɪs/ *n* smutek *m*

sae *n* = stamped addressed envelope

safari /sə'fɑːrɪ/ *n* safari *n inv*

safari park *n* park *m* safari

safe /seɪf/ **I** *n* sejf *m*, kasa *f* pancerna
II *adj* ① (free from threat) *[person, documents]* bezpieczny; *[job]* pewny; **~ and sound** cały i zdrów; **have a ~ journey!** szczęśliwej podróży! ② (risk-free) *[place, method, toy]* bezpieczny; *[structure, building]* solidny; *[method]* pewny; **the water is ~ to drink** tę wodę można bezpiecznie pić ③ (prudent) *[investment, choice]* bezpieczny; *[estimate]*

ostrożny ④ (reliable) *[driver, guide]* godny zaufania; **to be in ~ hands** być w pewnych rękach
IDIOMS: **better ~ than sorry** lepiej dmuchać na zimne; **just to be on the ~ side** (tak) na wszelki wypadek

safe bet *n* pewniak *m* infml; **it's a ~ that...** to pewne, że...

safe-conduct /ˌseɪf'kɒndʌkt/ *n* gwarancja *f* bezpieczeństwa

safe-deposit box /ˌseɪfdɪ'pɒzɪtbɒks/ *n* skrytka *f* bankowa

safeguard /'seɪfgɑːd/ **I** *n* zabezpieczenie *n* (**against sth** przed czymś)
II *vt* o|chronić *[interests]*; zabezpiecz|yć, -ać *[data]* (**against/from sth** przed czymś)

safe house *n* kryjówka *f*

safekeeping /ˌseɪf'kiːpɪŋ/ *n* **to give sth to sb for ~** powierzyć coś komuś

safely /'seɪflɪ/ *adv* ① (without harm) *[arrive, return, land]* bezpiecznie, szczęśliwie ② (without risk) *[assume, say]* spokojnie; *[locked, hidden]* bezpiecznie

safe sex *n* bezpieczny seks *m*

safety /'seɪftɪ/ *n* bezpieczeństwo *n*; **in ~** bezpiecznie; **to reach ~** dotrzeć w bezpieczne miejsce

safety belt *n* pas *m* bezpieczeństwa

safety net *n* siatka *f* asekuracyjna; fig zabezpieczenie *n*

safety pin *n* agrafka *f*

sag /sæg/ *vi [roof, mattress]* zapa|ść, -dać się; *[flesh]* obwis|nąć, -ać ② *[exports]* spa|ść, -dać

saga /'sɑːgə/ *n* saga *f*

sage /seɪdʒ/ *n* ① (herb) szałwia *f* lekarska ② (wise person) mędrzec *m*

Sagittarius /ˌsædʒɪ'teərɪəs/ *n* Strzelec *m*

Sahara /sə'hɑːrə/ *prn* Sahara *f*; **the ~ desert** Sahara

sail /seɪl/ **I** *n* ① (on boat) żagiel *m*; **to set ~** wypłynąć w morze; **a ship in full ~** statek pod pełnymi żaglami ② (on windmill) skrzydło *n*
II *vt* ① pływać na (czymś) *[ship]* ② przepły|nąć, -wać (statkiem) *[ocean, channel]*
III *vi* ① *[person]* po|płynąć; **to ~ around the world** opłynąć świat ② *[ship]* płynąć; **to ~ across sth** przepły|nąć (przez) coś *[ocean]*; **the boat ~s at 10** statek odpływa o godzinie dziesiątej ③ (as hobby) **to go ~ing** pojechać na żagle
■ **sail through**: wygr|ać, -ywać bez trudu

[match]; **to ~ through an exam** śpiewająco zdać egzamin *infml*

sailboard /'seɪlbɔːd/ *n* deska *f* windsurfingowa

sailboarder /'seɪlbɔːdə(r)/ *n* deskarz *m*

sailboat /'seɪlbəʊt/ *n* US żaglówka *f*

sailing /'seɪlɪŋ/ *n* żeglarstwo *n*

sailing ship *n* żaglowiec *m*

sailor /'seɪlə(r)/ *n* marynarz *m*

saint /seɪnt, snt/ *n* święty *m*, -a *f*

sake /seɪk/ *n* ① (purpose, end) **for the ~ of principle** dla zasady; **for the ~ of clarity** dla jasności; **to complain for the ~ of complaining** narzekać dla samego narzekania; **for old times' ~** ze względu na starą przyjaźń ② (benefit) **for the ~ of sb** or **for sb's ~** ze względu na kogoś; **for God's** or **heaven's ~** na miłość or litość boską!

salad /'sæləd/ *n* (of cooked vegetables) sałatka *f*; (of raw vegetables) surówka *f*; (of lettuce) sałata *f*; **ham ~** sałatka z szynką

salad bar *n* bar *m* sałatkowy

salad bowl *n* salaterka *f* *(na sałatki)*

salad dressing *n* sos *m* do sałatek, dressing *m*

salami /sə'lɑːmɪ/ *n* salami *n inv*

salary /'sælərɪ/ *n* pensja *f*

sale /seɪl/ *n* ① sprzedaż *f*; **for ~** na sprzedaż; **on ~** GB w sprzedaży ② (at reduced price) wyprzedaż *f*; **the ~s** wyprzedaż; **in the ~(s)** GB, **on ~** US na wyprzedaży

sale price *n* obniżona cena *f*

sales assistant *n* GB sprzedaw|ca *m*, -czyni *f*

sales executive *n* kierownik *m* handlowy

salesman /'seɪlzmən/ *n* (in store) sprzedawca *m*; (representative) akwizytor *m*

sales pitch *n* zachwalanie *n* towaru przez sprzedawcę

sales rep *n* infml przedstawiciel *m* handlowy, przedstawicielka *f* handlowa

saleswoman /'seɪlzwʊmən/ *n* (in store) sprzedaw-czyni *f*; (representative) akwizytorka *f*

saliva /sə'laɪvə/ *n* ślina *f*

salivate /'sælɪveɪt/ *vi* ślinić się

sallow /'sæləʊ/ *adj [complexion]* ziemisty

salmon /'sæmən/ *n* łosoś *m*

salon /'sælɒn, US sə'lɒn/ *n* salon *m*

saloon /sə'luːn/ *n* ① (also **~ car**) sedan *m* ② US knajpa *f* *(na Dzikim Zachodzie)*; (on train) salonka *f*

salt /sɔːlt/ **❶** *n* sól *f*

❷ *vt* po|solić *[food]*; zas|olić, -alać *[meat]*; po-syp|ać, -ywać solą *[road]*

saltcellar /'sɔːltselə(r)/ *n* solniczka *f*

salty /'sɔːltɪ/ *adj* słony

salutary /'sæljʊtrɪ, US -terɪ/ *adj [experience]* pożyteczny; *[advice]* zbawienny; *[lesson]* pouczający

salute /sə'luːt/ **❶** *n* pozdrowienie *n*; (military) salut *m*

❷ *vt* za|salutować (komuś)

❸ *vi* za|salutować

salvage /'sælvɪdʒ/ **❶** *n* ① (rescue) uratowanie *n* ② (rescued goods) uratowane mienie *n*

❷ *vt* ① (at sea) u|ratować *[belongings, cargo]* **(from sth** z czegoś) ② ocal|ić, -ać *[marriage, project, reputation]* ③ (save for recycling) odzysk|ać, -iwać

salvation /sæl'veɪʃn/ *n* (religious) zbawienie *n*; (rescue) ocalenie *n*

Salvation Army *prn* Armia *f* Zbawienia

salve /sælv, US sæv/ **❶** *n* balsam *m*

❷ *vt* **to ~ one's conscience** uspokoić sumienie

same /seɪm/ **❶** *adj* ① (identical) **the ~** taki sam; **people are the ~ everywhere** ludzie są wszędzie tacy sami; **to look the ~** wyglądać tak samo; **one wine is the ~ as another to him** dla niego każde wino jest takie samo; **it amounts** or **comes to the ~ thing** na to samo or na jedno wychodzi; **it's all the ~ to me** wszystko mi jedno; **at the ~ time** jednocześnie ② (unchanged) **the ~** ten sam; **she's not the ~ woman** to nie ta sama kobieta; **to remain** or **stay the ~** nie zmienić się

❷ the same *adv phr [act, dress]* tak samo; **I still feel the ~ about her** wciąż to samo do niej czuję; **life goes on just the ~** życie się toczy tak samo jak zwykle; **thanks all the ~** tak czy inaczej dziękuję

❸ the same *pron* to samo; **I'll have the ~** wezmę to samo; **the ~ applies to** or **goes for you** to samo dotyczy ciebie; **to do the ~ as sb** zrobić to samo co ktoś; **the ~ to you!** nawzajem!

same-day /ˌseɪm'deɪ/ *adj* **~ dry-cleaning** czyszczenie w ciągu jednego dnia; **~ delivery** dostawa tego samego dnia

sample /'sɑːmpl, US 'sæmpl/ **❶** *n* próbka *f*; **to take a blood ~** pobrać krew

❷ *vt* ① (taste) s|kosztować (czegoś) *[food, wine]* ② (test) pob|rać, -ierać próbki (czegoś) *[products]*; z|badać *[opinion, market]*

sanatorium GB /ˌsænə'tɔːrɪəm/, **sanitarium** US /ˌsænə'teərɪəm/ *n* sanatorium *n*; (in boarding school) ≈ izolatka *f*

sanctimonious /ˌsæŋktɪ'məʊnɪəs/ *adj* świętoszkowaty

sanction /'sæŋkʃn/ **❶** *n* sankcja *f*; **to impose ~ on sth** nałożyć sankcje na coś

❷ *vt* (make, legal) u|sankcjonować; (approve) za|aprobować

sanctity /'sæŋktətɪ/ *n* świętość *f*; (of life) nienaruszalność *f*

sanctuary /'sæŋktʃʊərɪ, US -tʃʊerɪ/ *n* ① (safe place) azyl *m* ② (church, temple) świątynia *f*; (of special importance) sanktuarium *n* ③ (for wildlife) rezerwat *m*; (for mistreated pets) schronisko *n*

sand /sænd/ **❶** *n* piasek *m*

❷ *vt* ① (also **~ down**) o|szlifować (papierem ściernym) *[woodwork]*; z|edrzeć, -dzierać (papierem ściernym) *[paintwork]* [2] posyp|ać, -ywać piaskiem *[icy road]*

sandal /'sændl/ *n* sandał *m*

sand castle *n* zamek *m* z piasku

sand dune *n* wydma *f*

sandpaper /'sændpeɪpə(r)/ [1] *n* papier *m* ścierny [2] *vt* oczy|ścić, -szczać papierem ściernym

sandpit /'sændpɪt/ *n* piaskownica *f*

sandstone /'sændstəʊn/ *n* piaskowiec *m*

sandwich /'sænwɪdʒ, US -wɪtʃ/ [1] *n* kanapka *f*, sandwicz *m*; **cucumber** ∼ kanapka z ogórkiem [2] *vt* **to be** ∼**ed (in) between sth and sth** być wciśniętym między coś a coś

sandwich bar *n* bar *m* kanapkowy

sandwich course *n* kurs *m* z praktykami

sandy /'sændɪ/ *adj [beach, soil]* piaszczysty; *[sediment]* piaskowy; *[water]* zapiaszczony; *[hair]* rudawozłoty; *[colour]* piaskowy

sane /seɪn/ *adj [person]* zdrowy psychicznie; *[policy]* rozsądny; *[judgment]* trzeźwy

sanitarium /ˌsænə'teərɪəm/ *n* US = **sanatorium**

sanitary /'sænɪtrɪ, US -terɪ/ *adj* [1] *[fittings, conditions]* sanitarny [2] *[place]* czysty

sanitary towel GB, **sanitary napkin** US *n* podpaska *f* (higieniczna)

sanitation /ˌsænɪ'teɪʃn/ *n* warunki *m pl* sanitarne; (toilets) urządzenia *n pl* sanitarne

sanity /'sænətɪ/ *n* zdrowie *n* psychiczne

Santa (Claus) /'sæntə(klɔːz)/ *prn* Święty Mikołaj *m*

sap /sæp/ [1] *n* (in plant) soki *m pl* [2] *vt* podkop|ać, -ywać *[confidence, health]*; osłabi|ć, -ać *[energy]*

sapling /'sæplɪŋ/ *n* młode drzewko *n*

sapphire /'sæfaɪə(r)/ *n* [1] (stone) szafir *m* [2] (colour) (kolor *m*) szafirowy *m*, szafir *m*

sarcasm /'sɑːkæzəm/ *n* sarkazm *m*

sarcastic /sɑː'kæstɪk/ *adj* sarkastyczny

sardine /sɑː'diːn/ *n* sardynka *f*

Sardinia /sɑː'dɪnɪə/ *prn* Sardynia *f*

sardonic /sɑː'dɒnɪk/ *adj [laugh, remark]* sardoniczny; *[person]* zgryźliwy

SAS *n* GB = **Special Air Service** jednostka *f* antyterrorystyczna

sash /sæʃ/ *n* (round waist) szarfa *f*; (ceremonial) szarfa *f*, wstęga *f*

Satan /'seɪtn/ *prn* szatan *m*

satanic /sə'tænɪk/ *adj [rites, practices]* satanistyczny

satchel /'sætʃəl/ *n* torba *f* na ramię

satellite /'sætəlaɪt/ *n* satelita *m*

satellite dish *n* antena *f* satelitarna

satellite TV *n* telewizja *f* satelitarna

satin /'sætɪn, US 'sætn/ [1] *n* atłas *m* [2] *adj [garment, shoe]* atłasowy; **paint with a** ∼ **finish** farba z połyskiem

satire /'sætaɪə(r)/ *n* satyra *f* (**on sth** na coś)

satiric(al) /sə'tɪrɪk(l)/ *adj* satyryczny

satirize /'sætəraɪz/ *vt* ośmiesz|yć, -ać

satisfaction /ˌsætɪs'fækʃn/ *n* zadowolenie *n*, satysfakcja *f*

satisfactory /ˌsætɪs'fæktərɪ/ *adj* zadowalający

satisfied /'sætɪsfaɪd/ *adj* [1] (pleased) zadowolony (**with** or **about sth** z czegoś); usatysfakcjonowany (**with** or **about sth** czymś) [2] (convinced) **to be** ∼ **that...** być przekonanym, że...

satisfy /'sætɪsfaɪ/ *vt* [1] (fulfil) zaspok|oić, -ajać *[need, hunger, desires, curiosity]*; zadow|olić, -alać *[person]* [2] (persuade) przekon|ać, -ywać [3] (meet) spełni|ć, -ać *[criteria, requirements, conditions]*

satisfying /'sætɪsfaɪɪŋ/ *adj [meal]* porządny; *[job]* dający dużo satysfakcji; *[relationship]* szczęśliwy; *[result, progress]* zadowalający

saturate /'sætʃəreɪt/ *vt* przem|oczyć, -aczać *[clothes]*; nawilż|yć, -ać *[ground]*; fig nasyc|ić, -ać *[market]* (**with sth** czymś)

saturation point *n* stan *m* nasycenia; **to reach** ∼ fig osiągnąć stan nasycenia

Saturday /'sætədeɪ, -dɪ/ *n* sobota *f*

Saturn /'sætən/ *prn* Saturn *m*

sauce /sɔːs/ *n* sos *m*

saucepan /'sɔːspən/ *n* rondel *m*

saucer /'sɔːsə(r)/ *n* spodek *m*

Saudi Arabia /ˌsaʊdɪə'reɪbɪə/ *prn* Arabia *f* Saudyjska

sauna /'sɔːnə, 'saʊnə/ *n* sauna *f*

saunter /'sɔːntə(r)/ *vi* (also ∼ **along**) przechadzać się; **to** ∼ **off** oddalić się niespiesznie

sausage /'sɒsɪdʒ, US 'sɔːs-/ *n* kiełbasa *f*; (small) kiełbaska *f*

sausage roll *n* ≈ krokiet *m* z mięsem

savage /'sævɪdʒ/ [1] *n* dzikus *m*, -ka *f* [2] *adj [blow, attack]* brutalny; *[criticism]* bezlitosny [3] *vt* *[dog]* za|atakować z furią; *[lion]* rozszarp|ać, -ywać

save /seɪv/ [1] *n* Sport obrona *f* (strzału) [2] *vt* [1] (rescue) u|ratować; **to** ∼ **sb from death** uratować kogoś od śmierci; **to** ∼ **sb's life** uratować życie komuś; **to** ∼ **the day** uratować sytuację [2] (keep) zachow|ać, -ywać *[goods, documents]*; zapis|ać, -ywać *[date, file]*; **to** ∼ **sb sth** or **sth for sb** zostawić coś komuś *[food]*; zatrzymać coś dla kogoś *[place]* [3] (economize on) oszczędz|ić, -ać *[money, energy, time, space]*; **you'll** ∼ **money** zaoszczędzisz trochę pieniędzy; **to have money** ∼ **d** mieć odłożone pieniądze; **it will** ∼ **us time** to nam zaoszczędzi czasu; **it'll** ∼ **you having to come back tomorrow** dzięki temu nie będziesz musiał przychodzić jutro [4] Sport o|bronić [3] *vi* [1] (put by funds) = **save up** [2] (economize) oszczędz|ić, -ać; **to** ∼ **on sth** oszczędzać na czymś *[energy, food]*

■ **save up** oszczędz|ić, -ać (**for** or **towards sth** na coś)

saver /'seɪvə(r)/ *n* ciułacz *m*, -ka *f*

saving grace *n* zaleta *f*; **it's his only** ~ to jego jedyna zaleta

savings *npl* oszczędności *plt*

savings account *n* rachunek *m* oszczędnościowy

savings bank *n* bank *m* oszczędnościowy

saviour GB, **savior** US /ˈseɪvɪə(r)/ *n* wybawca *m*

savour GB, **savor** US /ˈseɪvə(r)/ **Ⅰ** *n* (taste) smak *m*; (smell) zapach *m*

Ⅱ *vt* delektować się (czymś)

savoury GB, **savory** US /ˈseɪvərɪ/ *adj* (salty) słony; (spicy) pikantny; (tasty) smakowity

saw /sɔː/ **Ⅰ** *n* piła *f*

Ⅱ *vt* przepiłow|ać, - ywać, piłować; **to** ~ **down a tree** ściąć drzewo

sawdust /ˈsɔːdʌst/ *n* trociny *plt*

sawn-off /ˌsɔːnˈɒf/ *adj [barrel]* ucięty; **a** ~ **shotgun** obrzynek infml

saxophone /ˈsæksəfəʊn/ *n* saksofon *m*

say /seɪ/ **Ⅰ** *n* głos *m*, prawo *n* głosu; **to have one's** ~ **on sth** powiedzieć, co się myśli na temat czegoś; **to have a/no** ~ **in sth** mieć coś/nie mieć nic do powiedzenia w sprawie czegoś

Ⅱ *vt* ⒈ *[person]* powiedzieć, mówić *[hello, yes]* (**to sb** komuś, do kogoś); wypowi|edzieć, -adać *[words, line]*; zmówić *[prayer]*; **to** ~ **(that)…** powiedzieć, że…; **they** ~ **he is very rich, he's said to be very rich** (ludzie) mówią or mówi się, że jest bardzo bogaty; **she'll have something to** ~ **about that** będzie miała coś na ten temat do powiedzenia; **to** ~ **sth to oneself** powiedzieć coś do siebie; fig powiedzieć sobie coś; **let's** ~ **no more about it** nie mówmy już o tym; **it goes without** ~**ing that…** rozumie się samo przez się, że…; **let's** ~ **(that)…** powiedzmy, że…; **three days from now, that's to** ~ **on Monday** za trzy dni, czyli w poniedziałek; **how high would you** ~ **it is?** ile, według ciebie, to ma wysokości?; **I'd** ~ **she was about 25** powiedziałbym, że miała jakieś dwadzieścia pięć lat ⒉ *[sign, dial]* wskaz|ać, -ywać; *[gesture, signal]* oznaczać

Ⅲ *vi* **stop when I** ~ zatrzymaj się, kiedy ci powiem; **he wouldn't** ~ nie chciał powiedzieć IDIOMS: **it** ~**s a lot for him** to dobrze o nim świadczy; **there's a lot to be said for that method** wiele przemawia za tą metodą; **when all is said and done** w ostatecznym rozrachunku

saying /ˈseɪɪŋ/ *n* porzekadło *n*

scab /skæb/ *n* strup *m*

scaffolding /ˈskæfəldɪŋ/ *n* rusztowanie *n*

scald /skɔːld/ *vt* po|parzyć

scalding /ˈskɔːldɪŋ/ *adj* bardzo gorący, parzący

scale /skeɪl/ **Ⅰ** *n* ⒈ (extent) (of crisis, disaster, operation) skala *f*; (of support) stopień *m*; **on a large** ~ na dużą skalę ⒉ **pay** or **salary** ~ siatka płac; **on a** ~ **of 2 km to 1 cm** w skali 1 do 200 000 ⒊ (on thermometer, gauge) podziałka *f*, skala *f* ⒋ (for weighing) szala *f* ⒌ Mus gama *f* ⒍ (on fish, insect) łuska *f*

Ⅱ scales *npl* waga *f*

Ⅲ *vt* ⒈ wspi|ąć, -nąć się na (coś) ⒉ usu|nąć, -wać łuski z (czegoś)

■ **scale down:** ~ **[sth] down** zmniejsz|yć, -ać w skali *[drawing]*; fig ogranicz|yć, -ać

scale drawing *n* rysunek *m* w zmniejszonej skali

scallop *n* Culin muszla *f* świętego Jakuba

scalp /skælp/ **Ⅰ** *n* skóra *f* głowy

Ⅱ *vt* o|skalpować

scam /skæm/ infml *n* przekręt *m* infml

scamper /ˈskæmpə(r)/ *vi* (also ~ **about,** ~ **around**) *[child, dog]* po|truchtać; *[mice]* po|dreptać

scan /skæn/ **Ⅰ** *n* (CAT) tomografia *f*; (ultrasound) ultrasonografia *f*, USG *n inv*

Ⅱ *vt* ⒈ prze|jrzeć, -glądać *[paper, list]* ⒉ (examine) z|lustrować *[face, horizon]* ⒊ *[beam of light, radar]* przecze|sać, -ywać ⒋ Med z|robić badanie tomograficzne (czegoś) *[organ]*

Ⅲ *vi [poem, lines]* mieć rytm

scandal /ˈskændl/ *n* skandal *m*

scandalize /ˈskændəlaɪz/ *vt* z|gorszyć

scandalous /ˈskændələs/ *adj* skandaliczny

Scandinavia /ˌskændɪˈneɪvɪə/ *prn* Skandynawia *f*

scanner /ˈskænə(r)/ *n* (CAT) tomograf *m*; (for bar codes) czytnik *m*

scanty /ˈskæntɪ/ *adj [supply, swimsuit]* skąpy; *[audience]* nieliczny

scapegoat /ˈskeɪpɡəʊt/ *n* kozioł *m* ofiarny fig

scar /skɑː(r)/ **Ⅰ** *n* blizna *f*, szrama *f*

Ⅱ *vt* okalecz|yć, -ać; (with knife on face) oszpec|ić, -ać; **to** ~ **sb for life** oszpecić kogoś na całe życie; fig pozostawić trwałe ślady na psychice kogoś

scarce /skeəs/ *adj* rzadki; **money became** ~ zaczęło brakować pieniędzy

scarcely /ˈskeəslɪ/ *adv [credible]* niezbyt; *[remember]* ledwie; ~ **anybody** prawie nikt; **we have** ~ **any money** prawie nie mamy pieniędzy

scare /skeə(r)/ **Ⅰ** *n* ⒈ (fright) (prze)strach *m*; **to give sb a** ~ przestraszyć kogoś ⒉ (alarm) alarm *m*; **a bomb** ~ alarm bombowy

Ⅱ *vt* wystraszyć

■ **scare away, scare off:** odstrasz|yć, -ać *[trespassers]*; s|płoszyć *[burglar, animal]*

scarecrow /ˈskeəkrəʊ/ *n* strach *m* na wróble

scared /skeəd/ *adj* wystraszony; **to be** ~ bać się (**of sb/sth** kogoś/czegoś); **to be** ~ **stiff** infml śmiertelnie się bać

scaremongering /ˈskeəmʌŋərɪŋ/ *n* sianie *n* paniki

scarf /skɑːf/ *n* (long) szal *m*, szalik *m*; (square) chusta *f*, chustka *f*

scarlet /ˈskɑːlət/ **Ⅰ** *n* szkarłat *m*

Ⅱ *adj* szkarłatny

scarlet fever *n* szkarlatyna *f*

scary /ˈskeərɪ/ *adj* infml przerażający

scathing /ˈskeɪðɪŋ/ *adj [remark, tone, criticism]* zjadliwy; *[look]* jadowity

scatter /'skætə(r)/ **[I]** vt (also ~ **around, ~ about**) rozsyp|ać, -ywać [earth]; rozsi|ać, -ewać [seeds]; rozrzuc|ić, -ać [books, papers, clothes]

[II] vi [people, animals, birds] rozpr|oszyć, -aszać się

scatter-brained /'skætəbreind/ adj [person] roztrzepany; [idea] postrzelony infml

scattered /'skætəd/ adj [houses, population] rozproszony; [books, litter] porozrzucany; ~ **support** pojedyncze przypadki poparcia; ~ **showers** przelotne deszcze

scatty /'skæti/ adj GB infml roztrzepany

scavenge /'skævindʒ/ vi to ~ **in** or **through the dustbins for sth** [person, animal] grzebać w śmietnikach w poszukiwaniu czegoś

scavenger /'skævindʒə(r)/ n [1] (person) śmieciarz m [2] (animal) padlinożerca m

scenario /sı'nɑːrıəʊ, US -'nær-/ n scenariusz m

scene /siːn/ n [1] (in play, film) scena f; **behind the ~s** za kulisami [2] (location) miejsce n, scena f; **I need a change of** ~ muszę zmienić otoczenie [3] (sphere) **the jazz** ~ świat jazzu [4] (view) widok m

scenery /'siːnəri/ n [1] (landscape) krajobraz m; (as background for event, film) sceneria f [2] (on stage) dekoracje f pl

scent /sent/ **[I]** n [1] (smell) zapach m, woń f; (perfume) perfumy plt [2] (of animal) zapach m; (in hunting) trop m, ślad m

[II] vt zwietrzyć [animal]; zwęszyć [danger, scandal]

sceptic GB, **skeptic** US /'skeptik/ n scepty|k m, -czka f

sceptical GB, **skeptical** US /'skeptikl/ adj sceptyczny

scepticism GB, **skepticism** US /'skeptisizəm/ n sceptycyzm m

schedule /'ʃedjuːl, US 'skedʒʊl/ **[I]** n [1] (of work, events) harmonogram m; **to be ahead of** ~ wyprzedzać harmonogram; **to be behind** ~ [person] spóźniać się z terminem; [work] przebiegać z opóźnieniem; **finished on** ~ zakończony w terminie [2] (of train, coach) rozkład m jazdy; (of airline, plane) rozkład m lotów; **to arrive on/ahead of** ~ przybyć o czasie/przed czasem [3] (of charges) taryfa f; (of prices) wykaz m; **as per** ~ zgodnie z załącznikiem

[II] vt za|planować; **the station was ~d for completion in 1997** dworzec miał być gotowy w 1997 roku

scheduled flight n lot m rejsowy

scheme /skiːm/ **[I]** n [1] (arrangement) plan m, projekt m; **a** ~ **for (doing) sth** plan (zrobienia) czegoś; **pension** ~ program emerytalny [2] (plot) intryga f

[II] vi u|knuć intrygę, spiskować

scheming /'skiːmɪŋ/ **[I]** n machinacje f pl

[II] adj intrygancki

schizophrenic /ˌskɪtsəʊ'frenɪk/ adj [behaviour] schizofreniczny; [patient] ze schizofrenią

scholar /'skɒlə(r)/ n uczon|y m, -a f

scholarship /'skɒləʃɪp/ n stypendium n; **to win a** ~ **(to Eton)** uzyskać stypendium (w Eton)

school /skuːl/ **[I]** n [1] szkoła f; **there's no** ~ **today** dzisiaj nie ma lekcji [2] (university-level) szkoła f wyższa; **to go to medical** ~ studiować medycynę [3] (of fish) ławica f; (of whales) stado n

[II] adj [life, uniform, year] szkolny; ~ **outing** wycieczka szkolna; ~ **holidays** (in summer) wakacje; (in winter) ferie

schoolbag /'skuːlbæg/ n (case) teczka f szkolna; (traditional) tornister m

schoolboy /'skuːlbɔɪ/ n uczeń m

schoolchild /'skuːltʃaɪld/ n ucze|ń m, -nnica f

school fees n czesne n

schoolfriend /'skuːlfrend/ n kole|ga m, -żanka f z klasy

schoolgirl /'skuːlgɜːl/ n uczennica f

schooling /'skuːlɪŋ/ n nauka f, kształcenie n

school-leaver /ˌskuːl'liːvə(r)/ n GB absolwent m, -ka f szkoły

school leaving age n wiek m ukończenia szkoły średniej

school lunch n obiad m w szkole

school report GB, **school report card** US n semestralna lub roczna ocena pracy ucznia

schoolteacher /'skuːltiːtʃə(r)/ n nauczyciel m, -ka f

schoolwork /'skuːlwɜːk/ n nauka f

science /'saɪəns/ **[I]** n nauka f; (in opposition to arts) nauki f pl ścisłe

[II] adj [journal] naukowy; [subject] ścisły; ~ **teacher** nauczyciel przedmiotów ścisłych

scientific /ˌsaɪən'tɪfɪk/ adj naukowy

scientist /'saɪəntɪst/ n naukowiec m

scissors /'sɪzəz/ npl nożyce plt

scoff /skɒf, US skɔːf/ **[I]** vt GB infml (devour) wci|ąć, -nać infml

[II] vi kpić, drwić (**at sb/sth** z kogoś/czegoś)

scold /skəʊld/ vt z|rugać infml (**for doing sth** za zrobienie czegoś)

scoop /skuːp/ **[I]** n [1] (for measuring) dozownik m, miarka f [2] (of ice cream) gałka f [3] (piece of news) bomba f infml fig; **to get a** ~ zdobyć sensacyjny materiał

[II] vt infml zgarn|ąć, -iać infml [prize, sum, medal]

scooter /'skuːtə(r)/ n [1] (child's) hulajnoga f [2] (motorized) skuter m

scope /skəʊp/ n [1] (opportunity) możliwość f (**for sth** czegoś) [2] (range, extent) zakres m [3] (capacity) kompetencje f pl

scorch /skɔːtʃ/ **[I]** n (also ~ **mark**) ślad m po przypaleniu

[II] vt [sun] wypal|ić, -ać [grass, lawn]; [fire] osmal|ić, -ać [tree]; [iron] przypal|ić, -ać [fabric]

scorching /'skɔːtʃɪŋ/ adj infml (also ~ **hot**) [weather, day] skwarny, upalny; [sun] prażący

score /skɔː(r)/ **▯** *n* ⓵ Sport wynik *m*; (in cards) zapis *m*; **to keep (the)** ∼ notować wyniki; (in cards) prowadzić zapis ⓶ (in test, exam) wynik *m* ⓷ (written music) partytura *f*; (for film) muzyka *f* (do filmu) ⓸ (twenty) **a** ∼ dwudziestka *f*; **three** ∼ **years and ten** siedemdziesiąt lat ⓹ **on that** ∼ z tego powodu

▯▯ *vt* ⓵ Sport zdoby|ć, -wać *[points]*; strzel|ić, -ać *[goal]*; odn|ieść, -osić *[success, victory]*; **to** ∼ **9 out of 10** zdobyć 9 punktów na 10 możliwych ⓶ (cut) naci|ąć, -nać *[wood]*; po|nacinać *[meat]*

▯▯▯ *vi* (gain point) zdoby|ć, -wać punkt; (obtain goal) strzel|ić, -ać gola

(IDIOMS:) **to settle a** ∼ wyrównać rachunki

scoreboard /'skɔːbɔːd/ *n* tablica *f* wyników

scorn /skɔːn/ **▯** *n* pogarda *f* (**for sb/sth** dla kogoś/ czegoś)

▯▯ *vt* (despise) gardzić (czymś), pogardzać (czymś); (reject) wzgardzić (czymś) *[advice, invitation]*

scornful /'skɔːnfl/ *adj* pogardliwy

Scorpio /'skɔːpɪəʊ/ *n* Skorpion *m*

Scot /skɒt/ *n* Szkot *m*, -ka *f*

Scotch /skɒtʃ/ **▯** *n* (also ∼ **whisky**) szkocka (whisky) *f inv*

▯▯ *adj* szkocki

Scotch tape® *n* taśma *f* klejąca

scot-free /ˌskɒt'friː/ *adj* **to get off** ∼ (unpunished) wymigać się od kary *infml*; (unharmed) wyjść bez szwanku

Scotland /'skɒtlənd/ *prn* Szkocja *f*

Scottish /'skɒtɪʃ/ *adj* szkocki

scour /'skaʊə(r)/ *vt* ⓵ (scrub) wy|szorować ⓶ przeczes|ać, -ywać *[area, archives]* (**for sth** w poszukiwaniu czegoś)

scourer /'skaʊərə(r)/ *n* druciak *m*

scourge /skɜːdʒ/ *n* bicz *m*

scout /skaʊt/ *n* ⓵ (also **boy** ∼) skaut *m*, -ka *f*; (in Poland) harce|rz *m*, -rka *f* ⓶ (military) (person) zwiadowca *m*; (reconnaissance) zwiad *m* ⓷ (also **talent** ∼) łowca *m* talentów

■ **scout around**: robić rozpoznanie; **to** ∼ **around for sth** rozglądać się za czymś

scowl /skaʊl/ **▯** *n* grymas *m* niezadowolenia

▯▯ *vi* z|marszczyć brwi

scramble /'skræmbl/ **▯** *n* ⓵ (rush) szamotanina *f* ⓶ (climb) wspinaczka *f*

▯▯ *vt* za|szyfrować, za|kodować *[signal]*

▯▯▯ *vi* **to** ∼ **up sth** wdrapywać się po czymś; **to** ∼ **down sth** schodzić po czymś

scrambled egg *n* (also ∼**s**) jajecznica *f*

scrambling /'skræmblɪŋ/ *n* motokros *m*

scrap /skræp/ **▯** *n* ⓵ (of paper, cloth) skrawek *m*; (cutting from press) wycinek *m*; (of news, information) urywek *m*; (of conversation) strzęp *m* ⓶ (discarded metal goods) złom *m*

▯▯ scraps *npl* (of food) resztki *f pl*

▯▯▯ *vt* ⓵ infml odst|ąpić, -ępować od (czegoś) *[project, agreement]* ⓶ (dispose of) ze|złomować *[equipment, aircraft]*

scrapbook /'skræpbʊk/ *n* album *m* z wycinkami

scrape /skreɪp/ **▯** *n* infml **to get into a** ∼ wpakować się w tarapaty

▯▯ *vt* ⓵ (clean) o|skrobać *[vegetables, shoes]* ⓶ (damage) zadrap|ać, -ywać ⓷ (injure) ob|etrzeć, -cierać *[elbow, knee]*

▯▯▯ *vi* **to** ∼ **against sth** *[car part]* o|trzeć, -cierać się o coś

■ **scrape by**: poradzić sobie; **to** ∼ **by on £80 a week** przeżyć za 80 funtów tygodniowo

■ **scrape in**: (to university, class) z trudem dosta|ć, -wać się

■ **scrape out**: ∼ **[sth] out** wyskrob|ać, -ywać *[saucepan]*

■ **scrape through**: ¶ ∼ **through** z trudem da|ć, -wać sobie radę ¶ ∼ **through [sth]** z trudem zdać *[exam, test]*

scrap heap *n* złomowisko *n*; **to be thrown on the** ∼ fig zostać wyrzuconym na śmietnik fig

scrap iron *n* złom *m* żelazny

scrap paper *n* (for reuse) makulatura *f*

scrap yard *n* skład *m* złomu

scratch /skrætʃ/ **▯** *n* ⓵ (wound) zadrapanie *n* ⓶ (on polished surface, record, glass) rysa *f* ⓷ (of pen) skrzypienie *n*; (of lighted match) trzask *m* ⓸ infml **not to be up to** ∼ nie spełniać wymogów ⓹ **to start from** ∼ zacząć od zera

▯▯ *vt* ⓵ **to** ∼ **one's initials on sth** wydrapać swoje inicjały na czymś ⓶ *[cat, person, thorn]* po|drapać; *[person]* po|rysować *[car, furniture, record]*; **to** ∼ **sb's eyes out** wydrapać komuś oczy

▯▯▯ *vi* drapać się

scratch card *n* zdrapka *f*

scrawl /skrɔːl/ **▯** *n* gryzmoły *plt*, bazgroły *plt*

▯▯ *vt* na|gryzmolić

▯▯▯ *vi* gryzmolić

scrawny /'skrɔːnɪ/ *adj [person, animal]* wychudły

scream /skriːm/ **▯** *n* (of person, animal) krzyk *m*; (stronger) wrzask *m*; (of brakes, tyres) pisk *m*; ∼**s of laughter** wybuchy śmiechu

▯▯ *vt* wykrzyk|nąć, -iwać

▯▯▯ *vi* krzy|knąć, -czeć; (stronger) wrz|asnąć, -eszczeć

screech /skriːtʃ/ **▯** *n* wrzask *m*; (of tyres, brakes) pisk *m*

▯▯ *vi [person, animal]* wrz|asnąć, -eszczeć; *[tyres]* za|piszczeć

screen /skriːn/ **▯** *n* ⓵ (for display) ekran *m* ⓶ (panel) parawan *m*; (partition) przenośna ścianka *f* ⓷ US (in door) siatka *f*

▯▯ *vt* ⓵ (show) wyświetl|ić, -ać *[film]*; *[TV]* wy|emitować *[programme]* ⓶ (conceal) osł|onić, -aniać *[person, house]* (**from sth** od czegoś) ⓷ (test) sprawdz|ić, -ać *[applicant, candidate, baggage]*; **to**

~ **sb for cancer** poddać kogoś badaniom na obecność nowotworu

screening /'skri:nıŋ/ n ① (of film) pokaz m, projekcja f; (on TV) emisja f ② (of candidates) sprawdzanie n; (separating) selekcja f; Med badanie n przesiewowe ③ (of calls) kontrolowanie n

screenplay /'skri:npleı/ n scenariusz m

screen saver n Comput wygaszacz m ekranu

screenwriter /'skri:nraıtə(r)/ n scenarzyst|a m, -ka f

screw /skru:/ **I** n wkręt m; (screwbolt) śruba f

II vt **to** ~ **sth onto a door/to the floor** przykręcić or przyśrubować coś do drzwi/do podłogi

■ **screw up**: ① z|miąć; **to** ~ **up one's eyes** zmrużyć oczy; **to** ~ **up one's face** skrzywić się ② infml schrzanić infml [plan, task]

screwdriver /'skru:draıvə(r)/ n ① (tool) śrubokręt m ② (cocktail) wódka f z sokiem pomarańczowym

scribble /'skrıbl/ **I** vt na|bazgrać

II vi bazgrać, gryzmolić

scrimp /skrımp/ vi zaciskać pasa fig; **to** ~ **and save** odmawiać sobie wszystkiego

script /skrıpt/ n ① (for a film) scenariusz m ② GB (in exam) arkusz m egzaminacyjny

scripture /'skrıptʃə(r)/ n (also **Holy Scripture, Holy Scriptures**) (Christian) Pismo n Święte; (other) święta księga f

scriptwriter /'skrıptraıtə(r)/ n scenarzyst|a m, -ka f

scroll /skrəʊl/ **I** n (manuscript) zwój m; (painting) rolka f

II vt przewi|nąć, -jać [text]; **to** ~ **sth up/down** przewinąć coś w górę/w dół

III vi przewi|nąć, -jać się

scroll bar n Comput pasek m przewijania

scrounge /skraʊndʒ/ vt infml żebrać o (coś); **to** ~ **sth from** or **off sb** wyżebrać coś od kogoś; (by stealth) wycyganić coś od kogoś

scrounger /'skraʊndʒə(r)/ n infml pasożyt m fig

scrub /skrʌb/ **I** n ① (clean) **to give sth a (good)** ~ (dobrze) coś wyszorować ② Bot busz m

II vt wy|szorować [floor, vegetable]; **to** ~ **one's nails** wyszorować (sobie) paznokcie

■ **scrub up**: [surgeon] umyć się (do operacji)

scrubbing brush, scrub brush US n szczotka f do szorowania

scruff /skrʌf/ n **by the** ~ **of the neck** za kark

scruffy /'skrʌfı/ adj [person, clothes] niechlujny; [flat, bar] obskurny; [town] zaniedbany

scrum /skrʌm/, **scrummage** /'skrʌmıdʒ/ n (in rugby) młyn m

scruple /'skru:pl/ n skrupuły plt (**about sth** co do czegoś)

scrupulous /'skru:pjʊləs/ adj skrupulatny

scrutinize /'skru:tınaız, US -tənaız/ vt przypat|rzeć, -rywać się (czemuś) [face]; prze|analizować [motives]; sprawdz|ić, -áć [accounts, votes]; nadzorować [election]

scrutiny /'skru:tını, US 'skru:tənı/ n (of data) analiza f

scuba diving n nurkowanie n z akwalungiem

scuff /skʌf/ **I** n (also ~ **mark**) (on furniture, floor) rysa f; (on leather) zadrapanie n

II vt po|rysować [floor, furniture]; z|edrzeć, -dzierać z wierzchu [shoes]

scuffle /'skʌfl/ n przepychanka f

sculpt /skʌlpt/ **I** vt wy|rzeźbić

II vi rzeźbić

sculptor /'skʌlptə(r)/ n rzeźbia|rz m, -rka f

sculpture /'skʌlptʃə(r)/ n (object) rzeźba f; (art) rzeźbiarstwo n

scum /skʌm/ n ① (on pond, liquid) kożuch m ② (on bath) osad m brudu ③ **they are the** ~ **of the earth** to najgorsze męty

scuttle /'skʌtl/ **I** vt zat|opić, -apiać [own ship]; fig s|torpedować [talks, project]

II vi **to** ~ **away, to** ~ **off** zmykać

scythe /saıð/ n kosa f

sea /si:/ **I** n morze n; **beside** or **by the** ~ nad morzem; **the open** ~ otwarte morze; **to go to** ~ [boat] wypłynąć w morze; **a long way out to** ~ daleko na morzu; **to travel/send sth by** ~ podróżować/wysłać coś drogą morską

II adj [air, bird, water, voyage, creature] morski; [boot, chest] marynarski

seafood /'si:fu:d/ n owoce m pl morza

seafront /'si:frʌnt/ n bulwar m nadmorski

seagull /'si:gʌl/ n mewa f

seal /si:l/ **I** n ① Zool foka f ② (stamp) pieczęć f; **I need your** ~ **of approval** potrzebuję twojej zgody ③ (on container, door) plomba f; (on package, letter) pieczęć f

II vt ① (stamp) o|pieczętować [document] ② (close) zakle|ić, -jać [envelope]; szczelnie zam|knąć, -ykać [jar, tin]; uszczelni|ć, -ać [window, frame] ③ fig s|cementować, przypieczętow|ać, -ywać [friendship, alliance] (**with sb** z kimś); **to** ~ **sb's fate** przypieczętować los kogoś

■ **seal off**: oddziel|ić, -áć [section of building]; zam|knąć, -ykać dostęp do (czegoś) [building, area]; zam|knąć, -ykać [street]

sea lion n lew m morski

seam /si:m/ n szew m

seamless /'si:mlıs/ adj [transition] gładki; [process, whole] ciągły

seaplane /'si:pleın/ n hydroplan m

search /sɜ:tʃ/ **I** n ① poszukiwanie n (**for sb/sth** kogoś/czegoś); **in** ~ **of sth** w poszukiwaniu czegoś ② (examination) przeszukanie n (**of sb/sth** kogoś/czegoś) ③ Comput przeszukiwanie n

II *vt* przeszuk|ać, -iwać *[area, cupboard]*; dokładnie przej|rzeć, -glądać *[map, page, records]*

III *vi* [1] szukać; **to** ~ **for** or **after sb/sth** szukać kogoś/czegoś; **to** ~ **through sth** przeszukiwać coś *[cupboard, bag, file]* [2] Comput **to** ~ **for sth** szukać czegoś *[data, file]*

■ **search out**: ~ **[sb/sth] out**, ~ **out [sb/sth]** odszuk|ać, -iwać

search engine *n* wyszukiwarka *f*

searching /'sɜːtʃɪŋ/ *adj [look]* badawczy; *[question]* dociekliwy

searchlight /'sɜːtʃlaɪt/ *n* reflektor *m*, szperacz *m*

search party *n* ekipa *f* ratownicza

search warrant *n* nakaz *m* rewizji

sea salt *n* sól *f* morska

seashell /'siːʃel/ *n* muszla *f*

seashore /'siːʃɔː(r)/ *n* (beach) brzeg *m* morza; (part of coast) wybrzeże *n*

seasick /'siːsɪk/ *adj* **to feel** ~ cierpieć na chorobę morską

seaside /'siːsaɪd/ **II** *n* **at** or **by the** ~ nad morzem **II** *adj [town]* nadmorski; ~ **holiday** wakacje nad morzem

season /'siːzn/ **II** *n* **1** pora *f* roku; **strawberries are in/out of** ~ teraz jest/nie jest sezon na truskawki; **out of** ~ poza sezonem; **the holiday** ~ okres wakacyjny; **the Christmas** ~ okres świąt Bożego Narodzenia; **Season's greetings!** (on Christmas cards) Wesołych Świąt!

II *vt* Culin przyprawi|ć, -ać

seasonal /'siːzənl/ *adj [work, fruit]* sezonowy; *[rainfall]* okresowy

seasoned /'siːznd/ *adj [soldier]* zaprawiony w boju; *[politician]* wytrawny; *[campaigner, performer]* doświadczony; *[dish]* przyprawiony; **highly** ~ mocno przyprawiony

seasoning /'siːznɪŋ/ *n* przyprawa *f*

season ticket *n* (for travel) bilet *m* okresowy; (for theatre, sport events) abonament *m*

seat /siːt/ **II** *n* **1** (place) miejsce *n*; **take your** ~ **s please** proszę zająć miejsca **2** (object) siedzenie *n*; (on bicycle) siodełko *n*; **to take** or **have a** ~ usiąść **3** (of trousers) siedzenie *n*

II *vt* **1** posadzić *[person]* **2** **the car** ~ **s five** to jest samochód na pięć osób; **the cinema** ~ **s 130 people** kino może pomieścić 130 osób

seatbelt /'siːtbelt/ *n* pas *m* (bezpieczeństwa)

-seater /'siːtə(r)/ *in combinations* **a two** ~ (plane) samolot dwuosobowy; **a three** ~ (sofa) kanapa trzyosobowa

seating /'siːtɪŋ/ *n* miejsca *n pl* siedzące; **I'll organize the** ~ ja się zajmę rozmieszczeniem gości

sea urchin *n* jeż *m* morski

sea view *n* widok *m* na morze

seaweed /'siːwiːd/ *n* wodorosty *m pl* morskie

seaworthy /'siːwɜːðɪ/ *adj [ship]* zdatny do żeglugi

secateurs /ˌsekə'tɜːz, 'sekətɜːz/ *npl* GB sekator *m*

secluded /sɪ'kluːdɪd/ *adj [spot]* ustronny; *[house]* odosobniony

seclusion /sɪ'kluːʒn/ *n* odosobnienie *n*

second /'sekənd/ **II** *n* **1** (ordinal number) drug|i *m*, -a *f*, -ie *n* **2** (unit of time) sekunda *f*; (instant) sekunda *f*, chwila *f* **3** (date) **the** ~ **of May** drugi maja **4** GB (at university) **upper/lower** ~ ocena dobra/dość dobra *(na dyplomie ukończenia studiów)* **5** (also ~ **gear**) drugi bieg *m*; dwójka *f* infml **6** (inferior article) artykuł *m* w drugim gatunku

II *adj* drugi; **to have a** ~ **chance to do sth** mieć drugą szansę na zrobienie czegoś; **to have a** ~ **helping (of sth)** wziąć dokładkę (czegoś)

III *adv* **1** (in second place) *[come, finish]* na drugim miejscu, (jako) drugi; **the** ~ **longest bridge in the world** drugi co do długości most na świecie **2** (also **secondly**) po drugie

IV *vt* (support) pop|rzeć, -ierać *[motion]*

IDIOMS: **to be** ~ **nature to sb** być drugą naturą kogoś; **it is** ~ **to none** to nie ma sobie równych; **on** ~ **thoughts** po namyśle; **to have** ~ **thoughts** mieć wątpliwości

secondary /'sekəndrɪ, US -derɪ/ *adj* drugorzędny

secondary school *n* ≈ szkoła *f* średnia

second class **II** **second-class** *adj* **1** *[post, mail]* zwykły **2** ~ **carriage/ticket** wagon/bilet drugiej klasy **3** (second-rate) *[hotel]* podrzędny; ~ **goods** towary w drugim gatunku

II *adv* **to travel** ~ podróżować drugą klasą; **to send sth** ~ wysłać coś jako przesyłkę zwykłą

second hand /'sekəndhænd/ *n* (on watch, clock) wskazówka *f* sekundowa

second-hand /ˌsekənd'hænd/ **II** *adj [clothes, car]* używany; *[news, information]* z drugiej ręki **II** *adv [find out, learn]* z drugiej ręki; **to buy** ~ kupować rzeczy używane

secondly /'sekəndlɪ/ *adv* po drugie

second name *n* (surname) nazwisko *n*; (second forename) drugie imię *n*

second-rate /ˌsekənd'reɪt/ *adj [actor]* podrzędny; *[novel]* kiepski

seconds /'sekəndz/ *npl* infml repeta *f*

secrecy /'siːkrəsɪ/ *n* (secret nature) tajemnica *f*

secret /'siːkrɪt/ **II** *n* tajemnica *f*, sekret *m*; **to tell sb a** ~ wyjawić komuś tajemnicę **II** *adj* tajemny, sekretny **III** **in secret** *adv phr* w tajemnicy

secretarial /ˌsekrə'teərɪəl/ *adj [work, skills]* sekretarski; ~ **college** szkoła *f* sekretarek

secretary /'sekrətrɪ, US -rəterɪ/ *n* **1** (in office) sekreta|rz *m*, -rka *f* (**to sb** kogoś) **2** GB **Foreign Secretary** minister spraw zagranicznych **3** US **Secretary of State** sekretarz stanu

secretive /'siːkrətɪv/ *adj [nature]* skryty; *[conduct, smile]* tajemniczy, zagadkowy; **to be** ~ **about sth** robić z czegoś tajemnicę

secretly /'si:krɪtlɪ/ adv [meet] potajemnie; [hope] skrycie

secret weapon n tajna broń f

sect /sekt/ n sekta f

section /'sekʃn/ n ① (of train, aircraft, town) część f; (of pipe, tunnel, road) odcinek m; (of orange) cząstka f ② (of company, library, shop) dział m; (of organization) sekcja f ③ (of act, bill) ustęp m; (of newspaper) dział m

sector /'sektə(r)/ n (of land) strefa f; (of economy) sektor m

secular /'sekjʊlə(r)/ adj świecki

secure /sɪ'kjʊə(r)/ **①** adj ① [job, investment] pewny; [base, foundation] solidny ② [hiding place] bezpieczny ③ [lock, foothold] pewny; [knot] mocno zawiązany; [rope] dobrze umocowany; [door] zamknięty jak należy; **to be ~** [structure, ladder] być stabilnym ④ **to feel ~** czuć się bezpiecznie

② vt ① (get) uzysk|ać, -iwać [promise]; zdoby|ć, -wać [majority]; osiąg|nąć, -ać [objective] ② (fix) umocow|ać, -ywać [rope]; dobrze zam|knąć, -ykać [door, window]; ustawi|ć, -ać [ladder] ③ (make safe) zabezpiecz|yć, -ać [house, future] ④ (guarantee) zabezpiecz|yć, -ać [loan, debt]

secure unit n oddział m wzmożonego nadzoru (w szpitalu psychiatrycznym)

securities /sɪ'kjʊərətɪz/ npl papiery m pl wartościowe

security /sɪ'kjʊərətɪ/ **①** n ① bezpieczeństwo n; **job ~** gwarancja zatrudnienia ② (for prison, VIP) środki m pl bezpieczeństwa; **national ~** bezpieczeństwo narodowe ③ (guarantee) zabezpieczenie n (**on sth** czegoś)

② adj **~ measures** środki bezpieczeństwa; **~ camera** kamera nadzorująca; **~ firm** firma ochroniarska; **~ staff** ochrona

security guard n strażnik m, ochroniarz m

security leak n przeciek m poufnych informacji

sedate /sɪ'deɪt/ **①** adj [person, pace] stateczny; [lifestyle] spokojny

② vt poda|ć, -wać (komuś) środek uspokajający [patient]

sedation n **to be under ~** być pod działaniem środków uspokajających

sedative /'sedətɪv/ **①** n środek m uspokajający **②** adj [effect, drug] uspokajający

seduce /sɪ'dju:s, US -'du:s/ vt uw|ieść, -odzić

seductive /sɪ'dʌktɪv/ adj [smile] uwodzicielski; [person] ponętny

see /si:/ **①** vt ① zobaczyć, widzieć; **to ~ the sights** zwiedzać; **~ you next week!** infml do przyszłego tygodnia!; **do you ~ what I mean?** rozumiesz, o co mi chodzi?; **to ~ sb as a leader** widzieć w kimś przywódcę; **it remains to be seen if...** okaże się, czy... ② (make sure) **to ~ (to it) that...** dopilnować, żeby... ③ (accompany) **to ~ sb to the station** odprowadzić kogoś na dworzec; **to ~ sb home** odprowadzić kogoś do domu

② vi zobaczyć, widzieć; **I can't ~** nic nie widzę; **I'll go and ~** pójdę zobaczyć; **you'll have to wait and ~** to się dopiero okaże; **let me ~** niech pomyślę; **let's ~** zastanówmy się

■ **see off: ~** [sb] **off** po|żegnać

■ **see out: ~** [sb] **out** odprowadz|ić, -ać do drzwi

■ **see through:** ¶ **~ through** [sb/sth] przejrzeć [deception, lie, person] ¶ **~** [sth] **through** doprowadz|ić, -ać do końca

■ **see to:** do|pilnować [person, task]

seed /si:d/ n ① (of plant) nasienie n; (fruit pip) pestka f; (for sowing) nasiona n pl, ziarno n; **to go to ~** [plant] iść w ziarno; fig [person] zaniedbać się; [organization, country] podupadać ② Sport rozstawiony zawodnik m, rozstawiona zawodniczka f

seedling /'si:dlɪŋ/ n rozsada f, sadzonka f

seedy /'si:dɪ/ adj [hotel] obskurny; [person] zaniedbany; [area, club] podejrzany

seek /si:k/ vt ① szukać (czegoś) [solution, agreement, refuge]; zwr|ócić, -acać się z prośbą o (coś) [advice, help, backing] ② [police, employer] poszukiwać

■ **seek out:** odszuk|ać, -iwać [person]

seem /si:m/ vi ① wyda|ć, -wać się; **he ~s to be looking for something** chyba czegoś szuka; **the whole house ~ed to shake** wydawało się, że cały dom się trzęsie ② **it ~s to me that...** wydaje mi się, że...; **it ~s as if** or **as though...** wydaje się, że...; **I ~ to have offended him** chyba go obraziłem

seep /si:p/ vi sączyć się; **to ~ through sth** [liquid, light] sączyć się z czegoś/przez coś; [gas] ulatniać się z czegoś/przez coś; **to ~ away** [liquid] wyciekać

seesaw /'si:sɔ:/ **①** n huśtawka f (pozioma deska) **②** vi [prices, rates] skakać

seethe /si:ð/ vi ① [person] wrzeć z wściekłości ② (swarm) [crowd] kłębić się; **the country was seething with unrest** w kraju wrzało

see-through /'si:θru:/ adj [garment] prześwitujący

segment /'segmənt/ n segment m; (of orange) cząstka f

segregate /'segrɪgeɪt/ vt ① (separate) oddziel|ić, -ać (**from sb/sth** od kogoś/czegoś) ② (isolate) odseparow|ać, -ywać (**from sb/sth** od kogoś/czegoś)

segregated /'segrəgeɪtɪd/ adj [education, society, school] w którym obowiązuje segregacja rasowa

segregation /ˌsegrɪ'geɪʃn/ n (of races) segregacja f; (of rivals) rozdzielenie n; (of prisoner) odizolowanie n (**from sb/sth** od kogoś/czegoś)

seize /si:z/ vt ① chwyc|ić, -tać; **to ~ hold of sb/ sth** chwycić kogoś/coś [person, object] ② zaj|ąć, -mować [territory]; przej|ąć, -mować [power]; wziąć, brać [hostage]; **to ~ control of sth** przejąć kontrolę nad czymś

■ **seize up:** [engine] za|trzeć, -cierać się; [limb] odm|ówić, -awiać posłuszeństwa

seizure /ˈsiːʒə(r)/ *n* [1] (of territory) zajęcie *n*; (of power) przejęcie *n*; (of arms, drugs, goods) przechwycenie *n* [2] Med atak *m*

seldom /ˈseldəm/ *adv* rzadko

select /sɪˈlekt/ [1] *adj* [*group*] wybrany; [*restaurant*] ekskluzywny; [*club, school*] elitarny

[11] *vt* wyb|rać, -ierać; **to ~ from/from among sth** wybrać z/spośród czegoś

selection /sɪˈlekʃn/ *n* wybór *m*; (through elimination) selekcja *f*

selective /sɪˈlektɪv/ *adj* [*memory, recruitment*] wybiórczy; [*weedkiller*] selektywny; [*school, education*] dostępny nie dla wszystkich

self /self/ *n* [1] własne ja *n inv*; (in psychology) ego *n inv*; **he is back to his old ~** przyszedł już do siebie [2] (on cheque) **pay ~** wypłata własna

self-addressed envelope, SAE *n* zaadresowana koperta *f* zwrotna

self-adhesive /ˌselfədˈhiːsɪv/ *adj* samoprzylepny

self-assembly /ˌselfəˈsemblɪ/ *adj* do samodzielnego montażu

self-assured /ˌselfəˈʃɔːd, US -ˈʃʊərd/ *adj* pewny siebie

self-catering /ˌselfˈkeɪtərɪŋ/ [1] *n* GB własne wyżywienie *n*

[11] *adj* **~ accommodation** zakwaterowanie z możliwością korzystania z kuchni; **~ holiday** wczasy z wyżywieniem we własnym zakresie

self-centred GB, **self-centered** US /ˌselfˈsentəd/ *adj* egocentryczny

self-confessed /ˌselfkənˈfest/ *adj* zdeklarowany

self-confidence /ˌselfˈkɒnfɪdəns/ *n* wiara *f* w siebie

self-confident /ˌselfˈkɒnfɪdənt/ *adj* [*person*] ufny we własne siły

self-conscious /ˌselfˈkɒnʃəs/ *adj* [1] (shy) nieśmiały, skrępowany; **to be ~ about sth/about doing sth** wstydzić się czegoś/coś robić [2] [*style*] świadomy

self-contained /ˌselfkənˈteɪnd/ *adj* [*flat*] samodzielny

self-control /ˌselfkənˈtrəʊl/ *n* samokontrola *f*

self-defence GB, **self-defense** US /ˌselfdɪˈfens/ *n* samoobrona *f*; (in law) obrona *f* własna

self-destructive /ˌselfdɪˈstrʌktɪv/ *adj* autodestrukcyjny

self-determination /ˌselfdɪtɜːmɪˈneɪʃn/ *n* samostanowienie *n*

self-disciplined *adj* zdyscyplinowany

self-effacing /ˌselfɪˈfeɪsɪŋ/ *adj* skromny

self-employed /ˌselfɪmˈplɔɪd/ *adj* [*work*] na własny rachunek; **to be ~** pracować na własny rachunek

self-esteem /ˌselfɪˈstiːm/ *n* poczucie *n* własnej wartości

self-evident /ˌselfˈevɪdənt/ *adj* oczywisty

self-explanatory /ˌselfɪkˈsplænətrɪ, US -tɔːrɪ/ *adj* niewymagający wyjaśnienia

self-expression /ˌselfɪkˈspreʃn/ *n* wyrażanie *n* własnego „ja"

self-governing /ˌselfˈɡʌvənɪŋ/ *adj* samorządny

self-image /ˌselfˈɪmɪdʒ/ *n* wyobrażenie *n* o sobie

self-important /ˌselfɪmˈpɔːtnt/ *adj* zadufany w sobie

self-induced /ˌselfɪnˈdjuːst, US -ˈduːst/ *adj* [*vomiting*] sprowokowany przez samego siebie

self-indulgent /ˌselfɪnˈdʌldʒənt/ *adj* lubiący sobie dogadzać

self-interested /ˌselfˈɪntrestɪd/ *adj* [*person*] interesowny; [*behaviour*] wyrachowany

selfish /ˈselfɪʃ/ *adj* samolubny, egoistyczny

selfishness /ˈselfɪʃnɪs/ *n* egoizm *m*

selfless /ˈselflɪs/ *adj* bezinteresowny

self-portrait /ˌselfˈpɔːtreɪt/ *n* autoportret *m*

self-raising flour GB, **self-rising flour** US /ˌselfˈreɪzɪŋflaʊə(r)/ *n* mąka *f* z dodatkiem proszku do pieczenia

self-reliant /ˌselfrɪˈlaɪənt/ *adj* samodzielny

self-respect /ˌselfrɪˈspekt/ *n* szacunek *m* dla samego siebie

self-respecting /ˌselfrɪˈspektɪŋ/ *adj* szanujący się

self-righteous /ˌselfˈraɪtʃəs/ *adj* zadufany w sobie

self-rule /ˌselfˈruːl/ *n* autonomia *f*

self-sacrifice /ˌselfˈsækrɪfaɪs/ *n* wyrzeczenie *n*

self-satisfied /ˌselfˈsætɪsfaɪd/ *adj* zadowolony z siebie

self-service /ˌselfˈsɜːvɪs/ [1] *n* samoobsługa *f*

[11] *adj* samoobsługowy

self-sufficient /ˌselfsəˈfɪʃnt/ *adj* samowystarczalny

self-taught /ˌselfˈtɔːt/ *adj* **to be ~** być samoukiem

sell /sel/ [1] *vt* [1] sprzeda|ć, -wać; **to ~ sth for £5 each** sprzedawać coś po 5 funtów za sztukę; **'stamps sold here'** „sprzedaż znaczków" [2] (promote sale of) zapewni|ć, -ać zbyt (czemuś) [*product*]; zapewni|ć, -ać powodzenie (czemuś) [*film*] [3] przekon|ać, -ywać do (czegoś) [*idea, image, policy*]

[11] *vi* [1] [*person, shop, dealer*] sprzedawać [2] [*goods, product, house, book*] sprzeda|ć, -wać się

■ **sell off:** **~** [**sth**] **off** wyprzeda|ć, -wać [*goods, old stock*]

■ **sell out:** [1] [*merchandise*] sprzeda|ć, -wać się; **we've sold out of tickets** wyprzedaliśmy wszystkie bilety; **sorry, we've sold out** przykro mi, wszystko sprzedaliśmy; **the play has sold out** wszystkie bilety na sztukę zostały sprzedane [2] infml (betray one's principles) sprzeda|ć, -wać się (**to sb** komuś)

sell-by date /ˈselbaɪdeɪt/ *n* ≈ termin *m* ważności

selling /ˈselɪŋ/ *n* sprzedaż *f*; **telephone ~** telemarketing

Sellotape® /ˈseləʊteɪp/ [1] *n* taśma *f* klejąca

II **sellotape** *vt* przyklei|ć, -jać taśmą klejącą

sellout /'selaʊt/ **II** *n* **the match was a** ~ wszystkie bilety na mecz sprzedano

II *adj* **a** ~ **performance** występ, na który wszystkie bilety zostały sprzedane

semiautomatic /ˌsemɪɔːtə'mætɪk/ **II** *n* broń *f* półautomatyczna

II *adj* półautomatyczny

semicircle /'semɪsɜːkl/ *n* półkole *n*

semicolon /ˌsemɪ'kəʊlən/ *n* średnik *m*

semiconscious /ˌsemɪ'kɒnʃəs/ *adj* półprzytomny

semidarkness /ˌsemɪ'dɑːknɪs/ *n* półmrok *m*

semi-detached (house) /ˌsemɪdɪ'tætʃt(haʊs)/ *n* bliźniak *m*

semifinal /ˌsemɪ'faɪnl/ *n* półfinał *m*

semifinalist /ˌsemɪ'faɪnəlɪst/ *n* półfinalist|a *m*, -ka *f*

seminar /'semɪnɑː(r)/ *n* seminarium *n* (**on sth** na temat czegoś)

semi-skimmed /ˌsemɪ'skɪmd/ *adj [milk]* półtłusty

senate /'senɪt/ *n* senat *m*

senator /'senətə(r)/ *n* senator *m*; **the** ~ **for California** senator z Kalifornii

send /send/ *vt* ① wysył|ać, -yłać; **to** ~ **sth to sb, to** ~ **sb sth** wysłać coś komuś; **to** ~ **sb home** (from school, work) wysłać kogoś do domu; **to** ~ **sb to prison** posłać kogoś za kratki infml; ~ **her my love!** przekaż jej ode mnie pozdrowienia!; ~ **them my regards** przekaż im moje wyrazy uszanowania ② **to** ~ **shivers down sb's spine** przyprawiać kogoś o dreszcze; **to** ~ **sb into a rage** doprowadzić kogoś do wściekłości; **to** ~ **sb to sleep** *[rain, boring story]* uśpić kogoś

■ **send away**: ¶ ~ **away for [sth]** zam|ówić, -awiać ¶ ~ **[sb/sth] away** od|esłać, -syłać; **to** ~ **a child away to boarding school** posłać dziecko do szkoły z internatem

■ **send for**: w|ezwać, -zywać *[doctor, taxi, reinforcements]*

■ **send in**: przys|łać, -yłać *[letter, form, application]*; pos|łać, -yłać *[police, troops]*

■ **send off**: ¶ ~ **off for** zam|ówić, -awiać ¶ ~ **[sth] off** wysył|ać, -yłać *[letter]* ¶ ~ **[sb] off** Sport usu|nąć, -ać z boiska *[player]*

■ **send on**: wysył|ać, -yłać wcześniej *[luggage]*; przes|łać, -yłać na nowy adres *[letter, mail]*

■ **send out**: ① wysył|ać, -yłać *[light, signal]* ② wyrzuc|ić, -ać, kazać wyjść (komuś) *[pupil]*

■ **send up**: GB infml (parody) s|parodiować

(IDIOMS:) **to** ~ **sb packing** infml posłać kogoś do diabła infml

sender /'sendə(r)/ *n* nadawca *m*

send-off /'sendɒf, US -ɔːf-/ *n* pożegnanie *n*

send-up /'sendʌp/ *n* GB infml parodia *f*

senile /'siːnaɪl/ *adj* starczy

senile dementia *n* demencja *f* starcza

senior /'siːnɪə(r)/ **II** *n* ① starszy *m*; **to be sb's** ~ **by 5 years** być starszym od kogoś o 5 lat; **to be sb's** ~ (in business) być na wyższym stanowisku niż ktoś ② GB (student) uczeń *m*, -nnica *f* starszej klasy; US uczeń|ń *m*, -nnica *f* ostatniej klasy

II *adj* ① (older) *[person]* starszy ② *[civil servant]* wyższy rangą; *[figure]* ważny; *[position]* wysoki

senior citizen *n* emeryt *m*, -ka *f*

senior high school *n* US szkoła *f* średnia

seniority /ˌsiːnɪ'ɒrətɪ, US -'ɔːr-/ *n* ① (in years) starszeństwo *n* ② (in rank) wysokie stanowisko *n*; (in years of service) staż *m* pracy

senior management *n* wyższa kadra *f* kierownicza

senior school *n* szkoła *f* średnia

sensation /sen'seɪʃn/ *n* ① uczucie *n*; **to cause** or **create a** ~ wzbudzić sensację

sensational /sen'seɪʃənl/ *adj* sensacyjny

sensationalist /sen'seɪʃənəlɪst/ *adj [headline, story]* sensacyjny; *[journalist]* żądny sensacji

sensationalize /sen'seɪʃənəlaɪz/ *vt* z|robić sensację z (czegoś) *[event, story]*

sense /sens/ **II** *n* ① (faculty) zmysł *m*; **the** ~ **of hearing/sight/smell** zmysł słuchu/wzroku/powonienia; **a** ~ **of sth** poczucie czegoś *[duty, humour]*; **a** ~ **of direction** zmysł orientacji; **to lose one's** ~ **of time** stracić poczucie czasu ② (feeling) **a** ~ **of sth** poczucie n czegoś *[guilt, identity]*; **a** ~ **of purpose** cel w życiu ③ (practical quality) rozsądek *m*; **to have more** ~ **than to do sth** być zbyt rozsądnym, żeby zrobić coś ④ (reason) sens *m*; **there's no** ~ **in doing it** nie ma sensu tego robić; **to make** ~ **of sth** zrozumieć coś; **I can't make** ~ **of this article** nie rozumiem tego artykułu; **to make** ~ *[sentence, theory]* mieć sens; **in a** ~ w pewnym sensie

II **senses** *npl* **to bring sb to his** ~**s** przywieść kogoś do rozsądku

III *vt* ① wyczu|ć, -wać (**that...** że...); **to** ~ **danger** wyczuwać niebezpieczeństwo ② *[sensor]* wykry|ć, -wać

(IDIOMS:) **to see** ~ nabrać rozumu; **to talk** ~ mówić do rzeczy

senseless /'senslɪs/ *adj* ① *[idea, discussion, violence]* bezsensowny ② **to knock sb** ~ ogłuszyć kogoś

sensible /'sensəbl/ *adj [person, choice, diet]* rozsądny; *[clothing]* praktyczny

sensitive /'sensətɪv/ *adj* ① (responsive) wrażliwy (**to sth** na coś) ② *[matter, subject]* drażliwy; *[situation]* delikatny; *[information]* poufny

sensitivity /ˌsensə'tɪvətɪ/ *n* wrażliwość *f* (**to sth** na coś); (of instrument) czułość *f*

sensor /'sensə(r)/ *n* czujnik *m*

sensual /'senʃʊəl/ *adj* zmysłowy

sentence /'sentəns/ **II** *n* ① (in law) wyrok *m*; **to serve a** ~ odbywać karę ② (in grammar) zdanie *n* (niezależne)

II *vt* skaz|ać, -ywać (**sb for sth** kogoś za coś)
sentiment /'sentɪmənt/ *n* [1] (feeling) uczucie *n* (**for** or **towards sb/sth** do kogoś/czegoś) [2] (opinion) odczucie *n* (**about sth** w sprawie czegoś); **public ~** nastroje społeczne
sentimental /ˌsentɪ'mentl/ *adj* sentymentalny
sentry /'sentrɪ/ *n* wartowni|k *m*, -czka *f*
separate **II** /'sepərət/ *adj* (apart) oddzielny; (different) odrębny; **a ~ issue** odrębna kwestia; **she has a ~ room** ona ma osobny pokój; **they asked for ~ bills** (in restaurant) poprosili o oddzielne rachunki; **the flat is ~ from the rest of the house** mieszkanie jest oddzielone od reszty domu; **keep the knives ~ from the forks** trzymaj noże i widelce oddzielnie
II /'sepəreɪt/ *vt* [1] rozdziel|ić, -ać, oddziel|ić, -ać; **the child became ~d from his mother** dziecko i matka zostali rozłączeni [2] (sort out) po|dzielić *[people]*; oddziel|ić, -ać *[objects]*
III /'sepəreɪt/ *vi* **to ~ from sth** oddzielić się od czegoś
separately /'sepərətlɪ/ *adv* oddzielnie
separates /'sepərəts/ *npl* części *f pl* ubioru *(które można zestawiać)*
separation /ˌsepə'reɪʃn/ *n* (partition) oddzielenie *n*; (legal) separacja *f*
separatist /'sepərətɪst/ **II** *n* separatyst|a *m*, -ka *f*
II *adj* separatystyczny
September /sep'tembə(r)/ *n* wrzesień *m*
septic /'septɪk/ *adj* zakażony; **to go** or **turn ~** *[wound]* zostać zakażonym
septic tank *n* szambo *n*
sequel /'si:kwəl/ *n* (to novel, film) kontynuacja *f* (**to sth** czegoś)
sequence /'si:kwəns/ *n* [1] (of problems) pasmo *n*; (of events) ciąg *m*; (of photos) seria *f* [2] (order) kolejność *f* [3] (in film) sekwencja *f*
Serb /sɜ:b/, **Serbian** /'sɜ:bɪən/ **II** *n* Serb *m*, -ka *f*
II *adj* serbski
Serbia /'sɜ:bɪə/ *prn* Serbia *f*
serene /sɪ'ri:n/ *adj* pogodny
sergeant /'sɑ:dʒənt/ *n* sierżant *m*
serial /'sɪərɪəl/ *n* (film) serial *m*; (novel) powieść *f* w odcinkach
serialize /'sɪərɪəlaɪz/ *vt* nakręc|ić, -ać serial na podstawie (czegoś)
serial killer *n* seryjny morderca *m*
serial number *n* (of machine, car) numer *m* seryjny
series /'sɪəri:z/ *n* [1] (of books, stamps) seria *f*; (of concerts, lectures) cykl *m* [2] (film) serial *m*; (of programmes) cykl *m*
serious /'sɪərɪəs/ *adj* [1] *[person, discussion, approach, offer]* poważny; *[attempt, concern]* autentyczny; **to be ~ about sth** myśleć o czymś poważnie; **to be ~ about doing sth** naprawdę chcieć zrobić coś [2] *[accident, allegation, crime, error]* poważny

seriously /'sɪərɪəslɪ/ *adv* [1] (not frivolously) poważnie; **to take sb/sth ~** brać kogoś/coś (na) poważnie [2] *[ill, injured]* poważnie; *[underestimate]* bardzo
seriousness /'sɪərɪəsnɪs/ *n* [1] (of person, tone) powaga *f*; (of film, study) poważny charakter *m*; (of intention) szczerość *f*; **in all ~** z całą powagą [2] (of situation) powaga *f*; (of problem) waga *f*
sermon /'sɜ:mən/ *n* kazanie *n*
serrated /sɪ'reɪtɪd, US 'sereɪtɪd/ *adj [leaf]* ząbkowany; *[knife]* z ząbkami
serum /'sɪərəm/ *n* surowica *f*
servant /'sɜ:vənt/ *n* służący|y *m*, -a *f*
serve /sɜ:v/ **II** *n* Sport serw *m*, podanie *n*
II *vt* [1] (work for) służyć (komuś/czemuś) *[God, country]*; pracować dla (kogoś) *[employer, company]* [2] (attend to) obsłu|żyć, -giwać *[customers, guests]*; **are you being ~d?** czy ktoś już państwa obsługuje? [3] (offer food) poda|ć, -wać *[meal, wine]*; **to ~ sb with sth** podać komuś coś [4] (provide facility for) *[power station, public transport]* obsługiwać *[area, community]* [5] (satisfy) zaspok|oić, -ajać *[needs]*; **to ~ sb's interests** służyć interesom kogoś [6] **to ~ sb as sth** służyć komuś jako or za coś; **to ~ a purpose** być przydatnym; **it ~s no useful purpose** to do niczego nie służy [7] **to ~ a** or **one's sentence** odbyć karę więzienia [8] (in law) **to ~ a summons on sb** doręczyć komuś wezwanie (do sądu) [9] Sport za|serwować
III *vi* [1] (in shop) obsługiwać klientów; (in church) służyć do mszy; (at table) podawać do stołu [2] **to ~ on a committee** zasiadać w komisji [3] (in army) odbywać służbę wojskową [4] **this room ~s as a bedroom** ten pokój służy jako sypialnia or za sypialnię [5] Sport za|serwować; **Conti to ~** podaje or serwuje Conti
IDIOMS **it ~s you right!** dobrze ci tak!
server /'sɜ:və(r)/ *n* [1] Sport serwujący|y *m*, -a *f* [2] Comput serwer *m*
service /'sɜ:vɪs/ **II** *n* [1] (department) służba *f*; **emergency ~** pogotowie ratunkowe [2] (work done) usługa *f*; **to do sb a ~** wyświadczyć komuś przysługę; **we add on 15% for ~** dodajemy 15% za obsługę; **'out of ~'** (on machine) „nieczynne" [3] (transport facility) połączenie *n* [4] (overhaul) przegląd *m* [5] (religious) nabożeństwo *n*; **Sunday ~** nabożeństwo niedzielne; **marriage ~** ceremonia ślubna
II **services** *npl* [1] **the ~s** służba *f* wojskowa [2] (on motorway) stacja *f* obsługi
III *vt* z|robić przegląd (czegoś) *[vehicle, machine]*; **to have one's car ~d** oddać samochód do przeglądu
service centre GB, **service center** US *n* punkt *m* serwisowy
service charge *n* [1] (in restaurant) opłata *f* za obsługę; **there is a ~** opłata za obsługę nie jest

wliczona w rachunek [2] (in banking) prowizja *f* bankowa

service engineer *n* serwisant *m*

serviceman /'sɜːvɪsmən/ *n* wojskowy *m*

service station *n* stacja *f* obsługi (pojazdów)

servicewoman /'sɜːvɪswʊmən/ *n* kobieta *f* służąca w wojsku

serving /'sɜːvɪŋ/ *n* (helping) porcja *f*

serving dish *n* półmisek *m*

serving spoon *n* łyżka *f* do nakładania potraw

session /'seʃn/ *n* [1] (period of meetings) sesja *f* [2] (sitting) posiedzenie *n*; **the court is in** ~ trwa rozprawa [3] GB (year) rok *m* szkolny; US (term) trymestr *m*

set /set/ **I** *n* [1] (of keys) komplet *m*, zestaw *m*; (of golf clubs, cutlery) komplet *m*; (of coins, stamps, instructions) zbiór *m*; **a new** ~ **of clothes** nowe ubranie; **they're sold in** ~ **s of 10** są sprzedawane w zestawach or kompletach po 10; **a** ~ **of fingerprints** odciski palców; **a** ~ **of traffic lights** światła; **a** ~ **of false teeth** sztuczna szczęka [2] Sport (in tennis) set *m* [3] **TV** ~, **television** ~ odbiornik telewizyjny, telewizor [4] (scenery) (on stage) dekoracje *f pl*; (for film) plan *m* [5] GB (of pupils) grupa *f* [6] (hair-do) ułożenie *n* włosów **II** *adj* [1] *[pattern, procedure, task, time]* ustalony; **a** ~ **menu** gotowy zestaw dań; ~ **phrase** utarty zwrot; **to be** ~ **in one's ways** mieć swoje przyzwyczajenia [2] *[smile]* sztuczny, wymuszony; ~ **expression** kamienny wyraz twarzy [3] *[book, text]* obowiązkowy [4] (ready) gotowy (**for sth** na coś); **to be (all)** ~ **to leave** być gotowym do odjazdu [5] **to be (dead)** ~ **against sth/doing sth** być (zdecydowanie) przeciwnym czemuś/zrobieniu czegoś; **to be** ~ **on doing sth** być zdecydowanym zrobić coś [6] *[jam, jelly]* ścięty; *[honey]* gęsty; *[cement]* stwardniały, zastygły **III** *vt* [1] (place) umie|ścić, -szczać *[chair]*; oprawi|ć, -ać *[gem]*; **to** ~ **sth before sb** postawić przed kimś coś *[food]*; **to** ~ **the record straight** fig wyjaśnić sprawę; **a house set among the trees** dom stojący wśród drzew; **his eyes are set very close together** ma oczy osadzone bardzo blisko siebie [2] (prepare) zastawi|ć, -ać *[trap]*; **to** ~ **the table** nakryć do stołu [3] (establish) ustali|ć, -ać *[date, deadline, price, target]*; wy|lansować *[fashion, trend]*; nada|ć, -wać *[tone]*; stw|orzyć, -arzać *[precedent]*; ustan|owić, -awiać *[record]*; **to** ~ **a good/bad example to sb** dawać komuś dobry/zły przykład; **to** ~ **one's sights on sth** stawiać sobie za cel zdobycie czegoś [4] (adjust) nastawi|ć, -ać *[clock, alarm clock]*; włącz|yć, -ać *[burglar alarm]* [5] (start) **to** ~ **sth going** włączyć *[machine]*; **that set everyone laughing** to wzbudziło ogólne rozbawienie; **that set everybody thinking** to dało wszystkim do myślenia [6] (impose) zada|ć, -wać *[homework, essay]*; u|łożyć, -kładać *[exam,*

crossword puzzle] [7] *[author]* umiejsc|owić, -awiać; **the film is set in Munich** akcja filmu rozgrywa się w Monachium [8] **to** ~ **sth to music** skomponować muzykę do czegoś [9] (in printing) **to** ~ **sth in italics** złożyć coś kursywą [10] Med złożyć, składać *[broken leg]* [11] (style) u|łożyć, -kładać *[hair]*

IV *vi* [1] *[sun]* za|jść, -chodzić [2] *[jelly]* ścią|ć, -nać się; *[concrete]* zastyg|nąć, -ać; *[glue]* zas|chnąć, -ychać [3] *[fracture]* zr|osnąć, -astać się

■ **set about**: zab|rać, -ierać się do (czegoś) *[work]*; **to** ~ **about the job** or **task of doing sth** zabrać się do robienia czegoś

■ **set apart**: wyróżni|ć, -ać *[person, book]* (**from sb/sth** spośród kogoś/czegoś)

■ **set aside**: przeznacz|yć, -ać *[area, room, time]* (**for sth** na coś); od|łożyć, -kładać *[money, stock]*

■ **set back**: ¶ ~ **[sth] back** (delay) opóźni|ć, -ać ¶ ~ **[sb] back** infml uderzyć po kieszeni infml

■ **set down**: ~ **[sth] down** [1] określ|ić, -ać *[conditions]* [2] (record) odnotow|ać, -ywać *[fact]*

■ **set in**: *[infection]* wda|ć, -wać się; *[complications]* wywiąz|ać, -ywać się; *[despair]* zapanować

■ **set off**: ¶ ~ **off** wyrusz|yć, -ać; **to** ~ **off on a journey** wyruszyć w podróż ¶ ~ **[sth] off** [1] włącz|yć, -ać *[alarm]*; zdetonować *[bomb]*; wywoł|ać, -ywać *[riot, row, panic]* [2] (enhance) podkreślać *[colour, tan]* [3] **to** ~ **off loss against profits** równoważyć straty zyskami ¶ ~ **[sb] off** (cause to begin) **you've set the baby off** przez ciebie dziecko zaczęło płakać; **she laughed and that set me off** zaśmiała się i jej wesołość mi się udzieliła

■ **set on**: ¶ ~ **on [sb]** napa|ść, -dać (kogoś) ¶ ~ **[sb/sth] on sb** nas|łać, -yłać na kogoś *[police]*; **to** ~ **the dog on sb** poszczuć kogoś psem

■ **set out**: ¶ ~ **out** wyrusz|yć, -ać; **to** ~ **out for Paris** wyruszyć do Paryża; **to** ~ **out to do sth** *[person]* postanowić zrobić coś ¶ ~ **[sth] out** [1] roz|łożyć, -kładać *[goods, papers]*; rozstawi|ć, -ać *[chairs]*; wy|łożyć, -kładać *[food]* [2] przedstawi|ć, -ać *[ideas]*; określ|ić, -ać *[conditions]*

■ **set up**: ¶ **to** ~ **up in business** otworzyć interes; **to** ~ **up on one's own** otworzyć własny interes ¶ ~ **[sth] up** [1] (put) ustawi|ć, -ać *[stand, stall, equipment]*; postawi|ć, -ać, wzn|ieść, -osić *[statue]*; rozstawi|ć, -ać *[roadblocks]*; **to** ~ **up home** urządzić się; **to** ~ **up camp** rozbić obóz [2] (prepare) przygotow|ać, -ywać *[experiment]* [3] (establish) za|łożyć, -kładać *[business, company, charity]*; u|tworzyć *[committee]* [4] (start) z|organizować *[meeting]*; wszcz|ąć, -ynać *[procedures]* [5] (in printing) złożyć, składać *[page]* ¶ ~ **[sb] up** [1] **she set her son up (in business) as a tailor** pomogła synowi otworzyć zakład krawiecki [2] **that deal has set her up for life** ten interes ustawił ją na całe życie [3] GB infml (frame) wr|obić, -abiać infml *[person]*

setback /'setbæk/ *n* komplikacja *f* (**for sb** dla kogoś); **this would be a ~ to our plans** to by nam pokrzyżowało plany

settee /se'ti:/ *n* kanapa *f*

setting /'setɪŋ/ *n* [1] (location) sceneria *f*; **Milan will be the ~ for the film** miejscem akcji tego filmu będzie Mediolan [2] (in jewellery) oprawa *f* [3] (position on dial) ustawienie *n*

setting-up /ˌsetɪŋ'ʌp/ *n* (of committee, scheme) utworzenie *n*; (of business) założenie *n*; (of inquiry) wszczęcie *n*

settle /'setl/ **[]** *vt* [1] (seat) usad|owić, -awiać *[person]* [2] (calm) uspok|oić, -ajać *[nerves]* [3] załatwi|ć, -ać *[business]*; rozstrzyg|nąć, -ać *[matter, conflict]*; rozwiąz|ać, -ywać *[problem]*; **that's ~d!** załatwione!; **to ~ one's affairs** uporządkować swoje sprawy [4] (pay) u|regulować *[bill]*; spłac|ić, -ać *[debt]* [5] (people) zasiedl|ić, -ać

[] *vi* [1] *[bird, insect]* si|ąść, -adać, usiąść; *[dust]* osi|ąść, -adać [2] *[family]* osi|ąść, -adać; *[emigrant]* osiedl|ić, -ać się [3] *[wall]* osi|ąść, -adać; *[contents]* ubi|ć, -jać się [4] *[weather]* ustal|ić, -ać się [5] (end litigation) przysta|ć, -wać na porozumienie; **to ~ out of court** załatwić sprawę polubownie

■ **settle down**: [1] (sit down) usad|owić, -awiać się (**in/on sth** na/w czymś); (lie down) u|łożyć, -kładać się (**on/in sth** na/w czymś) [2] (calm down) *[person]* uspok|oić, -ajać się [3] (marry) ustatkować się

■ **settle for**: **~ for** *[sth]* zadow|olić, -alać się (czymś)

■ **settle in**: za|aklimatyzować się, za|adaptować się

■ **settle up**: [1] (pay) za|płacić [2] (sort out who owes what) rozlicz|yć, -ać się (**with sb** z kimś)

settlement /'setlmənt/ *n* [1] (agreement) porozumienie *n*, ugoda *f* [2] (in civil case) ugoda *f* [3] (dwellings) osada *f*, osiedle *n*

seven /'sevn/ *n*, *adj* siedem

seventeen /ˌsevn'ti:n/ *n* siedemnaście

seventeenth /ˌsevn'ti:nθ/ **[]** *n* [1] (in order) siedemnast|y *m*, -a *f*, -e *n* [2] (fraction) siedemnasta *f* (część) **[]** *adj* siedemnasty **[]** *adv [come]* na siedemnastym miejscu

seventh /'sevnθ/ **[]** *n* [1] (in order) siódm|y *m*, -a *f*, -e *n* [2] (fraction) siódma *f* (część) **[]** *adj* siódmy **[]** *adv [finish]* na siódmym miejscu

seventies /'sevntɪz/ *npl* [1] (era) **the ~** lata siedemdziesiąte [2] (age) **to be in one's ~** mieć siedemdziesiąt kilka lat

seventieth /'sevntɪəθ/ **[]** *n* [1] (in order) siedemdziesiąt|y *m*, -a *f*, -e *n* [2] (fraction) siedemdziesiąta *f* (część) **[]** *adj* siedemdziesiąty **[]** *adv [come]* na siedemdziesiątym miejscu

seventy /'sevntɪ/ *n* siedemdziesiąt

sever /'sevə(r)/ *vt* [1] (cut) przeci|ąć, -nać *[rope, artery]*; (cut off) odci|ąć, -nać *[branch]*; ur|wać, -ywać *[limb]* [2] fig z|erwać, -rywać *[relations, contact]*

several /'sevrəl/ **[]** *pron* **~ of them** (men) kilku z nich; (women, animals, objects) kilka z nich; (men and women, children) kilkoro z nich

[] *quantif* kilka; **~ books** kilka książek

severe /sɪ'vɪə(r)/ *adj* [1] *[problem, damage, shortage, illness]* poważny; *[shock, test]* ciężki; *[cold]* ostry; *[winter]* srogi; *[pain]* silny [2] (harsh) surowy (**with sb** dla kogoś) [3] *[haircut, clothes]* prosty

severely /sɪ'vɪəlɪ/ *adv* [1] *[restrict, damage]* poważnie; *[shock]* ciężko; *[ill]* poważnie; **~ disabled** dotknięty ciężkim kalectwem [2] *[treat, punish]* surowo; *[beat]* bezlitośnie

severity /sɪ'verətɪ/ *n* [1] (of situation) powaga *f*; (of damage, loss) dotkliwość *f* [2] (harshness) surowość *f*

sew /səʊ/ **[]** *vt* u|szyć *[garment]* **[]** *vi* szyć

■ **sew up**: zaszy|ć, -wać *[hole]*; zszy|ć, -wać *[tear, wound]*

sewage /'su:ɪdʒ, 'sju:-/ *n* ścieki *m pl*

sewer /'su:ə(r), 'sju:-/ *n* kanał *m* ściekowy

sewing /'səʊɪŋ/ *n* (activity) szycie *n*; (piece of work) szycie *n*, robótka *f*

sewing machine *n* maszyna *f* do szycia

sex /seks/ **[]** *n* [1] (gender) płeć *f* [2] (intercourse) (one act) stosunek *m* (płciowy); (repeated) współżycie *n* seksualne, seks *m* **[]** *adj [organ]* płciowy

sex change *n* **to have a ~** przejść operację zmiany płci

sex discrimination *n* dyskryminacja *f* ze względu na płeć

sex education *n* wychowanie *n* seksualne

sexism /'seksɪzəm/ *n* seksizm *m*

sexist /'seksɪst/ **[]** *n* seksist|a *m*, -ka *f* **[]** *adj* seksistowski

sex offender *n* winn|y *m*, -a *f* przestępstwa seksualnego

sexual /'sekʃʊəl/ *adj [preference]* seksualny; *[organ]* płciowy

sexual abuse *n* wykorzystywanie *n* seksualne

sexual harassment *n* molestowanie *n* seksualne

sexuality /ˌsekʃʊ'ælətɪ/ *n* seksualność *f*

sexually transmitted disease, STD *n* choroba *f* przenoszona drogą płciową

sexy /'seksɪ/ infml *adj [book]* erotyczny; *[person, clothing]* seksowny; sexy infml

shabby /'ʃæbɪ/ *adj [person]* obdarty; *[clothes]* wytarty; *[room, furnishings]* nędzny; *[treatment]* podły

shack /ʃæk/ *n* chałupa *f*

shade /ʃeɪd/ **[]** *n* [1] (shadow) cień *m* [2] (tint) odcień *m* [3] (also **lamp~**) abażur *m* [4] US (also **window ~**) roleta *f*

II *vt [tree]* ocieni|ć, -ać, osł|onić, -aniać od słońca;
to ~ one's eyes with one's hand przysłonić
oczy ręką
IDIOMS: **to put sb/sth in the ~** przyćmić kogoś/
coś

shadow /'ʃædəʊ/ **II** *n* cień *m*; **to have ~s under
one's eyes** mieć cienie pod oczami
II *vt [detective]* śledzić

shadow cabinet *n* GB gabinet *m* cieni

shadowy /'ʃædəʊɪ/ *adj* (dark) ciemny; (indistinct)
[form, outline] niewyraźny

shady /'ʃeɪdɪ/ *adj* ⓵ *[place]* ocieniony ⓶ *[deal,
business]* podejrzany

shaft /ʃɑːft, US ʃæft/ *n* ⓵ (of tool) trzonek *m*; (of arrow)
drzewce *n*; (of sword) rękojeść *f*; (in machine) wał *m*
⓶ (passage, vent) szyb *m* ⓷ **a ~ of light** snop
światła; **a ~ of lightning** zygzak błyskawicy

shaggy /'ʃægɪ/ *adj [hair, animal]* kudłaty; *[eyebrows]*
krzaczasty; *[carpet]* kosmaty

shake /ʃeɪk/ **II** *n* ⓵ **to give sb/sth a ~** potrząsnąć
kimś/czymś ⓶ (also **milk-~**) koktajl *m* mleczny
II *vt* ⓵ potrząs|nąć, -ać (kimś/czymś); **to ~
one's fist at sb** wygrażać komuś pięścią; **to ~
one's head** pokręcić głową; **to ~ sb's hand, to
~ hands with sb** uścisnąć komuś dłoń ⓶ *[event,
disaster]* wstrząs|nąć, -ać (kimś) ⓷ zachwiać
(czymś) *[faith, confidence, resolve]*
III *vi* ⓵ za|drżeć, za|trząść się; **to ~ with
emotion/cold/fear** drżeć z emocji/zimna/strachu
⓶ (shake hands) **they shook on it** uścisnęli or
podali sobie ręce (na znak zgody)
■ **shake off**: pozby|ć, -wać się (kogoś/czegoś)
[cough, habit, unwanted person]; otrząs|nąć, -ać się
z (czegoś) *[depression]*
■ **shake up**: ⓵ wstrząs|nąć, -ać *[mixture, bottle]*
⓶ wstrząsnąć (kimś) *[person]*

shaken /'ʃeɪkən/ *adj* wstrząśnięty

shake-up /'ʃeɪkʌp/ *n* restrukturyzacja *f*; Pol
przetasowania *n pl*

shaky /'ʃeɪkɪ/ *adj [chair, ladder]* chybotliwy; *[voice]*
drżący; *[relationship, position]* niepewny; *[argument]*
wątpliwy; *[memory]* zawodny; *[regime]* słaby; **my
French is a bit ~** mój francuski jest dosyć kulawy
infml; **my hands are a bit ~** ręce mi się trochę
trzęsą

shall /ʃæl, ʃəl/ *modal aux* ⓵ (in future tense) **I ~** or **I'll
go** pójdę; **we ~ not** or **shan't have a reply
before Friday** nie dostaniemy odpowiedzi przed
piątkiem ⓶ (in suggestions) **~ I set the table?** czy
mam nakryć do stołu?; **~ we go to the cinema?**
może pójdziemy do kina?; **let's buy some
peaches, ~ we?** kupmy trochę brzoskwiń,
dobrze?

shallot /ʃə'lɒt/ *n* ⓵ GB szalotka *f* ⓶ US szczypior *m*

shallow /'ʃæləʊ/ *adj [container, water, grave]*
płytki; *[knowledge]* powierzchowny

sham /ʃæm/ **II** *n* (person) oszust *m*; (ideas, views) lipa *f*
infml; (election, activity) cyrk *m*, szopka *f* infml
II *adj [election, democracy]* lipny infml; *[organiza-
tion]* fikcyjny; **a ~ building** atrapa
III *vi* uda|ć, -wać

shambles /'ʃæmblz/ *n* infml (of administration, room)
bałagan *m*

shame /ʃeɪm/ **II** *n* ⓵ (embarrassment) wstyd *m*; **~ on
you!** wstydziłbyś się! ⓶ (pity) **it's a ~ that...**
szkoda, że...; **it was such a ~ (that) she lost**
wielka szkoda, że przegrała
II *vt* ⓵ (embarrass) zawstydz|ić, -ać ⓶ (disgrace)
przyn|ieść, -osić wstyd (komuś/czemuś) (**by do-
ing sth** robiąc coś)

shameful /'ʃeɪmfl/ *adj [conduct]* karygodny; *[ignor-
ance]* żenujący

shameless /'ʃeɪmlɪs/ *adj [person, attitude]* bezwstydny

shampoo /ʃæm'puː/ **II** *n* szampon *m*
II *vt* u|myć głowę (komuś) *[customer]*; **to ~ one's
hair** umyć głowę

shamrock /'ʃæmrɒk/ *n* koniczyna *f* drobnogłów-
kowa

shandy /'ʃændɪ/ *n* piwo *n* z lemoniadą

shantytown /'ʃæntɪtaʊn/ *n* dzielnica *f* nędzy

shape /ʃeɪp/ **II** *n* ⓵ (form) (of object) kształt *m*; (of
person) figura *f*, sylwetka *f*; **a square ~** kwadratowy
kształt; **what ~ is it?** jaki to ma kształt?; **it is
round in ~** to jest okrągłe; **to take ~** *[plan,
project, idea]* nabrać kształtu ⓶ (condition) (of person)
forma *f*; (of machine, economy) stan *m*; **to be in/out of
~** *[person]* być/nie być w formie; **to get into ~**
nabrać formy; **to knock sth into ~** dopracować
[project, plan]
II *vt [person]* nada|ć, -wać kształt (czemuś) *[wind]*
u|kształtować *[rock]*; *[event, environment]* u|kształ-
tować *[character]*; określ|ić, -ać *[policy, future]*; **to
~ clay into sth** ulepić coś z gliny; **to ~ wood
into sth** wyrzeźbić coś z drewna
■ **shape up**: ⓵ (develop) *[person]* robić postępy
⓶ (meet expectations) popraw|ić, -ać się

-shaped /'ʃeɪpt/ *in combinations* **star-/V-~** w
kształcie gwiazdy/litery V

shapeless /'ʃeɪplɪs/ *adj* bezkształtny

shapely /'ʃeɪplɪ/ *adj [legs]* kształtny; *[woman]*
zgrabny

share /ʃeə(r)/ **II** *n* ⓵ (of money, profits, blame) część *f*;
to have a ~ in sth przyczynić się do (czegoś)
[success]; **to pay one's (fair) ~** zapłacić swoją
część ⓶ (in stock market) akcja *f*
II *vt* dzielić *[room]* (**with sb** z kimś); po|dzielić
się (czymś) *[sandwich, news]* (**with sb** z kimś);
podzielać *[opinion, enthusiasm]*; **they ~ an
interest in history** obaj interesują się historią
III *vi* **to ~ in sth** mieć swój udział w czymś
[success]
■ **share out**: rozdziel|ić, -ać *[food, profits,*

supplies]; **we ~d the cakes out between us** podzieliliśmy się ciastkami

shared /ˈʃeəd/ *adj [room, facilities, interest]* wspólny

shareholder /ˈʃeəhəʊldə(r)/ *n* akcjonariusz *m*

share option scheme *n* system *m* akcji pracowniczych

shark /ʃɑːk/ *n* rekin *m*

sharp /ʃɑːp/ **[I]** *adj* [1] *[knife, razor]* ostry [2] *[tooth, pencil]* ostry; *[nose, chin]* spiczasty [3] *[angle, bend]* ostry; *[drop, fall, rise]* nagły, gwałtowny [4] *[taste]* cierpki; *[smell]* ostry [5] *[pain, frost, wind]* przenikliwy; *[cry]* przeszywający; *[blow]* silny [6] *[tongue, tone]* ostry [7] *[person, mind]* bystry; *[hearing, ear]* wyostrzony [8] *[businessman]* cwany infml; **~ operator** cwaniak [9] *[image, picture]* ostry; *[difference]* wyraźny [10] Mus *[note]* z krzyżykiem, podwyższony o pół tonu

[II] *adv* [1] **to stop up ~** ostro zahamować; **to turn ~ left** skręcić ostro w lewo [2] **at 9 o'clock ~** punktualnie o dziewiątej [3] Mus *[sing, play]* za wysoko

sharpen /ˈʃɑːpən/ *vt* na|ostrzyć *[blade];* za|temperować *[pencil]*

sharpener /ˈʃɑːpənə(r)/ *n* (for pencil) temperówka *f*; (for knife) ostrzałka *f*

sharply /ˈʃɑːplɪ/ *adv* [1] *[turn]* ostro; *[rise, fall]* gwałtownie [2] *[speak]* ostro

shatter /ˈʃætə(r)/ **[I]** *vt* roztrzask|ać, -iwać *[glass];* zakłóc|ić, -ać *[silence];* z|rujnować *[life];* rozwi|ać, -ewać *[hopes];* z|niszczyć *[nerves]*

[II] *vi [window, glass]* roztrzask|ać, -iwać się

shattered /ˈʃætəd/ *adj* [1] (destroyed) *[dream]* rozwiany; *[life]* zrujnowany [2] *[person]* (devastated) zdruzgotany; infml (tired) wykończony infml

shave /ʃeɪv/ **[I]** *n* **to have a ~** ogolić się

[II] *vt [barber]* o|golić *[person];* **to ~ one's legs** ogolić (sobie) nogi

[III] *vi* o|golić się

(IDIOMS) **that was a close ~!** mało brakowało!

shaver /ˈʃeɪvə(r)/ *n* (also **electric ~**) maszynka *f* do golenia

shaving /ˈʃeɪvɪŋ/ *n* [1] (process) golenie *n* [2] (of wood, metal) strużyna *f*, wiór *m*

shaving brush *n* pędzel *m* do golenia

shaving mirror *n* lusterko *n* do golenia

shawl /ʃɔːl/ *n* (long) szal *m*; (square) chusta *f*

she /ʃiː, ʃɪ/ *pron* ona; **here she is** oto ona; **there she is** jest tam; **she's not here** nie ma jej tutaj, jej tu nie ma; **she's a genius** (ona) jest genialna

sheaf /ʃiːf/ *n* (of corn) snop *m*; (of flowers) pęk *m*; (of papers) plik *m*

shear /ʃɪə(r)/ *vt* o|strzyc *[sheep];* wystrzy|c, -gać, strzyc *[grass]*

shears /ʃɪəz/ *npl* (for garden, sheep) nożyce *plt*

shed /ʃed/ **[I]** *n* szopa *f*; (bigger) (at factory site, port) hangar *m*; (with no walls) wiata *f*

[II] *vt* [1] zrzuc|ić, -ać *[leaves, weight];* pozby|ć, -wać się (czegoś) *[inhibitions];* **to ~ tears** wylewać or ronić łzy; **to ~ skin** *[snake]* zrzucać skórę, linieć; **to ~ blood** przelewać krew [2] *[lamp]* rzucać *[light];* *[person]* rozt|oczyć, -aczać wokół siebie *[happiness]*

sheep /ʃiːp/ *n* owca *f*; **black ~** czarna owca

sheepdog /ˈʃiːpdɒg, US -dɔːg/ *n* pies *m* pasterski

sheepish /ˈʃiːpɪʃ/ *adj [expression]* zażenowany

sheepskin /ˈʃiːpskɪn/ *n* (hide) owcza skóra *f*; (coat) kożuch *m*

sheer /ʃɪə(r)/ *adj* [1] *[hypocrisy, stupidity]* czysty; *[boredom]* śmiertelny [2] *[cliff]* urwisty [3] *[silk]* delikatny; *[stockings]* przezroczysty, cienki

sheet /ʃiːt/ *n* [1] (of paper) kartka *f*; (of metal) blacha *f*; (thinner) folia *f*; (of glass) tafla *f*; **~ of stamps** arkusz znaczków [2] (for bed) prześcieradło *n* [3] **fact ~** ulotka informacyjna [4] **a ~ of ice** (thick) tafla lodu; **a ~ of flame** ściana ognia

sheet lightning *n* błyskawica *f* rozświetlająca całe niebo

sheet metal *n* blacha *f* karoseryjna

sheik /ʃeɪk, US ʃiːk/ *n* szejk *m*

shelf /ʃelf/ *n* półka *f*; **a set of shelves** regał

shelf-life /ˈʃelflaɪf/ *n* (of food) okres *m* przechowywania; (of technology, pop music) żywotność *f*

shell /ʃel/ **[I]** *n* [1] (of egg) skorupka *f*; (of nut) łupina *f*; (of tortoise, shrimp) skorupa *f*, pancerz *m*; (of snail, oyster) muszla *f*; **sea~** muszla (morska); **to come out of one's ~** wyjść ze swojej skorupy fig [2] Mil pocisk *m* [3] (of vehicle, building) szkielet *m* [4] (of building) szkielet *m*

[II] *vt* [1] Mil ostrzel|ać, -iwać *[town, installation]* [2] Culin łuskać *[peas, nuts];* wyj|ąć, -mować ze skorupki *[prawn]*

■ **shell out** infml: **~ out [sth]** wy|bulić infml *[sum]*

shellfish /ˈʃelfɪʃ/ *npl* [1] Zool (crustacea) skorupiaki *m pl*; (molluscs) małże *m pl* [2] Culin owoce *m pl* morza

shelter /ˈʃeltə(r)/ **[I]** *n* schronienie *n*; (against bomb) schron *m*; (for homeless) schronisko *n*; (for refugee) kryjówka *f*; **to take ~ from sb/sth** schronić się przed kimś/czymś *[storm]*

[II] *vt* [1] (against weather) osł|onić, -aniać (**from** or **against sth** od czegoś, przed czymś); (from criticism, reality) ochr|onić, -aniać, chronić (**from sth** przed czymś) [2] udziel|ić, -ać schronienia (komuś) *[refugee];* (hide) ukry|ć, -wać *[fugitive]*

[III] *vi* s|chronić się; **to ~ from the storm** schronić się przed burzą

sheltered accommodation *n* mieszkania dla osób wymagających częściowej opieki, starszych lub niepełnosprawnych

shelving /ˈʃelvɪŋ/ *n* półki *f pl*

shepherd /ˈʃepəd/ *n* pasterz *m*

shepherd's pie *n* potrawa *f* z mielonego mięsa i ziemniaków

sheriff /ˈʃerɪf/ *n* szeryf *m*

sherry /'ʃerɪ/ *n* sherry *n inv*

shield /ʃiːld/ **I** *n* [1] (of warrior) tarcza *f* [2] (screen) ekran *m* ochronny; (around gun) tarcza *f* kuloodporna [3] US (policeman's badge) odznaka *f*
II *vt* (from weather) osł|onić, -aniać; (from danger) ochr|onić, -aniać, chronić

shift /ʃɪft/ **I** *n* [1] (alteration) zmiana *f* (**in sth/of sth** w czymś/czegoś); **a ~ from agriculture to industry** przejście od rolnictwa do przemysłu [2] (period of time, group of workers) zmiana *f*; (in mine) szychta *f*; **to work an eight-hour ~** pracować na ośmiogodzinnej zmianie
II *vt* [1] przesu|nąć, -wać, przestawi|ć, -ać *[furniture, vehicle]*; zmieni|ć, -ać *[theatre, scenery]*; **to ~ sth away from sth** odsunąć coś od czegoś [2] usu|nąć, -wać *[stain, mark]* [3] zrzuc|ić, -ać *[blame, responsibility]* (**onto sb** na kogoś) [4] US Aut **to ~ gear** zmieniać biegi
III *vi* (also **~ about**) *[load]* przesu|nąć, -wać się; **to ~ from one foot to the other** przestępować z nogi na nogę

shift key *n* Comput klawisz *m* zmiany rejestru

shiftless /'ʃɪftlɪs/ *adj* (lazy) gnuśny; (lacking initiative) niezaradny

shift work *n* praca *f* w systemie zmianowym

shifty /'ʃɪftɪ/ *adj [manner]* niebudzący zaufania; **a ~ person** krętacz *infml*

shimmer /'ʃɪmə(r)/ *vi* [1] *[jewels, fabric, water]* mienić się [2] (in heat) *[landscape]* drgać

shin /ʃɪn/ *n* goleń *f*

shine /ʃaɪn/ **I** *n* połysk *m*
II *vt* [1] za|świecić (czymś) *[spotlight, searchlight]* [2] wy|polerować *[brass]*; wy|glansować *[shoes]*
III *vi* [1] *[light, sun]* świecić; *[hair]* błyszczeć; *[brass, floor]* lśnić; **to ~ through sth** przeświecać przez coś *[mist]* [2] *[eyes, face]* promienieć (**with sth** czymś) [3] (excel) błyszczeć fig; **to ~ at sth** wybijać się w czymś *[science, languages]*
(IDIOMS:) **to take a ~ to sb** *infml* od razu kogoś polubić

shingle /'ʃɪŋgl/ **I** *n* [1] (tile) gont *m* [2] (on beach) kamyki *m pl*
II shingles *npl* Med półpasiec *m*

shining /'ʃaɪnɪŋ/ *adj [car, hair]* błyszczący, lśniący; *[bald spot]* świecący; *[eyes]* błyszczący; *[face]* rozpromieniony
(IDIOMS:) **a ~ example of sth** wzór czegoś

shiny /'ʃaɪnɪ/ *adj [metal]* błyszczący; *[hair, shoes]* lśniący; *[nose]* świecący; *[seat of trousers]* wyświecony

ship /ʃɪp/ **I** *n* statek *m*; Mil okręt *m*
II *vt* przew|ieźć, -ozić; (by sea) przew|ieźć, -ozić statkiem; (send) wys|łać, -yłać

shipment /'ʃɪpmənt/ *n* (cargo) transport *m*, dostawa *f*; (sending) wysyłka *f*

ship owner *n* armator *m*

shipping /'ʃɪpɪŋ/ *n* żegluga *f*

shipping company *n* (sea) towarzystwo *n* żeglugowe; (road) firma *f* przewozowa

shipwreck /'ʃɪprek/ **I** *n* (event) katastrofa *f* morska; (ship) wrak *m*
II *vt* **to be ~ed** rozbi|ć, -jać się; **a ~ed sailor** rozbitek

shipyard /'ʃɪpjaːd/ *n* stocznia *f*

shirk /ʃɜːk/ *vt* uchyl|ić, -ać się od (czegoś) *[duty, responsibility]*; przemilcz|eć, -ać *[problem]*

shirt /ʃɜːt/ *n* (man's) koszula *f*; (woman's) bluzka *f* (koszulowa); (for sport) koszulka *f*

shirt-sleeve /'ʃɜːtsliːv/ *n* rękaw *m*; **in one's ~** bez marynarki

shirty /'ʃɜːtɪ/ *adj* GB *infml* **to get ~** (**with sb**) wkurzyć się (na kogoś) *infml*

shit /ʃɪt/ **I** *n* vinfml gówno *n* vulg
II *excl* jasna cholera! vinfml

shiver /'ʃɪvə(r)/ **I** *n* drżenie *n*; **to give sb the ~s** przyprawić kogoś o dreszcze
II *vi* (with cold, fear) za|drżeć (**with sth** z czegoś); (with disgust) za|trząść się (**with sth** z czegoś)

shoal /ʃəʊl/ *n* (of fish) ławica *f*

shock /ʃɒk/ **I** *n* [1] wstrząs *m*, szok *m*; **to get** or **have a ~** doznać wstrząsu or szoku; **to express one's ~** (indignation) wyrazić swoje oburzenie; (amazement) wyrazić swoje zdziwienie [2] (electrical) porażenie *n* (prądem); **to get a ~** zostać porażonym (prądem) [3] (of collision) wstrząs *m*; (of explosion) podmuch *m* [4] (of hair) gęsta czupryna *f*
II *vt* (distress) wstrząs|nąć, -ać (kimś); (scandalize) za|szokować

shock absorber *n* amortyzator *m* wstrząsów

shocking /'ʃɒkɪŋ/ *adj [sight]* wstrząsający; *[behaviour]* skandaliczny

shock wave *n* fala *f* uderzeniowa; **to send ~s through the stock market** wstrząsnąć rynkiem papierów wartościowych

shoddy /'ʃɒdɪ/ *adj [product]* tandetny; *[work]* niechlujny

shoe /ʃuː/ **I** *n* (footwear) but *m*; (for horse) podkowa *f*
II *vt* podku|ć, -wać *[horse]*

shoelace /'ʃuːleɪs/ *n* sznurowadło *n*

shoe polish *n* pasta *f* do butów

shoe shop *n* sklep *m* z butami

shoe size *n* rozmiar *m* obuwia

shoestring /'ʃuːstrɪŋ/ *n* US sznurowadło *n*
(IDIOMS:) **on a ~** za bardzo małe pieniądze

shoo /ʃuː/ *vt* (also **~ away**) przeg|onić, -aniać

shoot /ʃuːt/ **I** *n* (young growth) kiełek *m*; (offshoot) pęd *m*
II *vt* [1] wystrzeli|ć, -wać *[bullet, missile]*; wypu|ścić, -szczać *[arrow]*; **to ~ sth at sb/sth** wystrzelić czymś w kogoś/coś [2] postrzelić *[person, animal]*; (kill) zastrzelić *[person, animal]*; **she shot him in the leg** postrzeliła go w nogę; **to ~ sb dead** zastrzelić kogoś; **to ~ oneself** (kill) zastrzelić się; (wound) postrzelić się [3] **to ~ questions at sb**

bombardować kogoś pytaniami ④ (film) na|kręcić *[film, scene]*; s|filmować *[subject]* ⑤ **to ~ the bolt** (into a fastening) zasunąć zasuwę; (out of a fastening) odsunąć zasuwę ⑥ **to ~ the rapids** pokonać bystrze ⑦ US za|grać w (coś) *[pool]*

III *vi* ① strzel|ić, -ać **(at sb** do kogoś) ② **to ~ forward** wyrwać się do przodu; **the car shot past** samochód przemknął obok ③ Sport strzel|ić, -ać

■ **shoot down**: zestrzeli|ć, -wać *[plane, pilot]*

■ **shoot up**: ¶ *[flames, spray]* wystrzeli|ć, -wać; *[prices, profits]* podsk|oczyć, -akiwać gwałtownie ¶ ~ **[sth] up** infml (inject) wstrzyk|nąć, -iwać *[heroin]*

shooting /'ʃuːtɪŋ/ **I** *n* ① (killing) zabójstwo *n* ② (firing) strzelanina *f*

II *prp adj [pain]* rozdzierający

shooting range *n* strzelnica *f*

shooting star *n* spadająca gwiazda *f*

shoot-out /'ʃuːtaʊt/ *n* infml strzelanina *f*

shop /ʃɒp/ **I** *n* ① sklep *m*; **to go to the ~s** iść na zakupy ② (workshop) warsztat *m* ③ US (in department store) stoisko *n*

II *vi* **to go ~ping** iść na zakupy; (as browser) chodzić po sklepach

■ **shop around**: roz|ejrzeć, -glądać się **(for sth** za czymś)

IDIOMS: **to talk ~** rozmawiać o sprawach zawodowych

shop assistant *n* GB ekspedient *m*, -ka *f*, sprzedaw|ca *m*, -czyni *f*

shopkeeper /'ʃɒpkiːpə(r)/ *n* sklepika|rz *m*, -rka *f*

shoplifter /'ʃɒplɪftə(r)/ *n* złodziej *m* sklepowy, złodziejka *f* sklepowa

shopping /'ʃɒpɪŋ/ *n* zakupy *plt*

shopping bag *n* torba *f* na zakupy

shopping centre GB, **shopping center** US *n* centrum *n* handlowe

shopping trolley *n* wózek *m* sklepowy

shop-soiled /'ʃɒpsɔɪld/ *adj [garment]* zleżały *(na wystawie)*

shop steward *n* przedstawiciel *m* załogi *(z ramienia związków zawodowych)*

shop window *n* wystawa *f* sklepowa, witryna *f*

shore /ʃɔː(r)/ *n* (of sea, lake, island) brzeg *m*; **on ~** na lądzie

short /ʃɔːt/ **I** *n* ① GB infml (alcohol) mocny alkohol *m* ② (film) krótkometrażówka *f* infml

II **shorts** *npl* (krótkie) spodenki *plt*, szorty *plt*; US (underwear) bokserki *plt*

III *adj* ① (not long-lasting) krótki; **a ~ time ago** niedawno; **to work ~er hours** pracować krócej; **the days are getting ~er** dni robią się coraz krótsze ② (not of great length) krótki; **the suit is too ~ in the sleeves** ten garnitur ma za krótkie rękawy ③ *[person]* niski ④ (scarce) **books are in ~ supply here** tu jest mało książek; **time is getting ~** jest coraz mniej czasu ⑤ (lacking) **he is**

~ of sth brakuje mu czegoś; **she is ~ on talent** jest pozbawiona talentu; **my wages are £30 ~** dostałem o 30 funtów za mało pensji; **we are running ~ of sth** zaczyna nam brakować czegoś ⑥ (in abbreviation) **Tom is ~ for Thomas** Tom to zdrobnienie od Thomas ⑦ (abrupt) **to be ~ with sb** potraktować kogoś szorstko ⑧ *[pastry]* kruchy

IV *adv [stop]* nagle; **to stop ~ of doing sth** ledwie się powstrzymać od zrobienia czegoś

V **in short** *adv phr* krótko mówiąc

VI **short of** *prep phr* (except) oprócz (czegoś)

IDIOMS: **to sell oneself ~** mieć niską samoocenę; **to make ~ work of sth/sb** szybko coś/kogoś załatwić

shortage /'ʃɔːtɪdʒ/ *n* niedobór *m*, brak *m*; **housing ~** brak mieszkań

shortbread /'ʃɔːtbred/ *n* kruche ciastko *n*

short-change /ˌʃɔːt'tʃeɪndʒ/ *vt [shop assistant]* wyda|ć, -wać za mało *[customer]*; fig wyrolować infml

short circuit /ˌʃɔːt'sɜːkɪt/ **I** *n* zwarcie *n*, spięcie *n*

II **short-circuit** *vt* s|powodować zwarcie w (czymś)

III **short-circuit** *vi* **the lights short-circuited** doszło do zwarcia w oświetleniu

shortcomings /'ʃɔːtkʌmɪŋz/ *npl* braki *m pl*, wady *f pl*

shortcut /'ʃɔːtkʌt/ *n* skrót *m*; **to take a ~ through the park** iść na skróty przez park

shorten /'ʃɔːtn/ **I** *vt* skr|ócić, -acać *[garment, list, talk]*

II *vi [days]* sta|ć, -wać się krótszym

shortfall /'ʃɔːtfɔːl/ *n* niedobór *m*; (in budget, exports) deficyt *m*; (in accounts) manko *n*

shorthand /'ʃɔːthænd/ *n* stenografia *f*; **to take sth down in ~** stenografować coś

shorthand-typist /ˌʃɔːthænd'taɪpɪst/ *n* stenotypist|a *m*, -ka *f*

shortlist /'ʃɔːtlɪst/ **I** *n* lista *f* finalistów

II *vt* umie|ścić, -szczać na liście kandydatów branych pod uwagę *[applicant]*

short-lived /ˌʃɔːt'lɪvd, US -'laɪvd/ *adj [happiness, effect]* krótkotrwały

shortly /'ʃɔːtlɪ/ *adv* ① (very soon) wkrótce; **she'll be back ~** niedługo wróci ② (a short time) **~ before** na krótko przedtem; **~ after(wards)** wkrótce potem ③ *[reply]* szorstko

shortsighted /ˌʃɔːt'saɪtɪd/ *adj* ① **to be ~** być krótkowidzem ② fig *[person, policy, decision]* krótkowzroczny

short-sleeved /ˌʃɔːt'sliːvd/ *adj* z krótkimi rękawami

short-staffed /ˌʃɔːt'stɑːft, US -'stæft/ *adj* **to be ~** odczuwać brak personelu

short story *n* opowiadanie *n*

short term **I** *n* **in the ~** na krótką metę

II **short-term** *adj [solution]* tymczasowy; *[benefit]* krótkotrwały

shortwave /ˌʃɔːt'weɪv/ *n* fale *f pl* krótkie

shot /ʃɒt/ **❚** n ① (from gun) (wy)strzał m ② Sport (in tennis, golf, cricket) uderzenie n; (in football) strzał m ③ (snapshot) zdjęcie n ④ (in film-making) scena f; (filmed by one camera) ujęcie n; **to be in** ~ być w kadrze ⑤ (injection) zastrzyk m ⑥ (attempt) próba f; **to have a** ~ **at making a cake** spróbować upiec ciasto; **to be a good** ~ być dobrym strzelcem
❚❚ adj [silk] mieniący się

shotgun /'ʃɒtgʌn/ n śrutówka f

shot put n Sport pchnięcie n kulą

should /ʃʊd, ʃəd/ modal aux ① (ought to) **you** ~ **have told me before** powinieneś był wcześniej mi powiedzieć; **why shouldn't I do it?** dlaczego nie miałbym tego zrobić?; **we** ~ **be there by six o'clock** powinniśmy tam być o szóstej; **how** ~ **I know?** skąd mam wiedzieć?; **flowers! you shouldn't have!** kwiaty! nie trzeba było! ② (in conditional sentences) **had he asked me, I** ~ **have accepted** gdyby mnie poprosił, zgodziłbym się; **if you** ~ **change your mind...** jeżeli zmieni pan zdanie...; ~ **the opportunity arise** gdyby nadarzyła się okazja ③ (expressing purpose) **she simplified it in order that they** ~ **understand** uprościła to, żeby mogli zrozumieć ④ (in polite formulas) **I** ~ **like a drink** chętnie bym się czegoś napił; **I** ~ **like to go there** chciałbym tam pójść ⑤ (expressing opinion, surprise) **I** ~ **think so!** myślę, że tak!; **I** ~ **think not!** nie wydaje mi się!; **I** ~ **think she must be about 40** myślę, że ona musi mieć koło czterdziestki; **I** ~ **say so!** no pewnie!

shoulder /'ʃəʊldə(r)/ **❚** n bark m, ramię n
❚❚ vt fig wziąć, brać na swoje barki [responsibility, task, burden]
⟨IDIOMS⟩ **to rub** ~**s with famous people** stykać się ze sławnymi ludźmi

shoulder blade n Anat łopatka f

shoulder-length /'ʃəʊldəleŋθ/ adj [hair] do ramion

shoulder pad n (in jacket) poduszka f

shout /ʃaʊt/ **❚** n okrzyk m
❚❚ vt wykrzyk|nąć, -iwać [slogans, orders]
❚❚❚ vi krzy|knąć, -czeć; **to** ~ **at sb** krzyczeć na kogoś; **to** ~ **for help** wołać o pomoc
■ **shout out:** krzyk|nąć

shouting /'ʃaʊtɪŋ/ n krzyki m pl

shove /ʃʌv/ infml **❚** n **to give sb/sth a** ~ mocno popchnąć kogoś/coś
❚❚ vt ① (push) pop|chnąć, -ychać; **to** ~ **sth through the letterbox** wepchnąć coś do skrzynki ② (stuff hurriedly) wrzuc|ić, -ać (**sth into sth** coś do czegoś) ③ (jostle) potrącić [person]
❚❚❚ vi przep|chnąć, -ychać się
■ **shove up:** infml przep|chnąć, -ychać się

shovel /'ʃʌvl/ **❚** n (spade) szufla f, łopata f; (machine) koparka f
❚❚ vt **to** ~ **snow off the path** odgarniać śnieg ze ścieżki

show /ʃəʊ/ **❚** n ① (as entertainment) widowisko n; (in theatre) przedstawienie n; (in cinema) seans m; (on radio, TV) program m; (of slides) pokaz m; **a quiz** ~ (on TV) teleturniej ② (of flowers, crafts) wystawa f; (of cars) salon m; **a fashion** ~ pokaz mody ③ (of feelings) okazywanie n; (of strength, wealth) demonstracja f; **it was all for** or **just for** ~ to wszystko było tylko na pokaz
❚❚ vt ① pokaz|ać, -ywać [person, object, film]; okaz|ać, -ywać [ticket, feeling]; wskaz|ać, -ywać [direction]; **to** ~ **sb** pokazać coś komuś; **a dress that** ~**s her underclothes** sukienka, przez którą widać (jej) bieliznę ② (exhibit) wysta-wi|ć, -ać, pokaz|ać, -ywać [animal, flowers] ③ (prove) wykaz|ać, -ywać [truth, guilt] ④ (conduct) **to** ~ **sb to their seat** [usher] zaprowadzić kogoś na miejsce; **to** ~ **sb to their room** zaprowadzić kogoś do jego pokoju; **allow me to** ~ **you to the door** pozwól, że odprowadzę cię do wyjścia
❚❚❚ vi ① [label, stain] być widocznym; **terror** ~**ed on his face** na jego twarzy malowało się przerażenie ② [film] być pokazywanym
■ **show in:** ~ [sb] **in** wprowadz|ić, -ać
■ **show off:** ¶ ~ **off** infml popis|ać, -ywać się ¶ ~ **sb/sth] off** popis|ać, -ywać się (czymś [skill]; po|chwalić się (kimś/czymś) [car, baby]
■ **show out:** ~ [sb] **out** odprowadz|ić, -ać do wyjścia
■ **show round:** ~ [sb] **round** oprowadz|ić, -ać
■ **show up:** ¶ ~ **up** infml (arrive) pojawi|ć, -ać się ¶ ~ **up [sth]** ukaz|ać, -ywać ¶ ~ [sb] **up** z|robić wstyd (komuś)

show business n przemysł m rozrywkowy, show-biznes m

showcase /'ʃəʊkeɪs/ n gablota f wystawowa; **the programme is a** ~ **for young talents** ten program lansuje młode talenty

showdown /'ʃəʊdaʊn/ n ostateczna rozgrywka f

shower /'ʃaʊə(r)/ **❚** n ① prysznic m; **to be in the** ~ być pod prysznicem ② (rain) przelotny deszcz m
❚❚ vt **to** ~ **sb with sth** obsyp|ać, -ywać kogoś czymś [gifts, compliments]
❚❚❚ vi [person] wziąć, brać prysznic

show house n pokazowy dom m

show-jumping n skoki m pl przez przeszkody

show-off /'ʃəʊɒf, US -ɔ:f/ n infml pozer m, -ka f

show of hands n głosowanie n przez podniesie-nie ręki

showroom /'ʃəʊru:m, -rʊm/ n salon m wystawo-wy; **in** ~ **condition** [car] w idealnym stanie

shrapnel /'ʃræpnl/ n szrapnel m

shred /ʃred/ **❚** n ① fig (of emotion) strzęp m; (of truth) krztyna f; (of evidence) ślad m ② (of paper, fabric) strzęp m
❚❚ vt z|niszczyć [documents]; po|szatkować [vege-tables]; (cut) po|ciąć [paper]

shredder /'ʃredə(r)/ n niszczarka f dokumentów

shrewd /ʃruːd/ adj [person] bystry; [move] sprytny, mądry; [investment] trafny; [assessment] przenikliwy

shriek /ʃriːk/ **I** n ① (of person) wrzask m, pisk m; a ~ **of delight** radosny pisk ② (of animal) krzyk m **II** vi wrz|asnąć, -eszczeć; **to** ~ **with pain** wrzasnąć z bólu; **to** ~ **in delight** piszczeć z zachwytu

shrill /ʃrɪl/ adj [tone, cry, whistle] przenikliwy; [voice] wrzaskliwy

shrimp /ʃrɪmp/ n krewetka f

shrine /ʃraɪn/ n ① (place of worship) sanktuarium n ② (alcove in church) kaplica f; (building) kapliczka f

shrink /ʃrɪŋk/ **I** vt s|powodować kurczenie się (czegoś) [fabric]; zmniejsz|yć, -ać [budget] **II** vi ① [old person, funds] s|kurczyć się; [fabric] zbie|c, -gać się; [sales] z|maleć; **the staff has shrunk from 200 to 50** personel skurczył się z 200 do 50 osób ② (recoil) **to** ~ **from sth/doing sth** fig uchylić się przed czymś/zrobieniem czegoś

shrinking /ʃrɪŋkɪŋ/ adj [audience] malejący; [market] kurczący się; ~ **population** coraz bardziej spadająca liczba ludności

shrink-wrap /ʃrɪŋkræp/ vt za|pakować w folię

shrivel /ʃrɪvl/ **I** vt [sun, heat] wysusz|yć, -ać [skin, plant, leaf] **II** vi (also ~ **up**) [fruit, vegetable, leaf] wys|chnąć, -ychać; [skin] wysusz|yć, -ać się

shroud /ʃraʊd/ **I** n całun m **II** vt okry|ć, -wać [person, body] (**in sth** czymś)

Shrove Tuesday /ʃrəʊvˌtjuːzdeɪ, US tuːzdɪ/ n ostatki plt

shrub /ʃrʌb/ n krzew m

shrubbery /ʃrʌbəri/ n (in garden) krzewy m pl; (shrubs collectively) zarośla plt

shrug /ʃrʌg/ **I** n wzruszenie n ramion **II** vi (also ~ **one's shoulders**) wzrusz|yć, -ać ramionami ■ **shrug off**: z|lekceważyć [problem, rumour]

shudder /ʃʌdə(r)/ **I** n ① (of person) dreszcz m ② (of building) drganie n **II** vi ① [person] za|drżeć; **to** ~ **with fear** drżeć ze strachu ② **to** ~ **to a halt** [vehicle] szarpnąć i zahamować

shuffle /ʃʌfl/ vt ① poprzestawiać [furniture]; **to** ~ **one's papers** przerzucać papiery ② po|tasować [cards] ③ **to** ~ **one's feet** przestępować z nogi na nogę

shun /ʃʌn/ vt stronić od (kogoś/czegoś), unikać (kogoś/czegoś) [people, publicity]; wymigiwać się od (czegoś) [work]

shunt /ʃʌnt/ **I** vt przet|oczyć, -aczać [wagon, engine] (**into sth** na coś) **II** vi **to** ~ **back and forth** manewrować

shut /ʃʌt/ **I** adj [door, shop] zamknięty; **to slam the door** ~ zatrzasnąć drzwi; **to slam** ~ zatrzasnąć się; **to keep one's mouth** ~ trzymać język za zębami infml

II vt zam|knąć, -ykać [book] **III** vi ① [door, book, box, mouth] zam|knąć, -ykać się ② [office, factory] być zamykanym ■ **shut down**: ¶ ~ **down** [business] zosta|ć, -wać zamkniętym; [machinery] wyłącz|yć, -ać się ¶ ~ [sth] **down** zam|knąć, -ykać [business, plant]; wyłącz|yć, -ać [machinery] ■ **shut in**: [sb/sth] ~ **in** zam|knąć, -ykać (w środku) [person, animal] ■ **shut off**: [sth] ~ **off**, ~ **off** [sth] wyłącz|yć, -ać [motor]; odci|ąć, -nać [supply] ■ **shut out**: ① (keep out) nie wpu|ścić, -szczać do środka [animal, person]; zabezpiecz|yć, -ać przed (czymś) [noise]; uniemożliwi|ć, -ać dostęp (czegoś) [light]; **to be shut out** nie zostać wpuszczonym do środka ② (block) zasł|onić, -aniać [light, view] ■ **shut up**: ¶ ~ **up** infml zamknąć się vinfml; ~ **up about it!** przestań o tym gadać! ¶ ~ **up** [sb/sth], ~ [sb/sth] **up** ① infml (silence) ucisz|yć, -ać [person, animal] ② (confine) zam|knąć, -ykać [person, animal] ③ (lock) zam|knąć, -ykać [house, shop]; **to** ~ **up shop** infml zamknąć kramik infml fig

shutdown /ʃʌtdaʊn/ n (temporary) zamknięcie n (czasowe); (permanent) likwidacja f

shutter /ʃʌtə(r)/ n ① (on window) (folding) okiennica f; (rolling) żaluzja f ② (on camera) migawka f

shuttle /ʃʌtl/ **I** n ① (service) transport m wahadłowy ② (also **space** ~) wahadłowiec m, prom m kosmiczny **II** vt przew|ieźć, -ozić [people, goods]

shuttle service n transport m wahadłowy

shy /ʃaɪ/ **I** adj [person, look] nieśmiały; [animal] płochliwy; **to be** ~ **with** or **of sb** [person] być nieśmiałym wobec kogoś **II** vi [horse] **to** ~ **at sth** spłoszyć się na widok czegoś ■ **shy away**: **to** ~ **away from sth** cof|nąć, -ać się przed czymś

Siberia /saɪbɪərɪə/ prn Syberia f

sibling /sɪblɪŋ/ n (brother) brat m; (sister) siostra f; **I have five** ~**s** mam pięcioro rodzeństwa

Sicily /sɪsɪli/ prn Sycylia f

sick /sɪk/ adj ① (ill) chory; **to feel** ~ źle się czuć ② (nauseous) **to be** ~ wymiotować; **I feel** ~ jest mi niedobrze; **to be worried** ~ **about sth** być chorym z niepokoju o coś ③ [joke] niesmaczny; [mind, imagination] chory ④ (disgusted) **you make me** ~! jesteś obrzydliwy! ⑤ infml **to be** ~ **of sb/sth** mieć dosyć kogoś/czegoś

sick bay n izba f chorych

sicken /sɪkən/ **I** vt (disgust) wzbudz|ić, -ać odrazę w (kimś) **II** vi **I'm** ~**ing for a cold** bierze mnie przeziębienie

sickening /sɪkənɪŋ/ adj [sight, smell] obrzydliwy; [cruelty] odrażający

sick leave *n* zwolnienie *n* lekarskie; **to be on ~** mieć zwolnienie *n* lekarskie; być na zwolnieniu infml

sickly /'sɪklɪ/ *adj* [1] (often ill) chorowity [2] *[plant]* rachityczny [3] *[smell, taste]* mdlący; **~ sweet** przesłodzony

sickness /'sɪknɪs/ *n* [1] (illness) choroba *f* [2] (nausea) torsje *plt*, wymioty *plt*; **a bout of ~** napad mdłości or nudności

sick note *n* infml (for school) usprawiedliwienie *n*; (for work) zwolnienie *n* lekarskie

sick pay *n* wypłata *f* za czas choroby

sickroom /'sikru:m, -rʊm/ *n* (at home) pokój *m* chorego; (in school, institution) izba *f* chorych

side /saɪd/ **I** *n* [1] (of person's body, object) bok *m*; (of hill) zbocze *n*; (of boat) burta *f*; (of box) ścianka *f*; (of lake) brzeg *m*; **on my right ~** po mojej prawej stronie; **by her ~** u jej boku, koło niej; **~ by ~** tuż obok siebie; **at** or **by the ~ of the road** na poboczu, przy drodze [2] (of paper, record) strona *f* [3] (of problem) aspekt *m*; (of story) wersja *f* [4] (opposing group) **to take ~s** zajmować stanowisko; **to change ~s** przejść na drugą stronę [5] Sport (team) drużyna *f*

II *adj [door, window, entrance]* boczny

III **on the side** *adv phr* **a steak with salad on the ~** stek z sałatką; **to do sth on the ~** robić coś na boku

■ **side with**: **~ with [sb]** trzymać z (kimś)

sideboard /'saɪdbɔ:d/ *n* kredens *m*

sideboards /'saɪdbɔ:dz/ GB, **sideburns** /'saɪdbɜ:nz/ *npl* bokobrody *plt*, baki *plt*

side effect *n* efekt *m* uboczny

sideline /'saɪdlaɪn/ *n* [1] (of company) działalność *f* dodatkowa; (of person) zajęcie *n* uboczne [2] Sport linia *f* boczna; **to kick the ball over the ~** wybić piłkę na aut; **to be on the ~s** fig stać z boku fig

sidelong /'saɪdlɒŋ/ *adj [glance]* z ukosa, ukradkowy

side plate *n* talerzyk *m* (na chleb)

side-saddle /'saɪdsædl/ *n* siodło *n* damskie

sideshow /'saɪdʃəʊ/ *n* impreza *f* towarzysząca

sidestep /'saɪdstep/ *vt* unik|nąć, -ać (czegoś) *[issue]*; zejść, schodzić z drogi (komuś) *[opponent]*

side street *n* boczna uliczka *f*

sidetrack /'saɪdtræk/ *vt* odwr|ócić, -acać uwagę (kogoś) fig; **to get ~ed** (in debate) odejść od tematu

sidewalk /'saɪdwɔːk/ *n* US chodnik *m*

sideways /'saɪdweɪz/ **I** *adj [glance, look]* z ukosa

II *adv [move, look]* w bok; *[park]* bokiem

siding /'saɪdɪŋ/ *n* bocznica *f*

siege /si:dʒ/ *n* oblężenie *n*; **to lay ~ to sth** oblegać coś

siesta /sɪ'estə/ *n* sjesta *f*

sieve /sɪv/ **I** *n* (for draining) sito *n*; (for sifting) przetak *m*

II *vt* przesi|ać, -ewać *[flour]*

sift /sɪft/ *vt* [1] przesi|ać, -ewać *[flour]* [2] przeszuk|ać, -iwać *[information]*

■ **sift through**: przeszuk|ać, -iwać (coś)

sigh /saɪ/ **I** *n* westchnienie *n*

II *vi* w|estchnąć, -zdychać; **to ~ with relief** odetchnąć z ulgą

sight /saɪt/ **I** *n* [1] wzrok *m*; **at first ~** na pierwszy rzut oka; **to catch ~ of sb/sth** zauważyć kogoś/coś; **to lose ~ of sb/sth** stracić kogoś/coś z oczu; **to know sb by ~** znać kogoś z widzenia; **I can't stand the ~ of him!** nie mogę na niego patrzeć!; **to be in ~** *[town, land]* być w zasięgu wzroku; *[peace, freedom]* być blisko; **to be out of ~** (hidden) być niewidocznym; (having moved) zniknąć z pola widzenia; **don't let her out of your ~**! nie spuszczaj jej z oka! [2] (thing seen) widok *m*; **it was not a pretty ~** to nie był ładny or przyjemny widok

II **sights** *npl* [1] atrakcje *f pl* turystyczne (**of sth** czegoś); **to see the ~s** zwiedzać [2] (on gun, telescope) przyrządy *m pl* celownicze [3] fig **to set one's ~s on sth** stawiać sobie coś za cel

sightseeing /'saɪtsiːɪŋ/ *n* zwiedzanie *n*; **to go ~** zwiedzać

sightseer /'saɪtsiːə(r)/ *n* zwiedzający *m*, -a *f*

sign /saɪn/ **I** *n* [1] (symbolic mark) znak *m*; **the pound ~** symbol funta [2] (road sign) znak *m* (**for sth** czegoś); (outside shop) szyld *m*; (indicating opening hours) wywieszka *f* [3] (gesture) gest *m*, znak *m* [4] **to show ~s of sth** zdradzać oznaki czegoś *[stress, talent]*; **what ~ are you?** spod jakiego jesteś znaku?

II *vt, vi* podpis|ać, -ywać

■ **sign on**: [1] GB za|rejestrować się jako bezrobotny [2] (for course) zapis|ać, -ywać się (**for sth** na coś)

■ **sign up**: [1] (in forces) zaciąg|nąć, -ąć się [2] (for course) zapis|ać, -ywać się (**for sth** na coś)

signal /'sɪɡnl/ **I** *n* sygnał *m*; **a ~ for sb to do sth** sygnał dla kogoś, żeby zrobił coś

II *vt* **to ~ (to sb) that...** dać (komuś) znak, że...

III *vi* da|ć, -wać znak or sygnał

signature /'sɪɡnətʃə(r)/ *n* podpis *m*

signature tune *n* sygnał *m* dźwiękowy

significance /sɪɡ'nɪfɪkəns/ *n* [1] (importance) znaczenie *n*, waga *f* [2] (meaning) znaczenie *n*

significant /sɪɡ'nɪfɪkənt/ *adj* [1] (considerable) *[amount, influence]* znaczny [2] (important) *[event, victory]* znaczący [3] (meaningful) *[gesture, fact]* znaczący, znamienny

signify /'sɪɡnɪfaɪ/ *vt* oznaczać

sign language *n* język *m* migowy

signpost /'saɪnpəʊst/ *n* drogowskaz *m*; fig wskazówka *f*

silence /'saɪləns/ **I** *n* [1] (quietness) cisza *f*; **in ~** w ciszy [2] (absence of communication) milczenie *n*; **to break one's ~** przerwać milczenie

II *vt* ucisz|yć, -ać *[crowd, child]*

silencer /'saɪlənsə(r)/ *n* tłumik *m*

silent /'saɪlənt/ *adj* ① *[room]* cichy; **to be ~** *[person]* milczeć ② *[disapproval, prayer]* cichy ③ *[film]* niemy

silhouette /ˌsɪluː'et/ *n* (dark shape) sylwetka *f*; (contour) zarys *m*

silicon chip *n* (krzemowy) układ *m* scalony

silk /sɪlk/ *n* jedwab *m*

silky /'sɪlki/ *adj [hair]* jedwabisty

sill /sɪl/ *n* (of vehicle) próg *m*; (of window) parapet *m*

silly /'sɪli/ ① *adj [person, question, idea]* głupi; *[clothes]* śmieszny; **don't be ~**! nie bądź niemądry! ② *adv* **to drink oneself ~** upić się do nieprzytomności; **to bore sb ~** nudzić kogoś śmiertelnie

silo /'saɪləʊ/ *n* silos *m*

silt /sɪlt/ *n* muł *m*, szlam *m*

silver /'sɪlvə(r)/ ① *n* ① (metal) srebro *n* ② (silverware) srebra *plt* ③ (colour) (kolor *m*) srebrny *m* ④ (medal) srebro *n* ② *adj [ring, coin]* srebrny

silver birch *n* brzoza *f* biała

silver foil *n* GB folia *f* aluminiowa

silverware /'sɪlvəweə(r)/ *n* (solid) srebro *n* stołowe; (plate) srebrne platery *m pl*

similar /'sɪmɪlə(r)/ *adj* podobny; **~ to sth** podobny do czegoś; **~ in price** w podobnej cenie

similarity /ˌsɪmɪ'lærəti/ *n* podobieństwo *n* (**to** or **with sb/sth** do kogoś/czegoś)

similarly /'sɪmɪləli/ *adv [behave, dressed]* podobnie

simmer /'sɪmə(r)/ *vi* ① *[soup]* gotować się na wolnym ogniu; *[water]* wrzeć lekko ② *[person]* (with discontent) zaǁkipieć ze złości infml; (with revolt, violence) wrzeć (**with sth** czymś)

simple /'sɪmpl/ *adj* ① *[task, method]* prosty, łatwy; *[dress, lifestyle]* prosty, zwyczajny ② (dimwitted) ograniczony

simplicity /sɪm'plɪsəti/ *n* (of task) łatwość *f*; (of solution) prostota *f*

simplify /'sɪmplɪfaɪ/ *vt* uprǁościć, -aszczać

simplistic /sɪm'plɪstɪk/ *adj* nazbyt uproszczony

simply /'sɪmpli/ *adv* ① *[say, write]* prosto, w prosty sposób; *[dress]* z prostotą; **to put it ~ ...** mówiąc po prostu... ② (merely) po prostu

simulate /'sɪmjʊleɪt/ *vt* (feign) udaǁć, -wać *[interest, illness]*; (reproduce) symulować *[conditions]*

simulator /'sɪmjʊleɪtə(r)/ *n* symulator *m*

simultaneous /ˌsɪml'teɪnɪəs, US ˌsaɪm-/ *adj [event]* równoczesny; *[translation]* symultaniczny

sin /sɪn/ ① *n* grzech *m* ② *vi* zǁgrzeszyć (**against sth** przeciwko czemuś)

since /sɪns/ ① *prep* od (czegoś); **she's been a teacher ~ 1965** jest nauczycielką od 1965 roku; **she's been waiting ~ 10 am** czeka od 10 rano; **I haven't seen him ~ then** od tamtej pory go nie widziałem; **~ arriving** or **~ his arrival, he...** odkąd przyjechał or od swojego przyjazdu,...

② *conj* ① (from the time when) odkąd, od kiedy; **~ he's been away** odkąd wyjechał; **ever ~ I married him** odkąd za niego wyszłam; **it's 10 years ~ we last met** od naszego ostatniego spotkania minęło dziesięć lat ② (because) skoro; **you're so clever, why don't you do it yourself?** skoro jesteś taki mądry, dlaczego sam tego nie zrobisz? ③ *adv* (subsequently) od tej pory

sincere /sɪn'sɪə(r)/ *adj [person, apology]* szczery

sincerely /sɪn'sɪəli/ *adv* szczerze; **Yours ~, Sincerely yours** US (end of letter) z poważaniem; (less formally) pozdrawiam

sincerity /sɪn'serəti/ *n* szczerość *f*

sinew /'sɪnjuː/ *n* ścięgno *n*

sing /sɪŋ/ ① *vt* zaǁśpiewać; **to ~ sb's praises** wychwalać kogoś pod niebiosa ② *vi* zaǁśpiewać

Singapore /ˌsɪŋə'pɔː(r)/ *prn* Singapur *m*

singe /sɪndʒ/ *vt* przypalǁić, -ać *[clothing]*; opalǁić, -ać *[poultry]*

singer /'sɪŋə(r)/ *n* (in opera) śpiewaǁk *m*, -czka *f*; (of pop music) piosenkaǁrz *m*, -rka *f*

singing /'sɪŋɪŋ/ *n* śpiew *m*

single /'sɪŋgl/ ① *n* ① (also **~ ticket**) bilet *m* w jedną stronę ② (also **~ room**) pokój *m* jednoosobowy ③ (record) singel *m* ② *adj* ① (sole) jeden; **in a ~ day** w ciągu jednego dnia ② (not double) *[door, sheet]* pojedynczy; *[room, bed]* jednoosobowy ③ (unmarried) stanu wolnego ④ **every ~ day** codziennie; **not a ~ person** absolutnie nikt ■ **single out:** *[person]* wybǁrać, -ierać

single cream *n* śmietanka *f* o niskiej zawartości tłuszczu

single currency *n* jedna waluta *f*

single file *adv [walk]* gęsiego

single-handedly /ˌsɪŋgl'hændɪdli/ *adv* **to manage ~** dać sobie radę samemu

single market *n* jednolity rynek *m*

single-minded /ˌsɪŋgl'maɪndɪd/ *adj [person]* zdeterminowany

single mother *n* samotna matka *f*

single-parent *adj* **~ family** rodzina niepełna

singles /'sɪŋglz/ *npl* ① (in tennis) singel *m* ② (people) ludzie *plt* samotni

singles bar *n* bar *m* dla samotnych

singles charts *npl* lista *f* najlepszych singli

single-sex /ˌsɪŋgl'seks/ *adj [school]* (for males) męski; (for females) żeński

singlet /'sɪŋglɪt/ *n* GB ① Sport koszulka *f* ② (vest) podkoszulek *m*

singular /'sɪŋgjʊlə(r)/ ① *n* liczba *f* pojedyncza ② *adj* w liczbie pojedynczej

sinister /'sɪnɪstə(r)/ *adj [sign]* złowieszczy; *[look]* złowrogi

sink /sɪŋk/ **I** *n* (in kitchen) zlew *m*; (in bathroom) umywalka *f*

II *vt* ① zat|opić, -apiać *[ship]* ② wiercić *[oil well]*; kopać *[foundations]*; wbi|ć, -jać *[post, pillar]*; **to ~ one's teeth into sth** zatopić zęby w czymś

III *vi [object, ship]* za|tonąć; *[sun]* za|jść, -chodzić; *[cake]* opa|ść, -dać; *[building, wall]* osi|ąść, -adać; **to ~ to the floor** osunąć się na podłogę; **to ~ into a deep sleep** zapaść w głęboki sen; **to ~ into sth** zapaść się w coś, grzęznąć w czymś *[mud]*; pogrążyć się w czymś *[anarchy]*

■ **sink in:** it took several minutes for the truth to ~ in minęło kilka minut, zanim prawda dotarła do mojej świadomości

sinner /'sɪnə(r)/ *n* grzeszni|k *m*, -ca *f*

sinus /'saɪnəs/ *n* Anat zatoka *f*

sip /sɪp/ **I** *n* ły(cze)k *m*

II *vt* sączyć *[drink, wine]*

siphon /'saɪfn/ **I** *n* syfon *m*

II *vt* (also ~ **off**) spu|ścić, -szczać, ściąg|nąć, -ać *[water, petrol]*

sir /sɜ:(r)/ *n* ① pan *m*; **Dear Sir** (in letter) Szanowny Panie ② GB (in titles) sir *m inv*; **Sir James** Sir James

siren /'saɪərən/ *n* syrena *f*

sirloin /'sɜ:lɔɪn/ *n* polędwica *f* wołowa

sister /'sɪstə(r)/ *n* ① (sibling) siostra *f* ② GB Med siostra *f*

sister-in-law /'sɪstərɪnlɔ:/ *n* (sister of wife or husband) szwagierka *f*; (wife of brother) bratowa *f*

sit /sɪt/ **I** *vt* GB zdawać *[exam]*

II *vi* ① (u)siąść, siadać; **to ~ on the floor** (u)siąść na podłodze ② siedzieć; **to be ~ting reading** siedzieć i czytać; **to ~ still** siedzieć spokojnie ③ *[committee, court]* obradować ④ **to ~ on sth** zasiadać w czymś *[committee, jury]* ⑤ **to ~ on sth** *[bird]* wysiadywać coś *[eggs]*

■ **sit around, sit about:** siedzieć bezczynnie

■ **sit down:** usiąść, siadać; **to ~ down to dinner** siąść do obiadu

■ **sit in:** *[observer]* być obecnym; **to ~ in on sth** brać udział w czymś *[meeting]*

■ **sit up:** usiąść, siadać *(z pozycji leżącej)*; **to be ~ting up** siedzieć; **~ up straight!** usiądź prosto!

sitcom /'sɪtkɒm/ *n* infml sitcom *m (serial komediowy nagrywany z udziałem publiczności)*

site /saɪt/ *n* ① (also **building** ~) (before building) teren *m* pod budowę; (during building) plac *m* budowy ② (land for specific activity) teren *m*; **caravan** ~ pole kempingowe ③ (archaeological) stanowisko *n*

sitting /'sɪtɪŋ/ *n* ① (meeting) posiedzenie *n*; (for artist, photographer) sesja *f* ② **to serve dinner in two ~s** podawać obiad w dwóch turach

sitting room *n* salon *m*, pokój *m* dzienny

sitting target *n* łatwy cel *m*

situate /'sɪtjʊeɪt, US 'sɪtʃʊeɪt/ *vt* u|sytuować, z|lokalizować *[building]*; **to be ~d** być usytuowanym, znajdować się

situation /ˌsɪtjʊ'eɪʃn, US ˌsɪtʃʊ-/ *n* sytuacja *f*; (of town) usytuowanie *n*, położenie *n*

sit-ups /'sɪtʌps/ *npl* skłony *m pl* w pozycji leżącej; brzuszki *m pl* infml

six /sɪks/ *n, adj* sześć

sixteen /ˌsɪk'sti:n/ **I** *n* szesnaście

II *adj* szesnaście

sixteenth /ˌsɪk'sti:nθ/ **I** *n* ① (in order) szesnast|y *m*, -a *f*, -e *n* ② (fraction) szesnasta *f* (część)

II *adj* szesnasty

III *adv [come]* na szesnastym miejscu

sixth /sɪksθ/ **I** *n* ① (in order) szóst|y *m*, -a *f*, -e *n* ② (fraction) szósta *f* (część)

II *adj* szósty

III *adv [finish]* na szóstym miejscu

sixth form *n* GB Sch (lower) ≈ przedostatnia klasa *f*; (upper) ≈ ostatnia klasa *f*

sixth form college *n* GB dwuletnia szkoła *f* przygotowująca do egzaminu dojrzałości

sixth sense *n* szósty zmysł *m*

sixties /'sɪkstɪz/ *npl* ① (era) **the ~** lata sześćdziesiąte ② (age) **to be in one's ~** być po sześćdziesiątce

sixtieth /'sɪkstɪəθ/ **I** *n* ① (in sequence) sześćdziesiąt|y *m*, -a *f*, -e *n* ② (fraction) sześćdziesiąta *f* (część)

II *adj* sześćdziesiąty

III *adv [come]* na sześćdziesiątym miejscu

sixty /'sɪkstɪ/ **I** *n* sześćdziesiąt

II *adj* sześćdziesiąt

size /saɪz/ *n* ① (of person) wymiary *m pl*; (of animal, egg) wielkość *f*; (of building, room) wielkość *f*, powierzchnia *f*; (of photo, carpet) rozmiar *m*; (of sum of money) wysokość *f*; (of cheque) wartość *f*; (of tree) wysokość *f*; (of problem) rozmiar *m*, skala *f* ② (of population, company) wielkość *f* ③ (of jacket, bra) rozmiar *m*; (of shirt collar, shoes) numer *m*, rozmiar *m*

■ **size up:** ocenić, -ać *[person, problem, situation]*; z|mierzyć wzrokiem *[room]*

IDIOMS **to cut sb down to ~** przytrzeć komuś nosa

sizeable GB, **sizable** US /'saɪzəbl/ *adj [house, field]* spory; *[sum of money]* pokaźny

sizzle /'sɪzl/ *vi* za|skwierczeć

skate /skeɪt/ **I** *n* ① (ice) łyżwa *f*; (roller) wrotka *f* ② Zool płaszczka *f*

II *vi* (on ice) ślizgać się, jeździć na łyżwach; (on roller skates) jeździć na wrotkach

skateboard /'skeɪtbɔ:d/ *n* deskorolka *f*

skateboarder /'skeɪtbɔ:də(r)/ *n* deskorolkarz *m*

skater /'skeɪtə(r)/ *n* (on ice) łyżwia|rz *m*, -rka *f*

skating /'skeɪtɪŋ/ *n* (on ice) łyżwiarstwo *n*

skating rink *n* (ice) lodowisko *n*

skeleton /'skelɪtn/ *n* szkielet *m*

skeleton key *n* klucz *m* uniwersalny

skeptic *n, adj* US = **sceptic**
skeptical *adj* US = **sceptical**
skepticism *n* US = **scepticism**
sketch /sketʃ/ **▯** *n* ▯ (drawing, draft) szkic *m*; (hasty outline) zarys *m*; **rough** ~ wstępny szkic ▢ (comic scene) skecz *m*
▯▯ *vt* ▯ (make drawing of) na|szkicować ▢ (describe briefly) przedstawić zarys (czegoś)
sketchbook /'sketʃbʊk/ *n* szkicownik *m*
sketchpad /'sketʃpæd/ *n* blok *m* rysunkowy
sketchy /'sketʃɪ/ *adj [knowledge]* wyrywkowy; *[information]* pobieżny; *[memory]* mglisty
skewer /'skju:ə(r)/ **▯** *n* (for kebab) szpikulec *m*; (for joint) rożen *m*
▯▯ *vt* nadzi|ać, -ewać na szpikulec/rożen
ski /ski:/ **▯** *n* narta *f*
▯▯ *vi* (as hobby) jeździć na nartach; (move on skis) jechać na nartach; **to** ~ **down the slope** zjechać w dół stoku
ski boot *n* but *m* narciarski
skid /skɪd/ **▯** *n* (of vehicle) poślizg *m*
▯▯ *vi [vehicle]* wpa|ść, -dać w poślizg
skier /'ski:ə(r)/ *n* narcia|rz *m*, -rka *f*
skiing /'ski:ɪŋ/ *n* narciarstwo *n*; **to go** ~ wybrać się na narty
skiing holiday *n* wyjazd *m* na narty
ski jumping *n* skoki *m pl* narciarskie
skilful GB, **skillful** US /'skɪlfl/ *adj [person]* sprawny; *[portrayal]* zręczny; **to be** ~ **at doing sth** umiejętnie coś robić
ski lift *n* wyciąg *m* narciarski
skill /skɪl/ **▯** *n* ▯ (flair) biegłość *f*, wprawa *f* (**at sth** w czymś); (physical) sprawność *f* ▢ (special ability) umiejętność *f*, sztuka *f*; (gift) talent *m*
▯▯ **skills** *npl* (training) **computer** ~**s** znajomość obsługi komputera; **management** ~**s** umiejętność zarządzania
skilled /skɪld/ *adj* ▯ (trained) *[worker]* wykwalifikowany; *[work]* wymagający kwalifikacji ▢ (talented) *[negotiator]* zręczny; *[actor]* zdolny
skim /skɪm/ **▯** *vt* ▯ (remove cream from) z|ebrać, -bierać śmietankę z (czegoś) *[milk]*; (remove fat from) z|ebrać, -bierać tłuszcz z (czegoś) *[soup]* ▢ (touch lightly) *[bird, insect]* mus|nąć, -kać *[surface]* ▣ **to** ~ **stones** puszczać kaczki
▯▯ *vi* ▯ *[bird, plane]* **to** ~ **across sth** lecieć or szybować tuż nad czymś ▢ *[reader]* **to** ~ **over** or **through sth** prze|jrzeć, -glądać coś; **he** ~**med over the facts** tylko prześlizgnął się po faktach
skim(med) milk *n* chude or odtłuszczone mleko *n*
skimp /skɪmp/ *vi* **to** ~ **on sth** skąpić czegoś *[effort]*; oszczędzać na czymś *[food]*
skimpy /'skɪmpɪ/ *adj [portion, income]* skąpy; *[garment]* kusy
skin /skɪn/ **▯** *n* skóra *f*; (of fruit) skórka *f*; (of onion) łupina *f*

▯▯ *vt* ▯ Culin ob|edrzeć, -dzierać ze skóry *[animal]*; ob|rać, -ierać, zd|jąć, -ejmować skórkę z (czegoś) *[tomato]* ▢ (graze) **to** ~ **one's knee** obetrzeć (sobie) kolano
⟨IDIOMS⟩ **to have a thick** ~ być gruboskórnym; **to be** or **get soaked to the** ~ przemoknąć do suchej nitki; **by the** ~ **of one's teeth** cudem, z trudem
skin-deep /ˌskɪn'diːp/ *adj* powierzchowny
skin diving *n* płetwonurkowanie *n*
skinhead /'skɪnhed/ *n* GB skinhead *m*, skin *m* infml
skinny /'skɪnɪ/ *adj* infml chudy
skint /skɪnt/ *adj* GB infml *[person]* spłukany infml
skintight /'skɪntaɪt/ *adj* opięty
skip /skɪp/ **▯** *n* ▯ (jump) podskok *m* ▢ GB (container) kontener *m* na gruz
▯▯ *vt* opu|ścić, -szczać *[meeting, lunch, school]*
▯▯▯ *vi* ▯ (jump) podsk|oczyć, -akiwać ▢ (with rope) skakać przez skakankę
ski pants *npl* spodnie *plt* narciarskie
ski pass *n* karnet *m* na wyciągi
skipper /'skɪpə(r)/ *n* (of merchant ship, fishing boat) szyper *m*; (of yacht) kapitan *m*
skipping rope *n* skakanka *f*
ski resort *n* ośrodek *m* narciarski
skirt /skɜːt/ **▯** *n* spódnica *f*
▯▯ *vt [road, path]* okrążać *[wood, city]*; omi|nąć, -jać *[problem]*
skirting board *n* listwa *f* przypodłogowa
ski slope *n* stok *m* narciarski
ski suit *n* kombinezon *m* narciarski
skittle /'skɪtl/ **▯** *n* kręgiel *m*
▯▯ **skittles** *npl* (gra w) kręgle *plt*
skive /skaɪv/ GB infml *vt* (also ~ **off**) (shirk) wymig|ać, -iwać się od (czegoś); (be absent from) z|erwać, -rywać się z (czegoś) infml; (leave early) ur|wać, -ywać się z (czegoś) infml
skulk /skʌlk/ *vi* skradać się; **to** ~ **out** wykraść się na zewnątrz; **to** ~ **off** czmychnąć
skull /skʌl/ *n* czaszka *f*
skunk /skʌŋk/ *n* skunks *m*
sky /skaɪ/ *n* niebo *n*; **in the** ~ na niebie
skydiving /'skaɪdaɪvɪŋ/ *n* akrobacje *f pl* spadochronowe
sky-high /ˌskaɪ'haɪ/ *adj [prices, rates]* astronomiczny, niebotyczny
skyjacker /'skaɪdʒækə(r)/ *n* infml porywacz *m*, -ka *f* (samolotu)
skylight /'skaɪlaɪt/ *n* (window) świetlik *m*
skyline /'skaɪlaɪn/ *n* (in countryside) linia *f* horyzontu; (in city) linia *f* dachów (na tle nieba)
skyscraper /'skaɪskreɪpə(r)/ *n* drapacz *m* chmur
slab /slæb/ *n* (of stone, concrete) płyta *f*; (of cake, cheese, meat) kawał *m*; (of bread) pajda *f* infml; **a** ~ **of chocolate** tabliczka czekolady
slack /slæk/ **▯** *n* (in rope, cable) luz *m*

II adj 1 *[rope, cable]* luźny, poluzowany; *[skin, muscle]* zwiotczały 2 *[worker, work]* niedbały; *[student]* niezbyt pilny 3 *[period]* martwy; *[demand, sales]* niewielki

III vi (be careless) **to ~ on the job** opuszczać się w pracy

■ **slack off**: *[business, trade]* zw|olnić, -alniać tempo; *[rain]* usta|ć, -wać

slacken /'slækən/ **I** vt poluzow|ać, -ywać *[rope]*; popu|ścić, -szczać *[reins]*; zw|olnić, -alniać *[hold]*; **to ~ one's pace** zwolnić kroku

II vi *[rope, nut]* obluzow|ać, -ywać się; *[pressure]* zmniejsz|yć, -ać się; *[speed, sales]* zmniejsz|yć, -ać się; *[interest]* o|słabnąć; *[rain]* usta|ć, -wać

slalom /'slɑːləm/ n slalom m

slam /slæm/ **I** vt trzas|nąć, -kać (czymś) *[door]*; **to ~ sth shut** zatrzasnąć coś; **to ~ the door in sb's face** zatrzasnąć komuś drzwi przed nosem

II vi *[door]* trzas|nąć, -kać (**against sth** o coś); **to ~ shut** zatrzasnąć się

slander /'slɑːndə(r), US 'slæn-/ n oszczerstwo n; (in law) pomówienie n; **to sue sb for ~** wytoczyć komuś proces o zniesławienie

slang /slæŋ/ n slang m; **prison ~** gwara więzienna

slangy /'slæŋɪ/ adj infml slangowy

slant /slɑːnt, US slænt/ **I** n 1 (perspective) spojrzenie n (**on sth** na coś) 2 (slope) pochyłość f 3 (bias) skrzywienie n

II vi *[floor, handwriting]* być pochyłym; *[painting]* krzywo wisieć

III **slanting** prp adj *[roof]* pochyły; **~ing eyes** skośne oczy

slap /slæp/ **I** n (on back, leg) klepnięcie n; (on buttocks) klaps m; **it was a real ~ in the face for him** fig to był dla niego prawdziwy policzek fig

II vt trzepnąć *[person, animal]*; **to ~ sb on the back** poklepać kogoś po plecach; **to ~ sb in the face** uderzyć kogoś w twarz

slap bang /ˌslæp'bæŋ/ adv infml **he ran ~ into the wall** łupnął prosto w ścianę infml; **~ in the middle of sth** w samym środku czegoś

slapdash /'slæpdæʃ/ adj infml *[person]* niedbały; *[work]* byle jaki; **in a ~ way** byle jak

slash /slæʃ/ **I** n 1 (wound) cięcie n (**on sth** na czymś) 2 (in fabric, seat, tyre, painting) rozcięcie n 3 (in printing) ukośnik m

II vt 1 rozci|ąć, -nać *[cheek]*; po|ciąć *[painting, fabric]*; pod|erżnąć, -rzynać *[throat]*; **to ~ one's wrists** podciąć sobie żyły 2 (reduce) obniż|yć, -ać *[price, taxes, spending]*

slat /slæt/ n (of shutter, blind, floor) listwa f

slate /sleɪt/ **I** n (rock) łupek m; (for writing on) tabliczka f

II vt 1 pokry|ć, -wać łupkiem *[roof]* 2 GB infml (criticize) z|mieszać z błotem (**for sth** za coś)

IDIOMS **to wipe the ~ clean** zapomnieć o dawnych urazach

slaughter /'slɔːtə(r)/ **I** n 1 (in butchery) ubój m 2 (massacre) masakra f, rzeź f

II vt 1 (in butchery) ubi|ć, -jać 2 (massacre) wymordować 3 Sport infml rozgr|omić, -amiać

slaughterhouse /'slɔːtəhaʊs/ n rzeźnia f

Slav /slɑːv, US slæv/ **I** n Słowian|in m, -ka f **II** adj słowiański

slave /sleɪv/ **I** n niewolni|k m, -ca f

II vi (also **~ away**) tyrać, harować infml

slaver /'slævə(r)/ vi ślinić się

slavery /'sleɪvərɪ/ n (condition) niewola f; (system) niewolnictwo n

slaw /slɔː/ n US = **coleslaw**

slay /sleɪ/ vt zabi|ć, -jać *[dragon, enemy]*

sleaze /sliːz/ n infml brud m moralny

sleazy /'sliːzɪ/ adj infml *[place, hotel, café]* obskurny; *[character]* podejrzany, ciemny; *[story, aspect]* plugawy

sled /sled/, **sledge** /sledʒ/ GB **I** n sanie plt; (for children) sanki plt

II vi zjeżdżać na sankach

sledgehammer /'sledʒhæmə(r)/ n młot m dwuręczny

sleek /sliːk/ adj 1 *[hair]* lśniący; **~ animal** zwierzę o lśniącej sierści 2 *[shape]* foremny; *[figure]* kształtny; *[car]* elegancki

sleep /sliːp/ **I** n sen m; **to go to ~** zasnąć; **to go back to ~** ponownie zasnąć; **to send** or **put sb to ~** uśpić kogoś; **to have a ~** przespać się; **my leg has gone to ~** infml zdrętwiała mi noga; **to put an animal to ~** uśpić zwierzę

II vi spać; **to ~ at a friend's house** przenocować or spać u znajomego

■ **sleep in**: (stay in bed late) późno wsta|ć, -wać; (oversleep) zaspać

■ **sleep on**: **~ on sth** przespać się z (czymś) fig *[problem, decision]*

IDIOMS **to ~ like a log** or **top** spać jak zabity, spać jak suseł

sleeping bag n śpiwór m

sleeping car n wagon m sypialny

sleeping pill n tabletka f nasenna

sleepless /'sliːplɪs/ adj *[night, hours]* bezsenny

sleepwalk /'sliːpwɔːk/ vi chodzić we śnie

sleepy /'sliːpɪ/ adj *[person, animal]* śpiący, senny; *[voice, town]* senny; **I suddenly felt terribly ~** nagle poczułem straszną senność; **to make sb ~** *[fresh air, wine]* działać usypiająco na kogoś

sleet /sliːt/ n deszcz m ze śniegiem

sleeve /sliːv/ n 1 (of garment) rękaw m 2 (of record) okładka f; (of CD) pudełko n 3 Tech tuleja f; (for joining two tubes) złączka f rurowa

IDIOMS **to have something up one's ~** mieć coś w zanadrzu

sleeveless /'sliːvlɪs/ adj bez rękawów

sleigh /sleɪ/ n sanie plt

sleight of hand /ˌslaɪtəvˈhænd/ n ① (dexterity) zręczne ręce f pl ② (trick) sztuczka f

slender /ˈslendə(r)/ adj ① [person] szczupły; [neck] smukły; [waist] cienki ② [income, means] skromny, szczupły

sleuth /sluːθ/ n detektyw m

slew /sluː/ vi [mast] obrócić się; **the car ~ed from side to side** samochodem rzucało na wszystkie strony

slice /slaɪs/ ❶ n ① (of bread) kromka f; (of tart, cake) kawałek m; (of meat) plaster m; (of cheese, lemon, cucumber) plasterek m ② (of income, profits, territory) część f ③ (utensil) łopatka f
❷ vt ① po|kroić (w kromki) [loaf]; po|kroić (w plastry) [roast]; po|kroić (w plasterki) [lemon, sausage, onion] ② przeci|ąć, -nać [air] ③ Sport podci|ąć, -nać [ball]
❸ vi **to ~ through sth** ciąć coś [water, air]; wejść w coś [timber, meat]

sliced bread n chleb m pokrojony

slick /slɪk/ ❶ n (also **oil ~**) plama f ropy
❷ adj ① [production] zgrabny, zręczny; [operation] zręcznie przeprowadzony ② (superficial) płytki fig ③ [salesman] wygadany, sprytny; [answer] gładki, zgrabny ④ (slippery) [road, surface] śliski; [hair] przylizany

slide /slaɪd/ ❶ n ① (in playground) zjeżdżalnia f ② (photographic) slajd m, przezrocze n ③ (microscope plate) szkiełko n ④ GB (also **hair ~**) wsuwka f ⑤ (decline) spadek m; **a ~ in sth** spadek czegoś
❷ vt **to ~ sth forward/back** przesunąć coś do przodu/do tyłu
❸ vi ① [person] pośliznąć się, ślizgać się; [car] wpa|ść, -dać w poślizg; **the drawer ~s in and out** szuflada wsuwa się i wysuwa ② [prices, shares] spa|ść, -dać; **to let sth ~** infml zaniedbywać coś

slide projector n rzutnik m

slide rule GB, **slide ruler** US n suwak m logarytmiczny

slide show n pokaz m slajdów; (at lecture) demonstracja f przezroczy

sliding /ˈslaɪdɪŋ/ adj [door, roof] rozsuwany

sliding scale n skala f ruchoma

slight /slaɪt/ ❶ n afront m; **a ~ on sb** obraza dla kogoś
❷ adj [change, risk, danger] niewielki, nieznaczny; [hesitation] lekki, krótki; [pause] krótki; [figure, person] drobny; **not to have the ~est difficulty** nie mieć najmniejszych trudności
❸ vt ① (offend) ura|zić, -żać [person] ② US (neglect) zaniedb|ać, -ywać

slightly /ˈslaɪtlɪ/ adv [change] nieznacznie, nieco; [embarrassed, uneasy] nieco, trochę; **~ built** drobnej budowy

slim /slɪm/ ❶ adj [person, figure] szczupły; [book, volume] cienki; [watch, calculator] płaski; **to get ~** zeszczupleć
❷ vi odchudzać się; **I'm ~ming** odchudzam się

slime /slaɪm/ n maź f; (on river bed) muł m, szlam m; (of slug, snail) śluz m

sling /slɪŋ/ ❶ n ① (weapon) proca f ② Med temblak m; (for carrying baby) nosidełko n; (for carrying a load) pas m
❷ vt cis|nąć, -kać, miotać [object, insult]

slip /slɪp/ ❶ n ① (error) pomyłka f; **a ~ of the tongue** przejęzyczenie ② (receipt) paragon m; **a salary ~** pasek wypłaty; **a ~ of paper** kawałek papieru ③ (false step) potknięcie n ④ (petticoat) (full) halka f; (half) półhalka f
❷ vt ① **to ~ a note into sth** wsunąć liścik do czegoś; **she ~ped the shirt over her head** (put on) wciągnęła bluzkę przez głowę; (take off) ściągnęła bluzkę przez głowę ② [dog] z|rywać, -erwać się z (czegoś) [leash]; [boat] zerwać się z (czegoś) [moorings]; **it had ~ped my mind** wyleciało mi to z głowy; **to let ~ an opportunity (to do sth)** przepuścić okazję (zrobienia czegoś); **he let ~ a rude remark** wyrwała mu się nieuprzejma uwaga ③ Med **he ~ped a disc** wyskoczył mu dysk
❸ vi ① **to ~ into sth** wł|ożyć, -kładać coś [dress]; zapa|ść, -dać w coś [coma] ② **to ~ into/out of sth** wśliznąć się do czegoś/wymknąć się z czegoś [building, room] ③ [person] pośliznąć się; [vehicle] wpa|ść, -dać w poślizg; [knife, pen] ześliznąć się; [load] zsu|nąć, -wać się; **to ~ through sb's fingers** [opportunity] wymknąć się komuś ④ [rope, clutch] pu|ścić, -szczać; [wheel] ślizgać się

slipknot /ˈslɪpnɒt/ n węzeł m ruchomy

slip-on (shoe) /ˌslɪpɒn(ˈʃuː)/ n mokasyn m

slipped disc n wypadnięcie n dysku

slipper /ˈslɪpə(r)/ n pantofel m ranny or domowy

slippery /ˈslɪpərɪ/ adj [road] śliski

slip road n (for entering motorway) wjazd m; (for leaving motorway) zjazd m

slipshod /ˈslɪpʃɒd/ adj [person, worker] niedbały; [appearance] niechlujny

slip-up /ˈslɪpʌp/ n infml potknięcie n

slit /slɪt/ ❶ n szpara f; **to make a ~ in sth** naciąć coś
❷ adj **~ eyes** oczy jak szparki; **~ skirt** spódnica z rozcięciem
❸ vt (cut open) rozci|ąć, -nać; **to ~ sb's throat** poderżnąć komuś gardło; **to ~ one's wrists** podciąć sobie żyły

slither /ˈslɪðə(r)/ vi [person] ślizgać się; [snake] pełzać

sliver /ˈslɪvə(r)/ n (of glass) okruch m; (of soap) resztka f; (of food) kawałeczek m

slob /slɒb/ n infml (slovenly) flejtuch m infml; (lazy) nierób m infml

slog /slɒg/ vi infml (also **~ away**) mozolić się, harować infml

slop /slɒp/ ❶ vt rozl|ać, -ewać [liquid]
❷ vi (also **~ over**) [liquid] przel|ać, -ewać się

slope /sləʊp/ **Ⅰ** *n* (incline) nachylenie *n*; (hillside) stok *m*, zbocze *n*

Ⅱ *vi [ground, roof]* opadać (**towards sth** w kierunku czegoś); **his handwriting ~s** on ma pochyłe pismo

sloping /'sləʊpɪŋ/ *adj [ground]* nachylony; *[handwriting]* pochyły; *[ceiling]* skośny; *[roof]* spadzisty

sloppy /'slɒpɪ/ *adj* infml [1] *[work]* byle jaki; *[management]* nieudolny [2] (sentimental) *[film]* ckliwy

slot /slɒt/ **Ⅰ** *n* [1] (for coin, ticket, letters) otwór *m* [2] (in timetable) okienko *n*

Ⅱ *vt* **to ~ sth into a machine** wpasować coś do otworu maszyny

Ⅲ *vi* **to ~ into** *[coin, piece]* pasować do (czegoś); **to ~ into place** or **position** zaskoczyć

■ **slot together**: pasować do siebie

sloth /sləʊθ/ *n* Zool leniwiec *m*

slot machine *n* (game) automat *m* do gier; (for vending) automat *m* (*z papierosami, napojami*)

slouch /slaʊtʃ/ *vi* z|garbić się

Slovakia /slə'vækɪə/ *prn* Słowacja *f*

Slovenia /slə'viːnɪə/ *prn* Słowenia *f*

slovenly /'slʌvnlɪ/ *adj* niechlujny

slow /sləʊ/ **Ⅰ** *adj* [1] (po)wolny; **to be ~ in doing sth** wolno coś robić [2] *[market]* w zastoju; *[economic growth]* (po)wolny [3] (intellectually unresponsive) mało pojętny [4] **to be (10 minutes) ~** *[clock, watch]* spóźniać się (10 minut)

Ⅱ *adv* powoli

Ⅲ *vt, vi* (also **~ down**) zw|olnić, -alniać

slowly /'sləʊlɪ/ *adv* wolno, powoli

slow motion *n* zwolnione tempo *n*; **in ~** w zwolnionym tempie

slow-moving /ˌsləʊ'muːvɪŋ/ *adj* powolny

sludge /slʌdʒ/ *n* [1] (also **sewage ~**) osad *m* kanalizacyjny [2] (mud) muł *m*, osad *m*

slug /slʌg/ *n* ślimak *m* nagi

sluggish /'slʌgɪʃ/ *adj* [1] *[person]* niemrawy; *[circulation]* spowolniony [2] *[market, trade]* w zastoju

sluice /sluːs/ *n* [1] (also **~ gate**) wrota *plt* śluzy [2] (also **~ way**) śluza *f*

slum /slʌm/ *n* [1] (area) dzielnica *f* nędzy; **the ~s** slumsy [2] infml (messy house, room) chlew *m* infml fig

slumber /'slʌmbə(r)/ **Ⅰ** *n* sen *m*

Ⅱ *vi* spać

slump /slʌmp/ **Ⅰ** *n* (in trade, prices) gwałtowny spadek *m* (**in sth** czegoś)

Ⅱ *vi* [1] *[prices, trade, popularity]* gwałtownie spa|ść, -dać [2] *[business, economy]* zna|leźć, -jdować się w zastoju [3] *[person, body]* osu|nąć, -wać się

slur /slɜː(r)/ **Ⅰ** *n* [1] (in speech) mamrotanie *n* [2] (aspersion) oszczerstwo *n* [3] Mus legato *n*

Ⅱ *vi* **his speech began to ~** zaczął mamrotać or bełkotać niezrozumiale

Ⅲ **slurred** *pp adj [voice, speech]* bełkotliwy

slush /slʌʃ/ *n* (melted snow) breja *f*

slush fund *n* fundusz *m* łapówkowy

sly /slaɪ/ *adj* (cunning) przebiegły; (secretive) chytry

IDIOMS: **on the ~** infml ukradkiem, po cichu

smack /smæk/ **Ⅰ** *n* klaps *m*; (on face) policzek *m*

Ⅱ *vt* trzas|nąć, -kać (czymś) *[object]* (**on sth/ against sth** w coś/o coś); uderz|yć, -ać (czymś), da|ć, -wać klapsa (komuś) *[child]*

Ⅲ *vi* **to ~ of** trącić czymś *[irony]*

small /smɔːl/ **Ⅰ** *n* **the ~ of the back** krzyż

Ⅱ *adj* [1] mały; *[quantity, amount]* niewielki; **~ wonder he left!** nic dziwnego, że wyjechał! [2] (humiliated) **to feel ~** czuć się poniżonym; **to make sb feel ~** poniżyć kogoś

Ⅲ *adv [write]* drobnym pismem

small ad *n* GB ogłoszenie *n* drobne

small change *n* drobne *plt*

small talk *n* rozmowa *f* towarzyska; **to make ~** prowadzić rozmowę (towarzyską)

smart /smɑːt/ **Ⅰ** *adj* [1] (elegant) elegancki [2] (intelligent) *[child]* bystry; *[politician]* sprytny [3] (stinging) *[blow]* silny; *[rebuke]* bolesny; **to walk at a ~ pace** iść energicznym or szybkim krokiem [4] Comput inteligentny

Ⅱ *vi [cut, cheeks]* piec, szczypać

smart bomb *n* inteligentna bomba *f*

smart card *n* karta *f* chipowa

smarten /'smɑːtn/ *vt*

■ **smarten up**: poprawi|ć, -ać wygląd (czegoś) *[town, area]*; **to ~ oneself up** odszykować się

smash /smæʃ/ **Ⅰ** *n* [1] (of glass) brzęk *m*; (of vehicle) huk *m* [2] infml (also **~-up**) zderzenie *n*, kolizja *f* [3] infml (also **~ hit**) wielki przebój *m* [4] (in tennis) smecz *m*

Ⅱ *vt* [1] rozbi|ć, -jać *[glass, car]*; (more violently) roztrzask|ać, -iwać; rozwal|ić, -ać infml [2] (destroy) rozbi|ć, -jać *[drugs ring]*; rozn|ieść, -osić w puch *[opponent]* [3] Sport **to ~ the ball** ściąć piłkę

Ⅲ *vi* rozbi|ć, -jać się, roztrzask|ać, -iwać się

smashing /'smæʃɪŋ/ *adj* GB infml fantastyczny infml

smattering /'smætərɪŋ/ *n* powierzchowna znajomość *f* (**of sth** czegoś); **to have a ~ of French** znać parę słów po francusku

smear /smɪə(r)/ **Ⅰ** *n* [1] (mark) plama *f* [2] (defamation) oszczerstwo *n* [3] Med (also **~ test**) wymaz *m*

Ⅱ *vt* [1] (dirty) usmarować; **the baby's face was ~ed with jam** dziecko miało buzię usmarowaną dżemem [2] (spread) rozsmarow|ać, -ywać *[butter, lotion]*; rozmaz|ać, -ywać *[ink]*

Ⅲ *vi [ink, paint, lipstick]* rozmaz|ać, -ywać się

smell /smel/ **Ⅰ** *n* [1] (odour) zapach *m*; (unpleasant) smród *m* [2] (sense) węch *m*, powonienie *n*

Ⅱ *vt* (detect) po|czuć zapach (czegoś); (sniff deliberately) po|wąchać; **can you ~ burning?** czy czujesz zapach spalenizny?

Ⅲ *vi* pachnieć (**of sth** czymś); (unpleasantly) śmierdzieć (**of sth** czymś); **his breath ~s** czuć mu z ust

smelling salts *npl* sole *plt* trzeźwiące

smelly /'smelɪ/ adj śmierdzący

smile /smaɪl/ **I** n uśmiech m

II vi uśmiech|nąć, -ać się (**at sb** do kogoś)

■ **smile on**: ~ **on** [**sb/sth**] [luck, fortune] uśmiech|nąć, -ać się do (kogoś); [weather, person] sprzyjać (komuś)

smirk /smɜːk/ **I** n uśmieszek m

II vi (in a self-satisfied way) uśmiech|nąć, -ać się z wyższością; (knowingly) uśmiech|nąć, -ać się znacząco

smithereens /ˌsmɪðə'riːnz/ npl kawałeczki m pl; **in** ~ w kawałeczkach; **to smash sth to** ~ rozbić coś w drobny mak

smock /smɒk/ n bluzka f, koszula f

smog /smɒg/ n smog m

smoke /sməʊk/ **I** n dym m

II vt [1] palić [pipe] [2] u|wędzić [fish]

III vi (use tobacco) palić

IV **smoked** pp adj [food] wędzony

smoke alarm n czujnik m dymu

smoker /'sməʊkə(r)/ n palacz m, -ka f

smoke screen n Mil zasłona f dymna also fig

smoking /'sməʊkɪŋ/ **I** n palenie n; **to give up** ~ rzucić palenie; **'no** ~' „zakaz palenia"

II adj [compartment, section] dla palących

smoking-related /'sməʊkɪŋrɪleɪtɪd/ adj [disease] związany z paleniem tytoniu

smoky /'sməʊkɪ/ adj [room] zadymiony; [cheese, bacon] wędzony

smooth /smuːð/ **I** adj [1] (even) gładki; [sea] spokojny; [breathing] regularny; [movement] płynny [2] (pleasant) [taste] łagodny; [whisky, wine] gładki [3] (suave) [person, appearance, manners] gładki; ~ **operator** bajerant infml

II vt [1] (flatten out) wyrówn|ać, -ywać; (get creases out of) wygładz|ić, -ać [fabric] [2] ułatwi|ć, -ać [process, transition]

■ **smooth over**: ~ **over** [**sth**] zmniejsz|yć, -ać [differences]; usu|nąć, -wać [difficulties, problems]; **to** ~ **things over** załagodzić sprawę

smooth-running adj [organization] dobrze funkcjonujący; [event] gładko przebiegający

smother /'smʌðə(r)/ vt u|dusić [person]; z|dławić [opposition]; s|tłumić [laughter]

smoulder GB, **smolder** US /'sməʊldə(r)/ vi tlić się; **he ~ed with jealousy** zżerała go zazdrość

smudge /smʌdʒ/ **I** n plama f

II vt rozmaz|ać, -ywać [paint, make-up]; po|plamić [paper, cloth]

III vi [paint, make-up] rozmaz|ać, -ywać się

smug /smʌg/ adj zadowolony z siebie

smuggle /'smʌgl/ vt przemyc|ić, -ać [alcohol, drugs] (**into sth** do czegoś); **to** ~ **sb into Britain** nielegalnie wwieźć kogoś do Wielkiej Brytanii

smuggler /'smʌglə(r)/ n przemytni|k m, -czka f

smuggling /'smʌglɪŋ/ n przemyt m

smutty /'smʌtɪ/ adj [1] (crude) sprośny [2] (dirty) [face] umorusany sadzą

snack /snæk/ **I** n [1] (small meal) przekąska f; **to have a** ~ przekąsić coś [2] (crisps, peanuts) zakąska f

II vi podjadać

snag /snæg/ n [1] (hitch) szkopuł m (**in sth** w czymś) [2] (tear) rozdarcie n

snail /sneɪl/ n ślimak m

snail mail n infml poczta f (tradycyjna)

snake /sneɪk/ n wąż m

snap /snæp/ **I** n [1] (of branch, elastic) trzask m; (of fingers) pstryknięcie n [2] infml (photograph) fotka f infml [3] (card game) ≈ wojna f

II adj [decision, judgment] pośpieszny

III vt [1] pstryk|nąć, -ać (czymś) [fingers]; kłap|nąć, -ać (czymś) [jaws]; strzel|ić, -ać (czymś) [elastic] [2] (break) z|łamać [branch] [3] (say crossly) warknąć

IV vi [1] (break) złamać się [2] (speak sharply) warczeć

■ **snap at**: [1] (speak sharply) war|knąć, -czeć na (kogoś) [2] [dog] chwy|cić, -tać zębami

■ **snap up**: rozchwyt|ać, -ywać [bargains]

snappy /'snæpɪ/ adj [reply] natychmiastowy; [slogan] chwytliwy; [phrase] zgrabny; [clothes] szykowny

snapshot /'snæpʃɒt/ n zdjęcie n

snare /sneə(r)/ **I** n wnyki plt, sidła plt

II vt z|łapać [animal]; zastawi|ić, -ać sidła na (kogoś) [person]

snarl /snɑːl/ vi [animal, person] war|knąć, -czeć (**at sb** na kogoś)

snarl-up /'snɑːlʌp/ n (in traffic, distribution network) zator m

snatch /snætʃ/ **I** n [1] (of conversation) strzęp m; (of poem, tune) urywek m [2] (theft) kradzież f

II vt [1] (grab) (s)chwycić [book, key]; **to** ~ **sth from sb** zabrać or odebrać coś komuś [2] infml (steal) wyr|wać, -ywać [handbag] (**from sb** komuś)

sneak /sniːk/ vi **to** ~ **out** wymknąć się; **to** ~ **in** wkraść się; **to** ~ **up on sb** podkraść się do kogoś

sneaker /'sniːkə(r)/ n US tenisówka f

sneaking /'sniːkɪŋ/ adj **I have a** ~ **suspicion that...** coś mi się zdaje, że...

sneaky /'sniːkɪ/ adj przebiegły

sneer /snɪə(r)/ **I** n (szyderczy) uśmieszek m

II vi (smile) uśmiech|nąć, -ać się szyderczo; (speak) szydzić (**at sb** z kogoś)

sneeze /sniːz/ **I** n kichnięcie n

II vi kich|nąć, -ać

snide /snaɪd/ adj złośliwy

sniff /snɪf/ **I** n pociągnięcie n nosem

II vt [dog] obwąch|ać, -iwać; [person] wciąg|nąć, -ać [air]; po|wąchać [food]; wąchać [glue]

III vi [person] pociąg|nąć, -ać nosem; [dog] węszyć

snigger /'snɪgə(r)/ **I** n chichot m

II vi podśmiewać się (**at sb/sth** z kogoś/czegoś)

snip /snɪp/ *vt* przeci|ąć, -nać *[fabric, paper]*; przy-ci|ąć, -nać *[hedge]*

■ **snip off**: obci|ąć, -nać *[nail]*

sniper /'snaɪpə(r)/ *n* strzelec *m* wyborowy

snippet /'snɪpɪt/ *n* (of fabric) ścinek *m*; (of text, music) urywek *m*; (of conversation, information) strzęp *m*

snivel /'snɪvl/ *vi* pochlipywać

snob /snɒb/ *n* snob *m*, -ka *f*

snobbery /'snɒbərɪ/ *n* snobizm *m*

snobbish /'snɒbɪʃ/ *adj* snobistyczny

snooker /'snuːkə(r)/ **Ⅰ** *n* (game) snooker *m*

Ⅱ *vt* Sport (in snooker) za|blokować *[opponent]*; fig uniemożliwi|ć, -ać wykonanie ruchu (komuś)

snoop /snuːp/ infml **Ⅰ** *n* szpicel *m*

Ⅱ *vi* **to ~ on sb** szpiegować kogoś

■ **snoop around**: myszkować (**in sth** w czymś)

snooze /snuːz/ infml **Ⅰ** *n* drzemka *f*

Ⅱ *vi* zdrzemnąć się

snore /snɔː(r)/ **Ⅰ** *n* chrapanie *n*

Ⅱ *vi* za|chrapać

snorkel /'snɔːkl/ *n* (for diver) rurka *f*

snorkelling GB, **snorkeling** US /'snɔːklɪŋ/ *n* nurkowanie *n* z rurką

snort /snɔːt/ **Ⅰ** *vt* niuchać infml *[drug]*

Ⅱ *vi [person]* prych|nąć, -ać; *[horse]* parsk|nąć, -ać; *[pig]* chrząk|nąć, -ać

snout /snaʊt/ *n* (of most animals) pysk *m*; (of pig) ryj *m*

snow /snəʊ/ **Ⅰ** *n* śnieg *m*

Ⅱ *v impers* **it's ~ing** pada śnieg

snowball /'snəʊbɔːl/ **Ⅰ** *n* śnieżka *f*

Ⅱ *vi [profits]* wzr|osnąć, -astać lawinowo; *[plan]* po|toczyć się lawinowo

snowboard /'snəʊbɔːd/ **Ⅰ** *n* snowboard *m*

Ⅱ *vi* jeździć na snowboardzie

snowdrift /'snəʊdrɪft/ *n* zaspa *f*

snowdrop /'snəʊdrɒp/ *n* przebiśnieg *m*

snowfall /'snəʊfɔːl/ *n* opad *m* śniegu

snowflake /'snəʊfleɪk/ *n* płatek *m* śniegu

snowman /'snəʊmæn/ *n* bałwan *m* śniegowy

snowmobile /'snəʊməbiːl/ *n* sanie *plt* motorowe

snow plough GB, **snow plow** US *n* pług *m* śnieżny

snowshoe /'snəʊʃuː/ *n* rakieta *f* śnieżna

snub /snʌb/ **Ⅰ** *n* afront *m*

Ⅱ *vt* z|robić afront (komuś), z|lekceważyć *[person]*; wzgardzić (czymś) *[offer]*

snub-nosed /ˌsnʌb'nəʊzd/ *adj* z zadartym nosem

snuff /snʌf/ *n* tabaka *f*

snug /snʌg/ *adj [room, atmosphere]* przytulny; *[bed]* ciepły i przytulny

snuggle /'snʌgl/ *vi* przytul|ić, -ać się

so /səʊ/ **Ⅰ** *adv* ⒈ (so very) tak, taki; **he's so fat he can't get in** jest tak *or* tak gruby, że się nie mieści ⒉ (in such a way) tak; **so arranged/worded that...** tak zorganizowany/sformułowany, że...; **and so on and so forth** i tak dalej, i tak dalej ⒊ (for that reason) więc; **so it was that...** tak więc...; **she was**

young and so lacked experience była młoda, więc brakowało jej doświadczenia ⒋ (true) **is that so?** naprawdę?; **if (that's) so...** skoro tak,... ⒌ (also) również, też; **so is she** ona również *or* też; **if they accept, so do I** jeśli się zgodzą, to ja również *or* też się zgodzę ⒍ infml (thereabouts) **20 or so** 20 czy coś koło tego; **a year or so ago** mniej więcej rok temu ⒎ (other uses) **so that's the reason** (a) więc to dlatego; **so you're going, are you?** więc idziesz, tak?; **he dived and as he did so...** skoczył, a wtedy...; **I believe so** tak sądzę; **I'm afraid so** obawiam się, że tak; **so it would appear** na to by wyglądało; **so to speak** że tak powiem; **I told you so** mówiłem ci; **so I see** właśnie widzę; **I don't think so** nie sądzę; **who says so?** kto tak twierdzi?; **only more so** tyle że bardziej; **'it's broken' – 'so it is'** „to jest zepsute" – „rzeczywiście"

Ⅱ so (that) *conj phr* (in order that) (tak) żeby; **she fixed the party for 8 so that he could come** zaprosiła wszystkich na ósmą, (tak) żeby mógł przyjść

Ⅲ so as *conj phr* (tak) żeby; **so as to attract attention** żeby przyciągnąć uwagę

Ⅳ so much *adv phr*, *pron phr* **so much money** tyle pieniędzy; **so many friends** tylu przyjaciół; **I can pay so much** tyle mogę zapłacić; **I like it so much that...** tak bardzo to lubię, że...; **thank you so much!** bardzo dziękuję!

‹IDIOMS› **so much the better** tym lepiej; **so so** (as adjective) taki sobie; (as adverb) tak sobie

soak /səʊk/ **Ⅰ** *vt* ⒈ z|moczyć *[person, clothes]*; **to get ~ed** przemoknąć ⒉ nam|oczyć, -aczać *[clothes, dried foodstuff]*

Ⅱ *vi* ⒈ *[clothes, person]* moczyć się ⒉ **to ~ into sth** *[liquid]* wsiąknąć w coś *[earth, paper]*; **to ~ through sth** *[blood]* przesiąknąć przez coś *[bandages]*

Ⅲ soaked *pp adj* przemoczony; **to be ~ed to the skin** być przemokniętym do suchej nitki

■ **soak up**: ¶ **~ [sth] up, ~ up [sth]** *[earth, sponge]* wchł|onąć, -aniać ¶ **~ up [sth]** napawać się (czymś) *[atmosphere]*; **to ~ up the sun** chłonąć słońce

soaking /'səʊkɪŋ/ *adj* **~ wet** *[person]* całkowicie przemoczony; *[hair]* całkiem mokry

soap /səʊp/ *n* mydło *n*; **a bar of ~** kostka mydła

soap opera *n* telenowela *f*, opera *f* mydlana

soap powder *n* proszek *m* mydlany

soar /sɔː(r)/ *vi* ⒈ *[bird, plane, ball]* po|szybować w górę ⒉ (glide) unosić się ⒊ *[popularity]* (gwałtownie) wzr|osnąć, -astać; *[price, temperature, costs]* podsk|oczyć, -akiwać; *[hopes]* odży|ć, -wać ⒋ *[tower, cliffs]* wznosić się; *[sound]* narastać

soaring /'sɔːrɪŋ/ *adj [inflation, prices, temperature]* gwałtownie rosnący; *[hopes]* odżywający; *[skyscraper]* strzelisty

sob /sɒb/ **I** *n* szloch *m*

II *vi* za|szlochać

sober /'səʊbə(r)/ **I** *adj* [1] (not drunk) trzeźwy; **don't drive until you're** ~ nie siadaj za kierownicą, dopóki nie wytrzeźwiejesz [2] (serious) *[mood, expression, person]* poważny [3] (discreet) *[dress, colours]* spokojny

II *vt* *[news, reprimand]* otrzeźwi|ć, -ać *[person]*

■ **sober up:** wy|trzeźwieć

sobriety /sə'braɪətɪ/ *n* trzeźwość *f*

sob story *n* infml ckliwa opowieść *f*

soccer /'sɒkə(r)/ *n* piłka *f* nożna

sociable /'səʊʃəbl/ *adj [person]* towarzyski

social /'səʊʃl/ *adj* [1] *[background, class]* społeczny [2] *[call, visit]* towarzyski

social climber *n* karierowicz *m*, -ka *f*

social club *n* klub *m* towarzyski

social gathering *n* spotkanie *n* towarzyskie

socialism /'səʊʃəlɪzəm/ *n* socjalizm *m*

socialist /'səʊʃəlɪst/ **I** *n* (also **Socialist**) socja-list|a *m*, -ka *f*

II *adj* socjalistyczny

socialite /'səʊʃəlaɪt/ *n* bywal|ec *m*, -czyni *f*

socialize /'səʊʃəlaɪz/ *vi* udzielać się towarzysko; **to** ~ **with sb** utrzymywać kontakty towarzyskie z kimś

social life *n* (of person) życie *n* towarzyskie; (of town) życie *n* kulturalne

social science *n* nauki *f pl* społeczne

social security *n* (benefit) zasiłek *m*; **to be on** ~ być na zasiłku

Social Services *n* GB opieka *f* społeczna

social work *n* praca *f* w opiece społecznej

social worker *n* pracowni|k *m*, -ca *f* opieki społecznej

society /sə'saɪətɪ/ *n* [1] społeczeństwo *n*; **a multi-cultural** ~ społeczeństwo wielokulturowe [2] (for social contact) klub *m*; (for business contact) stowarzy-szenie *n*; (for intellectual contact) towarzystwo *n* [3] (upper classes) (also **high** ~) towarzystwo *n*

sociologist /ˌsəʊsɪ'ɒlədʒɪst/ *n* socjolog *m*

sociology /ˌsəʊsɪ'ɒlədʒɪ/ *n* socjologia *f*

sock /sɒk/ *n* skarpeta *f*

socket /'sɒkɪt/ *n* [1] (for plug) gniazdko *n*; (for bulb) oprawka *f* [2] (of joint) panewka *f* stawu; (of eye) oczodół *m*

soda /'səʊdə/ *n* [1] (chemical) soda *f* [2] (also **washing** ~) soda *f* do prania [3] (also ~ **water**) woda *f* sodowa; **whisky and** ~ whisky z wodą sodową [4] US (also ~ **pop**) napój *m* gazowany

sodden /'sɒdn/ *adj [clothes]* przemoczony; *[ground, towel]* całkiem mokry

sofa /'səʊfə/ *n* kanapa *f*, sofa *f*

sofa bed *n* rozkładana kanapa *f*

soft /sɒft, US sɔːft/ *adj* [1] *[ground, bed, butter]* miękki; *[muscle]* wiotki; *[breeze, climate]* łagodny; *[pressure, touch]* delikatny; *[heart]* miękki; *[eyes]* łagodny [2] (lenient) *[parent, teacher]* pobłażliwy

soft cheese *n* ser *m* miękki

soft drink *n* napój *m* bezalkoholowy

soft drug *n* narkotyk *m* miękki

soften /'sɒfn, US 'sɔːfn/ **I** *vt* [1] zmiękcz|yć, -ać *[hard water, skin, fabric, metal]*; rozmiękcz|yć, -ać *[soil, ground]*; **to** ~ **butter** podgrzać masło, żeby zmiękło [2] z|łagodzić *[impact, blow, pain]* [3] roz-my|ć, -wać *[contour, outline]*

II *vi* [1] zmięk|nąć; *[light, colour]* przy-gas|nąć, -ać; *[music]* przycich|nąć, -ać; *[outline]* s|tracić ostrość [2] *[person]* z|łagodnieć (**towards sb** w stosunku do kogoś)

■ **soften up:** ¶ ~ **up** z|mięknąć ¶ ~ **[sb] up** osłabi|ć, -ać *[enemy, opponent]*; ur|obić, -abiać *[customer]*

softly /'sɒftlɪ, US 'sɔːft-/ *adv [speak]* łagodnie; *[blow]* lekko; *[touch]* delikatnie; *[fall]* miękko

soft option *n* **to take the** ~ wybrać łatwe rozwiązanie

soft porn *n* infml miękkie porno *n inv* infml

soft spot *n* infml **to have a** ~ **for sb** mieć do kogoś słabość

soft-top /'sɒfttɒp, US 'sɔːft-/ *n* kabriolet *m* (*z dachem z materiału*)

soft touch *n* infml **she's a** ~ łatwo ją naciągnąć infml

soft toy *n* pluszowa *f* zabawka

software /'sɒftweə(r), US 'sɔːft-/ *n* oprogramowa-nie *n*

software house *n* producent *m* oprogramowania

software package *n* pakiet *m* oprogramowania

software piracy *n* piractwo *n* komputerowe

soggy /'sɒgɪ/ *adj [clothes]* przemoczony; *[food]* rozmoczony; *[ground]* grząski

soil /sɔɪl/ **I** *n* gleba *f*; **on foreign** ~ fig na obcej ziemi

II *vt* za|brudzić

soiled *adj* [1] (dirty) brudny, zabrudzony [2] (also **shop** ~) *[stock]* zleżały

solace /'sɒləs/ **I** *n* pociecha *f*

II *vt* przyn|ieść, -osić pociechę (**for sb** komuś)

solar /'səʊlə(r)/ *adj [battery, energy]* słoneczny

solar eclipse *n* zaćmienie *n* Słońca

solar power *n* energia *f* słoneczna

solder /'səʊldə(r), 'sɒ-, US 'sɒdər/ *vt* przylutow|ać, -ywać (**on** or **onto sth** do czegoś)

soldier /'səʊldʒə(r)/ *n* żołnierz *m*

■ **soldier on:** nie podda|ć, -wać się

sole /səʊl/ **I** *n* [1] (fish) sola *f* [2] (of foot, shoe) po-deszwa *f*; (of sock) stopa *f*

II *adj* [1] (single) jedyny [2] *[agent, importer]* wy-łączny

solely /'səʊlɪ/ *adv* (entirely) całkowicie; (exclusively) wyłącznie

solemn /'sɒləm/ adj [person, voice] poważny; [promise, occasion] uroczysty; **it's my ~ duty** to jest mój święty obowiązek

solicit /sə'lɪsɪt/ **[]** vt zwr|ócić, -acać się z prośbą o (coś) [money, help, opinion]; zabiegać o (coś) [investment, orders]

[II] vi [prostitute] nagabywać mężczyzn

soliciting /sə'lɪsɪtɪŋ/ n nagabywanie n mężczyzn w celach nierządu

solicitor /sə'lɪsɪtə(r)/ n GB (for documents) ≈ notariusz m; (for court, police work) adwokat m; **a firm of ~s** kancelaria adwokacka

solid /'sɒlɪd/ **[]** n ① (in geometry) bryła f ② (in chemistry, physics) ciało n stałe

[II] adj ① [substance] stały; **to go** or **become ~** zestalić się ② [oak, rock] lity; [tyre, rubber ball] pełny ③ [crowd] zbity; [earth] ubity ④ (unbroken) [line] ciągły; **four ~ days, four days ~** bite cztery dni ⑤ [investment] pewny; [advice] rozsądny; [worker] solidny

[III] adv [freeze] całkowicie; **the play is booked ~** bilety na tę sztukę są zarezerwowane do ostatniego miejsca

solidarity /ˌsɒlɪ'dærəti/ n solidarność f

solidify /sə'lɪdɪfaɪ/ **[]** vt zestal|ić, -ać [substance]

[II] vi [liquid] zestal|ić, -ać się; [semiliquid, fat] s|krzepnąć

solitary /'sɒlɪtrɪ, US -teri/ adj ① (unaccompanied) [occupation, walk] samotny; [drinking] w pojedynkę ② (lonely) [person] samotny; (by choice) lubiący samotność; [farm] samotny; [village] oddalony od świata ③ (single) jedyny

solitary confinement n więzienna izolatka f

solo /'səʊləʊ/ **[]** n Mus solo n inv; (in pop music) solówka f

[II] adj solowy

[III] adv [perform] solo; [fly] w pojedynkę

soloist /'səʊləʊɪst/ n solist|a m, -ka f

solstice /'sɒlstɪs/ n przesilenie n

soluble /'sɒljʊbl/ adj rozpuszczalny

solution /sə'lu:ʃn/ n (answer) rozwiązanie n; (mixture) roztwór m

solve /sɒlv/ vt rozwiąz|ać, -ywać [crossword puzzle, problem, mystery]; wyjaśni|ć, -ać [crime]; zna|leźć, -jdować sposób na (coś) [unemployment, poverty]

solvent /'sɒlvənt/ **[]** n rozpuszczalnik m

[II] adj [company] wypłacalny

sombre GB, **somber** US /'sɒmbə(r)/ adj [mood, news] ponury; [face] posępny

some /sʌm/ **[]** det, quantif ① (an unspecified amount or number) **~ cheese** trochę sera; **~ apples** kilka jabłek; **we need ~ money** potrzebujemy pieniędzy ② (certain) **~ shops won't sell this product** niektóre sklepy nie sprzedają tego produktu; **in ~ ways, I agree** w pewnej mierze się zgadzam; **~ people say that...** niektórzy twierdzą, że... ③ (a considerable amount or number) **she managed it**

with ~ difficulty poradziła sobie z tym z pewnymi trudnościami; **it will take ~ doing** to będzie wymagało pewnego wysiłku; **we stayed there for ~ time** zatrzymaliśmy się tam na jakiś czas ④ (a little, a slight) **the meeting did have ~ effect** to zebranie przyniosło pewne rezultaty; **there must be ~ reason for it** musi być jakiś tego powód; **to ~ extent** do pewnego stopnia ⑤ (an unknown) **~ man came to the house** do domu przyszedł jakiś człowiek; **a car of ~ sort, ~ sort of car** jakiś samochód ⑥ infml (a remarkable) **that was ~ film!** to dopiero film!

[II] pron ① (an unspecified amount) trochę; (an unspecified number) kilka; **I'd like ~ of those** poproszę kilka or parę tych; **(do) have ~!** weź sobie trochę/ kilka!; **(do) have ~ more!** weź sobie jeszcze! ② (certain ones) **~ (of them) are blue** niektóre (z nich) są niebieskie; **~ say that...** niektórzy mówią, że...

[III] adv ① (approximately) jakieś; **~ 20 people** jakieś 20 osób ② US infml trochę

somebody /'sʌmbədɪ/ pron (also **someone**) ktoś; **~ famous** ktoś sławny

somehow /'sʌmhaʊ/ adv ① (by some means) (also **~ or other**) jakoś (tam); **we managed it ~** jakoś (tam) nam się udało ② (for some reason) **~ it doesn't seem very important** to jakoś nie wydaje się bardzo ważne; **it was ~ shocking to see** to było na swój sposób szokujące

someone /'sʌmwʌn/ pron = **somebody**

somersault /'sʌməsɒlt/ **[]** n (of gymnast) przewrót m; (of diver) salto n; (of child) koziołek m; (of vehicle) dachowanie n

[II] vi [gymnast] wykon|ać, -ywać przewrót; [car] prze|koziołkować

something /'sʌmθɪŋ/ **[]** pron coś; **~ new** coś nowego; **there's ~ wrong** coś jest nie tak; **~ or other** coś (tam); **that house is quite** or **really ~!** to dopiero dom!; **in nineteen-sixty-~** w tysiąc dziewięćset sześćdziesiątym którymś roku; **she's gone shopping or ~** wyszła na zakupy czy coś takiego

[II] something of adv phr **she is ~ of an expert** jest, można powiedzieć, ekspertem; **it was ~ of a surprise** to było spore zaskoczenie

sometime /'sʌmtaɪm/ adv kiedyś; **we'll have to do it ~** kiedyś będziemy musieli to zrobić; **I'll phone you ~ tomorrow** zadzwonię do ciebie jutro

sometimes /'sʌmtaɪmz/ adv czasami, czasem

somewhat /'sʌmwɒt/ adv nieco; **things have changed ~** zaszły pewne zmiany

somewhere /'sʌmweə(r)/ adv ① (some place) gdzieś; **~ hot** gdzieś, gdzie jest gorąco; **~ or other** gdzieś tam; **~ between 80 and 100 people** jakieś 80 do 100 osób

son /sʌn/ n syn m

sonata /sə'nɑːtə/ *n* sonata *f*

song /sɒŋ/ *n* piosenka *f*; (solemn) pieśń *f*; (of bird) śpiew *m*

songwriter /'sɒŋraɪtə(r)/ *n* (of words) tekściarz *m* infml; (of music) kompozytor *m*, -ka *f* piosenek

sonic /'sɒnɪk/ *adj* dźwiękowy

sonic boom *n* US uderzenie *n* dźwiękowe

son-in-law /'sʌnɪnlɔː/ *n* zięć *m*

sonnet /'sɒnɪt/ *n* sonet *m*

soon /suːn/ *adv* [1] (in a short time) niedługo, wkrótce; **see you** ~! do zobaczenia! [2] (quickly) szybko [3] (early) wcześnie; **the** ~ **er the better** im wcześniej, tym lepiej; **as** ~ **as possible** jak najszybciej; **as** ~ **as I see him** jak tylko go zobaczę; ~ **er or later** prędzej czy później [4] (not long) zaraz, wkrótce; ~ **afterwards** zaraz or wkrótce potem; **no** ~ **er had I finished than...** ledwie skończyłem, kiedy... [5] (rather) raczej; **he'd** ~ **er die than do it** wolałby umrzeć, niż to zrobić

soot /sʊt/ *n* sadza *f*

soothe /suːð/ *vt* uspok|oić, -ajać *[person]*; z|łagodzić *[pain]*; u|koić *[nerves]*

soothing /'suːðɪŋ/ *adj* *[cream, music]* kojący; *[tone of voice]* uspokajający; *[medicine]* uśmierzający (ból)

sophisticated /sə'fɪstɪkeɪtɪd/ *adj* [1] (cultured) *[person]* wyrafinowany; (elegant) *[person, restaurant]* wytworny [2] *[taste, audience]* wyrobiony [3] *[equipment, technology]* wysokiej klasy

soporific /ˌsɒpə'rɪfɪk/ *adj* *[drug]* nasenny; *[effect]* usypiający

soprano /sə'prɑːnəʊ, US -'præn-/ *n* (person) sopran *m*, sopranist|a *m*, -ka *f*; (voice, instrument) sopran *m*

sorcerer /'sɔːsərə(r)/ *n* czarnoksiężnik *m*

sordid /'sɔːdɪd/ *adj* *[affair]* wstrętny; *[business]* brudny; *[room]* obskurny

sore /sɔː(r)/ **[I]** *n* rana *f* **[II]** *adj* [1] *[head, gums, muscle]* obolały; **I have a** ~ **throat** boli mnie gardło [2] *[subject, point]* drażliwy

sorrow /'sɒrəʊ/ *n* smutek *m*

sorrowful /'sɒrəʊfl/ *adj* *[person, voice]* smutny

sorry /'sɒrɪ/ **[I]** *adj* [1] (apologetic) **I'm terribly** ~! bardzo przepraszam!; **I'm** ~ **I'm late** przepraszam za spóźnienie; **we are** ~ **to hear that...** zmartwiła nas wiadomość, że...; **I'm** ~ **about your uncle** przykro mi z powodu twojego wuja [2] (regretful) **we are** ~ **to inform you that...** z przykrością zawiadamiamy, że... [3] (pitying) **to be** or **feel** ~ **for sb** współczuć komuś; **to feel** ~ **for oneself** użalać się nad sobą [4] *[sight, excuse]* żałosny; *[tale]* budzący litość or współczucie; **a** ~ **state of affairs** opłakany stan rzeczy **[II]** *excl* [1] (apologizing) przepraszam! [2] (failing to hear) ~? słucham?

sort /sɔːt/ **[I]** *n* [1] (kind) rodzaj *m*; **this** ~ **of fabric** ten rodzaj materiału; **machines of all** ~s wszelkiego rodzaju urządzenia; **I'm not that** ~ **of person** nie należę do takich osób; **it's some** ~ **of computer** to jest rodzaj komputera; **nothing of the** ~ nic podobnego [2] (type of person) **I know his** ~ znam takich jak on; **people of her** ~ ludzie jej pokroju **[II] of sorts, of a sort** *adv phr* infml **a duck of** ~s or **of a** ~ coś jakby kaczka; **progress of** ~s pewnego rodzaju postęp **[III] sort of** *adv phr* infml ~ **of eccentric** trochę jakby ekscentryczny; **he** ~ **of understood** mniej więcej zrozumiał; ~ **of blue-green** coś jakby niebieskawozielony; **it just** ~ **of happened** to się tak jakoś stało **[IV]** *vt* [1] po|sortować *[data, files, stamps]*; **to** ~ **books into piles** poukładać książki w sterty [2] (separate) **to** ~ **sth from sth** oddziel|ić, -ać coś od czegoś ∎ **sort out:** [1] rozwiąz|ać, -ywać *[problem]*; u|porządkować *[matters]*; **I'll** ~ **it out** załatwię to [2] ustal|ić, -ać *[details, arrangements]* [3] z|robić porządek w (czymś) *[cupboard]*; z|robić porządek na (czymś) *[desk]*; po|układać *[files, documents]*; u|porządkować *[finances, affairs]* [4] wyb|rać, -ierać *[photos]* IDIOMS **to be** or **feel out of** ~s (ill) źle się czuć; (grumpy) być nie w sosie infml; **it takes all** ~s **(to make a world)** różni są ludzie na tym (bożym) świecie

sort code *n* kod *m* bankowy

SOS *n* SOS *n inv*

so-so /'səʊsəʊ/ infml **[I]** *adj* taki sobie, jako taki **[II]** *adv* jako tako, tak sobie

sought-after /'sɔːtɑːftə(r), US -æf-/ *adj* *[type of employee]* poszukiwany; *[guest]* pożądany; *[actress]* wzięty; *[area]* cieszący się dużym zainteresowaniem

soul /səʊl/ *n* [1] dusza *f* [2] Mus (also ~ **music**) soul *m inv*

soul-destroying /'səʊldɪstrɔɪɪŋ/ *adj* śmiertelnie nudny

soulmate /'səʊlmeɪt/ *n* bratnia dusza *f*

soul-searching /'səʊlsɜːtʃɪŋ/ *n* **to do some** ~ zastanowić się głęboko

sound /saʊnd/ **[I]** *n* [1] dźwięk *m*; (noise) (of machinery, footsteps) odgłos *m*; (of voice, musical instrument) brzmienie *n*; **without a** ~ bezszelestnie; **a grating** or **rasping** ~ zgrzytanie; **to turn up/down the** ~ pogłaśniać/ściszać [2] fig **a 24-hour flight? I don't like the** ~ **of it** 24 godziny w samolocie? to nie brzmi zachęcająco; **he was in a bad temper that day by the** ~ **of it** zdaje się, że tego dnia był w złym humorze [3] Med zgłębnik *m*, sonda *f* [4] (strait) cieśnina *f* **[II]** *adj* [1] *[foundations]* mocny; *[heart]* zdrowy; *[constitution]* silny; **of** ~ **mind and body** zdrowy na ciele i umyśle [2] *[step]* rozsądny; *[argument]* mocny; *[reasoning]* logiczny; *[basis]* solidny; *[edu-*

cation] staranny; *[investment]* pewny; **let me give
you some ~ advice** pozwól, że dam ci dobrą
radę

III *vt* za|grać na (czymś) *[trumpet]*; uderz|yć, -ać
w (coś) *[gong]*; da|ć, -wać sygnał (czymś) *[siren]*;
the driver ~ed his horn kierowca zatrąbił; **to
~ the alarm** uderzyć na alarm

IV *vi* [1] (seem) **it ~s good** to brzmi nieźle; **it ~s
as if he's really in trouble** wygląda na to, że ma
poważne kłopoty; **that ~s like a good idea!** to
chyba niezły pomysł!; **it may ~ silly, but...**
może to zabrzmi głupio, ale...; **he ~s like an
American** mówi z amerykańskim akcentem
[2] *[alarm]* rozle|c, -gać się; *[bugle]* za|brzmieć;
[siren] za|wyć

V *adv* **to be ~ asleep** mocno spać
■ **sound out: ~ [sb] out** wybadać

sound barrier *n* bariera *f* dźwięku

sound bite *n krótki fragment nagranego wywiadu*

sound card *n* karta *f* dźwiękowa

sound effects *npl* efekty *m pl* dźwiękowe

soundly /'saʊndlɪ/ *adv [sleep]* mocno; **our team
was ~ beaten** or **defeated** przegraliśmy z kre-
tesem

soundproof /'saʊndpruːf/ *adj [room]* dźwięko-
szczelny; *[material]* dźwiękochłonny

sound system *n* aparatura *f* nagłaśniająca

sound-track /'saʊndtræk/ *n* ścieżka *f* dźwiękowa

soup /suːp/ *n* zupa *f*

soup kitchen *n* jadłodajnia *f* dla ubogich

soup plate *n* głęboki talerz *m*

soup spoon *n* łyżka *f* stołowa

sour /'saʊə(r)/ **I** *adj* [1] *[wine, fruit]* cierpki; *[milk]*
kwaśny, zsiadły; **to go ~** skwasić się, skwaśnieć
[2] (bad-tempered) *[person]* (permanently) zgorzkniały;
(temporarily) skwaszony

II *vt* zatru|ć, -wać *[relations, atmosphere]*

source /sɔːs/ *n* źródło *n*; **a ~ of sth** źródło czegoś
[anxiety, pollution]; przyczyna *f* czegoś *[error]*

sourdough /'saʊədəʊ/ *n* US zaczyn *m*

south /saʊθ/ **I** *n* południe *n*

II *adj [side, wind]* południowy

III *adv [move]* na południe; **to lie ~ of sth** leżeć
na południe od czegoś

South Africa *prn* Afryka *f* Południowa

South America *prn* Ameryka *f* Południowa

southeast /ˌsaʊθˈiːst/ **I** *n* południowy wschód *m*

II *adj [wall, side, wind]* południowo-wschodni

III *adv [move]* na południowy wschód; *[lie, live]* na
południowym wschodzie

southern /'sʌðən/ *adj [hemisphere, England, ac-
cent]* południowy; **a ~ town** miasto na południu

South Pole *prn* biegun *m* południowy

southwest /ˌsaʊθˈwest/ **I** *n* południowy zachód *m*

II *adj [side, coast, wind]* południowo-zachodni

III *adv [move]* na południowy zachód; *[lie, live]* na
południowym zachodzie

souvenir /ˌsuːvəˈnɪə(r), US ˈsuːvənɪər/ *n* pamiątka *f*

sovereign /'sɒvrɪn/ **I** *n* [1] (monarch) monarcha *m*
[2] (coin) suweren *m*

II *adj [state]* niezawisły, suwerenny

sovereignty /'sɒvrəntɪ/ *n* suwerenność *f*

Soviet Union /ˈsəʊvɪət ˈjuːnɪən, ˈsɒv-/ *prn* **the ~**
Związek *m* Radziecki

sow[1] /saʊ/ *n* locha *f*

sow[2] /səʊ/ *vt* [1] za|siać *[seeds, corn]*; **to ~ the
seeds of doubt in sb** fig zasiać w kimś wątpliwości
[2] obsi|ać, -ewać *[field, garden]* (**with sth** czymś)

soya /'sɔɪə/ *n* soja *f*

soya sauce *n* (also **soy sauce**) sos *m* sojowy

spa /spɑː/ *n* [1] (town) uzdrowisko *n* [2] US (health club)
centrum *n* odnowy biologicznej

space /speɪs/ **I** *n* [1] (room) miejsce *n*; **to take up a
lot of ~** zabierać dużo miejsca [2] (gap) odstęp *m*
[3] (area of land) teren *m*; **open ~s** otwarta
przestrzeń [4] (interval of time) odstęp *m* czasu; **in** or
within the ~ of five minutes w ciągu pięciu
minut [5] (in mathematics, physics) przestrzeń *f* [6] (also
outer ~) przestrzeń *f* kosmiczna

II *adj [programme, rocket]* kosmiczny

III *vt* rozstawi|ć, -ać *[objects]*

■ **space out:** rozstawi|ć, -ać *[objects]*; rozstrzeli|ć,
-wać *[words]*; rozł|ożyć, -kładać *[payments]*

space-bar /'speɪsbɑː(r)/ *n* klawisz *m* spacji

spaced out *adj* infml półprzytomny; (after drugs)
naćpany infml

spaceship /'speɪsʃɪp/ *n* statek *m* kosmiczny

space station *n* stacja *f* kosmiczna

spacesuit /'speɪssuːt, -sjuːt/ *n* skafander *m* kosmiczny

spacing /'speɪsɪŋ/ *n* (of payments) rozłożenie *n*; **in
double ~** (in printing) z podwójnym odstępem

spacious /'speɪʃəs/ *adj [room]* przestronny; *[gar-
ment]* obszerny; *[park]* rozległy

spade /speɪd/ *n* [1] (tool) łopata *f* [2] (in cards) pik *m*

Spain /speɪn/ *prn* Hiszpania *f*

spamming /'spæmɪŋ/ *n* Comput spamming *m*

span /spæn/ **I** *n* [1] (of time) okres *m*; **over a ~ of
several years** w przeciągu kilku lat [2] (across
wings) rozpiętość *f*; (of bridge) przęsło *n*

II *vt* [1] *[bridge]* spinać brzegi (czegoś) *[river]* [2] fig
[life] trwać; *[knowledge]* obl|jąć, -ejmować *[field]*

Spaniard /'spænjəd/ *n* Hiszpan *m*, -ka *f*

spaniel /'spænjəl/ *n* spaniel *m*

Spanish /'spænɪʃ/ **I** *n* [1] (people) **the ~** Hiszpa-
nie *m pl* [2] (language) (język *m*) hiszpański *m*

II *adj* hiszpański

spank /spæŋk/ *vt* da|ć, -wać klapsa (komuś)
[person]

spanner /'spænə(r)/ *n* GB klucz *m* (maszynowy)

spar /spɑː(r)/ *vi [boxers]* odby|ć, -wać sparing
(**with sb** z kimś)

spare /speə(r)/ **I** *n* (part) część *f* zamienna or
zapasowa; (wheel) koło *n* zapasowe

II *adj* **1** *[copy]* dodatkowy; *[ticket, chair, cash]* wolny **2** *[part, wheel]* zapasowy **3** *[time]* wolny; **do you have a ~ minute?** masz wolną chwilkę? **4** *[person]* szczupły; *[style]* oszczędny

III *vt* **1** **to have sth to ~** mieć coś w zapasie; **I caught the train with only a couple of minutes to ~** zdążyłem na pociąg w ostatniej chwili **2** (treat leniently) oszczędz|ić, -ać *[person]*; **to ~ sb sth** oszczędzić komuś czegoś *[trouble, worry]* **3** (be able to afford) poświęc|ić, -ać *[time]*; **can you ~ a pound?** możesz mi dać funta?; **to ~ no effort** nie szczędzić wysiłku (**to do sth** żeby coś zrobić) **4** (manage without) po|radzić sobie bez (kogoś) *[person]*

spare part *n* część *f* zapasowa or zamienna
spare room *n* pokój *m* gościnny
spare time *n* wolny czas *m*
spare tyre GB, **spare tire** US zapasowa opona *f*
sparingly /'speərɪŋlɪ/ *adv* *[use]* oszczędnie; *[eat]* niewiele
spark /spɑːk/ **II** *n* iskra *f*

II *vt* (also **~ off**) wywoł|ać, -ywać *[interest, controversy]*; zapoczątkow|ać, -ywać *[friendship, change]*
sparkle /'spɑːkl/ **II** *n* (of light, jewel) blask *m*; (in eye) błysk *m*

II *vi* *[flame, frost]* skrzyć się; *[jewel, water, metal, light]* lśnić; *[eyes]* błyszczeć; *[drink]* musować
sparkler /'spɑːklə(r)/ *n* (firework) zimny ogień *m*
sparkling /'spɑːklɪŋ/ *adj* **1** *[light]* iskrzący się; *[jewel]* mieniący się; **eyes ~ with joy** oczy skrzące się radością **2** *[wit]* błyskotliwy **3** *[drink]* gazowany; *[wine]* musujący
spark plug *n* świeca *f* zapłonowa
sparrow /'spærəʊ/ *n* wróbel *m*
sparse /spɑːs/ *adj* *[vegetation]* skąpy; *[hair]* rzadki
sparsely /'spɑːslɪ/ *adv* **~ wooded** skąpo zalesiony; **~ populated** (permanently) słabo zaludniony; (temporarily) wyludniony
spasm /'spæzəm/ *n* (of pain) paroksyzm *m*; (of panic, rage) atak *m*, napad *m*; (of energy) przypływ *m*
spate /speɪt/ *n* **1** **in full ~** GB *[river]* wezbrany; **he was in full ~** rozgadał się na dobre **2** **a ~ of sth** seria czegoś *[burglaries]*
spatula /'spætʃʊlə/ *n* (in kitchen) łopatka *f*; (used by painters) szpachla *f*; (doctor's) szpatułka *f*
speak /spiːk/ **II** *vt* **1** **to ~ English** mówić po angielsku, znać angielski **2** powiedzieć, mówić *[truth]*; wym|ówić, -awiać *[word, name]*; **he's the sort of person who ~s his mind** on zawsze mówi, co myśli

II *vi* **1** mówić (**of** or **about sb/sth** o kimś/czymś); **to ~ to sb** mówić do kogoś; **who's ~ing please?** (on the phone) kto mówi?; **(this is) Anna ~ing** mówi or tu Anna; **~ing as a layman...** jako laik uważam, że...; **generally** or **roughly ~ing** mówiąc ogólnie; **strictly ~ing** ściśle mówiąc **2** rozmawiać; **to ~ to** or **with sb about**

or **of sth** rozmawiać z kimś o czymś; **they are not ~ing (to each other)** nie rozmawiają ze sobą
■ **speak out**: mówić otwarcie
■ **speak up**: **1** (louder) mówić głośniej **2** (dare to speak) od|ezwać, -zywać się
speaker /'spiːkə(r)/ *n* **1** (person talking) mówiąc|y *m*, -a *f*; (public orator) mów|ca *m*, -czyni *f*; (lecturer) prelegent *m*, -ka *f* **2** **a Spanish-~** osoba znająca hiszpański **3** (loudspeaker) głośnik *m*
-speaking /'spiːkɪŋ/ *in combinations* **French-~ Canadians** francuskojęzyczni Kanadyjczycy; **an English-~ country** kraj anglojęzyczny
spear /'spɪə(r)/ *n* dzida *f*
spearhead /'spɪəhed/ *vtr* sta|ć, -wać na czele (czegoś) *[movement, offensive]*; za|inicjować *[reform]*
spearmint /'spɪəmɪnt/ *n* mięta *f* ogrodowa
special /'speʃl/ *adj* *[equipment, procedure]* specjalny; *[friend]* wielki; *[reason, treatment]* szczególny, specjalny; **I want to make this Christmas really ~** chcę, żeby to Boże Narodzenie było naprawdę wyjątkowe
special effect *n* efekt *m* specjalny
specialist /'speʃəlɪst/ *n* specjalist|a *m*, -ka *f*; **heart ~** kardiolog
speciality GB /ˌspeʃɪ'ælɪtɪ/, **specialty** US /'speʃəltɪ/ *n* specjalność *f*
specialize /'speʃəlaɪz/ *vi* specjalizować się (**in sth** w czymś)
specially /'speʃəlɪ/ *adv* **1** (specifically) specjalnie; **I made it ~ for you** zrobiłem to specjalnie dla ciebie **2** (particularly) wyjątkowo; *[like, enjoy]* szczególnie
special needs *npl* **children with ~** dzieci specjalnej troski
special school *n* szkoła *f* specjalna
species /'spiːʃiːz/ *n* (in biology) gatunek *m*
specific /spə'sɪfɪk/ *adj* *[example]* konkretny; *[information]* dokładny; **please be more ~** proszę wyrażać się jaśniej
specifically /spə'sɪfɪklɪ/ *adv* **1** (specially) specjalnie **2** (explicitly) wyraźnie **3** (in particular) w szczególności; **more ~** dokładniej
specify /'spesɪfaɪ/ **II** *vt* określ|ić, -ać *[reasons]*; *[contract]* przewidywać (**that...** że...)

II specified *pp adj* *[amount, date, value]* określony
specimen /'spesɪmən/ *n* (of species, plant) okaz *m*; (of urine, handwriting) próbka *f*; (of tissue) wycinek *m*; (of form, banknote) wzór *m*
speck /spek/ *n* (of dust, soot) drobina *f*; (of dirt, blood) plamka *f*; (of ink, mud, paint) kropeczka *f*
spectacle /'spektəkl/ **II** *n* widowisko *n*

II spectacles *npl* okulary *plt*
spectacular /spek'tækjʊlə(r)/ *adj* spektakularny
spectator /spek'teɪtə(r)/ *n* (at a game) kibic *m*; (in front of TV) widz *m*
spectre GB, **specter** US /'spektə(r)/ *n* widmo *n*

spectrum /'spektrəm/ *n* ① (of colours) widmo *n* ② (range) spektrum *n*

speculate /'spekjʊleɪt/ ❶ *vt* rozważać teoretycznie; **to ~ that...** domyślać się, że...

❷ *vi* spekulować (**on** or **about** sth na temat czegoś)

speculation /ˌspekjʊ'leɪʃn/ *n* ① (conjecture) spekulacje *f pl* ② (financial) transakcja *f* spekulacyjna

speech /spiːtʃ/ *n* ① przemówienie *n* (**on** or **about** sth na temat czegoś); **to give a ~** wygłosić przemówienie ② (faculty) mowa *f* ③ (language) język *m*

speech day *n* GB Sch uroczystość *f* rozdania nagród

speech impediment *n* wada *f* wymowy

speechless /'spiːtʃlɪs/ *adj* oniemiały; **he was ~ with horror** zaniemówił z przerażenia; **I was ~ at the sight** na ten widok odjęło mi mowę

speed /spiːd/ ❶ *n* ① (of vehicle, wind) prędkość *f*; (of response, reaction) szybkość *f*; **at top ~** *[run]* bardzo szybko; *[work]* w pośpiechu ② infml (drug) amfa *f* infml

❷ *vt* przyśpiesz|yć, -ać *[process, recovery]*

❸ *vi* ① (move quickly) pędzić; **to ~ away** *[car, driver]* szybko odjechać ② (drive too fast) przekr|oczyć, -aczać dozwoloną prędkość

■ **speed up:** ¶ **~ up** *[person, vehicle]* przyśpiesz|yć, -ać; *[activity]* nab|rać, -ierać tempa ¶ **~ [sth] up** przyśpiesz|yć, -ać *[process]*; zwiększ|yć, -ać tempo (czegoś) *[work]*

speedboat /'spiːdbəʊt/ *n* wyścigowa łódź *f* motorowa

speed camera *n* kamera *f* policyjna *(rejestrująca przypadki przekraczania dozwolonej prędkości)*

speed hump *n* próg *m* zwalniający

speeding /'spiːdɪŋ/ *n* przekroczenie *n* (dozwolonej) prędkości

speed limit *n* ograniczenie *n* prędkości

speedometer /spɪ'dɒmɪtə(r)/ *n* prędkościomierz *m*

spell /spel/ ❶ *n* ① (period) okres *m*; **a sunny ~** okres słonecznej pogody; **to go through a bad ~** mieć zły okres ② (magic words) zaklęcie *n*; **to be under a ~** być zaklętym or zaczarowanym; **to cast** or **put a ~ on sb** rzucić urok na kogoś; **to be under sb's ~** być pod urokiem kogoś

❷ *vt* ① (aloud) prze|literować *[word]*; (on paper) zapis|ać, -ywać ② zwiastować *[danger, disaster]*

❸ *vi [person]* pisać poprawnie; **he can't ~** on robi błędy ortograficzne

■ **spell out:** prze|literować *[word]*; przedstaw|ić, -ać *[details]*; **I had to ~ it out to him** musiałem mu to jasno wytłumaczyć

spellbound /'spelbaʊnd/ *adj* oczarowany (**by sb/sth** kimś/czymś)

spellcheck /'speltʃek/ *vt* Comput sprawdz|ić, -ać pisownię (czegoś)

spellchecker /'speltʃekər/ *n* Comput funkcja *f* sprawdzania pisowni

spelling /'spelɪŋ/ ❶ *n* pisownia *f*

❷ *adj [mistake]* ortograficzny

spend /spend/ ❶ *vt* ① wyda|ć, -wać *[money, salary]*; **to ~ money on clothes** wydawać pieniądze na ubranie ② spędz|ić, -ać *[time, day]*

❷ *vi* wyda|ć, -wać (pieniądze)

spending cut *n* ograniczenie *n* wydatków; Pol cięcia *n pl* w budżecie

spending power *n* siła *f* nabywcza

spending spree *n* szał *m* wydawania pieniędzy; **to go on a ~** zaszaleć infml *(na zakupach)*

spendthrift /'spendθrɪft/ *adj* rozrzutny

sperm /spɜːm/ *n* (cell) plemnik *m*; (semen) sperma *f*

sperm donor *n* dawca *m* spermy

spew /spjuː/ *vt* wypluć, -wać *[smoke, lava]*

sphere /sfɪə(r)/ *n* ① (shape) kula *f* ② (field) sfera *f*; **~ of activity** zakres działania; **~ of influence** strefa wpływów

spherical /'sferɪkl/ *adj* kulisty

spice /spaɪs/ *n* Culin przyprawa *f* (korzenna); **to add ~ to sth** fig dodać czemuś pikanterii

spick-and-span /ˌspɪkən'spæn/ *adj* nieskazitelnie czysty

spicy /'spaɪsɪ/ *adj* pikantny also fig

spider /'spaɪdə(r)/ *n* pająk *m*

spiderweb /'spaɪdərweb/ *n* US pajęczyna *f*

spike /spaɪk/ ❶ *n* szpic *m*; (on shoe) kolec *m*

❷ *vt* infml zaprawi|ć, -ać (alkoholem)

spiky /'spaɪkɪ/ *adj [branch, object]* kolczasty; *[hair]* nastroszony

spill /spɪl/ ❶ *n* (of oil) wyciek *m*; (liquid spilled) rozlana ciecz *f*

❷ *vt* rozl|ać, -ewać *[liquid]* (**on** or **over sth** na coś)

❸ *vi [liquid]* rozl|ać, -ewać się (**on** or **over sth** na coś)

■ **spill over:** *[liquid]* przel|ać, -ewać się (**onto sth** na coś); **to ~ over into sth** fig przerodzić się w coś *[looting, hostility]*

spin /spɪn/ ❶ *n* ① (of wheel) obrót *m*; (of dancer, skater) piruet *m* ② **to go into a ~** *[plane]* wejść w korkociąg ③ **to go for a ~** (in car) wybrać się na przejażdżkę

❷ *vt* ① za|kręcić (czymś) ② u|prząść *[thread, wool]* ③ *[spider]* u|snuć *[web]*

❸ *vi* ① obr|ócić, -acać się; *[dancer]* za|wirować; **my head is ~ning** kręci mi się w głowie

■ **spin out:** przeciąg|nąć, -ać *[visit, speech]*; oszczędnie gospodarować (czymś) *[money, food]*

■ **spin round:** ¶ **~ round** *[person]* obr|ócić, -acać się szybko; *[dancer, skater]* za|wirować; *[car]* obr|ócić, -acać się ¶ **~ [sb/sth] round** obr|ócić, -acać *[wheel]*

spinach /'spɪnɪdʒ, US -ɪtʃ/ *n* szpinak *m*

spinal cord /'spaɪnl kɔːd/ *n* rdzeń *m* kręgowy

spindly /'spɪndlɪ/ adj [legs, plant] patykowaty
spin doctor n rzecznik m prasowy partii
spin-drier, **spin dryer** /'spɪndraɪə(r)/ n wirówka f
spine /spaɪn/ n ①Anat kręgosłup m ②(prickle) kolec m ③(of book) grzbiet m
spineless /'spaɪnlɪs/ adj tchórzliwy
spin-off /'spɪnɒf/ n ①(incidental benefit) dodatkowa korzyść f ②(by-product) produkt m uboczny
spinster /'spɪnstə(r)/ n panna f; (derogatory) stara panna f
spiral /'spaɪərəl/ ❶ n spirala f
❷ adj [structure] spiralny
❸ vi [prices, costs] wzr|osnąć, -astać w szybkim tempie
❹ **spiralling** GB, **spiraling** US prp adj [costs] wzrastający
spiral staircase n schody plt kręcone
spire /'spaɪə(r)/ n iglica f
spirit /'spɪrɪt/ ❶ n ①duch m ②(courage) odwaga f; (determination) charakter m ③(drink) alkohol m wysokoprocentowy
❷ **spirits** npl nastrój m; **to be in good** or **high ~s** być w dobrym nastroju; **to keep one's ~s up** nie tracić humoru; **to raise sb's ~s** podnieść kogoś na duchu
spirited /'spɪrɪtɪd/ adj [performance] pełen werwy; [attack, defence] odważny; [debate] ożywiony; [horse] ognisty
spirit level n poziomnica f
spiritual /'spɪrɪtʃʊəl/ ❶ n Mus spirituals m inv
❷ adj duchowy
spit /spɪt/ ❶ n ①(saliva) ślina f ②(over open fire) rożen m; (in electrical device) szpikulec m rożna
❷ vt [person] wyplu|ć, -wać [food]; pluć (czymś) [blood]; [pan] strzel|ić, -ać (czymś) [oil]
❸ vi [person] splu|nąć, -wać, pluć; **to ~ at** or **on sb/sth** splunąć na kogoś/coś, opluć kogoś/coś; [oil, sausage] strzel|ić, -ać; [logs, fire] trzas|nąć, -kać
❹ v impers **it's ~ting (with rain)** kropi (deszcz)
IDIOMS **to be the ~ting image of sb** być do kogoś podobnym jak dwie krople wody
spite /spaɪt/ ❶ n złośliwość f
❷ **in spite of** prep phr (po)mimo (czegoś); **in ~ of the fact that...** mimo że...
❸ vt **to ~ sb** z|robić na złość komuś
spiteful /'spaɪtfl/ adj (malicious) złośliwy; (vindictive) mściwy
splash /splæʃ/ ❶ n ①(sound) plusk m ②(of mud, oil) plama f; (of colour) plamka f; (of drink) kapka f
❷ vt ochlap|ać, -ywać [person]; rozchlap|ać, -ywać [water]; **to ~ water onto one's face** chlusnąć sobie wodą w twarz
❸ vi [paint] chlap|nąć, -ać ②(in sea) pluskać się
■ **splash out** infml: (spend money) za|szaleć infml; **to ~ out on sth** szarpnąć się na coś infml [dress]

splay /spleɪ/ vt rozstawi|ć, -ać [feet]; rozczapierz|yć, -ać [fingers]
spleen /spliːn/ n śledziona f
splendid /'splendɪd/ adj [performance, idea] wspaniały; [occasion] doskonały
splendour GB, **splendor** US /'splendə(r)/ n wspaniałość f, świetność f
splice /splaɪs/ vt spl|eść, -atać [ropes]; skle|ić, -jać [tape, film]
splint /splɪnt/ n Med szyna f
splinter /'splɪntə(r)/ ❶ n (of glass) odłamek m; (of wood) drzazga f
❷ vi [glass, windscreen] rozprys|nąć, -kiwać się; [wood] rozszczepi|ć, -ać się; [alliance] rozpa|ść, -dać się
splinter group n odłam m
split /splɪt/ ❶ n ①(in fabric) rozdarcie n; (in wood) pęknięcie n; (in rock) szczelina f ②(in party, alliance) rozłam m (**into sth** na coś)
❷ **splits** npl (in gymnastics) szpagat m
❸ adj [log] pęknięty; [fabric] rozerwany; [seam] rozpruty; [lip] rozcięty
❹ vt ①rozłup|ać, -ywać [log, rock]; roz|edrzeć, -dzierać [garment] ②(cause dissent in) po|dzielić [party] ③(share) po|dzielić się (czymś) [cost]; **shall we ~ a bottle of wine (between us)?** wypijemy do spółki butelkę wina?
❺ vi ①[wood, log, rock] pęk|nąć, -ać, popęk|ać; [fabric, garment] roze|drzeć, -dzierać się; **my head is ~ting** głowa mi pęka ②[party] po|dzielić się (**on** or **over sth** w kwestii czegoś)
■ **split up**: ¶ **~ up** [couple, partners] rozsta|ć, -wać się ¶ **~ [sth/sb] up** po|dzielić [money] (**into sth** na coś)
split second n ułamek m sekundy
splutter /'splʌtə(r)/ vi [person] (stutter) bełkotać; (spit) za|charczeć; [fire] trzaskać; [fat] strzel|ić, -ać
spoil /spɔɪl/ ❶ vt ①(mar) po|psuć [event, evening, view]; z|niszczyć [place]; **it will ~ your appetite** to ci odbierze apetyt; **to ~ sth for sb** popsuć coś komuś ②(ruin) z|niszczyć [crop, garment] ③(pamper) rozpie|ścić, -szczać [person, pet]
❷ vi [product, foodstuff] po|psuć się, ze|psuć się
spoiled /spɔɪld/, **spoilt** /spɔɪlt/ GB adj [child, dog] rozpieszczony; **a ~ brat** infml rozpuszczony bachor infml
spoiler /'spɔɪlə(r)/ n Aut spoiler m
spoils /spɔɪlz/ npl łup m
spoilsport /'spɔɪlspɔːt/ n infml **he's a ~** on zawsze wszystkim psuje zabawę
spoke /spəʊk/ n szprycha f
spokesman /'spəʊksmən/ n rzecznik m
spokeswoman /'spəʊkswʊmən/ n rzeczniczka f
sponge /spʌndʒ/ ❶ n ①gąbka f ②(also **~ cake**) biszkopt m
❷ vt wy|trzeć, -cierać gąbką [material, stain, surface]

III *vi* infml **to ~ off** or **on sb/sth** pasożytować na kimś/czymś *[family, friend]*

sponge bag *n* kosmetyczka *f*

sponsor /'spɒnsə(r)/ **I** *n* [1] (advertiser, backer) sponsor *m*, -ka *f* [2] (patron) protektor *m*, -ka *f*

II *vt* sponsorować *[sporting event, team]*; finansować *[student]*

sponsorship /'spɒnsəʃɪp/ *n* sponsorowanie *n*, sponsoring *m*

spontaneous /spɒn'teɪnɪəs/ *adj* (impulsive) spontaniczny; (produced naturally) samorzutny

spontaneously /spɒn'teɪnɪəslɪ/ *adv* (impulsively) spontanicznie; (by natural process) samorzutnie

spoof /spu:f/ *n* infml (parody) parodia *f* (**on sth** czegoś)

spooky /'spu:kɪ/ *adj* infml *[house, atmosphere]* straszny; *[story]* z dreszczykiem

spool /spu:l/ *n* (of thread) szpulka *f*; (of tape) szpula *f*; (for fishing line) kołowrotek *m*

spoon /spu:n/ *n* łyżka *f*; (for tea, coffee) łyżeczka *f*

spoonful /'spu:nfʊl/ *n* łyżka *f*; (small) łyżeczka *f* (**of sth** czegoś)

sporadic /spə'rædɪk/ *adj* sporadyczny

sport /spɔːt/ *n* [1] sport *m* [2] **to be a good ~** umieć przegrywać

sporting /'spɔːtɪŋ/ *adj* [1] *[event, competition]* sportowy [2] *[offer, gesture]* szlachetny; **to have a ~ chance of winning** mieć szansę na wygranie

sports car *n* samochód *m* sportowy

sports centre GB, **sports center** US *n* kompleks *m* sportowy

sports club *n* klub *m* sportowy

sports ground *n* (large) stadion *m*; (in school, club) boisko *n*

sports jacket *n* GB sportowa marynarka *f*

sportsman /'spɔːtsmən/ *n* sportowiec *m*

sports star *n* gwiazda *f* sportu

sportswear /'spɔːtsweə(r)/ *n* odzież *f* sportowa

sportswoman /'spɔːtswʊmən/ *n* sportsmenka *f*

sporty /'spɔːtɪ/ *adj* infml wysportowany

spot /spɒt/ **I** *n* [1] (on fabric) groszek *m*; (on dice, domino) oczko *n*; (on animal) cętka *f* [2] (stain) plama *f* [3] (pimple) krosta *f*, pryszcz *m*; (on fruit) plamka *f* [4] (place) miejsce *n*; **to be on the ~** być na miejscu; **he decided on the ~** z miejsca się zdecydował [5] infml (small amount) odrobina *f* [6] infml **to be in a (tight) ~** znaleźć się w opałach

II *vt* [1] dostrze|c, -gać *[person]*; spostrze|c, -gać *[mistake]*; wykry|ć, -wać *[defect]* [2] (stain) po|plamić

spot check *n* (unannounced) niezapowiedziana kontrola *f*; (random) wyrywkowa kontrola *f*

spotless /'spɒtlɪs/ *adj [linen, kitchen]* nieskazitelnie czysty; *[reputation]* bez skazy

spotlight /'spɒtlaɪt/ *n* [1] (lamp) reflektor *m* punktowy; (light) światło *n* punktowe [2] (focus of attention) **to be in** or **under the ~** być w centrum uwagi; **to**

turn or **put the ~ on sb/sth** skierować uwagę na kogoś/coś

spotted /'spɒtɪd/ *adj [tie, dress]* w groszki; *[dog]* cętkowany; *[plumage]* nakrapiany, dropiaty

spotty /'spɒtɪ/ *adj* (pimply) *[face]* krostowaty, pryszczaty; (patterned) *[fabric]* w groszki; *[dog]* cętkowany

spouse /spaʊz, US spaʊs/ *n* małżon|ek *m*, -ka *f*

spout /spaʊt/ **I** *n* (of kettle, teapot) dziobek *m*

II *vt* [1] (spurt) *[fountain]* trys|nąć, -kać (czymś) [2] (recite) wyrzuc|ić, -ać z siebie *[figures]*; wygł|osić, -aszać *[advice]*

III *vi [liquid]* wytrys|nąć, -kiwać; **to ~ from** or **out of sth** wytryskiwać z czegoś

sprain /spreɪn/ **I** *n* Med skręcenie *n*

II *vt* skręcić *[ankle]*; nadwerężyć *[wrist, joint]*

sprawl /sprɔːl/ **I** *n* (of buildings) bezładne skupisko *n*; **urban ~** bezładna zabudowa miejska

II *vi [person]* rozł|ożyć, -kładać się

spray /spreɪ/ **I** *n* [1] (seawater) mgiełka *f*; **clouds of ~** mgiełka drobnych kropelek [2] (container) rozpylacz *m*, spray *m* [3] (of flowers) wiązanka *f*, bukiet *m*; (single branch) gałązka *f*

II *vt* rozprysk|ać, -iwać *[liquid]*; sprysk|ać, -iwać *[person]* (**with sth** czymś); **to ~ sth onto sth** (onto fire) polać coś czymś *[foam, water]*; (onto surface, flowers) opryskać coś czymś *[insecticide, water]*

spray can *n* spray *m*, aerozol *m*

spread /spred/ **I** *n* [1] (of disease, fire) rozprzestrzenianie (się) *n* [2] (of education, information) rozpowszechnianie (się) *n* [2] Culin pasta *f*; **cheese ~** serek do smarowania

II *vt* [1] (open out) rozł|ożyć, -kładać *[cloth, map, rug]* (**on** or **over sth** na czymś); **to ~ one's wings** rozprzestrzec skrzydła [2] rozsmarow|ać, -ywać *[jam, honey, paste]* (**on** or **over sth** na czymś) [3] (distribute) rozrzuc|ić, -ać *[fertilizer]*; rozn|ieść, -osić *[mud]*; rozł|ożyć, -kładać *[workload, responsibility]* [4] (also ~ **out**) rozł|ożyć, -kładać *[payments, meetings, course]* [5] rozprzestrzeni|ć, -ać *[fire]*; rozn|ieść, -osić *[disease]*; rozpowszechni|ć, -ać *[news]*; rozpowi|edzieć, -adać *[rumours]*; rozsi|ać, -ewać, siać *[confusion, panic]*

III *vi* [1] *[butter, jam, glue]* rozsmarowywać się [2] *[forest, town]* ciągnąć się, rozciągać się [3] *[epidemic, panic]* rozprzestrzeni|ć, -ać się; *[news, rumour]* roz|ejść, -chodzić się; *[pain, strike]* rozszerz|yć, -ać się

■ **spread out**: ¶ **~ out** *[group]* rozpr|oszyć, -aszać się; *[wings]* rozpo|strzeć, -ścierać się; *[landscape]* rozciągać się ¶ **~ [sth] out** rozł|ożyć, -kładać *[cloth, sheet, map]* (**on** or **over sth** na czymś)

spread-eagled /spred'i:gld/ *adj* **he lay ~ on the floor** leżał na podłodze z rozrzuconymi rękami i nogami

spreadsheet /'spredʃiːt/ *n* arkusz *m* kalkulacyjny

spree /spri:/ n **to go on a ~** (drinking) iść się napić; **to go on a shopping ~** iść zaszaleć w sklepach; **a drinking ~** popijawa infml

sprig /sprɪg/ n (of parsley) listek m; (of holly) gałązka f

sprightly /'spraɪtlɪ/ adj dziarski

spring /sprɪŋ/ **I** n [1] wiosna f; **in (the) ~** na wiosnę, wiosną [2] (coil) sprężyna f [3] (leap) skok m [4] (water source) źródło n

II vt [1] uruch|omić, -amiać [trap, mechanism]; **to ~ a leak** [boat, tank] zacząć przeciekać [2] **to ~ sth on sb** zaskoczyć kogoś czymś [proposal, piece of news]

III vi [1] (jump) sk|oczyć, -akać [2] (originate) [person] pojawić się; [idea] z|rodzić się (**from sth** z czegoś)

■ **spring up**: [building] wyr|osnąć, -astać

spring-clean /ˌsprɪŋ'kli:n/ vt z|robić gruntowne porządki w (czymś) [house]

spring onion n GB dymka f

springtime /'sprɪŋtaɪm/ n wiosna f

springy /'sprɪŋɪ/ adj [mattress, seat] sprężysty

sprinkle /'sprɪŋkl/ vtr **to ~ sth with sth** posypać coś czymś [salt, sugar, herbs]; **to ~ sth with water** pokropić or skropić coś wodą

sprinkler /'sprɪŋklə(r)/ n (for lawn) zraszacz m; (to extinguish fires) instalacja f tryskaczowa

sprint /sprɪnt/ **I** n (race) sprint m

II vi Sport po|biec sprintem; (run fast) bie|c, -gać bardzo szybko

sprout /spraʊt/ **I** n [1] (on plant, tree) pęd m; (of seed) kiełek m [2] (also **Brussels ~**) brukselka f

II vi [plant, tree] wypu|ścić, -szczać pędy; [buds, leaves] pojawi|ć, -ać się; [seeds] za|kiełkować

spruce /spru:s/ **I** n (also **~ tree**) świerk m

II adj [person] elegancki, wymuskany; [house, garden] wypielęgnowany, zadbany

■ **spruce up**: wy|stroić [person]; ogarn|ąć, -iać [house, garden]; **to ~ oneself up** ogarnąć się

spry /spraɪ/ adj dziarski, żwawy

spun /spʌn/ adj **~ gold** złote nici; **~ silk** przędza jedwabna; **~ sugar** wata cukrowa

spur /spɜ:(r)/ **I** n [1] fig bodziec m [2] (for horse) ostroga f [3] (of rock) boczna grań f

II vt pobudz|ić, -ać [person]; [rider] spi|ąć, -nać [horse]; **to ~ sb to sth/to do sth** pobudzić kogoś do czegoś/do zrobienia czegoś

IDIOMS **on the ~ of the moment** pod wpływem chwili or nagłego impulsu

spurn /spɜ:n/ vt odrzuc|ić, -ać [offer, help]; wzgardzić (czymś) [gift]

spurt /spɜ:t/ **I** n [1] (gush) (of water, oil, blood) wytrysk m; (of flame) słup m [2] (of energy, activity) przypływ m; (sudden acceleration) zryw m; **to do sth in ~s** robić coś zrywami; **to put on a ~** [runner, cyclist] przyśpieszyć

II vi (also **~ out**) [liquid] wytrys|nąć, -kiwać, trys|nąć, -kać (**from** or **out of sth** z czegoś)

spy /spaɪ/ **I** n szpieg m

II vt dostrze|c, -gać [figure, object]

III vi **to ~ on sb/sth** szpiegować kogoś/coś

spying /'spaɪɪŋ/ n szpiegostwo n

squabble /'skwɒbl/ vi sprzeczać się (**over** or **about sth** o coś)

squad /skwɒd/ n (of soldiers, police) oddział m; Sport kadra f, reprezentacja f

squad car n radiowóz m

squadron /'skwɒdrən/ n (of ships) eskadra f; (of cavalry) szwadron m; (of planes) dywizjon m

squalid /'skwɒlɪd/ adj zaniedbany, zapuszczony

squall /skwɔ:l/ n nawałnica f; (at sea) szkwał m

squalor /'skwɒlə(r)/ n (of house, surroundings) nędza f; **to live in ~** żyć w brudzie i nędzy

squander /'skwɒndə(r)/ vt roztrw|onić, -aniać [money]

square /skweə(r)/ **I** n [1] (in town) plac m; **town ~** rynek [2] (shape) kwadrat m; (on chessboard) pole n; (in crossword) kwadracik m; (on graph paper) kratka f [3] infml stary nudziarz m infml

II adj [1] (right-angled) kwadratowy; **four ~ miles** cztery mile kwadratowe [2] (quits) **to be (all) ~** (books, accounts) być w porządku; (players, teams) remisować; **I'll give you £20 and we'll be ~** dam ci 20 funtów i będziemy kwita

III vt [1] **to ~ one's shoulders** wyprostować ramiona [2] (settle) spłac|ić, -ać [debt]; uregulow|ać, -ywać [account]

■ **square up**: (settle accounts) rozlicz|yć, -ać się (**with sb** z kimś)

IDIOMS **to go back to ~ one** wrócić do punktu wyjścia

square bracket n nawias m kwadratowy; **in ~s** w nawiasie kwadratowym

square root n pierwiastek m kwadratowy

squash /skwɒʃ/ **I** n [1] Sport squash m [2] (drink) zagęszczony sok m owocowy [3] warzywo z rodziny dyniowatych; US kabaczek

II vt zgni|eść, -atać

■ **squash up** infml: [person] przycis|nąć, -kać się (**against sb/sth** do kogoś/czegoś)

squat /skwɒt/ **I** adj [person, structure, object] przysadzisty

II vi [1] (crouch) kuc|nąć, -ać [2] (inhabit) mieszkać na dziko

squatter /'skwɒtə(r)/ n dziki lokator m; squatter(s) m infml

squawk /skwɔ:k/ vi [parrot] za|skrzeczeć; [duck] za|kwakać; [hen] za|gdakać

squeak /skwi:k/ **I** n (of mouse, soft toy) pisk m; (of door, shoes, chalk, mechanism) skrzypnięcie n

II vi [child, mouse, soft toy] za|piszczeć; (repeatedly) popiskiwać; [door, chalk, shoes, mechanism] skrzyp|nąć, -ieć

squeaky /'skwi:kɪ/ adj [voice] piskliwy; [gate, hinge, wheel] skrzypiący

squeal /skwi:l/ vi [animal] za|kwiczeć; [person, brakes] za|piszczeć

squeamish /'skwi:mɪʃ/ adj **to be ~** (easily sickened) mieć delikatny żołądek; (by screen violence) być delikatnym

squeeze /skwi:z/ **Ⅰ** n ① infml (crush) ścisk m; **it will be a tight ~ with four of us** będzie nam ciasno we czwórkę ② **a credit ~** ograniczenie kredytów; **to feel the ~** [person, company] mieć trudności finansowe

Ⅱ vt ① ścis|nąć, -kać [tube, bottle]; wycis|nąć, -kać [tube, lemon]; uścisnąć [hand, arm]; nacis|nąć, -kać [trigger] ② wycis|nąć, -kać [juice, liquid] (**out of sth** z czegoś); fig wycisnąć [money] (**out of sb/sth** z kogoś/czegoś); **to ~ the truth out of sb** wycisnąć z kogoś prawdę ③ (fit) wcis|nąć, -kać [people] (**into sth** do czegoś); up|chać, -ychać [things] (**into sth** w czymś)

■ **squeeze in**: ¶ **~ in** [person] wcis|nąć, -kać się ¶ **~ [sb] in** [doctor] zna|leźć, -jdować czas dla (kogoś)

■ **squeeze past**: [car, person] przecis|nąć, -kać się

squelch /skweltʃ/ vi [water, mud] chlup|nąć, -ać, chlupotać; **to ~ along** brnąć z chlupotem

squid /skwɪd/ n kałamarnica f

squiggle /'skwɪgl/ n gryzmoły plt

squint /skwɪnt/ **Ⅰ** n zez m; **to have a ~** mieć zeza **Ⅱ** vi ① (look) z|mrużyć oczy ② (have eye condition) mieć zeza

squire /'skwaɪə(r)/ n ≈ dziedzic m

squirm /skwɜːm/ vi [snake] wić się; [person] (in pain) zwijać się; **to ~ with embarrassment** nie wiedzieć, gdzie się podziać ze wstydu

squirrel /'skwɪrəl, US 'skwɜːrəl/ n wiewiórka f

squirt /skwɜːt/ **Ⅰ** vt strzyk|nąć, -ać (czymś) [liquid] **Ⅱ** vi [liquid] trys|nąć, -kać (**from** or **out of sth** z czegoś)

stab /stæb/ **Ⅰ** n ① (act) dźgnięcie n; **a ~ in the back** fig nóż w plecy fig ② **a ~ of pain** kłujący ból **Ⅱ** vt pchnąć nożem [person]; **to ~ sb to death** zakłuć kogoś

stabbing /'stæbɪŋ/ n napad m z użyciem noża

stability /stə'bɪlətɪ/ n stabilność f; (of relationship) stałość f

stabilize /'steɪbəlaɪz/ **Ⅰ** vt u|stabilizować **Ⅱ** vi u|stabilizować się

stable /'steɪbl/ **Ⅰ** n stajnia f; **riding ~s** stajnie wyścigowe **Ⅱ** adj ① (steady) stabilny ② (psychologically) zrównoważony

stack /stæk/ **Ⅰ** n (of hay) stóg m; (of straw) sterta f; (of books, papers) stos m **Ⅱ** vt ① (also ~ **up**) (pile up) u|łożyć, -kładać w stosy or sterty [books] ② (fill) zapełni|ć, -ać [shelves] ③ kazać (czemuś) oczekiwać w kolejce [planes, calls]

stadium /'steɪdɪəm/ n stadion m

staff /stɑːf, US stæf/ n ① (employees) personel m; **to be on the ~ of a company** być pracownikiem firmy ② (also **teaching ~**) ciało n pedagogiczne; Univ pracownicy m pl dydaktyczni

staff meeting n Sch rada f pedagogiczna

staff room n Sch pokój m nauczycielski

stag /stæg/ n jeleń m

stage /steɪdʒ/ **Ⅰ** n ① (phase) etap m (**of** or **in sth** czegoś); (of illness) stadium n (**of** or **in sth** czegoś) ② (raised platform) podium n; (in theatre) scena f; (for pop singers) estrada f **Ⅱ** vt ① wystawi|ć, -ać [play] ② (organize) z|organizować [ceremony, protest] ③ (fake) od|egrać, -grywać, za|inscenizować [scene, quarrel]

stagecoach /'steɪdʒkəʊtʃ/ n dyliżans m

stage fright n trema f

stage-manager /ˌsteɪdʒ'mænɪdʒə(r)/ n inspicjent m, -ka f

stagger /'stægə(r)/ **Ⅰ** vt ① (shock) wprawi|ć, -ać w osłupienie [person] ② roz|łożyć, -kładać w czasie [visits, payments] **Ⅱ** vi (from weakness) za|chwiać się na nogach; (drunkenly) zat|oczyć, -aczać się

staggering /'stægərɪŋ/ adj [amount, increase, loss] olbrzymi; [news, event] zdumiewający; [success] oszałamiający

stagnant /'stægnənt/ adj [water] stojący; [economy] w stanie zastoju

stagnate /stæg'neɪt, US 'stægneɪt/ vi [economy] być w zastoju; [person, society] pogrąż|yć, -ać się w marazmie

stag night, stag party n wieczór m kawalerski

staid /steɪd/ adj [person] stateczny; [society] tradycyjny

stain /steɪn/ **Ⅰ** n ① (mark) plama f ② (for wood) bejca f; (for fabric) barwnik m **Ⅱ** vt ① (soil) po|plamić [clothes, carpet, fingers] ② (colour) zabarwi|ć, -ać [specimen]; za|bejcować [wood]

stained glass n szkło n witrażowe

stained glass window n okno n witrażowe

stainless steel /'steɪnlɪs stiːl/ n stal f nierdzewna

stain remover n odplamiacz m

stair /steə(r)/ **Ⅰ** n (step) stopień m **Ⅱ** stairs npl **the ~s** schody plt; **to fall down the ~s** spaść ze schodów

staircase /'steəkeɪs/, **stairway** /'steəweɪ/ n schody plt; (inside building) klatka f schodowa

stake /steɪk/ **Ⅰ** n ① (amount risked) stawka f; **to be at ~** (at risk) być zagrożonym; **hundreds of jobs are at ~** chodzi o setki miejsc pracy ② (investment) udział m (**in sth** w czymś) ③ (pole) słupek m; (thicker) słup m; (metal) pręt m **Ⅱ** vt postawić, stawić [money, property]; nara|zić, -żać [reputation, life]

■ **stake out**: **~ [sth] out** [police] obserwować [hide-out]

stale /steɪl/ adj [1] [bread, cake] czerstwy; [beer] zwietrzały; [odour] stęchły [2] [ideas] zwietrzały; [jokes] oklepany

stalemate /'steɪlmeɪt/ n [1] (in chess) pat m [2] (deadlock) impas m

stalk /stɔːk/ [1] n (of rose) łodyga f; (of leaf, apple) ogonek m; (of mushroom) nóżka f; (of cabbage) głąb m [1] vt [hunter animal] tropić, podchodzić; [murderer] śledzić [victim]

stall /stɔːl/ [1] n [1] (in market) stragan m; (at fair) stoisko n; (newspaper stand) kiosk m [2] (in stable) boks m [1] **stalls** npl GB (in theatre) parter m [1] vt I ~ed the engine/car zgasł mi silnik/samochód [1] vi [1] [car] z|gasnąć [2] (play for time) za|grać na zwłokę

stallholder /'stɔːlhəʊldə(r)/ n właściciel m, -ka f straganu

stallion /'stælɪən/ n ogier m

stalwart /'stɔːlwət/ adj [member] oddany; [defence] niezłomny

stamina /'stæmɪnə/ n wytrzymałość f

stammer /'stæmə(r)/ [1] n jąkanie się n [1] vi jąkać się

stamp /stæmp/ [1] n [1] (for envelope) znaczek m; **a 24 p** ~ znaczek za 24 pensy [2] (device) pieczątka f; (bigger) pieczęć f; **date** ~ datownik m [3] (mark) pieczątka f; (bigger) pieczęć f [1] vt [1] wbi|ć, -jać [name, number] (**on sth** do czegoś); ostemplow|ać, -ywać [passport, ticket]; przybi|ć, -jać pieczątkę na (czymś) [document] [2] **to** ~ **one's foot** (in anger) tupnąć nogą [1] vi [person] tup|nąć, -ać; [horse] grzebać nogą; **to** ~ **on sth** nadepnąć na coś [toy]; udeptać coś [soil, ground]

stamp-collecting /'stæmpkəlektɪŋ/ n filatelistyka f

stamped addressed envelope, sae n zaadresowana koperta f ze znaczkiem

stampede /stæm'piːd/ [1] n (rush) popłoch m [1] vi pędzić w popłochu or w panice

stance /stɑːns, stæns/ n (attitude) stanowisko n; (way of standing) postawa f

stand /stænd/ [1] n [1] (for tool, instrument) stojak m; (for coats) wieszak m; (for trophy) podstawka f; (for sheet music) pulpit m; (for lamp) statyw m [2] (stall) (in market) stragan m; (kiosk) budka f; (at exhibition, trade fair) stoisko n [3] (in stadium) trybuna f [4] (witness box) miejsce n dla świadka [5] (stance) **to take a** ~ **on sth** zająć stanowisko w kwestii czegoś [6] **to make a last** ~ stoczyć bój na śmierć i życie [1] vt [1] (place) postawić, stawiać [person, object]; ~ **it over there** postaw to tam [2] (bear) zn|ieść, -osić [person, insects, food]; **he can't** ~ **to do it** or **doing it** nie znosi tego robić; **she won't** ~ **any bad behaviour** nie będzie tolerować złego zachowania [3] infml postawić, stawiać [meal, drink];

to ~ **sb sth** postawić komuś coś [4] **to** ~ **trial** stanąć przed sądem [1] vi [1] (also ~ **up**) wsta|ć, -wać [2] (be upright) [person, object] stać; **to remain** ~**ing** stać nadal [3] [building] stać; [village] być położonym [4] (step) **to** ~ **on sth** nadepnąć na coś [5] (be) **as things** ~ ... w obecnej sytuacji...; **the total** ~**s at 300** suma wynosi 300; **where do you** ~ **on abortion?** jakie jest twoje stanowisko w kwestii aborcji?; **to** ~ **in sb's way** stać komuś na drodze also fig [6] (remain valid) [offer, agreement] obowiązywać, być aktualnym [7] (be a candidate) kandydować; **to** ~ **for parliament** kandydować do parlamentu ■ **stand back**: [person, crowd] cof|nąć, -ać się; **to** ~ **back from sth** odsunąć się od czegoś; fig wycofać się z czegoś ■ **stand by**: ¶ ~ **by** [doctor, army] być w pogotowiu ¶ ~ **by** [sb/sth] stać przy (kimś) [person]; być wiernym (czemuś) [principles]; trwać przy (czymś), trzymać się (czegoś) [decision]; dotrzym|ać, -ywać (czegoś) [promise] ■ **stand down**: [president] ust|ąpić, -ępować ■ **stand for**: [1] [person] opowie|dzieć, -adać się za (czymś); [initials] oznaczać [2] (tolerate) godzić się na (coś) ■ **stand in**: **to** ~ **in for sb** zast|ąpić, -ępować kogoś ■ **stand out**: [person, achievement] wyróżniać się; **to** ~ **out from** or **against sb/sth** wyróżniać się na tle kogoś/czegoś or spośród kogoś/czegoś ■ **stand up**: ¶ ~ **up** [1] (rise) wsta|ć, -wać [2] (stay upright) stać [3] [argument, theory] utrzym|ać, -ywać się; **to** ~ **up to sth** wytrzymywać coś [scrutiny] [4] **to** ~ **up to sb** stawić czoło komuś [5] **to** ~ **up for sb/sth** stanąć w obronie kogoś/czegoś ¶ ~ [sb/sth] **up** infml (fail to meet) wystawić kogoś do wiatru infml

standard /'stændəd/ [1] n [1] (level of quality) poziom m, standard m; **his work is not up to** ~ jego praca jest niezadowalająca [2] (official specification) standard m, norma f [3] (banner) sztandar m [1] adj [size] typowy; [procedure] standardowy; [rate, pay] normalny; **it's** ~ **practice** to ogólnie przyjęta praktyka

Standard Assessment Task n GB Sch ujednolicony sprawdzian m wiadomości

standardize /'stændədaɪz/ vt standaryzować, z|normalizować

standard lamp n GB lampa f stojąca

standard of living n poziom m życia

standby /'stændbaɪ/ n (person) zastęp|ca m, -czyni f; **to be on** ~ [army, emergency services] być w pogotowiu; (for airline ticket) być na liście rezerwowej

stand-in /'stændɪn/ n zastęp|ca m, -czyni f; (in film) dubler m, -ka f

standing /'stændɪŋ/ [1] n [1] (reputation) pozycja f (**among sb** wśród kogoś); **financial** ~ sytuacja finansowa [2] (length of time) **of long** ~ *[relationship]* długotrwały

II *adj [army, committee, invitation]* stały; **a** ~ **joke** stały temat żartów

standing charge *n* opłata *f* stała

standing order *n* zlecenie *n* stałe

stand-off /'stændɒf/ *n* US impas *m*

standpoint /'stændpɔɪnt/ *n* punkt *m* widzenia (**on sth** na temat czegoś); **from sb's** ~ z punktu widzenia kogoś

standstill /'stændstɪl/ *n* (in economy) zastój *m*; **to be at a** ~ *[traffic, factory]* stać; **to come to a** ~ *[person, car]* zatrzymać się; *[talks]* utknąć w martwym punkcie

stand-up /'stændʌp/ **I** *n* (also ~ **comedy**) występ *m* rozrywkowy jednego artysty

II *adj [comedian]* występujący solo

Stanley knife® /'stænlɪnaɪf/ *n* nóż *m* do wykładzin

staple /'steɪpl/ **I** *n* [1] (for paper) zszywka *f* [2] (basic food) podstawowe pożywienie *n*

II *adj [product, food]* podstawowy; **bread is their** ~ **diet** chleb stanowi podstawę ich pożywienia

III *vt* przypi|ąć, -nać (**to** or **onto sth** do czegoś)

stapler /'steɪplə(r)/ *n* zszywacz *m*

star /stɑː(r)/ **I** *n* [1] (in sky) gwiazda *f* [2] (person) gwiazda *f* [3] (asterisk) gwiazdka *f* [4] (award) (to hotel, restaurant) gwiazdka *f*; **a four-**~ **hotel** hotel czterogwiazdkowy

II *vt* **the play** ~**s Alan Bates** główną rolę w sztuce gra Alan Bates

III *vi [actor]* za|grać główną rolę (**in sth** w czymś)

starch /stɑːtʃ/ *n* [1] (carbohydrate) skrobia *f* [2] (for clothes) krochmal *m*

stardom /'stɑːdəm/ *n* status *m* gwiazdy; **to rise to** ~ stać się gwiazdą

stare /steə(r)/ **I** *n* (utkwione) spojrzenie *n*

II *vi* wpatrywać się (**at sb/sth** w kogoś/coś)

starfish /'stɑːfɪʃ/ *n* rozgwiazda *f*

stark /stɑːk/ *adj [landscape, decor]* surowy; **the** ~ **reality** brutalna rzeczywistość; **to be in** ~ **contrast to sth** jaskrawo kontrastować z czymś (ІDIOMS) **to be** ~ **naked** być zupełnie nagim or gołym *infml*

starry /'stɑːrɪ/ *adj [night, sky]* gwiaździsty

starry-eyed /,stɑːrɪ'aɪd/ *adj [person]* chodzący z głową w chmurach; ~ **about sb/sth** zauroczony kimś/czymś

star sign *n* znak *m* zodiaku

star-studded /'stɑːstʌdɪd/ *n* ~ **cast** gwiazdorska obsada

start /stɑːt/ **I** *n* [1] (beginning) początek *m*; **(right) from the** ~ od (samego) początku; **from** ~ **to finish** od początku do końca [2] (advantage) przewaga *f* na starcie [3] Sport (departure line) linia *f* startu [4] (movement) **she awoke with a** ~ poderwała się ze snu

II *vt* [1] (begin) zacz|ąć, -ynać *[day]*; napocz|ąć, -ynać *[bottle]*; **to** ~ **doing** or **to do sth** zacząć robić coś [2] (cause, initiate) zacz|ąć, -ynać *[quarrel, war]*; *[event]* zapoczątkow|ać, -ywać *[trouble]*; s|powodować *[fire]*; zał|ożyć, -kładać *[business]*; **to** ~ **a family** założyć rodzinę [3] uruch|omić, -amiać *[machine, car, motor]*

III *vi* [1] (begin) *[person]* zacz|ąć, -ynać; *[meeting]* zacz|ąć, -ynać się; *[fire]* wybuch|nąć, -ać; **to** ~ **again** zacząć od początku or od nowa; **to** ~ **by doing sth** zacząć od zrobienia czegoś; ~**ing Wednesday...** począwszy od środy [2] (depart) *[person]* wyrusz|yć, -ać; *[train]* odje|chać, -żdżać [3] (jump nervously) pod|erwać, -rywać się [4] *[car, engine]* zapal|ić, -ać; *[machine]* rusz|yć, -ać

IV to start with *adv phr* [1] (firstly) najpierw [2] (at first) początkowo [3] (first of all) przede wszystkim

■ **start off:** ¶ ~ **off** [1] (set off) *[train, bus]* rusz|yć, -ać; *[person]* wyrusz|yć, -ać [2] (begin) *[person]* zacz|ąć, -ynać (**with sth/by doing sth** od czegoś/od zrobienia czegoś); **to** ~ **off as a secretary** zaczynać jako sekretarka ¶ ~ **[sth] off** [1] zacz|ąć, -ynać *[visit, talk]* (**with sth** od czegoś) [2] uruch|omić, -amiać *[machine]*

■ **start out:** (on journey) wyrusz|yć, -ać

■ **start over:** US zacz|ąć, -ynać od początku or od nowa

■ **start up:** ¶ ~ **up** *[engine]* zapal|ić, -ać ¶ ~ **[sth] up** uruch|omić, -amiać *[car]*; za|łożyć, -kładać *[business]*; otw|orzyć, -ierać *[shop]*

starter /'stɑːtə(r)/ *n* [1] Sport (official) starter *m* [2] Culin przystawka *f* (ІDIOMS) **for** ~**s** infml na początek

startle /'stɑːtl/ *vt* [1] (take aback) zask|oczyć, -akiwać [2] (alarm) wystrasz|yć, -ać

startling /'stɑːtlɪŋ/ *adj* (surprising) zadziwiający; (alarming) alarmujący

starvation /,stɑː'veɪʃn/ *n* (hunger) głód *m*; (death) śmierć *f* głodowa; **to die of** ~ umrzeć z głodu

starve /stɑːv/ **I** *vt* [1] za|głodzić [2] (deprive) **to be** ~**d of sth** cierpieć na brak czegoś *[affection]*; **we're** ~**d for company** bardzo nam brakuje towarzystwa

II *vi* (suffer) głodować; (die) um|rzeć, -ierać z głodu

starving /'stɑːvɪŋ/ *adj* (hunger-stricken) głodujący; **I'm** ~! umieram or padam z głodu!

state /steɪt/ **I** *n* [1] stan *m*; **the present** ~ **of affairs** obecny stan rzeczy; **he is not in a fit** ~ **to drive** nie jest w stanie prowadzić [2] (nation) (also **State**) państwo *n* [3] (government) **the State** państwo *n*, władze *plt* państwowe

II States *npl* **the States** Stany *plt* (Zjednoczone)

III *adj* [1] *[school, enterprise]* państwowy; ~ **budget** budżet państwa [2] *[opening, banquet]* uroczysty

IV *vt* [1] (express, say) stwierdz|ić, -ać *[fact]*; wyra|zić, -żać *[opinion]*; poda|ć, -wać, określ|ić, -ać

[age, income]; **to** ~ **that...** oświadczyć, że...
$\boxed{2}$ (specify) określ|ić, -ać *[amount, place, time]*
$\boxed{\text{IDIOMS}}$ **to be in a** ~ być roztrzęsionym

State Department *n* US Departament *m* Stanu

state-funded /ˌsteɪtˈfʌndɪd/ *adj* finansowany przez państwo

stateless /ˈsteɪtlɪs/ *adj* bezpaństwowy

stately /ˈsteɪtlɪ/ *adj [mansion]* okazały; *[manner]* dostojny

stately home *n* GB rezydencja *f*

statement /ˈsteɪtmənt/ *n* $\boxed{1}$ twierdzenie *n*; **a** ~ **of fact** stwierdzenie faktu $\boxed{2}$ (formal announcement) oświadczenie *n* $\boxed{3}$ (also **bank** ~) wyciąg *m* z konta

state of the art *adj [technology]* najnowocześniejszy; *[laboratory]* supernowoczesny

statesman /ˈsteɪtsmən/ *n* mąż *m* stanu

static /ˈstætɪk/ $\boxed{\text{I}}$ *n* $\boxed{1}$ (also ~ **electricity**) elektryczność *f* statyczna $\boxed{2}$ Radio, TV zakłócenia *n pl*
$\boxed{\text{II}}$ *adj* $\boxed{1}$ (stationary) *[display]* statyczny; *[traffic]* zablokowany $\boxed{2}$ (stable) *[population, prices]* stały

station /ˈsteɪʃn/ $\boxed{\text{I}}$ *n* $\boxed{1}$ (also **railway** ~ GB) stacja *f*; (big) dworzec *m* $\boxed{2}$ Radio stacja *f* (radiowa); TV stacja *f* telewizyjna $\boxed{3}$ (also **police** ~) komisariat *m*; (small) posterunek *m* policji
$\boxed{\text{II}}$ *vt* postawić, stawiać *[guard, policeman]*; rozmie|ścić, -szczać *[troops]*

stationary /ˈsteɪʃnrɪ, US -nerɪ/ *adj [vehicle]* nieruchomy

stationer /ˈsteɪʃnə(r)/ *n* (also ~'s) sklep *m* papierniczy

stationery /ˈsteɪʃnərɪ, US -nerɪ/ *n* materiały *m pl* piśmienne; (for office) materiały *m pl* biurowe; (writing paper) papier *m* listowy

station wagon *n* US (estate car) kombi *n inv*

statistic /stəˈtɪstɪk/ *n* ~**s** dane *plt* liczbowe; **unemployment** ~**s** statystyki dotyczące bezrobocia

statistical /stəˈtɪstɪkl/ *adj* statystyczny

statue /ˈstætʃuː/ *n* posąg *m*, statua *f*

stature /ˈstætʃə(r)/ *n* $\boxed{1}$ (height) postura *f* $\boxed{2}$ (status) ranga *f*

status /ˈsteɪtəs/ *n* $\boxed{1}$ (position) status *m*; **financial** ~ sytuacja finansowa; **professional** ~ status zawodowy; **marital** ~ stan cywilny $\boxed{2}$ (prestige) status *m*

status quo /ˌsteɪtəsˈkwəʊ/ *n* status quo *n inv*

status symbol *n* atrybut *m* statusu społecznego

statute /ˈstætʃuːt/ *n* ustawa *f*; **governed by** ~ regulowany ustawą

statutory /ˈstatʃʊtərɪ, US -tɔːrɪ/ *adj [right]* ustawowy

staunch /stɔːntʃ, stɒntʃ/ *adj [supporter, defender]* zagorzały; *[ally]* wierny, oddany

stave /steɪv/ *n* Mus pięciolinia *f*
■ **stave off**: oszuk|ać, -iwać *[hunger]*; pokon|ać, -ywać *[fatigue]*; odsu|nąć, -wać *[threat]*

stay /steɪ/ $\boxed{\text{I}}$ *n* $\boxed{1}$ (visit) pobyt *m* $\boxed{2}$ **a** ~ **of execution** zawieszenie wykonania wyroku śmierci
$\boxed{\text{II}}$ *vi* $\boxed{1}$ (remain) zosta|ć, -wać; **to** ~ **for lunch** zostać na lunch; **to** ~ **calm** zachować spokój $\boxed{2}$ (have accommodation) zatrzym|ać, -ywać się; **to** ~ **in a hotel/at a friend's house** zatrzymać się w hotelu/u kolegi $\boxed{3}$ (spend the night) zatrzym|ać, -ywać się na noc; **to** ~ **overnight in Philadelphia** przenocować w Filadelfii
■ **stay in**: nie wyj|ść, -chodzić, zosta|ć, -wać w domu
■ **stay out**: **to** ~ **out late** wrócić późno; **to** ~ **out all night** nie wrócić do domu na noc; **to** ~ **out of trouble** nie pakować się w tarapaty
■ **stay up**: nie położyć się, nie kłaść się; **I** ~**ed up for him until two o'clock** czekałem na niego do drugiej w nocy; **he likes to** ~ **up late** lubi późno chodzić spać

staying-power /ˈsteɪŋpaʊə(r)/ *n* wytrzymałość *f*

steadfast /ˈstedfɑːst, US -fæst/ *adj [friend]* wierny; *[belief]* niezłomny; *[refusal]* stanowczy

steadily /ˈstedɪlɪ/ *adv* $\boxed{1}$ (gradually) *[increase]* stale $\boxed{2}$ *[work, rain]* bez przerwy

steady /ˈstedɪ/ $\boxed{\text{I}}$ *adj* $\boxed{1}$ (continual) *[speed, increase]* stały; *[pace]* równy; *[breathing]* miarowy; *[rain]* ciągły $\boxed{2}$ (firm) *[hand]* pewny; *[ladder]* stabilny; **to hold sth** ~ przytrzymać coś *[ladder]* $\boxed{3}$ *[voice]* opanowany; *[gaze]* spokojny $\boxed{4}$ (reliable) *[job, relationship]* stały; *[company]* solidny
$\boxed{\text{II}}$ *vt* **to** ~ **one's nerves** opanować nerwy

steak /steɪk/ *n* (of beef) befsztyk *m*; (of pork) kotlet *m*; (of fish) dzwono *n* (łososia, suma)

steal /stiːl/ $\boxed{\text{I}}$ *vt* u|kraść *[object]*; **to** ~ **sth from sb** ukraść komuś coś
$\boxed{\text{II}}$ *vi* $\boxed{1}$ (thieve) kraść; **to** ~ **from houses** okradać domy $\boxed{2}$ (creep) skradać się; **to** ~ **out of the room** wyjść się z pokoju; **to** ~ **up on sb** podkraść się do kogoś

stealing /ˈstiːlɪŋ/ *n* kradzież *f*

stealthy /ˈstelθɪ/ *adj [glance]* ukradkowy; *[steps]* skradający się

steam /stiːm/ $\boxed{\text{I}}$ *n* para *f* (wodna)
$\boxed{\text{II}}$ *vt* u|gotować na parze *[vegetables]*
$\boxed{\text{III}}$ *vi [food]* parować; *[kettle]* gotować się
■ **steam up**: *[window, glasses]* zaparow|ać, -ywać
$\boxed{\text{IDIOMS}}$ **to run out of** ~ *[campaign]* stracić impet; *[athlete]* opaść z sił; **to let off** ~ (use excess energy) wyładowywać się; (lose one's temper) wściekać się

steam engine *n* parowóz *m*

steamer /ˈstiːmə(r)/ *n* (boat) parowiec *m*

steamroller /ˈstiːmrəʊlə(r)/ *n* walec *m* parowy

steamy /ˈstiːmɪ/ *adj* $\boxed{1}$ *[window]* zaparowany; *[day]* parny $\boxed{2}$ infml *[film]* erotyczny

steel /stiːl/ $\boxed{\text{I}}$ *n* stal *f*
$\boxed{\text{II}}$ *vr* **to** ~ **oneself for sth/to do sth** przygotować się na coś/żeby coś zrobić

steelworks /'sti:lwɜ:ks/, **steelyard** /'sti:lja:d/ *n* huta *f* stali

steep /sti:p/ **[]** *adj* ① *[slope, hill, path, stairs, roof]* stromy ② (sharp) *[rise, fall]* gwałtowny ③ infml *[price]* wygórowany

[] *vt* na|moczyć *[fruit]* (**in sth** w czymś)

steeple /'sti:pl/ *n* (tower) wieża *f*; (spire) iglica *f*

steer /stɪə(r)/ **[]** *n* wół *m* opasowy

[] *vt* ① kierować (czymś) *[car]*; sterować (czymś) *[boat]* ② (guide) po|prowadzić, za|prowadzić *[person]*

[]] *vi* (in boat) płynąć; **the car ~s well** samochód dobrze się prowadzi

IDIOMS: **to ~ clear of sb/sth** trzymać się z daleka od kogoś/czegoś

steering lock *n* blokada *f* kierownicy

steering wheel *n* kierownica *f*

stem /stem/ **[]** *n* ① (of flower) łodyga *f*; (of mushroom) trzon *m*; (of leaf) ogonek *m*; (of fruit) szypułka *f* ② (of glass) nóżka *f*

[] *vi* za|tamować *[flow]*; powstrzym|ać, -ywać *[advance, tide]*

[]] *vi* **to ~ from sth** *[problem]* wziąć *or* brać się z czegoś; *[tradition]* wywodzić się z czegoś

stencil /'stensɪl/ **[]** *n* (card) szablon *m*; (in typing) matryca *f*

[] *vt* ozd|obić, -abiać za pomocą szablonu *[fabric, surface]*

stenography /ste'nɒgrəfɪ/ *n* US stenografia *f*

step /step/ **[]** *n* ① (pace) krok *m*; **to take a ~** zrobić krok ② fig (measure) krok *m*; **to take ~s to do sth** podjąć kroki zmierzające do zrobienia czegoś ③ (stair) stopień *m*; **~s** (small ladder) drabinka *f*

[] *vi* **to ~ on sth** nastąpić *or* nadepnąć na coś; **to ~ in sth** wejść w coś *[puddle]*; **to ~ into sth** wejść do czegoś *[lift]*; **to ~ off sth** zejść z czegoś *[pavement]*; **to ~ over sth** przejść przez coś *[fence]*

■ **step back** fig: nab|rać, -ierać dystansu (**from sth** do czegoś)

■ **step down**: ust|ąpić, -ępować; (as electoral candidate) wycof|ać, -ywać się

■ **step in**: wkr|oczyć, -aczać (**and do sth** żeby coś zrobić)

■ **step up**: zwiększ|yć, -ać *[production]*; nasil|ić, -ać *[campaign]*

IDIOMS: **one ~ at a time** wszystko po kolei

stepbrother /'stepbrʌðə(r)/ *n* przyrodni brat *m*

step-by-step /ˌstepbaɪ'step/ **[]** *adj [guide]* dokładny, krok po kroku; *[policy]* stopniowy

[] **step by step** *adv [explain]* punkt po punkcie

stepchild /'steptʃaɪld/ *n* (stepson) pasierb *m*; (stepdaughter) pasierbica *f*

stepdaughter /'stepˈdɔ:tə(r)/ *n* pasierbica *f*

stepfather /'stepfɑ:ðə(r)/ *n* ojczym *m*

stepladder /'steplædə(r)/ *n* drabina *f*

stepmother /'stepmʌðə(r)/ *n* macocha *f*

stepping stone *n* kamień *m* (ułatwiający przejście przez strumień); fig szczebel *m* w karierze

stepsister /'stepsɪstə(r)/ *n* przyrodnia siostra *f*

stepson /'stepsʌn/ *n* pasierb *m*

stereo /'steriəʊ/ *n* ① (technique) stereofonia *f*; **broadcast in ~** transmisja stereofoniczna *or* stereo ② (set) zestaw *m* stereo; **personal ~** osobisty odtwarzacz stereofoniczny

stereotype /'steriətaip/ *n* stereotyp *m*

sterile /'sterail, US 'sterəl/ *adj* ① *[person]* bezpłodny; *[land]* jałowy ② *[bandage]* sterylny

sterilize /'sterəlaiz/ *vt* ① wy|sterylizować *[person]* ② wy|sterylizować, wyjał|owić, -awiać *[instrument]*

sterling /'stɜ:lɪŋ/ *n* funt *m* szterling

stern /stɜ:n/ **[]** *n* (of boat) rufa *f*

[] *adj [look]* srogi; *[landscape]* surowy

steroid /'stɪərɔɪd, 'ste-/ *n* steroid *m*, steryd *m*

stew /stju:, US stu:/ **[]** *n* (with beef) mięso *n* duszone z jarzynami; (with chicken) potrawka *f*

[] *vt* u|dusić *[meat]*; u|gotować *[fruit]*; **~ed apples** (as dessert) kompot *m* z jabłek

steward /'stjuəd, US 'stu:ərd/ *n* (on plane, ship) steward *m*; (of estate) zarządca *m*; (of club) intendent *m*, -ka *f*; (at races) organizator *m*, -ka *f*

stewardess /'stjuədes, US 'stu:ərdəs/ *n* stewardesa *f*

stick /stɪk/ **[]** *n* ① (of wood) patyk *m*; (as weapon) kij *m*; (for ice cream) patyczek *m* ② (also **walking ~**) laska *f* ③ (of dynamite) laska *f* ④ (in hockey) kij *m*

[] *vt* ① wbi|ć, -jać *[spade, fork]* (**into sth** w coś) ② (put in) wsadz|ić, -ać; (put forward) wystawi|ć, -ać ③ (fix in place) przykle|ić, -jać *[stamp, poster]* (**on sth** na czymś)

[]] *vi* ① **the nail stuck in my finger** gwóźdź wbił mi się w palec ② *[stamp, label]* przykle|ić, -jać się; **to ~ to the pan** *[sauce, rice]* przywrzeć do dna ③ *[drawer, door, lift]* zaci|ąć, -nać się ④ *[name]* przylgnąć; *[habit]* przyj|ąć, -mować się; **to ~ in sb's mind** utkwić komuś w pamięci

■ **stick at**: **~ at [sth]** przy|kładać, -łożyć się do (czegoś) *[task]*

■ **stick out**: ¶ **~ out** *[nail, sharp object]* wystawać; **his ears ~ out** ma odstające uszy ¶ **~ [sth] out**: **to ~ out one's chest** wypiąć pierś; **to ~ one's tongue out** wystawić język

■ **stick to**: ① (keep to) trzymać się (czegoś) *[facts, plan, diet]*; **to ~ to the point** trzymać się tematu ② (stay close to) być przy (kimś) *[husband, friend]*

■ **stick together**: ¶ **~ together** ① *[pages]* skle|ić, -jać się ② infml (remain loyal) wspierać się nawzajem ③ infml (not separate) trzymać się razem ¶ **~ [sth] together** skle|ić, -jać *[objects, pieces]*

■ **stick up**: *[pole, mast]* wznosić się, stać; **to ~ up for sb** (defend) stanąć w obronie kogoś; (side with) stanąć po stronie kogoś

sticker /'stɪkə(r)/ *n* naklejka *f*

sticking plaster n plaster m opatrunkowy

sticky /'stɪkɪ/ adj ⓵ *[hand, substance]* lepki; *[label]* samoprzylepny ⓶ (sweaty) *[palm]* lepki

(IDIOMS:) **to have ~ fingers** mieć lepkie ręce or palce fig

sticky tape n infml taśma f klejąca or samoprzylepna

stiff /stɪf/ **Ⅰ** adj ⓵ sztywny; (after sport, sleeping badly) zesztywniały, zdrętwiały; **to have a ~ neck** mieć zesztywniały or zdrętwiały kark ⓶ *[drawer, door]* zacinający się; **to be ~** *[lever]* ciężko chodzić infml ⓷ *[manner, style]* sztywny ⓸ (harsh) *[sentence]* surowy; *[reply, warning]* ostry ⓹ (difficult) *[test, climb]* ciężki; *[competition]* silny ⓺ (high) *[charge, fine]* wysoki; *[price]* wygórowany ⓻ *[drink]* mocny

Ⅱ adv infml **to bore sb ~** zanudzać kogoś na śmierć; **to be scared ~** być sztywnym z przerażenia

stiffen /'stɪfn/ **Ⅰ** vt usztywni|ć, -ać *[fabric]*; wzm|ocnić, -acniać *[structure]*

Ⅱ vi ⓵ *[person]* ze|sztywnieć ⓶ *[mixture]* z|gęstnieć; *[jelly]* s|tężeć

stifle /'staɪfl/ vt powstrzym|ać, -ywać *[sneeze]*; s|łtumić, z|dusić *[fire, revolt]*

stigma /'stɪgmə/ n piętno n

stigmatize /'stɪgmətaɪz/ vt na|piętnować

stile /staɪl/ n (in wall, hedge) przełaz m

stiletto /stɪ'letəʊ/ n (also **~ heel**) (shoe, heel) szpilka f

still¹ /stɪl/ adv ⓵ (up to a point in time) wciąż; (as before) nadal; (expected to stop) (wciąż) jeszcze; **he's ~ as crazy as ever** jest zwariowany jak zawsze; **they're ~ in town** nadal są w mieście ⓶ (yet to happen) jeszcze; **I have four exams ~ to go** zostały mi jeszcze cztery egzaminy ⓷ (nevertheless) mimo to; **~, it's the thought that counts** w końcu liczą się intencje ⓸ (with comparatives) jeszcze; **better/worse ~ ...** jeszcze lepiej/co gorsze ...

still² /stɪl/ **Ⅰ** n ⓵ (photograph) fotos m ⓶ (for making alcohol) destylator m

Ⅱ adj ⓵ (motionless) *[air, water, person]* nieruchomy; *[day]* bezwietrzny ⓶ (peaceful) *[countryside, streets]* spokojny ⓷ *[drink, water]* niegazowany

Ⅲ adv *[lie, stay]* nieruchomo; **to sit/stand ~** siedzieć/stać spokojnie

still life n martwa natura f

stilted /'stɪltɪd/ adj *[style]* koturnowy

stimulant /'stɪmjʊlənt/ n środek m pobudzający; fig bodziec m, zachęta f (**to sth** do czegoś)

stimulate /'stɪmjʊleɪt/ vt pobudz|ić, -ać

stimulating /'stɪmjʊleɪtɪŋ/ adj *[lecture]* inspirujący; *[effect]* pobudzający

stimulus /'stɪmjʊləs/ n bodziec m

sting /stɪŋ/ **Ⅰ** n ⓵ (of insect) żądło n ⓶ (wound) ślad m użądlenia; **nettle ~** poparzenie pokrzywą

Ⅱ vt ⓵ *[insect]* u|kłuć, u|żądlić ⓶ *[wind]* smag|nąć, -ać

Ⅲ vi *[eyes, antiseptic]* za|szczypać; **it ~s!** (to) szczypie or piecze!

stingy /'stɪndʒɪ/ adj *[person]* skąpy

stink /stɪŋk/ **Ⅰ** n smród m

Ⅱ vi śmierdzieć, cuchnąć

stint /stɪnt/ **Ⅰ** n (period) **to do a three-year ~ with a company** przepracować trzy lata w firmie; **to do a six-month ~ as a teacher** być nauczycielem przez sześć miesięcy; **to finish a ~ of compulsory military service** zakończyć obowiązkową służbę wojskową; **I've done my ~ for today** zrobiłem już swoje na dzisiaj

Ⅱ vi **to ~ on sth** oszczędzać na czymś *[food]*

stipulate /'stɪpjʊleɪt/ vt określ|ić, -ać *[condition]*; **he ~d that...** zastrzegł (sobie), że...

stir /stɜ:(r)/ **Ⅰ** n **to cause a ~** wywołać poruszenie

Ⅱ vt ⓵ za|mieszać *[liquid, sauce]*; wy|mieszać *[paint, mixture]*; **to ~ sth into sth** zmieszać coś z czymś ⓶ *[breeze]* porusz|yć, -ać (czymś) *[leaves, papers]*

Ⅲ vi ⓵ *[leaves, papers]* porusz|yć, -ać się ⓶ (wake up) o|budzić się, wsta|ć, -wać

■ **stir up**: **~ [sth] up** wzniec|ić, -ać *[hatred, unrest]*; podburz|yć, -ać *[crowd]*; **to ~ things up** infml mieszać infml

stir-fry /'stɜ:fraɪ/ **Ⅰ** n Culin **a beef/vegetable ~** wołowina/warzywa na sposób chiński

Ⅱ vt szybko usmażyć, mieszając *[beef, vegetables]*

stirring /'stɜ:rɪŋ/ adj *[story]* pasjonujący; *[music, speech]* porywający

stirrup /'stɪrəp/ n strzemię n

stitch /stɪtʃ/ **Ⅰ** n ⓵ (in sewing, embroidery) ścieg m; (single loop in knitting) oczko n; (style in knitting) ścieg m ⓶ Med szew m ⓷ (pain) kolka f

Ⅱ vt przyszy|ć, -wać *[button]* (**to** or **onto sth** do czegoś); zszy|ć, -wać *[wound]*

stoat /stəʊt/ n gronostaj m

stock /stɒk/ **Ⅰ** n ⓵ towar m; **to be out of ~** *[product]* być wyprzedanym; *[shop]* nie mieć zapasów ⓶ (supply) zapas m; **while ~s last** do wyczerpania zapasów ⓷ Culin wywar m ⓸ (livestock) inwentarz m; (cattle) bydło n

Ⅱ **stocks** npl ⓵ (for punishment) **the ~s** dyby plt ⓶ (shares) akcje f pl; GB (government securities) obligacje f pl; **~s and shares** papiery wartościowe

Ⅲ adj *[size]* typowy; *[answer]* szablonowy; *[joke]* oklepany

Ⅳ vt ⓵ (sell) prowadzić sprzedaż (czegoś) ⓶ (provide with) zaopat|rzyć, -rywać *[fridge, shop]*; zapełni|ć, -ać *[shelves]*; **to ~ a lake with fish** zarybić jezioro

(IDIOMS:) **to take ~** zrobić bilans (**of sth** czegoś)

stockbroker /'stɒkbrəʊkə(r)/ n makler m giełdowy

stock-cube /'stɒkkju:b/ n kostka f rosołowa

stock exchange *n* the ~ giełda *f* papierów wartościowych

Stockholm /'stɒkhəʊm/ *prn* Sztokholm *m*

stocking /'stɒkɪŋ/ *n* pończocha *f*

stock market *n* 1 (stock exchange) giełda *f* papierów wartościowych 2 (prices, trading activity) rynek *m* papierów wartościowych

stockpile /'stɒkpaɪl/ *vt* z|gromadzić wielkie zapasy (czegoś) *[weapons, food, goods]*

stock room *n* magazyn *m*

stock-still /ˌstɒk'stɪl/ *adv* to stand ~ stać bez ruchu

stocktaking /'stɒkteɪkɪŋ/ *n* inwentaryzacja *f*, remanent *m*

stocky /'stɒkɪ/ *adj [person]* krępy

stodgy /'stɒdʒɪ/ *adj [food]* zapychający; *[person]* nudny

stoical /'stəʊɪkl/ *adj* stoicki

stoke /stəʊk/ *vt* (also ~ **up**) do|łożyć, -kładać do (czegoś) *[fire]*; palić w (czymś) *[furnace]*

stolid /'stɒlɪd/ *adj [person]* stateczny; *[book]* rozwlekły

stomach /'stʌmək/ **I** *n* (organ) żołądek *m*; (belly) brzuch *m*
II *vt* zn|ieść, -osić *[person, attitude]*

stomach ache *n* ból *m* brzucha; **I have (a)** ~ boli mnie brzuch

stone /stəʊn/ **I** *n* 1 kamień *m*; (pebble) kamyk *m* 2 (in fruit) pestka *f* 3 GB (weight) = 6,35 kg
II *vt* wy|drylować, wy|pestkować *[cherry]*

Stone Age *n* the ~ epoka *f* kamienia

stone circle *n* kamienny krąg *m*

stone-cold /ˌstəʊn'kəʊld/ *adj [meal]* zupełnie zimny

stonemason /'stəʊnmeɪsn/ *n* kamieniarz *m*

stonewall /ˌstəʊn'wɔːl/ *vi* prowadzić obstrukcję

stonewashed /'stəʊnwɒʃt/ *adj [jeans]* sprany

stony /'stəʊnɪ/ *adj [path, beach]* kamienisty; *[silence, look]* kamienny

stool /stuːl/ *n* stołek *m*

stoop /stuːp/ **I** *n* to have a ~ garbić się
II *vi* (be bent over) garbić się; to ~ **down** schylić się; to ~ to sth zniżyć się do czegoś *[blackmail]*; **I didn't think she would** ~ **so low as to sell the story to the newspapers** nie sądziłem, że upadnie aż tak nisko, żeby sprzedać te informacje prasie

stop /stɒp/ **I** *n* 1 przerwa *f*; (short stay) postój *m*, przystanek *m*; **to come to a** ~ *[vehicle, work]* zatrzymać się, stanąć; **to put a** ~ **to sth** położyć czemuś kres 2 (in telegram) stop *m*
II *vt* 1 (cease) *[person]* przer|wać, -ywać *[activity]*; **to** ~ **doing sth** przestać robić coś 2 (bring to a halt) zatrzym|ać, -ywać *[person, vehicle]*; przer|wać, -ywać *[match]* 3 (prevent) wstrzym|ać, -ywać *[publication]*; zapobie|c, -gać (czemuś) *[war]*; nie dopu|ścić, -szczać do (czegoś) *[event]*; **to** ~ **sb (from) doing sth** powstrzymać kogoś przed zrobieniem czegoś or od zrobienia czegoś 4 wstrzym|ać, -ywać *[allowance]* 5 (plug) zat|kać, -ykać *[hole, bottle]*
III *vi* 1 (halt) zatrzym|ać, -ywać się, sta|nąć, -wać 2 (cease) *[person]* s|kończyć; *[discussion]* ur|wać, -ywać się, za|kończyć się; *[bleeding]* usta|ć, -wać; (temporarily) *[person]* przer|wać, -ywać 3 (stay) zosta|ć, -wać; **to** ~ **for dinner** zostać na obiad
IV *vr* **to** ~ **oneself** powstrzym|ać, -ywać się
■ **stop off**: zatrzym|ać, -ywać się
■ **stop up**: ~ *[sth]* **up** zat|kać, -ykać *[hole]*

stopgap /'stɒpgæp/ *n* tymczasowe rozwiązanie *n*

stop-off /'stɒpɒf/ *n* przystanek *m*, postój *m*

stopover /'stɒpəʊvə(r)/ *n* przerwa *f* w podróży

stoppage /'stɒpɪdʒ/ *n* (strike) przerwa *f* w pracy, przestój *m*

stopper /'stɒpə(r)/ *n* (for bottle, bath) korek *m*

stop sign *n* stop *m*, znak *m* stopu

stopwatch /'stɒpwɒtʃ/ *n* stoper *m*

storage /'stɔːrɪdʒ/ **I** *n* (of food, fuel) przechowywanie *n*; (of heat) magazynowanie *n*; **to be in** ~ *[furniture]* być oddanym na przechowanie
II *adj* ~ **space** schowki

storage heater *n* piec *m* akumulacyjny

store /stɔː(r)/ **I** *n* 1 (shop) sklep *m* 2 (of food) zapas *m*; (of knowledge) zasób *m* 3 (place of storage) magazyn *m*; (for fuel) skład *m*; **I wonder what the future has in** ~ **(for us)** zastanawiam się, co nas czeka
II *vt* 1 przechow|ać, -ywać *[food, information]*; składować *[chemicals]* 2 Comput (enter) zapamięt|ać, -ywać; (retain) przechow|ać, -ywać

storekeeper /'stɔːkiːpə(r)/ *n* US właściciel *m*, -ka *f* sklepu

storeroom /'stɔːruːm/ *n* (in factory, shop) magazyn *m*; (in house) (for food) spiżarnia *f*; (for unnecessary things) schowek *m*

storey GB, **story** US /'stɔːrɪ/ *n* piętro *n*; **on the third** ~ GB na trzecim piętrze; US na drugim piętrze

stork /stɔːk/ *n* bocian *m*

storm /stɔːm/ **I** *n* burza *f*; (at sea) sztorm *m*
II *vt* (try to capture) szturmować *[castle]*; (capture) wziąć, brać szturmem *[castle]*
III *vi* **to** ~ **into/out of sth** wpaść do czegoś/wypaść z czegoś jak burza

stormy /'stɔːmɪ/ *adj [relationship]* burzliwy; *[temperament]* porywczy

story /'stɔːrɪ/ *n* 1 opowieść *f* (**about** or **of sb/sth** o kimś/czymś); **it's a true** ~ to prawdziwa historia; **a ghost** ~ opowiadanie o duchach 2 (in newspaper) artykuł *m* (**on** or **about sb/sth** o kimś/czymś) 3 (rumour) pogłoska *f* (**about sb/sth** o kimś/czymś); **the** ~ **goes that...** podobno... 4 US (floor) piętro *n*

storybook /'stɔːrɪbʊk/ n zbiór m opowiadań; (for children) historyjki f pl dla dzieci

storyteller /'stɔːrɪtelə(r)/ n autor m, -ka f opowiadań

stout /staʊt/ adj [1] (fat) [person] tęgi, korpulentny [2] (strong) [wall] gruby

stove /stəʊv/ n [1] (electric, gas) kuchenka f; (solid fuel) kuchnia f [2] (heater) piec m; (small) piecyk m

stow /stəʊ/ vt s|chować [luggage]

stowaway /'stəʊəweɪ/ n pasażer m, -ka f na gapę infml

straddle /'strædl/ vt siedzieć okrakiem na (czymś) [horse, bike, chair]; stać okrakiem nad (czymś) [ditch, stream]

straggle /'strægl/ vi [1] [houses] być rozrzuconym; **to ~ along a road** ciągnąć się wzdłuż drogi [2] (dawdle) wlec się

straggler /'stræglə(r)/ n maruder m

straggly /'stræglɪ/ adj [hair, beard] rozwichrzony, potargany

straight /streɪt/ **I** adj [1] [line, road, hair] prosty; **in a ~ line** w linii prostej [2] [wall] (upright) prosty; (level, even) równy; [bedclothes] równo położony; **your tie isn't ~** masz przekrzywiony krawat [3] (tidy, in order) uporządkowany [4] (clear) **to get sth ~** zrozumieć coś; **to set the record ~** wyjaśnić nieporozumienia [5] (honest, direct) [person] uczciwy; [answer, question] szczery; **to be ~ with sb** być szczerym wobec kogoś [6] [choice] prosty; [majority] zdecydowany [7] [spirits, drink] czysty; [theatre, role] tradycyjny

II adv [1] [walk, hang] prosto; **sit up ~!** usiądź prosto!; **to go/look ~ ahead** iść/patrzeć prosto przed siebie; **he headed ~ for the bar** skierował się prosto do baru [2] (without delay) prosto; **she went ~ back to Paris** wróciła prosto do Paryża; **she wrote ~ back** od razu odpisała [3] (frankly) wprost; **I'll tell you ~** powiem ci wprost; **I told him ~ out that he was wrong** powiedziałem mu wprost, że się myli [4] (neat) **to drink one's whisky ~** pić czystą whisky

IDIOMS: **to keep a ~ face** zachować powagę

straightaway /ˌstreɪtə'weɪ/ adv od razu

straighten /'streɪtn/ vt wy|prostować [arm, leg]; popraw|ić, -ać [picture, tie, hair, hat]

■ **straighten out:** **~** [sth] **out** [1] wy|prostować [crooked object, road] [2] **to ~ things out** uporządkować sprawy

■ **straighten up:** ¶ **~ up** [person] wy|prostować się ¶ **~** [sth] **up** (tidy) u|porządkować [objects, room]

straightforward /ˌstreɪt'fɔːwəd/ adj [person] prostolinijny; [answer] jasny; [question] prosty

straight-laced /ˌstreɪt'leɪst/ adj zasadniczy

strain /streɪn/ **I** n [1] (weight) obciążenie n (**on sth** czegoś) [2] (pressure) obciążenie n; (tension, stress) napięcie n; **to be under ~** [person] być narażo-

nym na stres; [relations] być napiętym; [system] być bardzo obciążonym [3] (of animal) odmiana f; (of virus) szczep m

II vt [1] to **~** one's **eyes/ears** wytężyć wzrok/słuch [2] obciąż|yć, -ać [finances]; wystawi|ć, -ać na próbę [patience] [3] (injure) nadweręż|yć, -ać [ankle, eyes, voice]; naciąg|nąć, -ać [muscle] [4] (sieve) przecedz|ić, -ać [tea, sauce]; odcedz|ić, -ać [vegetables, pasta]

III vi to **~** at the leash [dog] szarpać się na smyczy

strained /streɪnd/ adj (tense) [atmosphere] napięty; [smile] wymuszony; (injured) [eyes] nadwerężony; [muscle] naciągnięty

strainer /'streɪnə(r)/ n sitko n

strait /streɪt/ n cieśnina f; **to be in dire ~s** być w poważnych tarapatach

straitjacket /'streɪtdʒækɪt/ n kaftan m bezpieczeństwa

strand /strænd/ **I** n (of hair) kosmyk m; (of cable) żył(k)a f; fig (of story) wątek m

II vt to **be ~ed** [ship] osiąść na mieliźnie; **to leave sb ~ed** pozostawić kogoś własnemu losowi

strange /streɪndʒ/ adj [1] (unfamiliar) obcy; **don't talk to ~ men** nie rozmawiaj z nieznajomymi mężczyznami [2] (odd) dziwny; **it is ~ to be back again** to dziwne uczucie być tu z powrotem; **~ to say...** to dziwne, ale...

strangely /'streɪndʒlɪ/ adv dziwnie; **she looks ~ familiar** wygląda dziwnie znajomo; **~ enough...** o dziwo...

stranger /'streɪndʒə(r)/ n (unknown person) nieznajom|y m, -a f, obc|y m, -a f; **I'm a ~ here** (in company) nikogo tu nie znam; (in town) jestem nietutejszy

strangle /'stræŋgl/ vt (throttle) dusić; (kill) udusić

stranglehold /'stræŋglhəʊld/ n fig kontrola f

strap /stræp/ **I** n (of cloth, leather) pas m, pasek m; (on bus, train) uchwyt m; (on dress, bra) ramiączko n; (on trousers) strzemiączko n

II vt to **~** sth to sth przypiąć coś do czegoś

strapless /'stræplɪs/ adj [bra] bez ramiączek

strapped /stræpt/ adj infml **to be ~ for sth** odczuwać brak czegoś [cash, staff]

strapping /'stræpɪŋ/ adj **a ~ fellow** kawał chłopa infml

stratagem /'strætədʒəm/ n podstęp m, fortel m

strategic(al) /strə'tiːdʒɪk(l)/ adj strategiczny

strategy /'strætədʒɪ/ n strategia f

straw /strɔː/ n słoma f; (single stalk) słomka f

IDIOMS: **to clutch at ~s** chwytać się wszelkich sposobów (jak tonący brzytwy); **that's the last ~!** tego już za wiele!

strawberry /'strɔːbrɪ, US -berɪ/ **I** n truskawka f; **a wild ~** poziomka

II adj [jam, tart] truskawkowy

straw poll n sondaż m opinii publicznej

stray /streɪ/ **I** *n* (dog) bezpański pies *m*; (cat) bezdomny kot *m*

II *adj [animal]* zabłąkany; *[dog, cat]* bezpański

III *vi* 1 (wander) błąkać się; **to ~ from the road** zboczyć z drogi 2 *[eyes, mind]* błądzić

streak /striːk/ **I** *n* 1 (in character) element *m*; **he has a cruel ~** ma w sobie coś okrutnego 2 (period) okres *m*; **to be on a winning/losing ~** mieć dobrą/złą passę 3 (of paint) smuga *f*; (of light) promień *m*; **a ~ of lightning** zygzak błyskawicy 4 (in hair) pasemko *n*

II *vt* 1 (mark) pokry|ć, -wać smugami; **the rocks were ~ed with ore** skały poprzecinane były żyłkami rudy 2 **to get one's hair ~ed** zrobić sobie pasemka

III *vi* **to ~ past** przemknąć

streaky bacon /ˈstriːkɪ ˈbeɪkən/ *n* GB boczek *m*

stream /striːm/ **I** *n* 1 (small river) strumień *m*, potok *m* 2 **a ~ of sth** strumień czegoś *[people]*; lawina czegoś *[questions]*; rzeka czegoś *[cars]*; **a ~ of abuse** stek przekleństw

II *vi* 1 (flow) *[tears, blood]* płynąć; *[light]* lać się; **tears were ~ing down her face** łzy ciurkiem spływały jej po twarzy; **sunlight was ~ing into the room** do pokoju wlewało się słoneczne światło 2 (move) **the audience was ~ing out of the concert hall** publiczność wylewała się z sali koncertowej 3 *[banners]* powiewać; *[hair]* rozwiewać się 4 **her eyes were ~ing** oczy jej łzawiły; **my nose has been ~ing all week** od tygodnia cieknie mi z nosa

streamer /ˈstriːmə(r)/ *n* (of paper) serpentyna *f*

streamline /ˈstriːmlaɪn/ *vt* 1 nada|ć, -wać opływowy kształt (czemuś) *[aircraft, car]* 2 (make efficient) usprawni|ć, -ać *[procedure, production]*; (cut back) z|redukować personel

streamlined /ˈstriːmlaɪnd/ *adj* 1 *[cooker, furniture]* o nowoczesnej linii; *[hull, body]* opływowy, aerodynamiczny 2 *[production, system]* usprawniony

street /striːt/ *n* ulica *f*; **in** *or* **on the ~** na ulicy; **to live across** *or* **over the ~** mieszkać po drugiej stronie ulicy

street cred *n* akceptacja *f* grupy rówieśniczej

street lamp *n* latarnia *f* uliczna

street market *n* bazar *m* uliczny

street plan *n* plan *m* miasta

street value *n* cena *f* detaliczna (narkotyku)

streetwise /ˈstriːtwaɪz/ *adj* infml *[person]* cwany infml

strength /streŋθ/ *n* 1 (of person, wind) siła *f*; (of bulb, coffee, drink) moc *f*; (of electric current) natężenie *n* 2 (toughness) (of material, structure) wytrzymałość *f*; (of bond, feeling, reaction) siła *f*, moc *f*; **military ~** potencjał militarny

strengthen /ˈstreŋθn/ *vt* wzm|ocnić, -acniać *[material, muscle]*; um|ocnić, -acniać *[bond, currency,*

economy, position]; potwierdz|ić, -ać słuszność (czegoś) *[argument, claim]*

strenuous /ˈstrenjʊəs/ *adj [activity, job]* żmudny, mozolny; *[day]* ciężki; *[exercise, walk]* forsowny, wyczerpujący

stress /stres/ **I** *n* 1 (nervous) stres *m*, napięcie *n*; **emotional/mental ~** napięcie emocjonalne/ psychiczne; **to be under ~** być narażonym na stres 2 (emphasis) nacisk *m* (**on sth** na coś); **to lay ~ on sth** kłaść nacisk na coś 3 (pressure) obciążenie *n*; (tension) naprężenie *n* 4 (in linguistic, music) akcent *m*

II *vt* podkreśl|ić, -ać *[difficulty, advantage]*; **to ~ the importance of sth** podkreślić wagę czegoś

■ **stress out** infml: **~ [sb] out** ze|stresować

stressed /strest/ *adj* 1 (also **~ out**) zestresowany 2 *[syllable]* akcentowany

stressful /ˈstresfl/ *adj* stresujący

stretch /stretʃ/ **I** *n* 1 (of road, coastline, river) odcinek *m* 2 (of woodland, countryside) obszar *m* 3 (period) okres *m*; **to work for 12 hours at a ~** pracować 12 godzin bez przerwy

II *adj [fabric, pants]* elastyczny; **slacks with a ~ waist** spodnie na gumce

III *vt* 1 (extend) rozciąg|nąć, -ać *[rope, net]*; **to ~ one's arms** wyciągnąć ręce; **to ~ one's legs** rozprostować nogi *also fig* 2 rozciąg|nąć, -ać, naciąg|nąć, -ać *[elastic]*; powiększ|yć, -ać *[shoe]* 3 nagi|ąć, -nać *[truth]*

IV *vi* 1 (extend one's limbs) przeciąg|nąć, -ać się; (to reach sth) wyciąg|nąć, -ać się 2 *[road, track]* ciągnąć się; *[forest, water]* ciągnąć się, rozciągać się 3 *[elastic, garment]* rozciąg|nąć, -ać się

■ **stretch out**: ¶ **~ out** wyciąg|nąć, -ać się ¶ **~ [sth] out** wyciąg|nąć, -ać *[hand, leg]*; rozciąg|nąć, -ać *[net]*; rozłoż|yć, -kładać *[sheet]*

stretcher /ˈstretʃə(r)/ *n* nosze *plt*

strew /struː/ *vt* rozrzuc|ić, -ać *[litter, paper]*; rozsyp|ać, -ywać *[sand, flowers]* (**on** *or* **over sth** na czymś, po czymś)

stricken /ˈstrɪkən/ *adj* 1 *[face]* zbolały; *[region]* zagrożony; **~ by sth** dotknięty czymś *[illness]*; ogarnięty czymś *[fear]*; nękany czymś *[guilt]* 2 *[plane, ship]* uszkodzony

strict /strɪkt/ *adj* 1 *[discipline, person]* surowy; *[Catholic, Methodist]* ortodoksyjny 2 *[instruction]* ścisły; **in ~ confidence** w wielkim zaufaniu; **in ~ secrecy** w wielkiej tajemnicy

strictly /ˈstrɪktlɪ/ *adv* 1 *[treat]* surowo 2 *[confidential]* ściśle; *[forbidden]* surowo; **~ speaking** ściśle mówiąc

stride /straɪd/ **I** *n* krok *m*

II *vi* **to ~ in/out** wejść/wyjść zamaszystym krokiem; **to ~ across sth** przejść przez coś wielkimi krokami

IDIOMS: **to take sth in one's ~** nie przejąć się czymś

strife /straɪf/ n (conflict) konflikty m pl; (dissent) spory m pl

strike /straɪk/ **[]** n 1 strajk m; **to be on ~** strajkować 2 (attack) atak m, uderzenie n

[] vt 1 (hit) uderz|yć, -ać [person]; uderz|yć, -ać w (coś) [object]; [torpedo] trafi|ć, -ać w (coś) [vessel]; [car, person] uderz|yć, -ać w (coś) [rock, tree]; **he struck his head on the table** uderzył się głową o stół; **lightning struck the house** piorun uderzył w dom 2 (afflict) [disaster] dotk|nąć, -ykać [area, people] 3 [idea, thought] przy|jść, -chodzić (komuś) do głowy [person]; [resemblance] uderz|yć, -ać [person]; **to ~ the eye** rzucać się w oczy; **it ~ s me as odd that...** wydaje mi się dziwne, że... 4 (discover) (na)trafi|ć, -ać na (coś) [oil, gold] 5 (achieve) **to ~ an accord** dojść do porozumienia; **to ~ a deal** dobić targu; **to ~ a balance** znaleźć złoty środek 6 zapal|ić, -ać [match] 7 [clock] wybi|ć, -jać [time]

[] vi 1 (hit) uderz|yć, -ać 2 (refuse to work) za|strajkować

■ **strike down**: powal|ić, -ać [person]

■ **strike off**: ¶ ~ [sth] **off** (delete) skreśl|ić, -ać ¶ ~ [sb] **off** pozbawi|ć, -ać prawa wykonywania zawodu [doctor]; **to be struck off the roll** [barrister] zostać wykreślonym z rejestru

■ **strike out**: ¶ ~ **out** (hit out) uderz|yć, -ać; **to ~ out at sb** zaatakować kogoś also fig ¶ ~ [sth] **out** (delete) skreśl|ić, -ać, wykreśl|ić, -ać

■ **strike up**: [orchestra] zacz|ąć, -ynać grać; **to ~ up an acquaintance with sb** zawrzeć znajomość z kimś; **to ~ up a conversation with sb** zacząć rozmowę z kimś

strikebreaker /'straɪkbreɪkə(r)/ n łamistrajk m

strike force n oddział m uderzeniowy

striker /'straɪkə(r)/ n 1 strajkując|y m, -a f 2 (in football) napastnik m

striking /'straɪkɪŋ/ adj [contrast] uderzający; [pattern] rzucający się w oczy; [woman] uderzająco piękna; [man] niezwykle przystojny

string /strɪŋ/ **[]** n 1 (twine) sznurek m; **a piece of ~** kawałek sznurka 2 (on garment) tasiemka f; (on racket, guitar) struna f; (on puppet) sznurek m 3 (series) (of visitors) sznur m; (of crimes) seria f; (of successes) pasmo n 4 (set) **a ~ of pearls** sznur pereł

[] strings npl Mus the ~s instrumenty m pl smyczkowe

[] vt na|nizać, nawle|c, -kać [pearls, beads] (on sth na coś)

■ **string along** GB infml: ¶ **to ~ along with sb** zabrać się z kimś ¶ ~ [sb] **along** nab|rać, -ierać infml

IDIOMS: **to pull ~s** infml użyć wpływów

string bean n fasolka f szparagowa

stringed instrument n instrument m strunowy

stringent /'strɪndʒənt/ adj [measure] rygorystyczny; [ban] kategoryczny

strip /strɪp/ **[]** n (of material, paper) pas m; (smaller) pasek m

[] vt roz|ebrać, -bierać do naga [person]; opróżni|ć, -ać [house, flat]; zd|jąć, -ejmować pościel z (czegoś) [bed]; z|edrzeć, -dzierać farbę z (czegoś) [window, door, table]; rozł|ożyć, -kładać na części [gun, engine]; **to ~ a room of furniture** opróżnić pokój z mebli; **he was ~ped of his title** odebrano mu tytuł

[] vi roz|ebrać, -bierać się

strip cartoon n komiks m

stripe /straɪp/ **[]** n 1 (on fabric, wallpaper) pas m; (narrower) pasek m, prążek m 2 (on animal) pas m, pręga f; (smaller) pasek m, prążek m

[] striped pp adj [cloth] pasiasty; [animal] pręgowany

strip lighting n oświetlenie n jarzeniowe

stripper /'strɪpə(r)/ n striptizer m, -ka f

strive /straɪv/ vi **to ~ to do sth** usiłować coś zrobić; **to ~ for** or **after sth** dążyć do czegoś

stroke /strəʊk/ **[]** n 1 (blow) cios m, uderzenie n; (in tennis) uderzenie n; **at a single ~** za jednym zamachem; **a ~ of luck** uśmiech losu; **a ~ of bad luck** pech; **a ~ of genius** przebłysk geniuszu 2 (swimming movement) ruch m; (style) styl m 3 (of pen) kreska f; (of brush) pociągnięcie n 4 Med udar m

[] vt po|głaskać

stroll /strəʊl/ **[]** n przechadzka f

[] vi przechadzać się

stroller /'strəʊlə(r)/ n US (pushchair) wózek m spacerowy

strong /strɒŋ, US strɔːŋ/ adj 1 (powerful) [arm, person, wind, army, country] silny 2 [fabric, table] mocny; [heart] silny, mocny; [argument] mocny; [candidate] poważny; **spelling is not my ~ point** ortografia nie jest moją mocną stroną 3 [glue, tea] mocny; [medicine] silny, mocny 4 [smell, taste] wyraźny 5 [desire] silny; [reaction] zdecydowany; [objections] poważny 6 [chance] duży; **there is a ~ possibility that it's true** bardzo możliwe, że to prawda

IDIOMS: **to be still going ~** [person, company] wciąż dobrze się trzymać

strongbox /'strɒŋbɒks, US 'strɔːŋ-/ n sejf m, kasa f pancerna

stronghold /'strɒŋhəʊld, US 'strɔːŋ-/ n twierdza f; fig bastion m

strongly /'strɒŋlɪ, US 'strɔːŋlɪ/ adv 1 [push] mocno, silnie; [criticize] ostro; [deny] stanowczo; [advise, recommend] bardzo, gorąco; **I ~ disagree** absolutnie się nie zgadzam; **I feel very ~ about it** to jest dla mnie bardzo ważne 2 (solidly) [fixed] mocno; [made] porządnie, solidnie

strongroom /'strɒŋruːm, US 'strɔːŋ-/ n skarbiec m

strong-willed /ˌstrɒŋ'wɪld, US ˌstrɔːŋ-/ adj uparty

structure /'strʌktʃə(r)/ **[]** n 1 struktura f 2 (building) konstrukcja f

II *vt* s|konstruować *[argument, novel]*; z|organizować *[day, schedule]*

struggle /'strʌgl/ **I** *n* (battle, fight) walka *f*; (scuffle) bójka *f*

II *vi* ① (put up a fight) szamotać się (**with sb/for sth** z kimś/o coś) ② (try hard) **a young artist struggling for recognition** młody artysta walczący o uznanie; **to ~ to understand sth** usiłować coś zrozumieć

strum /strʌm/ *vt* brz(d)ąkać na (czymś) *[guitar]*; brząkać *[tune]*

strung out /ˌstrʌŋ'aʊt/ *adj* infml **to be ~ on sth** brać coś infml *[drug]*; **to be ~** (by drugs) być wyniszczonym (przez narkotyki)

strut /strʌt/ **I** *n* rozpórka *f*

II *vi* (also **~ about, ~ around**) kroczyć dumnie

stub /stʌb/ **I** *n* (of pencil) ogryzek *m* fig; (of cigarette) niedopałek *m*; (of cheque, ticket) odcinek *m*

II *vt* **to ~ one's toe** uderzyć się w palec (u nogi)

■ **stub out**: z|gasić *[cigarette]*

stubble /'stʌbl/ *n* (straw) ściernisko *n*, rżysko *n*; (on face) kilkudniowy zarost *m*

stubborn /'stʌbən/ *adj [person, animal]* uparty; *[resistance]* nieugięty; *[stain]* trwały; *[cough]* uporczywy

stuck /stʌk/ *adj [lift, door]* zablokowany, zaklinowany; **we were ~ in the traffic jam** utknęliśmy w korku; **I was ~ for an answer** kompletnie mnie zatkało infml

stuck-up /ˌstʌk'ʌp/ *adj* infml *[person]* nadęty infml

stud /stʌd/ *n* ① (on jacket, door) ćwiek *m*; (earring) kolczyk *m*; (on football boot) kołek *m*, korek *m* ② (stallion) ogier reproduktor *m*; (also **~ farm**) stadnina *f*

student /'stju:dnt, US 'stu:-/ *n* Univ student *m*, -ka *f*; US Sch ucze|ń *m*, -nnica *f* szkoły średniej

student grant *n* stypendium *n*

student ID card *n* legitymacja *f* studencka

student nurse *n* uczennica *f* szkoły pielęgniarskiej

student teacher *n* praktykant *m*, -ka *f* w szkole

student union *n* klub *m* studencki

studio /'stju:dɪəʊ, US 'stu:-/ *n* studio *n*; (of painter) pracownia *f*, atelier *n* inv

studious /'stju:dɪəs, US 'stu:-/ *adj [person]* pilny

study /'stʌdɪ/ **I** *n* ① (gaining of knowledge) nauka *f* ② (research) badania *n pl* ③ (room) gabinet *m*

II studies npl studia plt; **legal studies** studia prawnicze; **computer studies** informatyka

III *adj [group, visit]* naukowy; **~ trip** podróż naukowa

IV *vt* studiować *[physics]*; z|badać *[phenomenon]*

V *vi* (learn) uczyć się; (get one's education) studiować

study aid *n* pomoc *f* naukowa

stuff /stʌf/ **I** *n* ① (unnamed substance) coś *n*; **there's some black ~ stuck to my shoe** coś czarnego

przykleiło mi się do buta ② (unnamed objects) rzeczy *f pl*; **who wrote this ~?** kto to napisał?

II *vt* ① (fill, pack) wyp|chać, -ychać *[cushion, suitcase]* (**with sth** czymś); wy|słać, -ściełać *[furniture]* (**with sth** czymś) ② (pack in) w|epchnąć, -pychać, w|etknąć, -tykać *[objects]* (**in** or **into sth** do czegoś); (cram) up|chnąć, -ychać (**in** or **into sth** w czymś) ③ Culin na|faszerować, nadzi|ać, -ewać *[turkey, olives]* ④ wyp|chać, -ychać *[animal, bird]*

III stuffed *pp adj [chicken, tomato]* nadziewany, faszerowany; *[toy animal]* pluszowy; *[bird, fox]* wypchany

stuffing /'stʌfɪŋ/ *n* ① Culin farsz *m*, nadzienie *n* ② (of pillow) wypełniacz *m*; (of furniture) warstwa *f* wyściełająca

stuffy /'stʌfɪ/ *adj [room, atmosphere]* duszny ② *[person]* wyniosły, sztywny

stumble /'stʌmbl/ *vi* ① (trip) pot|knąć, -ykać się (**against** or **on** or **over sth** o coś) ② (in speech) zająk|nąć, -iwać się

■ **stumble across**: nat|knąć, -ykać się na (kogoś/coś) *[person, item]*

stumbling block *n* przeszkoda *f* fig

stump /stʌmp/ **I** *n* (of tree) pniak *m*; (of cigar, candle) ogarek *m*; (of tail, limb) kikut *m*; (of pencil) ogryzek *m*

II *vt* infml zabić klina (komuś) *[expert]*; **to be ~ed for an answer** nie potrafić znaleźć odpowiedzi

■ **stump up** GB infml: wy|łożyć, -kładać forsę infml (**for sth** na coś)

stun /stʌn/ *vt* ① *[blow]* ogłusz|yć, -ać; *[injection]* odurz|yć, -ać, osz|ołomić, -ałamiać ② *[news]* za|szokować; *[beauty]* olśni|ć, -ewać

stunned /stʌnd/ *adj* (by blow) ogłuszony; (by news) zaszokowany; (by beauty) olśniony

stunning /'stʌnɪŋ/ *adj* (beautiful) olśniewający; (amazing) szokujący; *[blow]* ogłuszający

stunt /stʌnt/ **I** *n* ① (for attention) chwyt *m* fig ② (in film) wyczyn *m* kaskaderski

II za|hamować *[growth, progress]*

stunted /'stʌntɪd/ *adj [tree, plant]* skarłowaciały

stuntman /'stʌntmæn/ *n* kaskader *m*

stupefying /'stju:pɪfaɪɪŋ, US 'stu:-/ *adj [effect]* otępiający; *[blow]* oszałamiający; *[news]* zaskakujący

stupendous /stju:'pendəs, US stu:-/ *adj [amount]* ogromny; *[achievement]* wspaniały, zdumiewający; *[film]* znakomity

stupid /'stju:pɪd, US 'stu:-/ *adj* głupi; **I've done something ~** zrobiłem coś głupiego

stupidity /stju:'pɪdɪtɪ, US stu:-/ *n* głupota *f*

stupor /'stju:pə(r), US 'stu:-/ *n* otępienie *n*; Med osłupienie *n*, stupor *m*; **in a drunken ~** w zamroczeniu alkoholowym

sturdy /'stɜ:dɪ/ *adj [person]* mocnej budowy; *[object]* solidny

stutter /'stʌtə(r)/ **I** *vt* wy|jąkać

II *vi* jąkać się

sty /staɪ/ *n* ①︎ (for pigs) chlew *m* ②︎ (also **stye**) Med jęczmień *m*

style /staɪl/ **①︎** *n* ①︎ (manner) styl *m*; **telling lies is not his** ~ kłamać to nie w jego stylu ②︎ (elegance) styl *m*, klasa *f*; **to marry in** ~ wziąć ślub z wielką pompą; **to live in** ~ żyć wystawnie ③︎ (design) (of clothing) fason *m*; (of car) model *m*; (of house) typ *m* ④︎ (fashion) moda *f*

②︎ *vt* (cut) ściǀąć, -nać *[hair]*; (set) uǀłożyć, -kładać *[hair]*

styling /'staɪlɪŋ/ **①︎** *n* ①︎ (design) projekt *m* ②︎ (in hairdressing) strzyżenie *n* i czesanie *n*

②︎ *adj* ~ **gel/mousse** żel/pianka do układania włosów

stylish /'staɪlɪʃ/ *adj [person, car, coat, resort]* elegancki; *[restaurant]* stylowy

stylist /'staɪlɪst/ *n* ①︎ (hairdresser) fryzjer *m*, -ka *f* ②︎ (designer) stylistǀa *m*, -ka *f*

stylistic /staɪ'lɪstɪk/ *adj* stylistyczny

stylus /'staɪləs/ *n* igła *f* (gramofonowa)

suave /swɑːv/ *adj [person]* gładki w obyciu

subconscious /ˌsʌb'kɒnʃəs/ **①︎** *n* **the** ~ podświadomość *f*

②︎ *adj* podświadomy

subcontinent /ˌsʌb'kɒntɪnənt/ *n* subkontynent *m*

subcontract /ˌsʌbkən'trækt/ *vt* zlecǀić, -ać podwykonanie (czegoś)

subcontractor /ˌsʌbkən'træktə(r)/ *n* podwykonawca *m*

subdivide /ˌsʌbdɪ'vaɪd/ *vt* poǀdzielić (na mniejsze części) *[land]*; rozdzielǀić, -ać *[work]*

subdue /səb'djuː, US -'duː/ *vt* podporządkowǀać, -ywać sobie *[nation]*; sǀtłumić *[rebellion]*

subdued /səb'djuːd, US -'duːd/ *adj [person]* przygaszony; *[reaction]* powściągliwy; *[voices, lighting]* przytłumiony

subheading /'sʌbhedɪŋ/ *n* podtytuł *m*

subject **①︎** /'sʌbdʒɪkt/ *n* ①︎ (topic) temat *m*; **to change the** ~ zmienić temat ②︎ (at school, college) przedmiot *m*; (for research, study) temat *m* ③︎ **to be the** ~ **of an inquiry** być przedmiotem śledztwa ④︎ (citizen) obywatel *m*, -ka *f*

②︎ /'sʌbdʒɪkt/ *adj* ①︎ (affected) podatny (**to sth** na coś); **the area is** ~ **to earthquakes** ten obszar jest narażony na trzęsienia ziemi ②︎ (liable) *[prices, goods]* podlegający; **to be** ~ **to sth** podlegać czemuś ③︎ (dependent) *[plan, decision, offer]* zależny, uzależniony (**to sb/sth** od kogoś/czegoś)

③︎ /səb'dʒekt/ *vt* (expose) wystawǀić, -ać (**to sth** na coś); **to** ~ **sb to torture** poddać kogoś torturom

subject heading *n* tytuł *m*

subjective /səb'dʒektɪv/ *adj* subiektywny

subjugate /'sʌbdʒʊgeɪt/ *vt* ujarzmiǀić, -ać *[country, people]*

subjunctive /səb'dʒʌŋktɪv/ *n* tryb *m* łączący

sublet /ˌsʌb'let/ *vt, vi* podnajǀąć, -mować *[room]*; poddzierżawiǀić, -ać *[land]*

sublime /sə'blaɪm/ *adj [beauty]* niezrównany; *[heroism]* najwyższy; *[indifference]* wyjątkowy

subliminal /sʌb'lɪmɪnl/ *adj [advertising]* podprogowy

submachine gun /ˌsʌbmə'ʃiːngʌn/ *n* pistolet *m* maszynowy

submarine /ˌsʌbmə'riːn, US 'sʌb-/ *n* okręt *m* podwodny, łódź *f* podwodna

submerge /səb'mɜːdʒ/ *vt [sea, flood]* zatǀopić, -apiać; *[person]* zanurzǀyć, -ać (**in sth** w czymś)

submission /səb'mɪʃn/ *n* (obedience) uległość *f* (**to sb/sth** wobec kogoś/czegoś); (of plan, proposal) przedǀłożenie *n* (**to sb** komuś); złożenie *n* (**to sb** komuś)

submissive /səb'mɪsɪv/ *adj [person]* uległy; *[behaviour]* pełen uległości

submit /səb'mɪt/ **①︎** *vt* przedstawiǀić, -ać *[budget]* (**to sb/sth** komuś/w czymś); złożyć, składać *[application, report]* (**to sb/sth** na ręce kogoś/w czymś); przedǀłożyć, -kładać *[proposal, plan]* (**to sb/sth** komuś/w czymś)

②︎ *vi* **to** ~ **to sth** poddać się czemuś *[medical examination]*; podporządkować się czemuś *[decision]*; ulec czemuś *[demand]*

subnormal /sʌb'nɔːml/ *adj [person]* niedorozwinięty

subordinate **①︎** /sə'bɔːdɪnət, US -dənət/ *n* podwładnǀy *m*, -a *f*

②︎ /sə'bɔːdɪnət/ *adj [issue]* podrzędny (**to sth** w stosunku do czegoś); *[official]* niższy rangą

subpoena /sə'piːnə/ *vt* wǀezwać, -zywać do sądu

subscribe /səb'skraɪb/ *vi* **to** ~ **to sth** (agree with) zgǀodzić, -adzać się z czymś *[opinion]*; (buy) zaǀprenumerować coś *[magazine]*; zaǀabonować coś *[TV]*

subscriber /səb'skraɪbə(r)/ *n* (to periodical) prenumerator *m*, -ka *f*; Telcom abonent *m*, -ka *f*

subscription /səb'skrɪpʃn/ *n* (to magazine) prenumerata *f* (**to sth** czegoś); (TV) abonament *m* (**to sb** za coś)

subsequent /'sʌbsɪkwənt/ *adj* (following) dalszy; (in time) późniejszy

subsequently /'sʌbsɪkwəntlɪ/ *adv* później

subservient /səb'sɜːvɪənt/ *adj* służalczy (**to sb** w stosunku do kogoś)

subside /səb'saɪd/ *vi* ①︎ *[storm, noise]* uǀcichnąć; *[fever, excitement]* opaǀść, -dać; *[pain, anger]* ustǀąpić, -ępować ②︎ *[building]* osiǀąść, -adać; *[land]* osuǀnąć, -wać się

subsidiary /səb'sɪdɪərɪ, US -dɪerɪ/ **①︎** *n* (also ~ **company**) jednostka *f* zależna

②︎ *adj* drugorzędny (**to sth** w stosunku do czegoś)

subsidize /'sʌbsɪdaɪz/ *vt* dotować

subsidy /'sʌbsɪdɪ/ *n* dotacja *f*

subsist /səb'sɪst/ *vi* utrzymywać się przy życiu

subsistence /səb'sɪstəns/ *n* utrzymywanie się *n* przy życiu

subsistence level *n* minimum *n* socjalne

substance /'sʌbstəns/ *n* [1] (matter) substancja *f* [2] (of argument, talks) istota *f*

substance abuse *n* nadużywanie *n* środków odurzających

substandard /ˌsʌb'stændəd/ *adj [goods]* niskiej jakości

substantial /səb'stænʃl/ *adj* [1] (in amount) *[sum, income]* znaczny; *[meal]* obfity [2] (solid) *[chair]* solidny; *[proof]* mocny

substantiate /səb'stænʃɪeɪt/ *vt* pop|rzeć, -ierać dowodami *[statement]*; *[evidence]* potwierdz|ić, -ać *[allegation]*

substitute /'sʌbstɪtjuːt, US -tuːt/ **I** *n* [1] (person) zastęp|ca *m*, -czyni *f*; Sport rezerwow|y *m*, -a *f* [2] (product, substance) substytut *m*
II *vt* zast|ąpić, -ępować; **to ~ dried sage for the fresh herb** zastąpić świeżą szałwię suszoną

subtitle /'sʌbtaɪtl/ **I** *n* podtytuł *m*
II subtitles *npl* (in film) napisy *m pl*

subtle /'sʌtl/ *adj [distinction, allusion, mind]* subtelny; *[change]* nieznaczny

subtotal /'sʌbtəutl/ *n* suma *f* częściowa

subtract /səb'trækt/ *vt* od|jąć, -ejmować (**from sth** od czegoś)

subtraction /səb'trækʃn/ *n* odejmowanie *n*

suburb /'sʌbɜːb/ **I** *n* dzielnica *f* podmiejska; **inner ~** dzielnica mieszkaniowa położona blisko centrum
II suburbs *npl* **the ~s** przedmieścia *n pl*

suburban /sə'bɜːbən/ *adj [street, train]* podmiejski

suburbia /sə'bɜːbɪə/ *n* przedmieścia *n pl*

subversive /səb'vɜːsɪv/ **I** *n* wywrotowiec *m*
II *adj* wywrotowy

subway /'sʌbweɪ/ *n* [1] GB (for pedestrians) przejście *n* podziemne [2] US (underground railway) metro *n*

sub-zero /ˌsʌb'zɪərəu/ *adj [temperature]* ujemny

succeed /sək'siːd/ **I** *vt* nast|ąpić, -ępować po (czymś) *[event]*; **she ~ed him as president** objęła po nim urząd prezydenta
II *vi [person]* (achieve success) osiąg|nąć, -ać cel; (go far in life) odn|ieść, -osić sukces; *[plan]* powieść się; **he ~ed in ending the conflict** udało mu się or zdołał zakończyć konflikt

succeeding /sək'siːdɪŋ/ *adj [day, generation]* kolejny; *[confusion]* wynikły

success /sək'ses/ *n* sukces *m*, powodzenie *n*; **to be a ~ with sb** podobać się komuś *[critics]*; **to be a ~ as sb** odnieść sukces jako ktoś *[actor]*

successful /sək'sesfl/ *adj [attempt, career, marriage]* udany; *[treatment, policy]* skuteczny; *[person]* odnoszący sukcesy; *[team]* zwycięski; **he was ~ in convincing everybody** udało mu się wszystkich przekonać; **a ~ film/writer** film/pisarz, który odniósł sukces

successfully /sək'sesfəlɪ/ *adv [end]* powodzeniem; *[argue]* skutecznie

succession /sək'seʃn/ *n* [1] (sequence) seria *f*; **a ~ of poor leaders** kolejni nieudolni przywódcy; **in ~** kolejno, z rzędu; **in close ~** jeden za drugim [2] (inheriting) dziedziczenie *n* (**to sth** czegoś)

successive /sək'sesɪv/ *adj [generation, day]* kolejny

successor /sək'sesə(r)/ *n* następ|ca *m*, -czyni *f*

success rate *n* (of treatment, method) skuteczność *f*

success story *n* sukces *m* życiowy

succinct /sək'sɪŋkt/ *adj [statement]* zwięzły

succulent /'sʌkjulənt/ *adj* soczysty

succumb /sə'kʌm/ *vi* **to ~ to sth** ulec czemuś *[persuasion, temptation]*

such /sʌtʃ/ **I** *det* (of kind previously mentioned) taki; (similar) podobny; (of similar sort) tego typu; **there's no ~ thing** nie ma czegoś takiego; **in ~ a situation** w takiej sytuacji; **and other ~ arguments** i inne argumenty tego typu; **a mouse or some ~ animal** mysz, czy jakieś podobne zwierzę; **you'll do no ~ thing!** niczego takiego or podobnego nie zrobisz!; **in ~ a way that...** w taki sposób, że...; **I was in ~ pain (that) I couldn't sleep** tak mnie bolało, że nie mogłem spać; **~ money as I earn I give to my parents** wszystkie zarobione pieniądze oddaję rodzicom; **dinner's ready, ~ as it is** obiad gotowy, jeśli to można nazwać obiadem
II such as *det phr, conj phr* taki jak; **~ a house as this, a house ~ as this** taki dom jak ten; **a person ~ as her** ktoś taki jak ona; **there's no ~ thing as the perfect crime** nie ma czegoś takiego jak zbrodnia doskonała
III *adv* (with adjectives) tak, tāki; (with nouns) taki; **in ~ a persuasive way** w tak or tak przekonujący sposób; **~ a nice boy!** taki miły chłopak!; **I woke up with ~ a headache!** obudziłem się z potwornym bólem głowy!; **don't be ~ an idiot!** nie bądź idiotą!; **~ a lot of problems** tyle problemów

such and such *det* **by ~ a date** do tego i tego dnia; **at ~ a time** o tej i o tej godzinie

suck /sʌk/ **I** *vt* [1] (drink in) *[person]* ssać *[liquid]*; *[machine]* zasysać *[air]* [2] (hold in mouth) ssać *[bottle, breast, thumb, toffee]*
II *vi* **to ~ at sth** ssać coś *[bottle]*; **to ~ on sth** pociągać *[pipe]*
■ **suck up: ¶ ~ up** *infml* podliz|ać, -ywać się *infml* (**to sb** komuś) **¶ ~ [sth] up** zas|sać, -ysać *[liquid]*; w|essać, -sysać *[dirt]*

sucker /'sʌkə(r)/ *n* [1] *infml* (dupe) frajer *m*, -ka *f infml* [2] (animal's pad) przyssawka *f*

suction /'sʌkʃn/ *n* ssanie *n*

suction pad *n* przyssawka *f*

sudden /'sʌdn/ *adj [death, decision]* nagły; (unexpected) niespodziewany; **all of a ~** nagle; (unexpectedly) niespodziewanie

sudden death play-off *n* Sport dogrywka do zdobycia pierwszego punktu

suddenly /'sʌdnlɪ/ adv nagle; (unexpectedly) niespodziewanie

suds /sʌdz/ npl (also **soap** ~) mydliny plt

sue /su:, sju:/ **I** vt poz|wać, -ywać (**for sth** za coś); **to ~ sb for damages** dochodzić od kogoś odszkodowania; **to ~ sb for divorce** wnieść sprawę rozwodową przeciwko komuś **II** vi wn|ieść, -osić sprawę do sądu

suede /sweɪd/ **I** n zamsz m **II** adj [shoe, glove] zamszowy

suffer /'sʌfə(r)/ **I** vt pon|ieść, -osić [loss, consequences]; cierpieć [hunger]; dozna|ć, -wać (czegoś) [injury]; **to ~ a heart attack** mieć atak serca **II** vi 1 **to ~ from sth** cierpieć na coś [malnutrition, rheumatism]; mieć coś [depression, headache]; cierpieć coś [hunger]; **to ~ from the heat** źle znosić upał 2 (do badly) [company, profits, popularity] u|cierpieć; **the country ~s from its isolation** kraj odczuwa skutki izolacji

sufferer /'sʌfərə(r)/ n ~**s from chronic disease** osoby cierpiące na przewlekłe schorzenia; **a leukemia ~** chory na białaczkę

suffering /'sʌfərɪŋ/ **I** n cierpienia n pl **II** adj cierpiący

sufficient /sə'fɪʃnt/ adj [amount] wystarczający; [evidence] dostateczny; ~ **money** wystarczająco dużo pieniędzy; **to be ~** wystarczać

sufficiently /sə'fɪʃntlɪ/ adv wystarczająco

suffocate /'sʌfəkeɪt/ **I** vt [fumes, smoke] dusić; [person, pillow] u|dusić **II** vi 1 u|dusić się 2 fig dusić się

suffocating /'sʌfəkeɪtɪŋ/ adj [smoke] duszący; [atmosphere] duszny; ~ **heat** duszący upał

suffrage /'sʌfrɪdʒ/ n prawo n wyborcze

sugar /'ʃʊgə(r)/ n cukier m; **brown ~** cukier brązowy

sugar beet n burak m cukrowy

sugar cane n trzcina f cukrowa

sugar-free /ʃʊgə'fri:/ adj [food] bez cukru; [diet] bezcukrowy

sugar lump n kostka f cukru

suggest /sə'dʒest, US səg'dʒ-/ vt za|sugerować [solution]; **to ~ that...** sugerować or proponować, żeby...; **can you ~ a place to eat?** czy możesz polecić jakąś restaurację?; **I ~ that you leave at once** uważam, że powinieneś natychmiast wyjść

suggestion /sə'dʒestʃn, US səg'dʒ-/ n 1 (proposal) propozycja f; **at sb's ~** zgodnie z propozycją or sugestią kogoś 2 (trace) element m (**of sth** czegoś); **there is no ~ of fraud** nic nie wskazuje na oszustwo

suggestive /sə'dʒestɪv, US səg'dʒ-/ adj [remark, smile] dwuznaczny; **to be ~ of sth** przypominać coś

suicidal /suːɪ'saɪdl, ˌsjuː-/ adj [mood] samobójczy; [person] o skłonnościach samobójczych

suicide /'suːɪsaɪd, 'sjuː-/ n (action) samobójstwo n; (person) samobój|ca m, -czyni f; **to commit ~** popełnić samobójstwo

suit /suːt, sjuːt/ **I** n 1 (man's) garnitur m; (woman's) kostium m 2 (lawsuit) proces m 3 (in cards) kolor m **II** vt 1 (flatter) **that dress ~s you** do twarzy ci w tej sukience; **red doesn't ~ her complexion** czerwony nie pasuje do jej karnacji 2 [date, arrangement] odpowiadać (komuś) **III** vr ~ **yourself!** rób, jak uważasz!

suitable /'suːtəbl, 'sjuː-/ adj odpowiedni; [time] dogodny; **the most ~ person for the job** najodpowiedniejsza osoba do tej pracy; **not ~ for human consumption** niezdatny do spożycia

suitably /'suːtəblɪ, 'sjuː-/ adv odpowiednio, stosownie

suitcase /'suːtkeɪs, 'sjuː-/ n walizka f

suite /swiːt/ n 1 (furniture) komplet m mebli 2 (rooms) apartament m

suited /'suːtɪd, 'sjuː-/ adj **to be ~ to sth** [place, person] nadawać się do czegoś; [clothes, conditions] być odpowiednim do czegoś; [format, style] pasować do czegoś; **they are ideally ~ (to each other)** są dla siebie stworzeni

sulk /sʌlk/ vi dąsać się (**about** or **over sth** z powodu czegoś)

sulky /'sʌlkɪ/ adj [person] nadąsany; **to look ~** mieć chmurną i obrażoną minę

sullen /'sʌlən/ adj ponury

sulphur GB, **sulfur** US /'sʌlfə(r)/ n siarka f

sulphuric acid n kwas m siarkowy

sultana /sʌl'tɑːnə, US -'tænə/ n Culin sułtanka f

sultry /'sʌltrɪ/ adj 1 [day, weather] parny 2 [voice, woman] zmysłowy

sum /sʌm/ n 1 (of money) suma f 2 (calculation) rachunek m
■ **sum up**: podsumow|ać, -ywać

summarize /'sʌməraɪz/ vt stre|ścić, -szczać [book, problem]; (sum up) podsumow|ać, -ywać

summary /'sʌmərɪ/ n (of plot) streszczenie n; (of main points) podsumowanie n

summer /'sʌmə(r)/ **I** n lato n; **in ~** w lecie, latem **II** adj [evening, clothes] letni

summer camp n US obóz m letni

summer holiday GB, **summer vacation** US n wakacje plt (letnie)

summerhouse /'sʌməhaʊs/ n altana f

summer school n szkoła f letnia

summertime /'sʌmətaɪm/ n lato n

summit /'sʌmɪt/ n szczyt m

summon /'sʌmən/ vt 1 w|ezwać, -zywać [doctor, police]; za|wołać [waiter] 2 (to court) w|ezwać, -zywać
■ **summon up**: z|ebrać, -bierać [energy, strength]

summons /'sʌmənz/ **I** n 1 (in law) wezwanie n do sądu 2 (order) wezwanie n (**from sb** od kogoś); **a ~ to do sth** wezwanie do zrobienia czegoś **II** vt w|ezwać, -zywać do stawienia się w sądzie

sumptuous /ˈsʌmptʃʊəs/ adj [meal] wystawny; [room] urządzony z przepychem

sum total n (of money) ogólna or łączna suma f; (of achievements) całość f

sun /sʌn/ n (also **the Sun**) Słońce n; **don't sit in the** ~ nie siedź na słońcu

sunbathe /ˈsʌnbeɪð/ vi opalać się

sunbed /ˈsʌnbed/ n (lounger) leżak m; (with sunlamp) łóżko n opalające or do opalania

sunblock /ˈsʌnblɒk/ n krem m z filtrem przeciwsłonecznym

sunburn /ˈsʌnbɜːn/ n oparzenie n słoneczne

sunburned, **sunburnt** /ˈsʌnbɜːnt/ adj [person, skin] (burnt) poparzony przez słońce; (tanned) GB opalony; **to get** ~ (burn) spalić się (na słońcu); (tan) opalić się

Sunday /ˈsʌndeɪ, -dɪ/ n niedziela f

Sunday best n (dressed) **in one's** ~ odświętnie ubrany

Sunday trading n handel m w niedzielę

sundial /ˈsʌndaɪəl/ n zegar m słoneczny

sundress /ˈsʌndres/ n letnia sukienka f na ramiączkach

sundry /ˈsʌndrɪ/ **I** **sundries** npl rozmaitości plt **II** adj [items] rozmaity, różny; **all and** ~ wszyscy bez wyjątku; (critical) byle kto

sunflower /ˈsʌnflaʊə(r)/ n słonecznik m

sunglasses /ˈsʌnglɑːsɪz, US -glæsɪz/ npl okulary plt (przeciw)słoneczne

sun hat n kapelusz m od słońca

sunken /ˈsʌŋkən/ adj [1] [treasure, wreck] zatopiony; [rock] podwodny [2] [cheek] zapadnięty [3] [bath] wpuszczony w podłogę; [garden] (położony) na niższym poziomie

sunlamp /ˈsʌnlæmp/ n lampa f kwarcowa

sunlight /ˈsʌnlaɪt/ n światło n słoneczne; **in the** ~ w słońcu

sunny /ˈsʌnɪ/ adj [1] [weather, day] słoneczny; [garden, room] (sunlit) nasłoneczniony; (facing the sun) słoneczny; **it's going to be** ~ będzie słonecznie [2] [person, temperament] pogodny

sunrise /ˈsʌnraɪz/ n wschód m słońca

sunroof /ˈsʌnruːf/ n szyberdach m

sunset /ˈsʌnset/ n zachód m słońca

sunshade /ˈsʌnʃeɪd/ n parasol m od słońca

sunshield /ˈsʌnʃiːld/ n Aut osłona f przeciwsłoneczna

sunshine /ˈsʌnʃaɪn/ n słońce n

sunstroke /ˈsʌnstrəʊk/ n udar m słoneczny

suntan /ˈsʌntæn/ n opalenizna f; **to get a** ~ opalić się

suntan lotion n emulsja f do opalania

suntanned /ˈsʌntænd/ adj opalony

suntan oil n olejek m do opalania

super /ˈsuːpə(r), ˈsjuː-/ adj, excl infml super infml

superb /suːˈpɜːb, sjuː-/ adj [player] znakomity; [view] wspaniały

supercilious /ˌsuːpəˈsɪlɪəs, ˌsjuː-/ adj wyniosły

superficial /ˌsuːpəˈfɪʃl, ˌsjuː-/ adj [wound, knowledge] powierzchowny; [person, book] płytki

superfluous /suːˈpɜːfluəs, sjuː-/ adj zbyteczny

superimpose /ˌsuːpərɪmˈpəʊz, ˌsjuː-/ vt nałożyć, -kładać [picture] (**on sth** na coś)

superintendent /ˌsuːpərɪnˈtendənt, ˌsjuː-/ n [1] (supervisor) kierownik m; (of park) nadzorca m [2] (also **police** ~) ≈ komisarz m [3] US (in apartment house) dozorca m [4] US (also **school** ~) kurator m

superior /suːˈpɪərɪə(r), sjuː-, sʊ-/ **I** n przełożony m, -a f **II** adj [1] [intelligence] ponadprzeciętny; [team] wyróżniający się; [product] pierwszorzędny [2] (condescending) wyniosły

superiority /suːˌpɪərɪˈɒrətɪ, sjuː-, US -ˈɔːr-/ n (in quality) wyższość f; (in amount, number) przewaga f

superlative /suːˈpɜːlətɪv, sjuː-/ **I** n stopień m najwyższy **II** adj doskonały

superman /ˈsuːpəmæn, ˈsjuː-/ n nadczłowiek m; fig superman m

supermarket /ˈsuːpəmɑːkɪt, ˈsjuː-/ n supermarket m

supernatural /ˌsuːpəˈnætʃrəl, ˌsjuː-/ **I** n **the** ~ siły f pl nadprzyrodzone **II** adj nadprzyrodzony

superpower /ˈsuːpəpaʊə(r), ˈsjuː-/ n supermocarstwo n

supersede /ˌsuːpəˈsiːd, ˌsjuː-/ vt zast|ąpić, -ępować [model]; wyp|rzeć, -ierać [theory]

supersonic /ˌsuːpəˈsɒnɪk, ˌsjuː-/ adj (po)naddźwiękowy

superstar /ˈsuːpəstɑː(r), ˈsjuː-/ n megagwiazda f

superstition /ˌsuːpəˈstɪʃn, ˌsjuː-/ n przesąd m

superstitious /ˌsuːpəˈstɪʃəs, ˌsjuː-/ adj przesądny

superstore /ˈsuːpəstɔː(r), ˈsjuː-/ n hipermarket m

supervise /ˈsuːpəvaɪz, ˈsjuː-/ vt nadzorować [activity, workers]; opiekować się (kimś) [student]; pilnować (kogoś) [child]; doglądać (kogoś) [patient]

supervision /ˌsuːpəˈvɪʒn, ˌsjuː-/ n (of staff, work) nadzór m; (of child, patient) nadzór m

supervisor /ˈsuːpəvaɪzə(r), ˈsjuː-/ n [1] (overseer) nadzorca m; (manager) kierowni|k m, -czka f; (foreman in factory) brygadzist|a m, -ka f [2] GB (for thesis) promotor m

supper /ˈsʌpə(r)/ n (evening meal) kolacja f; **to have** or **eat** ~ jeść kolację; **the Last Supper** Ostatnia Wieczerza

supple /ˈsʌpl/ adj [person, body] gibki; [limbs, mind] giętki

supplement **I** /ˈsʌplɪmənt/ n [1] (to diet, income) uzupełnienie n (**to sth** czegoś); **a vitamin** ~ suplement witaminowy [2] (extra charge) dopłata f [3] (to newspaper) dodatek m **II** /ˈsʌplɪment/ vt uzupełni|ć, -ać [diet, knowledge, staff]; **to** ~ **sth with sth** uzupełnić coś czymś

supplementary /ˌsʌplɪ'mentrɪ, US -terɪ/ *adj* *[income]* dodatkowy

supplier /sə'plaɪə(r)/ *n* dostawca *m* (**of sth** czegoś)

supply /sə'plaɪ/ **I** *n* ① (stock) zapas *m*; **cherries are in short ~** jest mało or brakuje wiśni; **to get in a ~ of sth** zaopatrzyć się w coś ② (source) źródło *n* zaopatrzenia; **~ of sth** (process of providing) dostarczanie czegoś, zaopatrywanie w coś; (act of providing) dostawa *f*; **the blood ~ to the brain** dopływ krwi do mózgu

II supplies *npl* ① (equipment) zaopatrzenie *n*; (food) prowiant *m*; (of natural resources) zasoby *m pl* ② **office supplies** materiały biurowe; **household supplies** artykuły gospodarstwa domowego **III** *vt* dostarcz|yć, -ać *[goods, oxygen]* (**to sb/sth** komuś/do czegoś); poda|ć, -wać *[answer]*; zaopat|rzyć, -rywać *[area, town, company]* (**with sth** w coś)

supply and demand *n* podaż *f* i popyt *m*

supply teacher *n* GB nauczyciel *m*, -ka *f* na zastępstwie

support /sə'pɔːt/ **I** *n* ① (backing) poparcie *n*; (financial, political, moral) wsparcie *n*; **to give sb/sth (one's) ~** udzielić poparcia komuś/czemuś, poprzeć kogoś/coś; **means of ~** środki utrzymania ② (sth to lean on) oparcie *n*, podparcie *n*; (person) podpora *f* (**to sb** dla kogoś) ③ (thing bearing weight) podpora *f*; (small) podpórka *f*

II *vt* ① (back) pop|rzeć, -ierać *[party, reform]* ② (financially, morally) w|esprzeć, -spierać; **the museum is ~ed by public funds** muzeum jest dotowane z kasy publicznej ③ (bear weight) podtrzym|ać, -ywać, utrzym|ać, -ywać ciężar (czegoś) ④ (show to be true) potwierdz|ić, -ać *[statement]*; przem|ówić, -awiać za (czymś) *[argument]* ⑤ (maintain) *[person]* utrzym|ać, -ywać *[family]*; *[land]* wy|żywić *[inhabitants]*

supporter /sə'pɔːtə(r)/ *n* zwolenni|k *m*, -czka *f*, stronni|k *m*, -czka *f*; Sport kibic *m*

support group *n* grupa *f* wsparcia

supporting /sə'pɔːtɪŋ/ *adj* *[part]* drugoplanowy; *[actor]* grający rolę drugoplanową

supportive /sə'pɔːtɪv/ *adj* *[person]* oddany; *[role]* wspomagający

suppose /sə'pəʊz/ **I** *vt* ① (think) **to ~ (that)...** sądzić, że...; **I ~ (that) she knows** przypuszczam, że ona wie ② (assume) za|łożyć, -kładać *[possibility]*; **let us ~ that it's true** załóżmy, że to prawda; **I ~ so/not** chyba tak/nie

II supposed *pp adj* **I'm ~d to be at work now!** powinienem być teraz w pracy!; **there was ~d to be a room for us** miał być dla nas pokój; **it's ~d to be a good hotel** to jest podobno dobry hotel

supposing /sə'pəʊzɪŋ/ *conj* przypuśćmy, że; **~ (that) he says no?** a jeśli powie nie?; **~ your income is X** przypuśćmy, że twój dochód wynosi X

suppress /sə'pres/ *vt* powstrzym|ać, -ywać *[smile]*; opanow|ać, -ywać *[anger, yawn]*; zatai|ć, -jać *[evidence, truth, information]*; s|tłumić *[rebellion]*; za|tuszować *[scandal]*; opóźni|ć, -ać *[growth]*

supreme /su:'pri:m, sju:-/ *adj* *[ruler, importance]* najwyższy; *[arrogance]* wyjątkowy

surcharge /'sɜːtʃɑːdʒ/ *n* dopłata *f*

sure /ʃɔː(r), US ʃʊər/ **I** *adj* (certain) pewny (**about** or **of sth** czegoś); **I'm not ~ when he's coming** nie jestem pewien, kiedy przyjdzie; **for ~** z całą pewnością; **we'll be there next week for ~!** na pewno będziemy w przyszłym tygodniu!; **nobody knows for ~** nikt nie wie na pewno; **he is, to be ~, a charming man** jest niewątpliwie czarującym człowiekiem; **to make ~ that...** (ascertain) upewnić się, że...; (see to it) dopilnować, żeby...; **he's ~ to fail** na pewno mu się nie uda; **to be ~ of oneself** być pewnym siebie

II *adv* (yes) **'you're coming?' – '~!'** „idziesz?" – „(no) pewnie!"; **~ enough** faktycznie, rzeczywiście

IDIOMS **~ thing!** US infml (no) jasne! infml; **as ~ as eggs is eggs** infml, **as ~ as fate, as ~ as I'm standing here** (pewne) jak dwa razy dwa cztery

sure-fire /'ʃɔːfaɪə(r), US ʃʊər-/ *adj* *[method]* niezawodny; *[success]* pewny

sure-footed /ˌʃɔː'fʊtɪd, US ʃʊər-/ *adj* zwinny

surely /'ʃɔːlɪ, US 'ʃʊərlɪ/ *adv* ① (expressing certainty) na pewno; **~ we've met before!** jestem pewien, że już się kiedyś spotkaliśmy! ② (expressing surprise, doubt) chyba; **you're ~ not going to eat that!** chyba nie zamierzasz tego jeść!

surf /sɜːf/ **I** *n* (waves) fale *f pl* przyboju; (foam) morska piana *f*

II *vi* Sport uprawiać surfing; Comput surfować po Internecie

surface /'sɜːfɪs/ **I** *n* ① (of water, land, object) powierzchnia *f*; (of road) nawierzchnia *f*; **on the ~ it was a simple problem** z pozoru sprawa była prosta ② (of solid, cube) ściana *f* ③ (worktop) powierzchnia *f* do pracy

II *vi* ① *[animal, submarine]* wynurz|yć, -ać się ② *[tension]* ujawni|ć, -ać się; *[problem]* wy|jść, -chodzić na światło dzienne

surface area *n* pole *n* powierzchni

surfboard /'sɜːfbɔːd/ *n* deska *f* surfingowa

surfer /'sɜːfə(r)/ *n* surfingowiec *m*

surfing /'sɜːfɪŋ/ *n* surfing *m*

surge /sɜːdʒ/ **I** *n* ① (of water) spiętrzona fala *f*; (of blood, energy, anger) nagły przypływ *m* ② (in demand, unemployment) gwałtowny wzrost *m* (**in sth** czegoś); (in prices) skok *m*

II *vi* ① *[waves]* przewal|ić, -ać się; *[water]* w|ezbrać, -zbierać; *[emotion]* w|ezbrać, -zbierać (**in sb** w kimś); **to ~ forward** *[crowd]* ruszyć do przodu ② *[prices, profits]* gwałtownie wzr|osnąć, -astać

surgeon /'sɜːdʒən/ *n* chirurg *m*

surgery /'sɜːdʒərɪ/ *n* [1] (operation) operacja *f*; (skill, study) chirurgia *f*; **to have** ~ mieć operację [2] GB (room) gabinet *m*; (building) przychodnia *f*

surgical /'sɜːdʒɪkl/ *adj [instruments]* chirurgiczny; *[boot]* ortopedyczny; *[stocking]* przeciwżylakowy

surgical spirit *n* spirytus *m (używany do dezynfekcji)*

surly /'sɜːlɪ/ *adj* gburowaty

surname /'sɜːneɪm/ *n* nazwisko *n*

surpass /sə'pɑːs, US -'pæs/ [1] *vt* (be better or greater than) przewyższ|yć, -ać; (go beyond) przekr|oczyć, -aczać *[expectations]*

[2] *vr* **to ~ oneself** prze|jść, -chodzić samego siebie

surplus /'sɜːpləs/ [1] *n* nadmiar *m*, nadwyżka *f*

[2] *adj* ~ **money/food** nadwyżka pieniędzy/żywności

surprise /sə'praɪz/ [1] *n* (unexpected event) zaskoczenie *n*; (experience, gift) niespodzianka *f*; **to take sb by** ~ zaskoczyć kogoś

[2] *vt* [1] zask|oczyć, -akiwać; **what** ~s **me most is...** mnie najbardziej dziwi to, że...; **it** ~**d them that...** zaskoczyło or zdziwiło ich, że... [2] (come upon) zask|oczyć, -akiwać *[intruder, thief]*

surprised /sə'praɪzd/ *adj* zaskoczony; **I'm not** ~ to mnie nie dziwi

surprising /sə'praɪzɪŋ/ *adj* (unusual) zadziwiający; (unexpected) niespodziewany; **it's** ~ **that...** to zaskakujące, że...

surprisingly /sə'praɪzɪŋlɪ/ *adv* zadziwiająco; ~, **they lost** niespodziewanie przegrali; **not** ~, **they rejected the offer** jak można było się spodziewać, odrzucili ofertę

surreal /sə'rɪəl/ *adj* surrealistyczny

surrealist /sə'rɪəlɪst/ [1] *n* surrealist|a *m*, -ka *f*

[2] *adj* surrealistyczny

surrender /sə'rendə(r)/ [1] *n* [1] (of army, town) kapitulacja *f* (**to sb** przed kimś); (of soldier) poddanie się *n* (**to sb** komuś) [2] (handing over) (of territory) oddanie *n* (**to sb** komuś); (of rights) zrzeczenie się *n* (**to sb** na rzecz kogoś); (of weapons) złożenie *n*; (of document) zwrot *m*

[2] *vt* podda|ć, -wać *[town]* (**to sb** komuś); wykup|ić, -ywać *[insurance policy]*; złożyć, składać *[firearm]* (**to sb** w ręce kogoś); odda|ć, -wać *[ticket]* (**to sb** komuś)

[3] *vi [army, soldier, country]* podda|ć, -wać się (**to sb** komuś)

surrogate /'sʌrəgeɪt/ [1] *n* [1] substytut *m* (**for sb/sth** kogoś/czegoś) [2] (also ~ **mother**) matka *f* zastępcza

[2] *adj* zastępczy

surround /sə'raʊnd/ *vt [trees]* ot|oczyć, -aczać *[garden]*; *[police]* ot|oczyć, -aczać *[building]*; osacz|yć, -ać *[person]*

surrounding /sə'raʊndɪŋ/ *adj [villages]* okoliczny; **the** ~ **area** okolica

surroundings /sə'raʊndɪŋz/ *npl* otoczenie *n*; (area) okolica *f*; **animals in their natural** ~ zwierzęta w ich naturalnym środowisku

surveillance /sɜː'veɪləns/ *n* nadzór *m*; (of spy, criminal) obserwacja *f*

survey [1] /'sɜːveɪ/ *n* [1] (of trends, prices) badanie *n*; (by questioning people) sonda *f*; (overview of work) przegląd *m* [2] GB (in housebuying) oględziny *plt* [3] (of land) pomiary *m pl*

[2] /sə'veɪ/ *vt* [1] z|badać *[market, trends]*; przeprowadz|ić, -ać sondaż wśród (kogoś) *[population]* [2] GB przeprowadz|ić, -ać oględziny (czegoś) *[house]* [3] przeprowadz|ić, -ać pomiary (czegoś) *[area]* [4] (look at) z|lustrować wzrokiem *[scene, audience]*

surveyor /sə'veɪə(r)/ *n* GB (of building) rzeczoznawca *m* budowlany; (of land) mierniczy *m*, geodeta *m*

survival /sə'vaɪvl/ *n* (of animal, custom) przetrwanie *n*; (of person) przeżycie *n*

survive /sə'vaɪv/ [1] *vt* [1] przeżyć *[accident, operation]*; przetrzym|ać, -ywać, przetrwać *[crisis, winter]*; *[furniture]* ocaleć z (czegoś) *[fire]* [2] przeży|ć, -wać *[person]*

[2] *vi [person]* przeży|ć, -wać *[company]* przetrwać; *[building]* ocaleć; **to** ~ **on £50 a week** żyć za 50 funtów tygodniowo

surviving /sə'vaɪvɪŋ/ *adj [person]* żyjący

survivor /sə'vaɪvə(r)/ *n* [1] (of accident) **he's the only** ~ tylko on ocalał; **the** ~**s of the accident** osoby, które przeżyły wypadek [2] (resilient person) **he's a** ~ on jest twardy

susceptible /sə'septəbl/ *adj* (to cold) wrażliwy (**to sth** na coś); (to persuasion) łatwo ulegający (**to sth** czemuś); (to disease) podatny (**to sth** na coś)

suspect [1] /'sʌspekt/ *n* podejrzan|y *m*, -a *f*

[2] /'sʌspekt/ *adj [person]* podejrzany; *[authenticity]* wątpliwy

[3] /sə'spekt/ *vt* [1] (believe) podejrzewać *[murder, plot]*; **to** ~ **that...** podejrzewać, że... [2] (doubt) wątpić w (coś) *[motives]* [3] (have under suspicion) podejrzewać *[person]* (**of sth** o coś)

suspend /sə'spend/ *vt* [1] (hang) zawie|sić, -szać [2] (call off) zawie|sić, -szać *[negotiations]*; wstrzym|ać, -ywać *[production]* [3] (remove) zawie|sić, -szać *[pupil]*

suspended sentence *n* wyrok *m* w zawieszeniu

suspender belt /sə'spendəbelt/ *n* GB pas *m* do pończoch

suspenders /sə'spendəz/ *npl* [1] GB (for stockings) podwiązki *f pl* [2] US (for trousers) szelki *f pl*

suspense /sə'spens/ *n* stan *m* napięcia or niepewności; (in film) suspens *m*; **to keep sb in** ~ trzymać kogoś w niepewności

suspension /sə'spenʃn/ *n* [1] (of negotiations) zawieszenie *n*; (of meeting) odroczenie *n*; (of aid) wstrzymanie *n* [2] (of pupil) zawieszenie *n* [3] Aut zawieszenie *n* [4] (mixture) zawiesina *f*

suspicion /səˈspɪʃn̩/ n (mistrust) podejrzliwość f; (of guilt) podejrzenie n; **to arouse** ~ wzbudzać podejrzenia; **to have** ~**s about sb/sth** mieć podejrzenia co do kogoś/czegoś

suspicious /səˈspɪʃəs/ adj [1] (wary) podejrzliwy; **to be** ~ **of sb/sth** odnosić się podejrzliwie do kogoś/ czegoś [2] *[person, vehicle]* podejrzany

sustain /səˈsteɪn/ vt [1] (maintain) podtrzym|ać, -ywać *[interest, growth]*; utrzym|ać, -ywać *[quality]*; kontynuować *[campaign]* [2] Mus przedłuż|yć, -ać *[note]* [3] (support) podtrzym|ać, -ywać *[regime, economy]*; **to** ~ **life** stwarzać warunki do życia [4] (suffer) odn|ieść, -osić *[injury]*; pon|ieść, -osić *[loss]*; dozn|ać, -wać (czegoś) *[burn]*

sustainable /səsˈteɪnəbl/ adj *[development]* zrównoważony; *[forestry]* nienaruszający równowagi ekologicznej; *[resource]* odnawialny; *[growth]* trwały

sustenance /ˈsʌstɪnəns/ n pożywienie n

swab /swɒb/ n (of cotton) wacik m; (of gauze) gazik m

swagger /ˈswægə(r)/ vi [1] (walk) kroczyć dumnie [2] (boast) puszyć się

swallow /ˈswɒləʊ/ [1] n [1] Zool jaskółka f [2] (of drink) łyk m; (of food) kęs m
[1] vt [1] (eat) poł|knąć, -ykać [2] (believe) da|ć, -wać wiarę (czemuś) [3] (suffer) przeł|knąć, -ykać *[insult]*; **to** ~ **one's pride** schować dumę do kieszeni
[1] vi przeł|knąć, -ykać; **to** ~ **hard** przełknąć ślinę

swamp /swɒmp/ [1] n bagno n
[1] vt *[water]* zal|ać, -ewać; **to be** ~**ed with sth** być zasypywanym czymś *[mail]*

swan /swɒn/ n łabędź m

swap /swɒp/ [1] n zamiana f
[1] vt zamieni|ć, -ać; **to** ~ **sth for sth** zamienić or wymienić coś na coś; **to** ~ **places (with sb)** zamienić się miejscami (z kimś)

swarm /swɔːm/ [1] n (of bees, flies) rój m
[1] vi *[bees]* wyr|oić, -ajać się; **to be** ~**ing with sb/sth** roić się od kogoś/czegoś *[tourists, ants]*

swarthy /ˈswɔːðɪ/ adj śniady

swat /swɒt/ vt pacnąć *[fly, wasp]* (**with sth** czymś)

sway /sweɪ/ [1] n **to hold** ~ dzierżyć władzę; **to hold** ~ **over sb/sth** mieć kontrolę nad kimś/ czymś
[1] vt [1] (influence) **to** ~ **sb** wpły|nąć, -wać na kogoś [2] (rock) za|kołysać (czymś)
[1] vi *[tree]* za|kołysać się; *[bridge]* za|chwiać się; *[person]* (from weakness) za|chwiać się na nogach; (to music) kołysać się

swear /sweə(r)/ [1] vt przysi|ąc, -ęgać *[loyalty]*; zaprzysi|ąc, -ęgać (kogoś) *[witness]*; **to** ~ **sb to secrecy** zobowiązać kogoś do dochowania tajemnicy
[1] vi [1] (curse) za|kląć [2] (attest) przysi|ąc, -ęgać
■ **swear by** infml: ~ **by [sb/sth]** ręczyć za (kogoś/coś) *[person, firm]*; święcie wierzyć w (coś) *[remedy]*

■ **swear in**: ~ **[sb] in** zaprzysi|ąc, -ęgać *[witness, president]*

swearing /ˈsweərɪŋ/ n przekleństwa n pl

swearword /ˈsweəwɜːd/ n przekleństwo n

sweat /swet/ [1] n pot m; **to break out into a** ~ oblać się potem; **in a cold** ~ zlany zimnym potem
[1] **sweats** npl US dres m
[1] vi *[person, hands]* s|pocić się

sweatband /ˈswetbænd/ n (on forehead) opaska f na czoło; (on wrist) frotka f

sweater /ˈswetə(r)/ n sweter m

sweat pants npl spodnie plt od dresu

sweatshirt /ˈswetʃɜːt/ n bluza f sportowa

sweatshop /ˈswetʃɒp/ n zakład m wyzyskujący siłę roboczą

sweaty /ˈswetɪ/ adj *[person, hand]* spocony; *[clothing]* przepocony; *[climb]* wyciskający siódme poty

swede /swiːd/ n GB brukiew f

Swede /swiːd/ n Szwed m, -ka f

Sweden /ˈswiːdn/ prn Szwecja f

Swedish /ˈswiːdɪʃ/ [1] n [1] (język m) szwedzki m [2] (people) **the** ~ Szwedzi m pl
[1] adj szwedzki

sweep /swiːp/ [1] n [1] **to give a room a** ~ zamieść pokój [2] (of arm) szeroki ruch m; (of axe) zamach m [3] (of land, woods) rozległa przestrzeń f; (of hills) rozległy obszar m [4] (also **chimney** ~) kominiarz m
[1] vt [1] zami|eść, -atać *[floor, room]*; przeczy|ścić, -szczać *[chimney]* [2] **to** ~ **sth off the table** zmieść ze stołu coś; **to** ~ **sb off their feet** *[sea, wave]* zwalić kogoś z nóg; (romantically) zawrócić komuś w głowie [3] *[beam, searchlight]* omi|eść, -atać *[sky, area]*
[1] vi [1] (clean) zami|eść, -atać [2] **to** ~ **in/out** *[person]* (quickly) wpaść/wypaść; (majestically) wkroczyć/wyjść dostojnym krokiem
■ **sweep aside**: odsu|nąć, -wać na bok *[person, protest]*
■ **sweep up**: zami|eść, -atać

sweeping /ˈswiːpɪŋ/ adj *[change]* szeroko zakrojony; *[cut]* radykalny; *[victory]* zdecydowany; ~ **generalization** nadmierne uogólnienie

sweet /swiːt/ [1] n GB (candy) cukierek m; (dessert) deser m; ~**s** słodycze
[1] adj [1] *[food, wine, taste]* słodki; **to have a** ~ **tooth** lubić słodycze [2] *[person]* miły; *[smile]* uroczy; *[baby]* słodki
[1] adv **to taste** ~ mieć słodki smak

sweet-and-sour /ˌswiːtənˈsaʊə(r)/ adj słodko-kwaśny

sweetcorn /ˈswiːtkɔːn/ n kukurydza f cukrowa

sweeten /ˈswiːtn/ vt [1] po|słodzić *[food, drink]* (**with sth** czymś) [2] uatrakcyjni|ć, -ać *[offer]*
■ **sweeten up**: ~ **[sb] up** przymilać się do kogoś

sweetener /ˈswiːtnə(r)/ n [1] słodzik m [2] infml (incentive) zachęta f; (illegal) łapówka f

sweetheart /ˈswiːthɑːt/ n ukochan|y m, -a f

sweetly /'swiːtlɪ/ *adv* słodko
sweet potato *n* batat *m*
sweet-talk /'swiːttɔːk/ *vt* infml przymilać się do (kogoś)
swell /swel/ **I** *n* (of waves) falowanie *n*; (wave) martwa fala *f*
II *vt* powiększ|yć, -áć *[membership, funds]*; s|powodować wezbranie (czegoś) *[river]*
III *vi [wood]* na|pęcznieć; *[ankle]* s|puchnąć; *[gland]* powiększ|yć, -áć się; *[river]* w|ezbrać, -zbierać; *[tyre]* wyd|ąć, -ymać się; *[balloon]* nad|ąć, -ymać się; *[stomach]* wzd|ąć, -ymać się; *[crowd]* powiększ|yć, -áć się
swelling /'swelɪŋ/ *n* (bump) opuchlizna *f*; (on head) guz *m*
sweltering /'sweltərɪŋ/ *adj [day]* duszny; *[climate]* gorący i wilgotny
swerve /swɜːv/ *vi* gwałtownie skręc|ić, -áć; **to ~ off the road** zjechać z drogi
swift /swɪft/ **I** *n* Zool jerzyk *m*
II *adj [reaction]* prędki; *[river]* bystry
swill /swɪl/ *n* (food) pomyje *plt*
swim /swɪm/ **I** *n* **to go for a ~** iść popływać; **to have a ~** popływać sobie
II *vt* przepły|nąć, -wać *[mile, Channel]*; płynąć (czymś) *[backstroke]*
III *vi* ① (without purpose) pływać; (in specific direction) po|płynąć; **to ~ across sth** przepłynąć (przez) coś ② **to be ~ming in sth** pływać w czymś *[cream, sauce]* ③ *[room, scene]* wirować przed oczami
swimmer /'swɪmə(r)/ *n* pływa|k *m*, -czka *f*
swimming /'swɪmɪŋ/ *n* pływanie *n*; **to go ~** (in sea, river) iść popływać; (in pool) iść na basen
swimming costume *n* GB kostium *m* kąpielowy
swimming pool *n* basen *m*
swimming trunks *npl* kąpielówki *plt*
swimsuit /'swɪmsuːt, -sjuːt/ *n* kostium *m* kąpielowy
swindle /'swɪndl/ **I** *n* oszustwo *n*
II *vt* oszuk|ać, -iwać *[person]*; **to ~ sb out of sth** wyłudzić coś od kogoś
swindler /'swɪndlə(r)/ *n* oszust *m*, -ka *f*
swing /swɪŋ/ **I** *n* ① (of pointer) drgnięcie *n*; (of pendulum) ruch *m*; (of hips, body) kołyszący ruch *m* ② (fluctuation) gwałtowna zmiana *f* (**in sth** czegoś); **market ~s** wahania rynkowe; **a ~ away from/ towards sth** (in opinion) odwrócenie się od czegoś/ zwrot w kierunku czegoś ③ (in playground) huśtawka *f*
II *vt* (to and fro) mach|nąć, -áć (czymś) *[stick]*; za|kołysać (czymś) *[hips]*
III *vi* ① (to and fro) (standing object) za|kołysać się; *[hanging object]* roz|bujać się ② (in a curve) **to ~ open** otworzyć się; **the car swung into the drive** samochód zakręcił na podjazd; **to ~ around** *[person]* obrócić się gwałtownie ③ (oscillate) *[mood, opinion]* wahać się (**between sth and sth**

między czymś a czymś); (change) zmieniać się; **to ~ from euphoria to despair** wpadać raz w euforię, raz w rozpacz; **the party has swung to the left** partia obrała kurs na lewo
IDIOMS: **to be in full ~** *[party]* trwać w najlepsze; *[work]* posuwać się pełną parą; **to get into the ~ of things** infml wciągnąć się
swing door GB, **swinging door** US *n* drzwi *plt* wahadłowe
swirl /swɜːl/ *vi [water]* wirować; *[snow]* kłębić się
Swiss /swɪs/ **I** *n* Szwajcar *m*, -ka *f*; **the ~** Szwajcarzy
II *adj* szwajcarski
switch /swɪtʃ/ **I** *n* ① (change) zmiana *f* (**in sth** czegoś); ② (for light) włącznik *m*, wyłącznik *m*; kontakt *m* infml; (on radio, appliance) włącznik *m*, wyłącznik *m*; (to change options) przełącznik *m*
II *vt* ① przen|ieść, -osić *[attention]* (**to sb/sth** na kogoś/coś); **to ~ lanes** Aut zmienić pas ② za|mieni|ć, -áć się (czymś) *[seats, roles]* ③ (also **~ round**) przestawi|ć, -áć *[objects]*
III *vi* ① **to ~ from sth to sth** przejść z czegoś na coś ② (also **~ over** or **round**) *[people]* zamieni|ć, -áć się (**with sb** z kimś)
■ **switch off**: wyłącz|yć, -áć *[appliance, light, engine]*; przer|wać, -ywać *[supply]*
■ **switch on**: włącz|yć, -áć *[appliance, light, engine]*
■ **switch over**: przełącz|yć, -áć (**to sth** na coś)
switchboard /'swɪtʃbɔːd/ *n* centrala *f* telefoniczna
switchboard operator *n* telefonist|a *m*, -ka *f*
switchover /'swɪtʃəʊvə(r)/ *n* przejście *n* (**from sth to sth** z czegoś na coś)
Switzerland /'swɪtsələnd/ *prn* Szwajcaria *f*
swivel /'swɪvl/ *vt* obr|ócić, -acać *[chair, camera, head]*; przewr|ócić, -acać (czymś) *[eyes]*
■ **swivel round**: obr|ócić, -acać się
swivel chair, **swivel seat** *n* fotel *m* obrotowy
swollen /'swəʊlən/ *adj [ankle]* spuchnięty; *[eyes]* zapuchnięty; *[gland]* powiększony; *[river]* wezbrany
swoop /swuːp/ *vi* ① (also **~ down**) *[bird, bat, plane]* za|nurkować; **to ~ down on sth** *[bird]* spaść na coś *[prey]* ② *[police]* z|robić nalot infml (**on sth** na coś); *[raiders]* napa|ść, -dáć (**on sth** na coś)
sword /sɔːd/ *n* szpada *f*; (curved) szabla *f*; (heavy) miecz *m*
swordfish /'sɔːdfɪʃ/ *n* Zool miecznik *m*
sworn /swɔːn/ *adj* ① *[statement]* złożony pod przysięgą ② *[enemy]* zaprzysięgły; *[ally]* wierny
swot /swɒt/ infml **I** *n* kujon *m* infml
II *vi* wku|ć, -wać infml
sycamore /'sɪkəmɔː(r)/ *n* sykomora *f*
syllable /'sɪləbl/ *n* sylaba *f*
syllabus /'sɪləbəs/ *n* program *m* nauczania
symbol /'sɪmbɒlɪk/ *n* symbol *m* (**of** or **for sth** czegoś)

symbolic /sɪmˈbɒlɪk/ *adj* symboliczny
symbolism /ˈsɪmbəlɪzəm/ *n* symbolizm *m*
symbolize /ˈsɪmbəlaɪz/ *vt* symbolizować
symmetric(al) /sɪˈmetrɪk(l)/ *adj* symetryczny
sympathetic /ˌsɪmpəˈθetɪk/ *adj* (compassionate) pełen współczucia (**to** or **towards sb** dla kogoś); (well-disposed) przychylny (**towards sb/sth** komuś/czemuś); życzliwie nastawiony (**to** or **towards sb/sth** do kogoś/czegoś)
sympathize /ˈsɪmpəθaɪz/ *vi* ⊡ (feel compassion) współczuć (**with sb** komuś); **I ~ with you in your grief** proszę przyjąć wyrazy współczucia ⊡ (support) sympatyzować (**with sb/sth** z kimś/czymś); **to ~ with sb's views** podzielać przekonania kogoś
sympathizer /ˈsɪmpəθaɪzə(r)/ *n* sympaty|k *m*, -czka *f*
sympathy /ˈsɪmpəθɪ/ *n* ⊡ (compassion) współczucie *n* ⊡ (solidarity) solidarność *f*; **what are her political sympathies?** jakie są jej sympatie polityczne?
symphony /ˈsɪmfənɪ/ *n* symfonia *f*
symphony orchestra *n* orkiestra *f* symfoniczna
symptom /ˈsɪmptəm/ *n* Med objaw *m*; fig przejaw *m*
synagogue /ˈsɪnəgɒg/ *n* synagoga *f*

synchronize /ˈsɪŋkrənaɪz/ *vt* z|synchronizować
syndicate /ˈsɪndɪkət/ *n* konsorcjum *n*
syndrome /ˈsɪndrəʊm/ *n* zespół *m*, syndrom *m*
synonymous /sɪˈnɒnɪməs/ *adj* synonimiczny; **to be ~ with sth** być synonimem czegoś
synopsis /sɪˈnɒpsɪs/ *n* streszczenie *n*
syntax /ˈsɪntæks/ *n* składnia *f*
synthesis /ˈsɪnθəsɪs/ *n* synteza *f*
synthesizer /ˈsɪnθəsaɪzə(r)/ *n* syntezator *m*
synthetic /sɪnˈθetɪk/ *adj* syntetyczny
syringe /sɪˈrɪndʒ/ Ⅰ *n* strzykawka *f* Ⅱ *vt* **to have one's ears ~d** przepłukać (sobie) uszy
syrup /ˈsɪrəp/ *n* syrop *m*
system /ˈsɪstəm/ *n* ⊡ system *m*; Pol ustrój *m*; **a road ~** sieć dróg ⊡ (digestive, reproductive) układ *m*; **to get sth out of one's ~** wydalić coś z organizmu; fig infml zapomnieć o czymś
systematic /ˌsɪstəˈmætɪk/ *adj* (efficient) systematyczny; (deliberate) planowy
systematically /ˌsɪstəˈmætɪklɪ/ *adv* [list, work] systematycznie; [destroy, undermine] systematycznie, planowo
systems analyst *n* analityk *m* systemowy

T

t, T /tiː/ *n* t, T *n*

tab /tæb/ *n* [1] (loop) pętelka *f* [2] (on can) uszko *n* [3] (label) etykietka *f*
IDIOMS: **to keep ~s on sb** infml mieć kogoś na oku

tabby (cat) /'tæbɪ/ *n* kot *m* pręgowany

table /'teɪbl/ **[I]** *n* [1] (furniture) stół *m*; **to set the ~** nakryć do stołu [2] (list) tabela *f*
[II] *vt* [1] GB (present) zgł|osić, -aszać *[bill, amendment]* [2] US (postpone) odł|ożyć, -kładać

tablecloth /'teɪblklɒθ, US -klɔːθ/ *n* obrus *m*

table manners *npl* **to have good/bad ~** umieć/ nie umieć zachować się przy stole

table mat *n* (under plate) mata *f*; (under serving-dish) podkładka *f*

tablespoon /'teɪblspuːn/ *n* [1] (object) łyżka *f* sto-łowa [2] Culin (also **~ful**) łyżka *f* stołowa

tablet /'tæblɪt/ *n* tabletka *f* **(for sth** na coś)

table tennis *n* tenis *m* stołowy; ping-pong *m* infml

tabloid /'tæblɔɪd/ **[I]** *n* brukowiec *m*; **the ~s** prasa bulwarowa
[II] *adj [press, journalism]* bulwarowy

taboo /tə'buː/ *n* tabu *n* *inv*

tacit /'tæsɪt/ *adj* cichy

tack /tæk/ **[I]** *n* [1] (nail) ćwieczek *m* [2] US (drawing pin) pinezka *f* [3] (approach) taktyka *f* [4] (in sailing) hals *m*
[II] *vt* [1] (nail) **to ~ sth to sth** przybić coś do czegoś [2] (in sewing) s|fastrygować
[III] *vi [sailor, yacht]* halsować
■ **tack on:** ~ **on [sth],** ~ **[sth] on** dołącz|yć, -ać *[clause, ending]*; dobudow|ać, -ywać *[porch]*

tackle /'tækl/ **[I]** *n* [1] Sport (in soccer, hockey) wejście *n* infml **(on sb** w kogoś) [2] (for fishing) sprzęt *m* wędkarski [3] (rigging) takielunek *m*; (for lifting) talia *f*
[II] *vt* [1] (handle) wziąć, brać się do (czegoś) *[task, problem]* [2] (approach) **to ~ sb about sth** zagadnąć kogoś o coś [3] Sport w|ejść, -chodzić w (kogoś) infml

tacky /'tækɪ/ *adj* [1] (sticky) lepki [2] infml (cheap) tandetny infml

tact /tækt/ *n* takt *m*

tactful /'tæktfl/ *adj* taktowny

tactical /'tæktɪkl/ *adj* taktyczny; **~ voting** głosowanie *n* taktyczne

tactics /'tæktɪks/ *npl* taktyka *f*

tactless /'tæktlɪs/ *adj* nietaktowny

tadpole /'tædpəʊl/ *n* kijanka *f*

---

tag /tæg/ *n* (on goods) metka *f*; (on luggage) przy-wieszka *f*; (on cat, dog) znaczek *m*; (on file) fiszka *f*
■ **tag along**: wlec się z tyłu infml

tail /teɪl/ **[I]** *n* ogon *m*
[II] tails *npl* [1] (tailcoat) frak *m* [2] (on coin) reszka *f*; **haeds or ~s?** orzeł czy reszka?
■ **tail off:** [1] *[figures]* zmniejszać się [2] *[voice]* u|cichnąć

tailback /'teɪlbæk/ *n* korek *m*

tailgate /'teɪlgeɪt/ *n* (of lorry) klapa *f* tylna; (of estate car) pokrywa *f* bagażnika

tail-off /'teɪlɒf, US -ɔːf/ *n* zmniejszanie *n* **(in sth** czegoś)

tailor /'teɪlə(r)/ **[I]** *n* krawiec *m*
[II] *vt* **to ~ sth to sth** dostosować coś do czegoś *[needs]*

tailor-made /ˌteɪlə'meɪd/ *adj* [1] (made to measure) *[suit, jacket]* szyty na miarę [2] *[machine, system]* dostosowany do potrzeb

tainted /'teɪntɪd/ *adj [food, water, air]* skażony **(with sth** czymś); *[reputation]* splamiony fig **(with sth** czymś)

take /teɪk/ **[I]** *n* (in film-making) ujęcie *n*
[II] *vt* [1] (take hold of) wziąć, brać *[object, money]*; chwy|cić, -tać *[rope]*; **to ~ sb by the hand** wziąć kogoś za rękę; **to ~ sth from sth** wziąć coś z czegoś *[shelf, table]*; wyjąć coś z czegoś *[pocket, box]*; **to ~ sth out of sth** wyjąć coś z czegoś [2] (have) wziąć, brać *[bath, shower]*; z|robić sobie *[holiday, break]*; **~ a seat!** proszę usiąść!; **to ~ an exam** zdawać egzamin [3] (carry along) zab|rać, -ierać *[object, person]*; **to ~ sb sth, to ~ sth to sb** zanieść komuś coś; **to ~ the car to the garage** odstawić samochód do warsztatu; **to ~ sth upstairs/downstairs** zanieść coś na górę/ znieść coś na dół [4] (accompany, lead) **to ~ sb to sth** *[bus]* zawieźć kogoś do czegoś *[place]*; *[path, road, person]* zaprowadzić kogoś do czegoś *[place]*; **to ~ a dog/child for a walk** wziąć psa/dziecko na spacer [5] (go by) po|jechać (czymś) *[bus, taxi, road]*; po|lecieć (czymś) *[plane]*; *[walker]* pójść, iść (czymś) *[path, road]* [6] (negotiate) *[car, driver]* wziąć, brać *[bend, corner]*; *[horse]* przesk|oczyć, -akiwać *[fence]* [7] (accept) przyj|ąć, -mować *[bribe]*; pod|jąć, -ejmować *[job]*; od|ebrać, -bierać *[phone call]*; *[machine]* przyj|ąć, -mować *[coin]*; honorować *[credit card, cheque]* [8] (require) *[activity, course of*

action] wymagać (czegoś) *[time, patience, skill, courage]*; **it ~s patience to do sth** zrobienie czegoś wymaga cierpliwości; **it ~s three hours to do sth** na zrobienie czegoś potrzeba trzech godzin; **it won't ~ long** to nie potrwa długo; **it took her 10 minutes** zajęło jej to 10 minut ⑨ (assume) **I ~ it that...** zakładam, że...; **to ~ sb for** or **to be sb/sth** wziąć kogoś za kogoś/za coś ⑩ (record) z|robić *[notes]*; z|mierzyć *[pulse, temperature]* ⑪ (hold) *[bus, hall, tank]* po|mieścić ⑫ (wear) nosić *[size]* ⑬ (subtract) od|jąć, -ejmować *[number, quantity]* (**from sth** od czegoś)

III *vi [drug]* za|działać; *[dye]* chwy|cić, -tać

■ **take aback**: zask|oczyć, -akiwać *[person]*

■ **take after**: być podobnym do (kogoś) *[parent]*

■ **take apart**: roz|ebrać, -bierać *[car, machine]*

■ **take away**: ① (remove) zab|rać, -ierać *[object, person]* (**from sth** z czegoś); **to ~ away sb's appetite** odebrać komuś apetyt ② (subtract) od|jąć, -ejmować *[number]*; **that doesn't ~ anything away from his achievement** to nie umniejsza jego zasług

■ **take back**: ① (to shop) zwr|ócić, -acać *[goods]* ② (accept again) przyj|ąć, -mować z powrotem *[employee, gift]*

■ **take down**: ① zd|jąć, -ejmować *[picture, curtains]*; roz|ebrać, -bierać *[scaffolding]*; zwi|nąć, -jać *[tent]* ② (write down) za|notować *[statement, name, details]*

■ **take hold**: *[disease, epidemic]* za|panować; *[idea, ideology]* rozprzestrzeni|ć, -ać się; **to ~ hold of sb/sth** (grasp) chwy|cić, -tać coś *[object, hand]*; z|łapać *[person]*

■ **take in**: ① (deceive) oszuk|ać, -iwać *[person]*; **I wasn't taken in by him** przejrzałem go ② (allow to stay) przyj|ąć, -mować pod swój dach *[person, refugee]*; przyj|ąć, -mować *[lodger]* ③ (understand) poj|ąć, -mować *[situation]* ④ (observe) zauważ|yć, -ać *[detail]* ⑤ (encompass) obj|ąć, -ejmować *[developments]* ⑥ (absorb) pob|rać, -ierać *[nutrients, oxygen]*; fig chłonąć *[atmosphere]* ⑦ *[boat]* nab|rać, -ierać (czegoś) *[water]* ⑧ (in sewing) zwę|zić, -żać *[dress, skirt]*

■ **take off**: ¶ **~ off** ① *[plane]* wy|startować ② *[idea, fashion, product]* przyj|ąć, -mować się ¶ **~ [sth] off** ① (deduct) **to ~ £10 off (the price)** obniżyć cenę o 10 funtów ② (have as holiday) **to ~ two days off** wziąć dwa dni wolnego ¶ **~ off [sth]** zd|jąć, -ejmować *[clothing, shoes, lid]* ¶ **~ [sb] off** infml (imitate) naśladować *[person]*

■ **take on**: ① (employ) zatrudni|ć, -ać *[staff, worker]* ② zmierzyć się z (kimś/czymś) *[player, team]*; (fight) sta|nąć, -wać do walki z (kimś) *[person, opponent]* ③ (accept) wziąć, brać na siebie *[responsibility]*; pod|jąć, -ejmować się (czegoś) *[task, work]*

■ **take out**: ¶ **~ [sth] out** ① (remove) wyj|ąć, -mować *[object]*; wyr|wać, -ywać *[tooth]*; wyci|ąć,

-nać *[appendix]*; (from bank) wyb|rać, -ierać *[money]* ② **to ~ it out on sb** wyładowywać się na kimś ¶ **~ [sb] out** wyj|ść, -chodzić z (kimś) *[person]*; **to ~ sb out to dinner** zabrać kogoś na kolację

■ **take over**: ¶ **~ over** ① *[army, faction]* przej|ąć, -mować władzę ② (be successor) **to ~ over from sb** przejąć obowiązki po kimś ¶ **~ over [sth]** opanow|ać, -ywać *[town, country]*; przej|ąć, -mować *[business, company]*

■ **take part**: wziąć, brać udział (**in sth** w czymś)

■ **take place**: odby|ć, -wać się

■ **take to**: ① (develop liking for) polubić *[person]* ② (begin) **to ~ to doing sth** zacząć robić coś ③ (go to) schronić się w (czymś) *[forest, jungle]*; **to ~ to the streets** *[strikers]* wyjść na ulice

■ **take up**: ¶ **~ up with sb** zaprzyjaźnić się z kimś *[person, group]* ¶ **~ up [sth]** ① (lift up) podn|ieść, -osić *[carpet, pavement, track]* ② (start) zainteresować się (czymś) *[golf, guitar]*; pod|jąć, -ejmować *[job]*; **to ~ up one's duties** zacząć pełnić swoje obowiązki ③ (continue) pod|jąć, -ejmować *[story, discussion, refrain]* ④ (accept) przy|jąć, -mować *[offer, invitation, challenge]* ⑤ **to ~ sth up with sb** zainteresować kogoś czymś *[matter]* ⑥ (occupy) zaj|ąć, -mować *[space, time]*; pochł|onąć, -aniać *[energy]* ⑦ (adopt) zaj|ąć, -mować *[position, stance]* ⑧ (shorten) skr|ócić, -acać *[skirt, curtains]* ¶ **to ~ sb up on sth** nie móc się zgodzić z czymś *[assertion]*; **to ~ take sb up on an offer** skorzystać z propozycji kogoś

IDIOMS **to ~ a lot out of sb** wyczerpywać kogoś

take-away /'teɪkəweɪ/ *n* GB (meal) jedzenie *n* na wynos; (restaurant) restauracja *f* sprzedająca dania na wynos

take-home pay /'teɪkhəʊmpeɪ/ *n* płaca *f* netto

taken /'teɪkən/ *adj* ① (occupied) **to be ~** *[seat, room]* być zajętym ② (impressed) **to be ~ with sth** być pod wrażeniem czegoś *[idea, person]*

take-off /'teɪkɒf/ *n* ① (by plane) start *m* ② infml (imitation) parodia *f* (**of sb** kogoś)

take-out /'teɪkaʊt/ *adj* US *[food]* na wynos

takeover /'teɪkəʊvə(r)/ *n* (of company) przejęcie *n*; (of power) przejęcie *n* władzy

takeover bid *n* oferta *f* przejęcia or wykupu

taker /'teɪkə(r)/ *n* chętn|y *m*, -a *f*

takings /'teɪkɪŋz/ *npl* wpływy *m pl* kasowe

talc /tælk/ *n* talk *m*

tale /teɪl/ *n* (story) opowieść *f*; (fantasy story) baśń *f*

talent /'tælənt/ *n* talent *m*

talent contest *n* konkurs *m* młodych talentów

talented /'tæləntɪd/ *adj* utalentowany

talisman /'tælɪzmən, 'tælɪs-/ *n* talizman *m*

talk /tɔːk/ **I** *n* ① (talking) gadanie *n* infml; (gossip) plotki *f pl*; **they are the ~ of the town** całe miasto mówi o nich ② (conversation) rozmowa *f*; **to have a ~ with sb** porozmawiać z kimś ③ (speech) wykład *m*; (informal) pogadanka *f*

II **talks** *npl* rozmowy *f pl*; **peace** ~**s** rozmowy pokojowe

III *vt* (discuss) **to** ~ **business** rozmawiać o interesach; **to** ~ **nonsense** mówić bzdury; **to** ~ **sb into sth** namówić kogoś do czegoś

IV *vi* (converse) mówić; **to** ~ **to oneself** mówić do siebie; **to** ~ **to** or **with sb** rozmawiać z kimś

talkative /'tɔːkətɪv/ *adj* gadatliwy

talking /'tɔːkɪŋ/ **I** *n* mówienie *n*; **I'll do the** ~ ja będę mówił; **'no** ~' „cisza!"

II *adj [doll, bird]* mówiący

talking book *n* książka *f* do słuchania

talking-to /'tɔːkɪŋtuː/ *n* bura *f* infml

talk show *n* talk show *m inv*

tall /tɔːl/ *adj [person, building, mast]* wysoki; **to be six feet** ~ *[person]* mieć 183 cm wzrostu; *[tree]* mieć 183 cm wysokości; **to grow** ~**(er)** rosnąć

tally /'tælɪ/ **I** *n* zapis *m*

II *vi [stories, amounts]* zgadzać się

tambourine /ˌtæmbə'riːn/ *n* tamburyn *m*

tame /teɪm/ **I** *adj* **1** *[animal]* oswojony **2** *[story, party]* nudnawy; *[film]* grzeczny fig; *[reform]* nieśmiały

II *vt* osw|oić, -ajać *[animal]*; poskr|omić, -amiać *[lion, tiger]*; fig u|temperować *[person]*

tamper /'tæmpə(r)/ *vi* **to** ~ **with sth** majstrować przy czymś *[machinery, lock]*; grzebać w czymś *[accounts]*

tan /tæn/ **I** *n* **1** (also **sun** ~) opal|enizna *f* **2** (colour) jasny brąz *m*

II *adj* jasnobrązowy

III *vt* **1** *[sun]* opal|ić, -ać **2** wy|garbować *[animal hide]*

IV *vi* opal|ić, -ać się

tandem /'tændəm/ *n* tandem *m*; **in** ~ wspólnie

tang /tæŋ/ *n* (taste) cierpki smak *m*; (smell) ostry zapach *m*

tangent /'tændʒənt/ *n* styczna *f*; **to go off on a** ~ (in speech) przeskoczyć na inny temat

tangerine /ˌtændʒə'riːn/ *n* mandarynka *f*

tangible /'tændʒəbl/ *adj* namacalny

tangle /'tæŋgl/ **I** *n* (of string, wire, weeds, streets) plątanina *f*; (of clothes, sheets) kłąb *m*

II *vi [hair, string, cable]* po|plątać się

■ **tangle up**: ¶ ~ **up** u|wikłać się ¶ **to get** ~**d up** *[hair, string, wires]* splątać się

tangy /'tæŋɪ/ *adj* (acid) cierpki; (spicy) pikantny also fig

tank /tæŋk/ *n* **1** (container) zbiornik *m*; (for fish) akwarium *n*; Aut bak *m* infml **2** Mil czołg *m*

tankard /'tæŋkəd/ *n* metalowy kufel *m* z przykrywką

tanker /'tæŋkə(r)/ *n* **1** (ship) tankowiec *m* **2** (lorry) samochód cysterna *m*; (railway) wagon cysterna *m*

tanned /tænd/ *adj* (also **sun** ~) opalony

Tannoy® /'tænɔɪ/ *n* GB **the** ~ megafon *m*

tantalizing /'tæntəlaɪzɪŋ/ *adj [smell, possibility, suggestion]* nęcący

tantamount /'tæntəmaʊnt/ *adj* **to be** ~ **to sth** być równoznacznym z czymś

tantrum /'tæntrəm/ *n* napad *m* złości; **to throw a** ~ wpaść we wściekłość

tap¹ /tæp/ **I** *n* (device to control flow) kurek *m*; (in sink, bath) kran *m*

II *vt* **1** (make use of) wykorzyst|ać, -ywać *[resources, energy]*; naci|ąć, -nać *[rubber tree]* **2** (install listening device) **to** ~ **the telephone (line)** założyć podsłuch telefoniczny

tap² /tæp/ **I** *n* (blow) stuknięcie *n*

II *vt* (knock) stuk|nąć, -ać w (coś) *[window, drum, floor]*

■ **tap in**: ~ **[sth] in** wbi|ć, -jać *[nail, peg]*; wstuk|ać, -iwać infml *[number]*; wklep|ać, -ywać infml *[data]*

tap dance *n* (also ~ **dancing**) stepowanie *n*

tape /teɪp/ **I** *n* **1** (for recording) taśma *f*; (cassette) kaseta *f*; (recording) nagranie *n* **2** (also **adhesive** ~) taśma *f* klejąca

II *vt* **1** (on cassette, video) nagr|ać, -ywać **2** (stick) **to** ~ **sth to sth** przykleić coś taśmą do czegoś

tape deck *n* magnetofon *m (bez wzmacniacza)*, deck *m*

tape measure *n* taśma *f* miernicza; (in sewing) centymetr *m*

taper /'teɪpə(r)/ *vi [sleeve, trouser leg, column]* zwężać się

tape recorder *n* magnetofon *m*

tapestry /'tæpəstrɪ/ *n* gobelin *m*

tapeworm /'teɪpwɜːm/ *n* tasiemiec *m*

tap water *n* woda *f* bieżąca

tar /tɑː(r)/ *n* smoła *f*; (in tobacco) substancje *f pl* smoliste

target /'tɑːgɪt/ **I** *n* **1** (in archery, shooting) tarcza *f* **2** (goal, objective) cel *m* **3** (butt) obiekt *m*; **to be the** ~ **of sth** być obiektem czegoś *[abuse, ridicule]*

II *adj [figure]* docelowy; *[date]* planowany

III *vt* **1** Mil (aim) wy|celować (czymś) *[weapon, missile]*; (choose as objective) wyb|rać, -ierać za cel ataku *[city, site, factory]* **2** (in marketing) **to be** ~**ed at sb** *[product, publication]* być adresowanym do kogoś

target language *n* język *m* przekładu

tariff /'tærɪf/ *n* (price list) cennik *m*; (list of duties) taryfa *f* celna; (duty) cło *n*

tarmac /'tɑːmæk/ *n* **1** (also **Tarmac**®) ≈ asfalt *m* **2** GB (of airfield) pas *m* kołowania

tarnish /'tɑːnɪʃ/ **I** *vt* fig s|plamić *[reputation]*

II *vi* **1** *[brass, copper]* za|śniedzieć **2** fig dozna|ć, -wać uszczerbku

tarpaulin /tɑː'pɔːlɪn/ *n* (material) brezent *m*; (sheet) plandeka *f*

tarragon /'tærəgən/ *n* estragon *m*

tart¹ /tɑːt/ *n* (small) tarteletka *f*; (large) tarta *f*

tart² /tɑːt/ *n* vinfml (woman) dziwka *f* vinfml
■ **tart up** GB infml: ¶ ~ **[sth] up** odpicow|ać, -ywać infml *[house, room]* ¶ ~ **oneself up** odpicow|ać, -ywać się infml
tartan /'tɑːtn/ *adj* w szkocką kratę
task /tɑːsk, US tæsk/ *n* zadanie *n*; **a hard** ~ trudne zadanie
task bar *n* Comput pasek *m* zadań
task force *n* [1] Mil siły *f pl* ekspedycyjne [2] (of police) odziały *m pl* specjalne [3] (committee) grupa *f* robocza
taskmaster /'tɑːskmɑːstə(r), US 'tæskmæstər/ *n* tyran *m* fig; **to be a hard** ~ być bardzo wymagającym
tassel /'tæsl/ *n* frędzel *m*
taste /teɪst/ **I** *n* [1] (of food) smak *m* [2] (sense of beauty) smak *m*, gust *m*; **that's a matter of** ~ to kwestia gustu; **to be in bad** ~ być w złym guście [3] (brief experience) smak *m*; (foretaste) przedsmak *m*; **to have a** ~ **of sth** skosztować czegoś
II *vt* [1] (try) s|próbować (czegoś); s|kosztować (czegoś) [2] (perceive flavour of) czuć smak (czegoś)
III *vi* *[food, drink]* smakować, mieć smak; **to** ~ **of sth** smakować jak coś
taste bud *n* kubek *m* smakowy
tasteful /'teɪstfl/ *adj* gustowny
tasteless /'teɪstlɪs/ *adj* [1] *[remark]* niesmaczny; *[garment, furnishings]* w złym guście [2] *[food, drink]* bez smaku
tasty /'teɪstɪ/ *adj* *[food]* smaczny
tatters /'tætəz/ *npl* **to be in** ~ *[clothing]* być w strzępach; *[career, life]* lec w gruzach
tattoo /tə'tuː, US tæ'tuː/ **I** *n* tatuaż *m*
II *vt* wy|tatuować (on sth na czymś)
tatty /'tætɪ/ *adj* infml *[appearance]* niechlujny; *[carpet, garment, book]* sfatygowany; zmatławy infml
taunt /tɔːnt/ *vt* drwić z (kogoś) *[person]*
Taurus /'tɔːrəs/ *n* Byk *m*
taut /tɔːt/ *adj* naprężony
tauten /'tɔːtn/ **I** *vt* napręż|yć, -ać
II *vi* napręż|yć, -ać się
tax /tæks/ **I** *n* podatek *m* (on sth od czegoś)
II *vt* [1] opodatkow|ać, -ywać *[profits, person]* [2] fig (strain) wystawi|ć, -ać na próbę *[patience]*
taxation /tæk'seɪʃn/ *n* [1] (imposition of taxes) opodatkowanie *n* [2] (revenue from taxes) wpływy *m pl* z podatków
tax bracket *n* przedział *m* podatkowy
tax collector *n* poborca *m* podatkowy
tax disc *n* Aut winietka *f*
tax evasion *n* uchylanie się *n* od płacenia podatków
tax exile *n* emigrant *m* podatkowy
tax-free /ˌtæks'friː/ *adj* wolny od podatku
tax haven *n* raj *m* podatkowy
taxi /'tæksɪ/ *n* taksówka *f*; **by** ~ taksówką
taxing /'tæksɪŋ/ *adj* wymagający wysiłku

taxi rank GB, **taxi stand** US *n* postój *m* taksówek
tax office *n* urząd *m* skarbowy
taxpayer /'tækspeɪə(r)/ *n* podatnik *m*
tax return *n* zeznanie *n* podatkowe
TB *n* = tuberculosis
tea /tiː/ *n* [1] (drink) herbata *f* [2] GB (afternoon meal) podwieczorek *m*; (evening meal) kolacja *f*
tea bag *n* torebka *f* herbaty ekspresowej
tea break *n* GB krótka przerwa *f*
teach /tiːtʃ/ **I** *vt* na|uczyć *[children, adults]*; uczyć (czegoś) *[foreign language, biology]*; **to** ~ **school** US być nauczycielem; **to** ~ **sb a lesson** *[person]* dać komuś nauczkę; *[experience]* być dla kogoś nauczką
II *vi* uczyć
teacher /'tiːtʃə(r)/ *n* nauczyciel *m*, -ka *f*
teacher training *n* kształcenie *n* nauczycieli
teaching /'tiːtʃɪŋ/ **I** *n* nauczanie *n*
II *adj* *[career, qualification]* nauczycielski; *[ability, skill]* pedagogiczny; *[materials, method]* dydaktyczny
teaching hospital *n* klinika *f*
teacup /'tiːkʌp/ *n* filiżanka *f* (do herbaty)
teak /tiːk/ *n* (wood) drewno *n* tekowe; (tree) drzewo *n* tekowe
team /tiːm/ *n* zespół *m*; Sport drużyna *f*
team member *n* członek *m* zespołu
team spirit *n* duch *m* współpracy
teamwork /'tiːmwɜːk/ *n* praca *f* zespołowa
teapot /'tiːpɒt/ *n* dzbanek *m* do herbaty
tear¹ /teə(r)/ **I** *n* Med pęknięcie *n*
II *vt* (rip) po|drzeć *[garment, paper]*; **to** ~ **sth out of sth** wyrywać coś z czegoś *[book, notepad]*; **to** ~ **a hole in sth** zrobić dziurę w czymś
III *vt* [1] (rip) po|drzeć się [2] (rush) gnać
■ **tear apart**: ~ (destroy) rozszarp|ać, -ywać *[prey, game]*; rozbi|ć, -jać *[relationship, organization, country]* [2] (separate) roz|erwać, -rywać [3] infml (criticize) zjechać infml *[film]*
■ **tear off**: od|erwać, -rywać
■ **tear open**: roz|erwać, -rywać *[envelope]*
■ **tear out**: od|erwać, -rywać *[coupon, cheque]*; wyr|wać, -ywać *[page, picture]*
■ **tear up**: po|drzeć *[letter, document]*
tear² /tɪə(r)/ *n* łza *f*; **to burst into** ~s wybuchnąć płaczem
tearful /'tɪəfl/ *adj* *[person, face]* zapłakany; *[voice]* płaczliwy
tear gas *n* gaz *m* łzawiący
tease /tiːz/ *vt* (annoy) dokuczać (komuś) *[person]* (**about sth** z powodu czegoś); drażnić *[animal]*; (make fun of) naśmiewać się z (kogoś)
teasing /'tiːzɪŋ/ *n* (joking) przekomarzanie się *n*; (malicious) dokuczanie *n*
teaspoon /'tiːspuːn/ *n* łyżeczka *f* (do herbaty)
teaspoonful /'tiːspuːnfʊl/ *n* łyżeczka *f* (of sth czegoś)

teat /tiːt/ *n* 1 (of cow, goat, ewe) dójka *m* 2 GB (on baby's bottle) smoczek *m*

teatime /ˈtiːtaɪm/ *n* pora *f* podwieczorku

tea towel *n* GB ścierka *f* do naczyń

technical /ˈteknɪkl/ *adj* 1 (mechanical) techniczny 2 (concerning rules) *[point, detail, defect]* formalny

technical college *n* uczelnia *f* techniczna

technical drawing *n* rysunek *m* techniczny

technical hitch *n* problem *m* techniczny

technicality /ˌteknɪˈkælətɪ/ *n* 1 (technical detail) szczegół *m* techniczny (**of sth** czegoś); (term) termin *m* fachowy 2 (minor rule) szczegół *m* formalny

technically /ˈteknɪklɪ/ *adv* 1 (strictly speaking) formalnie rzecz biorąc 2 (technologically) *[advanced, backward]* pod względem technicznym; *[possible, difficult]* technicznie

technician /tekˈnɪʃn/ *n* technik *m*

technique /tekˈniːk/ *n* technika *f*

technological /ˌteknəˈlɒdʒɪkl/ *adj* (of science) techniczny; (of method) technologiczny

technology /tekˈnɒlədʒɪ/ *n* 1 (applied science) technika *f*; **information** ~ informatyka 2 (method) technologia *f*

teddy /ˈtedɪ/ *n* (also ~ **bear**) miś *m* pluszowy

tedious /ˈtiːdɪəs/ *adj* nużący

teem /tiːm/ *vi* ~**ing with sth/sb** obfitujący w coś *[wildlife]*; pełen kogoś *[people]*

teenage /ˈtiːneɪdʒ/ *adj [person]* nastoletni; *[fashions]* młodzieżowy

teenager /ˈtiːneɪdʒə(r)/ *n* nastolat|ek *m*, -ka *f*

teens /tiːnz/ *npl* **to be in one's** ~ mieć naście lat

tee-shirt /ˈtiːʃɜːt/ *n* T-shirt *m* infml

teeter /ˈtiːtə(r)/ *vi* za|chwiać się

teethe /tiːð/ *vi* ząbkować

teething troubles *npl* fig początkowe problemy *m pl*

teetotal /tiːˈtəʊtl, US ˈtiːtəʊtl/ *adj* niepijący

teetotaller GB, **teetotaler** US /tiːˈtəʊtələ(r)/ *n* abstynent *m*, -ka *f*, niepijąc|y *m*, -a *f*

TEFL /ˈtefl/ *n* = **Teaching of English as a Foreign Language** nauczanie *n* angielskiego jako języka obcego

telecommunications /ˌtelɪkəˌmjuːnɪˈkeɪʃnz/ *n* telekomunikacja *f*

telecommuting /ˌtelɪkəˈmjuːtɪŋ/ *n* telepraca *f*

teleconference /ˈtelɪkɒnfərəns/ *n* telekonferencja *f*

telegram /ˈtelɪgræm/ *n* telegram *m*

telegraph /ˈtelɪgrɑːf, US -græf/ 1 *n* telegraf *m* 2 *vt* prze|telegrafować *[message]* 3 *vi* za|telegrafować

telegraph pole *n* słup *m* telegraficzny

telemarketer /ˈtelɪmɑːkɪtə(r)/ *n* osoba *f* zajmująca się telemarketingiem

telemarketing /ˈtelɪmɑːkɪtɪŋ/ *n* telemarketing *m*

telepathy /təˈlepəθɪ/ *n* telepatia *f*

telephone /ˈtelɪfəʊn/ 1 *n* telefon *m*; **to be on the** ~ (connected) mieć telefon; (talking) rozmawiać przez telefon 2 *vt* za|telefonować do (kogoś/czegoś) *[person, office]*; przekaz|ać, -ywać telefonicznie *[message, order]* 3 *vi* za|telefonować

telephone banking *n* system *m* telebanking (*usługi bankowe przez telefon*)

telephone booth , telephone box *n* (in the street) budka *f* telefoniczna; (inside a building) kabina *f* telefoniczna

telephone call *n* rozmowa *f* telefoniczna

telephone directory *n* książka *f* telefoniczna

telephone number *n* numer *m* telefonu

telephone operator *n* telefonist|a *m*, -ka *f*

telephonist /tɪˈlefənɪst/ *n* GB telefonist|a *m*, -ka *f*

telephoto lens /ˌtelɪfəʊtəʊˈlenz/ *n* teleobiektyw *m*

telesales /ˈtelɪseɪlz/ *n* telesprzedaż *f*

telescope /ˈtelɪskəʊp/ *n* (for astronomy) teleskop *m*; (hand-held) luneta *f*

teleshopping /ˈtelɪʃɒpɪŋ/ *n* telezakupy *plt*

televise /ˈtelɪvaɪz/ *vt* wy|emitować w telewizji *[programme]*; transmitować *[match, ceremony]*

television /ˈtelɪvɪʒn, -ˈvɪʒn/ *n* 1 (medium) telewizja *f*; **on** ~ w telewizji 2 (set) telewizor *m*

television licence *n* abonament *m* telewizyjny

television programme *n* program *m* telewizyjny

television set *n* telewizor *m*

teleworking /ˈtelɪwɜːkɪŋ/ *n* telepraca *f*

telex /ˈteleks/ 1 *n* teleks *m* 2 *vt* prze|teleksować *[message]*; za|teleksować do (kogoś/czegoś) *[person, company]*

tell /tel/ 1 *vt* 1 *[person]* powiedzieć, mówić *[truth]*; opowi|edzieć, -adać *[joke, story]*; przepowi|edzieć, -adać *[future]*; *[gauge, clock]* wskaz|ać, -ywać; **to** ~ **sb sth, to** ~ **sth to sb** powiedzieć komuś coś; **to** ~ **sb to do sth** powiedzieć komuś, żeby coś zrobił; **to** ~ **sb how to do sth** powiedzieć komuś, jak coś zrobić; **can you** ~ **me the time, please?** czy możesz mi powiedzieć, która godzina?; **I told you so!** a nie mówiłem?!; **I was told that...** powiedziano mi, że... 2 (deduce) **you can** ~ **(that)...** widać, że...; **you can** ~ **a lot from the clothes people wear** ubiór wiele mówi o człowieku 3 (distinguish) odróżni|ć, -ać; **to** ~ **the difference** dostrzec różnicę; **how can you** ~ **them apart?** jak ich odróżniasz?

2 *vi* 1 (reveal secret) **promise me you won't** ~! obiecaj, że nikomu nie powiesz! 2 (know) wiedzieć; **as far as I can** ~ o ile mi wiadomo; **how can you** ~? skąd wiesz? 3 (show effect) **her age is beginning to** ~ teraz zaczyna wyglądać na swoje lata

■ **tell off**: z|besztać infml *[person]*

■ **tell on**: 1 (reveal information about) don|ieść, -osić

na (kogoś) (**to sb** komuś) [2] (have effect) **the strain is beginning to** ~ **on him** widać już po nim skutki zmęczenia

telling /'telɪŋ/ adj [remark, detail, omission] znamienny

telltale /'telteɪl/ [I] n skarżypyta m/f infml
[II] adj [stain] znamienny; [sign] widomy

telly /'telɪ/ n GB infml telewizja f

temp /temp/ GB infml [I] n (substitute) (tymczasowy) zastępca m, (tymczasowa) zastępczyni f; (temporary) pracownik m tymczasowy, pracownica f tymczasowa
[II] vi pracować dorywczo

temper /'tempə(r)/ [I] n [1] (mood) humor m; **to be in a good/bad** ~ być w dobrym/złym humorze [2] (anger) **to be in a** ~ być złym; **to lose one's** ~ stracić panowanie nad sobą [3] (nature) usposobienie n
[II] vt [1] (moderate) z|łagodzić [rigours]; ostudz|ić, -áć [enthusiasm]; powściąg|nąć, -áć [emotion] [2] za|hartować [steel]

temperament /'temprəmənt/ n temperament m

temperamental /ˌtemprə'mentl/ adj (volatile) kapryśny

temperate /'tempərət/ adj [climate, zone] umiarkowany; [person, reply] powściągliwy

temperature /'temprətʃə(r), US 'tempərtʃʊər/ n temperatura f; **to have a** ~ mieć temperaturę

temper tantrum n napad m złości

tempest /'tempɪst/ n burza f

tempestuous /tem'pestʃʊəs/ adj [relationship, sea] burzliwy; [person] porywczy

template /'templeɪt/ n szablon m

temple[1] n /'templ/ (building) świątynia f

temple[2] n /'templ/ Anat skroń f

temporarily /'tempərərəlɪ, US -pərerɪlɪ/ adv (for a limited time) chwilowo; (provisionally) tymczasowo

temporary /'temprərɪ, US -pərerɪ/ adj [accommodation, certificate, manager] tymczasowy; [replacement, loss of memory] chwilowy; [job] dorywczy

tempt /tempt/ vt s|kusić; **to be** ~ **ed to do sth** [person] mieć ochotę zrobić coś

temptation /temp'teɪʃn/ n pokusa f

tempting /'temptɪŋ/ adj [offer, idea, discount] kuszący; [food, smell] apetyczny

ten /ten/ n, adj dziesięć

tenacious /tɪ'neɪʃəs/ adj [person] nieustępliwy; [memory] doskonały; [grip] mocny

tenancy /'tenənsɪ/ n dzierżawa f

tenant /'tenənt/ n (of land, building) dzierżawca m; (of apartment) lokator m, -ka f

tend[1] /tend/ vi [person] skłaniać się; **to** ~ **to do sth** [person] na ogół robić coś; [event] przejawiać tendencję do czegoś

tend[2] /tend/ vt opiekować się (kimś) [person]; zajmować się (czymś) [garden, store]

tendency /'tendənsɪ/ n (inclination) skłonność f (**to sth** do czegoś); (trend) tendencja f (**for sth** do czegoś)

tender[1] /'tendə(r)/ adj [1] [meat] kruchy [2] [kiss, smile, heart] czuły [3] [skin] wrażliwy; [spot] czuły; fig [subject] drażliwy

tender[2] /'tendə(r)/ [I] n oferta f przetargowa
[II] vt złożyć, składać [resignation, apology]

tendon /'tendən/ n ścięgno n

tendril /'tendrəl/ n (of plant) wąs m

tenement /'tenəmənt/ n kamienica f czynszowa

tenner /'tenə(r)/ n GB infml (note) banknot m dziesięciofuntowy; dycha f infml

tennis /'tenɪs/ n tenis m

tennis court n kort m tenisowy

tenor /'tenə(r)/ n Mus tenor m

tenpin bowling GB /ˌtenpɪn'bəʊlɪŋ/, **tenpins** US /'tenpɪnz/ n gra f w kręgle (dziesięcioma kręglami)

tense[1] /tens/ n czas m; **the present** ~ czas teraźniejszy; **in the future** ~ w czasie przyszłym

tense[2] /tens/ [I] adj [person] spięty; [atmosphere] napięty; [moment] pełen napięcia; **to make sb** ~ zdenerwować kogoś
[II] vt napi|ąć, -náć [muscle]; wy|prężyć [body]
■ **tense up**: (become nervous) [person] spi|ąć, -náć się

tension /'tenʃn/ n napięcie n

tent /tent/ n namiot m

tentacle /'tentəkl/ n (of squid, octopus) macka f; (of snail, polyp) czułek m; Bot włosek m

tentative /'tentətɪv/ adj [person, gesture, steps] niepewny; [offer, conclusion] wstępny

tenterhooks /'tentəhʊks/ npl
IDIOMS **to be on** ~ siedzieć jak na szpilkach; **to keep sb on** ~ trzymać kogoś w niepewności

tenth /tenθ/ [I] n [1] (in order) dziesiąt|y m, -a f, -e n [2] (fraction) dziesiąta f (część)
[II] adj dziesiąty
[III] adv [come, finish] na dziesiątym miejscu

tenuous /'tenjʊəs/ adj [link] luźny; [argument] słaby; [theory] naciągany; [distinction] subtelny

tepid /'tepɪd/ adj letni

term /tɜːm/ [I] n [1] (period of time) okres m; Pol kadencja f; (at school, university) (one of three) trymestr m; (one of two) semestr m; **autumn/spring/ summer** ~ trymestr jesienny/wiosenny/letni [2] (word, phrase) termin m; ~ **of abuse** obelga f
[II] **terms** npl [1] (contract) warunki m pl; (of will) zapisy m pl [2] **to come to** ~**s with sth** pogodzić się z czymś [death, defeat, failure, past]; załatwić coś [issue] [3] (relations) stosunki plt; **to be on good** ~**s with sb** być z kimś w dobrych stosunkach
[III] vt określ|ić, -áć
[IV] **in terms of** prep phr pod względem (czegoś)

terminal /'tɜːmɪnl/ [I] n [1] (station) stacja f końcowa; (in airport) terminal m; **ferry** ~ terminal promowy [2] Comput terminal m [3] (for electricity) końcówka f; (of battery) zacisk m

▥ *adj* ① *[disease]* (causing death) śmiertelny; (at final stage) w terminalnym stadium ② (last) *[stage]* końcowy

terminate /'tɜːmɪneɪt/ **▯** *vt* zak|ończyć, -ańczać *[meeting, phase, relationship]*; rozwiąz|ać, -ywać *[contract]*; wypowi|edzieć, -adać *[agreement]*; przer|wać, -ywać *[pregnancy]*

▥ *vi [agreement, contract, offer]* wygas|nąć, -ać; *[meeting, relationship]* za|kończyć się

termination /ˌtɜːmɪ'neɪʃn/ *n* ① (of contract) wygaśnięcie *n*; (discussion, relationship) zakończenie *n* ② Med zabieg *m* przerwania ciąży

terminology /ˌtɜːmɪ'nɒlədʒɪ/ *n* terminologia *f*

terminus /'tɜːmɪnəs/ *n* GB (of bus) przystanek *m* końcowy; (of train) stacja *f* końcowa

terrace /'terəs/ **▯** *n* ① (patio) taras *m* ② (row of houses) szeregowiec *m*

▥ terraces *npl* GB (in stadium) trybuny *plt* (stojące)

terrace(d) house *n* segment *m*

terracotta /ˌterə'kɒtə/ *n* ① (earthenware) terakota *f* ② (colour) kolor *m* terakoty

terrain /tə'reɪn/ *n* teren *m*

terrible /'terəbl/ *adj* ① (awful) *[pain, noise, sight, accident]* straszny ② infml (bad) *[performance, cook, player]* beznadziejny infml

terribly /'terəblɪ/ *adv* ① (very) *[pleased, easy]* szalenie; *[sad, hot]* strasznie ② (badly) *[play, sing]* okropnie; *[suffer]* straszliwie

terrific /tə'rɪfɪk/ *adj* ① (huge) *[amount, noise]* niesamowity; *[pleasure, speed]* ogromny; *[accident, problem, worry]* straszny ② infml (wonderful) świetny infml

terrifically /tə'rɪfɪklɪ/ *adv [difficult, hot]* niesamowicie

terrified /'terɪfaɪd/ *adj* przerażony; **to be ~ of sth** panicznie bać się czegoś

terrify /'terɪfaɪ/ *vt* przera|zić, -żać

terrifying /'terɪfaɪɪŋ/ *adj* przerażający

territorial /ˌterə'tɔːrɪəl/ *adj* terytorialny

territory /'terɪtrɪ, US 'terɪtɔːrɪ/ *n* terytorium *n*

terror /'terə(r)/ **▯** *n* ① (fear) przerażenie *n* ② (terrorism) terror *m*

▥ *adj* terrorystyczny; **a ~ campaign** fala terroru

terrorism /'terərɪzəm/ *n* terroryzm *m*

terrorist /'terərɪst/ *n* terrorys|ta *m*, -ka *f*

terrorize /'terəraɪz/ *vt* s|terroryzować

terry /'terɪ/ *n* (also **~ towelling** GB, **~ cloth** US) frotté *n inv*

terse /tɜːs/ *adj [style]* lapidarny; *[answer, article]* zwięzły; *[person]* oszczędny w słowach

tertiary /'tɜːʃərɪ, US -ʃɪerɪ/ *adj [education, college]* wyższy; *[sector]* usługowy

test /test/ **▯** *n* ① (of person, endurance, reliability) próba *f*; Sch, Univ (written) sprawdzian *m* pisemny; (multiple-choice) test *m*; (oral) sprawdzian *m* ustny; **to put sb to the ~** poddać kogoś próbie ② (of equipment, machine, new model) test *m* ③ Med (of blood, urine, organ) badanie *n* ④ Aut (also **driving ~**) egzamin *m* na prawo jazdy

▥ *vt* ① sprawdz|ić, -ać *[intelligence, efficiency]*; (in classroom) przepyt|ać, -ywać (**on sth** z czegoś); (at exam time) prze|egzaminować ② Tech prze|testować *[product]*; Med z|badać *[blood, urine]*; prze|badać *[new drug, vaccine]*; **to have one's eyes ~ed** zbadać sobie wzrok ③ (strain) wystawi|ć, -ać na próbę *[endurance, patience]*

testament /'testəmənt/ *n* ① (proof) świadectwo *n* (**to sth** czegoś) ② **the Old/the New Testament** Stary/Nowy Testament

test ban *n* zakaz *m* prób jądrowych

test case *n* precedens *m* sądowy

test-drive /'testdraɪv/ *vt* odby|ć, -wać jazdę próbną (czymś)

testicle /'testɪkl/ *n* Anat jądro *n*

testify /'testɪfaɪ/ **▯** *vt* to **~ that...** zaświadczyć, że...; (in court) zeznać, że...

▥ *vi [person]* zeznawać; **to ~ to sth** świadczyć o czymś

testimony /'testɪmənɪ, US -məʊnɪ/ *n* świadectwo *n*; (in court) zeznanie *n*

testing /'testɪŋ/ *n* ① (of vehicle, system, drug) testowanie *n*; (of blood, water) badanie *f*; Sch sprawdzanie *n* wiadomości

test paper *n* Sch sprawdzian *m* pisemny

test tube *n* probówka *f*

test-tube baby /ˌtesttjuːb'beɪbɪ, US -tuːb-/ *n* dziecko *n* z probówki

tetanus /'tetənəs/ *n* tężec *m*

tether /'teðə(r)/ *vt* uwiąz|ać, -ywać (**to sth** do czegoś)

[IDIOMS:] **to be at the end of one's ~** być u kresu wytrzymałości

text /tekst/ *n* tekst *m*

textbook /'tekstbʊk/ **▯** *n* podręcznik *m* (**about** or **on sth** czegoś)

▥ *adj [example, case]* podręcznikowy

textile /'tekstaɪl/ *n* tkanina *f*

texture /'tekstʃə(r)/ *n* (of substance) konsystencja *f*; (of surface) faktura *f*

Thames /temz/ *prn* **the (river) ~** Tamiza *f*

than /ðæn, ðən/ **▯** *prep* niż; **taller ~ me** wyższy niż ja or ode mnie; **he has more ~ me** on ma więcej niż ja or ode mnie; **more/less ~ 100** więcej/mniej niż 100; **more ~ half** ponad połowa; **temperatures lower ~ 30 degrees** temperatury poniżej 30 stopni

▥ *conj* ① (in comparison, expressing preferences) niż; **he's older ~ I am** jest starszy niż ja or ode mnie; **it took us longer ~ we thought it would** zajęło nam to więcej czasu, niż przypuszczaliśmy; **I'd sooner** or **rather do X ~ Y** wolałbym zrobić X niż Y ② (when) **no sooner had he left ~ the phone rang** ledwo wyszedł, jak zadzwonił telefon

3 US (from) **to be different** ~ **sth** różnić się od czegoś

thank /θæŋk/ vt po|dziękować (komuś) *[person, God]*; ~ **God!** dzięki Bogu!

thankful /'θæŋkfl/ adj (grateful) wdzięczny; (relieved) rad

thankfully /'θæŋkfəlɪ/ adv 1 (luckily) na szczęście 2 (with relief) z ulgą; (with gratitude) z wdzięcznością

thankless /'θæŋklɪs/ adj *[task, person]* niewdzięczny

thanks /θæŋks/ ∎ npl podziękowania n pl

∎∎ excl infml dzięki! infml; ~ **a lot** bardzo dziękuję; iron wielkie dzięki!; **no** ~ nie, dziękuję

∎∎∎ **thanks to** prep phr ~ **to sb/sth** dzięki komuś/czemuś

Thanksgiving (Day) /'θæŋksgɪvɪŋ, US θæŋks'gɪvɪŋ/ n US Święto n Dziękczynienia

thank you /'θæŋkju:/ ∎ n (also **thank-you, thankyou**) podziękowanie n; **to say** ~ **to sb** dziękować komuś

∎∎ adj *[letter]* z podziękowaniem; *[gift]* w podzięce

∎∎∎ adv dziękuję; ~ **very much** dziękuję bardzo

that ∎/ðæt, ðət/ det ten, ta, to; ~ **chair** to krzesło; **those chairs** te krzesła; **at** ~ **time** w tamtych czasach; **you can't do it** ~ **way** nie możesz tego robić w ten sposób; **he went** ~ **way** poszedł w tę stronę; ~ **lazy son of yours** ten twój leniwy syn

∎∎ /ðæt/ dem pron 1 (not this) tamten, tamta, tamto 2 (the thing or person observed or mentioned) to; **what's** ~ ? co to (jest)?; **who's** ~ ? kto to (jest)?; (on phone) kto mówi?; **is** ~ **Robert?** czy to Robert?; **who told you** ~ ? kto ci to powiedział?; ~ **'s how he did it** w ten właśnie sposób to zrobił; **what did he mean by** ~ ? co chciał przez to powiedzieć?; ~ **'s the kitchen** to jest kuchnia; **those who...** ci, którzy...

∎∎∎ /ðət/ rel pron który, -a, -e; **the woman** ~ **won** kobieta, która wygrała; **the book** ~ **I bought** książka, którą kupiłem; **the house** ~ **we live in** dom, w którym mieszkamy; **the man** ~ **I received the letter from** człowiek, od którego otrzymałem ten list; **the day** ~ **she arrived** dzień, w którym przybyła

∎∎∎∎ /ðət/ conj że; **he said** ~ **he had finished** powiedział, że skończył

∎∎∎∎∎ /ðæt/ adv (to the extent shown) (aż) tak; **it's about** ~ **thick** to jest mniej więcej takiej grubości; **I can't work** ~ **much** nie mogę aż tyle pracować; **he can't swim** ~ **far** nie potrafi popłynąć tak daleko

(IDIOMS) ~ **is (to say)...** to znaczy...; ~ **'s it!** (that's right) o to chodzi!; (that's enough) to wszystko!; (angrily) dość tego!; **I don't want to see you again and** ~ **'s** ~ **!** nie chcę cię już więcej widzieć i tyle!

thatched cottage /ˌθætʃt'kɒtɪdʒ/ n dom m kryty strzechą

thatched roof /ˌθætʃt'ru:f/ n strzecha f

thaw /θɔː/ ∎ n odwilż f

∎∎ vt rozt|opić, -apiać *[snow, ice]*; rozmr|ozić, -ażać *[frozen food]*

∎∎∎ vi 1 *[snow, ice]* s|tajać; *[ground, river]* rozmarz|nąć, -ać; *[frozen food]* rozmr|ozić, -ażać się 2 fig *[person]* rozluźni|ć, -ać się; *[atmosphere]* ociepl|ić, -ać się

the /ði:, ðɪ, ðə/ def art 1 (particular) **two chapters of** ~ **book** dwa rozdziały książki 2 (identifying) ten; **I've seen** ~ **man before** już gdzieś widziałem tego człowieka 3 (best) **THE French restaurant** najlepsza francuska restauracja 4 (with era) ~ **fifties** lata pięćdziesiąte 5 (with dates) **May** ~ **6th** szósty maja 6 (with weights and measures) **two pounds** ~ **yard** dwa funty za jard 7 (with adjectives) ~ **impossible** rzecz niemożliwa 8 (with comparative adjectives) **the news made her all** ~ **sadder** na wieść o tym jeszcze bardziej posmutniała; ~ **sooner** ~ **better** im prędzej, tym lepiej 9 (with superlatives) ~ **fastest train** najszybszy pociąg

theatre, theater US /'θɪətə(r)/ n 1 (place, art form) teatr m; **to go to the** ~ pójść do teatru 2 US (cinema) kino n

theatregoer /'θɪətəɡəʊə(r)/ n teatroman m, -ka f

theatrical /θɪ'ætrɪkl/ adj teatralny

theft /θeft/ n kradzież f (**of sth** czegoś)

their /ðeə(r)/ det ich; **they are wasting** ~ **time** marnują (swój) czas

theirs /ðeəz/ pron ich; **the green hats are** ~ zielone kapelusze są ich

them /ðem, ðəm/ pron (as direct object) je; (males) ich; (in negative sentence) ich; (as indirect object) im; **I know** ~ znam je/ich; **I don't like** ~ nie lubię ich; **some of** ~ niektórzy/niektóre z nich

theme /θiːm/ n temat m

theme park n tematyczny park m rozrywki

theme song, theme tune n (of film) temat m przewodni; (of radio, TV programme) sygnał m

themselves /ðəm'selvz/ pron 1 (reflexive) **they washed** ~ umyli/umyły się; **they bought it for** ~ kupili/kupiły to dla siebie 2 (emphatic) same; (men) sami; **(all) by** ~ (całkiem or zupełnie) sami/same

then /ðen/ adv 1 (at that time) wtedy; (implying more distant past) w tamtych czasach; **I was living in Dublin** ~ mieszkałem wtedy w Dublinie; **since** ~ od tej pory; **until** ~ do tego czasu 2 (afterwards) następnie, potem 3 (in that case) w takim razie, wobec tego 4 (therefore) a więc 5 (in addition, besides) ponadto

thence /ðens/ adv 1 (from there) stamtąd 2 (therefore) zatem

theology /θɪ'ɒlədʒɪ/ n teologia f

theorem /'θɪərəm/ n twierdzenie n

theoretical /θɪə'retɪkl/ adj teoretyczny

theoretically /θɪə'retɪklɪ/ adv teoretycznie; ~ **speaking...** teoretycznie...

theory /'θɪərɪ/ n teoria f

therapeutic /ˌθerə'pju:tɪk/ adj terapeutyczny

therapist /'θerəpɪst/ n terapeut|a m, -ka f

therapy /'θerəpɪ/ n terapia f, leczenie n

there /ðeə(r)/ **I** pron (as impersonal subject) ~ **is/are** jest/są; ~ **is't any room** nie ma miejsca; ~ **are many reasons** jest wiele powodów; ~ **is some left** trochę zostało; ~ **seems to be some mistake** wygląda na to, że to pomyłka

II adv ⊡ (at or to that place) tam; **up to** ~, **down to** ~ do tego miejsca; **put it in** ~ połóż to tam; **stand** ~ stań tam; **go over** ~ idź tam ⊡ (to draw attention) ~ **you are** (seeing sb arrive) jesteś; (giving object) proszę; (that's done) i sprawa załatwiona; ~'**s a bus coming** nadjeżdża autobus; **that paragraph** ~ ten akapit

III excl ~ ~! (soothingly) no już dobrze, dobrze; ~, **I told you!** no proszę, a nie mówiłem?!; ~, **you've woken the baby!** no widzisz, obudziłeś dziecko!

IV **there again** adv phr (on the other hand) z drugiej strony

thereabouts GB, **thereabout** US /ˌðeərə'baʊts/ adv ⊡ (in the vicinity) gdzieś (tam) w pobliżu ⊡ (roughly) **100 dollars or** ~ 100 dolarów, albo coś koło tego

thereby /ðeə'baɪ, 'ðeə-/ conj tym samym

therefore /'ðeəfɔ:(r)/ adv dlatego

thermal /'θɜ:ml/ adj [reactor, analysis] termiczny; [energy, insulation] cieplny; [spring] ciepły

thermal imaging n termografia f

thermometer /θə'mɒmɪtə(r)/ n termometr m

Thermos® /'θɜ:məs/ n (also ~ **flask**) termos m

thermostat /'θɜ:məstæt/ n termostat m

thesaurus /θɪ'sɔ:rəs/ n słownik m synonimów or wyrazów bliskoznacznych

these /ði:z/ npl → this

thesis /'θi:sɪs/ n ⊡ Univ rozprawa f; (doctoral) praca f doktorska; (master's) praca f magisterska ⊡ (theory) teza f

they /ðeɪ/ pron one; (including men) oni; **here** ~ **are** oto oni/one; **there** ~ **are** są tam

thick /θɪk/ **I** adj ⊡ [object, features] gruby; [forest, hair, fog] gęsty; **to be 6 cm** ~ mieć 6 cm grubości; ~ **with sth** pokryty grubą warstwą czegoś [dust, dirt] ⊡ infml (stupid) tępy

II adv [spread, slice, cut] grubo; **the snow lay** ~ **on the ground** śnieg okrywał ziemię grubą warstwą

IDIOMS: **to be in the** ~ **of sth** być w wirze czegoś [battle, fighting]

thicken /'θɪkən/ **I** vt pogrubi|ć, -ać [layer, wall]; zagę|ścić, -szczać [soup, sauce]

II vi [forest, fog, soup] z|gęstnieć

thicket /'θɪkɪt/ n gąszcz m

thickly /'θɪklɪ/ adv [spread] grubo

thickness /'θɪknɪs/ n (of piece, material) grubość f; (of snow, liquid) gęstość f

thickset /ˌθɪk'set/ adj [person] krępy, przysadzisty

thick-skinned /ˌθɪk'skɪnd/ adj niewrażliwy

thief /θi:f/ n złodziej m, -ka f

thieve /θi:v/ vt, vi u|kraść

thigh /θaɪ/ n udo n

thimble /'θɪmbl/ n naparstek m

thin /θɪn/ **I** adj ⊡ [nose, lips, strip] wąski; [wall, layer, line] cienki ⊡ [mud, mixture, liquid] rzadki ⊡ [person, arm] chudy; **to get** ~ chudnąć ⊡ fig **to wear** ~ [joke, excuse] spowszednieć

II vt rozcieńcz|yć, -ać [paint]; rozrzedz|ić, -ać [sauce, soup]

III vi (also ~ **out**) [fog, hair] przerzedz|ić, -ać się

thing /θɪŋ/ **I** n ⊡ (object) rzecz f; **the best** ~ (**to do**) **would be to go and see her** najlepiej byłoby pójść się z nią zobaczyć; **I couldn't hear a** ~ (**that**) **he said** zupełnie nie słyszałem, co mówi; **the** ~ **is** (**that**)... rzecz w tym, że...; **the only** ~ **is...** chodzi tylko o to, że...; **the funny** ~ **is that...** najśmieszniejsze jest to, że... ⊡ (person, animal) **she's a pretty little** ~ jest taka słodka; **you lucky** ~! infml szczęściarz z ciebie! infml

II **things** npl ⊡ (personal belongings, equipment) rzeczy f pl ⊡ (situation, circumstances, matters) sprawy f pl; **how are** ~**s with you?** co (u ciebie) słychać?; **all** ~**s considered** w sumie

IDIOMS: **for one** ~... (**and**) **for another** ~... po pierwsze..., a po drugie...; **I must be seeing** ~**s!** chyba mam przywidzenia!

think /θɪŋk/ **I** vt ⊡ (believe) myśleć; **I** ~ **so** myślę, że tak; **I don't** ~ **so** nie sądzę; **what do you** ~ **it will cost?** jak sądzisz, ile to będzie kosztować? ⊡ (imagine) pomyśleć; **I can't** ~ **how/why/where** nie mam pojęcia, jak/dlaczego/gdzie ⊡ (have opinion) **to** ~ **a lot/not much of sb** cenić/nie cenić kogoś; **what do you** ~ **of him?** co o nim sądzisz?

II vi ⊡ (engage in thought) po|myśleć; **to** ~ **about** or **of sth** myśleć o czymś; **I'll have to** ~ **about it** muszę się nad tym zastanowić; **to** ~ **hard** dobrze się zastanowić; **to be** ~**ing of doing sth** myśleć o zrobieniu czegoś ⊡ (consider) **to** ~ **of sb as sb** uważać kogoś za kogoś ⊡ (remember) **to** ~ **of sth** przypomnieć sobie o czymś

■ **think again:** (reflect more) zastan|owić, -awiać się poważnie; (change mind) zmienić zdanie

■ **think ahead:** po|myśleć naprzód

■ **think back:** sięg|nąć, -ać pamięcią wstecz

■ **think over:** ~ **over** [sth], ~ [sth] **over** rozważ|yć, -ażać [proposal]

■ **think through:** dobrze się zastanowić nad (czymś)

thinking /'θɪŋkɪŋ/ n (reflection) myślenie n; **current** ~ **is that...** GB obecnie uważa się, że...; **to my way of** ~ moim zdaniem

think-tank /'θɪŋktæŋk/ n zespół m doradców

thinly /ˈθɪnlɪ/ adv (sparingly) [cut, slice, spread] cienko; ~ **disguised** ledwie skrywany

thinner /ˈθɪnə(r)/ n rozcieńczalnik m

third /θɜːd/ **I** n ① (in order) trzeci m, -a f, -e n ② (fraction) trzecia f (część) ③ (also ~ **gear**) Aut trójka f infml ④ (also ~**-class degree**) GB Univ ≈ dyplom m z oceną dostateczną
II adj trzeci
III adv ① [come, finish] na trzecim miejscu ② (also **thirdly**) po trzecie

third-class /θɜːd'klɑːs, US -'klæs/ adj ~ **mail** przesyłka zwykła

third degree n infml **to give sb the** ~ [parent, teacher] wymagłować kogoś infml

third party /θɜːd'pɑːtɪ/ n osoby f pl trzecie

Third World n Trzeci Świat m

thirst /θɜːst/ n pragnienie n (**for sth** czegoś)

thirsty /ˈθɜːstɪ/ adj spragniony; **I'm** ~ chce mi się pić; **to make sb** ~ wywoływać u kogoś pragnienie

thirteen /θɜːˈtiːn/ n, adj trzynaście

thirteenth /ˌθɜːˈtiːnθ/ **I** n ① (in order) trzynastly m, -a f, -e n ② (fraction) trzynasta f (część)
II adj trzynasty
III adv na trzynastym miejscu

thirtieth /ˈθɜːtɪəθ/ **I** n ① (in order) trzydziestly m, -a f, -e n ② (fraction) trzydziesta f (część)
II adj trzydziesty
III adv na trzydziestym miejscu

thirty /ˈθɜːtɪ/ n, adj trzydzieści

thirty something n yuppie m po trzydziestce infml

this /ðɪs/ **I** det ten, ta, to; ~ **lamp/paper** ta lampa/ten papier; **do it** ~ **way, not that way** rób to tak, a nie tak
II pron to; **what's** ~? co to (jest)?; **who's** ~? kto to (jest)?; (on telephone) kto mówi?; **whose is** ~? czyje to (jest)?; ~ **is the dining room** to (jest) jadalnia; ~ **is Anna** (introduction) to (jest) Anna; (on telephone) mówi Anna; ~ **is not the right one** ten nie jest odpowiedni; **who did** ~? kto to zrobił?; ~ **is what happens when...** oto co się dzieje, gdy...
III adv tak; **it's** ~ **big** to jest takie duże
IDIOMS: **to talk about** ~ **and that** rozmawiać o tym i owym

thistle /ˈθɪsl/ n oset m

thong /θɒŋ/ n ① (of leather) rzemień m ② (on shoe, garment) rzemyk m ③ (underwear) figi pl t tanga

thorn /θɔːn/ n ① (on plant) cierń m ② (bush) ciernisty krzew m

thorough /ˈθʌrə, US ˈθʌrəʊ/ adj ① (detailed) [knowledge] gruntowny; [analysis, search] dokładny ② (meticulous) skrupulatny

thoroughbred /ˈθʌrəbred/ **I** n koń m czystej krwi
II adj rasowy

thoroughfare /ˈθʌrəfeə(r)/ n arteria f; **'no** ~' „droga zamknięta"

thoroughly /ˈθʌrəlɪ, US ˈθʌrəʊlɪ/ adv ① (meticulously) [check, search] gruntownie; [wash, prepare] dokładnie ② (completely) [clean, reliable] zupełnie; [dangerous, unpleasant] całkiem; [agree, approve] w pełni; [recommend] gorąco

those /ðəʊz/ npl → that

though /ðəʊ/ **I** conj chociaż; **strange** ~ **it may seem** chociaż może wydawać się to dziwne; **a foolish** ~ **courageous act** czyn odważny, choć głupi
II adv jednak

thought /θɔːt/ n ① (idea) myśl f ② (reflection) namysł m; **deep in** ~ zatopiony w myślach; **after much** ~ po długim namyśle; **to give** ~ **to sth** zastanowić się nad czymś

thoughtful /ˈθɔːtfl/ adj ① (pensive) [person, look] zamyślony ② (considerate) [person] troskliwy; [letter, gift, gesture] świadczący o życzliwości

thoughtless /ˈθɔːtlɪs/ adj [person, remark, act] bezmyślny; **to be** ~ **towards sb** nie myśleć o kimś

thought-out /ˌθɔːt'aʊt/ adj **well/badly** ~ **plan** przemyślany/nieprzemyślany plan

thought-provoking /ˈθɔːtprəˈvəʊkɪŋ/ adj skłaniający do refleksji

thousand /ˈθaʊznd/ n, adj tysiąc m; **a** ~ **and two** tysiąc dwa; **about a** ~ około tysiąca; **five** ~ **pounds** pięć tysięcy funtów; ~**s of people** tysiące ludzi

thousandth /ˈθaʊzndθ/ **I** n ① (in order) tysięczn|y m, -a f, tysiączn|y m, -a f ② (fraction) tysięczna f (część)
II adj tysięczny, tysiączny

thrash /θræʃ/ vt ① (whip) z|bić ② Mil, Sport roz|nieść, -nosić [opponent]
■ **thrash about, thrash around**: rzucać się
■ **thrash out**: rozpracow|ać, -ywać [problem]; wypracow|ać, -ywać [compromise, plan]

thrashing /ˈθræʃɪŋ/ n lanie n also fig

thread /θred/ **I** n ① (in sewing) nić f, nitka f ② (of screw) gwint m ③ (of argument, story) wątek m
II vt nawle|c, -kać [needle, beads]

threadbare /ˈθredbeə(r)/ adj [clothes] wytarty

threat /θret/ n (verbal abuse) groźba f; (danger) zagrożenie n

threaten /ˈθretn/ **I** vt (menace) za|grozić (komuś); **to** ~ **to do sth** grozić, że coś się zrobi; **they are** ~**ed with extinction** grozi im wyginięcie
II vi [danger, bad weather] grozić

three /θriː/ n, adj trzy

three-dimensional /ˌθriːdaɪˈmenʃnl/ adj trójwymiarowy

threefold /ˈθriːfəʊld/ **I** adj [meaning] potrójny; [increase] trzykrotny
II adv (three times) trzykrotnie; (triply) potrójnie

three-piece suit /ˌθriːpiːsˈsuːt, -ˈsjuːt/ n (for men) garnitur m trzyczęściowy; (for women) kostium m trzyczęściowy

three-piece suite /ˌθriːpiːsˈswiːt/ n komplet m wypoczynkowy

three-quarters /ˌθriːˈkwɔːtəz/ npl trzy czwarte; ~ **of an hour** trzy kwadranse

thresh /θreʃ/ vt wy|młócić

threshold /ˈθreʃəʊld, -həʊld/ n próg m

thrift /θrɪft/ n oszczędność f

thrifty /ˈθrɪftɪ/ adj [person] oszczędny (**in sth** w czymś)

thrill /θrɪl/ **I** n 1 (sensation) dreszcz m 2 (pleasure) ogromna przyjemność f
II vt u|radować
III vi [person] za|drżeć (z emocji)
IV **thrilled** pp adj (delighted) zachwycony (**with sth** czymś); (excited) podekscytowany (**with sth** czymś)

thriller /ˈθrɪlə(r)/ n thriller m, dreszczowiec m

thrilling /ˈθrɪlɪŋ/ adj [story] pasjonujący; [concert] porywający; [moment, sensation] fascynujący

thrive /θraɪv/ vi [person] mieć się świetnie; [plant] dobrze się rozwijać; [community, business] (dobrze) prosperować; kwitnąć fig

thriving /ˈθraɪvɪŋ/ adj [business, community] (dobrze) prosperujący; kwitnący fig; [person] kwitnący

throat /θrəʊt/ n gardło n; **a sore** ~ ból gardła; **I have a sore** ~ boli mnie gardło

throb /θrɒb/ vi 1 [heart, pulse] mocno bić; **my head is** ~**bing** głowa mi pęka 2 [machine] warkotać; [music, rhythm] pulsować; [building] drżeć

throbbing /ˈθrɒbɪŋ/ adj [ache, music] pulsujący

throne /θrəʊn/ n tron m

throng /θrɒŋ, US θrɔːŋ/ **I** n chmara f (**of sb/sth** kogoś/czegoś)
II vt wypełni|ć, -ać [street, room, town]

throttle /ˈθrɒtl/ n (accelerator) gaz m

through /θruː/ **I** prep 1 (from one side to the other) przez (coś); **the nail went right** ~ **the wall** gwóźdź przeszedł przez ścianę na wylot 2 (via, by way of) przez (coś); **to go** ~ **the town centre** jechać przez centrum miasta; **to look** ~ **sth** patrzeć przez coś [binoculars, hole, window]; **it was** ~ **her that I got this job** to dzięki niej dostałem tę pracę 3 (past) przez (coś); **to go** ~ **a red light** [driver] przejechać na czerwonym świetle; [pedestrian] przejść na czerwonym świetle; **to get** or **go** ~ **sth** przedostać się przez coś [barrier]; przejść przez coś [customs]; **she's been** ~ **a lot** wiele przeszła 4 (because of) ~ **carelessness** przez nieuwagę; ~ **illness** z powodu choroby 5 (until the end of) **all** or **right** ~ **the day** (przez) cały dzień 6 (up to and including) aż do; **from Friday** ~ **Sunday** od piątku do soboty
II adj 1 (direct) [train, freight] bezpośredni; '**no** ~ **road**' „ślepa ulica" 2 (successful) **to be** ~ **to the**

next round przejść do następnej rundy 3 infml (finished) skończony; **I'm not** ~ **with you yet!** jeszcze z tobą nie skończyłem! infml; **are you** ~ **with the paper?** przeczytałeś już gazetę?
III adv ~ **the water went right** ~ woda przeszła na drugą stronę; **to let sb** ~ przepuścić kogoś; **to read sth right** ~ przeczytać coś od początku do końca
IV **through and through** adv phr **to know sth** ~ **and** ~ znać coś jak własną kieszeń; **he is English** ~ **and** ~ jest Anglikiem w każdym calu

throughout /θruːˈaʊt/ **I** prep 1 (all over) ~ **Poland** w całej Polsce; ~ **the world** na całym świecie 2 (for the duration of) przez cały czas; ~ **his life** przez całe życie; ~ **history** w całej historii
II adv 1 (in every part) wszędzie 2 (the whole time) cały czas

throughway /ˈθruːweɪ/ n US droga f szybkiego ruchu

throw /θrəʊ/ **I** n rzut m
II vt 1 (send through the air) rzuc|ić, -ać (czymś) [ball, stone, spear] (**at sth** w coś); rzuc|ić, -ać [article of clothing, letter] (**onto sth** na coś); **to** ~ **a six** wyrzucić szóstkę 2 [horse] zrzuc|ić, -ać [rider] 3 (direct) rzuc|ić, -ać [question, look] (**at sb** komuś); rzuc|ić, -ać [image, shadow] (**on sth** na coś); pos|łać, -yłać [kiss]; zada|ć, -wać [punch] 4 fig (disconcert) [question] wprawi|ć, -ać w zakłopotanie; [news] porusz|yć, -ać 5 infml (organize) **to** ~ **a party** wydać przyjęcie 6 (in pottery) wyt|oczyć, -aczać [jug, vase]
III vi rzuc|ić, -ać

■ **throw away**: 1 wyrzuc|ić, -ać [paper, old clothes] 2 z|marnować [chance, life]; roz|trwonić [money]

■ **throw back**: wrzuc|ić, -ać z powrotem [fish]; odrzuc|ić, -ać [ball]

■ **throw in**: ~ **in** [sth], ~ [sth] **in** 1 (give free) do|łożyć, -kładać 2 (add) dorzuc|ić, -ać [ingredient, remark]

■ **throw out**: 1 wyrzuc|ić, -ać [rubbish, person] (**of sth** z czegoś) 2 odrzuc|ić, -ać [application, decision, bill]

■ **throw together**: ¶ ~ [sb] **together** zetknąć, stykać [people] ¶ ~ [sth] **together** s|klecić [artefact]; przygotow|ać, -ywać naprędce [meal]

■ **throw up**: ¶ ~ **up** infml z|wymiotować ¶ ~ **up** [sth], ~ [sth] **up** 1 (toss into air) wyrzuc|ić, -ać [arms]; wyrzuc|ić, -ać do góry [ball] 2 infml (abandon) porzuc|ić, -ać [job]

throwaway /ˈθrəʊəweɪ/ adj [packaging] jednorazowy; [society] rozrzutny; [remark] rzucony mimochodem or od niechcenia

throwback /ˈθrəʊbæk/ n relikt m also fig; **a** ~ **to sth** powrót do czegoś

thrush /θrʌʃ/ n Zool drozd m

thrust /θrʌst/ **I** *n* 1 (with weapon) pchnięcie *n*; (of body) ruch *m* do przodu; Mil natarcie *n*; Tech siła *f* ciągu 2 (of argument, narrative) zasadnicza myśl *f*
II *vt* **to ~ sth towards** or **at sb** pchnąć mocno coś w stronę kogoś; **to ~ sth into sth** wepchnąć coś do czegoś

thud /θʌd/ **I** *n* głuchy odgłos *m*
II *vi* wyda|ć, -wać głuchy odgłos; (fall) upa|ść, -dać ciężko

thug /θʌɡ/ *n* zbir *m*

thumb /θʌm/ **I** *n* kciuk *m*
II *vt* 1 przekartkow|ać, -ywać, kartkować *[book, magazine]* 2 infml **to ~ a lift** złapać okazję infml
[IDIOMS:] **to be under sb's ~** chodzić u kogoś na pasku; *[husband]* siedzieć u kogoś pod pantoflem

thumbs down /ˌθʌmzˈdaʊn/ *n* infml **to give sb/sth the ~** odrzucić kogoś/coś; **to get the ~** *[candidate, proposal, new product]* nie znaleźć uznania (**from sb** u kogoś)

thumbs up /ˌθʌmzˈʌp/ *n* infml **to give sb/sth the ~** zaakceptować kogoś/coś; **start the car when I give you the ~** zapal silnik, kiedy dam ci znak

thumbtack /ˈθʌmtæk/ *n* pinezka *f*

thump /θʌmp/ **I** *n* 1 (blow) walnięcie *n* infml 2 (sound) łomot *m*
II *vt* wal|nąć, -ić infml *[person]*; wal|nąć, -ić w (coś) *[table]*
III *vi* (pound) *[rhythm, music]* huczeć; *[heart]* walić infml

thunder /ˈθʌndə(r)/ **I** *n* 1 grzmot *m*; **a peal of ~** trzask pioruna 2 (of traffic, hooves) huk *m*; (of applause) burza *f*
II *v impers* grzmieć

thunderbolt /ˈθʌndəbəʊlt/ *n* piorun *m*

thunderclap /ˈθʌndəklæp/ *n* grzmot *m*

thunderstorm /ˈθʌndəstɔːm/ *n* burza *f* (z piorunami)

thunderstruck /ˈθʌndəstrʌk/ *adj* fig jak rażony gromem

Thursday /ˈθɜːzdeɪ, -dɪ/ *n* czwartek *m*

thus /ðʌs/ *adv* tak oto; **~ far** (of time) (jak) dotąd, dotychczas; (of place) dotąd, do tego miejsca

thwart /θwɔːt/ *vt* udaremni|ć, -ać *[efforts]*; po|-krzyżować *[plan]*; po|psuć szyki (komuś) *[person]*

thyme /taɪm/ *n* tymianek *m*

thyroid /ˈθaɪrɔɪd/ *n* (also ~ **gland**) tarczyca *f*

tiara /tɪˈɑːrə/ *n* (woman's) diadem *m*; (pope's) tiara *f*

Tibet /tɪˈbet/ *prn* Tybet *m*

tick[1] /tɪk/ **I** *n* 1 (of clock) tykanie *n* 2 (mark on paper) ptaszek *m* infml
II *vt* zaznacz|yć, -ać *[box, name, answer]*
III *vi* *[bomb, clock, watch]* tykać
■ **tick off**: odfajkow|ać, -ywać infml *[name, item]*

tick[2] /tɪk/ *n* Zool kleszcz *m*

ticket /ˈtɪkɪt/ *n* 1 (for travel, admission, participation) bilet *m*; (for cloakroom) numerek *m*; (for laundry, left luggage, pawn shop) kwit *m*; (label) etykietka *f*; **library**

~ karta biblioteczna 2 Aut infml (for fine) mandat *m* 3 US (of political party) lista *f* wyborcza; (platform) program *m* wyborczy

ticket office *n* kasa *f* biletowa

tickle /ˈtɪkl/ **I** *n* łaskotanie *n*
II *vt* 1 *[person, feather]* po|łaskotać; *[wool, garment]* gryźć fig 2 infml (gratify) po|łechtać fig *[person, vanity, palate]* 3 (amuse) rozśmiesz|yć, -ać *[person]*
III *vi* *[blanket, garment]* gryźć fig; *[feather]* łaskotać

tidal wave *n* fala *f* pływowa

tide /taɪd/ *n* 1 (in sea) pływ *m*; **the ~ is in/out** jest przypływ/odpływ 2 fig (of emotion) przypływ *m*; (of events, history) bieg *m*

tidy /ˈtaɪdɪ/ **I** *adj* 1 *[house, room, appearance, person]* schludny; *[writing, work, layout]* staranny 2 infml *[sum, portion, share]* ładny infml
II *vt, vi* = **tidy up**
■ **tidy up**: ¶ ~ **up** po|sprzątać; **to ~ up after sb** posprzątać po kimś ¶ ~ **up** *[sth]*, ~ *[sth]* **up** po|sprzątać *[house, room, objects]*; poprawi|ć, -ać *[hair, handwriting, appearance]*

tie /taɪ/ **I** *n* 1 (piece of clothing) krawat *m* 2 (bond) więź *f* 3 (constraint) zawada *f* 4 Sport remis *m*
II *vt* 1 (attach, fasten) przywiąz|ać, -ywać *[label, animal, prisoner]* (**to sth** do czegoś); (secure) związ|ać, -ywać *[parcel, hands, chicken]* (**with sth** czymś); za|wiązać *[scarf, laces, tie]* 2 fig (link) **to be ~d to sth** (linked to) mieć związek z czymś; (constrained by) nie móc rozstać się z czymś *[job]*; nie móc ruszyć się z czegoś *[house]*
III *vi* 1 (fasten) **the laces/rope won't ~** nie można zawiązać sznurowadeł/liny 2 (draw) (in match) z|remisować; (in race) osiąg|nąć, -ać ten sam rezultat; (in vote) uzysk|ać, -iwać taką samą ilość głosów
■ **tie back**: związ|ać, -ywać z tyłu *[hair]*
■ **tie down**: (hold fast) związ|ać, -ywać, s|krępować *[person]*; **she feels ~d down** fig odczuwa brak swobody; **to ~ sb down to sth** (limit) narzucić komuś coś
■ **tie in with**: (tally) zg|odzić, -adzać się z (czymś) *[fact, event]*
■ **tie up**: 1 (secure) związ|ać, -ywać *[prisoner]*; zawiąz|ać, -ywać *[parcel]*; uwiąz|ać, -ywać *[animal]* 2 (freeze) zamr|ozić, -ażać *[capital]* 3 (finalize) do|pracow|ać, -ywać *[details]*; s|finalizować *[deal]*; **to ~ up the loose ends** (explain) wyjaśnić wszystkie szczegóły

tie break(er) *n* (in tennis) tie-break *m*; (in quiz) runda *f* pytań dodatkowych

tier /tɪə(r)/ *n* (of cake, sandwich) warstwa *f*; (of organization) szczebel *m*; (of system) poziom *m*; (of seating) rząd *m*

tiff /tɪf/ *n* sprzeczka *f*

tiger /ˈtaɪɡə(r)/ *n* tygrys *m*

tight /taɪt/ **[]** **tights** *npl* (worn by women) rajstopy *plt*; (worn by acrobats, dancers) trykot *m*

[II] *adj* [1] *[fist, knot]* zaciśnięty; *[screw, nut]* mocno dokręcony; *[grip, grasp]* mocny; *[rope]* napięty; *[voice]* ściśnięty [2] *(constrictive)* *[space, shoes]* ciasny; *(closefitting)* *[jacket, shirt]* obcisły [3] *(strict)* *[security, discipline]* surowy; *[deadline, budget, schedule]* napięty

[III] *adv* (firmly) *[hold, grip]* mocno; *[fasten]* dokładnie; *[close]* szczelnie; **hold** ∼! trzymaj się mocno!; **sit** ∼ ! nie ruszaj się!

tighten /'taɪtn/ **[]** *vt* docis|nąć, -kać *[lid, spring]*; dokręc|ić, -ać *[screw]*; napi|ąć, -nać *[rope, strings, chain, muscles]*; zacieśni|ć, -ać *[grip]*; zacis|nąć, -kać *[belt, tie]*; zaostrz|yć, -ać *[security, restrictions]*

[II] *vi* *[lips]* zacis|nąć, -kać się; *[muscle]* napi|ąć, -nać się

tight-fisted /ˌtaɪt'fɪstɪd/ *adj* infml skąpy

tight-fitting /ˌtaɪt'fɪtɪŋ/ *adj* obcisły

tight-knit /ˌtaɪt'nɪt/ *adj [family]* zżyty; *[community]* zintegrowany

tightly /'taɪtlɪ/ *adv [grasp, hold, tied]* mocno; *[closed]* szczelnie

tightrope /'taɪtrəʊp/ *n* lina *f (do akrobacji)*

tightrope walker *n* linoskoczek *m*

tile /taɪl/ **[]** *n* (for roof) dachówka *f*; (for wall, floor) kafelek *m*

[II] *vt* pokry|ć, -wać dachówką *[roof]*; wy|łożyć, -kładać kafelkami *[wall, floor, room]*

till[1] /tɪl/ → **until**

till[2] /tɪl/ *n* kasa *f* sklepowa

tiller /'tɪlə(r)/ *n* rumpel *m*

till receipt *n* paragon *m*

tilt /tɪlt/ **[]** *vt* (slant) przechyl|ić, -ać *[table, chair, head]*; przekrzywi|ć, -ać *[hat, cap]*

[II] *vi* (slant) przechyl|ić, -ać się

timber /'tɪmbə(r)/ *n* [1] (wood) drewno *n* [2] (trees) drzewa *n pl (przeznaczone do wycinki)* [3] (beam) belka *f* drewniana

time /taɪm/ **[]** *n* [1] czas *m*; **as** ∼ **goes/went by** w miarę upływu czasu; **for a long** ∼ długo; **a long** ∼ **ago** dawno temu; **in five days'** ∼ za pięć dni [2] (hour of the day, night) godzina *f*; **what** ∼ **is it?**, **what's the** ∼? która godzina?; **10 am Polish** ∼ godzina dziesiąta w Polsce; **this** ∼ **last week** dokładnie tydzień temu; **on** ∼ na czas; **the** ∼**s of trains** godziny odjazdu pociągów; **it's** ∼ **for bed** pora spać; **it's** ∼ **we started** czas zaczynać; **about** ∼ **too!** najwyższy czas! [3] (era, epoch) czas *m*; **at the** ∼ wtedy; **there was a** ∼ **when...** kiedyś było tak, że...; **in former** ∼**s** w dawnych czasach; **it's just like old** ∼**s** jest jak za dawnych czasów [4] (moment) czas *m*, chwila *f*; **at** ∼**s** chwilami; **at the right** ∼ w odpowiednim momencie; **this is no** ∼ **for jokes** nie czas na żarty; **at all** ∼**s** przez cały czas; **any** ∼ **now** w każdej chwili; **the** ∼ **has come for action** przyszedł czas na działanie; **by**

the ∼ **I finished the letter it was dark** zanim skończyłem list, zrobiło się ciemno; **some** ∼ **next month** któregoś dnia w przyszłym miesiącu; **for the** ∼ **being** na razie [5] *(occasion)* raz *m*; **nine** ∼**s out of ten** dziewięć razy na dziesięć; **three** ∼ **a month** trzy razy w miesiącu; **three at a** ∼ trzy na raz; **from** ∼ **to** ∼ od czasu do czasu [6] *(experience)* **to have a hard** ∼ **doing sth** namęczyć się nad zrobieniem czegoś; **he's having a hard** ∼ przeżywa ciężkie chwile; **we had a good** ∼ świetnie się bawiliśmy [7] Mus takt *m*; (tempo) tempo *n* [8] *(in mathematics)* razy; **one** ∼**s two (is two)** jeden razy dwa (równa się dwa); **ten** ∼**s longer** dziesięć razy dłuższy; **eight** ∼ **s as much** osiem razy tyle

[II] *vt* [1] (schedule) za|planować godzinę *(czegoś)* *[attack]*; ustal|ić, -ać termin *(czegoś)* *[meeting, visit]*; wyb|rać, -ierać *[moment]* [2] (judge) uderz|yć, -ać w odpowiednim momencie *[ball]* [3] (measure speed) z|mierzyć czas *(komuś/czegoś)* *[athlete, speech]*

all in good ∼ wszystko w swoim czasie; **only** ∼ **will tell** czas pokaże; **to have** ∼ **on one's hands** (for brief period) dysponować wolnym czasem; (longer) mieć dużo wolnego czasu

time bomb *n* bomba *f* zegarowa

time-consuming /'taɪmkən'sjuːmɪŋ, US -s'uː-/ *adj* czasochłonny

time difference *n* różnica *f* czasowa

time-frame /'taɪmfreɪm/ *n* ramy *plt* czasowe

timeless /'taɪmlɪs/ *adj [beauty, quality]* ponadczasowy; *[laws]* wieczny

time-limit /'taɪmlɪmɪt/ *n* [1] (deadline) termin *m* (ostateczny) [2] (maximum duration) limit *m* czasu

timely /'taɪmlɪ/ *adj [arrival, intervention]* w (samą) porę

time off *n* (leave, free time) czas *m* wolny; wolne *n* infml

timer /'taɪmə(r)/ *n* (for cooking) minutnik *m*; (on bomb) zegar *m*; (for controlling equipment) regulator *m* czasowy

timeshare /'taɪmʃeə(r)/ *n* (house) dom *m* we współwłasności; (apartment) mieszkanie *n* we współwłasności

time-sheet /'taɪmʃiːt/ *n* karta *f* kontrolna *(pracownika)*

timespan /'taɪmspæn/ *n* okres *m*

timetable /'taɪmteɪbl/ **[]** *n* (schedule) Univ rozkład *m* zajęć; Sch plan *m* lekcji; (for plans, negotiations) kalendarz *m*; (for buses, trains) rozkład *m* jazdy

[II] *vt* ustal|ić, -ać godzinę *(czegoś)* *[class, lecture]*; ustal|ić, -ać termin *(czegoś)* *[meeting, negotiations]*

time zone *n* strefa *f* czasowa

timid /'tɪmɪd/ *adj* nieśmiały; *[animal]* płochliwy

timing /'taɪmɪŋ/ *n* [1] (scheduling) wybrany termin *m*; **the** ∼ **of the announcement was unfortunate** wybrano niefortunny moment na złożenia oświadczenia ☐2 Mus wyczucie *n* rytmu ☐3 Aut ustawienie *n* zapłonu

tin /tɪn/ *n* ☐1 (metal) cyna *f* ☐2 GB (can) puszka *f* ☐3 (container) (for biscuits, cake) pudełko *n* metalowe; (for paint) puszka *f*; (for baking) forma *f*; (small) foremka *f*

tin can *n* puszka *f* blaszana

tinfoil /'tɪnfɔɪl/ *n* folia *f* aluminiowa

tinge /tɪndʒ/ ☐ *n* odcień *m*; (of emotion) cień *m*
☐☐ *vt* ~**d with sth** zabarwiony czymś also *fig*

tingle /'tɪŋgl/ ☐ *n* (physical) mrowienie *n*; (psychological) dreszcz *m*
☐☐ *vi* ☐1 (physically) **my fingers are tingling** czuję mrowienie w palcach ☐2 (psychologically) **to** ~ **with sth** drżeć z czegoś *[fear]*

tinker /'tɪŋkə(r)/ *vi* **to** ~ **with sth** majstrować przy czymś *infml [car]*; poprawiać coś *[document]*

tinkle /'tɪŋkl/ ☐ *n* brzękanie *n*
☐☐ *vi* za|dzwonić

tinned /tɪnd/ *adj [meat, fruit]* puszkowy, w puszce

tinny /'tɪni/ *adj* ☐1 *[sound, music]* brzękliwy ☐2 (badly made) *[car, machine]* tandetny

tin opener *n* GB otwieracz *m* do konserw

tinsel /'tɪnsl/ *n* lameta *f*

tint /tɪnt/ ☐ *n* (trace) odcień *m*; (pale colour) (blady) kolor *m* pastelowy; (hair dye) szampon *m* koloryzujący
☐☐ **tinted** *pp adj [glass, spectacles]* przyciemniony; *[hair]* ufarbowany

tiny /'taɪni/ *adj* maleńki

tip¹ /tɪp/ *n* ☐1 (of umbrella, blade, pencil, spire) szpic *m*; (of nose, tongue, finger, shoe) czubek *m*; (of island, stick) koniec *m* ☐2 (protective cover) (of umbrella) okucie *n*; (of shoe heel) blaszka *f*

tip² /tɪp/ *vt* (tilt) przechyl|ić, -ać; (pour) wyl|ać, -ewać; (dump) wysyp|ać, -ywać *[waste, rubbish]*
■ **tip over**: przewr|ócić, -acać *[chair, pile]*

tip³ /tɪp/ ☐ *n* ☐1 (gratuity) napiwek *m* ☐2 (practical hint) wskazówka *f*; (in betting) typ *m*
☐☐ *vt* ☐1 (predict) **to** ~ **sb to win** typować kogoś na zwycięzcę ☐2 da|ć, -wać napiwek (komuś) *[waiter, driver]*
■ **tip off**: ~ **[sb] off** da|ć, -wać cynk (komuś) *infml*

tip-off /'tɪpɒf/ *n infml* cynk *m infml*

tiptoe /'tɪptəʊ/ ☐ *n* **on** ~ na palcach
☐☐ *vi* chodzić na palcach

tire¹ /'taɪə(r)/ ☐ *vt* z|męczyć
☐☐ *vi* ☐1 (get tired) z|męczyć się ☐2 (get bored) **to** ~ **of sth** znudzić się czymś
■ **tire out**: wyczerp|ać, -ywać *[person]*; **to be** ~**d out** być wykończonym

tire² /'taɪə(r)/ *n* US opona *f*

tired /'taɪəd/ *adj* ☐1 (weary) zmęczony ☐2 (bored) **to be** ~ **of sth/of doing sth** mieć dosyć czegoś/robienia czegoś; **to grow** ~ zaczynać mieć dosyć

tiredness /'taɪədnɪs/ *n* zmęczenie *n*

tireless /'taɪəlɪs/ *adj* niestrudzony

tiresome /'taɪəsəm/ *adj [child]* nieznośny; *[job, task]* męczący

tiring /'taɪərɪŋ/ *adj* męczący

tissue /'tɪʃuː/ *n* ☐1 (handkerchief) chusteczka *f* higieniczna ☐2 (also ~ **paper**) bibułka *f* ☐3 Anat, Bot tkanka *f*

tit /tɪt/ *n* Zool sikorka *f*
[IDIOMS:] ~ **for tat** wet za wet

titbit /'tɪtbɪt/ *n* GB (of food) smakowity kąsek *m*; (of gossip) ciekawostka *f*

title /'taɪtl/ ☐ *n* tytuł *m*
☐☐ **titles** *npl* (in film) napisy *m pl*
☐☐☐ *vt* za|tytułować *[book, play]*

titleholder /'taɪtlhəʊldə(r)/ *n* posiadacz *m*, -ka *f* tytułu mistrzowskiego

title role *n* rola *f* tytułowa

titter /'tɪtə(r)/ ☐ *n* chichot *m*
☐☐ *vi* za|chichotać

tizzy /'tɪzi/ *n infml* **to be in a** ~ być rozgorączkowanym

to /tə, before a vowel tʊ, tuː, emphatic tuː/
☐ *infinitive particle* ☐1 (expressing purpose) żeby; **to do sth to impress one's friends** zrobić coś, żeby zrobić wrażenie na znajomych ☐2 (linking consecutive acts) **he looked up to see...** spojrzał w górę i zobaczył... ☐3 (after superlatives) który; **the youngest to do sth** najmłodszy, który zrobił coś ☐4 (avoiding repetition of verb) **'did you go?' – 'no, I promised not to'** „poszedłeś" – „nie, obiecałem, że tego nie zrobię"; **'are you staying?' – 'I want to but...'** „zostajesz?" – „chciałbym, ale..." ☐5 (following impersonal verb) **it's difficult to understand** trudno to zrozumieć
☐☐ *prep* ☐1 (in direction of) do (kogoś/czegoś) *[shops, school, doctor's, dentist's]*; **she's gone to Mary** poszła do Mary; **to London/Poland/town** do Londynu/Polski/miasta; **the road to the village** droga (prowadząca) do wioski ☐2 (up to) do (czegoś); **to the end/this day** do końca/do dnia dzisiejszego ☐3 (in telling time) **ten (minutes) to three** za dziesięć trzecia; **it's five to** jest za pięć ☐4 (introducing direct or indirect object) **give the book to Anna** daj tę książkę Annie; **be nice to your brother** bądź miły dla brata; **to me it's just a minor problem** według mnie to nie jest wielki problem; **she gave it to them** dała im to ☐5 (in toasts) za (kogoś/coś); (in dedications) dla (kogoś); **to prosperity** za pomyślność; **to our dear son** (on tombstone) naszemu drogiemu synowi ☐6 (in accordance with) **is it to your taste?** czy ci smakuje?; **to dance to the music** tańczyć w takt muzyki ☐7 (in relationships) **to win by three goals to two** wygrać trzy do dwóch; **next door to the school** zaraz obok szkoły ☐8 (showing accuracy) **three weeks to the day** trzy tygodnie co do dnia; **to scale** w skali

|9| (showing reason) **to invite sb to dinner** zaprosić kogoś na obiad |10| (belonging to) **the key to the safe** klucz do sejfu; **a room to myself** pokój wyłącznie dla mnie; **personal assistant to the director** asystent dyrektora |11| (on to) *[tied, pinned]* do (czegoś) *[noticeboard, lapel]* |12| (showing reaction) **to his surprise/horror** ku jego zaskoczeniu/przerażeniu

toad /təʊd/ *n* ropucha *f*

toadstool /'təʊdstuːl/ *n* muchomor *m*

to and fro /ˌtuːən'frəʊ/ *adv* tam i z powrotem

toast /təʊst/ **▯** *n* |1| (bread) tost *m*, grzanka *f*; **a slice of** ~ grzanka, tost |2| (tribute) toast *m*; **to drink a** ~ wychylić toast
▯▯ *vt* |1| Culin opie|c, -kać *[bread, roll]* |2| (propose a toast to) wzn|ieść, -osić toast za (kogoś/coś)

toaster /'təʊstə(r)/ *n* toster *m*

tobacco /tə'bækəʊ/ *n* tytoń *m*

toboggan /tə'bɒgən/ *n* sanki *plt*; (for mountain rescue) tobogan *m*

today /tə'deɪ/ **▯** *n* dziś *n inv*, dzisiaj *n inv*; ~ **is Tuesday** dziś or dzisiaj jest wtorek
▯▯ *adv* dziś, dzisiaj also fig; ~ **week** od dziś za tydzień; **a month ago** ~ dokładnie miesiąc temu; **later** ~ później w ciągu dnia

toddler /'tɒdlə(r)/ *n* dziecko *n* uczące się chodzić

toe /təʊ/ *n* |1| Anat palec *m* u nogi; **big** ~ paluch; **little** ~ mały palec |2| (of sock) palce *m pl*; (of shoe) czubek *m*
IDIOMS **to** ~ **the line** podporządkować się; **from top to** ~ od stóp do głów

toehold /'təʊhəʊld/ *n* (in climbing) stopień *m*; **to get** or **gain a** ~ **in sth** zaczepić się w czymś *[organization]*; wejść na coś *[market]*

toffee /'tɒfɪ, US 'tɔːfɪ/ *n* toffi *n inv*

together /tə'geðə(r)/ **▯** *adv* |1| razem; **to get back** ~ **again** zejść się ponownie; **to be close** ~ *[objects, trees, plants]* być blisko siebie; **than all the rest of them put** ~ niż oni wszyscy razem wzięci; **they belong** ~ *[objects]* stanowią całość; *[people]* są stworzeni dla siebie; **the talks brought the two sides** ~ rozmowy zbliżyły do siebie dwie strony |2| (at the same time) razem, naraz
▯▯ together with *prep phr* (as well as, in the company of) razem z (kimś/czymś)
IDIOMS **to get one's act** ~ infml wziąć się w garść infml

togetherness /tə'geðənɪs/ *n* więź *f*

toil /tɔɪl/ **▯** *n* znój *m*
▯▯ *vi* |1| (also ~ **away**) (work) mozolić się |2| (move) **to** ~ **up the hill** wspinać się mozolnie pod górę

toilet /'tɔɪlɪt/ *n* (fixture) sedes *m*; (room, building) toaleta *f*

toilet bag *n* kosmetyczka *f*

toilet paper, **toilet tissue** *n* papier *m* toaletowy

toiletries /'tɔɪlɪtrɪz/ *npl* przybory *plt* toaletowe

toilet roll *n* |1| (roll) rolka *f* papieru toaletowego |2| (tissue) papier *m* toaletowy

token /'təʊkən/ **▯** *n* |1| (for machine, phone) żeton *m* |2| (on package) kupon *m*; (for product) talon *m*; **a book/record** ~ talon na książki/płyty |3| (symbol) znak *m*; **as a** ~ **of sth** w dowód czegoś *[esteem, gratitude]*
▯▯ *adj [resistance, payment, punishment]* symboliczny; ~ **gesture** zdawkowy gest

tolerable /'tɒlərəbl/ *adj* (bearable) znośny; (adequate) przyzwoity

tolerance /'tɒlərəns/ *n* |1| (broad-mindedness) tolerancja *f* |2| (resistance) odporność *f* |3| Med tolerancja *f* (**to sth** na coś)

tolerant /'tɒlərənt/ *adj* tolerancyjny

tolerate /'tɒləreɪt/ *vt* tolerować

toll¹ /təʊl/ *n* |1| (number) **the death** ~ liczba ofiar śmiertelnych |2| (charge) opłata *f* (za przejazd)

toll² /təʊl/ **▯** *n* (of bell) bicie *n* (dzwonu)
▯▯ *vt* bić w (coś) *[bell]*
▯▯▯ *vi [bell]* bić

toll call *n* US rozmowa *f* międzymiastowa

tomato /tə'mɑːtəʊ, US tə'meɪtəʊ/ **▯** *n* pomidor *m*
▯▯ *adj [sauce]* pomidorowy; *[salad]* z pomidorów

tomb /tuːm/ *n* grobowiec *m*

tomboy /'tɒmbɔɪ/ *n* chłopczyca *f*

tombstone /'tuːmstəʊn/ *n* nagrobek *m*

tomcat /'tɒmkæt/ *n* kocur *m*

tomorrow /tə'mɒrəʊ/ **▯** *n* jutro *n*; **I'll do it by** ~ zrobię to do jutra
▯▯ *adv* jutro; **see you** ~! do jutra!; ~ **week** od jutra za tydzień

tomorrow afternoon **▯** *n* jutrzejsze popołudnie *n*
▯▯ *adv* jutro po południu

tomorrow evening **▯** *n* jutrzejszy wieczór *m*
▯▯ *adv* jutro wieczorem

tomorrow morning **▯** *n* jutrzejsze rano *n*
▯▯ *adv* jutro rano

ton /tʌn/ *n* |1| (in weight) GB (also **gross** or **long** ~) tona *f* angielska (= *1016 kg*); US (also **net** or **short** ~) tona *f* amerykańska (= *907 kg*); **metric** ~ tona |2| infml (a lot) ~**s of sth** masa czegoś *[food, paper, time]*

tone /təʊn/ **▯** *n* |1| ton *m*; **his** ~ **of voice** ton jego głosu; **to set the** ~ nadawać ton (**for sth** czemuś) |2| Mus ton *m*; (on telephone) sygnał *m* |3| (of muscle) napięcie *n* mięśniowe
▯▯ *vt* (also ~ **up**) wzmoc|nić, -acniać *[body, muscle]*
▯▯▯ *vi* (also ~ **in**) (blend) *[colours]* współgrać (**with sth** z czymś)
■ **tone down**: s|tonować *[colour, light, attitude]*; z|łagodzić ton (czegoś) *[letter, statement]*

tone-deaf /ˌtəʊn'def/ *adj* niemuzykalny

tongs /tɒŋz/ *npl* szczypce *plt*

tongue /tʌŋ/ *n* |1| Anat język *m*; Culin ozór *m*; **to stick out one's** ~ **at sb** pokazać komuś język; **to**

lose one's ~ zapomnieć języka w gębie infml [2] (on shoe) język *m*

[IDIOMS] **to have sth on the tip of one's** ~ mieć coś na końcu języka; **a slip of the** ~ przejęzyczenie, lapsus

tongue-in-cheek /ˌtʌŋɪnˈtʃiːk/ [I] *adj* ironiczny, żartobliwy

[II] *adv* ironicznie, żartobliwie

tongue-tied /ˈtʌŋtaɪd/ *adj* oniemiały

tongue-twister /ˈtʌŋtwɪstə(r)/ *n* łamaniec *m* językowy

tonic /ˈtɒnɪk/ *n* [1] (also ~ **water**) tonik *m*; **gin and** ~ gin z tonikiem [2] Med lek *m* tonizujący

tonight /təˈnaɪt/ [I] *n* dzisiejszy wieczór *m*

[II] *adv* (this evening) dziś wieczorem; (after bedtime) dziś w nocy

tonne /tʌn/ *n* tona *f* metryczna

tonsil /ˈtɒnsl/ *n* Anat migdałek *m*; **he had his ~ s out** wycięto mu migdałki

tonsillitis /ˌtɒnsɪˈlaɪtɪs/ *n* zapalenie *n* migdałków

too /tuː/ *adv* [1] (also) też, także; **have you been to India** ~ ? (like me) czy ty też byłeś w Indiach?; (as well as other countries) czy byłeś też w Indiach? [2] (excessively) za, zbyt; ~ **big** za duży; **I ate** ~ **much** za dużo zjadłem; **you're** ~ **kind!** to zbytnia uprzejmość; **I'm not** ~ **sure about that** nie jestem tego zbyt pewien

tool /tuːl/ *n* narzędzie *n*

tool bar *n* Comput pasek *m* narzędziowy

toolbox /ˈtuːlbɒks/ *n* skrzynka *f* na narzędzia

tool kit *n* komplet *m* narzędzi

tooth /tuːθ/ *n* ząb *m*; **set of teeth** (one's own) uzębienie; (false) sztuczna szczęka

toothache /ˈtuːθeɪk/ *n* ból *m* zęba; **I have (a)** ~ boli mnie ząb

toothbrush /ˈtuːθbrʌʃ/ *n* szczoteczka *f* do zębów

toothpaste /ˈtuːθpeɪst/ *n* pasta *f* do zębów

toothpick /ˈtuːθpɪk/ *n* wykałaczka *f*

top¹ /tɒp/ [I] *n* [1] (of ladder, stairs, wave, wall) szczyt *m*; (of hill, mountain) szczyt *m*, wierzchołek *m*; (of head) czubek *m*; (of tree) wierzchołek *m*, czubek *m*; (of page, list) góra *f*; (of garden, field) (drugi) koniec *m*; (of box, chest) wierzch *m*; (surface) powierzchnia *f*; (of vegetable) nać *f*; **at the** ~ **of sth** u góry czegoś *[page, scale]*; na początku czegoś *[list]*; na końcu czegoś *[street]*; na szczycie czegoś *[hill]*; u szczytu czegoś *[stairs]*; **at the** ~ **of the building** na ostatnim piętrze; **at the** ~ **of the table** na honorowym miejscu [2] (highest, position) **to aim for the** ~ mierzyć bardzo wysoko; **to get to** or **make it to the** ~ zrobić wielką karierę; **to be** ~ **of the class** być najlepszym w klasie [3] (cap, lid) (of pen) skuwka *f*; (of bottle) zakrętka *f*; (with serrated edge) kapsel *m*; (of paint-tin, jar, box) wieczko *n*; (of saucepan) pokrywka *f* [4] (item of clothing) góra *f*

[II] *adj* [1] (highest) *[floor, step, shelf, gear]* najwyższy; *[layer, coat]* wierzchni; *[concern]* główny; *[priority]*

absolutny; **in the** ~ **left-hand corner** w lewym górnym rogu; **to get** ~ **marks** Sch dostawać najlepsze stopnie [2] (furthest away) *[bed, part, section]* ostatni [3] (leading) *[authority, agency]* największy; *[adviser]* główny; *[job]* najważniejszy

[III] *vt* [1] (head) znaleźć, -jdować się na czele (czegoś) *[pools, charts]* [2] (exceed) przewyższ|yć, -ać *[sum, figure]* [3] (finish off) zwieńcz|yć, -ać *[church]* (**with sth** czymś); zakończyć *[performance]* (**with sth** czymś); Culin pokry|ć, -wać *[cake]* (**with sth** czymś)

[IV] **on top of** *prep phr* [1] na (czymś) *[cupboard, fridge, layer]* [2] (in addition to) jako dodatek do (czegoś) *[salary, workload]*

■ **top up**: dopełni|ć -ać *[tank, glass]*

[IDIOMS] **on** ~ **of all this, to** ~ **it all** do tego wszystkiego; (after misfortune) na domiar złego; **from** ~ **to bottom** *[torn, zipped, drawn]* z góry do dołu; **to be over the** ~ or **OTT** infml *[reaction, comment]* być przesadnym; *[person]* przesadzać; **to feel on** ~ **of the world** być w siódmym niebie; **to shout at the** ~ **of one's voice** krzyczeć na cały głos or na całe gardło

top² /tɒp/ *n* (toy) bączek *m*

topaz /ˈtəʊpæz/ *n* topaz *m*

top hat *n* cylinder *m*

top-heavy /ˌtɒpˈhevi/ *adj* źle wyważony

topic /ˈtɒpɪk/ *n* temat *m*

topical /ˈtɒpɪkl/ *adj* *[issue, question]* aktualny; *[debate, play]* dotyczący aktualnych problemów

topless /ˈtɒplɪs/ *adj* *[model, waitress]* w stroju topless

top-level /ˌtɒpˈlevl/ *adj* *[talks, negotiations]* na najwyższym szczeblu

top management *n* ścisłe kierownictwo *n*

top-of-the-range /ˌtɒpəvðəˈreɪndʒ/ *adj* *[model]* najwyższej klasy

topping /ˈtɒpɪŋ/ *n* (of jam, cream) przybranie *n*; (icing) lukier *m*

topple /ˈtɒpl/ [I] *vt* przewr|ócić, -acać *[object]*; s|powodować zawalenie się (czegoś) *[building]*

[II] *vi* (sway) *[vase, pile of books]* za|chwiać się; (fall) (also ~ **over**) *[person, vase]* przewr|ócić, -acać się

top-ranking /ˌtɒpˈræŋkɪŋ/ *adj* wysoko postawiony; *[player]* wysoko notowany

top secret *adj* ściśle tajny

topsy-turvy /ˌtɒpsɪˈtɜːvɪ/ infml [I] *adj* postawiony na głowie infml

[II] *adv* do góry nogami infml

torch /tɔːtʃ/ *n* [1] GB (flashlight) latarka *f* [2] (burning) pochodnia *f*

torment [I] /ˈtɔːment/ *n* udręka *f*

[II] /tɔːˈment/ *vt* dręczyć

tormentor /tɔːˈmentə(r)/ *n* dręczyciel *m*, -ka *f*

torn /tɔːn/ *adj* rozdarty

tornado /tɔːˈneɪdəʊ/ *n* tornado *n*, trąba *f* powietrzna

torpedo /tɔːˈpiːdəʊ/ *n* torpeda *f*

torrent /'tɒrənt, US 'tɔːr-/ n strugi f pl; fig (of abuse, words) potok m fig

torrential /tə'renʃl/ adj [rain] ulewny

torrid /'tɒrɪd, US 'tɔːr-/ adj [weather] upalny, skwarny; [sun] palący; [climate] gorący

torso /'tɔːsəʊ/ n tułów m

tortoise /'tɔːtəs/ n żółw m lądowy

tortoiseshell /'tɔːtəsʃel/ n (shell) szylkret m

tortuous /'tɔːtʃʊəs/ adj [road] kręty; fig [explanation] pokrętny; [process, plot] zawiły

torture /'tɔːtʃə(r)/ **[]** n (infliction of pain) tortury f pl; fig katusze plt

[] vt torturować; fig dręczyć

Tory /'tɔːrɪ/ n GB torys m

toss /tɒs, US tɔːs/ **[]** n rzut m; **with a disdainful ~ of one's head** pogardliwie odrzucając głowę (do tyłu); **to decide sth on the ~ of a coin** rzucić monetę, żeby o czymś zdecydować

[] vt ① (throw) rzuc|ić, -ać [ball, stick]; rzuc|ić, -ać (czymś) [dice]; przerzuc|ić, -ać na drugą stronę [pancake]; wy|mieszać [salad]; **to ~ a coin** rzucić monetę ② (throw back) [animal] rzuc|ić, -ać (czymś) [head, mane]; **to ~ one's head** [person] odrzucić głowę (do tyłu) ③ [horse] zrzuc|ić, -ać [rider] ④ [wind] targać (czymś) [branches, trees]

[] vi ① (turn restlessly) [person] przewracać się; **to ~ and turn all night** przewracać się z boku na bok całą noc ② (flip a coin) [referee] rzuc|ić, -ać monetę; **to ~ for the first turn** rzutem monetą ustalać, kto będzie zaczynał

■ **toss off**: ~ [sth] off infml mach|nąć, -ać infml [letter, article]

■ **toss out**: ¶ ~ [sth] out wyrzuc|ić, -ać [empty bottles, newspaper] ¶ ~ [sb] out wyrzuc|ić, -ać (from sth z czegoś)

tot /tɒt/ n ① infml (toddler) brzdąc m infml ② GB (of whisky, rum) kapka f

total /'təʊtl/ **[]** n (of figures) (całkowita) suma f; (of people, things) ogólna liczba f; **in ~** ogółem

[] adj ① (added together) [cost, amount, profit] całkowity ② (absolute) [ignorance, silence] zupełny; [war] totalny; [effect] ogólny

[] vt ① (add up) zsumow|ać, -ywać [figures] ② (reach) wyn|ieść, -osić [sum]

totalitarian /ˌtəʊtælɪ'teərɪən/ **[]** n zwolenni|k m, -czka f totalitaryzmu

[] adj totalitarny

totally /'təʊtəlɪ/ adv całkowicie

totem /'təʊtəm/ n (pole) totem m; (symbol) symbol m

totter /'tɒtə(r)/ vi [person, child] iść chwiejnym krokiem; (drunkenly) zataczać się; [building, pile of books, government] za|chwiać się also fig

touch /tʌtʃ/ **[]** n ① (physical contact) dotknięcie n, dotyk m; **the ~ of her hand** dotyk jej dłoni ② (sense) dotyk m ③ (style, skill) wyczucie n; **the ~ of a master** ręka mistrza; **to lose one's ~**

stracić wyczucie ④ (little) **a ~ more/less (sth)** troszkę więcej/mniej (czegoś) ⑤ (communication) **to get/stay in ~ with sb** nawiązać kontakt/pozostawać w kontakcie z kimś; **he's out of ~ with reality** jest oderwany od rzeczywistości ⑥ Sport aut m

[] vt ① dot|knąć, -ykać (kogoś/czegoś) [object, person]; przylegać do (czegoś) [garden, property, land]; **to ~ sb on the shoulder** dotknąć ramienia kogoś; **I never ~ alcohol** nie biorę alkoholu do ust ② (affect) dotyczyć (czegoś); (move) porusz|yć, -ać; (with sadness, sympathy) wzrusz|yć, -ać; (adversely) dot|knąć, -ykać [person]

[] vi [wires, hands] zetknąć, stykać się

■ **touch down**: ① [plane] wy|lądować ② Sport (in rugby) zdoby|ć, -wać przyłożenie

■ **touch (up)on**: porusz|yć -ać [subject]

(IDIOMS:) **he is a soft ~** infml łatwo go naciągnąć infml; **it's ~ and go** na dwoje babka wróżyła

touchdown /'tʌtʃdaʊn/ n ① (of plane) lądowanie n ② Sport przyłożenie n

touched /tʌtʃt/ adj ① (emotionally) wzruszony ② infml (mad) szurnięty infml

touching /'tʌtʃɪŋ/ adj wzruszający

touch line n Sport linia f boczna

touchpad /'tʌtʃpæd/ n panel m dotykowy

touch screen n ekran m dotykowy

touch-tone /'tʌtʃtəʊn/ adj US ~ **telephone** telefon z klawiaturą

touch-type /'tʌtʃtaɪp/ vi pisać na maszynie metodą bezwzrokową

touchy /'tʌtʃɪ/ adj [person, subject] drażliwy

tough /tʌf/ **[]** adj ① (ruthless) [businessman, character, measures] twardy; [criminal] bezwzględny; [penalty, criticism] surowy; **a ~ guy** infml twardziel infml ② (difficult) trudny ③ (robust) [person, child, plant] odporny; [material] mocny; [skin, vegetable, meat] twardy ④ (rough) [area, place] niebezpieczny

[] excl infml trudno!

toughen /'tʌfn/ vt ① wzm|ocnić, -acniać [material, wall]; za|hartować [glass, person, character]; uelastyczni|ć, -ać [skin] ② (also ~ **up**) zaostrz|yć, -ać [law]

toupee /'tuːpeɪ, US tuː'peɪ/ n peruczka f, tupet m

tour /tʊə(r), tɔː(r)/ **[]** n ① (of country, city) wycieczka f; (longer) podróż f; (of building, castle) zwiedzanie n ② (by band) tournée n inv; Sport cykl m zawodów

[] vt ① zwiedz|ić, -ać [building, country, gallery] ② [band] odby|ć, -wać tournée po (czymś) [country]

[] vi [orchestra] odby|ć, -wać tournée

touring /'tʊərɪŋ, 'tɔː-/ n ① podróżowanie n; (in city) zwiedzanie n ② (by band, theatre company) tournée n inv

tourism /'tʊərɪzəm, 'tɔːr-/ n turystyka f

tourist /'tʊərɪst, 'tɔːr-/ n turyst|a m, -ka f

tourist class n klasa f turystyczna

tourist (information) office *n* biuro *n* informacji turystycznej

tourist trap *n* mekka *f* turystów

touristy /ˈtʊərɪstɪ, ˈtɔːr-/ *adj* infml nastawiony na turystów

tournament /ˈtɔːnəmənt, US ˈtɜːrn-/ *n* turniej *m*

tousle /ˈtaʊzl/ **[I]** *vt* z|mierzwić *[hair]*

> **[II] tousled** *pp adj [hair]* potargany; *[person, appearance]* niechlujny

tout /taʊt/ *n* **[1]** GB (selling tickets) konik *m* infml **[2]** (soliciting custom) naganiacz *m* infml **[3]** (racing) sprzedający *m* typy *(na wyścigach konnych)*

tow /təʊ/ **[I]** *n* (rope, cable) hol *m*; (act of towing) holowanie *n*

> **[II]** *vt* holować *[vehicle, boat]*; ciągnąć *[caravan, trailer]*

■ **tow away**: ~ **[sth] away** *[police, recovery service]* od|holować

toward(s) /təˈwɔːd(z), tɔːd(z)/ *prep* **[1]** (in the direction of) w kierunku (kogoś/czegoś); ~ **the east** na wschód; **he was standing with his back** ~ **me** stał odwrócony do mnie tyłem; ~ **the end of sth** pod koniec czegoś *[day, month, life]* **[2]** (in relation to) wobec (kogoś/czegoś); **to be friendly/hostile** ~ **sb** zachowywać się przyjaźnie/wrogo wobec kogoś **[3]** (as a contribution) na (coś); **the money will go** ~ **the cost of a new roof** pieniądze pójdą na nowy dach

towel /ˈtaʊəl/ *n* (for hands, body) ręcznik *m*; (for dishes) ścierka *f*

towelling /ˈtaʊəlɪŋ/ *n* tkanina *f* frotté

tower /ˈtaʊə(r)/ **[I]** *n* wieża *f*

> **[II]** *vi* **to** ~ **above** or **over sth** górować nad czymś *[village, countryside]*
>
> (IDIOMS) **to be a** ~ **of strength** być twardym jak stal

tower block *n* GB wieżowiec *m*

towering /ˈtaʊərɪŋ/ *adj [cliff, building]* wyniosły

town /taʊn/ *n* miasto *n*; (small) miasteczko *n*; **to go into** ~ wybrać się do miasta

> (IDIOMS) **to go to** ~ **on sth** wykosztować się na coś *[decor, catering]*; rozdmuchać coś infml *[story, scandal]*; **he's the talk of the** ~ wszyscy o nim mówią

town-and-country planning /ˌtaʊnənˌkʌntrɪˈplænɪŋ/ *n* planowanie *n* przestrzenne

town centre GB, **town center** US *n* centrum *n* miasta

town council *n* GB rada *f* miejska

town hall *n* ratusz *m*

town house *n* (as opposed to country seat) rezydencja *f* miejska; (urban terrace) dom *m* jednorodzinny *(w zabudowie szeregowej)*

town planning *n* GB urbanistyka *f*

township /ˈtaʊnʃɪp/ *n* społeczność *f* miejska; (in South Africa) getto *n* ludności kolorowej

towpath /ˈtəʊpɑːθ, US -pæθ/ *n* ścieżka *f* holownicza

tow truck *n* samochód *m* pomocy drogowej

toxic /ˈtɒksɪk/ *adj* toksyczny

toxin /ˈtɒksɪn/ *n* toksyna *f*

toy /tɔɪ/ **[I]** *n* zabawka *f*

> **[II]** *vi* **to** ~ **with sth** bawić się czymś *[object]*; rozważać coś *[idea]*; **to** ~ **with one's food** ledwie skubnąć jedzenia

toy boy *n* GB infml młody kochanek *m*

toyshop /ˈtɔɪʃɒp/ *n* sklep *m* z zabawkami

trace /treɪs/ **[I]** *n* ślad *m*

> **[II]** *vt* **[1]** (locate) odna|leźć, -jdować *[person, weapon, car, file]*; z|lokalizować *[fault]*; ustal|ić, -ać *[cause]*; **the call was** ~**d to a London number** ustalono, że telefonowano z londyńskiego numeru **[2]** (also ~ **back**) wyw|ieść, -odzić *[ancestry, origin]* (**to sth** od czegoś) **[3]** (draw) wykreśl|ić, -ać; (copy) przekalkow|ać, -ywać *[map, outline]*

tracing paper *n* kalka *f* kreślarska

track /træk/ **[I]** *n* **[1]** (print) (of person, vehicle, animal) ślad *m* **[2]** (course, trajectory) (of person) trop *m* also fig; (of missile, aircraft) tor *m*; **to keep** ~ **of sth/sb** *[person]* śledzić coś *[developments, events]*; śledzić przebieg czegoś *[conversation]*; *[police]* mieć kogoś na oku *[criminal]*; **to lose** ~ **of sb/sth** stracić z oczu kogoś/coś *[friend, aircraft]*; zgubić trop kogoś *[suspect]*; pogubić się w czymś *[conversation]*; **to lose** ~ **of (the) time** stracić poczucie czasu **[3]** (path) ścieżka *f*; (rough road) droga *f* **[4]** Sport (racing, speedway) tor *m*; (athletics) bieżnia *f* **[5]** (railtrack) tor *m* (kolejowy); US (platform) peron *m*; **to leave the** ~**(s)** *[train]* wykoleić się **[6]** Mus (on record, tape, CD) utwór *m* **[7]** US Sch (stream) grupa *f* *(utworzona z uczniów o określonym poziomie)*

> **[II]** *vt* wy|tropić *[person, animal]*; śledzić tor (czegoś) *[rocket, plane, comet]*

■ **track down**: wytropić *[criminal, animal]*; odna|leźć, -jdywać *[file, person]*

tracker ball *n* manipulator *m* kulowy

tracker dog *n* pies *m* tropiciel

track record *n* (of government, company) osiągnięcia *n pl*; (of professional person) życiorys *m* zawodowy

track shoe *n* kolec *m*

tracksuit /ˈtræksuːt, -sjuːt/ *n* dres *m*

tract[1] /trækt/ *n* **[1]** (of land) obszar *m* **[2]** Anat **respiratory** ~ drogi *plt* oddechowe

tract[2] /trækt/ *n* (pamphlet) traktat *m*

tractor /ˈtræktə(r)/ *n* traktor *m*

trade /treɪd/ **[I]** *n* **[1]** (activity) handel *m* (**in sth** czymś); **to do a good** ~ prowadzić korzystne interesy handlowe **[2]** (sector of industry) branża *f* **[3]** (profession) zawód *m*; (manual) fach *m*; **by** ~ z zawodu

> **[II]** *vt* wymieni|ć, -ać (**for sth** na coś)
>
> **[III]** *vi* handlować

■ **trade in**: da|ć, -wać w rozliczeniu; **he** ~**d in**

his Jeep for a Mercedes kupił mercedesa, w rozliczeniu oddając swojego jeepa

trade fair *n* targi *plt* (handlowe)

trade-in /ˈtreɪdɪn/ *n* wymiana *f* używanego towaru na nowy za dopłatą

trademark /ˈtreɪdmɑːk/ *n* znak *m* firmowy

trade name *n* nazwa *f* handlowa

trade-off /ˈtreɪdɒf/ *n* kompromis *m*

trader /ˈtreɪdə(r)/ *n* ①① (shopkeeper, stallholder) handlowiec *m* ② (at stock exchange) spekulant *m* giełdowy

tradesman's entrance *n* wejście *n* służbowe

Trades Union Congress, TUC *n* GB Kongres *m* Związków Zawodowych

trade union *n* związek *m* zawodowy

trade union member *n* związkowiec *m*

trading /ˈtreɪdɪŋ/ *n* ① (business) handel *m* ② (at stock exchange) transakcje *f pl*

trading estate *n* GB strefa *f* przemysłowa

tradition /trəˈdɪʃn/ *n* tradycja *f*

traditional /trəˈdɪʃənl/ *adj* tradycyjny

traditionalist /trəˈdɪʃənəlɪst/ 🞵 *n* tradycjonalist|a *m*, -ka *f*
🞶 *adj* tradycjonalistyczny

traffic /ˈtræfɪk/ 🞵 *n* ① ruch *m*; Aut ruch *m* uliczny ② (in drugs, arms, slaves, goods) handel *m* (**in sth** czymś)
🞶 *vi* **to ~ in sth** handlować czymś *[drugs, arms, stolen goods]*

traffic calming *n* ograniczenie *n* natężenia ruchu

traffic jam *n* korek *m*

trafficker /ˈtræfɪkə(r)/ *n* handla|rz *m*, -rka *f*

traffic lights *npl* sygnalizacja *f* świetlna; światła *n pl* infml

traffic warden *n* GB funkcjonariusz *m* kontrolujący, funkcjonariuszka *f* kontrolująca prawidłowość parkowania

tragedy /ˈtrædʒədɪ/ *n* tragedia *f*

tragic /ˈtrædʒɪk/ *adj* tragiczny

trail /treɪl/ 🞵 *n* ① (path) szlak *m* ② (of dust, slime, blood) smuga *f* ③ (trace) trop *m*
🞶 *vt* ① (follow) *[animal, person]* podąż|yć, -ać tropem (kogoś/czegoś); *[car]* jechać za (czymś) ② (drag) ciągnąć za sobą
🞷 *vi* ① *[garment, hair]* opadać; *[smoke]* snuć się; *[plant]* płożyć się ② (trudge) *[person]* wlec się ③ (lag)
to ~ badly *[racehorse, team]* wlec się w ogonie;
our team were ~ing by 3 goals to 1 nasza drużyna przegrywała trzy do jednego

trail bike *n* motocykl *m* terenowy

trailblazer /ˈtreɪlbleɪzə(r)/ *n* pionier *m*

trailer /ˈtreɪlə(r)/ *n* ① (vehicle, boat) przyczepa *f* ② US (caravan) przyczepa *f* kempingowa ③ (for film) zwiastun *m*

trailer park *n* US kemping *m* (karawaningowy)

train /treɪn/ 🞵 *n* ① (means of transport) pociąg *m*; **on** or **in the ~** w pociągu; **a ~ to London** pociąg do Londynu; **to go to Warsaw by ~** jechać

pociągiem do Warszawy ② (succession) (of events) łańcuch *m*; **a ~ of thought** bieg myśli ③ (procession) (of animals, vehicles, people) sznur *m* ④ (on dress) tren *m*
🞶 *vt* ① (instruct) wy|szkolić *[staff, worker, soldier]*; wy|kształcić *[engineer, doctor, teacher]*; wy|trenować *[athlete, player]*; wy|tresować *[circus animal, dog]* ② (aim) wy|mierzyć z (czegoś) *[gun]* (**on sb/sth** w kogoś/coś)
🞷 *vi* ① (for profession) *[student]* kształcić się; *[worker]* szkolić się; **he's ~ing to be a doctor** kształci się na lekarza ② Sport trenować

trained /treɪnd/ *adj [staff, worker]* wykwalifikowany; *[professional]* wykształcony; *[voice]* szkolony; *[singer, actor]* zawodowy; *[animal]* tresowany

trainee /ˌtreɪˈniː/ *n* praktykant *m*, -ka *f*

trainer /ˈtreɪnə(r)/ *n* ① (of athlete, horse) trener *m*, -ka *f*; (of circus animal, dogs) treser *m*, -ka *f* ② GB (shoe) ≈ adidas *m*

training /ˈtreɪnɪŋ/ *n* ① (instruction) szkolenie *n*; (as doctor, engineer) kształcenie *n* ② Sport trening *m*

training college *n* GB wyższa szkoła *f* zawodowa; (for teachers) kolegium *n* nauczycielskie

training course *n* szkolenie *n*

train spotter *n* hobbista zapisujący numery widzianych lokomotyw

trait /treɪ, treɪt/ *n* cecha *f*

traitor /ˈtreɪtə(r)/ *n* zdraj|ca *m*, -czyni *f* (**to sth** czegoś)

tram /træm/ *n* GB tramwaj *m*

tramp /træmp/ *n* (vagrant) włóczęga *m*; (urban) kloszard *m*

trample /ˈtræmpl/ *vt [person]* po|deptać; *[crowd, animal]* s|tratować

trampoline /ˈtræmpəliːn/ *n* batut *m*

trance /trɑːns, US træns/ *n* trans *m* also fig; **to go into a ~** wpaść w trans

tranquil /ˈtræŋkwɪl/ *adj* spokojny

tranquillizer, tranquilizer US /ˈtræŋkwɪlaɪzə(r)/ *n* środek *m* uspokajający

transaction /trænˈzækʃn/ *n* transakcja *f*

transatlantic /ˌtrænzətˈlæntɪk/ *adj [flight, crossing]* transatlantycki; *[countries]* zaatlantycki

transcend /trænˈsend/ *vt* (go beyond) wykr|oczyć, -aczać poza (coś); (surpass) przewyższ|yć, -ać

transcribe /trænˈskraɪb/ *vt* spis|ać, -ywać; Mus dokon|ać, -ywać transkrypcji (czegoś)

transcript /ˈtrænskrɪpt/ *n* ① (copy) kopia *f* ② US Univ ≈ wyciąg *m* z indeksu; Sch wykaz *m* ocen

transfer 🞵 /ˈtrænsfɜː(r)/ *n* ① (of power, skills) przekazanie *n*; (of employee, patient, civil servant) przeniesienie *n*; Sport transfer *m*; (telegraphic order) przelew *m*; (of property, debt) cesja *f* ② GB (on skin, china, paper) kalkomania *f*; (on T-shirt) nadruk *m*
🞶 /trænsˈfɜː(r)/ *vt* ① (move) przen|ieść, -osić *[data, prisoner, office, employee]* ② (hand over) przekaz|ać, -ywać *[land, power]*; przel|ać, -ewać *[money]*;

dokon|ać, -ywać cesji (czegoś) Jur *[property]*; przen|ieść, -osić *[allegiance, support, affections]*

III /træns'fɜ:(r)/ *vi* [1] (relocate) *[employee, player, student]* przen|ieść, -osić się [2] *[traveller]* przesi|ąść, -adać się

transferable /træns'fɜ:rəbl/ *adj [pension]* z możliwością przekazania; (in finance) zbywalny

transferred charge call *n* rozmowa *f* „R" *(płatna przez wzywanego)*

transfixed /træns'fɪkst/ *adj* (fascinated) urzeczony; (horrified) sparaliżowany

transform /træns'fɔ:m/ *vt* (change) odmieni|ć, -ać *[person, life, room]*; przekształc|ić, -ać *[equation, expression]*; (of electricity) prze|transformować

transformation /ˌtrænsfə'meɪʃn/ *n* zmiana *f*; (in person) przemiana *f*; (economic, political) transformacja *f*

transformer /træns'fɔ:mə(r)/ *n* transformator *m*

transfusion /træns'fju:ʒn/ *n* transfuzja *f*

transgenic /træns'dʒenɪk/ *adj* transgeniczny

transient /'trænzɪənt, US 'trænʃnt/ *adj [phase, population]* przejściowy; *[emotion, beauty]* przemijający

transistor /træn'zɪstə(r), -'sɪstə(r)/ *n* tranzystor *m*

transit /'trænzɪt, -sɪt/ *n* (of goods, people) przewóz *m*; (through a country) tranzyt *m*; **in** ~ *[goods]* w trakcie przewozu; *[people]* przejazdem

transition /træn'zɪʃn, -'sɪʃn/ *n* przejście *n*

transitional /træn'zɪʃənl, -'sɪʃənl/ *adj* przejściowy

transitive /'trænzətɪv/ *adj* przechodni

translate /trænz'leɪt/ **I** *vt* prze|tłumaczyć

II *vi [person]* tłumaczyć; *[phrase]* tłumaczyć się

translation /trænz'leɪʃn/ *n* tłumaczenie *n*

translator /trænz'leɪtə(r)/ *n* tłumacz *m*, -ka *f*

transmission /trænz'mɪʃn/ *n* [1] (of data, energy, knowledge, message) przekazywanie *n*; (of energy, light) przesyłanie *n* [2] (broadcast) transmisja *f* [3] Aut (gearbox) skrzynia *f* biegów

transmit /trænz'mɪt/ **I** *vt* (send, convey) przen|ieść, -osić *[disease]*; przekaz|ać, -ywać *[energy, message]*; transmitować *[programme]*

II *vi* nada|ć, -wać

transmitter /trænz'mɪtə(r)/ *n* [1] (in telecommunications) wkładka *f* mikrofonowa [2] (in radio, TV) przekaźnik *m*

transparency /træns'pærənsɪ/ *n* (slide) przezrocze *n*; (for overhead projector) foliogram *m*

transparent /træns'pærənt/ *adj [glass]* przezroczysty; *[water]* przejrzysty

transplant **I** /'trænspla:nt, -plænt/ *n* (operation, organ) przeszczep *m*

II /træns'pla:nt, US -'plænt/ *vt* przeszczepi|ć, -ać *[organ]*

transport **I** /'trænspɔ:t/ *n* transport *m*; **air/road** ~ transport powietrzny/samochodowy; **to travel by public** ~ korzystać z komunikacji miejskiej

II /træns'pɔ:t/ *vt* przew|ieźć, -ozić *[passengers, goods]*; prze|transportować *[prisoner]*

transportation /ˌtrænspɔ:'teɪʃn/ *n* US transport *m*

transpose /træn'spəʊz/ *vt* prze|transponować

transsexual /trænz'sekʃʊəl/ **I** *n* transseksualist|a *m*, -ka *f*

II *adj* transseksualny

transvestite /trænz'vestaɪt/ *n* transwestyt|a *m*, -ka *f*

trap /træp/ **I** *n* [1] (snare) pułapka *f* also fig [2] (vehicle) dwukółka *f*

II *vt* [1] z|łapać w pułapkę *[animal, person]* [2] (catch) uwięzić *[person]*; zatrzym|ać, -ywać *[heat]*; **to** ~ **one's finger in a door** przytrzasnąć sobie palec w drzwiach

trapdoor /'træpdɔ:(r)/ *n* klapa *f*

trash /træʃ/ *n* [1] US (refuse) śmieci *m pl* [2] infml (goods) chłam *m* infml [3] infml (nonsense) bzdury *f pl* infml; (literary, artistic) szmira *f* infml

trashcan /'træʃkæn/ *n* US kosz *m* na śmieci

trashy /'træʃɪ/ *adj* infml *[novel, firm]* szmirowaty infml; *[goods]* tandetny infml

trauma /'trɔ:mə, US 'traʊ-/ *n* uraz *m*

traumatic /trɔ:'mætɪk, US traʊ-/ *adj* traumatyczny; fig szokujący

traumatize /'trɔ:mətaɪz, US 'traʊ-/ *vt* s|powodować uraz u (kogoś)

travel /'trævl/ **I** *n* podróżowanie *n*; (trip) podróż *f*; **foreign** ~ podróże zagraniczne

II *vt* przeby|ć, -wać *[distance]*; przemierz|yć, -ać *[country, road]*

III *vi* [1] (journey) *[person]* podróżować; **he** ~**s widely** on dużo podróżuje; **to** ~ **abroad/to Brazil** jechać za granicę/do Brazylii [2] (move) *[person, car, plane, object]* poruszać się; *[news, light, sound, wave]* roz|ejść, -chodzić się; **to** ~ **back in time** cofać się w czasie [3] **to** ~ **well** *[cheese, wine]* dobrze znosić transport

travel agency *n* biuro *n* podróży

travel agent *n* pracowni|k *m*, -czka *f* biura podróży

travel card *n* GB bilet *m* wieloprzejazdowy

travel insurance *n* ubezpieczenie *n* na czas podróży

traveller GB, **traveler** US /'trævlə(r)/ *n* [1] podróżn|y *m*, -a *f*; (to distant places) podróżni|k *m*, -czka *f* [2] GB (gypsy) koczownik *m* fig

traveller's cheque GB, **traveler's check** US *n* czek *m* podróżny

travelling GB, **traveling** US /'trævlɪŋ/ **I** *n* (activity) podróżowanie *n*; (on single occasion) podróż *f*; **to go** ~ wybrać się w podróż; **the job involves** ~ w tej pracy trzeba podróżować

II *adj* [1] (mobile) *[actor, company, circus]* wędrowny [2] *[bag, rug]* podróżny; ~ **companion** towarzysz podróży; ~ **conditions** (on road) warunki na drogach ③ *[scholarship]* wyjazdowy; ~ **expenses** koszty podróży; ~ **allowance** dieta

travelling salesman *n* przedstawiciel *m* handlowy

travel-sick /ˈtrævlsɪk/ *adj* **to be** or **get** ~ cierpieć na chorobę lokomocyjną

trawler /ˈtrɔːlə(r)/ *n* trawler *m*

tray /treɪ/ *n* (for serving) taca *f*; (for baking) blacha *f*

treacherous /ˈtretʃərəs/ *adj* zdradziecki

treachery /ˈtretʃərɪ/ *n* zdrada *f*

treacle /ˈtriːkl/ *n* GB (black) melasa *f*; (golden syrup) syrop *m* z melasy

tread /tred/ **I** *n* (of tyre) (pattern) bieżnik *m*; (outer surface) powierzchnia *f* toczna

II *vt* kroczyć (czymś) *[path, road]*; przemierz|yć, -ać *[area]*; **to** ~. **water** pływać w miejscu; fig dreptać w miejscu fig

III *vi* (walk) stąpać; **to** ~ **on sth** (walk) stąpać po czymś; (squash) nadepnąć na coś; **to** ~ **carefully** fig postępować ostrożnie

treason /ˈtriːzn/ *n* zdrada *f*; **high** ~ zdrada stanu

treasure /ˈtreʒə(r)/ **I** *n* skarb *m* also fig

II *vt* ① (cherish) przechowywać pieczołowicie *[keepsake, gift]*; pielęgnować *[memories]* ② (prize) cenić wysoko *[independence, friendship, object]*

treasurer /ˈtreʒərə(r)/ *n* ① (on committee) skarbnik *m* ② US (in company) dyrektor *m* finansowy

Treasury /ˈtreʒərɪ/ *n* (also ~ **Department**) ministerstwo *n* finansów

treat /triːt/ **I** *n* (pleasure) przyjemność *f*; (food) smakołyk *m*; **I took them to the museum as a** ~ zabrałem ich do muzeum, żeby zrobić im przyjemność; **it's my** ~ infml ja płacę; (for food, drink) ja stawiam infml

II *vt* ① (act towards, handle) po|traktować *[person, animal, topic]*; ob|ejść, -chodzić się z (czymś) *[object]*; **to** ~ **sb well/badly** traktować kogoś dobrze/źle; **they** ~ **the house like a hotel** traktują dom jak hotel ② Med leczyć *[patient, disease]*; udziel|ić, -ać pomocy medycznej (komuś) *[casualty]* ③ (pay for) za|fundować (komuś) *[person]*; **to** ~ **sb to sth** fundować komuś coś; **to** ~ **oneself to sth** sprawić sobie coś

treatment /ˈtriːtmənt/ *n* ① (of person) traktowanie *n* ② Med leczenie *n*

treaty /ˈtriːtɪ/ *n* traktat *m*

treble /ˈtrebl/ **I** *adj* potrójny

II *vt* potr|oić, -ajać

III *vi* potr|oić, -ajać się

tree /triː/ *n* drzewo *n*; **an apple/a pear** ~ jabłoń/grusza

tree stump *n* pniak *m*

treetop /ˈtriːtɒp/ *n* wierzchołek *m* drzewa

tree trunk *n* pień *m* (drzewa)

trek /trek/ **I** *n* (long journey) wędrówka *f*; (laborious) wyprawa *f*

II *vi* wędrować

trekking /ˈtrekɪn/ *n* wędrówka *f*; **to go** ~ wybrać się na wędrówkę

tremble /ˈtrembl/ *vi* za|drżeć

tremendous /trɪˈmendəs/ *adj* *[crowd, success, effort]* olbrzymi; *[storm, explosion]* potężny

tremor /ˈtremə(r)/ *n* (in body, voice) drżenie *n*; (of delight, fear) dreszcz *m*; (in earthquake) wstrząs *m*

trench /trentʃ/ *n* rów *m*; Mil okop *m*

trench coat *n* trencz *m*

trend /trend/ *n* ① (tendency) tendencja *f* ② (fashion) trend *m*; **to set a new** ~ wylansować nową modę

trendsetter /ˈtrendsetə(r)/ *n* prekursor *m*, -ka *f*; **to be a** ~ lansować modę

trendy /ˈtrendɪ/ *adj* modny

trespass /ˈtrespəs/ *vi* wkr|oczyć, -aczać na teren prywatny; **'no** ~**ing!'** „wstęp wzbroniony!"

trespasser /ˈtrespəsə(r)/ *n* intruz *m*

trial /ˈtraɪəl/ **I** *n* ① (in court) rozprawa *f*, proces *m*; **to go on** ~, **to stand** ~ stanąć przed sądem ② (test) próba *f*; **on** ~ na próbę; **by** ~ **and error** metodą prób i błędów ③ Sport (in football) sprawdzian *m*; (horse, dog) zawody *plt* kwalifikacyjne ④ (trouble) udręka *f*; (less strong) problem *m*; **to be a** ~ *[person]* być uciążliwym

II *adj [period, separation]* próbny; **on a** ~ **basis** tytułem próby

trial run *n* próba *f*; **to take a car for a** ~ odbyć jazdę próbną samochodem

triangle /ˈtraɪæŋgl/ *n* trójkąt *m*

tribe /traɪb/ *n* plemię *n*

tribunal /traɪˈbjuːnl/ *n* trybunał *m*

tributary /ˈtrɪbjʊtərɪ, US -terɪ/ *n* dopływ *m*

tribute /ˈtrɪbjuːt/ *n* hołd *m*; **to pay** ~ **to sb/sth** złożyć hołd komuś/czemuś; **as a** ~ **to sb/sth** na cześć kogoś/czegoś; **floral** ~ (spray) wiązanka (kwiatów); (wreath) wieniec

trick /trɪk/ **I** *n* ① (to deceive) podstęp *m*; **a** ~ **of the light** złudzenie optyczne; **to play a** ~ **on sb** spłatać komuś figla ② (by magician, animal) sztuczka *f*; **to do** ~**s** robić sztuczki ③ (knack, secret) sztuczka *f*; **the** ~ **s of the trade** sekrety zawodowe ④ (in cards) lewa *f*; **to win** or **take a** ~ wziąć lewę

II *adj [photo, shot]* trikowy

III *vt* oszuk|ać, -iwać; **to** ~ **sb into (doing) sth** podstępem skłonić kogoś do (zrobienia) czegoś

[IDIOMS] **that'll do the** ~ to załatwi sprawę

trickle /ˈtrɪkl/ **I** *n* (of liquid, powder) strużka *f*; (of investment, orders) niewielka ilość *f*; (of people) niewielka liczba *f*

II *vi [water, blood]* sączyć się; *[people, orders]* napływać powoli; **to** ~ **down sth** spływać po czymś *[wall, cheek]*; **to** ~ **into sth** *[liquid]* wpływać do czegoś; *[people]* powoli napływać do czegoś

■ **trickle away**: *[water]* wycie|c, -kać; *[people]* roz|ejść, -chodzić się powoli

trick question *n* podchwytliwe pytanie *n*

tricky /'trɪkɪ/ adj ① *[decision, business, task]* trudny; *[problem]* złożony; *[situation]* delikatny ② (wily) *[person]* cwany

tricycle /'traɪsɪkl/ n (cycle) rower m trójkołowy

trifle /'traɪfl/ ❶ n ① (triviality) błahostka f ② GB Culin biszkopt m z owocami i bitą śmietaną
❷ vi **to ~ with sth** bawić się czymś *[feelings, affection]*; **to ~ with sb** stroić sobie żarty z kogoś

trifling /'traɪflɪŋ/ adj *[sum]* drobny; *[detail]* nieistotny

trigger /'trɪgə(r)/ n ① (on gun) spust m; cyngiel m infml ② (on machine) dźwignia f
■ **trigger off**: uruch|omić, -amiać *[alarm]*; wywoł|ać, -ywać *[debate, reaction]*

trilogy /'trɪlədʒɪ/ n trylogia f

trim /trɪm/ ❶ n ① (cut) (of hair, hedge) przycięcie n ② (good condition) forma f; **to keep oneself in ~** zachowywać formę
❷ adj *[appearance, person]* schludny; *[boat, house]* zadbany; *[figure, waistline]* szczupły.
❸ vt ① (cut) przyci|ąć, -nać *[branch, hair, hedge]* ② (reduce) obniż|yć, -ać *[budget, expenditure]* (**by sth** o coś) ③ Culin opraw|ić, -iać *[meat, fish]*; oczy|ścić, -szczać *[vegetable]* ④ (decorate) przyb|rać, -ierać *[tree, furniture]*; wyk|ończyć, -ańczać *[dress, handkerchief]*

trimming /'trɪmɪŋ/ n (on clothing) lamówka f; (on soft furniture) pasmanteria f; **~s** Culin (typowe) dodatki

trinket /'trɪŋkɪt/ n świecidełko n

trio /'triːəʊ/ n trio n

trip /trɪp/ ❶ n ① (journey) podróż f; (excursion) wycieczka f; **a business ~** podróż służbowa ② infml (drug experience) odlot m infml
❷ vt (also **~ over, ~ up**) podci|ąć, -nać *[person]*; (with foot) podstawi|ć, -ać (komuś) nogę
❸ vi ① (also **~ over, ~ up**) (stumble) pot|knąć, -ykać się; **to ~ on** or **over sth** potknąć się o coś ② (walk lightly) **to ~ along** iść lekkim krokiem

triple /'trɪpl/ adj *[thickness, gin]* potrójny; *[champion]* trzykrotny

triplet /'trɪplɪt/ n (child) jedno n z trojaczków

triplicate /'trɪplɪkət/ n trzecia kopia f; **in ~** w trzech egzemplarzach

tripod /'traɪpɒd/ n trójnóg m

triumph /'traɪʌmf/ ❶ n triumf m
❷ vi za|triumfować (**over sb/sth** nad kimś/czymś)

triumphant /traɪ'ʌmfnt/ adj *[person, team]* triumfujący; *[return]* triumfalny; *[success]* absolutny

trivia /'trɪvɪə/ npl drobiazgi m pl

trivial /'trɪvɪəl/ adj *[matter, error]* błahy; *[scale, offence, wage]* niewielki; *[film]* przeciętny; *[argument, conversation, person]* trywialny

trivialize /'trɪvɪəlaɪz/ vt s|trywializować

trolley /'trɒlɪ/ n ① (for shopping, luggage) wózek m; (table) stolik m na kółkach ② US (tram) tramwaj m

trolley bus n trolejbus m

trolley car n US tramwaj m

troop /truːp/ n (of people, animals) gromada f; Mil oddział m

trooper /'truːpə(r)/ n ① Mil (cavalryman) kawalerzysta m; (of armoured unit) pancerny m ② US (policeman) policjant m

trophy /'trəʊfɪ/ n trofeum n

tropic /'trɒpɪk/ n zwrotnik m; **in the ~s** w tropikach

tropical /'trɒpɪkl/ adj tropikalny

trot /trɒt/ ❶ n (of horse) kłus m; (jogging pace) trucht m; **at a ~** kłusem/truchtem
❷ vi *[horse, rider]* kłusować; *[person]* biec truchtem
■ **trot out** infml: **~ out [sth]** powtarzać w kółko *[excuse, explanation]*
(IDIOMS:) **on the ~** infml jednym ciągiem

trouble /'trʌbl/ ❶ n ① (problems) kłopoty m pl; **to get sb into ~** wpakować kogoś w kłopoty; **to get into ~** *[person, business]* popaść w kłopoty; **back ~** problemy z kręgosłupem; **what's the ~?** w czym problem?; **to have ~ doing sth** mieć trudności ze zrobieniem czegoś; **to get sb out of ~** wydobyć kogoś z tarapatów ② (effort, inconvenience) trud m; **it's not worth the ~** szkoda zachodu; **to take the ~ to do sth, to go to the ~ of doing sth** zadać sobie trud zrobienia czegoś; **to save sb the ~** oszczędzić komuś trudu zrobienia czegoś; **to go to a lot of ~** zadać sobie wiele trudu
❷ **troubles** npl (worries) kłopoty m pl; **money ~s** kłopoty finansowe
❸ vt ① (bother) *[person]* przeszk|odzić, -adzać (komuś) *[person]*; **may** or **could I ~ you to close the window?** czy mógłbym pana/panią poprosić o zamknięcie okna? ② (worry) niepokoić *[person]*; zaprzat|nąć, -ać *[mind]*; **don't let that ~ you** nie kłopocz się tym

troubled /'trʌbld/ adj *[person, mind, expression]* zatroskany; *[sleep, times, area]* niespokojny

troublefree /ˌtrʌbl'friː/ adj bezproblemowy

troublemaker /'trʌblmeɪkə(r)/ n wichrzyciel m

troubleshooter /'trʌblʃuːtə(r)/ n (in business, industry) konsultant m

troublesome /'trʌblsəm/ adj *[person]* nieznośny; *[pain, cough]* dokuczliwy; *[problem]* kłopotliwy

trouble spot n punkt m zapalny

trough /trɒf, US trɔːf/ n ① (for water) koryto n; (manger) żłób m ② (depression) (of river) koryto n; (on graph) minimum n ③ (in weather) niż m

trousers /'traʊzə(r)s/ npl spodnie plt

trout /traʊt/ n pstrąg m

trowel /'traʊəl/ n (bricklayer's) kielnia f; (plasterer's) packa f; (gardener's) rydel m

truancy /'truːənsɪ/ n (being absent) nieobecność f; (playing truant) wagary plt

truant /'tru:ənt/ n **to play** ~ pójść na wagary; (regularly) wagarować

truce /tru:s/ n rozejm m

truck /trʌk/ n ① (lorry) ciężarówka f ② (rail wagon) wagon m towarowy

truck driver n kierowca m ciężarówki

trudge /trʌdʒ/ vi iść noga za nogą; **to** ~ **through the snow** brnąć przez śnieg

true /tru:/ **Ⅰ** adj ① (based on facts) [news, story, fact] prawdziwy; **it is** ~ **to say that...** prawdą jest, że...; **that's** ~ (when agreeing) (to) prawda ② (real, genuine) [god, democracy] prawdziwy; [extent, nature, cost] faktyczny; **to come** ~ [dream, wish] spełnić się; [prediction] sprawdzić się ③ (heartfelt, sincere) [feeling, repentance, understanding, love] prawdziwy ④ (accurate) [copy] wierny; [assessment] sprawiedliwy ⑤ (faithful, loyal) [servant, knight, lover] wierny ⑥ Mus [note, instrument] czysto brzmiący

Ⅱ adv (straight) [aim, fire] precyzyjnie

true-life /ˌtru:'laɪf/ adj [adventure, story] z życia wzięty

truffle /'trʌfl/ n trufla f

truly /'tru:lɪ/ adv ① naprawdę; **well and** ~ całkowicie ② (in letter) **yours** ~ z poważaniem

trump /trʌmp/ n (suit) atu n inv; (card) atut m
[IDIOMS:] **to come up** ~**s** spisać się na medal

trumped-up /ˌtrʌmpt'ʌp/ adj [charge] sfingowany

trumpet /'trʌmpɪt/ n ① Mus (instrument) trąbka f; (person) trębacz m ② (elephant call) trąbienie n
[IDIOMS:] **to blow one's own** ~ chełpić się

trumpeter /'trʌmpɪtə(r)/ n trębacz m

truncheon /'trʌntʃən/ n pałka f

trunk /trʌŋk/ **Ⅰ** n ① (of tree) pień m; (of body) tułów m ② (of elephant) trąba f ③ (for travel) kufer m ④ US (car boot) bagażnik m

Ⅱ trunks npl kąpielówki plt

truss /trʌs/ n Med pas m przepuklinowy

■ **truss up**: obwiąz|ać, -ywać [chicken]; z|wiązać [person]

trust /trʌst/ **Ⅰ** n ① (faith) zaufanie n; **to put one's** ~ **in sb** obdarzać kogoś zaufaniem ② (arrangement) zarząd m powierniczy; (property) majątek m powierniczy

Ⅱ vt ① (believe, rely on) za|ufać (komuś/czemuś) [person, judgment]; polegać na (czymś) [device, method] ② (entrust) **to** ~ **sb with sth** powierzyć komuś coś ③ (hope) mieć nadzieję

Ⅲ vi **to** ~ **in sb/sth** zaufać komuś/czemuś [person, fortune]; **to** ~ **to luck** zaufać szczęściu

Ⅳ vr **to** ~ **oneself to do sth** wierzyć, że coś się potrafi zrobić

Ⅴ trusted pp adj [friend] zaufany; [method] niezawodny, pewny

trust company n spółka f powiernicza

trustee /trʌs'ti:/ n ① (who administers property in trust) powiernik m ② (board member) członek m zarządu

trust fund n fundusz m powierniczy

trusting /'trʌstɪŋ/ adj ufny

trustworthy /'trʌstwɜ:ðɪ/ adj [person, staff] godny zaufania; [source, witness, firm] wiarygodny

truth /tru:θ/ n **the** ~ prawda f; **there is some** ~ **in that** jest w tym nieco prawdy

truthful /'tru:θfl/ adj [person] prawdomówny; [account, version] prawdziwy

try /traɪ/ **Ⅰ** n ① (attempt) próba f; **to have a** ~ **at doing sth** spróbować zrobić coś ② Sport (in rugby) przyłożenie n

Ⅱ vt ① (attempt) s|próbować odpowiedzieć na (coś) [exam question]; **to** ~ **doing** or **to do sth** próbować zrobić coś; **to** ~ **hard to do sth** bardzo starać się zrobić coś; **to** ~ **one's best to do sth** ze wszystkich sił starać się zrobić coś ② (test out) wypróbow|ać, -ywać [method, recipe, person]; s|próbować (czegoś) [different solution, approach, plan]; [thief] s|próbować otworzyć [door, window]; spróbować przekręc|ić, -ać [door knob]; **to** ~ **one's hand at sth** spróbować swoich sił w czymś ③ (taste) s|próbować [food] ④ (consult) za|pytać [person]; sprawdz|ić, -ać w (czymś) [book]; ~ **the library** zapytaj w bibliotece ⑤ (subject to stress) wystawi|ć, -ać na próbę [patience, tolerance] ⑥ (in court) rozpat|rzyć, -rywać [case]; o|sądzić [criminal]

Ⅲ vi s|próbować; **to** ~ **again** spróbować jeszcze raz; **to** ~ **for sth** starać się o coś [loan, university place, promotion, baby]; próbować pobić [world record]; **keep** ~**ing!** nie rezygnuj!

■ **try on**: przymierz|yć, -ać [dress, hat]

■ **try out**: ~ [sth] out wypróbow|ać, -ywać

trying /'traɪɪŋ/ adj [person] męczący; [week, task] ciężki

T-shirt /'ti:ʃɜ:t/ n T-shirt m infml

tub /tʌb/ n ① (for flowers) donica f; (for water) ceber m; (for ice cream) kubek m ② US (bath) wanna f

tubby /'tʌbɪ/ adj infml przysadzisty

tube /tju:b, US tu:b/ n ① (cylinder) rura f; (small) rurka f ② GB infml **the** ~ metro n (londyńskie) ③ US infml (TV) telewizja f ④ Tech lampa f; (in TV set) kineskop m ⑤ (in tyre) dętka f

tuberculosis /tjuˌbɜ:kjʊ'ləʊsɪs, US tu:-/ n gruźlica f

tuck /tʌk/ **Ⅰ** n (in sewing) zakładka f

Ⅱ vt wsu|nąć, -wać; **to** ~ **one's shirt into one's trousers** włożyć koszulę do spodni

■ **tuck away**: ukry|ć, -wać [object]; **to be** ~**ed away** [object] być głęboko schowanym; [person] siedzieć w ukryciu; [village] leżeć na uboczu

■ **tuck in**: w|łożyć, -kładać do spodni [shirt]; wsu|nąć, -wać pod materac [bedclothes]; otul|ić, -ać [person]

Tuesday /'tju:zdeɪ, -dɪ, US 'tu:-/ n wtorek m

tuft /tʌft/ n (of grass, hair) kępka f; (of cotton) kłaczek m

tug /tʌg/ **I** *n* 1 (pull) szarpnięcie *n*; **to give sth a** ~ szarpnąć (za) coś 2 (also ~ **boat**) holownik *m* **II** *vt* (pull) szarp|nąć, -ać
III *vi* **to** ~ **at** or **on sth** szarpać za coś
tug-of-love /ˌtʌgəvˈlʌv/ *n* GB spór *m* o prawo opieki nad dzieckiem
tug-of-war /ˌtʌgəvˈwɔː(r)/ *n* przeciąganie *n* liny
tuition /tjuːˈɪʃn, US tuː-/ *n* (teaching) nauka *f*
tuition fees *npl* czesne *n*
tulip /ˈtjuːlɪp, US ˈtuː-/ *n* tulipan *m*
tumble /ˈtʌmbl/ **I** *n* 1 (fall) upadek *m*; **to take a** ~ wywrócić się 2 (of clown, acrobat) fikołek *m* infml
II *vi* 1 (fall) *[object]* upa|ść, -dać; *[person]* prze-wr|ócić, -acać się 2 *[price, share, currency]* spa|ść, -dać na łeb, na szyję 3 *[acrobat, clown, child]* fikać koziołki; *[rocket]* koziołkować
■ **tumble down:** *[wall, building]* zawal|ić, -ać się, walić się
tumble-drier, tumble-dryer /ˌtʌmblˈdraɪə(r)/ *n* suszarka *f* bębnowa
tumble-dry /ˌtʌmblˈdraɪ/ *vt* wy|suszyć w suszarce (bębnowej)
tumbler /ˈtʌmblə(r)/ *n* szklanka *f*
tummy /ˈtʌmɪ/ *n* infml brzuszek *m* infml
tumour GB, **tumor** US /ˈtjuːmə(r), US ˈtuː-/ *n* guz *m*
tumult /ˈtjuːmʌlt, US ˈtuː-/ *n* 1 (noisy) tumult *m* 2 (disorder) zamieszanie *n*
tuna /ˈtjuːnə, US ˈtuː-/ *n* (also ~ **fish**) tuńczyk *m*
tune /tjuːn, US tuːn/ **I** *n* 1 Mus melodia *f* 2 (accurate pitch) **to be in/out of** ~ być nastrojo-nym/rozstrojonym; **to sing in/out of** ~ śpiewać czysto/fałszować
II *vt* nastr|oić, -ajać, stroić *[musical instrument]*; dostr|oić, -ajać *[radio, TV, signal]*; wy|regulować *[engine]*
■ **tune in: ¶** ~ **in** włącz|yć, -ać odbiornik; **to** ~ **in to sth** nastawić odbiornik na coś *[channel]*
¶ ~ **[sth] in** nastawi|ć, -ać (**to sth** na coś)
tunic /ˈtjuːnɪk, US ˈtuː-/ *n* 1 tunika *f* 2 (uniform) (for nurse, schoolgirl) fartuch *m*; (for policeman, soldier) bluza *f* mundurowa ze stójką
tuning fork *n* kamerton *m*
tunnel /ˈtʌnl/ **I** *n* tunel *m*
II *vt* wy|drążyć *[passage, hole]*
III *vi* drążyć tunel
tunnel vision *n* **to have** ~ fig mieć klapki na oczach fig
turbine /ˈtɜːbaɪn/ *n* turbina *f*
turbo /ˈtɜːbəʊ/ *n* (engine) silnik *m* turbo; (car) samochód *m* z silnikiem turbo
turbocharged /ˌtɜːbəʊˈtʃɑːdʒd/ *adj* ~ **engine/car** silnik/samochód z turbosprężarką
turbot /ˈtɜːbət/ *n* turbot *m*
turbulent /ˈtɜːbjʊlənt/ *adj* 1 *[water, waves]* wzbu-rzony 2 *[times, career, history]* burzliwy; *[situation,*

times] niespokojny; *[mood, group, character]* buntow-niczy
tureen /təˈriːn/ *n* waza *f*
turf /tɜːf/ **I** *n* (grass) darń *f*; (peat) torf *m*
II *vt* pokryć, -wać darnią *[lawn, pitch]*
■ **turf out:** ~ **[sb/sth] out** wyrzuc|ić, -ać
Turk /tɜːk/ *n* Tur|ek *m*, -czynka *f*
turkey /ˈtɜːkɪ/ *n* 1 (bird) indyk *m* 2 US infml (failure) klapa *f* infml; (bad film) chała *f* infml
Turkey /ˈtɜːkɪ/ *prn* Turcja *f*
Turkish /ˈtɜːkɪʃ/ **I** *n* (język *m*) turecki *m*
II *adj* turecki
Turkish delight *n* rachatłukum *n* inv
turmoil /ˈtɜːmɔɪl/ *n* (political) wrzawa *f*; (emotional) podniecenie *n*
turn /tɜːn/ **I** *n* 1 (opportunity, in rotation) kolej *f*; **whose** ~ **is it?** czyja (teraz) kolej?; **it was his** ~ **to feel rejected** teraz on z kolei czuł się odrzucony; **to take** ~ **s at doing sth, to take it in** ~ **s to do sth** robić coś na zmianę 2 (circular movement) obrót *m*; **to give sth a** ~ przekręcić or obrócić coś; **to do a** ~ *[dancer]* zrobić obrót 3 (in vehicle, on ski) skręt *m*; **to make** or **do a right/left** ~ skręcić w prawo/lewo 4 (bend) zakręt *m*; **take the next left** ~, **take the next** ~ **on the left** skręcić w pierwszą (drogę) w lewo 5 (change, development) obrót *m*; (in weather) zmiana *f*; **to take a** ~ **for the better** *[situation, things, events]* zmienić się na lepsze; *[person]* poczuć się lepiej; **to take a** ~ **for the worse** *[situation]* zmienić się na gorsze; *[health]* pogorszyć się 6 GB infml (attack) atak *m*; **a dizzy** ~ zawroty głowy; **it gave me quite a** ~, **it gave me a nasty** ~ to był dla mnie prawdziwy szok 7 (act) numer *m*
II *vt* 1 (rotate) *[person, mechanism]* przekręc|ić, -ać *[screw, handle, wheel]* 2 (turn over, reverse) odwr|ócić, -acać *[mattress, person]*; przewr|ócić, -acać *[page, steak]*; wywr|ócić, -acać *[collar]*; **it** ~**s my stomach** robi mi się od tego niedobrze 3 (change direction of) odwr|ócić, -acać *[head, face, chair]* 4 (focus direction of) **to** ~ **sth on sb** skierować coś w stronę kogoś *[gun, hose, torch]* 5 (transform) **to** ~ **sth white/black** pobielić/poczernić coś; **it** ~**s the solution opaque** to sprawia, że roztwór mętnieje; **to** ~ **sth into sth** zamienić coś w coś; **to** ~ **a book into a film** zekranizować książkę; **to** ~ **sb into sth/sb** *[magician]* zamienić kogoś w coś *[frog]*; *[experience]* zmienić kogoś w kogoś *[extrovert, maniac]* 6 (deflect) **to** ~ **the conversa-tion towards sth** skierować rozmowę na coś 7 infml (pass the age of) **to** ~ **20** skończyć 20 lat 8 (on lathe) wyt|oczyć, -aczać *[wood, piece]*
III *vi* 1 (change direction) *[person, vehicle, ship, road]* skręc|ić, -ać; **to** ~ **down** or **into sth** skręcić w coś *[street, alley]*; **to** ~ **towards sth** skręcić w stronę czegoś 2 (reverse direction) *[vehicle, person]* zawr|ócić, -acać; *[tide]* zmieni|ć, -ać się; *[luck]* odwr|ócić,

-acać się ③ (revolve) *[wheel, key, person, planet]* obr|ócić, -acać się ④ fig (hinge) **to ~ on sth** *[argument, plot, discussion]* obracać się wokół czegoś *[point, issue]*; *[outcome]* zależeć od czegoś *[factor]* ⑤ (spin round angrily) **to ~ on sb** *[dog, person]* rzucić się na kogoś ⑥ fig (resort to) **to ~ to sb/sth** zwrócić się do kogoś/ku czemuś *[person, religion]*; **to ~ to drink/drugs** zacząć pić/zażywać narkotyki; **I don't know where to ~** nie wiem, co mam robić ⑦ (change) **to ~ into sb/sth** *[situation, evening]* zmienić się w coś *[farce, disaster]*; **to ~ to sth** *[substance]* zamienić się w coś *[ice, gold]*; *[fear, surprise]* przejść w coś *[horror, relief]* ⑧ (become by transformation) **to ~ white/green/red** zbieleć/zzielenieć/poczerwienieć; **the weather is ~ing cold/warm** robi się chłodno/ciepło ⑨ (go sour) *[milk]* s|kwaśnieć ⑩ *[leaves, trees]* po|żółknąć

IV **in turn** *adv phr [answer, speak]* po kolei; **she spoke to each of us in ~** rozmawiała z każdym z nas po kolei

■ **turn against**: ¶ ~ **against** [sb/sth] zwr|ócić, -acać się przeciwko (komuś/czemuś) ¶ ~ **sb against** [sb/sth] nastawi|ć, -ać kogoś przeciwko (komuś/czemuś)

■ **turn around**: ¶ ~ **around** ① (to face other way) *[person]* odwr|ócić, -acać się; *[vehicle, bus]* zawr|ócić, -acać ② (revolve, rotate) *[object, windmill, dancer]* obr|ócić, -acać się ¶ ~ [sth] **around** odwr|ócić, -acać *[object]*; zawr|ócić, -acać (czymś) *[vehicle]*

■ **turn aside**: zb|oczyć, -aczać (**from sth** z czegoś)

■ **turn away**: ¶ ~ **away** odwr|ócić, -acać się ¶ ~ [sb] **away** odprawi|ć, -ać *[applicant, salesman]*

■ **turn back**: ¶ ~ **back** ① (turn around) zawr|ócić, -acać; **there's no ~ing back** fig nie ma odwrotu ② (in book) cof|nąć, -ać się ¶ ~ [sth] **back** cof|nąć, -ać *[dial, clock]* ¶ ~ [sb/sth] **back** zawr|ócić, -acać *[people, vehicles]*

■ **turn down**: ① (reduce) przyga|sić, -szać *[volume, gas]*; przyciszyć, -ać *[radio]*; przyciemni|ć, -ać *[light]* ② (fold over) odwi|nąć, -jać *[collar, sheet]*; zagi|ąć, -nać *[page]* ③ (refuse) odrzuc|ić, -ać *[request, offer]*; nie przyj|ąć, -mować *[applicant]*

■ **turn off**: ¶ ~ **off** ① *[driver, walker]* skręc|ić, -ać ② *[motor, fan]* wyłącz|yć, -ać się ¶ ~ [sth] **off** wyłącz|yć, -ać *[light, oven, radio]*; zakręc|ić, -ać *[tap, water, gas]* ¶ ~ [sb] **off** infml odrzuc|ić, -ać

■ **turn on**: włącz|yć, -ać *[light, oven, radio]*; odkręc|ić, -ać *[tap, water, gas]*

■ **turn out**: ¶ ~ **out** ① (be eventually) **to ~ out well/badly** skończyć się dobrze/źle; **it depends how things ~ out** zależy, jak sprawy się ułożą; **she ~ed out to be wrong** okazało się, że się myli; **it ~s out that...** okazuje się, że... ② (come out) *[crowd, people]* przyby|ć, -wać ¶ ~ [sth] **out** ① (turn off) wyłącz|yć, -ać *[light, gas]* ② (empty)

opróżni|ć, -ać *[bag]*; wywr|ócić, -acać *[pocket]*; Culin wy|łożyć, -kładać (z formy) *[mousse]* ③ (produce) wy|produkować *[goods]*; wy|kształcić *[scientists, graduates]* ¶ ~ [sb] **out** (evict) wyrzuc|ić, -ać

■ **turn over**: ¶ ~ **over** ① (roll over) *[person]* przewr|ócić, -acać się na drugi bok; *[car]* przewr|ócić, -acać się na dach ② (turn page) odwr|ócić, -acać stronę ③ *[engine]* pracować ¶ ~ [sth/sb] **over** ① (turn) odwr|ócić, -acać *[page, card, object, mattress, soil]* ② (hand over) przekaz|ać, -ywać *[object, money, business, person]*

■ **turn round** GB = **turn around**

■ **turn up**: ¶ ~ **up** ① (arrive, show up) pojawi|ć, -ać się; **don't worry – it will ~ up** nie martw się, na pewno się znajdzie ② (present itself) *[opportunity]* nadarz|yć, -ać się; *[job]* znaleźć się ③ (point up) *[corner, edge]* wygi|ąć, -nać się ku górze ¶ ~ [sth] **up** ① (increase, intensify) podkręc|ić, -ać *[heating, volume, gas]*; pogł|ośnić, -aśniać *[music]* ② (point up) postawić, stawiać *[collar]*

IDIOMS. **to do sb a good ~** wyświadczyć komuś przysługę

turnaround /ˈtɜːnəraʊnd/ *n* (in attitude) zwrot *m*; (of fortune) odmiana *f* (**in sth** w czymś); (for better) zmiana *f* na lepsze, poprawa *f* (**in sth** czegoś)

turning /ˈtɜːnɪŋ/ *n* GB (in road) zakręt *m*

turning point *n* punkt *m* zwrotny (**in** or **of sth** w czymś)

turnip /ˈtɜːnɪp/ *n* rzepa *f*

turnoff /ˈtɜːnɒf/ *n* ① (in road) odgałęzienie *n*; (from motorway) zjazd *m* ② infml (person) **to be a real ~** budzić odrazę

turn of mind *n* usposobienie *n*

turn of phrase *n* (expression) wyrażenie *n*

turnout /ˈtɜːnaʊt/ *n* (attendance) frekwencja *f* (**for sth** na czymś); **there was a magnificent ~ for the parade** na defiladzie zjawiło się mnóstwo ludzi

turnover /ˈtɜːnəʊvə(r)/ *n* ① (of company) obrót *m* ② (of stock) obrót *m* towarowy; (of staff) rotacja *f*

turnpike /ˈtɜːnpaɪk/ *n* ① (tollgate) rogatka *f* ② US (toll expressway) autostrada *f* płatna

turnstile /ˈtɜːnstaɪl/ *n* kołowrót *m*

turntable /ˈtɜːnteɪbl/ *n* (on record player) talerz *m* (obrotowy)

turnup /ˈtɜːnʌp/ *n* GB (of trousers) mankiet *m*

turpentine /ˈtɜːpəntaɪn/ *n* terpentyna *f*

turret /ˈtʌrɪt/ *n* wieżyczka *f*

turtle /ˈtɜːtl/ *n* GB żółw *m* wodny; US żółw *m*

turtle dove *n* turkawka *f*

turtleneck /ˈtɜːtlnek/ *n* (also **~ sweater**) golf *m*

Tuscany /ˈtʌskəni/ *prn* Toskania *f*

tusk /tʌsk/ *n* kieł *m*

tussle /ˈtʌsl/ *n* bójka *f* (**for sth** o coś)

tutor /ˈtjuːtə(r)/, US ˈtuː-/ *n* ① (private teacher) korepetytor *m*, -ka *f* ② GB Univ ≈ opiekun *m* naukowy ③ US Univ asystent *m*, -ka *f*

tutorial /tjuːˈtɔːrɪəl, US tuː-/ n Univ (group) seminarium n; (individual) konsultacje f pl; (private) korepetycje plt

tuxedo /tʌkˈsiːdəʊ/ n US smoking m

TV n infml = **television** telewizja f; (set) telewizor m

TV dinner n gotowy posiłek m do spożywania podczas oglądania telewizji

TV screen n ekran m telewizyjny

twang /twæŋ/ n (of string, wire) brzdęknięcie n; (of tone) nosowe brzmienie n

tweak /twiːk/ vt **to ∼ sb's ear/hair** pociągnąć kogoś za ucho/włosy

tweezers /ˈtwiːzəz/ npl pinceta f

twelfth /twelfθ/ **[I]** n **1** (in order) dwunast|y m, -a f, -e n **2** (fraction) dwunasta f (część)
[II] adj dwunasty
[III] adv [come, finish] na dwunastym miejscu

twelve /twelv/ n, adj dwanaście

twentieth /ˈtwentɪəθ/ **[I]** n **1** (in order) dwudziest|y m, -a f, -e n **2** (fraction) dwudziesta f (część)
[II] adj dwudziesty
[III] adv na dwudziestym miejscu

twenty /ˈtwentɪ/ n, adj dwadzieścia

twice /twaɪs/ adv dwa razy; **∼ daily** or **a day** dwa razy dziennie; **she's ∼ his age** jest dwa razy starsza od niego; **∼ as much**, **∼ as many** dwa razy więcej

twiddle /ˈtwɪdl/ vt po|kręcić (czymś); **to ∼ one's thumbs** kręcić młynka palcami; fig zbijać bąki infml

twig /twɪg/ n gałązka f

twilight /ˈtwaɪlaɪt/ n zmierzch m also fig

twilight zone n (area) strefa f cienia fig

twin /twɪn/ **[I]** n (one of two children) bliźnię n; (boy) bliźniak m; (girl) bliźniaczka f
[II] adj **1** [brother, sister] bliźniaczy **2** [masts, propellers] bliźniaczy
[III] vt (link) po|łączyć w parę

twine /twaɪn/ n sznurek m

twinge /twɪndʒ/ n (of pain, jealousy, regret) ukłucie n; **a ∼ of conscience** wyrzut sumienia

twinkle /ˈtwɪŋkl/ vi [light, star, jewel] migotać; [eye] błyszczeć

twin town n miasto n bliźniacze

twirl /twɜːl/ **[I]** n obrót m
[II] vt za|kręcić (czymś) [lasso, baton]; obr|ócić, -acać [partner]; skręc|ić, -ać [hair, vine]
[III] vi [dancer] zakręcić się; **∼ round** (turn round) [person] obrócić się (na pięcie)

twist /twɪst/ **[I]** n **1** (in rope, cord, wool) skręt m; (in road) ostry zakręt m; (in river) zakole n **2** (in play, story, events) (zaskakujący) zwrot m **3** (small amount) **a ∼ of yarn/thread** kawałek m skręconej przędzy/nitki; **a ∼ of lemon** cienki plasterek cytryny
[II] vt **1** (turn) przekręc|ić, -ać [knob, cap, lid]; (open) odkręc|ić, -ać [cap, lid]; (close) zakręc|ić, -ać [cap, lid]; **to ∼ sb's arm** wykręcić komuś rękę; fig przycisnąć kogoś infml fig **2** (wind) skręc|ić, -ać; **to**

∼ the threads together skręcać nitki; **to ∼ sth round sth** okręcać coś wokół czegoś **3** (bend, distort) wykrzywi|ć, -ać [metal, rod, branch]; fig przekręc|ić, -ać [words, facts] **4** (injure) skręc|ić, -ać [ankle, wrist, neck]
[III] vi **1** **to ∼ round** [person] odwrócić się **2** [rope, flex, coil] skręc|ić, -ać się; [river, road] wić się; **the road ∼s and turns going up the hillside** droga pnie się zakosami po zboczu

twisted /ˈtwɪstɪd/ adj [wire, rope, metal rod] poskręcany; [ankle, wrist] skręcony; **a ∼ sense of humour** specyficzne poczucie humoru euph

twit /twɪt/ n infml cymbał m infml

twitch /twɪtʃ/ **[I]** n **1** (tic) tik m **2** (spasm) drgnięcie n
[II] vt szarp|nąć, -ać [curtain, fabric]
[III] vi (quiver) [person, animal] za|drżeć; [eye, limb, muscle, fishing line] drg|nąć, -ać

twitchy /ˈtwɪtʃɪ/ adj niespokojny

twitter /ˈtwɪtə(r)/ vi [bird] za|świergotać

two /tuː/ **[I]** n dwa; (pair) dwójka f; **in ∼ s** dwójkami
[II] pron (male) dwaj; (female) dwie; (male and female) dwoje
IDIOMS: **to be in ∼ minds about doing sth** wahać się, czy coś zrobić; **to put ∼ and ∼ together** skojarzyć fakty

two-faced /ˌtuːˈfeɪst/ adj dwulicowy

twofold /ˈtuːfəʊld/ **[I]** adj **1** (twice as great) [increase] dwukrotny **2** (of two parts) podwójny
[II] adv dwukrotnie

two-piece /ˌtuːˈpiːs/ n (also **∼ suit**) (woman's) kostium m (dwuczęściowy); (man's) garnitur m (dwuczęściowy)

two-seater /ˌtuːˈsiːtə(r)/ n (car) samochód m dwumiejscowy; (plane) samolot m dwumiejscowy

two-tier /ˌtuːˈtɪə(r)/ adj [bureaucracy, health service] dwupoziomowy; [society] dwuwarstwowy

two-time /ˈtuːtaɪm/ infml vt zdradz|ić, -ać [partner]

two-way /ˌtuːˈweɪ/ adj [street, traffic] dwukierunkowy; [communication, exchange] dwustronny

two-way mirror n lustro n weneckie

two-way radio n aparat m nadawczo-odbiorczy

tycoon /taɪˈkuːn/ n potentat m, -ka f, magnat m

type /taɪp/ **[I]** n **1** (variety, kind) typ m (**of sth** czegoś) **2** (in printing) czcionka f
[II] vt (on typewriter, computer) na|pisać [word, letter]; **a ∼d letter** list napisany na maszynie
[III] vi pisać na maszynie

typecast /ˈtaɪpkɑːst, US -kæst/ vt za|szufladkować [person]

typeface /ˈtaɪpfeɪs/ n krój m pisma

typewriter /ˈtaɪpraɪtə(r)/ n maszyna f do pisania

typhoid /ˈtaɪfɔɪd/ n dur m brzuszny

typhoon /taɪˈfuːn/ n tajfun m

typical /ˈtɪpɪkl/ adj typowy; **it's ∼ of him to be late** spóźnić się to do niego podobne

typically /'tɪpɪklɪ/ *adv* (usually) zazwyczaj; ~ **English** *[place, behaviour]* typowo angielski; **she's** ~ **English** jest typową Angielką

typify /'tɪpɪfaɪ/ *vt [feature, condition, work]* być charakterystycznym dla (kogoś/czegoś); *[person]* być uosobieniem (czegoś); *[institution]* symbolizować

typing /'taɪpɪŋ/ *n* pisanie *n* na maszynie; **two pages of** ~ dwie strony maszynopisu

typist /'taɪpɪst/ *n* osoba *f* pisząca na maszynie; (female) maszynistka *f*

typographic(al) /ˌtaɪpə'græfɪk(l)/ *adj [layout]* typograficzny; *[error]* drukarski

typography /taɪ'pɒgrəfɪ/ *n* typografia *f*

tyrannize /'tɪrənaɪz/ *vt* tyranizować

tyranny /'tɪrənɪ/ *n* tyrania *f*

tyrant /'taɪərənt/ *n* tyran *m*

tyre GB, **tire** US /'taɪə(r)/ *n* opona *f*; **spare** ~ koło zapasowe; fig fałdy tłuszczu w pasie

tyre pressure *n* ciśnienie *n* w oponach

U

u, U /juː/ *n* u, U *n*
udder /ˈʌdə(r)/ *n* wymię *n*
UFO *n* = **unidentified flying object** UFO *n inv*
ugly /ˈʌglɪ/ *adj* ① *[person, building]* brzydki ② *[situation]* groźny
UK *prn* = **United Kingdom** Zjednoczone Królestwo *n*
Ukraine /juːˈkreɪn/ *prn* the ~ Ukraina *f*
ulcer /ˈʌlsə(r)/ *n* wrzód *m*
ulterior /ʌlˈtɪərɪə(r)/ *adj [motive, purpose]* ukryty
ultimate /ˈʌltɪmət/ ❙ *n* the ~ szczyt *m*; the ~ in luxury/bad taste szczyt luksusu/złego smaku ❙❙ *adj [achievement]* najwyższy; *[challenge, success]* największy; *[destination, failure, result]* ostateczny
ultimately /ˈʌltɪmətlɪ/ *adv* ostatecznie
ultimatum /ˌʌltɪˈmeɪtəm/ *n* ultimatum *n*
ultramarine /ˌʌltrəməˈriːn/ ❙ *n* ultramaryna *f* ❙❙ *adj* w kolorze ultramaryny
ultrasound /ˈʌltrəsaʊnd/ *n* ultradźwięk *m*
ultrasound scan *n* ultrasonografia *f*, USG *n*
ultraviolet /ˌʌltrəˈvaɪələt/ *adj* ultrafioletowy
umbilical cord *n* pępowina *f*
umbrella /ʌmˈbrelə/ *n* parasol *m*
umpire /ˈʌmpaɪə(r)/ *n* Sport sędzia *m*
UN *n* = **United Nations** ONZ *f, m*
unable /ʌnˈeɪbl/ *adj* **to be ~ to do sth** (lacking the means or opportunity) nie móc czegoś zrobić; (lacking the knowledge or skill) nie umieć czegoś zrobić
unabridged /ˌʌnəˈbrɪdʒd/ *adj* nieskrócony
unacceptable /ˌʌnəkˈseptəbl/ *adj [terms]* nie do przyjęcia; *[behaviour]* niedopuszczalny
unaccompanied /ˌʌnəˈkʌmpənɪd/ *adj [person]* bez towarzystwa
unaccounted /ˌʌnəˈkaʊntɪd/ *adj* **the rest of the money is ~ for** brakuje reszty pieniędzy; **two of the crew are still ~ for** nadal nieznany jest los dwóch członków załogi
unaccustomed /ˌʌnəˈkʌstəmd/ *adj* **to be ~ to sth/to doing sth** być nieprzyzwyczajonym do czegoś/robienia czegoś
unaffected /ˌʌnəˈfektɪd/ *adj* ① (untouched) nienaruszony; **to be ~ by sth** nie odczuwać czegoś ② (natural) *[person, behaviour, style]* bezpretensjonalny
unafraid /ˌʌnəˈfreɪd/ *adj [person]* nieustraszony
unaided /ʌnˈeɪdɪd/ *adv [sit, stand, walk]* bez pomocy

unambiguous /ˌʌnæmˈbɪgjʊəs/ *adj* jednoznaczny
unanimous /juːˈnænɪməs/ *adj* jednomyślny
unanimously /juːˈnænɪməslɪ/ *adv* jednomyślnie
unannounced /ˌʌnəˈnaʊnst/ *adj [visit, changes]* niezapowiedziany
unanswered /ʌnˈɑːnsəd, US ʌnˈæn-/ *adj [letter, question]* pozostawiony bez odpowiedzi
unappetizing /ʌnˈæpɪtaɪzɪŋ/ *adj* nieapetyczny
unappreciative /ˌʌnəˈpriːʃətɪv/ *adj [person]* niewdzięczny; *[audience]* chłodno nastawiony
unapproachable /ˌʌnəˈprəʊtʃəbl/ *adj* nieprzystępny
unarmed /ʌnˈɑːmd/ *adj [person]* nieuzbrojony; ~ **combat** walka wręcz
unashamedly /ˌʌnəˈʃeɪmɪdlɪ/ *adv* otwarcie; *[deny]* bezwstydnie
unasked /ʌnˈɑːskt, US ʌnˈæskt/ *adv [come, attend]* bez zaproszenia; **to do sth ~** zrobić coś z własnej inicjatywy
unassuming /ˌʌnəˈsjuːmɪŋ, US ˌʌnəˈsuː-/ *adj* skromny
unattached /ˌʌnəˈtætʃt/ *adj* ① (single) samotny ② *[part, element]* luźny
unattainable /ˌʌnəˈteɪnəbl/ *adj* nieosiągalny
unattractive /ˌʌnəˈtræktɪv/ *adj [person]* nieatrakcyjny; *[idea]* nieciekawy
unauthorized /ʌnˈɔːθəraɪzd/ *adj* nielegalny
unavailable /ˌʌnəˈveɪləbl/ *adj* niedostępny
unavoidable /ˌʌnəˈvɔɪdəbl/ *adj* nieunikniony
unaware /ˌʌnəˈweə(r)/ *adj* ① (not informed) **to be ~ that...** nie wiedzieć, że... ② (not conscious) **to be ~ of sth** nie być świadomym czegoś
unawares /ˌʌnəˈweəz/ *adv* **to catch** or **take sb ~** zaskoczyć kogoś
unbearable /ʌnˈbeərəbl/ *adj* nie do zniesienia
unbeatable /ʌnˈbiːtəbl/ *adj [price, quality]* bezkonkurencyjny
unbeknown /ˌʌnbɪˈnəʊn/ *adv* ~ **to sb** bez wiedzy kogoś
unbelievable /ˌʌnbɪˈliːvəbl/ *adj* niewiarygodny
unbending /ʌnˈbendɪŋ/ *adj* nieugięty
unbias(s)ed /ʌnˈbaɪəst/ *adj* bezstronny
unblock /ʌnˈblɒk/ *vt* przet|kać, -ykać *[pipe, sink]*
unborn /ʌnˈbɔːn/ *adj [child]* nienarodzony
unbreakable /ʌnˈbreɪkəbl/ *adj [glass]* nietłukący; *[toy]* niezniszczalny

unbroken /ʌn'brəʊkən/ *adj* [1] (uninterrupted) *[series, sequence]* nieprzerwany [2] *[pottery]* nieuszkodzony

unbuckle /ʌn'bʌkl/ *vt* rozpi|ąć, -nać *[belt]*; rozpi|ąć, -nać sprzączkę przy czymś *[shoe]*

unbutton /ʌn'bʌtn/ *vt* rozpi|ąć, -nać

uncalled-for /ʌn'kɔ:ldfɔ:(r)/ *adj [remark]* nie na miejscu

uncanny /ʌn'kænɪ/ *adj* niesamowity

uncaring /ʌn'keərɪŋ/ *adj* obojętny

uncertain /ʌn'sɜ:tn/ **[]** *adj* [1] (unsure) niepewny; **to be ~ about sth** nie być pewnym czegoś [2] (changeable) *[weather]* niepewny; *[temper]* zmienny **[]** **in no ~ terms** *adv phr [state]* jasno i wyraźnie

uncertainty /ʌn'sɜ:tntɪ/ *n* niepewność *f*

unchallenged /ʌn'tʃælɪndʒd/ *adj* **to go ~** *[statement, decision]* nie zostać zakwestionowanym

unchanged /ʌn'tʃeɪndʒd/ *adj* niezmieniony

uncharacteristic /ˌʌnkærɪktə'rɪstɪk/ *adj* nietypowy; **it was ~ of him to leave like that** odejście w taki sposób było zupełnie nie w jego stylu

uncharitable /ʌn'tʃærɪtəbl/ *adj* nieżyczliwy

unchecked /ʌn'tʃekt/ *adv [develop, grow]* w sposób niekontrolowany

uncivilized /ʌn'sɪvɪlaɪzd/ *adj* [1] (inhumane) *[treatment, conditions]* nieludzki [2] (uncouth) prymitywny [3] (barbarous) niecywilizowany

uncle /'ʌŋkl/ *n* wuj *m*; (paternal) stryj *m*

unclear /ʌn'klɪə(r)/ *adj* [1] (not evident) *[motive, reason, circumstances]* niejasny; **it is ~ whether/how...** nie do końca wiadomo, czy/jak... [2] (not comprehensible) *[instructions]* niejasny; *[voice, handwriting]* niewyraźny

uncomfortable /ʌn'kʌmftəbl/, US -fərt-/ *adj* [1] *[shoes, seat]* niewygodny; *[heat, journey]* uciążliwy; **you look ~ in those clothes** chyba jest ci niewygodnie w tym ubraniu [2] (emotionally) *[silence, situation]* krępujący; *[feeling]* przykry

uncommon /ʌn'kɒmən/ *adj* rzadki

uncommunicative /ˌʌnkə'mju:nɪkətɪv/ *adj* niekomunikatywny

uncomplimentary /ˌʌnkɒmplɪ'mentrɪ/, US-terɪ/ *adj* niepochlebny

uncompromising /ʌn'kɒmprəmaɪzɪŋ/ *adj [person]* bezkompromisowy; *[standards]* surowy

unconcerned /ˌʌnkən'sɜ:nd/ *adj* (uninterested) obojętny (**with sth** na coś); (not caring) beztroski; (untroubled) niewzruszony

unconditional /ˌʌnkən'dɪʃənl/ *adj [surrender, obedience]* bezwarunkowy; *[offer]* bez żadnych warunków

unconfirmed /ˌʌnkən'fɜ:md/ *adj* niepotwierdzony

unconnected /ˌʌnkə'nektɪd/ *adj [incidents, facts]* niepowiązany ze sobą; **to be ~ with sth** *[event, fact]* nie mieć związku z czymś; *[person]* nie mieć powiązań z czymś

unconscious /ʌn'kɒnʃəs/ **[]** *n* **the ~** nieświadomość *f*

[] *adj* [1] (insensible) nieprzytomny; **to knock sb ~** (uderzeniem) pozbawić kogoś przytomności [2] (unaware, unintentional) *[bias, impulse]* nieświadomy; **to be ~ of sth** być nieświadomym czegoś

unconstitutional /ˌʌnkɒnstɪ'tju:ʃənl/ *adj* niezgodny z konstytucją

uncontested /ˌʌnkən'testɪd/ *adj [leader, fact]* niekwestionowany

uncontrollable /ˌʌnkən'trəʊləbl/ *adj [rage, laugh]* niepohamowany

uncontrollably /ˌʌnkən'trəʊləblɪ/ *adv [laugh, sob]* spazmatycznie

unconventional /ˌʌnkən'venʃənl/ *adj* niekonwencjonalny

unconvincing /ˌʌnkən'vɪnsɪŋ/ *adj* nieprzekonujący

uncooked /ʌn'kʊkt/ *adj* niegotowany

uncooperative /ˌʌnkəʊ'ɒpərətɪv/ *adj* niechętny do współpracy

uncoordinated /ˌʌnkəʊ'ɔ:dɪneɪtɪd/ *adj* nieskoordynowany; **to be ~** *[person]* poruszać się niezgrabnie

uncouth /ʌn'ku:θ/ *adj [person]* nieokrzesany

uncover /ʌn'kʌvə(r)/ *vt* odkry|ć, -wać *[evidence]*

uncritical /ʌn'krɪtɪkl/ *adj* **to be ~ of sb/sth** być bezkrytycznym wobec kogoś/czegoś

unctuous /'ʌŋktjʊəs/ *adj* nadskakujący

uncut /ʌn'kʌt/ *adj* [1] *[film]* w pełnej wersji [2] *[gem]* nieoszlifowany

undamaged /ʌn'dæmɪdʒd/ *adj [building, crops]* niezniszczony

undecided /ˌʌndɪ'saɪdɪd/ *adj [person]* niezdecydowany; *[outcome]* nierozstrzygnięty

undemanding /ˌʌndɪ'mɑ:ndɪŋ/, US -'mænd-/ *adj [task]* niewymagający wysiłku; *[person]* mało absorbujący

undemocratic /ˌʌndemə'krætɪk/ *adj* niedemokratyczny

undemonstrative /ˌʌndɪ'mɒnstrətɪv/ *adj* **to be ~** nie zdradzać się ze swoimi uczuciami

undeniable /ˌʌndɪ'naɪəbl/ *adj* niezaprzeczalny

under /'ʌndə(r)/ **[]** *prep* [1] (beneath) (location) pod (czymś); (movement) pod (coś); **~ a magnifying glass** pod lupą; **~ letter D** pod literą D [2] (less than) mniej niż (coś); **~ £10** poniżej dziesięciu funtów; **children ~ five** dzieci (w wieku) poniżej 5 lat; **a number ~ ten** liczba mniejsza od dziesięciu; **temperatures ~ 10°C** temperatury poniżej 10°C [3] (according to) zgodnie z (czymś); **~ the law** zgodnie z prawem [4] (subordinate to) pod (kimś); **I have 50 people ~ me** mam pod sobą 50 osób

[] *adv* [1] pod spodem; **to go/stay ~** *[diver, swimmer]* zniknąć/pozostawać pod wodą [2] (less) mniej; **£10 and ~** 10 funtów i mniej; **children of six and ~** sześciolatki i młodsze (dzieci) [3] (anaesthetized) **to put sb ~** podać komuś narkozę

underachieve /ˌʌndərəˈtʃiːv/ *vi* Sch osiąg|nąć, -ać wyniki poniżej swoich możliwości

underachiever /ˌʌndərəˈtʃiːvə(r)/ *n* Sch uczeń *m* osiągający wyniki poniżej swoich możliwości

underage /ˌʌndərˈeɪdʒ/ *adj* niepełnoletni

undercarriage /ˈʌndəkærɪdʒ/ *n* podwozie *n*

underclass /ˈʌndəklɑːs, US -klæs/ *n* margines *m* społeczny

underclothes /ˈʌndəkləʊðz/ *npl* bielizna *f*

undercoat /ˈʌndəkəʊt/ *n* (of paint) podkład *m*

undercooked /ˌʌndəˈkʊkt/ *adj* niedogotowany

undercover /ˌʌndəˈkʌvə(r)/ *adj [agent]* tajny

undercurrent /ˈʌndəkʌrənt/ *n* (in water) prąd *m* głębinowy; fig podtekst *m*

undercut /ˌʌndəˈkʌt/ *vt* **to ~ prices** stosować dumpingowe ceny

underdeveloped /ˌʌndədɪˈveləpt/ *adj [country, person]* słabo rozwinięty

underdog /ˈʌndədɒg/ *n* US -dɔːg/ *n* ① (in society) **the ~** najsłabsze jednostki *f pl* ② (in game, contest) przegran|y *m*, -a *f*

underdone /ˌʌndəˈdʌn/ *adj [food]* niedogotowany; *[steak]* GB lekko krwisty

underestimate /ˌʌndərˈestɪmeɪt/ *vt* nie doceni|ć, -ać (kogoś/czegoś)

underexposed /ˌʌndərɪkˈspəʊzd/ *adj* (in photography) niedoświetlony

underfed /ˌʌndəˈfed/ *adj* niedożywiony

underfoot /ˌʌndəˈfʊt/ *adv* pod stopami

underfunded /ˌʌndəˈfʌndɪd/ *adj* niedofinansowany

undergo /ˌʌndəˈgəʊ/ *vt* prze|jść, -chodzić *[change, test, training]*; podda|ć, -wać się (czemuś) *[operation, treatment]*

undergraduate /ˌʌndəˈgrædʒʊət/ *n* student *m*, -ka *f* na studiach licencjackich

underground ① /ˈʌndəgraʊnd/ *n* ① GB metro *n*; **to go on the** or **by ~** jechać metrem ② (secret movement) **the ~** podziemie *n* ③ (artistic) underground *m*
  ② /ˈʌndəgraʊnd/ *adj* ① (below ground) podziemny ② (secret) *[newspaper, movement]* podziemny ③ (artistic) **~ film/artist** film/artysta undergroundu
  ③ /ˌʌndəˈgraʊnd/ *adv* ① (below ground) pod ziemią ② (secretly) **to go ~** zejść do podziemia

underground train *n* metro *n*

undergrowth /ˈʌndəgrəʊθ/ *n* zarośla *plt*; (in forest) podszycie *n*

underhand /ˌʌndəˈhænd/ *adj* (also **underhanded** US) *[person, method]* krętacki; **~ dealings** ciemne interesy

underline /ˌʌndəˈlaɪn/ *vt* podkreśl|ić, -ać

underling /ˈʌndəlɪŋ/ *n* podwładn|y *m*, -a *f*

underlying /ˌʌndəˈlaɪŋ/ *adj* (basic) *[problem]* podstawowy

undermine /ˌʌndəˈmaɪn/ *vt* podkop|ać, -ywać *[foundations, authority, efforts]*; osłabi|ć, -ać *[confidence, position]*

underneath /ˌʌndəˈniːθ/ ① *n* **the ~** spód *m*
  ② *adv* pod spodem
  ③ *prep* (location) pod (czymś); (direction) pod (coś)

undernourished /ˌʌndəˈnʌrɪʃt/ *adj* niedożywiony

underpants /ˈʌndəpænts/ *npl* slipy *plt*

underpass /ˈʌndəpɑːs, US -pæs/ *n* (for traffic) przejazd *m* dołem; (for pedestrians) przejście *n* podziemne

underpay /ˌʌndəˈpeɪ/ *vt* płacić za mało (komuś) *[employee]*

underprivileged /ˌʌndəˈprɪvəlɪdʒd/ *adj* **socially/economically ~** społecznie/ekonomicznie upośledzony

underrate /ˌʌndəˈreɪt/ *vt* nie doceni|ć, -ać (kogoś/czegoś)

under-secretary /ˌʌndəˈsekrətrɪ, US -terɪ/ *n* (also **~ of state**) GB podsekretarz *m* stanu

undersell /ˌʌndəˈsel/ ① *vt* sprzeda|ć, -wać taniej niż (ktoś) *[competitors]*
  ② *vr* **to ~ oneself** nie umieć się dobrze sprzedać

undershirt /ˈʌndəʃɜːt/ *n* US podkoszulek *m*

understaffed /ˌʌndəˈstɑːft, US -ˈstæft/ *adj* cierpiący na niedobór personelu

understand /ˌʌndəˈstænd/ ① *vt* ① (intellectually) z|rozumieć; **I can't ~** nie rozumiem; **to make oneself understood** (using a foreign language) porozumieć się; (make oneself clear) wyrazić się jasno ② (believe) sądzić; **to ~ that...** sądzić, że...
  ② *vi* (comprehend) z|rozumieć; **no slip-ups, do you ~?** bez żadnych wpadek, rozumiesz?

understandable /ˌʌndəˈstændəbl/ *adj* zrozumiały

understandably /ˌʌndəˈstændəblɪ/ *adv* co zrozumiałe; **he is ~ disappointed** to zupełnie zrozumiałe, że jest rozczarowany

understanding /ˌʌndəˈstændɪŋ/ ① *n* ① (grasp of subject) rozumienie *n* ② (arrangement) porozumienie *n* (**about sth** co do czegoś) ③ (sympathy) zrozumienie *n* ④ (powers of reason) rozum *m*
  ② *adj [person, tone]* wyrozumiały

understatement /ˈʌndəsteɪtmənt/ *n* niedopowiedzenie *n*

understudy /ˈʌndəstʌdɪ/ *n* dubler *m*, -ka *f*

undertake /ˌʌndəˈteɪk/ *vt* ① podj|ąć, -ejmować się (czegoś) *[task, job]*; podj|ąć, -ejmować *[research]*; przedsię|wziąć, -brać *[journey]*; przyst|ąpić, -ępować do (czegoś) *[offensive]* ② (guarantee) **to ~ to do sth** podjąć się zrobienia czegoś

undertaker /ˈʌndəteɪkə(r)/ *n* przedsiębiorca *m* pogrzebowy; (company) zakład *m* pogrzebowy

undertaking /ˌʌndəˈteɪkɪŋ/ *n* (venture) przedsięwzięcie *n*; (promise) zobowiązanie *n*

under-the-counter /ˌʌndəðəˈkaʊntə(r)/ *adj [goods]* nielegalny; *[trade]* pokątny; *[payment]* z ręki do ręki

undertone /'ʌndətəʊn/ n [1] (low voice) ściszony głos m [2] (hint) odcień m

undervalue /ˌʌndə'væljuː/ vt [1] (financially) zbyt nisko wycenić, -ać [2] (not appreciate) nie docenić, -ać *[person, quality]*

underwater /ˌʌndə'wɔːtə(r)/ **[I]** adj *[exploration, world]* podwodny
[II] adv pod wodą

underway /ˌʌndə'weɪ/ adj **to get** ~ *[vehicle]* wyruszyć w drogę; *[preparation, season]* rozpocząć się

underwear /'ʌndəweə(r)/ n bielizna f

underweight /ˌʌndə'weɪt/ adj *[baby, person]* z niedowagą

underworld /'ʌndəwɜːld/ n (criminals) świat m przestępczy

undesirable /ˌʌndɪ'zaɪərəbl/ adj *[aspect, result, influence]* niepożądany; *[friend]* nieodpowiedni

undetected /ˌʌndɪ'tektɪd/ adv *[break in, listen]* niepostrzeżenie; **to go** ~ *[crime, error]* nie wyjść na jaw; *[person]* pozostać niezauważonym; *[cancer]* pozostać niewykrytym

undeterred /ˌʌndɪ'tɜːd/ adj niezrażony

undeveloped /ˌʌndɪ'veləpt/ adj *[person]* wątły; *[organ, limb]* niewykształcony; *[country]* nierozwinięty; *[land]* niezagospodarowany

undignified /ʌn'dɪgnɪfaɪd/ adj *[behaviour, fate]* niegodny

undisciplined /ʌn'dɪsɪplɪnd/ adj niezdyscyplinowany

undiscovered /ˌʌndɪ'skʌvəd/ adj *[secret]* nieujawniony; *[crime]* niewykryty; *[document, land, talent]* nieodkryty

undiscriminating /ˌʌndɪ'skrɪmɪneɪtɪŋ/ adj niewybredny

undisguised /ˌʌndɪs'gaɪzd/ adj *[anger, curiosity]* nieukrywany

undisputed /ˌʌndɪ'spjuːtɪd/ adj *[champion, leader]* niekwestionowany; *[fact]* bezsporny

undisturbed /ˌʌndɪ'stɜːbd/ adj *[sleep]* niezakłócony; *[quiet]* niezmącony

undivided /ˌʌndɪ'vaɪdɪd/ adj *[loyalty]* bezwzględny; **to give sb one's** ~ **attention** poświęcić komuś całą swoją uwagę

undo /ʌn'duː/ vt [1] (unfasten) rozwiązlać, -ywać *[knot]*; rozpiąć, -nać *[button, zip]*; otwlorzyć, -ierać *[lock, parcel]* [2] (cancel out) z|marnować *[good, effort]*; naprawić, -ać *[harm]*

undone /ʌn'dʌn/ adj *[button]* rozpięty; *[work]* niedokończony; **to come** ~ *[lace]* rozwiązać się; *[zip]* rozpiąć się

undoubtedly /ʌn'daʊtɪdli/ adv niewątpliwie

undress /ʌn'dres/ **[I]** vt rozlebrać, -bierać **[II]** vi rozlebrać, -bierać się

undrinkable /ʌn'drɪŋkəbl/ adj (unpleasant) nienadający się do picia; (dangerous) niezdatny do picia

undue /ʌn'djuː, US -'duː/ adj nadmierny

unduly /ʌn'djuːli, US -'duːli/ adv *[optimistic, surprised]* nadmiernie; *[flatter, worry]* zbytnio

unearthly /ʌn'ɜːθli/ adj *[sight, light, cry]* niesamowity; **at an** ~ **hour** o nieludzkiej porze

uneasily /ʌn'iːzɪli/ adv [1] (anxiously) niespokojnie [2] (uncomfortably) z zażenowaniem

uneasiness /ʌn'iːzɪnɪs/ n [1] (worry) niepokój m (**about sb/sth** o kogoś/coś) [2] (dissatisfaction) niezadowolenie n (**about sth** z powodu czegoś)

uneasy /ʌn'iːzɪ/ adj [1] (worried) *[person]* zaniepokojony (**about** or **at sth** czymś); *[conscience]* niespokojny [2] (precarious) *[alliance, compromise, peace]* niepewny; *[silence]* kłopotliwy [3] (worrying) *[sleep]* niespokojny

uneconomical /ˌʌniːkə'nɒmɪkl, -ekə-/ adj [1] (wasteful) *[method]* nieekonomiczny; *[person]* nieoszczędny [2] (not profitable) nieopłacalny

uneducated /ʌn'edʒʊkeɪtɪd/ adj *[person]* niewykształcony; *[tastes]* pospolity; *[speech]* zdradzający brak wykształcenia

unemotional /ˌʌnɪ'məʊʃənl/ adj *[person]* powściągliwy; *[approach]* pozbawiony emocji; *[account]* beznamiętny

unemployed /ˌʌnɪm'plɔɪd/ **[I]** n **the** ~ bezrobotni m pl
[II] adj bezrobotny

unemployment /ˌʌnɪm'plɔɪmənt/ n bezrobocie n
unemployment benefit GB, **unemployment compensation** US n zasiłek m dla bezrobotnych

unemployment rate n stopa f bezrobocia

unenthusiastic /ˌʌnɪnˌθjuːzɪ'æstɪk, US -ˌθuːz-/ adj nastawiony niezbyt entuzjastycznie

unenviable /ʌn'envɪəbl/ adj nie do pozazdroszczenia

unequal /ʌn'iːkwəl/ adj nierówny

unequivocal /ˌʌnɪ'kwɪvəkl/ adj *[attitude, answer, support]* jednoznaczny; *[person, declaration]* zdecydowany

unethical /ʌn'eθɪkl/ adj nieetyczny; Med niezgodny z etyką lekarską

uneven /ʌn'iːvn/ adj *[surface, hem, pulse, contest]* nierówny

uneventful /ˌʌnɪ'ventfl/ adj *[day, career]* spokojny; *[journey]* bez przygód; *[life]* zwyczajny

unexciting /ˌʌnɪk'saɪtɪŋ/ adj nieciekawy, monotonny

unexpected /ˌʌnɪk'spektɪd/ adj niespodziewany

unexpectedly /ˌʌnɪk'spektɪdli/ adv niespodziewanie; *[large, small]* nadspodziewanie

unexplored /ˌʌnɪk'splɔːd/ adj niezbadany

unfailing /ʌn'feɪlɪŋ/ adj *[support, remedy]* niezawodny; *[optimism, energy, source]* niewyczerpany; *[effort]* niesłabnący

unfair /ʌn'feə(r)/ adj *[person, action, verdict]* niesprawiedliwy (**to** or **on sb** dla kogoś); *[play]* nieprzepisowy; *[trading, competition]* nieuczciwy

unfair dismissal *n* nieuzasadnione zwolnienie *n* (z pracy)

unfairness /ʌnˈfeənɪs/ *n* niesprawiedliwość *f*

unfaithful /ʌnˈfeɪθfl/ *adj* niewierny (**to sb** komuś)

unfamiliar /ˌʌnfəˈmɪlɪə(r)/ *adj* ① (strange) *[face, name, place, situation]* nieznany (**to sb** komuś) ② **to be** ~ **with sth** nie znać się na czymś

unfashionable /ʌnˈfæʃənəbl/ *adj* niemodny

unfasten /ʌnˈfɑːsn, US -ˈfæsn/ *vt* rozpi|ąć, -nać *[buttons, zip, clothes]*; otw|orzyć, -ierać *[door, bag]*

unfavourable GB, **unfavorable** US /ʌnˈfeɪvərəbl/ *adj [conditions]* niekorzystny; *[reply, report]* nieprzychylny

unfinished /ʌnˈfɪnɪʃt/ *adj* niedokończony

unfit /ʌnˈfɪt/ *adj* ① (out of condition) nie w formie ② (sub-standard) *[housing, road, pitch]* w złym stanie; ~ **for (human) consumption** nienadający się do spożycia

unflattering /ʌnˈflætərɪŋ/ *adj [opinion]* niepochlebny; *[portrait]* niekorzystny

unfold /ʌnˈfəʊld/ **I** *vt* (open) rozł|ożyć, -kładać *[paper, arms]*; rozwi|nąć, -jać *[wings]*; rozstawi|ć, -ać *[chair]*
II *vi* ① *[flower]* rozwi|nąć, -jać się ② *[scene]* roz|egrać, -grywać się; *[mystery]* odsł|onić, -aniać się

unforeseeable /ˌʌnfɔːˈsiːəbl/ *adj* nie do przewidzenia

unforeseen /ˌʌnfɔːˈsiːn/ *adj* nieprzewidziany

unforgettable /ˌʌnfəˈgetəbl/ *adj* niezapomniany

unforgivable /ˌʌnfəˈgɪvəbl/ *adj* niewybaczalny

unforgiving /ˌʌnfəˈgɪvɪŋ/ *adj* bezlitosny

unfortunate /ʌnˈfɔːtʃənət/ *adj* ① (pitiable) nieszczęsny ② (regrettable) *[incident, choice, remark]* niefortunny ③ (unlucky) nieszczęśliwy

unfortunately /ʌnˈfɔːtʃənətlɪ/ *adv [end]* niefortunnie; ~, ... niestety...

unfounded /ʌnˈfaʊndɪd/ *adj* bezpodstawny

unfriendly /ʌnˈfrendlɪ/ *adj [attitude, place, climate]* nieprzyjazny; *[person, reception]* nieżyczliwy

unfulfilled /ˌʌnfʊlˈfɪld/ *adj [ambition, desire]* niespełniony; *[need]* niezaspokojony; **to feel** ~ czuć się niespełnionym

unfurnished /ʌnˈfɜːnɪʃt/ *adj* nieumeblowany

ungracious /ʌnˈɡreɪʃəs/ *adj* nieuprzejmy

ungrammatical /ˌʌnɡrəˈmætɪkl/ *adj* niegramatyczny

ungrateful /ʌnˈɡreɪtfl/ *adj* niewdzięczny (**towards sb** w stosunku do kogoś)

unhappily /ʌnˈhæpɪlɪ/ *adv* ① (miserably) smutno ② (unfortunately) na nieszczęście ③ (inappropriately) niefortunnie

unhappiness /ʌnˈhæpɪnɪs/ *n* ① (misery) nieszczęście *n* ② (dissatisfaction) niezadowolenie *n*

unhappy /ʌnˈhæpɪ/ *adj* ① (miserable) *[person, childhood]* nieszczęśliwy; *[face, occasion]* smutny ② (dissatisfied) niezadowolony; **to be** ~ **with sth** być

niezadowolnym z czegoś ③ (concerned) **to be** ~ **about sth** niepokoić się czymś

unharmed /ʌnˈhɑːmd/ *adj [person]* cały i zdrowy; *[building]* nieuszkodzony

unhealthy /ʌnˈhelθɪ/ *adj [person]* chory; *[complexion, economy, diet]* niezdrowy

unheard-of /ʌnˈhɜːdɒv/ *adj [levels, price]* niesłychany; *[actor, brand]* nieznany

unheeded /ʌnˈhiːdɪd/ *adj* **to go** ~ *[warning, advice]* zostać zlekceważonym

unhelpful /ʌnˈhelpfl/ *adj [employee, witness]* nieskory do pomocy; *[attitude]* nieżyczliwy

unhindered /ʌnˈhɪndəd/ *adj [freedom, access]* nieograniczony; ~ **by sth** nieskrępowany czymś *[rules]*

unhook /ʌnˈhʊk/ *vt* rozpi|ąć, -nać *[skirt]*; zd|jąć, -ejmować *[picture]* (**from sth** z czegoś)

unhurried /ʌnˈhʌrɪd/ *adj [pace, meal]* nieśpieszny; *[person]* spokojny

unhygienic /ˌʌnhaɪˈdʒiːnɪk/ *adj* niehigieniczny

unidentified /ˌʌnaɪˈdentɪfaɪd/ *adj* niezidentyfikowany

unification /ˌjuːnɪfɪˈkeɪʃn/ *n* (of a country) zjednoczenie *n*

uniform /ˈjuːnɪfɔːm/ **I** *n* mundur *m*
II *adj [size, shape, colour]* jednakowy; *[temperature]* stały

unify /ˈjuːnɪfaɪ/ *vt* (unite) z|jednoczyć

unilateral /ˌjuːnɪˈlætrəl/ *adj* jednostronny

unimaginative /ˌʌnɪˈmædʒɪnətɪv/ *adj [person]* pozbawiony wyobraźni; *[style]* bez polotu

unimpeded /ˌʌnɪmˈpiːdɪd/ *adj [access, influx]* wolny

unimportant /ˌʌnɪmˈpɔːtnt/ *adj* nieistotny

unimpressed /ˌʌnɪmˈprest/ *adj* (by person, performance) niewzruszony; (by argument) nieprzekonany

uninhabitable /ˌʌnɪnˈhæbɪtəbl/ *adj* nienadający się do zamieszkania

uninhibited /ˌʌnɪnˈhɪbɪtɪd/ *adj [person]* pozbawiony kompleksów (**about sth** na punkcie czegoś)

uninitiated /ˌʌnɪˈnɪʃɪeɪtɪd/ *n* **the** ~ niewtajemniczeni *m pl*

uninjured /ʌnˈɪndʒəd/ *adj* bez obrażeń

uninspired /ˌʌnɪnˈspaɪəd/ *adj [approach, performance]* sztampowy; *[person]* bez polotu; **to be** ~ *[writer]* nie mieć weny

unintelligible /ˌʌnɪnˈtelɪdʒəbl/ *adj* niezrozumiały; *[handwriting]* nieczytelny

unintended /ˌʌnɪnˈtendɪd/ *adj* niezamierzony

unintentional /ˌʌnɪnˈtenʃənl/ *adj* niezamierzony

uninterested /ʌnˈɪntrəstɪd/ *adj* niezainteresowany (**in sth** czymś)

uninteresting /ʌnˈɪntrəstɪŋ/ *adj* nieciekawy

uninvited /ˌʌnɪnˈvaɪtɪd/ *adj [attentions]* nieprowokowany; *[remark, guest]* nieproszony

uninviting /ˌʌnɪnˈvaɪtɪŋ/ *adj [place]* niezbyt zachęcający; *[food]* nieapetyczny

union /'ju:nɪən/ n 1 (also **trade** ~) związek *m* zawodowy 2 (in politics) unia *f* 3 (uniting) zjednoczenie *n*; (marriage) związek *m*

Unionist /'ju:nɪənɪst/ n unionista *m*

Union Jack n GB flaga *f* brytyjska

unique /ju:'ni:k/ adj wyjątkowy; **to be** ~ **to sb/ sth** być wyłączną cechą kogoś/czegoś

unisex /'ju:nɪseks/ adj uniseks

unison /'ju:nɪsn, 'ju:nɪzn/ n **in** ~ jednym głosem

unit /'ju:nɪt/ n 1 (whole) całość *f* 2 (group) komórka *f*; (in army, police) jednostka *f* 3 (building, department) oddział *m* 4 (of measurement) jednostka *f* 5 (piece of furniture) segment *m*

unite /ju:'naɪt/ 1 vt zljednoczyć (**with sth** z czymś)
2 vi zljednoczyć się (**with sth** z czymś)

united /ju:'naɪtɪd/ adj [nation] zjednoczony; [effort] wspólny

United Kingdom prn Zjednoczone Królestwo *n*

United Nations (Organization) prn Organizacja *f* Narodów Zjednoczonych

United States (of America) prn Stany *plt* Zjednoczone (Ameryki)

unit trust n fundusz *m* powierniczy

unity /'ju:nəti/ n jedność *f*

universal /ju:nɪ'vɜ:sl/ adj [acclaim, reaction, education] powszechny; [principle, truth] uniwersalny; [use] wszechstronny

universally /ju:nɪ'vɜ:səli/ adv [believed, loved] powszechnie

universe /'ju:nɪvɜ:s/ n wszechświat *m*

university /ju:nɪ'vɜ:səti/ n uniwersytet *m*

unjust /ʌn'dʒʌst/ adj niesprawiedliwy (**to sb** wobec kogoś)

unjustified /ʌn'dʒʌstɪfaɪd/ adj nieuzasadniony

unkempt /ʌn'kempt/ adj [person, appearance] zaniedbany; [beard, hair] rozczochrany

unkind /ʌn'kaɪnd/ adj [person, remark] niemiły; [thought] nieżyczliwy; **to be** ~ **to sb** być dla kogoś niedobrym

unknown /ʌn'nəʊn/ 1 n 1 **the** ~ (mystery) niewiadoma *f*; (place) nieznane *n* 2 (person) **the director gave the part to a complete** ~ reżyser powierzył rolę komuś zupełnie nieznanemu
2 adj nieznany

unlawful /ʌn'lɔ:fl/ adj niezgodny z prawem

unlawfully /ʌn'lɔ:fəli/ adv niezgodnie z prawem

unleaded petrol GB, **unleaded gasoline** US n benzyna *f* bezołowiowa

unless /ən'les/ conj (between clauses) chyba że, jeżeli nie; (in initial clauses) jeżeli nie; **he won't come** ~ **you invite him** nie przyjdzie, jeśli go nie zaprosisz; **she can't take the job** ~ **she finds a nanny** (ona) nie może podjąć pracy, chyba że znajdzie opiekunkę do dziecka

unlike /ʌn'laɪk/ prep 1 (in contrast to) w odróżnieniu od (kogoś/czegoś) 2 (different from) niepodobny do

(kogoś/czegoś) 3 (uncharacteristic of) **such behaviour is quite** ~ **her** takie zachowanie jest zupełnie do niej niepodobne

unlikely /ʌn'laɪkli/ adj 1 mało prawdopodobny; **it is unlikely that...** jest mało prawdopodobne, żeby... 2 (odd) niezwykły 3 [story] nieprawdopodobny

unlimited /ʌn'lɪmɪtɪd/ adj nieograniczony

unlined /ʌn'laɪnd/ adj 1 [garment] bez podszewki; [curtains] niepodszyty 2 [paper] gładki

unload /ʌn'ləʊd/ 1 vt 1 wyładow|ać, -ywać [goods]; rozładow|ać, -ywać [vessel] 2 rozładow|ać, -ywać [gun] 3 (get rid of) pozby|ć, -wać się (czegoś) [stockpile, goods]; **to** ~ **one's problems on(to) sb** zwierzyć się komuś ze swoich problemów
2 vi [truck, ship] być rozładowywanym

unlock /ʌn'lɒk/ vt otw|orzyć, -ierać; **to be** ~**ed** nie być zamkniętym (na klucz)

unluckily /ʌn'lʌkɪli/ adv niestety; ~ **for sb** na nieszczęście dla kogoś

unlucky /ʌn'lʌki/ adj [person, day, colour, number] pechowy; [coincidence, event] niefortunny; **it is** ~ **to walk under a ladder** przechodzenie pod drabiną przynosi pecha

unmade /ʌn'meɪd/ adj [bed] nieposłany

unmanageable /ʌn'mænɪdʒəbl/ adj [child, dog] nieposłuszny; [hair] niesforny; [problem] nie do rozwiązania

unmarried /ʌn'mærɪd/ adj [woman] niezamężna; [man] nieżonaty

unmistakable /ʌnmɪ'steɪkəbl/ adj 1 (recognizable) charakterystyczny 2 (unambiguous) jednoznaczny 3 (marked) wyraźny

unmotivated /ʌn'məʊtɪveɪtɪd/ adj [act] niczym nieumotywowany; [person] bez motywacji

unmoved /ʌn'mu:vd/ adj 1 (unperturbed) obojętny (**by sth** wobec czegoś) 2 (emotionally) nieczuły (**by sth** na coś)

unnamed /ʌn'neɪmd/ adj 1 (name not divulged) [person] niewymieniony z nazwiska; [source] nieujawniony; [buyer] anonimowy 2 (without name) **as yet** ~ jeszcze nienazwany

unnatural /ʌn'nætʃrəl/ adj 1 (odd) nienormalny 2 [style, laugh, colour] nienaturalny

unnecessarily /ʌn'nesəsərəli, US ʌnnesə'serəli/ adv niepotrzebnie

unnecessary /ʌn'nesəsri, US -seri/ adj 1 (not needed) [expense, effort] niepotrzebny; [superfluous] zbędny 2 (uncalled for) [remark, jibe] nie na miejscu

unnerve /ʌn'nɜ:v/ vt wytrąc|ić, -ać z równowagi

unnoticed /ʌn'nəʊtɪst/ adj niezauważony

unobstructed /ʌnəb'strʌktɪd/ adj [road, exit] przejezdny; [view] niczym nieprzesłonięty

unobtainable /ʌnəb'teɪnəbl/ adj [supplies] nieosiągalny; **the number is** ~ połączenie nie może być zrealizowane

unobtrusive /ˌʌnəb'tru:sɪv/ *adj [site]* dyskretny; *[object]* nierzucający się w oczy; *[person]* niezwracający na siebie uwagi

unoccupied /ˌʌn'ɒkjʊpaɪd/ *adj [house]* niezamieszkany; *[shop]* niewynajęty; *[seat]* wolny

unofficial /ˌʌnə'fɪʃl/ *adj* nieoficjalny

unorthodox /ʌn'ɔ:θədɒks/ *adj [teacher, approach]* niekonwencjonalny

unpack /ʌn'pæk/ *vt* rozpakow|ać, -ywać *[luggage, belongings]*

unpaid /ʌn'peɪd/ *adj [bill, tax]* niezapłacony; *[debt]* niespłacony; *[work]* nieodpłatny; ~ **leave** urlop bezpłatny

unpalatable /ʌn'pælətəbl/ *adj* ① *[truth, statistic, advice]* trudny do przełknięcia ② *[food]* niesmaczny

unparalleled /ʌn'pærəleld/ *adj* ① (unequalled) *[strength, success, luxury]* niezrównany ② (unprecedented) niespotykany

unpasteurized /ʌn'pɑ:stʃəraɪzd/ *adj [milk]* niepasteryzowany; *[cheese]* z mleka niepasteryzowanego

unperturbed /ˌʌnpə'tɜ:bd/ *adj [person]* nieporuszony

unplanned /ʌn'plænd/ *adj [stoppage, increase]* nieprzewidziany; *[pregnancy, baby]* nieplanowany

unpleasant /ʌn'pleznt/ *adj* nieprzyjemny

unpleasantness /ʌn'plezntnɪs/ *n* ① (of odour, experience, remark) przykry charakter *m* ② (bad feeling) nieprzyjemności *f pl*

unplug /ʌn'plʌg/ *vt* wyłącz|yć, -áć z sieci *[appliance]*; przet|kać, -ykać *[sink]*

unpopular /ʌn'pɒpjʊlə(r)/ *adj* niepopularny

unprecedented /ʌn'presɪdentɪd/ *adj* bezprecedensowy

unpredictable /ˌʌnprɪ'dɪktəbl/ *adj [event, weather]* nieprzewidywalny; *[person]* nieobliczalny

unpremeditated /ˌʌnpri:'medɪteɪtɪd/ *adj* nierozmyślny

unprepared /ˌʌnprɪ'peəd/ *adj* ① (not ready) *[person]* nieprzygotowany (**for sth** na coś) ② *[speech]* zaimprowizowany; *[translation]* na żywo

unprepossessing /ˌʌnpri:pə'zesɪŋ/ *adj* nieatrakcyjny

unpretentious /ˌʌnprɪt'enʃəs/ *adj* bezprentensjonalny

unproductive /ˌʌnprə'dʌktɪv/ *adj* bezproduktywny

unprofessional /ˌʌnprə'feʃənl/ *adj* nieprofesjonalny

unprofitable /ʌn'prɒfɪtəbl/ *adj* nierentowny

unprotected /ˌʌnprə'tektɪd/ *adj* niezabezpieczony (**from sth** przed czymś)

unprovoked /ˌʌnprə'vəʊkt/ *adj [assault, aggression]* nieuzasadniony

unqualified /ʌn'kwɒlɪfaɪd/ *adj* ① *[staff]* niewykwalifikowany; *[doctor, teacher, assistant]* nieposiadający pełnych kwalifikacji ② (total) *[support, ceasefire]* bezwarunkowy; *[respect]* bezwzględny

unquestionable /ʌn'kwestʃənəbl/ *adj* niewątpliwy

unravel /ʌn'rævl/ ① *vt* s|pruć *[knitting]*; rozpląt|ać, -ywać *[thread]*; rozwiąz|ać, -ywać *[mystery]* ② *vi [knitting]* s|pruć się; *[thread]* rozpląt|ać, -ywać się; *[mystery]* rozwikł|ać, -ywać się

unreal /ʌn'rɪəl/ *adj* ① (not real) nierzeczywisty ② infml (unbelievable) niewiarygodny

unrealistic /ˌʌnrɪə'lɪstɪk/ *adj* nierealistyczny

unreasonable /ʌn'ri:znəbl/ *adj* ① *[person]* nierozsądny; *[views, expectations]* niedorzeczny ② (excessive) *[price, demand]* wygórowany

unrecognizable /ʌn'rekəgnaɪzəbl/ *adj* nie do poznania

unrelated /ˌʌnrɪ'leɪtɪd/ *adj* ① (not connected) niezwiązany (**to sth** z czymś) ② (as family) niespokrewniony (**to sb** z kimś)

unrelenting /ˌʌnrɪ'lentɪŋ/ *adj [person]* nieubłagany; *[heat, stare]* bezlitosny; *[pressure, zeal]* niesłabnący

unreliable /ˌʌnrɪ'laɪəbl/ *adj [machine, method, scheme]* zawodny; *[evidence]* niepewny; **she is a bit ~** na niej raczej nie można polegać

unrepentant /ˌʌnrɪ'pentənt/ *adj* nieskruszony

unrequited /ˌʌnrɪ'kwaɪtɪd/ *adj [love]* nieodwzajemniony

unresolved /ˌʌnrɪ'zɒlvd/ *adj* nierozwiązany

unrest /ʌn'rest/ *n* (dissatisfaction) niepokój *m*; (active) rozruchy *plt*

unrestricted /ˌʌnrɪ'strɪktɪd/ *adj* nieograniczony

unrewarding /ˌʌnrɪ'wɔ:dɪŋ/ *adj* niewdzięczny

unripe /ʌn'raɪp/ *adj* niedojrzały

unrivalled /ʌn'raɪvld/ *adj* niezrównany

unroll /ʌn'rəʊl/ *vt* rozwi|nąć, -jáć

unruffled /ʌn'rʌfld/ *adj* ① (calm) niewzruszony ② *[hair]* gładko zaczesany

unruly /ʌn'ru:lɪ/ *adj* niesforny

unsafe /ʌn'seɪf/ *adj* ① (dangerous) *[environment]* niezdrowy; *[working conditions]* niebezpieczny; *[drinking water]* nienadatny do picia ② (threatened) zagrożony; **to feel ~** nie czuć się bezpiecznie

unsaid /ʌn'sed/ *adj* **to leave sth ~** przemilczeć coś

unsatisfactory /ˌʌnsætɪs'fæktərɪ/ *adj* niezadowalający

unsatisfied /ʌn'sætɪsfaɪd/ *adj [person]* niezadowolony; *[need]* niezaspokojony

unsatisfying /ʌn'sætɪsfaɪɪŋ/ *adj* niezadowalający

unsavoury GB, **unsavory** US /ʌn'seɪvərɪ/ *adj [individual]* podejrzany; *[smell]* nieprzyjemny

unscathed /ʌn'skeɪðd/ *adj* bez szwanku

unscheduled /ʌn'ʃedju:ld, US ʌn'skedʒʊld/ *adj [appearance, speech, performance]* nieplanowany; *[stop]* nieprzewidziany; *[flight]* pozarozkładowy

unscrew /ʌn'skru:/ *vt* odkręc|ić, -áć

unscrupulous /ʌn'skru:pjʊləs/ *adj [person]* pozbawiony skrupułów; *[tactic, method]* bez skrupułów

unseat /ʌn'siːt/ vt wysadz|ić, -áć z siodła

unseen /ʌn'siːn/ adv [escape, slip away] niepostrzeżenie

unselfconscious /ˌʌnself'kɒnʃəs/ adj [person] (spontaneous) nieskrępowany; (uninhibited) bez kompleksów

unselfish /ʌn'selfɪʃ/ adj [person] niesamolubny; [act] bezinteresowny

unsentimental /ˌʌnsentɪ'mentl/ adj [speech, account] rzeczowy; [person] chłodny

unsettled /ʌn'setld/ adj [weather] zmienny; [future] niepewny; [account] nieuregulowany

unsettling /ʌn'setlɪŋ/ adj [question, experience] niepokojący; [work of art] intrygujący

unshaken /ʌn'ʃeɪkən/ adj [person] niewzruszony; [belief, trust] niezachwiany

unshaven /ʌn'ʃeɪvn/ adj nieogolony

unskilled /ʌn'skɪld/ adj [worker] niewykwalifikowany; [job, work] niewymagający kwalifikacji

unsociable /ʌn'səʊʃəbl/ adj nietowarzyski

unsocial /ʌn'səʊʃl/ adj ~ **hours** nietypowe godziny pracy

unsolicited /ˌʌnsə'lɪsɪtɪd/ adj [advice] nieproszony; [violence] niesprowokowany

unsophisticated /ˌʌnsə'fɪstɪkeɪtɪd/ adj [person] prosty; [analysis] nieskomplikowany

unspeakable /ʌn'spiːkəbl/ adj [pain, sorrow] niewypowiedziany; [noise] nie do opisania

unspoken /ʌn'spəʊkən/ adj [1] (secret) niewypowiedziany [2] (implicit) milczący

unstable /ʌn'steɪbl/ adj [structure] chwiejny; (not secure) [government, prices] niestabilny; [person] niezrównoważony

unsteady /ʌn'stedɪ/ adj [legs, ladder] chwiejny; [voice, hands] drżący; **to be ~ on one's feet** chwiać się na nogach

unstoppable /ʌn'stɒpəbl/ adj [force, momentum] nie do zatrzymania; [athlete, leader] nie do pobicia

unstuck /ʌn'stʌk/ adj **to come ~** [stamp] odkleić się; [person, organization] ponieść porażkę

unsubstantiated /ˌʌnsəb'stænʃɪeɪtɪd/ adj [rumour] niepotwierdzony; [accusation] bezpodstawny

unsuccessful /ˌʌnsək'sesfl/ adj [1] [campaign, love affair, novel] nieudany; [effort, search] daremny; **to be ~** [attempt] nie powieść się [2] [candidate] (for job) odrzucony; (in elections) przegrany; [business person] pechowy; [artist] niespełniony; **to be ~ in doing sth** nie zdołać czegoś zrobić

unsuccessfully /ˌʌnsək'sesfəlɪ/ adv bez powodzenia

unsuitable /ʌn'suːtəbl/ adj nieodpowiedni; **to be ~ for sth** nie nadawać się do czegoś

unsupervised /ʌn'suːpəvaɪzd/ adj [workers] nienadzorowany; [child] bez opieki; [activity] bez nadzoru

unsure /ʌn'ʃɔː(r), US -'ʃʊər/ adj niepewny; **to be ~ about going/staying** nie wiedzieć, czy pójść/

czy zostać; **to be ~ of oneself** nie mieć pewności siebie

unsuspecting /ˌʌnsə'spektɪŋ/ adj [person, public] niczego niepodejrzewający

unsweetened /ʌn'swiːtnd/ adj niesłodzony

unsympathetic /ˌʌnsɪmpə'θetɪk/ adj [1] (uncaring) [person, attitude] obojętny [2] (unattractive) [person, character] antypatyczny

untaxed /ʌn'tækst/ adj nieopodatkowany

untenable /ʌn'tenəbl/ adj [standpoint, argument] nie do obrony

unthinkable /ʌn'θɪŋkəbl/ adj nieprawdopodobny

untidily /ʌn'taɪdɪlɪ/ adv [kept, strewn, scattered] nieporządnie; **to be ~ dressed** być niedbale ubranym

untidy /ʌn'taɪdɪ/ adj [person] nieporządny; (in appearance) niedbały; [habits, clothes] niechlujny; [room] niesprzątany

untie /ʌn'taɪ/ vt rozwiąz|ać, -ywać [knot, rope, hands]; **to come ~d** [laces, parcel] rozwiązać się

until /ən'tɪl/ (also **till**) [I] prep do (czegoś); ~ **Tuesday** do wtorku; ~ **the sixties** do lat sześćdziesiątych; ~ **now** dotychczas; ~ **then** do tego czasu; (up) ~ **1901** do 1901 roku; **from Monday ~ Saturday** od poniedziałku do soboty; **I won't know ~ Tuesday** dowiem się dopiero we wtorek; **it wasn't ~ the 50's that...** dopiero w latach pięćdziesiątych...

[II] conj (before fulfilment of condition) dopóki nie; **we'll stay ~ a solution is reached** zostaniemy, aż znajdziemy rozwiązanie; **let's watch TV ~ they arrive** pooglądajmy telewizję, dopóki nie przyjdą; **I'll wait ~ I get back (before doing sth)** poczekam (ze zrobieniem czegoś), aż wrócę; **she waited ~ she was alone** poczekała, aż zostanie sama

untimely /ʌn'taɪmlɪ/ adj [arrival, intervention] nie w porę; [moment] niefortunny; [death, end] przedwczesny

untold /ʌn'təʊld/ adj [1] (not quantifiable) ~ **millions** wiele milionów; ~ **damage** nieobliczalne straty [2] (endless) [joy, misery] nieopisany

untrained /ʌn'treɪnd/ adj [worker] nieprzeszkolony; [voice] nieszkolony; [eye] niewprawny

untranslatable /ˌʌntrænz'leɪtəbl/ adj nieprzetłumaczalny

untroubled /ʌn'trʌbld/ adj [face, life, person] spokojny; **to be ~ by sth** nie przejąć się czymś [news, threat]

untrue /ʌn'truː/ adj nieprawdziwy

untrustworthy /ʌn'trʌstwɜːðɪ/ adj [information, source] niewiarygodny; [person] niegodny zaufania

unused[1] /ʌn'juːst/ adj (unaccustomed) nieprzyzwyczajony; **to be ~ to sth/doing sth** być nieprzyzwyczajonym do czegoś/robienia czegoś

unused[2] /ʌn'juːzd/ adj nieużywany

unusual /ʌnˈjuːʒl/ *adj* niezwykły; **it is ~ to find...** rzadko można znaleźć...; **there's nothing ~ in it** nie ma w tym niczego niezwykłego

unusually /ʌnˈjuːʒəlɪ/ *adv* niezwykle

unwanted /ʌnˈwɒntɪd/ *adj* [*child*] niechciany; [*goods*] niepotrzebny; [*visitor*] niepożądany; **to feel ~** czuć się niepotrzebnym

unwarranted /ʌnˈwɒrəntɪd, US -ˈwɔːr-/ *adj* nieuzasadniony

unwary /ʌnˈweərɪ/ *n* **the ~** nieroztropni *m pl*

unwelcome /ʌnˈwelkəm/ *adj* [*visitor*] nieproszony; [*news*] niemiły

unwell /ʌnˈwel/ *adj* niezdrów; **he's feeling ~** nie czuje się dobrze

unwilling /ʌnˈwɪlɪŋ/ *adj* [*person*] niechętny; [*attention, departure*] wymuszony; **he is ~ to do it** nie ma ochoty tego zrobić; (*stronger*) nie chce tego zrobić

unwillingness /ʌnˈwɪlɪŋnɪs/ *n* niechęć *f* (**to do sth** do zrobienia czegoś)

unwind /ʌnˈwaɪnd/ **[]** *vt* rozwi|nąć, -jać [*rope*] **[]** *vi* [1] [*tape, cable, scarf*] rozwi|nąć, -jać się [2] (*relax*) [*person*] odpręż|yć, -ać się

unwise /ʌnˈwaɪz/ *adj* [*decision, choice*] niemądry; [*person*] nierozsądny

unwisely /ʌnˈwaɪzlɪ/ *adv* nierozsądnie

unwittingly /ʌnˈwɪtɪŋlɪ/ *adv* [1] (*innocently*) nieświadomie [2] (*without wanting to*) niechcący

unworthy /ʌnˈwɜːðɪ/ *adj* niegodny (**of sth** czegoś)

unwrap /ʌnˈræp/ *vt* rozpakow|ać, -ywać [*parcel*]

unwritten /ʌnˈrɪtn/ *adj* [*rule, agreement*] niepisany; [*tradition*] ustny

unzip /ʌnˈzɪp/ *vt* [1] rozpi|ąć, -nać [*dress, trousers*] [2] Comput rozpakow|ać, -ywać [*file*]

up /ʌp/ **[]** *adj* [1] (*out of bed*) **she's up** już wstała; **we were up very late last night** wczoraj siedzieliśmy do późna w nocy; **they were up all night** w ogóle się nie kładli (spać); **I was still up at 2 am** o drugiej nad ranem byłem jeszcze na nogach [2] (*higher in amount, level*) **prices are up (by 10%)** ceny wzrosły (o 10%); **numbers of students are up** wzrosła liczba studentów [3] *infml* (*wrong*) **what's up?** co się dzieje?; **what's up with him?** co mu jest? [4] (*erected, affixed*) **the notice is up on the board** ogłoszenie wisi na tablicy; **is the tent up?** czy namiot jest rozbity?; **he had his hand up for five minutes** przez pięć minut trzymał rękę w górze [5] (*open*) **he had his umbrella up** miał otwarty parasol; **the blinds were up** rolety były podniesione; **when the barrier is up you can go through** kiedy szlaban się podniesie, można jechać [6] (*finished*) **'time's up!'** „kończymy!"; **when the four days were up** po upływie czterech dni [7] (*facing upwards*) **'this side up'** (*on parcel*) „góra"; **he was floating face up** unosił się na wodzie, leżąc na plecach [8] (*pinned up*) **her hair was up** miała upięte wysoko włosy

[] *adv* [1] (*high*) **up here/there** tu/tam w górze; **up on the wardrobe** na szafie; **up in the tree/the clouds** na drzewie/w chmurach; **up on top of the mountain** na szczycie góry; **four floors up from here** cztery piętra wyżej; **I'm on my way up** idę na górę; **up to/in Scotland** do Szkocji/w Szkocji; **up North** na północ(y) [2] (*ahead*) **to be four points up (on sb)** mieć przewagę czterech punktów (nad kimś) [3] (*upwards*) **T-shirts from £2 up** podkoszulki od dwóch funtów wzwyż

[] *prep* **up the tree** na drzewie; **the library is up the stairs** biblioteka jest na piętrze; **he ran up the stairs** wbiegł po schodach; **she lives up that road there** ona mieszka trochę dalej przy tej ulicy; **he put it up his sleeve** wsunął to do rękawa

[] **up above** *adv phr, prep phr* w górze; **up above sth** ponad czymś

[] **up against** *prep phr* **up against the wall** (*oparty*) o ścianę; **to come up against opposition** napotkać sprzeciw

[] **up and about** *adv phr* [*be*] na nogach

[] **up and down** *adv phr, prep phr* [1] (*to and fro*) tam i z powrotem; **to walk up and down** chodzić tam i z powrotem [2] (*throughout*) **up and down the country** w całym kraju

[] **up to** *prep phr* [1] (*to particular level*) do (czegoś); **up to here/there** do tego/tamtego miejsca [2] (*as many as*) **up to 50 dollars** do 50 dolarów [3] (*until*) do (czegoś); **up to 1964** do 1964 roku; **up to 10.30 pm** do wpół do jedenastej wieczorem; **up to now** do tej pory [4] (*good enough for*) **I'm not up to it** (*not capable*) to przekracza moje możliwości; (*not well enough*) to ponad moje siły [5] (*expressing responsibility*) **it's up to you/her to make the next move** następny krok należy do ciebie/do niej; **'it's up to you'** „jak chcesz" [6] (*doing*) **what is he up to?** co on robi?; **they're up to something** oni coś szykują *infml*

(IDIOMS) **to be one up on sb** mieć nad kimś przewagę; **the ups and downs** wzloty i upadki (**of sth** czegoś); **to be (well) up on sth** znać się (dobrze) na czymś

up-and-coming /ˌʌp(ə)n(d)ˈkʌmɪŋ/ *adj* dobrze się zapowiadający

upbeat /ˈʌpbiːt/ *adj* optymistyczny

upbringing /ˈʌpbrɪŋɪŋ/ *n* wychowanie *n*

update /ʌpˈdeɪt/ *vt* [1] (*revise*) uaktualni|ć, -ać [*database, figures*] [2] (*modernize*) z|modernizować [*method, machinery*] [3] przekaz|ać, -ywać najświeższe nowiny (komuś) [*person*] (**on sth** na temat czegoś)

upfront /ʌpˈfrʌnt/ *adj* infml [1] (*frank*) otwarty [2] [*money*] płatny z góry

upgrade /ʌpˈɡreɪd/ *vt* [1] (*modernize*) z|modernizować [*machinery*] [2] Comput wprowadz|ić, -ać nową wersję (czegoś) *[software, hardware]* ③ (raise) awansować *[person]*; podn|ieść, -osić *[position]*

upheaval /ʌpˈhiːvl/ *n* wstrząs *m*; **political** ~ wstrząsy polityczne; **social** ~ wrzenie społeczne

uphill /ʌpˈhɪl/ **I** *adj* ① *[road, path]* (biegnący) pod górę ② (difficult) *[task]* ciężki

II *adv* pod górę

uphold /ʌpˈhəʊld/ *vt* stać na straży (czegoś) *[law, principle]*; utrzym|ać, -ywać w mocy *[decision]*

upholstery /ʌpˈhəʊlstəri/ *n* ① (covering) obicie *n* ② (stuffing) tapicerka *f*

upkeep /ˈʌpkiːp/ *n* ① (of property) utrzymanie *n* (**of sth** czegoś) ② (costs) koszt *m* utrzymania

uplifting /ʌpˈlɪftɪŋ/ *adj* podnoszący na duchu

upload /ʌpˈləʊd/ *vt* przes|łać, -yłać *[data]*

upmarket /ʌpˈmɑːkɪt/ *adj [hotel]* ekskluzywny

upon /əˈpɒn/ *prep* = **on** **I**

upper /ˈʌpə(r)/ **I** *n* (of shoe) wierzch *m*

II *adj* ① (in location) *[shelf, jaw, teeth, floor, deck]* górny; **the** ~ **body** górna połowa ciała ② (in rank) wyższy; (on scale) górny; **the** ~ **limit (on sth)** górna granica (czegoś)

IDIOMS: **to have/get the** ~ **hand** mieć/zyskać przewagę

upper case *adj* ~ **letters** wersaliki

upper class *n* **the** ~, **the** ~es warstwa *f* wyższa

uppermost /ˈʌpəməʊst/ *adj* ① (highest) *[branch, position]* najwyższy ② (to the fore) **to be** ~ być najważniejszym

upper sixth *n* US (in school) ostatnia klasa *f*

upright /ˈʌpraɪt/ **I** *adj* ① (physically) *[person, posture]* wyprostowany ② (honest) *[person, character]* uczciwy

II *adv* **to stand** ~ stać prosto; **to sit** ~ (action) usiąść prosto

uprising /ˈʌpraɪzɪŋ/ *n* powstanie *n* (**against sth** przeciwko czemuś)

uproar /ˈʌprɔː(r)/ *n* (noise) wrzawa *f*; (protest) oburzenie *n*

uproot /ʌpˈruːt/ *vt* wyr|wać, -ywać (z korzeniami) *[plant, flower]*

upset **I** /ˈʌpset/ *n* ① (setback) niepowodzenie *n*; (surprise) niespodzianka *f*; **to suffer an** ~ ponieść porażkę ② (upheaval) zamieszanie *n* ③ (distress) wstrząs *m* ④ Med **to have a stomach** ~ mieć rozstrój żołądka

II /ʌpˈset/ *adj* **to be** or **feel** ~ (distressed) martwić się (**at** or **about sth** czymś); (annoyed) denerwować się (**at** or **about sth** czymś); **to get** ~ (angry) zdenerwować się; (distressed) zmartwić się

III /ʌpˈset/ *vt* ① *[person, sight, news]* (distress) z|martwić; (annoy) z|denerwować ② (throw into disarray) po|krzyżować *[plan]*; ze|psuć *[calculation, pattern, situation]*; zachwiać *[balance]* ③ Med *[food, drink]* rozstr|oić, -ajać *[stomach]*

upsetting /ʌpˈsetɪŋ/ *adj* (distressing) przykry; (annoying) denerwujący

upside down /ˌʌpsaɪdˈdaʊn/ **I** *adj [picture, newspaper]* do góry nogami

II *adv* do góry nogami; **to turn the house** ~ przewrócić dom do góry nogami

upstage /ʌpˈsteɪdʒ/ *vt* przyćmi|ć, -ewać *[person, actor]*

upstairs **I** /ʌpˈsteəz/ *n* góra *f*, piętro *n*

II /ˈʌpsteəz/ *adj* ~ **room/flat** pokój/mieszkanie na piętrze or na górze

III /ʌpˈsteəz/ *adv* na górze, na piętrze; **to go** ~ iść na górę

upstart /ˈʌpstɑːt/ **I** *n* karierowicz *m*, -ka *f*

II *adj* karierowiczowski

upstream /ʌpˈstriːm/ *adv* w górę rzeki

uptake /ˈʌpteɪk/ *n*

IDIOMS: **to be quick/slow on the** ~ infml szybko/wolno się orientować

uptight /ʌpˈtaɪt/ *adj* infml (tense) *[person]* spięty; (reserved) skryty

up-to-date /ˌʌptəˈdeɪt/ *adj* ① *[music, clothes]* modny; *[equipment]* nowoczesny ② *[records, timetable]* aktualny; *[news, information]* najświeższy ③ *[person]* dobrze poinformowany

up-to-the-minute /ˌʌptəðəˈmɪnɪt/ *adj [information]* z ostatniej chwili

upward /ˈʌpwəd/ **I** *adj [push, movement]* do góry; *[path, road]* pod górę; *[trend]* zwyżkujący

II *adv* (also **upwards**) *[look, point]* w górę, do góry; **to go** or **move** ~ wznosić się; **from 5 years** ~ od pięciu lat wzwyż

upwardly mobile /ˌʌpwədlɪˈməʊbaɪl, US -bl/ *adj* pnący się po szczeblach drabiny społecznej

uranium /jʊˈreɪnɪəm/ *n* uran *m*

Uranus /ˈjʊərənəs, jʊˈreɪnəs/ *prn* Uran *m*

urban /ˈɜːbən/ *adj* miejski

urban planning *n* urbanistyka *f*

urban sprawl *n* aglomeracja *f* miejska

urchin /ˈɜːtʃɪn/ *n* łobuziak *m*

Urdu /ˈʊəduː/ *n* (język *m*) urdu *m inv*

urge /ɜːdʒ/ **I** *n* pragnienie *n* (**to do sth** zrobienia czegoś)

II *vt* (encourage) zalec|ić, -ać *[caution, restraint]*; nakł|onić, -aniać do (czegoś) *[resistance]*; **to** ~ **sb to do sth** namawiać kogoś do zrobienia czegoś; (stronger) popychać kogoś do zrobienia czegoś

urgency /ˈɜːdʒənsɪ/ *n* **the** ~ **of a situation** nagląca sytuacja; **as a matter of** ~ w trybie pilnym; **there's no** ~ nie ma pośpiechu

urgent /ˈɜːdʒənt/ *adj* ① (pressing) *[need]* naglący; *[demand, message]* pilny; *[measures]* podjęty w trybie nagłym ② (desperate) *[plea]* usilny; *[tone]* naglący

urgently /ˈɜːdʒəntlɪ/ *adv [plead, request]* natarczywie; ~ **needed** pilnie potrzebny

urinal /jʊəˈraɪnl, ˈjʊərɪnl/ *n* pisuar *m*

urinate /ˈjʊərɪneɪt/ *vi* odda|ć, -wać mocz

urine /ˈjʊərɪn/ *n* mocz *m*

URL n = Unified Resource Locator URL m
urn /ɜːn/ n urna f
us /ʌs, əs/ *pron* **they don't like us** oni nas nie lubią; **for us** dla nas; **with us** z nami; **without us** bez nas; **every single one of us** każdy/każda/ każde z nas; **some of us** niektórzy/niektóre z nas; **she's one of us** ona jest jedną z nas
US n = United States USA *plt inv*
USA n = United States of America USA *plt inv*
use [] /juːs/ n [1] (act of using) (of substance, object, machine) zastosowanie n; (of word, expression) użycie n; **the ~ of force** użycie siły; **for the ~ of sb** do użytku kogoś [customer, staff]; **for my own ~** do mojego użytku; **to make ~ of sth** wykorzystać coś; **to put sth to good ~** dobrze wykorzystać coś; **while the machine is in ~** podczas pracy urządzenia; **worn with ~** zniszczony od częstego używania; **this machine came into ~ in the 1950s** to urządzenie zaczęto stosować w latach pięćdziesiątych; **to have the ~ of sth** móc korzystać z czegoś [house, car, kitchen, garden]; **to lose the ~ of one's legs** stracić władzę w nogach [2] (way of using) (of resource, object, material) zastosowanie n; (of term) użycie n; **to have no further ~ for sb/sth** już więcej nie potrzebować kogoś/czegoś [3] (usefulness) **to be of ~ to sb** przydać się komuś; **to be (of) no ~** być bezużytecznym; **what's the ~ of crying?** płacz na nic się nie zda; **it's no ~** to nic nie da
[] /juːz/ *vt* (employ) [1] użyć|ć, -wać (czegoś); **to ~ sb as sth** posłużyć się kimś jako czymś; **to ~ sth for sth** użyć czegoś do czegoś; **to be ~d for sth** służyć do czegoś [2] (also **~ up**) (consume) zużyć|ć, -wać [fuel, food] [3] (exploit) wykorzyst|ać, -ywać [person]
[] **used** *pp adj* [car] używany
used /juːst/ [] *modal aux* **I ~ to do it** dawniej or kiedyś to robiłem; **didn't she use to smoke?** czy dawniej nie paliła?; **she ~ to smoke, didn't she?** dawniej paliła, prawda?; **there ~ to be a pub here** kiedyś był tu pub
[] /juːzt/ *adj* (accustomed) **to be ~ to sb/sth** być przyzwyczajonym do kogoś/czegoś; **to get ~ to sb/sth** [person, eyes, stomach] przyzwyczaić się do

kogoś/czegoś; **I'm not ~ to it** nie jestem do tego przyzwyczajony
useful /ˈjuːsfl/ *adj* [object, information] przydatny
useless /ˈjuːslɪs/ *adj* [1] (not helpful) nieprzydatny [2] (not able to be used) [object] niezdatny do użytku; [limb] niesprawny [3] infml (incompetent) [person] do niczego infml
user /ˈjuːzə(r)/ n użytkowni|k m, -czka f
user-friendly /ˌjuːzəˈfrendlɪ/ *adj* przyjazny dla użytkownika
usher /ˈʌʃə(r)/ *vt* **to ~ sb in/out** wprowadzić/ wyprowadzić kogoś
usherette /ˌʌʃəˈret/ n ≈ bileterka f
USSR n = Union of Soviet Socialist Republics ZSRR m *inv*
usual /ˈjuːʒl/ *adj* zwykły; **it is ~ for him do it** zwykle tak robi; **as ~** jak zwykle; **more/less than ~** więcej/mniej niż zwykle
usually /ˈjuːʒəlɪ/ *adv* zwykle
utensil /juːˈtensl/ n przyrząd m
uterus /ˈjuːtərəs/ n macica f
utility /juːˈtɪlətɪ/ [] n [1] (usefulness) użyteczność f [2] (also **public ~**) (service) usługa f komunalna [] **utilities** *npl* US akcje f *pl* zakładów użyteczności publicznej
utility company n zakład m użyteczności publicznej
utmost /ˈʌtməʊst/ [] n **to do** or **try one's ~ to do sth** starać się ze wszystkich sił coś zrobić; **she did it to the ~ of her abilities** zrobiła to najlepiej, jak potrafiła
[] *adj* (greatest) [caution, discretion, importance] najwyższy; [ease, secrecy] największy; [limit] maksymalny
Utopia /juːˈtəʊpɪə/ n utopia f
utter[1] /ˈʌtə(r)/ *adj* [disaster, amazement] kompletny; [boredom] śmiertelny; [despair] beznadziejny; [fool, scoundrel] skończony
utter[2] /ˈʌtə(r)/ *vt* wypowi|edzieć, -adać [word, curse]; wyda|ć, -wać z siebie [cry, sound]
utterly /ˈʌtəlɪ/ *adv* całkowicie
U-turn /ˈjuːtɜːn/ n **to make a ~** Aut zawrócić; fig zrobić zwrot o 180 stopni
UV *adj* = **ultraviolet** ultrafioletowy

V

v, V /viː/ *n* [1] (letter) v, V *n* [2] = **versus**

vacancy /'veɪkənsɪ/ *n* [1] (free room) wolny pokój *m*; **'vacancies'** „wolne pokoje"; **'no vacancies'** „brak wolnych miejsc" [2] (unfilled job) wolny etat *m*

vacant /'veɪkənt/ *adj* [1] (unoccupied) *[seat, place]* wolny; *[flat, room, office]* pusty [2] (available) *[post, job]* wolny [3] (dreamy) *[look, stare]* nieobecny

vacant possession *n* house with ~ dom do natychmiastowego objęcia

vacate /vei'keit, US 'veɪkeɪt/ *vt* zw|olnić, -alniać *[room, job]*; wyprowadz|ić, -ać się z (czegoś) *[house, flat]*

vacation /və'keɪʃn, US veɪ-/ *n* wakacje *plt*; (from work) urlop *m*

vacationer /və'keɪʃənə(r), US veɪ-/ *n* US urlopowicz *m*, -ka *f*

vaccinate /'væksɪneɪt/ *vt* za|szczepić (**against sth** przeciwko czemuś)

vaccination /ˌvæksɪ'neɪʃn/ *n* szczepienie *n* (**against sth** przeciwko czemuś)

vaccine /'væksiːn, US væk'siːn/ *n* szczepionka *f* (**against sth** przeciwko czemuś)

vacillate /'væsəleɪt/ *vi* wahać się

vacuum /'vækjʊəm/ **I** *n* [1] próżnia *f* [2] (also ~ **cleaner**) odkurzacz *m*
II *vt* (also ~**-clean**) odkurz|yć, -ać *[carpet]*; odkurz|yć, -ać w (czymś) *[room]*

vacuum pack *vt* o|pakować próżniowo

vagrant /'veɪgrənt/ **I** *n* włóczęga *m*
II *adj* wędrowny

vague /veɪg/ *adj* [1] (imprecise) *[account, rumour]* mętny; *[idea, memory]* mglisty; *[term]* niejednoznaczny; *[person]* mało precyzyjny; **to be ~ about sth** mówić ogólnikowo o czymś [2] (distracted) *[person, expression]* roztargniony

vaguely /'veɪglɪ/ *adv* [1] (faintly) *[resemble]* trochę, nieco; *[sinister, amusing]* z lekka [2] (distractedly) *[smile, gaze, say]* z roztargnieniem

vain /veɪn/ **I** *adj* [1] (conceited) próżny [2] (futile) *[attempt]* daremny; *[hope]* płonny
II in vain *adv phr* na próżno

valentine /'væləntaɪn/ *n* (also ~ **card**) walentynka *f*

Valentine('s) Day *n* walentynki *plt*

valet /'vælɪt, -leɪ/ *n* [1] (employee) służący *m* [2] US (rack) stojak *m* na ubrania

valet parking *n* odstawianie *n* samochodów na parking przez obsługę

valiant /'væliənt/ *n* *[soldier]* waleczny; *[effort]* śmiały

valid /'vælɪd/ *adj* [1] *[passport, licence, ticket, offer]* ważny [2] *[argument, point]* słuszny; *[comparison, method]* sensowny

validate /'vælɪdeɪt/ *vt* [1] potwierdz|ić, -ać *[theory, claim]* [2] (give legal force to) nada|ć, -wać ważność (czemuś) *[document]*

valley /'vælɪ/ *n* dolina *f*

valour GB, **valor** US /'vælə(r)/ *n* męstwo *n*

valuable /'væljʊəbl/ *adj* *[commodity, asset, advice]* cenny; *[ring]* kosztowny

valuables /'væljʊəblz/ *npl* kosztowności *plt*

valuation /ˌvæljʊ'eɪʃn/ *n* (of price) wycena *f*; (of quality) ocena *f*; **to have a ~ done on sth** zlecić wycenę czegoś

value /'væljuː/ **I** *n* wartość *f*; **family ~s** wartości rodzinne; **of no ~** bezwartościowy; **to be good/poor ~ for money** dostać towar wart swej ceny
II *vt* [1] (assess worth of) wyceni|ć, -ać *[assets, property]* [2] (regard highly) cenić (sobie) *[friendship, freedom]*

value pack *n* duże opakowanie *n*

valve /vælv/ *n* [1] (in machine, engine) zawór *m*; (on tyre, football) wentyl *m* [2] Anat zastawka *f*

van /væn/ *n* [1] (small, for deliveries) furgonetka *f*; (larger, for removals) furgon *m* [2] US (camper) przyczepa *f* kempingowa

vandal /'vændl/ *n* wandal *m*

vandalism /'vændəlɪzəm/ *n* wandalizm *m*

vandalize /'vændəlaɪz/ *vt* z|dewastować

van driver *n* kierowca *m* furgonetki

vanguard /'vænɡɑːd/ *n* Mil, fig awangarda *f*

vanilla /və'nɪlə/ *n* wanilia *f*

vanish /'vænɪʃ/ *vi* znik|nąć, -ać; **to ~ into thin air** ulotnić się jak kamfora

vanity /'vænətɪ/ *n* próżność *f*

vantage point *n* punkt *m* obserwacyjny; fig punkt *m* widzenia

vaporizer /'veɪpəraɪzə(r)/ *n* aerozol *m*

vapour GB, **vapor** US /'veɪpə(r)/ *n* para *f*

vapour trail *n* smuga *f* kondensacyjna

variable /'veərɪəbl/ **I** *n* zmienna *f*
II *adj* zmienny

variance /'veərɪəns/ n niezgodność f; **to be at ~ with sth** być sprzecznym z czymś [evidence, facts]

variant /'veərɪənt/ n wariant m (**of** or **on sth** czegoś)

variation /ˌveərɪ'eɪʃn/ n ① (change) zmiana f; (difference) różnica f ② (version) odmiana f

varied /'veərɪd/ adj różnorodny

variety /və'raɪətɪ/ n ① (diversity) różnorodność f (**in** or **of sth** czegoś); (interesting difference) urozmaicenie n; **for a ~ of reasons** z różnych powodów; **in a ~ of sizes/colours** w różnych rozmiarach/kolorach ② (type) rodzaj m; (of plant) odmiana f

variety show n rewia f

various /'veərɪəs/ adj (different) różny; (diverse) rozmaity; **on ~ occasions** przy różnych okazjach

varnish /'vɑːnɪʃ/ ❚ n lakier m
❚❚ vt po|lakierować; **to ~ one's nails** pomalować sobie paznokcie

vary /'veərɪ/ ❚ vt urozmaic|ić, -ać [menu, programme]; zmieni|ć, -ać [pace, route]; regulować [flow, temperature]
❚❚ vi ① (change) zmieni|ć, -ać się; **to ~ according to sth** zmieniać się w zależności od czegoś ② (differ) różnić się (**from sth** od czegoś)

varying /'veərɪɪŋ/ adj [amounts, degrees, opinions] różny

vase /vɑːz, US veɪs, veɪz/ n wazon m

vast /vɑːst, US væst/ adj [amount, sum, size, room] ogromny; [knowledge] bardzo rozległy; [wealth] nieprzebrany

vat /væt/ n kadź f

VAT /væt/ = **value-added tax** VAT m

Vatican /'vætɪkən/ prn Watykan m

vault[1] /vɔːlt/ n ① (roof) sklepienie n ② (basement) piwnica f; (of church) podziemia n pl; (in bank) skarbiec m

vault[2] /vɔːlt/ ❚ vt przesk|oczyć, -akiwać przez (coś) [barrier, fence, bar]
❚❚ vi sk|oczyć, -akać (**over sth** przez coś)

VCR = **video cassette recorder** n kamera f wideo

VD = **venereal disease**

VDU = **visual display unit** monitor m ekranowy, ekranopis m

veal /viːl/ n cielęcina f

veer /vɪə(r)/ vi [boat] obr|ócić, -acać się rufą do wiatru; [person] skręc|ić, -ać gwałtownie; [road] zakręc|ić, -ać ostro; **to ~ off course** zboczyć z kursu

vegan /'viːgən/ n wegan|in m, -ka f

veganism /'viːgənɪzəm/ n weganizm m

vegetable /'vedʒtəbl/ ❚ n warzywo n
❚❚ adj [soup, salad] jarzynowy; [fat, oil, matter] roślinny; [patch, garden] warzywny

vegetarian /ˌvedʒɪ'teərɪən/ n wegetarian|in m, -ka f

vegetarianism /ˌvedʒɪ'teərɪənɪzəm/ n wegetarianizm m

vegetate /'vedʒɪteɪt/ vi [person] wegetować; [plant] rosnąć

vegetation /ˌvedʒɪ'teɪʃn/ n wegetacja f

vegie burger n wegetariański hamburger m

vehement /'viːəmənt/ adj [gesture, attack] gwałtowny; [defence] zaciekły

vehicle /'vɪəkl, US 'viːhɪkl/ n pojazd m

veil /veɪl/ ❚ n ① welon m; (on hat) woalka f ② fig zasłona f
❚❚ vt [mist, cloud] spowi|ć, -jać
❚❚❚ prp adj **veiled** zawoalowany

vein /veɪn/ n żyła f; (on leaf, insect wing) żyłka f

velocity /vɪ'lɒsətɪ/ n prędkość f

velour(s) /ve'lʊə(r)/ n welur m

velvet /'velvɪt/ n aksamit m

velvety /'velvətɪ/ adj aksamitny

vending machine n automat m (z papierosami, napojami)

vendor /'vendə(r)/ n ① (in street, kiosk) sprzedaw|ca m, -czyni f ② (as opposed to buyer) sprzedający m, -a f

veneer /vɪ'nɪə(r)/ n ① (on wood) fornir m ② fig **a ~ of sth** pozory czegoś

venereal disease n choroba f weneryczna

Venetian blind n żaluzja f

Venezuela /ˌvenɪ'zweɪlə/ prn Wenezuela f

vengeance /'vendʒəns/ n zemsta f; **with a ~** [work, study] z wielkim zapałem

Venice /'venɪs/ prn Wenecja f

venison /'venɪsn, -zn/ n sarnina f

venom /'venəm/ n jad m also fig

venomous /'venəməs/ adj jadowity also fig

vent /vent/ ❚ n (shaft) przewód m wentylacyjny; **to give ~ to sth** dać upust czemuś [anger, feelings]
❚❚ vt da|ć, -wać upust (czemuś) [feeling, rage, frustration]

ventilate /'ventɪleɪt/ vt przewietrz|yć, -ać [room]

ventilation /ˌventɪ'leɪʃn/ n ① (system) wentylacja f ② (of patient) sztuczna wentylacja f

ventilator /'ventɪleɪtə(r)/ n Med respirator m

ventriloquist /ven'trɪləkwɪst/ n brzuchomówca m

venture /'ventʃə(r)/ ❚ n ① (undertaking) śmiałe przedsięwzięcie n; **a publishing ~** przedsięwzięcie wydawnicze ② (experiment) próba f
❚❚ vt za|ryzykować [opinion, suggestion]; **to ~ to do sth** ośmielić się coś zrobić
❚❚❚ vi **to ~ into the street** (odważyć się) wyjść na ulicę; **have you ~d outside today?** czy wychodziłeś dzisiaj?

venture capital n kapitał m wysokiego ryzyka

venue /'venjuː/ n miejsce n (spotkania, koncertu)

verb /vɜːb/ n czasownik m

verbal /'vɜːbl/ adj [agreement] ustny; [attack] werbalny; [suffix, form] czasownikowy

verbatim /vɜː'beɪtɪm/ ❚ adj [report, quotation] dosłowny
❚❚ adv [describe, record] dosłownie

verbose /vɜ:'bəʊs/ adj *[person]* wielomówny; *[article, style]* rozwlekły

verdict /'vɜ:dɪkt/ n ① (of court) wyrok m; (of jury) werdykt m; **a** ~ **of guilty/not guilty** wyrok skazujący/uniewinniający ② (opinion) opinia f; **well then, what's your** ~? no i co o tym sądzisz?

verge /vɜ:dʒ/ n ① GB (of road, path) skraj m; Aut pobocze n ② (brink) **on the** ~ **of sth** na progu czegoś *[adolescence, old age]*; **on the** ~ **of doing sth** bliski zrobienia czegoś

■ **verge on**: graniczyć z (czymś) *[stupidity, contempt]*

verification /ˌverɪfɪ'keɪʃn/ n weryfikacja f

verify /'verɪfaɪ/ vt (confirm) potwierdz|ić, -ać; (check) z|weryfikować

vermicelli /ˌvɜ:mɪ'selɪ, -'tʃelɪ/ n makaron m nitki

vermilion /və'mɪlɪən/ n cynober m

vermin /'vɜ:mɪn/ n (rodents) szkodniki m pl; (insects) robactwo n

verruca /və'ru:kə/ n brodawka f

versatile /'vɜ:sətaɪl/ adj *[person, mind]* wszechstronny; *[equipment, tool]* uniwersalny

verse /vɜ:s/ n ① (poems) poezja f ② (poem) wiersz m; **in** ~ wierszem ③ (part of poem) zwrotka f

version /'vɜ:ʃn, US -ʒn/ n wersja f

versus /'vɜ:səs/ prep ① (against) przeciwko (komuś/czemuś) ② (as opposed to) w przeciwieństwie do (czegoś)

vertebra /'vɜ:tɪbrə/ n Anat kręg m

vertebrate /'vɜ:tɪbreɪt/ n kręgowiec m

vertical /'vɜ:tɪkl/ adj *[line, column]* pionowy; *[cliff, drop]* stromy

vertigo /'vɜ:tɪgəʊ/ n zawroty m pl głowy; **to get** ~ dostać zawrotów głowy

verve /vɜ:v/ n werwa f

very /'verɪ/ Ⅰ adj ① (actual) właśnie ten; **at that** ~ **moment** w tej właśnie chwili; **the** ~ **thing I need** właśnie to, czego mi potrzeba ② (ultimate) sam; **at the** ~ **beginning** na samym początku; **in the** ~ **heart of the jungle** w samym sercu dżungli ③ (mere) sam; **the** ~ **mention of her name** sam dźwięk jej imienia; **the** ~ **idea!** cóż za pomysł!

Ⅱ adv ① (extremely) bardzo; **I'm** ~ **sorry** bardzo mi przykro; **that's all** ~ **well but...** no dobrze, ale przecież....; **I didn't eat** ~ **much** nie zjadłem dużo ② (absolutely) **the** ~ **best hotels** najlepsze hotele; **at the** ~ **latest** najpóźniej; **at the** ~ **least** przynajmniej; **the** ~ **next day** od razu następnego dnia; **did you do it on your** ~ **own** czy zrobiłeś to zupełnie sam?

vessel /'vesl/ n ① (ship) statek m ② Anat naczynie n; **blood** ~**s** naczynia krwionośne ③ (container) naczynie n

vest /vest/ n ① (underwear) podkoszulek m ② (for sport) koszulka f ③ US (waistcoat) kamizelka f

vested interest n **to have a** ~ **in sth** być osobiście zainteresowanym czymś

vestige /'vestɪdʒ/ n pozostałość f (**of sth** czegoś, po czymś)

vet[1] /vet/ n = **veterinary surgeon** weterynarz m

vet[2] /vet/ vt sprawdz|ić, -ać *[person]*; z|weryfikować *[application, proposal]*; podda|ć, -wać cenzurze *[publication]*

vet[3] /vet/ n US infml weteran m

veteran /'vetərən/ Ⅰ n weteran m, -ka f; (of war) kombatant m, -ka f

Ⅱ adj *[politician]* wytrawny; *[soldier]* zaprawiony w boju

veterinarian /ˌvetərɪ'neərɪən/ n US weterynarz m

veterinary surgeon n weterynarz m

veterinary surgery n klinika f weterynaryjna

veto /'vi:təʊ/ Ⅰ n ① (practice) weto n (**over** or **on sth** w sprawie czegoś) ② (also **the right of** ~) prawo n weta

Ⅱ vt za|wetować

vetting /'vetɪŋ/ n sprawdzenie n

vex /veks/ vt (annoy) drażnić; (worry) męczyć

vexed /vekst/ adj ① (annoyed) zirytowany (**with sb** na kogoś) ② *[question, issue]* dręczący

VHF n, adj = **very high frequency** VHF

via /'vaɪə/ prep ① przez (coś); ~ **London** przez Londyn; ~ **the motorway** trasą szybkiego ruchu; ~ **satellite** przez satelitę

viability /ˌvaɪə'bɪlətɪ/ n (of company) rentowność f; (of plan) wykonalność f

viable /'vaɪəbl/ adj (feasible) *[idea, plan]* realny, wykonalny; *[company]* rentowny; *[product]* opłacalny

viaduct /'vaɪədʌkt/ n wiadukt m

vibrant /'vaɪbrənt/ adj *[place, city]* tętniący życiem; *[person]* tryskający energią; *[personality]* pełen życia; *[colour]* żywy

vibrate /vaɪ'breɪt, US 'vaɪbreɪt/ vi drgać

vibration /vaɪ'breɪʃn/ n drganie n

vicar /'vɪkə(r)/ n (Anglican) pastor m

vicarage /'vɪkərɪdʒ/ n plebania f

vicarious /vɪ'keərɪəs, US vaɪ'k-/ adj *[knowledge]* z drugiej ręki

vice[1] /vaɪs/ n wada f; (weakness) słabostka f

vice[2] /vaɪs/ n (also **vise** US) imadło n

vice-captain /ˌvaɪs'kæptɪn/ n zastępca m kapitana drużyny

vice-chancellor /ˌvaɪs'tʃɑ:nsələ(r), US -'tʃæn-/ n GB Univ ≈ rektor m

vice-president /ˌvaɪs'prezɪdənt/ n (of country) wiceprezydent m; (of company) wiceprezes m

vice squad n policja f obyczajowa

vicinity /vɪ'sɪnətɪ/ n sąsiedztwo n; **in the** ~ w pobliżu (**of sth** czegoś); **in the immediate** ~ **of sth** w bezpośrednim sąsiedztwie czegoś

vicious /'vɪʃəs/ adj *[dog]* zły; *[criminal]* bezwzględny; *[attack]* wściekły; *[lie, rumour]* podły; *[sarcasm, words]* złośliwy

vicious circle *n* błędne koło *n*

victim /'vɪktɪm/ *n* ofiara *f*

victimization /ˌvɪktɪmaɪ'zeɪʃn/ *n* prześladowanie *n*

victimize /'vɪktɪmaɪz/ *vt* prześladować

victor /'vɪktə(r)/ *n* zwycięzca *m*, -żczyni *f*

Victorian /vɪk'tɔːrɪən/ *adj* wiktoriański

victorious /vɪk'tɔːrɪəs/ *adj* zwycięski

victory /'vɪktərɪ/ *n* zwycięstwo *n*

video /'vɪdɪəʊ/ **[I]** *n* [1] (also ~ **recorder**) magnetowid *m*; wideo *n inv* infml [2] (also ~ **cassette**) kaseta *f* wideo; **on** ~ na (kasecie) wideo [3] (also ~ **film**) film *m* wideo
[II] *adj [equipment]* wideo; *[footage, interview]* na wideo
[III] *vt* (from TV) nagr|ać, -ywać (na wideo); (on camcorder) s|filmować

video camera *n* kamera *f* wideo

video card *n* karta *f* wideo

video clip *n* wideoklip *m*

videoconference /'vɪdɪəʊkɒnfərəns/ *n* wideokonferencja *f*

videodisc /'vɪdɪəʊdɪsk/ *n* wideodysk *m*

video game *n* gra *f* wideo

video jock *n* infml disc jockey *m (prezentujący nagrania wideo w dyskotece lub TV)*

video nasty *n* film *m* wideo zawierający drastyczne sceny

videophone /'vɪdɪəʊfəʊn/ *n* wideotelefon *m*

video shop GB, **video store** US *n* sklep *m* wideo

videotape /'vɪdɪəʊteɪp/ *n* taśma *f* wideo

vie /vaɪ/ *vi* rywalizować (**with sb** z kimś); ubiegać się (**for sth** o coś)

Vienna /vɪ'enə/ *prn* Wiedeń *m*

view /vjuː/ **[I]** *n* [1] (scene, vista) widok *m*; **to block sb's** ~ zasłaniać komuś (widok); **to disappear from** ~ zniknąć (z pola widzenia); **in** ~ w zasięgu wzroku; **to do sth in (full)** ~ **of sb** zrobić coś na oczach kogoś [2] (of situation) ocena *f*; (prospect) widoki *plt*; **to have sth in** ~ (as prospect) mieć coś na widoku; (as aim) mieć coś na uwadze [3] (attitude) opinia *f*; **point of** ~ punkt widzenia; **sb's political** ~ **s** czyjeś poglądy polityczne; **in my** ~ według mnie
[II] in view of *prep phr* (considering) wobec (czegoś)
[III] with a view to *prep phr* **with a** ~ **to doing sth** mając zamiar coś zrobić
[IV] *vt* [1] (look at) o|bejrzeć, -glądać *[castle, exhibition, programme]*; zwiedz|ić, -ać *[exhibition, castle]* [2] (examine) rozpat|rzyć, -rywać *[matter, subject]* [3] (consider) patrzeć na (kogoś/coś); **to** ~ **sb with suspicion** traktować kogoś podejrzliwie

viewer /'vjuː:ə(r)/ *n* [1] (of TV) (tele)widz *m*; (of property) zainteresowan|y *m*, -a *f* [2] (for slides) przeglądarka *f*; (on camera) wizjer *m*

viewfinder /'vjuː:faɪndə(r)/ *n* wizjer *m*

viewing /'vjuː:ɪŋ/ **[I]** *n* (of exhibition, castle) zwiedzanie *n*; (of film, clothes collection) pokaz *m*
[II] *adj* ~ **habits/preferences** zwyczaje/preferencje widzów; ~ **figures** dane dotyczące oglądalności

viewpoint /'vjuː:pɔɪnt/ *n* punkt *m* obserwacyjny; fig punkt *m* widzenia

vigil /'vɪdʒɪl/ *n* czuwanie *n*

vigilant /'vɪdʒɪlənt/ *adj* czujny

vigilante /ˌvɪdʒɪ'læntɪ/ *n* członek *m* straży obywatelskiej

vigorous /'vɪgərəs/ *adj [person, attempt, exercise]* energiczny

vigour GB, **vigor** US /'vɪgə(r)/ *n* (of person) wigor *m*

vile /vaɪl/ *adj [smell, taste]* ohydny; *[language]* plugawy; *[mood, temper]* paskudny

villa /'vɪlə/ *n* (in the country) rezydencja *f* wiejska; (holiday house) dom *m* letni

village /'vɪlɪdʒ/ *n* miasteczko *n*; (farming) wieś *f*

village green *n* błonia *plt (w środku miasteczka, wsi)*

village hall *n* ≈ dom *m* ludowy

villager /'vɪlɪdʒə(r)/ *n* mieszkan|iec *m*, -ka *f* miasteczka; (farmer) mieszkan|iec *m*, -ka *f* wsi

villain /'vɪlən/ *n* (criminal) złoczyńca *m*; (child) łobuziak *m*; (in book) czarny charakter *m*

vindicate /'vɪndɪkeɪt/ *vt* potwierdz|ić, -ać słuszność (czegoś) *[action, decision]*; z|rehabilitować *[person]*

vindictive /vɪn'dɪktɪv/ *adj* mściwy

vindictiveness /vɪn'dɪktɪvnɪs/ *adj* mściwość *f*

vine /vaɪn/ *n* (grapevine) winorośl *f*; (climbing plant) pnącze *n*

vinegar /'vɪnɪgə(r)/ *n* ocet *m*

vineyard /'vɪnjəd/ *n* winnica *f*

vintage /'vɪntɪdʒ/ **[I]** *n* (wine) rocznik *m*
[II] *adj* [1] (wine) (z) dobrego rocznika; (port) stary [2] *[comedy, film]* klasyczny

vintage car *n* stary samochód *m*

vinyl /'vaɪnl/ **[I]** *n* winyl *m*
[II] *adj* winylowy

viola /vɪ'əʊlə/ *n* Mus altówka *f*

violate /'vaɪəleɪt/ *vt* [1] narusz|yć, -ać *[law, right, privacy]* [2] z|bezcześcić *[shrine, grave]*; zakłóc|ić, -ać *[peace]*

violation /ˌvaɪə'leɪʃn/ *n* (of law, agreement) naruszenie *n*; (offence) wykroczenie *n*

violence /'vaɪələns/ *n* przemoc *f*

violent /'vaɪələnt/ *adj* [1] *[person, behaviour, temper]* agresywny; *[death]* gwałtowny; *[crime, film]* brutalny [2] *[contrast]* uderzający [3] *[colour]* ostry

violently /'vaɪələntlɪ/ *adv* gwałtownie

violet /'vaɪələt/ **[I]** *n* [1] (flower) fiołek *m* [2] (colour) fiolet *m*
[II] *adj* fioletowy

violin /ˌvaɪə'lɪn/ *n* skrzypce *plt*

violinist /ˌvaɪə'lɪnɪst/ *n* skrzyp|ek *m*, -aczka *f*

VIP Ⅰ = very important person

Ⅱ *n* VIP *m*

Ⅲ *adj [area, lounge]* dla VIP-ów; ~ **guest** ważny gość; **to give sb (the)** ~ **treatment** przyjąć kogoś z honorami

viper /'vaɪpə(r)/ *n* żmija *f*

virgin /'vɜːdʒɪn/ Ⅰ *n* dziewica *f*

Ⅱ *adj* dziewiczy

Virgo /'vɜːgəʊ/ *n* Panna *f*

virile /'vɪraɪl, US 'vɪrəl/ *adj* jurny, męski

virtual /'vɜːtʃʊəl/ *adj* ① (almost complete) **it's a** ~ **impossibility** to praktycznie niemożliwe; **he was a** ~ **prisoner** był faktycznie więźniem ② Comput wirtualny

virtually /'vɜːtʃʊəlɪ/ *adv* praktycznie, w zasadzie

virtual reality *n* rzeczywistość *f* wirtualna

virtue /'vɜːtʃuː/ Ⅰ *n* ① (goodness) cnota *f* ② (advantage) zaleta *f*

Ⅱ **by virtue of** *prep phr* ze względu na (coś)

virtuoso /ˌvɜːtjʊ'əʊsəʊ, -zəʊ/ *n* wirtuoz *m*, -ka *f*

virtuous /'vɜːtʃʊəs/ *adj* prawy, cnotliwy

virus /'vaɪərəs/ *n* wirus *m*

virus checker *n* oprogramowanie *n* wykrywające wirusy

visa /'viːzə/ *n* wiza *f*

vis-à-vis /ˌviːzɑ'viː/ *prep* (in relation to) wobec (kogoś/czegoś); (concerning) co do (czegoś), względem (czegoś)

visibility /ˌvɪzə'bɪlətɪ/ *n* widoczność *f*

visible /'vɪzəbl/ *adj* ① (able to be seen) widoczny; **clearly** ~ wyraźnie widoczny ② (concrete) *[improvement, sign]* widoczny

visibly /'vɪzəblɪ/ *adv [moved, shocked]* wyraźnie

vision /'vɪʒn/ *n* ① (conception, idea, hallucination) wizja *f* ② (ability to see) wzrok *m* ③ (foresight) wyobraźnia *f*

visionary /'vɪʒənrɪ, US 'vɪʒənerɪ/ Ⅰ *n* wizjoner *m*, -ka *f*

Ⅱ *adj* wizjonerski

visit /'vɪzɪt/ Ⅰ *n* ① (call) wizyta *f*; (to see friend) odwiedziny *plt*; **a state** ~ wizyta państwowa; **to pay a** ~ **to sb, to pay sb a** ~ odwiedzić kogoś; (more official) złożyć komuś wizytę ② (stay) pobyt *m*; **on her first** ~ **to China** podczas jej pierwszego pobytu w Chinach

Ⅱ *vt* odwiedz|ić, -ać *[friend, patient, country]*; pójść, iść do (kogoś) *[doctor, solicitor]*; zwiedz|ić, -ać *[castle, exhibition]*

Ⅲ *vi* US (socially) **to** ~ **with sb** odwiedz|ić, -ać kogoś

visiting card *n* US wizytówka *f*

visiting hours *npl* godziny *f pl* odwiedzin

visitor /'vɪzɪtə(r)/ *n* ① (caller) gość *m* ② (tourist) zwiedzając|y *m*, -a *f*

visitor centre *n* informacja *f* turystyczna

visitors' book *n* księga *f* gości

visor /'vaɪzə(r)/ *n* daszek *m* przezroczysty; Aut osłona *f* przeciwsłoneczna

vista /'vɪstə/ *n* panorama *f*; fig perspektywa *f* (**of sth** czegoś)

visual /'vɪʒʊəl/ *adj [image, representation]* wizualny; *[perception, memory]* wzrokowy

visual aid *n* pomoc *f* wizualna

visual arts *npl* sztuki *f pl* plastyczne

visualize /'vɪʒʊəlaɪz/ *vt* wyobra|zić, -żać sobie

visually impaired *n* the ~ niedowidzący *m pl*

vital /'vaɪtl/ *adj* ① (essential) *[research, need]* podstawowy; *[service, help]* niezbędny; *[issue]* żywotny; *[role, factor, support, match]* decydujący ② (lively) *[person]* pełen życia

vitality /vaɪ'tælətɪ/ *n* witalność *f*

vitally /'vaɪtəlɪ/ *adv [needed]* absolutnie; *[important]* niezmiernie

vital statistics *n* hum (woman's) podstawowe wymiary *m pl*

vitamin /'vɪtəmɪn, US 'vaɪt-/ *n* witamina *f*

viva Ⅰ /'vaɪvə/ *n* GB egzamin *m* ustny

Ⅱ /'viːvə/ *excl* niech żyje!

vivacious /vɪ'veɪʃəs/ *adj* pełen życia

vivid /'vɪvɪd/ *adj* ① (bright) *[colour, light]* jaskrawy ② (graphic) *[imagination, memory]* żywy; *[detail, description, impression, language]* barwny

vividly /'vɪvɪdlɪ/ *adv [remember]* doskonale; *[describe]* barwnie

vivisection /ˌvɪvɪ'sekʃn/ *n* wiwisekcja *f*

vixen /'vɪksn/ *n* ① Zool lisica *f* ② (woman) jędza *f*

viz /vɪz/ *adv* = **videlicet** tzn.

V-neck /'viːnek/ *n* (neck) dekolt *m* w serek; (sweater) sweter *m* z dekoltem w serek

vocabulary /və'kæbjʊlərɪ, US -lerɪ/ *n* słownictwo *n*

vocal /'vəʊkl/ *adj* ① *[organs]* głosowy ② (vociferous) *[person, group]* głośno wyrażający opinię

vocalist /'vəʊkəlɪst/ *n* wokalist|a *m*, -ka *f*

vocals /'vəʊklz/ *npl* śpiew *m*; **to do the backing** ~ robić podkład wokalny

vocation /və'keɪʃn/ *n* powołanie *n*

vocational /və'keɪʃənl/ *adj* zawodowy

vocational course *n* szkolenie *n* zawodowe

vociferous /və'sɪfərəs, US vəʊ-/ *adj [person, protest]* hałaśliwy

vogue /vəʊg/ *n* moda *f* (**for sth** na coś)

voice /vɔɪs/ Ⅰ *n* głos *m*; **in a loud** ~ głośno; **in a cross** ~ gniewnym głosem; **he lost his** ~ (when ill) stracił głos; **at the top of one's** ~ na cały głos

Ⅱ *vt* wyra|zić, -żać *[concern, reservations]*

voicemail /'vɔɪsmeɪl/ *n* poczta *f* głosowa

voice-over /'vɔɪsəʊvə(r)/ *n* głos *m* lektora

void /vɔɪd/ Ⅰ *n* pustka *f*; **to fill the** ~ wypełnić pustkę

Ⅱ *adj* ① *[agreement, contract]* nieważny; *[cheque]* anulowany ② (empty) ~ **of sth** pozbawiony czegoś

volatile /'vɒlətaɪl, US -tl/ *adj [person]* wybuchowy; *[situation]* nieprzewidywalny; *[market, exchange rate]* niestabilny

volcano /vɒl'keɪnəʊ/ n wulkan m

volley /'vɒlɪ/ **I** n 1 Sport wolej m 2 (of shots) salwa f 3 (series) **a ~ of questions/stones** grad pytań/kamieni; **a ~ of insults** stek obelg

II vt Sport uderz|yć, -áć z woleja [ball]

volleyball /'vɒlɪbɔːl/ n siatkówka f

volt /vəʊlt/ n wolt m

voltage /'vəʊltɪdʒ/ n napięcie n prądu elektrycznego

volume /'vɒljuːm, US -jəm/ n 1 (book) książka f; (part of set) tom m 2 (of gas, liquid, object) objętość f (**of sth** czegoś); (of container) pojemność f 3 (bulk) **the ~ of sth** wielkość czegoś [production, sales, trade] 4 (sound quantity) głośność f

volume control n regulator m głosu

voluntarily /'vɒləntrəlɪ/ adv dobrowolnie

voluntary /'vɒləntrɪ, US -terɪ/ adj 1 (unforced) dobrowolny 2 (unpaid) społeczny

voluntary redundancy n odejście n z pracy na własną prośbę

volunteer /ˌvɒlən'tɪə(r)/ **I** n 1 (offering to do sth) ochotni|k m, -czka f 2 (unpaid worker) wolontariusz m, -ka f

II vt po|śpieszyć z (czymś) [information, advice]; **to ~ to do sth** zgodzić się coś zrobić

III vi zgł|osić, -aszać się na ochotnika

voluptuous /və'lʌptʃʊəs/ adj [woman] ponętna

vomit /'vɒmɪt/ **I** n wymiociny plt

II vt, vi z|wymiotować

voodoo /'vuːduː/ n wudu n inv

voracious /və'reɪʃəs/ adj żarłoczny

vortex /'vɔːteks/ n wir m also fig

vote /vəʊt/ **I** n 1 (choice) głos m; **to cast one's ~** oddać głos 2 (right to vote) **the ~** czynne prawo n wyborcze 3 (ballot) głosowanie n

II vt 1 (affirm choice of) za|głosować na (kogoś/coś); **to ~ sb into office** wybrać kogoś na stanowisko 2 infml (suggest) za|proponować

III vi głosować; **to ~ for** or **in favour of sth** głosować za czymś; **to ~ against sth** głosować przeciwko czemuś; **to ~ on sth** głosować w sprawie czegoś

vote of confidence n wotum n inv zaufania (**in sb** dla kogoś)

vote of thanks n podziękowania plt

voter /'vəʊtə(r)/ n wyborca m

voting /'vəʊtɪŋ/ n głosowanie n

voting age n wiek m uprawniający do głosowania

vouch /vaʊtʃ/ vt **to ~ that...** ręczyć, że...

■ **vouch for**: za|ręczyć za (kogoś) [person]; po|świadczyć [fact]

voucher /'vaʊtʃə(r)/ n bon m, talon m

vow /vaʊ/ **I** n (religious) śluby m pl; (of honour) ślubowanie n; **marriage** or **wedding ~s** przysięga f małżeńska

II vt ślubować [love, allegiance]; poprzysi|ąc, -ęgać [revenge]

vowel /'vaʊəl/ n samogłoska f

voyage /'vɔɪɪdʒ/ n podróż f morska

V-sign /'viːsaɪn/ n 1 (victory sign) znak m wiktorii 2 GB (offensive gesture) obsceniczny gest m

VSO n GB = **Voluntary Service Overseas** organizacja wysyłająca wolontariuszy do pracy w krajach rozwijających się

vulgar /'vʌlgə(r)/ adj 1 [person] nieokrzesany; [furniture, clothes] w złym guście; [taste] niewybredny 2 (rude) wulgarny

vulnerable /'vʌlnərəbl/ adj 1 (likely to be badly affected) narażony na niebezpieczeństwo; **~ to sth** narażony na coś [attack]; podatny na coś [infection] 2 (unable to defend itself) bezbronny

vulture /'vʌltʃə(r)/ n sęp m

w, W /'dʌblju:/ *n* w, W *n*

wad /wɒd/ *n* (of banknotes, papers) plik *m* (**of sth** czegoś); **a ~ of cotton wool** wacik

waddle /'wɒdl/ *vi* dreptać

wade /weɪd/ *vi* [1] (in water) **to ~ into the water** wejść do wody; **to ~ ashore** wyjść na brzeg; **to ~ across the river** przejść przez rzekę [2] *fig* brnąć (**through sth** przez coś); **I managed to ~ through the book** jakoś przebrnąłem przez tę książkę

waders /'weɪdəz/ *npl* wodery *plt*

wafer /'weɪfə(r)/ *n* [1] Culin wafel *m* [2] (in church) opłatek *m*

wafer-thin /ˌweɪfə'θɪn/ *adj* cienki jak opłatek

waffle[1] /'wɒfl/ *n* Culin gofr *m*

waffle[2] /'wɒfl/ *infml* **I** *n* (empty words) wodolejstwo *n* **II** *vi* (**also ~ on**) (speaking) ględzić *infml*; (writing) rozwodzić się

waft /wɒft, US wæft/ *vi* **to ~ up from somewhere** [sound, smell] dochodzić skądś

wag /wæg/ **I** *vt* mach|nąć, -ać (czymś) [tail] **II** *vi* [tail, finger, head] porusz|yć, -ać się; **tongues will ~** ludzie będą gadać

wage /weɪdʒ/ **I** *n* (**also ~s**) płaca *f* **II** *vt* prowadzić [campaign]; **to ~ (a) war against sb** prowadzić wojnę przeciwko komuś *also fig*

wage earner *n* [1] (person earning a wage) pracownik *m* najemny [2] (breadwinner) żywiciel *m* rodziny

wage packet *n* (envelope) wypłata *f* w kopercie; *fig* (money) wypłata *f*

wager /'weɪdʒə(r)/ *n* zakład *m*; **to make** *or* **lay a ~ that...** pójść o zakład, że...

wage slip *n* pasek *m* wypłaty

waggon GB, **wagon** GB, **wagon** /'wægən/ *n* [1] (horse-drawn) wóz *m* [2] GB (on rail) wagon *m* towarowy [IDIOMS:] **to be on the ~** *infml* odstawić alkohol

wail /weɪl/ **I** *n* (of person, instrument) zawodzenie *n*; (of siren) wycie *n* **II** *vi* [person, instrument] zawodzić; [siren] za|wyć

waist /weɪst/ *n* pas *m*, talia *f*

waistband /'weɪstbænd/ *n* pasek *m* wszywany

waistcoat /'weɪstkəʊt/ *n* GB kamizelka *f*

waist measurement *n* obwód *m* w talii

wait /weɪt/ **I** *n* oczekiwanie *n*; **an hour's ~** godzina czekania **II** *vt* [1] (await) czekać na (coś) [chance, turn] [2] US **to ~ table** podawać do stołu

vi czekać; **to keep sb ~ing** kazać komuś czekać; **to ~ for sb/sth** czekać na kogoś/coś; **~ for sb to do sth** czekać, aż ktoś coś zrobi; **(just you) ~ and see** zobaczysz; **she can't ~ to go on vacation** nie może się doczekać wyjazdu na wakacje

■ **wait around, wait about** GB: czekać (**for sb** na kogoś)

■ **wait behind**: zaczekać; **to ~ behind for sb** zaczekać na kogoś

■ **wait on**: obsłu|żyć, -giwać; **to ~ on sb hand and foot** skakać koło kogoś *infml fig*

■ **wait up**: [1] (stay awake) nie kłaść się spać; **to ~ up for sb** czekać na kogoś (do późna) [2] US **~ up!** zaczekaj!, chwileczkę!

waiter /'weɪtə(r)/ *n* kelner *m*

waiting game *n* gra *f* na przeczekanie

waiting list *n* lista *f* oczekujących

waiting room *n* poczekalnia *f*

waitress /'weɪtrɪs/ *n* kelnerka *f*

waive /weɪv/ *vt* uchyl|ić, -ać [rule]; odstąpić, -epować od (czegoś) [claim, demand]; zrze|c, -kać się (czegoś) [right]; z|rezygnować z (czegoś) [fee]

wake /weɪk/ **I** *vt* o|budzić *also fig*; **to ~ sb from a dream** przerwać komuś sen **II** *vi* o|budzić się; (from stupor, trance) ocknąć się

■ **wake up**: ¶ **~ up** o|budzić się; **~ up!** obudź się! ¶ **~ [sb] up** o|budzić

wake-up call /'weɪkʌpkɔ:l/ *n* budzenie *n* telefoniczne

Wales /weɪlz/ *prn* Walia *f*

walk /wɔ:k/ **I** *n* [1] (stroll) spacer *m*; (hike) wycieczka *f*; **it's about ten minutes' ~ to the castle** do zamku jest dziesięć minut drogi piechotą; **to go for a ~** pójść na spacer [2] (gait) chód *m* [3] (pace) krok *m* [4] (path) aleja *f*; (narrow) ścieżka *f* [5] Sport chód *m* sportowy

II *vt* [1] (cover on foot) prze|jść, -chodzić [distance, road, path] [2] prowadzić [horse, bicycle]; wyprowadz|ić -ać (na spacer) [dog]; **to ~ sb home** odprowadzić kogoś do domu

III *vi* iść, chodzić; (for pleasure or exercise) po|spacerować; (not drive or ride) iść na piechotę; **it's not very far, let's ~** to nie jest daleko, chodźmy piechotą; **to ~ down/up the street** iść ulicą

■ **walk around**: ¶ **~ around** po|spacerować; (aimlessly) po|wałęsać się ¶ **~ around [sth]** (to and fro) przej|ść, -chadzać się po (czymś) *[city, garden]*; (make circuit of) obj|ejść, -chodzić wkoło *[building]*

■ **walk away**: [1] odj|ejść, -chodzić (**from sb/sth** od kogoś/czegoś); fig (avoid) **to ~ away from a problem** uciekać od problemu [2] (survive unscathed) wyj|jść, -chodzić cało (**from sth** z czegoś) [3] (win easily) **to ~ away with sth** wygr|ać, -ywać coś *[game, election, prize]*

■ **walk back**: wr|ócić, -acać na piechotę; **we ~ed back (home)** wróciliśmy do domu na piechotę

■ **walk in**: w|ejść, -chodzić

■ **walk into**: ~ **into** [sth] [1] (enter) w|ejść, -chodzić do (czegoś) *[room, house]* [2] wpa|ść, -dać w (coś) *[trap, ambush]*; zna|leźć, -jdować się w (czymś) *[tricky situation]* [3] (collide with) wpa|ść, -dać na (kogoś/coś)

■ **walk off**: ¶ ~ **off** [1] (leave) odj|ejść, -chodzić nagle [2] infml **to ~ off with sth** (take) zab|rać, -ierać coś; (steal) podwędzić coś infml ¶ ~ [**sth] off** pozby|ć, -wać się (czegoś) podczas spaceru *[headache, hangover]*

■ **walk out**: [1] (leave) wyj|jść, -chodzić (**of sth** z czegoś) [2] fig *[spouse, partner, employee]* odj|ejść, -chodzić; **to ~ out on sb** rzucić kogoś; **to ~ out on a deal/contract** odstąpić od umowy/kontraktu [3] (as protest) opu|ścić, -szczać salę na znak protestu; (on strike) za|strajkować

■ **walk over**: ¶ ~ **over** (a few steps) pod|ejść, -chodzić (**to sth** do czegoś) ¶ ~ **over** [**sb**] infml [1] (defeat) po|bić (na głowę) [2] (humiliate) pomiatać (kimś) infml

■ **walk round**: ¶ ~ **round** pójść, iść ¶ ~ **round** [**sth**] (round edge of) obj|ejść, -chodzić naokoło; (visit) zwiedz|ić, -ać

■ **walk through**: przej|jść, -chodzić przez (coś) *[town, field, forest]*; prze|brnąć przez (coś) *[snow, mud]*

■ **walk up**: **to ~ up to sb** podejść do kogoś

walker /'wɔːkə(r)/ n (for pleasure) spacerowicz m, -ka f; (for exercise) piechur m

walkie-talkie /ˌwɔːkɪ'tɔːkɪ/ n krótkofalówka f

walking /'wɔːkɪŋ/ n spacerowanie n; (excursion) piesze wycieczki f pl

walking boots npl buty m pl turystyczne

walking distance n **to be within ~ of sth** być kilka minut marszu od czegoś

walking pace n **at a ~** spacerowym krokiem

walking stick n laska f

walkman® /'wɔːkmən/ n walkman m

walkout /'wɔːkaʊt/ n (strike) strajk m protestacyjny

walkover /'wɔːkəʊvə(r)/ n Sport łatwe zwycięstwo n

walkway /'wɔːkweɪ/ n przejście n

wall /wɔːl/ n [1] (of building, tunnel) ściana f; (of castle, town) mur m [2] Anat ściana f

wall chart n plansza f

walled /wɔːld/ adj otoczony murem

wallet /'wɒlɪt/ n (for notes) portfel m; (for documents) aktówka f

wallflower /'wɔːlflaʊə(r)/ n Bot lak m
IDIOMS **to be a ~** podpierać ściany *(podczas zabawy tanecznej)*

wall light n kinkiet m

wall-mounted /ˌwɔːl'maʊntɪd/ adj umocowany na ścianie

wallow /'wɒləʊ/ vi **to ~ in sth** taplać się w czymś *[mud]*; pławić się w czymś *[luxury]*; pogrążać się w czymś *[nostalgia]*; **to ~ in self-pity** rozczulać się nad sobą

wallpaper /'wɔːlpeɪpə(r)/ [1] n tapeta f also Comput [2] vt wy|tapetować

walnut /'wɔːlnʌt/ n [1] (nut, tree) orzech m włoski [2] (wood) orzech m

walrus /'wɔːlrəs/ n mors m

waltz /wɔːls, US wɔːlts/ [1] n walc m [2] vi za|tańczyć walca (**with sb** z kimś)

wand /wɒnd/ n różdżka f

wander /'wɒndə(r)/ [1] vt **to ~ the town** spacerować po mieście; **to ~ the streets** wałęsać się po ulicach [2] vi [1] (walk, stroll) przechadzać się; (aimlessly) wałęsać się [2] (stray) błąkać się; **to ~ away from the group** odłączyć się od grupy [3] (drift) *[mind, thoughts, eyes]* błądzić; **her mind ~ed back to her youth** powróciła myślami do czasów swej młodości

■ **wander about, wander around**: (stroll) przechadzać się; (when lost) błąkać się

wane /weɪn/ vi *[popularity, interest]* z|maleć, zmniejsz|yć, -ać się; *[enthusiasm, support]* o|słabnąć; **the moon is waning** księżyca ubywa

wangle /'wæŋgl/ infml [1] n (trick) sztuczka f [2] vt wycyganić infml *[gift, money]*; załatwi|ć, -ać sobie *[leave]*; **to ~ sth for sb** załatwić komuś coś

wannabe(e) /'wɒnəbiː/ n infml kiepski naśladowca m, kiepska naśladowczyni f

want /wɒnt/ [1] n [1] (need) potrzeba f [2] (lack) brak m; **for ~ of sth** z (powodu) braku czegoś; **it won't be for ~ of trying** to nie dlatego, że nie starał się [2] vt [1] (wish for) chcieć (czegoś); **I ~ it done today** to musi zostać zrobione dzisiaj; **to ~ to do sth** chcieć coś zrobić; **to ~ sb to do sth** chcieć, żeby ktoś coś zrobił [2] infml (need) *[person]* potrzebować (czegoś); *[object]* wymagać (czegoś) [3] (require presence of) potrzebować (kogoś); **if anyone ~s me** gdyby ktoś coś ode mnie chciał; **you're ~ed on the phone** jest do ciebie telefon; **to be ~ed by the police** być poszukiwanym przez policję [3] vi fml **you will never ~ for anything** niczego ci nie zabraknie

wanting /'wɒntɪŋ/ adj sb's ~ in sth komuś brak czegoś

wanton /'wɒntən, US 'wɔːn-/ adj [cruelty, damage, waste] niczym nieusprawiedliwiony

war /wɔː(r)/ n wojna f also fig; **in the** ~ na wojnie; **to wage** ~ toczyć wojnę

ward /wɔːd/ n ① (in hospital) (unit) oddział m; (room) sala f; **maternity** ~ oddział położniczy ②(electoral) okręg m wyborczy ③ (also ~ **of court**) (in law) **a child in** ~ dziecko pod opieką kuratora

■ **ward off**: zapobie|c, -gać (czemuś) [bankruptcy, disaster]; od|przeć, -pierać [attack, criticism]

warden /'wɔːdn/ n (of institution, college) ≈ dyrektor m administracyjny; (of castle, museum, park) strażni|k m, -czka f; (of estate) administrator m

warder /'wɔːdə(r)/ n GB strażnik m więzienny, strażniczka f więzienna

wardrobe /'wɔːdrəʊb/ n ① (piece of furniture) szafa f ② (set of clothes) garderoba f; (for theatre) kostiumy m pl

wares /'weəz/ npl towary m pl

warehouse /'weəhaʊs/ n magazyn m

warfare /'wɔːfeə(r)/ n wojna f

war game n gra f wojenna

warhead /'wɔːhed/ n głowica f bojowa

warlike /'wɔːlaɪk/ adj [people, mood] wojowniczy

warm /wɔːm/ ❚ adj ① (not cold) ciepły; **it's** ~ **today** ciepło dziś; **I'm** ~ ciepło mi ② (affectionate) [person, atmosphere, smile, welcome] ciepły; [applause] gorący; [support] entuzjastyczny ③ [colour] ciepły

❚❚ vt podgrz|ać, -ewać [water, milk, plate]; rozgrz|ać, -ewać [part of body, person]; ogrz|ać, -ewać [house, room]

❚❚❚ vi [food, liquid] podgrz|ać, -ewać się; [object] rozgrz|ać, -ewać się

■ **warm to, warm towards**: nab|rać, -ierać sympatii do (kogoś) [person]; przekon|ać, -ywać się do (czegoś) [idea]

■ **warm up**: ¶ ~ **up** ① [food, water] podgrz|ać, -ewać się; [place] ogrz|ać, -ewać się; [person] rozgrz|ać, -ewać się ② (become lively) [discussion, party, audience] ożywi|ć, -ać się ③ [athlete] rozgrz|ać, -ewać się; [orchestra, player] przygotow|ać, -ywać się ¶ ~ [sth] **up** podgrz|ać, -ewać [room, bed]; podgrz|ać, -ewać [food, water]; rozgrz|ać, -ewać [person]

warm-hearted /ˌwɔːm'hɑːtɪd/ adj serdeczny

warmly /'wɔːmlɪ/ adv [smile, greet] ciepło; [recommend, praise] gorąco

warmth /wɔːmθ/ n ciepło n also fig

warm-up /'wɔːmʌp/ n rozgrzewka f

warn /wɔːn/ ❚ vt ostrze|c, -gać; **to** ~ **sb about/ against** sth ostrzec kogoś o czymś/przed czymś

❚❚ vi **to** ~ **of** sth ostrze|c, -gać przed czymś

warning /'wɔːnɪŋ/ n ostrzeżenie n; (by an authority) upomnienie n; (by light, siren) sygnał m ostrzegawczy

warning light n światełko n ostrzegawcze

warning shot n strzał m ostrzegawczy

warning sign n (on road) znak m ostrzegawczy; (of illness, stress) sygnał m ostrzegawczy

warning triangle n Aut trójkąt m ostrzegawczy

warp /wɔːp/ ❚ vt wypacz|yć, -ać also fig [wood, character, personality]; odkształc|ić, -ać [metal]; z|wichrować [record]

❚❚ vi wypacz|yć, -ać się

warped /wɔːpt/ adj [wood, personality, judgment, view] wypaczony; [record, metal sheet] zwichrowany; fig [humour] osobliwy; [account] przeinaczony

warplane /'wɔːpleɪn/ n samolot m wojskowy

warrant /'wɒrənt, US 'wɔːr-/ ❚ n (in law) nakaz m

❚❚ vt da|ć, -wać podstawy do (czegoś) [action, measure]

warranty /'wɒrəntɪ, US 'wɔːr-/ n gwarancja f

warren /'wɒrən, US 'wɔːrən/ n ① (rabbits') królicza kolonia f ② (maze, building) labirynt m

warring /'wɔːrɪŋ/ adj [interests, ideologies] sprzeczny; **the** ~ **factions** walczące ze sobą frakcje

warrior /'wɒrɪə(r), US 'wɔːr-/ n żołnierz m; (of tribe) wojownik m

Warsaw /'wɔːsɔː/ prn Warszawa f

warship /'wɔːʃɪp/ n okręt m wojenny

wart /wɔːt/ n brodawka f

wartime /'wɔːtaɪm/ n **in** ~ w czasie wojny

war-torn /'wɔːtɔːn/ adj pustoszony przez wojnę

wary /'weərɪ/ adj ① (cautious) ostrożny; **to be** ~ mieć się na baczności (of sb/sth przed kimś/ czymś) ② (distrustful) nieufny; **to be** ~ nie ufać (of sb/sth komuś/czemuś)

wash /wɒʃ, US wɔːʃ/ ❚ n ① (clean) **to give sb/sth a** ~ umyć kogoś/coś; **to have a** ~ wymyć się, umyć się ② (laundry process) pranie n; (dirty clothes) brudy plt; **in the** ~ (being washed) w praniu; (with dirty clothes) w brudach ③ (sound of waves) plusk m

❚❚ vt u|myć, wy|myć [hands, hair, floor]; u|prać, wy|prać [clothes]; wy|kąpać [person, dog]; przemy|ć, -wać [wound, eye]; **to** ~ **one's face/hands** umyć (sobie) twarz/ręce; **to** ~ **the dishes** zmywać naczynia

❚❚❚ vi ① (clean oneself) u|myć się, wy|myć się ② (do laundry) prać, z|robić pranie; (do dishes) po|zmywać (naczynia)

■ **wash away**: ~ **away** [sth], ~ [sth] **away** ① (clean) zmy|ć, -wać [dirt, stains] ② (carry off) zn|ieść, -osić [bridge, village]; un|ieść, -osić [debris]; rozmy|ć, -wać [road, bank]; podmy|ć, -wać [cliff]

■ **wash up**: ¶ ~ **up** ① GB (do dishes) po|zmywać (naczynia) ② US (clean oneself) wy|myć się ¶ ~ [sth] **up** ① (clean) po|zmywać [dishes, cutlery]; u|myć [plate, pan] ② [tide] wyrzuc|ić, -ać na brzeg [body, debris]

washable /'wɒʃəbl, US 'wɔːʃ-/ adj zmywalny

washbasin /'wɒʃbeɪsn, US 'wɔːʃ-/ n umywalka f

washbowl /'wɒʃbəʊl, US 'wɔːʃ-/ n US umywalka f

washcloth /ˈwɒʃklɒθ, US ˈwɔːʃklɔːθ/ n US myjka f

washed-out /ˌwɒʃtˈaʊt, US ˌwɔːʃ-/ adj [1] [colour, jeans] sprany [2] (tired) wykończony infml

washed-up /ˌwɒʃtˈʌp, US ˌwɔːʃ-/ adj infml (finished) skończony infml

washer /ˈwɒʃə(r), US ˈwɔːʃər/ n Tech podkładka f

washer-dryer /ˌwɒʃəˈdraɪə(r), US ˌwɔːʃ-/ n pralka f z suszarką

washing /ˈwɒʃɪŋ, US ˈwɔːʃɪŋ/ n (laundry) pranie n; **to do the** ~ zrobić pranie

washing line n sznur m do bielizny

washing machine n pralka f

washing powder n GB proszek m do prania

washing-up /ˌwɒʃɪŋˈʌp, US ˌwɔːʃ-/ n GB (action) zmywanie n; (dishes) brudne naczynia n pl

washing-up liquid n GB płyn m do mycia naczyń

washout /ˈwɒʃaʊt, US ˈwɔːʃ-/ n (failure) klapa f infml

washroom /ˈwɒʃruːm, US ˈwɔːʃ-/ n umywalnia f

wash-stand /ˈwɒʃstænd, US ˈwɔːʃ-/ n US umy-walka f obudowana

wasp /wɒsp/ n osa f

waspish /ˈwɒspɪʃ/ adj [person, remark] uszczypliwy

wastage /ˈweɪstɪdʒ/ n [1] (of resources, energy) marno-trawstwo n; (of talent, opportunity) marnowanie n [2] (also **natural** ~) **the reduction in staff numbers by natural** ~ zmniejszanie liczby zatrudnionych z przyczyn naturalnych

waste /weɪst/ **[I]** n [1] (of food, money, energy, time) marnowanie n; **it's a go** ~ **of effort** szkoda wysiłku; **he let his talent go to** ~ zmarnował talent [2] (refuse) (also **wastes** US) odpady m pl
[II] wastes npl (wilderness) pustkowie n
[III] adj [1] [heat, energy] odpadowy; [water] brudny; ~ **materials** Med końcowe produkty przemiany materii [2] [land] (uncultivated) nieuprawiany; (barren) jałowy [3] **to lay** ~ **to sth** spustoszyć coś; obrócić coś w perzynę
[IV] vt [1] (squander) z|marnować [food, energy, talent, opportunity]; s|tracić [time] [2] [disease] wyniszcz|yć, -ać [person, body]

wastebasket /ˈweɪstbɑːskɪt, US -bæskɪt/ n kosz m na śmieci

wastebin /ˈweɪstbɪn/ n pojemnik m na śmieci

wasted /ˈweɪstɪd/ adj [1] [energy, time, life] zmarno-wany; [effort, care, journey] daremny [2] [person, face] wymizerowany

waste disposal n (removal) wywóz m odpadów; (management) zagospodarowanie n odpadów

waste disposal unit n GB kuchenny rozdrab-niacz m odpadków

wasteful /ˈweɪstfl/ adj [person, use] rozrzutny; [machinery, process] nieekonomiczny

wasteland /ˈweɪstlænd/ n (urban) teren m nieza-gospodarowany; (rural) nieużytek m

wastepaper /ˈweɪstpeɪpə(r)/ n makulatura f

wastepaper basket n kosz m na śmieci

waste pipe n rura f ściekowa

wasting /ˈweɪstɪŋ/ adj [disease] wyniszczający

watch /wɒtʃ/ **[I]** n [1] (timepiece) zegarek m [2] (sur-veillance) obserwacja f; **to keep** ~ trzymać straż; **to keep (a)** ~ **on sb/sth** pilnować kogoś/czegoś
[II] vt [1] (look at) o|bejrzeć, -glądać [TV, film]; przy|jrzeć, -glądać się [komuś/czemuś] [event, person]; (observe) obserwować [2] (monitor) obserwo-wać [career, progress, situation] [3] (keep under surveil-lance) obserwować [person, movements] [4] (pay atten-tion to) uważać na (kogoś/coś) [obstacle, dangerous object]; kontrolować [weight]; przestrzegać (cze-goś) [diet]; ~ **your step!** patrz pod nogi!; fig lepiej się pilnuj! [5] (look after) po|pilnować (czegoś) [property, child, dog]
[III] vi (look on) (po)patrzeć
■ **watch for**: czekać na (kogoś/czegoś)
■ **watch out**: (be careful) uważać; **to** ~ **out for sth** uważać na coś; ~ **out!** uwaga!
■ **watch over**: (protect) czuwać nad (kimś/czymś)

watchable /ˈwɒtʃəbl/ adj wart obejrzenia

watchband /ˈwɒtʃbænd/ n US pasek m do zegarka

watchdog /ˈwɒtʃdɒg/ n [1] (animal) pies m obron-ny; (kept outside) pies m podwórzowy [2] (organization) ciało n nadzorujące

watchmaker /ˈwɒtʃmeɪkə(r)/ n zegarmistrz m

watchman /ˈwɒtʃmən/ n (guard) stróż m

watch strap n pasek m od zegarka

watchword /ˈwɒtʃwɜːd/ n dewiza f

water /ˈwɔːtə(r)/ **[I]** n woda f
[II] vt pod|lać, -ewać [lawn, plant]; naw|odnić, -adniać [field, crop]; na|poić [horse, livestock]
[III] vi **the smell from the kitchen made my mouth** ~ ślin(k)a nabiegła mi do ust, gdy poczułem zapach z kuchni; **the smoke made my eyes** ~ oczy zaczęły mi łzawić od dymu
■ **water down**: [1] rozcieńcz|yć, -ać (wodą) [milk, paint, syrup] [2] fig z|łagodzić ton (czegoś) [article, criticism]; z|łagodzić [policy]; osłabi|ć, -ać [effect]

water bed n łóżko n wodne

water bird n ptak m wodny

water birth n poród m w wodzie

water bottle n bidon m

water cannon n armatka f wodna

watercolour GB, **watercolor** US /ˈwɔːtəkʌlə(r)/ n akwarela f

watercress /ˈwɔːtəkres/ n Bot rukiew f wodna; Culin rzeżucha f

waterfall /ˈwɔːtəfɔːl/ n wodospad m

water filter n filtr m do wody

waterfront /ˈwɔːtəfrʌnt/ n (on harbour) nabrzeże n; (by lakeside, riverside) nadbrzeże n

water-heater /ˈwɔːtəhiːtə(r)/ n terma f

watering can n konewka f

water jump n Sport rów m z wodą

water level n poziom m wody

water lily n lilia f wodna
waterlogged /'wɔ:tǝlɒgd/ adj [pitch] rozmokły
water main n główny przewód m wodociągowy
watermark /'wɔ:tǝmɑ:k/ n [1] (of sea) linia f poziomu wody [2] (on paper) znak m wodny
watermelon /'wɔ:tǝmelǝn/ n arbuz m
water power n energia f wodna
waterproof /'wɔ:tǝpru:f/ adj [coat] nieprzemakalny; [make-up] wodoodporny; [watch] wodoszczelny
water-resistant /ˌwɔ:tǝrɪ'zɪstǝnt/ adj wodoodporny
water-ski /'wɔ:tǝski:/ **[]** n narta f wodna
[] vi jeździć na nartach wodnych
water-skiing /'wɔ:tǝski:ɪŋ/ n narciarstwo n wodne
water slide n zjeżdżalnia f (na basenie kąpielowym)
water sport n sport m wodny
water supply n (in an area) zaopatrzenie n w wodę; (to a building) dopływ m wody
watertight /'wɔ:tǝtaɪt/ adj [1] [container, joint, seal] wodoszczelny [2] [alibi] niezbity; [argument, case] niepodważalny
water tower n wieża f ciśnień
water trough n koryto n
waterway /'wɔ:tǝweɪ/ n droga f wodna
water wings npl pływaczki m pl (zakładane na ramiona)
watery /'wɔ:tǝrɪ/ adj [1] [coffee, paint] wodnisty [2] [smile] blady; [colours] rozmyty
watt /wɒt/ n wat m
wave /weɪv/ **[]** n [1] (gesture) skinienie n; **to give sb a ~** pomachać komuś [2] (of water, light, in hair, on radio) fala f; **to make ~s** [wind] podnosić fale; fig (cause a stir) rozrabiać infml [3] (surge) fala f (**czegoś** of sth)
[] vt (shake, swing) po|machać (czymś) [hand, handkerchief]; potrząs|nąć, -ać (czymś) [stick]; **to ~ sb goodbye** pomachać komuś na pożegnanie
[] vi [1] (signal) **to ~ at** or **to sb** po|machać komuś or do kogoś [2] [flag] powiewać; [corn, branches] za|kołysać się
wave band /'weɪvbænd/ n pasmo n częstotliwości
wavelength /'weɪvleŋθ/ n (on radio) długość f fali
IDIOMS: **to be on the same ~ as sb** nadawać na tych samych falach infml
waver /'weɪvǝ(r)/ vi [1] (falter) [voice] za|drżeć; [courage, determination, love] o|słabnąć [2] (hesitate) za|wahać się
wavy /'weɪvɪ/ adj [hair] falujący; [line] falisty
wax¹ /wæks/ **[]** n (for candles) wosk m; (for skis) parafina f; (in ear) woskowina f
[] vt [1] na|woskować [floor, table, car]; na|smarować [skis] [2] wy|depilować woskiem [legs]
wax² /wæks/ vi **the moon ~es** księżyca przybywa
waxed jacket n GB kurtka f impregnowana

wax paper n papier m woskowany
waxwork /'wækswɜ:k/ n figura f woskowa
waxworks /'wækswɜ:ks/ n gabinet m figur woskowych
waxy /'wæksɪ/ adj [skin, texture] woskowaty
way /weɪ/ **[]** n [1] (road) droga f; **the quickest ~ to town** najszybsza trasa do miasta; **to ask the ~** zapytać o drogę; **there's no ~ around the problem** tego problemu nie da się obejść; **on the ~ back** w drodze powrotnej; **the ~ in** wejście (**to sth** do czegoś); (for vehicles) wjazd (**to sth** do czegoś); **the ~ out** wyjście (**of sth** z czegoś); (for vehicles) wyjazd (**of sth** z czegoś); **a ~ out of our difficulties** wyjście z naszych kłopotów; **on the ~** po drodze; **to be out of sb's ~** być komuś nie po drodze; **don't go out of your ~ (to do it)** nie zawracaj sobie głowy (robieniem tego); **out of the ~** (isolated) (położony) na uboczu; (unusual) niezwykły; **by ~ of sth** (via) przez coś; **to make one's ~ towards sth** zmierzać ku czemuś; **I made my own ~ home** sam dostałem się do domu [2] (direction) strona f, kierunek m; **that ~** w tamtą stronę; **come this ~** proszę tędy; **'this ~ up'** (notice on box) „góra"; **to look the other ~** (to see) patrzeć w drugą stronę; (to avoid seeing) odwrócić wzrok; fig (to ignore wrongdoing) przymykać oczy fig; **the other ~ up** drugą stroną do góry; **to put one's skirt on the wrong ~ around** włożyć spódnicę tył na przód; **you're Adam and you're Robert, have I got that the right ~ around?** ty nazywasz się Adam, a ty Robert, czy dobrze pamiętam?; **it was the other ~ around** to było odwrotnie; **she's coming our ~** ona idzie w naszą stronę [3] (space to proceed) droga f; (affording passage) przejście n; (for vehicle) przejazd m; **to be in the ~** zawadzać; **to be in sb's ~** zawadzać komuś; [person, large object] stać komuś na drodze; **to get out of sb's ~** zejść komuś z drogi; **to keep out of the ~** trzymać się z dala; **to keep out of sb's ~** nie wchodzić komuś w drogę; **to make ~ (for sb/sth)** zrobić miejsce (dla kogoś/czegoś) [4] (distance) droga f; **it's a long ~ to** daleko; **it's a long/short ~ into town** do miasta jest daleko/niedaleko; **to go all the ~ to China** pojechać aż do Chin [5] (manner) sposób m; **do it this/that ~** zrób to w ten sposób; **to do sth another ~** zrobić coś inaczej; **to do sth the French ~** robić coś na sposób francuski; **to do sth the right/wrong ~** robić coś dobrze/źle; **try to see it my ~** spróbuj spojrzeć na to z mojej strony; **they are nice people in their own ~** na swój sposób to mili ludzie; **to have a ~ with sth** znać się na czymś; **to have a ~ with children** mieć dobre podejście do dzieci; **there are other ~s of doing it** to można zrobić inaczej; **I like the ~ she dresses** podoba mi się jej styl ubierania się; **either ~, she's wrong** tak czy owak, ona nie ma racji;

one ~ **or another** tak czy inaczej; **I don't care one** ~ **or the other** mnie jest wszystko jedno; **you can't have it both** ~ **s** musisz wybrać: albo – albo; **no** ~**!** infml nie ma mowy! [6] (respect, aspect) sens *m*; **in a** ~ **it's sad** w pewnym sensie to smutne; **in many** ~ **s** z wielu względów; **in some** ~**s** pod pewnymi względami; **in no** ~, **not in any** ~ w żadnym razie [7] (custom) zwyczaj *m*; (person's) przyzwyczajenie *n*; **that's the modern** ~ to nowoczesny zwyczaj; **I know all her little** ~ **s** znam jej wszystkie przyzwyczajenia; **that's just his** ~ on taki już jest; **it's the** ~ **of the world** tak to w życiu bywa [8] (will, desire) **to get** or **one's own** ~ postawić na swoim; **she likes (to have) her own** ~ ona lubi stawiać na swoim; **if I had my** ~**...** gdyby to ode mnie zależało...; **have it your (own)** ~ niech ci będzie

II *adv* **to go** ~ **beyond what is necessary** wykraczać daleko poza granice tego, co konieczne; **to be** ~ **out in one's calculations** grubo się pomylić w obliczeniach; **that's** ~ **out of order** to za dużo powiedziane

III **by the way** *adv phr* [tell, mention] mimochodem; **by the** ~**,...** à propos...

waylay /ˌweɪˈleɪ/ *vt* (stop) zatrzym|ać, -ywać [person]; (attack) napa|ść, -dać na (kogoś)

waymark /ˈweɪmɑːk/ *n* tabliczka *f (wskazująca drogę)*

way-out /ˌweɪˈaʊt/ *adj* infml (unconventional) obłędny infml

wayside /ˈweɪsaɪd/ *n*
(IDIOMS:) **to fall by the** ~ (morally) zejść na złą drogę; (fail) [candidate] odpaść; [project] nie udać się; [marriage] nie ułożyć się

wayward /ˈweɪwəd/ *adj* [person, child, nature] krnąbrny; [husband, wife] niestały (w uczuciach)

we /wiː, wɪ/ *pron* my; **we saw her yesterday** widzieliśmy ją wczoraj; **we won't be here** nie będzie nas tutaj; **we Scots like the sun** my, Szkoci, lubimy słońce; **we all make mistakes** wszyscy popełniamy błędy

weak /wiːk/ *adj* [1] [person, animal, muscle, support, structure] słaby; (temporarily) osłabiony; [chest, bladder, stomach] delikatny; [ankle] nadwyrężony; **she was** ~ **with** or **from hunger/fear** słabo jej było z głodu/ze strachu; **to grow** or **become** ~**(er)** osłabnąć [2] (lacking authority, strength) [government, team, pupil, argument, excuse] słaby; (not firm) [parent, teacher] mało stanowczy [3] (faint) [light, tea, coffee] słaby; [laugh] lekki [4] [economy, dollar] słaby (**against sth** w stosunku do czegoś)

weaken /ˈwiːkən/ **I** *vt* osłabi|ć, -ać [person, heart, resistance, structure, beam] [2] fig osłabi|ć, -ać pozycję (kogoś/czegoś) [government, president]; osłabi|ć, -ać [authority, resolve, defence, morale]; zmniejsz|yć, -ać [support, power] [3] (dilute) rozcień-cz|yć, -ać

II *vi* [1] (physically) o|słabnąć [2] (lose power) [government, president, country] u|tracić silną pozycję; [resistance, support, alliance] o|słabnąć [3] [economy, market, currency] wykazywać tendencję zniżkową; [currency] o|słabnąć

weakling /ˈwiːklɪŋ/ *n* słabeusz *m* infml

weakness /ˈwiːknɪs/ *n* [1] (weak point) słaby punkt *m* [2] (liking) słabostka *f*; **to have a** ~ **for sb/sth** mieć słabość do kogoś/czegoś [3] (physical, lack of authority) słabość *f* [4] (of currency) niski kurs *m*

weak-willed /ˌwiːkˈwɪld/ *adj* **to be** ~ mieć słaby charakter

wealth /welθ/ *n* [1] (possessions, prosperity) bogactwo *n* [2] (large amount) **a** ~ **of sth** bogactwo czegoś [detail, illustrations, ideas]; mnogość czegoś [books, documents]

wealthy /ˈwelθɪ/ *adj* zamożny

wean /wiːn/ *vt* odstawi|ć, -ać od piersi [baby]; **to** ~ **sb away from** or **off sth** oduczyć kogoś czegoś [bad habit]; odwieść kogoś od czegoś [idea, belief]

weapon /ˈwepən/ *n* broń *f*

weaponry /ˈwepənrɪ/ *n* broń *f*

wear /weə(r)/ **I** *n* [1] (clothing) odzież *f*; **sports** ~ stroje sportowe [2] (use) **for everyday** ~ na co dzień; **to stretch with** ~ [shoes] rozciągnąć się w noszeniu [3] (damage) zużycie *n*; **normal** ~ **and tear** normalne zużycie; **to be the worse for** ~ [chairs, curtains] mieć już swoje lata; [person] mieć kaca infml

II *vt* [1] (be dressed in) być ubranym w (coś), mieć na sobie [garments]; (habitually) nosić [garment, jewellery]; **to** ~ **black** ubierać się na czarno; **to** ~ **one's hair short** mieć krótkie włosy [2] (use) nosić [make-up, glasses]; używać (czegoś) [perfume, suncream]; **to** ~ **make-up** malować się [3] (display) **he wore a puzzled frown** na jego twarzy malował się wyraz zaskoczenia [4] (damage by use) wy|trzeć, -cierać [step, clothes, carpet]; **to** ~ **a hole in sth** przetrzeć coś na wylot

III *vi* [carpet, clothes] wy|trzeć, -cierać się; [shoes, tyre] z|edrzeć, -dzierać się; [part] zuży|ć, -wać się; **my patience is** ~**ing thin** moja cierpliwość jest na wyczerpaniu

■ **wear away**: [inscription] za|trzeć, -cierać się; [rock, bank] ule|c, -gać erozji; [metal, stone] zetrzeć, ścierać się

■ **wear down**: ¶ ~ **down** [linings, heel] z|edrzeć, -dzierać się; [steps] zetrzeć, ścierać się ¶ ~ **[sth] down** z|edrzeć, -dzierać [linings, heels]; zetrzeć, ścierać [stone, steps]; fig osłabi|ć, -ać [resolve, will] ¶ ~ **[sb] down** [overwork, strain] wycieńczyć

■ **wear off**: [1] [drug] przesta|ć, -wać działać; [pain, sensation] ust|ąpić, -ępować [2] (come off) zetrzeć, ścierać się

■ **wear out**: ¶ ~ **out** [clothes, shoes] z|niszczyć się; [batteries] wyczerp|ać, -ywać się ¶ ~ **[sth] out** z|niszczyć [equipment, clothes]; z|edrzeć, -dzierać [shoes] ¶ ~ **[sb] out** wyczerp|ać, -ywać

■ **wear through**: *[elbow, trousers]* prze|trzeć, -cierać się na wylot; *[metal, glaze]* zetrzeć, ścierać się

weariness /ˈwɪərɪnɪs/ *n* znużenie *n*

wearing /ˈweərɪŋ/ *adj* (exhausting) *[day, journey]* męczący; (irritating) *[behaviour, person]* denerwujący

weary /ˈwɪərɪ/ **❶** *adj [person, mind, eyes]* zmęczony; *[smile, sigh, voice, gesture]* znużony; **to grow ~ of sth** znużyć się czymś

❷ *vi* znużyć się (**of sth/doing sth** czymś/ robieniem czegoś)

weasel /ˈwiːzl/ *n* [1] Zool łasica *f* [2] (sly person) krętacz *m*

weather /ˈweðə(r)/ **❶** *n* pogoda *f*; **the ~ is hot today** dziś jest upalnie; **in hot/wet ~** w upał/ deszcz; **what's the ~ like?** jaka dziś pogoda?; **~ permitting** jeśli będzie (ładna) pogoda; **in all ~s** bez względu na pogodę

❷ *vt* (withstand) przetrwać *[crisis, upheaval]*; **to ~ the storm** fig przetrwać najgorsze

IDIOMS: **to be under the ~** czuć się kiepsko

weatherbeaten /ˈweðəbiːtn/ *adj [face]* ogorzały; *[stone, brick]* skruszały

weathercock /ˈweðəkɒk/ *n* kurek *m* na dachu

weather forecast *n* prognoza *f* pogody

weather forecaster *n* (on TV) prezenter *m*, -ka *f* prognozy pogody; (in weather centre) meteorolog *m*

weatherproof /ˈweðəpruːf/ *adj [door, window]* szczelny; *[shelter, tent]* wodoszczelny; *[jacket, boots]* nieprzemakalny

weave /wiːv/ **❶** *vt* [1] u|tkać *[fabric, blanket, carpet]* [2] (interlace) u|pleść *[basket, wreath]*; spl|eść, -atać *[garland]*

❷ *vi* **to ~ in and out of the traffic** lawirować wśród samochodów; **she wove towards the door** (avoiding obstacles) przemknęła się w stronę drzwi; (drunk) zataczając się, dotarła do drzwi

❸ **woven** *pp adj [fabric]* tkany; *[mat]* pleciony

weaving /ˈwiːvɪŋ/ *n* tkactwo *n*

web /web/ *n* [1] (also **spider's ~**) pajęczyna *f* [2] fig **a ~ of ropes/lines** pajęczyna lin/linii; **a ~ of lies** plątanina kłamstw

Web /web/ *n* Comput sieć *f*

webbing /ˈwebɪŋ/ *n* (material) taśma *f* tapicerska

Web cam *n* kamera *f* sieciowa

web foot *n* stopa *f* z palcami połączonymi błoną pławną

Web page *n* strona *f* internetowa

Web server *n* serwer *m* internetowy

Website /ˈwebsaɪt/ *n* witryna *f* internetowa

wed /wed/ *n* **the newly ~s** nowożeńcy *plt*

wedding /ˈwedɪŋ/ *n* ślub *m*; **a church ~** ślub kościelny

wedding anniversary *n* rocznica *f* ślubu

wedding day *n* dzień *m* ślubu

wedding dress, **wedding gown** *n* suknia *f* ślubna

wedding reception *n* przyjęcie *n* weselne

wedding ring *n* obrączka *f*

wedge /wedʒ/ **❶** *n* [1] (block) klin *m*; (in rock climbing) hak *m* wspinaczkowy [2] (of cake, cheese, lemon) (trójkątny) kawałek *m*

❷ *vt* [1] (make firm) **to ~ sth in place** umocować coś; **to ~ a door open** zaklinować drzwi, żeby się nie zamykały [2] (jam) **to ~ sth into sth** wcisnąć coś do czegoś; **~d between two fat men** ściśnięta między dwoma grubasami

IDIOMS: **it's (only) the thin end of the ~!** to dopiero początek!

Wednesday /ˈwenzdeɪ, -dɪ/ *n* środa *f*

wee /wiː/ GB infml *vi* z|robić siusiu infml

weed /wiːd/ **❶** *n* (wild plant) chwast *m*; (in water) wodorosty *m pl*

❷ *vt* o|pleć

❸ *vi* pleć, opielać

■ **weed out**: pozby|ć, -wać się (kogoś/czegoś) *[employee, stock]*

weedkiller /ˈwiːdkɪlə(r)/ *n* środek *m* chwastobójczy

weedy /ˈwiːdɪ/ *adj* infml *[person, horse]* cherlawy infml; *[character]* słaby

week /wiːk/ *n* tydzień *m*; **this/last/next ~** w tym/ zeszłym/przyszłym tygodniu; **the ~ before last** dwa tygodnie temu; **the ~ after next** za dwa tygodnie; **every other ~** co dwa tygodnie; **~ in ~ out** tydzień w tydzień; **a ~ today** GB, **today ~** od dziś za tydzień; **the working** or **work** US **~** tydzień roboczy

weekday /ˈwiːkdeɪ/ *n* dzień *m* powszedni; **on ~s** w dni powszednie, w tygodniu

weekend /ˌwiːkˈend, US ˈwiːkˌ-/ *n* weekend *m*; **at the ~** GB, **on the ~** US w weekend; **at ~s** GB, **on ~s** US w weekendy

weekend bag *n* torba *f (podróżna)*

weekend cottage *n* letni domek *m*

weekly /ˈwiːklɪ/ **❶** *n* tygodnik *m*

❷ *adj [contract, payment]* tygodniowy; *[trip, meeting]* cotygodniowy

❸ *adv* (every week) co tydzień; (once a week) raz na tydzień

weep /wiːp/ *vi* [1] (cry) za|płakać; **to ~ over sth** płakać nad czymś [2] (ooze) **the wound is ~ing** sączy się z rany

weepy /ˈwiːpɪ/ *adj* płaczliwy; *[book, film]* łzawy

weigh /weɪ/ **❶** *vt* [1] (be particular weight) ważyć; (measure the weight of) z|ważyć *[object, person]*; **to ~ 10 kilos** ważyć 10 kilo; **how much** or **what do you ~** ? ile ważysz?; **to ~ oneself** zważyć się [2] (consider) rozważyć, -ać *[arguments, options, risks]*; **to ~ one's words** ważyć słowa

❷ *vi* (be a burden) **to ~ on sb** ciążyć komuś; **to ~ on sb's mind** leżeć komuś na sercu

■ **weigh down**: ¶ **~ down on [sb/sth]** przygni|eść, -atać ¶ **~ [sth/sb] down** obciążyć,

-ać *[vehicle]*; przycis|nąć, -kać *[papers]*; fig *[responsibility, anxiety]* przytł|oczyć, -aczać *[person]*; **to be ~ed down with sth** być obładowanym czymś *[luggage]*

■ **weigh in**: *[boxer, wrestler, jockey]* z|ważyć się

■ **weigh out**: odważ|yć, -ać *[ingredients, quantity]*

■ **weigh up**: rozważ|yć, -ać *[prospects, situation, options, risks]*; z|mierzyć (wzrokiem) *[person]*

weighing machine /ˈweɪŋməʃiːn/ n waga f

weight /weɪt/ **I** n waga f; **to put on/lose ~** przybrać/stracić na wadze; **what is your ~?** ile ważysz?

II vt (make heavier) obciąż|yć, -ać *[net, arrow]* ⟨IDIOMS⟩ **to not carry much ~ with sb** nie mieć większego znaczenia dla kogoś; **that's a ~ off my mind!** kamień spadł mi z serca!; **to pull one's ~** przykładać się do pracy; **to throw one's ~ about** or **around** szarogęsić się

weightlessness /ˈweɪtlɪsnɪs/ n (in space) nieważkość f

weight-lifter /ˈweɪtlɪftə(r)/ n ciężarowiec m

weight-lifting /ˈweɪtlɪftɪŋ/ n podnoszenie ciężarów

weight problem n problem m z nadwagą

weight training n ćwiczenia n pl siłowe

weighty /ˈweɪtɪ/ adj 1 *[problem, reason]* ważki 2 *[object, responsibility]* ciężki

weir /wɪə(r)/ n jaz m, tama f

weird /wɪəd/ adj (strange) dziwaczny; (eerie) niesamowity

welcome /ˈwelkəm/ **I** n powitanie n; **to give sb a warm ~** powitać kogoś serdecznie

II adj 1 (warmly greeted) *[relief, news]* upragniony; *[initiative, guest]* mile widziany; **to be ~** być mile widzianym (gościem); **to make sb ~** (on arrival) powitać kogoś serdecznie 2 **you're ~!** (acknowledging thanks) proszę bardzo!

III excl **~!** (to respected guest) serdecznie witamy!; (greeting friend) witaj!; **~ back!, ~ home!** witaj w domu!

IV vt po|witać *[person]*; przyj|ąć, -mować z zadowoleniem *[change, contribution, move]*

welcoming /ˈwelkəmɪŋ/ adj 1 *[atmosphere, person, smile]* serdeczny 2 *[ceremony, committee]* powitalny

weld /weld/ vt (also **~ together**) ze|spawać *[metal, joint]*; zgrz|ać, -ewać *[plastic]*; **to ~ sth to** or **on sth** przyspawać coś do czegoś

welfare /ˈwelfeə(r)/ **I** n 1 (well-being) dobro n; (interest) interes m 2 (state assistance) opieka f społeczna; (money) zasiłek m z opieki społecznej

II adj **~ system** system opieki społecznej; **~ meal** US darmowy posiłek

welfare benefit n zasiłek m z opieki społecznej

welfare services npl opieka f społeczna

welfare spending n wydatki m pl socjalne

welfare state n (as concept) państwo n opiekuńcze; (stressing state assistance) rozbudowany system m ubezpieczeń społecznych

well[1] /wel/ n 1 (for water) studnia f 2 (pool) sadzawka f ze źródlaną wodą

well[2] /wel/ **I** adj 1 (in good health) **to feel ~** dobrze się czuć; **are you ~?** czy dobrze się czujesz?; **she's not ~ enough to go to school** ona nie czuje się na tyle dobrze, żeby iść do szkoły; **to get ~** wyzdrowieć 2 (in satisfactory state) **that's all very ~, but...** wszystko to ładnie, ale...; **it would be just as ~ to check** nie zaszkodzi or nie zawadzi sprawdzić; **it would be as ~ for you not to get involved** dla ciebie byłoby lepiej, gdybyś się nie mieszał; **the flight was delayed, which was just as ~** odlot się opóźnił, na całe szczęście

II adv (satisfactorily) dobrze; *[pleased, satisfied, respected]* bardzo; **he isn't eating very ~** on za mało je; **to do ~ at school** dobrze sobie radzić w szkole; **mother and baby are both doing ~** matka i dziecko czują się dobrze; **to go ~** *[operation]* powieść się; **~ done!** brawo!; **you may ~ be right** możliwe, że masz rację; **we may as ~ go home** równie dobrze możemy iść do domu; **the museum is ~ worth seeing** stanowczo warto zwiedzić to muzeum; **to wish sb ~** dobrze komuś życzyć

III excl (expressing surprise) no proszę; (expressing indignation) no nie!; (expressing disappointment, hesitation) no cóż; (introducing topic) a więc; **~ then, what's the problem?** no więc, o co chodzi?

IV **as well** adv phr również

V **as well as** adv phr zarówno... jak (i)...; **they have a house in the country as ~ as an apartment in London** mają dom na wsi, a także mieszkanie w Londynie

⟨IDIOMS⟩ **to be ~ in with sb** infml być z kimś w dobrej komitywie; **to be ~ up in sth** infml być oblatanym w czymś infml; **to leave ~ alone** GB or **~ enough alone** US dać sobie spokój

well-balanced /ˌwelˈbælənst/ adj zrównoważony

well-behaved /ˌwelbɪˈheɪvd/ adj *[child]* dobrze wychowany; *[dog]* dobrze ułożony

well-being /ˌwelˈbiːɪŋ/ n dobro n

well-defined /ˌweldɪˈfaɪnd/ adj *[outline]* wyraźny; *[role, boundary]* wyraźnie określony

well-disposed /ˌweldɪˈspəʊzd/ adj przychylnie nastawiony (**towards sb/sth** do kogoś/czegoś)

well done /ˌwelˈdʌn/ adj *[steak]* dobrze wysmażony; *[task, job]* dobrze wykonany

well-educated /ˌwelˈedʒʊkeɪtɪd/ adj (having a good education) wykształcony; (cultured) kulturalny

well-heeled /ˌwelˈhiːld/ adj infml (na)dziany infml

well-informed /ˌwelɪnˈfɔːmd/ adj *[person]* dobrze poinformowany; **to be very ~** posiadać bardzo rozległą wiedzę

wellington (boot) /ˈwelɪŋtən/ n GB gumowiec m

well-kept /ˌwel'kept/ *adj [house, garden]* starannie utrzymany

well-known /ˌwel'nəʊn/ *adj* znany; **to be ~ to sb** być dobrze znanym komuś; **it is ~ that..., it is a ~ fact that...** powszechnie wiadomo, że...

well-liked /ˌwel'laɪkt/ *adj* powszechnie lubiany

well-made /ˌwel'meɪd/ *adj [object]* solidnie wykonany

well-meaning /ˌwel'miːnɪŋ/ *adj [person, act, remark]* pełen najlepszych intencji

well-meant /ˌwel'ment/ *adj [act, suggestion, offer]* w dobrej wierze

well-off /ˌwel'ɒf/ **[]** *n* **the ~** zamożni; **the less ~** ludzie niezamożni
[] *adj* zamożny; **to be ~ for sth** mieć pod dostatkiem czegoś

well-read /ˌwel'red/ *adj* oczytany

well-rounded /ˌwel'raʊndɪd/ *adj [education]* pełny; *[person]* gruntownie wykształcony

well-respected /ˌwelrɪ'spektɪd/ *adj* ogólnie szanowany

well-thought-out /ˌwelθɔːt'aʊt/ *adj* dobrze przemyślany

well-timed /ˌwel'taɪmd/ *adj [remark, suggestion]* na czasie; *[arrival, sale]* w odpowiednim momencie; **that was ~!** w samą porę!

well-to-do /ˌweltə'duː/ *adj* dobrze sytuowany

well-wisher /'welwɪʃə(r)/ *n* osoba *f* życzliwa

well-worn /ˌwel'wɔːn/ *adj [carpet]* wytarty; *[shoes, clothes]* znoszony; *[phrase, joke]* wyświechtany

Welsh /welʃ/ **[]** *n* [1] (people) **the ~** Walijczycy [2] (language) (język *m*) walijski *m*
[] *adj* walijski

welt /welt/ *n* (on skin) ślad *m* (po uderzeniu)

west /west/ **[]** *n* [1] (compass direction) zachód *m* [2] **the West** Zachód *m*
[] *adj* zachodni
[] *adv* na zachód; **~ of sth** na zachód od czegoś

West Bank *prn* **the ~** Zachodni Brzeg *m* Jordanu

western /'westən/ **[]** *n* (film) western *m*
[] *adj* zachodni

westerner /'westənə(r)/ *n* człowiek *m* z Zachodu; (representing western culture) człowiek *m* Zachodu

westernize /'westənaɪz/ *vt* narzuc|ić, -ać zachodnią kulturę (komuś/czemuś)

west-facing /'westfeɪsɪŋ/ *adj [window, room]* wychodzący na zachód; *[slope]* zachodni

West Indian **[]** *n* Antyl|czyk *m*, -ka *f*
[] *adj* antylski

West Indies /ˌwest'ɪndiːz/ *prn pl* **the ~** Indie *plt* Zachodnie

wet /wet/ **[]** *adj* [1] (damp) mokry; (not yet dry) wilgotny; **to get ~** przemoknąć; **to get one's feet ~** przemoczyć nogi; **to get the floor ~** nachlapać na podłogę; **~ through** (przemoczony) do suchej nitki [2] (freshly applied) mokry; **'~ paint'**
„uwaga! świeżo malowane" [3] (rainy) *[weather, day]* deszczowy; *[climate]* wilgotny; **it's been very ~** ostatnio dużo pada [4] GB *infml [person]* bezwolny; **don't be so ~!** nie bądź mięczakiem *infml*
[] *vt* z|moczyć *[hair, clothes]*; zachlap|ać, -ywać *[floor]*; **to ~ one's pants/the bed** *[child]* zrobić siusiu w majtki/do łóżka *infml*

wet blanket *n infml* smutas *m infml*

wet-look /'wetlʊk/ *adj [plastic, leather]* lśniący

wet suit *n* kombinezon *m* piankowy

whack /wæk, US hwæk/ **[]** *n* (blow) grzmotnięcie *n infml*
[] *excl* buch!, ryms!
[] *vt* [1] (hit) rąbnąć, walnąć *infml [person, ball]* [2] GB *infml* (defeat) spuś|cić, -szczać (komuś) łomot *infml*

whacked /wækt, US hwækt/ *adj infml* (tired) skonany *infml*

whacky /'wæki, US 'hwæki/ *adj infml [person]* szurnięty *infml*; *[joke]* dziwaczny; *[party, clothes]* wariacki *infml*

whale[1] /weɪl, US hweɪl/ *n* [1] Zool wieloryb *m* [2] *infml* **a ~ of a difference** kolosalna różnica; **to have a ~ of a time** doskonale się bawić

whale[2] /weɪl, US hweɪl/ *vt* US *infml* (thrash) da|ć, -wać łupnia (komuś) *infml*

whaling /'weɪlɪŋ, US 'hweɪlɪŋ/ *n* wielorybnictwo *n*

wharf /wɔːf, US hwɔːf/ *n* nabrzeże *n*

what /wɒt, US hwɒt/ **[]** *pron* (in questions) co; **with ~?** z czym?; **~'s her telephone number?** jaki jest jej numer telefonu?; **~'s his name?** jak on ma na imię?; **~ did it cost?** ile to kosztowało?; **~ for?** po co?, czemu?; **~'s that button for?** do czego służy ten guzik?; **~'s it like?** (weather) jak jest na dworze?; **do ~ you want** rób, co chcesz; **and ~'s more** a co więcej; **~ I need is...** potrzebuję...; **~'s worse** co gorsza; **he did ~?** co zrobił?; **Adam ~?** Adam, a jak dalej?
[] *det* (which) który, jaki; **~ time is it?** która godzina?; **do you know ~ train he took?** wiesz, którym pociągiem pojechał?; **~ a lovely dress!** jaka śliczna sukienka!; **~ a strange thing to do!** co za pomysł!; **~ use is that?** i po co to?; **~ belongings they had** wszystko, co mieli
[] *what about prh* [1] (to draw attention) **~ about the children?** a co z dziećmi? [2] (to make suggestion) **~ about a cup of coffee?** co powiesz na filiżankę kawy?; **~ about Tuesday?** może we wtorek?
[] *what if phr* **~ if she finds out?** co będzie, jeśli ona się dowie?; **~ if I bring the dessert?** może podam już deser?
[] *excl* co?!
(IDIOMS) **~ with one thing and another, I haven't had time** tyle było spraw, że nie miałem czasu

what-d'yer-call-it /'wɒtdjəkɔːlɪt, US 'hwɒt-/ *n infml* ten interes *m infml*

whatever /wɒt'evə(r), US hwʌt-/ **I** *pron* [1] (that which) wszystko (to) co; **to do** ~ **is required** zrobić wszystko, co potrzeba [2] (anything that) cokolwiek; **do** ~ **you like** rób, co chcesz; ~ **you say** (as you like) jak chcesz [3] (no matter what) cokolwiek; ~ **happens** cokolwiek się stanie; ~ **it costs, it doesn't matter** cena nie gra roli [4] (what on earth) ~**'s that?** cóż to takiego jest?

II *det* [1] (any) jakikolwiek (bądź); **they eat** ~ **food they can get** jedzą to, co mogą zdobyć [2] (no matter what) ~ **the reason** bez względu na powód; **for** ~ **reason** z jakichkolwiek powodów

III *adv* (also **whatsoever**) (at all) **none** ~ absolutnie żaden; **to have no idea** ~ nie mieć najmniejszego pojęcia

what's-her-name /'wɒtsəneɪm, US 'hwʌt-/ *n* infml jak jej tam infml

what's-his-name /'wɒtsɪzneɪm, US 'hwʌt-/ *n* infml jak mu tam infml

wheat /wi:t, US hwi:t/ *n* pszenica *f*

wheatgerm /'wi:tdʒ3:m, US 'hwi:t-/ *n* zarodek *m* pszenicy

wheatmeal /'wi:tmi:l, US 'hwi:t-/ *n* mąka *f* pszenna razowa

wheedle /'wi:dl, US 'hwi:dl/ *vt* **to** ~ **sth out of sb** wyłudzić coś od kogoś

wheel /wi:l, US hwi:l/ **I** *n* [1] (of vehicle) koło *n*; (on trolley, piece of furniture) kółko *n* [2] (for steering) (in vehicle) kierownica *f*; (on boat) koło *n* sterowe; **at** or **behind the** ~ Aut za kierownicą; Naut przy sterze [3] (in mechanism) kółko *n*; (for pottery) koło *n*

II *vt* pchać *[pram, trolley]*; prowadzić *[bicycle]*; **they** ~**ed me into the operating theatre** wwieźli mnie na salę operacyjną

III *vi* [1] (also ~ **round**) *[bird]* krążyć; *[windmill]* kręcić się [2] *[person]* odwr|ócić, -acać się gwałtownie; *[regiment]* z|robić zwrot o 180 stopni; *[car]* zawrócić

(IDIOMS) **to** ~ **and deal** kombinować infml

wheelbarrow /'wi:lbærəʊ, US 'hwi:l-/ *n* taczka *f*

wheelchair /'wi:ltʃeə(r), US 'hwi:l-/ *n* wózek *m* inwalidzki

wheelclamp /'wi:lklæmp, US 'hwi:l-/ *n* Aut blokada *f* (zakładana na koła pojazdu)

wheeler dealer *n* infml kombinator *m*, -ka *f* infml

wheelie bin /'wi:lɪbɪn, US 'hwi:lɪ-/ *n* pojemnik *m* na śmieci na kółkach

wheeze /wi:z, US hwi:z/ *vi [person]* oddychać chrapliwie

wheezy /'wi:zɪ, US 'hwi:zɪ/ *adj [voice]* chrapliwy; *[cough]* astmatyczny; **my chest is** ~ rzęzi mi w płucach

when /wen, US hwen/ **I** *adv* [1] (in questions) kiedy; **I wonder** ~ **the film starts** ciekawe, kiedy się zaczyna film; **I forgot exactly** ~ (time) zapomniałem, o której; (date) zapomniałem, kiedy; **say** ~ (pouring drink) mów, ile (nalać) [2] (as relative) kiedy;

at the time ~ **...** (precise moment) w chwili, kiedy...; (during same period) w okresie, kiedy...; **it's times like that** ~ **...** w takich właśnie chwilach... [3] (whenever) (za każdym razem) kiedy; **he's only happy** ~ **he's alone** jest szczęśliwy tylko, kiedy jest sam; ~ **necessary** w razie konieczności; ~ **possible** kiedy tylko możliwe

II *conj* [1] (temporal sense) kiedy; ~ **he was at school** kiedy był w szkole; ~ **sailing, wear a lifejacket** żeglując, noś kamizelkę ratunkową; ~ **I'm 18** kiedy będę miał 18 lat [2] (since) skoro, jeśli; **why go to a hotel** ~ **you can stay here?** po co iść do hotelu, skoro możesz tu przenocować?

III *pron* kiedy; **until/since** ~ **?** do/od kiedy?; **that's** ~ **I found out** właśnie wtedy się dowiedziałem

whenever /wen'evə(r), US hwen-/ *adv* [1] (no matter when) kiedykolwiek; ~ **you want** kiedy (ze)chcesz; **I'll come** ~ **it's convenient** przyjdę, kiedy tylko będzie ci to odpowiadać [2] (every time that) kiedy tylko; ~ **I see a black cat...** jak widzę czarnego kota...

where /weə(r), US hweər/ **I** *adv* (in what place) gdzie; (to what place) gdzie, dokąd; (which way) którędy; ~**'s my coat?** gdzie mój płaszcz?; ~ **is he from?** skąd on jest?; **the house** ~ **I was born** dom, w którym się urodziłem; **in several cases** ~ **...** w kilku przypadkach, w których...; **put it** ~ **you want** połóż to, gdzie chcesz; **it's cold** ~ **we live** tam, gdzie mieszkamy, jest zimno; ~ **necessary/possible** tam, gdzie to konieczne/możliwe

II *pron* **from** ~**?** skąd?; **near** ~**?** koło czego?; **this is** ~ **it happened** to tu się wydarzyło; **that is** ~ **he's mistaken** tu właśnie się myli

whereabouts /'weərəbaʊts, US 'hweər-/ *npl* **nobody knows his** ~ nikt nie zna miejsca jego pobytu

whereas /ˌweər'æz, US ˌhweər-/ *conj* podczas gdy; **she likes dogs** ~ **I prefer cats** ona lubi psy, podczas gdy ja wolę koty

whereby /weə'baɪ, US hweər-/ *conj* **a regulation** ~ **all staff will carry identification** przepis, na mocy którego personel będzie miał obowiązek noszenia identyfikatorów; **criteria** ~ **allowances are allocated** kryteria, według których przyznaje się fundusze

wherever /weər'evə(r), US hweər-/ *adv* [1] (as interrogative) gdzie(ż); (where to) dokąd; ~ **has he got to?** gdzież on się podział? [2] (no matter where) gdzie(kolwiek); (no matter where to) dokąd(kolwiek); ~ **she goes I'll go** gdziekolwiek pójdzie, tam pójdę i ja; ~ **you like** gdzie chcesz; **we'll meet** ~**'s convenient for you** spotkamy się, gdzie ci wygodnie [3] (whenever) ~ **necessary/possible** tam, gdzie jest to konieczne/możliwe

whet /wet, US hwet/ *vt* zaostrz|yć, -ać *[appetite]*; podsyc|ić, -ać *[curiosity, interest]*

whether /'weðə(r), US 'hweðər/ *conj* czy; **I wonder ~ it's true** ciekawe, czy to prawda; **~ you like it or not** czy ci się to podoba, czy nie

whew /fju:/ *excl* (in relief) uff!; (in surprise) fiu, fiu!

which /wıtʃ, US hwıtʃ/ **I** *pron* 1 (in questions) (also ~ **one**) który; **there are three skirts, ~ do you want?** są trzy spódnice, którą chcesz?; **~ of you...?** które or kto z was...?; **I don't mind ~** mnie wszystko jedno (który); **I can never remember ~ is ~** nigdy nie pamiętam, który jest który 2 (relative to preceding noun) który; **the contract ~ he's spoken about** umowa, o której mówił 3 (relative to preceding clause or concept) co; **from ~ they inferred that...** z czego wywnioskowali, że...; **~ reminds me...** co mi przypomina...
II *det* który; **~ books?** które książki?; **~ one of the children...?** które z dzieci...?; **she may wish to come, in ~ case...** ona może zechcieć przyjść, a w tym przypadku...

whichever /wıtʃ'evə(r), US hwıtʃ-/ **I** *pron* 1 (the one that) (ten) który; **'which restaurant?' – '~ is nearest'** „która restauracja?" – „ta, która jest najbliżej"; **come at 2 or 2.30, ~ suits you best** przyjdź o 2 lub 2.30, jak ci wygodniej 2 (no matter which one) którykolwiek; **'do you want the big piece or the small piece?' – '~'** „chcesz duży, czy mały kawałek?" – „obojętnie (który)"
II *det* 1 (the one that) ten który; **let's go to ~ station is nearest** pójdźmy na tę stację, która jest najbliżej 2 (no matter which) którykolwiek; **it won't matter ~ hotel we stay at** nie ma znaczenia, w którym hotelu się zatrzymamy

whiff /wıf, US hwıf/ *n* zapach *m*

while /waıl, US hwaıl/ **I** *conj* (also **whilst**) 1 (although) chociaż 2 (during) podczas gdy, podczas (czegoś); **he made a sandwich ~ I phoned** zrobił kanapkę, podczas gdy ja rozmawiałem przez telefon; **~ in Spain, I visited Madrid** kiedy byłem w Hiszpanii, zwiedziłem też Madryt; **I fell asleep ~ watching TV** usnąłem, oglądając telewizję; **close the door ~ you're at it** zamknij drzwi, skoro już tam jesteś 3 (whereas) natomiast
II *n* chwila *f*; **a ~ ago** przed chwilą; **a ~ later** chwilę potem; **it will take a ~ to** trochę potrwa; **after a ~ he fell asleep** po chwili usnął; **once in a ~** od czasu do czasu
■ **while away** skr|ócić, -acać sobie *[time]*

whilst /waılst, US hwaılst/ *conj* = **while** **I**

whim /wım, US hwım/ *n* kaprys *m*; **on a ~** ni z tego, ni z owego

whimper /'wımpə(r), US 'hwım-/ **I** *n* (of baby) kwilenie *n*; (of dog) skomlenie *n*
II *vi* 1 *[person]* za|jęczeć; *[baby]* za|kwilić; *[puppy]* za|skomleć 2 (whinge) lamentować

whimsical /'wımzıkl, US 'hwım-/ *adj* *[person]* kapryśny; *[play, tale, manner, idea]* dziwaczny

whine /waın, US hwaın/ *vi* (complain) marudzić (**about sb/sth** na kogoś/coś); (snivel) pochlipywać; *[dog]* zaskomleć

whinge /wındʒ/ *vi* infml biadolić infml

whining /'waınıŋ, US 'hwaın-/ **I** *n* (complaints) lamentowanie *n*; (of dog) skomlenie *n*
II *adj* (complaining) *[voice, letter]* płaczliwy; *[child]* marudny

whinny /'wını, US 'hwını/ *vi [horse]* za|rżeć cicho

whip /wıp, US hwıp/ **I** *n* 1 (for punishment, horse) bat *m* 2 Culin mus *m*
II *vt* 1 (hit) smag|nąć, -ać batem *[horse]*; wy|chłostać *[person]* 2 Culin ubi|ć, -jać *[cream, egg whites]* 3 infml (remove quickly) **he ~ped the plates off the table** prędko sprzątnął talerze ze stołu; **to ~ sth from sb** ściągnąć coś komuś infml; **I ~ped the key out of his hand** wyrwałem mu klucz z ręki

whiplash injury *n* Med uraz *m* kręgosłupa szyjnego spowodowany szarpnięciem

whip-round /'wıpraʊnd, US 'hwıp-/ *n* GB infml zrzutka *f* infml; **to have a ~ for sth** zrobić zrzutkę or zrzucić się na coś

whirl /wɜ:l, US hwɜ:l/ **I** *n* 1 (of air, sand) wir *m* also fig 2 (spiral motif) spiralny wzór *m*
II *vi [dancer, blade, propeller, snowflakes]* za|wirować; *[thoughts]* kłębić się
■ **whirl round** *[person]* odwr|ócić, -acać się gwałtownie
IDIOMS **to give sth a ~** infml spróbować czegoś

whirlpool /'wɜ:lpu:l, US 'hwɜ:l-/ *n* wir *m* (wodny)

whirlpool bath *n* wanna *f* do kąpieli z masażem wodnym

whirlwind /'wɜ:lwınd, US 'hwɜ:l-/ *n* trąba *f* powietrzna

whirr /wɜ:(r), US hwɜ:r/ *vi [motor]* za|warczeć; *[camera]* za|szumieć; *[fan, wings]* za|furkotać; *[insect]* za|brzęczeć

whisk /wısk, US hwısk/ **I** *n* (also **egg ~**) (manual) trzepaczka *f* do jaj; (electric) mikser *m*
II *vt* 1 Culin ubi|ć, -jać *[cream, eggs]* 2 (transport quickly) **I was ~ed into the operating theatre** błyskawicznie przewieziono mnie na salę operacyjną

whisker /'wıskə(r), US 'hwı-/ **I** *n* (of animal) włos *m* czuciowy
II whiskers *npl* (of animal) wąsy *m pl*; (of man) (beard) broda *f*; (moustache) wąsy *m pl*

whisper /'wıspə(r), US 'hwıs-/ **I** *n* szept *m*; **to speak in a ~** or **in ~s** mówić szeptem
II *vt* szep|nąć, -tać; **to ~ sth to sb** wyszeptać coś do kogoś
III *vi [person]* szep|nąć, -tać; *[water]* za|szemrać; **to ~ to sb** szeptać do kogoś

whistle /'wɪsl, US 'hwɪ-/ **[I]** *n* [1] (small pipe) gwizdek *m*; **to blow the** or **one's** ~ zagwizdać [2] (sound) gwizd *m*; (by referee) gwizdek *m* **[II]** *vt* zagwizdać **[III]** *vi* gwizd|nąć, -ać, zagwizdać; **to** ~ **for a dog** zagwizdać na psa (IDIOMS:) **to blow the** ~ **on sb** donieść na kogoś

white /waɪt, US hwaɪt/ **[I]** *n* [1] biel *f*, (kolor *m*) biały *m* [2] (part of egg, eye) białko *n* [3] (also **White**) (Caucasian) biały *m*, -a *f* [4] (in chess, draughts) białe *plt* **[II]** *adj* [1] (colour) biały; **to go** or **turn** ~ zbieleć; **to paint sth** ~ pomalować coś na biało [2] *[race, child, skin]* biały; **a** ~ **area** obszar zamieszkany przez białych [3] (pale) *[person, face]* blady; **go** or **turn** ~ **with fear** zblednąć ze strachu

whitebait /'waɪtbeɪt, US 'hwaɪt-/ *n* Culin *drobne szprotki lub śledzie smażone we fryturze*

whiteboard /'waɪtbɔːd, US 'hwaɪt-/ *n* tablica *f* suchościeralna

white coffee *n* kawa *f* z mlekiem

white-collar /ˌwaɪt'kɒlə(r), US ˌhwaɪt-/ *adj [job, staff, work]* biurowy; ~ **worker** urzędnik

white elephant *n* [1] (knick-knack) bibelot *m* [2] (project) kosztowne przedsięwzięcie *n*

white goods *npl* sprzęt *m* elektryczny *(w gospodarstwie domowym)*

white horses *npl* (waves) grzywacze *m pl*

White House *n* the ~ Biały Dom *m*

white-knuckle ride /ˌwaɪt'nʌklraɪd, US ˌhwaɪt-/ *n* szaleńcza jazda *f (na karuzeli)*

white lie *n* niewinne kłamstwo *n*

whitener /'waɪtnə(r), US 'hwaɪt-/ *n* [1] (for clothes) wybielacz *m*; (for shoes) środek *m* do bielenia [2] (for coffee) zabielacz *m*

whiteness /'waɪtnɪs, US 'hwaɪt-/ *n* biel *f*

white spirit *n* benzyna *f* lakowa

whitewash /'waɪtwɒʃ, US 'hwaɪtwɔː-/ **[I]** *n* [1] (for walls) wapno *n* [2] (cover-up) wybielanie *n* fig; (of mistakes) tuszowanie *n* **[II]** *vt* [1] pobiel|ić, -ać, bielić *[wall, building]* [2] (also ~ **over**) za|tuszować *[action, scandal]*; wybiel|ić, -ać *[person]*

white water *n* górska rzeka *f*

white water rafting *n* rafting *m (na górskiej rzece)*

white wedding *n* ślub *m* w bieli

Whitsun /'wɪtsn, US 'hwɪ-/ *n* (also **Whitsuntide**) Zielone Świątki *plt*, Zesłanie *n* Ducha Świętego

Whit Sunday *n* pierwszy dzień *m* Zielonych Świątek

whittle /'wɪtl, US 'hwɪt-/ *vt* ostrug|ać, -iwać *[piece of wood]*; wystrug|ać, -iwać *[figure, walking stick]*; **to** ~ **sth away** or **down** zmniejszyć coś *[advantage, lead, influence]*

whizz /wɪz, US hwɪz/ *vi* **to** ~ **by** or **past** śmig|nąć, -ać; *[bullet, arrow]* przel|ecieć, -atywać ze świstem

whizz-kid /'wɪzkɪd, US 'hwɪz-/ *n* infml cudowne dziecko *n*

who /huː/ *pron* [1] (interrogative) kto; ~ **knows the answer?** kto zna odpowiedź?; ~ **was she with?** z kim ona była?; ~ **did you get it from?** od kogo to dostałeś?; ~ **did you invite?** kogo zaprosiłeś?; ~ **did you buy it for?** dla kogo to kupiłeś? [2] (relative) (after noun) który; (after pronoun) kto; **the boy** ~ **won the prize** chłopak, który zdobył nagrodę; **this is Adam,** ~ **I told you about** to Adam, o którym ci mówiłem; **he/she** ~ **...** ten, kto... [3] (whoever) **bring** ~ **you like** przyprowadź, kogo chcesz; ~ **do you think you are?** za kogo właściwie się uważasz?

whodun(n)it /huː'dʌnɪt/ *n* infml kryminał *m* infml

whoever /huː'evə(r)/ *pron* [1] (the one that) ten, kto; ~ **did it must be insane** ten, kto to zrobił, musi być szalony [2] (anyone that) (as subject) każdy, kto; (other uses) kto; **I'll invite** ~ **I like** zaproszę, kogo (tylko) zechcę [3] (no matter who) ktokolwiek; **come out** ~ **you are** wychodź, kimkolwiek jesteś; **write to the prime minister or** ~ pisz do premiera, albo do kogoś takiego

whole /həʊl/ **[I]** *n* [1] (total unit) całość *f*; **as a** ~ (not in separate parts) jako całość; (overall) w całości [2] (all) **the** ~ **of the weekend** cały weekend; **the** ~ **of London is talking about it** mówi o tym cały Londyn **[II]** *adj* [1] (entire) cały; **a** ~ **day/hour** cały dzień/ cała godzina; **the** ~ **truth** cała prawda; **in the** ~ **world** na całym świecie [2] (emphatic use) cały; **a** ~ **new way of life** zupełnie inny tryb życia; **that's the** ~ **point (of the exercise)!** o to właśnie chodzi (w tym wszystkim)! [3] (intact) cały **[III]** *adv [swallow, cook]* w całości **[IV] on the whole** *adv phr* ogólnie rzecz biorąc

wholefood /'həʊlfuːd/ *n* GB zdrowa żywność *f*

wholehearted /ˌhəʊl'hɑːtɪd/ *adj [agreement]* całkowity; *[approval, support]* gorący

wholeheartedly /ˌhəʊl'hɑːtɪdlɪ/ *adv* całym sercem

wholemeal /'həʊlmiːl/ *adj* razowy

whole milk *n* mleko *n* pełne

wholesale /'həʊlseɪl/ **[I]** *adj* [1] (in commerce) hurtowy [2] (large-scale) *[destruction, attack, alteration]* masowy; *[acceptance, rejection, commitment]* całkowity **[II]** *adv* [1] *[buy, sell]* hurtem [2] fig *[accept, reject]* w całości

wholesaler /'həʊlseɪlə(r)/ *n* hurtownik *m*

wholesome /'həʊlsəm/ *adj* [1] (healthy) *[diet, food]* zdrowy [2] (morally good) *[advice]* zdrowy; *[entertainment, literature]* godziwy

wholewheat /'həʊlwiːt/ *n* = **wholemeal**

wholly /'həʊllɪ/ *adv* całkowicie

whom /huːm/ *pron* [1] (interrogative) kto; ~ **did she marry?** za kogo ona wyszła?; **to** ~ **are you referring?** kogo masz na myśli? [2] (relative) który;

the person to ~ **I spoke** osoba, z którą rozmawiałem

whooping cough /ˌhuːpɪŋ'kɒf, ˌwuː-, US ˌhwuː'pɪŋ'kɔːf/ *n* Med krztusiec *m*, koklusz *m*

whopper /'wɒpə(r), US 'hwɒpər/ *n* infml (large thing) kolos *m*

whopping /'wɒpɪŋ, US 'hwɒpɪŋ/ *adj* infml (also ~ **great**) gigantyczny

whorl /wɜːl, US hwɜːl/ *n* (on fingerprint) wzór *m* wirowy; (of shell, spiral) zwój *m*; (of cream, chocolate) zawijas *m*

whose /huːz/ **I** *pron* [1] (in questions) czyj; ~ **is this?** czyje to jest? [2] (relative) który; **the boy** ~ **father works here** chłopak, którego ojciec tu pracuje; **the woman** ~ **daughter he was married to** kobieta, z której córką się ożenił

II *det* czyj; ~ **book is this?** czyja to książka?; **do you know** ~ **house that is?** wiesz, czyj to dom?; **with** ~ **permission?** za czyją zgodą?

why /waɪ, US hwaɪ/ **I** *adv* [1] (in questions) (about reason) dlaczego; (to what purpose) po co; ~ **do you ask?** czemu or dlaczego pytasz?; ~ **bother?** po co się przejmować?; ~ **the delay?** skąd to opóźnienie?; **'tell them' – '** ~ **should I?'** „powiedz im" – „a po co?"; ~ **not?** czemu nie? [2] (making suggestions) ~ **don't we go away for the weekend?** może wyjechalibyśmy na weekend?; ~ **don't I invite them for dinner?** może zaprosić ich na kolację?

II *conj* dlatego; **that's** ~ **they came** dlatego właśnie przyszli; **I need to know the reason** ~ muszę wiedzieć dlaczego

wick /wɪk/ *n* (of candle, lamp) knot *m*

wicked /'wɪkɪd/ *adj* [1] (evil) *[person]* podły; *[intention, lie]* niecny; *[deed, plot]* haniebny; *[heart]* okrutny [2] (mischievous) *[grin, wink, stare]* szelmowski [3] (vicious) *[wind, weather]* paskudny; *[weapon]* groźny; **a** ~ **tongue** cięty język

wicker /'wɪkə(r)/ **I** *n* (also ~ **work**) wyroby *m pl* z wikliny

II *adj [basket, furniture]* wiklinowy

wide /waɪd/ **I** *adj* [1] (broad) szeroki; **how** ~ **is your garden?** ile szerokości ma twój ogród?; **the belt is 30 cm** ~ pasek ma 30 cm szerokości; **to make sth** ~**r** poszerzać coś; **her eyes were** ~ **with fear** oczy rozszerzyły jej się ze strachu [2] (immense) *[ocean, desert, sky]* bezkresny; *[panorama]* szeroki [3] (extensive) *[variety, range, interests]* szeroki; *[experience, choice]* bogaty [4] Sport *[ball, shot]* niecelny

II *adv* szeroko; **to open one's eyes** ~ otworzyć szeroko oczy; **open** ~**!** szeroko otwórz buzię!; **his eyes are** ~ **apart** ma szeroko rozstawione oczy; **to be** ~ **of the mark** *[ball, dart]* nie trafić

wide-angle lens /ˌwaɪdæŋgl'lenz/ *n* obiektyw *m* szerokokątny

wide awake *adj* **she was** ~ nie spała

wide-eyed /ˌwaɪd'aɪd/ *adj* [1] (out of fear, surprise) **to be** ~ wybałuszyć oczy; **to listen** ~ słuchać z wybałuszonymi oczami [2] (naïve) *[person]* naiwny

widely /'waɪdlɪ/ *adv* [1] (commonly) *[accepted, used]* powszechnie; ~ **available** powszechnie dostępny [2] (at a distance) *[planted, spaced]* szeroko [3] (significantly) *[differ, vary]* znacznie; (at a large distance) **she is** ~ **travelled** dużo podróżowała

widely-read /ˌwaɪdlɪ'red/ *adj [student]* oczytany; *[author]* poczytny

widen /'waɪdn/ **I** *vt* [1] poszerzyć, -ać *[road, path]*; zwiększyć, -ać *[gap]* [2] fig rozszerzyć, -ać *[scope, range]*; zwiększyć, -ać *[powers, lead]*

II *vi [river, road]* rozszerzyć, -ać się

widening /'waɪdnɪŋ/ *adj [division, gap]* powiększający się

wide open *adj* [1] *[door, window]* szeroko otwarty [2] **the game is** ~ Sport jeszcze wszystko może się zdarzyć

wide-ranging /ˌwaɪd'reɪndʒɪŋ/ *adj [poll, report, reforms]* szeroko zakrojony; *[interests]* szeroki

wide screen *n* szeroki ekran *m*

wide-screen TV *n* telewizor *m* panoramiczny

widespread /'waɪdspred/ *adj [epidemic]* szerzący się; *[devastation]* rozległy; *[belief]* rozpowszechniony

widow /'wɪdəʊ/ **I** *n* wdowa *f*

II *vt* **to be** ~**ed** owdowieć

widower /'wɪdəʊə(r)/ *n* wdowiec *m*

width /wɪdθ, wɪtθ/ *n* szerokość *f*; **to be 40 metres in** ~ mieć 40 metrów szerokości

wield /wiːld/ *vt* dzierżyć also fig *[weapon, tool, authority]*

wife /waɪf/ *n* żona *f*

wig /wɪg/ *n* (whole head) peruka *f*; (partial) (man's) tupet *m*; (woman's) treska *f*

wiggle /'wɪgl/ infml **I** *n* **a** ~ **of the hips** lekki ruch bioder

II *vt* poruszyć (czymś) *[tooth, object]*; kołysać (czymś) *[hips]*; kiwać (czymś) *[toe, finger]*

III *vi [snake, worm]* wić się

wild /waɪld/ **I** *n* **to live in the** ~ *[animal]* żyć na swobodzie; **to grow in the** ~ *[plant]* rosnąć dziko; **the call of the** ~ zew natury

II *adj* [1] (in natural state) *[animal, plant, landscape]* dziki; **the pony is still quite** ~ kucyk jest jeszcze ciągle narowisty [2] (turbulent) *[wind, storm]* gwałtowny; *[sea]* wzburzony; *[day, month]* burzliwy [3] (unrestrained) *[party]* szalony; *[imagination, laughter]* niepohamowany; *[person]* rozhukany; *[applause]* gromki; **to go** ~ *[fans, audience]* szaleć [4] infml (furious) wściekły; **he'll go** or **be** ~**!** wścieknie się! infml [5] infml (enthusiastic) **to be** ~ **about sth** mieć bzika na punkcie czegoś infml; **I'm not** ~ **about him** nie przepadam za nim [6] (outlandish) *[idea, plan]* szalony; *[claim, accusation]* niedorzeczny, absurdalny; *[story]* nieprawdopodobny

III *adv [grow]* dziko; **to run** ~ *[garden]* zdziczeć; **those children are allowed to run** ~ te dzieci są puszczane samopas; **to let one's imagination run** ~ popuścić wodze wyobraźni

wild boar *n* dzik *m*

wilderness /ˈwɪldənɪs/ *n* pustkowie *n*

wild-eyed /ˌwaɪldˈaɪd/ *adj [person]* o szalonym wzroku; (with fear, enthusiasm) oszalały

wildfire /ˈwaɪldfaɪə(r)/ *n* **to spread like** ~ *[news, rumours]* rozchodzić się lotem błyskawicy; *[disease]* szerzyć się w zastraszającym tempie

wild flower *n* kwiat *m* polny

wild-goose chase /ˌwaɪldˈguːstʃeɪs/ *n* szukanie *n* wiatru w polu; **to lead sb on a** ~ naprowadzić kogoś na fałszywy ślad

wildlife /ˈwaɪldlaɪf/ *n* (animals) fauna *f*; (animals and plants) fauna *f* i flora *f*

wildlife park, wildlife reserve, wildlife sanctuary *n* rezerwat *m* przyrody

wildly /ˈwaɪldlɪ/ *adv* 1 (recklessly) *[invest, spend]* lekkomyślnie; *[fire, run]* na oślep; **to hit out** ~ zadawać ciosy na oślep 2 (energetically) *[wave, gesture]* gwałtownie; *[applaud]* burzliwie; **to fluctuate** ~ gwałtownie się zmieniać; **her heart was beating** ~ serce biło jej jak szalone 3 (extremely) *[enthusiastic, happy, optimistic]* szalenie

Wild West *n* **the** ~ Dziki Zachód *m*

wilful GB, **willful** US /ˈwɪlfl/ *adj* 1 (headstrong) *[person]* nieposłuszny; *[behaviour]* samowolny 2 (deliberate) *[damage, disobedience]* umyślny 3 *[murder, misconduct]* popełniony z premedytacją

wilfully GB, **willfully** US /ˈwɪlfəlɪ/ *adv* 1 (obstinately) uparcie, z uporem 2 (deliberately) umyślnie, rozmyślnie

will[1] /wɪl, əl/ *modal aux* 1 (to express the future) **I'll see you tomorrow** do zobaczenia jutro; **it won't rain** nie będzie padać; ~ **there be many people?** będzie dużo ludzi?; **they'll come tomorrow** jutro przyjadą; **what** ~ **you do now?** co teraz zrobisz? 2 (expressing consent, willingness) ~ **you help me?** pomożesz mi?; **we won't stay too long** nie zostaniemy na długo 3 (in commands, requests) ~ **you pass the salt, please?** czy możesz podać sól?; ~ **you please listen to me!** czy możesz mnie wysłuchać?; **wait a minute,** ~ **you!** poczekaj chwilę! 4 (in offers, invitations) ~ **you marry me?** czy wyjdziesz za mnie?; **won't you join us for dinner?** zjesz z nami obiad?; **what** ~ **you have to drink?** czego się napijesz? 5 (in assumptions) **he'll be about 30 now** musi mieć około trzydziestki; **you'll be tired, I expect** pewnie jesteś zmęczony 6 (expressing custom or habit) **they** ~ **usually ask for a deposit** zwykle proszą o zaliczkę; **these things** ~ **happen** to się zdarza; **she** ~ **keep repeating the same old joke** stale powtarza ten sam stary dowcip 7 (in short answers and tag questions) **you'll come again, won't you?** przyjdziesz jeszcze,

prawda?; **you won't forget,** ~ **you?** nie zapomnij, dobrze?; **'they won't be ready'** – **'yes, they** ~**'** „nie zdążą" – „zdążą"; **'**~ **you help me?'** – **'yes, I** ~**'** „pomożesz mi?" – „tak"; **'she'll be furious'** – **'no, she won't'** „będzie wściekła" – „wcale nie"; **'I'll do it'** – **'no, you won't'** „ja to zrobię" – „wykluczone"

will[2] /wɪl/ **I** *n* 1 (mental power) wola *f*; **she has a** ~ **of her own** do niczego się jej nie zmusi; **to lose the** ~ **to live** stracić chęć do życia; **against one's** ~ wbrew własnej woli; **to do sth with a** ~ zrobić coś ochoczo 2 (in law) ostatnia wola *f*, testament *m*; **to leave sb sth in one's** ~ zostawić komuś coś w testamencie

II at will *adv phr [select, take]* do woli; (freely) na życzenie

III *vt* 1 (urge) **to** ~ **sb to do sth** siłą woli zmusić kogoś do zrobienia czegoś; **she** ~**ed him to live** modliła się, żeby przeżył 2 (wish, desire) chcieć 3 (in law) zapis|ać, -ywać (w testamencie) (**to sb** komuś)

willing /ˈwɪlɪŋ/ *adj* 1 (prepared) skłonny (**to do sth** coś zrobić); **I'm more than** ~ **to help** bardzo chętnie pomogę 2 (eager) *[pupil, helper]* chętny; *[accomplice, servant]* uległy; *[donation, sacrifice]* dobrowolny; **to show** ~ wykazać dobre chęci

willingly /ˈwɪlɪŋlɪ/ *adv [accept, help, work]* chętnie; **did she go** ~**?** (czy) poszła dobrowolnie?

willingness /ˈwɪlɪŋnɪs/ *n* gotowość *f* (**to do sth** zrobienia czegoś)

willow /ˈwɪləʊ/ *n* (also ~ **tree**) wierzba *f*

will power *n* siła *f* woli; **to have the** ~ **to do sth** mieć dość silnej woli, żeby coś zrobić

willy-nilly /ˌwɪlɪˈnɪlɪ/ *adv* chcąc nie chcąc

wilt /wɪlt/ *vi [plant, flower]* z|więdnąć; fig *[person]* (from heat, fatigue) opa|ść, -dać z sił; (at daunting prospect) upa|ść, -dać na duchu

wimp /wɪmp/ *n* infml mięczak *m* infml

win /wɪn/ **I** *n* (victory) zwycięstwo *n* (**over sb** nad kimś)

II *vt* 1 (be victorious) wygr|ać, -ywać *[match, battle, bet, money, election]* 2 (gain) dosta|ć, -wać *[scholarship, promotion]*; zdoby|ć, -wać *[medal, friendship, heart, support, votes]*; **to** ~ **sb's love/respect** zdobyć miłość/uznanie kogoś

III *vi* wygr|ać, -ywać, zwycięż|yć, -ać (**against sb** z kimś)

■ **win back:** ~ *[sth]* **back** odzysk|ać, -iwać *[support, affection, title]*; odbi|ć, -jać *[territory]*

■ **win over, win round:** przekon|ać, -ywać (**to sth** do czegoś)

wince /wɪns/ **I** *n* grymas

II *vi* s|krzywić się; (feel uncomfortable) wzdryg|nąć, -ać się

winch /wɪntʃ/ **I** *n* (for hoisting) wciągarka *f*; (for hauling) wyciągarka *f*

II *vt* to ~ sth down/up spuszczać/podciągać coś
wind[1] /wɪnd/ **I** *n* [1] wiatr *m*; **the** ~ **is blowing**
wieje wiatr; **which way is the** ~ **blowing?** skąd
wieje wiatr? [2] (breath) oddech *m*; **the news
knocked the** ~ **out of him** ta wiadomość poraziła
go; **to get one's** ~ złapać oddech [3] (flatulence)
wiatry *m pl*; **to break** ~ puszczać wiatry
II *vt* [1] (make breathless) zap|rzeć, -ierać (komuś)
dech w piersi [2] (burp) **she put the baby against
her shoulder to** ~ **him** przełożyła sobie dziecko
przez ramię, żeby mu się odbiło
wind[2] /waɪnd/ **I** *vt* [1] (coil up) nawi|nąć, -jać *[hair,
rope, wire]* (**on, onto sth** na coś); owi|nąć, -jać
(**round sth** wokół czegoś) [2] (also ~ **up**) nakręc|ić,
-ać *[clock, toy]* [3] przekręc|ić, -ać *[handle]* [4] **to** ~
one's or **its way** *[road, river]* wić się
II *vi [river, road, procession]* wić się; *[stairs]*
zakręcać

■ **wind down:** ¶ ~ **down** [1] *[organization]*
kończyć swoją działalność; *[activity, production]*
dobiegać końca; *[person]* odprężać się [2] *[clock-
work]* stawać ¶ ~ **[sth] down** [1] otw|orzyć,
-ierać *[car window]* [2] rozpocz|ąć, -ynać likwidację
(czegoś) *[organization]*; kończyć *[activity]*

■ **wind up:** ¶ ~ **up** [1] (finish) *[event]* za|kończyć
się (**with sth** czymś); *[speaker]* za|kończyć [2] infml
[person] s|kończyć, wy|lądować ¶ ~ **[sth] up**
[1] z|likwidować *[business, account]*; za|kończyć
[campaign, meeting, project] [2] nakręc|ić, -ać *[clock,
toy]*; zam|knąć, -ykać *[car window]* ¶ ~ **[sb] up**
[1] (tease) drażnić się z (kimś) [2] (annoy) z|denerwo-
wać

wind chimes *n* dzwoneczki *m pl* wietrzne
wind energy *n* energia *f* wiatru
windfall /ˈwɪndfɔːl/ *n* (fruit) spad *m*; fig nieoczekiwany przypływ *m* gotówki
windfall profit *n* nieoczekiwany zysk *m*
winding /ˈwaɪndɪŋ/ *adj [road, stairs]* kręty
wind instrument *n* instrument *m* dęty
windmill /ˈwɪndmɪl/ *n* wiatrak *m*
window /ˈwɪndəʊ/ *n* [1] (of house, room, vehicle) okno
n also Comput; (stained-glass) witraż *m*; (of envelope)
okienko *n*; **to look out of** or **through the** ~
wyglądać przez okno [2] (of shop) witryna *f*, wystawa *f* [3] (for service) okienko *n*
window blind *n* (roller shutter) roleta *f* okienna;
(Venetian) żaluzja *f*
window box *n* skrzynka *f* na kwiaty
window cleaner *n* (person) osoba *f* myjąca okna;
(product) płyn *m* do mycia szyb
window display *n* wystawa *f* sklepowa
window ledge *n* parapet *m*
windowpane /ˈwɪndəʊpeɪn/ *n* szyba *f*
window seat *n* [1] (in room) ławeczka *f* w oknie
[2] (in plane, bus, train) miejsce *n* przy oknie
window-shopping /ˈwɪndəʊʃɒpɪŋ/ *n* **to go** ~
oglądać wystawy (sklepowe)

windowsill /ˈwɪndəʊsɪl/ *n* parapet *m*
windpipe /ˈwɪndpaɪp/ *n* tchawica *f*
windpower /ˈwɪndpaʊə(r)/ *n* energia *f* wiatru
windscreen /ˈwɪndskriːn/ *n* GB Aut przednia
szyba *f*
windscreen wiper *n* GB Aut wycieraczka *f*
windshield /ˈwɪndʃiːld/ *n* US Aut = **windscreen**
windsurf /ˈwɪndsɜːf/ *vi* pływać na desce surfingo-
wej
windsurfer /ˈwɪndsɜːfə(r)/ *n* (person) windsurfer *m*;
(board) deska *f* surfingowa
windswept /ˈwɪndswept/ *adj [moor, hillside,
coast]* wystawiony na działanie wiatru; *[hair]*
potargany
windy /ˈwɪndɪ/ *adj [day]* wietrzny; *[place]* wystawiony na działanie wiatru; **it was very** ~ wiał
silny wiatr
wine /waɪn/ *n* [1] (drink) wino *n* [2] (colour) (kolor *m*)
bordowy *m*
wine bar *n* winiarnia *f*
wine box *n* karton *m* wina
wine cellar *n* piwnica *f* (na wino)
wine glass *n* kieliszek *m* do wina
wine grower *n* hodowca *m* winorośli
wine growing *n* [1] uprawa *f* winorośli
II *adj* ~ **region** region uprawy winorośli
wine list *n* karta *f* win
wine rack *n* stelaż *m* na butelki z winem
wine shop *n* sklep *m* z winami
wine tasting *n* degustacja *f* win
wine vinegar *n* ocet *m* winny
wine waiter *n* kelner *m* podający wino
wing /wɪŋ/ **I** *n* (of bird, insect, plane, building, party,
pitch) skrzydło *n*
II wings *npl* (in theatre) **the** ~**s** kulisy *plt*; **to be
waiting in the** ~**s** fig być w pogotowiu
winger /ˈwɪŋə(r)/ *n* infml GB skrzydłow|y *m*, -a *f*
wing nut *n* nakrętka *f* skrzydełkowa
wink /wɪŋk/ **I** *n* mrugnięcie *n* oka; **we didn't get
a** ~ **of sleep all night** całą noc nie zmrużyliśmy
oka
II *vi [person]* mrug|nąć, -ać; **to** ~ **at sb** puścić do
kogoś oko infml
winner /ˈwɪnə(r)/ *n* [1] (victor) zwycię|zca *m*, -żczy-
ni *f* [2] (success) **to be a** ~ *[film, book, song]* odnieść
olbrzymi sukces
winning /ˈwɪnɪŋ/ *adj* [1] (victorious) zwycięski
[2] *[smile]* ujmujący; **to have** ~ **ways** być ujmu-
jącym
winning post *n* meta *f*
winning streak *n* **to be on a** ~ mieć dobrą
passę
winter /ˈwɪntə(r)/ **I** *n* zima *f*; **in** ~ zimą or
w zimie
II *adj* zimowy
III *vi* prze|zimować
wintertime /ˈwɪntətaɪm/ *n* zima *f*

wipe /waɪp/ **▯** *n* ▯ **to give sth a** ~ wytrzeć or przetrzeć coś ▯ (for face) chusteczka *f* odświeżająca; **baby** ~**s** chusteczki pielęgnacyjne dla niemowląt **▯** *vt* wy|trzeć, -cierać *[table, glass, feet, nose]* ■ **wipe away**: o|trzeć, -cierać *[tears, sweat]*; zetrzeć, ścierać *[dirt, mark]*
■ **wipe out**: ▯ (clean) wy|trzeć, -cierać ▯ wy-wymaz|ać, -ywać *[memory, past]*; anulować *[debt]*; sprowadz|ić, -ać do zera *[chances, gains, losses]*; zmi|eść, -atać z powierzchni ziemi *[enemy, population]*
■ **wipe up**: ¶ ~ **up** po|wycierać naczynia ¶ ~ [sth] **up** wy|trzeć, -cierać
wipe-clean /ˌwaɪpˈkliːn/ *adj* łatwy w czyszczeniu
wire /ˈwaɪə(r)/ **▯** *n* ▯ (length of metal) drut *m*; (in plastic) kabel *m* ▯ US (telegram) telegram *m*
▯ *vt* ▯ **to** ~ **a house** założyć w domu instalację elektryczną; **to** ~ **a plug/lamp** podłączyć gniazdko/lampę ▯ (send telegram to) za|depeszować do (kogoś) *[person]*; przes|łać, -yłać *[money]*
wiring /ˈwaɪərɪŋ/ *n* (in house) instalacja *f* elektryczna; (in appliance) oprzewodowanie *n*
wiry /ˈwaɪəri/ *adj* ▯ *[person, body]* żylasty ▯ *[hair]* szorstki
wisdom /ˈwɪzdəm/ *n* mądrość *f*
wisdom tooth *n* ząb *m* mądrości
wise[1] /waɪz/ *adj [book, speech, person]* mądry; (prudent) mądry, rozsądny; **a** ~ **man** mędrzec; **to be none the** ~**r** (understand no better) nie być ani na jotę mądrzejszym; (not realize) nie mieć pojęcia
wise[2] /waɪz/ **▯** *n* fml (way) sposób *m*
▯ **-wise** *in combinations* ▯ (direction) **clock**-~ zgodnie z ruchem wskazówek zegara; **length**-~ wzdłuż ▯ (with regard to) jeżeli chodzi o; **work**-~ jeżeli chodzi o pracę
wisecrack /ˈwaɪzkræk/ *n* dowcipas *m* infml
wise guy *n* infml mądrala *m/f* infml
wisely /ˈwaɪzli/ *adv* mądrze
wish /wɪʃ/ **▯** *n* ▯ (request) życzenie *n* (**for sth** czegoś); **to make a** ~ wypowiedzieć życzenie; **her** ~ **came true** jej życzenie się spełniło ▯ (desire) pragnienie *n* (**for sth** czegoś); **I have no** ~ **to talk to you** nie mam zamiaru z tobą rozmawiać
▯ wishes *npl* życzenia *n pl*; **good** or **best** ~**es** najlepsze życzenia; (in letter) serdeczne pozdrowienia; **best** ~**es on your birthday** wszystkiego najlepszego z okazji urodzin; **please give him my best** ~**es** przekaż mu moje najserdeczniejsze życzenia
▯ *vt* ▯ (expressing longing) **I** ~ **he were here** szkoda, że go tutaj nie ma; **he** ~**ed he had written** żałował, że nie napisał ▯ (express congratulations, greetings) życzyć (komuś); **I** ~ **you happiness** życzę szczęścia; **to** ~ **sb well** dobrze komuś życzyć ▯ (want) życzyć sobie (czegoś)

▯ *vi* ▯ (desire, want) życzyć sobie fml (**for sth** czegoś); **just as you** ~ jak sobie życzysz ▯ (in fairy story) wypowi|edzieć, -adać życzenie
wishful thinking /ˌwɪʃflˈθɪŋkɪŋ/ *n* pobożne życzenia *n pl*
wishy-washy /ˈwɪʃiwɒʃi/ *adj* infml *[colour]* rozmyty; *[person]* nijaki
wisp /wɪsp/ *n* (of hair) kosmyk *m*; (of straw) wiązka *f*; (of smoke, fog) smuga *f*
wispy /ˈwɪspi/ *adj [hair, beard]* rzadki; *[cloud, smoke]* strzępiasty
wisteria /wɪˈstɪəriə/ *n* Bot wisteria *f*
wistful /ˈwɪstfl/ *adj* (sad) smutny; (nostalgic) tęskny
wit[1] /wɪt/ **▯** *n* ▯ (sense of humour) dowcip *m* ▯ (person) kpiarz *m*
▯ wits *npl* rozum *m*; **to collect** or **gather one's** ~**s** pozbierać się; **to frighten sb out of their** ~**s** śmiertelnie kogoś przestraszyć; **to live by one's** ~**s** kombinować; **to lose one's** ~**s** stracić rozum; **a battle of** ~**s** (argument) walka słowna; (rivalry) próba przechytrzenia się nawzajem
[IDIOMS] **to be at one's** ~**s' end** odchodzić od zmysłów
wit[2] /wɪt/ **to wit** *adv phr* (a) mianowicie
witch /wɪtʃ/ *n* czarownica *f*
witchcraft /ˈwɪtʃkrɑːft, US -kræft/ *n* czary *plt*
witch doctor *n* szaman *m*
witch-hunt /ˈwɪtʃhʌnt/ *n* polowanie *n* na czarownice also fig
with /wɪð, wɪθ/ *prep* ▯ (involving, concerning, accompanied by, as regards) z (kimś/czymś); **a discussion** ~ **sb** dyskusja z kimś; **a girl** ~ **long hair** dziewczyna z długimi włosami; **a boy** ~ **a broken leg** chłopak ze złamaną nogą; **take your umbrella** ~ **you** weź ze sobą parasol; **the frontier** ~ **Germany** granica z Niemcami; **to be patient** ~ **sb** być cierpliwym dla kogoś; **how are things** ~ **you?** co u ciebie?; **what's up** ~ **you?** co ci się stało?; **what do you want** ~ **another car?** po co ci jeszcze jeden samochód? ▯ (by means of) **to hit sb** ~ **sth** uderzyć kogoś czymś; **to walk** ~ **a stick** chodzić o lasce; **furnished** ~ **antiques** umeblowany antykami; **covered** ~ **mud** pokryty błotem; **wet** ~ **dew** wilgotny od rosy; **filled** ~ **sth** pełen czegoś ▯ (indicating manner) z (czymś); ~ **care** ostrożnie; ~ **a smile/sigh** z uśmiechem/westchnieniem ▯ (according to) w zależności od (czegoś); **to increase** ~ **time** wzrastać w miarę upływu czasu; **to vary** ~ **the temperature** zmieniać się w zależności od temperatury ▯ (owning) **passengers** ~ **tickets** pasażerowie z biletami; **people** ~ **qualifications** ludzie o odpowiednich kwalifikacjach; **somebody** ~ **your experience** ktoś z twoim doświadczeniem ▯ (because of) z (czegoś); **white** ~ **fear** pobladły ze strachu; **to be delighted** ~ **sth** być zachwyconym czymś; **I can't do it** ~ **you**

watching nie potrafię tego zrobić, kiedy mi się przyglądasz 7 (suffering from) **people ~ leukemia** ludzie chorzy na białaczkę; **to be ill ~ flu** mieć grypę 8 (employed by, customer of) **a reporter ~ the Gazette** reporter z „Gazety"; **I'm ~ Chemco** pracuję w Chemco; **I've been (banking) ~ them for years** mam u nich konto od lat 9 (in the same direction as) z (czymś); **to sail ~ the wind** żeglować z wiatrem; **to drift ~ the tide** unosić się z prądem

withdraw /wɪð'drɔː, wɪθ'd-/ **I** vt (remove, recall) cof|nąć, -ać *[hand, permission, support]*; pod|jąć, -ejmować *[money]*; wycof|ać, -ywać *[troops, motion]*; odwoł|ać, -ywać *[ambassador, diplomat, accusation]*; wycof|ać, -ywać się z (czegoś) *[offer, claim, aid]*
II vi 1 *[applicant, competitor, troops]* wycof|ać, -ywać się 2 (psychologically) zam|knąć, -ykać się w sobie

withdrawal /wɪð'drɔːəl, wɪθ'd-/ n 1 (of troops, candidate) wycofanie (się) n; (of cash) wypłata f; (of whole deposit) wycofanie n 2 (psychological) zamknięcie się n w sobie 3 (of drug addict) głód m narkotyczny

withdrawal symptoms npl objawy m pl abstynencyjne

withdrawn /wɪð'drɔːn, wɪθ'd-/ adj *[person]* zamknięty w sobie

wither /'wɪðə(r)/ **I** vt z|warzyć *[plant, leaves]*
II vi *[plant]* us|chnąć, -ychać

withering /'wɪðərɪŋ/ adj *[contempt, look, remark]* miażdżący

withhold /wɪð'həʊld/ vt wstrzym|ać, -ywać *[payment]*; odm|ówić, -awiać płacenia (czegoś) *[tax, rent]*; wstrzym|ać, -ywać wypłatę (czegoś) *[grant, funds]*; odm|ówić, -awiać (czegoś) *[consent, permission]*; zata|ić, -jać *[information]*

within /wɪ'ðɪn/ **I** prep 1 (inside) w (czymś); **~ the city walls** w obrębie miasta; **~ party** w partii 2 (in expressions of time) w ciągu (czegoś); **I'll do it ~ the hour** zrobię to w ciągu godziny or w godzinę; **15 burglaries ~ the week** 15 włamań w ciągu jednego tygodnia; **they died ~ a week of each other** zmarli w ciągu tygodnia jedno po drugim 3 (not more than) **to be ~ several metres of sth** znajdować się w odległości kilku metrów od czegoś; **it's accurate to ~ a millimetre** to jest odmierzone z dokładnością do milimetra 4 (not beyond the range of) w zasięgu (czegoś); **to be ~ sight** być w zasięgu wzroku; **to live ~ one's income** żyć skromnie
II adv wewnątrz; **seen from ~** widziany od wewnątrz

without /wɪ'ðaʊt/ **I** prep bez (kogoś/czegoś); **~ any money** bez pieniędzy; **~ saying a word** nie mówiąc słowa; **it goes ~ saying** to jest oczywiste
II adv na zewnątrz; **from ~** z zewnątrz

withstand /wɪð'stænd/ vt wytrzym|ać, -ywać *[attack, heat, pain]*

witness /'wɪtnɪs/ **I** n 1 (person) świadek m; **she was a ~ to the accident** była świadkiem wypadku; **~ for the prosecution/defence** świadek oskarżenia/obrony 2 (testimony) świadectwo n; **to be** or **bear ~ to sth** świadczyć o czymś
II vt 1 (see) być świadkiem (czegoś) 2 (at official occasion) być świadkiem przy (czymś) *[signature, signing]*; być świadkiem przy podpisywaniu (czegoś) *[document]*

witness box GB, **witness stand** US n miejsce n dla świadka

witticism /'wɪtɪsɪzəm/ n dowcipne powiedzenie n

witty /'wɪtɪ/ adj dowcipny

wizard /'wɪzəd/ n 1 (magician) czarnoksiężnik m 2 (expert) **to be a ~ at sth** być specem od czegoś infml *[computers, chess]*

wizened /'wɪznd/ adj pomarszczony

wobble /'wɒbl/ vi *[table, chair, tool, person]* za|chwiać się; *[voice]* za|drżeć

wobbly /'wɒblɪ/ adj *[chair, tooth]* kiwający się

woe /wəʊ/ n niedola f

wolf /wʊlf/ n wilk m; **she-~** wilczyca
IDIOMS: **to cry ~** podnieść fałszywy alarm

wolf-whistle /'wʊlfwɪsl, US -hwɪ-/ **I** n gwizd m *(na widok przechodzącej kobiety)*
II vi gwizd|nąć, -ać *(na widok przechodzącej kobiety)*

woman /'wʊmən/ n kobieta f; **a ~ Prime Minister** kobieta premier; **women drivers** kobiety za kierownicą

woman friend n przyjaciółka f

womanizer /'wʊmənaɪzə(r)/ n kobieciarz m

womb /wuːm/ n Anat macica f; fml łono n

women's refuge n schronisko n dla kobiet – ofiar przemocy w rodzinie

women's studies n studia plt feministyczne

wonder /'wʌndə(r)/ **I** n 1 (miracle) cud m; **(it's) no ~ that...** nic dziwnego, że...; **she has done ~s with that house** dzięki niej ten dom jest nie do poznania; **a change in diet can work ~s** zmiana sposobu odżywiania może zdziałać cuda 2 (amazement) zdumienie n
II vt (ask oneself) zastanawiać się; **I ~ how/why...** zastanawiam się, jak/dlaczego...; **I ~ if you could help me** mógłby mi pan pomóc?; **it makes you ~** to daje do myślenia; **it makes you ~ why/if/how...** nasuwa się pytanie, dlaczego/czy/jak...
III vi 1 (think) **to ~ about sth** zastanawiać się nad czymś 2 (be surprised) **to ~ at sth** dziwić się czemuś; (admiringly) zachwycać się czymś

wonderful /'wʌndəfl/ adj *[book, film, holiday, experience]* cudowny; *[meal, musician, teacher, achievement]* wspaniały

wonderfully /'wʌndəfəlɪ/ adv 1 (very) niezwykle 2 *[cope, behave, perform]* wspaniale

wonky /'wɒŋkı/ adj infml [1] (crooked) zwichrowany [2] (wobbly) [furniture, legs] chwiejny

wont /wəʊnt, US wɔːnt/ adj **to be ~ to do sth** mieć w zwyczaju coś robić; **as is his/their ~** jak to on/oni

woo /wuː/ vt zabiegać o względy (kogoś)

wood /wʊd/ [ ] n [1] (timber) drewno n [2] (forest) las m
[ ] woods npl las m
[ ] adj [smoke, fire] z palącego się drewna
[IDIOMS] **touch ~!** GB, **knock on ~!** US odpukać!;
we are not out of the ~ yet ciągle jeszcze nie wyszliśmy na prostą

wooden /'wʊdn/ adj drewniany; fig [acting, performance] [expression] beznamiętny

woodland /'wʊdlənd/ n las m

woodpecker /'wʊdpekə(r)/ n dzięcioł m

wood pigeon n grzywacz m

woodwind /'wʊdwınd/ n instrumenty m pl dęte drewniane

woodwork /'wʊdwɜːk/ n stolarka f

woodworm /'wʊdwɜːm/ n kołatek m

wool /wʊl/ n wełna f; **pure (new) ~** czysta (żywa) wełna
[IDIOMS] **to pull the ~ over sb's eyes** mydlić komuś oczy

woollen GB, **woolen** US /'wʊlən/ [ ] n (garment)
~s ubrania n pl wełniane
[ ] adj [garment] wełniany

woolly GB, **wooly** US /'wʊlı/ [ ] n infml sweter m
[ ] adj wełniany; [animal coat, hair] wełnisty; [cloud] pierzasty; fig [thinking] mętny

word /wɜːd/ [ ] n [1] (verbal expression) słowo n, wyraz m; **those were his very ~s** to właśnie powiedział; **with these ~s he left** to rzekłszy, wyszedł; **the last ~** ostatnie słowo; **to get a ~ in** wtrącić słowo; **a ~ of advice** dobra rada; **a ~ of warning** ostrzeżenie; **I believe every ~ he said** wierzę każdemu jego słowu; **I don't believe a ~ of it** absolutnie w to nie wierzę; **I mean every ~ of it** mówię poważnie; **too sad for ~s** tak smutny, że nie da się tego wyrazić; **a man of few ~s** człowiek małomówny; **not a ~ to anybody** nikomu ani słowa [2] (information) wiadomość f (**about sth** o czymś); **there is no ~ of the missing tourists** nie ma wiadomości o zaginionych turystach; **~ got out that...** rozeszły się wieści, że...; **to bring/send ~ that...** przynieść/przesłać wiadomość, że... [3] (promise, affirmation) słowo n; **he gave me his ~** dał mi słowo; **to keep one's ~** dotrzymać słowa; **to break one's ~** złamać słowo; **to take sb's ~ for it** uwierzyć komuś na słowo; **take my ~ for it!** słowo daję! [4] (rumour) pogłoski f pl ; **~ got round or around that...** krążą pogłoski, że...; **~ has it that he's a millionaire** mówi się, że jest milionerem [5] (command) polecenie n
[ ] words npl (of play) tekst m; (of song) słowa n pl

[ ] vt s|formułować [reply, letter, statement]
[IDIOMS] **my ~!** (in surprise) wielkie nieba!; (in reproof) ładne rzeczy!; **right from the ~ go** od samego początku; **to have a ~ with sb** zamienić z kimś kilka słów; **to have ~s with sb** posprzeczać się z kimś; **to put in a good ~ for sb** wstawić się za kimś

word for word /ˌwɜːdfə'wɜːd/ adv słowo w słowo

wording /'wɜːdıŋ/ n sformułowanie n

wordlist /'wɜːdlıst/ n lista f słów

word-of-mouth /ˌwɜːdəv'maʊθ/ [ ] adj [promise] ustny
[ ] by word of mouth adv phr ustnie

word processing, **WP** n przetwarzanie n tekstów

word processor n edytor m tekstu

work /wɜːk/ [ ] n [1] (physical or mental activity) praca f (**on sth** nad czymś); **it was hard ~ digging the garden** skopanie ogrodu wymagało wiele wysiłku or pracy; **to be hard at ~** ciężko pracować; **it's hot/thirsty ~** od tego robi się gorąco/chce się pić [2] (occupation) praca f; **to be in ~** mieć pracę; **to be out of ~** nie mieć pracy; **to be off ~** (on vacation) być na urlopie; **to be off ~ with flu** mieć zwolnienie z powodu grypy; **place of ~** miejsce pracy [3] (place of employment) praca f; **to go to ~** pójść do pracy [4] (building, construction) prace f pl, roboty f pl [5] (essay, report, study) praca f; (artwork, novel) dzieło n; (written, musical) utwór m (**on sth** na temat czegoś); **a ~ of reference** publikacja encyklopedyczna; **a ~ of fiction** utwór beletrystyczny; **this attack was the ~ of professionals** ten atak był dziełem zawodowców
[ ] works npl [1] (factory) zakład m [2] (building works) roboty f pl budowlane [3] infml (everything) **the (full** or **whole) ~s!** wszystko, co trzeba
[ ] vt [1] (drive) **to ~ sb hard** zmuszać kogoś do wysiłku [2] (labour) **to ~ days/nights** pracować na dziennej/nocnej zmianie; **to ~ a 40-hour week** mieć czterdziestogodzinny tydzień pracy; **to ~ one's way through university** pracować podczas studiów [3] (operate) [person] obsługiwać [machine] [4] eksploatować [oilfield, mine]; **to ~ the land** uprawiać ziemię [5] (bring about) **to ~ wonders** działać cuda also fig [6] (use to one's advantage) **to ~ the system** potrafić się ustawić infml [7] (fashion) ur|obić, -abiać [clay, dough]; formować [metal, gold] [8] (manoeuvre) **to ~ sth into sth** włożyć coś do czegoś [slot, hole]; **to ~ the lever up and down** poruszać dźwignią w górę i w dół [9] (exercise) ćwiczyć [muscles] [10] (move) **to ~ one's way through a crowd** przedrzeć się przez tłum; **to ~ one's hands free** wyswobodzić ręce; **his belt ~ed its way loose** pasek mu się rozwiązał
[ ] vi [1] (engage in activity) pracować; **to ~ for a living** zarabiać na życie [2] (strive) działać (**for sth** na rzecz czegoś); **to ~ towards sth** szukać

czegoś *[solution, compromise]*; starać się osiągnąć coś *[agreement]* ③ (function) działać; *[heart, brain]* pracować; **to ~ on electricity** działać na prąd; **the washing machine isn't ~ing** pralka nie działa ④ (act, operate) **it doesn't ~ or things don't ~ like that** to nie jest tak; **to ~ in sb's favour** działać na korzyść kogoś; **to ~ against sb** działać na niekorzyść kogoś ⑤ (be successful) *[treatment, drug, detergent]* działać (**against sth** na coś); *[plan]* powieść się; *[method, hypothesis]* sprawdz|ić, -ać się; **flattery won't ~ with me** pochlebstwami nic się u mnie nie wskóra

■ **work in:** ~ *[sth]* **in** ① wpl|eść, -atać *[joke, reference]*; wspom|nieć, -inać o (kimś/czymś) *[fact, name]* ② Culin doda|ć, -wać *[ingredient]*

■ **work off:** ① (remove) zd|jąć, -ejmować *[lid]* ② (repay) odpracow|ać, -ywać *[loan, debt]* ③ (get rid of) pozby|ć, -wać się (czegoś) *[excess weight]*; spal|ić, -ać *[excess energy]*; wyład|ow|ać, -ywać *[anger, frustration]*

■ **work on:** ¶ ~ **on** dalej pracować ¶ ~ **on** *[sb]* po|pracować nad (kimś) infml ¶ ~ **on** *[sth]* pracować nad (czymś) *[book, report, case, problem]*; poszukiwać (czegoś) *[cure, solution]*

■ **work out:** ¶ ~ **out** ① (exercise) ćwiczyć ② (go according to plan) powieść się ③ (add up) **to ~ out at** GB **or to** US *[total, share]* wyn|ieść, -osić ¶ ~ *[sth]* **out** ① (calculate) oblicz|yć, -ać, wylicz|yć, -ać ② (solve) zna|leźć, -jdować *[answer, reason, culprit]*; rozwiąz|ać, -ywać *[problem, riddle]*; rozgry|źć, -zać infml *[clue, problem]* ③ (devise) obmyśl|ić, -ać *[plan]*; ustal|ić, -ać *[route]* ¶ ~ *[sb]* **out** z|rozumieć; rozgry|źć, -zać infml *[person]*

■ **work up:** ¶ ~ **up** *[sth]* rozwi|nąć, -jać *[interest]*; zdoby|ć, -wać *[support]*; **to ~ up the courage to do sth** zdobyć się na odwagę, żeby coś zrobić; **to ~ up some enthusiasm for sth** wykrzesać z siebie odrobinę entuzjazmu dla czegoś; **to ~ up an appetite** zgłodnieć ¶ ~ **up to** *[sth]* przygotow|ać, -ywać się do (czegoś) ¶ ~ *[sb]* **up** ① (excite) podniec|ić, -ać *[person, crowd]* ② (make upset) **to get ~ed up, to ~ oneself up** zdenerwować się

workable /ˈwɜːkəbl/ *adj* ① (feasible) *[idea, plan]* wykonalny; *[system, arrangement]* nadający się do wykorzystania ② *[land]* nadający się do uprawy; *[mine, oil well]* nadający się do eksploatacji; *[cement]* obrabialny

workaholic /ˌwɜːkəˈhɒlɪk/ *n* infml pracoholik *m*

workbook /ˈwɜːkbʊk/ *n* (blank) zeszyt *m*; (with exercises) zeszyt *m* ćwiczeń

worker /ˈwɜːkə(r)/ *n* ① (employee) pracowni|k *m*, -ca *f*; (in manual job) robotni|k *m*, -ca *f*

work experience *n* doświadczenie *n* zawodowe

workforce /ˈwɜːkfɔːs/ *n* ① (in industry) siła *f* robocza; (in service sector) zatrudnieni *m pl*

working /ˈwɜːkɪŋ/ *adj* ① *[man, mother]* pracujący; *[day, breakfast, lunch]* roboczy; ~ **conditions/ environment** warunki/środowisko pracy; **during ~ hours** w godzinach pracy ② (provisional) *[definition, document, title]* roboczy ③ (functional) *[model]* sprawny; *[mine]* czynny; **in full ~ order** w pełni sprawny

working class ① *n* (also **the ~es**) klasa *f* robotnicza

② *adj [background, family]* robotniczy; *[culture, life]* klasy robotniczej

workings /ˈwɜːkɪŋz/ *npl* praca *f*

workload /ˈwɜːkləʊd/ *n* obciążenie *n* pracą

workman /ˈwɜːkmən/ *n* (worker) robotnik *m*; (craftsman) fachowiec *m*

workmanship /ˈwɜːkmənʃɪp/ *n* fachowość *f*; **a fine piece of ~** fachowa robota; **a company famous for sound ~** firma słynąca z produktów wysokiej jakości

workmate /ˈwɜːkmeɪt/ *n* kole|ga *m*, -żanka *f* z pracy

work of art *n* dzieło *n* sztuki

workout /ˈwɜːkaʊt/ *n* trening *m*

workpack /ˈwɜːkpæk/ *n* materiały *m pl* informacyjne *(dla uczniów, pracowników)*

work permit *n* pozwolenie *n* na pracę

workplace /ˈwɜːkpleɪs/ *n* miejsce *n* pracy

work-sharing /ˈwɜːkʃeərɪŋ/ *n* podział pracy pełnoetatowej pomiędzy dwie osoby zatrudnione na pół etatu

worksheet /ˈwɜːkʃiːt/ *n* Sch zestaw *m* zadań *(do pracy na lekcji)*

workshop /ˈwɜːkʃɒp/ *n* warsztat *m*; (training session) warsztaty *plt*

work station *n* Comput stacja *f* robocza

worktop /ˈwɜːktɒp/ *n* blat *m* kuchenny

work-to-rule /ˈwɜːktəˈruːl/ *n* strajk *m* włoski

world /wɜːld/ ① *n* świat *m*; **throughout the ~** na całym świecie; **to go round the ~** podróżować dookoła świata; **in the ~** na świecie; **the next ~** tamten świat; **to go up in the ~** piąć się w górę; **the Eastern/Western ~** Wschód/Zachód; **the ancient ~** świat starożytny; **he lives in a ~ of his own** żyje w swoim własnym świecie

② *adj* światowy; *[record, championship]* świata; *[cruise]* dookoła świata

⟦IDIOMS⟧ **to be on top of the ~** być w siódmym niebie; **to get the best of both ~s** ≈ upiec dwie pieczenie przy jednym ogniu; **a man of the ~** człowiek światowy; **out of this ~** nieziemski; **there's a ~ of difference** to ogromna różnica; **it did him the or a ~ of good** świetnie mu to zrobiło; **to think the ~ of sb** nie widzieć świata bożego poza kimś; **what/where/who in the ~** co/gdzie/kto u diabła?; **~s apart** całkowicie różny

world-class /ˌwɜːld'klɑːs, US -'klæs/ adj światowej klasy

World Cup n (in football) Puchar m Świata

World Fair n wystawa f światowa

world-famous /ˌwɜːld'feɪməs/ adj światowej sławy

world leader n [1] (in politics) światowy przywódca m [2] (athlete) mistrz m, -yni f świata; (company) światowy lider m

worldly /'wɜːldlɪ/ adj [1] (not spiritual) ziemski [2] (materialistic) zaradny

worldly-wise /ˌwɜːldlɪ'waɪz/ adj wyrobiony życiowo

world music n muzyka f świata

world power n światowe mocarstwo n

world-view /'wɜːldvjuː/ n światopogląd m

world war n wojna f światowa; **World War One/Two** pierwsza/druga wojna światowa

world-wide /ˌwɜːld'waɪd/ [] adj ogólnoświatowy [] adv na całym świecie

World Wide Web n ogólnoświatowa sieć f komputerowa, Internet m

worm /wɜːm/ n robak m

worn /wɔːn/ adj [carpet, stone, step] wytarty; [tyre] starty; [clothing, shoes] znoszony

worn-out /ˌwɔːn'aʊt/ adj [1] [carpet] wytarty; [brake] zużyty [2] [person] wycieńczony

worried /'wʌrɪd/ adj (distressed) zmartwiony; (anxious) zaniepokojony; **to be** ~ martwić się (**about sb/sth** o kogoś/coś); **he's** ~ **that he'll lose his job** martwi się, że straci pracę

worrier /'wʌrɪə(r)/ n **to be a** ~ zamartwiać się z byle powodu

worry /'wʌrɪ/ [] n [1] (anxiety) niepokój m (**about** or **over sth** o coś, w związku z czymś) [2] (problem) zmartwienie n (**about** or **over sth** w związku z czymś)

[] vt [1] (alarm) niepokoić; (upset) martwić; **I** ~ **that...** boję się, że...; **it worries me that...** martwi mnie, że... [2] (bother) przeszkadzać (komuś); **would it** ~ **you if I opened a window?** czy będzie ci przeszkadzało, jeśli otworzę okno? [3] (chase) [dog] zaganiać [sheep]

[] vi (be anxious) martwić się (**about** or **over sb/sth** o kogoś/coś); **don't** ~ nie martw się; **there's nothing to** ~ **about** nie ma powodu do zmartwienia

[] vr **to** ~ **oneself** martwić się (**about sb/sth** o kogoś/coś); **to** ~ **oneself sick over sth** zamartwiać się czymś na śmierć

■ **worry at**: [dog] szarpać [toy]; fig [person] zmagać się z (czymś) [problem]

worry beads n sznur m koralików (których przesuwanie palcami ma działać uspokajająco)

worrying /'wʌrɪɪŋ/ adj niepokojący

worse /wɜːs/ [] adj gorszy (**than sth** niż coś, od czegoś); **to get** ~ [conditions, weather] pogorszyć się; [noise, pressure] wzrosnąć; **he's getting** ~ czuje się coraz gorzej; **my cough is getting** ~ mam coraz gorszy kaszel; **to feel** ~ (more ill) gorzej się czuć; **it looks** ~ **than it is!** wygląda to gorzej, niż jest faktycznie!; **and what is** ~ a co gorsze; **and to make matters** ~, **he lied** a co gorsza, skłamał [] n **a change for the** ~ zmiana na gorsze; **there is** ~ **to come** będzie jeszcze gorzej

[] adv gorzej (**than sth** niż coś, od czegoś); **to behave** ~ sprawować się gorzej; **she could do** ~ **than follow his advice** nie wyszłaby źle na jego radach

worsen /'wɜːsn/ [] vt pog|orszyć, -arszać [situation, conditions]

[] vi [condition, weather, situation] pog|orszyć, -arszać się; [problem, crisis, shortage] sta|ć, -wać się poważniejszym; [pain] nasil|ić, -ać się

worsening /'wɜːsnɪŋ/ [] n pogorszenie się n

[] adj [situation] pogarszający się; [problem, shortage] coraz dotkliwszy

worse off adj [1] (less wealthy) gorzej sytuowany (**than sb** od kogoś, niż ktoś); **I'm £10 a week** ~ mam o 10 funtów tygodniowo mniej [2] (in a worse situation) **to be** ~ być w gorszej sytuacji

worship /'wɜːʃɪp/ [] n [1] (religious practice) kult m; **sun/ancestor** ~ kult słońca/przodków; **a place of** ~ miejsce kultu [2] (veneration) cześć f

[] **Worship** prn GB **Your Worship** (to judge) Wysoki Sądzie; (to mayor) Panie Burmistrzu

[] vt [1] czcić [god] [2] (idolize) wielbić [person]; wyznawać kult (czegoś) [money, success]

[] vi odprawiać obrzędy religijne

worshipper /'wɜːʃɪpə(r)/ n wiern|y m, -a f

worst /wɜːst/ [] n [1] (most difficult, unpleasant) **the** ~ najgorszy; **if the** ~ **came to the** ~ (in serious circumstances) w najgorszym wypadku; (involving fatality) gdyby się coś stało euph [2] (most negative trait) **to bring out the** ~ **in sb** wyzwalać w kimś najgorsze instynkty [3] (of the lowest standard, quality) **the** ~ najgorszy; **to be the** ~ **at French** być najgorszym we francuskim

[] adj [1] (most unsatisfactory, unpleasant) najgorszy; **the** ~ **book I've ever read** najgorsza książka, jaką kiedykolwiek czytałem; **and the** ~ **thing about it is that...** a najgorsze w tym wszystkim jest to, że... [2] (most serious) najgorszy; **the** ~ **mistake you could have made** najgorszy błąd, jaki można było popełnić

[] adv [smell, behave] najgorzej; [suffer, affect] najbardziej; ~ **of all, ...** a co najgorsze...

worth /wɜːθ/ [] n [1] (quantity) wartość f; **five hundred pounds'** ~ **of equipment** sprzęt (o) wartości pięciuset funtów; **thousands of pounds'** ~ **of damage** szkody sięgające tysięcy funtów; **a day's** ~ **of fuel** zapas paliwa na jeden dzień [2] (value) wartość f; **of no** ~ bez wartości

II *adj* [1] (of financial value) warty; **how much is it ~?** ile to jest warte?; **the pound is ~ 10 francs** funt jest wart 10 franków [2] (of abstract value) **to be ~ sth** *[person]* być coś wartym; **to be ~ a mention** zasługiwać na wzmiankę; **it's ~ a try** warto spróbować; **it was ~ it** warto było; **don't get upset, he's not ~ it** nie denerwuj się, on nie jest tego wart; **this book isn't ~ reading** nie warto czytać tej książki; **that's ~ knowing** to warto wiedzieć; **those little pleasures that make life ~ living** te (wszystkie) małe przyjemności, które nadają sens życiu
IDIOMS: **for what it's ~** cokolwiek to znaczy; **~ sb's while** wart zachodu

worthless /'wɜːθlɪs/ *adj* bezwartościowy; **he's ~** on jest nic nie wart

worthwhile /wɜːθ'waɪl/ *adj* interesujący; **it's ~ getting there early** warto być tam wcześniej

worthy /'wɜːðɪ/ *adj* [1] (deserving) **to be ~ of sth** zasługiwać na coś; **~ of note** godny uwagi [2] (admirable) *[cause]* szlachetny; *[citizen, friend]* godny

would /wʊd, wəd/ *modal aux* [1] (in conditional sentences) **it ~ be wonderful if they came** byłoby cudownie, gdyby przyszli; **if we'd left later, we ~ have missed the train** gdybyśmy wyszli później, spóźnilibyśmy się na pociąg; **we wouldn't be happy anywhere else** nigdzie indziej nie bylibyśmy szczęśliwi [2] (in reported speech) **she said she wouldn't come** powiedziała, że nie przyjdzie; **I was sure you'd like it** byłem pewien, że ci się to spodoba; **I wish you'd be quiet!** bądź cicho! [3] (expressing willingness) **she just wouldn't listen** ona po prostu nie chciała słuchać; **he wouldn't do a thing to help** nawet palcem nie kiwnął, żeby pomóc; **they asked me to leave but I wouldn't** prosili, żebym wyszedł, ale odmówiłem; **of course you ~ contradict him!** oczywiście musiałeś mu się przeciwstawić!; **the door wouldn't close** drzwi nie chciały się zamknąć [4] (in requests) **~ you help me to set the table?** mógłbyś pomóc mi nakryć do stołu?; **switch off the radio, ~ you?** możesz wyłączyć radio?; **~ you excuse me for a moment?** przepraszam na chwileczkę [5] (expressing wishes) **~ you like something to eat?** zjadłbyś coś?; **I'd like a beer** napiłbym się piwa; **we ~ like to stay another night** chcielibyśmy zostać na jeszcze jedną noc; **we'd really love to see you** bardzo chcielibyśmy cię zobaczyć; **she ~ have preferred a puppy** wolałaby szczeniaka; **I ~ much rather travel alone** zdecydowanie wolałbym podróżować sam; **I wouldn't mind another piece of cake** chętnie zjadłbym jeszcze jeden kawałek ciasta [6] (giving advice) **I wouldn't do it if I were you** na twoim miejscu nie robiłbym tego; **I ~ check the timetable first** najpierw radził-

bym sprawdzić rozkład jazdy; **wouldn't it be better to write?** czy nie lepiej napisać?; **it ~ be a good idea to wait** dobrze byłoby zaczekać [7] (in assumptions) **what time ~ that be?** która to mogła być godzina?; **it ~ have been about five years ago** to musiało być jakieś pięć lat temu [8] (used to) **she ~ sit for hours at the window** godzinami przesiadywała przy oknie

would-be /'wʊdbiː/ *adj* [1] (desirous of being) *[emigrants, investors]* potencjalny [2] (so-called) **~ intellectuals** tak zwani intelektualiści [3] (having intended to be) *[film star, poet, thief]* niedoszły

wound /wuːnd/ **I** *n* rana *f* also fig; **a ~ to** or **in the head** rana głowy; **bullet ~** rana postrzałowa **II** *vt* z|ranić also fig
IDIOMS: **to lick one's ~s** lizać rany; **to rub salt into the ~** ≈ dolewać oliwy do ognia

wounded /'wuːndɪd/ **I** *n* **the ~** ranni *m pl* **II** *adj* ranny; **~ in the arm** ranny w ramię

wrangle /'ræŋgl/ **I** *n* zatarg *m* **II** *vi* spierać się (**over** or **about sth/with sb** o coś/z kimś)

wrap /ræp/ **I** *n* (shawl) szal *m*; (stole) etola *f* **II** *vt* (in paper) zawi|nąć, -jąć; (in blanket) owi|nąć, -jąć; **would you like it ~ped?** zapakować panu?; **to be ~ped in mystery** fig być owianym tajemnicą
■ **wrap up:** ¶ **~ up** ciepło się ub|rać, -ierać ¶ **~ [sth] up** [1] owi|nąć, -jąć *[parcel]*; za|pakować *[gift, purchase]* [2] (involve) **to be ~ped up in sb** świata nie widzieć poza kimś; **to be ~ped up in sth** być pochłoniętym czymś *[work, activity, problem]* [3] ukry|ć, -wać *[meaning, ideas, facts]* (**in sth** w czymś)
IDIOMS: **to keep sth/to be under ~s** trzymać coś/być trzymanym w sekrecie

wrap-around /'ræpəraʊnd/ *adj [window, windscreen]* panoramiczny; *[skirt]* portfelowy

wrap-around sunglasses *npl* okulary *plt* przeciwsłoneczne z boczną ochroną

wrapper /'ræpə(r)/ *n* (of sweet, chocolate) papierek *m*

wrapping /'ræpɪŋ/ *n* opakowanie *n*

wrapping paper *n* (brown) papier *m* pakowy; (decorative) ozdobny papier *m* pakunkowy

wreak /riːk/ *vt* wyw|rzeć, -ierać *[revenge]* (**on sb** na kimś); **to ~ havoc** or **damage** dokonać spustoszenia; **to ~ havoc** or **damage on sth** zniszczyć coś

wreath /riːθ/ *n* wieniec *m*; **to lay a ~** złożyć wieniec

wreck /rek/ **I** *n* [1] (car, plane, sunken ship) wrak *m* [2] (person) **a human ~** wrak człowieka **II** *vt* [1] z|dewastować *[building, interior]*; rozbi|ć, -jać *[car, boat, train]* [2] fig z|rujnować *[career, health, life, marriage]*; zepsuć *[holiday, weekend]*

wreckage /'rekɪdʒ/ n [1] (of plane, car) szczątki *m pl*; (of building) gruzy *plt* [2] fig (of hopes, plan, attempt) resztki *f pl*

wrecked /rekt/ adj [1] *[vehicle, ship]* rozbity; *[building]* zdewastowany [2] fig *[plan, hope, life, career]* zrujnowany

wren /ren/ n strzyżyk *m*

wrench /rentʃ/ **I** n [1] (tool) klucz *m* francuski [2] fig **it was a real ~** to było naprawdę bolesne **II** vt szarp|nąć, -ać *[handle]*; **to ~ one's ankle** skręcić sobie kostkę; **to ~ sth from sb** wyszarpnąć coś komuś; **to ~ sth away from sth** oderwać coś od czegoś

wrestle /'resl/ **I** vt **to ~ sb for sth** walczyć z kimś o coś; **to ~ sb to the ground** powalić kogoś na ziemię **II** vi [1] Sport walczyć w zapasach [2] (struggle) mocować się; **to ~ with sb/sth** mocować się z kimś/czymś *[person, suitcase, lock]*; zmagać się z czymś *[problem, homework, temptation]*

wrestler /'reslə(r)/ n zapaśnik *m*

wrestling /'reslɪŋ/ n zapasy *plt*

wretched /'retʃɪd/ adj *[person]* nieszczęsny; *[existence, conditions, appearance]* nędzny; *[weather]* paskudny; **to feel ~** (due to illness, hangover) czuć się okropnie

wriggle /'rɪgl/ **I** vt **to ~ one's toes/fingers** przebierać palcami u nóg/palcami u rąk; **to ~ one's way out of sth** wydostać się z czegoś; fig wykręcić się od czegoś **II** vi *[person]* wiercić się; *[snake, worm]* wić się

wring /rɪŋ/ vt [1] (also ~ **out**) wyż|ąć, -ymać *[clothes]*; (by twisting) wykręc|ić, -ać [2] fig wycis|nąć, -kać *[confession, information, money]* (**from** or **out of sb** z kogoś) [3] (twist) **to ~ sb's/sth's neck** ukręcić komuś/czemuś łeb also fig; **to ~ one's hands** załamywać ręce also fig

wrinkle /'rɪŋkl/ **I** n (on skin) zmarszczka *f*; (in fabric) zagniecenie *n* **II** vt [1] z|marszczyć *[skin]*; **to ~ one's nose** krzywić się (**at sth** na coś) [2] po|gnieść *[fabric]* **III** vi *[skin]* pokry|ć, -wać się zmarszczkami; *[fabric]* po|gnieść się; *[wallpaper]* z|marszczyć się

wrist /rɪst/ n nadgarstek *m*, przegub *m* dłoni

wristband /'rɪstbænd/ n (for tennis) frotka *f*; (on sleeve) mankiet *m*

wristwatch /'rɪstwɒtʃ/ n zegarek *m* na rękę

writ /rɪt/ n nakaz *m* sądowy; **to issue** or **serve a ~ against sb** wydać nakaz sądowy przeciwko komuś

write /raɪt/ **I** vt [1] (put down on paper) na|pisać *[letter, novel, software, music, symphony]*; wypis|ać, -ywać *[cheque, prescription]*; przygotow|ać, -ywać *[legislation]*; **to ~ home** napisać do domu [2] US (compose a letter to) na|pisać do (kogoś) **II** vi na|pisać (**to sb** do kogoś)

■ **write back**: odpis|ać, -ywać (**to sb** komuś)

■ **write down**: zapis|ać, -ywać, za|notować

■ **write off**: **¶ ~ off** na|pisać (**to sb** do kogoś); **to ~ off for sth** napisać z prośbą o coś *[catalogue, information]* **¶ ~ [sth] off** [1] (wreck) s|kasować infml *[car]* [2] (in bookkeeping) odpis|ać, -ywać *[bad debt, loss]* [3] (end) um|orzyć, -arzać *[debt]*; anulować *[project]* **¶ ~ [sb] off** (dismiss) skreśl|ić, -ać infml *[person]*

■ **write out**: [1] (put down on paper) sporządz|ić, -ać *[list, report]*; wypis|ać, -ywać *[prescription, bill, cheque]* [2] (copy) przepis|ać, -ywać

write-off /'raɪtɒf/ n [1] US (in taxation) strata *f* *(odpisywana od przychodu)* [2] (car) pojazd *m* spisany na straty

writer /'raɪtə(r)/ n pisa|rz *m*, -rka *f*

write-up /'raɪtʌp/ n (review) recenzja *f*; (account) omówienie *n*

writhe /raɪð/ vi (also ~ **about**, ~ **around**) zwi|nąć, -jać się; **to ~ in agony** zwijać się z bólu

writing /'raɪtɪŋ/ n [1] (activity) pisanie *n* [2] (handwriting) charakter *m* pisma [3] (written material) pismo *n*; **to put sth in ~** przedstawić coś na piśmie [4] (literature) literatura *f*

writing pad n blok *m* listowy

writing paper n papier *m* listowy

writing table n biurko *n*

written /'rɪtn/ adj *[exam]* pisemny; *[guarantee, reply]* na piśmie; **~ evidence** or **proof** dowód na piśmie; **the ~ word** słowo pisane

wrong /rɒŋ, US rɔːŋ/ **I** n [1] (evil) zło *n* [2] (injustice) krzywda *f*; **to right a ~** naprawić krzywdę **II** adj [1] (incorrect) zły; (containing errors) błędny; *[note]* fałszywy; **he took the ~ key** wziął nie ten klucz, co trzeba; **it's the ~ glue for the purpose** to nie jest odpowiedni klej; **to go the ~ way** pomylić drogę; **to give the ~ answer** podać złą odpowiedź; **don't get me ~** nie zrozum mnie źle; **you've got the ~ number** (on phone) (to) pomyłka [2] (reprehensible) **it is ~ to lie** nie należy kłamać; **she hasn't done anything ~** nie zrobiła nic złego; **it was ~ of me to do it** nie powinienem był tego robić; **it is ~ that...** nie może tak być, żeby...; **there's nothing ~ with** or **in it** nie ma w tym nic złego; **(so) what's ~ with that?** (a) cóż w tym złego? [3] (mistaken) **to be ~** *[person]* nie mieć racji; **to be ~ about sb/sth** mylić się co do kogoś/czegoś; **to prove sb ~** dowieść, że ktoś nie ma racji [4] (not as it should be) **there's something (badly) ~** coś tu jest (bardzo) nie w porządku; **there's something ~ with the computer** coś jest nie w porządku z komputerem; **what's ~ with you?** (to a person suffering) co ci dolega?; (to a person behaving oddly) co się z tobą dzieje?; **what's ~ with your arm?** co ci się stało w rękę?; **your clock is ~** twój zegar źle chodzi **III** adv **to get sth ~** pomylić coś *[date, time, details]*; pomylić się w czymś *[calculations]*; **I think you've got it ~** chyba się pomyliłeś; **to go ~**

[person] pomylić się; *[machine]* zepsuć się; *[plan]* nie udać się

IV *vt* wyrządz|ić, -ać krzywdę (komuś) *[person, family]*

IDIOMS: **to be in the** ~ zawinić; **to get on the** ~ **side of sb** narazić się komuś; **his medicine went down the** ~ **way** zakrztusił się lekarstwem

wrongdoer /ˈrɒnduːə(r), US ˈrɔːŋ-/ *n* winowaj|ca *m*, -czyni *m*

wrongfoot /rɒŋˈfʊt, US ˌrɔːŋ-/ *vt* zmylić *[opponent, adversary]*

wrongly /ˈrɒŋlɪ, US ˈrɔːŋ-/ *adv* źle; **he had concluded,** ~**, that...** błędnie uznał, że...; **rightly or** ~ słusznie czy nie

wrought /rɔːt/ *adj [silver, gold]* kuty

wrought iron *n* kute żelazo *n*

wry /raɪ/ *adj [comment]* cierpki; *[look]* kpiarski; **a** ~ **humour** cierpki humor

X

x, X /eks/ *n* 1 (letter) x, X *n* 2 (standing for number, name) **for x people** dla or na iks osób; **Ms X** pani Iks; **X marks the spot** miejsce zostało oznaczone krzyżykiem 3 (kisses ending letter) całusy *m pl*

X-certificate GB *n [film]* dozwolony od lat osiemnastu

xenophobia /ˌzenəˈfəʊbɪə/ *n* ksenofobia *f*

xerox® /ˈzɪərɒks/ **I** *n* 1 (machine) ksero *n*, kserograf *m*, kserokopiarka *f* 2 (process) kserowanie *n* 3 (copy) ksero *n*, odbitka *f* kserograficzna, kserokopia *f* **II** *vt* s|kserować

Xmas /ˈeksməs/ *n* = **Christmas**

X-rated /ˈeksreɪtɪd/ *adj [film, video]* (dozwolony) od lat osiemnastu

X-ray /ˈeksreɪ/ **I** *n* 1 (ray) promień *m* X 2 (photo) zdjęcie *n* rentgenowskie; rentgen *m* infml; **he had an** ~ zrobiono mu prześwietlenie; **to give sb an** ~ zrobić komuś prześwietlenie **II** *vt* prześwietl|ić, -ać, z|robić prześwietlenie or rentgen infml

X-ray unit *n* pracownia *f* rentgenowska

Y

y, Y /waɪ/ *n* y, Y *n*

yacht /jɒt/ *n* jacht *m*

yachting /'jɒtɪŋ/ *n* żeglarstwo *n*, jachting *m*; **to go ~** pływać żaglówką

yachtsman /'jɒtsmən/ *n* żeglarz *m*

yahoo¹ /jɑːˈhuː, jə-/ *n* prymityw *m* pej; prostak *m* infml pej

yahoo² /jɑːˈhuː, jæ-/ *excl* hurra!

yak *n* /jæk/ jak *m*

Yale lock® /jeɪl/ *n* zamek *m* yale

yam /jæm/ *n* jams *m*, ignam *m*

yank /jæŋk/ **I** *n* szarpnięcie *n*; **to give sth a ~** szarpnąć (za) coś
II *vt* szarp|nąć, -ać *[person, rope]*
■ **yank out**: wyr|wać, -ywać

Yank /jæŋk/ *n* jankes *m*, -ka *f*

Yankee /'jæŋkɪ/ *n* jankes *m*

yap /jæp/ *vi [dog]* ujadać (**at sb/sth** na kogoś/coś)

yapping /'jæpɪŋ/ **I** *n* ujadanie *n*
II *adj [dog]* ujadający

yard¹ /jɑːd/ *n* (measure) jard *m* (= 0, 9144 m)

yard² /jɑːd/ *n* **1** (of house, farm, hospital) podwórko *n*, podwórze *n*; (of prison) dziedziniec *m* **2** US (garden) ogródek *m* **3** (for storage) plac *m* składowy; (for construction) plac *m* budowy; **builder's ~** skład materiałów budowlanych

yardarm /'jɑːdɑːm/ *n* nok *m* rei

yardstick /'jɑːdstɪk/ *n* fig miara *f*

yarn /jɑːn/ *n* **1** (fibre) przędza *f* **2** (tale) (barwna) opowieść *f*; **to spin a ~** opowiadać, snuć opowieść

yashmak /'jæʃmæk/ *n* czarczaf *m*, kwef *m*

yawn /jɔːn/ **I** *n* ziewnięcie *n*, ziewanie *n*; **to give a ~** ziewnąć
II *vi* **1** *[person]* ziew|nąć, -ać **2** *[abyss, chasm]* zionąć

yeah /jeə/ *particle* infml tak; **no** infml; **oh ~?** czyżby? also iron

year /jɪə(r), jɜː(r)/ **I** *n* **1** (period of time) rok *m*; **in the ~ 2000** w roku 2000; **every ~** co roku; **two ~s ago** dwa lata temu; **all (the) ~ round** przez cały rok; **over the ~s** przez (wszystkie te) lata; **the ~ before last** dwa lata temu; **they have been in Paris for ~s** od lat mieszkają w Paryżu; **for the first time in ~s** pierwszy raz od lat; **it's a ~ since I heard from him** od roku nie miałem od niego żadnej wiadomości; **to earn £30,000 a ~**

zarabiać 30 000 funtów rocznie **2** (indicating age) **to be 19 ~s old** or **19 ~s of age** mieć 19 lat; **a two-~-old child** dwuletnie dziecko **3** (pupil) **first/second ~** uczeń/uczennica pierwszej/drugiej klasy gimnazjum
II years infml *npl* (a long time) wieki *m pl*; **that would take ~s!** to będzie trwało wieki!; **it's ~s since we last met!** wieki się nie widzieliśmy!
(IDIOMS) **this job has put ~s on me!** przez tę pracę lat mi przybyło!

yearbook /'jɪəbʊk, 'jɜː-/ *n* **1** (directory) rocznik *m* **2** US księga *f* pamiątkowa

yearlong /jɪə'lɒŋ, US ˌjɜː'lɒŋ/ *adj [stay, course, absence]* roczny

yearly /'jɪəlɪ, 'jɜː-/ **I** *adj [visit]* coroczny, doroczny; *[account, income]* roczny
II *adv* corocznie

yearn /jɜːn/ *vi* **1** (desire) **to ~ for sb/sth** pragnąć kogoś/czegoś *[child, food, freedom, unity]*; **to ~ to do sth** bardzo pragnąć coś zrobić **2** (miss) **to ~ for sb/sth** tęsknić za kimś/czymś *[person, homeland]*

yearning /'jɜːnɪŋ/ **I** *n* pragnienie *n* (**for sth** czegoś); tęsknota *f* (**for sth** za czymś)
II yearnings *npl* pragnienia *n pl*, tęsknoty *f pl*

year out *n* roczna przerwa *f* w nauce (*poświęcona na pracę w wolontariacie lub naukę*)

year tutor *n* ≈ opiekun *m*, -ka *f* roku

yeast /jiːst/ *n* drożdże *plt*

yell /jel/ **I** *n* (shout) (of rage) ryk *m*; (of pain) krzyk *m*
II *vt* krzy|czeć, -knąć *[warning]*; wykrzy|czeć, -kiwać *[order, reply]*; **to ~ abuse** rzucać obelgi
III *vi* krzy|czeć, -knąć; **to ~ at sb** krzyczeć na kogoś

yelling /'jelɪŋ/ *n* krzyk *m*

yellow /'jeləʊ/ **I** *n* (kolor *m*) żółty *m*
II *adj* **1** (in colour) żółty; **to go** or **turn ~** zżółknąć, pożółknąć **2** infml (cowardly) tchórzliwy
III *vi* po|żółknąć, z|żółknąć

yellow-belly /'jeləʊbelɪ/ *n* infml cykor *m* infml

yellow card *n* Sport żółta kartka *f*

yellowish /'jeləʊwɪʃ/ *adj* żółtawy

Yellow Pages® *npl* branżowy wykaz *m* firm i instytucji; (part of telephone directory) żółte strony *f pl* infml

yelp /jelp/ **Ⅰ** *n* (of person) (of pain, anger, excitement) okrzyk *m*; (of animal) jazgot *m*; (of pain, fear) skowyt *m*, skomlenie *n*

Ⅱ *vi* (with pain, fear, excitement) *[person]* krzy|knąć, -czeć; *[animal]* (with pain, fear) za|skowyczeć, za|skomleć

Yemen /'jemən/ *prn* Jemen *m*; **North/South** ~ Jemen Północny/Południowy

yen[1] /jen/ *n* (currency) jen *m*

yen[2] /jen/ *n* infml (craving) **to have a** ~ **for sth/to do sth** mieć ochotę na coś/na zrobienie czegoś

yeoman /'jəʊmən/ *n* (also ~ **farmer**) drobny właściciel *m* ziemski

yeoman of the guard /'jəʊmən/ *n* GB żołnierz *m* królewskiej straży przybocznej

yep /jep/, **yup** /jʌp/ *particle* US infml tak

yes /jes/ **Ⅰ** *n* (affirmative reply) tak *n inv*; (in voting) głos *m* za; **to say** ~ zgodzić się; **the** ~**es and the nos** głosy za i przeciw

Ⅱ *adv* ⌐1⌐ (affirmative reply) tak; **please say** ~ zgódź się, proszę ⌐2⌐ (obeying order, request) ~ **sir/ma'am** tak, proszę pana/pani; **'be there by nine o'clock'** – '~, **OK'** „bądź tam przed dziewiątą" – „dobrze" ⌐3⌐ (answering call, inquiry) tak?; (on telephone) słucham; **'Fred'** – '~?' „Fred" – „tak?"; **'excuse me'** – '~, **what is it?'** „przepraszam" – „słucham, o co chodzi?" ⌐4⌐ (expressing interest, attentiveness) tak?; **'I went to see that new play last night'** – '**oh,** ~?' „poszedłem wczoraj na tę nową sztukę" – „naprawdę?" ⌐5⌐ (expressing pleasure, satisfaction) ~! **what a good idea!** tak! świetny pomysł!; (emphasizing) **you could win £5000,** ~, **£5000!** można wygrać 5 000 funtów, tak, 5 000!

yes-man /'jesmæn/ *n* infml potakiwacz *m* pej

yesterday /'jestədeɪ, -dɪ/ **Ⅰ** *n* wczoraj *n*; ~ **'s newspaper** wczorajsza gazeta; ~ **was a sad day for us all** wczorajszy dzień był dla nas wszystkich smutny; ~ **was the third of May** wczoraj był trzeci maja; **the day before** ~ przedwczoraj

Ⅱ *adv* wczoraj; **only** ~ zaledwie wczoraj; **all day** ~ cały wczorajszy dzień

yesterday afternoon **Ⅰ** *n* wczorajsze popołudnie *n*

Ⅱ *adv* wczoraj po południu

yesterday evening **Ⅰ** *n* wczorajszy wieczór *m*

Ⅱ *adv* wczoraj wieczorem

yesterday morning **Ⅰ** *n* (early) wczorajszy ranek *m* or poranek *m*; (before noon) wczorajsze przedpołudnie *n*

Ⅱ *adv* (early) wczoraj rano; (before noon) wczoraj przed południem

yet /jet/ **Ⅰ** *conj* ale, (a) mimo to

Ⅱ *adv* ⌐1⌐ (up till now, so far) jeszcze nie; (in questions) już; (with superlatives) jak dotąd; **it's not ready** ~ **to** jeszcze nie jest gotowe; **has he arrived** ~? czy już przyjechał?; **not** ~ jeszcze nie; **it's the best** ~ **to** jak dotąd jest najlepsze ⌐2⌐ (also **just** ~) (now)

don't start (just) ~ jeszcze nie zaczynaj ⌐3⌐ (still) jeszcze; **they may** ~ **come** oni jeszcze mogą przyjść; **he'll finish it** ~ jeszcze to dokończy; **he won't finish for hours** ~ przyjdzie dopiero za kilka godzin ⌐4⌐ (even, still) jeszcze; ~ **more cars** jeszcze więcej samochodów; ~ **another attack** jeszcze jeden atak; ~ **again** jeszcze raz

yew /ju:/ *n* (also ~ **tree**) cis *m*

Y-fronts /'waɪfrʌnts/ *npl* GB męskie slipy *plt*

YHA *n* GB = **Youth Hostels Association** Towarzystwo *n* Schronisk Młodzieżowych

yield /ji:ld/ **Ⅰ** *n* ⌐1⌐ (product) produkcja *f* ⌐2⌐ (in finance) dochód *m*, zysk *m* (**from** or **on sth** z czegoś)

Ⅱ *vt* ⌐1⌐ (produce) *[animal]* da|ć, -wać; *[land]* rodzić; *[mine, quarry]* dostarcz|yć, -ać ⌐2⌐ (provide) da|ć, -wać *[result]*; nada|ć, -wać *[meaning]*; dostarcz|yć, -ać *[clue]* ⌐3⌐ (surrender) odda|ć, -wać (**to sb** komuś); **to** ~ **ground to sb** fig ustąpić komuś pola

Ⅲ *vi* ⌐1⌐ (to person, temptation, pressure) ule|c, -gać (**to sb/sth** komuś/czemuś); (to threat) ust|ąpić, -ępować (**to sth** wobec czegoś) ⌐2⌐ (under weight, physical pressure) ust|ąpić, -ępować (**under sth** pod naporem czegoś) ⌐3⌐ (be superseded) **to** ~ **to sth** *[technology, phenomenon]* ust|ąpić, -ępować czemuś ⌐4⌐ US (driving) da|ć -wać pierwszeństwo przejazdu (**to sth** czemuś)

yob /jɒb/, **yobbo** /'jɒbəʊ/ *n* GB infml prymityw *m* pej

yodel /'jəʊdl/ *vi* jodłować

yoga /'jəʊgə/ *n* joga *f*

yoghurt /'jɒgət, US 'jəʊgərt/ *n* jogurt *m*

yoke /jəʊk/ **Ⅰ** *n* jarzmo *n*

Ⅱ *vt* (also ~ **up**) zaprzą|c, -ęgać

yokel /'jəʊkl/ *n* pej kmiot *m*, kmiotek *m* infml pej

yolk /jəʊk/ *n* żółtko *n*

yonks /jɒŋks/ *npl* GB infml **I haven't seen him for** ~ wieki go nie widziałem

you /ju:, jʊ/ *pron* ⌐1⌐ (singular) ty; (formal) pan *m*, pani *f*; **are** ~ **busy?** czy jesteś zajęty?; czy jest pan zajęty/ pani zajęta?; **oh, it's** ~ ach, to ty; **if I were** ~ na twoim/pana/pani miejscu; **poor** ~! biedaku!; ~ **liar!** ty kłamco!; **I saw** ~ **yesterday** widziałem cię/pana/panią wczoraj; **for** ~ dla ciebie/pana/ pani; **with** ~ z tobą/panem/panią; **without** ~ bez ciebie/pana/pani; **that's children for** ~! tak to już jest z dziećmi!; **there's manners for** ~! infml iron ładne mi maniery! iron; **she's taller than** ~ jest od ciebie/pana/pani wyższa ⌐2⌐ (plural) wy; (formal) pani zajęta/pani pani wyższa; (formal) (men) panowie *m pl*; (women) panie *f pl*; (mixed) państwo *plt*; ~ **English** wy, Anglicy; ~ **two can stay** wy dwaj/wy dwie/wy dwoje możecie zostać ⌐3⌐ (as indefinite pronoun) ~ **never know!** nigdy nie wiadomo!

you-know-what /ˌju:nəʊ'wɒt, US -'hwɒt/ *pron* infml wiesz co, wiecie co

you-know-who /ˌju:nəʊ'hu:/ *pron* infml wiesz kto, wiecie kto

young /jʌŋ/ **I** *n* 1 (young people) **the** ~ młodzi *m pl*, młodzież *f* 2 (animal offspring) młode *n pl*

II *adj* młody; ~ **at heart** młody duchem; **she is 10 years** ~ **er than him** (ona) jest od niego o 10 lat młodsza; **I feel 10 years** ~ **er** czuję się o 10 lat młodszy; ~ **lady** młoda dama; ~ **people** młodzi; ~ **person** młoda osoba; **the** ~ **er generation** młode pokolenie; **her** ~ **er brother** jej młodszy brat; **I'm not as** ~ **as I used to be** nie jestem już taki młody (jak kiedyś)

young blood *n* młoda krew *f*

youngish /'jʌŋɪʃ/ *adj* raczej młody

young-looking /'jʌŋlʊkɪŋ/ *adj* **to be** ~ wyglądać młodo

young offender *n* młodociany przestępca *m*

youngster /'jʌŋstə(r)/ *n* 1 (young person) (boy) młody chłopak *m*; (girl) młoda dziewczyna *f* 2 (child) dziecko *n*

your /jɔː(r), jʊə(r)/ *det* (to single addressee) twój; (formally) (to man) pana, pański; (to woman) pani; (to several people) wasz; (formally) (to men) panów; (to women) pań; (to men and women) państwa; (reflexive) swój (własny); **wash** ~ **hands** umyj ręce; **put on** ~ **shoes** załóż buty

yours /jɔːz, US jʊərz/ *pron* (to single addressee) twój; (formally) (to man) pana, pański; (to woman) pani; (to several people) wasz; (formally) (to men) panów; (to women) pań; (to men and women) państwa; **the money was not** ~ **to give away** to nie były twoje/wasze pieniądze, więc nie miałeś/nie mieliście prawa ich rozdawać; **is he a friend of** ~ **?** czy to twój/wasz znajomy; czy to pana/pani/państwa znajomy?; ~ **was not an easy task** nie miałeś/nie mieliście łatwego zadania

yourself /jɔː'self, US jʊər'self/ *pron* 1 (reflexive) **behave** ~ zachowuj się jak należy 2 (emphatic) sam; **you** ~ **said that...** sam powiedziałeś/sama powiedziałaś, że...; (formal) sam pan powiedział/ sama pani powiedziała, że... 3 (after preposition) **(all)**

by ~ (całkiem or zupełnie) sam/sama; **you must do it for** ~ musisz to zrobić dla siebie; **see for** ~ sam/sama zobacz; **speak for** ~ **!** mów (sam/sama) za siebie!; **you only think of** ~ myślisz tylko o sobie 4 (normal self) **you're not** ~ **today** nie jesteś dziś w formie

yourselves /jɔː'selvz, US jʊər'selvz/ *pron* 1 (reflexive) **have you hurt** ~ **?** skaleczyliście się? 2 (empemphatic) same; (men) sami 3 (after prepositions) **all by** ~ zupełnie or całkiem sami/same

youth /juːθ/ *n* 1 (young man) młodzieniec *m*; (boy) (młody) chłopak *m*; wyrostek *m* infml; **a gang of** ~ **s** banda wyrostków 2 (being young) młodość *f*, młody wiek *m*; **because of his** ~ ze względu na jego młody wiek 3 (young people) młodzież *f*

youthful /'juːθfl/ *adj* 1 (young) młody 2 (typical of youth) młodzieńczy; **his** ~ **looks** jego młodzieńczy wygląd

youth hostel *n* schronisko *n* młodzieżowe

youth hostelling *n* korzystanie *n* ze schronisk młodzieżowych

youth work *n* praca *f* z młodzieżą

youth worker *n* wychowawca *m* pracujący z młodzieżą

yo-yo® /'jəʊjəʊ/ **I** *n* 1 (toy) jo-jo *n* 2 US infml (fool) głupek *m* infml pej

II *vi* infml *[prices]* wahać się; *[inflation]* rosnąć i spadać

yuck /jʌk/ *excl* GB fu!, fuj!

yucky /'jʌkɪ/ *adj* GB infml ohydny, obrzydliwy

Yugoslavia /ˌjuːgəʊ'slɑːvɪə/ *prn* Jugosławia *f*

Yule log *n* duże polano spalane *w kominku w Boże Narodzenie*

yummy /'jʌmɪ/ infml **I** *adj* pyszny

II *excl* mniam, mniam! infml

yuppie /'jʌpɪ/ **I** *n* infml pej yuppie *m inv*; japiszon *m*, -ka *f* pej or hum

II *adj* *[image, style, fashion]* typowy dla yuppies

Z

z, Z /zed, US zi:/ n z, Z n
zany /'zeɪnɪ/ adj pocieszny
zap /zæp/ infml **[]** excl paff!
[] vt ⊡ (destroy) z|niszczyć, z|burzyć *[town]*; zabi|ć, -jać *[person, animal]* ⊡ (fire at) strzel|ić, -ać do (kogoś) *[person]* ⊡ (from computer screen) wy|kasować
[] vi to ~ **into town/a shop** skoczyć do miasta/ sklepu infml; **to ~ from channel to channel** przeskakiwać z kanału na kanał
zapper /'zæpə(r)/ n infml (TV remote control) pilot m
zeal /zi:l/ n ⊡ (fanaticism) gorliwość f; **religious ~** żarliwość religijna ⊡ (enthusiasm) zapał m
zealot /'zelət/ n fanaty|k m, -czka f
zebra /'zebrə, 'zi:-/ n zebra f
zebra crossing n przejście n dla pieszych; zebra f infml
zenith /'zenɪθ/ n fig apogeum n, szczyt m
zero /'zɪərəʊ/ **[]** n zero n
[] adj *[altitude, growth, inflation, voltage]* zerowy; *[investment, development]* na poziomie zerowym; ~ **confidence/involvement** kompletny brak pewności siebie/zaangażowania; **sub-~ temperatures** temperatury ujemne
■ **zero in: to ~ in on sth** nakierować się na coś *[target]*; otoczyć *[place]*; fig skoncentrować się or skupić się na czymś *[key issue, problem]*; skłaniać się ku czemuś *[option]*
zero hour n godzina f zero also fig
zest /zest/ n (enthusiasm) zapał m, ochota f; **his ~ for life** jego radość życia
zigzag /'zɪgzæg/ **[]** n zygzak m
[] adj *[design, pattern]* w zygzaki; *[line, road]* zygzakowaty
[] vi *[person]* iść zygzakiem; *[river]* płynąć zakolami; *[road]* biec zygzakami; **to ~ up/down** piąć się/schodzić zygzakiem
zilch /zɪltʃ/ n infml kompletnie nic
zimmer® /'zɪmə(r)/ n balkonik m (do rehabilitacji chorych)

zing /zɪŋ/ infml n (energy) wigor m; szwung m infml
zip /zɪp/ **[]** n ⊡ (also ~ **fastener, zipper** US) zamek m błyskawiczny, suwak m; **to do up/undo a ~** zapiąć or zasunąć/odpiąć zamek błyskawiczny ⊡ infml (energy) szwung m infml ⊡ US (also ~ **code**) kod m pocztowy
[] vt ⊡ (close) **to ~ sth shut** zamknąć coś na zamek błyskawiczny ⊡ (compress) dokon|ać, -ywać kompresji (czegoś)
[] vi infml **to ~ along, to ~ past** mknąć; pruć infml
■ **zip through** infml: **to ~ through one's work** szybko uporać się z robotą
■ **zip up:** ¶ ~ **up** *[garment]* zapinać się na zamek błyskawiczny; *[bag]* zamykać się na zamek błyskawiczny ¶ ~ **[sth] up** zapiąć zamek błyskawiczny (w czymś)
zipper /'zɪpə(r)/ n US = **zip** **[]**⊡
zip pocket n kieszeń f (zapinana) na zamek błyskawiczny
zloty /'zlɒtɪ/ n (currency) złoty m
zodiac /'zəʊdɪæk/ n zodiak m
zombie /'zɒmbɪ/ n zombi m inv; fig żywy trup m fig
zone /zəʊn/ **[]** n strefa f
[] vt (divide) po|dzielić na strefy
zonked /zɒŋkt/ adj (also ~ **out**) infml (tired) padnięty, wypompowany infml
zoo /zu:/ n zoo n inv
zoo keeper /zu:/ n dozorca m w zoo
zoologist /zəʊ'ɒlədʒɪst/ n zoolog m
zoology /zəʊ'ɒlədʒɪ/ n zoologia f
zoom /zu:m/ **[]** n (also ~ **lens**) zoom m, obiektyw m o zmiennej ogniskowej
[] vi infml ⊡ (move quickly) po|pędzić, śmig|nąć, -ać; **to ~ past** przemknąć obok; **to ~ around sth** krążyć z wielką szybkością po (czymś) *[streets, region]*; **he's ~ed off to Paris** pognał do Paryża infml ⊡ infml *[prices, profits]* silnie zwyżkować
zucchini /zu:'ki:nɪ/ n US cukinia f

English Irregular Verbs

Formy nieregularne, używane wyłącznie w specyficznych znaczeniach, oznaczono gwiazdką.

Pełna informacja dotycząca reguł użycia i wymowy jest podana w haśle danego czasownika.

infinitive/ bezokolicznik	past tense/ czas przeszły	past participle/ imiesłów czasu przeszłego
abide	abided, *abode	abided, *abode
arise	arose	arisen
awake	awoke	awoken
be	was/were	been
bear	bore	borne
beat	beat	beaten
become	became	become
befall	befell	befallen
beget	begot, (arch) begat	begotten
begin	began	begun
behold	beheld	beheld
bend	bent	bent
beseech	beseeched, besought	beseeched, besought
beset	beset	beset
bet	bet	bet
bid	*bade, bid	*bidden, bid
bind	bound	bound
bite	bit	bitten
bleed	bled	bled
bless	blessed	blessed, (arch) blest
blow	blew	blown, *blowed
break	broke	broken
breed	bred	bred
bring	brought	brought
broadcast	broadcast	broadcast
browbeat	browbeat	browbeaten
build	built	built
burn	burned, burnt	burned, burnt
bust	busted, (GB also) bust	busted, (GB also) bust
buy	bought	bought
cast	cast	cast
catch	caught	caught
choose	chose	chosen
cling	clung	clung
come	came	come
cost	*cost, *costed	*cost, *costed
creep	crept	crept
crow	crowed	crowed
cut	cut	cut
deal	dealt	dealt
dig	dug	dug
dive	dived, (US also) dove	dived
do	did	done
draw	drew	drawn
dream	dreamed, (GB also) dreamt	dreamed, (GB also) dreamt
drink	drank	drunk
drive	drove	driven
dwell	dwelt, dwelled	dwelt, dwelled
eat	ate	eaten
fall	fell	fallen
feed	fed	fed
feel	felt	felt
fight	fought	fought
find	found	found
flee	fled	fled
fling	flung	flung
floodlight	floodlit	floodlit
fly	flew	flown
forbid	forbade, forbad	forbidden
forecast	forecast, forecasted	forecast, forecasted
foresee	foresaw	foreseen
foretell	foretold	foretold
forget	forgot	forgotten
forgive	forgave	forgiven
forsake	forsook	forsaken
freeze	froze	frozen
get	got	got, (US also) gotten
give	gave	given
go	went	gone
grind	ground	ground
grow	grew	grown
hang	*hung, *hanged	*hung, *hanged
have	had	had
hear	heard	heard
hew	hewed	hewn, hewed
hide	hid	hidden, (arch) hid

English Irregular Verbs

infinitive/ *bezokolicznik*	past tense/ *czas przeszły*	past participle/ *imiesłów czasu przeszłego*
hit	hit	hit
hold	held	held
hurt	hurt	hurt
inlay	inlaid	inlaid
input	input, inputted	input, inputted
interweave	interwove, interweaved	interwoven, interweaved
keep	kept	kept
kneel	kneeled, knelt	kneeled, knelt
knit	knitted, *knit	knitted, *knit
know	knew	known
lay	laid	laid
lead	led	led
lean	leaned, (GB also) leant	leaned, (GB also) leant
leap	leaped, (GB also) leapt	leaped, (GB also) leapt
learn	learned, (GB also) learnt	learned, (GB also) learnt
leave	left	left
lend	lent	lent
let	let	let
lie	lay	lain
light	lighted, lit	lighted, lit
lose	lost	lost
make	made	made
mean	meant	meant
meet	met	met
miscast	miscast	miscast
misdeal	misdealt	misdealt
mishear	misheard	misheard
mishit	mishit	mishit
mislay	mislaid	mislaid
mislead	misled	misled
misread /'mɪs'riːd/	misread /'mɪs'red/	misread /'mɪs'red/
misspell	misspelled, (GB also) misspelt	misspelled, (GB also) misspelt
misspend	misspent	misspent
mistake	mistook	mistaken
misunderstand	misunderstood	misunderstood
mow	mowed	mown, mowed
outbid	outbid	outbid, (US also) outbidden
outdo	outdid	outdone
outfight	outfought	outfought
outgrow	outgrew	outgrown
output	output, outputted	output, outputted
outrun	outran	outrun
outsell	outsold	outsold

infinitive/ *bezokolicznik*	past tense/ *czas przeszły*	past participle/ *imiesłów czasu przeszłego*
outshine	outshone	outshone
overbid	overbid	overbid
overcome	overcame	overcome
overdo	overdid	overdone
overdraw	overdrew	overdrawn
overeat	overate	overeaten
overfly	overflew	overflown
overhang	overhung	overhung
overhear	overheard	overheard
overlay	overlaid	overlaid
overlie	overlay	overlain
overpay	overpaid	overpaid
override	overrode	overridden
overrun	overran	overrun
oversee	oversaw	overseen
overshoot	overshot	overshot
oversleep	overslept	overslept
overtake	overtook	overtaken
overthrow	overthrew	overthrown
partake	partook	partaken
pay	paid	paid
plead	pleaded, (US also) pled	pleaded, (US also) pled
prove	proved	proved, proven
put	put	put
quit	quit, quitted	quit, quitted
read /riːd/	read /red/	read /red/
rend	rent	rent
rid	rid	rid
ride	rode	ridden
ring	rang	rung
rise	rose	risen
run	ran	run
saw	sawed	sawed, (esp GB) sawn
say	said	said
see	saw	seen
seek	sought	sought
sell	sold	sold
send	sent	sent
set	set	set
sew	sewed	sewn, sewed
shake	shook	shaken
shear	sheared	*shorn, *sheared
shed	shed	shed
shine	*shone, *shined	*shone, *shined
shit	shit, shat	shit, shat
shoe	shod	shod
shoot	shot	shot
show	showed	shown, showed
shrink	shrank, shrunk	shrunk, shrunken
shut	shut	shut
sing	sang	sung
sink	sank	sunk

infinitive/ bezokolicznik	past tense/ czas przeszły	past participle/ imiesłów czasu przeszłego	infinitive/ bezokolicznik	past tense/ czas przeszły	past participle/ imiesłów czasu przeszłego
sit	sat	sat	swell	swelled	swollen, (esp US) swelled
slay	slew	slain			
sleep	slept	slept			
slide	slid	slid	swim	swam	swum
sling	slung	slung	swing	swung	swung
slink	slunk	slunk	take	took	taken
slit	slit	slit	teach	taught	taught
smell	smelled, (GB also) smelt	smelled, (GB also) smelt	tear	tore	torn
			tell	told	told
			think	thought	thought
sow	sowed	sowed, sown	thrive	thrived, (liter) throve	thrived, (arch) thriven
speak	spoke	spoken			
speed	*sped, *speeded	*sped, *speeded	throw	threw	thrown
spell	spelled, (GB also) spelt	spelled, (GB also) spelt	thrust	thrust	thrust
			tread	trod	trodden, trod
			typecast	typecast	typecast
spend	spent	spent	typeset	typeset	typeset
spill	spilled, spilt	spilled, spilt	typewrite	typewrote	typewritten
spin	spun, (arch) span	spun	undercut	undercut	undercut
			undergo	underwent	undergone
spit	spat, (esp US) spit	spat, (esp US) spit	underlie	underlay	underlain
			undersell	undersold	undersold
split	split	split	understand	understood	understood
spoil	spoiled, (GB also) spoilt	spoiled, (GB also) spoilt	undertake	undertook	undertaken
			undo	undid	undone
			unstick	unstuck	unstuck
spread	spread	spread	unwind	unwound	unwound
spring	sprang, (US also) sprung	sprung	uphold	upheld	upheld
			upset	upset	upset
			wake	woke	woken
stand	stood	stood	waylay	waylaid	waylaid
steal	stole	stolen	wear	wore	worn
stick	stuck	stuck	weave	wove, *weaved	woven, *weaved
sting	stung	stung	wed	wedded, wed	wedded, wed
stink	stank, stunk	stunk	weep	wept	wept
strew	strewed	strewn, strewed	wet	wet, wetted	wet, wetted
stride	strode	stridden	win	won	won
strike	struck	struck	wind	wound	wound
string	strung	strung	withdraw	withdrew	withdrawn
strive	strove	striven	withhold	withheld	withheld
sublet	sublet	sublet	withstand	withstood	withstood
swear	swore	sworn	work	worked, *wrought	worked, *wrought
sweat	sweated, (US also) sweat	sweated, (US also) sweat	wring	wrung	wrung
			write	wrote	written
sweep	swept	swept			